Encyclopedia of Emerging Industries

Sixth Edition

Encyclopedia of Emerging Industries

SIXTH EDITION

GALE
CENGAGE Learning™

Australia • Brazil • Japan • Korea • Mexico • Singapore • Spain • United Kingdom • United States

Encyclopedia of Emerging Industries, Sixth Edition

Product Management: Jenai Drouillard

Project Editor: Lynn M. Pearce

Editorial: Hillary Hentschel

Composition and Electronic Prepress: Evi Seoud

Manufacturing: Rita Wimberley

Gale, a part of Cengage Learning
27500 Drake Rd.
Farmington Hills, MI 48331-3535

ISBN-13: 978-1-4144-8687-1
ISBN-10: 1-4144-8687-1

This title is also available as an e-book.
ISBN-13: 978-1-4144-8688-8
ISBN-10: 1-4144-8688-X
Contact your Gale, a part of Cengage Learning, sales representative for ordering information.

Printed in Mexico
1 2 3 4 5 6 7 14 13 12 11

Contents

Introduction

Welcome to the sixth edition of the *Encyclopedia of Emerging Industries (EEI)*. In this volume readers will find essays covering specific businesses as well as broad business sectors that have, for the most part, shown evidence of significant growth in the recent past or potential for exemplary growth in the near future. In some cases, these areas of commerce fall within older, well-established industries—prominent examples include semiconductors, beverages, and tourism. More commonly, the essays focus on offshoots of relatively new industries, such as developments in software as a service (SaaS), "green" industries, and mobile apps. Students, entrepreneurs, investors, and job seekers alike will find information on technical subjects as arcane as optical sensing or encryption systems, and on topics as commonplace as gambling casinos.

Content and Arrangement Arranged alphabetically within the book, essay titles are cross-referenced in the General Index.

Supplementing the text are charts and graphs. In each essay, readers may expect to find some or all of the following aspects discussed:

- **Industry Snapshot.** Provides a brief overview of the topic and identifies key issues.

- **Organization and Structure.** Discusses the configuration and functional aspects of the business, including sub-industry divisions.

- **Background and Development.** Relates the genesis and history of the industry to date, including major technological advances, scandals, pioneering companies, major products, important legislation, and other shaping factors.

- **Pioneers.** Discusses individuals who have made significant contributions to the development of the industry.

- **Current Conditions.** Provides information on the status of the industry with an eye toward challenges on the horizon.

- **Industry Leaders.** Profiles major companies, and may include discussion of financial performance.

- **Work Force.** May contain information on the size, diversity, and characteristics of the industry's labor force, as well as discussion of skills needed by employees.

- **America and the World.** Contains information on the global marketplace in relation to the topic discussed.

- **Research and Technology.** Furnishes information on cutting edge developments, areas of research, and their potential to impact the industry.

- **Further Reading.** Provides users with specific source citations. These sources, many of which have been used to compile the actual essays, are publicly accessible materials such as articles from professional and academic periodicals and journals; books; corporate annual reports; and documents from government sources; as well as material supplied by industry associations. Included are references to numerous reputable Internet sites; whenever available, the URLs for these sources are included.

Indexes and Conversion Tables The General Index contains alphabetic references to items mentioned within the essays such as significant terms, companies, trade and professional associations, government agencies, names of individuals, significant court cases, and key legislation.

The Industry Index contains a listing of many 1987 Standard Industrial Classification (SIC) references, with page numbers as they pertain to the book's subject coverage.

Two industry classification tables allow cross-referencing of SIC categories used in the Industry Index with the 1997 North American Industry Classification System (NAICS) codes.

Topic Selection and Inclusion Criteria In determining topic selection, the editors found it best to rely upon several means, a portion of which were decidedly subjective. (Users will note that we have chosen to employ the term "emerging industries" rather loosely, often referring not only to entire *industries,* but to specific industrial and business *sectors,* discrete types of business *enterprises,* and sometimes simply to describe a particular *range of products or services.*) In considering inclusion, the questions we repeatedly asked ourselves revolved around these central points:

- Is the industry experiencing a period of significant growth, either financial or otherwise?

- Has the business been the recent focus of much public attention and, if so, why?

- Is the product or service being newly marketed in a particularly innovative way?

- Is the business involved in the use or production of cutting edge technologies?

Ideas for topics were culled, in part, from a wide assortment of variously ranked lists detailing the recent accomplishments of promising or well-established companies. Assorted content experts also provided myriad suggestions and assisted in refining the coverage within *EEI.* Finally, we relied to a certain degree on hunch, experience, and intuition, predicting to the best of our ability which emerging business areas our users would want and need to know more about.

Comments and Suggestions Comments and suggestions, including ideas for future essays, are most welcome. Readers are invited to send their thoughts to:

Managing Editor, *Encyclopedia of Emerging Industries*
Gale, a part of Cengage Learning
27500 Drake Rd.
Farmington Hills, MI 48331-3535
Telephone: (248)677-4253
Toll-Free: (800)347-GALE
Fax: (248)699-8070
Email: BusinessProducts@gale.com

ADULT AND RETIREMENT COMMUNITIES

■

SIC CODE(S)

6513

7041

INDUSTRY SNAPSHOT

The U.S. Census Bureau's population profile as of 2010 (using three assumptions about fertility, life expectancy, and net immigration) concluded that the nation's overall population, while continuing to grow, would slow down in *growth rate* during the next several decades. Between 2040 and 2050, for example, U.S. population growth is expected to be well below one percent, slower than ever before in the country's history. This projection is premised on the estimated number of natural deaths occurring in an aging "Baby Boom" generation (those born between 1946 and 1964, the years of prosperity following World War II). At the same time, notes the Census Bureau, *life expectancy* is expected to reach 82.6 years by 2050.

What all this means, in relative terms, is that the future median age of the U.S. population will be older than it is now, expected to peak around 2035, then decrease slightly through 2050. The increase in median age is also being driven by the large class of Baby Boomers, the first members of which will reach age 65 in 2011; at that time, the entire group will comprise roughly 25 percent of the total population. According to a study from the International Council on Active Aging, in 2004 there were 36.3 million U.S. residents age 65 and older; by 2030, that figure will more than double to over 71 million.

Who will support the needs of this aging population? Spending on entitlement programs, such as Social Security and Medicare, will rise sharply, noted the Population Reference Bureau in its 2010 World Population Data Sheet. Total spending on these two programs is projected to increase from 8.4 percent of the gross domestic product (GDP) in 2010 to about 12.5 percent in 2030. The two biggest drains on these funds will be for medical care and housing of an aging population.

However, financial housing assistance is only available to senior citizens who demonstrate financial need. For the vast majority of aging Americans (especially Baby Boomers), an increase in private-sector, for-profit adult and senior housing communities helped meet the demands during the relatively prosperous 1990s. Although the economic slump of the first decade of the twenty-first century later affected the adult and retirement community industry—as retirees worked longer or delayed moving into retirement communities while waiting for their houses to sell—companies involved in the business were able to at least maintain the industry, if not the momentum.

ORGANIZATION AND STRUCTURE

The adult and retirement community industry consists of a variety of facility options catering to the needs of residents aged 55 and older. While some income/needs-based public housing may be an option for certain seniors, by far the industry operates as a for-profit one that caters to Baby Boomers concerned about their futures. Retirement communities cover a wide spectrum of anticipated needs, from clusters of single-family residences for independent, active seniors, all the way through "assisted living" facilities that offer medical and/or custodial care for those needing physical assistance. According to the National Investment Center (NIC) in Annapolis, Maryland, which monitors

1

Percentage of Baby Boomers in Total U.S. Population

1994	30 percent of population
2011	25 percent of population
2029	16 percent of population

SOURCE: U.S. Census Bureau, Population Profile of the United States, National Population Projections, 2010.

growth in the seniors housing industry, the four categories of senior living are senior apartments, active adult communities, and owner-occupied housing; continuing care retirement communities (CCRCs), congregate-care facilities, independent living units in CCRCs, and board and care living facilities; assisted living in congregate and CCRCs and board and care facilities; and nursing homes and skilled nursing units in congregate, CCRCs, and hospitals. CCRCs often evolve with a certain theme; for instance, a resort community may offer recreational activities, while a health care community may offer nursing care.

Since 1992, the American Seniors Housing Association (ASHA) has followed and reported on the adult housing industry. The association was started by the National Housing Council and, along with Coopers & Lybrand, L.L.P, publishes annually the leading 25 managers and owners of seniors housing in the United States. ASHA also serves as a membership organization for companies involved in seniors housing and provides research and industry statistics. Another major resource and forecaster in the seniors housing industry is the National Investment Center (NIC), which held its first conference in 1991. The NIC offers information and data monitoring the financial state of the industry. Updates on loan volume, occupancy rates, move-in rates, and construction are available on a quarterly basis, and research publications are available for sale through its Web site.

The industry was initially developed by nonprofit organizations, religious orders, and social service groups. During the 1990s, Wall Street took notice, and there was an infusion of capital in the industry. By the early years of the twenty-first century, investors disappeared, and construction declined. This was not entirely an unwelcome development. Industry observers feared that the senior housing market had become too corporate, and not enough care was given to the needs of the residents.

Periodically, the industry has moved toward some type of government involvement. In the mid-1990s, the majority of senior housing was private pay, but some states had begun to allow Medicaid waivers for assisted living residences. Government involvement generally came in the form of regulations imposed as a condition of state and federal reimbursements. While many industry players, such as market leader Colson & Colson/Holiday Retirement Corporation, decried government intervention as a stifling intrusion, others, especially those in the nursing home sector, found themselves pushing for greater government involvement in the late 1990s. The federal role in the nursing home industry was diminished in some ways, particularly in federal budgetary cuts on sub-acute nursing home care, which would probably increase the pace at which nursing home operators scrambled to attract private investment. In the early years of the first decade of the 2000s, the industry was studying the European model, which can be described as a more socialized system. In Highland Park, Illinois, the local government donated a parcel of land to provide low-cost senior housing in the otherwise affluent suburb. However, this is not the norm, and the future of the industry continues to be linked to the economy and corporate investment.

Like the housing industry as a whole, the retirement communities and seniors housing industries are exceptionally cyclical. The industries' nearest relative is the hotel and multifamily sectors. In general, however, both occupancy rates and rents were slightly higher in the seniors housing industry than for either multifamily housing or lodging, thus yielding greater revenues.

BACKGROUND AND DEVELOPMENT

Adult and retirement communities first began as simple housing options for people entering their retirement years. The basic focus of these communities was to lure those seniors who were able to remain independent and who were willing to give up their homes in favor of living in a residential area with other people their age. Unfortunately, until the 1980s, the industry was not able to attract the number of seniors it had anticipated. Leaders in the seniors housing market discovered that seniors were not interested in giving up their homes as they grew older unless new adult communities could provide value-added services. Once builders and managers realized what it took to attract seniors, the industry, especially assisted living facilities, took off, increasing by 24 percent during the 1980s.

The dramatic growth in the retirement sector through the 1980s, however, resulted in a glut by the end of the decade, leading to massive financial restructuring. Analysts attributed the overbuilding to unchecked exuberance among investors and builders and to inadequate research into target markets and prospective rental rates. The industry took note and worked extensively to remedy such shortcomings.

In that spirit, the National Investment Center (NIC) was formed in 1991 to act as an information conduit between the investment community and the industry's owners and managers. The NIC mobilized quickly to provide comprehensive research and information to investors and lenders to help them understand the specific nature of the seniors housing market and particularly to spell out the tremendous growth opportunities it offered. Thus, the NIC took it upon itself to attract capital flows into the industry. The NIC conducts research independently and also jointly with other major senior resource organizations, including ASHA and the American Health Care Association. It also hosts an annual conference that provides industry information. Among the members of the NIC research projects committee are leaders in the field of real estate investment in housing for seniors.

These and similar efforts paid off handsomely, and the industry dusted itself off and charged into the 1990s full force. The market exploded throughout the decade, particularly beginning in the mid-1990s, as major investors dove in to make large profits.

While the tremendous industry growth through the 1990s attracted the attention of large institutional investors and lenders, the investment climate for the seniors housing industry remained tumultuous, leading to several large sell-offs in the late 1990s. Nevertheless, overall confidence in the industry remained exceptionally high, as returns remained healthy compared with other real estate-based investments.

As ever in the housing business, there were fears just below the surface of a possible glut in some geographic locations, particularly in the Northwest. For the most part, building and investment patterns, as well as demand for seniors housing, revealed little panic. The industry first started to register concern in late 1998 following the massive financial turmoil in foreign markets, after which investors started to flee the building industries, and thus many retirement-based companies saw their capital pulled out from under them. The market jolts of 1998 and 1999, however, may have even served as a preemptive strike against possible overbuilding, according to many analysts.

Some industry sectors learned the hard way that the sheer number of seniors was not enough to maintain a healthy market. Alterations to the Medicare payment systems cut into nursing home revenues and thus investor confidence. In the late 1990s, the sector was rife with executives calling for greater help from the government to provide more solid footing. Two leading nursing home operations, Assisted Living Concepts Inc. and Sunrise Assisted Living, Inc., achieved disappointing earnings, and some industry players feared an avalanche of bad news.

As Americans grow older and health care prolongs the lives of people suffering from chronic diseases, assisted living and continuing care facilities have had to expand their services to provide for residents who require additional care. According to some estimates, up to 30 percent of assisted living residents suffer from various degrees of Alzheimer's disease or other forms of dementia, and such communities are filled with growing numbers of frail residents who require the special assistance that trained specialists provide. As a result, costs are expected to rise, as these operations attempt to retain staff qualified to handle increasingly acute cases of such conditions.

In addition to self-contained retirement communities, or assisted living centers, the housing market began designing homes for retirement leisure. The increasingly youthful character of the retirement communities market, as 50-something empty nesters left the responsibilities of household maintenance behind them for the comforts of adult communities, forced an industry-wide shift in design and services. For starters, independent living facilities were among the fastest growing segments of the industry. Moreover, retirement communities were built adjacent to golf courses and other amenities that promoted an active lifestyle. As baby boomers move into retirement age in droves, industry analysts expected the 50-something market to fuel the industry's most dramatic growth and drive the next industry-wide building boom in the later years of the first decade of the 2000s. Fortunately, the younger residents were near the age of those designing and building the communities. Such relationships often saved the expense of research because the developers understood the people who had always been their customers. In a market ever-evolving due to the vastly diverse population of aging adults, sometimes the best investment was directed by the intimate knowledge of developers at the local level.

In addition, retirement communities operating with a focus on health care continued to alter their perspective at the end of the 1990s. Typical of some of these changes was The Washington House (TWH) in Alexandria, Virginia, which operates as a nonprofit corporation. TWH offers an array of options for living within the community. A companion program called "Community Washington House" was created to assist older adults in their own homes and to assist their caregivers. This program was a modification of what was predicted as a possible wave of the future: long-term care without walls. Membership, according to TWH president and CEO Judith Braun, RN, PhD, offers senior citizens the option of staying in their own homes longer. Community Washington House was unique as late as 1999 because it did not include an insurance component for payment of services, as did other similar programs. As past president and as a fellow of the National Gerontological Nursing

Association, Braun witnessed the changing landscape of retirement living beginning in the late 1970s.

Programs such as this one reflected the knowledge and commitment to ongoing care. Comprehensive membership in Community Washington House includes use of the fitness center, which is also offered for memberships separately; monthly wellness seminars; utilization of a personal liaison to coordinate home chores through the use of local service providers; and the benefit of social activities at the retirement community. Washington House gives seniors exercising this option the additional reassurance of priority placement on a waiting list.

Decision-making as people age and require additional care is a burden that many similar communities alleviated. Such arrangements encompassed three levels of care on the site, thus providing the security from upheavals at times when illnesses makes such moves unduly traumatic. The options of either living independently at home or retiring to a nursing home when a person could no longer deal with increasing frailty due to illness and age had been nudged aside by the end of the twentieth century. Braun noted that continuing care retirement communities (CCRCs) and nursing home facilities of the late 1990s looked very much like hospitals of the early 1980s. Length of stay was measured in weeks, rather than years.

A major development in the future of retirement living occurred on March 2, 1999. Residents of the Leisure World retirement community in Laguna Hills, California, voted to incorporate as a city. With an average age of 77, the 18,000 residents proved that aging Americans exercised political clout, in addition to their increasing economic influence. Other unincorporated communities, including the Sun City developments, continue to enjoy their status.

The business side of seniors housing had grown large and specialized enough to even work its way into the academic world at the end of the twentieth century. At the NIC Annual Conference in 1999, it was announced that the NIC Seniors Housing & Care Program had partnered with Johns Hopkins University to begin offering a graduate program dedicated to the field through the university's Real Estate Institute. A number of companies both inside and outside the industry, including Marriott Senior Living Services, GMAC Commercial Mortgage, and Senior Campus Living, contributed funding for the program. The courses, beginning in fall 2000, were open to the school's MBA students as a specialty field, which covers the issues of marketing, development, financing, quality of care, and other areas.

The adult housing market continued to experience consolidation as firms acquired one another in an effort to grow in size and gain market share. In addition,

publicly traded companies were becoming more common at the head of the pack. According to the American Seniors Housing Association's *2005 ASHA 50* report, while only 24 percent of the top 50 property owners were publicly traded firms, about 60 percent of the top 10 were public enterprises. Privately owned, for-profit companies were the most predominant overall, accounting for 56 percent of the top 50. Nonprofit organizations rounded out the industry, accounting for the remaining 20 percent of property owners. In all, ASHA listed 350,116 owned senior housing units in 2005, with a total of 379,203 units under management.

Traditionally, warm-weather states, such as Florida and Arizona, have been favored retirement venues. However, in the early years of the first decade of the 2000s, the term "aging in place" was coined to describe the growing sector of the elderly population refusing to move across the country. Research conducted by aforementioned developer Del Webb showed that only about 5 percent of retirees over the age of 65 will move across state lines. Instead, they choose to remain close to family and friends. Subsequently, more retirement communities are springing up on the outskirts of major cities, allowing residents to enjoy retirement living close to their former homes. One example is Webb's Sun City Huntley, a retirement community near Chicago.

Location is only one of many factors that leading architects and design teams are considering in future plans. The layout of retirement communities and the features of each unit are also carefully deliberated. Subtle differences include communities built with a "resort" or "vacation" look and those designed with a "village" style. The village style communities attempt to create the feeling of a close-knit town. Retail stores, shops, restaurants, and cafes offer residents a chance to mingle. Homes are also front-loaded with large porches and front lawns. This draws community members toward central areas and encourages informal contact with neighbors on sidewalks or promenades, as opposed to retreating to private backyard areas.

The interior design of each unit has also evolved. Traditionally, retirement housing has been synonymous with downsizing, but developers see this trend moving in the opposite direction. Potential buyers now want units that feature generous square footage. Floor plans often include a master suite, guest room, home office, den, or a great room. Luxurious bathrooms, exercise rooms, and wiring for Internet access are a few of the upscale amenities on the retirees' buying guide. Many of these options reflect the active lifestyles of the new wave of baby-boom retirees.

In addition to leading active lives, the new crop of retirees values independent living. With this in mind, architects are creating living spaces using a "universal design." Some features of this style include single-level homes; front-loading laundry appliances; wider, deeper stairs; and nonslip flooring with level thresholds. Most essential in this design is the subtle manner used to incorporate the special elements. Living quarters no longer have the look and feel of a geriatric ward. Design elements are seamlessly blended into the overall decor of the home and often go unnoticed.

Health and fitness are top priorities for future generations of retirees. Developers have implemented a number of measures to satisfy this requirement. Programs and activities, cuisine, and the environment all merit special attention. Activities that previously included bingo or movies have been eliminated in favor of yoga classes, book clubs, and golf outings. Many communities are equipped with fitness centers, spas, walking and bike paths, or even golf courses.

Traditional table service is quickly disappearing as the only dining option in about half of all CCRCs. Remodeled dining facilities in many communities now provide a wide array of options. The nursing home cafeteria, and its accompanying decor, are being replaced with cafes, bistros, and smaller, more intimate settings. Food selection has also undergone a radical change. Chicken and fish no longer dominate the menus. Instead, residents have low-fat, vegetarian options, ethnic foods, and salad bars. Take-out meals have also gained popularity, as research revealed that many retirees prefer to eat at home. Indeed, some upscale CCRCs offer residents four-star dining.

A healthy environment is another element of new developments. Construction features environmentally friendly materials that eliminate toxins, helping to minimize allergic reactions. Carpeting and central air systems are the primary culprits in floating potential allergens and are carefully selected for use.

Communities are also specializing in providing care or housing for retirees with similar lifestyles or needs. Gay retirement communities are one example. In the past, some same-sex domestic partners have felt unwelcome in tightly knit communities. This latest option allows couples to live together without the fear of discrimination that others have experienced in more traditional settings.

Alzheimer's communities are another model. Units in these villages are built with unique features to aid residents living in various stages of the illness. Closets are designed to position clothes in coordinated arrangements to facilitate dressing. Walls are painted different and contrasting colors to help differentiate rooms in the unit.

In late 2007, David Schless, president of the American Senior Housing Association, told *Time* magazine that "The senior-housing business has changed dramatically over the last seven or eight years." Some of the

changes include an emphasis on amenities that promote a physically active, rather than sedentary, lifestyle. These kinds of communities are sometimes called "active adult communities" and feature a vast array of activities that traditionally have not included retirement-age participants, including kayaking and skydiving. These developers are banking on the prediction that baby boomers will retire earlier and will have more financial resources to use toward retirement. The latter is necessary to live in some of the places long-time developers, including Del Webb, are creating. These luxury retirement communities, with fees of $500 to $2000 a month and homes starting at around $600,000, offer such services as concierges, personal trainers, and nutritionists. Del Webb had increased his management of such communities from 15 in 2001 to 59 in 2008, with several more planned. Some of these luxury senior housing developments are based on a theme. For example, those close to water may focus on sailing and scuba diving, whereas those in the mountains may offer skiing and hiking. A wellness-themed retirement community near Dallas, Texas, called Cooper Life at Craig Ranch offers, in addition to many other amenities, fitness centers, walking and cycling trails, medical facilities, prepackaged healthy meals, personalized vitamin regimens, and even regular CT scans. Fees are $2,000 a month with homes selling for up to $2 million.

Some luxury retirement housing is being built as high-rises near cities, another new trend in the early years of the first decade of the 2000s. For example, Pacific Retirement Services, based in Medford, Oregon, has created a 30-story continuing care community in Portland. The entry fee for the unit, which is charged in addition to rent, ranges from $400,000 to $1 million. Other companies building high-rise housing for seniors include Brookdale Senior Living, which charges around $4,200 a month for a unit in a 37-story building in the Lincoln Park area of Chicago, and Ziegler Capital Markets Group, which has 50 such buildings.

Yet another trend in the early years of the first decade of the 2000s in the retirement community industry is development on or near college campuses. Aimed at the baby boomers, who perhaps have not been on a campus since they went to college, these university-affiliated retirement communities offer residents the intellectual stimuli of a college campus, the opportunity to take or teach classes and to mentor young people, and a variety of other services not available in a typical retirement setting. Gerard Badler, managing director of Campus Continuum, a company that helps develop and market university-affiliated adult communities, distinguishes between two different kinds of communities built on the college model: continuing care retirement communities (CCRC), which include care for persons with some kind of medical condition, such as Alzheimer's, and the 55+ community, which includes persons age 55 to 70 who do not have medical concerns. Examples of the former are Lasell Village at Lasell College (Massachusetts), which opened in 2000, and University of Alabama-affiliated Capstone Village, which opened in 2005. The Praxeis Group (Jacksonville, Florida) expects to develop 8 to 10 not-for-profit university-affiliated communities for healthy retirees by 2010. Like other companies targeting active retirees, Praxeis prefers a term other than "retirement community"—in this case, "life-fulfilling centers"—in an attempt to emphasize the vibrant, active lifestyle aspect and de-emphasize age and degeneration. In the category of university-sponsored developments, 55+ communities are expected to be more popular than CCRCs in the later years of the first decade of the 2000s and are easier to fund and construct, according to Badler. Examples include Veridian Village at Hampshire College (Massachusetts), which is under construction, and University Commons (near the University of Michigan in Ann Arbor), among many others. Although alumni of the sponsoring universities or colleges are expected to be a targeted market, they are not the only prospective residents of such communities.

In practical terms, it is certain that in the coming years there will be more elder adults in the country than ever before, but the nature of their needs and preferences is unclear. This is the greatest challenge faced by the industry, which has been described as "on the brink of an identity crisis."

PIONEERS IN THE FIELD

A true pioneer of U.S. retirement living is Del Webb, who started to develop the idea in the late 1950s. A few years later, he was successful in finding retirees who were healthy enough to live independently in their own homes and luring them to the desert outside of Phoenix. In 1960, his Sun City, Arizona, development opened. Webb created the model for the United States's retirement communities. By the end of the 1970s, that idea had been successfully realized on 8,900 acres, when the first development came to fruition. Retirees fleeing the cold of the East Coast and Great Lakes flocked to the age-segregated, planned community. Until that time, many northern retirees went only to Florida. The Del Webb Corp. led the way to the future of comfortable living for people on fixed incomes—many of whom suffered through the Great Depression, fought in World War II, and worked hard in factories to save for a time of leisure as they aged. By the late 1970s, Sun City's 46,000 residents made it the nation's largest retirement community. Other Sun City retirement communities grew up elsewhere, including Tucson, Arizona; Hilton Head, South Carolina; and Roseville, California.

By 2004, the corporation had developed more than 10 Sun Cities, pushing into new geographical regions and expanding the range of services. In the late 1990s, Sun City moved north to the cold, bleak farmland of northern Illinois about 50 miles northwest of Chicago. Some Sun City communities are built around an 18-hole golf course and include an indoor recreation lodge, artificial lakes, and tennis courts. At least one of the resident spouses must be 55 or older. In the northern communities, natives were tied to the land and their grandchildren. The idea of living closer to the family they loved and the countryside that was familiar, not far from the city that might nurture them for many years to come, was seen as the crucial element in the success of Sun City in the Frost Belt. Meanwhile, the newest Sun Cities were equipped with spa facilities to supplement golf and other physical activities, providing a place to relax and stay fit with a wide range of holistic health treatments and facilities.

Moreover, the company was just getting going at the turn of the twenty-first century. In January 2000, Del Webb launched his very first branding campaign, a $7 million effort that included 60-second and 30-second television spots. By 2004, his company controlled or owned some 75,000 home sites. However, a relatively small number of these—approximately 8,000—were fully developed, providing ample capacity for future expansion.

CURRENT CONDITIONS

According to the American Association of Homes and Services for the Aging (AAHSA), as of 2010, there were 16,100 certified nursing homes, 39,500 assisted living facilities, and 1,900 continuing care retirement communities (CCRCs) operating in the United States. At the same time, there were more than 300,000 units of Section 202 affordable senior housing available nationwide. Notwithstanding, for every Section 202 affordable senior housing unit available, there were 10 eligible seniors on waiting lists for it. The average waiting time for such units is 13.4 months. By 2020, said AAHSA,12 million older Americans will need long-term services and support; for those who turned 65 in 2010, 69 percent will need some form of long-term services, whether in the community or in a residential care facility.

The number of available for-profit private housing units in senior living communities is harder to accurately trace. However, according to ASHA, the American Seniors Housing Association, in 2010, for-profit, privately-held entities made up almost half (48 percent) of the ASHA Top 50 seniors housing owners. Publicly-traded companies accounted for another one-fourth (24 percent). The National Investment Center for the Seniors Housing & Care Industry (NIC), calling itself "the most comprehensive database covering seniors housing and care," assessed the top 100 metropolitan-area markets in 2010, which represented nearly two-thirds of the 75+ population and over 12,500 properties. In 2010, the NIC reported that seniors housing occupancy rates had dropped in 11 of 12 quarters since 2007 (declining from a cyclical peak of 93 percent in the first quarter of 2007 to just 88 percent in the first quarter of 2010). Further analysis showed that assisted living properties fared better than independent living properties, which showed the steepest decline, likely due to the slumping economy. Continuing-care retirement communities (CCRCs) boasted the highest average occupancy rates in 2010, although they, too, suffered from slumping sales. According to the NIC, in 2010, the average entrance fee for each CCRC unit was $247,857, in addition to monthly fees.

Another indicator of a slumping economy affecting the industry in 2010 was the lack of new construction activity in adult/senior living communities. As of the first quarter in 2010, just 78 senior housing properties (with 8,897 units total) were under construction, compared to 159 properties (totaling 20,601 units) under construction in 2008. This translated to an overall decline in the construction pipeline of 57 percent from 2008 to 2010, reported NIC.

For investors, the slowdown in construction did not directly translate to a slowdown in supply growth or in profit. Through early 2010, the seniors housing inventory continued to grow at levels above 2000 units per quarter. Moreover, seniors housing was viewed as "outperforming" other asset classes, according to NIC, because year-over-year (YOY) rents continued to grow. In other words, notwithstanding the slowdown in new senior housing developments, existing units commanded higher monthly and yearly rental rates than in previous years (averaging 1.5 percent growth as of the first quarter of 2010). This compared with data provided by the Mortgage Bankers Association and PPR that showed office and multifamily YOY rents declining by nine percent and six percent, respectively, for the same time period (as of first quarter 2010).

On the other hand, between 2008 and 2010, two large seniors housing owners, Sunwest Management and Erickson Communities, filed for bankruptcy, and a third, Sunrise Senior Living, was reorganizing under heavy debt burden. A principal advisor to the industry, Mel Gamzon of Florida-based Senior Housing Investment Advisors, in a May 2010 article for *Multifamily Executive,* said that large seniors housing REITs (real estate investment trusts) such as Senior Housing Properties Trust, Nationwide Health Properties, and Healthcare Property Investors, were solidifying their balance sheets to quickly grasp opportunities in the market. He also indicated a rise in interest from equity providers, particularly foreign firms, looking to invest in seniors housing opportunities.

In August 2010, Health Care REIT and Merrill Gardens announced the formation of an $817 million partnership that will own and operate 38 seniors housing communities with approximately 4,300 units. The deal was considered one of the first major ones under the REIT Investment Diversification and Empowerment Act of 2007 (RIDEA). The Act allows healthcare REITs to receive rents as landlords as well as participate in operating profits as tenants. Other big transactions for 2010 include the $1.2 billion acquisition, by Blackstone Real Estate Advisors, of the 144-property portfolio previously owned by Salem, Oregon-based Sunwest Management.

INDUSTRY LEADERS

In September 2009, ASHA released its annual list of the top 50 seniors housing owners. Leading the list for the 16th consecutive year was Holiday Retirement Corporation (HRC), based in Salem, Oregon, with 296 properties and 34,657 units in 2009. Holding second and third place, respectively, were HCP, a publicly-traded REIT (formerly Health Care Property Investors; Long Beach, California), with 264 properties and 31,419 units; and Boston Capital (Boston, Massachusetts), with 595 properties and 30,249 units. Except for the number of properties and units, these rankings are unchanged from 2007.

The largest for-profit, privately-held seniors housing owners in 2010, according to ASHA, were Holiday Retirement and Boston Capital. The largest publicly-traded companies were HCP, Inc., Sunrise Senior Living, and Nationwide Health Properties. The largest not-for-profit ASHA Top 50 owners were Erickson Retirement Communities, ACTS Retirement-Life Communities, Inc., the Evangelical Lutheran Good Samaritan Society, and Presbyterian Homes & Services. (In 2010, Erickson Retirement Communities, seeking bankruptcy protection, was acquired and is now called Erickson Living.)

BIBLIOGRAPHY

Ascierto, Jerry. "Silver Opportunity: Investors Eye Opportunity in Independent Living Sector." *Multifamily Executive,* 5 May 2010.

Adler, Jane. "Game-Changing Partnership: Health Care REIT, Merrill Gardens Join Forces." *National Real Estate Investor,* 30 August 2010.

Adler, Jane. "Q&A with Granger Cobb: Acquisition of Sunwest Portfolio is Big Management Job." *National Real Estate Investor,* 30 August 2010.

American Seniors Housing Association. *ASHA 50.* September 2009. Available from www.seniorshousing.org.

———. "General Facts." Available from http://www.aasha.org/facts/

Andrews, John. "A Wave Like No Other: The Tide Has Never Been Higher for the Seniors Housing and Care Industry." *Assisted Living,* October 2007.

Angelo, Jean Marie. "Baby Boomers, Back to Campus: What Would It Be Like to Retire on a College Campus? More Older Adults Are About to Find Out." *University Business,* February 2008.

Berklan, James M. "Study: Broader Real Estate Woes Not Slowing Expansion." *McKnight's Long-Term Care News,* December 2007.

Bryjak, George. "Population Explosion: Part 2 of 2: Who Will Pay for Senior Boom?" *Adirondack Daily Enterprise,* 21 August 2010.

Greene, Kelly. "Continuing Care Retirement Communities: Weighing the Risks." Market Watch, the *Wall Street Journal,* 6 August 2010.

Hovanesian, Mara Der, and Deborah Stead. "Retire Here: We'll Help." *Business Week,* 14 April 2008.

International Council on Active Aging. " The U.S. Society Is All Grown Up," 2007. Available from www.icaa.cc/.

Kadlec, Dan. "Home Sweet Homes for Fiftysomethings." *Money,* January 2008.

National Investment Center. "1Q10 Market Signal: Construction Pipeline is Emptying, but...." *NIC MAP Market Signals,* May 2010. Available from http://www.nic.org/research/signals/signal1q10.aspx.

———. "1Q10 Market Signal: Three Year Occupancy Performance by Property Type." *NIC MAP Market Signals,* May 2010. Available from http://www.nic.org/research/signals/signal1q102.aspx.

———. "1Q10 Market Signal: What's in Store for Seniors Housing Rent Growth?" *NIC MAP Market Signals,* May 2010. Available from http://www.nic.org/research/signals/signal1q103.aspx.

———. "Seniors Housing Occupancy Falls, Rent Growth Continues." NIC Press Release, 13 May 2010. Available from http://www.nic.org/press/2010/May13.aspx.

Norwood, Graham. "Too Young to be Old." *Estates Gazette,* 11 February 2006.

O'Connor, John. "Finding Long-Term Solutions." *McKnight's Long-Term Care News,* May 2008.

Population Reference Bureau (PRB). "2010 World Population Data Sheet." Available from http://www.prb.org/Publications/Datasheets/2010/2010wpds.aspx.

Pristin, Terry. "Hot Niche in the Rental Market: Housing for the Elderly." *The New York Times,* 15 February 2006.

Serchuk, David. "Make Money in Real Estate." *Forbes,* 8 May 2006.

Smith, Jennette. "Boomers Changing the Face of Retirement Housing." *Crain's Detroit Business,* 26 June 2006.

Schultz, Sue. "Retirees Delay Moves as Home Sales Languish." *Baltimore Business Journal,* 25 January 2008.

"Tired Seniors Housing Communities Get a Makeover." *National Real Estate Investor,* 29 January 2007.

"Upscale High-Rises Attract Urban Seniors." *National Real Estate Investor,* 26 March 2007.

U.S. Census Bureau. "Population Profile of the United States: National Population Projections." Available from http://www.census.gov/population/www/pop-profile/natproj.html.

AGILE SOFTWARE

SIC CODE(S)

7371

7372

INDUSTRY SNAPSHOT

Agile software is an umbrella term for multiple innovative methods by which software developers organize and implement projects and communicate with their clients. Agile software development is an adaptive or incremental approach to software design and development that challenges more traditional, plan-based or engineering-based software practices. As the authors of "Agile Modeling, Agile Software Development, and Extreme Programming: The State of Research" explain, its concepts are intended "to strip away as much of the heaviness, commonly associated with the traditional software-development methodologies, as possible to promote quick response to changing environments, changes in user requirements, accelerated project deadlines and the like." Called by software engineer/researcher/consultant Hakan Erdogmus, founder and owner of Kalemun Research Inc. in Ottawa, Canada, "the most important paradigm that has swept the software development world over the last decade," agile software development, utilizing core principles of collaboration, coordination, and communication, has revolutionized planning, design, and implementation of software project development.

As opposed to traditional, predictive or plan-driven, sequential software development processes that follow the so-called waterfall model through the completed stages of conception, initiation, implementation, verification, and maintenance, agile software development methodology divides an entire software project into smaller segments with each portion the responsibility of a small team that takes the segment through a full software development cycle, from inception, coding, testing, and delivery of a working product to the client. Such an agile approach, emphasizing close collaboration between programmer and business experts, face-to-face communication, small working teams, and frequent deployment of workable software, agile proponents believe, leads to higher-quality software that better meets user needs more quickly and at a lower cost than traditional sequential software development methodologies.

A diverse collection of software designers met in 2001 to produce the Agile Manifesto, outlining the principles of agile software development. Subsequently the Agile Alliance, a nonprofit organization, was founded to advance agile development principles and practices through conferences, workshops, and academic research projects. The agile message has been further spread by agile software development consultants and a steady stream of book-length and journal articles. A 2010 search of the ISI Web of Science, for example, turned up 719 scientific publications on agile software development (627 conference papers and 92 journal articles) published between 1997 and 2009.

Despite widespread dissemination of agile principles and implementation of methodology by leading software development firms and major corporations, debate continues about what exactly agile software development is and its utility. As Hakan Erdogmus summarizes, "Agile software development is multi-faceted and poorly delimited. Is agility a general development philosophy? Is it about dealing with change and uncertainty? Is it a project management philosophy? A way of working with development teams?

A way of thinking about software? A way of life? A rebellion? A religion? A cultural revolution of the software intellectuals? Well, it's all of the above and none of the above at the same time." As Erdogmus makes clear, agile software development serves many functions and many masters as a means to streamline efficient software development and to change the ways software design has been achieved.

ORGANIZATION AND STRUCTURE

Agile software development as a concept grew out of several adaptive-oriented software design methodologies that evolved as early as the 1970s. To understand fully the techniques and methods of agile software approaches and practices, it is important to take into account these related processes that stand behind the agile movement.

Adaptive Software Development (ASD) Adaptive software development evolved from the concepts of rapid application development processes conceived by Jim Highsmith and Sam Bayer in the 1990s. ASD offered a new way of conceptualizing software development methods that emphasized an incremental approach and the replacement of the traditional waterfall method with continual learning and adaptation to the evolving project. Some of the key concepts of agile software development—collaboration, continual learning and adaptation, and short iterations of project segments—can be traced directly to ASD methodologies.

Agile Modeling (AM) As defined by author Scott W. Ambler, "Agile Modeling is a practice-based methodology for effective modeling and documentation of software-based systems" ("Agile Modeling (AM) Home Page"). AM extends the concepts of adaptive development to modeling practices, encouraging developers to produce sufficient models for design needs while keeping the number of models and amount of documentation as low as possible.

Crystal Methods Approach Based on the research of Alistair Cockburn in the 1990s, the Crystal is a process for selecting the most suitable design methodology for each individual project, factoring such components as risk, size of project, and staffing. Each level in the Crystal family is assigned a color indicating the required coordination and formality based on each project and team size. Using the concepts of Crystal, the application of agile development methods can be integrated in even the most complex projects to retain individuality and flexibility.

Dynamic Systems Development Method (DSDM) The Dynamic Systems Development Method was the work of a consortium of British software developers in the 1990s.

According to the authors of "Agile Software Development Methods: A Comparative Review," "The fundamental idea behind DSDM is that instead of fixing the amount of functionality in a product and then adjusting time and resources to reach that functionality, it is preferred to fix time and resources and then to adjust the amount of functionality accordingly. DSDM can be seen as the first truly agile software development method."

Extreme Programming (XP) The concepts of Extreme Programming, a collection of adaptive software engineering practices, developed out of the research of Kent Beck, one of the original signatories of the Agile Manifesto, for the Chrysler Corporation in the 1990s. Beck outlined the key principles of XP in his book *Extreme Programming Explained*. As defined by the authors of "Agile Software Development Methods: A Comparative Review," "Some of the main characteristics of XP are short iterations with small releases and rapid feedback, close customer participation, constant communication and coordination, continuous refactoring, continuous integration and testing, collective code ownership, and pair programming," all central features of agile software development practices.

Feature-Driven Development (FDD) FDD is the brainchild of Jeff De Luca in the 1990s. FDD is a methodology for achieving frequent deliveries of workable software in an adaptive environment that also includes accurate monitoring of the progress of each project. DeLuca's Web site (www.nebulon.com/articles/index.html) includes both the original FDD process and its latest refinements.

Scrum An adaptive project management methodology, Scrum originated from the work of two Japanese business management professors, Hirotaka Takeuchi and Ikujiro Nonaka, whose 1986 article in the *Harvard Business Review*, "The New New Product Development Game," likened a flexible project management process to rugby, in which the entire team cooperates to move the ball towards the goal. This process was later termed Scrum, as described by Jeff Sutherland and Ken Schwaber, both original signatories of the Agile Manifesto, in their work during the 1990s. Scrum calls for the creation of a small team of programmers, a ScrumMaster in place of a project manager, and a Project Owner, who represents the stakeholder and business interests. The incremental process of project development is divided into "sprints" of two to four weeks to create workable products for testing. Such an approach allows for incremental and adaptive project management, a cornerstone of agile software development methodology.

BACKGROUND AND DEVELOPMENT

It has been commonly claimed that agile software development is a return to the ways and means of the earliest software design that goes back to the 1950s with small teams of programmers working closely with their clients and adapting to evolving needs. As indicated in the Organization and Structure section, agile software development is a confluence of several adaptive, incremental software methodologies that came together as a collective concept in February 2001, in a ski resort in Utah, where a group of 17 software programmers, designers, and theorists met and drafted the so-called Agile Software Manifesto. They were, according to Jim Highsmith of the Agile Alliance in "History: The Agile Manifesto," "Representatives from Extreme Programming, SCRUM, DSDM, Adaptive Software Development, Crystal, Feature-Driven Development, Pragmatic Programming, and others sympathetic to the needs of an alternative to documentation driven, heavyweight software development processes." Later calling themselves "The Agile Alliance," the group formulated their credo of shared values:

- Individuals and interactions over processes and tools
- Working software over comprehensive documentation
- Customer collaboration over contract negotiation
- Responding to change over following a plan

Twelve principles were identified as standing behind the Agile Manifesto:

- Our highest priority is to satisfy the customer through early and continuous delivery of valuable software.
- Welcome changing requirements, even late in development. Agile processes harness change for customer's competitive advantage.
- Deliver working software frequently, from a couple of weeks to a couple of months, with a preference to the shorter timescale.
- Business people and developers must work together daily throughout the project.
- Build project around motivated individuals. Give them the environment and support they need, and trust them to get the job done.
- The most efficient and effective method of conveying information to and within a development team is face-to-face conversation.
- Working software is the primary measure of progress.
- Agile processes promote sustainable development. The sponsors, developers, and users should be able to maintain a constant pace indefinitely.

- Continuous attention to technical excellence and good design enhances agility.
- Simplicity—the art of maximizing the amount of work not done—is essential.
- The best architectures, requirements, and designs emerge from self-organizing teams.
- At regular intervals, the team reflects on how to become more effective, then tunes and adjusts its behavior accordingly.

In 2005, two of the original signatories of the Agile Manifesto, Alistair Cockburn and Jim Highsmith, co-authored with others a set of six management principles for agile software project managers, later called "The Declaration of Interdependence for Modern Management." These principles were:

- Increase return on investment by making continuous flow of value our focus
- Deliver reliable results by engaging customers in frequent interactions and shared ownership
- Expect uncertainty and manage for it through iterations, anticipation, and adaptation
- Unleash creativity and innovation by recognizing that individuals are the ultimate source of value, and creating an environment where they can make a difference
- Boost performance through group accountability for results and shared responsibility for team effectiveness
- Improve effectiveness and reliability through situationally specific strategies, processes, and practices

Subsequent efforts have been devoted to spreading the word of the value and utility of agile methodology by consultants and those who have worked in an agile environment and have profited by agile implementation.

PIONEERS IN THE FIELD

Kent Beck Kent Beck, one of the original signatories of the Agile Manifesto, is the creator of Extreme Programming and a leading proponent of Test-Driven Development software development methodologies. With an advanced degree in computer science from the University of Oregon, Beck is the founder and director of Three Rivers Institute, a software consultancy firm. His many books include *Extreme Programming Explained: Embrace Change* (1999), *Test-Driven Development: By Example* (2002), and *Implementation Patterns* (2008).

Alistair Cockburn Co-author of both the Agile Manifesto and the Declaration of Interdependence, Alistair Cockburn is an internationally renowned IT strategist who was voted in 2007 one of "The All-Time Top 150 I-Technology Heroes." A founder and consulting fellow of Humans and Technology, Cockburn is a recognized expert in use cases to determine the requirements of software design systems and business practices. His extensive field interviews with programmers at IBM in the 1990s led to his development of the Crystal family of adaptive methodologies.

Jim Highsmith Creator of Adaptive Software Development concepts, Jim Highsmith, an original signatory of the Agile Manifesto and a founder of the Agile Alliance, has served as the director of the Agile Project Management Advisory Service for the Cutter Consortium, an IT advisory research institute based in Arlington, Massachusetts. He is the author of *Agile Software Development: A Collaborative Approach to Managing Complex Systems* (1999), *Agile Software Development Ecosystems* (2002), and *Agile Project Management: Creating Innovative Products* (2004).

Ken Schwaber A signatory of the Agile Manifesto and a founder of the Agile Alliance, Ken Schwaber is one of the inventors, along with Jeff Sutherland, of the Scrum development process. He is the author of such books as *Agile Software Development with Scrum* (2002), *Agile Project Management with Scrum* (2005), and *The Enterprise and Scrum*.

Jeff Sutherland An inventor, with Ken Schwaber, of the Scrum development process, Sutherland is a graduate of the United States Military Academy at West Point and a former combat pilot during the Vietnam War. He received advanced degrees from Stanford University and a Ph.D. from the University of Colorado School of Medicine. He is chief executive officer of Scrum, Inc., in Boston and has worked as Scrum consultant to Microsoft, Yahoo, Adobe, GE Healthcare, and other companies.

CURRENT CONDITIONS

After a decade since the issuing of the Agile Manifesto, agile software development has gone from a contrarian's rebellion to mainstream practice. Few software development companies have resisted incorporating some aspects of agile methodology or practice. So pervasive has the agile movement become that many of its key concepts have moved beyond software development into general management theory and practice. The next phase in agile development is likely assessment by academics and others, measuring outcome and effectiveness of the many agile software development methodologies.

BIBLIOGRAPHY

Abrahamsson, Pekka, Nilay Oza, and Mikko T. Siponen. "Agile Software Development Methods: A Comparative View." In *Agile Software Development: Current Research and Future Directions,* edited by Torgeir Dingsøyr, Tore Dybå, and Nils Brede Moe. Berlin: Springer, 2010.

Ambler, Scott W. "Effective Practices for Modeling and Documentation." Agile Modeling (AM) Home Page: Effective Practices for Modeling and Documentation. 2010. Available from http://www.agilemodeling.com/.

Beck, Kent. *Extreme Programming Explained: Embrace Change.* Reading, MA: Addison-Wesley, 2000.

Cockburn, Alistair. *Agile Software Development: the Cooperative Game.* Upper Saddle River, NJ: Addison-Wesley, 2007.

Cohn, Mike. *Succeeding with Agile Software Development Using Scrum.* Upper Saddle River, NJ: Addison-Wesley, 2010.

Dingsøyr, Torgeir, Tore Dybå, and Nils Brede Moe. *Agile Software Development: Current Research and Future Directions.* Berlin: Springer, 2010.

Erickson, John, Kalle Lyytinen, and Keng Siau. "Agile Modeling, Agile Software Development, and Extreme Programming: The State of Research." *Journal of Database Management* 16:88-100.

Gonçalves, Marcus, and Raj Heda. *Fundamentals of Agile Project Management: an Overview.* New York: ASME Press, 2010.

Takeuchi, Hirotaka, and Ikujiro Nonaka. " The New New Product Development Game." *Harvard Business Review,* January-February 1986.137-146.

Highsmith, James A. *Adaptive Software Development: a Collaborative Approach to Managing Complex Systems.* New York: Dorset House Publishing, 2000.

Highsmith, Jim. *Agile Project Management Creating Innovative Products.* Upper Saddle River, NJ: Addison-Wesley, 2009.

Highsmith, Jim. "History: The Agile Manifesto." Manifesto for Agile Software Development. 2001. Available from http://agilemanifesto.org/history.html.

Martin, Robert C. *Agile Software Development: Principles, Patterns, and Practices.* Upper Saddle River, NJ: Prentice Hall, 2003.

"Nebulon—Articles." Nebulon Pty. Ltd. Available from http://www.nebulon.com/articles/index.html.

Schwaber, Ken. *Agile Project Management with Scrum.* Redmond, WA: Microsoft Press, 2004.

Sharp, Helen, and Hugh Robinson. "Three C's of Agile Practice: Collaboration, Co-ordination and Communication." In *Agile Software Development: Current Research and Future Directions*, edited by Torgeir Dingsøyr, Tore Dybå, and Nils Brede Moe. Berlin: Springer, 2010.

Shore, James, and Shane Warden. *The Art of Agile Development.* Beijing: O'Reilly Media, 2008.

Sliger, Michele, and Stacia Broderick. *The Software Project Manager's Bridge to Agility.* Upper Saddle River, NJ: Addison-Wesley, 2008.

AIDS TESTING, TREATMENT, AND SERVICES

———————■———————

SIC CODE(S)

8099

8011

8049

8062

INDUSTRY SNAPSHOT

Hampered for years by political complacency and social bigotry, AIDS testing, treatment, and services have blossomed into enormous industries scrambling to deal with the disease on a variety of levels, including research into a vaccine; development of drugs to combat symptoms; improvement of quality of life; faster, safer, less intrusive, and more accurate screenings; information resources for researchers, patients, and the public; and support centers for patients and their families.

According to statistics released in November 2009 by the Joint United Nations Programme (UNAIDS) on HIV/AIDS, an estimated 33.4 million people worldwide were living with HIV at the end of 2008, with women accounting for 50 percent of those affected. Unfortunately, persons newly infected with AIDS in 2008 (2.7 million) exceeded the number of AIDS-related deaths that year (2 million). More than 25 million people have died of AIDS since 1981.

Aside from the continuing scientific hurdles to developing more effective treatments, the central problems facing the industry are the economic and social dynamics of delivering care. Worldwide, only a small fraction of those who could benefit from human immunodeficiency virus or HIV-related services ever receives testing or treatment. According to UNAIDS, less than half of the estimated 9.5 million people in developing and transitional countries who are in immediate need of life-saving AIDS medicine are receiving help. Things are even worse on the prevention front: less than one in five at-risk individuals has access to prevention services, and testing is available to one in eight people.

Due to both the social stigma and uneven access to medical care, conventional wisdom holds that in the United States at any time, 50 percent of the HIV-infected population remains undiagnosed, risking potentially more severe symptoms for the carriers of the virus along with the attending danger of passing it to others. Infection rates are vastly higher abroad, particularly in sub-Saharan Africa, but new options for confidential testing and home-based sampling have shown some promising gains in earlier diagnosis and treatment of HIV/AIDS-related disease.

Once considered a life-threatening disease, likely fatal if not treated early, HIV/AIDS-related illness is now classified as a persistent condition that necessitates efficient disease management. According to Global Industry Analysts Inc., the optimistic upturn in prognosis has encouraged persons to increasingly adopt HIV testing procedures, resulting in a burgeoning testing and monitoring market expected to reach $3.9 billion by 2015.

ORGANIZATION AND STRUCTURE

Acquired Immune Deficiency Syndrome (AIDS) is the name given to the third stage of HIV infection in which the body's immune system has declined to the extent that complications develop, including unusual infections or

Percentage of U.S. Adults, Ages 18–64, Who Report Having Been Tested for HIV, by Race/Ethnicity, 2009

Total	53 percent of population
White	48 percent of White population
African American	73 percent of African American population
Latino	60 percent of Latino population

SOURCE: Kaiser Family Foundation, "HIV Testing in the United States." *HIV/AIDS POLICY*, June 2010.

cancers, severe weight loss, and mental deterioration (dementia). AIDS, caused by the human immunodeficiency virus (HIV), is often fatal, although thanks to rapidly developing drug treatments, patients are increasingly able to live healthy lives for well over a decade after contracting HIV.

HIV is a retrovirus that infects humans through its contact with tissues of the vaginal or anal linings, the mouth, eyes, or a break in the skin. HIV infection progresses slowly and the virus remains in the body during all three stages of the disease. The first stage, or primary infection stage, occurs within weeks of exposure to the virus, often appearing to be an illness such as the flu or mononucleosis with recovery in a few weeks. The second stage is a long period of infection without symptoms that lasts an average of 8 to 10 years. The third or symptomatic infection stage is known as AIDS.

There are four primary ways in which a person can become infected with HIV: through unprotected sexual contact with an infected partner; by sharing intravenous needles with an infected person; in the pre-natal stage from an infected mother; or by receiving infected blood through a transfusion. Especially in the United States and other industrialized nations, this last avenue of infection is now quite rare thanks to blood screening and related efforts. New treatments for protecting newborns from contracting the virus from their mothers have also reduced the incidence of prenatal transmission of the disease.

The United States's general AIDS policy is formulated through the Presidential Commission on AIDS, established under the administration of President Ronald Reagan in 1987. The commission has been a source of controversy since its inception. High profile members, such as basketball great Magic Johnson, have resigned from the commission, complaining the body was not serious about addressing all AIDS-related issues, including directing enough funding to research and development. During the early years of the disease's appearance on the national scene, both the Reagan and the George H.W. Bush administrations were roundly criticized for

what critics saw as a halfhearted commitment to finding a cure for AIDS.

Several elements of AIDS-related industries are more visible than others. Possibly the most visible of these are pharmaceutical companies. Research and development is the hub of the AIDS industry and accounts for the most spending, directed both at pure research into the disease's mechanics, as well as at shorter-term approaches to manage its symptoms.

A second major arm of the AIDS-related industries is not business but government agencies. In the United States, much of the focus of AIDS policy, as well as the source of research funding, has rested with two agencies, the National Institutes of Health (NIH) and the CDC. These agencies are part of the U.S. Department of Health and Human Services, which contributes to the underwriting of research at drug companies and at educational institutions throughout the country. NIH is the principal biomedical research arm of the federal government. The CDC, part of the U.S. Public Health Service's efforts to control infectious diseases, works with state health officials and is a repository of statistical information about AIDS and other diseases.

The third major segment of the AIDS-related industries involves the private and quasi-private, locally funded, and foundation-based enterprises classified as AIDS service organizations (ASOs). Some of the largest ASOs generate and distribute millions of dollars for research and education and prevention efforts. Smaller ASOs may be involved in work at the community level, such as distributing condoms or helping individuals find medical testing or housing. Although dwarfed by government agencies and the large pharmaceutical companies, ASOs generate funds used in research, provide direct services, and are beneficiaries of funding from government sources. Related businesses, such as condom manufacturers, medical supply companies, health food stores, and home healthcare aides, are also affected by AIDS, but do not generally break down the impact the disease has on their financial operations.

The CDC issues a handbook each year listing national organizations providing HIV and AIDS services. Virtually all of these are either governmental or nonprofit. Some are funded by significant private donors such as the Rockefeller Archive Center. Others are funded by religious organizations, such as the Presbyterian AIDS Network. Many are community-based, such as the Gay Men's Health Crisis Center in New York, the San Francisco AIDS Foundation, two of the largest, and the Madison, Wisconsin-AIDS Network. Although it is entirely inaccurate to characterize AIDS as only a homosexual disease, many ASOs are based in communities where substantial gay populations are located. The National Prevention

Information Network (formerly the National AIDS Clearinghouse) has reported more than 19,000 ASOs, many of which cropped up in the years 1982 to 1986, when the general public's awareness of AIDS also increased. Such organizations, however, have been subject to criticism as well. Some critics have suggested that the proliferation of AIDS-related organizations has a tendency to divert money from services and research into salaries and organization-based expenses.

Federal funds directed toward AIDS research, treatment, prevention, and education (other major elements of the AIDS industry) are the result of passage by the U.S. Congress of the Ryan White Act of 1990. Named for a teenager from Indiana who died as a result of receiving an HIV-contaminated blood transfusion, the act authorized $4.5 billion in federal spending for five years (from 1991 through 1996). Although the funding was authorized, the appropriation did not begin until 1994. The vast majority of the funding was directed toward research and development and treatment, although a portion was also directed toward education programs in schools and prisons and toward minorities.

Since that time, AIDS organizations have continued their private fundraising and continued to pressure the federal government to budget additional money to eradicate AIDS. In November 1999, however, the Ryan White Foundation was forced to close its doors due to lack of funding. Meanwhile, the Ryan White Act was due to expire in September 2000, leading to waves of outcry from interest groups and spurring movement in Congress to initiate legislation to extend the act and provide new money to the foundation. In October 2000 Congress easily passed legislation reauthorizing the act for five years, during which time Congress appropriated $1 billion annually for prevention and treatment programs. It has been funded annually since.

Insurance companies also comprise a major part of the AIDS-related industry. Although initial reports of HIV and AIDS generated considerable confusion and concern over possible impacts on the insurance industry, those impacts have not materialized. It was presumed that insurers would take a financial hit as the number of HIV-infected individuals and persons with AIDS grew. *Life Association News,* however, reported that AIDS has not had a significant negative impact on the insurance business. The debate is less over how much of the cost of HIV/AIDS treatments is covered (although that is a concern given the high cost of medications and care) than over what some have called the "buying off" of persons with AIDS.

This area, where insurance companies have found themselves in an unwanted spotlight, involves something called viaticals. The word is from the Latin *viaticum,* which refers either to the rites administered to dying persons in the Roman Catholic Church or to the provisions for a journey. It has come to mean a new growth segment of the AIDS-related insurance industry. A small number of companies—usually not an individual's life insurer—have entered into Living Benefits arrangements with AIDS patients. These individuals tend to be unable to find employment and may have to rely on assistance programs, such as Social Security disability payments or public relief payments. The viatical companies agree to "buy" the life insurance policy of an AIDS sufferer for between 50 and 80 percent of its face value. The policyholder gets access to needed money, and the viatical company collects on the life insurance policy when the individual with AIDS dies.

This approach has both supporters and detractors. Although someone with AIDS may not be able to work (either because of health considerations or because of de facto job discrimination), living expenses continue. Added to daily living costs are increasing costs for medicines and health-related services. Additionally, the ability to pay off student loans, make automobile payments, or be responsible for any kind of debt means the cost of having AIDS quickly mounts. The viatical approach has been viewed as a way for needed funding to get into the hands of those suffering from AIDS at a time when they really need the money—while they are still alive. The viatical insurance industry was generating an estimated $300 million in annual receipts in the mid-1990s. By 2000, however, the industry had decidedly slacked off, not only because of the increased life span of AIDS patients due to medical advances but also because of negative media attention directed at the industry.

Another element in the AIDS-related industry is equipment, ranging from extremely expensive machines used in the treatment of blood and blood-related products to disposable plastic gloves and condoms. Prior to the 1980s, condoms were rarely seen in public and were not widely marketed. With the onset of AIDS and public education campaigns, including announcements by then Surgeon General C. Everett Koop suggesting condom use was one way to minimize exposure to HIV, condoms became a product for mass marketing. With considerable fanfare (and inevitable controversy), condoms were advertised on television, with their regular use endorsed by sex therapist Dr. Ruth Westheimer. After basketball star Magic Johnson's November 1991 announcement that he was HIV-positive, stock in condom companies soared. Today, condoms are widely publicized and readily available.

There have been other, sometimes questionable, products and services resulting from AIDS. Author Elinor Burkett, who coined the phrase "AIDS Industrial

Complex" in her book *The Gravest Show on Earth,* listed a wide array of activities ranging from well-meaning failures to tasteless exploitation to outright scams. Some health food stores claimed certain vitamins could cure AIDS, and a Texas company peddled what it also claimed was an AIDS cure. There was an advertisement in a national magazine for Lasting Impression cards (sold for $19.95) for terminally ill patients to send to loved ones, and a $15.00 red rhinestone version of the AIDS ribbon often seen at entertainment events.

Virtually all branches of AIDS-related industries have come under criticism at one time or another for their failure to eradicate AIDS. Stories about advances seem to be balanced by stories of failures and rising death rates. Therefore it is unclear whether anything short of total eradication of HIV and AIDS would satisfy critics.

BACKGROUND AND DEVELOPMENT

The study of the origin of AIDS has been rather contentious. Although scientists have generally come to accept the theory that the disease has its origins in Africa, the precise timing and method of transmission to humans is still up in the air. While an examination of medical records suggests that people may have died of AIDS-like diseases throughout history, awareness of AIDS as an identifiable condition was first observed in the late 1970s. At that time, there were large population shifts in countries such as Zaire with thousands of rural dwellers moving to the cities, resulting in increased overcrowding and increased prostitution, which led to the spread of the disease. There had been plagues earlier in history, such as the Black Death that ravaged Europe in the Middle Ages and the worldwide influenza epidemic of 1918 to 1920 that killed more people than had died in World War I, but the causes of those plagues had long before been identified. That is not yet the case with AIDS.

Initially, it was believed this disease was spread only by inoculation, that the virus must somehow be injected into an individual's bloodstream. That thinking made intravenous drug users, who often shared needles, prime candidates for the syndrome. However, in 1981 physicians in New York and San Francisco began noticing a high death rate among gay males from such opportunistic diseases as Kaposi's sarcoma, a form of cancer thought to be isolated in Africa. Medical personnel also noticed that individuals who had exceptionally low T cell counts were virtually unable to fight off even simple infections. Initially, causes of death among this group of people were attributed to the infections. After these findings were revealed, other physicians reported that they had run into similar cases over the previous few years but these cases went unexplained.

AIDS was formally identified as a syndrome (or a series of diseases, opportunistic infections, and conditions) in 1981. It was believed that AIDS originated in Africa as a result of human-animal sexual activity and/or bites from infected animals, then spread to Western countries primarily through homosexual activity. By the late 1990s the debate heated up considerably. British journalist Edward Hopper revealed his findings suggesting that AIDS was born of early polio vaccine experiments in Africa in the 1950s that utilized infected chimpanzee cells. These findings were based on admittedly circumstantial evidence of the coincidence of the earliest AIDS cases and vaccine testing. The vaccine researchers vigorously denied using chimpanzee cells at all. Shortly thereafter, Los Alamos National Laboratory scientist Bette Korber reported that in light of her recent findings, Hopper's theory was highly unlikely, given that Korber traced the virus back to sometime between 1915 and 1941. The theory most widely accepted by scientists holds that the virus was transmitted via the hunting and butchering of chimpanzees infected with simian immunodeficiency virus (SIV, closely linked genetically with HIV), although direct connections between SIV and the dominant strains of HIV are still lacking.

In 1983 scientists identified HIV as the probable cause of AIDS, setting the stage for most subsequent research. Initially thought to be a gay male's or drug user's disease, AIDS deaths began to multiply among persons young and old who received blood transfusions from HIV-positive individuals, as well as those who engaged only in heterosexual practices. By the late 1980s AIDS was everyone's concern.

AIDS quickly became a sensitive political and social issue. President Ronald Reagan's administration was viewed as largely unresponsive to AIDS, prompting considerable protest and rhetoric. While President George H. W. Bush gave more attention to the problem, AIDS surfaced as a campaign issue in 1992, when Bush was challenged for the presidency by Arkansas Governor Bill Clinton. During Clinton's two terms as president, he greatly expanded the government's role in research, treatment, education, and prevention, with a substantial amount of money and effort still devoted to educating people about how AIDS is contracted and what should be done to minimize exposure to the disease. During this same period, the American Red Cross took extraordinary precautions to prevent the spread of AIDS through the blood supply.

In the mid-1990s there was an increase in AIDS-related lawsuits. One of the more significant lawsuits pitted Jackson National Life against Mrs. Frank Deramus, whose husband had died of AIDS. Mrs. Deramus sued the insurance company for not informing her husband that he had AIDS. A court ruled that insurers had no responsibility to notify those they insured of medical information to which the companies had access. Another significant set of cases involved a Japanese government AIDS researcher, Takeshi Abe, who in 1983 received donations from five different blood product manufacturers who were accused of having sold HIV-tainted products. Similar cases involving HIV-tainted blood were settled in Canada and France.

AZT, also known as azido-deoxythymidine, as zidovudine (ZDV), or by its trademarked name Ritrovir, was the first and probably the best known of the battery of drugs used to keep AIDS at bay. AZT combats the AIDS virus by interrupting its early stages of development.

Dramatic advances in AIDS treatments took place in the late 1990s with the development of new fusion inhibitors. In 1997 antiviral protease inhibitors were among the most promising of the new drugs in the expanding HIV/AIDS arsenal. These drugs interrupt the way HIV uses a healthy cell to make more viruses. In April 1999 the U.S. Food and Drug Administration (FDA) approved Agenerase, generically known as amprenavir, which remains one of the staples in its class of drugs.

The drug cocktail (drugs taken in combination) appears to be capable of eliminating nearly all detectable levels of HIV in the body tissues where the virus is known to reside, although traces still appear under intense magnification. Previous studies have shown that these drugs can reduce the level of HIV in the bloodstream, but the virus is known to hide in the tonsils, lymph nodes, spinal fluid, and semen. Canadian scientists have found that drug cocktails have been most effective with individuals who have not been ill with HIV for a long time. Unfortunately, while these protease inhibitors are highly effective in prolonging patients' lives when mixed in drug cocktails, the patients' HIV levels return to their high levels when the treatment is discontinued. Thus, the treatment curtails but does not destroy the virus.

One set of cocktail drugs is produced by GlaxoSmithKline and Abbott Laboratories and utilizes the drugs AZT, the first 3TC, and Norvir. A separate study found that the combination of AZT, 3TC, and Viramune (manufactured by Boehringer Ingelheim) had a similar effect. This approach, known as HIV therapeutics, was welcomed at the twelfth International Conference on AIDS held June 28 through July 3, 1998, in Geneva, Switzerland, and it generated optimism within the research community.

Although the use of drug cocktails in combination with other anti-HIV treatments is becoming the standard of care, it has not yet been determined which of the anti-HIV drug combinations is the most effective and consistent. What is clear is that the stronger the anti-HIV effects of a drug combination, the less likely it is that HIV will become resistant to the effects of the drugs. This will keep the world's drug manufacturers involved in research for the near future.

The cost of AIDS-related treatments was one of the industry's thorniest issues during the early 2000s, particularly in international markets, where companies have been accused of putting profits ahead of humanitarian interests. To diffuse mounting tension with governments and healthcare providers in a number of developing countries, leading pharmaceutical companies began offering their products near or at cost in certain areas. According to the international relief agency Doctors Without Borders, drug prices fall sharply as generic competitors enter the market. Such shifts can drastically alter the economics and logistics of providing treatment. In one example tracked by Doctors Without Borders and highlighted by President George W. Bush in his 2003 State of the Union address, the yearly cost per patient of a commonly used anti-retroviral (ARV) triplet of drugs dropped from $12,000 in 2000 to just $201 by 2003.

A like-minded effort to stabilize pricing of AIDS laboratory tests was announced in 2004 by former U.S. President Bill Clinton and five major industry players. Under a plan brokered through the Clinton Foundation HIV/AIDS Initiative, which had previously negotiated several drug price reductions, costs for essential tests to diagnose and monitor HIV were expected to decrease by as much as 80 percent in hard-hit regions such as Africa and the Caribbean. Participating firms, including Bayer Diagnostics, Beckman Coulter, Becton Dickinson, BioMericux, and Roche Diagnostics, planned to donate sophisticated equipment in addition to lowering their ongoing processing fees.

Because drug cocktails, or combinations of drugs, have regularly been shown to be helpful for controlling AIDS-related illnesses, some analysts believe a growing market will be found for combination pills such as GlaxoSmithKline's Combivir, a duet of AZT and 3TC offered as one pill. That product alone has reaped sales upward of $900 million a year, making it one of the multinational pharmaceutical giant's top 10 drugs and the world's best-selling AIDS medication. One analyst believed such combinations could account for as much as one-third of all AIDS-related drug sales by 2010.

A variety of drugs and treatments has proven successful in treating those infected from birth. Some of the oldest HIV-infected individuals in this category who were living in the first decade of the 2000s were nearly 20 years old, significantly older than doctors had predicted was possible. In the first decade of the 2000s, the National Institute of Allergy and Infectious Diseases in Uganda discovered that giving a dose of the anti-retroviral drug nevirapine to HIV-positive mothers during labor and a dose to their babies within three days of delivery cut the transmission of HIV to the babies by nearly 50 percent.

AZT, the first HIV drug to receive FDA approval, has been widely studied. Since there is no generic version of this drug, and since only one company manufactures it, GlaxoSmithKline has been in the forefront of AIDS-related industries. In July of 2002 the AIDS Healthcare Foundation filed suit against GlaxoSmithKline, alleging that the firm held no valid patent on the drug because part of its development costs were funded government grants. While a U.S. district court kept the case alive in 2003 by denying the company's motion to dismiss it, legal jousts continued into 2004 over whether the case would be heard at all. During the 1990s the U.S. Supreme Court declined to hear a similar case over AZT, effectively allowing the company to prevail.

New treatments involving anti-viral protease inhibitor drugs had mixed reviews, although the majority were positive. More alarming than mixed treatment prognoses are the financial aspects of AIDS. Many patients cannot get the costly medicines needed to keep their conditions under control because of restrictions imposed on them by their health maintenance organizations and state programs set up to assist low-income persons. The kinds of drug combinations recommended by doctors treating AIDS patients generally cost about $12,000 per year, a cost likely to remain prohibitive for as long as the individual is being treated for AIDS.

Since the introduction of the protease inhibitors around 1995, HIV/AIDS patients no longer have to endure long and painful stays in hospitals and are generally much more able to lead healthy lives. However, such patients are required to be meticulous about their daily medication, keeping to strict time and dosage regimens and continuously monitoring side effects. In 2003 Bristol-Myers Squibb received FDA approval for Atazanavir, a protease inhibitor that AIDS patients can take just once a day. The new drug also caused fewer cholesterol and triglyceride problems than similar treatments. However, the drug, like other anti-retroviral drugs, proved most effective as part of a combination of treatments.

According to many critics, one unfortunate side effect of improved drugs and treatments allowing for longer, healthier lives for those living with HIV and AIDS is that public visibility has diminished, and with it the sense of the disease's urgency. For instance, some surveys reported a decline in philanthropic donations to HIV/AIDS groups of 22 percent between 1997 and 2000, and "risky" behavior was generally viewed as on the upswing as the disease came to be conceptualized increasingly as a chronic condition, in the manner of diabetes, rather than as a fatal infection.

Most vaccination programs have focused on mimicking an infection in order to stimulate the immune system in one of two ways. First, the body's immune system can be taught to recognize an HIV invasion by injecting a protein that surrounds the HIV virus into the bloodstream, thereby causing the system to shoot antibodies at the intruder in attempts to neutralize it. While such experiments traditionally found that the stimulated antibodies were still far too weak to properly combat the virus, improved technologies have continued to maintain this technique as a viable option for vaccine development. The other route is to mimic an actual infection in order to prompt the body's T cells into action. In this case, a few HIV genes are injected, causing cells to create HIV proteins, thereby telling the body's T cells to carry out a seek-and-destroy mission. Recent years have witnessed the proliferation of such experiments whereby genetically engineered HIV proteins are injected on the backs of previously successful vaccine carriers, such as those for smallpox.

These methods, however, fail to focus the immune system's full attention on its target because the system will instinctively respond to the proteins from the carrier as well. For this reason, scientists have begun to utilize genetic engineering technology to introduce vaccines carrying DNA that interact with cells to produce HIV proteins. In the meantime, genetic manipulation has been successful in making the HIV genes more similar to human genes, thereby producing greater levels of HIV proteins and, as a result, greater T cell response.

One of the most advanced vaccination programs has been that developed by Dr. Donald P. Francis at VaxGen, Inc of Brisbane, California. After beginning human test trials in 1998, Francis oversaw the initial advanced-stage trial of a potential HIV vaccine called AIDSVAX in late 1999. The vaccine was administered to more than 8,000 patients in the United States and Thailand, endorsed by the UNAIDS. Most viewed the Phase III trial, which was conducted throughout 2002, as a crucial test to determine whether a viable vaccine was in sight. This was, in fact, the first AIDS vaccine to move into Phase III trials, the stage when a vaccine's effectiveness at preventing infectious disease is determined. When the results were released in 2003, the vaccine appeared to offer increased protection against infection among black and Asian subjects but fell far short of the FDA threshold of 30 percent effectiveness in the full panel of patients studied. The company was regrouping for further research into why the treatment appeared to work for some people but not others.

In 2001 Merck & Co. announced the results of AIDS vaccine studies that 30 of its scientists had conducted with monkeys. Merck scientists discovered that although vaccinated monkeys became infected when injected with the HIV virus, they remained healthy, unlike their unvaccinated counterparts. Merck scientists attributed the success of the vaccinated monkeys to increased production of T cells by their immune systems. One of the resulting vaccine candidates, known as the HIV-1 gag replication-defective adenovirus, began early human trials in certain countries in 2004. Administered to healthy subjects, the vaccine introduced a genetically engineered inert virus, rather than a live HIV variant, into the body in order to trigger the immune system. The trials were stopped when it was discovered that more subjects receiving the vaccine (24 of 741) were actually becoming infected than those who were receiving the placebo (21 of 762) were actually becoming infected.

In August 2006 scientists involved in the Antiretroviral Therapy Cohort Collaboration published the results of research involving 22,000 HIV positive individuals in North America who started drug treatment between 1995 and 2003. Despite previous fears that patients would develop a resistance to drug treatments, the research indicated that after 10 years of availability, this had not emerged as a problem. Combination drug "cocktails" remained effective at slowing the progression from HIV to AIDS and reducing mortality by 80 to 90 percent. The most pressing concern was that patients were not starting treatments soon enough, and that tuberculosis (TB) was becoming a more prominent infection among those with AIDS.

A major breakthrough came in 2006, when the FDA approved the very first once-a-day pill for AIDS. The new pill, named Atripla, was formed when competitors Gilead and Bristol-Myers Squibb partnered to develop a preparation that combined their separate drugs (Gilead's Emtriva and Viread and Bristol-Myers Squibb's Sustiva), which an estimated 20 percent of patients commonly mix together as part of their treatment regimens. The new combination pill was not expected to cost more than the sum of the three drugs purchased separately.

Unlike the 1990s, when patients had to take as many as 30 pills per day, by the early 2000s some patients could get by with six pills. However, remembering to take them was a problem for many. A report in the July 13, 2006, *Baltimore Sun* estimated that patients follow their treatment schedules as directed only 80 to 90 percent of the time. This was a concern because it increased the risk that the disease could form a resistance to the drugs. For this reason, FDA Commissioner Dr. Andrew C. von Eschenbach described the new pill as a "landmark" that was expected to "fundamentally change" HIV and AIDS treatment.

In the early 2000s, a number of new developments were on the horizon. In China, Tianjin Biochip Corp.

was developing a new biochip that was able to identify drug-resistant strains of AIDS. OraSure Technologies, which developed an oral swab test that hospitals and clinics could use to detect HIV, received FDA approval in 2004. Existing tests had required consumers to send a blood sample to a lab for analysis. HIV self-test kits were available for purchase on the Internet by 2007; however, regulators were concerned about improper use that could potentially generate a false positive and that some users might commit suicide following the test. As of 2008 self-test kits had not received FDA approval.

CURRENT CONDITIONS

In June 2010 the U.S. government's Centers for Disease Control and Prevention (CDC) released statistics indicating that in 2008 (the latest available collective data), an estimated 37,991 persons in the United States were newly-diagnosed with AIDS. One in five remained undiagnosed. Nearly 1.08 million people in the United States had been diagnosed with HIV/AIDS-related conditions since the beginning of the epidemic in the early 1980s. More than half of new infections occurred in gay and bisexual men, and Black/African-American persons were seven times more likely to be infected than whites. States reporting the highest number of AIDS diagnoses were California, Florida, and New York.

The first-ever coordinated strategy to address AIDs in its 30 years of known existence was announced by President Barack Obama in July 2010, directed, by memorandum, toward the heads of executive departments and agencies within the government. Obama outlined three goals encompassing the strategy: better prevention, better treatments, and "reducing health disparities" among those living with HIV/AIDS. He further reiterated the obligations of the federal government to "transcend barriers of race or station or sexual orientation or faith or nationality" in developing programs geared toward HIV/AIDS issues.

The memorandum designated six "lead agencies" to implement the strategy in conjunction with Obama's new healthcare reform programs. Under the new directive, the heads of the Departments of Health and Human Services, Justice, Labor, Housing and Urban Development, Veterans Affairs, and the Social Security Administration must submit reports detailing their respective agencies' plans for implementing the strategy to the Office of National AIDS Policy (ONAP) and the Office of Management and Budget (OMB) within the subsequent 150 days. Additionally, the chair of the Equal Employment Opportunity Commission (EEOC) must submit recommendations "for increasing employment opportunities for people living with HIV," as well as "a plan for addressing employment-related discrimination against people with HIV."

Putting action behind words, in September 2010 Health and Human Services Secretary Kathleen Sebelius announced two grants totaling $3.5 million to reach beyond the Ryan White Program. A three-year, $2.975 million grant went to HealthHIV in Washington, DC, to improve community health centers providing care and treatment services for minority patients impacted by AIDS. Another $550,000 went to Howard University for a three-year grant to establish an AIDS Education and Training Center (AETC) multicultural center, aimed at providing training and technical assistance to healthcare professionals and facilities serving the needs of people living with AIDS.

As of 2010, the available clinical tests used to diagnose HIV infection in the United States included conventional blood tests (with results available within hours in larger metropolitan areas); conventional oral fluid tests (OraSure being the only FDA-approved HIV oral fluid test at that time), with results taking several days; and a newer series of tests called "rapid tests." Rapid tests involve samples (usually blood or plasma) collected by healthcare providers, with results in as little as 10 minutes. However, positive results require additional testing for specific confirmation. As of 2010 there were six FDA-approved rapid tests: OraQuick Advance Rapid HIV-1/2 Antibody Test (sampling whole blood, plasma, or oral fluid); Reveal Rapid HIV-1 Antibody Test (using serum or plasma); Uni-Gold Recombigen HIV Test (blood, serum, plasma); Multispot HIV-1/HIV-2 Rapid Test (serum, plasma); and two Clearview tests (using blood, serum, or plasma). Calypte was the only approved HIV urine test, requiring up to two weeks for results.

As for the privacy and confidentiality of home testing kits, as of 2010 only one product classified as a home testing kit for the HIV/AIDS virus was approved by the FDA. Marketed as either The Home Access HIV-1 Test System or The Home Access Express HIV-1 Test System, the kit required users to collect blood samples and mail them to a laboratory for professional testing and analysis. A personal PIN was assigned to the sample, affording privacy and confidentiality, and the same PIN was used to access results. No test kits allowed consumers to self-diagnose or interpret results at home.

INDUSTRY LEADERS

A major participant in the industry is Abbott Laboratories, also a diversified drug maker. Abbott's Kaletra protease inhibitor was approved by the FDA in 2000. The company caused a stir at the end of 2003 when it raised the price of another protease inhibitor, Norvir, by some 400 percent to cover the firm's mounting development costs. The price jump prompted a hearing at the NIH over whether to allow other companies to produce generic equivalents because some of Abbott's research was funded by government grants. Abbott continued to market both Kaletra and Norvir in 2008. The company had 65,000 employees and more than $22 billion in sales for 2009.

OraSure Technologies was the emerging leader in rapid AIDS testing techniques. The company was created by the 2000 merger between STC Technologies Inc. and Epitope Inc. It pioneered OraQuick HIV screenings using only a drop of blood from a pin prick, rather than a whole vial required for conventional tests. Results could be ready in 20 minutes. The firm then developed the means to test for HIV using oral fluid, a process the company views as safer and easier to administer because it eliminates the use of needles and requires less training for healthcare workers. In 2010 OraSure became the first company to have a FDA-approved noninvasive oral test for HIV, marketed as the OraQuick-HIV test, which it hoped to market as over-the-counter. As of 2010 the company had 285 employees in three locations, and projected the U.S. market for its over-the-counter HIV test kits to exceed $500 million.

Calypte Biomedical Corporation is a smaller, rising competitor in the testing sector. The company markets a series of urine- and saliva-based tests that are less invasive than conventional blood-based methods, and as of 2010, had the only approved HIV urine test.

As of 2010 other key players in the industry included Adaltis Inc., Siemens Healthcare Diagnostics Inc., Bio-Rad Laboratories Inc., Gen-Probe Inc., the Celera Group, Medical Services International Inc., and Roche Diagnostics.

WORKFORCE

The front-line workers in the AIDS battle are clinical physicians, related clinic and hospital-based professionals, and home healthcare workers. Also part of the army of AIDS industry workers are the research scientists, pharmacists, related direct care providers, and the educators, outreach workers, and fundraisers who help keep the issue of AIDS in the public consciousness.

Biomedical researchers are the behind-the-scenes workers who rarely come into direct contact with AIDS patients. Many of them work for the NIH, the FDA, and the CDC. A substantial number of university-based researchers and individuals working for private pharmaceutical manufacturers also contribute to the $12 billion research industry.

A number of other occupations are also a part of AIDS-related industries. Particularly significant are manufacturing jobs, including those involved in the production of treatment equipment and items for prevention such as condoms and latex gloves. Except for doctors and other healthcare workers treating AIDS patients, very few persons in the AIDS industry run any risk of infection through their jobs.

Initially, there was dramatic fear that HIV and AIDS could be spread through casual contact with an infected individual. A number of medical workers became infected as a result of being stabbed by instruments that had touched virus-infected blood. While there are still some personnel who refuse to provide treatment to or come in contact with an HIV-positive, AIDS-infected individual—something the American Medical Association has condemned as a violation of its code of ethics—precautions in all areas of medical practice have improved to the point where the risk of accidental infection is almost nil.

AMERICA AND THE WORLD

By all measures, AIDS poses its greatest challenges outside the United States, particularly in sub-Saharan Africa. As of 2009, Africa, China, and India accounted for roughly 90 percent of the world HIV population, creating enormous potential for the marketing and use of HIV/AIDS testing and monitoring products. At that time, the United States and Europe accounted for more than 60 percent share of the global HIV/AIDS testing products market.

The number of people dying of AIDS worldwide declined slightly in 2009, but was still staggering at roughly 2 million persons. Africa alone had more than 14 million AIDS orphans by 2009, and an estimated 280,000 children died of AIDS in the preceding 12 months, while another 430,000 were infected.

At the biannual International AIDS Conference held in Vienna in July 2010, the HIV Vaccines and Microbicides Resource Tracking Working Group released its report that indicated global investment in HIV prevention research was level at approximately $1.17 billion for 2009 (it had actually declined 10 percent in 2008). The group warned that flat funding may limit the ability of researchers to quickly move promising new approaches forward. A large chunk of research funding continued to be supplied by philanthropist Bill Gates through his ongoing Bill and Melinda Gates Foundation.

RESEARCH AND TECHNOLOGY

In 2010, the FDA approved the first HIV diagnostic test that detected both antigens and antibodies for associated AIDS viruses. Antigens are components of the virus that trigger the production of antibodies. Testing for antigens allows for earlier detection of HIV, although there is still a short period of time after initial infection during which no available test can detect the virus. Referred to as the first "fourth-generation" test in the United States, these modern tests combine P24 antigen tests with standard antibody tests to reduce the "diagnostic window."

The biannual International AIDS Conference was held in Vienna in July 2010, and lauded scientific advancements in two key areas: vaccines and a HIV microbicide gel. In a U.S.-Thai joint trial effort conducted in Thailand that ended in 2009, an experimental AIDS vaccine proved 30 percent effective at protecting against HIV, but was not successful enough to advance to the next level of licensure. However, it did demonstrate that an effective AIDS vaccine could be made. Concurrently, U.S. researchers were able to identify, from the blood of infected individuals, a number of potent HIV antibodies that can neutralize many of the variants of HIV by attaching to the virus. Using these new clues and information, researchers were encouraged about how to design new vaccine candidates to elicit antibodies that would protect against the many different HIV varieties circulating worldwide.

Secondly, a clinical trial in South Africa used a vaginal gel (CAPRISA 004) containing experimental antiretroviral drugs, called microbicides, that resulted in a 39 percent effective rate in reducing HIV infection in women. According to the International AIDS Vaccine Initiative (IAVI), women accounted for half of all HIV infections globally and 60 percent of all persons living with HIV in Africa.

What may be the most welcome news to drug companies and AIDS researchers was a finding by Dr. Beryl Koblin and colleagues of the New York Blood Center that a 77 percent of individuals who are considered at high risk of HIV infection say they are willing to participate in HIV vaccine trials. The study included responses from homosexual men, intravenous drug users, and women at risk of HIV infection from heterosexual sex. An HIV vaccine, as well as a "day after" pill or medicine, remains the goal of researchers grappling with this frustrating disease.

BIBLIOGRAPHY

"Advances on HIV Prevention Tools Heralded at Conference." New York: International AIDS Vaccine Initiative Inc., 22 July 2010. Available from http://www.iavi.org/news-center/Pages/PressRelease.aspx?pubID=3181.

"AIDS Drugs Still Effective 10 Years On." *PAC-Pacific Islands Broadcasting Association,* 4 August 2006.

Anstett, Patricia. "25 Years of AIDS: Epidemic Scorns the Impact of Progress." *Detroit Free Press,* 4 June 2006.

"Biochip Which Identifies Drug Resistant AIDS Strains Could Hit Market Next Year." *China Business News,* 11 April 2006.

Centers for Disease Control and Prevention. "HIV/AIDS in the United States," March 2008. Available from www.cdc.gov/hiv/resources/factsheets/us.htm.

———. "HIV Surveillance Report, Volume 20," June 2010. Available from www.cdc.gov/hiv/surveillance/resources/reports/2008report/index.htm.

"Gates Commits 287 Million Dollars to AIDS Vaccine Research." *Xinhua News Agency,* 20 July 2006.

"Global HIV/AIDS Estimates, End of 2008." AVERT, 2009. Available from http://avert.org/worldstats/htm.

"HIV Blocking Gene Found." *Medical Laboratory Observer,* April 2008.

"HIV Fighters Gain Speed." *Wall Street Journal,* 30 August 2010.

"HIV/AIDS Policy Fact Sheet." The Henry J. Kaiser Family Foundation, June 2010. Available from http://www.kff.org.

"HIV/AIDS Testing Market to Exceed $3.9 Billion by 2015." *PR Newswire,* 23 October 2008.

Johnson, Steve. "Making Medicines Simpler: New AIDS Pill Combines Three Medicines." *San Jose Mercury News,* 23 May 2006.

Joint United Nations Programme on HIV/AIDS. "AIDS Epidemic Update," December 2007. Available from www.unaids.org.

———. "Fact Sheet: North America and Western and Central Europe," 24 November 2009. Available from http://dataunaids.org/pub/FactSheet/2009/20091124_FS_nacce_en.pdf.

———. "Global HIV Prevalence Has Leveled Off: AIDS Is Among the Leading Causes of Death Globally and Remains the Primary Cause of Death in Africa." 20 November 2007. Available from http://www.unaids.org.

McCarty, Mark. "Experts Say HIV/AIDS Vaccine Essential to Contain the Disease." *Medical Device Week,* 24 July 2007.

"Microbicide Design for AIDS Prevention." *USA Today,* February 2008.

"OraSure Changes the Landscape of the Diagnostic Medical Testing Market." Ben Franklin Technology Partners of Northeastern Pennsylvania, 29 January 2010. Available from http://nep.benfranklin.org.

"OraSure Technologies—OraSure in the News." OraSure Technologies Inc., 25 March 2010. Available from http://www.orasure.com/news-events/news-events-orasure-news.asp.

Osnos, Evan. "AIDS Winding its Way Through China." *Chicago Tribune,* 3 February 2006.

Rockoff, Jonathan D. "A Once-Daily Pill Becomes Option for HIV/AIDS Patients: FDA Approves Combination Drug after Accelerated 3-Month Review." *Baltimore Sun,* 13 July 2006.

Ruiguang, S., et al. "Estimation of HIV Incidence in the United States." *Journal of the American Medical Association, JAMA,* 2008.

Sachs, Jessica Snyder. "Rebooting The AIDS Vaccine." *Popular Science,* January 2008.

Simons, John. "Crunch Time for an HIV Test." *Fortune,* 29 May 2006.

Test Kits: HIV, AIDS: Component Database, 20 August 2010. Available from http://www.medibix.com/CompanySearch.jsp?.

U.S. Dept. of Health and Human Services. "HHS Awards $3.5 Million to Expand HIV/AIDS Care Capacity for Minorities," March 2008. Available from http://www.hrsa.gov/about/news/pressreleases/100901hhsawards35milliontoexpandhivaidscarecapacityforminorities.html.

Wareham, Hannah Clay. "New National HIV/AIDS Strategy an Example of Homegrown Activism." *Bay Windows,* 20 July 2010.

ALTERNATIVE ADULT EDUCATION

SIC CODE(S)

8249

8299

INDUSTRY SNAPSHOT

Adult education is defined in a variety of ways. The National Center on Education Statistics adopts a broad definition and includes voluntary and required educational activities that involve the presence of (or communication with) an instructor. These encompass courses teaching English as a second language (ESL), adult basic education, General Educational Development (GED) preparation classes, adult high school, and credential programs leading to a college or university degree or a post-secondary vocational or technical diploma.

In his first year of office, U.S. President Barack Obama outlined his plan for strengthening the nation's competitiveness by reasserting prominence in educational achievement. To that end, he established a goal of increasing the number of U.S. college graduates to 55 percent by 2025. With rising fuel costs and a slowly recovering economy, alternative and distance education will play a large role in achieving that objective.

In early 2009, the U.S. Department of Education's Institute of Education Sciences released a report showing that roughly two-thirds (66 percent) of the 4,160 public institutions granting two-year and four-year college degrees offered distance education courses in the 2006-2007 school year. Distance education was defined as a formal education process in which students and instructors were not in the same place, and most involved communication through the use of video, audio, or computer technologies (via both Internet and CD-ROM). Nevertheless, college-level distance education is just one example of the burgeoning market seeking alternatives to formal classroom instruction for adult students. The industry also encompasses basic education and learning skills as well as certain enrichment classes (e.g., second languages) and specific job-related training.

However, the need for continued education permeates all learning levels. According to U.S. Department of Labor data, 90 percent of the fastest growing jobs require some form of postsecondary or specialized education, and many jobs remain unfilled for this reason. Additionally, widespread unemployment associated with the economic slowdown of 2008 and 2009 has created the need for many individuals to pursue new careers. Still yet, new advancements in technology and economic globalization have created an even broader market for flexible, alternative learning options.

The popularity and proliferation of Internet-based, online learning (e-learning) represents the dominant trend in alternative adult education. As the cost of attending traditional educational institutions continues to escalate, many employers believe that online education for their employees makes simple mathematical sense. Also, the flexibility of Internet courses, accessible at all hours, meshes with the time constraints of many already overscheduled working adults. The trend has not gone unopposed, however, particularly among some members of the higher education community. Critics have argued that online education, particularly prepackaged online courses, dilute the quality of higher education and undermine the development of critical thinking skills. Nonetheless, a 2008 report supported by the Alfred P. Sloan

Foundation found that 75 percent of more than 2,500 colleges and universities agree that expanding the geographic reach of the institutions, in the course of competing for more students, was the primary reason for entering online education.

ORGANIZATION AND STRUCTURE

In the last three decades, over 100 traditional, four-year colleges in the United States closed. During the same period, the number of for-profit colleges or universities has increased from 400 to over 1,600. Many analysts say that in the future, higher education will continue to move away from traditional liberal arts studies—which, they charge, are aimed at elites—toward more practical education that stresses skills immediately applicable in the job market. The new trends target middle class working adults over 24, who make up an increasingly large percentage of the $200 billion per year higher education market.

Vocational Education. The 1990 Perkins Act defines vocational education as "organized educational programs offering a sequence of courses which are directly related to the preparation of individuals in paid or unpaid employment in current or emerging occupations requiring other than a baccalaureate or advanced degree." Postsecondary occupational curricula typically offer programs in the following categories: agriculture; business and office; marketing and distribution; health; home economics; technical education, including protective services and computers and data processing; engineering, science, and communication technologies; and trade and industry. Vocational education is also provided at the secondary level. By the millennium, almost six million students sought to improve career-related skills, and vocational education in the United States was on track to surpass traditional academic post-secondary education in enrollment, especially among students in non-baccalaureate programs.

Private, For-Profit Institutions. Proprietary, for-profit colleges set up campuses in locations such as shopping malls, near where working adults live, and schedule classes for evenings and weekends. Many focus offerings in business and technical fields and stress job placement. Examples include DeVry Technical Institute, the University of Phoenix, and ITT Educational Services, Inc. They pose a challenge to traditional colleges and universities, particularly the 1,250 U.S. community and technical colleges. Proprietary schools target under-served students such as working parents, returning students, and employees who need ongoing training.

Distance Instruction Two basic forms of distance instruction exist: traditional correspondence-based instruction, which is oriented for independent study; and telecommunications-based instruction, which offers the teaching and learning experience simultaneously. Some scholars distinguish between distance learning and distance education instead of using the term "instruction." Distance learning is exemplified by programs designed to encourage self-directed learning such as do-it-yourself books, while distance education requires formal evaluation and two-way communication with an institution as well as independent study.

Distance instruction is delivered through media such as audiotape, videotape, radio and television broadcasting, and satellite transmission. Increasingly, the Internet and the World Wide Web continue to shape distance learning and reach broader markets. Although broadcast television was often used for distance instruction in the earlier years, by the 2000s, most institutions had begun to adopt the Internet as the favored medium for computer-based instruction.

Two primary forms of communication are used to deliver distance instruction: asynchronous and synchronous. The main distinction between the two is whether teachers and learners are participating at the same time. Asynchronous methods use recorded instructional materials that allow participants to be separated in time and distance. Thus, telecommunications systems such as television or electronically-stored media such as video, audio, and computer software are among the technologies employed. Synchronous programs use technologies offering live, interactive instruction. Instructional Television Fixed Service and point-to-point microwave are among the most common live interactive systems linking classrooms within the regional area surrounding an institution. The students are able to see and hear one another as well as the instructor. Other examples of synchronous communications include audio conferencing and real time computer communications.

The organization and administration of distance instruction have varied according to the type of institution offering the instruction. Some universities offer distance learning programs exclusively, while others provide distance instruction as one of a number of program alternatives. Entire degree programs at both the undergraduate and graduate levels can be obtained via World Wide Web-based courses over the Internet.

Accreditation of distance instruction establishments varies by state and region. Institutions that also maintain a traditional campus often have the distance instruction component accredited as part of the main institution. One accrediting body specific to the industry is the Distance Education and Training Council (DETC), formerly the

National Home Study Council, founded in 1926 in Washington, D.C. The DETC is an association of distance learning and correspondence schools recognized by the U.S. Department of Education and the Commission on Recognition of Post-Secondary Accreditation.

Proprietary Colleges. Proprietary, for-profit colleges and universities emerged after World War II. While nonprofit universities reinvest surplus revenue in further educational efforts, proprietary institutions return it to shareholders. In 1972, amendments to the Higher Education Act allowed for-profit college students access to federal student loans to pay for their education. Their default rate, however, is higher than that of other students.

Perhaps the most well known such provider is the University of Phoenix, founded in 1976 by a former political science professor from San Jose State University and accredited since 1978. The university admits only employed students over 23 years old. Offering classes at about 150 locations, it enrolled more than 200,000 students in 2007, making it the largest private university in the United States. The university leases its classroom space and most faculty members are part-timers with M.A. degrees. The University of Phoenix also offers courses in a distance learning format via University of Phoenix Online.

The Higher Education Act of 1998 created a special liaison in the U.S. Department of Education to represent proprietary schools and it included them in the category of "institutions of higher education" that could benefit from Title IV federal financial aid funds. Prior to the act, proprietary schools were defined separately from other institutions of higher education, and were thus excluded from bills that affected post-secondary education overall. The 1998 act also allowed for-profits to appeal default sanctions that might imperil their access to financial aid because of high student loan default rates.

BACKGROUND AND DEVELOPMENT

For well over a century, a debate was fought in the United States over how to prepare students to become adult workers. Until the country's economy was transformed from an agricultural to a manufacturing base, children received a common core curriculum of academic subjects, and most left school before the end of the eighth grade. In 1900, 6.5 percent of students were graduated from high school, compared to about 78 percent in 2005, as reported by the National Commission on Adult Literacy.

As the manufacturing-centered economy took hold, changes in vocational education were required. Some policy makers proposed setting up separate vocational education programs to prepare young people for work. Others, especially John Dewey (1859–1952), urged the integration of academic and vocational instruction so that all students could learn the same academic material but in the context of occupations and adult experiences. The federal government, however, created distinct programs of vocational instruction when it passed the Smith-Hughes Act of 1917. Eventually, most schools divided students into "academic" and "vocational" tracks; and in the 1920s, many schools added a general track to give students a sampling of both. Although commissions and studies throughout the 20th century endorsed this approach to vocational education, many schools and school districts still designated vocational education as a separate track designed primarily to prepare students for work.

As high school graduates were increasingly seen as under-qualified to perform the technical jobs for which vocational education supposedly had trained them, adult vocational training took on added importance. In addition, improvements were sought in secondary school vocational training, notably in the Carl Perkins Vocational and Applied Technology Education Act of 1990, which promoted the integration of academic and vocational learning. The Perkins Act requires each state to use academic achievement as a measure of success, and it encourages linkages between secondary and post-secondary course work through "tech-prep" education. Another statute designed to improve vocational education was the School-to-Work Opportunities Act of 1994, which sought to raise educational standards and prepare students for post-secondary education.

The most utilized post-secondary vocational program of study remains business, with about 17 percent of all non-baccalaureate students declaring a major in that area. This is followed in popularity by health with 11 percent, and trade and industry with 8 percent. The combined technical fields—computers and data processing, engineering and science technologies, protective services, and communications technologies—account for 12 percent of all non-baccalaureate majors.

At the post-secondary level, community and technical colleges serve a broad range of students including those still in high school, recent high school graduates, college graduates returning for specific technical skills, adult workers returning for retraining, welfare recipients, and adults with limited basic skills. Community colleges and private proprietary schools redesign curricula to deal with a changing student body and the added burdens on adult education. In prior studies, public two-to-three-year institutions, including community colleges, enrolled about 60 percent of all non-baccalaureate, post-secondary students reporting a vocational major. The second largest providers were private proprietary institutions, which educated about 22 percent of non-baccalaureate vocational students.

In 1995 an estimated 76 million adults in the United States participated in adult education, including part time credential programs. By the turn of the century, this number had grown to roughly 87 million. According to the *2001 Digest of Education Statistics,* roughly 45 percent of the U.S. population participated in adult education. These adults were most likely to participate in work-related courses and personal development courses (22 percent for each). About 9 percent of adults participated in credential programs, about 2 percent in ABE/GED classes, about 2 percent in apprenticeship programs, and about 1 percent in English as a second language classes.

The Growth of Distance Instruction As early as 1728, advertisements appeared in the Boston *Gazette* soliciting students for shorthand lessons by mail. In 1840, Isaac Pitman (1813-1897) offered shorthand courses by mail in Bath, England. The 1880s saw the founding of private British correspondence colleges. Schools such as Skerry's College and University Correspondence College, established by the University of London, prepared students for post-secondary examinations. Correspondence schools also found fertile soil on the European continent. In Berlin, Germany, a modern language correspondence school was established by Charles Toussaint and Gustav Langenscheidt in 1856. This school still published instructional materials in the late 1990s.

U.S. academic distance learning began in 1874 at Illinois' Wesley University, which offered both undergraduate and graduate degrees by correspondence. In 1883 the Correspondence University was established in Ithaca, New York. Study outside the traditional classroom was furthered by Anna Eliot York, who founded the Society to Encourage Study at Home in 1873. Home reading circles for adults were created by John Vincent, who became a founder of the Chautauqua movement. The aim of this popular education society was to extend educational access to all Americans, and the movement has been called "the first significant distance education effort in America." Chautauqua continued to play a role in distance instruction when William Rainey Harper, called by many the father of American correspondence study, established a correspondence program for his students. Chautauqua later became an accredited university in New York State, and Harper became the first president of the University of Chicago and founder of the first university-level correspondence study division in the United States.

The growth of distance instruction centers spawned growth in other media. The first federally licensed radio station devoted to educational broadcasting, WHA, evolved from an amateur wireless station started by University of Wisconsin professors in 1919. The birth of educational television broadcasts occurred at the University of Iowa between 1932 and 1937.

A remarkable example of the potential for adult distance instruction can be seen in the Open University of the United Kingdom, established in 1971. In its first 10 years, the school enrolled 60,000 to 70,000 students per year. By the mid-1980s, more than 70,000 students had earned a Bachelor's degree from the university. U.S. attempts to emulate the Open University met with limited success. In 1974 the University of Mid-America was founded, aiming to create distance education in seven Midwestern states. The university, despite large enrollments over the years, closed its doors in 1982.

Of concern is the potential spread of "bogus" degrees from "diploma mills," especially on the Internet. Since accreditation is largely non-regulated, online colleges and universities can offer degrees costing thousands of dollars and offering little, if any, substantive education. Many people assume that the U.S. government regulates the industry and they are misled by advertisements boasting of full accreditation from an important-sounding accrediting entity; but as of the late 1990s, the only nationally recognized accrediting agency that evaluates distance education programs is the Accrediting Commission of the Distance Education and Training Council.

Despite continued growth in online education, also known as e-learning, the bursting of the Internet bubble in 2000 eventually forced many online education providers to shutter operations. For example, the University of California and New York University had canceled their online courses by mid-2002.

One dilemma facing the large numbers of traditional colleges and universities seeking to enter the online education market is the strain of managing a business enterprise necessary to a successful distance education program. Another difficulty is the great cost associated with the technology necessary to establish effective distance instruction. Access to education for students who do not attend classes on campus could be a question of their access to technology. Some critics wonder whether this could lead to a divide between the "technology rich" and the "technology poor."

Other critics of online education raise issues about the quality of the education itself. According to a May 2003 issue of *Journal of Industrial Technology,* "Many academics fear that turning college courses into prepackaged content for sale over the Internet compromises the spirit of free inquiry on which most academic institutions were founded." Adverse faculty reaction to the move away from classroom-based education to the Internet, a decision often made by university trustee boards without much initial faculty input, also includes fear of the loss of face-to-face relationships that characterize the best in traditional education. Skeptics raise questions about integrity and student cheating as well as concerns that the students able to succeed online will be limited to those who are self-motivated and highly disciplined.

The shift to online instruction also raises the issue of intellectual property rights. Although professors usually own their syllabuses and class materials and universities generally have no claim on royalties from books written by faculty members, the rules don't easily apply to online courses, the implementation of which requires input from programmers and other designers. Most colleges and universities making the leap to cyberspace in the early years of the first decade of the 2000s were only beginning to hammer out the policies that would govern their online offerings.

Business programs, health care, and education curricula seem to translate well to the online environment, while law schools have had more difficulty. Many business schools have entered e-learning with courses geared specifically to middle and upper level managers who want to pursue degrees for career advancement but who can't sacrifice the time away from the job to do so. The flexibility and cost savings have attracted many corporate employers who no longer have to send employees away from work for professional training. Furthermore, advances in technology have greatly enhanced the level of vitality and interactivity possible in virtual classrooms.

The *Chronicle of Higher Education,* citing data from BMO Capital Markets (a North American provider of commercial financial services) indicated that some 65,000 students participated in virtual schools, fueling a 30 percent annual growth rate that was expected to continue for several years.

Work-Related Education According to NCES data, some 40 percent of those over age 16 were engaged in work-related adult education of some kind in 2002-2003, including work-related courses (33 percent) and work-related degree programs (9 percent). Adults with higher levels of education were the most likely to be involved in this form of adult education. This was reflected in higher participation rates for those in management and professional capacities (70 percent) in comparison to workers in service, support, or sales roles (49 percent), or those in the trades (32 percent).

In terms of sources of work-related adult education, the NCES reported that 51 percent of participants from the business/industry sector received training, followed by colleges, universities, and vocational/technical schools (21 percent). Professional or labor organizations/associations and government agencies rounded out the list, with each category responsible for providing 19 percent of work-related education.

One positive development for the adult education industry was the approval of a House Education and the Workforce Committee bill authorizing $5 billion for job training programs in 2005, with additional funding as required through fiscal year 2011. The legislation provided funding for a system of community centers that would offer employment services and job retraining. According to the February 18, 2005, issue of *CongressDaily AM*: "The bill condenses three adult job training programs into one, increases accountability for adult education programs and expands job placement services. It also provides authorization for personal re-employment accounts, which can be used by the newly unemployed to purchase job training and other services."

Within the industry, ongoing corporate training, a $63 billion segment, did particularly well. The number of corporate universities such as General Electric Co.'s John F. Welch Leadership Center in Crotonville, New York and McDonald's Hamburger University grew from 400 in 1990 to about 2,000 by 2000, while enrollments increased about 30 percent each year. Typically, e-training costs about one half of what traditional classroom instruction costs.

CURRENT CONDITIONS

As the number of Internet-connected homes continues to grow and broadband connections become commonplace, online distance learning continues to dominate the market for alternative adult education. Statistics in *Staying the Course: Online Education in the United States, 2008* indicate that the number of online students in higher education had more than doubled in the previous five years, representing a compound annual growth rate of 19.7 percent (the overall higher education student body grew at an annual rate of 1.6 percent during the same period). The number of online students for the 2007-2008 academic year was estimated at 3.94 million.

Clearly, adult student enrollments in all categories remain significantly higher than non-adult enrollments, underscoring the continued need for alternative education technologies. In his Issue Paper for the Secretary of Education's Commission on the Future of Higher Education, Peter J. Stokes indicated that "traditional" 18 to 22 year-old full-time undergraduate students residing on campus accounted for only 16 percent of higher education enrollments; the vast majority of college and university students were non-traditional ones, particularly, working adults who needed to balance jobs, families, and educational needs. Stokes found that 58 percent of these enrolled students were aged 22 or older, and 40 percent (8 million) were studying part-time. Another 60 million adults were enrolled in work-related courses. He noted that many businesses had already made decisions to "off-shore" customer call centers and customer service. If higher education institutions fail to accommodate the needs of adult students, Stokes warned, the nation could face further risk of high-end service jobs (e.g., engineering, research and development) being moved off-shore as well, with dire consequences to the national economy. He went on to identify specific needs associated with adult students, including easier transfer of credits from institution to institution; more flexible course, certificate, and degree programs; and flexible financial aid policies.

Not only postsecondary education, but basic and remedial education needs also are expected to grow. The U.S. Department of Labor's Bureau of Labor Statistics' *Occupational Outlook Handbook* (2008–2009 Edition) noted that for the 2007-2008 school year (October 2007), approximately 3.3 million civilian noninstitutionalized 16 to 24-year-olds had not earned a high school diploma or alternative credential, and were not enrolled in high school for that school year. Employment prospects for adult literacy, remedial education, and GED teaching was expected to grow 14 percent by 2016, creating a need for another 11,000 instructors.

INDUSTRY LEADERS

Alternative education industry leaders are as diverse as the field itself. The market includes providers of vocational, career, and leisure/enrichment education for adults; traditional universities offering courses and degrees online; and institutions existing solely online. Distance instruction has caused some overlap. For example, providers of vocational education often provide coursework online or in some other distance environment, and traditional universities offering online courses may also teach career courses.

One industry leader in the area of vocational education is DeVry Inc., based in Oakbrook Terrace, Illinois. One of the largest publicly owned international education companies in North America, DeVry has offered technology-based career training to high school graduates for more than 65 years. Its DeVry University has 84 locations in the United States and Canada, with more than 49,000 students. DeVry's fiscal year 2009 profits were $165.6 million, with total revenues over $1.46 billion, an increase of 34 percent. DeVry's Keller Graduate School of Management is one of the nation's largest part-time graduate schools for working adults. DeVry also operates Ross University, a medical and veterinary school based in the Caribbean, as well as Becker Professional Review, a provider of preparatory materials for professional exams.

Another leader in alternative education is Baltimore, Maryland-based Laureate Education Inc. Formerly known as Sylvan Learning Systems Inc., Laureate provides undergraduate degrees, as well as master's and doctoral degrees, including such fields as medicine and law. Prior to becoming Laureate, Sylvan sold its Prometric division, which delivered computer-based testing for academic admissions and professional certifications—and which provided 60 percent of its revenues—to concentrate on its teaching operations. The company's global network included some 40 accredited institutions and nearly a half million students around the world in 2009. In 2007, Laureate Education Inc. agreed to be acquired by its CEO/founder and an investor consortium, after which time its stocks and value slightly flattened for 2008 and early 2009 while reorganization was undergoing.

Apollo Group of Phoenix, Arizona operates four subsidiaries that provide ongoing education for working adults: the University of Phoenix/University of Phoenix Online, the Institute for Professional Development, the College for Financial Planning, and Western International University. The company has established itself as a leading provider of higher education programs for working adults by focusing on servicing the needs of the working adult. Its University of Phoenix is the largest private university in the United States. The firm operates 160 sites and serves more than 300,000 students. Apollo reported a net revenue for the fiscal year ended August 31, 2009, of $4.0 billion, a 26.5 percent increase over fiscal 2008. Contributing to this increase was a 20.8 percent increase in University of Phoenix's average Degreed Enrollment for fiscal 2009 as compared with fiscal 2008. The University of Phoenix granted 55,400 Associates degrees, 31,700 Bachelors, 14,200 Masters, and 700 Doctorate degrees in its 2009 fiscal year alone.

Education Direct, formerly ICS Learning Systems, was operated by the Thomson Learning division of Thomson Corp. until 2007, when the business (along with Thomson Education Direct Ltd.) was acquired by Scranton, Pennsylvania-based Penn Foster, a leading consumer-based distance education provider. The company is recognized for being the first distance education provider to offer nationwide job placement opportunities to students. Education Direct provided programs that led to specialized associate degrees and career-specific diplomas. According to Penn Foster, its offerings range from high school and career diplomas to associate's degrees, with programs in areas such as business, finance, health care, industrial/corporate training, legal studies, and technology.

Based in Chicago, Cardean Learning Group began in 1998 as the $100 million startup UNext.com. From the beginning, the distance-learning provider partnered with some of the most prestigious names in traditional higher education, such as the University of Chicago, Columbia University, and the London School of Economics and Political Science. Faculty members from participating schools, including Stanford University and Carnegie Mellon University, create the content of Cardean's online courses. In 2007, the company had estimated sales of $5.8 million and 150 employees.

An expanding field is computer education for senior citizens. San Francisco-based SeniorNet is a nonprofit corporation offering classes from basic computer literacy skills to opening e-mail sites and surfing the Internet, still growing in 2009. In 1995, William Ashkin, then a 94-year-old retired dentist, created Century Club, a Web page and computer forum for adults over the age of 90. Over the Internet, seniors play bridge or exchange recipes with others from places such as Norway and London, and stimulate interest in other seniors to take basic courses in computer technology. In 2009, the company had more than 240 learning centers in 35 states, and in such international locations as Sweden and Japan.

AMERICA AND THE WORLD

China continues to be a lucrative market for alternative adult education. In 2008, China Distance Education Holdings became the first Chinese initial public offering (IPO) at the NYSE Arca. By 2009, it had reported a 48.4 percent increase in income with revenues of $17.6 million for 2008, and enrollments exceeding 743,000 (up 47 percent). The Chinese market for professional education and examination training was projected to reach 32.8 billion yuan (about US$5 billion) in 2010.

In particular, the country was ripe for English language training. In its April 30, 2007 issue, *PrimeZone Media Network,* a global newswire service for corporations, non-profits, and government agencies, cited data from the *2005-2006 China Education and Training Industry Research Report* indicating that English language training would be a $3.7 billion industry in China by 2010, up from $2.0 billion.

A study conducted by the European Center for the Development of Vocational Training and the Danish Teachers College found that Danes led all of Europe in adult education. Based on a survey of 18,000 people in 15 European countries, as well as Iceland and Norway, it was revealed that Danes attended more adult education classes and were the most willing to pay for lifelong learning pursuits. Half of all Danish respondents had been involved in some form of education or training within the year preceding the survey.

The United Nations Educational, Scientific, and Cultural Organization holds its International Conference of Adult Education annually, with attendees from around the world. The conference published a broad policy statement, the *Declaration of Adult Learning,* and more detailed proposals in its *Agenda for the Future.* The overall theme was to promote democratic understanding through education and making education accessible to all. The conference held several key seminars directed toward accessibility technology, women, global minorities, and the physically and developmentally challenged.

One topic that challenged the conference attendees concerned the state-of-the-art transmission of educational knowledge and information, not only from one global community to another but from one culture or subculture to another. New technology has employed the introduction of international symbols through media tools such as videotapes and interactive compact discs. These new devices could cut through the barrier of language as well as distance. The challenge of electronic transmission of educational materials to diverse adult cultures and peoples remained a global priority.

The Global Alliance for Transnational Education was formed in 1995 and remains a respected entity for certifying international institutions, both online and off. England's Labour Party gained wide support in its pre-election speeches addressing the "lifelong learning" needs of adults. In 1998, Britain's Department for Education proposed the University for Industry, a vocational and technical initiative comparable to the successful Open University, complete with governmental financial assistance in the form of "individual learning accounts." These proposals addressed the fact that while the majority of existing educational subsidies and post-school education budget funds go to universities, only one-fourth of the nation's five million over-16 learners attended universities.

BIBLIOGRAPHY

Burgess, Lesta A. and Shawn D. Strong. "Trends in Online Education." *Journal of Industrial Technology,* May 2003.

"ChinaCast Education Corporation Enters English Training Market in China." *PrimeZone Media Network,* 30 April 2007.

China Distance Education Holdings. Available from http://www.cdeledu.com/versions/pdf/PRESS_RELEASE_final_08_11_17_clean.pdf.

"Danes Best at Lifelong Learning: Report." *Xinhua,* 16 November 2004.

Devry Inc. Available from http://www.forbes.com/feeds/ap/2009/08/13/ap6777268.html.

Distance Learning Resource Network. "What Is Distance Learning?" Available from http://www.wested.org/tie/dlrn/distance.html.

"GE Invests in Leading Distance Learning Provider." *Business Wire,* 4 April 2007.

June, Audrey Williams. "Apollo Group Buys Online High School." *Chronicle of Higher Education,* 26 January 2007.

Johnson, Kimberley S. "After Buyout, eCollege Headquarters to Return to Denver. The Denver-Founded Company, Which Became Based in Chicago in 2005, Is Being Purchased by Pearson Plc for $538 Million." *The Denver Post,* 16 May 2007.

Klein, Alyson. "House Panel Approves Job Training Bill On Party-Line Vote." *CongressDaily AM,* 18 February 2005.

Kopf, David. "E-Learning Market to Hit $56B By 2010." *T.H.E. Journal,* 30 July 2007.

"Laureate Education Inc. News and INformation." 2009. Available from http://www.laureate-inc.com/pressreleaseID. php?releseID=86 .

Manzo, Kathleen Kennedy. "Study Urges Adult, Remedial-Ed. Programs to Join Forces." *Black Issues in Higher Education,* 10 February 2005.

Miller, M.H. "Report: Bush's Budget Cuts Threaten Work Force." *Community College Week,* 14 March 2005.

National Center for Education Statistics. "Digest of Education Statistics," 2001. Available from http://nces.ed.gov/pubs2002/digest2001/tables/dt359.asp.

———. "Distance Education at Degree-Granting Postsecondary Institutions: 2000-2001," July 2003. Available from http://nces.ed.gov.

———. "National Household Education Surveys of 2001," September 2004. Available from http://nces.ed.gov.

———. "Adult Participation in Work-Related Learning," 2004. Available from http://nces.ed.gov.

Salimi, Anwar Y. "The Promise and Challenges for Distance Education in Accounting." *Strategic Finance,* January 2007.

Sims, David. "Teleconferencing and Distance Learning: An Inside Look." *Customer Interaction Solutions,* January 2007.

"University of Phoenix Struggles to Grow; Traditional Colleges Compete for Online Enrollment." *The Grand Rapids Press,* 27 May 2007.

ALTERNATIVE ENERGY

SIC CODE(S)

2861

3511

3674

9611

INDUSTRY SNAPSHOT

The alternative energy industry is comprised of two main segments: renewable energy sources, such as wind, solar, and hydroelectric power, and alternative vehicle fuels, such as natural gas, electricity, and biodiesel. During the later years of the first decade of the twenty-first century, both of these segments were growing worldwide as countries sought sources of energy that were both environmentally friendly and economically viable.

Within the lifetimes of most who read this, the supply of world crude oil will have peaked (estimated around 2015), and natural gas liquids (NGL) will also have peaked (around 2020 to 2030), according to information presented at the September 2008 USA Conference of the Association for the Study of Peak Oil and Gas (ASPO). Discovery of new oil sources peaked 40 years earlier (in the 1960s). With a world population expected to reach nine billion by 2030 and the number of vehicles expected to double (to two billion) by 2025, the reality of a future energy crisis without alternative sources is self-evident.

In the United States alone, roughly 94 percent of energy came from traditional sources in 2008 (coal, oil, uranium, natural gas), despite the fact that the United States led the world in nuclear power. All traditional energy sources increased in price by 200 to 400 percent since 2003. With an aged and often collapsing infrastructure (bridges, roads, underground piping), failing electrical grids, and politically-volatile energy sources, the demand for alternative and renewable energy sources has never been greater.

Facing the long-term effects of global warming, carbon emissions, and the shorter-term consequences of extensive reliance on foreign oil supplies, U.S. automakers, researchers, environmentalists, and policy makers shared a common goal in the development of alternatives to the transportation sector's basis in gasoline and diesel fuels. Alternative fuels—including liquefied petroleum gas, methanol, ethanol, compressed natural gas (CNG), hydrogen, biomass, and mixtures of these with regular gasoline—gained increasing favor due to test results demonstrating their significantly more benign effects on the ozone layer and their reduction of pollutant emissions.

Nevertheless, the impact of a mass alternative fuel-based economic conversion remains a sticky issue, both domestically and globally. According to ASPO, 97 percent of the world's known oil reserves are located in 10 percent of existing oil fields, declining in production an average 10 percent each year. The tenuous balance of geopolitical power and international governmental alliances is intricately tied to control over energy supplies, which has served as the backdrop to wars as well as less dramatic international tensions. On the domestic front, some of the nation's largest enterprises have staked their fortunes on traditional energy sources slated for replacement by alternative fuels.

ORGANIZATION AND STRUCTURE

Alternative energy primarily focuses on clean, renewable energy sources that leave little or no carbon footprints on the earth (which contribute to depletion of the ozone, pollution, and global warming). Thus, the alternative energy field often incorporates the terms "clean energy" and/or "green energy." There are many alternative sources available, but the challenge requires an ability to produce alternative fuel in sufficient amounts to coincide with the depleting traditional sources, while still maintaining global and environmental stability and health.

Renewable Energy Sources An established source of clean, renewable energy, hydropower works by converting the kinetic energy produced from falling water into electricity. According to the National Hydropower Association (NHA), hydropower is the United States' leading renewable energy source. It outpaces other renewable forms of energy, such as wind and solar, to account for 80 percent of all renewable electricity generation. As a percentage of total U.S. electrical generation, NHA figures reveal that hydropower is responsible for 8 to 12 percent. This figure varies in different regions of the country. For example, hydropower accounts for 70 percent of all electricity generation in the Pacific Northwest. Worldwide, hydropower accounts for approximately one-fifth of all electricity generation. The United States is a world leader in hydropower production, second only to Canada.

According to the NHA, more than half of the nation's non-federal hydroelectric capacity will undergo the federal licensing process by 2017. Re-licensing is an expensive and lengthy process, taking 8 to 10 years, and is expected to impact U.S. hydroelectric production capacity.

Long the darling of renewable energy supporters, solar energy has yet to become a mainstay of the U.S. energy system, supplying less than one percent of energy needs in 2008. However, volatile energy markets in the first decade of the 2000s, coupled with increasingly pronounced environmental concerns among a growing segment of the population, made for a sunny long-term outlook for solar. With production costs inching downward and efficiencies rapidly improving, many observers expected the long-awaited solar energy boom to be just around the corner.

The untapped energy potential of the sun is enormous. For instance, scientists surmised that a single day's worth of sunlight, if properly harnessed and converted, could supply the entire energy needs of the United States for two years, and that the daily dose of solar energy outpaced that of the world's entire fossil fuel energy by a ratio of 1,000 to one.

Solar energy is harnessed by photovoltaic (PV) systems (see **Photovoltaic Systems**), which act as the mediator between the sun and the desired energy by converting sunlight directly to electricity. Research and development in the closing years of the twentieth century pushed the technology within the grasp of those wishing to market it to a mass audience in the consumer and industrial worlds. PV systems were finding increasing employment in households, automobiles, and remote power systems, and for telecommunications, lighting systems, and a range of other applications.

Wind power involves the generation of power using windmills of various sizes and types. Although wind power is used to provide energy for individual homes, it also is harnessed using enormous "wind farms" as well as large, utility-scale wind turbines. Single giant windmills capable of providing electricity to several thousand homes are operating in some areas of the United States; In October 2009, the world's largest wind turbine became operational in Texas. Wind power projects have received increased attention nationwide (and globally), but especially in areas of California where the state instructed utilities to obtain more power from renewable sources. New installation capital costs for wind power are expected to increase from $51.4 billion in 2008 to $139.1 billion in 2018, according to the research firm Clean Edge Inc.

Alternative Fuel Sources In the alternative fuels sector, a number of energy sources have shown promise in powering vehicles without reliance on gasoline. Electricity was used to power automobiles, vans, pickup trucks, motorcycles, buses, and forklifts. According to the Energy Information Administration (EIA), the official U.S. government provider of energy statistics, electric vehicles fall into one of three power source categories: batteries, hybrids, and fuel cells. As the EAI explains, "A battery-powered EV uses the electricity from onboard rechargeable batteries to run an electric motor, which turns the vehicle's wheels. A hybrid electric vehicle has two sources of motive energy. For example, it may use a lean burn gasoline engine in combination with batteries. A fuel cell vehicle uses electricity from fuel cells instead of batteries. A fuel cell operates like a battery in that it converts chemical energy directly into electricity."

Hydrogen remains a leading experimental vehicle fuel. It is created from hydrogen-rich materials such as water, renewable fuels, biomass, and fossil fuels. Potential hydrogen sources include natural gas, methanol, ethanol, petroleum, landfill waste, and coal. According to the EIA, high production costs and storage issues have been roadblocks to the mass adoption of hydrogen as an alternative fuel.

Two forms of natural gas are used as alternative vehicle fuels. Compressed natural gas (CNG) is used in light and medium-duty vehicles, while liquefied natural gas (LNG) is primarily used in heavy-duty vehicles as a diesel alternative.

Also known as propane, liquefied petroleum gas (LPG) is a byproduct of petroleum refining and natural gas processing. It is comprised of a mixture that contains 2.5 percent butane and higher hydrocarbons, at least 90 percent propane, and a balance of ethane and propylene. Propane is stored in liquid form, but is converted back to a gas before being burned by a vehicle's engine.

Ethanol is a liquid alcohol fuel made from corn. In addition to agricultural crops, it can be produced from agriculture and forestry waste, municipal waste, and wastepaper. According to the EIA, "As an alternative fuel, ethanol is most typically used as a blend of 85 percent ethanol and 15 percent gasoline, known as E85, which is appropriate for light-duty vehicles. Another less common ethanol/gasoline combination is a 95/5 percent blend called E95."

Methanol also is a liquid alcohol fuel. However, it is produced from natural gas, coal, and carbon-rich sources like seaweed, garbage, and waste wood. Methanol is largely used in light-duty, flexible-fuel vehicles that operate on gasoline, methanol, or a combination of each fuel type. M85, a mixture consisting of 85 percent methanol and 15 percent gasoline, is the most common mixture of this fuel type.

According to the National Biodiesel Board, the national trade association of the U.S. biodiesel industry, biodiesel is a clean burning alternative fuel that is made from domestic, renewable resources such as soybeans. It contains no petroleum, can be blended at any level with petroleum diesel, and requires few if any engine modifications. In addition, biodiesel fuel is both nontoxic and biodegradable.

Industry Legislation & Regulation The Clinton administration took a role in the attempt to convert to efficient energy with the issuance of Executive Order 13123 along with the Million Solar Roofs Initiative, which aimed at adding solar power systems to one million buildings throughout the United States by 2010. Shortly thereafter, a photovoltaic system was installed in the world's largest office building, the Pentagon, as part of the massive renovation of the structure. The system was expected to displace about 48,000 pounds of carbon dioxide per year. The Million Solar Roofs Initiative offered a 15 percent tax credit with a $1,000 cap for solar thermal panels and a $2,000 cap for photovoltaic (PV) panels.

The deregulation of the utilities industries set back efforts toward implementation of photovoltaic systems by the nation's power companies. Where before deregulation shareholder-owned utilities were guaranteed a profit and the development of new technologies like solar power was included in their allowable before-profit costs, deregulation eliminated much of this incentive by placing utilities under the squeeze of market forces, where development costs ate into short-term profits and market share. As a result, according to *Power Engineering,* a power generation magazine, industry utilities were less willing to spend significant funds to develop technologies that may take years to bring to term and turn a profit.

To stimulate interest, numerous laws and tax incentives are directed toward both producers and users of domestically produced alternative fuels, giving them a chance to compete with the oil industry and its monopolized hold on the global market. Some of the more important federal legislation supporting biofuels includes the Energy Security Act (1978); the Energy Tax Act (1978); the Gasohol Competition Act (1980); the Crude Oil Windfall Profit Tax Act (1980); the Energy Security Act (1980); the Surface Transportation Assistance Act (1982); the Tax Reform Act (1984); the Alternative Motor Fuels Act (1988); the Omnibus Budget Reconciliation Act (1990); the Clean Air Act Amendments (1990); the Energy Policy Act (1992); the Building Efficient Surface Transportation and Equity Act (1998); the Energy Conservation Reauthorization Act (1998); and the American Recovery and Reinvestment Act (2009). Most of these acts, or major portions thereof, are administered by the U.S. Department of Energy (DOE).

The manner in which these laws affect and interface with private industry can be summed up by the Alternative Motor Fuels Act of 1988. Its stated objective is to encourage the widespread development and use of methanol, ethanol, and natural gas as transportation fuels. Section 400AA requires the U.S. government to acquire the maximum number of alternative-fueled vehicles in its fleets as is practical. Importantly, the vehicles are to be supplied by original equipment manufacturers (OEMs), thus stimulating private industry. The act also mandates that the DOE must assist state and local governments in developing public transportation buses capable of operating with alternative fuels.

Concurrently, acts such as the Clean Air Act and its amendments continue to focus on reducing the amount of pollutants emitted from motor vehicles. The U.S. Environmental Protection Agency (EPA) also remains greatly involved in the monitoring of environmental effects caused by vehicular traffic and fuel byproducts. In the late 1990s, for example, the EPA ruled that particulates, microscopic specks of carbon emitted from diesel engines that can lodge in lungs and cause a host of medical complications (including death), constituted air quality health hazards.

To monitor progress under the Energy Policy Act of 1992 (EPAct), which extends the Alternative Motor Fuels Act by requiring the incorporation of Alternative Fuel Vehicles (AFVs) into the fleets of federal and state governments, the DOE reports to Congress annually on the progress of the act's focus, which is to encourage use of alternative fuels. Field researchers, OEM markets, and fuel suppliers complete lengthy annual surveys that primarily address the number and type of alternative fuel vehicles available; the number, type, and geographic distribution of those vehicles in use; the amount and distribution of each type of alternative fuel consumed; and information about the refueling/recharging facilities. As the data builds from year to year, the DOE paces its monetary funding and program initiatives accordingly.

Associations Because of its diverse nature, the alternative energy industry includes a very large number of trade associations and interest groups. Within the renewable energy segment, associations include, but are not limited to, the Boulder, Colorado-based American Solar Energy Society, as well as three Washington, D.C.-based organizations: the Solar Energy Industries Association, the National Hydropower Association, and the American Wind Energy Association.

The alternative vehicle fuels segment includes an even larger number of organizations, such as the American Methanol Institute (Arlington, Virginia); the Electric Auto Association (Palo Alto, California); the National Biodiesel Board and the National Ethanol Vehicle Coalition, both of Jefferson City, Missouri; and the Washington, D.C.-based National Hydrogen Association, the Natural Gas Vehicle Coalition, and the Renewable Fuels Association.

BACKGROUND AND DEVELOPMENT

Renewable Energy. Humankind's use of some renewable energy sources dates back thousands of years, while other uses are more recent. The first experimenter to successfully convert sunlight into electricity was French physicist Edmond Becquerel (1820–1891), who noted the photovoltaic (PV) effect in 1839 when he built a device that could measure the intensity of light by observing the strength of an electric current between two metal plates. For over 110 years following the initial discovery of the PV effect, scientists experimented with different materials in an attempt to find a practical use for PV systems. In the late nineteenth century, scientists discovered that the metal selenium was particularly sensitive to sunlight, and during the 1880s Charles Fritts constructed the first selenium solar cell. His device, however, was inefficient, converting less than 1 percent of the received light into usable electricity.

The Fritts selenium solar cell was mostly forgotten until the 1950s, when the drive to produce an efficient solar cell was renewed. It was known that the key to the photovoltaic cell lay in creating a semiconductor that would release electrons when exposed to radiation within the visible spectrum. During this time, researchers at the Bell Telephone Laboratories were developing similar semiconductors to be used in communication systems. By accident, Bell scientists Calvin Fuller and Daryl Chapin found the perfect semiconductor: a hybridized crystal called a "doped" cell, which was made of phosphorous and boron. The first solar cells using these new crystals debuted in 1954 and yielded a conversion efficiency of nearly six percent. Later improvements in the design increased the efficiency to almost 15 percent.

In 1957 Bell Telephone used a silicon solar cell to power a telephone repeater station in Georgia. The process was considered a success although it was still too inefficient to penetrate the general marketplace. The first real application of silicon solar cells came in 1958 when a solar array was used to provide electricity for the radio transmitter of Vanguard 1, the second U.S. satellite to orbit Earth. Solar cells have been used on almost every satellite launched since.

The oil crisis in the early 1970s and the nuclear accidents at Three Mile Island and in Chernobyl greatly enhanced the public's desire for alternative and renewable energies. As environmental consciousness grew, solar energy became the darling of the renewables category. It was not until the late twentieth century that solar energy became practical and economical enough to warrant its broad-scale marketing as one of the primary energy sources of the future. In the 1990s alone, the price of solar energy dropped 50 percent as technology continued to advance. It was during that period that PV applications went from a niche source of electricity to bringing solar technology to the threshold of big business. According to the Solar Energy Industries Association, over 10,000 homes in the United States were powered completely by solar energy in the late 1990s, and an additional 200,000 homes incorporated some form of photovoltaic system.

By the dawn of the twenty-first century, there were more than 100,000 people using solar power and living "off the grid," or independent of utility companies, in the United States, while worldwide, some 1.7 billion people lived outside of an electrical grid. However, solar power still represented only about one percent of all electric power in the United States that year, primarily due to its persistently high costs and the continuing availability of cheap energy via traditional sources. Thus there was little market-based incentive for customers to replace their existing energy technologies with photovoltaic systems.

Water has been used as an energy source for many centuries. Water turbines are essentially updated and more efficient versions of waterwheels, which were used for millennia. The first commercially successful water turbine design was developed by Frenchman Benoit Fourneyron (1802–1867) in the 1820s. More than 100 such turbines were eventually installed worldwide. These turbines were, however, costly to construct, physically unstable, and difficult to control for speed of rotation. They were eventually supplanted by the designs, developed in the 1830s, of American James Francis. Francis-type turbines remained one of the key turbine designs used in contemporary applications of the time. Water turbines were in widespread use by the mid-nineteenth century, primarily in powering saw and textile mills—though they were soon supplanted in these applications by steam engines.

The first use of water turbines to generate electricity on a commercial basis came in 1882, when a 12.5 kilowatt station in Wisconsin provided power to light two paper mills. The use of hydroelectric power grew rapidly thereafter, with the first 100,000-kilowatt installations built in the 1930s. From the 1940s to the early 1970s, a large number of small hydroelectric stations, most with less than 1,000-kilowatt capacity, were shut down due to their relatively high cost. Meanwhile, from the 1950s to the late 1980s, the production capacity of typical water turbine generators doubled, from 150,000 to 300,000 kilowatts, with the largest of modern units capable of producing 750,000 kilowatts.

A continuing issue for the hydroelectric industry in the United States is fish kills, particularly salmon and steelhead trout. These fish attempt to swim upstream, from the sea to a river, while spawning. However, when a hydroelectric station is along their path, the fish can get caught in the turbine blades. This is particularly problematic in the Pacific Northwest, in Washington's Columbia River Basin. Salmon and steelhead runs there declined from rates of 11 to16 million fish a year in pre-Colonial times to two million or fewer fish in the late 1990s.

Wind-powered generators offer an increasingly viable alternative power source. Since the mid-1980s, the cost of producing electricity with windmills has dropped more than fourfold, bringing wind power on a par with power produced using oil, coal, and natural gas. However, windmills had the disadvantages of being noisy and dangerous to birds. When properly situated, however, it is possible to mitigate these problems.

In 1992, the U.S. Department of Energy and the Electric Power Research Institute (EPRI) implemented a program to increase the commercial viability of wind power turbines by evaluating advanced turbines developed by U.S. electric companies. The first was a 6-megawatt facility in Fort Davis, Texas, which used 12 550-kilowatt wind turbines. The second, with 11 550-kilowatt turbines, began operating in Searsburg, Vermont, in 1997. Three 750-kilowatt wind turbines were installed in Algona, Texas prior to 2000, while other wind turbine projects were on tap for Nebraska, Texas, Oklahoma, New York, Wisconsin, and Alaska.

By 2003 wind power was the fastest growing segment in the energy generation industry, with annual 20 percent increases predicted through 2008.

During the middle of the first decade of the 2000s, *Business Week Online* reported that corporate investments in renewable energy were increasing. For example, annual sales hikes of 30 to 40 percent prompted the solar systems division of Sharp Electronics to plan an expansion of it solar panel fabrication plant in Memphis, Tennessee. In 2004 General Electric acquired AstroPower, the leading U.S. supplier of solar equipment. This followed the company's 2002 acquisition of Enron's wind power division. Private investments also were increasing. The same issue of *Business Week Online* indicated that, according to a PricewaterhouseCoopers Money Tree Survey, $76 million in venture capital investments were made in the first half of 2004 alone, outpacing the entire annual figures for 2003.

Wind power continued to garner increased attention as a combination of government support as well as advancements in wind turbine technology supported growth within this category. Examples included low interest loans for renewable energy initiatives from the U.S. Department of Agriculture, federal tax credits for wind-generated power, and some $300 million in state grants specific to renewable energy projects.

Alternative Vehicle Fuels It would be remiss not to begin the alternative fuel segment's history by emphasizing the enormous economic influence that gasoline has had over both Western and Eastern countries. In the United States, for example, gasoline supply disruptions between 1974 and 1984, such as those surrounding the 1973 Arab Oil Embargo and the 1979 Iranian Oil Embargo, cost Americans $1.5 trillion. In the late 1990s, petroleum imports accounted for nearly half of the U.S. trade deficit and were expected to rise to 60 to 70 percent within the next 10 to 20 years, even though Congress voted in 1990 that a dependence on foreign oil of more than 50 percent would constitute a "peril point" for the United States.

The additional cost in terms of military security and protection of foreign oil interests cost the United States an estimated $365 billion between 1980 and 1990. The Persian Gulf War alone cost $61 billion. These factors helped stimulate efforts toward near total replacement of gasoline fuels with renewable alternative fuels. Henry Ford himself, back in 1908, well expected his Model T automobile to be fueled by ethanol, the most viable alternative fuel at that time. In fact, an ethanol-gasoline mix (25 percent ethanol) was rather successfully marketed by the Standard Oil Co. in the 1920s. When high corn prices, combined with storage and transportation costs, made ethanol less feasible, federal and state initiatives were put in place to keep interest alive. Ford again re-entered the picture and joined others to establish a fermentation plant in the Corn Belt capable of producing 38,000 liters per day. However, the efforts could not effectively overcome the low petroleum prices, and ethanol production plants closed down in the 1940s.

Interestingly, at about the same time Ford was developing prototype vehicles, Rudolf Diesel was perfecting his diesel engines to run on peanut oil, with the intention that eventually they would be able to operate on several types of vegetable oils. It is unfortunate that both Ford's and Diesel's hopes were relegated to the back burners of a hot petroleum market with which these resourceful fuels could not then compete. It was not until the critical gasoline market in the 1970s that momentum was re-established. Ethanol-gasoline blends were again reintroduced to the U.S. market in 1979. These blends, however, were marketed not as gasoline replacement fuels but as "octane enhancers" or "gasoline extenders." This may have diminished any sense of urgency in the public's mind to accelerate conversion of a transportation economy so comfortable with inexpensive gasoline.

Complacency again reverted to a proactive attitude during the 1990s as Americans became more sensitive about environmental issues and economic dependency. The Clean Air Act Amendments of 1990 required that special fuels be sold and used in areas of the country with harmful levels of carbon monoxide. This resulted in the development and promotion of a cleaner-burning and lighter gasoline product known as "reformulated gasoline." California had its own formula. Again, ethanol blends and other alternative fuel choices caught the public's attention. Concurrently, the federal government continued to infuse money into numerous projects for biofuel development, also giving private industry a stake in the results. By the end of the 1990s, the alternative fuel industry had been resurrected.

The Clinton administration's Partnership for a New Generation of Vehicles (PNGV), established in 1993, created an industry-government consortium with the ultimate goal of phasing out gasoline engines over the next 20 to 30 years. The federal government pledged an annual investment of $500 million (half of which included direct federal funds) to help the industry. The University of Illinois received such a prize in 2000 to build a "biorefinery" devoted to the production and commercialization of Pure Energy Corp.'s P Series ethanol-based fuel.

One of the most intriguing possibilities for alternative fuels was the prospect of utilizing environmental waste, or "biomass," as an energy source. This subcategory of alternative fuels, known as "biofuels," converts agricultural and forestry residue, and even municipal solid and industrial waste, into bioethanol, biodiesel, biomethanol, and pyrolysis oil fuels. Biofuels are, by composition, alcohols, ethers, esters, and other chemicals made from cellulosic biomass.

The technology widely expected to achieve long-term dominance in the transportation sector was the fuel cell, a technology only beginning its steps toward commercialization by the middle of the first decade of the 2000s but which received a tremendous push in President Bush's call for a hydrogen-based economy in his 2003 State of the Union address. Pledging $1.7 billion to the development and commercial roll-out of fuel cell products for building, industrial, and vehicle power, the administration's announcement marked the most aggressive promotion yet of one particular alternative energy source. (See **Fuel Cells**.) However, all industry observers and players were unanimous in their estimation that the widespread deployment of fuel cell vehicles on U.S. highways was at least 15 years off, leaving short-term prospects to the crowded list of alternative fuel sources in development.

In October 2004, Shell introduced North America's very first hydrogen pump at a public service station in Washington, D.C. While this was an important milestone, the pump was used to fuel a small fleet of General Motors demonstration vehicles. In California, home to 65 hydrogen-powered experiment vehicles and 13 private refueling stations, Honda introduced a prototype of what it called "the world's first fuel-cell car certified by the U.S. Environmental Protection Agency and the California Air Resources Board for regular commercial use," according to the December 20, 2004, issue of the *San Diego Business Journal*.

Although hydrogen is a plentiful energy source and has great potential, its regular use is still a long way off. GM engineer Eric Raske estimated that the automaker would have a large fleet of hydrogen-powered vehicles by 2010. The National Hydrogen Association does not expect personal vehicles to be available until 2020. Mary Ann Wright of Ford Motor Co. estimated that it may not be until 2025 when hydrogen-powered vehicles are marketed for regular use, while other experts have pegged 2035 as the breakthrough year.

Industry observers noted mixed signals from government policies in the early years of the first decade of the twenty-first century. While the Bush administration stepped up its commitment to fuel cell technologies, major industry players and financiers noted that government backing for most types of alternative vehicle fuels remained well behind what competitors in Japan and Europe could expect from their governments. Moreover, in 2001 the administration announced that the United States was backing out of the international Kyoto Protocol, the cornerstone of global efforts toward the reduction of greenhouse gas emissions. The Government Accounting Office (GAO) determined that the nation would fail to meet the goals of 30 percent alternative-for-gasoline substitution by 2010.

U.S. auto manufacturers began investing in plants specifically devoted to alternative fuel vehicles. Ford Motor Co. broke new ground by initiating a new brand specifically devoted to ecologically friendly vehicles when it established its Th!nk Group. The Japanese auto giant Toyota introduced successive models of its Prius hybrid sedan, and planned a hybrid Lexus sports-utility vehicle. Similarly, rival Honda achieved impressive sales with hybrid versions of its popular Civic and Accord models. In 2002 Honda introduced its hydrogen-powered FCX, which became the first fuel cell vehicle to be certified for commercial use by the California Air Resources Board. By 2005, GM planned to begin manufacturing hybrid Saturn VUE SUVs with highway fuel efficiency improvements of 50 percent over conventional models, and other SUV makers were poised to follow suit, particularly in the face of skyrocketing fuel costs.

A host of AFV types existed, each with their own particular benefits and drawbacks. Dedicated alternative fuel vehicles, for instance, utilize only one alternative fuel, the most common being liquefied petroleum gas (LPG). Biofuel vehicles house separate tanks for regular gasoline and one type of alternative fuel. Flexible fuel models utilize a gas-alcohol mixture such as the popular E85, which blends a maximum of 85 percent ethanol and 15 percent gasoline, in one tank.

Many automobiles utilizing these alternative fuels met the criteria for Low Emissions Vehicles designed specifically to target the emissions standards established by the U.S. Environmental Protection Agency, which call for undercutting U.S. governmental standards by 70 percent in the field of smog-forming hydrocarbons and by 50 percent in the realm of nitrogen oxides.

Natural gas remained the most viable alternative fuel in the first decade of the twenty-first century. As the market awaited more sophisticated and affordable fuel cell vehicles, natural gas and alcohol fueling systems represented the most effective mass solution to the demand for more efficient and clean-burning vehicles. For all hydrocarbon emissions, compressed natural gas (CNG) vehicles save up to 48 percent and liquefied petroleum gas (LPG) cars cut emissions up to 31 percent.

Although they represented only a small portion of all vehicles on U.S. roadways and, despite special tax credits, were more expensive and difficult to service than traditional vehicles, the hybrid vehicle market continued to grow. Hybrid models were available from foreign players such as Toyota and Honda, including the Lexus and Acura brands. Domestically, General Motors, Ford, and DaimlerChrysler planned to introduce a range of new vehicles between 2004 and 2007. These included the Chevy Malibu, Chevy Tahoe, GMC Yukon, Ford Escape, Ford Fusion, Mercury Mariner, Saturn Vue, and Dodge Ram.

One critical element of a mass shift to alternative fuel was the development of an adequate fueling infrastructure. According to *State Legislatures,* by early 2005 every state offered some kind of alternative fueling site. California was the clear leader in electric fueling locations, ahead of Arizona and Florida.

Biodiesel fuel also was making inroads. In 2005 the National Biodiesel Board (NBB) reported that more than 500 major fleets used biodiesel fuels and that more than 300 biodiesel fueling sites were available throughout the United States. A 2004 NBB survey of 53 private and government fleet managers, representing some 50,000 vehicles, found that 91 percent were in favor of biodiesel fuel and 45 percent were already using it.

In March 2005, John Deere began using a blend of fuel that included two percent biodiesel as the "preferred factory fill" for its domestically produced diesel machinery. In a February 1, 2005, *Business CustomWire* release announcing the company's decision, John Deere's Don Borgman said: "Working with the National Biodiesel Board (NBB), we are promoting the use of B2 fuel because it is readily available and meets the high quality fuel standards that we have set for our engines, and it is a positive step toward adoption of renewable fuels. If B2 were used in all diesel engines in the U.S., the United States could displace the equivalent of about one billion gallons of foreign oil per year. That could, in turn, translate to some very significant increases in the demand for crops from which biodiesel is made, like soybeans and other natural fats and oils."

CURRENT CONDITIONS

According to the EIA, in 2008, renewable sources of energy produced only about 7.3 percent of total U.S. energy consumption and 9 percent of electricity generation. However, the economic slump of 2008 and 2009, part of which was characterized by $4/gallon gasoline, could have been the best thing for triggering renewed interest in alternative energy.

Renewable Energy. President Obama's Economic Stimulus bill, officially known as the American Recovery and

Reinvestment Act of 2009, directly allocated approximately $47 billion for renewable energy initiatives, smart grids, and other energy efficient programs. In addition, $20 billion was made available for tax incentives and new investment tax credits for manufacturers of renewable energy technology. For individual taxpayers, tax incentives and credits were authorized for homeowners who adopted geothermal heat systems and solar hot water heaters, and the popular "Cash for Clunkers" program offered large rebates for new car purchases that included trade-ins of old gas-guzzling cars. A similar program in some states, through governmental grants, offered rebates on household appliance purchases accompanied by the return of an older energy-inefficient model.

The federal bill provided $17 billion for improved public transit, including high-speed rail, $5 billion to weatherize old buildings, and $6 billion for new loan guarantees on wind and solar projects. Moreover, manufacturers became eligible for a 30 percent tax credit on new projects certified by the Secretary of the Treasury through a bidding process.

Regarding solar energy, a sudden oversupply in silicon in 2008 (following decreased demand during the global recession) sent prices tumbling and temporarily flattened the market. Renewed interest in the U.S. market followed the passage of the Economic Stimulus Bill, laden with incentives. According to Clean Edge Inc., the solar photovoltaics industry (modules, system components, and installation) was worth $29.6 billion in 2008, but was forecast to grow to $80.6 billion in 10 years (2018).

Wind power also was expected to grow from $51.4 billion in 2008 to $139 billion in 2018. In fact, 2008 proved a banner year for new U.S. global wind power installations, accounting for more than 8,000 MW and representing more than 40 percent of total new electricity generating capacity brought online in 2008. This achievement caused the United States to trump Germany as the world's leading generator of wind energy, culminating in October 2009, when the world's largest wind turbine began operating in Texas.

The U.S. Bureau of Land Management (BLM) announced in early 2009 that several western states together could generate as much as 5,500 MW of geothermal energy from 110 plants by 2015, rising to 6,000 MW by 2025. To that end, the Obama administration slated over $400 million for geothermal projects in its economic stimulus package. Over 100 confirmed and unconfirmed projects were on the line for funding. The Geothermal Energy Association (GEA) reported that BLM also intended to open 111 million acres for geothermal leasing in 2009.

Alternative Vehicle Fuels. The Energy Information Administration (EIA) estimated that over 1.2 million alternative fuel and hybrid vehicles (AFVs) cruised U.S. highways in 2008. Liquified petroleum gas (LPG) vehicles accounted for 7,932 of that total, with their compressed natural gas (CNG) cousins totaling 2,765. While electric fuel cell vehicles were widely expected to emerge as the AFV of choice sometime over the next decade, such vehicles totaled only 4,066 in 2008. However, the gasoline-electric hybrid vehicles totaled 320,293. The number of vehicles powered by the E85 ethanol-gasoline mixture grew from 12,788 in 1998 to 884,379 in 2008.

Global production and wholesale pricing of ethanol and biodiesel fuels reached $34.8 billion in 2008, according to Clean Edge Inc., and was projected to grow to $105.4 billion by 2018. This figure represented the production of more than 17 billion gallons of ethanol and 2.5 billion gallons of biodiesel worldwide.

AMERICA AND THE WORLD

Renewable Energy. According to Clean Edge Inc. research, global revenues for clean energy solar photovoltaics, wind power, and biofuels combined were $115.9 billion in 2008. Wind power revenues exceeded $50 billion. New global investments in energy technologies grew nearly five percent, to $155.4 billion. This included venture capital, private equity investments, project finance, asset finance, public markets, and research/development. The rate was expected to be higher, but many projects were cancelled due to the severely tightened credit markets following the global recession in 2008. Notwithstanding, the global wind market is projected to grow some 143 percent between 2008 and 2015, according to a 2009 article in *Energy and Capital.*

Some pending world energy projects in 2009 included the Three Gorges Dam hydro project in China (600 feet tall, 1.5 miles long); a huge offshore wind farm in Copenhagen; Brazil's sugarcane ethanol facility; an Iowa corn ethanol facility; a Palm Springs wind farm; the controversial nuclear reactor in Iran; and the Alberta tar sands project.

Germany had the largest solar market in the world as of 2008. As credit markets began to improve throughout Europe, financing for new energy projects was put back on the table at many banks. The Italian solar market was slated to grow over 3000 percent between 2009 and 2015, according *Energy and Capital.* As a whole, the global solar market was projected to grow 374 percent in the same time.

Chevron Corporation remained the largest producer of geothermal energy in the world as of early 2009, with 1,273 MW produced, primarily in the Philippines and

Indonesia. But the Philippines Energy Development Corporation placed bids for two plants, the addition of which would make it the largest producer.

Alternative Vehicle Fuels According to ASPO, vehicle travel continues to grow at a rate faster than the population. While U.S. consumption of oil has increased 70 percent since 1965, China's has increased more than 3000 percent. But biofuel contenders have some downsides. The market for corn ethanol has created a food vs. fuel crisis in some countries. Sugarcane ethanol has worked well in tropical countries, but not truly viable for the U.S. market. Cellulosic ethanol shows potential but requires too much consumption of trees to sustain itself over years. Algae biodiesel also shows potential but is too costly in the current market. Many analysts believe that alternative fuels can only be produced in sufficient quantities to replace petroleum products if there is a concurrent reduction in consumption through the crisis years (2015 through 2030).

RESEARCH AND TECHNOLOGY

Continuous advancements in the renewable energy segment of the industry resulted in improvements upon existing technologies, such as smaller and more affordable solar panels, as well as better software controls, conversion technology, and blades for wind turbines.

The development of enhanced geothermal resources (EGS) has spawned new investment interest, after a 2008 MIT study commissioned by the DOE revealed that EGS could add 100,000 MW of power. EGS involves the pumping of water into hot dry rock formations. Following release of the study, the DOE awarded $3.4 million to Ormat Technologies to demonstrate EGS's viability.

The 2008 collapse of the U.S. auto industry will hopefully propel new vehicle manufacturing toward conversions to electric drive propulsion. Additionally, the new low carbon fuel standards will accelerate a transition to alternate fuels.

There has been increased research into development of what is known as the "pod car," a single-occupant vehicle that was the brainchild of a Swedish government think-tank. The solar-powered pod cars do autonomous driving (some may implement bio-mimicry), are lightweight, reasonably-priced, and practical for the needs of the vast majority of travel: work, school, shopping, and leisure. By 2009, ten cities in Sweden had joined forces to implement them, and over $10 billion in capital was committed from POSCO S. Korea, Masdar UAE and others.

Cost and an adequate refueling infrastructure remain roadblocks to hydrogen-powered cars. For example, some demonstration cars carry price tags of approximately $1

million. In addition, GM estimated that the cost of modifying 12,000 gas stations in 100 major cities could cost $12 billion. Because the practical use of hydrogen was a long way off, some scientists argued that government resources should be devoted to energy sources that will have a more immediate positive impact on the environment.

The Massachusetts Institute of Technology (MIT) Plasma Science and Fusion Center devised a plasmatron hydrogen-enhanced engine, which aimed to make traditional vehicle engines runs more cleanly by converting some gasoline to hydrogen-rich gas. Estimating the technology could boost fuel efficiency by some 20 percent, the MIT researchers discovered the plasmatron while studying fusion power. Fuel entering the device is sparked with electricity, transforming the fuel and the surrounding air into electrically charged gas, according to *The Engineer,* a magazine serving U.K. technological engineers, which then produces hydrogen-rich gas that can boost fuel efficiency while running on about one kilowatt of electricity.

Breakthroughs in the use of biomass for fuel have been at the forefront of industry development. Scientists at the University of California at Berkeley, sponsored by the DOE, discovered a process by which green algae, known affectionately as "pond scum," ceases oxygen production in favor of hydrogen. Algae-generated hydrogen was known to scientists for years but dislodging the element under controlled circumstances proved troublesome. The Berkeley team found that the answer not in the molecular structure of hydrogen but in its diet. By effectively starving the algae of the sulfur it requires to produce protein, the scientists halted its oxygen production, thereby forcing the algae to switch its emissions to hydrogen to survive. As a bonus, they found that hydrogen was emitted in much greater quantities when sulfur was cut off than researchers had believed possible. The team added that the metabolic switch does not kill the algae, which can be reused over and over. After a few days of sulfur starvation, all the plant's production capacity is exhausted, at which point sulfur is reintroduced to its diet allowing it to regenerate its necessary carbohydrates for protein production.

Although the integration of this process into a large industrial framework remains to be configured, requiring alternative land-use strategies, its potential benefits include vastly more efficient, cost-effective, and ecologically sound energy production than oil drilling and coal mining. A researcher on the project, Michael Seibert of the National Renewable Energy Laboratory, surmised that algae-production lands covering the size of New Mexico would sufficiently supply all the energy needs in the United States.

The expanding market for alternative fuels has inevitably led to a market for alternative fuel components.

Among the most potentially useful of these are hydrogen sensors. In the form of tiny chips, hydrogen sensors monitor the amount of hydrogen circulating through a fuel system, sending signals to the engine to adjust its operations accordingly. Most analysts expect that hydrogen sensors will be a standard component of any hydrogen-fueled vehicle, especially on fuel cell cars. Thus, as the alternative fuel market grows, so goes the sensor market.

BIBLIOGRAPHY

"A Jump Start for Alternatives." *State Legislatures,* February 2005.

"Alternative Energy. Government Initiatives Continue Expanding Renewable Energy Markets." *RBC Capital Markets,* 14 September 2004.

"Alternative Fuels." Energy Information Administration, 2003. Available from http://www.eia.doe.gov.

"Alternative Fuels Data Center." Office of Transportation Technologies, 2003. Available from http://www.afdc.doe.gov.

"Alternative to the Hydrogen Economy." *The Engineer,* 7 November 2003.

Baker, David R. "Sales Soar at Green-tech Companies." *San Francisco Chronicle,* 7 March 2007.

"Biodiesel Basics." National Biodiesel Board, 3 April 2005. Available from http://www.biodiesel.org/resources/biodiesel_basics/default.shtm.

Broderick, Pat. "Fueling the Future." *San Diego Business Journal,* 20 December 2004.

Carey, John. "Alternative Energy Gets Real; Pricey Oil and Gas are Heating Up Industrial Interest in Renewable Sources." *Business Week,* 27 December 2004.

"Carmakers Look for Alternative Fuel." *Energy CustomWire,* 2 March 2005.

Clean Edge Inc., "Clean Energy Trends 2009." Available from http://www.cleanedge.com/reports-trends2009.asp

The Current Status of the Wind Industry. Belgium: European Wind Energy Association, 2004. Available from http://www.ewea.org/documents/factsheet_industry2.pdf.

De Aenlle, Conrad. "Future Energy that Generates Profits Today." *The New York Times,* 21 July 2007.

"Engines and Turbines." *Encyclopedia of Global Industries,* Online Edition. Thomson Gale, 2005. Reproduced in Business and Company Resource Center. Farmington Hills, Mich.: Gale Group. 2005. Available from http://galenet.galegroup.com/servlet/BCRC.

"Ethanol Plants Need More Corn." *Southeast Farm Press,* 9 March 2007.

"Green Fuel: Germany's Hydrogen Highway." *Business CustomWire,* 1 March 2005.

Halperin, Alex. "Taking Stock of Green Energy Options." *Business Week Online,* 19 March 2007. Available from www.businessweek.com.

Hatcher, Charles L. "Biodiesel as a Renewable Energy Source: A New Direction?" *Spectrum,* Summer 2004.

Healey, James R., Sharon Silke Carty, and Chris Woodyard. "Alternative-Fuel Vehicles Star, but Wide Use Is Miles Away." *USA Today,* 12 January 2005.

———. "2009 Solar Energy Overview: Examining the Solar Profit Process." *Energy and Capital,* 20 February 2009.

Hodge, Nick. "Investing in Clean Energy." *Energy and Capital,* 6 March 2009.

———. "Renewable Energy Market Growth." *Energy and Capital,* 26 August 2009.

"John Deere to Use B2 Biodiesel Fuel in US Manufacturing Plants; Natl. Biodiesel Board Appluads John Deere's Announcement at Biodiesel Conf." *Business CustomWire,* 1 February 2005.

Johnson, Jim. "Truck Fleets Support Biodiesel, Survey Says." *Waste News,* 10 May 2004.

Kay, Barry. "Will the U.S. be Less Dependent on Gasoline in Future Years? The Latest News on Hybrids & Diesels." *Anton Community Newspapers,* September 2004.

Kharif, Olga, and Steve Rosenbush. "Racing to Energy's Great Green Future; From Hybrid Autos and Solar Panels to Fuel Cells and Beyond, Alternative Energy Is Fast Going from Fringe to Mainstream." *Business Week Online,* 8 October 2004. Available from www.businessweek.com.

Nelder, Chris. "Notes from the 2008 ASPO-USA Peak Oil Conference." 20 February 2009.

"Markets, Funding Increasing for Alternative Energy Sources." *Wireless News,* 22 March 2005.

"Oil Prices Rise Above US$76 a Barrel Ahead of US Oil Data." *International Herald Tribune,* 6 September 2007.

"Ontario to Increase Water, Wind Power Capacity." *Renewable Energy Today,* 11 March 2005.

"Photovoltaic Systems." *Encyclopedia of Emerging Industries,* Online Edition. Thomson Gale, 2005. Reproduced in Business and Company Resource Center. Farmington Hills, Mich.: Gale Group. 2005. Available from http://galenet.galegroup.com/servlet/BCRC.

Randerson, James. "Hydrogen: Saviour or Fatal Distraction?" *New Scientist,* 21 August 2004.

"RenewableEnergy Consumption and Electricity Preliminary 2006 Statistics." Energy Information Administration, August 2007. Available from http://www.eia.doe.gov.

Schoen, John W. "Gas Prices Seen Peaking in May. Drivers Hit By Surging Crude Prices, Strong Demand." MSNBC, 7 April 2005. Available from http://www.msnbc.com/id/7407519/.

Simms, Andrew. "It's Time to Plug into Renewable Power: Fossil Fuels Not Only Wreck the Climate, They Also Keep the Poor World Poor." *New Scientist,* 3 July 2004.

Thurston, Charles W. "Geothermal Market Update: Steady Growth in 2009." *Renewable Energy World,* 29 January 2009.

"USDA to Offer Low-Interest Loans for Renewable Projects." *The Kiplinger Agricultural Letter,* 18 March 2005.

U.S. Dept. of Energy, Energy Information Administration. "Projected Number of Onroad Alternative Fuel and Hybrid Vehicles: 2008." April 2009. Available from http://www.eia.doe.gov/cneaf/alternate/page/atftables/attf_s7.html

U.S. Dept. of Energy, Energy Information Administration. "Renewable & Alternative Fuels FAQs." 2009. Available from http://www.eia.doe.gov/ask/renewables_faqs.asp

"Venture Capitalists Betting on Biofuels." *UPI NewsTrack,* 7 March 2007.

"Vietnam Explores Alternative Energy Sources." *AsiaPulse News,* 16 March 2005.

"Wind-powered Electricity Output: 2010 Outlook." *The Kiplinger Letter,* 10 December 2004.

ALTERNATIVE MEDICINE

—■—

SIC CODE(S)

8049

2833

8041

8099

INDUSTRY SNAPSHOT

Alternative medicine is for the most part a Western term. Worldwide, the use of such methods as acupuncture, aromatherapy, herbal remedies, homeopathy, and hypnotherapy has been part of the medical mainstream for centuries. For this reason, the undeniable growth of the alternative medicine industry in the United States represents a dramatic shift not only in the traditional Western medical industry but in Western thought itself. Historically, alternative therapies such as those mentioned above were used by only a small portion of the population in the United States and were considered by many Western doctors to be opposed to traditional Western medical practice.

However, a growing dissatisfaction with conventional treatments and therapies has led an increasing number of patients to seek practitioners of alternative medicines. In the *2009 Survey of Health Care Consumers,* published by the Deloitte Center for Healthcare Solutions, 19 percent of consumers reported treating a health problem with an alternative approach or natural therapy in the preceding 12 months; the percentage was slightly higher for Baby Boomers and the uninsured. This coincided with a one in five ratio of consumers who preferred alternatives to traditional medicine, including homeopathic, chiropractic, and naturopathic approaches and remedies. Thirteen percent of consumers reported consulting an alternative healthcare practitioner in the previous year, up slightly from the 12 percent reported in 2008. Of interest, those who chose alternative approaches did so primarily to try a different approach (49 percent), or preferred such treatment over conventional medicine (43 percent). Additionally, 31 percent responded that reduced cost was important.

A majority of private insurance companies now cover at least some CAM therapies, namely acupuncture and chiropractic care, pushing utilization to an all-time high. Leading medical institutions such as Duke and Harvard have established centers for complementary and alternative medicine (CAM). Many hospitals offer alternative medicine treatments to their patients, usually at a financial loss, and employers often turn to alternative treatments as one way to help contain skyrocketing medical costs. This increased acceptance in the medical community has combined with a new wealth of information and alternatives, made available by increased access to the Internet. The result is a growing trend away from traditional Western medicine as a sole solution. From this synergy of traditional or conventional medicine along with alternative approaches comes a new term in medical jargon, "integrative medicine."

ORGANIZATION AND STRUCTURE

While the term "alternative medicine" encompasses a wide range of loosely related therapies and practices, the common denominator of all alternative medicines is their holistic focus: the treatment of an illness by considering the role played by both the body and the mind. The leading fields of alternative medicine include mind/body

Types of Complementary and Alternative Medicine Therapies Used

Nonvitamin, nonmineral, natural products	17.7%
Diet-based therapies	3.8%
Chiropractic or osteopathic manipulation	8.6%
Massage	8.3%
Meditation	9.4%
Deep-breathing exercises	12.7%
Yoga	6.1%
All other/misc	33.4%

SOURCE: Center for Disease Control and Prevention, National Center for Health Statistics.

medicine, chiropractic therapy, massage therapy, homeopathy, and acupuncture. An additional term being increasingly used is "naturopathy," which refers therapies that rely exclusively on natural remedies, such as sunlight combined with diet and massage. In addition, the overall field frequently encompasses preventive medicine regimens (e.g., nutritional supplements and vitamins) in addition to therapies, treatments, and remedies for existing conditions.

Although the industry is essentially a private, for-profit one, in 1995 the federal Office of Alternative Medicine (OAM) appointed a new director, Wayne Jonas, a retired military physician who had run the Medical Research Fellowship program at Walter Reed Army Institute of Research in Washington, D.C. Of interest to proponents of alternative medicine was that Dr. Jonas himself had been trained in bioenergetics, homeopathy, acupuncture, and spiritual healing, and he had used such treatments in his family medical practice. When Jonas addressed the first International Congress on Alternative and Complementary Therapy, he cautioned against self-conclusions about the efficacy of alternative medicine without the support of corroborative data.

Shortly thereafter, in October 1995, OAM announced the funding of eight additional centers for alternative medicine research. Of these, at least two were cited for specific research in homeopathy: The University of California-Davis and Harvard Medical School's Beth Israel Deaconess Medical Center in Boston, Massachusetts. In 1998, the OAM was transformed into a full federal agency and renamed the National Center for Complementary and Alternative Medicine (NCCAM). With a budget of $100 million, NCCAM began conducting broad-based clinical trials to determine the efficacy of various alternative therapies. It continues as a clearinghouse for information as well as a sponsor for various clinical trials, surveys, and therapeutic testing.

Mind/Body Medicine Mind/body medicine is among the most popular forms of alternative medicine, according to the *New England Journal of Medicine*. While traditional Western medicine focuses solely on reactions in the body, mind/body medicine explores the role the mind plays in healing, as well as the role the body plays in healing the mind. Although mind/body medicine is not a treatment in the traditional sense of the word, it is a method of influencing and controlling the reactions and responses of the body. The ultimate goal of all forms of mind/body medicine is to achieve relaxation or the reduction of stress, which is considered the catalyst for many kinds of illness. Consequently, mind/body medicine is largely a complementary form of treatment, not a primary form. Standard medical testing procedures can demonstrate the power of the mind to overcome poor health. For example, patients participating in medical studies who have been given placebos such as sugar pills often report feeling relief from their symptoms.

Mind/body techniques include meditation; progressive relaxation, which is similar to meditation; autogenic training, which is the use of auto-suggestive phrases, such as "I'm calm"; hypnosis; and biofeedback or amplification of body signals so that patients can hear or see signs of stress and learn how to control stress. All of these techniques seek to counteract the body's reaction to stressful situations. When experiencing stress, the body releases various chemicals that affect the body by causing the heart rate to speed up, blood pressure to rise, and the muscles to become tense. Frequent and long-term stress impairs the immune system and can cause insomnia, high blood pressure, and depression, among other things. Although biofeedback therapy requires special training and a state license, other forms of mind/body medicine do not. However, practitioners of these other therapies often hold licenses in other fields.

Chiropractic Therapy Chiropractic therapy, the second most popular form of alternative medicine, assumes that an inherent healing mechanism strives to return the body to a state of balance and therefore health. Chiropractic theory holds that the nervous system is responsible for maintaining the body's balance, and that subluxations (bones out of alignment within joints) and fixations (motion anomalies or irregularities) obstruct the flow of nervous impulses and consequently the body's natural healing system. By manipulating the bones and their respective joints and muscles, especially the spine, chiropractic therapy seeks to undo motion anomalies. Chiropractic therapy is employed to relieve or alleviate a wide range of illnesses, including arthritis, asthma, back pain, carpal tunnel syndrome, headaches, premenstrual syndrome, and tendonitis.

While still considered an alternative form of medicine, chiropractic therapy is widely accepted. Chiropractic services are covered by Medicare and Medicaid in many states as well as by most of the large private insurers. In addition, the practice is licensed in all 50 states and taught at special chiropractic colleges. Chiropractic licenses are governed by the Council of Chiropractic Education and the Federation of Chiropractic Licensing Boards. Nearly one-third of the U.S. population has used chiropractic therapy at least once, and 10 percent have undergone chiropractic therapy on a continuing, regular basis. Moreover, chiropractors make up the second largest group of primary care providers (approximately 60,000, according to the American Chiropractic Association) behind physicians.

Daniel David Palmer, originally a magnetic healer, founded the practice of chiropractic therapy in 1895. Palmer manipulated a man's ill-aligned vertebra and cured his deafness. He considered this proof that misaligned spines could cause poor health and that manipulation of the spine could restore health by correcting the flow of nervous impulses. In 1897 Palmer established the first chiropractic school, which his son managed.

However, one of the school's instructors, John Howard, disputed Palmer's contention that subluxations caused disease. Consequently, he left Palmer's school and founded his own, the National College of Chiropractic. Howard's school relied on some of Palmer's basic teachings but tempered them with standard scientific and medical thought and evidence. Hence, the split created two camps of modern practitioners: the straights, who follow Palmer, and the mixers, who follow Howard. Straights focus solely on the manipulation of the spine whereas the mixers integrate other techniques such as massage and nutritional therapy.

Massage Therapy Massage therapy is another frequently used form of alternative medicine. In the first decade of the 2000s, more than 55,000 massage therapists were in practice and the American Massage Therapy Association was one of the fastest-growing associations of healthcare professionals. Numerous schools or forms of massage therapy exist, including shiatsu (acupressure), deep tissue massage, neuromuscular massage, Swedish massage, and Esalen massage.

The myriad forms of massage therapy are based on a series of common tenets: circulation of blood, release of tension, release of toxins, and reduction of stress. Massage therapy holds that proper blood circulation is essential for health. Tension can impede circulation, thus interfering with the flow of nutrients and the removal of waste and toxins and possibly causing psychological and immune system problems. Hence, by releasing tension in muscles and other soft tissues, massage therapists strive to improve the circulation of blood, which will bring about the removal of toxins and the reduction of stress that some believe cause over 80 percent of all illnesses.

Considered by many to be one of the oldest healthcare techniques, mention of massage use can be found in Chinese records dating back about 3,000 years, but its use probably predates these documents by many years. Physicians and healthcare practitioners from many cultures and from many eras have practiced massage therapy. In Germany, Japan, and China, for example, massage therapy has continued to be used as it has for centuries, and massage therapists work alongside doctors.

The medical use of massage began to decline in the United States in the early part of the twentieth century as surgical and pharmaceutical approaches to medicine began to blossom. Physicians began to view massage as too time-consuming so they delegated it to aides, who evolved into modern-day physical therapists. Massage therapy began to turn professional in 1943 when the graduates of massage schools decided to found the American Massage Therapy Association. A majority of U.S. physicians believed massage to be effective in reducing stress, boosting immune system function, and alleviating chronic pain.

Homeopathy Homeopathy represents another one of the largest sectors of the industry. The word homeopathy comes from the Greek words *homios* meaning "like" and *pathos* meaning "suffering." Thus the term implies its conceptual underpinnings, to treat "like with like." Contrary to traditional Western (allopathic) medicine, which hastens to suppress, alleviate, or obliterate symptoms, homeopathy works with a patient's symptoms, not against them. Homeopaths view a sick person's symptoms, such as a dry cough or runny nose, as the body's attempt to heal itself. The remedies therefore attempt, by administration of minute, highly-diluted doses of natural substances, to trigger the sick body's natural healing responses to cure the patient.

Because homeopathic remedies are based on such inexpensive natural substances as plants, herbs, or minerals, homeopathy is often conflated with other forms of alternative medicine such as aromatherapy, acupuncture, massage, herbal medicine, and chiropractic care. In its purest form, homeopathy is not really aligned with these other forms, many of which are allopathic in approach and methodology. Nonetheless, the association has hardly hurt the industry, as a "back to basics, back to nature" mentality swept across the United States and the world. Continually barraged with news of oil spills, toxic exposures, hormonal additives in food sources, chemical and often carcinogenic sprays and herbicides on fresh produce, and untoward side effects of conventional pharmaceutical and prescriptive medications, the public's resurgent interest in and search for homeopathic and other natural alternative medicines was all too apparent and predictable. This resurgence conveniently combined with a renewed interest in preventive rather than palliative medicine as people learned how to prolong their health and life expectancies through natural diet, exercise, and therapy. Health food stores became one of the hottest industries, with shelves loaded with herbal teas, megavitamins, natural mood enhancers, stimulants, depressants, aphrodisiacs, and purportedly natural cures for everyday ailments. Caught up in the momentum of all this, "homeopathy" became a household term.

Homeopathic methods have remained popular for more than two centuries despite criticism from some doctors that these methods rely more on anecdotal than empirical knowledge. Since the 1970s, many people suffering from common chronic ailments found relief through homeopathy, leading some doctors, researchers, lawmakers, and insurance carriers to become more open to sanctioning homeopathy. Led by consumer demand, homeopathy and homeopathic medicine are poised for even greater public acceptance and new growth.

A survey of homeopathic practitioners found homeopathy most effective in treating common ailments such as colds and flu, chronic headaches, arthritis, allergies, asthma, premenstrual syndrome, and menopause. Homeopathic treatments have also been used for depression and anxiety as well as common childhood conditions such as earaches, colic, and teething. Patients can get these remedies from mainstream pharmacies, natural pharmacies, and health food stores, or from catalogs featuring alternative healthcare products. Several catalogs and pharmacies sell home treatment kits that contain 20 or more vials of common homeopathic remedies. Included in these kits are reference materials that can be used to explain which remedy to use to treat specific ailments. Homeopathic remedies typically come in liquid, tablet, or granule form.

Roughly 3,000 medical doctors and licensed healthcare providers practice homeopathy in the United States. To operate as a homeopath in the United States, one must be a licensed healthcare provider. All states have laws that allow medical doctors (MDs) and osteopathic doctors (DOs) to diagnose and treat illnesses. A few states—including Alaska, Arizona, Connecticut, Hawaii, Montana, New Hampshire, Oregon, Utah, and Washington—license naturopathic doctors (NDs) to do the same. An MD or DO can be certified as competent to practice homeopathy through the American Board of Homeotherapeutics, which grants a DHt certification. NDs go through the Homeopathic Academy of Naturopathic Physicians, which grants a DHANP certification. All healthcare providers can be certified through the Council for Homeopathic Certification. The Council on Homeopathic Education monitors these educational programs. The U.S. Food and Drug Administration regulates all homeopathic remedies, but because homeopathic products contain little or no active ingredients, many are exempt from the same regulations as other drugs.

In 2005 the homeopathy profession commemorated the 250th anniversary of founder Samuel Hahnemann's birth. In November of that year, the *Journal of Alternative and Complementary Medicine* devoted a large portion of its issue to homeopathy. Among its contents were the results of a landmark Six-year University Hospital Outpatient Observational, involving approximately 6,500 patients, in which 70 percent of patients reported significant positive health changes.

Acupuncture Like other forms of traditional Chinese medicine, acupuncture dates back roughly 4,500 years. While its practice in the West has been slow to catch on, it has received steady interest. A 1971 *New York Times* story acted as the catalyst that led to growth of acupuncture in the United States. Acupuncture is based on the concept of *chi,* which is the life force that circulates through the body within 14 channels called "meridians." According to the concept, when *chi* flows freely, people experience good health; and when *chi* is blocked or flows slowly, people experience poor health.

Consequently, the goal of acupuncture is to stimulate proper flow of *chi.* To do so, acupuncturists insert very thin sterilized needles to penetrate the area just under the surface of the skin, where the *chi* passageways, or acupoints, are said to be located. Acupuncturists insert the needles less than an inch into the skin in some cases and three to four inches in others. They also rotate the needles. The entire procedure causes little pain. Acupuncture, in Western parlance, builds host resistance, which is the body's natural defenses and its ability to fight illness.

Acupuncture's primary application in the United States has been the alleviation of pain caused by a plethora of illnesses including arthritis, back pain, headache, gout, stress pain, and toothache. Nevertheless, acupuncturists are beginning to use this technique to relieve symptoms of other kinds of illnesses, such as those of addiction and stroke. Of the many acupuncturists in the United States, about one fourth are licensed medical doctors. Many doctors of traditional Western medicine, however, still find it hard to accept the theory of invisible flowing energy and contend that acupuncture produces nothing more than a placebo effect. Despite the criticism, scientific research indicates that acupuncture helps to improve health and relieve pain by stimulating the body's production of natural pain killers (endorphins and enkephalins) and a natural anti-inflammatory substance (cortisol). Acupuncture also was gaining acceptance as a treatment for nausea associated with chemotherapy.

BACKGROUND AND DEVELOPMENT

Because alternative medicine is such a broad term and encompasses so many specialized fields that are often hard to track, exact figures regarding the value of the industry have been hard to come by. For example, some statistics include sports nutrition and vitamins under CAM, while others exclude nutritional or preventive regimens and focus only on treatments/therapeutics/remedies (alternative medicine approaches used as interventions for already-identified medical conditions or problems).

In February 2005, *Chain Drug Review* reported that "a vast majority of insurers" covered at least some CAM therapies, namely acupuncture and chiropractic care. Blue Cross and Blue Shield of Florida gave its members 45 percent discounts on mail order vitamins and herbal supplements. Healthcare experts indicated that more insurance companies were covering CAM therapies in an effort to control healthcare costs, since many CAM treatments were more affordable alternatives to conventional ones.

The government also was exploring the viability of CAM approaches. For example, Medicare beneficiaries in Virginia, New Mexico, Maine, and Illinois were able to receive coverage for chiropractic care for neuromusculoskeletal conditions. This was part of a special demonstration project that would be used to determine if such coverage would be extended to all Medicare beneficiaries.

Another important development in the growth of alternative medicine was the introduction of the Access to Medical Treatment Act. The federal bill, proposed in the late 1990s, would allow consumers to choose any medical treatment that was not proven to be dangerous, had fully disclosed side effects, and fell within the scope of a provider's expertise. It would also allow for a new definition of healthcare providers as "any properly licensed medical doctor, osteopath, chiropractor or naturopath." As of 2009 it was still pending in the 11th Congress (2009–2010 session).

By 2010 about 25 percent of U.S. hospitals offered complementary and alternative medicine treatments to their patients, according to an American Hospital Association survey involving 1,390 facilities. Most of the time, hospitals offered these services at a financial loss, choosing to provide them in an effort to increase patient satisfaction, rather than turn a profit. Reporting the results of the survey in its September 2006 issue, *Health Care Strategic Management* indicated that massage therapy was the most commonly provided form of alternative medicine, offered to 37 percent of inpatients and 71 percent of outpatients.

The economic slump of 2008 and 2009 was a pressing issue for employers, who searched for ways to offer health insurance to staff at a reasonable price. In addition to increasing deductibles and supporting disease management programs, employers viewed alternative medicine treatments as one additional measure to contain costs.

In early 2009 the *Nutrition Business Journal* assessed the CAM industry at $39 billion, with an additional $1.9 billion value for the U.S. practitioner supplements market. The journal's *2009 Supplement Business Report* broke down 2008 supplement sales by product: vitamins represented 34 percent of market sales; herbs and botanicals at 19 percent; sports nutrition at 11 percent; specialized meal replacement products at 10 percent, and minerals at 8 percent. Another 18 percent was listed as miscellaneous/specialty products. The report noted that these statistics followed 13 years of continuous market research.

In April 2009 a medical information clearinghouse known as *TheMedica* cited information gleaned from a December 2008 national governmental survey regarding the use of therapeutic CAM (acupuncture, homeopathy, naturopathy, ayurveda) in the United States. Survey results indicated that approximately 38 percent of adults and 12 percent of children used some form of CAM. The results also disclosed that usage increased with annual incomes of more than $100,000, and was more common with adults who possessed post graduate education. The most common reason cited for using alternative medicine was to promote general health, and the most common ailment or condition for which users employed CAM was musculoskeletal problems. The survey also found decreasing use of CAM for head or chest colds. In fact, back, neck, and joint pain combined accounted for 65 percent of CAM use.

CURRENT CONDITIONS

The Health Care Reform bill President Barack Obama signed into law in March 2010 had little immediate impact on alternative medicine practices or policies, but could impact the future of the industry, said Jane Hoback in an April 2010 article for *Natural Foods.* This was premised on the fact that prior to enactment, many persons had turned to CAM or herbal remedies because they did not have health insurance. Under the new law, requirements to carry healthcare insurance may cause more persons to bypass CAM and head for doctors' offices or hospitals first rather than last.

On the other hand, Sections 5101 and 3502 of the new law create a National Healthcare Workforce Commission and provide for "community health teams" that include "licensed complementary and alternative medicine practitioners." This inclusion of CAM and integrative medicine in the total healthcare package could provide opportunities for more licensed practitioners and products. Another provision in Section 4206 sets up a pilot program for wellness plans and includes grants for up to ten community health centers. The wellness plans will concentrate on nutrition and exercise, cessation of smoking and excess alcohol, stress management, and dietary supplements (focal points in most CAM practices).

Integrative Medicine In its statistical reporting, the *Nutrition Business Journal* (NBJ) began using the term "integrative medicine" to replace what it formerly referred to as the *CAM Report.* In its *2009 Integrative Medicine Report,* NBJ estimated the U.S. integrative medicine market to be worth between $39 and $45 billion, in addition to what it identified as the $1.9 to $2 billion practitioner channel supplement market. The relative reduced cost and availability of over-the-counter alternative medicines (primarily herbs and vitamin supplements) grew to nearly $639 million between October and December 2009, a nearly 10 percent increase from the same period in 2007, reported *Natural News.* Sales of herbal supplements alone grew 6 percent. It also reported that the British market had grown 18 percent from 2007 to 2009, and was expected to rise yet another 33 percent in the subsequent four years.

Homeopathy Perhaps the biggest news in the field was the pending opening of The American Medical College of Homeopathy, which was slated to begin offering a doctoral program in early 2011. Prior to this, the last homeopathic medical school in the United States had closed in the 1930s. Until 2010, homeopathic education had been through diploma/certificate programs following an average training regimen of about 700 hours.

Homeopath Tom Rowe, in his 2010 report on the status of the profession, noted that there was neither uniform licensing nor uniform professional standards for the practice of homeopathy in the United States. In Arizona, Connecticut, and Nevada, licensure as a homeopathic physician was available only to licensed medical doctors (MDs) and doctors of osteopathy (DOs). Arizona and Nevada also licensed homeopathic assistance who performed medical services under the supervision of a homeopathic physician.

Twelve states and the District of Columbia licensed naturopathic physicians, under which the scope homeopathy is included. These included Arizona, California, Connecticut, Idaho, Kansas, Maine, Minnesota, Montana, New Hampshire, Oregon, Utah, Vermont, and Washington, D.C. In all states, veterinary practice includes homeopathic practice. Rowe further noted that several states (including California, Minnesota, Oklahoma, Rhode Island, Idaho, and New Mexico) had adopted legislation granting the right to practice to anyone who gives full disclosure of his or her training and background.

Chiropractic According to the 2010–2011 edition of the *Occupational Outlook Handbook,* published by the U.S. Department of Labor, Bureau of Labor Statistics, there were approximately 49,100 chiropractors employed in the United States in 2009. As of 2010, 16 chiropractic programs were accredited by the Council on Chiropractic Education.

Mind/Body Medicine Research published in 2010 in the *Proceedings of the National Academy of Sciences* reported a new meditation technique used by researchers at the University of Oregon, in collaboration with a team of Chinese researchers from Dalian University of Technology. The technique induced positive structural changes in brain connectivity. Experiments involved brain-imaging equipment to track the effects of integrative body-mind training (IBMT) between subjects receiving IBMT and the control group. The results indicated that after 11 hours of learning IBMT, students experienced a boost in efficiency in the part of the brain that helps regulate behavior in accordance with their goals. The new technique was not yet available for academic training or credit as of 2010.

Acupuncture As of 2010, the Accreditation Commission for Acupuncture and Oriental Medicine (ACAOM) listed more than 60 schools and colleges with accredited or candidacy status with the commission. Since its inception, the National Certification Commission for Acupuncture and Oriental Medicine (NCCAOM) has issued more than 19,000 certificates in acupuncture, Oriental medicine, Chinese herbology, and Asian bodywork therapy. In Arkansas, Florida, and New Mexico, homeopathic medicine is included in the scope of practice for acupuncturists. The sub-industry's sustainability is attributed to wider acceptance by both public and private entities, and many national health insurance plans now cover acupuncture as an accepted therapy.

INDUSTRY LEADERS

American HealthChoice Inc. is ranked among the leading providers of alternative medicine therapies, offering these therapies along with conventional healthcare services. By 2007 the company owned or managed 50 medical centers, including primary care, urgent care, physical therapy, and chiropractic clinics, in Tennessee and Texas. However, it became embroiled in continuing patent litigation that flattened its resources in 2008 and 2009. In 2010 the Securities and Exchange Commission suspended the company's license to publicly trade its stock, pending further investigation for alleged trading violations and reporting failures.

In the homeopathy sector, two of the highest-grossing remedy makers include the Boiron Group and Dolisos Homeopathic Pharmacology Laboratories, which was acquired by Boiron of France in 2005. Boiron had operations in France as well as Australia, Africa, the Middle East, and both North and South America. The Boiron Group produces roughly 100 million single and multi-dose tubes of homeopathic medicine each year, covering a range of 200 homeopathic remedies. It was formed in 1932 by three French homeopathic pharmacists. Since the mid-1990s the company has maintained the Institute Boiron, an independent homeopathic laboratory staffed with more than 100 clinical physicians working on research and development of products for veterinary and medical prescriptions and guidelines for pharmacies and home medication.

Dolisos was founded in 1937 by Dr. Jean Tetau, a French pharmacist. It began selling and researching homeopathic veterinary drugs during the mid-1990s. Its plant produces active ingredients for pharmacists to blend or finished products ready for the patient. In 1996 the world's leading seed-producing company, Groupe Limagrain, acquired Dolisos, allowing its new subsidiary to keep its own name.

BIBLIOGRAPHY

"2009 Survey of Healthcare Consumers: Key Findings, Strategic Implications." Deloitte Center for Healthcare Solutions, 6 May 2009. Available from: http://www.deloitte.com/assets/Dcom-UnitedStates/Local%20 Assets/Documents/us_chs_2009SurveyHealthConsumers_ March2009.pdf.

"About AMTA." American Massage Therapy Association, 13 February 2007. Available from http://www. amtamassage.org/about/about.html.

"Alternative Medicine." *Modern Health Care,* 7 August 2006.

"Alternative Medicine Starts to Go Mainstream." *Chain Drug Review,* 28 February 2005.

Deardorff, Julie. "Doctors Going Alternative." 2009. *Chicago Tribune,* 14 January 2009.

DeVries, George. "Using Complementary and Alternative Medicine Insurance to Contain Health Care Costs." *Benefits and Compensation Digest,* September 2006.

"Facts and Figures." American Chiropractic Association, 2007. Available from http://www.amerchiro.org.

Gutierrez, David. "Sales of Alternative Medicine Products Are Booming." *Natural News,* 9 June 2010.

Hoback, Jane. "Health Care Reform to Impact CAM, Supplements." *Natural Foods,* 6 April 2010.

"Integrative Body-Mind Training (BMT) Meditation Found to Boost Brain Connectivity." *Science Daily,* 18 August 2010.

"Integrative Medicine Report 2009." *Nutrition Business Journal,* Available from http://nutritionbusinessjournal.com/alternative-medicine/market-research/0227-nutrition-business-journal-integrative-medicine-complementary-alternative-report.

"Many Hospitals Offer Alternative Therapies; Few Profit from Them." *Health Care Strategic Management,* September 2006.

"National Acupuncture & Oriental Medicine Day Aims to Educate Consumers about Benefits of Using Certified Practitioners." *Business Wire,* 24 October 2006.

National Certification Commission for Acupuncture and Oriental Medicine, 19 August 2010. Available from http://www.nccam.org/about/index.html.

Occupational Outlook Handbook, 2010–11 Edition. U.S. Department of Labor, Bureau of Labor Statistics. Available from http://www.bls.gov/oco/ocos071.htm.

Rowe, Todd. "Homeopathic Legal and Regulatory Practice in the United States." *Homeopathy,* 12 August 2010. Available from http://www.hpathy.com.

Saper, R.B., et al. "Lead, Mercury, and Arsenic in U.S. and Indian-manufactured Ayurvedic Medicines Sold Via the Internet." *Journal of the American Medical Association (JAMA),* Vol. 300 (8) 2008.

"Shareholders and Investors Area." Boiron Pharmaceutical Laboratories Worldwide, 20 August 2010. Available from http://www.boiron.com/en/Shareholders-and-investers-area/Group-information.

"Traditional Chinese Medicine Enjoys Fast Growth in Revenue." *AsiaPulse News,* 13 November 2006.

"The U.S. Alternative Medicine Industry Overview." *TheMedica,* 29 April 2009. Available from http://www.themedica.com/articles/2009/04/alternative-medicine-industry.html.

ALTERNATIVE VEHICLE FUELS

SIC CODE(S)

2861

INDUSTRY SNAPSHOT

With skyrocketing gas prices, the threat of global warming, and the consequences of extensive reliance on foreign oil supplies, U.S. automakers, researchers, environmentalists, and policy makers shared a common goal in the development of alternatives to the transportation sector's basis in gasoline and diesel fuels . Alternative fuels—including liquefied petroleum gas (LPG), methanol, ethanol, compressed natural gas (CNG), hydrogen, biomass (plant or animal waste), and mixtures of these with regular gasoline—gained increasing favor due to test results demonstrating their significantly more benign effects on the ozone layer and their reduction of pollutant emissions; however, mass commercialization was another issue.

The extensive resources, in terms of private investment and public policy, required to maintain the stability of the U.S. oil supply create an enormous incentive for the introduction of viable alternative fuel technologies on a mass level. Political factors, including increasing concern—particularly following the terrorist attacks of September 11, 2001, and U.S. military involvement in an unstable Middle East, home to 90 percent of the world's proven oil reserves—over the country's dependency on foreign energy sources, as well as evolving attitudes toward environmental stability, have played the leading role in the push toward alternative vehicle fuels.

The impact of a mass alternative fuel-based economic conversion is a sticky issue, both domestically and globally. The tenuous balance of geopolitical power and international governmental alliances is intricately tied to control over energy supplies, which has served as the backdrop to wars as well as less dramatic international tensions. On the domestic front, some of the nation's largest enterprises have staked their fortunes on traditional energy sources slated for replacement by alternative fuels. Power companies, electricians, coal companies, and oil firms are just a handful of the players throughout the economy that will need to scramble for a meaningful place in a dramatically changed market.

Market forces, as a result, are unlikely to be the primary motivating factor in the rollover from oil-based fuels to alternative vehicle energy sources. AFVs (alternative fuel vehicles) typically cost several thousand dollars more than conventional vehicles, and the fueling station infrastructure to accommodate AFVs has been sorely lacking.

Thus, one of the biggest challenges facing the alternative fuels industry has been how to incorporate such fuels into vehicles and power systems on a mass scale cheaply and without sacrificing everyday conveniences and comforts. The question of how best to accomplish this task amidst the range of hurdles—logistic, economic, and environmental—is not so easily answered and remains the most nebulous aspect of the alternative fuels industry.

ORGANIZATION AND STRUCTURE

Because of the interrelationship and interdependency between transportation fuels and the national economy as well as national security, both the gasoline and alternative fuel industries are heavily structured, controlled, and regulated by federal and state interests. Control spills

E85 Flexible Fuel Vehicles in Use in the United States

1998	140,000
2002	2.07 million
2004	3.43 million
2006	5.08 million
2007	6.15 million
2008	7.30 million
2009	8.35 million

SOURCE: U.S. Department of Energy, Alternative Fuels & Advanced Vehicles Data Center.

over into the user market in that private industry must not only produce AFVs that can compete with the price and efficiency of traditional gasoline-fueled vehicles but must also meet strict emissions and other environmental regulation standards.

The Energy Information Administration (EIA) reports that the primary determinant of the choice and scale of alternative fuel production is governmental policy, noting that use of such technology takes off only following public policy initiatives, whereas incentive seems to be in short supply absent government spurs. Not surprisingly, then, federal funding remains a cornerstone of alternative fuels development programs.

Industry Regulation. To ease the pain of regulation as well as stimulate interest, numerous laws and tax incentives are directed toward both producers and users of domestically produced alternative fuels, giving them a chance to compete with the oil industry and its monopolized hold on the global market. Some of the more important federal legislation supporting biofuels includes the Energy Security Act (1978); the Energy Tax Act (1978); the Gasohol Competition Act (1980); the Crude Oil Windfall Profit Tax Act (1980); the Energy Security Act (1980); the Surface Transportation Assistance Act (1982); the Tax Reform Act (1984); the Alternative Motor Fuels Act (1988); the Omnibus Budget Reconciliation Act (1990); the Clean Air Act Amendments (1990); the Energy Policy Act (EPAct; 1992); the Building Efficient Surface Transportation and Equity Act (1998); the Energy Conservation Reauthorization Act (1998); and the Energy Independence and Security Act (2007). The latter, also known as the Energy Bill, set new vehicle fuel efficiency standards and requires refiners to replace 36 billion gallons of gasoline with biofuel by 2022.

The manner in which these laws affect and interface with private industry can be summed up by the Alternative Motor Fuels Act of 1988. Its stated objective is to encourage the widespread development and use of methanol, ethanol, and natural gas as transportation fuels. Section 400AA requires the U.S. government to acquire the

maximum number of AFVs in its fleets as is practical. Importantly, the vehicles are to be supplied by original equipment manufacturers, thus stimulating private industry. The act also mandates that the DOE must assist state and local governments in developing public transportation buses capable of operating with alternative fuels.

Concurrently, acts such as the Clean Air Act and its amendments continue to focus on reducing the amount of pollutants emitted from motor vehicles. The U.S. Environmental Protection Agency (EPA) also remains greatly involved in the monitoring of environmental effects caused by vehicular traffic and fuel byproducts. In the late 1990s, for example, the EPA ruled that particulates, microscopic specks of carbon emitted from diesel engines that can lodge in lungs and cause a host of medical complications (including death), constituted air quality health hazards.

To monitor progress under the EPAct of 1992, which extends the Alternative Motor Fuels Act by requiring the incorporation of AFVs into the fleets of federal and state governments, the DOE reports to Congress annually on the progress of the act's focus, which is to encourage use of alternative fuels. Field researchers, original equipment manufacturers markets, and fuel suppliers complete lengthy annual surveys that primarily address the number and type of AFVs available; the number, type, and geographic distribution of those vehicles in use; the amount and distribution of each type of alternative fuel consumed; and information about the refueling/recharging facilities. As the data builds from year to year, the DOE paces its monetary funding and program initiatives accordingly.

BACKGROUND AND DEVELOPMENT

It would be remiss not to begin the industry's history by emphasizing the enormous economic influence that gasoline has had over both Western and Eastern countries. In the United States, for example, a single dollar increase in the price per barrel of crude oil could lead to a $1 billion change in oil imports. In fact, gasoline supply disruptions between 1974 and 1984, such as those surrounding the 1973 Arab Oil Embargo and the 1979 Iranian Oil Embargo, cost Americans $1.5 trillion. In the late 1990s, petroleum imports accounted for nearly half of the U.S. trade deficit and were expected to rise to 60 to 70 percent within the next 10 to 20 years, even though Congress voted in 1990 that a dependence on foreign oil of more than 50 percent would constitute a "peril point" for the United States.

The additional expense in terms of military security and protection of foreign oil interests cost the United States an estimated $365 billion between 1980 and 1990. The Persian Gulf War alone cost $61 billion. Factoring in these energy security costs results in the reality that the true financial cost of oil consumption in the late 1990s was approximately $5 per gallon.

These factors helped stimulate efforts toward near total replacement of gasoline fuels with renewable alternative fuels. Henry Ford himself, back in 1908, well expected his Model T automobile to be fueled by ethanol, the most viable alternative fuel at that time. In fact, an ethanol-gasoline mix (25 percent ethanol) was rather successfully marketed by the Standard Oil Co. in the 1920s. When high corn prices, combined with storage and transportation costs, made ethanol less feasible, federal and state initiatives were undertaken to keep interest alive. Ford again entered the picture and joined others to establish a fermentation plant in the Corn Belt capable of producing 38,000 liters per day. However, the efforts could not effectively overcome the low petroleum prices, and ethanol production plants closed down in the 1940s.

Interestingly, at about the same time Ford was developing prototype vehicles, Rudolf Diesel was perfecting his diesel engines to run on peanut oil, with the intention that eventually they would be able to operate on several types of vegetable oils. It is unfortunate that both Ford's and Diesel's hopes were relegated to the back burners of a hot petroleum market with which these resourceful fuels could not then compete. It was not until the critical gasoline market in the 1970s that momentum was reestablished. Ethanol-gasoline blends were again re-introduced to the U.S. market in 1979. These blends, however, were marketed not as gasoline replacement fuels but as "octane enhancers" or "gasoline extenders." This may have diminished any sense of urgency in the public's mind to accelerate conversion of a transportation economy so comfortable with inexpensive gasoline.

Complacency again reverted to a proactive attitude during the 1990s as Americans became more sensitive about environmental issues and economic dependency. The Clean Air Act Amendments of 1990 required that special fuels be sold and used in areas of the country with harmful levels of carbon monoxide. This resulted in the development and promotion of a cleaner burning and lighter gasoline product known as "reformulated gasoline." California had its own formula. Again ethanol blends and other alternative fuel choices caught the public's attention. Concurrently, the federal government continued to infuse money into numerous projects for biofuel development, also giving private industry a stake in the results. By the end of the 1990s, the alternative fuel industry had been resurrected.

The Clinton administration's Partnership for a New Generation of Vehicles, established in 1993, created an industry-government consortium with the ultimate goal of phasing out gasoline engines over the next 20 to 30 years. The federal government pledged an annual investment of $500 million (half of which included direct federal funds) to help the industry. The University of Illinois received such a prize in 2000 to build a "biorefinery" devoted to the production and commercialization of the Pure Energy Corp.'s P-Series ethanol-based fuel. Pure Energy Corporation, headquartered in Paramus, New Jersey, develops and commercializes cleaner burning fuels and technologies to produce bio-chemicals that are components of those fuels, and patents its fuel formulations.

Other direct government efforts to boost the commercialization of AFVs include the Job Creation and Worker Assistance Act of 2002, which provides for a 10 percent credit up to $4,000 for the purchase of hybrid (conventional internal combustion engine combined with an electric battery-powered motor), fuel cell, or electric vehicles before December 31, 2006, while the Internal Revenue Service allowed for a tax write-off of up to $2,000 for the purchase or conversion of engine components for the utilization of clean fuels.

The Southwest remains a leading center of AFV deployment. Long a leader in the development and employment of environmentally friendly energy, California launched an ambitious zero emission vehicle program to aggressively boost fuel economy and mitigate periodic price fluctuations like the one that so angered consumers in the summer of 2004. A study by the California Air Resources Board conservatively concluded that zero emission vehicles consumed about 25 percent less energy than conventional vehicles. Arizona, meanwhile, offered attractive incentives to individuals and businesses to convert to AFVs utilizing various fuels, including dollar-for-dollar tax credits to consumers reaching up to $5,000 or 30 percent of the total vehicle cost.

Initial Corporate Efforts U.S. auto manufacturers took the new technology seriously enough as a fixture in their operations that they began to bypass the traditional outsourcing methods for gas power conversions in favor of investment in plants specifically devoted to AFVs. Ford Motor Co. also broke new ground by initiating a new brand specifically devoted to ecologically friendly vehicles when it established its Th!nk Group. Ford, which manufactures about 90 percent of the AFVs sold in North America, committed over$1 billion in research to develop its alternative fuel capacity. It appeared to pay off for the industry giant, which produced ten different E85 models in 2010, in addition to its popular Ford Fusion.

Toyota aggressively pushed ahead with its plans to boost long-term market share by producing AFVs. The Japanese auto giant introduced successive models of its Prius hybrid sedan. Rival Honda achieved impressive sales with hybrid versions of its popular Civic and Accord models. In 2002, Honda introduced its hydrogen-powered FCX, which became the first fuel cell vehicle to be certified for commercial use by the California Air Resources Board and the EPA. The city of Los Angeles agreed to lease nine FCX vehicles from Honda by 2003 for roughly $500 per month. The deal marked the first U.S. retail agreement for a fuel cell vehicle.

Early Hurdles Cost remains a primary impediment to mass consumption of AFVs. Vehicles powered by natural gas, for instance, cost about $3,000 to $5,000 more than standard gasoline vehicles, according to the U.S. General Accounting Office. However, while alternative fuel technology was still more or less in the gestation process in the first decade of the 2000s in terms of achieving mass viability of AFVs, competition was already intense. Most auto manufacturers as well as the research firms they forged contracts with were becoming notoriously tight-lipped about their development programs for fear of tipping off competitors or breaching restrictive confidentiality agreements.

Hampering the proliferation of automobiles powered by LPG and CNG was the finding by researchers from BP Amoco and Ford that the retrofitting of traditional fueling systems for use of LPG and CNG can in fact lead to more rather than less net emissions. Similarly, skeptics of alcohol-based fuels such as ethanol have called for studies of the entire production process. That is, while studies have found significant emission reduction in ethanol fuels, critics have claimed that the entire process from development to delivery to emission actually results in a net increase in greenhouse gases.

While a host of alternative fuel types vied for long-term viability heading into the late years of the first decade of the 2000s, the commercial market that did exist was filled primarily with what were seen as short-term solutions, in the form of hybrid vehicles. In particular, politicians and automakers alike were looking to gasoline-ethanol blends and vegetable oil based biodiesel as a way to reduce the nation's dependence on foreign oil. The slow economy and high gas prices of 2007 and 2008 prompted automakers to focus their advertising dollars on fuel-efficient automobiles as well as AFVs.

Each AFV type has its own particular benefits and drawbacks. Dedicated AFVs, for instance, utilize only one alternative fuel, the most common being compressed natural gas (CNG). Biofuel vehicles house separate tanks for regular gasoline and one type of alternative fuel. Flexible fuel models utilize a gas-alcohol mixture such as the popular E85, which blends a maximum of 85 percent ethanol and 15 percent gasoline in one tank.

Many automobiles utilizing these alternative fuels met the criteria for low emissions vehicles designed specifically to target the emissions standards established by the EPA, which call for undercutting U.S. governmental standards by 70 percent in the field of smog-forming hydrocarbons and by 50 percent in the realm of nitrogen oxides.

Natural gas remained the most viable alternative fuel in the first decade of the twenty-first century. As the market awaited more sophisticated and affordable fuel cell vehicles, natural gas and alcohol fueling systems represented the most effective mass solution to the demand for more efficient and clean-burning vehicles. For all hydrocarbon emissions, compressed natural gas (CNG) vehicles save up to 48 percent and liquefied petroleum gas (LPG) cars cut emissions up to 31 percent.

The Emergence of Biofuel One of the most intriguing possibilities for alternative fuels was the prospect of utilizing environmental waste, or "biomass," as an energy source. This subcategory of alternative fuels, known as "biofuels," converts agricultural and forestry residue, and even municipal solid and industrial waste, into bioethanol, biodiesel, biomethanol, and pyrolysis (chemical change by heat) oil fuels. Biofuels are, by composition, alcohols, ethers, esters, and other chemicals made from cellulosic (of cellulose, the main part of the cell wall) biomass.

Biodiesel, made from animal fats and soybean oil, emerged as the most promising alternative fuel in the early years of the first decade of the 2000s. The National Biodiesel Board reported that 35 U.S. biodiesel plants supplied more than 1,400 distributors nationwide in 2005. In turn, these distributors served 450 retail pumps. The most widely used biodiesel was a mixture of 20 percent biodiesel with 80 percent petrodiesel called B20, though lower grades such as B5 or B2 were used as well. Biodiesel was approved as an alternative fuel by the DOE in 1998 under amendments to the EPAct of 1992 that allow regulated fleets to use up to 450 gallons of biodiesel per vehicle per year to qualify for EPAct credit.

An EPA study found that biodiesel surpasses petrodiesel's emissions reductions of particulate matter by 47 percent, while further reducing unburned hydrocarbons 67 percent and carbon monoxide 48 percent. Increasingly, it is replacing traditional fuel in work environments that require exposures to diesel exhaust such as near airports or locomotive systems. The nation's first biodiesel fueling station opened in 2001 in pioneer Biodiesel Industries Inc.'s hometown of Las Vegas, which purchased 1 million gallons of the firm's fuel each year and used it exclusively in 325 fleet vehicles.

By 2005, the National Biodiesel Board reported that all major branches of the U.S. military were using biodiesel in their fleet operations. Other users included more than 100 U.S. school districts, NASA, Yellowstone

National Park, the city of Seattle, Washington, and public utility fleets. According to the National Biodiesel Board, as of 2008, the United States had the capacity to produce 2 billion gallons of biodiesel per year, which would be enough to satisfy the renewable fuels requirement of the 2007 Energy Bill. In 2007, the United States produced 500 million gallons of biodiesel, nearly double the production of 2006. Eighty percent of the fuel came from soybeans.

Ethanol remained the most widely marketed biofuel. Made from brewed starch crops such as corn or, in the case of bioethanol, from cellulosic biomass, it was marketed in the late 1990s as an octane booster and a cleaner emissions fuel additive. In 2005, a record 4 billion gallons of ethanol were produced by 95 refineries in 19 states. By 2007, those figures had increased to 6.5 billion gallons, 26 states, and 139 refineries.

Ethanol can be used in its pure form or blended as E10 (10 percent ethanol) and up to E85 (85 percent ethanol) blends. Ethanol derived from biomass generates emissions reductions of up to 90 percent and can be used in traditional vehicle infrastructures, thus making it a popular alternative for auto manufacturers who would prefer that the overhaul of their production processes be kept to a minimum.

Government Involvement A national Renewable Fuels Standard was implemented in August 2005, when President George W. Bush signed the EPAct of 2005. Beginning with a baseline of 4 billion gallons of renewable fuel in 2006, production must reach 7.5 billion gallons by 2012. According to data from global expert services firm LECG, LLC cited in the Renewable Fuels Association's *Ethanol Industry Outlook 2006,* one goal of the legislation was to cut crude oil imports by 2 billion barrels by 2012, at the same time keeping $64 billion from foreign producers. The legislation was expected to be especially beneficial to ethanol producers, according to the Renewable Fuels Association, causing domestic ethanol production to double by 2012.

While Congress and automakers like General Motors and Ford were supportive of the president's push for more flexible fuel vehicles (FFVs), oil companies like ConocoPhillips, Exxon Mobil, and Royal Dutch Shell were skeptical of E85's ability to compete with regular gas. According to Manimoli Dinesh in the February 22, 2006 issue of *The Oil Daily,* the naysayers cited the limited number of cars that were E85-ready, the need for a separate fuel storage infrastructure at filling stations, adding complexity to the supply chain, and poor fuel economy among their reasons.

Other critics charged that the president was not supporting the research and development needed to support his alternative fuel plan. For example, before hitting the road to promote his agenda, Dinesh noted that the Bush administration quickly reversed several cuts that had been made to the National Renewable Energy Laboratory's budget, which would have resulted in the elimination of scientist positions.

Corporate Efforts The Big Three automakers were all engaged in the movement toward FFVs (flexible fuel vehicles) heading into the second decade of the 2000s. In 2006, DaimlerChrysler, General Motors, and Ford sent a letter to Congress pledging to double their annual FFV production by 2010, according to the National Ethanol Vehicle Coalition. They met this goal, and in 2007, there were 15 different FFV vehicles available to U.S. consumers; in 2010, there were at least 35, in addition to several hybrid/electric models.

Toyota had plans to double the number of hybrid vehicles it offered by the early 2010s. *Automotive News* revealed that the company would increase the number of models it offered from 7 to 14 in that time. Toyota also was stepping up its research in the area of plug-in hybrid cars.

Hybrid SUVs were later coming on the market, but by 2007 Toyota was producing two such models: the Lexus 400 Rh and the Toyota Highlander Hybrid. Ford joined the game with its Ford Escape and Mercury Marina Hybrid, and Saturn manufactured the Saturn VUE Green Line. Chevy, Dodge, and GMC also had hybrid SUVs on the market by 2008. In addition, that same year, GM announced plans to produce a hybrid Cadillac Escalade in 2009, along with FFV models of the GMC Denali, Chevrolet HHR, Buick Lucerne, and Hummer H2 and H2 SUT. These planned rollouts were part of GM's goal of providing half of their vehicle line as E85 compatible by 2012.

While hydrogen-powered vehicles were still far from ready for the mass market, Ford was one company that made clear its intent to continue research into the technology. Its new vehicle, called the Ford Edge, was, according to the company's Web site, "the world's first drivable fuel cell hybrid electric plug-in that combines an onboard hydrogen fuel cell generator with lithium-ion batteries to deliver more than 41 mpg with zero emissions." Ford had already produced hydrogen-powered shuttle buses, which were leased to airports in Florida and California beginning in 2005. According to *Automotive News,* production of the vans, leased at a price of $250,000 each, was being limited to 100 so that the vans could be monitored. BMW also released a combination hydrogen/gasoline engine in its 7-series sedan.

In May 2008, oil prices reached an all-time high of $130 a barrel, and the top five big oil companies were under the gun from the government and the public to use some of their profits toward researching renewable energy sources. A report produced by the House Select Committee on Energy Independence and Global Warming found that one of the Big Five, ExxonMobil, spent $76 million of its $40 billion in profits in 2007 on pay raises for its top five executives and invested only $10 million in renewable energy alternatives. By 2010, oil was again trading below $100 a barrel, but the Gulf of Mexico oil spill involving BP Corporation was enough to keep enthusiasm strong for alternative energy sources.

Earlier, in May 2008, the Grocery Manufacturers Association (GMA) launched a multimillion-dollar campaign against the production of ethanol. The GMA's position is that too much of the food supply is being used to produce biofuels and that the production of such fuels is the cause of the rise in food prices. National Biodiesel Board CEO Joe Jobe responded to the GMA's claims by stating that "Less than five percent of the world's soybeans are used for U.S. biodiesel production. Soy-based biodiesel is made from the plant oil, leaving 80 percent of the soybean—the protein—for animal feed and food uses." Moreover, much interest has gone into the development of non-food feedstocks which are sustainable and low-cost, such as algae, jatropha, castor, used vegetable oil, and tallow, all of which represented excellent prospects for biodiesel fuels.

CURRENT CONDITIONS

In March 2010 President Barack Obama signed an executive order requiring federal fleet consumption to drop 30 percent by 2020. Under the American Recovery and Reinvestment Act, the GSA invested more than $300 million to obtain 17,000 fuel-efficient vehicles in 2009, including hybrids, flex-fuel, and four cylinder models. In 2010, the federal fleet increased from 5,522 vehicles to 11,125 hybrid trucks and cars, mostly hybrid Ford Fusions, Ford Escapes, and Chevrolet Silverados. The overall federal fleet was not increased in size, as the initiative merely allowed agencies to swap their least efficient vehicles for hybrids. This is expected to save taxpayers more than $40 million over the next seven years. Another 6,500 new vehicles went to the U.S. Postal Service, the largest civilian fleet in the United States, with 43,000 alternative fuel vehicles as of 2010.

Overall, U.S. E85 flexible fuel vehicles in use more than doubled from 4.12 million in 2005 to 8.35 million in 2009 (the latest figures available). (This coincided with a jump in hybrid-electric vehicle sales, more than 275,000 sold in 2009 alone). Domestic vehicle manufacturers churned out more E85 flexible fuel models in 2010 than ever before, with Ford Motor Company and General Motors producing at least 10 models each. The 2010 model year also showcased

Honda's new FCX Clarity, a hydrogen fuel cell sedan with a fuel economy of 60/60 mpkg (it first introduced a version of FCX in 2002). This model was the only one introduced in 2010 to qualify for the emissions class of AT-PZEV (advanced technology partial zero emission vehicle). American Honda Motor Corporation was also the only manufacturer to introduce a compressed natural gas (CNG) vehicle in 2010, a special Civic GX.

According to the U.S. Department of Energy, U.S. production of fuel ethanol jumped from about four billion gallons in 2005 to nearly 11 billion in 2009. Equally impressive was that U.S. consumption equaled production in 2009, whereas in 2008, about 350 million gallons were imported in order to meet U.S. demand.

For naysayers as well as environmentalists and the general public, the 2010 BP oilrig explosion and subsequent spill of millions of barrels of crude oil into the Gulf of Mexico was enough to dampen enthusiasm for more domestic gasoline production and proved to be a shot in the arm for the future of alternative fuels.

Finally, although media attention generally goes to vehicle, truck, or bus fleets using alternative fuels, progress in the use of alternative jet fuels in the aviation industry during 2010 was characterized as "stunning," according to environmental executives from Boeing, Airbus, and IATA. According to Billy Glover, Boeing Commercial Airplane's Managing Director for Environmental Strategy, most of the technical barriers and fuel standards were in place for up to 50 percent blends of drop-in hydrotreated Renewable Jet (HRJ) fuels (although sustainable commercialization was still several years away). However, one brand of biofuel, Bio-SPK/HRJ, was expected to be certified for use in 50 percent blends by the end of 2010. Overall, global jet fuel demand in 2010 was about 5 million barrels per day, or 5.8 percent of total global oil consumption.

AMERICA AND THE WORLD

In 2007, there were only 20 oil-producing countries supplying the needs of 200 nations. By 2010, nearly 200 nations were producing or supplying biodiesel fuels around the world. Moreover, there has been a shift from increasingly expensive first generation biofuels, using soy, rapeseed and palm oil, to a new generation of nonfood feedstocks grown specifically for use as fuel. These feedstocks not only represent lower costs for production, but also do not compete for foodstock sources such as soy and rapeseed (used for hydrogenated and partially-hydrogenated cooking oils in many food products).

Globally, the biggest gain in production of biodiesel fuels has been in non-food feedstocks. According to Will Thurmond in his *Biodiesel 2020: A Global Market Survey,* China had set aside enough land to cover the size of

England for the production of jatropha, and India had up to 60 million hectares of non-arable land also available for jatropha. India has declared that it intends to replace at least 20 percent of diesel fuels with jatropha-based biodiesel. In Africa, as well as Brazil, significant programs were dedicated to the development of non-food crops (jatropha and castor) for use as biodiesel fuels.

Notwithstanding, the rapidly-expanding market for vehicles using E85 fuel has created an ongoing market for ethanol. In 2010, ethanol production replaced the need for the equivalent of 370 million barrels of oil globally. The Global Renewable Fuels Alliance (GRFA), an international federation representing more than 65 percent of global renewable fuels from 30 countries, predicted that global production of ethanol at the end of 2010 would reach 85.9 billion litres, growing by 16.2 percent from the 2009 production of 73.9 billion litres. Edible vegetable oil remained the major feedstock used to produce biodiesel in 2010. However, its share in total biodiesel production was expected to decrease from almost 90 percent over the base to about 75 percent by 2019. Sugar cane used for ethanol production at the worldwide level is expected to reach almost 35 percent by 2019. The United States was still the leader of ethanol production in 2010, projected to be more than 45 billion litres in 2010. On the other side of the world, countries like Nigeria and Malawi were turning to ethanol production to boost their economies and secure future energy needs as their countries developed. At least three countries were producing commercial cellulose ethanol in 2010.

In 2009, the International Energy Agency acknowledged the build-up of global biofuels production as a necessary component of meeting future global energy needs as well as decreasing dependence on diminishing crude oil and fuel imports, and contributing to green energy. Total global biofuels production in 2010 was estimated at more than one million barrels per day, according to GRFA spokesperson Bliss Baker.

RESEARCH AND TECHNOLOGY

As of 2010, there were several new substances tested and developed, some becoming the latest alternative fuel possibilities to complete successful trial runs. The Cambridge, Massachusetts-based biotech company, Joule Unlimited, announced that it had succeeded in obtaining a patent (No. 7,794,969) for a genetically modified bacterium that photosynthesized diesel-like chemicals. The company referred to its hopeful product as "liquid fuel from the sun," as it relied solely on freely available natural energy sources such as sunlight and excess carbon dioxide ($CO2$) already in the air, rather than on more limited resources like specific biomasses or natural gas. The granted patent is "Methods and Compositions for the Recombinant

Biosynthesis ofn-Alkanes." The company hoped that its new bacterium would ultimately be capable of producing ethanol or another novel fuel quickly and cost-effectively. However, scientists cautioned that breakthroughs in alkane-secreting bacteria represented only the first step toward commercial manufacturing of a viable alternative fuel, which could take years.

Student researchers at Northeastern University, under the direction and leadership of distinguished professor Yiannis Levendis, designed and developed a waste combustor capable of breaking down waste (non-biodegradable) plastics into clean fuel products. The prototype was featured at the annual MIT Energy Conference in March 2010. The double-tank combustor first processed waste plastic through pyrolysis, which converted the solid plastic to a gas. The gas then flowed to a lower tank, where it was burned with oxidants to generate heat and steam. The heat sustained the combustor while the steam could be used to generate electric power.

Perhaps the most creative new fuel idea was the coffee-powered car, dubbed the "car-puccino." In March 2010, it successfully completed a 260-mile trial run from London to Manchester, England, using up the equivalent of more than 10,000 expressos (about five expressos per mile). The vehicle, a converted 1988 Volkswagen Scirocco, utilized a system that converted coffee grounds into flammable gas. The novel car did require test drivers to stop every 40 to 60 miles to add more coffee granules and clear coffee filters of soot and tar that were generated from the burn process.

In the aviation industry, researchers were looking to create a 100 percent renewable jet fuel by using solid biomass to create pyrolysis oil, which would then be upgraded to make aromatic hydrocarbons in the jet fuel range. Aromatics, naturally present in conventional jet kerosene but not in biofuels, is required for aircraft engine seal swell. The fuel has already been tested in the Boeing Hydroplane in 2009. Also in 2009, a successful Qatar Airways gas-to-liquid (GTL) commercial flight was completed between London and Doha. The first Airbus biofuel test flight was scheduled for November 2010 in a joint project with Brazilian carrier TAM and other partners.

The expanding market for alternative fuels has inevitably led to a market for alternative fuel components. Among the most potentially useful of these are hydrogen sensors. In the form of tiny chips, hydrogen sensors monitor the amount of hydrogen circulating through a fuel system, sending signals to the engine to adjust its operations accordingly. Most analysts expect that hydrogen sensors will be a standard component of any hydrogen-fueled vehicle, especially on fuel cell cars. Thus, as the alternative fuel market grows, so goes the sensor market.

Other technologies deal with pollutant emissions after the fact. A process called Gas-to-Liquids, patented by Colorado-based Rentech, Inc., was developed to capture solid, liquid, and gas carbon dioxide industrial emissions for conversion into hydrocarbons. The process was slated for use in the manufacturing facilities of Oroboros AB, a Swedish steel firm. Whereas industrial greenhouse gases are typically flared into the atmosphere at standard facilities, the Gas-to-Liquids process will capture hydrogen and carbon monoxide and convert the materials into safe, usable energy, reducing by an estimated 200 tons the plant's carbon dioxide emissions.

One of the original criticisms of alternative fuels was their ostensibly lower "energy density," technical jargon for the formularized relationship between weight or mass of the energy source and the energy it would produce. Historically, gallon for gallon, alternative fuels have offered shorter driving ranges, less acceleration capability, and more vulnerability at high speeds or in heavy traffic situations than their gasoline counterpart. However, most of the energy in gasoline and diesel fuel was burned off as combustible heat and friction, not as locomotive power. Nevertheless it was true that gasoline engines were distinguishable for rapid acceleration capability, a desirable quality in a nation with as many freeway systems as the United States.

Conversely, alternative fuels such as ethanol and methanol burned cleaner than gasoline, an important consideration in urban areas plagued with smog. Beginning in the late 1990s, federal Clean Air laws began to require automobile manufacturers to increase the number of vehicles offered that met the newly mandated Ultra Low Emissions Vehicles standards. Ultimately, vehicles will be required to meet Zero Emissions Vehicle standards, and clearly, AFVs held the competitive edge in this arena. In fact, combustible natural gas was so clean burning that the only byproducts were carbon dioxide and water vapor.

BIBLIOGRAPHY

"Coffee, an Alternative Fuel?" *USA Today,* 11 March 2010.

"Global Ethanol Production to Reach 85.9 Litres in 2010." *Commodities,* 22 March 2010.

"2007 Flexible Fuel Vehicles Announced." National Ethanol Vehicle Coalition, 31 July 2006. Available from http://www.e85fuel.com.

Alexander, Sheryll. "Hybrid Vehicles and Diesel Trucks and Cars." *AOL Autos,* June 2008. Available from http://autos.aol.com.

"Alternatives to Traditional Transportation Fuels 2006." Energy Information Administration, May 2008. Available from http://www.eia.doe.gov.

"Alternative Fuels and Advanced Vehicles Data Center." Office of Transportation Technologies, 2008. Available from http://www.afdc.doe.gov.

"Big Food's Big Food Fight Finally Featured." *Roll Call,* 15 May 2008.

"Big Three Promise to Double FFV Production." National Ethanol Vehicle Coalition, 30 June 2006. Available from http://www.e85fuel.com.

"Biodiesel Best, Says Study." *Chemistry and Industry,* 17 July 2006.

"Biodiesel Push for South Korea." *ICIS Chemical Business,* 10 July 2006.

Cheong, Theresa. "Transforming Waste Plastic into an Alternative Fuel." *Renewable Energy World,* 3 June 2010.

Ethanol Industry Outlook 2008. Renewable Fuels Association, 2008. Available from http://www.ethanolrfa.org/.

"EU Urges More Biofuels Research." *Agra Europe,* 9 June 2006.

"Ford First to Offer E85 Hybrid." National Ethanol Vehicle Coalition, 25 January 2006. Available from http://www.e85fuel.com.

Gordon, Michael. "US Biodiesel Outputs to Double." *ICIS Chemical Business,* 22 May 2006.

Halliday, Jean. "Auto Giants Find Themselves Firing on Just Four Cylinders." *Advertising Age,* 2 June 2008.

Hargreaves, Steve. "Bush Signs Energy Bill." CNNMoney, 19 December 2007. Available from http://www.money.CNN.com.

Industry Statistics. Renewable Fuels Association, 2008. Available from http://www.ethanolrfa.org/industry/statistics/.

Kautz, Michelle. "2009 Cadillac Escalade to be E85 Compatible." National Ethanol Vehicle Coalition, 9 June 2008. Available from http://www.e85fuel.com.

Markus, Frank. "Diesel Revolution." *Motor Trend,* July 2008.

Newman, Lily. "Patented Bacterium Aids Alternative Fuel Research." *Science & Tech,* 16 September 2010.

"Oil Companies' Record Profits Going to Execs and Stock Buy-Backs, Leaving Energy Alternatives Behind." Select Committee on Energy Independence and Global Warming, 21 May 2008.

"President Bush Calls for Investment in Alternative Fuels." National Biodiesel Board, 25 April 2006, Available from http://www.biodiesel.org.

"Progress on Alternative Jet Fuels Stunning, Says Aviation Industry, but Commercialization is Now the Major Challenge." *GreenAir,* 2 August 2010. Available from http://www.greenaironline.com/news.php?viewStory=894.

"Obama to Double Federal Hybrid Fleet in 2010." *GreenBiz,* 31 March 2010. Available at http://www.greenbiz.com.

"OECD-FAO Agricultural Outlook 2010-2019: Information on Biofuel Production." Available from outlook.org/.../0,3343, en_36774715_36775671_45438665_1_1_1_1,00.html.

"Research to Begin On Sludge-into-Biodiesel." *Bulk Transporter,* 16 June 2008.

"The Problem is Energy." National Biodiesel Board, 10 June 2008.

Thurmond, Will. *Biodiesel 2020: A Global Market Survey.* 2d Edition, 2008. Available from http://www.emergingmarkets.com/biodiesel.

Treece, James B. "Toyota Buys into Biofuel Vehicles; Flex-fuel Autos Set for U.S.; Plug-in Research Planned." *Automotive News,* 19 June 2006.

U.S. Department of Energy, "Model year 2010: Alternative Fuel Vehicles and Advanced Technology Vehicles." Available from http://www.afdc.energy.gov/afdc/pdfs/my2010_afv_atv.pdf.

ANTI-AGING PRODUCTS AND SERVICES

SIC CODE(S)

2844

2833

2834

INDUSTRY SNAPSHOT

The new millennium brought with it the country's largest class of approximately 77 million baby boomers, and along with them, an unprecedented demand for anti-aging products and services. Extended longevity and relative financial stability have given aging U.S. consumers the desire and the means to purchase cosmetics, nutritional supplements, and surgical procedures that promise to mask, stave off, or even reverse the effects of growing older.

Anti-aging products encompass items meant to be taken internally, such as "nutraceutical" vitamin and mineral dietary supplements, and items applied externally, such as skin care and cosmetic preparations. Many of the latter have moved beyond traditional cosmetics into the realm of "cosmeceuticals." Cosmeceuticals don't simply camouflage the signs of aging; instead, they contain ingredients intended to reduce or delay those signs. Such ingredients include vitamins, antioxidants, hormones, amino acids, and botanicals (plant parts or extracts). In general, anti-aging products have become more scientific and technical in their makeup.

Drugstores continue to dominate the channels for sales of cosmeceuticals and other anti-aging products, along with department stores and mass merchandisers such as Wal-Mart and Kmart. Although grocery stores do not perform competitively in this sector, consumer-direct sales through such venues as Internet sites are claiming an increasing presence in the anti-aging sales landscape.

ORGANIZATION AND STRUCTURE

Large pharmaceutical companies and cosmetics manufacturers produce most cosmeceuticals. Many of the largest cosmetics companies are part of multinational personal hygiene and home care product manufacturers. Both the large cosmetics companies and the pharmaceutical manufacturers have access to internal research and development resources, giving them an inestimable advantage in the ever-evolving anti-aging products market.

Hormonal compounds used for medicinal purposes are manufactured primarily by pharmaceutical companies and are subject to U.S. Food and Drug Administration (FDA) scrutiny and approval. Hormonal preparations used in dietary supplements, such as dehydroepiandrosterone (DHEA), are not subject to governmental regulation at present, and, as such, are manufactured by a wide range of companies.

Amino acids and enzymes, including alpha- and beta-hydroxy acids, are essential components of many cosmeceuticals and dietary supplements. Like cosmeceuticals, these substances are produced primarily by large pharmaceutical and cosmetics manufacturers, although some independent chemical laboratories and a few small firms are also engaged in their production.

Herbal anti-aging preparations and dietary supplements are manufactured primarily by small companies. As is the case with hormones used in dietary supplements, herbal supplements are not subject to governmental regulation, which enables companies to develop new products with far less expenditure on research and development (See also **Dietary Supplements**).

Within the anti-aging products industries, a strict dichotomy exists between those sections of the market that come under federal regulatory scrutiny and those that do not. Under the provisions of the Food, Drug, and Cosmetic Act of 1938, the FDA must approve pharmaceutical preparations only. The distinction between cosmetics and pharmaceuticals was quite clear at the time of the act's passage, but modern cosmeceuticals have made changes in the act a possibility. Many countries, including Japan, have amended similar regulatory rules to classify cosmetics that alter physiology as pharmaceuticals subject to regulation. While companies in the anti-aging products industries dread increased regulation, the trend in the United States has not been in this direction. In fact, the Dietary Supplement Health and Education Act of 1994 exempted "natural substances—including human hormones, herbal compounds, amino acids, and enzymes—from regulation so long as these substances were included in dietary supplements rather than medicines." Increasing reports of dangerous side effects and drug interactions suffered by people taking herbal and hormonal dietary supplements, however, may trigger increased regulatory scrutiny of these products.

BACKGROUND AND DEVELOPMENT

Medical science has been aware of the therapeutic uses of hormones since the 1930s, but they were not widely used in over-the-counter preparations until the Dietary Supplement Health and Education Act of 1994. While estrogen replacement continued to be the primary therapy to reduce menopausal symptoms during the middle of the first decade of the 2000s, it was no longer prescribed to create cardiovascular protection. In addition, the effectiveness and safety of hormonal dietary supplements remained questionable. Small manufacturers produce most of these substances. In fact, many local health food stores are able to manufacture their own DHEA, a human hormone synthesized by the adrenal glands. DHEA was one of the first hormones recognized to play a role in the aging process, in that its level drops markedly as individuals age. DHEA replacement, however, has not been demonstrated to slow or reverse the aging process, and has caused troubling side effects in those who ingest more than 50 milligrams per day. Other popular, and controversial, hormone replacement therapies include human growth hormone injections, which are said to boost stamina, sex drive, and muscle mass; testosterone for men; and melatonin. The National Institute on Aging has criticized the use of hormone therapy to combat aging until further studies have been undertaken.

During the mid-1970s, the popular solution of alpha-hydroxy acid was first used in cosmetic preparations, but it did not attract widespread consumer attention until the 1992 release of Avon's Anew line of skin care products. The Anew product line achieved sales of over $190 million in 1997, and its phenomenal success led other major cosmetics manufacturers to launch competing compounds. Industry growth has slowed since the initial onslaught of alpha-hydroxy products, but new innovations have enabled individual companies to post fabulous growth rates with still newer products.

Antioxidants and vitamins, including beta carotene and vitamins A, C, E, and K, have long been observed to protect cells from certain forms of damage caused by environmental factors. As customers became increasingly concerned about the potential effects of environmental degradation on their health, and in particular the effects of increased ultraviolet radiation on their skin, demand for skin treatment products that incorporated antioxidant vitamins soared. Antioxidants are useful in treating far more aging problems than previously thought: research conducted in 1998 found that antioxidants showed great promise for preventing chronic aging diseases, such as Alzheimer's, cataracts, heart disease, and cancer. This study later came under scrutiny and mixed opinions concerning the efficacy of antioxidants dominated published information for the next decade.

Hair restoration services traditionally did not involve medication but rather physical replacement of hair. The introduction of Rogaine with minoxidil by the Upjohn Co. in 1988 revolutionized this portion of the anti-aging industry, enabling individuals suffering hair loss to enjoy some renewed growth through application of the product. Rogaine's limited efficacy allowed hair weave and other services to survive, but the product continued to post steady success.

The problem of impotence received its first medicated treatment when Pfizer Inc. introduced its new impotence drug, Viagra, in the United States in 1998 and received instant phenomenal success, instantly garnering worldwide sales of $193 million. One in three U.S. doctors has written a prescription for Viagra, and it has been approved in 77 countries around the world. Research has shown that while Viagra doesn't increase libido or boost sexual desire, it does enhance normal physiological response.

Passage of the Dietary Supplement Health and Education Act of 1994 provided great impetus to the herbal remedy and dietary supplement industries. Herbs have been used to treat a variety of maladies from prehistoric times. While the therapeutic properties of some herbs, including gingko biloba and aloe vera, were proven, many others were subject to question. Of particular concern were the effects of ingesting high concentrations of the active ingredients present in herbs, as these ingredients often interact harmfully with medications. Such concerns notwithstanding, small manufacturers readily filled the huge public demand for herbal anti-aging remedies, dietary supplements, and skin care products.

Since nearly 90 percent of skin aging results from photo damage, increased consumer concern over the effects of ultraviolet radiation on the skin led to a booming market for sunscreens and related products. In spring 2000, the first internal sunscreen appeared. Developed by Protective Factors, Inc. of Boston, the patent-pending sun protectant—an oral supplement, Sunray Defense—contained antioxidants such as lutein, which help cells to absorb ultraviolet (UV) rays and block the formation of UV-induced free radicals.

Alpha and beta-hydroxy acids, Retin-A, and the antioxidant vitamins A, C, and E continue to dominate the mass skin care market. Products also featured natural ingredients in anti-aging preparations, especially grapeseed extract, olive leaf, and green sea moss. D Polyhydroxides were introduced as milder versions of alpha and beta-hydroxies; similarly, new polymer and protein-based delivery systems made vitamin-enhanced formulations much less irritating to skin.

Although the only anti-aging skin care products with established scientific backing are the prescription retinoic acids (such as Retin-A and Renova), which have received FDA testing, and the alpha-hydroxy acids, numerous manufacturers touted new, "breakthrough" ingredients in their product roll-outs. For example, copper peptide emerged as a new formulation in skin care products. ProCyte Corp. debuted its Neova line of skin products and touted the role of its peptide copper complexes in tissue repair. The Neova line included eye gel, skin lotions, and creams. The Japanese company Kosei promoted the marine carotenoid astaxanthin, an anti-oxide, in its skin care line, noting that the ingredient could reverse photo damage to the skin.

Botanicals were another prominent new ingredient category. ICN Pharmaceuticals, Inc. launched its highly successful Kinerase skin products that contained the plant growth factor N6-furfuryladenine, which it claimed resisted the results of photo-aging. In its first four months on the market, the product line generated sales of about $6 million. Soliance was investigating wheat soramides and Mu Laboratoires was investigating pine bark and black currants. Even the sap of the *Acer saccharum* tree, used to make maple syrup, found its way into a Canadian skin care line. Chemist Ben Kamins included the sap in B. Kamins' Menopause Cream and Revitalizing Booster Concentrate for sunburn, reasoning that if the sap helped maple trees survive harsh northern winters, it might also improve the condition of aging boomers' skin.

Other producers such as Christian Dior, RoC, and Plenitude all launched preparations containing nonprescription doses of the proven anti-wrinkle ingredient retinol. Another development was the introduction of home use versions of products usually applied only in dermatologists' offices, such as Fairchild's YouthfulYou facial peel.

Special multipurpose anti-aging centers also sprang up to deliver clinical services alongside cosmetic ones. For example, John Sperling, the founder of the for-profit University of Phoenix, unveiled the Phoenix Kronos Clinic, the first in a planned string of nine such centers to be opened in retiree-dense Arizona and California. Clinic patients submit themselves to a comprehensive series of tests intended to generate their complete aging profile, including their hormone levels, risk of various cancers, and cardiac health. The clinic then can tailor and provide a full battery of remedies, ranging from cosmeceutical preparations and nutrition to more advanced medical procedures, to help them stave the effects of time.

Nutrition science has played an increasing role in the attempts to slow the aging process from the inside out. Reliv International, Inc., a nutritional supplements manufacturer, released in 2000 a dietary supplement it claimed replenished key anti-aging hormones. The product, ReversAge, was designed to "promote longevity, enhance wellness, and reduce the effects of aging at the cellular level." The mix included 7 KETO, symbiotropin, antioxidants such as coenzyme Q10, and herbs such as gingko biloba and maca. Also in 2000, Royal Body-Care of Irving, Texas announced the introduction of a new mineral antioxidant, which it sold under the name Microhydrin, and which it claimed improved cell hydration and reduced lactic acid accumulation during exercise. Fairchild brought out a YouthfulYou supplement line to complement its cosmeceuticals of the same name, including Lover's Delight-V for sexual enhancement and an anti-aging dietary supplement that contains L-lysine, glucosamine, and chondroitin. Liddell Laboratories' Age Defying line was the first anti-aging supplement to be delivered in oral spray form. Liddell announced that the product, which was hormone-free, "supports the body's release of human growth hormone." Other ingredients included ginseng, amino acids, and pituitary extract. Debates over whether these products actually work continued into the first decade of the 2000s. Skeptics point out that no empirical data exists to support the anti-aging claims of such products.

At the low-tech end of the nutritional spectrum, the humble blueberry was also trumpeted for its anti-aging virtues. A study by Dr. James Joseph of the Human Nutrition Center on Aging at Tufts University linked blueberries and their active ingredient anthocyanine to a reversal of age-related dysfunctions, such as balance and memory loss, in lab mice. Blueberries were ranked first in antioxidant activity among 40 fruits and vegetables.

Vitamins, it was said, were also meant to be applied to the exterior of bodies to prevent aging. Vitamin C moved to the forefront as the vitamin of choice. Added to skin products at doses of more than 20 percent, however, it tended to create irritation. Nevertheless, Murad Inc. introduced its 30 percent Vitamin C Home Facial, which it claimed delivered antioxidant benefits directly into the skin without irritation. Vitamins A, C, and E were particularly prominent in skin care products.

Hormone replacement therapy, delivered both orally and transdermally, also emerged as a means—though a controversial one—to combat aging. Going beyond the familiar estrogen replacement therapies available for menopausal and postmenopausal women, the field encompassed the genetically-engineered human growth hormone (HGH). Though it is promoted as an injectable anti-aging treatment that retards loss of muscle and bone density, it may represent a cancer risk, according to Dr. Samuel Epstein, chairman of the Cancer Prevention Coalition. Among the risks associated with HGH were colon, prostate, and breast cancers. Although approved by the FDA in 1994 for limited medical disorders, such as dwarfism, HGH has not been endorsed by the FDA for anti-aging therapies. When the National Institutes of Health canceled clinical trials for hormone replacement therapies in 2002, thousands of women stopped using the drugs, a trend which some analysts believed would weaken this sector of the anti-aging industry.

Pharmacia & Upjohn, Inc.'s domination of the hair restoration medication market with Rogaine was challenged in 1998 with the introduction of Propecia, an orally administered hair-restoring pharmaceutical by Merck & Co., Inc. Although sales of Rogaine slumped in 1997 and 1998, increased advertising and the introduction of Rogaine for Women helped mitigate the slump.

Researchers also uncovered more anti-aging powers of simple aspirin. In addition to its well-publicized work in fighting the risk of heart attack, it also helps promote blood flow in diabetics, reduces the likelihood of bowel cancer, and may stave off Alzheimer's disease.

It has been estimated that more than half of dermatologists sell cosmetics in their offices, and many offer treatments in spas and author books on how to have more youthful skin. Some even attached their names to lines of specialized skin care products. According to the November 30, 2004 issue of *Business Week Online,* "As a result, patients increasingly see dermatologists as having the skills and tools to reverse or halt the aging process." The publication noted that patients looked to dermatologists to help them navigate a vast array of treatments, including peels, laser treatment, collagen implants, and Botox injections.

In addition to concerns over false or misleading advertisements, some industry observers were concerned that as more dermatologists focused on the cosmetic side of their specialty, fewer medical dermatologists would be on hand to treat serious skin diseases and cancers. Groups such as the American Academy of Dermatology were concerned that a shortage of medical dermatologists would prompt patients to seek treatment for skin problems from doctors who were not specialized in dermatology. Research conducted by the academy found that just 13 percent of dermatologists interviewed saw the need for more cosmetic dermatologists, while 90 percent saw the need for more medical dermatologists.

The U.S. Census Bureau predicts that by 2030, the number of Americans over the age of 65 will reach more than 70 million, representing one fifth of the entire population. There will be 9 million people over 85, and by 2050 some 40 percent of Americans will be 50 or older. While the general population is expected to grow at a rate of 13 percent by 2010, FIND/SVP Inc., a New York-based business consulting and research company, predicts that the population of those aged 45 and older will grow by 38 percent.

In its January 2007 issue, *Global Cosmetic Industry* cited figures from the research firm Datamonitor indicating that nearly 64 percent of women over age 50 were expected to spend more on cosmeceutical preparations. This same eagerness was driving growth in a number of niche categories within the industry. The publication reported that the anti-aging and nourishing products segment was projected to reach $15.8 billion by 2010. In addition, it revealed that the market for anti-aging chemicals and ingredients in cosmetics was expected to reach $4.1 billion by 2009, according to figures from the market research firm Freedonia Group.

It is not only aging baby boomers who are fueling industry growth. Increasingly younger consumers, especially affluent women between 20 and 30 years old, are investing in preparations that will act as preventive "medicine" in the battle against aging. Even teens are becoming more willing to spend money on such products.

In 2006 Procter & Gamble launched its Olay Definity line of anti-aging skin care products. Supporting the brand with $50 million in advertising, first-year sales of $115 million were not out of reach, according to the June 5, 2006, issue of *Chain Drug review,* which said the Definity introduction was "being billed as the biggest skin care launch ever in the mass market." Aveeno also planned to enter the market in 2007, with its Positively Ageless line of products.

CURRENT CONDITIONS

From BCC's 2009 technical market research report came a finding that the global market for anti-aging products and services was worth $162.2 billion in 2008, with an expected increase to $274.5 billion by 2013. The report broke the market down into three sector: for appearance, disease, and fitness. The sector addressing medical conditions and diseases (joint and bone health, sexual dysfunction, metabolic disorders, cardiovascular and eye conditions, etc.) took the lion's share of the market with $66.0 billion in 2008, projected to grow to $119.2 billion by 2013. The appearance sector (facial rejuvenation, skin rejuvenation, hair care and body shaping) was worth almost as much, $64.4, in 2008, with a projected market of $105.4 billion by 2013. The fitness sector had the third largest market share, at $31.8 billion for 2008, and was expected to generate $49.8 in 2013. Cumulatively, the market is projected to average a compound annual growth rate (CAGR) of 11.1 percent by 2013.

Breaking the market down between products and services (cosmetic surgeries or procedures, alternative medicine therapies, spa treatments, gym services, etc.), the service market accounted for the major portion of the anti-aging market, 54.2 percent in 2008. The 2008 value of just the products market was $73.3 billion, brojected to rise to just under $200 billion by 2013.

Despite a very good consumer outlook, there are some legal issues looming on the horizon. In the United States, Congress continues working on the prospect of the cosmeceutical industry, especially products carrying the "natural" or "natural ingredients" label, being regulated by the FDA. This issue is being addressed globally, as the European Union (EU) also proposed legislation on the restriction of ingredients which claim active changes to skin, for example. Controversy remains over the fine line between medicine and cosmeceuticals, exacerbated by the sometimes enhanced claims of the products.

The International Association for Physicians in Aesthetic Medicine (IAPAM) predicted several new anti-aging trends in 2009. They included the increased use of minimally invasive procedures over surgical options; an increase in eye appearance procedures, including and incorporating the use of Allegan's new FDA-approved Latisse product, which claims to support the growth of new, darker eyelashes; and a surge on new over-the-counter cosmeceuticals with innovative ingredients such as caffeine and peptides.

INDUSTRY LEADERS

The cosmeceutical portion of the skin care industry was dominated by cosmetic firms Estée Lauder, Procter & Gamble, Cosmair, Maybelline, and Avon Products, Inc., each of which has incorporated anti-aging substances in product lines to some degree.

Large cosmetics companies, some owned by multinational pharmaceutical manufacturers, have continued to dominate the cosmeceuticals industry. Avon Products Inc., originator of Anew, the first cosmetic product to include alpha-hydroxy acids, remains a major player. Avon's competitive position was enhanced when it added retinol, a vitamin A-based compound said to help protect skin from ultraviolet radiation, to its original Anew formula.

L'Oréal SA, of Clichy, France, remains the world's leading beauty products manufacturer. Its product lines included Maybelline, Biotherm, and Lancôme. Corporate subsidiaries operate in medical and pharmaceutical research and development, and support L'Oréal's creation of new cosmeceutical products.

Estée Lauder Companies Inc. accounts for roughly half of the sales of prestige women's cosmetics in the United States. Estée Lauder's Diminish Retinol eye cream has ranked among the biggest sellers in anti-aging skin care. Estée Lauder's brand lines include Clinique, Aveda, and Origins. Revlon Inc. also has entered the anti-aging cosmetics market with its Almay and Color Stay product lines, as well as Age Defying Makeup with Botafirm for women with dry skin.

Large, diversified consumer goods manufacturers also play a key role in the anti-aging products industry. Procter & Gamble (P&G), whose brand names include Cover Girl, Olay, Max Factor, and Noxema, is one such corporation. P&G's rival, the consumer products behemoth Unilever, included among its truckload of brands the Chesebrough Pond's line of cosmetics and toiletries. Health care product manufacturer Johnson & Johnson (J&J), of New Brunswick, New Jersey, is a leading pharmaceutical maker, It participates in the cosmeceuticals industry through its Neutrogena product line, which it purchased in 1994. In addition to cosmeceuticals, J&J developed Retin-A and the anti-wrinkle treatment Renova, which won FDA approval in 1996.

Small, independent laboratories and other corporations continue to produce the majority of the non-pharmaceutical hormones and hormone-based dietary supplements and cosmeceuticals.

Two companies dominate the hair replacement portion of the anti-aging products industry: McNEIL-PPC Inc., manufacturer of Rogaine, and Merck & Co. Inc., manufacturer of Propecia.

As is the case with hormonal anti-aging products, herbal-based anti-aging compounds are primarily produced by small, independent concerns. Natrol Inc., a California-based producer of melatonin, is typical of these concerns.

AMERICA AND THE WORLD

Demand for anti-aging products is centered in the West and the economically developed areas of Asia, particularly Japan, which represents one of the strongest cosmetic and skin care markets in the world. The European cosmeceutical market was prjected to reach $4 billion in 2009, up five percent from 2008, according to BCC's 2009 technical market research report. According to *Euromonitor International* in 2009, the facial anti-aging market was expected to grow by 8 percent a year from 2007 to 2012. India's market was on the rise, due to a more affluent middle class, with the Indian beauty and cosmetic market valued at $950 million for 2008, according to figures provided by the Confederation of Indian Industries and reported in *Nutraceuticals World.*. Japan had a large skin care market, but spending on anti-aging products remains low. In South America, Brazil led with 2007 sales of $927 million, according to *Euromonitor International,* in 2009, as reported by a comprehensive article in *Nutraceuticals World.*

Manufacturing of anti-aging products is also concentrated in Europe and the United States. Multinational giants Unilever, P&G, and their subsidiaries play a prominent role in the industry globally. Production of herbal and hormonal cosmetics and dietary supplements is fragmented among small manufacturers, although Europe accounted for approximately one half of worldwide demand for herbal remedies in the early years of the twenty-first century's first decade.

RESEARCH AND TECHNOLOGY

The buzz word in the industry was "nano-technology," referring to products and/or services that are capable of genetically altering the appearance or function of human tissue. The latest trend in research has been to develop products that combine clinically proven ingredients with scientifically-patented delivery systems, such as through nanoparticles or nanospheres. The industry giant L'Oréal, the leader in nanopatents, devotes about $600 million annually to reserach. Another leader, Dow Corning, has been offering delivery systems incorporating the use of microencapsulation and phospholipid-based liposomes.

A team of Purdue University scientists, in collaboration with Utah-based NuSkin, identified an age-related enzyme, arNOX, which they believe is linked to typical skin damage that appears with age. This discovery was expected to trigger a new series of developments designed to address the control of arNOX to prevent skin discoloration or loss of elasticity. As always, a key research objective is the development of products that contain stable ingredients that will continue to perform over the use of the product.

In Italy, European industry leader Dermophisiologique introduced its newly-developed Maschera al Ferro (Iron Mask), containing iron microspheres, omega 3s and ceramides that ostensibly simulate magnets to draw impurities out of the skin.

Finally, another research initiative is directed at slowing down the signs of aging by increasing energy production in cells, which then increase cellular production of elastin, collagen, and keratin, and also increase cellular repair and protection. Dr. Dilip Ghosh reported in a 2009 *Nutraceuticals World* article that one such ingredient, a synthetic tripeptide, claimed to increase ATP (adenosine triphospate) levels in *in vitro* studies.

BIBLIOGRAPHY

Alvarez, Dr. Manny. "Anti-Aging Conference Offers new Ideas for Not Getting Old." *Fox News,* 26 November 2006.

"Antiaging Skin Care: No Mere Wrinkle in Time." *Global Cosmetic Industry,* January 2006.

"Big Launch Planned for Olay Definity." *Chain Drug Review,* 5 June 2006.

De Guzman, Doris. "C&T Trends: Emerging Markets, Man's Products and Natural Ingredients Top the List." *CMR,*9-15 May 2005.

Edgar, Michelle. "Aveeno Entering Antiaging Market." *WWD,* 20 October 2006.

"Estee Lauder, Other Firms, Face Suit Over Ads of Anti-aging Products." *Knight Ridder/Tribune Business News,* 12 January 2005.

Geria, Navin M. "Enhancing the Properties of Anti-aging Products." *Household & Personal Products Industry,* October 2004.

Ghosh, Dilip. "Anti-aging Fuel the Cosmeceuticals Boom..." *Nutraceuticals World,* September 2009.

Gogoi, Pallavi. "An Ugly Truth about Cosmetics." *Business Week Online,* 30 November 2004. Available from www.businessweek.com.

Jeffries, Nancy. "The New Face of Beautiful Aging." *Global Cosmetic Industry,* January 2007.

"New Survey Reveals Consumers Confused About, but Overwhelmingly Use, Anti-Aging Products and Procedures; Education Needed: National Consumers League Launches Campaign to Help Consumers Make Good Choices About Efforts to Turn Back the Clock." *PR Newswire,* 13 May 2004.

Russell, Jeff. "Top Anti-Aging Trends for 2009." International Assn. for Physicians in Aesthetic Medicine, 27 January 2009. Available from http://www.IAPAM.com.

Sherwood, Tracy. "Antiaging: Beyond Wrinkles." *Global Cosmetic Industry,* January 2007.

Stephens, Gregory. "The Anti-aging Market." *Nutraceuticals World,* October 2009.

Tsao, Amy. "The Changing Face of Skin Care." *Business Week Online,* 30 November 2004. Available from www.businessweek.com.

Weil, Jennifer. "Growth Seen in Aging Population." *WWD,* 4 June 2004.

ANTI-BACTERIAL PRODUCTS

SIC CODE(S)

2841

2842

INDUSTRY SNAPSHOT

Anti-bacterial products have enjoyed rising popularity as consumers aspire to eradicate germs from their surroundings. Between 1996 and 2002, the number of new antimicrobial products in the U.S. market grew from 150 to more than 700, rising to over 3,000 by 2009.

The global fear of bacteria and germs continued to drive sales of products designed to neutralize them. In fact, health scares such as the 2009 H1N1 virus (Swine Flu) and earlier 2008 Avian Flu (H5N1 virus) were causing large organizations to examine their level of emergency preparedness in the event of a pandemic. Some were developing business continuity strategies that included the use of equipment like masks and respirators, but also anti-bacterial cleaners for hard surfaces and hands. A September 2009 research report run by Mintel with Toluna indicated that while people responded that they did not change their personal hygiene habits in the wake of publicity over the swine flu pandemic, they did appear to be more aware of germs, e.g., buying personal hand sanitizers and being more sensitive to others who appeared symptomatic. For these consumers antibacterial products offered a barrier for them and addressed their fears of becoming ill or infected.

The mix of products with anti-bacterial properties extends well beyond household cleaners and hand sanitizers to a surprising array of merchandise, including everything from pillows and diapers to toothbrushes and touch screen displays. While manufacturers of these products sometimes shy away from making overly specific claims for fear of regulatory headaches, the marketing behind anti-bacterial products assures users that their homes and businesses will be cleaner, safer places thanks to embedded germ-killing agents.

Some medical and health experts caution, however, that the flood of anti-bacterial products could be encouraging development of more resistant strains of harmful bacteria. Moroever, there has been increasing negative press (continuing through 2009) about the active ingredient triclosan and its dangers to the environment, causing many manufacturers to find new and effective alternatives to keep up with needs in the global market. Notwithstanding, the industry continued to produce a broadening range of innovative materials and products, some of which were potential tools in the effort to detect and destroy biological weapons.

ORGANIZATION AND STRUCTURE

The U.S. Food and Drug Administration (FDA) oversees the production of pharmaceuticals or any products that include regulated, approved medicinal or health benefits. With such a product as soap, for instance, the FDA has very clear guidelines. According to the FDA Office of Cosmetics Safety, there are two categories of soap: "true" soaps, made up solely of fats and an alkali, and synthetic "detergent products." "True" soaps are regulated by the Consumer Product Safety Commission, not the FDA, so they do not require labeling. Most synthetic soaps come under the regulation of the FDA, as do any "true" soaps that make a so-called cosmetic claim, such as having moisturizing or deodorizing properties. Words such as "anti-bacterial" push a product into the drug category, which is subject to additional regulation. In June, 2009, FDA pulled alcohol-free Clarcon Antimicrobial Hand Sanitizer from the U.S. market after it found that the product contained high levels of various bacteria, including those which could cause "opportunistic infections of the skin and underlying tissues and could result in medical or surgical attention as well as permanent damage."

Products with disinfectant qualities that are used on inanimate surfaces (in other words, not on or in the human body) fall under the purview of the U.S. Environmental Protection Agency (EPA). That agency's involvement stems from the federal government's classification of disinfectants as pesticides, which are also under the EPA's jurisdiction. Disinfectants are thus registered through the Anti-microbials Division of the EPA's Office of Pesticide Programs. The agency has been criticized for taking too long to review products and costing manufacturers too much.

Anti-bacterials classified as homeopathic, or alternative medicine, are not regulated by the FDA. In essence, they are unregulated and could make any claim, valid or questionable, regarding their effectiveness in fighting bacteria. In the area of plastics that use anti-bacterial protections, all industry standards pertaining to their occupational safety, along with consumer protection guidelines, direct production.

BACKGROUND AND DEVELOPMENT

The market for anti-bacterial products owes its success to the origins of bacterial study and Sir Alexander Fleming, a Scottish researcher who joined the research department of St. Mary's Hospital in London in 1906. Fleming's experiences during World War I as a soldier in France presented him with the terrible reality of infectious wounds.

World War I brought horrors that other wars had not, due to modern artillery, machine guns, and bombs. Physical disfigurements, infections, and wounds that resulted from the new technology inspired many medical breakthroughs. In addition to Fleming's commitment to finding medicines that would attack infections, much of modern-day plastic surgery underwent its earliest experiments during this time. According to Ted Gottfried for *Scotsmart Books* in an online biography, "Fleming discovered in 1928 that an unwashed and bacterially infected flask appeared to be disinfected by mold, which had grown from airborne spores. Penicillin's use in combating bacterium had been discovered." After World War II, thanks to Fleming's discovery, penicillin began to be used to treat people in the fight against infections.

The onset of the use of antibiotics such as penicillin and its derivatives, administered orally or intravenously,

remained the focus of medical research and pharmaceutical companies. Products that employed anti-bacterial safeguards in surgical products such as heart catheter tubes were crucial in hospitals and other medical care settings to offset the chance of spreading disease. In alternative medical arenas, various herbal compounds and natural plants were the basis for homeopathic remedies and beauty products. As far back as ancient times, natural poultices, creams, and herbal drinks were used or taken for the cure of infections.

Although the industry had supplied anti-bacterial items to hospitals and medical supply companies, not until Safeguard, a soap from the Procter & Gamble Co., was introduced in the early 1970s did most Americans see the term "anti-bacterial" appearing on any product, even though products such as Lysol disinfectants and Listerine mouthwash had been available for decades. Safeguard soap was introduced into hospitals first and was then advertised to the U.S. consumer. Procter & Gamble kept it on the market due to its well-received response in terms of sales.

Despite warnings of the possible harmful aspects of non-traditional practices, the alternative medicine industry managed to grow into an $18 billion market by 1996, as reported by the *Nutrition Business Journal* and as referenced in a series of investigative articles in the *Los Angeles Times*. They reported that even insurance companies began to look at various alternative treatments as viable and offered some reimbursement for certain procedures. Every one of hundreds of natural health companies offered some line of anti-bacterial products, both for personal and household use. The products included soaps, lotions, herbs, teas, vitamins, and household cleaning products, all thought to improve physical health and immunity.

Not all anti-bacterial products have experienced unqualified success. Anti-bacterial toothbrushes, for instance, have proven a problematic category. Johnson & Johnson ran into a roadblock with its anti-bacterial Reach toothbrush in 1998 when the EPA fined the company for misleading consumers about its health benefits. In a retreat, the company could claim only that the anti-bacterial agent in the plastic handle could protect the user's hands from transmitting bacteria. Another anti-bacterial category with a troubled history is diapers. Drypers Corp., the first company to market such a product, announced in 1999 it was ceasing production of its Drypers Supreme with Germ Guard because of disappointing sales. A company representative acknowledged that the product had a small but loyal following.

Widespread use of anti-bacterial products began to draw pointed criticism from certain scientists and medical experts in the late 1990s. An October 1998 article in the *Tufts University Health & Nutrition Letter* entitled

"Anti-bacterial Overkill" laid out some of their objections. According to a growing number of medical researchers, said the article, "Using a special anti-bacterial cleanser when ordinary soap will do the job just as well (and it will) is a form of overkill that can backfire. It can lead to the development of bacteria that will be able to withstand the action of anti-bacterial agents should they ever really be needed."

"It's the same with anti-bacterial compounds used in common household cleaners," the article continued. "The more they're used, the more the bacteria that they are supposed to destroy—*E. coli, Salmonella,* and other germs that make their way into food—will undergo mutations that only serve to strengthen them by allowing them to 'resist' the anti-bacterial attacks. The upshot: the germs will thrive on kitchen counters, floors, sinks, dishes, and hands, and more people could potentially be sickened by bacteria contaminated food." The piece argued, moreover, that anti-bacterial compounds wouldn't work at times when they're needed most, such as when a patient's immune system is weakened.

The root of the problem, a number of researchers concluded, was with triclosan, the major ingredient in anti-bacterial cleansing agents, soaps, and lotions. Stuart B. Levy, M.D., director of the Center for Adaptation Genetics and Drug Resistance at the Tufts University School of Medicine, probed to find the way triclosan actually works. It was first thought that triclosan worked simply by "punching holes" in bacterial membranes, but when Levy published his results in *Nature,* he reported that his research group determined that the agent destroys *E. coli* by simply killing a single gene. If that gene underwent a mutation, the *E. coli* bacteria would be able to fight off the force of the triclosan and continue to live and grow. More importantly, a gene similar to the mutated one in the Tufts experiment was found in a strain of bacteria that caused tuberculosis.

Levy, a microbiologist whose work on triclosan has been widely cited, admitted that such a condition had not yet been observed outside of a laboratory environment. Still, he and others have warned that before all of the evidence was examined over a long period, caution should be used; that anti-bacterial products are sometimes necessary but not always. He also noted that while bleach and chlorine-containing products were not labeled as anti-bacterial products, they were still effective in wiping out entire bacteria colonies.

Manufacturers have continued to unveil a spate of new products with anti-bacterial and disinfectant properties. By 2005, anti-bacterial products were expanding beyond the realm of soaps, detergents, and hand sanitizers to include garbage bags, sponges, flooring material, and touch screen displays for kiosks and computer systems. Microban International Ltd.'s product, Microban, was used by manufacturers in a wide range of industries to build anti-microbial properties into products for industrial, medical, and consumer markets. Applications for Microban ranged from paper and textiles to polymers, coatings, and adhesives.

New product development continued to be of primary importance to industry players. In 2006 the Australian company Biosignal, which produces anti-bacterial medical devices and implants as well as anti-bacterial contact lenses, forged an 18-month licensing and development agreement with Ciba Specialty Chemicals, which makes anti-microbial products for both industrial and consumer markets. Together, the two firms hoped to pool their resources and expertise to introduce new products to the market, potentially applying Biosignal's anti-biofilm compounds in markets such as paints, paper and fiber products, coatings, and plastics. One specific new product was a spray-based hand sanitizer from Handborne Inc. that could also be used on hard surfaces like telephones and restaurant tabletops. In addition, the new product contained emollients that moisturized skin.

Trade organizations such as the Soap and Detergent Association continued to stand behind the safety and effectiveness of such products when used as directed, while new studies periodically emerged that raised concerns. For example, a study released by the journal *Emerging Infectious Diseases* in March 2006 found that some hand sanitizers (mainly homemade preparations, but at least one commercially sold product) were not effective because they did not contain the 60 percent alcohol concentration needed for killing germs.

Another example was a risk assessment conducted by the EPA, which found that the commonly used biocide orthophenylphenol, as well as group I and II quaternary ammonium compound sanitizers and disinfectants known as quats, posed environmental risks, as well as risks to unprotected workers and children, in specific situations. The risks associated with using these sanitizers, commonly used in home, institutional, and agricultural applications, were being evaluated by the EPA as part of a re-registration eligibility process. Examples such as these are clear indications that the industry's products will continue to be scrutinized for the foreseeable future.

While increasing use of anti-bacterial products was good news for product manufacturers, it continued to be a source of concern among portions of the medical community. In March 2004 the Saint Louis University Health Sciences Center issued a statement arguing that anti-bacterial soaps were harmful. Peggy Edwards, chair of the department of clinical laboratory science at the university's Doisy School of Allied Heath Professions, stated a number of reasons. Leading the list were continuing concerns that anti-bacterial products promote the growth of bacteria that resist antibiotic medications. Another concern centered on the impact anti-bacterial agents have on the environment once products have been discarded.

The university's statement prompted a joint rebuttal from the Soap and Detergent Association and the Cosmetic, Toiletry & Fragrance Association. The two trade groups countered that when used properly, anti-bacterial soaps and waterless sanitizers are safe. The groups further argued that independent research from a variety of organizations had failed to produce evidence that anti-bacterial products produced antibiotic-resistant bacteria and that the phenomenon was instead caused by the over-prescription of antibiotics by physicians. The trade associations also stated that anti-bacterial products were formulated to be safe for disposal.

In November 2004, *American Family Physician* reported the results of a double-blind clinical trial conducted by Larson and Associates, which found that for the general population, the use of anti-bacterial cleansers does not have any benefits, and that "The potential value of anti-bacterial cleansers in household use should not be overestimated by zealous manufacturers."

Despite these concerns, truly cutting-edge anti-bacterial products were in the development pipeline heading into the middle of the first decade of the 2000s. One example was an anti-microbial "nanocarpet" developed by researchers at the University of Pittsburgh. Comprised of groupings of nanotubes, this material resembled the fibers of a carpet or rug. When exposed to bacteria such as E. coli, the nanotubes changed color and then killed the bacteria. In the October 2004 issue of *Nanoparticle News,* Alan J. Russell, director of the McGowan Institute for Regenerative Medicine and professor of surgery at the University of Pittsburgh School of Medicine, indicated that this substance might be used to detect and diffuse biological weapons. Researchers also were attempting to develop a paint with similar properties.

CURRENT CONDITIONS

According to healthcare market research publisher Kalorama Information's 2009 "Worldwide Market for Anti-Infectives (Antifungals, Antibacterials and Antivirals)," the total world market for antibacterial drugs, which represents almost half of the anti-infectives market, was estimated at $24.5 billion for 2009, up just 0.7 percent from 2008. Growth was flat and in some cases, sales were declining, the report indicated. However, the over-the-counter antibacterial products market, as opposed to the overall therapeutic antibacterial market, did well. According to a June 2008 ICIS article, global sales of the biocide component of personal care products was estimated at

$350 million to $400 million a year, and was rising at a rate of 3 to 7 percent annually.

Amid fears of the H1N1 flu virus in 2008 and 2009, the number of global shipments of antibacterial products, particularly hand sanitizers and wipes, skyrocketed threefold in the third quarter of 2009 (September), according to trade-tracking firm Panjiva. The market for personal wipes, according to *Euromonitor International* 2008 data, was valued at $623.9 million and household care wipes at $3.08 million. Not all these contained antibacterial agents, but a large percentage did.

The controversy over the use of triclosan continued, particularlly after the Environmental Working Group (EWG) in 2008 published its survey of personal care product ingredient labels, showing triclosan in 112 of 259 liquid hand soaps. The Center for Disease Control and Prevention (CDC) detected triclosan in urine samples of 75 percent of persons 6 years of age and higher (Calafat 2008). According to a study published in the August-September 2009 issue of the journal *Environmental Pollution,* the presence of triclosan was detected in the blood of 31 and 23 percent of bottlenose dolphins in South Carolina and Florida respectively, suggesting contamination from downstream sewage systems. In 2008, a powerful lobbying coalition, including the Sierra Club, American Bird Conservancy, and Breast Cancer Fund, petitioned the EPA to ban triclosan.

INDUSTRY LEADERS

All of the top global players in household care wipes have a traditional surface care product portfolio. Procter & Gamble, Reckitt Benckiser (London) and SC Johnson led the category, driving sales through an association with their established cleaning products. Intense price competition has focused on adding multi-purpose and anti-bacterial properties to wipes in line with wider household care trends. Reckitt Benckiser added Lysol Dual Action Disinfecting Wipes to its all-purpose cleaning wipes product portfolio, with one textured side for scrubbing and one smooth side for wiping.

The Procter & Gamble Co. (P&G), one of the world's largest consumer products firms, has rolled out an extensive line of new products and brand extensions with anti-microbial claims, including dish detergent, hand soap, hand sanitizer, face soap, laundry detergent, cleaning towelettes, and produce wash. The company's sales totaled $68.2 billion in 2006, up more than 20 percent from 2005.

Once part of P&G, The Clorox Co. manufactures Clorox bleach, Pine-Sol, and Clorox Disinfecting Wipes Kitchen, among many other products. The company's traditional bleach products all have anti-bacterial properties, and Clorox has used these to its advantage in marketing. It competes head-on with P&G in several anti-bacterial product categories. Sales reached $4.6 billion in 2006, up almost 6 percent from the previous year.

GoJo Industries was one of the industry's category-defining companies in the late 1990s with its introduction of Purell waterless hand sanitizer. The product, which contains alcohol in a moisturizing gel, appeals to people at work, in transit, or in other places where they might not have access to washing their hands by conventional means. As of 2007, GoJo was still the leader in the consumer hand sanitizer segment. The company reported estimated sales of $83.3 million.

Through a patented blend of pure botanicals, the San-Francisco-based company CLeanwell now offers hand sanitizers and washes claiming the same 99.99 percent germ-killing properties as the mass-marketed products of the larger companies.

RESEARCH AND TECHNOLOGY

In 2008, researchers at the University of California-Davis published a new study in the journal *Endocrinology* ("Triclocarban enhances testosterone action: A new type of endocrine disruptor?") indicating that in lab studies, triclocarban (of which an estimated 1 million pounds of are imported annually for the U.S. market) mimics hormones. Clearly, an alternative to its use in antibacterial personal products was pressing on manufacturers. The newer science of nanotechnology promises the possibility of protective coatings that bind and synergize with human cells to provide antibacterial barriers to skin.

BIBLIOGRAPHY

"About Us." Microban International Ltd. 11 January 2005. Available from http://www.microban.com/americas/about_us/?lang=en.

"Anti-bacterial Overkill." *Tufts University Health & Nutrition Letter,* October 1998.

"Biotechnology News: Anti-microbial Nanocarpet Detects and Destroys Toxins." *Nanoparticle News,* October 2004.

"Don't Wash Your Hands Without Reading This: Avoid Anti-bacterial Soaps." Food Safety Network, 29 March 2004. Available from http://archives.foodsafetynetwork.ca/fsnet/2004/3-2004/fsnet_march_29-2.htm.

"Germ Warfare: Recent World Health Scares Have Made Cleaning Equipment Manufacturers Very Popular with OP Resellers. With Hygiene High on the Agenda, Those at the Forefront of This Category Have Found Themselves Involved in One of the Most Exciting and Innovative Markets in the OP Industry." *Office Products International,* June 2006.

Gottfried, Ted. "Famous Scots: Sir Alexander Fleming." 2 May 1999. Available from http://scotsmart.com.

"Joint Statement: The Soap and Detergent Association and The Cosmetic, Toiletry, & Fragrance Association." The Soap and Detergent Association and The Cosmetic, Toiletry, & Fragrance Association, 31 March 2004. Available from http://www.germsmart.com/html/new3.31.04.html.

"Latest Hand Sanitizers More Consumer Friendly." *MMR,* 18 September 2006.

McMmenamin, Helen. "EPA Finds Risks in Some Uses of Sanitizers." *Pesticide & Toxic Chemical News,* 1 May 2006.

Neufeld, Sonya. "WRAP-Biosignal to Develop Anti-bacterial Products with Ciba." *AAP News,* 3 April 2006.

Roach, Mary. "Germs, Germs Everywhere. Are You Worried? Get Over It." *The New York Times,* 9 November 2004.

Sadovsky, Richard. "Does Use of Anti-bacterial Products Reduce Infections?" *American Family Physician,* 1 November 2004.

"SDA: Common Sense Needed in Discussions Over Hand Sanitizer Use." Cleaning 101, 12 February 2007. Available from http://www.cleaning101.com/newsroom/02-12-07.cfm.

APPLICATION SERVICE PROVIDERS

SIC CODE(S)

7371

7372

7374

INDUSTRY SNAPSHOT

The fact that market analysts cannot agree on a consistent definition of this industry points to the broader debate in the business over what exactly constitutes an application service provider (ASP). The ASP Industry Consortium, the leading trade group for the fledgling industry, defines an ASP broadly as any firm that hosts and manages applications over a wide area network (usually the Internet) for multiple clients.

Previously, ASPs attempted to build on the long-established paradigms of high-end software rental and computer time-sharing by challenging the supremacy of user-licensed and user-maintained software in the corporate information technology market. This ASP model represented a shift both in pricing and in the total cost of owning (or using) software. Traditional software licensing involved buying application licenses based on the number of simultaneous users, sometimes called seats, of the program. Copies of the application were then installed and maintained on each machine that needed to run the program. In an effort to exploit the World Wide Web's nearly universal connectivity, ASPs attempted to position themselves as a remedy for the ills of software ownership by hosting software applications remotely and allowing companies (and individuals) to tap into them through a secure Internet site. All software maintenance was done by the ASP. The customer simply needed a computer equipped with a compatible Web browser. However, the high costs associated with the infrastructure needed to provide such services proved to be a major downfall for this ASP model, and many ASP start-ups found themselves on the brink of folding when the technology market crashed in 2000.

The ASPs who survived the fallout began focusing their efforts on software management services, leaving software licensing to the software vendors themselves. Many ASPs were following the "software as a service' model, whereby the focus was on the service provided and not so much the specific application. The ASP function was increasingly described using other terms, such as business process outsourcing and e-sourcing, and ASPs themselves were referred to as business service providers or hosted service providers.

Despite the trend toward software as a service, some observers argued that the service-oriented approach was not likely to replace traditional enterprise software, in which companies had made significant investments. Hosted services were instead expected to develop into a solid industry niche and co-exist alongside traditional options.

ORGANIZATION AND STRUCTURE

Defining ASPs. Most businesspeople seem to understand the concept in more specific terms, according to a survey by the Information Technology Association of America (ITAA), an influential trade organization. The ITAA's study found that two-thirds of respondents defined ASPs as companies that provide "specific business applications on a subscription basis via the Internet or other networked arrangement." The key difference here is the assumption that software is leased on a subscription basis, such as through a flat monthly payment, whereas the ASP Industry Consortium doesn't consider pricing structure a defining feature. It is also interesting to note that survey respondents' most common definition assumes ASPs are geared toward businesses, not consumers.

In the same survey, two other competing definitions were espoused by a noteworthy minority of survey respondents. The first, supported by 15.2 percent of respondents, held that ASPs are for-profit entities that offer aggregated IT resources over a network to remotely connected customers. This notion encompasses a wider array of services such as hardware management and even programming services that some view as part of a complete ASP package. The third most common definition of an ASP, chosen by 12.9 percent of respondents, was simply a company that offers "outsourcing/hosting of hardware and/or software," again a broader definition that doesn't specify pricing method or even mode of delivery.

Technical Portrait. In simplest terms, an ASP consists of a Web site that provides some user-oriented application or function. Familiar consumer applications on the World Wide Web include free Web-based e-mail services, such as Hotmail and Yahoo! Mail, and personal calendar/scheduling applications by the same vendors.

Application hosting for businesses follows a similar approach on a much grander scale and is usually more lucrative for the ASP. At a minimum, the ASP provides packaged or custom applications through a secured portal. The software in question might be a familiar desktop productivity suite such as Microsoft Office or StarOffice. More often, it might be a high end program tailored to some business process or functional department: order processing, sales force management, accounting and finance, human resources, manufacturing systems, or supply-chain management.

Indeed, some of more popular packages served up by such leaders as USInternetworking Inc., which was acquired by AT&T in 2006, are the so-called enterprise resource planning (ERP) suites by software developers such as Lawson Software Inc. These multi-application suites, often industry specific, are designed to provide broad, efficient, and powerful functionalities that all organizations of a certain type might need (say, banks or telecommunications companies), but without the costs of developing a set of completely custom applications. With the rise of ASPs, ERP has become a leading candidate for outsourcing because, in theory, corporations can leave the implementation and maintenance to the ASP and simply enjoy the benefits of the software.

In addition to merely providing a networked conduit to popular applications, ASPs handle scores of back end system management tasks. In fact, ASPs began focusing on this segment of services more than any other. System management tasks range from routine data backups and software upgrades to software customization and hardware maintenance. Often, an ASP commits to a minimum level of service as measured in application availability ("up time") or some other performance gauge. If the ASP fails to deliver as promised, the customer is usually entitled to some type of discount or credit. This guarantee is formalized in a contract frequently called a service-level agreement, a document that both ASPs and customers alike must scrutinize to ensure they're not leaving themselves open to tremendous liabilities or insufficient remedies should problems arise.

While access via public World Wide Web space is most commonly associated with ASPs, many also furnish their services over private networks using high speed leased lines or fiber-optic cable. Having a private connection is especially important when the customer has large amounts of mission-critical data flowing into and out of the remote application. The application interface may still be viewed through a Web browser but the communications channel is not the World Wide Web.

Market Structure. All ASPs aren't for all companies. While some cast their nets widely during the industry's formative stages, fundamentally there are separate markets for different kinds of applications and a single ASP is unlikely to serve all markets equally well. For instance, there are applications geared toward big businesses and others aimed at small businesses. Large companies typically require much more elaborate functions and the ability to effectively manage tremendous amounts of data—and need deep pockets to pay for it all. Many large corporations could afford to go it alone if they had to, but choose ASPs for the sake of long-term efficiency and cost savings. Small businesses by contrast tend to have simpler needs and more limited means. They possibly don't possess or can't afford the expertise needed to effectively manage a slew of different applications and would be satisfied to get reliable access to a few good programs without many bells and whistles.

Thus, not all ASPs offer the same applications or levels of service. They likewise differ in the kinds of bundled services they offer, such as connectivity, maintenance, consulting, customized programming, Web site hosting, and the like. ASPs that concentrate on applications hosting are often termed "pure-play" ASPs because subscription applications are their primary line of business.

A similar breed of outsourcing services is known as application maintenance outsourcing providers or application hosts. These firms differ from the common definition of an ASP in that the customer still purchases an ordinary software license from a software vendor, but the application host takes responsibility for running the software and providing remote access. In essence, the application maintenance provider acts as a manager of the client's own software, which is typically run on the provider's hardware.

Nevertheless, market segmentation by ASPs remains somewhat blurred as providers get a feel for what market needs are out there and how they can profitably meet those needs. Clearly, there are already some ASPs directed solely at small businesses or larger organizations, and the process of specialization is likely to accelerate once the most capable ASPs begin building a meaningful presence in the market.

BACKGROUND AND DEVELOPMENT

As they are understood today, ASPs are of very recent vintage, dating only to 1998 or so. Many of the underlying principles and practices, however, are firmly rooted in high end computer sales and service conventions set forth as early as the 1950s and 1960s.

Before 1969, when a bit of trust-busting by the U.S. Justice Department forced IBM Corp. to uncouple its software and hardware distribution, software acquisition was generally tied to the purchase or rental of hardware. Since computers in those days were phenomenally expensive by today's standards, combined software and hardware rental was a regular occurrence in the business world. And because computers were such large investments and so few people were familiar with them, high end systems tended to come with a great deal of support and ongoing service that later began to be scaled back and billed separately.

System manufacturers and software writers such as IBM weren't the only ones involved in high end computer support. A cadre of service providers, including Electronic Data Systems Corp. (EDS) and Remington Rand (maker of the path-breaking UNIVAC computers and forebear to present-day Unisys Corp.), became involved in outsourced data processing and computer facilities management.

Time-Sharing Services Thrive Remote data center and application hosting flourished in the 1970s as a bevy of service providers made inroads into the market by offering so-called computer time-sharing services. Under these arrangements, customers accessed databases and software applications maintained by the time-sharing company through a network connection (often a dial-up connection). The end user typically did so via a "dumb terminal," one that had no processing or storage capacity of its own. This meant that users often could only view information on their screen, but not print it or store it locally.

What's more, the software interfaces were universally text-based and non-graphical.

"Time-sharing" was then a general computing term for multi-user systems, and in this case carried the special significance that different customers were sharing access to the same computer, often being billed for the amount of time they used it. Soon the phrase also carried the negative connotation that users had to wait their turn for using the remote system, as they didn't always possess 24-hour access to the remote computers.

While such limitations are apparent in hindsight, they didn't stop time-sharing from becoming a fast-growing, multibillion-dollar enterprise during the 1970s and early 1980s. Some of the era's big names included Tymshare, EDS, General Electric Information Services, Comshare, and Automatic Data Processing. They didn't all fare so well by the mid-1980s, but their vision was strikingly similar to that of present day ASPs: an economical, scalable alternative to owning software and hardware.

PC Revolution, Software Licensing Overshadow Time-Sharing As companies began adopting personal computers (PCs) wholesale in the 1980s, interest in time-sharing waned. Personal computers were seen as relatively inexpensive and surprisingly powerful tools that some believed would curtail the need for high end, multi-user systems in general. Although that prediction did not pan out, companies focused on developing in-house information technology (IT) infrastructure using PCs. Many chafed at the lack of control in time-sharing arrangements and yearned for the independence and ease of use that PCs seemed to promise. Coupled with time-sharing firms' poor marketing and seemingly stagnant offerings, time-sharing was relegated to an increasingly obscure and ridiculed niche by the late 1980s.

With PCs, the software paradigm was almost entirely license-driven from the get-go. This occurred in part because PCs relied more heavily on packaged software and third party software than had larger systems. Moreover, a different breed of software developers—Microsoft, for one—began catering to the PC market and their dominant mode of distribution was licensing.

Since PCs were considered relatively small-ticket items (at least on an individual basis) and were always located on premises, companies focused on acquiring legions of PCs for their employees and, as a consequence, outfitting each machine with the requisite operating systems, spreadsheets, word processors, and so on. The licenses, and later, support needs, began racking up. In addition, PC networks quickly came into vogue, creating demand for client/server and networking software, which was also primarily licensed and run on internal servers.

Internet and Thin-Client Computing Open New Possibilities Commercialization of the Internet in the mid and late 1990s provided an opportunity to revisit outsourcing software and hardware. The Internet provided nearly universal connectivity across far-flung locations. Moreover, its primary mode of access, Web browsers, enabled the same content and functions on a Web site to be shared on disparate computers without installing or maintaining any software locally aside from the browser. Growing antipathy toward aggressive software publishers, especially Microsoft, which by the late 1990s had become the world's biggest software company, also fueled interest in alternatives to software licensing.

At the same time, larger companies lamented the expense and complexity of maintaining the sprawling PC networks they had assembled. Upgrading software was commonly a major ordeal, and troubleshooting PC and network problems consumed corporate IT staff hours. Some dissatisfaction with distributed computing was channeled toward so-called network computers (NCs) and NetPCs, bare bones network—centric workstations that run centralized applications off a network server. NCs and similar devices were part of a broader "thin client" movement, where full-featured PCs running their own space-hungry applications are known as "fat clients." Web browsers are considered thin clients in the software realm.

The ultimate extension of thin client computing in fact was the adoption of updated versions of the once-derided dumb terminal. Late 1990s terminal systems such as Windows-based terminals were a far cry from the brooding monochrome text screens of yesteryear, however. They supported graphical interfaces, Web browsing, local printing, and point-and-click operations, and in large part provided the look and feel of a PC—and at a fraction of the cost.

While thin client hardware was making its revival, a complementary and much bigger movement began to unfold on the software side. As Web programming grew more robust and stable, various parties began developing software applications that could be accessed through browsers. Corporate intranets put common internal information and functions—employee information, message boards, operating data—within reach of any Web browser. Extranets did the same for sharing information and data with suppliers and customers.

ASPs Emerge With electronic commerce (e-commerce) on a steep rise, it was just a short leap to online application hosting and subscription services being conducted over the World Wide Web. The first companies dedicated to serving up applications over the World Wide Web (and browser-friendly private networks) sprang up in 1998 with the formation of leading pure-play ASPs such as USInternetworking, Inc. and Corio, Inc. These companies marketed themselves as solutions to the hassles of licensing software and maintaining it on unwieldy and resource-sapping internal PC networks. Although sales were not immediately off the board—USInternetworking generated less than $5 million in revenue in 1998—nascent ASPs met with strong interest and even stronger growth prospects in future years. Venture capitalists poured millions into ASP startups, and a few of the larger ones began going public in 1999.

The year 1999 proved a watershed for the industry, with a huge influx of new investors, competitors, and customers. In addition to service providers focused solely on application hosting, a large number of IT service and consulting firms and Internet access companies began touting themselves as ASPs. Software publishers such as Oracle Corp. and Sun Microsystems, Inc. also became outspoken proponents of Web-enabled software rental. The industry received extensive coverage in the business and technology press, and by the end of the year even Microsoft, which had publicly criticized the ASP model, began to warm up to the idea of letting its titles be rented online.

While ASPs made immeasurable gains in public awareness during 1999, the market for online application hosting remained subdued in dollar terms, as many services were just coming on line that year. Worldwide ASP revenues in 2000 approached $2 billion, according to research by International Data Corp., but were expected to grow at a furious 90 percent rate per year well into the first decade of the 2000s. Other organizations estimated that the market would be worth significantly more than that.

As customers test-drove the new technology and began to demand more immediate return on their ASP investments than had thus far been realized, ominous rumblings threatened the industry. When the technology industry crash of 2000 forced many dot-com companies into bankruptcy, ASPs saw a large portion of their client base simply disappear. Lacking the critical mass necessary to offset the costs associated with licensing software, ASPs such as USInternetworking and Corio were forced to rethink their business model. The Gartner Group predicted that fully 60 percent of existing ASPs would collapse by the end of 2001.

This dire forecast appeared imminent in the early years of the first decade of the 2000s as industry leader USInternetworking filed for Chapter 11 bankruptcy protection and another leading player, Corio, saw its stock price plunge from $22 per share in July of 2000 to 70 cents per share in mid-2002. However, like many other ASPs, both firms managed to stay afloat by narrowing their focus to software management. This shift in focus prompted Gartner to assert that most ASPs would be more appropriately dubbed AMOs, or applications management outsourcers. According to an October 2002 issue of *CFO, The Magazine for Senior Financial Executives,* "Most ASPs, in fact, now concentrate on managing software versus renting it. Whereas they once harbored dreams of a one-to-many model in which they licensed software from vendors and then rented it to many clients, that has proved unfeasible (although software makers themselves do offer this option). Instead, ASPs now tout their implementation and managerial expertise; they are hired guns, not wholesalers."

Despite its more narrowed focus, or perhaps because of it, the ASP sector remains one of the fastest-growing U.S. markets in the IT services arena. One main trade-off that companies continue to contend with is the lack of customization offered by many ASPs. By offering one service to many customers, many ASPs lacked the ability to customize their offerings to suit very specific needs of clients. Therefore, companies were required to balance potential savings with the need for customization.

According to columnist Stan Gibson in the October 25, 2004, issue of *eWeek,* analysts from the research firm Gartner indicated that one major IT trend was the movement toward flexible system architectures that allow companies "to run applications of the moment." This focus on agility marked a departure from architectures designed to run specific software applications.

In line with the concept of the agile enterprise was the Agility Alliance spearheaded by Electronic Data Systems Corp. (EDS). According to EDS, the alliance is "a federation of market-leading infrastructure, application and business process providers chartered with driving industry innovation and cost leadership through the development and delivery of EDS' Agile Enterprise Platform." The alliance consisted of six partner companies: Cisco, Dell, EMC, Microsoft, Sun, and Xerox. By working with these select industry heavyweights, EDS hoped to impact the development of its customers' IT architectures.

After weathering difficult times during the 1990s and early years of the first decade of the 2000s, ASPs were still very much in demand during the decade's middle years. However, rather than simply reselling applications from other vendors on a hosted basis, many ASPs were following the "software as a service' model, whereby the focus was on the service provided and not so much the specific application. The ASP function was increasingly described using other terms, such as business process outsourcing and e-sourcing, and ASPs themselves were referred to as business service providers or hosted service providers.

In a March 6, 2007, *Business Wire* release, Gartner Research Vice President Ben Pring provided insight into the current state of affairs, explaining, "Due to the law of large numbers, traditional IT solution models are becoming victims of their own success, while the relative smallness of new approaches facilitates growth much more easily. For large, established IT solution providers, the SaaS market so far has not appeared to have enough incremental growth potential to meaningfully contribute to revenue growth. As a result, they have tended to ignore it. This has left the door open for smaller, newer players, who are now pouring into this gap. Incumbent IT solution providers are slowly waking up to this and are entering the market to leverage SaaS market interest."

According to some industry observers, any service that was not among a company's core competencies was an excellent candidate for outsourcing via the ASP model. Examples include expanded customer services, the payroll function, as well as logistics and transportation management and regulatory/corporate compliance. In the financial sector, money management firms used hosted software to ensure compliance with trading and ethics policies, and to safeguard against potential infractions such as insider trading.

CURRENT CONDITIONS

Technological advances in both software and hardware have forced the market to continue to constantly redefine itself and reinvent its products. This fact limits overall market forecasting and reporting because of the varying definitions of services and products. However, certain sectors of the market have provided some insight. For example, in 2008, Global Industry Analysts, Inc. predicted that the global ASP hosting service market would exceed $45 billion by 2010.

Within the ASP subgroup, the T3i Group reported in September 2009 that during the next five years, all seven umbrella managed/hosted telecommunications service groups are expected to generate positive year-over-year growth. These would be led by Hosted IPT & Applications and Business Continuity Services, followed by Managed PBX & Voice Applications,include Managed Access Services, Managed Network Services, Managed Security Services, Business Continuity Services and Managed KTS/Hybrid. Year-over-year, double-digit revenue growth worldwide was projected for Hosted IPT & Applications in particular. In 2008, the U.S. government alone spent $26.7 million on Internet service providers (including ASP services), awarding 317 contracts to 77 companies, the average contract value being $347,557.

A 2009 report from market research firm DMG Consulting predicted that the SaaS-based call center software market would grow 30 percent in 2009, 35 percent in 2010 and 20 percent in 2011. The report indicated

2008 was actually a good year for vendors offering hosted or Web-based call center solutions, despite the down economy.

Overall, revenue from all telecom services and equipment grew by 5.7 percent to $1.9 trillion in 2008, as the historic shift between mobile and fixed services continued to grow, with rollout into emerging markets. The total market was projected to exceed $2.1 trillion in 2013, according to research reporter Dataquest in July 2009. Notwithstanding, Gartner reported that enterprise IT spending worldwide was expected to decline by about 6.8 percent in 2009 and not return to 2008 levels until 2012. Gartner estimated that 2009 worldwide enterprise IT spending would total some $2.3 trillion compared to $2.5 trillion in 2008. Part of the problem was the delayed scheduled replacements of servers, expected to reach 10 percent by 2010.

INDUSTRY LEADERS

An interesting two-year Internet Observatory Report was presented in October 2009 at the NANOG47 Conference in Dearborn, Michigan. Key findings included the conclusion that during the previous five years, most Internet content traffic had migrated to a very small number of very large hosting, cloud, and content providers. These included Facebook, Google, Microsoft, and YouTube, all of which provided hosting and other ASP services. The study found a core group of international transit providers had moved away from previous business models (IP wholesale transit) to client enterprise services, content hosting, and VPNs.

As this small cluster of cloud companies dominated much of the sector, still others were able to rise alone in the industry as leaders. Some noteworthy ASPs include Colorado-based Cetrom (SaaS-based) with 2008 sales of $25 billion and only 35 employees; Colorado-based Level 3 Communications (a networking giant), with 2008 sales of $4.3 billion and 5,300 employees; CDNetworks Co;, Inc., based in South Korea, with 2008 sales of $54.4 million and 244 employees; and Massachusetts-based Akamai Technologies, with 2008 sales of $790.0 million and 1,500 employees. Texas-based Affiliated Computer Services Inc. continued to make headlines, as did ASP segments of AT&T and IBM.

BIBLIOGRAPHY

"Arbor Networks, the University of Michigan and Merit Network To Present Two-Year Study of Global Internet Traffic At NANOG47." 14 October 2009. Available from http://www.arbornetworks.com/en/arbor-networks-the-university-of-michigan-and-merit-network-to-present-two-year-study-of-global-int-2.html

"ASP Option Has Bite." *Precision Marketing*, 3 December 2004.

Barnard, Patrick. "The Advantages of SaaS-based Call Center Solutions, Part 1." TMCNet article dated 16 October 2009, available from http://www.tmcnet.com/channels/call-center/articles/66842-advantages-saas-based-call-center-solutions-part-1.htm.

"Corporate Overview." BlueStar Solutions Inc., 3 February 2005. Available from http://www. bluestarsolutions.com/about.

"EDS Agility Alliance." Electronic Data Systems Corp,. 1 February 2005. Available from http://www.eds.com/services/alliances/agility.

"Gartner Says Service Providers Must Prepare Now for the Software as a Service Wave." *Business Wire*, 6 March 2007.

Gibson, Stan. "Improving On ASPs. Gartner: Time Is Finally Right for Software as a Service." *eWeek*, 25 October 2004.

"Global Application Service Provider (ASP) Hosting Services Market to Reach $45 Billion by 2010...," 23 April 2008. Available from http://computing.pressreleasewatch.com/global-application-service-provider-asp-hosting-services-market-to-reach-45-billion-by-2010-according-to-new-report-by-global-industry-analysts-inc-51684/

Hahn, WIlliam L. "Dataquest Insight: Global Telecommunication Market Take, June 2009." *Dataquest*, 2 July 2009.

"Hoover's Company Profiles." *Hoover's Online*. Available from http://www.hoovers.com.

Information Technology Association of America. *The ITAA ASP Customer Demand Survey*. Information Technology Association of America, 2000.

Kissell, Joe. "The Google Office." *Macworld*, August 2007.

Leibs, Scott. "ASPs: Alive and ...Well, Alive." *CFO, the Magazine for Senior Financial Executives*, October 2002.

Meredith, Simon. "ASPs Snake Back into Hosting Limelight." *Computer Reseller News*, 11 September 2006.

Middlemiss, Jim. "The ABCs of ASPs: The Application-Service-Provider Model Is Gaining Momentum as Firms Seek Ways to Lower the Cost of Technology Adoption." *Wall Street & Technology*, September 2004.

"SAAS Route Could Be Bumpy." *eWeek*, 23 April 2007.

Schoenfeld, Anita, and Martha A. Winslow. "A Brave New World: Are You Ready to Host Your System?" *Risk Management*, June 2006.

Schwartz, Ephraim. "REALITY CHECK: REALITY CHECK: Applications, Supplied on Demand—There Is Value in Software as a Service if You Can Look Beyond the Hype." *InfoWorld*, 5 July 2004.

Scott, Robert W. "The Return of the ASP." *Accounting Technology*, December 2004.

Sturdevant, Cameron. "Hosted Apps Pick Up Steam." *eWeek*, 18 June 2007.

T3i Group, LLC. "The 2009-2014 Global Managed Services Market Forecast, " Available from http://www.telecomweb.com/marketresearch/enterprisesvcs/IES/GlobalManagedServicesMarketForecast.

Thibodeau, Patrick. "Budget Cuts Could Increase Server Failures, Warns Gartner." *ComputerWorld*, 19 October 2009.

"Welcome to Google Apps." Google Inc., 19 July 2007. Available from http://www.google.com.

ARTIFICIAL INTELLIGENCE

SIC CODE(S)

7371

7373

7379

INDUSTRY SNAPSHOT

In the very simplest of terms, the artificial intelligence (AI) industry seeks to create machines that are capable of learning and intelligent thinking. It includes the development of computer-based systems that can learn from past behaviors and apply that knowledge to solving future problems. AI draws from a variety of academic fields, including mathematics, computer science, linguistics, engineering, physiology, philosophy, and psychology, and predates the modern computer age. Although it did not truly emerge as a stand-alone field of study until the late 1940s, logicians, philosophers, and mathematicians formed the foundation upon which modern AI rests during the eighteenth and nineteenth centuries.

The field of artificial intelligence gradually evolved during the last half of the twentieth century, when major research departments were established at prominent U.S. universities, beginning with the Massachusetts Institute of Technology (MIT). The U.S. government has been a dominant player in this market for many years, providing significant funding for military projects. However, private enterprise also is a major stakeholder. AI technology is used in such varied fields as robotics, information management, computer software, transportation, e-commerce, military defense, medicine, manufacturing, finance, security, emergency preparedness, and others.

After years of frequent failures and narrow successes, artificial intelligence was going mainstream, according to Gary Morgenthaler's 2010 article, "AI's Time Has Arrived." Morgenthaler attributed this to a "confluence of trends," including expanding broadband capability, cloud computing, improved AI algorithms, smartphones, and the steady expansion of raw processing power dictated by Moore's Law.

ORGANIZATION AND STRUCTURE

The AI industry is powered by a blend of small and large companies, government agencies, and academic research centers. Major research organizations within the United States include the Brown University Department of Computer Science, Carnegie Mellon University's School of Computer Science, the University of Massachusetts Experimental Knowledge Systems Laboratory, NASA's Jet Propulsion Laboratory, MIT, the Stanford Research Institute's Artificial Intelligence Research Center, and the University of Southern California's Information Sciences Institute.

In addition, a large number of small and large companies also fuel research efforts and the development of new products and technologies. Software giants such as IBM Corp., Microsoft Corp., Oracle Corp., PeopleSoft Inc., SAS AB, and Siebel Systems Inc. are heavily involved in the development and enhancement of business intelligence, data mining, and customer relationship management software.

Large corporate enterprises often have their own research arms devoted to advancing AI technologies. For example, Microsoft operates its Decision Theory and Adaptive Systems Group, AT&T operates AT&T Labs-Research (formerly AT&T Bell Labs), and Xerox Corp. is home to the Palo Alto Research Center.

Associations. The artificial intelligence industry is supported by the efforts of the Association for the Advancement of Artificial Intelligence, or AAAI (formerly the American Association for Artificial Intelligence), a nonprofit scientific society based in Menlo Park, California. According to the AAAI, which was established in 1979, it is "devoted to advancing the scientific understanding of the mechanisms underlying thought and intelligent behavior and their embodiment in machines. AAAI also aims to increase public understanding of artificial intelligence, improve the teaching and training of AI practitioners, and provide guidance for research planners and funders concerning the importance and potential of current AI developments and future directions." Along these lines, the AAAI included students, researchers, companies, and libraries among its more than 6,000 members.

In addition to its annual National Conference on Artificial Intelligence, the AAAI hosts fall and spring symposia, workshops, and an annual Innovative Applications of Artificial Intelligence conference. It awards scholarships and grants, and publishes the quarterly *AI Magazine*, the annual *Proceedings of the National Conference on Artificial Intelligence*, and various books and reports.

BACKGROUND AND DEVELOPMENT

The history of artificial intelligence predates modern computers. In fact, its roots stretch back to very early instances of human thought. The first formalized deductive reasoning system—known as syllogistic logic—was developed in the fifth century B.C. by Aristotle. In subsequent centuries, advancements were made in the fields of mathematics and technology that contributed to AI. These included the development of mechanical devices such as clocks and the printing press. By 1642 the French scientist and philosopher Blaise Pascal had invented a mechanical digital calculating machine.

During the eighteenth century, attempts were made to create mechanical devices that mimicked living things. Among them was a mechanical automaton developed by the mechanician Jacques de Vaucanson that was capable of playing the flute. Later, Vaucanson created a life-sized mechanical duck that was constructed of gold-plated copper. In an except from *Living Dolls: A Magical History of the Quest for Mechanical Life* that appeared in the February 16, 2002, issue of *The Guardian*, author Gaby Wood described the duck this way: "It could drink, muddle the water with its beak, quack, rise and settle back on its legs and, spectators were amazed to see, it swallowed food with a quick, realistic gulping action in its flexible neck. Vaucanson gave details of the duck's insides. Not only was the grain, once swallowed, conducted via tubes to the animal's stomach, but Vaucanson also had to install a 'chemical laboratory' to decompose it. It passed from there into the 'bowels, then to the anus, where there is a sphincter which permits it to emerge.'"

Other early developments included a form of binary algebra developed by English mathematician George Boole that gave birth to the symbolic logic used in later computer technology. About the same time, the Analytical Engine was developed. This programmable mechanical calculating machine was used by Ada Byron (Lady Lovelace) and another English mathematician named Charles Babbage.

British mathematician Alan Turing was a computing pioneer whose interests and work contributed to the AI movement. In 1936 he wrote an article that described the Turing Machine—a hypothetical general computer. In time, this became the model for general purpose computing devices, prompting the Association of Computing Machinery to bestow an annual award in his honor. During the late 1930s Turing defined algorithms—instruction sets used during problem solving—and envisioned how they might be applied to machines. In addition, Turing worked as a cryptographer to decipher German communications for the Allied forces during World War II, creating a machine named Colossus that was used for this purpose. In 1950 he developed the now famous Turing Test, arguing that if a human could not distinguish between responses from a machine and a human, the machine could be considered "intelligent."

Thanks to the efforts of other early computing pioneers, including John von Neumann, the advent of electronic computing in the early 1940s allowed the modern AI field to begin in earnest. However, the term "artificial intelligence" was not actually coined until 1956. That year, a Dartmouth University mathematics professor named John McCarthy hosted a conference that brought together researchers from different fields to talk about machine learning. By this time the concept was being discussed in such varied disciplines as mathematics, linguistics, physiology, engineering, psychology, and philosophy. Other key AI players, including MIT scientist Marvin Minsky, attended the summer conference at Dartmouth. Although researchers were able to meet and share information, the conference failed to produce any breakthrough discoveries.

A number of milestones were reached during the 1950s that set the stage for later developments, including an AI program called Logic Theorist. Created by the research team of Herbert A. Simon and Allan Newell, the program was capable of proving theorems. It served as the basis for another program the two men created called General Problem Solver, which in turn set the stage for the creation of so-called expert systems. Also known as rule-based systems, experts systems consist of one or more computer programs that focus on knowledge of a specific discipline or field (also known as a domain). The system then functions as an expert within the domain. Another noteworthy development was the creation of the List Processing (LISP) programming language in applications.

The AI field benefited from government funding during the 1960s, including a $2.2 million grant to MIT from the Department of Defense's Advanced Research Projects Agency. A number of new AI programs were developed in the 1960s and 1970s, including the very first expert systems. DENDRAL was created to interpret spectrographic data for identifying the structure of organic chemical compounds. MYCIN, another early expert system, was developed at Stanford University and introduced in 1974. It was applied to the domain of medical diagnosis, as was the INTERNIST program developed at the University of Pittsburgh in 1979.

By the 1980s, the AI industry was still very much in development. However, it had established links to the corporate sector and continued to evolve along with technology in general. Of special interest to the business market were expert systems, which were in place at the likes of Boeing and General Motors. One estimate placed the value of AI software and hardware sales at $425 million in 1986. By 1993 the U.S. Department of Commerce reported that the AI market was valued at $900 million. At that time some 70 to 80 percent of *Fortune* 500 companies were applying AI technology in various ways.

According to the AAAI, important AI advancements during the 1990s occurred in the areas of case-based reasoning, data mining, games, intelligent tutoring, machine learning, multi-agent planning, natural language understanding, scheduling, translation, uncertain reasoning, virtual reality, and vision. In addition to private sector adoption, AI continued to evolve within the defense market during the 1990s. Applications included missile systems used during Operation Desert Storm. Some of the more dramatic AI milestones during the late 1990s included chess champion Garry Kasparov's 1997 loss to the Deep Blue chess program, as well as the creation of an interactive, drum-playing humanoid robot named COG by the MIT Artificial Intelligence Lab's Rodney Brooks in 1998. Heading into the new millennium, AI technology was being adopted at a rapid pace in computer software, medicine, defense, security, manufacturing, and other areas.

In the early 2000s terrorism and fraudulent business behavior such as insider trading were among the most pressing problems worldwide. AI technologies were being used to address both these and other issues. Following the terrorist attacks against the United States of September 11, 2001, teams of graduate students brought robots to Ground Zero and joined in the search and rescue efforts there. This was the first time robots had been used in a real situation such as this, according to Dr. Robin Murphy, a computer science professor at the University of South Florida who was involved in the search and rescue efforts. The robots proved useful, leading to the discovery of ten sets of remains.

AI technology also was being used to combat bio-terrorism. Realtime Outbreak and Disease Surveillance (RODS), a system developed by Carnegie Mellon University and the University of Pittsburgh, was capable of analyzing statewide data from immediate care facilities and hospital emergency rooms for patterns indicative of bio-terrorism. In the event that a pattern was found, RODS was configured to notify the appropriate public health officials via pager. This system was used in Salt Lake City for the 2002 Olympics. For that project, 80 percent of the health systems in the Salt Lake region were connected to share data. The system eventually covered 80 percent of the state of Utah.

AI also was being used to monitor the investment world for fraud. For example, in December 2001 the National Association of Securities Dealers began using an AI application called Securities Observation, News Analysis and Regulation (SONAR) to monitor the NASDAQ, as well as the over-the-counter and futures markets, for questionable situations. SONAR won an Innovative Applications of Artificial Intelligence Award from the AAAI. In a news release, the AAAI explained that each day, SONAR monitors some 1,000 quarterly and annual corporate SEC filings, between 8,500 and 18,000 news wire stories, and some 25,000 securities price-volume models. This analysis results in 50 to 60 daily alerts, a few of which are ultimately referred to federal authorities. SONAR used AI technologies such as knowledge-based data representation, data mining, intelligent software agents, rule-based inference, and natural language processing.

By 2004 companies like Sony marketed intelligent consumer robot toys like the four-legged AIBO, which could learn tricks, communicate with human owners via the Internet, and recognize people with AI technology such as face and voice recognition. Burlington, Massachusetts-based iRobot sold a robotic vacuum cleaner called Roomba for $200.

Some other applications included business intelligence and customer relationship management, along with defense and domestic security, education, and finance. Technical concentrations that were growing the fastest included belief networks, neural networks, and expert systems.

Discussions have continued regarding the day when machines would become conscious. Although some disagreed, several leading researchers argued that it was only a matter of time and that human beings were themselves only complex machines. Although science had yet to develop a machine capable of passing the Turing Test,

AI technology was being incorporated into systems and tools that, it was asserted, made the world a better, more enjoyable, and safer place. These applications included everything from hearing aids and digital cameras to systems that analyzed enormous volumes of data to find patterns that human beings might not otherwise see.

Heading into the mid-2000s, leading AI researchers such as Ray Kurzweil and Jeff Hawkins continued to cast their respective short- and long-term visions of the future. In 2005 Kurzweil published *The Singularity Is Near: When Humans Transcend Biology*, and Hawkins published *On Intelligence*. In the January 2006 issue of *Strategic Finance*, Hawkins indicated that intelligent machines were perhaps only ten years away, remarking: "It took fifty years to go from room-size computers to ones that fit in your pocket. But because we are starting from an advanced technological position, the same transition for intelligent machines should go much faster."

New developments in artificial intelligence continued on a daily basis toward the end of the decade. For example, in June 2008, Roadrunner, a supercomputer built by IBM and housed at Los Alamos National Laboratory, became the world's first computer to achieve sustained operating speeds of one petaflop (a petaflop is a million billion, or a quadrillion). In other words, Roadrunner could process a million billion calculations per second. One of the new supercomputer's potential applications was to perform calculations to certify the reliability of the U.S. nuclear weapons stockpile, with no need for underground nuclear tests. It also was slated to be used for other complex science and engineering applications. In the week after Roadrunner achieved its petaflop speed, researchers tested the code known as PetaVision, which models the human vision system, and found that, for the first time, a computer was able to match human performance on certain visual tasks such as distinguishing a friend from a stranger in a crowd of people or faultlessly detecting an oncoming car on a highway. Said Terry Wallace of the Los Alamos National Laboratory, "Just a week after formal introduction of the machine to the world, we are already doing computational tasks that existed only in the realm of imagination a year ago."

An area in which AI was growing rapidly was robotics. Robots were being used to perform a vast array of tasks, particularly those related to military and industrial operations. In the manufacturing industry, robots perform such duties as assembling, packing, loading, and transferring items. As of 2008 approximately 178,000 robots were working in U.S. factories, making the United States second only to Japan in robot applications. According to the Robotic Industries Association, robotics companies based in North America saw a 25 percent increase in orders in 2007, one of the largest increases in years. About 65 percent of orders go to automakers and suppliers. Worldwide, the population of robots was more than 1 million, with more growth expected.

Experts predict that robots will become more common in the life of the everyday consumer as well, not just in military and industrial settings. ABI Research forecast that by 2015, the personal robot market will reach $15 billion, and many people will be willing to pay as much for a multitasking humanoid robot as they would for a new car. These updated personal robots will not only be able to perform household chores but will entertain users and help with personal care. Nissan has even developed a robot that will ride along in the car with a driver and monitor his or her mood, then offer encouragement or suggestions.

In addition to robots being used in more applications and settings, experts predict that they will become more human-like. For example, a robot from MIT, Nexi, can display a range of facial expressions, in addition to being able to see and hear. A researcher at the Delft (Netherlands) University of Technology has developed a robot, Flame, which walks like a human. Although walking robots have been around since the 1970s, Flame uses a more fluid, human-like stride, rather than the rigid, careful movement of earlier walking robots. Another new robot, named Zeno and produced by Hanson Robotics in Dallas, Texas, can lie down, rise to a standing position, gesture with its arms, smile, make eye contact, and open and close its eyes and mouth. Using computer software, Zeno's creators claim he can "think" and grow smarter with time, as more data is input into the system.

PIONEERS

John McCarthy Many consider John McCarthy to be the father of modern AI research. Born on September 4, 1927, in Boston, McCarthy's father was a working-class Irish immigrant and his mother was a Jewish Lithuanian. Both were politically active and were involved with the Communist party during the 1930s. McCarthy subsequently developed an interest in political activism, although he rejected Marxism.

After skipping three grades in public school, McCarthy graduated from the California Institute of Technology in 1948. A doctoral degree in mathematics followed from Princeton in 1951, where he also accepted his first teaching position. In 1953, McCarthy moved to Stanford to work as an acting assistant professor of mathematics. Another move came in 1955, when he accepted a professorship at Dartmouth.

The following year, McCarthy made a significant mark on the field of artificial intelligence by coining its very name. He did this at a summer conference, which he hosted to explore the concept of machine learning with researchers from other institutions and disciplines. Another milestone was reached in 1958, when McCarthy joined MIT as an associate professor and established the first research lab devoted to AI.

At MIT, McCarthy developed the List Processing Language (LISP), which became the standard language used by the AI community to develop applications. His work at MIT involved trying to give computers common sense. After moving back to Stanford University in 1962, McCarthy established an AI research lab there and continued to work in the AI concentrations of common sense and mathematical logic.

In honor of his accomplishments, the Association for Computing Machinery presented McCarthy with the Alan Mathison Turing Award in 1971. He also received the Kyoto Prize in 1988, the National Medal of Science in 1990, and the Benjamin Franklin Medal in Computer and Cognitive Science in 2003. In addition to assuming the Charles M. Pigott Chair at the Stanford University School of Engineering in 1987, McCarthy accepted a professorship in the university's Computer Science Department and was named director of the Stanford Artificial Intelligence Laboratory. In addition to his academic work, McCarthy also is a former president of the AAAI.

Marvin Minsky Another founding father of the AI movement, Marvin Lee Minsky was born in New York on August 9, 1927, to eye surgeon Dr. Henry Minsky and Zionist Fannie Reiser. After attending the Bronx High School of Science and then graduating from the Phillips Academy in Andover, Massachusetts, Minsky spent one year in the Navy. In 1946 he enrolled at Harvard with the intent of earning a degree in physics. Instead, he pursued an eclectic mix of courses in subjects such as genetics, mathematics, and psychology. He became intrigued with understanding how the mind works, and was exposed to the theories of behavioral psychologist B.F. Skinner. Minsky did not accept Skinner's theories and developed a model of a stochastic (pertaining to a family of random variables or a probability theory) neural network in the brain, based on his grasp of mathematics. Minsky then switched his major, and ended his time at Harvard in 1950 with an undergraduate mathematics degree.

Next, Minsky attended Princeton, where he and Dean Edmonds built an electronic learning machine called the Snarc. Using a reward system, Snarc learned how to successfully travel through a maze. Upon earning a Doctorate in mathematics in 1954, Minsky worked briefly as a research associate at Tufts University and then accepted a three-year junior fellowship at Harvard, where

he was able to further explore theories regarding intelligence. In 1958 Minsky joined MIT, where he worked on the staff of the Lincoln Laboratory. The following year he made a significant impact on AI when, along with John McCarthy, he established the Artificial Intelligence Project. Minsky worked as an assistant professor from 1958 to 1961, and then served as an associate professor until 1963, when he became a professor of mathematics.

Several important developments in Minsky's career occurred in 1964. That year, he became a professor of electrical engineering, and the project he started in 1959 with McCarthy evolved into MIT's Artificial Intelligence Laboratory. Minsky served as the lab's director from 1964 to 1973, and it became a place where researchers were allowed to be adventurous. It was there that some of the first automatic robots were developed, along with new computational theories. In recognition of his efforts, Minsky received the Alan Mathison Turing Award from the Association for Computing Machinery in 1970.

In 1974 Minsky was named the Donner professor of science in MIT's Department of Electrical Engineering and Computer Science. While he also continued to serve as a professor in the Artificial Intelligence Laboratory, Minsky began conducting his own AI research when the lab's work went in theoretical directions that differed from his own. Indeed, he became critical of some of the lab's research as being too narrow in focus.

Minsky has shared many of his thoughts about AI with the public by penning articles in magazines like *Omni* and *Discover*. In addition, his 1986 book, *The Society of Mind*, provides a mechanized and detailed theory about how the mind functions and how it may be duplicated one day. Minsky moved to MIT's Media Laboratory in 1989 and was named the Toshiba Professor of Media Arts and Sciences. In 1992 he co-authored a science fiction novel with Harry Harrison titled *The Turing Option*, which was based on his theory. Beyond his academic work, Minsky founded several companies, including General Turtle Inc., Logo Computer Systems Inc., and Thinking Machines Corp.

CURRENT CONDITIONS

According to a 2009 published report by Global Industry Analysts Inc., the global artificial intelligence market is expected to exceed $36 billion by 2015. While the Asia-Pacific region is expected to offer the highest growth potential, the United States remains the largest market for AI. The market was aimed at improving existing applications to enhance capabilities in such domains as finance, transportation guidance systems, and medical technology.

By 2010 artificial intelligence had grown at such an accelerated pace that the AI field had developed its own disciplines (machine learning, computer vision, speech recognition, natural language understanding, etc.), which worked both independently and in concert with one another. According to author Gary Morgenthaler, by 2013 to 2015, virtual personal assistants (VPAs) with improved AI will know one's personal social graph and habitual patterns, even to the point of making suggestions (i.e., "Do you want me to invite your accountant to this meeting?"). People will be able to manage business and social calendars by having their VPAs handle more complicated tasks, such as finding the most convenient time for a four-person meeting in the upcoming week or reserving a 2:00 tee time.

Owners of newly-capable Roombas will be able to text ahead to tell their vacuum cleaners to vacuum specific rooms, knowing that the machines will recognize and avoid hazards like steps, pets, etc. Smartphones will allow people to locate the restaurants that are closest to their hotels and which offer specific menu items (e.g., ethnic favorites); the smartphone will then translate languages to allow placing an order in the ethnic language requested (e.g., Chinese, Latino, Hungarian). Moreover, most new smartphones will be voice-enabled rather than relying on thumb-typing. Customers will be able to search, text, e-mail, collaborate, purchase, and schedule simply by talking to their smartphones. Even search engines on PCs will be enabled to answer very specific queries directly, instead of providing pages of hyperlinks.

Most of these developments are the result of cloud computing. Companies such as True Knowledge scour databases such as Wikepedia, Freebase, etc., and create deep pools of this easily accessed data, thus facilitating data mining and crowd sourcing. These data pools are intelligently sorted into categorical common sense facts about everyday life, taking into account language usage rather than literal meaning (e.g., "I want to drop off my car."). Machine-learning algorithms automatically recognize such complex patterns of words and make intelligent decisions based on facts drawn from the data pools. The result is rapid feedback and clearly enhanced performance. Speech recognition companies such as Nuance and Vlingo draw on the data pools in the cloud to compare and analyze millions of speech utterances and then feed results back into their systems. As of 2010 there was commercially available dictation software that could capture virtually all words in the entire English language with nearly 100 percent accuracy.

In music and the performing arts, North Carolina-based Zenph Sound Innovations models the music performances of great musicians from old scratchy records and creates new recordings as though the original musicians were alive and performing. Zenph has designed special robotic pianos that take high resolution MIDI files created by software that simulates the style of the old classical and jazz performers, literally by depressing the piano keys using between 12c and 24 high-resolution MIDI attributes. To critical acclaim in live settings at Carnegie Hall, Steinway Hall, and the *Live from the Lincoln Center* shows, the robotic pianos have stunned and amazed crowds with their note-for-note renditions of historic performances of the past. Zenph hoped to develop clear versions of other muddy or distorted old recordings and convert them to software that would allow musicians to jam with virtual versions of famous musicians.

In 2010 engineers at the University of California, Berkeley, announced the development of a pressure-sensitive electronic material, made from semiconductor nanowires, which functions like human skin. It is the first material to be made from inorganic single crystalline semiconductors. Scientists first grew the germanium/silicon nanowires on a cylindrical drum, which was then rolled onto a sticky substrate, causing their impression to be imprinted on the material. The nanowires were then printed onto an 18-by-19 pixel square matrix containing a transistor. The nanowires' transistors were then integrated with apressure-sensitive rubber coating to provide the sensing function. Intended to address one of the key challenges in robotics (adapting the amount of force needed to grip, hold, or manipulate objects of differing degrees of hardness, softness, or temperature), the "e-skin" may eventually be used to restore the sense of touch to persons with prosthetic limbs.

INDUSTRY LEADERS

Some emerging newcomers in 2010 included San Jose, California-based Siri, which licensed DARPA-funded SRI technology and developed a VDA operated by voice commands and queries, such as restaurant reservations and movie tickets, from the Web. Computer giant Apple acquired Siri in 2010. Google later announced its Voice Actions application for Android, seen by industry analysts as a response to Apple's Siri acquisition.

Honda still maintained its lead in the most technically-advanced human-like robot, ASIMO, that continued to wow audiences with its varying capabilities and human-like responses, but the gap in technology between competitors was closing. Enter Watson, IBM's supercomputer, which was dubbed as the world's most advanced question-answering machine. In 2010 the company announced that the producers of *Jeopardy!* had agreed to pit Watson against some of the game's best former players.

Kurzweil Technologies Inc. Based in Wellesley Hills, Massachusetts, Kurzweil Technologies Inc. (KTI) is a private research and development enterprise headed by visionary, inventor, and entrepreneur Ray Kurzweil, author of such best-selling works as *The Age of Intelligent Machines, The Age of Spiritual Machines, When Computers Exceed Human Intelligence,* and *The Singularity Is Near: When Humans Transcend Biology.* KTI includes a number of Kurzweil's various enterprises, including KurzweilAI. net, Ray & Terry's Longevity Products, FatKat, Kurzweil Music Systems, Kurzweil Educational Systems, Kurzweil CyberArt Technologies, Kurzweil Computer Products, and Kurzweil AI. According to KTI, it is involved in "developing and marketing technologies in pattern recognition, artificial intelligence, evolutionary algorithms, signal processing, simulation of natural processes, and related areas."

In terms of breakthrough commercial developments, Ray Kurzweil has been recognized for achieving a number of notable firsts. Among them are the first commercial large vocabulary speech recognition system, omni-font optical character recognition, a print-to-speech reading machine for blind individuals, the text-to-speech synthesizer, and the CCD flat-bed scanner. For his efforts, Kurzweil received the National Medal of Technology from President Clinton in 1999. His many other honors include the Association for Computing Machinery's Grace Murray Hopper Award, as well as Inventor of the Year from MIT.

Southwest Research Institute Based in San Antonio, Texas, the Southwest Research Institute (SwRI) is a leading independent, nonprofit organization devoted to applied research and development. SwRI employs approximately 3,000 workers in 13 states and China. The institute's 1,200-acre campus includes labs, offices, and other facilities that collectively span almost 2 million square feet.

SwRI has concentrated on several key research areas, including automotive products and emissions research; chemistry and chemical engineering; mechanical and materials engineering; training, simulation, and performance improvement; automation and data systems; engine and vehicle research; space science and engineering; nuclear waste regulatory analyses; applied physics; signal exploitation and geolocation; and aerospace electronics and information technology. In this latter category, the company has conducted research in AI and knowledge systems.

RESEARCH AND TECHNOLOGY

The buzzword for the early 2010s was cloud computing. As of 2010 data mining and processing speeds could increase the procession power of a single server by a factor of 1 million, compared to capabilities in the 1990s. Conversely, cloud computing may multiply AI-related processing power by a factor of 1 billion by 2020. Open source programs such as Hadoop (developed by Yahoo!) permitted AI systems to run data and algorithms simultaneously across multiple servers. This capability also will facilitate merging of the various parallel AI disciplines (speech recognition, dialog management, machine learning) and reassemble them into artificial-based logic.

Researchers in the AI field have dubbed these colonies of computers that gather cloud data as a new phenomenon: swarm Intelligence. One of the earliest applications of this was the joint effort of SRI International, DARPA, and several leading university research subcontractors to reassemble AI subdisciplines into an integrated whole. The resulting development will be applied to assist warfare with a mobile, VDA-like battlefield assistant.

In addition to Apple's Siri efforts, both Google and Microsoft made intelligence-at-the-interface a key focus for research and development plans in 2010.

In the field of medicine, scientists have been making strides with robo-infants, different from other AI models in that they focus on simulating the reasoning processes of infants rather than mathematical problem solving, much the way that infants learn about their bodies and environments. Two ongoing projects involving robo-infants were Xpero (2010) and iCub (2006). A starfish-like robot was able to resort information about its body after several of its mechanical limbs were removed, and quickly redirected its remaining limbs to walk away. This successful experiment is expected to feed data mining efforts to find a cure for conditions such as Parkinson's disease.

The U.S. Department of Defense funded a research team at the University of Texas at Dallas to improve existing facial recognition software for national security applications. As of 2010, algorithms varied greatly between software developers and most had not faced real-world challenges. Face Perception and Research Laboratories was working on combining millions of faces captured within databases and examining them under different conditions (e.g., illumination, angle, changes in facial and head hair, eyewear, etc.), to combine results for algorithm determinations.

At the University of Arizona's Artificial Intelligence Lab, Dr. Hsinchun Chen and his team were designing computer software to mimic a financial analyst. As of 2010, the program performed text mining to scan stock prices and financial news to buy or sell stocks that it believed would gain more than 1 percent in the subsequent 20 minutes. (The system sold the stocks after 20 minutes.) When first tested (using 2005 stock price data) it accomplished a return of 8.5 percent.

Beyond a host of research projects with very practical applications, the climate of technological advancement seemed to indicate a future that was both exciting and frightening. Several of the world's leading academic minds, including astronomer Stephen Hawking, predicted that machine intelligence would surpass human intelligence within only a few decades. As the processing speed and storage capacity of computers increased exponentially, and as projects to create biological microelectromechanical systems (bioMEMs) and nanobots—machines of microscopic size that can be inserted into the human body—were developed, other experts took a view that tested the very limits of human imagination.

On *KurzweilAI.net*, entrepreneur, author, and visionary Ray Kurzweil painted a picture of a posthuman world, where technology will allow humans to either eliminate many of their biological organs or replace them with artificial ones. In Kurzweil's future, the distinction between man and machine becomes difficult to discern. In his February 17, 2003, article, "Human Body Version 2.0," Kurzweil claims that by 2030—following the nanotechnology revolution and reverse engineering of the human brain—biological brains will merge with nonbiological intelligence, which will allow individuals to share conscious experiences, fully immerse themselves in virtual environments, and expand the limits of memory and thought.

Although AI pioneer Marvin Minsky once placed Kurzweil among the leading modern-day futurists, no one can completely predict the future of AI or the further evolution of mankind. However, it seems fairly certain that a number of very interesting developments can be expected during the first several decades of the twenty-first century.

AMERICA AND THE WORLD

Although the United States has historically led the world in AI research, the industry is a global one. For example, the Artificial Intelligence Applications Institute at the University of Edinburgh is a leading AI player in the United Kingdom. Through the university's School of Informatics, AIAI offers both undergraduate and postgraduate degrees in artificial intelligence, and works to transfer a number of AI technologies to the commercial, industrial, and government sectors in four key areas: adaptive systems; bioinformatics; knowledge systems and knowledge modeling; and planning and activity management.

Since 1969, the International Joint Conference on Artificial Intelligence (IJCAI) has been the main conference for AI professionals throughout the world. It is hosted every other year in cooperation with one or more national AI societies from the hosting country. The IJCAI presents distinguished AI professionals with a number of awards and honors. These include the Award for Research Excellence, the IJCAI Computers and Thought Award for outstanding young AI scientists, the Donald E. Walker Distinguished Service Award, and the Distinguished Paper Awards.

BIBLIOGRAPHY
"About AAAI," 20 June 2008. Available from http://www.aaai.org.

"AI Today and Tomorrow." *Strategic Finance*, January 2006.

"A Robot that Can Smile or Frown: MIT Debuts Nexi." *Industry Week*, June 2008.

"Engineers Make Artificial Skin Out of Nanowires." *Science Daily*, 13 September 2010. Available from http://www.sciencedaily.com/releases/2010/09/100912151550.htm.

Gaudin, Sharon. " Personal Robot Market Expected to Balloon to \$15B by 2015." *Computer World*, 31 December 2007.

Global Industry Analysts Inc. "Global Artificial Intelligence Market to Exceed \$36 Billion by 2015, According to New Report by Global Industry Analysts, Inc." 23 June 2009. Available from http://www.strategyr.com/Artificial_Intelligence_AI_Market_Report.asp.

Lomas, Natasha. "Artificial Intelligence: 55 Years of Research Later—and Where Is AI Now?" *Silicon*, 8 February 2010.

Maloney, Lawrence. "A Tale of Two Robots." *Design News*, 2 June 2008.

MIT Computer Science and Artificial Intelligence Laboratory. "CSAIL in the News." January–February 2008. Available from http://www.csail.mit.edu/events/news/inthenews.html.

Moltenbrey, Karen. "Brain Power: An Inventor Uses Massive's Software to Make his Creation Think." *Computer Graphics World*, May 2008.

Morgenthaler, Gary. "AI's Time Has Arrived." *BusinessWeek*, 21 September 2010.

"Roadrunner Supercomputer Puts Research at a New Scale." PhysOrg.com, 12 June 2008. Available from http://www.physorg.com.

Spice, Byron. "Over the Holidays 50 Years Ago, Two Scientists Hatched Artificial Intelligence." *Pittsburgh Post-Gazette*, 2 January 2006.

Teresko, John. "The Future Is Now for the Robot Revolution: The Next Wave of Robots Will Be Remarkably Human in Appearance and Function." *Industry Week*, June 2008.

"The New AI: Turn Robnots Into Infant Scientists." *Discover Magazine*, 25 August 2010.

Thompson, Clive. "Smarter Than You Think—Who Is Watson?" *New York Times*, 16 June 2010.

"TU Delft Robot Flame Walks Like a Human." *Space Daily*, 3 June 2008.

Valentino-DeVries, Jennifer. "Using Artificial Intelligence to Digest News, Trade Stocks." *Wall Street Journal*, 21 June 2010.

Von Buskirk, Eliot. "Virtual Musicians, Real Performances." *Wired*, 2 March 2010.

ARTS AND CRAFTS STORES

SIC CODE(S)

5945

INDUSTRY SNAPSHOT

The U.S. arts and crafts industry serves a very diverse population of artisans, artists, crafters, and hobbyists. These individuals engage in a variety of creative pursuits using paper, fabric, leather, metal, wood, stone, glass, plastic, and other materials to produce unique handmade items.

Arts and crafts have existed in U.S. culture for hundreds of years. In the 1770s, dissenting Quakers, who chose to retain violent trembling or shaking in their worship services, became known as Shakers. They established their own communities and became well known for crafting woven goods and furniture of the highest quality. Their culture and religion still impact the United States.

During economic downturns when discretionary income may be more limited, the arts and crafts industry has managed to maintain itself as a viable alternative to more expensive hobbies and interests. Although the industry primarily attracts adult women as recurring customers/clients, it is broad enough in scope to cover the interests of men, as well as entire families who wish to exercise their creativity in either individual or community settings.

ORGANIZATION AND STRUCTURE

A handful of very large public and private companies dominates the retailing side of the arts and crafts industry. These include traditional brick-and-mortar enterprises such as Michaels Stores Inc., Hobby Lobby Stores Inc., and A.C. Moore Arts & Crafts Inc. However, companies such as QVC Inc., which sells goods via television and the Internet, and catalog-based enterprises such as Oriental Trading Company Inc., also hold significant shares of the market. Beyond these major players, the industry is home to thousands of smaller, independently owned hobby and craft stores, many of which focus on particular types of arts and crafts such as scrapbooking or rubber stamping.

Beyond the aforementioned retail channels, direct selling also has a significant place within the arts and crafts industry. Independent demonstrators peddle products on behalf of companies such as St. Cloud, Minnesota-based Creative Memories, which markets a popular line of scrapbooking products. Another leading direct seller of arts and crafts products is Salt Lake City, Utah-based Stampin' Up! With annual revenues of roughly $181 million during the late 2000s, the company sells its rubber stamping products via a network of approximately 50,000 independent demonstrators throughout the United States and Canada.

Independent demonstrators normally earn a percentage of the sales they make for arts and crafts companies. Most of these sales are made by soliciting people to host small in-home classes or workshops, also known as "parties." The person hosting the party invites friends, family members, and co-workers to enjoy food, fellowship, and demonstrations showing how to create items (scrapbooks, gift cards, and other related items) with products offered by the demonstrator's company. While a large number of independent demonstrators work on a part-time basis, investing most of their earnings back into their hobbies, for others it is a full-time endeavor. For example, in the December 2003 issue of *Stampin' Success,* Stampin' Up!

Market Share of Arts & Craft Customers

Novice	56%
Intermediate	28%
Expert	16%
Collector	1%

SOURCE: Scrapbooking.com's *2010 Magazine Profile.*

profiled one highly successful demonstrator who averaged more than $10,000 in monthly sales.

The end market for arts and crafts products is incredibly broad, reflecting the industry's diverse customer base of artisans, artists, crafters, and hobbyists. Many of these individuals engage in arts-and-crafts-related activities for enjoyment or to earn a secondary income by peddling their wares at craft shows, malls, bazaars, yard sales, expositions, and via the Internet. A smaller number actually earn their livings by making handcrafted goods for others.

Because of the industry's diverse customer base, the finished products produced by end users vary widely in type and quality, ranging from crudely constructed items made from Popsicle sticks to breathtakingly beautiful works of fine art produced by master craftspeople, including ironwork and blown glass vases. Broad arts and crafts categories include children's crafts; home décor; the needle arts, including quilting, crocheting, embroidery and needlepoint; paper crafting approaches such as rubber stamping and scrapbooking; jewelry and other wearable goods; holiday crafts; soap, candles, and body products; and even doll-making and toy-making. However, even within these large categories there is considerable diversity in the items produced and the techniques used to produce them.

Of great benefit to manufacturers in a variety of industry sectors is the wide range of materials crafters use. Common materials include paper, textiles, metal, clay, wood, plastic, leather, rubber, glass, stone, and wax. Crafters even take discarded items such as computer circuit boards and turn them into items such as Christmas ornaments, coasters, and so on.

Associations. In February 2004 the Hobby Industry Association (HIA) and the Association of Crafts & Creative Industries (ACCI) combined to form a new trade association called the Craft & Hobby Association. In addition to supporting its membership base and operating two industry trade shows, the new association sought to make its mark internationally through research and educational activities.

According to the CHA, its vision is "to create a vibrant industry with an exciting image, an expanding customer base and successful members. The goal is to stimulate the sales growth of the craft and hobby industry worldwide by creating consumer demand, helping members succeed and leading the industry."

CHA translates its vision into reality via national promotional events that increase knowledge and awareness of craft industry products, as well as two annual craft and hobby trade shows, which the association claims are the largest of their kind worldwide.

The CHA's predecessors played a hand in the industry for many years. HIA's roots stretch back to 1940, with the formation of the Model Industry Association. Eventually, the association's focus broadened and it was renamed the Hobby Industry Association. Representing hobby and craft supply designers, manufacturers, and distributors, HIA's main objective was to increase industry sales. To accomplish this, the association conducted research on consumer participation, demographics, and more, and sought to heighten members' awareness and knowledge of industry products. HIA also helped to promote the industry through National Craft Month. At the time of its conjugation with ACCI, more than 4,900 companies from every segment of the hobby and craft industry were HIA members.

ACCI was founded in 1976 as the Mid-American Craft and Hobby Association, which initially served members in the Midwestern United States. However, by 1984 it had evolved into a national body called the Association of Crafts & Creative Industries. ACCI played a major role in the area of industry research, and arranged the industry's first Gallup survey in 1992. In addition, the association drove consumer outreach efforts, including the establishment of National Craft Month in 1988. At the time of its merger with HIA, ACCI had approximately 6,000 members in 40 countries.

In addition to the CHA, there are a number of other industry associations. Formed in 1897, the Society of Arts and Crafts (SAC) is the nation's oldest nonprofit craft organization. According to SAC, its mission is "to support excellence in crafts by encouraging the creation, collection, and conservation of the work of craft artists and by educating and promoting public appreciation of fine craftsmanship. SAC has been at the forefront of the American craft movement, fostering the development, sales, recognition and education of crafts for over one hundred years." The SAC operates a two-story gallery in Boston that includes retail and exhibition space.

The American Craft Council (ACC) is another national, nonprofit organization serving the industry. According to the ACC, the council is "dedicated to promoting understanding and appreciation of contemporary American craft," and is "the leading voice for the crafts in America, celebrating the remarkable achievement of the many gifted artists working in the media of clay, fiber, glass, metal, wood and other materials." The ACC was established in 1943 by Aileen Osborn Webb. The council's endeavors include the hosting of workshops and seminars, operation of a contemporary craft library, publication of a bimonthly magazine, the issuance of educational grants, and more.

BACKGROUND AND DEVELOPMENT

Men and women have been crafting handmade items for thousands of years. In early U.S. history, the Shakers—dissenting Quakers who chose to retain violent trembling or shaking in their worship services, and whose culture and religion still impact the United States—were well known for crafting woven goods and furniture of the highest quality.

In his book *The American Soul, Rediscovering the Wisdom of the Founders,* Jacob Needleman states, "We need to appreciate the important role that innovative religious communities played in the formation of our country—remembering that, for many of the Founding Fathers, America itself was envisioned as a new land, a new community defined not only politically but also spiritually." A small group of Shakers came to America in 1774 and settled north of Albany, New York. They won tolerance of their religion and many converts until they were about 6,000 strong by the Civil War, eventually creating 19 village communities in the Northeast, Ohio, and Kentucky.

The Shakers saw America as their chance to form a more perfect society, or Utopia, on earth. They lived agriculture-based lives, forming rural village communities where they practiced common ownership of property and goods and celibate purity, which necessitated them adopting children or accepting converts. At age 21, the adopted children were free to remain in their Shaker community or go into the larger world. The Shakers believed in equality between the sexes and races, a very advanced notion in their time; living away from the corruption of cities; good sanitation; simplicity of dress, speech and behavior; and opportunities for intellectual and artistic development within their society. Shakers improved the plow and adopted other labor-saving techniques; invented metal pen nibs, a washing machine, the flat broom, waterproof and wrinkle-free cloth, and a metal chimney cap that kept out rain. A Shaker woman invented the circular saw. Shaker communities became known for the quality of the goods, including furniture, which they produced. Shakers were also pacifists and Lincoln exempted Shaker men as conscientious objectors from fighting in the Civil War.

After the Civil War, industrialization of the economy made it difficult for the Shakers to compete. Their falling prosperity made it increasingly difficult to find converts. Shaker communities began failing and closing.

Only the Sabbathday Lake Shaker Community actively existed in Sabbathday, Maine.

For many years, a relatively clear distinction existed between art and crafts, and the latter emphasized the creation of functional items. As arts and crafts became increasingly popular during the twentieth century, this distinction began to disappear. This especially was true in the latter part of the century as handcrafted items became more whimsical, sometimes foregoing function altogether.

While the Shakers played an important role in early U.S. history, the specific term "arts and crafts" originated in England during the late 1800s with the formation of the Arts and Crafts Movement. According to the SAC, the Arts and Crafts Movement emerged in direct response to the Industrial Revolution. By the mid-1800s quality handcrafted items, once a marketplace staple, had been largely replaced with cheap, machine-made products. This caused artists and craftspeople to lose market share and forced many of them to forego their skilled trades for other pursuits.

In England, Thomas Carlyle, William Morris, and John Ruskin spearheaded the Arts and Crafts Movement. As Patricia Leigh Brown explained in the January 25, 1995 issue of the *New York Times,* "Repelled by the effects of the Industrial Revolution, they called for a return to home and family and the spiritual values of the medieval guild system. They lamented the soulessness of the machine and its products, drawing design inspiration from the Middle Ages, when craftsmanship and a deep commitment to work constituted what was perceived to be a purer and simpler life."

In the United States, the Arts and Crafts Movement was headed up by millionaire Elbert Hubbard, a soap salesman turned direct marketing pioneer who founded a crafts and publishing community near Buffalo, New York. Another pioneer was Gustav Stickley, a former furniture salesman who eventually went bankrupt.

In 1897 a handful of educators, collectors, craftspeople, and architects held the nation's first crafts exhibition in Boston's Copley Hall, showcasing the works of more than 100 different artists. The SAC was formed that same year and explains that Boston became a hub for the Arts and Crafts Movement. In 1900 the society opened a shop to sell goods made by craftspeople. Two years later it began publishing a magazine called *Handicraft.* In 1907, 33 craft societies from 20 states joined together to form the National League of Handicraft Societies. Another noteworthy development occurred in 1939 when the SAC established the American Handcraft Council, predecessor to the American Craft Council.

Although the Industrial Revolution proceeded unchecked, the Arts and Crafts Movement was not a wasted effort. By the latter half of the twentieth century Americans were pursuing arts and crafts in growing numbers. Following World War II, university art departments began to offer crafts to an influx of interested veterans as part of their curriculums. This set the stage for a period of new creativity, when arts and crafts would depart from the traditional and move toward the experimental.

During the 1950s crafting was still quite reserved. In the January 28, 1982, *New York Times,* writer Grace Glueck described this period as "pure, holy and classical," explaining that crafters emphasized the functionality and utility of the items they made: "A thing of clay, however experimental, had to reflect the pot tradition; fiber work was strictly two-dimensional, bearing the mark of the loom, and wood knew its place, largely in furniture and salad bowls. What's more, crafts were crafts and art was art, and never the twain would meet."

By the 1960s the United States' view of arts and crafts had relaxed, moving more toward the fine art end of the spectrum and away from functionality. The so-called hippie movement furthered this trend, as some youth engaged in communal living arrangements and created handmade jewelry and art that had no creative limitations.

By the 1970s arts and crafts had exploded in popularity. The field gained national recognition in 1972 when crafts became an official department within the National Museum of American Art and the Smithsonian opened Renwick Gallery. The inclusion of crafts in university programs several decades before had helped to further the sharing of information about crafting techniques through books, lectures, classes, and workshops. Subsequently, the number of full-time, professional craftspeople began to grow. In addition to traditional, functional crafts, during the 1970s crafters continued to make more whimsical items. In addition, they began using more non-traditional materials. For example, during this period one artist developed a wall hanging that included both neon tubing and fabric. According to the National Endowment for the Arts, during the 1970s the number of artisans producing crafts was in the 375,000 to 400,000 range.

The popularity of crafts during the 1970s caused handcrafted items to appear on display in corporate headquarters, museums, and even shopping malls. This trend continued into the 1980s, as a growing number of professional and amateur crafters sold their creations at bazaars, craft fairs, festivals, and more. Marking a drastic departure from the Arts and Crafts Movement, some merchandisers even began commissioning crafters to create handmade goods that could be mass-produced.

By 1980 grants to craftspeople from the National Endowment for the Arts totaled $1.3 million, up from $102,000 in 1973 when the organization began to formally support crafts. During the late 1980s two companies that would go on to make huge impacts on the arts and crafts industry were established. In 1987 Rhonda Anderson and Cheryl Lightle formed Creative Memories, which would become a major player in the burgeoning scrapbook market in the coming decades. A future rubber stamp heavyweight was born in 1988, when Shelli Gardner established Stampin' Up! with her sister.

Crafts continued to gain in popularity during the 1990s. According to the HIA, in 1990 some 90 percent of U.S. households had at least one crafter or hobbyist. In 1993 the industry celebrated the Year of American Craft, and select items from leading artisans were used to decorate the White House. By 1995 the White House Collection of American Crafts had become an exhibit at the Smithsonian's National Museum of Art. The following year, the number of crafters and hobbyists per U.S. household had dropped to 84 percent, according to the HIA. At that time, individuals spent an average of 7.4 hours per week on hobby-related activities. In terms of participation rates, leading craft and hobby categories were cross-stitch/embroidery (48 percent), crocheting and apparel/fashion sewing (29 percent), and home décor painting and accessorizing (20 percent). According to *Forbes,* arts and crafts industry revenues nearly doubled between 1992 and 1997, reaching $14 billion.

Americans faced some truly difficult times during the twenty-first century's first decade. In addition to weak economic conditions and rising unemployment, the nation endured devastating terrorist attacks on September 11, 2001. Together, these developments had a negative impact on the manufacturing and retail sectors alike. However, the arts and crafts industry was something of an exception. According to the HIA, sales within the hobby and craft industry increased 11 percent in 2001 and 13 percent in 2002, reaching $29 billion. Of this amount, the general crafts category was responsible for the majority of sales (43 percent), followed by needlecrafts (29 percent), painting/finishing (18 percent), and floral crafts (10 percent).

In 2002 the HIA reported that 27 percent of industry sales were made by large discount chains, followed by craft chains (20 percent), and fabric/craft chains (12 percent). That year, 77 percent of U.S. households had at least one member engaging in crafting, down from the 90 percent high recorded during the 1990s but up from 2001 levels of 76 percent. In terms of usage, the HIA indicated that the most popular reason for making crafts was to make gifts (79 percent), followed by personal use (69 percent), home decorating (61 percent), holiday decorating (43 percent), and making items for sale (15 percent).

Following the terrorist attacks, many Americans opted to spend more time at home instead of traveling. Longing for what seemed to be simpler and safer times, there also was a renewed interest in more nostalgic pursuits. These factors benefited the arts and crafts sector. According to *DSN Retailing Today,* five of the leading public craft companies saw their average stock prices jump in the five-month period following September 11 to the tune of 75 percent. Unemployment also benefited the industry in some respects. As families became more mindful of expenses, crafting was viewed as a way to save money by making affordable homemade gifts for friends and loved ones.

The industry's strong growth during 2001 to 2004 was due in part to the rising popularity of scrapbooking. HIA figures reveal that scrapbooking sales quadrupled from 1998 to 2003, reaching $2 billion. *DSN Retailing Today* reported that scrapbooking supplies accounted for about 7 percent of hobby and craft supply sales during the early 2000s. With 3,000 independent scrapbooking stores and some 1,600 products manufacturers operating in late 2003, industry observers anticipated this segment would grow at an annual rate of 40 to 80 percent through 2008. While an estimated 98 percent of scrapbookers were women, a growing number of men were participating in the hobby as of 2004.

Amidst this optimistic forecast, in 2003 Michaels Stores Inc. opened two stand-alone, 6,000-square-foot scrapbooking stores called Recollections. Staffed by scrapbooking enthusiasts and offering some 10,000 different product SKUs (stock-keeping units), the new stores were to include space for classes and other amenities such as kiosks for printing digital photos. Beyond traditional industry players, mass merchandisers and office supply giants such as Wal-Mart, Target, Office Depot, and Office Max also were expanding their offerings of scrapbooking products. In addition to attending conventions, scrapbooking enthusiasts even embarked on cruises or took special trips to resorts to work on their scrapbooks with other like-minded individuals, spending as much as $1,000 for the pleasure.

Scrapbooking's popularity was evident by the naming of March 4 as International Scrapbooking Day, as well as a bevy of new products and magazines that had appeared on the market. Nevertheless, this niche was no longer growing as explosively as it had during the late 1990s and the early 2000s. The continual introduction of the "latest" new product, heightened competition, and the growing foothold of leading "big box" stores were factors that led to the demise of many independent scrapbooking stores. In addition, many independent retailers simply did not have the business skills to make the grade, despite their passion for the hobby. Despite these challenges, industry players argued that the scrapbooking category would continue to thrive for years to come.

Scrapbooking was driving sales of other papercraft supplies, including embellished gift tags, announcements,

and cards. As Debbie Howell wrote in the January 23, 2006, issue of *DSN Retailing Today,* "The expansion of scrapbooking into related papercrafting hobbies also translates into a positive outlook. Some crafters that may not be as interested in traditional scrapbooking could be to attracted to related hobbies such as cardmaking, home décor projects involving photos or sewing and knitting projects using digital images."

Finally, another industry trend was the development of scrapbooking products aimed at specific niche markets. In particular, manufacturers were offering products for different ethnic groups. One example is the availability of Spanish-language stickers. Teens and pre-teens were two other popular target markets for manufacturers, such as RoseArt, which was finding success with its Scrapfabulous line.

By 2008 more than 5,900 retail stores in the United States sold scrapbooking materials, with 2,700 independent retailers devoted to serving the needs of scrapbookers. *Scrapbooking.com Magazine,* one of the largest sources of scrapbooking information in the industry, estimated that it had 350,000 visitors per month in 2008 and more than 1 billion hits per year. Many other Web sites were devoted to scrapbookers as well.

Digital, or "hybrid," scrapbooking was the hottest trend. In digital scrapbooking, hobbyists build pages on-screen using digital photos and design elements instead of cutting and pasting elements onto paper pages. Finished pages are either printed onto glossy paper and put into a regular album or maintained in digital form on Web sites or CD-ROMs. Basically, everything that can be done in traditional scrapbooking can be done in digital scrapbooking, minus the physical elements of cutting tools, embellishments, and so on. Shari Sentlowitz, marketing manager of the Digital Photofinishing Division of Sony Electronics, said, "Digital scrapbooking is growing, with many websites dedicated to the art, companies producing software for it, and new magazines emerging. I anticipate this market will increase tremendously in the next few years."

Digital scrapbookers can take onsite or online courses to learn techniques and gain new ideas. Tracy Watson, cofounder of digital crafting graphics company Curvy Line Creative and an instructor for such classes, told *PMA Magazine,* "Enrollment ranges from a couple hundred worldwide students to several thousand at a time. They are extremely popular." Courses are also available for retailers who are interested in getting involved in digital crafting but are not sure how to get started.

Those who stuck to traditional scrapbooking had more "green" options as several stores began to offer recycled scrapbooking materials. For example, in 2008, K&Company, one of the largest retailers of scrapbooking papers, albums, and embellishments, launched the first widely available paper crafting line comprised of recycled and reusable product and packaging. Wal-Mart followed suit in offering its ReMake line, made up of 100 percent recycled materials in addition to recycled, reusable, and biodegradable packaging and materials printed with soy ink.

In addition to scrapbooking, paper crafting and card-making also were very popular. The use of rubber stamps to make greeting cards also crossed over into the scrapbooking realm. Other popular arts and crafts endeavors of the early twenty-first century included knitting and the production of homemade candles, soaps, and body care products. Cross-stitching and home décor painting also remained popular crafts.

CURRENT CONDITIONS

The NPD Group put total U.S. toy sales (under which arts and crafts are often listed) for 2009 at $21.47 billion, down slightly from $21.65 billion in 2008. Despite flat overall sales, however, arts and crafts revenues increased 7 percent. Anita Frazier, industry analyst for the NPD Group, attributed this increase to the category's entertainment value and cost effectiveness.

In a 2010 article for the Craft & Hobby Association's *CHA Portfolio* magazine, noted artist and author Suzanne McNeill, creator of *Design Originals* and *Zentangle* designs, was asked to characterize industry trends. She described 2009 as an economic rollercoaster year that focused on personalization crafts, hands-on activities, artcrafters groups, and creative classes. According to McNeill, new products and techniques for 2010 centered on crafts that were inspirational, nostalgic, spiritual, and/or that expressed values. In addition, *Design Originals'* Dean Rohlfing noted that "Personalized projects like Quilting, Scrapbooking, Cards, beading, Gifts, Art, Needlework and Zentangle can be a source of comfort and reassurance during troubled times."

According to McNeill, in 2010 shop owners around the country noted a resurgence of creativity as a basis for community. Arts and crafts classes and clubs were increasingly popular and profitable. Although sales of supplies were slightly off, revenues generated from art and craft classes kept stores profitable. "Now that people are living with less, they enjoy their relationships more," McNeill explained. In addition to group craft meetings at art shops, studios, churches, or private homes, retreats and seminar getaways were growing in popularity.

For artists and crafters who sold their own works, the Philadelphia Museum of Art Craft Show conducted a nationwide survey of more than 1,200 craft artists in 2009. According to the survey, 69 percent of respondents indicated sales declines from the previous year; however, less than half had declined more than 25 percent, and 31 percent of respondents indicated that sales were equal or better.

Scrapbooking remained the leading hands-on and digital activity in 2010. Retail sales for the scrapbooking category were roughly $1.65 billion in 2009. The industry was expected to grow to $4 billion by 2020. Both *Scrapbooking.com Magazine* and the SMART Group reported that only 1.6 percent of Americans engage in scrapbooking as a hobby (4.4 million persons, mostly women).

As of 2010 the scrapbooking category was represented in more than 5,900 retail stores. A Scrapbooking.com study showed that, on average, dedicated scrapbookers spent $120 monthly on their hobby. The biggest spenders were novices. In addition, more than 94 percent of scrapbookers had PCs in their homes, and nearly 73 percent of them have purchased scrapbooking supplies online.

Online photo-imaging brought in about $7.8 billion in 2008, and the Photo Marketing Association estimated that more than 24 billion photographs were taken that year, with 16.5 billion of them being printed. This represented a huge marketplace for creative presentation of these photos, either online or offline.

In 2010 opportunities to work from home in the arts and crafts industry paid up to $10,000 annually, according to N. Nayab and Jean Scheid at *BrightHub*. They listed the five top home opportunities as gift baskets, picture framing, faux painting, stained glass, and scrapbooks.

INDUSTRY LEADERS

Michaels Stores Inc. Michaels Stores is the nation's leading arts and crafts retailer, offering virtually every kind of art and craft supply imaginable, as well as framing services, classes, workshops, and more. Growing from only 16 stores in 1984 to more than 500 in the mid-1990s, the company expanded at an aggressive pace in the late 1990s and 2000s. By 2009 it operated 1,035 Michaels stores in 49 states and Canada, 165 Aaron Brothers Stores, and 11 ReCollections scrapbooking stores. Michaels also owned a frame and molding manufacturing operation called Artistree and four Star Decorators Wholesale Warehouses serving interior decorators, party planners, and professional crafters. The company also operated seven U.S. distribution centers. Michaels' sales reached $3.82 billion in 2009, on the strength of 39,000 employees.

Jo-Ann Stores Inc. With 2009 sales of more than $1.99 billion, Jo-Ann Stores Inc. is the nation's leading fabric retailer, with approximately 760 Jo-Ann Fabrics and Crafts stores in 47 states nationwide. The company embarked on a superstore strategy in the late 1990s, and had more than 200 superstores in place by 2008. "As we serve and inspire our guests every day, we serve to be their number one creative resource," says Jo-Ann's

CEO, Alan Rosskamm, revealing some of the company's customer service philosophy. "We aim to meet all of our customers' creative needs, not only with the latest high-quality products from around the world, but also by providing the ideas, inspiration and advice to help their projects succeed." In its 2011 fiscal year, the company intended to open 30 new stores and close 30 others.

Hobby Lobby Stores Inc. Hobby Lobby was another leading industry player, with 435 stores, 9,600 employees, and 2009 sales of approximately $2.3 billion. The company's roots stretch back to 1970, when president and founder David Green operated a miniature picture frame company called Greco Products. Green added 300 square feet of retail space to his company in August of 1972, giving birth to Hobby Lobby. By January of 1973 his enterprise had moved to a house in Oklahoma City where retail space increased to cover 1,000 square feet.

By 2004 the company offered 60,000 items at its stores and operated a 1.7 million-square-foot headquarters that included a distribution center and 725,000 square feet of manufacturing space to produce picture frames, candles, scented products, and more. Sister companies based at Hobby Lobby's headquarters include Mardel; Hemispheres; Crafts, Etc!; H.L. Construction; Bearing Fruit Communications; and Hong Kong Connection. In 2010 the company announced a minimum hourly wage of $11 for all employees (several dollars more than federal minimum wages).

A.C. Moore Arts & Crafts Inc. A.C. Moore Arts & Crafts was another leading arts and crafts marketer on the scene. Like Hobby Lobby, A.C. Moore grew from a single store into a large chain. Founded in Moorestown, New Jersey, in 1985 by Jack and Pat Parker and William Kaplan, by 2008 the company had more than 135 stores in place in the eastern United States. Its stores carry about 60,000 SKUs (stock-keeping units) throughout the year, with some 45,000 items offered at any given time. For its fiscal year ending January 2, 2010, A.C. Moore reported $468.9 million in sales, down 12.3 percent from the previous year. The company employed more than 4,400 workers.

Creative Memories Based in St. Cloud, Minnesota, Creative Memories is a leading industry player, even though it has no retail outlets. In 2006 the company relied on more than 90,000 independent sales reps (up from 60,000 in 2004) in the United States, Canada, the United Kingdom, Germany, Australia, New Zealand, Taiwan, and Japan to market its products. A subsidiary of the Antioch Co., Creative Memories serves the world's growing legions of scrapbookers. According to the company, its consultants "teach the importance of and techniques for organizing, documenting and preserving their photographs and memorabilia in safe, meaningful, keepsake albums. Consultants educate and provide hands-on assistance during Home Classes, Workshops and other events." Creative Memories was established in 1987 by Montana housewife Rhonda Anderson and the Antioch Co.'s Cheryl Lightle. In addition to its World Headquarters and Technology Center, Creative Memories also operates a distribution center and album manufacturing plant in St. Cloud.

Stampin' Up! Another direct seller of arts and crafts materials is Riverton, Utah-based Stampin' Up! With 2007 sales of $181 million and 560 employees, Stampin' Up! relies on more than 50,000 independent demonstrators in the United States and Canada to sell its rubber stamp sets and accessories, which are used for paper card-making, scrapbooking, to make unique home décor items, and more. Shelli Gardner and her sister established the company in 1988. In addition to its 40,000-square-foot headquarters and demonstrator support call center in Salt Lake City, where the company also operates a 110,000-square-foot warehouse and distribution center, Stampin' Up! has a rubber stamp manufacturing plant in Kanab, Utah. The company began manufacturing stamp sets in 1992. By 1997 it only sold stamp sets from the Stampin' Up! line. As of 2008, Stampin' Up! had more than 50,000 demonstrators throughout North America, many of whom resided in California, Michigan, Minnesota, Washington, and Wisconsin.

BIBLIOGRAPHY

"2008 Magazine Profile." *Scrapbooking.com Magazine,* 2008. Available from http://scrapbooking.com.

"About Stampin' Up!" Stampin' Up!, 20 June 2008. Available from http://www.stampinup.com.

"About Us." A.C. Moore Arts & Crafts Inc., 20 June 2008. Available from http://www.acmoore.com.

"About Us." Creative Memories, 20 June 2008. Available from http://www.creativememories.com.

"About Us." Michaels Stores Inc., 20 June 2008. Available from http://www.michaels.com.

"All About CHA." Craft & Hobby Association, 20 June 2008. Available from http://www. hobby.org/allaboutcha.html.

"The American Craft Council," 20 June 2008. Available from http://www.craftcouncil.org.

"Attitude and Usage Study." Hobby Industry Association, 2008. Available from http://www.hobby.org.

Clairmont, Kristy. "Data Watch: There Is Growth Potential in the Scrapbooking Industry, Despite Shrinking Market." *PMA Foresight,* 21 January 2008. Available from http://pmaforesight.com.

"Company Information." Hobby Lobby Stores Inc., 20 June 2008. Available from http://www.hobbylobby.com.

"Creative Leisure News Update on A.C. Moore, Hancock, HobbyLobby, and Provocraft." CHA PR Manager, 20 April 2010. Available from http://www.craftandhobby.wordpress.

Gretzner, Bonnie. "Defining Digital Scrapbooking." *PMA Magazine,* February 2007.

Howell, Debbie. "Retailers Piece Together New Crafting Opportunities." *DSN Retailing Today,* 23 January 2006.

"Jo-Ann Fabrics Stores," 21 August 2010. Available from http://www.marketwatch.com.

"K&Company Launches Recycled Paper Crafting Line." *Scrapbooking Manufacturer News,* 14 May 2008.

McNeill, Suzanne. "Trends in the Crafts Industry." *CHA Portfolio,* 4 March 2010. Available from http://www.blog.suzannemcneill.com/2010/03/.../trends-in-the-craft-industry.

"Michaels Stores, Inc.," 21 August 2010. Available from http://www.marketwatch.com.

Nayab, N. "Work from Home Opportunities in Arts and Crafts," 14 June 2010. Available from http://www.brighthub.com.

Philadelphia Museum of Art Craft Show. "The Philadelphia Museum of Art Craft Show Conducts Nationwide Craft Industry Survey," 3 November 2009. Available from http://www.pmacraftshow.org/news/news_018.php.

"Scrapbooking.com 2010 Magazine Profile," 21 August 2010. Available from http://www.scrapbooking.com/sales/files/MagazineProfile.pdf.

The Shaker Historic Trail. National Park Service, 20 June 2008. Available from http://www.nps.gov/history/nr/travel/shaker/shakers.htm.

"The Society of Arts and Crafts," 20 June 2008. Available from http://www.societyofcrafts.org/about.asp.

"Toy & Craft Supplies Wholesaling Industry Research in the US by IBISWorld," 21 August 2010. Available from http://www.ibisworld.com/industry/default.aspx?indid=954.

"U.S. Toy Industry Sales Generate $21.47 Billion in 2009." Port Washington, NY: The NPD Group Inc., 21 August 2010. Available from http://www.npd.com/pressreleases/press_100201a.html.

Walker, Andrea K. "Michaels May Go on Block." *Baltimore Sun,* 21 March 2006.

"Who Is the Scrapbooker?" *DSN Retailing Today,* 23 January 2006.

Yeager, Amanda. "Behind Digital Scrapbooking." *PMA Magazine,* December 2007.

AVIATION SECURITY

———— ◼ ————

SIC CODE(S)

7381

INDUSTRY SNAPSHOT

Airport security: it is a buzzword for the media, a political minefield for politicians and lawmakers, and a headache for travelers. No matter which camp you are in, the controversy surrounding airport security isn't going away. Since the terrorist attacks of September 11, 2001, against the United States, the safety, or lack thereof, of U.S. airports has become the subject of considerable debate. In June 2009, the International Air Transport Association (IATA) forecast $9 billion in revenue losses for the global aviation industry, while at the same time airlines were spending $5.9 billion a year on security. Despite these concerns, the U.S. Congress made certain to fund aviation security in its 2009 stimulus bill.

On November 19, 2001, President George W. Bush signed the Aviation and Transportation Security Act (ATSA), which created the Transportation Security Administration (TSA) within the Department of Transportation. The goal of this new legislation was to create an authority charged with the task of securing the air travel system in the United States. The first major initiatives for the organization included replacing all private sector security screeners with a workforce of federal employees and equipping all airports with the machinery needed to screen every single piece of checked baggage. The time frame for implementing these sweeping changes was immediate. One year was allocated to complete the transition from civilian to federal employees and a December 31, 2002, deadline was adopted in regard to the checked baggage mandate.

By January 2003 the business of airport security in the United States had received a complete overhaul. The November 19, 2002. deadline for deploying federal baggage handlers was honored, resulting in the termination of millions of dollars in contracts with private security firms. The goal of installing electronic systems to screen 100 percent of checked baggage was nearly achieved by the established deadline. Only 30 or 40 of the nation 429 airports waited for equipment deliveries.

These improvements represented the beginning of a new wave of potential security measures for airports around the country. Different options have been proposed and challenged by many groups that have a stake in the future of airline security. As new proposals are reviewed and adopted, new corporate players in the industry will emerge.

ORGANIZATION AND STRUCTURE

A review of the inner workings of airport security sheds some light on the challenges facing the industry. First, the very word "industry" suggests a group of comparable companies and organizations competing to serve or fill a need. In the complicated world of aviation security, nothing could be further from the truth. Providing airport security is a Herculean task and can be divided into four main categories: facilities, employee and vendor supervision, equipment, and procedures. The responsibility for keeping travelers safe has historically been divided among various factions: airport authorities, who manage the facilities; airlines, who control maintenance and access to the planes; the Federal Aviation Authority (FAA), who monitors the skies and determines safety standards; and a mix of public and private sector companies patrolling the areas in between. The division of duties has long posed a challenge to the authorities trying to safeguard the traveling public.

The creation of the Transportation Security Administration (TSA) was intended to provide a single governing body to monitor the safety of U.S. airports. The first priority of the TSA was achieved in December 2002 when it successfully hired and trained over 40,000 federal passenger screeners. These screeners replaced all private sector employees and effectively eliminated the role of private security firms in this capacity.

In addition to staffing facilities with federal employees, the Aviation and Transportation Security Act (ATSA) mandated the use of sophisticated baggage screening devices for all airports. The private sector was able to regain a piece of the airport security business by bidding on the contracts to install the new screening equipment. Defense and electronics companies competing to install the new equipment designed to detect explosives included Northrop Grumman Corp. and Raytheon Co. Northrop eventually won a large portion of the assignment, including providing training for screeners using the devices. Other contracts related to installing security upgrades in airports have received bids from a number of companies specializing in defense electronics such as Boeing Co., Lockheed Martin Corp., and TRW Inc. The explosive detection/screening devices are manufactured by a handful of companies, such as L-3 Communication Holdings and Invision Technologies.

In 2003 the TSA placed the control and structure of the airport security industry firmly in the hands of the federal government. Acting with the authority of congressional legislation and the cooperation of the FAA, the agency determines necessary safety measures and moves to implement them. As of 2007, the mandate that all TSA and airport security personnel must be federal employees remained in place. Private sector companies now provide services as equipment manufacturers and train federal employees on proper use of the equipment, but private security firms are no longer a strong presence in U.S. aviation security.

BACKGROUND AND DEVELOPMENT

Airport security traces it roots back to 1926, the year the U.S. Congress passed the Air Commerce Act. The goal of the legislation was to create safety standards for air travel, thus making it more appealing to the public. The Department of Commerce, operating from its newly formed Aeronautics Branch, assumed oversight authority for the nation's airports, air traffic control, and regulations governing pilot training and certification. At that time, guaranteeing the safety of air travel meant focusing on the pilot certification process and the procedures for safety inspections of aircraft. Lighted runways and radio beacons were introduced to serve as navigation aids.

In 1934 the Aeronautics Branch was renamed the Bureau of Air Commerce in response to the growing popularity of commercial air flight. In 1936 the federal government established and operated three air traffic control centers. The first air traffic controllers used maps and blackboards to plot flight paths between destinations. They also performed the necessary mathematical calculations by hand. In 1938 air travel was on the rise and the responsibility for monitoring it was transferred to a new agency, the Civil Aeronautics Authority. The government became further involved in the industry by claiming the right to regulate travel routes and air fares.

Only two years later, the new department would again undergo a reorganization, this time at the behest of President Franklin Roosevelt. The agency was divided in two in an attempt to eliminate conflicting interests within the unit. In place of the Civil Aeronautics Authority, the Civil Aeronautics Administration (CAA) and the Civil Aeronautics Board (CAB) were created. The CAA assumed responsibility for air traffic control and safety regulations and certifications. The CAB was accountable for making the rules, investigating accidents, and managing the economic policies of the airlines. Prior to World War II, the CAA implemented the use of radar screens in air traffic control protocols and monitored all takeoffs and landings at national airports.

On June 30, 1956, a Trans World Airlines jet and a United Airlines DC-7 collided in midair over the Grand Canyon. Everyone on both planes died instantly. The Federal Aviation Act of 1958 was enacted in response to this incident and a wave of other in-flight collisions between airliners. The Federal Aviation Agency (FAA) was born and given broad authority to regulate the industry. The first head of the FAA was Elwood Quesada, who would lead the agency in its reform efforts. The FAA functioned as an autonomous body until 1967, when the new Department of Transportation, a cabinet level department, emerged. The Federal Aviation Agency became a unit of the Department of Transportation and underwent only a slight name change to become the Federal Aviation Administration. The National Transportation Safety Board was also founded to investigate accidents.

During the 1960s, a series of hijackings caused the FAA to become more active in security issues. In 1970, Palestinians hijacked four planes and promised to blow them up if their demands went unanswered. In the aftermath of this incident, President Nixon mandated the use of "sky marshals" on certain high-risk flights. This precaution did not deter would-be saboteurs, and in 1971 perhaps the most unusual hijacking occurred. A man named Dan Cooper boarded a flight in Portland, Oregon, and then threatened to blow up the plane with a bag full of explosives if the airline did not pay him $200,000.

The airline succumbed to the threat, and with ransom money in hand, Cooper then parachuted from the plane, using the back stairs as an escape route. After this incident, the "Cooper Vane" was designed and installed in all aircraft to prevent the back stairs from being lowered while planes are airborne.

By 1972 it was obvious that none of the prescribed safety measures were effective against would-be assailants. In December 1972 the Federal Aviation Administration (FAA) ordered the airlines to begin searching all luggage and passengers boarding each flight. The first rudimentary metal detectors were installed in airports. The scanning equipment was created using technology borrowed from the timber industry, which used it to detect metal deposits in logs harvested by timber mills. Staff from the FAA's security offices haphazardly conducted the first inspections. The random selection of passengers angered the public and became the focus of legal action. Lawsuits claimed that the use of metal detectors violated passengers' Fourth Amendment rights banning illegal searches and seizures. The courts ruled that the searches could be construed as a violation of Fourth Amendment rights but permitted them with certain stipulations. All passengers were searched to avoid prejudice and these searches could only be used to uncover hidden weapons or explosives.

The 1988 downing of Pan Am Flight 103 near Lockerbie, Scotland, shocked the world and reminded everyone of the potential dangers of an inadequate security system. A bomb smuggled on board destroyed the aircraft and killed all 270 passengers and crew on board. The FAA again upgraded security measures. Laptop computers and other carry-on electronics received greater scrutiny in the search for incendiary devices. The new rules also mandated baggage matching, which required that each piece of baggage must be traceable to a passenger present on the airplane at takeoff.

Throughout the history of aviation and airport security, the greatest reforms have almost always happened as the result of serious security breaches. Unfortunately, this pattern held true in the wake of the terrorist attacks of September 11, 2001. Members of the al Qaeda terrorist network hijacked two commercial airliners en route to the West Coast from Boston's Logan Airport, one from Newark International Airport in Newark, New Jersey, and one from Dulles International Airport outside Washington, D.C.. Two of the planes crashed into the twin towers of the World Trade Center in New York City, one hit the Pentagon building in Washington, D.C., and the fourth crashed in a field in rural Pennsylvania. These tragic events triggered a comprehensive review of the state of airport security and a complete restructuring of the industry.

Congress implemented legislation aimed at preventing future attacks. In the following months, more new laws were passed regulating aviation security than in any other time in history. For perhaps the first time, the laws went beyond merely introducing new safety measures and took notice of the personnel hired to implement the measures. The FAA determined safety standards for aviation and airport security, but each airport, airline, or municipality was responsible for the day-to-day operations of the equipment and facilities. A review of practices uncovered some distressing facts. The majority of airline security personnel had been hired through contracts with private security firms, and in many cases, neither the airport authority nor the airlines had played a part in the process. An investigation revealed that employees hired to fill these positions had lied about criminal records or qualifications, and had sometimes provided false identification or social security numbers to obscure their true identities. These findings signaled the demise of traditional airport security firms.

The Aviation and Transportation Security Act of 2001 was passed by a House and Senate Conference resolution to address the inadequacies of the system and was signed by President George W. Bush on November 19, 2001. The bill required all checked baggage to be screened and the personnel hired for these jobs to be federal employees. This final provision was a huge blow to the private firms with contracts to provide staff for the nation's airports. The industry was granted one year to adopt the changes and the Transportation Security Administration (TSA) was formed within the Department of Transportation to ensure compliance. In 2002 the TSA worked tirelessly to meet federal mandates for upgrading security practices. With days to spare, the new agency successfully completed the first phase of its mission, leaving behind the remains of the airport security industry.

In 2003 the TSA entered its second year of operation after a rather rocky beginning. The agency met government deadlines for upgrading security checkpoints at airports and hiring federal employees as screeners, but improvement was still needed in many areas. With the elementary measures in place, the focus shifted to reviewing and refining procedures and devising a plan to manage costs. In the future, travelers can expect continued scrutiny as new electronic databases are employed to track the movement of passengers and search for indicators of hostile intent. It may not be long before biometric devices are used to identify and record personal information about those who fly frequently.

In April 2003 the airlines met the deadline for installing reinforced cockpit doors to bolster in-flight security. By mid-decade, the TSA had programs in place to test the use of non-federal screeners in U.S. airports. Called the Screening Partnership Program (SPP), this initiative paved the way for private corporations to re-establish a presence in the industry. After implementing test programs in San Francisco, Kansas City, Jackson Hole, Rochester, and Tupelo, in November 2004 the TSA had started taking applications from all 450 commercial U.S. airports that were interested in reverting back to private contractors for airport screening.

The TSA had a program in place to test the use of non-federal screeners in U.S. airports. Called the Screening Partnership Program (SPP), this initiative paved the way for private corporations to re-establish a presence in the industry. By late 2009 the TSA had expanded its Screening Partnership Program to 15 airports, including the San Francisco International Airport, Kansas City International Airport, Greater Rochester International Airport, Sioux Falls Regional Airport, Jackson Hole Airport, Tupelo Regional Airport, Key West International Airport, Charles M. Schultz-Sonoma County Airport, Roswell Industrial Air Center, Gallup Municipal Airport, and the 34th Street Heliport.

However, airports were not quick to opt out of the federal screening program. In fact, by September 2005 the San Francisco International Airport announced that it would stop using private screeners on May 7, 2006 because of liability concerns. Because other airports shared these concerns, they were reluctant to apply for the SPP until the Congress provided liability protection, according to the September 7, 2005, issue of *Airport Security Report*. The San Francisco airport indicated that it would consider remaining in the program if Congress provided liability protection by January 20, 2006.

The aforementioned issue of *Airport Security Report* further indicated that San Francisco's decision was an important one for the industry, explaining, "A pull-out from SPP by San Francisco could put the program's future in jeopardy. Twenty-five airports remain interested in joining the program, but none are moving forward because of the liability issue, according to the Airports Council International-North America (ACI-NA). Four others besides SFO have been part of a pilot program, and one more has opted in since last fall." (In October 2009 the Glacier Park International Airport in Montana decided to opt back out of federal security screening and privatize its security workforce afterexperiencing staffing and customer service problems, according to dailyinterlake.com.

Some observers noted that the (TSA) was potentially moving away from a heavy emphasis on bag and passenger checking and toward a more scientific, risk management approach involving forecasting techniques and cost-benefit analyses. This approach centers on identifying the most significant threats and then prioritizing resources accordingly. While a number of analysts were supportive of this

approach, some were concerned that the TSA would not implement it properly.

According to a report from M2 Communications, in August 2005 the TSA proposed a number of measures to make air travel more convenient for passengers. These included lifting the requirement that all passengers remove their shoes at security checkpoints, scaling back the number of pat-down searches, and allowing travelers to once again carry items such as razors, small knives, and scissors on flights. In February 2009, the House of Representatives passed the FAST Redress Act of 2009 by a vote of 413-3, designed to eliminate the confusion associated with erroneously-challenged travelers who have appeared on a terrorist watch list.

However, proposed legislation called for more stringent security measures. For example, in the U.S. House of Representatives, Rep. Nita Lowey (D-NY) proposed a bill, H.R. 2688, that "would require the physical screening of all people, goods, property, vehicles, and equipment before they are allowed into the secure area of an airport," according to the September 2005 issue of *Security Management*. Additionally, Rep. Edward Markey (D-MA) introduced H.R. 2649, a bill that proposed to increase aviation security by mandating basic security for flight attendants, requiring airport operators to complete vulnerability assessments and action plans related to their facilities, and requiring the Department of Homeland Security (DHS) to develop an inspection system to screen all cargo transported on passenger aircraft.

In addition to traditional security measures, new technologies have emerged that promise to play a critical role in shaping industry practices. On June 21, 2005, the Orlando International Airport became the first in the nation to offer a privately sponsored, DHS-approved Registered Traveler program. In about one month's time, 4,000 people signed up for the program, which is operated jointly by the Greater Orlando Airport Authority, the DHS, Verified Identity Pass Inc., and Lockheed Martin Corp. After submitting to an in-depth background investigation and paying an $80 annual fee, qualifying passengers receive biometric smart cards that allow them to bypass regular airport screening practices. Although the program is designed as an incentive for travelers and is intended to reduce travel time and inconvenience, many view it as an invasion of personal privacy.

Public safety versus personal privacy will continue to be dominant issues within the industry. During the early 2000s, the TSA proposed a system comparable to current credit profiling practices in an effort to gauge the threat level posed by individual travelers. The system involved the creation of a central database that would store a vast array of personal information collected by various methods. The American Civil Liberties Union voiced its disapproval of this system, known as Computer Assisted Passenger Prescreening System (CAPPS), as well as its successor, CAPPS II, calling it an invasion of privacy. The system eventually was replaced by a new proposed program, called Secure Flight, in August 2004.

There were a number of differences between CAPPS II and the new program. While Secure Flight initially planned to use commercial data sources to verify the identities of air travelers, the TSA tabled that aspect of the program after criticism from the Government Accountability Office (GAO) and privacy activists. In addition, passenger names would be cross-referenced only against terrorist lists, and not listings of all criminals. While these differences pleased some industry observers, others were concerned that Secure Flight would become more stringent after it was implemented. One analyst raised the possibility that the voluntary Registered Traveler program, which required travelers to divulge more private information than Secure Flight did, could one day become a mandatory program for all travelers.

The TSA planned to roll out Secure Flight in the summer of 2005. However, delays pushed the projected launch until late 2005 or early 2006. Some observers were concerned that based on a March 2005 GAO report, the TSA had not met the bulk of program criteria set by Congress. Six months later, it appeared that the TSA still had work to do before launching Secure Flight. In its September 22, 2005, issue, *The Wall Street Journal* noted that a forthcoming report from the Secure Flight Working Group was "highly critical of the TSA." According to the report, it said, the agency did not have a clear understanding of the new program's goals, which served as a roadblock to addressing issues regarding security and privacy.

A number of key developments were unfolding within the industry as it headed into the latter part of the decade. In August of 2007 the U.S. Department of Homeland Security (DHS) issued an announcement about the implementation of two regulations, stemming from the 9/11 Commission's recommendations, which aimed to bolster aviation security.

DHS's Advance Passenger Information System (APIS) Predeparture Final Rule allows the department "to collect manifest information for international flights departing from or arriving in the United States prior to boarding." Secondly, DHS announced it was taking first steps toward the implementation of the Secure Flight program via its Secure Flight Notice of Proposed Rule Making (NPRM), which "lays out DHS plans to assume watch list matching responsibilities from air carriers for domestic flights and align domestic and international passenger prescreening."

Part of the 2004 Intelligence Reform and Terrorism Prevention Act, implementation of the Advance Passenger Information System was in line with a congressional mandate that required the DHS's Customs and Border Protection to receive advance information about international air passengers. The new regulations will "require air carriers to transmit manifests 30 minutes prior to departure of the aircraft or provide manifest information on passengers as each passenger checks in for the flight, up to the time when aircraft doors are secured. . . . For vessels departing from foreign ports bound for the United States, current requirements to transmit passenger and crew arrival manifest data between 24 to 96 hours prior to arrival will remain unchanged, but requires vessel carriers to transmit APIS data 60 minutes prior to departure from the United States."

Regarding the Secure Flight program, DHS announced it would begin taking steps to uniformly prescreen passenger data by comparing it to federal government watch lists both domestic and international flights. The eventual transfer of this function's responsibility from air carriers to the Transportation Security Administration (TSA) was marked by a voluntary testing period in the fall of 2007, aimed at ensuring the Secure Flight System's validity. Specifically, this involved the TSA comparing its matching activities with those of carriers.

According to the DHS announcement, the department eventually plans to merge Secure Flight with the list matching system for international flights, creating "one master system, operated by DHS, that would be used to perform prescreening for all aviation passengers.

Other important aviation security developments in 2007 resulted in more convenience for passengers and security professionals alike. On August 4, the TSA announced it would no longer ban common cigarette lighters in carry-on luggage. Although bans of torch lighters remained in place, this freed TSA officers from collecting 22,000 common lighters, which were no longer considered to be a threat, from passengers each day. This development was made possible on October 4, 2006, when Congress passed the Department of Homeland Security Appropriations Act allowing the TSA administrator to not enforce the lighter ban. In addition, the TSA announced new rules that allowed a mother, either with or without her child, to carry more than 3 ounces of breast milk through security checkpoints. Breast milk was added to the same category as liquid medication, allowing it to be carried past checkpoints as long as it was declared before screening.

A number of key developments were unfolding within the industry as it headed into the latter part of the decade. In August of 2007, the U.S. Department of

Homeland Security (DHS) issued an announcement about the implementation of two regulations, stemming from the 9/11 Commission's recommendations, which aimed to bolster aviation security. These included the Advance Passenger Information System (APIS) Predeparture Final Rule, which was related to the collection of manifest data for international flights, as well as the first steps toward the implementation of the Secure Flight program.

In 2007, conditions became more convenient for passengers and security professionals alike when, on August 4, the TSA announced it would no longer ban common cigarette lighters in carry-on luggage. In addition, the TSA announced new rules that allowed a mother, either with or without her child, to carry more than 3 ounces of breast milk through security checkpoints.

Earlier in 2007, President George Bush signed the Implementing the 9/11 Commission Recommendation Act (the 9/11 Act), P.L. 110-53, requiring the Secretary of Homeland Security to establish a system that would ultimately result in the screening of 100 percent of cargo transported on passenger aircraft. The new law was to be sequentially implemented within three years, with full compliance by 2010. Furthermore, the Narrow Body Screening Amendment became effective in October 2008, requiring 100 percent screening of all cargo on narrow body aircraft.

CURRENT CONDITIONS

In October 2009 the IATA reported that airlines were spending $5.9 billion a year on security. It formally called upon governments and regulators to work smarter with the aviation industry to eliminate costly duplications of aviation security procedures. To meet the challenge of delivering cost-effective yet safety-effective security measures, IATA and the Aviation Security Group developed a five-part strategy. It recommended the adoption of a threat-based and risk management approach, utilizing its Security Management System (SeMS) integrated with national regulations; working with industry instead of in isolation; exercising care not to implement even small regulatory or procedural changes which may cost airlines millions to test or implement; affirmatively employing innovative technology for improvements; and implementing measures judged in terms of added value, cost effectiveness, and common sense.

Within the United States, Congress and Obama administration, in February 2009, finalized the Stimulus Bill (American Recovery and Reinvestment Act), which included $1 billion to TSA for explosives detection systems to be used at airports. In a statement accompanying the bill, lawmakers estimated that more than 3,500 new jobs would be created for the TSA inspection equipment, expected to be installed at 20 airports.

TSA's proposed new rules, published in the Federal Register on October 30, 2008, were met with such opposition and skepticism that it decided to hold several public hearings in early 2009. The proposed rules would prohibit general aviation aircraft from carrying many different items, such as tools, hardware and various technical devices. Most opposition came from owners and operators of small corporate, charter and privately owned aircraft. In February 2009 the TSA announced that it had sought input from 3,000 general aviation airport operators across the country to complete threat and vulnerability assessments surveys, which the TSA would consider before finalizing its rules.

INDUSTRY LEADERS

The events of September 11, 2001, clearly illustrated that in order to provide the highest levels of airport and aviation security, advanced technology and equipment and competent employees to operate it are needed. There are few, if any, companies that can supply both components of the ideal security model. In the field of airport security, two distinct types of companies emerged. The first group of companies includes Boeing, Raytheon, Northrop Grumman, and others who manufacture sophisticated electronic equipment used in screening and surveillance. The second group of companies is comprised of private security firms that contracted to staff the screening checkpoints. Prior to the terrorist attacks on September 11, 2001, Argenbright Security was the largest security firm providing staff to airports across the nation. Other notable companies were Huntleigh USA, Securicor, Securitas, and Garden Security Services Solutions (GS-3). In January 2009 New Jersey-based Safeguards Technology received a contract to install a perimeter intrusion detection system (which it produces) for an unspsecified airport in India.

WORKFORCE

The employees of the airport security industry were thrust into the public spotlight in the aftermath of the September 11, 2001, terrorist attacks. A government inquiry revealed that the private security firms holding the contracts to maintain security at U.S. airports used inadequate pre-employment screening practices and provided minimal training for employees. It also was discovered that a significant number of personnel employed as security screeners had failed to accurately provide authentic identification and personal information. As a consequence of this investigation, legislation was passed mandating that all security screening personnel employed at the nation's airports must meet federal hiring standards.

The original law passed by Congress in November 2001 called for 30,000 federal screeners to be hired. That number eventually climbed to 73,000 employees when the entire scope of the undertaking was clear. Each U.S. airport will be under the direction of a Federal Security director who will receive a salary in the range of $105,000 to $150,000. A number of assistant directors will be employed for larger airports. The budget for staff has grown tremendously since its inception and steps are being taken to trim the excess personnel from the system. Staff cutbacks began in 2003 and may continue as features such as self-closing doors and surveillance cameras replace the need for live personnel at every corner.

Heading into the later part of the decade, the Transportation Security Administration (TSA) issued a number of facts about its workforce as part of an effort to counter myths regarding employment conditions within the agency. In addition to outlining details of its Model Workplace Program, which includes employee councils for dealing with grievances, the TSA indicated that it had issued some $58 million in job-performance-related pay increases and bonuses. In 2006 the agency paid out some $20 million in retention bonuses to its staff. However, a Government Accountability Office (GAO) report released in February 2009 noted that TSA had been unable to provide documentation identifying how its inspectors (TSIs) spent 49 percent of their time, which the TSA listed as "other." when describing what the TSIs did with their time. The "other." activities represented ones not captured in TSA's regulatory reporting system, but represented the largest single category measured.

RESEARCH AND TECHNOLOGY

In January 2009 TSA announced that it was working with companies with the ability to design and produce scanning devices that could detect explosives or weapon parts concealed inside shoes and other clothing items. It was also working on more sophisticated walk-through detectors capable of detecting metallic objects. No more details were provided.

Technology will play a defining role in the future of airport security systems. Biometrics are considered the most promising of all protocols for developing new identification technologies. Biometrics do not attempt to profile or identify a potential security threat based on external data, but instead attempt to provide foolproof verification of an individual's identity. This is done by scanning and measuring specific body parts and then comparing those measurements to a previously recorded scan. The most common example of biometrics is fingerprinting. More sophisticated methods include scanning of the irises or measuring finger geometry.

Biometrics already are in use in European airports. Gatwick Airport in London began using smart cards to store passenger information in 2002. Each card contained the scan of the passenger's fingerprints and stored the image on the card. Passengers would then present the card to security officials and submit to finger scans before boarding their flight. If the biometric image recorded at the gate matches the image stored on the card, the identity of the passenger is confirmed. Early trials show the error rate for false matches comes in at less than 1 percent. These smart cards may also one day contain information which will not only confirm a traveler's identity but also provide officials with profiling information.

The use of profiling as part of any screening process is controversial, but many expect it to emerge as a viable option. Privacy concerns continue to factor into the decision-making process. Airports in Amsterdam have also issued security cards that store a template of a passenger's iris, but the cards must remain in possession of the individual; the government is not allowed to collect and compile a database of biometric information for use in any other endeavor. The biometric information remains with the passenger and is only presented for inspection when needed. France's privacy commission also is concerned about biometric data being divulged to other commercial, government, or law enforcement agencies.

Scientists at the University of Buffalo were working with support from the Federal Aviation Administration to develop a tool that could possibly thwart security threats before they reached the nation's airports. These scientists were developing a special search engine that could be used to scan disparate public Web sites and identify possible patterns that were indicative of potential terrorist threats. According to the September 2005 issue of *USA Today Magazine*,: "The system permits users to find the best trail of evidence through many documents that connect two or more apparently unrelated concepts. Existing search engines process individual documents based on the number of times a key word appears. In contrast, the new system is based on the construction of concept chain graphs that search for the best path connecting two concepts within a multitude of documents." Beyond aviation security, this technology may have applications in areas such as medical research.

AMERICA AND THE WORLD

In May 2009 the European Commission adopted a proposal for a Directive on aviation security changes in Europe concerning the financing of aviation security, recovery of which was regulated at the national level but mostly passed on to passengers. Among other things, the proposal aimed at ensuring transparency and non-discrimination in charges to passengers or specific airlines; the assurance that airlines would be consulted on security charges; ensuring the use of security charges for de facto security costs; and establishing an independent supervisory authority for the resolution of disagreements.

On a global scale, international companies continue to pioneer new systems for monitoring and controlling the flow of passengers and cargo throughout the industry. London's Heathrow Airport is the largest international airport in the world and has been a leader in security for almost two decades. In the aftermath of the bombing of Pan Am Flight 103 over Lockerbie, Scottish and British airports tightened security and introduced many safety protocols used today. Norman Shanks, the airport security manager at Heathrow from 1986 to 1991, described the differences between U.S. and British screening processes in a 2002 edition of *Airport Security Report*: "In the U.S., there is a tendency to rely too much on what officials believe they know about the individual. This may be either because the trusted staff member is so well embedded into the thinking of the TSA or because they believe it's a way of overcoming some form of trade/staff disputes." As part of the British system, all personnel, including staff, are subject to search at any time. Shanks also believes that U.S. security is experiencing some of the same difficulties that foreign carriers had previously encountered.

The U.S. government continued to work out terms regarding the sharing of passenger data on European passengers traveling to the United States. Many EU lawmakers were opposed to the United States's desire for 34 facts about all passengers, including details about credit cards and where tickets were purchased. In the meantime, the two government bodies continued to operate under the terms of an interim agreement signed in October of 2006.

Europe continued to experience rapid growth in its aviation security market in the wake of standard EU security standards being imposed throughout Europe, according to the research firm Frost & Sullivan. According to the June 27, 2007, issue of *Airline Industry Information*, the report further indicated that 36 European airports will undergo upgrades between 2006 and 2010, and 20 new airports will be constructed. These developments were expected to support growth of more than 34 percent.

BIBLIOGRAPHY

Anderson, Teresa. "Airport Biometrics Preparing to Take Flight in France; The French Civil Aviation Authority Is Beginning a Six-Month Analysis of Fingerprint, Iris, and Facial-Recognition Data; The Objective: Decide Which Biometric Technology Is Most Reliable." *Informationweek,* 29 December 2004.

Anderson, Teresa. "Airport Security." *Security Management,* September 2005.

"Directive on Aviation Security Charges in Europe." *TravelDaily News,* 13 May 2009.

"Aviation Security and Border Security Favored in Senate Stimulus Bill's $4.7B DHS Package." 6 February 2009 Available from http:///www.homelandsecurityresearch.com/2009/02/aviation-security-and-border-security-favored-in-senate-stimulus bills-47b-dhs-package/.

"Computer Search Engine Thwarts Terrorism." *USA Today Magazine,* September 2005.

"DHS Announces Predeparture Screening of International Passengers and First Step Toward Secure Flight." Transportation Security Administration, U.S. Department of Homeland Security, 9 August 2007. Available from http://www.tsa.gov/press/releases/2007/press_release_08082007.shtm.

Doherty, Brian. "Privacy in the Skies: CAPPS II: The Sequel." *Reason,* December 2004.

"European Airport Security Market Expected to Grow." *Airline Industry Information,* 27 June 2007.

The Federal Aviation Administration. "A Brief History of the Federal Aviation Administration and Its Predecessor Agencies," March 2003. Available from http://www1.faa.gov.index.cfm/apa.html.

"Frequently Asked Questions about FAA History." Available from http://www1.faa.gov.index.cfm/apa.html. March 2003.

"General Aviation Airport Operators Asked to Perform Vulnerability Assessments. *Government Security News Magazine,* 10 February 2009. Available from http://www.gsnmagazine.com/cms/market-segments/aviation-security/1510.html

"Hawley to Head TSA." *The Journal of Commerce,* 22 August 2005.

Meckler, Laura. "Air-Traveler Screening to Launch Without Commercial Databases." *The Wall Street Journal,* 22 September 2005.

Meller, Paul. "EU Oficial Says Pact on Airline Data Is Near." *Computerworld,* 21 May 2007.

"Opt-Out Screening Program Begins to Take Shape." *Airport Security Report,* 6 October 2004.

PBI Media, LLC. "Building Airport Security Requires A Wide View." *Airport Security Report,* Volume 9, No. 23. 6 November 2002.

"Montana Airport to Privatize Scurity Screening." 22 October 2009. Available from http://www.privatizationwatch.org/index.php?/archives/425-October-22,-2009.html

"Registered Traveler Takes Off from Florida." *Washington Technology,* 1 August 2005.

Sanchez, Julian. "Ten Percent Solution: TSA Reforms Stall at the Gate." *Reason,* July 2005.

Segal, Geoffrey F. "Private Screening: Airports Opt Out." *Reason,* April 2005.

"SFO Begins Its End Game with TSA over Private Screeners." *Airport Security Report,* 7 September 2005.

"TSA Can't Document How Security Inspectors Spent Nearly Half Their Time in 2007." *Government Security News Magazine,* 6 February 2009.

U.S. Department of Homeland Security, Transportation Security Administration, "Myth vs. Fact on TSO Workforce," 9 September 2007. Available from http://www.tsa.gov/approach/people/myths.shtm.

U.S. Department of Homeland Security, Transportation Security Administration, "New Policies for Lighters, Electronics, and Breast Milk," 4 August 2007. Available from http://www.tsa.gov/travelers/sop/index.shtm.

U.S. Department of Homeland Security, Transportation Security Administration, "Screening Partnership Program," 9 September 2007. Available from http://www.tsa.gov/what_we_do/optout/spp_faqs.shtm.

"U.S. Authorities Consider Relaxing Aviation Security Procedures." *Airline Industry Information,* 15 August 2005.

U.S. Department of Homeland Security, Transportation Security Administration, "TSA: Programs and Initiatives," 2009. Available from http://www.tsa.gov/what_we_do/tsnm/air_cargo/programs.shtm.

"U.S. Transportation Security Administration." *Air Transport World,* October 2004.

BIOMETRICS

———— ■ ————

SIC CODE(S)

7382

3829

INDUSTRY SNAPSHOT

In the wake of the September 11, 2001, terrorist attacks against the United States, security concerns, both in the physical world and in cyberspace, took on a renewed prominence. Calls for increasingly high-tech and fool-proof safeguards led to identity verification technologies designed to restrict access to buildings, computer systems, accounts, and so on. Biometrics technology was increasingly viewed as a major barrier against security threats of various kinds, from identity theft to terrorism. Biometrics measures physical characteristics unique to each human being, such as fingerprints, retinal and iris patterns, facial structure, and even vocal inflections and the rhythms of an individual's signature and typing strokes. These measurements are then stored in a computer database and used in security applications to recognize or verify a person's identity.

The surge in identity theft, stolen passwords, and other forms of electronically based mischief provided another impetus to the adoption of biometrics technologies. Biometrics verifies actual individuals, rather than cards, passwords, or personal identification numbers, all of which can be shared or stolen. Unlike other forms of identification, such as passwords, biometrics identity verification systems require the subject's physical presence, thus making illicit use a much more complicated affair. With acts of computer crime at an all-time high and companies, governments, and consumers increasingly wary of their sensitive personal or financial information

falling into the hands of unscrupulous individuals, biometrics makers were poised to tap into ripe market conditions.

For several years, demand lagged behind the technology's maturity. Prohibitive implementation costs, lingering technical problems, fears of privacy invasion, and concerns over system accuracy stalled mass implementation. Biometric systems were well entrenched in some sectors, particularly government and health care, but penetration was meager for other industries that were long on promise, such as financial services and the travel industry. Governmental applications remained the predominant market for biometrics, while certain types of biometrics systems enjoyed overwhelming dominance. Together, fingerprint and hand scanners represented the majority of all deployed biometrics technologies.

However, heightened security consciousness was making a noticeable impression on the industry's prospects. Decreasing costs and increasing technical sophistication of products meant that biometrics was gradually penetrating many kinds of transactions. Biometrics technology has thus enjoyed a period of modest but promising growth, moving out of the realm of science fiction and into everyday life.

ORGANIZATION AND STRUCTURE

Once relegated to the realm of comic books, science fiction films, and Orwellian predictions of oppressive governmental surveillance of civilian populations, biometrics systems have been used for some time by sectors such as law enforcement, defense installations, and nuclear facilities because of the extremely high level of security they

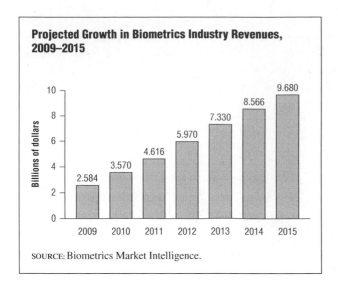

Projected Growth in Biometrics Industry Revenues, 2009–2015

Year	Billions of dollars
2009	2.584
2010	3.570
2011	4.616
2012	5.970
2013	7.330
2014	8.566
2015	9.680

SOURCE: Biometrics Market Intelligence.

demand. The rapid proliferation of electronic record keeping, ATM banking, e-commerce, and widespread air travel created new demands for increased security in many venues of ordinary life. Producers of biometric devices are rushing to meet those needs; and also to provide identification systems that monitor those entering college dormitories, seeking driver's licenses, claiming welfare payments, or trying to immigrate.

Verification and Identification Biometric devices record and store a template of unique biological or behavioral features. That template is later matched against features obtained from an individual for purposes of verification or identification. In the former case, a person uses two forms of input (for example, a personal identification number, or PIN, and a biometric), and a computer verifies whether the data match. In the latter, a person provides a biometric (such as a picture taken at a border crossing), and a computer uses that data to identify the person.

Most biometrics systems can only verify. Identification systems have to be more powerful because they don't involve cues from PINs or access cards. The computer has to search its entire database and compare biometric data for all its enrolled users—a time-consuming enterprise—until a match is made or the data is rejected as unidentified.

Biometric systems often include safeguards to ensure that a live person is the source of the data. A fingerprint system, for example, may require the detection of body heat before it will validate a fingerprint. Similarly, a voice recognition system may look for air pressure to prevent the use of a recording.

Types of Biometrics Fingerprints With as many as 60 variations to analyze and compare, fingerprints are the most widely used biometric in forensic and government databases. The trend is toward compiling databases into national, statewide, and regional networks. Technology is becoming available to allow sharing of fingerprint data from dissimilar systems. The Federal Bureau of Investigation (FBI) maintains the integrated Automated Fingerprint Identification System. With 630 million images, it is the world's largest fingerprint database. Biometric devices may measure prints, dimensions, patterns, or topography of fingers, thumbs, or palms. At one time fingers were inked and pressed on paper to create a print, but by the late 1990s fingerprint scanners, such as those used by the California Department of Motor Vehicles, required no ink. With a mere touch of a glass plate or silicon chip, details of one's print are recorded and stored in an electronic database. Scanners can be integrated into keyboards, notebooks, and mice.

Fingerprinting is gaining popularity. Many banks use thumbprints to identify customers. Toronto-based Mytec Technologies Inc. developed a fingerprint scanner used by the Royal Canadian Mounted Police to identify individuals and by the Louvre museum in Paris to control access to secured areas. Fingerprint readers at an Amsterdam airport let frequent flyers avoid long lines at passport control. In addition, many state governments in the United States use fingerprint data to verify eligibility for welfare. The city of Oceanside, California, purchased 2,400 finger scanners and BioLogon software from Identix, Inc. to evade the costs and hassles of having to change forgotten municipal employee passwords. The city often received as many as 75 password change requests per day before the switch to biometrics. According to the research firms Gartner Group and Forrester, password management can cost an organization an average of $200 per year per user. By 2006 fingerprint technology accounted for 43.6 percent of the overall biometrics market, according to the International Biometric Group (IBG).

Hand Geometry To measure hand geometry, two infrared photos of a person's hand—one shot from above, one from the side—record more than 90 measurements such as length, width, thickness, surface area, finger shape, and joint positions. First developed for nuclear power plants, hand scanners were eventually adopted in prisons, universities, airports, and hospitals. Many manufacturing and construction sites rely on hand scanners to provide a biometric "time card" to verify attendance. Nicks and dirt do not significantly alter readings.

National research labs were among the first users of Recognition Systems Inc.'s ID3D HandKey Biometric System, but industry soon followed. For example, Hand-Key identified workers at L.L. Bean, parents at a day care center run by Lotus Development Corp., and people trying to get free food at the University of Georgia's cafeteria. In addition, HandKey controlled the access of more than 65,000 athletes, trainers, and support staff to the Olympic Village in Atlanta, Georgia. A similar technology measuring finger geometry was used to grant access to season pass holders at some Walt Disney facilities. Hand scanners also are used to monitor employee attendance and punctuality. IBG indicated that hand geometry technology accounted for almost 9 percent of the biometric market in 2006.

Facial Recognition Individual face patterns are unique, even between identical twins. While some systems evaluate shadow patterns on a face illuminated in a specific way, others use an infrared camera to record multiple heat patterns (thermal images) at points around the cheekbones and eyes. Face recognition is growing in popularity because the hardware is inexpensive. Manufacturers are already building camera lenses into computer monitors to accommodate videoconferencing. IBG reported that facial recognition technology accounted for almost 19 percent of the biometric market in 2006.

Although, thanks in part to interest from the U.S. Department of Homeland Security, the technology faced some major setbacks earlier in the decade. For example, in 2001 the police department in Tampa, Florida, installed security video cameras equipped with facial recognition technology alongside a database of some 24,000 criminals, but the program was aborted two years later after failing to lead to any arrests and turning out a number of false identity matches.

Eye Scans Retina scanners flash an infrared light into the eye and examine the distinct pattern of blood vessels behind the retina. Retinal scanning data occupies less memory space in a computer than does fingerprinting data, so it could be useful in decreasing the time necessary to search the large databases used for identification. Retina scanning, however, is perceived as intrusive by some. When military pilots were first subjected to retinal scans, they refused them, thinking the scans might impair their visual acuity (despite the fact that no evidence indicated this would happen). Both the iris and retina contain more identification points than a fingerprint. At distances up to 12 inches, for instance, iris scans can measure 400 unique characteristics such as freckles, contraction furrows, rings, and darkened areas, which remain stable from infancy. Even identical twins do not have the same features. Iris scans convert the distinct details of the colored part of the eye into a biological "bar code" that acts as a unique identifier. Positive identification can be made through glasses, contact lenses, and most sunglasses.

Iris scanning debuted at the 1998 Winter Olympics in Nagano, Japan, when security officials required biathletes to undergo scans to check out their rifles. The iris also can be scanned without the knowledge of the subject, which could be useful in applications such as airport security and terrorist detection. Sensar, Inc. licensed the camera technology from Sarnoff Corp. in Princeton, New Jersey, who originally designed it for taking ground surveillance photos from high-flying military helicopters. According to Sensar, the matching probability of their iris scanning process is greater than that of DNA technology. In fact, they argue that iris identification is the only form of personal electronic identification that has never granted a false acceptance.

Spring Technologies supported iris recognition programs at the 2000 Summer Olympics in Sydney, Australia; the Charlotte/Douglas International Airport in North Carolina; and on airlines in Europe, the United States, and Latin America. Other iris scan tests included consumer authorization for individuals who initiated e-commerce purchases with debit cards.

Bank United of Houston was the first U.S. institution to test iris recognition. It installed iris-scanning ATMs in supermarket branches in the Texas communities of Dallas, Fort Worth, and Houston. Consumer response was favorable, with 98 percent of the 130 users surveyed reporting a positive first experience. Iris scan technology accounted for 7.1 percent of biometrics industry revenue in 2006, according to the International Biometric Group (IBG).

Voice Verification Voices may sound similar, but no two are alike. The unique topography of a person's mouth, teeth, and vocal chords produces inimitable pitch, tone, cadence, and dynamics. Character, expression, and regional dialects also influence voice patterns. Voice systems are an obvious choice for phone-based applications. They are also suitable for use with personal computers (PCs). IBG reported that voice scan technology accounted for 4.4 percent of biometrics industry revenue in 2006.

Signature Dynamics The speed and style with which a person signs his or her name is a unique behavioral biometric. Signature dynamics measure the pressure, angle of attack, and stroke characteristics with which a person writes. They have been used to verify identity for banking transactions, insurance forms, and electronic filing of tax returns. Chase Manhattan was the first bank to test this technology. Signature scan technology accounted for 1.7 percent of biometrics industry revenues in 2006, according to IBG figures.

Future identifiers may include measurements of lip and ear shape, knuckle creases, wrist veins, and even vibrations from major body organs. IBM's Blue Eyes was researching "attentive user interfaces" such as gaze tracking. This technology involves a computer camera mounted to a display that follows the user's iris movements and calls up information from sites when the eye focuses on the monitor, without the need to click a hyperlink.

Biometrics

Applications Biometric devices were first developed to keep unauthorized persons out of military installations and nuclear power plants. The FBI's Automated Fingerprint Identification System (AFIS) came next, drawing upon technologies developed by defense industries. In 1968 a Wall Street brokerage became the first financial institution to apply biometrics when it used fingerprints to open vaults that stored stock certificates. Biometrics currently plays a role in security and identification across industry lines.

Finance A number of banks have tested or used finger-based biometrics. These included the Bank of America, Citicorp, Mellon Bank, Bankers Trust, and Chevy Chase Savings and Loan Association. Perdue Employees' Federal Credit Union in West Lafayette, Indiana was the first U.S. bank to implement finger imaging to identify customers. As of 2006, *Bank Systems + Technology* reported that, according to data from the Boston-based consulting firm Aite Group, about 5 to 7 percent of financial institutions were using biometric technology in the United States. By this time, the cost of biometric technology was decreasing and well-known financial service companies were buying or forming alliances with biometric companies, making banks more comfortable. Indeed, consumer acceptance was the main barrier standing in the way of widespread adoption.

Retail Biometrics may eliminate the need for cashiers and baggers at retail outlets and grocery stores. Such systems already were being utilized by some retailers, including the Cub Foods supermarket chain owned by Supervalu. However, biometric technology has been met with resistance in the retail sector.

E-Commerce E-commerce may provide the most amenable entry for wide biometrics penetration of American markets, in the form of swipeable smart cards encoded with digital signature technology to be used with card readers and the appropriate software when making online purchases. Although often preloaded with a monetary value, virtually any type of biometrics data can be stored on the card, allowing security systems to verify without storing the information in large databases. In addition to e-commerce, smart cards are useful in PC security and regulating medical prescriptions. Encryption and digital signature authorization safeguard the sensitive information embedded in the cards.

Airports Airport entryways in several metro areas, including San Francisco, New York, and Toronto, were equipped with HandKey hand geometry readers for access control. Authorized personnel swiped access cards, then placed their hands into entryway readers to gain access. In 1997, Malaysia's Langkawi Airport installed the first face recognition technology to increase airport security. The system, developed by Visionics Corp. and TL Technology, matched a passenger's face with an image encoded in the boarding pass during check-in. Unisys developed iris pattern scanners to permit frequent flyers to bypass long airport lines. The International Civil Aviation Organization was assessing various biometric technologies that might be used to establish international airport standards. The September 11, 2001, terrorist attacks sparked increased interest in this sector of the biometrics industry as U.S. government officials sought ways to improve airport security.

Correctional Institutions Inmates in some prisons speak a password into a phone to verify their presence. Since the early 1990s, a federal Georgia prison has used a hand geometry biometric system to monitor staff and inmate movements. The first six months of use of fingerprint readers in the Pima County, Arizona, jail exposed 300 inmates who had given false identities.

In Great Britain, a partnership between the Advanced Fingerprint Recognition system (AFR), the world's largest, and several technology providers has brought live-scan fingerprinting at low cost to its prisoner handling centers. Processing nearly 83,000 sets of fingerprints exposed 3,800 prisoners as having given false identities. Upon release, former inmates can use a biometric system to report to their parole officers without actually meeting in person. At a prearranged time, the parolee goes to a kiosk similar to an ATM, enters an identification number, and is verified by a hand geometry reader. The parolee receives messages from the parole officer on a display terminal. The kiosk system has a better attendance rate than personal meetings. If a parolee fails to appear for a check-in, an intense follow-up is initiated.

Colleges and Universities With hand templates encoded in photo identification cards, colleges and universities can better manage physical access for large student populations. At the University of Georgia, hand geometry readers allow access to the student cafeteria. Since 1992, hand readers have controlled security turnstiles at New York University dormitories. At the University of Montreal, students use a hand scanner to enter an athletic complex. Similar arrangements are in use at health clubs and day care centers.

Government The government's surging interest in biometrics was marked in 2003 by the U.S. Department of Homeland Security's awarding of a three-year, $2.2 million contract to research the effects of biometrics applications on security and border management issues. The U.S. Department of Defense was looking into smart card technology utilizing finger scan biometrics for military and civilian personnel, while the Government Services Administration (GSA) conducted a multi-application smart card pilot with 400 employees to determine the feasibility of rolling out smart cards to all federal government employees.

The government also considered adopting public key infrastructure technology to boost security capabilities. Finally, the U.S. government in 2003 announced plans to begin scanning non-citizens' fingerprints upon entering the country in an effort ostensibly aimed to combat terrorism.

Other Applications One of the most innovative applications of biometrics technology emerged in the wake of tragic U.S. school shootings in the late 1990s. Responding to public calls for improved gun safety features, gun maker Smith & Wesson announced in early 2000 its prototype "smart gun"—at least two years away from commercial development—that used a biometric verification system developed by Mytec to prevent anyone but an authorized user from firing the weapon. The prototype was equipped with a cartridge attachment that can be removed only when the user slides his or her fingerprint across a tiny, battery-powered optical scanner. The ammunition clip can then be inserted into the handgun and the gun can be fired.

Governmental Regulation and Privacy Concerns Americans are renowned for their intense focus on protection of personal privacy, a trait less marked in some other parts of the globe. This national characteristic has hampered the biometrics industry's efforts to expand its presence in U.S. markets. The pressure to view increased biometric identification as an unwelcome intrusion even led the European Union to take the lead in calling for international privacy standards with its Data Protection Directive.

Biometrics industry advocates counter that biometric verification, since it circumvents such easily tampered-with items as passwords and physical credit cards or keys, works as a "privacy protection tool" rather than a privacy menace. However, the industry will have to make some decisive statements to allay the fears of those who believe that increasing digitalization of personal data will lead to lost control over financial and medical records and thus perhaps cost them jobs, credit, or health insurance. In response, the industry formed the International Biometrics Industry Association in 1998 to draft statements on ethics, security, and privacy that would help win skeptical members of the consuming public to its side. In May 1999 the group announced a four-pronged statement on privacy principles that it vowed would govern future industry developments.

The industry itself began promoting self-regulation to stave off more burdensome governmental legislation. In 1999 the BioAPI Consortium and the Human Authentication Application Programming Interface Working Group merged to supervise all biometric applications and programming interface efforts under one organization.

BACKGROUND AND DEVELOPMENT

The September 11, 2001, terrorist attacks were a major catalyst to biometrics firms, as companies were increasingly inclined to launch expensive efforts toward high technology security measures in the light of evolving threats and fears. According to International Biometric Group, between 2002 and 2007 civil identification and PC/network access were expected to be the most commonplace biometric applications, securing roughly $2 billion in combined annual revenues in 2007. Physical access and time and attendance applications were expected to account for $245 million in annual revenues in 2004, while surveillance and screening applications garnered roughly $49 million in sales that year. The government was the leading biometric customer, followed by the financial, travel, and transportation sectors.

In December 2003 President Bush signed the Fair and Accurate Credit Transaction (FACT) Act into law, committing the federal government to the implementation of biometrics in the financial services industry by enforcing safeguards against electronic identity theft. In addition, the act charges the Treasury Department with amassing information from various industry players and analysts on the costs, risks, and uses of biometrics. By committing the government to mass implementation of biometrics across an industry, the act was expected to play a major role in pushing biometrics into general acceptance, and industry analysts expected it would spur other industries and companies to comply with the emerging standard.

The U.S. Visitor and Immigrant Status Indicator Technology (US-VISIT) program went into effect in January 2004 at airports and seaports all over the country, with plans to expand into Mexico and Canada in 2005. Foreign visitors to the United States were thus required to present machine-readable passports with biometric data such as fingerprints or digital photographs. The U.S. Department of Homeland Security aimed to eventually expand the biometrics component to U.S. consular offices abroad, hoping it would act as an early check on possible terrorist or criminal elements trying to enter the United States.

The Immigration and Naturalization Service (INS) awarded Digital Biometrics Inc. a contract for 276 TENPRINTER live-scan fingerprint systems valued at in excess of $8.8 million. The INS's IDENT border control program scans left and right index fingerprints and photographs of recidivist individuals and stores them in a database. Fingerprint and facial recognition readings taken of persons suspected of criminal activity are compared with the stored images. The system is designed to easily identify individuals accused of repeatedly crossing the border into the United States in violation of immigration laws.

Privacy Concerns Fears of an all-out governmental scheme to map citizens' identities down to the last gene strand may be overblown, but they do point out the need for policy guidelines and regulations about exactly what information can be measured and stored about whom and by whom. The extent to which both government and business may peer into the identities of ordinary individuals is a question that industry and government finally started to address. For instance, the International Biometrics Group began work on a set of best practices and informal regulations for the use of biometrics. The group noted that some biometrics technologies, such as finger scanning and facial recognition systems, carried greater privacy risks, particularly as the information from such scans is stored in public sector data banks. It recommended as a starting point issuing rating systems for the varying levels of privacy risk among biometrics applications.

Advocates of the increased security that biometrics technology can provide pointed to the events of September 11, 2001, as evidence that tighter security was more important than a potential erosion of some individual privacy. By 2003, 14 state legislatures were considering bills that called for the insertion of biometrics technologies into drivers' licenses, though privacy concerns and legal action brought by the American Civil Liberties Union scuttled many such efforts out of fears of the creation of state or nationwide databases of citizens.

During the early 2000s, there continued to be a number of obstacles that were preventing rapid and widespread adoption of biometrics. In March 2006, the *Security Director's Report* revealed that, according to results from the National Biometric Security Project, the main barrier (cited by 29 percent of those surveyed) was unproven technical performance. Uncertain return on investment was a close second, at 28 percent, followed by distrust of the technology (24 percent). A variety of other reasons accounted for the remainder.

From a technology perspective, users have long been concerned by a lack of standards. With hundreds of products marketed by a diverse pool of vendors, consumers and businesses maintained concerns over privacy, accuracy, integration with existing systems, and long-term support. However, as the market consolidates and device vendors team up with software makers, these issues are gradually being resolved.

Biometric standardization continued to evolve. In the early 2000s the national standards organization for the financial services industry, the Accredited Standards Committee (ASC), issued a biometrics standard for the verification of customers and employees involved in financial services. By late 2005 the U.S. Department of Commerce's National Institute of Standards and Technology was testing the interoperability of biometric products from 14 different vendors. In addition, biometric vendors were working to make the biometric templates (digital representations of one's physical features) used by their products compatible.

Privacy continued to be a pressing issue. With looming fears among the public of mass-scale privacy invasion, many businesses have been wary of aggressively implementing biometric technologies that could prove to be extremely risky. Many consumers associate fingerprint scanning with criminal law enforcement. Thus, by 2006 some industry players were using the term "finger image" instead of fingerprint. Also, the scanning, comparison, and storage of unique biological traits makes some feel their privacy is being violated. As of early 2006, leading privacy groups were concerned that biometric technology was advancing faster than related laws governing its use.

One prime example of consumer resistance to biometrics was the rollout of a biometric retail authentication system by Piggly Wiggly. After launching the system in early 2005, the retailer's chain-wide rollout was met with resistance from consumers. This was especially true within the conservative Christian community, where some compared the implementation of the fingerprint-based system to the "mark of the beast" described in the Bible's book of Revelation. In the story, those without the mark are limited in what they can buy or sell.

On a purely practical level, some consumers voiced concerns that their fingerprints could be lifted from ordinary items and used to violate their privacy or engage in illegal activity. In fact, vendors were forced to address the potential for criminals to use severed fingers, or false fingerprints made in latex or other material, in an attempt to fool biometric systems. Therefore, a number of systems had pulse detection capabilities, which could differentiate between real and false fingerprints.

The definition of biometrics has evolved. According to Peter Higgins, a leading expert in the field, the current definition of biometrics is "automated methods of recognizing a person based on a physiological or behavioral characteristic." Such behaviors can include the way a person walks or how he or she types his or her name into a computer. Physiological characteristics had also expanded to include such factors as the shape of a person's ears. According to Higgins, the term "living person" had previously been part of the definition, until it was discovered that irises can be scanned up to 48 hours after a person dies. Higgins told *National Defense* that such new information shows how fast the field is changing.

Governments remain the main users of biometric devices. Biometrics were being used extensively in Iraq to catalog as many Iraqis as possible and help distinguish the "good guys" from the "bad guys." By May 2008 the Army had collected information on more than 2.2 million people, mostly using fingerprints, eye scans, and digital mug shots. This data is then uploaded into the Defense Department's database at the Biometrics Fusion Center in West Virginia.

In addition to the Defense Department, the FBI was very interested in biometrics. In 2008 it awarded Lockheed Martin a contract to design and build a biometric identification system that can be used to identify and arrest criminals. The contract, which can be renewed for up to nine years, is valued at approximately $1 billion. In an announcement regarding the contract, an FBI representative said, "Due to the many issues associated with identity theft, lost and stolen documents, and the ability to spoof standard name-based identity management systems, coupled with the rapid advances in technology and the national focus on combating terrorism, there are increasing needs for new and improved identification services."

Another new development in the industry occurred on February 6, 2008, when West Virginia University (WVU), in Morgantown, became the FBI's leading academic partner in biometric research. WVU is the first institution in the world to offer a bachelor of science degree in biometric systems, in addition to a graduate-level certificate and master's degree emphasis.

CURRENT CONDITIONS

As of 2010, biometrics—the viability of which was deemed essential in both public and private sectors—was expected to enjoy sustained growth for the foreseeable future. Acuity Market Intelligence (AMI) reported total industry revenues of $2.58 billion for 2009, a figure that was expected to reach $3.57 billion by the end of 2010. In five years (2015), AMI projected revenues of $9.68 billion.

AMI further reported a 61 percent compound annual growth rate for biometric surveillance through 2017, representing $872 million in annual revenue. The ePassport and eVisa markets were particularly slated for marked growth; AMI reported global ePassport and eVisa revenues of $3.19 billion in 2009, which were projected to reach $5.1 billion by the end of 2010. By 2014 the top ten nations were expected to issue 133 million documents, with an ePassport market adoption (valued at $7 billion) of 88 percent at that time.

According to "Global Biometric Forecast to 2012," the world market for biometrics was forecast to grow at a 22 percent CAGR between 2011 and 2013. The report noted the expansion of applications, especially increasing security concerns ranging from individual identity theft to corporate and national security. The report also confirmed that the government sector continued to account for the lion's share of the biometrics market in 2010, with the health care and financial sectors emerging as potential adopters and assimilators of biometrics systems.

Trends for the industry include the integration of two or more biometric technologies into a single verification unit, especially in security applications where more accurate authentication is required. For example, with the integration of smart cards and biometrics, verification can be done on the chip in the card in real time, without the need for any online verification, and providing a higher level of security. Such technology already was being implemented for government IDs, border control, and (especially rural) banking.

In mid-2010 S.I.C. Biometrics announced the introduction of its Fingerprint Mobile Identification Device (iFMID), the first biometric fingerprint solution for all things that were Apple wireless. The device facilitates identification of people from an iPhone or iPod touch through an application running on an Apple device and a remote matching server. The remote server was capable of matching the template against a database of 25,000 other templates in less than a second.

AMERICA AND THE WORLD

In March 2010 Frost & Sullivan's Asia-Pacific research analyst, Navin Rajendra (who studied Smart Cards and AutoID), reported that the biometrics industry saw healthy growth "in the government vertical, with numerous national ID card projects being thrown into the limelight." Voice biometrics were boosted in 2009 by banks in Asia (India, China, and Malaysia) and Europe that began testing this technology for banking verification. However, according to Rajendra, 70 percent of 2009 biometric revenues in the Asia Pacific region were still coming from fingerprint biometrics. This region also was investing in contactless palm vein biometrics, as many people "were not comfortable with touching a scanner that had been touched by a number of other individuals," said Rajendra.

Japan and Korea have readily accepted contactless palm scanner technology, as have other regions where a contactless medium is required. In the United States, hospitals have begun to express interest in the technology as a means to facilitate more sterile environments.

INDUSTRY LEADERS

AuthenTec Inc. of Melbourne, Florida, was a leader in the fingerprint sensor market. In fact, market research firm Frost & Sullivan has awarded the company its Market Leadership Award on three occasions. The firm focused primarily on the consumer electronics market, building fingerprint-scanning chips for implementation into electronic components, including computers. By 2006 AuthenTec had developed a prestigious base of partners and customers, including APC, Fujitsu Computer, Computer Associates, HP, IBM, LGE, Microsoft, Samsung, and Texas Instruments. Ninety percent of AuthenTec's sales came from the Asia/Pacific region. In 2010 AuthenTec announced a merger with UPEK, a biometrics software vendor. UPEK had 2009 revenues of $18 million, and the combined company was expected to generate more than $10 million for 2011.

L-1 Identity Solutions Inc., formerly Viisage, of Stamford, Connecticut, was formed in 2006 due to a merger of Viisage Technology and Identix Incorporated. L-1's face, finger, and iris recognition technologies are targeted mostly to the federal, civil, criminal, commercial, border, and management markets. In 2010 L-1 announced that it would soon be acquired by a larger biometrics company, Safran, which was a leader in the defense industry. Safran intended to merge L-1 into one of its business units known as Morpho. However, part of the agreement was that, prior to the sale, L-1 would sell its intelligence services businesses to BAE Systems Inc. The remaining L-1 businesses (Secure Credentialing Solutions, Biometric and Enterprise Access Solutions, and Enrollment Services) were expected to have a combined revenue value of $486 million.

BAE Systems, another industry leader, and further strengthened by the L-1 acquisition, had a growing intelligence and security business in 2010. Its main customer missions were intelligence and counterintelligence, homeland security, law enforcement, and support to military operations.

Other key industry players included New York-based SiVault Systems Inc., which specialized in signature recognition technologies, and Iridian Technologies, based in Moorestown, New Jersey, a major manufacturer of iris-scanning systems. In 2006 Iridian was purchased by Viisage, which was subsequently merged with Identix to create L-1 Identity Solutions.

BIBLIOGRAPHY

"Biometrics Market Intelligence: Biometrics Industry Revenues 2009–2017." Acuity Market Intelligence, 20 August 2010. Available from http://www.biometricsmi.com.

"Biometrics: Payments at your Fingertips; Fingerprints and Iris Scans Will Replace Keys and Credit Cards if Outfits Like Pay By Touch Succeed in their Biologic Mission." *Business Week Online,* 28 March 2006. Available from www.businessweek.com.

Biometrics Security News and Information, August–September 2010. Available from http://www.biometricnews.typepad.com/biometric_news_and_infor/.

"Biometrics: The Eyes Have It." *Airport Security Report,* 30 January 2008.

Bruno-Britz, Maria. "Back to the Future: Banks Are Revisiting Biometrics, Study Says." *Bank Systems + Security,* March 2006.

"Consumers Resist Retail Biometrics." *eWeek,* 30 January 2006.

Federal Bureau of Investigation. "West Virginia University Named National Leader for FBI Biometrics Research," 8 February 2008. Available from http://www.fbi.gov/pressrel/pressrel08/wvu_fbi_020608.htm.

"Fingerprint Technology Is Biometric of Choice." *Security Director's Report,* March 2006.

"Frost & Sullivan Finds Vast Potential for Biometric Industry in APAC." Frost & Sullivan, 2 March 2010. Available from http://www.frost.com/prod/servlet/press-release.pag?docid=194455857.

Kingsbury, Alex. "Figuring Out Who's Who: The Army Ramps Up Biometrics as It Maps the Human Terrain." *U.S. News & World Report,* 12 May 2008.

"Lockheed Gets $1 Billion FBI Biometrics Contract." *InformationWeek,* 13 February 2008.

Magnuson, Stew. "Proof of Identity: U.S. Government Driving the Advance of Biometric Technologies." *National Defense,* November 2007.

"Poised for Growth Beyond North America: Frost and Sullivan Inc. Predicts the Growth for Fingerprints and Biometric Identifier." *Card Technology,* February 2006.

"Report Addresses Biometric Investment Landscape through 2010." *PR Newswire,* 23 January 2006.

Rodier, Melanie. "The Value of Biometrics." *Wall Street & Technology,* May 2008.

Vijayan, Jaikumar. "Little Progress on Government-Wide Smart Card Initiative." *New York Times,* 14 November 2007.

Woodward, Kevin. "E-Passports Await Real-World Tests." *Card Technology,* March 2006.

BIOREMEDIATION

———◼———

SIC CODE(S)

8011

8031

8093

INDUSTRY SNAPSHOT

Bioremediation, a term coined by scientists in the early 1980s, is sometimes referred to as biotreatment, remediation, or natural attenuation. It is an environmental biotechnology which describes natural cleansing systems that introduce living microorganisms into a chemically altered area in order to degrade and reduce or remove pollutants (also known as hazardous or toxic waste), so that the contaminated environment can recover, become less toxic, or, in an optimal scenario, return to its original and natural condition. The bioremediation industry treats most forms of hazardous waste. Bioremediation is achieved through the use of bacterial microbes, surfactant enhanced oxidation, yeast, fungi (mycoremediation), plant matter or their enzymes (phytoremediation), algae, and nitrate and sulfate fertilizers. Targets of bioremediation include such contaminants as metals, crude oil and its derivatives, and a variety of chemicals and solvents like PCBs, explosives, and some radioactive material. These contaminants are most often found in industrial and farm waste present in air, ground and surface waters, soil and sediment in landfills, underground storage tanks, and some building materials. *In situ* bioremediation technology treats contaminated material at the site; removal of the contaminated material to another site to be treated is known as *ex situ* bioremediation. Abandoned or underused industrial and commercial facilities that contain hazardous waste and are considered for redevelopment are known as brownfield sites, or brownfields.

Bioremediation Techniques and Terms

- **Bioaugmentation**. An enhanced bioremediation process in which specific strains of microorganisms or enzymes are isolated or produced *ex situ* and then introduced into polluted material in order to enhance the degradation and biotransformation of biomasses in wastewater and soil.

- **Bioreactor**. A vessel or a landfill constructed to rapidly transform and degrade polluted groundwater and soil with microorganisms. In some cases, bioreactors can minimize greenhouse gas emissions. Bioreactors can work aerobically, anaerobically, or as a hybrid of the two. Liquid such as wastewater is often used to enhance the microbial process. Explosives in soil and soils with a high clay content can be degraded by use of a bioslurry reactor.

- **Biosparging**. An *in situ* process that uses indigenous microorganisms to remediate organic components by injecting air, oxygen, and/or nutrients into saturated soil.

- **Biostimulation**. A bioremediation process in which nutrients, oxygen, or electron donors or receptors such as phosphorus, nitrogen, oxygen, or carbon are added to toxic environments to enhance the effectiveness of microorganisms already present in the site. These additives can be delivered through the use of injection wells, a still-emerging bioremediation technology. The remediation of oil and gas spills can be aided by the use of biostimulation.

- **Bioventing**. A form of biostimulation that enhances the effectiveness of bacteria in contaminated soil and hastens biodegradation of hydrocarbons through the inducement of air or oxygen flow that may be injected into the site. Bioslurping uses a combination of bioventing and vacuum pumping to remediate soils. Targets of bioventing include adsorbed fuel residue and volatile organic compounds (VOCs).

- **Landfarming**. Soils, sludges, and sediments contaminated by heavy metals and organic waste are excavated, spread on the ground, and aerated through tilling or plowing to allow the growth of microorganisms.

- **Mycoremediation**. This bioremediation process uses fungal mycelia to secrete enzymes and acids, which break down contaminants such as diesel oil in soil. The process of using fungi mycelia used to filter pollutants from water in soil is known as mycofiltration.

- **Phytoremediation**. A popular, cost-effective, easily monitored bioremediation method that uses hyperaccummulative plants to bioaccumulate, degrade, and detoxify a variety of contaminants, including metals, pesticides, solvents, explosives, crude oil, and oil products from soil, water, and air. Examples of phytoremediation processes are phytoextraction, phytostabilization, phytotransformation, phytostimulation, and phytovolatilization. Rhizofiltration involves the use of root mass to adsorb (remove) or absorb (assimilate) toxic material.

Bioremediation has proven to be an important tool for the worldwide environmental industry. An increasing number of contaminants can be treated through bioremediation technology at comparatively low costs and with no toxic results and less post-treatment cleanup, and new technologies within the industry, such as genetic engineering, have great potential to expand and enhance the effectiveness of bioremediation. In the United States, the Environmental Protection Agency offers stimulus money through its agencies, including the EPA's Superfund program, and through other grant initiatives that help to fund bioremediation research and provide incentives for industries to take advantage of bioremediation solutions, as well as more traditional technologies, to reduce or remove hazardous waste.

ORGANIZATION AND STRUCTURE

The bioremediation market operates according to the processes needed by individual industries for pollution cleanup and control. Environmentalexpert.com, an online marketplace specializing in the environmental industry, lists more than 300 companies offering a wide range of bioremediation products and services. These include consultants; suppliers of bioremediation technology, processes, and equipment; and companies engaged in biotechnology research programs. Many companies offer a combination of products and services. Companies that provide market research and those which manufacture and market pollution monitoring devices and software for remediation models comprise a subset within the industry.

- **Consultants**. Consultants evaluate the pollution issues of individual companies, provide input on bioremediation options and cost-benefit analyses, and assist companies in fulfilling their regulatory obligations.

- **Technology and Processes**. These companies supply and apply bioremediation technology and techniques. Some specialize in certain processes, while others offer a variety of methods to treat a range of contaminants. One example of a company that treats a wide array of contaminants and provides bioremediation solutions for soil, sediment, and groundwater is Aventus Americas, one of the world's largest bioremediation companies.

- **Equipment**. Bioremediation equipment runs the gamut from bioreactor to vegetable oil emulsion products that enhance the *in situ* remediation of such anaerobically degradable contaminants as solvents and some toxic metals. Other examples of bioremediation equipment are products that trap and treat contaminants, oxygenation systems, liquid suspension products that contain beneficial microorganisms, and equipment that delivers bioremediation processes such as the tubular Waterloo Emitter, which allows a steady stream of oxygen into contaminated groundwater.

- **Research**. Bioremediation research has been encouraged and often funded by the EPA. An example from 2009 is Agave BioSystems, a Texas company awarded $70,000 in funding from the EPA's Small Business Innovation Research program to develop an enzyme engineering system. The Environmental Services Division at NASA has also undertaken research to identify the most effective microorganisms to reduce contamination levels. The U.S. Department of Energy, through its National and Accelerated Bioremediation Research (NABIR) program, promotes the training of and research among scientists engaged in bioremediation technology.

Regulations and the Bioremediation Industry. The bioremediation industry is affected by the environmental statutes and regulations administered by federal and state environmental programs and agencies, each with its own requirements. In the United States, the Environmental Protection Agency oversees regulation and compliance. The EPA works with the Department of Justice and state and tribal governments to ensure compliance with federal environmental laws. The EPA's position on regulation is clear: "Compliance with the nation's environmental laws is the goal, but enforcement is a vital part of encouraging governments, companies and others who are regulated to meet their environmental obligations. Enforcement deters those who might otherwise profit from violating the law, and levels the playing field with environmentally compliant companies." Companies within the bioremediation sector face the challenge of helping their end users to fully satisfy regulatory demands.

BACKGROUND AND DEVELOPMENT

Naturally-occurring bioremediation has been utilized for centuries in such forms as composting, phytoremediation, and desalinization. Michael Sims, the author of *Bioremediation: Nature's Cleanup Tool,*observes, "Research into hydrocarbon-consuming bacteria was documented in scientific circles as early as 1913, according to J.B. Davis in his book *Petroleum Microbiology.* In the 1930s, a Soviet petroleum geologist suggested that oil-eating microbes be used 'as a prospecting tool.'" The 1970s saw the first successful application of microbes to degrade organic pollutants present in soil through landfarming techniques. In 1971 *in situ* Sun Oil scientists applied bioremediation technology to a drinking water aquifer contaminated by gasoline. Soon afterwards, protocols for *in situ* remediation of hydrocarbons in groundwater began to appear in literature concerning pollution control. As Stephen P. Cummings of the School of Applied Sciences, Northumbria University, observed, "However, subsequent events, particularly the decline of heavy industry and the end of the cold war, led to large areas of land on which industrial or military activity was conducted becoming available for redevelopment. In these areas, the anthropogenic pollution had occurred over decades and involved an array of both organic and nonorganic contaminants. In order to effectively treat these large areas of land in which the extent and type of pollution was often poorly defined and heterogeneous, a range of new techniques were developed that relied on multidisciplinary approaches to define the problem, treat the pollutants, and effectively monitor the consequences of these activities."

The development of the bioremediation industry in the United States was driven in large part by federal environmental laws, such as the Clean Air Act, Clean Water Act, and the Comprehensive Environmental Response Compensation and Liability Act of 1980 (CERCLA), more widely known as the Superfund Act, which were created and/or expanded to regulate the storage and removal of toxic waste and the subsequent need to discover more effective methods of removing, reducing, and controlling contaminants in air, water, and soil. A highly publicized example of pollution that became a lightning rod for environmental regulation was Love Canal, a neighborhood in Niagara Falls, New York, which had become heavily contaminated with chemical waste dumped there since the 1940s and which caused serious health problems for residents of the area. The 1989 *Exxon-Valdez* oil spill in Prince William Sound, Alaska, which affected marine life and habitats over 1,300 miles of coastline and 11,000 square miles of ocean, similarly caused a public outcry, which helped lead to the Oil Pollution Act of 1990. The EPA accepted a proposal from Exxon to use microorganisms enriched with fertilizers to help clean up the spill. Encouraged by the qualified success of this technique, the EPA began to fund bioremediation research. By the 1990s, small firms that had pioneered bioremediation methods began to grow and new companies entered the market. Industry expansion received a boost in the first decade of the twenty-first century due to greater public interest in so-called "green technology," together with increased awareness and concern regarding the environment and its ecosystems. A recent example is the vigorous public and governmental response to the near-ecological disaster caused by the BP oil spill of April 2010.

PIONEERS IN THE FIELD

George M. Robinson Robinson, the assistant petroleum engineer for the city of Santa Maria, California, in Santa Barbara County during the 1960s, is credited with the invention of the bioremediation process. Robinson's home experiments with bacteria cultures led to his treatment of a crude oil spill from an oil well pump in the area in 1969. This was the first commercial use of naturally occurring microbes to remediate a toxic site. By 1972, an enhanced version of Robinson's technology was used at more than 4,500 oil pump sites in the state. Robinson went on to engineer the cleanup of municipal sewage and other sites and to form several environmental companies serving a range of clients, including Exxon, Shell Oil, Standard Oil, and Texaco. Robinson's daughter, Mery, inherited the technology developed by her late father and subsequently founded XyclonyX, a successful microbial technology company specializing in the development, application, and licensing of patented hazardous waste treatments through microbial bioremediation. In 1997 XyclonyX was acquired by Robert Brehm of Global Venture Funding, who formed U.S. Microbics, Inc., a business development company for bioremediation firms. U.S. Microbics is known on its pink sheets as BUGS.

Paul Stamets Stamets is a mycologist, who has researched the use of fungi, specifically mushroom mycelia, for use in bioremediation. He coined the terms mycoremediation and mycofiltration to describe the application of fungi in bioremediation processes. The recipient of several awards for his research over the last two decades, Stamets is the founder and president of Fungi Perfecti.

Stephen S. Koenigsberg A pioneer in the development and commercialization of advanced bioremediation and chemical oxidation technologies and a receiver of the *Wall Street Journal* Technology Innovation Award, Koenigsberg began his career as cofounder of the environmental services company, Regenesis in 1992. There, he co-invented and developed the bioremediation products Oxygen Release Compound and Hydrogen Release Compound, used on over 16,000 sites worldwide. Koenigsberg directed the development of the chemical oxidation product RegenOx, the Metals Remediation Compound, and pioneered the development of biotechnology tools for the assessment of site microbial ecology. The publisher of over 150 articles on bioremediation and advanced site diagnostics, Koenigsberg has worked at the ENVIRON and Adventus Group environmental companies.

Ronald M. Atlas Professor of Biology at the University of Louisville, a fellow of the American Academy of Microbiology, and a recipient of the ASM Award for Applied and Environmental Microbiology, Atlas began research into hydrocarbon biodegradation while a graduate student at Rutgers University. This research helped pioneer the field of petroleum bioremediation. Atlas has served as a consultant to ExxonMobil and BP oil companies.

Robert C. Borden A professor of Civil, Construction, and Environmental Engineering at North Carolina State University, Borden pioneered the development, application, and assessment of monitored natural attenuation and advanced *in situ* bioremediation for groundwater remediation, as well as such contaminants as petroleum hydrocarbons and chlorinated solvents. Since 1999, his patented emulsifier oil products have been used for a variety of bioremediation applications in hazardous waste sites around the world. He is currently affiliated with the bioremediation company EOS Remediation.

CURRENT CONDITIONS

The bioremediation industry faces some challenges: the resistance of certain heavy metals to absorption or capture; the incompatibility of hydro-geological conditions with bioremediation methods at some contaminated sites; the relatively longer length of time it takes for some bioremediation techniques to degrade and/or fully cleanse a site, together with questions on how long a site will remain contaminant free; the costs of research and development; the need for many countries to fully pinpoint and assess contaminated sites; and the tendency for end users to use traditional technologies through lack of awareness of bioremediation solutions and consideration of the issues listed above. Scientific opinion has been divided concerning the feasibility and advisability of using microbes to clean up oil spills, despite widespread enthusiasm for oil bioremediation solutions, especially in the wake of the BP oil spill in the Gulf of Mexico and the presence of patented, genetically engineered hydrocarbon-consuming microbes. Naturally occurring microbes remain the solution of choice, whenever possible. Daniel Biello, writing in a May 25, 2010, article in *Scientific American* on the BP oil spill, notes that a week before the publication of his article, geneticists at the J. Craig Venter Institute in San Diego synthesized the first self-replicating microbe using a synthetic genome, but pointed out that so far, "there are no signs of such organisms put to work outside the lab." However, an encouraging development regarding oil bioremediation came in November 2010 with the announcement that Thomas Wicker, the inventor and patent-holder of the OsmoSorb Type A Oil Remediation Filter Cartridge, had refined his device so that it safely separates and captures oil from water.

Despite ongoing challenges, the stability and potential growth of the bioremediation industry looks promising. As the editors of Advances in Applied Bioremediation comment, "It is difficult to evaluate this market with any specificity, but the international market for remediation is estimated to be around U.S $25–30 billion. It is challenging to establish such estimates, as many countries have not undertaken comprehensive identification of contaminated sites. Remediation markets usually develop after a country had addressed its air, water and waste management priorities. The United States, Canada, Western Europe, Japan and Australia are considered to be the dominant international markets for remediation, with an established presence of a large number of environmental companies, products and services. Emerging economies of some developed Asian, Eastern European and Latin American countries will represent significant medium-term remedial market opportunities."

INDUSTRY LEADERS

Adventus Americas Founded in 2003 and based in Freeport, Illinois, Adventus Americas is an international environmental services company that provides patented biotechnology-based remedial solutions to treat such contaminants as chlorinated solvents, heavy metals, petroleum hydrocarbons, and nitrates in soils, sediment, and groundwater. As of 2010, the company had successfully treated millions of liters of groundwater and over

8,000,000 metric tons of soil at more than 1,000 sites across North America, South America, Europe, Asia, and Oceana. Adventus Americas is part of the Adventus Group, which includes the groundwater remediation firm EnviroMetal Technologies and works with field contracting companies and the independent third party biotechnology laboratories CH2M Hill, Kemron, and Spectrum Analytical. Adventus Americas has a reported revenue of approximately U.S. $14 million to $140 million.

Regenesis Based in San Clemente, California, Regenesis has developed, manufactured, marketed, and distributed bioremediation technologies for soil and groundwater for over 16,000 remediation sites since its formation in 1994. The company's patented bioremediation products include Controlled Release Technology, the Oxygen Release Compound (ORG), the Hydrogen Release Compound (HRC), the chemical oxidation product RegenOx, and 3-D Microemulsion (3-DMe), which Regenesis debuted in the fall of 2010. Land Science Technologies, a division of Regenesis, was created in 2007 to support brownfields developments. Regenesis advises regulatory agencies worldwide and works with its partnered firms to develop specialized bioremediation equipment. The company's reported revenue is $1 million to $10 million.

Osprey Biotechnics An industrial microbiology company headquartered in Sarasota, Florida, Osprey Biotechnics isolates, characterizes, grows, stabilizes, and markets beneficial microbial products for remediation and for manufacture by other companies. Its product line includes the Munox system of oils that break down a variety of organic compounds, including those related to oil spills, and Ready-to-Use (RTU) bioremediation products. The company was founded in 1963 as Microlife Technics to develop vat starter microbial cultures marketed to the food industry. In 1990, Microlife's environmental division began operating as Osprey Biotechnics. The company partners with the EPA to develop products under the Design for the Environment (DfE) Program. Osprey's Cincinnati-based partner, C.L. Solutions, provides bioremediation for soil and groundwater. Osprey's reported revenue is $2.20 million.

Terra Systems, Inc. (TSI) Founded in the 1970s and based in Wilmington, Delaware, TSI provides a wide range of patented bioremediation products for groundwater and soil, including monitored natural attenuation, *in situ* anaerobic bioremediation and chemical oxidation, plate counts that can determine the number of culture-worthy bacteria, and petroleum hydrocarbon degraders. TSI has received a U.S. Department of Agriculture permit to receive and assess foreign soils for treatment. The company's reported revenue is $1.5 million.

General Environmental Science, Inc. GES develops and manufactures bacterial-based products for the remediation and nitrification of municipal wastewater, as well as lakes and ponds, though its aquaculture system technologies. Founded in 1974 to address the increasing problem caused by municipal wastewater, GES is headquartered in Cleveland, Ohio. The company's technologies are used at sites worldwide and it is the patent-holder of four bioaugmentation processes. Its joint venture partner, Ascenda Environmental Science Corporation (AES), oversees the company's markets in China. The company's reported revenue is $2.5 million to $5 million.

Alabaster Corporation Founded in 1989 and headquartered in Pasadena, Texas, the Alabaster Corporation provides environmental consulting, as well as a range of chemical, microbiological, technological, and emergency response products and processes to remediate contaminants in water and soil. Its products include the Petro-Clean Emergency Response Solution. The company has worked on more than 1,000 bioremediation projects since its inception, is listed on the U.S. Department of Defense Central Contractor Registration list with a standing Blanket Purchase Approval, and has provided microbial chemical solutions to such clients as the Panama Canal Commission, the Norfolk Naval Station, and Langley Air Force Base. The company's reported revenue is $580,000.

WORKFORCE

The bioremediation industry employs staff who have been educated in a variety of interdisciplinary applied sciences, including microbiology, chemistry, biochemistry, geology, hydrogeology, chemical and environmental engineering, soil and plant sciences, and ecology. Companies may require previous experience in field work and certification or licensing in a field in addition to a four-year degree in the relevant sciences. Some companies offer career mentoring and training for new hires, and some schools, such as the University of Hawaii, offer courses to strengthen the bioremediation skills of students interested in pursuing a career in the industry. Salaries in the industry depend on the level of education and experience. Schoolsintheusa.com, an online career search engine for students, lists entry-level to maximum salaries in the environmental sector, within the applicable scientific disciplines, that range from $29,920 to $133,310.

RESEARCH AND TECHNOLOGY

Research to develop more effective microorganisms and to enhance the technology necessary to deliver them to hazardous waste sites has been an ongoing aspect of the bioremediation industry and research institutions. In

October 2010, Genetic Engineering & Biotechnology News (GEN) cosponsored a roundtable discussion by a panel of scientists at the Boston campus of the University of Massachusetts, to discuss biological solutions to man-made or natural disasters, with a special emphasis on oil spills. Recent examples of research projects and new bioremediation products include an EPA-funded research project at Agave BioSystems, Inc., to develop a new enzyme engineering system intended to remediate contaminated sites; a low-cost microbial bilge pad, available from Young Enterprises, which digests hydrocarbons and turns them into harmless water-soluble fatty acids ingested by fish and plants; a bioremediation product for petrochemicals, developed by Mariner's Choice International, Inc.; and research conducted by scientists at Japan's Tohoku Gakuin University to detoxify organic mercury in polluted soil and transform it into harmless volatile elemental mercury.

BIBLIOGRAPHY

Atlas, Ronald M., and Jim Philp. *Bioremediation: Applied Microbial Solutions for Real World Environmental Cleanup.* Washington, D.C.: ASM Press, 2005.

Bhattacharyya, Bimal C., and Rintu Banerjee. *Environmental Biotechnology.* New Delhi: Oxford University Press, 2007.

Biello, David. "Slick Solution: How Microbes Will Clean Up the Deepwater Horizon Oil Spill." *Scientific American.* May 25, 2010. Available from http://www.scientificamerican.com/.

"Biodegradable OsmoSorb(SM) Type A Oil Remediation Filter to Safely Separate and Bioremediate: *PR Newswire,* 17 November 2010, Available from http://www.prnewswire.com/news-releases/biodegradable-osmosorbsm-type-a-oil-remediation-filter-to-safely-separate-and-bioremediate-oil-from-water-is-ready-to-clean-up-contaminated-water-ways-108662604.html

"Bioremediation." In *Plant Sciences,* edited by Richard Robinson. New York: Macmillan Reference USA, 2009.

Borém, Aluízio, Fabrício R. Sanatos, and David E. Bowen. *Understanding Biotechnology.* Upper Saddle, NJ: Prentice Hall, 2003.

Crawford, Ronald L., and Don L. Crawford. *Bioremediation: Principles and Applications.*Cambridge: Cambridge University Press, 2005.

Cummings, Stephen P. *Bioremediation: Methods and Protocols.* New York, NY: Humana Press, 2010.

Environmental Expert. The Environmental Industry Online. Available from http://www.environmental-expert.com.

King, R. Barry., Gilbert M. Long, and John K. Sheldon. *Practical Environmental Bioremediation: the Field Guide.* Boca Raton, FL: Lewis Publishers, 1998.

Molecular Plant Biotechnology Techniques, Methods, Applications, Procedures, Genes, DNA Replication and Repair, Animal Biotechnology. Available from http://www.molecular-plant-biotechnology.info.

Prasad, M. N. V., Kenneth S. Sajwan, and R. Naidu. *Trace Elements in the Environment: Biogeochemistry, Biotechnology, and Bioremediation.* Boca Raton, FL: CRC/Taylor and Francis, 2006.

Scragg, A. H. *Environmental Biotechnology.* Oxford: Oxford University Press, 2005.

Shah, Vishal. *Emerging Environmental Technologies.* Berlin: Springer, 2008.

Sims, Michael, Tricia Clark, and Charles Worth Ward. *Bioremediation: Nature's Cleanup Tool.* Darby, PA: Diane Pub., 1993.

Singh, Ajay, Ramesh C. Kuhad, and Owen P. Ward, eds. *Advances in Applied Bioremediation.* Berlin: Springer, 2009.

Singh, Ajay, and Owen P. Ward. *Biodegradation and Bioremediation.* Berlin: Springer, 2004.

Singh, Shree N., and R. D. Tripathi. *Environmental Bioremediation Technologies.* Berlin: Springer, 2007.

Thieman, William J., and Michael Angelo Palladino. *Introduction to Biotechnology.* San Francisco: Pearson/Benjamin Cummings, 2009.

U.S. Environmental Protection Agency. "Enforcement | Compliance and Enforcement | US EPA." Available from http://www.epa.gov/compliance/index-e.html.

Wang, Lawrence K. *Environmental Biotechnology.* New York: Humana Press, 2010.

BOUNTY HUNTING

—■—

SIC CODE(S)

7389

INDUSTRY SNAPSHOT

When people are arrested for committing a crime, they often post bail in order to avoid jail time before their trial. Because most people cannot personally afford the high cost of bail, many turn to bail bonds companies to cover their bail in exchange for a fee. In the event that someone skips bail by failing to appear in court, the bail bonds company can be held liable for covering the entire cost of his/her bail. To avoid this, bail bonds companies rely on bounty hunters to locate, apprehend, and recover so-called bail jumpers or skips. Also known as bail enforcement or fugitive recovery officers, most bounty hunters work as independent contractors and usually receive 10 to 15 percent of the posted bail as a fee for successfully recovering the skip. A great many of these individuals work on a part-time basis and hold other jobs in addition to working in the field of fugitive recovery.

Because only a minority of states license agents, as of 2010 there was no way to accurately track the number of agents nationally, most of whom were employed by private bond companies. Best estimates are that there are several thousand bounty hunters/bail enforcement agents (distinguished from bail agents) in the United States, who account for 30,000 to 50,000 arrests per year. Although a growing number of states have required bounty hunters to obtain licenses or meet certain professional standards, they are not required to produce warrants as police do when pursuing fugitives. This is because bounty hunters enforce private contracts with bail bonds companies as opposed to laws. Some assert that bounty hunters have more power than the police but far less training and accountability.

ORGANIZATION AND STRUCTURE

The business of bounty hunting grew rapidly in the late twentieth century, partially because of overcrowding in the nation's prisons that led to lower bail rates, a greater number of people who post bail, and a higher number of bail jumpers. Despite strong industry growth, most bounty hunters also held other jobs or worked for more than one bail bonds company. Some industry observers indicated that the number of full-time bounty hunters was only in the hundreds.

Even into the new century, the bounty hunting trade was completely unregulated in about half of the United States, where bounty hunters were not required to hold a professional license or insurance policy, undergo a background check, demonstrate psychological stability, be a certain age, or demonstrate that they had obtained any training that qualified them for their job. In fact, bounty hunters in most of these states were able to work even if they had criminal records.

However, at least 12 states required bounty hunters to obtain a license. These included Indiana, Nevada, Mississippi, New York, South Dakota, Connecticut, Arizona, Utah, Iowa, Louisiana, California, and West Virginia. Seven states—New Hampshire, Georgia, Colorado, Tennessee, Arkansas, Texas, and Oklahoma—imposed restrictions on bounty hunters in areas such as age, criminal history, training, and experience. Bounty hunting was illegal in Wisconsin, Illinois, Oregon, and Kentucky. A few states, including Florida, North Carolina, and South Carolina, prohibited the use of freelance agents, meaning that bail bonds companies could only use regular employees to locate and recover fugitives.

How Bounty Hunting Works When someone is suspected of breaking the law and is arrested, they often have the option of posting bail until they must appear in court as opposed to waiting in jail. To cover the required bail amount, suspects usually seek out a bail bonds company that will post the 10 percent of bail they need to avoid incarceration. This 10 percent is refunded to the bonds company if the suspect appears in court. Suspects must pay a fee for this service, usually 10 percent of the bail amount, and instead often obtain the money from a friend or relative. In some cases, suspects use their house or other valuable items as collateral.

In addition to paying a fee to the bail bonds company, suspects sign paperwork agreeing to give up many of their rights in the event that they do not appear in court, a situation known as bail forfeiture. In such cases, bond companies often rely on bail enforcement agents, or bounty hunters, to find fugitive suspects. If he is not able to do so successfully within a period of about 180 days, the bounty hunter earns no commission and the bonds company must pay the remaining 90 percent of the suspect's bail to the court.

While bail bonds companies have a great incentive for recovering bail jumpers, they must be careful in choosing bounty hunters because they could potentially share in the liability for illegal or excessive behavior. However, because bounty hunters are considered independent contractors, legal experts say that in most cases, bail bonds companies are free from liability.

The field of bounty hunting has developed a somewhat glamorous image in the public's mind. In 1988, actor Robert Deniro starred as a bounty hunter in the movie *Midnight Run,* and USA Networks' television series *The Huntress* showcased a mother-daughter bounty hunting team. However, while many believe the bounty hunting field to be filled with constant danger and excitement, many within the trade claim that most of what they do is dull and routine, with about 3 to 5 percent of their time devoted to activities that are considered dangerous or risky.

Indeed, much of a bounty hunter's time is spent doing detective work to uncover information about fugitives that will lead to an arrest. This involves conducting computer research and driving around to speak with so-called snitches or informants, or people with whom the fugitive is associated. While a fugitive's enemies would appear to be an obvious source of information, friends, colleagues, and family members often are willing to assist bounty hunters in their search. Even though some of these individuals may have ill feelings toward the fugitive, others believe that he or she would be safer if taken into custody. Bounty hunters also may conduct long stakeouts that require several days of sitting in one location.

Bounty hunters often begin by looking for fugitives in obvious places, such as at their home address or the addresses of family members or significant others. Because they either do not try very hard to avoid detection or else make foolish mistakes, most fugitives are easy to find. However, those who are clever can make the bounty hunter's job a difficult one. In such cases, hunters must employ equally creative strategies to find them. One such strategy involves sending a letter to the fugitive's family from a non-existent organization that offers to drop all charges against the suspect if they simply call a toll-free number. Another strategy is notification that the fugitive has won the lottery. When the fugitive dials the number, his call is traced and the bounty hunter is able to pinpoint his location and apprehend him. Another clever tactic is the use of disguises to get close to the target. A skip trace, which involves using the fugitive's Social Security number to locate places where he might be working, is another approach.

Even when a fugitive has been located, bounty hunters often are not required to break down doors or use force to apprehend them, contrary to popular belief. Many bounty hunters report that suspects come willingly, and some are even relieved to have been found. According to first-hand accounts, it is rare that a bounty hunter must use force to apprehend someone. While some bounty hunters wear body armor and carry guns for protection, many report that they have never drawn their weapons to apprehend a suspect. However, dangerous situations do arise, especially when the fugitive has a history of committing serious crimes. Once an apprehension has been made, bounty hunters are normally required to bring fugitives before a judge or to a detention facility within 48 hours.

Associations There are a number of trade organizations within the bail bonds industry. A few are exclusive to bounty hunters, while others serve the needs of bail bonds organizations in general.

Based in Spring Grove, Illinois, the National Institute of Bail Enforcement (NIBE) is devoted to producing "the finest and most efficient bail fugitive investigators in the United States." The institute has trained more than 2,000 agents since its inception, teaching them to avoid unsavory practices like the use of excessive force, false entry, and false arrest. In addition to training bounty hunters, the institute publishes a bi-monthly newsletter called *Track-down.* It also established the National Enforcement Agency (NEA) to promote networking among professional bail enforcement agents. NEA membership comes with professional credentials and access to a toll-free number agents can give law enforcement officials for the purpose of validating their statu and s as professional bounty hunters.

Based in Washington, D.C., the American Bail Coalition is comprised of companies that underwrite criminal court appearance bonds. Its members include Underwriters Surety Inc., International Fidelity Insurance Co., Associated Bond and Insurance Agency, American Surety Co., and Allegheny Casualty Co. The coalition focuses on representing the interest of its members' agents and educating local government about commercial bail bonding's many advantages. In addition to its headquarters, the coalition has regional offices in the eastern, central, and western United States. In 2010 the organization was accused of heavy lobbying in Arizona's new anti-immigration laws, enjoined by a federal district court later that year.

The Professional Bail Agents of the United States (PBUS), also based in Washington, D.C., was founded in 1981. Representing approximately 14,000 bail agents in the early 2000s, the PBUS is focused on providing all agents with information, education, and national representation. According to the PBUS, in cooperation with state associations it has "advanced the profession through legislative advocacy, professional networking, continuing education, support of bail agent certification, enhanced liability insurance and development of a code of ethics." The PBUS holds two conventions each year, maintains a hall of fame, sponsors a professional bail agent certification program, and publishes a quarterly magazine entitled *Bail Agents Perspective.*

In addition to these national groups, there are numerous state organizations within the bail bonds industry, including the California Bail Agents Association, Professional Bail Agents of Arizona, the Florida Surety Agents Association, Bail Agents Independent League of Florida, the Georgia Association of Professional Bail Agents, the Indiana Surety Bail Agents Association Inc., the Oklahoma Bondsmen Association, the Tennessee Association of Professional Agents, and Professional Bail Agents of Texas.

BACKGROUND AND DEVELOPMENT

The modern bounty hunting profession's roots date back to medieval England. At that time in history, English prisons were filthy places where suspects often died before standing trial. As *Texas Lawyer* explained in its September 22, 1997, issue, as an alternative to detention, sheriffs began placing defendants in the legal custody of sureties. "A surety's custody was deemed to be a continuation of the sheriff's initial imprisonment, and a surety seeking to recapture an accused enjoyed rights of search and arrest identical to those possessed by a sheriff seeking to catch an escaped prisoner. That system of bail and the rights of bounty hunters to arrest persons on bail were adopted in America following the Revolution."

In the 1872 case of *Taylor v. Taintor,* the U.S. Supreme Court issued a ruling that essentially gave bounty hunters the expansive powers they have enjoyed into the early twenty-first century. According to the same *Texas Lawyer* article: "The Supreme Court said that regardless of whether a defendant's trial date has passed, bounty hunters as bondsmen's agents have the authority to break into the home of a person on bail at any time to make an arrest. In fact, they are entitled to break into the home of a third party to arrest a defendant who is inside. They also may imprison the accused until custody can be returned to the state. And like sheriffs pursuing escaping prisoners, they are entitled to use all necessary force, including deadly force, to obtain custody over a defendant. 'The bail bondsmen have their principal on a string, and may pull the string whenever they please, and render him in their discharge,' the court wrote."

This ruling ultimately led to the formation of a legal presumption that suspects agree to let bail bondsmen, or anyone else who bails them out of jail, arrest, and detain them should they fail to appear in court. This is generally the case even in the absence of formal written or verbal agreements.

More than 100 years later, critics questioned why the 1872 court ruling had not been revisited. Legal experts, including the National Association of Criminal Defense Lawyers, indicated that there has been little reason to do so. For many years, the number of full-time bounty hunters in the United States was relatively small and the High Court's attention has been focused on other, more pressing matters. However, a number of high-profile incidents involving bounty hunters eventually led to increased attention on the profession.

In 1997 masked criminals posing as bounty hunters used sledge hammers to break into the home of an Arizona family. Upon entering, the criminals bound three children, one teenager, and an adult and held them at gunpoint. When another resident fired shots at the intruders in self-defense, they fired back, killing him and his girlfriend. That same year, seven other incidents were reported across the country in which real bounty hunters either killed, apprehended, or entered the homes or hotel rooms of innocent people.

For many years bounty hunting was virtually unregulated. However, incidents like these led to public outcry and promises from states to regulate or even ban for-profit bounty hunting. By 1997 six states had some kind of licensing requirement for bounty hunters. However, proponents argued that total bans would be ineffective, given the large number of fugitives that are recovered each year at no cost to taxpayers. Instead, they advocated more stringent regulations, such as mandated training, required liability insurance, and background checks. Because bounty hunting often involves pursuing fugitives across state lines, some suggested that Congress evaluate the industry and issue appropriate federal laws.

A growing number of states required bounty hunters to hold a license or meet certain criteria. One example of state bounty hunter legislation is California's Bail Fugitive Recovery Persons Act of 2000. This law prohibits bounty hunters from having criminal records and requires them to notify police six hours prior to taking a fugitive into custody. In addition, bounty hunters in that state are required to undergo 79 hours of training and carry proof of completion with them while working.

Such license requirements were not without good reason. In late 2003, New Jersey bounty hunters faced attempts to prevent them from breaking into homes or carrying firearms. In its September 7, 2003, issue, *The Record* reported that Kenneth Wickliff, a bounty hunter in Gloucester County, had been convicted of criminal trespassing after breaking into the home of a woman whose son had skipped bail. Wickliff's boss, Rodger Jones, also found himself in a legal tangle when a panel of three judges ruled that he could no longer carry a gun while bounty hunting. Jones reportedly had incurred some $40,000 in legal fees related to the case. New Jersey Deputy Attorney General Lori Linskey indicated that the state appellate court did not give a great deal of weight to *Taylor v. Taintor* in Jones' case.

New York State also was cracking down on bounty hunters. In that state, Governor George Pataki signed a law on April 1, 2001, that required bounty hunters to provide the state with proof that they possessed $500,000 in collateral in the form of a surety bond. In addition, they were required to successfully complete 25 hours of basic training approved by the New York Secretary of State in order to obtain a license that allowed them to apprehend fugitives in New York and transport them to other states. Several months after the law went into effect, no bounty hunter had applied for a state license. The state indicated that many New York bounty hunters were possibly already covered under a clause that grandfathered in private investigators, but it did not deny the possibility that the absence of applicants was a form of protest.

While the New York bill generated an outcry from some bounty hunting industry players who considered it an undue financial hardship, some supported the measure. In the June 5, 2001, issue of *The Times Union,* Professional Bail Agents of the United States Executive Director Steve Kreimer said, "New York state is to be commended for passing training legislation, because before this any

yahoo could call himself a bounty hunter and pretend he was in some Wild West show. We've long said we want to regulate or eliminate those loose cannons. Frankly, it's the Rambos who scare us and tarnish our profession."

While overcrowding in jails and prisons supported growth within the bail bonds industry, thereby benefiting bounty hunters, the industry faced more stringent regulation than ever before. In addition to a growing number of states that required bounty hunters to carry licenses or meet other standards, some states were cracking down on the methods bounty hunters used to recover fugitives—despite the 1872 Supreme Court ruling in *Taylor v. Taintor* that has granted the industry so much freedom.

Along with stricter regulations, the general public demonstrated a growing level of interest in the bounty hunting trade during this mid-decade period. This was evident by the popularity of A&E's program, *Dog The Bounty Hunter.* The series chronicles the efforts of legendary bounty hunter Duane "Dog" Chapman as he pursues fugitives, with the assistance of his brother, son, and wife. According to the October 25, 2004, issue of *Television Week,* some 3.2 million viewers tuned in for the show's premiere, which was a record for A&E. By 2006 the average number of viewers per episode was estimated at 4.2 million. In November 2007 A&E suspended the program after the *National Enquirer* posted an audio tape of a phone conversation in which Chapman made racial remarks. Chapman apologized and conducted a series of appearances and other reconciliatory acts through African American organizations. By the summer of 2008, the show was back on the air.

Other broadcasting stations picked up on the trend as well. HBO debuted its reality show about bounty hunters with the September 2004 premiere of *Family Bonds,* which followed the life of the Evangelista family, bounty hunters in New York City and Long Island. The popularity of the genre did not wane, as evidenced by the premier of yet another bounty hunting show in 2007. The women's channel, WE, aired *Wife, Mom, Bounty Hunter* for the first time in April 2007.

States continued to vary on what was considered lawful in the bounty hunting business. Four states—Illinois, Wisconsin, Kentucky, and Oregon—ban bounty hunting altogether, whereas others, such as Florida, North Carolina, and South Carolina, allow it only on a very restricted basis. Eleven states require licensing, and most others have requirements regarding age, certification, gun control, clothing (i.e., wearing clothing that identifies one as a bounty hunter), and other issues.

Many were tightening their restrictions on bounty hunting, including Washington, where a bill introduced in 2008 would increase the number of hours of training bounty hunters must receive. In 2006 licensing regulations required 4 to 12 hours of training; the new bill raises that figure to 32 hours. It also requires bounty hunters to report directly to the Department of Licensing every time they enter a home by force. The latter requirement addresses an issue that has arisen several times in the industry: that of bounty hunters entering homes forcibly without permission and/or arresting the wrong person.

In response to the increased need for training, institutions such as the U.S. Recovery Bureau, based in New Jersey, offered classes to the aspiring bounty hunter. For about $400, individuals can take a 30-hour course during which they can learn the proper way to "speed cuff," strike a fugitive, and administer mace. Other topics include legal aspects, street survival, and prisoner transport.

Bill Kreins, the Safety National Casualty Corp. contact for the Professional Bail Agents of the United States, told *Hawaii Business* in 2006 that the bounty hunting industry was growing at a rate of 13 to 15 percent per year. According to Kreins, although criminal activity has increased, the growth rate in the industry is largely due to rapidly rising bail schedules instituted by courts around the country. Varying sources place the amount of penal liability in the United States at $7 billion to $10 billion, with 14,000 bail agents and approximately 15 insurance companies collecting 10 percent. Another study by Eric Helland and Alexander Tabarrok found that if people released to commercial bond agencies decided to run, they were 50 percent more likely to be caught if chased by a bounty hunter. According to Helland and Tabarrok, bounty hunters catch about 25,000 to 35,000 fugitives a year.

On the federal regulation front, in 2008 the Bail Bond Fairness Act was making its way through Congress. The act mandated that bail bonds be forfeited only if a defendant does not appear in court as ordered. Previously, federal judges had the authority to attach behavioral conditions to bail bonds, a situation over which bail bond agents had no control.

CURRENT CONDITIONS

In March 2010 President Obama issued a memorandum calling on agency heads and executive departments to enhance their efforts to recapture improper payments; he declared his support for the Improper Payments Elimination and Recovery Act (S.1508) introduced by Senator Thomas Carper (D-DE) that would require all government agencies to pay more than $1 million for recovery audits for their programs. At the same time Congress (the Joint Economic Committee and the House Ways and Means Committee minority staff) proposed a need for up to 16,500 new IRS "bounty hunters" to audit, examine, and collect tax information needed for new tax provisions and the newly-enacted healthcare

plan. The IRS continued to make use of its Private Debt Collection (PDC) program, fully implemented in 2008, to employ private agencies/debt collectors, who would be paid up to 25 cents on every dollar collected in unpaid taxes, in addition to a $100 bonus for every account closed.

In July 2010 the Dodd-Frank financial reform bill was signed into law, representing a more aggressive approach to securities frauds and securities law violations. New provisions require the Securities and Exchange Commission (SEC) and the U.S. Commodity Futures Trading Commission (CFTC) to award a bounty payment of 10 to 30 percent to any whistleblower who provides information about securities fraud that results in a judgment in excess of $1 million. The relevant information may relate to either a publicly-traded company, or a private company owned by a public company.

On July 23, 2010, the SEC granted an unprecedented $1 million bounty to a couple in Connecticut. The case involved a former spouse who allegedly was involved in insider trading relating to a hedge fund. The SEC successfully won a $28 million settlement, including a $10 million penalty, against the hedge fund. Congress gave the SEC and CFTC until April 2011 to propose and approve new regulations regarding the bounty program, including a period for public comment.

In Britain, the consumer credit reporting entity known as Experian (also operating in 37 countries, including the United States) announced plans to help reduce Britain's annual benefit-fraud budget by catching fraudulent disability and housing benefits claims.

In *United States v. Poe,* a federal appeals court considered whether bounty hunters were "state actors," or agents of a governmental entity acting on behalf of that government. It held that they were not. There were significant consequences attached to such rulings, because bounty hunters generally enjoy greater powers of search and arrest than do police officers. Not being state actors, they are not constrained by the same constitutional or regulatory safeguards as law enforcement officers are (i.e., the Fourth Amendment's prohibitions against illegal searches and seizures).

WORKFORCE

While most bounty hunters are males in their 30s, the National Institute of Bail Enforcement (NIBE) indicates that males, females, and people of all racial and ethic backgrounds are attracted to the fugitive recovery business. In fact, a growing number of women are involved in this profession. One female bounty hunter in New Mexico, who repossessed cars by day, spent evenings and weekends bounty hunting with her husband. A number of industry insiders argue that women are more successful than men at skip tracing and bounty hunting. In addition to being more meticulous researchers, they say that male suspects are more likely to open their doors for women, and may in fact be somewhat disarmed by them.

Most bounty hunters are independent contractors and freelance for one or several bail bonds companies. However, some work exclusively for one bail bonds agent on a full- or part-time basis—a mandatory situation in states that prevent bounty hunting for profit. The majority of freelance bounty hunters hold other jobs in addition to recovering fugitives. The relatively small number of bounty hunters who work at the profession full-time do so on a national basis, since there often is not enough work in any one location to support them. These individuals rely on advertising and networking with other bounty hunters to be as successful as possible. The most successful bounty hunters usually have legitimate backgrounds, are adept at conducting research, possess a certain amount of so-called street smarts, and dedicate themselves to operating in an ethical manner. These legitimate bounty hunters adhere to all applicable state and local laws.

Contrary to popular belief, although some bounty hunters have military or law enforcement backgrounds, bounty hunting is not analogous to being a Navy Seal or serving on a S.W.A.T. team. This is reflected in the training the NIBE offers to its students. As the institute explains, "Since one's size, shooting skills, knowledge of self-defense, martial arts, or driving skills play little role in locating bail fugitives, the schooling offered at the National Institute of Bail Enforcement focuses on the skills necessary to succeed as a bail enforcement agent, such as: telephone skills, national networking with other bounty hunters, understanding laws applicable to fugitive recovery, arrest contracts, the where and why of advertising, cross-border operations, etc."

AMERICA AND THE WORLD

For many years, bounty hunters within the United States were free to pursue fugitives across the Mexican border. In fact, law enforcement agents and bounty hunters could once count on assistance from Mexican "federales" to apprehend U.S. fugitives who sought refuge there. This changed in 1993 when Mexico revised an extradition treaty with the United States that made the abduction and cross-border transport of criminal suspects illegal.

The catalyst for this treaty change came in 1990, when the United States Drug Enforcement Administration hired Mexican bounty hunters to apprehend Dr. Humberto Alvarez Machain, a physician from Guadalajara, so that he could stand trial in the United States, angering Mexicans in the process. Following the 1993 revision, the United States was required to obtain the Mexican government's consent before apprehending a fugitive. This required obtaining an expulsion or deportation order or going through the extradition process— procedures used for only the most serious crimes. Mexican police caught assisting bounty hunters risked severe punishment for doing so.

By the early 2000s, several U.S. bounty hunters wound up in Mexican prisons for violating the new law. In 1999 bounty hunter Christopher James Levi was charged with kidnapping and sentenced to 15 years in La Mesa State Penitentiary in Tijuana, along with two associates, for apprehending drug smuggler Joseph William Swint. A more high-profile case took place in 2003 when convicted-felon-turned-bounty-hunter Duane Lee (Dog) Chapman was jailed for arresting Andrew Luster, heir to the Max Factor fortune, in Puerto Vallarta, Mexico. Luster, who was convicted of drugging and raping women, was extradited to the United States and incarcerated in California. Chapman, along with a cameraman, his agent, and his son, faced kidnapping charges for arresting Luster in violation of Mexican law. They were later acquitted.

BIBLIOGRAPHY

Cave, Andrew. "Experian Chief Don Robert on Bounty Hunting and Catching Fraudsters." *The Telegraph* (UK), 21 August 2010.

Choo, David K. "Dog Inc.: Inside the Business of Bail Bonds and Bounty Hunting." *Hawaii Business,* June 2006.

"Corporate Con Game." *In These Times,* July 2010.

Drimmer, Jonathan. "Bounty Hunter Laws." American Bail Coalition, 25 June 2008. Available from http://www.americanbailcoalition.com/new_html/.

"Groudhog Day for Medicare Audits?" *HomeCare Magazine,* 15 March 2010.

"H.R. 2286: Bail Bond Fairness Act of 2007," 15 June 2008. Available from http://www.govtrack.us/congress/bill.xpd?bill=h110-2286.

Kouri, Jim. "Health Care Mandate to Be Enforced by IRS Bounty Hunters." *Mens News Daily,* 21 March 2010.

Lowry, Brian. "Wife, Mom, Bounty Hunter." *Daily Variety,* 19 April 2007.

"The Mission of the Professional Bail Agents of the United States." Washington, DC.: Professional Bail Agents of the United States, 20 June 2008. Available from http://www.pbus.com.

"National Institute of Bail Enforcement." National Institute of Bail Enforcement, 20 June 2008. Available from http://www.bounty-hunter.net.

Nichols, Katherine. "A&E Lets Dog Out of the Pound." *Star Bulletin,* 14 May 2008.

Royval, Adam M. "*United States v. Poe*: A Missed Opportunity to Reevaluate Bounty Hunters's Symbiotic Role in the Criminal Justice System." *Denver University Law Review,* May 2010.

U.S. Immigration and Customs Enforcement. "Joint Investigation Leads to Arrest on Charges of Distributing False Badges," 1 July 2008. Available from http://www.ice.gov/pi/nr/0807/080701newark.htm.

BOUTIQUE WINERIES

SIC CODE(S)

2048

5182

INDUSTRY SNAPSHOT

Compared to larger wineries, which have more of a commercial focus, "boutique" wineries typically limit their annual production to a small number of cases (often 2,000 or less). In addition, the owners and employees of boutique wineries are known for being especially passionate about winemaking. While some boutique wineries are newer operations, others can trace their heritage as grape producers or winemakers back over several generations. Most are operated by individuals, families, or small partnerships.

While many boutique wineries are located in charming, rural areas, some are located in more unusual settings. For example, one boutique winery located near Sonoma, California, operated from an industrial park. Instead of holding wine tastings in an elegant setting, the owner opted to host them in the parking lot. In addition, some boutique wineries have unique reputations and quirky offerings. During the late 2000s the Whitmore Wine Co. offered comforting, laid-back wines with names like Leftover Meatloaf Mourvedre and Fuhgetaboutit Barbara.

Although there may not be a concrete definition, many have tried to describe what makes a winery "boutique." According to a March 17, 2010, passage from Chloe Mathieu Phillips and Dennis Phillips on www.eatboutique .com, "perhaps boutique is more a state of mind that a number of bottles. It's more of an attitude than a location."

Elaborating further on boutique wines in an August 18, 2002, article on www.supermarketguru.com, writer Dennis Manuel explained: "There are boutique wines from all over the world. What you are looking for in a boutique wine is not just a small winery, because there are many small wineries that are not producing good wine or interesting wines, but due to their size they have to charge more for a wine you can get for less from a bigger winery. What you're looking for is the reason why a passionate winemaker makes a slightly different wine. A good winemaker has a passion for a specific expression of a specific grape or blend of grapes. That's what you want to try."

In a July 29, 1989, *Globe & Mail* article, David Lawrason added: "Specialization is a common thread. Boutique winemakers tend to be dreamers, zealots and perfectionists. To make the best of any one type of wine—say the great California pinot noir, or the great Australian Chardonnay—is their calling. Many disdain commercialism, avoiding pressures to increase quantities or expand their range of wines, but it's hard to resist the forces of success."

ORGANIZATION AND STRUCTURE

Winemaking. The making of wine begins with the grape harvest, which generally occurs from August through November, depending on the grape variety and the weather. The grapes are placed in a crusher that separates the stems from the fruit and breaks up the berries. The stems are then discarded, leaving a combination of juice, seeds, pulp, and skins, called "must." Juice from red or white wine grapes is colorless.

119

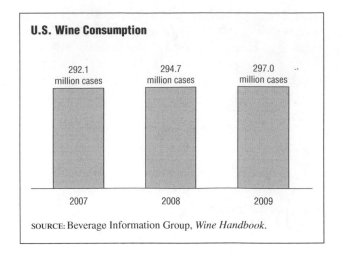

U.S. Wine Consumption

292.1 million cases — 2007

294.7 million cases — 2008

297.0 million cases — 2009

SOURCE: Beverage Information Group, *Wine Handbook.*

To make white wine, the skins and seeds usually are removed from the must after a few hours. The remaining juice is called "free-run." The discarded skins also are pressed to extract the "press juice." Both juices then are filtered, placed in storage, and given yeast to facilitate the fermentation process. White wine fermentation can last anywhere from three days to three weeks. Upon completion, the wine is filtered for solids or remaining yeast. The wine then is aged for a period of one week to a year in stainless steel, oak, or redwood containers. It also can be aged in the bottle. After aging, the wine can be blended with other wines to create a desired style or can be sent to be finished (a process that stabilizes and filters the wine before bottling).

Production of red wine is slightly different than the process of making white wine. Red wine is fermented at warmer temperatures than white wine. For red wine production, the skins are fermented with the crushed juice to give it color and flavor. The skins float to the top and are moistened regularly with juice to extract color and flavor. Red wine usually is fermented for 5 to 10 days and then is filtered, clarified, and preserved with sulfites. Red wine commonly is aged in oak barrels for one to two years.

Champagne is made in one of two ways: by method champenoise or the charmat process. In method champenoise, still wine is blended with a mixture (called triage) of still wine, yeast, and a sugar substance. This blend is resealed in bottles where it is fermented for a second time and aged. Carbon dioxide collects in the bottles, which is released in a rush of bubbles when the bottles are uncorked. In the charmat, or bulk, process, the still wine, yeast, and sugar are fermented in a pressurized tank rather than in bottles.

Related Services. Beyond winemaking, boutique wineries often engage in a wide range of secondary services.

For example, many offer special rooms devoted to wine tastings. In addition, some host concerts, weddings, private parties, food tastings, picnics, and movie nights on their premises. Other boutique wineries have educational offerings that enable people to learn about winemaking and culture.

Types of Wines. Wines sold in the United States generally are divided into the following categories: champagne, aperitif, dessert wine, table wine, and varietal wine. Also included are brandy and other fortified wines. Wines can be named one of four ways: by variety, which tells the predominant type of grape; by a generic name describing the color, such as blush; by the region that originally inspired the wine, such as Chablis; or by a proprietary name, which is a label created by the winery.

Champagne and sparkling wines are names used interchangeably in the United States for wines with effervescence. These wines range from very dry (natural), to dry (brut), to slightly sweet (extra dry), to sweet (sec and demi-sec). Aperitifs are appetizer wines usually served prior to a meal and can include champagnes and sherries. Dessert wines are officially classified as those with an alcohol content of 17 percent to 21 percent. They can be sweet or dry and include sherries and ports.

Table wine is a term commonly used to describe all red, white, blush, and rose wines that contain 7 to 14 percent alcohol. These wines are still rather effervescent and are served mainly with meals. Table wines can be made from any grape or combination of grapes and in any style that the winemaker chooses. Varietal wines are table wines that are made from a minimum of 75 percent of a particular grape variety; they carry the name of the grape variety from which they are produced, such as chardonnay or merlot.

The red table wine category has been led by cabernet sauvignon, a full-bodied, rich, intense wine with noticeable tannins. A leading prestigious varietal, cabernet sauvignon has been one of the most widely available wines from California. Other red varietals include merlot, petite sirah, and zinfandel. Merlot is a medium- to full-bodied wine that originally was made for the sole purpose of blending with cabernet sauvignon. Petite sirah is a wine with deep color, full body, and a fresh-berry taste. Zinfandel, known as the classic California wine, is known too for its versatility, range of style, and raspberry-spicy aroma and flavor.

White table wines have been dominated by chardonnay. It is a dry wine that has a balance of fruit, acidity, and texture. Depending on what the winemaker uses for storage, chardonnay can range from clean and crisp wines to rich, complex, oak-aged wines.

Other white varietals include French columbard, sauvignon blanc, Johannisberg reisling, gewurztraminer, and pinot blanc. French columbard is generally fresh and fruity, ranging from light to medium in body. Sauvignon blanc has been one of the fastest-growing varietals in California; sometimes called fume blanc, it is best known for its grassy, herbal flavors and is often consumed with fish and shellfish. Johannisberg Riesling, from the German Riesling grape, is aromatic, delicate, and slightly sweet. Late harvest Rieslings are good accompaniments for dessert. Gewurztraminer offers spicy aromas and flavors and a slight wisp of residual sweetness. Often this wine goes well with Asian food. Pinot blanc is a unique, dry white wine, with styles ranging from bold and oak-aged to crisp and medium-bodied.

Brandy is "burnt wine" or fruit wine that is boiled and aged in wood. Virtually any type of fruit can be used to make brandy, although grapes have been the most common. Brandy has been produced primarily in Spain, Italy, and France, and most recently in the United States. Cognac has been considered to be the best of all brandies. Cognac's discerning characteristic has been its blending, often created from a number of different cognacs coupled carefully to achieve an appropriate mixture.

Fortified wines were the creation of the Spanish and Portuguese and included port, sherry, and Madeira. Sherry is made by blending younger sherries with older sherries in oak casks. It varies in dryness levels and in hues.

Port is red wine fortified with grape brandy. It was created unintentionally in the seventeenth century when Portugal tried to ship its table wine to England. In order to stabilize the wine during its voyage across the Atlantic, the wine needed the addition of grape brandy. England has remained the most popular market for port.

Madeira comes from a tropical island of the same name and is a raisiny, sweet wine. Madeira has been closely linked with the history of the United States, according to the *New York Times Magazine*. It was considered to be the wine of choice for American Revolutionary notables such as Thomas Jefferson, George Washington, and Ben Franklin. Unlike other wines that soured during the long, hot voyage across the Atlantic, Madeira was the only wine known to improve dramatically with the introduction of heat.

BACKGROUND AND DEVELOPMENT

California winemaking began in 1769 when Father Junipero Serra planted vines at Mission San Diego. In September 1772 the grapes were harvested and pressed, creating California's first vintage. These early wines were produced for sacramental purposes and personal consumption at the missions.

The commercial era of wine production began in 1830 with the efforts of Frenchman Jean Louis Vignes

from Bordeaux, France. His vineyard was located in what is now downtown Los Angeles. The wine industry boomed as an ancillary result of the discovery of gold in California in 1848. A surge of Europeans came to the state seeking their fortune. Immigrants from Italy, France, and Germany who had no luck finding gold turned to a trade they already knew—winemaking.

Between 1860 and 1880 the industry grew rapidly as numerous wineries were established. By 1890 several of the state's famous wine regions already had taken shape and the industry was producing 25 million gallons of wine per year. After suffering losses from a vine pest called phylloxera, the industry virtually disappeared with the passage of Prohibition in 1919. The repeal of Prohibition in 1933, however, prompted the industry to rebuild. Growth was steady between 1949 and 1960, with annual output increasing from 117 million gallons to 129 million gallons. By the 1970s the demand for California table wines had doubled.

As the industry evolved, so did consumer preferences. From 1933 to 1967 dessert wine was the most popular kind of wine in the United States. During the 1970s wineries such as Sutter Home and Mondavi, which would evolve into major operations producing millions of cases annually, were boutique wineries.

At this time generic table wines, like California Chablis and California Burgundy, dominated sales. The popularity of boutique wineries was garnering national attention by the mid-1980s. For example, *Harper's Bazaar* ran a story titled "A Vine Romance: America's Boutique Wineries" in September 1986. By the late 1980s varietal wines, those labeled with the name of the grape, had become the most popular.

After posting a 6.5 percent loss in 1993, wine sales in the United States continued to rise, while per capita consumption remained steady at 1.8 gallons. According to the San Francisco-based Wine Institute, consumer demand for premium varietal wines spurred a 5 percent increase in California table wine sales in 1994. This was the strongest performance in more than a decade.

After a time of record growth throughout the 1990s, U.S. winemakers began seeing wine sales flatten in the early 2000s. With a shaky economy made all the more so by the terrorist attacks against the United States on September 11, 2001, the wine industry, like many U.S. industries, was affected by the decrease in consumer spending on travel and recreation, which is tied to wine drinking. Another factor in the state of the wine industry from 2000 to 2003 was the overproduction of grapes and the ensuing drop in grape prices by as much as 75 percent in 2001 and 2002. Wine prices dropped during this time while sales flattened.

By the mid-2000s the U.S. wine industry was improving. California wineries shipped a record amount of products, with approximately 428 million gallons shipped domestically, from a total of 522 million gallons shipped worldwide. While so-called "extreme value" varieties continued to sell well, expensive premium wines also were seeing increases, accounting for 64 percent of industry revenues. Following the trend across nearly all U.S. retail industries, the middle variety sales were flat, with the majority of the industry growth occurring at either extreme end of the price spectrum. In 2004 sales of red outpaced white for the first time in years.

In 2006 major changes were taking place throughout the winemaking industry. In response, a new partnership named Vintage Point was established in California to help boutique wineries in a number of areas. These ranged from channel management and merchandising to forecasting/planning, advertising, Web site development, and package design.

In the March 10, 2006, issue of just-drinks.com, David Biggar, one of the partners, explained: "Above all, we want to help small, independent boutique wineries get to market. The way wine is marketed and sold in the US is changing so quickly, with consolidation happening in all parts of the business—retail, wholesale and supplier. As a result, we see that these wineries are getting lost in the system. Our aim is to partner with these wineries so that their businesses remain viable, profitable and strong."

The following year, boutique wineries benefited from the establishment of a partnership between BoutiqueWineCellar.com and Inertia Beverage Group. The partnership resulted in an online marketplace that brought together offerings from multiple boutique wineries and enabled direct-to-consumer sales. In addition to making purchases, consumers were able to make recommendations and share comments on different wines.

During the late 2000s, many boutique wineries were struggling in the wake of difficult economic times. Those selling high-priced wines were hit especially hard as consumers scaled back on luxury purchases. In addition, sponsorship funding for wine festivals also hurt wineries that depended on large events for sales. One example was California-based Loose Goose, which closed its doors in 2009.

CURRENT CONDITIONS

Wineries continued to operate in difficult economic times during the early 2010s. Mirroring conditions in the housing market, a number of prime vineyards and wineries faced foreclosure, or were sold under distress as property owners defaulted on their loans. In the March 22, 2010, issue of *BusinessWeek,* Silicon Valley Bank Wine Division Manager Bill Stevens indicated that, according to 250 of the bank's vintner clients, the economic downturn was the worst they had experienced in two decades.

Nevertheless, factors such as a consumer shift to lower-priced wines helped minimize the economic impact on the overall wine industry during the recession. Looking ahead, the future looked promising. According to the August 4, 2010, issue of *OfficialSpin,* the online business information aggregator Companiesandmarkets.com revealed that the U.S. wine market would reach $33.5 billion in 2013, driven by sales of 871 million gallons.

In addition to making wines available for sale online, many boutique wineries were taking advantage of technology in order to maintain a competitive edge during the difficult economy. For example, some were maintaining blogs, adding live chat functionality to their Web sites, and offering video clips for online viewing. The importance of interactive marketing comes into focus when one considers that online-based wine sales increased 29 percent in 2009, according to a survey of 3,500 U.S. wineries conducted by the firm VinterActive LLC.

Boutique wineries were contending with an important political challenge in 2010 called House Resolution 5034, also known as the Comprehensive Alcohol Regulatory Effectiveness Act. Supported by the Wine and Spirits Wholesalers Association and the National Beer Wholesalers Association (trade organizations backing wholesale distributors), the act proposed to give states the power to eliminate or limit direct-to-consumer wine sales from other states. In addition, the legislation proposed to overrule the interstate commerce clause found in the Constitution, which places control of inter-state sales with the federal government.

Instead of being able to sell directly, under HR 5034 wineries would be forced to sell their selections through distributors. Because low-volume boutique operations would likely be a low priority for distributors, this option would not be feasible for most small wineries. In addition, boutique operations offering a variety of selections would not be able to make them all available via a distributor, according to some observers. In an April 20, 2010, *Business Wire* article, the organization Family Winemakers of California called the bill "a naked attempt to dominate the marketplace and change consumption patterns," and argued that it "puts at risk most of the 7,000 wineries in the nation."

AMERICA AND THE WORLD

Boutique wineries are an international phenomenon. For example, in France and Italy, small wineries that produce unique wines are held in high esteem. Australia also is known for passionate boutique winemakers who produce distinct handcrafted wines. Successful boutique operations even exist in India, which in 2010 was preparing to become the first Asian member of the International Organisation of Vine and Wine. Mirroring developments in the United States, online sales have come to the fore in other international markets. In October 2009 Top Wines announced an online wine store that was created to make boutique wines from Australia and New Zealand more easily available throughout Australia.

BIBLIOGRAPHY

Alegria, Andrea. "Loose Goose, Another Casualty of the Economy: Consumers Cut Luxuries When the Economy Sours." *San Fernando Valley Business Journal,* 27 April 2009.

Arora, Cindy. "Boutique Label Offers Wine without Pretension." *Record,* 10 January 2007.

Berkowitz, Natalie. "A Vine Romance: America's Boutique Wineries." *Harper's Bazaar,* September 1986.

"Family Winemakers of California Opposes H.R. 5034." *Business Wire,* 20 April 2010.

Fujii, Reed. "Lodi Boutique Wineries Grow through Direct Sales." *Record,* 7 February 2008.

"India First Asian Nation to Join OIV." *Indian Wine Academy,* 30 March 2010.

Jett, Cathy. "Vintners See Bill as Bad Idea." *Free Lance-Star,* 3 June 2010.

Kalish, Geoff. "WINE; For Vineyards, Small Can Be Superior." *New York Times,* 12 September 1993.

Lawrason, David. "Micro Craze: Sonoma's Boutique Wineries Are Pumping Out Blockbuster Bottles." *Toronto Life,* September 2009.

———. "ON WINE Boutique Wineries: Mosey On Up, Pardner, and Sip a Chardonnay." *Globe & Mail* (Toronto), 29 July 1989.

Levy, Dan. "Napa Valley's Grapes of Wrath." *BusinessWeek,* 22 March 2010.

Macias, Chris. "Wine Buzz: New Head of California's Wine Institute Has a Barrel Full of Challenges." *Sacramento Bee,* 30 June 2010.

Manuel, Dennis. "Boutique Wines." *Supermarket Guru,* 18 August 2002. Available from http://archive.supermarketguru.com.

"New Online Marketplace Created by BoutiqueWineCellar.com." *Internet Business News,* 15 March 2007.

Obra, Joan. "Boutique Wineries Are Offering More to Sample Than Just Wines: Industry Uncorks Many Events." *Fresno Bee,* 26 August 2008.

"Online Wine Sales Grew 29% Last Year: Survey." *Direct,* 29 April 2010.

Phillips, Dennis, and Chloe Mathieu. "What Is Boutique Wine?" 17 March 2010. Available from: http://www.eatboutique.com.

"Top Wines, a New Online Wine Store to Buy Boutique Wine at Competitive Price." *PRWeb Newswire,* 3 November 2009.

"US: Boutique Winemaking Partnership Formed." just-drinks.com, 10 March 2006.

"U.S. Wine Consumption Continues to Grow." *PR Newswire,* 14 September 2009.

"U.S. Wine Consumption Maintains Growth Trend." *PR Newswire,* 5 August 2010.

"U.S. Wine Consumption Still Climbing with No End in Sight." *PR Newswire,* 22 August 2008.

"US Wine Market Forecast to 2012—New Market Report Published; New Report Provides Detailed Analysis of the Food and Drink Market." *OfficialSpin,* 4 August 2010.

"US Wine Sales to Jump 13% through 2013." *M2 Presswire,* 11 May 2010.

"Wines, Brandy, and Brandy Spirits." *Encyclopedia of American Industries.* Farmington Hills, MI: Gale Group, 2009.

BUSINESS CONTINUITY AND DISASTER RECOVERY PLANNING

INDUSTRY SNAPSHOT

According to the Association of Contingency Planners, "Business continuity planning should be an integral part of every business . . . Every business should plan for how it would continue to operate in the face of interruption from a variety of natural or manmade hazards." However, surveys continue to show that many companies do not have a business continuity plan, despite a plethora of natural disasters and other unforeseen events that should serve as warnings.

Natural disasters, acts of terrorism, and other unfortunate happenings have threatened cities, towns, and commercial markets throughout history. Devastating fires in cities such as Chicago spurred growth in the vital records preservation industry during the early twentieth century, and companies began storing important documents in fireproof safes and vaults. Insurance policies also offered some protection against catastrophic loss. For many years,

businesses were content to simply deal with disasters if and when they occurred, with little or no resources devoted to proactive planning.

In time, the storage and transmission of data became critical to the continuation of commercial and financial markets. The terms *business continuity/disaster recovery* and *emergency preparedness* emerged as public and private organizations began devoting resources to ensuring their survival in the wake of potential catastrophes.

In *Total Contingency Planning for Disasters,* author Kenneth N. Myers wrote: "The primary function of business insurance is to provide a hedge against loss or damage. A disaster recovery and business continuation plan, however, has three objectives: (1) prevent disasters from happening, (2) provide an organized response to a disaster situation, and (3) ensure business continuity until normal business operations can be resumed."

Business continuity and disaster recovery planning has now emerged as its own industry. Serving the companies in need of such services were hundreds of consultants and service providers of all sizes, as well as government agencies and nonprofit organizations. The industry's growth was supported by heightened concerns over terrorism and other disasters in the wake of the terrorist attacks on September 11, 2001, a massive blackout that affected the eastern United States and portions of Canada on August 14, 2003, and the U.S. military presence in Iraq and Afghanistan. Other disasters included Hurricane Katrina, one of the deadliest hurricanes in American history, which decimated the city of New Orleans, Louisiana, as well as much of the north central Gulf Coast, in the summer of 2005, and the Gulf

Status of Business Continuity Management Programs

A crisis management process and plan is in place.	79.06%
A crisis communications program is in place.	73.54%
Policies and procedures are in place to interact and coordinate with external agencies in times of disaster.	64.59%
A full functioning Emergency Operations Center is in place.	50.98%
Currently developing and implementing BC and/or IT DR plans that meet the needs of the organization.	49.72%
Off-site data recovery only.	8.80%
There are no business continuity and/or IT disaster recovery plans in place.	1.97%

SOURCE: International Business Continuity Program, *Management Benchmark Report.*

of Mexico BP oil spill of 2010, which put thousands of companies out of business for the better of three months (some forever).

ORGANIZATION AND STRUCTURE

Climate The business continuity and disaster recovery planning industry's emergence and growth can be attributed directly to the environment of unprecedented risk that existed in the early twenty-first century. U.S. organizations of every type and size faced premeditated human acts such as arson, sabotage, embezzlement, fraud, terrorist attacks involving chemical and biological weapons, theft, and vandalism. Environmental risks included everything from explosions, hazardous materials spills, broken water mains, labor strikes, and civil uprisings to power outages and transportation-related accidents involving airplanes, trucks, automobiles, and trains. These risks were in addition to a host of natural threats, such as earthquakes, wildfires, floods, hurricanes, and tornadoes.

Organizations Within this uncertain environment, U.S. organizations without sound business continuity strategies had much to lose. In addition to critical assets such as buildings, equipment, telecommunications systems, network infrastructures, and human resources, paper and digital assets also were at risk. These included multiple kinds of strategic, operational, and vendor data ranging from contracts, deeds, check ledgers, and credit applications to customer lists, employee files, invoices, legal documents, and titles.

In order to mitigate risks and ensure the continuance of operations, U.S. organizations employed a number of different tactics. Many companies simply relied on business insurance policies to cover potential losses. However, more progressive firms engaged in formal business continuity planning that addressed three principal areas. First was the aspect of disaster preparedness, which involved an organization's ongoing efforts to ensure readiness in the

event of a disaster. Second was disaster response, which pertained specifically to a company's critical actions in the immediate wake of a disaster. Finally, disaster recovery encompassed the procedures required for maintaining or restoring operations.

The process of developing a business continuity plan varies from company to company, depending on an organization's size and focus, the industry in which it operates, available financial resources, and so on. It may involve completing a simple questionnaire, in the case of a smaller company, or involve several teams of staff and consultants in larger enterprises. In any case, the process often begins with some form of a risk assessment, whereby major vulnerabilities are identified in such key areas as telecommunications, computer networks, physical infrastructure, and equipment.

At some point, major business continuity goals and objectives are established. Virtually all organizational plans will share at least a few similar goals and objectives. These include preventing potential disasters, containing disasters that do occur, ensuring staff and customer safety, protecting assets, preserving data through backup systems or network redundancy, identifying the exact manner in which the organization will respond during a disaster and how resources will be utilized, and minimizing or preventing disruptions to market share and cash flow. Beyond these, organizations may identify other goals and objectives that are specific to their enterprise or industry.

After goals and objectives have been identified, a period of information gathering often occurs, as key staff members or departments provide input regarding how their respective areas can preserve operations and continue to function in the event of a disaster. Once this critical information has been compiled, the business continuity plan is formulated. Following this, businesses must ensure that all employees are aware of the plan's existence and familiar with its contents. This is especially true of staff at the management level who may be required to fulfill a leadership role during a disaster. As part of their business continuity and disaster planning efforts, some organizations engage in regular disaster drills to familiarize staff with all elements of the plan.

Consultants Consultants play a critical role assisting businesses of every type and size to engage in business continuity planning. In addition to a very big number of independent consultants and small consulting firms, virtually every large consulting enterprise was involved in business continuity planning by the early 2000s.

In addition to traditional business consultants, some consultants specialized exclusively in the business continuity and disaster planning arena. As the U.S. Department of Labor's *Occupational Outlook Handbook* explains: "These consultants provide assistance on every aspect of security, from protecting against computer viruses to reinforcing buildings against bomb blasts. Logistics consulting firms also are finding opportunities helping clients secure their supply chain against interruptions that might arise from terrorist acts, such as the disruption of shipping or railroad facilities. As security concerns grow, rising insurance costs, as well as the threat of lawsuits, are providing added incentives for businesses to protect the welfare of their employees."

Product and Service Providers Beyond traditional consulting players such as Ernst & Young, many of the largest global technology and telecommunications firms offered business continuity services ranging from consulting to services for protecting and preserving data networks and digital assets. These included the likes of AT&T Inc., Hewlett-Packard Co., International Business Machines Corp. (IBM), and Electronic Data Systems Corp (EDS). They were joined by a vast array of small, medium, and large firms offering everything from business continuity plan software to safety products such as disaster kits and fire extinguishers.

Government Agencies A number of different government agencies play important roles in preventing and dealing with disasters. For example, low interest disaster loans are provided by the U.S. Small Business Administration. However, the U.S. Department of Homeland Security (DHS) arguably has the largest responsibility of any government agency. DHS carries out much of its emergency preparedness and emergency management efforts through the independent Federal Emergency Management Agency (FEMA), which became part of DHS in 2003. In addition to management of the U.S. Fire Administration, FEMA is responsible for administering the National Flood Insurance Program, providing training to those who first respond to emergencies, and initiating proactive emergency mitigation activities.

FEMA had more than 2,600 full-time employees stationed across the United States as of 2006, as well as some 4,000 disaster assistance workers who were on standby in the event of an emergency. According to FEMA, its mission is "to lead the effort to prepare the nation for all hazards and effectively manage federal response and recovery efforts following any national incident." One important resource that FEMA offered to the business sector was its *Emergency Management Guide for Business & Industry,* which it developed and distributed with support from a large number of industry trade groups and corporations, including the American Red Cross, the American Insurance Association, Building Owners and Managers Association International, the National Association of Manufacturers, and the National Emergency Management Association.

Described by FEMA as a "step-by-step approach to emergency planning, response and recovery for companies of all sizes," the guide was divided into four main sections. Section 1 walked organizations through the disaster planning process. Section 2 discussed operations-related emergency management issues, including administration and logistics, communications, and property protection. Section 3 provided details on common hazards ranging from fires and hazardous material spills to tornadoes and technological emergencies. Section 4 gave readers a listing of additional resources, including further reading materials, and even brochures in a ready-to-print format.

Although FEMA focused specifically on emergency management issues, other government agencies also impacted the work of business continuity and disaster recovery professionals through various regulations and/or publications that often pertained to the financial sector. One example is the "Interagency Paper on Sound Practices to Strengthen the Resilience of the U.S. Financial System" issued by the U.S. Securities and Exchange Commission (SEC), the Board of Governors of the Federal Reserve System, and the Office of the Comptroller of the Currency. According to the SEC, "The paper identifies three new business continuity objectives that have special importance in the post-September 11 risk environment for all financial firms. The paper also identifies four sound practices to ensure the resilience of the U.S. financial system, which focus on minimizing the immediate systemic effects of a wide-scale disruption on critical financial markets."

In addition to IRS regulations regarding the retention of tax records, the financial sector also was called on to comply with regulations from other regulatory bodies. These included the National Association of Securities Dealers, the New York Stock Exchange, and the Federal Deposit Insurance Corp.

Another example of government-mandated business continuity requirements involved the Federal Energy Regulatory Commission (FERC). In 2002 the FERC set forth standards specific to the protection and maintenance of the nation's power grid. In essence, the standards required energy players to have security plans in place to protect the grid and the larger energy market from accidental or intentionally harmful acts.

According to the FERC, "Wholesale electric grid operations are highly interdependent, and a failure of one part of the generation, transmission or grid management system can compromise the reliable operation of a major portion of the regional grid. Similarly, the wholesale electric market, as a network of economic transactions and interdependencies, relies on the continuing reliable operation of not only physical grid resources, but also the operational infrastructure of monitoring, dispatch, and market software and systems. Because of this mutual vulnerability and interdependence, it is necessary to safeguard the electric grid and market resources and systems by establishing minimum standards for all market participants, to assure that a lack of security for one resource does not compromise security and risk grid and market failure for the market or grid as a whole."

Government regulations regarding business continuity and disaster recovery also existed for other industry sectors including healthcare, consumer product manufacturing, and transportation. The *USA PATRIOT Act of 2001,* formerly titled *Uniting and Strengthening America by Providing Appropriate Tools Required to Intercept and Obstruct Terrorism* (Public Law 107-56), also included a section devoted to protecting the nation's critical infrastructures.

Associations Located in the Minneapolis-St. Paul area, the nonprofit Business Continuity Planners Association (BCPA) is a mutual benefit association for professionals in the business continuity field. According to the BCPA, its mission is "to provide a professional and educational environment for the exchange of experience, dissemination of information, professional growth, and for added value of mutual interest to the membership." The BCPA indicates that its members are involved or interested in initiatives related to business recovery, contingency planning, crisis management, disaster preparedness planning, or emergency management. In addition to seasonal luncheons, the BCPA hosts regular monthly meetings for members that include expert presentations and panel discussions on a variety of topics.

Another nonprofit trade association within the business continuity industry is the Association of Contingency Planners (ACP). Incorporated in California, the ACP serves local and regional members through various chapters across the United States. The association's purpose is "to provide an environment for the exchange of experiences and information. This includes identification of common planning needs and potential recovery response solutions as well as networking opportunities through local and national alliances." The ACP's roots stretch back to 1983, when it began as an informal professional group. Within two years, the ACP had submitted its articles of incorporation and was on the road to becoming an international organization.

Headquartered in Falls Church, Virginia, DRI International (DRII) was another leading industry organization during the early 2000s. Known as the Disaster Recovery Institute International when it was formed in 1988, DRII serves to "promote a base of common knowledge for the business continuity planning/disaster recovery industry through education, assistance, and publication of the standard resource base; certify qualified individuals in the

discipline; and promote the credibility and professionalism of certified individuals. DRII sets standards that provide the minimum acceptable level of measurable knowledge, thus providing a baseline for levels of knowledge and capabilities." DRII's important contributions to the profession include the establishment of an international standard in 1997 known as Professional Practices for Business Continuity Planners. In addition to publishing its quarterly *DRI International* newsletter, DRII hosted an annual meeting and conference.

BACKGROUND AND DEVELOPMENT

Natural disasters have presented great risks to mankind throughout human history. For example, the Virginia settlement of Jamestown was devastated by a hurricane in 1667, and 8,000 people died when a hurricane hit Galveston, Texas, in September of 1900 in what some have called the nation's deadliest natural disaster. During the early years of the twentieth century, fires wreaked havoc on major cities such as Chicago, San Francisco, and Baltimore. This effectively gave birth to the vital records preservation industry, as businesses sought to preserve important documents and records with fireproof safes and vaults.

Beyond natural disasters, the United States also has experienced its share of terrorist attacks. One event in particular revealed the need for disaster preparedness within the financial sector. On September 16, 1920, anarchists bombed 23 Wall Street in New York, then home to the venerable financial powerhouse J.P. Morgan & Co. The attack killed and wounded many people and shattered windows in a zone that spanned a half mile. In the September 20, 2001, issue of *TheStreet,* financial journalist Daniel Gross summarized the tragedy, explaining: "Wall Street ran red with blood . . . Thirty people were killed instantly: messengers, stenographers, clerks and brokers. Thomas Joyce, the chief Morgan clerk, died at his desk. Three hundred more were injured, among them Junius Morgan, Jack Morgan's son."

Describing New York's quick response to this tragedy, Gross said: "A bell rang out on the floor of the exchange, which halted trading—the first time trading had ever been halted by violence. Within minutes, 1,700 New York City policemen and 75 Red Cross nurses, many of them World War I veterans, rushed to the scene by horse, car, subway and foot. Troops from the 22nd Infantry, garrisoned on Governor's Island, marched through Lower Manhattan, rifles and bayonets at the ready. Mayor John Hylan rushed from his office to supervise. A 17-year-old office boy, James Saul, loaded injured people into a car that he commandeered, and he ferried more than 30 casualties to Broad Street Hospital. Order was quickly restored, as bodies were laid out on the sidewalk and covered with white sheets. Undaunted by the unprecedented act, the NYSE governors met at 3:30 p.m. and decided to open for business the next morning."

As the century progressed, a growing amount of attention was paid to the issue of disaster recovery. Insurance policies offered some protection against catastrophic loss. However, for many years, businesses were perfectly content to deal with disasters if and when they happened and little or no resources were devoted to proactive planning. As the business world became more complex, so did plans to mitigate risks and survive disasters.

By the 1980s business continuity planning had emerged as a standard practice within the banking industry. In addition, the issue was receiving more attention from members of the business and academic communities. This was evident by the establishment of the Disaster Recovery Institute International (DRII) in 1988. DRII evolved from the efforts of professionals—including members of Washington University in St. Louis—who foresaw the need for business continuity education, research, and professional certification.

The first attack on the World Trade Center in 1993, followed by the unprecedented attacks of September 11, 2001, only supported the case for increased levels of disaster recovery and business continuity planning. The 2001 attacks dealt a strong blow to world financial markets. For example, they caused the first multi-day shutdown of the New York Stock Exchange since President John F. Kennedy was assassinated in 1963, as well as closure of the NASDAQ, the bond and equity markets, and scores of companies. The loss of human life, economic productivity, and business information was astronomical.

Amidst the chaos of September 11, 2001, some companies with established disaster recovery plans were able to minimize their losses and resume operations quickly. These included Fiduciary Trust Co. International, which had established a plan some 14 years before amidst concerns over power outages. Responsible for the management of $44 billion in securities for endowments and pensions, Fiduciary's preparedness enabled it to restore minimal functionality the day after the attacks. In fact, by week's end the company had signed a 15-year lease on new office space.

By mid-2004 discussions regarding the business world's level of preparedness for disasters continued among government officials, industry players, and the news media. Although estimates varied, it seemed clear that a greater level of business continuity planning was needed.

According to the New York-based Business Network of Emergency Resources Inc. (BNet), although most businesses were cognizant of the importance of having a disaster recovery plan, many had yet to develop one by

the middle of the twenty-first century's first decade. BNet reported that most companies devoted a mere 3 percent of their budget to the aspect of business recovery planning. In addition, the network revealed that of those companies that experience a significant loss of data, more than 90 percent close their doors within five years.

The level of preparedness among small and medium-sized businesses during the early 2000s also left much room for improvement. This was a concern for several reasons. Although smaller enterprises did not have the same amount of assets at stake as large corporations, they existed in greater numbers. In addition, small and medium-sized businesses were more vulnerable to disasters because all of their assets were often located at only one or two sites. The August 2003 issue of *Best's Review* reported results of a Hartford Financial Services Group survey, which suggested that disaster planning increased with a company's size. According to the study, of those companies with 51 to 500 workers, 62 percent had disaster plans in place, compared to 50 percent of companies with 21 to 50 workers and 30 percent of operations employing three to 20 people. The study also revealed that in the absence of a plan, 40 to 50 percent of businesses affected by disasters do not recover.

Businesses of every size were put to the test on August 14, 2003, when a massive power blackout affected portions of the Midwest, Northeast, and parts of Canada, including that nation's capital in Ottawa, Ontario, and Toronto. Following the blackout, which lasted more than one day, some experts said that while companies did a good job of preventing data loss, the same was not true of business processes.

In its March 15, 2004, issue, *National Underwriter Property & Casualty-Risk & Benefits Management* reported the results of a study that revealed the blackout's impact. Issued by Strongsville, Ohio-based consulting firm Mirifex Systems LLC, the study found that of 142 survey respondents, approximately 66 percent lost at least one day's worth of business because of the blackout and 25 percent lost at least two days. In terms of hourly downtime costs, 22 percent of respondents placed this figure at $50,000 or more. Surprisingly, more than half of those surveyed said they did not plan to increase investment in disaster recovery or business continuity planning.

Business continuity planning became more visible on the corporate radar screen in the wake of unfortunate natural disasters (Hurricanes Katrina, Rita, and Wilma) that hit the Mississippi-Louisiana Gulf Coast region of the United States during the summer of 2005. With damage estimates ranging as high as $75 billion, Hurricane Katrina is recognized as the costliest hurricane in U.S. history. In addition to the financial costs, at least 1,336 people were estimated to have lost their lives, and many more were injured. The economic impact of the

2005 hurricane season was felt worldwide, as oil refineries were damaged or destroyed and the operations of many businesses were interrupted.

These natural disasters highlighted how critical good planning and coordination are during times of crisis. In addition to role of government at the local, state, and federal level, other agencies played a key role in responding to the 2005 hurricane season. For example, the American Red Cross provided assistance through the efforts of 233,760 relief workers, opened 1,196 shelters, and served 34 million meals. Financial assistance was given to 3.7 million people. Donations for Hurricanes Katrina, Rita, and Wilma alone totaled $2.07 billion. Efforts such as these are critical for restoring order and dealing with matters of public health and safety.

Following Hurricane Katrina, many businesses were able to restore operations thanks to existing business continuity and disaster recovery plans. However, the sheer magnitude of the disaster caused problems for which even the best laid plans were not prepared. These include the long-term lack of fuel, power, communications, mail service, and reliable transportation.

In 2006 banking regulators were advising businesses to prepare for a possible global bird flu pandemic. In May, President George W. Bush issued a 227-page plan to contend with such an outbreak, which could kill as many as 2 million U.S. citizens. Issues such as these prompted businesses to consider as many contingencies as possible.

A survey by Symantec Corp. in 2007 showed that although 91 percent of IT (information technology) organizations worldwide carry out full scenario testing of their disaster recovery plans, 50 percent of those plans fail. In addition, of the companies that did have disaster plans, almost half of them had had to deploy them at some point. The same study found the most feared consequences of disasters among IT professionals were negative impact on customer loyalty, harm to their company's brand and reputation, damage to their standing in the market, and loss of company information. Another study, conducted by the EDUCAUSE Center for Applied Research, also found that half of the educational institutions surveyed had used their emergency response plans in the past five years. Lack of funding was reported as the primary barrier to disaster planning.

The latter half of the first decade of the 2000s provided many examples of why businesses need disaster recovery plans. The number of tornadoes in the first quarter of 2008 exceeded the previous four-year average. Research company A.M. Best found that losses of $1 billion and more from single tornadoes and related severe storms were becoming more frequent. Although hurricanes and earthquakes historically have tended to generate higher losses per event,

in 2007 tornadoes and related storms accounted for 67 percent of total insured catastrophe losses.

The storm known as the Super Tuesday Tornado Outbreak in the mid-South on February 5 and 6 resulted in damages of $850 million; damages from a tornado that struck Atlanta on March 14 were estimated at $340 million. Tornadoes causing extensive damage hit almost every part of the nation in early 2008, including Oklahoma, Kansas, Colorado, North and South Carolina, Mississippi, Alabama, Iowa, Oregon, and others. In June 2008 heavy rains caused massive flooding in Indiana, Wisconsin, and Iowa, with damages in the latter state, including crop damage, estimated at more than $4 billion. Wildfires also swept across the southwest; as of May 2007, 21,000 wildland fires had broken out, burning more than 1.3 million acres, twice the 2001–2008 average.

The unusual number of weather disasters gave some companies the opportunity to prove the value of disaster response plans. For example, telecommunications giant Qualcomm Inc. and MiraCosta Community College both reported on the success of their plans in reaction to the October 2007 wildfires in the San Diego area that caused $1.1 billion in damages and the displacement of 500,000 people. According to Lyn Hall of Qualcomm, the most important aspects of their plan were establishment of an emergency operations center and an employee communication plan, as well as an automated alert system.

According to some reports, continuity planning evolved in 2007 and 2008, moving from a focus on infrastructure and IT to one focused on employees. The human element became a more pressing issue in disaster response plans. Alexander Tabb of the Tabb Group, a strategy and planning firm for financial groups, told *U.S. Banker,* "We all understand technology; we all understand backup and recovery. To deal with the human psyche and all the elements that go along with that is much more challenging." The article went on to say that "understanding how employees might react and having plans and technology in place for communicating with them, is crucial in the early hours of a crisis."

Other experts concur. In a 2008 *Business Wire* interview, Amir Moussavian, president and CEO of MIR3, a provider of intelligent notification systems, said: "Instant, two-way communication with employees and administration can be the difference between success and failure when it comes to execution of a business continuity or disaster recovery plan." Equipping employees with the devices and technology they need to work from another site also was an important consideration.

CURRENT CONDITIONS

In May 2010 AT&T published the results of a study it conducted involving companies with annual revenues of more than $10 million and international operations. According to the results, 83 percent of businesses surveyed indicated that they had a business continuity plan in place, up 14 percent since 2005. Gulf Coast companies were more likely to have their plans tested in the past year, compared to other regions, given the susceptibility to hurricanes and floods (and the 2010 BP Gulf of Mexico oil spill).

The survey also found that 63 percent of companies had included wireless network capabilities as part of their plan, and 77 percent included the use of mobile devices. About 50 percent had virtualized their computing infrastructure, and 40 percent required outside suppliers or vendors to have BCPs in place as a criterion for doing business with them. Another key finding was that three out of four executives expressed concern about the increased usage of social networking capabilities and mobile networks/devices, and their potential impact in the way of security threats. Seventy percent indicated they would be investing in new technologies during 2010.

In 2010 the Business Continuity Institute had 5,000 members, hailing from 2,500 organizations in 90 countries. The Institute conducted an online survey between November 20, 2009, and January 14, 2010, to assess the perceived and actual substantive benefits that BCM programs were bringing to the organizations that had implemented them. Ninety-four percent of selected respondents (220) said their organizations had experienced some level of disruption in the preceding 12 months. The top five events were swine flu, IT and/or telecom disruption, adverse weather, lack of energy supply, and computer virus/cyber attacks.

Respondents indicated that the key advantages to having the BCMs were "reduced impact of incidents" and "faster recovery from incidents," and 82 percent agreed that the plans mitigated the effects of the disruptions. Most companies claimed that they were implementing BCM two to five times annually for a variety of events/incidents. Interestingly, some BCM programs now consider industry or market events in their applications.

Another (more comprehensive) study was published in July 2009 by Business Continuity Management Inc. Although it was intended as an international benchmark study, 71 percent of respondents represented U.S. companies. Among U.S. respondents, the average business continuity management budget (approximate or estimated expenditures) was $3.9 million. Average dedicated full-time employees numbered 15 and there were 45 part-time employees. More than 79 percent of international respondents indicated they had a crisis management process and plan in place, and 73 percent had a crisis communication program in place. Sixty-four percent indicated they had policies and procedures in place to enable interaction and coordination with external agencies in times of a disaster. About half indicated they had a fully functioning emergency operations center in place. Less than 2 percent stated there were no business continuity and/or IT disaster recovery plans in place, and about 8 percent indicated they had off-site data recovery only.

INDUSTRY LEADERS

Preparis A relative newcomer, Atlanta, Georgia-based Preparis was formed in 2007 to enable organizations to better withstand crisis situations. It provides expert information, training, certification, and emergency communications tools delivered through online platforms accessible from both desktop and mobile devices. The company hoped to offer more accessible replacement material than earlier competitors, who published binders of BCM information that customers would leave on bookshelves or in cars. In just three years the company grew from a personal investment of $100,000 plus credit card debts to a seven-figure-revenues success. In September 2009 it closed a $4.6 million Series A led by Fulcrum Ventures.

SunGard Data Systems Inc. Based in Wayne, Pennsylvania, SunGard Data Systems Inc. is a leading provider of processing solutions and integrated software. The company is a major player in the business continuity and disaster recovery industry. With approximately 16,600 employees, SunGard served more than 25,000 clients in 50 countries, mainly in the financial services industry. The company's systems process approximately 70 percent of NASDAQ trade orders and account for approximately $15 trillion in investment assets. As SunGard explains, "Wherever financial assets are managed, traded, processed or accounted for, SunGard offers a software or processing solution." Although SunGard specializes in the financial sector and counts the world's 50 largest financial service firms among its client base, it also serves the education and public sectors.

SunGard provides business continuity services via its Availability Services division to roughly 10,000 clients throughout Europe and North America, offering everything from availability engineering services and availability planning software to business continuity planning, continuity program management, end-user recovery, hosting infrastructure, information security services, and IT (information technology) outsourcing.

According to SunGard, it has written 5,000 business continuity plans, performed 100,000 simulated continuity tests, and achieved a recovery rate of 100 percent during 1,500 recoveries. Of those U.S. companies with revenues exceeding $1 million, more than 90 percent are located within a 35-mile radius of a SunGard facility.

International Business Machines Corp. Armonk, New York-based International Business Machines Corp. (IBM) was another leading player within the business continuity and disaster recovery market. The company's IBM Crisis Management Services unit offered consultants and technology to help companies manage disasters and other emergency situations.

With experience in a wide range of disasters, including earthquakes, fires, floods, and the Oklahoma City bombing, IBM's business continuity consulting team helped companies to develop total business continuity programs that were based on sound security and risk management principles. This involved the integration of a crisis management plan, IT recovery plan, and emergency response plans with an organization's overall strategies. In addition, attention was devoted to communications with local, state, and federal authorities.

IBM's related services included a Subscription Retainer Service that provided on-call access to an IBM Crisis Response Team during emergencies, as well as a Disaster Management Service that offered on-site analysis; recovery coordination efforts including employee, customer, government, and media relations; and site relocation. The service also offered site recovery expertise specific to water, smoke, chemical, and fire damage, as well as document salvage and mechanical, structural, and electrical systems. IBM even helped clients to acquire replacement equipment ranging from generators, emergency supplies, and telephones to computer hardware and peripherals.

In June of 2004 IBM acquired London-based Schlumberger Business Continuity Services, which operated 40 recovery sites worldwide for leading multinational corporations, government agencies, and the financial community. This included Europe's largest business recovery site. As part of the deal, IBM added 260 employees from Schlumberger.

AT&T Inc. San Antonio, Texas-based AT&T Inc. also offered a range of business continuity and disaster recovery services. The company's AT&T Business Continuity Professional Services unit offers services such as business impact analysis and risk assessment; disaster recovery and business continuity consulting; and business continuity program management.

Beyond the services it made available to other businesses, AT&T's own disaster recovery infrastructure—upon which it relied to ensure that the United States maintained critical telecommunications service—was especially impressive. In the event that a disaster compromised or destroyed one of the company's own central offices, AT&T developed the Network Disaster Recovery (NDR) program. According to AT&T, the NDR program's three main goals are to "route noninvolved communications traffic around an affected area, give the affected area communications access to the rest of the world, and recover the communications service to a normal condition as quickly as possible through restoration and repair."

The NDR program involves a team of approximately 90 specially trained AT&T technicians, engineers, and management personnel who are on standby in the event of an emergency. At their disposal during the mid-2000s was a massive, 100-piece mobile recovery fleet that could be deployed to any U.S. location within two hours. The fleet, which was utilized during the September 11, 2001, terrorist attacks on the World Trade Center in New York, includes custom trailers containing all of the equipment needed to restore communications to an affected area. The NDR team participates in drills on a regular basis to ensure its readiness for a wide range of disasters, including blizzards, earthquakes, explosions, floods, forest fires, hurricanes, mudslides, and tornadoes.

Other Industry Leaders Leading consultancies, especially those in the IT sector, also play a dominant role in the business continuity and disaster recovery industry. One example is Stamford, Connecticut-based Gartner Inc., whose services included executive risk assessments, business impact analysis, IT recovery strategy development, IT disaster recovery planning, and business continuity planning. Another leading player was Plano, Texas-based Electronic Data Systems Corp., which operated an Emergency Management Services Practice. Traditional business consultancies such as New York-based Ernst & Young L.L.P. also offered business continuity and disaster recovery advisement for their clients. The business continuity and disaster recovery industry also is served by a vast array of independent consultants, as well as numerous product and service providers.

WORKFORCE

Although business continuity efforts cross virtually all organizational lines and usually involve everyone from low-level workers up to the CEO, some companies employ professional safety engineers whose responsibilities range from occupational health and safety initiatives to disaster and emergency preparedness planning.

In addition to safety engineers, some organizations employ emergency management specialists who, according to the U.S. Department of Labor's *Occupational Outlook Handbook,* "coordinate disaster response or crisis management activities, provide disaster preparedness training, and prepare emergency plans and procedures for natural (e.g., hurricanes, floods, earthquakes), wartime, or technological (e.g., nuclear power plant emergencies, hazardous materials spills) disasters or hostage situations." This profession was expected to grow faster than average through 2014.

Those interested in pursuing careers in business continuity, disaster planning, or emergency management had many academic programs to choose from. According to *Disaster Resource Guide,* programs were offered by more than 30 institutions throughout the United States, including community colleges and leading universities. Of these, 11 institutions offered individual certificate programs, 18 offered certificate programs in which courses were offered as part of a concentration of study or minor, nine offered associate's degree programs, 10 offered bachelor's degrees, and 12 had post-graduate programs.

AMERICA AND THE WORLD

Business continuity and disaster preparedness planning are not unique to the United States. Indeed, these issues are even more pressing for companies operating in areas such as the Middle East, where the likelihood of violence and terrorist attacks was much higher. Heading into the late 2000s, the global nature of the economy was prompting more attention to the impact that a disaster in one part of the globe could have elsewhere. One prime example was the impact a potential bird flu outbreak, natural disaster, major industrial accident, or terrorist attack in Asia would have on China's manufacturing and shipping operations, and the devastating economic effects that would stem from a disruption of the global supply chain. For this reason, in June of 2006 China's legislature was in the process of discussing an emergency management bill that would address the country's response to these and other serious situations.

According to BC Management Inc. in its 2009 benchmark report of the international community, the countries whose companies were dedicating the largest budgets to BCM were the United States, Canada, Japan, the United Kingdom, Singapore, Australia, and Brazil. Of noted interest were the comparatively low budgets dedicated by Chinese companies.

RESEARCH AND TECHNOLOGY

In 1997, a federal, state, and private sector study called the Joint Loss Reduction Partnership (JLRP) was conducted to study the needs of businesses following disasters. The study revealed that better communications were needed between government and private enterprise. In addition, it was determined that businesses were very concerned about the ability to access their facilities as soon as safety permitted. Behind this concern was a need to recover everything from "vaulted assets," including cash, checks, securities, and stock certificates, to valuable documents, records, and equipment.

From the results of this research, the nonprofit Business Network of Emergency Resources Inc. (BNet) was established to further partnerships and solutions between the private and public sectors in the area of crisis and emergency management. The network's main focus is to help businesses resume operations as quickly as possible following disaster-related interruptions in order to minimize or prevent any negative economic impact. As BNet explains, "The coordination of business and government in emergency management efforts on a region wide basis will make a significant difference between major economic losses and rapid economic recovery for business, industry and other organizations."

BNet allows businesses in the New York area to tap into resources beyond their individual emergency response and disaster mitigation plans and access a regional and statewide business continuity communications program. In support of the needs identified by the JLRP, as soon as BNet was formed, it sought to improve workplace access for businesses that were involved in emergency events. This led to the development of the Corporate Emergency Access System (CEAS), which assists member organizations to communicate with public sector officials, regain entry to restricted sites with the approval of local authorities, and more. CEAS was implemented in Buffalo, New York, in 2001, and a pilot program was implemented in New York City several years later.

BIBLIOGRAPHY
"About DRI International." DRI International, 20 June 2008. Available from http://drii.org/displaycommon.cfm?an=1.

Allen, Mike. "A Plan for a Pandemic." *Time,* 15 May 2006.

"A.M. Best Special Report: Tornado Losses Approach Those of Hurricanes." *Business Wire,* 11 April 2008.

"AT&T Study: U.S. Businesses Improving Continuity Planning," *PR Newswire,* 28 May 2010. Available from http://www.prnewswire.com.

"BCP 101." Association of Contingency Planners, 20 June 2008. Available from http://www.acp-international.com.

Booth Thomas, Cathy. "You're On Your Own." *Time,* 29 May 2006.

"Climate of 2008." National Climatic Data Center, 13 June 2008.

Cole, Jim. "Pandemic Risk: Banks' Perspective Taking Shape." *American Banker,* 17 May 2006.

"Companies Exposed from Inadequate Disaster Recovery Planning, Testing." *Internet Wire,* 16 October 2007.

Devitt, Caitlin, and Yvette Shields. "Midwesterners Assess Flood Damage: Bush to Approve $2B Relief Funding." *The Bond Buyer,* 19 June 2008.

"Educational Institutions." *Disaster Resource Guide,* 20 June 2008. Available from http://www.disaster-resource.com/content_page/edu_train.shtml.

"Enterprises Urged to Address Business Continuity and Disaster Recovery Plans." *Business Wire,* 15 May 2008.

"Executives Focus on Business Continuity Management." *Executive's Tax & Management Report,* June 2006.

Federal Emergency Management Agency. *Emergency Management Guide For Business & Industry,* 18 May 2006. Available from http://www.fema.gov/business/guide/index.shtm.

Golden, Cynthia, and Diana G. Oblinger. "The Myth about Business Continuity and Disaster Recovery." *EDUCAUSE Review,* May/June 2007.

Goodchild, Joan. "Business Continuity Planning Still on the Upswing." *Network World,* 3 June 2010.

Hobson, Katherine. "Are We Ready?" *U.S. News & World Report,* 1 May 2006.

"Human Risk Is Neglected in Disaster Plans, Warns Study." *Computer Weekly,* 13 November 2007.

Hunt, Kristin Gunderson. "Wildfires Put Disaster Recovery Plans to the Test." *Business Insurance,* 5 May 2008.

"IBHS President Places Priority on Preventing Losses in Keynote Address." Institute for Business and Home Safety, 5 May 2008. Available from http://www.disastersafety.org/newsroom.

"International Business Continuity Program Management Benchmarking Report." BC Management Inc., July 2009. Available from: http://www.bcmanagement.com.

O'Marah, Kevin. "The Real Disaster: Inadequate Preparation; Globalization's Growing Impact Means Disruptions in One Place Are Felt Far and Wide. Few Companies Make Adequate Preparations." *Business Week Online,* 21 June 2006. Available from www.businessweek.com.

O'Mitra, Sramana. "Deal Radar 2010: Preparis," 26 April 2010. Available from http://www.sramanamitra.com/2010/04/26/deal-radar-2010-preparis.

"Organizations Spending More on Disaster Preparedness." *Access Control & Security Systems Integration,* 9 May 2006.

Sausner, Rebecca. "Disaster Planning: Plans Focus on Employees Instead of Infrastructure." *U.S. Banker,* May 2007.

"Study Finds One in Five Businesses Lacks Continuity Plan." *Access Control & Security Systems Integration,* 3 June 2008.

"The Business Case for BCM." Caversham, United Kingdom: The Business Continuity Institute, 2010 Available from: http://www.thebci.org.

"URGENT: China Mulls Emergency Management Law." *Xinhua News Agency,* 23 June 2006.

U.S. Department of Labor, Bureau of Labor Statistics. *Occupational Outlook Handbook, 2008–09,* December 2007. Available from http://bls.gov.

"What Is the BCPA?" St. Paul, MN: Business Continuity Planners Association, 20 June 2008. Available from http://www.bcpa.org.

CALL CENTERS

———■———

SIC CODE(S)

7389

INDUSTRY SNAPSHOT

The experience is familiar to most: you call a company to inquire about your latest bill and you are routed through a series of push button options before you speak to a customer service representative with the inside scoop on your account. This represents call centers in action. The 2008 and 2009 economic downturn apparently did not quell contact center growth. Despite market threats of nearshoring and offshoring—whereby operations are moved to countries with less expensive labor and operating costs—for more and more companies, call centers were positioned as the hub of all customer service operations. The list of services provided via call centers also continued to expand. Used by banks, airlines, health care operations, telemarketers, retailers, catalog companies, industrial firms, and a host of other industries, call centers remain the most used medium of contact between companies and customers. According to one estimate, there were over 10,000 Emergency call centers (answering and routing 911 emergency calls) operating in the United States in 2009. Roughly 5 percent of Gross Domestic Product (GDP) transactions in the United States are routed through call centers.

While lower labor costs of offshore centers continue to attract companies looking for ways to survive a tight economy, there are tempering factors in force. The CFI Group's "2009 Contact Center Satisfaction Index" noted that survey respondents who had called a contact center and believed they had reached an offshore call center were three times more likely to defect as customers.

Conversely, if they believed they had reached a domestic call center, they were twice as likely to recommend the company or organization (serviced by the call center) to others. Another survey concluded that handling a customer call in an offshore center took 25 to 35 percent longer than one handled at a U.S. call center, and first-call resolution was 20 to 30 percent lower (and abandonment rates 5 to 10 percent higher) in offshore centers. These statistics shed some light on the true cost of lower labor in offshore centers.

ORGANIZATION AND STRUCTURE

Call centers typically are highly automated telephone systems that customers call with a service or billing question, purchase request, or some other inquiry, depending on the nature of the company. Conversely, many firms also use their call centers to place calls to customers, including those with regular accounts and those targeted as potential new business. In a way, call centers are indicative of the never-ending race to squeeze costs and boost the volume of business. More broadly, however, call centers serve as a central buffer between the company and the public, filtering questions and requests so as to free other workers to concentrate on their particular areas.

Most indicators for measuring call center performance included the amount of time devoted to the average call, the number of calls each agent handled, and so on. In this way, the emphasis tended to rely far more on quantity than on quality. The logic goes that by squeezing the average time per call and expanding the number of calls per agent, the company will reap higher benefits from its call center. Many analysts were seriously challenging that logic, however, noting that it betrays an outlook on call centers from a cost-centered rather than revenue-centered perspective. Instead, such critics contended that the call center could be more fruitfully utilized as a creative new business strategy that aimed to generate increased revenue through enhanced quality and expansion of available services, not to mention promoting new sales.

Indeed, a growing number of companies were beginning to catch on to that possibility. About one-third of call centers surveyed by Ernst & Young in 1999 planned to devote more resources to gearing their call centers toward customer access and sales opportunities rather than simply handling customer service inquiries. Nevertheless, by the middle of the first decade of the 2000s some industry players stressed the need to measure more meaningful aspects of call center performance, such as contribution to an organization's revenue, value, or profit.

BACKGROUND AND DEVELOPMENT

The call center as a major component of the U.S. business environment had its genesis in the mid and late 1980s during the massive downsizing and corporate restructuring trends. In part, call centers offered firms undergoing such transformation a cost-effective way to process a greater number of customer services and requests, since a large number of employees could be accommodated in a small office space, thus cutting down on overhead. As call centers moved ever closer to the mainstream, customers came to expect the quick access and convenience they offered, though call centers certainly generated their share of complaints related to the long periods customers spent on hold, a reputation that centers were far from shaking off by 2000.

By the late 1990s, the call center market was growing about 40 percent each year, though within that surging growth, assessments were mixed. Ernst & Young LLP conducted a survey in 1999 comparing call centers by industries and found, unsurprisingly, that banking companies and health care operations housed the most sophisticated and successful call centers. The varying nature of industries, however, ensured that call centers were more easily integrated into some industries than into others. For example, the study found that utilities were among the least successful industries in the application of call centers. In large part, this was due to the large amount of information, such as service schedules and payment histories, that must be verified and processed before utilities customers could be provided with information.

The American Bankers Association conducted a study in 2000 of call centers in the banking industry, which found that nearly a quarter of all U.S. banks considered their call centers to be top of the line. A mere 14 percent of those banks surveyed, however, considered the call center a source of profit in itself, and, perhaps as a result, a majority of banks failed to allocate the resources necessary to adequately train call center managers or keep tabs on customer satisfaction with call centers.

Banking call centers were relied upon to handle a range of products and services, including general account information and maintenance, mortgages, credit cards, and home equity lines of credit. One of the banking industry's most pressing problems with call centers is that they are famously troublesome to integrate into the strict data-handling environments that banks rely on. Moreover, call centers were generally viewed by banks as extra to or outside of their normal operations, and as a result, few were reaping the types of benefits proponents claimed were waiting to be realized.

The managed health care industry was another hotbed for call centers. One of the central features of demand management among health maintenance organizations (HMOs) was the nurse call center, versions of which were used by more than half of all HMOs to reduce costs and boost efficiency. Nurse call centers provide customers with 24-hour access to health professionals. Many industry analysts, however, felt that nurse call centers, too, fell short of their potential, even though customers reported satisfaction rates exceeding 90 percent, and despite the fact that HMOs typically figured that call centers drastically reduced both emergency room and physician visits. Critics held that HMOs had done too little to promote nurse call centers to make them a regular recipient of patient requests. Still, the HMO industry remained confident in the utility of call centers, noting that some 30 to 40 percent of all physician visits were in fact unnecessary and positioning call centers as a potential remedy for that problem.

The rise of Internet technology has significantly impacted call center services, altering how call centers interact with customers as well as widening the range of services that a call center can provide. The dramatic rise in business conducted over the Internet in the late 1990s and early 2000s eventually spawned the development of Web-enabled call centers, which offer consumers both telephone and online service. Many businesses have connected their call centers to their Web sites to provide more immediate customer service options to Internet surfers. In particular, banking firms were among those most likely to integrate their call centers with their Web sites as the online financial market burgeoned.

Online technology allowed for call center enhancements such as instant chat, which allows online customers instantaneous access to a service representative via a text-based communications program. Some Web-enabled call centers also began offering an Internet call-back service that allowed customers to submit a real time request online if they wished to have a customer service representative call them via telephone momentarily. Although it is less immediate, Web-based call center services also typically offer e-mail as a communication medium.

Online businesses began using Web-enabled call centers after watching potential customers abandon their purchases before completing a transaction due to the limited availability of service online. In some cases, although the answer to a question about a product or service was prominently located on a company's Web site, customers still chose to abandon the purchase rather than sift through information. Many businesses believed that offering advanced call center services on their Web sites could help to turn these lost sales into profits. As stated in the April 2001 issue of *Informationweek.com,* "The ability of Web-enabled call centers to enhance customer service and to close sales more quickly isn't only appealing, it can be crucial to the bottom line. Call center agents who use e-mail, instant chat, and Web collaboration to interact with customers are able to more quickly and completely handle questions and resolve problems." Forrester Research predicted that Web sites and e-mail would each account for more than 17 percent of a typical company's communication with customers by the end of 2002.

In 2000, the cost for developing an integrated call center was roughly $4,500 per agent, not including integration and implementation expenses. Because this was well beyond the financial reach of many small companies, technology firms targeting small and mid-sized businesses began to develop less expensive options. In 2001 Qwest Communications and AT&T Corp. both began working to develop network-based call centers that would allow small businesses to tie into an existing call center network, eliminating the need to purchase new equipment. Via this type of structure, calls that come in to a networked call center, either by telephone or by a link from a company's Web site, are first sent to a network server and then routed to a specific call center that can handle the request. In 2002, call center technology specialist Rockwell introduced FirstPoint Business Edition, a Web-enabled call center solution for small and medium-sized businesses, at a price of $1,625 per agent.

Research and analysis company Gartner Group forecast that small and medium-sized business would account for roughly 88 percent of the call center marketplace by 2005. As a result, technology firms were expected to continue developing new call center services designed specifically for smaller enterprises.

By early 2005, the practice of relocating call center services to foreign markets with lower labor and operational costs, known as offshoring or nearshoring, was having a significant impact on the call center industry. As more companies relocated operations, the number of call centers

based in the United States began to fall. By 2008 the research firm Datamonitor forecast U.S. call centers would decline from 50,600 to 47,500, largely because of offshoring.

Offshoring has become necessary for many organizations to remain competitive, and the practice has resulted in significant cost savings. Nevertheless, it is far from being a silver bullet. Indeed, the practice has its own set of challenges, and some call center clients have been disappointed with their decision to move operations offshore. Cultural differences are a major roadblock in the call center offshoring game. According to a study conducted by TMC Research, summarized in the January 2003 issue of *Customer Interaction Solutions,* 62 percent of potential teleservices customers were concerned about offshoring. Leading the list of concerns were call center agents with foreign accents (18 percent), management/setup/training costs (15 percent), inexperience on the part of outsourcers (14 percent), global turmoil (13 percent), loss of campaign control (12 percent), and a lack of familiarity with the practice of offshoring (9 percent).

Consistent with previous trends, call centers continued to concentrate more on customer relationship management functions. In fact, beginning in the early 2000s the industry's focus began to shift away from customer acquisition and more toward customer retention. This was furthered by federal do-not-call laws that allowed consumers to evade telemarketers by placing their name on a centralized Do Not Call List. This shift was especially evident within the banking industry, where institutions began to up-sell and cross-sell financial products and services to existing high-value customers.

According to the research firm Datamonitor, during the first decade of the 2000s, the United States was home to 50,600 call centers. However, in the wake of nearshoring and call center and agent totals were expected to fall off in later years. Other factors contributing to this decline included the federal government's Do Not Call List, which severely impacted the telemarketing industry by allowing consumers to remove their phone numbers from call lists, and call center technologies that continued to automate interactions with customers.

By 2007, one significant emerging trend was "homeshoring," or the use of home-based call center staff—sometimes as an alternative to offshoring. A number of leading companies—including Sears Holdings, J. Crew, Office Depot, Victoria's Secret, and Wyndham Hotels—were discovering that the use of freelance, home-based call center staff had numerous advantages. One major plus was the fact that freelance staff often supplied their own computers, telephone equipment, office space, and Internet connections. In addition, the approach was an effective way to tap talented workers from a larger geographic area who simply need more flexible schedules, such as stay-at-home mothers, college students, and disabled individuals.

According to the January 2007 issue of *HRMagazine,* homeshoring can result in technology and property savings of up to 80 percent over offshoring, based on figures from The Telework Coalition's Senior Vice President Jack Heacock. Citing figures from the research firm Gartner, the publication explained that 70 to 80 percent of home-based call center staff hold college degrees. This stands in comparison to 30 to 40 percent of workers at physical call centers. The research firm IDC Corp., which reportedly coined the term homeshoring, forecasts that the number of home-based call center staff will grow from 112,000 in 2007 to more than 300,000 by 2010, "all but replacing the offshore call center trend of the past 10 years," as reported by Martha Frase-Blunt of *HRMagazine.*

CURRENT CONDITIONS

The National Association of Call Centers (NACC), which publishes quarterly reports on the status of the industry, noted in early 2009 that in the fourth quarter of 2008, more call center jobs were lost in the United States than were gained. This was the first time for such an occurrence since the data was first collected in 2005. The report identified the U.S. recession as the leading causative factor, but noted that some industry sectors, such as medical services, showed a net positive growth.

The flattened or downturned trend did not last long. By mid-2009, a new report by CB Richard Ellis (CBRE)'s Labor Analytics Group showed significant net gains in American call center employment in the first five months of 2009, resulting in 17,000 additional jobs. A particularly pronounced spike occurred in June and July 2009. The growth rate was also 45 percent greater than it was for the same period last year. Overall, during the 12-month period ending May 2009, the U.S. contact center industry added approximately 29,331 jobs, more than doubling the level from the 12-month growth through May 2008, which netted only 14,126 jobs. At the same time, the U.S. captured approximately 43 percent of all new worldwide contact center jobs.

According to a July 2009 industry article by Malcolm Carlaw, some of the growth in call center business was attributable to the Census Bureau, which hired 4,925 people to support the 2010 census. While these jobs do not represent permanent industry growth, they will last at least a few years as the Census Bureau collects data and then responds to questions from the public. Interestingly, 250 of these jobs were created overseas to count Americans living in other countries. The Telecommunications industry added 1,880 employees, likely to support iPhones technology. The Financial Services industry added 2,330 new jobs, despite the 2008-2009 banking sector crash.

Another rising trend in 2009 was the growth of home-based customer service. In July 2009, *Executive Insights*

published an article for businesses to prepare an at-home service model in the event of a swine flu pandemic. Even without such a possibility, home-based call center services were seen as cost-effective in light of rising gasoline prices and the fact that most agents use their own computers. As customers demanded rapid response, 24/7, to their queries or concerns, round-the-clock home-based agents could address these issues.

In October 2009, an IBISWorld Industry Report combining telemarketing and call centers valued the overall industry at $18.5 billion for 2008. It predicted that this industry would continue to face some tough competition from overseas. The industry's former strong growth could be affected as companies move their operations from the United States to India and China. The report also identified Convergys, Applica Inc., and TeleTech Holdings as industry leaders.

AMERICA AND THE WORLD

Offshoring remained a key business practice in the call center industry during the late 2000s. By many accounts, India remained the leading market for call center outsourcing at this time. Other key markets were the Philippines, Latin/South America, the Caribbean, Europe, China, and Canada. The Philippines, in particular, was fast becoming a hot market for offshore call center operations, especially the city of Manila. The BPO/call center industry in the Philippines expected to create 130,000 jobs in 2009. Part of this growth was due to the November 2008 announcement by Citibank that it planned to expand its Philippines BPO operations and hire 1,000 more workers in the Philippines in 2009.

In May 2009, Sitel and TeleTech opening 2,000 call-center seats in The Philippines, followed by Medtronics with a 1,400 seat center in San Antonio, Texas. In auto industry depressed Detroit, General Warranty Services opened the fourth largest center worldwide with a 1,000-seat facility in Detroit. Egypt was the location of the fifth largest new contact center: a 700 seat center in Cairo opened by Stream Global Services.

Offsetting these new or expanded offshore centers was the rise in reports of poor customer service in offshore centers. While it remains hard to track the number of companies moving their call centers back to the United States, it was widely reported in 2009 that both United Airlines and Delta were moving several call center jobs in India back to U.S. soil. Additionally, AT&T moved 5,000 jobs back to centers in North Carolina, Louisiana, Alabama, Florida, and Kentucky.

A relatively new player in the call center outsourcing game, China was fast becoming an ideal location for U.S. and international firms. By 2005 China's economy continued to boom, supporting the need for customer service and support centers. In April 2004, *Telecom Asia* cited the results of a study from Frost & Sullivan that indicated consumer durable goods were driving immediate growth in Chinese call centers, but that emerging telecommunications and financial industries would spur growth in subsequent years. By locating call centers in China, companies were able to support customers in locations such as Taiwan and Hong Kong, which were home to Chinese-speaking peoples. Japanese companies also found value in China, because Chinese cities such as Dailan were home to Japanese-speaking residents.

During the late 1990s and early 2000s, many U.S. firms looked to European markets to establish their call center operations. Frost & Sullivan, a business and consulting firm that offers market analysis and research services, predicted that the number of European call centers with at least 11 agents would soar from 12,750 in 1999 to nearly 28,300 in 2006, and that the portion of those centers that are Web-enabled would skyrocket from one percent to 80 percent. Largely due to favorable tax conditions, Holland contained the highest concentration of call centers in Europe. Major U.S. firms, such as Adobe, Apple, Cisco Systems, Hewlett-Packard, IBM, Microsoft, and many others, have established major call centers in Holland. Other factors contributing to Holland's strong presence in the international call center market were its advanced telecommunications infrastructure and a relatively strong labor pool for such operations. The United Kingdom was also experiencing rapid growth in its call center market.

RESEARCH AND TECHNOLOGY

In his 2009 industry report for the National Association of Call Centers, David Butler noted that Internet Protocol (IP) continued to make inroads, with 43 percent of 2008 respondents currently using the technology in their contact centers. Butler noted that the greatest usage ws in centers configured with 75 or fewer agent seats. His report also noted the steady growth in 2008 of Workforce Optimization, defined as a group of products designed to optimize agent performance with such tools as e-learning and quality monitoring of productivity.

The National Association of Call Centers, in its 2009 report, indicated that the "Millennial generation" of call center employees (who will replace Baby Boomer employees) will demand Web 2.0 services, along with the growing use of UC (unified communications), to service their customers.

A technology called "presence" was very much on the call center industry's radar screen. Although call center workers have long had the ability to see what other staff are available to accept different types of calls, presence technology takes this concept further by extending it to

an entire enterprise, in theory making it possible for any employee (not just call center staff) to visually see what staff members within a company are available to accept calls and serve as information resources during a call. The key challenge, according to industry experts, is to get staff to make themselves available and participate in the system.

Call center software packages were growing in sophistication. This was especially true of quality assurance applications. In addition to monitoring call center agent performance, one application enabled management to view the impact that certain types of calls had on the larger organization. This was possible by tracking customer calls that were transferred to multiple agents within the call center, providing a more global view of how certain situations were handled. In addition to a higher degree of sophistication, quality assurance applications also were becoming more affordable, so that smaller companies were able to take advantage of software tools that at one time were only within the reach of larger call center operations.

Related technologies include auto dialers and predictive dialers. Auto dialers simply relieve the representative of having to actually dial the phone, saving valuable seconds that add up to hours after a few hundred calls. Predictive dialers anticipate the representative's next call; thus, when the agent hangs up with one customer, the predictive dialer automatically moves to the next person on the list and the call can be waiting for the representative as soon as the first call is completed.

BIBLIOGRAPHY

Barnard, Patrick. "The Advantages of SaaS-based Call Center Solutions, Part 1." TMCNet, 16 October 2009. Available from http://www.tmcnet.com/channels/call-center/articles/66842-advantages-saas-based-call-center-solutions-part-1.htm.

"BPO Industry and Call Centers in Asia—2009. " Available from http://aprgsso.wordpress.com/.

Butler, David. "North American Contact Center Industry 2008-2009: The Year in Review and a Look Ahead." National Association of Call Centers, 2009.

———. "State of the Call Center Industry Report: 4th Quarter 2008 Data." National Association of Call Centers, 2009. Available from http://www.nationalcallcenters.org/pubs/SOIR/.

Carlaw, Malcolm. "Good News for the Call Center Training Industry!" *Impact Learning,* July 2009.

"China's New Engine for Growth—Call Center Outsourcing." *TelecomWeb News Digest,* 1 March 2004.

"Circle of Winners—Our 2004 Products of the Year Award-Winners Represent the Most Innovative and Useful Products that the Call Center Industry Has to Offer." *Call Center,* 1 March 2004.

Frase-Blunt, Martha. "Call Centers Come Home: Using Home-Based Call Center Workers Can Offer Employers Significant Financial and HR Advantages over Offshoring." *HRMagazine,* January 2007.

Goolsby, Kathleen. "Enabled Offshored Call Centers to Move Back on Shore." *Outsourcing Journal,* September 2009.

Greenlees, Donald. "Filipinos Are Taking More Calls in Outsourcing Boom." *The New York Times,* 24 November 2006.

Guerrero, David. "The World: Insider's View—The Philippines." *Campaign,* 6 October 2006.

Magee, Thomas David. "How Well Are the 911 Call Centers in the United States?" Associated Content, 28 October 2009. Available from http://www.associatedcontent.com/article/2316148/how_well_are_the_911_call_centers_in.html.

"New Engine of Growth in China." *Telecom Asia,* April 2004.

"Protect Your Business Against a Pandemic with the At-Home Service Model." *Executive Insights,* July 2009.

Read, Brendan B. "Contact Center Employment Growing: CB Richard Ellis." *Call Center,* 24 July 2009. Available from http://www.tmcnet.com/channels/call-center-hiring/articles/60643-contact-center-employment-growing-cb-richard-ellis.htm.

———. "Stay in the USA?-The Best Place for Your Call Center May Be in Your Backyard. Here's Why, and Where to Locate." *Call Center,* 1 July 2004.

Sablosky, Tanja Lian. "'Hello!' 'This Is Your Call Center. I'm Evolving Into a More Dynamic Channel for Banks to Interact with Their Customers.' If Your Call Center Could Ring You Up, That Is Probably What It Would Say." *Bank Marketing,* October 2004.

Stockford, Paul. "Contact Center 2007: Exciting, Electrifying, Innovative, Thrilling, Exhilarating ... Not.—Will This New Year Bring Revolutionary Changes in the Industry? The Outlook Is Trending Against That Scenario." *Call Center,* 1 January 2007.

"Study: Offshore Costs Vary Widely; The Movement of Customer Care Services Offshore Will Continue Unabated Due To Labor Arbitrage." *CommWeb,* 8 November 2004.

Tehrani, Nadji. "The Next 25 Years in CRM and Call Centers." *Customer Interaction Solutions,* July 2006.

———. "The State of the Industry: Time to Look at the Crystal Ball (Publisher's Outlook)." *Customer Interaction Solutions,* January 2003.

Telemarketing and Call Centers Industry Report, IBISWorld Industry Reports, October 24, 2009. Available from http://www.ibisworld.com/.

"The Vanishing American Call Center; One Research Group Thinks That There Will Be At Least 3,000 Fewer Call Centers in the US By 2008. And Not Just Because of Offshore Outsourcing." *CommWeb,* 21 September 2004.

Wallace, Bob. "The Modern Call Center." Informationweek, 9 April 2001. Available from http://www.informationweek.com/832/call.htm.

CHARTER SCHOOLS

—■—

SIC CODE(S)

8211

8299

INDUSTRY SNAPSHOT

While charter schools continue to enjoy growth in enrollments, the future of the industry remains uncertain. The topic generates heated arguments from proponents and critics alike, from the grassroots level to the halls of Congress. In the short term, their growth is all but certain as more states adopt legislation to grant charters to organizations wishing to establish an educational alternative, but the ability of charter schools to deliver superior educational results and to spur competitive innovation among mainstream public schools remains undetermined. Assessments of the industry to date have been highly mixed.

Although publicly funded, charter schools are free from many of the restrictions that govern other public schools. In exchange for such autonomy, a charter school agrees to abide by the terms regulating its operations as set forth in a contract or "charter" between the school and the authority that sponsors it—either the local school board, the state, or a public university. If the charter school fails in its obligations, its charter may be revoked and the school closed down. Charter schools must be tuition-free and nonsectarian and observe open admissions policies. Most charter schools are run by parent or educational groups, but several for-profit companies have become involved in this arena as "education management organizations," hoping to mimic the success of health maintenance organizations in the health care industry.

Advocates promote charter schools as a welcome remedy to what they see as the excessive bureaucracy and stifling regulatory atmosphere in the failing public school system that hinders educational creativity. A more competitive, market-oriented climate would, according to proponents, foster innovation and efficiency in moribund public schools. Detractors counter that the independence of charter schools paves the way for plummeting accountability, financial mismanagement, and diminishing educational standards, jeopardizing children's right to a decent education.

ORGANIZATION AND STRUCTURE

As of 2009, 40 states, the District of Columbia, and Puerto Rico had passed legislation permitting charter schools. Despite charter schools operating in the majority of states, charter school enrollments still accounts for a very small fraction (2 percent or less) of all public school students. However, according to the National Alliance for Public Charter Schools, in 2009, charter schools enrolled more than one in five public school students in 14 major metropolitan communities, including Detroit, St. Louis, and Kansas City.

There is no federal law creating public charter schools. Each state determines its own set of regulations stipulating how a charter school may be organized, receive funding, and assess its students' performance. Charter schools may be newly created institutions or existing public or private schools that have converted to charter status. In addition, some states allow charters to hire only state-accredited teachers while other states are more lax about qualifications. Some proposed schools must win support in their local communities, while others are not so required; and some states allow only public schools or public school personnel to set up such schools. Others place a cap on the maximum number of charter schools in the state. All of these differences make it hard to determine an overall financial analysis for this field.

Perhaps one of the most important yet least clear aspects of charter schools is how they receive their funding. Some districts give charter schools 100 percent of the per-pupil funding that the other public schools receive, while others allot only a portion of that amount. In addition, charters may or may not be eligible for or permitted to receive monies for special education students or other entitlement programs. Minnesota totally funds its charter schools while Louisiana state-approved charter schools do not receive any district funding.

Most charter schools are relatively small, with a median enrollment of 137 students, compared to 475 for public schools overall. Thus, start-up capital has been one of the greatest problems facing such schools. The "typical" charter is also mission-driven. Beyond that, drawing generalizations about charters becomes difficult. Successful charters enjoy a high degree of parental and community involvement in their ongoing operations. According to the U.S. Department of Education, three-fifths of charter schools enroll a higher percentage of non-white students than the regular public schools, but fewer special needs students than public schools overall. Charters also possess a slightly lower student-to-teacher ratio than other public schools—16 to 1 versus 17.2 to 1. Finally, charters include a larger grade span than public schools.

Many charter schools have found a niche serving at-risk students, those students who often fall through the cracks in a traditional school setting. Charter schools can be more responsive to these students because the schools have greater flexibility and can accommodate individual student needs. According to the U.S. Department of Education, one-fourth of all new charters are created to target a distinct student population. Conversion schools often find that receiving a state charter provides additional financial resources. Notably, however, education management organizations (EMOs) frequently steer away from special needs students since they cost more to educate than other students.

BACKGROUND AND DEVELOPMENT

In 1988, politicians as well as some private citizens started calling for more "choice" in public education in the form of vouchers, waivers, and alternative schools. In 1991, Minnesota passed legislation allowing the formation of charter schools and numerous other states soon followed. According to the North Central Regional Educational Laboratory—part of a national network of 10 private non-profit educational laboratories funded by the U.S. Department of Education to provide research and development, technical assistance, and training to education,

government, community agencies, business and labor—over 50 percent have been set up in Arizona, California, Michigan, and the District of Columbia, all places with "strong" charter laws.

Support for charter schools has come from diverse sources. Reasons for supporting charters range from a desire for public school options to a belief that such competition will strengthen all public schools. Proponents also hope that since they are free of bureaucratic strictures, these schools will initiate reforms not possible at other public schools and that education will improve because these schools are held accountable for student performance.

Critics are just as vocal and diverse. They argue that charter schools will destroy standard public education, are too limited in scope, and do not serve children with special needs. In addition, critics believe that charter schools are not adequately accountable for financial viability and students' academic improvement since they do not face the same scrutiny as public schools.

By 1992 private education management companies were eyeing the charter school field. That year, the Baltimore Board of Education signed an agreement with Education Alternatives, Inc. (EAI) to run nine of the district's schools for a five-year period. In just three short years, however, the board ended its relationship with EAI, citing continued antagonism between EAI and the Baltimore teachers union and EAI's failure to disclose financial information to the Baltimore City Council. Student scores had also not shown the improvement originally anticipated. In fact, EAI admitted to having inflated student test scores. In 1995, EAI also contracted to run all of the 52 schools in the Hartford, Connecticut school district, but the deal was canceled a few months later.

Even the Edison Project, started in 1991 by Chris Whittle of Whittle Communications, found that it would have to rein in its originally ambitious plans. Whittle initially proclaimed he would set up 1,000 schools within a few years of launching his operation. By the 2000-2001 academic year, the Edison Project, now known as Edison Schools, Inc., was operating only about 80 public charter schools nationwide.

In the late 1990s it remained unclear if charter schools would prosper in more affluent areas where good public school systems were already in place. While charter schools in the city of Chicago had waiting lists, the outlying suburban areas were less enthusiastic about the charter concept. For example, Jefferson Charter School in the northwest suburbs of Chicago faced an uphill battle since organizers announced their intentions to create the school. Despite opposition from the local Elk Grove Township Elementary District 59, Jefferson School finally received its charter from the state of Illinois after three years of legal wrangling. When Jefferson School finally opened enrollment for the

1999–2000 school year, however, the response was lukewarm. During two days of advance registration in January 1999, 50 students signed up, far short of the 96 needed to satisfy state requirements, and much less than the 220 that Jefferson School officials had hoped for.

In 1998, according to the Reason Public Policy Institute and John M. McLaughlin, head of the Education Industry Group (EIG), charter schools had become the fastest growing portion of the approximately $310 billion spent annually on public kindergarten through 12th grade education. EIG reported that only about 10 percent of these charter schools are managed by larger private companies intent on making a profit from running them.

Several major foundations assisted charter schools in the 1990s. Donald and Doris Fisher, founders of Gap, Inc., pledged $25 million to help San Francisco schools bring in The Edison Project, while A. Alfred Taubman, chairman of Sotheby's, put up $680 million to launch his own for-profit charter school management company, the Leona Group. Moreover, Walton family members offered $350,000 of their Wal-Mart fortune to promote charter schools. Manufacturer J. C. Huizenga bankrolled the National Heritage Academies, a for-profit education management firm that runs Michigan charters that stress moral values along with academics in their curricula.

Companies were also looking at other ways to fund and support these schools. For example, Charter School USA's CEO John Hage has launched what he termed the "second generation" of charter schools and depends on his clients to pay for school buildings. Thus, Ryder System Inc. financed the construction of a charter school across from its headquarters in Florida. In exchange, children of Ryder employees will be given first chance at the spaces in the new school. Such an arrangement, however, would not work in the many states that, unlike Florida, prohibit preferential access to charter enrollments.

Charter schools have received some strong criticism from teachers and other educational organizations. The American Federation of Teachers (AFT) concluded in a 2002 study that the majority of charter schools spent more money on administration and less on instruction than traditional public schools. The study also indicated that student performance in charters showed no improvement over student performance in public schools and that charter schools tend to be markedly less diverse than public schools. However, the Charter Schools Development Center released a 2003 study that demonstrated higher Academic Performance Index scores (708, compared to the public school average of 689) by students attending California-based charter schools that had been in operation for five years or longer. According to United Press International, "Similar surveys in Michigan, Minnesota, and other states suggest that charter schools are holding

their own, if not out-performing the rest of the public school system. These average score results are all the more impressive if we consider that in many cases, charters are taking in kids that the public schools don't seem to be able to educate."

According to many analysts, sweeping assessments of charter school effectiveness were premature and most preliminary findings highly mixed because charters hadn't been operating long enough to generate meaningful assessment data. However, the pressure brought down on mainstream public schools by charter school competition seems to have spurred some change. For example, the Toledo school district declined an offer from Edison to run a local charter, opting instead to set up the Grove Patterson Academy charter school under its own auspices with help from the Toledo Federation of Teachers. The kindergarten through fourth grade, 220-student school provides early instruction in foreign languages, home computers for the students, and boasts a waiting list of about 400. Research conducted by Berkeley education graduate student Eric Rofes on the impact of competition from charters in 25 school districts in eight states and Washington, D.C., discovered that the presence of charters had led half these districts to institute moderate to substantial changes in attempts to retain student enrollments and hence, educational funds. Rofes's conclusions were reinforced by findings of similar studies undertaken by researchers at Western Michigan University, James Madison University, and for the Pioneer Institute. The latter study of 10 Massachusetts districts revealed that it took the loss of 2 to 3 percent of the student population to galvanize traditional public schools to imitate charter schools' educational strategies to staunch the outflow of students.

Sometimes institutions that provide much needed services for at-risk children can find themselves at risk. According to the Center for Education Reform, by the end of 2002, 194 of the 2,874 charter schools founded in the United States since 1991, roughly 6.7 percent, had closed. In some cases, the reasons for closure were simply financial. In other cases, a failure to meet academic standards prompted a school to shutter operations. Mismanagement was also the culprit at some failed charter schools. In response to closures, which in many cases proved more harmful to students than to anyone else, some states began establishing a more stringent qualification process for applicants. For example, the Charter School Resource Center of Texas only approved two out of 44 charter school applicants in 2002.

The success of a charter school program dubbed the Knowledge is Power Program (KIPP) began gaining attention. When nearly all of the students enrolled in the KIPP program began to pass standardized tests, KIPP schools began to secure additional financing. Students enrolled in a KIPP school attend classes for 10 hours a day, as well as every other Saturday and in the summer. Equipped with cell phones, teachers are available to students any time they need assistance. KIPP planed to open another 19 schools in 2004, bringing its total to 38. As stated in a March 2003 issue of *Newsweek,* "Education reformers say KIPP represents the second wave of charter schools."

Beyond funding-related challenges, a number of obstacles challenged charter startups during the middle of the first decade of the 2000s. Little advance lead time to get up and running, uneven cash flow even when funds are available, and frequent opposition from local school boards and teachers unions hamper efforts to implement often experimental curricula and upgrade substandard facilities. In the May 2004 issue of *World & I,* Myron Lieberman criticized many charter schools for lacking innovation, which he attributed to a conservative mindset in many schools that emphasized a "back to basics" classroom approach.

Although conclusive research regarding the effectiveness or ineffectiveness of charter schools had yet to be published, some states were losing patience with charter schools that failed to meet state standards. In Texas, Education Commissioner Shirley Neeley began imposing stricter requirements on the schools and threatened to close schools that consistently produced low scores on state exams. This came in the wake of rapid charter school growth in the Lone Star state. In Massachusetts, opponents have resorted to intense public relations campaigns to impact public opinion of charter schools in the city of Cambridge. In addition, opponents in some communities have filed lawsuits against the Massachusetts Board of Education in an attempt to stop new charter schools from opening. Finally, the Ohio Congress of Parents and Teachers filed a motion with their state's Supreme Court asking it to hear their case challenging the constitutionality of Ohio's charter school program.

The absence of comprehensive accountability guidelines in many state charter laws has long injected uncertainty for charter school personnel into the process of determining exactly what information and how much of it should be tracked and disclosed. In order to assist school boards, nonprofit groups, universities, and other organizations involved with the authorization of charter school programs, the Alexandria, Virginia-based National Association of Charter School Authorizers issued a voluntary set of standards in 2004. Entitled Principles and Standards for Quality Charter School Authorizing, the standards addressed such issues as application process design and oversight, contract negotiation, school evaluation and oversight, and decision-making regarding contract renewal.

The debate over the effectiveness of charter schools raged on. In a July 10, 2007, *Washington Post* online article,

Jay Mathews summarized a new book entitled *Charter Schools: Hope or Hype* by Jack Buckley and Mark Schneider. A detailed analysis of charter schools in Washington, D.C., Mathews described the book as "one of the deepest and most even-handed examinations of charter schools I have ever read," and explained that it was a good reflection of what was happening nationally.

In the article, Mathews explained that Buckley and Schneider "reach some conclusions that sound like they are on the anti-charter side. They find that although parent satisfaction with D.C. charter schools is at first higher than parent satisfaction with regular D.C. public schools, that level of charter satisfaction declines over time to something close to the regular public school level.

"But they also point out that their conclusion is the result of complex extrapolation of their data. They concede there is merit on the other side of the argument, and indicate what further research is necessary. They also reveal that charter schools do a better job than regular schools in promoting citizenship and point out some particular charter schools that, they say, are 'doing wonderful things.'"

Setbacks Beyond schools that failed to meet academic standards, districts across the country also faced situations involving mismanagement and ethical dilemmas. The Philadelphia School District was forced to take action against the Raising Horizons Quest Charter School when auditors "found inadequate bookkeeping, inaccurate enrollment data, a shortage of certified teachers, and a staff where a third of employees were related to the founder," according to the December 11, 2006, issue of the *Philadelphia Inquirer.*

In California, problems occurred on a larger scale at California Charter Academy—which served some 10,000 students on 60 campuses and at one time was the state's largest network of charter schools. In 2007 Charles Steven Cox, the organization's founder, was charged with stealing approximately $5.5 million and 100 counts of misappropriating school funds, which were alleged to have been used to purchase luxury items such as concert tickets and spa services.

Funding Funding is crucial for charter schools, and funding shortfalls continued to challenge many programs during the middle to late years of the first decade of the 2000s. The U.S. Department of Education acknowledged that one of the most difficult tasks facing proponents of charter schools was raising the needed capital. Some schools became extremely innovative with ways to cut initial start-up costs by holding classes in churches, local YMCA facilities, and other spaces, including—in the case of Cesar Chavez Public Charter School in Washington, D.C.—a few rented rooms in a shopping mall basement. In addition to federal support, several states, including Louisiana,

Minnesota, Pennsylvania, and Ohio, have allocated either low or no-interest loans for charters. To minimize operating expenses, charters often contract with outside vendors to supply food and transportation services or forego them altogether.

Innovation Nevertheless, heading late into the first decade of the 2000s, charter schools continued to offer innovative approaches to education. One example was the Pennsylvania Distance Learning Electronic Academy (PDELA). A publicly-funded charter school for K-12 (kindergarten through 12th grade) students, PDELA had 680 students throughout the state in late 2006, according to *Government Video*. The program, which included virtual classroom experiences, was an alternative instruction option that was especially targeted at highly motivated students who were easily bored with traditional classroom instruction. The state provided participants with the equipment and Internet connection required for participation, as well as access to databases containing electronic articles, books, and some 10,000 online videos. In addition to field trips, students were allowed to partake in sports and music programs at their nearest public school location.

CURRENT CONDITIONS

As of 2009, 40 states, the District of Columbia, and Puerto Rico had passed legislation allowing charter schools. The ten states still without charter schools were: Alabama, Kentucky, Maine, Montana, Nebraska, North Dakota, South Dakota, Vermont, Washington, and West Virginia. That status had not changed in several years. During the 2008-2009 school year, approximately 4,700 charter schools collectively served some 1.4 million students.

In June 2009, a fairly comprehensive national assessment of charter schools (covering just 15 states and the District of Columbia, but representing 70 percent of U.S. charter school students) was released by the Center for Research on Education Outcomes (CREDO) at Stanford University. Considered the first national assessment of charter schools, the study compared state achievement test scores of charter students in reading and math with scores of their peers in regular public schools.Results showed that 37 percent of charter schools posted math scores significantly lower than what students would have shown if enrolled in local traditional public schools. Moreover, 46 percent of charter schools showed math scores statistically indistinguishable from those of their public school counterparts. The bottom line was that only 17 percent of charter schools exceeded traditional public schools in math achievement. Likewise, in reading skills, charter schools realized a growth that was less (but not statistically significant) than public schools. The study's lead author, Margaret Raymond, stated at a news conference, "This study

shows that we've got a 2-to-1 margin of bad charters to good charters."

The report came on the heels of a pledge from the Obama administration to direct nearly $5 billion of the $100 billion federal stimulus funds allocated for education to be used in encouraging charter school development (the Race to the Top Fund). In June 2009, the Center for Education Reform (CER) announced the winners in the Race to the Top for charter school growth as the District of Columbia, Minnesota, and California, the only three winning top marks for strong, rigorous charter laws. The CER's 2009 Ranking and Scorecard found that the most important factors influencing the creation of a high number of successful charter schools were independent authorizing entities, fiscal equity and operational independence.

In its *Public Charter School Dashboard: 2009 edition,* the National Alliance for Public Charter Schools reported that 62 percent of public charter school students were non-white and 48 percent qualified for free and reduced price lunch (compared with 45 percent non-white and 45 percent free and reduced price lunch in all public schools). While 56 percent of students attend public charter schools in large cities, a growing percentage of students are enrolled in them in rural areas (14 percent compared with 11 percent five years ago). Nationally, the average public charter school has been open 5.9 years. This data-laden report provides numerous statistics on each jurisdiction with public charter schools.

INDUSTRY LEADERS

In 2009, the CREDO report listed five states where charter schools had achieved significant gains in learning over their public school counterparts: Arkansas, Colorado, Illinois, Louisiana, and Missouri. According to the National Alliance for Public Charter Schools, in 2009, the largest market share of public charter school communities (including ties) were: New Orleans, LA (57 percent); Washington, D.C. (36 percent); Detroit, MI (32 percent); Kansas City, MO (29 percent); Dayton, OH (27 percent); Youngstown, OH (26 percent); St. Louis, MO (25 percent); Flint, MI (24 percent); Gary, IN (23 percent); Phoenix Union High School District, AZ (22 percent); and Minneapolis, MN (22 percent). Not only were charters in New Orleans serving a higher percentage of public school students than anywhere else in the nation, but they also were the highest performing sector of public schools in the city. More importantly, the city's public schools as a whole are outperforming the pre-Katrina system.

As for specific chartered schools, New York-based EdisonLearning, Inc., formerly Edison Schools, Inc., was founded in 1991. The largest and most widely known for-profit company involved in charter school management, Edison derives much of its recognition from its founder,

Chris Whittle, of Whittle Communications. A former owner of *Esquire* magazine, Whittle in 1989 created Channel One, an electronic news system that beams educational programming, along with commercials, into classrooms. Even though Edison did not take off as quickly as Whittle had hoped, the company has continued to expand, growing from 4 schools in 1995 to more than 137 as of 2008. Edison has invested heavily in these schools, which supply computers to their students for home use and telephones and televisions in the classrooms.

Another leading manager of charter schools was Arlington, Virginia-based Imagine Schools Inc. The company rose to a leadership position in mid-2004 when it acquired Chancellor Beacon Academies. The acquisition gave Imagine, which was founded in 2004 by multimillionaire executive Dennis Bakke and his wife Eileen, more than 70 charter schools in nine states and the District of Columbia. Collectively, these schools served some 20,000 students. Formerly known as Alternative Public Schools, Beacon Education Management LLC was formed in 1997. Beacon merged with Chancellor Academies in 2002 to become the second largest school management group in the United States, behind Edison. In 2006 Imagine became a not-for-profit enterprise. The company opened 26 schools in 2008, and revenue increased to $196 million.

Among publicly traded education management organizations (EMOs), West Chester, Pennsylvania-based Nobel Learning Communities Inc. had some 180 facilities operating in 17 states as of 2009. Its fiscal year 2009 revenues were $220.1 million, representing a 7.8 percent increase from fiscal year 2008.

BIBLIOGRAPHY

Borja, Rhea R. "Multimillionaire Buys Major Charter School Manager." *Education Week,* 9 June 2004.

Careless, James. "Pennsylvania Supports Home Schooling with Distance Learning." *Government Video,* 1 December 2006.

Center for Education Reform (CER), "The Final Ten." 1 February 2007. Available from http://www.edreform.com/_upload/CER_FinalTenCharterStates.pdf/

Center for Research on Education Outcomes (CREDO), *Multiple Choice: Charter School Performance in 16 States.* June 2009. Available from http://www.credo.stanford.edu/

Cortez, Dan. "Charter School Criticism Grows." *Detroit Free Press,* 1 April 2007.

"Ed-Biz: Charter Schools—Parent Certified." United Press International, 8 April 2003.

EdisonLearning, Inc. Available from http://www.edisonschools.com/edison-schools/about-us/

"Founder of Charter School Network Indicted." *American School & University,* 5 September 2007.

Gehring, John. "Debate Over Charter Schools Rages in Mass." *Education Week,* 26 January 2005.

"Imagine Schools charter operator, contractor in dispute over $3M." *Columbus Business Journal,* April 13, 2009. Available from http://columbus.bizjournals.com/columbus/stories/2009/04/13/story13.html

Johnston, Robert C. "Anti-Charter Group Seeks Ohio Supreme Court Ruling." *Education Week,* 20 October 2004.

Kantrowitz, Barbara. "Not Head of the Class." *Newsweek,* 30 August 2004.

Lieberman, Myron. "Charter Schools: Facts, Fictions, Future." *World & I,* May 2004.

Mathews, Jay. "An Honest Look at Charter Schools." *Washington Post,* 10 July 2007. Available from www.washingtonpost.com.

Miners, Zach. "Charter Schools Might Not Be Better." *U.S News & World Report,* 17 June 2009.

Murphy, Victoria. "Where Everyone Can Overachieve." *Forbes,* 11 October 2004.

"National Charter Schools Week, 2007." The White House, President George W. Bush, 27 April 2007. Available from http://www.whitehouse.gov.

Nobel Learning Communities, Inc., 2009. Available from http://biz.yahoo.com/e/090909/nlci10-k.html.

Olson, Lynn. "Standards for Authorizers of Charter Schools Issued." *Education Week,* 26 May 2004.

"Proclamation 7777—National Charter Schools Week, 2004." *The Federal Register,* 5 May 2004.

Radcliffe, Jennifer. "Decade of Change for Charter SchoolsL: Experts Say Spotty Success Keeps Them from Competing with Traditional System." *Houston Chronicle,* 17 December 2006.

Richard, Alan. "New Texas Policy Cracks Down on Charters." *Education Week,* 26 January 2005.

Sacchetti, Maria, and Tracy Jan. "S. Boston Charter School Faces Closure over Scores." *Boston Globe,* 16 December 2006.

Viadero, Debra. "Federal Report Examines Charter Schools." *Education Week,* 1 December 2004.

Wingert, Pat. "At the Top of the Class." *Newsweek,* 24 March 2003.

Woodall, Martha. "Overhauled Charter Still Scrutinized. The District Cleaned House after Finding a Financial and Administrative Mess. Its Audit has Gone to U.S. Authorities." *Philadelphia Inquirer,* 11 December 2006.

CHILDREN'S EDUCATIONAL FRANCHISES

SIC CODE(S)

8211

INDUSTRY SNAPSHOT

Beyond the basics of reading, writing, and arithmetic, children's education has become increasingly viewed as big business. Although for-profit educational franchises accounted for less than 10 percent of the monies spent in the United States on K-12 (kindergarten through twelfth grade) education, the franchise "education industry" continued to prosper through the tough economy of 2008 and 2009. Fueling this steady market were U.S. demographics—enrollments that were expanding and expected to outstrip even the numbers of the baby boomers in their school days. Further, the adoption of new technology in educational practice, as well as the federal No Child Left Behind (NCLB) Act's supplemental educational service provision, continued to drive spending on services such as technology integration, test preparation, educational assessment, and tutoring. By the 2008-09 school year, Eduventures, the Boston-based leader in education market research, estimated the K-12 supplier market at about $28 billion.

For-profit charter schools were among the most visible—and controversial—components of the children's educational franchise industry. Likened to health maintenance organizations, these so-called EMOs, or education management organizations, were promoted as a panacea for the ills of an ineffective and inefficient national public school system. Education is the last large segment of the economy controlled by the government, and penetration by the private sector accelerated at the twentieth century's end. Their overall effectiveness remained to be seen as the industry headed into the late years of the first decade of the twenty-first century.

Virtual schools were an emerging trend. According to a report issued by the Commercialization in Education Research Unit (CERU) at Arizona State University's Education Policy Studies Laboratory, four EMOs operated 17 virtual schools in 2003-2004, serving a combined student body of 10,500 students in 11 states. While virtual high schools in particular represented a promising industry niche, by mid-2007 they had not yet emerged as a major profit center, according to a July 2007 *Business 2.0* article. However, the January 2007 acquisition of Portland, Oregon-based Insight Schools by The Apollo Group, which owns the University of Phoenix, was a major industry development. Insight had plans to double its online high school enrollment in Oregon from 600 students in 2006-07 to 1,200 students in 2007-08. With initial plans to expand into Wisconsin and southern California, Apollo was positioned to expand the virtual high school concept.

Other industry providers specialized in delivering computers, tutoring, Internet-based curricula, textbooks, and other instructional aids to both school districts and individual parents. At-risk youth, often expelled from public schools for drug and weapons violations, formed a challenging and emerging target population for specialized educational franchises.

ORGANIZATION AND STRUCTURE

According to Eduventure's overview entitled "The Education Industry: Markets and Opportunities," the industry can be divided into three segments: schools, educational products, and educational services.

The most prominent component of the schools sector was for-profit charter schools—schools that, although publicly funded and tuition-free, can be managed by organizations that seek to generate a profit from their operation. Charter schools operate according to a charter drawn up between the school and its sponsoring organization, usually a local school board or the state. In exchange for freedom from the restrictions that govern other public schools, the charter school must live up to the terms of its charter or its administering organization could lose the contract. For-profits receive the same per-pupil allotment as public schools in a district. After operating costs are deducted from that amount, the company keeps the remainder. Though for-profit charters have been enthusiastically backed by Wall Street investors and many parent groups and school boards, profits have been somewhat elusive for industry players and the very arrangement has drawn heavy criticism, especially from teachers' organizations that argue that profit is inimical to the very idea of an equal opportunity, public education for all U.S. schoolchildren.

Some non-educational corporations also sponsor elementary and secondary public schools. For example, the American Bankers Insurance Group (ABIG) operates a "learning center" for kindergarten through second grade in Miami, Florida. Although the building belongs to ABIG and only children of its employees attend the center, the Dade County public school district provides the books, teachers, furniture, and other supplies. Florida law permits property tax exemptions for corporation-owned buildings that house such educational endeavors. Honeywell ran a similar operation in Clearwater. The Walt Disney Co.'s Celebration School in Celebration, Florida operates in tandem with the Osceola County school district.

The products sector encompasses producers of educational supplies and equipment for classroom and home use such as instructional materials developers Harcourt Education and Scholastic Corp. Heading into the late years of the first decade of the 2000s, many educational resources were marketed online. One example was Pearson plc's Family Education Network (FEN). With offices in New York City, Boston, Chicago, and Parsippany, NJ, FEN offered resources for parents (FamilyEducation.com), teachers (TeacherVision.com), and students (FEkids.com and FunBrain.com).

The services sector contains not only more traditional tutoring endeavors but also specialized providers who serve at-risk students. For example, Community Education Partners began to operate two campuses for approximately 2,000 students who required extra surveillance in the Houston school district; one opened in 1997 and one in 1998. Security and supervision are much greater than at ordinary district schools and much of the learning that occurs is self-paced, often taking place on computers. Furthermore, teachers are more likely to have backgrounds in corrections work, counseling, or communications than in education. Although all possess at least a Bachelor's degree, only about 15 percent are certified instructors.

PIONEERS IN THE FIELD

One of the leaders in the move to privatize elementary and secondary education is Christopher Whittle, the media entrepreneur who developed Channel One, a commercial educational news program intended for broadcast within school classrooms. By the early 1990s, Whittle was airing the idea of creating a company that would operate public schools and turn a profit, in somewhat the same manner as health maintenance organizations operate health care facilities. Although Whittle's initial projection of building 1,000 such schools within the first few years of operation turned out to be premature, his new venture, Edison Schools Inc. (initially The Edison Project), became the largest manager of for-profit public schools by 2000. It went public in November 1999, raising $109 million in the process. In 2000, Edison signed its first contract with a state government when it agreed to run three low-performing schools in the Baltimore school district. (See also **Charter Schools.**)

BACKGROUND AND DEVELOPMENT

The privatization of K-12 education was spurred in the late 1990s by a huge infusion of private venture capital, which quadrupled to $3.3 billion in 1999 and was projected to rise to $4 billion in 2000, according to Eduventures. Parental clamor for more school choice and changing American demographics were also behind industry development. Nonetheless, the sector's stock performance was shaky, despite the runaway success of the U.S. economy overall. Eduventures tracked an index of 30 major education stocks and reported they were down by 25 percent by December 1999. In November 1999, Edison Schools, the largest of the for-profit K-12 school operators, went public, though the stock market's response was lukewarm. Despite the less than spectacular performance of its stocks, Wall Street warmly backed the education industry. In particular, the role of the Internet and other technology applications in education had generated a new focus among investors on the education sector. Sylvan Learning Systems, for instance, sold off its testing business in 2000 to generate funds for a new Internet-related strategy, a move of which many investors took notice.

When the technology industry crashed in 2000, however, investors became increasingly leery of investing in any Internet-based venture, including those related to education. In fact, investors began scrutinizing investments of all kinds more closely. In the early years of the first decade of the 2000s, private support for charter schools began to wane. Private equity invested in education ventures of all kinds fell 73 percent to $800 million in 2001 and dropped another 67 percent to $255 million in 2002.

During this time, public funding for education remained a bit more stable. In 2001, President George W. Bush earmarked $182 million for charter schools, and in January of 2002, he requested another $150 million from Congress to be included in the fiscal year federal budget to support continued expansion of charter schools and school choice nationwide. Bush also declared the last week in April National Charter Schools Week in both 2002 and 2003.

Charter schools had emerged from the school choice movement, which was concerned with combating the problems of overcrowding and substandard achievement that characterized many of the U.S. public K-12 school facilities. For-profit charters multiplied from fewer than 100 nationwide in 1994, the first year they went into operation, to approximately 2,700 in 2003, according to The Center for Education Reform. These schools were operating in 36 states and the District of Columbia, educating about 700,000 students. Despite this rapid growth, however, charter school enrollments still accounted for only one percent of all public school students. Also, besides opposition from many teachers' groups, charter schools have had to contend with many of the same negative factors that hinder the performance of regular public schools, such as a shortage of qualified teachers and tight funds for building maintenance and classroom supplies.

At-risk students and those who have been expelled from public schools constituted a population that children's educational franchises increasingly sought to address. Many alternative for-profit schools designed to serve this population were filled to capacity and expanding to meet increasing demand as public schools failed to adequately grapple with students who had been removed from the public system for drug use or carrying weapons. Schools for troubled youth often set up in such states as Utah and Montana, whose relaxed regulatory climates and remote locations are well adapted for the purpose. No single type of institution predominates in this young industry sector and the total number of such schools in operation is unknown. Facilities range from small, independent home schooling ventures to large corporations that provide psychiatric and therapeutic services in addition to academic instruction and room and board. Complete costs can range up to $40,000 per year per pupil.

Such schools have come under scrutiny for focusing too heavily on drug rehabilitation and job training and not enough on academics. A common pedagogical practice is to stress individual, often computer-based learning at the expense of class lectures and collaborative projects. Many schools individualize lesson plans because students enter the schools on a rolling basis rather than all together at the beginning of the semester.

Sometimes institutions that provide much-needed services for at-risk children can find themselves at risk. By the end of 2002, 194 or approximately 6.7 percent of the 2,874 charter schools founded in the United States had closed, according to the Center for Education Reform. Financial woes proved to be the culprit in some cases. Failure to meet academic standards prompted other schools to shut down. In other cases, mismanagement was to blame. To reduce the number of closures, which often were more harmful to students than to anyone else, some states began establishing more stringent guidelines for applicants. In Texas, for example, the Charter School Resource Center only approved two out of 44 charter school applicants in 2002.

Some analysts believe that the future of public education will include extensive collaboration between traditional public schools and for-profit education providers. A report released by the Commercialization in Education Research Unit (CERU) at Arizona State University's Education Policy Studies Laboratory revealed that 51 education management organizations (EMOs) operated 463 public schools in the 2003-2004 school year, collectively serving 200,400 students in 28 states and the District of Columbia. Entitled *Profiles of For-Profit Education Management Companies,* the report revealed that 81 percent of EMO-managed institutions were charter schools. Online schools also were emerging. The CERU's report indicated that four EMOs operated 17 virtual schools in 2003-2004, serving a combined student body of 10,500 students in 11 states.

Although conclusive research regarding the effectiveness or ineffectiveness of charter schools had yet to be published, some states were losing patience with charter schools that failed to meet state standards. In Texas, Education Commissioner Shirley Neeley began imposing stricter requirements on the schools and threatened to close schools that consistently produced low scores on state exams. This came in the wake of rapid charter school growth in the Lone Star State. In Massachusetts, opponents have resorted to intense public relations campaigns to impact public opinion of charter schools in the city of Cambridge. In addition, opponents in some communities have filed lawsuits against the Massachusetts Board of Education in an attempt to stop new charter schools from opening. Finally, the Ohio Congress of Parents and Teachers filed a motion with their state's Supreme Court, asking it to hear their case challenging the constitutionality of Ohio's charter school program.

The private tutoring sector of the for-profit education industry stood to benefit considerably from the federal No Child Left Behind (NCLB) Act's supplemental educational service provision. According to the act, schools that fail to measure up to state achievement standards for three consecutive years are required to use part of their Title I budgets (aid for disadvantaged students) to provide free tutoring services. Some 1,500 private companies, which states include on approved tutor lists, were eager to tap into a pool of government dollars that totaled $2 billion. According to the December 8, 2004 issue of *Education Week,* Eduventures Inc. Senior Analyst J. Mark Jackson indicated that NCLB could double the $2 billion private tutoring market.

Considering that many school districts had not done an effective job of communicating the availability of tutoring to qualifying parents, there appeared to be considerable growth potential within the market. However, for-profit tutoring providers faced criticism from some education industry players who were concerned about lax state oversight. The same issue of *Education Week* revealed that although states were required to evaluate tutors after a period of three years, most had not done so.

By 2005, for-profit education companies continued to draw criticism from the likes of teachers unions, educators, and school administrators, who charged that the companies put the interests of stockholders before students, deliver mixed academic results, shy away from special needs children who require more resources than other children, and are more expensive to operate than regular public schools.

Faced with such opposition, some of the for-profit education industry's largest firms created their own trade group in 2004 called the National Council of Education Providers, with a goal of leveling the playing field and making their concerns heard among legislators in Washington. The council's founders included New York-based Mosaica Education; Charter Schools USA of Fort Lauderdale, Florida; Chancellor Beacon Academies of Coconut Grove, Florida; New York-based Edison Schools Inc.; Grand Rapids, Michigan-based National Heritage Academies; and Akron, Ohio-based White Hat Management.

Virtual high schools represented a promising industry niche, although by mid-2007 they had not yet emerged as a major profit center, according to a July 2007 *Business 2.0* article. However, the January 2007 acquisition of Portland, Oregon-based Insight Schools by The Apollo Group, which owns the University of Phoenix, was a major industry development. Insight had plans to double its online high school enrollment in Oregon from 600 students in 2006-07 to 1,200 students in 2007-08. With initial plans to expand into Wisconsin and southern California, Apollo was positioned to expand the virtual high school concept.

Beyond creating compelling content that could keep Web-driven adolescents interested and engaged, the market for virtual high schools also was supported by socioeconomic factors. According to the aforementioned *Business 2.0* article, a Bill and Melinda Gates foundation study, conducted in March of 2006, found that 5 million U.S. high school-aged students were not enrolled in courses. Of these, 4 million were not enrolled because of the need to provide care for a family member or to earn income for their families. By offering high school curricula online, students such as these would have additional options for balancing work, life, and educational responsibilities.

In mid-2006, Adam Newman, Eduventures' managing vice president of industry solutions, gave a brief synopsis of the conditions facing industry players, explaining, "The K-12 market is under a lot of pressure right now with increased demands for accountability, a shift to outcome-based performance measurement, and efforts to more effectively integrate technology into instruction and administrative processes. As the pressure increases on schools, it creates more demand for innovative and cost-effective solutions from the businesses that support these schools."

CURRENT CONDITIONS

According to Cory Barber in a June 2009 *Cape Business News* education review from *Franchise Times Magazine,* the child education industry generates about $60 billion in annual revenue and provides more than 3.5 million jobs. Just the consumer-based tutoring businesses and test-prep services alone fetch $3 billion to $5 billion each year in the United States, according to Boston-based education information company Eduventures, as reported in "The ABCs of educational franchises" in *Franchise Times* magazine.

In her September 2009 article, "20 Recession Resistant Franchise-Promising Picks to Choose From—Even in This Economy," Tennille Robinson noted that even with the tight economy leading into 2010, people are still hesitant to cut back on spending and/or coompromise on services for their children. Robinson noted that child tutoring and supplemental education services ballooned in recent years into a $69 billion industry, quoting IBISWorld Research (www.ibisworld.com). The sector saw 11 percent average unit growth over the past three years and looked to be on a curriculum to score even higher.

Helping the sector get there were its biggest companies: Kumon Math & Reading Centers, Sylvan Learning, and Huntington Learning Center. While the Japanese import Kumon offers subsidized rent to qualifying franchisees, Sylvan went on record to note that prospective franchisees in specific markets such as Atlanta, Chicago, and Sacramento, California, could potentially earn $200,000 to $1 million in revenues.

Technology-related products and services continued to represent a key area of opportunity for industry players. Specifically, more schools were using virtual classroom technology and interactive assessment tools, according to Eduventures. In addition, opportunities existed for those who could help school districts integrate and manage administrative and academic data from disparate computer systems as the education sector began pursuing an enterprise data approach that was already common in the corporate sector.

INDUSTRY LEADERS

A focused article appearing in *Entrepreneur* magazine in 2008 identified the "Top Ten" children's educational franchises as Kumon Math, Sylvan Learning Center, Huntington Learning Centers, Club Z!, Goddard School, The Little Gym, Tutoring Club, Primrose, Enopi-Daekyo North America Inc,. and Mathnasium Learning Centers.

Japan-based Kumon was created in 1958 by a math teacher. The Kumon method focuses on daily practice and self-paced advancement to improve children's math and reading skills, from simple addition and letter sounds to differential calculus and literature. As of November 2008,the Kumon Math and Reading franchise has grown to 4.2 million students in 26,138 centers around the world. There were 250,000 students enrolled in more than 1,800 units in the United States. From 2003 to 2008, its North American revenue rose more than 10 percent a year. For its 2008 fiscal year, the company reported net income of $38.4 million worldwide on $758.4 million in revenue. It attributed much of its sales growth to the No Child Left Behind Act, which for the first time forced all public schools to report how well their students were performing. Low-performing students were now easily identified. Meanwhile, many high-performing students wanted to keep their edge as schools focused more on raising the test scores of under-achievers. Kumon's reading students in the United States more than doubled since 2001, while the company saw a 56 percent jump in math students.

Sylvan Learning Center is a nearly 30-year-old franchising system that provides personalized instructional services for students in grades K-12. Franchisees can provide tutoring services in their main center, online and in students' homes. There are almost 800 franchises in the United States, and 76 in Canada. (Baltimore, Maryland-based Laureate Education Inc., formerly known as Sylvan Learning Systems Inc., provides undergraduate degrees, as well as master's and doctoral degrees, including such fields as medicine and law).

Huntington Learning Centers assists K-12 students with reading, writing, math, study skills, phonics, SAT/PSAT and ACT prep. Likewise, Club Z! helps students by tutoring services to take place at the student's home, library, school or after-school facility; subjects vary from the core three (reading, writing and arithmetic) to foreign languages, computers and music.

Goddard School is a year-round educational facility for children from six weeks to six years old. Its programs also include after-school and summer programs for older elementary school students. Each school is a licensed childcare facility and staff members are trained in Early Childhood Education or Childhood Development.

During the early 2000s, Educate Inc. emerged as a new player in the K-12 education market, but it consisted of established parts. With financial backing from Apollo Management L.P., the company purchased Sylvan Learning Systems' K-12 businesses in 2003. Sylvan turned its focus on the higher education market and sold Sylvan Learning Center, Catapult Learning, eSylvan, and Schülerhilfe to Educate. Educate operated 1,000 Sylvan Learning Centers throughout North America, enjoying a leadership position within the tutoring sector. In addition, eSylvan provided live, online tutoring to students in grades three through nine. Educate also operated more than 900 Schülerhilfe centers in Europe and offered research-based supplemental education services to school districts and individual schools via Catapult Learning. Educate subsidiary Progressus Therapy offered professional services in the areas of speech-language, occupational, and physical therapy. A $535 million management buyout of Educate occurred in 2007, which resulted in the company being divided into five independent businesses. These included Educate Online, Educate Corporate Centers, Hooked on Phonics, Progressus, and the holding company Educate Services (Catapult, Schülerhilfe, and Sylvan).

Nobel Learning Communities, which was founded in 1984 to run a string of child care centers, later expanded to operate elementary and high schools. In 2007 it ran a system of 150 schools in 12 states, including private pre-elementary, elementary, middle, and specialty high schools, as well as schools for learning-challenged children. In early 2000 it announced a five-year contract to manage the Philadelphia Academy Charter.

KinderCare Learning Centers Inc. led the United States in providing child care and educational services for preschool-age children. In 2005, the Portland firm operated more than 1,250 learning centers. The company served approximately 120,000 children from as young as six weeks old to age 12 in 39 states.

WORKFORCE

Many of the driving personalities behind the new for-profit education ventures are the so-called education entrepreneurs: business professionals who are seeking to transform and privatize public education. They are spurred by the belief that free market forces will boost the efficiency of school performance, increase the range of educational options available to parents and students, and improve the quality of instruction through competition. In the process, they feel that public schooling can be made to turn a profit and that under-performing schools will be weeded out.

Many workers in the new for-profit educational franchises are former elementary and secondary teachers who are unsatisfied with making relatively low wages after years of teaching service or are frustrated by the layers of bureaucracy that come with public school systems. They have decided to jump on the entrepreneurial bandwagon and move into the sector of the educational industry that seems most likely to bring financial rewards for risk-taking, innovation, and a more "businesslike" approach to teaching youngsters. One example is Paul Wetzel, a former middle school teacher in Greenville, South Carolina, who started Wetzel Educational Services, a private tutoring firm that provides test preparation and individual and group tutoring for both elementary and secondary students.

At the other end of the spectrum are businesspeople, some of whom have prior experience working for investment banking or venture capital firms. Among such businesspeople is J.C. Huizenga, cousin of H. Wayne Huizenga, the former AutoNation chairman and Miami Dolphins football team owner. J.C. Huizenga created National Heritage Academies as a for-profit educational franchise with a curriculum that stresses discipline, morals, and character development along with academics. Based in Grand Rapids, Michigan, National Heritage Academies expanded from one fledgling charter school of about 200 students to 61 schools in six states with more than 38,000 students in 2009.

Many schools have similarly sought out high level industry executives to serve as school administrators. The Michigan-based Leona Group recruited former General Motors marketing manager Rod Atkins to serve as principal of its Voyageur Academy elementary school in Detroit despite his lack of experience in the educational field. Moves such as these highlight for-profits' desire to operate less like a traditional educational institution and more like a modern business.

Ironically, for-profit educational franchises often pay less than their public school counterparts and thus tend to hire inexperienced teachers. Some critics charge that stock options and merit pay can't compensate for the lower salaries that are often coupled with longer days and school years than those of the public school system. When Edison's Boston Renaissance school, which enrolls primarily low-income minority kindergarten through eighth grade students, raised salaries and shortened the academic calendar, teacher turnover decreased and student performance improved.

BIBLIOGRAPHY

"About Us." National Heritage Academies. Available from http://heritageacademies.com/about-us/. Applied Research Center. "The Education Industry Fact Sheet." Available from http://www.igc.org/trac/feature/education/industry/fact.html.

Barber, Cory. "Franchise Opportunities—Children's Education Businesses." *Franchise Times,* June 2009. Available from http://www.cbn.co.za/pressoffice/business_education/fullstory/1654.htm

Bergman, Becky. "The ABCs of Educational Franchises" *Franchise Times,* January 2008.

Borja, Rhea R. "Education Industry Eyes Opportunities in 'No Child' Law." *Education Week,* 7 April 2004.

————. "For-Profit Education Firms Pick Up More Schools." *Education Week,* 25 February 2004.

Datta, Saheli. "High School Goes Online." *Business 2.0,* July 2007.

Davidson, Alex. "Sticking to Basics." *Forbes,* 10 November 2008.

"Eduventures Expands its Service Offerings for the K-12 Market." Eduventures Inc., 10 May 2006. Available from http://www.eduventures.com.

"For-profits See Growth, Adjust Marketing and Add Programs." *Educational Marketer,* 4 September 2006.

Fredrickson, Tom. "Lower Education; Enrichment Centers for Under-5 Set Are Booming." *Crain's New York Business,* 26 February 2007.

Friel, Brian. "For-Profit Educators Unite." *National Journal,* 7 February 2004.

Gehring, John. "Debate Over Charter Schools Rages in Mass." *Education Week,* 26 January 2005.

Hurst, Marianne D. "Edison Schools Inc. Reports Growth in Number of Students Served." *Education Week,* 24 September 2004.

Johnston, Robert C. "Anti-Charter Group Seeks Ohio Supreme Court Ruling." *Education Week,* 20 October 2004.

Kantrowitz, Barbara. "Not Head of the Class." *Newsweek,* 30 August 2004.

"Laureate Education Inc. News and Information," 2009. Available from http://www.laureate-inc.com/pressreleaseID.php? releseID=86.

Lieberman, Myron. "Charter Schools: Facts, Fictions, Future." *World & I,* May 2004.

Miller, Kimberly. "Investment Firm Sees Profit in Disabled Students." *The Palm Beach Post* (West Palm Beach, Fla.), 22 February 2005.

Murphy, Victoria. "Where Everyone Can Overachieve." *Forbes,* 11 October 2004.

Olson, Lynn. "Standards for Authorizers of Charter Schools Issued." *Education Week,* 26 May 2004.

"Proclamation 7777—National Charter Schools Week, 2004." *The Federal Register,* 5 May 2004.

Reid, Karla Scoon. "Federal Law Spurs Private Companies to Market Tutoring." *Education Week,* 8 December 2004.

Richard, Alan. "New Texas Policy Cracks Down on Charters." *Education Week,* 26 January 2005.

Robinson, Tennile M. "20 Recession Resistant Franchise-Promising Picks to Choose From—Even in This Economy ." *Black Enterprise,* September 2009.

Russell, Jeanne, and Jenny LaCoste-Caputo. "Just How Well Have Charter Schools Worked?" *San Antonio Express-News,* 28 January 2007.

"Supplemental Content, Assessment, Tutoring and Test Prep Drive Spending in K-12 Educational Market." Eduventures Inc., 4 March 2006. Available from http://www.eduventures.com.

Tiffany, Laura. "Top 10 Children's Franchises." *Entrepreneur,* 19 June 2008.

"Trends in K-12 Enterprise Management: Districts Are Crossing the Chasm with Trepidation." Eduventures Inc., 13 March 2007. Available from http://www.eduventures.com.

Viadero, Debra. "Federal Report Examines Charter Schools." *Education Week,* 1 December 2004.

COMPETITIVE INTELLIGENCE

SIC CODE(S)

8732

INDUSTRY SNAPSHOT

Loosely defined as the legal and ethical collection of information regarding the operations of rival corporations, the term "competitive intelligence" implies an almost academic quest for knowledge. In pursuit of competitive intelligence, analysts, librarians, and research specialists study documents and survey computer databases in an attempt to identify trends and help manufacturers produce safer and otherwise improved products. In some cases, competitive intelligence may more correctly be called "corporate espionage." This second application entails a variety of possibly illegal and largely unethical practices, such as foraging through trash cans, bribing employees, and wiretapping phones and offices, with an ultimate goal of undermining a company's opposition. Eventually the industry of information gathering, in its various formations and practices, was elevated to a professional pursuit.

More than 3,500 professionals belonged to the Strategic and Competitive Intelligence Professionals (SCIP) in 2010 (formerly named the Society of Competitive Intelligence Professionals), and many more were employed by companies of various sizes to scope the competition. Most large companies, such as Motorola, Procter & Gamble, AT&T, and Kraft, had dedicated internal resources to the endeavor. Called by various names, including competitive intelligence (CI), market research and analysis, and strategic planning, these departments had a single goal: to stay one step ahead of the competition. Mid-sized firms, which cannot justify the expense of full-time staff, often contracted with independent firms on a project basis. The increasing number of firms established primarily to scope the competition signaled the growing market for this service.

Modern business philosophy dictates that some form of competitive intelligence is considered a key part of a company's operations. According to *Information Management Journal,* "CI is so critical that it can literally make the difference between a corporation's success or failure." Accordingly, all companies participate in CI to some degree, whether formally or informally, and whether they call it competitive intelligence or not.

ORGANIZATION AND STRUCTURE

Not every company relied on hired professionals to provide competitive intelligence. Small business owners did it themselves or relied on informal networks to gather feedback on competitors. Operating on a large scale, this word-of-mouth process could yield incredible results. Countries had also joined the ranks of business information gatherers and often depended on members of the business community to pass corporate information to government contacts for analysis. Japan was a recognized leader in the art of competitive intelligence, and used it without benefit of a designated state intelligence agency.

Executives of corporations and trading companies regularly collected and disseminated strategic information to appropriate officials in policy-making roles within the Japanese government. Other nations pursued their fact-finding initiatives in a more institutional manner. Government agencies were enlisted to procure sensitive, useful data, such as financial statements or patent applications, or any information that might secure an advantage for the companies

Percentage of Companies That Are Vulnerable to:

Information theft, loss, or attack	71%
Vendor, supplier, or procurement fraud	51%
Theft of physical assets or stock	50%
IP theft, piracy, or counterfeiting	47%
Corruption and bribery	44%
Internal financial fraud or theft	44%

SOURCE: Kroll Global Fraud Survey 2009–2010.

driving their nations' economies. The United States had traditionally distanced itself from such government-business collusion, although increased global trading may eventually sway policy makers to assist corporate efforts.

The services offered by competitive intelligence (CI) companies varied depending on the specific industry and the scope of operations. The most basic corporate intelligence work included research, data collection, and analysis. This information gathering translated into hours of searching public documents, databases, and tracking media coverage. As global competition for consumer dollars intensified, so did the need for information. Cutting-edge techniques were developed that promised to identify and deliver warnings of competitors' important developments and revolutionary technologies. Corporate war games allowed company executives to implement hypothetical situations to determine the most prudent course of action. Patent tracking provided a glimpse into what new products might be just beyond the competitive horizon. Trade shows provided "target rich environments" and could offer access to the inner workings of a rival's operation or plans. Some companies even went so far as to commission psychological profiles of top executives in their industry in an attempt to predict behavior.

In the realm of corporate spying, or at least snooping, the professionals might operate as independent entities without ties to any one firm. Unlike employees of a particular company, such as IBM, who spend their days studying every nuance of the computer business from high-speed processors to shipping costs, these individuals or companies had no loyalty to a particular brand or employer. They could be hired to provide analysis of the corporate environment in any industry. The goal was to amass information rather than produce a detailed analysis. Competitive intelligence agents were experts at ferreting out the desired facts and figures, but the client generally possessed the specific industry knowledge to place that information in a useful context.

At first glance, it might seem impractical and even cumbersome to involve a third party in such confidential matters, but there are reasons for using outside personnel. It can prove more cost effective to pay for the temporary services of trained professionals as opposed to covering the overhead costs involved with recruiting, training, and benefits administration for an in-house staff of employees. Companies that find themselves in time-sensitive negotiations with suppliers, vendors, or employees may also choose to seek the aid of experts who can launch an operation quickly and without risk of internal leaks. Finally, some companies opt for autonomous agencies simply because the subject matter being investigated is questionable or even litigious. In these extreme cases, mainstream corporations do not want to be perceived as "playing dirty" and so they pay others to do so. If the contracted party does engage in illegal or unethical behavior, the company is able to maintain deniability of any wrongdoing.

In the early 2000s, the practice of competitive intelligence or corporate spying raised many legal and ethical questions. Since the industry was relatively new, practitioners were not bound by established professional guidelines, such as the Hippocratic Oath for doctors or the Oath of Admission for attorneys. However, the Society of Competitive Intelligence Professionals (SCIP) authored a code of conduct for its membership. According to the SCIP Web site, the code encouraged its constituents to do the following: to continually strive to increase the recognition and respect of the profession; to comply with all applicable domestic and international laws; to accurately disclose all relevant information, including one's identity and organization, prior to all interviews; to fully respect all requests for confidentiality of information; to avoid conflicts of interest in fulfilling one's duties; to provide honest and realistic recommendations and conclusions in the execution of one's duties; to promote this code of ethics within one's company, with third-party contractors, and within the entire profession; and to faithfully adhere to and abide by one's company policies, objectives, and guidelines.

Ultimately, though, there is no regulatory agency to police the practice of information gathering. Should a member of SCIP or anyone else violate the aforementioned guidelines, there is no mechanism for sanction or discipline, except in the case of illegal activity. Even then, it is likely to be difficult to seek retribution.

Laws governing economic crimes were virtually nonexistent before the mid-1990s. Until that time, legal recourse at the national level was available under the Computer Fraud and Abuse Act, the Interstate Transportation of Stolen Property Act, or the Mail and Wire Fraud statutes. None of these laws specifically addressed the crime of economic espionage, and this omission resulted in failed prosecutions. Finally in 1996, after two years of debate, President Bill Clinton signed the Economic Espionage Act of 1996 to stop the proliferation of corporate spying. The act protected trade secrets and took aim at both foreign and domestic culprits. The new law applied uniformly to individuals and organizations, but it provided stiffer penalties for the latter.

Unfortunately, comprehensive laws and guidelines could not be enacted rapidly enough to keep pace with ingenious ploys used by top corporate spies. In 2001 Patrick Grayson, a consultant to corporations on security issues, was quoted in the *Financial Times* as saying that "much of the law on intelligence gathering is a muddle. Some activities are clearly illegal. 'You can assume bugging or breaking and entering is off-limits pretty much anywhere you go' ... Rules on claiming to be someone else differ from country to country, as do laws on rifling through rubbish. 'There should be a whole international law practice on garbage collection,' he says."

Within the United States, laws differ from state to state. In some states, it is perfectly acceptable to root through a company's trash, which is categorized as abandoned property. Additional restrictions can come into play depending on whether the rubbish is inside or outside a building or in a covered receptacle.

Members of SCIP frown on any attempt to recycle garbage into research material and consider it unnecessary and unethical behavior. However, in the late 1990s and early 2000s, several large companies were caught engaging in the practice. Two noteworthy cases involved computer giant Oracle and home products conglomerate Procter & Gamble. In each instance the offending organization had hired an independent firm to gather intelligence on a competitor. Oracle was endeavoring to help federal prosecutors in their antitrust suit against its chief rival, Microsoft. The contractors employed offered bribes to provide testimony to custodians of affiliate groups in return for access to trash barrel contents. The bribes were not accepted, and the operative reported to the authorities. Despite the fact that bribery is practically always a crime, Oracle defended its actions as being a necessary means to an end. On the other hand, Procter & Gamble acknowledged the impropriety of its actions and voluntarily disclosed the ethics breach. Its hired help had salvaged trash from Dutch rival Unilever. Both incidents provided embarrassing evidence about the evolving world of corporate espionage.

BACKGROUND AND DEVELOPMENT

The first act of corporate espionage occurred during the Industrial Revolution in 1811, when Francis Cabot Lowell journeyed to England and absconded with plans for building a weaving loom. Lowell was able to gain admittance to a factory and memorized the design of the Cartwright loom during his visit. Upon his return to Massachusetts, he opened his own business, and the region became

famous as the home of the textile mill. The city of Lowell, Massachusetts, was named in his honor.

Much has changed in the corporate spy world since that first incident. Since many suspected cases go unreported, it is difficult to offer proof in the form of facts and figures concerning this practice. However, reports of wrongdoing date back to 1943, when Procter & Gamble was fined $5.6 million in a lawsuit alleging patent infringement. The company was found guilty of bribing an employee of Lever Brothers to steal bars of a new soap product. Several other episodes were reported during the early 1900s, with most resulting in legal action.

The practice of corporate information gathering became more sophisticated as foreign governments embraced the concept. Whereas earlier occurrences typically involved rival corporations committing obvious acts of theft and bribery, government sponsored spying was less conspicuous.

The end of the cold war displaced many government operatives already schooled in the practice of intelligence gathering. Recruited and coached in the art of corporate espionage, former KGB agents found new careers. They collected information on foreign businesses and economic plans, and passed it along to officials of the newly formed regional governments—for a price. Other countries followed suit. In the 1960s and 1970s the Japanese routinely raided U.S. technology by photographing the layout of factories during plant tours. Germany and France also entered the spy business, using less than admirable tactics. German officials used confidential bank records to gather information on competitors. The French techniques were the most intrusive and included searching the briefcases of foreign businessmen staying in local hotels and possibly using agents as French flight attendants to eavesdrop on international business travelers.

The intense global competition caused some to question whether the Central Intelligence Agency (CIA) should reinvent itself as a corporate intelligence agency. In the late 1980s and early 1990s there was a push to convert the agency and establish a new mission for its vast network of operatives. In 1991 David L. Boren (D-OK), chairman of the Senate Intelligence Committee, lobbied for an expanded role for the CIA and was quoted in *Business Week* as saying: "Going into the next century, our position of world leadership will depend more on our economic strength than even our military strength."

Many questioned whether there was a need for the CIA in the post-cold-war period and argued that it would be worth the expense to reposition satellites and listening devices toward civilian targets. The information gathered would be laundered and then passed along to U.S. corporations via the Department of Commerce. In a 1991 story for *Business Week* magazine, Admiral Stansfield Turner, head of the CIA under President Jimmy Carter, advocated using CIA agents to actively steal intelligence from foreign competitors, writing: "We steal secrets for our military preparedness. I don't see why we shouldn't to stay economically competitive."

The notion of government-sponsored spying never gained enough popular support to be granted a trial. It was not feasible in light of the potential conflicts. Spying on U.S. allies would surely cause relations to suffer and cause an escalated response. Even if the operations could be completed in a covert manner, the larger question would be which U.S. companies should be given the misappropriated information and consequently the competitive advantage. Every possible scenario would have caused an uproar in both the business and political arenas.

During the mid-1980s private intelligence firms began springing up across the country, many founded by former government or military agents. The economic community had awakened to the world of intelligence gathering, and with no government support, it turned to consultants for hire. The Society for Competitive Intelligence Professionals, founded in 1986, experienced sudden membership growth. By 1998 a survey conducted by The Future Group reported that 82 percent of companies with revenues over $10 billion had organized internal intelligence departments, and 60 percent of companies with revenues of over $1 billion had done the same. In 2000 some 77 percent of SCIP members worked directly for corporations and 17 percent worked for independent agencies. In terms of budgetary allocations, at least one fourth of respondents in a SCIP survey reported spending at least $100,000 for intelligence. Additionally, about 14 percent indicated a budget of over $500,000, and 5 percent said they spent over $1 million dollars annually.

Competitive intelligence gained acceptance in a growing number of industries. It also became part of the business landscape for companies large and small, as well as those working in the fields of academia and government. By 2006 one trend was the movement of library and information science professionals into the area of CI, either on an occasional project-based basis or full-time.

At one time, only industry leaders were engaged in the research and planning activities designed to ensure their position as the frontrunner. However, the increased need for information at all levels was responsible for the creation of independent CI firms. Professionals in this field are in demand as companies rush to join the ranks of corporations who regularly scope the competition.

In addition to more than 3,000 members of SCIP, there were many more unregistered practitioners working in the corporate world. The top industries using competitive intelligence professionals were professional services, such as accounting, consulting, and legal; financial services, such as insurance, lending, and banking; pharmaceuticals;

manufacturing; information technology; telecommunications; healthcare; aerospace; biotechnology; and energy/utilities.

Despite recent growth, many firms had yet to implement CI initiatives or were not sure about the best way to do so. The good news was that companies were considering CI programs in growing numbers. Among those with established initiatives, the trend was toward integrating them across various business areas, including distribution, manufacturing, research and development, marketing, and sales.

Leaders in the CI field have stressed the need to turn their occupation into a professional pursuit and encourage formal degree programs as a means for accomplishing this goal. As the industry continues to evolve, education and standards for the profession will present the greatest challenges to practitioners, who realize the need to overcome the negative connotations associated with competitive intelligence.

Although technology continues to provide new avenues for data collection and data theft, experts in the field agree that human intelligence is invaluable. Sophisticated satellites, listening devices, and computer viruses may make it possible to penetrate the defenses of almost any organization, but they cannot replace the information gleaned through interviews or carefully orchestrated conversations. Companies who lose their competitive advantage often do so because of the actions of their own employees. In recognition of this fact, companies train internal employees to manage and control the flow of information within the company and to outside vendors or consultants. As this trend continues, it is reasonable to expect that competitive intelligence issues will become a part of daily life for many employees, suggesting a prosperous future for those in the industry.

PIONEERS IN THE FIELD

Jan Herring Jan Herring is credited as one of the founding fathers of competitive intelligence. Like many of the early CI professionals, Herring began his intelligence career in government service. He logged 20 years of duty with the CIA, completing various assignments dealing with national intelligence issues. Upon his departure, he was honored with the Medal of Distinction and multiple letters of commendation. Herring then turned his attention to the corporate world and created the first CI department at Motorola Inc., modeled after government programs. It was considered a top-rate unit, viewed by many other groups as the prototype when they set up their own operations.

In 1986 Herring was a founding member of the Society of Competitive Intelligence Professionals (SCIP). He continued to work as a consultant for almost a decade and earned the respect of the intelligence community. In 1996 he again assumed the role of leader when he co-founded the Academy for Competitive Intelligence, a private institution that offers training and certification for intelligence professionals. He also lectured at the nation's top business schools, such as The Wharton School, Stanford University, Tufts University, Massachusetts Institute of Technology, and Northwestern University, furthering the acceptance of competitive intelligence in the academic community.

Leonard Fuld Leonard Fuld, another charter SCIP member, made lasting contributions to the profession. He started his own CI firm, Fuld and Company, in 1979, and more than half of the Fortune 500 companies have hired him to consult on intelligence questions. He gained national prominence as a lecturer and has published books and articles shedding light on CI practices.

John Nolan John Nolan joined the field after completing two decades of service in military operations performing intelligence and counterintelligence work. In 1991 he founded the Phoenix Consulting Group, named after an intelligence operation conducted during the Vietnam War. The company provided consulting service to the federal government and maintained a host of corporate clients. In fact, Nolan's company was named as the perpetrator of the corporate espionage scandal involving Procter and Gamble and Unilever, though Nolan was not permitted to comment on this matter under confidentiality agreements. In 1997 Nolan launched the Centre for Operational Business Intelligence, which taught intelligence gathering methods. The most well known technique was "elicitation," the art of gathering information through conversation without asking direct questions. Nolan also published material on the subject of corporate espionage.

Marc Barry Marc Barry was perhaps the most shadowy figure in the world of corporate intelligence. Author of the book, *Spooked: Espionage in Corporate America,* he represented the cutting edge of intelligence gathering. He reportedly had a background in intelligence gathering in Southeast Asia, but little was known about this endeavor and he had no known affiliation with a government agency. He was the founder of C3I Analytics, a New York-based consulting firm specializing in corporate assignments. Barry openly spoke about the dark side of CI, the unethical practices and theft of information. He maintained that many companies were guilty of these practices but tried to distance themselves from actual wrongdoing by hiring him to conduct questionable operations. His guerrilla tactics made him unpopular among some in the SCIP community who would like to bury the whole notion of corporate espionage. In his book, which was published in 2000, Barry detailed operations that allegedly crossed many of the ethical guidelines set out by SCIP.

CURRENT CONDITIONS

By 2010 the new industry buzzword was social media. Not only were there Web sites offering instructions to analysts regarding how to search social media sites for key information (e.g., what Tweeters or Facebookers were saying about products or competitors), industry blogs and bloggers also shared a wealth of information. The Marketing Executives Networking Group (MENG), a group of senior-level marketing professionals with more than 2,000 members, launched such a blog in July 2010, the *MENG Blend.* Co-authored by 18 marketing professionals, the password-protected blog planned to offer and share some of the best marketing strategies among members.

Earlier in 2010, MENG published results of a survey revealing the top 20 blogs that marketing executives read and found to contain the most valuable marketing content. The top blog belonged to Seth Godin, followed by *Mashable,* Chris Brogan, and Guy Kawasaki. While not totally dedicated to competitive intelligence, MENG has increasingly dedicated blog and press space to promote better intelligence strategies.

Business intelligence contributor Kroll Inc. released its Global Fraud Report in late 2009, indicating that the 2008–2009 economic downturn had affected business behavior and business exposure to fraud. The highest percentage of companies vulnerable to fraud was in the area of information theft, loss, or attack. Greater vulnerability was attributed to higher staff turnover, reductions in internal controls, and reduced revenues across the board.

According to a previous MENG survey, competitive intelligence ranked fourth in the list of the top 10 marketing trends for 2008, as evidence of its rising importance. Results of a study by Cutting Edge Information published in *Internet Wire* revealed that, in 2008, the average CI budget for U.S. companies was $448,000, as compared to $335,000 in 2005. The highest reported CI budget in 2005 was $1 million, whereas by 2008 it had increased to $2 million. David Richardson of Cutting Edge said: "As the role of CI continues to expand and gain leverage, companies must equip their CI teams with adequate budgets that match their increasingly strategic roles."

As competitive intelligence grew as an industry, it also became a field of study. A small number of universities offered undergraduate and graduate course work in competitive intelligence. Some notable examples are Brigham Young University, California Institute of Technology, Indiana University, Rutgers University, Trinity College, and the University of California at Los Angeles. In addition, several pioneers in the field of competitive intelligence joined forces to create the Fuld Gilad Herring Academy of Competitive Intelligence, which offered certification programs.

Other companies followed suit. The Institute for Competitive Intelligence, the Academy of Competitive Intelligence, and many others offered competitive intelligence certificate programs and training. Programs also became available in specific fields, such as pharmacy, library science, and law. The latter is evidenced by the Special Libraries Association's Click University, which offers its members continuing education credit for its three CI courses.

In order to gain acceptance as a respected profession, the CI industry still needed to move forward in its efforts to define educational, practical, and ethical standards for its members. It had yet to distinguish itself from the world of government intelligence and spy scenarios.

INDUSTRY LEADERS

Kroll Inc. Based in New York and a subsidiary of Marsh & McLennan Companies, Kroll Inc. was founded in 1972. With operations in more than 60 cities in over 29 countries worldwide, not all of the company's employees were engaged in traditional competitive intelligence activities. In fact, technically classified as a risk consulting company, the firm was something of a hybrid, serving clients in areas such as corporate advisory and restructuring; electronic evidence and data recovery; financial accounting, valuation and litigation; and security services.

According to Kroll, its business intelligence and investigations unit "uncovers fraud committed by client employees and vendors. Kroll's investigators also scrutinize potential business opportunities and evaluate the clout of clients' competitors. Kroll often develops evidence and other intelligence for attorneys to support case-specific legal strategies. The firm also evaluates whether a client's business practices are in compliance with legal and ethical standards in the United States and abroad.

In November 2002 Kroll's investigative unit generated only 18 percent of total revenues. This amount represented a reduction from 40 percent in the prior year and was a far cry from several years earlier, when investigative work accounted for almost 100 percent of company revenues. Yet the revenues continued to soar. By 2003 the company reported record revenues of over $485 million and a record income of nearly $38 million. A portion of the company's growth could be attributed to the elevated level of interest in corporate security as a result of the September 11, 2001, terrorist attacks on the United States. Corporations wanting to establish more stringent internal controls and crisis management programs turned to the experts, and Kroll answered their call. In 2004 Kroll became a business segment of the global professional services firm Marsh & McLennan. However, despite $667 million in 2009 revenues, Kroll was slated for sale by Marsh & McLennan in 2010.

The Phoenix Consulting Group The Phoenix Consulting Group began in 1990 as the brainchild of John Nolan, former federal intelligence operative. The privately held firm, headquartered in Huntsville, Alabama, accepted consulting assignments and also provided training and development programs for corporations interested in fashioning internal CI departments. As of 2010 the group did not release detailed revenue information. However, in recent years it reported that more than 80 percent of its revenues were generated from corporate assignments rather than government intelligence work. Initially, the opposite scenario was true. All work performed by the company was shrouded in confidentiality agreements and management did not divulge client names.

Of course, occasional news reports linked the company to corporate activities, as in the case of the much publicized legal battle between Procter & Gamble and Unilever, which resulted in Procter & Gamble paying a substantial amount of money to Unilever to settle a case of trade secret theft. In 2006 Phoenix indicated that its Commercial Practice had "completed over 2,100 engagements—domestically and internationally—for client firms ranging from the Fortune 50 to the Inc. 500 and everywhere in between, across a variety of industries."

Fuld and Company Another prominent firm in the field of CI is Fuld and Company, located in Cambridge, Massachusetts. Leonard Fuld started the firm in 1979 and it soon became the first company to offer public seminars on competitive intelligence. Throughout its history, the company maintained its commitment to research and education, along with fulfillment of its consulting assignments. Its aim was completing numerous case studies and benchmarking studies that established guidelines and parameters for intelligence gathering. In the late 1990s the Fuld War Room became the first interactive tool used for predicting competitor behavior. Fuld offered seminars in conjunction with the Academy of Competitive Intelligence, where Leonard Fuld was on the faculty. The company named more than half of the Fortune 500 companies as clients and claimed that a staggering 90 percent of all clients re-sign with the firm for subsequent CI assignments.

Another good source of business intelligence information is the Economist Intelligence Unit, the business information arm of The Economist Group, publisher of *The Economist* magazine. With a global network of 700 analysts in 2010, it assesses and forecasts political, economic, and business conditions in 200 countries, and claims itself as the world's leading provider of country intelligence.

WORKFORCE

Although observers in the early 2000s described competitive intelligence as a new occupational field, industry experts disagreed. Claiming roots that went back 15 years to the founding of SCIP, members argued that it was time to recognize the discipline as a profession. SCIP boasted worldwide membership of more than 3,230 practitioners by 2006. The organization consisted of chapters in 71 different countries, where members met regularly to share experiences. Despite these impressive statistics, the industry had not received the respect that members believed it deserved.

Competitive intelligence employees came from varied backgrounds, including market researchers, librarians, analysts, and former government intelligence officers. Nonetheless, it was believed that the profession would improve credibility by gaining acceptance in the academic world and establishing accredited training programs, which remained scant. There was no degree or program of study required to work in the field. Adding to the confusion was the fact that there was no standard nomenclature for positions within the profession. More often than not, CI professionals are branded as "spies" or "spooks," terms offensive to legitimate businesspeople.

According to a SCIP/Lexis-Nexis survey, the average salary for CI professionals in 2003–2004 was $78,064. This marked an increase of 16 percent over a prior survey conducted in 2000–2001. By 2006 the CI profession remained in a state of flux. While many firms had established CI programs, many more had not. Employment opportunities varied in the midst of these conditions, and many CI professionals were waiting for an expected hiring surge.

In the April 15, 2006, issue of *Library Journal,* Cynthia Cheng Correia described some of the skills needed to work in the CI field, explaining: "CI is specialized and not for everyone. Each intelligence function requires specific and often dedicated skills and qualities that may be mutually exclusive. For example, the characteristics for a crack literature searcher may not translate easily to human source interviewing or analysis. Good intelligence literature searching requires skills, judgments, and techniques that are not only logical, precise, and detailed but highly creative. Human source collection requires excellent social skills and/or the ability to elicit information from people, often strangers. Analysis requires the ability to discern patterns and trends from seemingly disparate sets of data and information—a knack for details and the big picture. Many practitioners suggest that, while skills may be learned, essential qualities for the distinct CI functions are instinctive."

AMERICA AND THE WORLD

Globalization has produced intense competition for world consumers. Virtually all economically developed countries admit to corporate spying or intelligence gathering in some form. Some perceive the United States as a leader in the field, but Britain, France, Germany, Japan, and Canada are rapidly expanding their CI practices.

According to a 2009 report from the Kroll Group, more than 30 percent of global companies reported that the economic downturn had directly increased their exposure to fraud during the previous 12 months. Hardest hit was the financial services industry. According to Kroll, North America experienced the highest incidence of fraud, but the Middle East and Africa experienced the worst fraud levels, with companies losing an average $11.5 million. Information theft ranked highest in vulnerability.

RESEARCH AND TECHNOLOGY

Research was becoming increasingly important within the CI field. This was evident by SCIP's establishment of the Competitive Intelligence Foundation in 2005. According to SCIP, the foundation's objective is to "develop, maintain, and promote the body of knowledge for the competitive intelligence community through research and education, and to improve the ability of its practitioners to support organizational decision-making. The foundation's primary initiatives are to conduct and support research on emerging trends and issues in the practice of competitive intelligence and to make existing and developing knowledge visible and available to CI practitioners through targeted publications, including books, studies, and survey reports." By 2008 the organization's publications included *Competitive Intelligence Magazine* and the *Journal of Competitive Intelligence and Management,* an academic journal, as well as *SCIP.online.*

Jules B. Kroll, of Kroll Inc., told *Leaders Magazine* that while technology is important to the business, it is only one important part of service and operations. For example, Kroll spends a considerable amount of R & D time and money in electronic evidence discovery, because that segment is all about technology.

A discussion of the use of research and technology in corporate intelligence work can venture into sensitive areas. When the role of technology is mentioned, the conversation immediately turns to wiretapping devices, computer hacking, and the use of satellites and sophisticated scanning equipment to monitor the competition. Professionals who consider themselves ethical, fair-minded business executives eschew this type of conduct. The CI purists argued that the secret to successful CI would not be found in the next wave of electronics that could allow one competitor to steal from another. Instead, they placed a premium on human intelligence gathering. Many of the seminars taught by leaders in the field stressed the importance of gathering information through dialogue. The technique of elicitation was mentioned frequently and experts were willing to teach novices how to encourage strangers to disclose valuable business information in the course of casual exchange.

Trade shows were often mentioned as a best bet for getting a peek at the competition. Employees running trade show booths and exhibits were encouraged to sell their company and its products to potential investors and customers. When this goal was pursued indiscriminately, the result could be a research and development nightmare. An enthusiastic employee could be drawn into conversation with a skilled intelligence analyst and end up revealing privileged information concerning upcoming product releases. A competitive advantage, years in the making, might vanish in one afternoon. Even those who favored this form of information gathering objected to the exchange of information under false pretenses, asserting that an ethical intelligence analyst should not misrepresent himself as an investor, potential employer, student, or journalist in an attempt to collect data.

Despite the legal and ethical questions, electronic surveillance does have a place in CI. While it may not be considered honorable or ethical, satellites can be employed to conduct overhead sweeps of a competitor's operations. The information can be as simple as the number of cars in the parking lot, the square footage of a factory, or types of materials being delivered to a site. As of 2010, electronic eavesdropping and computer hacking were illegal. Although they did happen, both could be difficult to trace. Reputable companies were reluctant to engage in this type of activity directly or indirectly due to the risk of exposure. The punishment for corporate espionage and the potential for a public relations debacle served as deterrents.

BIBLIOGRAPHY

"Average Budget for Global CI Departments Surpasses $1 Million." *Internet Wire*, 3 June 2008.

"Click University CI Program Now Open for Class of 2008." *Information Outlook*, January 2008.

"Competitive Intelligence Helps Identify Market Risks as Well as Business Growth Opportunities." *Business Wire*, 24 June 2008.

"Competitive Intelligence in Law Firms." *Marketing the Law Firm*, 1 April 2008.

Correia, Cynthia Cheng. "Getting Competitive: Competitive Intelligence Is a Smart Next Step for Information Pros." *Library Journal*, 15 April 2006.

"Financial Services Industry Hit Hardest by Fraud According to Global Report." The Kroll Group, 19 October 2009. Available from http://www.kroll.com/about/library/fraud/Oct2009.

"Global Fraud in the Economic Downturn—2009 Survey by Sector." The Kroll Group, October 2009. Available from http://www.kroll.com/about/library/fraud/Oct2009/downturn_and_fraud.aspx.

"Marketing Executives Networking Group Launches Blog to Advance Shared Best Practices in Marketing." *PR Newswire*, 29 July 2010.

"MENG Survey Reveals the Top 20 Marketing Blogs That Marketing Executives Read." *PR Web*, 12 January 2010. Available from www.mengonline.com/visitors/newsroom.

Progress and Performance. Society of Competitive Intelligence Professionals, 2006. Available from http://www. scip.org.

"Top 10 Marketing Trends for 2008." *Print Ambassador*, 13 June 2008.

COMPUTER ANIMATION
ENTERTAINMENT

■

SIC CODE(S)

3571

7812

7999

INDUSTRY SNAPSHOT

The first decade of the new century proved to be a high-growth one for computer animation, which remained a multi-billion-dollar business. Once aimed at children's entertainment, the industry has expanded to adult audiences on cable and satellite television as well as the Internet. The use of digital technology has become more pervasive throughout the motion picture industry as well, accounting for as much as half of the $150 million typically spent to make a feature film. Competition continues to heat up as major studios increase production and rely more heavily on computer animation for both animated and regular feature films.

Animation, the art of producing the illusion of movement from a sequence of two-dimensional drawings or three-dimensional objects, has long been a staple of the entertainment industry. Animation can take on many shapes, ranging from primitive drawings in television cartoons such as *The Flintstones* to complex dinosaurs in *Jurassic Park*. Computer animation's entertainment uses are spread far and wide. From the dreamlike landscapes of *What Dreams May Come* to the intricately detailed talking mouse of *Stuart Little* to lifelike digital characters and imaginary landscapes in 2005's *Star Wars: Episode III—Revenge of the Sith*, computer animation continues to transform the face of cinematic reality.

Movie and television audiences can now watch celestial collisions pulverize Earth, realistic dinosaurs hunting terrified scientists around an island, and insects and toys living out their own dramatic fantasies in feature-length films. Moreover, all of this looks perfectly normal. Elaborate computer-generated special effects have become the motion picture industry's standard. Developments in computer animation had reached a fever pitch by the turn of the twenty-first century, and studios raced to employ the latest developments in order to showcase the most dazzling, amusing, and terrifying effects Hollywood had to offer.

In their zeal to wow audiences, directors and studios took turns beating each other over the head with their checkbooks. Early on, films such as Twister, The Matrix, Titanic, and a host of others all carried computer animation budgets that alone would have made studios of yesteryear blanch. Later, these budgets were par for the blockbuster course. At the same time, however, advances in technology were allowing movie producers to make less expensive animated films.

ORGANIZATION AND STRUCTURE

Animation has always been a labor-intensive process, and as a consequence, most animation projects are collaborative efforts integrating the talents of animators, technical directors, producers, artists, and engineers. Even though computer animation is technology driven, the workflow for an animated feature movie is still essentially the same as it was in the earliest days of animation. While the computer has replaced some hand drawings, it has not entirely eliminated pen-and-ink sketches. An animation project begins with the creation of a storyboard, a series of sketches outlining the important points of the story and some of the dialogue. When animation was strictly done by hand, the workload would then be distributed between senior artists, who sketched the frames where the most action was occurring, and junior artists, who filled in the in-between frames. When computers are used, artists use the storyboard sketches to create clay figures that are made into digitalized three-dimensional (3D) characters, which are then manipulated by animation artists who also create the background fill. Altogether, an animated feature is the collective work of many people, including animators, lighting experts, story writers, and sound technicians.

BACKGROUND AND DEVELOPMENT

From the very beginning, studios employed animation artists, people who could painstakingly draw quirky animated characters by hand. Before the arrival of computers, in fact, all animation was created in this way. Production teams simulated motion by drawing a series of successive, incrementally altered frames. In order to trick the eye into seeing motion, each second of animated sequence for film required 24 frames. In the earliest cartoons, each one of the frames was hand drawn, thereby creating a tremendous workload just to complete a short cartoon. For instance, the 1910 cartoon *Gertie the Trained Dinosaur,* which was primitive compared to later animation, required 10,000 separate drawings. In 1915, Earl Hurd streamlined the process by developing a time-saving method known as cel animation whereby each individual character was drawn on a separate piece of transparent paper while the background was drawn on a piece of opaque paper. When the animation was shot, the transparent paper was overlaid on the opaque. With this method, the background was drawn once and only the parts that needed to be changed had to be redrawn instead of the entire frame. The animation industry flourished this way from the 1930s to the 1950s, largely through the efforts of pioneer Walt Disney, who produced such full-length animated movies as Dumbo, Bambi, and *Snow White and the Seven Dwarfs.*

Thus, for many decades, hand-drawn animation was the industry standard. Filmmaker John Whitney began to change that in the late 1950s and early 1960s. Whitney pioneered motion graphics using equipment that he purchased at a government war surplus auction. These precise instruments allowed Whitney to develop motion control of the camera, zoom, and artwork. Later these techniques would be used to create the star-gate slit-scan sequence in Stanley Kubrick's *2001: A Space Odyssey* (1968). In 1986, Whitney received an Academy of Motion Pictures Arts and Sciences "Medal of Commendation for Cinematic Pioneering" in recognition of his contribution.

The 1960s saw another development that led to the eventual rise of computer animation. In 1963, Ken Knowlton,

who worked at Bell Laboratories, created a programming language that could generate computer-produced movies. It was not until 1982, however, with the release of Disney's *Tron,* that computer-generated imaging (CGI) would be explored as a serious moviemaking technique. The widespread arrival of computers in the 1980s marshaled in teams of new workers (namely scientists, engineers, and programmers) capable of developing complex animation software. Computers thus revolutionized the animation process, supplementing traditional animation methods with hardware and software capable of creating realistic on-screen characters.

Before 1995, conventional wisdom held that computer-generated imaging (CGI) was too inexact a science to replace hand-drawn animation, which many felt was the only way to capture small, quirky facial and body movements. In 1995, however, Pixar Animation Studios and its partner, The Walt Disney Co., showed that computer animation wasn't just an ancillary technique with the release of *Toy Story,* the first fully computer-animated feature length movie. The success of *Toy Story,* which grossed $350 million in worldwide box office sales, proved that computer animation was a viable moviemaking art form and one that required constant research and development. Pixar had already greatly advanced its computer animation techniques by the time it began work on its next project, *A Bug's Life,* which was released in 1998. The movie's director, John Lasseter, noted that *A Bug's Life* utilized 12 times the computing power employed in *Toy Story.*

The release of *Toy Story 2* in 1999 showcased the collaborative efforts of over 250 artists, animators, and technicians using 1,200 individual models, 18 virtual sets, and about 10,000 painted images used to define skin characteristics. The film's digital innovation was such that because shading and rendering technology had improved facial mobility and realism to such a great extent, most of the cast had to be completely redesigned. The release of *Toy Story 2* capped the most highly animated year in film history, which included *The Prince of Egypt* and *Tarzan,* among others. The following year, a record five animated features hit the nation's screens during the summer blockbuster season, and no less than a dozen animated features were expected by year's end. In addition to feature length cartoons, nearly all the major blockbusters were augmented with, or even written around, computer-animated special effects. Before Jar Jar Binks was a ubiquitous mass merchandising item, he was the computer-generated amphibian comic relief in the highly successful *Star Wars Episode One: The Phantom Menace,* which also featured enormous battle scenes between computer-animated creatures.

In 2001, 8 of the top 10 box office films either used digital effects in certain scenes or were shot entirely with CGI. The animation industry even won Academy prestige in 2002, when Best Animated Feature Film became the first new Oscar category since 1981. DreamWorks

PDI landed the award for *Shrek,* its second 3D feature animation film.

Animators continued to push the limits of CGI's capabilities with, for example, *Star Wars: Attack of the Clones,* which employed roughly 2,000 digital effects during 95 percent of the movie. The movie's battle among hundreds of thousands of Storm Troopers, battle droids, and Jedi is the largest scene to date in the *Star Wars* series. In 2002, *Lord of the Rings: The Fellowship of the Ring* secured an Oscar for visual effects. Industry leaders such as Pixar and DreamWorks continued to compete with the likes the likes of Disney and Lucasfilm, as well as Sony Pictures Imageworks. This resulted in a host of new films that relied on computer animation, including *The Lord of the Rings: The Return of the King; I, Robot; The Polar Express, Spider-Man 2,* and *Star Wars: Episode III—Revenge of the Sith.*

Computer animation also offered a glimmer of hope for the democratization of film production. As CGI fuels further sophistication of interactive video games, high-tech moviemaking capabilities creep ever closer to the hands of the average amateur tech wizard. By 2003, an animation technique known as Machinima, which draws from the rendering techniques employed in 3D video games, provided amateur filmmakers with the ability to create nearly Hollywood quality short animated films.

PIONEERS IN THE FIELD

There is perhaps no name more well known in the field of animation than that of Walt Disney, the cartoon artist who founded the mega-entertainment empire that bears his name. Disney, who was born in Chicago in 1901, left school at 16 and later studied briefly at art schools in Chicago and Kansas City, Missouri. Disney's 1928 cartoon *Steamboat Willie* was a first on two accounts. It was the first cartoon that was synchronized with sound and it also introduced Mickey Mouse, his enduringly popular cartoon character. Disney would go on to many other firsts in the field of animation. In 1932 he used full color in a cartoon for the first time in the film *Flowers and Trees.* He also created the first full length animated feature with his 1937 *Snow White and the Seven Dwarfs,* which was produced with 400,000 sketches. Disney's production company ushered in the golden age of animation with film classics such as *Pinocchio* (1940), *Fantasia* (1940), and *Bambi* (1942). At that time, all animation work was done by hand with Disney overseeing the productions. Before he died in 1966, Disney had expanded his enterprise to include the Disneyland Theme Park in Anaheim, California; numerous syndicated comic strips featuring his cartoon characters; and television programs such as *The Mickey Mouse Club* and *Walt Disney's Wonderful World of Color.* Disney himself received 32 Academy Awards.

One particular advancement in computer animation centered around the human face. In the September 2004 issue of *Technology Review,* writer Gregory T. Huang explained: "Photorealistic digital faces—ones that can pass for real in still pictures or on the big screen—are among the last frontiers of computer graphics. Until recently, digital faces have looked fake when examined closely and have therefore been relegated to quick cuts and background shots. The problem is that we're extraordinarily sensitive to how human faces should look; it's much easier to fool people with a computer-generated T. rex than with a digital human. But advances in rendering skin, lighting digital scenes, and analyzing footage of real actors for reference are now allowing artists and programmers to control the texture and movement of every tiny patch of pixels in a computerized face."

As the industry used a growing number of computer-generated characters in films, some continued to suggest that this trend was a threat to human actors. However, others argued that the main benefit of using digital actors was to complement live actors and create scenes that they could not film using conventional methods and cameras. In the same *Technology Review* article, Sony Imageworks Visual Effects Supervisor Scott Stokdyk, whose credits include the *Spider-Man* blockbusters, explained, "In the past, directors and editors have basically massaged the cut around different quick actions and camera angles to convey a story. Now they don't have those kinds of limits." In addition to creating "impossible" scenes, computer animation now enables moviemakers to recreate deceased actors and make living ones appear to be a different age. Although the ability to create intimate levels of realism was not yet ready to push such virtual actors onto the big screen, developers were working toward the day when screen stars could be created to feature all the ideal visual characteristics as well as the ability to perform superhuman feats.

The computer animation entertainment industry continued to produce a seemingly endless array of new films, including DreamWorks's *Over the Hedge* (2006) and *Shrek the Third* (2007); Sony Pictures Imageworks' *Monster House* (2006); and Warner Brothers' *Happy Feet.* Beyond feature films such as these, CGI was becoming more commonplace in television commercials. This was evident during Super Bowl XLI in 2007, when Budwesier unveiled its well-received spot, "King Crab," a commercial showing a host of animatronic crabs produced with CG. Coca-Cola aired a commercial called "Videogame," inspired by the well-known game Grand Theft Auto, which was produced entirely in CG. In addition, FedEx aired a piece involving computer animation titled "Moon Office," which showed astronauts standing on the moon.

While growth in computer animation was good news for the industry, it also increased competition as more players flooded the market. This ultimately meant that consumers were forced to choose from films that were often quite similar. This led some studios to cut back staff, such as the Walt Disney Co., which in December 2006 announced plans to trim approximately 160 jobs from its 800-employee animation division.

The industry continued to pursue what once seemed like a seemingly unattainable goal: creating truly lifelike digital characters. During the latter part of the decade, improvements in motion-capture technology and digital face creation were quickly turning this goal into reality. In the November 2006 issue of *Computer Graphics World*, Debbie Denise, Sony Pictures Imageworks' executive producer and executive vice president of production infrastructure, commented on what filmmakers armed with this new technology were focused on, saying that: "A Holy Grail is to be able to capture a performer, face, and body, on set without infringing on principal photography, without an additional setup. Directors want to employ the best actors they can; they don't want to have to worry about who is playing that character. And, they don't want to be encumbered by the needs of visual effects."

The latest motion-capture techniques gave filmmakers the ability to capture the live-action movements of human actors, which were then applied to digital characters. This breakthrough approach was being accomplished in different ways. At one end of the spectrum, they could film actors in body suits adorned with special sensors, like LED lights, as they performed on stage in a specifically designed, controlled environment. However, developments such as Industrial Light & Magic's I-Mocap system, allowed the use of off-the-shelf video cameras to capture the movements of actors in just about any environment. Technology had even advanced to the point where filmmakers could shoot a scene and then immediately see how the movements of human figures translated when applied to digital characters, such as the animated penguins in *Happy Feet*.

To accompany the realistic, human-like movement, the industry was quickly gaining the ability to give digital characters realistic faces. One industry breakthrough was Contour, a system developed by WebTV founder Steve Perlman. After applying glow-in-the-dark makeup to an actor's face, filmmakers and videogame producers could use Contour to convert facial features into 3D images, and ultimately into a digital version of the actor's face.

Other digital face advancements included Sony Pictures Imageworks' proprietary Facial Action Coding System, which was used for the creation of *Monster House*. In the July 2006 issue of *Computer Graphics World*, Troy Saliba, the company's animation supervisor, described the system by saying, "Imagine it is a library of over 100 facial poses, such as 'inner eyebrow up' or 'outer

eyebrow up.' It harnesses the complete facial range of a person and divides it into individually numbered poses, so that it can choose any number of them, such as 4, 36, 37, and 94, and combine them in different percentages to create a complete facial shape."

Creating animated characters out of thin air is a long, laborious process. While computers play a large role in animation, hand drawings are still the first step. Artists' sketches develop the story line and characters. As an example, it took 27,000 such sketches to define the plot and personalities of the characters in *A Bug's Life*. The design department then used these sketches to model clay figures of the insects. These clay figures gave the animators an idea of how the characters moved. From there, the clay figures were transformed onto a computer screen as 3D wire-frame models. Technical directors put opaque-surfaced polygons over the wire-frame models. The purpose of the opaque surfaces was to show the animators how light would reflect off the figures. Afterward, animators brought the 3D images to life, while technical artists filled in the background and applied the final touches to the characters. When animators want to create animated human figures, they use a motion capture booth, which records a person's movements and translates them into 3D images. Rainbow Studios has an 800-square-foot motion capture booth that it uses in the development of animated video games for Microsoft.

One of the difficulties for animators, even with high-level computers, was the need to get the complete drawings exactly correct or else spend valuable time re-creating the animation sequence from scratch. In 1999, New York-based Improv introduced its Siggraph technology, which animators can use to store animation sequences for use in overlaying various scenes and activities. In this way, if a certain portion of an animation sequence is not to a director's liking, the particular components can simply be overlaid with a new component pulled from a stored sequence library, saving the time, effort, and money of re-creating the entire sequence. After building up a library over time, animators could conceivably create entirely new scenes using a simple cut-and-paste approach.

CURRENT CONDITIONS

As of 2009, the industry sub-sector of interactive and digital media (including animation, video games, online/mobile media and new forms of digital entertainment) had sky-rocketed into a multi-billion dollar business. According to PriceWaterhouse Coopers' "Global Entertainment & Media Outlook," the global videogames industry was expected to swell from $53.9 billion in 2009 to $68.3 billion by 2012, with Asia leading the pack in rapid growth. As of May 2009, Sony's PlayStation Network had more than 24 million registered accounts worldwide. The overall animation industry was estimated at $160 billion in 2008.

Interactive Entertainment has become one of the fastest growing industries in the world, in 2008 yielding more than $10 billion in revenues. In addition, gamers, the target market for interactive entertainment products, are now reaching beyond the traditional 8-34 old male target demographic to include women, Hispanics, and African Americans, a pattern observed in several markets, including Japan, China, Korea, and India. The success of Nintendo Wii and Guitar Hero are but a few examples of the spectacular growth in this industry sector, growing 15 percent year over year. Overall 2008 software revenue rose to $11 billion, an increase of 26 percent over 2007.

INDUSTRY LEADERS

Many of the leading animation firms bring together powerhouse names from the entertainment and computer fields. The cofounders of Microsoft Corp. and Apple Computers Inc. have both paired up with influential filmmakers to produce animated movies. The results of these ventures have generally been financial successes and, as a consequence, new animation studios and production companies have started to form around the world.

DreamWorks SKG Inc. DreamWorks Animation SKG Inc., based in Glendale, California, co-produced the highly successful animated features *Shrek, Shrek 2, Shrek the Third, Antz,* and *Shark Tale.* In 2004, DreamWorks Animation became a public company when it was spun off from DreamWorks LLC. Its former parent company is the collaborative effort of three founding partners—movie producer Steven Spielberg, former Disney executive Jeffrey Katzenberg, and music industry mogul David Geffen—who each received a 22 percent share of the company for individual investments of $33 million. The main shareholder, at 24 percent, is Paul Allen, the cofounder of computer software giant Microsoft.

Industrial Light & Magic Filmmaker George Lucas's Industrial Light & Magic (ILM), part of Lucas Digital, is an outgrowth of the special effects team that worked on the box office smash *Star Wars* and has been ranked as the world's largest digital production facility. The San Rafael, California-based company has been supplying special effects in Hollywood since the mid-1970s. ILM was responsible for creating dinosaurs in Steven Spielberg's *The Lost World,* rampaging fire in *Backdraft,* and water for *The Abyss.* Overall, ILM provided the special effects for 8 of the 15 highest grossing box office hits of all time, raking in 14 Academy Awards for best visuals. In 2003, George Lucas established Lucasfilm Animation, which operates separately from ILM. During the mid-

years of the first decade of the 2000s, ILM was involved in such films as *The Hulk* and *Finding Nemo.* Heading into the late years of the decade, the company was creating digital characters with human-like-movement faces with its I-Mocap system, which allowed the use of off-the-shelf video cameras to capture the movements of actors in just about any environment.

Pixar Animation Studios Steve Jobs, cofounder of Apple Computers, put up $50 million of his own money to purchase Emeryville, California-based Pixar Animation Studios from George Lucas. Under Jobs's leadership, Pixar went on to create *Toy Story,* the first fully computer-animated movie, in partnership with The Walt Disney Co. *Toy Story,* created by a team of 60 Pixar animators, was the highest-grossing film released in 1995. Pixar has developed proprietary software in the areas of modeling, animating, lighting, production management, and image rendering. Pixar's RenderMan software was used to create dinosaurs in *Jurassic Park.* Its Marionette and Ringmaster software programs complement RenderMan to control the entire range of animated production.

Pixar licenses its software to other production companies. In 1997, Pixar and Disney announced a five-movie deal. As part of the agreement, Disney handles marketing and distribution of the movie while Pixar maintains creative control. The first fruit of the arrangement was *A Bug's Life,* released in 1998. Much of Pixar's initial success was credited to John Lasseter, who worked for Disney and for George Lucas's special effects company before overseeing creative development at Pixar. *Toy Story 2,* released in late 1999, cheated the dreaded sequel curse, garnering tremendous acclaim and financial rewards. In 2001 Pixar completed the next installment in its Disney co-productions, *Monsters, Inc.* In mid-decade, the company added the 2004 film *The Incredibles* to its list of features. In a $7.4 billion deal, Disney acquired Pixar in 2006.

Walt Disney Co. The Walt Disney Co., headquartered in Burbank, California, was an early pioneer in full-length animated feature movies and continued its dominance in the first decade of the 2000s. Disney produced two of the top-grossing animated features of all time: *The Lion King,* which had grossed nearly $400 million by 2000, and *Aladdin,* which recorded domestic box office sales of $250 million. In 1991 Disney entered into a three-movie deal with Pixar Animation Studios that resulted in the 1995 animated feature *Toy Story,* a film that earned $1 billion in box office, video, and licensing sales. The companies renegotiated and signed a five-picture agreement in 1997, allowing Disney to purchase 5 percent of Pixar. Subsequent successes included *A Bug's Life, Toy Story 2,* and *Finding Nemo.* Disney ranked as one of the world's largest media companies heading into the late years of the first decade of the twenty-first century, with operations that include theme parks, television and film studios, publishing companies, a cruise line, and professional sports teams. In December 2006 the company announced plans to trim approximately 160 jobs from its 800-employee animation division, not including Pixar.

WORKFORCE

The computer animation industry is characterized by a well-educated workforce, populated with people who combine computer expertise and creative ability. While there is some on-the-job training—to learn an individual company's proprietary software programs, for instance—production studios generally don't train employees in technical areas such as creating special effects or programming languages. These skills, in addition to basic animation drawing, are learned in specialized computer animation programs offered by colleges, universities, and art schools. Most animators enter the job market with degrees in computer animation; a typical computer animation program includes the following classes: life drawing, character animation, color and design, character design, animation layout, storytelling, 3D character computers, and background painting. Because of the high level of technical sophistication required, many workers with advanced degrees come from disciplines such as mathematics or computer programming. Often, these programs work closely with companies in the industry and tailor their curricula to meet the marketplace's needs. For instance, in addition to funding an animation program at the California Institute of the Arts (CalArts), Disney Studios hires graduates of the program.

One benefit enjoyed by those pursuing a career in the computer animated entertainment industry was the ability to use their skills in a myriad of different ways. In a March 31, 2006, news release from the Entertainment Industry Office and Louisiana Department of Economic Development, Stacey Simmons, director of Baton Rouge's Red Stick International Animation Festival, explained: "The thing about the digital media industry is even though the individual jobs are very specialized, they're transferable. If you know how to do digital lighting, for example, you can go into a video game and light it. You can also do lighting for special effects on a film or on an animated feature. Those skills transfer very easily."

AMERICA AND THE WORLD

In its "Global Animation Industry: Strategies, Trends and Opportunities 2009" report, the Research and Markets group identified the major markets for computer animation as the United States, Canada, Japan, France, Britain, and Germany. In addition to computer animation itself, licensing operations for T-shirts, caps, and other products bearing media characters or symbols have provided another major source of revenue for the industry. In Japan, single computer games have advanced to animated series such as Pokemon, Monster Farm, Power Stone, and Detective Conan.

Another trend noted by the report was the increase in outsourcing of animation, particularly to Asia. This market, particularly tapped by North American film and television program producers, has been stimulated by economic factors of low labor costs in the Asia/Pacific region, as well as advanced animation platforms for 2D animation content along with some amount of 3D content. France was known for animation schools such as Supinfocom, which had campuses in Arles and Valenciennes. Students from these and other schools won awards for their work at venues such as the SIGGRAPH 2005 Computer Animation Festival.

Canadian companies also have demonstrated innovation in animation technology. In the late 1990s, Toronto-based Nelvana Ltd. and Vancouver-based Mainframe Entertainment Inc. both created 3D computer-generated television shows for children. Nelvana created, along with partner French MediaLab, *Donkey King Country*, a 3D cartoon series. Nelvana also partnered with another French company, Sparx, to create a series of half-hour 3D television shows called *Rolie Polie Olie*. It took a team of 20 employees one year to complete the show's 13 episodes. Mainframe contracted with Hasbro Properties Group to create a series of half hour *Action Man* cartoons created exclusively with CGI technology. In 2003, Mainframe worked with Sony Picture Television to produce 13 episodes of *Spider-Man*.

International partnerships also hoped to improve on the prehistoric realism of one of the most utilized purposes of CGI, dinosaur creation. In early 2000, the BBC in the United Kingdom hooked up with the Discovery Channel to re-create the Jurassic lizards in "Walking with Dinosaurs," a miniseries that recaptured dinosaurs as they lived in their natural habitat. By touching up the California redwood forest, Chilean volcanoes, and the Arizona desert with animation effects, the digital dinosaurs were layered over authentic photographic backgrounds. The animation team at London-based Frame-Store created scale dinosaurs, scanned them into computers, and refitted the creatures' actions to suit the scenery. The computerized material was then shot again with the cameras to create lifelike scenes of dinosaurs in their own habitat. After its British debut on the BBC, the ambitious miniseries, which cost $9.8 million, made its rounds into more than 30 international markets, attracting record ratings in several of them. In 2001, the two firms partnered to create a similar miniseries dubbed "Walking with Beasts."

RESEARCH AND TECHNOLOGY

Now that 3D animation rules in the industry, thanks to a new camera mapping tool called Zenviro, computer animators can build synthetic worlds around static matte paintings and models. CG supervisors can build a 3D scene using multiple image planes and 3D models, all textured with photographic elements that are projected onto the 2D and 3D geometry and then touched up, when needed, in Adobe's Photoshop. In other words, Zenviro artists are able to project high-resolution textures—2D images—onto 2D cards and onto 3D geometry within a 3D environment, paint on the textures, and move the camera around inside the resulting environment."

Another cutting-edge tool enhancing computer animation was Machinima, an animation technique that uses the rendering techniques employed in 3D video games. This technology essentially allows filmmakers to create movies within a video game engine, and considered nearly Hollywood quality.

BIBLIOGRAPHY

"Animation Asia Conference 2009 Sets the Tone..." 5 November 2009. Available from http://www.animenewsnetwork.com/press-release/2009-11-05/animation-asia-conference-2009-sets-the-tone-with-kadokawa-opening-keynote-address/.

Barker, Robert. "A Hollywood Play for Dreamers Only." *Business Week,* 1 November 2004.

Galloway, Stephen. "Dream Weavers. With a Mantel Full of Oscars and a Hot IPO, the Founders of DreamWorks SKG Have Turned Their Fantasy into Reality." *Hollywood Reporter,* 2 November 2004.

"Global Animation Industry: Strategies, Trends and Opportunities 2009..." Research and Markets report, Reuters, 23 April 2009. Available from http://www.reuters. com/article/PressRelease/idUS187119=23-Apr-2009+BW 20090423.

Holson, Laura M. "Disney Will Trim 160 Jobs from its Animation Unit." *The New York Times,* 2 December 2006.

Huang, Gregory T. "The New Face of Hollywood." *Technology Review,* September 2004.

Kaufman, Debra. "Cool Commercials: This Year's Super Bowl Spots Covered the Field of Animation, with the Goal of Scoring Big with Viewers." *Computer Graphics World,* March 2007.

McEachern, Martin. "This Old House: Imageworks Uses Performance Capture and Hand Animation to Create 'Dollhouse' Realism." *Computer Graphics World,* July 2006.

Moltenbrey, Karen. "Portfolio: DreamWorks' Matte Department." *Computer Graphics World,* March 2006.

Puig, Claudia. "'Shark Tale' Leads Computer-Animation Charge." *USA Today,* 30 September 2004.

Roberts, Johnnie L. "Working the Dream." *Newsweek,* 16 May 2005.

Robertson, Barbara. "Acorns & Aliens: Despite their Focus on Feature Films, Pixar and Blue Sky Studios Once Again Create Oscar-worthy Short Animations." *Computer Graphics World,* February 2007.

———. "Big Moves: Visual Effects and Motion-capture Studios Push the State of the Art for Mocap Technology and Techniques." *Computer Graphics World,* November 2006.

———. "Dark and Stormy Knight. ILM Creates New Tools to Craft a Galaxy Far, Far Away." *Computer Graphics World,* June 2005.

———. "Locomotion. Live-Action Film Techniques Transport Tom Hanks and Cast into the CG World of The Polar Express." *Computer Graphics World,* December 2004.

PlayStation. Available from http://vizeurope.com/uk/news/2009/06/news-392/.

Roncarelli, Robi. "Animation Industry Barrels Along." *Computer Graphics World,* April 2001.

Schlender, Brent. "The Man Who Built Pixar's Incredible Innovation Machine." *Fortune,* 15 November 2004.

"Toon Town." Entertainment Industry Office and Louisiana Department of Economic Development, 31 March 2006. Available from http://www.lafilm.org/media/index.cfm?id=626.

Peckham, Matt. "Wii Tops December Video Game Sales, Overall 2008 Revenue" *PC World,* December 2008.

Wingfield, Nick. "Digital Replicas May Change Face of Films." *The Wall Street Journal,* 31 July 2006.

Wolff, Ellen. "A Blend of Art and Science. The SIGGRAPH 2005 Computer Animation Festival." *SIGGRAPH 2005.*

COMPUTER NETWORK
SUPPORT SERVICES

———■———

SIC CODE(S)

7378

7379

7372

7376

INDUSTRY SNAPSHOT

Complicated technology, rising costs, and a dearth of information technology (IT) workers have made network support services a fast-moving business. However, as advances in networking software and hardware continued to integrate voice and data technology, the basic definition of network support services began to change and the differences between network support services and more general IT support services were scant. During the mid to late years of the first decade of the twenty-first century, a number of key trends were driving industry growth. These included rising security concerns, the adoption of radio frequency identification (RFID), increasing use of wireless technology, and growing acceptance of voice over Internet Protocol (VOIP).

Although many customers have approached IT outsourcing with trepidation, fearing poor service and lack of accountability, service level agreements (SLAs)—detailed contracts specifying a minimum quality of service and monetary penalties for the service vendor if the standard is not met—have done much to allay concerns. Businesses that use outside network support are also increasingly selective about which tasks they farm out, so they are less likely to find themselves in an unsatisfactory blanket arrangement. Cost savings remain a key motivator for companies that hire network support services.

With service options proliferating and quality improving, some analysts envision IT services growing ever more pervasive in network computing—to a point where a company doesn't need its own network but relies entirely upon services. High speed fiber-optic networks, the ubiquity of the Internet, and new networking paradigms such as virtual private networks, have all helped make this possible on a limited scale and point to a future where network services figure prominently.

ORGANIZATION AND STRUCTURE

In a typical network support agreement, the service provider may assume daily responsibility of a local area network or wide area network and guarantee a specified response time to all problems and difficulties. Additional services may include 24-hour/seven-days-a-week support; planning for optimal capacity; and preventive maintenance activities, such as scheduled upgrades. Help desk services include handling trouble calls, resolving problems, and staging or coordinating inventories. Often the network support services provider becomes the liaison contact with other computer vendors involved with the contracting company, including software, hardware, and telecommunications providers. Profit comes only with experienced personnel and volume, as additional customers are incremental costs to a support operation.

Companies supplying computer network support services range in size from large vendors, such as IBM Global Services and HP Technology Solutions Group, down to much smaller resellers. Resellers, often called value-added resellers (VARs), may partner with larger corporations. That is, the VAR enters into a reseller agreement with the large corporation and the giant wholesales its hardware and/or software to the reseller. VARs customize products channeled from the vendor, bundle them with network and other services, and add value in other ways. VARs serve as the distribution channel for vendors and are often the primary source of computer equipment and services for small and medium-sized companies.

Due to growing client demand for support services and escalating hardware and software complexity, the interaction between large vendors and VARs is not always clearly defined. There is money to be made in services, and it seems everybody wants to take advantage of the opportunity. In response to the demand, and in an effort to boost revenues, vendors such as Hewlett-Packard Co. and IBM Corp. run integration, consulting, and service units or divisions that often compete with their channel partners for customers.

To gain an edge on the competition, a VAR can concentrate on available niche opportunities that are more appropriate for its smaller, more tightly focused organization, or the reseller can work in a joint venture or subcontract mode with a large services provider. A third option, which allows the reseller firm to be acquired by the giant, nets a nice profit for the business owner at the cost of the VAR's independent existence.

Telephone companies and their subsidiaries perform network support and systems integration without a direct stake as reseller or vendor channel. Telecommunications companies such as AT&T have become active in providing network support services and systems integration.

Finally, consulting firms such as Accenture Ltd. and staffing service firms such as Adecco provide network support services from a large pool of technical personnel.

BACKGROUND AND DEVELOPMENT

In the 1980s and early 1990s, the word network, as used in the term computer network, was a simple noun referring to "a group of computers and associated devices that are connected by communications facilities." It was easy to define and easy to visualize. A network's activities, which consisted mostly of making shared files and printers available to network members, were coordinated by a network operating system installed on a server. The network's activities were fairly limited and routine, and a few information technology professionals could tame, control, and manage them.

By the mid-1990s, hardware and software advances had gradually expanded the basic network, as local area networks (LANs) supported more and more users and demand for wide area networks (WANs), metropolitan area networks (MANs), and other configurations surged. Networks were the infrastructure for the fast-growing client/server paradigm. Added to the mix was a range of

Internet technologies that gobbled up resources on both the public network and the private networks that interfaced with it. The Internet's popularity brought an onslaught of new traffic to private networks in the form of e-mail, Internet browsing, and related applications.

Stretched to the limit, companies turned to vendors or third party companies for help installing, configuring, managing, maintaining, and troubleshooting their increasingly complex networks. By 1996, according to a *PC Week* feature, all Fortune 1000 companies had implemented outsourcing contracts with third party companies for network support services. Computer network support service was becoming a rapidly growing, highly profitable industry niche.

A larger shift by corporations toward outsourcing nonessential functions also gave the industry a boost. According to a 1997 survey, almost 73 percent of IT managers reported outsourcing some of their technical needs. The top function outsourced was network maintenance (46.6 percent), followed by software development (42.5 percent), mainframe/legacy migrations (37 percent), software maintenance (32.9 percent), and Web site hosting (24.7 percent). According to another study, 27 percent of surveyed companies were considering outsourcing remote network management services as well.

The foremost problem with external service and support, according to a 1996 survey, was cost. Outsourcing expenses depended on the services required and the system's complexity. One company, NetSolve, offered a service called ProWatch Exchange at $5,500 per month for a 30-site network. Other companies offered more configurable pricing arrangements. AT&T Managed Network Solutions charged a base rate of $225 per site per month for a managed router contract, but it added $50 for each additional LAN or WAN connection. Additional problems identified in the same survey were poor responsiveness and lack of multi-vendor expertise.

The market was fueled by the spate of companies wishing to build or enhance their e-commerce capabilities. In doing so, they needed anything from consulting and design services to integration services to hosting and management services. Primary network concerns shifted from engaging in e-commerce to increasing security, particularly after several highly publicized Internet-based viruses brought business to a standstill at several large organizations. The proliferation of wireless network availability and related integration added a boost to outsourcing demand.

The fast-growing market for network support services has enticed a number of large players to bolster their presence through acquisitions and joint ventures. Market analysts at International Data Corp. (IDC) suggested that as the computer hardware business grows less profitable, top hardware companies will gravitate toward services to sustain their business. Providing one example,

Cisco Systems, the network hardware colossus, weighed in with heavy investments in the IT consulting wings of Cap Gemini and KPMG. The deals gave Cisco a hand in the service business and potentially opened new distribution channels for its hardware. In 2002 Cisco acquired AYR Network Inc., a distributing networks services provider. Similarly, Lucent Technologies made a pair of acquisitions that added substantial heft to its already large network services.

The line between network support and general information technology support began to blur because, as stated in the April 2003 issue of *Computer Weekly,* "Networks have become mainstream and integrated with the rest of the IT department and the company. Not that the role has been downgraded: networks have become increasingly important to business along with experienced network people with the relevant skills." This blurring of boundaries is due mainly to the convergence of voice and data technology.

A number of key trends were driving industry growth. These included rising security concerns, the adoption of radio frequency identification (RFID), increasing use of wireless technology, and growing acceptance of voice over Internet Protocol (VOIP).

In the security realm, market research firm Gartner noted that while spending on security was beginning to level off, so-called "disruptive technologies" ensured growth in this area. In a June 6, 2005, news release, Gartner managing Vice President Victor S. Wheatman stated, "Each wave of technology obliterates the security architecture appropriate for its predecessor. Enterprises will often rely on outside support, such as consultants and outsourcers, at the onset of any change. Security funding will shift from traditional solution purchaser to a broader, better-defined risk management process involving investment in three objectives: keeping the bad guys out, letting the good guys in, and keeping the wheels on (maintaining operations)."

Radio frequency identification (RFID) was another key technology that was increasing the volume and complexity of data moving across corporate networks. This technology involves the use of small radio tags that are able to communicate with a networked device known as a reader. These tags, which vary in size, price, and capability, consist of a digital memory chip and a transponder. They are affixed to or embedded within a wide range of items that manufacturers, retailers, and other parties wish to track. Much more than mere tracking devices, RFID tags contain actual data that is transmitted back to the reader. This data may include serial numbers and other specifications, such as the date and time that a product was manufactured or purchased.

Leading retailer Wal-Mart, as well as the U.S. Department of Defense (DOD), required vendors to use RFID technology as a condition of doing business with them. Mandates such as these were expected to fuel strong growth within the RFID market. Allied Business Intelligence Inc. (ABI) projected that the overall RFID market would grow from $1.4 billion in 2003 to $3.8 billion by 2008.

Despite these optimistic projections, many organizations were evaluating the returns they would get from RFID investments. In addition, they faced the task of integrating RFID into existing systems without disrupting the flow of business. Amidst these conditions, consultants and companies that could help on the integration front stood to benefit. In December 2004, International Data Corp. (IDC) indicated that the market for RFID-related consulting, implementation, and managed services was expected to reach $2 billion by 2008.

In the wireless segment, the industry witnessed a rise in the use of wireless networks capable of moving larger amounts of data. At the same time, this increased the need for equipment and services devoted to troubleshooting and real-time monitoring. One reason for this was the complexity of protocols used in wireless data transmission, which was increasing as the industry planned to transition to 3G technology—a third generation wireless global telecommunication system with roaming, broad bandwidth, and high speeds focused on a shift from voice-centric to multi-media (video, voice, data, fax) services.

During the middle of the decade, the integration of voice and data technology continued, as more companies adopted voice over Internet protocol (VOIP), which allows voice communications to be transmitted over the Internet instead of traditional telecommunications networks. According to *User Plans for IP Voice, North America 2005,* a study conducted by Infonetics Research, large, medium, and small organizations reported average Internet protocol (IP) voice spending of $117,000 in 2003, an increase of 46 percent from the previous year. In addition, participating organizations indicated that they would increase spending by an additional 9 percent in 2005. According to the study, while 29 percent of large North American organizations indicated that they would be using VOIP during 2005, the same was true for only 16 percent of medium-sized firms and four percent of small firms.

According to statistics from the U.S. Department of Commerce and the National Association of Software and Service Companies, of the 505,000 outsourcing jobs listed for India in 2004, more than 250,000 were IT workers. The statistics illustrated that the number of IT jobs being outsourced to India has increased steadily since 2000, when the total was slightly more than 100,000. While IT workers accounted for roughly two-thirds of all the outsourcing jobs listed in these figures for that year, by 2004 they accounted for about half. This seems to suggest the growth of other types of outsourcing to India, beyond just IT.

A controversial 2004 report from the Information Technology Association of America (ITAA), based on research conducted by Global Insight Inc., predicted that U.S. spending on offshore outsourcing would increase from $10 billion in 2003 to $31 billion by 2008, with related savings rising from $6.7 billion to $20.9 billion during the same time period. While the ITAA saw off-shoring as a positive factor and indicated that more economic growth would occur as a result, others were skeptical. In particular, critics were concerned about the loss of productive white collar jobs to nations overseas.

In a May 15, 2007, news release, Gartner Research Vice President Kathryn Hale commented, "Core business process outsourcing (BPO) services had a strong showing in 2006. These process management services grew 8.6 percent worldwide, and several market leaders grew faster than the overall market. Still, development and integration services represent the backbone of IT services, accounting for 30 percent of the market."

Separate research from IDC, which evaluated the global market for enterprise network consulting and integration services, projected explosive growth into the coming decade. Bolstered by compound annual growth of 12.3 percent, IDC's July 2007 forecast predicted this market segment would be valued at $36 billion by 2011.

Commenting on the research in an overview of the study, IDC Senior Analyst Wu Zhou explained: "Enterprise customers need high-performing, scalable, and secure networks that are global, distributed, and always available. Vendors that can leverage strategic partnerships and develop vertically focused and repeatable service offerings will have an above-average chance of becoming trusted partners to the enterprise segment."

CURRENT CONDITIONS

The economic downturn palpably affected sales in the networking industry in 2008 and early 2009, according to Infonetics Research, which showed a gradual decline is sales of service provider switches and IP core and edge routers. The December 2008 report indicated that the North American carrier router and switch market declined significantly, while the Europe, Middle East, and Africa Region was slightly up. The Asia-Pacific region was also flat.

In October 2009, an IBISWorld Industry report broke down IT support, CRM, and Data Processing Services products and services by percent of total market. It reported that business process management held roughly a fourth of the market, with data management services and application service provisioning each holding about 10 to 12 percent. IT technical support services, IT computer network management services, collocation services, and Web site hosting services collectively held about 28 to 30 percent. This report valued the entire industry as worth $101.9 billion in 2008.

The overall computer hardware market was valued at $537.3 billion in 2008. As for the U.S. sector of computer hardware and equipment used in networking services, First Research, Inc. noted that about 1,000 U.S. companies were active within the industry, with combined annual revenues of $50 billion. However, in a November 2009 interview for the *New York Times,* Ann M. Livermore, executive vice president of Hewlett Packard, described U.S. computer networking as a $40 billion a year market with a high profit margin.

INDUSTRY LEADERS

Cisco Systems Cisco continued to lead the market in 2008 and 2009, with fiscal 2008 revenues of $39.5 billion, an increase of 13 percent year over year, reported the company in its annual report to shareholders. Cisco's share of the networking market is well-grounded, in that it provides end-to-end solutions and also leads the market in more than 20 product areas. Nevertheless, Cisco's margin of market share began to slip during the above period, as competitors such as Juniper, Alcatel Lucent, Hewlett Packard, and others began to merge or acquire smaller concerns to gain market share. A report on the service provider router market published by Dell'Oro Group found that Cisco's market share had dropped 6 percent in the second and third quarter of fiscal year 2008, while competitors' shares grew. Synergy Research Group also reported that Cisco's share in service provider edge routers began to slip in late 2008.

Hewlett-Packard Co. In an effort to provide a more integrated offering of solutions to its customers, Hewlett-Packard (HP) had merged its HP Services and Enterprise Systems units in 2004 to form the HP Technology Solutions Group, headed by Ann M. Livermore, who remained at the helm in late 2009. According to HP, its services division employed 69,000 people in 2007. At that time, the division's operations included 112 call centers/service desks, 82 outsourcing data centers, 80 customer education centers, 64 business recovery centers, 42 remote management centers, and 14 global delivery application services centers. In November 2009, HP announced that it would acquire 3Com for $2.7 billion in an effort to equalize the market with Cisco. Newly-acquired 3Com, with strong ties in China, manufactured networking gear such as routers and switches, as well as provided security and networking management services. It was expected to add $1.3 to 2 billion to HP's portfolio in the future.

Alcatel-Lucent Best known as a hardware vendor, Alcatel-Lucent (formerly Lucent Technologies Inc.) is also a prominent provider of network support services, and ranked No. 2 in the edge router market for 2008. In 1997 the company formed Lucent NetCare Services, which offered clients consulting, management, and maintenance services for enterprise voice, data, and video networks. By 1999 Lucent had expanded its NetCare support capabilities to customers in 93 countries. The same year, it acquired International Network Services and Ascend Communications, which added 2,200 employees to NetCare and bolstered its strength in network technologies such as asynchronous transfer mode (ATM) and Internet protocol (IP). Eventually, NetCare was renamed Lucent Worldwide Services. In late 2006, Lucent was acquired by Alcatel in an $11.6 billion deal. The company remained a major industry player, with 2007 revenues of $26.2 billion and 89,370 employees. For 2008, the company reported losses and was still under massive restructuring going into 2009.

Juniper Networks Juniper was considered Cisco's main networking competitor going into 2009. With a 2008 annual revenue of $3.57 billion (up from $2.7 billion just a year prior), the company was holding a 25 percent market share going into 2009. The company was heavily engaged in industry research and development.

AT&T As of 2009, AT&T remained a true industry giant, providing what seemed to be every type of computer or telecommunications service that corporate end users could want via its Enterprise Business division. These services included long distance voice services, domestic and international toll-free inbound services, virtual private network applications, audio and video teleconferencing, and Web-based video conferencing, as well as local voice and data telecommunications. AT&T Business Services provided integrated voice, data and IP services that involved the use of high capacity digital circuits, giving users with high-volume data needs a direct connection to one of AT&T's switches and enabling them to create internal data networks and access the Internet and other external data networks. The company also offered data networks that utilized packet switching and transmission technologies to economically and securely transmit large amounts of information. Other offerings included contact center and business continuity services.

IBM Global Services The world's largest IT services vendor, IBM's Global Services division posted 2005 revenues of $47.4 billion. Network support, however, makes up only a small portion of IBM's service portfolio, which in 2007 included a full array of consulting, programming, maintenance, and integration services. Specific offerings included business continuity and resiliency, integrated communications, IT strategy and architecture, maintenance and technical support, middleware, outsourcing, security and

privacy, servers, and storage/data management. In 2000, former IBM services chief Douglas T. Elix expressed his wish to turn Global Services into IBM's biggest division by doubling sales within four years through the integration of clients' systems into an e-business network. In 2002, IBM bought PwC Consulting and folded it into its Global Services unit.

A few other industry up-and-runnings to watch were Asia's Huawei, Polycom (with 2008 revenues of $1.1 billion) and Redback.

WORKFORCE

At the end of the twentieth century, the United States was experiencing a dramatic shortage of IT workers. The Information Technology Association of America estimated that there were 346,000 unfilled IT positions at U.S. firms in 1999. The U.S. Bureau of Labor Statistics (BLS) predicted in 1998 that computer scientists, computer engineers, and systems analysts would be the three fastest growing occupations through 2006. The forces cited by BLS as driving the demand for systems analysts included the expansion of client/server environments and increasing demand for networking to share information. However, the slowdown in the technology industry in the early 2000s, coupled with the flagging U.S. economy, offset this job shortage considerably. During the mid-years of the first decade of the 2000s, the trend of outsourcing and offshoring led to further job losses within the IT sector, which was expected to continue.

According to a national salary survey by J & D Resources, Inc., typical salaries for network administrators ranged from $40,000 to $58,000, while network analysts, managers, and LAN/WAN specialists averaged between $50,000 and $75,000. For help desk support technicians, average salaries ranged from $35,000 to $42,500. At the higher end, network architects typically earned $60,000 to $80,000 and systems architects pulled in $70,000 to $95,000.

AMERICA AND THE WORLD

According to expert Sramana Mitra in his February 2009 report on the networking sector, total U.S. revenues grew 18 percent in 2008, but the international Americas growing 77 percent year over year. The Asia Pacific region grew 10 percent, led by Japan and China.

Outsourcing or offshoring remained a major trend within the IT industry. Companies sought tremendous labor cost savings—as much as 20 to 70 percent—by moving operations to low-cost nations like China and India. In December 2003 alone, IBM transferred almost 5,000 programming jobs to those two nations.

Heading into the second decade of the 2000s, India was projected to experience continued growth from outsourcing, infrastructure expansion, and growth in other IT areas. According to the research firm IDC, the country's IT industry experienced growth of 31 percent in 2006 alone and was expected to grow at a compound annual rate of 18 percent through 2011, reaching $100 billion.

Regarding computer hardware used in networking services, the global industry was valued at $537.3 billion in 2008. Asia-Pacific optical networking (ON) sales were $4.39 billion in 2008, up 21 percent, according to Industry Market Research Report; the increase was attributed to systems and services that supported higher data transfer and storage. According to IDC, the Western European IP PBX market reached $2.1 billion in 2008. Datamonitor's 2009 Computer Hardware Report showed that the market for what it referred to as BRIC (Brazil, Russia, India, and China) increased by 15.4 percent between 2004 and 2008 to reach a value of $35.6 billion. Datamonitor forecast this market to reach $64.2 billion by 2013. It also reported that Russia had the fastest growing market between 2004 and 2008.

BIBLIOGRAPHY

"About HP Services." Hewlett-Packard Co., 8 September 2007. Available from http://h20219.www2.hp. com/services/cache/13424-0-0-225-121.html.

"Annual Report 2008" Cisco Systems. Available at http://www.cisco.com/web/about/ac49/ac20/ac19/ar228/letter_to_shareholders/index.html.

"AT&T: Enterprise Business: Products and Services." AT&T Inc., 8 September 2007. Available from http://www.business.att.com.

"Business Profile Lucent Worldwide Services." Lucent Technologies, 8 June 2005. Available from http://www.lucent.com/corpinfo/ws.html.

Frauenheim, Ed. "HP Merges Services, High-End Computing Units." CNET News, 4 May 2004.

"Frost & Sullivan: 3G Brings New Opportunities for Wireless Network Monitoring and Protocol Analyzer Vendors." *Wireless News,* 2 May 2005.

"Gartner Says Disruptive Technologies Create Continuing IT Security Challenges." Gartner Inc., 6 June 2005. Available from http://www.gartner.com.

"Gartner Says Worldwide IT Services Revenue Grew 6 Percent in 2006." Gartner Inc., 15 May 2007. Available from http://www.gartner.com.

"Gartner Says Worldwide IT Services Revenue Grew 6.7 Percent in 2004." Gartner Inc., 8 February 2005. Available from http://www.gartner.com.

"HP to Acquire 3Com for $2.7 Billion." *New York Times,* 12 November 2009.

"IDC: India IT Industry Grows by 31% in 2006." *Wireless News,* 4 April 2007.

"India Builds Global Business Role on an IT Advantage: Economic Reform Breeds Strategic Growth in Industry." *Institutional Investor,* March 2005.

"Infonetics: Enterprise IP Voice Spending Up 46% in 2004." *Wireless News,* 6 May 2005.

Marion, Larry. "At Your Service; Expanding Services Industry." *PC Week,* 15 January 1996.

Mitra, Sramana. "Networking Sector Cisco, Juniper, Polycom." *Entrepreneur Journeys,* 5 February 2009.

———. "Sector Overview: Networking." *Entrepreneur Journeys,* 8 December 2008.

"Networks Market Research Reports." Available from http://www.marketresearch.com

Porter, Eduardo. "Outsourcing Is Becoming a Harder Sell in the U.S." *The New York Times,* 6 March 2004.

Reingold, Jennifer. "A Brief (Recent) History of Offshoring." *Fast Company,* April 2004.

———. "Into Thin Air: These People Lost High-Tech Jobs to Low-Wage Countries. Try Telling Them That Offshoring Is a Good Thing in the Long Run." *Fast Company,* April 2004.

"Strong Growth Expected in RFID Consulting Services." *TechWeb,* 6 December 2004. Available from http://www.techweb.com/wire/ebiz/54800641.

Thibodeau, Patrick. "More IT Jobs to Go Offshore, Controversial ITAA Report Says: Concludes that U.S. Economy will Benefit from Growing Trend." *Computerworld,* 5 April 2004.

Weston, Rusty. "Why Fight IT?" *PC Week,* 22 July 1996.

Woolnough, Roisin. "Finding the New Breed of Network Manager." *Computer Weekly,* 29 April 2003.

"Worldwide Network Consulting and Integration Services 2005-2009 Forecast." IDC, May 2005. Available from http://www.idc.com.

"Worldwide and U.S. Enterprise Network Consulting and Integration Services 2007-2011 Forecast and Analysis." IDC, July 2007. Available from http://www.idc.com.

COMPUTER SECURITY

SIC CODE(S)

7372

7379

INDUSTRY SNAPSHOT

As businesses, individuals, governments, and institutions grow into an increasingly interconnected web of computer networks, computer security has become a rapidly growing concern in the twenty-first century. By the latter half of the twenty-first century's first decade, an inestimable volume of crucial transactions—financial and otherwise—were transmitted over the Internet and other networks every day, and the effects of a disruption to any one of these networks threatened to ripple through the wider economic and social fabric.

Information was among the most valued assets a company could claim. As such, the protection of that information was of primary concern to owners and managers, who eyed, with worry, reports of the damages stemming from data theft. Business intelligence contributor Kroll Inc. released its *Global Fraud Report* in late 2009, indicating that the 2008–2009 economic downturn had affected business behavior and business exposure to fraud. The highest percentage of companies vulnerable to fraud was in the area of information theft, loss, or attack. The greater vulnerability was attributed to higher staff turnover, reductions in internal controls, and reduced revenues across the board.

Internet-based fraud, sophisticated viruses, illicit network access, and computer-network-based sabotage were among the industry's chief enemies. Worms, viruses, malicious codes, security breaches, and cyber-attacks grew stronger and more sophisticated each year, with no end in sight. Providers of computer security software and services found themselves in a sort of arms race with hackers, online thieves, and others seeking to invade or disrupt the operation of computers and networks. Moreover, following the security shock of the terrorist attacks against the United States on September 11, 2001, intelligence reports revealed burgeoning interest among terrorist groups in U.S. computer networks. Thus, computer and network security measures were increasingly folded into broader national security efforts, including measures embedded in the Homeland Security Act.

ORGANIZATION AND STRUCTURE

The field of computer security is extremely diverse and thus opportunities are abundant for those with a wide range of skills. There are three main levels of computer security: physical, software, and administrative controls. Each level is addressed by a different specialist using different skills.

Physical security addresses problems such as fire, theft, sabotage, and malicious pranks. Systems analysts and security officers typically address these types of problems.

Software security involves factors such as accidental disclosures caused by partially debugged or poorly designed programs and the active or passive infiltration of computer systems. Active infiltration includes such activities as using legitimate access to a system to obtain unauthorized information, obtaining identification to gain access through improper means, or getting into systems via unauthorized physical access. Passive infiltration includes activities such as wiretapping on data communications lines or databases

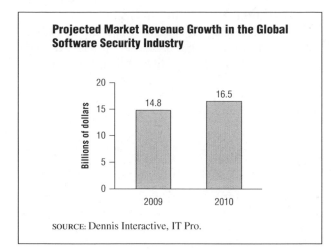

Projected Market Revenue Growth in the Global Software Security Industry

SOURCE: Dennis Interactive, IT Pro.

and using concealed transmitters to send or retrieve data in central processing units, databases, or data communications lines. People involved in software security include analysts, network administrators, programmers, auditors, and security officers.

Administrative controls involve issues such as controls on personnel for fraud protection, controls on sensitive programs, security of remote terminal access, software security, and file reconstruction capability. Auditors, programmers, systems analysts, security officers, and network administrators are involved in addressing the development and implementation of administrative controls.

While different specialists often address all of these security issues, the need for multilevel controls is increasing as the number of computers grow—one more indication that additional computer security is a continuing demand. The industry will no doubt grow to accommodate the problem.

Most applications and systems software—Internet browsers, e-mail programs, operating systems, databases, and the like—have historically provided only rudimentary security at best and are often easily vulnerable to devastating attack or misappropriation. While security in ordinary desktop applications is improving, to help users withstand such intrusions, computer security companies market a diverse range of products and services to combat fraud, sabotage, and other unauthorized uses of computer resources. These consist of security consulting services; virus detection software; firewall hardware and software; encryption software; intrusion detection and analysis software; and specialty devices for user authentication, such as biometrics and voice recognition.

Computer Security and the Law One of the unique aspects of the computer security industry is its connection to the criminal justice system. Many of the activities

computer security deals with are illegal. Thus, these activities fall under the broad heading of computer crime.

There are three primary areas of computer crime: data security and integrity, national security threats, and protection of software copyright. Heading into the twenty-first century's second decade, there was a technological gap between the criminal justice system and the enforcement of laws designed to prosecute computer criminals. This lag opens the door for more computer security experts among attorneys, law enforcement agencies, the military, and government organizations.

In August of 1998 the nation's top anti-terrorism chief discussed the threat of computer warfare that could cripple the United States. Potential targets included banks, airports, stock markets, telephones, and power suppliers. Richard Clarke, the first national coordinator for security, infrastructure protection, and counter-terrorism, proposed backup plans and vigilance to foil a coordinated multi-pronged attack from a foreign military, terrorist, or intelligence group.

On the legislative front, the controversial Cyberspace Electronic Security Act, under consideration since 1998, was finally passed by the Senate as an amendment to the Homeland Security Act in November 2002. The bill, a counterpoint to the Clinton administration's easing of encryption software exports in 1999, gave law enforcement new powers to access encrypted information and conduct electronic searches. In 2003 the White House augmented this legislation with its National Strategy to Secure Cyberspace, which listed a series of recommendations to businesses and network administrators detailing needed system improvements and strategies. In addition, in the wake of the e-commerce explosion, a slew of privacy, data integrity, and other federal and international computer security laws and regulations sprang up to enforce minimum security standards to protect the flow of information through and between industries and networks.

The National Vulnerability Database is the U.S. government repository of standards-based vulnerability management data. NVD includes databases containing security checklists, security related software flaws, misconfigurations, product names, etc. As of September 2010, it was processing 11 CVE vulnerabilities daily, with a database of 43,772 total CVE vulnerabilities.

BACKGROUND AND DEVELOPMENT

Computers for commercial use date back to the 1940s. Since that time, computers have evolved from gigantic board-wired, cathode-ray-tubed, card-deck-operated machines that literally filled climate-controlled glass houses into desktop machines that are many times more powerful than their larger predecessors.

By the 1990s people in every walk of life were using computers to perform a variety of tasks ranging from mixing recipe ingredients to desktop publishing. In many cases, they were tied into networks such as wide area networks, local area networks, and the Internet. The increasing reliance on networks has created a greater demand for security since networks allow for more opportunities to compromise files and databases.

Businesses in particular have been using more powerful computers for every function possible. Naturally, the almost infinite growth in data processing has led to computer-related problems such as crime, terrorism, harassment from hackers who break into computer systems, and crackers who deliberately damage others' computers. The need for protection against hackers and crackers has prompted corporations and individuals to seek the help of security specialists.

The development of computer security procedures paralleled developments in the data processing industry. Each succeeding generation of computers has been accompanied by concomitant developments in security measures. Originally, computer security involved controlling access to computer rooms. It was concentrated in the industrial arena, since computers were rarely found outside industry. Computer security specialists were generally senior level members of a company's data processing staff.

In the early days, computers were generally stand-alone units. Gradually, manufacturers added components such as modems that allowed computers in remote locations to communicate with one another. In the 1980s and 1990s, businesses rapidly deployed legions of personal computers (PCs) and Unix-based workstations, often networking them so information and resources could be shared.

Hackers, Crackers, and Thieves Along with its many benefits, the rise of networking brought with it a multitude of security risks, as each computer on a network is a potential entry point for outside hackers and internal miscreants. In most cases, the technology to exchange data between computers greatly outpaced the technology to keep them secure, and aside from a few rudimentary measures, security was often an afterthought.

Hackers and online thieves frequently crack into e-commerce sites looking for customer credit card and other information. Other vulnerable targets include customer relationship management systems, which store potentially valuable details about a firm's customer base, and supply chain systems, which govern the movement of products and supplies through a firm's infrastructure and also contain sensitive information about prices, payments, exchange terms, and production schedules. Some hackers breached computers just for the fun of it, while others hoped to gain wealth or information, cause harm, or wreak havoc.

In 1998 the research firm International Data Corp. reported that roughly 70 percent of Fortune 1000 companies had hired an ethical hacker to try and break into their own computer system. Such penetration testing to check firewalls will become a necessary part of every security consulting package in the future, according to the market research firm.

In April 1999 the FBI initiated the largest Internet manhunt ever to catch the world's fastest-spreading computer virus to date. The virus, known as Melissa, replicated itself through e-mail. All totaled, the FBI estimated that the virus infected more than 100,000 computer systems in commercial, government, and military installations, forcing some administrators to shut down their e-mail systems for a week. Investigators tracked down the originator with the help of a controversial serial identification number called a Global Unique Identifier or GUID. In the end, authorities charged a 30-year-old computer programmer with creating Melissa. The following summer, a similar virus was spread to computers around the world via an attachment with the disarming name of "I Love You." Beginning in Asia, the virus spread by infecting entire e-mail systems of its recipients, who then inadvertently sent it on to others. The damage to individuals, businesses, and institutions was estimated at roughly $10 billion.

A much different kind of attack was mounted in February 2000, when several popular Web sites were disrupted with so-called denial-of-service attacks. The sites, including such mainstays as Amazon.com, eBay, and Yahoo!, were effectively taken offline when the host computers were inundated with bogus traffic generated by a handful of computers. As a result, legitimate users weren't able to access the sites. These sorts of attacks had erupted before periodically, but never on the same scale or with the same coordination. The episode highlighted the vulnerability of even the biggest sites.

Each year saw a handful of super viruses and worms win particular notoriety for the extent of their damage, the breadth of their spread, the innovation of their design, or the means of their attack. In July of 2001 a worm entitled "Code Red" began attacking Microsoft Internet Information Server (IIS) systems. The worm infected servers running Windows NT 4, Windows 2000, Windows XP, and IIS 4.0, and defaced Web sites. Various versions of the worm were powerful enough to shut down Web sites and slow Internet traffic in general. Research firm Computer Economics estimated the cost of the worm at nearly $2 billion. While computer security experts were able to eradicate the worm, authorities were unable to pinpoint its origin. In August of 2003 a worm dubbed Blaster, the most rapidly spreading e-mail virus to date, infected more than 1 million systems and shut down several corporate networks. Moving into 2003 and 2004, incidents of such viruses grew so frequent that they tended to cause little sensation. However, while the number of highly visible computer security breaches like these continued to rise, their actual financial impact had begun to decline by 2002, according to the Computer Security Institute.

The increase in computer crime in turn gave rise to a new breed of law enforcement officials who became experts in computer use. The need for specialists who could help law enforcement officials and others involved in the criminal justice system, such as lawyers and judges and who could familiarize themselves with security procedures concerning computers, also grew. These technical advisers and consultants have been responsible for much of the research and new product development in the industry today.

The Adaptive Network Security Alliance, a coalition of 40 hardware and software vendors, tries to promote and enforce industry-wide standards to ensure all security products work well together. With the integration of automated tools, network administrators can plug a breach in a firewall in nanoseconds.

Extent of Risks A prominent annual survey found that 62 percent of respondents from government and private industry in 1999, at the height of the dot-com boom, reported computer security breaches within the previous year. The study, conducted by the Computer Security Institute (CSI) and the FBI, pegged total losses due to security breaches at more than $123 million for the 163 organizations that disclosed losses. Heisted proprietary information and financial fraud were the most expensive breaches.

Consistent with previous research, the survey found that disgruntled workers represented the most likely source of attacks on business computer systems. Independent hackers placed second, and domestic industry competitors ranked as the third most likely source. Ranked fourth and fifth were foreign competitors and foreign governments, respectively. The Internet was blamed as the most frequent point of attack, reflecting a steady increase of incidents involving the Internet, but illicit access through internal systems and remote dial-up also were common.

Meanwhile, the federal government itself was found to be seriously lagging behind in the effort to create secure computer environments. A study by the Subcommittee on Government Management, Information and Technology of the federal government's 26,000 separate computer systems found them to be in need of a serious security overhaul. Issuing letter grades, the committee awarded no As, while about half the agencies received Ds and Fs. The General Accounting Office concluded that the government was riddled with serious and widespread security weaknesses.

On the bright side, these massive efforts finally began to reverse the trend of financial damage stemming from computer attacks. According to the *2003 Computer Crime and Security Survey,* by the Computer Security Institute and the FBI, total losses from digital attacks fell from $455.8 million in 2002 to $201.8 million in 2003. Indeed, most forms of security breaches were pushed back in 2003. Losses stemming from financial fraud plummeted from $100 million in 2002 to less than $10 million in 2003, among the survey's 530 respondents. Theft of proprietary information, which emerged as the most expensive security issue facing businesses, cost about $170.8 million in 2002; a year later, security efforts cut that figure to $70.2 million. Losses due to penetration by unauthorized users fell from $13.1 million to $2.8 million, while internal sabotage of network data fell from $15.1 million to $5.1 million. Only denial-of-service attacks continued to outpace efforts to stem them, increasing from $18.4 million in 2002 to $65.6 million in 2003.

Not all of this turnaround was a result of improved security measures, however. According to the Yankee Group, while incidents of computer security breaches didn't decline over that period, firms were strengthening their ability to correctly assess the value of their proprietary information. Thus, they more modestly estimated the damage done by theft and other forms of compromised data. Not to underestimate the value of improved security systems and procedures, the Yankee Group further noted that they were increasingly characterized by mutual cooperation between businesses, with sharing of best practices and security knowledge.

During the early 2000s the Internet was the most frequent avenue of attack, with 78 percent reporting security breaches via that method. The *2003 Computer Crime and Security Survey* found that the most common defensive actions taken were anti-virus software and firewalls, which were utilized by nearly all respondents. Access control and physical computer security measures were in place at about 85 percent of firms. About 75 percent implemented intrusion detection systems, and two-thirds reported using encrypted files. Biometrics also was gaining in popularity; 11 percent of firms reported implementing such technologies. Internal system regulation was as much a priority as firewalls and other measures to keep out possible intruders. Ominously, the survey found that over half of all data theft benefits from assistance from within the company.

Emerging Business Models One of the fastest-growing trends among industry players was the movement toward subscription-based services. Market leaders like Symantec and Network Associates' McAfee increasingly expanded their services to include Internet-based computer scanning systems, whereby users order a scan of their computers for possible vulnerabilities. When the scan is complete, the vendor recommends improvements—such as downloads of newer, stronger versions of their proprietary software—that will bolster the user's defenses against disruptions such as e-mail worms and other malicious codes.

This development also opened a less obvious new area of competition between market leaders. The ability to scan customers' computers also afforded these firms the opportunity to sniff for their competitors' products and to point out their weaknesses to customers. While McAffee and Symantec mutually pledged not to use their ability to root around users' hard drives in unethical or secret information collection, according to the *Wall Street Journal,* the pressures to gain a foothold in this burgeoning market niche were evident in such practices.

Other Trends Computer security continued to be a critical issue for organizations and consumers during the mid-2000s. The *2005 CSI/FBI Computer Crime and Security Survey,* conducted by the Computer Security Institute (CSI) and the San Francisco Federal Bureau of Investigation's (FBI) Computer Intrusion Squad, detailed the impact of computer crime on organizations. The report was compiled with input from 700 computer security professionals at corporations, financial institutions, government agencies, universities, and medical institutions. According to the survey, computer crime cost organizations more than $130.1 million in 2005. At nearly $42.8 million, viruses caused the greatest dollar loss, followed by unauthorized computer access ($31.2 million), and theft of proprietary information ($7.3 million).

However, these figures only tell part of the story. In a separate survey of 2,000 public and private organizations, the FBI revealed that 10 percent of known attacks were not reported to authorities. Factors such as market pressures, the threat of negative publicity, and declines in consumer confidence prohibit firms from calling excessive attention to security breaches within their networks. The FBI report estimated that some 64 percent of the companies it surveyed withstood some form of financial loss, totaling $32 million.

While the impact of computer security breaches at the organizational level is significant, consumers also suffered substantial losses. This was especially true in the case of cyber scams. In its April 3, 2006, issue, *Business Week Online* cited a report from the research firm Gartner indicating that financial losses related to the theft of personal or financial information totaled $1.5 billion in 2005, up from $690 million in 2004.

Computer criminals were becoming more sophisticated, using blackmail and other psychological tactics to trick individuals into releasing money or financial information. For example, hackers often watch news headlines for stories about tragic events and mergers between financial institutions to devise realistic financial scams that fool computers users into donating money or providing sensitive account information. One trend was to send one or more e-mails with legitimate information and no request for action on the part of the recipient, in an effort to build trust, followed by later communications requesting personal information. Such non-technical methods made the job of security professionals harder than ever before.

Needless to say, computer security is a growth industry. The growing list of security threats was a welcome boon to providers of computer security systems and services. In terms of the most promising markets, the aforementioned *2005 CSI/FBI Computer Crime and Security Survey* found that firewalls were the most widely used form of computer security during the middle years of the first decade. Some 97 percent of respondents indicated that their organization used that form of security, followed by anti-virus software (96 percent), intrusion detection systems (72 percent), server-based access control lists (70 percent), the encryption of data during transmission (68 percent), reusable account log-ins or passwords (52 percent), file encryption (46 percent), and smart cards/one-time password tokens (42 percent). Intrusion prevention systems and public key infrastructure were each used by 35 percent of respondents, while biometrics were used by only 15 percent.

Software behemoth Microsoft Corp. was getting into the security act as well. Widely criticized in the industry for issuing new versions of its operating systems filled with bugs for users to report, thereby allowing Microsoft to remain the first to market while only gradually updating its security on a piecemeal basis, the firm started incorporating anti-virus features in the Windows operating system, which was the largest target for hackers and virus makers. Microsoft's Windows Security Center, launched in 2004, scanned users' systems to assess the effectiveness of their current anti-virus and other security software.

CURRENT CONDITIONS

In its *Security Industry Association 2009 Annual Report,* the SIA reported the value of the electronic security market to be $17.9 billion (based on 2007 and 2008 data), with $8.2 billion of that coming from installers and integrators of security products. However, industry analyst Gartner forecast the global software security market alone would exceed $16.5 billion in 2010, up from $14.8 billion in 2009. Gartner also indicated that products delivered via the software-as-a-service (SAAS) model and/or via appliances would sell at a greater pace than those purchased through traditional software licenses.

In the comprehensive 2010 edition of CSI's annual *Computer Crime and Security Survey,* respondents reported sharp rises in password sniffing, financial fraud, and malware infection. However, average losses resulting from security incidents fell once again (from $289,000 to

$234,244 per respondent), although still above 2006 figures. Other reported facts: one-third of respondents' organizations were fraudulently represented as the senders of phishing messages, but 25 percent of overall respondents believed that the majority of their financial losses were due to non-malicious actions by insiders. A previous CSI survey had reported that the most prevalent security problem was insider abuse of network access or e-mail, an incident that 59 percent of the companies experienced. Virus incidents occurred at 52 percent of companies.

In its September 2009 "Top Cyber Security Risks" report, the SANS Institute noted that two risks dwarfed all others: unpatched client-side software and vulnerable, Internet-facing Web sites. In the first, targeted e-mail attacks (i.e., spear phishing) used programs such as Adobe PDF Reader, QuickTime, Adobe Flash, and Microsoft Office as the primary initial infection vendors to compromise computers that had Internet access. Infected computers were then used to propagate the infection and compromise other internal computers and sensitive servers. The report noted that, on average, major organizations took at least twice as long to patch client-side vulnerabilities as they did to patch operating system vulnerabilities. In the second risk, attacks against Internet applications constituted more than 60 percent of total attack attempts observed on the Internet. Vulnerabilities such as SQL Injection or Cross-Site Scripting account for the majority. Most Web site owners failed to scan effectively and became unwitting vehicles to infect visitors that trusted those sites.

PC Magazine published its top picks for the best security suites of 2010, with Editor's Choice recognition going to Norton Internet Security 2010, along with Norton 360 v4.0. These products had good anti-malware and anti-spam scores, and Norton 360 added PC tune-up along with a powerful backup system. High scores also went to McAfee Total Protection 2010, with an especially strong anti-spam module, as well as an overall impressive suite. Other good products included AVG Internet Security 9.0, avast! Internet Security 5.0, and PC Tools Internet Security 2010, which included anti-malware features. BitDefender scored high in anti-spam and parental controls, but dragged system performance with its bonus features. ZoneAlarm Extreme Security also scored high, with its ForceField virtualization technology and system tune-up (ZoneAlarm had been the 2009 Editor's Choice.)

Hacking has become a hobby with its own social network. In 2008 the Web site "House of Hackers" had more than 4,000 members. Although the site's creator, Petko D. Petkov, includes a note that criminal behavior is not promoted, many of the threads of discussion relate to what people hack and how they go about it. According to the site's home page, "The House of Hackers community is established to support the hacker culture, mindset, way of life, ideologies, political views, vision, etc."

INDUSTRY LEADERS

Symantec Corp. Symantec, based in Cupertino, California, is a giant security software firm, hawking systems that shield computer systems from viruses, detect intrusion by unauthorized network users, and enable users to manage systems from remote locations. The company's Norton Antivirus and Norton Utilities suites generate enormous consumer sales. Symantec claimed 64 percent of the consumer market by 2004, according to International Data Corp., and the company leveraged that strength to expand into services such as consulting, security management, and security assessment.

Founded by artificial intelligence scientist Gary Hendrix in 1982, the company steadily grew through a series of acquisitions of smaller, niche market software vendors. In the late 1990s Symantec picked up IBM's and Intel's anti-virus operations and acquired rival AXENT Technologies, a top seller of risk assessment and intrusion detection products with roughly 40 percent of that category's global market. Its acquisition pace slowed in the mid-1990s to focus on the emerging Internet market. After liquidating its Web access management operations in 2001, Symantec purchased Resource Technologies, SecurityFocus, and Riptech in 2002, in an attempt to steal market share from rival Network Associates. To beef up its online subscription service, in 2004 Symantec announced a partnership with Internet service provider Earthlink Inc. to offer anti-virus and firewall software to Earthlink subscribers for a small monthly fee.

In mid-2005 Symantec merged with VERITAS in a deal valued at approximately $11 billion. A string of acquisitions followed, beginning with WholeSecurity Inc. and Sygate in October 2005. Others included Blindview in January 2006 and both IMlogic and Relicore the following month. Symantec boasted record revenues of $6.15 billion for 2009 and maintained a payroll of 17,100 employees.

McAfee Inc. Another leading security software vendor, McAfee Inc. of Santa Clara, California, was created as Network Associates in 1997, through the merger of virus detection software manufacturer McAfee and Network General, which didn't compete in the security market. Many of its offerings feature personalized security and services, based on the user's specific system, software, and peripherals.

The company's origins in the computer security market date back to the founding of McAffee Associates by John McAffee. Its initial anti-virus products were offered as shareware, counting on users to pay for the software if it proved helpful. The strength of the offerings was such that this method enabled McAffee to grow into a major provider of enterprise security systems, with a rapidly expanding client base. Early in 1998, Network

Associates acquired Trusted Information Systems, a supplier of firewalls and intrusion detection software. That same year, Network Associates spun off its McAfee.com consumer virus detection software site as a separate, publicly traded company. The firm later repurchased McAfee.com in an effort to consolidate operations.

The company made aggressive inroads into the intrusion detection market in the early 2000s with the purchase of IntruVert Networks and Entercept Security Technologies, indicating it intended to directly confront its rivals in this market niche. With 3,700 employees, its online service, McAfee.com, claimed some 4.5 million subscribers in 2004, while International Data Corp. reported Network Associates' share of the consumer market at 15.3 percent. By mid-decade, consulting and support services represented about 45 percent of total revenues. Network Associates then changed its name to McAffe Inc. as part of its shift toward an exclusive focus on security offerings. The firm sold off the last of its non-security businesses in 2004. In August of 2010 hardware and chip giant Intel purchased McAfee Inc. for $7.68 Billion in cash.

Check Point Software Technologies Ltd. Check Point Software Technologies, based in Israel, is one of the world's top producers of firewall software and other security programs. Formed in 1993, the firm made early inroads by securing distribution deals with heavy hitters like Hewlett-Packard and Ingram Micro. With operations in more than 20 countries, Check Point generated 43 percent of its sales in the United States. Software subscriptions accounted for 31 percent of sales, while licenses and consumer and enterprise products represented 60 percent. The remainder derived from its service operations, including consulting, support, and training. Among other new products, the company was targeting software at users of household broadband connections such as digital subscriber line (DSL) and cable Internet services, which are particularly vulnerable to intrusion. Check Point maintained a large client base, including all of the *Fortune* 100. It reported 2009 revenues of $924.4 million, representing a 14 percent increase from 2008, with particularly strong growth in the Asia-Pacific region. During 2009 the company acquired technology from FaceTime that offered detection and security for more than 4,500 Internet applications and 50,000 Web 2.0 widgets. It also introduced its new Softward Blade architecture and WebCheck and OneCheck products.

Internet Security Systems Inc. Internet Security Systems (ISS) is a leader in the risk assessment, intrusion detection, and adaptive security software segments. Headquartered in Atlanta, ISS was established by Christopher W. Klaus in 1994 and went public in March of 1998. ISS brought in revenues of $730.9 million in 2007, up from $329.8 million in 2005, with operations including consulting, training, and online security research. The firm purchased German-based Cobion AG in 2004 to bolster its content protection line with Cobion's anti-spam and content filtering products.

RSA Security Inc. RSA Security Inc. of Bedford, Massachusetts, protected networks with its line of user monitoring and management software and hardware, which track and protect the use of networks and other enterprise applications. In addition, the firm was a leading provider of digital certificate and Internet access management software, and was the originator of digital signature technology. In mid-2006 RSA's client base included nearly 20,000 enterprises and institutions in the telecommunications, finance, and healthcare sectors, among others. The company acquired authentication software provider Cyota in December of 2005 and was subsequently purchased by EMC for $2.1 billion in 2006. RSA remained EMC's security division heading into 2011.

WORKFORCE

The computer security industry is a component of the larger computer and data processing industry and it is only recently that computer security technicians (or their equivalent) have become specialists within the industry. As the number of computers in use grows, so will the number of security analysts. Employment in the industry was projected to grow 90 percent between 1990 and 2005, making it the third-fastest-growing industry in the economy. One out of every four employees in the industry is a computer programmer or computer systems analyst. Three of every four workers are between the ages of 25 and 44. The average firm in the industry employs only 18 workers.

Computer security specialists are also responsible for detecting illegalities in software copyright and bringing them to the attention of the proper authorities. In some cases, law enforcement agencies offer employment opportunities for security analysts. In other cases, computer security experts act alone to detect illegal or fraudulent activities. The variety of available experience illustrates the numerous opportunities available to security experts who wish to become consultants in the field.

AMERICA AND THE WORLD

In an increasingly globalized and networked world, computer security knows no boundaries. The CERT Coordination Center (CERT/CC), based in Pittsburgh at the Carnegie Mellon University Software Engineering Institute, is a U.S. government-funded center used to coordinate communication during major computer security breaches. Established in 1988, CERT/CC strives to minimize the threat of future incidents by operating a 24-hour point of contact that can respond to security emergencies anywhere on the global Internet. The organization also facilitates communication among experts around the world who are working to solve security problems.

CERT/CC-developed incident response procedures have become the model for more than 70 incident response teams worldwide, including the Forum of Incident Response and Security Teams (FIRST). FIRST consists of individual incident response teams that focus on special national, industrial, and/or academic communities. Each FIRST team establishes contacts within its community, making it possible for FIRST members to meet the community's security needs, collaborate on incidents that cross national boundaries, and post transnational alerts and advisories on problems with local and/or global relevance. More than 50 FIRST teams work together in this global effort, including groups from Australia, Germany, the United Kingdom, Israel, and France.

In its *Security Industry Association 2009 Annual Report,* the SIA reported the value of the electronic security market in South America to be about $704 million (based on 2008 data), primarily coming from Argentina, Chile, Columbia, Mexico, Panama, and Venezuela.

RESEARCH AND TECHNOLOGY

Information security consultants and companies use a number of strategies to counter the threat of computer crime. The most commonly used security technologies are anti-virus software programs that detect and nullify the effect of software "viruses" programs that destroy or garble data when they run on an unsuspecting victim's computer system by accessing control procedures, including the use of passwords and other user authentication techniques; physical security such as locked doors, guarded rooms, and other barriers to physical access; firewalls or software programs that restrict incoming and outgoing network traffic; and encryption or coding messages to make data illegible without the decoding key.

There is a constant need for new security-related computer products. One contemporary way of improving computer security is through keystroke analysis. This system, developed by New Mexico State University professor Juris Reinfelds and two associates, allows computer access only to individuals based on their typing styles. The system is relatively simple. It monitors the pace of users' keystrokes. A timing device or box traps keyboard signals before they reach the computer processor. The box then sends out two signals. One goes to the computer and the second shows how many milliseconds have elapsed since the last keystroke. If the typing patterns do not match, the computer denies further access. The developers say the system detects impersonators 99 percent of the time.

Moreover, it detects unauthorized users even after they enter legitimate passwords.

The use of biometrics to fend off intruders continued to increase. One example of this technology is a system that records the faces of authorized personnel to build a database of users. To log on to a personal computer or workstation, a user must face an attached video camera so the computer can compare the facial image to stored images. Fingerprint identification devices that plug into the home or office computer also are available, and they are becoming increasingly affordable.

Firewalls have remained a leading method of monitoring access to computers and computer networks. However, there is some debate as to how effective firewalls can actually be. Some experts believe they are easy for hackers and crackers to get around. Even though there is much debate over their effectiveness, this has not prevented firewalls from becoming popular. Different types of firewalls offer different levels of security. The lowest-level firewall uses a technology called "packet filters." The system examines the address from which data enters a system or the address to which it is going. It decides whether to let the data pass through based on its analysis.

Mid-level firewalls are circuit-level gatekeepers that prevent systems from coming into direct contact with the outside world. More advanced systems go well beyond examining the addresses or prohibiting direct contact. High-level programs look at the content of messages as well as the "To" and "From" addresses. Of course, prices of such packages and ease of installation are based on the level of the firewall, ranging in cost from $3,000 to $100,000. Installation of the more expensive packages can be time-consuming and must be performed by security experts.

Computer technologies change so rapidly that researchers are not always able to keep up. The concern about computer security is prompting people in diverse fields to develop new products designed to enhance network, individual PC, and stand-alone integrity. This continued focus guarantees an expansion of computer security efforts to protect owners and users against problems.

BIBLIOGRAPHY

"Check Point Software Reports Record Fourth Quarter and Fiscal Year 2009 Financial Results." Check Point Software Technologies Ltd., 28 January 2010. Available from http://www.checkpoint.com.

CSI/FBI Computer Crime and Security Survey. New York: Computer Security Institute, 2009. Available from http://gocsi.com/survey.

"Cyber-Blackmail and Mobile Viruses Increase—Report." *Internet Business News,* 24 April 2006.

"Financial Services Industry Hit Hardest by Fraud According to Global Report." The Kroll Group, 19 October 2009. Available from http://www.kroll.com/about/library/fraud/Oct2009.

Grow, Brian, Keith Epstein, and Chi-Chu Tschang. "The New E-Spionage Threat." *Business Week,* 21 April 2008.

"Hackers Join Social Network Craze With House of Hackers." *Information Week,* 7 May 2008.

"Intel Buys Cyber Security Giant McAfee for $7.68 Billion in Cash." *TechCrunch,* 19 August 2010. Available from http://techcrunch.com/2010/08/19/intel-buys-cyber-security-giant-mcafee-for-7-68-billion-in-cash.

Murray, Mike. "Can Cell Phones Compromise Your Network? Simply by Carrying a Mobile Phone, Employees May Inadvertently Be Walking, Talking Network-Security Risks. Here's How Companies Can Respond." *Business Week Online,* 13 April 2006. Available from www.businessweek.com.

Neal, David. "Hackers to Concentrate on Moving Targets." *IT Week* (UK), 19 May 2008.

"Number of Hackers Attacking Banks Jumps 81%." *Information Week,* 2 August 2007.

"Online Fraud Trends." *Security Management,* April 2006.

"Phisher Kings Court Your Trust; Computer-Based Fraudsters Are Finding New Ways to Trick People—Not Technology— to Get the Information They Seek." *Business Week Online,* 3 April 2006. Available from www.businessweek.com.

Richardson, Robert. *2007 CSI Computer Crime and Security Survey.* Computer Security Institute, 2007.

Rubenking, Neil J. "The Best Security Suites for 2010." *PC Magazine,* 25 February 2010.

Schmidt, Andreas U. *Long-Term and Dynamical Aspects of Information Security: Emerging Trends in Information and Communication Security.* Hauppauge, NY: Nova Science Publishers, 2007.

Security Industry Association 2009 Annual Report. Security Industry Association. Available from http://www.siaonline.org.

"Software Security Revenue to Hit $16.5 Billion in 2010." *IT PRO,* 16 August 2010.

"Top Cyber Security Risks—Executive Summary." The SANS Institute, September 2009. Available from http://www.sans.org/top-cyber-security-risks.

CONCIERGE SERVICES, CORPORATE AND PERSONAL

SIC CODE(S)

7299

7389

INDUSTRY SNAPSHOT

In today's busy world, few people have time for such headaches as picking up the laundry from the dry cleaners or returning that overdue library book. If corporate and personal concierge service firms had their way, the no one would. While most people had not yet forsaken routine personal chores and opted to hire professionals, the concierge industry, known as lifestyle management in the United Kingdom, had become an increasingly popular option. Concierge services have since gained credibility as bona fide business ventures and not just a passing fad for the super rich.

Katharine Giovanni, president and co-founder of the International Concierge and Errand Association (ICEA), stated in a 2008 article for *Crain's Cleveland Business,* "The concierge service business has grown rapidly in the United States, driven by consumers who are overwhelmed by basic tasks and with their increasingly hectic lives and long commutes." Whereas there were only about 50 such businesses in the United States during the 1990s, a decade later were thousands.

The concierge industry serves several different markets: hotels, individuals or families in need of an extra set of hands, corporations offering the service as an employee benefit, and residential or commercial buildings hoping to attract tenants. Initially, the realm of the concierge was limited to luxury hotels and the homes of the power elite. This is no longer the case. The corporate world had embraced the industry, and it was no longer unusual to see this type of service listed as a company-sponsored employee benefit along with health insurance and pension plans.

ORGANIZATION AND STRUCTURE

Concierge services are quite varied in their organization. Some corporations hired their own staff to function as part of their payroll, while others contracted with local concierge firms to provide services on call. Concierge companies sometimes employed as many as 200 professional concierges, whereas others were staffed by retirees and students trying to earn extra cash by offering to run errands part-time.

For ongoing concierge services, a corporation would typically pay a retainer fee ranging from $1,000 to $5,000 a month depending on the size of the corporation and number of employees covered. Multinational corporations might pay much more for services that are more extensive. Companies negotiated a variety of deals with concierge firms, tailoring the range of services and payments to suit their needs. Companies would decide which services they wanted to make available and which employee requests they would subsidize. Some companies simply set up an account with a concierge firm and allowed employees to use the personal services at their own expense, but paid a discounted rate brokered by the employer. Other firms might pay all or part of an employee's expense, in which case the company would typically put a limit on the type and extent of services an employee might request. Though concierge services were most heavily used by larger corporations, they were quite popular among smaller businesses in several major cities, such as New York, Boston, Washington, Atlanta, Chicago, Los Angeles, and San Francisco.

A combination of the hotel and corporate concierge position, the building concierge launched a new division of concierge services. The building concierge could be found in both commercial office complexes and residential apartment buildings. Sometimes the concierge operated from offices within the building, but often a separate location was maintained. A residential building concierge handled the typical assignments of package deliveries, repair appointments, or reservation arrangements. Duties might also include researching and selecting vendors for building maintenance contracts, securing group discounts for residents, and acting as a liaison between real estate agents and building management. A concierge serving a commercial office building would also oversee renovations to office space for clients and process parking permits. In each instance, the building owners believed that the concierge saved money by attending to tenants' needs, which contributed to fewer vacancies.

By 2003 the Internet allowed independent concierge firms to offer services directly to the public, although positive word of mouth remained a must in this sector. Many individuals were encouraged to contract with a personal concierge firm. Independent firms had established networks of partners and generated referrals in this manner. It remained extremely important for customers to check the credentials of potential concierges before turning over any personal information or granting access to a home or property.

The industry was served by the National Concierge Association and the International Concierge and Errand Association, both of which sponsor annual conferences for members.

BACKGROUND AND DEVELOPMENT

The concierge connection to the hospitality industry actually dates back to the Middle Ages, when concierges were charged with catering to royal visitors and maintaining the keys to the royal palaces. The word "concierge" stems from the French term *comte des cierges,* meaning "keeper of the candles." The definition evolved over time to cover other positions such as doorkeeper, building manager, and palace custodian. When trains and ships became suitable means of transportation for the wealthy and privileged, leisure travel became popular. Guests would travel from country to country, staying at the finest hotels. These hotels discovered that they needed a concierge just as palaces had in historical times. The first hotel concierges served in fine hotels in Switzerland and France.

The position of concierge did not appear in the United States until the mid-1970s. The first U.S. chapter of *Les Clefs d'Or* (The Gold Keys) formed in San Francisco. *Les Clefs d'Or* is an international organization for hotel concierges with over 4,000 members worldwide. The association helped solidify the reputation of the industry in the United States, and concierges assumed an influential role in hotel management.

During the 1990s the U.S. economy prospered, and corporations made every effort to capitalize on favorable market conditions. Doing so meant greater demands on employees, longer workdays, and more business travel. Entrepreneurs noticed this trend and decided to copy the concierge model used by hotels and to offer the service to corporations. Services were customized and offered directly to individuals or to companies seeking to augment their benefits packages and extract harder, higher-quality work from their employees. The industry kicked into high gear beginning in the early 1990s, mainly at large companies such as PepsiCo and Andersen Consulting. Notoriously on-the-go consultants were among the earliest recipients of concierge services in the corporate world. Soon the practice spread to other industries as part of employee benefit packages.

Such concierges were hired to perform an almost limitless array of tasks tailored to individuals' particular needs. Usually, assignments consisted of basic chores, such as grocery shopping, feeding pets, and running routine errands. However, the tasks could include more personalized requests, such as researching golf course locations, locating good insurance deals, and sending flowers to spouses. The division of labor, so the theory went, generated increased workplace productivity and boosted employee satisfaction. According to Katherine Giovanni, president of the International Concierge and Errand Association (ICEA), concierge benefits are one of the most cost-effective benefits employers can provide. They give organizations looking for good workers an edge on the competition, as not all workplaces are offering such benefits.

Even if concierge services were not an employment perk, they were available to regular working people by the early years of the first decade of the 2000s. A number of companies marketed their products directly to active professionals. These companies, with names like 2 Places at 1 Time, offered to do anything that was "legal, moral, and feasible." These parameters could entail handling the details of a move to a new home, arranging vacations, shopping for gifts, or even organizing photo albums. Billing themselves as "lifestyle managers," no task was too big or too small.

The "building" concierge had also become more common in real estate circles. Once thought of as an amenity found at five-star hotels, the concierge found a new home in office and apartment buildings. The duties of a building concierge might be different from one hired to serve individual families or employees, but the bottom line remained the same. Building concierges were retained because they added value to a property and often resulted in cost savings for the building owners. Like their corporate counterparts, professional building concierges were credited with cost cutting and lowering the turnover rate of tenants. With the industry expanding into this new field, it appeared that concierge services would continue to prosper.

The terrorist attacks of September 11, 2001, negatively affected almost every sector of the U.S. economy. The travel and tourism industries suffered dramatic losses, which created new challenges for the concierge industry. In the aftermath of the events, hotel concierges became extremely visible. The typical concierge duties were expanded to include security, public relations, and sales. Many people were reluctant to travel, and those who did posed tough questions of their hosts. Questions related to airport security, travel times, and safety measures for visiting national monuments had never been part of the job description before, but suddenly they had become a priority.

Security was the first priority for hotels, corporations, and residential and commercial tenants. Companies providing concierge services were given the added responsibility of stepping up protective measures. Caution became the buzzword, as building owners were watchful of any type of suspicious activity. It was no longer acceptable for a suitcase to sit abandoned in a hotel lobby or for strange deliverymen to wander into buildings unsupervised. Vendors and suppliers for parties and business meetings needed to be screened diligently, and most of these new responsibilities fell to the concierge.

Despite a struggling economy in the early 2000s, the concierge industry continued to grow and attract new clients, particularly as the decrease in the workforce put more pressure and workload on those who remained employed. The concierge industry emerged as a pivotal player in rebuilding local and regional sales among customers. Members of concierge services reported a greater number of invitations to sales meetings with potential clients. They assumed a support role in the sales process, responding to questions about logistics, vendors, and security. A concierge with a well-developed network of partners could recommend a caterer or delivery service based on years of experience. This knowledge provided comfort and security to prospective guests and tenants. In addition to selling a specific building or service, the concierge industry was instrumental in generating positive publicity for various cities through regional associations. These groups played a key role in convincing tourists to return to New York City and continued to partner with government officials in bringing events such as political conventions, Super Bowls, or Olympic Games to a city.

However, the New York market was not all rosy for those in the hotel industry. By late 2003 travel to the city was back up to near pre-September 11 levels, but the travelers were neither the royal international visitors nor the ultra wealthy Americans of years past. Rather, the travelers were middle-income tourists and business travelers on a strict budget. Some concierges, who typically earned $35,000 to $80,000 annually, of which 30 percent came from tips, saw their incomes cut by half. Others retained the same level of salary but for far more work. Hotel guests were far more likely to ask the concierge for directions to a tourist attraction than for a private jet to an island for the weekend.

According to travel expert Richard Turen, travelers simply do not understand what a concierge can offer guests, let alone how much they should tip. "The problem is that Americans have just learned to pronounce the word and, I suspect, not a few of our clients are intimidated by the entire concept. The industry should do a better job at getting its message of service out to the public," Turen said in *Travel Weekly*. "As long as it's legal and moral we'll pretty much do anything," said the head concierge at London's Landmark Hotel.

According to the International Concierge & Errand Association, the industry was valued at more than $1 billion worldwide. Concierge services continued to meet the needs of everyone from vacationing teenagers and busy working parents to senior citizens with mobility problems. In addition, a growing number of progressive companies were offering concierge services for their time-strapped employees. In fact, leading publications such as *Fortune Magazine* reported that among the top companies to work for, some 33 percent offered concierge services for their workers.

While many regular concierge services could be utilized for $20 to $40 per hour, luxury services cost as much as $15,000 per year. Such high end services employed staff members with connections in the fields of hospitality and entertainment, including former personal assistants to A-list celebrities.

Attention to detail is a requirement for any first rate concierge service. Whether working at a hotel, corporation, or for an individual client, the concierge must treat each request with the utmost care. Though it might seem like taking a good thing too far, specialty niches have opened in the concierge market. It is possible to contact a pet concierge to attend to all the needs of a beloved animal. In Florida resorts, the title "citrus concierge" was coined to describe the experts in charge of fruit juices and beverages. A "sleep concierge" excelled at making a client's dreams come true. The person in this job designs the perfect sleep experience for clients. Doing so might entail selecting the correct pillow, bed linens, and lighting, or suggesting the perfect late night snack.

Teen concierge services at leading hotel chains represented an emerging niche in the early 2000s. Four Seasons

Hotels, Embassy Suites Hotels, and Loews Hotels were a few chains that employed local teens who could tell visiting peers about cool places to hang out and fun things to do, such as cafes, skate parks, and shopping destinations. In addition, some of these hotels offered teens amenities like private adjoining rooms, as well as age-appropriate books, video game system rentals, snacks, product samples, and copies of magazines like *Teen People.*

In 2008, one of the new trends in the concierge industry was the development of "one-stop-concierge shops," operating much like convenience stores but offering more products and services, such as dry cleaning, gift wrapping, banking, and prepared meals. One such store was JGA's C-Course, which provided both drive-up options and a relaxing in-store environment for stressed consumers. Another place concierge services were showing up was grocery stores, such as West Seattle's Metropolitan Market, where customers could consult the onsite concierge service, called the Red Coats, with questions about recipes, menus, or meal preparation.

Although concierge services were most often used by dual-earner couples or corporate stay-at-home wives, single men were also looking to them for help. Some concierge businesses provided home decorating or personal shopping, with a targeted market of single, divorced, or widowed men who needed help getting organized or settling into a new place. Hemancipation, in Beverly Hills, California, was one such company. Akilah Kamaria founded the company in 2005 and told *Newsweek International,* "Our services are pretty customized, but fall into the arena of men in transition."

Heading into the mid-2000s, healthcare continued to be a growing market niche for the industry. Faced with a shortage of nurses and other skilled caregivers, hospitals and healthcare systems implemented concierge services as a tool to recruit these hard-to-find professionals and retain the ones they already employed. In the February 2006 issue of *Trustee,* Todd Wheeler wrote, "On average, a single nurse will save as many as five hours per month by using a hospital's concierge service. When that number is multiplied by an average of 500 requests per month placed by a hospital's staff, a hospital can save its nurses as much as $300,000 per year in personal time (when multiplied by a $25 per hour salary)."

The healthcare industry also offered concierge services to patients. A major motivation for this, according to a representative of St. Clair Hospital in Pittsburgh, which began offering a menu concierge program in 2008, was patient satisfaction. Patients receive one-on-one consultation about the foods that will best help their particular health condition.

CURRENT CONDITIONS

In 2009 Mr. Tom Wolfe, chief concierge at the Fairmont San Francisco, was officially honored by the Northern California Concierge Association as the first concierge in the United States. Wolfe, who trained as a concierge in Europe, set up a concierge desk in the hotel lobby at the Fairmont in the 1970s. He later founded the U.S. chapter of the international organization of hotel lobby concierges. In 1989 Ivana Trump appointed him executive chief concierge and director of guest services at New York's Plaza Hotel, where he stayed for four years before returning to Europe. He later returned to the Fairmont to resume his statured position.

The competitive environment in hotel bookings actually helped the industry through the turmoil of 2008 and 2009. According to PriceWaterhouseCoopers, notwithstanding lackluster occupancy rates for the 2009 fiscal year (hovering around 50 percent, well below 60.3 percent in 2008), people were still willing to pay for, and in fact desired, personal attention and service. Accordingly, high-end hotels not only retained their concierges, but kept them busy.

Looking to maintain high-value customers in an increasingly competitive world, large and small businesses increasingly turned to the use of personal concierge services. According to the 2010 American Express Global Customer Service Barometer, Americans were willing to spend 9 percent more with companies that provided excellent service. An astounding 98 percent of consumers said that personal experience was the most influential factor in doing business with a company.

In healthcare, CareCloud announced the national launch of its new CareCloud Concierge, a software suite and service package for medical practices, to manage appointments, verify benefits eligibility, handle registration, billing, and document imaging directly over the Internet. Such services are expected to grow in coming years, as medical practices consolidate to handle increased patient bases under the new healthcare reform plans.

INDUSTRY LEADERS

Many concierge services firms serve only local markets, due in part to the nature of the business. An outstanding concierge service depends on a network of contacts and partners that takes years to build. It is understandably difficult to simply open shop in a new city and expect customers to come knocking. Nevertheless, several firms have established national reputations.

2 Places at 1 Time One such firm is aptly named 2 Places at 1 Time. The company was founded in 1991 by Andrea Arena, who, with only $5,000 in savings, opened a personal errand service for individuals. Located in Atlanta, Georgia, by 2001, 2 Places at 1 Time employed 119 concierges in 66 offices throughout the United States and Canada, the majority working for corporations on site. The firm charged corporations a monthly retainer of several thousand dollars plus a nominal hourly fee for services. In 2008 the company launched its senior life-style management program, called Second Half.

Capitol Concierge Capitol Concierge, based in New York, focused on both individual and corporate clients throughout the greater New York area and was founded by Mary Naylor in 1987 for only $2,000. Naylor delegated management responsibilities of the $6 million dollar operation to senior staff and went on to create Internet start-up VIPdesk.com. She later dropped the dot-com from the company name. Known in 2003 simply as VIPdesk, Naylor continued to operate this growing firm. By 2004 VIPdesk was offering services via e-mail, Web-enabled PDAs and phones, toll-free numbers, and instant answers. In 2008 the company continued to offer its clients' employees or customers "the high-valued gift of time and convenience by fulfilling their requests for Anything, Anytime, Anywhere." Naylor sold Capitol Concierge in 2007 and continued VIPDesk with a new line of home-based customer care centers, a concept called "home-shoring." Capitol Concierge continued under new ownership and both concerns were thriving as of 2010.

Les Concierges Les Concierges was founded in San Francisco, California, in 1987. Linda Jenkinson became CEO in the late 1990s after a stint at a Web-based concierge firm. In 2006 the business served more than 5 million customers worldwide and had offices in 35 different cities. The company catered to corporate executives and busy professionals, and described itself as a "world leader." Services included travel planning, relocation assistance, nanny referrals, and other acceptable services that might be requested. Les Concierges offered round-the-clock service to its customers via the Internet and e-mail. Clients included six of *Fortune's* "100 Best Companies to Work For." In November 2010 the 22-year-old company announced a joint venture with AXA Group, subsidiary of a French insurance giant, to build a global concierge entity. The new venture was anticipating revenues of $30 million for 2010.

WORKFORCE

A typical concierge combines outstanding personal skills with resourcefulness and organization. A degree is not required, but many in the field do have a college education and work experience in the hospitality or travel industry. In 2006 the Bureau of Labor Statistics estimated that there were 20,000 concierges employed in the United States, with faster-than-average growth expected from through 2016. Although the concierge stirs images of wealth and grandeur, the average salary figures were not upper bracket. However, there were non-monetary perks associated with the profession, such as hard-to-get tickets and choice tables in restaurants.

AMERICA AND THE WORLD

Les Clefs d'Or International is a global association of hotel concierges designed to advance the profession on an international level. An annual congress to promote education, professionalism, and friendship among peers is held each year in a different country. The meetings began in the early 1950s and continued regularly. In order to be accepted as a member, a concierge must be nominated by a fellow concierge with eight years or more in the industry, be employed full time at a hotel, have at least three years experience, and be 21 years of age. The organization has approximately 3,000 members in 50 countries worldwide.

RESEARCH AND TECHNOLOGY

A majority of one's personal chores could be conducted via cyberspace, a fact that has not been lost on the concierge services industry. Cyber-concierges, also known as "compcierges," have cropped up in hotels to help travelers establish Internet connections from their laptops. Compcierges offered a full range of computer support to hotel guests, and these services were offered as features catering to the business traveler. Other businesses, meanwhile, have placed their entire concierge operations online, inviting individual users to fill out requests on the World Wide Web. This industry segment was consolidating in a hurry, providing one-stop shopping sites where consumers could upload a list of requests in one neat package. By the early 2000s companies such as VIPdesk were offering clients a real-time "virtual personal assistant," available 24 hours a day, seven days a week.

BIBLIOGRAPHY

"About ICEA." International Concierge and Errand Association, 20 June 2008. Available from http://www.iceaweb.org.

"About NCA." National Concierge Association, 20 June 2008. Available from http://www.nationalconciergeassociation.com.

Andrews, Michelle. "An Experiment With Concierge Medical Care." *U.S. News & World Report*, 8 May 2008.

Bertram, Cindy. "The New Concierge." *The Northwest Indiana and Illinois Times*, 18 May 2007.

Brandes, Heidi. "Stressed Workers Turning to Personal Concierge Services." *The Journal Record (Oklahoma City)*, 2 April 2010.

"CareCloud Launches Concierge: A Modernized Physician Revenue Cycle Experience." *Marketwire*, 18 May 2010. Available from http://www.marketwire.com/press-release/CareCloud-Launches-Concierge-A-Modernized-Physician-Revenue-Cycle-Experience-1262465.htm.

"C-Course: JGA Creates a Concierge Service Center of the Future Catering to Time-Starved Consumers." *Chain Store Age*, March 2008.

"Cottage-Style Concierge Industry Is Flourishing." *PRLog*, 25 June 2008.

Cunningham, Jaime. "Helping Men Get Back in the Game." *Newsweek International*, 26 November 2007.

Gaudette, Karen. "Concierge Service—At the Grocery Store." *Seattle Times*, 28 March 2007.

Glagowski, Elizabeth. "Personal Concierge Services Expand Across All Industries." *1to1 Magazine,* 2 August 2010.

Hoge, Patrick. "Big Partnership Helps LesConcierges Serve Itself." *San Francisco Business Times,* 16 November 2009.

Hoholik, Suzanne. "Concierge Service Saves Workers Time, Trouble." *Ohio Dispatch,* 13 May 2006.

Kibbe, Cindy. "Concierges Can Bring Order to Busy Lives." *New Hampshire Business Review,* 16 March 2006.

"May I Help You? Concierge Services Popping Up to Assist Clients who are Struggling to Juggle Hectic Work and Personal Lives." *Crain's Cleveland Business,* 10 March 2008.

"Pittsburgh Hospital Hires Cura as foodservice Provider: Menu Concierge Program Implemented to Heal Patients through Food." *Food Service Director,* 15 May 2008.

Robbins, McLean. "At Your Service: Concierge Benefits Are a Low-Cost Way to Bring High-Value Services to SMB Employees." *Employee Benefit News,* 1 April 2008.

Scordo, Lizbeth. "Can't Always Get What You Want? Some Can." *San Diego Business Journal,* 12 December 2005.

"Tom Wolfe, America's First Concierge, Honored." *Hotel World,* 6 January 2009.

U.S. Department of Labor, Bureau of Labor Statistics. *Occupational Outlook Handbook, 2008–09 Edition,* December 2007. Available from http://bls.gov.

"VIPdesk CEO Mary Naylor Hires Home-Based Talent." *Washington Business Journal,* 27 April 2009.

CREDIT CARD ISSUING

SIC CODE(S)

6141

INDUSTRY SNAPSHOT

As of March 2009, U.S. revolving consumer debt, almost entirely constituting credit card debt, was about $950 billion. Under traditional economic conditions, this would not be astounding or alarming. However, following the economic downturn of 2008 into 2009, along with double-digit unemployment, rising bankruptcies, and government loans to the banking and auto industries, such a statistic seemed worrisome at best. According to a report before the U.S. Congress' Joint Economic Committee in May 2009, in the fourth quarter of 2008, 13.9 percent of consumer disposable income went to service credit card debt. Even that figure was misleading, because consumers were increasingly using credit cards to purchase necessities such as food and gasoline. Therefore, credit card payments were not quite coming from "disposable income" *per se.*

This did not deter credit card issuers, who simply made existing accounts more profitable by raising interest rates and fees. In pursuit of new cardholders, not only did they rely on old recruitment techniques such as direct mailings and telemarketing, they also turned to ad campaigns aimed at tech savvy generation X-ers and offered nearly "instant" credit approval via online applications. They stepped up efforts to cross-sell new programs to current cardholders. In addition, they courted untapped pools of potential card issuees such as the newly affluent and small business owners. They even approached heretofore off-limits demographic pools such as college students, teens, and those they formerly shunned—individuals with poor credit histories.

Changes in consumer spending habits also spurred new credit card products and marketing strategies. The growing popularity of online financial transactions and shopping, which offer alternate modes of payment to conventional credit cards, meant that card companies had to adapt quickly to the world of Internet commerce. Credit cards must contend with stored value cards, electronic checks, and direct electronic bill payment options. Chip-embedded "smart cards," already used in many countries, emerged in the United States as the most promising new card technology. Issuers and participating merchants were strongly supporting the use of contactless smart cards for signature-free payments under $25.

Even with Congress passing the Credit Card Accountability, Responsibility and Disclosure Act of 2009, banks and card issuers scrambled to beat the effective date (February 2010) by immediately raising interest rates on many accounts, reducing credit lines/limits on existing accounts, and raising fees for over-limit charges and late payments. The Federal Reserve had made a special point to ask banks about the impact of the sweeping pro-consumer reforms contained in the new law. Approximately half of banks said the legislation had already or would lead to reduced credit limits for both prime and subprime customers. About 40 percent responded that it would lead to hiked annual fees for those with good credit scores; even more banks would raise fees for those with poor credit. About 30 percent expected to increase the use of variable rates, which allow them to more easily raise rates in the future without interference from the reform law. Roughly 47 percent respondedd that they intended to or have already raised minimum credit score requirements for prime customers applying for a credit card (even higher for subprime customers).

ORGANIZATION AND STRUCTURE

Credit, Charge, and Debit Cards Traditional credit cards—magnetic stripe plastic cards that, when accompanied by the holder's signature, entitle the bearer to draw on a revolving line of credit—still dominate the landscape of non-cash transactions in the United States. Cardholders who carry over part of their balances to the next pay period are charged an annual rate of interest that varies according to their income and past credit history. Card firms often also levy an annual fee for use of their cards, plus additional penalties and other fees for charging over the approved card limit such as making purchases outside of the United States or failing to use the card within a specified period.

Some credit cards are affinity cards, which are offered jointly by two organizations, one a financial institution and the other a non-financial group such as a university or sports team. Co-branded cards are issued by financial institutions and collaborating retailers such as department stores or airlines. The cards bear the names of both organizations. MBNA Corp. dominates the domestic affinity card market.

Charge cards are similar to credit cards except outstanding balances must be paid in full by each due date. No interest is charged for their use. American Express and Diners' Club are the most well-known charge card brands.

Debit cards are bank cards that, like checks, draw funds directly from the holder's bank account. The amount is taken out immediately with online cards but is delayed by up to 72 hours with offline versions. Both MasterCard and Visa offer debit cards in addition to credit cards.

Private Label Cards Retailers can issue private label cards, which bear the retailer's logo. They are accepted only by the issuer, which partners with financial companies to back the cards. About 10 percent of mass market retailer Target Corp.'s $8.56 billion sales in 1999 were processed through its private label card. Also in 1999, the world's number one retailer, Wal-Mart, jumped on the private label bandwagon for the first time in its 37-year history. In February 2000, Staples debuted a no-fee private label credit card targeted at small business owners. Ford Motor Co. also developed a private label card for small businesses—cardholders who service their cars at participating dealers earn discounts toward the purchase or lease of their next Ford.

The Internet and Smart Cards Smart cards (or chip cards) contain computer chips with a given amount of memory or storage capacity. When read by special terminals, the terminals can access data stored on the chip. They can be used as cash cards, identification cards, or credit cards, and offer potential for enhanced security for online financial transactions. By 2000, most smart cards functioned as memory-only cards with stored monetary values and thus served as a replacement for cash at photocopying machines, subways, and public phones. Smart cards have already been implemented in over 90 countries. Germany, for example, has 85 million national insurance smart cards. Smart cards are widely viewed as the next wide-scale development in the card industry. (See also **Smart Cards.**)

Heading into the late years of the first decade of the 2000s, contactless smart cards were poised for strong growth as merchants and issuers alike supported and promoted their use for micro-payments (payments less than $25). Contactless cards allowed consumers to simply wave their card at a special wireless sensor and pay for their purchase without signing. While the transactions are encrypted, card issuers backed the technology up with the same fraud protection as standard cards. By March of 2007, issuers such as Chase and American Express offered this technology to cardholders regardless of whether they requested it.

PIONEERS IN THE FIELD

Frank McNamara The man behind the first widely accepted charge card was Frank McNamara, a World War II veteran who founded Diners' Club in 1950. McNamara claimed he dreamed up the idea of presenting an authorized cash substitute, the value of which the carrier would pay at a later date, one evening in New York City when he couldn't foot the dinner bill while entertaining a business client. Dubbed the "last supper," the incident was later revealed to be a promotional yarn.

McNamara, however, did persuade a group of New York restaurateurs to take cardboard cards in lieu of hard cash from customers on the understanding that the cards were backed by a financially reliable third party, Diners' Club. Diners' Club paid the restaurant bills, retained a 7 percent service fee, and then in turn was paid by its cardholders. Within two years, approximately 150,000 diners had become card-carrying members.

In the long run, this scheme didn't benefit McNamara, though. He sold his interest in Diners' Club in 1952 for $500,000, believing that charge cards were merely a passing trend. After having tried his luck at real estate, in 1957 he died penniless of a heart attack at age 40.

BACKGROUND AND DEVELOPMENT

In 2000 the modern credit card completed its fifth decade. The concept of credit cards appeared much earlier, in Edward Bellamy's futuristic 1888 novel, *Looking Backward.* Proprietary credit cards, honored only at a single establishment, appeared in the 1920s, when a California gas station chain issued cards to its regular customers. Departments and hotels followed suit. In 1947, Flatbush National Bank collaborated with nearby retailers in an arrangement that permitted customers to charge their purchases. The result was the first known third party charge card.

The charge card burst onto the national scene in 1950 with the Diners' Club card, which a number of hotels and restaurants agreed to accept. In 1958, American Express (AmEx) created its own charge card to rival the industry pioneer. Although early versions were made of cardboard, AmEx introduced plastic cards and computerized billing in the 1970s.

Also in 1958, Bank of America premiered Bank Americard (known as Visa since 1976), the first true credit card. With it, customers didn't have to pay off their card balances each month. Instead, they could make a minimum payment and be charged interest on the remaining revolving balance. The initial offer of a $500 line of credit with an 18 percent interest rate drew about 60,000 members. In 1966, Bank of America started licensing the card to other financial institutions. Competition grew with the creation of Master Charge (now MasterCard) in 1977, a new credit card backed by a consortium of Midwestern banks.

Governmental regulation of the industry really began with congressional passage of the Truth in Lending Act (TILA), part of the Consumer Protection Act, in 1968. The TILA was intended to protect consumers against abusive lending practices and to mandate comprehensible disclosure of credit terms so that consumers could make more informed credit decisions. The act has been amended numerous times. Other important legislation includes the Equal Credit Opportunity Act. Enacted in 1974, it prohibits creditors from discriminating against consumers on the basis of sex or marital status. Two years later, its scope was enlarged to bar additional discrimination based on race, color, religion, national origin, age, or receipt of public assistance. In 1989, Senator Charles Schumer won approval for Regulation Z to become part of the Fair Credit and Charge Card Disclosure Act. It required that key credit information, such as annual interest rate, fees, and grace periods, be grouped together on applications and displayed in what became known as the "Schumer box." Some issuers circumvented the regulation by printing the box in small type and placing it in an unobtrusive location on the forms. In May 2000, the Federal Reserve Board proposed an amendment to Regulation Z stipulating that the Schumer box must appear in "reasonably understandable form" and be "prominently located."

Visa and MasterCard were enmeshed in several lawsuits in the 1990s. Wal-Mart led a group of four million retailers in a lawsuit against the two companies attacking their debit card policy. Debit card issuers require that merchants accept their debit cards as readily as credit cards and charge similar fees to process both. However, debit cards, unlike credit cards, don't encourage shoppers to spend more than they can immediately afford, so retailers find little reason to pay high fees on the Visa and MasterCard debit cards, especially when regional networks such as STAR, Cirrus, or NYCE charge much less. The plaintiffs sought compensatory damages for the difference, which estimates placed at $8.1 billion to $63 billion. In June 2000, the U.S. Department of Justice (DOJ) took Visa and MasterCard to court for antitrust violations, complaining that the two prohibited their shared network of banks from issuing the cards of competitors such as American Express and Discover. In August, the DOJ issued its proposed final judgment, calling on the companies to require of their respective board members exclusive dedication to their companies and to repeal their exclusionary practices. A third antitrust lawsuit was filed against Visa and MasterCard in the California State Superior Court of Alameda County. It contested the one percent fee that they charge for currency conversion (incurred when purchases are made abroad). The lawsuit alleged that "there is no rational relationship between the additional cost to the defendants of a foreign card charge and the currency conversion fee defendants levy," and violated the Truth in Lending Act as it was not disclosed to consumers.

Credit card fraud remained a serious problem. More effective security measures have led to an overall decline in fraud. Citing data from *The Nilson Report, Business Week* indicated that credit card fraud totaled $1.05 billion in 2005. As computer hackers and insiders became more sophisticated, that number rose dramatically. By 2008, the total annual fraud amount jumped to $48 billion, with 9.9 million adult U.S. identity fraud victims in just that year alone, reported Javelin Strategy & Research in February 2009. Women were 26 percent more likely to be victims of identity fraud than men, the report noted. Fraud remained a very pressing problem in the e-commerce sector. As large e-tailers and auction sites such as eBay became more adept at battling fraud and working with law enforcement, criminals targeted the more vulnerable class of small businesses.

Credit card fraud also occurs when slip-ups temporarily expose otherwise protected data. According to *InformationWeek,* in 2005 alone, HSBC North America indicated that the account numbers of some 180,000 of its customers may have been lifted in one incident; Bank of America lost tapes containing 1.2 million card numbers; and Citigroup lost tapes that contained sensitive information on 3.9 million customers. Additionally, in June 2005, MasterCard International reported that a security breach at the third party payment processor CardSystems Solutions Inc. may have exposed 40 million accounts to fraud, including 13.9 million MasterCards as well as a number of Visa, Discover, and American Express Cards. In August 2009, the Justice Department indicted Miami resident Alberto Gonzalez for what the Department referred to as the largest case of computer crime and identity theft ever prosecuted. Gonzalez, along with two unnamed Russian conspirators, had accessed more than 130 million credit and debit card numbers between 2006 and 2008. Some were used for unauthorized purchases and bank withdrawals, while others were sold online. Of note, Gonzalez had previously been arrested in 2003 for a similar crime, but worked with prosecutors and the Secret Service to identify his former online conspirators who traded and sold card numbers in the black market.

In summary, consumers love plastic. The April 2009 Nilson report showed that 78 percent of U.S. households (roughly 91.1 million households) had one or more credit cards at the end of 2008 (there were 90.4 million households with cards in 2007). In fact, consumers held an average of 5.4 cards, said Experian's Marketing Insight Snapshot of March 2009. The *New York Times* on February 23, 2009, noted that a stack of all those credit cards would reach more than 70 miles into space and would be almost as tall as 13 Mount Everests. The U.S. Census Bureau projected that the number of U.S. cardholders would grow to 181 million persons by 2010.

New Products Affinity cards remained a popular means of generating accounts. First USA pledged $16 million to the University of Tennessee, payable over seven years, in exchange for exclusive rights to market its Visa affinity cards to the university's students, staff, and alumni. In addition, the university received 5 percent of every transaction charge. Schools are often paid $20 to $50 for each account generated. Sometimes issuers earmark contributions for specific endeavors, such as tutoring centers, athletic programs, or campus radio stations, raising concerns that they may exercise at least indirect influence over the functioning or content of such programs. MBNA, the foremost affinity issuer, entered a marketing agreement with Virtual Communities, Inc. of New York to issue affinity cards focused on the ethnic identity groups featured on each of its ethnic Web sites. Other tried and true draws were rebates or discounts on selected products or other incentives for card members. Perhaps the most well known of these are frequent flier miles.

In the early years of the first decade of the 2000s, credit card firms scrambling to retain market share in the increasingly saturated U.S. credit card market began to experiment with new card shapes and designs, extending their efforts beyond 0 percent interest offers. For example, in 2002, Bank of America introduced the "mini VISA." Half the size of a regular credit card, the mini VISA can be attached to a key chain. Similarly, Discover launched its oval-shaped "2GO Card," which is protected by a plastic case that clips to a key chain or belt. In May of 2003, Capital One released its "See-Through Designs" line of seven cards that are available in seven translucent colors.

Some issuers began offering online procedures that featured anonymity and accelerated approval. According to a report issued by Change Sciences Group, more than 9 million U.S. consumers applied for credit cards online during 2002. The group predicted that more than half of all credit cards would be obtained online in 2003. The leading online credit card issuers in 2002 were Discover, National City, Chase, Fleet, and Bank of America.

New Targets Issuers also strove to reach new groups of potential members. For example, small businesses were identified as an underserved and very promising market. Of the 14 to 20 million small business owners in the United States, only 17.3 percent used business cards for transactions in 1992. However, usage tripled by the century's end, according to a survey by National Small Business United and Arthur Andersen's Enterprise Group. Only 100 of the 21,000 financial institutions that issued Visa cards offered debit or credit cards tailored for small businesses in the late 1990s. Visa tried to persuade existing consumer credit members with small businesses to take on business-only cards. American Express (AmEx) courted small businesses with card-related product and service discounts with retailers such as IBM, Federal Express, Mobil, and Hertz, as well as a Blue Business card. In 1999, LiveCapital.com was the first institution to offer small-business-oriented cards on its online site. In 2003, American Airlines and American Express launched a corporate card targeting mid-sized companies. Known as the American Express Business ExtrAA Corporate Card, the co-branded card offers a cash rebate on airline tickets as well as points for all American Airlines purchases.

Potential customers that issuers used to approach with caution drew increased attention. So-called tweeners—people with emerging credit such as recent immigrants and formerly good customers whose credit ratings slipped because of temporary financial difficulties—form the exclusive market for some card companies such as CompuCredit of Atlanta. However, after personal bankruptcies began to climb in the wake of the U.S. economic recession in the first decade of the 2000s, analysts began to predict that firms offering credit to those individuals labeled credit risks would curb their marketing expenditures.

In particular, prepaid cards were an especially promising market for the industry, which looked to the nation's roughly 14 million "unbanked" households for growth, according to the aforementioned *Bank Technology News* article. The publication revealed that this sector was valued at approximately $300 billion. Specific examples of prepaid cards included ones linked to savings accounts, payroll accounts, and health savings accounts.

The Federal Reserve reported that total consumer debt was a record $2.41 trillion in January of 2007. A study conducted by the Federal Reserve Board in the wake of 2005's bankruptcy law reforms found that credit card companies were not to blame for high consumer debt levels. The report indicated that issuers were not careless in extending credit card offers, and that most cardholders made timely payments.

Even so, some industry players were predicting a rise in delinquencies in 2007 and 2008. One such report came from Bernstein Research, which forecast that net loss ratios for credit card portfolios—which had declined from nearly 4.7 percent in 2005 to 3.2 percent during the first half of 2006, following bankruptcy law reforms—would total 3.5 percent in 2007 and almost 6 percent in 2008, The research firm also forecast that weekly bankruptcy filings would surge from 8,000 during the first half of 2006 to 27,000 during the last half of 2008. Reasons for the increase included lax underwriting during 2003 and 2004, a decline in the use of home equity loans to pay off credit card debt (due to rising interest rates), as well as rising unemployment.

CURRENT CONDITIONS

As of 2009, credit cards were responsible for more than $2.5 trillion in transactions annually and cards were accepted at more than 24 million locations in more than 200 countries and territories, according to the American Bankers Association. The Association also estimated that there were 10,000 payment card transactions made every second around the world. According to an April 2009 Nilson Report, the top 10 U.S. credit card issuers held an 87.55 percent market share of $972.73 billion in general purpose card outstandings (card charges still owed) in 2008. That included Visa, MasterCard, American Express, and Discover card accounts. According to Visa.com, as of March 31, 2009, there were 318 million Visa credit cards and 346 million Visa debit cards in circulation in the United States. According to Master-Card.com, as of June 30, 2009, there were 220 million MasterCard credit cards and 127 million MasterCard debit cards in circulation in the United States. A Sallie Mae report in April 2009 indicated that 84 percent of the student population overall have credit cards, an increase of approximately 11 percent since the fall of 2004.

The April 2009 Nilson Report found the average outstanding credit card debt for households that have a credit card was $10,679 at the end of 2008, about the same as the previous year. The National Foundation for Credit Counseling, in its April 2009 Financial Literacy Survey, reported that in the preceding 12 months, 15 percent of American adults, or nearly 34 million people, had been late making a credit card payment and 8 percent (18 million people) had missed a payment entirely. Twenty-six percent of Americans, or more than 58 million adults, admitted to not paying all of their bills on time. In September 2009, the *New York Times* reported that late payment penalty fees from credit cards would amount to about $20.5 billion in 2009, according to R.K. Hammer, a consultant to the credit card industry.

According to the American Bankruptcy Institute, personal bankruptcies surged to more than one million filings in the United States in 2008, the most since amendments to the bankruptcy laws took effect in 2005. For the second straight year, Tennessee had the distinction of having the overall highest per capita rate of filings; Alaska retained its title as the state with the fewest personal bankruptcies, as per the Automated Access to Court Electronic Records or AACER, January 2009.Young Americans now have the second highest rate of bankruptcy, just after those aged 35 to 44.

A 2008 National Small Business Association survey reported that credit cards are now the most common source of financing for the United States' small-business owners, with 44 percent of them identifying credit cards as a source of financing that their company had used in the previous 12 months. According to Nilson Reports, in 2008, JPMorgan Chase was the largest issuer of small business credit cards with $34.5 billion in total card volume. Bank of America was second with $26.31 billion and Capital One was third with $20.7 billion.

INDUSTRY LEADERS

Industry leaders can be defined by several different factors, but just a handful of entities continually appear at or near the top, irrespective of criteria. According to 2009 Nilson Reports, the top U.S. general purpose card issuers based on outstandings (credit card debt still owing) as of June 30, 2009 were Chase (with $165.87 bilion in outstandings); Bank of America ($150.82 billion); Citi ($102.54 billion); American Express ($78.16 billion); Capital One ($55.46 billion); and Discover ($48.9 billion). Other leaders included Wells Fargo, HSBC, and U.S. Bank. The companies with the greatest number of general purpose credit cards in circulation in 2008 were Chase (119.4 million), Citi (92 million), Bank of America (80.2 million), Discover (48 million), and American Express (46.5 million).

With respect to profit, the March 2009 Nilson Report indicated that the leading credit card issuers in 2008 were Chase ($780 million profit); Bank of America ($520 million profit); American Express ($850 million profit); Capital One ($1 billion profit); Discover ($710 million profit); Wells Fargo ($990 million profit); HSBC ($520 million profit); and US Bank ($1.07 billion profit). Citibank, although a leader, reported a $530 million loss for 2008. (It should be noted that most of these leaders received federal "bailout" loans in late 2008 under the Obama administration's economic stimulus package.)

Visa International, based in Foster City, California, remained the reigning monarch of the consumer loans industry with 60.25 percent of the global market share (by purchase volume) and 47.2 percent of the U.S. market (by outstandings) for 2008, according to the April 2009 Nilson Report. About 20,000 banks own Visa Corp. and each issues and markets its own Visa cards. The VisaNet payment system authorizes and processes transactions for all the owner banks. Besides plastic credit cards, Visa offers debit cards, value-stored cards, and online payment systems.

Number two MasterCard International Inc. in Purchase, New York, held 28.3 of the global market and 35.3 percent of the domestic market in 2008. It is owned by more than 25,000 financial institutions. Like VisaNet, MasterCard handles marketing and account approval and processing for all its products, including its MasterCard credit and debit cards and its European Maestro debit cards. In 2002 MasterCard expanded its European operations with the purchase of Europay International.

Third-ranked American Express Co. (AmEx), with 10 percent of the global market and 11 percent of the domestic market, is headquartered in New York City. In the late 1990s, it broadened its palette of card offerings (the standard green American Express card and its upscale cousin AmEx gold) with the launch of smart card AmEx Blue and super-elite AmEx Centurion (the AmEx Black card) in the United Kingdom. AmEx spun off its Ameriprise Financial business in 2005.

DiscoverCard (with 6.3 percent of the domestic market in 2008), the credit card issuer for Morgan Stanley Dean Witter & Co. of New York, claimed about 50 million members and formed the largest independent credit network in the United States. The card is well known for its annual CashBack bonus.

New York's Citigroup Inc., created by the merger of Citibank and Travelers Group, is one of the world's largest financial services companies and credit card issuers. In 2007 the firm had operations in more than 100 countries. Sales totaled $146.6 billion in 2006, up nearly 22 percent from the previous year. Its AAdvantage card has been ranked as one of the most successful co-branded cards in the industry. Chairman Sandy Weill, the architect behind the creation of Citigroup, retired in 2006.

AMERICA AND THE WORLD

Near the end of the first decade, India was an especially promising market for the credit card industry. In its January 11, 2007, issue, *Cards International* reported that some 15.5 million credit cards were in circulation in that country by mid-2006, according to data from the Reserve Bank of India. During the first 10 months of that year, credit card transactions made in India totaled $6.88 billion. Domestic leaders in India included ICICI Bank, which

enjoyed a commanding 29 percent share of the market and had about 5 million credit cards in force, followed by the State Bank of India/GE, the nation's largest bank, with 3 million cards in force. However, global players were making quick inroads in India. With 2.85 million cards, Citibank was the country's third largest card issuer, and companies such as HSBC, GE Money, and Standard Charter were quickly establishing themselves.

China was another emerging market for the industry. MBNA announced in 2004 that it had opened an office in Shanghai, which it would use "to conduct market research, to further develop relationships with Chinese regulators and the banking community in China, and to design long-term strategies for entering China's credit card market." In mid-2005, Bank of America announced that it had acquired a 9 percent share of China Construction Bank, which is one of the largest lenders in China.

By the end of the 1990s, Iceland had become the world's most "cashless" society—only 14 percent of all financial transactions involved the use of hard currency; even parking meters would accept stored value cards.

Around the rest of the globe, however, the acceptance of plastic has been less all-embracing. Most European cards are debit cards like Maestro rather than credit cards. With the proliferation of smart cards, some countries previously not receptive to credit cards seemed poised to avoid their implementation altogether. Instead, they were moving directly to the adoption of smart card technology. Visa was pursuing collaborations with 22 global vendors to develop off-the-shelf packages for smart chip card compatibility that included cards, terminals, and software. MasterCard's European affiliate Europay required that all of its 170 million Maestro cards, 2.3 million point-of-sale terminals, and 234,000 automated teller machines be smart card compliant by 2005.

American Express introduced its super-elite Centurion or AmEx Black card in the United Kingdom, which was available by invitation only. Intended for the extremely wealthy, it is delivered in a velvet-lined box by private security personnel and comes with such perks as upgrades on the Concorde and private shopping hours at Saks and Neiman Marcus. Visa signed on with the French smart card firm Gemplus to permit mobile payment services on cell phones, and with the Swedish mobile phone company Ericsson and Finnish phone company Nokia to embed credit card data directly into the phone. This technology verifies the identity of the phone user.

RESEARCH AND TECHNOLOGY

As fraud remained a pressing issue during the middle years of the twenty-first century's first decade, especially online, the industry developed new technology to combat the problem. One such technology, which MasterCard International used as part of its Operation STOP IT initiative, was VigilActive. An offering of Madison, Wisconsin-based NameProtect Inc., this service helped card issuers identify so-called phishing scams, in which malicious parties attempted to trick consumers into revealing sensitive data. One way VigilActive accomplished this was by reviewing new domain name registrations to identify the possible fraudulent use of legitimate brand names. In addition, the service allowed issuers to monitor chat rooms where criminals trade stolen account data. The service also was used by Visa USA and a number of banks.

Visa USA had developed new technology called Advanced Authorization that analyzed credit card transaction data on individual and batch levels to identify patterns of possible fraud. On June 14, 2005, *Informationweek* explained that "with the emergence of phishing attacks, Internet E-commerce, and the opening of new accounts using stolen identities, more instances of card fraud are part of a broader scheme. The Advanced Authorization system examines transactions both vertically, based on risk behaviors associated with the individual cardholder, and horizontally, based on similarities occurring across the Visa network. For example, a fraud ring might be simultaneously testing hundreds of stolen or counterfeit account numbers; the system will detect that pattern of activity and alert Visa and the issuing banks to halt the transaction at the point of sale." Visa expected the technology would allow the company to prevent some $164 million in fraud through 2010.

According to MasterCard International, the near future could see a refrigerator capable of monitoring the freshness of its contents and generating lists it could electronically communicate to a "thinking" countertop that keeps a shopping list. The "smart" countertop could trigger a message to the supermarket so the week's groceries could be waiting at the store. MasterCard would be the payment vehicle for that transaction.

In a less science fiction-like scenario, in the early years of the first decade of the 2000s, Wells Fargo & Co. developed an arrangement with e-Bay, the online auction house, to create an entirely new credit card niche: consumer-to-consumer credit card transactions. Through Billpoint, a payment service provider, customers who sell on e-Bay can accept payments directly from their online customers. Such payments go directly into the sellers' checking accounts.

In early 2007, a sobering research report titled "Borrowing to Stay Healthy" was released by Mark Rukavina, executive director of Boston's Access Project, and Cindy Zeldin of the non-partisan New York think tank Demos: A Network for Ideas & Action. The report found that a growing number of Americans were using credit cards to pay their medical bills. Specifically, the report revealed that

credit card debt in low- and middle-income households with medical bills was 46 percent higher than similar households with no medical debt. In its January 22, 2007, issue, *American Banker* quoted an excerpt from the report, which read: "The use of credit cards for medical expenses can be problematic because the resulting debt is lumped in with all other consumer debt, making this debt not only invisible as a medical debt, but also subject to a maze of interest rates and penalty fees."

BIBLIOGRAPHY

Ackerman, Andrew. "News In Brief: Consumer Credit Up $1.3B in April." *The Bond Buyer,* 8 June 2005.

Adler, Joe. "In Brief: Fed Study Defends Credit Card Issuers." *American Banker,* 5 July 2006.

Bandy, Justin. " India's Card Market Poised for Growth: New Products, Foreign Participation and a Booming Tourism Industry Are Combining to Create High Levels of Growth in India's Nascent Cards Sector, Helped by Product Innovation and a Supportive Regulatory Environment." *Cards International,* 11 January 2007.

"Bank of America to Buy MBNA for $35 Billion." *Baseline,* 30 June 2005.

Berner, Robert, and Adrienne Carter. "Swiping Back at Credit Card Fraud; Bogus Transactions Are Falling Overall, but e-Tailers Are Still Feeling the Pain." *Business Week,* 11 July 2005.

"Bernstein Sees Rising Credit Losses Through 2008." *Cardline,* 3 November 2006.

Bigda, Carolyn. "Wave and You've Paid." *Money,* March 2007.

"Citigroup, the World's Biggest Credit-Card Issuer, Will Begin Issuing American Express Cards, Probably in Late 2005." *Chain Store Age,* January 2005.

"Consumers Lose Confidence in Credit." *In-Store,* 10 May 2005.

Crutsinger, Martin. "Consumer Credit Up in January." Herald Sun, 7 March 2007. Available from http://www. heraldsun.com/business/21-826833.cfm.

Der Hovanesian, Mara. "Tough Love for Debtors; Credit-Card Rules that Raise Minimum Monthly Payments Could Hurt Banks and Debt-Burdened Consumers Alike." *Business Week Online,* 14 April 2005. Available from www.businessweek.com.

"Cards: Opportunities Abound in Crowded Payments Field: Although Credit and Debit Card Usage Accounts for More Than Half of All In-Store Purchases, a Multi-Trillion Dollar Slice of the Payments Market Remains for the Taking." *Bank Technology News,* February 2007.

Jalili, H. Michael. "In Brief: Report Ties Card Debt to Medical Costs." *American Banker,* 22 January 2007.

Karash, Julius A. "Medical Fees Boost Debt on Credit Cards: People Who Charge Health-Care Expenses Are Getting Deeper into Trouble, a Report Says." *Kansas City Star,* 17 January 2007.

"Largest U.S. Visa and MasterCard Issuers: At Yearend, Ranked by Outstandings." *American Banker,* 19 May 2006.

Launder, William. "In Brief: Discover's Sign-Up Share Rises to 15%." *American Banker,* 2 January 2007.

Lim, Paul J. "A National Credit Spree." *U.S. News & World Report,* 11 April 2005.

Lindenmayer, Isabelle. "Amex Files Suit vs. Visa, MC, and 8 Bank Issuers." *American Banker,* 16 November 2004.

Lindenmayer, Isabelle. "In Brief: Delinquencies Fall To a 10-year Low." *American Banker,* 13 June 2005.

"MasterCard Plots Smartcard Trial." *Marketing,* 22 June 2005.

"MBNA Opens Representative Office in China; World's Largest Independent Credit Card Issuer Plans Entry in China." *PR Newswire,* 16 April 2004.

"New Visa Technology Detects Fraud Rings; Advanced Authorization Detects Transactions Using Numbers Acquired Through Phishing and ID Theft." *InformationWeek,* 14 June 2005.

Nilson Reports 2009. Available from http://www.creditcard. com.

Sallie Mae. "How Undergraduate Students Use Credit Cards." April 2009. Available from http://www.salliemae.com.

"Security Breach Exposes Data on Millions of Payment Cards; As many as 40 Million Cards May Have Been Exposed, Making It the Largest Breach of Personal Financial Data in a String of Recent Cases." *InformationWeek,* 17 June 2005.

Simon, Jeremy M. "Banks Continue to Tighten Credit Card Lending Standards." 2009. Available from http://www.credit cards.com/credit-card-news/2009-q3-senior-loan-officers-survey-lending-standards-tighten.php.

Talcott, Sasha. "MBNA to be Sold to Bank of America." *Denver Post,* 1 July 2005.

U.S. Department of Justice. 2009. "Alleged International Hacker Indicted for Massive Attack on U.S. Retail and Banking Networks." Press Release, August 17, 2009. Available at http://www.usdoj.gov/opa/pr/2009/August/09-crm-810.html.

Wolfe, Daniel. "MasterCard Claims Victories in Fight Against Web Fraud." *American Banker,* 16 May 2005.

Woolsey, Ben and Matt Schulz. "Credit Card Statistics, Industry Facts, Debt Statistics." 2009. Available from http://www.credit cards.com/credit-card-news/credit-card-industry-facts-personal-debt-statistics-1276.php.

DATA MINING

———— ■ ————

SIC CODE(S)

7372

INDUSTRY SNAPSHOT

Data mining is a process in which special software applications are used to analyze multiple sets of information and find patterns or relationships between them. Once patterns or links have been established between information sets (normally large databases), data mining techniques enable users to make informed decisions or predictions based on the results of their analyses.

Data mining applications use algorithms to produce desired results. Simply stated, an algorithm is a problem-solving method that uses a sequence of steps or actions to achieve an objective. In recent years, this software classification has grown more powerful due to the increased processing power and data storage capacity of modern computer systems.

During the 1980s, the earliest data mining applications were somewhat limited in scope. While applications were more robust by the mid-1990s, they still required expert users who were versed in statistical analysis. By the early years of the first decade of the twenty-first century, things had changed. Everyday professionals were able to personally use a new, more user-friendly generation of data mining software for a variety of purposes. Corporate professionals used these applications to solve the most pressing business problems, law enforcement agencies used them to predict crime patterns and catch wrongdoers, and financially strapped state governments used them to identify tax delinquent individuals and businesses.

Data mining applications are marketed by leading software industry heavyweights, including IBM, Oracle, SPSS, and SAS Institute Inc. The overall industry is often referred to as business intelligence (BI), which includes technological strategies such as advanced analytics and data warehousing.

ORGANIZATION AND STRUCTURE

Data mining applications comprise but one of the many segments within the larger software industry. To best understand this emerging segment, one need only look to the end users who apply data mining applications to a wide swath of challenges. It is they who drive the development of new products and services.

In mid-2005, *KDnuggets*, a leading newsletter about data mining, knowledge discovery, Web mining, and related topics, conducted a survey to determine the industries and fields where data mining techniques were being applied. Of the 421 votes received, the leading 10 categories were customer relationship management (12 percent), banking (12 percent), credit scoring (8 percent), direct marketing/fundraising (8 percent), fraud detection (7 percent), retail (6 percent), insurance (6 percent), telecommunications (5 percent), manufacturing (5 percent), and science (4 percent). More recently, the medical and pharmaceutical industries have bought into the industry (e.g., pharmaceutical companies interested in physicians's prescription-writing histories), but in 2009, legal challenges on grounds of privacy dampened that market.

In terms of the specific types of data mining techniques employed by end users—many of which are highly technical—an April 2006 *KDnuggets* poll of 176 voters revealed that the leading techniques were decision trees rules (51.1 percent), clustering (39.8 percent), and regression (38.1 percent) led the top 10, followed by statistics (36.4 percent), association rules (30.7 percent), visualization (21.6 percent), SVM (17.6 percent), neural networks (17.6 percent), sequence/time series analysis (13.6 percent), and Bayesian (13.6 percent).

Some industry observers estimate that roughly half of data mining users come from larger companies with annual revenues exceeding $1 billion, while nearly 20 percent are from smaller organizations or consultancies with revenues of less than $500,000.

Regardless of the industry in which it is used, the size of the organization using it, or the specific techniques being applied, data mining is more suitable for certain purposes than it is for others. According to the November/December 1999 issue of *IEEE Intelligent Systems,* "Good data mining application areas require knowledge-based decisions; have accessible, sufficient, and relevant data; have a changing environment; have sub-optimal current methods; will not be obsoleted by imminent new technology; and provide a high payoff for the correct decisions."

Applications of Data Mining While the basic principle behind data mining is essentially the same, the types of benefits vary depending on the context in which the technique is applied. In the business realm, companies use data mining to gain new insight about their customers. For example, research from consumer goods giant Procter & Gamble revealed that fathers often purchased beer during after-work trips to the store for items like milk and diapers. This type of intelligence is extremely useful to store planners, who determine where to place merchandise. One leading national clothing retailer stopped stocking all of its stores the same way when data mining revealed that demand for colors and sizes of the same garments varied considerably among major metropolitan markets. The company was thus able to sell more effectively by tailoring the product mix to each individual market.

Pizza Hut is one example of how a leading restaurant chain used data mining to increase sales. By late 2003, Pizza Hut laid claim to the fast food industry's largest consumer data warehouse, containing information on some 40 million households (40 to 50 percent of the U.S. market). Pizza Hut's initial database included approximately 10 years of telephone pizza orders. Using Teradata Warehouse Miner software, the chain was able to improve the accuracy of its data and increase the profitability of its direct marketing efforts.

Businesses also use data mining to up-sell or cross-sell customers. This works extremely well online, where leading retailers like Amazon.com and L.L. Bean combine detailed data about customers' viewing and purchase histories to recommend other relevant products. However, recommendations that appear to be irrelevant can irritate customers. This is one reason why some leading retailers continue to combine data mining and human insight to produce meaningful recommendations.

The business sector's use of data mining extends beyond customer interactions. For example, the sheer size of some companies has been known to cause duplication of effort. Data mining was used to prevent one division of a leading aerospace company from embarking on a multi-million dollar project that was already being conducted in another division. Data mining also is employed by the NASDAQ to prevent illegal stock trades, which are sometimes attempted in advance of negative company information disclosures.

Within the education market, school administrators use data mining to identify patterns among a wide range of data—including teacher seniority, attendance, disciplinary action, immigration patterns, student demographics, test scores, grades, and medical problems—and determine which students are likely to have trouble or drop out of school. Such analysis also enables educators to tailor curricula to students in a more individualized way and choose which new programs to develop. Some systems enable educators to analyze more than 200 different combinations of data. One of the main drawbacks to using data mining in the education market is the cost. This especially was true during the early and middle years of the twenty-first century's first decade, when many school districts faced budget deficits.

Dire financial circumstances also were a factor in data mining investments for many state governments, but for the opposite reason. Despite budget shortfalls that in many cases exceeded the $1 billion mark, many states pressed on with multi-million-dollar data mining projects because of their potential to maximize tax collections. States like Iowa, Texas, and Virginia used data mining to compare tax collection records with a diverse array of private and public information sources—including federal tax returns, property tax records, drivers license records, aircraft and boat registrations, credit reports, state contract listings, building permits, customs declarations, and unemployment insurance records—and identify tax delinquent individuals or companies. Some systems were capable of comparing information from as many as 100 different databases in one search.

On May 8, 2002, the *Wall Street Journal* reported that this technique allowed Texas to collect $158 million between 1999 and 2001 alone. Iowa and Virginia reported collections in the $30 million range over a three- to five-year period. States were expected to begin using similar data mining approaches to detect welfare fraud. In these cases, eligibility records could be compared with information about house or car purchases. Data mining was especially attractive to many states because leading industry vendors were willing to provide or upgrade data mining systems at no cost in exchange for a cut of tax recoveries over a specified time period.

Government use of data mining to identify lawbreakers led to outcries from consumer privacy proponents, including the Washington, D.C.-based Electronic Privacy Information Center. These groups asserted that governments did not have the right to cull through non-public information sources, and that such behavior was an invasion of privacy. The same criticisms were applied to the federal government's efforts to use data mining in the war against terrorism. This was especially true of the Pentagon's Total Information Awareness (TIA) project, a $64 million effort headed by retired Admiral John Poindexter to develop a system for analyzing public and private records for terrorist information.

In addition to government initiatives directed at uncovering terrorists, federal, state, and local law enforcement agencies were using data mining to solve and reduce other types of crime. Law enforcement officials use data mining to reveal trends or patterns among large volumes of data, including leads stored in police databases. When police databases from multiple cities, states, or jurisdictions are linked together, the artificial intelligence and algorithms of data mining applications can deliver results that would be impossible with human analysis. In addition to identifying patterns, these applications can be used to predict when a crime is likely to occur.

BACKGROUND AND DEVELOPMENT

While the term data mining did not emerge until the 1980s, data mining software applications include elements from three fields that stretch back many years, according to *A Brief History of Data Mining*. These include classical statistics, artificial intelligence, and machine learning. Basic statistical concepts like regression analysis, cluster analysis, discriminant analysis, confidence levels, and standard deviation constitute the basic platform for exploring relationships between data and are at the heart of more complex statistical methods.

Because of the massive (and thus, expensive) computer processing power it required, for many years the field of artificial intelligence (AI) was inaccessible to most organizations, save the government and certain research institutions. However, some of the concepts that emerged from AI were useful to the data mining field, including a problem-solving method called heuristics, and the query features of relational database management systems (RDBMS).

Machine learning involved the conjugation of AI and statistics. *A Brief History of Data Mining* explains that "Machine learning could be considered an evolution of AI, because it blends AI heuristics with advanced statistical analysis. Machine learning attempts to let computer programs learn about the data they study, such that programs make different decisions based on the qualities of the studied data, using statistics for fundamental concepts and adding more advanced AI heuristics and algorithms to achieve its goals."

As early as the 1960s, computer users stored relatively static data on tape, disks, and large mainframe systems. By the 1980s, flat-file databases had evolved into relational database management systems that stored data in related tables, allowing the data to be viewed or queried in a large number of different ways. However, according to the November/December 1999 issue of *IEEE Intelligent Systems,* during the 1980s data mining software systems were still somewhat limited in that they were applied to individual tasks. The publication explained that "Such tools addressed a generic data analysis problem, and their intended user had to be technically sophisticated. Also, using more than one tool on the same data set was difficult and required significant data and metadata transformation."

The evolution of data mining applications continued into the 1990s, resulting in multi-dimensional databases, data warehouses, and decision support systems. This was made possible by multi-dimensional analytic software tools collectively known as online analytic processing (OLAP). By the middle of the twenty-first century's first decade, data mining software programs were marketed as suites that included multiple tools. As *IEEE Intelligent Systems* explained, "These tools were driven by the realization that the knowledge discovery process requires multiple types of data analysis and most of the effort is spent in data cleaning and preprocessing."

By the late 1990s, data mining software had evolved into applications that everyday businesspeople could use to solve specific problems—without advanced knowledge of statistical analysis. This ease of use propelled industry revenues into the billion dollar range.

By the dawn of the twenty-first century, the information age had truly arrived. The value of knowledge and information had increased exponentially with the advent of personal computing and the Internet. The processing power and storage capacity of computers, as well as advanced algorithms, allowed information workers to use data in more proactive and powerful ways than ever before.

During the early years of the first decade of the 2000s, government use of data mining technology was giving the field something of a bad name in the United States, as concerns about invasion of privacy emerged. In addition to individual citizens, groups like the Washington, D.C.-based Electronic Privacy Information Center (EPIC) were leery of government initiatives that might violate civil liberties.

In 2003, public concern led Congress to cancel the Pentagon's Total Information Awareness (TIA) project, a $64 million effort headed by retired Admiral John Poindexter to develop a system for analyzing public and private records for terrorist information. According to the February 22, 2004, issue of the *Atlanta Journal Constitution*: "Poindexter aimed to predict terrorist attacks by identifying telltale patterns of activity in arrests, passport applications, visas, work permits, driver's licenses, car rentals and airline ticket buys as well as credit transactions and education, medical and housing records. The research created a political uproar because such reviews of millions of transactions could put innocent Americans under suspicion. One of Poindexter's own researchers, David D. Jensen at the University of Massachusetts, acknowledged that 'high numbers of false positives can result.'"

However, it appeared that the U.S. government was continuing similar efforts under the guise of an office called Advanced Research and Development Activity (ARDA), which curiously received similar funding of $64 million. In the February 23, 2004, issue of the *Christian Science Monitor,* Steve Aftergood of the Federation of American Scientists called the move a "shell game," explaining, "There may be enough of a difference for them to claim TIA was terminated while for all practical purposes the identical work is continuing."

According to ARDA, it is "an Intelligence Community (IC) center for conducting advanced research and development related to information technology (IT) (information stored, transmitted, or manipulated by electronic means). ARDA sponsors high risk, high payoff research designed to produce new technology to address some of the most important and challenging IT problems faced by the intelligence community. The research is currently organized into five technology thrusts: Information Exploitation, Quantum Information Science, Global Infosystems Access, Novel Intelligence from Massive Data and Advanced Information Assurance."

By 2009, the FBI's data mining system contained more than 1.5 billion government and private sector records concerning U.S. citizens and foreigners, drawing data from a wide variety of sources, including records of international travel, hotel bookings, car rentals, department store transactions and active aircraft pilots. The database was kept at the FBI's National Security Branch Analysis Center (NSAC) near Washington, according to documents acquired under a Freedom of Information (FOIA) request by *Wired* magazine.

At the state level, another data mining project that concerned privacy advocates like EPIC and the American Civil Liberties Union was the Multi-State Anti-Terrorism Information Exchange (MATRIX). Developed by the Institute for Intergovernmental Research (IIR) working group in the wake of the September 11, 2001, terrorist attacks, MATRIX assists law enforcement agencies to investigate criminal or terrorist activity and develop leads by combining private databases with public records from various states. The institute claims that MATRIX does not involve the collection of new information or the connection of criminal intelligence databases. Instead, existing data sources—including incarceration records and criminal histories, vehicle registration and driver's license information, and even digital photos—are connected in order to expedite investigations. Both the Justice Department and the U.S. Department of Homeland Security have contributed funding for MATRIX, which was being used by the states of New York and Florida in early 2004.

By late 2003, data mining technology was evolving beyond the analysis of highly structured databases and onto the World Wide Web. That September, IBM announced that WebFountain, a data mining tool it had been developing for three years at its Almaden Research Center, would be available on a subscription basis through Factiva. Going beyond the capabilities of a regular Web search engine, WebFountain actually performs analysis on the vast sea of information available online, searching for trends and patterns. According to IBM, WebFountain is a useful tool for companies engaging in reputation and brand management, providing them with one more tool to use in an increasingly competitive marketplace. The *San Jose Mercury News* reported that WebFountain was powered by approximately 500 servers at IBM. The system used a massive half-terabyte of space to store data. Subscription costs were expected to range from $150,000 to $300,000 per year.

Text mining applications also had appeared on the market by late 2003. Like Web mining applications, these tools also marked a departure from the use of data mining techniques on highly structured data. Leading industry firms, including SPSS, offered software capable of processing as many as 250,000 pages of text per hour, helping researchers analyze the contents of e-mails, memos, transcripts, journal and news articles, and reports in order to find patterns among them. These applications put article information into different categories and displayed the connections between documents in visual maps. In the process, researchers were able to discover associations between topics or concepts that, without such analysis, might have gone undiscovered. While their significant cost limited text mining applications to large companies and academic institutions, industry observers expected that affordable versions eventually would be available to individual users.

Privacy remained a pressing issue for the data mining industry during the middle of the twenty-first century's first decade. This was especially the case within the government realm, where privacy advocates criticized federal agencies for using technology to snoop on everyday citizens while trying to uncover potential terrorist threats. Tension peaked in December 2005 when the *New York Times* revealed that President George W. Bush had authorized a surveillance program allowing the National Security Agency (NSA) to monitor e-mails and telephone calls in the United States without a warrant. This news drew charges that the administration had violated the Foreign Intelligence Surveillance Act of 1978 (FISA), which requires warrants for eavesdropping, not to mention citizens' Fourth Amendment rights.

Technology initially developed as part of the Pentagon's Total Information Awareness (TIA) project, which Congress cancelled in 2003 amidst privacy concerns, was a focal point of privacy watchdogs. According to the Massachusetts Institute of Technology's *Technology Review,* in early 2006 it became known that the Advanced Research and Development Activity (ARDA) office, located somewhere within the National Security Agency's Fort Meade, Maryland headquarters, had acquired key components of the former TIA program. One example was the Information Awareness Prototype System. Renamed "Basketball," the publication described this component as "the core architecture that would have integrated all the information extraction, analysis, and dissemination tools developed under TIA." *Technology Review* further explained that ARDA had obtained technology called Genoa II, which "used information technologies to help analysts and decision makers anticipate and pre-empt terrorist attacks," and renamed it "Topsail."

By the middle of the first decade of the twenty-first century, the NSA reportedly had access to the records and switches of all major U.S. telecommunications companies. A prime example was AT&T, which maintained a data center in Kansas housing records of nearly 2 trillion telephone calls spanning several decades. By cooperating with the NSA, telecommunications companies gave the NSA unprecedented access to the communications of U.S. citizens, as well as international callers whose calls traveled over U.S. communications networks.

This situation ultimately prompted the Electronic Frontier Foundation, a privacy group, to file a class action lawsuit against AT&T. However, the federal government quickly decided to intervene in the matter. Specifically, on April 28, 2006, Assistant Attorney General Peter D. Keisler, United States Attorney Kevin V. Ryan, Deputy Assistant Attorney General Carl J. Nichols, and other attorneys for the United States of America filed a first Statement of Interest on behalf of the government advising the United States District Court for the Northern District of California that the United States planned to move for the case's dismissal. In addition, the government planned to "assert the military and state secrets privilege" in the action.

In its Statement of Interest, the government's counsel stated, "The United States cannot disclose any national security information that may be at issue in this case. However, the fact that the United States will assert the state secrets privilege should not be construed as a confirmation or denial of any of Plaintiffs' allegations, either about AT&T or the alleged surveillance activities. When allegations are made about purported classified government activities or relationships, regardless of whether those allegations are accurate, the existence or non-existence of the activity or relationship is potentially a state secret. Therefore, the assertion of the state secrets privilege, as a general matter, does not mean that any particularallegation is true but is a reflection of the subject matter at issue." The United States indicated that it would file its motion by May 12, 2006, prior to a hearing date that was scheduled for June 21.

As Mark Williams wrote in the aforementioned issue of *Technology Review,* "With access to much of the world's telecom traffic, the NSA's supercomputers can digitally vacuum up every call placed on a network and apply an arsenal of data mining tools. Traffic analysis, together with social network theory, can reveal patterns indiscernible to human analysts, possibly suggesting terrorist activity. Content filtering, applying highly sophisticated search algorithms and powerful statistical methods like Bayesian analysis in tandem with machine learning, can search for particular words or language combinations that may indicate terrorist communications."

There were other indications that the NSA planned to monitor communications traffic and mine related data. For example, in September 2005 the agency obtained a patent for a technique that could be used to identify an Internet address's physical location. Heading into the second half of the decade, it was clear that data mining was an invaluable tool for identifying terrorists. However, it appeared that privacy was one cost for using this technology. Moving forward, some industry players, privacy advocates, and ordinary citizens were hopeful that a delicate balance between privacy and national security could be found.

PIONEERS IN THE FIELD

Usama Fayyad, Ph.D. One of the data mining field's founding fathers is Usama Fayyad, Ph.D., whose educational background is rooted in the fields on which data mining is based: computer science, engineering, and mathematics. After earning undergraduate degrees in electrical and computer engineering in 1984, Fayyad received an MSE in computer science and engineering in 1986, and a Master's in mathematics in 1989. He then earned a Ph.D. in engineering from the University of Michigan, Ann Arbor, in 1991.

In 1989, Fayyad established the Jet Propulsion Laboratory's (JPL) Machine Learning Systems Group at the California Institute of Technology. In that role, he developed data mining systems that were used to solve significant scientific problems by analyzing large databases. In recognition of his efforts, Fayyad received a U.S. Government Medal from NASA, as well as a most distinguished excellence award from Cal Tech/JPL.

Although he would maintain his relationship with JPL as a Distinguished Visiting Scientist, Fayyad joined Microsoft Research in 1996 and established the software giant's Data Mining & Exploration (DMX) Group. Fayyad's biography explains that his work at Microsoft Research "included the invention and development of scalable algorithms for mining large databases and customizing them for server products such as Microsoft SQL Server and OLAP Services. These components were shipped in Microsoft SQL Server 2000 as part of the new industry standard in data mining, Microsoft's OLE DB API, which Dr. Fayyad also helped establish and promote. He also led the development of predictive data mining components for Microsoft Site Server (Commerce Server 3.0 and 4.0)."

In 2000, Fayyad co-founded digiMine, Inc. with two other Microsoft employees. With Fayyad at the helm as president and CEO, this new, privately held enterprise developed data mining and business intelligence solutions. The company changed its name to Revenue Science, Inc. in 2003, with venture capitalist Bill Grossman serving as CEO and Fayyad as chairman.

In addition to editing two books and publishing hundreds of technical articles on data mining, Fayyad has served as editor in chief of several technical journals. He also has been involved with leading academic and technical conferences, both as a speaker and in leadership roles.

By 2007, the use of data mining technology continued to increase at the government level, with some 200 different programs in operation. In keeping with the climate that existed during the middle part of the decade, the government's use of data mining remained a double-edged sword. On the upside, data mining enabled the government to crack down on fraud, and thus save taxpayers money. For example, by 2006 the U.S. Department of Agriculture's Risk Management Agency (RMA) revealed that since 2001, data mining had enabled the agency to save taxpayers $456 million by identifying suspect crop loss claims from producers and avoiding

payment on those claims. Data mining allowed the government to compare reported crop losses from a given producer to those of neighboring producers, and see if the losses were consistent. According to the RMA, it saved $23 for every $1 spent on data mining.

However, concern about government use of data mining, along with a perceived need for safeguards, appeared to be more top-of-mind with the public and industry watchdogs. In the January 11, 2007, issue of the *Atlanta Journal-Constitution,* former Georgia Republican Representative Bob Barr commented, "Data mining is completely out of control. Americans have no idea what is going on with these programs."

While proponents indicate that data mining has enabled the government to reveal criminals and registered sex offenders working in youth service organizations, locate missing children, and profile possible terrorists, others argued that the efforts result in many false positives, which cause difficulty for innocent people. Watchdogs argue that data mining technology has advanced beyond the scope of existing privacy laws.

In the same *Atlanta Journal-Constitution* article, Senator Patrick Leahy (D-VT), chairman of a Senate Judiciary Committee conducting an investigation of the Bush administration's terrorist surveillance programs, said, "The federal government's use of data mining technology has exploded without congressional oversight or comprehensive privacy safeguards."

Heading toward the end of the decade, government use of data mining promised to remain a controversial issue. The National Council of State Legislatures indicated that approximately 12 states had proposals regarding data mining and privacy pending in 2007, In addition, Nevada voted to ban the sale of prescription data from physicians to outside parties such as pharmaceutical firms. This followed a similar move by New Hampshire in 2006 that was challenged by data mining companies in federal court, on the grounds of being unconstitutional.

CURRENT CONDITIONS

According to research group Forrester, business intelligence (BI) software was the tip of the data mining application software pyramid in 2009. Based on deep data analysis, BI became even more important in economically challenging times. As such, the BI market was much less affected by the economic crises in 2008 and 2009 than most other software markets. Forrester prdicted that advanced analytics would drive market growth to $14 billion by 2014. Research analyst firm Gartner agreed, reporting in June 2009 that the market for BI tools defied the recession and showed revenue growth of almost 22 percent in 2008. Gartner reported that worldwide sales for BI platforms, analytic applications and performance management software went from $7.2 billion in 2007 to $8.8 billion in 2008.

The 2008 and 2009 global economic downturn did produce some palpable changes in the market. Wayne Eckerson, Director of Research and Service for The Data Warehousing Institute, noted that software as a service (SaaS) picked up, as an on-demand packaged analytic applications. This was an economical option for mid-market or smaller departments in larger companies that did not have IT resources for packaged applications. In his trends forecast for *TechTarget* in January 2009, Eckerson opined that SaaS applications from LucidEra, PivotLink, Xactly Analytics, Autometrics, Oco, and Business Objects would gain traction. He also noted that many companies would likely invest in new analytic database products, the platforms for which employed massively parallel processing (MPP) databases and servers that would dramatically improve performance and lower cost.

Gartner Inc. analysts also predicted in early 2009 that through 2012, over 35 percent of the top 5,000 global companies will fail to keep pace with significant changes in their business and markets, and will therefore fail to make insightful decisions. However, Gartner also noted that by 2010, 20 percent of organizations would have industry-specific analytic applications delivered via SaaS as a standard component of their BI portfolio. The company also opined that by 2012, business units would control at least 40 percent of future budgets for BI, increasing spending on packaged analytic applications that target specific functions, such as finance or corporate performance management.

Gartner reported significant revenue growth in both BI platforms and analytics applications software for 2008, totalling approximately $3.1 billion and $5.7 billion respectively. It listed the 2008 leading companies (see below) as SAP ($2.09 million); SAS Institute ($1.28 million); Oracle ($1.28 million); IBM ($996 million); and Microsoft ($681 million).

INDUSTRY LEADERS

In June 2009, Gartner analyst Dan Sommer, in an article appearing in *Information Age,* attributed industry growth to industry consolidation and a focus on sales and marketing by large stack vendor, particulary towards new acquisitions.The 2009 Gartner report showed that, thanks to its 2007 acquisition of Business Objects, SAP accounted for almost a quarter of the market, followed by the SAS Institute and Oracle (both at 14.6 percent), IBM (11.3 percent) and Microsoft (7.7 percent).

SAS Institute Inc. Founded in 1976, SAS leads the data mining industry pack and is recognized as the world's largest privately owned software enterprise. SAS had nearly 10,000 employees around the world, located in some 400 offices. SAS is devoted to furthering the evolution of its products and invests about 25 percent of its revenues into research and development. According to SAS, its software is used at more than 40,000 locations. Among its customers are 96 of the top 100 companies on the *Fortune* 500, as well as the Department of Defense.

SAS holds roughly one-third of the world data mining software market. Its applications included SAS Enterprise Miner, an application that "reveals significant patterns and trends, explains known outcomes and identifies factors that can secure a desired effect—all from collected demographic data and customer buying patterns." In conjunction with Enterprise Miner, SAS also offered an add-on module called SAS Text Miner, intended for use on unstructured data sources like documents, e-mails, notes, and reports.

In 2006 SAS made *Fortune's* 100 Best Companies to Work For list for the ninth year in a row and was ranked at number six as *Computerworld's* Best Places to Work in IT. In 2007 the company was voted Best Data Mining Toolset vendor for the third consecutive year in the Intelligent Enterprise Readers' Choice Awards.

International Business Machines Corp. (IBM) International Business Machines Corp. (IBM) is a leading information technology company with offerings that range from computer systems and software to storage systems and micro-electronics. In addition to its status as the leading computer products and services provider, IBM is the second leading software manufacturer after Microsoft. IBM is a pioneer within the data mining industry, thanks in part to the efforts of its Intelligent Information Systems Research (Quest) group at the company's San Jose, California-based Almaden Research Center.

Quest played a role in creating IBM's scalable DB2 Intelligent Miner for Data software suite, which according to IBM provides users with a single data mining framework that "supports the iterative process, offering data processing, statistical analysis, and results visualization to complement a variety of mining methods." With DB2 Intelligent Miner for Data, users are able to employ a variety of algorithms and techniques—including clustering, associations, sequential patterns, and time sequences—in order to glean useful information from a wide variety of enterprise data.

Oracle Corp. Founded in 1977, Oracle is a world heavyweight in the realm of database management systems software, including applications for data mining. In 2009, research company IDC named Oracle as the leader in the data warehouse platform market, with 2008 sales of $2.3 billion and more than 56,000 employees. It reported

2008 sales of more than $100 million in packaged analytic applications, giving it nearly a 40 percent share in that market for 2008. In 2007 the company announced its acquisition of the business intelligence software maker Hyperion Solutions Corp. for $3.3 billion.

Oracle's data mining product, named Oracle Data Mining, was offered as part of the company's Oracle 10g Database Enterprise Edition (EE). According to Oracle, its offering "embeds data mining functionality for making classifications, predictions, and associations, as well as extracting new features from data, clustering data and ranking relative attribute importance. All model building and scoring functions are accessible through either a Java interface or PL/SQL interface. A graphical interface, the ODM Client supports 'point and click' data mining with the benefit of generating Java code to expedite application development." By 2006, Oracle Data Miner Release 10gR2 had been released, offering new algorithms such as Decision Tree and Anomaly Detection. In 2008, it released Oracle Exadata.

SPSS Inc. Another leader in the data mining industry is Chicago-based SPSS Inc. SPSS serves customers within the corporate, academic, government, and health care sectors with predictive analytics software. Users apply SPSS software in the areas of customer acquisition and retention, up-selling and cross-selling, fraud detection, and patient outcome improvement. Clementine, SPSS's data mining "workbench," is available in seven languages besides English and is designed around a standard called CRISP-DM, which allows for the application of data mining technology to specific business problems.

WORKFORCE

While non-technical workers were using data mining applications in growing numbers during the middle of the decade, many end users and software developers had formal training in the field of computer science. Common occupations in this field include database administrators, computer systems analysts, and computer scientists. According to the 2006-2007 edition of the U.S. Department of Labor's *Occupational Outlook Handbook,* this broad professional group included approximately 994,000 workers in 2004. Of this total, 487,000 were computer systems analysts, 104,000 were database administrators, and 22,000 were computer and information research scientists. Computer systems analysts earned median salaries of almost $66,460 in 2004, while database administrators earned median salaries of about $60,650, and computer and information research scientists' median salaries were $85,190.

The U.S. Department of Labor estimates that through 2014, database administrators, computer scientists, and computer systems analysts will be among the nation's fastest growing occupations. Employment of these computer specialists is expected to grow much faster than the average for all occupations as organizations continue to adopt and integrate increasingly sophisticated technologies.

In its March 2006 issue, *KDnuggets* reported that among 173 respondents to a data mining salary poll, 15.6 percent were students; 11 percent earned less than $30,000; 19.7 percent earned $31,000 to $60,000; another 19.7 percent earned $61,000 to $90,000; 15.6 percent earned $91,000 to $120,000; and 18.5 percent earned more than $120,000. The best salaries were earned in the United States and Canada, with a median of approximately $100,000.

RESEARCH AND TECHNOLOGY

According to Forrester Research Group in its 2009 market analysis, new categories of advanced analytics will fuel the growth and merge into the core BI market, including business performance solutions, text analytics, predictive analytics, and complex event processing. Each of these market sectors will grow at its own pace and will converge over time into core BI as new sectors emerge. Success in each sector will require differing strategies, but opportunity for smaller, nimbler players is clearly there despite the recent surge of mergers and acquisitions (M&A) activity.

Innovation and research are at the heart of the data mining field's continued evolution. Next-generation dashboards will allow users model and simulate reality using historical data, and more companies were expected to create analytical sandboxes for analysts to play with data, using Teradata and other vendors, said Data Warehousing Institute's Wayne Eckerson in early 2009.

Two groups that play an instrumental role in this process are the From Data To Knowledge (FDK) research unit at the University of Helsinki and the Intelligent Information Systems Research (Quest) group at IBM's Almaden Research Center.

From Data To Knowledge Research Unit As its name implies, FDK is devoted to "developing methods for forming useful knowledge from large masses of data." According to FDK, its research focuses on four distinct but inter-related areas: data mining and machine learning, computational methods in medical genetics and expression data analysis, combinatorial pattern matching and information retrieval, and computational structural biology. An important aspect of FDK's work is the combination of theory and practice, and that researchers work on multiple projects in order to further the transfer of information.

Designated as one of the Academy of Finland's centers of excellence from 2002 to 2007, FDK's research has been used internationally to benefit a wide variety of different fields, including ecology, genetics, molecular biology, natural language processing, process industry, and telecommunications. The results have attracted wide international attention. Many concepts created by the group are used by the scientific community. In addition, the unit's findings have been used to develop new commercial software and appear in educational texts.

IBM Almaden Research Center The Intelligent Information Systems Research (Quest) group at IBM's San Jose, California-based Almaden Research Center was a pioneering force in the data mining field. The group was involved in the development of IBM's Intelligent Miner software, and also developed other tools in the areas of e-business, Web hosting, and content sharing. In addition to holding approximately 40 patents, Quest has published a large number of research papers. As of 2004, the group was involved in the creation of information systems that protected data privacy without hindering the flow of information. This work included data mining, but also extended to data and databases in general, including query execution methods, encryption techniques, and relational data rights management.

Technological Advancement During the early years of the first decade of the twenty-first century, competition was heating up in the market for computer processors. Subsequently, 64-bit chips—capable of moving and accessing larger amounts of data than common 32-bit chips—were coming down in price. This was good news for data mining professionals, especially those in small and mid-sized organizations. Traditionally restricted to large, custom computer systems developed by the likes of IBM and Sun Microsystems, by 2004, Advanced Micro Devices (AMD) offered a 64-bit chip that not only would run older 32-bit programs but cost business users as little as $2,800. Market leader Intel also offered a 64-bit chip called Itanium. The company claimed that Itanium was targeted specifically at the kinds of large 64-bit systems developed by Sun and IBM, which cost anywhere from $10,000 to more than $100,000. While Itanium was not capable of running 32-bit applications, industry observers expected that Intel would ultimately release a chip with the same 32-bit/64-bit flexibility found in AMD's version.

BIBLIOGRAPHY
"A Brief History of Data Mining." Data Mining Software, 23 February 2004. Available from http://www.data-mining-software.com/data_mining_history.htm.

"About Our Company." SAS Institute Inc., 5 April 2007. Available from http://www.sas.com.

"About SPSS Inc." SPSS Inc., 2 May 2006. Available from http://www.spss.com.

"An Introduction to Data Mining. Discovering Hidden Value in Your Data Warehouse," 23 February 2004. Available from http://www.thearling.com/text/dmwhite/dmwhite.htm.

Ashford, Warwick. "FBI Database Holds Records on 1.5 Billion People." *Computer Weekly,* 24 September 2009.

Carr, Rebecca. "Privacy Advocates Blast Data Mining: 'Completely Out of Control.' Senate Panel Told Feds' Programs Infringe on Individuals' Rights." *The Atlanta Journal-Constitution,* 11 January 2007.

Chordas, Lori. "Data-mining Saves Federal Crop Insurance Program $456 Million, Director Says." *Best's Review,* August 2006.

"Computer Scientists and Database Administrators." *Occupational Outlook Handbook, 2006-07 Edition.* Washington, D.C.: U.S. Department of Labor, Bureau of Labor Statistics.

"Computer Software & Services." *Value Line Investment Survey.* Value Line Publishing Inc., 2004.

"Computer Systems Analysts." *Occupational Outlook Handbook, 2006-07 Edition.* Washington, D.C.: U.S. Department of Labor, Bureau of Labor Statistics.

"Data Miner Income (Salary) by Region." *KDnuggets,* March 2006. Available from http://www.kdnuggets.com.

"Data Mining and Analytic Technologies." 23 February 2004. Available from http://www.thearling.com.

"Data Mining Methods." *KDnuggets,* April 2006. Available from http://www.kdnuggets.com.

"DB2 Intelligent Miner." IBM Corp., 2 May 2006. Available from http://www-306.ibm.com/software/data/iminer/.

"First Statement of Interest of the United States, Case 3:06-cv-00672-VRW Document 82-1." Washington, D.C.: U.S. Department of Justice, Civil Division, Federal Programs Branch, 28 April 2006. Available from http://www.eff.org/legal/cases/att/USA_statement_of_interest.pdf.

"From Data To Knowledge (FDK) Research Unit." University of Helsinki, Department of Computer Science, 11 March 2004. Available from http://www.cs.helsinki.fi/research/pmdm/introduction.html.

Gavin, Robert. "States Turn Super Tax Sleuths. Officials Peruse Millions of Records in Just Minutes With Data-Mining Systems." *Wall Street Journal,* 8 May 2002.

Harris, Shane. "How Does the NSA Spy?" *National Journal,* 21 January 2006.

Hentoff, Nat. "Investigating the NSA." *The Washington Times,* 16 January 2006.

"Independent Research Report Documents SAS' Strength in Data Mining." *LocalTechWire.com.* 26 January 2004. Available from http://www.localtechwire.com/printstory.cfm?u=6810.

"Intelligent Information Systems." IBM Almaden Research Center, 2 May 2006. Available from http://www.almaden.ibm.com/software/disciplines/iis.

Kelly, Jeff. "Experts Forecast Business Intelligence Market Trends for 2009." *TechTarget,* 7 January 2009. Available from http://searchdatamanagement.techtarget.com/news/article/0,289142,sid91_gci1344197,00.html.

Kessler, Michelle. "AMD Follows Own Path to Success." *USA Today,* 17 February 2004.

Market Overview: The Business Intelligence Software Market. Forrester Research, 2009. Available from http://www. forrester. com/go%3Fdocid%3D55034.

Markoff, John. "Government Looks at Ways to Mine Databases." *The New York Times,* 25 February 2006.

Mullin, Joe. "Nevada: Panel Votes to Ban Data-Mining." *Houston Chronicle,* 3 April 2007.

"Multistate Anti-Terrorism Information Exchange (MATRIX)." Institute for Intergovernmental Research, 10 March 2004. Available from http://www.matrix-at.org.

"Number of Data Mining Projects in 2006 (January 2007)." *KDnuggets,* January 2007. Available from http://www. kdnuggets.com.

"Oracle Data Mining." Oracle Corp., 2 May 2006. Available from http://www.oracle.com.

Piatetsky-Shapiro, Gregory. "The Data-Mining Industry Coming of Age." *IEEE Intelligent Systems,* November/December 1999.

Regan, Tom. "US Still Funding Powerful Data Mining Tools." *The Christian Science Monitor,* 23 February 2004. Available from http://www.csmonitor.com.

Robinson, J.J. "Business Intelligence Market Grows 22%, Says Gartner." *Information Age,* 15 June 2009.

"SAS Ranked Best in Data Mining." *Business Wire,* 29 January 2007.

Sniffen, Michael J. "U.S. Pressing for High-Tech Spy Tools." *The Atlanta Journal-Constitution,* 22 February 2004.

"Successful Data Mining Applications." *KDnuggets,* July 2005. Available from http://www.kdnuggets.com.

Tsai, Jessica. "Worldwide BI Revenue Reached $8.8 Billion in 2008" *CRM Magazine,* 29 July 2009.

"Usama Fayyad, Ph.D." Revenue Science Inc., 7 March 2004. Available from http://www.revenuescience.com/about/fayyad.asp.

"WebFountain Advanced Analytic Solutions." IBM Almaden Research Center., 10 March 2004. Available from http:// www.almaden.ibm.com/webfountain.

Williams, Mark. "Information Awareness Project Lives On." *Technology Review,* 26 April 2006.

Zuckerman, Mortimer B. "Using All the Tools." *U.S. News & World Report,* 27 February 2006.

DIGITAL AUDIO ENTERTAINMENT

SIC CODE(S)

3651

3652

3663

3695

7379

7929

INDUSTRY SNAPSHOT

Digital audio entertainment—including services that allow consumers to download individual songs or entire albums, as well as portable media players—has significantly impacted the larger music industry. Traditional music recording and distribution continued to struggle as illegal sharing of music files, CD copying, and heightened competition for consumers' entertainment dollars reduced compact disc sales. The music industry continued to lose more than $2 billion annually due to piracy alone. Then in March 2007, citing Nielsen SoundScan data, *The New York Times* reported that sales of plastic CDs were surpassed by digital tracks for the very first time.

Amidst these difficult times, the music industry witnessed a number of significant changes, including mergers and ownership changes. Developments included the combination of Sony's recorded music business with that of rival BMG, creating Sony BMG Music Entertainment, as well as the sale of Warner Music Group by Time Warner.

Many industry observers noted that Apple Computer's introduction of the iPod digital music player in 2002, followed by the opening of its iTunes Music Store

in April 2003, were two factors that catapulted digital music into the realm of mass acceptability. Apple's iTunes store was responsible for some 70 percent of all legal music downloads, selling some 2 billion digital songs in 2007. In August 2009, NPD Group figures revealed that iTunes dominated the digital music sales market with 25 percent of all songs sold. Retail giant Walmart took second place.

Moving forward, the main challenge for major record labels was to convert illegal file sharers into customers of legitimate digital music services. One well-respected report from IFPI estimated that 95 percent of music downloads in 2008 were illegal and unpaid for. While the future was uncertain, some observers foresaw a radical transition in which the music industry would become purely service-oriented. As digitized files became the principal format for distributing music, they indicated that the production and distribution of CDs would cease, and physical retail space for new music would likewise disappear. In addition, these futurists posited that a more direct link would emerge between creative artists and music lovers.

ORGANIZATION AND STRUCTURE

Consumer Market. According to NPD Group research, by late 2004, some 62 percent of Internet- connected homes in the United States had digital music files stored on their personal computers. This figure demonstrated the sheer size of the digital music market, which continued to grow at an explosive pace into the latter part of the decade.

A sizable portion of the digital music market consisted of younger consumers, ranging in age from 13 to

35. The *Hitwise Online Music Report* found that while traditional music shopping sites like BMG Music Service were frequented more heavily by those in the 25 to 44 age group, 51 percent of online music site users were males in the 18 to 34 age bracket with annual incomes of $30,000 to $60,000. Within the teenage market sector, Jupiter Research found that teenage girls were an especially strong user category, spending 15 percent more per month on online music than boys.

By 2004, traditional online music retailers still held more of the consumer market than digital music download sites, but they were quickly losing share. According to Hitwise, download sites saw their share of the market skyrocket 20.6 percent between January and July of 2004 alone, while traditional music retailers saw their market share fall 9.1 percent during the same time frame.

Digital Music Sources The digital music industry was in a state of flux during the middle of the first decade of the 2000s. A great many consumers still opted to illegally trade digital music via popular file-sharing networks. However, legal pay services were making strong inroads while illegal file sharing began to decline. As of 2007, consumers were able to choose from a range of pay services, including Apple Computer's iTunes Music Store, RealNetworks' Rhapsody, and offerings from the likes of Napster and Wal-Mart.

Converting consumers from illegal file-sharing network users to customers of legitimate pay services was a major industry challenge. According to NPD Group research, only 2 percent of Internet-connected homes in the United States had tried a for-pay service by late 2004. Twenty percent of those who "trialed" a pay service ended up actually subscribing, compared to a 50 percent conversion rate for those who trialed a free peer-to-peer (P2P) service. NPD also found that many P2P users who tried pay services continued to use free P2P services.

Although they once had a firm grasp on music distribution, traditional music retailers were negatively impacted by the advent of digital music. As retail sales of recorded music fell, some retailers (including National Record Mart) closed their doors, while others—such as Tower Records and Wherehouse—filed for bankruptcy protection. Industry leader Musicland Group responded by scaling back its base of stores.

As major music distributors moved to form their own digital distribution platforms, such as Pressplay and MusicNet, retailers were concerned about being cut out of the loop. In response, Best Buy was involved in the establishment of a retail consortium called Echo in early 2003 that eventually included Virgin Entertainment, Trans World Entertainment, Tower Records, Hastings Entertainment, and Borders Group. According to the *Hollywood Reporter,*

each retail member reportedly contributed $150,000 apiece to the consortium, with an ultimate goal of raising $10 million to $12 million to build a digital distribution infrastructure. By working together, the retailers hoped to leverage their collective clout with the music industry.

When Apple Computer unveiled its iTunes service in April 2003, the dynamics of the game changed. With the potential cost of building a rival service pegged at $30 million to $100 million, this effectively sounded the death knell for Echo. By mid-2004, Echo's members were either pursuing their own individual strategies for surviving in the digital music world, or, in the case of Borders, were taking time to evaluate their options. As of early 2005, retailers were aligning with established digital music providers. For example, Best Buy partnered with Rhapsody and Napster to provide customers with digital music via in-store kiosks.

Some industry analysts argued that simply installing in-store kiosks was not enough to cure the music retail sector's ills. In the March 2004 issue of *Business 2.0,* Forrester Research principal analyst Josh Bernoff remarked, "I think retailers understand the change that's taking place in their business. There's just not that much they can do. It's beginning to look very scary for them." On a positive note, following the closure of more than 1,000 stores the previous year, the retail sector experienced improvement in 2004. Industry analysts attributed this to improved sales of CDs, combined with a decrease in piracy. Nevertheless, the popularity of digital music appeared to be an irreversible trend.

Digital Rights Management As for-pay music services grew in popularity and the use of digital audio tracks extended to everything from cell phone ring tones and Internet radio to TV commercials, the issue of managing digital copyrights and tracking royalties on behalf of artists developed into a prime concern.

By the middle of the first decade of the 2000s, a number of solutions for tracking digital copyrights began to emerge. One example was Royalty Services LP, a $30 million joint venture between San Francisco-based Exigen Group, Universal Music Group, and Warner Music Group that offered a technology platform for managing the royalty distribution process traditionally handled by record labels. The new offering, which tracked how royalties from a 99-cent song download got divided among multiple parties such as singers, composers, song writers, and record labels, was based on existing Exigen technology that had been used to track transactions for stock brokers and insurance companies. This was an important industry development, since Universal and Warner accounted for about 42 percent of sales within the record industry.

Europe's BT Group and Blueprint offered another platform for managing digital rights and tracking royalties. The two companies created a service for hosting, managing, and distributing digital music and other content that was based on Blueprint's Open Royalty Gateway and Song Centre software. According to a November 24, 2004, news release from *M2 PressWire,* the service "enables rights holders—artists, writers, publishers and record companies—to host their songs, videos, ring tones and other digital media files while allowing direct commercial relationships with retailers to drive far more innovative product offerings to the consumer."

Finally, Bedford, Massachusetts-based RSA Security also was developing digital rights management technology. RSA's offering pertained to mobile devices and was intended to offer copyright protection for digital music as well as games and video.

Although piracy remained a major concern for industry players in 2007, consumers were demanding music tracks that were free of digital rights management (DRM) protection. In response, Apple announced it would begin selling tracks from EMI and other labels without copy protection. Major labels, such as Warner Music, Sony BMG, and Universal Music, were reluctant to move into the DRM-free realm. However, Amazon.com's announcement that it would unveil a download service to rival iTunes in late 2007 or early 2008, with DRM-free tracks from some 12,000 different labels, put added pressure on the majors to move in this direction.

Artists Rather than passively watching the music industry's digital transformation, some artists have taken an active role in defining the future. Perhaps the prime example of this is the Magnificent Union of Digitally Downloading Artists (Mudda), spearheaded by rock stars Peter Gabriel and Brian Eno. According to a statement from Gabriel on Mudda's Web site, "The relationship of artist to the business has most often been one of contract and servitude. We believe the way forward must be a partnership in which the artist can take a much bigger role in how their creations are sold, but also have the chance to stand at the front of the queue when payments are made instead of the traditional position of being paid long after everyone else." Mudda issued a manifesto that urged artists to band together and take greater control over the content, length, marketing, and distribution of their creative works. This included urging artists to offer content to fans via their own Web sites, including different states of songs as they are developed, as opposed to only a single finished product, and direct licensing agreements for works that are not tied to a particular recording company.

In addition to his work with Mudda, Gabriel cofounded a digital downloading service called On Demand

Distribution (OD2) during the late 1990s with Charles Grimsdale. By the middle of the first decade of the 2000s, OD2 had become the leading digital music distributor in Europe. In addition to working with independent labels, the company also partnered with the industry's leading recording companies. OD2 also formed a corporate partnership with Coca-Cola and released a Windows Media Player plug-in called Sonic Selector that, according to the January 27, 2004, issue of *Variety,* allowed the media player to function as a digital music store.

Associations Based in Washington, D.C., the Recording Industry Association of America (RIAA) promotes the mutual interests of recording companies, manufacturers, and distributors. Founded in 1952, it represents the music industry through government relations, anti-piracy activities, intellectual property protection, public relations, and research initiatives. The RIAA's roughly 250 members create, market, and distribute an estimated 90 percent of all legitimate sound recordings produced and sold in the United States. In addition to representing the recording industry's interests, the RIAA is the official certification agency for gold, platinum and multi-platinum awards. The RIAA has committees devoted to numerous industry topics including engineering, labor relations, legal issues, market research, marketing, traffic/freight, and more. Formerly known as the Record Industry Association of America, the RIAA has evolved with the industry overall, and during the first decade of the twenty-first century has been at the forefront of prosecuting individuals engaged in illegal file sharing.

Legislation Signed into law by President Clinton on October 28, 1998, the Digital Millennium Copyright Act is an important piece of legislation affecting the digital music industry. The act covers more than just digital music, and was created as a means of implementing treaties signed at the World Intellectual Property Organization (WIPO) Geneva Conference in 1996. In addition to requiring Webcasters to pay licensing fees to recording companies, it initially gave the Recording Industry Association of America (RIAA) the power to obtain federal court subpoenas without the approval of a judge in order to obtain the names of file sharers from Internet service providers. By the fall of 2003, the RIAA had used this power to subpoena thousands of names, and had actually filed lawsuits against several hundred file sharers, according to the *Washington Post.* However, this approach came to an end in December 2003 following an appellate court decision in Washington that the RIAA could not force ISPs to give up the names of their customers.

By early 2005, the RIAA was appealing a subsequent 2 to 1 federal ruling by an 8th Circuit Court of Appeals panel. In the meantime, the association took a different—and more expensive—approach to sue alleged violators. According to the Associated Press, the trade group had resorted to filing civil lawsuits against nameless defendants, using their Internet addresses as a starting point and embarking upon a complicated legal process to eventually learn their real identities.

On the international front, in 2008, France and the United Kingdom both took affirmative measures to work with ISPs in addressing Internet piracy. France created a draft Creation and Internet Law to set up a system of graduated response to persistent copyright abusers, starting with written warnings and leading up to loss of Internet access for 1 to 12 months. In July 2008, the UK government brokered a joint Memorandum of Understanding to bind members of the recording and film industries and the six largest ISPs in working together to achieve significant reductions in unauthorized file-sharing. The government further requested advice on legislative options to sanction internet piracy. In New Zealand, ISPs will now be required to implement policies of terminating accounts of repeat infringers, and legislative review continues in Australia, Hong Kong, Italy, Japan, South Korea, and the United States.

BACKGROUND AND DEVELOPMENT

The rise of digital music can be attributed to a number of main factors. First was the advent of digital compact discs in the early 1980s, which inspired music lovers to replace their analog record and tape collections with a new digital format that, theoretically, could be reproduced without compromising sound quality. The first CD players, which did not include copy protection capabilities, were released in 1982 by Sony and Phillips. CD-ROM drives first became available for personal computers in the mid-1980s. Eventually it became possible for consumers to convert or "rip" traditional compact disc audio tracks to individual digital files that produced similar or equal sound quality with a comparatively smaller file size. The most popular digital file format was MP3, which was patented in 1995.

The introduction of writable CD drives, which enabled users to "burn" customized collections of digital tracks to CDs, was another critical growth factor. However, it was Internet file sharing networks that attributed to the rapid rise of online music trading. The pioneering Napster, which came onto the scene in 1999, used centralized servers for file sharing. Other "peer to peer" (P2P) networks allowed users to share a variety of digital files directly between their computers.

These factors quickly began to impact the music industry's financial health. In fact, during the early years of the first decade of the 2000s, a number of industry

analysts questioned whether the industry would remain intact in its current form. A number of developments occurred on the legal front. In 2000, the heavy metal band Metallica sued Napster, and a lawsuit against the Web site MP3.com resulted in a $250 million award to record label Universal. Traditional music shipments fell more than 10 percent in 2001, from 1.08 billion units in 2000 to 968.58 million units in 2001, according to the RIAA. Total "album" sales fell 11 percent again in 2002. That year, legal pressure caused Napster to fold as a file-sharing service. Kazaa, which had formed in Amsterdam two years before, then became the leading file sharing network. Kazaa would go on to withstand legal assaults in later years.

According to some industry observers, rising Internet connectivity and the pervasiveness of digital technology—namely writable CD drives and MP3 players—had much to do with the industry's troubles. In January of 2003, *Internet Business News* reported that the number of Web pages and peer to peer (P2P) applications devoted to file sharing had increased 300 percent from 2001 levels. Citing findings from Forrester Research, *The Economist* revealed that some 27 percent of Americans were engaged in downloading music by the early years of the decade. Referring to May 2002 survey results from Peter D. Hart Research Associates, the RIAA indicated that "by a more than two-to-one margin, consumers who say they are downloading more also say they are purchasing less."

In 2003, Nielsen SoundScan began charting digital music downloads from the leading for-pay music services. NPD Group research revealed that 64 percent of Web-connected homes had computers containing at least one digital music file, according to the September 13, 2003, issue of *The Online Reporter*. File sharing was responsible for 66 percent of all digital music file acquisitions, with the remainder attributed to consumers ripping music directly from CDs. Of all digital music files, the research firm estimated that half existed in homes with high-speed Internet connections. This revealed the impact that broadband service was having on the industry.

Amidst these conditions, major recording companies were all struggling to stay afloat. In its February 2003 issue, *Wired* published an article by Charles C. Mann entitled "The Year Music Dies," which discussed the possibility that the industry, as it existed, would collapse in less than five years.

As digital music formats exploded in popularity, the industry was taking a number of different measures to address piracy One tactic involved putting greater pressure on hardware manufacturers to implement anti-piracy technology. While this protection action was called for in proposed legislation like the *Consumer Broadband and Digital Television Act*, it led to wrangling between players in the electronics and recording industries. In addition, both domestic and international recording companies were calling for Internet service providers to take measures to stop music piracy by monitoring their networks. Other tactics included making CDs that were not playable—and thus not recordable—on personal computers, as well as other technology that simply prevented consumers from copying CDs.

The recording industry eventually moved toward "legitimate" digital music subscription services such as MusicNet (RealNetworks) and Pressplay (Universal Music Group and Sony Music Entertainment), which allowed consumers to download music for a fee. In a similar move, six of the leading U.S. music retailers attempted to establish their own service called Echo, but the initiative ultimately failed. Such services usually limited downloaded music to one device or medium, which many music lovers found irritating.

Apple Computer changed the game with the release of its iTunes Music Store in April 2003, which allowed customers to download songs to iPod music players, up to three computers, and an unlimited number of CDs for 99 cents per track. Before long, Apple had 80 percent of the legal digital music market, according to Nielsen SoundScan. By this time, other legitimate music download services had emerged including Roxio's new Napster service, which replaced Pressplay, as well as offerings from Listen.com, Liquid Audio, and MusicNet.

Buoying industry growth was the emergence of totally new markets for digital music. The $300 million mobile entertainment segment was a prime example. This included cell phone ring tones, which represented new revenue streams for creative artists and record companies alike. Cell phone ring tones became so popular that *Billboard* magazine began publishing a weekly top 20 chart for the hottest ring tones in November 2004.

By 2007, Apple had become an even more dominant force within the industry, with more than 2 billion digital songs sold via its ever popular iTunes store. In July of 2007, NPD Group figures revealed that iTunes had surpassed Amazon.com to become the nation's third largest music retailer with a 9.8 percent of retail music sales, according to the *Colorado Springs Business Journal.* iTunes was second only to Best Buy (13.8 percent) and Wal-Mart (15.8 percent).

Heading into 2008, industry players were desperately trying to preserve the album format. The aforementioned article in *The New York Times* revealed that digital single purchases outpaced digital album sales by 19 to 1. Furthermore, *eWeek* reported that both CD and digital album sales were down 10 percent in the first quarter of 2007, based on data from Nielsen SoundScan. Apple came to the industry's aid in early 2007 when it announced a service that would give consumers credit for tracks they already owned if they wanted to purchase

a complete album. However, some analysts were skeptical about the ability of such promotions to reverse the movement away from complete albums. They argued that albums will still be relevant for some genres, such as opera, classical, and psychedelic rock. However, rap, pop, and country enthusiasts are more likely to stick with only those popular songs that interest them.

Although piracy remained a major concern for industry players, consumers were demanding music tracks that were free of digital rights management (DRM) protection, which limited the devices on which they could store and play their digital music. In response, Apple announced it would begin selling tracks from EMI and other labels without copy protection. Although the tracks were slightly more expensive than protected tracks, the DRM-free selections had enhanced sound quality. Major labels such as Warner Music, Sony BMG, and Universal Music, were reluctant to move into the DRM-free realm. However, Amazon.com's announcement that it would unveil a download service to rival iTunes in late 2007 or early 2008, with DRM-free tracks from some 12,000 different labels, put added pressure on the majors to move in this direction.

Mobile music continued to hold promise for the industry. Apple was positioned to play a hand in this niche as well, with the introduction of its iPhone, a combination mobile phone and iPod, in June of 2007. The music industry was hopeful that the device would increase the purchase of music sales. In its June 28, 2007 issue, *eWeek* reported that 28 million music-ready photos would exist in the U.S. market by the year's end, according to figures from JupiterResearch. However, only a small portion of consumers were expected to actually take advantage of the feature.

One drawback to the iPhone is that, when launched, it did not support wireless over-the-air (OTA) song downloads, which is supposed to be a lucrative emerging market. Instead, users had to synch their device with iTunes to load music files. The research firm International Data Corp. (IDC) forecasts that OTA services will generate more than $1 billion in revenues by 2010, when the number of users reaches the 50 million market. By that time, some 60 percent of all mobile phones sold will be music-ready.

Looking to the future, some industry observers foresee a radical transition, in which the music industry would become purely service oriented. As digitized files became the principal format for distributing music, they indicate that the production and distribution of CDs will cease and physical retail space for new music will disappear. In addition, these futurists posit that a more direct link will emerge between creative artists and music lovers.

CURRENT CONDITIONS

In its *Digital Music Report 2009,* IFPI advised that in 2008, the international digital music industry had grown to $3.7 billion, representing about 25 percent growth and a sixth year of expansion. Digital platforms now accounted for 20 percent of recorded music sales, which was at the forefront of the online and mobile revolution.

According to Nielsen SoundScan, the United States is still the world leader in digital music sales, holding roughly 50 percent of the global digital music market value.

Despite these numbers, the music industry was still burdened with massive amounts of unlicensed music distribution online. After reviewing and collating information from 16 countries over three years, IFPI concluded that over 40 billion files were illegally file-shared in 2008, constituting a piracy rate of around 95 percent.

Meanwhile, a new generation of music subscription services, social networking sites, and new licensing channels was emerging. In 2008, these were led by Nokia Comes With Music phone, MySpace Music (in September 2008), and several partnerships with Internet Service Providers (ISPs), such as TDC in Denmark (PLAY), Neuf Cegetel in France, TeliaSonera in Sweden (launching a bundled music service in six countries), and BSkyB in the United Kingdom (announcing plans to bundle broadband and music). Sony Ericsson's PlayNow plus also emerged in 2008. TDC reported a decrease in "churning" (the rate at which customers switch to competitors) after it bundled music with its mobile and broadband services. AmazonMP3 also joined the European market, and more stores became licensed to sell DRM-free music tracks.

Single track downloads, extremely popular in the United Kingdom and up 24 percent globally, continued to drive the online market, with 1.4 billion units in 2008, the first year they passed the one billion mark. The top-selling digital single for 2008 was Lil Wayne's "Lollipop," with sales of 9.1 million units. Digital albums sold 66 million units, up 32 percent, as noted in the IFPI report.

Music companies increasingly granted licenses to third parties, such as music game proprietors. Music games accounted for more than 15 percent of overall game sales in the first half of 2008, according to NPD Group, with Guitar Hero and its sequels selling more than 23 million copies in three years (worth $1 billion in North America alone).

INDUSTRY LEADERS

To survive revenue-cutting illegal activities, the music industry witnessed a number of significant changes, including the emergence of legitimate digital music sales and a number of mergers and ownership changes. Developments included the combination of Sony's recorded music business with that of rival BMG, creating Sony BMG Music Entertainment, as well as the sale of Warner Music Group by Time Warner. Universal Music Group (UMG) and Sony BMG were key leaders in the recording

side of the industry, while Apple Computer and RealNetworks were leading providers of digital music services and, in the case of Apple, portable music players.

Universal Music Group Universal Music Group (UMG), a subsidiary of Vivendi Universal, remains a key leader in the recording industry along with Sony BMG Music Entertainment. Analysts estimated that each company held about 25 percent of the global recording industry market. In 1998, when former Universal parent company Seagram acquired PolyGram and combined the two recording companies, the result was Universal Music Group. By the early years of the first decade of the 2000s, the company had established itself as a market leader in more than 70 percent of the markets in which it conducted business. The company's record labels include Decca, Deutsche Grammophon, Interscope Geffen A & M, Island Def Jam Music Group, MCA Records, MCA Nashville, Mercury Nashville, Polydor, Universal/Motown Records Group, and Verve Music Group.

Some analysts indicated that UMG, with 2005 sales of nearly $5.8 billion, held roughly 31 percent of the online music market. From this leadership position, the company launched a new label called UMe Digital in November 2004 that intended to distribute music exclusively through digital providers such as Apple iTunes and Napster. According to *Billboard*, UMe Digital was established to help market music from established artists who no longer generated significant sales through traditional retail channels. In 2007, UMG made headlines when it opted to not sign a long-term agreement with Apple's iTunes Music Store. Alternatively, the company opted to continue with a month to month arrangement, giving it more flexibility to negotiate with other services, such as Amazon's new digital download service that was expected to open in the late 2007 or early 2008.

Sony BMG Music Entertainment Sony BMG Music Entertainment was formed in 2004 when Sony Corp. combined its recorded music business with that of rival Bertelsmann (BMG). Although the split ownership arrangement was expected to save the companies $350 million, some insiders foresaw a difficult transition period as executives from each company adjusted to working together.

Sony Corp., one of the best-known names in consumer electronics, was established shortly after World War II. Its early products, tape recorders and transistor radios, sold well. In the 1960s, the company led the international electronics industry with its miniaturized products based on the transistor. After faltering sales growth in the mid- 1970s due to increasing competition, Sony once again came to dominate the market in 1978 with the introduction of the portable stereo system, the Walkman. Within another three years, the company broke new ground again when it developed and introduced the CD in conjunction with the Dutch electronics firm Philips.

Sony established itself as the largest record producer when it formed its subsidiary, Sony Music Entertainment International, and bought CBS Records in 1987. By the millennium, Sony Music Entertainment Inc. was the second largest global music company. In 2006, a European court nullified the approval of the Sony-BMG venture that had been granted by the European Union, adding a degree of uncertainty to the company's future, but in October 2008, the acquisition was complete. In mid-2009, Sony announced corporate losses for the third consecutive quarter, but, after fully taking over the 50 percent interest in Sony Music Entertainment from Bertelsmann, the world's second largest music label made Sony $1.11 billion), representing 96 percent more than it made from the Sony BMG joint venture in 2008.

Apple Computer Apple Computer is well known for being the most visible dissenter to the Windows/Intel standards that dominate the PC business. Based in Cupertino, California, Apple was a pioneer in PC technology when it was founded in 1977 and, after several short-lived models, introduced its immensely successful Macintosh line of computers in 1984. From the beginning, Apple's marketing efforts were aimed at the school, college, and home markets. It was never as successful in the business market.

Apple's introduction of the iPod digital music player in 2002, followed by the opening of its iTunes Music Store in April 2003, effectively changed the digital music game. By June of 2004, Apple had sold three million iPods and the device had become the market's most popular portable music player. In addition, its iTunes store was responsible for some 70 percent of all legal music downloads. Digital music became so important to Apple that the company established a separate iPod division. By early 2005, Apple sold eight different iPod models, ranging in price from $99 for the iPod Shuffle to $450 for its iPod Photo model. Two years later, Apple had become an even more dominant force within the industry, with more than 2 billion digital songs sold via its iTunes store.

Despite Apple's early success, many industry players predicted that its dominance would be eroded as other major players—such as Microsoft—stepped up competition with their own services and portable devices. One major threat to its dominance was a new digital music download service that Amazon.com planned to introduce in late 2007 or early 2008. In 2006, Apple's sales totaled almost $19.3 billion, up 38.6 percent from the previous year, and its net income surged 49 percent, to $1.98 billion.

In 2009, prices for iTunes were increased, but unit sales fell. In October 2009, Google Music Service announced that it was partnering with Imeem, Amazon MP3 and iTunes (also iLike and LaLa) to stream songs from LaLa.com, song samples from iLike.com, and song purchasing options from Apple's iTunes and from Amazon MP3. Revenue from the service will be split between the music services and the record labels.

RealNetworks Inc. With the release of its RealAudio and RealPlayer software in 1995, RealNetworks Inc. cemented its position as an Internet media pioneer. Some 10 years later, approximately 300 million people had downloaded the company's media player to stream multimedia content over the Internet. In addition to RealNetworks' media player, the company's RealRhapsody service provided consumers with access to more than 900,000 songs. Its RealPlayer Music Store offered some 700,000 songs for download, and its RadioPass service allowed customers to stream more than 3,200 Internet radio stations, including 90 subscription-based stations that were free from advertisements. RealNetworks' other offerings included a games service called RealArcade, as well as news and entertainment via RealOne.

RealNetworks also provided digital content delivery services to the corporate market. During the middle of the first decade of the 2000s, the company was marketing its Helix Servers and RealProducer product families, touting, "We continue to lead the way in delivering the highest quality Internet media experience delivering any media format, from any point of origin, across any network transport, running any OS to any person on any Internet-enabled device anywhere in the world." Revenue trends in the third quarter of 2009, including the effects of foreign currency exchange rate changes, compared with the year-earlier quarter were: a slight increase in Media Software and Services revenue to $24.6 million, offset by a 7 percent decrease in Music revenue to $38.8 million, an 8 percent decrease in Technology Products and Solutions revenue to $47.4 million, and a 14 percent decrease in Games revenue to $29.5 million.

RESEARCH AND TECHNOLOGY

Because the recording industry is highly reliant on electronics technology, research and technological development in the electronics industry has a large impact on digital audio technology. The developments with the greatest impact have been newer electronic formats with greater sound fidelity.

In the early 1990s, two new formats were introduced, the mini disc and the digital compact cassette (DCC). Both of these formats brought CD quality fidelity to home recording. Industry analysts in 1992 claimed the new formats would benefit long-term growth prospects, encouraging customers once again to replace their older recordings in the new format. The new formats worried many in the industry, however, and artists and companies alike feared the loss of copyright revenues from home recordings. Indeed, piracy has always been the major form of income loss. In 1992, however, the consumer electronics industry worked out compromise legislation with government and industry leaders that provided compensation for prospective copies done on the digital machines by imposing royalty fees on the equipment sales. By early 1993, both formats had been released. Due to high initial equipment costs, sales started slowly, but analysts agreed that once prices came down, both formats would do well. While many agreed that one format would eventually dominate the other, none could predict which format would win.

As it turned out, such speculation turned out to be moot. Consumers once again confounded the experts by failing to show any interest in the new formats. As with the earlier digital audiotape format (DAT), sales languished and consumer enthusiasm was lukewarm at best. The failure of the digital compact cassette (DCC) in particular came as a surprise, because this format at least offered backward compatibility with conventional analog cassettes, allowing users to play their old tapes on their new digital decks. Nevertheless, consumers seemed far more interested in convenience and affordability than in improved quality, staying away from the new formats in droves. The failure of these formats was puzzling to many in the industry, given the success of CDs. The success of the CD, however, probably had as much to do with its convenient small size and durability as with its improved sound quality. In fact, many audiophiles still insisted that analog sound (as represented by vinyl records) was superior to digital sound.

By the early years of the first decade of the twenty-first century, the home computer operator could easily become his or her own independent label, thanks to recordable and erasable CDs. Recordable CDs (called CD-Rs) and recording units were first widely marketed in 1996, although the recorders took some experience to operate because they depended heavily on the type of source material. Assuming the source had digital optical output, it could be recorded as input and dubbed much like an audiotape. Erasable CDs first appeared on the market in 1997 but were initially too expensive for the average individual. Erasable or rewritable CDs (called CD-RWs) were useful for data storage because old data could be erased and overwritten. In music applications, similarly, yesterday's "Hit Parade" could be erased and replaced with today's hottest tunes.

During the middle of the new century's first decade, MP3 continued to be the most popular file format for storing digital music tracks on CD, on one's computer, and especially on portable music players. However, other formats were making inroads. Advanced Audio Coding (AAC), which was part of the Motion Picture Expert Group's (MPEG) MPEG4 specification, was marked as MP3's likely successor by some industry observers. AAC was the format of choice for Apple's iTunes store. According to Apple, AAC offered better sound quality than MP3 with a smaller file size. MP3 PRO was another potential successor to MP3. However, acceptance of this format had been somewhat slow. Microsoft's Windows Media Audio (WMA) format was another popular file format for storing and playing digital music, namely with the Windows Media Player.

BIBLIOGRAPHY

"8% of Households Have 56% of the Music Files." *The Online Reporter,* 13 September 2003.

"62% of Net-Enabled Homes Store Digital Music." *The Online Reporter,* 18 December 2004.

Adegoke, Yinka. "Digital Single Sales Could Make Up a Third of Market." *New Media Age,* 13 May 2004.

———. "Teenage Girls Bigger Users of Online Music than Boys." *New Media Age,* 12 February 2004.

Allen, Jenny. "School Considers Legal File-Sharing." *Stanford Daily,* 3 March 2005. Available from http://daily.stanford.edu.

"Amazon Launch Against iTunes has a Sting in Tail." *The Birmingham Post* (England), 22 May 2007.

Amdur, Meredith. "Legal Tune Downloads Up Sharply This Year." *Daily Variety,* 18 May 2004.

"Americans Believe Personal Downloading Is OK." *The Online Reporter,* 14 February 2004.

"Apple Computer." New York: Prudential Equity Group LLC. 3 March 2005.

"Apple Gets Behind the Album Format with New Offer." *eWeek,* 29 March 2007.

Banerjee, Scott. "Music Retailers' Digital Music Alliance Fails." *The Hollywood Reporter,* 19 June 2004. Available from http://www.hollywoodreporter.com.

Burba, Chris. "iPod: How Long Will It Reign? S & P Counsels Caution on Apple's Stock as its Digital Music Player's Dominance May Be Challenged by New Devices from Sony and Others." *Business Week Online,* 3 December 2004. Available from www.businessweek.com.

Burrows, Peter. "Rock On, iPod—What Jobs Must Do to Maintain Apple's Dominance." *Business Week,* 7 June 2004.

"Digital Music Timeline." *Internet Magazine,* April 2004.

"Digital Purchases Rise as Album Sales Fall." *The New York Times,* 5 July 2007.

"Earnings: Sony Down On Falling Gadget Sales, High Yen 30," July 2009. Available from http://paidcontent.org/article/419-earnings-sony-down-on-falling-gadget-sales-high-yen/.

Evangelista, Benny. "Digital Music's Niche Industry Business Software Firms Marching to a New Number." *San Francisco Chronicle,* 1 November 2004.

Fiveash, Kelly. "iTunes swallowed a quarter of US music sales." *The Register* (UK), 18 August 2009.

Fritz, Ben. "Real Trying to Take a Bite Out of Apple iPod." *Daily Variety,* 17 August 2004.

Gallo, Phil. "Gabriel, ENO Lead Digital Charge." *Daily Variety,* 27 January 2004.

Garrity, Brian. "Music Biz Gets a Makeover in 2004: Label Shifts, Piracy Efforts and Digital Distribution Give the Business a New Look." *Billboard,* 25 December 2004.

Green, Heather. "Downloads: The Next Generation Music Merchants Are Trying New Ways to Make an Honest Buck Off the Internet." *Business Week,* 16 February 2004.

Hamilton, Anita. "Punching at iTunes: How Rivals Are Taking Aim at Apple's Dominance in Digital Music." *Time,* 16 August 2004.

"IDC Says Wireless Mobile Music Users Could Surpass Online Music Service Users by 2010." *Business Wire,* 15 June 2006.

"IFPI Publishes Digital Music Report 2009," 16 January 2009. Available from http://www.ifpi.org/content/ section_resources/dmr2009.html. and http://www.ifpi.org/ content/library/DMR2009-key-statistics.pdf.

"Imeem, Amazon MP3 and iTunes partner in Google Music next to iLike and LaLa 22," October 2009. Available from http:// www.muztec.com/itunes/imeem-amazon-mp3-and-itunes- partner-in-google-music-next-to-ilike-and-lala.html.

"Innovative Distribution Service Set to Accelerate Growth of Global Digital Music Industry." *M2 PressWire,* 24 November 2004.

Johnson, Joan. "iTunes Takes Over No. 3 Ranking for Online Sales." *Colorado Springs Business Journal,* 6 July 2007.

Keegan, Paul. "Is the Music Store Over? The Big CD Retail Chains May Have Only a Few More Years Before the Downloading Craze Buries Them. They Can Survive, But Only by Becoming Like No Store You've Seen Before." *Business 2.0,* March 2004.

Leeds, Jeff. "Sony and BMG Start Building Their Odd Music Club." *The New York Times,* 30 July 2004.

———. "With CD Sales Falling, Labels Seek New Deals with Apple." *The New York Times,* 26 March 2007.

Mann, Charles C. "The Year the Music Dies." *Wired,* February 2003.

McGuire, David. "Song-Swap Networks Unveil Code of Conduct." *Washington Post,* 29 September 2003 Available from www.washingtonpost.com.

"MUDDA. The Magnificent Union of Digitally Downloading Artists." MUDDA, 6 March 2005. Available from http:// www.mudda.org/index.lasso?page=home.

"The Music Business Could Become a Purely Service Industry." *The Futurist,* November-December 2004.

"Music Downloads Take Market Share from Record Retailers." *Research Alert,* 17 September 2004.

"Music File Formats." *Internet Magazine,* April 2004.

"Music Industry Calls on ISPs to Fight Piracy." *Internet Business News,* 27 January 2003.

"Music Industry Hopes for, Yet Fears, iPhone Effect." *eWeek,* 28 June 2007.

"Music Sales Up 1.6 %, Universal Leads." *The Online Reporter,* 8 January 2005.

"North American Music Sales to Reach $26.5b in 2011." *The Online Reporter,* 12 May 2007.

"Online Music Sales to Hit $6 Billion in 2010." *The Online Reporter,* 4 December 2004.

"RealNetworks Announces Third Quarter 2009 Results." Real Networks, 29 October 2009. Available from http:// www.realnetworks.com/pressroom/releases/2009/ q309_results_lkj946kjh75.aspx

"Research and Markets: The Global Digital Music Market Will Grow from $4.8 Bn to $13.74 Bn by 2012." *Business Wire,* 19 August 2009. Available from http://www.allbusiness.com/ media-telecommunications-sound-r . . . /12693479.htm

Siklos, Richard. "Music Industry Fails to Turn Tables on iTunes." *Australasian Business Intelligence,* 9 July 2007.

Suhr, Jim. "RIAA Appeals Ruling in Legal Flap Over Copyright Subpoenas." Associated Press, 24 February 2005.

"Unexpected Harmony—Online Music." *The Economist,* 25 January 2003.

Walsh, Chris M. "Source: UMG Snubs iTunes Deal." *Billboard,* 14 July 2007.

DIGITAL IMAGING

INDUSTRY SNAPSHOT

Driven by voracious demand for digital cameras, digital imaging is swiftly becoming a mass market phenomenon after years of languishing in the exclusive domain of imaging professionals and technophiles. Falling prices have fueled the market, as have technical strides and the wider use of the Internet for disseminating personal photographs and the like. The easy transferability of digital images from one medium to another, either directly or via memory card (e.g., from digital camera or mobile cell phone download to PC or printer, provided the fabric to weave an integrated, connected, and massive digital imaging industry that penetrated all countries, age groups, and specialties.

However, perhaps the biggest story in recent years was the mid-2009 conversion of all analog television signals and stations in the United States to digital image high definition television (HDTV) (see Current Conditions below). Additionally, the rapid growth of mobile cell phones with camera capability, new 3D and even 4D medical imaging for diagnostic and treatment purposes, and digital media social-sharing over Internet sites such as FaceBook all contributed to an industry still growing exponentially near the end of the century's first decade.

This reality had its fallout as well. In addition to the transition from analog to digital television, digital electronics manufacturers continuously churned out new features on their products, making some computers, cameras, and phones technically and stylishly "dated" within months or weeks of purchase. Consumers rapidly discarded old cameras, cell phones, and now useless analog televisions, creating massive environmental concerns (E-waste) for local landfills and offshore dump sites. The Consumer Electronics Association (CEA) estimated that over 26.8 million digital TVs were sold in the United States in 2008, reaching 34.5 million in 2009. Roughly 138 million were sold worldwide. Added to this was an estimated 1.18 billion cell phones sold worldwide in 2008 alone. The EPA estimated that less than 15 percent of old discarded phones and televisions (and computers) would be recycled in 2009 (i.e., stripped of valuable components and materials and/or refurbished and resold).

On the upside (environmentally), digital imaging contributed to a slow but steady decline in the printing industry, as cost-conscious consumers and businesses transferred documents and images in digital format instead of by printed matter. Amidst the economic downturn, companies adopted practices of seeking the most cost effective means to producing documents. Once these electronic practices are in place, they will not likely return to print. The printing industry, two-thirds into 2009, posted a -8.8% decline.

In addition to digital still cameras, digital imaging technologies include digital camcorders for capturing digital video; so-called personal computer or Web cameras, used mostly for live low-resolution video teleconferencing; and a range of still-image scanners for converting printed material into digital format. Most of these gadgets are designed for transferring ready-to-use yet editable graphics to a computer where they can be customized with graphics software and then shared with others via e-mail or over the World Wide Web.

Businesses have discovered new applications for digital imaging as well. While such activities as creating image libraries, scanning forms, and publishing product catalogs have long relied on digital imaging, the technology has spread to new applications such as insurance claims verification and real estate marketing.

Digital imaging was being utilized by medical specialists, optometrists, dentists, and hospitals to capture and store patients' anatomical images. One key example of how digital imaging was revolutionizing healthcare was the Picture Archiving and Communications System, commonly referred to as PACS, which allowed healthcare providers such as hospitals and doctors' offices to electronically capture, store, and send images like X-rays. Instead of having to mail film, PACS made transmitting and sharing images virtually instantaneous, thereby improving the quality and efficiency of care.

ORGANIZATION AND STRUCTURE

Traditional film photography relies on tiny crystals of light-sensitive silver compounds suspended in a coating that surrounds a transparent film. As the shutter of the camera opens, light from the brightest parts of an image is thrown onto the film and the crystals start breaking down. In developing the film, a chemical called a "developer" changes the crystals exposed into black silver, while another chemical called a "fixer" dissolves the unexposed crystals. The resulting negative shows black silver where the scene was brightest and nothing where the film was left dark (no image was recorded).

The wet chemistry required to develop photographs, however, has many disadvantages. It is messy and environmentally hazardous since most of the chemicals are toxic. In addition, the wet chemistry process is time-delayed; the entire developing process makes instant viewing and editing impossible. Finally, there is always a risk of spoilage: film that is overdeveloped or underdeveloped results in poor images.

Still images, such as photos, slides, transparencies, and paintings have traditionally been converted to digital format using a scanner. The scanner "copies" the image and translates it to a binary format. Scanner accuracy is defined in two ways: by resolution and color information. Resolution is referred to as dpi (dots per inch) or ppi (pixels per inch). Color information is defined by the number of bits of information per color. For example, 24 bits per pixel (8 bits each of red, green, and blue) creates 1.6 million colors. The size of a pixel varies from one device to another and is essentially a single square unit of the same size. Digital cameras rely on the same measurements of resolution and color information.

Digital cameras don't require wet chemistry, lab processing, or scanning. Instead, digital imaging cameras create a binary image directly by recording the image on a charge-coupled device (CCD). The CCD sensor is an opto-electronic element that records light as a charge in a condenser. Developed originally by Bell Laboratories, the CCD contains an array of cells representing a picture element. Each cell converts light into an electrical charge. Pixels arranged in a straight row are called linear arrays. In the late 1990s, CCDs accounted for about half the cost of a digital camera. Together, CCDs and storage accounted for more than three-quarters of the cost. According to Nicholas van den Berghe, vice president and general manager of the consumer division at Live Picture Inc., the combined cost of the CCD and storage needed to be around 15 percent of the system cost before digital cameras would take off with the consumer market. Digital images created by digital cameras measure resolution in the same manner as a scanner.

BACKGROUND AND DEVELOPMENT

In the early years of the first decade of the 2000s, technological advances that increased resolution from a standard 300,000 pixels to 2 million pixels (two megapixels) transformed the digital camera from a personal computer accessory for those who liked to e-mail pictures to friends and relatives to a full-fledged rival to the standard 35-millimeter camera. Declining prices, from about $500 for a 300,000-pixel camera in the mid-1990s to $200 for a two-megapixel device by the mid-2000s also fueled digital camera sales.

When digital camera sales began to outpace film-based camera sales at the turn of the twenty-first century, new players had begun to enter the industry. Traditional camera makers like Eastman Kodak were suddenly forced to compete with electronics giants like Sony Corp. In fact, in 2002 Sony held a 23 percent share of the global digital camera market compared to the 14 percent held by Kodak. However, Kodak's introduction that year of the EasyShare system for transferring images from digital cameras to PCs boosted its market share in the fourth quarter of the year to 17 percent, placing it ahead of both Olympus and Hewlett-Packard and moving it close to Sony.

By 2005 the digital revolution was well under way. Personal computers continued to come down in price, making technology more accessible to the masses than ever before. At the same time, the processing power and storage capacity of personal computers increased dramatically, making it feasible for the average person to store large collections of digital photographs, and even edit digital video footage to create home movies on DVD.

According to the PMA, online services, which allow customers to send their photos to a local lab via e-mail and either have them delivered by mail or made ready for pickup, were experiencing the most rapid growth during the middle of the first decade of the 2000s, followed by retail services. However, home printing still represented the largest portion of the market.

Despite all of these options, the vast majority of digital photographs taken mid-decade were stored in digital form and never printed. According to PMA figures, in 2004 some 64.8 percent of digital photos were kept in digital form only. In 2005, this percentage was expected to fall to 61.5 percent as more consumers took advantage of print services.

The use of online services to order prints of digital photos continued to explode in popularity, according to the Photo Marketing Association (PMA). In 2006, the number of all prints made from digital still cameras increased 48 percent. The greatest increase in utilization was seen in online photo services, which increased 129 percent. Prints made at a local retailer increased 51 percent, followed by digital self-service kiosks (41 percent), and prints made at home (25 percent). In terms of a percentage of all digital printing, prints made on a home computer or related device led the way, with 40.3 percent share, followed by orders sent to mini-labs (23.7 percent), instant prints via kiosks (13.8 percent), prints ordered online and received via mail (11.7 percent), and those ordered online and picked up at a retail location (8.8 percent).

In 2007 more consumers were expected to buy cameras in the 8 to 12 megapixel range, according to *PC Magazine Online*. In order to accommodate the larger file sizes that resulted from higher resolution images, the capacity of storage media (such as memory sticks and memory cards) continued to increase as well, ranging from 4GB to 8GB in early 2007. Cameras also were offering consumers more in the way of standard capabilities right out of the box. One example was Nikon's L6 COOLPIX camera, which was capable of taking 1,000 photos on one set of Energizer e2 Lithium AA batteries.

Perhaps the most exciting aspect of digital imaging technology was the bevy of features that were available to users—especially in the digital camera category. Examples included face detection software that allowed cameras to recognize and focus on up to 10 human faces at once, even adjusting the depth of field to capture faces located at varying distances. In addition, some cameras came with imaging software that allowed photographers to improve lighting conditions in a photo after exposure. Another cutting-edge feature was wireless connectivity (WiFi), which enabled the transfer of images from cameras to computers without using cables. Finally, other advancements included anti-shake technology, as well as

Global Positioning System (GPS) accessories that allowed photographers to insert latitudinal and longitudinal data into image files, capturing the exact location in which a given photo was taken.

CURRENT CONDITIONS

According to the Consumer Electronics Association, U.S. consumers purchased $172 billion in consumer electronics in 2008, despite the economic downturn. Sales were expected to remain similar in 2009, at $171 billion. By far, the lion's share of the market went to digital televisions, digital cameras, and digital camera mobile (cell) phones.

The Camera and Imaging Products Association (CIPA), which represents the various Japanese camera manufacturers, reported that units shipped in 2008 rose 19.3 percent, to 119,757,000. Digital SLRs constituted the majority of units with a year-on-year increase of 29.7 percent. However, overall camera shipments were expected to drop for 2009 by 0.7 percent, then increase in 2010 and 2011. Shipments of interchangeable lens digital SLR cameras were increasing while shipments of digital cameras with built-in lens were declining. The forecast for shipments in both 2010 and 2011 anticipated economic recovery as well as growth potential in Asia and other areas in showing slow but continued growth with year-on-year increases of 2.9 percent.

In the United States alone, Digitimes estimated digital camera sales for 2008 at 42 million. It also noted that IDC reporteding that digital photo frame shipments grew 6.3 percent to 9.1 million units in 2008, with the United States being the dominant region of nearly 5.9 million units, according to IDC. Declines of 10 to 11 percent were predicted for the 2009 (8.2 million units) and 2010 years, with single digit growth resuming in 2011. Overall, this market was expected to show only a 0.4 percent CAGR (compound annual growth rate) for 2008-2013.

A conflicting report came from InfoTrends, a leading worldwide market research and strategic consulting firm for the digital imaging and document solutions industry. which found digital photo frames to be " A Bright Spot in the Consumer Imaging Market." it projected this market segment to achieve a compound annual growth rate of nearly 22 Ten-to-eleven percent from 2008-2013, surpassing 21 million units. It also reported that just over 15 percent of all digital photo frames shipped were wireless in 2008, but this percentage is expected to jump to almost 35 percent by 2012.

In May 2009, InfoTrends released its study on photo merchandise trends, noting that the photo merchandise market currently offered the highest growth potential of any segment within the consumer digital imaging market. It projected that the U.S. photo merchandise market will achieve a CAGR of 22 percent from 2007 through

2013. While 21 percent of the total surveyed population said they purchased photo merchandise within the past year, 56 percent of those purchasers were young adults, followed by the second highest category of mothers with minor children. In April 2009, InfoTrends reported that young adults between the ages of 18 and 24 captured more digital photos (female users more than males) than any other age group reported, and having more than 900 digital photos stored in memory. It also reported (in August 2009) that U.S. consumers place a high value on having the ability to take photos with their mobile phones, with young adults being the most active camera phone users. In September 2009, it reported that nearly 78 percent of consumers aged 18 to 24 and just over 68 percent of consumers aged 13 to 17 were regular users of social networking, and nearly 60 percent of female teenagers and young adults stated that they frequently posted pictures for their friends to see.

With respect to digital television, Title III of the Deficit Reduction Act of 2005 (P.L. 109-171) mandated that all free local television stations turn off their analog channels and continue broadcasting only in digital format. In order for non-cable or satellite television viewers to continue watching television, three choices were available. They could purchase new televisions formatted for digital signals (DTVs); attach their old analog televisions to a converter box (similar to the old cable boxes that sat on the tops of televisions) to receive the new signal; or purchase cable or satellite television broadcasting. Despite three years of preparation and publicizing, it became increasingly evident that insufficient numbers of U.S. consumers would be prepared for the transition by the February 19 deadline date, which was then revised to become effective on June 12, 2009. A massive public information campaign was launched, and on June 12, analog television became history, with little sequelae.

INDUSTRY LEADERS

Most digital imaging hardware is fairly sophisticated technology, and as such, the industry has been dominated by major international corporations specializing in consumer electronics, semiconductors, and other forms of photographic and imaging equipment. Particularly in the digital camera segments, a handful of producers dominate the market. These include Sony Corp., Canon Inc., FUJIFILM Holdings Corp., Eastman Kodak Co. (after major restructure), Olympus Corp., and Nikon Corp.

In the Webcam segment, Logitech International SA is one of the market's leading firms. Best known for its mice and other pointer devices, the company bought its way into the Webcam business in 1998 when it purchased the Webcam operations of Connectix Corp.

AMERICA AND THE WORLD

The results of InfoTrends' 2009 European Digital Photography Survey revealed some intriguing variations for each of the countries surveyed, which included France, Germany, the United Kingdom, Poland, and Russia. Despite the considerably lower household incomes of those in Eastern Europe, digital SLRs were more prevalent in Poland and Russia than in Western Europe. Noting that Russian consumers are notable photo enthusiasts, InfoTrends found that Russian respondents reported capturing the most photos, printing the most photos, spending the most on their cameras and using the video-clip feature on their cameras most frequently.

According to a report from Global Industry Analysts Inc. of San Jose, California, the worldwide 3-D medical imaging market was projected to be worth $3.9 billion by 2012. Europe represents the largest market, with sales estimated at $935 million in 2008. The United States represented the single largest market, holding an estimated 34.6 percent share in 2008. Since 2000, the Asia-Pacific region, the fastest-growing segment, experienced a CAGR of 20 percent, expected to continue through 2010.

RESEARCH AND TECHNOLOGY

APS Attempts to Bridge the Digital Divide The Advanced Photo System (APS) is a digital/print hybrid that was initially backed by Kodak, Fuji, Canon, Minolta, and Nikon. APS cameras, film, and processing equipment have the ability to "communicate" with each other and to compensate for conditions such as light and film speed. APS technology allows for switching between different size photographs on the same roll of film and imprints digital information about the shot, lighting conditions, date, and other data that facilitate the developing process.

The growing success of digital cameras did not bode well for Advanced Photo Systems, and they had all but disappeared from the market by 2007. In the early years of the decade, leading camera manufacturers, including Konica Corp., Olympus Optical Co., and Minolta Co., all shuttered their APS camera operations. Both Nikon Corp. and Asahi Optical Co. reduced their APS activities in favor of digital technology. This trend continued as Kodak announced it would cease worldwide distribution of APS cameras by the end of 2004. While this was no surprise to some industry observers, the company did garner attention with its decision to stop marketing regular 35mm cameras in the United States, Canada, and Western Europe. However, despite what appeared to be a waning APS market, both Fuji and Canon, two of the world's leading APS camera makers, remained committed to the technology. Fuji planned to launch a new APS model in 2004 and Canon planned to continue marketing its four APS models.

Digita Software Enables On-Camera Applications One industry innovation continuing to be developed as of the early years of the twenty-first century's first decade is a software application environment for digital cameras and related devices known as Digita. The software, developed by Flashpoint Technologies Inc., allows users to run mini-applications on specially equipped cameras. For instance, a photographer taking standardized pictures for a company catalog could instruct the camera to automatically modify the images to meet the project's needs—say to automatically place the company logo in the right bottom corner of the image and adjust the color balance to remove the pallor of fluorescent lighting. More sophisticated uses might create a Web page directly on the camera using a template and a set of pictures. The applications rely on a scripting language that users can learn and program themselves, or predefined scripts can be purchased from developers.

International Imaging Industry Association Works on Standards The Digital Imaging Group (DIG) was launched in October 1997 with nine members: Adobe Systems Inc., Canon, Inc., Eastman Kodak Co., Fuji Photo Film Co., Ltd., Hewlett-Packard Co.. IBM Corp., Intel Corp., Live Picture Inc., and Microsoft Corp. Two months after its formation, DIG more than tripled its membership. In 2001, DIG merged with the Photographic and Imaging Manufacturers Association (PIMA) to form the International Imaging Industry Association (I3A).

The group is an open industry consortium whose mission is to communicate the benefits of digital imaging and digital technology and monitor market response and developer recommendations. Membership gives companies the opportunity to help define the future of digital imaging technology, promote solutions, and have the opportunity to collaborate. The first annual DIG Congress was held in Burlingame, California, in June 1998. That year, DIG began the process of defining the next versions of the FlashPix and Internet Imaging Protocol (IIP) specifications. FlashPix is an incredibly powerful tool for users of digital images. It uses flexible compression and color management options to offer a universal storage and exchange platform for digital imaging. By transferring to random access memory or RAM, FlashPix reduces the amount of time it takes to manipulate and send a file. In 2003, I3A released the CPXe standard, which is essentially a series of interoperability specifications, and created the Picture Services Network (PSN).

BIBLIOGRAPHY

"Brand Mot." *Brand Strategy,* November 2004.

DeBat, Alfred. "Three Smart Things New Digital Cameras Can Do." PMA, 2007. Available from http://www.pmai.org/index.cfm/ci_id/33127/la_id/1.htm.

"CIPA Makes Camera Sales Predictions For 2009 and Beyond." 27 January 2009. Available from http://www.dcresource.com/news/newsitem.php?id=3862.

"Digital Photo Frames: A Bright Spot in the Consumer Imaging Market." InfoTrends Report, 14 November 2008. Available from http://www.digitalimagingconference.com/public/Content/Press/2008/11.14.2008.html.

"Digital Camera Takes 1,000 Pictures on One Set of Batteries." *Product News Network,* 2 October 2006.

"Digital Camera Tips." *Electronics News,* 16 December 2004.

"Digital Camera Usage." *Studio Photography & Design,* September 2006.

"Digital Camera's Evolution Slowing Down." *PC Magazine Online,* 11 March 2007.

"Facts and Figures on E Waste and Recycling." 21 September 2009. Available from http://www.computertakeback. com/Tools/Facts_and_Figures.pdf.

"InfoTrends Survey Shows Variations across European Digital Photography Market." 16 October 2009. Available from http://www.digitalimagingconference.com/public/Content/Press/2009/10.16.2009.2.html.

"Manufacturers, Retailers React to Kodak's Decision to End Distribution of Cameras." *Photo Marketing Newsline,* 28 January 2004.

Les, Caren B. "Medical Imaging Market: Moving Up." *BioPhotonics,* February 2009.

Matsumoto, Yukihiko, Dimitrios Delis, and Emily Fassanella. *Photo Industry 2005: Review and Forecast,* Jackson, Michigan: Photo Marketing Association International, February 2005.

"PMA Monthly Printing and Camera Trends Report. Highlights and Overview through December 2006." PMA, 26 February 2007. Available from http://www.pmai.org.

"US Digital Camera Market to Reach 40 Mln in 2008, 2.5 Mln of Them to be SLRs." 26 August 2008. Available from http://www.digitimes.com/tag/revenues/001813.html.

U.S. Census Bureau. *Manufacturers's Shipments, Inventories, and Orders (M3) Report.* August 2009. Available from http://www.census.gov/indicator/www/m3/hist/naicsvsp.bd

"Younger Consumers Embrace Photo Sharing Through Social Networks." InfoTrends Research report, 22 September 2009. Available from http://www.digitalimagingconference.com/public/Content/Press/2009/09.22.2009.html

Yu, Yvonne. "Digital photo frame market to decline in 2009 and 2010, says IDC." Press Release, DIGITIMES, 29 October 2009.

DIGITAL MAPPING

SIC CODE(S)

7379

4899

3829

3812

5043

INDUSTRY SNAPSHOT

A rapidly growing and widely diversified field, the digital mapping industry emerged in the late 1990s and almost immediately found ready application in industries as diverse as education, automobile navigation, agriculture, banking, railroading, and telecommunications. Though the idea of integrating and displaying complex data on digital maps was already several decades old at the time, the rapid increases in computer processing power brought business geo-graphics (the use of digital mapping databases for business applications) into the mainstream business world.

By 2000, the number and variety of applications for digital mapping had grown by leaps and bounds compared to just a decade earlier, with an estimated 85 percent of all businesses having some geographic component able to be mapped and utilized. The maps created by using these components are typically linked to large databases, often called geographic information systems (GISs), making it possible to access, arrange, and view an ever wider range of information.

Some industry players began using the term geospatial to better describe what formerly was included under the geographic information system (GIS) banner. In October 2004 the consulting firm Daratech Inc. explained: "This broader definition recognizes that engineering data from CAD systems, billing information from ERP systems, facilities management and many other types of enterprise content must be brought together with the traditional spatial data from a GIS in order to efficiently make decisions."

The increasing use of mobile devices (mobile phones and portable navigation devices, or PNDs) further expanded the field and created new sub markets for location-based services (LBS) and products, and by 2009, this became the fastest-growing segment of the industry. With the rapid growth of LBS and UGC markets came a new market opportunity, geotagging. This involves identifying people, objects, or data by their geographic locations through the process of adding geographic metadata to various media such as videos, Web sites, photographs, RDF or RSS feeds.

ORGANIZATION AND STRUCTURE

Digital maps differ greatly from traditional paper maps. First, while printed maps are painstakingly hand drawn by patient mapmakers, digitized maps are made up of millions of pixels, the tiny colored dots that make up graphic images on computer screens. Secondly, printed maps are static, based on a single interpretation of a single set of data, while digital maps are dynamic, created out of individually selected layers of data and images. The digital map used by a farmer, for example, might show an area's various soil types in one view and then, with a click of a mouse, layer the various types of crops being grown in the same area. The digital map for a

221

railroad might at one moment display a map showing the signals, switches, and alternate routes along the track a train is traveling on and then call up a window showing the train's exact longitudinal and latitudinal location based on a satellite signal beamed to the train's cab. The user might even call up a recorded full-motion video image of the terrain and region of track the train is passing over at the time. In short, the digital map is often interactive, an image that can be changed at the user's discretion.

Mapmaking Models Digital maps store data in layers of visual information that have been constructed using one of two models, the vector or the raster. The vector model uses standard geometry to plot a map's features—such as buildings or roads—using the specific longitudinal and latitudinal position in space that each object occupies. This method is ideal for plotting discrete objects or features on a map, but it is also expensive. The raster model is less expensive and more useful for mapping continuously and/or subtly changing features such as soil type. With this model, a map is created by dividing the terrain into equal-sized cells and then combining scanned or photographed images of these terrain cells together into a grid. Simply put, the vector method builds maps out of individual points while the raster method builds them out of rectangular blocks of terrain images. With the advent of high-resolution satellites that photograph the earth in precisely this rectangular, cell-by-cell manner, the raster method has become the dominant method for digital mapmaking.

Building a GIS Building a geographic information system (GIS) involves five distinct phases. First, the printed (or analog) map is digitized. This is by far the most time-consuming phase of the digital mapmaking process. It can be done using scanners that create photographic images of the source map and then turning them into the binary ones and zeros a computer can understand or by using a specialized digitizing table. In the latter process, the paper map is taped to the table, then the operator selects an object on the map to digitize, and then he/she traces it with a pen-like instrument that reads or converts the object into digital information. Since a typical map has anywhere from 5,000 to 10,000 objects, digitizing is a laborious and expensive process that has traditionally been outsourced to countries in developing parts of the world.

The second phase in making a GIS is manipulating the newly digitized geographic data so it conforms to the needs of the mapmaker. For example, an analog map converted into digital data may need to have its scale (or degree of accuracy) adjusted or the mapmaker may decide that some of the information included on the original analog map is irrelevant and can therefore be deleted.

In the third stage, a database management system (DBMS) is used to store, organize, and manage the digitized map data. The most popular DBMS is the "relational" method, which allows data to be stored in rows and columns of tables so that different types of data can be compared and combined.

The fourth stage in the construction of a functioning GIS is the query and analysis phase: the posing of questions to the geographic database so that certain views or maps of information are displayed or hypothetical situations explored. It is at this stage that the digital map truly becomes a GIS, offering customized maps that answer or visualize the user's questions. Two common types of analysis are proximity analysis and overlay analysis. In a proximity analysis, the user might ask the GIS how many switches or signals separate a train from the next station. In an overlay analysis, however, the user might ask the GIS to integrate two different types of data, or data layers, such as all the road crossings as well as all the switches that separate a train from the next station. Once the analysis is complete, the final stage of the GIS process occurs: the requested information is displayed graphically.

Related Technologies A geographic information system (GIS) involves several related but distinctly different technologies, all of which may be used to create the GIS. Desktop mapping programs are GISs that have been tailored for the desktop personal computer (PC) and therefore have more limited data management and customization features than GISs. Computer-aided design systems are often used by architects, engineers, and builders to create designs and plans, but lack the data management and analytical features of GISs. Remote sensing and the Global Positioning System (GPS) are aspects of the data-gathering arm of a GIS, using cameras or radar, for example, to generate digital images of the earth that can be used in a GIS. The GPS is a network of orbiting satellites and earthbound receivers developed by the U.S. Department of Defense to provide users with pinpoint time and position information from anywhere on the globe. While the GPS can provide a GIS with the specific location data to create highly accurate digital map databases in real time, it cannot provide the context ("What's over the next hill?") that a good GIS offers.

Another source of data for a GIS is photogrammetry, which the Merriam Webster's Collegiate Dictionary, 11th Edition, defines as "The science of making reliable measurements by the use of photographs and especially aerial photographs (as in survey)." It is commonly thought of as the use of aerial photographs to provide geographic images. GPS differs from photogrammetry in at least two important respects: GPS requires that the user actually be at the location coordinates provided by GPS satellites; also, photogrammetry does not provide location coordinates, but it can provide remote imaging of inaccessible places.

Industry Segments The digital mapping and GIS industry consists of four segments: services, hardware, software, and data. The services segment, which generates about one-fifth of the industry's revenues worldwide, is comprised of firms that offer GIS-related consulting, GIS integration, analog-to-digital conversion, photogrammetry and ortho-photography, and satellite imagery. Consulting firms provide project direction to companies trying to implement GISs, including project feasibility studies, GIS database design, and GIS project management. System integrators (Intergraph Corp., for example) design and build entire GISs by integrating the often proprietary or stand-alone GIS products of software and hardware, and database vendors. In other words, they make a customer's GIS components work together. The conversion services firms convert or digitize data so it can be used within the digital GIS environment. These firms may fix errors or omissions in the primary or analog data or assure that the conversion is clean and accurate. Because it involves the snail-paced digitization process, this segment of the GIS services industry is highly labor intensive and therefore lucrative. Unfortunately for these firms, however, conversion generates little repeat business as data needs conversion only once. Moreover, as the world moves inexorably toward digital-only mapping, prospects for future growth in the data conversion market are slim.

The photogrammetry and orthophotography segments of the GIS services segment can transform aerial photos into clean, sequenced map data. Photogrammetry might be considered the science of surveying terrain from the air and orthophotography as the process of digitizing aerial photos. Gislounge.com, a GIS Web site, defines orthophotograpy as "digital imagery in which distortion from the camera angle and topography have been removed, thus equalizing the distances represented on the image." In particular, orthophotography involves smoothing out the distortions that inevitably arise from taking aerial photos of terrain so that the resulting image has a resolution of one meter—that is, making it sharp enough to identify objects 1 meter in size or larger. Both photogrammetry and orthophotography firms must have expensive equipment and a highly skilled workforce, and they generally offer services only in the geographic regions covered by their photo archives. Nevertheless, the photogrammetry segment is among the most profitable sectors of the GIS services industry.

The last segment of the GIS services industry is satellite imagery. A relatively new field, satellite imagery arose only after the conclusion of the Cold War made it possible for high-resolution spy satellites to seek commercial markets. By offering extremely fine-grained images for customers building digital maps, satellite imagery firms pose a threat to the aerial photo (photogrammetry) segment of the industry. However, the satellite segment is expected to remain rather small. According to Teal Group, only 43 earth-imaging satellites, or 3 percent of all satellites, were expected to be built and launched between 2001 and 2010. (See also **Satellites.**)

The hardware—computers, workstations, and peripherals such as printers and scanners—used in the digital mapping and GIS industries is manufactured mainly by large computer equipment firms, such as IBM, Hewlett-Packard, and Unisys. A few industry-specific firms, however, such as Intergraph and Trimble Navigation, also manufacture workstations and GIS-related hardware.

The software segments of the digital mapping and GIS industries produce design or mapmaking software used to create digital maps or to manipulate and display them. The customers of this industry segment have traditionally been the industries—energy, utilities, railroads, and governments—whose mapping needs were such a vital part of their businesses that they had no choice but to buy the expensive, highly specialized software products that were once the sole niche of industry firms. With the rapid emergence of powerful desktop computers, however, the digital mapping software segment began to ply its wares to a wider marketplace: mainstream business and consumers. A host of software firms in the 1990s offered relatively inexpensive digital mapping products that allowed users to insert maps into their publications, multimedia presentations, animation, and Web sites. Among these firms were companies such as Autodesk, Inc., Eagle Point Software, MapInfo Corp., and Magellan Geographix. By 2000, some of these firms offered digital maps via the traditional CD-ROM format and through electronic commerce sites on the World Wide Web. Similarly, high quality maps were made available in such popular desktop graphics formats as Adobe Illustrator, Photoshop, Macromedia Freehand, and CorelDraw.

Applications As the industry developed, it became apparent that the range of applications for digital mapping and GIS was nearly limitless. In agriculture, for example, GIS technology is used to find the best soils for growing crops; to plan and optimize shipping routes for transporting food and agricultural chemicals and fertilizers; to monitor and analyze crop production trends; to rate and market crop insurance policies; and to plan the application of chemicals or pesticides. By 2000, more than 80 countries worldwide used GIS technology for agronomy and food planning purposes.

In banking and finance applications, GIS is used to ensure compliance with federal lending regulations; to maintain geographic distribution information on automated teller machines or competitors' locations; to create demographic profiles of existing and prospective customers; and to perform site analysis studies to locate branches at the best possible locations.

In police work and public safety, GIS is used to optimize the computer-aided dispatch of emergency vehicles through route planning and in-cab navigation systems; to track police and fire vehicles in real time as they respond to emergencies; and to analyze crime incidence records with map displays to learn and predict crime patterns. Firefighters also use digital maps to give them valuable information about hydrant and fire station location, hazardous materials hot spots, and building occupancy. Disaster planning agencies use GIS to create on-the-spot emergency action plans to help evacuate a region, track damaged structures for repair, or generate computer models to predict the behavior of natural disasters such as floods and tornadoes.

Electric utilities use digital mapping and GIS to manage their "Call before you dig" telephone systems for warning construction crews of buried power lines. They also use them to determine the appropriate rates for the sale of excess energy to other utilities, to automate equipment inventory procedures, and to map out the joint use of utility poles by telecommunications firms. Similarly, oil and gas pipeline firms employ digital mapping technology to perform market analysis, manage risk, and analyze complex pipeline routes so as to take into account environmentally sensitive areas and land use conflicts, and to make appropriate decisions regarding terrain and geology.

The U.S. government, historically quick to adopt digital mapping technology, ran approximately 250,000 GIS applications annually between 1994 and 2000, from disaster planning and natural resource preservation to traffic planning projects and the planning and tracking of census statistics. Other industries that have found uses for digital mapping include petroleum (analyzing the placement of filling stations), customer service businesses (automating call center responses), and railroads (tracking train deployment and safety).

BACKGROUND AND DEVELOPMENT

Although the science of mapmaking can be traced back to such pioneers as Ptolemy, Eratosthenes, Mercator, and Cassini, its modern development really began with the invention of the airplane at the start of the 20th century.

To be sure, the invention of printing enabled maps to be widely disseminated for the first time, and the application of mathematical and statistical methods introduced greater accuracy, but the airplane enabled mapmakers to map previously unknown regions. Industrialist Sherman Fairchild (1896–1971) pioneered commercial aerial surveying after World War I. After the end of World War II, military surveillance techniques were adapted for use in civilian mapmaking and the science of photogrammetry began to come into its own.

In the 1960s, the first rough computer maps came into use, and industries such as energy, utilities, and the railroads—as well as the federal government—employed computerized maps for such purposes as plotting pipeline routes, tracking population movements, and mapping the mineral content of geologic formations. Because computing power was still an expensive commodity, however, it took several millions of dollars just to create a customized map showing, for example, piping networks or infrastructure. Government offices and utilities could not afford to do without such mapping data, however, and still comprised three-quarters of the digital mapping industry's customer base well into the mid-1990s.

The U.S. spy satellite program of the 1950s and 1960s bore fruit for the digital mapping industry in 1972 when the National Aeronautics and Space Administration initiated the Landsat program to survey the earth with multi-spectral scanner technology, a development that marked the beginning of the systematic use of space-based remote sensing as a source of raw data for cartographers. With Landsat, mapmakers could create rapidly updatable, photo-based "thematic" maps for such specialized needs as mapping water pollution, mineral deposits, or crop health. For many years, Landsat and its French counterpart were the only source of space-based imagery available to private mapping firms.

The birth of the desktop computer and advances in microchip manufacture and design in the late 1970s and early 1980s transformed the landscape of digital mapping. With computer processing power doubling every eight months (a phenomenon that came to be known as Moore's Law), previously impractical digital mapping applications were suddenly possible. By 1984, GIS-based vehicle navigation systems were already being used in marine and aeronautic applications, and companies such as Motorola and Rockwell Automotive were hard at work on navigation systems for automobiles. In 1985, digital mapmaker Etak introduced its Navigator map display and vehicle positioning system, and rival Navigation Technologies demonstrated a similar routing system, DriverGuide, the same year. By the mid-1990s, such systems were already a reality at rental car companies such as Hertz and Avis.

By 1986, Thomas Bros. Maps, the largest mapmaker in California, sensed the change afoot in the mapping industry and began digitizing its entire map collection. With the launching of the new trade magazine *GIS World* in the late 1980s, it was clear that a new industry, digital mapping, had come into its own. For the first time in history, maps were suddenly easy and inexpensive to make. By the late 1990s, a typical government mapping project, such as mapping a state's population distribution, could be completed in a matter of weeks, or even days. Moreover, digital cartographers began systematizing the analytical foundations of the new GIS science by striving for standards for calculating distances and technical parameters, such as terrain surface slope and aspect.

In 1990, the American Automobile Association, General Motors, the Federal Highway Administration, and the Florida Department of Transportation launched a project known as TravTek to develop one of the most important early demonstrations of on-board navigation and route guidance for the auto industry. The geographic data was provided by Navigation Technologies and Etak, both "street level" digital map database providers. By 1995, Navigation Technologies had thoroughly mapped all the major metropolitan areas of the United States for the system and Etak had completed a less detailed mapping of the rest of the country.

The collapse of the Soviet Union in the early 1990s opened a potentially major new niche for the digital mapping industry. As Russia began privatizing its military satellite system, its high-resolution images of the earth suddenly became available to commercial mapmakers. Not to be outdone, the U.S. government responded by permitting U.S. firms to plan high-resolution satellite systems for commercial mapping purposes. In 1995 the U.S. Navy also declassified its secret radar charts, and two U.S. entrepreneurs began preparing a comprehensive, high-accuracy map of the ocean floor for sale to non-military markets. By the late 1990s, three U.S. companies had announced plans to launch and operate small commercial satellites they claimed would deliver images at resolutions of three meters or less for a few hundred dollars an image and could be used for urban planning, agricultural and environmental monitoring, making and revising maps, and even vacation planning.

By the early 1990s, major corporations such as McDonald's and Dunkin' Donuts were already using GIS technology to determine where to build restaurants. At the same time, Cincinnati began reducing mapping costs by sharing its GIS with local utilities. Furthermore, the U.S. Bureau of Land Management and the U.S. Forest Service each discussed allocating $1 billion to GIS public land information services, and the U.S. Census Bureau sold a rough digital city block map of the United States for $10,000. By early 1992, map users in the United States could choose from 100 different geographic databases plotting everything from streets to soil types, and from over 200 different software packages.

The emergence of the Global Positioning System (GPS)—originally developed by the U.S. government to guide missiles—as a consumer product in the late 1990s enabled industry firms to offer real time, high precision mapping information for customers, and GPS receivers were quickly integrated into some automobile navigation systems. At this same time, the former Federal Defense Mapping Agency had been reorganized as the National Imaging and Mapping Agency with a new mandate to promote the application of formerly military mapping capabilities to the commercial market.

As early as 1991, the U.S. GIS industry had enjoyed revenues of $3.5 billion, with Pentagon spending alone accounting for one fourth of that figure. A 1992 estimate predicted that the demand for GIS products and services by utility companies and local governments alone ensured that the GIS industry would grow 25 percent annually through 2002—with even faster growth if applications could be found to entice corporate customers and consumers. By the mid-1990s, the GIS market was one of the fastest growing computer application markets, with an estimated value of $2 billion in 1995 and an 18 percent annual growth rate. In 1995 the remote sensing arm of the digital mapping/GIS market (which included both satellite imaging and traditional aerial photography) was valued at $550 million, and it was estimated that it would reach $2.7 billion by 2000.

Total GIS spending reached $7.7 billion in 2001, of which software accounted for $1.1 billion and services accounted for $5.4 billion, according to market research company Daratech Inc. As stated in the February 2003 issue of *Electric Light & Power,* "The largest market for GIS software was the utilities industry, which accounted for 21 percent of all software revenue, followed closely by state and local governments, the telecommunications industry, and organizations involved in earth resources management."

PIONEERS IN THE FIELD

Among the pioneering firms in the digital mapping industry are Etak Inc., Navigation Technologies, the Environmental Systems Research Institute, and GeoSystems Global. Founded in 1983 by Stanley Honey, Etak produced the world's first automated car navigation system, the Navigator, in 1985, and has licensed navigation technology to some of the biggest makers of automotive dashboard electronics. Although the sales of Navigator were limited to business customers such as restaurant guides, taxi companies, and vendors of PC mapping software,

Etak (a subsidiary of Sony Corp.) was the only major company in the digital map business prior to 1985. By 1999, the company offered a GPS-based map generator to run on notebook computers with coverage across the United States, and traffic report services via cellular phones and cellular phone-connected screens.

A pioneer in the route guidance segment of the digital mapping industry was Navigation Technologies (NavTech), founded in Sunnyvale, California, in 1985. In 1988 NavTech partnered with Holland-based electronics giant Philips Electronics N.V. to develop its auto navigation system, in which it had invested more than $200 million. By the late 1990s, it had accumulated detailed databases for North American and European metropolitan areas covering a population of 350 million, and less detailed coverage of sub-metropolitan areas representing another 270 million people. The company supplies vehicle databases for factory or dealer-installed systems on vehicles from such makers as Acura, BMW, and Mercedes-Benz. Aftermarket systems using NavTech databases include the Philips Carin Navigation System and Hertz NeverLost.

The Environmental Systems Research Institute (ESRI) was founded in 1969 in Redlands, California, by Jack and Laura Dangermond. In the 1970s, ESRI concentrated on developing GIS applications used in urban renewal projects. In the 1980s, ESRI became a digital mapping/GIS software company and, in 1981, released ArcInfo, the first modern GIS integrated into a single system. ArcInfo remained the company's flagship product and was modified to work in Unix, Windows NT, and network computer environments. In the early 1990s, ESRI unveiled ArcView GIS, a mainstream desktop mapping and GIS tool; ArcData, to provide users with ready-to-use GIS data; and ArcCAD, which integrated computer-aided design and GIS technologies. ESRI released its first consumer mapping product in 1994. In the late 1990s, it positioned itself to capitalize on the "live mapping" technology made possible by the Internet and in 1999 enjoyed total sales of roughly $340.9 million and software revenues of $296.6 million for a commanding 35 percent of the GIS software market. That year, the company began to contribute software and support to federal and local livability programs and to the National Oceanic and Atmospheric Sustainable Seas Expeditions project. In 2009, ESRI still commanded a dominant market share at 30 percent, according to Daratech.

GeoSystems Global of Mountville, Pennsylvania was founded in 1967 as the cartographic services division of publisher R.R. Donnelley & Sons. In the 1970s and 1980s, it expanded into customized mapping services for textbook, atlas, travel, directory, and reference publishers, and became the largest custom mapping business in the United States. In 1989 Donnelley formed a joint venture with Spatial Data Sciences and two years later acquired selected assets of Spatial Data to form GeoSystems. In 1992, GeoSystems released GeoLocate, its flagship mapping and routing software program, and in 1993 Donnelley's Cartographic Services and GeoSystems were merged as GeoSystems to form a total GIS services company. In 1996 GeoSystems entered the online publishing business with MapQuest, the first interactive mapping service on the Internet. MapQuest immediately became a World Wide Web hot spot as consumers used the service to call up "zoomable" maps of locations throughout the United States. In 1999 the company changed its name to Mapquest.com and moved its headquarters to New York City, reflecting an increased commitment to the Internet.

Some industry players began using the term geospatial to better describe what formerly was included under the GIS banner. This information is gathered from remote sensing, mapping, and surveying and other technologies. Geospatial technologies capture, store, manage, integrate, display, analyze and otherwise assist in the interpretation of this data in its entire context for better decision-making. This broader definition recognizes that engineering data from CAD systems, billing information from ERP systems, facilities management and many other types of enterprise content must be brought together with the traditional spatial data from a GIS in order to efficiently make decisions."

According to Daratech, worldwide GIS revenues totaled $1.84 billion in 2003, an increase of 5.1 percent over 2002. Software represented 64 percent of this total ($1.18 billion), followed by services with 24 percent ($447 million), data products with 8 percent ($147 million), and hardware with 4 percent ($70 million). Daratech expected worldwide GIS revenues to climb 9.7 percent in 2004, reaching $2.02 billion. Growth was supported by increased investment by government agencies in areas like homeland security. During the middle of the first decade of the 2000s, Daratech reported that 44 percent of industry revenues came from the regulated sector, followed by the public sector (29 percent) and the private sector (24 percent).

Within the regulated segment of the market, field automation technologies used by the likes of electric utilities continued to represent a significant growth area. In its January/February 2005 issue, *UA* provided data from the market research firm InfoNetrix indicating that annual geospatial and field automation expenditures totaled nearly $200 million in 2004, up from $150 million in 2002. In 2005, expenditures were projected to exceed $275 million and then climb to nearly $400 million by 2007. Total expenditures include field automation solutions, technical and integration services, and geospatial systems. Heading into the late years of the first decade of the 2000s, steady growth was projected within the geospatial systems segment, with the majority of expenditures occurring within the other categories, especially technical and integration services.

In 2006 Daratech reported that during 2004, three companies (ESRI, Bentley, and Intergraph) generated about half of the industry's software-related revenues. However, it also reported that growth was being driven by an influx of new companies and customers, especially in the specialized software segment. In addition, growth was stemming from the increasing availability of both private and public data. The need for integration services also was increasing due to the availability of new multimedia technology, database systems, applications, services, and mass market user interfaces.

In fact, the number of interfaces through which users could access digital maps was growing rapidly. This was especially the case online. According to Nielsen/Net Ratings, in October 2006 alone, some 27 million people used Google Maps. In addition, 19 million people used Yahoo Maps. Nielsen reported that in general, the use of online mapping services increased 28 percent in 2005.

Beyond online maps, more consumers were accessing digital maps via navigation systems in their cars, cell phones, or special hand-held devices. In the June 4, 2006, issue of *The Star-Ledger,* Phil Magney, a principal analyst at Minnetonka, Minnesota-based Telematics Research Group, estimated that 4.5 million navigation systems were in use during 2006. Magney forecast this number to increase 50 percent in 2007, reaching 6.7 million, and then mushroom to 25 million in 2011. In addition, he predicted that the number of GPS-equipped phones would double from 2006 to 2007, to 2.6 million.

Heading into the late years of the first decade of the 2000s, digital maps continued to grow in richness and utility. Via its free Google Earth software, search engine heavyweight Google combined its Google Search tool with satellite images, terrain, maps, and 3D visuals of buildings. On its Web site, the company prompted users to "Fly to your house. Just type in an address, press Search, and you'll zoom right in. Search for schools, parks, restaurants, and hotels. Get driving directions. Tilt and rotate the view to see 3D terrain and buildings. Save and share your searches and favorites." Google offered more robust versions of Google Earth, including one aimed at business users, for a fee.

In addition to 3D maps, companies like Tele Atlas continued to add more lifelike attributes to digital maps. For example, navigation systems will be eventually able to provide users with a picture of an intersection at which they are supposed to turn, or instruct a driver to turn left after passing a landmark like a restaurant instead of requiring one to search for a hard-to-see street sign.

The industry was contending with a number of GIS and geospatial-related challenges during the first decade of the 2000s. Among these was a continued lack of standardization. This problem was more pronounced as more organizations began sharing and trying to link various types of data through geospatial systems. Some observers argued that consumers would ultimately demand technology suppliers to ascribe to established data format standards. Another challenge was information management. Specifically, this included ensuring that data shared between geospatial and GIS systems was synchronized and up to date, and presented in the proper format for different groups of end users. Issues such as these continued to grow in importance as GIS data was increasingly linked to other types of information systems, such as those used for enterprise resource planning.

CURRENT CONDITIONS

The global growth of the GIS/Geospatial industry as a whole slowed down to only one percent in 2009, according to Daratech, down from 11 percent in 2008 and a more robust 17.4 percent in 2007. Due to recurring applications in homeland security and investments in GIS in the public sector, North America was not as adversely affected by the economic downturn as other areas.

The most dramatic slowdown, according to Daratech in its October 2009 press release, was in the private sector, forecast to shrink to $1.4 billion by the end of 2009, down 0.7 percent from 2008. Daratech attributed this to the broader pulling back from major investments in new IT technologies by private sector entities. Conversely, Daratech expected public sector sales to carry the industry, growing 4.1 percent in 2009 to almost $957 million. The outlook for 2010 was positive.

According to ABI Research, revenues for the LBS segment of the industry grew a staggering 156 percent in 2009, from $1.7 billion in 2008 to $2.6 billion one year later. It predicted that LBS revenues would surpass $14 billion by 2014. One of the main reasons was the growth in LBS applications as part of one-off fee smartphone platforms. Apple's iPhone led the industry, followed by Blackberry, Nokia, and Android. Many carriers in both the United States and Europe began adopting more open LBS strategies. For example, Verizon increased the number of unlocked GPS phones and Vodafone acquired navigation software vendor Wayfinder.

The GPS segment of the market, particularly the number of GPS-enabled LBS subscribers, was expected to grow by leaps and bounds, with market revenues reaching US $9.8 billion in 2013, according to a 2009 market research report by RNCOS. The positive forecast was directly attributed to the rapid development and refinement of digital mapping software. The report also predicted the gradual shifting from PNDs (which dominated the GPS device market with a 90 percent share) to GPS-enabled handsets, accounting for approximately 70 percent market share by 2013.

INDUSTRY LEADERS

In its October 2009 released study, Daratech identified ESRI as still dominating th market (30 percent) in the traditional GIS segment. Intergraph was listed as the second largest player, with a 16 percent market share in 2009, followed by GE Energy, the market leader in the utilities market with a 24 percent share.

In the larger GIS/Geospatial market, MacDonald Dettweiler and Associates (MDA) controlled 21.8 percent of the market in 2009. MDA focused on geospatial data and engineering services for imaging, GIS, geology, weather, and defense. ESRI and Bentley Systems were also listed. Bentley carried a 42 percent share in GIS/Geospatial market software and services, as well as the geo-enabled engineering applications market.

Intergraph Corp., based in Huntsville, Alabama, is a diversified producer of hardware, software, consulting, and support services for the information technology field. During the middle of the twenty-first century's first decade, Intergraph underwent a transformation process that reduced its corporate divisions from four to two. These included Process, Power & Marine (PP&M) and a new division called Security, Government & Infrastructure (SG&I). The latter division included businesses formerly included in the company's Intergraph Public Safety (IPS), Intergraph Solutions Group (ISG), and Intergraph Mapping and Geospatial Solutions (IMGS) divisions. In 2004, Intergraph's revenues totaled $551.1 million, a 4.5 percent increase over 2003. Net income totaled $159 million in 2004, a whopping 585.3 percent increase over the previous year. In 2005, the company's sales increased 4.7 percent to $576.8 million, but its net income fell 28 percent, to $114.4 million. Hellman & Friedman LLC and Texas Pacific Group acquired Intergraph in 2006 for approximately $1.3 billion.

Based in Troy, New York, MapInfo Corp. generated sales revenue of $165.5 million in 2005, a 10.8 percent increase from 2005. Its products enable insurance companies and sales organizations to translate complex corporate data into easily understood maps to simplify the process of performing marketing analysis, selecting business sites, managing corporate assets and risk, and optimizing delivery routing and logistics. By the middle of the first decade of the 2000s, MapInfo offered a wide range of software, products, and consulting services. The company's scope of operations had grown to include such areas as asset/facilities management, e-government, homeland security, logistics, network planning, sales force automation, service pre-qualification and provisioning, risk management, and target marketing. MapInfo's growth and expansion was achieved through a continuing list of acquisitions, including Thompson Associates (2003), Southbank Systems Ltd. (2004), and GeoBusiness Solutions Ltd. (2005).

Analytical Surveys Inc. (ASI) produces high-accuracy digital maps that are integrated with databases in GIS applications to store, retrieve, analyze, and display information about the characteristics of utilities networks, natural resources, transportation systems, and residential and commercial communities. ASI creates maps using aerial photography, ground surveys, and existing printed maps. It also focuses on four aspects of the GIS business: digital mapping of physical plants such as power generation facilities; photogrammetric mapping for utilities using aerial photos that have been processed to remove distortions; cadastral mapping showing property lines, property zoning, and use restrictions for local governments; and digital orthophotography for creating high-accuracy maps that look like aerial photos. In mid-1999, ASI was an integral player in the building of New York City's first photogrammetric land base. However, its many acquisitions that year caused some accounting turmoil and the company was forced to restate its earnings and slash some of its workforce. In 2002 the SEC launched a formal investigation into the firm's accounting practices from 1998 through the end of 2001. ASI recorded revenues of $19.1 million and employed 200 workers in 2002. Revenues continued to decline during the middle of the first decade of the 2000s, falling to $11.6 million in 2004 and $4.3 million in 2006. The company's employee count also fell, to 109 in 2004 and 82 in 2005. During the late years of the decade, heavy competition in other areas prompted ASI to specialize in the oil and gas industry.

AMERICA AND THE WORLD

The U.S. digital mapping industry remained the world's largest, and its long history of government and private initiatives in GIS, digital mapping, and satellite sensing technologies gave it a competitive edge in the world market. The United States was estimated to account for roughly one quarter of the total world demand for GIS-related products and services. As globalization increased and more countries began to share GIS and geospatial data, this presented the same types of standardization challenges that existed within various U.S. industry segments.

Daratech's 2009 study concluded that growth in the United States would top 2.1 percent in 2010, representing more than twice the growth in the Asia Pacific region, and five times as great as in Europe. The study noted that the 2008–2009 global economic downturn resulted in many European governments cutting back on purchases involving geospatial technology; this did not hold true in the United States.

Despite the lead enjoyed by the U.S. digital mapping industry, however, several world regions were also at the cutting edge of GIS technologies. Japan, for example, quickly embraced auto navigation technology and was hear the head of the pack to mas produce more than a million Japanese cars manufactured with navigation systems. Europe was also a leader in the use of digital mapping to aid auto navigation, led by companies such as European Geographic Technologies and TeleAtlas. Germany was the first country in the world to complete a full mapping of its roadways for integration into in-vehicle navigation systems, and Germany's BMW was the first European car company to offer navigation technology as an option. According to a 2009 market research report by RNCOS, markets in India and China were expected to grow rapidly with the adoption of GPS technology combined with low-cost GPS-enabled mobile handsets.

Great Britain played a major role in pushing digital mapping technology by launching, under the auspices of its Ordnance Survey (the national mapping agency), a complete digital database of all 70 million topographical features of the British Isles. When the mammoth project was completed, the British government explored the option of privatizing the Ordnance Survey—a clear reflection of the worldwide trend toward finding private, commercial uses for previously military or strictly governmental satellite technologies.

Russia also played a major role in the trend toward privatization. When the Soviet Union unraveled, its previously top secret, high resolution satellite photos became available to commercial international mapmakers. Soon after, the private Russian company in charge of managing this satellite data reached an agreement with Sweden's Satellitbild to sell two-meter resolution satellite images to Western buyers. About the same time, India's IRS-1 six-meter resolution satellite images were also made available for commercial use. These developments prompted the United States to relax its restrictions on the commercial use of high resolution satellite images, encouraging consortia of international companies to form ventures to launch commercial imaging satellites for the world market. The U.S.-based Lockheed and Raytheon teamed up with Mitsubishi to form Space Imaging, which promptly announced plans to launch a one-meter resolution commercial satellite. However, by 2003, due to waning demand for imagery in the commercial sector, Lockheed and Raytheon opted not to finance Space Imaging's high resolution satellite.

One global challenge the industry faced was how to adapt geospatial information so that it was understood across many cultures. This situation was complicated by the addition of non-geographic information, including images and documents, into GIS displays. Thus, the industry continued to work toward a better understanding of how individual users understand, perceive, and process information. This was expected to remain a challenge for the foreseeable future.

RESEARCH AND TECHNOLOGY

Advances in digital mapping technology center around the standardization of the map objects that comprise the content of digital maps, new applications for digital mapping technology, the growth of the Internet as a platform for "live" interactive mapping, and the likelihood that high resolution, military quality satellite images will soon become available to consumers and businesses alike. The profusion of digital mapping platforms and concerns over how to ensure the integrity of digital maps spurred the digital mapping industry to undertake its largest research project ever in an attempt to find objective guidelines for communicating map data. Such guidelines would include standardized or codified classification techniques for grouping map data "attributes" and logic-based systems for selecting the right graphic symbols to represent different types of map data.

The Internet seemed to offer an increasingly natural environment for digital mapmakers, and the growing availability of such mapping technology on the World Wide Web was regarded as one of the key factors in the eventual emergence of a true electronic yellow pages in which users could not only search out addresses and phone numbers but also detailed maps pointing out the best routes to a business. High-precision satellite images became available for only a few hundred dollars as 11 companies were given licenses for consumer GIS satellite systems, some with resolutions as sharp as 85 centimeters. A complete high-resolution mapping of the world, however, remained an unaccomplished goal by the early years of the first decade of the 2000s when, according to the National Imaging and Mapping Agency, less than 50 percent of the earth had been mapped with 10 meter or better resolution.

The World Wide Web continued to play a critical role in the GIS and geospatial realm, as governments, corporations, and utilities all sought to provide customers and constituents with online data. In some cases, online digital mapping technology enabled organizations to increase efficiency levels and serve customers with fewer staff members. During the later years of the decade, user expectations of Internet-based digital maps continued to rise. This was evident by the advent of 3-D digital maps, such as those offered via Google Earth.

BIBLIOGRAPHY

Bray, Richard. "Painting the Big Picture." *CIO Canada,* 1 February 2007.

Cassar, Ken. "The Other 95 Percent of our Time." *Nielsen/ NetRatings NETREPORTER,* January 2007. Available from http://www.netratings.com/.

"Digital Maps Help Spot Historic Sites." *Europe Intelligence Wire,* 2 January 2007.

Essex, David. "DHS Special Report: FEMA Maps Out a Better Response." *Government Computer News,* 19 June 2006.

"The Evolving GIS/Geospatial Industry." Daratech Inc., 1 August 2006. Available from http://www.daratech.com/press/releases/2006/060801.html.

"GIS/Geospatial Industry Worldwide Growth Slows to 1% in 2009." Daratch Inc. report, 20 October 2009. Available from http://openpr.com/news/102216/GIS-Geospatial-Industry-Worldwide-Growth-Slows-to-1-in-2009.html.

"GIS In Our World." ESRI, 16 February 2007. Available from http://www.esri.com/company/about/facts.html.

"GIS Software Market Sees Dynamic Growth." *Electric Light & Power,* February 2003.

"GIS/Geospatial Market Grew 17% in 2005 to Top $3.3 Billion; Sales Led by Growth in Data Products." Daratech Inc., 6 July 2006. Available from http://www.daratech.com/press/releases/2006/060706.html.

"Global Space Revenue Tops US$251 Billion." 8 September 2008. Available from http://www.albawaba.com

"Google Earth." Mountain View, Calif.: Google Inc., 18 February 2007. Available from http://earth.google.com/.

Gopwani, Jewel. "Navigating Digital Maps; Demand for Location Gizmos Fuels Niche." *The Star-Ledger,* 4 June 2006.

"High Growth Reported for the World GPS Market Forecast to 2013." Market Reseaerch report, April 2009. Available from http://www.reportlinker.com/p0116472/World-GPS-MArket-Forecast-to-2013.html.

Howell, Donna. "Jack Dangermond's Digital Mapping Lays It All Out." *Investor's Business Daily,* 14 August 2009.

Jesdanun, Anick. "Digital Maps Going Beyond the Roads." *The America's Intelligence Wire,* 29 December 2005.

"Lack of Standards, Web-Proliferation, Homeland Security, Information Management Needs Changing the Face of GIS and Geospatial Industries." Daratech Inc. Available from http://www.daratech.com/press/releases/2005/050328.html.

"LBS Revenues to Reach $2.6 Billion in 2009." ABIResearch, 7 September 2009. Available at http://www.abiresearch.com

Lowe, Jonathan W. "Web GIS Gets Flashy." *Geospatial Solutions,* May 2005.

Pulusani, Preetha. "The Globalization of Data Sharing." *Geospatial Solutions,* January 2005.

Smith, Mike. "The Evolution of Utility GIS: From 'Good-Looking Maps' to Mainstream Application." *UA,* January/ February 2005.

Stover DeRocco, Emily. "The Emerging Geospatial Workforce." *Geospatial Solutions,* January 2005.

"Technology Issues Confronting the GIS/Geospatial Industry." Daratech Inc., 28 August 2006. Available from http://www.daratech.com/press/releases/2006/060828.html.

"Worldwide GIS Revenue Forecast to Top $2.02 Billion in 2004, Up 9.7% Over 2003." Daratech Inc. Available from http://www.daratech.com/press/releases/2004/041019.html.

DIRECT BROADCAST SATELLITE TELEVISION

---■---

SIC CODE(S)

3663

3679

4841

INDUSTRY SNAPSHOT

Buoyed by innovative programming and consumers' disenchantment with their cable companies, direct broadcast satellite (DBS) services made sizable inroads into the U.S. pay television market, as cable continued to lose ground to DBS. New technologies and features remain a primary catalyst for growth of DBS services. For more than a decade, DBS providers have been locked in what is largely a battle of attrition against cable, and insiders of all stripes stress the importance of staying ahead of the technology curve. As of 2010, the newest services included high-definition television (HDTV), Internet Protocol Television (IPTV), video on demand (VOD), digital video recording (DVR), and HD-3DTV.

ORGANIZATION AND STRUCTURE

Satellite signals are transmitted in a single digital stream to reception dishes mounted on rooftops, in backyards, and atop industrial buildings. Direct broadcast satellites orbit 22,300 miles above Earth. At this height, the orbital period coincides with the earth's daily rotation about its axis. The result is that the satellite seems to hang at a constant position in the sky, allowing subscribers to point their reception dishes in a fixed direction and reducing the cost and complexity of the home system. As of 2010, the major U.S. space transport company offering satellite television services was the Space Explorations Technology Corporation (SpaceX). SpaceX also is a major contractor with NASA.

The rights to telecommunications satellite orbital positions and transmission frequencies are assigned to individual nations by the Geneva-based International Telecommunications Union. The Federal Communications Commission (FCC), which controls U.S. slots, has reserved a portion of the broadcast spectrum and eight orbital positions for DBS. In order to allow higher powered transmissions for interference-free reception by smaller dishes, the DBS orbital positions are spaced nine degrees apart rather than two degrees apart as are conventional communications satellites.

Originally, four of the eight DBS orbital positions were intended to serve the eastern United States, with the others serving the west. With current technology, however, three of the positions (101, 110, and 119 degrees west longitude) can transmit to the entire continental United States. Abbreviated as "Full CONUS" slots, they are by far the most coveted since they generate the greatest range for providers.

Each orbital slot is assigned 32 transponder frequencies. The number of channels a DBS provider can offer depends on how many transponders the FCC has licensed it to use. Generally these rights are purchased at FCC auctions. Satellite owners buy slots in space and lease assigned transponder frequencies to service providers. Each transponder frequency can accommodate a number of channels depending on how compactly the signal can be digitally compressed, which varies with the type of programming. Sports events, with small objects moving quickly against complex backgrounds, can only

2009 Revenues for the Satellite Industry	
Satellite services revenues (satellite television leading this sector)	$71.8 billion
Satellite manufacturing revenues	$13.5 billion
Satellite launch revenues	$ 1.9 billion
Satellite ground equipment revenues	$49.9 billion

SOURCE: Satellite Industry Association (SIA).

be compressed seven or eight to a transponder. Talk shows might be squeezed nine to a transponder. Since film is shot at a slower frame rate than video, it can be compressed still further, up to 11 per transponder. High definition television (HDTV), however, requires a great deal of compression, allowing only about two channels to a transponder. With the current mix of program types and compression technology, each orbital position provides about 200 channels from its 32 transponders.

The compression and processing of the signal happen before it ever gets to the satellite. DBS service providers maintain advanced, highly automated broadcast centers that receive programming via standard communications satellites, landlines, and videotape. From the broadcast centers, the material is encrypted for security and transmitted to the satellite using large uplink antennas. Taped programming goes through a careful editing and quality control process before transmission, including optimization for digital compression. By contrast, live satellite programming received by the broadcast centers is generally retransmitted immediately, so the quality of the signal is dependent on that of the incoming "feed."

To receive a signal, the customer needs a small dish antenna and a set-top receiving/decoding unit approximately the size of a VCR. This unit decrypts and decompresses the signal, usually for only one channel at a time. Watching or recording multiple programs simultaneously requires multiple decoders. The receiver is individually addressable by means of a telephone connection and a "smart card" programmed with a unique serial number. With this capability, DBS providers can activate and deactivate programming options packages, track pay-per-view services, and implement electronic countermeasures to thwart unauthorized access or "piracy."

Industry Regulation Congress and the FCC traverse tenuously between the competing interests of cable and DBS, and the relationship of those industries with broadcast television. The Satellite Home Viewer Act of 1994 stipulated that DBS providers could sell local service only to customers who could not receive acceptable broadcast television reception off the air and who were not cable television subscribers within the past 90 days. The loose

definition of "acceptable broadcast" fueled no small amount of controversy between cable, broadcasting, and DBS companies, including a number of lawsuits to prevent DBS players from moving into local markets.

The problem was greatly alleviated, at least from the DBS industry's point of view, when in November 1999 Congress passed the Satellite Home Viewer Improvement Act, allowing DBS to directly offer rebroadcast local network signals to customers. This was a significant blow to cable companies, given that access to local programming was a key advantage they enjoyed over DBS providers. Knowing the legislation was likely to lead to a whole new round of fighting, the FCC ruled that after May 29, 2000, DBS carriers retransmitting local signals must obtain permission from the local station.

BACKGROUND AND DEVELOPMENT

Satellite dishes have been showing up in backyards for many years, as hobbyists set up receiving stations to intercept traditional analog satellite television downlinks transmitted on the "C-band" as feeds to local stations. However, the ten-foot diameter antennas needed to pull in these signals and the complications of swiveling the big dishes around to track the various satellites limited the appeal of this technology.

In 1986 the National Rural Telecommunications Cooperative (NRTC) was formed to address a need to provide reliable and affordable services to 25 million residents of rural communities across the United States. DBS was not yet feasible because of high costs and immature compression and encryption techniques. The NRTC approached GM Hughes, a leader in satellite communications, about a partnership, but Hughes was working on a deal of its own with Australian media mogul Rupert Murdoch, NBC, and Cablevision. Called Sky Cable, the project was to provide a 75-channel service, but the partnership collapsed.

Having worked out some of the bugs, Hughes launched the first DBS satellite in 1993 and negotiated a deal with NRTC that would attract more than 100,000 rural customers to Hughes' DirecTV service in its first year. These customers, spread out all over the country, received a basic package of 20 channels using 18-inch fixed dish antennas. This provided much wider exposure than DirecTV otherwise would have received in a few test markets. Provisions in the Cable Act of 1992 assured that programming would be available to DBS.

Meanwhile, Primestar had established itself as the first direct-to-home service in 1990, operating from a conventional satellite and therefore requiring a larger (three-foot) dish antenna. In 1995 an improved compression scheme, MPEG-2, increased the number of channels available to provide viewers a full complement of offerings.

Since the signals are transmitted in digital packets, the medium is capable of sending signals as video, audio, and computer data, making it ripe for Internet and other interactive capabilities. In 1997, Hughes Network Systems launched DirecDuo, a service combining the company's 400 kilobit-per-second Internet service called DirecPC with its DirecTV offerings, using a single dish antenna. EchoStar developed similar technology shortly thereafter.

DBS companies continued to aggressively pursue new business areas. America Online partnered with DirecTV, Hughes Network Systems, Philips Electronics, and Network Computer to work on developing "AOL TV." DirecTV and AOL worked together on a service to combine digital satellite television programming and AOL TV's enhanced interactive TV Internet service. EchoStar teamed up with WebTV Networks Inc. for similar purposes.

DirecTV and EchoStar lost no time taking advantage of the Satellite Home Viewer Improvement Act to stake their claims in many local markets. DirecTV enjoyed early take rates of up to 55 percent in markets such as Washington, D.C., and Atlanta, and offered local channels in about 22 markets. DirecTV enjoyed an advantage over its rival in one key area pertaining to local broadcasts: in most of its markets, DirecTV subscribers did not need to acquire new dishes to receive the local signals.

While EchoStar offered free hardware upgrades, the shipping time of about six weeks was a drawback in this rapidly growing market sector. Nonetheless, EchoStar was slightly better positioned in local markets, pitching its products in 35 cities in the summer of 2000. By that time, both DBS companies were wrapping up their first phase of local service launchings and were busily signing carriage agreements with TV stations in mid-sized markets. Limited satellite bandwidth, however, prevented the local signals from reaching all subscribers.

Perhaps the DBS industry's most prominent, if not unexpected, event of the early 2000s was the acquisition of industry leader DirecTV by the Australian media conglomerate News Corporation. Despite its track record of growth and vast marketing prowess, DirecTV had endured as an odd duck in the General Motors (GM) family at GM's Hughes Electronics subsidiary. That arrangement has been blamed for stifling DirecTV's advance, and for years, a variety of suitors were said to be eyeing its purchase.

In 2001 and 2002, its junior competitor EchoStar briefly vied to purchase DirecTV, only to be blocked by federal regulators on antitrust grounds. In 2003 News Corporation came forward at last with a $6.8 billion bid that was accepted by General Motors and green-lighted by the FCC. The new ownership, under the watch of Rupert Murdoch, was expected to rejuvenate DirecTV and allow it to compete more aggressively for a commanding share of the market.

Even as the DBS industry grew markedly faster than most sectors of the economy, a number of analysts suggested the heady growth was liable to settle at a more moderate pace. Although relatively low, customer churn, the turnover of subscribers who often leave to take a competitor's offer, had been on the rise, nearing 1.5 percent a month in 2004 for the two dominant providers, DirecTV and Echo Star. Aside from potentially cannibalizing other satellite customers, DBS companies had three primary growth opportunities: winning over business from cable, selling to established households that don't pay for TV services, and gaining new customers as the population naturally expands.

The first option had always been the most viable, but DBS companies were preparing for stiffer contests with cable operators as they methodically rolled out new technologies that had been in development for some time. DBS had proven its mass appeal, but still faced competitive disadvantages versus cable in that cable was readily accessible in 97 percent of U.S. households and, for many consumers, cable remained the obvious, low-risk choice. Deeper market penetration has also been a remarkably effective strategy, but posed greater challenges given that more than 80 percent of U.S. homes already subscribed in one form or another. Meanwhile, natural growth of the market due to new households forming was limited, on average, to less than 2 percent a year. All of these factors seemed to point toward a deceleration in growth.

Highlighting the consumer dynamic is evidence of just how readily they will switch services. Lacking strong allegiance to any particular technology or company, a significant share of the market is motivated by price and a compelling service offer. A 2004 survey by Leichtman Research Group found that equal proportions of cable and DBS subscribers—around 10 percent—said they were apt to change services within six months. The same study singled out cost as the leading gripe consumers have about subscription TV.

As of 2004 DBS customers typically paid monthly fees starting at $30 for the most basic package, while premium services pushed the tally easily above $60 a month. The national average was just below $50, according to a 2003 consumer survey by J.D. Power and Associates. While DBS firms have often wielded price as a competitive weapon against cable companies, their own fees edged up slightly in the early 2000s as the major DBS firms carried more local broadcasts. Some expected this trend to continue, particularly as DirecTV hinted it may style itself more as a topflight service aiming for premium rates.

In order to prevail in this price-sensitive climate, industry participants increasingly look to two areas of cost containment: content and taxes. Both EchoStar and DirecTV had indicated willingness to engage in contentious—and often public—negotiations with studios and content vendors. In a notable example, in the winter of 2004 EchoStar halted all Viacom programming, including such mainstays as MTV, Comedy Central, and CBS broadcasts, amid contract talks with Viacom. Upon News Corporation's purchase of DirecTV, executives at the company likewise said they planned to use the parent company's heft to negotiate better deals on programming, of which News Corporation is also a supplier.

At the same time, the industry has opposed vigorously any new taxes on its services, even challenging some state laws in court. Most states impose some form of sales tax on DBS services, sometimes more than 5 percent, and several state legislatures were looking at new rounds of taxation to shore up their treasuries. While it has fought all such taxes, the industry has focused on bills that would tax satellite TV disproportionately relative to cable.

Cable continued to lose ground to DBS, as the segment of cable subscribing households fell from 62 percent in 2004 to 60 percent in 2005, while DBS saw its share of subscribing households climb from 19 percent to 27 percent during the same timeframe, according to data from J.D. Power and Associates. However, in the fourth quarter, industry leaders saw subscriptions fall as cable providers made significant headway with consumers by offering them package deals that bundled Internet access, phone, and cable television. While only one of the largest publicly traded cable providers saw a basic subscriber dip in the fourth quarter, EchoStar saw subscriptions fall 23 percent and DirecTV experienced a 55 percent reduction.

Cable providers looked to steal market share from the DBS industry by offering high definition television (HDTV), video on demand, and digital video recorders. However, DBS players were not resting on their laurels. By early 2006 both DirecTV and Echostar were expanding HDTV offerings. In the April 17, 2006, issue of *Satellite News,* DirecTV Chief Technology Officer Romulo Pontual described the company's HDTV expansion as "one of the cornerstones of our brand strategy." By 2008 DirecTV offered 95 national HD channels and provided local HD broadcast channels in almost 80 cities.

There was no question that HDTV was the direction in which the market was heading. The aforementioned issue of *Satellite News* further explained that the number of households with access to HDTV was expected to rise from 4 million in 2006 to 52 million in 2009. By 2010

analysts anticipated that approximately 500 channels would be broadcast in HD, according to Northern Sky Research.

One emerging source of competition for DBS providers was Internet Protocol Television (IPTV), in which broadband Internet subscribers use special set-top boxes to receive programming via the Internet. Telecommunications firms and cable TV companies were positioned to offer this service.

In 2008 a split in shares caused the creation of two companies out of Echostar: Echostar and DISH Network. DISH Network was a brand name that Echostar established in 1996 to market its satellite TV system, and in 2008 it became the corporation that dealt with the satellite TV part of the business, whereas Echostar retained ownership of the technology segment, including the satellites.

In 2008 DirecTV remained the largest DBS company in the United States, with almost 17 million customers in the United States and 4.8 million in Latin America. DirecTV reported 2008 first quarter revenue increases of 17 percent, after having gained 275,000 new U.S. subscribers. The company attributed most of the increase in revenue to the 40 percent surge in its HD and DVR (digital video recording) subscription base, which had topped 7 million subscribers. DirecTV supplied 95 national HD channels, the most of any DBS provider.

DISH Network was the second largest DBS company, with 13 million subscribers. In May 2008, DISH launched 22 new national HD channels. However, that same month it canceled 15 special-interest Voom channels, causing some subscribers to complain.

DBS providers faced customer satisfaction challenges during the late 2000s. According to the 2008 American Customer Satisfaction Index, put out by the University of Michigan, both DBS and cable TV providers were at the low end of the rankings across all sectors, beating out only the oft-bemoaned airline industry. Regarding customer satisfaction, analyst Craig Moffett told *Hollywood Reporter,* "The picture is not pretty. The pay TV group is, overall, a disaster, ranking worse on average than the IRS."

Another development that affected DBS providers was the federal government's scrutiny of early-termination fees. In mid-2008 the FCC was scheduled to hold a hearing to consider restrictions on the penalties, and possible legislation regarding the fees was pending in Congress. The target of the investigations was the charges DBS providers, as well as cell phone companies, place on subscribers who cancel their contracts early.

For example, subscribers who canceled their service with DirecTV before the predetermined contract was up paid $20 a month for the remainder of the time. According to FCC spokesman Robert Kenny, "We want to make sure this [the early-termination penalty] isn't being used as an artificial means of locking consumers into a particular service provider." At the same time, the legal system was dealing with scores of disputes regarding such fees, as customers exerted their right to cancel a service without a financial penalty.

The DBS industry continued to compete with cable TV for viewers, particularly Comcast, the nation's largest cable provider in 2008. Both types of providers used newer services and features such as high definition television (HDTV), video on demand (VOD), and digital video recording (DVR) to draw customers. DirecTV Executive CEO Chase Carey told *Television Week* in late 2007, "We're not seeing a slowdown in advanced products. We're continuing to see demand that exceeds my expectations. I think once people have DVRs, they're not going back to a world without it."

CURRENT CONDITIONS

On Sunday, February 7, 2010, the largest TV audience in history (an average of 106.5 million viewers) tuned in to a CBS broadcast, transmitted via satellite, of the Super Bowl. This new record speaks to the power of the technology that is capable of bringing (to most subscribers) more than 200 different media channels into one's home or business at the touch of a button.

In April 2010 the *APSCC Newsletter* summarized the state of the industry to date: 130 million subscribers to satellite pay-TV and 2009 industry revenues of $70 billion, according to data from the Euroconsult report, Satellite TV Platforms, World Survey and Prospects to 2019. The Satellite Industry Association quoted slightly higher revenues of $71.8 billion for all satellite services, which included satellite television as the leader in that sector. At the end of 2009 there were 113 TV platforms in service, covering more than 100 countries. In the United States satellite TV platforms DirecTV and Dish Network succeeded in displacing cable TV delivery networks as the leading pay-TV providers.

Notwithstanding the overall positive global forecast for the industry, for the first time ever the number of U.S. cable, satellite, and telecommunication services dropped in the second quarter of 2010, according to research firm SNL Kagan. Specifically, the television market lost 216,000 customers (compared to a gain of 378,000 one year prior). The number of total subscribers fell to 100.1 million in the second quarter. Although the firm pointed to economic factors and unemployment as contributing to subscriber declines, it also noted that the decline could signal a new market trend where subscribers turned to Internet-television for programming.

In February 2010 Global Industry Analysts Inc. announced its newest report on the global mobile satellite TV market, forecasting industry revenue growth of nearly $11 billion by 2015. The success was attributed to the growing popularity of TV services, especially mobile handhelds and phones that supported general image quality and high data transfer rates.

INDUSTRY LEADERS

The DirecTV Group Inc. The DirecTV Group, an El Segundo, California-based subsidiary of News Corporation, was the dominant player in the DBS industry during the late 2000s, with almost 17 million subscribers in the United States and 4.8 million in Latin America. The company originated as a unit of Hughes Electronics Corporation, a diversified high-tech subsidiary of General Motors. Hughes shed the last of its military contracting business in early 2000, selling its satellite manufacturing business to Boeing and paving the way for further expansion of DirecTV.

To gain greater channel capacity and further seal its lead in the market, the company bought U.S. Satellite Broadcasting for $1.3 billion in 1998 and Primestar for $1.8 billion in early 1999. Immediately after its buying spree, DirecTV carried all three services under its umbrella. In an effort to expand its subscriber base in 1999, the DBS giant signed marketing agreements with Bell Atlantic, GTE, and SBC Communications that allowed DirecTV to offer its satellite services to the companies' customers. The company further signed up electronics manufacturing giants Panasonic and Samsung to produce set-top boxes with DirecTV reception capability.

Through its partnership with Wink Communications, DirecTV worked to create a sharper and more efficient broadcast signal, and it was working with America Online to develop a TV-based Internet service. In October 2001 EchoStar bid $26 billion for DirecTV parent Hughes Electronics. The Federal Communication Commission nixed the deal, however, leaving DirecTV open to other offers. In 2003 News Corporation took a controlling interest in Hughes Electronics for $6.8 billion in cash and stock. The company was renamed DirecTV Group in 2004 and held under News Corporation's Fox Entertainment division. DirecTV reported sales of $18.6 billion in 2009 with 12,300 employees.

DISH Network DISH (Digital Information Sky Highway) Network originated in Echostar Corporation as a brand name in 1996, before becoming its own company in 2008. In 1999 the company developed significant new capacity through a $1.46 billion purchase of coveted satellite space from MCI Worldcom and News Corporation. DISH Network transmits more than 500 channels from a Full-CONUS orbital slot and also owns rights to East Coast and West Coast transponders that deliver local data services, foreign language programming, and other channels via an additional antenna dish. The firm also offers Internet access and has moved into satellite-generated Internet data transmission with its purchase of Media4, now called EchoStar Data Networks. Plans in 2001 to acquire Hughes Electronics, the parent of DirecTV, dissolved after the FCC squashed the deal. In 2009 DISH Network's total satellite TV customers numbered 14.3 million and the company was rated number one in customer satisfaction, according to the American Customer Satisfaction Index (ACSI). At that time the company employed 23,000 people.

AMERICA AND THE WORLD

In its April 2010 quarterly newsletter, Asia Pacific Satellite Communications (APSCC) covered the burgeoning market in that region, indicating that Asia alone had gained 8.7 million new subscribers in 2009. The organization anticipated that total subscribers would reach 43 million by the end of 2010 and 74 million by 2014. New satellite TV platforms were appearing in India and the Philippines, and for most countries, these platforms had become the leading pay-TV providers (e.g., Sky PerfecTV, Tata Sky, and Dish TV India in Asia).

Malaysia was the only country in the Asian market showing a satellite pay-TV penetration of greater than 30 percent. In fact, the only markets in which satellite TV failed to take lead positions were ones with strong historical cable penetration, such as in the Netherlands and Hong Kong. The situation in China remained unclear; APSCC indicated that satellite pay-TV services were unlikely prior to 2011. Russian operator RSCC was another company poised to grow, with eight satellites scheduled to launch by the end of 2013. Overall, including the January 2010 launch of K+ in Vietnam, there were 31 platforms operating in Asia, enabling that market to grow an impressive 35 percent in 2009.

North America, Europe, and Asia-Pacific dominated the global market for mobile satellite TV in 2009. Their growth was driven by the conversion of television signals to digital formats and free Wi-Fi technologies such as MediaFLO and DVB-H. The market was expected to benefit from developing countries including Brazil, China, and India. Leading companies in the global satellite-based mobile TV were Alcatel-Lucent, AT&T, DiBcom, DISH Network Corporation, KVH Industries Inc., Nagravision SA, and RaySat Inc.

In early 2010 SES Astra announced that, for the first time, the number of satellite TV homes had overtaken cable homes in Europe, reaching 77 million households (6 million more than cable). Both SES and Entelsat also were gearing up for 3D-HDTV, Entelsat already dedicating an all-3D channel on Eurobird 9A. It already had

broadcast live coverage of a Six Nations rugby match between France and England in 3D to 30 cinemas in France.

Satellites orbit the globe and beam programming signals heedless of national borders. Among U.S. DBS providers, DirecTV has been by far the most active in pursuing joint ventures and other opportunities abroad, establishing a significant foothold, especially in Latin American markets.

Canada, Mexico, and some South American countries hold some of the orbital slots over the Western Hemisphere that could service the United States. If any of these choose to auction off transponder rights, U.S. companies can bid for them. Likewise, U.S. companies can potentially service other markets in the Americas from their own slots. Nations may attempt to control the industry by regulating the sale of decoders. In 1998 Argentina temporarily halted DirecTV from competing in its market while it tried to get its own system in place.

In general, the European DBS market is well served by companies such as the Luxembourg-based Sociét&eacute Européenne des Satellites S.A. (SES), which operates ASTRA, and British Sky Broadcasting (BSkyB). Thus, Europe does not represent a particularly attractive market for U.S. DBS firms. In 2005 satellite providers added some 2 million subscribers in Europe, despite competition from emerging IPTV players and established cable providers. Of these new customers, some 25 percent were attributed to Sky Italia, the second-leading European provider (behind BSkyB) with a total of 3.6 million total subscribers.

RESEARCH AND TECHNOLOGY

In early 2010 the United States and Europe launched SES Astra Satellite TV Company's 3D demo channel. Europe used the 23.5 E orbital position on the Astra satellite television broadcast, hosted by the German Cable Operators Association (ANGA) in Cologne. In the United Kingdom, BSkyB has been using Astra 2A Satellite (28.2 E) to transmit kyHD 3D TV there and in Ireland.

DBS was born of advanced compression schemes allowing multiple streams of programming along with the ability to control information per transponder frequency. Still, one technological hurdle was to mitigate the trade-off between picture quality and the number of channels offered, since to date the heavy compression necessary to deliver a large number of channels can result in picture softness. Squeezing down the signal even more would be an advantage, but providers also want to eliminate the occasional blocky digital compression artifacts that some viewers find distracting. Moreover, both DirecTV and EchoStar began to offer a handful of HDTV channels, but were reined in somewhat by the massive compression required to deliver these signals. In the long run, this represents a significant hurdle for the DBS industry because it risks running out of bandwidth, particularly once local broadcasts begin to flood HDTV.

One answer to bandwidth limits is to adopt new spectrum. One area under development is known as multichannel video distribution and data service (MVDDS), a new technology that opens significant unchartered bandwidth for satellite service providers. MVDDS in fact does not require satellite dishes, but rather resembles a cellular phone network using a system of terrestrial towers. In 2004 the FCC auctioned a series of MVDDS licenses for the entire country, and the buyers included affiliates of EchoStar and Rainbow DBS (Cablevision). At the time, the systems were only starting to be conceived, but industry watchers speculated that MVDDS would offer a ready outlet for local-into-local broadcasts alongside national programming via DBS.

Besides improving compression, other areas of technological development include higher power transponders that allow more information to pass through existing bandwidth because less error-correcting coding is required. Signal polarization, controlling the orientation of the electromagnetic wave transmissions, is used to isolate adjacent transponder slots and allow more of them within a fixed-frequency spectrum. Statistical multiplexing maximizes the use of existing bandwidth by assigning it upon demand depending on the information density of a particular program being carried by a channel at a given time.

Beyond just television delivery, the drive toward telecommunications integration was a prime area of research and competition in the first decade of the 2000s. EchoStar introduced a new satellite dish in 2001, integrating two-way satellite Internet and television service developed through its partnership with StarBand Communications Inc. and Microsoft Corp. The dish can receive signals from three separate satellites simultaneously, allowing for interactive Internet capability, as well as satellite television. More companies engaged in such alliances throughout the decade, bundling bundle video, voice, and high-speed Internet access for residential phone customers. This bundling of services, according to many analysts, which followed the introduction of cable-based Internet access and telephone service, heralds the next stage in the battle between cable companies and the DBS industry.

DISH Network announced a new technology in 2008 that would allow apartment dwellers easier access to satellite TV. Such individuals face challenges in gaining access due to restrictions on mounting satellite dishes on property they do not own. With DISH's "fiber-to-the-home"

technology, programming is delivered via satellite to a base system that can support up to 128 subscribers in a multiple unit building; the signals are then sent to individual apartments through fiber lines. The company also planned research into mobile broadcast technology, which would allow delivery of TV service to handheld devices. DirecTV already offered such services, allowing the broadcast of certain programs on laptop computers and mobile phones.

BIBLIOGRAPHY

Coonan, Clifford. "Satellite TV Catching On in Asia." *Daily Variety,* 11 April 2006.

"DirecTV Holdings LLC—Amended Annual Report." DirecTV Holdings LLC, 18 August 2010. Available from http://apps.shareholder.com/.

"DirecTV Q1 Earnings Rise 10% on HD Sub Growth." *TelevisionWeek,* 12 May 2008.

"Dish Network, Bring Back Voom!" TV Predictions, 15 May 2008. Available from http://www.tvpredictions.com/dishvoom051508.htm.

"Dish Network News." DISH Network Corp., 18 August 2010. Available from http://www.dishnetwork.com/news/acsi/aspx.

El Bouzegaoui, Mounia, and Dimitri Buchs. "Dynamic Growth of Satellite Pay-TV Market in Asia." *APSCC Quarterly Newsletter,* April 2010.

"Frost & Sullivan Sees Increased Revenue in Mobile Satellite TV Markets." *Wireless News,* 13 May 2008.

"Global Mobile Satellite TV Market to Reach 11000000000 to 2015, According to a New Report by Global Industry Analysts, Inc." *Business Wire,* 22 February 2010. Available from http://www.coercs.com/2010/09/14/global-mobile-satellite-tv-market-to-reach-11000000000-to-2015-according-to-a-new-report-by-global-industry-analysts-inc/.

"HDTV Content Options In United States Growing." *Satellite News,* 17 April 2006.

Moran, Andrew. "Number of Subscribers to Cable, Satellite TV Services Fall in Q2." *DigitalJournal,* 26 August 2010.

Moss, Linda. "DirecTV Is Outpacing Dish." *Multichannel News,* 19 May 2008.

Richgels, Jeff. "New Technology to Help DISH Network Serve Apartments." *The Capital Times,* 1 May 2008.

Salzman, Avi. "Hanging Up on Early-Exit Fees." *Business Week Online,* 6 June 2008. Available from www.businessweek.com.

"SIA...A Positive Orbit For Satellite Industry Revenues." *SatNews Daily,* 8 June 2010.

Smith, Jeff. "Dish Comes Back Fighting." *Rocky Mountain News,* 15 May 2008.

Szalai, Georg. "Dissatisfaction Guaranteed: Consumer Survey Gives Cable, Satellite TV Firms Rotten Grades." *Hollywood Reporter,* 21 May 2008.

"The Sky's the Limit." Digital TV Europe, 25 May 2010. Available from http://www.digitaltveurope.net/feature/25_may_10/the_skys_the_limit.

Waldman, Allison J. "Moguls Take an Expansionist View." *TelevisionWeek,* 24 September 2007.

DISTANCE LEARNING

———— ■ ————

SIC CODE(S)

3571

7812

7999

INDUSTRY SNAPSHOT

Whether knowledge seekers are around the corner or around the world, distance learning offers a viable alternative to traditional learning methods. Also known as distance education, this approach features a wide array of training formats including print, audio, video, satellite, and Internet-based courses. These may be combined in creative ways using prerecorded or interactive technology.

Distance learning involves the provision of educational programs to students who are not located on a school's physical campus. This broad definition allows for a diverse group of students to participate in options that are synchronous (classes that take place at specific times only) or asynchronous (classes that occur at flexible times).

Distance learning makes it possible for people with limited time or local options to efficiently achieve their goals. Still others are taking advantage of technology applications to update their skills for the workplace. The training site might be a satellite classroom, boardroom, community center, or home.

In early 2009, U.S. President Barack Obama outlined his plan for strengthening the nation's competitiveness by reasserting prominence in educational achievement. To that end, he established a goal of increasing the number of U.S. college graduates to 55 percent by 2025. With rising fuel costs and a slowly recovering economy,

alternative and distance education will play a large role in achieving that objective.

ORGANIZATION AND STRUCTURE

Views regarding the value of distance learning have changed for the better. According to the United States Distance Learning Association (USDLA), corporate America was one of the principal users of distance learning, using such methods for every aspect of internal and external training. Because of this, the types of courses available in most college catalogs are frequently available through distance learning programs. Exceptions include some areas of advanced study and training requiring lab work or performance.

Distance learning providers include traditional colleges, universities, community colleges, technical schools, vocational schools, high schools, specialized companies, and online resources. In fact, by the early years of the first decade of the twenty-first century, online courses, also known as e-learning, provided the biggest area for growth.

The fees for distance learning courses are typically comparable to those for other educational/training alternatives. Some institutions require technology fees. Many students take classes part-time while working to pay remaining related costs not covered by financial aid or their employers.

The Distance Education and Training Council (DETC) receives many calls about the accreditation status of distance learning institutions. DETC offers the following definition of accreditation: "Distance Education accreditation is certification by a recognized body that a distance education institution has voluntarily undergone a comprehensive study and peer evaluation that has demonstrated that the institution does in fact meet the established standards." Evaluation involves making sure an institution performs the function it claims, such as setting educational goals for students, offering formal and organized learning experiences/services customized for students, and showing proof that learning experiences are beneficial for students and graduates. The process gives public recognition to institutions meeting certain standards.

U.S. legislators' quest to ensure the freedom of distance education resulted in a new law. On October 10, 2001, the Internet Equity and Education Act, H.R. 1992, was passed with a strong bipartisan vote of 354-70. Representative Johnny Isakson, who sponsored H.R. 1992, said that community leaders and legislators had a responsibility to ensure that new technologies were enhancements, not hindrances, in meeting educational challenges with innovative solutions.

Highly debated in 2003, The College Affordability in Higher Education Act sought to create a new "College Affordability Experimentation Site" designation. This would provide institutions with the freedom to expand distance education programs without violating federal laws. One prohibitive law was the "50 Percent Rule" requiring 50 percent of student instruction to occur in real versus virtual classrooms. Opposition came from the American Council on Education, which denounced the proposal due to tuition limitations.

The Council for Higher Education Web site, www.chea.org, provides links to regional and professional accreditation agencies, as well as government relations updates.

BACKGROUND AND DEVELOPMENT

There was a time when distance learning required a lot of waiting by the mailbox and trips to the post office. Correspondence courses were print-based and did not offer many opportunities to interact with instructors or fellow students.

Online Learning recalled that a 1964 essay, entitled "The Banishment of Paperwork," contained a prediction by Arthur L. Samuel of IBM's Watson Research Center that "all computers would be connected to a vast database of knowledge, from which 'it will be entirely possible to obtain an education at home, via one's own personal computer.'"

In the May 2002 issue of *Online Learning*, Patti Shank discussed reasons why what happened fell short of making the vision a reality, explaining that many online courses were little more than blocks of text that had been posted online. Shank described an evaluation continuum created by Rod Sims, associate professor of instructional technology at Australia's Deakin University. Sims evaluated self-paced e-learning in terms of interaction. At the lowest end was "object interactivity" (clicking on something to get a response), and at the highest end was "contextual interactivity" (content similar to the learner's work environment). Although most courses ranked low on the Sims continuum, there were some notable exceptions.

In the business world's pre-distance learning period, business people attended live training sessions and referenced materials organized in three-ring binders. There was minimal flexibility in scheduling, even though attendance was often mandatory.

"Our training system was paper-based and decentralized, so we spent a lot of time and money duplicating and managing classes for our employees," Gundersen Lutheran's Manager of HRIS Jay Fernandez said, according to *Health Management Technology*. "If we had had Web-based education, then employees could leapfrog over material they already knew." Results showed that during the first six months of using learning management system (LMS) software called Pathlore to deliver OSHA courses online, the La Crosse, Wisconsin-based healthcare network saved $700,000 in employees' time, plus instructors' fees and travel costs.

Technology had greatly improved distance learning by the early years of the first decade of the 2000s, providing the business community with innovative learning solutions. In addition to meeting corporate e-learning needs, technologies such as online conferencing provided additional benefits, as they also could be used for general business purposes.

Several industry insiders cited blended learning as being a "hot trend" with great potential. This winning combination united the best of e-learning and classroom courses, such as flexibility and face-to-face interaction. Results thus far have been excellent, including enhanced knowledge acquisition and higher student retention. At the same time, many experts believed the success of distance learning was greatly impacted by whether expectations were realized by learners and their level of computer expertise.

In March 2005, the National Center for Education Statistics (NCES) released what it called the first federal study of distance learning among K–12 schools. The study found that during the 2002–2003 school year, approximately 36 percent of the nation's 15,000 U.S. public school districts had students enrolled in distance education classes. While the majority of these (76 percent) were high school students, the study found that distance learning also was used by middle school (7 percent) and elementary school (2 percent) students.

Distance education was especially valuable to high school students in remote or rural areas. Some 43 percent of U.S. public schools are located in rural communities, which often struggle to attract teachers. The NCES study found that 46 percent of rural school districts had students enrolled in distance learning. This rate was much lower in suburban districts (28 percent) and urban districts (23 percent).

Through distance learning, students in these areas are able to pursue courses, especially those of an advanced nature, that otherwise would not be available to them. During the middle of the first decade of the 2000s, states such as Oklahoma, Minnesota, North Carolina, Nebraska, and West Virginia shared teachers to provide courses in subjects such as advanced mathematics and physics and to offer virtual field trips.

In addition to benefiting rural students, distance education also has been a blessing to rural teachers and administrators. In rural districts, educators are able to pursue much-needed continuing education and meet certification standards mandated by the No Child Left Behind Act. In addition, teachers also can pursue advanced degrees in the subjects they teach. Finally, distance education technology has been used by some rural school districts to enable discussions between educators and professionals, including school psychologists.

On the post-secondary front, colleges and universities continued to embrace distance learning. In addition to making it possible for them to offer enrollment to more students than their existing physical campuses could accommodate, distance learning enabled institutions of higher learning to literally save millions of dollars by avoiding costly physical expansion projects.

In its October 18, 2004, issue, *U.S. News & World Report* revealed that the corporate sector also was saving considerable money from distance learning during the middle of the first decade of the 2000s. For example, IBM education head Sean Rush attributed annual savings in the amount of $350 million to putting courses online. The publication explained, "From IBM to the Mayo Clinic to Bay Area Rapid Transit in San Francisco, organizations that need to teach lots of workers quickly about new products or new insurance regulations—or even how to evacuate in a terrorist attack—have rushed to replace expensive and disruptive class time with 'just in time' instruction at the employee's desk."

While there were many advantages to distance learning, the industry was not without its challenges. At the high school level, some educators were concerned about how instructor workloads are calculated for distance learning courses in comparison to traditional classroom workloads. Others feared that distance learning would remove the element of social interaction from education, compromise the quality of instruction, or become an excuse for schools to rid themselves of problematic or challenging students.

On more than one level, funding was another issue. Of concern to school administrators was the prospect of losing per-pupil funding if students pursuing courses from other school districts were not counted as being enrolled in their home district. In addition, course development and equipment costs were frequently cited as roadblocks to implementing distance learning programs, especially in cash-strapped school districts.

An important development occurred in 2006 when Congress revoked the so-called 50-percent rule, which excluded institutions that offered more than half of their courses at a distance, or that had more than half of their students enrolled at a distance, from receiving Title IV student aid. While some distance education programs already had special exemptions to the 50 percent rule, this change came as good news to most industry players. Even so, by early 2007 only a few colleges had taken advantage of it. Instead, most were treading cautiously until they were familiar with eligibility requirements, according to the Distance Education Training Council.

PIONEERS IN THE FIELD

Three institutions that created distance learning blueprints adapted by others were the University of Southern California (USC) School of Engineering's Distance Education Network (DEN), Capella University, and The University of Phoenix.

The Distance Education Network (DEN) was founded in 1972 as a means of offering USC School of Engineering instructional content off-campus. By mid-2003, some 800 students were pursuing advanced degrees through DEN nationwide. Companies such as Boeing, General Dynamics, Motorola, and NASA offered tuition reimbursement to employees enrolled in this program. Through the use of Webcasting technology, DEN offered some 20 different graduate degrees to full-time working engineers via distance learning.

Since 1993, Capella has been a fully online academic accredited institution serving adult learners and employers. Educating more than 6,000 learners across the United States and internationally, it uses the Internet to remove institutional and logistical barriers. Central to Capella's approach is the high degree of online interaction between expert faculty, achievement-oriented learners, and university staff. Capella Chancellor and Founder Stephen Shank has testified before Congress on behalf of the distance learning community.

The University of Phoenix was among the first accredited universities to provide college degree programs via the Internet. Unlike other programs, 100 percent of the curriculum can be completed via the Internet, including registration and administration services.

Distance learning also was being utilized in a growing number of U.S. high schools, as well as in middle and elementary schools. In fact, by 2007 full-fledged K-12 programs and virtual high schools were operating in several states. In October of 2006, University of Phoenix parent The Apollo Group acquired Insight Schools, a Portland, Oregon-based company operating a public online high school with 600 students in Washington State.

Another example is the Pennsylvania Distance Learning Electronic Academy (PDELA). A publicly-funded charter school for K-12 students, its program, which included virtual classroom experiences, was an alternative instruction option that was especially targeted at highly motivated students who were easily bored with traditional classroom instruction. The state provided participants with the equipment and Internet connection required for participation, as well as access to databases containing electronic articles, books, and some 10,000 online videos. In addition to field trips, students were allowed to partake in sports and music programs at their nearest public school location.

Looking ahead, some industry observers expected considerable growth within the distance learning industry. In its November/December 2004 issue, *Futurist* revealed that according to William E. Halal, 30 percent of training programs would be delivered via distance learning by 2008. The publication also forecast that 30 percent of college courses would be delivered in this manner by 2014.

CURRENT CONDITIONS

As the number of Internet-connected homes continues to grow and broadband connections become commonplace, online distance learning continues to dominate the market for alternative adult education. Statistics in *Staying the Course: Online Education in the United States, 2008* indicate that the number of online students in higher education had more than doubled in the previous five years, representing a compound annual growth rate of 19.7 percent (the overall higher education student body grew at an annual rate of 1.6 percent during the same period). The number of online students for the 2007-2008 academic year was estimated at 3.94 million.

Not only postsecondary education, but also basic and remedial education needs through distance learning is expected to grow as well. The U.S. Department of Labor's Bureau of Labor Statistics' *Occupational Outlook Handbook* (2008–2009 Edition) noted that for the 2007-2008 school year (October 2007), approximately 3.3 million civilian noninstitutionalized 16- through 24-year-olds had not earned a high school diploma or alternative

credential, and were not enrolled in high school for that school year. Employment prospects for adult literacy, remedial education, and GED teaching was expected to grow 14 percent by 2016, creating a need for another 11,000 instructors.

INDUSTRY LEADERS

Apollo Group of Phoenix, Arizona operates four subsidiaries that provide ongoing education for working adults: the University of Phoenix/University of Phoenix Online, the Institute for Professional Development, the College for Financial Planning, and Western International University. The company has established itself as a leading provider of higher education programs for working adults by focusing on servicing the needs of the working adult. Its University of Phoenix is the largest private university in the United States. The firm operates 160 sites and serves more than 300,000 students. Apollo reported a net revenue for the fiscal year ended August 31, 2009 of $4 billion, a 26.5 percent increase over fiscal 2008. Contributing to this increase was a 20.8 percent increase in University of Phoenix's average Degreed Enrollment for fiscal 2009 as compared with fiscal 2008. The University of Phoenix granted 55,400 Associates degrees, 31,700 Bachelors, 14,200 Masters, and 700 Doctorate degrees in its fiscal 2009 year alone.

Mountain View, California-based Docent was a leading provider of integrated software solutions tailored to address the unique requirements of vertical markets including government, life sciences, energy, high-tech, telecommunications, financial services, retail, and manufacturing. Docent customers included Cingular Wireless, Harley-Davidson, Wachovia Corp., Lucent Technologies, Kelly Services, and Eaton Corp. Docent maintained offices throughout the United States, Europe, and the Asia-Pacific.

WORKFORCE

In a January 2002 *Journal of European Industrial Training* article, Robert W. Taylor recognized that instructors face steep learning curves with the advent of Internet-based education. Conversations with experts, including IBM Mindspan Solutions Director of Strategy and Ventures Margaret Driscoll, revealed that changes in the training and development field were calling for workers with new skills. These included knowledge of and proficiency in adult learning principles, instructional design, and cognitive psychology. In addition, educators also required specialized skills such as content authoring, videography, project management, and database design.

In the same article, Willie Horton, president of William Horton Consulting, pointed out that online communication requires different skills than those required of traditional educators. More than being a good speaker or writer, those designing distance education courses must have the ability to put complex information in terms that are easy to understand. In addition, it was becoming more commonplace for educators to become versed in technical e-learning standards, including metadata and extensible markup language (XML).

AMERICA AND THE WORLD

It is clear from the body of literature published by sources around the world that distance learning is considered to be a convenient option by many and a necessity by others.

In mid-2006, *Africa News Service* reported that Nigeria's National Universities Commission had began collaborating with the state of Georgia in the United States in areas of research and capacity expansion in regard to distance education. Nigeria had some 30,000 students participating in distance education programs, and the country was looking to expand its offerings. In terms of enrollment, the University Abuja led with 15,000 students. The remainder was divided between universities in Ibadan and Lagos.

China's Ministry of Education had previously launched a national initiative called the National Program for Invigorating Education Towards the 21st Century. The Chinese Minister of Education Zhou Ji later stated that China was promoting its compulsory nine-year education program in rural areas of the country, some eight percent of which did not have access to the program. China continues to be a lucrative market for alternative adult education. In 2008, China Distance Education Holdings became the first Chinese initial public offering (IPO) at the NYSE Arca. By 2009, it had reported a 48.4 percent increase in income with revenues of $17.6 million for 2008, and enrollments exceeding 743,000 (up 47 percent). The Chinese market for professional education and examination training was projected to reach 32.8 billion yuan (about US$5 billion) in 2010.

According to an *Educational Technology* article by Insung Jung, South Korea's Presidential Commission on Education Reform defined the twenty-first century Korean Education System as an "Edutopia" in which every citizen has easy access to government-sponsored education at any place or time throughout their lifetime. Distance learning was considered to be an important tool for realizing this vision.

RESEARCH AND TECHNOLOGY

According to the January 5, 2007, edition of the *Chronicle of Higher Education* a study released by Vault Inc. in December found that 55 percent of managers gave preference to candidates with traditional degrees, while 41 percent indicated that they would consider online and traditional degrees equally. Bias against online

degrees was strongest among managers unfamiliar with such programs, and in cases where candidates held degrees from programs that were offered exclusively online, as opposed to degrees from traditional universities that offered some courses or degrees via distance education.

The same *Chronicle of Higher Education* article summarized the results of a study conducted by Florida State University Associate Professor Jonathan Adams, which sought to determine whether, in the case of two equally qualified candidates, employers would choose someone with an online degree or a traditional one. Of 269 respondents, 96 percent indicated they would choose the traditionally degreed candidate. The results of these studies indicate that distance education still had hurdles to overcome in terms of conveying an image of quality comparable to traditional degree programs.

The *Chronicle of Higher Education* has summarized findings from the non-profit Alliance for Higher Education Competitiveness in its report entitled *Achieving Success in Internet-Supported Learning in Higher Education.* The alliance found that those distance education programs offering complete degrees, as opposed to only a few courses, were the most successful. This was attributed to complete degree programs garnering a greater degree of institutional support for both online students and faculty.

A study featured in the *Journal of Education for Business* examined barriers to successfully delivering distance learning courses and how to overcome them. The study involved 81 business professors who taught distance learning at 61 U.S. business schools. Researchers summarized findings indicating that the professors primarily used self-training for the design and delivery of online courses. They believed that the technology was not sufficiently reliable and that the greatest benefit of distance learning was flexibility for students. In addition, the professors perceived a student-centered teaching approach as being necessary for successful distance education courses.

Technology helps distance learning evolve and reach more learners with innovative applications. Satellite is but one example. A number of distinctive applications have been developed involving one-way and two-way satellite carriers, equipment manufacturers, and distance learning applications providers.

BIBLIOGRAPHY

2004 Distance Education Survey. A Report on Course Structure and Educational Services in Distance Education and Training Council Member Institutions. Washington, D.C.: Distance Education and Training Council, 2004.

"AMD Chips at heart of China Long-Distance Education Project." *Electronic News,* 17 January 2005.

Byassee, Jason. "Virtual Seminary." *Christian Century,* 22 February 2005.

Capella IPO Makes the Grade with Investors: Rather than Capital, Online University Seeks Visibility." *Saint Paul Pioneer Press,* 11 November 2006.

Careless, James. "Pennsylvania Supports Home Schooling with Distance Learning." *Government Video,* 1 December 2006.

Carnevale, Dan. "Employers Often Distrust Online Degrees." *Chronicle of Higher Education,* 5 January 2007.

———. "Offering Entire Degrees Online Is One Key to Sucess Distance Education, Survey Finds." *Chronicle of Higher Education,* 4 February 2005.

"ChinaCast Education Corporation Enters English Training Market in China." *PrimeZone Media Network,* 30 April 2007.

China Distance Education Holdings Ltd. Available from http://www.cdledu.com/ versions/pdf/PRESS_RELEASE_final_08_11_17_clean.pdf.

"Chinese Minister of Education Vows to Promote Rural Education." *Business CustomWire,* 27 January 2005.

"Danes Best at Lifelong Learning: Report." *Xinhua,* 16 November 2004.

Devry Inc. Available from http://www.forbes.com/feeds/ap/2009/08/13/ap6777268.html.

"Distance Education Growing in Popularity." *Business CustomWire,* 2 March 2005.

"E-learning Replaces Classroom: Wisconsin Healthcare Network Uses LMS to Educate Staff and Track Federally Mandated Training." *Health Management Technology,* April 2003.

Field, Kelly, and Dan Carnevale. "End of Ban on Federal Student Aid for Most Online Institutions Provokes Few Changes." *Chronicle of Higher Education,* 19 January 2007.

"Frequently Asked Questions." Distance Education and Training Council, 26 March 2007. Available from http://www.detc.org/frequentlyQust.html.

June, Audrey Williams. "Apollo Group Buys Online High School." *Chronicle of Higher Education,* 26 January 2007.

Jung, Insung. "Online Education for Adult Learners in South Korea." *Educational Technology,* May-June 2003.

Kingsbury, Alex. "Remote Access." *U.S. News & World Report,* 18 October 2004.

Kopf, David. "E-Learning Market to Hit $56B By 2010." *T.H.E. Journal,* 30 July 2007.

McGrath, Anne. "Bricks & Clicks." *U.S. News & World Report,* 18 October 2004.

Mupinga, Davison M. "Distance Education in High Schools. Benefits, Challenges, and Suggestions." *The Clearing House,* January/February 2005.

"Nigeria, US Collaborate on Distance Education." *Africa News Service,* 11 July 2006.

"Outlook 2005." *Futurist,* November/December 2004.

Perreault, Heidi, et al. "Overcoming Barriers to Successful Delivery of Distance-Learning Courses." *Journal of Education for Business,* July-August 2002.

"Research Info. & Statistics." Distance Learning Association, 28 March 2005. Available, from http://www.usdla.org/html/aboutUS/researchInfo.htm.

Shank, Patti. "No More Yawns: The Majority of Self-Paced Learning May Be Boring, but There's a Lot to Be Learned from the Exceptions." *Online Learning,* May 2002.

Sims, David. "Teleconferencing and Distance Learning: An Inside Look." *Customer Interaction Solutions,* January 2007.

Vaishali, Honawar. "Education Department Tracks Growth in Distance Learning." *Education Week,* 9 March 2005.

E-COMMERCE: BUSINESS TO BUSINESS

SIC CODE(S)

7371

7372

7379

INDUSTRY SNAPSHOT

Following the dot-com fallout of the late 1990s and early 2000s, a smaller core of key business-to-business (B2B) e-commerce players remained in such major industries as retail, automotive, chemicals, technology, insurance, and metals.By the late years of the first decade, it was abundantly clear that B2B e-commerce continued to be an important business tool for both large companies and small businesses. It also remained a powerful economic force.

Business-to-business (B2B) e-commerce offers a range of practical benefits for companies, including increased efficiency, improved responsiveness to market shifts, reduced costs, and the maximization of profits. Such benefits are gleaned in several ways. For one, e-commerce can rid a company of any number of stages of manual order placement and tracking. Another is the ability to reach new suppliers, or at least old ones in new ways, so that the cost of merchandise is lower than what would have been paid otherwise. If these benefits seem abstract, consider that some large firms that only do a moderate amount of e-commerce with their suppliers have saved millions of dollars, and by some estimates, a few have already saved billions over time.

ORGANIZATION AND STRUCTURE

Business-to-business (B2B) e-commerce encompasses a curious mix of business models and activities. For purposes of this discussion, there are four main categories of B2B activities: those who conduct some aspect of their normal line of work, whether it's manufacturing sprockets or providing astrological management consulting services, over the Internet; online retail sites that cater primarily or exclusively to business clientele, such as office supply portals; business exchanges or electronic marketplaces that provide a forum and tools to facilitate transactions among a range of participant companies; and, serving in sort of a meta-B2B role, e-commerce software and services providers, which provide systems that enable other firms to engage in one of the other forms of B2B e-commerce.

General E-Commerce The "everything else" category, general B2B e-commerce, is really not an industry unto itself so much as it is a new territory being settled by a host of different industries. In effect, it's merely an extension of those industries, often well established, into a new medium of transactions. What might be more interesting to consider is how they go about setting up their e-commerce. To the extent they buy software or use the services of e-commerce-oriented providers, they are providing revenues to e-commerce firms. Otherwise they're simply conducting their usual line of business in a new way.

This is not to say what these firms do or don't do isn't important for the more narrowly defined B2B e-commerce industry. Quite the opposite, the route these firms take toward enabling electronic transactions has a dramatic effect on the fortunes of firms whose business it is to facilitate e-commerce. In other words, if ordinary firms go it alone and develop their own e-commerce systems without using the software and services of specialists, it will diminish opportunities for specialist firms. On the other hand, if ordinary businesses use e-marketplaces and e-commerce software packages extensively, it will mean tremendous growth for firms specializing in e-commerce products and services.

Retail B2B Retail sites serving the business market are fairly easy to recognize and understand. They're often the online equivalents of the real-life storefronts providing similar products. In some cases, they're directly related, as is staples.com to the online offerings of office supply giant Staples Inc. Likewise, there are scores of Internet-only merchants that focus on various needs of businesses large or small, general or specific.

Exchanges and E-Marketplaces Electronic exchanges and marketplaces all share one goal: to bring together companies that are buying and selling some type of product or service. Exactly how they do it varies considerably.

Some e-marketplaces—for instance, VerticalNet—focus on establishing an online community that serves particular interests, such as food ingredients. They develop extensive Internet content centered on that business with the aim of bringing people in the industry back regularly even if they're not coming to make a purchase. In addition, of course, they also provide software tools that allow firms to hold auctions, place orders, submit bids, and manage other aspects of the purchasing process.

B2B exchanges take a more utilitarian approach. They provide an Internet-based forum and a mechanism for conducting online transactions, but don't attempt to make their sites destinations in their own right.

Most exchange venues have some reasonably well-defined focus, be it chemicals or metals or public utilities. These are commonly known as vertical segments or industries. Certain exchanges also focus on specific types of transactions, such as eliminating excess inventory, as opposed to general procurement activities.

Exchanges and marketplaces earn money in different ways. Some charge a per-transaction surcharge, occasionally as high as 20 percent of the selling price, for the privilege of using their system. However, this practice hasn't been received well and there's some evidence that it has led to a loss of business for such services. Sellers who submit bids on the exchange are sometimes also charged a transaction fee. Other exchanges levy some type of annual fee or membership fee. Still others are joint ventures run by the companies that use them.

E-Commerce Software and Services One of the fastest growing and closely watched segments of e-commerce, software and service providers provide technical infrastructure for other firms' electronic endeavors. For example, vendors like Ariba develop software packages with predetermined functions that companies are likely to

want for conducting business online. These packages are then customized for individual clients to fit their particular needs, giving them the look and functions that are appropriate for what the client does.

BACKGROUND AND DEVELOPMENT

Electronic commerce between businesses in the modern sense has its roots in a variety of earlier practices. One of the most important precursors was the development of electronic data interchange (EDI) systems, a breakthrough championed in the 1980s.

Using EDI, which was often complex and expensive to implement, two or more businesses would create an interface between their respective inventory and procurement systems. The network link would then be used to place orders for new supplies. In the more advanced EDI systems, the process would be highly automated so that when the customer's inventory dropped below a certain threshold, the system would automatically order an appropriate amount of new stock. For example, if a grocery store's inventory of paper towels fell below a certain level, the system might generate an order for 12 new cases of paper towels on a wholesaler's or manufacturer's system. The system might also factor in other stock depletion concerns such as seasonal variation.

In practice, however, things were never quite so easy on a large scale. A big company gets its supplies from myriad vendors, so the task of integrating with everyone could quickly become daunting. Added to the challenge was the multitude of different software packages and data standards used by different firms in the supply chain. And this is to say nothing of the features needed from the EDI application, which differed by company.

All this spelled only limited success for EDI. Enterprises, who implemented it successfully and swore by it, but it certainly didn't fill everyone's needs and rarely even reached medium and small companies. As the Internet gained commercial viability, procurement visionaries began pondering—and some began implementing—Internet-based commerce. One thrust of this activity was to adapt the old EDI model to an Internet-based system, which promised to be cheaper and faster to deploy than home-grown software and networking. However, a more profound vision was that of using the Internet to completely revamp and simplify the business purchasing process.

Some important first attempts at Internet-based commerce between businesses began quietly in 1995 and 1996, when much attention was being paid to consumer applications and setting up business "brochure" sites: Web pages that described companies and their marketing messages but didn't allow for any kinds of transactions online. Meanwhile, fledgling companies like FreeMarkets, Inc., and

VerticalNet, Inc., both founded in 1995, were charting new territory by trying to harness the vast public network to bring together disparate buyers and sellers into an efficient online exchange of goods, services, and information.

By 1997, billions of business-to-business (B2B) dollars were flowing through the Internet. The majority of the activity then was concentrated in a handful of sites of very large companies like Cisco Systems Inc. that had seized on the Internet as an efficient conduit through which to conduct their already thriving businesses.

Needless to say, B2B transactions of all types continued growing at a torrid pace, reaching $43 billion in 1998 according to an estimate by Forrester Research. Again, much of the dollar value was driven by relatively few companies—the Ciscos, Dells, and Intels of the world.

By this time, industry watchers also grew increasingly enamored with B2B exchanges, which were expanding frantically and, ever important in the Internet economy, issuing public stock. The next year saw much of the same, with massive stock buildups and soaring revenue projections bringing legions of new entrants into the business. E-commerce exchanges and so-called online vertical industries sprang up left and right, backed by venture capitalists, Fortune 500 companies, and existing players in the B2B arena.

By early 2000, however, things began looking a little dicey for smaller start-ups. The B2B exchanges, in particular, were doing paltry business compared to earlier growth projections and, for the publicly traded ones, compared to their stock valuations. As the general stock market reeled from sharp downturns in the spring of 2000, cash for smaller B2B operations dried up rapidly. Venture capital firms pulled back and stopped giving new money, public investors sold in droves. Within months, the shares of B2B high fliers like Commerce One and VerticalNet lost 75 percent and even 90 percent of their value. For companies throughout the technology sector, and especially the Internet sector, a shakeout was under way.

The damage to Internet companies was considerable. By one estimate, over 200 Internet businesses of all types had failed in 2000 and another tally found 17 e-marketplaces shuttered. Layoffs abounded, and segments of the business had clearly not lived up to their optimistic growth predictions. For example, one jubilant estimate in 1999 had forecast 10,000 online B2B commerce sites in 2000, whereas the final tally peaked closer to 1,500 and then dropped.

PIONEERS IN THE FIELD

In such a young business, it's of little surprise that two of its trailblazers are still intimately involved in the industry. Mark B. Hoffman, CEO and chairman of Commerce One, and Keith Krach, his counterpart in both positions at Ariba, both have left an indelible mark on business-to-business commerce over the Internet.

Hoffman was already prominent in the software world when he founded Commerce One in 1997. More than a decade earlier, he co-founded Sybase, Inc., an influential maker of relational database software. After being forced out of Sybase in 1996 amid declining revenues and rising losses, Hoffman, an ex-Army officer, quickly took an interest in an obscure, closely-held electronic cataloging business. He saw in it potential to revolutionize the supply chain by using software and the Internet to connect buyers and sellers in a highly efficient marketplace. His venture, which originally concentrated on the vertical niche of selling business supplies, quickly obtained venture funding and began marketing a more generalized Internet procurement product in 1998. In another year, Commerce One, by that time publicly traded, had become a darling of Wall Street and grew its sales tenfold. Hoffman, who was separately involved in the publicly traded startup Intraware, remained at the helm during a turbulent 2000, when sales rocketed more than tenfold again.

Keith Krach also had a noteworthy career before his e-commerce venture. With academic credentials in engineering and management, Krach had a successful tenure at General Motors, where he was something of a boy wonder. Later, he plied both of his talents at a software firm that sold innovative design automation applications. In 1996, Krach teamed up with several other entrepreneurs from engineering and venture funding backgrounds to form Ariba Inc. with the vision of using Internet software to automate procurement. The firm swiftly developed a pedigreed clientele of Fortune 100 companies, thanks in part to Krach's contacts and stature, and by 1999 became another stock market favorite following its public offering.

Following the slowdown between 2000 and 2002, B2B e-commerce initiatives were expected to return to a growth rate, and this time to a more broadly based growth. One key difference in demand, according to the October 2002 issue of *E-commerce Times,* was that "companies now tackle technology improvements in much smaller increments than in bygone days. By dividing implementation into smaller-scale projects, companies clearly are seeking to deflect the risks of new investments in technology. For vendors, that means big-ticket contracts will be few and far between."

Some B2B failures were perhaps victims of their own marketing myths. Intoxicated by lofty market projections and by the popular folklore that on the Internet, startup companies can easily unseat entrenched corporations, executives at B2B ventures—and not a small number of their equity investors—plunged forth into the market with ill-defined products, unreal pricing structures, and inadequate buy-ins from the big customers that could make or break their ventures.

Mid-sized companies did not take to B2B exchanges quickly. In addition, packages from leading software vendors did not always synch with the products that many exchanges were established to trade. One observer noted that instead of flocking in droves to online exchanges and dealing with a bevy of new suppliers, many businesses opted to remain with existing suppliers, ones they had forged strong relationships with. While this was not good news for emerging B2B exchanges, the practice of B2B e-commerce still benefited because many companies began transacting business electronically with their trusted partners.

In the September 2004 issue of *KMWorld,* Zap Think senior analyst Jason Bloomberg gave his take on the general state of affairs, commenting, "All the tourists have gone home, as we say. Those that are left are doing real business. The technology is a lot better, and the business models are a lot better. The Internet for e-business is what the roads were for Rome. You couldn't do business without it, but once you have it, the sky's the limit."

One major example of B2B consolidation was the 2005 merger of two major, and profitable, retail exchanges: the WorldWide Retail Exchange (WWRE) and Global-NetXchange (GNX). WWRE was created in 2000 by a group of major retail players that included Best Buy and Target. GNX was established the same year and included Kroger and Sears among its founders.

Early on, large companies of *Fortune* 1000 stature dominated B2B e-commerce. This especially was true of manufacturers in the electronics and technology sectors. By 2003, 84 percent of large firms procured materials and services via the Internet.

Nonetheless, small and medium-sized companies also have benefited from B2B e-commerce. Long denied the luxuries of highly efficient electronic transactions that very large enterprises can afford, smaller companies are likely to take advantage of exchanges and other e-commerce venues that can simplify their procurement processes and improve their bargaining power with suppliers.

Believing this niche market would grow, online auction powerhouse eBay Inc. created eBay Business, a B2B exchange targeting small and mid-sized companies, in 2003. Early the following year, some 70 percent of small businesses using eBay Business said the service had helped to maximize their profitability. By mid-2005, eBay Business offered a wide array of items for businesses. Organized under the heading of Industrial Equipment & Supplies, these items fell under the following categories: Agriculture & Forestry, Industrial Electrical & Test, Construction, Industrial Supply, MRO, Food Service & Retail, Manufacturing & Metalworking, Healthcare, Lab & Life Science, and Office, Printing & Shipping. Under the Other Business Products heading, eBay Business also offered items in the Computers, Networking & Software,

Professional Gear, and Business Vehicles & Parts categories.

Heading toward the end of the decade, businesses continued to conduct business with one another electronically in growing numbers. However, the absence of standards continued to hinder the pace at which adoption was taking place. One example was the execution of electronic payments between companies. In a March 2007 *Bank Systems + Technology* article, Alenka Grealish of the Boston-based consulting firm Celent indicated that many businesses continued to rely on manual payment processes and use legacy computer systems with their own unique data formats to engage in electronic data interchange (EDI).

A transition to Extensible Markup Language (XML), which allows users to code information in a way similar to how Web pages are coded in HTML, has long been seen as one solution that will enable companies to exchange data in a standard way regardless of the computer systems involved. However, a report from Celent indicated that the mass migration from EDI to XML could take as long as 20 years. Therefore, in contrast to the business to consumer (B2C) side of the industry, where many consumers had shifted to electronic payments, progress was likely to unfold at a slow pace in this area in the B2B realm.

Usability problems also were a challenge for B2B e-commerce participants in the late years of the first decade of the 2000s. A 2007 report from Forrester Research found that while many companies had made great strides to make their B2C sites user friendly, such was not the case on the B2B side of the fence, where issues like text legibility (a problem faced by both categories), logical organization, and relevant functionality were common sources of frustration for site users.

In addition, B2B sites tended to not focus on users as individuals with specific needs. In the April 23, 2007, issue of *B to B,* John Underwood, e-channel commercial manager for Caterpillar Inc., commented on the need for companies to take a more personalized approach with customers online, asking: "Are they a new customer? Are they an existing customer? Are they looking for a new product or to better take care of the product they've got? Are they looking to solve a business problem? . . . You've really got to understand those things about your customer. And then you've got to really focus what you attempt to deliver to them so they don't get lost in the shuffle."

CURRENT CONDITIONS

In September 2009 the annual global Commercial Consumption Expenditure (CCE) Index, recognized as an industry benchmark for measuring commercial spending, was released by Visa. The index tracks B2B purchases to acquire goods and services used in the production, wholesale, and retail market, as well as business capital expeditures (excluding construction and durable defense spending) and government spending on goods and services. The CCE report estimated that global e-commercial spending grew to $90.2 trillion in 2008. This represented a global increase of 10.9 percent from the $81.3 trillion spent in 2007. According to the U.S. Census Bureau in 2008, B2B activity accounted for 93 percent of all e-commerce in 2006 (the latest statistic available).

Tech Crunchies reported in the 2008 "Internet Statistics and Numbers" that online spending for B2B advertising was estimated at $4.4 billion for 2008, $5.3 billion for 2009, and $6.4 billion for 2010.

INDUSTRY LEADERS

Based in Sunnyvale, California, Ariba Inc. is a leading provider of Internet procurement software and services. Within ten years of its beginning in 1996, the company's xAriba Supplier Network was accessed on some 4 million desktops worldwide. The network connected approximately 145,000 suppliers with distribution channels, buyers, and partners. Among Ariba's customers were one third of the Fortune 500 firms, including Hewlett-Packard, Colgate-Palmolive, Cisco Systems, BMW, and ABN AMRO. In 2001 the company acquired Agile Software Corp., a maker of software for managing manufacturing supply chains. Ariba increased in size in 2004, after acquiring FreeMarkets, a global supply management firm, in a combination cash/stock deal valued at $493 million, and a few years later acquired Procuri, Inc. The company employs approximately 1,500 workers and recorded total GAAP revenues for fiscal year 2008 of $328.1 million.

On the international front, Alibaba, the world's leading business-to-business e-commerce company, announced 2008 total revenue of RMB3 billion, an increase of 39 percent as compared to 2007. EPS (diluted) was up 31 percent year-on-year to 26.71 Hong Kong cents and net income (profit attributable to equity owners) was up 25 percent year-on-year to RMB1.2 billion. The number of registered users and online storefronts on Alibaba.com's marketplaces increased by 10.5 million and 1.7 million respectively. Registered users grew by 3.5 million during the year to 7.9 million, up 80 percent year-on-year, and it added 126,000 paying members to its marketplaces in just 2008 alone. The company reported that China contributed 36 percent to its 2008 revenues.

Agentrics is a massive business to business exchange that provides services ranging from supply chain collaboration and product lifecycle management to global data synchronization and sourcing. The company's customers included the likes of Best Buy, Campbell's Soup, Kroger, Radio Shack, Safeway, and Walgreen's as of mid-2007. According to the company, by this time its customers had realized more than $2 billion in cost savings through their use of Agentrics' services and technology. With headquarters in both Alexandria, Virginia, and Chicago, as well as office locations in Tokyo and the United Kingdom, in 2007 Agentrics LLC received an Achievement Award from the Voluntary Interindustry Commerce Solutions Association for being the Most Innovative Third Party Technology Provider. In 2008, Brazilian software firm Datasul founder Miguel Abuhab (MAP) acquired a majority share in Agentric for $50 million. In 2008, Agentrics and Neogrid represented the operating companies of MAP. With over 450 people working in 15 languages across 24 countries, they provided business solutions to retailers and manufacturers, representing more than $1.5 trillion in consumer spending.

AMERICA AND THE WORLD

A growing share of business to business Internet commerce continues to come from outside the United States, particularly from Asia. B2B sites in Asia suffered some of the same setbacks as U.S.-based sites did in the early years of the twenty-first century's first decade. There was a buildup of new sites targeting the gamut of business interests, and gradually the startups faced tightening funding and increased competition from large, established firms. This trend was expected to play out like the U.S. trend, where large, well-known players are most likely to survive.

The 2008 CCE Index found the strongest growth rates in Central and Eastern Europe, Middle East, and Africa, averaging about 23.7 percent. The Latin America and Caribbean region sowed a 17.4 percent growth rate. Nevertheless, Europe held the largest share of global B2B spending, and B2B spending in the Asia Pacific region surpassed the United States for the first time.

Heading toward the end of the decade, China was experiencing explosive economic growth. Earlier hard data on the state of B2B e-commerce in China was hard to obtain. However, the *International Journal of E-Business Research* reported that some estimates indicated that B2B transactions were far more dominant in the country in comparison to B2C. In 2008, the China Internet Association DCCI Data Center reported 2008 B2B e-commerce at an estimated $6.17 billion yuan, and 2009 at $8.98 billion yuan (one yuan equals 100 cents, but not 100 U.S. cents).

Another international hotbed for B2B e-commerce was the United Arab Emirates (UAE), according to a report from Madar Research. According to an August 8, 2006, *Global News Wire-Asia Africa Intelligence Wire* release, revenues from B2B e-commerce are projected to reach $36 billion by 2010, up from $4 billion in 2005. Driving annual growth of 55 percent were factors like new security laws in the UAE, as well as a business climate that supported the movement toward e-procurement.

BIBLIOGRAPHY

"$90.2 Trillion in Global Commerce Spending for 2008." *Payment News,* September 2009. Available from http://www.paymentsnews.com/2009/09/902-trillion-in-global-commercial-spending-for-2008.html.

Agentrics. Available from http://www.agentrics.com/web/agentrics/home.

"Agentrics, Best Buy Win VICS Achievement Awards." Agentrics LLC, 4 June 2007. Available from http://www.agentrics.com.

Alibaba. Available from http://b2b-trade-international.com/2009/03/alibabacom-year-2008-results-announced.html.

"Ariba Reports Results for Fourth Quarter and Fiscal Year 2008." Available from http://www.ariba.com/company/investor_finReleases.cfm?pressid=2785.

"B2B Transactions in UAE Expected to Soar Until 2010." *Global News Wire-Asia Africa Intelligence Wire,* 8 August 2006.

Bills, Steve. "Amex Augments Supply, Payment B-to-B Services." *American Banker,* 9 May 2007.

"Commerce One Completes its Final Transaction." *Information Age* (London, UK), 10 December 2004.

"Commerce One Patents Go to Mystery Bidder." *Client Server News,* 13 December 2004.

"E-business in Developing Countries: A Comparison of China and India." *International Journal of E-Business Research,* January 2007.

Fusco, Patricia. "Study: Online Business Proving Profitable for Small Firms." internet.com 24 March 2004. Available from http://www.ecommerce-guide.com/news/print.php/3330871.

"GNX and WWRE Complete Merger Transaction to Form Agentrics." Agentrics LLC, 15 November 2005. Available from http://www.agentrics.com.

"Gmarket Reports 4Q08 GMV of Yuan 1.1 Trillion..." Reuters, 30 January 2009. Available from http://www.reuters.com/article/pressRelease/idUS161363%2B30-Jan-2009%2BMW20090130.

Gross, Grant. "B2B Retail Hubs Join Forces." *CIO Magazine,* 15 June 2005.

Hirsh, Lou. "The Incredibly Quiet B2B Resurgence." *E-commerce Times,* 18 October 2002. Available from http://www.ecommercetimes.com.

Kabir, Nowshade. "Why Suppliers Should Use B2B Exchanges." *WebProNews,* 15 June 2004. Available from http://www.webpronews.com.

Kohler, Olivier. "E-business and B-to-B Strategy: Where Are we Now?" *B to B,* 13 June 2005.

Liedtke, Michael. "Bankrupt Commerce One Fetches $15.5 Million for Prized Patents." *America's Intelligence Wire,* 7 December 2004.

"AMarketTooFar." Economist,15May2004.

Morrison, Mary E. "Usability Problems Plague B-to-B Sites; Text Legibility, Functionality, Task Flow Among Web Sites' Biggest Failures." *B to B,* 23 April 2007.

"Growth of B2B Online Advertising in the United States." Tech Crunchies, 10 January 2008. Available at http://techcrunchies.com/growth-of-b2b-online-advertising-in-us/.

E-COMMERCE: CONSUMER PRODUCTS

SIC CODE(S)

5399

INDUSTRY SNAPSHOT

Business to consumer (B2C) electronic commerce (e-commerce) was the darling of the much-heralded New Economy in the late 1990s, generating a flood of new business and a great deal of hype. It seemed as though everyone was setting up new dot-com enterprises to hawk virtually any type of good; and typically, once a new product category was established on the Internet a bevy of copycat vendors scurried to claim their share. This was certainly the case in the crowded sectors for consumer products such as computers, books, apparel, toys, and other retail items. The highly publicized rush of cash to back new e-commerce ventures was one of the top stories on the covers of business pages. Online retailers could not have avoided having money thrown in their direction by avaricious investors dying to join the rest of the market in its euphoria.

Nonetheless, by early 2000 it appeared that the honeymoon was over, particularly in the business to consumer (B2C) sector, and online retailers became subject to the market discipline from which they were famously immune in the financing splurge of the late 1990s. A multitude of B2C exchanges went bankrupt in 2000 and 2001 as investors, increasingly concerned about profitability, proved reluctant to continue funding unprofitable dot-com businesses. The e-commerce market thus showed its first signs of maturity as investors began to make solid distinctions between those online merchants that had established a durable presence and those that had not, and to evaluate prospective companies in terms of business plans rather than starry-eyed glamour. By the middle of the first decade of the 2000s, business to consumer e-commerce was clearly on solid footing

Thanks to the Internet's capacity to reach new markets, B2C e-commerce not only survived the dot.com fallout but actually claimed double-digit increases and some 4.3 percent of overall retail sales by the decade's end.

ORGANIZATION AND STRUCTURE

Development. One of the most inviting characteristics of the e-commerce world, and a major factor in the overcrowding that began to take its toll in 2000, is the exceptionally low barrier to entry. It may take as little as finding someone to create an attractive Web page, setting up an Internet domain, and attracting a retailer by emphasizing the importance of establishing an online presence.

Nevertheless, it is not always that easy, as many e-tailers (electronic retailers) found out to their dismay. Though there was an exceedingly wide range of development costs, depending on innumerable variables—such as whether a company was an established retailer—a survey by the Gartner Group found that the cost of setting up an e-commerce Web site ran about $1 million, a cost that was expected to rise 25 percent annually in the early years of the first decade of the 2000s. The survey of mid-sized to large corporations also found, revealingly, that companies routinely underestimated the amount of money and time they would spend in setting up an e-commerce infrastructure, no matter whether their e-tail (electronic retail) plans were modest or ambitious.

E-Shopping. There are a number of virtual outlets where consumer e-commerce takes place. The most basic is the

251

direct, brochure-style corporate site at which customers can order products directly from the company via e-mail or an online order form. This was often referred to as first generation e-commerce, though many firms still enter into the online marketplace by this method.

The largest proportion of consumer products, however, are sold through large online retailers such as Amazon.com, Inc., which feature a number of departments for different product categories. These retailers develop deals with manufacturers to market and sell products through centralized Web sites, and the largest of these benefit from the vast interlinking network between various sites under their names.

There also were a number of sites designed to allow quick and easy comparison shopping. Junglee Corp. and MySimon.com Inc. made their mark by collecting pricing information from various Web sites and compiling them for their visitors, who could then assess prices across a broad range without having to hop from one Web site to another, compiling lists of their own. Both of these companies were eventually bought by Internet behemoths—Junglee by Amazon.com and MySimon by CNet. One of the largest remaining independent "shopbots," as they are known, was DealTime. While e-tailers originally resisted such sites, they eventually began to accept them as not only an inevitability but even a positive force that can funnel more business their way.

Online auctions provided another avenue for online sales of consumer goods, whereby companies establish a deal with an auction site to provide a listing for their products, which customers then bid on. This method was particularly attractive to online merchants since it tends to generate higher selling prices, but was not exceptionally lucrative for most consumer products that were widely available elsewhere. Since consumers generally hope to find the best bargain they can, it made little sense to go to an auction site and bid up the price of a product they could purchase for a lower fee from a major retailer. Nonetheless, the auction site was a valuable supplement to business to consumer e-tailing (electronic retailing) operations, particularly in the collectibles market. Major online auction companies included eBay, Amazon.com, uBid, and Yahoo .com. (See also **E-commerce: Online Auctions**.)

Finally, by 2000, new sites were popping up that enabled consumers to engage in online haggling with companies. Firms such as NexTag, HaggleZone, and Respond launched sites where customers could search for products in select categories, such as computers or consumer electronics, and the site would then return a list of companies with whom the firm has established a contract. Customers could directly contact the prospective merchant suggesting a lower price, and the negotiation process would ensue until a satisfactory price was reached. Like shopbots, many companies originally saw these negotiation sites as a threat but have since come to value them as a marketing tool.

Taxation. At the political level, perhaps the most contentious issue was that involving state and national legislators as well as both e-commerce and brick-and-mortar firms regarding taxation of e-commerce sales. Despite pressure from the National Governors' Association, which drafted a resolution demanding the taxation of Web-based transactions, the U.S. Congress passed the Internet Tax Freedom Act in 1998 that prohibited discriminatory taxes—taxes implemented by brick-and-mortar businesses to discourage e-commerce—and established a moratorium on interstate e-commerce taxes through 2001, declaring that an appropriate and integrated tax policy would have to be in place before companies could be expected to apply taxes to online sales.

By May 2000, however, Republicans in Congress were already devising legislation to extend the tax ban through 2006, despite an outcry from state governments and established retailers of all sizes. Democrats at the federal level also wanted to maintain a tax-free Internet. Opponents feared that such measures would leave state governments, which provide the bulk of government services, without crucial revenues, thus forcing them to scale back spending programs. Others simply contended that pushing back the end of the moratorium would provide a disincentive for state governments to streamline and coordinate their labyrinth-like tax policies so as to more easily facilitate e-commerce.

The sales tax issue continued to be of concern during the middle of the first decade of the 2000s. According to the September 2004 issue of *Purchasing*, professors at the University of Tennessee's Center for Business and Economic Research reported that local and state governments lost approximately $15.4 billion in 2003, a number that could possibly reach $33.7 billion by 2008. While these estimates, from Professors William E. Fox and Donald Bruce, included both consumer and business purchases, they revealed the huge base of potential tax revenues that could result from e-commerce.

As a result of these missed revenues, some states were engaged in legal action against retailers. For example, in late 2004, Wal-Mart, Office Depot, and Target paid the state of Illinois $2.4 million stemming from a lawsuit over sales taxes that began in 2003. A potential long-term solution called the Streamlined Sales Tax Project, an 18-state network that hoped to influence Congress to mandate a nationwide e-commerce sales tax, appeared in 2005. As part of the voluntary program, which began on October 3, 2005, the network provided free software to merchants who agreed to collect and remit sales taxes to the member states. It also created an amnesty period for sellers who member states had not contacted for auditing.

A press release issued by the collaborative on the agreement's effective date hailed it as "the culmination of a multi-year, nationwide effort by 44 states, the District of Columbia, local governments and members of the business community to develop measures to design, test and implement a system that radically simplifies sales and use tax collection and administration by retailers and states.... The simplified system reduces the number of sales tax rates, brings uniformity to definitions of items in the sales tax base, significantly reduces the paperwork burden on retailers, and incorporates new technology to modernize many administrative procedures."

By mid-2007, the network included 15 states that had amended their laws to comply with the project—Indiana, Iowa, Kansas, Kentucky, Michigan, Minnesota, Nebraska, New Jersey, North Carolina, North Dakota, Oklahoma, Rhode Island, South Dakota, Vermont, and West Virginia—and the "associate member states" of Arkansas, Nevada, Ohio, Tennessee, Utah, and Wyoming.

BACKGROUND AND DEVELOPMENT

In the early 1990s, the World Wide Web was just beginning to flower and was touted as the new information superhighway that would spread knowledge and ideas to individuals at the click of a mouse. Up until the mid-1990s, the main users of the Internet were academic scientists and other technology specialists. It wasn't long, however, before talk of the information superhighway was drowned out by the buzz of e-commerce. By creating a stir over the potential windfall that online shopping could portend, venture capitalists poured billions of dollars into new firms, essentially paying for the infrastructure to make online commerce a reality.

One of the first online retailers to make waves was Amazon.com. The company's Web site went up in 1995 and the company, aware that most major bookstores and publishing companies maintained extensive electronic lists of titles, began selling books with a surprisingly good deal of success. In 1997 the company began to generate substantial revenues, much to the chagrin of established book retailers such as Barnes & Noble, which scrambled furiously to establish its own Web site to try to mitigate some of the damage.

In 1997, however, many companies were still weighing the prospective costs and benefits of establishing a Web site devoted to commerce and an appropriate business model was far from resolved. As more and more new start-ups popped up in the late 1990s, however, companies were left with little choice but to either establish their own e-tail operation or align with an existing one. The frenzy also happened to coincide with and contribute to the sustained stock market boom of the period; and from there, the avalanche of dot-coms ensued.

According to a 1999 study by CDB Research and Consulting Inc., books were the largest consumer product category in terms of online sales, accounting for about 33 percent of online purchases, while computer equipment brought in 13 percent. Apparel manufacturers meanwhile continued to grow on the Internet, although sales were expected to remain relatively modest according to Jupiter Communications. The greatest difficulty facing apparel retailers was how to make clothing look as attractive on the Web as on a catalog page. In addition, customers remained wary of many dot-coms' shipping and return policies, a crucial element of this sector as customers searched for the perfect look and fit.

Some of the fastest growing product categories in 1999 were automotives—including automobiles sold directly to customers online—in which revenues leapt 2,300 percent; toys, which saw revenues increase 440 percent; and health and beauty products, which grew by 780 percent in 1999.

Entrepreneurs launching new shopping sites faced a number of profound challenges. First off, through the late 1990s, such merchants had to face down the scads of competition in any given field. For instance, there were more than a half dozen commerce sites revolving around the "pets.com" theme in early 2000. In addition, the industry is particularly tied to the wax and wane of technology stocks. Through the late 1990s, the industry largely floated itself on the copious flow of venture capital, but investors have grown weary of companies languishing for years without significant revenues.

In the late 1990s, traditional brick-and-mortar retailers such as Barnes & Noble, Wal-Mart, and Kmart all moved aggressively to mark out their territory on the Web. Kmart, for instance, announced the launch of BlueLight.com in December 1999 with the help of SoftBank Venture Capital. A month later, Wal-Mart rolled out Wal-Mart.com Inc. in conjunction with the venture outfit Accel Partners.

Shakeout. Throughout 2000, the market finally registered the effects of what many analysts decried as over-exuberance on the part of investors and venture capitalists. For several years, the industry gained notoriety for its seemingly bottomless financing for firms that barely posted revenues much less registered a profit. Market analysts chalked this behavior up to the feeling among financiers that something new, profound, and potentially lucrative was in the works in the economy, and investors scrambled to get in on the ground floor on almost any venture that came their way. Moreover, this craze came at a time in the U.S. economy when investors had the disposable income to throw at new dot-com ventures, and the stratospheric trajectory of the stock market only encouraged these players that nothing could go wrong.

These rosy projections proved unfounded. The panic in the stock market's technology sector in the spring of 2000 crushed a good number of e-commerce firms, especially among the also-rans in the consumer goods sector. Since for almost any given consumer product category the industry's successes tended to concentrate in one or two firms, the shakeout did away with much of the dead weight, the firms that many analysts expected had to go at some point.

As an illustration of the mounting difficulties, the ten business to consumer firms that went public in the second quarter of 1999 brought in a combined net of $2.5 billion while the eight companies that did so in the same period in 2000 mustered only about $1 billion. Unfortunately for the industry, such trends were the rule rather than the exception for much of 2000.

However, the damage was hardly limited to second rate companies. Major e-tailers were forced to close their virtual doors as well. Boo.com, a leading sports clothing retailer, announced its liquidation in May 2000 after several weeks of unsuccessful fundraising. Even market linchpins were feeling the heat. Amazon.com and eToys watched their stock prices fall 60 percent between January and August 2000, and eToys eventually declared bankruptcy. With the future of capital financing in doubt, a large segment of the business to consumer e-tailing market was expected to either shut down or be absorbed by other companies by the end of 2001.

Nevertheless, many observers insisted that the shakeout was inevitable and was in fact part of many firms' business plans all along; that the idea was to build up a strong financial base by dramatizing the glamour and potential of the Internet so as to position oneself for a buyout when push came to shove. In addition, the online retailing sector registered more real success stories than its reputation might indicate. Boston Consulting Group released a study in August 2000 reporting that nearly 40 percent of the 221 online retailers studied were already profitable.

Impact of the Shakeout on Remaining Businesses. In the early years of the first decade of the 2000s, with funding sources scarce, only the most solid businesses remained operational. Even those based on ideas that appeared promising, such as online grocer Webvan Group, proved unable to stay afloat if they could not satisfy investors' demands for a business model that had already produced profits or would produce profits in the very near future. In the case of Webvan, many analysts agree that the firm, in its quest to secure as many customers as possible, expanded too rapidly into other goods before stabilizing its core grocery delivery operations.

Founded in 1999, Webvan had made several sound marketing and customer service decisions according to several market analysts. For example, to draw repeat business and to encourage larger orders, Webvan offered free delivery for orders over $50. Also, customers with questions about their orders could call a toll-free customer service line. As a result, within six months, Webvan had managed to reach 47,000 customers in a single market, compared to the 110,000 clients secured by its largest competitor, Peapod, which had operations in eight markets. However, despite the firm's impressive growth, its continued losses began to concern investors in 2000. Like many other business to consumer exchanges, Webvan launched new operations rather than curb spending and focus its efforts on minimizing losses. Unable to secure additional financing, Webvan declared bankruptcy in July of 2001.

Venture capitalists still willing to invest in business to consumer exchanges sought businesses planning to peddle products or services likely to sell in current and future market conditions. For example, after the bursting of the dot-com bubble, online luxury item merchants continued to secure funding simply because investors believed that individuals able to afford those items were not likely to be affected by the recession. As a result, online jewelry retailer Bluenile.com secured a $7 million round of financing from Bessemer Venture Partners, Kleiner Perkins Caulfield & Byers, and other venture capitalists in 2001. In addition, Winetasting.com secured a $5 million loan from an individual investor. While luxury retailers were not the only online companies securing financing in the early years of the decade, their success does reflect the importance venture capitalists had begun to place upon favorable market conditions.

The middle of the First Decade of the 2000s. By the middle of the first decade of the 2000s, business to consumer e-commerce was clearly on solid footing. According to *Business Week,* data from the National Retail Federation's Shop.org unit and Forrester Research revealed that e-commerce sales were expected to reach $172 billion in 2005, representing 7.7 percent of all retail sales. The data further indicated that sales growth was slowing in comparison to the early years of the decade and appeared to be leveling off into a steady, stable pattern. Compared to growth of 51 percent in 2003, e-commerce sales grew 24 percent in 2004 and were expected to grow 22 percent in 2005.

Other consumer e-commerce sales reports were more conservative. For example, an eMarketer study titled *E-commerce in the U.S.: Retail Trends,* estimated that U.S. consumers would invest $84.5 billion in online retail goods and services in 2005, a number that was projected to reach $139 billion in 2008, according to *Twice*. A separate report from JupiterResearch estimated that online retail sales would grow from $66 billion in 2004 to $79 billion in 2005, according to *Wireless News*.

In addition to sales growth, more online retail companies were turning a profit. According to *Twice*, data from eMarketer indicated that while 70 percent of online retailers were profitable in 2002, this number had increased to 79 percent in 2003. Profit margins also were increasing for many industry players. The aforementioned *Business Week* article revealed that after reaching 21 percent in 2003, average operating profit margins for online retail rose to 28 percent in 2004.

As the volume and size of e-commerce transactions continued to grow mid-decade, Internet security remained a major industry concern. So-called "phishing" scams, in which criminals attempt to trick consumers into providing sensitive data such as bank or credit card account numbers, cost more than one million consumers $929 million between May 2004 and May 2005 alone, according to data from the research firm Gartner.

By mid-2005, a new form of scam was emerging that undermined a portion of the Internet's infrastructure. Called "pharming," the technique involves the use of computer code that affects domain name servers (devices that translate Web site names into numeric Internet Protocol or IP addresses) by automatically redirecting consumers to bogus Web sites. Once directed to these sites, connected computers are vulnerable to spyware programs, which enable the monitoring of one's online activities and possible compromise by hackers.

Marketers were concerned about the impact that spyware was having on e-commerce volume. Fearful that their data could be compromised in some way, the threat of spyware infection prompted some individuals to shy away from online shopping altogether, while others shopped more conservatively. While data from the Pew Internet & American Life Project indicated that some 78 percent of consumers were aware of what spyware is, about one-third were not confident in their ability to do anything about it. According to the July 11, 2005, issue of *Network World*, some 90 percent of respondents to a Pew survey had changed their behavior because of such concerns. The publication explained that "48% of the 1,336 people surveyed have stopped visiting particular Web sites; 34% have stopped downloading software; 18% say they no longer open e-mail attachments; and 18% say they have changed browsers to try to avoid surreptitious software installation."

A study from FGI Research and ForeSee Results involving the top 40 grossing online retailers found that multi-channel retailers were not utilizing the online channel to its fullest potential. In addition, the research found

that many top e-tailers were missing the mark with consumers in terms of delivering the right kind of experience. Although price trumped factors like product selection and navigation, site experience played a critical role in customer satisfaction—and sales. According to the June 20, 2005, issue of *Twice,* on a 100-point scale, Amazon.com ranked first in customer satisfaction with a score of 84. Following Amazon.com were QVC.com, also with a score of 84, TigerDirect.com (81), Apple.com (80), HSN.com (79), Dell.com (77), HPShopping.com (77), OfficeDepot.com (75), Staples.com (75), BestBuy.com (75), Wal-Mart.com (75), and Overstock.com (75).

Following a strong finish in 2006, e-commerce continued to grow at a healthy clip in 2007, accounting for an increasingly larger share of overall consumer spending. U.S. Census Bureau figures revealed that e-commerce sales in the fourth quarter of 2006 were nearly 25 percent higher than in the final quarter of 2005. According to the March 5, 2007, issue of *Business Week,* e-commerce sales totaled $108 billion in 2006.

During the latter part of the decade, several key trends applied to the online sale of consumer products, as well as many other e-commerce categories. Perhaps the most important was the increasing importance of consumer feedback. By 2007 it had become clear to marketers that adding the ability for customers to rate products and leave comments was a key tactic for driving sales. In addition, negative feedback helped retailers to quickly identify flawed or poor quality products and remove them from the site.

In the February 13, 2007, issue of *Business Week Online,* writer Pallavi Gogoi explained that the trend in so-called social computing, marked by the popularity of sites like MySpace and FaceBook, which allowed people to share information about themselves, was helping to fuel the popularity of online product feedback and reviews. Gogoi indicated that according to the research firm MarketingSherpa, 23 percent of e-commerce sites allowed customers to leave feedback at the close of 2005. One year later, this percentage had mushroomed to 43 percent.

Another key trend was offering consumers the ability to engage in an online chat with representatives. Especially in the case of more expensive items, retailers such as The Home Depot discovered that offering customers the ability to ask questions was an important tool for closing the sale. In addition, some online chat tools allowed representatives to see the location from which users were chatting, allowing them to direct potential customers to a physical store for hands-on assistance when needed. A number of companies using this technology were convinced of its effectiveness at converting prospects to customers.

Security remained a pressing concern for e-commerce firms of all stripes. In early 2007 the Internet security firm

ScanAlert issued the results of a study involving 27,000 online retailers. The report revealed that half of the sites studied were vulnerable to being compromised by various forms of database attacks. This study followed a November 2006 survey of 5,000 U.S. adults by the research firm Gartner, which found that security fears cost online retailers nearly $2 billion in 2006. Nearly $1 billion of these estimated losses came from consumers who avoided e-commerce altogether, and a similar amount was attributed to consumers who avoided sites that simply appeared to be unsafe. These two pieces of research pointed to the continued need to address real vulnerabilities, as well as those that only existed in the minds of consumers. Each held great importance in terms of lost sales.

CURRENT CONDITIONS

According to research firm eMarketer's November 2008 report, retail e-commerce B2C sales were valued at $136.8 billion in 2008, representing a 7.2 percent increase from 2007. 2009 B2C sales were estimated at $142.4 billion, with only a 4.1 percent increase from 2008. The report further opined that e-commerce sales would continue to increase at only a single-digit pace through 2012. These figures excluded travel sales, digital downloads, and event tickets.

Notwithstanding, market research firm yStats.com, in its "Global B2C E-Commerce Report-September 2009," opined that U.S. revenues were expected to drop by 1.5 percent in 2009, due to the economic crisis. At the same time, noted the report, Europe (particularly Germany, Great Britain, and France) could expect double-digit increases.

In September 2009, the U.S. Census Bureau released its *Quarterly Retail E-Commerce Sales 2nd Quarter 2009* report, confirming a continuing decline in the overall U.S. retail sector since the third quarter of 2008. This paralleled the economic crisis that overtook the nation during those months. However, since January 2009, there has been a slow but steady increase in e-commerce sales. The report showed U.S. online sales for the third quarter rising to $32.4 billion, accounting for 3.6 percent of all retail sales, despite a 0.4 percent decline in total retail sales.

Google and Yahoo! sites remained the most popular Web sites for 2008 in the United States as well as Japan, the United Arab Emirates and Germany (the four regions studied), according to Australian-based research group BuddeComm's report, "2008 Global Digital Economy-M-Commerce, E-commerce & E-payments." The firm predicted that B2C spending would reach $1 trillion by 2012. The fastest growing retail e-commerce categories in 2008, as reported by com.Score, were video games and accessories (29 percent), followed by home and garden (25 percent) and sports/fitness (25 percent).

Meanwhile, U.S. online advertising dropped 7 percent in 2009, from $6.6 billion to $6.2 billion over the same period in 2008, according to the IDC in August 2009 in the *Worldwide and U.S. Internet Ad Spend Report 2009.*

INDUSTRY LEADERS

Amazon.com Amazon.com, based in Seattle, Washington, is one of the most recognizable names on the Internet and is nearly synonymous with e-commerce. One of the earliest Internet-related retail success stories, The world's leading online bookseller, Amazon expanded beyond that category in 1998, and by decade's end its retail lines were virtually without end, also leading the way in music and videos and everything from jewelry to groceries to sporting goods. With its tremendous—and growing—leverage in the e-tailing market, Amazon.com was considered able to withstand market jolts such as those that hit the industry in 2000. Sitting at the center of a vast, diversified e-tail empire, Amazon.com could direct traffic through its disparate e-commerce operations, thus giving the company a leg up on competitors in those arenas. The company reported 2008 revenues of $19.17 billion, up 20 percent from the previous year, and expected a 9 to 19 percent increase for 2009.

Overstock.com Inc. Overstock.com was another major e-commerce player heading into the late years of the first decade of the 2000s. The company sold brand name goods at discounts of 40 to 80 percent in nine major categories, including bedding, clothing, entertainment, furniture, home, jewelry, sports, watches, and electronics. Overstock.com leverages its partnerships with manufacturers to obtain products at low prices due to factors such as inventory reduction, overproduction, canceled retail orders, and downsizing. Established as Discounts Direct in 1997, the company held its initial public offering (IPO) in 2002. In 2008 Overstock.com's sales totaled $834.3 million, with a net profit of $142.9 million, after three negative years. Patrick Byrne, Overstock.com's chairman and president, has an ownership stake of approximately 40 percent.

GSI Commerce Inc. Global Sports catapulted to the top of the online sporting goods heap with its purchase of market leader Fogdog Inc. in 2000. Fogdog was the leading online retailer of sporting goods apparel, footwear, and equipment. Amid mounting competition in the sporting goods sector, Fogdog went public in late 1999, in the process granting Nike a 10 percent stake in the company in exchange for a special discount on Nike products and an exclusive online marketing deal with Nike. The technology sector stock plunge in the spring of 2000 forced Fogdog to seek a partner. That year, the firm acquired Ashford.com, a retailer of luxury goods online, and changed its name to GSI Commerce Inc. to better reflect its broader focus. By mid-2005, GSI was involved in site design, hosting, and merchandising. At that time the company served Sport Chalet, RadioShack,

Aeropostale, Polo Ralph Lauren, Reebok, and about 50 other leading retailers and entertainment companies, including HBO. The company remained an e-commerce heavyweight heading into the late years of the first decade of the 2000s. Net revenues for 2008 were $966.9 million an increase of 29 percent from $750 million in 2007.

Buy.com Inc. Buy.com Inc. was a leading online superstore during the middle of the first decade of the 2000s. Its sales were concentrated particularly in computer hardware, software, and peripherals, but the firm also generated strong sales in books, consumer electronics, and a number of other product categories. Founded in 1997, Buy.com was based in Aliso Viejo, California. The company's portal provides links to its sixteen specialty stores, selling products from leading manufacturers in each respective field. Founder Scot Blum repurchased Buy.com from investors in 2001, taking the firm private. In 2007 the company offered the digital *BuyMagazine,* which provided prospective buyers with product reviews.

AMERICA AND THE WORLD

Notwithstanding, market research firm yStats.com, in its "Global B2C E-Commerce Report- September 2009," opined that U.S. revenues were expected to drop by 1.5 percent in 2009, due to the economic crisis. At the same time, noted the report, Europe (particularly Germany, Great Britain, and France) could expect double-digit increases. In Poland, the number of online shoppers increased 12 percent in 2008. In Japan, mobile shopping by mobile phone, on the rise, was expected to account for 20 percent of all e-commerce sales in 2009.

The growth of consumer e-commerce in China has been staggering. In 2008, China had the largest number of Internet users in the world (worldwide, it reached approximately 1.4 billion in 2008.). According to the IDC, China B2C e-commerce maintained a growth rate of 30 percent in 2008, surpassing B2B growth of 20 percent. Total China e-commerce transaction volume in 2008 was 1.951 trillion Yuan (one yuan equals 100 cents, but not 100 U.S. cents, depending on the exchange rate), and was expected to reach 2.51 trillion Yuan for 2009. China uses Google and Yahoo! as well as Baidu and Alibaba for online retail searches.

Among the biggest hurdles to international e-commerce were the differences between nations in privacy laws and restrictions relating to the Internet and commercial transactions. U.S. laws safeguarding consumer privacy are in general far more relaxed than those of European nations, allowing companies to engage in extensive trade of consumer data, and thus transAtlantic e-commerce was stuck in limbo until early 2000, when the U.S. Department of Commerce negotiated a deal with the European Commission to guarantee European customers of U.S. online merchants the same privacy protections they expect under European laws, which decree that no company may share customer data with another firm without the customer's permission. U.S. retailers operating in Europe have the option of attempting to prove that U.S. laws are in sync with those of Europe in their sector of operation, placing themselves under the jurisdiction of a European regulatory authority, or participating in a self-regulating organization approved by the U.S. Federal Trade Commission.

RESEARCH AND TECHNOLOGY

In September of 2006, the research firm Harris Interactive issued the results of a survey which found that when engaging in e-commerce, consumers were easily frustrated by Web site errors. Such irritation came with a $9 billion price tag for retailers, in terms of lost sales. The survey of 2,790 people included customers buying products at retail, as well as those engaging in transactions related to travel, banking, and insurance. The research indicated that almost one-third of frustrated customers will take their business to a competitor. Of special interest to retailers was the fact that some 88 percent of respondents indicated they had trouble conducting an online transaction at some point during the year.

BIBLIOGRAPHY

"2008 Global Digital Economy-M-Commerce, E-commerce & E-payments." Available from http://www.budde.com.au/Research/2008-Global-Digital-Economy-M-Commerce-E-Commerce-E-Payments.html

Amazon. Available from http://phx.corporate-ir.net/.

"$90.2 Trillion in Global Commerce Spending for 2008." *Payment News,* September 2009. Available from http://www.paymentsnews.com/2009/09/902-trillion-in-global-commercial-spending-for-2008.html.

Barboza, David. "Yahoo! Pays $1 Billion for Stake in Chinese E-commerce Site." *Seattle Post-Intelligencer,* 11 August 2005.

"Brazil: E-commerce Market to Reach US$4 Billion in 2005." IPR Strategic Information Database, 6 June 2005.

"Brazil's E-commerce Closed 2004 with Revenues of US$636.5 Million." *Latin America Telecom,* February 2005.

"Cash Registers Are Ringing Online." *Business Week,* 5 March 2007.

Cervini, Lisa. "Shoppers Flock to Internet, Driving Sales, Earnings, Share." *Twice,* 20 June 2005.

Dix, John. "Spyware Changing the Way the 'Net..." *Network World,* 11 July 2005.

"E-commerce Growth Spurs More Sophisticated Scams; As Electronic Commerce Increases on the Internet, So Does the Sophistication of Technology Used by Scam Artists, with a New Tactic Called 'Pharming' Being The Most Dangerous." *InternetWeek,* 14 June 2005.

"Gartner: $2 Billion in E-Commerce Sales Lost Because of Security Fears." *Baseline,* 27 November 2006.

"Gmarket Reports 4Q08 GMV of Yuan 1.1 Trillion..." Reuters, 30 January 2009. Available from http://www.reuters.com/article/pressRelease/idUS161363%2B30-Jan-2009%2BMW20090130.

Gogoi, Pallavi. "Retailers Take a Tip from MySpace; E-commerce Sites Are Letting Customers Post Comments, Reviews, and Even Photos—and Finding Out A Lot about their Products in the Process." *Business Week Online,* 13 February 2007. Available from www.businessweek.con.

"GSI Commerce: News Releases—GSI Commerce Reports Fiscal 2008." Available from http://www.gsicommerce.com/index.php/en/article/560/.

"Half of Web Sites Vulnerable to Hackers According to New Study of 27,000 Online Retailers; SQL Injection and Cross Site Scripting Dangers Widespread for Online Retailers." *Internet Wire,* 6 February 2007.

"JupiterResearch: 2004 Online Holiday Retail Spending Exceeded $22 Billion." *Wireless News,* 7 February 2005.

Krebs, Brian. "States Move Forward on Internet Sales Tax." *Washington post,* 1 July 2005. Available from www.washingtonpost.com.

Murphy, Samantha. "IM: Need Help? Instant Messages from Retailers Build Revenue, Retailer Productivity." *Chain Store Age,* July 2006.

"Overstock.com Reports Fourth Quarter and Fiscal Year 2008 Financial Results." Available from http://www.reuters.com/article/pressRelease/idUS172432+30-Jan-2009+PRN20090130

Powell, Bill. "Why Yahoo! Fancies Its Chances in the Race for China's eBillions." *Time,* 11 August 2005.

Power, Denise. "Retail Site Errors Create $9B Risk." *WWD,* 26 September 2006.

"Retail E-Commerce Update." Emarketer.com, 2008. Available at http://www.emarketer.com/Reports/All/Emarketer_2000545.aspx.

"Sales Tax Simplification Agreement Becomes Effective Today and Launches Key Element: Amnesty Program," 3 October 2005. Available from http://www.streamlinedsalestax.org.

"State and Local Governments Lost More Than $15.4 Billion." *Purchasing,* 2 September 2004.

"Study: Many Web Sites Don't Meet Expectations." *Fairfield County Business Journal,* 27 June 2005.

Tedeschi, Bob. "Online Swindlers Shift Focus to Smaller Retailers." *The New York Times,* 11 December 2006.

"Transaction Volume of B2C Maintain 30% Growth Rate in 2008." *PRLog,* 16 June 2009, available from http://www.prlog.org/10259145-transaction-volumes-of-b2c-maintain-30-growth-rate-in-2008.html.

"Why E-tailers Are E-lated." *Business Week,* 6 June 2005.

E-COMMERCE: ONLINE AUCTIONS

—■—

SIC CODE(S)

5999

INDUSTRY SNAPSHOT

Garage sales may not yet be obsolete, but folks wishing to unload their attic collectibles have discovered a new way in which just about anything can be sold to anyone with an Internet connection. As a bonus, sellers are relieved of the ominous chore of hauling their wares to the flea market or to the end of the driveway, and they could reach millions of customers rather than the handful they would attract in a physical setting, thereby assuring greater and more lucrative sales. Online auction sites, which put prospective buyers of virtually any product in touch with those with that item to sell, emerged as a cornerstone of the surging electronic commerce (e-commerce) market. Unlike many e-commerce business models that disappeared when the Internet bubble burst in 2000, the online auction demonstrated its staying power by evolving into one of the few profitable e-commerce models.

Whether searching for elusive Beanie Babies to complete one's collection or for the Mercedes of one's dreams, "netizens," i.e., individuals, businesses, and even traditional auction houses all acknowledge the benefits of conducting auctions on the Internet rather than in a physical location where only a relative handful of people can attend. Since more potential buyers can participate in online auctions, the prices of the goods sold generally go up with more competing bids, generating enhanced revenues. Conversely, the sheer number of auctions taking place and the availability of comparative information on the Internet help keep prices in check.

ORGANIZATION AND STRUCTURE

There were thousands of online auction sites in 2009, including massive generalist sites as well as those specializing in certain kinds of products or certain forms of transactions, such as business to business. Typically, users register on a Web site and upload descriptions of the products they have to sell, which are then sorted into product categories. Often these descriptions include photographs and a starting bid price. As prospective buyers roam around the site, they begin to register bids, which are continuously updated. The highest bidder at the time the auction closes is obligated to purchase the product. Sellers then contact the buyers directly via any communication method and work out payment and shipment plans. Some of the larger sites, moreover, maintain listings of recently completed auctions, detailing the number of bids and final sales prices so users can get a feel for what they can expect to spend or receive at an auction.

Sites typically charge a listing fee. Market leader eBay Inc., for instance, charges based on the value of the item sold, although other sites, such as Yahoo!, charge no listing fee, relying on advertising and other sources for revenue. Most sites also ask a small percentage, usually no more than 5 percent, of the final sale price, although configurations vary.

Although the large sites such as eBay promote themselves as enterprises more akin to swap meets than retail outlets, their huge stores of consumer products of all varieties effectively place them in direct competition with traditional retailers, a fact to which those retailers quickly awoke.

Unlike the major online auction sites, merchant auction sites do not provide space for individuals to auction off their products. Instead they acquire items unsold by other vendors and then auction the merchandise for their own revenues. As a result, they open themselves to a great deal more liability, and indeed some have engendered tremendous controversy for taking money for products that never reached their buyers, issuing fraudulent bid victory notices, or misplacing or short-changing shipments. In most cases, customers who encounter a problem with such sites are forced to take up the issue with the vendors rather than the auction sites, who often fail to guarantee that the products are actually in stock.

BACKGROUND AND DEVELOPMENT

The online auction industry didn't exactly have the most dramatic or profound of beginnings. Pierre Omidyar apparently met with great frustration at his inability to locate Pez brand candy dispensers on the Internet and decided that something had to be done. Thus he began Auction Web in 1995, which began charging fees for item listings a year later. By 1997 the company was known as eBay and was well on its way to becoming synonymous with online auctions, spreading its name around the Internet with banner ads and overseeing some 800,000 auctions daily. Although the fees were miniscule, the sheer volume of activity raked in tremendous revenues, making other Internet companies, both established and fledgling, sit up and take notice.

Originally known for auction listings featuring mainly quirky collectibles, the online auction industry grew in the late 1990s to include hundreds of specialized sites and sub-sites selling everything from jewelry to automobiles to real estate. By 2000, hundreds of online auction sites graced the Internet, including some of the biggest and most established names in the New Economy such as Amazon.com, Inc. and Yahoo! Inc.

The industry also managed to earn a darker image, gaining notoriety for online hucksters and snake oil artists. The National Consumer League (NCL) reported that in 1999, online auction-related gripes were the number one complaint of all Internet users, accounting for 90 percent of all NCL phone calls. Typically, the problems centered on damaged or unreceived goods, according to the Federal Trade Commission. Generally, it was up to the auction sites to check out their sellers, and many required credit card numbers or other identification that could help stave off would-be scam artists.

Nonetheless, product and service complaints gave rise to a great deal of skepticism and dissatisfaction among consumers, and auctioneers attempted to shield themselves from these complaints and potential lawsuits by adding extensive disclaimers on their Web sites in order to pre-emptively wash their hands of any misdeeds related to

products and shipments. Thus analysts advised caution, noting that for the time being, the customer would have to maintain responsibility for assessing the validity of auction sites, the products they post, and the vendors and sellers from whom they wanted to buy.

The level of responsibility placed on the shoulders of online auctioneers for the products that were auctioned on their sites was far from clear. In late 1999, eBay was slapped with a lawsuit by a San Francisco man alleging that the company failed to take adequate steps to prevent the trading of illegal bootleg music recordings. While all parties were agreed that bootlegs were in fact bought and sold through eBay, at issue was whether eBay had a right to conduct auctions of them. eBay's defense relied on its insistence that it was not an actual retailer but rather more of a giant classified advertising collection and was thus not responsible for the dealings between its customers.

In part to stave off such illegal trading on its site, eBay initiated its Verified Rights Owners Program in summer 1999, which invited over 200 interested parties, including companies, individuals, trade groups, and others, to regularly log on and monitor the Web site for illegal or inappropriate activities. Some of the hardest-hit industries, including computer software, music, and movies, took eBay up on the offer to try to force pirates and scam artists off the site.

By the turn of the twenty-first century, even old-fashioned business giants had gotten into the act. The business-to-business auction model was expected to assume increased importance in equipment and supply transactions, as it carried the benefit of reducing transaction costs for all parties. General Motors Corp. (GM) teamed up with the Canadian auction house Commerce One to launch Trade-Xchange, which GM used to sell off manufacturing equipment. Likewise, Ford Motor Co. conducted its first auction in early 2000 to purchase tires. The scheme brought together five tire manufacturers to bid on prices at which they would sell their products to Ford. This type of business-to-business (B2B) auction generated a great deal of hype in business circles, leading to proclamations that the practice would reconfigure the very matrix of supply and demand. Investors took the news to heart and poured money into new online B2B auction startups. However, when the technology industry crashed in 2000, venture capital for such startups vanished. Because the technology was relatively undeveloped, most sites like TradeXchange had been unable to secure the number of customers they needed to actually turn a profit before the downturn. As a result, the number of business to business auction sites plummeted from 1,000 in 2000 to a mere 50 in 2002.

Scams continued to plague the industry. The U.S. Federal Trade Commission (FTC) logged roughly 51,000 online auction complaints in 2002, up considerably from

20,000 in 2001. To combat the growing instances of fraud, the FTC developed the "Operation Bidder Beware" program to help protect consumers and it publicly urged online shoppers to conduct considerable research on sellers before sending payment for items purchased via an online auction.

According to the *IC3 2004 Internet Fraud Crime Report,* issued in 2005 by the National White Collar Crime Center and the Federal Bureau of Investigation, the Internet Crime Complaint Center (IC3) referred 103,959 online fraud complaints to enforcement agencies in 2004. Collectively, these cases represented a total loss of $68.14 million. Of the referred cases, 71.2 percent were related to Internet auction fraud, followed by non-delivered merchandise and payment (15.8 percent), credit/debit card fraud (5.4 percent), and check fraud (1.3 percent). Some 87 percent of those who complained of online auction fraud reported a monetary loss, with individual losses averaging $200.

Reverse auctions, in which sellers compete for buyers in real time, also experienced notable growth. The December 20, 2004, issue of *Federal Computer Market Report* indicated that states like Wisconsin, Texas, Pennsylvania, Minnesota, and Massachusetts were pioneers in the use of reverse auctions to cut procurement costs. The publication reported that at the federal level, the U.S. General Services Administration (GSA) had realized savings of 12 to 48 percent since starting reverse auctions in fiscal year 2003. While this form of auction works well for raw materials and standard goods, some analysts indicated that the same was not always true for professional services and custom work, such as the development of IT systems.

In early 2007, the Dallas/Fort Worth International Airport used an online auction to sell more than 2,000 merchandise lots that contained everything from surplus goods left over from construction projects to office equipment, vehicles, and portable buildings. As reported in *Airline Industry Information,* some 18 million page views were generated during the auction, which raised nearly $1.8 million for the airport.

Finally, more than 600 police departments from Los Angeles to New York used PropertyRoom.com, an online auction service operated by Mission Viejo, California-based Property Room Inc., to sell "seized, found, stolen, recovered and surplus items." While the business, established by a former law enforcement officer named Thomas Lane, took about half of the proceeds from items sold, it provided law enforcement with a turn-key way of unloading items. In many cases, PropertyRoom.com enabled law enforcement agencies to make more than they otherwise would through a traditional auction, and with less hassle. In addition to its auction service, Property Room operated a free registry that helped people to recover lost or stolen items.

CURRENT CONDITIONS

According to Forrester Research's 2008 estimate, online consumer auction sales will reach $65 billion by 2010. In fact, said Forrester, history showed that one in five online consumers had already purchased from an online auction in the preceding 12 months (2007 to 2008). The September 16, 2009 IBIS World Industry Report for e-commerce and online auctions forecast that over the outlook period, the industry would experience strong growth. This was due in large part, according to IBIS, to more consumers becoming familiar with PayPal and establishing a broadband connection.

cMarket Network, the leader in online auction fundraising for nonprofit organizations, announced a 44 percent increase in the number of auctions run in 2008, bringing the total to over $53 million raised for nonprofits since 2003. It reported 2,259 online auctions in 2008, generating $20,459,687 in revenue for a wide variety of worthy causes. The single largest auction of the year, South Beach Food & Wine Festival, raised $266,414. Eleven chapters of the Muscular Dystrophy Association combined their auctions and raised $580,000 on top of the annual Jerry Lewis Labor Day Telethon event. As traditional funding sources continued to decline, cMarket Network increasingly relied on Internet auctions and had already booked 58 percent more charity auctions in the first quarter of 2009.

In an attempt to address continued fraud and theft, the Retail Industry Leaders Association, a lobbying group that represent the biggest retail chains in the United States, lobbyied Congress in mid-2008 to start regulating what can be sold on online auction sites. The association's articulated concerns included the transfer of stolen goods and counterfeit products. As of September 2009, Congress had not passed legislation addressing this.

With sluggish retail sales, manufacturers and wholesalers continued to utilize online auctions to decrease surplus and salvage supplies and merchandise, and the reverse logistics market was predicted to reach $63.1 billion in 2008, according to research by D.F. Blumberg Associates.

Sedo UK, the leading online marketplace for buying and selling Internet domains, experienced an increase of 44 percent in the number of domains sold in 2008 compared to 2007 and an increase of over 180 percent in the number of bidders participating.

INDUSTRY LEADERS

eBay Inc. The leading online auction company in 2007 was eBay Inc. Founded in 1995, the San Jose, California-based firm employed approximately 12,600 workers, listed roughly 50,000 product categories, hosted some 300,000 online stores, and generated millions of dollars in auction sales each day. In addition to dominating online auctions, the company was home to powerful related businesses and technologies including its lucrative PayPal payment service; the Internet telephone service Skype; and StubHub, a ticket business it acquired in 2007 for $310 million.

In order to make the purchase of bulky items such as automobiles simpler for customers, eBay also established local marketplaces throughout the United States. In the late 1990s, the company purchased a six percent stake in business to business (B2B) surplus retailer TradeOut.com and rolled out its own B2B unit called eBay Business Exchange for small businesses.

Despite the extremely challenging economic environment in 2008, including a slowdown in global e-commerce, eBay reported $8.5 billion in revenues for 2008, an 11 percent increase from the prior year. The eBay marketplace continued to be the largest in the world with nearly $60 billion of gross merchandise volume (the total value of goods sold in all of its Marketplaces) in 2008. PayPal continued to experience strong growth, both on eBay and across e-commerce, and Skype had a great year, reported the company, growing both revenues and user base.

Amazon.com Amazon.com's name, like that of eBay, was synonymous with a form of e-commerce, though Amazon.com earned its fame through book retailing. Nonetheless, Amazon.com was giving eBay a run for its money. Founded in 1994, the Seattle, Washington-based firm quickly established itself as one of the darlings of the Internet's emerging commerce sector, and began its online auction operations in early 1999. With operations in about 150 countries, the company was poised to capitalize on the rapidly expanding global cyberspace auction market. By 2007, Amazon.com's auction service included a wide range of categories, including Art and Antiques; Books; Cars and Transportation; Coins and Stamps, Collectibles, Comics, Cards and Sci-Fi, Computers and Software, Electronics and Photography, Jewelry, Gems and Watches, Movies and Video, Music, Sports, and Toys and Games. In 2008, Amazon.com reported revenues of $19.17 billion, up 29 percent from 2007.

Yahoo! Inc. One of the Internet's premier Web portals, Yahoo! Inc. moved into the online auction business in the late 1990s, attempting to take financial advantage of its position as the most heavily trafficked site on the Web. The company boasted a portfolio of over one million auction listings. The firm sold its European auction business to eBay in 2002. In 2007, Yahoo! announced that it would shutter its auction sites in the United States and Canada on June 16. The company, which reported sales of $7.2 billion in 2008, continued to operate Yahoo! Auction sites in Singapore, Taiwan, and Hong Kong.

UBid.com UBid.com, a Chicago-based merchant auction site with approximately 5 million registered users, was another auction leader heading into the late years of the first decade of the 2000s. UBid conducted auctions for a variety of products with a particular focus on closeout and refurbished computer hardware and electronic items. Though criticized for its often unpredictable merchandise availability, the company maintained a strong and loyal customer base. Seventy percent of the company's business was generated by repeat customers. UBid was spun off from its parent company Creative Computers in 1999 after beginning its auction operations in 1997. The company expanded with a focus on specific B2B markets beginning in 2000 when it unveiled its new Ironmall.com, which conducted auctions of construction equipment. In 2002, UBid generated revenues of roughly $200 million. The following year uBid was acquired by Petters Group Worldwide. By this time, the company claimed to have sold more than $1 billion worth of merchandise. In 2008, UBid.com. Holdings Inc. became Enable Holdings, Inc., holding itself out as "the world's leading excess inventory solutions company that links brand name sellers with customers around the globe."

AMERICA AND THE WORLD

The premier online auction companies were not particularly quick to move into foreign markets, and when they did, the moves were not without their complications. In France, for instance, the law stipulated that only a handful of certified auctioneers could operate. Similar cultural and legal barriers existed in other countries as well. Nonetheless, the major companies, especially Yahoo!, eBay, and Amazon.com, were spreading across the globe, setting up shop abroad by a variety of methods. eBay, for instance, bought its way into the German market by acquiring that country's Alando and quickly surpassed Ricardo.de to achieve German dominance. In the United Kingdom, the company struck out on its own; in Australia, it established a joint venture; and in Japan it sold a percentage of its Japanese operations to its industrial partner NEC.

China was a hotbed of online auction activity. Specifically, the country was dominated by Taobao, a subsidiary of the Alibaba Group, which claimed approximately 80 percent of China's consumer to consumer e-commerce, according to China IntelliConsulting Corp. reported in the April 18, 2007, issue of *China Business News*. In 2009, it was expected to double its 2008 revenues of about 400 million yuan ($58.6 million).

RESEARCH AND TECHNOLOGY

As pressures mounted on online auction companies to protect customers from fraudulent sales pitches, the companies scrambled to implement measures that could perform that duty at a minimum of extra work and expense to themselves. eBay partnered with Austin, Texas-based InfoGlide to implement InfoGlide software to weed out auction fraud. Designed to sniff out similarities between different files and databases, InfoGlide acted essentially as an exceptionally scrutinizing search engine, turning up information such as whether a particular eBay user was previously barred from the site for prior shenanigans. As a bonus, the software also proved useful in tracking and organizing information relating to the site's sales and statistics, such as best-and-worst lists of sales and customers. Previous incarnations of Info-Glide's software were used by the U.S. military to track terrorist threats and by police departments to try to catch criminals by identifying similarities between seemingly disparate crimes.

BIBLIOGRAPHY

"About uBid.com Holdings, Inc." Available from http://www.ubid.com.

"Alibaba's Taobao Unit May More Than Duble (sic) Revenue This Year." *HaoHao Report,* 20 September 2009. Available from http://www. haohaoreport.com/ChinaNews/Alibaba-s-Taobao-Unit-May-More-Than-Duble-Revenue-This-Year/.

Burke, Steven. "Betting On eBay—For Small System Builders, Online Auction Channel Can Pay Off in More Ways Than One." *Computer Reseller News,* 4 October 2005.

"China's Leading Auction Website Reports Surging Transaction Volume." *Xinhua News Agency,* 18 January 2007.

"eBay Trounces Expectations; the Online Auctioneer Reported a 52% Increase in Profits, Thanks in Part to its Paypal Unit, and Plans for Additional Stock Buybacks." *Business Week Online,* 19 April 2007. Available from www.businessweek.com

"Dallas/Fort Worth Airport Completes Latest Online Auction." *Airline Industry Information,* 7 February 2007.

"Fast Facts about PropertyRoom.com." Property Room Inc., 6 May 2007. Available from http://about.propertyroom.com.

Hof, Robert D. "The eBay Economy; The Company Is Not Just a Wildly Successful Startup. It Has Invented a Whole New Business World." *Business Week,* 25 August 2003.

IC3 2004 Internet Fraud Crime Report. Internet Fraud Complaint Center (IFCC), 2005. Available from http://www.ifccfbi.gov/strategy/2004_IC3Report.pdf.

Milbourn, Mary Ann. "Hundreds Take a Day to Learn the eBay Way." *The Orange County Register,* 6 May 2007.

"Online Auctions: Benefit Buying in Cyberspace." *Employee Benefit Advisor,* 1 January 2007.

"Online Reverse Auctions by State Governments to Grow 300 Percent By FY07." *Federal Computer Market Report,* 20 December 2004.

Seibel, Jacqueline. "Police Property Going Once, Going Twice...: Departments Turn to Online Auctions to Clear Unclaimed Goods." *Milwaukee Journal Sentinel,* 16 June 2006.

Stone, Brad. "Sold on eBay, Shipped by Amazon.com." *The New York Times,* 27 April 2007.

"Taobao Leaves Rivals Far Behind—Report." *China Business News,* 18 April 2007.

"Top Auction Web Sites." *ADWEEK,* 13 December 2004.

"Yahoo 2008 Revenue Profit 2009 *Fortune* 500 Rank : Finance." 25 April 2009. Available from http://finance.econsultant.com/yahoo-2008-revenue-profit-2009-fortune-500-rank/.

E-COMMERCE: ONLINE BROKERAGES

SIC CODE(S)

6211

INDUSTRY SNAPSHOT

During the first decade of the new century, online brokerages began hobbling back toward the aggressive competition that characterized the industry in the late 1990s, when the stock market was soaring and online brokerages were all the rage. The earlier (2000) collapse of the stock market and subsequent shakeout dramatically transformed this once hotshot industry. Forcing about 100 online brokerages out of business and producing several years of losses, layoffs, severe cost cutting, and boosted fees, the shakeout left behind a handful of well entrenched industry leaders with solid foundations, although no firm clearly dominated. Following the 2008 Wall Street shakeup and global economic meltdown, only 16 viable online brokerages existed in the United States in 2009, but they were rapidly gaining new clients and defectors from full-service brokers.

The U.S. brokerages offering online services were roughly divided into two camps. The first was comprised of online-oriented firms that focused primarily, even exclusively, on electronic accounts. These included the likes of E*TRADE Group, Inc. and TD Ameritrade Holding Corp. The second group consisted of traditional brokerage houses and investment firms that expanded into the online arena. Some, like Charles Schwab, had done so on a monumental scale, amassing a million or more online accounts in just a few years. Big high-end houses such as Merrill Lynch lumbered into the online business belatedly.

Many online brokerages, including discounters, increasingly emphasized offering a range of content and services beyond simple online trading. For some, the ultimate prize was to become a one-stop financial services site, offering banking, bill payment, retirement account management, and investment opportunities beyond stocks and mutual funds. When the technology industry bottomed out in 2001, online trading activity slowed drastically and online brokerages were forced to broaden their focus. Charles Schwab, for example, began to sell research reports and investment advice, along with online trading services. E*TRADE began to diversify into banking. Brokerage firms were also forced to trim their ranks to cut costs and alter their fee structure to generate increased revenues.

ORGANIZATION AND STRUCTURE

Online brokerages function in much the same way as conventional brokerages and are governed by mostly the same laws and regulations. Customers often set up most aspects of their accounts by filling out and submitting forms electronically and they fund their accounts by mailing a check or ordering a wire transfer to the brokerage. Most brokerages enforce a minimum balance, which can be as low as $1,000 at deep discount outfits or as high as $100,000 or more for full-featured accounts. Basic accounts at discount brokerages may provide only the ability to place orders and monitor the account, whereas pricey accounts boast of such features as detailed research reports, stock recommendations, and access to financial advisers.

Regulation All online brokerages are subject to federal oversight and regulation, principally by the Securities and Exchange Commission (SEC) as well as state jurisdiction and self-regulation from bodies such as the National Association of Securities Dealers (NASD). Federal regulations, for instance, charge brokers with the duty of finding the best execution for a trade—a vague concept that means the broker should seek to maximize the customer's returns in market transactions, not simply its own. Brokerages must also take reasonable steps to provide timely execution of orders (although no time limit exists) and inform customers that delays are possible. Myriad regulations cover the kinds of communications and assertions a brokerage can make to its customers. These laws and regulations are aimed at curbing fraud and ensuring that investors have ample information before entrusting their money to a brokerage and its computer system.

A Price for Everyone Online brokerages make their money in several ways and their pricing structures can be complex. Most obviously, they charge a commission on each trade their customers execute, although several industry players began resorting to free or deeply discounted trades in 2006 and 2007 as a competitive measure, if clients met certain criteria. While customary commissions are a percentage of the dollar value being traded, easily amounting to hundreds or thousands of dollars on a single transaction by a larger investor, the battle cry of discount brokers has been flat commissions. Under a flat pricing structure, customers pay a fixed surcharge on each trade, ranging between $8 and $30 at the most popular brokerages. Some firms also levy account management fees, typically assessed on an annual basis, which are either a flat rate or a percentage of the assets in the account. Most online brokerages—Ameritrade was a major exception in the early and middle years of the first decade of the 2000s—apply a handling or processing fee on top of the base trading cost.

Even under flat pricing, though, there are often some exceptions. For one, different types of stock orders can yield different fees. The most common distinction is between market orders, where the customer agrees to buy or sell shares at the prevailing current price, and limit orders, which allow the investor to specify a maximum or minimum price that must be met for the transaction to be executed. Limit orders usually cost a few dollars more than market orders.

A number of online brokerages instituted a graduated flat rate structure whereby people who trade more frequently pay lower fees. For example, E*TRADE gave its heavy traders a $5 rebate for each trade in excess of 29 per quarter, and a $10 rebate for each trade beyond the seventy-fourth. In effect, for the 75-plus share traders, the commission on trading popular NASDAQ stocks drops from $19.95 to $9.95 after completing 29 trades at $19.95 and another 45 at $14.95, at which point the brokerage has already collected $1,250 in commissions.

Other special pricing situations include trading in unlisted, over-the-counter stocks, which tend to be more speculative; thinly-traded issues at very low per-share prices; and very large orders, such as moving more than 5,000 shares in one trade. These sorts of transactions often include a per-share surcharge. If a customer requires a broker to help complete a trade, typically an additional fee is charged.

Margin Lending Lastly, brokerages earn money by lending their customers investment funds through margin accounts. Use of margin lending soared with the advent of online trading, with total margin debt leaping about 75 percent in 1999 alone. With these accounts, qualifying customers can buy or sell shares that are worth more than the total value of their own assets. In theory, if the customers get in on a profitable trade, they can reap most of the profits of having invested a greater sum. Of course, as does any lender, brokerages charge interest on the value of the margin trades, and margin transactions are regulated somewhat strictly to reduce the likelihood of investors losing too much money that isn't theirs. In a so-called margin call, the brokerage forces customers whose margin positions are losing money to either increase their own equity stake in the shares or sell the shares at a loss to pay back the brokerage. While this can be a setback for the investors, it tends to be profitable for brokerages, which may obtain 20 percent or more of their revenue from margin lending.

BACKGROUND AND DEVELOPMENT

The movement that ultimately gave rise to online brokerages in the 1990s dates to the mid-1970s deregulation of the securities industry. Until that time, full-service brokerages had a stranglehold on the business and their commissions were fixed by the securities exchanges they traded on. In 1975, the SEC deregulated the securities business, opening it up to new competition.

Originally a full-service brokerage like all the rest, Charles Schwab & Co., headed by its namesake, jumped on the opportunity to compete in the new era. The company is widely credited with launching the discount brokering business. The concept was simple: give customers access to affordable stock trades and let them fend for themselves (or simply pay extra) when it comes to researching investments and planning their portfolios. Schwab started offering no-frills investment services at deep discounts in 1974 and rapidly became the dominant player in that niche.

By most measures, online brokerages didn't exist until 1995, although companies such as Schwab and E*TRADE offered some form of electronic trading since the mid-1980s. The rapid growth of online services such as America Online and, increasingly, Internet-based information accessed over the Web, made for compelling market prospects. Using the eSchwab brand, Schwab was one of the first to set up shop online, quickly amassing 337,000 online accounts by 1995.

E*TRADE, which was founded in the 1980s as an electronic service for other brokerages, began offering retail online brokerage services in 1992 through the self-contained networks of America Online and CompuServe. Unlike Schwab, which had millions of accounts to draw on from its huge offline discount operation, E*TRADE was one of the first pure play (selling only over the Internet) online brokerages. It launched its Internet presence in 1996 and, taking a page from Schwab, began to compete on price with Schwab and other players in the nascent business.

As Internet use exploded in the 1990s and the U.S. stock market began a steep ascent, investors flocked to online brokerages. By 1997, more than a million online accounts had been opened, with nearly half at Schwab, and $50 billion in assets floated through cyber accounts. Swift growth continued through the late 1990s. At the end of 2000, the industry supported some 15 million online investment accounts, adding over a million new accounts each quarter, while the size of assets reached $1.6 trillion, according to International Data Corp. At that time, online brokerages were averaging as many as 500,000 trades each day, at times representing up to one-fifth of total market volume. However, online trading consumers had yet to maintain significant online financial resources. A study by McKinsey & Company showed that while over one-third of all trades were made online, those trades represented only five percent of total assets invested.

Old-school brokerages, such as Merrill Lynch & Co., Inc., Morgan Stanley Dean Witter & Co., and Donaldson, Lufkin & Jenrette, Inc. continued to lag in the online arena but were expected to slowly grab a larger share of the market. Many of these full service brokerages never quite took to the discounting revolution spearheaded by Schwab decades earlier so they considered mass market online accounts unprofitable and outside their league. Still, all the major brokerages did begin to offer online services, often with a mix of the traditional handholding of big firms and the self-empowerment of the startup services. Their commissions and account fees tended to be as large as ever, but some moved closer to the discount model while still insisting on substantial balances—easily $20,000 or more at a minimum. As a measure of the big firms' lag, Merrill Lynch's online accounts in early 2000 were at about the same number that Schwab had three years earlier.

Customer service proved to be the industry's albatross at the beginning of the twenty-first century. In part victims of their own success, online brokerages sometimes failed to invest adequately in their technical and corporate infrastructures. As a result, when trading activity surged, their systems became sluggish and frustrating to use—a woeful liability in a fast-moving market—and occasionally crashed. Consequently, online brokerages were inundated with technical support and general customer service requests that they labored to keep up with, again often failing in their customers' eyes. Surveys reported high levels of customer dissatisfaction with some aspects of online services and suggested that many online investors contemplated switching brokerages because of perceived bad service.

End of the GoldenAge The NASDAQ experienced the largest one-year drop in its history in 2000, and many Dow Jones Industrial Average stocks posted losses. When the market failed to stabilize in 2001, online trading activity dipped precipitously, forcing online brokerages to broaden their focus. For example, Datek pledged to offer enhanced services that would keep its online trading customers informed of market conditions. To this end, Datek announced a strategic partnership with MarketWatch.com, a leading Internet-based provider of financial news and information. The March 2001 deal enabled Datek customers to access CBS MarketWatch.com's financial news and real time headlines via Datek's News Center. Industry leader Charles Schwab began to sell research reports and investment advice along with its online trading services, and E*TRADE began to diversify into banking. By 2002, E*TRADE's banking segment, which offered a wide variety of consumer banking products and services, had become the largest Internet bank in the United States with 490,913 accounts.

Along with forcing online firms to broaden their focus, trim their ranks, alter their fee structures, and pursue new markets, the stock market "crash" of 2000 also sparked a wave of industry consolidation. In 2001, Ameritrade paid $40 million for TradeCast Ltd. The addition of TradeCast's business to business operations prompted the eventual reorganization of Ameritrade into two units serving different clients, individual investors and institutional investors. Rival E*Trade acquired online mortgage originator LoansDirect, which it renamed E*TRADE Mortgage; PrivateAccounts Inc., which it renamed E*TRADE Advisory Services; and online brokerage firm Web Street Inc. The purchase of Dempsey & Company LLC, a market-making services firm, enabled E*TRADE to handle all aspects of equity trading. In 2002, E*Trade acquired Tradescape and, in September of that year, Ameritrade paid $1.3 billion for Datek Online to become the leading online brokerage based on volume.

After the stampede to online trading in the late 1990s, online trading tailed off in the early years of the first decade of the 2000s. In the winter of 2000, for instance, Internet-based trading represented 45 percent of daily trading volume. By late 2002, this figure fell to just 15 percent, according to *Barron's,* which further reported that online accounts increased 5 percent in 2002, while total customer assets fell 10 percent, as did daily trading activity. The novelty of online trading having long since worn off, and with competition extremely tough, online brokerages increasingly waged their battle for customers in the realm of customer satisfaction, differentiating themselves from the competition via value-added services and the convenience of one-stop shopping for financial products and information.

However, making customers happy wasn't the only way leading online brokerage firms competed. Through the early years of the twenty-first century's first decade, several of the largest players pushed aggressive ads, often naming competitors' names while painting unflattering portraits of them. Shortly after backing off attempts to sell its online trading business to E*TRADE or Charles Schwab, TD Waterhouse launched an aggressive ad campaign knocking its competition for their alleged high prices. For its part, Charles Schwab pushed a commercial spot depicting an unnamed rival attempting to dress up a worthless stock to encourage customers to buy. Though making for ugly competition, by 2004, such strategies appeared to be paying off: TD Waterhouse reported the commercials were its most successful ever, quickly bolstering its client roster.

Brokerage firms were also forced to trim their ranks in an effort to cut costs. Between 2000 and 2003, Charles Schwab reduced its workforce from 26,000 to less than 19,000. Many firms also increased their fees in an effort to offset the impact of fewer trades. In 2002, Datek implemented a $10.99 fee for each trade, a $2.99 increase over its $8.00 fee established in 2000. And after shareholders publicly criticized E*TRADE CEO Christos Cotsakos for his allegedly exorbitant salary, E*TRADE trimmed his compensation by roughly $25 million. Cost cutting continued into the middle years of the first decade of the 2000s. In a move that surprised many observers, Schwab even announced in 2003 its plans to cease matching employee payments into 401(k) plans.

The legions of online investors include many small investors who never had brokerage accounts before the online craze. The online brokerages welcomed—and often depended on—this broadening of the investment market to build up their businesses. Because most of these firms charged flat rates for trading, their business depended on getting lots of customers who make lots of trades. However, when small investors began to bail out of the trading market in the early years of the first decade of the 2000s, online brokerages began to set their sites on wealthier

clients. Forrester Research estimated in 2002 that roughly 80 percent of U.S. citizens with more than $1 million to invest had Internet access and were more likely than less wealthy Internet users to use the Internet to obtain financial information.

According to an estimate from one industry player, the number of online brokerages stood at approximately 100 in 2005. This number was expected to fall to about 50 by the end of the decade and then level off, amidst the backdrop of industry consolidation. By late 2005, the financial research and consulting firm TowerGroup estimated that consumers had placed about $1.7 trillion in assets with online brokerages, according to *Business Week.*

There were numerous examples of consolidation in the first decade of the 2000s. After more than two years of discussion between the two firms, Ameritrade acquired TD Waterhouse from TD Bank Financial Group in January 2006 for $2.9 billion, forming a new company named TD Ameritrade Holding Corp. In May and June of 2005, E*TRADE made two unsuccessful bids to buy Ameritrade. While those deals, which included a $6 billion-plus offer, never materialized, E*TRADE made other acquisitions that year. These included JP Morgan's online discount brokerage, BrownCo, for $1.6 billion, and the U.S. online operations of BMO Financial Group's Harrisdirect for $700 million.

Online brokerages enjoyed a growing base of subscribers heading toward the end of the twenty first century's last decade, according to *Electronic Information Report.* In its June 4, 2007, issue, the publication's Brokerage & Financial Information Services Online Subscriber Survey revealed that online brokerages had 1.32 million subscriptions in the first quarter of 2007, following an annual increase of 5.2 percent in 2006.

Competition in the online brokerage segment reached a boiling point of sorts in late 2006 when Zecco.com, a start-up brokerage in Ontario, California, allowed customers with a minimum balance of $2,500 to make free trades. Established financial companies like Bank of America and Wells Fargo quickly followed suit, offering free trades to customers who met certain criteria. For example, this perk was available to Bank of America customers who carried a $25,000 minimum balance in their savings, checking, or money market account. Still other brokerages were offering deeply discounted trades. In all, these developments meant that regular players like TD Ameritrade and E*Trade were feeling the heat as other firms vied for their share of the online investment pie.

Some industry regulars downplayed the impact of free trades, arguing that investors value more than just the cost of trades and consider factors such as investment advice and service when dealing with a broker. Others said the strategy simply was not an effective way to entice long-term investors who were not frequent traders, since the savings would not amount to very much money. However, industry observers countered that the latter was not necessarily true. They contended that a segment of long-term investors that had avoided exchange-traded funds—over concerns that fees would outweigh or cancel out any meaningful returns—would be called to action.

Security remained a pressing problem for the industry as hackers developed ever more sophisticated techniques to steal from online investors. While *Business Week* estimated that losses from online brokerage theft were less than $20 million annually, the SEC was concerned enough to issue an investor guide in late 2005 outlining steps investors could take to protect their financial data. The problem, according to experts, was not the security of the brokers themselves, which had virtually flawless security measures in place to protect customers. Rather, it was a lack of adequate protection on individual investors' PCs, such as the absence of a personal firewall or anti-spyware software. In addition, cyber criminals used elaborate phishing schemes in an attempt to trick investors, with seemingly legitimate e-mails, into revealing personal account information and/or passwords. The best defense for such schemes was often common sense.

In March 2007 *USA Today* reported on two separate security-related developments involving online investors, both of which resulted in action by the Securities and Exchange Commission (SEC). One incident involved 25 companies that were suspected of using unsolicited e-mail campaigns to artificially inflate their stock prices. Another complex scheme involved criminals who used stolen passwords to access online accounts at Merrill Lynch, Fidelity Investments, Vanguard, Charles Schwab, E*Trade, and TD Ameritrade. Once logged on, the thieves sold victims' portfolios and used the money to buy additional shares of penny stocks they owned, causing the share price to artificially jump. They then sold off the penny stocks for a nice profit. The latter scheme resulted in the SEC freezing nearly $733,000 in allegedly stolen assets connected to crooks in countries such as Russia and Latvia. Both of these incidents indicated a continued need for investor vigilance.

CURRENT CONDITIONS

The financial crisis of 2008 (the S&P 500 fell 38 percent and Lehman Brothers collapsed in September) accelerated a downward spiral for large investment banks as investors pulled more than $100 billion from traditional full-service brokerages like Citigroup's Smith Barney and Bank of America/Merrill Lynch. Conversely, $32 billion moved into the two largest online brokerages, TD Ameritrade Holding and Charles Schwab, said Rachel Chang in her July 2009 article for Reuters. Referring to data

from Gartner Research, she noted that for 2008, 43 percent of investors worked with full-service brokers while 24 percent were with online ones. However, the trend was clearly and convincingly toward online outfits. As of 2009, there were 16 established Internet brokerages operating in the United States, Chang noted.

INDUSTRY LEADERS

TD Ameritrade Holding Corp. Prior to its $1.3 billion purchase of Datek in 2002, Ameritrade Holding Corp. was a smaller deep discount operation that nonetheless ranked among the top five or six brokerages in terms of account numbers and trading volume. Following the merger, Ameritrade managed to retain 90 percent of its new customers, an extraordinary feat in the industry. The company continued to diversify and cater to several types of investors, such as Ameritrade Plus and Freetrade.com services specialized in more experienced traders. Further expanding its online trading volume, Ameritrade purchased SWS Group's Mydiscountbroker.com accounts and those of BrokerageAmerica in 2003, and some 100,000 such accounts via its acquisition of Bidwell & Company in 2004.

After more than two years of discussion between the two firms, Ameritrade acquired TD Waterhouse from TD Bank Financial Group in 2006 for $2.9 billion, forming a new company named TD Ameritrade Holding Corp. Controlled by Canada's Toronto Dominion Bank, before the sale TD Waterhouse had boasted 3.2 million online brokerage accounts overall in 2004, making it the fourth largest online brokerage in daily trades and third in terms of total accounts, although it ranked first by trades-per-day in 2009. The company saw a 46 percent year-on-year rise in new accounts during the last quarter of 2008, bringing in $7.8 billion in new assets. Overall, it reported $240 billion in managed funds with 2008 revenues exceeding $2.7 billion.

Charles Schwab One of the biggest fish in the online brokerage sea, San Francisco-based Charles Schwab gained its position through its market leadership in the closely related discount brokerage business, specializing in accounts for self-serve investors. Although Schwab was able to command as much as half of the entire online brokerage business in the mid-1990s, by 1999 the flood of other entrants had trimmed its share to less than 20 percent. Schwab purchased heavyweight online brokerage CyberTrader in 2000, further entrenching its industry leadership. In its movement toward one-stop financial shopping, the firm launched Charles Schwab Bank. In 2005 the company filed a lawsuit against TD Waterhouse over an ad that made negative claims about its service and prices. By 2007 the company had client assets totaling $1.3 trillion, 6.8 million brokerage accounts, and

1.1 million corporate retirement plan participants. Schwab reported 2008 revenues of $5.3 billion.

ETRADE Financial Corp. With more than 4 million accounts in 2007, E*TRADE Financial Corp. was another online brokerage powerhouse. The company advertised aggressively to make its site one of the premier finance destinations on the Internet. During E*TRADE's short history, its strategy focused on growth via the use of cutting-edge technology. When the hype surrounding dot-com start-ups began to die in 2000, however, E*TRADE was forced to retool its products and services to decrease its dependency on online trading revenues. E*TRADE opened E*TRADE Financial Centers in New York, Boston, Beverly Hills, Denver, and San Francisco. The firm purchased Tradescape's online trading business in 2002 for $280 million, immediately on the heels of rival Ameritrade's purchase of Datek. In May and June of 2005, E*TRADE made two unsuccessful bids for buy Ameritrade but made other acquisitions that year. These included JP Morgan's online discount brokerage, BrownCo, for $1.6 billion, and the U.S. online operations of BMO Financial Group's Harrisdirect for $700 million. Because of its risky loan portfolios, the company reported a net loss of $832 million for its third quarter in 2009, which followed two previous 2009 quarterly losses.

BIBLIOGRAPHY

Borrus, Amy, Mike McNamee, Brian Grow, and Adrienne Carter. "Invasion of the Stock Hackers; An Alarmed SEC Says that Teams of Thieves are Lifting Passwords from Home PCs—and Emptying Online Brokerage Accounts." *Business Week*, 14 November 2005.

Braham, Lewis. "The Best E-Broker for You." *Business Week*, 31 July 2006.

Carey, Theresa W. "Squeezed Down." *Barron's*, 3 March 2003.

Chang, Rachel. "Investors dump brokers to go it alone online." Reuters, 24 July 2009. Available from http://www.reuters.com/article/wtUSInvestingNews/idUSTRE56N63H20090724.

Charles Schwab. Available from http://www.schwab.com.

Craig, Suzanne, and Robin Sidel. "E*TRADE, Toronto Dominion Unit End Merger Talks." *Wall Street Journal*, 19 January 2004.

"E*Trade to Acquire Harrisdirect; The Consolidation of Online Stock Trading Firms Continued Monday as E*Trade Financial Announced It Will Acquire the U.S. Online Brokerage Operations of Harrisdirect for $700 Million." *InternetWeek*, 8 August 2005.

"E*TRADE FINANCIAL Corporation Announces Third Quarter 2009 Results." Reuters, 27 October 2009. Available from http://www.reuters.com/article/pressRelease/idUS220087+27-Oct-2009+BW20091027.

"Financial Segment Posts 4.5% Subscriber Increase." *Electronic Information Report*, 4 June 2007.

"JupiterResearch Ranks Ameritrade the Top Online Brokerage and Sees Mixed Impact of Merger with TD Waterhouse." *Business Wire*, 26 July 2005.

Lugo, Denise. "TD Waterhouse Gets Pushy." *The Investment Dealers' Digest*, 16 February 2004.

"Online Brokers Step Up Competition with Free Trades." *USA Today*, 16 January 2007.

"Price War Erupts as BofA Offers Free Trades." *USA Today*, 12 October 2006.

"SEC Suspends Trading for 35 Companies, Cites Spam Activity." *USA Today*, 9 March 2007.

"SEC Urges Investors to Protect their Online Brokerage Accounts from Identity Thieves." *Banking & Financial Services Policy Report*, February 2006.

Stovall, Sam "S&P Cuts Telecom Services Sector; Also: Comments on E-Trade's Plans to Buy JP Morgan's Online Brokerage, a Downgrade of Forest Labs, and More Analyst Opinions." *Business Week Online*, 30 September 2005. Available from www.businessweek.com.

Strasburg, Jenny. "Ameritrade-TD Waterhouse Merger Took a Long Time; Chief Executive Moglia Foresees Additional Consolidation in Online Brokerage Business." *San Francisco Chronicle*, 5 July 2005.

TD Ameritrade, 2008. Available from http:// www.amtd.com.

"TD Ameritrade Transaction Complete; TD Bank Financial Group Gains Ownership Stake in Leading Online Brokerage Player TD Ameritrade." *CNW Group*, 25 January 2006.

Wolfe, Daniel. "Online Brokerages Getting Ready for 'A Small Y2K.'" *American Banker*, 8 March 2007.

E-COMMERCE: ONLINE GROCERY SHOPPING

———■———

SIC CODE(S)

5411

INDUSTRY SNAPSHOT

In the closing years of the twentieth century, no one could have predicted a headline that read "Online grocery shopping isn't dead." The industry was born in the early 1980s, when various firms made tentative forays into computer-based grocery shopping. Nevertheless, it was not until the late 1990s that a new breed of well-funded Internet-based services held promise for tapping into the potentially massive U.S. market for online grocery services. It was a promise they could not deliver. By 2003, the pioneers in the online grocery business had all but vanished.

The spectacular failure of the emerging industry took many in the business world by surprise. Online grocers had to compete with both traditional supermarkets and, to a lesser degree, restaurants—especially those offering takeout and delivery. It was an uphill battle to take customers from either side, but online grocers believed that the customers would come in large numbers. Online grocer Webvan spent millions of dollars constructing elaborate warehouse and distribution systems without first securing a single customer. The crowds never came, and one by one, the lineup of online players went out of business.

However, online grocers were poised to make a comeback. This time they were moving slowly and with a new plan. According to the Nielsen Company's Maya Swedowsky, Associate Research Director, and Alex Burmaster, Communications Director for the United Kingdom and European markets, in their October 2009 Nielsen newswire, "Consumer Opportunities Abound for Online Grocers," there were four key megatrends that would carry the market beyond 2010: (1) the convenience of online shopping; (2) the coming of age of computer-raised Generation-Y shoppers; (3) broadband Internet, with almost two-thirds of Americans having access; and (4) customization and personalization of shopping experiences through the use of online digital platforms.

Nevertheless, as of early 2009 online grocery sales attributed to less than one percent of the total food and beverage industry. Plunkett Research estimated the 2009 U.S. food industry (including but not limited to retail food stores and supermarkets, convenience stores, restaurants, and farming) at $1.57 trillion.

ORGANIZATION AND STRUCTURE

In the mid-1990s, the biggest obstacle to running a successful Web-based grocery service was logistics—getting the product to the customer. This hurdle was undeniably a factor when it came to perishable goods. At least four business models had been tested: opting to sell only non-perishables and ship them via express delivery vendors such as FedEx; affiliating with physical grocery stores in certain regions and thereby relying on the old-fashioned grocer to handle logistics down to the city or even neighborhood level; developing independent distribution systems, complete with a system of regional and local warehouses and a fleet of delivery trucks; and offering perishables and non-perishables, but only with very limited stock (often snacks or convenience foods), in limited distribution areas (often within one city), and accompanied by such non-grocery services as video rental and laundry services. At that time, only two models, grocery store-affiliated online ventures and using independent express delivery for non-perishables, continued to support active business ventures.

The oldest and perhaps most obvious way to organize a home grocery delivery service is around the ample infrastructure of the bricks-and-mortar grocery industry. This strategy was industry founder Peapod's approach. The online grocer signs agreements with various supermarket chains and has its own fleet of delivery trucks deliver groceries from the store to its customers' homes. Several supermarkets, including Safeway, Shaw's, and Pink Dot, launched online order and delivery systems.

For the most part, though, store-affiliated online grocery ventures did poorly as partnerships between independent entities. A number of programs sponsored by stores were canceled in the mid-1990s because of low demand. Peapod, for all its perseverance, never made a profit from 1989 to 2000 and was teetering on insolvency by the end of that period, though it managed to hang on through an alliance with Netherlands-based grocer Royal Ahold NV.

Part of the problem may be inefficiencies in store logistics, which are optimized for consumers to see, smell, touch, and squeeze their favorite groceries in stores. Some believe that if delivery is the object, a specially designed warehouse is better suited for rapid order assembly and shipment. NetGrocers.com used the first model and only shipped nonperishable items via Federal Express. Using an independent freight shipper saved the company the cost of hiring employees to pack and deliver orders. Some analysts did not consider this a true online grocery model, since the customers' item selections were restricted.

BACKGROUND AND DEVELOPMENT

Directly or indirectly, grocery stores have allowed people to place and receive orders at home for decades. Neighborhood grocers have provided delivery service to customers since at least the nineteenth century. Moreover, since the 1960s, third party services have offered phone-in or dial-in ordering and delivery services in local areas.

More often than not, it seems these services have not caught on. They were often unavailable or unappealing to a wide number of consumers; and even more frequently, they were not profitable for the vendors. In the 1980s, for example, a number of delivery services sprang up claiming to be the solution for overworked, dual income couples. With services couched in terms such as "teleshopping," they allowed consumers within local service areas to phone in grocery orders and have them delivered at an appointed time. This practice never gained widespread acceptance.

By the middle to late 1980s, a number of local grocery delivery services also allowed consumers to browse listings and place orders by computer. Several marketing strategies were employed during this time and were revived in the late 1990s, such as catering to suburban families and using price promotions to attract new customers. Observers were enthusiastic that grocery delivery would be commonplace by 1990.

Out of this environment grew one of the more enduring online grocery services, Peapod, based in suburban Chicago. Founded in 1989, Peapod was one of the biggest and best-known services to rely solely on computer-based orders. Peapod subscribers used the company's proprietary software and a modem to dial into its local systems, originally in Chicago and San Francisco, where it had alliances with the Jewel and Safeway chains respectively. Once an order was placed, Peapod staff would go to the local store, select the requested items, and deliver them to the customer.

Publicity over Peapod and similar services, coupled with the fear of missing some great technological leap forward, caused many supermarkets to launch their own versions of home-based order and delivery. Safeway considered expanding its use of Peapod in order to cover a wider area of northern California and part of Nevada. Other chains linked their catalogs to consumer online content services, such as the Prodigy network, and dispatched their own employees to fill orders.

By the mid-1990s, much of the expected promise had failed to materialize. Stores often found the arrangements unprofitable when their own workers were given the responsibility of assembling orders. In some cases where both phone and personal computer (PC) orders were accepted, computer orders were negligible, while the more labor-intensive phone orders predominated. Specialty services such as Peapod experienced growing demand, with sales nearly doubling each year, but costs kept mounting as well, leaving it with recurring losses and escalating debt.

Meanwhile, other competitors surfaced. Streamline Inc., of Westwood, Massachusetts, became one of the more aggressive players that did not rely on existing supermarkets. The suburban Boston firm, founded in 1993, focused instead on developing its own warehouse and relationships with wholesalers and distributors in a bid to keep costs down and efficiency high. Streamline's model was also unique because it offered dry cleaning and other non-grocery services as well. A separate innovation was its use of pre-packed service boxes with freezer and refrigerator compartments, so delivery staff could drop off groceries in a customer's basement or garage without the customer being there. In effect, Streamline created a blueprint that others followed once the Internet was integrated into the model.

Companies such as Streamline, Peapod, and HomeRuns (operated by the Maine grocery chain Hannaford Bros.) began setting up shop on the Web in 1996. This move came just as Internet use was skyrocketing and the Web was being positioned as a resource for ordinary consumers and families rather than technophiles. The Internet provided a familiar and almost universal platform on which firms could build their order-taking systems, in contrast to the murky world of proprietary software running on the customer's PC and dialing into a delivery service's computer.

Perhaps the final pivotal event to influence the nascent online shopping business was the Internet stock craze and the infusion of cash into "dot-com" companies. Emboldened by Netscape's phenomenal stock launch, venture capitalists and investors began combing the Internet for the next blockbuster concept. Entrepreneurs stepped up to try to grab the brass ring as well. Against this backdrop emerged competitors such as HomeGrocer.com and Webvan.

Separately, a number of analysts attempted to attach a price to the potential market for online grocery shopping. There was some agreement that the potential market was vast and would go untapped for some years, but the specific estimates again varied. Forrester believed the total market potential in the early years of the first decade of the 2000s was approaching $40 billion. Gazing further out, a senior executive at Streamline pegged the market's potential at $60 billion by 2007. To whatever extent the industry realizes this market potential, nearly all of its gains were expected to come at the expense of traditional grocery retailers.

One of the biggest challenges for online grocers was to tap into the peculiar customer attitudes toward online grocery shopping. A survey by PricewaterhouseCoopers in 2000 found that 21 percent of Internet users insisted that nothing could persuade them to buy their groceries online. Interestingly, price seemed to be a much bigger factor than convenience for online grocery shoppers. Only 11 percent of survey respondents said they would pay more for groceries even if ordering online saved them time. Nearly half wanted free delivery as an inducement to order online.

As newer firms flush with capital entered the online grocery arena, some of the old-timers, such as Peapod, stumbled. Some argue that Peapod's store-dependent model, one it was belatedly trying to break from in the late 1990s, was simply flawed. Although the company went public in 1997, it never achieved the levels of market capitalization and private funding that firms such as Webvan garnered. The situation began to deteriorate in 1999, when Peapod admitted it had cash flow problems. The announcement unnerved the stock market and sent Peapod's shares tumbling, just when it needed money most. By early 2000, Peapod had lined up a hefty $120 million deal with a group of corporate investors, but the deal caved in when Peapod's chief executive, William Malloy, fell ill and abruptly resigned in March 2000. On the brink of insolvency, Peapod stared at a dismal future. Then, in April, the Netherlands-based

grocery firm Royal Ahold NV came to Peapod's rescue, paying $73 million to Peapod in exchange for a 51 percent share of the company. Royal Ahold saw the move as an expansion of its domestic online grocery business into the United States. Peapod went on to rebuild and thrive under new management.

However, Peapod's troubles were only the beginning. In the next year and a half, all leading online grocers disappeared. Shoplink.com, Streamline.com, Homegrocer.com, Kozmo.com, HomeRuns.com, and Urbanfetch.com, all smaller regional players, were forced out of business. In July 2001, the industry was flattened when Webvan.com declared bankruptcy after running through almost one billion dollars in venture capital.

The Webvan story was described by an uncommon number of business and media types as a "tragedy"—not simply a business failure, but a real debacle. Not only did the company manage to lose $1 billion in record time, but its failure was seen as an indication that online grocery shopping could not succeed. In the aftermath of the bankruptcy, explanations and analysis were plentiful. What made this story so unfortunate in the eyes of many was that Webvan genuinely seemed to have the potential to be a blockbuster concept. It was not some get-rich-quick scheme perpetuated by a dot-com company with no visible product or revenue stream, so how it failed remained the question.

After the initial shock of the collapse, conventional wisdom said the business model for online grocery shopping was just not effective and should be laid to rest. A closer look suggested that the management team driving Webvan might have suffered from poor judgment. Executives were criticized for planning on a grand scale. In 1999, the company set out to spend $1 billion on distribution centers around the nation. Those who observed the results firsthand described the centers as inefficient with much wasted space. They were also costly to maintain and had expanded into too many regions at one time. Spending spiraled out of control, and there were not enough customers to generate profitable revenues. Many reports noted that the grocery business operates with a very small profit margin, and it is difficult under any circumstance to make money. The additional costs of warehouses, vans, and delivery employees did nothing to reduce the overhead. Another obstacle to success was the merger in September 2000 of Webvan.com and HomeGrocer.com. The two operations did not mesh well, and some later said that the merger was the beginning of Webvan's undoing. The executives at the dot-com company eventually knew the company was in trouble and began pulling out of certain geographic areas in order to stop the flow of cash. Just months before declaring bankruptcy, the company launched a rebranding campaign. It was too late, however, and in July 2001, Webvan filed for Chapter 11 bankruptcy.

In early 2003 there were only a few names remaining in the online grocery sector, but regional bricks-and-mortar grocery stores were lining up to try their luck with the Internet option. Surprisingly, Peapod weathered the storm of dot-com failures and remained in business, although their operation was scaled down. Netherlands retailer Royal Ahold purchased 58 percent of Peapod in 2000 and installed Marc van Gelder as CEO. Royal Ahold remained optimistic about the opportunities in the lucrative online market and purchased the remaining stake in Peapod. In May 2002 van Gelder claimed that all of Peapod's markets except one had reached profitability. He credited the partnership with Ahold as the critical element in the company's success. Ahold owned traditional grocery stores throughout the nation, including the popular names Stop & Shop and Giant Foods, which served as order fulfillment sites.

Others watched from the sidelines and eagerly entered the marketplace. Albertson's opened online outlets in the Seattle, Washington and San Diego areas. Using existing stores and employees to fill orders, the company slowly created a profitable niche for itself. Publix Supermarkets also launched an online shopping option based in the southeastern states. In August 2002 Vons began offering online shopping in Southern California. The chain's parent company, Safeway, already offered the service in Northern California and Oregon. All of these enterprises worked in conjunction with brick-and-mortar partners, thus eliminating the need for costly warehouse construction.

Tesco, a British grocer, also met with good fortune online. Tesco, a top supermarket chain in the United Kingdom, used the hybrid model of online ordering and order fulfillment through its traditional grocery stores. Some analysts attributed Tesco's success to the thickly populated London landscape. Seven or eight deliveries could be completed in an hour due to the close proximity of customers' homes. This situation contrasted with the typical U.S. market in which drivers had to contend with extensive suburbs and commuter traffic, limiting them to three or four deliveries an hour. In the early years of the first decade of the 2000s, Tesco did not believe the United States was a lost cause in the online grocery industry. In June 2001 Tesco formed a partnership with Safeway and its online arm, Groceryworks.com.

By 2004, online grocery shopping continued to be better received in the United Kingdom than in the United States. At the close of 2003, there were about 2 million shoppers registered in the United Kingdom alone, with 170,000 of them placing regular weekly orders. The challenge was not in attracting customers but in converting shoppers into "regulars," which appeared to happen after the fourth order.

However, traditional brick-and-mortar grocery stores have the advantage of a variety of marketing ploys to encourage impulse buys of generally high-profit merchandise, which typically comprises 20 percent of a customer's order. Once shoppers became regulars, the online grocery stores were challenged to attract shoppers to their version of these high-profit items, not just to the staple 80 percent of each grocery order that generally does not differ from week to week. Promotions such as coupons, recipes, and bundles were used for marketing tools, the online version of promotional end-cap display (merchandise displays at the end of isles, often for high margin, impulse items).

Domestically, Florida-based PublixDirect shut down in 2003. On the opposite coast, Vons was seeing growth in the Southern California market. Most successful of all that year, Joe Fedele launched Fresh Direct in New York City, a gourmet online grocery store, which was already making a profit by 2004. The company was succeeding by what Fedele described to *Business Week* as "mass production of customized orders." Fresh Direct's formula was to eliminate intermediaries by purchasing directly from producers, elevating quality and reducing prices. Because costs were lower, prices were lower. At the close of 2003, Fresh Direct employed 600 workers and handled well over 3,000 orders each day.

A number of noteworthy industry developments occurred in 2006. In May, e-commerce heavyweight Amazon.com made its entry into the sector by launching an online grocery store. By mid-2007, the store had a growing selection of approximately 22,000 non-perishable items (down to 14,000 in 2009), including some 7,000 organic choices. The company offered shipping at no charge to customers who took advantage of its Amazon Prime, Super Saver Shipping, and free standard shipping options. In addition to everyday choices like Kellogg's cereal, Amazon.com also offered specialty selections like Zico Pure Coconut Water.

Another major industry development occurred in October 2006 when Safeway Inc. acquired full ownership of GroceryWorks, the online grocery service in which it already had a 56.2 percent stake. The remaining shares were acquired from Tesco plc and other shareholders. Following the transaction, GroceryWorks became a wholly owned subsidiary of Safeway.

Moving toward 2008, the industry's leading players continued to prosper, despite occasional predictions of their eventual demise. Behind their staying power was a strategy of slow, measured growth. A departure from the early dot-com days, this approach seemed to be working as a growing base of customers—especially busy two-income families in urban markets—turned to online grocers to make their lives easier.

One key strategy for the industry was an emphasis on prepared meals, wine, and fresh meats and vegetables. Fresh-Direct indicated that a major source of its growth came from prepared meals. The company competed with area restaurants by offering its customers specialties such as chocolate soufflé and cassoulet. In Minnesota, SimonDelivers forged alliances with popular bakeries, caterers, and pizzerias to offer its customers a choice of tasteful selections, and also offered fish fillets from a supplier that flew in seafood from the West Coast on a daily basis. Smaller players in other markets concentrated on natural and organic products in order to compete with larger competitors.

As the industry moved forward, it no longer faced the early dot-com hurdle of wooing customers to use the Internet for placing orders online. Instead, the major challenge appeared to be logistical in nature, as players struggled to find the best fulfillment model. Existing approaches ranged from picking orders off the shelves of traditional supermarkets to dedicated distribution centers. Each approach had different advantages and disadvantages, and it remained to be seen which would win out as the gold standard.

CURRENT CONDITIONS

Despite the rosier outlook than in previous times, online grocery sales still accounted for less than one percent of all food and beverage sales in 2008, as reported by Nielsen Company's Maya Swedowsky and Alex Burmaster in their October 2009 Nielsen newswire, "Consumer Opportunities Abound for Online Grocers." According to Nielsen research, the industry was more developed and diversified in Europe (particularly the UK) than in the United States. Another interesting Nielsen finding: on average, online shoppers tended to spend twice as much as offline when making food and beverage purchases. Two reasons cited as contributing to this finding were that many online grocers offered free shipping and had minimum order requirements.

Nielsen also reported that total online grocery industry sales reached approximately $3.75 billion in 2008, but were still poised for growth. (Datamonitor had reported sales of $3.47 billion for the year previous, 2007.) The Datamonitor report (August 2008) also revealed that actual food was the primary focus of online sales (as opposed to other items sold by online grocers), 53 percent of total online sales in the United States compared to 43 percent in Europe.

With the growth of the Internet and broadband, 94 percent of U.S. consumers have shopped online, noted online grocery network giant, MyWebGrocer. This represents a captive consumer market ready to tap. Moreover, a 2008 study by Coupons, Inc., and Simmons Market Research showed that the number of Americans using online coupons rose from 26 million in 2005 to 34 million in 2007 (estimated 36 million in 2008).

INDUSTRY LEADERS

MyWebGrocer MyWebGrocer (MyWebGrocer.com), a provider of online commerce software and digital media services for grocery stores and consumer goods companies, was one of the first to launch online Software as a Service for retail grocers in 1999. MyWebGrocer increases basket size (the average 2009 online order was $140, increasing with best class retailers to $160+), acquires new customers, retains current customers, and drives revenue in-store and online business for their clients. MyWebGrocer has the largest grocery advertising network in the country covering 85 percent of the US, earning their clients direct ad revenue. Some of their clients include Shoprite, Lowes Food Stores, Big Y, Food Lion, and 90 other leading grocery chains. In January 2009, MyWebGrocer announced the addition of Peapod to its network, bringing the total number of retailers it served to 93, collectively representing more than $90 billion in grocery sales. Roughly $46 billion of that had just been added in the previous six months with the addition of new partners such as A&P, Piggly Wiggly, Lunds, Roche Brothers, Big Y, and then Peapod. With the addition of Peapod, the majority of retail grocery online transactions occur within the MyWebGrocer advertising network.

Peapod Based in Skokie, Illinois, Peapod is one of the oldest firms in the online grocery industry. Founded in 1989 by brothers Andrew and Thomas Parkinson, Peapod was first offered in the Chicago area, where it teamed up with the large Jewel supermarket chain. Later, Peapod expanded to the San Francisco Bay area; Boston; Columbus, Ohio; and Dallas, Houston, and Austin, Texas. Slow to adapt from its inefficient store shopping service model, Peapod was blindsided in the late 1990s by mounting costs and competition. It failed to hold investors' imaginations the way feisty Webvan did, and because of its funding and management crises, Peapod in 2000 was forced into the arms of Netherlands-based Royal Ahold NV.

By 2009, Peapod, which turned 20 that year, was serving 14 major U.S. markets and had achieved over 13 million deliveries since its inception. Although parent Dutch retail company Ahold would not release financial numbers, industry sources estimated Peapod's 2008 sales to be about $373 million, according to Jon Springer in *Supermarket News,* (quoting the Internet Retailer Top 500 Guide). The Guide estimated an average 900,000 unique visitors to Peapod each month, with around 1.5 million total visits per month. Average basket ticket was $158.

Tesco Tesco is another Internet success story. Operating with a base in the United Kingdom, this old-fashioned grocer managed to lead the way in cyber shopping. The company pioneered online delivery in London to great approval. It used its traditional markets to supply the needed food items and then sent out the delivery trucks. The delivery fee ran about $10 dollars per order, which helped recoup the cost of processing expenses. Tesco contended it also saved money when fewer cashiers and baggers were needed in its stores. Some analysts also attributed the company's European success to an easier marketplace, saying it is relatively simpler to establish a brand identity in smaller European regions than in the United States. Apparently, Tesco did not place much importance on that observation, as it chose to expand its business to the United States by forming a partnership with Safeway and Groceryworks.com.

Tesco changed its name from Tesco Direct to Tesco Home Shopper in 2003, a hybrid online/offline service that would operate in conjunction with its established online grocery store. However, Tesco Home Shopper would encourage customers to discontinue ordering by phone or fax, and move to online ordering instead. The company reported in 2004 that both profit and sales continued to rise each year, beginning with 1999. Tesco was doing so well, in fact, that it was also operating in the United States on the West Coast by 2003. At home in the United Kingdom, Tesco processed over 110,000 orders each week. By 2006, Tesco and Safeway's e-grocery service was available in nine U.S., and was the fastest-growing part of Safeway, according to Chief Operating Officer Dave Lauffer. However, a major industry development occurred in October 2006, when Safeway Inc. acquired full ownership of GroceryWorks by buying out Tesco and other investors. As of 2009, Tesco remained the top online grocer in the United Kingdom, with over 465,000 employees and 4,226 stores operating in 14 markets across Europe, Asia, and North America. It reported 2008 revenues of $54.3 billion.

Other Rising Stars to Watch. In June 2009, the Plunkett Research Group reported "Ten Major Trends Affecting the Food and Beverage Industry." One of them was the rising success of some online grocers, notably Manhattan's (New York) FreshDirect, launched in 2001. In 2009, it offered more than 3,000 products online in the New York City area (part of its success was attributed to the dense urban area), and had a customer base of more than 250,000. Fiscal 2007 revenues were $200 million.Grocery Shopping Network's (GSN) reach expanded to 6.2 million consumers monthly and over 75 million impressions per month in the grocery shopping category in 2009.

BIBLIOGRAPHY
"About Peapod." Peapod LLC, 5 May 2007. Available from http://www.peapod.com.

"Cash Registers Are Ringing Online." *Business Week,* 5 March 2007.

Coupons Inc. & Simmons Markeet Research Bureau. "2008 Printable Coupon Consumer Pulse." Coupons Inc., 25 April 2008. Available from http://www.couponsinc.com/corp/pdf/2008_Consumer_ Pulse_Survey.pdf.

"Gartner: $2 Billion in E-Commerce Sales Lost Because of Security Fears." *Baseline,* 27 November 2006.

Mehta, Trupti."BG Group Net Falls; Tesco Net Rises." 1 July 2009. Available from http://www.ticker.com/earnings-story/BG-Group-Net_falls;-Tesco-Net-Rises/33555/.

"Online Grocery Shoppng Patterns." Report No. DMC4629. Datamonitor, August 2008. Available from http://www.scribd.com/doc/10316107/Online-Grocery-Shopping-Patterns.

"Peapod and Wild Oats Come to D.C. Lunds/Byerly's Does E-commerce." *Progressive Grocer,* 1 October 2006.

"Plunkett Research Reports the 10 Major Trends Affecting the Food and Beverage Industry." Plunkett Research, 2 June 2009. Available from http://plunkettresearch.com/AboutUs/News/tabid/403/Default.aspx

Power, Denise. "Retail Site Errors Create $9B Risk." *WWD,* 26 September 2006.

"Safeway Buys Out its Portland Delivery Service." *Daily Journal of Commerce,* 4 October 2006.

"Safeway Goes Grocery Shopping." *Internet Retailer,* 4 October 2006.

Springer, Jon, Mary Wedowsky, and Alex Burmaster. "Staying Power: Peapod Turns 20." *Supermarket News,* 2 November 2009. Available from http://supermarketnews.com/retail_finacial/staying-power-1102/.

Swedowsky, Mary, and Alex Burmaster. "Consumer Opportunities Abound for Online Grocers," 6 October 2009. Available from http://blog.nielsen.com/nielsenwire/consumer/opportunities-abound-for-online-grocers/.

"Tesco Company History," April 2004. Available from http://81.201.142.254/companyInfo/sales_profit.asp?section=1.

E-COMMERCE: ONLINE MUSIC AND FILM DISTRIBUTION

INDUSTRY SNAPSHOT

Consumers love their music. NPD research indicated that total music consumption in the United States rose one-third between 2003 and 2007, and the recorded music industry generated a greater percentage of its revenues through digital sales that the film, magazine, and newspaper industries combined. According to Casey Johnson in an August 2009 article for ArsTechnica, "If current trends hold, U.S. digital music downloads will rake in more money than physical formats next year. Worldwide, digital will overtake physical by 2016."

However, downloads were only part of the story, according to a report from the Insight Research Corp. The market for on-demand digital content—including music, video, and Internet Protocol Television (IPTV)—streamed to a user's computer or mobile device was poised for explosive growth. The revenue derived from content sales, as well as related advertising, was forecast to reach $27 billion by 2011 in the United States alone. Insight explained that these conservative estimates represented a compound annual growth rate of almost 32 percent.

Although initially met with a harsh reaction from music industry behemoths, online music distribution was quickly adopted by the major music business players. Short of sparking a revolution, the start-up firms who led the e-music drive were largely absorbed by those very companies whose wrath they aroused in the late 1990s. When the e-commerce shakeout ensued in the early years of the twenty-first century's first decade, most music dot-coms lacked the leverage to survive on their own. The music industry, meanwhile, after much grumbling, came to accept digital downloads as the inevitable future of music distribution and rolled out their own online music operations.

While nearly all new Hollywood film releases were accompanied by extensive Web-based promotion, film distribution remained a small though rapidly growing niche market, with all the major Hollywood studios taking steps to embrace and incorporate film downloads as another arm of their operations. Major television networks, in particular, were moving quickly to capitalize on the online video market.

ORGANIZATION AND STRUCTURE

The online music distribution industry included a varied group of companies. CNET Networks' MP3.com offered space for the digital distribution of unknown or established artists. Others, such as online retailer Amazon.com, allowed consumers to order physical products through a central online site. In the early 2000s, the major record labels ceased dragging their feet over online distribution and moved to offer both online retailing and digital distribution.

Some sites, moreover, offer "personalized" music packages, which come in a number of varieties. In general, the idea behind customized music is that customers can pick and choose from a catalog of music only those selections that they want and then have the compilation made and sent to them either digitally or as a physical compact disc (CD). CD customization companies, however, were not given free rein to collage artists as they pleased. Most major artists' contracts, according to *Billboard,* include coupling clauses that grant the artists the final say on their music's appearance on compilations, typified by Ozzy Osbourne's insistence that "You'll never put me on the same CD with Hanson!"

While one of online distribution's most profound impacts on the music industry has been the inauguration of marketing schemes that directly target consumers rather than radio and music video stations and record stores, some Internet-based music companies offer their distribution or customization services to brick-and-mortar music retailers.

Like most e-commerce industries, online music distribution carried no sales tax, a fact of great consternation on Capitol Hill and in state legislatures where lost tax revenues threatened to cut into government spending programs. The Advisory Commission on Electronic Commerce, created by Congress to study Internet taxation, issued a proposal in 2000 to temporarily eliminate the sales tax on CDs in order to create tax parity between tangible and digital music media. The proposal, warmly embraced by the music industry, constituted an effort to placate various industry sources as the precise taxation legalities of Internet sales were ironed out. Some analysts, however, insisted that the attempt to reach some kind of compromise on Internet taxation wasn't worth the effort, noting that sales tax collection for mail order distribution was barely enforceable and that Internet sales taxes would prove even more difficult to collect.

Although the traditional record industry was coming around to online music, tension was far from alleviated. The Recording Industry Association of America, while not hostile to online distribution itself, vigorously monitored the wide proliferation of digital downloads to try to mitigate the massive black market for online music. The RIAA's efforts included its high profile lawsuit against Napster in 2000 on behalf of the major record companies, Napster's shutdown in 2001, lawsuits against peer to peer sites like Kazaa and Morpheus, and even suits against the users of such sites in September of 2003.

Film distribution in general is a far more complicated affair, since the movie industry's products pass through several layers of distribution, including theater, pay-per-view, video, cable, and so on, creating a complex web of contracts and methods that would require untangling before online distribution could become widely accepted in the mainstream.

BACKGROUND AND DEVELOPMENT

Music was one of the earliest commodities for which the Internet became a popular distribution medium, beginning especially in the mid-1990s. At first, however, the Internet hardly generated enthusiasm in the music industry. In fact, some of the earliest users of the Internet for music distribution were college students who figured out how to transfer CD-quality recordings to a digital

format. Before long, people were sending artists' songs to their friends via e-mail.

Such digital music files, however, were generally so large and slow to transfer that mass distribution was nearly impossible. Not until compressed music formats such as MP3 came along did digital music distribution become a viable activity, not to mention a burgeoning new industry. According to Wikipedia, MP3's audio-specific compression format uses different bit rates to make high-quality recordings that take up much less space. Quickly, sites popped up all over the Internet at which folks could download the latest releases by major music artists for free or for a cut-rate pirate fee, and "MP3" quickly became the most popular term for Internet searches.

Aside from piracy, one of the more positive uses of MP3 technology was by fledgling artists trying to get their music heard by promoting themselves on the Internet. In this way, they hoped to generate an audience base that they could then use for leverage in trying to attract a label. MP3.com, the creator of the MP3 format, launched its Web site for this purpose, allowing artists to upload their songs for general distribution while MP3.com kept half of the revenues for downloads.

Historically, the music industry has not earned a reputation as a leading supporter of cutting-edge technology. Prior to the advent of MP3, the common wisdom held that the Internet was of little concern to major record labels. As soon as their catalogs, however, appeared all over the Internet without their permission and without generating any revenues for the companies, they sprang into action, at first crying foul and calling for more stringent anti-piracy measures.

One of the most obvious signs that the music industry planned to fully embrace online music distribution was the mega merger between America Online and Time Warner Inc. in 2000. Even in this deal, however, the tension between traditional and online distribution was rather apparent. Later that year, America Online placed downloadable software on its Web site that was ideal for music piracy, a move that got the Time Warner brass up in arms, causing AOL to then quickly remove the software. AOL also hoped to develop a subscription-based distribution system whereby consumers would be granted access to entire catalogs for a flat monthly fee, which Warner feared would lead to diminished CD sales.

At any rate, with the major labels in full online distribution mode, established e-music sites were likely to depend for their survival on their ability to shore up their content and promote heavy traffic in an attempt to attract a major label acquisition. Consolidation began to heat up in 2000, and several small distributors were swallowed by their larger counterparts.

A series of lawsuits plagued the industry in the early years of the first decade of the 2000s. MP3.com and the music-trading Web site Napster—which at its peak boasted some 50 million visitors trading up to 30 million songs each day—were both slapped with copyright infringement lawsuits by the record industry in early 2000. MP3.com was found guilty of copyright infringement and ordered to pay Universal Music Group $120 million in damages, and Napster was forced to shutter its operations. However, such suits did not deter unlicensed downloading. Without a clearinghouse of music like Napster available, users simply began to use peer-to-peer networks such as Kazaa, Morpheus, and Grokster. Eventually, those sites faced lawsuits. In September of 2003, the Recording Industry Association of America (RIAA) filed copyright infringement lawsuits against 261 Internet users, targeting those who were sharing more than 1,000 music files via sites like Kazaa. While the 261 users targeted represented a miniscule fraction of the 57 million Americans using the peer-to-peer network to share music files, the RIAA claimed it was attempting to send a message that piracy would not be tolerated.

Forrester Research estimated the market for music downloads at about $269 million in 2004, greatly disappointing the more ambitious predictions earlier in the decade. After years spent dragging their feet and resisting the new technology, major record labels reorganized to make digital downloads a complementary, rather than antagonistic, aspect of their business. These moves were perfectly timed to meet the avalanche of new high-speed Internet transmission technologies, including digital subscriber lines and cable modems, which had achieved widespread popularity by then. Indeed, perhaps the clearest predictor of whether an individual downloaded music or film was the type of Internet access a user possessed.

Computer giant Apple seemed poised to become a major music industry force when it introduced its iPod portable music player, exploding in popularity following its launch in October 2001. Through an alliance with major record companies, Apple launched the iTunes Music Store in 2003. Hoping to appeal to Internet users who had been downloading music for free, Apple charged only $9.99 for full albums and 99 cents for individual songs. While at that time the files downloaded from Apple's store were compatible only with the iPod player, the firm struck a deal with Hewlett-Packard whereby HP computers would be sold equipped with Apple's iTunes jukebox software pre-installed. Other major players from various industries coveted Apple's early lead. Sony, Microsoft, and Wal-Mart busily developed their own systems combining online music stores with portable players.

While online music stores typically still lacked the rights to sell many major artists' songs,they were creating a profitable niche selling studio outtakes, live recordings, remixes, and songs generally considered throwaways by the artists themselves. Since artists were usually less likely to try to capitalize on such recordings in the same way as their more official releases, they were generally more willing to cooperate with online music distributors in the release of such songs. In addition, because online music distribution was so inexpensive, it was easier for Internet music stores to offer tracks that were unlikely to reach a mass audience. Major record labels embraced the practice as another vehicle to promote their artists' wares. Warner Bros. allowed Apple's iTunes store to release rehearsal outtakes from R.E.M., while Atlantic partnered with iTunes on a remixed version of the Jewel hit "Intuition." iTunes quickly offered for download a tune by Green Day produced for a Super Bowl commercial, and the song became an instant online success. Artists also increasingly turned to downloads of singles, live tracks, or unreleased material as a way to build momentum for a forthcoming release.

With the cost of DVD players steadily falling—and with many of the new models being portable—users by and large saw little advantage in the time-consuming and as yet untrustworthy online distribution method. However, industry analysts noted a light at the end of the tunnel for online film distribution in that the next generation of DVD players would likely come equipped for wireless Internet, specifically tailored to digital film downloads.

On the other hand, Internet-based ordering of DVDs and videos skyrocketed, largely on the heels of Netflix, the online start-up that offered its stock of films online for delivery via regular mail. Unlike established video stores, Netflix's arrangement allows users to hold on to the titles as long as they wish and to contribute to Netflix operations with ratings of the titles, allowing Netflix to build a proprietary recommendation system, similar to that of Amazon.com. Video store behemoth Blockbuster, facing a decline in rentals, took note of Netflix's encroachment and planned its own online rental service.

Since the movie industry is characterized by different copyright holders for different regional markets, ownership and distribution rights as they pertain to the Internet were complicated, further stalling the industry's acceptance of online distribution. Also, the Motion Picture Association of America expressed concern that peer to peer networks would pose the same issues for online movie distribution as they had for music distribution.

Nevertheless, in much the way that online distribution allows independent musicians a forum to have their music heard outside the confines of the massive music industry, online film distribution with its fast-improving technologies gives independent film producers an entry into a market where they can acquire an audience on a budget and at a level of artistic concessions that doesn't even begin to compare with those working within the mainstream film industry.

The skyrocketing popularity of broadband Internet connections was helping to fuel the market for online music and video. In March 2006, *Mediaweek* reported that according to Nielsen/NetRatings, the number of broadband users in the United States reached almost 100 million in February 2005, up 28 percent from the previous year. Broadband users accounted for 68 percent of all Web surfers—an increase from 55 percent in 2004 and 33 percent in 2003.

According to a report from the Insight Research Corp. The market for on-demand digital content—including music, video, and Internet Protocol Television (IPTV)—streamed to a user's computer or mobile device was poised for explosive growth. The revenue derived from content sales, as well as related advertising, was forecast to reach $27 billion by 2011 in the United States alone. Insight explained that these conservative estimates represented a compound annual growth rate of almost 32 percent.

Wireless over-the-air (OTA) was an emerging distribution platform for the music industry, according to the research firm International Data Corporation (IDC). OTA involves the downloading of music and related audio content to a mobile phone or handheld device. OTA mobile music storefronts, which first appeared in late 2005, are expected to flourish by 2010, at which time revenues will exceed $1 billion and users will number more than 50 million. While the limited availability of compatible handsets initially limited growth, IDC projected that by 2010, some 60 percent of handsets would support OTA.

In the area of online film distribution, a number of important developments occurred midway through the twenty-first century's first decade. In 2005, Apple Computer introduced a version of its popular iPod that was capable of playing video on a 2.5-inch color screen. At the same time, the company's iTunes service began offering approximately 2,000 music videos as well as episodes of the popular television programs *Desperate Housewives* and *Lost* for $1.99. Apple later revealed that iTunes service had sold more than 1 million videos in less than 20 days.

By the end of the first decade, a number of studio-supported movie download sites were in operation, including MovieLink with 1,700 titles (MGM, Paramount, Sony, Universal, and Warner Bros.) and CinemaNow (Microsoft, Blockbuster, Lion's Gate) with more than 4,000 titles. In partnership with IT giant Intel, Revelations Entertainment—a production company owned by actor Morgan Freeman—was preparing to launch a film download venture called ClickStar that, unlike the studio-backed firms, would make movies available for download shortly after their theater premier.

Some industry players remained skeptical about a quick shift to online feature film distribution. In the May 26, 2006, issue of *Business Week Online,* Netflix CEO Reed Hastings argued that DVD sales would continue to dominate for at least another 10 years, given that studios garnered 60 percent of revenues from DVD sales and rentals. Although he did not foresee a large market for Web distribution, Hastings nevertheless said his company would roll out this option by the year's end.

Even though a growing number of consumers had broadband Internet access, the research firm International Data Corporation (IDC) reported that a mere 2.5 million U.S. homes used computers in the living room for television and movie viewing in 2006. The number was projected to increase heading into the latter part of the decade, reaching 3.9 million in 2007. This transition was expected to set the stage for further online entertainment distribution.

The online sale of digital content continued to benefit from continuing trends, namely growth in broadband adoption and the proliferation of portable music and video players such as Apple's iPod. According to figures from Verdict Research, reported in the December 7, 2006, issue of *New Media Age,* digital piracy set the market for online music and video back 5 percent in 2005 and 1.7 percent the following year. However, the market was expected to benefit from growing sales of legitimate downloads into the early years of the next decade, with annual increases of 1.3 percent expected through 2011.

By 2007 it was clear that the market for online video in particular was blossoming. That year, the research firm eMarketer projected that online video advertising would triple by 2010, growing from an estimated $775 million to $2.9 billion. Major media networks were expected to claim about three-fourths of this revenue. The beefy revenue projection was supported by a growing base of viewers; in late 2006, Forrester Research indicated that some 45 percent of those over the age of 18 watched videos online.

Further proof of the online video market's potential was marked by some important industry developments. In October of 2006, Internet behemoth Google acquired the video-sharing site YouTube. This was followed by Viacom's $1 billion lawsuit against Google, which alleged that users had watched approximately 160,000 clips of the media company's content on YouTube some 1.5 billion times, according to the March 19, 2007, issue of *RCR Wireless News.*

Following the Google/YouTube Deal, in March of 2007 NBC Universal and News Corp. announced plans to create what they described as the "largest Internet video distribution network ever assembled with the most sought-after content from television and film.' Developed in partnership with AOL, MSN, MySpace, and Yahoo!, the new venture had backing from advertisers such as Intel, General Motors, Cadbury Schweppes, Cisco, and Esurance, and was expected to reach some 96 percent of Internet users. With a projected launch date of late summer 2007, NBC Universal and News Corp. revealed that the site would include "full-length programming, movies and clips, representing premium content from at least a dozen networks and two major film studios."

The network announced a comprehensive distribution agreement with Comcast Corp., the largest U.S. cable provider, in mid-April. In late May, the as yet unnamed venture, which will have offices in both New York and Los Angeles, had added SPEED, Sundance Channel, FUEL TV, Oxygen, and TV Guide as content partners.

A number of key trends were evident on the digital music front. Proprietary mobile communications networks continued to be of great interest to the industry, offering a channel for selling digital content that was both legal and carried a lower risk of piracy, since users were not able to transfer and swap music content. However, a potentially negating factor was that more and more mobile providers were offering subscribers unrestricted access to the Internet. As more cities and towns rolled out municipal wireless Internet networks, this served to dissolve any advantage associated with peddling content via the providers' closed mobile networks.

Another trend involved the way that people purchase their music. Unlike in the past, when people purchased entire albums by their favorite artists, the online music industry had led to the dominance of individual track sales over album sales. Referring to Nielsen SoundScan data, *The Online Reporter* indicated that sales of digital singles surpassed CD sales for the first time in 2006.

Finally, marketers within the industry were forced to contend with the new ways in which consumers discovered music. The online environment lessened the power of written music reviews and radio promotion by allowing people to discover similar artists or genres via music discovery tools. Some tools, such as Musicovery, took music discovery to new levels by allowing users to find songs with similar harmonies or rhythm.

CURRENT CONDITIONS

The International Federation of the Phonographic Industry's (IFPI) much-anticipated *IFPI Digital Music Report 2009* revealed that in 2008, the global digital music industry grew by approximately one-fourth to reach US $3.7 billion, with digital platforms now accounting for about 20 percent of recorded music sales (quoting the 2008 PWC Global Entertainment and Media Report). The digital share of revenues for films was only four percent. 2008 single-track downloads were 1.4 billion units globally, up 24 percent from 2007. In fact, single

track downloads crossed the one billion mark for the first time in 2008. The top selling single in 2008 was Lil Wayne's *Lollipop*. Additionally, digital albums showed a healthy 33 percent hike for the year, with 66 million units sold.

By 2012, digital music is expected to account for 40 percent of all music sold, said Eliot Can Buskrk, referring to data from InStat in his April 2008 article for *Wired* magazine. He also noted a contemporaneous Digital Music News finding that iTunes was installed on nearly 30 percent of all computers worldwide.

INDUSTRY LEADERS

Apple Computer, Inc. Midway through the twenty-first century's first decade, Cupertino, California-based Apple Computer had emerged as a major player in the market for digital music and video. This was evident by the success of the company's line of iPod portable music and video players, as well as the Apple iTunes store, which offered more than 5 million songs, 350 TV programs, and 500 movies, as well as a wide range of audiobooks, podcasts, and music videos for downloading in mid-2007. Apple introduced the iPod in 2002 and launched iTunes the following year. By 2004, iPod sales surpassed 2 million units. That year, the company unveiled the iPod mini, which allowed users to store up to 1,000 songs, and iPod sales constituted 35 percent of the company's revenues.

Apple's impact on the industry continued in 2005. That year the company replaced the iPod mini with the iPod nano, a media player that was thinner than a pencil but could hold 500 to 1,000 songs. In addition, Apple unveiled an iPod capable of playing video on a 2.5-inch color screen. Apple's iTunes service began offering approximately 2,000 music videos in 2005 as well as episodes of the popular TV programs *Desperate Housewives* and *Lost* for $1.99. In only 20 days time, iTunes sold more than 1 million videos. In 2006, Apple Corps Ltd., The Beatles recording company, sued Apple Computer for copyright infringement related to the use of its apple logo on the iTunes Music Store, charging that Apple Computer violated a prior licensing agreement between the two companies. While the courts initially sided with Apple Computer, Apple Corps vowed to take the case to Britain's Court of Appeal.

In April of 2007 Apple announced that it has sold its 100 millionth iPod, which had become "the fastest selling music player in history," according to a company news release. In April 2008, it announced that it had sold more than four billion iTunes since their debut, now accounting for roughly 70 percent of all digital music sold worldwide. According to *Wired* magazine in April 2008, despite the fact that Amazon was compatible with iPod, it was not taking customers from iTunes; less than ten percent of Amazon MP3 customers had purchased iTunes in the past.

CNET Networks, Inc. San Francisco-based CNET purchased MP3.com in 2003, adding to its vast network of technology content and products. MP3.com was an industry pioneer, specializing in offering downloadable music files for little-known artists, giving them a space to store and promote their own music. Established in 1997, MP3.com insisted it was not a record label, but rather that artists simply filled out forms and uploaded their tracks and artist information. In 2000, the company generated a wave of industry controversy when it announced the introduction of My.MP3.com, a digital storage locker whereby customers with an account could log on and access music from any Internet connection, relieving them of lugging around bulky CD collections. While several sites offered such services, MP3.com's innovation was to save customers the time of uploading their CDs by reproducing CDs themselves to create a vast library of popular music, an activity that many record industry executives insisted amounted to copyright violations. The company lost a high-profile lawsuit in 2000 to Universal Music Group, requiring MP3 to pay Universal $120 million for copyright violations.

Vivendi Universal acquired MP3 in 2001 and began downsizing its operations. Two years later, CNET purchased MP3.com from Vivendi. As of 2007, the company maintained the site as a music information center to complement CNET's free independent site, Download.com. In early 2009, CNET was acquired by CBS Corporation.

Emusic.com. Emusic.com, based in New York, offered digital downloads of both single tracks and entire albums and was the leading distributor of independent music, holding licensing deals with hundreds of independent record labels. The company's library boasted some 2 million songs for download in 2007. In 2001 the firm was acquired by Vivendi Universal, but Vivendi sold it two years later to Dimensional Associates, JDS Capital Management's private equity arm, which maintained ownership.

Online Film Companies. IFILM.com specialized in streaming independent short films and feature film clips as well as edgier, experimental shorts and commercials. As of 2007, 10 million viewers accessed IFILM's massive collection of short films and movie clips every month. During the early years of the first decade of the 2000s, the firm forged a deal with RealNetworks whereby the latter handled IFILM's subscription service. At that time, the firm enjoyed financial backing from the likes of Sony, Kodak, Yahoo!, and other entertainment industry bigwigs. IFILM was acquired by Viacom International Inc. in October of 2005 and organized under the company's MTV Networks division.

Movielink, LLC, headquartered in Santa Monica, California, was a joint venture between major movie studios MGM, Paramount, Sony, Universal, and Warner Bros. offering Internet downloads of feature-length Hollywood films. Though its launch was stalled for several years due to those studios' concerns over piracy and the quality of Internet-distributed film, Movielink was finally rolled out in 2002 with a library of about 200 films. Through Movielink, major film studios hoped not to repeat the drama faced by the music industry in the late 1990s and early part of the first decade of the 2000s by embracing digital downloading early on and trying to get customers in the habit of paying for the service. By 2007, the service had expanded its offerings to include more than 3,500 titles.

Another firm offering on-demand Internet film downloads was CinemaNow, Inc., based in Marina del Rey, California. Employing a tough encryption code to prevent digital piracy, CinemaNow started out distributing films only from independent studios, but in 2002 it became the first online film distribution service to offer Hollywood fare when it inked an agreement with Warner Bros. Though a competitor to MovieLink, the two firms enjoyed the backing of many of the same major Hollywood studios by 2004. As of mid-2007, CinemaNow offered more than 4,000 titles for downloading, ranging from feature-length films and shorts to television programs and music concerts from approximately 250 different licensors.

Netflix, Inc. of Los Gatos, California, emerged in the early years of the first decade of the 2000s with a business model designed to draw customers away from video stores. With a Web site offering an ever-expanding range of film titles, Netflix allowed customers to order films online, aided by its proprietary recommendation service, to be delivered straight to their homes via regular mail. For a flat monthly fee, Netflix's 6.8 million subscribers can receive a pre-determined number of films (according to their subscription plan) and keep them as long as they want, thereby eliminating late fees. The firm operated through 44 distribution centers throughout the United States in 2007. By this time, Netflix allowed its customers to view certain television programs and movies online. In all, the company's 80,000 titles made it the world's largest online movie rental enterprise.

AMERICA AND THE WORLD

In 2008, the United States was the world leader in digital music sales, representing some 50 percent of global value for the digital music market, said IFPI's 2009 report. In Japan, a mostly mobile music market, 140 million mobile singles were sold in 2008 (quoting RIAJ). Sales were up 45 percent in the United Kingdom, with 110 million single tracks downloaded in 2008, and digital albums selling 10.3 million. In France digital music sales were up hearly

50 percent, with 14.5 million singles downloaded and 1.4 million digial albums sold in 2008. Germany's market also experienced rapid growth with 37.4 million single track downloads and 4.4 million digital albums sold (IFPI's report referring to Media Control GfK International for this data).

In both the music and film markets, international online piracy was of great concern to distributors. IFPI collated separate reports from 16 countries around the world over a three-year period, concluding that more than 40 billion files were illegally file-shared in 2008. This figure constitutes a staggering 95 percent piracy rate. IFPI's cumulative 2009 report, referring to research by Jupiter, noted that in Europe, 16 percent of Internet users regularly swapped infringing music on file-sharing services. Even more startling, P2P filesharing, the vast majority of which represents unauthorized copyrighted film and music, accounts for up to 80 percent of all traffic on ISP networks, said IFPI (referring to information from ipoque).

The film industry also showed effects from online infringements, IFPI referring to information from Equancy and Co. as well as Tera Consultants, showing that in France alone, 13.7 million films were distributed on P2P networks in May 2008, compared to 12.2 million cinema tickets sold.

Since copyright laws and distribution rights often vary considerably between countries, the borderless world of the Internet posed particularly pressing difficulties. In the United States, the Digital Millennium Copyright Act granted the Recording Industry Association of America the authority to track and sue violators of copyright laws. On a global scale, the Secure Digital Music Initiative brought together 120 firms, including record companies and music publishers, to establish an open global standard for online music distribution and security.

Through global education efforts and litigation, the industry had made progress in the fight against piracy. IFPI reported that in 2008, it removed three million Internet links to infringing music (as compared to 550,000 in 2007), focusing on pre-release piracy which hits at the most damaging time of album release cycles.

BIBLIOGRAPHY

"Apple Sells a Million Videos in New Service." *eWeek,* 31 October 2005.

"Broadband Has 64% Internet Share in UK." *The Online Reporter,* 25 February 2006.

Deeken, Aimee. "Broadband Connections Soar 28%." *MEDIAWEEK,* 20 March 2006.

"The Digital Redemption. Can Morgan Freeman Persuade Hollywood to Stop Worrying and Love the Internet?" *Forbes,* 3 July 2006.

"Generator Research: Apple Music Revenues to Hit $15 Billion by 2010." *Wireless News,* 17 May 2006.

"Growth of Digital Music Sales Triples in Last Year." *The Computer & Internet Lawyer,* December 2005.

"IDC: Wireless Mobile Music Users Poised to Pass Online Music Service Users by 2010." *Wireless News,* 16 June 2006.

"IFPI Digital Music Report 2009: Key Statistics." 16 January 2009. Available from http://www.ifpi.org/content/section_resources/dmr2009.html

Johnston, Casey. "US Digital Music Sales to Eclipse CDs by 2010." *ArsTechnica,* 14 August 2009. Available from http://arstechnica.com/media/news/2009/08/global-digital-music-sales-to-overtake-physical-by-2016.ars

Kapko, Matt. "Coo." *RCR Wireless News,* 19 March 2007.

"Market for Paid Music Downloads Grows." *Research Alert,* 5 May 2006.

Mullaney, Timothy J. "Netflix. The Mail-order House that Clobbered Blockbuster." *Business Week Online,* 25 May 2006. Available from www.businessweek.com.

"NBC Universal and News Corp. Announce Deal with Internet Leaders AOL, MSN, MySpace and Yahoo! to Create a Premium Online Video Site with Unprecedented Reach." News Corp. and NBC Universal, 22 March 2007. Available from http://www.newscorp.com/news/news_329.html.

"News Corporation, NBC Universal and Comcast Reach Strategic Online Video Distribution and Content Agreement." News Corp. and NBC Universal, 16 April 2007. Available from http://www. newscorp.com/news/news_331.html.

"News Corporation/NBC Universal Joint Venture Inks Deals with Troupe of Premier Content Partners." News Corp. and NBC Universal, 30 May 2007. Available from http://www.newscorp.com/news/news_337.html.

"Only True Fans Are Buying Full Albums." *The Online Reporter,* 30 March 2007.

"Overview of the Digital Music Industry in 2007." *The Online Reporter,* 10 March 2007.

Tait, Matthew. "Music 2.0: The Technology of Web 2.0—Combined with the Potential Demise of DRM—Spells More Freedom and Autonomy for Music Lovers." *PC Magazine,* 10 April 2007.

Van Buskirk, Elliot. "iTunes Store May Capture One-Quarter of Worldwide Music by 2012." *Wired* Magazine, 27 April 2008.

Whitney, Daisy. "Searching for Web Video Riches." *Television Week,* 19 March 2007.

ELECTRIC VEHICLES

—•—

SIC CODE(S)

3711

INDUSTRY SNAPSHOT

Electricity can be used to power a wide range of vehicles, including automobiles, vans, pickup trucks, motorcycles, buses, forklifts, and scooters. According to the Energy Information Administration (EIA), the official U.S. government provider of energy statistics, electric vehicles, sometimes referred to as EVs, fall into one of three power source categories: batteries, hybrids, and fuel cells. An EIA report released in April 2010 indicated that there were approximately 1.5 million alternative fuel and hybrid vehicles on the road in 2008, of which approximately 2,800 were electric vehicles.

As the EIA explains: "A battery-powered EV uses the electricity from onboard rechargeable batteries to run an electric motor, which turns the vehicle's wheels. A hybrid electric vehicle has two sources of motive energy. For example, it may use a lean burn gasoline engine in combination with batteries. A fuel cell vehicle uses electricity from fuel cells instead of batteries. A fuel cell operates like a battery in that it converts chemical energy directly into electricity."

A variety of companies are engaged in the manufacture and production of electric vehicles and batteries. However, many of the same domestic and global organizations that dominate the traditional automotive manufacturing industry also are leaders within the electric vehicle sector. During the late 2000s skyrocketing energy costs and environmental concerns caused many industry players to focus more heavily on alternative fuel vehicles. Although several major automotive manufacturers were preparing to introduce electric cars in 2010, the high cost of batteries was expected to

be a limiting factor in their widespread adoption through 2020. Until that time, hybrid vehicles were expected to outpace vehicles powered solely by electricity.

ORGANIZATION AND STRUCTURE

Vehicles produced by this industry may be either entirely electric-powered or gas-electric/diesel-electric hybrids. While some are designed for use by individual consumers, others are developed for commercial or recreational purposes. In addition, vehicles may fall into one of several different categories. Two-wheeled vehicles are typically light-duty and include the likes of electric motorcycles and scooters. Four-wheeled vehicles, of which there are many types, can be further subdivided into the classifications of light-duty, medium-duty, and heavy-duty.

A wide range of companies are engaged in the manufacture and production of electric vehicles and batteries. Many of the same domestic and global companies that dominate the traditional automotive manufacturing industry also are leaders within the electric vehicle sector. During the late 2000s skyrocketing energy costs and environmental concerns caused many industry players to focus more heavily on alternative fuel vehicles.

Following the success of its Prius gas-electric hybrid vehicle, Toyota had plans to introduce a compact electric vehicle in the early 2010s. Ford was at work on a battery-powered commercial van and a battery-powered electric passenger sedan, slated for introduction in 2010 and 2011, respectively. In addition, Nissan was preparing to introduce its electric-powered Nissan Leaf. Midway through 2010 the company broke ground on a plant in Smyrna, Tennessee, to produce batteries for its electric vehicles.

Consumer Likelihood of Purchasing an All-Electric Vehicle	
Very likely	6%
Somewhat likely	11%
Not very likely	40%
Not at all likely	35%

SOURCE: Rasmussen Reports, *Brandweek*, April 19, 2010.

Finally, General Motors introduced its Chevy Volt plug-in hybrid in 2010.

Because they deliver the power required by electric vehicles, utilities are key industry players. In the June 2010 issue of *Public Utilities Fortnightly*, Hugh McDermott, vice president of the electric vehicle infrastructure company Better Place, indicated that roughly 60 to 75 percent of the energy required to power electric vehicles will be delivered at home, while another 10 to 20 percent may be delivered at a driver's workplace. Although this is valuable information, electric utilities will require additional information in order to anticipate the specific demands that electric vehicles will place on the power grid.

Based on factors such as outside temperature, humidity, building size, and day of the week, utilities can predict traditional energy loads with a high degree of accuracy. However, anticipating energy demand for electric vehicles is another matter, due to the high degree of variability associated with vehicle use. In addition, when charging, electric vehicles may do so at a rate of either 120 or 240 volts, adding yet another degree of variability to the equation.

One solution may be the use of demand-response software. According to the aforementioned *Public Utilities Fortnightly* article, companies such as GridPoint offer applications to manage electric vehicle charging within a specific service territory. In the article, GridPoint's Will Cousins explained that while the development of new power plants may not be necessary, careful use of the existing utility infrastructure will be needed, with consideration devoted to balancing energy demands placed on the power grid.

Over the years, automotive manufacturing and electric utility professionals have taken steps to better understand the complexities associated with both industries. In the same *Public Utilities Fortnightly* article, Steve Andersen described simplifications and misconceptions that have occurred in both camps: "Car companies thought of electricity simply as fuel, with little understanding of how utilities make money, the vagaries of rate commissions and state regulators or the nuances of investor, public and cooperative ownership. By the same token, utilities often compared EVs to appliances, not fully considering that these machines draw power at varying voltage and intermittent times, then drive across town and plug in somewhere else—completely unlike a close dryer or air conditioner." Developments such as the formation of the Infrastructure Working Council have led to the creation of standards pertaining to electric vehicles and greater inter-industry collaboration.

BACKGROUND AND DEVELOPMENT

Electricity was not readily available on a large scale until the 1880s. This gave impetus to the development of storage batteries, used for more than 35 years while alternating current systems were developed and perfected. The batteries used were large enough to power more than 2 million homes for an hour. Although AC power began to carry more of the load, storage batteries continued to be used in the operation of electrical switches in power networks. The appearance of "horseless carriages" in the 1890s also fueled demand for storage batteries.

In the early days of the automobile, storage batteries were seriously considered as an alternative to horses and internal combustion engines. Storage batteries powered horseless racing carriages and electric cabs. However, the batteries could not compete in long-distance travel and use declined as roads improved. However, they continued to be well suited for town travel since gasoline vehicles had to be hand-cranked, which was a risky prospect. Storage batteries helped provide a solution for this difficulty, making the electric passenger car obsolete. The first automobile to use an electric starter as standard equipment was the 1912 Cadillac.

The use of electric street trucks continued into the 1930s. By this time storage batteries powered household appliances, boats, and the first submarines. In World War II they also powered torpedoes, aircraft radios, and commercial broadcast stations. In addition, they were used to power local telephone exchanges and intercontinental repeater stations. Storage batteries excelled in other industrial uses, such as powering electric shuttles in mines and battery-powered trains, which became quite popular in Germany. Golf carts provided an important market for the batteries as well.

Issues of general ecology and global warming continued to drive the development of alternative fuel vehicles, including those utilizing electric power. The limiting factor in efforts to create such vehicles was the creation of storage batteries that were light and powerful, yet cost effective. Automakers resisted the demand of buyers and government for many years, citing the high cost of fuel cells and the business and marketing risks involved, but legislative changes worldwide forced investment in the technology. In the United States, under the Alternative Motor Fuels Act of 1988, manufacturers of alternate-fuel vehicles were to be included "favorably" in the Corporate Average Fuel Economy program, and otherwise encouraged to build environmentally-friendly vehicles.

The State of California passed a law requiring any automaker that sold more than 5,000 vehicles annually in the state to guarantee 2 percent Zero Emission Vehicles (ZEV) by 1998 and 10 percent ZEV by 2003, emitting no harmful substances into the atmosphere. Electric vehicles presented the most feasible technology for meeting California standards, and manufacturers worldwide began investigating ways to produce a practical electric car. Early models were unpopular because of slow cruising speeds and lack of performance, but by the end of the century electric car production began to be realistic.

Nissan's electric R'nessa was able to reach 80 kilometers per hour (km/h) in 12 seconds, with a maximum speed of 120 km/h. In 1998 an electric race car debuted at the Le Mans race in France. Toyota combined an internal combustion engine with an electric motor-driven car to reduce pollutants without sacrificing automobile performance. The same year, GM introduced a number of ecofriendly concept cars at the North American International Auto Show, the most notable of which was the Parallel Hybrid performance car.

By 2001 Toyota and Honda were selling gas-electric hybrid vehicles at the retail level. The four-door Toyota Prius, priced in the low $20,000s, got 55 miles per gallon (mpg) on city roads. By comparison, the two-door Honda Insight, priced between $15,000 and $16,000, boasted 70 mpg on highways.

During the mid-2000s Toyota developed a leadership position with the Prius sedan. According to the Alliance of Automobile Manufacturers (AAM), 2004 "Tier 2" vehicle models were almost 100 percent cleaner than those of three decades before. In fact, more than one-third of all new vehicles met the strict mandatory 2009 standards five years early. R.L. Polk & Company reported that registrations for hybrid electric vehicles in the United States were 81 percent higher in 2004 than in 2003, with 83,153 registered new vehicles. The Toyota Prius captured 64 percent of that market, with 53,761 new registrations, followed by the Honda Civic Hybrid, which had 31 percent of the market with 25,586 registered hybrid cars in 2004.

Alternative fuel vehicles were not limited to passenger cars. In Germany, the Mercedes Nebus (new electric bus) was developed in the laboratories of Daimler-Benz during early 2000s. Midway through the decade, Hybrid Electric Buses (HEBs) had moved from development into commercial production and use. There were nearly 700 HEBs in regular service in North America in 2005–2006, operated by more than 40 transit agencies. Another 400 HEBs were operational in late 2006. The Plug-In Hybrid Electric Vehicle (PHEV), which can be renewed by plugging into a community electric grid to recharge the batteries, rather than the more typical hybrid method of using a gasoline or diesel engine to help keep batteries charged, was being demonstrated in Kansas City and North Hempstead, New York, in 2006.

By the late 2000s the question was not if electric vehicles would achieve widespread adoption, but when, according to some industry analysts. Dialogue between major industry players, namely electric utilities and automotive manufacturers, began to intensify. This was evident by the formation of the Infrastructure Working Council in 2007, which sought to develop standards related to electric vehicles. One example was the creation of a universal charging system, the Electric Vehicle Supply Equipment (EVSE), which the council helped to develop in partnership with the Society of Automotive Engineers.

CURRENT CONDITIONS

According to the U.S. Energy Information Administration's report, "Alternatives to Traditional Transportation Fuels, 2008," released in April 2010, there were approximately 1.5 million alternative fuel and hybrid vehicles on the road in 2008. Of these, approximately 2,800 were electric vehicles (2,740 light-duty vehicles, 58 heavy-duty vehicles, and 4 medium-duty vehicles). Gasoline-electric hybrids accounted for 324,801 vehicles (324,779 light-duty vehicles and 22 heavy-duty vehicles). Finally, diesel-electric hybrids accounted for approximately 1,000 vehicles (2 medium-duty vehicles and 1,001 heavy-duty vehicles).

Despite all of the hype about electric vehicles, the high cost of batteries was a major limiting factor in their widespread adoption during the early 2010s, according to several analysts. Hybrid-electric vehicles were expected to outpace pure electrics, at least in the short term. According to a study from the Boston Consulting Group, profiled in the January 8, 2010, issue of *The New York Times*, the high cost of batteries would keep pure electric vehicles out of reach for the majority of consumers until the 2020s. By that time, electric cars were expected to represent 6 percent of the global market.

Although a small segment of the population was projected to purchase electric vehicles, regardless of price, analysts indicated that a quadrupling of oil prices, or major government incentives, would be needed to encourage more widespread adoption. Boston Consulting Group's research indicated that the cost of an electric vehicle would not be comparable to a gas-powered vehicle until about 2025. Nevertheless, major automotive manufacturers continued to sing the praises of their products, including the Chevy Volt, which was slated to go on sale in late 2010. Other proponents included Energy Secretary Steven Chu, who in the aforementioned *New York Times* article commented: "We urgently need to change how we power our cars and trucks. America has fallen behind in the race to build cars of the future."

By 2010 Rep. Jose E. Serrano (D-NY) had introduced legislation (the American Electric Vehicle Manufacturing Act) requiring the U.S. Postal Service (USPS) to adopt at least 20,000 electric vehicles in an effort to reduce fuel consumption. In addition, Rep. Serrano was seeking to allocate $1.86 billion that the USPS and Department of Energy could use for electric mail trucks. Along these lines, the USPS contracted with the electric vehicle firm ZAP to convert one of its standard mail trucks to run on electric power. The vehicle was slated to undergo field testing in Washington, D.C., in 2010.

INDUSTRY LEADERS

Many of the same domestic and global companies that dominate the traditional automotive manufacturing industry also are leaders within the electric vehicle sector. During the late 2000s, skyrocketing energy costs and environmental concerns caused many industry players to focus more heavily on alternative fuel vehicles. In addition to automotive manufacturers, the industry also includes companies focused on the development and production of batteries and other components used in electric vehicles.

Toyota Motor Corporation A major development in the electric vehicle market took place in October of 1997 when Toyota unveiled the Prius. A hybrid vehicle, the Prius combined a highly efficient gas engine with a self-regenerating electric motor, reducing carbon dioxide emissions by half. Although initial estimates showed that production would have to surpass 200,000 vehicles a year for the Prius to turn a profit, by March 1998 demand was surpassing supply, and the future of the eco-car on the domestic market looked promising. Prius finally hit the U.S. and European markets in late 2000, amid increased fuel prices and mounting concerns over global warming.

Toyota had started work on the Prius in the late 1990s. In a profile of the brand, *Fortune* magazine (March 6, 2006) claimed the Prius offered the first "serious alternative to the internal combustion engine since the Stanley Steamer ran out of steam in 1924." The Prius prototypes, however, suffered undignified difficulties. They would not start consistently and could not take cold weather, and the bulky battery ran the danger of catching on fire. When the first models arrived in the United States, testers found they could not fit a baby stroller in the trunk. The cars were noisy, slow to get up to speed, and the savings in gas did not actually make up for the higher sticker price.

After only a year, however, Hollywood celebrities were driving the Prius, proud to make a statement about saving energy. A redesigned model came out in the

United States in 2003, and production could not keep up with demand. U.S. sales doubled in 2004 and almost doubled again the next year. Toyota had a significant advantage over all other carmakers. It had a head start on hybrid technology, and it had its enormous and flexible global manufacturing capability to take advantage of the new turn toward radically more fuel-efficient cars.

During the mid-2000s the Prius was sweeping the European and U.S. markets. However, the vehicle was not without its problems. For example, in October of 2005 Toyota recalled 160,000 Prius vehicles after receiving reports of periodic stalling in the gas portion of the hybrid engines. In 2008 Toyota President Katsuaki Watanabe revealed plans to introduce a compact electric vehicle in the early 2010s. The following year, the company announced that it would introduce a compact gas-electric hybrid car, with better fuel efficiency than the Prius, sometime around 2011. In addition, Toyota indicated that it also would roll out a hydrogen fuel cell vehicle by 2015. In 2010 Toyota generated sales of $217.9 billion, and the company employed 320,590 workers.

Ford Motor Company Among the United States' leading auto manufacturers, Ford has made a significant commitment to the development of hybrid and electric vehicles. In 2006 the company revealed plans to increase annual production of hybrid vehicles from 20,000 units in 2006 to 250,000 by 2010. That same year, the company announced that it would invest $1.8 billion to develop hybrid cars capable of 70 miles per gallon. By 2009 Ford had offered a hybrid version of its Escape SUV for a number of years.

Ford made plans to introduce a hybrid version of the Ford Fusion in 2010, which was expected to achieve fuel economy of 36 miles per gallon in the city, and 41 miles per gallon on the highway. The company introduced a battery-powered commercial van, the Trans Connect Electric, in 2010, followed by plans to introduce a battery-powered electric Focus in late 2011. Additional hybrid vehicles were slated for introduction in 2012.

In January 2006 Ford announced a major restructuring plan called "Way Forward," involving the elimination of 25,000 to 30,000 jobs and up to 14 plant closures by 2012. In September 2006, Alan Mulally was named president and CEO. At that time the company announced plans to eliminate 10,000 white-collar jobs and reduce costs by $5 billion. After losing $2.7 billion in 2007, Ford eliminated one-third of its North American jobs and sold Aston Martin in 2007, as well as Jaguar and Land Rover in 2008, to Tata Motors. Ford generated sales of $118.31 billion in 2009, at which time the company had 198,000 employees.

General Motors Co. Like most leading automotive manufacturers, General Motors (GM) has its hand in the production of electric vehicles and associated alternative energy technology. In early 2008 the company established a renewable energy start-up enterprise in Warrenville, Illinois, in partnership with Coskata. That year GM also revealed plans to introduce its Chevy Volt plug-in hybrid in 2010, which was expected to retail for approximately $32,500. By 2009 the company had pledged to devote $758 million to technology associated with the Volt, which could run solely on electricity for the first 40 miles. In addition, the company developed a concept luxury sedan, named the Cadillac Converj, based on Volt technology.

As the economy faltered and auto sales plummeted to unprecedented levels during the late 2000s, GM faced the possibility of bankruptcy and asked Congress for financial assistance. After receiving billions of dollars as part of a bailout package for the entire U.S. auto industry, the company suspended production at all 30 of its plans for a month in December 2008. General Motors filed for bankruptcy in June 2009, and the company received an additional $30 billion from the government. As a result of the bankruptcy, General Motors Corp.'s name was changed to General Motors Company.

After filing for bankruptcy, China-based Sichuan Tengzhong Heavy Industrial Machinery Company Ltd. acquired GM's Hummer brand, and plans were put in place to significantly reduce the number of manufacturing plants. Compared to 47 plants in 2008, GM was expected to have 31 plants by 2012. In addition, some 21,000 hourly workers were expected to be eliminated from the company's workforce. As of 2009, GM employed 217,000 people, and reported revenues of $104.59 billion.

Nissan Motor Co. Ltd. Nissan is another leading global manufacturer that is involved in electric vehicle production. In 2008 the company revealed that it would introduce an electric car in both Japan and the United States by 2010. At the same time, the scope of its commitment to environmentally-responsible vehicles came into focus when Nissan indicated it would roll out a global lineup of electric vehicles by 2012. More specifically, Nissan indicated it would try to sell 500,000 electric cars annually beginning in 2013.

In April 2010 Nissan began accepting orders for an electric vehicle called the Nissan Leaf. With a range of approximately 100 miles on a full charge, the Leaf had a sticker price of $32,780. The federal government offered consumers a $7,500 federal tax credit for purchasing the vehicle, slated for availability in December, and a number of states also offered tax credits ranging from $2,000 to $5,000. In May 2010 the company broke ground on a plant in Smyrna, Tennessee, which would manufacture batteries for Nissan's electric vehicles starting in 2012. At that time, the company already had received 6,000 pre-

orders for the vehicle in Japan, and 13,000 pre-orders in the United States.

Difficult economic conditions led Nissan to announce a major restructuring initiative in 2009. At that time, the company announced that it would eliminate 20,000 jobs worldwide. Nissan generated sales of $86.7 billion in 2009, at which time it employed 160,422 people.

WORKFORCE

In 1990 there were 271,400 employees in the auto industry. By 2005 there were only 249,700 employees, which was a loss of 8 percent. Heading into the late 2000s industry employment continued to plummet in the wake of dire economic conditions and massive workforce reductions. By 2007 employees engaged in motor vehicle manufacturing totaled 179,885. Of this total, 155,300 were production workers. In 2008 employment fell to 163,025, of which 139,525 were production workers. Beyond automotive manufacturing, the industry also employs workers engaged in storage battery manufacturing. In 2008 this sector of the industry employed approximately 19,417 people, 14,869 of whom were production workers.

The United Auto Workers (UAW) union represents many employees within the automotive industry. In 2009 there were 390,000 active members and 600,000 retirees. By comparison, the UAW had 710,000 active and approximately 500,000 retired union members in 2005. In 2010 the UAW represented approximately 750 local unions, compared to about 950 in 2005.

AMERICA AND THE WORLD

Heading into the early 2010s the market for electric vehicle production and infrastructure development was valued at $49 billion, according to a December 18, 2009, *Internet Wire* release. The publication reported that Europe held 60 percent of the market. However, some observers questioned the strength of European power grids over the long haul. Strong growth was projected in both North America and China, according to research from SBI Energy. By 2014 North America was expected to account for approximately 20 percent of the electric vehicle infrastructure manufacturing market. Meanwhile, Asia was expected to account for 24 percent of the market. By that time European market share was projected to fall slightly, reaching 56 percent.

In June 2010, *Public Utilities Fortnightly* reported that, according to the electric vehicle infrastructure company Better Place, some 120 different electric vehicle models had been announced worldwide in the previous year. In North America alone, approximately 36 models were expected to become available. Some global markets had more ambitious plans than others. For example, the publication indicated that Israel was working toward a goal of 100 percent electric vehicle adoption by the year 2020.

Most growth in the Asian market was expected to occur in China. In mid-2010 BYD Auto, a Chinese manufacturer of cars and batteries, announced it would increase its output of electric vehicles by 1,000 units for 2010. In addition, the world's largest manufacturer of electric bicycles, Jiangsu Xinei E-VEHICLE Co., announced that it had established a strategic partnership with Dongfeng Citroen to develop and produce electric cars in China.

RESEARCH AND TECHNOLOGY

According to the July 5, 2010, issue of *Automotive News*, Nissan Research Center Mobility Service Laboratory General Manager Takeshi Mitamura indicated that, through 2050, macro trends, such as the aging population and growing levels of urbanization, will accelerate the transition from fossil fuels to electrically powered vehicles. By 2010 General Motors had developed a concept vehicle called the EN-V (Electric Networked Vehicle) in partnership with China-based Shanghai Automotive Industry Corp. that was based on a future transportation system model.

Specifically, the EN-V was developed for a transportation system based on smaller, intelligent vehicles capable of communicating with the electric grid, road and parking infrastructures, and other vehicles, as described in the aforementioned issue of *Automotive News*. Programmed to independently drive from one point to another, avoid collisions, and even identify available empty parking spaces, such vehicles essentially would allow drivers to become passengers. However, because every vehicle would need to be networked in order for the system to work, universal adoption within a defined territory would be required. Some observers foresaw the initial adoption of networked vehicles in dedicated lanes, or in specific zones such as college campuses or city centers.

BIBLIOGRAPHY

2008 Annual Survey of Manufactures. U.S. Census Bureau, 30 March 2010. Available from: http://factfinder.census.gov.

"Alternatives to Traditional Transportation Fuels 2008." U.S. Energy Information Administration, April 2010. Available from: http://www.eia.doe.gov.

Andersen, Steven. "Tipping Point: Industry Giants Start the EV Revolution." *Public Utilities Fortnightly*, June 2010.

Bunkley, Nick. "Nissan Says Electric Car Is Sold Out for This Year." *The New York Times*, 26 May 2010.

———. "Study Raises Cost Estimate for Electric Cars." *The New York Times*, 8 January 2010.

Chappell, Lindsay. "Spiffs will Slice Price of Nissan EV." *Automotive News*, 19 April 2010.

"China Economic News in Brief: New Airports in Xinjiang, Dongfeng Citroen Electric Car Partnership with Xinri E-Vehicle." *Xinhua News Agency*, 18 June 2010.

"China's BYD Auto Raises Electric Vehicle Output Target for 2010." *AsiaPulse News*, 14 June 2010.

Dolliver, Mark. "Six Percent Said It's 'Very Likely' and 11 Percent 'Somewhat Likely' That the Next Car They Will Buy will Be an All-Electric Model." *Brandweek*, 19 April 2010.

Ehart, William. "Not Your Father's MPG; New Fuel Cost Ratings Needed in the Era of Plug-ins." *The Washington Times*, 20 November 2009.

Ford Motor Co. *Notable Corporate Chronologies*. Online Edition. Farmington Hills, MI: Gale Group, 2009.

"Fuel Cells." In *Encyclopedia of Emerging Industries*. Online Edition. Farmington Hills, MI: Gale Group, 2009.

General Motors Corp. *Notable Corporate Chronologies*. Online Edition. Farmington Hills, MI: Gale Group, 2009.

Henry, Jim. "Hostile Territory? Tomorrow's Tightly Packed Cities May Force Radical Changes to the Automobile—and How It's Used." *Automotive News*, 5 July 2010.

Joyce, Mary. "Developments in U.S. Alternative Fuel Markets." U.S. Energy Information Administration. Available from: http://www.eia.doe.gov.

"Motor Vehicles." *Encyclopedia of Global Industries*. Online Edition. Farmington Hills, MI: Gale Group, 2009.

"Motor Vehicles and Passenger Car Bodies." In *Encyclopedia of American Industries*. Farmington Hills, MI: Gale Group, 2008.

Murray, Charles J. "What Would It Take to Make You Buy an EV?" *Design News*, 1 January 2010.

Nissan Motor Company Ltd. *Notable Corporate Chronologies*. Online Edition. Farmington Hills, MI: Gale Group, 2010.

"North America and Asia Gaining Ground in Global Electric Car Infrastructure Manufacturing Market." *Internet Wire*, 18 December 2009.

"North American Grid Operators Assess Impact of Electric Vehicles." *Transmission & Distribution World*, 1 April 2010.

"Storage Batteries." *Encyclopedia of American Industries*. Online Edition. Farmington Hills, MI: Gale Group, 2010.

"Toyota Motor Corp." *Notable Corporate Chronologies*. Online Edition. Farmington Hills, MI: Gale Group, 2010.

"Toyota Motor Corporation." *International Directory of Company Histories*, Vol. 100. Farmington Hills, MI: St. James Press, 2009.

"UAW Quick Facts." Detroit, MI: UAW, 30 June 2010. Available from: http://uaw.org.

"ZAP to Design Electric Vehicle for Postal Service." *Fleet Owner*, 22 February 2010.

Zoia, David E. "High Battery Costs to Keep Lid on EVs." *Ward's Auto World*, 1 February 2010.

ELECTRONIC COMMUNICATIONS NETWORKS

SIC CODE(S)

6211

6231

INDUSTRY SNAPSHOT

Electronic Communications Networks (ECNs) are computerized trading systems that link buyers and sellers of stocks (some have also delved into other securities and financial instruments). ECNs take the place of broker-dealers on the Nasdaq Stock Market, who are often large brokerages and investment banks such as Goldman Sachs and Merrill Lynch, and the so-called specialists on the New York Stock Exchange (NYSE), who include many of the same firms but have a monopoly on the market for a specific NYSE-listed-company's shares. In short, ECNs cut out the middlemen.

Complicating matters are the many similarities between ECNs and stock exchanges. Indeed, starting in 1999, several ECNs filed with the Securities and Exchange Commission (SEC) for exchange status. In 2002, Archipelago Holdings, one of the smaller ECNs, merged with the Pacific Stock Exchange to create the first hybrid ECN exchange. Archipelago was thus in the highly favorable position of actively trading NYSE stocks while functioning as an exchange.

While ECNs initially tried to unseat customary exchanges, or at least give them a run for their money, by the middle of the twenty-first century's first decade, they were blending with traditional floor-based trading. Following the Archipelago/Pacific Stock Exchange merger, the NYSE agreed to merge with Archipelago Holdings in April 2005, creating a new company called NYSE Group Inc. Only days after the Archipelago deal, the Nasdaq Stock Market agreed to buy Instinet Group Inc. from Reuters Group Plc. The $1.88 billion deal effectively brought together the two largest U.S. equities markets.

One important ECN-related development during the middle of the first decade of the 2000s was the SEC's April 2005 adoption of Regulation NMS, a trade-through rule that included proposals related to market data, inter-market access, sub-penny stock pricing, and order protection. In particular, the regulation mandated that investment firms obtain the best price for consumers engaged in electronic stock trading, even if that price happens to be on a different exchange.

By late 2006, many exchanges were in the process of upgrading their equity trading systems to comply with Regulation NMS and improve trading efficiency. The SEC had initially set the compliance date for Rules 610 and 611 of Regulation NMS as June 29, 2006. However, on May 18 of that year, the commission extended the deadline, setting a series of five different compliance dates that began on October 16, 2006 and ended with a final completion date on October 8, 2007.

ORGANIZATION AND STRUCTURE

ECNs are one of several possible links between buyers and sellers of stocks. In securities industry lingo, they serve as over-the-counter markets for securities that may or may not be listed on the major exchanges such as Nasdaq or the NYSE. As their rather nondescript moniker suggests, ECNs at their core are computer networks devoted to listing and matching stock orders. Users may connect to the system directly or, more often for smaller traders, through a participating brokerage that sends orders to the system.

Once an ECN receives an order, it's posted anonymously on a list of open orders and the system searches other open orders for a match. If a match is found—that is, if a buyer is willing to pay a seller's price—the order is executed within the network. This can happen within seconds. When no match is waiting, the order remains on the system's list, often called a notebook or an order book, and in the case of NASDAQ shares, is sent for listing on the Nasdaq Level II quotation system. There, anyone inside or outside the ECN can fill the open order.

Until recently, most ECNs have been closed systems, meaning that only users of the same service are matched in the system's notebook. Archipelago led the charge toward open systems. Given that market liquidity—access to buyers or sellers when you need it—is paramount to most traders, the trend toward open systems is likely to accelerate.

Setting up a basic ECN is relatively inexpensive as far as capital expenses go. According to one estimate, a firm can build for less than $10 million a credible system that can support 15 transactions per second. It is not quite pocket change, but the fairly low entry barriers (others being mostly regulatory) have led numerous companies to seek a piece of the action. Although there were only a dozen functioning ECNs in the early 2000s, several more were in the works and as many as 140 companies had approached the SEC about establishing an ECN.

Unmaking the Market Makers ECNs are most similar to market makers and dealers on the NASDAQ. These are brokerages, investment banks, and related firms that compete with each other to fill open orders at terms favorable both to themselves and the party who placed the order. Whose interests come first is a matter for debate. Market makers may keep an inventory of some companies' shares and engage in both buying and selling as the situation dictates. In effect, traders buy from or sell to market makers, who fill orders and provide liquidity to the market. Sometimes market makers have a particular interest in a company's shares, such as when they've underwritten the company's public offering, and because of their size they are able to manipulate a stock's price. Any market maker, however, can deal in any stock on the NASDAQ, and there are an average of 11 market makers per the NASDAQ issue.

The premise behind an ECN is that in a large, reliable electronic environment, buyers and sellers can find each other just fine without any go-between. If market makers function as wholesalers and retailers to the securities business, ECNs are akin to a trader cooperative, or perhaps a simpler brokering system in which buyers and sellers are brought together.

In order to compete with market makers, ECNs tend to make trading cheaper with the hope that heavy volume will keep them afloat. Whereas market makers, like retailers, usually skim a profit from the difference between what they pay for shares and what they sell them for, ECNs levy on every trade a very small surcharge, much as an exchange would. ECN commissions may run less than a hundredth of a cent to a few cents per share. Even so, some ECN fees have drawn criticism from former SEC chairman Arthur Levitt, among others.

The NASDAQ fought back with SuperMontage, a quote aggregation and execution system designed to draw market makers by displaying the top three quotes for best bid and ask price on a trading system. This would effectively match orders in the manner of an ECN but with vastly greater liquidity. ECNs, of course, fiercely resisted this effort. They were aided in Congress by House Commerce Committee Chairman Tom Bliley (R-VA), who sent a letter to Levitt expressing extreme concern over SuperMontage and the potentially unfair advantages it would afford Nasdaq.

NYSE Could Be Nicer The comparison is similar with the New York Stock Exchange (NYSE), which has about twice the market capitalization of the NASDAQ. On the NYSE, each company's shares are delegated to a so-called specialist, a firm that exercises in effect a monopoly on making a market for a given issue. As a result, these firms tend to reap even richer profits when they deal. In heavy trading, though, it's possible for orders to be matched on the NYSE without bringing in a specialist. This kind of trading is executed at very favorable terms that ECNs would have trouble meeting.

For a long time, few ECNs needed to worry about meeting costs on the NYSE because they were excluded from trading its shares. The NYSE's onerous Rule 390 forbade trading of shares that had been listed on the NYSE since before 1979. That made up about 30 percent of NYSE's shares, but half of its trading volume, including the IBMs and AT&Ts of the world. ECNs were thus restricted from trading many of the largest, most demanded stocks listed on that exchange. Rule 390, under heavy pressure from the SEC, was repealed in 2000, much to the delight of the ECN industry.

BACKGROUND AND DEVELOPMENT

ECNs trace their modern form to 1996, when the SEC meted out new order-handling regulations in the wake of a Nasdaq price-fixing scandal. In the mid-1990s and earlier, Nasdaq market makers allegedly conspired to pad their pockets by not filling orders that weren't particularly profitable to them or by filling orders at less than optimal prices to the customer. All of this was fairly easy to pull off because market makers were not required to publicize every order they received.

In its new Order Handling Rules, which took effect in 1997, the SEC forced market makers to publish all their orders to the NASDAQ or an ECN that would in turn post orders to the NASDAQ Level II bulletin board, an electronic queue of orders waiting for takers. This new order transparency, along with a weighty $1 billion civil settlement by the market makers, was intended to ensure fairer trading and better order executions for investors.

At the time, Instinet Corp., a unit of global news and financial data titan Reuters Group PLC, was about the only ECN around. Founded in 1969, Instinet was something of a private trading club for institutional investors, letting them trade after market hours and offering various other features. However, part of the SEC ruling mandated that ECNs also post their orders to Nasdaq Level II, bringing Instinet's activities out in the open.

The order-handling rules created an easy opening for other ECNs to jump through: they were effectively guaranteed to be listed on the NASDAQ. Provided that they could attract a loyal following of users to post orders on their systems, new ECNs could readily divert business away from traditional market makers and other intermediaries.

They wasted little time. Island and Bloomberg's TradeBook (later renamed B-Trade and merged with a service called Posit) set up shop in 1996, followed by Archipelago and RediBook ECN the next year. Companies such as Island, majority-owned by online brokerage Datek Online Holdings Corp., had roots in the day trading business, which was resurgent around the same time and provided a natural user base for ECNs. By 1999, those four firms plus Instinet dominated the ECN turf with an assortment of other players scrambling for their own niches.

By 2000, ECNs were churning about a third of all Nasdaq share volume and an even greater proportion of its individual trades. The higher number of trades indicated that the average ECN trade was still smaller than the hefty institutional transactions that still relied on other channels. Still, for hotly traded stocks such as those of Internet companies, the ECNs' share was even greater. Although estimates of ECN market share vary, the volume of shares handled through ECNs grew easily by 50 percent in less than a year.

Despite occasional insults lobbed by partisans of ECNs and traditional market players, the ECN business was heavily funded by mainstream Wall Street concerns. Archipelago, an innovative ECN, received backing from Merrill Lynch, Goldman Sachs, and J.P. Morgan, among others. Spear, Leeds & Kellogg, majority owner of RediBook ECN, was an old-school NYSE market specialist. Several big name brokerages, including Merrill Lynch and Morgan Stanley Dean Witter, hedged their bets by investing in more than one ECN. All told, brokerages and investment houses poured into ECNs upwards of $200 million by 2000. Because the ECN model threatened comfy brokerage margins, though, cynics suggested that some long-time players would have just as soon lost their investments.

Even as new ECNs were in the works, industry analysts predicted in 2000 that the increasingly crowded ECN field would soon be ripe for consolidation. In fact, some of that had begun by then. In late 1999, Bloomberg announced plans to merge its B-Trade system with Posit, a minor ECN for institutional investors, to create a "SuperECN." Soon after, BRUT and Strike, a pair of ECNs funded by a cadre of Wall Street bigwigs, made known their plans to merge. Some industry observers felt that as few as two ECNs could be left once consolidation swept through. In the meantime, however, market conditions were conducive to new entrants and the number of functioning ECNs was expected to rise in the short term.

In the early years of the twenty-first century's first decade, ECNs like Instinet, Island, and Archipelago faced competition not only from other ECNs but also from more traditional operations as well. Determined to compete in the new landscape carved out by ECNs, the NASDAQ and the New York Stock Exchange (NYSE) both began considering public offerings of their own. In addition, Nasdaq, which saw more than one-third of its transactions being processed by ECNs, began working on the Super Montage, an ECN that would display stock buy and sell prices on a single system. Despite charges by Instinet and other ECNs that the Super Montage would eliminate competition, the SEC approved the NASDAQ's plans to build the new system in 2001.

In 2000, Archipelago agreed to merge with Pacific Stock Exchange into a new electronic stock exchange that would compete with the NASDAQ and the (NYSE). After much debate, the deal was completed in March of 2002. Archipelago's battle to become an exchange reflects a much larger clash between ECNs in general and Wall Street itself. The success of ECNs has taken a definite bite out of the business of traditional brokerages and trading houses. In 2000, the SEC launched a one-year investigation of what the major Wall Street players refer to as fragmentation in the marketplace, which makes it more difficult for smaller investors to get the best price, they assert. One proposed solution is the creation of a Central Limit Order Book (CLOB), through which all orders would be processed on a first come/first served basis. In contrast, ECNs argue that what Wall Street calls market fragmentation is simply competition and, they say, a CLOB would undercut a key factor in the success of ECNs: the ability to execute orders quickly.

A major merger took place in the ECN industry in July of 2002 when Instinet acquired Island for $508 million in stock. The merged entity accounted for a whopping 22 percent of NASDAQ transactions. As reported in a June 2002 issue of *Computerworld*, "Island, which had been pursuing exchange status on its own, said it will continue to do so jointly with Instinet. The move, analysts said, will likely force the U.S. Securities and Exchange Commission to redefine what an exchange is, something it has shown reluctance to do in the past."

A number of important ECN-related developments took place during the middle of the first decade of the 2000s. One was the Security and Exchange Commission's April 2005 adoption of Regulation NMS, a trade-through rule that included proposals related to market data, inter-market access, sub-penny stock pricing, and order protection. In particular, the regulation mandated that investment firms obtain the best price for consumers engaged in electronic stock trading, even if that price happens to be on a different exchange. Regulation NMS was scheduled to become effective in 2006, with the best price aspect of the rule effective in June of that year.

Prior to Regulation NMS, brokers trading NYSE-listed stocks were required to pass their orders through the NYSE. Critics argued that this unfairly benefited the NYSE, and that the new rule would boost investor confidence through greater transparency and liquidity. However, the new rule was opposed by large institutional investors such as TIAA-CREF and Fidelity, who charged that investors would lose the right to consider factors such as transaction costs and market data. Additionally, institutional investors were opposed to the fact that the rule also pertained to NASDAQ stocks.

In an April 25, 2005, *National Underwriter Life & Health* article, Jim Connolly detailed a statement from Fidelity to the House Committee on Financial Services, which asserted that "'so long as bids and offers are made available to investors on a timely and continuous basis, and investors have ready access to competing market centers, the government need not—and should not—deprive investors of the freedom to choose among markets.'"

Some ECNs were opposed to any kind of trade-through rules. For example, in the January 31, 2005, issue of *Securities Industry News,* Bloomberg Tradebook President and CEO Kim Bang expressed skepticism as industry players considered how the new rule would impact them. In the article, Bang stated, "We think the existing trade-through rule as we know it has proven unsuccessful in terms of providing for a better market structure and market environment for market participants and investors. There is little reason to believe that the new trade-through rule proposals will lead to a better market structure."

Instead of competing with traditional stock exchanges, during the middle of the first decade of the 2000s, ECNs were being integrated with floor-based trading. This trend, which began in 2000 when Archipelago agreed to merge with Pacific Stock Exchange, continued when The New York Stock Exchange agreed to merge with Archipelago Holdings Inc. in April 2005, creating a new company called NYSE Group Inc. In an April 21, 2005, *Regional Business*

News article, Brendan Caldwell, CEO of Caldwell Securities, said the combination would "provide the exchange with a new 'vibrance' and 'purpose.'"

Only days after the Archipelago deal, the Nasdaq Stock Market agreed to buy Instinet Group Inc. from Reuters Group Plc. The $1.88 billion deal effectively brought together the two largest U.S. equities markets. While Nasdaq retained INET ECN, it sold Instinet subsidiary Lynch, Jones & Ryan to the Bank of New York Co. and its brokerage arm to Silver Lake Partners.

By 2006, many exchanges were in the process of upgrading their equity trading systems to comply with Regulation NMS and improve trading efficiency. The SEC had initially set the compliance date for Rules 610 and 611 of Regulation NMS as June 29, 2006. However, on May 18 of that year, the commission extended the deadline, setting a series of five different compliance dates. Specifically, these included a specifications date on October 16, 2006; a trading phase date on February 5, 2007; a pilot stocks phase date on May 21, 2007; an all stocks phase date on July 9, 2007; and a completion date on October 8, 2007.

By mid-2006, the competition between ECNs and the Nasdaq for liquidity had risen to a boiling point. The NASDAQ, which had acquired its own ECNs (Inet and Brut ECN), moved to kick ECNs off as part of a move to merge its three trading platforms to one named Single Book. By taking away the ability of ECNs to display quotes and proposing to shift order delivery fees from order delivery firms to ECNs with no cap, ECNs' existence was placed in jeopardy.

According to the January 15, 2007, issue of *Securities Industry News,* in October of 2006, ECNs were "booted off" the NASDAQ. Subsequently, they began turning to regional stock exchanges and equity exchanges, "hoping to win them over with roughly 450 million shares of daily order flow." Developments began with Track ECN and BATS Trading quoting and printing trades on the National Stock Exchange (NSE). However, there were technical challenges to contend with, such as the fact that the NSE's display system did not reveal which ECN an order was originating from.

"Double execution" was another consideration. In the same *Securities Industry News* article, writer Patrick Ruppe explained: "If the ECN routes to the exchange and the exchange and the ECN find a buyer for the same quote at the same time, either the exchange or the ECN will be faced with a double-booked trade and forced to find extra shares or cancel the transaction, which could result in lost revenue. The ECNs want the exchanges to commit to double-checking the displayed orders, but the exchanges aren't keen on doing so because it could slow them down." Moving forward, it was clear that issues such as these needed to be resolved.

CURRENT CONDITIONS

In November, 2008, the New York Stock Exchange changed its pricing for accessing its order delivery system pursuant to which it no longer pays rebates for adding liquidity to its book. As a result, ECNs could only pay their subscribers for adding liquidity when there was an internal match on their own books. This change resulted in some deterioration of trading volumes.

In September 2008, Kansas City-based BATS Trading Inc., the largest U.S. electronic communications network still standing independent, announced that it had received SEC approval in August to become the 11th U.S. stock exchange. The exchange status will now put them on the same plane as NYSE and the NASDAQ. As an ECN, it needed to display its orders on exchanges, which involved a small time lag that put it at a disadvantage in a world of subsecond execution. The new status will greatly enhance transactional speed and increase market share. BATS was the first ECN whose exchange application was approved by the SEC. At the time, it already controlled about ten percent of U.S. equity trading.

INDUSTRY LEADERS

Instinet Corp. and Archipelago Holdings LLC played pioneering roles in the industry before they were acquired by leading stock exchanges.

Instinet Corp. The granddaddy of all ECNs, Instinet began operation in 1969, before the NASDAQ market even existed, when the trading system was known as Institutional Networks. While it was perceived as a maverick at points in its history, by the time new ECNs were being conceived amid the SEC's order-handling shakeup in the mid-1990s, Instinet seemed a stodgy near-monopoly. Under control of Reuters Group PLC since 1987, New York-based Instinet continued to serve its core institutional clientele through the late 1990s, gradually adding a number of additional services beyond basic trading. It continued to command the largest market share of any ECN, often double that of its nearest competitor. In 1999 the company decided to pursue a brokerage strategy and made plans to roll out an international retail brand in 2000.

In 2002 Instinet acquired competitor and Datek subsidiary The Island ECN Inc. for $508 million in stock, gaining a 22 percent share of the Nasdaq market. Sales reached $1.05 billion that year, and increased to $1.2 billion in 2004. In April 2005 the Nasdaq Stock Market agreed to buy Instinet Group Inc., the holding company for Instinet and several other concerns, from Reuters for $1.88 billion, bringing together the two largest U.S. equities markets. While the NASDAQ retained INET ECN, it sold Instinet subsidiary Lynch, Jones & Ryan to the Bank of New York Co., and also sold Instinet's brokerage arm to

Silver Lake Partners. Meanwhile, in August 2009 Instinet announced that it would acquire substantially all the business and assets of TORC Financial, LLC, a leading provider of derivatives trading technologies.

Instinet was honored throughout 2009 with a total of six different industry recognitions, including "Best Electronic Brokerage House" from *Asset*'s Triple A Transaction Banking Awards for 2009; "Best Agency Broker" from *Financial News*'s Awards for Excellence in I.T. Trading & Technology, Europe 2009; and "Best Execution-Only Broker" from *AsianInvestor*'s 2009 Service Provider Awards.

Archipelago Holdings LLC Formed in 1996, Chicago-based Archipelago boasted revenues of $541.3 million in 2004, up more than 18 percent from the previous year. The company has courted both institutional and retail accounts, and was one of the first to adopt an open system. Archipelago had lagged behind several ECNs in terms of its share volume, but it one-upped Island's bid to become an exchange by merging with one in 2002. Archipelago merged with the ailing Pacific Stock Exchange to create a new national electronic exchange. While some viewed it as a dubious combination of two also-rans, Archipelago—whose private investors have included the likes of Instinet, the online brokerage E*TRADE Group Inc., financial channel CNBC, and Wall Street pillars Goldman Sachs and J.P. Morgan—ultimately evolved into a strong player. With its Archipelago Exchange, called ArcaEx, the company offered listings on the Pacific Exchange, as well as the NYSE, the NASDAQ, and AMEX. After Archipelago was acquired by the New York Stock Exchange, a new company was created under the name of NYSE Group Inc.

RESEARCH AND DEVELOPMENT

In October 2009, Instinet announced that its European SmartRouter routing technology offered by its European brokerage unit, Instinet Europe Limited, had been named "Best Broker-Supplied Tool/Technology" by *Buy-Side Technology* magazine in the 2009 Buy-Side Technology Awards. The highly-sophisticated routing technology connected to all new venues from the moment they became available, and as a result delivered significant price improvement and savings to Instinet clients. (Price improvement is defined as the difference between execution price and the best quoted price on the primary exchange at that time.)

BIBLIOGRAPHY

"BATS ECN Approved as Newest Securities Exchange." *Pensions and Investments,* September 2008. Available at http://www.pionline.com/article/20080901/PRINTSUB/309019991.

Bresiger, Gregory. "The Nasdaq-ECN War Is Off for Now." *Traders Magazine,* October 2006. Available from http://www.tradersmagazine.com/.

Chapman, Peter. "BATS Says it Wants to Apply to SEC for Exchange Status." *Traders Magazine,* April 5, 2007. Available from http://www.tradersmagazine.com/.

Cohn, Michael. "ECNs Ponder Changing Rules of the Game." *Securities Industry News,* 31 January 2005.

Connolly, Jim. "SEC Adopts Trade-Through Rule." *National Underwriter Life & Health,* 25 April 2005.

Farrell, Greg. "SEC Expected to Alter Rule on Buying, Selling." *USA Today,* 6 April 2005.

Hintze, John. "Remaining ECNs at Mercy of Nasdaq Initiatives: Anticipating Restrictions, Independents Explore Alternative Quote Venues." *Securities Industry News,* 22 May 2006.

"Instinet Agrees to Acquire TORC Financial, LLC." *Fox Business News* Release, 26 August 2009. Available from http://www.fox business.com/story/markets/industries/finance/instinet-agrees-acquire-torc-financial-llc/.

"Instinet's European SmartRouter Again Wins Buy-Side Technology's "Best Broker-Supplied Tool/Technology" Award." Reuters, 22 October 2009. Available from http://www.reuters.com/article/pressRelease/idUS67337+22-Oct-2009+BW20091022.

Krantz, Matt. "Nasdaq, NYSE Wage 'Interesting Battle' over ECNs." *USA Today,* 25 April 2005.

Massaro, Kerry. "Reinventing Themselves." *Wall Street & Technology,* August 2004.

Mearian, Lucas. "Merged Electronic Trading Net to Set Sights on Nasdaq." *Computerworld,* 17 June 2002.

"Nasdaq Goes After the Competition." *USA Today,* 25 April 2005.

"Nasdaq to Buy Reuters' Instinet for 1.88 Billion Dollars." *Finance CustomWire,* 22 April 2005.

"NYSE Goes Public in Merger with Archipelago." *Finance CustomWire,* 21 April 2005.

Ruppe, Patrick. "ECNs Seeking to Shop Order Flow." *Wall Street Letter,* 15 January 2007.

"SEC Extends Compliance Dates for Regulation of NMS." *Banking & Financial Services Policy Report,* August 2006.

"Trading Trends Favor Electronic Avenues." *Informationweek,* 16 February 2004.

Tully, Shawn. "The One Man the NYSE Should Fear." *Fortune,* 22 March 2004.

ELECTRONIC PUBLISHING

SIC CODE(S)

2741

3571

INDUSTRY SNAPSHOT

Although an anathema to some literary purists, the explosive future of electronic publishing seemed etched in stone by the new millennium. With communication and commerce rapidly shifting to the Internet, publishers of all genres were increasingly forced to look to this channel as a way of augmenting sales or risk being left behind. Most of the world's classics, from Shakespeare to Virginia Woolf to James Baldwin, already could be retrieved on the World Wide Web. Retail book giants, such as Barnes & Noble, were forced into the electronic commerce market to hedge against market encroachment from such upstarts as Amazon.com. By 2000, all major newspapers and magazines in the United States had an Internet strategy, and the market was poised for a booming new reading medium: the electronic book or e-book.

While there was a market for fiction titles and other works that people read for enjoyment, non-fiction appeared to be the most promising e-book market during the mid to late years of the first decade of the 2000s. Specifically, the industry was focused on works in the genres of education, corporate/institutional training, and reference. Heading into the latter part of the decade, this trend was bolstered by growing e-book collections at libraries throughout the world, especially in Asia.

Electronic publishing clearly benefited from the rapid adoption of broadband Internet connectivity, which had reached more than half of Internet-connected homes in the United States by mid-2005, according to data from Nielsen/NetRatings. Without having to dial up for a connection, more consumers had instant access to the Web at any time of the day for a steady stream of content on virtually any subject.

So-called "citizen journalism," also called distributed journalism, reality media, and grass-roots media, was another major development in the electronic publishing realm during the mid to late years of the twenty-first century's first decade. This phenomenon saw a growing number of common people sharing uncensored electronic news as it happened from points throughout the world. To distribute information, blogs were the platform of choice for most citizen journalists. Short for "Web log," a blog is a one-to-many Web-based form of communication. It is similar in many respects to a personal Web site, online journal, or diary that readers can respond to, and often includes links to other places on the World Wide Web. Effectively bringing together people that otherwise would be separated by the boundaries of politics, geography, and time, blogs are 24/7 soapboxes that people use to express their opinions, complaints, and musings on any conceivable topic—in chronological order.

ORGANIZATION AND STRUCTURE

Generally, online publishers gain revenue from three sources: ad banners, subscriptions, and pay-per-view. Advertising revenue can be generated in several different ways. For instance, advertisers might pay a fee each time their banner is displayed on the publisher's site. In another method, publishers receive a payment each time one of their site users clicks on an ad and is taken to the advertiser's Web site. Finally, the publisher can receive a payment when the user buys an advertised product. This type of arrangement, which is becoming more popular, gives the publisher a percentage of the purchase price. Online sellers who have used these kinds of programs include Amazon.com, Barnes & Noble, and Ticketmaster.

While print publishers routinely charge for their magazines or newspapers, subscription-based publications on the Internet are unusual. With only a few publishing exceptions—notably the *Wall Street Journal* and *The Economist*—Internet users have shown a reluctance to pay for online content. Publishers have another option to raise revenues in the form of pay-per-view, which requires readers to pay in order to download material. This method is commonly used for online fiction books and article archives such as those of *The New York Times*. In the case of an archive, users can usually search for free but are charged a fee, running anywhere from 50 cents to several dollars, for each article they view.

BACKGROUND AND DEVELOPMENT

Modern publishing dates back to the 1440s and a German printer named Johannes Gutenberg, who is believed to be the first European to print with hand-set type cast in molds. For the most part, printing technology remained fairly static over the next centuries, but the rise of computers in the 1970s changed that. During the 1980s, almost all printing functions such as creating artwork, setting type, and scanning photographs, became automated. There were several electronic publishing advancements in 1984. That year saw the first computer-based CD-ROM (compact disk-read only memory); the first online magazine featuring short science fiction and fantasy stories on the BITNET network at the University of Maine; and the appearance of desktop publishing systems that integrated high quality images and graphics with text. The 1970s and 1980s also gave birth to the Internet, a global communication system composed of thousands of interconnected networks. In 1990, Tim Berners-Lee, working at CERN, a particle physics lab in Geneva, Switzerland, developed the World Wide Web. The accelerated growth of the Web in the 1990s can be attributed in part to its use of hypertext, the non-sequential form of writing created by Ted Nelson in 1968.

While much Internet activity has focused on trying to make money, at least one early Internet pioneer saw the value of providing online content at no charge. Project Gutenberg, which was founded in 1971 by Michael Hart of Urbana, Illinois, continues to this day making public domain books available for free in an electronic format, boasting more than 10,000 titles in 45 languages by mid-2005. Hart's goal is to have 20,000 books online by July of 2006. The works of authors such as Leo Tolstoy,

Rudyard Kipling, and Nathaniel Hawthorne are featured on the site.

Early electronic book publishers used diskette and CD-ROM formats. In 1994 there were five or six publishers, including Chicago-based Spectrum Press, which offered books on 3.5-inch and 5.25-inch floppy disks. Daniel Agin, who owned Spectrum, called these products "e-text" books. Even by 1994, however, disks were being replaced by CD-ROMs that could hold 300,000 pages of text and had tracks for sound and motion pictures. Because of the vast amount of space available on CD-ROMS, reference publishers such as Grolier Interactive adopted the technology.

In 1995, U.S. newspapers were jumping on the Internet bandwagon. That year, 70 daily newspapers (three times as many as in 1994) established an Internet presence. As reported by Steve Alexander in a June 12, 1995 article in the *Minneapolis Star Tribune,* an American Opinion Research study found that 19 percent of newspaper editors and publishers believed that the Internet would be the main competitor for advertising revenue by 2000. Early on, the *San Jose Mercury News,* owned by Knight Ridder, and the *Raleigh News and Observer* were leaders in gaining an online identity. The *Mercury News* made use of on-screen graphics and hyperlinks to related Internet sites to build a national readership. The site received 250,000 to 300,000 hits a day in 1995.

The phenomenal growth of electronic publishing raised questions in the areas of copyright laws and pornography. Legislators, educators, citizens' groups, and Web site owners are grappling to find solutions to these complex issues. The enormity and easy access of the Internet makes it nearly impossible to regulate, much less monitor. Recognizing this fact, the Digital Millennium Copyright Act, passed by Congress in August 1998, provided immunity to Internet service providers, such as America Online, for the copyright infringements of its customers. Even so, the vastness of the Internet has not deterred some from believing that it needs controls. For instance, many people are bothered by the fact that children can readily find pornography on the Internet. The Child Online Protection Act, signed into law by President Bill Clinton in 1997, was designed to combat this problem by requiring commercial Internet publishers of certain types of sexually explicit material to verify the age of Web site readers or face a penalty. Many mainstream Internet publishers, however, were bothered by this federal law and challenged it in court. The publishers argued that the age verification procedures would be too difficult and costly to implement, and as a result, many publishers would practice self-censorship— even if their material had not been intended to be prurient—to ensure that they did not break the law.

As electronic publishing grew, virtually all sectors related to the publishing operations were forced to adapt to rapidly changing market conditions. Newsprint was slated to be the prime casualty of the electronic publishing boom. The online classifieds sector alone grew astronomically—240 percent in 1997 and 118 percent in 1998. By 2003, a full 15 percent of the U.S. classified market was expected to be online, according to the Boston Consulting Group. Online news services will similarly eat into the news printing market, as more and more customers look to the Internet rather than to the printed page to keep up with world developments. Printed magazines and catalogs were expected to suffer a similar fate, though not to the same extent as newspapers.

After their much-heralded launch in late 1998, e-books enjoyed only lukewarm sales during their first years on the market, due in large part to their high costs. During this time, e-book reading devices generally cost between $200 and $600. Moreover, their displays usually were monochrome and fairly drab, while most high quality texts require color capability. Many analysts noted that manufacturers hadn't done enough to create a market for e-books. While there were some modest success stories, e-book companies were forced to the realization that for the time being, authors, not technologies, sell books. (The number one title for 2008 was O'Reilly's *Mac OS X Leopard: The Missing Manual.*)

By the end of 2000, only 25,000 e-book reading devices had been sold and e-book sales were less than $5 million. Along with sluggish demand, the e-book industry was also forced to deal with limited supplies. E-book availability was growing at a much slower pace than e-book reading device makers had anticipated. In 2001, the number of e-books compatible with Gemstar's RocketBook, the industry's leading platform, had reached only a few thousand. Concerned that e-book sales might undermine print sales, particularly on the new releases likely to make the best seller lists, many publishers were only willing to offer electronic versions of classics like *Moby Dick* and *Romeo and Juliet.*

Incompatible formats posed another problem for the e-book industry. By 2001, each of the three e-book industry leaders—Gemstar, Adobe, and Microsoft—was working to position its format as the industry standard. The lack of standards left many publishers leery about committing to any single format and many decided to wait and see which format proved dominant before investing in the e-book industry. For the same reason, consumers resisted spending money on e-book reading devices, most of which could read only one format.

Copyright issues also proved daunting to many publishers. Despite legislation like the Digital Millennium Copyright Act, which made the manufacture or sale of products designed to dodge copyright laws illegal, many publishers were unsure how to go about protecting copyrighted books offered electronically. At the same time, publishers unwilling to release electronic versions of their copyrighted books also worked to prohibit other companies from doing so. For example, although authors like Kurt Vonnegut and Robert Parker granted RosettaBooks permission to publish electronic versions of their books, questions arose as to whether or not RosettaBooks needed to gain permission from Random House, the copyright holder of the traditional print books written by those authors. In February of 2001, Random House filed a copyright infringement lawsuit. In December of 2002, the two parties settled out of court. RosettaBooks retained the right to publish electronic versions of the books in question, but the company was required to pay royalties to Random House.

Although the e-book market grew more slowly than anticipated, some major publishers continued to pursue new e-book ventures. Many industry experts believe that the future of e-books is in niche markets, such as children's books, textbooks, and reference publications.

Electronic textbooks also seem poised for growth in the early years of the first decade of the 2000s. Online courseware, the smallest segment of the industry, was estimated to increase at an annual rate of 31 percent. Reasons for this rapid rise include the increased use of the Internet in classrooms and the acceptance of electronic publishing in the learning process.

Online newsletters became increasingly popular in the early 2000s. While many companies make online newsletters available on their Web site, the most popular online newsletter delivery method is e-mail. For example, CNET.com, a site covering the computer and technology industries, had more than 40 free online newsletters, all sent to subscribers via e-mail. The Motley Fool, known for its witty investment advice, also offered members free weekly newsletters, including *FoolWatch Weekly* and *Investing Basics,* via e-mail.

While some online newsletters are published to simply convey information, many are published to generate additional sales for the publisher. In fact, a 2001 study conducted by *Opt-in News* revealed that one out of three online newsletter publishers used newsletters to generate advertising revenue. Advertising in online newsletters is growing in popularity mainly because it is often more effective than placing a banner ad on a Web site. According to Forrester Research, ads in e-mailed newsletters had an average response rate of 18 percent in 2001 compared to a Web site banner ad response rate of less than 1 percent.

Online periodical publishers were still trying to find out how to make their services profitable in the early years of the first decade of the 2000s. The only publisher to actually make money from an online newspaper was WSJ.com, the online version of *The Wall Street Journal.* When online advertising revenues plummeted in 2000, WSJ.com was able to rely on its base of nearly 600,000 paying subscribers for revenue. In fact, subscription sales began to account for more than advertising revenues in 2001.

By mid-decade, the electronic publishing market continued to grow. One indication of its good health was online advertising. Citing data from the Interactive Advertising Bureau, *American Journalism Review* reported that online advertising revenues grew 21 percent from 2002 to 2003, reaching $7.3 billion, and then jumped approximately 32 percent in 2004 to $9.6 billion. The publication revealed that leading media companies faced a shortage of online advertising space. To remedy the situation, many firms sought established online properties to acquire rather than building new ones from scratch. While some of these properties offered news, others were simply a means to build a more sizable advertising base. Examples include the Washington Post Co.'s acquisition of *Slate* from Microsoft; Dow Jones' $529 million purchase of the financial news site MarketWatch; and the $410 million acquisition of online reference destination About.com by the New York Times Co. In addition, newspaper industry giants Gannett, Knight Ridder, and the Tribune Co. all took 25 percent ownership shares in news aggregator Topix.net.

The rising popularity of online news was another key electronic publishing development. Traditional newspapers were challenged by the changing tastes of younger readers, who preferred getting their news online instead of in print. Despite the aforementioned acquisitions by major news companies such as Dow Jones and the Washington Post Co., some observers criticized major newspapers for not investing enough in their online editions. In the June-July 2005 issue of *American Journalism Review,* Barb Palser wrote: "Every paper has a Web site, but spending on content and development is still paltry. In its annual report on the state of the news media, the Project for Excellence in Journalism found that despite growing audiences, news organizations are reluctant to invest in the Web and 'have imposed more cutbacks in their Internet operations than in their old media.' Instead of investing forward, news managers are still fixated on figuring out how to get a generation of young people to subscribe to the print edition. If that's the question burning in their brains, they still don't get it."

Some newspapers were experimenting with electronic editions that were truly interactive. One example was BlufftonToday.com, a site linked to a free daily paper in the city of Bluffton, South Carolina. Unlike the traditional online edition of a printed paper, BlufftonToday used online contributions from readers as a content source for the regular paper's reporting staff. As the concept of "citizen journalism," also called distributed journalism, reality media, and grass-roots media, caught on, possibly piquing the interest of leading media companies, some observers suggested that one day, papers might offer citizens the ability to write their own versions of certain local stories, providing views that differed from or complemented those of staff reporters.

Efforts by established media companies to make news more interactive was only the tip of the citizen journalism iceberg. In fact, this phenomenon saw a growing number of common people sharing uncensored electronic news as it happened from points throughout the world. To distribute information, blogs were the platform of choice for most citizen journalists. Short for Web log, a blog is a one-to-many Web-based form of communication. It is similar in many respects to a personal Web site, online journal, or diary that readers can respond to, and often includes links to other places on the World Wide Web. Effectively bringing together people that otherwise would be separated by the boundaries of politics, geography, and time, blogs are 24/7 soapboxes that people use to express their opinions, complaints, and musings on any conceivable topic—in chronological order.

According to the non-profit, non-partisan Pew Internet & American Life Project, 32 million Americans read blogs during the middle of the twenty-first century's first decade. Blogs have been called everything from personal broadcasting systems to glorified electronic dictionaries. As Francine Fialkoff wrote in the April 1, 2005, issue of *Library Journal,* "While blogs can disseminate news from many sources, they also can generate news and be news, too. They reflect tremendous energy, often creating niches for and drawing together likeminded readers. As with any written words, however, in their immediacy, blogs can make mistakes."

The relationship of blogging to traditional media coverage can be illustrated by several key examples. The tsunami that wreaked havoc on Southeast Asia on December 26, 2004, was documented by bloggers, who, in addition to providing photos, video, and news of the disaster, also shared casualty and missing person lists and provided links to government agencies and disaster/relief organizations. During the 2004 presidential race, several political bloggers were given highly prized press credentials and allowed to report from the Republican and Democratic national conventions along with traditional media heavyweights. In addition, Howard Dean leveraged his *Blog For America* site as a successful fundraising and volunteer recruitment tool.

"Rather-Gate," also referred to as "Memogate," is another example of the impact that bloggers have on traditional media. When CBS News' Dan Rather claimed on September 8, 2004, to have memos proving President George W. Bush compromised the terms of his military service during the Vietnam War, bloggers proved the documents were forged. The controversial *60 Minutes II* story led to the termination of several CBS staff members, an apology from Rather, and an internal review at CBS.

Blogs continued to experience strong growth. This was evident by the number of people who were still unaware of its existence. For example, the aforementioned Pew Internet & American Life Project memo indicated that blogs were still relatively unknown during mid-decade. In the memo, Pew explained that 62 percent of all Internet users surveyed did not understand what the term "blog" means.

After a rough start during the late 1990s and the early years of the first decade of the 2000s, e-books were finding a niche during the middle of the decade. From 288,400 units sold in the first quarter of 2003, sales had increased 46 percent by the first quarter of 2004, totaling 421,955 units sold. However, this was still a small fraction of the total U.S. book market at that time, which consisted of well over two billion books sold. eReader.com claimed to offer the largest e-book store in the world, offering more than 13,000 selections that could be viewed on personal digital assistants (PDAs) and pocket computers. Companies like OverDrive, which specialize in digital rights management technology, also allowed libraries to offer e-books and other digital media to their patrons via a secure channel.

By late 2006, the electronic publishing market was buoyed upward by the rapid adoption of broadband Internet connectivity, which had reached nearly 80 percent of Internet-connected homes in the United States, according to data from Nielsen/NetRatings. Without having to dial up for a connection, more consumers had instant access to the Internet at any time of the day for a steady stream of content on virtually any subject.

More Internet users were relying on the Web for content, according to a Nielsen/NetRatings study released in August 2007. Conducted on behalf of the Online Publishers Association, the study found that higher-quality content and the availability of more video caused U.S. Internet users to devote about 47 percent of their online time to content sites, an increase from 34 percent in 2003. At 33 percent, e-mail received a smaller share of users's online time, falling from 46 percent in 2003.

CURRENT CONDITIONS

The future direction of electronic publishing can be summarized by looking at the publishing industry as a whole. In February 2009, Datamonitor released its *Publishing: Global Industry Guide,* which reported that the global publishing market grew by 2.6 percent in 2007 to reach

a value of $426.2 billion. It forecast that in 2012, the global publishing market woould have a value of $487.8 billion, an increase of 14.4 percent since 2007. Advertising was the leading segment in the global publishing market, accounting for 33.4 percent of the markets value. The Americas accounted for 40.8 percent of the global publishing market value, the report indicated.

Rudiger Wischenbart, in "The Global Ranking of the Publishing Industry 2008: An overview and analysis," made note that the new leader of the industry, the professional information giant Thomson (renamed Thomson Reuters after the acquisition of the news wire agency in early 2008) flatly boasted on its Web site that "ca. 88 percent of total revenues derived from electronic products, services and software." This followed the previous year's announcement by industry leader Reed Elsevier that growth as well as profits were being driven clearly by digital products, and that preferably the company would rely on continuous streams of income from subscribers rather than on volatile advertising markets.

Online Advertising Online advertising continued to be a strong indicator of electronic publishing's good health during the decade's late years. In March 2009, the Interactive Advertising Bureau (IAB) reported that Internet advertising revenues exceeded $23 billion in 2008, reaching a record high. It was the fifth consecutive year of record results. (Conversely, the wounded U.S. newspaper industry lost $7.5 billion in print and advertising advertising revenues in 2008 according to Technorati. 2008 totals were $37.85 billion, for comparison.)

Blogs By 2009 the number of blogs on record at Technoratia, a blog search service, since it started tracking them in 2002, was estimated at 133 million. The average number of blog posts in a 24 hour period was given as 900,000. Factoring in private blogs, as well as those found on the popular site MySpace, the grand total of existing blogs could be much higher. (A 2008 estimate from comScore estimated the number of people globally who read blogs as 346,000,000.) Roughly 77 percent of active Internet users read blogs.

The 2008 presidential elections brought a new high to the number of blog commentaries as well as readers. While it remains true that virtually anyone can establsh a blog site, the election campaigns brought more established, well-respected news media and commentators out into the blogs, such as the *Chicago Tribune*'s "TheSwamp." U.S. President Barack Obama will go down in history as the first president to make widespread use of electronic publishing to reach millions of people during his campaign.

Among professional and self-employed bloggers, 17 percent of the total respondents to a Technorati survey said they derived their primary income from blogging. For bloggers who generated revenue from their blogs, by far the greatest source of revenue was from display ads or search ads. The mean annual advertising revenue was $42,548. Over 70 percent of bloggers talked about brand products they liked or disliked.

E-Books E-books continued to benefit from the efforts of libraries to expand their electronic holdings. In public, academic, and private libraries, librarians were central players in acquiring and digitizing e-content, and helping their patrons understand and take maximum advantage of what e-book collections had to offer. A press release in June 2009 announced that the Association of American University Presses (AAUP), a nonprofit organization of academic publishers, entered into a cooperative agreement with iPublishCentral, a self-service e-content publishing, marketing, warehousing and delivery platform from Impelsys, to support its 130 members in pursuing electronic publishing. For its part, iPublishCentral will allow participating AAUP members to market books on the Internet, sell content online, and promote brands and titles across the World Wide Web. "Scholars are increasingly looking for content on electronic platforms, and university presses want to serve those readers and writers as best as possible," said Peter Givler, Executive Director of AAUP.

In October 2009, Forrester Research raised its original projection of 2 million U.S. e-Reader sales in 2009 up 50 percent. Forrester later expected that three million e-Readers would be sold in 2009 and that 30 percent of those would be sold during the 2009 holiday season. Faster than expected sales were attributed to falling prices, better retail distribution, and the media buzz that currently surrounded eBooks and eReaders. For 2010, Forrester projected e-Reader sales of up to ten million. For 2010, Forrester predicted that Barnes & Noble would become serious competition for Amazon with the Nook and the forthcoming Nook Color.

As the competition among e-Reader manufacturers was heating up, a larger number of U.S. retailers, including Best Buy, Costco, Target, and Wal-mart started to devote shelf space to eReaders. As more content was available and manufacturers like iRex and Sony were backing the open ePub standard. According to the Association of American Publishers (AAP), e-Book sales since June 2009 went up 149 percent for the year and the industry was now generating $14 million in sales every month (Forrester). AAP collected e-Book sales statistics in conjunction with the International Digital Publishing Forum (IDPF). Jeff Bezoz, Amazon's CEO and founder, noted in an October 2009 interview with the *New York Times* that whenever Amazon offered both a Kindle and paper version of a book, 48 percent of total sales came from the digital Kindle edition.

According to a study completed by the Book Industry Study Group, the total annual revenue of U.S. book publishers for 2008 was $40.32 billion. This study included Internet sales and sales of books in electronic format, which were not included in previous years. Within the e-book sector, wholesale sales for 2008 were $52 million for 13 participating trade publishers, suggesting retail sales around $100 million.

Leading publishers and booksellers like HarperCollins were experimenting with ways to offer content, such as the first chapter of a book, available via mobile devices, as a way of introducing readers to new print releases. Publishers also were considering the sale of additional factual content, such as recipes, via mobile channels, as a way of extending print titles. Another example of this type of approach involved a deal between ICUE, a developer of technology that makes it easy to read mobile content on cell phones, and Borders. The deal made first chapters of forthcoming books available to customers, who could then download a coupon for 20 percent off the title once it was released.

INDUSTRY LEADERS

CNET Networks Inc., headquartered in San Francisco, is a leading content network in terms of audience size and revenues. The company operates a range of Web sites that offer information about computers, the Internet, and digital technologies. As of 2007, its brands included BNET, CNET, CNET Channel, FameFAQs, GameSpot, International Media, MP3.com, mySimon, Search.com, TechRepublic, TV.com, Webshots, and ZDNet. In early 2009, CNET was acquired by CBS Corporation.

Dow Jones & Co. Inc.'s flagship publication, the *Wall Street Journal,* appears in both print and online form. The company offered *The Wall Street Journal Online* at WSJ.com via The Wall Street Journal Digital Network of Web sites. According to the company, the network, WSJ.com had 983,000 subscribers in 2007, making it the world's largest paid subscription news site. In addition to *The Wall Street Journal Online,* The Wall Street Journal Digital Network offered content sites such as CareerJournal.com, OpinionJournal.com, CollegeJournal.com, StartupJournal.com, and RealEstateJournal.com.

Knight Ridder Inc. was ahead of the times in 1993 when it launched its first Web site, Mercury Center, an offshoot of its newspaper franchise, the *San Jose Mercury News.* Over the next four years, the company poured $70 million into online ventures without seeing any profit on its investment. Despite losses from Internet operations, Knight Ridder remained committed to technology; and to that end, in 1998 the company moved its headquarters from Miami to San Jose to be closer to its new media division. Amidst declining stock value, Knight Ridder announced in March 2000 that it would launch

KnightRidder.com, a collection of portals for cities in which Knight Ridder publishes and the home of all its online operations. The company operates 30 daily and 50 non-daily newspapers across the United States, including the *Miami Herald* and the *Philadelphia Inquirer*. In 1997 the company launched the Real Cities network, which included 37 Web sites in association with its newspapers. By mid-2005, the Real Cities network reached approximately 18 percent of the U.S. online adult population. In 2006 Knight Ridder was acquired by The McClatchy Co. In early 2009, several newspapers formerly owned by McClatchy filed for bankruptcy under Chapter 11 of the Bankruptcy Code, making amounts owed to McClatchy likely uncollectible. As a result, the company reported only $1.9 billion in revenues for 2008.

Salon Media Group Inc., publisher of the San Francisco-based online magazine Salon.com, decided to go public in 1999. In April of that year, the publication announced an initial public offering of 2.5 million common shares. Salon is a media company that produces original content in a variety of categories. It also is home to online communities like Table Talk and The WELL, which it acquired in 1999. That year, the firm struck a deal with Bravo Networks in which Salon traded over a million shares in exchange for $11.8 million in airtime on Bravo's cable television programming for Salon's news, interviews, and cultural coverage. Like many online publications, Salon's main source of revenue comes from advertising. The company boasted some 60,000 paying subscribers in 2007 and revenues of $7.8 million.

The Chicago-based Tribune Co., a newspaper and entertainment conglomerate, paired up with AOL in 1996 to build Digital Cities, an online network providing services in cities across the United States. The Tribune Co. invested $20 million and owned 20 percent of the venture. The purpose of Digital City was to offer local content such as news, weather, and entertainment guides tailored specifically to each of its 88 U.S. markets. By 1998, however, the online city guide field had become so crowded and competitive that Digital City laid off 80 staff members. The Tribune Co. publishes 11 newspapers, including the *Chicago Tribune* and the *Los Angeles Times*. Its Tribune Interactive operations maintain the Web sites for the company's newspapers and television outlets.

RESEARCH AND TECHNOLOGY

Piracy remains a pressing concern for e-book makers and merchants. Since such books are downloaded from the Internet, the potential for a sophisticated hacker to engage in unauthorized duplication is omnipresent. To assist in copyright protection, Adobe Systems developed and made available its PDF Merchant to encrypt electronic content and distribute the certificates required for access to electronic documents. Adobe's product was likely to be especially well received since most electronic books already used Adobe's PDF format, causing easy conversions and thus faster market penetration.

BIBLIOGRAPHY
"34 Years of Project Gutenberg." Project Gutenberg Literary Archive Foundation, 31 August 2005. Available from http://www.gutenberg.org/events/34-years.txt.

Alexander, Steve. "More Newspapers Across the Country Are Launching Electronic Editions." *Minneapolis Star Tribune,* 12 June 1995.

"ANALYSIS: Will Consumers Read a Book on Mobile?" *New Media Age,* 12 July 2007.

Bloggers. A Portrait of the Internet's New Storytellers. Washington, DC: Pew Internet & American Life Project, 19 July 2006. Available from http://www.pewinternet.org.

Book Industry Study Group. "Book Industry Trends: 2009." Available from http://www.bisg.org/news-5-363-book-industry-trends-2009-indicates-publishers-net-revenue-up-10-in-2008-to-reach-4032-billion.php

"Booksellers, Libraries See Growth in Ebooks; After Years of Hype, Ebooks Are at Last Becoming a Popular Reading Format, Particularly for Commuters, Vacationers, and Business Travelers. Both Online Booksellers and Libraries Are Using Ebooks to Expand Their Reach." *InternetWeek,* 19 July 2004.

Brynko, Barbara. "Global Survey Offers Insight into Libraries' Use of eBooks." *Information Today,* July-August 2007.

Dilworth, Dianna. "$16.8b Spent on Net Advertising in '06: I.A.B." *DM News,* 19 March 2007.

Dorror, Jennifer. "Dotcom Bloom: The Web Seems Poised to Blossom with Stand-Alone News Sites." *American Journalism Review,* June/July 2005.

Green, Heather. "The Big Shots of Blogdom." *Business Week,* 7 May 2007.

Hawkins, Donald T. "Ebooks Make a Comeback." *Information Today,* January 2007.

Hendrickson, Mike. "State of the Computer Book Market 2008." February 2009. Available from http://radar.oreilly.com/2009/02/state-of-the-computer-book-mar-24.html.

Holahan, Catherine. "The Twitterization of Blogs; Most Bloggers Prefer Mundane Tidbits to Deep Thoughts, and Backed by Voice Transcription and Video Sharing, the Cell Phone May Soon Be the Tool of Choice." *Business Week Online,* 5 June 2007. Available from www.businessweek.com.

"iPublishCentral, AAUP Make E-Book Publishing Available to 130 University Presses." Press Release, 19 June 2009. Available from http://www.ipublishcentral.com/news_detail.php?id=42.

Interactive Advertising Bureau (IAB). "Internet Advertising Revenues Surpass $23 Billion in '08, Reaching Record High." Press Release, 30 March 2009. Available from http://www.iab. net/about_the_iab/recent_press_releases/press_release_ archive/press_release/pr-033009.

Israel, Shel. "Why Gartner's Blog Estimates Are Shortsighted." *Communication World,* May-June 2007.

King, Ivory. "E-Books Reach 10% of Total Books Sold in Q1 2009." 20 May 2009. Available from http://www.atelier-us.com/facts-and-figures/article/e-books-reach-10-of-total-books-sold-in-q1-2009.

Levith, Will. "Hearst, Blog to Host Journo Competition." *MEDIAWEEK,* 14 May 2007.

Lardinois, Frederic. "Holiday Outlook for eReaders and eBooks: Even Better Than Previously Thought." *EContent,* 7 October 2009. Available from http://www.readwriteweb.com/archives/ holiday_outlook_for_ereaders_and_ebooks_much_bette.php

"McClatchy Files Form 10-K and Reports Final Results for 2008: Reports Additional Loss from Discontinued Operations." 2 March 2009. Available from http://www.mcclatchy.com/ pressreleases/story/2228.ht.

"Over Three-Fourths of U.S. Active Internet Users Connect ViaBroadband at Home in November, According to Nielsen// Netratings." Nielsen//Netratings, 12 December 2006. Available from http://www.nielsen-netratings.com/pr/ pr_061212.pdf.

Palser, Barb. "Bridging the Gap: Newspapers Must Invest Much More Heavily in their Web Sites." *American Journalism Review,* June/July 2005.

Reid, Calvin. "E-books Go to School. Reality Sets In, but Survival Seems Assured." *Publishers Weekly,* 30 May 2005.

Salon Media Group financials taken from SEC filings, Aughst 2009. Available at http://www.faqs.org/sec-filings/091119/ SALON-MEDIA-GROUP-INC_10-Q.A/.

Schonfield, Erick. "The Wounded U.S. Newspaper Industry Lost $7.5 Billion in Advertising Revenues Last Year." 29 March 2009. Available at http://www.techcrunch.com/2009/03/29/ the-wounded-us-newspaper-industry-lost-75-billion-in-advertising-revenues-last-year/.

"State of the Blogsphere 2009." Technorati, 19 October 2009. Available from http://technorati.com/blogging/article/state-of-the-blogosphere-2009-introduction/.

Tedeschi, Bob. "Ad Costs on the Web Are Rising, but Perhaps a Bit Irrationally." *The New York Times,* 25 December 2006.

"Web Users Read More Content Online." United Press International, 14 August 2007. Available from http://www. imedinews.ge/en/news_read/57728.

Wischenbart, Rudiger. "The Global Ranking of the Publishing Industry 2008: An Overview and Analysis," *Livres Hebdo,* June 2008. Available from www.wischenbart.com/ publishing

Wood, Christina. "The Myth of E-books." *PC Magazine,* 1 July 2001.

ENCRYPTION SYSTEMS AND DIGITAL CERTIFICATES

SIC CODE(S)

7371

7372

INDUSTRY SNAPSHOT

Although for some it may bring to mind cereal box decoder rings and sundry childhood sleuthing paraphernalia, data encryption is increasingly pervasive in the digital economy. Whether protecting wireless data from interception or vouching for a Web site's authenticity, digital certificates and encryption technologies are fast becoming staples of the networked life.

As an example, in 2005, the certification authority service VeriSign Inc., a provider of digital certificates that vouch for a site's or a user's authenticity, had bestowed more than 400,000 of its certificates, and supporting security infrastructure, on Web sites around the world. These certificates are used to verify that a site is being operated by the company that registered the site and to provide a channel for secure communications. By mid-2007, that number had increased to 750,000 Web servers throughout the world, including 93 percent of those operated by Fortune 500 companies.

As an economic enterprise, however, digital security software and services have a lamentable reputation for over-promising and under-delivering. In particular, public key infrastructure (PKI) systems, a widely used model of data encryption and exchange, have been alternately championed and lampooned. For several years running, industry soothsayers proclaimed that PKI sales would skyrocket into the multibillion-dollar stratosphere. However, estimates in 2000 by the Gartner Group pegged global PKI sales at $300 million, a "paltry" sum to one observer. A dearth of widely accepted standards and the sheer cost and complexity of implementing PKI systems were to blame. Added to those troubles was a slowdown in corporate information technology (IT) spending during 2000 and 2001, seen as another impediment to PKI's takeoff. Since then, a number of encryption schemes have emerged that are simpler and more affordable alternatives to PKI.

Setbacks aside, there is still a strong market for PKI-based encryption. The technology has become a large part of daily life. Transactions on secure e-commerce Web sites, for example, routinely use basic PKI behind the scenes. The rising popularity of technologies like virtual private networks (VPNs), used to securely access corporate networks from remote locations, likewise spells more sales of certificate-based technologies. New laws and government regulations are also easing the move toward legally binding digital transactions. In addition, mergers and partnerships are giving certificate issuers access to new customers and new business models.

ORGANIZATION AND STRUCTURE

Broadly speaking, data encryption is a branch of computer security that deals with the secure transmission of documents, authorizations, and other electronic communications. Companies active in the encryption field provide software and services, sometimes hardware as well, mostly to other firms. In many cases, encryption products are components used in other applications. They appear, for instance, in e-mail applications, Internet browsers, networking applications, and on Web sites that require a secure exchange of information.

Of IDs, Signatures, and Algorithms There was a time when a unique user name and a hard-to-guess password were considered a good security system. Today, however, a great number of security systems, especially for the Internet, are based on digital certificates and public key infrastructure (PKI). These technologies tend to provide multiple layers of encryption and authentication compared with only one line of defense in simple password systems.

Although the implementation can be incredibly complex, at their core, PKI systems are, in the words of one industry veteran, a "glorified messaging system." Public key systems are security architectures that use two encryption keys (in technical parlance, asymmetric cryptography) in any exchange to protect electronic information and verify its authenticity.

One key is public, meaning that the encryption scheme is published in a central directory and accessible to all users of the system. More precisely, it is accessible for retrieval by all users' security software, as it isn't the kind of directory an individual would like to peruse. The public key is used by the sender's software to encrypt the outgoing information for a particular recipient. Then, for each user or site, a related private key is used by the recipient to decrypt the message—less fun, admittedly, than a decoder ring, but serving the same purpose. The private key normally isn't shared with anyone else and is based on a complex algorithm that links it to the public key.

Certificates are a central component in any PKI security system. Digital certificates, or digital IDs, are secure electronic documents that identify their owner as a valid user of the system. These credentials are used to provide access to a system, authenticate users, and disseminate encryption keys. In a typical configuration, the certificate is sent to the user as a digitally signed message. A digital signature adds another layer of encryption to ensure that the document—in this case, a certificate—wasn't altered between the sender and the recipient. If the document has changed, it's not valid. Once a certificate is issued successfully, it enables the user to send and receive communications—submitting online transactions, for example—within the secure system. Those of a technical persuasion call this process binding the certificate to the user.

PKI systems also involve certification authorities (CAs) and registration authorities (RAs), which are systems (often third party services like VeriSign) that assign, validate, track, and revoke certificates for both individuals and Web sites. Once a PKI system is launched, CAs and RAs, which can be one and the same, provide the service backbone to keep it all running. RAs perform the initial certification, determining who should be allowed on the system and assigning unique certificates to users. They also usually determine who should no longer be using the system by revoking certificates. Meanwhile, CAs perform validation and authentication services on every transaction, making sure (via encrypted exchanges) that each user is who he says he is and has permission to do what he's trying to do. CAs and RAs must be highly trusted sources because while they aren't giving away keys to the kingdom, they do give out security keys that could compromise a system's integrity if they fall into the wrong hands.

Equally important, the public key infrastructure contains policies for managing certificates. How long is a certificate good? When can a certificate be revoked? Do different uses of the system require different levels of security? These are all questions that must be answered when defining a public key system. The answers typically take the form of rules or procedures the system follows under certain conditions or under all conditions.

Ode to Standards and Regulations As with most new technologies, PKI and digital certificates suffer from a shortage of standards on how exactly the infrastructure should work, which elements of a system are essential and which are optional, and what protocols should be used for transmitting information. Some progress has been made toward better standardization and consistent regulation of the system, but experts believe more work will be necessary before PKI can reach its potential.

The most widely acknowledged standard to date has been proposed by the International Telecommunication Union (ITU), a United Nations-affiliated body concerned with telecommunications standards and practices. Known as X.509, in perhaps a small tribute to cryptography, it defines what information a digital certificate should contain and how the different components of a PKI system should work together. For example, X.509 requires certificates to encode, among other things, who the issuer is, what the start and expiration dates are, and what algorithm was used to create the certificate.

While this is all good on paper, in practice different companies have implemented the standard in different ways. Web browsers of recent vintage, for instance, are capable of accepting and transmitting certificates. However, a Microsoft browser may not work with X.509 certificates designed for Netscape and Netscape may choke on X.509 certificates created with Internet Explorer in mind.

Meanwhile, a pair of legal developments facilitated the use of highly secure encryption systems to conduct authoritative transactions electronically. First, in September 1999, the Clinton administration announced an easing of the long-standing ban on exporting powerful encryption software. The ban, often decried by the software industry, had prevented firms from shipping abroad any software with encryption beyond a certain level. That level, according to security experts, was unreasonably low and impeded sales of products with state-of-the-art encryption. The new policy, while still restricting some activities, placed a much higher ceiling on the allowable level of encryption and reduced other burdens for selling strong encryption products.

Then in June 2000, President Clinton signed into law, digitally, new legislation prescribing how electronic signatures may be used in legally binding transactions. The law, known as the E-Sign Act or the Electronic Signatures in Global and National Commerce Act, essentially gives electronic signatures the same legal standing as paper signatures for transactions and agreements in the private sector. This was seen as a major milestone toward treating important and complex electronic transactions on equal footing with traditional paper contracts. Within the federal government, a previous law allowed for a similar ability.

The problem is, some observers say, that the law barely defines what constitutes an electronic signature. Within some technical circles, there's an understanding that an electronic signature consists of a digital signature, a mark or symbol with encoding to ensure no tampering after it's issued, coupled with some form of authentication that the issuer is not an imposter. As it turns out, you can have a digital signature that's not authenticated or an authentication without sealing it with a digital signature. In theory, an imposter could use someone's digital signature to authorize a purchase, and the rightful owner of the signature could deny responsibility. The law is silent about these issues. The implications are that individual businesses will have to decide for themselves what an electronic signature consists of; and absent further legislation to clear the air, the exact boundaries may be tested in court.

BACKGROUND AND DEVELOPMENT

Within the financial and health care sectors, regulatory requirements resulting from the Graham-Leach-Bliley Act and the Health Insurance Portability and Accountability Act (HIPAA) called for organizations to ensure the security of sensitive data. While traditional PKI-based encryption schemes involving digital certificates were effective from a security standpoint, organizations in industries such as these were in need of a simpler approach that could work easily with e-mail communications.

One emerging alternative to PKI was Identity-Based Encryption (IBE), developed by Stanford University Cryptographer Dan Boneh and University of California Davis Professor Matt Franklin. As columnist Andrew Conry-Murray explained in the October 2004 issue of *Network Magazine*, "IBE essentially does away with the notion of

digital certificates. Using a master secret and a set of public parameters derived from an eliptical curve cryptography algorithm, IBE can use an arbitrary string, such as an e-mail address, to create a public key."

According to Conry-Murray, IBE is far easier for large organizations to use because it does not require the cumbersome process of managing digital certificates for an entire workforce. In addition, it enables secure communications with a company's vendors and customers without the need for them to possess digital certificates. Voltage Security was a leading provider of IBE-based encryption during the middle of the decade.

While some believed that IBE was a solid alternative to PKI, industry analysts voiced a need for caution. As one analyst explained, an entire system could be compromised if an authentication server, which contains the system's master key, is compromised. In addition, some felt the need for further testing and review because IBE is a relatively new encryption scheme. Beyond IBE, other PKI alternatives involved gateway servers that resided between an organization's e-mail server and the Internet, as well as other Web-based methods of secure communication.

Federated identity management was another alternative to PKI encryption developed by the Liberty Alliance, a consortium of 150 organizations including Wells Fargo, IBM, American Express, Fidelity, Citigroup, ABN Amro, and Swedbank. In the February 2004 issue of *ABA Banking Journal*, columnist Bill Orr explained: "In the Liberty worldview, each party to a transaction can be identified by a set of attributes, which, taken together, define that party's multifaceted business personality. Hence, there is no need for a single identity for all purposes, stored in a central place. Indeed, privacy and protection from identity theft are enhanced when attributes are scattered in autonomous circles of trust. When a member of a trust circle asks the identity provider (IdP) to authenticate another member, the IdP doesn't send back a full identity package; it generates a coded token or pseudonym that authorizes the transaction according to previously agreed terms. This protocol enables a user to transact business with any member of the trust circle by entering a single sign-on without having her PIN, password, or other sensitive data."

When the GAO issued its Federal Computer Security Scorecard in 2003, as required by the Federal Information Security Management Act, it gave the government an overall grade of D in the area of information security. Eight agencies received a failing mark. By mid-2004, a number of government agencies were testing PKI-based encryption systems to bolster security. For example, the Drug Enforcement Administration (DEA) was using PKI to communicate with pharmaceutical companies, and the FBI was piloting the technology to send documents securely. Finally, the U.S. Navy was implementing a system that involved the use of smart cards and PKI to authenticate users for network access. With spending on e-government initiatives expected to reach $575 million by 2008, according to market intelligence from INPUT, the government market for encryption technology appeared to be on solid footing.

Research firm Gartner expected the market for digital certificate and public key infrastructure to reach approximately $1 billion by 2010, according to the March 2007 issue of *SC Magazine*. Security breaches as well as regulatory requirements within the financial and health care sectors continued to bolster the need for more security. In addition, digital certificates were being employed in new niches. Examples included the Gem Certification & Assurance Lab's use of digital certificates for diamond grading certificates, as well as Equifax's use of the technology for the online lending industry.

While public key infrastructure (PKI) began to decline in popularity, the technology was still very much a key component of the industry during the latter part of the first decade of the 2000s. In fact, while PKI was not necessarily exploding in popularity, many analysts were optimistic about PKI, arguing that the technology had no inherent flaws and attributing some of the early resistance to unrealistic expectations. Factors supporting a renewed affection for PKI included a more transparent and less cumbersome employment of the technology and a simpler approach to certificate management. Importantly, more discretion was being used in PKI employment instead of using it in cases where encryption was not really required.

In its May 21, 2007, issue, *Computerworld* cited the results of a survey conducted by Ponemon Institute LLC, in which 768 business and IT professionals revealed why they did or did not employ encryption technology. The leading reason for encrypting data, at 66 percent, was to prevent data breaches. This was followed by regulatory compliance (51 percent), protecting a company's reputation or brand (40 percent), avoiding the need to notify others about a security breach (13 percent), and to honor privacy commitments (7 percent).

The same *Computerworld* article also cited the results of a similar survey that shed light on the flipside of the coin. Polling 227 IT security professionals in North America, research from Enterprise Strategy Group Inc. cited performance implications as the leading hindrance to encryption employment (64 percent). Cost was a close second at 60 percent, followed by management-related concerns (37 percent), disaster recovery implications (36 percent), and the effort involved in making needed changes to applications (32 percent).

CURRENT CONDITIONS

In September 2009 research firm Gartner forecast the global security software market to reach US$14.5 billion

for the year, up 8 percent from 2008 (at which time a 17 percent growth rate was recorded). Gartner expected the global security software market to reach $16.3 billion in 2010, representing a 13 percent market growth. In Europe, the security software market was expected to end 2009 at $3.2 billion, representing a 7 percent growth from 2008.

Notwithstanding the economic downturn, security remained a critical area not affected by cost-cutting measures for most companies. Ruggero Contu, principal Gartner research analyst, opined that software as a service (SaaS) would control the greatest growth opportunities, especially for small to medium businesses. According to Ellen Messmer for *Network World,* IT security budgets increased in 2009 to consume 12.6 percent of the entire IT operating budget (citing a survey by Forrester Research of 942 IT and security managers in North America and Europe).

Consumer security dominated the industry in 2009, representing about 25 percent of market share. Another large chunk of the market was dedicated to the enterprise security software market, formed by a number of segments such as endpoint protection platform, e-mail security boundary, and user provisioning.

Another recent market study released by Ovum (commissioned by Cisco) reported that the global market for four managed services (metro Ethernet, IP VPNs, IP voice, and security) was growing at a compound annual growth rate of 18 percent and would reach $66 billion by 2012.

The 2008 year was one of consolidation for several high-level entities, including McAfee's purchase of Secure Computing, Symantec acquiring MessageLabs, and Sophos acquiring Ultimaco. Gartner analyst Contu anticipated further consolidation into 2010, telling *Homeland Security Newswire*'s John Kennedy that "End-users are gradually moving to to better-integrated multi-products, particularly in areas such as endpoint security and identity and access management."

INDUSTRY LEADERS

Entrust Technologies Inc. of Addison, Texas, is one of the largest firms competing in the digital certificate and data security arena. Originally part of Nortel Networks Corp., Entrust gained its independence in 1997 just as Internet use was skyrocketing.

Another big player is VeriSign Inc. of Mountain View, California. The firm, founded in 1995, is a leading certification authority service, and also licenses its services through authorized resellers. By mid-2007, the company's digital certificates protected some 750,000 World Wide Web servers throughout the world, including 93 percent of those operated by Fortune 500 companies. Perhaps its boldest initiative was its purchase in 2000 of Network

Solutions Inc., then a near-monopoly in the Internet domain name registration business. The purchase was seen as a strategic move into providing a suite of Web site life cycle management services that extends from registering the domain name to certifying the site operator and managing certificates throughout the site's operation.

Based in Bedford, Massachusetts, RSA Security Inc. is a leading provider of the hardware and software organizations used to manage access to their networks and information assets. Functioning as a security provider for approximately 90 percent of Fortune 500 companies, RSA's products cover the areas of identity and access management, secure enterprise access, secure mobile and remote access, and secure transactions. In addition to digital certificates, the company offers development tools used to create encryption software components. In 2006, RSA was acquired by EMC Corp. Together with Network Intelligence, the company became part of EMC's Security Division.

Other notable leaders include PGP Corp., a global leader in enterprise data protection which launched a new managed service (MSP) network in late 2008; Mozilla (owner of the popular Firefox, which held a global market share, as of November 2009, of 25 per cent); and Safend, an end-point data protection global company that grew 50 percent in 2008. Zix Corporation was a top leader in 2009 for email encryption and payor sponsored e-prescribing services.

RESEARCH AND DEVELOPMENT

In 2009, Irish company Beyond Encryption Technologies announced its pending patents in the United States for technology that would change the access end of encryption functions. Many encryption products rely on users who must remember a password to unlock their data. The approach of Beyond Encryption is to have access controlled by an administrator, making the data centrally protected wherever it goes. The company's core product is available in three formats. The first is a hosted service for protecting up to 100 devices. The second is aimed at organizations with in-house IT staff who can install and manage the software, while the third is a customized service aimed at very large enterprises or industry sectors with specific data protection needs.

BIBLIOGRAPHY

"About Entrust." Entrust Inc., 4 September 2007. Available from http://www.entrust.com/corporate/factsheet.htm.

"About the Liberty Alliance." 10 February 2005. Available from http://www.projectliberty.org/about/index.php.

"About RSA." RSA Security Inc., 4 September 2007. Available from http://www.rsasecurity.com.

"About VeriSign." VeriSign Inc. 4 September 2007. Available from http://www.verisign.com.

Anthes, Gary. "Encryption: It's Time; The Need has Never Been Greater, and the Technology Is Ready." *Computerworld,* 21 May 2007.

Chabrow, Eric. "PKI Has Its Price, Feds Say." *InformationWeek,* 19 January 2004.

Chickowski, Ericka. "PKI Redux: After Losing Favor a Short While Ago, Digital Certificates and PKI have Made a Quiet Comeback, Reports Ericka Chickowski." *SC Magazine,* March 2007.

"Company." RSA Security Inc. 11 February 2005. Available from http://www.rsasecurity.com.

Conry-Murray, Andrew. "Secure E-mail and Public Key Cryptography: Together at Last?" *Network Magazine,* October 2004.

"Corporate Overview." VeriSign Inc. 10 February 2005. Available from http://www.verisign.com.

"Equifax Brings Digital Certificates to Online Lending Market." *M2 Presswire,* 4 July 2006.

"GCAL's Certificates Go Digital." *National Jeweler,* 1 September 2006.

Kennedy, John. "Global Security Software Market to Hit US $14.5 bn." *Homeland Security Newswire,* 3 November 2009. Available at http://homelandsecuritynewswire.com/growth-trends-software-security-favor-beyond-encryption

LaMonica, Martin. "IBM Has Joined the Internet Security Consortium Liberty Alliance at the Request of a Customer, European Mobile Telecommunications Provider Orange." CNET News, 21 October 2004. Available from http://news.zdnet.com/2100-9588_22-5420814.html.

Maselli, Jennifer. "Making the Security Grade: Agencies Shore Up Systems After Flunking GAO Assessments." *Government Enterprise,* June 2004.

Messmer, Ellen. "Encryption Top IT Security Initiative in 2009." *Network World,* 5 January 2009.

Orr, Bill. "Who Are You—Really?" *ABA Banking Journal,* February 2004.

Mehling, Herber. "PGP Recruits Channel to Take Encryption to Managed SaaS Model." 27 October 2008. Available from http://www.itchannelplanet.com

"VeriSign Presented the 2004 Frost & Sullivan Award for Market Leadership in the Certificate Market." *Business CustomWire.* 12 January 2005.

ENTREPRENEURIAL TRAINING AND ADVISORY SERVICES

SIC CODE(S)

8299

8742

INDUSTRY SNAPSHOT

Entrepreneurial training and advisory services focus on practical business skills and strategies, going beyond traditional theory-centered business classes. Entrepreneurial training courses are generally taught by instructors who have had substantial entrepreneurial success themselves—i.e., success starting and managing their own businesses—and therefore they are able to provide guidance and mentorship to people starting or wishing to expand their own businesses or seeking to apply entrepreneurial skills in a corporate environment.

While the number of U.S. college and university entrepreneurial training programs stood at only 16 in 1970, by 2009 there were more than 1,600 programs offering more than 2,200 entrepreneurship courses. The influx of entrepreneurial programs and the booming demand for them stemmed in part from the remarkable success of small businesses and computer-related start-ups. The strong interest in entrepreneurial training goaded colleges and universities throughout the country to revamp their business programs to instill and promote entrepreneurial skills more vigorously.

Furthermore, many consulting firms, including industry giants such as Andersen Consulting, which was later renamed Accenture, and PricewaterhouseCoopers, began offering entrepreneurial advisory services as the trend of entrepreneurship began to pick up speed. These services provide guidance to entrepreneurs through various stages of development, from planning to going public. Although entrepreneurs may receive general insights or confront specific business problems of other companies in entrepreneurial training programs, they receive help with specific problems they are facing with their businesses—such as widening the search for financial backing—from advisory services. Besides these primary forms of entrepreneurial training and advisory services, many government agencies and community organizations also offer an array of services designed to teach entrepreneurial skills and help people plan, launch, and maintain businesses.

By the start of the new century, many members of the younger generation looked to starting their own businesses instead of taking traditional jobs while large numbers of baby boomers were expected to launch their own businesses upon retirement. This interest in entrepreneurship created significant demand for entrepreneurial training and advising services. Even when the technology industry downturn of the early years of the first decade of the 2000s forced many of the dot-coms launched in the late 1990s into bankruptcy, interest in entrepreneurship remained high, due perhaps to rising unemployment levels, a phenomenon which traditionally increases demand for all types of training.

ORGANIZATION AND STRUCTURE

Generally speaking, entrepreneurial training concentrates on inculcating general real-world business skills and strategies, whereas entrepreneurial advising focuses on resolving specific entrepreneurial problems. Entrepreneurial education begins with the premise that entrepreneurship is a learnable skill, even though many renowned entrepreneurs had little formal training. Colleges and universities are the primary sources of entrepreneurial training. Nevertheless, some private training institutes and organizations offer entrepreneurial training, too.

Colleges and universities offer entrepreneurial training as part of undergraduate and graduate degree programs, as well as part of continuing education programs. Some universities report in fact that entrepreneurship has become one of the leading majors in Master of Business Administration (MBA) programs, surpassing longtime favorites such as marketing and finance. Some university entrepreneurial programs are even run as small businesses themselves.

Courses in an entrepreneurial degree program may include evaluating business and growth opportunities, developing a business plan, obtaining financing, and managing small businesses. Such courses frequently are supplemented by internships in startup businesses, offering students an opportunity to apply what they have learned and to learn new skills by solving actual problems that entrepreneurial ventures confront.

Entrepreneurial advising, on the other hand, is frequently provided by consulting firms. These firms may provide advice in areas of entrepreneurship such as business product, financial planning, market analysis, and management assistance. In addition, such service providers also may offer transitional support to expanding startups, furnishing chief financial and technology officers to ensure that financial strategies and development plans are executed properly. In addition, since entrepreneurial advisory services tend to focus on the various business situations entrepreneurs face when starting a new business, they may render guidance during initial public offerings, mergers and acquisitions, business negotiations, and selecting investment banks.

Alternatively, organizations such as The Entrepreneurial Development Institute provide entrepreneurial training to low income and otherwise disadvantaged high school students. The goal of such programs is to offer students an opportunity to transcend any setbacks they may have had by launching their own businesses. The Entrepreneurial Development Institute alone has had over 25,000 participants in its program, and 80 percent of these students went on to found their own businesses.

In addition, other entrepreneurial organizations promote the training of under-represented groups. For example, the Women's Network for Entrepreneurial Training strives to teach women entrepreneurial skills beginning in high school, and the National Minority Supplier Development Council as well as the U.S. Hispanic Chamber of Commerce offer various forms of entrepreneurial training and advice. Moreover, local community organizations, departments of commerce, and employment commissions also often offer entrepreneurial training. In particular, the U.S. Department of Commerce, the U.S. Chamber of Commerce, and the U.S. Small Business Administration all provide and promote entrepreneurial training, advice, and assistance.

Another form of this kind of entrepreneurial service is the business incubator. Business incubators offer entrepreneurs low rent facilities to help them develop their products and services and offer them shared business services and equipment and management help. As a result, entrepreneurs have the accounting, computer programming, and other business services they need, as well as the equipment necessary to develop their business ideas. The concept involves an entrepreneur moving into the incubator facility and working with the assistance of the incubator staff and co-tenants for a year or two before moving on and launching the business. Public, private, and public/private partnerships have established business incubators throughout the nation.

Business incubators are served by the National Business Incubation Association (NBIA), which had approximately 800 members by 2007. At that time, the NBIA reported that 47 percent of incubation programs were for mixed uses, while 37 percent were aimed specifically at technology, 7 percent at manufacturing, 6 percent at the service sector, and 4 percent at other uses. Finally, online communities such as JumpUp.com allowed entrepreneurs to engage in social networking and locate those in similar industries or geographic areas.

BACKGROUND AND DEVELOPMENT

The success of startup companies in the late 1990s as well as unprecedented levels of corporate downsizing in the first decade of the 2000s worked to boost the popularity of entrepreneurship as a career pursuit for people of all ages. College students and business veterans alike showed greater interest in entrepreneurship beginning in the early 1990s and extending through the early years of the decade. As a result, more schools, organizations, and training institutes started to offer entrepreneur training and advisory courses and services. Indeed, the period of the late 1990s and the early years of the first decade of the 2000s has been called the Entrepreneurial Age by some, and a survey by Ernst & Young LLP indicated that entrepreneurship would be a key trend in the twenty-first century. Moreover, the National Foundation for Teaching Entrepreneurship found that entrepreneurial training has been one of the fastest growing areas of education ever.

Federal and state governments have also sponsored entrepreneurial training because entrepreneurship is an important source of job creation. For example, small businesses accounted for about 75 percent of all new

U.S. jobs, according to the U.S. Small Business Administration. The roughly 26 million small businesses operating in the United States in 2009 (according to the American Small Business League) employed more than 50 percent of the private work force.

About 33 percent of all U.S. business schools offered concentrations in entrepreneurship and U.S. colleges and universities had established some 100 entrepreneurship centers to promote entrepreneurial training. Some MBA programs, including one offered at the Cox School of Business at Southern Methodist University, actually required students to successfully complete an entrepreneurship course. In addition, numerous entrepreneurial courses were offered as continuing education classes, enabling students to enhance existing skills or pick up some new skills quickly without devoting a substantial amount of time to obtaining a degree, a convenient option for people already running businesses.

According to a 2009 *Entrepreneur* article listing the top 25 undergraduate colleges for entrepreneurial training (using information provided by *The Princeton Review,* Babson College's Arthur M. Blank Center for Entrepreneurship again ranked first, followed by the University of Houston's Wolff Center for Entrepreneurship, the University of Arizona's McGuire Entrepreneurship Program, and Baylor University's Baylor Entrepreneurship Program. Temple University's Innovation & Entrepreneurship Institute completed the top five in this ranking. The essential ingredients of a quality entrepreneurship program are mentoring, access to capital, and the ability to provide training that is easily applied to real world business situations, according to Robert H. Smith, director of the University of Maryland's Dingman Center for Entrepreneurship. To be sure, obtaining an MBA is the first step to starting a new business, as evidenced by the fact that 99 percent of the MBA applicants to Stanford indicated in their admissions essays that they planned to pursue entrepreneurial ventures after graduation. Obtaining entrepreneurial training prior to starting a business helps new business owners avoid common mistakes made while running a new business or running a business for the first time.

The demand for entrepreneurial training and the need for it in the marketplace is also evident from the number of corporate donations business schools receive to start entrepreneurial centers. Furthermore, university professors play an active role in helping entrepreneurial students obtain funding and manage their companies. Sometimes professors even invest their own money in their students' ventures and sit on their companies' boards of directors. According to *Inc.,* business professors at schools such as Harvard, Stanford, the University of California at Los Angeles, and Cornell frequently invest in their students' entrepreneurial ventures. Although some schools prohibit professors from directly investing in their students'

businesses while they are in the professors' classes, they do not extend the prohibition to investments made after students have left professors' classes. As of the early years of the first decade of the 2000s, the London Business School was maintaining its own venture capital fund to finance student start-ups.

In addition, budding entrepreneurs in entrepreneurial training courses can obtain funding through search funds. With this funding mechanism, entrepreneurs receive funding from investors, who might include university professors, for a few years while the entrepreneur looks for a business to purchase or start. After the new business is bought, the entrepreneur repays the search fund investors by selling shares of the new company to them at an advantageous rate.

The Premier FastTrac training program, created by the Entrepreneurial Education Foundation of Denver and adopted by entrepreneurial foundations and organizations around the country, also played an important role in the education of entrepreneurs. These training programs provide business neophytes with crash courses in business, allowing entrepreneurs to take courses at night while running their businesses by day. The program, however, encourages business planning in its first phase and then focuses on business expansion in its second phase. Moreover, numerous private, for-profit schools specializing in business and entrepreneurial education have continued to grow in number, according to Eduventures.com, a research firm that monitors the education industry.

State governments also promoted entrepreneurship. At least eight states—California, Delaware, Maine, Maryland, Oregon, New Jersey, New York, and Pennsylvania—offered programs where the unemployed could use their unemployment benefits to launch their own businesses. However, selection for these self-employment assistance programs is extremely competitive and those who qualify are required to attend entrepreneurial education classes as well as entrepreneurial counseling sessions. In addition to these basic requirements, individual states may impose other requirements.

In order to stimulate their economies, states also continued to offer a number of resources to encourage entrepreneurial development and connect new entrepreneurs with service providers and capital sources. For example, in mid-2005, Arkansas was home to organizations like the Fund for Arkansas' Future, Accelerate Arkansas, the Arkansas Institutional Fund, the Arkansas Venture Forum, and Techpreneur.

With the Internet and advanced information services, entrepreneurs can obtain some training, advice, and information for free. Entrepreneurs can access this information at home or at a local library via a computer and a modem. In addition, library reference staff usually can help entrepreneurs explore various sources of financing and research specific markets.

Besides appealing to people who want to start their own businesses, entrepreneurial education may also be sought by people wish to apply these skills and strategies to a corporate environment. Such people have been called "intrapreneurs." Intrapreneurs do not face some of the challenges entrepreneurs confront, such as obtaining funding. Instead, they may lead a team of a corporation's workers in a quasi-independent project funded by the corporation to launch a new product or service.

The strength of entrepreneurship was evident by the growth and success of related resources. For example, *Entrepreneur* magazine had a readership of 2.1 million in 2005. The publication was produced by Entrepreneur Media Inc., which also operated a book publishing enterprise called Entrepreneur Press, with some 50 new titles released each year; the Entrepreneur.com Web site, which received approximately 30 million monthly page views; and other information resources such as *Be Your Own Boss* magazine.

As offshoring and outsourcing saw many U.S. jobs move overseas, especially within the manufacturing sector, the economy was counting on a new generation of entrepreneurs to create new markets and spark employment growth. New resources were being developed to target this demographic group. One such resource was *The Young Entrepreneur's Guide to Business Terms,* a 128-page book with alphabetically ordered technical definitions and terms that targeted teenaged entrepreneurs.

America's interest in and passion for entrepreneurship continued to grow at a strong clip. In the February 2007 issue of *FSB: Fortune Small Business,* Phaedra Hise indicated that according to data from the Small Business Administration, an unprecedented 672,000 new companies with employees were formed in the United States in 2005—a 30,000-count jump from the previous year and 12 percent higher than the dot-com boom of 1996. In addition, many more Americans were planning to start a new enterprise. As Hise wrote in the article, "Everybody Wants In.... We are in the midst of the largest entrepreneurial surge this country has ever seen."

Even though entrepreneurship came with an element of risk, factors such as lower interest rates and falling computer prices, as well as declining job security and cutbacks in the corporate world, all helped to fuel America's interest in business ownership. The appeal of being an entrepreneur was not limited to the working ranks, but extended all the way down to middle and high school students. According to *FSB: Fortune Small Business,* in 2006 nearly 71 percent of students between the ages of 13 and 18 indicated a desire to become an entrepreneur.

That year, some 15,970 students within this same age bracket took part in entrepreneurship programs offered by the National Foundation for Teaching Entrepreneurship in 2006—up from 2,600 students in 1995. Interest in entrepreneurship also remained strong at the college level. Data from the Kauffman Foundation found that 19 American colleges and universities had actual departments devoted to entrepreneurship, up from 7 such departments five years before. Educational incentives abounded, including the $100K Business Plan Competition at the Massachusetts Institute of Technology (MIT).

In addition to familiar publications like *Entrepreneur* magazine, which saw its circulation jump 450 percent since 1986 and enjoyed a base of 2.4 million readers each month, the Internet continued to grow in importance. The Web site Entrepreneur.com was used by some 6 million unique visitors daily, offering news, information, and expert how-to video content on a variety of topics. Finally, online communities such as JumpUp.com allowed entrepreneurs to engage in social networking and locate those in similar industries or geographic areas.

In its November 2009 issue, *Entrepreneur* magazine published its 2010 Top Trends list, detailing the leading trends and markets where entrepreneurs were finding great success. Leading the publication's list were so-called "clean energy" or environmentally friendly products, chocolate, and education/tutoring services for children. Other popular business/market areas included healthy food, nanotechnology, wine, and virtual economies.

CURRENT CONDITIONS

The serious rise in national unemployment following the 2008–2009 economic downturn had an upside: a wealth of opportunity for small businesses and entrepreneurial ventures. One of the worst-hit was the automotive industry, leaving thousands of former auto workers in need of job retraining. In June 2009, the Obama administration appointed Dr. Ed Montgomery as executive director of the White House Council on Automotive Communities and Workers. To that end, Montgomery endorsed the work of the Kauffman Foundation in sponsoring entrepreneurial training programs in Detroit, funded by the New Economy Initiative, which consists of a consortium of ten foundations in southeast Michigan. In conjunction with this initiative, the June 24, 2009, "FastTrac to the Future" event in Detroit announced that more than 500 aspiring entrepreneurs had been selected to receive entrepreneurial and leadership training in preparation for new careers.

Indeed, reported *Entrepreneur* magazine in November 2009, the bad economy was truly inspiring entrepreneurs. "Results from Challenger, Gray & Christmas's job market index revealed that 8.7 percent of job seekers gained employment by starting their own businesses in second quarter 2009—way, way up from the record low of 2.7 percent during the last quarter of 2008," said the magazine.

The Obama administration's American Recovery and Reinvestment Act (the economic stimulus) included some $730 million allocated for small-business loans and other assistance, all good news for budding entrepreneurs. The benefits for small-business borrowers were a reduction in loan fees, higher guarantees in some cases, and incentives to encourage the secondary market.

Moreover, the mood in Washington, D.C., seemed to encourage entrepreneurial self-interest. A plethora of political initiatives were proposed in Congress, including the Job Creation Through Entrepreneurship Act of 2009 (H.R. 2352); the Small Business Development Centers Modernization Act of 2009 (H.R. 1845); the Expanding Entrepreneurship Act of 2009 (H.R. 1842); a proposal to amend the Small Business Act to modify certain provisions relating to women's business centers, and for other purposes (H.R. 1838); the Native American Business Development Enhancement Act of 2009 (H.R. 1834); the Educating Entrepreneurs through Today's Technology Act (H.R. 1807); and the Veterans Business Center Act of 2009 (H.R. 1803). As of late 2009, none of these had yet been signed into law.

INDUSTRY LEADERS

While colleges and universities are the leading providers of entrepreneurial training and education, large financial consulting and accounting firms such as Accenture and PricewaterhouseCoopers as well as specialty firms such as Euro Worldwide Investments Inc. offer entrepreneurial advisory services.

Accenture Ltd., formerly Andersen Consulting, is the largest consulting firm in the world. In addition to many other services, Accenture provides diverse advisory services of use to entrepreneurs and entrepreneurial companies, helping them secure financing, go public, outsource various functions, and develop and execute plans.

PricewaterhouseCoopers International Ltd. was formed after the 1998 merger of Price Waterhouse and Coopers & Lybrand, creating the second largest accounting and consulting firm in the country. Both Price Waterhouse and Coopers & Lybrand offered entrepreneurial advisory services. Through its nearly 770 offices worldwide, PricewaterhouseCoopers has a strong presence in the industry.

Based in San Francisco, Euro Worldwide Investments Inc. (EWI) counsels entrepreneurs and small businesses at each step of the business development process. EWI's advisors can help take entrepreneurs from the planning of a product and a market to target to executing those plans. EWI offered planning services in four categories: business, financial, product, and liquidity.

Through its franchised network of Sandler Sales Institutes, Sandler Systems Inc. is one of the major non-college or university players in the entrepreneurial training industry with over 160 affiliates throughout the country. Founded by David Sandler in the 1960s, the company began franchising in 1983. Although the company's founder died in 1995, the Sandler Sales Institute continues to provide entrepreneurial and sales training via its network of trainers and consultants.

idealab! ranked among the leading business incubators in the middle of the first decade of the 2000s. The Pasadena, California-based company boasts of successful alumni such as eToys Inc., GoTo.com, CitySearch, NetZero, and Tickets.com. Bill Gross founded the company in an effort to launch his online business, eToys. The company provides funding, materials, working space, and other amenities in addition to its entrepreneurial advisory services. In 2000, the company announced its plan to go public, although it remained private as of 2007, at which time it was focused on renewable energy, Internet businesses, robotics, and wireless communications.

AMERICA AND THE WORLD

The United States is the leading provider of entrepreneurial training and education with an abundance of public and private colleges, universities, schools, organizations, institutes, and consulting firms offering such services. Nevertheless, other countries, particularly those in Europe and Asia, have adopted entrepreneurial training programs. For example, German business schools began offering classes on entrepreneurship in the late 1990s and established entrepreneurial departments. Despite efforts to teach entrepreneurship in Europe, critics contend that obstacles to entrepreneurship such as business restrictions on where companies can operate and the timidity of European venture capitalists must be removed first. Nevertheless, many Europeans began following the U.S. trend of quitting secure jobs and pursuing entrepreneurial ventures, especially in the technology industries.

In Asia, the financial crisis of the mid to late 1990s brought increased interest in entrepreneurship. Entrepreneurs who could deliver products or services that helped cash-strapped consumers and companies fared well during this period. In 2003, Japan's Ministry of Economy, Trade and Industry (METI) passed a law that reduced requirements for startup capital from 10 million yen to just 1 yen. The exemption will last until 2008 and is designed to foster the creation of 360,000 new companies per year.

Globalization had become a key consideration for American entrepreneurs, according to the January 9, 2007 issue of *Business Week Online*. Some industry observers noted that waiting too long to address the international aspect of a start-up business could cause delays and problems later, when quick expansion and rapid sales cycles call for quick action. Therefore, learning how to work with foreign engineers and manufacturing partners was something that experts recommended doing sooner rather than later.

RESEARCH AND TECHNOLOGY

Computer and information service technology holds the potential for facilitating the delivery of entrepreneurial training and advisory services. Students could take a wide range of classes over the Internet and Internet universities began to crop up. Online entrepreneurial courses included degree program courses for undergraduate and graduate degrees as well as individual classes to acquire specific skills related to entrepreneurial ventures. In addition, with the high penetration of Internet access, the Internet proved to be a convenient tool for networking, sharing advice, querying other entrepreneurs, and communicating with advisory services.

BIBLIOGRAPHY

"2010 Trends: 10 (and 1/2) Trends to Watch." *Entrepreneur,* Fall 2009. Available from http://www.entrepreneur.com/trends/index.html.

"America's Best Graduate Schools." *U.S. News & World Report,* January 2003. Available from http://www.usnews.com/usnews/edu/grad/rankings/mba/brief/mbasp06_brief.php.

Beck, Susan. "Professors Get Their Shares." *Inc.,* March 1998.

Betz-Zall, Jonathan, and Stephan Schiffman. "The Young Entrepreneur's Guide to Business Terms." *School Library Journal,* July 2004.

"*Entrepreneur's* 2007 Hot List of Business Trends: What to Get In On Now." *PR Newswire,* 13 December 2006.

Gumpert, David E. "What Entrepreneurs Need to Know." *Business Week Online,* 9 January 2007. Available from www.businessweek.com.

Hise, Phaedra. "College Can Wait." *FSB: Fortune Small Business,* February 2007.

"H.R. 2352, The Job Creation Through Entrepreneurship Act of 2009." *Washington Watch.* Available from http://www.washingtonwatch.com/bills/show/111_HR_2352.html.

———. "Everybody Wants In." *FSB: Fortune Small Business,* February 2007.

"Leading Business Experts Help Entrepreneurs Face to Face on Entrepreneur.com." *PR Newswire,* 26 February 2007.

Lesonsky, Rieva. "Entrepreneur Evolution." *Entrepreneur,* February 2007.

"Making Millions Before Making It to 40." *PR Newswire,* 26 September 2006.

Minniti, Maria, William D. Bygrave, Andrew L. Zacharakis, and Marcia Cole. "National Entrepreneurship Assessment, United States of America." *Global Entrepreneurship Monitor.* Arthur M. Blank Center for Entrepreneurship, Babson College, 2004. Available from http://www.gemconsortium.org/download/1117999034734/GEMUSReport 8.5x11.pdf.

Newton, David. "Can Entrepreneurship Be Taught?" *Entrepreneur,* 01 April 2003.

Norman, Jan. "Stimulus Act Gives Modest Help to Small-Business." *Orange County Register,* 18 February 2009.

Rosenberg, Yuval. "Building a New Nest." *Fast Company,* April 2007.

Shea, Peter. "Sunny Franchise Days Ahead." *Franchising World,* January 2005.

Smith, Mike Jr. "Next-Generation Entrepreneur." *Arkansas Business,* 16 May 2005.

"Top 25 Undergraduate Colleges for Entrepreneurial Programs." *Entrepreneur.* Available from http://www.entrepreneur.com/topcolleges/undergrad/0.html.

"What Is Business Incubation?" National Business Incubation Association, 5 June 2005. Available from http://www.nbia.org/resource_center/what_is/index.php.

"White House Expresses Support for Kauffman-New Economy Initiative to Revitalize Detroit." Kauffman Foundation Press Release, 24 June 2009. Available from http://www.kauffman.org/newsroom/white-house-expresses-support-for-kauffman-new-economy-initiative-to-revitalize-detroit.aspx.

Zwaniecki, Andrzej. "Entrepreneurship Spreads Across U.S. University Campuses." 25 March 2008. Available from http://www.america.gov/st/econ-english/2008/March/20080320172 503saikceinawz0.2316095.html.

ENVIRONMENTAL REMEDIATION

————■————

SIC CODE(S)

9511

9512

INDUSTRY SNAPSHOT

Much of the U.S. population lives within close range of sites that have been contaminated with hazardous materials. The U.S. government estimates that about one-third of all Americans live within four miles of a location federally designated as in need of environmental cleanup. In fact, 80 percent of all sites marked for cleanup under the Superfund, or Comprehensive Environmental Response, Compensation, and Liability Act (CERCLA), are located in residential areas. The process of removing harmful substances from the soil and water in such areas is known as environmental remediation. In addition, remediation efforts can also remove harmful substances such as asbestos from buildings.

For decades, U.S. industries released a wide array of harmful or potentially harmful chemicals into the atmosphere with little or no monitoring. Among those substances are trichloroethylene (from dry cleaning and metal degreasing), lead (from gasoline), arsenic (from mining and manufacturing), tetrachloroethylene (from dry cleaning and metal degreasing), benzene (from gasoline and manufacturing), and toluene (from gasoline and manufacturing). Remediation efforts can require ten years or more and millions of dollars to complete.

Environmental remediation has constituted a volatile political topic since the introduction of CERCLA in 1980 by the Carter administration. The Superfund toxic waste cleanup program, once funded by taxes paid by chemical and petroleum companies, relied on a relatively flat level of federal funding in the wake of inflation and increasingly complex remediation projects. In fact, federal, state, and local governments account for roughly half of the industry's revenues, while the private sector accounts for the remaining half.

According to *The Global Market for Hazardous Waste Remediation,* a market research report issued by BCC Research, the hazardous waste remediation technology market was expected to reach $16.6 billion worldwide by 2011. In a news release summarizing its research, BCC wrote, "Hazardous waste remediation is not only an ecological issue but an economic one as well. The design of equipment as well as the distribution of goods and services represent a multi-billion dollar industry, generating profit for investors, shareholders, and employees with personal interest." Hazardous waste containment technologies remained the largest segment in 2009, and was expected to total nearly $3.8 billion by 2011. Next was the separation segment ($2.65 billion by 2011), followed by chemical treatment ($2.34 billion in 2011). It should be noted that containment was projected to drop in the future, and recycling/re-use was the fastest-growing segment, projected to grow at nearly a 19 percent rate heading toward 2011.

ORGANIZATION AND STRUCTURE

Environmental remediation services seek to remove hazardous substances that are toxic, corrosive, ignitable, explosive, infectious, or reactive, thereby making contaminated sites comply with state and EPA standards. Lead, arsenic, and metallic mercury rank among the leading hazardous substances found in the ground and in water, and all pose serious health risks. In addition, scientific literature is rife with examples of afflictions such as lung disorders and cancer that humans suffer as a result of exposure to noxious substances in the environment.

Types of Remediation Environmental remediation operations rely on four general methods: thermal, chemical, biological, and physical remediation. Thermal remediation, which includes a variety of incineration techniques, subjects hazardous materials to high temperatures to decompose them. Traditional chemical remediation relies on the "pump and treat" technique for cleaning contaminated water: a remediation company pumps the water into a treatment tank where contaminants are removed or neutralized and then the water is pumped back into its natural basin. Newer techniques allow remediation services to treat the water chemically on site, thereby obviating transportation and storage and alleviating some of the costs. Biological remediation covers techniques such as using indigenous or genetically-engineered insects or micro-organisms to decompose hazardous materials. Physical remediation entails collecting and containing the contaminated or toxic substances and burying them in containers. This method, however, draws criticism from environmentalists who fear the containers could break, releasing dangerous substances into the ground and water.

EPA and state-sanctioned remediation processes usually include three steps. First, the remediation contractor assesses the risks of the site and studies the soil and water contaminants. During this step, the investigator determines the site's possible hazards to the environment and to the public. Secondly, the remediation contractor decides which remedial method will adequately and efficiently purge the site and considers which of the four general approaches to remediation will successfully accomplish the goal. In the third step, the contractor undertakes the cleanup of the site.

The EPA, along with state governments, sets contamination and pollution standards as well as criteria for establishing the risk posed by contaminated sites. Ranges in the criteria reflect the different uses or locations of the contaminated areas. For residential areas, many states require that the probability of infection be one out of one million, whereas for an industrial site, states may require only one out of 10,000.

Key Legislation The primary legislation governing and motivating environmental remediation includes the Comprehensive Environmental Response, Compensation, and Liability Act of 1980 (CERCLA) and the Resource Conservation and Recovery Act of 1976 (RCRA). CERCLA, also known as Superfund, established a list of high-priority industrial sites needing remediation. Environmental agencies and remediation firms refer to such locations as "brownfields" or contaminated sites no longer usable for industrial purposes that pose a risk to neighboring communities. CERCLA concentrates on the cleanup and redevelopment of already contaminated sites, not on creating contemporary environmental standards. Superfund constitutes the driving force behind environmental remediation. CERCLA entitles government agencies to several key enforcement prerogatives. They can use money from the Superfund Trust Fund to clean sites on Superfund's National Priorities List (NPL), require responsible parties to finance the necessary remediation, and pursue reimbursement for Superfunded cleanups from responsible parties.

Under Superfund, sites that are identified for possible hazardous substance releases are entered into a Comprehensive Environmental Response, Compensation, and Liability Information System (CERCLIS) database, a computerized log of all potentially hazardous sites. The cleanup process itself involves nine separate steps, from preliminary site inspections and assessments through remedial investigation and feasibility study, implementation of cleanup plans, and post-operation evaluation. As of 2007, a total of 1,245 uncontrolled hazardous waste sites were included on Superfund's National Priorities List (NPL) of sites, down from 1,604 in 2005.

CERCLA relies heavily on liability and the so-called Polluter Pays principle. Pollution-contributing past and present owners of a contaminated site bear the responsibility for cleaning the brownfield and government agencies can pursue any or all of them for reimbursement of cleanup costs. With Superfund's structure of strict liability, governments do not need to demonstrate negligence on the part of site operators. Furthermore, the government is not required to identify the exact source of the wastes located at a contaminated site. This joint and several liability forces companies to implement waste and pollution reducing technologies and to clean up any hazardous materials as soon as possible to avoid the escalating remediation costs. In 1986 the Superfund Amendments and Reauthorization Act was passed, which granted any potentially responsible party who settled with the U.S. government the right to seek contributions from other liable parties while obtaining contribution protection for itself.

The Resource Conservation and Recovery Act (RCRA) of 1976 amended the Solid Waste Disposal Act of 1970 that contains four key focal points: solid waste, hazardous waste, underground storage, and medical waste. This act regulates the usage, storage, and disposal of over 200 toxic substances such as heavy metals, insecticides, and herbicides. With amendments in 1984, RCRA works in conjunction with CERCLA by imposing deadlines on brownfield remediation. In contrast to CERCLA, RCRA largely governs the management of waste substances so that no further brownfields and Superfund priority sites are created. The act concentrates on companies that transport, treat, dispose of, and store potentially harmful forms of waste. Under the land disposal restrictions of RCRA, the EPA establishes standards for wastes found in landfills. CERCLA and RCRA, however, overlap in some ways, which promotes confusion in enforcement of and compliance with these acts. In addition to these federal laws, each state develops legislation regarding environmental remediation and air, water, and soil cleanliness standards that work with the federal statutes.

The EPA also promotes remediation through initiatives such as the Brownfields Economic Redevelopment Initiative (BERI), which promotes the sustainable re-use of brownfields. Faced with a dwindling budget and congressional pressure to impose policies that do not inhibit economic growth, the EPA started a campaign to marry economic development to environmental remediation in the mid-1990s. By the early years of the first decade of the 2000s, BERI had funded 3,600 Brownfields Assessment Pilots. Government support in this area continued into the late years of the decade. In 2006, the EPA announced that communities in 44 states, 2 territories, and 3 tribal nations would share in Brownfields grants totaling $69.9 million. By that time, the EPA had awarded 883 assessment grants totaling $225.4 million, another 202 revolving loan fund grants ($186.7 million), and 238 cleanup grants ($42.7 million).

Environmental Remediation and the Economy As part of the growing link between the environment and economics, companies' environmental records play a role in their ability to borrow money. When environmental laws became tougher with the enactment of bills such as CERCLA, lenders began to avoid doing business with companies that frequently handle toxic substances or began to require thorough assessment of environmental liability prior to approving loans, thereby circumscribing their involvement in projects of companies dealing with toxic substances. While bankers' policies curb the environmental degradation by companies prone to release hazardous substances, they also impede remediation since they approach such projects with caution or even refuse to finance them.

Other incentive packages designed to encourage environmental remediation and urban redevelopment include Community Development Block Grants (CDBG) offered by the U.S. Department of Housing and Urban Development. Cities eligible for CDBG can use the funds for hazard assessment and cleanup if the result of the remedial efforts promotes significant housing-related needs such as those benefiting lower income households or eradicating slums and urban blight. The Economic Development Administration (EDA) also provides grants that can help stimulate environmental remediation. The EDA's public

works grants, for example, allow cities to clean up and renovate contaminated or otherwise unusable industrial sites. Finally, tax incentives such as industrial development bonds stimulate environmental remediation by offering private companies tax-exempt bonds to launch redevelopment and cleanup projects.

BACKGROUND AND DEVELOPMENT

Events such as the establishment of Earth Day on 20 April 1970 and the environmental disaster at Love Canal in New York galvanized public awareness of the dangers of uncontrolled hazardous waste disposal. Over 40 pieces of environmental legislation, including laws governing air and water quality, hazardous wastes, chemicals, and pesticides were subsequently introduced. In December 1970, the Environmental Protection Agency (EPA) also was established to research environmental destruction, recommend policies to combat the contamination of natural resources, and prevent environmental degradation. The EPA estimated that by 1979, the United States contained between 30,000 and 50,000 abandoned hazardous waste sites.

Legislation enacted in the 1980s requiring hazardous site cleanups and limiting the release and disposal of harmful substances spawned a burgeoning industry, with companies vying to cash in on federally mandated and subsidized environmental remediation projects. Moreover, companies' environmental records slowly became associated with their financial capabilities. In 1989 the Securities and Exchange Commission (SEC) began requesting disclosure of environmental liabilities from companies, which forced businesses to exercise more caution and discretion when disposing of hazardous substances. As the industry's success continued in the 1980s, numerous companies offered remediation and consulting services, creating a glutted market by the 1990s.

The competitive industry climate forced companies to reduce fees, and therefore environmental remediation companies began operating with very slim profit margins. Smaller companies also started specializing in one area or another of remediation in an attempt to stand out. In addition, numerous mergers and acquisitions took place as companies attempted to achieve economies of scale necessary to win contracts from major clients such as chemical manufacturers and governments.

Because environmental remediation has grown less risky with the development of advanced technology, clients have sought fixed-sum contracts instead of flexible-sum contracts. Furthermore, private sector companies realized that their cleanup expenditures were greater than they anticipated, which made them more frugal, demanding lump-sum prices with no surprises.

To cope with the flooded market, many companies developed innovative practices, such as outsourcing, to stay ahead in the environmental cleanup business. Environmental operations started offering released waste testing and monitoring of corporate compliance with environmental policies. In addition, they purchased sites requiring remediation, such as wastewater plants and oil wells, remediated and renovated them, then leased them back to operators. Environmental remediation companies also shifted their focus from the development of remediation plans—the sector of the industry that thrived in the 1980s—to the execution of remediation. They have also turned their attention increasingly to foreign markets, particularly Mexico, Eastern European countries, and the former East Germany.

Several factors hindered the industry's progress. For example, lawyers advised some companies to postpone environmental remediation projects until Congress finished haggling over the Superfund re-authorization, a process that had been ongoing for several years. Financing Superfund was a particular point of contention between the parties. Until 1995, an excise tax on the oil and chemical industries funded the project, but Congress subsequently refused to renew the tax. Superfund was up for revision in 2000, but analysts were confident reforms would fizzle prior to that year's elections before picking up again in the following legislative session, when House appropriators awarded only $1.27 billion. The political tone of the debates was typified by the two wildly differing reports of Superfund's performance in 2000, one of which was flaunted by Republicans in the U.S. Congress as a sign of the program's failure while the EPA pointed to the other as proof of the program's success.

By the early years of the first decade of the 2000s, Superfund had assessed 44,418 sites and spent over $14 billion for site cleanups. Of all designated sites, cleanup was completed on 56 percent and underway on 43 percent. A total of 11,312 sites remained active with the site assessment program or were on the Superfund National Priority List (NPL). The number of Superfund National Priority List sites requiring remediation totaled 1,560. As of December 31, 2002, a total of 61 sites were proposed to the NPL. Despite the legislative hurdles, Superfund demonstrated progress in identifying and remediating contaminated sites in the 1990s and the first decade of the 2000s. The Government Accounting Office estimated that cleanups at 85 percent of all identified Superfund sites would be completed by 2008 and that total operations would cost from $8.2 billion to $11.7 billion more than has already been spent on the work. The EPA's estimate for time required to complete remediation of an average site was eight years. However, to pump and treat groundwater may require 30 years or more.

The U.S. Commerce Department's Office of Technology Policy, in an industry overview entitled *Meeting the Challenge of the 21st Century,* characterized the industry as being in a state of transition from one focused on pollution control and waste remediation to one that should stress resource productivity and preventive measures. Average annual returns since 1991 of the 240 leading environmental companies listed by the *Environmental Business Journal* hovered at about 6 percent, with investment in research and development very low. The Office of Technology Policy advocated "market-based" approaches to environmental management such as environmental management systems, pollutant trading, brownfield redevelopment, and privatization to combat the industry slump.

The efficacy of Superfund came under increased scrutiny as the trust declined in value from $2.4 billion in 1995 to $370 million in 2002. Supporters of the fund advocated for renewing authority to collect taxes from chemical and petroleum companies to pay for cleanup of toxic waste sites. Opponents of such taxation argued that the risks associated with many Superfund sites were relatively low and hence, they asserted, Superfund cleanup costs were quite inefficient. They argued that Superfund site decisions were often determined by political exigencies such as percentage of voters in a specific location or high levels of media attention rather than by solid cost-benefit analyses. They also asserted that many of the companies taxed by Superfund had never been known to create toxic waste problems, and that burdening these companies with additional taxes would only serve to weaken an already struggling economy.

According to the General Accounting Office, the EPA became aware of 500 new hazardous waste sites per year. Recognizing that it might not be able to rely on federal support much longer, the EPA also took steps to encourage more private investment in environmental remediation by removing 33,106 contaminated sites from its database of potential Superfund sites in 2002. In 2003, the U.S. Senate rejected a bill to reinstate taxation of chemical and petroleum companies to fund the Superfund trust.

In the next three decades, analysts predict that between $373 billion and $1.6 trillion will be spent on environmental remediation, mostly funded by government agencies such as the U.S. Department of Energy and the U.S. Department of Defense. In total, Frost & Sullivan projects the U.S. remediation market will grow at a compound annual rate of 7.2 percent through 2010. In addition to major industry segments such as brownfields revitalization, Superfund sites, and underground storage tank removal, the water remediation sector has begun to grow, and industry analysts expect the discovery of methyl tertiary butyl ether (MTBE), a gasoline oxygenate, in drinking water to boost demand for environmental remediation services.

CURRENT CONDITIONS

Through 2013, the EPA expected to add about 28 new sites to its National Priorities List each year. While most experts agree that a program like Superfund is needed to address such sites—because cleanup initiatives often go beyond the means of private organizations—there also is broad agreement that the program is in trouble. This mainly is because about one third of Superfund sites either cannot be linked to a responsible entity or the responsible party is unable to pay the cost of remediation. Because Superfund no longer is fed by taxes on chemical and petroleum companies, it receives funding from the general budget. Although funding levels have been largely steady, factors such as more complex cleanup efforts and inflation are major concerns. Experts have different views on a solution to these challenges, including a greater level of investment from the private sector.

The American Recovery and Reinvestment Act of 2009 (part of the Obama administration's economic stimulus package) provided the EPA with $600 million in funding to help clean up Superfund sites across the nation. The $600 million in stimulus money virtually doubled the amount available for Superfund work in the 2008 fiscal year, officials said. President Obama also made known his wishes to restore the former tax; he has assumed that it will provide $1 billion in revenues for his 2011 budget. The 2009 funding will accelerate ongoing cleanup activities or initiate new construction projects at 51 Superfund sites. It was expected to not only boost local economies by creating and maintaining jobs, but also to enhance the protection of human health and the environment.

In a May 2009 press release, the EPA announced its 2009 Brownfields grants of $111.9 million would go to communities in 46 states, four Tribes, and two U.S. Territories. These grants will be used to help convert former industrial and commercial sites (problem properties) into productive community sites. The grants included $37.3 million from the American Recovery and Reinvestment Act of 2009 and $74.6 million from the EPA brownfields general program funding. Since the beginning of the Brownfields Program, the EPA has awarded 1,450 assessment grants totaling $337.5 million, 242 revolving loan fund grants totaling $233.5 million and 538 cleanup grants totaling $99 million. As of 2009, the nation had nearly 1,600 Superfund sites.

Overall, design and construction markets related to environment, infrastructure, and facilities grew in 2008, despite deteriorating market conditions during the second half of the year, according to the 21st annual State-of-the-Industry Report delivered by management consultants Farkas Berkowitz & Company. The firm's report estimated that the remediation consulting market grew 12 percent in 2008 after contracting 2 percent in 2007.

"Cost cutting among nearly all industries, the collapse of the brownfields market, and a sharp reduction in merger and acquisition activity all contributed to a sudden down-turn in the industrial remediation market in the fourth quarter," said Mr. Farkas.

INDUSTRY LEADERS

Bechtel Group Inc. ranked high in the industry with overall revenues of $31.4 billion in 2008. Environmental remediation services account for roughly 20 percent of the company's sales. The construction company employs 40,000 workers and specializes in hazardous waste and nuclear waste remediation, including Chernobyl and Three Mile Island. Approximately 63 percent of the company's clients were in the private sector and roughly 60 percent of its sales come from international customers. Bechtel's construction division has also worked on the Alaskan pipeline, the Hoover Dam, and San Francisco's rapid transit system. The Bechtel family continues to control the private company, with Riley P. Bechtel as its CEO and chairman.

Waste Management Inc. of Houston, Texas, was ranked at the top of the solid waste industry and serves clients throughout North America. It collects, transfers, and disposes of solid wastes and manages landfills and recycling services. Sales in 2008 were nearly $13.4 billion and the company employed 50,000 people. In the early years of the first decade of the 2000s, Waste Management divested the operations of Waste Management International, which it purchased in 1998, in an attempt to decrease its debt.

Safety-Kleen Systems Inc. (formerly known as Safety-Kleen Corp. and Laidlaw Environmental Services Inc.) specializes in environmental remediation and related services, collecting and re-refining more than 200 million gallons of used oil annually. The company has more than 200 branches in the United States and Canada. Laidlaw Inc. owned 44 percent of the company in 1999, and forestalled plans to sell its holdings after Safety-Kleen's stock value decreased. An internal investigation of the firm's accounting practices was launched and three top officials, including CEO Kenneth Winger, were suspended. Safety-Kleen eventually filed for Chapter 11 bankruptcy protection as it reorganized its operations. After reorganizing as a private company, the firm adopted the name Safety-Kleen Systems Inc. It posted revenues of $1.7 billion for 2008.

RESEARCH AND TECHNOLOGY

In 2009, a new patent has been awarded to Professor Barry Goodell and B. and J. Jellison of the University of Maine for "Oxidation using a non-enzymatic free radical system mediated by redox cycling chelators." The technology permits new ways of generating oxygen radicals that can be used to clean up organic pollutants. The same oxygen radicals have been used to activate lignin and to make new adhesives and bond together composite products. The chemical treatment share of the remediation market is around 18 percent. The oxidation process developed in this patent is one of the most effective technologies in the chemical treatment segment.

Another advancement involved the use of seaweed to break down the now-banned pesticide dichlorodiphenyl-trichloroethane, commonly known as DDT. DDT has proven difficult to remove from the environment, with some research indicating the substance may remain in the environment for as many as 15 years before decomposing. According to the February 2005 issue of *Civil Engineering*, Australian and U.S. researchers discovered that adding dried, pulverized seaweed to moist contaminated soil may expedite the decomposition of DDT. Seaweed, which is inexpensive and readily available, is effective at decomposing DDT because it contains a combination of dissolved organics, nutrients, and sodium. According to the researcher, in some types of soil, seaweed may lower DDT levels by 80 percent in only three to six months.

As environmental remediation firms sought more effective and cost-efficient technologies and methods of remediation, environmental engineers discovered they could use compact directional drilling, a horizontal drilling technique, for environmental remediation and testing for underground contamination. Unlike vertical drilling, it does not destroy surface objects and formations such as trees and sidewalks. It also lets workers access contaminated underground areas that cannot be reached by other means, facilitates bio-remediation of leaking underground tanks, and obviates bringing contaminated soil and water to the surface.

Engineers at Lawrence Livermore National Laboratory in Livermore, California, announced a new technology that could reduce the time required for cleanup of underground contaminants from decades to months. Dynamic underground stripping uses steam to heat the soil and groundwater, thus freeing up pollutants. The technology was employed by Southern California Edison Corp. (SCE) at its Visalia pole yard, a four-acre Superfund site heavily contaminated with creosote and pentachlorophenols (PCPs). Southern California Edison reported that it removed about 1.2 million pounds of contaminants in only 30 months, a 1,500-fold increase in speed.

Environmentally friendly approaches to remediation are gaining ground. For example, Envirogen Inc. announced commencement of a National Science Foundation-funded project to research a bacterium that feeds on methyl tertiary butyl ether (MTBE), an oxygenated additive in gasoline that contaminates drinking water systems. MTBE captured public attention when it was featured in January 2000 on the

television news magazine *60 Minutes*. It was also the focus of a class action lawsuit brought by several environmental groups in the New York State Supreme Court. Several MTBE suits filed in California were underway as of early in the first decade of the 2000s.

Environmental remediation companies also used short-term crops such as alfalfa and sunflowers for cleaning up sites. Likewise, researchers experimented with using the bacterium *Deinococcus radiodurans* to clean up nuclear waste sites containing radioactive and toxic contaminates. Researchers hope these genetically engineered bacteria will be able to degrade the toxins yet withstand the radiation. Research on *Deinococcus radiodurans* continued into 2003.

Some companies mix high and low tech options in their cleanup operations. At the Tibbetts Road Superfund site in New Hampshire, the cleanup effort directed by ARCADIS Geraghty & Miller Inc. involved "thyto-remediation," in which a pumped vacuum-enhanced recovery system extracted chemicals from the soil and water on the site. Afterward, hybrid poplar trees were planted on the site, which acted as a natural filtration system to siphon the remaining low levels of chemicals from the soil and groundwater. The approach also reduced completion time for the project to three years, down from an estimated 22 years if more traditional methods had been used. U.S. Microbics employed its Bio-Raptor system to wash contaminated soil with microbially-treated water in situ (in place) rather than hauling the soil off-site. The Bio-Raptor includes a mechanism for shredding and breaking up the soil so it can easily be treated on the premises. The procedure involves no gases and is much quieter than traditional soil cleaning methods. In 2001, Bio-Raptor was able to reduce more than 96 percent of the total petroleum hydrocarbons in 1,000 cubic yards of petroleum-impacted soil in approximately 30 days.

BIBLIOGRAPHY

Berg, David, and Grant Ferrier. "Meeting the Challenge of the 21st Century: The U.S. Environmental Industry." U.S. Department of Commerce, Office of Technology Policy, September 1998. Available from http://www.ta.doc.gov/reports.htm#mcs.

Broder, John M. "Without Superfund Tax, Stimulus Aids Cleanups" *New York Times,* 25 April 2009.

"Communities in 46 States, Four Tribes, and Two U.S. Territories Will Share $111.9 Million in EPA Brownfields Grants." EPA Press Release, 8 May 2009. Available from http://epa.gov/brownfields/archive/newsevents/announcg_06_09.htm.

"EPA to Cut Pollution by a Billion Pounds." *Pollution Engineering,* January 2005.

"GlobalMarkets for Waste Remediation Technologies." 2006. Summary available from http://www.bccreserch.com/report/ENV006A.html.

Geiselman, Bruce. "What a Mess: Superfund Growing as a Financial Supernightmare." *Waste News,* 28 March 2005.

Goodell, Barry. "Environmental Clean-up and Adhesives from Forest Bioproducts." In *University of Maine Wood Utilization Research Impact Statements 2008-2009*. Available from http://woodscience.umaine.edu/UMWUR/UMaine%20WUR%20Research%20Impacts%202008-2009.htm.

"Growth for Design and Construction Markets Stops in 2009." Press Release, 8 November 2009. Available from http://www.ewire.com/display.cfm/Wire_ID/5270.

"Hazardous Waste Remediation Market to Reach $11.4 Billion by 2011." Research Studies-Business Communications Inc., 23 March 2006.

Nilkanth, Kshitij. "Fields of Gold for the US Remediation Services Industry." *Frost & Sullivan Market Insight,* 1 March 2005. Available from http://www.frost.com.

"Nanotechnology in Environmental Applications: The Global Market." BCC Research Report, July 2009. Available from http://www.bccresearch.com/report/NAN039B.html.

Oliver, Felicia. "Mining for Green in Brownfields." *Professional Builder,* 1 February 2007.

"Research Indicates Seaweed Helps Break Down DDT." *Civil Engineering,* February 2005.

U.S. Environmental Protection Agency. "Communities in 44 States, 2 Territories and 3 Tribal Nations Share $69.9 Million in Brownfields Grants," 30 June 2006. Available from http://www.epa.gov.

———. "EPA's FY 2008 Budget Focuses on Next Phase of Environmental Progress," 5 February 2007. Available from http://www.epa.gov.

———. "New Final NPL Sites," 7 March 2007. Available from http://www.epa.gov.

———. "Superfund Information Systems." 12 July 2005. Available from http://www.epa.gov.

———. "Superfund National Accomplishments Summary Fiscal Year 2006 as of December 2006," December 2006. Available from http://www.epa.gov.

———. "Superfund Program Implements the Recovery Act" May 2009. Available from http://www.epa.gov/superfund/eparecovery/index.html.

EXTREME SPORTS

—■—

SIC CODE(S)

7999

3949

INDUSTRY SNAPSHOT

Although sales of particular products such as in-line skates have been lethargic, sales of extreme sports products overall continue to outstrip those of more traditional sporting goods. Along with all the gear directly related to the sports, a slew of apparel, accessories, and media content is marketed to a willing audience of extreme sports enthusiasts, many of whom are in their teens and early twenties. And even as the growth of such well-established activities as in-line skating slows, newer extreme contests such as wakeboarding, kiteboarding, and street luging continue to amass new followers.

According to statistics released by the Sporting Goods Manufacturers Association, tens of millions of Americans engaged in extreme or alternative sports during the twenty-first century's first decade. At that time popular activities included in-line skating, skateboarding, paintball, artificial wall climbing, snowboarding, mountain biking, and trail running. Rounding out the list were BMX bicycling, wakeboarding, roller hockey, mountain/rock climbing, and boardsailing/windsurfing.

Extreme sports continued to evolve. A host of new activities were emerging, providing ample opportunities for marketers of related products and services. For example, stores specializing in extreme sporting apparel, accessories, and equipment were becoming more commonplace in the retail sector. Among the newest activities was zorbing, a sport in which enthusiasts (dubbed zorbonauts) are harnessed into transparent, double-hulled, plastic balls and roll downhill at speeds of up to 25 miles per hour. (In 2007, space diving was touted as the next extreme sport. However, two years later, in 2009, there was an acute absence of developments to report.)

The industry serving extreme sports devotees includes a diverse mix of companies. They range from multibillion-dollar mainstream sporting companies, such as Nike and adidas to scores of small start-ups run by fervent athletes. Brands marketed by the latter group tend to have more credibility with avid extreme athletes, who often identify with individualist and anti-establishment values.

ORGANIZATION AND STRUCTURE

As an industry, extreme sports tend to vary considerably in both structure and organization. In general, the sports player has four points of contact with the industry: purchase of basic equipment, purchase of safety equipment, training, and locating a place to practice the sport. The great explosion in extreme sports participation during the 1990s led to a proliferation of sport organizers and providers. Most new extreme sports business opportunities are in the service sector—providing equipment and opportunities for sports enthusiasts to practice and enjoy their pastimes.

Some aspects of extreme sports industries are regulated in part by government agencies. Bungee jumping from hot air balloons, for instance, requires a license from the Federal Aviation Administration. Bungee jumping from a crane requires licensing from the Occupational Safety and Health Administration to assure protection for the workers at the top of the crane. These sports have developed safety codes and organizations to ensure that safe practices are in place. The British Elastic Rope Sports Association and the North American Bungee Association both oversee safety standards within their industry.

Rock Climbing and Wall Climbing Rock climbing and its man-made counterpart, artificial wall climbing, are among the most popular extreme sports. Heading into the middle years of the first decade of the 2000s, the number of U.S. rock climbers totaled 2.1 million, while wall climbers totaled 8.6 million. There are two types of rock climbing practiced in the United States today. The first, and the most extreme, is called free climbing. Many rock-climbing enthusiasts prefer free climbing to all other forms of the sport. In free climbing, the climber uses only hands and feet for the actual climbing process. A rope is attached to pitons (spikes, wedges, or pegs) or chocks (wedges or blocks) in the cliff in case of accidents. The second type of rock climbing is called direct-aid climbing, whereby the climber attaches a rope ladder to pitons or chocks in the rock and uses the ladder to assist in the climb. Some climbers specialize in a particular type of ascent, such as vertical walls; others specialize in different types of terrain, such as ice climbing, which involves ascending frozen waterfalls or glaciers. These types of climbs usually require additional equipment.

Of course, as rock climbing has become more mainstream, the definition of the sport has broadened. Many weekend adventurers enjoy walking on rocks on the weekends without necessarily scaling a 90-degree granite wall. Regardless of whether they are climbing straight up or walking on a slight incline, rock climbers need, and seem to love, the attendant gear. The rock climbing industry has boomed in the last decade as demand for what were once specialty items such as climbing boots, backpacks, and dehydrated food are now available at the local Wal-Mart. The Outdoor Recreation Coalition of America, a trade organization, estimates that sales for rock climbing and hiking equipment grew from just $1 billion in the early 1990s to over $5 billion by the end of the decade. Much of the industry's growth has relied on the proclivity that many consumers have for wearing hiking or climbing gear to the park or on a city stroll even if they never intend to climb a mountain.

In-line Skating In-line skating is one of the most popular modern sports. The Sporting Good Manufacturers Association (SGMA) estimated that participation in the sport has grown over 850 percent since the mid-1980s. Admittedly, the sport has grown so common that many of today's casual practitioners don't qualify as extreme athletes. Indeed, it has almost entirely eclipsed the traditional, sub-extreme pastime of roller skating.

The concept of in-line skates, in which the wheels are arranged in a single line like ice skate blades, dates back to the eighteenth century. Around 1750, an enthusiastic Belgian skater named Joseph Merlin devised a set of roller skates by fastening wooden spools to the bottom of his shoes. In 1823 an Englishman named Robert John Tyers created the Rolito, a set of skates with five wheels per shoe in a line. The idea of the Rolito traveled to the Netherlands, where dry-land skaters, nicknamed "skeelers" made the sport popular for a period of 20 years. In 1863, an American named J.L. Plimpton developed the first roller skate using the pattern of two wheels in front and two in back. Plimpton's pattern dominated the market in the United States for almost 120 years.

Hockey players and brothers Scott and Brennan Olson developed the first modern in-line skates in 1980. In 1983, Scott Olson formed Rollerblade, Inc.; and because the company was the only manufacturer for a long time, "rollerblading" became the term for in-line skating. After Olson sold the company, its new owners improved the Rollerblade design with the launch of the very successful Lightning TRS. Other in-line skate companies—such as Ultra Wheels, Oxygen, and K2—followed. The sport has since attracted more than 30 million skaters around the world and has grown into a billion-dollar international industry.

In-line skaters vary from individuals interested only in skating as a hobby or an exercise to serious, aggressive skaters who compete by skating up vertical surfaces. Simple in-line skating, like traditional roller skating, can be performed on public streets and sidewalks. Aggressive skating, however, can require special surfaces. Both kinds of skating require safety equipment, including helmets, elbow pads, and knee pads. Manufacturers of skates usually also offer safety equipment geared to the interests of the people who buy their skates. Aggressive skating enthusiasts require different forms of protection than neighborhood skaters.

Many traditional manufacturers of roller skates turned to in-line skating when the craze began in the 1980s. The in-line skates manufactured and sold today generally have four wheels arranged in a straight line and attached to a solid plastic or leather boot. The chassis, which holds the wheels, is usually made from aluminum, glass-reinforced nylon, or a composite. The wheels themselves are polyurethane.

Most advances in the field are technical innovations to the skate itself. Rollerblade Inc. introduced two important modifications: active brake technology (ABT) in 1994 and the Xtenblade in 1996. ABT allows the skater to brake simply by pointing a toe, while traditional skate brakes require the skater to press down with the heel. The Xtenblade is a children's skate that can be stretched through four sizes, allowing the skate to grow with the child.

In-line skating grew faster than any other extreme sport for much of the 1990s. Although 1999 sales associated with the sport fell 30 percent to $305 million, the market for in-line skating equipment still exceeded those of more traditional sports such as baseball, tennis, bowling, and downhill skiing. Between 1998 and 2002, the number of in-line skating participants fell 20 percent to 21.5 million. This number continued to decline in 2003, reaching 19.2 million.

Bungee Jumping Bungee jumping remains one of the most controversial of the extreme sports and one of the least widely practiced. The inspiration for it came from Pentecost Island in the New Hebrides chain in the South Pacific. According to legend, a woman tried to escape from her abusive husband by climbing to the top of a banyan tree. When he started to climb after her, she tied vines to her ankles and jumped from the top of the tree. The vines kept her safe, but her husband fell to his death. By the time the first *National Geographic* article appeared in 1955 describing the islanders' practice of diving from the top of a tower, the practice had changed into a ritual performed by the men of the tribe, partly as a rite of manhood and partly as a fertility ceremony to ensure a good crop of yams.

On April 1, 1979, the modern sport of bungee jumping was born when members of the Oxford Dangerous Sports Club jumped from Clifton Bridge in Bristol, England. A member of the same group set a world record in 1980 by dropping from the Royal Gorge Bridge in Colorado. Although bungee jumping overall has a low total number of fatalities, the sport has attracted a lot of notoriety because of the inherent danger involved. For instance, an exhibition jumper named Laura Dinky Patterson died in preparation for a jump at the 1997 Super Bowl in New Orleans.

The Kockelman brothers were among the fathers of bungee jumping in the United States. John and Peter Kockelman, engineering graduates of California Polytechnic State University in San Luis Obispo, formed Bungee Adventures Inc. in 1998. Bungee Adventures was North America's first commercial bungee operation, according to the company's Web site, and the Kockelman brothers popularized the sport of bungee jumping by leaping from bridges over deep ravines in the Sierra Nevadas. The brothers have jumped from many diverse structures, including redwood trees, indoor coliseums, office atriums, the Golden Gate Bridge, and hot air balloons. In 1993 Bungee Adventures released the Ejection Seat, a patented human slingshot ride. The Kockelman brothers have also been active in planning safety regulations for the industry.

By and large, however, bungee jumping is a fairly unregulated sport. Jump sponsors can range from unlicensed pirate jumpers to large companies. The sites of the jumps also vary widely. Jumping from public bridges is perhaps the most popular because the sites require little preparation and are plentiful. Safety concerns, however, have made bungee jumping from public bridges legal only in the states of Oregon and Washington. Jump sponsors can legally work from privately owned bridges, but the regulations against public bridge jumping have led to many illegal pirate jumps. Hot air balloon jumps are also popular, but they are dependent on weather and time of day. Balloons can fly safely only in relatively still air, usually in the early morning or evening. A third option is crane jumping. However, cranes that can support the repetitive shock caused by bungee jumping are expensive and hard to find. A jump sponsor can spend between $70,000 and $150,000 for a used crane and then has to obtain permission from local agencies to set it up and use it for the business of jumping.

Snowboarding and Ski-boarding Snowboarding is arguably the fastest-growing extreme sport. Ski resorts, once hesitant to allowing snowboarders in, are now embracing them, especially during the off- season. Since the snowboard course tends to be smaller, resorts manufacture the snow (usually shaved ice) during periods of limited snowfall, much like ski resorts. At the turn of the twenty-first century, nearly two-thirds of ticket sales at Southern California ski resorts came from snowboarders. A recent variation called ski-boarding, which involves smaller boards that allow higher speeds and more tricks, has gained popularity as well. A late 1990s estimate pegged the U.S. snowboard market at $2 billion a year, while the number of participants grew from 1.4 million in 1990 to 7.8 million in 2003. For the 2005–2006 season, the National Ski Areas Association reported that a record 58.9 million visits were made by skiers and snowboarders. Snowboarders represented 30.4 percent of the visit total, an increase of 3 percent from 2004–2005.

Wakeboarding Wakeboarding, performed in the wake of powerboats, is fastest-growing water sport. The sport is similar to water skiing, only a board is used rather than skis. The board makes it easier for daring athletes to perform flips and jumps, and wakeboarding shares some techniques with surfing, skateboarding, and snowboarding, making this newer sport a popular warm weather substitute for those more established extreme activities. A number of leading wakeboard manufacturers are snowboard makers who branched into the wakeboard business.

Street Luging Another of the newer entrants to the world of extreme sports, street luging is inspired by the winter sled-based luge. In the street variety, the lugers, sometimes called "riders," lie face up and feet first on a board similar to a skateboard. Donning helmets and other protective gear, riders race each other on downhill courses, steering with subtle body movements and braking with their feet. Street luge boards, which are specially engineered, can reach speeds up to 90 miles an hour.

Freestyle Motocross Freestyle motocross is an amalgamation of various motorbike stunt and race events that have been around for decades. The version that has gained favor lately, as featured in such competitions as the Gravity Games and the X Games, usually involves a dirt track with large ramps and obstacles. Motocross bikers attempt to pull off high jumps and other difficult and original tricks while maintaining style and continuity in their performance.

BACKGROUND AND DEVELOPMENT

The increasing popularity of extreme sports, both from a participant and spectator standpoint, is apparent by the continued media coverage devoted to such ventures. In addition, marketers have gone to great lengths to incorporate the "extreme" element into their brands. In August 2004, *Esquire* reported that nearly 1,400 products were on the market that included the word "extreme," in their name, including X-treme Jell-O.

Eventually, ESPN's X Games grew into an entire franchise. In addition to X Games, Winter X Games, and All Access, the X Games brand had evolved to include international X Games events, retail products, skateparks, as well as an Ultimate X large format film, EXPN.com, and EXPN Radio. On April 27, 2005, ESPN Inc. and AEG announced a five-year agreement to keep the X Games in Los Angeles through 2009. After hosting the games in 2003 and 2004, the city was chosen as the site for five additional games, beginning with X Games 11 in August 2005. Aspen/Snowmass, Colorado was chosen as the site for the Winter X Games through 2007.

In February 2005, *Daily Variety* reported that NBC and Clear Channel had teamed up to create the 2005 Dew Action Sports Tour. Dubbed "an extreme-sports media extravaganza," the tour was to include monthly weekend competitions in five cities between June 9 and October 16. Categories included BMX dirtbiking, skateboarding, and freestyle motocross. NBC planned to air 22 hours of coverage, with USA airing 10 hours.

Extreme sports enthusiasts also had access to their very own cable network during the middle of the first decade of the 2000s. Epic Sports Channel created new and original extreme sports content, relying on skilled action sports producers and cinematographers. According to Epic, the channel "created a content grid that has been targeted at two generations and appeals to both children and adults." Epic's lineup included Epic Kids and Trix and Tips, as well as profiles of action sports pioneers, music videos, news, behind-the-scenes programming, and more.

According to its 2004 "Superstudy of Sports Participation," the Sporting Goods Manufacturers Association reports that tens of millions of Americans engage in extreme or alternative sports, depending how the category is defined. In-line skating is by far the most common, with 19.2 million people slipping on a pair of skates at least once in 2003 (down from nearly 28 million in 1999). The number of skateboarders in the United States climbed to 3.44 million in 2002 (up 66 percent from 1998), and then skyrocketed to 11 million in 2003. Other leading sports associated with the extreme moniker included paintball (9.8 million), artificial wall climbing (8.6 million), snowboarding (7.8 million), mountain biking (6.9 million), and trail running (6.1 million). Rounding out the list were BMX bicycling (3.3 million), wakeboarding (3.3 million), roller hockey (2.7 million), mountain/rock climbing (2.1 million), and boardsailing/windsurfing (777,900).

A number of small entrepreneurial companies have marketed adventure vacation packages to exotic locations specifically for the purpose of pursuing extreme sports. Many foreign countries have fewer regulations than the United States governing extreme sports. In March 2005, entrepreneur Bill Lee launched eXtreme Hotels and opened the company's first location, a 20-room extreme sports hotel in Cabarete, Dominican Republic. The location offered instructors, storage space for sports equipment, and provided access to surfing, skateboarding, and kiteboarding.

Kiteboarding was a newer extreme sport in the early years of the first decade of the 2000s. It involves riding small, kite-propelled boards over water, snow, sand, or grass. The sport's growing popularity was evidenced by the formation of national and state associations as well as the Kiteboard Riders Association World Cup Tour. Kiteboarding schools staffed by professional instructors catered to thousands of enthusiasts, ranging in age from eight to seventy years old. In addition, relatively inexpensive equipment made the sport accessible to a wide range of income groups.

Another emerging extreme sport was Parkour, also known as urban running. In the May 21, 2007, issue of *WWD*, writer Rosemary Feitelberg explained: "Parkour is defined by purpose-getting somewhere swiftly and efficiently using the human body to sidestep any obstacles, and free running is defined by the art of moving through your environment regardless of the path you choose to take. Parkour is akin to tearing through an obstacle course—albeit, an urban one—using the most effective movements with the least loss of momentum; free running involves more flair, complete with acrobatics, flips and spins." This type of sport was exemplified by so-called "urbanathalons," which were beginning to gain in popularity.

CURRENT CONDITIONS

What was new in 2009 in the extreme sports industry was not the introduction of new sports, but rather the introduction of new access to existing extreme sports. Adventure sports resorts were springing up all over the world, reported Keith Miller in his November 2009 *Funworld* magazine article. He noted that while many of the most popular extreme sports had been in existence for at least ten years, *access* to enjoy them had been limited. Not so anymore, according to Miller. Some of the new or pending complexes included Wake Nation Waveboarding Park in Cincinnati, Ohio, which opened in May 2009. Set on a 10-acre man-made lake, the complex also featured other extreme sporting venues including BMX biking. Wake Nation allows guests to wakeboard, water ski, and kneeboard without the need of a boat because participants are pulled along the water's surface by the use of a cable.

Waveyard is a 160-acre development planned for Mesa, Arizona; construction on phase one of the $500 million project was expected to begin in 2010. The park plans to offer a variety of sport and adventure activities, including surfing, wakeboarding, kayaking, scuba diving, zip lining, canyoneering, and whitewater rafting. It will also feature a large sand beach, resort hotel, villas, an indoor waterpark, a conference center, an amphitheater, restaurants, retail shops, and office space. The park is expected to play host to world-class competitions and special events.

VentureXtreme (www.venture-xtreme.com), which is based in the United Kingdom, was developing several extreme sports complexes there; in Europe, there are already more than 100 cable waveboarding parks. In Miller's article, Roy Higgs of Baltimore, Maryland's Development Design Group (DDG) said he was not certain why there was more significant growth in areas outside the United States. He suggested, "it may have something to do with the fact that the Extreme Sports Channel is carried in 70 countries, but not in the U.S." He also noted that the hottest markets for the DDG/Extreme Group partnership were the United Kingdom, South Africa, and Japan. "Commercial property developers are looking for something unique," Higgs said. "Developers see the interactive nature of extreme sports and retail is very powerful, and it's relatively low-cost entertainment."

INDUSTRY LEADERS

Retailers On the retail side of the business, the DDG teamed with London-based Extreme Group to bring extreme sports together with leisure brands and food and beverage in a retail environment, a concept they call Expo-Xplore. Extreme Group produces the Extreme Sports Channel (www.extreme-international.com), which was broadcast 24 hours a day in some 70 countries in 2009. The partnership has U.S.-based projects in various stages of development in Hawaii, Tennessee, Florida, Georgia, and New Jersey, and internationally based projects in Hungary, China, the United Kingdom, Turkey, Japan, and South Africa.

Kent, Washington-based Recreational Equipment Inc. (REI) is among the leaders. The member-owned cooperative retailer, which markets many general line sporting goods as well, posted sales of $1.4 billion in 2008, up slightly from 2007.

Another influential player, The North Face Inc., is both a manufacturer and a retailer, operating as a subsidiary of VF Corp. The California-based company makes everything from hiking gear for frigid polar expeditions to backpacks for use on an afternoon stroll. Another VF Corp. subsidiary is Vans Inc., one of the more visible apparel and accessory makers and retailers catering to the extreme sports crowd. Its main product line is a diverse selection of athletic shoes, mostly targeted at skateboarders. Vans also operates 160 stores in the United States and Europe and sponsors extreme sporting events. In September 2009, Reuters reported that the U.S. Environmental Protection Agency (EPA) filed suit against VF Corp. for failure to register with EPA more than 70 styles of shoes advertised as containing "bacteria-killing" properties. Such claims are required to be tested by EPA, which then registers the pesticide and product. VF Corporation reported revenues of $7.64 billion for fiscal year 2008.

Known as much for its trendy style and chic designs as for its high quality equipment, Lost Arrow Corp. is the holding company for the pricey Patagonia brand retail outlets and merchandise. Patagonia also markets gear under the brand names Water Girl, Lotus Designs, and Great Pacific Iron Works.

Manufacturers Manufacturers devoted to alternative sports include the world's biggest snowboard maker, Burton Snowboards. The company was founded by snowboarding pioneer Jake Burton. In addition to snowboards, Burton Snowboards also produces apparel and accessories. During the late years of the first decade of the 2000s, the Burlington, Vermont-based private company held an estimated 40 percent share of the U.S. snowboarding market.

One of the leading manufacturers of surfing, skating, and snowboarding apparel and accessories, Billabong International Ltd. sells its branded merchandise at sporting shops throughout Australia, Europe, Japan, South America, and North America. In 2001, Billabong acquired Element, a skateboarding apparel and accessories brand made by U.S.-based Giant International. Because it had already been successfully established, Billabong planned to preserve the Element brand name. The firm also acquired the sunglasses and snow goggles brand Von Zipper, which had been created in 1999. Having operated retail shops of its own in Australia, Europe, Japan, and South Africa for several years, Billabong opened three U.S. stores, all located in California, in 2002. In 2008 the company's sales were $A1.67 billion.

For in-line skating equipment, the leader in the field is still its founder, Rollerblade USA Corp. By midway through the first decade of the 2000s, the company marketed a skate with inflatable wheels that allowed enthusiasts to skate on different types of terrain. Tecnica, based in Italy, bought Rollerblade in mid-2003.

Rock climbing and bungee jumping use similar equipment, and major manufacturers for both sports overlap. One of the most prominent manufacturers of climbing and jumping equipment in Europe is Petzl Ltd. Petzl makes and sells harnesses that are used by both private individuals and service companies. Its Crux harness is among the most popular and most copied safety devices used in sports today.

BIBLIOGRAPHY

"About Us." Epic Sports Channel. 8 May 2005. Available from http://www.epicsportstv.com.

Browne, David. "Random Knowledge about Extreme Sports." *Esquire,* August 2004.

Cajueiro, Marcelo. "Turner Teams On Sports Net." *Variety,* 4 December 2006.

Chang, Julia. "The Need for Speed: Risk-taking Executives Turn to Extreme Sports to Unwind." *Sales & Marketing Management,* March 2006.

Clark, Jayne, Jerry Shriver, and Jennifer Vishnevsky. "Hotel Goes Head Over Heels for Extreme-Sports Fans." *USA Today,* 18 February 2005.

"Extreme Participation." *American Fitness,* March/April 2005.

"Extreme Sports Have National Appeal." *Parks & Recreation,* October 2004.

Feitelberg, Rosemary. "Adrenaline Rush; Boating Too Boring? Tennis Too Polite? Take a Run on the Wild Side." *WWD,* 21 May 2007.

Frase, Nancy. *Bungee Jumping for Fun and Profit.* Merrillville, IN: ICS Books, 1992.

Gonzalez, Isabel C. "Go Fly a Kiteboard." *Time,* 21 June 2004.

Gunn, Eileen P. "Easy Doesn't Do It." *U.S. News & World Report,* 13 November 2006.

Huo, Emily. "Great Balls of Plastic." *Business 2.0,* October 2006.

Johnston, Turlough, and Madeleine Hallden. *Rock Climbing Basics.* Mechanicsburg, PA: Stackpole Books, 1995.

"Key Developments For VF Corporation." Reuters, 26 October 2009 and 22 September 2009. Available from http://www.reuters.com/finance/stocks/keyDevelopments?symbol=VFC.N.

Lipke, David. "Urban Adventure." *Daily News Record,* 9 October 2006.

Mehta, Trupti. "Earnings Analysis: APN News, Billabong Net Falls." 21 August 2009. Available from http://australia.123jump.com/australia/earnings-story/APN-News-Billabong-Net-Falls/34223/.

Miller, Keith. "Industry News: Adventure Sports Resorts are Springing Up All Over the World." *FunWorld,* November 2009.

"National Statistics for the 2005/06 Ski and Snowboard Season." American Recreation Coalition, 30 August 2007. Available from http://www.funoutdoors.com.

"NBC Goes to Clear Extreme." *Daily Variety,* 9 February 2005.

Outdoor Industry Association. "REI Announces 2008 Revenues and Member Dividend." 11 February 2009. Available from http://www.outdoorindustry.org/media.outdoor.php%3Fnews_id%3D4978.

Parks, Liz. "New Wave in Retailing." *Stores Magazine,* February 2007.

"The U.S.A. at Play—Annual Participation Topline Report Released." Sporting Goods Manufacturers Association, 8 April 2005. Available from http://www.sgma.com/index.html.

"X Games in L.A. Through 2009." ESPN Inc., 27 April 2005. Available from http://expn.go.com/expn/story?pageName=050427_xgames_2009.

"'X' No Longer Marks Extreme-Sports Startup." *Multichannel News,* 26 July 2004.

FERTILITY MEDICINE: PRODUCTS AND SERVICES

———————■———————

SIC CODE(S)

2834

2835

8071

INDUSTRY SNAPSHOT

Use of drugs and clinical procedures in the pursuit of bearing children has been on a steady incline in the United States for two decades. Although such treatments led to successful childbirth in only a minority of cases, technological advances have edged up the success rates of assisted reproductive techniques. Likewise, sales of fertility drugs have flourished.

Statistics suggest that more than 6.1 million U.S. couples are faced with infertility, often defined as the inability to conceive after one year of unprotected intercourse. While the percentage of couples who are infertile is believed to remain stable over time, the proportion of those obtaining treatment has possibly doubled since the 1980s as treatments have become more widely available. The industry encompasses fertility clinics, sperm banks, egg donors, fertility drugs, and surrogacy programs.

Not surprisingly, social trends have also influenced demand for infertility treatments. For decades, many U.S. couples have been waiting longer to have children, and the evidence is clear that the older women are, the harder it is for them to get pregnant. In addition, as the general public has grown more comfortable with the idea of procedures such as in vitro fertilization (IVF), institutional support for infertility treatments has risen. Private health insurance plans increasingly cover infertility treatment (although coverage of the most expensive procedures decreased

slightly and may be limited). According to Kaiser Family Foundation's State Health Facts, as of January 2009 at least 15 states mandated insurance companies to provide infertility treatment as a benefit in all of their policies.

The industry remains largely unregulated and provocative, receiving more than its share of publicity in 2009 following the controversial "Octomom" case and new threats of designer baby clinics. Despite the improvements in technology, the overall failure rate for fertilization procedures is roughly 70 percent. Yet another downside to fertility treatment started to become apparent in the late 1990s. Using baseline data that had been accumulated for more than two decades, research appeared to show correlations between fertility drugs and certain cancers, such as breast and ovarian cancer, in women. Although some early studies failed to show any link between fertility treatments and ovarian cancer, one study published by the American Society for Reproductive Medicine did indicate a slightly increased risk of breast cancer in women who used certain fertility drugs for a period of longer than six months. Other potential drawbacks with some infertility treatments include a greater chance of multiple births and the risk of passing on infertility to children.

ORGANIZATION AND STRUCTURE

The fertility industry can be divided into two broad sectors, pharmaceutical and medical. The pharmaceutical sector is dominated by two companies, Merck Serono S.A. and Organon Inc. Both firms manufacture drugs used primarily to stimulate or regulate ovulation. The drugs can be prescribed on their own as a low tech treatment to assist conception. More and more, however, they are used in conjunction with a high tech procedure such as in vitro fertilization (IVF), in which the drugs stimulate ovulation and then eggs are collected and fertilized in vitro before being implanted in a woman's uterus or fallopian tubes.

Selling fertility drugs is an extremely profitable undertaking for pharmacies. A typical prescription for a woman undergoing IVF includes 12 different products, including as many as eight drugs, prenatal vitamins, and paraphernalia such as syringes and swabs. Profit margins are also higher in infertility care than for other categories of drugs that pharmacists dispense. While most pharmacies make a 20 to 22 percent profit on drug sales, they earn 30 to 35 percent on infertility products.

The medical sector of the industry is far more complex. It includes private obstetrics and gynecology (OB/GYN) and urology practices, fertility clinics, hospitals, and laboratories. Statistics on fertility clinics are difficult to come by. One reason is the lack of agreement as to what constitutes a "fertility clinic." The American Society for Reproductive Medicine (ASRM), which for years has single-handedly assembled statistics on fertility in America, prefers the term "ART (assisted reproductive technology) practice." ART encompasses high tech methods of fertilization such as IVF, gamete intrafallopian transfer, and intracystoplasmic sperm injection, all of which arose after the first test tube babies were born in the late 1970s and early 1980s. ASRM's professional organization, the Society for Assisted Reproductive Technology, had more than 392 member practices in early 2007. That figure, according to the American Society for Reproductive Medicine (ASRM), accounts for about 85 percent of the assisted reproductive technology (ART) practices in the United States. The Centers for Disease Control and Prevention (CDC) has released annual reports on fertility clinics, giving consumers, researchers, and lawmakers access to success rate rankings of more than 300 clinics that provided data for its studies.

ART practices can be small or large, independent or affiliated with other institutions such as hospitals or universities. The larger practices have staffs of physicians, embryologists, andrologists, nurses, lab technicians, and advanced laboratory facilities where the latest techniques of micromanipulation can be performed. A small ART practice might consist of just one or two reproductive endocrinologists, a staff of a few nurses and technicians, and a small lab capable of basic fertility analyses. When it performs high tech treatments, such a clinic generally uses a hospital lab.

Fertility treatments can be classed as low tech or high tech. Low tech treatments might be relatively new—fertility drugs, for example, have been in use for only 30 years or so—but they rely on traditional medical techniques. The most common treatments include artificial insemination, surgery, and basic drug therapies. They have varying success rates, generally lower than high tech treatments. Success in fertility is defined as a cycle of treatment that results in the birth of a live baby.

Artificial insemination is the oldest and most common low tech treatment. Semen, either from a woman's partner or an anonymous donor, is inserted into the vagina through a catheter. Insertion is timed to occur just after ovulation to maximize the chances of fertilization. Since the 1970s, most donor sperm have been supplied by sperm banks, where they have been cryogenically preserved.

Surgery has been most often used when a woman has no fallopian tubes or when they have been blocked or damaged. Until the advent of in vitro fertilization (IVF), surgery was the only possible treatment for tubal infertility. Surgery, however, is more costly and invasive and less effective than IVF, and during the 1990s its use declined by 50 percent.

Fertility drugs are one of the simplest low tech methods. They can be taken orally, by injection or subcutaneously (under the skin), and they work by stimulating the ovaries to produce eggs. After approximately 36 hours, fertilization is attempted via sexual intercourse or artificial insemination. The use of fertility drugs is complicated by their powerful effects on the endocrine and reproductive systems as well as their link to ovarian cancer. Furthermore, a large percentage of pregnancies stemming from fertility drugs result in multiple fetuses. Nationwide, about 38 percent of the live births from fertility enhanced pregnancies in 1996 involved more than one fetus.

As a means of achieving pregnancy and birth, these low tech methods seem to be unpredictable when used on their own. Statistics for the U.S. population as a whole are not available, but studies on small sample groups suggest that simple artificial insemination has a success rate of around 6 percent. When accompanied by fertility drugs, however, that rate can nearly triple. Fertility drugs alone have a success rate of approximately 10 percent. There are conditions when neither drugs nor artificial insemination can be used, such as when a woman has tubal problems or when a man has a low or nonexistent sperm count.

Assisted reproductive technology (ART) is at the high tech end of the fertility treatment scale. The most common treatments are IVF, gamete intrafallopian transfer (GIFT), zygote intrafallopian transfer (ZIFT), and increasingly, intracytoplasmic sperm injection. Freezing of sperm and embryos (known as cryopreservation) and drug therapies are often used in tandem with these techniques.

IVF is the most common high tech assisted reproductive technology. In this procedure, eggs are removed from the prospective mother's ovaries, usually after stimulation with fertility drugs, or donor eggs are obtained. The eggs are then fertilized in a laboratory dish with sperm from the partner or a donor. Two to four of the resulting embryos are implanted in the woman's uterus. Other embryos can be cryogenically preserved for use in future IVF if the first attempt at conception is unsuccessful. IVF can be used in practically all cases of infertility, though at first it was used primarily for women with fallopian tube disorders or endometriosis, a condition in which tissue from the lining of the uterus exists and functions elsewhere in the abdomen.

In gamete intrafallopian transfer (GIFT), gametes (sperm and eggs) are collected and the sperm prepared as in IVF. They are introduced separately, however, into the fallopian tubes rather than the uterus, and fertilization takes place in vivo—that is, in the body. It is believed that a large number of eggs and high concentrations of sperm at the natural site of fertilization would increase the likelihood of conception. As IVF is refined, use of GIFT is dropping. Its slightly higher success rates do not seem to outweigh the more difficult surgical intervention that is required.

Zygote intrafallopian transfer (ZIFT) is a hybrid of IVF and GIFT. Fertilization takes place in vitro as in IVF. The zygote is introduced immediately into the fallopian tube, as in GIFT, where the normal cycle of conception then runs its course. ZIFT is most often used when a male's sperm count is low or when anti-sperm antibodies are present in the woman.

Non-surgical embryonic selective thinning and transfer (NEST) is a newer technique that helps IVF embryos live a day or so longer. This allows extra time to determine which one is the strongest and healthiest for implantation. The embryonic shell is then hatched to make it easier to attach to the uterine lining. Some experts believe this process may boost IVF success rates from about 24 percent to as high as 80 percent.

Intracytoplasmic sperm injection (ICSI), first used successfully in Belgium in 1992, is one of the latest high tech procedures to be used on a mass scale. A single sperm cell is injected directly into an egg. ICSI enables men with very low sperm counts or inactive sperm—80 percent of infertile men—to father their own children. The procedure also allows men who have had vasectomies to have genetic offspring. ICSI is seen as a useful tool for many conditions because it largely eliminates sperm as a factor in fertilization and allows physicians to concentrate on the conditions for pregnancy in a woman's body. By 1999, tens of thousands of babies had been born through ICSI.

The chance that a healthy, reproductively normal couple will conceive a child in a given month is estimated at around 20 percent. Success rates of assisted reproductive technology (ART) procedures are as good as or often better than that, ranging from about 22 to 28 percent.

Fertility treatment is expensive. A single attempt with artificial insemination usually costs between $300 and $500. One cycle of fertility drug treatment, which typically involves multiple drugs, can cost $2,500, and patients typically need drug treatment for two to four monthly cycles. ART procedures typically cost between $8,000 and $12,000 per treatment. Given that the most effective treatment results in a child barely one in four times, a high percentage of infertile couples inevitably go through more than one round of treatment. According to Kiplinger Online, it is not unusual for a couple to spend at least $30,000 trying to have a child.

In 2002, fewer than half of U.S. medical insurers covered infertility. Even when they did, reimbursements were often limited to diagnostic costs, or coverage was frequently limited to treatments that were ineffective for some patients or less cost-effective than others. As of 2007, a total of 15 states mandated insurance for infertility, but coverage varied widely. Some states required a round of low tech treatments before IVF could be attempted. Some excluded HMOs from providing coverage. Hawaii mandated nothing more than a one-time outpatient diagnostic visit. In Texas, a couple was required to try unsuccessfully for five years before they were considered infertile, although most physicians considered one year the defining period. Lack of insurance combined with high costs has made ongoing infertility treatments a realistic option for only the well-to-do.

Infertility treatment has long been something of a gray area with insurers, but increasing demand coupled with lawsuits by those without insurance coverage seems to be leading to a more standardized approach. In June 1998, the U.S. Supreme Court issued a ruling stating that reproduction is "a major life activity." This cleared the way for patients denied infertility coverage by insurers to sue under Title VII of the Civil Rights Act of 1964 or under the Americans with Disabilities Act of 1990. However, between 1997 and 2002, the percentage of U.S. medical insurers covering IVF fell from 21 percent to 17 percent.

Patients find fertility services in a variety of ways. Many are referred by personal physicians. Some clinics advertise. Consumer groups are a valuable source of information. The most important one in the fertility area is RESOLVE: The National Infertility Association. Besides having local offices throughout the United States, RESOLVE maintains a national help line and compiles a detailed referral list of fertility specialists in the United States and Canada. Another important source of information is patient support groups. Members share the names of doctors and their experiences, suggest solutions to those with problems, and help newcomers navigate the complex and often impersonal medical bureaucracy.

The Internet has become an important resource as well, enabling individuals to gain access to information about new techniques and medications that their own doctors may be unwilling to share. The number of fertility-related chat rooms is growing and a few fertility doctors have set up Web pages to answer questions and discuss the latest medical developments. Some pharmacies sell fertility drugs online. The Web site for the InterNational Council on Infertility Information Dissemination also provides a wealth of material.

The field is beginning to see the development of a market for donated eggs. From 1989 to 1994, the number of births that resulted from the implantation of donated eggs grew from about 120 to nearly 1,300. Cumulatively, by 1999, upwards of 10,000 babies were produced from donor eggs. In an extraordinary example, 63-year-old Arceli Keh gave birth in 1996 to a healthy baby who grew from a donor egg. By 2007, roughly 55.2 percent of births resulting from assisted reproductive technology treatment started with donor eggs, according to the Advanced Fertility Clinic of Chicago, citing information posted in 2009 by the CDC and and the Society for Assisted Reproductive Technology (SART). As these successes continue to multiply, donor eggs will be in increasingly high demand. It can be a lucrative business. Donors can earn up to $5,000 for donating eggs, and an egg that is suitably matched to an infertile couple may cost the couple as much as $6,000 or more.

Industry growth has been marked by the emergence of specialized niches formed by entrepreneurs, often as a result of personal experience, according to *Business Week Online*. For example, because Jewish donors are difficult to find in the United States, a woman named Ruth Tavor formed New York Lifespring, a business that secures eggs from Israeli donors for implantation into her clients.

In addition, New Jersey lawyer Melissa Brisman established a business to help women who are unable to carry a fetus to term find third-party "gestational carriers." In this case, a couple's fertilized egg is implanted in woman who serves as the carrier.

Another niche was egg freezing, which, as the name implies, involves the removal and freezing of a woman's eggs. Traditionally used for cancer patients facing chemotherapy, by 2006 fertility clinics were marketing this approach as a means by which women could save eggs for pregnancy attempts at a later age.

Regulation and Legislation The Food and Drug Administration (FDA) regulates the manufacture and sale of all fertility drugs in the United States. Like other pharmaceuticals, such drugs must undergo a series of stringent clinical trials and reviews before they are approved for use. According to the Pharmaceutical Research and Manufacturers of America, it takes an average of 15 years for a

drug to move from the experimental stage to pharmacy shelves, a long process that contributes to high costs. Drugs are usually available in other countries years before they reach the United States but remain unavailable to American consumers. Occasionally the FDA will relax restrictions on foreign drugs. When two common American fertility drugs, Pergonal and Metrodin, were in very short supply between February 1996 and February 1997, the FDA allowed the import of substitutes from foreign suppliers.

Andrology laboratories, which work with sperm, are regulated at the federal level by the Clinical Laboratory Improvement Amendments of 1988 (CLIA-88). The law spells out strict standards of specimen control and technical supervision for labs performing "high complexity" procedures and tests, such as those connected with sperm handling. Labs are required to register with the Health Care Financial Administration and are subject to inspection by that body or an equivalent such as the College of American Pathologists. Embryology labs, where in vitro fertilization takes place, do not fall under CLIA-88 regulation.

The American Society for Reproductive Medicine (ASRM) together with the College of American Pathologists has drawn up andrology (a branch of medicine concerned with treatment of male reproductive diseases) and embryology lab guidelines for its member clinics. There also are attempts in Congress to include andrology labs under CLIA-88, a move ASRM opposes because the CLIA was written for diagnostic facilities and their specific conditions. Embryology and andrology labs, the ASRM argued, engage in treatment rather than diagnosis and should be regulated accordingly.

The Fertility Clinic Success Rate and Certification Act of 1992 (FCSRCA) directed the U.S. Department of Health and Human Services, in cooperation with the Centers for Disease Control and Prevention (CDC), to develop a model program for the certification of embryology labs. Unlike CLIA-88, such programs would be voluntary and would be made available to the states to adopt at their discretion. Lack of funding has prevented the model program clause from ever being implemented.

The FCSRCA also includes a provision requiring fertility clinics to report success rates for IVF, GIFT, ZIFT, and other procedures to the CDC. The CDC issued such a report in 2002, based on data collected in 2000. Previously, the American Society for Reproductive Medicine (ASRM) collected and distributed this information itself. The 2000 data show that nationwide, IVF (without intracytoplasmic sperm injection or ICSI) had a 28.6 percent success rate, GIFT 24.5 percent, ZIFT 29.2 percent, and IVF with ICSI 31 percent (where success is live birth rate per retrieval procedure). Despite the above-mentioned federal policies, the use of assisted reproductive technology by physicians and clinics is largely unregulated and a variety of doctors dabble in fertility treatments. Since 1978, the number of clinics has increased from about 30 to over 300. Although the drug therapies are approved by the FDA, the actual practice of fertility medicine is unstructured and highly variant.

In the mid-1970s, federal funding of research on human embryos was halted in the United States when the Congress failed to fund an ethics board to review research proposals. Although the law was nullified by later legislation, it still prompted the National Institutes of Health (the major source of federal funding for medical research) to deny financial support for human embryo research. Therefore such research must depend on private funding, some of which comes from grants established by two drug companies, Serono and Organon. Much of the research is conducted at fertility clinics and is paid for from clinic revenues.

BACKGROUND AND DEVELOPMENT

The first documented case of artificial insemination in humans was in 1790. The development of infertility treatment as a discrete sector of the contemporary economy is directly linked to technological development. The most important clinical practices of the 1990s have their roots in the discoveries of the past 40 years.

The 1950s and 1960s were largely a period of research advances that only slowly made their way into practice. The first modern fertility-inducing substances were discovered and developed during the 1960s, when gonadotropins (hormonal substances that stimulate ovulation) were extracted from human pituitary tissue. Mass scale production was made possible when researchers learned they could also be produced from the urine of postmenopausal women. So-called menotropins are the active ingredients in the most widely used fertility drugs such as Pergonal, Humegon, and Metrodin.

Clomiphene citrate was also first introduced in the 1960s. Unlike menotropins, however, which had to be injected, it was an oral medication. Another advantage of clomiphene citrate was the considerably lower incidence of multiple births that resulted from taking it—about 8 percent as opposed to between 25 and 50 percent for the menotropins. In 1977, Andrew V. Schally and Roger Guillemin won the Nobel Prize in physiology for their discovery of the gonadotropin-releasing hormone (GnRH), a substance that enables the pituitary gland to secrete gonadotropins, which in turn stimulate the gonads (reproductive glands). GnRH restored ovulation in women for whom it had apparently ceased completely.

Cryopreservation techniques date from the late 1940s, and the first successful artificial inseminations using sperm that had been frozen were reported in 1954. An increase in oral contraception and legalized abortion decreased the number of babies available for adoption during the 1970s, helping create a demand for donor sperm. As a result, sperm banks, which could preserve sperm cryogenically, proliferated.

The major landmark in the history of fertility was achieved in England's Bourn Hall clinic on July 25, 1978, when Patrick Steptoe and Robert Edwards delivered the world's first "test-tube baby" conceived via in vitro fertilization (IVF). The first in vitro fertilization (IVF) baby in the United States was delivered in 1981 by Drs. Howard and Georgiana Jones. The 1980s were subsequently marked by breathtaking progress. Among the new developments was trans-vaginal ultrasound, a procedure that involved inserting a wand vaginally to collect eggs needed for IVF. It required only a local anesthetic, and no laparoscope was necessary. The first pregnancies were achieved using frozen embryos and the first births were from donor eggs. Late in the decade, the first gamete intrafallopian transfer (GIFT) and zygote intrafallopian transfer (ZIFT) babies were born.

During the early 1990s, intracytoplasmic sperm injection (ICSI) was developed, and further refinements of the procedure continue. With this method, if there is no sperm in a man's semen, it can be surgically removed from testicular tissue and implanted using ICSI. New technologies are also being perfected that enable physicians to recognize a potent, live sperm cell among sperm that are apparently dead.

The impact of these new technologies can be seen in the growth of assisted reproductive technology (ART) since the early 1980s. In 1985, four years after the first U.S. IVF baby, the Society of Assisted Reproductive Technology had 30 member clinics. By 1993, that number had grown to 267 clinics, and by 1999 the figure had climbed to more than 335.

The fertility industry has suffered occasional embarrassments. During the summer of 1996, a scandal erupted when it was revealed that three doctors at the University of California at Irvine were suspected of having taken eggs and embryos from patients without their consent. As many as ten babies may have been delivered from the "undonated" eggs and embryos. The physicians were sued by 39 patients and the incident led to the closure of the university's Center for Reproductive Health. In Virginia, another fertility doctor inseminated nearly 75 patients with his own semen and not with semen from anonymous donors as he had told them. He was sentenced to a five-year prison term for fraud.

Cloning is a result of assisted reproductive technology (ART). In 1997 a sheep named Dolly was cloned from a single adult cell. While this was a tremendous milestone in the annals of science, it was also a development fraught with ethical and moral issues. For instance, doctors are researching the transfer of the nucleus from an older woman's egg into a younger donor egg, the nucleus of which has been removed. The donor egg would then be transferred to the uterus of the older patient for gestation. Using de-nucleated eggs is very similar to the process that led to Dolly the sheep, and this kind of ART makes the cloning of humans very possible. President Bill Clinton responded to the controversy surrounding such procedures by calling for a five-year ban on any experiments related to human cloning.

Cloning was a key industry issue during the early years of the twenty-first century's first decade. In June 2001, the U.S. House of Representatives voted to ban human cloning for both reproductive purposes as well as for research purposes. However, after a few months of debate, the U.S. Senate rejected the bill arguing that issuing such a broad-based ban could stunt promising medical research.

Despite concerns related to potential side effects of taking fertility drugs, a growing number of infertile couples continued to opt for drugs or procedures that could help them to produce children. The number of clinics devoted to high tech assisted reproductive technology (ART) jumped from only 30 in 1985 to over 400 in the early years of the first decade of the 2000s. IVF continued to be the most common form of ART, accounting for more than 70 percent of all procedures, while the more invasive GIFT and ZIFT methods were on the decline. IVF has been shown to yield live birth rates similar to those of the other two procedures.

An ironic side effect of many infertility treatments is the prevalence of multiple births. Couples who have trouble conceiving a single child find themselves rearing twins, triplets, or even greater numbers of multiple siblings. Couples using ART procedures, for example, experience multiple births in 38 percent of all pregnancies—10 times the rate of the general population.

Newer procedures such as blastocyst transfer, a refined form of IVF that allows an embryo to develop in vitro a few more days than ordinary IVF before transferring it to the uterus, greatly reduce the likelihood of more than two births per medically assisted pregnancy. Blastocyst transfer, which has been practiced since only the late 1990s, also may lead to higher live birth rates than other IVF techniques. Some observers believe that improving success rates and falling multiple birth rates will win infertility treatments greater protections under the law and better coverage by health insurance plans.

Improved pharmaceuticals also play a significant role in infertility treatment. Some are used alone and others are used in conjunction with artificial insemination, IVF, or other medical procedures. In the early years of the first decade of the 2000s, two follitropin-based drugs,

Gonal-F from Serono and Follistim from Organon, rapidly gained market share as they made it easier for women to take a follicle-stimulating hormone to enhance egg production. The follitropin compounds are easier to administer and reduce certain side effects that can impair embryo development.

Another new fertility aid employs high frequency sounds to determine whether a woman is in ovulation. In 2000, Fertility Acoustics Inc., with backing from consumer products giant Kimberly-Clark, was developing a hearing test that let women know if they were ovulating. The technology was based on a finding that women's sound perception changes during ovulation. The company believed the family planning product could eventually be used in homes without a prescription, but the test kit had yet to be approved for marketing by the FDA. In 2001, Appro Healthcare Inc. acquired Fertility Acoustics and continued developing its fertility monitoring technology.

Medical professionals continued to research the link between various forms of cancer and fertility drugs. On a positive note, some studies released in the early years of the first decade of the 2000s failed to show any link between fertility treatments and increased risk of ovarian cancer. However, one study published by the American Society for Reproductive Medicine (ASRM) did indicate a slightly increased risk of breast cancer in women who used certain fertility drugs for a period of longer than six months. The ASRM believed that these results, while considered inconclusive, did reflect a need for additional research.

In 2005 the industry witnessed an important legal development when a judge in Cook County, Illinois, allowed a couple to proceed with a wrongful death lawsuit against a fertility clinic that accidentally threw away their frozen embryo. According to *National Catholic Reporter,* the judge indicated that the state's legislature intended embryos to be considered human beings. This legal development concerned fertility doctors, who indicated that it could have grave implications for the industry.

CURRENT CONDITIONS

Estimates vary on exactly how much is spent on fertility medicine, but in late 2009 Marketdata Enterprises Inc., an independent market research publisher, released a 221-page report entitled *U.S. Fertility Clinics & Infertility Services: An Industry Analysis.* The report estimated the value of the U.S. industry to be about $4 billion at that time. According to Marketdata Enterprises in its 2009 study, *U.S. Fertility Clinics & Infertility Services: An Industry Analysis,* the typical or "average" U.S. fertility clinic has revenues estimated at $3.2 million.

Being, for the most part, a self-regulated for-profit industry, separate subsectors found themselves lumped together under heightened scrutiny following several highly-publicized stories in 2009. Perhaps the most widely-publicized was that of Nadya Suleman, dubbed the "Octomom" by the media. A single mother who already had six children (two with special needs) Suleman gave birth to octuplets in January 2009 following the implantation of six viable embryos by Dr. Michael Kamrova, a fertility specialist. Public outrage against both Suleman, who had already been on public assistance, and Dr. Kamrova, dominated the media for weeks and prompted public and professional inquiry and scrutiny.

In March 2009, Marcy Darnovsky of the Center for Genetics and Society (CGS), in a CGS article, noted that the industry's voluntary guidelines on the implantation of embryos were violated by at least four out of five clinics, with the highest transgression in California (90 percent of clinics in violation). Darnovsky also noted that there were no meaningful sanctions within the self-regulating industry. In fact, it was not until September 2009 that the American Society for Reproductive Medicine (ASRM) quietly announced that it had expelled an unnamed member "for cause." Nearly a month after that, Rita Rubin at *USA Today* revealed that the unnamed "member" was Kamrova. In any event, ASRM membership is not required to practice the specialty; the expulsion simply made Kamrova the most visible transgressor.

In October 2009, after heated controversy following the octuplet births, the ASRM announced tightened practice guidelines as well as a willingness to work with policymakers to put teeth into its recommendations. In his follow-up article for the American Medical Association's news publication, Kevin B. O'Reilly noted that the organization did not alter its guidance on the number of embryos to transfer based on different patient prognoses, but requested that doctors who exceed the recommendation transfer only one additional embryo, make note of the decision in the medical record, and caution their patients about the risks of multi-fetal pregnancies. At least three states considered legislation in 2009 to regulate IVF clinics, but none was passed, noted O'Reilly.

Meanwhile, and almost concurrent with this early 2009 saga was the advertised service by a fertility clinic in Southern California offering to use an embryo screening technique to select hair color, eye color, and complexion of future children. There was near unanimous condemnation by other fertility practitioners and bio-ethicists, and the clinic suspended its advertisement in March 2009. A CGS examination of data reported by fertility clinics to the CDC revealed that many clinics continue to advertise nonmedical gender selection in fertility treatments, another practice contrary to ASRM guidelines.

As of 2009, the states that mandated insurance companies to provide infertility treatment as a benefit in all of their policies were Arkansas, California, Connecticut, Hawaii, Illinois, Louisiana, Maryland, Massachusetts, Montana, New Jersey, New York, Ohio, Rhode Island, Texas, and West Virginia.

INDUSTRY LEADERS

Two pharmaceutical companies dominate the fertility drug industry: Merck Serono S.A. and Organon International Inc. Merck Serono (formerly Serono S.A.) offers a wide range of products primarily for reproductive medicine but also in the areas of growth, metabolism, and immunology/oncology. Altogether, the company, with its flagship Gonal-F drug, is believed to control as much as 65 percent of the global fertility drug market. The company became Merck Serono in January 2007, when Merck KGaA acquired Serono in a $13 billion deal.

Serono has an impressive list of research achievements. The company launched the world's first human menotropin, Pergonal, in the 1960s; the first gonadotropin containing the follicle-stimulating hormone Metrodin in the 1980s; and Fertinex, the world's first gonadotropin that could be injected subcutaneously instead of intramuscularly, in the late 1980s. In 1995 the company developed the world's first recombinant (genetically recombined) menotropin, Gonal-F. With this revolutionary discovery, the active ingredient in the most important fertility drugs can be synthesized. Thus, production is no longer dependent on world supplies of human menopausal urine. Gonal-F (follitropin alpha) is a hormone that stimulates follicle development, which leads to egg production. Gonal-F was the first drug approved by the European Union, and the FDA approved its use in 1997. In 2000 the company purchased the marketing rights to Asta Medica's fertility treatment Cetrotide, which is used to prevent premature ovulation for women using other fertility medicines. Serono also licenses drugs to other manufacturers, including Organon, its leading competitor in the fertility field.

Organon International manufactures a number of fertility drugs. During the middle of the first decade of the 2000s, the company offered a new product called Orgalutran, which reduced treatment times for in vitro fertilization patients from four weeks to less than two weeks. Other offerings included Pregnyl, an injectable preparation of human chorionic gonadotropin, as well as the recombinant follicle-stimulating hormone Puregon. Organon also offered a wide range of drugs for contraception, anesthesiology, and central nervous system disorders. The company is a subsidiary of the Dutch chemical manufacturer Akzo Nobel. However, Schering-Plough agreed to acquire Organon in 2007.

Organon was founded in Europe in the early 1920s to develop human pharmaceuticals from the hormones present in animal organs. In addition to creating the world's first fast-acting insulin, Organon was the first to isolate and identify the male hormone testosterone in 1935 and the first to standardize the hormone progesterone in 1939. The fertility drug Humegon was introduced in Europe in 1963, but FDA approval was not granted until 1994. Organon also received FDA approval in 1997 for its Follistim (follitropin beta), a hormone that helps stimulate the growth of follicles. In 1999, Organon beat out its larger competitor by gaining the FDA's blessings on Antagon, the first of a new generation of gonadotropin-releasing hormone (GnRH) treatments.

One of the leading U.S. fertility clinics is the Jones Institute for Reproductive Medicine in Norfolk, Virginia. The Jones Institute was founded in 1981 by Drs. Howard and Georgiana Jones. They delivered America's first IVF baby at the institute in 1981 and have used various assisted reproductive technology (ART) methods, including in vitro fertilization (IVF), to deliver approximately 3,650 babies since then (as of 2009). The institute offers a full range of fertility techniques. In June 1993 the institute delivered the first baby that had been screened for Tay-Sachs disease, a fatal condition, using pre-implantation genetic testing. Jones Institute prides itself on attracting sizable research funds from private sources and the pharmaceutical industry. As of 2007, the institute offered advanced technology such as 3D Ultrasound, performed robotically assisted gynecological surgery, and was engaged in a clinical research study with Eastern Virginia Medical School.

Another leading U.S. fertility clinic is the Genetics and IVF Institute (GIVF) in Fairfax, Virginia. GIVF was founded in 1984 and has achieved more than 1,400 pregnancies utilizing assisted reproductive technology (ART) procedures. In 1984 GIVF conducted its first prenatal genetic testing, and it does ongoing research on sperm separation, DNA testing, and other advanced technologies. GIVF was the first clinic to use non-surgical, trans-vaginal ultrasound for the retrieval of eggs for IVF in 1985. In the early 1990s, it became the first fertility center in the United States to offer cryopreservation of ovarian tissue. GIVF offered the Origins Drug Benefit Program to patients with no insurance coverage or whose insurance did not cover IVF. The program provided Gonadotropin drugs at no cost to a range of new and existing patients, reducing cycle costs by about 33 percent. By 2009 the institute was responsible for more than 20,000 IVF pregnancies worldwide, and had published more than 500 peer-reviewed original medical articles and abstracts.

WORKFORCE

There are no reliable statistics on precisely how many U.S. physicians currently treat infertility. The American Society for Reproductive Medicine (ASRM) has approximately 10,500 members. Roughly 90 percent of them are obstetrician-gynecologists and 7 percent of them are urologists. Most of these members have general practices rather than fertility clinics and offer reproductive services together with other related treatments. Such practitioners provide most first-tier fertility treatments.

Various reproductive specialists work in ART practices. The most common are reproductive endocrinologists (REs), specialists who treat female infertility. An RE completes a normal medical school education, usually as an obstetrician/gynecologist, followed by a two-year fellowship in a certified RE program. A reproductive urologist diagnoses and treats male-factor infertility and completes a similar two-year, post- medical-school fellowship program on reproductive medicine. Larger clinics often have a reproductive immunologist on their staff who is also a medical doctor and whose presence, considering the growing importance of immunological factors in fertility, can be critical to treatment.

Fertility clinics employ other specialized personnel. The embryologist is responsible for preparing embryos before and after cryopreservation. Embryologists may be medical doctors or have advanced degrees in biology, biochemistry, or a related science. Andrologists—lab technicians with degrees in biochemistry, endocrinology, or physiology—prepare sperm for freezing and fertilization procedures. Geneticists advise couples with potential genetic abnormalities and generally have an advanced degree in biology or genetics.

AMERICA AND THE WORLD

Globally, cloning remained a controversial issue through the first decade of the 2000s. In March 2005 the U.N. General Assembly approved a non-binding resolution to entirely ban human cloning, still in effect in 2009. While the United States and other nations supported the ban, which according to MSNBC.com labeled cloning as "an affront to human dignity," nations such as South Korea and Britain indicated that they planned to continue cloning for purposes of therapeutic research.

In general, U.S. reproductive science lags behind that conducted in Europe due to the stringent U.S. regulation of pharmaceuticals and the financial and societal restrictions placed on research. Drugs are usually available overseas 10 to 15 years before they can be purchased by U.S. patients; and when they finally become available for sale in the United States, they are frequently much more expensive than in Europe or Latin America. Because of high fertility drug costs, a certain percentage of Americans prefer to buy them abroad (in Mexico, for example) despite the risks involved in smuggling them back into the country.

U.S. fertility research also comes up short versus its European counterpart because so little of it is publicly funded. The most imposing foreign presence in the U.S.

fertility industry consists of the two drug companies, Serono and Organon, whose parent companies are both European. Another European company, Cryos, based in Aarhus, Denmark, is considered one of the world's largest sperm banks. It even exports to a number of countries, including the United States.

Differences in health insurance between the United States and other countries also account for differences in reproductive technology. For example, medical insurance in Sweden pays for numerous cycles of IVF and allows doctors to transfer just one embryo as opposed to the two to four (or even more) typically transferred in the United States. This gives Swedish clinics a lower success rate of births per egg transfers, but it greatly reduces the risk of multiple births, the rate of which some observers find disturbingly high in the United States.

In 2005 a new law in the United Kingdom gave children born from donated sperm and eggs the right to trace their biological parents once they reach the age of 18. The new law intended to give these children the same rights as adopted children, so that they can obtain a sense of identity. This development concerned many in Britain's fertility sector. With donations already in short supply, they feared that the new law would reduce the number of willing donors. According to research from the London Fertility Centre, donors and recipients alike prefer anonymity. Some hinted that the law could encourage the development of a black market for sperm and egg donors, or an exodus to clinics in other European countries. However, others noted that in countries with similar laws—including Sweden, which implemented a like measure in 1985—donor rates were only affected temporarily. Instead of declining, the makeup of the donor pool shifted from younger donors to older donors who already had families of their own.

RESEARCH AND TECHNOLOGY

Research conducted at the University of Pennsylvania School of Veterinary Medicine showed that sperm stem cells, or spermatogonia, can be transplanted successfully from fertile mice into sterile mice. Spermatogonia are the cells that manufacture sperm. The once sterile mice can then have healthy offspring. These sperm stem cells can also be frozen, thawed, and transplanted. The initial success in these animal trials holds promise for reversing fertility problems in men.

Some techniques are being perfected in clinical research. A handful of clinics can perform pre-implantation genetic diagnosis, which is used when a couple is at risk for X-linked recessive diseases such as cystic fibrosis or spinal muscular atrophy. In this procedure, researchers do a single-cell genetic analysis on cells taken from embryos until they find one that does not have the genetic defect. Some clinics are able to

perform clinical sperm separation, distinguishing sperm by the X or Y chromosome they carry. When perfected, this treatment will enable physicians to control over 350 X-linked recessive disorders such as hemophilia, a disease that strikes primarily males. Fewer than 100 children have been born using this process, but it has allowed parents to avoid passing along serious genetic disorders.

Another advance was in the use of laser technology to aid fertilization. Noting that many IVF failures occur because the fertilized embryo doesn't get embedded in the womb, researchers based in Hungary and Belgium explained to the European Society of Human Reproduction and Embryology conference in Bologna, Italy their laser-aided fertilization technique. In this process, lasers were used to precisely drill the membrane surrounding the human egg to allow for easier implantation of the embryo.

One additional area of research was ovarian transplantation, which focused on preserving the fertility of the growing number of young women receiving high-dose chemotherapy or radiation, both of which often destroy ovaries. Research has shown that ovarian function can be preserved in primates whose ovaries are removed and frozen prior to treatment. When ovaries are re-implanted, quite often egg production resumes. Human clinical trials for such a procedure began in the early years of the first decade of the 2000s.

BIBLIOGRAPHY

"About INCIID." The InterNational Council on Infertility Information Dissemination, 23 June 2005. Available from http://www.inciid.org.

"About Us." RESOLVE: The National Infertility Association, 23 June 2005. Available from http://www.resolve. org/main/national/help/help.jsp?name=help.

Alperowicz, Natasha. "Serono: Big Ambitions in Biotech: Expansion Drives a Boost in Biologics Capacity." *Chemical Week,* 27 April 2005.

American Society for Reproductive Medicine. "National Average Egg Donation Statistics from the 2007 CDC Report." Available from http://www.advancedfertility. com/donor-egg-success-rates.htm.

"Cell Phone Use Affects Fertility, Study Shows." *eWeek,* 27 October 2006.

"A Cook County, Ill., Judge Ruled that Alison Hiller and Todd Parish Can Go Forward with a Lawsuit for Wrongful Death—Against a Fertility Clinic that Mistakenly Discarded a Frozen Embryo from the Chicago Couple." *National Catholic Reporter,* 25 February 2005.

"Facility Centers Are Marketing Egg-Freezing." *Marketing to Women: Addressing Women and Women's Sensibilities,* August 2006.

"Fast Facts about Infertility" RESOLVE: The National Infertility Association, 13 March 2007. Available from http://www.resolve.org/site/PageServer?pagename=fmed_ mcff_ffi.

"Genetics & IVF Institute Launches the Origins Drug Benefit Program." Genetics & IVF Institute, 26 June 2005. Available from http://www.givf.com.

Grady, Denise. "Report of First Birth for Cancer Survivor In a Tissue Implant." *New York Times,* 24 September 2004.

———. "Woman Has Child After Receiving Twin's Ovarian Tissue." *New York Times,* 8 June 2005.

Gumpert, David E. "The Business of Life; The Emerging Industry of Helping to Facilitate Pregnancy May Be a Hot Field in the Near Future, but it Comes with Plenty of Questions." *Business Week Online,* 23 August 2006. Available from www.businessweek.com.

Kaiser Family Foundation. " Kaiser State Health Facts Mandated Coverage of Infertility Treatment." January 2009. Available at http://www.statehealthfacts.org/.

"Legislative History." Bethesda, MD: RESOLVE: The National Infertility Association, 25 June 2005. Available from http://www.resolve.org/main/national/advocacy/insurance/facts/history.jsp?name=advocacy&tag=insurance.

"Making Babies: Will a New UK Law Stop People Donating Eggs and Sperm?" *New Scientist,* 12 March 2005.

Marketdata Enterprises, Inc. *U.S. Fertility Clinics & Infertility Services: An Industry Analysis.* August 2009.

"No Coverage through Work?" RESOLVE: The National Infertility Association, 13 March 2007. Available from http://www.resolve.org/site/PageServer?pagename=ta_ic_empmain.

O'Reilly, Kevin B. "Fertility Doctors Tighten Guidelines in Wake of Octomom Controversy." *AmedNews, 9 November 2009.*

"Patients Get the Present . . ." *Newsguide,* 10 July 2009. Available from http://www.newsguide.us/health-medical/general/Patients-Get-the-Present-When-Genetics-IVF-Institute-Celebrates-25th-Anniversary/ .

"Products." Organon International Inc., 26 June 2005. Available from http://www.organon.com/products/index.asp.

"Recombinant Products Make Strides in $1.5B Infertility Market." *Pharma Marketletter,* 23 May 2005.

Reynolds, Jesse. "CGS : Assisted Reproduction A New Line From the Fertility Industry?" *Biopolitical Times,* 21 October 2009. Available from http://geneticsandsociety.org/section.php%3Fid%3D89

"Success Rates." Jones Institute for Reproductive Medicine, November 2009. Available from http://www.jonesinstitute.org/success_ivf_rates.html.

"U.N. General Assembly Backs Cloning Ban. Nonbinding Resolution Approved After 4-Year Struggle." MSNBC.com, 8 March 2005. Available from http://msnbc.msn.com/id/7133378.

"U.S. 'Baby Business' (Infertility Services) Worth $4 Billion." 17 August 2009. Available athttp://www.tmcnet.com/usubmit/2009/08/17/4326513.htm.

"What We Do." RESOLVE: The National Infertility Association, 23 June 2005. Available from http://www.resolve.org/main/national/index.jsp?name=home.

"Young Women Seek Fertility Treatments." *Marketing to Women: Addressing Women and Women's Sensibilities,* August 2006.

Zepf, Bill. "Nationwide Success Rates at Fertility Clinics Are Increasing." *American Family Physician,* 1 February 2005.

FIBER OPTICS

———■———

SIC CODE(S)

1731

3357

8011

5065

INDUSTRY SNAPSHOT

Intense jockeying for market share in the high speed communications markets drove the breakneck rollout of fiber optics technology in the late 1990s as demand outstripped supply in many segments. When the technology industry crashed in late 2000, demand for fiber optics equipment and systems waned and the market began to suffer from overcapacity. However, many analysts began to once again view fiber optics as a growth market, driven by demand for broadband technology.

Rigging homes and small businesses with fat bandwidth fiber-optic cabling—known as fiber to the home (FTTH), or fiber to the premises (FTTP) in the case of businesses—was once considered extravagant and excessively costly. However, through 2009, it has enjoyed a steady and consistent presence within the overal broadband industry, with modest growth. Cable modems, the most common form of individual broadband access, typically made use of metal coaxial cables rather than fiber optic cables; and digital subscriber lines (DSL), an increasingly popular broadband technology, used traditional copper phone wires. This was beginning to change as telecommunication giants unveiled plans to bring fiber optic connections directly to more businesses and homes, providing high-speed voice, data, and video services.

Although DSL and cable still commanded a much greater share of the market, fiber to the home (FTTH) and fiber to the business (FTTB) remained a popular and growing architecture for broadband service delivery. In the wake of expanded broadband service rollouts by players such as AT&T and Verizon, as well as the desire for services such as Internet Protocol Television (IPTV) and video on demand (VOD), the technology was poised to experience rapid growth. A report from the research firm Parks Associates cited in the March 5, 2007, issue of *Broadcast Engineering* projected that the number of U.S. subscribers with fiber connections would reach 18 million by 2011, up from a base of 3 million.

Looking forward, the industry was expected to benefit from the overall growth in broadband. A report from In-Stat cited in the May 30, 2007, issue of *Telephony* projected that global broadband subscriptions would double by 2011, reaching 567 million. Of this total, some 10 percent of subscriptions were expected to be fiber to the home (FTTH), while DSL was expected to hold a much larger (58 percent) share of the market.

ORGANIZATION AND STRUCTURE

Fiber optics for telecommunications can be broadly cleaved into two industry segments: cable and equipment. While it's not exactly inexpensive compared to other transmission media, fiber-optic cable is largely a commodity and represented just 16 percent of the world's fiber-optic hardware market. The equipment side, which includes devices for transmitting, multiplexing, switching, amplifying, and decoding optical data, accounted for the other 84 percent. The larger segment also includes relatively low tech wares such as connectors and adapters. Companies that manufacture cable and equipment are usually separate from those that install fiber-optic networks and operate them.

Fiber-optic technologies are likewise used in a host of special instruments and other devices. These include medical instruments, industrial sensors, testing equipment, and a variety of other industrial applications.

Fiber Fabrication The manufacturing of optical fibers consists of coating the inner wall of a silica glass tube with 100 or more successive layers of thin glass. The tube is then heated to 2,000 degrees Celsius and stretched into a thin, flexible fiber. The result is called a clad fiber, which is approximately 0.0005 inches in diameter. By comparison, a human hair typically measures 0.002 inches.

Optical fibers operate on the principle of what is called total internal reflection. Every medium through which light can pass possesses a certain refractive index, the amount by which a beam of light is bent as it enters the medium. As the angle at which the light strikes the medium is decreased from the perpendicular, a point is reached at which the light is bent so much at the surface that it reflects completely back into the medium from which it originated. Thus the light will bounce back rather than escape.

In an optical fiber, total internal reflection is accomplished by a layer of material known as cladding that has a lower refractive index than glass alone. Once light enters the fiber, it is internally reflected by the cladding. This prevents light loss by keeping the beam of light zigzagging inside the glass core.

Markets and Applications The manufacturers sell their products to organizations that use fiber-optical equipment to supply a service such as telecommunications or cable television stations; to run an information/communication network, such as that used by the U.S. government; or to other industry segments for various uses. Businesses are turning to fiber optics when they install in-house computer networks, and at least one local government started wiring an entire city with fiber.

Since the invention of the telegraph in the nineteenth century, most data sent along lines has consisted of electrical impulses transmitted along copper wires. Fiber optics differs in two fundamental respects: the medium of transmission is a line of glass or plastic, not copper; and pulses of light, not electricity, are the means. Lasers send pulses of light down the glass strand in an information stream that can be either analog or digital. The stream is slightly faster than an electrical current on copper and it is unaffected by electrical disturbances that can create static in the line.

Different information streams travel down the same fiber strand separated by their wavelengths. The number of wavelengths available on a line determines how much information can be transmitted. That amount is referred to as the medium's bandwidth, and the essential difference between fiber-optic line and copper line is fiber-optic's enormously higher bandwidth. A fiber strand can transmit 4,200 times more information than copper at one time and transmit it thousands of times faster due to the higher volume of data that can be packed into the higher frequency wavelength. Copper relays, for example, can handle 24 simultaneous phone calls per second. By 2000, laser and fiber optics systems were nearing capacity. This capacity is increasingly important as videos, sound, and other space-hungry files get transmitted back and forth across the Internet. Copper can transmit a mere 64,000 bits per second compared to fiber-optic's 10 gigabits per second, or 10 billion bits. Higher bandwidth means not only more information but faster information. For example, a Web page that takes 70 seconds to load by copper will be nearly instantaneous by fiber, and an X-ray that requires 2.5 hours by conventional lines takes only 2 seconds on fiber.

BACKGROUND AND DEVELOPMENT

Medicine was the first application of fiber optics. In the late 1950s, Dr. Narinder S. Kapany hit upon the idea of building an endoscope capable of seeing around twists and turns in a patient's body by using fiber-optic bundles. His device, which came to be called the fiberscope, consisted of two bundles of fiber: one incoherent bundle, where there is no relationship between the order of fibers from one end of the bundle to the other; and one coherent bundle, in which the individual fibers have the same position at both ends of the bundle to carry a color image back to the physician.

Optical fibers were first used in telecommunications in the late 1960s when it became apparent that data transmitted by laser light could be broken up and absorbed by uncontrollable elements such as fog and snow. The first optical fibers produced contained flaws that resulted in significant amounts of light loss. To boost the range of the light signal, energized atoms from rare elements were used to amplify the signal at 1.54 micrometers, the wavelength at which the fibers are able to transmit light the farthest.

Paul Henson of United Telecommunications in Kansas was perhaps the first to gamble on fiber optics in the telecommunications field. He invested $1 billion in the late 1970s. By 1982, United Telecom had one of the largest fiber optic networks in the world, outstripping even AT&T.

The technology took off with the first deregulation of the telephone industry in 1982. Carriers competing with AT&T for long distance business, such as MCI and Sprint, began planning their own state of the art fiber-optic phone networks. By 1984 Henson was chairman of Sprint, which announced plans for a 100 percent fiber-optic long distance network. The same year, MCI laid its first fiber-optic line from Washington, D.C., to New York. By 1988, Sprint's entire network was fiber-optic and, in 1989, the company made the first transatlantic phone call along fiber-optic line. Currently, fiber-optic technology forms the backbone of the long distance telephone industry.

Full implementation of the Telecommunications Act of 1996 was expected to stimulate the industry. Passed in February of that year, the law completed the deregulation of the telecommunications industry that started with AT&T's breakup in the early 1980s. The law did away with the monopoly of local phone service that had been in place since 1934 and allowed anyone to compete in the market, including long distance servers, local companies, cable television companies, and utility companies. The law also reversed the AT&T consent decree that forbade regional Bell companies from providing long distance service or manufacturing telephone equipment. The law was intended to stimulate competition and the quick implementation of new technology. Fiber-optic companies were expected to benefit from the new situation.

Optical fibers have also been demonstrated as an ideal method of transmitting high-definition television (HDTV) signals. Because its transmissions contain twice as much information as those of conventional television, HDTV allows for much greater clarity and definition of picture. Standard transmission technology, however, is not capable of transmitting so much information at once. Using optical fibers, the HDTV signal can be transmitted as a digital light pulse, providing a nearly flawless image reproduction that is far superior to broadcast transmission.

While the conversion to fiber optics first began in earnest during the 1980s, spending on fiber and equipment escalated sharply in the 1990s. Every segment of the fiber-optic manufacturing industry was growing. From 1987 to 1997, fiber-optic cable was laid at a rate of about 4,000 miles a day; and by the late 1990s, more than 25 million miles of it had been installed. Nonetheless, 60 percent of that was "dead fiber," which is completely unused fiber optic line. The remainder was used at only a small fraction of its total capacity—a reflection of fiber's enormous potential.

As both national and local network build-outs continue, metropolitan areas are where most of the world's fiber cable is being laid. Statistics released by Corning Inc. cited that as much as 70 percent of all cable deployment in 1999, about 3 million miles, was for metropolitan area networks, including access lines for businesses and homes. A range of carriers has been targeting this market, including cable operators, local Bell companies, and independent

phone and data carriers. Fueling the expansion has been the insatiable appetite for Internet bandwidth as well as heightened interest in integrated communications packages. At the end of 2002, as the fiber optics industry began to slowly recover from the economic downturn, it was this type of local or "last mile" access that continued to fuel growth.

The challenge for the fiber optics industry was to replace old, cumbersome copper line systems with a faster, more powerful type of electronic transmission without interrupting or slowing down a service people have come to expect. Communications companies must also weigh the cost, load, and signal differences of upgrading and revamping obsolete switching equipment from copper to optical cable versus replacing everything with a completely new fiber-optic system.

A hybrid approach was considered the solution by the telecommunications industry. The plan was to use copper at one level and patch into fiber optics at another level. Later, the copper lines could be removed, and the system could be upgraded to fiber optics. Fiber-optic equipment is rapidly being installed for computer network backbone infrastructure based on asynchronous transfer mode optical switches, following the lead of the telecommunications industry. Nonetheless, not everyone sees copper as obsolete.

Costs and competitive dynamics will no doubt affect the rate and extent that fiber optics penetrate local access markets. Cable operators use fiber optics as the backbone of their TV systems, but generally use metal coaxial cables to connect individual customers to the network. They've already made significant strides toward offering cable Internet service. In addition, most of the big operators have unveiled some form of digital interactive TV or similar service (See also **Internet Service Providers**).

Some industry insiders believe a union between cable and copper wire phone carriers would be ideal. Cable companies would possess bandwidth-rich "dumb" networks or networks unencumbered by complex switching equipment. Phone companies, on the other hand, have extensive two-way networks—and money. Upgrades to digital cable in many metropolitan areas has narrowed the communications gap, affording some cable systems two-way capabilities, but the process has demanded vast sums of cash.

Meanwhile, phone companies and several independent carriers are aggressively pushing an alternative high speed data format that relies on old-fashioned copper phone wires. Known as digital subscriber line (DSL), the service involves upgrades at phone companies' central offices but lets consumers access high-bandwidth service using just a DSL modem and a phone line. DSL accounted for 33 percent of the 19.1 million U.S. broadband users in 2002.

The telecommunication industry was recovering following a period of several difficult years. In particular, the industry was looking to packages that offered bundled "triple play" services such as video, voice, and broadband Internet as a source of new growth. Fiber-optic leaders such as Corning claimed that fiber-optic cable was the medium of choice for service providers who were seeking to roll out these services to consumer markets. In addition to incredible bandwidth, they claimed that fiber-optic cable provided service providers with an infrastructure that was "future-proof."

The United States lagged behind many other nations in terms of penetration levels. For example, in mid-2005, data from Nielsen/NetRatings placed U.S. broadband penetration at 58.8 percent, while Canada enjoyed a rate of about 77 percent.

Rigging homes and small businesses with fat bandwidth fiber-optic cabling—known as fiber to the home (FTTH) or fiber to the premises (FTTP)—was once considered extravagant and excessively costly. However, it was beginning to gain considerable momentum by the middle of the first decade of the 2000s. Telecommunication giants such as Verizon and SBC unveiled plans to bring fiber-optic connections directly to more businesses and homes, providing high-speed voice, data, and video services.

Despite these ambitious plans, telecommunications providers faced a number of roadblocks. One particular sticking point were the franchise fees levied by individual communities that allow utilities and cable companies to run cables underground and on public land. As new service providers who would increase competition, "telcos" such as SBC argued that they should be exempt from such fees. Cable companies, which pay $2.4 billion in these fees annually, felt differently, claiming that any exemption would be unfair. Many cash-strapped municipalities also were calling on the telcos to pay up. While groups like the National Association of Telecommunications Officers & Advisors saw an unwillingness to pay as a violation of telecommunication law, some telcos claimed they were exempt from paying franchise fees based on an FCC ruling that freed voice over Internet telephone services from regulation at the local level. Moving ahead, this appeared to be an issue that would be interpreted by and resolved in the courts.

A second hurdle also involved cities and towns that telcos were trying to enter. While telcos sought to lay fiber-optic cable in upscale areas where customers could afford to pay for fiber-optic service, some cities called for the same "access for all" provision that regular telephone service and other utilities are subject to. In the midst of this situation, some rural and underserved areas of the United States were laying the groundwork to develop their own fiber-optic networks. Two such initiatives were OpportunityIowa, a $3.5 million non-profit group involving more than 80 communities in Iowa, and iTown Communications, a non-profit serving communities in West Virginia.

Optical Components: The Next Wave, a report from research firm CIR, estimated that optical components used for data communications and telecommunications would reach $6.6 billion by 2011, up from $1.5 billion in 2006, according to the September 2006 issue of *Lightwave*. In addition, a report from Infonetics Research revealed the global market for passive optical network (PON) equipment grew 71 percent in 2006, to $308 million, according to the May 2007 issue of *Lightwave*. Infonetics Research Analyst Jeff Heynen explained, "Service providers of all shapes and sizes are pushing fiber deeper into their access networks to support the demand for video, online gaming, P2P networking, and other bandwidth-intensive applications."

CURRENT CONDITIONS

As of August 2009, there were 227 million Internet users in the United States, or roughly 74 percent of the population, according to Nielsen Online. Internet broadband provider companies and Leichtman Research Group, Inc. reported that as of June 30, 2009, total broadband subscribers totaled about 69.9 million nationally.

Broadband penetration was a topic highlighted in President Obama's American Recovery and Reinvestment Act, signed into law in early 2009. The Act provided a total of $7.2 billion to the Commerce Department's National Telecommunications and Information Administration (NTIA) and the U.S. Department of Agriculture's Rural Utilities Service (RUS) to accelerate broadband deployment in areas of the country that have been without the high-speed infrastructure; the national broadband plan was due to Congress in February 2010.

In August 2009, comScore, Inc. released a study on broadband growth in rural, micropolitan and metropolitan areas in the United States. Results indicated that while broadband penetration was much higher in the metropolitan and micropolitan areas, broadband had experienced the most significant gains in rural areas during the prior two years, growing 16 percent in this time.

Although DSL and cable still commanded a much greater share of the market, fiber to the home (FTTH) and fiber to the business (FTTB) remained a popular and growing architecture for broadband service delivery. In the wake of expanded broadband service rollouts by players such as AT&T and Verizon, as well as the desire for the services Internet Protocol Television (IPTV) and video on demand (VOD), the technology was poised to experience rapid growth. A report from the research firm Parks Associates cited in the March 5, 2007, issue of *Broadcast*

Engineering projected that the number of U.S. subscribers with fiber connections would reach 18 million by 2011, up from a base of 3 million. In fact, according to the latest update to the global ranking of FTTH/B economies, jointly issued by the three FTTH Councils, the number of FTTH/B subscribers grew 15 percent in the first six months of 2009, with more than 5.5 million new subscribers added worldwide.

According to a 2009 MarketResearch report, the fiber-optic cable maufacturing sector of the industry brought in $1.9 billion in revenues for 2008. Author Asif Anwar, in his August 2009 report, *Fiber Optic Analog IC Market Forecast 2008-2013,* noted that "Consumer demand for high bandwidth applications like VOD, HDTV, high speed internet access and social networking, coupled with traffic demands from emerging 3G and 4G networks has created a re-birth of the fiber optic market." To satisfy these needs, said Anwar, 10 Gbps (gigabits per second) networks will become the de facto standard network. Moreover, 40 Gbps networks will also appreciate dramatic growth. Anwar forecast that the overall market for analog ICs (TIAs, laser drivers, limiting amps) will grow to $492 million during his forecast period.

INDUSTRY LEADERS

Corning Corning Inc., one of the founders of fiber optics, remains the world's leader in the production and sale of fiber-optic cable. In 2000 the company solidified its lead in that market with the purchase of Siemens AG's fiber optics units, and the combined businesses were christened Corning Cable Services. The company, which has deep roots in the glass industry, averaged nearly 20 million miles of cable annually during the late 1990s. The acquisition of Rochester Photonics Corp. (with 1998 revenue at $3 million) gave Corning access to new fiber-optic technology such as "microlenses," which increased network performance through improved in-fiber laser focus and had transmitters and receivers that were more temperature resistant. The company reported 2008 revenues of $5.9 billion, with 23,000 employees worldwide.

Alcatel-Lucent Lucent Technologies Inc. of Murray Hill, New Jersey was split off from AT&T in November 1995. It took with it about three-quarters of the world-famous Bell Labs and went on to become one of the leading designers and manufacturers of conventional and wireless telecommunications equipment as well as fiber optics. In late 2006, Lucent was acquired by Alcatel in an $11.6 billion deal. The company remains one of the world's leading producers of fiber cable, and it also produces a variety of other fiber-optic components, systems, and fiber/copper telecommunications systems.

Lucent's fiber-optic production grew fivefold between 1991 and 1999. In 1999 the company agreed to supply its TrueWave RS fiber for Viatel Inc.'s European Network, an ambitious project to link several major European cities. That endeavor was followed in 2000 with Lucent's hefty $3 billion purchase of Ortel Corp., a producer of opto-electronic components that allow speedy two-way communications over cable TV systems. Analysts viewed the latter move as a strategic commitment to serving the fiber-optic needs of the cable TV broadband market. The Alcatel-Lucent total revenue for 2008 was $16.98 billion (euro), a slight year-on-year decline.

Ciena Ciena Corp. of Linthicum, Maryland, is a smaller developer of optical networking gear. The company's primary products are dense wavelength division multiplexing (DWDM) systems for leading telecommunications companies. DWDM systems give optical fiber the ability to carry up to 40 times more data, voice, and graphic information than usual. The company is also a major supplier of erbium-doped fiber amplifiers, one of the key technologies in the change to a 100 percent optical system. In 2000 the company made two major acquisitions, Omnia Communications Inc. and Lightera Networks Inc., two other fiber-optic equipment makers, after which sales plunged. Ciena reported 2008 revenues of $902 million, following its acquisition of World Wide Packets, a supplier of carrier Ethernet switches, for $300 million earlier in the year.

ADC Telecommunications ADC Telecommunications Inc. of Eden Prairie, Minnesota, is a leader in the design and manufacture of fiber-optic connectivity products, including routers, switches, transmitters, receivers, couplers, patch cords, panels, and Internet working products. The company has customers in the public, private, and government sectors, as well as foreign nations building telecommunications infrastructures. Net sales fell 56 percent in 2002, to $1.04 billion. This decline had worsened by 2004, when sales totaled $784.3 million. In addition to sales to the regional Bell companies, ADC has made acquisitions and has entered the wireless and international markets. ADC reported full year revenues of $1.5 billion for 2008, representing a 10.4 percent growth.

JDS Uniphase Formed in the 1999 merger between Uniphase Corp. and JDS FITEL Ltd., JDS Uniphase Corp. is a major manufacturer of both passive and active fiber-optic components. Its line includes lasers, switches, transmitters, and amplifiers. The company went on a buying spree in the wake of the 1999 merger, the biggest deal coming in 2000 with the $15 billion acquisition of E-Tek Dynamics, another equipment maker. The rich price was made possible by JDS Uniphase's high-flying stock, which had been a favorite on Wall Street because of the industry's expected growth rate. Fiscal 2009 revenues (ending June 27, 2009) were $1.29 million, with the company undergoing major restructure.

AMERICA AND THE WORLD

As of June 2009, according to the FTTH (fiber to the home) Councils of Asia-Pacific, Europe, and North America, at least 21 global economies had more than one percent of households with an FTTH/B connection. All of the top 10 ranked economies (including the United States) had more than 5 percent of their households connected with FTTH/B. The Asia-Pacific region still leads the global ranking with South Korea, Hong Kong, Japan, and Taiwan taking the first four places, followed by the Nordic countries of Sweden and Norway.

FTTH was responsible for some 65 percent of the European fiber-optic market, according to a KMI Research report cited in the September 2006 issue of *Lightwave*. The remainder of growth was attributed to fiber deployments to network nodes and buildings. In particular, municipal utilities and municipalities were the key drivers of growth, especially in rural areas overlooked by existing service providers.

Japan's FTTH market was especially strong during the late years of the first decade of the 2000s, according to the January 2007 issue of *Lightwave*. Based on a report from Tokyo's Yano Research Institute Ltd., FTTH subscriptions increased 88 percent from March of 2005 to March of 2006, reaching 5.4 million. The firm attributed this increase to explosive demand for Internet telephone service, which had become more affordable than regular phone service, as well as falling broadband fees. By 2011, Japan was expected to have 27 million FTTH subscribers, representing half of the country's households.

One promising market for fiber-optic providers was Asia. Compared to relatively mature Internet markets like Europe and the United States, approximately 70 percent of Asian Internet backbones were upgraded in 2003. In its December 2004 issue, *Laser Focus World* reported that "a huge portion of international fiberoptic bandwidth still goes unused, according to TeleGeography. On trans-Atlantic routes, for example, only about a quarter of currently lit capacity is actively deployed to carry voice, Interent, and corporate traffic. The remainder lies idle, either unsold or unused by service providers." The publication indicated that this supply imbalance would likely exist for a number of years.

The United States had a significant lead on foreign companies in the fiber optics race. The U.S. companies Corning and Lucent sold about 80 percent of the world's fiber cable, and companies such as Ciena and ADC were at the cutting edge with erbium doped fiber amplifiers (EDFA) and dense wavelength division multiplexing technology. Two European companies, Pirelli of Italy and Alcatel Telecom of France, were involved in development and production to the same extent as the leading American firms. Pirelli introduced the first commercial erbium doped fiber amplifier (EDFA) through its North American subsidiary in North Carolina. The company once formed a partnership with MCI to install wavelength division multiplexing (WDM) technology on a fiber-optic line from St. Louis to Chicago. Alcatel produces EDFA and WDM as well, but its penetration into the American market has not been as pronounced. The annual revenue growth for optical transmission systems in Europe was estimated at 40 percent in the early years of the first decade of the 2000s.

Countries that have virtually no existing telecommunications networks are a major market—perhaps the primary market—for fiber optics. The People's Republic of China was a major consumer of optical cable and required millions of core kilometers of fiber optics, buying wavelength division multiplexing (WDM) systems from Lucent and Japan's NEC. Alcatel and Fujitsu Ltd. were preparing an18,000-mile undersea WDM cable that would run from Australia and New Zealand to the United States and then loop back through Hawaii and Fiji to Australia.

RESEARCH AND TECHNOLOGY

Asif Anwar, in his August 2009 report, *Fiber Optic Analog IC Market Forecast 2008-2013,* noted that GaAs, Silicon CMOS, SiGe and InP devices will all compete for market share with the market for compound semiconductor devices driven by higher value, higher growth market demand from 10Gbps and above. Two technological breakthroughs had transformed fiber optics to meet this expected demand: the erbium-doped fiber amplifier (EDFA) and wavelength division multiplexing (WDM). The EDFA grew out of the fundamental incompatibility of electronics and fiber optics. The optical pulses must be amplified as they travel along the fiber or else they dissipate and no longer register as signals. In the past, because they could not match fiber optics' larger bandwidth, electronic amplifiers acted as a bottleneck on the fiber-optic flow. Bell Laboratories demonstrated that a short length of fiber treated with the mineral erbium and excited with a laser acted as an optical amplifier. With the use of this type of system, electronics are no longer necessary and fiber optics' huge data capability can be exploited in full.

Wavelength division multiplexing (WDM) was developed at Bell Labs in the mid-1980s. In WDM, laser signals generate light pulses that can be as short as a billionth of a second in length. Each wavelength opened can be used to transmit data. The first WDMs opened transmission lines that could carry up to 2.5 gigabits per second (Gbps). They were integrated into the standard fiber-optic systems. In the early 1990s, researchers discovered dense wavelength division multiplexing, which squeezes more pulses into shorter wavelengths. At the decade's end, amplifier design advances such as Lucent's WaveStar Optical Line System 400G expanded the operating region, thus bringing more than 40 channels operating at 10 Gbps each.

A number of interesting fiber-optic developments were taking place on the military front. These included a partnership between Morristown, New Jersey-based Honeywell International and Allentown, Pennsylvania-based SiOptical to develop components for next generation communications networks.

Smaller companies also were involved in military fiber-optic research initiatives. For example, Middletown, Rhode Island-based KVH Industries was awarded a $730,000 Phase II Small Business Innovation Research grant to continue developing its ActiveFiber technology. According to the November 2004 issue of *Laser Focus World,* this technology "uses the company's patented D-shaped fiber and electro-optic polymers to create components inside the fiber itself, making the fiber an active element within an optical system." There was continued development of KVH's "fiberoptic gyro-based inertial measurement unit technology" as well as its vehicle navigation system used by the military in Afghanistan and Iraq.

In addition to military applications, fiber-optic technology also was being developed for homeland security purposes. For example, Northrop Grumman was testing a harbor defense system called Centurion that used fiber-optic sonar sensors to detect potential incoming surface or underwater threats—even individual divers. According to the January 2005 issue of *Laser Focus World,* the system used fiber-optic hydrophone array technology that, while providing wide-area coverage, had low power requirements. The publication explained that "The next step in maturation of the technology involves optimizing the fiber-optic sonar arrays for the harbor environment, integrating additional sensors into the system, and demonstrating the enhanced integrated harbor picture that results from these improvements."

The development of plastic optical fiber brought a number of advantages over glass. It is less expensive to produce and easier to work with as well as being equal to glass in performance, flexibility, and reliability. Landmark discoveries continue to flow from the laboratory to the marketplace. Where most were impressed by the terabit (1 trillion bits) speeds reached in 1996, Alastair Glass, head of photonics research at Bell Labs, envisioned the day when one fiber optic cable carries thousands of WDM beams with a capacity of 200 terabits per second, enough to transmit all the contents of the Library of Congress within one second.

BIBLIOGRAPHY

ADC Telecommunications. Available from http://investing. businessweek.com/research/stocks/.

Alcatel-Lucent. 4 February 2009. Available from http:// www.channelweb.co.uk/cm/news/2235716/alcatel-lucent-2008-losses-top 5bn/.

Anwar, Asif. *Fiber Optic Analog IC Market Forecast 2008-2013.* 4 August 2009.

Ciena. Available from http://www.straightstocks.com/stock-watch/ciena-takes-over-nortels-unit/.

"Corning Sees Bright Future Fiber to the Premises." *Laser Focus World,* March 2005.

"Fiber-Optic Costs Lower Than Expected." *Underground Construction,* December 2004.

"Fiberoptic Sonar Sensors Detect Harbor Threats." *Laser Focus World,* January 2005.

Fleck, Ken. "Optical Downturn: Not a Pretty View." *Electronic News,* 29 April 2002.

Fuller, Meghan. "European Municipalities Lead FTTH Charge." *Lightwave,* September 2006.

———. "FTTH Boosts Overall Optical Market Growth in Japan." *Lightwave,* January 2007.

Grow, Brian, Roger O. Crockett, and Cathy Yang. "The Fiber-Optic Quagmire." *Business Week,* 6 December 2004.

Gubbins, Ed. "Broadband Subscriber Base to Double by 2011." *Telephony,* 30 May 2007.

Hardy, Stephen M. "Counting Chickens." *Lightwave,* May 2007.

"Honeywell and SiOptical Target Next-Generation Networks." *Laser Focus World,* November 2004.

"Internet Growth Slows in USA, Europe." *Laser Focus World,* December 2004.

"JDSU Announces Fiscal 2009 Fourth Quarter and Year End Results." Press Release, 19 August 2009. Available from http://www.jdsu.com/news/news-release/2009/jdsu-announces-fiscal-2009-fourth-quarter.

"KVH Secures $1 Million in Defense Contracts." *Laser Focus World,* November 2004.

MarketResearch Inc. *Fiber Optic Cable Manufacturing Industry.* Available from http://www.marketresearch.com/procut/display.asp%3Fproductid%3D2432144.

"Optical Components Market to Net $6.6 Billion by 2011." *Lightwave,* September 2006.

Pease, Bob. "Optical WDM Networking Takes to the Air." *Fiberoptic Product News,* July 2004.

Tanner, John C. "Fiber Comes Home." *Telecom Asia,* May 2005.

"United States Broadband Statistics Update." August 2009. Available from http://www.internetworldstats.com/am/us.htm

"US-Canadian Broadband Penetration Gap at 20 Points—US Broadband Penetration Crawls to 58.8% in May-June 2005 Bandwidth Report." *WebSiteOptimization.com,* 2 August 2005. Available from http://www.websiteoptimization.com/bw/0506.

"U.S. Fiber Optic Market to Grow 10 Percent Annually Through 2006, Reaching $22 Billion." *Lightwave,* October 2002.

"U.S. Fiber Subscribers to Hit 18 Million by 2011." *Broadcast Engineering,* 5 March 2007.

"Verizon: Time for FTTP Is Now." *Underground Construction,* December 2004.

"Worldwide PON Equipment Neared $1b in 2006." *Lightwave,* May 2007.

Yang, Catherine and Ira Sager. "Hometown Broadband Heroes." *Business Week,* 22 November 2004.

FINANCIAL PLANNING SERVICES

SIC CODE(S)

6282

8748

INDUSTRY SNAPSHOT

Financial planning is a holistic approach to personal financial management that has flourished since the mid-1980s. Rising levels of wealth and consumer sophistication about finances have fueled the upswing, as has deregulation of the financial services industry. Experts predict the pace of growth will remain brisk, and even increase, as baby boomers near retirement and as large institutions target planning services at middle and lower income people.

The financial planning industry has experienced a number of significant trends. These included millions of baby boomers who were not adequately prepared for retirement, Social Security benefits that were expected to run out of funding by 2042, a volatile stock market, and skyrocketing health care costs. Perhaps most significantly, the responsibility for retirement planning was rapidly shifting to the individual and away from employers. This boded well for financial planners, who were faced with the difficult task of helping people from a wide range of demographic and socioeconomic backgrounds make difficult choices about an uncertain future.

Nevertheless, the 2008–2009 economic downturn clearly hurt many associations that represent financial planners, investment advisers, and big brokerages, according to Sara Hansard in her November 9, 2009, article for *Investment News*. Membership fell about 10 percent at both the Financial Planning Association (FPA) and the Investment Adviser Association (IAA), and was off slightly at the Securities Industry and Financial Markets Association. The National Association of Personal Financial Advisors (NAPFA) also experienced a slowed membership growth as well as a loss of conference revenues.

Scope of Activities. Financial planners, sometimes called advisers, analyze a person's complete financial situation and develop a strategy to optimize personal resources and meet life goals. They consider a number of factors, including income, assets, present and future expenses and investments, as well as personal data such as age, health, and number of dependents. Planners use the detailed information they get from meeting with clients to make financial recommendations, including advice on budgeting, saving, insurance, taxes, investments, and retirement planning. They often assist customers by directly managing assets. Some financial planners focus on only one financial issue, but most work on many.

Financial planning services originated in the early 1960s. It wasn't until 1970, however, that the first fee-only planners—now a quasi-standard—appeared. As an industry, financial planning came of age as the United States' corporations gradually replaced traditional corporation-managed pension plans with employee-managed 401(k)s and other retirement savings alternatives, forcing individuals to take on more responsibility for long-term fiscal planning. Concerns about the viability of Social Security and Medicare, coupled with growth in the number of small businesses and the self-employed, have forced many individuals who had given very little thought to retirement planning to become more knowledgeable about estate plans, insurance, home ownership, taxes, and the multitude of new financial products and investments.

Brisk Growth The number of firms and individuals offering various forms of consumer financial advice has skyrocketed since the late 1980s. Because there is neither a single definition of what a financial planner is nor a consistent set of boundaries between the profession and related activities such as investment advising or accounting, estimates of the industry's size vary considerably. A 1997 *Barron's* report pegged the count of financial planning firms at 25,000, while more recent estimates entertain figures as high as 300,000 for the total number of professionals offering financial advice. The number of those with formal accreditation is much smaller. The Certified Financial Planner Board of Standards, one of the largest and most visible professional licensure bodies for the industry, reported over 42,200 active licensees in 2003, a figure nearly four times that of the mid-1980s. By 2007 this number had grown even more, exceeding 55,000.

The growth of the financial planning industry parallels the increasing accumulation of assets by Americans and greater sophistication about investments. The change in savings patterns illustrates the trend. The 61 percent of personal savings that were held in banks, savings and loans, and credit unions during the 1970s had declined to less than 38 percent by the mid-1990s. Through pension and mutual funds, households and businesses increasingly participate in huge, diversified portfolios of stocks, bonds, real estate, and even commodities. As reported in the *Washington Times,* pollster Peter Hart said that it took 25 years for stock ownership among Americans to double, from 10.4 percent in 1965 to 21.1 percent in 1990, and that it took only seven years for stock ownership to double again. The article also reported that by the end of 2001, 51.9 percent of U.S. families owned stock, marking the first time that more than half of U.S. households owned stocks; that most of these families owned stock indirectly through their retirement funds; and that only 21.3 percent of families owned stock directly.

As rising wealth widened demand for financial planning, large financial services firms jockeyed for shares of the highly fragmented market. Such captains of finance as Citigroup and American Express launched new financial planning services in the late 1990s and the early years of the first decade of the 2000s, and tax preparation giant H&R Block was readying a major retail thrust that could make planning service outlets as ubiquitous as its tax centers. Even discount broker Charles Schwab forayed into planning-related territory by rolling out a planner referral service for its investment clients. Meanwhile, some smaller firms that specialized in planning began to merge and consolidate in hopes of building a more recognizable presence in this traditionally localized business.

Competency Concerns Increasing apprehension over the competency and legitimacy of individuals practicing financial advising has accompanied the industry's growth. As a *Barron's* writer quipped, "Can't cut it as a hairstylist? Try financial planning." In the absence of universal professional or legal credentials distinguishing financial planners, several professional organizations and recent laws have sought to impose a baseline of competency and heighten public awareness of the meaning of a bewildering array of financial planning credentials.

ORGANIZATION AND STRUCTURE

Financial planning is the process of establishing financial goals and creating a way to realize them. The process involves taking stock of all personal resources and needs, developing a plan to manage them, and systematically implementing the plan to achieve financial objectives. Financial planning is an ongoing process. A plan must be monitored and reviewed periodically so that adjustments can be made to assure that it continues to meet individual needs.

The profession involves expertise (or access to experts) in various disciplines such as estate planning, taxation, benefit plans, pension plans, insurance, investments, and real estate. Thus the consumer financial planning market has come to be fragmented across several disparate service professions in addition to those just practicing planning, and many of these services specialize in certain aspects of financial planning to the exclusion of others.

The Certified Financial Planner Board's Web site, www.cfp.net, provides a wealth of information for those confused by the many definitions of "financial planner." There were more than 55,000 certified financial planner (CFP) licensees working in the United States in 2007. According to the CFP Board, the following list of professions may provide financial planning services: Accountant, Broker/Dealer, Certified Financial Planner Licensee or CFP Practitioner, Chartered Financial Analyst (CFA), Chartered Financial Consultant, Estate Planning Professional, Fee-based Financial Adviser, Fee-only Financial Adviser, Financial Adviser, Financial Consultant, Financial Counselor, Financial or Securities Analyst, Financial Planner, Insurance Agent, Investment Adviser, Investment Adviser Representative, Investment Consultant, Money Manager, Personal Financial Specialist, Portfolio Manager, Real Estate Broker, Registered Investment Adviser, Registered Representative, and Stockbroker

Adding to the confusion about the variety of financial planning services, a CFP Board survey showed that consumers have many misconceptions about the role of a financial planner. The survey, conducted in February 1999 by Bruskin-Goldring Research for the CFP Board, was nationwide and included 1,016 adults. Among the misconceptions, 36 percent of those surveyed believed that financial planners would automatically put their assets into the best-performing stocks and mutual funds; 17 percent expected assurances from a financial planner that they would become rich; another 16 percent expected that they would be asked to pay up front for a financial planner's services.

Fees and Commissions Financial planners are paid in a variety of ways, usually depending on the planner's affiliations. The methods are fee only, commission only, fee offset, combination fee/commission, and salary. Ethical standards mandate that planners disclose who pays them if they are earning commissions, but this is not always observed.

Aside from fee only, the balance of these payment schemes imply that financial planning is being offered in conjunction with other products or services such as investment brokering, banking, accounting, or underwriting. These planners are often described as product-driven, as opposed to fee-only planners who are called process-driven. Less delicately put, critics of financial planners who accept commissions call them salespeople, not advisers.

Because fee-only planners are paid by the client and don't receive commissions, they have fewer conflicts of interest when they recommend investment vehicles and thus are sometimes considered more impartial than other types of planners. Still, despite a major push in the industry toward fee-only compensation, the most common pay structure among CFP certificate holders is combination fee and commission.

The problem of identifying a planner's potential conflicts of interest is aggravated by a dearth of openness and clarity about the compensation of many planners. Guy Halverson, writing in the *Christian Science Monitor,* described the results of a study released in 1997 by the Consumer Federation of America and the National Association of Personal Financial Advisors, the trade association for fee-only planners (which has trademarked the phrase "fee only"). Of 288 Washington, D.C.-area planners and firms in a random survey, "two-thirds claimed to offer fee-only services. Of those, three out of five were earning commissions or other financial incentives from undisclosed third parties, such as mutual fund companies or insurance firms." Consumer wariness about conflicts of interest may be part of the reason for a planner's reluctance to reveal sources of income, the study suggested. The organization has been perhaps the most aggressive advocate of true fee-only planning and has developed visibility programs such as its Fiduciary Oath and the fee-only trademark to make consumers aware of the distinction.

Regardless of the type of planner retained, fees can vary widely. An article in *Money* magazine by Ruth Simon reported that fee-only advisers often charge a flat fee to develop a plan, typically from $500 to $6,000, depending on complexity. Hourly fees range between $75 and $225, and the average for certified financial planners is about $120. Some use a sliding scale, charging more to customers with higher incomes or greater assets. Many also charge an annual fee equal to .5 percent to 1.5 percent of total assets to manage a portfolio.

Regulation In part reflecting the fragmented market, government regulation of financial planning has been uneven and complex. That, however, is changing. A law amending federal securities laws, the National Securities Market Improvement Act, became effective 8 July 1997 and divided regulation between the federal government and the states. Firms with $25 million or more in managed assets remain under the jurisdiction of the U.S. Securities and Exchange Commission (SEC), while the remaining investment advisers, an estimated 16,500, revert to state regulation.

In the past, some states licensed advisers. Financial planners were not required to register with the SEC unless they recommended specific stocks or bonds, in which case they had to be registered investment advisers. The SEC required no test, however, with the result that registration reflected little about the adviser's competency. Applicants simply paid a fee and submitted a form listing their disciplinary history, educational background, and investment philosophy. Even as many states do not require licensure of financial planners, most state securities agencies do not regulate individuals associated with investment of financial planning firms, whether or not those firms are registered with the SEC or with a state agency.

Under the new regulations, the SEC retained jurisdiction within any state that had not enacted its own regulations but had no plans for testing or enforcing competency requirements. Many states, however, have begun to coordinate some testing requirements for new entrants to the field. As of June 1998, the American Institute of Certified Public Accountants reported that 15 states had a 150-hour education requirement for planners in effect with another 29 scheduled to follow suit on a future date; and that in addition, 22 states prohibit commissions and contingent fees.

The states present a mixed picture. David Weidner wrote in a *Wall Street Journal* report that some are adapting faster than others to the new order of things, saying, "Pennsylvania, along with [Connecticut and Washington], is considered a model in dealing with the new responsibility." Like Connecticut and Washington, Weidner said, Pennsylvania had an active regulatory agency that worked with the SEC before the act went into effect.

Associations Professional associations have been key to developing standards of ethics and raising the bar for who qualifies as a financial planner. A number of associations have emerged to promote education, expertise, professionalism, and ethics in the field. These groups provide professional financial planners with information and continuing education. Many will also recommend reliable firms and individuals who are knowledgeable in financial planning.

The Financial Planning Association (FPA), www. fpanet.org, was formed in 2000 through the merger of two of the industry's foremost associations, the Institute of Certified Financial Planners (ICFP) and the International Association for Financial Planning (IAFP). Although the two organizations, which were roughly the same size, had previously disagreed on licensing and other matters, in 1999 they agreed to merge. The ICFP had allowed only members who held the CFP designation or were in the process of getting it, whereas the IAFP consisted of a more diverse group. Under the merger, the FPA was opened to non-CFP holders as well, although members were encouraged to seek the designation.

The Association for Financial Counseling and Planning Education (AFCPE), www.afcpe.org, headquartered in Upper Arlington, Ohio, is a nonprofit professional organization comprised of researchers, academics, financial counselors, and planners. The AFCPE administers certification programs for financial counselors, including the national Accredited Financial Counselor program, as well as certification programs for housing counselors, including Accredited Housing Counselor and Certified Housing Counselor. It offers education and training programs at an annual conference and publishes a professional journal devoted to financial counseling and planning, as well as a newsletter with a guide to resources, including Web sites, publications, and industry trends.

The CFA Institute (formerly the Association for Investment Management and Research) had 94,588 members in 133 countries as of 2007. The organization, which grants the prestigious Chartered Financial Analyst designation, sets the highest standards in education, ethics, and advocacy for investment professionals, their employers, and their clients.

The Certified Financial Planner Board of Standards Inc. (CFP Board) was founded in 1985. The CFP Board administers the CFP exam and regulates professional behavior for holders of that credential. It creates professional and ethical standards and disciplines CFP holders who violate its tenets.

Members of the National Association of Independent Public Finance Advisors (NAIPFA), www.naipfa. com, include firms that specialize in financial advice on bond sales and financial planning to public agencies. Headquartered in Montgomery, Illinois, the NAIPFA seeks to build credibility and recognition of financial advisory firms and maintains high ethical and professional standards. It maintains a board of review to ensure member compliance with standards, provides educational materials to independent financial advisers, and responds to legislative needs of member firms and the public agencies they serve.

Founded in 1983, the National Association of Personal Financial Advisors (NAPFA) is headquartered in Arlington Heights, Illinois. With more than 1,000 members and affiliates in 50 states, it serves as a network for fee-only planners to discuss practice management, client services, and investment selections. The association works to encourage and advance the practice of fee-only planning by developing the skills of members, increasing awareness of fee-only financial planning, and fostering interaction with other professional groups.

The Registered Financial Planners Institute (RFPI) is headquartered in Amherst, Ohio. The institute promotes professionalism in financial planning for individuals and businesses. RFPI offers classroom seminars and correspondence courses and sponsors a research program and referral service. The institute bestows the designation of Registered Financial Planner (RFP) on qualified members.

The Society of Financial Service Professionals (SFSP) is headquartered in Bryn Mawr, Pennsylvania. SFSP was formerly the American Society of CLU & ChFC. It is a national membership organization representing 23,000 financial services professionals who have earned the chartered life underwriter or chartered financial consultant designation from the American College also in Bryn Mawr. Members specialize in estate planning, investments, tax planning, wealth accumulation, and life and health insurance.

The financial planning industry faced a number of significant trends during the late years of the first decade of the 2000s. Perhaps the most pressing issue was that Americans were simply not saving for their golden years, or saving enough. According to the Principal Financial Well-Being Index, released by the Principal Financial Group and Harris Interactive, 42 percent of adult workers in the United States save between 5 and 10 percent of their pay for retirement, falling short of the 15 percent needed to replace 85 percent of their income after the conclusion of their working years. A mere 8 percent of workers were saving the recommended amount. Another 21 percent of eligible employees choose not to participate in their employer-sponsored 401(k) plan at all. The top regret among working adults (45 percent) and retirees (32 percent) was starting to save for retirement too late.

This trend was especially evident among the approximately 76 million baby boomers who were approaching retirement age. However, due to poor saving habits, many boomers were not adequately prepared for retirement. According to one estimate, some 65 percent of this demographic group had not saved sufficiently for retirement at the traditional age of 65. Additionally, boomers were more likely to have racked up higher levels of debt than past generations. In its July 25, 2005 issue, *Business Week* reported that of those households headed by individuals aged 50 to 59, some 50 percent had $10,000 or less in a 401(k) account.

While this was an important consideration for financial planners of all stripes, more significant issues loomed on the horizon. In addition to Social Security benefits that were expected to run out of funding by 2042, as well as a more volatile stock market, the responsibility for retirement planning was rapidly shifting to the individual and away from employers that once offered generous pension plans. In fact, one estimate indicated that a mere 12.5 percent of employees will be guaranteed a pension by 2025.

Exacerbating the burden of individual responsibility for health care were rising life expectancies. According to some observers, many individuals were not cognizant of the fact that they would be living much longer than previous generations. This poses the very real possibility of one outliving his or her retirement savings. Faced with this challenge, financial companies were struggling to develop investment products that provided retirees with adequate security.

In addition to these burdens, many Baby Boomers were contending with the need to care for and support elderly parents, and pay college tuition for their children. Outlays such as these often put a strain on retirement savings. Because of the significant financial impact these situations were expected to have, many financial planners were preparing to have serious conversations with their clients.

The need to save more for retirement was not limited only to Baby Boomers. Generations X and Y, as well as the so-called Millennials, which will constitute the majority of the U.S. workforce by 2050, also needed to save more According to data from the Employee Benefits Research Institute, cited in the December 1, 2006, issue of *Employee Benefit News,* approximately 33 percent of those aged 21 to 30 participated in their company's 401(k) plan. The publication cited challenges such as college loan payoffs and credit card debt, as well as a tendency to focus on immediate gratification, as roadblocks that hindered younger people from saving for their future.

Looking ahead, the only certain thing appeared to be that, as a whole, individuals were being challenged to assume more responsibility for and invest more heavily in their own retirement than ever before. This boded well for financial planners, who were faced with the difficult task of helping people from a wide range of demographic and socioeconomic backgrounds make difficult choices about an uncertain future.

CURRENT CONDITIONS

According to First Research, Inc., there were about 25,000 U.S. companies engaged in financial planning and advising in 2009. Their combined annual revenues were approximately

$115 billion. On a global level, in March 2009, the Financial Planning Standards Board Ltd. (FPSB) announced that the number of CFP (certified financial planner) professionals had roughly doubled in the previous eight years to a 2009 total of 118,506, concentrated in about 20 global territories. The majority of them (59,676), according to FPSB, were doing business outside of the United States. Certification and/or professional affiliation of planners and advisors is increasingly requested or demanded.

The severe rise in national unemployment in 2009, coupled with the downturned economy stemming from a year earlier, created both problems and business for the industry. In his December 2009 article for *Financial Planning* magazine, Robert Menchaca noted that data showed the Dow Jones Index finished 2008 down 35 percent, while the S&P 500 and Nasdaq were off even more, nearly 40 percent. However, since the market low in March 2009, all of the major indices/indexes have been up over 50 percent. That kind of roller-coast ride has led investors to second-guess their planners, their plans, and their futures. The historic reliance on a portfolio heavy with stocks and bonds, such as 60/40 splits, was giving way to the old but often ignored rule of heavy diversification.

The bank failures also triggered an interest in having the industry more regulated. In late 2008, the FPA, NAPFA, and the Certified Financial Planning Board coalesced to lobby Congress for a more clearly-defined and regulated financial planning industry, much opposed by securities and investment concerns. Among issues dividing the groups was the desire for a statutory definition of "fiduciary." Increasingly, stockbroker arbitration was being invoked to help investors who had lost money due to ineptitude or stock fraud on the part of financial advisors, and professional malpractice suits were on the rise. In March 2009, investment banker Bernard ("Bernie") Madoff pleaded guilty to essentially creating false investment accounts and privately pocketing funds received from investors, periodically paying returns to some of them with money received from other prospective investors under a giant "Ponzi" scheme. He was sentenced to 150 years in prison in June 2009. In connection with this case, the accounting firm of Friehling & Horowitz and its partner David G. Friehling, C.P.A. were also charged with fraud and various SEC violations for falsely representing that they had conducted legitimate company audits of Madoff's investment firm over the years, when in fact they had not.

RESEARCH AND TECHNOLOGY

Beyond impersonal online advice systems that dish out recommendations based on prefabricated problems and solutions, some planning services companies envision a future where a majority of planners and advisors will videoconference with customers over the Web via home personal computers and public kiosks. Another possibility for the service would be to bring together several specialists—say a lawyer, an accountant, and an insurance broker—to work together with a customer instead of making the client visit each one separately. Real-time information from the exchanges and faster access to global markets will make the industry challenging but rewarding for those who demand the best.

BIBLIOGRAPHY

"2010-2015: The Future of Financial Planning." *Financial Planning,* April 2005.

Becker, Ramey "CFP Certification Top Choice for Financial Planners Globally." Press Release, 6 March 2009. Available from http://www.free-press-relesae.com/news/200903/1236362125.html

Carey, Theresa W. "Beyond Cool: Online Trading Goes Mainstream as Quality Rises and Commissions Plunge." *Barron's,* 16 March 1998.

Connolly, Jim. "When the Sandwich Starts to Fall Apart." *National Underwriter Life & Health,* 15 January 2007.

"Do-It-Yourself Retirement; The Burden of Funding One's Later Years Has Shifted Irrevocably." *Business Week,* 25 July 2005.

First Research, Inc. *Financial Planners and Investment Advisors.* 26 October 2009.

Gleckman, Howard, and Rich Miller. "More Risk—More Reward; Now More than Ever, Retirees Are On Their Own." *Business Week,* 25 July 2005.

Halverson, Guy. "Warning: Few Planners Are Really 'Fee Only.'" *Christian Science Monitor,* 14 January 1997.

Hansard, Sara. "Industry Gropus Feeling the Pinch from the Economy." *Investment News,* 8 November 2009.

Jamieson, Dan. "Regulation of Financial Planning Industry Facing New Opposition, Leaders Predict." *Investment News,* 18 October 2009.

Kelly, Ross. "A Clear Future for Financial Planning." *Money Management,* 7 October 2004.

Liddich, Betty. "Employers Addressing Women's Unique Needs in Planning Retirement; Financial Education Programs Speak to Special Challenges Raised by Cultural Factors and Longer Life Expectancy." *Workforce Management,* 1 January 2005.

"Life-stage Benefits: Wooing the MTV and Internet Generations." *Employee Benefit News,* 1 December 2006.

Menchaca, Robert."Think Different." *Financial Planning,* 1 December 2009.

"More Capital Gains, Less Urge to Tax Them." *Washington Times,* 7 July 1998.

Simon, Ruth. "The Big Bad News about Fee-only Financial Planners: Some Are Wolfing Down Commissions on the Products They Recommend." *Money,* December 1995.

"The Retirement Gap." *Research,* May 2004.

Toth, David. "Baby Boomers Not Saving Enough for Retirement, Planners Say." *Westchester County Business Journal,* 26 June 2006.

Weidner, David. "Oversight of Financial Planners Is Mixed." *Wall Street Journal,* 15 September 1997.

"Workers Cite Biggest Financial Planning Regrets: Saving Too Little, Too Late in Early Working Years, According to Latest Principal Financial Well-Being Index." *Business Wire,* 13 September 2006.

FUEL CELLS

SIC CODE(S)

2679

2296

3629

3069

3674

INDUSTRY SNAPSHOT

Following a decade of advances in fuel cell technology, the fuel cell industry remained poised for eventual mass commercial deployment in vehicles, power plants, and homes as the solution to dependence on fossil fuels and dirty or inefficient energy sources. According to the Freedonia Group, the fuel cell market would continue to grow, reaching $975 million by 2012.

The automobile industry continued to be a developing arena for fuel cell use. In 2010 several companies, including Honda, Mercedes-Benz, and Toyota, developed hybrid vehicles that run on fuel cells. Fuel cell use in other vehicles, including lift trucks at manufacturing facilities, also was emerging. Giants such as Wal-Mart, General Motors, FedEx, Bridgestone, and Michelin used fuel cell-powered vehicles to move materials. Cost and access to hydrogen sources was one main challenge to the widespread adoption of fuel cell vehicles.

Less attention has been paid to the industrial and commercial use of stationary fuel cells, which actually represented a sector of the market showing more promise than vehicular use. By 2010 several local government entities, as well as a growing number of private companies, where incorporating fuel cell technologies into their power and energy budgets as appreciable rebates and other government incentives inspire transfers to more "green" options.

ORGANIZATION AND STRUCTURE

The introduction of fuel cells to the mass market was stalled somewhat by ambivalence over the proper configurations for their various applications. Fuel cells use one of a number of possible electrolytes, including phosphoric acid, solid oxide, molten carbonate, polymer, and alkaline, which determine the operating temperature and thus the efficiency of the fuel cell. Electrolysis is the process whereby water's component elements, hydrogen and oxygen, are physically separated by an electric current shot through the molecule. After electrolysis, the elements are shuttled toward battery electrodes, the hydrogen toward the anode and the oxygen toward the cathode. A catalyst then kicks the hydrogen atom, forcing it to release its electron into the cathode, while the remaining positively charged hydrogen proton is also shot toward the cathode. The electrodes then run through an external circuit, such as a motor, to yield an electric charge. When the current returns to the cathode, the hydrogen electrons recombine with the oxygen to generate heat and water. As long as a stream of fuel is provided, the fuel cell can run indefinitely, requiring no recharging.

How They Work. Fuel cells produce electricity from the electrochemical interaction of hydrogen and oxygen, resulting in a clean and efficient energy source fit for a wide variety of applications. While the exact method of extracting hydrogen varies and can influence the emission composition, the most efficient fuel cells produce only clean—even drinkable—water as a byproduct.

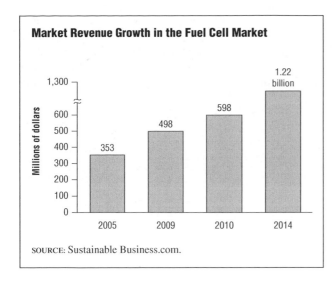

Market Revenue Growth in the Fuel Cell Market

Millions of dollars

- 2005: 353
- 2009: 498
- 2010: 598
- 2014: 1.22 billion

SOURCE: Sustainable Business.com.

There are four major types of fuel cells. Solid oxide fuel cells (SOFCs) and molten carbonate fuel cells (MOFCs) pull hydrogen out of methane, which requires particularly high operating temperatures (in this case, reaching 600 degrees Celsius and 1,000 degrees Celsius, respectively). As a result, these fuel cells necessitate dangerous and expensive materials to build component parts capable of withstanding such temperatures. Mainly for that reason, these types of fuel cells receive relatively little practical attention.

Phosphoric acid fuel cells (PAFCs) find their most extensive use in stationary power systems and indeed were the only type of fuel cells in significant commercial use during the early 2000s. Like SOFCs and MOFCs, PAFCs utilize methane rather than pure hydrogen, but PAFCs operate at only 200 degrees Celsius and thus are practical for stationary use. Such temperatures, however, still require heavy components, thus making PAFCs of limited use for vehicles.

For vehicles, proton exchange membrane (PEM) fuel cells are the order of the day. With comparatively quick power conversion at temperatures of 80 degrees Celsius, PEM fuel cells are the crown jewel of the auto industry's fuel cell research, although they still pose significant difficulties. The membrane that gives the fuel cell its name is a thin, Saran Wrap-like electrolyte coated with a catalyst and it is permeable to hydrogen protons. Such cells, however, result in only about 0.6 volts of electricity. In order to effectively power an electric motor, a series of cells is stacked together. PEM fuel cell stacks are also finding increasing favor among manufacturers devoted to stationary power systems.

Hydrogen is the most widely used fuel for fuel cells, although it poses its share of difficulties. The low energy density of hydrogen calls for a great deal of storage space, which can be impractical in an automobile. Liquefied hydrogen, moreover, necessitates cryogenic (very low temperature)

storage, resulting in significant energy losses. As a result, great strides must be forthcoming in hydrogen storage before such vehicles can hit the mass market. A temporary solution favored by oil companies and automakers is to generate hydrogen inside the vehicle by reforming methanol or light hydrocarbons, though such methods continue to result in dirty emissions. While reformers will likely provide manufacturers with an more immediate market entry strategy, most analysts expect that the ability to implement effective and practical direct hydrogen fueling is just around the corner.

There were three basic designs for automobile reformers. The first, steam reforming, combines traditional fuels such as gasoline or methanol with heat and steam to produce hydrogen. Second, partial oxidation reformers produce hydrogen and carbon monoxide by combining fuel with oxygen, thereby yielding even more hydrogen as the carbon dioxide mixes with the steam. Finally, auto-thermal reforming involves both steam and oxygen to produce a reaction derived from the balance of heat.

Industry Regulation and Legislation Fuel cells have been nurtured by a regulatory climate increasingly aimed at curtailing U.S. dependence on foreign energy supplies and reducing pollutant emissions. For example, a national Renewable Fuels Standard (RFS) was implemented in August 2005 when President George W. Bush signed the Energy Policy Act (EPACT) of 2005. Beginning with a baseline of 4 billion gallons of renewable fuel in 2006, production must reach 7.5 billion gallons by 2012. According to data from LECG LLC, cited in the Renewable Fuels Association's (RFA) *Ethanol Industry Outlook 2006,* one of the legislation's goals was to cut crude oil imports by 2 billion barrels by 2012, at the same time keeping $64 billion from foreign producers.

A host of laws, regulations, and initiatives are in place fostering the development of fuel cells in one way or another, including the Clean Air Acts of 1963, 1970, and 1990; the Energy Policy Act of 1992; the Omnibus Budget Reconciliation Act of 1993; the National Appliance Energy Conservation Act of 1987; the Tax Payer Relief Act of 1997; the Federal Highway Bill of 1998; and the Climate Change Action Plan. The U.S. Department of Energy (DOE) aims to eliminate 10 percent of all petroleum-based vehicle fuels by 2010 and 30 percent by 2030, while the international Kyoto Protocol calls for the United States to reduce greenhouse gas emissions.

The Congressional Climate Change Technology Initiative is a massive project aimed at reducing emissions, improving air quality, and reducing U.S. dependence on foreign energy supplies. Programs included tax credits for implementing efficient, renewable energy technologies in buildings, automobiles, and power plants. The program provided for a 10 percent tax credit for the purchase of fuel cell or other highly efficient electric vehicles.

The DOE also runs the Vision 21 program designed to streamline power plant operations toward more ecologically sound practices. The DOE began dispersing money to fuel cell companies and research centers in 2000 with an eye toward completing a clean Vision 21 power plant infrastructure for commercial use by 2015. Another key DOE program was the Partnership for a New Generation of Vehicles, which partnered the federal government with three leading automakers (DaimlerChrysler, Ford, and General Motors) to develop low emissions vehicles. In 2003 the DOE awarded some $75 million to educational and research institutions for fuel cell development to solve the technical problems blocking their way to commercialization, particularly high production costs and heat utilization.

Nevertheless, government efforts remained well below the levels industry players deemed necessary to achieve the leadership position in the global fuel cell market, according to a major study by the Breakthrough Technologies Institute, "Fuel Cells at the Crossroads." Whereas industry financers, manufacturers, and analysts noted that Japanese and European companies could develop comfortably atop a plentiful supply of government funding, they complained that the U.S. industry was strapped with too little government support, as the federal government spread its dollars over too wide a range of possible alternative energy sources rather than picking one to focus on.

BACKGROUND AND DEVELOPMENT

While fuel cells were touted as one of the most significant emerging energy technologies, they have had an extremely long shelf life in the laboratory. The principle of deriving electricity from hydrogen was discovered as early as 1839, but since generating an electrochemical current proved especially problematic, the principle failed to yield any significant breakthrough and was put back on the shelf for a century. With the rise of the internal combustion engine and its reliance on fossil fuels, the discovery was simply written off.

Not until the U.S. National Aeronautics and Space Administration (NASA) employed General Electric to develop alkali fuel cells for its Gemini and Apollo spacecrafts did the technology re-emerge. While the fuel cells proved successful on these missions, only an enormously resourceful organization such as NASA could afford to use them because in order to generate high power at an appropriately low weight, the fuel cells were outfitted with high amounts of platinum and gold.

Spurred by the energy crisis of the 1970s, the American Gas Association and the Institute of Gas Technology set out to study the possibility of a hydrogen-based

energy infrastructure. The next major breakthrough came in the early 1980s when researchers at the Los Alamos National Laboratories eliminated the need for much of the precious metals in fuel cell components, thus paving the way for the popular PEM cell that stood at the industry's forefront in 2000.

Meanwhile, the range of fuel options for fuel cells was expanded with breakthroughs in the reforming process. Working with the U.S. Department of Energy, industry leader Plug Power Inc. in 1997 found a way to capture sulfur from gasoline before it reached the fuel cell. Gasoline had been considered unusable for fuel cells since sulfur acts to poison the cells. With a specialized catalytic converter, the company worked to expand reformer capabilities to facilitate multiple fuel sources.

While the immediate impetus behind the search for alternative energy sources was the pending depletion of the world's oil supplies coupled with the jolts to the nation's economy generated by foreign political turmoil, recent years have witnessed a gradual shift of rationale. With oil reserves currently deemed stable for decades to come, perhaps the most pronounced motive for the development of new fuel technologies is the evolving public attitude toward environmental sustainability. The high cost, in terms of political initiative and military security, of the nation's foreign oil dependence further spurred calls for improved energy technologies in the United States.

In his State of the Union address in 2003, President George W. Bush called for $1.7 billion in federal funds to be allocated to hydrogen research, particularly for use in powering automobiles. By endorsing the move to a hydrogen economy, the Bush administration committed the U.S. government's support for various research and development programs to bring fuel cells to prominence. This was certainly welcome news to industry players, who felt a lack of support compared to their foreign rivals. From 1996 to 2002, private sector funding clearly outpaced U.S. government investment in fuel cell development, peaking at $1.1 billion at the tail end of the economic boom in 2000, although private sector funding fell off nearly 50 percent from that point by 2002. Federal government spending, according to a report by the Breakthrough Technologies Institute, increased incrementally from $114 million in 1996 to $159 million in 2002.

However, the U.S. economic downturn put the brakes on the rapid development of the late 1990s, as corporate cost-cutting measures were felt particularly in research and development expenditures, where immediate returns to ensure short term viability were less readily identifiable. Combined with the drying up of venture capital for smaller fuel cell companies, the sputtering economy translated into a general lack of funding as compared with the free-flowing capital of the late 1990s.

The net effect of the downturn was to drive many industry players—particularly those built on the plentiful seed money of the 1990s—out of the market altogether, or into the arms of larger firms that enjoyed the economies of scale to wait out the period of lackluster investment.

Several major events in the early years of the first decade of the twenty-first century positioned the industry in the public eye as never before. The U.S. economic downturn reduced consumer demand for large trucks and sport utility vehicles while at the same time rising gasoline prices sparked consumer interest in more fuel-efficient vehicles. Growing concerns over the country's reliance on foreign oil, particularly following the terrorist attacks of September 11, 2001, and the subsequent wars in Afghanistan and Iraq, afforded the industry political support as public pressures mounted for alternative energy sources, as did evolving attitudes regarding environmental sustainability. In addition, in August 2003 the largest power blackout in U.S. history left the majority of the northeastern United States and parts of Ontario without power for anywhere from eight hours to two days, heightening interest in hydrogen fuel cells as a utility power source.

However, the biggest questions remain unanswered and harbor the real excitement. Most prominently among these is the degree of technical and commercial viability of fuel cells in the short term. Predictions for the future of the fuel cell market have been dependent on a host of variables, and thus the near-term future of the fuel cell market could be very different depending on the factors considered.

Of particular concern to industry players was the perception among the buying public and, significantly, the financial community, that fuel cells constituted a replacement rather than additive technology, according to a study by the Breakthrough Technologies Group. In other words, fuel cell makers and marketers had their work cut out for them to create demand for their products, particularly when customers were not especially dissatisfied with the current alternative.

Environmental and even growing political pressures notwithstanding, there was little in the way of a mass market outcry against the use of gasoline or fossil fuels generally, and thus it would be difficult to convince customers of a need to change the kinds of vehicles they drove or the means by which they powered their homes. Without a clear demand for the technology itself, fuel cells needed to compete with traditional fuels in price, service, and convenience, where, during the mid-2000s, they remained at a disadvantage. A major change in this dynamic was not likely in the absence of major upheavals, such as a national energy crisis.

The industry faced self-induced hurdles in the middle of the first decade of the 2000s as well. Chief among these obstacles was overcoming its reputation for hype and false promises. Extraordinary claims about imminent market prominence in the late 1990s led to a windfall of venture funding at the time, but when the bottom fell out of the technology market in the spring of 2000 and investors re-examined their portfolios, they saw a string of companies with little product and extraordinary debt working in a market for which there was extremely little demand. Although new technological developments arose with increasing frequency as the industry entered the late 2000s, concerns remained as to just when the technical and production cost problems nagging the industry would be sufficiently overcome as to enable mass production for a demanding public.

Portable electronic devices were one of the hottest areas for fuel cell application during the late 2000s. Research company Frost & Sullivan predicted that the worldwide micro fuel cell industry would produce 72 million unit shipments by 2010, a figure that the company expected would quadruple by 2013. According to a 2007 *Industry Week* article, direct methanol fuel cells (DMFC) are the "technology of choice" to power portable consumer devices, due to their small size and weight, quiet operation, and environmental benefits.

The adaptation of vehicles to more efficient fuel technologies is expected to be a primary focus of the automotive industry well into the twenty-first century. Although natural gas fuels such as methanol and ethanol and hybrid vehicles combining such fuels with standard gasoline remained the most common alternatives (see entry on Alternative Vehicle Fuels), analysts were virtually unanimous in their prediction that fuel cells would eventually be on their way to dominance over the alternative fuel market, to be followed within decades by dominance of the auto market itself. Emitting only water vapor, fuel cell vehicles were about 50 percent more efficient and 90 percent cleaner than gasoline-powered vehicles.

In mid-2008 Honda Motor Co. began production on its FCX Clarity fuel cell vehicle, the first vehicle built to U.S. specifications. The vehicle is manufactured at the Honda Automobile New Model Center in Tokyo, which has a dedicated fuel cell vehicle assembly line. Other companies followed suit. Mercedes-Benz expected to release a fuel-cell vehicle by 2010 that will be at full power within 15 to 20 seconds of ignition (start-up time has previously taken up to one minute). Toyota also began production on its HCHV-adv model, which was expected to get 516 miles on one tank of hydrogen.

The lack of a refueling infrastructure, and the heavy costs involved in building one, topped the list of challenges as the industry headed into the latter part of the decade. A complete overhaul of refueling stations to include hydrogen pumps would undoubtedly be prohibitively expensive, and smaller gas stations fear that such a restructuring would put them out of business. The National Hydrogen Association estimated that 70 percent of all Americans could be within 2 miles of a hydrogen fueling station for about $10 billion to $15 billion; Shell Company put the figure at $20 billion.

Proposed alternatives have included the installation of small electrolysis centers alongside traditional gasoline pumps or even the implementation of photovoltaic cells, which produce electricity directly from sunlight and yield no pollutants, atop service stations to facilitate the local production of hydrogen. While such solutions would mitigate some of the environmental impact, cost and technology hang-ups remain.

The reforming process is pivotal to the choice of fuel. Since reformers add weight to an automobile, the more refined the process, the more feasible the technology. Down the road, reforming will likely be unnecessary, but if companies want to start to introduce fuel cells to the automotive marketplace, some compromise will have to suffice. For this reason, the earliest fuel cell cars will not be completely devoid of pollutant emissions, either, as the most common alternative, on-board conversion of methanol into hydrogen, will release some carbon dioxide.

Standard gasoline, a possible reforming source thanks to recent innovations, could take advantage of both filling stations' and vehicles' existing infrastructures. This, however, is a dubious benefit in the eyes of environmentalists since gasoline is so laden with carbon dioxide. In that respect, methanol is greatly preferred, but then the infrastructure difficulties re-emerge. However, outfitting the nation's filling stations with methanol pumps poses nowhere near the costs associated with the implementation of pure hydrogen pumps.

Reformers are also problematic because they typically require up to a minute to warm up after starting, and add time between a driver's action, such as flooring the gas pedal, and the engine's response. With performance demands at an all-time high, such restrictions are not likely to win over many customers. While reformers could instead be installed at filling stations, thereby eliminating many of the size and time restrictions (since these reformers could run continuously), in the end the problem of on-board storage will not go away.

The cost of the catalyst necessary for fuel cells to produce energy is also an issue. The most efficient catalyst discovered as of mid-2008 was platinum, which cost approximately $1,500 per ounce. At this price, the platinum catalyst contributes about $3,000 to the cost of a small fuel cell-powered vehicle. According to Peter Strasser at the University of Houston, "The automobile companies have been asking for a platinum-based catalyst

that is four times more efficient, and, therefore, four times cheaper, than what is currently available." Research involving alternatives continues.

Despite advances, some industry observers remained skeptical about any rapid developments taking place in the near future, noting that scientists and futurists have been making long-term predictions about the arrival of fuel cell powered vehicles since the mid-1980s. In a 2006 *Tire Business* article, Mark Rechtin wrote: "Every major auto maker has created a gazillion-dollar prototype that wheezes to 80 mph and gets great fuel economy but has a limited range. I know. I've driven them. They're nice enough vehicles, great public relations gambits—but I sure wouldn't want to live with one. The true challenge is creating a fuel cell version that sacrifices nothing to today's cars in performance and packaging and outdoes them in equivalent fuel economy and emissions."

Several factors will affect the overall transition to fuel cell powered vehicles. The level of pressure applied to companies by consumers will have the most immediate impact on the industry's willingness to invest heavily in the commercialization of fuel cell vehicles. The world's oil and gas prices, which skyrocketed in the first decade of the 2000s, are subject to dramatic fluctuation and political wrangling, which could in turn affect the pace at which companies are inclined to speed fuel cells to market. These factors also influence and will be influenced by progress in implementing processes and facilities capable of delivering low-cost mass production of fuel cell vehicles.

Fuel cells also began to impact the utility industries, promising "grid-busting" power distribution whereby customers need only make a trip to their local appliance store to acquire the only energy source they need. The turnover to stationary home power systems was likely to be gradual, however, with fuel cells first emerging as a niche market, particularly in areas with troubled grid reliability and excessive peak loads at power plants.

Energy companies and fuel cell manufacturers positioned fuel cells to facilitate what is known as "distributed generation," an industry buzzword signifying the production of energy at or near the location of use. The relationship between fuel cell technology and public utilities received unprecedented public attention in August 2003 after the largest power outage in U.S. history left millions of residents in the northeastern United States and Ontario without power for up to two days.

According to the U.S. Fuel Cell Commercialization Group, when fully developed, fuel cells will provide household efficiency levels (measured by the amount of power generated as a percentage of fuel consumption) of over 50 percent, possibly reaching as high as 70 percent if the steam and heat outputs are also harnessed for productive use. By way of comparison, traditional coal-burning sources yield efficiencies of about 30 to 40 percent.

The Freedonia Group reported that electric power generation will be the first large-scale commercial application of fuel cell technology. In fact, through 2014, this application was projected to account for more than 50 percent of global demand for fuel cell products and services. Nevertheless, despite increased funding and support for fuel cell research, skeptics view the viability of hydrogen as a public utility a distant possibility at best. Electrical grids covered nearly everyone in the United States, and combined with relatively low energy costs, there were few demands for a major conversion in the offing. As with the transportation sector, stationary fuel cells were primarily relegated to competing not in terms of environmental, social, or technological advantages, but in basic market points such as price, convenience, and reliability, all of which were likely to remain among the industry's weak points.

PIONEERS IN THE FIELD

The principle underlying fuel cells was first uncovered in 1839 by the colorful British physicist Sir William Grove while he was experimenting with electrolysis. Grove found that not only could its elements be broken apart, but they could be combined in a sort of reverse electrolysis to yield water and electricity. Despite his insistence that he had no interest in the potential uses of his discovery, Grove described in great detail exactly how the reverse electrolysis would generate electricity.

Nearly 150 years later, a Canadian geologist named Geoffrey Ballard propelled the technology into the industry we know today. After the General Electric/NASA fuel cell successes, Ballard worked in a government laboratory in the United States as well as on various government-subsidized alternative energy products before settling in Vancouver, British Columbia, to work on the development of lithium electric car batteries. Ballard Power Systems Inc. built on the early PEM technology by General Electric to develop fuel cell stacks with sheets of graphite, thereby generating increased power output. Ballard's research team's big break came from the Canadian military, which found that the team's PEM fuel cells could be of use in battlefield communications equipment.

CURRENT CONDITIONS

The fuel cell industry got a shot in the arm from the Obama administration's clean energy initiatives that included investment tax credits (ITCs) for use of fuel cells in the private sector. Under the incentive, businesses that purchased a fuel cell for a highly-efficient combined heat and power (CHP) application were eligible for an ITC of up to 30 percent of

the cost (up to $3,000 per kilowatt). Senator Christopher Dodd (D-CT) offered a new 2010 proposal to increase the ITC to up to 40 percent of cost, urging both federal agencies and private businesses to increase their use of fuel cells as a source of electricity.

In 2010 SBI Energy research estimated that the fuel cell market would reach $598 million by the end of that year, and then grow to $1.22 billion by 2014. This projection incorporated 2009 results of $498 million, followed by an estimated compound annual growth rate (CAGR) of 20 percent. The United States and Japan were the two largest financial segments of the market in 2009. SBI believed that fuel cell technology was poised to become an international heavyweight in alternative energy in the coming years.

According to SBI the portable sector of the fuel cell market was the fastest growing market in 2009. Growth was attributed to toys and educational devices powered by low-watt fuel cells. With the advance of portable electronics (e.g., mobile phones, PDAs, medical diagnostic devices, etc.), the small-cell market was expected to maintain its momentum for the foreseeable future.

However, the largest demand for fuel cells was in the stationary front, with commercial and public entities turning to green alternatives for power generation units. Most purchasers were using new power fuel cells as backup or additional power sources, although it is hoped that in the future, fuel cells will actually do the work of currently-overloaded power grids, particularly in large metropolitan areas. A breakout market in 2009 was the use of fuel cells for niche transport needs (e.g., forklifts and other materials handling vehicles) where such off-the-road vehicles could be tested in a more controlled environment.

With respect to use in vehicles, the development of hydrogen fuel cells was not advancing at the pace of other alternative fuel technologies. A December 2009 study at UC Davis, published in the *Journal of Power Sources,* found that over their lifetimes, hydrogen vehicles would emit more carbon than gasoline vehicles. Another critical article appeared in *The Washington Post,* asking: "But why would you want to store energy in the form of hydrogen and then use that hydrogen to produce electricity for a motor, when electrical energy is already waiting to be sucked out of sockets all over America and stored in auto batteries...?" It dismissed a commercialized hydrogen vehicle as a tailpipe dream. Both Ford and Nissan announced curbed efforts for hydrogen cars in favor of hybrid-electric models. The estimated number of hydrogen-powered vehicles in the United States was only around 200 as of late 2009, and these were mostly in the temperate climate of California.

This followed an earlier announcement in May 2009 by U.S. Secretary of Energy Stephen Chu that the government would cease funds for development of hydrogen vehicles (but would continue to fund research for stationary fuel cells). The announcement explained that hydrogen vehicles "[would] not be practical over the next 10 to 20 years." The decision was met with widespread criticism in academia and industry.

The industry experienced a small setback in August 2009. At that time a hydrogen refueling station in Rochester, New York, exploded during a fuel supply transfer. Although hydrogen fuel is technically no more flammable than gasoline, the fiery incident gave pause to fuel cell advocates to, at a minimum, proceeded with caution in their advocacy.

Progress continued among leading automakers. In September 2009 Daimler, Ford, GM, Honda, Hyundai, Kia, Nissan, Renault, and Toyota issued a joint statement committing themselves to further development and launch of fuel-cell electric vehicles as early as 2015.

INDUSTRY LEADERS

Ballard Power Systems Inc. A pioneer in fuel cell technology, Ballard Power Systems specializes in the cells, their systems, and their related components. Ballard developed its fuel cells both for stationary power systems and for the transportation market. Ballard's first released product was its 1995 275-horsepower fuel cell bus engine. The firm rolled out the first commercial fuel cell product in 2002, a methanol-based PEM unit for use as a portable generator. For several years, the Canadian company maintained partnerships with the world's major automakers to produce the fuel cells around which they developed vehicle infrastructures.

In 2007, Ballard sold its automotive fuel cell assets to Daimler and Ford and began to refocus its efforts on commercial applications for fuel cells. Based in Vancouver, British Columbia, Ballard employed 500 employees in 2007, down from 1,300 workers in 2003. In 2007 the company saw revenues of $65.5 million and had yet to make a profit due to the lag in adoption of fuel cells in the automobile industry; the company sold the remaining stake in its automotive fuel cells business in December 2009. According to Reuters, analysts generally expected the company to achieve about the same financial performance in 2010 as in 2007: $65.7 million.

In August 2010 Ballard announced its contract with Ohio's FirstEnergy Generation Corp., allowing that power company to activate Ballard's CLEARgen fuel cell generator during peak demand periods with its customers, taking strain off the power grid. Ballard also announced that its prior agreement with Plug Power Inc., scheduled to expire in December 2010, would be extended to 2014. Under its terms, Ballard would remain the exclusive supplier of fuel cell stacks for Plug Power GenDrive power units. In return, Plug Power would become the exclusive systems integrator for Ballard's fuel cell stack for addressing solutions in North America's material handling market.

Plug Power Inc. Plug Power, of Latham, New York, has focused on distributed power systems for commercial and residential buildings with its PEM fuel cell stacks. Plug Power was born of the joint venture between a subsidiary of DTE Energy Co. and Mechanical Technology Inc. and went public in late 1999. Its research and development partnership with Albany NanoTech promised new fuel cell systems incorporating nanotechnology, and it is also working on backup power systems for the telecommunications and industrial sectors. With clients in the United States, Europe, and Japan, the firm shipped 145 different fuel cell systems in 2003. In 2009 sales were $12.3 million and the company employed 390 workers.

FuelCell Energy Inc. FuelCell Energy of Danbury, Connecticut, focused on fuel cell stacks with a generating capacity of over 250 megawatts, mainly for power plants. The electrochemical technologies firm Energy Research Co. spun off its batteries operations in 1998 before renaming itself FuelCell Energy Inc. In its hometown in 1999, the company commissioned its first commercial plant, which supplied power to its own manufacturing facilities and the local power grid. FuelCell's development projects include its Direct FuelCell (DFC), which generates hydrogen from natural gas and other sources without needing an external reactor. Although the firm operated 40 DFC power plants around the world in 2007, the U.S. market accounted for two-thirds of sales. FuelCell announced revenues of $88 million for its 2009 fiscal year, and $50.1 million for the first nine months of 2010. In 2010 it announced four new major projects with California universities.

QUANTUM Fuel Systems Technologies Worldwide Inc. Based in Irvine, California, QUANTUM brought in sales of $146.7 million in 2007, thanks largely to General Motors, an owner of the company, which accounted for 87 percent of QUANTUM's revenues. Toyota is another important customer. A spin-off from IMPCO Technologies, QUANTUM produced fuel cells mainly for the automotive market, having sold some 14,000 vehicle fuel systems by 2004, but the firm also laid a path to the stationary and portable power sectors. QUANTUM's primary products in the first decade of the 2000s were hydrogen storage tanks, delivery regulators, injectors, valves, and electronic pressure controls. The firm essentially quadrupled in size in 2006, following the acquisition of Tecstar Automotive.

Bloom Energy Inc. A newcomer with promising products is Bloom Energy Inc. In 2010 Adobe became the company's biggest fuel cell site customer with the installation of 12 Bloom fuel cells in its parking garage. Also making use of its generator units in 2010 were Bank of America, the Coca-Cola Company, and Google.

AMERICA AND THE WORLD

FC Expo, the world's largest fuel cell exhibition, took place in Tokyo in 2010, with more than 500 exhibits. According to sponsors, the event was very well attended, with 47 countries participating and overbooked conference attendance. Two major exhibits caught the attention of most participants. First, the Honda FCX Clarity car was available for test drives. It contained Honda's revolutionary Vertical Flow Fuel Cell Stack (52 liters and weighing 67 kilograms). The stack gave 100kW peak power and up to 30kW steady power, making it the first fuel cell to challenge the power density of an internal combustion engine. The back of the fuel stack led to a DC/DC converter with the 270V battery beneath the rear seat.

The second big exhibition was the Japanese Domestic CHP Fuel Cell Program, which introduced the development of SOFC (solid oxide) at the New Energy Foundation. The introduction of high temperature SOFCs brought Japan into the competitive market with other major players, such as ceramic fuel cells. The New Energy Foundation installed 132 units for trial tests between 2007 and 2010. The units operated on a variety of fuels, including natural gas, LPG, and kerosene. Particularly popular was the Japan Hydrogen and Fuel Cell Ride and Drive exhibit, with eight vehicle types available for test drives.

Ceramic fuel cells were on the German pavilion at the event, and the UK entity, ACAL Energy, exhibited its FLOWCATH System, similar to a PEM fuel cell, but using a stack/regenerator instead of a stack/humidifier. Australia's Ceramic Fuel Cells Ltd. boasted an electrical efficiency of 60 percent in its SOFC products, and when heat was recovered from the electricity production process, total efficiency rose to 85 percent.

Although the United States was a leader in the portable and stationary sectors, and a strong competitor with Japan in the automotive sector, its leadership role was far from certain as the industry moved into the second decade of the 2000s. Whereas European and Japanese fuel cell makers enjoyed long-term and deeply entrenched support from their governments, the United States was slower to lend a hand to its domestic industry. Japan's first hydrogen fuel filling station opened in June 2003 in Tokyo. The Japanese government called for the production of 50,000 fuel cell-powered vehicles on the roads by 2010, to be followed a decade later by 5 million, according to *Business Week*. To this end, in 2003 the Japanese government increased its allocation of funding to fuel cell products by 40 percent to $280 million.

For years, Western Europe has heavily taxed fuel as a way of raising revenue and safeguarding the environment by cutting consumption and emissions. In recent years, the United Kingdom, moreover, announced that it would continue to increase gasoline and diesel taxes at a rate of 6 percent annually above the rate of inflation. The European Union as a whole meanwhile planned to reduce its emissions by 8 percent from 1990 levels by 2010, in keeping with the Kyoto Accords, which the United States opted not to honor in 2001.

Meanwhile, Iceland took the leading role on the world's fuel cell stage in 1999 when it announced its plans to become the first hydrogen-powered economy, immediately attracting the likes of DaimlerChrysler, Shell's new hydrogen division, and the Norwegian energy firm Norsk, all hungry to test their newest fuel cell vehicles in what was seen as a dress rehearsal for the future. Daimler's first fuel cell buses hit the Reykjavik streets in late 1999. Iceland hopes to eventually replace its entire automotive population with fuel cell vehicles and is well positioned to move toward its goal, given that the country is already accustomed to relying on renewable or alternative energy sources, gleaning 72 percent of its total energy from renewable sources and all of its electricity. The country has ambitiously aimed to be completely fossil fuel free by 2030.

WORKFORCE

Most fuel cell companies, particularly those firms primarily engaged in research and development and built on venture capital, employed a few hundred people at most, according to the Breakthrough Technologies Institute. Public companies exclusively focused on fuel cells employed about 2,000. Looking ahead, the Institute predicted total industry employment would total some 168,000 by 2021, including those directly and indirectly associated with fuel cell development. The largest share of these employees would likely be based in the stationary sector, with a sizable proportion involved in the transportation and component development segments. Only a fraction of total industry employment was likely to based in the portable sector by 2021.

RESEARCH AND TECHNOLOGY

New developments in fuel cell technology were occurring in all areas. For example, in June 2010 chemical engineers at Purdue University announced a new process for storing and generating hydrogen used to run fuel cells. The process, called hydrothermolysis, uses ammonia borane, a powdered chemical having one of the highest hydrogen contents (19.6 percent) of all solid materials. This is important because it allows a relatively smaller quantity and volume to store large amounts of hydrogen.

It also was important because the U.S. Department of Energy had set a 2015 target of 5.5 weight percent hydrogen for hydrogen storage systems (i.e., available hydrogen should be at least 5.5 percent of a system's total weight). By using a concentration of 77 percent ammonia borane in a process combining hydrolysis and thermolysis, researchers hoped to efficiently produce hydrogen for fuel cells to recharge batteries in electronics applications (cell phones, PDAs, notebook computers, etc.) and handheld medical diagnostic devices (also defibrillators).

Other hot research and/or trial projects going on in 2010 included ClearEdge Power's stationary cell running on natural gas or propane; Ceres Power's $75 project to develop stationary fuel cells that use methane to heat homes and generate electricity; ACAL Energy's startup project of membrane exchange fuel cells with cathodes that use only one-fifth the platinum of traditional membrane fuel cells; CellEra, an Israeli company working on a stationary cell that totally eliminates platinum, using instead proprietary electrode technology; and Electro Power System's development of a stationary cell aimed at the mobile phone backup market. This Italian company reverses the process: fuel cells would convert hydrogen to electricity when grid power is down, then convert water back to hydrogen via electrolysis using grid power once it is returned.

In 2008 researchers at the Massachusetts Institute of Technology improved power output of DMFCs by 50 percent using a new, lower-cost material. Acumentrics Corp. received a $15.6 million grant from the Department of Energy to continue to study its tubular solid oxide fuel cell (SOFC) technology, which, according to Norm Bessette, senior vice-president of the company, "is the highest-efficiency low-emission alternative for providing power and heat for homes, small and medium size businesses, remote locations and military applications while using conventional and alternative fuels."

The largest fuel cell installation worldwide to date was scheduled to begin in New York in 2009. The New York Power Authority contracted UTC Power to supply 12 fuel cells, totaling 4.8 megawatts of power, to the new towers under construction at the World Trade Center site in Manhattan. Also, in 2008 Versa Power Systems was selected by the U.S. Department of Defense to develop an ultra-long endurance unmanned aircraft using fuel cell technology.

Driven by its goal to be completely fossil fuel free by 2030, Iceland was an important center of fuel cell research in the 2000s' first decade. In its September 2005 issue, *Modern Power Systems* reported that the Technological Institute of Iceland was in the process of starting a hydrogen technology center that could be used for testing purposes. In addition, studies underway at the University of Iceland touched upon many facets of hydrogen research. Initiatives included geothermal hydrogen energy production and storage systems, the chemistry of hydrogen bonds in compounds, and the nanostructural aspects of hydrogen storage. The country's research activities even explored socioeconomic implications of a hydrogen-based economy.

Mississauga, Ontario-based Hydrogenics, meanwhile, partnered with General Motors to develop fuel cell diesel hybrid engines for use by the U.S. Army in some 35,000 light tactical vehicles. Lasting longer than batteries and independent of supply lines, fuel cells were highly attractive to military planners, who also eyed the technology's water emissions, which could come in handy when fighting in harsh desert climates such as in the Middle East.

The United Kingdom's Morgan Fuel Cell devised the ElectroTech technique to boost the power generated by a fuel cell's bipolar plates to up 16 percent. The ElectroTech technique consciously mimics the basic breathing processes of plants and animals, distributing the reactants through a branch of flow fields to the electrodes the way a living organism distributes oxygen through a number of smaller channels to its useful source. The end result was a more even distribution of gas through the bipolar plate, thereby boosting fuel cell production and efficiency.

BIBLIOGRAPHY

"Acumentrics Receives $15.6 Million DOE Fuel Cell Development Contract." Westwood, MA: Acumentrics Corporation, 4 June 2008. Available from http://www.acumentrics.com.

Aichlmayr, Mary. "Fuel-Cell Power Payback." *Material Handling Management,* May 2008.

"Alternative & Advanced Fuels." U.S. Department of Energy, Alternative Fuels and Advanced Vehicles Data Center, 2007. Available from http://www.eere. energy.gov.

"Alternative & Renewable Fuels." Energy Information Administration, 2007. Available from http:// www.eia.doe.gov.

Baker, Erin. "Mercedes Joins the Fuel-Cell Race." *Daily Telegraph,* 28 June 2008.

"Ballard Power Systems Inc. Comment on H2 2010 Reuters, 28 July 2010. Available from http://www.reuters.com/finance/stcks/keydevelopments.

Birch, Stuart. "Fuel Cells and Diesel Hybrids Are the Future, Says Zetsche." *Automotive Engineering International,* May 2008.

"BTI Releases New Report on State Fuel Cell, Hydrogen Activity." *Fuel Cells Today,* 4 May 2006.

"Ceramic Fuel Cells Limited FY2010 Directors Report and Accounts." Ceramic Fuel Cells Ltd., September 2010. Available from http://www.cfcl.com.au.

Evans, Jon. "Fuellng the Future." *Chemistry and Industry,* 5 May 2008.

"FuelCell Energy's Proposals for Distributed Energy." Fuel Cell Markets Ltd., September 2010. Available from http:// www.fuelcellmarkets.com.

"FuelCell Energy Reports Fourth Quarter and Fiscal Year Results." FuelCell Energy, August 2010. Available from http://www.fuelcellenergy.com/files/12-09-09.

"Fuel Cell Market Powering Up." *Plant Engineering,* June 2006.

"Fuel Cell Market to Reach $1.2B by 2014." *Sustainable Business,* 24 September 2010. Available from http://www.sustainablebusiness.com/index.cfm/go/news.

"HARC Publishes Fuel Cell Industry Assessment Report." *Business Wire,* 22 March 2006.

"Hydrogen Cars' Lifecycle Emits More Carbon Than Gas Cars, Study Says." *Digital Trends,* 1 January 2010.

"Hydrogen Fuel Cell Generator Set to Deploy Ballarod Power Systems Proton Exchange Membrane Technology." Reuters, 11 August 2010. Available from http://www.reuters.com/finance/stcks/keydevelopments.

"Hydrogen Powered Car Still Seems Improbable." *The Washington Post,* 17 November 2009.

Jusko, Jill. "Micro Possibilities: Power-Hungry Portable Devices Fuel the Drive to Develop Micro Fuel Cell Technology." *Industry Week,* April 2007.

Morrison, David. "Are Fuel Cells Ready for Takeoff?" *Power Electronics Technology,* 1 May 2008.

"New Process Is Promising for Hydrogen Fuel Cell Cars." *Science Daily,* 18 June 2010.

"New York Power Authority Selects UTC Power to Supply Fuel Cells for World Trade Center Site." UTC Power Company, 11 June 2008. Available from http://www.utcpower.com.

"Plug Power Inc. and Ballard Power Systems Inc. Extend Supply Agreement Through 2014." Reuters, 15 July 2010. Available from http://www.reuters.com/finance/stcks/keydevelopments.

"Plug Power Inc. (PLUG: US) Earnings Estimates." *Business Week,* 10 September 2010.

"Production Begins for the New FCX Clarity Fuel Cell Vehicle." Honda Motor Company, 16 June 2008. Available from http://www.fuelcells.org/news/updates.html.

Rechtin, Mark. "Fuel Cell Vehicles? Don't Hold Your Breath; Somehow, Success Always Seems to be Just 20 Years Away." *Tire Business,* 27 February 2006.

"Report from FC Expo 2010, the World's Largest Fuel Cell Exhibition." Fuel Cell Markets Ltd., September 2010. Available from http://www.fuelcell markets.com.

"Report Predicts Fuel Cell Industry Will Top $18 Billion by 2013." *Fuel Cells Today,* 17 April 2006.

St. John, Jeff. "10 Fuel Cell Startups Hot on Bloom Energy's Trail. *Earth2Tech,* 22 February 2010. Available from http://www.earh2tech.com/2010/02/02/22/10-fuel-cell-startups.

Teresko, John. "A New Material Benefits Fuel Cells." *Industry Week,* July 2008.

"Toyota Motor Has Developed the FCHV-adv." *Automotive Business Review,* 9 June 2008.

Truett, Richard. "Ford V-10 Runs on Hydrogen." *Automotive News,* 24 July 2006.

"Versa Power Systems Selected by Boeing to Develop Ultra-Long Endurance Aircraft Technology." Versa Power Systems, 3 June 2008. Available from http://www.versa-power.com.

Wald, Matthew L. "U.S Drops Research Into Fuel Cells for Cars." *New York Times,* 7 May 2009.

GAMBLING RESORTS AND CASINOS

7011

7993

7999

INDUSTRY SNAPSHOT

Gambling as an industry is growing, noted an article in the November 2009 issue of *The Economist*. In fact, said the article, in the four years from 2004 to 2008, global revenues increased by 24 percent. The United States is fast becoming a nation of high rollers. Approximately one in four adult U.S. citizens, or 54.6 million Americans, visited casinos in 2008. Despite a waning economy, the industry earned steady (but slightly decreased) revenues that year. Issues such as possible tax increases at the state level and uncertainty regarding how the riverboat segment of the industry would tap into the burgeoning baby boomer demographic led analysts to label the industry as "stable."

Gambling has received increasing, though hardly universal, acceptance as a socially-acceptable form of entertainment over the years, with about 81 percent of Americans holding that the practice is a matter of personal choice and is acceptable for themselves or for others, according to a national survey by pollsters Peter D. Hart Research Associates, Inc., and The Luntz Research Companies. As legalized gambling continues to spread, the industry faces a period of transition, its structure yet to be ironed out. The biggest, glitziest names have been consolidating in order to boost efficiency and secure market position, while the smaller gambling houses and riverboat casinos have tried to boost their image and diversify their services to attract high rollers to their niche market.

Online gambling in the United States remained a hot issue, although still not legal as of December 2009. Another hot trend was the growth of non-gaming amenities with commercial casinos as their nucleus. According to the American Gaming Association (AGA), multi-component entertainment venues offering a wide variety of diversions such as retail shopping, fine dining spas, and golf courses have buoyed the gambling industry during leaner days when differentiation from competitors is important. According to the Nevada Gaming Control Board, non-gaming revenue on the Las Vegas Strip accounted for more than 60 percent of total revenue in 2008, compared to just 40 percent 15 years earlier.

In short, according to an October 2008 report from Global Betting and Gaming Consultants (GBGC), in spite of the global financial crisis gripping the end of the decade, the world's gambling market was poised for continued growth for several years, with the Internet sector trumping land-based gambling businesses, and Asia leading the pack.

ORGANIZATION AND STRUCTURE

Casinos are the biggest moneymakers and the driving force in the gambling industry. They have completely changed from their inception, moving from purely gaming houses to adult theme and fantasy parks, often with such services as childcare and video arcades. Casino gambling is now interlaced with 24-hour shopping malls and visual attractions such as talking statues, erupting volcanoes, and mock ocean battles with pirate ships. Slot machines are generating mounds of new business. Slots appeal to novice gamblers because they are easily understandable and fast-paced. Originally, casinos devoted only about 30 percent of their space to slot machines, but this eventually changed to about 90 percent.

Casino gambling stretches well beyond the havens of Las Vegas, Nevada, and Atlantic City, New Jersey. Shortly after New Jersey approved gambling in 1976, Native American tribes, exempt from local laws as sovereign nations, realized that they too could profit. Gambling also spread to several waterfront and river states such as Iowa, Mississippi, and Illinois after state legislatures authorized gambling on cruise ships and paddlewheel riverboats.

Casinos are subject to federal, state, and local regulations. Before operating a casino, gambling companies must acquire a license or reach an agreement with a state. Some states, such as Illinois, limit the number of licenses they issue, while other states simply conduct reviews and background checks on all applicants for casino licenses. The Indian Gaming Regulatory Act (IGRA) of 1988 is the key piece of legislation governing casinos run by Native Americans. This act led to tremendous growth of such facilities, especially in states such as North Dakota, Iowa, New York, South Dakota, and North Carolina. The IGRA permits Native American tribes to engage in and regulate gambling on their lands if their lands are located in a state that allows gambling and if federal law allows for such gambling.

The industry's primary organizations are the AGA and the National Indian Gaming Association (NIGA). Based in Washington, D.C., the AGA provides the industry with statistics and information on the gambling industry around the country. Besides promoting the economic success of the industry, the AGA also promotes casino safety and responsible gambling. Providing its members with national representation, the AGA pushes for legislation to stimulate the gambling industry.

The NIGA comprises 184 Native American nations and strives to protect and advance the Native American casino industry. The broader, stated purpose of NIGA is to propel advancement of the economic, social, and political lives of all Native Americans, promoting the gaming industry as one remedy for the crippling poverty suffered by Native American communities. Also based in Washington, D.C., NIGA trains tribal members to run casinos and offers seminars on improving casino business and safety.

BACKGROUND AND DEVELOPMENT

According to Dr. John Findlay, author of *People of Chance*, gambling in America really evolved in the 1800s during the westward migration. With little other entertainment and a belief in luck and risk-taking, many U.S. pioneers embraced all forms of gambling. Between 1800 and 1840, towns along the Mississippi River became ports for the riverboats transporting goods and people. The riverboats were transformed into moving gambling parlors.

Further west in the mining camps and small towns, public organized systems of gambling evolved. Most of the gambling involved such card games as monte and poker, but some wheel games existed.

As emerging cities in the Midwest, South, and West became bigger, wealthier, and more sophisticated, they sought acceptance from the East by tackling their "problems." Since the East viewed gaming as vulgar, many cities passed ordinances banning dealers and gamblers, and those caught were arrested.

While U.S. cities started turning against gambling in the mid-1800s, a new, elegant, upscale form of gaming evolved in Europe among the aristocratic classes—casino gambling. Casinos were different because they used large tables and machinery such as roulette wheels. Casinos were found in elegant vacation resorts and mineral spa areas such as Baden Baden and Bad Homburg, Germany, along with Nice, Cannes, and Monte Carlo on the French Riviera.

In 1863, Francois Blanc, a successful Parisian casino manager who was jailed for stock fraud, arrived in Monaco to build and run a casino there despite wavering and resistance from his patron, Prince Charles II. Blanc brought wealth to Monaco and is considered the father of today's casinos. His management theories and rules for customer relations are used today in Las Vegas casinos as faithfully as they were in the 1850s.

While casino games such as baccarat and roulette became popular and gained wide acceptance in Europe, a series of irregularities in U.S. lotteries and horse racing caused national scandals in the late 1800s. By 1910, almost all U.S. forms of gambling had been outlawed.

Regulated betting on horses, overseen by strict state laws, eventually returned in the 1930s. During Prohibition, private clubs in cities offered various forms of illegal gambling—crap pits, poker, blackjack, and slot machines. After World War II, Las Vegas started using its gambling resorts to attract tourists. During the 1950s, Benjamin "Bugsy" Siegel, a known gangster, saw an opportunity to elude California's strict ban on gambling and quench its citizens' thirst for gaming. Siegel traveled to Nevada, since the state had tolerated gambling in the 1930s during the construction of the Hoover Dam, and built a luxury Caribbean style hotel and casino called the Flamingo. Siegel contributed to Las Vegas's reputation as a rough town operated by organized crime from New York and Chicago, but with his casino, he had started something that would eventually contribute to the development of a new reputation. To attract gamblers, Las Vegas began offering inexpensive hotel rooms, food, free drinks, and famous entertainment. Soon, Las Vegas became one of the regular stops for such performers as Frank Sinatra and Elvis Presley.

Howard Hughes became an investor in Las Vegas after he and his entourage moved into the Desert Inn in

1976, renting an entire floor of the hotel to stay out of range of photographers and the public. The Desert Inn management decided Hughes and his crew were a detriment to the business since they didn't gamble and so they evicted him. Hughes responded by buying the hotel. He then began buying land on the Las Vegas Strip, which prompted large East Coast corporations such as Hilton to do the same.

In 1978, casinos spread to Atlantic City, and they later cropped up in states such as Colorado, Louisiana, and South Dakota. The early 1980s saw casino resorts become more popular for guests and businesses alike, and casino growth increased dramatically by the decade's end. Casino gambling was approved in South Dakota, Iowa, Illinois, Mississippi, Missouri, and on many Native American reservations. In 1989 Iowa became the first state to officially allow gambling on riverboat casinos.

Also in the late 1980s, Stephen A. Wynn almost single-handedly changed Las Vegas by taking gambling to its next step when he built the Mirage resort. The casino resort boasted a shark tank, a wild animal haven, and an artificial erupting volcano. Other major casino operators soon followed suit. Old casinos such as the Sands, the Hacienda, and the New Frontier were demolished. New casinos like the Luxor—a glass version of the great pyramid with copies of Egyptian monuments and statues of pharaohs—were built to attract tourists looking for entertainment.

Although many new casinos were introduced in various cities in the early to mid-1990s, Las Vegas and Atlantic City still claimed approximately two thirds of 1994's gross revenues. To attract visitors, these casino resorts were becoming ever more elaborate. Some even had features such as malls, roller coasters, and golf courses.

Casino companies spent the early 1990s scaling back operations and plunging themselves into serious debt in an effort to rebuild their operations with an eye toward a more lucrative late-1990s market, a gamble that paid off.

Following the release of the National Gambling Impact Study Commission report, initiated in 1997 by President Bill Clinton, a good deal of heated political debate ensued in Washington and in state legislatures about how to properly regulate the casino industry and the activity of gambling itself. Proposals included everything from a legal gambling age of 21 nationwide to banning automatic teller machines (ATMs) from casinos to cigarette-style warning labels on all gambling products about the potential risks of addiction.

The commission recommended a federal ban on Internet gambling and wagering on college sports. The report also urged a limit on casino industry political contributions at the state and local levels. Overall, however, analysts expected that the report was unlikely to lead to any drastic changes to the industry, and thus casino

companies' widespread worries springing from the creation of the commission would prove unwarranted.

Perhaps the most significant element of the report was its call for a moratorium on the expansion of legal gambling in the United States. Particularly concerned were Native American casino industries, which noted that casinos constitute a cornerstone of their economies and that a ban would entail a drastic cutback in social services. The release of the commission's report nonetheless had the industry claiming victory. AGA President Frank J. Fahrenkopf, Jr., trumpeted the report's failure to validate concerns over the gambling industry's connection to organized crime or casino-propelled increases in crime rates.

In efforts to stave off compulsive gambling and the massive losses that accompany it, several proposals cropped up aimed at restricting the ease of cash access. In light of growing awareness of gambling addiction and its dangerous social side effects, critics argued that the presence of ATMs in or near gaming facilities greatly increases the likelihood that individuals would get in over their heads. The industry was heartened, however, when Illinois state legislators struck down an attempted ban on the installment of ATMs inside the state's casinos.

Despite all the continued debate and controversy, the industry's financial supporters were apparently feeling lucky. Bank of America Corp., the leading casino lending operation in the late 1990s, closed the biggest bank financing deal the casino industry had ever seen in 1999 when it agreed to lend $3 billion to Park Place Entertainment for its purchase of Caesar's World and other gaming operations from Starwood Hotels and Resorts Worldwide, Inc. The major casino operators, meanwhile, with more leverage to invest, continued to offer new resorts in efforts to capture the broadest number of customers.

After years of fighting in Atlantic City, Las Vegas, and other cities, the casino industry scored a major victory in June 1999 when the Supreme Court struck down a 65-year-old prohibition against broadcast advertising of casino gambling. Resting on First Amendment provisions, the court stated that the ban "sacrifices an intolerable amount of truthful speech about lawful conduct." Casinos were particularly eager to be rid of the ban, following a 1988 amendment in Congress legalizing such ads for Indian tribes pitching their resorts as vacation spots.

Tribal casinos found some friends in the federal government in the late 1990s. The Department of the Interior issued a controversial ruling in April 1999 under the Indian Gaming Regulatory Act allowing alternative procedures for gaming compacts between states and Native American tribes. The alternative proposal mandates judicially supervised mediation in the case of a state's failure to negotiate gaming compacts in good faith.

Since tribes can claim sovereign immunity under the 11th Amendment to the Constitution, states had little incentive to negotiate compacts with Native American gaming interests. The ruling gives equal footing to tribes in negotiations by reinforcing them with the possibility of a federally enforced non-negotiated compact with the state, thus making it in the interests of the state to engage in good-faith bargaining. Some states, however, such as Alabama and Florida, where casino gambling has been rejected, decried the ruling as an usurpation of states' rights.

Following several major deals in the gaming industry, such as MGM Grand Inc.'s $6.5 billion purchase of Mirage Resorts Inc. in May of 2000, consolidation continued into the early years of the first decade of the 2000s. In April 2001, Colony Capital paid $140 million for the Resorts International Hotel & Casino. In December of that year, Majestic Star Casino paid $149 million for three properties from Fitzgeralds Gaming. American Real Estate Partners paid $38.1 million for the bankrupt Stratosphere Corp. in 2002. Also, in September of 2003, Harrah's Entertainment Inc. bid $1.45 billion for Horseshoe Gaming Holding Corp., which operates casinos in Louisiana, Indiana, and Mississippi. One reason for continued consolidation is the downturn in air travel following the terrorist attacks of September 11, 2001, which prompted the large gaming companies based in Las Vegas, a destination most often reached via air travel, to expand into other geographic areas.

Improved economic conditions, as well as the growing popularity of Las Vegas (especially as a major convention site), benefited the gaming industry. However, even though the industry was prospering, several leading analysts were reluctant to say anything more than that the industry was "stable." Among analysts' concerns was the opinion that most of the gaming industry's discretionary cash flow would go toward expansion and not debt reduction. Other concerns included the impact of potentially negative legislation, possible tax increases at the state level, and uncertainty regarding how the riverboat segment of the industry would tap into the burgeoning baby boomer demographic that was flocking to major casinos.

Despite these concerns, *Bank Loan Report* indicated that investment banks were quite interested in loaning money to the gaming industry. In its May 23, 2005 issue, the publication stated, "Bankers are craving a sector with a strong resilience to market trends, and gaming fits the bill perfectly. At a time when everything from textiles to transportation has been shaken up due to spiking energy costs and soft economic conditions, the gaming industry remains generally profitable, fairly free from regulatory concerns and has positive growth predictions almost across the board. As a result, banks are jockeying to fulfill gaming companies' every financing desire." Banks even

were extending financing to Native American casinos, which previously had difficulty obtaining loans or were forced to do so at high interest rates.

In mid-2004, Caesars Entertainment Inc. announced that it had agreed to be acquired by Harrah's Entertainment Inc. in a deal valued at $9.4 billion. The deal, which was subject to government and shareholder approval, was expected to go through some time in 2005. A second megadeal saw Mandalay Resort Group acquired by MGM MIRAGE for $4.8 billion. In addition, MGM assumed $3.1 billion of Mandalay's debt. Following this activity, the industry was quiet through mid-2005. Because additional merger and acquisition opportunities were limited in the upper echelon of the gambling industry, many industry observers were waiting for the acquisition wave to hit second-tier casinos, possibly during the second half of 2005. Meanwhile, newly formed industry giants looked to international markets for additional growth.

By late 2006, online gambling had become a lucrative niche for the industry, with an estimated 2,000 Web sites accepting bets for poker and sports alone. The United States accounted for about half of the segment's estimated annual revenues of $12 billion. However, a major industry development took place on October 13, 2006, when President Bush signed the Unlawful Internet Gambling Enforcement Act, which makes it unlawful for banks to electronically transfer funds to gambling sites.

The new law had devastating results for regulated, publicly traded companies like 888Holdings plc and PartyGaming plc, which stopped accepting bets from the United States. Based in the United Kingdom, these companies garnered anywhere from50 percent to 70 percent of their revenues from U.S. gamblers. According to *The Cincinnati Post,* publicly traded Internet gambling companies lost approximately$7 billion in market capitalization as a result of the legislation.

It was unclear what the total impact of the Unlawful Internet Gambling Enforcement Act would be. While it certainly impacted publicly traded companies and the manner in which gamblers placed their bets, analysts, gamblers, and gambling firms all doubted that it would stop online wagering. In fact, those engaging in online gambling simply turned to other payment channels, namely e-wallets like NETeller, Click2Pay, and CentralCoin. Some e-wallets allowed customers to accept payments from pre-paid phone cards, making payments virtually impossible to track.

In fact, many observers argued that the act will encourage criminal activity. In the October 19, 2006 issue of *Business Week Online,* Catherine Holahan indicated that the existence of established, regulated players could "make way for private gambling companies and banks based in nations where such industries are loosely policed at best. As a result, the new law could ultimately make billions of dollars in U.S. online gambling transactions more difficult to trace, and increase the likelihood that funds end up in criminal hands."

Despite the Unlawful Internet Gambling Enforcement Act, mobile gambling was still forecast to experience significant growth. In January 2007, the firm Jupiter Research forecast that worldwide, gross bets placed via mobile gambling channels (including sports betting, lotteries, and casinos) would reach $16.6 billion by 2011, up from $1.35 billion in 2006. While Europe was the top market in 2006, with bets totaling $665 million, the most explosive growth was expected in the Asia-Pacific region, which was expected to overtake Europe in 2008 and reach $6.7 billion in bets placed by 2011.

CURRENT CONDITIONS

Revenues for the global gambling industry increased by 24 percent in the four years from 2004 to 2008, noted an article in the November 2009 issue of *The Economist.* The year 2008 saw revenues totaling some $358 billion. Revenues from online betting were a small share of the total, at $20.2 billion, but were increasing fast. However the global economic recession hit the industry in several communities. For example, by the end of 2008, the number of people visiting Las Vegas dropped 4.4 percent to 37.5 million for the year. While the economy appeared to be the most obvious reason, some pointed to the rise in statewide smoking bans as a deterrent.

Nevertheless, two racinos (racetrack casinos) opened in Indiana in 2008, bringing the number of states with racinos to 12. At the same time, voters in Maryland passed a statewide referendum in 2008 legalizing 15,000 slot machines throughout the state. On the global level, gross gaming revenues from Macau in Asia continued to surpass those of the Las Vegas strip. Other Asian markets like Taiwan and Korea were considering casino gambling, and new casino properties in Singapore further expanded the Asian market, said the AGA.

The *2009 AGA Survey of Casino Entertainment* indicated that gross gaming revenues in the United States totaled $32.5 billion, about four percent less than 2007 but still the second highest ever. Sixty percent of survey respondents did say that they were cutting back on gambling activity because of the economy, proportionately similar to those who responded that they were cutting back on restaurant-eating and weekend trips.

According to the AGA, state and local governments were paid $5.7 billion in direct tax revenues from the gaming industry in 2008. The industry was also a major employer, with 357,314 employees during 2008, earning $14.1 billion in wages, benefits, and tips. About 29,600 persons were employed by the gaming equipment manufacturers, which reported $12.7 billion in economic output for 2008. The racetrack casino sector employed 29,000 individuals and reported $2.59 billion in 2008 revenues, growing 17 percent in one year. However, the poker boom of the early decade appeared to be on the wane.

However, in fiscal year 2009, state revenues from all sources of authorized gambling fell 2.8 percent, according to a report from the Rockefeller Institute of Government released in September 2009. It was the first decline in data going back at least 20 years. The report broke down revenues by sector. Lottery income, the largest source of state gambling revenues, fell 2.6 percent. It was the first annual drop in lottery revenue going back to 1970, according to the group. Casino revenues fell 8.5 percent, while revenue from pari-mutuel wagering (including dog and horse racing) was down nearly 15 percent. The bright spot was racinos. The revenue from race tracks that also hosted electronic gambling machines such as slot-machines increased by 6.7 percent, largely because of the new racinos that opened in Indiana and Pennsylvania, the report said.

INDUSTRY LEADERS

Harrah's Entertainment Inc., which accepted a $17 billion buyout offer from Apollo Management and Texas Pacific Group in December of 2006, was the industry's largest player in 2007, following its $9.4 billion acquisition of Caesars Entertainment Inc. in 2005. The company operated or managed 50 casinos and gambling resorts, garnering revenues of $9.67 billion in 2006 and employing approximately 85,000 people. The company sold its East Chicago and Harrah's Tunica casinos to Colony Capital as part of the Caesars deal. In 1999 the company merged with Rio Hotel and Casino and purchased riverboat casino operator Players International. In 2003, Harrah's bid $1.45 billion for Horseshoe Gaming, which operates casinos in Louisiana, Indiana, and Mississippi. The company reported 2008 revenues of $10.1 billion.

Before its acquisition by Harrah's, Caesars Entertainment Inc., which was once named Park Place Entertainment Corp., boasted 24 casinos in five countries in 2005, including such behemoths as Caesar's Palace and the new Paris Las Vegas. Park Place employed 50,000 worldwide and garnered revenues of $4.2 billion in 2004. The company's purchase of Starwood Hotels & Resorts' gaming operations in 1999 brought Caesar's Palace into its empire, adding to its high profile operations like the Flamingo, Bally Entertainment Casinos, and Hilton Casinos. The company's gambling operations included resorts in Las Vegas, Atlantic City, New Orleans, Indiana, and Mississippi, as well as Australia and Canada. Park Place changed its name to Caesars Entertainment Inc. in January 2004, in order to take advantage of its most famous resort's name recognition.

Industry heavyweight MGM MIRAGE had grown even larger with its 2005 acquisition of Mandalay Resort Group, which it obtained for $4.8 billion and the assumption of $3.1 billion of Mandalay's debt. The company was formed in 2000, with the $6.5 billion takeover of Mirage Resorts Inc. by MGM Grand Inc. MGM MIRAGE's properties include some of the most high-profile and glitzy resorts in the business. Before the two firms were united, MGM Grand ran casinos in Australia and South Africa in addition to its U.S. strongholds in Detroit and Atlantic City and operated Nevada casinos through its subsidiary Primadonna Resorts. Its famous New York-New York Hotel and Casino apes the Manhattan skyline. But MGM's pride and joy was its flagship 5,000-room MGM Grand Las Vegas hotel and casino. Mirage Resorts featured everything at its Las Vegas casinos from tigers and dolphins to fine art galleries to themes of pirate ships and a tropical paradise. Under the leadership and colorful personality of Steve Wynn (who chose not to stay on board after the purchase), Mirage grew into one of the largest casino companies in the world. MGM MIRAGE's total sales reached $7.2 billion in 2008, and the company employed 66,500 workers.

Trump Entertainment Resorts Inc. features another colorful personality at the helm. After filing for Chapter 11 bankruptcy protection in 2004, Trump Entertainment emerged in 2005. Following the bankruptcy, the notorious billionaire Donald Trump owned 29 percent of the company, down from 47 percent in 2002. The company, which in 2004 recorded a net loss of $191.3 million on revenues of $1.1 billion, employed 8,450 workers at its casinos, which include Trump Plaza Hotel and Casino, Trump's Marina, and the Trump Taj Mahal in Atlantic City. In December of 2005, the company sold its Indiana riverboat casino to The Majestic Star Casino LCC in a $253 million deal. In March of 2007, Merrill Lynch was retained to help the Trump Entertainment Resorts (TER) identify and evaluate strategic corporate options in the areas of value creation, capital structure, and financing. In February 2009, declining revenues forced Trump Entertainment to file for Chapter 11 bankruptcy.

WORKFORCE

The American Gaming Association reported that in 2008, the industry had 357,314 workers in occupations as diverse as poker dealers, slot attendants, cocktail waiters and waitresses, security guards, and hospitality workers dressed in novelty costumes. They earned $14.1 billion in wages, benefits, and tips. About 29,600 persons were employed by the gaming equipment manufacturers, and the racetrack casino sector (racinos) employed 29,000 individuals.

In some markets, at least, union representation can have a significant impact on wage levels. In two cities in the casino-heavy state of Nevada, Las Vegas and Reno, studies revealed significant wage differentials between the highly represented Las Vegas hotel, gaming, and recreational employees and those in the less unionized market in Reno, with wages substantially higher in the former.

RESEARCH AND TECHNOLOGY

Online gaming continued as a hotly contested issue. In May 2009, the industry's push to legalize online betting got a significant boost from Rep. Barney Frank, D-Mass., who also was head of the House Financial Services Committee. Frank and others argued that online gambling would continue regardless of its legal status and could be regulated and taxed if not outlawed. Opponents centered their objections mostly on moral grounds.

At $12 to $20 billion annually—half of which was attributed to Americans—it also was big business. Much of the segment's popularity was driven by online poker. According to Ben Meyerson in his May 2009 article for the *Chicago Tribune,* a 2007 study for the gambling industry claimed that Frank's 2007 bill, which, though similar to the 2009 bill but was not identical, could have brought in $8.7 billion to $17.6 billion from 2008 to 2017.

However, the moral grounds of expanding gambling to boost a sagging economy remained viable. In January 2009, Reuters announced that Britain's gambling industry faces a compulsory 5 million pound ($7.3 million) a year levy for research into problem gamblers unless it funds a voluntary scheme. In the government announcement, Sports Minister Gerry Sutcliffe, publishing a consultation on how to collect the levy, said it was very disappointing that the industry had failed to agree to a voluntary arrangement. Since 2002 operators had been voluntarily contributing to fund research, education and treatment of problem gambling in an organized effort administered by the Responsibility in Gambling Trust (RIGT). In the United States, casinos, many as part of their state charters, have established similar funds.

BIBLIOGRAPHY

American Gaming Association. 2009 AGA Survey of Casino Entertainment. August 2009. Available from http://www.americangaming.org/assets/files/AGA_Facts_Web.pdf.

———. "Casino Employment," 25 March 2007. Available from http://www.americangaming.org/Industry/factsheets/general_info_detail.cfv?id=28.

———. "Gaming Revenue: Current-Year Data," October 2006. Available fromhttp://www.americangaming.org/Industry/factsheets/statistics_detail.cfv?id=7.

———. "Gaming Revenue: 10-Year Trends," June 2006. Available from http://www.americangaming.org/Industry/factsheets/statistics_detail.cfv?id=8.

———. "States with Gaming," April 2006. Available from http://www.americangaming.org/Industry/factsheets/general_info_detail.cfv?id=15.

———. "Top 20 U.S. Casino Markets by Annual Revenue," April 2006. Available from http://www.americangaming.org/Industry/factsheets/statistics_detail.cfv?id=4. "Experts Debate Impact of Big Gaming Mergers."

———. "U.S. Commercial Casino Industry: Facts at Your Fingertips." August 2009. Available at http://www.americangaming.org/.

Ablott, Matt. "U.S. Outlaws Offshore Credit Card Gambling." *Cards International,* 1 July 2003.

Castle, Tim, and Matt Scuffham. "PDATE 1-UK Gambling Industry Faces 5 Million Pound Levy." Reuters Press Release, 6 January 2009. Available from http://www.reuters.com/article/idUSL660934320090106

"Company Profile." Caesars Entertainment Inc., 2 June 2005. Available from http://www.caesars.com/Corporate/AboutUs/.

"Harrah's Entertainment to Acquire Caesars Entertainment, Create World's Largest Distributor of Casino Entertainment." Harrah's Entertainment Inc., 15 July 2004. Available from http://investor.harrahs.com/releaseDetail.cfm?ReleaseID=139189.

"Harrah's Entertainment, Caesars Entertainment Certify 'Substantial Compliance' With FTC Information Requests." Harrah's Entertainment Inc., 1 January 2005. Available from http://investor.harrahs.com/releaseDetail.cfm?ReleaseID=153187.

"Hitting the Jackpot." *The Economist,* 18 November 2009.

"Experts Debate Impact of Big Gaming Mergers." *Meeting News,* 24 January 2005.

Findlay, John M. *People of Chance.* New York: Oxford University Press, 1986.

"Gaming Industry Looks Stable, but Some Risks Do Exist." *Bank Loan Report,* 23 May 2005.

Habib, Daniel G. "Online and Obsessed." *Sports Illustrated,* 30 May 2005.

Holahan, Catherine. "Online Gambling Goes Underground: A U.S. Law Aimed at Cracking Down on Internet Gambling May Drive the Practice More Into the Shadows and Do Little to Deter Betters." *Business Week Online,* 19 October 2006 Available from www.businessweek.com.

"High Stakes/Anti-gambling Bill Threatens Growth of Popular Online Gambling Industry." *The Cincinnati Post,* 28 October 2006.

"Jokers Wild." *Economist,* 16 April 2005.

Meyerson, Ben. "Gambling Industry Pushes Efforts to Legalize Online Betting." *Chicago Tribune,* 13 May 2009.

"MGM Mirage Reports Revenue Down 6 Percent in 2008." *Hotel & Resort,* 18 March 2009.

"Mobile Gambling Forecast to Top $16 Billion Globally by 2011, Despite Bleak Prospects for US Market." *Internet Wire,* 15 January 2007.

"Recession Creates A Perfect Storm for Internet Gambling." *Business Wire,* 4 October 2008. Available from http://www.highbeam.com/doc/1G1-186324924.html

Rooney, Ben. "Report Shows State Gaming Revenue Fell as the Economy Slumped, Raising Concerns for States Betting Big on Casino and Lottery Income." CNNMoney, 21 September 2009. Available from http://money.cnn.com/2009/09/21/news/economy/gambling/index.htm.

Swartz, John. "3 States Move Toward Legalizing Online Gambling." *USA Today,* 16 March 2005.

"Trump Entertainment Files for Chapter 11." Reuters Press Release, 17 February 2009. Available from http://www.cnbc.com/id/29220893.

"Wall Street Plays Odds in Gaming Sector." *Bank Loan Report,* 23 May 2005.

GAME DESIGN & DEVELOPMENT

——— ■ ———

SIC CODE(S)

7371

7372

INDUSTRY SNAPSHOT

Video game developers produce titles for everything from traditional arcade games to "boxed" games for PC, Macintosh, and popular console systems such as the Sony PlayStation 3, Nintendo Wii, Nintendo DS, and Microsoft Xbox 360. These may be sold online, through traditional brick-and-mortar stores, or in downloadable electronic formats. Online and mobile games, especially those available through popular social media channels, are another major market for video game developers.

During the early 2010s, the video game industry was struggling amidst difficult economic conditions. According to data from NPD Group, reported in the October 16, 2010, issue of *eWeek,* total video game sales were $1.18 billion in September of 2010, down from $1.28 billion in September of 2009. Video game software sales totaled $614 million, down from $649 million the previous year, while hardware sales totaled $383 million, down from $472 million in 2009.

ORGANIZATION AND STRUCTURE

Video game development occurs across a broad spectrum. In addition to amateur "bedroom programmers," large publishing companies employ entire staffs of developers, designers, and artists to produce hit titles. In between independent developers and industry heavyweights are a wide range of small and mid-sized studios.

Developers create games that are distributed via a number of different channels. In addition to traditional arcade games, some titles are distributed as "boxed" games for PC, Macintosh, and console systems such as the Sony PlayStation, Nintendo Wii, Nintendo DS, and Microsoft Xbox 360. These may be sold online, through traditional brick-and-mortar stores, or in downloadable electronic formats.

Online and mobile games were another major market for video game developers during the early 2010s. Consumers were able to download and play a variety of free or low-cost games from leading application stores. In addition, gaming on popular social media sites, such as Facebook, also had become very popular.

Historically, young males have accounted for a large percentage of video game enthusiasts. However, by 2010 an estimated 114 million American adults were video game players, according to information from the Simmons Market Research Bureau National Consumer Survey, reported in the January 25, 2010 issue of *OfficialSpin.* Specifically, this total included 28 million grandparents, 25 million adults over the age of 55, and 13 million retirees.

BACKGROUND AND DEVELOPMENT

Although many consider video games to be a relatively recent phenomenon, the industry's roots stretch back to the first half of the 20th century. In 1940 a coin-operated amusement business named Service Games was formed to provide entertainment on military bases for American servicemen. After relocating to Japan in 1951 the business combined the first two letters of the words "service" and "games" to become Sega.

In 1957 Massachusetts Institute of Technology (MIT) engineers Ken Olsen and Harlan Anderson established Digital Equipment Corporation (DEC) and eventually unveiled a solid-state "personal computer" called the PDP-1, which cost $110,000. MIT purchased a PDP-1 in 1961. Although the computer was utilized for nuclear weapon simulations and other complicated calculations, faculty and student members of the University's Tech Model Railroad Club began tinkering with the device during off hours and eventually created a game called Spacewar!

DEC began putting Spacewar! on all of its PDP-1 computers, and utilized the game as a final test before shipping out the devices to customers (usually universities). Users quickly discovered Spacewar! in the PDP-1's magnetic memory and, according to the December 1, 2008, issue of *Game Developer,* the program "spread across the country's higher education system inspiring new groups of young hackers to expand and refine its gameplay." The article further revealed that Nolan Bushnell was among the college students who discovered Spacewar! Inspired by Spacewar!, which he discovered while attending both the University of Utah and Stanford University, Bushnell developed his own game called Computer Space in 1971. Computer Space has been recognized as the first coin-operated arcade game. According to an article in the August 9, 2001, issue of *The New York Times,* the futuristic-looking game, which resembled a pod from Woody Allen's movie *Sleeper,* was included in the 1973 science fiction film *Soylent Green.*

In later years, various versions of the game (of which 2,000 were made) would be exhibited in modern art museums. In the same *New York Times* article, Bushnell commented, "I knew Computer Space would be in a museum just because of its look, and because it's the first one like it. I was quite aware at the time that we were breaking interesting new ground. But I didn't really perceive that it would become as big and mainstream as it did."

Another major industry development occurred in 1966 when an engineer named Ralph H. Baer, who worked for the firm Sanders Associates Inc., was working on projection and circuit board technology. Along with his partner, Bill Harrison, Baer constructed a chassis with transistors inside. Following a 1967 demonstration, which led management to consider how the device might generate revenue for the organization, Baer and Harrison subsequently developed an interactive prototype called the Brown Box, which enabled users to interact with a screen image.

Baer's original attempt to sell the video game idea to cable companies and manufacturers was an uphill battle. Cable companies were not interested, and television companies were lukewarm. RCA backed out, but Magnavox eventually produced the device, introducing the Odyssey

in May of 1972. The Odyssey, which allowed a player to shoot at targets or play simple ball and stick games such as volleyball and table tennis, was the first video game manufactured and marketed for home use. Six months after the Odyssey became available, 100,000 units were sold. By the end of 1975, 700,000 Odyssey units were in homes across the nation.

Industry developments continued when Nolan Bushnell established Atari Inc. with a $500 investment and introduced an arcade game named Pong in 1972, of which 150,000 units were sold. In 1975 Atari introduced a home version of Pong in response to Magnavox's Odyssey. Because the company was short of funds, Atari formed an agreement with Sears, Roebuck & Co. in which the retailer not only helped fund Atari's inventories, but also agreed to purchase all 100,000 home Pong machines.

In 1976 Atari was sold to Warner Communications Inc. for $28 million, of which Bushnell received about $15 million. The following year the Atari 2600 game system was introduced. In addition to the Combat game cartridge, which was sold with the game system, a flurry of game cartridges were ultimately developed for the 2600 including Adventure (1978), Bowling (1979), Space Invaders (1980), Asteroids (1981), Pac-Man (1981), Pitfall! (1982), Berserk (1982), Mario Bros. (1983), and Pitfall II (1984). Cartridges were developed by Atari, as well as a range of other companies (e.g., Activision, Coleco, Mattel, Imagic, and others).

Atari kicked off the 1980s by introducing Asteroids, an arcade game that competed with Bally's popular arcade game, Space Invaders. A cartridge version of the game was soon introduced, and by the following year more than 1 million units had been sold. By 1981 Atari was the largest producer of video games in the world, with an estimated 80 percent market share in the United States alone.

Although sales totaled approximately $2 billion in 1982, Atari fell upon difficult times, marked by ownership changes and lawsuits. Warner Communications eventually sold the company to former Commodore International Ltd. head Jack Tramiel in 1984 for approximately $240 million. Atari merged with the California-based hard disk drive manufacturer JTS Corp. in 1996, and the company was de-listed from the American Stock Exchange. Infogrames acquired rights to the Atari license in 2000 and ultimately changed its name to Atari Inc.

Video games exploded in popularity during the 1980s. The 1980 release of Pac-Man inspired a hit song two years later called Pac-Man Fever, which captured the enthusiasm of gamers everywhere. Following the debut of *Electronic Games,* the first magazine devoted exclusively to video games, *Time* magazine featured them on its cover in 1982. That same year Disney broke new ground by producing Tron, a feature movie about video games starring Jeff Bridges. Other popular arcade games during the decade would include Defender, Pole Position, Spy Hunter, and Dragonslayer.

First introduced to North America in 1985, the Nintendo Entertainment System (NES) and its successor, the Super Nintendo Entertainment System, were extremely popular game console systems during the last half of the 1980s and into the 1990s. An "arcade" version of the NES, which retailed for $199, came equipped with the popular game Super Mario Bros. Ultimately, more than 70 million NES units were sold throughout the world.

During the 1980s, video game development also accelerated for the popular Commodore 64 (C-64) personal computer. Based on its predecessor, the VIC-20, the C-64 ultimately generated unit sales of approximately 17 million between its 1982 debut and end of production 10 years later. Ease of programmability led to a flurry of games for the C-64, from leading manufacturers such as Electronic Arts. In addition, young hackers began "cracking," copying, and trading games, further accelerating their popularity. The C-64 was later succeeded by the C128 Personal Computer.

By the early 1990s controversy had surfaced regarding violence in video games, prompting a Senate investigation into the matter. In 1993 the breakthrough game Myst was introduced, providing a non-violent, visually stunning gaming experience to consumers.

Nintendo continued to have a major impact on video game development during the remainder of the 1990s. In 1995 the company celebrated the sale of its 1 billionth video game. The popularity of game consoles was furthered by the availability of game cartridge rentals at many video stores. The introduction of the Sony PlayStation in 1995 and Sega Dreamcast in 1998 assured the continued popularity of home video game systems.

In addition to game consoles, PC games also were extremely popular during the 1990s. Games became major productions, with soundtracks featuring well-known recording artists and voice talent from leading celebrities like Dennis Hopper. One popular game during the late 1990s was Tomb Raider, which concentrated on the adventures of archaeologist Lara Croft.

The new millennium was accompanied by the debut of a strategic life simulation game called The Sims. By this time, unit sales of Nintendo's popular Game Boy handheld gaming system reached 100 million. As a testament to their continued popularity, video games received their own television network in 2002 called G4.

The video game console market remained extremely competitive during the first decade of the 2000s. Following Sony's release of PlayStation 2, Sega stopped manufacturing game consoles in 2001. That year Microsoft got in the game with the release of its Xbox game system, which was succeeded by the more robust Xbox 360 in late 2005. In addition to Sony and Microsoft, Nintendo continued introducing new game systems throughout the remainder of the decade. For example, the Nintendo GameCube debuted in 2001, followed by the Nintendo Wii in 2006. By 2009 Wii sales exceeded 50 million, and sales of the company's Nintendo DS system totaled more than 100 million.

PIONEERS IN THE FIELD

Nolan Bushnell Born in 1943, Nolan Bushnell, who has been called the "Father of the Video Game Industry," is one of the most active entrepreneurs of his time. After inventing the video game Computer Space in 1971, Bushnell established Atari in 1972. He earned the nickname "King Pong" after the hugely successful table-tennis video game he invented that year. In 1976 Bushnell sold Atari to Warner Communications.

Bushnell has founded more than 20 companies. In 1978 he established Pizza Time Theaters and the well-known character, Chuck E. Cheese. Catalyst Technologies was established in 1981, three years before Bushnell resigned from Pizza Time. He joined Aristo International (later Play-Net Technologies) in 1996 and formed uWink.com in 1999, at which time he also joined Wave Systems Corp.'s board of directors.

For all of his success in establishing companies, however, Bushnell has had a spotty record of long-term corporate growth. Several of his companies have failed and he earned a reputation for losing interest in those that did succeed. Despite this, he remained a creative force in Silicon Valley's competitive atmosphere.

Ralph H. Baer Ralph Baer is the inventor of what is widely recognized as the first home video game played on a television. Ralph Baer knew his "Brown Box," the predecessor to the 1972 Magnavox Odyssey, would be a hit when he first envisioned it in 1966. Allowing the user to play volleyball, football, and table tennis, as well as shoot at targets, his patented "Television and Gaming Training Apparatus" was in 700,000 homes by 1975.

Baer immigrated to the United States in 1938, at the age of 16. He found a job in a factory and began working while simultaneously taking courses with the National Radio Institute (NRI). Baer completed his studies in 1940 when he became a radio service technician. For the next three years, Baer serviced televisions and radios in multiple New York shops, before being drafted to fight with the army in World War II.

Baer served for three years, two of them in France, until the war ended in 1946. He became an expert in weapons, particularly small arms, and spent much of his enlisted time training troops about the technology. At the end of the war, however, he opted to return to civilian life rather than remain with the army. Baer did not return to New York, instead choosing to enroll in the American Television Institute of Technology (ATIT) in Chicago. Baer graduated in 1949, earning a bachelor of science degree in television engineering, the first degree of its kind.

After completing school, Baer took a position as an engineer for several New York firms: Wrapper Inc. (1949–1950), Loral Electronics (1951–1952), and Transitron Inc. (1952–1956). Transitron relocated to Manchester, New Hampshire, in 1955, and Baer went with the company. In 1956 he joined Sanders Associates Inc., in Nashua, New Hampshire. He remained with Sanders until the 1990s, even after forming his own company, R.H. Baer Consultants, in 1975.

As he climbed the corporate ladder, Baer worked on such products as surgical cutting machines, time punch clocks, radar test equipment, electrostatic loudspeakers, military intelligence snooping equipment, high speed picture tube deflection components, and high-density multi-layer printed circuit boards. In 1966, however, the invention that would change the course of his career came to fruition, with the development of the Brown Box.

After the Odyssey came a variety of Baer-created hand-held and table top video games and electronic toys and products, such as Smarty-Bear, Computer Perfection, MANIAC, Talking Tools, and SIMON, which was created in the 1970s and was still in production in the second decade of the twenty-first century. In the middle of the first decade of the 2000s, Baer donated a functional replica collection of experimental video game models to the Museum of the Moving Image in New York, and gave his collection of all the original game units to the Smithsonian Institution in Washington, DC. For his important contribution to video game technology, Baer was awarded the National Medal of Technology by President George Bush in 2006, and the Developers Choice Pioneer Award by the video game industry in 2008.

CURRENT CONDITIONS

During the early 2010s, the video game industry was struggling amidst difficult economic conditions. According to data from NPD Group, reported in the October 16, 2010 issue of *eWeek,* total video game sales were $1.18 billion in September of 2010, down from $1.28 billion in September of 2009. Video game software sales totaled $614 million, down from $649 million the previous year, while hardware sales totaled $383 million, down from $472 million in 2009.

Some analysts indicated that the growing popularity of game systems such as the Nintendo Wii, which appealed to a broad audience, meant that the industry was more sensitive to economic cycles that in the past, when hard-core gamers accounted for the majority of sales. In addition, many consumers begin purchasing second-hand games and playing free online games, including those on popular social networking sites such as Facebook. Another consideration was that while traditional video game hardware and software sales were struggling, growth was taking place in other channels. This especially was the case with digital downloads. In its September 25, 2010, issue, *eWeek* reported additional data from NPD Group indicating that during the first half of 2010, the number of PC full-game digital downloads exceeded physical games sold at retail for the very first time.

After a flurry of hit video games in 2008, the industry experienced a lull in 2009 until the latter part of the year. "Modern Warfare 2" became the fastest-selling game in history in November, when 7 million copies were sold on its release day. Other popular titles included NCAA Football 11, Starcraft II, and Lego Harry Potter.

In order to compete in the marketplace, industry leaders have been offering video game consoles with extended features. For example, in mid-2010, rumors began circulating that both Microsoft and Sony would enhance their game consoles by adding access to the popular online video site Hulu. By this time Sony, Microsoft, and Nintendo all offered access to the online movie service Netflix on their devices, enabling consumers to stream movies and popular television programs via the Internet. In a March 30, 2010, *Internet Wire* release, a report from the research firm Parks Associates, titled "Digital Lifestyles: 2010 Outlook," found that the number of U.S. households with Internet-connected game consoles increased 64 percent from 2008 to 2009. In October 2010, *PC Magazine Online* referred to reports that Sony would be offering a smartphone version of the PlayStation Portable.

Violence in video games was a hot topic in 2010. At that time the industry was fighting a 2005 California law that would prohibit the rental or sale of violent games to minors. Questions over the law's constitutionality and free-speech limitations catapulted the case, Schwarzenegger v. Entertainment Merchants Association, to the U.S. Supreme Court in November, at which time the high court heard related arguments.

In its November 11, 2010, issue, *The New York Times* provided further insight into the issue of violence in video games. Referring to several games that it deemed "grotesquely violent," (including Duke Nukem 3D and Grand Theft Auto: Vice City), the publication said that some games "graphically depict mutilation, torture, rape and murder. Players don't read about violence or just see it. They act it out. Parents worry that young people may engage in violent behavior or suffer psychological harm."

INDUSTRY LEADERS

The video game development industry is dominated by a number of heavyweights. Companies such as Sony Corp. (PlayStation 3) and Microsoft (Xbox 360) have operations that extend well beyond the video game market. Other leaders, such as Nintendo Company Ltd., have concentrated on video games more exclusively, and for a much longer period of time.

Nintendo Company Ltd. traces its roots back to 1889, when Fusajiro Yamauchi established Marufuku Co., Ltd. to produce Hanafuda, traditional Japanese playing cards. In 1951 the company adopted the name Nintendo Playing Card Company Ltd. The word "Nintendo" is a proverbial expression meaning "you work hard but, in the end, it's in heaven's hands." President Hiroshi Yamauchi believed this name was a more accurate reflection of the company's product line.

Nintendo released its first electronic product, the Beam Gun Series, in 1970. Three years later, people were playing the company's simulated clay-pigeon shooting game, which utilized a laser beam gun and computer-projected "pigeons." In 1975 Nintendo and Mitsubishi Electric combined their technologies and creativity to produce the first video game in which a human could compete against a computer. To further expansion into the United States, Nintendo of America Inc. was formed in 1980. During the early 1980s the company introduced the Family Computer (Famicom), which later was called the Nintendo Entertainment System (NES).

In 1989 Nintendo celebrated its centennial with the release of Game Boy, a hand-held version of its NES. Nintendo of America Inc. sold its 1 billionth video game in 1995 and its 100 millionth Game Boy unit five years later. The company continued to dazzle consumers with new game systems, such as the Nintendo GameCube console in 2001, the Nintendo DS in 2004, and the interactive Nintendo Wii in 2006. In 2009 Wii sales exceeded the 50 million mark, and Nintendo DS sales surpassed 100 million. Nintendo generated sales of $17.56 billion during its 2010 fiscal year, at which time the company employed 4,130 people.

Another industry leader with a long heritage is Redwood City, California-based Electronic Arts Inc., which traces its roots back to 1982, when it was formed as Amazin' Software. Backed by $5 million in private capital, the company (headed up by three former Apple Computer managers) began producing video game titles for a variety of computer systems. These included the Atari 800 and the Commodore 64. Later, Electronic Arts began producing titles for video game systems such as the

Sega Genesis and Super Nintendo Entertainment System. In particular, Electronic Arts became known for its EA SPORTS games, including John Madden Football.

By the mid-1990s, Electronic Arts was an international leader in the video game market. During the early years of the first decade of the 2000s, the company began producing titles for the Sony PlayStation 2. In addition, it acquired a casino/parlor card games site called Pogo.com in 2001, broadening its opportunities. Other titles during that decade included games associated with Harry Potter, James Bond, and Lord of the Rings.

By the middle of the first decade of the 2000s, Electronic Arts was enjoying success from its hit title, The Sims. After establishing a partnership with Hasbro in August of 2007, the company went on to produce Hasbro-branded games. The popularity of family-friendly titles made the venture a success, and by 2010 it had introduced 20 different Hasbro games for 18 different platforms. Electronic Arts generated sales of $2.95 billion in 2004, at which time it held a 22 percent share of the North American video game market. Electronic Arts' operating revenue reached $3.65 billion during the company's 2010 fiscal year, when Electronic Arts employed 7,800 people.

In addition to the very largest industry players, a large number of video game development companies drive success and innovation within the industry. In its June 1, 2010, issue, *Game Developer* produced a list of the industry's leading 30 developers for 2009. Heading up the list were: ThatGameCompany (Los Angeles); Bio Ware Edmonton (Edmonton, Alberta, Canada); From Software (Tokyo, Japan); 5th Cell (Bellevue, Washington); CCP Games (Reykjavik, Iceland); Infinity Ward (Encino, California); Yuke's (Osaka, Japan); Playfish (London); and Gearbox (Plano, Texas).

AMERICA AND THE WORLD

The impact of difficult economic conditions on the video game industry was not unique to the United States. According to data from the consultancy Screen Digest, reported in the March 27, 2010, issue of *The Economist*, video game sales fell 6.3 percent worldwide in 2009. The largest sales drop took place in America (9.3 percent), followed by Europe (3.5 percent), and Japan (2 percent).

Looking ahead, one promising market for video games was China. This was especially true of mobile gaming applications. In a January 20, 2010, *Wireless News* release, Pyramid Research projected that between 2009 and 2014, the country's mobile gaming market would expand to $2.5 billion on the strength of a 51.5 percent compound annual growth rate. The research firm identified several conditional factors that were essential in order to achieve this growth, including affordable data access, more robust handsets, and better 3G coverage.

In addition to mobile games, online games were another strong market. In its January 29, 2010, issue, *Daily Variety* indicated that China was home to 66 million online game players in 2009. This was an increase of 33 percent from the previous year. Looking forward, the Chinese online gaming population was projected to reach 123 million by 2014.

RESEARCH AND TECHNOLOGY

The topic of violence in video games remained at the forefront in late 2010. In August of that year, a national non-profit organization named Common Sense Media conducted a nationwide poll in order to gain insight into the issue. Performed by Zogby International, the survey of 2,100 adults found that 72 percent "would support a law that prohibits minors from purchasing ultraviolent or sexually violent video games without parental consent," according to the September 29, 2010, issue of *Electronics Business Journal.*

On the technology front, Wi-Fi-equipped gaming consoles were exploding in popularity. According to a report from the firm Research and Markets, shipments of Wi-Fi-equipped devices were projected to reach 177.3 million units by 2013, up from 108.8 million units in 2009. Although these figures include devices such as personal media players and cameras, the majority of shipments were expected to be attributed to handheld gaming devices and gaming consoles, as reported in the January 2010 issue of *Wi-Fi Wireless LAN.*

BIBLIOGRAPHY

"72 Percent of Adults Support a Ban on the Sale of Ultraviolent Video Games to Minors." *Electronics Business Journal,* 29 September 2010.

"Atari Corp." *Notable Corporate Chronologies.* Online Edition. Farmington Hills, MI: Gale Group, 2001.

"Atari Inc." *Notable Corporate Chronologies.* Online Edition. Farmington Hills, MI: Gale Group, 2009.

Coonan, Clifford. "Gamer Population Growing Rapidly." *Daily Variety,* 29 January 2010.

"EA Touts Sales of More Than 8 Million Units of Hasbro-Branded Video Games in One Year." *Wireless News,* 17 February 2010.

"Electronic Arts Inc." In *International Directory of Company Histories,* Vol. 85. Farmington Hills, MI: St. James Press, 2007.

Fleming, Jeffrey. "Boston, Massachusetts." *Game Developer,* 1 December 2008.

Glaser, Mark. "The Space Age Game That Set the Stage." *The New York Times,* 9 August 2001.

Grossman, Lev, and Kristina Dell. "From Geek to Chic in 33 Years: Three Decades after Video Games Invaded Our Space, It's Finally Hip to Be Square." *Time,* 23 May 2005.

Kendall, Brent. "High Court to Hear Video game Case; Justices Agree to Decide Constitutionality of California Bid to End Sales of Violent Content to Minors." *The Wall Street Journal Eastern Edition,* 27 April 2010.

Matthews, Ian. "The Commodore 64: Machine of Destiny," 2 June 2007. Available from http://commodore.ca/products/c64/commodore_64.htm.

Neild, Barry. "Space Invaders." *Computer Weekly,* 13 January 2000.

"Nintendo Company, Ltd." In *International Directory of Company Histories,* Vol. 67. Farmington Hills, MI: St. James Press, 2005.

"Nintendo Company Ltd." *Notable Corporate Chronologies.* Online Edition. Farmington Hills, MI: Gale Group, 2010.

"Nintendo Famicom/NES," 10 November 2010. Available from http://www.cyberiapc.com/vgg/nintendo_nes.htm.

"Nolan Bushnell." *Business Leader Profiles for Students.* Detroit: Gale, 1999.

"Nolan Bushnell." *Newsmakers.* Detroit: Gale, 1985.

"PC FullGame Digital Downloads Surpass Retail Unit Sales." *eWeek,* 25 September 2010.

"Pyramid Research: Mobile Gaming in China to Reach $2.5 Billion by 2014." *Wireless News,* 20 January 2010.

"Ralph H. Baer." *Biography Resource Center.* Detroit: Gale, 2010.

"Report: PlayStation 3 May Get Hulu Service." *Seattle Post-Intelligencer,* 28 June 2010.

"Report: Sony PlayStation Phone Is Coming." *PC Magazine Online,* 27 October 2010.

"Research and Markets: Wi-Fi-Enabled Entertainment Device Shipments Will Increase from 108.8 million in 2009 to 177.3 million in 2013." *Wi-Fi Wireless LAN,* January 2010.

"SEGA: Company History." *Marketing Week,* 13 July 2006.

Sheffield, Brandon, and Jeffrey Fleming. "Top 30 Developers." *Game Developer,* 1 June 2010.

"Still Playing; Video Games in the Recession." *The Economist,* 27 March 2010.

"The Video gamer Population Includes 25 Million Adults in the 55+ Age Bracket, 13 Million Retirees and 28 Million Grandparents; New Report Provides Detailed Analysis of the Leisure Market." *OfficialSpin,* 25 January 2010.

"Total Share: Personal Computer Market Share 1975–2005," 11 November 2010. Available from http://jeremyreimer.com.

"U.S. Households Using PCs and Game Consoles to Extend Online Video to the TV." *Internet Wire,* 30 March 2010.

"Video Game Industry Slumps Despite Surge in Hardware Sales." *eWeek,* 14 August 2010.

"Video Game Odyssey: The Long Journey from Brown Box to Xbox." *Technology Review,* March 2002.

"Video Game Sales Slip Again in September." *eWeek,* 16 October 2010.

"Video Games and the First Amendment." *The New York Times,* 11 November 2010.

GENEALOGY PRODUCTS AND SERVICES

SIC CODE(S)

2721

2741

7372

7379

7389

8999

INDUSTRY SNAPSHOT

The pursuit of genealogy involves searching for one's ancestors; the validation, verification, and documentation of related facts; and often the publication of such information in the form of family trees, books, videos, Web sites, or presentations. Once a relatively obscure pastime, genealogy has evolved into the United States' second most popular hobby (behind gardening), according to the National Genealogical Society. Rhonda McClure, author of *The Complete Idiot's Guide to Online Genealogy,* further noted that genealogy was the nation's leading year-round hobby. Tracking site comScore Media Metrix reported that in a single month, April 2009, more than 8 million unique worldwide visitors spent more than 4 million hours on the Ancestry Web site.

In their quest to identify ancestors, build family trees, and learn more about their roots, genealogists, also known as family historians or "rooters," employ a variety of tactics. While they engage in old-fashioned archival research by combing through public records, obituaries, and local history collections at libraries, genealogists also take advantage of a growing base of products and services

that include computer software, online databases, books, and videos.

Genealogy enthusiasts spend anywhere from $700 to $20,000 per year in their effort to uncover the past, according to Everton Publishers, a leading provider of genealogy publications and services. Driven by the spending of some 80 million genealogists, genealogy products and services constitute a billion-dollar industry. The industry marketed its wares to a wide range of customers in virtually every age, ethnic, and demographic group. The aging baby boomer segment of the population, which had ample spending cash and a growing amount of leisure time, was an especially lucrative market.

ORGANIZATION AND STRUCTURE

Market Overview. At one time, genealogy and family history were largely stereotyped as a hobby pursued by older adults, Civil War enthusiasts, Mormons, and, in the words of *The Washington Times'* Lisa Rauschart, "straight-laced Mayflower descendants." While these segments of the population represent a sizeable share of the family history market, children, teenagers, and younger adults from a wide range of demographic and socioeconomic backgrounds were pursuing genealogy.

In particular, the aging baby boomer demographic, with money to spend and growing amounts of free time, represented a lucrative customer base for genealogy product and service providers. In the April 2001 issue of *Utah Business,* Paul Nauta, manager of the planning and communications office of the Mormon Church's Family and Church History Department, explained, "In the United States, as the baby boomers approach retirement age, it seems they are becoming increasingly interested in capturing their family histories as a legacy for their posterity. The urbanization of America and the breakdown of the traditional nuclear family have also left many longing for the close family bonds of their youth. Many are finding that using technology to discover and verify their heritage provides a deep feeling of belonging and meaning."

While some companies specialize in one area or another, many of the genealogy industry's major players offer a range of products and services in multiple categories. These include subscription-based online services, publications, and computer software. In addition, the industry includes local, state, and federal archives and libraries; government agencies that provide copies of vital records and other documents; professional genealogists; tour operators; and associations for both amateur and professional genealogists.

Online Resources Of the leading genealogy sites in 2008, eight were operated by The Generations Network Inc. (now Ancestry.com). These included RootsWeb.com, one of the oldest message board communities; Geneaolgy. com, a membership site providing access to a variety of records and family histories; and Ancestry.com, which offered 23,000 searchable databases, approximately 5 billion records, free software, message boards, and a variety of forms, charts, and other resources. Ancestry. co.uk gave users access to more than 200 million names and ecclesiastical, civil, and immigration records from Wales, Scotland, Ireland, and England. Finally, the company's namesake site, MyFamily.com, allowed families to build and maintain password-protected family Web sites that were useful for sharing historical information, planning family events, and even having online discussions.

In addition to general genealogy Web sites that offered something for just about everyone, there were numerous Web sites that catered to specific racial and ethic groups. These sites helped researchers to overcome roadblocks or deal with subtleties unique to each group. For example, prior to the Civil War, African American slaves were not always listed in records by their names. Making matters even more complicated, after the war, many former slaves assumed new names.

One major player in the world of Internet genealogy resources is the Church of Jesus Christ of Latter-day Saints (LDS). Also known as the Mormon Church, LDS operates the Family History Library System, which consists of the world's largest family history library and a network of branch locations called family history centers (including approximately 1,800 in the United States). The church's Web site, familysearch.org, provides useful information about compiling family histories and allows users to search the church's record collections, which

contain more than two million rolls of microfilm with digitized documents from countries throughout the world. In addition, the site gives genealogists the ability to share their data with fellow researchers and connect through e-mail collaboration lists.

Operated by the Statue of Liberty-Ellis Island Foundation, a non-profit organization dedicated to the restoration and preservation of the Statue of Liberty and Ellis Island, ellisislandrecords.com was another useful online resource for genealogists. In addition to serving as a channel through which the public could make donations to the foundation and buy genealogy-related items, this site allowed researchers to conduct searches among records of immigrant passengers who entered through the Port of New York and Ellis Island between 1892 and 1924. In addition, users could view historical information and photos about Ellis Island, create and search family scrapbooks, learn more about genealogy, and download useful forms.

Books and Publications A strong market existed for books devoted to family history and genealogy. Online retailer Amazon.com has listed more than 66,000 titles in this subject area. While the sheer number of titles may seem overwhelming, many selections were written for specialized reader groups. For example, Amazon.com offered titles specifically for readers interested in Jewish or Italian genealogy. Other niche titles included books specifically for women, such as Christina Schaefer's *The Hidden Half of the Family: A Sourcebook for Women's Genealogy,* and Rachael Freed's *Women's Lives, Women's Legacies: Passing Your Beliefs and Blessings to Future Generations.* Other titles applied to conducting genealogical research on the Internet using popular brands of genealogy software, while many more were aimed at individuals who were new to the hobby and needed advice getting started. Books that provided solid general overviews of genealogy included *The Complete Idiot's Guide to Genealogy* by Christine Rose and Kay Germain Ingalls, as well as *The Everything Family Tree Book: Finding, Charting, and Preserving Your Family History* by William G. Hartley. In addition to its wide range of online offerings and CD-ROM database products, The Generations Network Inc. published some 50 book titles during the late years of the first decade, as well as magazines like *Genealogical Computing Magazine* and *Ancestry Magazine.*

Computer Software Before the advent of the Internet, genealogists were forced to travel in person to conduct their research. This started to change during the 1980s with the adoption of personal computing. As part of this trend, libraries and other organizations began digitizing records and storing them on CD-ROMs and consumers started investing in genealogy software applications that allowed them to store their data in electronic format, build family trees, and more. According to the September 23, 2002, issue of *The New York Times,* even before the emergence of the Internet, the genealogy software industry was worth approximately $30 million. By the turn of the new century, genealogy software had evolved into an established segment of the larger software industry. While some basic genealogy software applications, such as Personal Ancestral File from the Mormon Church, were available for free, software companies marketed many programs with more extensive features. These applications helped family history enthusiasts to find their ancestors, document their findings, organize everything from text-based information and digital images to video clips, and print family trees and other types of reports. Most genealogy applications allowed users to store their family tree information in a common file format called GEDCOM, which stands for Genealogical Data Communications.

Vital/Public Records Government agencies at the federal, state, and local levels are another group of important genealogy industry players. For many years, government offices ranging from county clerks and state vital records departments to the National Archives charged genealogy researchers nominal fees for copies of death, birth, and marriage certificates, as well as census records and land deeds. However, many cash-strapped government agencies sought to capitalize on genealogy's burgeoning popularity and turn records into a significant revenue source.

On an August 22, 2003, Minnesota Public Radio broadcast, Marion Smith, senior historian of the Immigration and Naturalization Service, said, "Certainly, the sticker shock is going around, because government at every level is raising the fees on this sort of thing. So it becomes a little bit expensive here to start doing this genealogy that used to be a tank of gas to go to the courthouse or whatever." Citing just one example of rising government fees, reporter Rachel Dornhelm indicated that the National Archives had increased its fees for copies of Civil War pension records to $37, up from $10 just a few years prior.

Professional Genealogists Software companies, book publishers, and government agencies are not the only parties benefiting from the burgeoning market for genealogy and family history. Professional genealogists, who earn anywhere from $20 to $100 per hour (plus expenses) for their services, are another key segment of the industry. Many reputable professionals belong to the Association of Professional Genealogists, which had some 2,000 members worldwide in 2009. In addition to professional genealogists, translators are another key group of service providers who translate records, correspondence, articles, and other media for people who do not have a grasp of their ancestors' ethnic language.

Specialty Travel The travel industry also has a hand in the business of family history. Genealogy enthusiasts frequently plan everything from short day trips to lengthy international vacations in order to comb archives for records, visit the locations where their ancestors once lived and worked, locate gravestones and battlefields, and more. Publications that cater to specific ethnic groups commonly include advertisements for trips with a genealogy theme. For example, *Nordic Reach,* a quarterly magazine dedicated to Scandinavian culture, regularly includes classified advertisements for personalized and group "heritage tours" and genealogy research trips in Sweden. Many of these tours promise to take travelers off the beaten path via foot, bicycle, and even kayak to visit places of interest. In addition to tours, advertisements promote translation services, museums and research centers, and other places of importance to travelers.

Associations The genealogy market includes numerous clubs and societies at the state and local levels. A number of national organizations represent the interests of both amateur and professional genealogists alike, and serve to promote the field as a meaningful pursuit. These include the National Genealogical Society, the United States Internet Genealogical Society, and the Association of Professional Genealogists.

Established in 1903, the non-profit, Arlington, Virginia-based National Genealogical Society (NGS) includes amateurs and advanced family historians among its members. In addition to research trips and its annual NGS Conference in the States, the NGS publishes *NGS NewsMagazine* and *NGS Quarterly.* The association also offers its members an online resource center and various home study courses.

According to the NGS, its objectives include "Providing genealogical skill development through education, information, publications, research assistance, and networking opportunities; establishing and promoting the highest standards of ethical research principles and scholarly practices; establishing important links with other groups worldwide; providing depth and breadth of knowledge and opportunities for our members; creating programs to increase public awareness of opportunities to discover family history; and, promoting interest in the fascinating field of genealogy and family history."

Although it benefits many of the same enthusiasts as the NGS, the United States Internet Genealogical Society (USIGS) is focused on making primary source documents freely available to genealogists and historians via the Internet. According to the USIGS, it accomplishes its mission via: "Recognition of those projects with primary source records already online for FREE access; encouragement of other projects both online and off to persuade them to copy primary source records and to post them online for FREE access; education of individuals and projects in all aspects of the process of finding, copying and posting primary source records online; acquisition of funds to support ourselves and other projects in all aspects of finding, copying, posting, and storing primary source documents; storage of documentation, web pages, databases, and archives which are generated in all aspects of the operation of our organization; and encouragement of membership in our organization."

As its name suggests, the non-profit Association of Professional Genealogists (APGEN) represents individuals who have either chosen genealogy as their vocation or are aspiring to do so. In addition, it serves to protect members of the public who use the services of professional genealogists. Based in Westminster, Colorado, APGEN was founded in 1979 with nineteen members. By 2009 its ranks had grown to 2,000, up from 1,300 earlier in the decade. The association publishes a quarterly journal and a biennial membership directory and hosts an annual professional conference. Its objectives are "To promote international awareness of, and interest in, professional genealogical services; to promote professional standards in genealogical research, writing and speaking; to engage in activities which improve access, facilitate research and preserve records used in the fields of genealogy and local history; to promote awareness of activities and/or laws which may affect genealogical and historical research; to educate the membership and public through publications and lectures; and to provide support for those engaged in genealogical pursuits as a business."

BACKGROUND AND DEVELOPMENT

The tracing of family lineages dates back thousands of years. The establishment of the National Genealogical Society (NGS) in 1903 marked the beginning of a more formal approach to this endeavor in the United States. Three years after it was founded, the NGS had 37 resident members, 40 non-resident members, and 23 honorary members. As genealogy became a popular pastime for residents across the country, non-resident members eventually represented the majority of the AGS membership base. The association celebrated its fiftieth anniversary in 1953 and was still flourishing as of the middle of the first decade of the 2000s.

By the mid-1990s, genealogy was quickly becoming popular with millions of Americans. A May 1996 Maritz Marketing Research poll, conducted by the University of Connecticut's Roper Center, found that of 777 respondents, 38 percent were somewhat involved with genealogy while 7 percent were involved a great deal. America's interest in genealogy continued to grow into the new millennium, supported by the growing availability of information on the World Wide Web. A subsequent Maritz poll, conducted in

association with Genealogy.com in May of 2000, found that 60 percent of Americans were somewhat interested in genealogy by this time.

The rapid availability of online data led to concerns regarding identify theft. For example, in December 2001, California Governor Gray Davis blocked the sale of the state's database of birth and death records. The data included sensitive details, such as mothers' maiden names, which could be used by malicious parties to access financial information for individuals who were still living. While this aggravated some genealogists, the move was welcomed by privacy advocates.

Genealogy continued to explode in popularity. Just as the Internet did much to accelerate the progress of family historians during the previous decade, new advancements continued to help some researchers overcome long-standing roadblocks in their search to uncover the past. One such advancement was the use of DNA testing to determine one's ancestry. A number of companies sold do-it-yourself genetic testing kits that people could use to collect DNA samples and mail them back to a laboratory for analysis.

Generally speaking, DNA testing seeks to identify certain genetic markers that are passed down from generation to generation. These markers either correspond to mitochondrial DNA (mtDNA) that people inherit from their mothers, or to markers on the Y chromosome that males pass from generation to generation. If two individuals have the same markers, it is likely they share a common ancestor at some point in their past. By comparing one's DNA to a database of DNA samples collected from people throughout the world, genetic testing seeks to identify which geographic region someone comes from.

Based in Salt Lake City, Utah, the Sorenson Molecular Genealogy Foundation (SMGF) was one player in the arena of DNA analysis. Led by entrepreneur James LeVoy Sorenson, the foundation hoped to map the entire world family tree using genetic technology. In early 2004 the foundation allowed individuals to trace their paternal ancestry by entering the results of their DNA analysis online and comparing their information against a database of 5,000 DNA samples. These samples were obtained from people who provided ancestry records going back four or more generations. According to a March 1, 2004, *Business Wire* release, the SMGF uses Y chromosome information to link surnames with geographic locations and birth dates prior to the 1900s (in order to protect individual privacy). The aforementioned 5,000 samples pertained to some 205,000 people. This dataset was a mere fraction of the 40,000 DNA samples the foundation claimed to have collected.

DNA tests hold the potential to help some researchers fill in blanks about their past. However, a number of scientists are skeptical about their reliability. They argue that such tests have a number of limitations, and that a genetic match does not necessarily prove that individuals hail from the same place. Although DNA analysis is useful in tracing the large-scale migration patterns of clans or ethnic groups, using this same approach at the individual level may not be as effective. One criticism is that the DNA databases used for comparison are largely incomplete. As more samples are collected from different ethic groups, it will become possible to offer more specific results. In addition, these tests only look at limited genetic information, which in some cases is not always specific to a particular ethic group or geographic region.

As genealogy grew in popularity, so did the number of resources available to genealogists of all stripes. Of appeal to a wide swath of hobbyists were new database products like Proquest's Genealogy Center, which allowed libraries to hand-pick from a variety of information products in order to create custom resources for patrons. In addition, ProQuest had plans to offer a massive 10 million-record database of death notices, dating back to 1851, from leading newspapers like *The Boston Globe, Chicago Tribune, The Washington Post, The New York Times, Los Angeles Times,* and the *Atlanta Journal-Constitution.*

In addition to resources such as these, which appealed to large audiences, new offerings continued to hit the market for those with very specific needs. One example was the book *Medieval Genealogy: How to Find Your Medieval Ancestors,* by Paul Chambers. The tome helped family research enthusiasts trace their roots back to the time period from 1066 to 1603. Another niche resource was the Jamestowne and Colonial Virginia Genealogy and DNA Project, a collaboration between three Utah firms—Relative Genetics, GenealogyFound, and Heirlines Family History & Genealogy. Beginning in 2007, the project planned to use both genetics and traditional genealogy methods to help ancestors trace their roots back to early colonial America.

Finally, in September 2006, the Sorenson Molecular Genealogy Foundation made its database of some 5,000 mitochondrial DNA samples available to amateur genealogists at no charge. The database allowed those who had already undergone DNA testing to match their results against Sorenson's database, in order to trace their maternal ancestors. Sorenson also offered mitochondrial DNA tests at a discount to those who had not had the test performed.

CURRENT CONDITIONS

In December 2009, Ancestry.com announced that President Barack Obama and investment billionaire Warren Buffett were seventh cousins three times removed. They were related through a 17th century Frenchman named Mareen Duvall. According to genealogists, Duvall, who immigrated to Maryland from France in the 1650s, was Obama's ninth great grandfather and Buffett's sixth great grandfather.

In August 2009, Ancestry.com announced plans for the potential introduction of the TV show 'Who Do You Think You Are?' in early 2010, following a similar show on BBC in 2006.

INDUSTRY LEADERS

Ancestry.com (formerly The Generations Network Inc.) In July 2009, The Generations Network announced that it would now be known as Ancestry.com. Based in Provo, Utah, the company is a true heavyweight in the business of genealogy and family history. Ancestry.com, which advertised that it was the world's leading online family history resource as of 2009, had more than 4 billion records, proprietary search technologies, an engaged community of 950,000 subscribers and more than 3.5 million active members. Ancestry.com claimed the only completely indexed online U.S. Federal Census Collection (1790–1930), the most comprehensive online compilation of U.S. ship passenger lists (1820–1960), the largest online collection of African-American historical documents, and the most comprehensive online collection of U.S. military records, among other things. In August 2008, Ancestry launched a dedicated Chinese family history Web site, jiapu.com. In addition to Ancestry.co.uk, which offered access to names and ecclesiastical, civil, and immigration records from Wales, Scotland, Ireland, and England, the company operated other country-specific sites. These included Ancestry.ca (Canada), Ancestry.com.au (Australia), and Ancestry.de (Germany).

Ancestry.com DNA now extends the Ancestry service into the field of genetic genealogy. MyCanvas, a digital publishing platform integrated into Ancestry.com, gives persons the ability to create completely unique, professionally printed family history books. Family Tree Maker(R) 2009, the highest-selling family history software package, is available online and in major retail stores throughout North America and Europe.

In mid-2009, Ancestry.com filed for an IPO, hoping to raise about $75 million according to an SEC filing. The present Ancestry.com has many owners, but the majority stake was held by Spectrum Equity Investors, a media/communications firm, which paid about $300 million for its share of the company. The other investors included Sorenson Media, CMGI@Ventures, and EsNet Group. Revenues increased to $197.6 million in 2008, a CAGR of of 12.7 percent. For the first six months of 2009, it had revenues of $99.9 million, compared to $87.4 million in revenues in the first six months of 2008.

RootsMagic Inc. With roots dating back to 1986, RootsMagic Inc. (formerly FormalSoft Inc.) was established by

Bruce Buzbee in San Jose, California. Among the different software programs the company developed was a genealogy application called Family Origins. Although it licensed Family Origins to Parsons Technology in 1990, FormalSoft continued to serve as the program's developer until it was discontinued in 2003. FormalSoft relocated to Springville, Utah, in 1993. In March of 2004, the company changed its name to RootsMagic Inc. At that time, the same development team behind Family Origins created a new genealogy program called RootsMagic. In October of 2006, RootsMagic released a new software application called Family Atlas, which allows users to make custom family maps based on their genealogy data.

Everton Publishers Serving the genealogy market for more than 50 years, Logan, Utah-based Everton Publishers was established in 1947. The company's founder, Walter M. Everton, sought to fill a perceived void in the marketplace for genealogy-related publications, research, and continuing education. Driven by this mission, Everton Publishers became well known among both professional genealogists and hobbyists as a leading provider in these areas. According to the company, its *Genealogical Helper* magazine "became the 'bible' of periodicals for family history researchers." The company focused on improving the publication's focus on providing valuable content. In addition to its magazine, Everton also provided content from its Everton Genealogical Library as well as searchable databases. In February of 2007, the company was planning to launch a redesigned version of its Web site.

AMERICA AND THE WORLD

In August 2009, UK-based Brightsolid, owner of British subscription and pay-per-view genealogy site FindMyPast.com, announced it was acquiring the Friends Reunited Group for 25 million pounds (about $42 million). The deal was still subject to clearance by British competition authorities. Friends Reunited was a 20.6 million-member British social network launched in 2000. Its sister site Genes Reunited, the United Kingdom's largest genealogy site with 9 million members and 650 million names in records, was launched in 2003.

Especially in the case of U.S. residents, genealogy frequently requires obtaining records from other nations. This once meant that family historians had to physically travel to faraway locations to conduct their research, with no promise of meaningful results. For those who were unable or unwilling to travel, the only alternatives were expensive international telephone calls or correspondence with libraries, records offices, or researchers via regular mail. The Internet did much to speed up this process. Not only did Web sites allow researchers to search for and identify information sources in faraway countries, e-mail enabled faster communication. In addition, genealogists gained the ability to obtain digital copies of records and pay for them online.

RESEARCH AND TECHNOLOGY

Increasingly in 2008 and 2009, genealogical searches were conducted for medical reasons as well as ancestral curiosity. New DNA testing of interleukin promised to predict genetic (inherited) risks for heart, dental, and dietary diseases. In 2007, Ancestry.com had partnered with Sorenson Genomics for ancestral DNA testing. By February 2009, Sorenson reported its gross revenues had grown 240 percent in just one year (2008) and it had to hire ten more scientists to keep up with demand (the company conducts forensic and paternity DNA tests as well).

In November 2008, the American Society of Human Genetics (ASHG) issued a statement critical of genetic genealogy testing companies. The organization, whose 8,000 members include geneticists, scholars, genetic counselors, nurses and others, issued a statement with recommendations for the genetic genealogy industry. Specifically, it faulted tests that were designed to determine ethnic ancestry, rather than the Y-DNA tests that estimate whether a person is related to someone else. "Rarely can definitive conclusions about ancestry be made beyond the assessment of whether putative close relatives are or are not related," reported the statement. It was prompted by the rising popularity of genetic genealogy. According to the ASHG, a half-million Americans would spend $100 to $1,000 per test in 2008.

BIBLIOGRAPHY

"About." Association of Professional Genealogists, 30 November 2009. Available from http://www.apgen.org.

"About the Foundation." Statue of Liberty-Ellis Island Foundation, 23 January 2005. Available from http://ellisislandrecords.com/EIinfo/about.asp.

"About Us." Everton Publishers, 10 February 2007. Available from http://www.everton.com/about_us.

Berson, Tara Rummell. "DIG INTO YOUR Roots." *Redbook,* September 2006.

Bonham, Nicole A. "Genealogy Pays Off for Utah: Barking Up the Family Tree." *Utah Business,* April 2001.

"Corporate Overview." The Generations Network Inc., 10 February 2007. Available from http://www.tgn.com.

Dornhelm, Rachel. "Genealogy Going from Popular Hobby to Money-Making Industry." *Marketplace Morning Report.* Minnesota Public Radio, 22 August 2003.

"Everton NewsLine." Everton Publishers, 4 February 2007. Available from http://www.everton.com/newsline/weekly_index.php?id=2435.

"Genetic Genealogy Companies Under Fire." *Family Tree Magazine,* November 2008.

Greene, Kylie. "Links to the Past; The Internet Opens Up a World of Genealogical Records." *Telegraph Herald* (Dubuque, Iowa), 1 February 2004.

"History." National Genealogical Society, 18 January 2005. Available from http://www.ngsgenealogy. org/ahistory.htm.

"Merger Creates Britain's Leading Genealogy Company." *Family Tree Magazine,* August 2009.

Mims, Bob. "Provo, Utah-Based Online Genealogy Company Seeks to Expand." *The Salt Lake Tribune,* 15 April 2004.

"Mission Statement." The United States Internet Genealogical Society, 23 January 2005. Available from http://www. usigs.org/about_us/mission.html.

"MyFamily.com Inc. Changes Corporate Name to The Generations Network." The Generations Network Inc., 19 December 2006. Available from http://www.tgn.com.

"Obama Says Hi Cuz to Investment Guru Buffet." Reuters Press Release, 15 December 2009. Available at http:// www.reuters.com/article/idUSTRE5BE0PB20091215.

"ProQuest Debuts Genealogy Center." *Library Journal,* 1 May 2006.

Rauschart, Lisa. "Searching for One's Roots Fills Bare Spots in Family Tree; Genealogists Dig Deep Into Archives." *The Washington Times,* 20 March 2003.

"RootsMagic Inc. Releases Family Atlas Genealogy Mapping and Publishing Software." RootsMagic Inc., 31 October 2006. Available from http://www.rootsmagic.com/ newsFamilyAtlas.htm.

"Searching Through History." *New Scientist,* 1 July 2006.

"Sixty Percent of Americans Intrigued by their Family Roots." Maritz Research Inc., May 2000. Available from http:// www.maritzresearch.com/release.asp?rc=195&p=2& T=P.

"Sorenson Molecular Genealogy Foundation Launched First-of-its-Kind Ancestry Database." *Business Wire,* 1 March 2004.

Taylor, Debbi. "Three Utah Firms Partner to Create Genealogical Database." *The Enterprise,* Aug. 28-Sept. 3 2006.

Tedeschi, Bob. "Tapping the Family Tree in the Digital Era Is Now as Easy as Typing a Surname into the Computer." *The New York Times,* 23 September 2002.

"Who Are We?" RootsMagic Inc., 8 February 2007. Available from http://www.rootsmagic.com/about.htm.

Willing, Richard. "DNA Database to Open Doors to Amateur Genealogists." *USA Today,* 14 September 2006.

GENETIC ENGINEERING

SIC CODE(S)

8731

8733

2836

INDUSTRY SNAPSHOT

Genes are basic biological units of heredity composed of DNA. Genetic engineering transfers a gene from one or more cells to another cell, thereby transforming the target cell's genetic makeup. The physical jiggling of genes offers humans more control, posing the potential to alter almost every aspect of human life, to say nothing of life in general. According to Dr. W. French Anderson, a pioneer in the field of genetic engineering, the ability to alter a human's genetic blueprint could theoretically afford interested parties the ability to alter genes related to any human characteristic, including intelligence, hair loss, docility, or aggression. While the ability to make sweeping changes to the human infrastructure was years away, concerns were already pronounced by the turn of the twenty-first century, and many scientists, ethicists, and others hoped to generate more discussion about genetic engineering (GE) possibilities and their consequences.

With applications spanning from curing human diseases to boosting crop yields to creating alternate sources of energy, GE has long been on the cusp of scientific revolution—and popular suspicion. Genetically altered foods have become remarkably commonplace, with a hearty share of such staples as corn and soybeans being sown in genetically tweaked varieties. At the same time, public resistance has made the idea, if not the fact, of genetic modification a live political wire, particularly outside the United States, and has forced companies to tread lightly when marketing such products.

ORGANIZATION AND STRUCTURE

Human genetic engineering has been touted as the fourth major medical revolution of the modern age, on a par with the discovery of the cause of cholera infection that led to remodeled sanitation systems in the 1850s, the use of anesthesia in surgery, and the development of vaccines and antibiotics to treat infections. Unlike these remedies, however, genetic engineering proposes to solve the underlying human biological causes of diseases and ailments. Gene therapy is built on the knowledge that human genes play a pivotal role in the body's ability to withstand and adapt to conditions forced on it by nature, such as diseases. Understanding genes, the logic goes, will help us to understand and control our susceptibility to diseases and infections.

Merriam-Webster's Collegiate Dictionary, Eleventh Edition, defines genome as a set of chromosomes with the genes they contain or, more broadly, the genetic material of an organism. The human genome, as explained on MedicineNet, Inc.'s "doctor-produced" Web site of medical terms and information, consists of all DNA that a person has in his/her chromosomes (microscopically visible rod-shaped carriers of DNA and proteins that make up genetic material) and mitochondria (rod-shaped chromosomes outside the nucleus of a cell responsible for converting food into energy). MedicineNet added, "Each of us has, in fact, two genomes—a large chromosomal genome and a much smaller mitochondrial genome. Our genome also includes every gene we own plus all of our junk DNA. The human

Global Growth of Biotech Crops, in Number of Hectares Planted	
2007	114 million hectares
2008	125 million hectares
2009	134 million hectares

SOURCE: International Service for the Acquisition of Agri-Biotech Applications (ISAAA).

genome is both 'the treasury of human inheritance' and a vast dump (or recycling center)."

Regulation Genetic engineering research, development, and marketing are highly regulated in the United States. For genetically engineered foodstuffs, direct oversight is primarily the responsibility of the manufacturers, who are then required to consult with the U.S. Food and Drug Administration (FDA), which retains the authority to issue a recall of products it deems unsafe. The FDA has maintained a policy of strictly monitoring and testing genetically engineered food products if they vary in nutritional value or genetic makeup. The FDA also reserves the right to require labeling of any genetically engineered food product that contains allergens that the conventional food product does not contain, or any product the nutritional content of which is altered via the GE process. In light of increasingly heated protests against genetically engineered crop production, both foreign and domestic, the U.S. Department of Agriculture (USDA) issued tightened rules to scale back the latitude it had afforded marketers of genetically engineered foods for employing the organic label on products. Most of the policies pertaining to genetically engineered food products stem from the federal Food, Drug, and Cosmetic Act of 1938 (and its amendments), which stipulate the type of labeling various kinds of products must have.

Furthermore, a USDA branch, the Animal and Plant Health Inspection Service, monitors the research and testing of genetically engineered products such as seeds and livestock. The U.S. Environmental Protection Agency (EPA) also plays a role in regulating the industry. It establishes standards for the performance of genetically altered products in conjunction with the USDA. These last two government agencies try to ensure that genetically engineered products do not pose any environmental risks such as introducing undesirable characteristics to naturally occurring plants and wildlife. These agencies have a particular concern for the possibility that a genetically modified plant might outcross with wild plants, creating new weed-like species.

Patents In 1995 President Bill Clinton helped open new financial doors for the industry by amending the U.S. Code of Patents with the Biotechnology Process Patent Act, extending its scope to include the development of a novel product from a specific gene in a specific cell line. Although gene patents were first issued in the mid-1970s, a former ruling contended that a process for creating biotechnological materials could not be patented. The 1995 policy allowed the patenting of procedures that yield genes and genetic materials.

This policy has subsequently met with controversy, however, as geneticists faced pressure and rushed to patent the general section of genetic code they were sequencing before that section was patented by someone else and the work lost. The issue heightened in early 2000 when Human Genome Sciences, Inc., received a patent for a new gene that the human immunodeficiency virus (HIV) exploits when it attacks a cell. While major biotech firms held that such intellectual property rights were necessary to protect research and maintain incentive to engage in expensive research, opponents of more liberal patent rules charged that such protection would actually slow innovation as companies are prohibited from entering into areas of research patented by other companies. More broadly, some ethicists were concerned over the right to own discoveries related to the human genome.

BACKGROUND AND DEVELOPMENT

Genetic engineering of sorts has taken place for centuries. Breeding of plants and animals traces back many centuries as farmers have often experimented with various crossbreeding and grafting techniques to create hybrids with more desirable features. Wheat, for example, is a hybrid of several wild grasses. However, as a discipline of modern science, it emerged around the end of the 19th century, becoming more pronounced and codified throughout the twentieth century. Early interest and later motivation for interest in genetics came from the work of Gregor Mendel, an Austrian botanist who studied the hereditary features in peas, pumpkins, beans, and fruit flies. In 1865 Mendel established laws of genetic traits, characterizing those most likely to be transferred through breeding as dominant and those less likely to be transferred as recessive. His work led to theories and methods of crossbreeding.

Before genetic engineering proper could come about, scientists needed an understanding of genetics itself. In *The Epic History of Biology,* Anthony Serafini reported that genetics pioneer T. H. Morgan introduced the formal study of genetics to the twentieth century. Beginning with the work of his predecessor, William Bateson, Morgan ascertained that chromosomes were the bearers of genetic data. In 1911, Morgan and some colleagues published the first substantive article on chromosomes and genes. Morgan made other crucial discoveries including sex-linked (male and female chromosomes carry different information) and sex-limited (certain genetic characteristics are realized only in one sex, not both) genetic information. In 1926, Morgan sketched an early picture of how parents passed traits to their offspring in his book titled *The Theory of the Gene.*

The 1920s brought discoveries of ribonucleic and deoxyribonucleic acids, RNA and DNA, which are essential to genetic communication. RNA holds the genetic information for some viruses while DNA carries it for most organisms. Viruses are submicroscopic plant, animal, or bacterial parasites that can replicate only when they invade a host cell, often causing diseases. Organisms are life forms (plant, animal, bacterium, fungus) that work together to carry on various life processes. In the 1940s, scientists proved that genes carried genetic information, not proteins as some had believed. In the 1950s, researchers James Watson and Francis Crick used x-rays to photograph DNA, leading to further understanding of the acid. As a result, they determined that DNA contained four kinds of smaller molecules hooked together in spiral chains. (A molecule is the smallest particle of a substance that retains its chemical and physical properties. It is composed of two or more atoms, the chemical properties of which cannot be broken down.) At this point, genetic engineering began to accelerate. Max Delbruck of Vanderbilt University and Alfred Hershey created a hybrid virus by combining the chromosomal material from two different viruses—a creation that had a powerful impact on genetic engineering research as other scientists began to attempt more arduous genetic manipulations, according to Serafini.

By 1977, a gene manufactured by researchers was used for the first time to create a human protein in bacteria. This procedure used a recombinant gene—one made from the combination of the genes from two separate organisms—to clone the protein. This feat helped to launch the industry. Biotech companies and universities began to flood the field with attempts to produce marketable products, leading to the development of many recombinant DNA (rDNA) projects throughout the country in the middle to late 1970s. One of the first was in 1978, when Genentech, Inc. and The City of Hope National Medical Center created a center for developing human insulin for diabetics using the rDNA technology. The FDA approved of the sale of genetically engineered insulin in 1982. A wave of gene and protein cloning also took place within this period, such as proteins from hepatitis B in pursuit of a cure or treatment, and genes for human growth hormones in the hope of unlocking the door to growth and development. This flurry of interest in genetic engineering provoked Congress to attempt regulating the industry by forcing researchers to concoct

specimens that could not escape from their laboratories, but none of these legislative proposals ever passed.

In the 1980s, the genetic engineering industry received the patent support it needed when the U.S. Supreme Court decided that genetically engineered products could be patented. Thus businesses could pursue years of research and investment without the worry that other companies could capitalize on their research by producing a similar product. Also in the 1980s, Kary Mullis and others at Cetus Corp. in Berkeley, California, created a technique called a polymerase chain reaction for multiplying DNA sequences in laboratories. In 1986, the FDA approved the first genetically engineered crop, genetically modified tobacco. In 1990, Calgene Inc. began testing modified cotton that was designed to have a genetic structure resistant to herbicides. That year, GenPharm International Inc. developed the first transgenic cow, which produced human milk proteins for infant formulas, by deliberately modifying its genetic makeup.

Criticism of and controversy about genetic engineering of crops and animals grew steadily through the 1990s. A 1997 EPA ruling raised the ire of Greenpeace and other international environmental activist organizations as well as EPA scientists for what they saw as a systematic leniency toward the GE industry at the expense of consumer and environmental protection. The EPA's approval of the genetically engineered bacteria *Rhizobium meliloti* ignored the advice of its own Biotechnology Scientific Advisory Committee (BSAC), resulting in the resignation of one BSAC biologist, Dr. Conrad Istock, who decried the relegation of the committee's research to a mere formality. Shortly afterward, a release from EPA scientists criticized the lack of objectivity in the EPA's final release, which, the white paper concluded, amounted to a de facto endorsement of the bacteria.

On its February 4, 2000, NPR broadcast, Science Friday reported that in late January, after a week of round-the-clock bargaining in Montreal, 130 government and U.N. representatives from around the world ratified an agreement "governing trade in genetically modified organisms (GMOs). In the end, the agreement hinged on two points. First, major biotechnology-using countries, including the U.S. and Canada, agreed to label shipments of seeds, grains, and plants that 'may' contain genetically modified material. An earlier version, requiring that exporters certify shipments as definitely containing GMOs and listing specific seed types and varieties, was dropped after criticism from U.S. negotiators that it would be extremely difficult to adopt. Under current practice, many varieties of certain grain crops are often blended together in a single shipment. The second major hurdle involved the amount of scientific evidence of harm needed to ban a GMO—or conversely, the amount of evidence needed to prove that a genetically modified organism was 'safe.' Eventually, the delegates settled on language that left both sides claiming victory: 'Lack of scientific certainty due to insufficient relevant scientific information and knowledge ... shall not prevent [a country] from taking a decision' on the wisdom of importing GMOs, either pro or con."

Following the success and furor over a sheep named Dolly, the first successfully cloned large mammal, scientists at the University of Hawaii cloned several mice in June 1998. The copying of large mammals, however, seemed to be based on somewhat of a fluke, but that changed in late 1999 when a research partnership between the University of Connecticut in Storrs and the Prefectural Cattle Breeding Development Institute in Kagoshima, Japan cloned four calves from skin cells derived from a bull. The cells were allowed to grow in a dish before gene DNA was pulled from their nuclei and then injected into cows' egg cells before being inserted into the cows' uteri. The use of skin cells rather than cells from reproductive organs offers a far more practical method of deriving the genetic material for cloning. In addition, since the cells were preserved for several months instead of injected freshly into the host animal, the new techniques offered greater possibilities for genetic manipulation of the material to be injected.

Researchers from countries around the world banded together in 1990 in an effort to develop a map of all the estimated 20,000 to 25,000 human genes and make them available for further biological study. Known as the Human Genome Project (HGP), this grand endeavor was backed by the U.S. government with $3 billion. The U.S. Department of Energy (DOE) Human Genome Program and National Institutes of Health (NIH) National Human Genome Research Institute sponsored and coordinated the project. The United Kingdom's Wellcome Trust shortly became a major partner and other important contributors were scientists from Japan, France, Germany, China, and other countries. By the late 1990s, profit incentives had spurred the race, with pharmaceutical companies and even some private laboratories competing with the federal project. Completion of the map of human genetic information entailed identifying the 23 pairs of chromosomes, then sequencing all the DNA contained in the chromosomes to discover the protein each gene produces and for what purpose. By translating the entire human genetic code, scientists hoped to gain an understanding of the precise nature and function of human genes, including the isolation of malfunctioning genes that could then either be replaced or directly modified to resume functioning. In 2003, the sequencing of the human genome, which refined the earlier mapping work, was completed. According to MedicineNet, it "covered about 99 percent of the human genome's gene-containing regions."

On their Web pages about the Human Genome Project, the U.S. Department of Energy and the National Institutes of Health state, "Another project goal was to determine the complete sequence of the 3 billion DNA subunits (bases in the human genome). As part of the HGP, parallel studies were carried out on selected model organisms such as the bacterium E. coli and the mouse to help develop the technology and interpret human gene function." Additional project goals listed were to "store this information in databases; improve tools for data analysis; transfer related technologies to the private sector; and address the ethical, legal, and social issues that may arise from the project."

TWENTY-FIRST CENTURY DEVELOPMENTS

Genetically Modified Food In a September 4, 2006, *NewScientist.com* article titled "Instant Expert: GM Organisms," writer John Pickrell reported that consumer furor over GM foods erupted in the United Kingdom in February 1999 when "a controversial study suggested that a few strains of GM potatoes might be toxic to laboratory rats. Those experiments, subsequently criticized by other experts, were carried out in Scotland by biochemist Arpad Pustzai. What followed was a European anti-GM food campaign of near religious fervor. Spearheaded in the United Kingdom by environmental groups and some newspapers, the campaign had far-reaching consequences. It culminated in an unofficial moratorium on the growth and import of GM crops in Europe and led to a trade dispute with the United States. GM crops are today very rare in Europe, strict labeling laws and regulations are in place for food (DNA bar codes), and public opinion towards the technology remains largely negative. Several U.K government reports have offered qualified support for GM crops and produce, though they argue that the economic benefits of the technology are currently small. Some African nations have also opposed engineered crops, even to the point of rejecting international food aid containing them. GM produce has been taken up with far less fuss in the United States, India, China, Canada, Argentina, Australia, and elsewhere. However, controversy over a type of GM corn—only approved for animal feed—that turned up in taco shells and other products stirred opinion in the United States."

Controversy over genetically engineered crops in the United States began to catch up to that of Europe when a study at Cornell University found that corn engineered to withstand pesticides, carrying a gene producing *Bacillus thuringiensis* (Bt) toxins, killed monarch butterflies and caterpillars, validating some environmentalists' fears that such technology posed a threat to natural ecosystems. The Cornell team, while clarifying that such findings were preliminary, advocated that seed companies encourage their client farmers to plant a buffer zone of traditional corn around their genetically engineered crop fields, thus preventing pollen-carrying Bt toxins from finding their way into butterfly habitats. By the early years of the twenty-first century's first decade, scientists were still working to determine the toxicity of Bt corn to monarch populations.

Critics also decried the possible centralization of the world's food supply that could result from continued dominance of seed technology by a handful of large biotech firms. Not only would such centralization afford such firms an alarming degree of influence over the world's population, opponents contended, but it could also expose the food system to a catastrophe should mishaps occur within such a tightly systematized production process.

While defending the safety of genetically engineered crops and food products, a number of major food companies, including Frito-Lay Inc., Seagram Co., Gerber Products Co., and H.J. Heinz Co., took the threat of declining sales to heart, announcing they would refrain from using genetically engineered crops in their products. Militant environmental and consumer activists, meanwhile, perturbed at what they saw as the cozy relationship between the Clinton administration and the biotechnology industry, took to trashing a number of research labs. In 2003, Greenpeace protested the use of genetically engineered crops by occupying test fields and blocking researchers from getting into the fields.

By 2003, more than 50 genetically engineered crops had been approved for sale in the United States. The vast majority of soybeans and a rising share of corn output was genetically modified, translating into a mountain of food products from soft drinks to pasta to ice cream, as well as livestock products from animals fed with genetically engineered crops. Livestock, for instance, consume about 75 percent of corn production. Worldwide, genetically engineered croplands in 2003 expanded by 15 percent, nearing 170 million acres.

The labeling of genetically engineered food was a hotly contested issue. In 2003, several bills were proposed that addressed this issue, including the Genetically Engineered Food Safety Act and the Genetically Engineered Food Right to Know Act. The former subjected all genetically modified food components to pre-market review by the FDA, whereas the latter required food products with any genetically modified materials to be labeled as such. A number of companion measures were proposed to provide additional protections for farmers and consumers. However, the bills stalled in committees and most members of Congress have been wary of the issue. Indeed, in 2003 the House passed a resolution praising the Bush administration for its

vigorous attempts to loosen European Union regulations on genetically modified foods. That year, the European trade bloc eased its long-standing ban on GE crops and instituted a new labeling system for GE products.

Such a climate persuaded some makers of genetically modified foods and seeds to scale back plans. In 2004, industry leader Monsanto announced it would not introduce a new line of engineered wheat it had planned because of a wave of negative reactions to the product by conventional wheat growers. A company representative speculated that the marketing effort might return in five to ten years if the market was more open to it. Regulatory hurdles likewise have convinced some firms to abandon what seemed to be promising developments.

In June 2005 Kirsten Schwind, program director at the Institute for Food and Development Policy, and biologist Hollace Poole-Kavana wrote "We Need GM food Like a Hole in Our Kidneys" for the CommonDreams.org, explaining that genetically modified plant and animal foods are not the answer to world hunger. In addition, according to Schwind and Poole-Kavana, GM foods may threaten human health and even be a "risky technology" that does not meet human needs. Their writing was based on a 2001 Monsanto study indicating blood and kidney abnormalities in rats fed a strain of Bt corn eaten every day by Americans, along with the FDA's approval of GM foods for public consumption after comparing their nutritional content to non-GM foods and then checking a database for known allergens. They added that GM crops cannot end hunger because hunger is caused by poverty, inequality, and racism. Thus, a world food shortage cannot be overcome by GM technology because small, diversified farms can grow several times more food per acre than GM seeds, which were developed for large, mechanized farms as an attempt to lower production costs.

Schwind and Poole-Kavana's last argument addresses ethical and legal problems that GM seeds can cause farmers worldwide: "For as long as humans have grown food, farmers have developed better seeds through natural cross-breeding and exchanged seeds to share the best varieties. Seeds are a common good of human civilization. When biotech companies convinced the U.S. Patent Office to allow them to patent seeds, single companies claimed ownership of entire cultural legacies with just one laboratorial tweak. As farmers buy GM seeds from Monsanto, they must sign a contract recognizing the company's intellectual property rights over the seed and promise not to share or save any to use the next year. However, plants breed naturally with no knowledge of who signed a contract, and pollen from GM corn blows easily into neighboring fields."

Most segments of genetic engineering meet with conflicting public support, as consumers typically appreciate the technology's benefits but also have numerous fears. Particularly regarding foods, U.S. consumers have voiced principled objections to GE products, yet most have not been moved enough to demand special labeling. Some observers interpret the response as ambivalent, noting the simultaneous surge in production of both GE and organic produce. Such ambiguity was likely to characterize the industry's market for the foreseeable future.

In fact, many U.S. consumers were simply uninformed about GE. This was especially the case regarding genetically engineered food. Despite the fact that the majority of large U.S. farming operations in the middle years of the first decade of the 2000s planted GE crops and did not make efforts to separate them from non-GE crops, a Pew Initiative on Food and Technology study, released in November 2005, found that of every 10 adults, six were unaware of the existence of GE crops. In addition, a mere quarter of respondents knew that GE foods had been sold in the United States for a decade. In fact, according to *New Scientist,* in the United States and Canada alone, GE foods had been consumed by approximately 300 million people since the mid-1990s.

In mid-2006, *Farm Journal* reported that each year, some 200 million acres of biotech crops are planted worldwide, and in all, approximately 1 billion acres had been planted since the mid-1990s. The publication indicated that since 1995, the use of biotech crops had caused yields to rise 21 percent, and pesticide use to fall by 379 million pounds; and that together, these factors had resulted in farm income growth of $27 billion. Despite benefits such as these, and evidence that GE crops are helpful to poor farmers in developing countries, many people continued to oppose GE crops, arguing that they are harmful to the environment and pose a threat to organic farmers. Critics called for further analysis and testing of GE foods, as well as product labeling.

So far, genetically engineered food has generally not been required to carry any labeling distinguishing it from other foods, despite public uproar and laws in Europe to that effect. In May 2006, the issue of labeling genetically engineered foods resurfaced in Congress. At that time, Rep. Dennis Kucinich (D-OH) re-introduced the Genetically Engineered Food Safety Act (GEFRKA) along with five other measures as part of a biotech labeling bill. According to the June 5, 2006 issue of *Food Chemical News,* when he introduced the legislation, Kucinich stated, "The bills will protect our food, environment, and health. They are a common sense precaution to ensure genetically engineered foods do no harm. Genetic engineering is having a serious impact on the food we eat, on the environment, and on farmers. To ensure we can maximize benefits and minimize hazards, Congress must provide a comprehensive regulatory framework for all genetically engineered products."

Genetic Engineering in Animals Meanwhile, developments continued in the area of cloning. Just two and a half years after Dolly's birth, her "parents" at Scotland's PPL Therapeutics moved closer to genetically copying a human being by creating cloned triplet piglets, which scientists had been attempting for years. Pigs are more difficult to clone than sheep or mice. The most widely publicized purpose for cloned animals, particularly pigs, is for the development of xenotransplantation or the transplant of animals' organs into humans. Such organs would require genetic manipulation to survive in a human being. Another purpose is for drug treatments. Dolly the sheep was engineered with human genetic data, thus allowing her to produce human proteins through milk that can then theoretically be used to treat human illnesses. Scientists in the early years of the first decade of the 2000s continued to attempt to successfully clone animals in an effort to achieve xenotransplantation.

A number of other breakthroughs occurred in the GE industry during the early years of the first decade of the 2000s. The actual creation of artificial life from scratch came closer to fruition with the discovery of the minimal number of genes required to maintain a living organism. Using scientifically created genes and chromosomes, researchers at the Institute of Genomic Research (TIGR) in Rockville, Maryland, successively knocked out genes until they isolated those necessary to sustain the world's simplest known organism, the *Mycoplasma genitalium* bacterium. Although ethical and technical questions loomed large, the next step was to synthesize a new life form from scratch building on this knowledge.

Some GE discoveries, however, did please environmentalists. Michael Daly at the Uniformed Services University of the Health Sciences in Bethesda, Maryland genetically enhanced the bacterium *D. radiodurans,* known to withstand an enormous level of radiation, to help break down nuclear waste by reducing the toxicity of ionic mercury. The development offered the potential to help in the bioremediation of the nation's 113 federal nuclear waste sites, which cover a combined area about the size of Delaware and Rhode Island and have contaminated alarming amounts of water and soil, according to the U.S. Department of Energy. By stabilizing the metal compounds, the bacteria can alleviate the spread of contamination. While early tests revealed no adverse effects to humans, it had yet to be actively tested in the field, and researchers suggested it would take at least five or six years before testing could be completed and the bacteria modified to effectively treat the waste at the different sites.

Gene Therapy Gene therapy has faced similar difficulties. It involves the injection of one or more genes as a replacement for absent or failing genes in the human body. Scientists discovered that inserting genes into cells could also be used to change cell function, broadening the range of disorders that can be treated genetically. Another technique, usually known as small molecule therapy, alters the gene's functions by adding molecules via drugs into the patient's system. As of the middle of the twenty-first century's first decade, gene therapy remained largely in the experimental stage and was fraught with controversy and complications.

Other Applications Promising developments continued in the area of xenotransplantation, whereby organs from animals are adapted for use in humans. Organs from pigs continued to hold special promise because they are similar in function and size to their human counterparts. One challenge is that the presence of a sugar molecule makes the organs impossible to use. In 2006, the biotechnology start-up Revivicor had produced pigs whose organs did not have the molecule. In addition, the company's researchers were adding human genes to the pigs to make their organs more compatible for xenotransplantation.

The use of genetic engineering in crops and food remained an issue of great controversy in the latter half of the first decade of the 2000s, even as the industry grew. According to a report by the International Service for the Acquisition of Agri-Biotech Applications (ISAAA), in 2007 the number of acres planted in biocrops increased by 12 percent to 114.3 million hectares, the second highest increase since 2002 (see updated figures below). The number of farmers planting GE crops also increased by 2 million, bringing the worldwide total to 12 million. The principal biotech crop was soybeans, taking up 51 percent of the total hectares planted, followed by maize (31 percent), cotton (13 percent), and canola (5 percent). Of the 23 countries in which the crops were planted, 12 were developing and 11 were industrial; in addition, a majority of the farmers were resource-poor. These facts, according to Clive James of the ISAAA, point to the importance of biotech crops in the efforts to alleviate poverty. James also said, "With increasing food prices globally, the benefits of biotech crops have never been more important" and that "If we are to achieve the Millennium Development Goals (MDGs) of cutting hunger and poverty in half by 2015, biotech crops must play an even bigger role in the next decade."

The ISAAA predicted that growth in biotech farming would continue and that by 2015, 100 million farmers in 45 countries would plant 200 million hectares of biotech crops. The organization noted that farmers in such countries as China, India, and South Africa would experience increasingly greater benefits.

Despite the support of such organizations as ISAAA, some countries, such as those in the European Union—where few GE crops are approved for use and a number of countries have bans on planting them—and organizations such as Greenpeace and Friends of the Earth continue to vehemently oppose the use of GE crops and food, citing harmful effects on human health and the environment.

CURRENT CONDITIONS

According to First Research, Inc., the U.S. biotechnology industries, encompassing roughly 1500 companies, had combined annual revenues of $70 billion in 2009. Major U.S. companies included Amgen, Genentech (owned by Switzerland-based Roche) Genzyme, Life Technologies, and Monsanto.

In 2010, the U.S. Supreme Court ruled that a lower court had overstepped its authority in issuing an injunction on the planting of GM alfalfa by the Monsanto Company, (*Monsanto v. Geertson Seed Farms*). As background, Monsanto owned the intellectual property rights to the subject alfalfa variety, known as Roundup Ready Alfalfa (RRA). RRA was an alfalfa seed that had been genetically engineered to resist the active ingredient (glyphosate) weed/plant killer in the herbicide Roundup brand (that Monsanto also produced). The U.S. Department of Agriculture's Animal and Plant Health Inspection Service (APHIS) had originally classified RRA as a regulated article, but in 2004, Monsanto petitioned for non-regulated status of two strains of RRA. APHIS did prepare a draft EA assessing the likely environmental impact, published a notice in the Federal Register inviting public comment on the EA, and after considering those comments, issued a Finding of No Significant Impact. It also authorized nearly 300 field trials of RRA conducted over eight years. Geertson Seed Farms, joined by several other traditional farms as well as environmental groups, filed suit to stop RRA from polluting (from cross-field contamination, i.e., GM seed being redistributed on pure fields through cross-pollination, wind, rain, etc.) their pure (and often organic) traditional alfalfa fields. Monstanto won, as the high court found the permanent injunction too severe a remedy, in summary.

Following this, more than 50 members of Congress called on the USDA to keep Monsanto's RRA, genetically modified to resist Monsanto's own Roundup herbicide, out of alfalfa fields. Moreover, this spawned a revived interest in GMO food labeling. Reprentative Dennis Kucinich (D-OH) introduced three bills, one relating to labeling food containing genetically engineered material; one relating to the cultivation and handling of GM crops, and one; establishing farmers's rights regarding genetically engineered animals, plants, and seeds. They are H.R. 5577 (the Genetically Engineered Food Right to Know Act), H.R. 5578, and H.R. 5579.

Another significant GMO food battle in 2010 was over farm-raised GM salmon, genetically altered to grow twice as fast as wild caught salmon. AquAdvantage Salmon produced by AquaBounty Technologies was seeking FDA approval to offer the salmon for human consumption. Amid strong public and industry outcries regarding the lack of labeling as well as insufficient data to support safe consumption, the FDA was to schedule public hearings on the matter in September 2010 and make final determinations thereafter.

Significant resistance continues. The Institute of Science in Society (I-SIS) offered a series of lectures in 2010, including in Switzerland, the United Kingdom, and Sweden, before a variety of organizations (e.g., the 5th European Conference on GMO-Free Regions, the Swedish International Agricultural Network Initiative, etc.) that warned of the dangers of GMO crops in particular. Some of the scientific evidence reported at these lectures/seminars pointed to significant dangers in the use of Monsanto's Roundup product, showing that over 40 plant diseases had been reported following the use of glyphosate (the key ingredient), including the release of a mycotoxin that could enter the food chain from cereal crops. Moreover, scientists reported that glyphosate prevents mineral nutrients from being absorbed by plants and also kills beneficial bacteria and fungi.

In the medical arena, the industry took note of the increasingly nebulous line between pharmaceutical and biopharmaceutical companies; they are no longer distinct. Specialist companies like Amgen and Genzyme were in direct competition with traditional pharma companies, while Pfizer, Merck, and Novartis presented themselves as biopharma/pharma companies and have aggressively pursued strategic acquisitions and partnerships with biotech companies, or advanced their own biotech projects in-house. Oncology products and treatments was the fastest growing segment in the overall industry, due not only to an increase in adjunct therapies but also effective biotherapies. Many top pharmaceutical companies now include biologic cancer treatments as part of new projects. Roche's takeover of Genentech is a good example: Genentech had three cancer therapies (Avastin, Rituxan, and Herceptin) that brought in sales of $15.6 billion in 2009. The oncology industry sector grew from $30 billion in 2005 to a projected $65 billion for 2010.

INDUSTRY LEADERS

Genentech Inc. Founded in 1976, biotechnology pioneer Genentech develops and markets pharmaceuticals made from recombinant DNA. Genentech markets an expanding range of drugs in the United States to treat congenital disorders and serious illnesses. Some of its best-selling products include Protropin, a hormone for children suffering from growth impediments; Nutropin, a hormone for children with renal trouble and growth insufficiency; and Activase, an agent that dissolves blood clots in heart attack patients. In 1998 the company launched Herceptin, an antibody for certain breast cancer patients. That year was also a profitable first full year of sales for the non-Hodgkin's lymphoma drug Rituxan. In the late 1990s, Genentech suffered legal difficulties, resulting in a $50 million lawsuit settlement following charges that it sold human growth hormone for improper purposes. The South San Francisco-based company had 11,174 employees and reported sales of $11.7 billion in 2007. Swiss drug giant Roche Holding, whose subsidiary, Hoffmann-La Roche, Inc., markets Genentech's products internationally, purchased the remaining interest. The company brought in $13.4 billion in 2008 sales, but in 2009, Roche finalized its (friendly) takeover of Genentech, making Roche the world's largest biotech firm, displacing Amgen Inc.

Amgen Inc. Amgen has also led the genetic engineering industry with its two products that exploit GE recombinant DNA technology: Epogen, the world's leading anti-anemia drug, and Neupogen. Epogen simulates red blood cells and is used to treat the kidney problems of renal dialysis patients, while Neupogen simulates white blood cells and is used by cancer patients undergoing chemotherapy. The firm has expanded its line considerably since the late 1990s. Amgen's treatments for anemia, Epogen and Aranesp, account for more than one third of sales. In Amgen's pipeline were products for several forms of cancer, rheumatoid arthritis, and bone marrow disorders. Its research into the human genome also yielded the discovery of material that aids the spread of cancer cells. In 2006 the company acquired human therapeutic antibody manufacturer Abgenix for $2.2 billion.

Monsanto Co. With many other major GE agriculture firms backing out of the business, Monsanto remained the world's leading player in this field. A former chemical firm, St. Louis-based Monsanto Co. spent the 1990s transforming itself into a leading life sciences company. In its agricultural sector, the potential to patent seed technology spurred Monsanto to spend over $8 billion in the late 1990s buying up seed companies. With a work force of 12,600, Monsanto is best known for its flagship chemical Roundup, a leading herbicide. It also has developed a variety of genetically engineered agricultural products. Roundup Ready brand soybeans, canola, and cotton are genetically resistant to Roundup brand herbicides. Seeds genetically designed to prevent insect damage include Bollgard and Ingard brands of cotton, Yieldgard and Maisgard brands of corn, and

NewLeaf brand potatoes. In 2000 Monsanto was acquired by Pharmacia & Upjohn for $53 billion. The following year, Pharmacia decided to spin off Monsanto as a public company. Monsanto reported $11.7 billion for fiscal 2009, *Forbes* reported.

AMERICA AND THE WORLD

Dr. Clive James, executive director of ISAAA, stated in a keynote address before the 2010 Agricultural Biotechnology International Conference that "In the next 50 years, the global population will consume two times as much food as humans have consumed since the beginning of agriculture 10,000 years ago." He opined that conventional farming will not meet these startling needs, and that biotechnology/GMO crops specifically could help alleviate food poverty. James further stated that 85 million farmers were now using GMO crops.

ISAAA's 2009 report, released in February 2010, indicated that in 2009, 14 million farmers planted 134 million hectares (330 million acres) of GM/biotech crops in 25 countries. This was up from 13.3 million farmers and 125 million hectares in 2008. More importantly, 13 million of the 14 million farmers (90 percent) were small and resource-poor farmers, mostly from developing countries. Brazil passed up Argentina as the second largest grower of biotech crops globally.

The largest market growth (1,350 percent) was in biotech cotton grown in the small African country of Burkino Faso. Overall, the rest of Africa grew by 17 percent, and Egypt by 15 percent, mostly in biotech maize. In India, 5.6 million farmers planted 8.4 million hectares of biotech cotton. The 87 percent adoption of biotech cotton had another effect: India reported a reduction by 50 percent of insecticide use. In November 2009, China rendered a landmark decision to issue biosafety certificates for the growing of GM insect-resistant rice and phytase maize; however, the crops must complete two to three years of standard registration field trials before being commercialized. China is the largest rice-producing country and suffered significant crop losses in the past from the rice borer insect. The biotech rice had the potential to reduce pesticides by 80 percent in addition to increasing crop yields by eight percent.

In Europe, Germany discontinued biotech plantings. Conversely, 80 percent of all biotech maize in the European Union was planted in Spain in 2009. Overall, the top five countries growing biotech crops were the United States, Brazil, Argentina, India, and Canada, followed by China and Paraguay. In July 2010, the European Commission proposed an overhaul of the European Union's policy for approving GMOs. The policy in effect prior to amendment allowed licensed crop cultivation across 27 countries as part of European Union's single market. The new proposed policy would allow individual countries the autonomy to block GMO cultivation within their territory, such restrictions only allowed under the strict conditions of the existing policy.

As background, at the turn of the twenty-first century, an embittered trade war had followed the European Union's decision to slap import restrictions on genetically engineered U.S. crops out of health and environmental concerns. Meanwhile, the United Nations Food Safety Agency in September 1999 endorsed the European Union's moratorium on bovine somatotropin, a genetically engineered hormone injected into cattle to stimulate milk production that was banned by the European Community in 1990. Approximately 30 percent of U.S. dairy cattle received the hormone treatment, according to Monsanto.

Farmers in the developing world, moreover, were beginning to take matters into their own hands. In India, home to one-quarter of the world's farmers, a coalition of 2,000 organizations representing farmers, environmentalists, scientists, and religious groups initiated Operation Cremate Monsanto, digging up cotton fields and setting Monsanto-brand seed crops afire. Long-suffering Indian farmers were furious over Monsanto's perceived attempts to dictate their farm production.

The United States produces roughly 75 percent the world's GE crops. Unlike Europe, Japan, Russia, and Australia, however, the United States does not yet require any sort of labeling for GE food products. In 2003, the European Parliament passed a law requiring the labeling of all GM food and animal feed containing more than 0.9 percent of GM materials.

By 2008, the International Service for the Acquisition of Agri-Biotech Applications reported that genetically engineered crops were grown in 23 countries by approximately 12 million farmers. The United States, Argentina, Brazil, Canada, India, and China continued to be the principal adopters of biotech crops globally.

On October 18, 2005, the *Associated Press* reported in an article titled "Mexico Rejects Biotech Corn" that Mexico had just stopped Monsanto and other biotech companies from "planting genetically engineered corn, rekindling fierce debate in that country over the technology. Environmentalists said the government's decision will help prevent biotech corn from contaminating corn native to Mexico, the birthplace of corn and still a storehouse of genetically valuable native species. But the decision angered some biotech supporters who said it would limit access to plants that could reduce pesticide and herbicide use and have other advantages for local farmers. Even environmentalists don't think [the decision] is the last word. Mexico imposed a moratorium on the planting of genetically modified crops in 1998, but in 2005, President Vicente Fox signed a bill that set out a framework for approving such planting in the future."

Corn originated in Mexico about 8,000 years ago and there are at least 59 native corn species in existence there today. The Organic Consumers Association in its October 2006 newsletter *Organic Bytes* stated, "The law is designed to protect native varieties from being contaminated by biotech varieties. The Monsanto Corporation, the biggest seller of genetically engineered corn, vows it will reverse this law when president-elect Calderon takes office. Monsanto claims Mexico's 59 varieties of corn, many of which have been grown for thousands of years, will not be at risk of contamination if genetically engineered varieties are approved."

In September 2006, in response to a May 2005 public interest petition by four activists to allow field trials of genetically modified crops only after rigorous scientific, reliable and transparent biosafety testing, India's Supreme Court banned any new field trials of genetically modified crops in country until it could review whether the approval process contained conflicts of interest. The attorney for the petitioners said that India was allowing field trials to precede such testing along with unacceptable monitoring and accountability, which was causing irreversible crop contamination. The petition arose out of civil unrest over the safety of field trials of India's first GM food crop, Bt brinjal (eggplant), which forced the Genetic Engineering Approval Committee (GEAC), whose prior permission is necessary for field trials to be conducted, to put the final decision in the hands of five experts that it appointed. However, the five experts and the GEAC were both criticized by civil society groups for being insufficiently independent. The court asked the government to respond with its objections and any other experts it wished to propose.

On October 12, 2006, the Supreme Court, headed by its Chief Justice, ruled that the ban on further approval of field trials would continue but allowed an exception: Delhi University would be allowed to carry out trials of a specific variety of GM mustard in a limited area so that it would not lose a year of research. India had so far not allowed any GM crop to be commercially grown for human consumption; only GM cotton was being grown on a commercial scale. The court directed Delhi University to ensure that the gene involved does not escape the trial area. In a October 14, 2006, article, Reuters reported that India's prime minister "underlined the need to balance possible health and environmental dangers from the development of new genetically modified varieties with the need to feed the country's more than 1 billion people."

In its October 2006 online newsletter *FEED,* the environmental advocacy organization Union of Concerned Scientists (UCS), announced that Kraft Foods, the second largest food producer in the world, told Greenpeace China in a letter dated December 13, 2005, that it agreed to sell only non-genetically engineered foods in China starting January 1, 2007. The UCS went on to say that "More than a hundred food brands, including those made by companies like PepsiCo, Coca-Cola, and Danone, already offer only non-GE foods in China. Kraft's decision suggests that if the company can provide non-GE food to a market as large as China, it could offer non-GE food to its U.S. market as well—where the GE status of food is not labeled, but where most processed foods are probably made with GE crops (half the corn and most soybeans grown in the United States are GE crops)."

This UCS announcement was based on an article posted on AP-Foodtechnology.com on February 1, 2006, which also revealed that "Kraft's move came as several Chinese newspapers criticized Nestle, the world's number one food firm, for not adopting a non-GM stance in China. The group does not use GM ingredients for its products sold in the European Union or Russia, largely because of consumer opposition." The article went on to point out that although 107 food brands had a non-GM policy in China by October 2005, there is concern about increase in costs if GM-free supplies dwindle globally. However, a Greenpeace China activist said, "The growing concerns of the Chinese consumers have started to reshape the GE ingredient policy of top food companies."

RESEARCH AND TECHNOLOGY

One of the new technological developments in the industry in the early years of the first decade of the 2000s was represented by Dow AgroSciences' agreement with Sangamo BioSciences regarding research into the "zinc finger," which is, according to a 2008 article in *Forbes,* "a naturally occurring protein that can be used in a cell nucleus like an editor's red pencil" and that "can turn specific genes off or on or to some point in between, delete genes altogether or add new genetic material." Commenting on the new technology, Edward Lanphier of Sangamo said, "We can target and regulate genes inside any cell in any organism. This is enormously powerful science." Dow's focus for the zinc finger involved crop applications, such as turning inedible crops into edible versions and creating plants that could survive severe drought. The first results of the project were not expected for several years.

Another emerging area within the field of genetics was synthetic genomics, which involves the use of synthetically designed and engineered DNA to produce cells and viruses. This approach held promise for the development of drugs that relied on rare natural agreements. In 2006 Amyris Biotechnologies, based in Emeryville, California, was founded, which sought to develop a version of the rare drug artemisinin, used to treat malaria, from bacteria. As of 2008, the company was also working on producing renewable biofuels. Another company working in synthetic genomics was Synthetic Genomics Inc, based in Rockville, Maryland, and formed by Human Genome Project codeveloper J. Craig Venter in 2005. In its research on GE and the creation of biofuels, according to *Earth2Tech,* the company was "looking to do no less than overthrow the petrol industry and create an artificial life form."

In the first decade of the 2000s, GE researchers scurried to find new ways to propel their technology forward while circumventing negative publicity. Scientists at the Center for the Application of Molecular Biology to International Agriculture in Canberra, Australia, built on the knowledge of naturally occurring mutations, noting particularly the overwhelming similarity of the genes that produce the proteins giving corn and rice their distinct characters. Because of the great genetic overlap, which research leader Dr. Richard A. Jefferson said generalizes to all living things, actual gene swapping may be unnecessary. Dr. Jefferson surmised that the same effects, such as resistance to cold, achieved by gene transfers could be generated by spurring genetic mutations inherent in the original crop or species.

Essentially, this process, called transgenomics, involves the rapid shuffling and mutating of genes, thus speeding the process of evolution in order to bring desired inherent traits into prominence centuries before natural processes would bring them about. As a result, the transfer of genes that has protesters up in arms is avoided altogether in favor of a controlled acceleration of evolution and genetic mutation. In a way, this simply brings farmers' traditional practices of selective breeding to the molecular level, letting nature do most of the work, albeit egged on by scientists. r. Jefferson claimed that in addition to helping third world countries meet their food necessities, the process would also help small seed and biotechnology companies sidestep the overwhelming obstacle of patents produced by the seed acquisition frenzy at Monsanto, DuPont, and other large corporations.

Meanwhile, computer-generated research not only analyzed genetic material but made use of it. In an evolution fit for Silicon Valley, researchers developed micro-arrays, or biochips, which use genes or gene fragments and their DNA in the manner of computer chip semiconductors to power computerized biochemical experiments. The chips were beginning to find extensive use at companies engaged in research related to the genomics industry.

After all the difficulties surrounding gene therapy, scientists were intent on building the field's experimental sector on studies of hemophilia, widely viewed as the simplest illness to treat with gene therapy. In March 2000, researchers at the Children's Hospital of Philadelphia in conjunction with the biotech firm Avigen Inc. announced success with two of three hemophiliac patients who received gene treatments based on the spherical adeno-associated virus (AAV). Although for years it was thought impossible to manufacture, AAV was genetically engineered by Avigen and Targeted Genetics and readied for testing in humans. Although the experiment proved both safe and successful, the researchers stressed that results were preliminary and that the research required further trials, which continued throughout the latter part of the decade.

In 2006, a $1.4 million Nobel Prize in medicine was awarded to Craig Mello, a University of Massachusetts Medical School professor, and Andrew Z. Fire, a professor at Stanford University, for discovering a process capable of silencing specific genes. Genes work by transmitting molecules known as messenger RNA to a cell's protein-making function. Through the introduction of certain molecules that destroy or deactivate that genetic protein production, the target gene is rendered inoperable. Mello and Fire published their research on the process, called RNAi for RNA interference, in 1998, which also determined that RNAi occurs in plants, animals and humans, and that it is important in the regulation of gene activity and defense against viruses. Their research has been adopted by scientists everywhere and has become a standard procedure for studying genes in the laboratory, as researchers work to develop treatments for a host of diseases. Mello said that his daughter's diabetes is the force that drives him to continue working on RNAi. Fire observed that the Nobel award reflected the value of government-funded research in areas that take a long time to come to fruition.

Another $1.4 million Nobel Prize was awarded to Stanford University School of Medicine Professor Roger D. Kornberg for his research on how cells take information from genes to produce proteins. According to the *Detroit Free Press,* " Kornberg's work is important for medicine, because disturbances in that process are involved in illnesses like cancer, heart disease and various kinds of inflammation. And learning more about the process is key to using stem cells to treat disease." Kornberg's work has resulted in several promising drugs and therapies with many more predicted to come.

BIBLIOGRAPHY
Anderson, Clifton E. "Biotech on the Farm." *The Futurist,* September-October 2005.

"Biologics Pipeline Set to Replenish Coffers." August 2010. Available from http://www.genengnews.com/gen-articles/.

"Biotechnology Labeling Bill Introduced in House." *Food Chemical News,* 5 June 2006.

"Biotechnology Sector." First Research, Inc. report published 7 June 2010. Available from http://www.marketreseach.com.

"Chemistry Professor, Like Father, Wins Nobel Prize." *Detroit Free Press,* 5 October 2006.

Clive, James. "Global Status of Commercialized Biotech/GM Crops: 2007." ISAAA Brief No. 37-2007. International Service for the Acquisition of Agri-Biotech Applications, 13 February 2008.

Coghlan, Andy. "Genetic Engineering: A Decade of Disagreement." *New Scientist,* 21 January 2006.

Definitions of human genome, chromosome, mitochondrial genome, DNA, RNA, cytoplasm, gene, atom, molecule. MedicineNet, Inc. 1 July 2008. Available from www.medicinenet.com.

Dolan, Kerry A. "A Whole New Crop." *Forbes,* 2 June 2008.

"EU Governments Slam Brussels's GM Crops Plan." *EurActiv,* July 2010.

Fatka, Jacqui. "Biotech Acres Keep Increasing." *Feedstuffs,* 3 March 2008.

"FDA Advisers Weigh Approval of Genetically Modified Salmon." *Business Week,* 20 September 2010

Fehrenbacher, Katie. "Venter's Synthetic Genomics Is Gearing Up." *Earth2Tech,* 23 April 2008. Available from http://earth2tech.com/2008/04/23/venters-synthetic-genomics-is-gearing-up/.

Finck, Charlene, Pam Henderson, and Wayne Wenzel. "Tailgate Talk." *Farm Journal,* 13 May 2006.

"Gene Research to Treat Diseases Wins Nobel Prize." *Detroit Free Press,* 3 October 2006.

"Genentech Culture Intact After Roche Takeover." *San Francisco Gate,* 2010.

"Genetic Engineering—Lectures." ISIS. Available from http://www.i-sis.org.uk/GE-debates.php.

Gertsberg, Deniza. "Lawmakers Propose Labeling in Response to Supreme Court's Monsanto Decision." *GMO Digest,* 14 July 2010.

"Indian Court Allows GM Mustard Trial for Research." Reuters, 14 October 2006. Available from http://in.today.reuters.com/misc/PrinterFriendlyPopup.aspx?type=businessNews&storyID.

"ISAAA Brief 41–2009" Press Release. 23 February 2010. Available from http://www.isaaa.org

"Kraft Will Sell Nongenetically Engineered Foods in China." *FEED,* Union of Concerned Scientists October 2006.

Lane, Jim. "ISAAA Chief Said Biotech Crops Only Way Out of Global Poverty, Food Crises." *Biofuels Digest,* 17 September 2010.

O'Neill, Graeme. "Gaining Ground: Debating the Growing Impact of GM Agriculture." *Ecos,* February-March 2007.

Mercer, Chris. "Kraft to Scrap GM ingredients in China." *Decision News Media,* 1 February 2006. Available from http://www.ap-foodtechnology.com/news/printNewsBis.asp/id=64831.

Minowa, Craig, and Ronnie Cummins. "Mexico Bans GE Corn." *Organic Bytes #93,* 25 October 2006. Organic Consumers Association.

"Online Extra: Side of Valves, Hold the Bacon; Someday, Organs from Pigs May Save Human Lives. But Solving the Genetic Engineering Problems Is Turning Out to be Tricky." *Business Week Online,* 11 January 2006 Available from www.businessweek.com.

"Presentations and Financial Reports." Monsanto, 2008. Available from http://www.monsanto.com/investors/presentations.asp.

Pickrell, John. "Instant Expert: GM Organisms." NewScientist, 4 September 2006. Available from http://newscientist.com/article.ns/id=dn9921&print=true.

Rosenthal, Elisabeth. "Questions on Biotech Crops with No Clear Answers." *The New York Times,* 6 June 2006.

Sreelata, M. "Indian Supreme Court Bans GM Crop Trials." *Science and Development Network,* 31 October 2006.

Stevenson, Mark. "Mexico Rejects Biotech Corn." *Associated Press, Straight to the Source,* 18 October 2006. Available from http://www.organicconsumers.org/2006/article_3178.cfm.

"Supreme Court of India Clears Trial of GM Mustard." *Economic Times,* 14 October 2006.

Swedin, Eric G. "Designing Babies: A Eugenics Race with China? The Rapid Pace of Genetic Research, the Author Argues, Guarantees that We Will See Genetically Manufactured Babies Before the End of the Century." *The Futurist,* May-June 2006.

"The Planet Versus Monsanto." *Forbes,* 18 January 2010.

"USA 2008: GM Cultivation Almost at 60 Million Hectares." *GMO Compass,* 1 July 2008.

U.S. Department of Energy Office of Biological and Environmental Research and the National Institutes of Health National Human Genome Research Institute. *History of the Human Genome Project.* 2008. Available from http://www. ornl.gov/sci/techresources/Human_Genome/project/hgp.shtml.

"U.S. Using Food Crisis to Boost Bio-Engineered Crops." *Chicago Tribune,* 14 May 2008.

Walter, Patrick. "EU Could (Bio)Fuel GM Growth." *Chemistry and Industry,* 9 April 2007.

GEOGRAPHIC INFORMATION SYSTEMS

———— ■ ————

SIC CODE(S)

7389

INDUSTRY SNAPSHOT

Location, location, location. Once the exclusive motto of real estate agents, now location is a critical aspect of retailing, weather reporting, and even national security, thanks to geographic information systems (GIS). Geographic information systems allow geographic and land survey information to be combined with descriptive, nonspatial data and displayed in the form of a coded map. A simple example is a city map divided into political precincts and then coded to provide information detailing age, gender, and race of registered voters for each block. All of the information is merged and users are able to query the database of stored information, producing maps displaying any combination of attributes.

The National Center for Geographic Information and Analysis (NCGIA) defines GIS as "a computerized database management system for capture, storage, retrieval, analysis, and display of spatial (locationally defined) data." Two of the industry's professional associations, the American Society for Photogrammetry and Remote Sensing (ASPRS) and the American Congress on Surveying and Mapping (ACSM), established a more comprehensive definition along with a set of principles explaining the important concepts. This collaboration resulted in the following definition: "A system of hardware, software, data, people, organizations, and institutional arrangements for collecting, storing, analyzing, and disseminating information about areas of the earth." The unique feature of GIS, cited in both definitions, is the system's ability to link geographical images to information from a collection of sources.

GIS software customers include those in the regulated sector (water, gas, and electric utilities; telecommunications; transportation; and education), which together account for nearly half of industry revenues. Federal, state, and local governments accounted for 30 percent of revenues, while private sector firms in fields like cartography and earth resources accounted for 24 percent. As the technology to power GIS became more affordable, its applications expanded into the for-profit world of retail as well. GIS can be used for projects as disparate as identifying utility lines, oil and gas exploration, mining, mapping census data, establishing property ownership, or planning a housing development or shopping center. As organizations become more knowledgeable concerning the cost and time-saving capabilities of GIS, the demand for services is expected to continue to grow.

According to the Geospatial Information & Technology Association (GITA) in Aurora, Colorado, the two most common uses of geographic information system technology were managing land records and tracking utility infrastructure. Geospatial data sharing among public sector agencies was also common, and mobile applications were increasing. The GITA report, published in March 2008, found that, whereas the creation of land records such as address lists and tax assessment maps was the most common application, water and sewer line tracking was second and address maintenance was third. Asset management was fourth, and community planning was fifth. The report also found that 74 percent of GIS users in the public sector had been using the technology since the 1980s and 1990s and that 75 percent of users utilized mobile applications, up from 63 percent the year before, and 15 percent used wireless communications to share GIS data, an increase from 4 percent

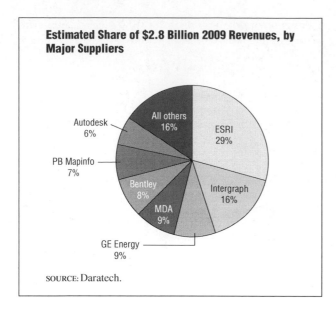

Estimated Share of $2.8 Billion 2009 Revenues, by Major Suppliers

- All others 16%
- ESRI 29%
- Autodesk 6%
- PB Mapinfo 7%
- Bentley 8%
- MDA 9%
- Intergraph 16%
- GE Energy 9%

SOURCE: Daratech.

in 2006. According to Robert Samborski of GITA, "The uptake of mobile technology in field operations is resulting in increasing productivity levels and significantly streamlined operations... This is a major trend that will continue as mobile technology continues its rapid evolution and more governments and utilities use it."

ORGANIZATION AND STRUCTURE

During the 1960s and 1970s, geographic information systems were developed almost exclusively for use by governmental or environmental agencies. As technology became more sophisticated and affordable, so did GIS. When this new tool became widely available to the business community, a host of new applications emerged. GIS revolutionized planning processes, which previously required months of labor. Spurred by the public interest in GIS, companies and consultancies began to emerge as a growth industry; there was no shortage of options for those seeking expertise in the field.

Companies in need of GIS services evaluate their needs and decide what type of commitment they are willing to make to fulfill those requirements. By its very nature, GIS brings together parcels of information that normally would not overlap. In most cases, different departments or agencies are responsible for collecting and disseminating the various types of information needed to implement a successful GIS. There are four important components in the creation of a viable GIS: geographic information (maps), nonspatial information (demographics, descriptive data), technology (hardware, software, or even satellites), and people. When deciding whether to form an in-house GIS department or hire an independent consultant, all four of these resources are considered.

It is also important to note that GIS is only truly effective when a long-term commitment exists. Typically it takes several years to lay the groundwork for a functional system. Once the system is operational, land maps have a life cycle of almost 100 years, but the accompanying non-geographic data must be updated constantly. Along with the need for a stream of current data that reflects changes to a region, technology and personnel must also adapt to meet new challenges. Often the initial start-up costs of such an initiative are overwhelming, and corporations elect to hire outside consultants to supply GIS expertise. Consultants can provide the training and technology required to build an in-house staff or perform the work themselves and provide the client with maps and analysis.

GIS customers come from a wide variety of industries. Retailers may hire a consultant to help find the perfect location for a new store opening. Matching the geographic requirements to the merchant's target demographic, a possible list of sites can be quickly generated. Cities and towns use GIS to plan transportation lines and roadways, emergency vehicle routes, school district boundaries, and land development projects. GIS has even been employed by pest control companies to identify target markets. By creating a map system that identifies regions with large termite populations and matching that data with information on income and new home sales, a marketing plan can be developed.

Not every organization opts to contract out the work. Many government agencies and businesses discovered that GIS can provide support for long-term initiatives and they formed internal departments. An important benefit of GIS is information sharing between groups. In order for a GIS project to be effective, all parties must be willing to establish new standards for data, coding, and access. Incorporating GIS into an existing operation often requires restructuring roles and functions and orienting employees.

The global positioning system (GPS) is a location-based GIS technology that exploded in the early years of the first decade of the 2000s. Created and funded by the U.S. Department of Defense and originally designed to help U.S. forces locate targets and move quickly, GPS is now used by thousands of civilians worldwide. Using specially coded satellite signals, GPS can enable a user to compute position, velocity, and time. Outside of the military, one of the system's most popular uses is in vehicles as navigation tools. According to one report published in *Space Daily,* more than 90 percent of the GPS market share in 2007 went to such devices. However, the same report stated that GPS-enabled handsets will overtake the market by 2012 and account for 78 percent of the market share by the end of that year. Growth in the GPS sector of the GIS industry was expected to continue at a breakneck speed into the next decade.

BACKGROUND AND DEVELOPMENT

Researchers and practitioners offer different perspectives on the evolution of the science based on their own areas of specialization. In an effort to define the field, the GIS History Project was launched in 1996. The following initiatives were cited as the primary goals of the study: to foster research on the history of GIS by all scholars, whether or not they are directly involved in the project; to document the history of Geographic Information Systems (GIS), especially the early days of the technology; to develop and maintain a professionally-managed archive of materials related to the history of GIS; to coordinate research on the history of GIS and act as a clearing house whereby GIS history researchers can find out what research has been completed, what is underway, and which topics have not yet been addressed; and to disseminate results and findings as broadly as possible in a variety of forms to reach educational and scholarly communities and the general public.

Geographic information systems utilize physical, cultural, biological, demographic, and economic information merged with geographic data, which are then analyzed and manipulated via technology. Because of their diverse roots in many disciplines, there is no single version of their evolution that satisfies all scholars. However many agreed there have been certain significant milestones for the industry.

The origins of GIS can be traced back to the very first maps that appeared as drawings on cave walls. These rudimentary pictures documented day-to-day events, changes in seasons, and movement of animal life. Another noteworthy example occurred during the American Revolution. French cartographer Louis-Alexandre Berthier created maps to chart the movement of British troops during the war. Almost a century later, in the 1850s, mapping was used to assist with railroad construction. The "Atlas to Accompany the Second Report of the Irish Railway Commissioners" combined data regarding geology, topography, population, and traffic patterns to provide a blueprint for the project. In 1854 in London, Dr. John Snow used maps to study the outbreak of cholera that was ravaging the city. His work went beyond merely charting the progress of the disease. By adding an overlay of the city's water system, he was able to study the relationship between the spread of the disease and the location of public wells, thus identifying a contaminated well as the source of the outbreak.

Late in the nineteenth century, technology made its first appearance in the annals of GIS history. Herman Hollerith invented a computer card that automated the U.S. Census for the first time in history. Illustrating the impact of his invention, using the Hollerith card allowed people to determine the results of the 1890 Census before the results of the 1880 Census. Hollerith went on to found IBM, a company that became a computer giant.

Contemporary GIS began to emerge in earnest with the advent of mainframe computers. Improvements in computer technology were the catalysts for changes in the use of mapping techniques. Public awareness of social and cultural factors led to greater efforts to collect data on social issues, the environment, and education, which were needed to complement the geographic component. GIS was largely confined to government agencies that were among the few who could afford the large-scale technology required to run a GIS network. In the 1950s and 1960s, city planners in Detroit and Chicago employed GIS when they designed transportation plans. The mapped models allowed them to plan routes, map times, and destinations, and implement measures to control traffic flow.

The 1960s gave birth to a number of organizations that would become key players in the evolution of GIS. In 1963, the Canadian Geographic Information System (CGIS) was created to compile a land inventory for the country, which still boasted acres of undeveloped land and needed a tool to aid in land management. Maps of the terrain were scanned and converted to usable size and scale. In order to include supplementary information, "layers" were added to the map: overlays were created showing soil type, roads, wildlife, and other information. The project made inroads in methods for scanning maps, organizing internal data, and creating overlays. The project proved to be long and costly and failed to meet some of its stated objectives in a timely manner. However, the work done by this organization provided the groundwork for many subsequent innovations in the field.

In 1964 Harvard University opened the Harvard Laboratory for Computer Graphics and Spatial Analysis. The lab was a magnet for talent and some of the most important scholars in the field got their start in this program. The lab was founded by Howard Fisher, and among his students were David Sinton, the founder of Intergraph Inc., and Jack Dangermond, the force behind industry leader ESRI Inc. The lab created groundbreaking software capable of handling the large stores of data processed in GIS undertakings. The software packages developed at the lab dominated the field for the following decade. Some of the notable programs included SYMAP, an early map-making package that allowed amateurs to make their own maps with the aid of computers. CALFORM was similar to the SYMAP system but provided better quality images and legends for interpretation. In the late 1960s, SYMVU produced the first three-dimensional images.

A decade later, the burgeoning supply of information collected by the Census Bureau mandated further modifications to available software packages. POLYVRT allowed data to be entered into the system with fewer restrictions and provided file-sharing capabilities. The most prolific achievement of the Harvard Lab was the release of the ODYSSEY program in the late 1970s. This package incorporated all the applications of previous offerings in the first comprehensive system.

In 1967 the U.S. Census Bureau concluded that it needed a new system for matching geographic locations with street addresses and census data. In 1970 the agency released the first geo-coded Census data created using DIME files. This method coded street blocks in urban areas and assigned coordinates to each location. DIME files became popular among government users and became the basis for improvements in emergency vehicle dispatch, garbage collection routes, and automobile navigation and driver guides. The success of the 1970 census marked the beginning of an important time for GIS. The ability to map urban areas and provide matching demographic information caught the attention of the corporate world, which realized that the new technology could be a useful tool. Applications began to appear allowing retailers to use maps for sales and marketing plans.

The late 1960s saw the emergence of the first corporate GIS entities. In 1969, two companies, ESRI and Intergraph, which were still industry leaders as of 2004, were launched. After they worked at the Harvard Lab, Jack and Laura Dangermond founded Environmental Research Systems Institute (ESRI). The new endeavor grew slowly during the 1970s but flourished in the 1980s. Its first major success came with the release of the ARC/INFO program. The program did not require the cumbersome mainframe system on which previous systems had relied. It also provided a toolbox for user interface, which allowed applications to be built on top of the primary application.

Satellites became pivotal in acquiring geographic information during the 1980s. In 1981, the Global Positioning System became operational. In 1982, SPOT Image became the first commercial company to offer worldwide geographic footage using the Earth Observation Satellite. The ETAK, MapInfo, and Smallworld commercial mapping companies were all launched during the 1980s as the field became increasingly commercialized. In 1988 the U.S. Bureau of Census released the first public copy of Topologically Integrated Geographic Encoding and Referencing (TIGER), the geo-encoded census report.

The use of the work station and personal computers significantly altered the field of GIS and greatly increased their ease of use during the 1990s. The first Web-based interactive map was developed by Steve Putz. It accepted user requests for map renderings and returned an HTML document including a Graphics Interchange Format (GIF) image of the requested map.

This event marked the beginning of the migration to Internet-based programs. MapInfo Professional released a version of its software for Windows 95. In 1998 the most ambitious research project in years was completed with the launch of TerraServer (www.terraserver.com). TerraServer was a joint effort between Aerial Images, the USGS, Compaq Computers, and Microsoft. The project began as a software trial for Microsoft. The company wanted to test the operating capacity of its SQL software running only Windows NT. In order to perform the experiment, the company needed a tremendous amount of data to process. Enter USGS with its global collection of satellite footage housed at the University of California in Santa Barbara. Microsoft decided to use data that would have some value to users around the world as opposed to countless unrelated files of data. Additional photos were obtained from SPIN-2, a Russian space agency satellite. The result was a huge global atlas that is searchable over the Internet by all users. It is possible to enter a city name or street address and view satellite footage of the ground below.

By the early years of the first decade of the 2000s, GIS was being used in new and interesting ways. For example, in its November 11, 2003, issue, *Computer Weekly* reported that the Tower of London was employing GIS technology to monitor and slow the rate of the landmark's deterioration. The historic tower accommodated some two million visitors annually, and GIS software from industry leader ESRI allowed officials to "plot statistics showing the relationship between visitor numbers, humidity, temperature and damage to the stone construction." Intelligence gleaned from such analysis could be used to manage how visitors access the tower.

In 2004 Google launched a similar program called Earth Viewer—renamed Google Earth in 2006. Google Earth is a virtual globe program that uses a combination of satellite images and aerial photos and allows users to see virtually anything on the earth from a bird's eye view. By 2008, users could also view many locations from a street-level view, as well as see structures in some locations in 3D format. Google Earth was released to the public in mid-2006, causing a more than tenfold increase in media coverage on virtual globes and related applications.

GIS technology proved its worth to governments in the wake of the September 11, 2001, terrorist attacks and outbreaks of West Nile Virus. GIS continued to provide significant benefits to humans in need. This was evident following Hurricane Katrina, one of the deadliest natural disasters in U.S. history. The economic and human impact of Katrina was devastating. In addition to decimating areas of Mississippi, the hurricane flooded the city of New Orleans and damaged oil refineries in the Gulf of Mexico. GIS technology proved to be an invaluable tool in disaster recovery, relief, and rebuilding efforts. It was used by the federal government, state governments, and agencies such as the American Red Cross to help rescue workers locate victims and determine where to send supplies and establish shelters and relief centers.

The most common example of map-based technologies can be found online at such portals as MapQuest and Google Maps. These Web sites allow the average Internet user to map a location, request driving instructions from place to place, or locate a specific retail outlet by name. Similar navigation systems are installed in cars rolling off the assembly lines. There are drawbacks to using these cyber route-finders. In what is becoming a common refrain, the product output is only as good as the quality of the data that are placed into the system. Despite the high quality of existing aerial photography, mistakes are made. A stream or footpath can be mistaken for a road, a shadow mistaken for a bridge. Even when roads and byways are accurately identified, characteristics such as one-way streets can be missed. Many mapping sites contain warnings and advise that users call ahead to verify directions and pay close attention to all roadside directions.

By 2008, GIS had expanded to become "location-based." Location-based GIS allows a user to access the technology from a computer or cell phone in a wireless manner. It also allows merchants to capture information and transfer it to a GIS system, for example, whenever a customer swipes a credit card at the checkout counter, which is valuable for marketing campaigns. One example of a location-based GIS system is Citysense, which can be downloaded to BlackBerry phones or iPhones. Created by Sense Networks, Citysense highlights the busiest nightspots in San Francisco in real time using data from cell phones. Users can see what places have a high activity level at any given moment or view locations that historically draw large crowds. The company also introduced Macrosense, software that analyzes historical and real-time location data from mobile devices and cars. Tony Jebara of Sense Networks told *Information Week,* "Sense Networks has indexed the real places in a city and characterized them by activity, versus proximity or demographics, to better understand the context of consumers' offline behavior."

More companies were using GIS technology to gain information that would be useful to their organization. For example, Lamar Advertising, a leading vendor of billboard marketing, used information gathered on traffic patterns and driver demographics to make sales presentations; Chico's, a women's clothing chain, used it to determine site locations and make better use of its mail order campaign; and Colonial Pipeline, a company that ships 100 million gallons of fuel products a day in the eastern United States, utilized data from GIS to ensure the product was moving safely and efficiently. Emergency responders were also using the technology to more quickly locate people in

need of help, find the fastest route, and make better-informed decisions regarding where to take them.

Government agencies adopted new applications for GIS. In the aftermath of the terrorist attacks against the United States on September 11, 2001, a premium was placed on security and disaster preparedness. GIS entered the war on terrorism and bio-terrorism. In January 2002, GIS leader MapInfo released a Homeland Security Program. The program is designed to assist government agencies and local authorities respond to emergency situations. It provides an overview of regional landmarks, transportation centers, communications lines, and power plants as well as non-spatial data on population and resources to allow authorities to fashion the most efficient rescue and recovery efforts.

Geographic information systems (GIS) were being employed by all levels of government to address a wide range of public health concerns. Particularly at the county and city levels, such systems were used to combat outbreaks of West Nile Virus, monitor harmful bacteria levels near beaches, study the incidence of breast cancer in relation to environmental factors, and track the spread of water-borne illnesses. Hospitals also were employing GIS technology as part of electronic bulletin board systems. These allowed hospitals to better manage how patients were assigned to or transferred between rooms and to improve the efficiency with which they were discharged.

The Centers for Disease Control and Prevention uses maps to track the outbreak of diseases or threats of bio-terrorism. Maps provide the basis for decision making among emergency responders. GIS professionals have proposed a more elaborate model that would link a wide variety of data sources. Instead of monitoring only hospital emergency rooms, the new system would solicit information from private practice physicians, managed care, insurance companies, labs, public health officials, hospitals, poison control centers, 911 calls, schools, medical examiners, and veterinarians and animal hospitals. Collectively, this data would capture emerging patterns or identify at-risk areas. Although the proposed plan was laudable in its goals, it might prove difficult to implement. The quality of data would be difficult to guarantee since there is no unique identifier when dealing with medical patients and records. Social security numbers are used in some instances, but many patients are reluctant to provide this information in light of privacy concerns. A universal patient identification system could be created to eliminate duplicate records, but doing so would require thousands of records to be amended to include the new data. Confidentiality of medical records could also be compromised in such a far-reaching system.

Although the GIS community continued to face issues regarding privacy and security, and even how to make GIS systems more user friendly, there was a growing convergence of "business intelligence" and GIS.

Business intelligence (BI) can include everything from market research and competitive analysis to consumer behavior patterns and customer demographics. Historically, many BI analysts have preferred to view data in spreadsheet form. However, GIS applications were becoming more affordable and user-friendly, allowing a growing number of business users to look at data in a visual way and glean new insights.

Retailers and corporations can employ GIS to gather critical intelligence on customers and competitors. A detailed map combined with demographic information can provide a potential business owner invaluable information for evaluating a potential store location. The number of households in an area, median income, number of competitors, and travel and traffic patterns can identify the positive and negative aspects of a planned venture. Retail profiling is the most common use of GIS, excluding actual land location services. Retailers go to great lengths to pinpoint the geographic location of customers. One popular method for achieving this information is to request ZIP code information with each in-store sale. Other industrious business owners actually record the license plate numbers of cars in the parking lot and trace the home addresses of the owners. Retail applications for GIS are surprisingly not limited to brick-and-mortar stores.

Government and consumer use of GIS technology is also expanding. A greater number of state and local agencies are adopting GIS models to enhance municipal services. Communities and school districts pool resources to create new systems to serve multiple users. Much of the data used by state officials is common to more than one agency. Agreements to share information eliminate the redundancies in data collection and ultimately can save taxpayer dollars. In order to achieve this level of collaboration, staff must be willing to forgo proprietary claims on information and outline a uniform set of standards for maintaining data. Even the most sophisticated GIS model is only as reliable as the data that is put into the system. Employees working in different branches of government must follow the same protocol when editing information or the benefit of the entire project is diminished.

PIONEERS IN THE FIELD

Jack Dangermond attended the California Polytechnic College in Pomona and graduated with a B.S. in Environmental Science. He continued his studies and received an M.S. in urban planning from the Institute of Technology at the University of Minnesota before heading east to Harvard University. At Harvard, he earned an M.S. in landscape architecture from the Graduate School of Design and worked in the Laboratory for Computer Graphics and Spatial Design where he began his career in GIS. He founded ESRI in 1969 with his wife and

continued his career as the company CEO. He was an advisor on international projects such as the United Nations Environmental Programme and the Digital Chart of the World Project for the National Imagery and Mapping Agency. He is the recipient of numerous awards and prizes including the Cullum Geographical Medal of Distinction from the American Geographical Society. He has consulted for NASA's Science and Technology Advisory Committee, the EPA, the National Academy of Sciences, and the National Science Foundation. His most noteworthy contribution may be the success of his company, ESRI. As of 2004, its software packages were in the hands of thousands of customers around the world.

GIS has experienced several transformations. In the 1970s, GIS applications were housed on large mainframe computers. During the 1980s, stand-alone workstations emerged on personal computers. By 2003 the Internet had become the wave of the future for GIS, with files located on servers and distributed on the Internet. However, as Dr. Sam Batzli, a geography professor at Michigan State University, described this new delivery method in *Software Development,* "A lot of things are called Web-GIS, but they are not doing any analysis; they're just for display." He cited a map-based database housed at Michigan State that catalogues and displays foliage as an example of display-only technology. Users are able to view aerial photographs of different regions but cannot submit queries or manipulate data. In contrast, the Tropical Rain Forest Information Center offers an application, also based at Michigan State, which does allow users to interact and work with the stored data. The ability for users to modify or add data to existing maps continues to be a challenge for the industry. Ideally, viewers would have the ability to select a map online and merge that geographic image with data from his or her computer desktop.

Technology is not the only hindrance to public recognition of GIS as a valuable tool. Dr. Michael Goodchild, the director of the Center for Spatially Integrated Social Sciences at the University of California/Santa Barbara, noted four other factors affecting the development of the GIS industry. In its infancy the cost of GIS was prohibitive and only large clients could afford to hire or train experts to perform the work. The arrival of digital technology produced a glut of inexpensive, high quality maps and photographic datasets, which allow even very small companies to perform their own mapping surveys without outside consultants. In addition, these new image services are charging for maps and data that were previously available free of charge from government sources. Some photos and maps are no longer considered public domain, as private companies and foreign governments claim ownership of worldwide images. In light of the first two developments a third concern, privacy, has emerged. With this newfound capability to photograph and sell captured images, is it possible to keep one's home or property out of the public view? There are standards regulating the resolution of images that can be released to the public. They are more restrictive than those for government-commissioned satellite photography, which is powerful enough to read the newspaper on a person's front step. After the terrorist attacks of September 11, 2001, the concern turned from privacy to security. Many photos and maps of water and transportation systems and land formations were removed from the public domain as a matter of national security.

Goodchild's final observation echoed the sentiments of others in the field: how to create the best user interface? Achieving the perfect level of functionality without making the process too cumbersome for the user was an ongoing struggle. In order for the industry to sustain growth, it had to continue to serve customers with very different needs. Three distinct groups were identified: GIS professionals, business professionals from many commercial sectors, and the average online user seeking driving directions.

CURRENT CONDITIONS

Cambridge, Massachusetts-based market research firm Daratech, Inc., published an extensive report in August 2009, indicating, among other things, that overall GIS/Geospatial industry growth had slowed in 2009 to just one percent globally. This compared with 11 percent in 2008 and even higher growth in 2007. Notwithstanding, industry CEOs who were interviewed by Daratech expressed high optimism for the full 2010 year: that the 11 percent compound annual growth rate (CAGR) of the previous six years would return. The report noted that North American growth rate (2.1 percent) was not as adversely affected as other regions because of ongoing national security needs and continuing investment by governmental entities. (According to Daratech, European governments had cut back on GIS purchases in anticipation of lower tax revenues, and 2010 growth was expected to be less than one percent in that region.) Daratech estimated global revenues for the entire GIS/Geospatial industry at roughly $5.3 billion in 2009. Of that figure, it estimated that North America was responsible for nearly $2.8 billion. (Daratech's reports encompassed an expanded umbrella of GIS and its related services to include data, geo-enabled engineering, GPS, photogrammetry, and remote sensing.)

The most dramatic global slowdown, consistent with the above data results, was in the private sector, where investment in IT technologies was significantly curbed. However, public sector sales grew about 4.1 percent, especially in the software sector.

Worldwide GIS/geospatial *software* sales in 2009 were estimated at roughly $2.3 billion. Of that, the public sector carried the load with just under an estimated $1 billion in

revenues ($957 million). Both regulated and unregulated private sector revenues made up the remainder.

In February 2010, market researcher RNCOS released its report, *GPS Market to Grow by 20%,* concerning the GPS segment of GIS. RNCOS predicted that the number of subscribers of GPS-enabled location-based services would grow substantially, with market revenue close to $10 billion by 2013. Formerly, the GPS device market was dominated by portable navigation devices (PNDs), but RNCOS forecast a continuing shift to GPS-enabled handsets that would eventually account for two-thirds of the market by 2013. Overall, considering the projected 20 percent CAGR and increasing use in automotive and consumer applications, the mobile location technologies market could reach $70 billion by 2013.

INDUSTRY LEADERS

ESRI continued to dominate the market in 2009, holding a 30 percent stake. Intergraph, the second largest stakeholder in the traditional segment, held a 16 percent share. Other key players included GE Energy (the leader in the utilities market), MDA, Bentley, PB MapInfo, Autodesk, Leica Geosystems, Logica, and SICAD Geomatics.

Environmental Systems Research Institute, Inc. (ESRI), was founded in 1969 by Laura and Jack Dangermond. Jack Dangermond gained experience in the field at the Harvard Lab in the 1960s. With very little money, he and his wife Laura launched the company and headquartered it in Redlands, California. Since its inception, ESRI has been an innovative company, releasing numerous GIS software packages and upgrades. The company's ArcGIS products dominate the field, and its clients include those from the government and the forestry, oil and gas, and transportation industries. The Bureau of Land Management, the Environmental Protection Agency, and the U.S. Forest Service use ESRI products along with approximately 300,000 other organizations worldwide. 2009 revenues exceeded $800 million, and the company employed 2,500 people. Almost 40 years after its humble beginnings, the company remained privately owned by the Dangermonds.

Intergraph Corp. is another prominent force in GIS. Founded the same year as ESRI, Alabama-based Intergraph counted nearly 20 percent of all GIS users as clients. Founded by David Sinton, an alumnus of the Harvard Lab, Intergraph was a publicly traded company that posted just under $450 million in sales in 2009. With approximately 3,450 employees worldwide in 2008, the company provided technical systems and support to local and national governments, utilities, and private industry. It also had clients in the transportation, process plant design, power, marine, public safety, and utilities industries. In 2006 the company was sold to Texas Pacific Group and Hellman & Friedman LLC for about $1.3 billion.

WORKFORCE

The benefits of GIS are indisputable, and a growing number of public and private organizations have integrated the discipline into corporate planning and development initiatives. In 1999 the first known position of Geographic Information Officer was created at the U.S. Geological Survey. Other job titles in the field include computer programmer, database administrator, system administrator, and cartographic designer. Training and education for a career in GIS is available at over 400 universities in the United States. In addition to academic degree programs, training is available online or through corporate training programs. Specializations include mapping, global positioning, and cartography.

AMERICA AND THE WORLD

According to Daratech, worldwide industry growth slowed in 2009 to just one percent, but North America grew closer to 2.1 percent, mostly in the public sector. The Asia Pacific region fared average (around one percent), whereas the European market came in at less than one percent growth, with total sales coming in at approximately $1.7 billion. (Asia Pacific regional revenues were roughly estimated at $400 million. The rest of the world brought in a little over $300 million in 2009.

Outside the United States, Canada was an early leader in the GIS movement. The establishment of the Canadian Geographic Information System was a landmark event. The Canadian project attempted to inventory the rural land that blanketed the country's more populated regions. The Canadian project defined three distinct tiers for study: political, census, and postal data. The political component divided the country into municipalities, towns, or districts used to distinguish authority from one parcel of land to the next. Political boundaries are useful for users who need to know what laws or regulations are in force in a region. Census data provide the essential population demographics, and postal data provide the addresses to match. The last two sets are of great importance to marketers. The Canadian project was ambitious in scope and plagued by delays and deficits but was highly regarded for its contributions to GIS. The huge infrastructure, however, made the work difficult to upgrade and maintain, and by the 1980s the group's status had declined. The emergence of GIS consultants offering smaller, less expensive solutions was the undoing of the organization, which could not compete with the new products.

India, in particular, is forecast to grow by leaps and bounds in GIS technology. In 2008, Japan had the highest number of in-vehicle GPS systems, followed by North American and European countries. The 2008 Olympics were expected to give a boost to the industry in China, whereas Taiwan was a major manufacturer of GPS systems.

RESEARCH AND TECHNOLOGY

According to Eric Gakstatter in a December 2009 article for *GPS World,* industry software suppliers ESRI, Small-World, and MapInfo designed their software from the world of GIS, whereas Autodesk, Intergraph, and Bentley designed their software from a CAD perspective. Pure GIS, and the infrastructure upon which it is based, said Gakstatter, will remain in the hands of highly technical professionals. However, geospatial data and services in general have taken on an expanded definition. When Google Earth, Mapquest, Bing Maps, and Yahoo! maps paved the way, they were followed by GPS navigators. The technology poised to explode, therefore, was with the wireless service providers. New applications for mobile phones and other handhelds appear on the market on a daily basis. A new company, TeleNav, began to write navigation software for mobile phones. In addition to navigation software, a plethora of new software in the social networking arena, which falls under location-based-services (LBS), further muddies a purist, scientific definition of GIS.

GIS is a technology-driven industry, and new developments occur at a rapid pace. One example of the benefits of the increases in technological advancements in the field was evidenced by the Richmond, Virginia, Police Department in 2008. Using business intelligence, predictive analysis, and GIS technologies, the Department created a GIS software application that can, according to an *American City & County* article, "predict the likelihood of crimes occurring based on variables such as time of day, weather and the coincidence of public events, and sometimes prevent crimes." Other advances in GIS technology were affecting a number of fields, including agriculture, business, forestry, health care, real estate, and many others.

BIBLIOGRAPHY

Belgaumkar, Badrinath. "Geospatial Information Systems (GIS) Become Increasingly Relevant to Idia as Several State Organs Tap its Potential." ARC Advisory Group, 1 February 2010. Available from http://www.arcweb.com/manufacturingIT-India/.

Baxter, Roberta. "More than Mapping: Some Innovative Uses of GIS." *Journal of the American Planning Association,* July 2008.

Carberry, Sonja. "Map Out Opportunities." *Yahoo! News,* 3 July 2008.

"Citysense Uses Mobile Data To Pinpoint Night Life Hot Spots." *InformationWeek,* 9 June 2008.

"Explore, Search, Discover." Google Earth, 1 July 2008. Available from http://earth.google.com.

Gakstatter, Eric. "Who is Geospatial? *GPS World,* 8 December 2009.

Gillette, Becky. "Geospatial Companies Hit Ground Running in Katrina's Wake." *Mississippi Business Journal,* 9-15 January 2006.

"GIS/Geospatial Industry Worldwide Growth Slows to 1% in 2009." Prress Release, Daratech Inc. 19 August 2009. available from http://www.daratech.com/press/releases/2009/091908.html.

"GIS In Our World." ESRI Inc., 1 July 2008. Available from http://www.esri.com.

"GIS News: GPS Market to Grow by 20%." 24 February 2010. Available from http://www.gisdevelopment.net/news.

McDaid, Cathal. "GPS Overview." *Palowireless,* July 2008. Available from http://www.palowireless.com/.

Monroe, Rodney. "High-Tech Crime Fighting." *American City & County,* 1 January 2008.

"Precision Agricultural Practices with GIS." *GEO: Connexion,* May 2008.

Shankland, Steven. "GIS Exec Works to Unlock Hidden Geographic." *Webware,* 13 May 2008. Available from http://www.webware.com.

"Technology Trends in Mobile GIS." Environmental Systems Research Institute, 2008. Available from http://www.esri.com/.

"World GPS Market Forecast to 2013—Report." Abstract and summmary, 24 February 2010. Available from http://www.educationgis.com/2010/02/world-gps-market-forecasat-to-2013.html.

Wyland, Jessie. "GIS Portal Streamlines Aquaculture and Fisheries in Africa." African Geo Information Research Network, 10 June 2008.

GREEN CONSTRUCTION

—■—

SIC CODE(S)

1521

INDUSTRY SNAPSHOT

Green construction or green building is the practice of envisioning, building, and maintaining structures that are sustainable in their creation and in their upkeep. This can be done with energy-efficient siting, design, construction, operation, maintenance, renovation, and demolition. The primary focus of green construction is to efficiently use water, energy, and other resources to protect occupant health and improve employee productivity, and to reduce waste, pollution, and environmental degradation.

Green construction seeks to reduce the environmental impact of new buildings by siting, designing, building, and operating the structure and site with smart, safe, and effective energy-efficient practices that reduce their influence over land use, water and energy consumption, and air and atmosphere alterations. Because new buildings significantly impact many or all of these factors, green construction has been an area of much study and improvement in the past few years.

According to the Environmental Protection Agency, the new building sector accounts for 30 to 40 percent of global energy use. When these buildings are in use, they produce more than 80 percent of the most harmful environmental emissions. Those statistics alone have made green construction a high-profile emerging industry.

Critics have cited the extra expense as a reason to not use green construction. However, the World Business Council for Sustainable Development reports that green building costs are overestimated. Experts in real estate and construction point out that the estimates for green construction are around 17 percent higher than typical construction, when in reality the cost of green construction is about 5 percent higher than typical construction.

Green construction joins a variety of practices and techniques that reduce and will perhaps one day eliminate the impact of new building on the environment and human health. This includes utilizing renewable resources (e.g., passive solar, active, solar, and photovoltaic sources and using plants and trees through green roofs, rain gardens, and for reduction of rainwater run-off). Other perma-care techniques, such as using packed gravel or permeable concrete instead of conventional concrete or asphalt, helps the replenishment of ground water.

The actual practices and technologies used in green building may be different from region to region. However, there are several foundations, including site and structure design efficiency, energy efficiency, water efficiency, materials efficiency, indoor environmental quality enhancement, operations and management optimization, and waste and toxin reduction. The goal of green construction is to optimize one or more of these fundamentals with the goal of weaving each technology together to create a great overall effect.

Green construction also takes into account the philosophy of designing a building that is in harmony with the natural features and resources surrounding the site. This can be accomplished by several key steps in designing sustainable buildings. These include specifying green building materials from local sources, reducing loads, optimizing systems, and generating on-site renewable energy.

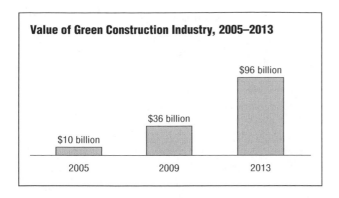

Value of Green Construction Industry, 2005–2013

$96 billion
$36 billion
$10 billion
2005   2009   2013

ORGANIZATION AND STRUCTURE

The green construction industry is largely a part of the construction industry itself. As environmentally friendly policies grow and more and more consumers are aware of the need to conserve energy in every area of their lives, green construction will become more and more mainstream. Al Gore's 2006 documentary, *An Inconvenient Truth*, helped to further the trend to go green. The growth of recycling, use of CFL bulbs, and the use of local food growers to provide more ingredients to local restaurants and supermarkets are several examples.

Consumers also have become interested in building homes that are energy-efficient in various ways. Xeriscaping helps a local environment by eco-friendly landscaping and design, which encourages natural heating and cooling rather than using nonrenewable energy. Another example is environmentally-friendly upkeep, which encourages employees to turn off lights, recycle waste, and carpool or use environmentally-friendly public transportation. All of these ideas are key drivers with the green construction industry.

Regulation of the green construction industry is mostly overseen by a collection of organizations, including the International Green Construction Code, the U.S. Green Building Council (which hands out LEED certification), the Living Building Challenge, Green Globes, Build it Green, and the National Association of Home Builders National Green Building Standard (NAHB NGBS). The U.S. Green Building Council certifies buildings for their design, their energy efficiency, and their overall energy savings with a LEED standard, in various levels (certified, silver, gold, and platinum). The NAHB NGBS provides a template for builders and consumers who seek to build a green home from the ground up by providing a guideline on how to site, design, build, operate, and deconstruct residential buildings throughout the United States.

BACKGROUND AND DEVELOPMENT

Green construction got its start in the energy crisis in the 1970s. It was during those events that first made government and consumers think seriously about the effects of building on the environment. Since then, federal agencies, such as the Occupational Safety and Health Administration (OSHA) and the Environmental Protection Agency (EPA) have represented consumers with ongoing concerns about environmental issues related to new building construction, renovation, clean-up and demolition, and upkeep and operations. The EPA introduced the Clean Air Act, the Clean Water Act, and Superfund, and in 2010 seeks to introduce legislation to introduce standards related to indoor air quality.

Green construction is a huge piece of helping to preserve our environment and our health. Human beings spend a majority of their day inside a building, whether in their own homes or at work or at school. The idea of building new construction to sustain a healthy environment and healthy consumers appeals to many consumers, builders, and the government. A safer building is a better building, and will save money by lowering health care costs, focusing renovation expenses on sustainable measures, and altogether building for efficiency.

PIONEERS IN THE FIELD

Paul Hawken is an entrepreneur, environmentalist, and author. He is cofounder of retailer Smith & Hawken, which sells organic and eco-friendly home and garden furnishings throughout the United States and the world. Hawken has authored six books including *The Next Economy* (1983), *Growing a Business*, and *The Ecology of Commerce* (1993), wherein he coined the term the "restoration economy." His book, *Natural Capitalism: Creating the Next Industrial Revolution* (1999), coauthored with Amory Lovins and Hunter Lovins, popularized the now-standard idea of natural capital and direct accounting for natures services. *Natural Capitalism* has been translated into 26 languages.

Blessed Unrest, How the Largest Movement in the World Came into Being and Why No One Saw It Coming, published by Viking Press in May 2007, argues that a vast world-changing "'movement with no name' is now forming, which Hawken believes will prevail. He conceives of this 'movement' as developing not by ideology but rather through the identification of what is and is not humane, like an immune system."

Hellmuth, Obata, and Kassabaum (now HOK) is a global design firm that consults on global architecture, interiors, engineering, and planning. "HOK is the largest U.S.-based architecture-engineering firm and the world's fourth-largest architectural firm. HOK also is the country's leading design firm in terms of non-U.S. fee growth and the second-largest interior design firm." HOK is an innovator in architecture design, thanks to its software development aimed at assisting architects by encouraging the vision of sustainable development and its consulting on a wide variety of new building projects in the past 30 years. The firm has published the *HOK Guidebook to Sustainable Design*, a guidebook encouraging LEED-certified design and construction.

Mitchell Joachim is "acknowledged as an innovator in ecological design and urban design. He also is a researcher and architectural educator. Mitchell Joachim's specific professional interest has been adapting principles of physical and social ecology to architecture, urban design, transport, and environmental planning."

Joachim is a cofounder of Terrefuge and Terreform One, an ecological design group. He graduated with a Ph.D. from the Massachusetts Institute of Technology in the Department of Architecture, Design, and Computation program. He was named to *Popular Science*'s list of environmental visionaries in the publication's "Future of the Environment" segment in 2010. Other pioneers include Buckminster Fuller, James Tennant Baldwin, Dr. Ken Yeang, and Alexander Thomson.

CURRENT CONDITIONS

Green construction is no longer just a trend for many construction companies. They see the demand for sustainable, environmentally-friendly design, construction, and upkeep at an all-time high (for both residential and commercial projects). The value of green construction was estimated at $10 billion in 2005. This figure increased to approximately $36 billion in 2009 and was expected to reach to $96 billion by 2013.

These figures confirm that consumers and businesses care about the environment. This is either from public opinion or from a national consciousness that is finally pierced with the knowledge that unhealthy building practices lead to higher health care costs, exorbitant retrofits, and/or dangerous cleanup of degraded structures and landscaping. Rather than face bigger costs down the road, green construction seeks to minimize future concerns by front-loading the costs and increasing the insurance against later disasters. This includes sustainable design practices, low-energy or zero-energy building practices, water conservation, materials efficiency, sustainable architecture, and indoor air quality. It also includes operations and maintenance optimization and waste reduction.

While cost is an upfront consideration with green construction, estimates may be three times as high as they are in reality, leading many businesses and consumers to mistakenly think that they cannot afford to go with green construction methods. In actuality, the costs of not going green may be three times as much as anticipated. Rather than saving money at the outset, some companies think they can just hedge their bets against the costs of not going green later on. Not seeking the highest quality in

environmental protections may cost much more in the long run, when one considers government regulations, such as Superfund.

INDUSTRY LEADERS

Turner Construction was founded in 1902 with just $25,000 of startup capital. Since then it has become an $8.2 billion dollar construction company and the largest in the United States. Turner Construction is a subsidiary of HOCHTIEF Germany. Projects include Yankee Stadium, Madison Square Garden, and the World Trade Center cleanup (New York City); Quest Field (Seattle, Washington); and Nintendo of America Headquarters (Redmond, Washington). Turner Construction's national segment groups include Green Building, Justice, Pharmaceutical, Sports, and Transportation and Aviation.

McCarthy Building Companies is ranked eleventh nationally in the number of LEED accredited professionals on staff. It brings in $4 billion worth of construction each year. Based in St. Louis, Missouri, McCarthy began in 1864 and, nearly 150 years later, was still 100 percent employee-owned. During the early 2000s McCarthy's Green Team formalized its "in-house green knowledge network to capture and build upon the best green practices on its projects and in its offices."

WORKFORCE

The construction world was hit hard between 2008 and 2010. Plans for a true "green construction" movement slowed down in response to difficult economic conditions. Many new building plans were put on hold, and domestic international development slowed down. However, construction has persevered. One of the ways the industry has responded is with a renewed commitment to environmentally-friendly building practices. In the midst of this economic downturn, commercial and residential builders have turned their focus toward green construction, as evidenced by the emergence of agencies and for-profit companies seeking to help educate or regulate the adherence to green construction standards.

Examples of this include the California Department of Resources Recycling and Recovery (CalRecycle), a Web site geared toward new building contractors and residential developers who are seeking information on green construction and green operations. Another example is *GreenSource, the Magazine of Sustainable Design*, an online magazine with the latest information about trends and new R&D technologies for both commercial and residential construction. Oikos, a service of Iris Communications Inc., seeks to serve professionals whose work "promotes sustainable design and construction." ConstructionGreenBook.com offers a listing of general contractors who work toward sustainable development and building practices. The National Association of Home Builders has its NAHBGreen program, which is a trade organization made up of contractors who seek to bring the best innovations and technologies for green construction into the mainstream. The NAHB has a listing of general contractors and builders for developers and consumers to choose from.

As consumers continue to note the importance of safe building practices, both for their own health and for the health of our planet, green construction will soon become a mandate. Construction workers who have worked in the field for years will have to learn new skills and new ways of building. New construction workers will need to understand the importance of green construction as they enter the workforce. Because construction is such a big industry, many labor unions have begun to offer training that will allow their members to stay competitive. However, many construction workers are non-union. Therefore, they must assume responsibility for staying current on the latest green construction technologies and learn to adapt to a changing construction world.

AMERICA AND THE WORLD

Beyond the United States, green construction appears to have progressed more quickly. The United Kingdom, Canada, and Europe (especially northern Europe) have taken drastic, pioneering steps to standardize their building regulations in consideration of human, animal, and environmental health.

Although in the 1970s and 1980s, new building construction had little aesthetic design quality, it was an attempt by designers and developers to build differently than they had before. Rather than use standard materials that cost a lot more in annual upkeep and operation, contractors wanted to try something new. They used a variety of non-sustainable, mostly manmade materials. As a result, the structures that were built only 30 or 40 years ago have not withstood the test of time as well as those built 100 years earlier.

Now that aesthetics have changed, buildings in Europe seek to become timeless, both by their energy efficiency and by their shape and design. Rather than destroy the surrounding environment, the building site seeks to blend in better. Rather than use materials that do not withstand the test of time and cost a fortune to replace, builders are returning to an older material that does not require as much upkeep, in cooperation with emerging technology that helps that material to function for a longer time period.

In Canada, GreenCA, reports on the latest developments in green construction (both for commercial and residential building projects). In the United Kingdom,

the Green Register highlights companies and design technologies that can help builders to put up buildings to stand the test of time. GreenSpec provides a gallery of green building projects, materials, technologies, and feature products. The National Building Specification provides the latest in regulatory and government guidelines about green construction and building.

RESEARCH AND TECHNOLOGY

Green construction has made tremendous progress, which will likely continue in coming decades. When choosing to site and design a building, many factors come into play. The location and situation of a building impacts the ecosystem and atmosphere around it. With green construction, the goal is to introduce the least amount of disturbance to the surrounding wildlife and ecosystem. How the building is situated is of the utmost importance, because it affects everything concerning the building up until the day the building may be demolished years into the future. The design of a building needs to take into account many features: energy conservation in windows and doorways, lighting, heating and cooling, indoor air quality, and waste removal and cleaning. Reducing water consumption and maintaining high water quality are vital impact issues in green construction. Materials and new technologies also are key considerations. Renewable materials are preferred, but production costs and the time and distance required to ship materials to the building site also must be taken into account. Indoor air quality seeks to reduce volatile organic compounds (VOCs) in a new building after its completed.

Green construction also addresses the issue of water waste. This pertains to both construction and operation of the building. "Greywater" usage involves taking nonpotable water and cleaning it just enough so that it can water vegetation and landscaping, or be used for flushing toilets. Ultimately, this helps to reduce the impact on wastewater facilities and the effect on local groundwater.

The loudest argument against green construction is the price. The cost of green construction is at least 5 percent higher than in typical construction. However, analysts estimate that the costs incurred upfront may ultimately prove to be minimal. Energy savings over the lifetime of a new building are substantial. Studies of buildings over a 20-year period have shown a $53 to $71 per square foot savings on energy costs. If these numbers are anywhere near to what is actually saved over the lifetime of a new building, green construction is actually the only choice. While it may appear to cost more initially, contractors would do well to encourage green construction practices as much as possible in the early stages of their projects. Green construction may mean the resurgence of construction as a power industry as our economy comes back to life.

BIBLIOGRAPHY

California Department of Resources Recycling and Recovery (CalRecycle), 2010. Available from http://www.calrecycle.ca.gov/greenBuilding.

Construction Green Book, 2010. Available fromhttp://www.constructiongreenbook.com.

GreenSource, 2010. Available from http://greensource.construction.com.

Hawken, Paul. *Blessed Unrest, How the Largest Movement in the World Came into Being and Why No One Saw It Coming.* New York: Viking, 2007.

Mendler, Sandra F., William Odell, and Mary Ann Lazarus. *HOK Guidebook to Sustainable Design.* New York: Wiley, 2005.

Oikos, a Division of Iris Communications Inc., 2010. Available from http://oikos.com/about/index.html.

GREEN RETAILING

———————————— ■ ————————————

SIC CODE(S)

5999

INDUSTRY SNAPSHOT

The practice of green retailing reduces the carbon footprint of brick-and-mortar or Internet stores through the use of sustainable buildings and design, eco-friendly maintenance, efficient supply chains, and the provision of information to consumers regarding the transportation and manufacture of products. Green retailing raises the bar for companies who have sold products and services to consumers without being required to communicate how those products or services were displayed, produced, or replenished.

The U.S. Green Building Council awards different levels of LEED (Leadership in Energy & Environmental Design) Green Building Rating System certification in several categories. These include sustainable building sites, water efficiency, energy and atmosphere, materials and resources, indoor environmental quality, location and linkages, awareness and education, innovation and design, and regional priority. In late 2010 the Council was preparing to unveil a LEED standard specifically for the retail industry. Called LEED for Retail Rating Systems, the new standard made it easier for retailers to achieve certification. Previously, certification had to be obtained via the LEED for Commercial Interiors program, which included requirements that were somewhat prohibitive, such as the inclusion of staff facilities for showering and bike storage.

Green retailing appears to be a permanent indicator of how consumers spend their hard-earned cash. In 2009 the *Christian Science Monitor* reported that discount giant

Wal-Mart had "a plan to display eco-ratings alongside its products...Wal-Mart chairman and CEO Mike Duke said the company was developing an electronic indexing system, which would help customers choose products that are healthy for the planet. The software, he said, could in the future become the basis for an international eco-rating system."

Other retail companies are following Wal-mart's lead, including REI, The North Face, Bass Pro Shops, Smith & Hawken, and Timberland, which have received awards in the past few years because of their LEED-certified retail space, energy-efficient lighting and power, water efficiency, innovation, and design. By 2010 other LEED-certified new construction buildings in various locations across the United States included Chipotle (platinum LEED rating); Denny's (gold); McDonald's (gold); Best Buy (silver); and Kohl's (silver).

As demand for green retailing grows, so do the opportunities. For those working in retail, the pressure has always been about sales; things may be different in the near future. While stocking shelves, employees may be asked about how various products affect the environment or customers may express concern at the amount of power required to light up a store parking lot when there are no customers during the night. There may be new employment opportunities in the future as well, including green retailing specialists who help customers pick out the most energy-efficient choices. At the senior executive level, companies may employ a chief of green operations who projects the future "green" choices the company will make.

Some companies are using the opportunity to go green as a chance to simply make more profits. "Greenwashing"

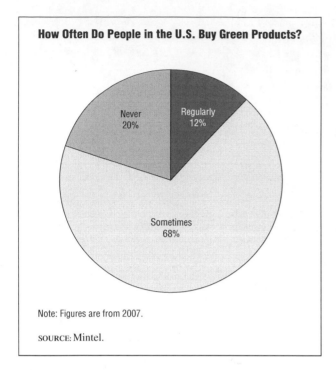

How Often Do People in the U.S. Buy Green Products?

Never
20%

Regularly
12%

Sometimes
68%

Note: Figures are from 2007.

SOURCE: Mintel.

includes practices that are held up to be green retailing, but in fact are simply putting money back in the pockets of the retailer because they appear to be green. More and more consumers are expressing their preference for consumer goods that 1.) are sustainable (i.e., not harvesting animal populations for food or other products), 2.) don't contain harmful components that can't be safely recycled or absorbed by either humans or natural composting (i.e., jewelry with high amounts of lead or cadmium), 3.) don't waste energy by overuse of power sources, shipping resources, or waste management, and 4.) don't push "greenwashing."

ORGANIZATION AND STRUCTURE

Organizations such as the Center for Environmental Health; local, state, and federal government agencies; the U.S. Green Building Council; the Humane Society; and FishWise seek to educate consumers and take upon themselves the responsibility to point out (either in lawsuits or in public service announcements) if retailers are not living up to their green promises. In addition, city law has banned the use of plastic grocery bags in the city of San Francisco. The city of Los Angeles was expected to follow suit with a similar city-wide ban. Beyond these organizations, the weight of keeping consumers safe has fallen on the shoulders of the Food and Drug Administration.

How can consumers know which products and services are actually good for the environment? Heading into 2011, the level of available information was still growing. Industry organizations were often specific as to the type

and scope of information that they provided. One example was the U.S. Green Building Council.

According to the council, "USGBC does not certify, endorse or promote products, services or companies, nor do we track, list or report data related to products and their environmental qualities. LEED is a certification system that deals with the environmental performance of buildings based on overall characteristics of the project. We do not award credits based on the use of particular products but rather upon meeting the performance standards set forth in our rating systems. It is up to project teams to determine which products are most appropriate for credit achievement and program requirements." As things progress, especially as consumer advocacy groups get louder, it is possible that the public will have a rating system that is verified at the state or federal government level and held to the highest of standards.

BACKGROUND AND DEVELOPMENT

In 2006 former Vice President Al Gore was featured in a documentary about his campaign to educate citizens about global warming. The documentary was called *An Inconvenient Truth* and later won two Academy Awards while Al Gore himself won the Nobel Peace Prize in 2007 (along with the Intergovernmental Panel on Climate Change). This documentary changed the public's perception about global warming (now more commonly referred to as climate change) irrevocably.

Never before had the subject received so much nationwide attention. Many individuals eventually began carrying their own reusable shopping bags to the grocery store and exchanging their old incandescent light bulbs for compact fluorescent light bulbs that used less energy. Homeowners put their televisions, computers, and toasters on power strips to save on energy. Consumers also became more interested in energy-efficient washers and dryers, dishwashers, refrigerators, home-building materials, and cars. People began considering their own carbon footprint, not simply because of *An Inconvenient Truth*, but because it became trendy to be seen as green. It was a status symbol to drive an energy-efficient car, to get rid of perfectly good working appliances in order to upgrade to energy-efficient models, and to replace serviceable windows, doors, and heat pumps for new models that were seen as essential to saving the planet.

One negative result was that the trend overcame the need. Rather than continue to drive a car that had plenty of use left, many consumers bought new cars. Rather than simply turning off the lights when they left the room, some consumers put in CFL bulbs and continued to leave every light in their home blazing for hours even though no one was left at home. This is another example of the greenwashing now present in retail. The hope is

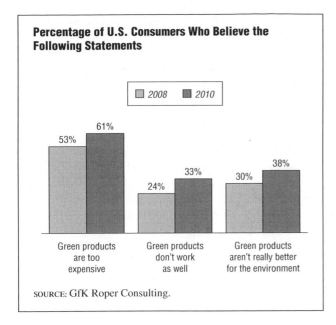

Percentage of U.S. Consumers Who Believe the Following Statements

▢ *2008* ■ *2010*

Green products are too expensive: 53% / 61%
Green products don't work as well: 24% / 33%
Green products aren't really better for the environment: 30% / 38%

SOURCE: GfK Roper Consulting.

that this abates as people get smarter and more cost- and energy-efficient in the years to come.

With the election of Barack Obama as president of the United States in 2008, many in the United States felt that new legislation would help to regulate some of these simple changes that could make so much difference. However, the recession and lingering bad economy, the 2010 Gulf of Mexico oil disaster, and legislative disagreements among Congressional leaders were limiting factors. One positive development took place in October 2010 when the Federal Trade Commission (FTC) proposed revisions to its "Green Guides" in an effort to stem misleading green marketing.

Consumer awareness groups, on the other hand, are actively working to get legislation passed at the local, state, regional, and federal levels that is focused on curbing energy waste or pushing through enough signatures to change government regulations. There also is disagreement regarding environmental solutions. Some green activists insist that most, if not all, retailing is not energy-efficient and wish to decrease the amount of goods available for sale in stores. Other activists simply want to further educate the public about how much we consume and how much is really necessary.

PIONEERS IN THE FIELD

Born in Washington, D.C, in 1948, Al Gore Jr. was the son of a U.S. representative who later served as a Tennessee senator. The younger Gore went to Harvard, where during his junior and senior years he learned about oceanography and global warming from environmental activist Roger Revelle. After a brief stint in the army, Gore went to graduate school and began work as an

investigative journalist at *The Tennessean*. He later enrolled in law school, but never finished due to his run for his father's vacant House of Representatives seat.

At 28, Gore was elected to Congress and stayed there for the next 17 years, serving in both the House (1976–1984) and the Senate (1984–1993). He ran with Bill Clinton on the Democratic ticket in the 1992 presidential election and then served as vice president of the United States for eight years (1993–2001). In 2000 Gore lost a controversial president election to George W. Bush by an electoral college count of 271–266, but won the general election recount in Florida by 500,000 votes.

By 2002 Gore began to speak out against the Bush administration and the growing war cadence toward Iraq and Afghanistan. Gore's interest in the environment began as a young freshman representative and continued throughout his political career. Surprisingly, his greatest accomplishments in environmental awareness came after his political life; in 2006, *An Inconvenient Truth* brought the concept of global warming (climate change) to the forefront of the American conscience.

Rachel Carson (1907–1964) changed the conversation in the United States about the environment with her best-selling book, *Silent Spring*, which was a pivotal tool in the modern environmental movement. Carson was born in 1907 in Springdale, Pennsylvania. She wrote stories as a young child; her first story was published at age 11. Her favorite story material was the nature surrounding her small family farm. She attended Pennsylvania College for Women, first studying English and then switching to biology. Carson earned a master's degree in zoology in 1932.

At her job at the U.S. Bureau of Fisheries, Carson gave a weekly educational broadcast to generate the public's interest in fish biology. After publishing three books about the sea, Carson's interest turned to conservation, primarily pesticide overuse. Her book was a powerful force for the grassroots environmental movement fighting against pesticides use, including DDT. It is noted that the creation of the Environmental Protection Agency (EPA) and the rise of eco-feminism are directly related to her work. Carson died in 1964 at the age of 56 from breast cancer.

CURRENT CONDITIONS

Although green retailing remained popular and trendy, in 2010 the continuing economic recession made it difficult for businesses to keep up with consumer demand, and widespread job loss cooled consumers' ability to choose green. According to some observers, this underscored the importance of education. They were hopeful that consumer attitudes would ultimately change through a greater realization of the long-term impacts of purchasing decisions.

In 2010 President Obama was frustrated by a lack of Congressional action to affect federal environmental legislation. In addition, many of Obama's supporters were frustrated by his administration's lack of openness and transparency on the subject. A *Huffington Post* report talked about how the Obama administration covered up the worst-case scenario of the BP oil spill in the Gulf of Mexico in April 2010 because it would cast a long shadow on the president's plans for environmental reform. Many of the president's constituents saw this as a shortsighted plan. Although the BP oil spill may have dampened enthusiasm for the Obama administration, some argued that consumer demand for environmental protection could readily get louder as public perceptions change and new legislation is proposed.

INDUSTRY LEADERS

A growing number of retailers are modifying their business practices, and the products and services they offer, in order to be more environmentally friendly. As *Financial Express* explained in its July 21, 2009, issue: "Large retailers such as Tesco, Wal-Mart, Kohl's, Office Depot and many more have adopted green strategies and realized the significant benefits accruing from them. Green initiatives include, among others, green buildings, efficient consumer and delivery systems, efficient lighting systems, the use of mobile power such as solar, wind and biomass and promotion of green products."

Wal-Mart Wal-Mart Stores Inc. started in 1962, when the first Wal-Mart Discount City opened in Rogers, Arkansas. The company was incorporated in Delaware in October 1969. The first three Sam's Clubs were opened in 1984, the first supercenter opened in 1988, and the first Neighborhood Market was opened in 1999. Wal-Mart retail stores specialize in providing a broad assortment of quality merchandise and services at everyday low prices. The company operates in three business segments: Wal-Mart Stores, Sam's Club, and International. By 2010 Wal-Mart operated more than 8,400 stores. These included 803 discount stores, 3,100 supercenters, and 595 Sam's Clubs in the United States. Outside of the United States, the company enjoyed a leadership position in Mexico and Canada. In addition, its operations extended to Europe, South America, China, and Japan. In 2010 Wal-Mart enjoyed sales of $408.2 billion on the strength of 2.1 million employees.

Wal-Mart has made sustainability a significant part of its corporate strategy. Because of its size and influence, the company's practices often have a major impact on the retail industry overall. The issue of sustainability was very much on the company's radar screen by the mid-2000s. According to the December 1, 2008, issue of *Supermarket*

News, in October 2005 Wal-Mart CEO Lee Scott gave a presentation titled Twenty-First Century Leadership "in which he outlined the company's short- and long-term commitment to make a zero waste, use 100% renewable energy and sell sustainable products. Through several initiatives, Wal-Mart set in motion a trend that was quickly adopted by other retailers and is raising the bar for what it means to be green."

In 2007 Wal-Mart began measuring the energy used to produce and distribute a number of its own products. In addition, the company unveiled a pilot energy-reduction initiative with select suppliers in specific categories (beer, milk, soap, vacuum cleaners, DVDs, soda, and toothpaste). Wal-Mart's commitment was further exemplified in July of 2010. At that time the company established a long-term strategic partnership with Seventh Generation, a provider of non-toxic and environmentally friendly household products. The partnership called for Seventh Generation's products to become available at approximately 1,500 Wal-Mart stores nationwide, and also via Wal-Mart.com.

According to a July 26, 2010, *Internet Wire* release, the partnership between the two organizations goes beyond product availability. As part of the alliance, "Wal-Mart will collectively encourage families to live better through concrete expressions of education to nearly three and a half million consumers through initiatives such as Walmart's mom bloggers, Facebook and the 7GenBlog. This is designed to give customers the tools and information they need to lead a healthier and more environmentally friendly lifestyle."

Winn-Dixie Stores Inc. Headquartered in Jacksonville, Florida, Winn-Dixie Stores Inc. was founded in 1925 by William Milton Davis who purchased Rockmoor Grocery in Miami, Florida. He changed the name to Table Supply in 1927. The company went public in 1952 and changed its name to Winn-Dixie in 1955 after the acquisition of Dixie Home Stores. Winn-Dixie filed for Chapter 11 in 2005. On November 21, 2006, the company emerged from bankruptcy protection. By 2010 Winn-Dixie Stores ranked as one of the nation's largest food retailers, with approximately 515 stores in Alabama, Georgia, Florida, Louisiana, and Mississippi. At that time the company employed 49,000 people and generated sales of $7.25 billion.

As of 2010 Winn-Dixie was taking a practical approach to green retailing. As Wes Bean, the company's senior director of strategic sourcing, explained in the May 17, 2010, issue of *Supermarket News*: "Our focus is very much on sustainability built around sound business cases in a rational payback period." Examples of the company's efforts include the optimization of trucking routes, reducing empty trailer miles, and cutting down its waste hauling costs. The latter effort involves sending nearly 3 million pounds of food slated for disposal to the Feeding America initiative.

Whole Foods Market Inc. Headquartered in Austin, Texas, Whole Foods Market Inc. is a major retailer committed to green retailing. Most of its products are healthy for the environment, easily recycled or disposed of, and healthy for humans and animals. Whole Foods doesn't just sell products that help the environment, its stores also are environmentally-friendly. Filled with natural lighting and materials, a Whole Foods store is often like walking into an open-air market. Minimal energy expenditures mark each level of usage throughout a Whole Foods store.

Whole Foods Market was founded in 1980 and began trading on the NASDAQ in January 1992. The company operates retail supermarkets specializing in natural and organic foods, with an emphasis on perishables and prepared foods. Wholly-owned subsidiaries such as bakehouse operations, seafood processors, a confectionary, and a specialty tea and coffee operation, exist to supply the company's single business segment. In 2003 Whole Foods Market became the first American grocer to be independently certified as organic.

In August 2007 Whole Foods Market acquired Wild Oats Markets Inc., which operated stores in the United States and Canada under four names: Wild Oats Marketplace, Henry's Farmers Markets, Sun Harvest, and Capers Community Market. The 55 stores netted from this acquisition were all rebranded with the Whole Foods name and are part of the company's 295-store total. Among Whole Foods Market's numerous private-label brands are Allegro Coffee Company, Mrs. Gooch's, and Fresh Fields. The company also carries control brands such as Eternal Water. In 2010 the company generated sales of $9 billion on the strength of 58,300 employees. At that time it operated nearly 300 stores in the United States, Canada, and the United Kingdom.

WORKFORCE

The National Retailing Federation (NRF) and the Association of Retail Environments (A.R.E.) offer conferences and training seminars for people wishing to learn about green retailing and sustainability. Several major retailers, including Whole Foods, Lowes, Home Depot, and REI, specifically hired employees who not only are knowledgeable about their products, but also can share how those products can help to reduce a shopper's carbon footprint.

Industry employers walk a fine line by trying to sell enough products to remain profitable, while at the same time attempting to limit overconsumption and its related negative environmental impact. For workers interested in becoming skilled in the area of green retailing, a look at the NRF and the A.R.E. are worthwhile. Current jobs related to green retailing may be limited, but a growing number of jobs will likely be designated as green in the future.

In fact, retail workers will devote a growing percentage of their work time to green retailing practices, according to SAP's Jim Sullivan, who spoke at the NRF's Sustainable Retail Consortium in September 2010. He was interviewed on NRF's Big Retail blog afterward, stating: "The first area which is common among all retailers is improving the bottom line due to cost savings from business process efficiencies. Typically savings of 30% or more can be achieved by a focused look at benchmarking operations around energy and climate change (particularly electricity and fuel use in stores and warehouses, fuel use in fleets, lift trucks, and logistics operations, refrigerant and cooling use, etc.). The second is improving top line revenues through increased market share (more loyal customers, increased product differentiation), new market entry (new eco-friendly products), or margin improvement (higher brand values)."

AMERICA AND THE WORLD

While the United States may have the idea to bring in a wave of green retailing, other countries are more advanced in this area and are sharing their ways of doing "green" business and utilizing innovative energy-reducing practices. Sweden has brought to us more than just techniques for small living through its IKEA stores; the retailer now encourages the use of CFL bulbs and reusable shopping bags, as well as fully recyclable materials used to build a great many of its products.

Environmental sustainability also is high on the radar screen in India. In mid-2008 the Indian government unveiled a national climate change action plan. India's Bureau of Energy Efficiency designated the retail industry as being energy-intensive. The adoption of green supply chains, or the improvement of existing supply-chain infrastructures, became a top priority heading into the early 2010s.

In November 2010, *Computing* reported that the United Kingdom was placing a sharp focus on the use of enterprise technology to minimize retailing's environmental impact. One example was the retailer Tesco, which established a goal of becoming a carbon-free operation by 2050. One practical approach that the company was taking to accomplish this goal was the use of virtual servers, as opposed to physical computer hardware. This enabled Tesco to use fewer physical machines, thereby reducing electricity and the need for additional air conditioning at its data centers. In addition, the company was using specialized software to analyze energy consumption across its chain of 4,700 stores.

RESEARCH AND TECHNOLOGY

By 2010 manufacturers had yet to take advantage of significant opportunities for reducing their respective carbon footprints. In the April 10, 2010, issue of *Grocer,* Xavier Vital explained that Bureau Veritas had completed 10 years of research, involving thousands of consumer products, in order to identify and assess carbon footprint reduction opportunities. The company's research found that, in the case of many consumer products, carbon footprints could be reduced by as much as 60 percent using processes that result in cost savings for the manufacturer.

In its July 21, 2009, issue *Financial Express* described the results of a survey of 23,000 consumers in 17 developing countries. The survey found that the majority of respondents viewed global warming as a threat. Furthermore, a significant number of those surveyed revealed a willingness to pay higher prices for green products.

BIBLIOGRAPHY

Association of Retail Environments. "Sustainable Retail," 28 November 2010. Available from http://www.retailenvironments. org/RETAILENVIRONMENTS/RETAILENVIR ONMENTS/ARESectors/SustainableRetail/Default.aspx.

Gallagher, Julie. "Going Green Makes Sense—and Cents." *Supermarket News,* 17 May 2010.

"Green Retailing." *Financial Express.* 21 July 2009.

Hawken, Paul, Amory Lovins, and L. Hunter Lovins. *Natural Capitalism: Creating the Next Industrial Revolution.* New York: Back Bay Books, 2008.

Laszlo, Chris. *Sustainable Value: How the World's Leading Companies Are Doing Well by Doing Good.* Stanford, CA: Stanford Business Books, 2008.

National Retail Federation. "Retail's BIG Blog," 27 September 2010. Available from http://blog.nrf.com/2010/09/27/how-going-green-can-save-you-money/.

———. "Sustainability Headquarters," 28 November 2010. Available from http://www.nrf.com/.

Schendler, Auden. *Getting Green Done: Hard Truths from the Front Lines of the Sustainability Revolution.* New York: Public Affairs, 2010.

"Seventh Generation and Wal-Mart Announce Strategic Partnership to Offer Environmentally Friendly, Sustainable Products at More Than 1,500 Stores." *Internet Wire.* 26 July 2010.

Shaerr, Matthew. "Wal-Mart Takes the Lead in Green Retailing. Yes, that Wal-Mart." *Christian Science Monitor,* 16 July 2009. Available from http://www.csmonitor.com/Innovation/Horizons/2009/0716/wal-mart-takes-the-lead-in-green-retailing-yes-that-wal-mart.

Stern, Neil, and Willard Ander. "Green Retailing Is Here to Stay." *Supermarket News,* 1 December 2008.

"Technology Makes Retailers See Green." *Computing.* 4 November 2010.

U.S. Green Building Council. "Help Topics," 2010. Available from https://www.usgbc.org/FAQConsolidation/FAQ_Main.aspx.

Vital, Xavier. "Simple Methods Can Reduce Carbon by 60%: Cutting Products' Carbon Footprint Is Easier Than You Think—and It Can Even Help Save Money." *Grocer,* 10 April 2010.

Weinstein, Nathalie. "U.S. Green Building Council to Launch LEED for Retail This Fall." *Daily Journal of Commerce, Portland,* 20 September 2010.

"Wal-Mart: Measuring Just How Green; The Retailing Giant Launched a Potentially Groundbreaking Initiative to Measure Suppliers' Energy Use. How Hard Will It Push for Change?" *Business Week Online,* 26 September 2007. Available from www.businessweek.com.

Yudelson, Jerry. *Sustainable Retail Development: New Success Strategies.* New York: Springer, 2009.

HANDHELD COMPUTING DEVICES

—■—

SIC CODE(S)

3571

INDUSTRY SNAPSHOT

Handheld and palmtop computers are the lightest and smallest computing devices for the mass market. Features common to these devices include color flat-panel display screens; built-in touchpads or other pointing devices in lieu of a separate mouse; specialized versions of software; and expansion slots for a variety of external devices. Many PDAs (personal digital assistants) use a stylus or pen instead of a keyboard for input.

After a decade and a half of false starts and sputters, the handheld computing industry had finally come of age with features and performance paired with true portability. After peaking in 2001, shipments of handheld computers registered three consecutive years of decline. Analysts attributed this decline to competition from so-called "smart" mobile phones. By the middle of the decade, smart phones offered users many of the same basic and advanced features as PDAs, including MP3 file playback, at a much lower price.

While early handhelds were little more than glorified calendars and organizers, both software and hardware have come a long way. However, top-of-the-line PDAs have evolved into a class of more powerful handheld computers. These machines included operating systems such as Microsoft Windows and were capable of running popular productivity software suites such as Microsoft Office, taking digital photos, and playing video clips and MP3 files. Most were equipped for wireless Internet access and were capable of sending e-mail and viewing regular Web pages.

The distinction between PDAs and smartphones became increasingly nebulous, as smartphone technology incorporated all tasks that PDAs could perform. Smaller chips and faster speeds for data transfer contributed to a convergence of technologies, making older PDAs rapidly obsolete. The time had come for development of a single handheld device incorporating digital camera and video, cellular telephone, GPS, MP3 music, games, location services, social networking, and Web access capabilities. However, as of December 2009, most techno-savvy consumers still had a minimum of two separate devices: a smartphone and a small netbook computer or electronic notebook.

BACKGROUND AND DEVELOPMENT

Short History of Portable Computing. The Osborne I, developed in 1980 by Adam Osborne of Osborne Computer Corp., included innovations that led the way in the evolution of truly portable computers. Weighing 17 pounds, it had a detachable keyboard, a five-inch black and white display, and two floppy disk drives. It used a Zilog Z-80 microprocessor chip, an improved clone of Intel's 8080. The Osborne I not only pioneered portability, it was also credited with being the first to bundle software packages with the computer, an idea that became fundamental to selling hardware in the industry. Tens of thousands of the Osborne I portable computers were sold before it became the victim of the company's own success. In 1983, the company announced that it would build an IBM-compatible portable called the Vixen, causing buyers to stop buying the Osborne I in anticipation of the new machine. The announcement, however, was premature, and without incoming orders to fund the new product's manufacture, Osborne was forced to file for bankruptcy protection. By the time the Vixen was ready to market,

413

consumers had been wooed away by the products of a new leader, Compaq, that had been able to meet their demand.

According to Les Freed's *The History of Computers,* Compaq's opportunity to successfully take the portable computer market lead was largely due to a gaping hole in IBM's product line. In 1983, Compaq shipped the Compaq Transportable and Compaq Plus, both fully functional, IBM-compatible, portable PCs weighing a not so svelte 30 pounds. During its first year in business, the company sold 53,000 portables and took in revenues of $111.2 million, giving Compaq the highest first-year sales in the history of American business.

In 1984 Gavilan Computer developed a truly portable machine that did not have to be plugged in. Industry commentator Tim Bajarin wrote, "The computer's clamshell design and battery-power capability made it the first serious mobile computing system." Gavilan, however, could not manufacture them in sufficient quantity and went out of business.

Apple Computer's PowerBook models, introduced in 1991, set a new standard for portables. They combined long battery life with excellent display quality and a built-in pointing device. The PowerBook 170 contained an optional internal modem slot, again redefining the meaning of a mobile office computer. Apple's Duo 210, released in 1992, featured the DuoDock, an innovation that allowed hookup to a docking station that might contain more system RAM, a larger hard drive, or more video RAM for a color monitor. The Duo could thus function fully as a desktop computer when in the DuoDock and as an excellent portable at other times.

Emergence of Handhelds In 1993 another Apple innovation was the Newton MessagePad, a new type of portable known as a personal digital assistant (PDA). It was the first mass market handheld computer and was offered as a personal information manager. The Newton solved the problem of keyboard size by using a stylus for input, but it promised more of this new pen-based technology than it could deliver. Apple promoted the Newton's ability to interpret handwriting with disastrous results because at the time, its capability was relatively primitive. By 1997, when the next-generation Newton, the MessagePad 2000, reached the market, its handwriting recognition was much improved. Reviewers praised the revamped MessagePad for its robust communication and computing features. However, with Apple mired in losses, and profits from the Newton not imminent, in 1998 Apple dropped the curtain on the Newton line—the MessagePad, eMate (a Newton-based clamshell notebook for the education market), and the Newton operating system.

In the meantime, another competitor with greater staying power was emerging. In 1994, inventor Jeff Hawkins

came up with a design for a new kind of PDA that would become the PalmPilot. At the time, he was working at a software firm developing handwriting recognition technology for handheld devices, but the sparse handhelds at the time lacked many useful features, and to Hawkins, an engineer, they were poorly designed. He believed an effective handheld device should be extremely light and portable, ought to synchronize readily with desktop computers, and should be simple in features and purpose. With his innovative design and support from the company's management, Hawkins helped transform the company into a hardware designer and maker, Palm Computing.

In 1995 the private company was sold to modem manufacturer U.S. Robotics in order to finance the product's debut. The first PalmPilot was shipped in early 1996, and by year's end, over 350,000 units had been sold. Within another year, over a million PalmPilots had been sold and the product began attracting a devoted following of users, software writers, and corporate partners. Palm became part of 3Com Corp. with its 1997 purchase of U.S. Robotics, and by that time Palm was becoming entrenched as the market leader in the nascent PDA category.

By then Palm was not alone, though. Numerous models of handhelds, palmtops, and other PDAs came on the market around the same time. These included computers running Microsoft's Windows CE operating system. Windows CE, although less functional than desktop Windows versions, was easy to learn for those familiar with the PC versions. Windows CE devices included modified versions of the popular Microsoft Word and Excel software, along with Microsoft's Internet Explorer browser. The Casio Cassiopeia, for instance, was able to transmit faxes, access e-mail, and receive information via a one-way pager in addition to being able to link and synchronize data through a docking station to a Windows 95 desktop computer. Hewlett-Packard introduced its 1000CX palmtop PC and Philips Electronics North America Corp. unveiled the Velo 1 in early 1997.

Still, others resisted the Windows product. They were the Toshiba Libretto, the ill-fated Newton, and most importantly, PalmPilot. Although some Palm devices were capable of running CE, for strategic and other reasons Palm preferred to use its own operating system, Palm OS.

Before the introduction of color screens during the early years of the first decade of the 2000s, handheld computers were equipped with flat liquid crystal displays (LCDs). These were either passive matrix or active matrix displays, and some were backlit for clarity. Passive matrix displays used grids of horizontal and vertical wires, the intersections of which were LCD elements, single pixels that either admitted or excluded light. Active matrix, or thin film transistor displays, had much better resolution but were more expensive to produce. LCD technology was developed in the United States, but Japan, Korea, and Taiwan produced almost all of the world's LCD screens.

After surging past $1 billion for the first time in 1998, worldwide handheld sales continued their sharp uptick in 1999, when sales reached an $2.3 billion, according to estimates by the information technology (IT) and telecom market research firm Dataquest. The U.S. market accounted for about 45 percent of global handheld sales. In 1999, handheld shipments were estimated at 5.7 million units.

Shipments of handheld devices increased 88 percent to 13.6 million in 2000. The U.S. market accounted for nearly half of this total. Growth slowed to 43 percent in 2001, according to International Data Corporation (IDC), which forecast an annual growth rate of roughly 40 percent through 2005, when shipments were expected to reach 70.9 million. By then, the United States was expected to account for only 38 percent of the global market.

Besides continued technological innovation and product enhancement, probably the biggest issue facing the industry during the early years of the first decade of the 2000s was the shift toward wireless communications. In that domain, handhelds began to compete with smart phones and other specialized gadgets that offer access to e-mail and Internet content. Palm embarked on the wireless path at the turn of the twenty-first century with the introduction of its topflight Palm VII model, which included built-in wireless connectivity through the company's Palm.net subscription service. Until the Palm VII, most handhelds could gain access to Internet communications only through expensive add-on devices. Other high-end handhelds began to include modems as well, and a bevy of phone-based wireless Internet devices were being positioned to provide comparable and even more advanced services. IBM developed a line of wireless-enabled Thinkpad notebooks, PDAs, and servers in 2001. The firm also began offering software, support, and services designed to allow customers to access applications from remote locations as well as from any device.

Advancing performance and versatility of handhelds was another key trend. Technical hurdles for handheld makers included improving battery life, increasing speed and processing power, and upgrading graphics. A regular gripe about Palm PDAs, for instance, was that their monochrome screens did't fare well in dim light or in very bright light. Palm's answer was its first color screen model, introduced in 2000, which featured a very modest, low-resolution screen despite its premium price. By 2003 PDAs also had begun to include built-in cameras and MP3 players.

As stated earlier, after peaking in 2001, shipments of handheld computers registered three consecutive years of decline. Unit shipments fell from 10.6 million in 2003 to 9.6 million in 2004, according to the research firm IDC. Analysts attributed this decline to competition from so-called "smart" mobile phones. Because of technological advancements, by the middle of the decade, smart phones offered users calendar and address book functionality as well as more advanced features such as MP3 file playback. These features were offered at a lower price than PDAs, some of which cost $600 or more. Analysts from the research firm Gartner indicated that smart phone sales were expected to eclipse PDA sales for the first time in 2004.

Another factor driving this decline was the fact that PDA users tended to retain their device for its lifetime, as opposed to upgrading to newer units. What's more, those buying new PDA units for the first time often purchased cheaper, entry-level models. This trend caused market saturation for top-line PDAs. Increased competition from the likes of Research In Motion (BlackBerry), Dell, and Hewlett-Packard also made for a more challenging industry landscape.

Amidst these trends, the handheld computing industry witnessed both consolidation as well as the exit of several formidable competitors. In 2003, Palm acquired Handspring and changed its name to palmOne. With the exception of the Japanese market, Sony and Toshiba both exited the PDA business in 2004. Although most analysts expected that there would continue to be a market for handhelds, there were many questions about the industry's future heading into the second half of the first decade of the 2000s.

Despite tough market conditions, PDAs and handheld computers continued to evolve, offering stronger batteries, larger and brighter screens, as well as advanced capabilities such as Global Positioning System (GPS) functionality. In addition to streaming video and audio capabilities, some PDAs were capable of controlling other digital devices in one's home or office, such as viewing regular Web pages and more. Some analysts struggled to define what constitutes a handheld computer, as smart phones began incorporating additional functionalities. Adding to the confusion, by the middle of the first decade of the 2000s, some PDAs were equipped with both cellular communication and Wi-Fi (wireless fidelity) capabilities.

According to the research firm Gartner Inc., the desire to access e-mail and other data wirelessly pushed worldwide shipments of personal digital assistants (PDAs) to a record 17.7 million units in 2006, up 18.4 percent from the previous year. According to preliminary shipment estimates, the market leader was Research In Motion, manufacturer of the Blackberry, with 3.51 million units sold and a 19.8 percent share of the market, followed by Palm (1.97 million, 11.1 percent), Hewlett-Packard (1.72 million, 9.7 percent), Mio Technology (1.52 million, 8.5 percent), and Sharp (1.43 million, 8 percent). Other vendors accounted for about 7.60 million units, for 42.8 percent of the market.

In a February 6, 2007, news release, Todd Kort, a principal analyst in Gartner's Computing Platforms Worldwide group, commented, "60 percent of all PDAs shipped in 2006 offered cellular connectivity, up from 47 percent in 2005. Forty-eight percent of all PDAs shipped in 2006 were purchased by enterprises. This was about the same percentage as one year ago due to the strong sales to consumers and prosumers of devices, such as the Sidekick 3, Mio Technology GPS devices and the Motorola Q."

CURRENT CONDITIONS

The years 2008 and 2009, despite economic parsimony, will go down as years caught in the web of exponentially-growing wireless technology, rendering some handheld devices near obsolescence even as they were being manufactured. The convergence of cellular voice with traditional PDA functions led to increasingly sophisticated smartphones. From there, nothing seemed valuable unless it incorporated "mobile" applications to accommodate the needs of technologically-savvy consumers looking for ways to stay continuously connected, with data, image, voice, Internet and location, 24/7. With the explosion of wireless broadband in 2008, in combination with high-speed downlink packet access and high-speed uplink packet access, cellular technology became cost-attractive to a wider range of consumers. The performance of high-speed packet access (HSPA) provided a megabit or two of bandwidth in uplink and downlink directions, also increasing new potential uses. A stand-alone significant driver behind the growth was mobile Internet users. BIA's Kelsey Group anticipated "a tenfold increase in the number of mobile Internet users during the forecast period—from 5.2 million in 2008 to 56.2 million in 2013."

To that end, in January 2009, research giant Gartner, Inc. published eight mobile technologies that it predicted would evolve significantly through 2010, impacting short-term mobile strategies and policies. First on its list was Bluetooth 3.0 technology, with the first devices being released in 2010. They will likely include features such as ultra-low-power mode that will enable new devices, such as peripherals and sensors, and new applications, such as health monitoring. "Bluetooth 3.0 is intended to support three bearers: classic Bluetooth, Wi-Fi and ultrawideband (UWB)," noted the Gartner report.

Second, Gartner identified mobile user interfaces (UIs) as an area of intense competition in 2009 and 2010, with newer applications for business-to-employee (B2E) and business-to-consumer (B2C) communications. The addition of Location Sensing will also enhance applications, particularly in conjunction with Wi-Fi technology. Third, Gartner identified 802.11n as the first Wi-Fi technology to

offer performance on a par with the 100 Mbps Ethernet commonly used for wired connections to office PCs. Gartner also forecast that during 2009 and 2010, several new display technologies would impact the marketplace, including active pixel displays, passive displays and pico projectors. Pico projectors enable new mobile use cases (for example, instant presentations projected on a desktop to display information in a brief, face-to-face sales meeting).

In a November 2009 article for *PDA Street,* Michelle Menga listed the top trends for mobile handheld (smart-phone) applications to include money transfers, location-based services (LBS), and mobile searches. Mobile browsing and health monitoring also ranked high. These expanded uses brought new security risks for compromised privacy. Indeed, by the third quarter of 2009, smartphone shipments worldwide were up 4.2 percent with 43.3 million in just that quarter. Nokia retained the No. 1 spot worldwide.

In addition to security concerns, safety issues grew commensurately with handheld use. In January 2009, the National Safety Council urged a total ban on cell phone or PDA use while driving, and indeed, several states followed suit by passing legislation prohibiting such use.

INDUSTRY LEADERS

According to analyst Toni Sacconaghi of Bernstein Research, Apple was doing to the handset industry in 2009 what it had done to the PC industry with the Mac: claiming an inordinate share of profits relative to revenue. She estimated that Apple (AAPL), though it was only the fifth-largest handset vendor, claimed nearly a third of handset industry profits in the first half of 2009, noted John Paczkowski in his November 2009 post for *Digital Daily.* According to Sacconaghi, Bernstein Research's analysis indicated that Apple's iPhone accounted for only 8 percent of the handset industry revenues but 32 percent of industry operating profits in the first half of 2009.

Other major players in the handheld market include several of the top computer makers as well as specialists. In addition to the vendors discussed below, leading manufacturers include Research In Motion (RIMM), Nokia, Sony Ericsson, LG, Mio Technology, Dell Inc., IBM, NEC Corp., Sharp Electronics, Casio Computer, and Panasonic.

Palm Inc. In 2003, Sunnyvale, California-based Palm Inc. acquired Handspring Inc., a former competitor led by two of Palm's founders, Jeff Hawkins and Donna Dubinsky. Following the acquisition, Palm spun off its operating system business, which became PalmSource Inc.

Early in its history, Palm had an uneasy relationship with its parent, 3Com Corp., which acquired Palm through the 1997 buyout of U.S. Robotics. To give Palm greater autonomy and value separate from that of 3Com, primarily a networking equipment company, Palm was spun off from

3Com in 2000. Palm was criticized for a lack of innovation since its first products were introduced. It was slow to adopt color displays and other new features that competitors rolled out. Part of Palm's strategy was to keep its brand clear and devices simple, but skeptics assert the firm lost customers based on its limited product offerings.

In the early years of the first decade of the 2000s, Palm's generous lead in the market was diminished as new competitors shipped handhelds that had more features and in some cases were cheaper than Palm's line. During the middle years of the decade, Palm marketed its Zire line of handheld computers, which sported color screens and wireless Internet capabilities. In 2006 the company's PDA shipments dropped 29 percent as it focused more on smart phones, namely its Treo. That year, Gartner reported that Palm shipped about 1.97 million PDAs. Total revenues for just the second quarter of its fiscal year 2009 were $191.6 million, the company reported. Its full-year revenues for fiscal year 2008 were $1.3 billion.

Hewlett-Packard Co. Early on, Hewlett-Packard (HP) was a leading contender in the handheld arena through its Jornada line. Aimed at higher-end users, Jornada handhelds delivered color graphics and fast processing speed relative to PDAs, and also supported multimedia and wireless communications. The Windows CE (Pocket PC) based devices, which looked like tiny notebook computers, received high ratings for performance and versatility, and challenged Palm's market dominance.

After Hewlett-Packard merged with Compaq Computer Corp. in a $23 billion deal in 2002, the firm nixed the Jornada line in favor of the Compaq iPAQ. Retailing from $350 to $600 during the middle of the first decade of the 2000s, iPAQ mobile computers were among the most popular on the market. In addition to basic features, iPAQs were capable of storing digital photo albums, controlling home entertainment devices, streaming content over Wi-Fi (wireless fidelity) networks, and viewing Web pages. HP even offered a device with integrated three-way wireless capabilities, including Bluetooth, GSM/GPRS, and Wi-Fi, that was used in conjunction with T-Mobile phone service. In 2006 HP shipped 2.3 million PDAs, according to the research firm Gartner. The company's iPAQ 68xx and 69xx accounted for about 33 percent of these shipments. HP recorded revenues of $114.6 billion for fiscal year 2009, but this represented a 15 percent decline from $118.4 billion in 2008.

RESEARCH AND TECHNOLOGY

Looking forward into the second decade of the new century, The use of portable PCs and intelligent non-PC devices (smartphones and PDAs) are expected to give way to devices with applications that will both enable and make use of pervasively networked computing. New technology has drastically reduced the size of semiconductor chips, making the addition and convergence of separate systems into one, such as MP3 players/video, digital cameras, GPS, and mobile cell phone functionality all in one handheld device.

According to Research in Motion (RIMM), the maker of Blackberry, data transfer speeds have increased significantly as well. As the wireless industry moved from second generation (2G) mobile to third generation (3G), developers were already working on 4G as of 2009. This created a somewhat parallel battle of industry standards comparable to the Sony/BetaMax video format dilemma of the 1980s. In the wireless world, one of the leading standards going into development and implementation of 4G technology was WiMax. As of 2009, WiMax was competing with two major 3G systems, CDMA2000 (EV-DO) and UMTS (W-CDMA). It was estimated that WiMax could offer speeds nearly five times as fast as either of the other two. WiMax and W-CDMA networks are incompatible with one another, and as of December 2009, it was not known which one would prevail as the new industry standard. Only Sprint was strongly supporting WiMax; however, in 2009 it made a $3 billion investment into WiMax technology, so the battle was expected to continue for awhile.

A major technology challenge in the handheld computing market continues to be security. As handheld devices grew more powerful, their use for storing and transmitting business-related data increased. However, the vast majority of these devices (as many as 70 percent, according to some research analysts) were not officially approved by corporate information technology (IT) departments. This posed a significant security risk in that sensitive corporate data could be stolen, compromised, or destroyed by hackers or malicious viruses.

In November 2009, another iPhone worm came on the scene, targeted at mobile banking transactions and personal data, according to several security firms. The worm was also capable of hijacking the handhelds for use as botnets. As of November 30, 2009, the worm was isolated to "jailbroken" iPhones and iPod Touches, those whose owners had hacked into them to enable them to run applications not approved by Apple, noted Michelle Menga in her article for *PDAStreet.* Nevertheless, it served to remind users of the vulnerability which still existed in these devices even now.

According to the December 2004 issue of *Business Communications Review,* the consequences of compromised security were significant. The publication explained, "Privacy regulations like Sarbanes-Oxley, Gramm-Leach-Bliley, HIPAA and Japanese and EU Data Protection Directives now require many companies to protect private data from unauthorized access (and, in some cases, alteration). But companies scrambling to comply by safeguarding confidential data on servers, desktops and laptops often give little thought to the same data stored on PDAs and smart phones. A lost, stolen or hacked handheld that leads to breach of privacy can have significant regulatory, legal or financial consequences, no matter what kind of device stores the data, or even who owns the device."

In order to address these issues, analysts indicated that corporate IT departments would need to gain control over devices used to store and transmit company data. In addition to file encryption schemes and a host of common sense measures, the technical solutions used to protect mobile devices and mobile networks were often the same being used to protect laptops. These included file and folder encryption, secure remote access (VPN) clients, firewalls, virus scanners, and intrusion detection tools. Manufacturers also offered the Wi-Fi Protected Access (WPA) standard, which offered greater data security (encryption) than previous standards.

The same technological advances that have allowed handheld computing devices to become increasingly sophisticated also made more urgent a major drawback of handheld devices: the limitations imposed by battery life. In an effort to address this dilemma, technology giant Intel Corp. created a unit charged with developing a longer lasting lithium-ion battery by 2004. Other industry players began examining fuel cells that use methanol to produce electricity and last two to three times longer than lithium-ion batteries. Personal device users would simply replace methanol cartridges instead of recharging batteries.

BIBLIOGRAPHY

Baig, Edward C. "Pricey Little iPaqs Aim to Be Much More than Organizers." *USA Today,* 29 July 2004.

Boonnoon, Jirapan. "HP Banking on New Pocket PCs." *The Nation,* 3 December 2004.

Bostrom, Johan. "Worldwide Handheld Market Declines Again. PDAs in Third Straight Year of Weakening Sales, Research Firm Says." *PC World,* 2 February 2005.

Brooks, Jason. "Handhelds Capitalize on Pocket PC." *eWeek,* 13 December 2004.

"Cattleman's Calculator Software." *Beef,* October 2004.

Engelhardt, Jim. "Handhelds Get Rugged." *Geospatial Solutions,* September 2004.

Freed, Les. *The History of Computers.* Emeryville, CA: Ziff-Davis Press, 1995.

"Gartner Says Worldwide PDA Shipments Top 17.7 Million in 2006." Gartner Inc., 6 February 2007. Available from http://www.gartner.com/it/page.jsp?id=500898.

"Gartner Reveals Eight Mobile Technologies to Watch in 2009 and 2010." Press Release, 28 January 2009. Available from http://www.gartner.com/it/page.jsp?id=867012

Graves, Brad. "Cops Turning to PDAs to Fight Crime." *San Diego Business Journal,* 20 September 2004.

Lewis, Peter. "HP's Beast with Three Brains." *Fortune,* 23 August 2004.

Menga, Michelle. "Second iPhone Worm TargetPersonal Data." 30 November 2009. Available from http://www.pdastreet.com/articles/2009/11/2009-11-30-Second-iPhone-Worm.html.

———. "Smartphone Shipments Up, Profits Down." 9 November 2009. Available at http://www.pdastreet.com/articles/2009/11/09/Smartphone-shipments-up.html.

———. "Top Ten Mobile App Trends to Come." 30 November 2009. Available from http://www.pdastreet.com/articles/2009/11/2009-11-30-Top-10-Mobile-Trends-to-Come.html.

"Mobile Handheld,Winning Media Strategies." BIA/Kelsey Press Release, 29 April 2009.

Palm Inc. Available from http://investing.businessweek.com/researech/stocks/earnings/earnings.asp%3Fric%3DPALM.O.

Phifer, Lisa. "Portable Security: Safeguarding PDAs and Smartphones." *Business Communications Review,* December 2004.

"Research Shows Handheld Computers in Classrooms Enhance Student Achievement; GoKnow Learning Unveils Landmark Studies at National Educational Computing Conference." *Business Wire,* 5 July 2006.

"Sony Corp to Introduce Blu-ray and Handheld Computers." *Telecomworldwide,* 17 May 2006.

Thomas, Daniel. "Coca-Cola Rolls Out 28,000 Handheld PCs." *Computer Weekly,* 27 April 2004.

HEALTH SPAS

—■—

SIC CODE(S)

7011

7231

INDUSTRY SNAPSHOT

By the twenty-first century, Americans no longer considered spas as places to go for lavish pampering. Guests viewed their spa vacation as one component of a healthy lifestyle. More so than ever before, the American public was health conscious. Health spas had previously enjoyed booming popularity and this trend grew in the new millennium. The spa industry remained the fourth largest leisure industry in the United States, according to the International Spa Association (ISPA)

The general atmosphere of health spas has shifted focus from strict regimented programs with emphasis on strength and fitness training. While such aspects remained a vital component of the health spa experience, they were part of a broader plan that emphasized wellness, relaxation, holistic health, and therapy. Many spas dispensed with gymnasiums altogether, instead offering expansive outdoor retreats for exercise in a more natural and, presumably, less stressful environment.

Instead of being merely an added benefit to a destination, spas were becoming a destination in and of themselves as they marketed themselves to a broader range of patrons. In fact, the spa industry experienced such growth into the 2000s that the International Spa Association (ISPA) began to focus on continuing education for supervisors and managers, teaming with the Educational Institute of the American Hotel & Lodging Association. Together, the organizations would customize the program used to certify hospitality industry supervisors so that it specifically addressed the spa industry.

Spas addressed a wide range of concerns related to health and fitness, or wellness, including skin care, muscle relaxation, weight loss, fitness, stress relief, and others. Clients rated relaxation as the chief reason for their spa attendance, according to the International Spa Association, and they voiced a desire for relief from the stress of everyday life. A trend toward medical spas, which saw doctors and wellness educators on staff, continued to grow.

ORGANIZATION AND STRUCTURE

Spas draw from techniques used by ancient peoples as well as those from the modern world. Ideally, the spa experience focuses on a client's total physical, mental, and spiritual well-being. In fact, many spas actually requested that patrons leave all "necessities" at home, including clothing, makeup, cellular phones, and hair dryers. The resorts provided loose, comfortable clothing and products for personal hygiene.

Destination spas provided the complete wellness experience. Fitness programs were offered along with programs and lectures to educate and nurture. Typical meals consisted of spa cuisine with an emphasis on balanced, nutritious foods. Resort spas were situated on the grounds of vacation resorts that specialized in activities such as horseback riding, golf, or tennis. The menu was less restrictive than a traditional spa setting with most operating bars and lounges on the premises.

Wellness and weight management spas spotlighted methods for dealing with medical ailments or injuries. Visitors sought a healthier lifestyle and often worked with

Where Are the Spas?

	Percent of total spas	Number of spas
Day/Club salon spas	64.3%	45,113
Hotel/Resort spas	16.4%	11,489
Medical spas	6.1%	4,274
All others	13.2%	9,310

SOURCE: SpaFinder.com.

physicians and health care professionals to devise routines that could be used in daily living at home.

Spas abroad and day spas represented the opposite ends of the spectrum for customers. For those who wanted to travel to an exotic paradise, there were many top-notch spas scattered throughout the world. Services reflected the culture of the host country and offered a peek into customs of the region. Day spas continued to soar in popularity, as clients sought refuge from the pressures of everyday life. Most visits were a full or half day in duration, although the emergence of the hotel spa encouraged an overnight stay on the premises.

Cruise ship spas and hot springs are unique forms of destination spas. The increasingly popular cruise ship spa experience typically lasted from three days to two weeks, depending on the destination. Spas developed around natural hot springs experienced resurgence in popularity. As generations of people have known, therapeutic minerals such as sulfur, iron, calcium, and magnesium found in these waters can alleviate discomfort from arthritis, sore muscles, and chronic back pain.

Many luxury hotels and resorts were adding spas and outdoor recreation facilities to their properties. Surveys revealed that vacationers and business travelers who patronized higher end hotels and resorts had come to expect spa amenities and treatments. Hotel and resort owners unanimously agreed that having full spa facilities gave them an edge over the competition in attracting clients. Fitness facilities with saunas, whirlpools, steam rooms, and juice bars were usually available, not to mention salons for pampering and rooms for massage, aromatherapy, and other treatments.

Day spas became the industry's hottest sector in the late 1990s and continued to gain popularity into the later years of the first decade of the 2000s. Affluent clients leading hectic lifestyles shared the public's growing interest in alternative health therapies, and many beauty salons offered these spa services in conjunction with traditional beauty services. At a day spa, clients might purchase full- or half-day packages, or selected services à la carte. Along with manicures, pedicures, and hair styling, the day spa client could experience facials, yoga, various types of massages, aromatherapy, hydrotherapy, acupuncture, meditation,

light and sound therapy, and other treatments that were offered at destination spas.

Health spas offered many types of treatment. Innovative therapies frequently gained loyal followers. According to *Spa Finder,* the hippest new trends include yoga, Pilates, Neuromuscular Integrative Action (NIA), hot stone therapies, and polarity exercises. Pilates and NIA workouts benefit both the mind and body. Pilates were developed by a German gymnast and can be performed on an exercise mat or by using weight-training machines. The ultimate goal is to condition the body and increase core body strength. NIA is a low impact discipline that is often compared to Tai Chi for its flowing dance-like moves. Polarity and stone therapies are both body treatments designed to balance the energy of the mind and body. In the case of the latter, warm, smooth stones are actually placed on the body to relieve tension and increase the flow of energy.

Traditional treatments such as massages, facials, manicures, and pedicures remained preferred treatments. Each of these services was also available in conjunction with aromatherapy, which employs oils, herbs, and flowers for relaxation or stimulation. Other desired body treatments were the Ayurvedic relaxation treatment that combines oil and massage, dripping oil on energy centers while massaging it in; body wraps consisting of the application of herbs, seaweed, or mud, followed by a wrap, as the substance penetrates the skin; and hydrotherapy, which may include any treatment that takes place in water or milk, with underwater music frequently accompanying these treatments. Shower hydrotherapy includes the Vichy shower with seven nozzles that hit nerve spots along the spine and Scotch hose therapy that hits the skin in a high-pressure massage.

Reflexology is the massage of the feet. Its practitioners believe pressure points on the foot relate to systems throughout the body. Massage is the manipulation of the skin and underlying muscles, and its practitioners believe it improves circulation, rids the body of toxins, and relieves stress. Lymphatic massage manipulates the muscles to drain the lymph nodes and move waste out of the system. Reiki uses healing touch to direct universal healing energy into the body's energy centers. Swedish and sports massages get blood flowing for relaxation and get lactic acid out of the system. Acupuncturists use needles, finger pressure, or electrodes to stimulate different points on the body. These points are said to release energy flow and correspond to different body systems.

The success of the health spa industry has created a ripple effect in other market sectors. Treatments traditionally reserved for spas cropped up in new venues. Barbershops offered back massages, health clubs featured massage treatments and Pilates and yoga classes, and department stores offered aromatherapy makeovers.

The fastest growing segment in the industry was the medical spa, as the focus and purpose of spa-going switched from pampering to wellness. While some physicians tried to appeal to customers by offering spa-like treatments in a traditional medical office setting, true medical spas were emerging that integrated medical services such as physicals, dentistry, and dermatology treatments with traditional spa services such as body wraps. For example, whereas a spa-goer may visit a traditional spa for a relaxing facial, he or she may go to a medical spa to undergo additional treatments performed by a plastic surgeon, such as a chemical peel. The number of medical spas in the United States increased 69 percent between 2003 and 2005, and growth continued throughout the latter part of the decade. Regulation is still an issue with medical spas, however, and more statewide guidelines dictating who can do what at a medical spa are expected. For example, Florida is the first state that defined the practice of medicine in a medical spa in such a way that only a plastic surgeon or a dermatologist may actually operate a medical spa, according to a 2007 article in *Plastic Surgery Products*. Other examples of services a medical spa might offer include those related to hormone replacement therapy, weight management, and anti-aging therapies.

BACKGROUND AND DEVELOPMENT

Twenty-first century spas evolved from public baths, a tradition going back over 4,500 years. The Dead Sea Scrolls reveal that the site around Qumran, Jordan, was famous for its hydrotherapy and herbal medicines. The Greeks, Romans, and Egyptians incorporated hydrotherapy into their healing practices. Public baths have also been discovered in the ruins of Pakistan and in Babylonia (present-day Iraq, south of Baghdad). Popularity of the public baths declined in the Middle Ages, but in the seventeenth and eighteenth centuries, physicians began prescribing baths and their popularity rose again. Spa popularity continued to rise with the endorsement of Vincent Priessnitz, often referred to as the father of the modern hydrotherapy movement, and wealthy Europeans in the 1800s visited spas for months, both for treatments and for socializing. Massage therapy has been an important part of Chinese healing for 3,000 years.

Spa-going was introduced to the United States in the 1840s by Robert Wesselhoeft and became more popular as prices began to fall and day spas began to open, allowing those with modest means to try the spa experience. By the 1930s, the American Medical Association maintained a committee whose focus was spas. Spas benefited from the growing acceptability of alternative medicines and therapies in the 1980s. Some Baby Boomers reported that doctors seemed unreceptive to treating "creeping complaints," such as arthritis, back pain, and high blood pressure, in nontraditional

ways. Many people who preferred not to be on long-term medication or to undergo surgery turned to massage therapy, acupuncture, biofeedback, hypnosis, and reflexology.

The *ISPA 2002 Spa Industry Study* published in October 2002 reported that 156 million guests patronized spas in the United States in the year 2001. This figure was an enormous increase from a reported 30 million people in the year 1999. Revenues grew from $5 billion dollars in 1999 to $10.7 billion in 2001, an increase of 114 percent. Approximately 9,600 spas operated in the United States in 2002, with day spas accounting for 75 percent of all locations. Resort and hotel spas comprised the second largest group. Predictably, the majority of spa clients selected day spas as the site for services. Almost 70 percent of reported visits occurred at day spas throughout the country.

Despite poor overall economic conditions, the industry sustained an extraordinary level of growth in the early twenty-first century. In the aftermath of the terrorist attacks of September 11, 2001, there was a sharp decline in non-essential travel. Virtually every sector of the travel and tourism industry experienced a decline in sales, but it was only a temporary setback for the spa industry. As of 2003, facilities reported normal or improved occupancy rates as compared to 2001 figures. Several trends in attendance resulted from the events of 2001. Facilities noticed an increase in group outings, both personal and professional. Families and friends coordinated travel plans. Companies began scheduling employee retreats and board meetings at spa locations. In addition, management noted that guests were increasingly local and were selecting destinations within driving distance as opposed to flying to another area of the country.

Customers recognized the benefits of the spa experience but had a limited amount of free time to partake of services. In light of this fact, many day spas offered special half-day or lunchtime packages for busy professionals. Developers used day spas to attract consumers to shopping malls. Although a shopping mall does not offer a scenic locale, it does offer convenience, which became an important consideration for successful ventures.

Who are the owners of this new wave of establishments? The ISPA survey shows that people already firmly established in the field operated much of the new construction. "Branding" was the buzzword in spa circles. For example, in the world of hotel spas, The Four Seasons moved to the forefront of competitors. It operated spas in its hotels in most major U.S. cities and earned a reputation for quality and style. Within each spa or chain of spas, there was fierce competition for product placement. Cosmetic and hair care product suppliers vied for the distinction of an "exclusive" contract. It was a coup to be named the sole supplier for a high end spa.

By the year 2000, several subdivisions emerged within the spa industry. In recognition of this fact, ISPA sponsored three distinct user surveys in the year 2001. For the first time, data were collected separately for each market: day spas, destination spas, and hotel/resort spas. The studies gathered information on customer demographics, user preferences, treatments, and activities. The statistics offered the following profile. The average spa guest was college educated and employed full time with an annual household income of six figures. Household income varied slightly among user groups. Day spa guests tallied the lowest income, averaging $96,000 per year. Resort/hotel spas and destination spas finished virtually even, with user income of $122,000 and $125,000 respectively. The majority of participants had no children living at home. Many spa visitors indicated that they intended to return within the following year to one of the three types of spa facilities being studied. Day spas and destination spas tied for the highest percentage of repeat business with 81 percent giving a positive response. The most important factors named when deciding on a specific spa were environment or setting and the spa treatments. The least important criteria when choosing a spa were the educational programs. Favorite spa treatments named were facials, massage therapy, manicures, pedicures, and hair treatments.

According to *Spa Finder,* 2003 brought the spa industry record growth as spas began to attract a larger variety of patrons. No longer just for the ultra-wealthy, many spas began marketing services specifically to middle income Americans, a move that paid big dividends in growth and revenues. Other emerging trends in the industry included spas as healing centers, a push for the spa industry to adopt environmentally friendly practices, and marketing to men. According to a study by the ISPA, 29 percent of U.S. spa-goers in 2003 were men, and this number was increasing.

One of the types of spas seeing enormous growth was the "destination day spa," which offered all of the amenities of a full service spa with the convenience and lower cost of a day spa experience. In addition, businesses had begun to turn to spas for employee and client rewards as well as corporate meeting locations.

Men continued to represent a growing target market for the industry heading into the later years of the first decade of the twenty-first century. In the December 2005 issue of *Club Management,* Glenn Colarossi explained that according to a survey conducted for KSL Resorts, approximately 25 percent of male respondents had made at least one visit to a spa. For 20 percent, the visit was their first to a spa in 12 months. ISPA research found that men represented anywhere from 23 to 29 percent of spa visits in the middle of the decade.

Spas targeting men were going to great lengths to ensure their comfort. Beyond specialized shaving products developed just for male skin, some spas began to offer everything from beer and single malt scotch to sporting events on big-screen TVs.

Distinct market segments emerged within the industry. *Spa Finder* identified six categories: destination spas, resort spas, wellness spas, weight management spas, spas abroad, and day spas. Management at top spas strove to separate their establishment from the crowded field by cultivating a reputation for excellence in a specific discipline. Some examples of specialization were tennis, golf, or hiking programs. Yoga also was becoming a major force in spa curriculums. With a little research, potential guests could identify the ideal locale for an upcoming visit.

Analysts attributed the explosion of spa popularity in the 1990s and the first decade of the 2000s to a variety of factors: the increasingly technological setting of the workplace; the greater number of individuals reaching middle age; the strong U.S. economy that was creating more leisure spending; and the growing acceptance of alternative therapies and treatments combined with awareness of health and fitness. Spas were increasingly used as a retreat from job-related stress and a fast-paced culture. Many companies took it upon themselves to send their employees to day spas, and some even took advantage of spas as a way to combine meetings with relaxation.

The wellness factor affected the spa industry in other ways as well as spas catered to consumers' desires to stay healthy by incorporating nutritious food, various forms of exercise, and stress-relieving activities. According to the ISPA, in 2008, 51 percent of U.S. spas offered educational programs and nutritional consultations, 40 percent offered healthy eating classes, and 26 percent offered classes on obesity or weight gain issues.

Another trend in the industry was the creation of resident spas, where spas are integrated into communities or neighborhoods. For example, Canyon Ranch, one of the most popular spas in the world, created condo communities in Miami and other locations that include a spa and wellness center, restaurants with light, nutritious food, and a concierge service. SpaFinder indicated there were 250 such spas in the United States by 2008. Specialized spas were also becoming more common, such as those that cater to a new mom and baby or couples, as well as spas that have a specific theme, such as the Asian-inspired spa at the Mandarin Oriental hotel in Miami.

Some corporations were offering spa benefits to their employees as a way to reduce absenteeism and improve productivity. For example, Google, which was chosen by *Fortune* magazine as the No. 1 company to work for in 2007, offers on-site massages to its employees; General Mills sent workers to the Hotel Ivy Spa Club in downtown Minneapolis for a break during a two-day meeting; and TPG Credit Management sent several employees to the same spa as a reward for their hard work. According to ISPA President Lynne McNees, "A spa experience is the perfect way for employers to show their team that they care about their health and well-being."

Globally, the industry was estimated to be worth $250 billion in 2008. The more than 71,600 spas worldwide employed approximately 1.2 million workers. The United States was the top earner in the industry, followed by Japan, Germany, France, Italy, the United Kingdom, and China. In addition, capital investment in spas increased to $13 billion worldwide.

According to figures from the ISPA, there were 14,615 spas employing 234,600 people in the United States in 2007. Revenues of all U.S. spas totaled $9.4 billion. Approximately 32 million people were regular spa-goers, culminating in a total of 110 million visits annually. These figures represented a slight drop from the previous year. Top growth areas by spa type were medical spa (19 percent), resort/hotel spa (16 percent), and destination spa (13 percent).

CURRENT CONDITIONS

The 2010 Global Spa Summit, held in Istanbul, Turkey, drew record numbers of delegates from a record number of countries (40); the conference reported that it was "sold out." At the summit, the results of several 2010 reports from industry analysts were presented. The entire "Wellness" industry was valued at close to $2 trillion, but one report, *Spas and the Global Wellness Market,* by SRI International, specially commissioned for the summit, reported a global revenue estimate of $60 billion for just the spa segment. Another finding: the top three things that consumers were most likely to do to improve their wellness were exercise, better nutrition, and spa visits. Moreover, consumers were more likely to visit spas (and more frequently) if the visits were linked to research studies demonstrating that treatments delivered measurable health benefits.

Why spa visits? Also presented were the results of a consumer survey by Coyle International focusing on what drives consumers to spas. An overwhelming majority (89 percent) indicated for relaxation/stress management. Other findings: spa consumers visited websites to find spa deals (62 percent), view spa menus (57 percent) and check out customer feedback (48 percent). Top online resources were SpaFinder.com (44 percent), search engines (43 percent), and Facebook (25 percent). Sharing spa experiences via social media was on the rise: 59 percent e-mail friends, while 48 percent would write online reviews. Eighty-eight percent would be comfortable with follow-up communications from a spa, especially if it inquired about their satisfaction with the visit.

Smith Travel Research (STR), in its 2010 report, "Latest in Benchmarking Hotels and Luxury Spas," found that luxury hotel spas were more resilient during the 2008-2009 recession than room occupancy at the hotels. Spa treatment room usage actually increased in 2009 by 3.5 percent, whereas overall hotel room occupancy dropped 8.7 percent. This spoke to the ability of spas to capture and/or attract hotel guests as well as attract a local audience. STR also reported an upward trend during the first quarter of 2010 in both spa treatment rates and room utilization, but discounts continued, from an average luxury spa treatment in 2008 of $149 to $142 in 2009, and down again to $136 in early 2010.

Finally, a live poll of summit attendees showed that despite a tough recession in 2009, 47 percent of spa and wellness respondents reported gains over 2008, and another 17 percent at least stayed even. Nearly 80 percent expected revenues to increase for the full 2010 year.

INDUSTRY LEADERS

Conde Nast Traveler magazine, a leading resource for the spa industry, conducted a poll of vacationers, published in 2006, to discover the most popular spas and resorts. The survey differentiated between various types of spas and collected opinions on best destination, resort, and hotel spas. The results also included information on the best spa cruises and singled out individual accomplishments, such as best spa cuisine or best treatments. The five most popular spas included the Four Seasons Resort Hualalai Spa in Big Island, Hawaii (resort spa); the Miraval Life in Balance in Catalina, Arizona (destination spa), the Peninsula Spa in Chicago (urban hotel spa), and Regent Seven Seas Cruises (cruise spa). In October 2009, Conde Nast announced it would close four magazines, and speculation circulated that lost advertising revenues might cost it close to $1 billion. Shifting to an online format, the company hoped that new devices, like the kPad, would make up roughly one-third of its publishing revenues from this source.

Canyon Ranch is one of the best-known spas in the world and offers an enormous array of services, from aquatic therapy to exotic massage treatments to dance classes to fitness training. Canyon Ranch's men-only fitness classes, outdoor sports classes, and medical treatments geared toward men make it the most popular spa among men in the United States. The company also opened the largest day spa in the United States, covering some 61,000 square feet, at the Venetian Resort Hotel Casino in Las Vegas. In 2008 the company had spas in Tucson, Arizona; Lenox, Massachusetts; Las Vegas; and Kissimmee, Florida; as well as on the *Queen Mary 2* cruise ship.

One industry resource for locating leading spas was *The Spa Finder Worldwide Directory: Guide To Spas,* published by *Luxury Spa Finder* magazine. The publication listed spas in multiple categories, from day spas and medical spas to luxury resorts and spa residential communities, and included detailed information and photographs about each location.

WORKFORCE

All types of people work for health spas. In the hotel/resort/destination end, there are managers, marketers, salespeople, human resource specialists, receptionists, maids, concierges, and maintenance people. Professionally, chefs, nutritionists, massage therapists, acupuncturists, reflexologists, fitness trainers, cosmetologists, and other treatment specialists all contribute to and make their living from the spa industry. In 2008, the International Spa Association reported that the industry employed 234,600 people: 118,000 full-time; 73,600 part-time; and 42,900 contract. Notably, a shortage of high-quality, trained labor was cited as one of the major challenges facing the spa industry, according to experts that attended the first Global Spa Summit in New York in 2007.

In addition, in 2008, the American Massage Therapy Association claimed a membership of 57,000 massage therapists in 27 countries. While not all worked in the spa industry, the industry tended to hire licensed or certified therapists. Accredited massage therapy schools required 500 or more hours of course work. Recertification required 200 hours of work experience and 50 hours of appropriate continuing education. The national exam required proficiency in the following areas: human anatomy, physiology, and kinesiology; clinical pathology and recognition of various conditions; massage therapy and bodywork theory, assessment, and application; and professional standards, ethics, and business practices.

Cosmetologists perform a variety of functions at health spas, including facials, manicures, pedicures, waxing, and other pampering treatments. Cosmetologists are regulated by states, most of which require graduation from a cosmetology school, successful completion of an exam, and continuing education. Other professionals employed by health spas might or might not be regulated under state or local laws. There are, however, a growing number of professional societies, such as the American Alliance of Aromatherapy and the Awakenings Institute, which offers a Reiki Certification course, attempting to self-regulate with ethical and professional standards.

Massage therapy was one of the most popular treatments at spas during the first decade of the 2000s, and the field continued to grow. Many massage schools have adjusted coursework to reflect the fact that the majority of students train to work at spas rather than in private practice. Massage therapists in spas were expected to be knowledgeable in the latest treatments and products. Some portion of a therapist's salary was dependent upon his or her ability to sell products to guests. Along with these new requirements came improved salaries and benefits. Although there was still a gap in expectations among spa owners and therapists, the demand for trained masseuses was high. Skilled therapists were an integral part of building and retaining a loyal customer base.

AMERICA AND THE WORLD

Industry analysts Ernst & Young in their "Middle East Spa Benchmarking, 2010" report indicated that Dubai and the United Arab Emirates (UAE) represented one of the hardest hit regions in the global recession. Nevertheless, the hotel spa economy in that region came roaring back in later 2009, with aggregate spa revenues in the fourth quarter 2009 roughly 48 percent higher than during the first quarter. Moreover, first quarter 2010 revenues were up 45 percent year over year (YOY). In the first quarter of 2010, spa treatment revenues shot up 70 percent and treatment bookings jumped 62 percent YOY.

EuroMonitor International reported that in 2009, spa travel packages outperformed standard retail travel packages, based on performance data from 45 luxury hotels for the full year 2009 and the first quarter of 2010. Moreover, it forecast about a 4 percent growth each year for 2012, 2013, and 2014.

During the first decade of the twenty-first century, women and men around the world were rediscovering the many advantages of spa treatments. More Asian women were taking advantage of spas that traditionally catered to male clientele. Among the most popular spa treatments in Asia are Thailand, massage; Japan, bathing; Korea, exfoliation; China, herbal medicine and acupuncture; and Indonesia, herbal body treatments.

In Europe, spas were once the province of the wealthy, who might spend months on end at their retreat. However, by the middle of the twenty-first century's first decade, European spas were increasingly taking on the role of vacation and health destinations rather than physician-prescribed, government-subsidized visits. As a result, the customer base was getting younger and more mainstream. European spas then had begun to take on the look and feel of U.S. spas, which blended European and Asian practices and augmented them with particularly American features. Still, the cultural differences were apparent among the clientele. In the United States, Americans expected results and overscheduled themselves, partaking in treatments, fitness, and classes back-to-back. European spas encouraged a slower pace, one with little or no exercise, the emphasis being on terrific cuisine and pampering treatments such as facials, massages, and body wraps.

BIBLIOGRAPHY

"2008 Spa Industry Trend Watch." International Spa Association, 1 July 2008. Available from http://www. experienceispa.com.

"About AMTA." American Massage Therapy Association, 1 July 2008. Available from http://www. massagetherapy.org/.

"Global Spa Summit 2010." 14 June 2010. Available from http://globalspasummit.org/2010/06/2010-global-spa-summit-draws-record-numer-of-delegates-from-record-number-of-nations/.

Colarossi, Glenn. "Spa Marketing for Your Male Members." *Club Management,* December 2005.

Colburn, Jonathan D. "Spa Owner Boosts Offerings, Revenue." *San Fernando Valley Business Journal,* 24 October 2005.

Crosby, Jackie. "Recession? Relax." *Star Tribune,* (Minneapolis, MN), 13 May 2008.

Ellis, Susie. "Spas and Medical Tourism." Available from http://spafinder.com/medical-tourism/spa-medical-tourism.

Glickman, Elyse. Worldwide Wellness Boosts Spa Biz: Propelled by the Growing Wellness Trend, the US $11.2 Billion-Plus Spa Industry Is Targeting Both High-End and Mainstream Clients in an Increasingly Sophisticated Spa Market." *Global Cosmetic Industry,* September 2005.

"Global Spa Economy Estimated at $255 Billion a Year, According to First-Ever Study Unveiled at 2008 Global Spa Summit." Spa Finder, 22 May 2008.

"Global Spa Summit 2010." 14 June 2010. Available from http://globalspasummit.org/2010/06/2010-global-spa-summit-draws-record-numer-of-delegates-from-record-number-of-nations/.

"Hotel Fitness & Spa Expert Glenn Colarossi Unveils b spa Brand for Hotels." *PR Newswire,* 14 April 2008.

Howells, Rhianon. "What's Next for the Spa Industry?" *Leisure Management,* January-February 2008.

"Just How Much Did Conde Nast Lose?" *Newsweek,* 8 October 2009.

Manson, Emily. "Spas on the Rise as Offer Is Increased." *Caterer & Hotelkeeper,* 2 March 2006.

"Middle Eastern Spa Benchmarking." Ernst & Young, June 2010. Available from http://globalspa summit.org/2010/06/2010-global-spa-summit-draws-record-numer-of-delegates-from-record-number-of-nations/.

Salley, Hope. "More Than Just a Massage and a Shvitz: It's Not Your Mom's Spa Anymore." *Fairfield County Business Journal,* 10 January 2005.

Sass, Eric. "MediaPost Publications Digital Dollars: 40% of Conde Revs From Apps in Future." *Media Daily News,* 21 September 2010.

Sears, Diane. "Ma's, Pa's and Spas." *Florida Trend,* February 2008.

"SpaFinder's Research Division Releases First Annual Day Spa Industry Report." Spa Finder, 10 November 2007.

"Spas and the Global Wellness Market." SRI International, 2010. Available from http://www.imtjonline.com/news/?EntryId82=247129.

"Spas Have Arrived." *Global Cosmetic Industry,* September 2005.

"The New Consumer Mindset." *Euromonitor International,* June 2010. Available from http://globalspasummit.org/2010/06/2010-global-spa-summit-draws-record-numer-of-delegates-from-record-number-of-nations/.

"With Spa Industry Booming, Delegates at First-Ever Global Spa Summit Cite Labor Shortage as Top Industry Challenge." Spa Finder, 30 May 2007.

Whitman, Cheryl. "A Work in Progress: A Look at the Present and Future Growth of the Medical-Spa Industry." *Plastic Surgery Products,* February 2007.

HIGH SPEED INTERNET SERVICE PROVIDERS

———————■———————

SIC CODE(S)

7375

INDUSTRY SNAPSHOT

The explosion in popularity of the Internet in the closing decade of the twentieth century and the opening years of the new millennium fueled a strong public demand for ever faster connections with the Information Superhighway. This demand continued, as the Internet played a central role in an increasing number of business and personal activities.

Growing even more spectacularly than Internet use in general has been the number of users accessing the World Wide Web via high speed, or broadband, connection. The most common broadband technologies were DSL (digital subscriber line) and cable. The most widely used broadband technology worldwide was DSL, although newer technologies such as WiMax (Worldwide Interoperability for Microwave Access and W-CDMA (Wideband Code Division Multiple Access) were set for explosive growth. Fiber-optic broadband service (FiOS) was also a threat to DSL and cable providers: the number of people worldwide using fiber optics to connect to the Internet—4.2 million—surpassed those who used cable or DSL, according to a report by U.K-based Point Topic.

The industry was served by the United States Internet Service Provider Association (USISPA). In 2002 the former Commercial Internet eXchange disbanded in order to change membership and focus. Founded by Verizon, America Online, and EarthLink, among other internet service provider (ISP) companies, the USISPA is a lobbying group specific to the needs and concerns of the giants in the high tech ISP industry. Despite the differences and rivalries between and among the companies, there is much common ground in policy and service decisions.

ORGANIZATION AND STRUCTURE

The line between dial-up (narrowband) and high-speed (broadband) Internet service providers (ISPs) is somewhat blurred, with most of the major nationwide ISPs offering both types of access. Other players in the Internet service market include hundreds of small local and regional telephone companies. However, the lion's share of all Internet access in the United States is supplied by the large, nationwide ISPs, including America Online (AOL), AT&T, EarthLink, MSN, and Verizon. The market also includes a limited number of ISPs that provide only broadband access. The two major segments of the high-speed Internet access market are cable and DSL (digital subscriber line). While cable dominated the broadband access market in mid-2002, holding a 54 percent share, DSL was growing at an even more impressive rate. By March 2006, the Consumer Electronics Association indicated that DSL and cable each held 29 percent of the broadband market. By 2007, DSL had overtaken cable in market share.

Cable modem access to the Internet is provided by the network of a local cable television provider, using the same coaxial cable that brings television signals into the home. Although Internet connections via cable generally provide greater bandwidth than DSL, multiple users must share this bandwidth. As the number of a provider's subscribers increases, the speed of the connection may be somewhat degraded. Major players in the cable Internet

Cable vs. DSL Internet in 2009

Cable providers	39.3 million subscribers
DSL providers	32.5 million subscribers
Total broadband	**71.8 million subscribers**

SOURCE: High Speed Internet Access Guide, "Broadband Statistics 2009—Even Fewer New Internet Subscriber".

service market include the nation's leading cable television providers, including CableVision and Comcast.

DSL uses the same copper wiring that brings telephone service into the home to provide high-speed data transfer between the subscriber's home and the nearest Telephone Central Office. Typically, most residential DSL service is asymmetric and provides higher speeds in downloading data to the home from the Internet than in uploading data from the home to the Internet. For most users, this is not a problem, as their need to download information from the World Wide Web far exceeds any need to send data in the other direction. The major players in the DSL market include nationwide and regional telephone service providers, including AT&T and Verizon, as well as other companies that provide not only Internet access but also Internet content. Leaders in this latter category include AOL and MSN.

A shrinking share of the broadband access market is held by Integrated Services Digital Network (ISDN) services, which integrate both analog and voice data with digital data over the same telephone network. Far slower than cable or DSL but faster than regular dial-up service, ISDN uses a special adapter in place of a modem to speed up the transmission of data between user and the Internet.

BACKGROUND AND DEVELOPMENT

Although the Internet has been around since the early 1970s, it was not really until the final decade of the twentieth century that it came into wide use by the general public. Originally conceived as an inter-network architecture that would allow packet networks of different types to communicate with one another, the Internet in its earliest form was used largely by government agencies and academic users and was not ready for prime time until the early 1990s. However, once residential and business users got a sample of what the Internet could offer them, the World Wide Web was quickly embraced and grew at exponential rates. As the content on the Web grew in both volume and sophistication, users rapidly grew frustrated with the time it took to access data and graphics online. Thus was born the demand for progressively higher speeds to access the riches of the Internet.

Although broadband technologies were discovered almost nearly half a century ago, for much of that time they were not available for general use largely because of regulatory constraints and the high cost of accessing such technologies. Until relatively recently, such technologies have been chiefly the domain of large telecommunications networks and cable television services, which used coaxial cable for one-way delivery of television signals. The emergence of the Internet into the public realm in the 1990s intensified the demand for high-speed access to the World Wide Web, fueling the drive to make broadband technologies more widely available. First to seize upon broadband technologies to meet this growing demand was the cable television industry. Under deregulation, the industry found it imperative to invest in new technologies to hold off competition from telecommunications services and direct broadcast satellite.

Helped immensely by massive investments in broadband technologies by such giants as AT&T and Microsoft, cable operators in the late 1990s began introducing new interactive services designed to attract Internet users frustrated by slow dial-up connections. Most interactive services were offered in partnership with companies like Road Runner and Excite@Home, a high-speed network that in late 2001 was sold to AT&T. By the close of the twentieth century, cable companies had signed up approximately 1.5 million cable modem subscribers and were adding 2,500 new subscribers daily. The merger of AOL and Time Warner in late 1999 also helped to intensify the push for interactive cable services.

Digital subscriber line (DSL) access to the Internet has grown rapidly in spite of a slower start than high speed cable service. The basic technology employed in DSL has been around since the late 1980s but was not put into service by large telecommunications companies for fear that it might hurt their existing businesses. After deregulation of the telecommunications industry in 1996, these same companies moved aggressively to deploy DSL capability. At the end of 1999, DSL subscribers numbered less than 1 million, but in the early years of the new millennium, that figure grew significantly, reaching 6.8 million subscribers by the end of the first quarter of 2003, according to Leichtman Research Group. Cable subscriptions also continued to show robust growth, Leichtman reported, climbing to nearly 12.3 million by the end of March 2003.

Although high speed Internet service providers (ISPs) made giant strides in growing their segment of the industry, there remained a good deal of demand that had not yet been satisfied. In some cases, this demand had not yet been met because the DSL and cable infrastructure necessary to supply high-speed Internet access was not in place at many locations. Such locations can be served by satellite, but the costs are generally higher than the other two options.

Through the first quarter of 2003, according to data from Leichtman Research Group Inc., the leading U.S. cable and DSL Internet service providers had increased their total subscribers to just over 19 million. Of that total, nearly 12.3 million accessed the Internet via cable while the remaining 6.8 million used DSL. To accelerate DSL expansion, a number of the leading providers trimmed prices in an effort to attract more subscribers, but DSL had a long way to go to overcome the lead of cable providers, which held nearly two-thirds of the total market.

As broadband access to the Internet has grown, there has been a resulting decline in the number of Americans connecting to the Internet via dial-up, or narrowband, lines. In March 2006 the Consumer Electronics Association (CEA) released the results of a new study that found dial-up accounted for only 36 percent of all connections, down from 60 percent in 2003 and 74 percent in 2000. By 2007, cable broadband dominated the U.S. market, but DSL soon caught up to cable as the primary Internet technology.

The CEA study reported that digital subscriber lines (DSL) and cable each held a 29 percent share of the broadband market during the middle years of the first decade of the 2000s. However, a smaller segment of the high speed Internet market belonged to satellite service providers. The service, delivered via satellite, is somewhat slower than that available from cable and DSL access. More significantly, the costs for satellite service were sharply higher, with set-up costs approaching $1,000 and monthly charges of approximately $70. Satellite Internet service was not expected to expand robustly because of its high costs.

High-speed ISPs had a strong ally in the White House under President George W. Bush, who assigned high priority to easing the way for rapid deployment of broadband infrastructure throughout the United States. Assessing the outlook for broadband at the Broadband Outlook 2002 Conference in Washington, D.C., Nancy Victory, Assistant Secretary of Commerce for Communications Information, said, "There is no question that broadband technology has great promise. Whether it develops into a critical new medium or a completely new media remains to be seen. But either way, Americans' enjoyment of the full benefits of broadband appears to depend at least in part on a regulatory policy that eliminates unnecessary impediments to deployment and promotes full and fair competition—a regulatory policy that is comprehensive and coordinated, with all of its elements in balance."

PIONEERS IN THE FIELD

Two of the companies that played a significant role in laying the groundwork for growth of broadband access to the Internet were AT&T and Microsoft. AT&T recognized early on the vast potential offered by the Internet and by the late 1990s moved aggressively to promote the adoption of Internet Protocol (IP) Telephony by the telecommunications industry worldwide. At the 1998 Fall Internet World trade show in New York City, the telecommunications giant announced a series of innovative moves and unveiled a power set of capabilities to help Internet Protocol (IP) win favor across the global industry. "AT&T strongly believes that IP is the unifying protocol for transforming the telecommunications industry worldwide," said Kathleen B. Earley, vice president of AT&T Internet Services. "These actions will help jump-start IP Telephony, which has enormous potential for networking around the globe." AT&T demonstrated its confidence in the future of broadband access to the Internet with its 1999 acquisition of Tele-Communications Inc. (TCI) at a cost of $55 billion. The purchase gave AT&T a major foothold in both cable Internet and television services. In the wake of the TCI acquisition, AT&T announced the formation of AT&T Broadband, the business unit responsible for overseeing all of the company's cable ventures. In the fall of 2002, AT&T Broadband was acquired by rival Comcast.

So confident was Microsoft that broadband represented the wave of the future that in 1994 it called a summit meeting of more than 100 companies likely to keenly feel the impact of the new technology. According to Microsoft representatives, the software giant's aim in calling the meeting was to outline its software architecture and business model for digital broadband networks. To encourage the involvement of third party developers in preparing for the services, applications, and content for the emerging platform, Microsoft announced that it would make available its user interfaces for broadband and also offer developers other assistance to help them hop on the broadband bandwagon. More recently, Microsoft further secured its hold on the broadband market by helping finance Comcast's acquisition of AT&T Broadband in late 2002. In exchange for its help, Comcast gave Microsoft the right to offer Internet access over Comcast's broadband cables.

In 2004, some companies were building wireless networks in an attempt to gain subscribers who had no other broadband option. Networks were built first, and then the connection would be distributed wirelessly. The top five wireless Internet Service Providers in 2004 were DTN SpeedNet of Omaha, with 5,100 subscribers; CommSpeed of Prescott, Arizona, with 4,579 subscribers; Prairie Inet of West Des Moines, Iowa, with 4,001 subscribers; AMA TechTel of Amarillo, Texas, with 4,000 subscribers; and FirstStep Internet of Moscow, Idaho, with 2,709 subscribers.

Spam, or unsolicited junk e-mail, was an ongoing problem in the first decade of the 2000s, and high speed ISPs were challenged to help subscribers manage the problem. Despite the federal anti-spam law, which took effect on January 1, 2004, the amount of spam continued to increase, largely due to the sheer number of spammers and the increasing success spammers have had in covering their tracks.

Soon, Internet connections were quickly becoming the norm. *New Scientist* indicated that as of August 2005 approximately 42 percent of the U.S. population had broadband Internet access at home. According to the publication, this was an increase from 36 percent only eight months before and represented two of every five people. In March 2006, *Mediaweek* reported that, according to Nielsen/NetRatings, the number of broadband users in the United States reached almost 100 million in February 2005, up 28 percent from the previous year. Broadband users accounted for 68 percent of all Internet surfers—an increase from 55 percent in 2004 and 33 percent in 2003.

While broadband adoption was skyrocketing, dial-up Internet connections were rapidly fading from the scene. In March 2006 the Consumer Electronics Association released the results of a new study, "Broadband and the Home of Tomorrow," which revealed that dial-up accounted for only 36 percent of all connections, down from 60 percent in 2003 and 74 percent in 2000. Among broadband users, the study found that DSL and cable each held a 29 percent share of the market.

Online entertainment was a key factor driving industry growth. As the baby boomer segment of the population continued to grow older, some analysts predicted that this well funded demographic group would desire to get a large amount of their entertainment at home. As oil prices reached record highs in 2006, skyrocketing gasoline costs only added to the popularity of home entertainment options available via the Internet, including on-demand video, music, and gaming services. In its February 4, 2006 issue, *The Online Reporter* cited research from Park Associates indicating that U.S. consumers were expected to spend almost $9 billion on online entertainment—an increase of 260 percent since 2006.

In an effort to keep ahead of the increasingly fast technology game, several companies, including Comcast, Time Warner Cable, Bright House Networks, Sprint Nextel, Clearwire, Intel, and Google, joined together to create an ISP that would deliver a nationwide WiMax network by 2010. Comcast's Steve Burke told *Multichannel News* in July 2008 that the companies hoped to "get a two- to three-year head start" ahead of competitors AT&T and Verizon Wireless in high-speed mobile services. Burke also said, "It would be great to imagine a world where we have wireless broadband, at speeds our competition couldn't match."

Fiber-optic service (FiOS) networks were also on the rise in the latter part of the 2000s' first decade. According to a 2008 *Information Week* article titled "Forget DSL or Cable, Broadband Users Want Their Fiber," the use of fiber-optic broadband services surpassed DSL and cable worldwide in the first quarter of 2008 for the first time. The United States held the top spot in fiber-optic installations, followed closely by China, which continued to add more fiber-optic subscribers as compared to cable and DSL. Verizon, the largest provider of FiOS in the United States, with 1.8 million subscribers at the beginning of 2008, had plans to spend $23 billion to replace its copper wires with fiber-optic lines. The company hoped to have 7 million FiOS customers by 2010.

One issue with broadband Internet connections involved concerns that the United States had not reached the same infiltration rates as several European and Asian countries. Based on a rating by the Organization of Economic Cooperation and Development (OECD), in 2008 the United States ranked 15th globally in broadband penetration measured against population. In other words, although 70 million people had access to the technology in the United States, that represented only 23 out of 100 people, or about 20 percent. The top five countries had rates of at least 30 percent. In addition, a Pew Internet & American Life Project survey found that only 25 percent of American households with annual incomes of $20,000 or less had broadband connections at home, and there was no growth in broadband adoption among poor people in the United States from May 2007 to May 2008. Ways to increase accessibility in the United States—especially for the U.S. poor and those living in rural areas"were issues in the industry as the first decade neared a close.

CURRENT CONDITIONS

As of early 2010, the growth of the high speed Internet industry continued to slow, according to the *High Speed Internet Access Guide*. Contributing factors included a slowing economy, high unemployment, and a U.S. broadband Internet market reaching maturity, the publication said. The major DSL and cable ISPs in the United States added 4.1 million new subscribers in 2009, but that was 1.3 million less new subscribers than in 2008. The only viable markets still available were in rural areas where ISPs would face high costs and technical challenges.

The American Recovery and Reinvestment Act under the Obama administration provided the U.S. Department of Commerce with grant money through the National Telecommunications and Information Administration. Most grants were going to state and local governments to provide high speed service to governmental units and employees, Denver, Colorado, being a mid-2010 example. Broadband plan adviser Blair Levin, a former FCC employee and associated with the Aspen Institute think tank in 2010, announced his plans to push for a new proposal to expand broadband coverage to 97 percent of the United States within 10 years for $10 billion.

There was a palpable shift in the market, however, as U.S. cable Internet providers continued to grow at a faster pace than DSL providers. Comcast High Speed Internet pulled ahead of AT&T in 2009 to become the largest broadband provider in the United States, with nearly 16 million Internet subscribers. Most ISPs focused on development of wireless Internet service (see below). In any event, in 2009, cable providers served 39.3 million subscribers, whereas DSL served 32.5 million subscribers. Total broadband subscriptions were 71.8 million.

New developments going into 2010 were centered around 4G LTE wireless networks, with Verizon Wireless and AT&T Wireless in the lead. With much faster connection speeds than 3G networks, they hoped to attract new home users for both mobile and home use. However, in September 2010, Sprint and Clearwire announced their launch of faster 4G wireless broadband service in both Pittsburgh and Minneapolis, bringing the total to 55 cities serviced nationwide, according to Sprint. Plans were also announced to add New York City, Los Angeles, San Francisco, Denver, Miami, Cincinnati, and Cleveland before the end of 2010.

Plunkett Research Ltd., an industry analyst group that publishes detailed industry studies, offered several statistics reflecting high speed internet activity during 2009 and early 2010. For example, as of June 2010, there were 150 million high speed internet lines (including 50 million wireless) in the United States. Monthly global Internet traffic in 2009 was 14,686 PetaBytes, according to Cisco VNI, with a global projection of 63,904 PetaBytes by 2014. U.S. broadband revenues in 2008 were $34.7 billion, according to the telecommunications Industry Association (TIA). That revenue is expected to reach 49.2 billion by 2012.

Wireless Internet services were poised for explosive growth. Free Wi-Fi (wireless fidelity) networks had been put in place in cities throughout the United States, and users could access the network in "hot spots" such as coffee houses, libraries, or hotels. Two other technologies on the scene were WiMax (Worldwide Interoperability for Microwave Access), which was similar to Wi-Fi but had several advantages, such as greater speed and longer range, and W-CDMA (Wideband Code Division Multiple Access), a type of 3G cellular network that grew out of the mobile voice technology. According to a May 2008 *Multichannel News* article, "WiMax is a relatively new technology but has the potential to surpass Wi-Fi, the current wireless-broadband flavor of the day. A single WiMax tower can offer service over a 30-mile radius—compared to a four- to six-mile radius for Wi-Fi—and at higher speeds." WiMax speeds were actually far faster than those delivered by any other wireless service: WiMax could deliver data at a rate of 70 Mbps (millions of bits per second). WiMax also had the

potential to deliver Internet services to people who did not have access to DSL or cable. One industry estimate predicted that mobile WiMax would connect 8 percent of the world's 1.1 billion mobile broadband subscribers by 2012, accounting for nearly 88 million users worldwide.

INDUSTRY LEADERS

Many of the major high speed ISPs also offer dial-up services. As the demand for faster access to the Internet grows, so will the share of the total market held by high speed providers. The leading providers of high speed access include the following.

AT&T Inc. In November 2005, SBC Communications purchased AT&T Corp., creating the nation's then-largest telecommunications company, as well as the leading U.S. provider of broadband DSL service. Headquartered in San Antonio, Texas, the company employed a workforce of 310,000 and reported 2009 related sales of $16 billion. AT&T merged with BellSouth in the first decade of the 2000s.

Verizon Communications Inc. Headquartered in New York City, Verizon not only ranks second among DSL access providers but also provides narrowband access to the Internet for millions of users. As of 2008, Verizon had 8 million broadband subscribers. With 235,000 employees, Verizon revenues for a trailing 12 months (TTM) through June 30, 2010, were $108 billion.

Comcast Corp. Headquartered in Philadelphia, Comcast was the largest cable television company in the United States and had 13 million Internet subscribers. With roughly 100,000 employees, Comcast reported 2009 sales of $35.76 billion.

Time Warner Cable. A unit of Time Warner, Time Warner Cable also was a top provider of high speed cable access to the Internet, reporting 3.9 million subscribers in March 2006—up from almost 2.7 million subscribers three years before. The company owns Road Runner, a cable-based Internet access service.

Cox Communications Inc. With 3 million Internet access subscribers in 2008, Cox Communications ranked in the top cable-based ISPs. A unit of Cox Enterprises, the Atlanta-based company anticipates increasing its hold on the high-speed Internet access market by moving aggressively into the telecommunications field. To pave the way for this move, the company deployed fiber-optic networks and upgraded its hybrid coaxial fiber networks.

EarthLink Inc. With 4 million Internet subscribers, EarthLink was moving to bridge the gap between dial-up and high speed Internet users. The company, based in

Atlanta, has moved aggressively to make premium high speed Internet access available on a wide basis. In 2009 Earthlink reported sales of $723 million.

WORKFORCE

Because almost all the companies providing high speed Internet access also supply other services, including narrowband access and telephone and cable television service, it is difficult, if not impossible, to identify the size of the workforce engaged in this business. In many cases, employees of these companies provide overlapping services. The tasks involved in installing a cable television hookup or a cable connection for Internet access are virtually identical, as is the installation of telephone service or a DSL connection.

AMERICA AND THE WORLD

The Asia Pacific region was poised for steady growth through 2014, and China was experiencing the fastest growth in the industry, with an estimated 80 million broadband subscribers, followed by the United States with 71.8 million. Previously the United States had been ranked number one. Japan held third place, with 28.6 million users. Germany was fourth, although it experienced a much higher growth rate in 2008 than Japan—23 percent as compared to 4 percent—mostly due to Japan's already high penetration rate. Other countries in the top 10, in order of number of broadband subscribers, were the United Kingdom, France, Korea, Italy, Canada, and Spain. The Asian-Pacific region overall was expected to experience a fast growth rate in broadband revenue, according to a study by Frost & Sullivan. The research group predicted an annual growth rate of 7.1 percent, with total broadband revenues in the region reaching $42 billion by 2013, up from $28.1 billion in 2007.

RESEARCH AND TECHNOLOGY

The fast development of WiMAX, a 4G wireless digital communications standard, being incorporated into home, business, and mobile applications, kept the industry excited. WiMAX (also known as IEEE 802.16) was not widely available yet in mid-2010, but new developments were being announced all year. This next-generation high speed wireless technology is expected to be accessed widely by PCs, smartphones, gaming devices, etc., bringing about an estimated 60 percent increase in wireless traffic by 2013. WiMAX speeds may be as fast as 2 Mbps to 4 Mbps for downloads, which represents a dramatic increase in speed compared to the average of 700 Kbps on existing WiFi networks, making WiMAX the mode of choice for fast online applications. Clearwire Corporation was the main deployer of WiMAX, and announced its new Clear

Spot portable WiFi router that will connect Wi-Fi-enabled smartphones and cameras to the 4G wireless network. The router was manufactured by CradlePoint.

BIBLIOGRAPHY

"63m Broadband Users in China by 2008." *The Online Reporter,* 14 January 2006.

"Asia Pacific Broadband Revenues to Touch US$42 Bln by End 2013." *AsiaPulse News,* 10 July 2008.

AT&T Offers Nation's Fastest 3G Network." *PR Newswire,* 10 July 2008.

Bode, Karl. "Levin Wants to Wire 97% of U.S. for $10 Billion." 30 September 2010. Available from http://www.broadbandreports.com.

———. "Sprint Launches 4G in Pittsburgh, Minneapolis." 30 September 2010. Available from http://www.broadbandreports.com.

"Broadband Has 64% Internet Share in UK." *The Online Reporter,* 25 February 2006.

"China's Broadband Market to Double." *InternetWeek,* 18 January 2006.

"China Tops U.S. Broadband Totals." *TelecomWeb News Digest,* 6 June 2008.

Comcast financial data accessed 18 September 2010 at http://www.cnbc.com/id/36333877/Comcast_CEO_Received_Pay_of_25_million_for_2009.

"Continued Slow Broadband Growth in 2009." *High Speed Internet Access Guide,* 13 March 2010. Available from http://www.high-speed-internet-access-guide.com/articles/broadband-statistics-for-2009.html.

Deeken, Aimee. "Broadband Connections Soar 28%." *MEDIAWEEK,* 20 March 2006.

Farrell, Mike. "WiMax Takes Flight." *Multichannel News,* 12 May 2008.

"Forget DSL Or Cable, Broadband Users Want Their Fiber." *InformationWeek,* 3 July 2008.

Holahan, Catherine. "The Sad State of U.S. Broadband." *Business Week Online,* 23 May 2008. Available from www.businessweek.com.

"Home Broadband Adoption Stalls Among Some Americans." *InformationWeek,* 3 July 2008.

"Latest Developments in WiMAX Technology." 8 September 2010. Available from http://www.broadbandinfo.com/wireless/high-speed-internet/latest-developments.

"New CEA Study Finds 43 Million American Households Now Have Broadband Internet Access." *Business Wire,* 30 March 2006.

"Online Entertainment Spending to Reach $9b in 2010." *The Online Reporter,* 4 February 2006.

Rougeot, Jonathan. "Tech Giants Make Big Investment in WiMax Wireless Networking." *Computer Shopper,* July 2008.

"Rural Broadband Access Grows to 24%." *The Online Reporter,* 4 March 2006.

"Sowing Seeds of WiMax." *Multichannel News,* 7 July 2008.

"Telecommunications Industry Almanac 2011." Plunkett Research, Ltd., 2010. Available from http://www.plunkettresearch.com.

"Time Warner Cable Beats Estimates, Subscription Revenue Up," 28 January 2010. Available from http://seekingalpha.com/article/185146-time-warner-cable-beats-estimates-subscription-revenue-up.

HIGH TECH PR FIRMS

—————■—————

SIC CODE(S)

8743

INDUSTRY SNAPSHOT

Even (or perhaps especially) in the world of high tech wizardry, it is often how a product is portrayed rather than how it works that makes or breaks a company. With the surge in high tech industries, more and more companies came to realize this essential truth, and in so doing, gave a dramatic boost to the high tech public relations industry. The rush of dollars into high tech start-ups flooded the industry with new business as companies sought to grow at an accelerated pace while scrambling to differentiate themselves from competitors through the employment of public relations (PR) firms. The high tech sector of the PR industry easily outpaced other major sectors such as finance and health care during this period.

Meanwhile, those traditional PR agents who specialized in high tech issues and who felt confident enough to brave the rapidly consolidating high tech PR environment struck out on their own, setting up their own PR boutiques catering to dot-coms and other sectors.

Public relations firms create a buzz around a new product, getting media, and thus customers, talking and thinking about the item. At the same time, PR firms devote themselves to digging up sales leads. In addition to product placement, high tech PR firms are often called on for crisis management, investor relations, publicity related to mergers and acquisitions, and a range of other tasks. In the early 2000s, this information could effectively be communicated via pop-ups on the Internet or blog articles. By 2008 and 2009, trends such as using real-time communications (e.g., "Twitter") and online/social media applications became increasingly effective PR tools.

ORGANIZATION AND STRUCTURE

PR firms sell their services to clients in the high tech industry and work with those clients to develop public relations strategies that are then implemented by the PR firm itself. In effect, then, PR firms act as consultants and as media concierges. Companies contract with PR firms to acquire the kind of specialized knowledge of product placement and media savvy they may not be able to muster within their own organizations.

Of course, not all agencies are right for all firms all the time, and a good deal of specialization exists even within the high tech sector. The selection of a PR agency is often a major undertaking in itself, and many companies bring in outside consultants to aid in the selection process.

Generally, a well-prepared company will draw up a precise outline of the problems and deficiencies in its internal public relations efforts, a clear and specific list of the objectives and expectations it hopes to realize with the PR firm, and a team of internal contacts to work with the PR firm on an ongoing basis.

For their part, high tech PR firms maintain inside contacts with the media and analysts, sending e-mails, attending trade shows, initiating meetings, and generally keeping the public abreast of goings-on within client firms regarding new products and business developments, including placing the desired spin on the events to create a positive image of the company in the public mind.

BACKGROUND AND DEVELOPMENT

When the high tech PR industry first began to take off in the 1970s and 1980s, it was a world of glitz and glamour centered around highly publicized trade shows featuring the latest gadgetry. By the late 1980s, however, things began to cool off as the economy slowed, the industry matured, and its customer base became more fragmented.

Partly as a result of these late 1980s changes, the mid-1990s were characterized by furious merger activity. Beginning with Porter/Novelli International's high-profile purchase of Waltham, Massachusetts-based Brodeur & Partners in 1993, the industry's leading firms consolidated over the next several years, reshaping the high tech PR market in the process. GCI Group acquired Jennings & Co., Manning, Selvage & Lee bought up Rourke & Co., and other leading firms were forced into similar deals in order to keep up with these competitors. Smaller firms meanwhile were continually squeezed by the industry giants and scrambled to make themselves attractive for larger suitors to acquire them.

Propelling the trend was the realization that PR companies were beginning to outgrow the niche markets to which smaller PR firms catered and needed a more integrated, holistic PR approach that only the larger players could generate. And as high tech gadgetry and services increasingly became a part of the average consumer's daily life, clients demanded a more consumer-oriented PR approach.

The development of the Internet and the World Wide Web through the early and mid-1990s had a two-fold effect on the high tech PR industry. First, the Internet brought about a flurry of new businesses, as dot-com start-ups began popping up in droves, which demanded the services of PR firms. At the same time, the Internet gave PR firms a new medium to consider in their PR strategies, as companies used the Internet for advertising and product placement and generally quickened the pace at which the crucial PR-related information moved throughout the market.

In addition, as the news cycle speeded up and media outlets deployed fewer reporters to cover regular beats, reporters increasingly requested packaged news stories containing the bulk of the information they required to complete an article. High tech companies were often too strapped for time, cash, or personnel to get such information to the press in the most articulate, timely, and favorable fashion.

Thus, in the startup-crazy New Economy of the late 1990s high tech PR firms found a gold mine. So firmly established were these agencies that it was not unusual for a high tech start-up to pay between $20,000 and $40,000 in monthly fees to their PR firms. In addition, because the nature of the Internet fostered the faster movement of information, PR firms were able to procure clients by convincing them that they needed outside professional help in getting the latest information and spin to media outlets.

Nevertheless, the high tech PR industry was in a somewhat dubious position at the start of the first decade of the 2000s. As the New Economy continued its meteoric ascendancy and money poured into Internet and high tech start-ups, the demand for high tech PR firms was by all accounts at a stratospheric level. While this was obviously good news for those with a stake in the industry, demand far outpaced the industry's ability to supply quality people and services, alarming many industry players who were caught between the desire to capitalize on the booming market and the need to foster knowledge and skills among their employees. In leaning toward the former, firms were forced to speed new recruits through the training process, generating calls for greater training resources for PR firms. In particular, the industry was inundated with pleas for a greater number of face-to-face meetings between PR trainees and reporters as well as heightened knowledge among PR agents of the contours of the media itself.

Indeed, one of the crucial relationships in the PR industry, that with the media, was far from intimate. A poll conducted by *Softletter* in late 1999 revealed that journalists specializing in high tech issues were displeased with the service they were getting from PR firms and that many journalists and analysts registered a sense of alienation stemming from a lapse in PR quality. Some respondents, such as Michael Vizard at *Infoworld,* concluded that PR clients were not actually receiving the access to the media that they thought they would get when they contracted with PR firms. Denny Arar of *PC World* added that PR reps typically failed to acquire a good sense of the publications and the kinds of issues and products they covered before trying to do business with those publications.

Other complaints were based on the industry's growing client list and subsequent inability to accommodate all the demand at premium levels of quality. For instance, much of the personal nature of the PR process was lost to mass e-mail distributions that failed to differentiate between publications, much less between writers of varying specialties.

For every negative report, however, there was a PR firm insisting that their agents did their homework, were articulate, and were knowledgeable about the product and the media outlet. Sure enough, the high tech PR industry, though clearly not without its difficulties, was in strong shape in 2000, and the market for such services was expected to prove exceptionally lucrative well into the decade.

These growth projections proved false, however, after the air was finally let out of the dot-com tire by the end of 2000 and PR firms were forced to sift through the rubble to find viable clients. At first, most analysts believed that the sudden grounding of the dot-com industry would not have a devastating effect on PR firms. They reasoned that the Internet was here to stay and companies would always need agents to help with their images. However, as the economy remained weak into the early years of the first decade of the 2000s, a growing number of high tech PR firms began to feel the pinch.

After peaking at a rate of 32.9 percent in 2000, the growth rate of the $4.2 billion PR industry declined 2.65 percent in 2001. The reason for this abrupt downturn had to do with the industry's dependence on technology's meteoric rise. High tech accounts had accounted for 40 percent of the PR industry's revenues by 2000. As a result, when the technology industry crashed, the PR industry as a whole was particularly vulnerable to the downturn, and the high tech sector was hit even harder. In the early years of the first decade of the 2000s, the general economic malaise in the United States also prompted firms in other industries to cut costs, which quite often meant trimming PR budgets. In fact, according to Impulse Research, PR budgets fell an average of 21 percent in 2001, from $4.8 million to $3.8 million.

To offset the decline, many PR firms, particularly high tech PR firms, began reducing their workforces. At the same time, some larger PR firms began to compete for smaller accounts in an effort to generate new sources of revenue. To gain a competitive advantage, some companies also reduced their rates, a practice which undercut profitability.

According to an April 2002 article by the Council of Public Relations Firms, the economic downturn had a profound effect on public relations firms: "The biggest firms are laying off employees, slashing their prices for the first time in five years and chasing small accounts that they wouldn't have bothered with in the late 1990s boom." One industry giant, Burson-Marsteller, laid off 15 percent of its workforce in 2001. Another large pubic relations firm, Edelman, trimmed its ranks by 10 percent after sales dropped 5 percent that year. Porter/Novelli saw its revenues dip 13 percent and initiated its first staff reduction program in nearly a decade.

By the middle of the first decade of the 2000s, the technology sector was improving along with the overall economy, both domestically and globally. Following the tumultuous period of the decade's early years, many tech companies were evaluating and reevaluating their strategic objectives and the very nature of their businesses. For assistance, many companies continued to seek advisement from high tech PR firms. However, as companies wrestled with identity issues and sought to reposition their organizations and their brands, PR agencies were challenged to be more in tune with the views of senior executives, including CEOs and CFOs, not just technology managers.

In addition, high tech PR firms were becoming more involved in helping their clients to communicate with all of their constituencies, not just the news media. As firms were engaged to help their clients more effectively communicate with such key stakeholders as customers and analysts, they saw the need to hire staff with broader experience and to offer training that related to what technology companies do. For example, going beyond training in creativity, a high tech PR firm might offer training in data storage and security issues. However, as one industry executive noted, high tech PR firms were still tasked with boiling down key messages from the likes of scientists and engineers and effectively transmitting them to the right target audiences—which often included people with limited knowledge of technology.

During the middle of the first decade of the 2000s, blogs represented a hot niche within the high tech PR industry. Short for Web log, a blog is a one-to-many, Web-based form of communication. It is similar in many respects to a personal Web site, online journal, or diary that readers can respond to, and often includes links to other places on the Internet. Effectively bringing together people who otherwise would be separated by the boundaries of politics, geography, and time, blogs are 24/7 soapboxes that people use to express their opinions, complaints, and musings on any conceivable topic—in chronological order. According to the non-profit, nonpartisan Pew Internet & American Life Project (PIP), 32 million Americans read blogs during the middle of the decade. In addition, 7 percent of U.S. adult Internet users (8 million people) had created a blog or Web-based diary. Additionally, 12 percent (14 million people) had posted comments or other material on another person's blog.

As the use of blogging grew, companies quickly recognized the wealth of honest feedback that existed within blogs regarding their products, brands, and organizations. In order to harvest and analyze this valuable market intelligence, marketers turned to high tech PR firms as well as specialized business intelligence companies like Intelliseek, Factiva, and Techdirt. In addition to serving as a feedback mechanism, blogs also are a channel that companies can use to address rumors and concerns being circulated by customers. Therefore, they are a newer tool that companies can use to employ effective brand and reputation management strategies.

Blogs also had emerged as a tool that high tech PR professionals could use to gain insight into the mechanics of their trade. For example, Alan Weinkrantz, president of San Antonio, Texas-based high tech PR firm Alan Weinkrantz And Co., created a blog in which he shared news, reflection, observation, and analysis with colleagues around the world. In addition to insight and tips, this blog included links to other industry professionals, news about trade shows, articles, photos, and more.

As the industry passed into the second half of the decade, high tech PR firms continued to embrace new ways to reach increasing wired and "wi-fied" audiences. "We are living in Boom 2.0—our media now are wired people, social networking and consumer-generated, inter-dependent communications," Abby Carr of Bliss, Gouverneur and Associates and committee chairperson for the Council of Public Relations Firms (CPFR) noted in the CPFR 2006 Annual Report. "We will help rewire the way human beings connect to each other, how they talk about our clients and their brands. And we will do so in a way that trust and authenticity prevail."

While the largest firms continued to embrace blogs as a means for both internal and external communication, smaller firms began to abandon their internal blog sites. According to CPFR, whereas firms valued at over $50 million increased blog use from 33 percent in the third quarter of 2005 to 67 percent in third quarter of 2006, the number of smaller firms (valued at less than $3 million) maintaining blogs dropped sharply during the same time period from 86 percent to 14 percent. Overall, PR industry blog sites dropped from 68 percent to 32 percent.

Blogs continued to be offered as a customer tool to the industry's clients, with approximately 67 percent of all firms providing blog services to customers. Podcasts also became a hot trend, with about half of all firms offering podcast services in 2006 (up from just 25 percent in 2005). Podcasting uses media files, which are transmitted over the Internet via syndicated feeds. Podcasts are unique from other downloadable material because they can be accessed automatically, without manual download, using syndicated feeds, such as RSS. A Podcast, which takes it name from Apple's original iPod scheme, allows consumers to access a wide variety of information.

The PR industry picked up steam, with the high tech sector leading the way, followed by consumer products and services and healthcare. According to a CPFR survey in early 2007, a majority of PR firms experienced positive growth in 2006 and almost all expected business to continue to be strong through 2007. As a result, over half of firms added staff in 2006, with the majority of firms continuing to hire into 2007.

CURRENT CONDITIONS

The role of mobile technology for high-tech PR communications, and its role in media and Internet companies' multiplatform business models cannot be overstated. In an April 2009 forecast, BIA's Kelsey Group, a division of BIA Advisory Services, LLC, predicted that U.S. mobile search advertising revenues would grow from $39 million in 2008 to $2.3 billion by 2013. One of the drivers behind the forecast was the growth of mobile Internet users. The report anticipated "a tenfold increase in the number of mobile Internet users during the forecast period-from 5.2 million in 2008 to 56.2 million in 2013."

The potential to reach expanded audiences through sophisticated electronic means has helped the PR industry. Electronic social conversation and social networking have become viable media choices for plugging products and services. The potential audience is staggering. For example, a 2009 study referenced by Techcrunchies indicated the number of U.S. Twitter users will cross the 25 million mark by 2010. According to the same study, there were 6 million in 2008, but 2009 users were expected to reach 18 million. Likewise, by 2009, the number of blogs indexed by Technorati, a blog search service, was estimated at 133,000,000 since it started tracking in 2002. The average number of blog posts in a 24-hour period was given as 900,000. A 2008 estimate from comScore estimated the number of people globally who read blogs as 346,000,000, or roughly 77 percent of active Internet users. O'Dwyer's Public Relation News reported in late 2009 that total Internet ad revenues for the first half of 2009 reached nearly $11 billion.

Another medium with high-tech PR potential was the reality of mobile TV. An enabling factor has been the growth of mobile broadband such as 3G networks. This is analogous to the broadband penetration that has made online video explode, and to the next generation fiber networks that will bring IPTV. As television broadcasters considered the many different uses of the spectrum bandwidth now possible through digital television (DTV), the BIA Financial Network estimated that the industry could reap an additional $2 billion in annual revenues by 2012 through the delivery of content to mobile and/or handheld receivers. Additionally, the new flow of revenues could potentially create $9.1 billion in incremental market value for broadcasters.

INDUSTRY LEADERS

Omnicom is the world's largest media services holding company. Its PR holdings include Brodeaur Worldwide, CONE, Fleishman-Hillard, Ketchum, and Porter Novelli International. The company's total revenues were $11.4 billion in 2006. Its public relations sector accounts for roughly 10 percent of total company sales.

Porter Novelli, a business unit of Omnicom, was one of the world's top public relations firms during the mid-years of the first decade of the 2000s, and its Technology Division was a high tech PR leader. The company grew about 25 percent each year in the late 1990s, bringing in annual fees of $85 million. Formerly known as Brodeur Porter Novelli, the company wrote its own software, designed extranets for clients, and built and maintained Web sites. In January 2000, Porter/Novelli International merged with Copithorne & Bellows Public Relations to form the Porter/Novelli Convergence Group, which was one of the world's largest high tech PR operations, working in Europe, Asia Pacific, and the Americas.

During the middle of the first decade of the 2000s, Porter Novelli's Technology Practice continued to leverage its experience in such tech segments as consumer electronics, enterprise hardware and software, semiconductors, telecommunications and infrastructure, and wireless devices and technologies. According to the firm, its clients ranged from "promising venture capital-funded start-ups to mid-sized, fast-growth companies to *Fortune* 100 global enterprises." This broad lineup included the likes of Analog Devices Inc., BMC Software Inc., People-Soft Inc., EMC Corp., Hewlett-Packard Co., and QUALCOMM Inc. In mid-decade, Porter Novelli generated approximately $109 million in revenues.

St. Louis-based Fleishman-Hillard, Inc., also a leading U.S. PR firm, is another Omnicom-owned heavy hitter. Fleishman-Hillard maintains about 80 offices worldwide, and its clients include Dell and Nortel.

Edelman, based in Chicago, Illinois, is a privately held company spread over various PR sectors, including sports, government, and financial, in addition to its high tech operations. Founded in 1952, Edelman maintained a client list that included AT&T, IBM, Microsoft, the Gartner Group, NCR, Samsung, Texas Instruments, and other heavy hitters. In its 2005 fiscal year, Edelman had 42 offices throughout the world and collected $239 million in fees. Edelman's Interactive Division was anchored in Chicago and New York, but had sites in such major cities as Los Angeles, London, and Dublin. Recognized as a technology leader, Edelman was the first of the major agencies to have its own Web site. In 1999, the firm acquired Wham Communications of Seattle. In 2007, the company hired nearly 50 staffers dedicated solely to new media. Global revenues for its 2009 fiscal year declined slightly to about $446 million from more than $448 million in fiscal 2008, the agency reported.

Waggener Edstrom, one of Silicon Valley's last independent PR agencies, works with such companies as Advanced Micro Devices and T-Mobile, but its meal ticket was its role as Microsoft's public relations agency, which was responsible for about half the company's annual fees of over $40 million—enhanced, no doubt, by Microsoft's high-profile fight with the Justice Department over alleged antitrust violations. The company's relationship with Microsoft made it a coveted object for the larger PR firms, which were increasingly eyeing the firm for acquisition. Founded in 1983, the Lake Oswego, Oregon-based company remained privately held.

A division of Interpublic's McCann WorldGroup, Weber Shandwick Worldwide was one of the world's leading communications management and public relations firms, with more than 75 offices worldwide. At that time, the firm's technology practice continued to set standards within the PR business, drawing from hundreds of agency professionals in cities across the globe. Weber Shandwick served every sector within the technology industry, providing marketing and PR services, as well as reputation management. According to Weber Shandwick, its technology experience "extends from electronic components to general consumer products, including electronics, digital media, enterprise software and systems, networking, semiconductors, storage, wireless/mobile, telecom and cable."

WORKFORCE

High tech PR agents ideally are personable folks with a good inside knowledge of the relevant media. Not only should PR agents command extensive knowledge of their clients' products, but they're charged with knowing which media outlets are appropriate placement venues for those products and services, the precise nature and editorial slant of those outlets, and even which editors or contacts are the best in a given situation or for a given type of product. Hiring prospects were strong as the PR industry experienced bottom line growth.

RESEARCH AND TECHNOLOGY

To capitalize on the growth wealth of consumer and business information found in Web logs, or blogs, high tech PR firms and business intelligence firms were being hired to analyze these online data threads for their clients. In particular, PR firms sought to harvest references to their clients' companies, brands, and products in an attempt to obtain unbiased feedback. Software applications called aggregators, also known as newsreaders, were among the technology tools that firms used to perform this analysis. Using technology known as Really Simple Syndication (RSS), aggregators combine content feeds from multiple blogs onto one Web page. This allows blogs to syndicate their content, and eliminates the need for readers to visit the individual blogs they are interested in. Other widely available tools included BlogPulse, a Web site offered by Intelliseek and used to track, search, and analyze millions of blog postings every day.

To take advantage of the Podcast and content feed boom, by the end of 2006 approximately 46 percent of firms offered RSS service in increasing numbers (up from 29 percent in 2005). By the second half of the first decade of the 2000s, many major marketing outlets used content feeds, including USAToday.com, ABCNews, BBC News Headlines, and CNET. Advertisers benefit because RSS feeds avoid problems with spam filters and ad blockers.

BIBLIOGRAPHY
"About Us." Weber Shandwick Worldwide, 26 May 2005. Available from http://www.webershandwick.com/overview/index.cfm.

Boland, Mike. "Mobile Handheld, Winning Media Strategies." BIA/Kelsey Traditional Media Perspective, Press Release, 29 April 2009. Available from http://blog.bia.com/bia/category/mobilehandheld/.

Brown, Caraline. "Did I Really Want It All Back Again?" *Management Today,* October 2004.

"Company." San Francisco: Blanc Otus, 26 May 2005. Available from http://www.bando.com/company/index.html.

Council of Public Relations Firms. "2006 Annual Report," 2007. Available from http://prfirms.org/docs/AnnualReports/CPRF-Annual-Report-2006.pdf.

———. "Council of Public Relations Firms Survey Shows Growth in Industry for 2006," 2 February 2007. Available from http://prfirms.org.

Howorth, Vikki. "Tech PR More Issue than Product Based as Market Recovers." *Media Asia,* 27 August 2004.

"Life in the Fast Lane of High Tech PR Revealed in Weinkrantz Web Log; International Strategic PR Consultant Alan Weinkrantz Offers Observation, Reflection, News, Analysis, and More in Fast-Paced Blog." *PR Newswire,* 7 February 2005.

"Number of Twitter Users in USA." Tech Crunchies Available from http://techcrunchies.com/number-of-twitter-users-in-usa/.

"Profile: Waggener Zorkin Has Tech PR Down to a Science." *PR Week,* 29 November 2004.

"Technology." Weber Shandwick Worldwide, 26 May 2005. Available from http://www.webershandwick.com/capabilities/index.cfm.

Washkuch, Frank. "Edelman's 09 Revenues Flat; Organic up 3.7%." *PR Week,* 31 July 2009.

"Welcome." Edelman, 26 May 2005. Available from http://www.edelman.com/about_us/welcome.

"What We Do." Porter Novelli, 26 May 2005. Available from http://www.porternovelli.com.

HOLOGRAPHY

———————————— ■ ————————————

SIC CODE(S)

3559

3674

3699

INDUSTRY SNAPSHOT

While people could not yet use holography to re-enact scenes from their favorite novels as promised on *Star Trek: The Next Generation,* by the twenty-first century, holographic technology was boldly going where no one had gone before. The technology was expanding into numerous alien territories such as solar weather forecasting, three-dimensional (3D) information storage and sound projection, and the production of lifelike images of objects that exist only in virtual reality. Such applications move light years beyond the more familiar holographic uses on credit cards, packaging, compact discs, and in fields such as computer-aided design, medical imaging, and security.

Holography permits the recording and reproducing of 3D images called holograms. This can be achieved via two methods. Transmission holograms are created by splitting a laser beam into two sections. The first, or reference beam, is bounced off a mirror and strikes a photographic plate, but the waves of the reference beam remain unchanged. The second, or object beam, encounters the holographic subject before also striking the same side of the photographic plate. The intervening object alters the object beam's waves and the plate records the difference between the two beams. Known as the interference pattern, this difference is accounted for by the shape of the holographic subject, which is imprinted on the photographic plate in three dimensions. A laser that is shone through the film permits the image to be viewed.

The newer, and more common, reflection holograms are generated in much the same manner. The laser beams, however, strike the opposite sides of the holographic plate. Reflection holograms can be seen in white light without the aid of an additional laser. The interference pattern recorded on the plate distorts the silver material within the film, creating varying depths within the image. Unlike the stereoscopic views created by toy View Masters, holographic images are genuinely three-dimensional. The viewer's eyes refocus on different depths; and rotating the image permits one to see around and behind the object.

ORGANIZATION AND STRUCTURE

Characterized initially by individual artistic shops and museum marketers, the holography industry has continued to be dominated by private companies. Like most new industries, it experienced some volatility among its corporate players. The most active industry leaders are in the areas of advertising, engineering, medicine, mass storage media, and security. Several other companies have found specialty niches in producing holographic foil supplies or equipment. The holography industry tends to be grouped largely by function: design, origination, production, utilization, distribution, and marketing or sales of holographic products—although several companies are vertically integrated.

Advertising and Packaging. Advertising holograms have eye-catching appeal that results in an exceptional rate of retention as compared with other advertising media. Universal Studios commissioned a custom-made hologram watch to commemorate the 100th anniversary of Alfred Hitchcock's birth. The face of the watch contained a holographic version of the director's unmistakable silhouette surrounded by birds. McDonald's full-page hologram on the back of *National Geographic*'s centennial anniversary issue cost more than $1 million for space that normally sold for $200,000. The ad ran worldwide in 10.5 million copies.

In 1995 Ford Motor Co. began generating full-size, full-color, photographic quality holograms of new cars directly from computer images that allowed a clinical view without the historic clay model. As early as 1973, General Motors Corp. used holography for measuring clay models prior to making press dies. Virtual reality will allow test drives without prototypes in the future. In 1999 Ford used stereograph technology to display a full-blown prototype car, the P2000, at the Detroit Auto Show. The impressive P2000 appeared on the display floor in living color, a demonstration of future innovations planned by the auto manufacturer. The P2000 was generated exclusively from an array of holographic images that created the illusion that a solid object (the car) was on display. Zebra Imaging of Austin, Texas, which assembled the resource-intensive P2000 display, processed approximately three terabytes of digital data for nearly two weeks to create the final image. Zebra Imaging predicted that pending technology improvements will reduce that time-consuming process from 300 hours to a mere five minutes in the foreseeable future.

Security Devices The production of holograms requires expensive, specialized, and technologically advanced equipment, so they are considered a good security device. Holograms cannot be easily replicated by color copiers, scanners, or standard printing techniques since they are governed by light diffraction as opposed to light reflection. Visa and MasterCard have used holograms for more than a decade. They are also used on passports in several European countries and on some government bonds and certificates in the United States. The market for optically variable devices, such as those used on credit cards, is anticipated to expand by 30 to 40 percent a year. The sector is highly fragmented, with over 350 producers worldwide.

Microsoft adopted an anti-counterfeiting label, the 3M Authentication Label, which first appeared on MS-DOS 6.0 packages in 1993. In 1996 the holographic seal on Microsoft's MS-DOS and Windows software helped break up a $4.7 million counterfeit operation, the largest ever in the United States. The Windows 2000 software contained a full-surface holographic security image generated by Applied Optical Technologies.

U.S. military applications include the development by the U.S. Department of Energy's Pacific Northwest Regional Lab in Richland, Washington of a holographic 3D radar camera. The device can record images of fighter planes before and after repair work to verify that radar-absorbing material that coats stealth bombers (to help them remain stealthy) has not been damaged, thus jeopardizing their security.

Data Storage Holographic storage developments reached a watershed by 2000, and the first commercial release of a holographic memory device appeared in 2006. Holographic data storage surpasses magnetic storage technology because of its ultrahigh storage density, rapid data transfer capability, short data access time, and exceptional reliability. In 1995, to develop the holographic storage technology, the U.S. Department of Defense funded half of a $64 million joint industry, academic, and government venture that consisted of two branches. The Holographic Data Storage System Consortium, with participants including IBM, Rockwell, and Stanford University, investigated hardware development for a commercially viable storage system in which, ideally, a gigabyte of data would fit on a pencil eraser and could be retrieved at one billion bits per second. The Photorefractive Information Storage Materials project worked on materials research.

Medical Field The Voxcam, developed by Voxel Inc., is part of a system designed to interface with existing medical scanners to produce 3D X-rays, and consists of a camera to convert computerized axial tomography—or simply computerized tomography (CT)—and magnetic resonance scans into holograms that provide an accurate interactive "road map" for physicians prior to surgery. The system converts complicated conventional CT scans or X-rays, which normally require a radiologist's interpretation, into a virtual model that is readily understandable by any physician. The hologram enables the physician to interact in, around, and through the image as if it were a real specimen. It allows doctors to peer inside blood vessels and assists in pelvic surgery and treating brain tumors and carotid arteries as the viewer moves around within the image.

BACKGROUND AND DEVELOPMENT

A theoretical procedure for holography (which comes from the Greek *holo*, meaning "whole," and *gram*, meaning "recording") was originally conceived by Dennis Gabor in 1948 as a means of improving the resolution of electron microscopes. Where conventional photography captures only the amplitude or brightness of reflected light, a hologram also records the interference of light waves between a single coherent light split into two beams of light waves that converge on a recording plate or film. The reference beam travels directly to the recording medium and the other beam is reflected off the object. The recorded intersection of straight un-reflected light waves and the light waves reflected from an object allows a hologram to reproduce a virtual image that includes parallax viewing, an apparent change in perspective or viewpoint that occurs with different angles of viewing.

The invention was ignored for several decades except for attempts by Albert Baez and Hussein El-Sum at Stanford University to use X-rays to make holograms in the 1950s. Interest in holography ebbed because of the lack of a coherent light source of consistent, unvarying wavelengths with the equal crests and troughs essential to the success of the process. In the 1960s, Emmett Leith and Juris Upatnieks at the University of Michigan produced several holograms by combining Gabor's principles with Theodore Harold Maiman's laser. However, it was not until 1991 that physicists were able to use electron holography to reconstruct a crystal's structure, fulfilling Gabor's original goal.

In 1994 Lambertus Hesselink, John Heanue, and Matthew Bashaw developed the first holographic storage system to store digital data. Initially, commercialization was expected to take three to five years, but that outcome has yet to be achieved. The combination of the storage of millions of data bits per page, fast retrieval rates, and rapid random access make this a highly practical storage method.

Sources for holograms include light waves, X-rays, electron beams, and microwaves. Waves other than light waves have successfully used holographic principles in an increasing variety of applications. In 1994 a new holographic system for displaying 3D images of internal anatomy was developed. Microwaves that penetrate a variety of media have been used to detect unseen flaws in layered metal parts. X-ray technology, using the same principles, allowed 3D imaging of live organisms. A new family of organic materials such as peptide oligomers appears promising in offering erasable holographic storage. Energy X-ray holography, which was developed by Charles Fadley and Dietlef Bahr, relied on fluorescent atoms as detectors rather than sources in order to look at the structure of minute materials to make the first hologram of an atom in a solid.

Engineering applications of holography include stress analysis, checking for cracks or voids in layered or composite surfaces such as aircraft fuselages or wings, and vibration analysis. Acoustic holography is applied to geophysical and underwater explorations. Microwave holography can also provide detailed surface maps. A heterodyne Mach-Zehnder interferometer was first built by students to show the feasibility of detecting sound waves in a small cell.

Other applications include a digital scale, developed by Sony Magnescale, Inc. in 1995, which can measure plus or minus .0086 micrometers by monitoring and measuring the phase change of a laser beam as it passes through a hologram grating. IBM Corp. introduced its 3687 holographic supermarket checkout station that could read universal product code information on standard and irregularly shaped articles in 1982. HoloScan introduced its first holographic bar code scanner in 1994.

Scientists are now examining the possibility of using holograms to display 3D images, creating true 3D television and movies. In fact, Gabor himself began such research late in his life. The fruits of these efforts can be found in the appearance of holographic goggles and even a hologram simulation video game.

PIONEERS IN THE FIELD

Dennis Gabor studied in Berlin, earning his doctorate in engineering in 1927. After World War II, Gabor turned his attention to the electron microscope. His earlier attempts to develop the instrument had failed and he was determined to make a comeback in the field. His goal was to be able to "see" individual atoms by taking an electron picture. In initial attempts, the image was distorted by problems with the lens. Gabor theorized that this could be corrected by optical means using light. He published his theory in scientific papers in 1947, in which he first coined the term *hologram*. Its implications for beams of light, however, awaited only the invention of the laser.

The invention of the laser in 1960 sparked renewed interest in holography, since a constant narrow light source where all waves were in phase was now available to experimenters. The first laser hologram in 1962 ensured Gabor's reputation. In 1967 he retired from the Imperial College of Science and Technology in London, where he had worked since 1949, but continued his research. He was able to show the application of holography to computer data processing, where it has been particularly useful in data compression. He received his highest honor in December 1971, when he was awarded the Nobel Prize in physics for his work in holography. His Nobel lecture concerned the issues that dominated his later years: the role of science and technology in society.

After Gabor was awarded the Nobel Prize, Lawrence Bartell of the University of Michigan set out to develop a holographic electron microscope. He shared his work with Gabor in 1974, and Gabor immediately began designing his own holographic electron microscope. In the summer of that year, however, Gabor suffered a stroke that left him unable to read or write. Despite this he was able to maintain contact with his colleagues. He even visited the Museum of Holography in New York City when it opened in 1977. He died in a London nursing home in February 1979.

In 2000, several Holographic Data Storage System (HDDS) Consortium partners proclaimed they were pursuing technical developments that would speed holographic storage to market. The IBM Almaden Research Center, Rockwell Science Center, and Jet Propulsion Labs were developing optical associative memories that combined holographic storage capacities with optical correlation, which would permit the retrieval of data by association performed in parallel for a speedy perusal of large volumes of information. It would also enable complex queries involving multiple variables. Any holdups in debuting the system were credited to insufficiencies in available storage media.

According to the August 2003 issue of *The Economist,* "After years of development, researchers are on the verge of using holograms to store data in memories that are both fast and efficient...the first commercial holographic memory should be on the market next year and more are expected to follow." Along with 1,000 gigabytes, or one terabyte, of storage space, these new holographic memory devices were also expected to operate at a speed of one billion bits per second, roughly 60 times the speed of a DVD.

By 2005, holograms were being applied in very practical ways. For example, holographic packaging materials were being used to thwart tampering and counterfeiting for expensive products such as electronics, pharmaceuticals, perfume, cosmetics, and liquor. Alcan Packaging's HoloAuthentica enabled manufacturers to print diffraction patterns, as well as attractive custom images.

Holographic technology also was being used in the security sector. One application included biometric identification and authentication devices. Aprilis Inc. used holograms as part of a cutting-edge fingerprint reader that, when combined with special software, provided performance that was superior to traditional systems. Because they were virtually counterfeit-proof, holographic ID cards were another practical application for holograms during the middle years of the first decade of the 2000s.

Holographic data storage had not hit the marketplace by 2005, but its introduction was closer than ever before. A number of important developments had occurred by this time. In January 2005, Longmont, Colorado-based InPhase Technologies announced that it had developed a prototype of the world's first holographic storage drive and claimed that holographic storage was about to transition from research to commercialization. The InPhase prototype was to serve as the basis for a line of holographic drives capable of storing 200 gigabytes to a massive 1.6 terrabytes on one disk.

Named Tapestry, InPhase's holographic drive was developed in partnership with government agencies and the private sector. The National Geospatial-Intelligence Agency's National Technology Alliance program (NTA) partially funded certain automation aspects of the manufacturing process for Tapestry, as well as the drive's holographic media. Another leading investment and development partner was Hitachi Maxell Ltd., which designed a cartridge to protect the drive's light-sensitive recording material, and was developing a high volume manufacturing process for InPhase's patented recording media.

Another important industry development was the formation of the Holographic Versatile Disc (HVD) Alliance in February 2005. Comprised of six companies—CMC Magnetics Corp.; FUJI PHOTO FILM CO. LTD.; Nippon Paint Co. Ltd.; Optware Corp.; Pulstec Industrial Co. Ltd.; and TOAGOSEI CO. LTD.—the alliance was created to develop the market for HVD and promote HVD products. A potential successor to high definition DVD (HD DVD) and related technologies, HVD discs will allow the average consumer to store as much as one terrabyte of data on one disc, holding the capacity of 200 regular DVDs. With data transfer rates of more than one GB per second, HVD was expected to find quick acceptance among consumers wishing to record high definition TV broadcasts. In December 2004, a technical committee was formed to discuss the HVD standardization.

Highly sensitive, yet very affordable, biosensors were an emerging application for holograms during the mid-years of the first decade of the 2000s. In its February 19, 2005 issue, *eWeek* reported on the development of so-called "smart labels" that could measure and accurately display properties specific to biological organisms and products. According to the publication, "Prototypes have already been made for contact lenses that monitor glucose levels, thin badges that detect alcohol levels, and sticks that can tell, instantly, if milk has spoiled or become contaminated. The technology promises to be quicker and cheaper than tests used today. It will also require less training, because the hologram itself can be designed to show results graphically." *eWeek* further revealed that Cambridge University Professor Chris Lowe had established a company called Smart Holograms that was devoted to holographic technology with bio-sensing applications.

North American Products Corp. announced it had designed a holographic cloning amplifier technology (HCAT) to reconstruct distortion-free sounds in acoustic holograms. The technology creates a "virtual map" of the physical locations from which sounds are generated during recording that are embedded deep in audio signals. With HCAT, sounds seem to the listener to come out of the surrounding air rather than being projected from speakers. HCAT has promising applications in 3D movies, videos, and high-definition television (HDTV) in theme parks, movie theaters, military simulations for training exercises, and home entertainment systems.

The market for embossed and display holograms experienced nothing short of phenomenal growth between 1986 and 2006. In 1986, sales of embossed and display holograms were an estimated at $25 to $30 million, and the industry was dominated by just a few producers, including American Banknote Holographics, which accounted for over one-third of industry revenues. According to a 2007 estimate by *Holography News,* the market value for embossed holograms neared $2 billion in 2006. In 2010 dollar value, that means that the industry grew 40 to 50 times larger in 20 years. In addition, prices declined significantly, as much as 75 percent for packaging materials and 50 percent for security applications. As a result, production numbers actually increased by one hundredfold. The industry makeup also changed, with over 250 hologram firms operating globally by 2007.

The largest growth in the embossed hologram market was in document authentication, product authentication, and packaging. Newer applications included gift wrap and store decor. Currency use was also increasing. By the middle of the first decade of the 2000s, 93 issuing authorities used holograms (or the related kinegrams) on almost 250 banknote denominations.

The industry turned another corner in late 2006 when InPhase Technology, under a production contract with Maxwell Hatachi, released its first generation of holographic drives. The Tapestry 300M disc, which uses the volume of the disc rather than just writing to the surface, can hold 300 gigabytes on one disc, with a transfer rate of 160 megabytes per second—about 10 times faster than a DVD. The company expected to release even higher volume discs in the future, with hopes of reaching 1.6 Tbyte capacity by 2010. The first systems are aimed at commercial customers as prices were $15,000 for drives and $120 to $150 for each disc. Consumer applications, with lower capacities of 75 to 100 gigabytes, are anticipated by the end of the decade.

In a technological breakthrough, in February 2007 Dai Nippon Printing announced the development of "Motion Image," a hologram for credit card and security use on branded goods that appears to move similar to an animated image. According to *Innovative New Packaging in Japan,* "Unlike conventional embossed holograms, which have become increasingly easy to counterfeit, the new type consists of data of several images recorded onto a special material—making the counterfeit process extremely difficult."

CURRENT CONDITIONS

It seemed the holography industry came of age in 2008 and 2009 with major technological advances that helped expand applications and reduce production and development costs in many areas. In the manufacturing arena, the global use of holograms to brand products and prevent counterfeit reproductions experienced palpable growth. One example was the use of holographic tax stamps on alcohol and tobacco products. The use on alcoholic spirits increased by 34 percent and by 2009 covered 26 billion bottles annually. This also helped authorities correlate alcohol sales with tax revenues received. Advanced holographic packaging also enhanced the sporting goods industry to fight counterfeit sports merchandise.

Data storage remained a promising area for growth. By 2009, nanotechnology had expanded holographic memory capability by leaps and bounds. The overall nanophotonic field produced components and products such as nanophotonic LEDs, organic LEDs (OLEDs), near-field optics, photovoltaic cells, optical amplifiers and switches, and holographic data storage systems. The nanophotonics technology market was expected to grow rapidly because of such attributes as low weight, high thermal stability, power efficiency and long working life. This meant a significant increase in the number of applications in near-field optics, holographic memory and optical amplifiers. According to a 2009 MarketsandMarkets report, *Nanophotonics: Advanced Technologies and Global Market (2009-2014),* the optical amplifier and holographic memory device segments were estimated to have a compound annual growth rate (CAGR) of 239 percent and 234.6 percent, respectively, from 2009 to 2014.

INDUSTRY LEADERS

Holographics North, Inc., produces some of the world's largest holograms and claims to be the only U.S. company capable of producing large format (42-by-72-inch), color, high resolution holograms. They are generally used in trade shows, museums, space centers, and educational centers. The firm also creates animated stereographs, which include computer graphics, reduced or enlarged images, and on-site recordings. Their work is custom-produced. The company is located in Burlington, Vermont.

OpSec Security Group (formerly Applied Optical Technologies) is a U.K.-based company that was created when Applied Holographics acquired the U.S. companies Optical Security Group and Bridgestone. Optical Security specialized in security laminates and it counted the U.S. National Football League and several state driver's license issuers among its customers. The company reported revenues for the six months ending September 30, 2009 as $16.3 million British pounds and employed more than 250 workers. The company maintained customer strongholds in Europe and the Far East.

An international presence in the manufacture of holographic packaging materials was U.S. chemical coating producer CFC International. Like OpSec Security Group, CFC's holographic offerings cut across several industry sectors, although they center primarily in the high security and premium packaging arenas. Headquartered in Chicago Heights, Illinois, CFC also has office locations in England, France, and Germany. The company has designed materials for such industry heavyweights as Colgate-Palmolive Co. and Glaxo SmithKline. By 2005, the company had more than 5,000 customers worldwide. At the end of 2006, CFC was purchased by Illinois Tool Company for $76 million.

Elmsford, New York-based American Bank Note Holographics Inc. (ABNH), a spin-off of American Bank Note, specialized in holographic images for security and promotional applications. In 2005 about 85 percent of ABNH's revenues were generated by credit card companies, including MasterCard (30 percent) and Visa (35 percent). However, Visa cancelled its contract with ABNH.

Zebra Imaging is an Austin, Texas-based company that devises large format, full color holograms. For its first commission, it created Ford's virtual P2000 for the Detroit Auto Show. In 1999 Ford acquired an equity interest in the firm, whose customers also include the Walt Disney Co., DuPont, Starbucks, and Warner-Lambert. In December of 2001, Zebra Imaging created the largest publicly displayed holographic image in the world for the Austin-Bergstrom International Airport.

Mid-decade, Zebra had raised $14 million in equity offerings. At that time, the company's main investors included Ford, Convergent Investors, and DuPont. According to the company, it was "focused on visualization applications of its current technologies, with primary markets in automotive and manufacturing design and engineering, petroleum and gas exploration, and defense, aerospace, and military areas." In 2007 Zebra owned 23 patents, with 13 U.S and eight foreign patents pending.

WORKFORCE

Due to the diversity of applications, unique niche products, and the private nature of many of the companies, it is difficult to estimate the total size of the workforce in the holography industry with any degree of accuracy. Like all new and emerging industries, however, holography will likely create jobs that do not exist today. The growth of affiliated medical and computer fields is well documented. Trends for employment in areas associated with holography products in medicine, manufacturing, research, and advertising appear to be strong and growing. The skill level and compensation range from that of engineers, physicists, and optical scientists in research and development to machine operators.

RESEARCH AND TECHNOLOGY

New on the scene in 2009 was the commercial development of holographic discs (HVD), similar to DVDs but holding 20 times as much data as a dual-layer Blu-ray disc (which can store 50 gigabytes). The use of new materials that made reading and writing 3D holograms more reliable, i.e., larger, branched polymer molecules, made this technology a reality, with far-reaching possibilities for applications. As of 2009, there were about 20 pioneering companies developing holographic data-storage devices and holograph-based data drives in the world. It was hoped that the new technology would allow

them to fit at least 1000 gigabytes of data onto a standard disc. One such company was Colorado-based InPhase Technologies.

In 2008, the U.S. Patent and Trademark Office granted patent rights to Indian industry leader Infosys for a holographic mobile handset capable of projecting, capturing, and sending 3D images. The machine can build a series of 2D shots taken, for example, from a digital camera, into 3D holograms using algorithms (called "Fourier" transformations) to calculate the extra third dimension. Potential applications for 3D snapshots caught on the portable machines would include helping accident investigators, teachers, and doctors work remotely by instantly relaying realistic depictions of car damage, injuries, medical scans, or educational aids. By 2010, the devices will routinely bring 3D films, games, and virtual goods into consumers' homes, according to Infosys.

In 2009, Prism Solar Technologies fine-tuned a solar panel that consists of silicon strips spaced out by holographic film. The film concentrates sunlight onto the cells to produce a module that will be 18.7 percent efficient by 2015. Prism expected to sell both complete modules as well as holographic film that other manufacturers will be able to insert into their products.

Researchers at the Massachusetts Institute of Technology (MIT) developed a working prototype of a holographic videoconferencing system. This sci-fi staple, according to the head of MIT's Spatial Imaging Group, Stephen Benton, uses holographic data storage and fiber optics to create real time, three-dimensional, computer-generated holograms. Having mastered the reduction of information and image scanning, the next trick for scientists is to take the compressed digital signals and scale them up to a practical size. Researchers expect to tackle this problem with micro-electro mechanical systems (MEMS), or micromachines, which combine sensors, actuators, electronics, and mechanical components on a tiny silicon substrate. Also see the essay entitled "Micromachines/Nanotechnology."

New holographic probe technology to take non-contact measurements of 3D cross-sections from any angle of complex objects and parts that contain many blind spots and holes was under development by Optimet. The Conoscan 3000 used a laser probe technology called conoscopic holography to produce finely detailed analyses of angles, radii, and the distance between points on objects made of most opaque materials, even under low-light conditions. A laser beam is shot into a blind hole and bounced off a mirror to gauge the piece's internal angles. Measurement precision equals more than one eight-thousandth (1/8,000) of the working range. The technology would benefit quality control operations for clients such as the auto industry, which must inspect engine blocks, and the plastics industry.

Even predicting the weather on the far side of the solar surface emerged as a holographic application. Physicists Charles Lindsay of Solar Physics Research Corp. and Douglas Brown of Northwest Research Associates, Inc. announced in 2000 that they had devised a means of using seismic holography to track the path of sound waves as they travel through the inside of the sun. Although under normal conditions sound waves make the interior journey in about three and one-half hours, when they bump into areas of high magnetic activity, their path is distorted and they advance about six seconds out of synchronization with the undisturbed waves. Following the wave paths permits space weather forecasters to predict the emergence of solar storms that are brewing on the far side of the sun, which is hidden from normal viewing, about one week before they would appear. Though the researchers proposed the forecasting technique a decade earlier, it was only with the construction of the Michelson Doppler Imager for the Solar and Heleospheric Observatory, a space-based observatory operated from a permanent point 1.5 million kilometers sunward of the earth, that a sophisticated enough device was available to register the recordings. Routine tracking is not yet possible but is anticipated to be by 2006. Knowing the solar weather report in advance would help earthlings prepare for the damage solar storms can inflict on power grids, telecommunications systems, and space station workers.

An unlikely pair of inventors—two London sculptors working in a de-consecrated church-turned-studio and bar—developed a highly effective auto-stereoscopic, holographic display device that can produce a remarkably impressive image for little more than five dollars over the cost of a conventional liquid crystal display (LCD). Working on a virtually non-existent budget, artists Edwina Orr and David Trayner developed the technology to create holographic art at their Studio 291—so christened for the former church's address and in homage to pioneering photographer Alfred Stieglitz's path-breaking gallery at 291 Fifth Avenue in New York. They also founded a company, Reality Vision Ltd., and intended to market a scaled-up version of their device that was produced using an LCD module from IBM. One of the device's greatest strengths was its compatibility with ordinary two-dimensional viewing. Adding the modestly priced holographic optics to a conventional LCD module permits the user to turn it off for normal viewing, then switch it on for use in computer-aided design, medical imaging, or computer games applications.

BIBLIOGRAPHY

Baker, M.L. "Holograms Poised to Reveal Bio Data." *eWeek,* 19 February 2005.

Barras, Colin. "Holographic Discs Set to Smash Storage Records." *New Scientist,* 22 January 2009.

Bjelkhagen, Hans. "SPIE's Practical Holography." *Holography News,* February 2007.

"Company." Aprilis Inc., 14 March 2005. Available from http://www.aprilisinc.com.

"'Cost-Effective' Holograms." *Packaging Today International,* December 2004.

"Currency Continues as Growth Market for Holograms." *Holography News,* January 2007.

Heath, Nick. "Infosys: Holograms on Handsets by 2010." CNET News, 20 July 2008. Available from http://news.cnet.com/Infosys-Holograms-on-handsets-by-2010/2100-1041_3-6242143.html.

"Hologram-based Security Fights counterfeit Sports Merchandise." *Packaging Digest,* 1 November 2009.

"Holographic Firm Claims Data Storage Density Record." *InformationWeek,* 24 March 2006.

"Holographic Tax Stamps Protect Alcohol and Tobacco Brands..." *Package Design,* 4 December 2008.

"Holographic TV: Ready for Survivor 3D? Harold Garner Is Creating Technology That Could Make Holographic TV—and a Long List of Other Holo-Devices—a Reality." *Technology Review,* June 2004.

"Holographic Versatile Disc (HVD) Alliance Formed." *LinuxElectrons,* 5 February 2005. Available from http://www.linuxelectrons.com/article.php/20050205201554958.

"How Large is the Holography Industry?" *Holography News,* January 2007.

"InPhase Enters OEM Deal With DSM for Holographic Storage." *Broadcast Engineering,* 8 January 2007.

"InPhase Technologies Introduces the World's First Holographic Drive Prototype." InPhase Technologies, 4 January 2005. Available from http://www.inphase-technologies.com/news/firstholoproto.html.

Les, Carin B. "Nanophotonics market: Upward bound." *Photonics,* Fall 2009. Available from http://www.photonics.com/Content/ReadArticle.aspx?ArticleID=40066.

"Light on the Horizon: Holographic Data Storage." *The Economist,* 2 August 2003.

"Moving Holograms." *Innovative New Packaging in Japan,* 25 February 2007.

"Out of This World; 3D Television." *The Economist,* 13 November 2004.

"Photopolymer Data Storage Business Heats Up." *Holography News,* September 2006.

Young, Ken. "300GB Holo Discs 'On Sale in 2006.'" *Personal Computer World,* 1 February 2006.

Zalud, Bill. "Go Beyond What's Enough." *Security,* January 2005.

HOME HEALTH CARE SERVICES

SIC CODE(S)

8082

INDUSTRY SNAPSHOT

Health care organizations recognized a number of advantages in offering home health care services. First and foremost, such services offered significant cost savings compared with similar services conducted inside hospitals. Patients, moreover, tend to prefer to receive treatment in the comfort of their own homes rather than in a hospital or nursing home, provided adequate and appropriate care is maintained.

Home health care, however, faced a grim reality as a number of setbacks rocked the industry and caused its players to seriously rethink their home-oriented operations. The industry was devastated by the implementation of the Balanced Budget Act in 1997, which included measures to slash Medicare and Medicaid reimbursements to home health care providers. In part this was seen as an effort to reduce the levels of fraud—a charge leveled frequently at the industry—and in part as indicative of Congressional leaders' calls for reduced government spending. However, no matter what the intentions, the effect on the industry was clear. More than 3,500 agencies had either closed their doors or simply no longer accepted Medicare patients by early 2002, according to the National Association for Homecare.

Significant challenges continued to face the industry, including heightened competition, reimbursement cuts, skyrocketing gas prices, and bad press stemming from industry fraud. However, the most profound challenge of all was the Medicare Prescription Drug, Improvement and Modernization Act of 2003. Also known as the Medicare Modernization Act (MMA), this legislation included sweeping Medicare reimbursement changes for providers of home medical equipment, which represents a large share of business for many home care agencies.

Despite these conflicts, demographic realities—namely the graying of 77 million baby boomers—ensured that home health care services would remain popular well into the twenty-first century. According to *Home Care Magazine*, by the middle of the first decade of the 2000s, some 24 million baby boomers had reached age 50. By 2030, members of the 66 to 84 age bracket will constitute an estimated 20 percent of the U.S population, requiring treatment for a variety of chronic diseases and age-related conditions.

According to a January 2008 report prepared by the National Association for Home Care & Hospice, at that time, approximately 7.6 million persons were receiving home care from 17,000 providers. The 2007 annual expenditures (the latest available) were projected to be $57.6 billion.

ORGANIZATION AND STRUCTURE

Home health care service is generally administered by a nurse or aide, and can include part time or intermittent skilled care, physical therapy, the administration of medicine, rehabilitation, durable medical equipment and supplies, home health aide services, family and patient education, and other services. Supported by technology, home care is considerably less expensive than institutional or hospital care. Home care agencies providing health care services fall into three main categories: private or proprietary, hospitals, and public or not for profit. Services are differentiated by the type and level of activity, such as home health aides, nursing care, and physical therapy. The home health care services industry is structured along the lines of prevention, diagnosis, infusion therapy, skilled and unskilled care, and durable medical equipment. The three largest of these segments are infusion therapy, skilled care, and durable medical equipment. Infusion therapy consists of intravenous products and services such as antibiotics and immunoglobulins. Skilled care includes nurses, home health aides, and therapists, all under the direction of a physician. Durable medical equipment includes ventilators, respirators, and wheelchairs.

If a person is homebound and requires skilled care, Medicare pays for medically necessary home health care, including part time or intermittent nursing care; physical, speech, and occupational therapy; medical social services; and equipment and supplies. For terminally ill patients, Medicare will pay for care provided by a Medicare-certified hospice where specialized care includes pain relief, symptom management, and supportive services in lieu of curative services.

To qualify for Medicare home health care, a patient's doctor must determine that medical care is needed in the home, that the care be intermittent, and that the patient must be homebound except for infrequent trips of short duration. Skilled nursing for wound care or injections, home health aides for personal care and physical assistance, physical, speech, and occupational therapy, and medical social services, supplies, and equipment are all included. A maximum of 28 hours per week, including a mix of all of the various providers, is allowed to qualify as part time care.

The Joint Commission on Accreditation of Healthcare Organizations serves as the accrediting body for home care agencies. Participation is voluntary, but agencies must still meet accepted industry standards. State and local governments also serve to regulate the industry.

Nearly every segment of home health care services is determined heavily by public policies and funding, and there is a growing need to reconcile the aging population with the call for reduced government expenditures. Some states are now imposing bans on new nursing home construction, which should channel more patients to home care.

BACKGROUND AND DEVELOPMENT

Beginning in 1965, the federal government funded Medicare for home health care services, structured primarily to cover short term services following hospital discharge. Since this home health coverage allowed health care organizations to shift some of the fixed hospital overhead to cost-based services, home health care services sprouted up in droves in the 1970s and 1980s. By 1994 it was the fastest growing segment of health care, and the second fastest growing segment of the economy at large. Contributing to this growth were new advances in medical

devices and high technology that made home care a viable alternative to institutional care. For example, respiratory patients who previously would have been hospitalized or nursing-home-bound were able to conduct normal working and living activities with the aid of portable oxygen systems. In addition, cancer patients, who were once confined to hospitals, could live at home and even return to work.

The industry's fortunes changed suddenly in 1997 as Medicare, mandated by the Balanced Budget Act, began implementing massive cuts in reimbursements to home health care companies. The federal agency planned to decrease home care spending by $16 billion over five years. Between 1989 and 1996, the number of beneficiaries receiving home health care and the number of visits per user more than doubled. In an effort to hold down costs, Medicare changed its payment system. Before October 1997, the agency reimbursed home care companies on a visit-by-visit basis with no limitations. The new system paid based on an average cost basis. Depending on the service, payment reductions to home care agencies ranged from 15 to 50 percent. The decreased payments devastated home health agencies, leaving the industry in a state of crisis. Critics argued that that method didn't adequately cover chronically ill patient care.

Home health care appeals to insurance companies. The Medicare cuts of 1997 created a market for supplemental home health care benefits in addition to, or coordinated with, long term care benefits. When the baby boom generation reached 50 years old, they began taking care of their parents and therefore were aware of the need for insurance to cover some of the cost. Few in that generation wished to move into nursing homes as they aged. They wanted to stay in their own homes as long as they could and use home care policies. Insurance companies moved into this niche market. Bankers Life and Casualty, along with long term care insurance companies, pursued the home health care segment of the market.

The Health Care Financing Administration (HCFA) noted that while the number of home health care providers receiving Medicare benefits jumped from 5,656 in 1990 to 10,500 in 1997, a significant proportion of that increase was attributed to wasteful practices and fraud, a factor that contributed heavily to the implementation of the Balanced Budget Act. In addition to the new Medicare fee restructuring, therefore, the HCFA took several steps to reduce Medicare and Medicaid fraud. In response to the increasing home health care share of Medicare expenditures, the HCFA worked to cut costs, implementing rulings establishing salary equivalency guidelines for physical, occupational, respiratory, and speech therapists providing home health services. These rulings were projected to save Medicare $1.7 billion from 1997 to 2001. The HCFA also proposed revisions to regulations that would require Medicare home health providers to conduct criminal background checks on home health aides.

Meanwhile, legislative help was on the way in the form of the Medicare Balanced Budget Refinement Act, which was signed into law in late 1999. Both houses of Congress and the White House even reached a tentative agreement in advance of the bill to pass reform legislation. The act restored about $1.3 billion in federal funding to home health care agencies. In addition, the further 15 percent Medicare payment reduction was delayed another year, scheduled to be enacted in October 2001.

Political wrangling and lobbying by industry leaders continued to delay the additional 15 percent Medicare payment reduction for home health care services. In fact, in June of 2002, the U.S. House of Representatives voted to repeal the scheduled cut, and as of 2003, the issue remained under debate in the U.S. Senate. Supporters of the 15 percent cut argued that the home health care industry, which operated with profit margins of 20 percent, according to the General Accounting Office, could easily withstand some belt-tightening. Opponents insisted that the industry, which had lost nearly 35 percent of its home health agencies since 1997, would be severely stressed by more cutbacks.

On July 31, 2001, the Health Care Financing Administration changed its name to the Centers for Medicare and Medicaid Services (CMMS). The CMMS spent the early years of the first decade of the 2000s shifting from open-ended reimbursement for home care agencies based on numbers—rather than the nature of the service—to a prospective payment system (PPS). The PPS plan set regional limits on reimbursement rates based on the cost history of providers in a given area. Thus, for more severe cases, the agency received greater set amounts for administration of care services to that patient. In this way, agencies had a precise idea of their incoming funding and could schedule costs accordingly, although it was not yet determined exactly how much money would be offered up front.

Under the prospective payment system (PPS), companies could no longer count on their home health programs to produce revenues, and as a result, the industry was expected to see a large-scale shakeout. Those companies opting to remain in the game could still use home health care as a way of reducing overall costs, and such services could still contribute to health care profitability, provided the services were effectively integrated into the organizations' cost-based hospital departments.

For those health care organizations that opted to get rid of their home health care operations, patients were left with severely restricted options. Most local home health operations shy away from patients requiring higher cost

and longer term care, and as a result, many such patients may simply wind up in long term care inside the organizations' hospitals, which would severely boost the organizations' costs and would defeat the purpose of divestiture.

The new PPS was first implemented nationwide in October 2000. Until then, agencies had been reimbursed on the interim payment system (IPS), which was a flat sum per patient and involved a yearly per-patient cap. One problem with the IPS was that that payment was not adjusted by the severity of the illness. If the cost of care went over the cap, the agency lost money. If the cost was under the cap, however, the agency did not get the difference. A number of analysts contended that the IPS policy was the primary reason many home health care agencies had failed. While the prospective payment system (PPS) was expected to force companies to make difficult decisions, it was largely seen as an improvement over the IPS, precisely because companies have a more specific idea of the kind of funding they can expect against a detailed indication of what kinds of costs they can expect to accrue.

Analysts argued that health care companies would be able to keep their home health care operations afloat if they streamlined their structures, instituted innovative programs, and in some cases merged with other agencies to create larger, more effective units. According to analysts, clinical programs must be adapted to serve the patients who have the greatest need for their services, and to deal with the most prevalent diseases in the areas they serve.

Legal Woes The home health care industry was rocked by a series of lawsuits and scandals in the late 1990s, and the industry was trying diligently to dust itself off in the early years of the new decade, but the damage to the industry's reputation and to its leading players was likely to be felt for some time.

Industry leader Apria Healthcare Group met with trouble in the late 1990s from the U.S. Attorney's office in Sacramento, California, which had filed a suit that stemmed from suspicions regarding Apria's Medicare and Medicaid billing practices. Though the government closed the case without taking action in summer 1999, Apria continued to face legal woes.

In 1997, federal officers raided the hospital facilities of Columbia/HCA (also known as HCA—The Healthcare Co.) in El Paso, Texas, seizing billing records and other documents on suspicion of fraudulent billing practices, including for home health care services. In the wake of this drama, the company was completely remade, highlighted by a boardroom coup that did away with the chairman and other chief company officers. The federal suit was settled in December 2000, when Columbia/HCA agreed to pay $840 million to the U.S. government. In the meantime, the company was forced to restructure entirely, selling off its home health care business. In June 2002, without making any arrests, the U.S. Justice Department announced the formal end of its criminal investigation of Columbia executives.

Tenet Healthcare Corp., a company that had exited the home health care sector in 1998, also found itself facing a fraudulent billing suit in the early year of the first decade of the 2000s. Tenet's 1995 acquisition of Palmetto General Hospital brought with it allegations that Palmetto had fraudulently billed Medicare between 1994 and 1997 via its home health agencies. In July of 2002, although Tenet denied any legal wrongdoing, it agreed to pay $29 million to settle the case.

CURRENT CONDITIONS

The U.S. home health care market was driven by an ever-expanding and aging population, a critical need for cost-effective solutions for servicing patients with long-term chronic conditions, and an increasing use of technology to meet the needs of those receiving home-based medical care. According to Medtech Insight's January 2009 report, *U.S. Markets for Home Health Care Products,* sales revenues for the major home health care product segments, including respiratory therapy products, durable medical equipment, wound care products, peritoneal dialysis, infusion therapy, and enteral nutrition delivery systems, were expected to grow at a combined compound annual rate (CAGR) of about 4.3 percent, reaching $5.2 billion in 2012.

Some interesting statistics were published in 2008 and 2009 from the National Association for Home Care & Hospice and the Hospice Association of America, respectively. In their published reports, the total national health care expenditures for 2008 were projected to be $2.38 trillion. The home health care segment of those expenditures was estimated to be $57.6 billion (2007). Medicare remained the highest single payer of home health care services, but home health benefits in 2007 represented only 3.6 percent of total Medicare spending. As of January 2008, there were 9,284 Medicare-certified home healthcare agencies and 3,346 Medicare-certified hospices (January 2009). Perhaps the most startling statistic in the NAHCH report was contained in Table 12: "Comparison of Hospital, SNF [skilled nursing facility], and Home Health Medicare Charges, 2005-2007." According to the Table, in 2007, a single day in hospital was charged at $5,765, while a single day in a SNF was charged at $544. A once-a-day home healthcare visit, conversely, was charged at $132 a day.

Opportunities In 2009, respiratory therapy products and services accounted for a very large segment of this market and were expected to continue to dominate going forward. This segment included mechanical ventilator systems, nebulizers, obstructive sleep apnea (OSA) therapy systems, and oxygen therapy systems, which together were expected to generate sales of nearly $1.8 billion in 2012. Within the respiratory segment, OSA represented the largest and fastest growing opportunity, with OSA therapy system sales expected to reach $988 million for 2009 and nearly $1.2 billion by 2012. According to the American Sleep Apnea Association, more than 12 million people in the United States suffer from sleep apnea and 10 million or more remain undiagnosed.

Another area of opportunity within the industry was the providing of of hospice services. The Hospice Association of America said in its September 2009 report that more than 80 percent of its payment sources comes from Medicare. In 2009, that was projected to represent $12.5 million, up from an estimated $11.4 million in 2008 according to CMMS. In addition, stock prices for hospice operations were rising at a noteworthy clip. Because of this trend, non-profit home care agencies, long term care facilities, and health care systems were expected to either establish hospice programs or expand existing hospice operations.

Technological Advancements The nature of home health care also was changing due to advancements in technology. Faced with a shortage of nurses and other health professionals, home care agencies were relying on technology that, while costly, allowed providers to care for patients more efficiently—especially those living in remote or rural areas. Examples include laptop computers that enable caregivers to enter data directly into electronic medical records, as well as the use of digital photography to send images of healing wounds to doctors for remote evaluation.

Analysts at Forrester Research expect the rise in home care, and the demands of independence-minded baby boomers, to fuel strong demand for providers of home networking services, high-tech medical devices, and remote health services. In fact, the market for this type of technology is projected to reach $34 billion by 2015.

In fact, there were several new technological developments in 2009, including The 3M Littman Electronic Stethoscope that uses Bluetooth technology to send sounds from the body to computer software where it can be analyzed, and Bayer AG's Contour USB monitor to check the blood glucose levels of diabetics while plugged directly into a personal computer.

Significant Challenges While the growing markets for home care and technological advancements were both promising developments, the industry faced significant challenges. These ranged from heightened competition and reimbursement cuts to skyrocketing gas prices and bad press from industry fraud. However, the most profound challenge of all was the Medicare Prescription Drug, Improvement and Modernization Act of 2003. When President George W. Bush signed this legislation in December of 2003, it set the stage for major changes within the home health care industry. Also known as the Medicare Modernization Act (MMA), this legislation included sweeping Medicare reimbursement changes for providers of home medical equipment, which represents a large share of business for many home care agencies.

Among the ways that the MMA impacted the home medical equipment (HME) industry were reimbursement cuts for durable medical equipment (DME) effective in January 2005. Cuts applied to manual and power wheelchairs, beds and air mattresses, nebulizers and oxygen, as well as diabetic lancets and test strips. In a November 1, 2004, article summarizing some of the MMA's effects, *Home Care Magazine* reported that cuts could range from 2 to 14 percent. In addition, payment for certain types of durable medical equipment, such as prosthetic devices, was frozen at 2003 levels until 2008.

The Medicare Modernization Act (MMA) also introduced the element of competitive bidding. The Centers for Medicare and Medicaid Services (CMMS) began a demonstration program using competitive bidding for clinical laboratory services in April 2007, with a second trial to begin one year later. As part of this program, suppliers bid competitively for contracts to provide durable medical equipment (DME) to Medicare beneficiaries in so-called "competitive acquisition areas." Although it is possible for multiple suppliers within a given area to win contracts, Medicare beneficiaries are only able to obtain DME from winning suppliers. This program was expected to expand to 80 metropolitan statistical areas (MSAs) in 2009, after which time it likely will be introduced to the rest of the nation. Excluded from the competitive bidding program were rural areas or those with low population densities. The MMA also authorized the CMMS to develop a pilot program that would use performance-based contracting to provide disease management services to those in the elderly, fee-for-service Medicare population, which was begun in 2005. The program focuses on those with diabetes and/or congestive heart failure, due to the fact that the former accounts for 32 percent of Medicare spending and the latter 43 percent.

One other result of the MMA was mandatory accreditation, whereby Medicare durable medical equipment (DME) suppliers are required to meet certain quality standards and obtain accreditation from one or more accrediting organizations designated by the Department of Health and Human Services (HHS). Under the act, HHS has up to one year after the introduction of the quality standards to name the accrediting bodies.

In conclusion, the Medicare Modernization Act (MMA) posed many significant challenges for the home care industry—namely those who rely on home medical equipment (HME) sales. More than 1 in 10 respondents to

Home Care Magazine's annual Forecast Survey, released in December 2004, indicated that the MMA would result in the closure or sale of their business sooner than expected. However, 75 percent of respondents indicated that they planned to remain in business through 2009, when the MMA is fully implemented. According to the forecast, HME providers planned to meet these challenges in a number of ways. Some planned to diversify their business in 2005 by moving away from Medicare and toward other payment sources, including retail. Providers also planned to increase the efficiency of their operations to cut costs. This included buying equipment directly from manufacturers instead of distributors, doing a better job of inventory control, offering new products, entering new markets, taking on more patients, and affiliating with hospitals and physicians.

INDUSTRY LEADERS

American HomePatient Inc., headquartered in Brentwood, Tennessee, reported sales of $328.1 million in 2006. Reeling from the Balanced Budget Act, the company froze its acquisitions schedule and trimmed its staff early in the first decade of the 2000s. In 2002 the company filed for Chapter 11 bankruptcy protection but emerged the following year. By 2009, American HomePatient had 270 branches in 34 states, with 2008 sales of $266.9 million.

The Lake Forest, California-based Apria Healthcare Group was one of the largest home health care companies in the United States. Services carried out through its more than 500 branches include home respiratory and infusion therapy and the rental and sale of home medical equipment. The company acquired 27 businesses in 2003, contributing to 12 percent annual growth within its respiratory care business. Apria planned to continue expanding its respiratory business, in spite of government funding cutbacks. The company also piloted a cash-and-carry durable medical equipment (DME) store in a Dallas area Wal-Mart, mirroring a move by other industry players. In 2008, after struggling with Medicare cuts, it agreed to go private with a $1.6 billion buyout from private equity leader Blackstone Group.

Lincare Holdings Inc. is an aggressive provider of oxygen and other respiratory services in the home. The company serves 625,000 patients through some 880 home care sites in 47 states, making it one of the largest respiratory services in the nation. The company also offers infusion therapy and sells and rents home medical equipment. In 1999, Lincare purchased the nursing firm Healthcor Holdings. As part of an ongoing expansion effort, the company expanded in 2003 by opening 85 new operating centers. In 2008, Lincare raked in $1.66 billion in sales and employed more than 8,300 workers.

With 3,479 employees, the Norcross, Georgia-based Pediatric Services of America Inc. (PSA) has found a niche in providing home pediatric nursing and therapy to medically fragile children, along with infusion therapy and other home services and equipment. PSA operates in 18 states and, since January 1997, has acquired more than 10 health care companies, including a New Jersey nursing company, a Florida pediatric company, a North Carolina home health agency, and an Illinois pharmacy. In 2006, PSA sold its respiratory therapy and equipment business to Lincare.

WORKFORCE

According to the U.S. Bureau of Labor Statistics, home health aides were listed among the fastest-growing occupations through 2014. As of 2006 there were approximately 867,100 persons employed as home health care workers. These included home care aides, registered nurses, LPNs, physical and occupational therapists, and social workers. Workers are usually paid minimum wage and generally visit two clients a day; however, they are not paid for commuting time while traveling to homes of clients. Largely due to such conditions, the industry was characterized by heavy personnel turnover, a factor that industry analysts warned could damage public perception of service quality.

The National Association for Health Care Recruitment, a 1,400-member organization, seeks to provide information, education, and networking for facility-based health care center recruiters and human resources professionals. Additionally, the Cooperative Home Care Associates assists home health aides in finding above-minimum-wage jobs.

RESEARCH AND TECHNOLOGY

With expenditures expected to continue their rise over the next several years, health care organizations were under increasing stress to effectively implement information technology strategies into their home health care operations. The Outcome and Assessment Information Set (OASIS) data collection requirements, sponsored by the HCFA, systematize the key data that factor into the assessment of home patient care and outcomes. Home health care agencies are required to report OASIS data to their state survey agencies, typically by electronic means. These requirements may in fact benefit the industry in ways that extend beyond basic accountability. As health care organizations assess the future of their home health care operations, such streamlined, automated data sets can be used to determine which aspects of those operations integrate on a cost and service level with their core operations.

Whereas the Internet provided a more efficient way to communicate between home health care patients and their providers, other technology benefited the home health care industry as well, including medical devices such as glucose readers, digital thermometers, stethoscopes, and videoconferencing tools. According to Parks Associates, the digital home health services market will grow to $2.1 billion in 2010, up from $461 million in 2005, and affect 64 million people. The main drivers of this growth will be in wellness monitoring services, e-mail and Internet messaging, and online consultation services. Other examples of the technology at use in the home health care environment are devices that let patients self-monitor weight, blood pressure, blood sugar, and oxygen and then send results via the Internet to their provider, and a wireless motion sensor system that tracks daily movements and notifies a caregiver via a computer of changes in routine movements.

BIBLIOGRAPHY

"A New Twist on Home Health Care." *EC&M Electrical Construction & Maintenance,* 1 September 2006.

"Baby Boomers to Boost Home Care." *Health Management Technology,* August 2004.

"Basic Statistics about Home Care." National Association for Home Care & Hospice. 2004. Available from http://www.nahc.org/NAHC/Research/research.html.

"Blame It on MMA." *Home Care Magazine,* 1 December 2004.

"CMS Approves DME Accreditors." *Home Care Magazine,* 1 January 2007.

Craver, Martha Lynn. "Home Health Care Poised to Grow Despite Obstacles." *Kiplinger Business Forecasts,* 20 January 2005.

"Health Care Costs Expected to Grow Faster than Economy." *Chain Drug Review,* 1 May 2006.

Helman, Christopher. "Breathe Easier." *Forbes,* 14 April 2003.

"Home Care Industry Prepares for Power Shift in Congress." *Home Care Magazine,* 1 December 2006.

Hospice Association of America. "Hospice Facts and Statistics." September 2009. Available from http://www.nahc.org/facts/HospiceStats09.pdf.

"Hospice Companies Benefit from Favorable Medicare Rates." *Health Care Strategic Management,* January 2004.

"Industry In Focus: US Home Health Care Revenues Set to Exceed $5 Billion by 2012." *MedTech Insight,* August/September 2009.

"Machines to the Rescue." *Crain's New York Business,* 21 August 2006.

"The Market Is Out There." *Home Care Magazine,* 1 April 2004.

National Assn for Home Care & Hospice. "Basic Statistics About Home Care." Updated 2008. Available from http://www.nahc.org/facts/08HC_Stats.pdf.

Ulman, Kurt. "Medicare Dives into Disease Management: Pilot Program Coordinates Care of Diabetes, Other Chronic Illnesses." *DOC News,* September 2006.

U.S. Department of Labor. Bureau of Labor Statistics. *Occupational Outlook Handbook,* May 2008. Available from http://www.bls.gov/.

Waters, Robert J. "The Outlook for CMS Competitive Bidding: Part II." *Medical Laboratory Observer,* October 2006.

Weeks, Wallace. "Preparing for MMA." *Home Care Magazine,* 1 November 2004.

Welbel, Jenny. "Productive Aging: As the American Population Continues to Get Older, Home Health Care Manufacturers Focus in on These Aging Consumers and Achieve Great Success." *Private Label Buyer,* October 2006.

HOME MEDICAL EQUIPMENT

———— ◼ ————

SIC CODE(S)

3841

3842

7352

8082

INDUSTRY SNAPSHOT

The medical device industry is by far the most diverse segment of the larger health care industry. Its product categories number in the hundreds of thousands, ranging from the most basic items such as thermometers and crutches to highly advanced life support equipment used by hospitals. The medical device industry is expected to grow as the U.S. population continues to age.

Medical devices marketed to consumers for their personal/in-home use was a growing category. Historically, a sizable share of home medical equipment (HME) has been provided to consumers via home health care agencies that also provide related health care services such as skilled nursing care, respiratory and physical therapy, and intravenous infusion services.

A number of trends fueled growth within the HME industry. Leading the list was the graying of 77 million baby boomers. According to *Home Care Magazine,* during the first decade of the twenty-first century, some 24 million baby boomers had reached age 50. After the first members of this generation reach age 65 in 2011, those over age 65 will continue to represent a larger share of the overall population. By 2020, more than 54 million people in the United States will be over age 65. In fact, by 2030, members of the 66 to 84 age bracket will constitute an estimated 20 percent of the U.S. population.

In addition to a larger number of older citizens, people also were living longer due to advancements in medicine and public health. Coupled with this trend was an increased incidence of chronic diseases and other age-related conditions, including heart disease, diabetes, Alzheimer's disease, and arthritis.

Another industry growth factor was simply the rise in home health care, as more people received medical treatment outside of hospitals and other institutions. This rise in home care, coupled with general technological advancement, has led to an increasingly sophisticated array of medical devices intended for personal use. This spells opportunity for companies marketing devices directly to consumers.

The industry faced numerous challenges as producers were confronted with increased regulatory requirements and proposed budgetary cuts to Medicare, which would significantly alter the makeup of the industry. Home medical equipment and care was already the most cost-effective, slowest-growing portion of Medicare spending, increasing only 0.75 percent per year according to the most recent National Health Expenditures data. That compared to more than 6 percent annual growth for Medicare spending overall. Home medical equipment represented only 1.6 percent of the Medicare budget in 2009. Under President Bush's Medicare Modernization Act (MMA), the home medical equipment sector was subjected to a 9.5 percent reimbursement cut that took effect on January 1, 2009.

ORGANIZATION AND STRUCTURE

Because medical device manufacturers market their products to hospitals and integrated health care systems, which often own home health care agencies, and to retailers and

451

individuals, it is difficult to provide an exact overview of the home medical equipment industry. According to First Research Inc., in its September 2009 report, the overall U.S. medical supplies and devices manufacturing industry included about 12,000 companies with combined annual revenue of $78 billion. Major companies include Baxter, Boston Scientific, Johnson & Johnson, and Medtronic.

Significant barriers to entry exist in the medical device industry, since companies must fund significant research and development programs, overcome regulatory hurdles related to product safety, contend with liability issues, and fight patent-related legal battles with other industry players. Regulatory compliance issues alone can be significant within this industry. Examples of legislation that has affected the manufacture of medical devices include the Federal Food, Drug, and Cosmetic Act of 1938; the Medical Device Amendments of 1976; the Safe Medical Device Act of 1990; the FDA Modernization Act of 1997; and the Medical Device User Fee and Modernization Act of 2002.

Sales Channels Unlike medical devices that are marketed directly to hospitals, clinics, and other health care providers, the home medical equipment (HME) industry has a strong consumer focus. Industry players market their wares via health care providers who deliver related care, but have increasingly employed a direct to consumer (DTC) approach.

In the August 2003 issue of *MX,* Mal Mixon, chairman and CEO of home medical equipment distributor and manufacturer Invacare Corp., commented, "A company is not going to increase the number of heart valves sold by marketing them on TV. But our products clearly are different from certain medical devices—more like pharmaceuticals—in that they enable people to do things that they want to do and otherwise couldn't. They may not know a product exists to help them do it, or may not realize that it is an item that they could get reimbursement for if they have a certain medical condition and their physician writes a prescription for the product. So there is tremendous education that can go on in this field."

Historically, home health care providers have been a key HME sales channel. However, traditional channel lines were beginning to blur as companies that once sold products exclusively via caregivers began engaging in direct to consumer (DTC) advertising, including print and television advertising, Internet promotion, and even county fair exhibits. In February 2004, the Food and Drug Administration issued draft guidance for medical device manufacturers wishing to market certain restricted devices to consumers via traditional marketing channels. Once approved, the guidance would allow a greater level of manufacturer-sponsored advertising, similar to that found within the pharmaceutical industry.

While manufacturers' direct to consumer (DTC) advertising was of concern to many traditional HME providers, namely home health care agencies, some felt that it actually helped their business. They argued that consumers who are reluctant to order via telephone or the Internet instead ask their home care providers about products they have seen advertised. In any case, it was clear that medical device companies were stepping up their efforts to directly reach a burgeoning consumer market for home medical equipment (HME).

On the retail front, leading drug stores also were increasing their efforts to market medical devices, namely durable medical equipment (DME), to consumers. Walgreen's was a prime example of this approach. In addition to selling DME items via its retail stores, Walgreen's was a leading player in the home care market via its Walgreen's Health Initiatives service, which included medical equipment, as well as home care services such as respiratory therapy and home infusion.

End Users Individuals with health problems, and the people who care for them outside of medical settings, are the obvious end markets for HME. However, the industry serves a number of key target groups. These include disabled individuals, but also those with chronic health conditions. As the population ages, the incidence of chronic health conditions—which often lead to secondary medical problems—is expected to rise. A number of chronic medical conditions were especially prevalent, including heart disease, osteoarthritis, diabetes, and chronic obstructive pulmonary disease (COPD). Other prevalent conditions included sleep apnea, obesity, and Alzheimer's disease.

The medical device industry was poised to benefit from the aging baby boom generation. Industry observers have noted that members of this generation are less willing to accept being homebound, thereby fueling demand for new products that increase mobility and lessen the lifestyle impact associated with certain medical conditions. In many cases, this means increased demand for products that are not medically necessary, but which provide added comfort or convenience. Manufacturers were encouraged by the significant amount of discretionary income baby boomers had at their disposal to purchase these types of products.

While baby boomers spelled opportunity for the industry, it was clear that this generation would have high expectations in regard to quality and product innovation. Members of this demographic group were well informed about diseases, symptoms, and treatments, thanks to the Internet, increased coverage of health issues by the press, and rising levels of direct advertising on the part of drug companies and medical equipment manufacturers. In addition, they were well versed in various forms of technology, including cell phones, home computer networks, and handheld computing devices. These trends paved the way for a new generation of home medical equipment (HME) products that were stylish, convenient, and cutting-edge.

Another lucrative industry category was over-the-counter (OTC) diagnostics, which includes such devices as blood glucose monitors. According to the January 24, 2005 issue of *MMR,* the research firm Kalorama Information indicated that this category was valued at $1.53 billion in 2003, following a period of 9.8 percent annual growth since 1999. Blood glucose monitors were the leading device type, with sales of $518 million. By 2008, OTC diagnostic device sales were reaching $2.4 billion.

Product Segments Citigroup Smith Barney sub-categorizes the home medical equipment (HME) industry into three segments: durable medical equipment (DME), home infusion equipment, and home respiratory equipment.

Durable medical equipment (DME) is intended for repeated use in the home by individuals with an illness or injury. It is not intended to be used merely as a comfort or convenience, and usually requires a physician's prescription. DME includes traditional devices such as walkers, crutches, canes, traction equipment, beds, bedpans, special toilet seats, lifts, cushions, pads, scooters, and wheelchairs. This category also includes more complex devices such as kidney machines, ventilators, home dialysis systems, blood pressure monitors, and insulin pumps. Also included are various forms of oxygen equipment such as concentrators, tank systems, and liquid oxygen for patients with chronic lung problems or congestive heart failure. This segment represented about 23 percent of industry sales ($6 billion), according to Citigroup Smith Barney.

DME equipment use varies among patients with different conditions. For example, diabetic patients require devices such as blood glucose monitors and insulin pumps. Patients with cardiac disease often require devices to monitor their blood pressure. Individuals suffering from Alzheimer's may need special equipment to avoid injury in the home, such as locks, barriers, alarms, grab bars, cushions, and pads. Severely obese individuals rely on special walkers that are equipped with seats and oxygen tank holders, as well as special mechanical lifts and mobility products like scooters.

Home infusion equipment includes devices such as feeding pumps and intravenous (IV) infusion pumps. At $5 billion, this segment was responsible for 38.5 percent of industry sales. The home respiratory segment, which includes equipment needed for the administration of breathing treatments, accounted for the remaining 38.5 percent of industry sales ($5 billion).

Industry Associations The Washington, D.C.-based Health Industry Manufacturers Association (HIMA) includes more than 800 manufacturers of medical devices, medical information systems, and diagnostic products among its members. According to HIMA, its members "manufacture nearly 90 percent of the $69 billion [of the] health care technology products purchased annually in the United States, and nearly 50 percent of the $147 billion purchased annually around the world."

Based in Alexandria, Virginia, the American Association for Homecare (AAH) was an industry trade group representing all elements of home health care services, including providers of HME, infusion and respiratory therapy, telemedicine, and rehab/assistive technology. The association was formed in 2000, when the National Association for Medical Equipment Services combined with the Health Industry Distributors Association, the Home Care Market Group, and the Home Health Services and Staffing Association. The American Homecare Association also became part of AAH in December 2001. With 3,000 members and an annual budget of $2.7 million, the AAH includes committees dedicated to a number of industry issues including education, regulatory affairs, ethics, and legislative policy, as well as a special technology task force.

BACKGROUND AND DEVELOPMENT

When President George W. Bush signed the Medicare Prescription Drug, Improvement and Modernization Act of 2003 in December 2003, it set the stage for major changes within the home health care industry. Also known as the Medicare Modernization Act (MMA), this legislation included sweeping changes for providers of HME who relied on Medicare reimbursements..

Among the ways that the MMA impacted the HME industry were reimbursement cuts for durable medical equipment (DME) effective in January 2005. Cuts applied to manual and power wheelchairs, beds and air mattresses, nebulizers and oxygen, as well as diabetic lancets and test strips. In a November 1, 2004, article summarizing some of the MMA's effects, *Home Care Magazine* reported that cuts could range from 2 to14 percent. In addition, payment for certain types of DME, such as prosthetic devices, was frozen at 2003 levels until 2008.

The MMA also introduced the element of competitive bidding. Beginning in 2007, a competitive acquisition program was slated for introduction in 10 metropolitan statistical areas (MSAs). As part of this program, suppliers will bid competitively for contracts to provide durable medical equipment (DME) to Medicare beneficiaries in so-called "competitive acquisition areas." Although it was possible for multiple suppliers within a given area to win contracts, Medicare beneficiaries would only be able to obtain DME from winning suppliers. This program was expected to expand to 80 metropolitan areas in 2009, after which time it would be introduced to the rest of the nation. Excluded from the competitive bidding program were rural areas or those with low population densities.

One other result of the Medicare Modernization Act (MMA) was mandatory accreditation, whereby Medicare durable medical equipment (DME) suppliers will be required to meet certain quality standards and obtain accreditation from one or more accrediting organizations designated by the U.S. Department of Health and Human Services (HHS). Under the Act, HHS had up to one year after the introduction of the quality standards to name the accrediting bodies.

Similar accreditation and licensure requirements were being implemented or pursued at the state level during the middle of the first decade of the 2000s. For example, in June 2004, Ohio Governor Bob Taft signed legislation that required all home medical equipment (HME) providers to obtain a state license. In Florida, where Medicare fraud had been an ongoing problem, a bill was introduced in January 2005 that would require all HME providers to become accredited in order to maintain state licenses.

In conclusion, the Medicare Modernization Act (MMA) posed many significant challenges for the home medical equipment (HME) industry. More than one in ten respondents to *Home Care Magazine's* annual Forecast Survey, released in December 2004, indicated that the MMA would result in the closure or sale of their business sooner than expected. However, 75 percent of respondents indicated that they planned to remain in business through 2009, when the MMA is to be fully implemented.

CURRENT CONDITIONS

Indeed, 2008 and 2009 were years of adjustment as two major pieces of legislation served to affect the industry. On January 1, 2009, two new policies, in the form of a 36-month cap on payments for home oxygen therapy and a 9.5 percent across-the-board payment cut (for the home medical equipment sector) took effect (pursuant to the above MMA). Industry protest was pronounced. In August 2009, *Forbes* revealed the high stakes associated with lobbying in Washington with its article, "Medtronic Spends $1 Million Lobbying Congress In Second Quarter." Other publications revealed similar lobbying efforts by many other medical device providers. The efforts were primarily focused to block a requirement for comparison tests with other devices. Medtronics also lobbied against efforts to change the law to allow personal injury lawsuits against device makers.

Another issue before Congress was a proposed total tax to the device industry of $20 billion over 10 years to help cover health care reform spending, but the final structure of the tax and how it would be allocated remained pending as of November 2009. The Senate released its consolidated health care reform package on November 18, which included not only a fee targeting the device industry as a whole, but also a new tax in the form of a 5 percent-per-procedure levy on elective cosmetic procedures. In any event, the tax, proposed for a spread of $2 billion per year over 10 years, was half of the previous amount ($40 billion) approved by the Senate Finance Committee a month prior.

One of the biggest opportunities in 2009 for the industry was in continuous glucose monitoring (CGM). As of June 2009, Medtronic held about 90 percent of the CGM market (in which DexCom Inc. and Abbott also operate) with just over $100 million in sales. However, that represented only a tiny fraction of a blood glucose monitoring market, estimated as worth almost $3 billion in 2008 and forecast to grow to nearly $4 billion by 2013, according to *U.S. Markets for Diabetes Management Products,* a report published in May 2009 by the Medtech Insight division of Elsevier Business Intelligence. This new market faced some reimbursement problems, but that was expected to dissipate with more widespread use and popularity.

According to Mary Stuart in her August 2009 article for *Start Up* magazine, several small companies were targeting continuous glucose monitoring (CGM), including OrSense Ltd., with its non-invasive OrSense NBM-200G that used occlusion spectroscopy to measure analytes in blood from a finger cuff. Echo Therapeutics, Inc. had a needle-free wireless device called the Symphony Transdermal CGM system, using ultrasonic permeation technology to create reversible channels in the skin. Echo was in clinical trials and hopes to file a PMA within 24 months (2011).

INDUSTRY LEADERS

In industry news, Stryker announced in late November 2009 that it planned to acquire Ascent Healthcare Solutions for $525 million. Ascent, which was privately held, led the market in recycling (reprocessing and remanufacturing) medical devices. Ascent was formed in 2005 with the merger of Vanguard Medical Concepts and Alliance Medical.

Lake Forest, California-based Apria Health care Group had more than 10,500 employees and provided home care services to almost 500 locations across the United States. It was one of the largest national home health care service providers in the U.S. Services included home respiratory and infusion therapy and the rental and sale of home medical equipment (HME). The firm agreed to pay the government $1.7 million to settle a claim filed in 1995 charging that it improperly paid physicians for patient referrals. The company acquired 27 businesses in 2003, contributing to 12 percent annual growth within its respiratory care business. The company also piloted a cash-and-carry durable medical equipment (DME) store in a Dallas area Wal-Mart, mirroring a move by other industry players. In 2008, after struggling with Medicare cuts, it agreed to go private with a $1.6 billion buyout from private equity leader Blackstone Group.

Lincare Holdings Inc. is an aggressive provider of oxygen and other respiratory services in the home. The company serves 700,000 patients through some 880 home care sites in 48 states, making it one of the largest respiratory services in the nation. Lincare also offers infusion therapy, and sells and rents home medical equipment (HME).

Elyria, Ohio-based Invacare continued to be a leading home medical equipment (HME) manufacturer and distributor. The company claimed to offer the broadest product offering in the world to some 15,000 independent HME providers. In addition to its Ohio headquarters, the company had manufacturing plants in the United States and several countries. Invacare's product offerings focus on non-acute care and include manual and power wheelchairs (including custom chairs and high-performance chairs used for sports and recreation), as well as scooters, mobility aids, bath safety products, patient transport equipment, home care beds, oxygen concentrators, nebulizer compressors, portable oxygen systems, and more. Invacare reported revenues of $1.75 billion for fiscal year 2008.

Based in Northridge, California, Medtronic MiniMed Inc. is a subsidiary of Medtronic focusing on products used to treat and manage diabetes, including glucose monitors and insulin pumps. Founded in 1983, Minimed Inc. went public in July 1995 and assumed its current name in December of 2002, when it was acquired by Medtronic and combined with its Medical Research Group.

The home medical equipment (HME) industry also was home to numerous specialty manufacturers. For example, Archbol, Ohio-based Gendron Inc. designed, developed, and manufactured patient care products for the obesity or bariatric market. These products included shower chairs, bath safety products, a variety of bariatric stretchers, patient beds and scale beds, lift and transfer products, and custom tilt-and-recline power wheelchairs.

RESEARCH AND TECHNOLOGY

Invention and innovation are at the heart of developing and improving medical devices. According to the Health Industry Manufacturers Association (HIMA), the medical device industry is a leader in the area of research and development. In fact, the HIMA reports that in the United States, research and development (R&D) investments by

medical technology companies outpace that of the aerospace and telecommunications industries.

In August 2009, 3M Health Care and Zargis Medical unveiled The 3M Littman Electronic Stethoscope that uses Bluetooth technology to send sounds from the body to computer software where it can be analyzed. Initial applications were expected to include enabling health-care providers to confirm the diagnoses of clinicians, as well as to aid in gathering a second opinion on diagnoses.

One month later, in September 2009, Bayer AG's Diabetes Care Unit announced that it had received FDA clearance for its Contour USB monitor to check the blood glucose levels of diabetics while plugged directly into a personal computer. It is designed to provide instant access to information to help patients manage their diabetes. Bayer expected to begin selling them within months.

In an unrelated but similar development, Steven Kelly, a diabetic student at Creighton University, invented a iPhone-based device to watch blood-sugar levels for Type 2 diabetics, which could also work with iPod. In November 2009, Kelly announced that Johnson & Johnson was being targeted as the likely company to license his invention. Kelly saw his iDrop glucose reader, marketable for $62.50, as a good match with Johnson & Johnson and its application for both devices that would correlate with his invention.

BIBLIOGRAPHY

"3M Releases Stethoscope With Bluetooth Capability." *Minneapolis St. Paul Business Journal,* 19 August 2009.

"All About Diabetes." American Diabetes Association, 29 March 2007. Available from http://www. diabetes.org/about-diabetes.jsp.

"Alzheimer's Disease Facts and Figures 2007." Alzheimer's Association, 29 March 2007. Available from http://www.alz.org.

Babyak, Richard J. "Fighting Unhealthy Design." *Appliance Manufacturer,* July 2004.

"Bayer Gets FDA Approval For Diabetes Monitor That Plugs Into PC." *Medical Devices Today,* 24 September 2009.

"Blame It on MMA." *Home Care Magazine,* 1 December 2004.

"Breaking into the US Market: Taking a New Medical Device to the US Market Place Can Be Challenging, but the Rewards Can Be Great If Appropriate Strategic Planning Is Applied." *Medical Device Technology,* July-August 2004.

"Electromedical and Electrotherapeutic Apparatus Manufacturing: 2002." *2002 Economic Census.* U.S. Census Bureau, December 2004. Available from http://www.census.gov/prod/ec02/ec0231i334510.pdf.

"Facts about Arthritis." Arthritis Foundation, 29 March 2007. Available from http://www.arthritis.org/resources/gettingstarted/default.asp.

"FDA Wants Reform of Medical Device Ads." *Broadcasting & Cable,* 16 February 2004.

Filmore, David. "Health Reform Taxes: Senate Reduces Device Fee, Adds Cosmetic Surgery Tax." Reprinted from "The Gray Sheet," *Medical Devices Today,* 23 November 2009.

First Research, Inc. *Medical Supplies and Devices,* 21 September 2009.

"Florida HME Accreditation Bill Introduced." *Home Care Magazine*, 1 February 2005.

Grilliot, Rebecca. "Growing Expectations (bariatrics products)." *Home Care Magazine*, 1 January 2005.

Gundersen, J. "Trowbridge Brings His 'Wisdom' to RDI." *HME News*, August 2004. Available from http://www.hmenews.com/2004.08/depts/news/topstory3.htm.

Halasey, Steve. "Looking Ahead to Golden Years." *MX*, July/August 2003. Available from http://www.devicelink.com.

"Health Care: Products & Supplies." *Standard & Poor's Industry Surveys*, New York: The McGraw-Hill Companies Inc., 23 September 2004.

Heart Disease and Stroke Statistics—2007 Update. American Heart Association, 2007. Available from http://www.americanheart.org.

"The Health Industry Manufacturers Association (HIMA) and Its Members." The Health Industry Manufacturers Association, 29 March 2007. Available from http://www.advamed.org/publicdocs/whoarewe.html.

Heiner, Christine, and Paula Stankovic. "Decade of Excellence: With the Creation of the Human Engineering Research Laboratories, the Science of Wheelchairs Was Never the Same Again—and for the People Who Use Them, a Bright Future Began to Dawn." *Paraplegia News*, December 2004.

Heston, Tim. "HME Issues Scorecard." *Home Care Magazine*, 1 November 2004.

"HME Mergers and Acquisitions Down." *Home Care Magazine*, 29 January 2007. Available from http://www.homecaremag.com.

"HME Providers Move into Wal-Mart." *Home Care Magazine*, 1 April 2004.

"Home Care Groups Bash Bush 2008 Budget Proposal." *Home Care Magazine*, 1 March 2007.

"Home Medical Equipment Industry." *Equity Research: United States, Small/Mid Cap Health Care Services*, Citigroup Smith Barney, 13 April 2004.

"Home Tests Way of Life for Many." *MMR*, 24 January 2005.

Hopkins, Susanne. "Power Play (wheelchair market)." *Home Care Magazine*, 1 May 2004.

"Industry Dodges Bullet During Lame-Duck Congress." *Home Care Magazine*, 11 December 2006. Available from http://www.homecaremag.com.

"Industry Statistics Sampler: NAICS 339113, Surgical Appliance and Supplies Manufacturing." *2002 Economic Census Industry Series Report*. U.S. Census Bureau, 20 March 2005. Available from http://www.census.gov/epcd/ec97/industry/E339113.HTM.

"Information about Sleep Apnea." Washington, DC: American Sleep Apnea Association. 20 March 2005. Available from http://www.sleepapnea.org/geninfo.html.

Jancin, Bruce. "Advances in Insulin Pump Therapy Are on the Horizon." *Internal Medicine News*, 1 January 2005.

"Lincare Posts Profit Gain." *Tampa Bay Business Journal*, 9 February 2009.

"The Market Is Out There." *Home Care Magazine*, 1 April 2004.

———. "Moving Forward and Making Sense (Chronic Obstructive Pulmonary Disease)." *Home Care Magazine*, 1 January 2004.

McClinton, Denise H. "Cents & Sensitivity." *Home Care Magazine*, 1 March 2005. Available from http://homecaremag.com/mag/medical_cents_sensitivity/.

———. "An Overnight Success. Obstructive Sleep Apnea Continues to Rise, Making This a Lucrative, Yet Challenging, Opportunity for the Home Medical Equipment Industry." *Home Care Magazine*, 1 March 2004.

"Medical Device TV Commercials Coming Soon." *Biomedical Safety & Standards*, 1 April 2004.

"Medical Industry Outlook 2005." U.S. Census Bureau. Available from http://www.census.gov.

"Medicare Modernization Act (MMA) of 2003: Payment for DME and Competitive Acquisition of Items & Services." National Association of Chain Drug Stores, October 2004.

"Medtronic Spent Over $1 Million Lobbying Government In 2nd Quarter" *Forbes*, 17 August 2009.

"NOW SHOWING Facts & Figures." *Home Care Magazine*, 1 July 2004.

"Obesity in the U.S." American Obesity Association. Available from http://www.obesity.org/subs/fastfacts/obesity_US.shtml.

"Ohio Passes HME Licensure Law." *Home Care Magazine*, 1 July 2004.

"Oxygen Reform Plan Moves Ahead with 'Provider' Change Intact." *Home Care*, 13 April 2009. Also available at http://homecaremag.com/oxygen/aahomecare-15-point-oxygen-reform-plan-20090413/.

Patch, Paula. "Beyond the Test Strip. A Look on the Diabetes Therapy Equipment Industry Forecasts." *Home Care Magazine*, 1 March 2004.

"Patients See Medicare Home Oxygen Cuts for 2009." *EMS Responder*, Available from http://www.emsresponder.com/web/online/Top-EMS-News/Patients-See-Medicare-Home-Oxygen-Cuts-for-2009.

Peisner, Lynn. "A Fair Deal." *Home Care Magazine*, 1 October 2004.

"Providers Look to Build Sales in HME Retail." *Home Care Magazine*, 26 March 2007.

"Stryker To Buy Ascent Healthcare For $525 Million." *Wall Street Journal*, 30 November 2009.

Stuart, Mary. "Opportunity for Start-Ups in Continuous Glucose Monitoring ." *Start Up*, August/September 2009.

"Students Have The Touch For Business Success." *Omaha Herald*, 21 November 2009.

U.S. Department of Health and Human Services, Food and Drug Administration. *Draft Guidance for Industry and FDA Consumer-Directed Broadcast Advertising of Restricted Devices.*, Center for Devices and Radiological Health Office of Compliance, 10 February 2004. Available from http://www.fda.gov/cdrh/comp/guidance/1513.pdf.

"VC Firms Invested $6.33 Billion in Health Industries in 2004." *Diagnostics & Imaging*, 3 February 2005.

Verespej, Mike. "Decrepit Populace Keeping Health Care Fit." *Plastics News*, 8 January 2007.

"Vladeck Predicts HME Markets will Double by 2020." *Home Care Magazine*, 1 April 2004.

Weeks, Wallace. "Preparing for MMA." *Home Care Magazine*, 1 November 2004.

White, Jennifer. "Try This at Home; More High-Tech Medical Equipment Is on the Market, but Some Wellness Wanes." *HFN , The Weekly Newspaper for the Home Furnishing Network*, 7 February 2005.

Williams, David T. "HME at Your Service." *Home Care Magazine*, 1 October 2004.

HOME NETWORKING EQUIPMENT

SIC CODE(S)

3577

3663

INDUSTRY SNAPSHOT

In the digitized twenty-first century, U.S. households are placing a premium on connectivity. Home networking equipment as a result emerged out of the "someday" mindset and into the mainstream. Home networking electronically links devices throughout the home in an integrated, seamless network. Networked computers share peripherals, file storage, and Internet connections over a single system. As home offices flourished and the Internet became increasingly central to daily activities, from news to research to shopping to communication, home networks began to fill households at a rapid pace. Many households today enjoy broadband Internet connection, used not only for e-mail and browsing, but also to stream music and video, play online games and/or make voice calls using a VoIP (Voice over Internet Protocol) service. They also may have several PCs on a home network, as well as some combination of a gaming console like the Xbox 360, an iPhone or other handheld device, a streaming music player such as the Squeezebox or a streaming video player such as the Roku. While some of these devices may have a wired connection to a network router, most tap in wirelessly.

Most of the biggest names in computers, electronics, and communications have thrown themselves full force into the home networking arena and some currently reside atop the home networking equipment industry's list of leading companies. As a result, products in virtually all high-tech home consumer product categories will be manufactured with the integrated home network in mind.

In the long run, visionaries see home networking equipment leading to the advent of smart homes in which appliances will speak to each other to generate maximum household efficiency and even talk to the household's members, sensing their presence to optimize lighting and upgrade home security. Eventually, analysts claim, personal computers (PCs), stereos, telephones, digital video recorders, and even refrigerators will be in constant communication with each other.

ORGANIZATION AND STRUCTURE

At its most basic (and, with current technology, practical), home networking is simply the connection of multiple computers to a central workstation that includes everything from a printer, fax machine, scanner, server, and so on, all connected to the Internet. Networks are activated by plugging an interface card into a computer and then connecting the system's requisite power source, as in plugging into a phone jack. Since most home networks utilize existing infrastructures, they can be quite simple to set up. Still, a variety of configurations exist. Choosing the appropriate systems for one's home poses a great many challenges, depending on the household's current equipment and the users' specific needs. This is further exacerbated by the uncertainty over developing standards.

The most common home networking method involved channeling data signals through the home's existing phone lines, typically resulting in data transmission speeds of one megabit per second (Mbps). Since speed was a primary concern, companies worked fast at trying to outdo one another in this area. The phone line network configuration, however, suffered from the limitation of

457

phone jack locations throughout the house, and the quality of phone line data transmission could be highly erratic.

Home networks could also be installed by routing signals through the house's existing electrical wiring. While this makes for easy adaptation to the infrastructure, the electrical wiring method was sometimes problematic due to signal interference from large electrical appliances, limiting data speeds to only about 400 kilobits per second (Kbps).

A more recent network method involves wireless communication of networked appliances over radio frequencies. Not surprisingly, wireless systems find their greatest utility in households relying extensively on battery-powered notebook computers and handheld electronic devices. The data transmission speed is typically on par with phone line systems. The most prohibitive drawback for wireless systems thus far is the high cost necessitated by the sophisticated transmission system, which can rise to about twice those of phone line networks.

Another configuration is the Ethernet local area network protocol, which offers speeds of 10 to 100 megabits per second (Mbps) and exceptionally clear signals. Ethernet, however, requires some infrastructure alterations in the form of new wiring between each network node, which can prove prohibitive to most potentially networked households.

BACKGROUND AND DEVELOPMENT

Perhaps the earliest home networks were the intercom systems of the early 1900s, developing eventually into the novelty of centrally controlled, distributed systems of the 1950s that handled light, climate, and audio and video appliances. However, the modern home network featuring the transmission of digital information between household locations did not emerge until the massive influx of PCs into the mainstream household in the 1980s. A handful of companies at that time developed central security systems and electronics controls within reach of only the extremely wealthy. However, such systems were generally clunky and communicated awkwardly with the components since the various technologies were nowhere near a universal communication standard. At that time, the emphasis lay more on home automation than home networking as it is conceptualized today. By the mid-1990s, however, home offices and Internet connections fueled the transformation of the industry into a viable and mass-marketable commodity.

Like many emerging high-tech industries, home networking equipment evolved rapidly. Whereas in the late 1990s it seemed that power line networks were poised to rise to market dominance, by 2000, several formats offered a host of advantages and disadvantages and there were no set criteria by which a broad market could base a sound decision. Moreover, since nearly all major electronics manufacturers maintained some kind of commitment to home networking, a number of competing standards developed that threatened to contain its potentially explosive emergence into the mainstream consumer market.

Phone wire networking teetered between two competing standards. The Home Phone Networking Standards Association (HomePNA) standard used a device that plugged into a phone jack and transmitted information to all connected home phone lines. Developed by Tut Systems, the HomePNA standard was modeled on the digital subscriber line (DSL) and was endorsed by such leading firms as Intel, 3Com, Compaq, and Hewlett-Packard. The MediaWire standard, created by Avio Digital, required additional wiring but featured data speeds up to 100 Mpbs and its own application interfaces. Although Microsoft cofounder Paul Allen invested in Avio, MediaWire's standard enjoyed only limited support throughout the industry. The increasingly common USB ports installed on PCs had their own standard, but as of 2000 it was not widely supported by other electronic devices except for cable modems. Wireless home networking enjoyed a fairly stable and widely supported standard in Home RF, which utilized an Ethernet-based protocol developed by Proxim Inc. Its most recent incarnation, however, failed to provide for broad multimedia support. Such confusion was expected to maintain many consumers' ambivalence about diving into home networking until a clear, lasting standard was accepted. Microsoft's release in 2000 of Windows XP, considered by many the first operating system designed to support a home network, eased some concerns regarding home networks.

With 23 percent of all multiple-PC homes having broadband access in 2002, the home networking industry appeared to be on the brink of explosive growth. According to a 2003 Industry White Paper published by Motive Communications Inc., "Home networking products and services are on track to gain mass market acceptance during the next several years." While the "smart home" dream remains vivid in the minds of developers, most networking, at least in the short term, will likely center around PCs and home entertainment devices. The steamrolling proliferation of the Internet may prove to be just what this long-heralded "industry of the future" needs to finally become the industry of the moment. While industry observers have long held that home automation would propel home networking into the mainstream, it is the desire for perpetual Internet connectivity, the preponderance of information and commerce on the Web, and the proliferation of multiple-PC households that will take the home networking equipment industry to a wide audience. One of the developing Internet technologies spurring the growth of home networking is high speed broadband connection, which offers 24-hour Internet access and thus serves as a justification for a home network setup allowing the simultaneous connection of two or more PCs to the Internet. Moreover, as PC and peripheral prices fall, more homes will inevitably contain the equipment for which a home network becomes practical and even necessary.

Because each home's setup and equipment are unique—due to the use of components from a variety of vendors—networked homeowners are generally on their own to troubleshoot bugs and difficulties. To get around such problems, many companies have embarked on the development of systems that stand behind a simple principle: no new wires. Wireless networks continued to explode in popularity along with the rise in broadband Internet connections. By 2003, broadband providers were working to develop support services for home networking customers. Looking forward, the industry was expected to benefit from the overall growth in broadband. A report from In-Stat cited in the May 30, 2007 issue of *Telephony* projected that global broadband subscriptions would double by 2011, reaching 567 million. Of this total, some 10 percent of subscriptions were expected to be fiber to the home (FTTH), while DSL was expected to hold a much larger (58 percent) share of the market.

Although there was no one magical home networking setup by the middle of the first decade of the 2000s, the industry was moving steadily toward more seamless technology. The formation of the Digital Home Networking Group in June 2003—comprised of such industry heavyweights as Sony, HP, Philips, Samsung, and Nokia—served to further this evolution, as leading manufacturers worked to develop compatible electronic devices. With approximately 20 percent of new homes being constructed with structured wiring packages, builders began partnering with consumer electronics retailers like Best Buy and industry groups like the Internet Home Alliance to study ways in which builders could effectively market networked homes. This was accomplished by conducting research to better understand consumer wants and needs.

Networking household appliances other than entertainment equipment was also not only a possibility but an available option by the first decade of the 2000s. The Internet Home Alliance, a network of companies involved in collaborative research regarding home networking, introduced a program called Laundry Time in 2006, which would alert consumers via their televisions, cell phones, or computers when a load of wash was completed, dried, and so on. Microsoft was including Laundry Time as part of its Windows XP Media Center Edition 2005; other companies on board included Hewlett-Packard, Panasonic, Proctor and Gamble, and Whirlpool.

CURRENT CONDITIONS

According to a 2009 report published by market research firm In-Stat, home network users were continuing to migrate toward newer and faster home networking connectivity technologies, including Gigabit Ethernet, 802.11n and alternative wire technologies such as coax, powerline and phone wiring. In 2008, 10/100 Ethernet was still the leading technology in use with home networks worldwide, but by the end of 2009, it was expected that 802.11x networks would outnumber 10/100 Ethernet. The Wi-Fi users were transitioning from 802.11b to the more robust 802.11g, while those with 802.11g were upgrading to draft 802.11n-compatible products. In-Stat analyst Joyce Putscher, quoted by Anamika Singh in an article for IP Comunications, stated that "the use of home networks for more than just Internet sharing among North American users increased from 41.8 percent in 2008 to 49.7 percent in 2009."

In-Stat's report further declared that worldwide installed home networks would surpass 300 million households in 2011, and that home networks with Gigabit Ethernet would more than quadruple through 2013 to nearly 90 million households worldwide. It was expected that the Asia/Pacific region would lead in Wi-Fi home network penetration by 2012. However, Europe led in networked households with alternative wire technologies, both currently and throughout the forecast period.

In-Stat/MDR also estimated the total value of home connectivity networking equipment as reaching around US$17.1 billion by the end of 2008.

By way of connected populations, 2008 research by MultiMedia Intelligence group found that among the top designated marketing areas (DMAs), San Francisco, Miami and Los Angeles were the most connected cities, based on home networking adoption. Mark Kirstein, President of MultiMedia Intelligence, noted, "San Francisco has the highest household home networking adoption rate of 28% among the top DMAs. In contrast, the San Antonio, Chicago and Cleveland DMAs have among the lowest home networking adoption. This reflects, in part, the varying regional demographics."

Finally, in July 2009, In-Stat reported that coax and phoneline networking was becoming increasingly important among home network connectivity alternatives, particularly for service provider provisioned networks. Cumulative households with an in-home provider network utilizing coax/phoneline technology was likely to more than double from 2008 to 2010, it reported.

INDUSTRY LEADERS

3Com Corp. of Marlborough, Massachusetts, poured extensive research and development resources into home networking equipment in the late 1990s and became well established as a major force in the young industry. Its

Personal Connectivity unit built interface cards that enabled the connection of computers to a network, while the Network Systems unit produced structural equipment such as routers, switches, and network management software. The firm also specialized in handheld computing equipment. Founded in 1979, 3Com employed 11,000 workers by 2000. However, in 2004 this number had declined to 1,924 employees, which was a near 42 percent decrease from 2003 levels. In March 2000, 3Com sold off its modem business and ceased to manufacture high-end networking equipment for large businesses so as to focus networking production on the home and small business market. Largely for this reason, the company's sales dropped from $5.7 billion in 1999 to $4.3 billion in 2000. In 2003, 3Com received $100 million for the sale of CommWorks, which offered IP (Internet protocol) infrastructure software and tools to the likes of Internet service providers and communications carriers. By the middle of the first decade of the 2000s, 3Com's focus had shifted to the enterprise market. Reported revenues for fiscal year 2009 were $1.31 billion.

Cisco Systems Inc. of San Jose, California, was a leading manufacturer of computer networking equipment, although its main area of concentration was the high-end business networking market. In addition to its top-selling routers and switches, the firm also developed servers and network management software. By 2000, Cisco was focusing increased attention on the growing home networking market in hopes of winning market share from its rival 3Com. Cisco spent the mid and late 1990s on a buying spree, acquiring dozens of companies to expand its product lines, and maintaining partnerships with top computer industry players Microsoft, IBM, and Sun Microsystems. In 1999 the firm acquired fiber-optic network equipment maker Cerent as well as routing software producer GeoTel. Cisco also was developing gateways with GTE, Whirlpool, and Sun Microsystems and was working toward the integration of home appliances into high-speed networks. The firm's revenues totaled $18.8 billion in 2003, and it employed 34,000 workers. At that time, Cisco paid $500 million in stock for home networking equipment manufacturer Linksys Group Inc. Net sales for fiscal Year 2009 were $36.1 billion with 38,413 employees.

Intel Corp., based in Santa Clara, California, was the number-one producer of semiconductors in the country in 2007. In the early years of the first decade of the 2000s, Intel had also emerged as a leader in the networking market, building hubs, servers, and routers. Founded in 1968, Intel maintained a payroll of 99,900 employees in 2006. The firm invested heavily in networking in 1999 with its purchase of Shiva Corp., which it renamed Intel Network Systems, and its subsequent acquisitions of Dialogic, DSP Communications, and Level One. The

company's two largest customers, PC giants Dell and Hewlett-Packard, together accounted for roughly one-third of sales, which in 2008 were $38.3 billion.

Other leading computer industry names figured prominently in home networking equipment as well. Hewlett-Packard Co. offered its customers network cards, network adapters, routers/base stations, and equipment for networking printers. In May of 2002, HP acquired Compaq Computer Corp., which had developed portable systems and corporate servers, in a deal worth $19 billion. Apple Computer Inc.'s Airport product line, developed in collaboration with Lucent Technologies, was a leader in the wireless technology market. IBM Corp., meanwhile, spun off its Home Director networking product into its own separate company in late 1999.

BIBLIOGRAPHY

3comCorp., 2009. Available from http://www.3com.com/corpinfo/.

Brown, Michael. " Home Networking: How to Avoid Traffic Jams." *Computer World,* 30 November 2009.

"Cisco Reports Fourth Quarter and Fiscal Year 2009 Earnings." Cisco, September 2009. Available from http://newsroom.cisco.com/dlls/2009/fin_080509.html

Edwards, Cliff, Arlene Weintraub, Irene M. Kunli, and Andy Reinhardt. "Digital Homes; Net Hookups are Spreading from the Study to the Living Room, Bedroom, and Kitchen." *Business Week,* 21 July 2003.

"Home Networking: The Challenge and Opportunity for Broadband Service Providers." Motive Communications Inc., 2003.

"Home Networking Revenue Will Top $20 Billion in 2009." *Residential System,* 1 October 2005.

"Hoover's Company Capsules." *Hoover's Online.* 20 March 2007. Available from http://www.hoovers.com.

"Know The Industry: IT in Focus." 30 November 2009. Available from http://www.netacadadvantage.com/connection.htm.

Kirstein, Mark. "San Francisco, Miami and Los Angeles are the Most Connected Cities, Based on Home Networking Adoption, According to MultiMedia Intelligence." MultiMedia Intelligence Press Release, 30 September 2008. Available from http://www.multi mediaintelligence.com/.

McCune, Heather. "Big Blue Builds Home Network Technology." *Professional Builder,* April 2003.

McNamara, Paul. "Your Washer"s Calling and the Dryer's on IM." *Network World,* 17 July 2006.

"Networking Equipment May Need More Test." *Test & Measurement World,* 1 February 2007.

"North American Households with Home Networking over Coax & Phone Wiring to Double in Two Years." 8 July 2009. Available from http://www.instat.com.

Quail, Jennifer. "Wired Science; Slowly but Surely, Technology Is Taking Control of the House." *HFN, The Weekly Newspaper for the Home Furnishing Network,* 1 December 2003.

"Sales of Home Network Gear to More than Double." *Business Communications Review,* October 2005.

Sanchez, Rick, Heidi Collins, and Carol Costello. "US—U.S. Broadband Use Continues to Climb." *The America's Intelligence Wire,* 29 December 2004.

Singh, Anamika. "According to In-Stat, Consumers are Migrating to Faster Home Networking Technologies." TMCnet, 15 September 2009. Available from http:// ipcommunications.tmcnet.com/topics/ip-communications/ articles/64360-according-in-stat-consumers-migrating-faster-home-IP Communications@tmc.net.

"United States Broadband Statistics Update." August 2009. Available from http://www.internetworldstats.com/am/us.htm.

Zurier, Steve. "Network Research: Looking to Strengthen the Home Technology Market, Builders Will Team with the Internet Home Alliance and Major Retailers to Study Consumer Trends. *Builder,* December 2003.

INFANT AND PRESCHOOL PRODUCTS

—■—

SIC CODE(S)

2032

3944

INDUSTRY SNAPSHOT

The infant and preschool products industry is not child's play. In fact, the various sectors comprising this industry amount to an enormous and fiercely competitive market. In general, the industry can be broken into two large, diversified sectors: toys and non-toys.

The global toy market generated sales of $78 billion in 2008 (of which about $21.7 billion was represented by U.S. sales), according to a July 2009 report from The NPD Group, market researchers. The infant and preschool toy sector of the industry, representing about 46 percent of total industry sales through August 2009, continued its shift toward more educational and high-tech items, and this was the demographic group expected to grow the most over the next few years.

The market for non-toy products aimed at infants and preschoolers includes children's furniture such as child seats, high chairs, and bedding; "functional" items such as strollers, baby carriers, and similar accessories; and everyday items such as bath toys, bibs, and diapers.

By all accounts, the single most recurring factor affecting the industry was child safety, irrespective of economic slump, item novelty, or price. Product recalls reached an all-time high in 2007 and 2008, prompting legislators to tighten regulations on imports and product testing. The recalled products involved not just the widely-publicized lead-tainted toys, but also (among other things) defective cribs, car seats, rattles, necklaces, baby food items, and a few medicinal goods.

ORGANIZATION AND STRUCTURE

By far the leading retail outlets for infant and preschool products were mass merchandisers. According to Harris Nesbitt Retail Analyst Sean P. McGowan, in 2004, Wal-Mart Stores Inc. was the leading toy retailer, with a market share of 25 percent, followed by Toys "R" Us (16 percent), and Target (12 percent). Roughly two-thirds of total toy industry sales occur in the fourth quarter when many toys are bought as holiday gifts. This is beginning to level out, however, as toy manufacturers market products all year through movie and fast food chain tie-ins.

Retail giants like Wal-Mart and Target also were leaders in the baby care category, which includes baby soaps, ointments and bath powders, oils and lotions, bottles and nipples, and nursing accessories. By the start of the twenty-first century, the largest percentage of nursing accessories, bottles and nipples, oils and lotions, and baby bath soaps were sold through mass merchandisers, as opposed to baby powder and baby ointments, which had the heaviest sales in supermarkets. According to the Juvenile Products Manufacturers Association, in 2005, sales of non-toy products such as these totaled $6.02 billion during the middle of the first decade of the 2000s.

Baby superstores were another way to sell juvenile products. In the latter part of the 1990s, Toys "R" Us introduced its new Babies "R" Us stores focusing on juvenile products, furniture, apparel, and toys. Through these stores, Toys "R" Us was expected to become an even larger retailing force for young families. In the middle of the first decade of the 2000s, Toys "R" Us had 218 Babies "R" Us stores throughout the country.

Juvenile products and toys are also sold through catalogs. Many parents find this an easy and convenient way to shop. There are also parent information and resource centers on the Internet as well as shopping directories pointing online shoppers to products for children.

Licensing Toy licensing began during the twentieth century, when Richard Felton Outcault's design of the comic character The Yellow Kid was placed on toys. Since then, toy licensing has become increasingly sophisticated and is reaching ever deeper into children's lives. Licensed products, such as Disney and Winnie-the-Pooh, have contributed greatly to sales in such areas as baby bottles and toys. In 2002 the Toy Manufacturers of America estimated that over 46 percent of all toys sold were licensed products. Even youngsters under the age of three are affected by the onslaught of commercials and characters they encounter as part of daily television viewing, and companies continue to initiate new ways to reach these youngsters through electronic media.

Almost anywhere children go, they find products reflecting the characters they know from popular television shows and movies. *Barney, Teletubbies, Blue's Clues, Sesame Street,* and *Sponge Bob Square Pants* are among the most universal, but there are many more. In the late 1990s, Hasbro, Inc., entered into a fierce bidding war with Mattel, Inc., to maintain Hasbro's longtime license for *Star Wars* products, which Hasbro finally won in 1997 for $600 million plus a 7.4 percent share of Hasbro for *Star Wars* mastermind George Lucas. In 2002, Hasbro extended its *Star Wars* licensing contract through 2018. The *Star Wars* Electric Light Saber sword from Hasbro proved to be one of the best-selling toys in the United States in 2002. Mattel meanwhile managed to secure the licensing rights to the 2002 Olympic games, allowing the company to produce toy mascots for the events.

Nevertheless, not all vendors agree that licensing is the best avenue. Some juvenile bedding vendors pinned product hopes on non-licensed looks and patterns that stayed clear of major films or cartoon and comic book characters, believing that licensing is becoming a high-risk proposition.

Product Safety Safety is the primary concern of parents with infants and young children. The Juvenile Products Manufacturers Association developed a Certification Program that tests products for compliance with the American Society for Testing and Materials (ASTM) standards and issues a certification seal after the product passes rigorous testing. The ASTM Certification Program covers high chairs, play yards, walkers, carriages and strollers, gates and enclosures, full-size cribs, and portable hook-on chairs. They continue to develop standards for additional categories, including toddler beds, bath seats, bedding products, and non-standard-sized cribs.

As with other juvenile products, child safety is fundamental to the development and manufacture of toys. Together with the U.S. government, the Toy Manufacturers of America leads the world in the development of toy safety standards by investing heavily in child development research, dynamic safety testing, quality assurance engineering, risk analysis, and basic anthropometric (human body measurement) studies of children.

Toys are closely monitored and highly regulated by the federal government. The basic law covering toy safety is the federal Hazardous Substances Act and its amendments, notably the Child Protection and Toy Safety Act of 1969. This legislation was supplemented by the Consumer Product Safety Act in 1972. These regulations were incorporated by reference in the industry's voluntary standard, ASTM F963. While toy makers are not compelled to abide by ASTM F963, many retailers require compliance with voluntary standards, and many manufacturers, especially the larger ones, have in-house testing laboratories that ensure that all products meet or exceed government standards for safety.

BACKGROUND AND DEVELOPMENT

There is archeological evidence that simple toys were made thousands of years ago in Greece, Rome, and ancient Egypt. Later, during the Middle Ages, the colorful world of knights and fair ladies was reproduced for the pleasure of medieval children. From the end of the Middle Ages on, toy production increased rapidly, and by the middle of the 18th century, central Europe had become the heart of the world's toy industry. Germany, particularly the city of Nuremberg, was the established toy manufacturing center of the world. In the early 20th century, Japan, Great Britain, and the United States also began to manufacture toys on a large scale.

Toys are an important part of every child's life starting in infancy. Children learn through play, and today we know that a child's education begins long before he or she enters school. Babies become familiar with shapes and sounds by playing with rattles and bell toys. They learn to distinguish colors by watching mobiles. Toddlers enjoy and learn from pull toys, pegboards, puzzles, and blocks. And the preschooler uses paints, crayons, and clay to express emotions.

Revolutionary educational methods, such as those of Maria Montessori (1870–1952) and Friedrich Froebel (1782–1852), with their precepts of learning by doing, have taught that an interested child is a happy one. Each year, more and more toys are designed to educate as well as to amuse. For example, wooden clocks with movable hands teach children how to tell time, and alphabet blocks help them learn to spell. In addition, new methods of teaching in kindergarten influenced the pattern of toys and introduced building blocks, constructor sets, educational puzzles, and many of the toys we now take for granted. In the twentieth century, soft toys also became popular. The teddy bear made its debut in 1903 and remains a favorite. Advanced technology in vinyl, plastic, and foam rubber also helped to revolutionize the toy industry.

Child Safety Of concern to the industry during the late 1990s and early years of the first decade of the 2000s was a claim made by some public interest groups that polyvinyl chloride (PVC), a vinyl used in toys and infant products such as teethers and pacifiers, posed environmental hazards as well as dangers to children, who could ingest lead, cadmium, and phthalates into the bloodstream if they chewed on these products. The European Union also took consumers' fears to heart, issuing a formal ban in late 1999 on phthalates from PVC-based toys that manufacturers expected children to chew on. Meanwhile, Mattel announced that it would phase out production of toys containing PVC and would switch instead to plant and vegetable-based plastics.

However, those plans have yet to materialize, possibly because of a June 2001 Report to the U.S. Consumer Product Safety Commission by the Chronic Hazard Advisory Panel on Diisononyl Phthalate (DINP), which concluded that DINP was carcinogenic to rodents but humans were not receiving from DINP-containing products enough exposure to represent a significant increase in cancer risk, and that "Children 0-18 months old who mouth PVC plastic toys containing DINP for three hours a day exceed the recommended ADI (average daily intake). This implies that there may be a risk of health effects from DINP exposure for any young children who routinely mouth DINP-plasticized toys for 75 minutes a day or more. For the majority of children, theexposure . . . would be expected to pose a minimal to non-existent risk of injury." The Commission added, "Further research addressing topics listed above could reduce the uncertainty associated with this characterization of DINP risk from consumer products." In 2003, the U.S. Consumer Product Safety Commission (CPSC) denied a petition to ban PVC in toys and other children's products intended for children under age five, asserting that no scientific evidence existed to support such a ban. The Juvenile Products Manufacturers Association publicly supported the CPSC decision.

Car seat safety also emerged as a concern in the late 1990s and early years of the first decade of the 2000s. A study by the National Safe Kids Campaign found evidence that eight out of ten child safety car seats were used incorrectly. Infants under 20 pounds and one year of age were required to be placed in a rear-facing seat at a 45-degree angle to best support their necks. From 20 to 40 pounds, children could be seated in forward-facing car seats; and from 40 to 80 pounds, they could use booster seats. Adding to the problems was the sheer proliferation of car seat styles and automobiles, making it difficult for manufacturers to ensure a proper fit. In hopes of correcting some of these problems, federal laws began requiring auto manufacturers to add special bars, bolts, and tethers to make it easier for parents to secure the car seats. Automakers and the government also teamed up to offer roadside clinics and seat checks to verify child safety seats were correctly installed.

Twenty-First Century Innovation Infant and preschool toy sales grew 14 percent in 2001, significantly outpacing the 1.7 percent growth experienced by the U.S. toy industry as a whole. Even when the toy industry saw sales decline by 1 percent in 2002, due in large part to weak economic conditions in the United States, the infant and preschool sector continued to see gains, albeit a more modest 2.1 percent growth. Analysts predicted that infant and preschool product sales would continue to grow, if for no other reason than the fact that the number of kids in the United States is growing. The U.S. Department of Health and Human Services reported roughly 4 million births in 2001.

By the end of the 1990s, traditional toy sales were beginning to level off in favor of more sophisticated alternatives such as advanced computer programs and other electronic equipment, even for preschool children. As technology assumed an ever-increasing role in American daily life and thus in children's education, parents increasingly sought out toys that provide educational content and early familiarity with gadgetry in addition to entertainment.

Toy manufacturers' high-tech efforts geared for tots often built upon their existing successes. For instance, to move into the interactive, computer-based market for preschoolers, Mattel Interactive rolled out *Elmo's Deep Sea Adventure* and *Ernie's Adventure in Space,* two CD-ROMs packaged with small toy spaceships or submarines. These were the follow-ups to Mattel's successful *Reader Rabbit* and *Baby & Me,* the company's first ventures into the interactive baby market. Hasbro meanwhile created an interactive Barney, called *My Barney,* which plugs into the Internet. Parents can download specific activities and games from the My Barney Web site. Once *My Barney* is programmed, children can play with it without the computer. Fisher-Price and other companies had similar products in the works, and industry analysts expected such toddler products to get even more "whiz-bang" in coming years.

The increasingly tech-savvy toddler was forcing a major revitalization effort among the industry's leaders and prospective entrants alike. Toy manufacturers embraced new market possibilities that stemmed from the latest research, contending that children can take steps toward becoming better learners and get a leg up on their peers by starting younger. Industry players stepped up their efforts to pitch their products to parents not only as entertainment but also as a means toward helping children reach their full potential. Interactive toys typically targeted at older children were being adapted for use by their younger siblings. According to a review of the 2002 U.S. toy industry by the NPD Group, sales of infant and preschool toys reflected "an emerging trend of educational products that increase a child's ability to learn while at play. The top two products in this category, LeapPad and LeapPad books, were also the top two overall products for the year."

By far the most radical innovation in juvenile products during the late 1990s was the very controversial extension of packaged entertainment in the form of television shows and video games for children under the age of two. The lovable purple dinosaur Barney got the ball rolling by appealing to youngsters from two to five years old in the mid-1990s, but by the late 1990s, the British import *Teletubbies* was marketed to infants under the age of one. Along with television programs came computer programs such as Jump Start Baby, which offers children as young as nine months old their first formal introduction to the sun, bears, shapes, and capitalism.

The larger toy industry suffered through difficult times during the early years of the first decade of the 2000s as children turned away from traditional toys in lieu of video games, digital music players, and cell phones, and amidst price wars with retail giants such as Wal-Mart and Target. According to the NPD Group, overall toy industry revenues fell 3 percent, from $20.7 billion in 2003 to $20.1 billion in 2004.

Toy industry conditions led to Toys "R" Us's decision to sell its toy business and retain its Babies "R" Us, which was more profitable year-round. However, investment groups began bidding on both, or the entire company. In early 2005, a real estate investment consortium comprised of Kohlberg Kravis Roberts & Co., Bain Capital Partners LLC, and Vornado Realty Trust emerged as the winner, buying Toys "R" Us for $6.6 billion. While it remained to be seen what the consortium did with the company, it generally was seen as a positive development by industry players. Free from Wall Street, the now privately held firm had the flexibility to reinvent itself without outside input. Many analysts agreed that at least 100 under-performing stores would close, while others estimated the number could be as high as 250.

In a March 17, 2005, *Business Custom Wire* release, Jim Silver, publisher of the *Toy Book* industry magazine, foresaw Toys "R" Us evolving into a family entertainment store that sold items of interest to both parents and children, including low-end digital cameras and iPods. Other industry players suggested that the store would incorporate more participatory elements, like those found in stores where children build their own dolls and teddy bears.

Engaging and interactive new products in the infant/preschool segment included the Laugh & Learn Learning Home from category leader Fisher-Price, which was rated as one of 2004's best toys. Fisher-Price also announced a new "Elmo Knows Your Name" doll, which parents could download personal information to (including a child's name and favorite food) via a USB cable while the toy was still in the box. LeapFrog Enterprises offered its LeapFrog Baby product line, which included the Learn & Groove Activity Station, the *Touch & Tug Discovery Book,* and the Magic Moments Learning Seat.

The extension of marketing to babies has spawned a great deal of controversy, with some arguing that it is unethical to market products to children who cannot even speak the name of the item they are being encouraged to desire. Nevertheless, marketers themselves argued that infants watch television anyway, and they are simply filling a market niche with appropriate material. There were no figures available for how large a market the three-and-under set represented, but it continued to draw the attention of toy and entertainment producers during the early years of the first decade of the 2000s.

Benefiting the manufacturers of these products was Cartoon Network's introduction of a two-hour, preschool-focused programming block in 2005. While this offered advertisers more opportunities to promote their offerings, cable networks remained cautious to avoid violating FCC guidelines regarding children's advertising. According to *Advertising Age,* during the early years of the first decade of the 2000s, guidelines for children's advertising were set by the FCC, the Children's Advertising Review Unit, and the National Association of Broadcasters. In its February 28, 2005, issue, the publication explained that "Toys must be presented literally and realistically, animation is limited to about 10 seconds a spot and marketers must disclose a full level of honesty about whether other parts are sold separately or if batteries are not included." In 2004, the FCC fined Disney's ABC Family $500,000 and Nickelodeon $1 million for violations.

In the earliest stages of product development, many designers use information from sources that include parents, psychologists, educators, and other child development specialists. This background provides valuable clues to what consumers are looking for when they purchase toys and how children learn through play. Some toy manufacturers maintain in-house, year-round nursery school facilities for this purpose, while others establish relationships with universities or other research facilities.

CURRENT CONDITIONS

According to The NPD Group, in 2009 the United States and Europe represented 9 percent of total children in the population, but 57 percent of the world's toy consumption. In October 2009, NPD reported that U.S. toy industry sales fell 3 percent during the 12 months ending August 2009 compared to the same point in 2008 and were off 2 percent year-to-date through the year's first eight months. Despite the drop, the traditional toy industry's $21.5 billion haul for the August 2008 to August 2009 period outperformed other consumer product categories like apparel, consumer technology and video games, according to NPD Group analyst Anita Frazier. A decline in sales of toys for infants and preschoolers (down 6 percent) was considered troublesome for the U.S. toy business, considering this category was considered the sweet center for the toy industry. "Kids 3-5 are especially thought to represent the core toy consumer, and in fact they account for more than a quarter of total toy sales, but this age group declined 5 percent in dollar sales and comprises a smaller share of the toy industry than it did a year ago," Frazier said.

Despite legislative measures and tightened import controls, recalled products continued to plague the industry in 2009, including lead-tainted items. On November 24, 2009, Fisher-Price recalled close to another million toys containing lead-based paint. This despite the fact that in August 2008 President Bush signed into law the Consumer Product Safety Improvement Act (H.R. 4040), which, among other things, addressed concerns over the safety of children's products, and, specifically, it limited the level of hazardous materials allowed in toys. Under the new law, lead and cadmium levels in toys must be 40 parts per million or less, while levels of plasticizing chemicals called phthalates in toys must be 100 parts per million or less. These chemicals have been linked to mental and physical developmental defects in research animals and humans. The bill also outlined clear penalties for non-compliance. Earlier in 2008, Washington had approved the nation's strongest toy standards for lead, cadmium and phthalates.

In *Toy Directory* (TD) Magazine's December 2009 issue, Julie Jones listed the top 10 most wanted school supplies and educational toys. For the preschool group, this was Snap-n-Learn Number Bugs by Learning Resources. The chunky, snap-together pieces (for small hands) were designed to introduce children to numbers, counting 0 to 5, addition and color matching.

INDUSTRY LEADERS

Mattel Headquartered in El Segundo, California, Mattel Inc. was the world's leading toy manufacturer in 2007. Mattel's second largest core brand (after Barbie) is Fisher-Price, the leader in the infant and preschool market with a history that spans more than 70 years. Mattel also includes Disney infant and preschool See 'N Say talking toys; Tyco Toys, which has an infant preschool line based

on *Sesame Street* characters; and Magna Doodle and View-Master toys.

Barbie's popularity in the late 1990s culminated with the celebration of the doll's 40th birthday in 1999. According to the company, 1 billion Barbie dolls had been sold since the doll was introduced in the 1960s, making Barbie the best-selling fashion doll worldwide. Barbie software continued to expand to meet the new demands of Barbie fans. In addition, the company's Barbie Web site allows its mostly preteen customers to shop for PlayStation 2, Game Boy, Xbox, and PC Barbie games, as well as a variety of electronic devices and learning aides, including the Barbie My Secret Diary; Barbie Video Cam Wireless Video Camera; Oregon Scientific Barbie Digital Camera; the Barbie 35mm Camera Kit; Barbie B-Book; and the Barbie B-Bright Learning Laptop. Mattel's sales grew to $5.9 billion in 2008. The company maintained a workforce of 26,000 employees.

Hasbro Hasbro Inc., the second largest toy company, began as a family-owned company in 1923. In more than 70 years, it has grown from eight family members to a company with almost 6,000 employees in facilities around the world. By 1985, Hasbro was the world's largest toy company, gaining access to the European market and uniting four strong divisions: Hasbro Toy, Milton Bradley, Playskool, and Playskool Baby. The entire line of infant products was part of the well-recognized Playskool division. The Playskool line offers fun and educational items ranging from baby care products to clothing and preschool toys, including such classics as Mr. Potato Head, Play-Doh, and Lincoln Logs. The company also maintained industry staples, such as the Nerf, Tonka, and G.I. Joe lines. In addition, Hasbro produced *Star Wars* products and Milton Bradley (e.g., Candy Land) and Parker Brothers (e.g., Monopoly) board games. The 1998 purchase of Tiger Electronics gave Hasbro one of the biggest hits of the late 1990s in the talking Furby doll, which turned multilingual in the early years of the first decade of the 2000s. Company net revenue was $4.02 billion for fiscal year 2008, an increase of 4.8 percent from $3.8 billion in Fiscal year 2007.

WORKFORCE

Toy production is labor intensive, requiring procedures such as painting, assembly, inspection, packaging, and detailing for authenticity. The costs associated with this type of production in the United States are often very high. Since the early 1950s, U.S. manufacturers have combined domestic operations with overseas production in developing countries (where labor is inexpensive) to lower costs. It was estimated that 75 percent of toys sold in the United States were manufactured either wholly or in part overseas.

Activist pressure was brought to bear on major toy manufacturers such as Mattel for what was decried as abusive labor practices in factories overseas. Mattel responded by dismissing several of its Chinese contractors for harsh treatment of workers and poor working conditions, including low wages, child and prison labor, and unsanitary and unsafe working environments. Mattel also was a co-signatory, along with apparel manufacturers Levi Strauss and Reebok, of a "bill of rights" for foreign factory workers. Such actions were not quite enough, however, to placate critics of these companies' labor practices, who argued that such gestures were primarily formal and provided for little substantive change.

AMERICA AND THE WORLD

The United States represented nearly a third in global toy industry revenue in 2008, followed by Europe at 29 percent and Asia at 27 percent, according to The NPD Group. According to the July 2009 report, about 65 percent of the world's toys were consumed by just ten countries. The United States also leads the world in toy development and in such sales support areas as marketing, advertising, and special promotions. Moreover, Asia and Africa were expected to gain market share, with Asia likely overtaking the United States and Europe by the end of 2012, said the report.

While Europe and the United States share some similarities, these markets also differ in a number of ways. During the middle of the first decade of the 2000s, some analysts indicated that European children were not as tech savvy as their U.S. counterparts, but that this trend was changing. Also, some European countries are much more vigilant than the United States in combating toy advertising aimed at small children. Greece, Sweden, and Norway restrict at least some forms of toy advertising, and Sweden even announced its intention to propose such a ban throughout the entire European Union when it assumed the European Union presidency in 2001. In the summer of 1999, the European Commission dropped its attempts to fight Greece's advertising ban as little progress had been made to repeal the Greek government's decision, which the commission feared would spread to other countries.

Global alliances have proven an attractive option for leading toy makers seeking a competitive edge in new markets. The leading manufacturer in the $8.4 billion Japanese toy industry, Bandai Co., partnered with Mattel in 1999 to market the latter's products in Japan, while Mattel agreed to market Bandai's products throughout Latin America. In the future, the two companies planned to collaborate on the development of new toys.

BIBLIOGRAPHY

"2005 vs. 2006 State of the Industry." Toy Industry Association Inc., 20 March 2007. Available from http://www. toy-tia.org/.

"2005 American International Toy Fair Reports a 16% Increase in Buyer Attendance; Hot Trends Include Infant/Pre-School, Learning and Toys That Inspire Active Play." Toy Industry Association Inc., 16 March 2005. Available from http:// www.toy-tia.org/.

"About JPMA." Juvenile Products Manufacturers Association, 27 May 2005. Available from http://www.jpma.org/about/ AboutJPMA.htm.

"About Toy Fair." Toy Industry Association. 20 March 2007. Available from http://www.toyfairny.com.

Desjardins, Doug. "KKR Sweeps In to Save Toys 'R' Us—and U.S. Toy Business." *DSN Retailing Today,* 28 March 2005.

Ebenkamp, Becky. "Got Identity Issues? Have I Got a Toy for You." *Brandweek,* 19 February 2007.

Elkin, Tobi. "Licensing Now Drives $20 Billion Toy Industry." *AdAge.com,* 17 February 2003. Available from http://www. adage.com.

French, Dana. "Developmental Toys Continue Growth." *Kids Today,* April 2005.

Frenck, Moses. "Toy Treatment: Bilingual Playthings Mean Big Business for Industry Bent on Marketing to Latinos." *ADWEEK,* 19 February 2007.

Hasbro. Available from http://www.wikinvest.com/stock/ Hasbro_(HAS).

Hayes, Dade. "Invasion of the Techie Tots." *Variety,* 19 February 2007.

"Hoover's Company Capsules." *Hoover's Online.* 20 March 2007. Available from http://hoovers.com.

"House Passes To Safety Legislation." *TD Magazine,* 20 February 2008.

Jones, Julie L. "Top-10 Most-Wanted School Supplies & Educational Toys." *TD Magazine,* December 2009.

Juvenile Products Manufacturers Association. "Top 10 Most Innovative Juvenile Products Announced at the 2006 International JPMA Show." 8 May 2006.

Klassen, Abbey. "Toy Industry Looks to Tots for Boost." *Advertising Age,* 28 February 2005.

"NPD: US toy sales dipped in first 8 months." *Playthings,* 1 October 2009. Available from http://www.playthings.com/ article/CA6699830.html.

Palmeri, Christopher. "Happier Times in Toyland." *Business Week Online* 13 February 2007. Available from www.businessweek.com.

———. "Stand Down, Wooden Soldier." *Business Week Online,* 17 July 2006. Available from www.businessweek.com.

"Toys R Us Buyout May Re-Ignite Industry." *Business CustomWire,* 17 March 2005.

"Trouble in Toyland." *Economist,* 23 October 2004.

"U.S. and U.K. Are Biggest Toy Markets." *Duty-Free News International,* 1 May 2006.

"U.S. Toy Industry: Where It's Been—Where It's Heading." *Business Wire,* 12 February 2003.

"U.S. Toy Sales Dipped in First 8 Months.'s *PlayThings,* 1 October 2009.

"World Toy Sales in 2008 were $78 Billion, a Decrease of Less Than 1 Percent from 2007." NPD Research Group, 29 July 2009. Available from http://www.npd.com/press/releases/ press_ 090729.html

"A Year in Review: 2005." Toy Industry Association. 20 March 2007. Available from http://www.toy-tia.org.

INFOMERCIALS

———————————•———————————

SIC CODE(S)

7319

INDUSTRY SNAPSHOT

Entrepreneur.com defines the infomercial, or direct response TV (DRTV), as a commercial with a toll-free telephone number that allows the consumer to buy the product being advertised. The infomercial industry has generally grown away from its often tacky late-night spots hawking novelty items and get-rich-quick schemes, though its former tendencies still periodically manifest themselves. Production values have grown slick and sophisticated; products have become mainstream and functional. By the first decade of the twenty-first century, the medium's reputation was considered stable enough for well-established giants in major industries. Indeed, by this time, *Fortune* 1000 firms accounted for roughly 20 percent of all new infomercial production.

The most intensive and "intimate" of the more than 500 commercial messages absorbed by the average American each day, infomercials were marketing not only through the media, but also in supermarkets and discount stores through "as seen on TV" sales. Analysts noted that while only 10 percent of consumers actually buy directly from an infomercial or other television advertisements, the infomercial medium develops pent-up demand that releases itself in standard retail channels. In fact, "as seen on TV" has developed from an occasional novelty promotion to a standard in-store marketing scheme, with some outlets even opening entire departments devoted to "as seen on TV" products. Although only about 1 in 20 infomercials have proved financially successful, a hit could have producers rolling in money.

An infomercial is usually a 28.5-minute block of programming that resembles a television show and is designed to explain and sell anything from kitchen gadgets to advice from psychic friends. An infomercial's purpose is to show consumers how a product would satisfy a need, benefit their lives, motivate them, or solve a problem. Fitness devices are among the most successful infomercial products because they are easily demonstrated by fit, photogenic people. The more sophisticated infomercials often have a celebrity spokesperson, testimonials from satisfied customers, location shooting, a musical soundtrack, and a well-developed script. Production costs vary widely, depending on the amount and quality of special effects, talent salaries (which for celebrities can be astronomical), and a host of other considerations.

The industry's history is littered with its share of hucksters, prompting the creation of an organization to regulate it and project a professional image. The Electronic Retailing Association (formerly known as NIMA International and the National Infomercial Marketing Association) represents the electronic retailing industry in the United States and overseas.

ORGANIZATION AND STRUCTURE

Most electronic retailers do not invent products themselves but instead scout trade shows and fairs or accept submissions for easily marketable, new inventions. For instance, Guthy-Renker Corp. and e4L Inc. often buy the rights to a product from inventors and pay them a 10 percent (or less) royalty fee. In return, infomercial producers assume all the financial risk—and most of the payoff—for launching a product.

After finding a prospective product, the company produces an infomercial. Costs vary widely, depending on quality, but general estimates run between $100,000 and $600,000. These costs could include $4,000 to $20,000 for the script and the same range for a director; $3,000 for props; $30,000 to $60,000 for editing; and $25,000 to $50,000 for crew and equipment. For kitchen items, a chef and a food stylist are also necessary, and live audiences add even more expense. Costs for location and a host (who may be a celebrity) are vastly divergent and can run into the hundreds of thousands of dollars.

Industry firms usually test finished ads on focus groups before airing infomercials in specific markets. If the product generates enough response, industry firms buy more media time in diverse markets. Because response is so rapid—customers either call in or the phones are quiet—industry firms know within days if the infomercial is working or if it needs rewriting and reshooting. If the product receives positive responses, it eventually goes to home shopping channels, the Internet, and, finally, to traditional retailers. If the product receives negative responses, industry firms often pull it from the air and move on to promoting other products. Due to expanding television markets, the largest firms have plenty of media time available and can launch 30 or more products per year.

While major success stories are few and far between, the potential payoff can be great. Once an infomercial's product generates good sales, electronic retailers display the product on television, usually on the home shopping channels. Some products may also be shown on channels related to the product, as when a fitness machine and exercise video are featured on sports channels. The final sales venue is the retail store, where the original infomercial runs on a store's videocassette player, repeating and reinforcing the product's benefits to potential buyers.

Fortune 500 companies, such as Lexus, Microsoft, Apple Computer, Magnavox, Sears, AT&T, Volvo, Fannie Mae, and Fidelity Investments, added infomercials to their marketing strategies during the late 1990s, but they worked with industry firms differently than did struggling entrepreneurs. Major corporations typically contract with a direct-response marketer to produce the infomercial or spot, establish both the supporting telemarketing and fulfillment structure, buy media time, and provide operational management. Or the marketer might provide just one or a group of these services. The advantage of this approach is maximum flexibility and control of the project while still retaining all the upside potential. The disadvantage, of course, is that the investor's capital is at risk.

The infomercial production industry reaches consumers by purchasing air time on broadcast, satellite, and regional and national cable television. Infomercials are not tracked by Nielsen ratings in the manner of traditional broadcast programs, so the number of viewers is unknown. About 4 percent of the U.S. adult population, however, purchased items from an infomercial in 1999, according to the Infomercial Marketing Service.

Beginning in 2000, all infomercials longer than 10 minutes were required by the Telecommunications Act of 1996 to be close-captioned. Direct marketers generally viewed this as a welcome development, noting that the inclusion of closed-captioning opened the door for about 24 million new consumers who were untapped by the infomercial industry due to hearing impediments. The National Captioning Institute further noted that such consumers are often influenced in their purchasing decisions by the drive to include them in marketing campaigns, that 66 percent of this market is more likely to purchase from captioned advertisements, and that 35 percent will exhibit brand loyalty to a company that offers captioning over a company that does not. The investment was attractive to many infomercial producers. Captioning a 30-minute spot cost an average of $520 and usually no more than $1,000, a pittance when factored into a $400,000 production budget.

Infomercials, and the products they sell, stand or fall on consumer reaction. Gene Silverman, president of Hawthorne Communications, advised prospective electronic retailers that at virtually every moment, an infomercial must grab the viewer's attention and convince that viewer that it is necessary to continue watching, and that only about 1 percent of viewers will actually call the toll-free number to place an order or request information so a company must reach a large audience to keep the response level high. Some suggested tips included to avoid telling the whole story right up front. That is, to consider how to tease an audience. For instance, using a "grabber" that keeps an audience watching, such as "In the next half hour you will..." or "Stay tuned to witness an amazing..." to give the viewer an opportunity to subconsciously think, "I want to see this." The formula for success, Silverman said, could be summed up in a few words: to first engage a viewer emotionally, then convince the viewer intellectually that buying the product is a smart deal.

The Electronic Retailing Association (ERA) member firms must agree to comply with all laws, from federal to local, that cover advertising and selling consumer goods. In addition, they must accurately portray their own business operations, including revenues and profits, and avoid libel or slander of competitors. Most importantly for consumers, member firms must promise "To honor all warranties and money-back guarantees, and to establish and maintain a fair and equitable distribution system for handling customer complaints." Unlike the Federal Trade Commission (FTC), however, the ERA cannot really punish violators.

BACKGROUND AND DEVELOPMENT

Infomercials began during the 1950s when television grew popular. In those days, television had little regulation and some shows became intertwined with the sponsors. For example, some analysts believe the late 1990s corporate infomercials owe a debt to 1950s shows such as the *Bob Hope Texaco Star Theater*. The show featured the Texaco logo prominently throughout, and Bob Hope interrupted the program with commercial breaks pitching Texaco's products.

In 1963 the Federal Communications Commission set a two-minute limit on television ads, which effectively killed the infomercial. The two-minute limit, however, allowed marketers to refine the short form to pitch straightforward items such as K-Tel records.

When the Reagan administration deregulated the broadcast and cable television industry in 1984, cable subscriptions expanded and infomercials reappeared. From 1984 to 1987, few federal guidelines existed and this sometimes led to misleading ads and fraudulent claims. FTC guidelines issued in the late 1980s halted most deceitful ads by forbidding false claims and misleading presentations, noting that such regulatory measures were necessary since so many infomercials constituted deliberate attempts to fool customers into believing they were watching regular programs. From 1987 to 1997, the FTC charged over 100 people or companies with false advertising in an infomercial. Joel Winston, an assistant director of the FTC's Division of Advertising Practices, commented that the FTC filed fewer charges each year because the industry had "matured" and become more mainstream.

The prestige of the *Fortune* 500 found its way into the infomercial industry in the 1990s. Their products accounted for 10 percent of infomercials on television. In the mid-1990s, Microsoft Corp. anointed the genre by using an infomercial to help launch Windows 95, using actor Anthony Edwards from television's ER to explain the new operating system to consumers. High-tech and financial products lent themselves especially well to the 28-minute television format since their features were not easily summed up in a 30-second television spot. The motive was to educate consumers, fix a brand name in their minds, and point potential customers to the nearest retailer. The aim of Fortune 500 spots is to generate sales leads rather than to sell products over the phone. For example, the Lexus infomercial explained its used car program and included a toll-free number. Over one year, the infomercial generated 40,000 phone calls and 2 percent of those callers eventually bought a used Lexus. Sears, Roebuck & Co. also ran infomercials during the mid-1990s and claimed to have doubled in-store sales on items featured in the spots.

PIONEERS IN THE FIELD

One industry trailblazer was Ron Popeil, who began as a television pitchman for his father's kitchen inventions, the Chop-O-Matic and the Veg-O-Matic, during the 1950s. These products made over $1 million and drew Popeil into a career marketing his own inventions on television. Under the Ronco brand name, Popeil marketed such gadgets as the Ronco Spray Gun, the Pocket Fisherman, and Mister Microphone. Considering himself an inventor, Popeil is indeed acknowledged to have invented the new advertising medium. The highly successful Chop-O-Matic spot is today considered the first infomercial. After a series of financial setbacks, Popeil rebounded with a new 30-minute spot hawking his Ronco Electric Food Dehydrator. By the late 1990s, Popeil was back at it, reaping rewards from his infomercials for GLH Formula #9 Hair Spray, a tinted spray used to conceal men's bald spots, and for Ronco Showtime kitchenware.

Other industry pioneers started during, and have survived, the unregulated days of the 1980s. For example, Tyee Productions of Portland, Oregon, a private company headed by John Ripper, produced a very successful infomercial for Soloflex in 1987. By 1999, Tyee had clients such as Philips Magnavox, Home Depot, and Target and generated sales of $60 million. Another 1980s pioneer was Tim Hawthorne of Fairfield, Iowa-based Hawthorne Communications. Hawthorne represented the infomercial's first mainstream client when the company brought Time Life Music to the air in 1986. By the late 1990s, Time Life had grown so comfortable with the genre that it sold ad time within its infomercials to other companies.

Infomercials owed a good deal of their strength to health and fitness products, including training equipment, exercise videos, and dietary and nutritional supplements, which, combined, accounted for half of the top ten infomercials produced in 1999. American Telecast's Total Gym, the Cyclone Cross Trainer from Quantum/Direct.-America, and the Tae-Bo video series all placed near the top of the *Greensheet Annual Review* in 1999. The market for such products generally coincides with general societal levels of prosperity, one clue to their success in the late 1990s. The combination martial arts and aerobics Tae-Bo series was in fact such a knockout that the infomercial graduated to pay-per-view status in late 1999. While cosmetic infomercials suffer from the consumer's inability to actually try the products, infomercials promising consumers a quick route to a healthy and beautiful body flourish. With more than one third of all Americans qualifying as overweight according to the National Center for Health Statistics and with most of them opting for self-treatment, the direct "one-to-one" nature of infomercials fits perfectly. For the future, the continued increase in fitness consciousness among more affluent older audiences offers the infomercial industry a promising future in this long-time staple category.

Despite years of effort to improve the image and integrity of infomercials, the medium remained one of the least trusted in the eyes of consumers. A survey conducted by Wirthlin Worldwide found that only 9 percent found infomercials to be "very believable" and 48 percent figured them to be "somewhat believable." An unfortunate 42 percent completely distrusted infomercials as an advertising medium. By way of comparison, 27 percent found product information in news articles to be very believable and 68 percent found it somewhat believable. Interestingly, however, infomercials ranked just above regular TV commercials in the eyes of the public. In 2003, in a move likely to increase viewer skepticism, the Federal Trade Commission levied fraudulent advertising charges against Slim Down Solution LLC for its infomercials marketing D-Glucosamine weight loss supplements.

By 2003, nearly two-thirds of all U.S. residents over the age of 16 had seen at least one infomercial and over one fourth had actually made a purchase. However, a survey conducted by *American Demographics* revealed that of the 63 percent of Americans who watch direct response television advertising—which includes home shopping shows and direct response commercials—only 35 percent watched infomercials in 2003 compared to 47 percent in 1994.

The infomercial celebrated its twentieth anniversary in 2004 and appeared to be on solid footing heading into the second half of the decade. The industry was expected to be buoyed somewhat by demographic luck. One of its largest sales demographics was the category of empty-nest baby boomers, especially those re-outfitting their homes to suit changing lifestyles. This market will grow about 19 percent by 2009, while similar growth will occur in nontraditional households of childless couples and singles, another prime infomercial target.

In June 2005, *Business 2.0* reported that the average infomercial viewer is between 30 and 50 years of age, has some college education, and an annual household income of approximately $50,000. In addition, women represent 60 percent of all viewers. According to research from Hawthorne Direct, only one in 100 viewers will respond to an infomercial by dialing their phone, following an average of 13 to 15 minutes of viewing.

Expo TV is a 24/7 infomercial channel that started in October 2004 as a video-on-demand offering via the Insight Communications cable service. In the middle of the first decade of the 2000s, it became the first channel dedicated exclusively to infomercials, offering information to consumers about the products and the process of purchasing them. Developed by Daphne Kwon, former chief financial officer of the Oxygen cable network, Expo TV offers themed programming segments around

infomercial spots. While some industry players are skeptical about Expo's future success, the new venture has a number of formidable backers, including former HBO President Thayer Bigelow and former Time Warner CEO Nick Nicholas.

In an effort to help protect consumers' rights and boost the image and reliability of infomercials and DRTV, the Electronic Retailing Association established an independent self-regulation program in 2004, the Electronic Retailing Self-Regulation Program (ERSP). The program is administered by the Council of Better Business Bureaus and protects consumers from false advertising on direct response radio, TV, and Internet ads. According to the ERA, in the first two years of operation the program tracked 3,800 infomercials and made 102 judgments. In 94 percent of the cases, the marketer agreed to modify or discontinue the advertisement in question.

CURRENT CONDITIONS

In 2009, a year of record-high unemployment and record-low consumer confidence, the recession lowered the cost of television and radio advertising, creating a golden opportunity for infomercials. According to the U.S. Census Bureau, newspapers and radio stations lost revenues in 2008, but cable and other subscription programming (e.g., producing and broadcasting television programs for cable and satellite television systems) continued to see increased revenues, growing from $40.9 billion in 2007 to $45.1 billion in 2008. According to Telemarketing.com, the entire telemarketing industry (which included not only DRTV/radio spots, but also direct mail, emails, faxes, print ads, and websites) was expected to reach $480 billion by the end of 2009. The most recent report by Direct Marketing Association forecast that business to consumer (B2C) telemarketing revenues would reach $212.9 billion for 2009, while business to business (B2B) telemarketing sales would leap to $268.3 billion.

Sadly, the industry lost one of its most famous personalities on TV infomercials, Billy Mays, of OxiClean and Mighty Putty fame, who passed away suddenly in June 2009 at the age of 50. However, by then, the industry was no longer regarded as TV's second-class citizen, but increasingly became the very subject of prime time television. Popular new faces, like talk-TV host Montel Williams, were now part of the infomercial family. However, perhaps the most famous infomercial in recent years was the October 2008 half-hour program produced and paid for by the Obama campaign and aired on three networks and select cable channels, during which then-presidential candidate Barrack Obama introduced himself to the American public.

In its April 2009 prime-time hour-long news documentary, "As Seen On TV," CNBC described DRTV as a $150 billion a year industry. Using research provided by Infomercial Monitoring Service (IMS) and others, sports business reporter Darren Rovell provided the business community with facts and figures about the big business of direct response that has helped make Oxi-Clean, the Snuggie, ShamWow, and the Ginsu Knife household names.

Additionally, The Discovery Channel, which had directly benefited from two decades of infomercial broadcasting, six hours per night, 365 days a year, produced a 12-episode reality TV series about the DRTV industry in 2009 that featured the late Mays and his business partner, Anthony Sullivan. The show, "Pitchmen," took viewers behind the curtain to watch Mays and Sullivan help everyday entrepreneurial men and women succeed. Meanwhile, IMS analyst Robert Hoffman, in a December 2009 article for *Response Magazine,* said, "At IMS, we can predict with absolute certainty that next year we'll see around 500 new infomercials and 1,200 new spots, but we have no idea when or if we'll ever see or hear the likes of Billy Mays again." (The greatest percentage of new spots and new infomercials in 2010 will go to health and fitness products, followed by household products.)

INDUSTRY LEADERS

Among the leading U.S. infomercial producers during the middle of the first decade of the 2000s, Guthy-Renker Corp. had sales of approximately $1.8 billion in 2008. According to the company, it had enjoyed an average annual growth rate of 33 percent over the prior decade. Guthy-Renker markets skin care and cosmetic products, including Proactive Solution, as well as fitness and motivational items. Founded in 1988 by Bill Guthy and Greg Renker, the Palm Desert, California company was at one point 38 percent owned by TV mogul Rupert Murdoch after Murdoch purchased World Communications, with whom Guthy-Renker had formed an alliance in 1993. However, in 1999 the company repurchased its stock from Murdoch and became 100 percent privately owned again. Guthy-Renker also operates the Guthy-Renker Television Network, which runs commercials on cable around the clock. A series of strategic alliances over the years has afforded Guthy-Renker privileged access to a number of consumers and resources that have helped build its reputation as a leading producer of winning infomercials. In 1999 the firm allied with the San Francisco-based Internet firm Looksmart. Some of their infomercial products included Personal Power by Tony Robbins, which generated $250 million in sales over several years, and the Power Rider fitness machine. Other hosts appearing in Guthy-Renker infomercials include Kathy Lee Gifford, Cindy Crawford, and Victoria Principal.

Another industry leader was Thane International Inc., a privately held firm that was established in 1990 by Bill Hay and his wife, Denise DuBarry-Hay. With a distribution network that includes 90 countries, the company specializes in consumer product multi-channel direct marketing in such categories as housewares, fitness, and health and beauty. Some of the products Thane markets are the Ab Revolutionizer, California Beauty Cosmetics, and the FlavorWave Oven. Thane operates by acquiring the production and distribution rights for products and then arranging for their manufacture at a low cost. While the company uses infomercials to reach consumers, it also leverages other channels including retail, catalogs, credit card inserts, print advertisements, and the Internet. Headquartered in La Quinta, California, Thane also operates Thane Direct-Canada, a subsidiary based in Toronto, Ontario, as well as the Thane Product Group in Santa Monica, California.

AMERICA AND THE WORLD

Industry observers are optimistic about the global potential of infomercials. European customers in particular have signaled their increased receptiveness to direct response television and Internet commerce. During the first decade of the 2000s, European customers had a growing number of television viewing options at their fingertips, giving direct response marketers increasing levels of access to peddle their wares. Some industry observers compared the emerging European market mid-decade to the U.S. market of the mid-1990s. However, Europe was different from the United States in that regulations were more stringent. In addition, there were language and cultural issues that resulted from a population that was less homogenous than that of the United States. One bonus was that European marketers had the Internet to use as an integrated tool with DRTV promotions. This gave them the ability to cross-sell or up-sell consumers with tactics such as e-mail marketing. The increased activity was partially reflected in a 35 percent increase in Asian membership in the ERA from 2005 to 2006.

RESEARCH AND TECHNOLOGY

Enhanced interactivity and convergence were the buzzwords in the infomercial industry in the first decade of the 2000s, both of which pointed to further integration with Internet commerce. With this thought in mind, the ERA worked to shore up its relationship with the Internet industry by creating an Internet industry liaison to help familiarize the Internet community with direct response retailing and vice versa.

The Internet-infomercial cooperative efforts were mutual. Florida-based Reliant Interactive Media Corp. launched a global computer marketing concern called "As Seen on TV PC," and one of the most common new features in infomercial campaigns is the inclusion of retail Web sites specifically designed to supplement traditional direct response sales. Less directly, the Internet has aided the infomercial industry by providing a whole new spectrum of market research focusing on nontraditional shopping venues.

BIBLIOGRAPHY

"2004 Marks the 20th Anniversary of Infomercials." Arlington, VA: Electronic Retailing Association, 1 March 2004. Available fromhttp://www.retailing.org/new_site/default.asp.

2005-2006 Annual Report. Electronic Retailing Association, 20 March 2007. Available from http://www. retailing.org/.

"About Expo." Expo TV, 20 March 2007. Available from http://www.expotv.com.

"Analysis: Can DRTV Really Build Brands Better than Image Ads?" *Precision Marketing,* 9 February 2007.

Canlen, Brae. "Beyond Infomercials: Home Channel Manufacturers Discover the Benefits and Extra Revenues of Direct Response TV. *Home Channel News,* 22 August 2005.

"Direct Response TV Expanding in Europe." *Market Europe,* 1 December 2004.

Fetto, John. "As Seen on TV." *American Demographics,* 1 June 2003.

"FTC Slams Weight-Loss Infomercials." *Broadcasting & Cable,* 27 January 2003.

"FTC's Busy Summer Continues with New Filings, Findings, Injunctions." *Response,* September 2004.

Guthy-Renker. Available from http://www.guthy-renker.com.

Hoffman, Robert. "A Year of Growth and Sadness." *Response Magazine,* December 2009.

"Hoover's Company Capsules." *Hoover's Online.* 20 March 2007. Available from http://hoovers.com.

"Industry Research, Facts and Figures, 2005." Electronic Retailing Association, 20 March 2007. Available from http://www.retailing.org.

"Jordan Whitney's Infomercial Rankings, 2006." 20 March 2007. Available from http://www.jwgreensheet.com.

Koleva, Gergana. "As Infomercials Move to Mainstream TV, Stay Alert For Scams." *MarketWatch,* 24 January 2008.

Mannes, Tanya. "Infomercials standing by!" *San Diego Union Tribune,* 22 May 2009.

Mucha, Thomas. "Stronger Sales in Just 28 Minutes: Done Right, a Good Pitch Really Pays Off. That's Why Mainstream Firms Are Lining Up to Learn the Art of the Effective Infomercial." *Business 2.0,* June 2005.

Paul, Delila J. "N.J. Has Grownas the Capital of the TV Informercial Industry." *Star-Ledger,* 12 July 2009.

"Telemarketing Services, Outbound Telekarketing, Inbound." 2009. Available at http://www.telemarketing.com/.

"U.S. Census Bureau: Newspaper Publishers Revenues Decline in 2008." Public Information Office Press Release, 16 December 2009.

Whitney, Daisy. "Infomercials Get Their Day, Night; 24/7 Ad TV: Expo TV Adds to Options in Growing Field of Multibillion-Dollar Direct TV." *Advertising Age,* 9 May 2005.

INFORMATION MANAGEMENT SYSTEMS

—■—

SIC CODE(S)

8742

7373

INDUSTRY SNAPSHOT

The field of information management systems, like so many industries based on computer technology, is characterized by consistent change. Whether as the result of improvements in hardware and its underlying software, the evolution of the World Wide Web as a medium of information delivery, or fundamental shifts in thinking about the role and use of information in business and industry, information management and the systems used to implement it function in an environment that is rarely the same from one day to the next.

Information management is the means whereby information is collected, identified, and analyzed, then distributed to the points within an organization where decisions are made and customers are served. Information management systems streamline and automate the often complex processes of coordinating a company's many activities with employees, suppliers, and customers.

During the twenty-first century's first decade, the field was populated by computer industry giants such as IBM Corp. and Microsoft Corp.; smaller but powerful companies such as Sybase and Oracle; and as yet unknown startups with large doses of technological savvy and the fierce desire to reap the benefits of redefining the possibilities of what can be accomplished through technology.

Ours is an increasingly global society wherein rapid, accurate access to vast amounts of disparate information is not only demanded but increasingly taken for granted.

Timely, accurate information is what fills the inevitable gaps created by the necessity to do more with less. In that context, information management systems will continue to assume greater prominence while businesses, governments, and individuals become increasingly reliant upon them.

ORGANIZATION AND STRUCTURE

An information management system is built on workflow software, groupware, and reporting tools. Workflow software automates the division and assignment of work and removes unnecessary steps along the way. Examples of workflow software include project management, billing, or integrated payroll systems. Groupware incorporates a variety of software (including e-mail and Internet browsers) and hardware (including fax machines and voice mail) to allow employees direct access to the information management system and each other. Reporting tools enable users to retrieve information from the information management system. Examples of reporting tools include online analytical processing tools associated with data warehouses.

With the rise of the Internet and the World Wide Web as ubiquitous and fundamental research tools, issues related to retrieving and organizing information have become increasingly important to a wider and more varied population of information consumers. Libraries, once the primary users of information management systems, no longer have exclusive claim to the need to manage vast pools of wide-ranging data. Businesses, governments, and similar institutions have developed an unrelenting need to use the tools available for controlling a steady, massive inflow and output of information.

Data warehousing and online analytical processing (OLAP) are information repositories and reporting tools that enable users to convert raw data to valuable information. Data warehousing is a variation of data migration that involves moving and transforming data from a variety of systems into a single repository. OLAP software provides interactive access to multi-dimensional analysis of the data. There is a symbiotic relationship between the data warehouse and the OLAP tools used to mine the information since the repository structure and querying tools operate interdependently.

A data warehouse in essence is a large collection of data with the tools to sort and analyze the data or, as defined by founding father William H. Inmon, it centers around a subject orientation, includes normalized data, and incorporates non-volatile content (archival data that does not change once recorded). The subject orientation of a data warehouse may include, for example, products, customers, and inventory. The data warehouse receives information on these subjects from a variety of operational databases within the organization such as transactionals (invoice databases) or records (marketing databases). The data received from these different databases is frequently coded and described in different ways and must be normalized prior to use. Disparate databases, data types, and data elements can be handled by a gateway within the information management system to integrate enterprise-wide knowledge into one usable whole. Structured query language (SQL) translators accomplish the task of interpreting a variety of database types, elements, and messages from standard relational databases. Essentially, a database begins by talking to an SQL server such as Oracle 7 or IBM's DataJoiner. The SQL server provides the necessary translation using a global data dictionary and passes the information on to the next database. The internal formats of different databases vary according to the business concepts behind the database design. Thus, while the translation may be technically accurate, the SQL solution means data may require additional manipulation.

Alternately, Internet based information management systems rely on the system architecture of the client-server and a common user interface to integrate information between disparate databases. A client-server system consists of a server (a computer that contains information and serves it up at the request of a client computer) and a client (a computer that asks for information from a server). Client-server solutions can result in a lack of data cohesiveness. While operational databases are updated regularly with deletions and insertions, the data warehouse is a read-only environment in which information is loaded and then read through a series of snapshots. As the snapshots are stacked together, it becomes possible to examine data across layers of geography or time as well as across the traditional two-dimensional columns and rows of the single snapshots. The content of the data warehouse includes integrated data, detailed and summarized data, historical data, and metadata. Metadata describe the context of the information.

Online analytical processing (OLAP) tools extend the architecture of the data warehouse by reading and aggregating large groups of diverse data. Richard Finkelstein, president of Performance Computing Inc., noted that the objective of OLAP is to analyze these relationships and look for patterns, trends, and exceptional conditions. The key characteristic of an OLAP tool is that it provides a multi-dimensional conceptual view of the data. Variations of OLAP include relational online analytic processing (ROLAP) and desktop online analytical processing (DOLAP). Data mining, another form of online analysis, creates a model from current information and projects this model onto another scenario where information is non-existent. One drawback to an OLAP system is that it often requires the use of a proprietary OLAP database or warehouse without the same capacity as a standard relational database. ROLAP software allows users to make queries of a relational data warehouse.

Decentralized data and different databases abound in corporate America. Information management systems piece together information from disparate sources. Simple component information management systems link databases together based on their involvement with a part or product. For example, an inventory re-order system is a kind of information management system that tracks inventory stock and updates all databases for re-order, shipment, and payment. Because component information management systems are based on a pre-existing product or need, such as the search for a part, gateways and search engines are pre-coordinated. Evolving from these product-based systems, a more complex information management system emerges to allow employees to post-coordinate their information retrieval needs. Workflow software, groupware, and reporting tools share information with each other so that, for example, employees can specify what kind of information is desired and in what format it will appear. This integration of information represents a progressive movement from piecemeal business data toward business knowledge for employee, supplier, and customer alike.

Trends Many companies were looking to one of the spin-offs of that technology: intranets. An intranet is an internal information system based on Internet technology, such as Web services, transfer protocols, and the Hypertext Markup Language (HTML). Although intranets use technological concepts that are prevalent on the Internet and World Wide Web, the information contained on an intranet stays securely within the company or organization managing it. Intranets are private business networks based on Internet and World Wide Web standards, but they are designed to be used internally. In other words, random Internet users cannot access a company's intranet. Only those individuals granted specific access to an intranet can use it.

Like the Internet, intranets often require little or no training, as people who are familiar with navigating the Internet can usually become equally proficient at using intranets. Intranets can be easily maneuvered within graphics-based Internet browsers, which are standard on every hardware platform in the intranet. This facilitates greater remote access without the use of wide area networks.

The connection between intranets and information management systems is twofold. First, information management systems are fundamental for any company trying to take advantage of intranets since they provide the freedom to fine-tune access to data, facilitate the targeting of specific information to specific people, simplify delivery of information, and incorporate databases. Second, using intranets in conjunction with information management systems reduces the costs of software, hardware, and maintenance. Indeed, the two systems are so well suited that most information management vendors are now adapting their products for intranet use. With ever more information to manage and share, it is a trend that is sure to continue.

Emerging from the use of intranets is the trend toward the next level: extranets. Extranets are business-to-business networks operating over the Internet. When two companies allow each other access to parts of their intranets, they have created an extranet. Extranets can provide regulated and secure communications between companies and are frequently used to aid in customer service, to facilitate transaction processing, and as an adjunct to marketing.

A number of software applications making it easier to set up and use extranets were introduced at the turn of the twenty-first century. With increased ease of use and the convenience to customers and business partners of unimpeded access to a company's communications and information core, it is expected that extranet use will continue to increase dramatically until extranets become as prevalent in corporate information management systems as networks. The ease with which they let companies and customers interact will be a dominant factor in the increased use of extranets.

Applications Information management systems appear in a variety of ways and for a variety of reasons. A human resource information management system, for example, concentrates its focus on payroll, benefits, and status information. Laboratory information management systems (LIMS) are typically designed specifically for the analytical laboratory. LIMS connect the analytical instruments in the lab to one or more workstations or personal computers (PCs). When data are collected by these instruments, they are forwarded by an interface to the PC where the data are stored, sorted, and organized into reports and other meaningful forms of output based on the type of information requested by the system users. Financial institutions benefit greatly from information management systems when customer account data and transaction histories are integrated. Businesses that rely heavily on statistical analysis, such as real estate investment firms, also benefit from information management systems. Many buy-sell decisions are made according to a wide variety of market indicators. Viewing data multidimensionally across time and geography can provide invaluable information for investment decisions using an information management system.

Among their advantages, information management systems provide quick access to multiple databases holding information such as engineering parts, financial transactions, textbook titles, and customer contacts. Information management systems also encourage design reuse and reduce the time necessary to set up a new part, coordinate schedules, or change workflow processes. The Internet and the World Wide Web have spurred innovation and development of information management systems by capitalizing on the inherent network functionality of the Internet and the universality and ease of the Internet browser. It is possible for all workers, suppliers, and customers to enjoy the same common interface without regard to physical location or time. Reduced hardware and software costs are prime benefits of a Web-based information management system. The formerly separate processes of document management and workflow are two applications now merging into one larger system on the Internet.

BACKGROUND AND DEVELOPMENT

The first functioning document retrieval system to use electronics was demonstrated in Dresden, London, and Paris in 1931, according to Michael Buckland, a professor at the University of California-Berkeley's School of Information Management and Systems. Well before digital computers, Emanuel Goldberg's "statistical machine" combined photocell, circuitry, and microfilm for document retrieval.

Nevertheless, even if Goldberg's machine provided the first hints of what an electronic information management system could do, it was not until the advent of the computer that information management began to evolve and increasingly complex systems became necessary to handle the large amounts of data generated.

The first prototype of a working business computer, the 409, was introduced in 1951. Information was fed to the 409 via a refrigerator-sized punch card unit. Punch cards—stiff cards in which holes were actually punched via machine—provided the programming and data for early computers as they "read" the sequence of holes. This physical means of introducing data to a computer, however, created an environment in which an error could result in many lost hours of work. Early computer operators did not have the convenience of a backspace or delete key.

However, information management systems evolved from the punch card machines to mainframes and spools of magnetic tape. Structured query language (SQL) was introduced in the 1970s via a database system called System R. The Multics Relational Data Store was released in June 1976 and is believed to be the first relational database management system offered by a major computer vendor—in this case, Honeywell Information Systems, Inc.

In the 1970s, IBM mainframe computers were the prevalent systems found in business usage, whereas minicomputer platforms such as AS/400 and VAX/VMS dominated in the 1980s. The 1980s also saw the rise of the personal computer as both an individual and business tool. It is, however, the evolution of the Internet and World Wide Web in the 1990s as a medium of information archiving and dissemination that continues to have the greatest impact upon the field of information management systems.

The financial services and manufacturing industries led the information management systems boom in the early years of the first decade of the 2000s with heightened demand for information technology and services. It was these industries, along with utilities and telecommunications industries, that were forecast to drive the information management systems industry through the first decade of the new century.

The leading applications of information management systems included record and archival capacity, accounts payable and receivable, customer service, human resources, and litigation information management. Some of the leading motivations for implementing information management systems included the growth of e-commerce, the influx of information and data, and the popularity of the Internet. At the same time, in the wake of the technology industry downturn of the early years of the decade, businesses sought the increased efficiency afforded by most information management systems.

The growth of e-commerce also spawned a new segment of the industry: application service providers (ASPs) that create Web-based systems for providing information on product availability and current customer orders, processing orders and payments, arranging delivery, and storing names and addresses. While smaller companies such as Digital River Inc. were some of the first providers of this technology, industry giants such as Oracle and SAP AG formed application service provider (ASP) divisions. The ASP sector is one of the most significant growth markets for information management system providers. In 2006 AT&T broke into the ASP business by purchasing Usinternetworking for $300 million.

To combat the information overload, a growing technique used for Web-based information management systems was the development of portals. Similar to Web sites such as Yahoo!, the portal organizes information on a Web page replete with graphs, images, tables, charts, and other objects to make the tangle of information on the Internet more accessible and manageable. Portals are often used with intranets, integrating and organizing applications, files, and data from throughout a company and its departments. In 1999, only about 16 percent of companies had implemented portals, but by 2002 more than 90 percent were using or building portals, according to a January 2003 Jupiter Research Executive Survey. Roughly 40 companies offered portals during this period, including Plumtree Software, Viador, SAP AG, and PeopleSoft Inc.

Several information management systems players began to consolidate, a sign that the somewhat fragmented industry was maturing. For example, in 2001, IBM paid $1 billion for Informix and its database management systems. In 2003, Cognos Inc. paid $160 million for Adaytum Inc., a financial planning application software maker; Hyperion Solutions paid $142 million for Brio Software Inc., a query and reporting application developer; and Business Objects SA paid $820 million for Crystal Decisions Inc., an enterprise reporting software vendor. Also in 2003, in one of the industry's largest deals, Oracle bid $7.5 billion for PeopleSoft, which attempted to stave off the hostile overture by paying $1.8 billion to buy J.D. Edwards & Co. The Oracle and PeopleSoft merger was finally completed in January 2005. The reason for the consolidation, according to the July 2003 issue of *Information Week,* was that "Vendors are trying to build complete lines of reporting and analysis apps…vendors also are expanding beyond mainstream business intelligence into areas such as performance management because IBM, Microsoft, and Oracle are providing more basic reporting and analysis capabilities built into their database software."

The efficient and cost effective management of information continued to be a key factor in business. Consequently, companies large and small continued to invest in information technology (IT). According to a report from the research firm International Data Corporation, (IDC), IT spending in the United States was expected to increase.

According to the April 15, 2005, issue of *Wireless News,* the IDC report further indicated that IT spending growth in the areas of content and process management were being driven primarily by the banking, government, and manufacturing sectors, as well as insurance, health care, and media. Part of this growth was attributable to the need to meet compliance standards. For example, in the health care and insurance industries, this was evident in the Health Insurance Portability and Accountability Act. In addition to a growing need to share data across different platforms and systems, the need for data mobility was another major information management issue, especially in health care, manufacturing, education, and banking.

As greater amounts of information moved across a growing number of platforms, mobile and otherwise, security issues were more pressing than ever. Some observers were very concerned about the vulnerability of the United States's IT infrastructure. An article in the September 8, 2005, issue of *Space Daily* revealed that the U.S. information technology infrastructure—including everything from military and intelligence networks to financial systems, power grids, and air traffic control systems—is "highly vulnerable to terrorist and criminal attacks." Citing the existence of some 100,000 different worms and computer viruses, the publication revealed that according to the President's Information Technology Advisory Committee, "there is little federal budgetary support for fundamental research to address the security vulnerabilities of the civilian IT infrastructure, including defense systems."

Application Service Providers (ASPs) continued to gain momentum during the middle of the first decade of the 2000s. One factor driving growth in the ASP space was related to document management. Specifically, a number of companies sought to enable collaborative document sharing among staff, allowing remote, Internet access and increasing security through greater information control. This especially was true of companies in the accounting and financial sectors. This particular application of ASP technology came to the forefront in the wake of Hurricane Katrina and other natural disasters, as companies focused on disaster recovery.

Within the information technology sector, leading industry players began acquiring ASP firms. One prime example was IBM's acquisition of Corio Inc. in early 2005. Based in San Carlos, California, Corio provides enterprise resource management and customer relationship management software from the likes of SAP and Siebel Systems on a hosted basis. Following the acquisition, Corio became part of IBM Global Services. Another key example was Sun Microsystems' 2005 acquisition of Ashburn, Virginia-based managed services provider Seven-Space Inc.

CURRENT CONDITIONS

According to research published in 2008 by International Data Corporation (IDC), as of 2007 the digital universe was 281 exabytes in size. It predicted that the digital universe would reach nearly 3,000 exabytes by 2010 (3,000,000,000,000 gigabytes; one exabyte is equal to 1

billion gigabytes). This represented an increase from its earlier projection of an annual growth rate of 57 percent in the amount of information created and copied, resulting in an output of 988 exabytes by 2010. The revised forecast underscores just how fast this industry is growing—exponentially. It also represented a conservative estimate, which excluded specialized data from scientific experiments such as the Large Hadron Collider and digital telescopes that generate several exabytes per week.

This increase in information will have a major impact on society, said John Gantz of IDC. "The incredible growth and sheer amount of the different types of information being generated from so many different places represents more than just a worldwide information explosion of unprecedented scale... From a technology perspective, organizations will need to employ ever-more sophisticated techniques to transport, store, secure, and replicate the additional information that is being generated every day." He also said that the growth will change the way organizations and IT professionals do their jobs, in addition to the way consumers use information.

Nevertheless, the overall IT industry suffered some decline in 2008 and early 2009. IBM, like SAP, had experienced layoffs, with more than 1,400 employees trimmed from the Information Management business. However, by late 2009, the industry appeared to have leveled its losses and stabilized. In November 2009, *Information Age* (publishers of the Information Age Index) reported that after 12 months of consistent decline, the rate of revenue decline among the IT industry's key suppliers slowed in October 2009.

INDUSTRY LEADERS

Microsoft, with fiscal 2009 revenues of $58.44 billion, remains the number-one software provider in the world. Sybase Inc., IBM, and Oracle Corp. also provide structured query language (SQL) gateways and online analytical processing (OLAP) software for use in an information management system. Sybase is headquartered in Dublin, California, and the employer of 3,715 people. Giant IBM, based in Armonk, New York, had 366,345 employees. The service sector of IBM is the largest in the world and accounts for more than half of the company's sales. Oracle, based in Redwood City, California, had 56,133 employees. In June of 2003, Oracle launched a $5.1 billion hostile bid for rival PeopleSoft, which attempted to thwart the takeover effort by acquiring a majority stake in J.D. Edwards. Unfazed, Oracle upped its bid to $7.25 billion. The deal was finally completed in January 2005. Other entities purchased by Oracle included Siebel Systems and Portal Software.

Other players in this market niche include Cognos Inc. and Hyperion Solutions Corp. Cognos offers PowerPlay and Impromptu (a reporting and querying package), and Hyperion Solutions makes Essbase. In 1996 Arbor Software (which merged with Hyperion Software in 1998 to form Hyperion Solutions) integrated Essbase with a reporting tool called Crystal Info and Crystal Reports from Seagate Software Co. In 2003 Cognos released ReportNet, a business intelligence reporting platform.

In early 2008, IBM completed its acquisition of Cognos, and made it known that it was happy with the results, said Doug Henschen of *Intelligent Enterprise.* Cognos is now one of four parts of IBM's "Information On Demand" strategy, and IBM said revenue growth for the business in 2008 was a healthy 18 percent, reported Henschen.

CA Inc. (formerly Computer Associates International) is a world leader in mission-critical software for a variety of applications, including life cycle and service management, operations, security, and storage. According to CA, its "solutions touch many areas of everyday life, from ATM transactions to airport security to online sales, customer service and medical information. . . . Our integrated solutions help manage the infrastructures of more than 95 percent of the *Fortune* 500 companies and more than 80 percent of the Global 1000, as well as government organizations and hundreds of other companies in diverse industries worldwide." Headquartered in Islandia, New York, the company reported in May 2009 that its fiscal year sales were $4.27 billion. The company employed about 16,000 people.

AMERICA AND THE WORLD

The United States accounts for roughly 50 percent of the global information management market, while Europe makes up about 30 percent and Asia 10 percent. Furthermore, although many of the major players in the information management systems industry have headquarters in the United States, these providers also maintain an extensive worldwide presence. Cognos, for example, has corporate headquarters in Ottawa, Canada, with U.S. sales headquarters in Burlington, Massachusetts. In mid-2005, the company served customers in more than 135 countries and had locations in approximately 25 countries, from Australia to Taiwan. Lotus maintains offices in several different countries. Sybase has its world headquarters in Dublin, California but has other departments located in approximately 63 countries, including France, Canada, Italy, Germany, and the People's Republic of China.

One of the industry's major software providers, SAP AG, is headquartered in Walldorf, Germany, but also maintains several international offices. As of 2009, SAP had more than 92,000 customers, including Microsoft and General Motors, in over 120 countries. It reported revenues of $7.48 billion for first nine months of 2009.

RESEARCH AND TECHNOLOGY

In February 1998, the World Wide Web Consortium approved the Extensible Markup Language (XML) as a standard. XML, a meta-language that provides information about data, comes from the same common background as Hypertext Markup Language (HTML), but is considerably more powerful and permits more efficient structure and easier exchange of data than HTML.

Along with streamlining e-commerce, making it easier for companies to conduct business in the online world, Extensible Markup Language (XML) also eased existing difficulties in sharing information on an intranet and allowed Internet searches to become more detailed and sophisticated. In addition, whereas Hypertext Markup Language (HTML) allows users to only view data, XML allowed the manipulation of data inside a browser.

One area in which XML is predicted to prove particularly lucrative is streamlining supply chains for manufacturers. Some analysts estimate that new developments based on XML will save manufacturers across the globe as much as $90 billion per year. One firm already reaping these benefits is Maytag Corp., which began using XML to tag its product specification data in 2001. Prior to adopting the new technology, Maytag programmers had to download the data from the firm's mainframe system and then manually key it into a spreadsheet program before they could send it off to their retailers. Now, explains *Business Week* columnist Jim Kerstetter, "Maytag's mainframe zips out the specs to retailers and trading partners. Their XML-savvy computers automatically pick out each spec and insert it in the proper column. The price information, for instance, will wind up in the price column, no matter whether the price column is named B or E, or whether the document is an Excel spreadsheet or an entry form for a database from Oracle Corp."

One downside to XML is that for it to truly revolutionize supply chain processes, each industry must develop a standard set of tags. Because the companies within each industry tend to be intense rivals, working together on such a process poses issues of trust as well as other problems. These problems prevented most industries from developing standard XML tags. In the September 2005 issue of *Intelligent Enterprise,* writer Doug Henschen remarked, "Switching to XML-based content, management can save big money in the long run by promoting content reuse and multichannel delivery. It can also be an expensive, time-consuming challenge akin to building a house from a pile of lumber." Henschen further explained that emerging standards, such as the Darwin Information Typing Architecture, were making XML content management less frustrating.

Intranets and data warehouses will continue to proliferate, Lotus predicted, and push technology will make it easier to establish customized methods for delivering exactly what information a person wants from the vast store of material available electronically, even if a customer does not really know what might be available.

Information management researchers focused on issues such as record-keeping software, electronic records retention, and archiving electronic records, according to John T. Phillips in *Information Management Journal.* Since e-mail and computer-generated documents constitute the major business records, companies require information management systems that are designed to organize and store these kinds of documents, not paper documents. Electronic documents also create a problem of how long they should be stored and so information management applications must address this problem, too. Some methods being explored to solve this problem include developing retention schedules for different departments (for example, ones for accounting, human resources, and production) so that certain types of documents are retained for specific periods depending on the department. Finally, given the potential for loss of electronic documents through computer malfunctioning, viruses, and environmental factors, researchers are exploring issues of media compatibility, data transfer rates, and data recording methods, while simultaneously considering their effect on information retention.

BIBLIOGRAPHY

"ASPs Prepare to Make Comeback." *Network World,* 18 August 2003.

"AT&T Buys into the ASP Market by Acquiring Usi." *Network World,* 18 September 2006.

Azua, Maria. "Dawn of the Social Age." *InformIT,* 14 August 2009. Available from http://www.informit.com/articles/article. aspx%3Fp%3D1388957%26seqNum%3D6

Buckland, Michael. "Emanuel Goldberg and His Statistical Machine, 1927." Available from http://www.sims.berkeley.edu/~buckland/statistical.html.

———. "Emanuel Goldberg, Pioneer of Information Science." Available from http://www.sims.berkeley.edu/~buckland/goldberg.html.

"Businesses Adopting Mobile Apps Faster than Anticipated, Security a Major Concern." *Wireless News,* 11 July 2005.

CA Inc. Available from http://www.ca.com/us/press/release.aspx%3Fcid%3D205816.

"Consolidation Time." *Information Week,* 28 July 2003.

"The Digital Universe Created 161 Exabytes Of Data Last Year." *InformationWeek* 7 March 2007.

Gantz, John F., et al. "The Diverse and Exploding Digital Universe, An Updated Forecast of Worldwide Information Growth Through 2011." IDC Report, March 2008. Available from http://www.emc.com/collateral/analyst-reports/diverse-exploding-digital-universe.pdf.

Henschen, Doug. "Emerging Standard Eases Content Modeling Headaches." *Intelligent Enterprise,* September 2005.

———. "IBM-Cognos One Year Later." *Intelligent Enterprise,* 6 February 2009.

"Hoover's Company Capsules." *Hoover's Online,* 20 March 2007. Available from http://hoovers.com.

"IDC: U.S. IT Spending Will Reach $497 Billion by 2008." *Wireless News,* 15 April 2005.

"Information Age Index: A return to growth?." *Information Age,* 19 November 2009. Available from http://www.information-age.com/channels/information-management/company-analysis/1095157/information-age-index-a-return-to-growth.thtml.

"IT Think Tank Thinks IT Is Good For The Economy." *InformationWeek,* 13 March 2007.

SAP. Available from http://www.sap.com/about/investor/press.epx?pressid=12109.

Scott, Robert W. "The Return of the ASP." *Accounting Technology,* December 2004.

Thibodeau, Patrick. "Buyout Wave Pushes ASPs into Deals with Big Vendors: Users Anticipate Potential Benefits of Increased Efficiencies and Lower Costs." *Computerworld,* 21 March 2005.

"US IT Systems Highly Vulnerable to Attack." *Space Daily,* 8 September 2005.

Wilcox, Joe. "Microsoft Takes Big Hit: Q4 Revenue Falls For All Products." *BetaNews,* 23 July 2009. Available from http://www.betanews.com/joewilcox/article/Microsoft-takes-big-hit-Q4-revenue-falls-for-all-product-divisions/1248389279.

INTERNET SERVICE PROVIDERS

SIC CODE(S)

7375

INDUSTRY SNAPSHOT

U.S. Internet services continue to migrate toward high-speed options and premium services in an industry that has consolidated sometimes in surprising ways. In the consumer market, basic Internet access has grown rapidly into a commodity service. As a result, the industry is maturing rapidly as its customer base continues to swell. Intense price pressures, heavy infrastructure spending, and changing competitive dynamics are forcing many Internet service providers (ISPs) to merge, dragging the total count of ISPs down.

To differentiate themselves and to mine for new revenue streams, ISPs of all stripes are looking for new value they can bring to customers beyond getting them connected and delivering their e-mail. Because they're usually less pedestrian than basic access service, value-added services can offer greater opportunities for profit. Different approaches include offering Internet telephone service through Voice Over Internet Protocol (VoIP), unified messaging (receiving voice, fax, and e-mail messages all from one source), instant messaging (text-based chats with others online), online security software and software applications for rent, and unique content by partnering with media and entertainment outlets.

By the twenty-first century's first decade, dial-up connections had become nearly obsolete, replaced instead by broadband. The most common broadband technologies were DSL (digital subscriber line) and cable. Internet service providers fought for market share, and DSL was the broadband technology most used worldwide. However, another technology involving fiber optics had appeared on the scene that held possibilities for tremendous growth and surpassed the number using DSL or cable, according to U.K. research firm Point Topic. Wi-Fi and the even faster and longer range WiMax were other new technologies that were expected to gain greater public interest and use into the second decade of the twenty-first century.

ORGANIZATION AND STRUCTURE

Internet service is delivered in myriad ways and is required by several distinct markets. Mode of access often varies by market.

Cable Cable system operators and their specialized partners deliver broadband Internet services to customers using coaxial cable and a special cable modem. These services, run through the same wires that supply cable television programming, can support speeds up to one megabit per second (Mbps), although the norm is considerably lower. Cable Internet services effectively connect households to a local area network that's shared with other subscribers in their area. This allows consumers to maintain a constant connection—no dialing in—but as marketers of competing broadband services are quick to point out, the cable network structure makes the medium one of the least secure, leaving the average subscriber's personal computer (PC) vulnerable to hacking unless the subscriber takes special measures to shore up security.

DSL Cable's main broadband challenger is a collection of technologies known as digital subscriber line (DSL). DSL variants include symmetric DSL (SDSL), where upload and download speeds are the same, and asymmetric DSL

(ADSL), where downloads are faster than uploads. DSL sends a digital signal over ordinary telephone lines and requires special equipment at the local phone switching center and a DSL modem for the subscriber's computer. DSL services are offered by local phone companies as well as specialty distributors such as Covad Communications Group that have deployed DSL infrastructure in metropolitan areas. The technology can support speeds up to 800 Kbps, but the common consumer speed is closer to 128 Kbps. Unlike cable, DSL service does not degrade as quickly when more users are on the local system and ISPs are able to guarantee a minimum level of service, but it faces some of the same security and local overload issues.

Dial-up Services Analog dial-up service over standard phone lines, which supports download speeds of up to 56 kilobits per second (Kbps), is usually both the slowest and cheapest way to reach the Internet. As broadband access to the Internet has grown, there has been a resulting decline in the number of Americans connecting to the Web via dial-up, or narrowband, lines. Those users who had not already switched to broadband connections were opting for discount dial-up services.

Speed limitations, however, have rendered dial-up access ineffective for transmitting the vast pools of data that popular Internet applications increasingly require. Downloading high-resolution graphics, animations, sound files, and video clips as well as large software application files are all problematic over a 56 Kbps line. Typically, upload speeds are even slower.

Wireless Options Wireless was poised for explosive growth. Free Wi-Fi (wireless fidelity) networks had been put in place in cities throughout the United States, and users could access the network in "hot spots" such as coffee houses, libraries, or hotels. By 2008, two other technologies had come on the scene: WiMax (Worldwide Interoperability for Microwave Access), which was similar to Wi-Fi but had several advantages, such as greater speed and longer range, and W-CDMA (Wideband Code Division Multiple Access), a type of 3G cellular network that grew out of the mobile voice technology.

Internet service providers scrambled to offer the newer options in an effort to gain market share.

Business Market Needs Higher Performance All the connection types available to consumers are options for businesses, but usually medium and large companies require even greater bandwidth to support Internet connectivity for legions of employees and to accommodate electronic commerce (e-commerce) needs.

Some of the most common formats are leased lines such as T—1 or T—3 connections, which can achieve transfer rates of 1.5 Mbps and 45 Mbps respectively. The technology is similar to that of DSL, only these connections have much greater capacity, and consequently cost more. Indeed, T—3s are what connect much of the Internet backbone, the core high-speed network that forms the central nervous system of the Internet. T—1s and T—3s can also be bundled or divided to tailor the amount of bandwidth available. Fiber optics, even faster and more costly, provide another alternative.

Service Providers Vary Just as connection types vary, so do the companies offering them. The industry can be segmented broadly into three types of carriers. Consumer-oriented ISPs such as America Online (AOL) and EarthLink focus on residential service and frequently offer their own content. Business-oriented providers and many local phone companies meanwhile provide high-speed connections along with such services as Web hosting and network consulting. Finally, wholesale providers sell Internet access and related services to resellers rather than end users.

BACKGROUND AND DEVELOPMENT

The History of Computer Networks Forbears of the Internet began as limited network systems for organizations to communicate either internally over short distances or externally over long distances by using computers. In the late 1970s, computer networking started to grow. Organizations could afford to use this technology due to the advent of microcomputers that had the power to support several user terminals at once. With local area networks (LANs), companies or organizations could connect a cluster of microcomputers because the technology was relatively inexpensive and easy to install. LANs, however, had their disadvantages, too. They required expensive hardware to transmit large quantities of information quickly. Also, certain kinds of LAN systems could not work with others. Therefore, if an organization had a special LAN for its warehouse and another for its accounting department, they would not be compatible. Moreover, LAN cables could extend only about 500 meters without harming performance.

The LAN counterpart, wide area networks (WANs), existed since the late 1960s and early 1970s and used modems to send messages through regular telephone lines instead of through directly-linked cables such as LANs. WANs also required a host computer at each participating site that was devoted to connecting transmission lines and maintaining the operation of the system. The host computer, often called a server, functioned independently of computers using the WAN. On the other hand, WAN technology cost substantially more than LAN technology because WANs required transmission lines, modems, a special computer, and WAN software, whereas LANs simply required cabling and software. Furthermore, as with LANs, most WANs were incompatible with other WANs and with LANs.

This background created a need for a less expensive, long and short range expandable networking system. The U.S. Department of Defense's Advanced Research Projects Agency (ARPA) endeavored to resolve the problems with existing networking technology and developed a working model of what came to be called the Internet. ARPA interconnected LANs and WANs, using this model to provide the features of each computer networking system. In the mid-1970s, commercial computer companies began to develop their own closed, or proprietary, networks, which would work only with the vendor's software and hardware, although ARPA had conceived of the Internet as an open network that could allow users to communicate no matter whose software and hardware they used. Companies changed their minds, however, as computer hardware technology advances spurred new sales. The cost of computers also decreased, so companies could expect an expanding customer base as well.

By 1982, researchers had a working version of the Internet in operation, and some major technological universities and industrial research organizations began using it. Computer science departments in particular led a campaign to connect all researchers in computer science via the Internet. In addition, the U.S. military also started to rely on the Internet as a standard means of communication and information transmission. At this point, the Internet became an actual tool for communication as opposed to being just an experiment. After the military began using the Internet, the number of computers connected doubled to about 500, though the amount was small relative to the number of computers connected to the Internet in the 1990s. By 1984, the number of Internet users doubled again as more government agencies, including the U.S. Department of Defense and the National Aeronautics and Space Administration, started to take advantage of computer network communication.

Researchers, however, realized that the existing system was becoming flooded and could not hold many more connections. Consequently, the National Science Foundation (NSF) launched an effort to renovate the Internet. Although the NSF could not fund the campaign itself, it served as a clearinghouse by devising a plan and soliciting the help of IBM Corp., the long distance carrier MCI, and MERIT, a Michigan school consortium that had developed its own computer network. By 1988, the cooperative effort of these companies and organizations laid the foundation of the Internet. However, in 1991 this network reached its capacity, too.

The same participants plus Advanced Networks and Services (later ANS Communications and originally a non-profit company until bought by AOL in 1995) set out to revamp the network once more, expanding it to hold substantially more connections. This renovation also took the majority of the funding away from the federal government, turning it over to private industry instead. Between 1983 and 1993, the number of computers connected to the Internet increased from 562 to 1.2 million. By 1994, the number soared to 2.2 million. Around this time, the Internet became a means of communication and information transmission for private individuals because of the expanded network and the decreasing prices of PCs.

Emergence of Internet Access Services In the mid-1980s, online services that would provide a model for ISPs began to emerge. CompuServe, an H&R Block subsidiary, had accommodated businesses with proprietary information services since 1969. Prodigy, a joint venture between Sears, Roebuck & Co. and IBM, began offering proprietary online services to the general public in 1984, and AOL (under the name Quantum Computer Services, a network for Commodore computers) went online in 1985. Netcom On-line Communications Services, Inc., one of the first true Internet services, emerged in 1988, originally providing Internet service to university students and later expanding to include residential and business clients. PSI-Net, Inc., founded in 1989, was one of the early Internet services to focus on business and commercial users and sold Internet access to residential providers to resell to their clients. General Electric also launched an online venture called GEnie, although the company later divested itself of the service when it failed to capture a wide following.

Technological advances in 1993, particularly the introduction of graphical internet browsers, brought mass appeal to the World Wide Web, an area of the Internet that was previously navigable only via text-based browsers. As a result, small ISP operations cropped up all over, in major cities as well as in rural areas that the larger companies neglected. Phone companies also wanted part of the action. The regional Bell operating companies petitioned the Federal Communications Commission to allow them to participate. Long distance phone carriers Sprint and MCI also vied for customers in the booming market of the mid-1990s.

As use of the Internet expanded, proprietary online services such as AOL came under pressure to offer general access as other companies started offering this service. The closed network was becoming obsolete because the Web featured more diverse content and its access wasn't dependent on a captive subscriber base. As a result, companies moved away from this format. IBM jettisoned its share of Prodigy and offered general Internet access instead called Internet Connection. Finally, in 1995 Microsoft introduced the Microsoft Network (MSN), which at the outset provided proprietary services in addition to general access. It briefly opted to abandon the proprietary service and focus exclusively on Internet service, but MSN later decided to stay with exclusive content offerings and to expand them to distinguish its service from that of other companies. Most of the proprietary networks, most notably AOL, followed a similar hybrid approach, keeping some unique content and a distinct user interface but also allowing general access to the Internet.

Free dial-up service for consumers was one of the fastest growing segments of the industry, not to mention one of the most controversial, in the late 1990s and the early years of the first decade of the twenty-first century. Such services, which included among their ranks Alta Vista, NetZero, Juno, and FreeInternet.com, let consumers access the Internet for free after filling out a detailed registration form. Advertisers then used information gleaned from subscribers to target well-defined consumer groups with their sales pitches. In addition to feeding subscribers a heavy dose of advertising, some free ISPs required users to click on an ad every so often, say once an hour, in order to stay connected. Some free ISPs also tracked what sites users visited and stored that information in marketing profiles of the users.

As the U.S. economy in the early years of the first decade of the 2000s worsened, free ISPs found themselves under mounting pressure from shareholders to produce profits. Not only were sources of funding disappearing, but as many firms, dot com and otherwise, began tightening their online advertising budgets, free ISPs also saw their main source of revenue drying up. As a result, firms like Juno began experimenting with ways to convince users to switch to fee-based services. In 2001, Juno began making it more difficult for its most frequent users to log on to the free service. According to *BusinessWeek Online,* "The misconnects were no technical glitch. Juno was deliberately curbing heavy hitters' access to prod them into switching to its $14.95-a-month plan. The reason: a survey of its subscriber base revealed that a mere five percent of users of its free service accounted for more than half of Juno's online costs. By the end of 2001, several free ISP rivals had declared bankruptcy and many analysts began to call into question the viability of the free ISP model, but by 2003,

United Online was making the model work with a good mix of both paying and non-paying customers.

Before the advent of relatively low monthly fees for unlimited access, providers such as AOL and MSN charged a base monthly fee ranging from $5 to $10 per month that included 10 or 15 hours of access. After the monthly hour allocation was spent, these services charged additional fees for each subsequent hour. In 1994, these rates ranged as high as $9.80 per hour; by 1995, many were closer to $2.95 per hour; and in 1996, the flat rate of $19.95 for unlimited hours became widespread.

Although new ISPs continued to spring up throughout the turn of the twenty-first century, the total number began to decline due to stiff competition and increasing consolidation. Although estimates vary, Infonetics Research estimated the head count at just over 4,200 at the end of 2000, down from 4,500 a year earlier, with further decline predicted for following years. In June of 2001, Juno and NetZero announced their intent to merge and the deal was completed three months later. The newly merged firm, named United Online, became the third largest Internet access provider in the United States, only later to be surpassed by Comcast.

Internet service revenues soared as more households and businesses got connected. In 2004 there were an estimated 80 million home Internet users in the United States. Roughly 66 percent of North Americans had Internet access. Cable modem revenues alone reached $11 billion in 2002. That year, cable modems accounted for 58 percent of the broadband market, while DSL accounted for 33 percent.

Broadband remained the industry's brightest spot, with more than 7 million new customers signing on to cable, DSL, or other high-speed services for the first time in 2003. In January of 2002, broadband access accounted for 51 percent of the 2.3 billion hours Americans spent online, compared to 38 percent in January of 2001. This marked the first time broadband had outpaced traditional dial-up methods of accessing the Internet in the United States. By the first quarter of 2003, Comcast had secured the largest broadband customer base with four million subscribers. Time Warner followed with 2.7 million. In third place was SBC, with 2.5 million. Verizon held the fourth place spot with 1.8 million and Cox Communications boasted 1.6 million subscribers.

By the middle of the first decade of the twenty-first century, broadband Internet connections were quickly becoming the norm. *New Scientist* indicated that as of August 2005, approximately 42 percent of the U.S. population had broadband Internet access at home. According to the publication, this was an increase from 36 percent only eight months before and represented two of every five people. In March 2006, *Mediaweek* reported that according to Nielsen/NetRatings, the number of broadband users in the United States reached almost 100 million in February 2005, up 28 percent from the previous year. Broadband users accounted for 68 percent of all Internet surfers, an increase from 55 percent in 2004 and 33 percent in 2003. Heading into 2007, those who had not already switched to broadband were opting for discount dial-up services.

Online entertainment was a key factor driving industry growth. As the Baby Boomer segment of the population continued to grow older, some analysts predicted that this well-funded demographic group would desire to get a large amount of their entertainment at home. As oil prices reached record highs, skyrocketing gasoline costs only added to the popularity of home entertainment options available via the Internet, including on-demand video, music, and gaming services. In its February 4, 2006, issue, *The Online Reporter* cited research from Park Associates indicating that U.S. consumers were expected to spend $2.6 billion on online entertainment in 2006. By 2010, this figure was projected to reach almost $9 billion, an increase of 260 percent. Internet telephone service offered through Voice Over Internet Protocol (VoIP) also was driving the need for broadband heading into the late years of the first decade of the 2000s.

By 2006, a decline in dial-up subscribers and more level growth in the area of broadband subscriptions was affecting large and small ISPs in different ways. Following a loss of 2.8 million subscribers, AOL's subscriber base fell to 19.5 million in 2005 and continued to shrink. These conditions have forced larger players to seek other sources of revenue, such as new service offerings and advertising. In fact, some observers have suggested that ISPs will transition to a new business model, in which they operate more like advertising-supported television stations.

AOL is an excellent example of the movement away from subscription revenues. During the middle years of the twenty-first century's first decade, the company acquired a number of firms to support its expansion and growth in various service areas. After acquiring advanced wireless technologies provider Wildseed Ltd. in August of 2005, AOL acquired blogging company Weblogs Inc. two months later. This was followed by the purchase of Music Now LLC, a digital music subscription company, in November, and video search engine developer Truveo Inc. in December. That same month, Google acquired a 5 percent stake in AOL from Time Warner for $1 billion cash as part of an advertising partnership.

Dial-up's demise has forced many small ISPs out of business. Among the survivors, some have turned to consulting, while others have begun to offer Internet service to rural areas that larger players have overlooked. Although a few smaller players have been able to move into the broadband arena, this is a difficult task. When

independent DSL providers move into a new market, they must secure the cooperation of the local phone company in order to add their equipment to its local switching offices. While phone companies tend to perform both the retail marketing and technical development, many independent DSL outfits specialize in one or the other, relying on a distributor-retailer arrangement. During the middle years of the first decade of the twenty-first century, the ability to offer broadband cable service was essentially limited to cable providers, as they were not required to share access to their lines the way telecommunications firms do.

By the latter part of the decade, experts agreed that, due mostly to their speed and mobility, wireless Internet services such as Wi-Fi, WiMax, and third-generation (3G) cellular services would experience the fastest growth in the industry. According to a May 2008 *Multichannel News* feature, "WiMax is a relatively new technology but has the potential to surpass Wi-Fi, the current wireless-broadband flavor of the day. A single WiMax tower can offer service over a 30-mile radius—compared to a four- to six-mile radius for Wi-Fi—and at higher speeds."

In 2008, Internet service providers (ISPs) worked to keep pace with technology and consumers' demands for faster connections. AT&T announced in July of that year that it offered the fastest 3G mobile broadband network in the United States. The network was available in 300 U.S. cities by mid-2008, and the company had plans to add 50 more cities by the end of the year. AT&T also boasted the best 3G global service, with availability in more than 200 countries.

Other ISPs rallied around different technologies. For example, also in 2008, a joint venture among Comcast, Time Warner Cable, Bright House Networks, Sprint Nextel, Clearwire, Intel, and Google was announced that aimed to offer a nationwide WiMax network. The companies were hoping to reach between 120 million and 140 million users by 2010. Indeed, mobile WiMax appeared to be the wave of the future. According to a report by TelecomView, mobile WiMax will connect 8 percent of the world's 1.1 billion mobile broadband subscribers by 2012, accounting for nearly 88 million users worldwide and $43 billion in system spending.

Besides keeping up with breaking technology, ISPs were dealing with other issues as well as the first decade of the twenty-first century neared a close. For instance, child pornography on the Internet had become a major public concern in the United States. New York State Attorney General Andrew Cuomo said in a news announcement in June 2008, "The pervasiveness of child pornography on the Internet is horrific and it needs to be stopped." In response, Verizon, Time Warner Cable, and Sprint agreed to purge their servers of child porn Web sites and to block newsgroups that allowed users to upload and download child pornography. Cuomo told *Information Week,* "I commend the companies that have stepped up today to embrace a new standard of responsibility, which should serve as a model for the entire industry." The three ISPs also agreed to block Web sites identified by the National Center for Missing & Exploited Children and to develop a new, more efficient response system for user complaints about child pornography. In addition, the ISPs together made a commitment to contribute $1.125 million to stopping child pornography on the World Wide Web through the National Center for Missing & Exploited Children and the Attorney General's office.

In addition to child pornography, the United States Internet Service Provider Association (USISPA) listed several other pressing issues in the industry in 2008, including law enforcement cooperation, cybersecurity, liability, and upcoming state legislation.

CURRENT CONDITIONS

In 2010, First Research, a major industry intelligence company, released results of its latest study of U.S. internet service providers. The report indicated that as of 2010, there were about 4,000 ISP companies that together generated about $20 billion for the industry. Major companies providing services at that time included AOL, AT&T, Comcast, Microsoft, and Verizon. (Internet access operations of telecommunications carriers were included in the study, although telecommunications companies themselves constitute part of a separate industry.) The report also found the industry highly concentrated: the 50 largest companies (out of 4,000) generated roughly 80 percent of all revenues, and even more revealing, the four largest companies generated more than 50 percent.

Companies that provide internet access account for about 75 percent of all industry revenues (the other major segments being web site design and hosting, and technical support services). In September 2010, Reportlinker announced a new market research report, "Internet Access: Global Industry Almanac." According to the report, the global internet access market grew 9.4 percent in 2009, reaching $159.3 billion in value. This figure represented a subscriber base of 500.8 million globally, a 9.6 percent growth in numbers. Americans accounted for 41.9 percent of market value. The report forecast that the market would grow 49.3 percent by 2014, reaching revenues of $230.7 billion. Further, the number of subscribers was forecast to reach 732.9 million at that time.

According to the "Telco 2.0 Strategy Report" published in 2010, the global broadband access market would reach $274 billion by the end of the year. The report proposed three new broadband business models that would evolve: bulk wholesale, "a new approach to mobil data roaming" loop-unbundling and open fiber access in fixed market, such as Amazon's Kindle where a product vendor or service provider contracts for data capacity with a broadband provider and bundles it in a combined offer; and "slice and dice" wholesale (more controversial) in which operators sell data capacity in parcels to other-than-users, the users also paying for access. This two-sided business model might involve deals with device vendors for inclusion of data in bundled M2M offers or to content/application providers who pay for data transmission rather than the end users.

Going into the second decade of the 2000s, perhaps one of the most pressing issues facing ISPs was not delivery of service but rather, liability for having done so, especially in media markets. Globally, several governments are working toward legislation requiring ISPs to curb digital piracy over the Internet. For example, in early 2010, the United Kingdom announced the passing of the Digital Economy Bill in the U.K. House of Commons. It contained provisions requiring ISPs to disconnect persons accused of illegal file-sharing, and moreover, to reveal their names in pending legal actions. The bill contained provisions for the future powers of the secretary of state to seek court injunctions to block any Web site "which the court is satisfied has been, is being or is likely to be, used for, or in connection with, an activity that infringes copyright."

In the United States, the Digital Millennnium Copyright Act (DMCA), and specifically, the Safe Harbor provision as codified in Section 512 of the U.S. Copyright Act, afforded protection to ISPs for unknowingly transmitting copyrighted digital music products through P2P (person to person) illegal downloading and filesharing. However, the Act has come under increasing criticism, now that there is data to show its effects, for providing no incentive to ISPs to cooperate with content providers when they, in fact, enjoy greater revenues from Internet activity. It is well established that existing access to copyrighted music, and now, movies, are the main attractions of the Internet. The ongoing litigation between Viacom, YouTube, and Google speak to the seriousness of the problem, as in 2010 it remained easy for anyone to upload, access, transmit, or store any piece of digital content, copyrighted or not.

Not all was hostile. In June 2009, Universal Music and Virgin Media announced a deal offering unlimited download service. Geoff Taylor, BPI Chief Executive, stated in a related press release, "It is very encouraging to see an ISP and a record label working together as creative partners." Music companies have reached out to offer new ways for consumers to buy and access music, such as ISP subscription services that bundle in music services with broadband, streaming services with applications for mobile devices, and online music video services.

Between 2009 and 2010, IFPI reported that, music companies had partnered with advertising-supported services including Deezer, MySpace, Music, Spotify, and We7; ISPs including Terra in Brazil, TDC in Denmark, and Sky in the UK; mobile operators including Vodafone; handset makers such as Nokia and Sony Ericsson; and online video channels including Hulu and VEVO.

Finally, on the national security front, a bill, discussed in the U.S. Congress in 2010 but not to be formally introduced until 2011, intends to make all online services available for wiretapping. The delay in action was related to the pending need for ISPs to redesign several services from the ground up. For example, some ISPs offer peer to peer (P2P) messaging that even the ISPs cannot unscramble. There would also be a need to establish a domestic office for foreign-based providers to perform required interception services. Under existing law, ISPs are subject to wiretap orders but are not required to have interception capability. Historically, most ISPs have waited until the order is served before they try to develop a means to intercept the communications. Opponents to the new proposed law cite both security and privacy concerns.

INDUSTRY LEADERS

AOL LLC Founded in 1985, America Online (AOL) was the United States' largest consumer ISP, with 8.5 million subscribers by 2008. The company, which merged with media conglomerate and cable operator Time Warner in 2001, held a commanding lead in the U.S. market, but in 2003 suffered heavy subscriber defections and a leadership crisis.

In the mid-1990s, it launched a massive campaign to recruit ordinary consumers who weren't necessarily technology mavens. AOL originated as a closed network with proprietary content, and it remains a hybrid between an online content provider and an ISP. Soon, AOL fashioned itself as the blue chip ISP, a reference to its vaunted stock traded on the New York Stock Exchange, and made numerous acquisitions worldwide. In 1998, it took over rival CompuServe (with 2.2 million customers of its own as of 2000) and bought Internet browser developer Netscape later the same year. AOL has also been a major force in international markets, with millions of subscribers in Europe and a growing base in Latin America. In the spring of 2000, the company purchased Bertelsmann's half interests in AOL Europe and AOL Australia.

In the early years of the first decade of the 2000s, the company struggled as it got demoted in the Time Warner merger and as its dial-up business model eroded amid surging demand for high-speed service. Long-time CEO Stephen M. Case departed active duty in 2003 while new management tried to redirect the flagging behemoth. Following a loss of 2.8 million subscribers, AOL's subscriber base fell to 19.5 million in 2005. Late that year, a dissatisfied Case resigned from Time Warner's board of directors and called for the break-up of AOL and its parent company.

Following a global online advertising partnership with Google in late 2005 in which Google acquired a 5 percent stake in AOL from Time Warner for $1 billion cash, AOL began seeking other revenue sources. In 2006, the company launched a number of new services, including In2TV, which served up free, ad-supported access to 14,000 classic TV programs from Warner Bros. and an Internet telephone service called AIM Phoneline. In 2006, the company partnered with cable and telecommunications firms to launch a nationwide broadband network. The company was reorganizing in 2010 and expected a 15 to 20 percent loss in revenues.

AT&T In November 2005, SBC Communications purchased AT&T Corp., creating the nation's largest telecommunications company, as well as the leading U.S. provider of broadband DSL service. Headquartered in San Antonio, Texas, the company employed a workforce of 310,000 and reported 2009 sales of $16 billion. AT&T merged with BellSouth in the latter half of the decade.

EarthLink Created by the 2000 merger between EarthLink Network and MindSpring Enterprises, the new EarthLink Inc. remained one of the largest U.S. ISPs in 2006, with five million subscribers. EarthLink and MindSpring were both founded in 1994. By 2004, EarthLink was aiming for the discount broadband market, piloting a program with California proprietary DSL start-up Digitalpath Networks. Heading into the latter part of the decade, the company was quickly establishing a leadership position in the development of Wi-Fi broadband networks. Following a partnership with Google to develop a Wi-Fi network in San Francisco, during the fourth quarter of 2005, EarthLink was chosen to build city-wide municipal Wi-Fi broadband networks in Anaheim, California, and Philadelphia. EarthLink gained a strong position as a supplier of broadband to small and medium-sized businesses with its December 2005 acquisition of New Edge. The $144 million cash and stock deal gave EarthLink one of the nation's largest communications and data networks. By 2008 the company was also offering services such as Web hosting and advertising. In 2009, EarthLink had approximately 2 million subscribers, about 1 million of which were broadband. With roughly 1,000 employees, sales reached $723 million.

Comcast Corp. Headquartered in Philadelphia, Comcast had 13 million broadband subscribers in 2008, up from just over 4 million in 2003. Comcast grew rapidly in late 2002 with its acquisition of AT&T Broadband. In addition to its leadership position in terms of Internet access subscribers, Comcast Cable is the largest cable television company in the United States, with 24 million subscribers. In 2008 the company also offered Comcast Digital Voice, a Voice over Internet Protocol (VoIP) telephone service, which has about 4 million customers. With roughly 100,000 employees, Comcast reported 2009 sales of $35.76 billion.

United Online Inc. United Online has at its roots one of the biggest of the free ISPs, NetZero Inc., which was founded in 1997 and began offering service in late 1998. Advertisers picked up the tab for NetZero's free, unlimited access, but the catch was that users had to divulge details about themselves and have ads streaming onto their computer screens the entire time they were online. The formula allowed NetZero to rack up 3 million users, half of whom were considered active, by 2000. However, although the company had $55.5 million in sales that year, it remained far from turning a profit. Like many other free ISPs, NetZero began looking for ways to convince its customers to pay for something they had previously received for free. In September of 2001, NetZero merged with Juno Online Services Inc. to form United Online. The company made a smooth transition to profitability and by 2004 was the fourth largest consumer ISP, with 5 million paid subscribers. United Online also offered additional services, including Internet telephone service and Web hosting. The company also had acquired Classmates Online Inc.

Other Companies Several other companies were significant ISPs in the industry in 2010. According to the USISPA, Sprint, Time Warner Cable, Yahoo!, Microsoft, and Verizon were also in the top 10.

AMERICA AND THE WORLD

International Internet piracy of copyrighted or unauthorized data remained a major concern in 2010. In addition to the proffered legislation in the United Kingdom, France, South Korea, and Taiwan had already adopted new laws to address this in 2009. New Zealand also had pending legislation in 2010.

Although the United States is the world's largest national market for Internet services, other regions are proving significant markets as well, and some have higher penetrations of broadband. Although broadband was growing at a rapid pace in the United States, the country still lagged behind other countries in terms of penetration. For example, a March 2006 study from the Consumer Electronics Association (CEA) found that broadband penetration exceeded the 50 percent mark in South Korea, Hong Kong, Singapore, and Taiwan, and had reached nearly 50 percent in Japan. The CEA study ranked the United States 15th worldwide, behind these and other countries, including the Netherlands, Denmark, France, Sweden, and Canada.

Internationally, China was poised for rapid growth. The country was home to a growing number of high-income workers with the means to access DSL (the most popular form of broadband in China) and cable Internet services. In January 2006, *Internetweek* reported that according to Chinese wireless and telecommunications equipment manufacturer ZTE Corp., the number of broadband subscribers in China was expected to exceed 113 million by 2009, up from 50 million users in 2006.

Growth also was taking place in the United Kingdom during the middle years of the twenty-first century's first decade. According to the country's Office of National Statistics, broadband penetration totaled 64 percent in 2006. Helping matters was a government decision that British Telecom needed to lease its infrastructure, which would serve to increase competition in Britain.

Human Rights Watch argues that since the Internet has the potential to unite thousands and thousands of people from all over the world, allowing them to engage in political discussion among other things, some countries see the Internet as a threat to their autonomy and their policies. Hence, some countries have enacted strict regulations. For example, China requires all Internet service providers to register with the government, while Saudi Arabia and Vietnam provide only government-controlled access.

Although affluent citizens of countries such as the United States, Japan, and Germany can afford PCs and the other requisite technology for using the Internet, elsewhere in the world access is considerably less common due to cost. Nonprofit organizations in some countries, such as the Peruvian Scientific Network in Peru, however, have created public computer facilities that offer Internet access in addition to classes on Internet navigation for $15 a month, according to Calvin Sims in the *New York Times*. The United Nations provided initial subsidies to the organization, which at the time had 22,000 members and was ranked the fourth-fastest-growing network in the world behind Brazil, Mexico, and Chile, according to Sims.

BIBLIOGRAPHY
"63m Broadband Users in China by 2008." *The Online Reporter,* 14 January 2006.

"AOL Links VoIP Service To AIM; The Online Portal Is Planning a New Internet Phone Service That'll Give Users of Its Instant Messaging a Free VoIP Number." *InternetWeek,* 11 May 2006.

"AOL: Lower Numbers, Increased Optimism." *The Online Reporter,* 4 February 2006.

"AOL's 2009 By the Numbers: $190 M Reorg Charges; Sold Buy.at For $17M: Patch's $50M 2010." Available from http://paidcontent.org.

AT&T Offers Nation's Fastest 3G Network." *PR Newswire,* 10 July 2008.

Barraclough, Chris, and Dean Bubley. "Mobile, Fixed and Wholesale Broadboard Models: Best Practice Innovation..." Telco 2.0 Strategy Report, 2010. Available from http://www.telco2research.com/articles/AN_Happy-Pipes-416Bn-2020_Full.

Beck, Julie. " Federal Bill Calls For Redesign of Internet, To Make It Wiretappable." *Popular Science,* 27 September 2010.

"Broadband Has 64% Internet Share in UK." *The Online Reporter,* 25 February 2006.

"China's Broadband Market to Double." *InternetWeek,* 18 January 2006.

Comcast. Available from http://www.cnbc.com/id/36333877/Comcast_CEO_Received_Pay_of_25_million_for_2009.

"Current Issues." United States Internet Service Providers Association, 2008.

Deeken, Aimee. "Broadband Connections Soar 28%." *MEDIAWEEK,* 20 March 2006.

Farrell, Mike. "Competition Pays Off." *Multichannel News,* 16 April 2007.

———. "WiMax Takes Flight." *Multichannel News,* 12 May 2008.

"Forget DSL Or Cable, Broadband Users Want Their Fiber." *InformationWeek,* 3 July 2008.

"IFPI Publishes Digital Music Report - 2010." 21 January 2010. Available from http://www.ifpi.org/content/section_resources/dmr2010.html

"Importance of IPTV, Video Services Grows among Service Providers, Says Study." *Broadcast Engineering,* 27 May 2008.

"In2TV Bringing 14,000 Warner Bros Titles to AOL." *The Online Reporter,* 25 February 2006.

"ISPs Agree To Block Child Porn Sites, Newsgroups." *InformationWeek,* 10 June 2008.

Kharif, Olga. "EarthLink's Big Bet on Broadband; Will Building Municipal Wi-Fi Networks Pull the Company Out of its Dial-up Doldrums?" *Business Week Online,* 2 June 2006. Available from www.businessweek.com.

"New CEA Study Finds 43 Million American Households Now Have Broadband Internet Access." *Business Wire,* 30 March 2006.

"Online Entertainment Spending to Reach $9b in 2010." *The Online Reporter,* 4 February 2006.

"Reportlinker Adds Internet Access: Global Industries Almanac." *PR newswire,* 21 September 2010. Available from http://www.prnewswire,com/news-releases/reportlinker-adds-internet-access-global-industry-almanac-103445954.html.

Rougeot, Jonathan. "Tech Giants Make Big Investment in WiMax Wireless Networking." *Computer Shopper,* July 2008.

"Rural Broadband Access Grows to 24%." *The Online Reporter,* 4 March 2006.

"Sowing Seeds of WiMax." *Multichannel News,* 7 July 2008.

"Universal Music and Virgin Media Announce Unlimited Download Service." BPI Statement, 16 June 2009. Available at http://www.bpi.co.uk/categories/news.

"The US Internet Service Provider (ISP) Industry Includes About 4,000 Companies That Generate Combined Annual Revenue of About $20 Billion. *TMC News* M2 Press WIRE, 29 April 2010. Available from http://www.tmcnet.com.

"WiMax vs. DSL." *Wireless Weblog,* 19 June 2006.

Worth, Dan. "ISP Industry Protests UK Disconnection Laws." *iTnews,* 9 April 2010. Available from http://www.iTnews.com/au/news/171629.

IT CONSULTING

SIC CODE(S)

7371

INDUSTRY SNAPSHOT

Only one segment of the larger information technology (IT) services continuum, IT consulting is the weighty and highly competitive business of telling companies what technologies to buy and how to deploy them. Paradoxically, although IT consulting has relatively few entry barriers—it is largely just a matter of having some expertise in an area of technology—serving top tier clients like the Fortune 500 is an opportunity usually accessible to only a handful of consultancies, themselves often among the Fortune elite.

The consulting side of information technology (IT) has evolved with the onset of e-business or Internet-enabled business processes such as e-commerce, supply chain integration, and sales force automation. Early on, large firms like Andersen, KPMG, and EDS were perceived sometimes as old-school vendors who were not proficient in cutting-edge Internet technologies. This was a boon in the late 1990s for emergent e-business specialty houses like MarchFirst, Razorfish, and Scient, which quickly racked up revenues in the hundreds of millions and stock valuations in the billions.

By 2000, however, as dot-com stocks toppled and high-flying upstart consultancies teetered on insolvency, momentum began shifting back to traditional vendors serving traditional clients. The shakeout proved to be a double-edged sword, since Internet companies can be both providers and sizable customers of IT consulting. In the meantime, the large, established vendors had gone to great lengths to prove their relevance in the changing market. Many of the big operations set up specialized e-commerce units, sometimes treating them as independent companies, as if to underscore how much things were changing. In an effort to maximize their market power and quell rising fears that integrated accounting and consulting firms have intrinsic conflicts of interest, there also was a wave of separations and mergers among top tier consulting firms.

All of these changes played out against a backdrop of tremendously strong sales. Demand for IT consulting was hard to satisfy, propelled by Internet-related projects, year 2000 preparations, and generally strong business conditions that left many corporate budgets replete with funds for technology consultation. Nevertheless, buoyant sales at the macro level couldn't hide the tumult facing some of the industry's finest. The revenue decelerations of 2000 were devastating, as were the bitter losses in market capitalization. By one estimate, based on government filings, publicly traded Web services firms laid off some 5,000 employees during the latter half of 2000 in the wake of financial shortfalls.

As a result, consultancies on shaky financial footing were prey to acquisition or worse. Thought to be most vulnerable were firms focusing on sleek designs and simple e-commerce deployments rather than meat-and-potatoes competencies like legacy system integration and large-scale process re-engineering. By 2001, IT consulting demand had begun to slow. The industry was characterized by both fee reductions and continued layoffs into the early years of the first decade of the twenty-first century. Consultancies such as MarchFirst, Sapient, Razorfish, iXl, and Scient had faded from the scene by the middle of the decade, while traditional players such as IBM and Accenture remained.

Conditions within the IT consulting sector were showing signs of improvement by the middle of the first decade of the 2000s as the economy mended and companies began to consider and contract for unavoidable technology projects. Analysts indicated that signs of recovery, primarily in the United States but in Europe as well, were first apparent in late 2004. Conditions were expected to improve at a moderate clip, according to Standard & Poor's. Factors driving growth included increased spending on homeland security and defense technology, a shortage of qualified IT consultants, and increasing economic globalization.

ORGANIZATION AND STRUCTURE

IT consulting encompasses many types of computer work and its boundaries with other industries are often vague. Although the word consulting may suggest primarily an advisory role, in practice, IT consultants often are the implementers of technology development, deployment, and training.

The field ranges from large multi-national management consulting firms with billion dollar budgets to one-person shops that bring in $100,000 or less a year. What they all have in common is a client who contracts with them as outside service providers to work on a computer problem on a project basis. A project may be a day or two in length or a year or longer. Some contracts are renewed indefinitely until a consultant becomes, in many respects, indistinguishable from a normal full-time employee.

The most visible side of the industry consists of large firms. Traditionally these have included the so-called Big Six accounting firms and big hardware and software producers like Hewlett-Packard and IBM.

In the late 1990s, however, a series of mergers, spin-offs, and acquisitions changed the character and form of the industry, particularly with regard to the independent consulting firms. Price Waterhouse, for example, merged in 1998 with Coopers and Lybrand, another Big Six firm, to become PricewaterhouseCoopers (PwC). In 2002, in response to fears about conflicts of interest, PwC sold its consulting arm to IBM Corp. for $3.5 billion.

Other large consulting firms also transformed themselves. The consulting arm of Ernst & Young LLP, a member of the remaining Big Five, was sold in 2000 to Cap Gemini SA of France, forming Cap Gemini Ernst & Young. Also in 2000, KPMG LLP spun off its consulting business as KPMG Consulting LLC. KPMG Consulting received major funding from networking giant Cisco Systems Inc., which also had a financial stake in the Cap Gemini Ernst & Young venture. Meanwhile, after a bitter and drawn-out separation, Andersen Consulting, later renamed Accenture, gained its independence from Arthur Andersen. However, confusingly, Arthur Andersen has another internal IT consulting practice that was not spun off with Andersen Consulting.

These firms are distinguished from the thousands of smaller consultancies, which often provide only a fraction of the breadth of services offered by a top tier firm. Nonetheless, in the United States, a major share of IT consulting is performed by small companies, partnerships, or individuals. Companies often begin as one-or-two-person operations and grow as their reputation builds. If they are offered more work than they are able to handle alone, they then expand to take on extra employees. These smaller operations generally have from 1 to 10 employees and tend to specialize in a few particular types of projects. They can be in a particular business sector involving specific applications, computer languages, and operating systems that are within their expertise.

Staying current or even ahead of technology is a critical ongoing process for IT consultants. Consultants' fees relate directly to the demand for the skills mastered and it is the new and uncommon abilities that are in greatest demand. Familiarity with SAP software, a popular but relatively new set of business applications in the United States, brings significantly higher fees than familiarity with UNIX, a system that is important but with which a great deal of consultants are conversant. Consultants frequently accept work outside their skill set at a fraction of the rates normally paid in order to get experience in a new application. According to the Software Contractors' Guild, the software side of consulting alone encompasses numerous abilities: in all, more than 500 skill classifications, including 171 different applications, 55 computer languages, and 24 operating systems.

Consultants find clients in different ways. Some advertise or have Web pages. However, word of mouth plays an important role. A sizable number of consultants get new clients only through referrals. Once consultants or companies have completed an impressive job, they can rely on new client referrals because there are so few consultants in relation to the amount of work at any given time. One group of independent consultants, known as contractors, does not organize its own jobs. These contractors rely instead on placement agencies similar to temporary employment agencies to find work for them. Contractors provide to an agency a resume that describes in depth their skill set, are interviewed, and indicate their availability. When work is available, usually within a few days, the agency notifies the contractor. Clients pay the contractor's fee, which has been specified or negotiated in advance, plus an additional 30 to 60 percent to the agency.

Staffing agencies play a large role in the consulting business. All of the major temporary staffing firms, including Adecco, Kelly, and Olsten, have technical units geared to placing consultants and other technical specialists in interim positions.

The Software Contractors' Guild acts as a job clearinghouse for contractors, consulting companies, agencies, and clients. For a $20 annual membership, contractors can post resumes online, noting their skill-set items and relocation options. According to observers, listing with the Guild brings more work offers than most members can single-handedly manage, and the organization has steady turnover. Contractors frequently have their own Web pages to advertise their special skills.

Although both are self-employed and work for clients, a few rough distinctions can be drawn between contractors and consultants. Contractors in general work through agencies, at least while they are getting started in the business; they tend to work exclusively on site at the client's place of business; their projects range from a day to indefinite renewal; the projects they work on tend to be more clearly defined and of more limited scope; and they tend to spend more time "writing code," which is creating computer programs. Contractors, who number in the tens of thousands, constitute the majority of the consultant labor force. Consultants tend to work on a project for three to nine months. Oftentimes, they are required to take an active role in a client's problem definition and needs analysis. The first weeks or even months of a project at a mid-to-large-sized company usually involve a series of meetings and interviews with different members of staff. Only afterward can the technical problems be approached.

The technical work performed by IT consultants varies. Sometimes older software is modified to run in a different system or in an ensemble of different applications. Other times programs are written from scratch or may be patched together from routines a consultant keeps in his or her "tool kit."

The decision to outsource an IT function is increasingly viewed not just as a quick fix but as an integral part of a company's long term business strategy. According to Frank Casale, executive director of the Outsourcing Institute of Jericho, New York, "An organization needs to analyze its core competency. Anything from that point on could be a candidate for outsourcing." Among the reasons for increased outsourcing are: to be able to react quickly to market shifts, to have access to highly skilled personnel, and—most importantly—to cut costs. Companies considering the outsourcing of an IT function are cautioned to carefully determine the cost of that function. "Estimating cost is more complicated that people think," Casale says.

For corporations that outsource IT functions, the benefits may be either obvious or difficult to quantify. Some of the benefits, such as improved performance, the ability of the company's full time staff to concentrate on its core competency, and a reduction of operating costs, can readily be seen and measured. However, some of the more subtle benefits of outsourcing may take time to become apparent. "If four years ago you had told someone you could use outsourcing to increase morale, you would have been laughed at," Casale says. Today, however, most top IT executives realize that outsourcing one or more functions can reduce the pressure on an overtaxed staff, creating a more hospitable working environment for full-time employees in the IT department. "Then it becomes a tool to create a good work environment," says Casale. "It's tough enough to keep these people as it is. It becomes a perk."

Regulation Section 1706 of the Internal Revenue Code is the most troublesome regulation for consultants because they fall into three tax classes: 1099 workers, W-2 workers, and those who have incorporated. The latter two are legally uncomplicated, but the former falls into the IRS's gray zone. W-2 workers are paid by the placement agency for which they work. The agency collects the fees from the client and cuts the contractor a paycheck with income tax already deducted. The advantage of not having to keep track of taxes is offset by the numerous tax breaks not available to W-2 employees. Self-employed consultants who have not incorporated are considered 1099 workers. Although they are ostensibly independent, by working on site and using the client's equipment, they may be considered for tax purposes regular employees of the client (i.e., as workers who should be in the W-2 class). As such, 1099 contractors risk being audited and forced to repay deductions made as self-employed workers. Their clients also are at risk of litigation for unpaid benefits or failure to withhold income taxes.

Thus, it is to an independent consultant's advantage to incorporate, even if he or she works completely on his/her own. Incorporation as a business sidesteps these problematic income tax questions. The Software Contractors Guild expressly advises clients looking for contractors to hire only those who have incorporated or who are W-2 employees of a contract placement agency.

There are certain contractual restrictions on software consultants. Because of the sensitive client information to which they have access, consultants are usually required to sign confidentiality agreements. Their placement agency contract requires them to wait a year after the conclusion of such a contract before accepting independent work with the same client. Professional ethics require that when a contractor is offered the same job by different agencies, the first offer is accepted.

BACKGROUND AND DEVELOPMENT

The rise of technology consulting as a profession parallels the expansion of computers throughout the business world. Not long after this expansion began, computer manufacturers began to realize that they had to provide many more services to the companies installing their computers than was possible for them. Their in-house programming and computer departments soon realized they were incapable of maintaining the cutting-edge skills necessary to adapt to the swiftly evolving computer industry.

Led by pioneers like Jerry Weinberg and Ed Yourdan, the first independent software consulting firms opened in the 1960s. They arose in response to software packages that were difficult to use and in response to software vendors who offered inadequate support for complex projects. Software consulting began mediating between inflexible software and the increasingly helpless software user.

IT consulting services also grew out of support businesses run by leading hardware vendors such as IBM, Hewlett-Packard, and Unisys. These firms developed extensive support and maintenance services because their systems were usually proprietary and outsiders often lacked the knowledge needed to manage them on their own. Later, these services grew into full-fledged consulting and systems integration operations, often handling machines and software produced by their competitors. Indeed, by the mid-1990s, services became key to sustaining business growth and profitability at large hardware makers like IBM and Compaq, which faced declining margins on their hardware sales due to falling computer prices.

IT consulting had turned into a phenomenal growth industry by the late 1990s. Not surprisingly, one of the biggest growth drivers has been Internet-related technology. Barely on the consulting map in the mid-1990s, business initiatives involving the Web or derived technologies funneled billions of dollars into consulting.

Related and perhaps equally as profound was an altered paradigm regarding technology's role in business. Technology, once the means toward implementing corporate strategy, or perhaps merely the mundane but necessary infrastructure for operating the business, has become ever more strategic. In the most visible examples, the famous and infamous Web start-ups of the 1990s, superior technology was sometimes the entire strategy. The implications were unparalleled productivity and efficiency, the forging of new markets, and formidable competitive advantage.

Impact of the Dot-com Fallout The IT consulting industry experienced record cutbacks and layoffs early in the twenty-first century. The advent of Internet start-up consultancies like Scient and Viant in the late 1990s had presented a new form of competition to traditional consultancies, forcing them to compete both for new clients seeking to incorporate Internet technology into their business practices and for a rapidly shrinking pool of qualified employees. As a result, many firms began boosting their compensation packages to retain existing employees as well as to attract new help. When the Internet market began to falter in 2000, weakening the U.S. economy, many consultancies were left overloaded with highly paid help. According to a July 2001 issue of *The Economist,* "Consultants are finding that their rate of attrition—the rate at which people leave voluntarily—has shrunk dramatically as rival jobs (such as joining an Internet start-up or venture-capital operation) have become less attractive." When revenues began to wane in the early years of the first decade of the 2000s, many firms reduced headcount in an effort to bolster earnings.

Attrition at two of the industry's leading firms, Accenture and McKinsey, fell from 20 percent in 2000 to 12 percent in 2001. Accenture laid off 4 percent of its workforce and asked hundreds of employees to take a leave of absence that year. Pricewaterhouse Coopers also lightened its workforce and reduced pay to all U.S. consulting employees by 7 percent. Similarly, Cap Gemini Ernst & Young cut 4 percent of its global workforce, KPMG Consulting trimmed 7 percent of its staff, and upstart Scient laid off nearly half of its workforce. Consequently, between October 2000 and October 2001, the worldwide consulting industry saw its ranks fall by nearly 5 percent, from a total of 600,000 employees to 572,000 employees.

As well as trimming their ranks, many consultancies lowered their fees in an effort to remain competitive. *Consultants News* predicted that fee increases would likely remain under 5 percent in the early years of the first decade of the 2000s compared to 12 percent in 1998. The sluggish market conditions also left some consultancies with no choice but to shutter operations. For example, Cambridge, Massachusetts-based A.D. Little declared bankruptcy in early 2002.

Conditions within the IT consulting sector were showing signs of improvement by mid-decade, as the economy mended and companies began to consider and contract for unavoidable technology projects. Analysts indicated that signs of recovery, primarily in the United States but in Europe as well, were first apparent in late 2004.

Applications like wireless networking and the melding of computing and communications benefited the industry. Another trend benefiting consultants was the rise of so-called enterprise software. These heavy duty systems, often aimed at companies with many thousands of employees, attempt to provide the advantages of off-the-shelf software with sufficient customization to meet a company's unique requirements. They are designed to serve enterprise-wide functions like human resources, accounting, inventory management, and sales management. The software category is commonly known as enterprise resource planning (ERP) because one of the bigger selling points is the software's ability to give management detailed information about corporate resources. Authored by such vendors as SAP and Oracle, these programs have pre-defined features and their own development environments for customizing the software.

CURRENT CONDITIONS

Due to its status as the largest technology enterprise, IBM's performance serves as one metric to assess the tech industry's general health. The company indicated that this strong performance was partially attributable to demand for its consulting services. Notwithstanding, the overall IT industry suffered some decline in 2008 and early 2009. IBM had experienced layoffs, with more than 1,400 employees trimmed from the Information Management business. Yet, by late 2009, the industry appeared to have leveled its losses and stabilized. In November 2009, *Information Age* (publishers of the Information Age Index) reported that after 12 months of consistent decline, the rate of revenue decline among the IT industry's key suppliers slowed in October 2009.

Wyatt Matas and Associates, in its "Government IT Consulting Industry M&A Report Summer 2009," predicted that IT revenue in the management-consulting sector would increase by 3.4 percent during the final three quarters of 2009. The government segment, which makes up almost 30 percent of the sector, was expected to outperform the private sector. Furthermore, President Obama's proposed 2010 budget would increase information technology spending throughout most government agencies, noted the firm. The Department of Homeland Security (DHS) will receive over $400 million more in 2010 for systems that help protect infrastructure IT, and Department of Defense (DOD) (which spends the most on IT) will receive over $57.2 billion for communications and mission support systems, along with $10.5 billion for command, control, and computer systems. Finally, the budget includes $1.2 billion in new, across-the-board, broadband spending. Because President Obama made it his goal for every American to have electronic health care records by 2014, a significant investment in healthcare IT will be assured.

Merger and acquisition activity in the IT consulting sector will likely be high in 2010, said Wyatt Matas and Associates. It predicted that IT firms without data storage or healthcare IT capabilities will acquire smaller concerns that already have that capability. It opined that the economy will continue to improve, motivating private equity firms to add to their portfolios those IT government contracting companies that had recurring revenue streams and well-defined technological competence.

INDUSTRY LEADERS

Numerically speaking, the industry is dominated by small firms that typically cater to small businesses or highly specialized, low-volume needs of larger businesses. However, much more visible are the large companies active in the industry.

Successors to the reconfigured Big Five accounting/consulting firms form a major part of the industry at the top tier. These include Accenture (formerly Andersen Consulting), KPMG International, and Capgemini (formerly Cap Gemini Ernst & Young). These firms, and others like them, are distinct in that they are very well-established, multinational enterprises and are largely independent of any hardware or software vendor (although some have financial ties to hardware concerns). They are also unique in their extensive offering of management and technical consulting services. All of them have (or had) ties to financial and accounting services, but most have taken great pains to distance their consulting businesses from their accounting and auditing responsibilities.

Accenture, a Bermuda company with headquarters in New York, was the world's largest consulting firm. IT consulting is one of its five groups of services. Including all services, Accenture brought in $21.58 billion in sales in its fiscal year 2009. The company employed 180,000 people in 50 countries. Another giant, KPMG International, based in the Netherlands, had 2009 sales of $20.1 billion and 103,621 employees. Capgemini, which is based in Paris but has a subsidiary in New York (Capgemini U.S.), was smaller than the previous two, with 61,036 employees and $8.2 billion in 2006 sales, but still considered one of the world's leaders in IT consulting.

Another group of large players consists of firms with ties to the hardware and software sectors. Examples include IBM Global Services, the world's largest IT services firm in the middle of the first decade of the 2000s, which acquired PwC Consulting in 2002, and HP Technology Solutions Group. IBM Global of Armonk, New York, offers services in such areas as networking, data storage, application development, technical support, and infrastructure management. In 2007, IBM landed a 10-year contract worth $800 million with India's fifth biggest wireless operator, Idea Cellular. In early 2008, it completed its acquisition of Cognos, which is now one of four parts of IBM's "Information On Demand" strategy. HP Technology Solutions Group in Palo Alto, California, is the largest business sector of Hewlett-Packard. These companies are sometimes seen as not being independent enough and too focused on pushing their own platforms. They also are perceived more as technical experts rather than comprehensive consulting firms that can advise on strategy, branding, or other business issues.

Consulting also is done by a number of large, independent IT outsourcing firms such as Computer Sciences Corp. (CSC) and Electronic Data Systems (EDS). These firms may perform anything from operating a data center to deploying very large custom systems for corporations or governments. Companies like CSC and EDS are often chosen for long- term, highly complex projects involving legacy systems and scads of data. CSC, in El Segundo, California, and Plano, Texas-based EDS were also in the running.

WORKFORCE

Precise statistics regarding the number of active IT consultants are scarce. Technology consultants usually have a college degree, and often an advanced degree as well, in computer science, engineering, or business. Independent consultants generally require about two years experience working in a company before they generate work on their own. Some have professional engineering licenses issued by states, but clients do not generally expect such licensing. A large number of consultants also have systems certification issued by software companies like Novell Inc., Microsoft, or Oracle.

One of the main challenges for consultants and contractors is keeping up to date with the rapid changes in the computer world. To this end, many read the latest computer periodicals and maintain personal reference libraries of the latest computer manuals. A great deal of information is available from the Internet. All of the major computer magazines have Web sites and all of the businesses associated with computers and software maintain an online presence where they publish press releases and other updates. Many seek out work that will bring them into practical contact with technologies and systems of interest, and many also complete training or certification courses to develop new skills.

It is not unusual for a qualified consultant to earn $100,000 or more per year. Even contractors who work primarily through agents do not find it difficult to earn a six-figure income. Average income for newcomers to independent practice—consultants or contractors who have put their time in with a firm and have struck out on their own—is around $55,000 per year. In addition, because consultants tend to work on short-term projects, usually no longer than nine months, they have more flexibility to schedule vacations. On the other hand, as self-employed persons, consultants have to take responsibility for their own taxes, health insurance, and retirement plans.

AMERICA AND THE WORLD

Being a profession in which so much work is distributed by referral and personal reference, consulting depends on establishing face to face, individual relationships with clients. For that reason, domestic workers do most software consulting in the United States. What foreign competition does exist is as yet unorganized and poses little threat to Americans, if only because of the serious shortage of qualified personnel that currently exists in the United States.

However, the Internet has made it easier for international consultants to work for U.S.-based customers. For instance, some consultants come from India, Indonesia, or Eastern Europe. These consultants find clients that transmit the work electronically, which is becoming easier to do. It is then distributed to a crew of workers who finish the job much more quickly—and for a much lower price—than domestic manpower. Software workers in India, as an example, do extremely high quality work and many charge much less than U.S. consultants.

U.S. consulting also has a tremendous global reach. Top providers like Accenture and KPMG have large international operations that serve multinational corporations and government agencies throughout the world. Likewise, European firms like Cap Gemini have global presence as well.

BIBLIOGRAPHY

"Accenture Beats Profit Estimates, Raises Forecast." Reuters, 27 March 2007. Available from http://www.earthtimes.org.

"Accenture Eyes Chinese City for Key Base." *AsiaPulse News,* 14 June 2005.

"Accenture Reports Fourth-Quarter and Full-Year Fiscal 2009 Results." 1 October 2009. Available from http://newsroom.accenture.com.

"ACS: A Private Affair?" *Business Week Online,* 21 March 2007. Available from www.businessweek.com.

"Capgemini Sees Margin Pressure but Revenue Holds Steady." *Computer Business,* 30 July 2009. Available from http://www.cbronline.com/news/capgemini_sees_margin_pressure_but_revenue_holds_steady_090730.

"China's IT Service Market Likely to Top US$8.7 BLN in 2005." *AsiaPulse News,* 25 August 2005.

Crane, Stephanie S. "Accenture Awaits a Turning Tide." *Business Week Online,* 27 June 2005. Available from www.businessweek.com.

"IBM Wins Key Deal With India Mobile Player; The 10-year Contract with Idea, India's Fifth-Largest Wireless Operator, Boosts Idea's Competitiveness and Increases IBM's Lead in IT Services and Consulting." *Business Week Online,* 22 March 2007. Available from www.businessweek.com.

"IDC Study Reveals IT Spending." *Telecomworldwide,* 3 August 2005.

"Information Age Index: A return to growth?." *Information Age,* 19 November 2009. Available from http://www.information-age.com/channels/information-management/company-analysis/1095157/information-age-index-a-return-to-growth.thtml.

Kessler, Michelle. "Investors Relieved by IBM's Solid Earnings." *USA Today,* 19 July 2005.

McGee, Marianne Kolbasuk. "Generation Gap: Who Will Step Up as IT Vets Retire?" *InformationWeek,* 13 June 2005.

U.S. Department of Labor, Bureau of Labor Statistics. "Management, Scientific, and Technical Consulting Services." *Occupational Outlook Handbook, 2006-07 Edition,* 20 March 2007. Available from http://www.bls.gov/.

Wyatt Matas and Associates. "Government IT Consulting Industry M&A Report Summer 2009." Available from http://www.articlesbase.com/finance-articles/government-it-consulting-industry-ma-report-summer-2009-1025591.html.

KNOWLEDGE MANAGEMENT SOFTWARE AND SERVICES

SIC CODE(S)

7370

INDUSTRY SNAPSHOT

The wealth of information available and necessary to companies' early success spawned an industry devoted to organizing and navigating the efficient flow of information and knowledge through and between firms in a knowledge-centered economy. Knowledge management software and services gained prominence as firms grew increasingly aware of the competitive advantages available in the possession and efficient use of information. Knowledge management products have grown increasingly sophisticated in the twenty-first century, as demand and expanded application warrants. Increased government contracts, particularly from the U.S. Department of Homeland Security, are expected to help fuel the continued growth.

Market research by Merrill Lynch estimated that approximately 85 percent of all digital information owned by businesses was in the form of unstructured data, which in that form was of little financial or strategic value. And the exponential increase of electronic data flows through the Internet and within and between company networks only enhanced the need for companies to bring this raw information under some kind of control.

Untold millions of pieces of data were thus felt to be going to waste embedded in company software, systems, libraries, data banks, work processes, and hardware, as well as the implicit knowledge employees bring to their work. Knowledge management promised to boost firms' intellectual capital by unleashing these hidden gems and systematizing them efficiently in a company's strategic interest. By uprooting such knowledge and preparing it for seamless sharing across company networks, knowledge management puts to work the information and data that firms were only barely aware they even possessed. Companies utilize knowledge management software and services to quantify and classify problem-solving techniques and approaches to various business situations, and take an inventory of the kinds of expertise existing among employee ranks. In addition, many companies establish an entire digital library to store all vital documents and the available knowledge accumulated through these means.

A 2010 report by KnowledgeBusiness.com found that by 2012, there will be 3 to 5 global companies in each of the major business sectors (e.g., airlines, computers, defense, energy, IT, pharmaceuticals, etc.), each in control of nearly incalculable amounts of accumulated data. Those companies that have strong knowledge-based strategies will be the most likely to survive.

The specific aspect of knowledge management known as content management is the processes and technologies that allow companies to track, organize, and manage all their information. Content management is driven by the challenges of companies to comply with increasingly strict regulations regarding data as they strive to be successful in a fiercely competitive business market. Datamonitor reported that between 2008 and 2012, the e-mail archiving market will grow faster than any other business application. Most of the investment worldwide in content management, according to the same report, will come from the small and mid-market segments.

ORGANIZATION AND STRUCTURE

Knowledge management, or KM, seeks to solve common problems such as one employee developing a solution to a

497

Global Knowledge Management Revenues

Services	67.6 percent
Software/related	32.4 percent

SOURCE: Global Industry Analysts, Inc. 2008.

problem that an employee in another department has already solved. Knowledge management strives to pool a company's knowledge and best practices to promote greater efficiency, avoid redundancy, and retain knowledge and practices within the company after key employees and officers leave. Knowledge management also encompasses adopting successful business practices of other companies, even of competitors. Knowledge management theorists distinguish knowledge from information and data.

Data and information lack any specific context, existing merely as potentially useful facts or observations. They cannot be used to solve a problem until they have been intelligently processed and converted into knowledge. Knowledge organizes those facts into strategically important details with specific meaning within a specific context. For example, a company may design a database to extract knowledge from a mass of information; knowledge management then seeks to implement that knowledge in the best possible manner to advance the company, determining how that knowledge can continue to be accessed, used, and manipulated. Managing this flow involves seeing that information gets to the right person in the quickest manner possible.

A firm's knowledge management operations must account for both explicit and tacit knowledge. According to the *Journal of American Academy of Business,* explicit knowledge covers tangibles such as customer data as well as proprietary information covered by patents and trademarks. Tacit knowledge, the less easily defined component, refers generally to the layers of processes and practices of companies and the individuals within it, as well as the untapped connections among the various realms of raw data and information housed in companies' various sorts of data storage.

The key participants in the industry include software companies such as Microsoft and IBM and consulting firms such as Accenture and Bearing Point, as well as their smaller counterparts. The goal of knowledge management software is to categorize information in an easily accessible format and to facilitate the exchange of information. The foundation of many knowledge management software applications is the use of portals or pages similar to Web sites such as Yahoo! that organize information into different categories. Knowledge management consultants, on the other hand, help companies achieve similar results by recommending software or cultural and structural changes, or a combination of the two, to bring about a more manageable organization of knowledge that can be readily shared with others.

Knowledge management applications usually are accessible, searchable, and shareable repositories of knowledge. To create such repositories, companies often create a centralized network where all this knowledge and information is stored and can be accessed by all employees. The benefit of knowledge management is the reusability of knowledge and information: a solution to a specific problem is developed only once (unless a better solution is needed). In addition, knowledge management is frequently characterized as "leveraging" information to new applications or uses. However, most industry observers agree that knowledge management involves more than just technology; that corporate culture also plays a role in the exchange of knowledge. Hence, knowledge management ultimately is a meld of information sharing practices (accessing and retrieving information) and technology that facilitates this process.

BACKGROUND AND DEVELOPMENT

Knowledge management emerged as a central concern among businesses in the late 1980s and early 1990s, although the field's theoretical history itself dated back to the 1970s, when researchers at Stanford University and the Massachusetts Institute of Technology collaborated on a study of information transfer within organizations. These studies examined how knowledge was produced, used, and transferred in organizations. By the late 1980s, the field had developed to such an extent that industry observers grew increasingly aware that businesses needed to take notice in order to utilize their resources efficiently and remain competitive. The increasingly global nature of major companies, along with corporate downsizing and restructuring, also brought with it a massive turn toward knowledge management as companies strove to eliminate redundancy and coordinate their efforts over a broader area.

At the end of the 1980s and the beginning of the 1990s, "knowledge management" became a bona fide term in the business lexicon. In 1989, a group of companies established the Initiative for Managing Knowledge Assets in an effort to develop technological solutions for knowledge management. Simultaneously, consulting firms began offering knowledge management services. All these factors combined to create a thriving trend in management by the mid-1990s, which included the creation of chief knowledge officers or chief intelligence officers as new corporate executives.

The knowledge management software and services industry also is a product of computer and information technology innovations and the movement to a knowledge-based economy in the 1990s. Advances in computer and information technology brought about the rapid-fire transmission of information, and inter-firm competition expanded to include these grounds. During the mid- to late 1990s, businesses could easily access prodigious quantities of information via the Internet and massive databases. Unstructured data on the Internet is particularly problematic for companies because of the labor needed to locate and analyze it. Employees who then bring information in off the Internet tend to keep it for personal use, even though it may be of use to others in the company. These varied developments and events all contributed to the growth of knowledge management as an industry and not just an academic theory.

The information overload of the late 1990s and very early 2000s proved to be fertile ground for the industry, which saw spectacular growth in the late 1990s and anticipated even greater growth in the early years of the new century. Ovum, an industry analyst, estimated that knowledge management software sales would reach $3.5 billion and services would reach $8.8 billion worldwide in 2004, creating a $12.3 billion industry. The U.S. Bureau of Labor Statistics predicted that there would be about 10,000 knowledge management workers by 2006. Research by Teltech Resource Network Corp. indicated that companies invested most of their knowledge management dollars in their production (30 percent) and product development (25 percent) departments. Other key departments included customer service (15 percent), strategic planning (10 percent), and sales (5 percent). International Data Corp. research demonstrated that 50 percent of U.S. corporations with over 500 employees planned to implement some form of knowledge management program in the near future.

Software makers began to roll out knowledge management applications in earnest. Industry big boys, such as Microsoft and IBM (especially through its Lotus subsidiary), all entered the knowledge management fray. Lotus touted its knowledge management software, code-named Raven, as the first genuine knowledge management application. Raven's innovations included discovery engines that categorized data and user profiles that facilitated moving important information into prominent areas. Raven complemented earlier IBM/Lotus efforts to promote knowledge sharing, including their Lotus Notes client and Domino server. Microsoft's venture into knowledge management included the Digital Dashboard of its Outlook 2000 as well as its Office and BackOffice software suites. Digital Dashboard technology integrates various applications and functions according to user preferences. Digital dashboards combine personal, department, corporate, and outside information and resources according to user specifications.

However, with knowledge sharing at an all-time high, companies found their knowledge increasingly vulnerable to compromise from unscrupulous employees, cyber thieves, and hackers. Alongside comprehensive knowledge management software, firms implemented stronger and more powerful security measures and systems. According to the Computer Security Institute, internal sabotage and unauthorized access as well as external network attacks were on the rise, though the financial damage stemming from such attacks was finally dropping, thanks to bolstered security efforts.

After the initial explosion of knowledge management technology, companies began to sort out and come to terms with just what was involved in managing their intellectual capital. In that regard, companies increasingly moved away from utilizing technological components as a panacea for organizing company information and expecting financial windfalls to follow in short order. Instead, firms took a more sober and nuanced view of knowledge management, recognizing that true knowledge management efficiency involved corporate culture as much as it did technical fixes or innovation. The trick, according to many industry analysts, was to find a way of seamlessly integrating new software systems with both existing networks and applications and, crucially, business practices and communication flows that derive from the corporate structure and culture.

Moving into the second half of the decade, some industry observers noted that knowledge management was not only an established part of the organizational world, it was evolving quickly. In the April 2005 issue of *Information Services & Use,* Michael E.D. Koenig noted, "The KM movement has gone through a number of stages, and it is now moving into a stage of recognizing the importance of and incorporating information and knowledge external to the parent organization."

By 2006, this trend was presenting librarians and other information industry professionals with new career opportunities. Because of their expertise working with external information, some librarians were becoming involved in the design of KM systems for organizations, which placed great importance on so-called "competitive intelligence" (CI). In the April 15, 2006 issue of *Library Journal,* Cynthia Cheng Correia explained: "CI has become an attractive concept for LIS pros, as information and research functions have become commoditized by end users, and financial, competitive, and performance pressures increase the need to demonstrate value. In the current competitive and cost-cutting environment, business stakes are higher. Many corporate info pros find that CI is a way to broaden their skills, raise their visibility, and more directly contribute to their firms' operations and direction."

Government spending and consulting were among the key drivers of the knowledge management industry in early 2006. According to market research firm INPUT, the government sector in particular was expected to have a continued impact on growth through 2010, with federal spending projected to reach $1.3 billion by that time. In addition, as large and complex implementations became the norm at government agencies, as well as large corporations, consultants were expected to be in demand to conduct needs assessments and help clients with the tasks of design and implementation.

The U.S. Federal Bureau of Investigation was among the leading proponents and users of knowledge management. With federal funding for security on the rise following the terrorist attacks of September 11, 2001, the FBI and other intelligence services utilized knowledge management software and practices to track, store, and share information within its ranks and with other agencies and governments throughout the world. Of particular use to such efforts was knowledge management's ability to sniff out connections between seemingly unrelated bits of data. Moreover, if different investigators were following similar leads, each one's work was brought to the others' attention, enabling the investigation to avoid duplicating efforts and to make connections individuals might have missed.

KMWorld noted two trends in the knowledge management (KM) industry in a 2008 article titled "KM Past and Future." First, according to the author, KM has evolved to become more flexible and accessible, having in the past been very limiting and hard to navigate. For example, software programs for KM tended to be complicated and understood only by the members of an organization's IT department. If a change needed to be made in the KM program, it took a considerable amount of time in addition to a commitment from one of the few people in the organization who knew how to make the modifications. Now, however, the industry is moving closer to the early vision of KM as "providing free-flowing, vital information in a way that is adaptive and user-driven." Another change that has occurred regards the focus of KM: whereas information storage and access was the primary goal initially, the people factor has become much more important. According to Jerome Nadel, CEO of Human Factors International, "KM is no longer just about connecting people to content; it is also about connecting people to people." In other words, KM now has a much broader user base, involving all employees in a company, not just the higher-ups. KM is no longer primarily concerned with meeting rules for compliance, although that may still be one of the basic goals. Said Nadel, "KM environments are no longer measured only on how well they lead users to relevant knowledge; the new measure is how effectively they promote participation."

Others agree that the people factor is important. They contend that although software is a critical component of knowledge management, the value of these applications is questionable, and knowledge management is still too theoretical. Knowledge management isn't just a series of technological innovations. For a company to truly reap the benefits of knowledge management, it must be an integral part of the corporate culture. That is, the internal practices, communications, structures, habits, and atmosphere of the company must be conducive to the kind of knowledge sharing on which knowledge management depends. Employees must be encouraged to share knowledge between themselves, either informally or by working in teams that continually interact; and employers must remain open to accepting ideas from and continually interacting with their subordinates.

Despite advances in knowledge management technology and software, many companies remain without a plan for KM. According to a 2008 Monster Worldwide survey, only 20 percent of companies have formal strategies to manage and preserve organizational knowledge, despite the fact that one third of the companies predict that 20 percent of their workforce will be eligible for retirement within 10 years. The question of how—or if—information will be transferred from these baby boomers to the next generation of workers is a major concern. Another report by Tandberg found that 61 percent of U.S. federal managers do not have a KM policy or any plan for training staff for when the so-called brain drain occurs. Of the 39 percent of managers who do have a plan, 74 percent said their staff was unaware of the policy. According to Joel Brunson of Tandberg's federal market business department, organizations "can't afford a single gap of knowledge," and when a large number of people leave the workforce at the same time, " it's about losing day-to-day knowledge, tricks of the trade," as well as an accumulation of what's been learned over the past two or three decades.

CURRENT CONDITIONS

According to Global Industry Analysts, Inc., global revenues in knowledge management will exceed $157 billion by 2012. The United States led the global market in 2009. Knowledge management services accounted for two-thirds of industry revenues, followed by knowledge management software.

By 2010, KM was already manifesting in specialty applications. For example, in 2009, knowledge management formed the largest submarket (worth $1.3 billion) in the biometrics industry. In the automotive industry, new EPA regulations for vehicles and trucks, aimed at reducing carbon and increasing mileage per gallon, created a new demand in the aftermath market that will need KM expertise to handle compliance tracking and testing, among other things. According to Frost & Sullivan, the 2010 EPA regulations will result in greater levels of distributed electronics in currently-compliant trucks and vehicles, as well as those in the future. This, in turn, will create a tremendous specialty market reliant upon knowledge-management expertise to benefit the emerging revenue growth opportunity.

Despite overall positive prospects, during the economic downturn in 2009 and early 2010, corporate cost-cutting was in order, and many companies, with other pressing priorities, moved information management to a "wish list" rather than a "must have." It was clearly with cautious optimism rather than a "full steam ahead" attitude that the KM industry proceeded into 2010. Following the bankruptcy filing of industry leader BearingPoint Inc. in February 2009, the KM industry began to increasingly specialize and/or fragmentize into specialties. Forecasts and results of overall industry revenues were hard to come by, as individual industry leaders reorganized or renamed their focus, e.g., e-learning, customer experience management, social networking-based KM, etc.

The KNOW Network, via knowledgebusiness.com, published its 2009 Global MAKE (Most Admired Knowledge Enterprises) Report, basing its distinction of industry leaders not so much on individual entity total revenues, but rather on its approach to the most valuable way to maximize business strategies based on knowledge leadership. The 2009 Global MAKE Report found that its named winners that traded on the NYSE/NASDAQ showed total returns to shareholders (TRS) in the preceding ten years to be 9.6 percent, which represented about four times the average *Fortune 500* company median. Its final list of the top twenty were Accenture, Apple, British Broadcasting Corporation (BBC), Deloitte Touche Tohmatsu, Ernst & Young, Fluor, General Electric, Google, Hewlett-Packard, IBM, Infosys Technologies, McKinsey & Company, Microsoft, Nokia, PricewaterhouseCoopers, Samsung, Schlumberger, Tata, Toyota, and Wipro Technologies. Several of these are focused below.

INDUSTRY LEADERS

This industry's top companies include some of the world's leading consulting and software firms. Nevertheless, smaller concerns also play an important role in providing knowledge management counseling and in developing knowledge management software.

The world's largest consulting firm, Accenture Ltd., formerly Andersen Consulting, of New York ranks among the leading providers of knowledge management services. Accenture specializes in knowledge management of the pharmaceutical, chemical, energy, food,

automotive, and financial services industries. The company strives to help clients identify best practices, expedite innovation, reduce risk, and increase value. Accenture's clients have included British Petroleum, MCC, and the U.S. Department of Housing and Urban Development. The consulting firm partnered with Microsoft, using the latter's software products to provide companies with technical consulting services. Accenture has a strong global presence in business and technology fields with some 150 offices in 50 countries, and the company derived just over half its sales from overseas ventures. Sales in 2009 were $21.6 billion, representing an 8 percent drop from 2008, while the firm employed 170,000, including its technological consultants highly trained in the latest knowledge management systems.

BearingPoint Inc., (in Chapter 11 bankruptcy as of 2010) was another major provider of knowledge management services. The McLean, Virginia-based BearingPoint customizes its services based on particular business needs. It has focused on helping companies optimize the use of Microsoft products such as Office and Outlook as knowledge management tools. According to BearingPoint, the company offers a variety of integrated solutions its clients can use to address knowledge management challenges. These solutions are concentrated in the areas of business intelligence, business process management, collaboration, document and content management, learning management, and portal frameworks. BearingPoint services six primary industries—the public sector, financial services, communications, technology, health care, and consumer and industrial markets—with a global client list exceeding 2,000 firms and governments in 60 countries. About 30 percent of the company's revenues came from U.S. government agencies, with the U.S. Department of Defense accounting for 11 percent of that total.

Deloitte Touche Tohmatsu, a global company in which 168,000 staff members in independent firms collaborate under the brand name "Deloitte," collectively offer audit, consulting, financial advisory, risk management, and tax services to their global clients. Named in the top 20 for the 2009 Global MAKE list, DTT was recognized for developing knowledge-based products/services/solutions and delivering value based on stakeholder knowledge. Aggregate member firm revenues under DTT reported $26.1 billion for fiscal year 2009.

Sopheon Plc was another knowledge management service provider. Sopheon, which merged with the knowledge management firm Teltech Resource Network Corp. in late 2000, concentrates on supplying companies with systems for organizing and sharing their knowledge. In 2000, the firm launched Intotaa, a Web-based knowledge resource, to facilitate business-to-business knowledge transactions in the technical and scientific fields.

Headquartered in the United Kingdom, Sopheon's product line was particularly suited to companies whose operations were heavily involved in research and development. The firm sold off its Teltech division in 2003.

In the software sector, IBM's Lotus Development Corp. and Microsoft are two of the most prominent companies. Lotus considers itself the first mover in the knowledge management software sector. In 2006 Lotus continued to offer software—including its well-known Lotus Domino—that clients used for collaboration and productivity. The company's offerings ranged from solutions focused on e-forms and the management of documents and Web content to messaging, learning, and both team and real time collaboration.

IBM has a presence of its own in the industry with its software and its consulting services. Some of IBM's knowledge management applications have included IBM Enterprise Information Portal and Visual Warehouse. In addition, the company provides knowledge management services through its IBM Global Services consulting arm, which focuses on three primary aspects of companies to bring about improved knowledge management: content, infrastructure, and culture. In January 2006, *KM World* recognized IBM with its KM-World Award. The publication praised IBM for its efforts within the industry, commenting that its knowledge management initiatives "were developed to emphasize and facilitate knowledge exchange within its various business units and to promote reuse of assets. Furthermore, the past few years have seen that emphasis exchange knowledge across the various business units to provide integrated solutions for its customers and clients." In 2009, IBM reported overall sales of $95.8 billion, down from $103.6 billion in 2008.

As the largest software maker in the world, Microsoft, Inc.'s approach to knowledge management is not to create a bunch of new applications but to use existing software. Microsoft contends that some of its core products, including its Office suite, BackOffice, and in particular its Outlook application, are all knowledge management tools. Company founder and chairman Bill Gates considers Microsoft Outlook a quintessential knowledge management application with its Digital Dashboard that facilitates communication among employees and the organization of critical company knowledge. In addition, Microsoft manufactures programs such as Visual Studio that allow users to develop knowledge management applications to augment its Office suite. Moreover, Microsoft plans to continue integrating functions, enabling users to combine information and applications according to their needs. This vision includes continuing production of software with collaboration, searchability, information management, and data warehousing capabilities.

Microsoft worked with Groove Networks to develop a set of collaboration tools based on knowledge management theories. Microsoft planned to shift its operations increasingly into Web-based applications and services. Its knowledge management operations are built upon the universal data-exchange meta-language Extensible Markup Language (XML). Microsoft acquired Groove Networks in March of 2005, adding the firm to its Information Worker Business. The company also released a new collaboration tool called Office Communicator.

Another Global MAKE leader, Pricewaterhouse-Coopers (Global) was the world's leading professional services network. It provides tax and advisory servies in 757 cities in 151 countries. Its recognition in the KM arena focuses on more than 163,000 persons across the PwC network who share their thinking, expertise, and solutions to develop practical advice and a fresh perspective. PwC reported global revenues of $26.2 billion for its fiscal 2009 year.

An impressive smaller company, Infosys Technologies (India), provides consulting and IT services to global clients. It uses a low-risk Global Delivery Model (GDM) to accelerate schedules and has made a concerted effort to provide integrated solutions to meet KM needs for the organization and has developed key KM workers through senior management. For its fiscal year 2009, the company reported sales of $4.7 billion, with 100,000 employees.

Another small player, Open Text, is the maker of the Livelink program. The Canadian firm designs software to mine through corporate data banks to extract and manage useful knowledge, direct workflow, and coordinate scheduling and knowledge sharing. Among its top-selling knowledge management offerings are its search and management program Livelink; its library automation software Techlib; and BASIS, a data mining and management tool. The firm bolsters its product line with professional and technical services, which was leading its expansion.

AMERICA AND THE WORLD

One of the biggest trends in knowledge management has been offshore outsourcing. An April 2010 report by Evaluserve, found that legal process outsourcing (LPO) to India and the Philippines was the fastest growing subsector in the knowledge process outsourcing (KPO) domain. Law firms have tremendous overhead expenses (40 percent) in legal and ligrary research, paralegal, clerical, accounting, marketing, IT, and knowledge management, etc. that cannot transfer to billable hours. Even during 2008 and 2009, the LPO sector grew 40 percent, according to Evaluserve. At least 90 percent of the work came from the United States and the United Kingdom. Evaluserve predicted that knowledge management would be a growth area for the LPO industry, estimating that between 2010 and 2015, revenues from legal outsourcing will grow 26 percent each year, from $300 million to $960 million.

Knowledge process outsourcing (KPO) services to the global market are predicted by KPMG to reach $17 billion for 2010, with India controlling the lion's (70 percent) for the foreseeable future, and China gaining over the long run.

As some industry analysts frequently point out, knowledge management practices are not new. In fact, some of its theories and practices were developed in the United States after observing the structure of Japanese companies. While researching their customs, Ikujiro Nonaka discovered that some Japanese companies were structured so that information and knowledge of different departments overlapped, which circulated company know-how among a broad range of employees, as described in the article "The Knowledge-Creating Company." The advantages these companies experienced included faster product development and more efficient problem solving.

Furthermore, European companies have followed U.S. companies in implementing knowledge management initiatives. These efforts mirror their U.S. counterparts with a combination of technology and business practices to promote the exchange of knowledge and best practices. Global U.S. companies such as IBM also have taken their knowledge management practices abroad. Like U.S. companies, European companies have found that information sharing is not an intuitive employee activity and instead it must be taught and induced with incentives.

RESEARCH AND TECHNOLOGY

New software packages to manage data and help businesses keep track of their information continued to be developed were being developed every day, and organizations in an increasing number of diverse industries were using KM echniques. According to Ovum, a central area of research and expansion in the knowledge management industry will be creating virtual communication within and without corporate intranets. Achieving this kind of communication would involve converting intranets to extranets, which enable people outside of a company to communicate with those inside. To maintain the confidentiality of information, however, companies must ensure that adequate security measures are taken so that only the appropriate users can access the networks.

BIBLIOGRAPHY

"2009 Most Admired Knowleddge Enterprises (MAKE) Report." Executive Summary, 2010. Available from http://www. knowledgebusiness.com.

Britt, Phil. "Banks Invest in KM." *KMWorld,* July-August 2008.

———. "KM Makes Inroads into Retail." *KMWorld,* 8 February 2008.

Byrne, Tony. "The WCM Marketplace—2008." *KMWorld,* June 2008.

"China's Software Outsourcing Industry Divergence." 14 June 2010. Available from http://www.forexarbitrage.org/chinas-software-outsourcing.

Cleslak, David. "Paper Erasure: Going Paperless." *California CPA,* June 2008.

Correia, Cynthia Cheng. "Getting Competitive." *Library Journal,* 15 April 2006.

"Coveo Reports 55 Percent Increase in Q1 2010 License Revenue; SIgns 24 Deals with New & and Existing Customers." 2010. Available from http://www.coveo.com/en/news-and-events/coveo/news/2010.

"Enterprise Investments in Content Management Set to Scale New Peaks." *Database and Network Journal,* December 2007.

"Global Knowledge Management Market Revenues to Exceed $157 Billion by 2012, According to a New Report by Global Industry Analysts." 3 November 2008.

Federal Managers Think Agencies Aren't Ready For Boomer Exodus." *InformationWeek,* 13 November 2007.

Koenig, Michael E.D. "KM Moves Beyond the Organization: The Opportunity for Librarians." *Information Services & Use,* April 2005.

Lamont, Judith. "Consulting Firms Play a Key Role in Context of KM." *KMWorld,* January 2006.

"LPO and the Great Recession." *Law Without Borders,* 29 April 2010.

———. "KM Past and Future." *KMWorld,* 28 December 2007.

McKellar, Hugh. "100 Companies that Matter in Knowledge Management." *KMWorld,* March 2008.

"Online Publishing, e-Learning, and Knowledge Management - Part 2." Semantico.

St. Clair, Guy, and Dale Stanley. "Knowledge Services: The Practical Side of Knowledge." *Information Outlook,* June 2008.

LASERS AND LASER APPLICATIONS

SIC CODE(S)

3674

3845

3699

INDUSTRY SNAPSHOT

The very same qualities that made lasers so potently frightening in grade B sci-fi flicks from the 1950s—their speed, precision, and ability to vaporize anything in their path—are precisely the things that have given them such versatility. Their applications span the fields of medicine, the military, electronics, machine processing, and cosmetics, to name a few. For examples, see the essays on Digital Video Discs, Holography, Optical Laser Surgery, Photonics, and Smart Cards.

The term "laser" is an acronym for light amplification by stimulated emission of radiation. A laser is a narrow, extremely focused, powerful beam of monochromatic light that can be used for a variety of functions. For instance, lasers etch information onto the surface of compact discs. Lasers used in the production of CD-ROM disks condense large amounts of information, such as a set of encyclopedias or the New York metropolitan phone book, onto one disk. Another example of laser etching is in digital video discs (DVDs), which by the middle of the first decade of the twenty-first century had largely replaced videocassettes as the means of providing home movie entertainment. Holograms, three-dimensional images, also are examples of laser technology at work. In the middle of the decade, many credit card companies affixed holograms to their cards to discourage would-be counterfeiters, and some world governments used them on passports for the same reason.

Public speakers employ laser pointers when giving presentations. Laser light shows were abundant in entertainment, often as alternatives to fireworks displays at public events.

At the forefront of laser-oriented research are attempts to perfect high-speed, high-density storage of digital data using the newly discovered blue or violet laser. In the realm of medicine, promising procedures for the quick diagnosis of cancer and highly accurate methods to target tumors in treatment have emerged. Scientists at the University of Wisconsin-Madison discovered that infrared lasers could image not only molecules but even the smaller bonds that hold them together. At the opposite end of the scale, astronomers scanned the skies for laser pulses as a clue to the existence of extraterrestrial life, and physicists attempted to control the weather with lasers by issuing preemptive laser strikes at storm clouds to generate lightning bolts on demand. Breakthroughs in the field occurred more quickly than technology could evolve to support many promising new laser applications.

ORGANIZATION AND STRUCTURE

Lasers have become indispensable. Fiber-optic communications use pulses of laser light to send information on glass strands. Before the advent of fiber optics, telephone calls were relayed on thick bundles of copper wire. With the appearance of this new technology, a glass wire no thicker than a human hair could carry thousands of conversations. Lasers also are used in scanners, in price code checkers at supermarkets, in tags to prevent book thefts from libraries or clothing thefts from stores, and in inventory systems in company warehouses. Heating lasers can drill through solid metal in an industrial setting. They remove gallstones in

505

operating rooms and cataracts in outpatient surgery. They are able to precisely remove an oxidized outer layer and thus restore an art object to its original beauty. In the late 1960s and early 1970s, measuring lasers assisted scientists in calibrating the distance between Earth and the moon to within two inches. They continue to provide surveyors with assistance in making much smaller measurements as well. Lasers are used for guiding missiles. They aid building contractors to assure that walls, floors, and ceilings are in proper alignment. See the essay on Fiber Optics.

Several interest and advocacy groups foster technological advances. These organizations include the Laser Institute of America (formerly the Laser Industry Association), and the IEEE Lasers & Electro-Optics Society, operated by the Institute of Electrical and Electronics Engineers. Many significant laser manufacturers belong to the Laser and Electro-Optics Manufacturers' Association (LEOMA). LEOMA plays a key role in representing the industry in Washington and in settling disputes between companies. For example, LEOMA lobbies in Washington to maintain funding for laser research. LEOMA also possesses an alternative dispute resolution agreement whereby members agree not to initiate legal action against one another without first attempting to resolve the conflict with the help of a mediator. According to LEOMA, its 30 member companies represent 90 percent of the industry's annual North American sales.

While the federal government oversees laser research through the Technology Reinvestment Program, the National Institute of Standards and Technology has an interest in the laser industry, especially through its Advanced Development Program. The U.S. Department of Energy, the National Institutes for Health (NIH), the Food and Drug Administration (FDA), and the National Aeronautics and Space Administration (NASA) are also interested in various laser applications.

BACKGROUND AND DEVELOPMENT

Laser light is produced by the process of stimulated emission, which involves bringing many atoms into an excited state. When light travels through a normal material containing more ground-state atoms than excited-state atoms, it is more likely to be absorbed than amplified. To make a laser, energy must be delivered to produce more excited-state atoms than ground-state atoms. This situation is called a population inversion. If light traveling through the material is more likely to collide with excited atoms than ground-state atoms, it causes stimulated emission. The material or medium then becomes an amplifier.

A laser consists of three components: an optical cavity, an energy source, and an active medium. The optical cavity, two mirrors facing one another, contains the active laser medium. One of the mirrors fully reflects light from the stimulated emission whereas the other is only partially reflective. Light, generated and amplified by the medium, resonates back and forth between the mirrors in a constant flux between the background and excited energy states. Some of the light transmitted by the less reflective mirror is diverted as a highly focused beam, the laser. Generally, electricity is the energy source. The active medium can be solid state, semiconductor, gas, or dye. One example of a solid state laser is a ruby crystal.

PIONEERS IN THE FIELD

Albert Einstein (1879–1955) first considered the idea of stimulated emission, a key element in laser technology, in 1917. In 1954 Charles H. Townes (1915-) supplied another key element by producing population inversion in a microwave device, which he called a microwave amplification by stimulated emission of radiation, or maser. During the 1950s, the United States and the Soviet Union entered into a technology race to develop a laser, and on May 16, 1960, Theodore Harold Maiman (1927-), a U.S. scientist, operated the first solid state laser. In 1964, Townes and two Soviet physicists shared the Nobel Prize in physics for their work in laser development.

The gas laser also made its appearance in 1960. That was the creation of Ali Javan, a Bell Laboratories engineer working in New Jersey. In 1962, semiconductor lasers were developed. The dye laser made its first appearance in 1966.

During the 1960s, some people within the scientific community called lasers "a solution without a problem" because they could not conceive of a practical use for them. Lasers began having commercial applications in 1961 when Maiman formed the industry's first laser company, Quantatron. Other laser companies also made their appearance, primarily producing ruby solid state lasers. In 1999 Bell Labs in Murray Hill, New Jersey, created the first bi-directional semiconductor laser, which can emit two beams of light of widely divergent wave lengths—a feat previously accomplished using two different lasers.

The military took a keen interest in the use of lasers for missile guidance and other applications such as the development of nuclear fusion. The federal government became a major player in laser development during the 1970s and 1980s as it tried to augment the laser's existing uses. One of the most famous plans for a military application of lasers was the highly publicized Star Wars Defense system, championed by President Ronald Reagan, which did not come to fruition during his administration. By the 1990s, laser applications were rapidly expanding in both the military and automotive fields for vehicle position sensing, crash avoidance, and profiling object surfaces from long distances. The military used laser guidance systems in smart bombs during the Persian Gulf War of 1991.

LASERS IN THE TWENTY-FIRST CENTURY

The laser and laser applications industry continued to grow quickly in the middle of the first decade of the 2000s. One factor driving industry growth was homeland security. Following the terrorist attacks of September 11, 2001, in 2003 the U.S. military began developing a system of green and red lasers for use in the airspace around Washington, D.C. In operation by 2005, these visible beacons are visible up to 25 miles away and are used to warn pilots who enter the 2,000-square-mile air defense identification zone surrounding the nation's capital. The zone encompasses a region bordered by the Ronald Reagan Washington National Airport, the Washington Dulles International Airport, and the Baltimore-Washington International Airport.

From a secret command center, officials are able to shine a laser on a specific unauthorized aircraft without disrupting other airplanes that may be nearby. According to the *Washington Times,* each laser cost approximately $500,000. The laser system issues two red bursts, followed by a green burst, and then repeats itself. By mid-2005, pilots had accidentally violated the restricted airspace more than 1,700 times, and the laser system sought to reduce the number of military aircraft deployments needed to counter potentially threatening aircraft. One of the system's limitations is operating in cloudy weather.

Lasers continue to be used in many types of surgery because of their guaranteed precision. The cauterizing effect of the beam greatly reduces blood loss during procedures. Laser eye surgery continued to be one of the most widely implemented applications of laser medical technology, although medical insurance frequently does not cover it. A laser "smart scalpel" was developed by the U.S. Department of Energy's Sandia National Laboratories. The instrument—a biological microcavity laser—identifies the presence of cancerous cells while a surgeon operates by shining a laser beam on a stream of cells as they are pumped from the operation site into a spectrometer. Cancerous cells, which contain a higher density of protein than regular cells, change speed when the laser illuminates them, thus alerting the surgeon when all the malignancy has been removed.

Dr. Harry Whelan and his colleagues at Milwaukee's Children's Hospital successfully adapted light-emitting diode (LED) light to treat brain cancer. The procedure, FDA-approved for clinical trials, is called photodynamic therapy (PDT). The surgeon directs LED light with a pinhead-sized diode onto the tumor, which has been treated with the anti-cancer drug photofrin. The light activates the drug, which destroys the malignant cells but leaves surrounding healthy tissue unaffected. Interim trials of a similar PDT for age-related macular disintegration, which causes loss of eyesight, were underway at Johns Hopkins. In those studies, doctors activated the drug verteporfin with lasers. The drug slows the growth of choroidal blood vessels in the eyes that leads to sight impairment. In ophthalmology, laser scanning was also introduced to map the contours of the eye in three dimensions, thus enabling physicians to identify retinal diseases much earlier than with previous diagnostic methods. Researchers at Dartmouth College discovered that cancerous cells fluoresce more quickly, but less brightly, than normal cells. This aid for early detection was 5 percent more accurate than the surgical biopsies it was intended to replace and was expected to be in increased use, pending clinical trials results. Along these same lines, in 2002 a group of United Kingdom-based researchers developed a laser-based ophthalmoscope able to produce color images of the back of the eye, allowing for easier identification of different retinal diseases.

Since the FDA approved lasers for the removal of facial wrinkles in 1996, the use of lasers for cosmetic treatments has boomed. Applications also include the removal of unwanted hair, tattoos, and spider veins. However, in June 2005 *Cosmetic Surgery Times* reported that a number of surgeons were foregoing laser treatments and shifting to chemical peels, which offered more consistent results and fewer side effects for skin resurfacing patients.

Just as lasers are used to resurface humans, they also find applications for treating industrial surfaces. They can harden, anneal, and alloy surface materials in targeted areas with great precision. Laser cutting of manufacturing parts creates a milled-quality edge and eliminates the need for secondary operations such as grinding and deburring, thereby reducing production costs.

Laser printers, CDs, and other products featuring lasers continue to be fast-selling items. By 2000, network-ready color laser printers were on the market. While the machines approached ink jet printers' color performance and delivered much faster results, their prohibitive prices initially kept them out of the reach of most consumers for home use. However, in 2003, Minolta became the first in the industry to price a networked color laser printer under $700, and by mid-2005 models from Samsung and Konica sold for $399.

There have been reported cases of laser abuse. Basketball fans have used lasers to distract players on the free throw line. More seriously, police worry that they're the target of snipers when they see the laser light on their chests. For reasons such as these, lasers are banned or restricted in Philadelphia; New York City; Dearborn, Michigan; Virginia Beach, Virginia; Ocean City, Maryland; Chicago Ridge, Illinois; Westchester County, New York; and in Seattle's public schools.

One of the major events in the laser industry in 2006 was the introduction of the next generation of high-capacity optical-storage technology, the Blu-ray disc. The first blue semiconductor laser for commercial use was introduced by Shuji Nakamura of the small Japanese firm Nichia Chemical Industries in 1998. Because it sported a shorter wave length than the conventional infrared lasers used for decades, the blue laser permitted digital data to be packed much more densely on storage media such as digital video discs. Blue lasers could also turn up in longer lasting, more energy efficient lights; in large scale, high-precision video displays; and in extremely accurate medical instrumentation. By mid-2005, Disney and Sony Pictures were backing the Blu-ray laser optical disc format along with leading electronics and computer manufacturers such as Dell, Apple, Hewlett-Packard, Pioneer, Hitachi, and Samsung.

According to Jim Reeves of *Military and Aerospace Electronics*, "Laser communications technology is still in its infancy for military and aerospace applications that call for extended range, security, and portability. Commercial laser communication systems today lack the attributes most necessary to assist ground and air forces in a battlefield environment." At this point, the laser communications market consisted mainly of free-space optics, or systems that can communicate information from one point to another with very large bandwidth capacities. However, the new technology of adaptive optics was enhancing the possibility of using laser communications in airborne and ground-based military systems. With adaptive optics lasers, a user can obtain data and link the data to a point as far away as 12 miles in a matter of seconds—all with almost guaranteed non-detection and noninterference.

CURRENT CONDITIONS

In December 2008, *Laser Focus World* magazine announced its annual review and forecast of the laser market for the entire year 2009. It forecast that 2009 global laser revenues (including both diode and non-diode lasers for applications as varied as metal cutting, vision correction, fiber communications, and DVD players) would decline by 11 percent compared to 2008 ($7.1 billion). Manufacturers had reported extremely poor visibility for 2009. However, the long-term prospects for the industry were very positive, especially in light of the promotion of renewable energy under the Obama administration, creating a green revolution for the larger laser and photonics industry.

According to ReportLinker.com, the global market for cosmetic surgery services will reach the $40 Billion mark by 2013, up from $31.7 Billion in 2008. This could bolster the overall laser industry slightly, although less cosmetic and more therapeutic applications were in order (e.g., spider veins, mole removal, etc.)

The 2009 North American merchant machine-vision market was expected to decline about 30 percent, according to Nello Zuech, consultant in machine vision. He expected revenues to fall to an estimated $1.13 billion from $1.6 billion in 2008. However, North American machine-vision companies were expected to sell $2.4 billion in the global machine-vision market in 2009 (but still a decrease of 34 percent from 2008's $3.6 billion).

In January 2010, guest speakers at the annual Laser and Photonics Marketplace Seminar (San Francisco) were scheduled to usher in the era of high-power quantum cascade lasers (QCLs) with their widespread potential for applications in civilian, military, and homeland security. Among other speakers, Dr. Tom Hausken, Director of Optoelectronic Components at Strategies Unlimited, was scheduled to discuss the market for lasers in micro-materials processing, one of the fastest growing segments in the laser business. The technology uses sub-kilowatt lasers for precision processes like repairing semiconductor wafers, scribing solar cells, drilling printed circuit boards, making microwelds in medical devices, engraving industrial parts, and many other applications.

INDUSTRY LEADERS

The Laser and Electro-Optics Manufacturers' Association includes most of the major players in the North American laser industry. Many laser manufacturers produce a wide variety of instruments for industrial to military to medical operations. A former leader in the industry, Lucent Technologies, was sold to Alcatel-Lucent of Paris in 2006 for $11.6 billion.

Prominent in the industry are Coherent Inc. and Candela Corp. Coherent, of Santa Clara, California, produces roughly 150 kinds of lasers for a variety of commercial and scientific uses. Coherent, with customers in 80 different countries, reported 2008 sales of $599.3 million with 1,700 employees. Candela, of Wayland, Massachusetts, is producing systems for tattoo removal, treatment of dermal abnormalities (age spots, birthmarks), and hair removal. In August 2009, it announced full-year revenues of $116 million. Medical lasers for dental procedures form the basis of BioLase Technology Inc.'s production. PhotoMedex Inc. develops lasers used in dermatological and medical procedures (urology, gynecology, orthopedics, and general surgery).

Nortel Networks Corp. manufactures extremely high-precision lasers for high-speed fiber-optic transmission of traffic on the Internet. In 1999 the company reported that it had to triple its production capacity, adding 5,000 new jobs worldwide to keep pace with demand. However, due in large part to the technology industry's downturn, revenues in 2002 fell 40 percent to $10.5 billion and the number of employees fell 31 percent to 37,000. In 2009 Nortel was in bankruptcy and selling off pieces of its operations.

Symbol Technologies Inc. was a leading maker of laser bar code scanners and merged with Motorola in 2006. Among Symbol's innovations are a handheld laser scanner, a scanner-integrated computer, and a portable self-checkout shopping system. Finally, II-VI Corporation, which had absorbed the former Laser Power Optics company posted revenues from continuing operations for the year ended June 30, 2009, as $292 million. Plymouth, Michigan and Hamburg, Germany-based ROFIN-SINAR Technologies Inc. announced full year revenues of $575 million for its fiscal year ending on September 30, 2009.

RESEARCH AND TECHNOLOGY

By the end of 2009, disk technology was well established in many industrial laser processes and fast becoming the key enabler for generating green laser light starting in the picosecond regime, producing hundreds of watts in the nanosecond pulse regime and in the cw mode. The various pulsing characteristics were well suited for a variety of materials and associated application, e.g. scribing of thin film solar cells with picosecond lasers, drilling of Silicon, and welding of copper, in the electronics industries.

As of 2009, nearly every aspect of the photonics industry had gone or was going "green," with a heavy emphasis on environmentally sustainable processes and products. Light-emitting diodes (LEDs) were penetrating the lighting market, organics LEDs (OLEDs) were making a splash in displays, photovoltaics continued to make advances in on-par fossil fuel performance, and even laser fission/fusion was looking to become a viable long-term energy source. Other green technologies employing lasers included optical sensors for environmental monitoring and laser processing for solar cells.

The 2009 announcements by Sumitomo and Osram that they each had developed green-emitting laser diodes (at 531 and 515 nm respectively) raised the specter of a "true green" semiconductor laser light source competing in the marketplace very soon. At the same time, Coherent announced that its OPSL was available in a 5W green version targeted at Ti:sapphire pumping. Other technologies in the green-emitting arena include fiber, disk, and DPSSL lasers.

The search to employ lasers for enhanced digital data storage remained on the cutting edge of developments in laser-enhanced technology. This promising application could permit storage densities of one trillion bits per cubic centimeter and increase the speed of data loading and retrieval to over 10 gigabits per second. Several organizations pursued this line of development, among them SRI International in Menlo Park, California, which announced its coherent time-domain optical memory. This technology, which incorporates semiconductor processing techniques and dye lasers, was being overseen by the Defense Advanced Research Projects Agency.

In Chicago, physicians at Rush-Presbyterian-St. Luke's Medical Center pioneered a new, if somewhat controversial, laser-based treatment for angina, the pain that accompanies heart disease. The researchers reported that drilling tiny holes into the heart muscle with a laser—a process called transmyocardial laser revascularization—improved blood flow to the heart muscle, thus greatly reducing pain and increasing mobility in 72 percent of the patients treated, compared with 13 percent of patients given only drugs to treat the condition. Transmyocardial laser revascularization was used to treat cardiac patients and was accepted by most insurance companies.

As far back as the 1990s, scientists had hoped for a breakthrough in the area of nuclear fusion. Nuclear fusion promised to provide cheap and abundant power without the dangers associated with nuclear fission, the conventional form of nuclear reaction. In May 2000, the federal budget for development of this technology was increased when $245 million was earmarked for the National Ignition Facility at Livermore Lab. The project, which involves the world's largest laser, is intended to aim 192 laser beams at a target the size of a pellet. If successful, it would permit scientists to test the possibility of generating fusion energy and to simulate nuclear weapons without actual detonation. The project deadline was pushed back to 2008. However, as of late 2009, scientists had not yet achieved a major goal of ignition-net energy production from thermonuclear fusion.

BIBLIOGRAPHY

"2002 National Totals for Cosmetic Procedures." American Society for Aesthetic Plastic Surgery. Available from http://www.asaps.org/press/national_totals.pdf.

"2010 Conference Agenda: Laser and Photonics Marketplace Seminar." Available from http://www.market placeseminar.com/index.html.

"Candela Announces Results for the Fourth Fiscal Quarter and Full Year." 18 August 2009. Available from http://news.moneycentral.msn.com.

"Coherent." *Hoover's Online.* Available from http://www.hoovers.com.

"Cosmetic Surgery Industry to Exceed $40 Billion in Revenues by 2013." 11 September 2009. Available from http://www.reportlinker.com/p0132720/Cosmetic-Surgery-Markets-Products-and-Services.html.

Croal, N'Gai. "The Battle of the Video Discs." *Newsweek,* 6 June 2005.

Cuenco, Candy. "An Amazing Player." *Camcorder & Computer Video,* April 2007.

"Feature: Combat Lasers Becoming a Reality." *United Press International,* 11 December 2002.

"Laser Revenues to Decline 11% in 2009 Based on Laser Focus World Annual Review." *Laser Focus World,* 19 December 2008.

"Machine-vision Sales Slowly Improving for North American Companies, Competition Increasing." *Vision Systems Design,* 16 December 2009.

Glanz, William. "Lasers Set to Help Protect D.C. Airspace." *Washington Times,* 18 May 2005.

"Growth in Plastic Surgery Slows." *Research Alert,* 1 April 2005.

Jasper, Paul. "Cool Color Lasers for Under $700." *PC World,* June 2003.

"Laser Could Rival Energy from Sun's Center." *Business CustomWire,* 22 May 2005.

Levine, Jenny. "Blue Laser Discs and Storage." *Library Journal,* July 2003.

"Motorola Completes Acquisition of Symbol Technologies." 9 January 2007. Available from http://www.symbol.com.

Nash, Karen. "Many Factors Fuel Continued Cosmetic Surgery Boom." *Cosmetic Surgery Times,* 1 June 2005.

"New Warning System Not Used in D.C. Scare." *Finance CustomWire,* 24 May 2005.

Reeves, Jim. "Have Bandwidth, Will Travel." *Military & Aerospace Electronics,* May 2005.

"Rofin-Sinar Announces Three Month and Fiscal Year Results." *PR Newswire,* 5 November 2009.

Star, Lawrence. "Haircut, Manicure, and a Little Medicine." *Medical Economics,* 8 October 2004.

Steele, Robert V. "Diode-Laser Market Takes a Breather." *Laser Focus World,* February 2007.

LIFE COACHING

◼

INDUSTRY SNAPSHOT

Life coaches are professionals who, through planning and human interaction, assist people to navigate the jungles of life and career. They aid in the establishment and attainment of goals, helping a client to effectively deal with change and discover what he or she believes to be his/her life's purpose. Much as someone might rely on a personal trainer for tips on diet and exercise or on an athletic coach to improve performance in a particular sport, people from all walks of life—including blue collar workers, stay-at-home moms, middle managers, top executives, creative artists, teachers, and students—rely on life coaches to identify and achieve specific personal or professional goals.

According to the International Coach Federation (ICF), "Professional coaches are trained to listen and observe, to customize their approach to the individual client's needs, and to elicit solutions and strategies from the client. They believe that the client is naturally creative and resourceful and that the coach's job is to provide support to enhance the skills, resources, and creativity that the client already has. While the coach provides feedback and an objective perspective, the client is responsible for taking the steps to produce the results he or she desires."

Although some professional life coaches also are medical doctors, psychologists, or licensed clinical therapists, life coaching does not focus on diagnosing or treating mental or emotional disorders. Rather than dealing with issues from a person's past that may be causing life problems, life coaching concentrates on human potential, desired outcomes, and future possibilities. Skilled life coaches are adept at knowing when they must refer a client to a professional therapist to work through issues that fall outside of their expertise or capability.

There were at least 30,000 life coaches, also known as life planners or life strategists, practicing on a part-time and full-time basis in the United States in the 1980s. However, their popularity swelled during the late 1990s and early years of the twenty-first's first decade. By this time, life coaches appeared on such noteworthy talk shows as the Oprah Winfrey Show. For example, Dr. Phil McGraw was a highly popular life strategist who used coaching techniques as a guest on the Oprah Winfrey show and later on his own television program.

ORGANIZATION AND STRUCTURE

According to the International Coach Federation, personal/life coaching is one of four broad coaching categories. Other related types of coaching include career and transition coaching, which helps people to make decisions about staying in a particular job, changing careers, or adjusting to a new career. Small business coaching can involve working with budding, existing, or would-be entrepreneurs regarding new business ventures or offering assistance to business owners, private practitioners, and telecommuters. Executive and corporate coaching usually involves working with top- level executives and managers on various matters, such as strategy and vision development or burnout prevention. Coaches in this area also may help companies to implement their own internal coaching programs by training managers to coach others. While these are all distinct categories, considerable overlap can exist between them, and some life coaches practice in several or all of these areas. Within the personal/life coaching concentration, coaches may specialize in or prefer to work with certain types of people, such as women, minorities, or those with disabilities.

The Life Coaching Process Many life coaches do not meet with their clients in person on a regular basis as clinical therapists do. Some meet in person for the first session and then conduct future sessions via telephone, while others meet exclusively by phone. In both cases, coaches frequently include e-mail and fax communication as part of their services. Many coaches and clients prefer this approach because it is informal and relaxed, not to mention convenient. Proponents argue that conducting sessions this way takes the focus off of the immediate physical environment and allows coach and client to concentrate more clearly on the matters at hand.

The life coaching process often begins with a simple inquiry. About 70 percent of life coaching clients result from word-of-mouth referrals. Inquiry is followed by an initial consultation regarding what a prospective client hopes to accomplish working with the life coach. At this stage, both parties must determine if a synergistic, mutually beneficial relationship is possible. Once a client agrees to move ahead, assessments may be used to help him/her zero in on his/her life skills and interests.

At this early stage, the focus is quite broad in scope, looking at the development of big picture, top-level goals that vary considerably from person to person. Some individuals may wish to stop procrastinating, make more effective decisions, become better time managers, write a novel, or gain financial freedom. Others seek to discover and use their natural strengths, identify core values and limiting beliefs, increase self-awareness, or formulate motivational strategies. Still others might have goals that focus on diet, health, fitness, creativity, spirituality, interpersonal and/or family relationships, or organizational skills. Coaches may have clients rank major life areas by importance, including work, education, family, spirituality, and fun. As simple as it sounds, a big first step for many clients is to slow down and take time to think about who they are, where they are going, and what they ultimately want from life. This involves asking lots of questions, and the willingness to look at life from a different perspective.

From this point on, the coaching process usually becomes more specific, as coach and client focus on concrete short term and long term goals, the steps required to attain them, and techniques for staying focused. In addition to reflective verbal discussions, this process often involves journaling or writing goals down on paper, assignments that must be completed in between sessions, and even collage creation. Coaches may ask clients to identify three to five important goals they would like to accomplish in as many months, followed by a list of things that could hinder or take energy away from achieving them. The focus often centers on what people want (things that motivate them), as opposed to what they think they should be doing (things that are expected of them).

One key aspect of the entire life coaching process is that it is client-driven. Clients assume responsibility for putting plans into action and pursuing goals, while coaches act as cheerleaders, guides, and organizers, offering insight, encouragement, and motivational assistance. In addition, clients largely determine the length and frequency of the sessions they have with coaches, as well as how long the overall coaching relationship will last. Some clients use the services of a coach for only a few sessions, while others use them for several years. On average, most clients use coaching services for 6 to 24 months.

In the February 16, 2004, issue of the *Indianapolis Star*, one life coach commented on the heart of her dealings with clients, explaining, "I find out what clients want to do. Many times, they have no clue about their gifts. I have some assessments I use to help them figure out what their gifts are. To be a client and have someone like a life coach who has never met you tell you how you think and how you feel can be an overwhelming experience. It's almost holy to get down to someone's absolute core and find out who they are. And that their gifts are so unique and see how they are packaged. It's so unique. I feel like I'm launching people into life. It's honoring, humbling and exciting."

Cost While personal coaches have been known to charge clients anywhere from $70 to $500 per hour, the International Coach Foundation (ICF) reports that most place their hourly fees in the $100 to $150 range. Weekly half-hour sessions are the most common arrangement, costing clients $200 to $450 per month. Corporate coaching normally commands a higher fee, ranging from $1,000 to $10,000 per month. Some coaches offer group sessions at a lower cost to clients, and a few have been known to offer a select number of scholarships to needy clients each year.

Concerns Because no universally accepted certification is required for life coaching, anyone can assume this title and seek out clients. The fact that state requirements are more stringent for barbers and plumbers than for life coaches—whose work is the very stuff of clients' lives—has been a point of criticism regarding this self-regulated profession. Some critics argue that the services of life coaches really don't differ all that much from those offered by licensed counselors and therapists. In addition, those who are skeptical of life coaching argue that the same kind of advice can be obtained from a self-help book or from friends at no charge. Their position is that much of the advice and strategies offered by life coaches is mere common sense. While some life coaches agree with this argument, they counter that some clients either lack the necessary motivation, perspective, or support to go it alone, or simply prefer to hire an objective outsider for assistance.

Some estimates indicate that as many as 50 percent of those seeking life coaches have psychological problems, including depression. Because most life coaches are not professional therapists and the very focus of life coaching is on moving forward as opposed to dealing with problems, life coaches do not diagnose or treat mental illness. While some life coaches see patients who are receiving separate professional mental health counseling, the ICF's ethical guidelines frown upon such practices. The reason for this is that patients who are vulnerable or unstable may be harmed by the life coaching process, which can involve calculated risk-taking and pushing the boundaries of so-called comfort zones. For this reason, life coaches must be skilled at determining the suitability and stability of prospective clients.

Associations The International Coach Federation (ICF), which includes personal and business coaches among its members, is the primary professional association for the life coaching industry. The nonprofit ICF was established in 1992 and began accrediting coaches in 1998. The organization offered certifications as an associated certified coach (ACC), professional certified coach (PCC), or master certified coach (MCC). In 2002 the organization had 71 chapters and some 5,000 members worldwide. By the end of 2009, those figures had grown to more than 16,000 members in 90 countries. According to the federation, in addition to connecting people with coaches, it "supports and fosters development of the coaching profession; has programs to maintain and upgrade the standards of the profession; conducts a certification program that is the gold standard for coaches worldwide; and conducts the world's premier conference and other educational events for coaches." As of 2010, ICF was the oly organization that awarded a global credential, held at that time by 4000 coaches.

Other, smaller associations that supported the industry included the International Coaching Council, which offered a Certified Master Coach certification from its Graduate School of Master Coaches; the International Association of

Coaching, through which one could become a IAC Certified Coach; and the European Coaching Institute, which also offered an accreditation program. Such organizations as the FranklinCovey Institute, the Life Coach Institute, and the Institute for Life Coach Training, among many others, also offered training to be a life coach.

PIONEERS

For many years, a key figure in the life and business coaching industry was Thomas J. Leonard. A native of the San Francisco area, Leonard worked as a financial planner before helping establish coaching as a profession. Leonard's pioneering work involved the establishment of several educational programs and organizations related to coaching. These included a leading training center called Coach University; the Graduate School of Coaching, which had 1,400 students in 35 countries; and a virtual university called TeleClass.com, which served more than 20,000 students with courses delivered via telephone and the Internet.

In addition to writing nearly 30 different personal and professional development programs, Leonard wrote six books on coaching, including *Becoming a Coach,* the *Coaching Forms Book, The Distinctionary, The Portable Coach, Simply Brilliant,* and *Working Wisdom.*

In addition to his impact on the educational side of coaching, Leonard was instrumental in establishing coaching as a bona fide profession. He formed an industry association called the International Coach Federation (ICF) in 1994, which within a period of 10 years had more than 130 chapters throughout the world. In addition, Leonard also founded the International Association of Certified Coaches.

When he died at age 47, Leonard was the CEO of CoachVille.com, which claimed to be the world's largest training network for coaches, with some 20,000 member coaches and graduates from 85 countries. For his work, Leonard was featured in various news broadcasts and articles in such outlets as *Fortune, Newsweek, Time, NBC Nightly News, The Times (London),* and *The Los Angeles Times.*

Another key industry pioneer is George D. Kinder, a Harvard-trained tax advisor and financial planner who many consider the father of life planning. Unlike traditional financial planning that begins with a focus on financial goals, life planning helps clients to identify major life goals and then use financial planning to achieve them. In the March 3, 2003, issue of *Business Week,* Kinder summarized the approach, explaining, "We begin by asking three questions: If you had all the money you needed, what would your life look like? If you had 5 to 10 years to live, what would you do with your life? If you had only 24 hours left to live, what do you think you would most regret not having accomplished? Usually, it's in that last question people come out with their true goals."

Leading financial publications have named Kinder as one of the nation's top financial planners and as one of the financial services industry's most influential people. Kinder is the director of life planning for Boston-based Abacus Wealth Management. In addition, he is founder of the Kinder Institute of Life Planning.

Kinder is also the author of *The Seven Stages of Money Maturity,* which is considered a landmark book about life planning. In addition, he also is the co-founder of the Nazrudin Project, which according to his Web site is "a vital and influential think tank of national financial advisors dedicated to exploring the human and spiritual aspects of money and personal finance."

BACKGROUND AND DEVELOPMENT

Some life coaches refer to themselves as mentors, and the life coaching process is like mentoring in many ways. As a process, mentoring has been going on for more than 3,000 years. During much of the twentieth century, individuals were often employed by the same organization for long periods of time. This scenario was conducive to formalized mentoring, whereby workers—be they skilled tradesmen or business professionals—benefited from the wisdom of mentors who helped to guide them through different stages of their careers. Additionally, as various historians have noted, previous generations were more complacent regarding their work/life situations and were more content to accept things as they were.

Business conditions later changed and workers began switching employers and careers with greater frequency. Society and life itself became increasingly complex, resulting in higher levels of stress and uncertainty. These conditions were very favorable to the birth and evolution of life coaching, which first emerged during the 1980s. At that time, a growing number of U.S. residents became interested in personal fulfillment.

In the beginning, the business of life coaching was mainly conducted by the likes of financial planners, psychologists, and business consultants, often as part of other services. However, much like marriage and family counseling developed as a specialty during the 1970s, life coaching ultimately emerged as its very own field. By 1992, the nonprofit International Coach Federation (ICF) was formed to serve the needs of personal and business coaches. It began accrediting coaches in 1998, at which time the life coaching industry was exploding in popularity.

This popularity was due in part to the media attention life coaches received in the late 1990s and the early years of the first decade of the 2000s. During this time period, the subject of life coaching began appearing on the likes of the Oprah Winfrey show. Oprah's guests included people such as author Cheryl Richardson, who penned the best-selling book *Life Makeovers* and advocated the use of life coaches. Dr. Phil McGraw was another highly popular life strategist who used coaching techniques as a guest on the Oprah Winfrey Show and also on his own television program.

As with many emerging fields, life coaching was engaged in a process of definition and trailblazing in the early 2000s. By 2004, regulation had become a hot topic for life coaches. According to the ICF, a certain degree of confusion still existed about the relationship between coaching and mental health services. In addition, states like Arizona, New York, and Minnesota were concerned about a growing number of unlicensed individuals who were practicing counseling and therapy. In Colorado, this led coaches to proactively seek exclusion from the Colorado Mental Health Boards. Coaches sought to avoid any possibility that they would be considered unregistered psychotherapists and forced to register with the state.

In the April 2004 issue of *Coaching World,* ICF Executive Director Daniel Martinage, CAE, said, "Coaching is not part of the mental-health profession, and these laws are not intended for coaches. However, if an unlicensed individual performs counseling and calls himself/herself a coach, this would be of concern to the states, as well as to the ICF."

As an alternative to state or federal regulation, the ICF supported continued self-regulation of the life coaching industry. The organization claimed that its Code of Ethics, Ethical Conduct Review Process, ICF Core Competencies, and Credentialing Program represented a strong foundation on which self-regulation could exist. In 2007 the ICF received a record 1,411 certification applications and granted certification to 1,118 professionals.

In the middle part of the first decade of the 2000s, the life coaching industry continued to contend with the issue of regulation. In the September 7, 2005, edition of *Training Magazine,* Guy Sheppard summarized the current state of affairs, explaining: "Self-regulation is spreading fast in coaching, but the direction it will take is difficult to predict. Some coaches argue that a common set of standards is needed to help weed out unscrupulous operators, while others believe that the profession is too diverse for this option to work. There is also an argument that, unlike other branches of training, the qualities required for good coaching are just too complex to codify."

During 2005, ICF President Steve Mitten explained that a great deal of confusion remained in the market over what coaching is about, the profession's benefits, and how to choose a coach. Confusion also existed among coaches themselves in regard to credentialing and educational standards. Mitten further indicated that "Individuals with no intention of becoming properly trained are joining the ICF and calling themselves ICF coaches, thus adversely affecting the integrity of both our profession and our professional association." The ICF sought to address these challenges and promote the elements of trust in and respect for the coaching profession.

Life coaching was catching on internationally by 2006. In Europe, the profession was gaining recognition as a valuable tool the legal profession could use to physically, emotionally, and psychologically prepare individuals for courtroom appearances. In addition, life coaching was seen as a beneficial tool that barristers could use to improve their personal and professional lives.

Growth of the International Coach Federation (ICF) was one sign of the steady rise of the industry in the first decade of the 2000s. From 1999 to 2008, the organization experienced a 600 percent growth in membership and had more than 15,000 members by 2008. It had also expanded membership to 90 countries and hosted 162 chapters in 49 countries. A majority of members (62 percent) resided in North America; 25 percent were in Europe and the Middle East, and 10 percent in the Asia-Pacific region.

As the industry evolved and expanded, some coaches carved out niches, targeting certain groups other than business executives or people who wanted to gain better control over their money, time, career, or life in general. For example, in 2006, Kevin Ryan, a professional in the publishing business in the United Kingdom, created the concept of Moving On, which involved coaching for creative people in the business—artists, writers, and so on. Ryan said in a *Bookseller* article, "Creative people have to struggle with many things that can frustrate and block their creativity or make them lose sight of their goals. I can help them find their way, as I have dealt with many of the same problems myself." In individual coaching sessions, Ryan works with people to overcome a creative block or find alternative solutions to problems.

Another new niche involved the dating scene. Dating coaches work with people to improve their interpersonal relationship skills and their success in the dating scene. Many dating coaches are already certified as life coaches and chose dating as their area of specialty. In fact, according to a survey of 6,000 life coaches by the ICF, 20 percent of them specialized in some type of relationship coaching. As of 2008, dating coaches charged anywhere from $75 to $125 an hour and provided services through workshops, seminars, and one-on-one consultations using the Internet, telephone, and face-to-face meetings.

CURRENT CONDITIONS

2010 figures from the ICF indicated that its membership was up to 16,000 in over 90 countries. (These are professional members of ICF. Globally, it was estimated (by the Spencer Institute) that there were about 40,000 persons practicing in that capacity.)

In 2009, ICF published its *ICF Global Coaching Client Study,* considered a landmark report. Highlights included a finding that 96 percent of coaching clients stated they would repeat their coaching experience, and nearly 83 percent reported they were "very satisfied " with their coaching experiences. Interestingly, the majority of clients possessed advanced college degrees, mostly female, and the largest cluster of all clients fell within the age bracket of 36 to 45 (although that cluster only constituted 35.9 percent of the total). The top three motivating factors for seeking coaching were self esteem/self confidence issues (40 percent), work/lofe balance (35 percent), and career opportunities (26 percent). The duration of a coaching experience or coaching relationship for survey participants was 12.8 months.

As of 2010, the industry remained unregulated, and there was no national (United States) or international standard for credentialing or licensing. Notwithstanding the slumping economy, life coaching as an industry continued to enjoy steady revenues into 2010. A 2009 report by Pricewaterhouse Coopers LLP (PwC) indicated that the approximate global revenue produced annually by the coaching industry was $1.5 billion. At that time, part-time coaches averaged related income of $26,150, and full-time coaches averaged $82,671 per year. Further, PwC found that the average professional coach was 46 to 55 years old and had been coaching for 5 to 10 years. Almost 70 percent of life coaches were female. The majority of coaches maintained an average of 10 to 12 clients at any given time.

The Spencer Institute, in its 2010 rundown of latest trends and state-of-the-profession, noted that in the United States, remuneration for the average life coach was roughly $400 monthly per client (for four 45-minute sessions). Corporate clients warranted higher fees, about $150 to $200 per hour. About 70 percent of coaches, according to the Spencer Institute, worked mostly by telephone and email, with a nationwide practice. The Instutute estimated that the industry continued to grow at about 20 percent annually.

WORKFORCE

Life coaches come from diverse backgrounds. Prior to becoming coaches, these professionals may have worked as teachers, trainers, accountants, interior designers, consultants, hospital administrators, real estate developers, engineers, executives, or nurses. In addition to their roles as life coaches, some may work concurrently as professional trainers, licensed therapists, or even medical doctors. Still others are certified financial planners who help clients to develop sound investment and money management strategies that support broader life goals.

Specific credentials or training programs were not required for one to become a life coach. While this was a cause of concern for some industry observers, by 2006 the ICF had accredited approximately 24 coach training programs throughout the world. In addition, a growing number of coach programs, many of which focus on business coaching, have emerged at prestigious colleges and universities in recent years. George Washington University and Duke University were two such institutions in the latter years of the decade.

In addition to completing one of the aforementioned certificate-based programs, successful coaches possess a certain degree of intelligence and are critical thinkers. They also have a number of other attributes that oftentimes come from previous career paths. In the January 17, 2004, issue of *The Australian,* Dr. Anthony Grant, director of the coaching psychology unit at the University of Sydney, said good coaches "have an understanding of the following areas: behavioural science (why people think, behave and feel the way they do); adult education (adult developmental life cycles); business or systems (how businesses or human systems such as families function); and philosophy (most of the deep questions are philosophical)."

RESEARCH AND TECHNOLOGY

Critics of the life coaching profession have named lack of industry research as a drawback to proving its effectiveness. However, the ICF's Research & Development Committee had posted an indexed bibliography of published coaching research on the ICF Web site. The bibliography was described as the first phase of a larger online repository. Therefore, the possibility existed that both industry players and observers would have access to additional research materials heading into the second half of the decade.

Technology had its hand in the industry. In 2008 the U.S. consulting group Accenture launched its Personal Performance Coach, a software system that ran on any Windows-based smartphone paired with a Bluetooth headset. The system, which was targeted toward business executives, could provide instant feedback on everything from conversational style to fitness regime. Accenture researcher Dana Le described the device in a *Business 2.0* article as "an angel on your shoulder telling you how you should behave." For example, for an executive who wants to be a better listener, the system can be programmed to track how much time he or she talks during a meeting or conversation. If the exec goes over the amount of time that has been programmed in, the device will whisper a reminder to "talk less."

BIBLIOGRAPHY

2007 Annual Report. International Coach Federation, 2008.

"2010 Trends: 10 and 1/2 Trends to Watch." *Entrepreneur,* Available from http://www.entrpreneur.com/trends/index.html.

"About Coaching." Spencer Institute of Life Coaching, 2010. Available from http://www.spencerinstitute.org/aboutcoaching.

"A Capital Idea for Women." *Newsweek,* July 2007.

Blakely, Lindsay. "The Life Coach in your Headset." *Business 2.0,* July 2007.

"Coaches FIGHT for Credibility." *Training Magazine,* 7 September 2005.

"Coaching in the Library." *American Libraries,* 18 February 2010.

"Dating Coach: A Booming Field." *Wisconsin State Journal* (Madison), 6 July 2008.

Dueease, Bill. "NY Times Reports Women Owners' Success Due to M3 Program and TCC Coaching." *The Coach Connection,* 5 October 2007.

Ellin, Abby. "The Dating Coach Is In ($125/Hour)." *The New York Times,* 27 September 2007.

"First Global Survey of Coaching Clients Reveals High ROI/Satisfaction." *Market Wire,* 6 July 2009. Available from http://www.marketwire.com/press-release/First-Global-Survey-of-Coaching-Clients-Reveals-High-ROI-Satisfaction-1012958.htm.

"George Kinder." *Financial Planning,* January 2005.

Global Coaching Study. International Coach Federation, February 2008.

"International Coach Federation Dispels Common Misconceptions About Professional Coaching." International Coach Federation, 30 April 2008.

"Life Coaches—Who Are They to Tell Us How to Live?" Live Radio Talk Show, WKPCC Southern California Public Radio, 11 August 2010. Transcript available from http://www. scpr.org/programs.

O'Donovan, Gerard. "Courtroom Appearance. The Life-Coaching Industry Has a Valuable Role to Play in Preparing for Court." *The Lawyer,* 14 November 2005.

"Results of Landmark ICF Global Coaching Client Study Released." BNET Market Wire, February 2009.

Williams, Patrick. "The Evolving Profession of Life Coaching." *Personal Fitness Professional Magazine,* August 2006.

LOGISTICS OUTSOURCING SERVICES

—■—

SIC CODE(S)

4731

INDUSTRY SNAPSHOT

Logistics refers to supply chain services such as the transportation of goods from manufacturers to retailers and distributors. Logistics outsourcing services enable companies to dispense with their own fleets and rely on third party shipping services to transport their goods.

The decision to outsource logistics has long been driven by the desire to reduce costs, and some progressive companies were viewing logistics outsourcing as a key part of their long-term corporate strategy. Therefore, efficient logistics became a means to increase market share, customer satisfaction levels, and more.

Because so many goods and products are imported from other countries, the industry increasingly encompasses a global market, wrought with complex issues involving international communications and coordination, contractual fulfillments, border inspections and delays, taxation, customs, and other concerns that can affect both time and condition upon arrival at the final destination point. One example, in 2008 and 2009, was the manifold increase in the number of cargo ships (destined for ports all over the globe) attacked by modern-day pirates off the coast of Somalia who made exorbitant ransom demands. This created, at best, delayed deliveries, insurance payouts, lost or damaged cargo, backlogged inventory, and unhappy end-users. At worst, it created threats to life, loss of carriers and goods, and international tensions.

ORGANIZATION AND STRUCTURE

Logistics outsourcing services provide an array of supply chain services including warehousing, transportation, and inventory management. Warehousing refers to the storage and management of products usually in the third party service provider's warehouse. Typically, these warehouses have information technology in place that enables both parties to monitor inventory. Transportation services include the shipment of goods from warehouses to customers, such as the shipment of goods from manufacturer to distributors or retailers. Third party logistics (or 3PL) transportation services include truckload, less-than-truckload (shipping freight that does not completely fill a truck), inter-modal (truck, train, air), dedicated contract carriage (dedicated fleet for a contract), and express delivery.

Finally, inventory management involves keeping track of customers' inventories, often using inventory control software. Logistics services manage freight and information about freight for everything from raw materials to finished products.

Most companies that use logistics outsourcing services rely on bidding processes to determine which logistics service will be awarded a contract. A minority of firms negotiate with individual logistics companies to reach an agreement on outsourcing logistics tasks.

BACKGROUND AND DEVELOPMENT

The modern logistics outsourcing services industry grew out of warehousing and shipping services of Europe. Venice was home to the first major European commercial warehouse and transportation nexus. As trading spread out from the Mediterranean, port cities cropped up with their own warehouses. By storing goods at port city warehouses, transportation time decreased because ships spent less time at each port.

In the United States, the growth of the railroad industry spurred the development of the logistics industry. Freight train cars themselves served as warehouses; but the dearth of cars led to the construction of warehouses throughout the country. Since the railroads controlled both transportation and warehousing, it had a monopoly on logistics services. To court large corporations, the railroads would offer them free warehousing in exchange for using their transportation services.

The American Warehousing Association, formed in 1891, fought to end free warehousing by the railroads, lobbying for the Hepburn Act of 1906. The Hepburn Act terminated warehousing by railroads, facilitating the development of separate warehousing businesses.

The Industrial Revolution also contributed to the growth of the early logistics industry. Companies started to use mass production techniques, creating a large supply of goods that had to be shipped around the country. While companies initially stored their products in their own warehouses, they started to move their products closer to the markets for the products and to use warehousing services to achieve this goal.

Advances in transportation technology such as the development of the truck and the airplane also drove the industry as it evolved from just railroads and warehouses. Although companies tended to handle their own warehousing and transportation, they frequently began to outsource these tasks beginning in the late 1980s and early 1990s, spawning the logistics outsourcing services industry. During this period and in subsequent years, companies determined what their core competencies were. If these competencies did not include logistics, then they outsourced these tasks to third party service providers.

At the turn of the century, outsourcing logistics tasks had become a significant trend among U.S. companies. Although the logistics outsourcing services industry had not skyrocketed into the colossal industry some forecasted in the early 1990s, it had become a strong and growing industry that etched a permanent place in the economy. In the late 1990s, total U.S. logistics costs reached $862 billion annually, and by 2000 saved the companies an estimated $5 billion. Total revenues for the industry that year were an estimated $50 billion to $55 billion, according to the *Journal of Commerce,* up from $45.3 billion in 1999. In 1999, dedicated contract carriage services accounted for $7.2 billion, other domestic transportation services for $6.6 billion, warehousing for $16.6 billion, international services for $12 billion, and logistics software for $3 billion. During the late 1990s, the industry grew at a rate of roughly 20 percent annually.

The outlook for the logistics outsourcing services industry also appeared favorable because most customers seemed pleased with these services according to various surveys. For example, a survey by University of Tennessee's Center for Logistics Research, Exel Logistics, and Ernst & Young found that nearly 100 percent of the customers surveyed believed objectives such as asset reduction, strategic flexibility, employee reduction, and expanded global presence were being fulfilled. In addition, over 90 percent felt they were accomplishing their goal of supply chain integration via logistics outsourcing services and about 90 percent of those surveyed indicated overall satisfaction with third party logistics companies. However, respondents were less satisfied with logistics services in meeting objectives such as facilitating e-commerce and implementing changes and new technology quickly. Nevertheless, the survey revealed several key benefits of outsourcing: reduced logistics costs, shortened order cycles, and reduced inventories.

The industry also witnessed heightened merger and acquisition activity in the late 1990s. For example, the industry's leading company, Exel Plc, had come about via the merger of Ocean Group Plc and NFC Plc. Exel went on to acquire over 12 other logistics service providers. In the United States, UPS acquired Rollins Logistics and Finon Sofecome, FedEx bought Caliber Logistics and GeoLogistics, and Schneider added Tranzact to its portfolio. Furthermore, six logistics outsourcing services, including J.B. Hunt Logistics and Covenant Logistics, pooled their efforts together to form Transplace.com.

Surveys and reports indicated that 80 percent of the *Fortune* 500 companies were outsourcing at least some of their logistics tasks by the turn of the new century. Nevertheless, a study by the industry publication *Logistics Management Distribution Report* found that many companies only farmed out a portion of their logistics functions, thereby failing to realize greater savings achieved when entire logistics functions are outsourced. A report by the University of Maryland's Best Practices Group demonstrated that companies that outsource their entire logistics functions save approximately 21 percent the first year. Furthermore, their savings increase proportionately with the number of tasks they outsource. That is, the more they outsource, the more they save. The report also revealed that about 10 percent of all major U.S. companies outsourced their entire functions and that the savings these companies realized did not dilute the quality and reliability of warehousing and transportation. According to a survey conducted by *Purchasing* magazine in late 2001, 66 percent of companies anticipated increasing their logistics outsourcing in the near future.

Trends included the movement toward one-stop logistics services, the increased profitability of third party logistics companies, and greater global expansion. One-stop logistics, or integrated logistics companies, provide a host of services and oversee the entire logistics process. If they are unable to provide particular services, integrated logistics companies form partnerships with other third party providers to offer their clients a single outsourcing solution with one contact, bill, and computer interface. These bundled services may include packaging, assembly, warehousing, transportation, and information systems. Nevertheless, integrating services has led to rising costs among third party logistics services, which forces them to increase their rates. However, logistics services have been wary of raising rates too high out of fear that customers will shop around to find lower rates.

The Internet was an important tool for third party logistics services in the early years of the decade. The Internet enabled logistics services to provide their customers with access to information and pricing, online dispatch and ordering of services, online tracking systems, and expedited communication via e-mail. During this period, the Internet and software expenditures constituted one of the most substantial investments of the industry, driven by customer demand for real time information and easy accessibility to it.

Logistics also grew increasingly important to the trucking and courier services industry. In one case, UPS used its expertise in logistics to transport 4.5 million vehicles to North American automobile dealers for Ford Motor Company, reducing delivery time by 25 percent and saving the automaker roughly $240 million. In fact, logistics sales at UPS jumped 58 percent to exceed $1 billion for the first time as UPS completed work on major projects like those for Ford. A similar project for National Semiconductor Corp. proved equally successful. As stated in a May 2001 issue of *Business Week,* UPS designed and constructed a Singapore-based warehouse for National Semiconductor that uses "a delivery process that is efficient and automated, almost to the point of magic." Once new products, such as computer chips, are manufactured and sent to the Singapore warehouse, "it is UPS's computers that speed the box of chips to a loading dock, then to truck, to plane, and to truck once again. In just 12 hours, the chips will reach one of National's customers, a PC maker half a world away in Silicon Valley. Throughout the journey, electronic tags embedded in the chips will let the customer track the order with accuracy down to about three feet." By outsourcing its shipping, inventory management, and other logistics processes to UPS, National Semiconductor reduced expenses by an estimated 15 percent by 2002. To compete, smaller trucking companies like Yellow Corp. and Roadway Express Inc. began offering similar just-in-time services to their clients.

One area that still offered room for growth was Internet-based logistics, which is essentially the use of Internet technology to coordinate all aspects of freight shipping, from ordering and pick-up to payment and delivery. Yellow Corp. was considered a leader in this market segment. In 2001 the firm transformed Transportation.com from an online transportation marketplace to a marketer of the transportation management software developed internally by Yellow Corp. Transportation.com also began offering logistics and transportation management consulting services. In 2002, Yellow Corp. created transportation technology management unit Meridian IQ to house its Internet-based logistics services.

In 2005, the IWLA indicated that third party logistics providers (3PLs) accounted for $78 billion of the U.S. gross domestic product, with annual growth estimated at 15 to 20 percent. In only a few years, the industry had achieved remarkable growth. According to *The Journal of Commerce,* the logistics outsourcing market increased from $30.8 billion in 1996 to $76.9 billion in 2003. In addition, 90 percent of *Fortune* 100 companies had relationships in place with logistics outsourcing firms.

The logistics outsourcing industry was on solid footing during the middle of the twenty-first century's first decade. A report by the IWLA in 2007 indicated that one-fifth of third party logistics providers (3PLs) had seen revenue increases of 20 percent or more in 2006. Eight percent saw increases of 15 to 20 percent, and another 25 percent reached double-digit increases of 10 to 15 percent. In addition, the survey found more than half of 3PLs were planning to add employees in 2007 and 61 percent planned to add warehouse space.

Looking ahead, the IWLA's study indicated that its members saw the greatest growth potential for logistics outsourcing in the following industries: food, beverage, and grocery; paper and related products; retail/general merchandise; pharmaceuticals; and computers/high technology.

According to the IWLA, the industry was growing not just in terms of services provided and outsourced but in also in terms of volume. As global trade became more commonplace, the importance of logistics outsourcing increased. According to *Forbes* magazine, total merchandise exported from the United States increased from $782 billion in 2000 to $904 billion in 2005.

For most companies, the decision to outsource the logistics function was still driven mainly by potential cost savings. However, this was beginning to change as some organizations saw logistics outsourcing as a way to achieve broader strategic goals such as improving customer service or increasing market share. For example, by outsourcing logistics to a more efficient third party provider, companies might be able to shorten delivery times, reduce late deliveries, and improve inventory flow. For these reasons, logistics executives were more often included in high-level strategic planning discussions. This shift required companies to look beyond short-term cost savings and take a longer and broader view of logistics outsourcing. Other factors influencing the industry included the growth of e-commerce and the general trend toward outsourcing.

Despite the positive growth, logistics outsourcing providers were also facing the challenge of higher costs. According to Rosalyn Wilson of CSCMP, "Logistics costs have gone up over 50 percent during the last decade. Transportation costs, mostly trucking, accounted for much of the increase." The rise in fuel costs had the biggest impact on the increase in costs, with the trucking industry spending $87.7 billion on diesel fuel in 2005 as compared to $65.9 billion in 2004. The cost of insurance for truck drivers also went up. Wilson cited the increase in disruptions such as terrorism, political upheaval, and natural disasters as a factor that challenged the logistics industry in the latter years of the first decade of the 2000s.

CURRENT CONDITIONS

Clearly the global economic slump of 2008 and 2009 created excess inventories, delayed shipments, and headaches around the world. In past recessions, enterprises increased both IT and business process outsourcing (BPO) initiatives to drive out cost, said Phil Fersht and Dana Stiffler of AMR Research, in their July 2009 report of the industry. However, starting in the fall of 2008 through the first six months of 2009, they noted, most enterprises put outsourcing plans on the back burner while they tackled fundamental issues, including contemplating their very survival. However, AMR predicted the industry would move forward with more caution and global focus.

In August 2009, *Logistics Quarterly Magazine* published its August survey of the top forty 3PLs in North America, 72 percent of which indicated that gross revenues were down 12 percent for the year, while 24 percent reported increased revenues. The market segments differed in results, with value-added warehousing (contract logistics) revenues declining by just 2.8 percent, while transportation management segments uniformly saw greater reductions in revenue. Domestic transportation managers (including freight brokers) reported gross revenues down by nearly 13 percent. International transportation management (including freight forwarding) was down 16 percent. Especially hard hit was air freight, where volumes were running 20 to 25 percent less.

Automotive logistics tended to pull the industry down, with a negative -37.5 percent as of mid-2009, according to *Logistics Quarterly Magazine.* These numbers reflected the collapse of GM and Chrysler as well as the reduced sales of other automakers. Michigan and Ontario, along with several of their "old line" 3PL operations, were hit particularly hard.

Economic recovery in North America should continue throughout 2010, said *Logistics Quarterly's* Richard Armstrong. He predicted that by year end, 3PL activity would be close to 2008 levels. Further, outsourcing to 3PLs should proceed at two to three times the increase in GDP. He also expected more big company "carve-outs" like the IBM/Geodis deal.

INDUSTRY LEADERS

Exel Plc is one of the world's largest logistics service providers based on revenue. The company formed after the merger of Ocean Group Plc and NFC Plc and is a global player with strong sales from e-commerce. The company has more than 500 offices in 120 countries and provides air courier, trucking, warehousing, and express courier services.

C.H.Robinson (CHR) dominated North American domestic transportation management with more than 20 percent of total revenue and 40 percent of EBIT in 2009. It expected to have a net revenue increase of 3 percent for 2009, but Expeditors International, a leading freight forwarder in North America, unfortunately reported gross revenues down 35 percent for the first six months of 2009.

Menlo Worldwide, a subsidiary of Conway Inc. (formerly CNF), is another major player in the logistics outsourcing services industry. In addition to managing the logistics tasks of other companies, Menlo Logistics also develops logistics software. In 2008 the parent company reported revenues of $5 billion ($1.5 in 3PL), and it employed 9,200 workers. In 2004 CNF sold part of Menlo Worldwide, Menlo Worldwide Forwarding, to UPS.

Ryder System Inc.'s Ryder Integrated Logistics also ranks among the leading logistics outsourcing companies. Operating on both the domestic and global fronts, Ryder specializes in distribution management and transportation management. In 2008 Ryder Integrated Logistics had sales of $2.2 billion in 3PL turnover with 18,500 dedicated 3PL employees, 200 warehouses, and 58,000 tractors. The parent company brought in $6.2 billion.

Schneider Logistics, a division of Schneider National Inc., played a key role in the industry. The company's core services included freight management, supplier management, inbound freight conversion and control, and express shipment services.

J. B. Hunt Logistics, a subsidiary of J. B. Hunt Transport Services, Inc., was another industry leader. However, in 2000, J. B. Hunt merged its logistics arm with the logistics units of five other companies—Covenant Transport, Inc., Inc., M.S. Carriers, Inc., Swift Transportation Co., Inc., U.S. Xpress Enterprises, Inc., and Werner Enterprises, Inc.—to form Transplace Inc. The company's Web-based platform, Transplace.com, remained a useful tool for shippers and carriers to work together to plan logistics services including truckload, less-than-truckload, inter-modal, and express delivery services worldwide. Sales for the parent company totaled $3.5 billion ($927 million 3PL) in 2008 with 5,500 JBH employees and 10,080 tractors.

Other major logistics outsourcing services included FedEx Logistics and UPS Worldwide Logistics, specializing in both domestic and international airfreight distribution.

AMERICA AND THE WORLD

According to a 2009 report from ARC Advisory Group, economic development in the Middle East and North Africa (MENA) was prompting increased demand for outsourced logistics. Report author Adrian Gonzalez said the region's 3PL sector remained fragmented with local regulations and constraints presenting providers and customers with "unique challenges." The Gulf Cooperation Council (GCC), a subset of the larger MENA region, had a transport and logistics market worth $18 billion in 2008 and one consulting firm (Booz) expected the market to reach $27 billion by 2012. ARC noted that other sources valued the entire MENA region at $120 billion in 2009. With a regional GDP averaging 5.5 percent, Gonzalez said the non-oil sector was beginning to take off. He cited Saudi Arabia's $80 billion investment in the King Abdullah Economic City (KAEC) as an example.

The Associated Chambers of Commerce and Industry of India (Assocham) said in its September 2009 report that third party logistics (3PL) business in India was likely to reach $90 million by 2012 from $58 million in 2009. According to the chamber, India's logistics market size would reach $125 billion by 2010 from $105 billion in 2009, growing at an average rate between 16 to 17 percent for the next two years.

RESEARCH AND TECHNOLOGY

Computer networking and information technology have been areas of significant research by the logistics outsourcing services industry. Collaborative Planning Forecast and Replenishment (CPFR) software, for example, enables manufacturers and retailers to share their forecasts on the production of and demand for certain products and to develop sales targets together. This software, referred to as advanced planning and scheduling (APS) software, allows manufacturers and retailers to respond to fluctuating demand by alerting each other of possible changes in demand through computer software.

Other computer networking and Web-based software, such as transportation management software (TMS) and warehouse management software (WMS), lets companies purchase products and arrange shipping via the Internet.

With this software, companies can also monitor the inventory of their trading partners. In addition, some developers of Web-based logistics software rent their applications for a monthly fee or service charge, making it possible for small and medium logistics outsourcing services to employ this kind of supply, scheduling, and inventory software. Besides these kinds of Web-based applications, logistics companies developed new programs that allowed users to create custom contracts, execute these contracts, and automatically pay for services online.

BIBLIOGRAPHY

Armstrong, Richard. "The Top 40 3PLs 2009: A Very Differend Year in 3PL Land." *Logistics Quarterly Magazine,* August 2009. Available from http://www.logisticsquarterly.com/issues/15-4/agility.html.

Biederman, David. "Outsourcing's Strategic ROI: Cutting Costs Is One Way of Measuring Logistics Outsourcing, but Looking At the Strategic Value May Show the Real Return On Investment." *The Journal of Commerce,* 27 September 2004.

Doherty, Kathy. "Logistics Costs Skyrocket." *Food Logistics,* 15 October 2006.

Fahey, Jonathan. "I'll Handle That." *Forbes,* 16 April 2007.

Fersht, Phil, and Dana Stiffler. "State of the Outsourcing Industry in Mid-2009: Activity To Resume With a More Cautious and Global Focus." *AMR Research Report,* 23 July 2009.

Hannon, David. "What's Hot." *Purchasing,* 9 December 2004.

"Hoover's Company Capsules." *Hoover's Online.* 1 April 2007. Available from http://hoovers.com.

"Industry Background." Des Plaines, IL: International Warehouse Logistics Association, 1 April 2007. Available from www.iwla.com.

"IWLA Members Predict Continued Double-Digit Growth for the 3PL Warehouse Logistics Industry." International Warehouse Logistics Association, 9 April 2007. Available from www.iwla.com.

"Logistics Outsourcing on the Rise in China." *Purchasing,* 5 October 2006.

"Logistics Outsourcing to Reach $90 mn by 2012: Assocham." 27 September 2009. Available from http://taragana.com/index. php/archive/logistics-outsourcing-to-reach-90-mn-by-2012.

MacDonald, Andrea. "Ground Transport Upscales into Supply Chain Management." *World Trade,* October 2006.

"New 3PL Study Offers Industry Insights." *Logistics Today,* November 2006.

"Now Is the Right Time to Explore Logistics Outsourcing." *Purchasing,* 20 March 2003.

Tirschwell, Peter. "Danger Signs." *The Journal of Commerce,* 25 December 2006.

Trunick, Perry A. "The Many Faces of Logistics in China." *Logistics Today,* January 2007.

MASS MERCHANDISING

———————— ■ ————————

SIC CODE(S)

7829

5945

5999

INDUSTRY SNAPSHOT

Mass merchandising, or tie-ins, which may have begun as a technique to bolster sales on occasion, has become a veritable industry in its own right. With advertising costs increasing, competition heating up, and markets peaking, companies turn to tie-ins—movie, television show, video game, recording artist, or sports star—to revitalize aging products and brands and to propel new ones. Going into the second decade of the new century, Disney and Warner Brothers were among the top tie-in campaign companies, releasing several blockbuster movies coupled with cross-promotions in the fast food, toy, apparel, and other industries.

Mass merchandising, such as spin-offs, tie-ins, cross-promotions, and merchandise licensing played an increasingly important role in the entertainment industry. Licensed entertainment properties, such as action figures, clothing, and plush dolls, along with marketing campaigns tied to fast food chains and soft drink companies, not to mention musical soundtracks, books, and computer games, have become just as important as the original source material. Some high-profile blockbuster films have earned more in merchandise revenue than in ticket sales, while successful movie soundtracks often stay on the charts months after the films disappear from theaters.

In the last two decades of the twentieth century, the practice of licensing—when companies pay a fee to use the image of a sports team or an animated character—exploded. Businesses as diverse as fast food restaurants and T-shirt makers discovered the benefits of aligning themselves with high-profile characters and images that literally sell themselves.

Licensing and tie-ins continued to drive growth within the mass merchandising industry. Factors affecting growth included the continued release of blockbuster movies, new TV licensing opportunities, and emerging global markets in countries such as China, India, Russia, Poland, and Brazil. Consumer demand was also expected to continue, as was retailers' willingness to participate in selling the products.

Product placement itself, a tactic that gained great favor in the 1980s and 1990s, gained a new outlet in the form of a new television genre: the highly successful "reality programming" shows that became a dominant force in the early twenty-first century. Brand names were in very plain sight in living spaces of MTV's *Real World* subjects and CBS's *Big Brother* houseguests, and *Survivor* contestants competed in physical activities for popular soft drinks. Reality programming continued to be a strong outlet for product placements heading into the second decade of the 2000s.

Merchandisers also exploited the possibilities of new technical developments such as wireless technology (including cell phones) and, of course, the Internet. As new technology developed, merchandisers continued to employ traditional techniques, but in new ways. When movie tie-ins became a somewhat risky proposition, merchandisers turned to television, particularly to target the growing pre-school and adolescent markets that were

Estimated 2009 Revenues by Licensed Property Type	
Art	$ 136 million
Characters	$ 2,400 million
Collegiate	$ 200 million
Fashion	$ 705 million
Music	$ 110 million
Non-profit	$ 35 million
Sports	$ 660 million
Trademarks	$ 880 million
Publishing	$ 34 million
Other	$ 5 million
Total	**$5,165 million**

SOURCE: Licensing Industry Merchandisers' Association (LIMA).

drawn to the medium in increasing numbers, thanks to the thriving "Kids TV programming" as well as the popularity of pop stars such as Hannah Montana and the Jonas Brothers. After television, merchandisers turned to the hugely popular video game market and the new breed of merchandising: cross-promotions. More than simple product placement, video games moved toward plot lines that kept the gamers interacting with the virtual product.

ORGANIZATION AND STRUCTURE

Generally, after a product, movie, television show, recording artist, or athlete achieves fame or popularity, companies attempt to tap into this popularity with tie-ins (although many movie tie-ins are planned before the movies are released). In doing so, companies create a network of brands, each capitalizing on the strength of the other, at least in theory. For example, toy maker Hasbro, Inc., ties different toys with different fast food restaurants, which allows the restaurants to get Hasbro toys and allows Hasbro to use the chain names on its toys.

Because of the explosive popularity and substantial revenues of Disney movies, having a tie-in with a Disney movie means the likelihood of a successful centerpiece promotion. Soaring revenues have come with greater expectations and some growing pains, however. Some critics worry that movies are being made simply to sell more licensed gadgets rather than the other way around. Meanwhile, advertisers with a growing stake in the promotion of movies have even been known to propose script changes to maximize tie-in potential or press for earlier release dates.

Conversely, high profile box office releases, such as *Godzilla* and *Babe: Pig in the City*, proved disappointing when it came to tie-ins. With licensing costs rising, such promotional ventures have become more risky. Rising costs on both sides of the licensing fence might push movie studios and restaurant chains into unprecedented

alliances, enabling chains to consider films while they are still in the development stage.

Meanwhile, manufacturers who pinned hopes on a product as seemingly solid as sports merchandise—shirts, hats, and trash bins with team logos—faced losses when the major sports organizations experienced labor trouble such as the baseball strike of 1994 and the National Basketball Association lockout during the 1998-99 season. Nonetheless, for both large and small businesses, mass merchandising in its various forms continues to offer important benefits to firms that spend wisely, whether it be to put the latest Disney character on a pair of socks or a *Star Wars* character on a pencil sharpener. As media companies continue to merge and expand, and books and soundtracks based on film and television become increasingly popular, marketing such spin-offs using different media is expected to become more frequent and sophisticated.

BACKGROUND AND DEVELOPMENT

Mass merchandising has been around for quite a long time, although the industry was not always as lucrative as it has been since the late 1970s. In the early twentieth century, actors and baseball players often appeared on cigarette cards, and children purchasing chewing gum would also get free trading cards.

Upon analysis, it was the cards, not the gum or cigarettes, that collectors came to desire. A 1909 cigarette card of Hall of Fame baseball player Honus Wagner is rare because Wagner quickly demanded that his image be removed from the package so he would not appear to encourage smoking. The card has an estimated worth of $500,000.

Toy executive Cy Schneider asserted in his book *Children's Television* that the first licensing agreement arranged with a toy manufacturer came in 1913 when the Ideal Toy Co. introduced the world to the "teddy" bear, having first sought permission from former president Teddy Roosevelt. Companies would later use popular radio characters from the 1920s and 1930s to sell products and licensed goods. Ralston Cereals, for example, offered the "Ralston Straight Shooter Manual," which told readers, presumably young boys, about the real adventures of the popular cowboy character Tom Mix. It even included the "Tom Mix Chart of Wounds," which illustrated 12 bullet wounds and nearly 50 bone fractures the cowboy purportedly suffered. The General Mills cereal company organized several promotions around the *Lone Ranger* radio series, as did Quaker Oats with the famed detective Dick Tracy. Ovaltine, meanwhile, targeted girls with "Little Orphan Annie's Very Own Shake-Up Mug," based on the famous character who got her start in the Sunday comics, then moved to radio, and later starred in movies and on Broadway.

High marketing costs and market unpredictability still fueled the tie-ins and cross-category promotions in the late 1990s and the early years of the first decade of the 2000s. Because tying a product in with a universally recognized character such as Mickey Mouse can substantially reduce the need for advertising, companies continued to launch tie-in campaigns. Similarly, however, tie-ins proved not to be fail-safe, as some tie-ins do not strike a chord with consumers and hence result in losses. For example, many companies put their advertising eggs in the *Star Wars Episode I: The Phantom Menace* basket in 1999, and the movie was not the cornucopia they anticipated. While action figures sold well, the numerous other products concocted to capitalize on the movie—such as clothes, linens, and cookware—had slumping sales according to *Entertainment Weekly*. Moreover, fast food companies that did tie-ins—Tricon's KFC, Pizza Hut, and Taco Bell—realized only a 1 or 2 percent increase in revenues, which amounts to somewhat of a phantom flop.

The Phantom Menace debacle had a lingering after-effect on movie tie-ins as marketers took a harder look at such deals and scaled back considerably. Previously, movie tie-ins were considered the optimum licensing arrangement, but throughout 2000 and 2001, retailers and licensees remained wary. By 2000, retail sales of licensed goods dropped 1 percent to $73.8 billion, while sales of entertainment/character-based product dropped 5 percent to $15.2 billion, according to *The Licensing Letter*. In the new environment of tighter advertising budgets, marketers had to readjust and become more selective. As a result, even a mega-movie event like Warner Brothers' *Harry Potter* only attracted one partner, the Coca-Cola Company.

In 2002, PepsiCo Inc., which previously would invest hundreds of millions of dollars into tie-ins, only bought a single TV spot for Pepsi Twist that featured "Austin Powers" star Mike Myers. Dawn Hudson, PepsiCo's senior vice-president for marketing, said the new tack was to be smarter with money while keeping the program simple. Taco Bell, one of the Phantom Menace casualties, decided to drop movie tie-ins entirely.

This caused some movie producers to seek previously untapped areas for new sponsors. As a result, unlikely new names such as Kellogg, Hershey, and Reebok began to align themselves with prospective blockbusters like the *Spiderman* movie. For a while, at least, movie producers would have to do without the product giants. Marketers, being marketers, tried to place a positive spin on the situation. "Having more partners is a positive," said Ira Mayer, publisher of the *Entertainment Marketing Letter*, about the new attitude. "People are paying more attention

to what they are doing, trying for more measurable results, and are more sophisticated about their promotions."

The toy industry, however, was still able to land some successful merchandising agreements with films like *The Scorpion King, Austin Powers in Goldmember, Spirit: Stallion of the Cimarron, Lilo and Stitch, Scooby-Doo,* and, ironically enough, *Star Wars Episode II: Attack of the Clones.* Nevertheless, for every success, there seemed a significant failure. Poor performers included *Lara Croft: Tomb Raider, Jurassic Park III,* and *The Mummy Returns.* The success of the 2001 *Star Wars* film was attributed to the more subdued approach taken, which included only the basic toys and video games. Spin-offs were reduced to less than 50 as opposed to 85 for *The Phantom Menace*) and fewer toys were shipped. No one was stuck with unsold products on their shelves as was the case for *Phantom Menace*.

Through it all, Disney has persistently done well with tie-ins. Continuing its legacy of churning out hit after hit, Disney remained in the vanguard of the tie-ins industry at the beginning of 2000. With its May 2000 release, *Dinosaurs,* Disney positioned itself to reap the benefits of another tie-in campaign, which included licensing rights to McDonald's for its Happy Meals. These rights are so important to McDonald's that it considered the *Dinosaurs* promotion the crux of its summer 2000 marketing program, according to *Advertising Age*. In addition to providing dinosaur toys with its Happy Meals, McDonald's offered its "Hatch, Match, and Win" game, which featured prizes such as a $25,000 diamond, $1 million in cash, and Hawaiian vacations.

McDonald's was not the only company to climb aboard Disney's gravy train. Many companies try to set a Mickey Mouse trap to bolster sales. General Mills, for example, struck a two-year deal with Disney in 2000 to fortify its Betty Crocker fruit snacks. The agreement provides for General Mills Mickey Mouse Peel-Outs, Winnie the Pooh Fruit Snacks, and *Dinosaur* fruit rolls. With this agreement, General Mills hopes to cut advertising costs and continue to dominate the fruit snack market.

Because of tie-in campaigns such as these in previous years, a *Nation's Business* writer said Disney "sets the gold standard" when it comes to success in the area of mass merchandising. Mickey Mouse, as Cy Schneider wrote, remains "the greatest salesman of them all." Disney's track record is impressive. Nearly every year in the 1990s Disney produced a lucrative animated film, from 1992's *Aladdin,* which made about $500 million worldwide at the box office, to *Hercules* in 1997. *The Lion King,* released in 1994, has reaped estimated total sales of $1.5 billion from theater tickets, merchandise, and related products. Animated films are secure foundations for a wide variety of marketing possibilities and revenue sources since they appeal to the whole family and tend to include characters that can easily become cute toys or other licensed properties.

Disney has easily shown itself to be the top player in the animation game. "Aside from extensive use of the usual avenues of publicity, Disney finds promo tools through toy store displays, record albums, and merchandising and fast food tie-ins. It's impossible to troll the mall without multiple exposures to the Disney blitz," reported *Variety* in an article entitled "High Noon for Toon Boom," which described increasing competition in the animation field.

Indeed, other entertainment companies are jumping into the animation business. After decades spent watching Disney run away with the animation market, rival companies have decided to invest heavily in an effort to wrest some of the market from Disney's grip. While this is an expensive and risky maneuver, the potential rewards for a successful campaign are almost too tempting to ignore; and each company realizes that any opportunity it fails to jump on will be taken by some other company.

In an effort to keep up with Disney and McDonald's, Universal Pictures teamed up with Burger King in a tie-in deal for Universal's *The Flintstones in Viva Rock Vegas,* which opened in May 2000. The $20 million promotion included Burger King commercials with footage from the movie and Flintstone toys in its Kids Meals. Later in 2000, Burger King put its efforts into tie-in promotions with *Rugrats in Paris—The Movie* and *Pokemon 2,* while the latter also drew in such heavy hitters as Target, Kmart, Sears, Kellogg, Clorox, and others. Moreover, the fast food mogul agreed to sponsor the fall 2000 tour of the Backstreet Boys, which included the release of a compact disc (CD) with five new songs and a video.

Television has been another important catalyst for the tie-in industry. Animated television shows in particular perform well as vehicles for creating and promoting tie-ins. As Cy Schneider wrote, "Television can do what movies cannot by virtue of its enormous reach and frequency of exposure." However, this has been reversed completely. As *Advertising Age* reported, these days, "most TV properties don't have the revenue potential of feature film blockbusters." Consider MTV's raunchy cartoon characters Beavis and Butt-Head. Paramount Pictures expanded on the cartoon's television popularity and created a blockbuster film, *Beavis and Butt-Head Do America,* which then led to several profitable tie-ins, from books to a successful soundtrack. Nevertheless, while generally not as lucrative as blockbuster films, successful TV shows are typically a much safer gamble for tie-ins than the uncertain movie market.

Moreover, there is growing potential in television for selling everything from computer games to clothes to videos, especially to and for children. From the *Mickey Mouse Club* to *Sesame Street,* television has had its long-term lucrative franchises. The Tickle Me Elmo doll, which rocked the toy industry, was a *Sesame Street* spin-off. Almost all popular television shows from the 1970s and 1980s produced tie-ins such as lunch boxes, comic books, and toys. In the late 1980s, *The Simpsons* brought television merchandising possibilities to a higher level, and the scale has only grown since then.

A leader in the field, not surprisingly, is the children's network Nickelodeon. Popular shows such as *Rugrats* and *Blue's Clues* have become spin-off bonanzas for the network. *Rugrats* even made the transition to the big screen in 1998. Two years earlier, meanwhile, Paramount Home Video, Nickelodeon's sister company, released a home video based on *Blue's Clues,* a "detective show" for kids aged two to six. The video release attracted 7,000 fans to the FAO Schwarz store in Manhattan and 480,000 videos sold in just nine days. Two CD-ROM titles based on the show were also highly successful. *The Rugrats* show also spun off a CD that can be used for music and computer activities. Of course, each of these Nickelodeon-based products line the shelves of toy and children's clothing stores.

As with blockbuster films, the success of television cartoons has also raised the stakes in the industry, and many competitors have been seeking to imitate Nickelodeon's success. The Fox Family Channel reported that it would spend some $500 million to reach into this market using, among other things, the Fox Kids Network. Fox even hired a prominent executive, Rich Cronin, away from Nickelodeon to become chief executive officer of the Fox Family Channel.

The competition has even led marketers to target younger and younger children. British exports of the *Teletubbies* have spurred a "Beatlemania for 2- to 5-year-olds," according to *Advertising Age.* The Teletubbies—four teddy-bear-like, live-action figures who speak like infants and have televisions for stomachs—are designed for children as young as 18 months. Again, typical products such as videotapes, bath toys, and puzzles have proven lucrative. Tie-ins stretch all the way to TubbieCustard, a ready-to-eat, yogurt-like product based on what the Teletubbies eat on the show.

The president and CEO of Itsy Bitsy Entertainment, which licenses *Teletubbies* for broadcast in the United States, outlined the keys to a successful children's entertainment product. "For a hit, you need a property that children really like, parents approve of and that retailers will support, plus a little innovation," Ken Viselman told *Advertising Age.*

Of course, that is not as easy as it sounds. Already the increasing competition of the tie-in merchandising market has claimed casualties. For years, Equity Marketing made promotional items that were given away free by other marketers such as Coca-Cola and Exxon. Equity produced toys based on *Small Soldiers* and *The Rugrats Movie,* for example, which were given away free with the purchase of children's meals at Burger King. Looking to expand, Equity attempted to directly sell products based on the films *Godzilla* and *Babe: Pig in the City,* both of which failed to generate big merchandising sales and were viewed as critical and commercial failures. Equity subsequently announced it would drop out of the movie licensing business. According to *Advertising Age,* Equity's "misfortunes are an example of the risks smaller marketers are forced to take in hopes of riding the coattails of potential blockbusters. . .Such marketers as Hasbro and Mattel, for instance, do a broader array of license and non-license toy making, which enables them to sustain the ups and downs of the film business." This also suggested that despite worries that the quality of films will suffer in the zeal to snare tie-in deals, it still takes a good movie to sell products. As one analyst told *Advertising Age,* "If you don't succeed on the silver screen, it's very hard to have merchandise jump off the shelves."

Some feel that the advertisers and merchandisers are tinkering excessively with what in the end may be the most important product: the movies themselves. According to *Time,* Universal's 1996 summer movie *Flipper* was ready for theaters when studio executives approached the film's writer and director with concerns that there were only three main animal characters in the film. Toy manufacturers wanted a fourth, to round out a line of dolls. The director said it was simply too late to add another character. A compromise was forged when the studio found a turtle who appeared literally in one shot, turned it into Sam the Turtle, and then shipped him out to toy stores nationwide. Similarly, when McDonald's expressed strong interest in the Disney film *George of the Jungle,* the studio promptly doubled the film's budget to increase the special effects and the number of animals that could be turned into toys.

As Pat Wyatt, president of licensing for Fox, acknowledged to *Time,* "Not every film is a great merchandising opportunity." Importantly, *Time* added that "not all spin-offs are aimed at junior." Indeed, almost everyone eats candy and cereal, also popular tie-in products. Hershey Foods ran a theater concession promotion with the DreamWorks film *Antz* and launched five dinosaur-themed products to go with *The Lost World: Jurassic Park.*

Substantive tie-in growth for all ages has also occurred in publishing, especially with musical soundtracks. While acknowledging that "most movie tie-in books are crass rehashings of the films," *U.S. News and World Report* highlighted a trend toward higher quality tie-in volumes during the 1998 holiday season.

Meanwhile, a front page headline for a *Billboard* article announced, "Soundtracks Spark Chart Heat." As reporter Catherine Applefeld Olson wrote, "The staying power of soundtracks in [the 1990s], which kicked off with *The Bodyguard* in 1992 and has gained momentum with *Waiting to Exhale, Space Jam,* and *Titanic,* to name a few, has given record companies a new perspective on the potential of film music." Most recording companies now have departments dedicated to soundtracks, Olson explained, and "several are even outperforming the films from which they were culled." Soundtracks also serve as useful venues to debut a record company's new bands. Even television shows such as *Ally McBeal* have spawned successful albums.

The *Billboard* report continued, "With this popularity has come escalated bidding wars," as well as "increased cooperation between record labels and film studios." This is where mass merchandising seems to be headed: cooperation, synergy, or convergence—call it what you will. Larger and larger media companies, not to mention online technology, have made marketing and selling tie-in merchandise increasingly sophisticated. The Web site for the hit Warner Brothers network television show *Dawson's Creek* has a complete list of songs played on the show, many available through the Warner Brothers recording arm. A media empire such as Time Warner can promote a movie and soundtrack using print media, cable television, and books, since it has its own film, recording, publishing, and broadcasting arms. Feature stories and interviews on entertainment products can even pop up on a network's newscasts.

Also on the music front, tie-ins and product promotions began appearing on MTV in music videos. For instance, in 2003, General Motors Corp. paid $300,000 to place its Hummer H2 in a video starring rapper Ms. Jade. This represented a new trend, as the top record labels, hurt by poor sales, began teaming up with advertisers in a mutually beneficial arrangement. The advertisers would supply the money to produce the video, while the record company would allow product placement. MTV was not very happy with the arrangement, as the cable channel had always disallowed any advertising in the videos it broadcast. However, the development seemed a natural one, as music videos, which are produced very much like commercials in the first place—and even made by directors who formerly worked in commercials—are essentially commercials to begin with, designed to sell an artist's latest product.

PIONEERS IN THE FIELD

Television and film spurred real growth in this industry. The first big success is familiar enough. In 1928, Walt Disney brought the character Mickey Mouse to life for the first time in a film titled *Steamboat Willie* co-starring Minnie Mouse. Within five years, Pluto, Goofy, and Donald Duck joined Mickey and Minnie as treasured characters. By the mid-1930s, one million Mickey Mouse watches were sold annually, and 10 percent of Disney's revenues came from licensing its cartoon characters, according to *The Disney Touch* by Ronald Grover. *Snow White and the Seven Dwarfs,* the first full-length animated film, released in 1937, was a huge licensing success as well.

Animated films produced in the 1940s and 1950s, such as *Pinocchio, Fantasia, Dumbo,* and *Bambi,* came with a line of products and cross-promotions, such as books and music. The Disneyland theme park in California, which had fledgling television network American Broadcasting Co. (ABC) as a big investor, added to Disney's already considerable ability to market its own products.

With ABC backing, Disney was also one of the first companies to use television to sell related products. The *Davy Crockett* series, part of ABC's *Disneyland* series, inspired a famous national craze for coonskin caps, and "The Ballad of Davy Crockett" sold 10 million copies. Building on the success of *Disneyland,* the *Mickey Mouse Club* hit television airwaves in 1955. A small toy company, Mattel, also jumped on the Disney bandwagon, advertising on the *Mickey Mouse Club* and later marketing successful tie-in products such as "Mousegetars,"—musical instruments for kids. Such early successes helped Mattel become the nation's top toy manufacturer.

Warner Brothers cartoon characters—Bugs Bunny, Porky Pig, Daffy Duck, among others—also proved to be licensing and tie-in hits for their creators. Disney hit it big again in 1964 with the mostly non-animated feature *Mary Poppins,* which produced not only inexpensive trinkets but also entire clothing lines and even shoe polish.

Despite Disney's success, "licensed products coming from hit movies had not been big winners" into the 1970s, Cy Schneider wrote. The release of George Lucas' *Star Wars* in 1977 changed that. The *Star Wars* trilogy, as well as the later Indiana Jones productions, generated billions in licensed product sales. In 1976, licensed toys accounted for 20 percent of all toy sales. By the mid-1980s, that figure rose to 80 percent. Then, according to the Toy Manufacturers of America (TMA), it settled at about 40 percent—although in his 1999 annual address, TMA President David A. Miller predicted an upswing "with the introduction of the new *Star Wars* prequel series."

Before the release of the original *Star Wars,* Kenner toys signed an exclusive deal to produce toys, games, and other products based on the film for $100,000 annually, a fairly risky venture at the time. The deal made Kenner hundreds of millions of dollars through the 1980s.

The effect of this on the entire toy industry should not be underestimated. By 1991, when Hasbro bought Kenner, there had not been a *Star Wars* movie in nearly a decade, and merchandise sales lagged, yet Lucas was still receiving $100,000 every year. Hasbro ended the relationship. A year later, San Francisco-based Galoob Toys was able to successfully launch its own *Star Wars* line. Hasbro later returned to the *Star Wars* fold. Some industry analysts have speculated, though, that Galoob's successful marketing of older *Star Wars* merchandise spurred Lucas's decision to reissue the original trilogy in theaters, thus kicking off the anticipation and marketing frenzy for *The Phantom Menace.*

For a large company such as Hasbro, which was earning over $3.5 billion annually, the *Star Wars* line represented a significant but not overwhelming portion of its revenue. Galoob, on the other hand, earned up to one-third of its $360 million annual revenue from *Star Wars* merchandise. Although licensing fees for *The Phantom Menace* were around the once unthinkable 15 percent of wholesale revenues from the goods sold, the involvement with Lucas seemed to help Galoob's stock rebound from earlier losses. Hasbro's purchase of Galoob in 1998 may have helped as well, since it consolidated the nation's second- and third-largest toy makers, not to mention both major *Star Wars* toy license holders.

In 2003, licensed Yu-Gi-Oh merchandise was the top-selling branded toy, generating $2 billion in the U.S. alone. Beginning with Pokemon, and followed by Digimon, Dragon Ball Z, and other similar brands, the new century's craze for Japanese anime (a colorful, action-filled, starkly graphic style of animation) even reached back several decades for new licensed products. The television show *Astro Boy,* first broadcast in the 1960s, made a comeback in 2004 on both Kids' WB and the Cartoon Network. Licensed Astro Boy products were set to include toys, linens, and stationary, as well as other items from the 45 U.S. licensees.

In 2004, the diversification of tie-ins was apparent with the release of the Scooby-Doo movie sequel, *Scooby Doo 2, Monsters Unleashed.* On board for licensing agreements were such diverse companies as Burger King, Oscar Mayer Lunchables, Del Monte foods, Dannon Sprinkl'ins, Sparkle paper towels, General Mills Fruit Snacks, Bayer vitamins, Kellogg's cereal, Keebler crackers, and Kraft Macaroni & Cheese.

Ironically, some of the movie tie-in products that were most successful were books. Four book tie-ins to the

Tolkien movies sold over 750,000 copies in 2002. In 2003, *Seabiscuit* sold 2.6 million copies in the mass market edition and 1.5 million copies in trade paperback. *The Hours* sold 636,000 copies. In addition, *Cold Mountain, Girl with a Pearl Earring,* and *Under the Tuscan Sun* each sold over 500,000 copies. Even the landing of the Mars rover prompted a series of product tie-ins.

However, tie-ins are not just for children. For example, the *SpongeBob SquarePants* television show, which is the most watched children's program in television history, has a wide range of appeal from young children up to older adults. In fact, one-third of the billions of dollars worth of SpongeBob merchandise was purchased by adults for adults in 2003.

In addition to television, in 2004, the multi-billion dollar video game industry (video games and consoles account for one-half of annual toy sales) that appealed to the principally male video game player in his late twenties to early thirties was on the cutting edge of tie-ins. Unlike the dozens of video games based on movies, such as *The Lion King, The Matrix, Monsters Inc., Terminator, The Hulk, Goldeneye,* and *The Lord of the Rings,* the new licensing phenomenon is cross-promotions. For instance, the wildly popular Tony Hawk Pro Skater skateboard video games sparked the release of a new volume to the series, "Tony Hawk's Underground." In this version, gamers do tricks on banisters outside a McDonald's. In other games, players rip off a Puma store, groove with hot hip-hop artists Killer Mike and Nas, step into the Playboy mansion, snowboard on premium dnL equipment, or tear off in a customized Volvo S40. In other games, players see products including Colgate, Sprite, Procter & Gamble, AutoZone, Butterfinger candy, and Honda.

In the closing decades of the twentieth century, video game creators had to pay for the privilege to include images of branded products or people in the scenery or as characters in the games. However, the first decade of the twenty-first century saw a completely different story, with products lining up for incorporation into the "new Hollywood" of video games. In fact, 2004 saw a partnership form between Pixar animation, the creator of *Toy Story* and *Finding Nemo,* and THQ, a video game creator, so that the companies collaborate on cross-promotion products from the outset.

By 2006, licensing and tie-ins continued to drive growth within the mass merchandising industry. According to data from *License Magazine's 2005 Industry Annual Report,* global retail sales of licensed products totaled $175 billion. Included in this estimate were entertainment/character licensing revenues of $60.0 billion; corporate brands and trademarks, including food and beverage licensing revenues of $35.5 billion; art licensing revenues of $18.6 billion; and sports licensing revenues of $18 billion.

Licensed content for digital and mobile devices was a strong, emerging category during the middle years of the first decade of the 2000s, with revenues of nearly $5.1 billion. Sales of licensed sports merchandise in the United States and Canada totaled $13.2 billion in 2005, according to the *Licensing Letter.*

As a testament to the unfading popularity of product tie-in and licensing deals, during the middle of the first decade of the 2000s, leading retailers, brand owners, and manufacturers continued to congregate at their own trade show. In 2006, the 26th annual Licensing International trade show drew some 23,000 attendees from 100 different countries, including leading movie studios, book publishers, and *Fortune* 500 brand managers. More than 500 exhibitors represented approximately 6,000 intellectual properties, making the show "the most comprehensive presentation of brands in one place at one time, anywhere in the world," according to a June 20, 2006 *Business Wire* release.

Leading the entertainment licensing sector in 2006 were movie companies such as Warner Bros. Consumer Products, Viacom, Universal Studios Consumer Products, Sony Pictures Consumer Products, MGM, New Line Cinema, LucasFilms, DreamWorks, and Disney Consumer Products. Top television production firms included the likes of HIT Entertainment, Nickelodeon, and Sesame Workshop. In September of 2005, Kellogg apparently terminated a 15-year agreement with Disney when it partnered with DreamWorks to promote the company's films. The multi-year agreement called for the cereal giant to promote DreamWorks releases via licensing and promotional programs, television ads, and in-store and online programs.

Heading into 2007, entertainment licensing was experiencing additional growth from the demand for downloadable digital content. A host of new movie-related licensing opportunities were created in 2006, including Warner Brothers' *Superman Returns* and Disney's *Cars, Pirates of the Caribbean,* and *High School Musical.* In its June 2006 issue, *Promo* reported that tie-ins for *Superman Returns* exceeded $280 million, including $80 million in domestic support and a staggering $200 million in international support. In May 2006, the *Hollywood Reporter* revealed that promotional support for Disney's *Cars* totaled $125 million. Both studios indicated that their respective promotional campaigns for these films were the largest to date.

However, 2008 was no different, with blockbusters such as Disney's *The Chronicles of Narnia: Prince Caspian, WALL-E,* and *High School Musical 3.* Other companies were not to be left out of the licensing game, as DreamWorks Animation's *Kung Fu Panda,* Lucasfilm Ltd.'s *Indiana Jones and the Kingdom of the Crystal Skull* and the CGI-animated *Star Wars: The Clone Wars,* and Marvel Entertainment's *Iron Man* and *The Incredible Hulk* all generated scores of licensed products.

Indeed, targeting the adult market was a new trend in the mass merchandising and licensing industry in the latter part of the decade. *Promotions & Incentives* cited deals made for brands related to the TV shows *24, Heroes,* and *Desperate Housewives* as examples. According to Ian Downes, director of Start Licensing, "Broadcasters are becoming more adept at marketing that sort of show [*24*]. There are very recognizable demographics associated with them, making the targeting of products easier for brands." Downes also cited the wide range of possible products for licensing, as well as the larger variety of venues in which the products could be sold, as positive features of the adult market. Retro products, such as those related to Paddington Bear (which celebrated its 50th anniversary in 2008), were also experiencing popularity in both the children's and adult licensing markets.

CURRENT CONDITIONS

The International Licensing Industry Merchandisers' Association (LIMA), in its 2010 "Licensing industry Survey," reported that industry brand owners collected roughly $5.2 billion in licensing royalty revenues for 2009. This representedd and 8.7 percent decline from 2008 and the second year of decline. (The first year of decline was 2008, which was, down 5.6 percent, after years of steadily rising revenues since LIMA first began collecting data.) The annual survey is based on responses from companies directly involved in the licensing business, examination of public documents, and interviews with licensing industry executives. Most respondents cited sluggish consumer spending on non-essential products and a generally conservative climate for most of 2009. They expressed optimism for 2010 and beyond, and indicated they would continue a growing trend to diversify distribution among a broader spectrum of retailers. These included specialty stores as well as general and large mass merchandisers, supermarkets, drug stores, online retailers, and even dollar stores.

By far, the leading segment in the industry was Characters, responsible for almost half (46 percent) of all revenues, at $2.4 billion for 2009. This segment includes all characters from the entertainment business, animated and real. Notwithstanding a lead in the industry, licensed character sales were actually off by 7.9 percent from 2008. Corporate trademarks and brands, at 17 percent market share, brought in $880 million in 2009. Fashion brands came in third, at 14 percent of market share, with $705 million in 2009 sales. The sports licensing merchandise came in fourth, at $660 million, representing a 10.8 percent drop from 2008. Other leaders in the industry included collegiate licensed

merchandise at $200 million, art at $154 million, and music at $110 million. Publishing royalties brought in $34 million, and all others/miscellaneous brought in an additional $6 million.

The LIMA released key findings from its report at the opening session of the LIMA-sponsored Licensing International Expo 2010, held during June 2010 at the Mandalay Bay Convention Center in Las Vegas. Many of the more than 30 seminars presented during the three-day event were eligible for credit under LIMA's Certificate of Licensing Studies (CLS) program.

Leading the collegiate top-selling universities/manufacturers in 2009 was The University of Texas at Austin, marking the fifth consecutive year that its licensed merchandise led sales. The University of Alabama, after success in its National Championship season, moved up to second place. The University of Kentucky was the biggest mover, jumping five positions to come in at number eight Royalty revenues from collegiate T-shirts represented 25 percent of all apparel revenues. Top collegiate apparel categories for the 2009-2010 season included T-shirts, performance, headwear, and youth. Knights Apparel Inc. was the number one collegiate apparel licensee. It supplied merchandise to Wal-mart and the mass/discount retail channel. Nike had previously held the No.1 slot for several years. For non-apparel licensees (e.g., video games, housewares, home furnishings, etc.), EA Sports took the lead.

In other industry news, the U.S. Olympic Committee signed a licensing agreement with Outerstuff in September 2010 to develop and push merchandise in Target, Kohl's, JCPenney, and other mass-market retailers. Although USOC was still working on creating primary marks to be associated with the U.S. team, the primary slogan will be "Team USA London 2012." Licensed merchandising revenues account for about $30 million a quadrennium, according to USOC Chief Marketing Officer Lisa Baird in *The Sports Journal.*

Finally, in June 2010, store chain Wal-mart announced plans to work with NASCAR team and league officials to develop a partnership that would involve Wal-mart becoming NASCAR's exclusive licensee and retailer in the mass merchandise market. Such a direct license would give Wal-mart the right to choose suppliers and set its own prices for such items as NASCAR hats and T-shirts. Concurrent with these negotiations, NASCAR was exploring its ability to roll its team and licensing rights into a trust, which would create a centralized licensing agency for this sport.

WORKFORCE

Importantly, mass merchandising is not merely for Hollywood movers and shakers and global fast food chains. Many small and mid-sized clothing manufacturers, for example, do a large portion of their business through licensing and other mass merchandising methods. There are potential pitfalls, of course. Disney, for example, can bring manufacturers profits, but according to *Nation's Business,* they can be very demanding. A product may also be tied to an overexposed character, as many who invested in a license for the purple dinosaur Barney eventually discovered. Sports merchandise has also been a fickle investment given that three of the major four sports experienced labor troubles in the 1990s.

RESEARCH AND TECHNOLOGY

Nation's Business made several suggestions for prospective licensees. "Make the initial contact," to find out a licenser's requirements. This inquiry might involve hiring a consultant or attorney who specializes in the field. Be prepared to "document your qualifications," since licensers may not want to risk selling their product to an unsound firm. Knowing the market and finding a niche are also important, according to *Nation's Business.* It also suggested that potential players "consider taking a risk;" that being in on the ground floor of an unproven property could be lucrative. A less costly way to play this game is to "try a knockoff." That is, if a film such as *Jurassic Park* hits it big, rather than license characters from the film itself, look into products related to dinosaurs. *Nation's Business* noted that, for example, generic wildlife products did well following the release of Disney's *The Lion King.*

On the development front, participants in the mass merchandising industry have begun to exploit the tie-in capabilities of the Internet. As part of a plan to cash in on the projected $2.4 trillion e-commerce industry by the middle of the next decade, television producers experimented with marketing items seen in their shows via the Internet. Through the site AsSeenIn.com, viewers could obtain the clothes and furniture seen in popular shows such as *Melrose Place* and *Friends.* The site also featured links to other sites. For example, clicking on a game in a *7th Heaven* room would transport users to eToys, according to *Variety.* In a parallel endeavor, TVStyle.com would enable users to search for clothing they had seen worn by their favorite actors on television shows. Other Internet tie-ins aimed at bringing kids online to the product Web sites, such as the 2004 tie-in to DC Comics' super heroes on cereal boxes, which directed kids to the Post Web site to work on their own comic books.

Game and movie tie-ins involving cellular phones were projected to be the next trend in technology. The most highly visible promotion involved a "Spider-Man" spin-off with Cingular Wireless Inc. that included a series of games, screen-savers, logos and ring tones to coincide with the movie's release. The trick, the experts said, of making such a promotion a success was finding the right content.

BIBLIOGRAPHY

Aclin, Justin. "Pitching the Tentpoles: With Big Movies Driving So Much Licensed Product, *License! Global* Takes a Look at Upcoming Potential Blockbusters and the Promotional Partnerships They're Inspiring." *License!* April 2008.

"The Collegiate Licensing Company Names Top Selling Universities and Manufacturers." Prress Rerlease, 26 August 2010. Available at http://www.clc.com/clcweb/publishing.nsf/Content/Rankings+Annual+2010.

"Disney Consumer Products at Licensing International Expo 2010–Cars 2 Merchandise." 5 June 2010. Available from http://www.toyexplosion.com/2010/06/disney-consumer-products-at-licensing-international-expo-2010-cars-2-merchandise/.

Johannes, Amy. "Superman Soars with Over $280 MM in Tie-Ins." *Promo,* June 2006.

"Licensing 2006 International: The Crystal Ball to Retail Trends for 2007." *Business Wire,* 20 June 2006.

"Licensing: Breathing New Life into the Oldies." *Promotions & Incentives,* 20 November 2007.

"Licensing Royalty Revenues Decline: Industry Develops Avenues for Future Growth." 12 June 2010. Available from http://www.lvtsg.com/imho/2010/06/licensing-royalty-revenues-decline-industry-develops-avenues-for-future-growth.

"Licensing: Something for the Grown-Ups." *Promotions & Incentives,* 1 January 2008.

Lisanti, Tony. "A Bullish Forecast through 2010." *License!* October 2007.

Mickle, Tripp. "New USOC Agreement to Put Merchandise in Mass Retailers." *Sports Business Journal,* 6 September 2010.

Pomphrey, Graham. "Disney Deluxe: DCP's Latest European Plan Targets an Older Market with Luxury Products to Sell into High-End Retailers." *License!* 15 April 2007.

"Retail Sales of Licensed Sports Merchandise, by Product Category, U.S. & Canada 2005." *Licensing Letter,* 6 March 2006.

Schiller, Gail. "Brave New World for Summer Tie-Ins." *Hollywood Reporter—International Edition,* 30 May 2006.

"Top 100 Global Licensors." *License!* 1 April 2008.

"Walmart, NASCAR Explore Wide-Ranging Licensing Deal." Press Release, 8 June 2010. Available from http://www.nascar.com

Wasserman, Todd. "DreamWorks, Kellogg Ink Multiyear Deal: Alliance Comes After Kellogg-Disney Pact Evaporates." *Brandweek,* 26 September 2005.

"Youngsters Gravitate to Licensed Products." *MMR,* 23 June 2008.

MEDICAL SELF-TESTING PRODUCTS

————— ■ —————

SIC CODE(S)

2835

INDUSTRY SNAPSHOT

Medical self-testing products are quietly usurping the doctor's office as the checkup of first resort. With an increasingly health-conscious and aging populace more at ease with technology, and with prohibitive medical costs forcing individuals to consider health from a preventive standpoint, the market for over-the-counter diagnostic products, increasingly referred to as self-test point-of-care products (POC), continues to grow. Privacy issues, cost of healthcare, and patient autonomy all played a role in a complex picture of consumer desire for more control and independence in matters of healthcare.

With the growth of general medical knowledge, consumers have become far more aware of the importance of early disease detection. Using the large, and growing, number of medical self-testing products currently on the market, preventive-minded "patients" can test themselves for a wide range of ailments and conditions, including high cholesterol and glucose levels, HIV, high blood pressure, and pregnancy.

Industry proponents noted that while medical self-testing cannot replace a visit to a doctor altogether, it does offer individuals the opportunity to assume a proactive role in the physician-patient relationship, allowing patients to catch a problem early in the process and come to the doctor's office with an idea of what's in store. Most importantly, however, the industry players pitch their products as a cost-saving medical strategy. While the cost of medical kits is often as expensive as an actual checkup, the benefits of early detection can drastically cut massive medical expenses that would result from late-stage detection.

ORGANIZATION AND STRUCTURE

There were literally hundreds of U.S. Food and Drug Administration (FDA) approved over-the-counter home diagnostic tests on the market during the middle of the twenty-first century's first decade, and they came in many shapes and sizes.

Blood pressure monitors could be purchased as the old-fashioned model, which featured a stethoscope and inflating armband, while the newer models were diminishing in size and encompassed digital technology. Diabetes tests involved obtaining a small blood sample and placing it on a strip of paper, which could then be monitored by a small electronic device to determine glucose levels.

Diagnostic tests for colon cancer and for urinary tract infections involved placing a specially designed strip into the toilet after using. The strip would then change color to denote a potential problem. Doctors stressed, however, that a colored strip for a colon cancer test did not necessarily mean that the user in fact had colon cancer, only that there was something wrong with the stool sample and that a potential problem might exist.

Meanwhile, home diagnostic tests for HIV infection, approved by the FDA in the mid-1990s, actually involved outside input. Users simply sent a dried sample of their own blood to a laboratory and awaited the results, usually delivered by a trained counselor over the telephone. Hepatitis C tests functioned in much the same manner.

Although pharmacies remained the primary retail outlet for medical self-testing products, a growing proportion of total product sales were garnered through specialty stores, including Sharper Image and Brookstone, which carried everything from body fat monitors to cholesterol tests. In addition, general retailers such as Walgreen's and Safeway cleared shelf space for diagnostic kits.

Medical self-testing products are subject to approval by the FDA before they hit the market. The extensive clinical tests each product must wade through to meet approval generally mean that product accuracy is rarely a problem once it hits store shelves. The much more pressing difficulty for manufacturers of home medical self-testing products is generating significant enough margins on their sales. Typically, manufacturers thus concentrate on the mass production of a small number of products, usually in the same general health area. By the first decade of the 2000s, firms were devising all sorts of creative marketing strategies to bolster margins, and their efforts were beginning to pay off.

BACKGROUND AND DEVELOPMENT

While some home diagnostic equipment, like the thermometer, have been around for ages, the modern medical self-testing product industry dates back to the early 1970s, when home testing kits for diabetes were introduced. The sharp rise of medical self-testing through the late 1980s and 1990s was closely tied to the growth of managed health care, which strongly encourages preventive medical practices as a way of trimming medical costs. Meanwhile, the movement of many baby boomers into middle age—a time at which health concerns such as blood pressure and cholesterol begin to assume crucial proportions—along with the aging of the population in general and an enhanced understanding of preventive medicine, provided a natural marketplace for home diagnostics.

Home diagnostic kits originally were sold almost exclusively through doctors' offices or, occasionally, behind the counter at pharmacies. In general, pharmacies were reluctant to carry such items because they tended to be bulky and sales were so slight. Through the 1990s, the technology and production of medical self-testing products improved dramatically, thus bringing costs down and causing over-the-counter sales to skyrocket. By the late 1990s, revenues for manufacturers of home diagnostic tests were growing between 10 and 15 percent each year, according to Frost & Sullivan.

A high-profile breakthrough came when the first home access tests for HIV were approved by the FDA in the mid-1990s. This development was part of a massive effort to boost the numbers of individuals who tested their HIV status. At the time, U.S. surveys found that 60 percent of Americans engaged in behavior that put them at risk of infection, but only a small minority had actually been tested. With the relatively high degree of anonymity of home testing, it was hoped that more people would be inclined to keep track of their sero status.

Blood glucose monitors comprised the leading industry category in 1999, with sales totaling $386 million, according to ACNielsen. Product innovation in this sector was a leading factor in its strong sales. By 2000, glucose test kits capable of measuring blood sugar in a matter of seconds were beginning to hit the market.

Blood pressure monitors were another strong category for medical self-testing products, with sales topping $330 million by the late 1990s as the technology was refined, producing more accurate readings and eliminating a lot of the guesswork that characterized earlier models. Competition in this sector was heating up, with new players such as Panasonic and Braun throwing their hats into the ring. Meanwhile, the American Heart Association reported that about one quarter of all adults in the United States suffer from hypertension but about 32 percent of them are unaware of the condition. The challenge for blood pressure kit manufacturers has been to create greater awareness of the extent and severity of this problem while positioning their products as a part of the arsenal to combat it.

Home pregnancy tests have been another mainstay in the medical self-testing product industry. They first went on the market in 1977, courtesy of Warner-Lambert. More recently, ovulation monitoring kits have emerged as a significant market sector, designed to test fertility and denote when a woman is most likely to get pregnant, are marketed toward women who hope for positive results. Meanwhile, a growing number of women over 35 years of age have been attempting to get pregnant for the first time and the industry has predicted growing demand for ovulation testing kits.

In *Best's Review,* former Lincoln Reinsurance Company Vice President and Chief Underwriting Officer Barry A. Wilkinson posed a hypothetical scenario. It involved a man who used at-home medical tests and obtained a positive reaction for diabetes. He kept that discovery to himself. His wife, doctor, and potential insurance agent were kept in the dark. This scenario pointed out the challenge tests outside the doctor's office can cause for insurers. "Insurers can't underwrite properly for something that's kept hidden from us. The only solution is knowledge, and that means testing—thorough, accurate blood and urine testing."

Straight Goods reported that members of the Canadian Medical Association expressed concerns about the safety and accuracy of testing kits, how they are marketed and whether results are reported to doctors. In the article, Group Director of Policy and Advocacy for the American Pharmaceutical Association Susan Winckler was credited as saying, "Self-testing may raise questions best answered by a pharmacist, physician or other health professional. In many states, pharmacists help consumers navigate the use of these tests by either performing the test in the pharmacy or helping consumers learn to use the equipment at home." Winckler also noted that prescription medications require a doctor's prescription to be obtained legally and yet by buying prescriptions from companies on the Web, Canadians were getting around this and doing so could result in incorrect self-medicating.

The Independent reported that a panel of specialists and a laboratory manager convened by *Health Which?* magazine examined 11 home testing kits available from pharmacies and Internet shops and called for four of them to be removed from sale because they were "misleading and unreliable." Those tests were cholesterol tests sold by Boots and BodyWATCH, an osteoporosis risk assessment kit from BodyWatch, and an Early Alert Alzheimer's home screening test from Homechec.

The market for medical self-testing products was exceptionally fertile as manufacturers began to engage in sophisticated marketing strategies to capture a share of the potentially lucrative market. With the baby boomer generation spanning middle age and possessing a relatively high level of education and income, concern over health and fitness was at an all-time high.

This represented a profound change in the demographic market for home diagnostic kits. Traditionally, such products were pitched toward individuals over 55 years of age and suffering from chronic medical conditions. In addition, due to the high costs of self-testing products, most of those customers brought in annual incomes exceeding $60,000, according to ACNielsen Corp. Most such customers also made their purchases on the recommendations of their doctors. By 2000, all that had changed. Home diagnostic kits were geared especially for baby boomers but also toward individuals as young as 25.

As the market grows more sophisticated, so do merchandising strategies. It is commonplace to see diagnostic kits and health monitors marketed in conjunction with over-the-counter treatments for a respective condition. In this way, manufacturers hope to lure more customers who have not been advised by a doctor to seek out diagnostic kits.

Industry reports suggest that diagnostic kits do in fact aid significantly in personal medical monitoring. One third of home diagnostic customers reported that the kits led to early detection of a disease or condition, according to a national survey of over 1,000 such

customers by LifeSource. Forty-two percent answered that the kits spurred them to take their medications on a regular basis. The two biggest factors in the purchase of home diagnostic equipment seemed to be convenience and cost. Sixty-four percent responded that the primary reason for their purchase was that using such kits was easier than going to a doctor, while half said that the affordability of testing kits makes them a practical monitoring method.

Industry sales were being driven by a number of factors, including the continued aging of the nation's 77 million baby boomers, growing rates of chronic disease, and rising levels of health consciousness. In addition, the skyrocketing cost of professional medical services spurred an unprecedented number of consumers to purchase self-diagnostic kits. Subsequently, a number of leading pharmacies expanded their range of offerings in this category in order to meet demand.

Self-testing products included everything from thermometers, blood pressure monitors, pregnancy tests, and ovulation predictors to menopause monitors, cholesterol tests, and a number of urine tests. Urine tests were especially strong sellers for drugstores. In particular, metabolism test strips were popular among consumers adhering to low-carbohydrate diets. By 2005, consumers even had access to an inexpensive home allergy test that could indicate hay fever allergies in 30 minutes.

Pregnancy test kits continued to be strong sellers. According to *MMR: Mass Market Retailers*—a biweekly global newspaper serving headquarters personnel of supermarkets, drug stores and discount chains and featuring industry reports—data from Information Resources Inc. revealed that pregnancy test kits generated $230 million in sales in 2006. This figure, which includes discount stores, supermarkets, and drug stores, was an increase of 2 percent from the previous year. In terms of unit volume, 19.7 million kits were sold, marking a 2.6 percent increase.

The market for family planning kits, which can be used to avoid or increase a couple's chance of conceiving, also was substantial. In addition to kits that predict ovulation through the measurement of luteinizing hormone levels in a woman's urine, other tests detected the presence of salts in saliva. Special thermometers that measured basal body temperature were yet another method. Finally, because males are responsible for some 40 percent of infertility cases, one company offered a kit that males could use in the home to measure their sperm count, thereby avoiding a potentially embarrassing doctor visit.

According to *MMR*, Information Resources also reported that ovulation prediction kits achieved sales of $32.5 million during the 12 months ended March 20, 2005. This figure, which includes discount stores (except

Wal-Mart), supermarkets, and drug stores, was a 12.9 percent decrease from the previous year. Total unit sales were 1.3 million. Private label brands accounted for $7.8 million of category sales. The leading brand was Clearblue Easy ($9.7 million), followed by Clearplan Easy ($6.7 million), First Response ($3.4 million), Answer Quick & Simple ($2.5 million), and Inverness Medical ($1.3 million).

While the availability of a growing number of home testing kits was, in many cases, a positive thing, the need for caution remained. Medical experts were concerned about the fact that some marketers were promoting bogus or misleading test kits. For example, one company sold a kit via its Web site that claimed to predict a baby's gender. In the October 2004 issue of *Prevention,* New York University School of Medicine Endocrinologist Dr. Frederick Licciardi claimed that a technique involving in vitro fertilization was the only real way to ensure that a woman would give birth to a child of a specific gender.

In April 2005, the FDA issued a consumer warning about test kits marketed by Montreal-based Globus media. The kits, which included tests for HIV, Syphilis, Dengue Fever, Marijuana, Cocaine, and Amphetamines, were not approved for sale in the United States. The FDA was concerned about the possibility—and consequences of—false results stemming from the tests.

According to *Chain Drug Review,* by 2007 even some insurance companies were recognizing the advantage of self-test kits and the resulting lowering of costs for trips to the doctor's office. The journal attributed the self-test kits' convenience, technology, and privacy factor to the increase in demand. Experts predicted that in the future, devices will simultaneously test for multiple conditions and that more different conditions will be testable at home. An example is the introduction of the product called DUO-CARE, which is the first product to combine a home-use blood glucose and wrist blood pressure monitor, eliminating the need for two separate devices. The demand for self-test home diagnostic products had even extended into the heart health arena, with the introduction of home cholesterol test meters. With 107 million Americans living with high cholesterol, a risk factor for heart disease, the device was expected to be well received.

As Jodie Root of Cardiocom told *Diagnostic Update,,* "America is an aging population," and with the increased rates of diabetes, heart failure, asthma, and other diseases, "the industry is now understanding that [these devices] are cost-effective because you [can] use fewer nurses, and you're more efficient, so you can interact with more patients."

CURRENT CONDITIONS

In November 2009, Espicom Healthcare Intelligence released a comprehensive report on the industry, "Point

of Care Diagnostics—*Players,* Products & Future Market Prospects," giving a detailed evaluation of over 150 companies. According to the source, in 2008, patient self-testing accounted for 71 percent ($8.9 billion) of the POC (point-of-care) market, and grew at a faster rate than the professional care sector. The overall POC market grew by 11 percent in 2008 and was valued at $12.6 billion, said Epsicom.

The self-test market continued to be dominated by blood glucose testing, and the increasing incidence of Type II diabetes in both developed and emerging markets ensured continued expansion. By 2014, blood glucose testing could account for more than 60 percent of the POC market. Coagulation monitoring and pregnancy testing also show positive growth. New on the market were prostate screening home test kits, which screen for the detection of prostate specific antigen (PSA) in the diagnosis and monitoring of prostate cancer and benign prostatic hyperplasia (BPH). With the swine flu pandemic of 2009, ABAXIS announced, in December 2009, an exclusive worldwide OEM Agreement for an Avian Influenza Antigen Test Kit. For dog lovers, ABAXIS also announced that it had received USDA approval to launch the first fully automated canine wellness profile test that includes a canine heartworm antigen test. The new product, about the size of a shoebox, can perform 25 canine wellness tests right in the veterinary clinic with about two drops of blood.

Self-testing away from home was also on the rise, with an increasing number of Lifeclinic automated self-testing health stations (primarily for blood pressure and weight) appearing in workplaces, shopping malls, and chain stores around the country. By 2009, 32 million persons were testing themselves in over 35,000 stations every month, including 5,000 worksites. A study appearing in the January 2009 issue of *Postgraduate Medicine* found that Lifeclinic automated self-testing health stations in the workplace were indeed a valuable tool for employees and employers in the management of hypertension and obesity. The study found that over 21 percent of the employees voluntarily used worksite health stations to measure their blood pressure or weight. Approximately half of the employees with hypertension and 10 percent of the employees with obesity successfully reduced their health risks.

In November 2009, Ionian Technologies, Inc. announced that it had received additional funding from the Bill & Melinda Gates Foundation to develop POC diagnostic tests for use in the developing world. The grant from the Foundation will extend the total commitment to this program, initiated in November 2008, to $3 million over two years. The program will continue to focus on utilizing Ionian's proprietary isothermal nucleic acid amplification technology, the NEAR Assay, to develop a platform for various global health diseases unique to the needs of the developing world. The initial diseases that will be targeted are tuberculosis, chlamydia, and gonorrhea. However, the platform may be easily adapted to other priority global health diseases in subsequent efforts.

INDUSTRY LEADERS

Roche Diagnostics, based in Indianapolis, Indiana, is a subsidiary of the Basel, Switzerland-based Roche Holding Ltd., one of the world's leading pharmaceutical companies. Roche's Accu-Chek blood glucose monitor has been one of the largest-selling items in the home diagnostics industry. While its diagnostic products business was traditionally a lower priority for Roche, the firm bought its way to the position of the world's largest diagnostics company with the $10.2 billion purchase of Corange in 1988. 2003 marked the launch of Roche's first direct-to-consumer advertising of prescription medications, which highlighted Accu-Chek in the $40 million integrated effort, as reported by *Advertising Age*. In 2005 Roche was named one of the 100 best companies to work for by *Fortune* magazine. In 2009, its leading self-testing products included blood glucose monitors, test strips, lancing devices, pregnancy and ovulation tests, and CoaguChek.

One of the largest manufacturers of health care products in the world, employing some 115,600 workers in 2006, Johnson & Johnson was home to several brands in the medical self-testing market. Topping the list was LifeScan. Purchased by Johnson & Johnson in 1986, LifeScan produces One Touch Strips, a blood glucose diagnostic kit that was the industry's top selling product in 2000 and that constituted about 70 percent of LifeScan's revenues. LifeScan also manufactures palm-sized monitors for blood glucose levels. In 2000 LifeScan Inc. lost a lawsuit it brought against Home Diagnostics Inc. for patent violation. In March 2003, *Investment Dealer's Digest* announced that Johnson & Johnson agreed to pay $2.4 billion for the Sunnyvale, California-based Scios biotech company, which was still generating revenues through sales.

Based in Abbott Park, Illinois, Abbott Laboratories, a diversified drug and nutritional product manufacturer, is engaged in the production of a wide range of non-invasive monitoring technologies. In all, the firm employed about 59,700 workers in 2006. Founded in the home of Dr. Wallace Abbott in 1888, Abbott Laboratories dove headfirst into the home diagnostic products market in 1996 with the purchase of MediSense, a manufacturer of blood sugar tests. Products include tests for HIV, strep throat and pregnancy. The company was embroiled in controversy in the late 1990s, culminating in a $100 million fine from the FDA, which ordered that

Abbott pull 125 diagnostic products from the shelves as a result of serious questions of quality assurance at its Chicago manufacturing plants. Nonetheless, Abbott was able to boost its overall sales in 1999 to $13.2 billion from $12.5 billion in 1998. After that, Abbott faced more "road blocks," which *Med Ad News* attributed to "unresolved manufacturing problems of Abbott's diagnostics, a devaluation of Argentinean currency, and questions surrounding the side effects of the obesity drug Meridia." Consequently, Abbott was forced to restate 2002 earnings expectations. Abbott had total sales of $29.5 billion in 2008.

Omron Healthcare, based in Bannockburn, Illinois, is the medical products subsidiary of Japan's Omron Corp. The company has been operating in the United States since 1988. Omron's Body Logic Pro fat analyzer was geared especially toward younger consumers as a fitness product. The firm has been expanding its marketing efforts by developing new diagnostic kits and monitors, such as its wrist blood pressure monitor, for sale in sporting goods stores and health clubs. Its wrist blood pressure monitor features the company's patented IntelliSense technology, which enables the monitor to adjust itself to the user's optimal compression setting, thereby reducing discomfort and speeding up the time before a reading is obtained. In 2002, the HEM-637 wrist monitor was introduced, which uses Omron's patented Advanced Positioning Sensor technology. The company also offers a variety of thermometers, heart rate monitors and pedometers. Omron Healthcare's research and development staff included more than 90 engineers and support staff, who were located in Kyoto, Japan.

Home Access Health Corp. of Hoffman Estates, Illinois, produces home HIV and hepatitis C tests. "These are high-anxiety tests. So many people don't find out at all, but with these tests, they can find out early when there's still time to do something about it," said Home Access President Richard Quattrocchi with regard to the hepatitis C tests, according to *Newsweek*. Through the late 1990s, Home Access maintained an agreement with Abbott Laboratories to collaborate on the manufacturing and marketing of a range of new diagnostic kits using Home Access's Telemedicine technology. Telemedicine, pioneered by Home Access in the late 1990s, provides anonymous test information and professional consultation to the customer's home via the telephone, and accounted for the rapid sales of their Home Access HIV Test System. Abbott also bought a minority interest in Home Access as part of the agreement. Home Access has provided hepatitis awareness and testing services for California, Delaware, Florida, and Illinois. It delivered a West Nile hotline service to the state of Florida. Abbott also worked with public health officials on the development of an interactive bio-terrorist response service related to the threat of future attacks. Home Access has processed more than 300,000 home HIV tests, and was the only organization with FDA approval to offer them. The company was also in the process of developing products for allergy screening and cholesterol monitoring.

Unipath Diagnostics, a division of Inverness Medical Innovations Group of Waltham, Massachusetts, manufactures home pregnancy and ovulation tests. In 1999 Unipath received FDA approval for its ClearPlan Easy Fertility Monitor, which earmarks a six-day span for high fertility as opposed to the usual two days for ovulation tests. The Unipath Bedford, U.K. facility serves as the headquarters for a worldwide network. More than 500 people work at the facility that also houses the R&D and manufacturing facilities. The company maintains sales offices in the United States, Scandinavia and Germany, and its products were sold in more than 80 countries worldwide.

RESEARCH AND TECHNOLOGY

Size and speed were among the key criteria for innovation of medical self-testing products as companies scrambled to create smaller, more lightweight products that can perform their tasks in less time. Thus, medical self-testing products have grown more user friendly over time. In the old days, kits and monitors tended to be bulky and not especially mobile. These days, a number of products are designed to fit in the user's palm. This is especially true for monitors of blood pressure and heart rates, with which customers can keep tabs on their readings while they are working out on the exercise bike or treadmill.

Chain Drug Review cited the following as being reflective of the "ever-improving" high blood pressure products now available: PrecisionSensor wrist blood monitors marketed by the Gillette Company through its Braun division; Mark of Fitness's MF-75 blood pressure monitor, a watch-style device incorporating IQ; and Omron's 630 model, which offers results in seconds. It also stated that Sunbeam debuted an advanced manual-inflate digital blood pressure monitor at the National Hardware Show.

In another *Chain Drug Review* article, B-D Inc. (Becton Dickinson) was applauded for its BD Sensability breast self-examination aid designed to assist women with performing their monthly breast exams. It is a light, soft plastic pad with a lubricant sealed inside to help users' fingers glide across the breast. Users found it to be easier and more comfortable to perform their exams.

The Internet has also played a subtle but significant role in boosting the popularity of medical self-testing products. The sheer level of information widely available as a result of Internet distribution affords customers an abundance of health and medical knowledge, thereby encouraging greater sales of products designed to monitor personal health. *Pacific Business News* argued that more people turning to the Web for answers is not always the best thing, positing that "Cyberchondria" is a new condition that functions like a "high-tech hypochondria" caused by increased access to medical information and self-diagnosis practices.

Innovation among some of the industry's leading product sectors, especially blood pressure and blood glucose monitoring kits, is directed toward the integration of monitoring and treatment, often via high tech means. For example, several companies such as Lifescan and Roche developed software packages to supplement their diagnostic monitors by tracking trends over time for use in the development of treatment plans.

BIBLIOGRAPHY

"ABAXIS Announces Exclusive Worldwide OEM Agreement For A Lateral Flow Avian Influenza Antigen Test Kit." Press Release, 12 December 2009. Available from http://www.medcompare.com/news.asp?typeid=45.

"ABAXIS Announces Launch of the First Fully Automated Canine Wellness Profile That Includes a Canine Heartworm Antigen Test." Press Release, 8 October 2009. Available from http://www.medcompare.com/news.asp?typeid=45.

Abbott. Available from http://www.abbott.com/static/content.

"At-Home Heart Health Tests Gaining Traction." *Chain Drug Review,* 19 February 2007.

"Banks' Lesser Role in M & A Deals: In Two Recent Drug Mergers, Only One Adviser Was Hired." *Investment Dealers' Digest,* 10 March 2003.

Carmichael, Mary. "Medical Testing at Home." *Newsweek,* 19 May 2003.

"Eliminating the Guessing Game." *MMR: Mass Market Retailers,* 9 May 2005.

"Glucose Test Gets Ad Push." *Advertising Age,* 28 April 2003.

Hanlon, Toby. "Say No to Gender Selection Kits." *Prevention,* October 2004.

"Home Tests Way of Life for Many." *MMR: Mass Market Retailers,* 24 January 2005.

"Ionian Technologies, Inc. Receives Additional Funding from the Bill & Melinda Gates Foundation to Develop Point-of-Care Diagnostic Tests for the Developing World." Press Release, Ionian Technologies, Inc., 18 November 2009.

"Hoover's Company Capsules." *Hoover's Online,* 15 April 2007. Available from http://www.hoovers.com.

Johnsen, Michael. "Synova Health." *Drug Store News,* 11 September 2006.

"Johnson & Johnson's Net Soars." *Wall Street Journal,* 22 January 2003.

"Jury Still Out on Feasibility of Self-Testing Chlamydia." *Chemist & Druggist,* 21 May 2005.

Munro, Aria. "Reduce Obesity and Hypertension." Press Release, 13 February 2009. Available from http://www.lifeclinic.com/products.aspx.

Omron. Available from http://www.omron.com/ir/news/2009/20090420.html.

"Omron Helps Retailers Find Missed Opportunity." *Chain Drug Review,* 9 June 2003.

Pesman, Curtis. " Patient, Diagnose Thyself—Carefully." *Money,* October 2006.

"Point of Care Diagnostics—Players, Products & Future Market Prospects." Espicom Healthcare Intelligence, 12 November 2009.

"Pregnancy Test Kits." *Chain Drug Review,* 1 January 2007.

Schultz, John. "Patients, Chains Embrace an Idea Whose Time Has Come." *Chain Drug Review,* 14 August 2006.

"Self-Test in the Supermarket." *Community Pharmacy,* 12 May 2005.

"Self-testing INR Achieves Good Results." *Chemist & Druggist,* 19 April 2003.

Simonsen, Michael. " POC Testing, New Monitoring Strategies on Fast Growth Paths in European Healthcare Arenas." *Biomedical Business & Technology,* 1 January 2007.

Wachter, Kerri. "FDA Warns Consumers about Imported Test Kits." *Internal Medicine News,* 15 April 2005.

Walden, Geoff. "When Possible, Self-Monitoring Is the Way to Go." *Chain Drug Review,* 16 August 2004.

"What Makes Pregnancy Test Kits Good." *MMR: Mass Market Retailers,* 9 May 2005.

Young, Karen. "Cardiocom Launches Devices for Telemonitoring of Diabetes." *Diagnostic Update,* 23 November 2006.

MEDICAL TOURISM

SIC CODE(S)

4724

4725

7011

7999

INDUSTRY SNAPSHOT

Medical tourism (also called by the terms medical travel, health tourism, or global health care) was created as a term by travel agencies and the media to describe the rapidly growing practice of traveling into other countries to obtain health care. It may also refer to the instances of health care providers traveling out of the country to deliver health care services that cannot otherwise be received.

U.S. citizens used to travel internationally for cancer treatments not found in the United States. However, now, typical treatments sought by travelers include elective procedures as well as complex specialized surgeries such as joint replacements (both knee and hip), cardiac surgery, dental surgery, and cosmetic surgeries.

Because the practice has grown so much in the past few years, now, virtually every type of health care, including psychiatry, convalescent care, and burial services are sought. Because these services are often found in countries that have little governmental oversight, health care providers and health care customers are able to utilize less-formal means of billing and payment.

Currently, over 50 countries have identified medical tourism as a national industry. However, a lack of accreditation and other measures of quality are extremely wide-ranging around the world, and the subsequent risks

and ethical issues make this medical care very controversial. Some destinations where U.S. citizens go to receive health care are still considered hazardous or dangerous.

However, because of the popularity of medical tourism, similar services found in other countries have wound up being offered after a time in the United States, including cancer care centers for patients fighting off the illness and needing a place to heal, and streamlined and less expensive laser surgery to improve eyesight.

In the context of global health, medical tourism is often seen as risky to extend outward to other countries, because on such trips, health care providers may practice outside of their areas of expertise or hold to a different standard of care. Currently, greater numbers than ever before of student volunteers, health profession trainees, and researchers from resource-rich countries are working temporarily as well as anticipating future work opportunities in resource-starved areas, including hurricane-stricken Haiti, refugee-overcrowded Sudan, and war-torn Congo.

ORGANIZATION AND STRUCTURE

Cancer patients used to have one choice: go to Mexico or die a painful, agonizing death. Then Europe became the destination for specialty cancer care centers, until the United States began opening the same within our borders. The same can be said about inexpensive laser surgery (as controversial as it may seem to cut into eyeballs while renting out space from a low-income strip mall or in the back of a discount store), which came about after many Americans went to Canada to get their eyes fixed for half the price.

While still a big option for U.S. citizens trying to save money on their health care expenses, the growing medical tourism trade comes with some major concerns. Are the procedures that are received in other countries as safe? Does a lack of regulation only mean a lack of paperwork and bureaucratic red tape? What if it means life or death? What if medical tourism becomes even more commonplace? Currently, Americans visit European or Central American cities for procedures and then relax and live it up getting to know a beautiful foreign city afterward. does it not?

Medical tourism carries some risks that U.S. medical care does not. Some countries, such as India, Malaysia, or Thailand, have very different infectious disease-related epidemiology than North America. Exposure to diseases in those countries without having built up natural immunity can be a hazard for weakened individuals. Gastrointestinal diseases prevalent in those countries (e.g., hepatitis A, amoebic dysentery, paratyphoid) could weaken progress in a post-surgical patient and lead to mosquito-transmitted diseases, influenza, and tuberculosis.

The quality of post-operative care in a foreign country can also vary dramatically, depending on the hospital and country (ask anyone who's spent time in a foreign hospital before deciding to take the plunge), and are often very different from what patients are used to by U.S. standards. Traveling long distances right after surgery can increase the risk of complications. Long flights and decreased mobility in a cramped airplane are a known risk factor for developing blood clots in the legs. Other post-procedure vacation activities can be problematic, too. Scars may become darker and more noticeable if they sunburn while healing. To minimize these problems, medical tourism patients often combine medical trips with vacation time specifically for rest and recovery in the same country where they underwent their procedures.

Health facilities treating medical tourists may lack an adequate complaint policy to deal with complaints made by dissatisfied patients, especially patients who are visiting from a foreign country.

Because of the popularity of medical tourism, differences in health care provider standards around the world are noted by the World Health Organization. In 2004, it launched the World Alliance for Patient Safety, a group that assists hospitals and governments around the world in setting patient safety policy and practices that can become particularly relevant when providing medical tourism services.

BACKGROUND AND DEVELOPMENT

Medical tourism dates back centuries to when pilgrims from Greece travelled to the Mediterranean in order to visit a sacred place said to heal all visitors by the power of the god Asklepios. In the eighteenth century, England sent many medical tourists to spas around the world rumored to cure gout, liver disease, and bronchitis. England welcomed medical tourists to the fabled healing waters of Bath (site of the Roman baths built centuries earlier) that promised to heal illness with a single sip.

The concept of medical tourism actually isn't all that innovative. The idea of traveling to get good medical care happens wherever there is a war, closed borders because of a government's outlook on a neighboring country, or even citizens living right at the border of two connecting countries and choosing to turn right or left on their way to the doctor.

PIONEERS IN THE FIELD

Florence Nightingale was the first medical tourism pioneer. Nightingale was born May 12, 1820, and was a celebrated English nurse, writer, and statistician. A Christian universalist, Nightingale believed that God had called her to be a nurse. She came to prominence for her pioneering work in nursing during the Crimean War, where she tended to wounded soldiers. She was dubbed "The Lady with the Lamp" after her habit of making rounds at night.

Nightingale established her nursing school in 1860, at St. Thomas's Hospital in London, which was the first secular nursing school in the world. Nightingale is credited with laying the foundation for the modern nursing profession. The Nightingale Pledge taken by new nurses is done so in her honor and the annual International Nurses Day is celebrated around the world on her birthday.

The Crimean War became Nightingale's focus after news of the suffering was relayed to Britain. On October 21, 1854, she and 38 other women volunteer nurses were sent to the Ottoman Empire to Selimiye Barracks, the main British camp, in Scutari (now a modern-day neighborhood in Istanbul), about 295 nautical miles across the Black Sea. Nightingale and her nurses discovered an overworked medical staff overwhelmed with too many wounded soldiers to care for and ignored by British high command. Medicine was limited, there was little to no hygiene being practiced, and mass infections were common, many of them fatal. There was not a way to adequately produce enough food for all the patients.

The 1911 first edition of the *Dictionary of National Biography* claimed that Nightingale reduced the mortality rate significantly, but the second edition in 2001 did not. Death rates did not drop; on the contrary, they increased. In fact, the death count was the highest of all hospitals in the region. During Nightingale's first winter at Scutari, 4,077 soldiers died and ten times more soldiers died from illness—typhus, typhoid, cholera, and dysentery—than from battle wounds. Conditions at Scutari were grim because of overcrowding and defective sewers and lack of ventilation. A Sanitary Commission had to be sent by the British government to Scutari in March 1855, almost six months after Florence Nightingale arrived, to flush out the sewers and improve the ventilation. Only then were death rates sharply reduced. Nightingale did not recognize hygiene as the predominant cause of death during the Crimean War, and she never claimed credit for helping to reduce the death rate.

In fact, Nightingale firmly believed the death rates were because of poor nutrition and supplies and over-working of the soldiers. It was not until she returned to Britain and began collecting evidence to appear before the Royal Commission on the Health of the Army that she realized that most of the soldiers at the hospital were killed by poor living conditions. This was the experience that most influenced her later career, when she advocated sanitary living conditions as of greater importance. Consequently, she reduced deaths in the army after the war and turned her attention to the sanitary design of hospitals for most of her later life. Nightingale died August 13, 1910.

CURRENT CONDITIONS

Currently, medical tourism lies in two distinct categories: people traveling to foreign countries to receive medical care and people traveling to foreign countries to give medical care. Both are growing trends.

In recent years, over 600,000 people have traveled from both the United States and the United Kingdom to Thailand for joint replacements, cosmetic surgery, organ transplants, and dental treatments in just one 12-month period. Slightly smaller numbers of people traveled to Jordan for fertility treatments, cardiac care, and organ replacement. Other popular places for medical tourism to receive treatment are India, Malaysia, and South Africa. Countries receiving medical tourists include Haiti, Sudan, Congo, Thailand, and Mexico.

For example, in India, medical tourism to receive treatment is slated to become a $2.3 billion business by the year 2012. Currently, over 60,000 cardiac surgeries are done every year with outcomes on par with international standards. Multi-organ transplants are completed in one-tenth the time in comparison to procedures in the West in patients from 55 countries. The cost of heart surgery in India is $8,000, whereas the cost of the same heart surgery in the United States is $30,000. The Indian health care industry expects a 30 percent growth annually just from giving medical tourism health care services. The Indian government spent about 8 percent of its annual Gross Domestic Product (GDP) on the health care sector.

INDUSTRY LEADERS

United Group Programs is a health plan administration company located in Florida founded in 1968. UPG is an "innovative team of employee benefit specialists with a high degree of expertise in the design, communication, and administration of benefit programs." UPG is also a leading provider of services for self-funding through their Third Party Administration (TPA) sector. UPG "has a long and solid history as a consultant in the arena of employee benefits that include fully insured major medical plans and partially self-funded programs, Health Savings Accounts and Retirement Plans." UPG can custom design solutions with every product or service an employer may wish to include in a benefits package and is "a full-service benefits organization and a licensed third party administrator. The long-term relationships with these carriers enables us to meet the specific benefit needs of a company and save valuable premium dollars." UPG often offers health care plans that allow employees to travel to other countries to receive medical procedures that are covered under UPG's policies.

The Joint Commission International (JCI) "has been working with health care organizations, ministries of health, and global organizations in over 80 countries since 1994." The JCI's focus is on "improving the safety of patient care through the provision of accreditation and certification services as well as through advisory and educational services aimed at helping organizations implement practical and sustainable solutions."

In September 2007, JCI received accreditation by the International Society for Quality in Health Care (ISQua). "Accreditation by ISQua provides assurance that the standards, training and processes used by JCI to survey the performance of health care organizations meet the highest international benchmarks for accreditation entities."

The world's first World Health Organization (WHO) Collaborating Centre, dedicated exclusively to patient safety solutions, is a joint partnership between the WHO, The Joint Commission, and JCI.

In 2009, the first hospital accredited by JCI, Hospital Israelita Albert Einstein, a private, non-profit, non-governmental facility in Sao Paulo, Brazil, celebrated its tenth anniversary. Since then, more than 300 public and private health care organizations in 39 countries have been accredited by JCI. "JCI provides accreditation for hospitals, ambulatory care facilities, clinical laboratories, care continuum services, medical transport organizations, and primary care services, as well as certification for disease or condition specific care."

The World Health Organization (WHO) was founded on April 7, 1948, one of the first official acts of the newly formed United Nations. The WHO acts as a coordinating authority on international public health. With headquarters in Geneva, Switzerland, the agency inherited the mandate and resources of its predecessor, the Health Organization, which had been an agency of the League of Nations.

The WHO coordinates efforts to control outbreaks of infectious diseases, such as SARS, malaria, tuberculosis, swine flu, and AIDS, around the world. The WHO also sponsors programs to prevent and treat those diseases, and supports the development and distribution of safe vaccines, pharmaceutical diagnostics, and drugs. After over two decades of fighting smallpox, the WHO in 1980 declared that the disease had been eradicated. Smallpox was the first disease in history to be eliminated by human effort.

WORKFORCE

Estimates about the future of medical tourism vary greatly, but as more and more people discover the health care options available from all around the world, the practice of medical tourism will continue to grow. As more and more U.S. workers seek opportunities to live and work overseas, health care standards that are common in the United States will be spread around the entire world.

This also holds true for U.S. medical volunteers and professionals who travel abroad to give out medical care. More and more students are seeking out volunteer opportunities as sort of a "gap year" experience during their secondary education. As they travel and work in health care fields, they also spread more affluent standards throughout other countries. The end result is that the students realize how lucky they have been to have good health care for their entire lives and can share as much of that knowledge and experience with as many people around the world as possible.

Critics cite the "affluence drift" carried around the world by these medical tourists as dangerous. Other countries often have different customs and cultural expectations around their health care. Americans acting like their way of doing health care is the best and only way can be problematic. However, if the goal is to save lives through lessening mortality rates, providing pain relief, and easing suffering by American-based procedures, medical tourism can be a positive thing.

Americans often use their entitlement as a battering ram with which to force their way of life onto other cultures. Some cultures have no desire to be like the United States. They also do not understand why their health care needs to be improved. Often, seeking to improve a country's health care is seen as an attempt to improve that country's culture and customs and way of living and may be with resentment and anger. As medical tourists, Americans must remember to be especially tolerant of other cultures that have been practicing their health care customs for centuries longer than the Western world.

AMERICA AND THE WORLD

While estimates predict that medical tourism of Americans to other countries will increase in coming years, the rest of the world also uses medical tourism as a reason to receive better health care options. They come to the United States for procedures, including joint replacement, cancer treatment, organ transplants, and cosmetic surgery. This is of no surprise to most Americans since we have often considered our health care system the best in the world. What is surprising is that now more and more of the world have already discovered better health care procedures elsewhere and have long wondered when the United States would follow their lead. Countries like Thailand, India, Costa Rica, and many countries in Europe offer cost-effective health care options that patients from around the world can utilize.

Critics of medical tourism point out that many struggling countries have countless medical patients who have no means to travel outside their homeland to get better medical care. This is why another definition of medical tourism also stands for volunteers, both laypeople and medical professionals, who go into those countries to provide health care that can't otherwise be found (or traveled to). As more and more of the world's citizens begin to call for health care to be a basic right of all humanity, health care in both forms of medical tourism will continue to increase.

RESEARCH AND TECHNOLOGY

As health care tools and procedures become more and more accessible to all countries around the world, the desire to travel outside of a citizen's own country for medical treatments will continue to increase. Technology of health care machines continues to accelerate at a terrific pace; iPhones loaded with diagnostic tools are available to ambulatory care professionals. This has eased the pressures on medical professionals working in refugee camps and on medical tourism volunteers who travel the world to give health care to less fortunate countries.

Suddenly, now an expensive cardiac procedure also exists on a "flat world" paradigm: lowest price wins. Capitalism has graduated to the entire world, including countries that offer the lowest price and forget about safety conditions. In addition, for patients who care more about price and convenience, concerns about safety are better left up to their good judgment. Many medical tourists point out that they have successfully traveled for health care procedures without incident; they also insist that the standards are on par or better than those found in U.S. hospitals. This experience varies among medical tourism patients. There have been bad experiences for many Americans; however, there are not statistics to indicate American lives were lost while undergoing medical procedures on foreign soil.

The question of whether or not medical tourism (receiving treatment) is a smart choice is often a personal one. Before committing, patients are encouraged to do their research, find reputable health care organizations that are accredited by the World Health Organization or the Joint Commission International, and take every precaution to ensure their health and safety.

For those interested in medical tourism (giving), volunteers are encouraged also to use their good judgment to find reputable health care organizations to serve with that have a good track record of giving high-quality medical care in the countries they serve. Volunteers should also take precautions when they travel and serve, taking care to consider other cultures and to be tolerant of other cultures's belief systems.

All in all, medical tourism has been around for a long time and looks to be around for a long time into the future.

BIBLIOGRAPHY

"About Us." Joint Commission International, 2010. Available from http://www.jointcommissioninternational.org/about-jci/.

Goldberg, James R. *The American Medical Money Machine: The Destruction of Health Care in America and the Rise of Medical Tourism.* London: Homunculus Press, 2009.

"Home Page." Med Retreat, 2010. Available from http://www.medretreat.com/.

"Home Page." Medical Travel and Tourism Guide, 2010. Available from http://medicaltravelandtourismguide.com/.

"Home Page." United Group Programs, 2010. Available from http://www.ugpinc.com/.

MICROMACHINES AND NANOTECHNOLOGY

———■———

SIC CODE(S)

3674

3599

3699

INDUSTRY SNAPSHOT

Broadly speaking, micromachines and nanotechnology refer to gadgetry and systems on a Lilliputian scale. A nanometer is one-billionth of a meter. A single sheet of paper is about 100,000 nanometers thick. Newer scanning electron and transmission electron microscopes have enabled scientists to better understand the physical, chemical, and biological properties of matter at this level. However, the impact of this pint-sized technology—financial and otherwise—is anything but small. Indeed, by the turn of the new century, nanotechnology was widely touted as one of the most revolutionary and innovative developments on the horizon. By manipulating and organizing matter at the atomic and molecular levels, nanotechnology promised to transform nearly every major industry, generating not only a slew of new products but processes as well, leading to entirely new engineering paradigms. Some of the sectors most immediately affected by nanotechnology and micromachines included health care, automotive, energy, telecommunications, and computing. Analysts predicted major gains in biotechnology, the military, the environment, waste management, and consumer goods as well. Down the road, researchers expected the field to reach its Holy Grail of self-assembling manufacturing components, a feat that would carry almost unimaginable social, technological, and economic implications.

While market penetration was extremely modest early on, few analysts claimed anything less than an extraordinary future for nanotechnology. The Foresight Institute, a major nonprofit educational group of leading scientists devoted to preparing society for adaptation to advancing technologies, noted that nanotechnology's bottom-line promise was "that almost any chemically stable structure that is not specifically disallowed by the laws of physics can in fact be built."

The field of nanotechnology grew out of increased scientific understanding of the way in which tiny structures, such as atoms and molecules, come together and interact to form highly complex systems. Nanotechnology refers specifically to materials, devices, and systems built on the scale of a nanometer, which is equal to one ten-millionth of a centimeter, 500 times smaller than the width of a human hair. Nanotechnology involves manipulating and harnessing chemical reactions and the molecular processes of living cells in a design aimed at a specific technological function. One of the most stifling roadblocks in nanotechnology development is that at the nano scale, different laws of physics must be taken into account. Instead of everyday forces such as gravity, researchers working with nanotechnology must be able to negotiate quantum variables. The National Science Foundation predicted that by 2015 the annual global market for nanotechnology would reach $1 trillion.

ORGANIZATION AND STRUCTURE

The field devoted to manipulating, transforming, and controlling nano-scale materials was populated by a wide range of large companies, small startups, universities,

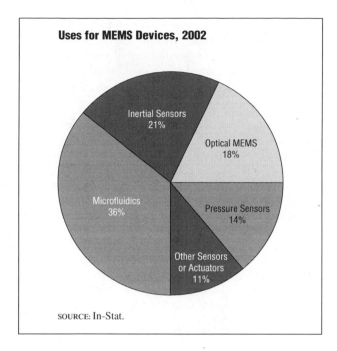

Uses for MEMS Devices, 2002

- Inertial Sensors 21%
- Optical MEMS 18%
- Microfluidics 36%
- Pressure Sensors 14%
- Other Sensors or Actuators 11%

SOURCE: In-Stat.

production is larger than that of ICs, start-up companies are often able to purchase obsolete production equipment from IC manufacturers.

As the MEMS industry began to grow, a small group of satellite concerns grew around it: businesses from other sectors devoted to the specific needs of MEMS. A small group of marketing professionals, for example, specializes in the area. More significant is the computer software industry where new computer-aided design (CAD) software and other design tools are being developed for MEMS.

The fruits of the micromachine industry's labors are sold to other manufacturers for use as components in the fabrication of more complex systems. According to the MEMS Industry Group, most U.S. MEMS companies developed and/or offered products in either sensors or telecommunications. Many were starting to move away from the transportation and industrial markets to focus more tightly on the growing telecommunications and medical markets. New MEMS and nanotechnology applications were likely to be heavily concentrated in the sciences. Also by that time, MEMS technology itself had created a laboratory of sorts in which biotechnology researchers could test biochemical reactions for the study and manipulation of DNA strains. Moreover, one of the most ambitious nanoprojects is DNA computer technology, and data storage in general. DNA computing was hailed as a new and ultra-powerful development intended to rival high-speed supercomputers in the storage and processing of large amounts of complex information.

The industry received support from the NanoBusiness Alliance, a membership organization for nanotechnology companies that was founded in 2000, and the International Association for Nanotechnology. The Alliance's members ranged from small start-ups and large corporations to nonprofit organizations, universities, and service firms worldwide. Several other organizations also provided information and support, including the Center for Biological and Environmental Nanotechnology at Rice University, the Center for Responsible Nanotechnology, the International Council on Nanotechnology, and the Project on Emerging Nanotechnologies.

research institutes, and government agencies. Some of the biggest names in the corporate world maintained nanotechnology development efforts, including Motorola, Samsung, IBM, Hewlett-Packard, Intel, Lucent, Siemens, NEC, and General Electric. Scores of smaller firms, floating largely on venture capital, were devoted exclusively to the development of micromachines or any number of approaches to nanotechnology.

The leading consultancy, McKinsey, reported the number of nanotechnology startups at 837 in 2003, up from 462 just two years earlier, while roughly 100 U.S. companies were active in the micromachines or MEMS area at the start of the twenty-first century. MEMS usually comprise a very small percentage of the total production of the larger firms, though some, notably Motorola Inc. and Texas Instruments Inc., have been working in the field since the 1970s. The remaining U.S. MEMS and nanotechnology companies were small businesses with annual production of less than $10 million—and in most cases, less than $5 million—per year. These companies in general focused exclusively on MEMS and a small number of products, or on one or another branch of nanotechnology, such as nanoelectronics, nanomechanics, nanomaterials, or bionanotechnology.

The most common MEMS production techniques are essentially the same as those used to produce integrated circuits (ICs). Material is deposited on a silicon disk. A pattern is imposed lithographically and material around the pattern is removed, revealing the mechanism. Companies use this process to mass produce large numbers of inexpensive micromechanisms, including micromachines with moving parts. Because the scale of MEMS

Regulation Aside from the restriction of high-technology exports the president of the United States could impose for national security reasons, the only regulation of micromachines required is FDA approval for material used in medical applications. On the other hand, federal regulation of the auto industry presented opportunities for the micromachine industry. Federal fuel economy and pollution standards in the 1970s led to the development of the micromechanical manifold air pressure sensor, a critical element in the system that regulates a car's fuel to air ratio. Similarly, air bag laws created a market for the small, accurate accelerometers used in passenger safety systems. Finally, the increasing development of fuel cell systems in automobiles provided a new opportunity for MEMS sensors.

BACKGROUND AND DEVELOPMENT

Micromachines have their roots in the miniaturization processes that led to the development of the transistor in the 1950s, followed later by the integrated circuit and the microprocessor. The potential benefits of micromachine technology include vastly expanded functionality and eventually dramatic savings in production costs, although to date production is relatively expensive since the processes and system architecture are so varied throughout the industry. Karen Lightman, managing director for the MEMS Industry Group, cited the top market opportunities for MEMS (micro-electro-mechanical systems) in 2008 as automotive, consumer goods—especially mobile devices—and industrial and medical devices, according to the *MEMS Investor Journal.*

The first real impetus toward the development of the micromachine and nanotechnology came from physicist Richard Feynman in a talk at the California Institute of Technology in 1959, but the industrial world was already moving in this shrinking direction. The first technological advance toward the micromachine was the discovery of a piezoresistive effect—a resistance charge created in silicon when it is under stress—at Bell Labs in 1954, a factor that made silicon an ideal candidate for sensors and accelerometers. Development continued apace throughout the 1960s and 1970s. Spurred mainly by funding from NASA, the first silicon pressure sensors were created. The National Science Foundation provided funding as well in the 1970s, albeit on a limited scale. Electronic imaging technology company Fairchild Imaging spawned a number of spin-off companies in the Silicon Valley that pursued silicon sensor technology: ICTransducers (now Foxboro/ICT) and National Semiconductor Sensor Group (now SenSym) were founded in 1972, Cognition (now Rosemount) in 1976.

Micromachines A major turning point in the micromachine field was the publication in 1982 of *Silicon as a Mechanical Material* by Kurt Peterson, who is called "the father of MEMS." The paper described the unique mechanical-structural properties of silicon (metals such as iron, steel, and aluminum have too many structural irregularities at a microscopic level to be viable micromachine materials). The paper was followed by the first two MEMS (micro-electo-mechanical systems) start-up companies in Silicon Valley: Transsensory Devices (1982) and NovaSensor (1984). Meanwhile, researcher

K. Eric Drexler (later the cofounder and chairman of the Foresight Institute) introduced the term "nanotechnology" in 1986 in his highly influential book, *Engines of Creation,* which discussed the possibility of manufacturing systems and products based on the manipulation of atomic and molecular matter.

Pressure sensor designs were modified throughout the 1980s, with a great deal of impetus for these modifications coming from the automotive and medical industries. Full commercialization was finally reached around 1990. Sales of micromachine pressure sensors increased from about 3 million units a year in 1983 to over 50 million units by 1995 and continued to grow at double-digit rates.

Micromachined accelerometers, used primarily as crash sensors in automotive air bag systems, are the other micromachine application brought to market on a mass scale, though nowhere near the degree of the pressure sensor. First developed between 1985 and 1990, sales grew from about $200,000 in 1992 to $13 million to $15 million in 1995. A few other micromachined products then entered the marketplace, including ink jet heads for printers, read/write heads for magnetic hard drives, fuel injection nozzles for autos, and video chips for high-resolution television.

In the late 1990s, the micromachine industry ended a childhood characterized by a long period of research "push" and began an adolescence where a growing commercialization would create market "pull," drawing the industry into a period of sustained growth. The lithography-based techniques of silicon batch processing developed by use of the integrated circuit (IC) were considered the key to low-cost micromachining in the United States. The present infrastructure—adapting old IC production facilities to MEMS' needs—was advantageous for small firms wishing to enter the market, but wasn't considered optimal for generating or supporting the manufacturing energy needed to push beyond the prototype stage to the mass production stage. With the limited effect of MEMS on IC manufacturers, there was no need felt in those quarters to create new solutions to the problems facing the MEMS industry. With relatively low revenues, most of which are tied up in applications research and product development, the micromachine industry was unable to pursue those solutions on its own.

By 2003, as micro-electro-mechanical systems (MEMS) became an enabling technology for such applications as DNA sequencing, wireless communications, and fiber optic signal routing, the market neared the $5 billion level, according to the market research firm In-Stat. European estimates of the 2002 world market for micromachines, meanwhile, were much higher, ranging from $15 billion to $38 billion, according to *Electronic Times.*

The market breakdown for MEMS devices in 2002 was as follows: 36 percent of the MEMS products sold were for microfluidics, 21 percent were inertial sensors, 18 percent were optical MEMS, 14 percent were pressure sensors, while the rest were other sensors or actuators.

Companies in the automotive and medical sectors accounted by far for the largest part of MEMS sales as the twentieth century drew to a close. In medicine, for example, micromachines were employed for invasive surgery, and the future of nanotechnology promised molecule-sized robots trained to enter and repair internal body systems. While the automotive industry was long considered one of the most potentially lucrative outlets for MEMS products, auto companies were slow to integrate them on a mass scale. According to In-Stat, while only a handful of devices were incorporated at a high volume, the number of MEMS devices per car would likely double from 5 to 9.1 between 2002 and 2007, while revenues from the automotive sector would climb from $1 billion to almost $1.5 billion over the same period, particularly as a result of the integration of biometric sensors, tire-pressure monitoring systems, and entertainment displays.

Optical and magnetic sensors received even further refinement following a grant by the U.S. government's Small Business Innovative Research Program awarded to NanoSciences Corp., which aimed at the development of micromachines for burrowing holes in silicon so as to convert light rays. This technique was intended for the creation of self-contained position sensors for MEMS devices, using a magnetic field to get a precise position fix by reading a system's voltage. Such systems find use in medical, security, and industrial applications.

As research projects developed, many remarkable science fiction fantasies began to turn into reality. A team of Japanese electronics firms developed microscopic plumbers, rolling out micromachines designed to probe pipes, especially in power plants, and isolate and repair them. Expected to experience their first duties in Japanese power plants, these robots, at a weight of about one-seventieth (1/70) of an ounce each, will invade leaky pipes and end up acting as component parts by connecting to the pipes with couplings affixed to their sides.

While the industry saw strong unit shipments of MEMS (micro-electro-mechanical systems) devices in 2005 (1.8 billion units), revenues fell considerably, to $7 billion, according to a report from the firm In-Stat. Reasons for the decline ranged from weakness in critical market segments and below-average prices to inventory backlogs.

Looking ahead, In-Stat projected that unit shipments would grow 11 percent through 2010, while revenues would only increase 6.8 percent. In an April 17, 2006, *Business Wire*

article, the firm cited several reasons for the revenue declines, including "continued price reductions, as well as the introduction of new MEMS devices with commodity-like pricing." One important trend during the aforementioned time period was that industrial and communications markets were expected to surpass computing and automotive as the leading industry categories. Other important categories were aerospace, defense, and homeland security. According to Munich, Germany-based Wicht Technologie Consulting, the market for MEMS applications in these segments was expected to reach $265 million in 2009, up from $100 million in 2005.

Established industries in the United States barely recognized the potential impact of MEMS technology on their products. Micromachine producers still had to prove themselves in the market against entrenched conventional products. Characteristics that may make MEMS products profitable in the long run include size, weight, the ability to solve "unsolvable" problems, and extremely low cost. As new, viable microtechnologies developed, the industry was expected to expand into the profitable areas of consumer electronics, data storage, and micro-instrumentation, and to buttress its hold on the auto and medical industries.

Nanotechnology By 2000, there still was basically no commercial market for nanotechnology, while only a few micromachine applications such as inertial and medical sensors and automotive systems began to reap significant rewards. At that time, the realms of micromachines and nanotechnology were moving toward the marriage altar, whereby the tiny chemical processes of nanotechnology were precisely guided by MEMS-based machines.

The U.S. government, meanwhile, saw tremendous promise in nanotechnology. President Bill Clinton called for the creation of the National Nanotechnology Initiative (NNI) in January 2000 to integrate nanotechnology and information technology. While the bulk of this money went toward basic research, approximately $100 million was earmarked for "grand challenges," as the White House called them, including such pet projects as cancer-treating nanobots, machines to clear up water pollution, the boosting of computer speed by a factor of millions, and "shrinking the entire Library of Congress into a device the size of a sugar cube." By the early 2000s, the NNI was the leading public funding source for nanotechnology and micromachine development.

Between 2000 and 2003, the U.S. government more than tripled its investment in nanotechnology research. The NNI, with the support of the National Science Foundation (NSF), furthered nanoscale science and engineering through investments in research by individual investigators and small interdisciplinary teams; in large science, technology, engineering, and materials research centers; and in instrumentation at facilities such as the National Nanofabrication Users Network and the Network for Computational Nanotechnology. The NSF focused its investments in seven areas: biosystems on the nanoscale; nanoscale structures; novel phenomena and quantum control; device and system architecture; nanoscale processes in the environment; multi-scale, multi-phenomena modeling and simulation on the nanoscale; nanoscale manufacturing; and the convergence of nanotechnology with information technology, biology and the social sciences.

Testament to the promise of vast riches in nanotechnology's future, the hype generated by advancements produced a flood of investment, and some industry observers warned that the term nanotechnology was in danger of suffering from overuse. In particular, investors and legislators feared that firms were misusing and misapplying the word to describe their operations in an effort to attract funding and inflate their stock prices. Investment firm Asensio & Company complained to Merrill Lynch and to the New York Attorney General, charging that firms with an extremely tenuous connection to nanotechnology were included in Merrill Lynch's nanotechnology index, as those companies attempted to promote their stocks fraudulently.

The U.S. military eyed developments in nanotechnology and micromachines with keen interest. One of its earliest financial supporters, by 2003, the Department of Defense allotted $243 million to nanotechnology research and development. Most immediately, the military planned to incorporate into their operations ultradurable munitions, widely dispersed sensors, and communications systems enabled with micromachines and nanomaterials.

More ambitiously, the U.S. government created the NBIC initiative. Short for "Nano-Bio-Info-Cogno," this program aimed to integrate biotechnology, information technology, and cognitive neuroscience by perfecting engineering at the nano level. Mihail Roco of the National Science Foundation headed the initiative, as he did the National Nanotechnology Initiative. Such a "megatechnology" would massively overhaul most of the scientific industries developed through the twentieth century. The June 2002 publication of a report compiled by panelists from industry, academia, and the government, titled "Converging Technologies for Improving Human Performance," announced the NBIC initiative, which grew out of the exploration of ways in which these converging fields could enhance human physical and cognitive abilities, according to *The Ecologist*.

Prospects for the nanotechnology industry were very promising. In April 2006, the firm Research and Markets released a report titled "Nanotechnology—The Coming Revolution," which indicated that the industry was valued at $225 million in 2005. Predictions of long-term future growth varied, but even the lowest estimations portended astonishing growth in the coming decades. Indeed, the National Science Foundation famously predicted a trillion-dollar market for nanotechnology by 2015. Of that total, about $600 billion would derive from electronics and informatics, $340 billion would flow from nanostructured materials and processes, and pharmaceutical applications would account for $180 billion. The consulting firm Freedonia Group predicted more modest growth, to about $35 billion by 2020.

Carbon nanotubes, which were integrated into industrial production in the early 2000s, offer a wide range of potential uses and were the among the technology's most fundamental materials. Carbon nanotubes conduct electricity and heat highly efficiently through tiny strips of graphite with unpaired electrons, exhibiting exceptional mechanical strength, stability, and density. Some applications for carbon nanotubes included acting as wires for micromachine computer components, flat screen televisions, and computer monitors, and as hydrogen storage units in fuel cells. They also served as the backbone of biochips used to identify DNA molecules for use in biomedical procedures, and researchers at IBM continued to make progress in the area of nanotube research.

Challenges Difficulties were in finding new applications for micro-electro-mechanical systems (MEMS), creating a group of basic products that can be simply and easily modified to meet a broad range of customer needs, and establishing a manufacturing infrastructure to support a large market. In short, establishing the silicon-based MEMS techniques in the market was to depend on volume production. Micromachine companies must develop low-cost, accurate, and implementable product-testing techniques on a mass scale if potential clients are to be convinced of the reliability of MEMS products.

One of the most serious questions to be addressed by the industry was micromachine packaging—the outer case of the micromachine that must insulate its sensitive inner workings from external factors (chemicals or electrical conductivity) without interfering with other operations of the machine. In addition, the lithographic and etching methodologies of the integrated circuit (IC) industries will have to be modified to reflect micromachining's need for greater 3-D focus (in contrast to integrated circuitry's drive toward ever greater degrees of miniaturization). MEMS need their own specialized design tools in order to continue product development. New firms were already creating computer-aided design software specifically for the micromachine industry. By 2008, the field had evolved so that, according to Karen Lightman, managing director of the MEMS Industry Group, "while most people are still working with traditional packaging, we are seeing a definite migration towards MEMS integration with CMOS [complementary metal oxide semiconductor] processes," as reported by *MEMS Investor Journal*.

The production process was a limiting factor for mass market availability of nanotechnology at the turn of the century, since the customization process required for each design necessitated extensive research and production costs. The standard micromachining technique involves the application of a series of layers of materials on silicon in a high temperature setting, and requires a great deal of intensive labor from skilled technicians. The entire process of physically creating a new micromachine typically takes over two months. In total, it typically takes two to three years to develop a prototype and another one to three years to design the larger system for which the microcomponent is intended.

As with many highly advanced scientific developments, nanotechnology and MEMS were not immune from fears of misuse and ethical violations. The science fiction overtones of some of the potential developments, particularly medical nanobots, aroused concerns over the ability of these tiny machines to carry viruses or other destructive materials. Such fears were not limited to the fringes of society or to technophobes, moreover. The cofounder of Sun Microsystems, Bill Joy, announced his concerns that such technology, if not properly controlled, could find its way into the hands of extreme individuals, affording them too much capacity for mayhem. In addition, Joy feared more generally that the convergence of GNR (genetics, nanotechnology, and robotics) technologies could unleash unintended consequences proving disastrous to humanity and the environment. Joy's dire warnings were particularly startling, given that they came from one of Silicon Valley's leading innovators.

Concerns about a nanotechnology backlash continued into 2006. In late 2005, the research firm Jupiter issued a report titled "Knowing Nano" indicating that nanotechnology was evolving more quickly than guidelines for safety and ethics. The report raised concerns about criminal abuse, as well as the potentially harmful effects nanoparticles could have on health and the environment. However, many scientists held that such fears were grossly overstated and premature, contending that for the time being, most of the research was invested in simply learning how the technology really works in the first place, and thus the ability to unleash Armageddon was a long way off.

Safety concerns regarding nanotechnology did not readily abate. According to David Rejeski of the U.S. Project on Emerging Nanotechnologies, quoted in a 2008 *Chemistry and Industry* article, "public trust is the dark horse in nanotechnology's future." and industry and the government must work harder to prove to the public that the technology is safe or consumers may reach for the products marked "no nano." Rejeski pointed to the effect public mistrust can have on an industry and cited the example of the European Union's ban on genetically modified foods, driven largely by public concerns, which cost U.S. farmers an estimated $300 million annually in lost sales. European countries tend to be more cautious about new technology, and one report showed that in 2006 they were spending almost twice as much ($24 million) than the United States ($13 million) on research into the safety of nanotechnology.

One of the upcoming applications for MEMS in 2008 was their use in cell phones and other devices as accelerometers, which are motion-sensing tools. Some of the possible applications made capable by accelerometers include allowing users to input commands through gestures, utilize GPS indoors, and not worry about turning off their phone—the device will shut down automatically when it is not used. As of 2008, the Apple iPhone used an accelerometer to sense the movement of the phone and automatically change the display from portrait to landscape when it is rotated. The popular Wii video game system also used accelerometers to judge the movements of players and cause corresponding movements on the screen. Although the potential for MEMS use in cell phones was there, most industry experts did not see it happening any time soon due to the cost of the technology. Although the price of accelerometers had decreased, the consensus was that they would need to cost less than $1 before mass market infiltration was probable; as of 2008, the devices were priced at about $1.50. Douglas McEuen of ABI Research told *Electronic Engineering Times* in April 2008 that MEMS accelerometers will not go under the $1 barrier until at least 2010. In the same article, Marlene Bourne of Bourne Research said, "I do believe we are experiencing a slow integration of sensors into everything—with slow being the operative word." Indeed, the use of MEMS accelerometers in cell phones was in its infancy in 2008. According to Mathieu Potin of Yole Development (Lyon, France), MEMS accelerometers were used in only 1 to 2 percent of cell phones shipped in 2007. However, McEuen predicted that between 2007 and 2012, shipments of accelerometers for cell phones would grow by 139 percent to 437 million units. This figure represents between 30 and 40 percent of all cell phones by 2012.

CURRENT CONDITIONS

The use of nanotechnology and micromachines grew so rapidly in the first decade of the new century that it could more appropriately be perceived not as an industry in itself, but rather, as state-of-the-art technology used in an increasingly wide spectrum of applications across many industries. For this reason, statistics and numbers vary, according to what is included in the industry. In any event, according to a 2010 report by BCC Research, total worldwide revenues (sales only) in 2009 were approximately $11.67 billion, expected to increase to $26 billion by 2015, with a compound annual growth rate (CAGR) of 11 percent. An even higher CAGR was anticipated for the nanomaterials segment (14.7 percent), which was the largest sales segment in 2009 (more than $9 billion) and expected to grow to $19.6 billion by 2015. Another hot area was nanotools, accounting for sales of $2.6 billion in 2009. BCC Research also reported that the global market for nanofiber products was $80.7 million in 2009, but had an anticipated 34 percent CAGR through 2015, accelerating to 37 percent CAGR by 2020.

Nanostructured coatings, mainly used in construction and exterior protection (e.g., anti-weather coatings), military and defense (anti-corrosion for vehicles and protective textiles for soldiers), and automotive (anti-corrosion, hydrophobic and thermal barrier coatings) brought in just under $1 billion for 2009, according to research group Future Markets, Inc. It reported global revenues for polymeric nanocomposites at approximately $223 million in 2009. Clay nanocomposites took the largest share, with about $89.6 million in 2009. The largest applications in 2009 were in plastics and packaging ($49.5 million); aerospace and aviation ($45.4 million, including military); and automotive ($28.3 million).

Just within the consumer products area, nanomaterials have been incorporated in golf clubs and ski wax, as well as in advanced display technologies in electronics and self-cleaning surfaces in the home. In its 2010 report, technology publisher Future Markets, Inc. reported that revenues for nanotechnology and nanomaterials in consumer products were approxmately $1.54 billion in 2009, with automotive, electronic, and household care segments generating the greatest sales. However, revenues were expected to triple in just five years; by 2015, according to Future Markets Inc., the nano-market for consumer products alone will reach $5.33 billion. Further, said the report, advanced material properties in 2009 had been achieved by adding nanoparticles either in the bulk material or applied to the surface. Next generation products are expected to incorporate nanomaterials with multi-functional "smart" capabilities.

Federal government involvement remains primarily channeled through the National Nanotechnology Initiative (NNI), which had a 2010 fiscal year budget (spread among 13 of its 25 agencies) of $1.6 billion, mostly slated for research. The 2011 fiscal year budget request was for $1.8 billion. The new budget request called for FDA and the Consumer Products Safety Commission (CPSC) to be added to the list of other agencies that fund nanotechnology research.

INDUSTRY LEADERS

Involvement in MEMS and nanotechnology is spread across a wide range of companies, all with varying degrees of research and product development in the industry. Larger, diversified electronics companies devoted enormous sums to research and development initiatives, and often partnered with the fast-growing crop of smaller specialist firms. As of 2010, reported Future Markets, Inc., most multi-national companies with products related to surfaces (especially paint, varnish, lacquer products and household care products) were heavily involved in research using nanotechnology.

International Business Machines Corporation IBM was a leading nanotechnology researcher, using its vast economy of scale to invest heavily in MEMS and nanoprocesses for use in information technology. Its work on carbon nanotubes yielded promising results for the improvement of integrated circuits and data storage equipment; IBM's Millipede project was devoted to the expansion of storage density. Other projects included the development of photonic bandgap materials using nanotechnology and processes to redirect lightwaves for computer and telecommunications networking. In 2008, the company announced plans to invest $1.5 billion in nanotechnology chip projects, including a new research site in New York.

Intel Corporation The world's leading semiconductor manufacturer, Intel began production of nano-scale silicon computer chips in 2000. In late 2003, the firm rolled out 90-nanometer silicon-based transistors that were the most advanced commercial employment of nanotechnology in the semiconductor manufacturing process. Intel maintained a number of in-house and external research programs aimed at the refinement of its silicon nanotechnology processes for chip development. Intel continued its involvement in nanotechnology research. In particular, the company was focused on using nanotechnology to develop transistors that were faster, smaller, and more power-efficient.

Hewlett-Packard Company The computer and peripheral giant Hewlett-Packard's HP Labs research arm boasted an innovative nanotechnology division, which won the 2000 Feynman Prize in Nanotechnology, along with its research partners at Georgia Tech and UCLA, for its theoretical work on computer modeling for nanostructure material science. HP Labs' Quantum Science Research group maintained a number of patents seeking to render molecular electronic devices practical to manufacture.

General Electric Company GE got into the nanotechnology act as well, partnering with the Palo Alto, California-based Molecular Nanosystems on a three-year, $5.8 million program to devise a platform for manufacturing processes enabling the precise and cost-effective control of nano-scale materials. GE Global Research's nanotechnology program worked to incorporate the science into

GE's wide range of products. The program carried a hefty research and development budget, which was used to fund research in ten core areas, including micro and nanostructures technologies.

Motorola With MEMS research efforts stretching back to the 1970s, Motorola was one of the earliest large electronic firms to invest in micromachine technologies. Its first MEMS pressure sensor rolled out in the mid-1980s. The firm's MEMS sensors were widely used in the automotive and medical sectors. In 2002, Motorola picked Dalsa Corp. to manufacture MEMS-based sensors for its Semiconductor Products Sector. The following year, its Sensor Products Division launched a new MEMS package for inertial sensors about 70 percent smaller than standard. Motorola was investing in technology that could lead to the first-ever use of carbon nanotube technology in flatscreen TVs. The company continued its research in the nanoelectronics realm via its Embedded Systems and Physical Sciences Research Center.

Texas Instruments Inc. Texas Instruments (TI) began work on MEMS in 1977, and its first micromachine print chip for printing airline tickets and boarding passes was introduced a decade later. That research also yielded TI's big micromachine application, the digital micromirror device (DMD). The DMD, based on a million fluctuating mirrors acting to project a screen image, was designed as a video component for home television, teleconferencing, and projection theaters, and comprised a sizeable share of the video display market. In conjunction with Advanced Micro Devices (AMD), Freescale, IBM, Intel, and Micron, Texas Instruments contributed funds in conjunction with a Semiconductor Industry Association grant for the establishment of the Western Institute of Nanoelectronics. The new research organization consisted of representatives from Stanford University, UCLA's Henry Samueli School of Engineering and Applied Science, the University of California-Santa Barbara, and the University of California-Berkeley.

Analog Devices, Inc. Analog Devices, a leading manufacturer of micromachined accelerometers and digital integrated circuits, was founded in 1965 as an electronic module company. Its first MEMS product was an air bag crash sensor integrated into the 1994 Saab 900. By 2000, its accelerometer had also been designed into an earthquake sensing device, a vehicle security system, navigation devices, computer game pads, computer peripherals, and a device to guard against back injuries. By 2004, the firm was the world's largest volume supplier of single-chip MEMS accelerometers.

Industrial Nanotech, Inc., a global nanoscience company, reached record highs in revenues in 2010 with its patented Nansulate product, a thermal insulating product with widespread applications, including pipelines and roofing materials. The startup company, based in Naples, Florida, estimated its 2009 revenues at \$15.5 million, boasting major contracts with Mexico, Saudi Arabia, and Alaska, in addition to U.S. business.

Nanogen, Inc. Nanogen geared its NanoChip system and other nanotechnology-based offerings toward the health care industry, particularly for use in genomics and biomedical research. Its research efforts centered on the production of analyte specific reagents (ASRs) to seek out genetic variations that lend themselves to certain types of diseases, using the information derived from the Human Genome Project. A partnership with drug giant Aventis aimed to produce consumable pharmacogenomic drugs. (See also **Pharmacogenomics.**) Other clients included the U.S. Department of Defense, which contracted with Nanogen to build nanotechnological warfare applications. In mid-2006, the company's products included such next-generation products as the NanoChip Molecular Biology Workstation and NanoChip 400 instruments for DNA-based analyses.

AMERICA AND THE WORLD

In its 2010 *Report to the President and Congress on the Third Assessment of the National Nanotechnology Initiative,* the NNI advised that "The United States remains a leader in nanotechnology based on various metrics, including R&D expenditures and outputs such as publications, citations, and patents. However, the European Union has more publications and China's output is increasing." However, leading researchers indicated that without continued investment, the United States might lose its leadership status. For example, according to *PhysOrg.com,* in his June 2005 testimony before U.S. House of Representatives Science Subcommittee on Research, Motorola Vice President of Technological Commercialization Jim O'Connor remarked, "Thanks to public-private partnerships between Federal and State governments, business and academia, our nanotechnology position has become strong. However, the relative lead the U.S. currently holds is in jeopardy because the rest of the world is catching up to the U.S. in a variety of measurements. In government funding, for example, the rate of increase in the European Union and Asia is higher than that of the U.S."

China was an especially attractive location for new nanotechnology research centers, due to its affordability and access to educated workers. In April of 2006, German chemical heavyweight BASF—which had earmarked about \$223 million for its global nanotechnology research initiatives between 2006 and 2008—announced that it had opened the Competence Center for Nanostructured Surfaces in Singapore. Focused on nanostructured surfaces that sought to reduce fuel costs and keep ship hulls cleaner, the center would benefit from \$16 million in funding from BASF through 2009, according to *Xinhua News Agency.*

A further indication of China's growing importance in the area of nanotechnology was the publication of the *China Industrial Nanotechnology BlueBook* by the firm Research and Markets. Following an analysis of the nanotechnology and nanotechnology-enhanced products that were commercially available in China, the firm worked from a universe of 600 companies to ultimately compile a report of the "80 most active and to be watched firms," according to an April 26, 2006, *Business Wire* article.

RESEARCH AND TECHNOLOGY

According to the 2010 *Report to the President and Congress on the Third Assessment of the National Nanotechnology Initiative,* the promise and optimism of nanotechnology had manifested in several significant developments. In electronics, the semiconductor industry was cited as the most successful and extensive adopter of nanotechnology. As of 2010, integrated circuits were using components and structural features in the 30-nanometer range or smaller, about 1000 times smaller than typical biological cells. Laptops and iPods contained chips loaded with nano-scale features.

In the field of energy, the catalyst and catalytic process industry had employed nanotechnology to develop liquid fuels and plastics with cleaner environmental effects. Carbon nanotubes were being incorporated into high-strength composites, then woven into yarns to produce lighter and more conducive electrical wires and harnesses.

The 2010 report to the president and congress also noted that new nanoparticulate formulations of conventional drugs were being used in clinical trials, especially for imaging agents and treatments that targeted only cancer cells or arterial plaques. nano particles were increasingly added to sunscreen products and cosmetics as well.

One of the most significant areas of research in the nanotechnology industry was in the medical field. According to a March 2008 article in *Small Times,* "the next generation of nano-based medical applications have the potential to obsolete existing technology." An example of new research efforts was the partnership between STMicroelectronics and Debiotech in which researchers sought to develop a miniaturized insulin-delivery system. The Nanopump, as it is called, is a tiny pump, mounted on a disposable skin patch, that delivers continuous insulin infusion for diabetics. As of mid-2008, the first prototype had been developed and samples were in production. According to a 2008 article in the *Indiana Business Journal,* "Biomarkers within the body could be quantitatively and qualitatively identified with nanoparticles, leading to easier identification of cancers, heart attacks and infections." Nanotechnology was also being used to design drug delivery systems that targeted only the disease-affected cells within the body, such as when treating cancer.

Another exciting research project involving nanotechnology in the medical field was being conducted by Dr. Mauro Ferrari at the University of Texas Health Science Center in Houston. Ferrari, a pioneer in the field of biomedical nanotechnology, and his research team were working on developing nano-textured chips that could detect cancerous cells. Ferrari told *Small Times,* "Of the millions of molecular species some are a billion times more concentrated than we want. If we can single out key markers at the nanoscale, we can develop a predictive method that lets us change our approach to cancer. Instead of responding to crises, we can prevent them." Ferrari hoped to have the product ready for phase one clinical trials by 2010. He stated that the real challenge when developing such nanoparticles is to get them to recognize their target, such as a cancerous tumor, and be able to cross all the barriers in the body to get to it. "When we achieve this," said Ferrari, "we will change the world."

Many other research projects involving nanoparticles and cancer, as well as other diseases, were also under way. Aura Biosciences was investigating using nanoparticles to treat liver cancer in a safer and more effective way. Researchers there had developed a particle called a Nanosmart, an organic envelope that carries chemotherapy drugs directly to cancer cells. Whereas traditional chemotherapy kills all the cells—both healthy and malignant—the Nanosmart keeps the drugs in a capsule until it reaches the tumor cells inside the liver, where it then releases them. The capsule also carries a fluorescent ink that can be seen by magnetic resonance imaging (MRI), thus allowing doctors to judge the size of a tumor and whether it has spread. Researchers had not begun clinical trials so could not guarantee that the Nanosmart would work, but, if it does, the company hoped to market the particle for use in bladder and breast cancer as well. Cutting-edge technology in the industry was resulting in vast improvements in the fields of medical diagnosis and detection and drug development. According to one report, the market for nanotechnology-enabled drug delivery was $3.4 billion in 2007 and was expected to increase to $26 billion by 2012 and even $220 billion by 2015.

In May of 2006, an exciting industry development took place when the state of New York, IBM, and Rensselaer Polytechnic Institute announced a $100 million partnership to create the world's most powerful university-based supercomputing center. Called the Computational Center for Nanotechnology Innovations, the new center was planned to drive nanotechnology developments in the areas of semiconductors, arts, medicine, energy, and biotechnology. According to the May 10, 2006, issue of *Internet Wire,* the center would be one of the top 10 of any kind throughout the world. The slated completion date was 2011.

Researchers insisted that for the full potential of nanotechnology to be realized, engineers would need to devise processes and design paradigms that transcend those developed in the silicon era of the mid and late twentieth century. Meyya Meeappan, the director of nanotechnology for NASA's Ames Research Center, opined that integrated circuit (IC) lithography, the dominant silicon design process, would be insufficient for generating patterns that most fully harness materials at the nano level. The hope among researchers was that nano-scale materials could be arranged flexibly and cheaply, utilizing processes that lead most efficiently toward the self-assembly model, where manufacturing costs are pushed downward mostly to the costs of the materials themselves and the energy spent to manipulate them.

Innovative production processes boosted the efficiency and usefulness of MEMS. Sandia National Laboratories pioneered a production process whereby nanotechnology components assimilate five layers of polysilicon, the highest number of layers yet attainable. The benefits of more layers include the ability of micromachine components to perform more complex tasks. According to *Machine Design,* three layers allow for the creation of gears with hubs, while four layers can generate linkage arms throughout the plane of gears. With the five-layer process developed by Sandia, complex, interactive components can be manipulated on moving platforms. Adding layers of polysilicon is tricky because each new layer inherits the textural qualities of those underneath it, thereby adding surface protrusions that can interfere with the gears if not factored into the design. Sandia solved this problem by implementing a process that smooths out the protrusions with chemical oxide before each new layer is added.

An important development at the Berkeley Sensor and Actuator Center was I-MEMS—integrated MEMS—developed in conjunction with Analog Devices. I-MEMS are an array of linked microdevices, gyros, accelerometers, and other sensors built around a chip that is linked to a computer. Other current research includes work on computer-aided design for MEMS, a MEMS mass spectrometer, and micromirrors to miniaturize scanner technology.

At the University of Southern California's Information Science Institute, a production process was developed that could make the fabrication of micromachines far more efficient. The process, known as Efab, for "electrochemical fabrication," employs a unit small enough for a desktop that accepts images from a computer to reproduce three-dimensional (3-D) complex shapes for the production of new micromachines. A similar process was used for years in the 3-D design of planes and automobiles.

Durability was another serious concern among micromachine manufacturers, and research efforts were spearheaded to find more wear-resistant materials that were also compatible with the precise functions for which they were intended. In that spirit, Sandia National Laboratories pushed research on amorphous diamonds, the second-hardest material on Earth after crystalline diamond. Researchers have long coveted diamond as a nanotechnology material due to its durability and biocompatibility. In 2000, Sandia announced that it successfully developed the first diamond micromachine, which added the benefit of compatibility with existing manufacturing techniques. Amorphous diamond, essentially a form of chemically benign carbon, was slated as a potentially useful material in medical nanotechnology, as it would not generate allergic reactions.

According to *Electronic Design,* researchers speculated that amorphous diamond could enhance durability in wear applications by a factor of 10,000. Moreover, since the material was compatible with silicon chips already in production, Sandia even suggested that silicon micromachines with diamond layers could wind up replacing polysilicon machines. Sandia's premier diamond micromachine was a diamond comb driver to be used in a micro-engine piston.

Scientists also harnessed the information storage capabilities of DNA molecules for use in micromachine technology that could potentially generate information systems far more powerful than the current generation of supercomputers. Researchers at the University of Wisconsin pushed this technology ahead several steps toward the production of DNA-based computers, which will harbor hundreds of millions of DNA molecules, each carrying tremendous amounts of data and memory. In DNA computing, any specific problem can be solved by a process of elimination, in which the molecules, each identified as carrying a possible answer to a particular problem, are weeded through until only the DNA molecule with the correct answer is left standing. To spur this process, the molecules are exposed to catalysts designed to execute a particular operation.

The University of Wisconsin team successfully employed hybridization chemistry to facilitate this identification process. Initial tests found that the DNA chips were capable of solving multi-step mathematical problems. As the technology is further refined, it is expected to tackle far more complex problems than can currently be solved by digital technology. The full potential of such tiny DNA supercomputers will not be realized, however, until researchers discover an appropriate architecture in which to store the millions of molecules.

BIBLIOGRAPHY

Addison, Brad. "Nanotechnology Presents an Enormous Opportunity." *Indianapolis Business Journal,* 23 June 2008.

"Agile MEMS Robots 100 Times Smaller than Previous Robotic Designs." *Next Big Future,* 3 June 2008.

BCC Research. "Nanofibers: Technologies and Developing markets." *Market Research,* 2010. Available from http://www.marketresearch.com.

———. "Nanotechnology: A Realistic Market Assessment." *Market Research,* 1 July 2010. Available from http://www.marketresearch.com.

Eisberg, Neil. "No Nano Labels Could Become Reality." *Chemistry and Industry,* 5 May 2008.

Fister Gale, Sarah. "A Slow Road to Big Impact: Small Tech in Medicine." *Small Times,* March 2008.

Future Markets, Inc. *The World Market for Nanostructured Coatings.* 1 August 2010. Available from http://www.marketresearch.com.

———. *The World Market for Nanotechnology and Nanomaterials in Consumer Products 2010-2015.* 1 May 2010. Available from http://www.marketresearch.com.

"IBM to Invest $1.5 Billion in Nanotech." *PC Magazine Online,* 16 July 2008.

"Industrial Nanotech, Inc. Patented Nansulate Certified for Mexico." Press Release, 15 June 2010. Available from www.industrial-nanotech.com/INTK_Press_release-06152010.htm.

McGrath, Dylan. "Analysts Split on Near-Term Prospects for MEMS Accelerators in Cell Phones." *Electronic Engineering Times,* 5 May 2008.

———. "Riding Wii's Wake, Consumer Camps Get Moving on Motion Sensors." *Electronic Engineering Times,* 7 April 2008.

"MEMS Industry Challenges and Trends." *MEMS Investor Journal,* 18 June 2008.

"MEMS Market for Defense and Aerospace to Hit $265 Million by 2009." *Military & Aerospace Electronics,* April 2006.

"MEMS Sensor/Actuator Growth Forecast to Double." *Motion System Design,* July 2008.

Merritt, Richard. "Gold, DNA Combination May Lead To Nano-Sensor." Duke University, 20 June 2008.

"MIT Uses Nanotubes to Detect Deadly Gases." *PC Magazine Online,* 11 June 2008.

"Nano Institute Forms." *Electronic Engineering Times,* 13 March 2006.

National Science and Technology Council. *Report to the President and Congress on the Third Assessment of the National Nanotechnology Initiative,* February 2010. Available from www.nano.gov/html/res/FINAL_NANO_REPORT.pdf.

———. "The National Nanotechnology Initiative- Supplement to the President's FY 2011 Budget." February 2010. Available from www.nano.gov/NNI_2011_budget_supplement.

"New Supercomputing Center to Advance the Science of Nanotechnology; $100 Million Partnership Will Create World's Most Powerful University-Based Computing Center." *Internet Wire,* 10 May 2006.

"SEMI Report Forecasts $4.2 Billion Nanoelectronics Market by 2010." NanoBusiness Alliance, 29 May 2006. Available from http://www.nanobusiness.org.

Wittmann, Art. "Big Blue Thinks Small." *Network Computing,* 13 April 2006.

"The World Market for Nanotechnology and Nanomaterials in Consumer Products, 2010-2015." Future Markets, Inc., 1 may 2010. Available from http://www.marketresearch.com/productid=2683148.

Zimmerman, Eilene. "A Tiny Cure for Cancer?" *FSB,* July 2008.

MICROWAVE APPLICATIONS

—■—

SIC CODE(S)

3663

3679

3825

INDUSTRY SNAPSHOT

Microwave technology applies to many industries other than the most obvious one—food preparation. Radar, medicine, chemistry, and telecommunications have increasingly relied on this form of electromagnetic energy. The entire electromagnetic range, in order of increasing frequency, includes radiowaves, infrared radiation, visible radiation (light), ultraviolet radiation, X-rays, and cosmic radiation. Within the telecommunications industry, microwave technology is used for some conventional mobile radios and telephones, all cellular telephones, all television broadcast channels above Channel 13, satellite communications systems, and high-speed computers. This segment of the industry expanded quickly because of heightened demand for high-speed Internet access, wireless handhelds, and GPS.

Microwave energy has been applied to food preparation since 1950. Conventional heating combines two disadvantages, slowness and inefficiency, because it warms food gradually with heat entering from the outside. In contrast, microwaves create heat only when absorbed by the object they cook, resulting in rapid, even heating. Microwave technology works best on materials that hold some water and don't conduct electricity particularly well. Since microwaves focus energy, much less floor space is necessary in comparison to conventional heating and drying equipment.

Many other industries have reaped the benefits of microwave technology for heating and drying purposes. The chemical industry employed microwave technology in curing coatings, cross-linking polymers, and plasma polymerization. Printers and photographers have used microwave drying of film and ink curing to work more efficiently. Also, a microwave kiln for processing of ceramic raw materials has been successful. Despite its success, however, microwave energy to heat materials is not as widespread as some of its proponents believe it should be. One reason is that radio frequency heating, a related and more established technology, was more popular than microwave technology in such processes as plastics welding and wood gluing. Secondly, there is a great variety of microwave uses with different kinds of equipment. Some companies are understandably reluctant to invest in one microwave-related product only to realize they should have chosen another.

ORGANIZATION AND STRUCTURE

Microwave applications are found in a number of industries including telecommunications carriers, electronic device and component manufacturers, and the appliance industry. Certain firms, generally smaller companies, focus more exclusively on microwave applications, but large electronics firms such as Matsushita and telecommunications giants, such as Motorola, have a great impact on the industry overall.

Most of these systems used an analog signal to provide multiple television channels to consumers, competing with wire line cable providers or filling gaps where conventional cable was not available. These systems primarily

555

operated in the 2.1 to 2.3 gigahertz (GHz) spectrum. At the end of the 1990s, the Federal Communications Commission (FCC) ruled that two-way communication could be used in this spectrum. When a new spectrum became available at 24 GHz, new possibilities were opened up. In addition, manufacturers and software developers continued to make improvements that increased the capabilities of microwave systems. The industry looked toward broadband communication of data such as Internet access as its future and these developments attracted the attention of the broader telecommunications industry.

By 1999, microwave ovens had reached the status of a household necessity in the United States. A study conducted by the Yankelovich Partners, a marketing consultant firm, indicated that Americans ranked the microwave oven as the number one technology that made their lives easier, beating out the telephone answering machine and automatic teller machines. According to a report cited in *Forecast* magazine, 93 percent of homes in the United States had a microwave. All major appliance lines included microwaves of various sizes, wattage, and features. Larger and sometimes more sophisticated models were made for commercial kitchens.

Regulation Like the rest of the telecommunications industry, regulation of wireless cable companies was drastically reduced by the Telecommunications Act of 1996. Most radio frequencies, however, including most microwave frequencies, are licensed by the FCC, although some telecommunications companies operate on unlicensed frequencies. This gives them easier access to the frequency but also makes interference more likely. The FCC continues to regulate the telecommunications industry to some degree in order to promote orderly development and proper competition.

Microwave ovens have been regulated by the U.S. Food and Drug Administration (FDA) since 1971. Medical devices that use microwave energy are also regulated by the FDA.

BACKGROUND AND DEVELOPMENT

The term "microwave region" is generally defined as falling in the upper section of the radio frequency range of the electromagnetic spectrum, under that of infrared radiation. Microwave is defined differently by different groups. The FCC identifies the lower end of the range at a frequency of 890 megahertz (MHz), or 890 million cycles per second. The Institute of Electrical and Electronics Engineers defines microwave frequencies beginning at 1,000 MHz. More general definitions extend the range from 300 MHz to 300 GHz—equivalent to 300 billion cycles per second. Regardless of the definition, the term "microwave" in general pertains to one segment of the whole electromagnetic spectrum.

German physicist Heinrich Rudolph Hertz (1857–1894) was the first person who intentionally generated electromagnetic energy at microwave frequencies in his experiments to verify the existence of electromagnetic waves. By 1920, other scientists were generating frequencies exceeding 3700 GHz. These relatively low energy levels, however, could not be easily controlled. In 1931, the first microwave radio link for telephone use connected Dover, England and Calais, France.

During World War II, major microwave innovations began in earnest. Microwave technology generated the higher frequencies necessary for the use of radar in airplanes. In 1947, the first point-to-point microwave radio relay system began, connecting Boston and New York City. By 1951 the first coast-to-coast system was in effect. By the 1960s, microwave technology (specifically, two-way wireless communications) manifested itself in the citizens band radio trend. Eventually, though, because of its reputation for undependable analog transmission quality, microwave technology faced tougher times in the 1980s. Many local telephone companies also deployed high bandwidth digital services around this time.

By the 1990s, however, microwave communication technology made something of a comeback. With access to an electromagnetic spectrum formerly reserved to the military sphere, many established and start-up companies took advantage of the digital compression of video channels in the telecommunications industry. This development allowed wireless cable systems to deliver up to 200 virtual channels of video. From 1980 to the mid-1990s, the total number of licensed microwave radio stations in the United States rose from about 22,000 to more than 100,000.

The telecommunications landscape in the 1990s appeared very different from that of any other time in history. In 1996 nearly two-thirds of all long distance telephone calls were delivered via microwave. Pager and cellular telephones represented two of the most successful examples of wireless technology. The widespread application of both products prompted many telephone companies to worry about exhausting their supply of telephone number exchanges (also see the essay entitled Wireless Communications).

The microwave spectrum is an enormous domain with 100 times as much frequency space for communications in the microwave range as in the whole spectrum beneath that bandwidth. A wireless cable is a broadband service that may deliver addressable, multi-channel television programming, access to the Internet, data transfer services, and other interactive benefits. The wireless cable system has three main components: the transmit site, the signal path, and the receive site. These systems receive their programming from satellites that transmit a signal downward to the cable operator's receiving station. The operator then converts that signal to a microwave frequency and broadcasts it to subscribers from a transmitting tower. These signals can travel up to 50 miles.

Wireless cable customers have a rooftop antenna, a piece of equipment that receives the signal and transforms it into a cable frequency. The rooftop antenna may be installed on a single dwelling unit or on a multiple dwelling unit. These antennas generally fall into two categories, microwave antennas to capture the wireless cable signals and VHF/UHF antennas to receive the local broadcast channels. The signal is then decoded and unscrambled for viewing. Some analog wireless cable systems use microwaves to deliver local channels.

The FCC set up rules and regulations for wireless cable operators in 1983, and the first wireless cable system emerged in 1984. For several years, the wired cable industry thwarted its program subsidiaries' attempts to sell on fair and nondiscriminatory terms to new competitors. That changed in 1992 when Congress passed the Cable Competition and Consumer Protection Act, which allowed fair access to programming for cable rivals.

Until 1996, the FCC gave each wireless cable licensee the legal right to operate particular multipoint, multichannel distribution service channels within a protected service area (PSA). Generally, a PSA's radius was 15 miles and was shielded from signal interference of other close transmissions. In 1996 the FCC overhauled this system and divided the United States into 493 basic trading areas (BTAs), each of which was auctioned to the greatest bidder. Under the new rules, each licensee operated as before, although with the implementation of BTAs, the incumbent PSAs were enlarged to cover 35 miles.

In July 1996, the FCC issued a declaratory ruling that allowed wireless cable operators to digitize their licensed channels as long as neighboring wireless cable systems suffered no interference from the analog-to-digital conversion procedure. One result of this ruling was that wireless cable could transmit up to 200 digitized channels of video, a considerable improvement over the original 33 analog channels per market.

In the United States, the wireless cable industry ballooned from about 200,000 subscribers in 1992 to one million by the mid-1990s. According to the Wireless Cable Association International, by 1997, roughly 5 million people in 80 countries subscribed to wireless systems. At the same time, more than 200 wireless cable systems existed in the United States. Mexico City, Mexico, particularly thrived on wireless cable with more than 600,000 subscribers in its service area.

By 2002, according to a report by Alexander and Associates, Inc., the percentage of U.S. households with cable television connections declined significantly. In the early months of that year, households subscribing to one of the direct-to-home satellite services increased about 18 percent. The firm indicated that this represented an important shift in the wired and wireless delivery of electronic home entertainment.

In its ninth annual report on competition in the Multi-Channel Video Program Distribution (MVPD) marketplace released in 2003, the FCC reported that the total number of subscribers to both cable and noncable MVPDs increased to 89.9 million households, an increase of 1.8 percent over the previous reporting period. In addition, the study revealed that 76.5 percent of all Multi-Channel Video Program Distribution (MVPD) subscribers received their programming from a franchised cable operator, down from 78 percent a year earlier. The FCC also said that it believed that 2002 represented the first year that the cable industry, as a whole, suffered a net loss of subscribers. As far as noncable MVPD subscribers, the numbers reached the 21.1 million mark by June 2002, the FCC said. This represented an increase of more than 9 percent over the previous reporting period. For the year, direct broadcast satellite services represented 20.3 percent of all MVPD. In addition, the FCC noted that the number of direct broadcast satellite (DBS) subscribers grew from almost 16 million households to about 18 million households in the span of a year.

Microwave Cooking In 1946, the Raytheon Co. filed a patent applying microwaves to cook food. An oven that heated food with microwave energy was put in a restaurant in Boston, Massachusetts, for testing. The original weighed more than 750 pounds and cost more than $5,000. Given its bulkiness and expense, initial sales were not impressive.

In 1962, Dr. Roberta Oppenheimer perfected the world's first Underwriters Laboratories-approved microwave oven. While unsophisticated by the standards of this new century, it could prepare a 12-pound turkey in slightly less than two hours as compared to six hours in a conventional oven. With this development making international headlines, the U.S. government proceeded with plans to install the new ovens in homes and restaurants.

The U.S. Department of Health and Welfare eventually took responsibility for production of microwave ovens, while many scientists worried about the potential abuse of other nations latching onto microwave cooking. By the mid-1960s, the Soviet Union had its own microwave ovens. By the late 1960s, many more countries were producing microwave ovens of their own.

In 1972, the North Atlantic Microwave Organization (NAMO) was founded in an attempt to prevent franchised microwave ovens produced in communist countries from infringing upon models made in the Western world. NAMO also created standards for maximum power levels and radioactivity. By 1975, sales of microwave ovens outdistanced sales of gas ranges. By the 1980s, the United States and Europe were manufacturing microwave ovens in record numbers.

Microwave ovens remained a key industry segment in the late 1990s and early years of the first decade of the 2000s. According to a survey by the Harris Corp., U.S. consumers ranked the microwave among the five most important household technologies. In addition, consumers were getting more value for their money when purchasing a microwave oven in the late 1990s and the beginning of the new decade. New models of microwaves had more features and more power at nearly the same prices as earlier models. According to *Appliance* magazine's shipment statistics, 1999 shipments of household and commercial microwaves in the United States reached 11,421,900 units, up 10 percent from 1998. Consequently, microwave ovens represented the best-selling major cooking appliance. Over 90 percent of U.S. households had a microwave oven, and demand throughout the rest of the world was climbing. Worldwide microwave oven shipments were expected to climb another 3.7 percent in 2000 to reach 31 million units.

Communications During the 1990s and early years of the first decade of the 2000s, the telecommunications segment of the microwave application industry experienced expansion and consolidation. The explosive popularity of the Internet during this period drove the expansion of microwave-based telecommunications, leading many in the telecommunications industry to recognize the need for the capability to transmit large volumes of data without the use of landlines. With the newly granted right to use two-way digital signals, existing wireless cable companies took steps to move into this market by converting their systems to digital, an expensive proposition. Many of them found themselves in debt beyond their capability to maintain.

By the late 1990s, the FCC helped wireless cable operators branch out into high-speed digital data applications, including Internet access. In 2000, some of the U.S. cities that offered such access included Washington, D.C.; Las Vegas, Nevada; Lakeland, Florida; Colorado Springs, Colorado; Dallas/Fort Worth, Texas; Santa Rosa, California; New York City; Seattle, Washington; Rochester, New York; San Jose/Silicon Valley, California; and Nashua, New Hampshire. Hence, by 2000, wireless cable telecommunications providers had

garnered over 1 million subscribers in 250 U.S. systems and 5 million subscribers in 90 countries.

By 1997, a new group of products applied microwave technology to connect local area networks (LANs) at speeds of 10,000 bits per second and at distances of up to 15 miles. Companies such as Southwest Microwave, Inc. and Microwave Bypass Systems, Inc. in particular capitalized on this relatively low-risk, low-cost trend. Unfortunately, some shortcomings in using microwave technology to connect LANs exist. These include forests, which, like high-rise buildings, can obstruct communication, poor weather, and long distances, all of which can create similar problems.

At the end of the 1990s, the FCC put up for auction 986 licenses for local multipoint distribution service systems. These licenses for frequencies in the 28 GHz range opened up still more possibilities and attracted the interest of wireless entrepreneurs such as Craig McCaw, called "the father of cellular." Given the very large amount of transmission capability of these frequencies and their fiber-like reliability, the primary use of these licenses was expected to be for high speed data transmission and Internet access.

The possibilities of broadband wireless communication in the lower frequencies used by the older wireless cable operators also attracted the interest of telecom giants, goading a spate of consolidations at the brink of the new century. In 1999, Sprint Corporation, the third largest U.S. long distance company, agreed to acquire People's Choice TV, American Telecasting, Wireless Holdings, Transworld Telecommunications, Inc., and Videotron USA, all wireless cable companies. At the same time, MCI WorldCom (which became known as WorldCom in mid-2000) agreed to purchase CAI Wireless Systems and Wireless One. Besides Internet access and data transmission, these assets could be developed to enable these companies to bypass the local telephone company to reach the individual home or business for regular telephone service. In early 2000, MCI WorldCom proposed a merger with Sprint, which shareholders of both companies approved. This merger would have created a global wireless telecommunications powerhouse. However, the merger was shot down by the antitrust team at the U.S. Justice Department. The proposed merger also sparked harsh criticism from the European Commission.

When the new technology industry suffered its great collapse in 2000 and 2001, the telecommunications industry was obviously greatly affected as it touched so many other technology-related business sectors. Previous to the collapse, during the technology explosion of the late 1990s, an expected high demand for broadband access generated a great deal of optimism for the future. Plunkett Research, Ltd., the Texas-based firm that provides industry analysis and market research, reported that in 1999 and 2000, a remarkable 12 to 15 percent of all capital investments among the Standard & Poor's 500 firms was in the area of telecommunications. Opportunities seemed endless and technological possibilities almost limitless. However, the bubble burst in the early part of the new century. The repercussions were profound. Large, established companies such as AT&T and Lucent endured great financial losses and were forced to lay off a large number of their workers. Smaller companies and start-ups went out of business.

When the dust settled, however, it was believed a better structured and less reckless industry arose. Obviously the need for services still existed and continued to grow. According to Plunkett, in 2001 there were 101.7 million U.S. households with telephone service, up by 11 million since July 1992. Likewise, demand increased for telecommunications services and products such as cellular phones and Internet connections, but at a lower rate than in the boom years. Another era of growth was predicted, but it would require increased broadband access in the typical consumer home. This new era would most likely arrive, Plunkett indicated, between 2007 and 2010.

By 2002, approximately 10 million U.S. homes had cable modem access to the Internet, while 5 million were connected to digital subscriber lines (DSLs), according to Plunkett. Less homes were connected to broadband through fixed wireless or satellite methods, but it was predicted that by 2010, nearly 100 million households would have broadband access, reported Plunkett.

Plunkett indicated that an alternate technology that could help drive the new era in growth would be fixed wireless systems based on line: site microwave transmission to a special receiver installed at the consumer's home or office. Another alternate technology, said Plunkett, would be satellite broadband transmission.

Medicine By the late 1990s, medicine increasingly used microwave applications. In 1996, the Prostatron became the first microwave device to treat an enlarged prostate (benign prostatic hyperplasia) in men. Manufactured by EDAP Technomed Group, this piece of machinery uses microwaves to eradicate excess prostate tissue. Restricted to medium-sized prostate glands, the procedure usually lasts an hour and can be done on an outpatient basis with local anesthetic. The FDA has approved of this procedure, which provides people suffering from benign prostatic hyperplasia a third treatment option. While medications sometimes cause substantial side effects and surgery requires anesthesia, an extended stay at a hospital, and a longer recuperation period, the microwave therapy can often be performed in a doctor's office without side effects, an extended stay, or a long recuperation period, according to *RN*.

In the late 1970s, Augustine Cheung, a microwave engineer, was exploring possibilities in microwave hyperthermia (heat therapy) to eventually cure cancer. Undeterred by the lack of research funds, he started Cheung Laboratories in the early 1990s to sell microwave hyperthermia systems. Even though his company experienced a $1.3 million loss on revenues of $157,618 in 1995, Cheung remained committed to his own original purpose, encouraged by studies that indicated a 90 percent response rate in applying extreme heat to destroy cancerous cells. The side effects caused by burning surrounding tissue, however, often outweighed the technology's benefits. To eliminate such side effects, Cheung began applying an adaptive focusing technique called adaptive phased array, developed by the Massachusetts Institute of Technology.

A third medical microwave application in the 1990s was for dissolving varicose veins. In 1996, Dynamic Associates Inc., a holding company that contains two subsidiaries—P & H Laboratories Inc. and Microwave Medical Corp.—owned the patent for a technology in which a metal wand is employed to focus microwave energy on varicose veins. The procedure disintegrates the tissue, then collapses the vein. It is generally less painful than the more established practice of relying on a needle to insert a saline or acidic solution in the vein.

Microwave technology was also used in the late 1990s to treat menorrhagia, a form of abnormal uterine bleeding. A *Lancet* article described a study in which microwave therapy was compared to laser, diathermy, and radio frequency electromagnetic waves. With the latter three therapies, the failure rate ranged from 19 to 56 percent and many complications ensued. By contrast, microwave therapy achieved an 83 percent success rate six months after treatment. In terms of safety, microwave proved superior to the other therapies, and medical staff found it easy to learn and perform.

In the mid-1990s, Drs. Theodore and Wendy Guo, both employed by Potomac Research Inc., received a patent for microwave imaging technology that could eventually replace the much more expensive CT scans and magnetic resonance imaging (MRI). The National Institutes of Health and the U.S. Department of Energy have funded some of Potomac Research's efforts. Until the mid-1980s, microwaves, with relatively massive wavelengths, were considered ineffective for probing the human body. Since X-rays and CT scans had shorter wavelengths, they were the preferred technology of choice. After the Guos helped to produce an algorithm to decipher microwaves' images, however, a new microwave application seemed imminent.

By 2000, microwave therapy emerged as a possible long-term cure for those suffering from symptoms of hepatitis called hepatocellular carcinoma. Researchers at

Ehime University's School of Medicine in Japan conducted a study that indicated "microwave coagulation therapy can cure some patients with multiple bipolar hepatocellular cancer," according to Charles Henderson in *Hepatitis Weekly*. He reported that after one patient's tumors were removed with microwave therapy, none had recurred four years later.

In the early part of the first decade of the twenty-first century, clinical trials were being conducted that demonstrated potentially successful applications of microwave radiation and microwave thermal therapy in the treatment of breast and prostate cancer. In 2001, researchers studied the viability of using microwave radiation focused externally on the breast to kill tumor cells. The microwave radiation would be delivered before lumpectomy and radiation therapy to reduce the need for additional surgery. Results from clinical trials proved promising as most of the patients treated with the microwave heat therapy showed significant tumor necrosis before lumpectomy. The technology for the treatment was invented by Dr. Alan J. Fenn, a senior staff member at MIT Lincoln Laboratory. Fenn originally researched the technology for use in missile detection. He later realized that, in theory, the technology also could serve as a useful weapon in the war against cancer. Celsion Corporation licensed the technology from MIT, then developed a clinical thermotherapy system and funded clinical studies.

In the same year, studies involving interstitial microwave thermal therapy indicated that the technology could be a safe and effective treatment for prostate cancer. Researchers at the Ontario Cancer Institute in Toronto evaluated the safety and efficacy of microwave therapy in 25 patients with prostate cancer in whom external beam radiation had failed. The thermal therapy was delivered through five antennae inserted percutaneously (through the skin) under ultrasound guidance and offered promising results.

General Microwave technology was being employed by the manufacturing sector to cure paint film on newly manufactured products. This involved special lamps that generated high-intensity ultraviolet (UV) light. Microwave UV lamps were an alternative to classic arc lamps, and had a number of advantages, including the ability to start almost instantly and no need to maintain an idle power level. Unlike the metal reflectors used in other lamps, microwave UV lamps employed borosilicate glass reflectors that were transparent to microwaves and reduced the need for waveguides to direct energy to the bulb, according to the *Asia Pacific Coatings Journal*. Glass also provided other advantages, including the ability to use reflectors of different shapes "without influencing the tuning of the microwave cavity and coupling of the microwave field to the bulb."

The middle part of the first decade of the 2000s also saw the emergence of WiMAX (Worldwide Interoperability for Microwave Access). WiMAX (also known as 4G, or "fourth generation") is a wireless Internet broadband technology similar to Wi-Fi but with a much greater range. WiMAX can provide wireless data over long distances in a variety of different ways, ranging from point to point links to full mobile cellular type access, and it allows for very high-speed Internet access from laptops, phones, or other mobile devices over greater distances than previous technologies. WiMAX promises a data transfer speed of as much as 2 to 4 mbps (megabits per second) as compared to current 0.4 and 0.7 mbps wireless speeds. The disadvantage of WiMAX over Wi-Fi, however, is that WiMAX networks require a dedicated, licensed wireless spectrum in the 2.5GHz band, which is expensive. However, many companies were considering WiMAX for "last mile" connectivity at high data rates, which was expected to result in lower pricing for customers due to competition. Companies planning to offer the service through mobile phones beginning in 2008 included Sprint Nextel, Nokia, and Motorola. Other devices besides phones and the Internet with the potential to benefit from WiMAX included digital cameras, video players, and even automobiles.

Of the myriad of uses of microwaves in the early twenty-first century, another application that greatly affected consumers was the cell phone. According to Wikipedia, in the United Kingdom there are more cell phones than people, and experts predict there will be 400 million cell phone users in China by 2008. The highest mobile phone penetration rate in the world is attributed to Luxembourg, with 164 percent as of December 2005. Hong Kong's penetration rate was 117 percent in September 2004, and the Cellular Telecommunications and Internet Association estimated there were 219 millon cell phone subscribers in the United States in 2006. Worldwide, about 80 percent of the population has mobile phone coverage, and this number is expected to be 90 percent by 2010. India boasts the most growth numerically, adding 6 million cell phones a month in 2006.

At the start of the twenty-first century, many other applications of microwave technology were emerging. For example, a group of scientists at Boston-based Invent Resources were working on such innovations as a microwave clothes dryer that tackles metal zippers and buttons and a microwave cooking device that allows for a crispier texture.

A Cornell University study demonstrated how moisture, heating rate, and food's porosity interact during microwave cooking. By understanding these interactions, scientists hope they can improve microwave technology to produce tastier foods. Ashim Datta, an associate professor of agricultural and biological engineering at Cornell, explained, "The microwave is grossly underused. Up until now, we haven't really understood much of the physics that occur during the microwave processing of food. This research shows us the quantitative physics as to why microwave food can be soggy and sometimes unappealing and also why sometimes excessive amounts of moisture can be lost."

According to Datta, previous research on microwave technology did not calculate the interrelationship between porosity and the internal pressures that develop because of evaporation of water inside food. With the impact of internal pressure, much more moisture reaches the food's surface, while air inside a microwave oven stays at room temperature. This sometimes causes sogginess in foods. "Through understanding the true physics of microwave cooking, companies can use this information to provide better tasting and better texture of food, as well as to provide more convenience to consumers by promoting increased use of microwave cooking," said Datta.

In 1999, General Electric Co. introduced a new method of browning and achieving crispier food via the microwave: the Advantium, which featured a 950-watt microwave coupled with 4,500-watt halogen bulbs. This combination not only browned food but also cooked it quickly. The Advantium was also preprogrammed to cook more than 100 recipes.

Packaging for microwavable meals was increasingly important in the early to middle of the first decade of the 2000s. The most sophisticated packaging used susceptors (surface layers) to minimize the flaws of microwave cooking. These devices consisted of a plastic film metalized usually with aluminum and laminated to paper or paperboard. They often made foods crispier by improving their texture. Since producers of packaging materials continually explore methods to improve the design of susceptors, monitoring of high-temperature materials is extremely important.

In 1998, Microwave Science LLC, a Georgia software company, received a patent for a system that would allow microwave ovens to prepare food to consistent standards. This system used software and sensors in the oven that would enable the user to input simple codes that would adjust the oven during cooking to match the actual conditions of voltage, altitude, type of food, and other factors.

Developers also created more portable microwaves at the turn of the century. For example, Samsung rolled out its battery-operated microwave oven in 2000 for the trucking, recreational vehicle, and marine markets.

Sharp Corp. launched a trendier innovation in microwave oven technology in Japan: the Internet-ready microwave, which connects to a computer through a special adapter and enables users to locate recipes on Sharp's Web site. The oven's video display then shows the recipe and the oven automatically adjusts itself for the preparation of the selected dish.

CURRENT CONDITIONS

In May 2009, market research firm Infonetics Research released its *Microwave Equipment: Market Size, Market Share, and Forecast* report. Among other things, the report tracked access and backhaul/transport PDH/SDH microwave equipment and Ethernet and dual Ethernet/TDM microwave equipment. Infonetics reported that worldwide microwave equipment sales hit $4.9 billion in 2008, up 23 percent from the previous year. Mobile operators continued to invest in mobile backhaul to accommodate rapidly rising mobile broadband traffic (the primary driver behind microwave equipment market growth)

In 2009, the big trend in the microwave equipment market was the transition from TDM to Ethernet. Microwave enables mobile operators to make phased upgrades of their backhaul networks from TDM-only to hybrid TDM/Ethernet systems and then to packet-based all-Ethernet solutions in the future. According to Infonetics, this offers a scaleable and cost-effective way to manage the escalating bandwidth demands caused by the mobile broadband boom and future 4G deployments. Typically, operators will keep legacy TDM microwave for another 5 to 10 years to support 2G/3G voice while they deploy Ethernet for growing volumes of data traffic, the report noted.

Fred Schindler, chairman of IMS 2009 and director of RF Micro Devices, in an interview published in the June 2009 issue of *Wireless Design and Development Asia,* was asked about new trends in the microwave industry. Schindler said that commercial applications such as wireless communications and GPS were having more impact on the industry than before because of new diversification of applications as more opportunities to use RF and microwave technologies came to market. This included areas such as RFID, automotive radar, electronic toll collections, and automated meter reading, creating many opportunities in the industry. Schindler also mentioned the growing importance of Asia to the market.

In its December 2009 issue, *Microwave Journal* noted that The Strategy Analytics RF & Wireless Component market research service predicted that the market for power amplifiers (PA) in cellphones and related mobile devices would grow to $2.8 billion over the next five years. In its report, "Cellular PA Forecast 2009 to 2014," it attributed this in part to the continued spread beyond conventional handsets into notebook and netbook computers, and machine-to-machine systems such as automatic meter readers.

INDUSTRY LEADERS

According to Infonetics Research, Ericsson and NEC were neck-and-neck battling for the lead in the fast growing microwave equipment market in 2008. Ericsson reported full year revenues for 2008 growing by 11 percent to SEK 208.9 billion. Converesely, NEC reported that its revenues dropped 8.7 per cent to 4.22 trillion yen ($46.4 billion) and the company posted a net loss of 296.6 billion yen ($3 billion), compared to a tiny profit of 22.7 billion yen in fiscal 2007.

Agilent Technologies Inc. Based in Palo Alto, California, Agilent Technologies Inc. was a leader in the microwave industry during the middle of the first decade of the 2000s. A leading manufacturer of scientific equipment and instruments, Agilent's products in the microwave and RF sector helped customers to "create designs, generate waveforms, measure and analyze signals, and build systems for a wide range of applications," according to the company. Its range of microwave and radio frequency (RF) product offerings included spectrum analyzers, signal generators, network analyzers, signal source analyzers, electronic design automation software, microwave and RF frequency counters, power meters and power sensors, impedance analyzers, and a host of microwave and RF test accessories. In July 2009, Agilent announced it would acquire Varian Inc. for $1.5 billion. Varian had annual revenue of $1 billion in its fiscal year 2008. Meanwhile, Agilent report $5.8 billion in sales 2008 and employed more than 20,000 workers.

L-3 Communications Holdings Inc. New York-based L-3 Communications was another industry leader, supplying both custom and commercial microwave and RF components, instruments, and assemblies. With 59,500 employees, L-3 served U.S. Government intelligence agencies, the Department of Defense, and the Department of Homeland Security, as well as clients in the aerospace, commercial telecommunications, and wireless markets. The company offered products used for microwave and telemetry applications, as well as surveillance and reconnaissance, intelligence, avionics, secure communications, and space and navigation. According to L-3, it provides "microwave vacuum electron devices and power modules for manned and unmanned airborne radars, F-14, F-16, Predator and Global Hawk platforms, and for missile applications for the AMRAAM and Patriot."

RESEARCH AND TECHNOLOGY

In an interview published in the June 2009 issue of *Wireless Design and Development Asia,* Fred Schindler, chairman of IMS 2009 and director of RF Micro Devices, cited metamaterials, which in the extreme are hyped for potential cloaking properties, as flagships of the future. Gallium Nitride (GaN) was also a hot topic with a number of very impressive power amplifier results showing very high power levels, he said. A secondary technology trend of the microwave market in 2009 was the transition from point-to-point (P2P) to point-to-multipoint (P2MP) architectures, which further enabled cost-saving benefits.

Infonetics Research reported in May 2009 that microwave was increasingly used as an access technology in developing countries where there were viable wireline access alternatives for enterprises and organizations with growing bandwidth needs.

CHA Corp. was developing microwave technology that removed harmful pollutants from both the air and water. According to the March 2004 *Journal of Environmental Engineering,* the company's process for cleaning the air works by using microwave energy to regenerate adsorbents (solid substances that absorb another substance) that, as part of a fume hood exhaust system, have been saturated with pollutants, including non-chlorinated and chlorinated volatile organic compounds (VOCs). According to the journal, these compounds are common at both military and industrial sites. The company's microwave air purification process has been used at air force bases to remove harmful gasses and other elements from the air, and also during remediation projects to remove substances from extracted soil vapor. Because of successful demonstrations and technological advancements, CHA hoped to commercialize its air purification technology during the last half of the first decade of the 2000s.

Environmental Risks in Telecommunications From the mid-1970s to the mid-1990s, there were thousands of journal articles and research studies on the subject of the correlation between electromagnetic field (EMF) exposure and cancer in human beings. Although the research data were not conclusive, several studies in different countries indicate the possibility that electromagnetic field (EMF) exposure may at least contribute to some cancers in humans. The studies that explore a possible link between cancer and EMF exposure are entirely different from other studies that focus on whether the microwave radiation can contribute to cancer. According to the Electromagnetic Energy Association, there were more than 100,000 microwave radio stations in the United States in the mid-1990s. Harmful exposure of the public and the worker to microwave energy from these sources was extremely low. The output power of the average transmitter employed for microwave radio is fairly comparable to that of a citizens band radio.

By the early 1980s, U.S. measurements done in close proximity to microwave towers and on the rooftops of buildings near microwave antennas indicated a very positive scenario. Even in the most troubling cases, the recorded microwave levels were thousands of times below exposure limits set by the American National Standards Institute and the National Committee on Radiation Protection. There are several epidemiological studies, however, of people who have been exposed to above average levels of radio frequency/microwave radiation in their jobs. Through their medical records and other health-related data, researchers have found some correlation between high radiation exposure and physical symptoms such as heart disease, cancer, birth abnormalities, and miscarriages. To what extent these workers' problems are due to radiation exposure or to other factors (such as work or stress), however, is not always easy to ascertain.

With the worldwide popularity of cellular telephones in the 1990s, scientists began studying whether the radioactive effects of these devices actually posed a health threat to users. In 1994 Australian researchers concluded from their experiments that cancer-susceptible mice that had been exposed to cellular phones' radio frequency/microwave radiation experienced two times the number of cancers as other mice. Since the Australian cellular phone industry participated in this study and had not anticipated its disturbing results, other scientists praised the validity of the study, many of them following up on its results. In the late 1990s, however, it was still not known whether the study's results and conclusion are applicable to the health of humans.

In 1995, Debbra Wright, a 42-year-old mother of three children and an employee of Bell Atlantic Mobile, sued Motorola, Inc., claiming that the cell phones she had used since the late 1980s had caused a brain tumor. The cancer, diagnosed in 1993, was close to her left ear. While at the time there were at least eight other lawsuits seeking to tie cellular phones to cancer, *Microwave News* claimed Wright's was reportedly the first by a service provider employee.

By 2000, concerns about cell phone use increased as more than 80 million Americans used the devices as their primary form of communication. That number jumped to 97 million by 2001. In response, the Cellular Telecommunications Industry Association formed Wireless Technology Research (WTR) to study the effects of cellular phones. Following its research, WTR said it found several health problems related to radiation exposure due to phone use. At the time, the FDA said it knew of no proven ill effects of cellular phone use. The WTR study was one of many conducted on the dangers of cell phone use. However, the studies have only increased and not concluded the debate.

Nevertheless, growing evidence suggested that the perceived danger of cellular phones was indeed real. Studies involving mice indicated an increase in cancer cells as well as memory loss. Other studies, including several conducted by the FDA, indicate that there is no strong evidence that suggests that cell phone use negatively impacts users' health. The FDA itself admitted it couldn't say whether cellular phones are safe or not, but it agreed that studies should continue.

A study performed in Denmark and released in 2001 tracked the health of 420,000 Danish cell phone users and found no sign the phones increase the risk of cancer. The study, published in the *Journal of the National Cancer Institute,* was the largest one ever performed to date to look at the issue. The researchers concluded that cell phone users are no more likely than anyone else to suffer the kind of cancers that critics were concerned about, including brain or nervous system cancers, leukemia or salivary gland tumors. Around the same time, two smaller U.S. studies found no cancer risk, either. In 2007 a Japanese study concluded that radio-frequency radiation from base stations does not cause damage to human cells, and a European study published in the *International Journal of Cancer* did not find a link between cell phone use and the risk of glioma, a type of brain cancer. However, that study did find a 40 percent increased tumor risk for long-term cell phone subscribers. In view of the mixed results and ongoing controversy, no government agency has been willing to go on record as saying that without question the devices are completely safe. The only danger that everyone seems to agree on is that cell phone use while driving can cause accidents.

While many environmental concerns about microwave energy have not been completely resolved, many if not most of its applications have been proven reasonably safe. While microwave technology's most traditional purposes revolved around heating and drying, some of its most innovative uses have been in telecommunications and medicine.

BIBLIOGRAPHY

"Agilent Had Net Revenues of $5.8 billion in fiscal 2008." February 2009. Available at http://www.investor.agilent.com

"Agilent Technologies to Acquire Varian Inc. for $1.5 Billion." 27 July 2009. Available from http://www.agilent.com/about/newsroom/presrel/2009/27jul-gp09016.html.

Browne, Jack. "Frequency Synthesizers Fit Many Modular Formats." *Microwaves & RF,* March 2007.

Cha, Chang Yul, et al. "Microwave Technology for Treatment of Fume Hood Exhaust." *Journal of Environmental Engineering,* March 2004.

"Ericsson Revenues Grow 11 Percent, Net Profit Drops 48%." 21 January 2009. Available from http://www.telecompaper.com/news/article.aspx?cid=654222.

Gross, Grant. "Government Policies Add to Japan's Broadband Success." IDG News Service, 4 April 2007. Available from http://www.networkworld.com/.

Higgins, Kevin T. "Safe, Effective Microwave Cooking." *Food Engineering,* June 2004.

"Hoover's Company Capsules." *Hoover's Online.* 15 April 2007. Available from http://www.hoovers.com.

Las Marias, Stephen. "IMS 2009 to Highlight Latest RF/ Microwave Technologies, Applications and Trends." *Wireless Design and Development Asia* June 2009.

Maitland, Dr. John. "From Pizza to Paint." *Asia Pacific Coatings Journal,* August 2004.

"Mobile to the Max: New Broadband Technology Foreshadows Content Evolution." *Billboard,* 14 April 2007.

Morgan, Timothy Prickett. "Hitachi Scores Largest Loss in Japanese Manufacturing History; NEC Optimistic." *Financial News,* 12 May 2009.

"MRC Link HD Microwave Systems Get Presidents Day Workout." *Broadcast Engineering,* 15 March 2007.

"OECD Broadband Statistics to December 2006." Organisation for Economic Co-operation and Development, 2007. Available from http://www.oecd.org/.

"Oxymoron or Not, Mobile Broadband Is Hot." *CT Reports,* 13 April 2007.

"RFID Growth Strong." *Purchasing,* 15 February 2007.

Rosen, Christine. "Our Cell Phones, Ourselves." *The New Atlantis,* Summer 2004.

Silva, Jeffrey. "Pair of Health Studies Show Mixed Results." *RCR Wireless News,* 29 January 2007.

"United States Broadband Statistics Update." Internet World Stats, 12 April 2007. Available from www.internetworldstats.com/.

"Warp-Speed Wireless." *Popular Science,* May 2007.

Webb, Richard. "Microwave Equipment Market Hits $4.9 billion in 2008, Led by Ericsson and NEC." Press Release, Infonetics Research. 14 May 2009.

"What's New?—Microwaves." *Catering Update,* December 2003.

Wilson, J.R. "RF and Microwave Industry Struggles to Meet the High Demands of the Military." *Military & Aerospace Electronics,* August 2004.

MINIMALLY INVASIVE TECHNOLOGIES

SIC CODE(S)

3845

8011

INDUSTRY SNAPSHOT

Minimally invasive technologies include a wide array of medical devices designed to perform complex surgeries that forego traditional medical procedures that rely on massive incisions. Also called minimal access or keyhole surgery, minimally invasive surgery (MIS) has proven successful in a wide range of operations, from the removal of gall bladders—one of its most common procedures—to kidney transplants, and new applications for these technologies were being found at an increasing rate. Among doctors who routinely use minimally invasive technologies are gastroenterologists (a doctor who specializes in digestive diseases), internists, gynecologists, cardiovascular surgeons, plastic and reconstructive surgeons, orthopedic surgeons, and veterinarians.

Some of the equipment used in minimally invasive surgeries consists of guide wires, which connect the surgical devices with their operators and help guide the instruments to their proper location; steerable catheters, soft-tipped flexible tubes designed to offer greater maneuverability within the body; sutures, the tiny thread-like materials used to sew together small incisions; micro-sized needles, staplers, scissors, and similar surgical tools; and supplemental equipment such as monitors, cables, lighting equipment, and computer consoles. Perhaps the most developed submarket, however, is that of endoscopes. An endoscope is a medical instrument, typically a hollow tube, which can be either rigid or flexible, with a tiny video camera inside or with light-transmitting glass fibers, that is inserted through a natural body opening and allows a live picture of the inside of a patient's organ to be viewed and evaluated in the operating room during surgery.

By making two small holes in the patient's body, rather than the large incisions used in traditional open surgery, minimally invasive surgeons greatly simplify the procedure. In one hole, they insert the endoscope, and they maneuver their tiny medical instruments in the other. The internal images are projected and magnified by the endoscope onto an operating room video screen, where doctors monitor progress and their manipulation of the instruments. This high-tech procedure offers a number of advantages to patients, particularly the speed of recovery time, since patients need not heal from large incisions. In addition, minimally invasive surgery (MIS) drastically reduces patient pain and scarring, cost of surgery, and post-surgical complication.

ORGANIZATION AND STRUCTURE

In the early stage of development of minimally invasive technologies, the competition revolved primarily around bringing out new tools, systems, and equipment that simply make operations easier for surgeons to perform while keeping cumbersome costs to a minimum. By the early years of the first decade of the twenty-first century, most equipment was still fairly expensive and primitive, greatly limiting minimally invasive surgery's applicability over a wide range of conditions. Still, competition in this area was increasing, as more open surgeries were converted to MIS procedures. The use of minimally invasive surgery continued to grow during the middle years of the decade. In March 2006, the *The New York Times*

Minimally Invasive Surgeries, by Type	
Cardio-thoracic	70%
Orthopedic	12%
Gastrointestinal	10%
Gynecologic	3%
Miscellaneous	5%

SOURCE: BCC Research, 2009.

reported that approximately 4.4 million Americans undergo laparoscopic (located within the abdomen or pelvic cavity) procedures alone each year. Surgeons in a variety of medical specialties were using the approach, when appropriate, instead of traditional surgical techniques. In addition, advancements in minimally invasive surgery allowed it to be used in a widening array of medical applications.

In the middle of the first decade of the 2000s, advancements were allowing the technology to be used for spinal surgery and neurosurgery (surgery on the brain, spinal cord, nervous system), in addition to minute tasks such as reconnecting ligaments in the knee, operating on infected sinuses, performing tubal ligation (female sterilization by surgically tying a woman's fallopian tubes, which carry eggs from ovaries to uterus or womb), repairing heart valves, and removing gall bladders. Companies sell their equipment to hospitals and research laboratories by emphasizing not only the efficiency of the operating process itself, but also the savings in administrative and logistic costs as well.

The leading manufacturers of minimally invasive technologies are either large, multinational firms (often specializing in both medical and optical instruments) or smaller specialty companies engaged in partnerships with larger medical and diagnostic firms. Johnson & Johnson's subsidiary Ethicon Endo-Surgery has been a long-time market leader, and so has Tyco International's United States Surgical Corp. Multinational Japanese firms Olympus Optical Co., Inc. and Fuji Photo Optical Co., Ltd. (also known as Fujinon) have produced many of the top-selling endoscopes. These companies enjoy the built-in credibility of their established lines of scientific instruments as well as their expertise in camera equipment, research that can easily be applied to endoscopic technology. Other significant players in the industry include Boston Scientific Corporation, Endoscopic Technologies, Inc., and endoscopy pioneer Karl Storz GmbH & Co.

Endoscopy Proves Flexible Endoscopes have been adapted to enter many regions of the body that were previously accessible only via large incisions. Endoscopy, which literally means looking inside, can be performed

for diagnostic or therapeutic reasons. These might include evaluating a source of pain, taking biopsies, removing foreign bodies and abnormal growths, arresting bleeding, reshaping or reconstructing tissue, and placing tubes or stents.

Endoscopes may be either rigid or flexible. Rigid endoscopes contain a solid rod lens developed by Harold Hopkins, a physicist, who was largely responsible for making modern medical endoscopy a practical reality. Flexible endoscopes use a fiber-optic bundle, also developed by Hopkins, which maneuvers around curves and bends but provides poorer resolution than the solid rod lens. The most common endoscopes, named after the body part interior they examine, are called colonoscopes (entire colon and rectum), cystoscopes (bladder and urethra), fiberscopes (fiber-optic endoscope), gastroscopes (stomach), hysteroscopes (cervix and uterus), laparoscopes (abdomen, pelvis), sigmoidoscopes (sigmoid colon area), peritoneoscopes (abdominal, pelvic), and proctosigmoidoscopes (anus, rectum, colon).

Although minimally invasive surgery (MIS) is considered the "gold standard" in diagnosing and treating some diseases, it is nonetheless still an invasive technique that carries risks and requires a level of training that is not yet standardized. Because the manual and visual skills required for these procedures can be very different from those required for conventional surgery, the surgeon's skill and experience, as well as careful patient selection, are especially important in determining a successful outcome.

According to a memo in *Health Care Strategic Management,* several factors impact endoscopy growth. A growing population of older Americans will be more likely to require medical procedures using endoscopes for virtually all medical specialties. Additionally, Medicare and managed health care organizations have experienced savings resulting from reduced recovery time and related costs.

BACKGROUND AND DEVELOPMENT

Minimally invasive technology traces its roots back to the earliest endoscopes, employed in the early twentieth century, that were basically small telescopes with a light on the front end through which doctors peered. The widespread use of endoscopy was challenged by determining how to safely get enough light into a body cavity and how to transmit realistic visual images. These considerations served to limit the initial scope of application for endoscopic procedures and many old-school physicians remained skeptical. Karl Storz is recognized as the father of cold light endoscopy, developed in the 1960s, which made incandescent bulb mounting obsolete. Storz's discovery opened the door for capturing diagnostic findings in images. He also built the first extracorporeal (outside the body) electronic flash. Eventually, as the hardware developed, so did the attitudes of the collective medical community, who eventually came to accept the technology for diagnostic and therapeutic application.

In 1988, the field finally got onto its present course when doctors first used a tiny endoscopic camera and tiny medical tools to remove a gall bladder, after which the use of MIS became more accepted. Though the use of the procedure spread quickly, the established medical community remained slow to accept it. A meeting of leading professionals called by the National Institutes of Health (NIH) in 1992 resulted in a rather hesitant approval for laparoscopic invasive surgery. A statement issued still held that traditional, open surgery "remains a standard against which new treatments should be judged." Moreover, despite the boom in demand in the late 1980s and early 1990s, the onset of managed care pushed pricing considerations to the forefront, thus holding industry growth in check as firms struggled to get their latest products to the market at affordable prices and drove out many smaller competitors in the process.

Because of such economic pressures, claims were made asserting the superiority of some MIS techniques that were later disproved by long term studies. For example, in the rush to offer laparoscopic gall bladder removals in the early 1990s, surgeons attempted the procedures after attending a weekend course, and numerous complications occurred as a consequence of inadequate training. Minimally invasive appendectomies did not reduce the length of hospital stays or complications, and many arthroscopic (endoscopic examination of the interior of a joint) orthopedic procedures continued to be less successful than their traditional open surgery equivalents.

However, as medical schools began adding MIS procedures to their clinical programs, the level of skill and experience in the medical community greatly changed in the 1990s. In 1997, the American Gastroenterological Association (AGA) issued a policy statement to guide hospitals in making decisions about extending endoscopic surgery privileges to physicians. In the late 1990s, many metropolitan hospitals and clinics were well equipped with both hardware and knowledgeable professionals who were well seasoned in multiple areas of MIS.

Since minimally invasive technology exploded in the early 1990s, the amount of equipment required to support it turned operating rooms into obstacle courses of computers, monitors, lighting equipment, and other gadgetry. In large part, this was due to hospitals adding minimally invasive technologies piecemeal to their facilities as the equipment became available, rather than overhauling hospital infrastructure from the start to more easily and efficiently integrate the new equipment.

In order to reduce the crowding and clutter, some hospitals began to take ambitious steps toward constructing entirely new operating facilities to seamlessly integrate the array of minimally invasive medical technologies. One of the most advanced facilities was opened at ValleyCare Medical Center in Pleasanton, California, in the summer of 2000. This MIS center highlighted the added benefit of integration, which is the ability to access medical records, files, and data, both from inside the hospital and across networks outside the hospital, for use and referral right inside the operating room. This convenient access for doctors can save valuable time during an operation, while contributing to the overall efficiency of the hospital. The technology facilitates research and educational procedures as well, because the procedures can be viewed by teleconference in remote locations, providing surgeons and students with a firsthand look inside the operating room irrespective of location.

On the cutting edge of MIS technologies in 2000 was robotic surgery employing highly sensitive surgical consoles and three-dimensional (3-D) imaging. The U.S. Food and Drug Administration (FDA) gave approval in the summer of 2000 to a system developed by Mountain View, California-based Intuitive Surgical Devices Inc. that was immediately used to remove a gall bladder. The system builds on the science of "haptics," derived from the Greek word meaning "to touch," which builds the sense of feeling into computer consoles. Since one of the biggest drawbacks of MIS surgery was the loss of the surgeon's physical contact with the patient's organs, developers were hopeful that such technology could breathe new life into MIS. Robotic MIS devices coupled with non-invasive imaging that shows tissue in three dimensions allowed surgeons to attempt intricate procedures in previously inaccessible places and to target tissue more accurately. In addition, streamlined approval procedures for new medical devices made it easier for manufacturers to develop and bring new products to market in step with the pace of technological changes.

One potentially valuable haptics device that was under development early in the first decade of the 2000s was the CyberGlove, engineered by Dr. Mark Cutkosky of Stanford University's Dexterous Manipulation Lab. The CyberGlove is linked to a robotic arm that mimics the user's movements. The arm in turn returns a tactile sensation to the fingers. While the device is still fairly primitive—it will take much stronger impulses to convince the fingers they are actually feeling objects during an operation—such technology promised to greatly enhance the surgeon's remote command of the operating procedure and room.

Some see such developments as inevitably moving toward surgical practices in which the surgeon is in fact several hundred miles away from the operating table, controlling the robotic surgical tools by remote control. While such prospects make some observers uneasy, most analysts agree that while such projections may be partly true, it is more likely that only the most difficult and specialized procedures will be performed by doctors from afar, while more basic work will be the jurisdiction of a doctor in the operating room. Thus, the patient will not be entirely separated from a competent surgeon.

Another promising application of endoscopic technology was the treatment known as endoscopic photodynamic therapy, which technically involves the use of light-activated chemotherapeutic reactions to destroy abnormal tissue. In trial applications during the late 1990s, it was used to halt, and in some cases cure, early gastrointestinal cancers. Despite some initial problems with systemic photosensitization (untoward patient reaction), the future of endoscopic photodynamic therapy in contrast with the more conventional thermal (heat) laser therapy remained promising.

In April 1999, Endoscopic Technologies, Inc. (ESTECH), a company less than three years old, received a major U.S. patent for its "multichannel catheter," to be used in minimally invasive cardiac surgery. Technically referred to in the field as a "remote access perfusion (RAP)" cannula, it took the place of the several catheters previously needed in any cardiac surgery. Prior to RAP, several different catheters and multiple incisions were needed to perform the separate but simultaneous functions of delivering oxygenated blood to the body, stopping blood flow to the heart with a balloon, and delivering drugs to the heart. RAP allows all of these procedures to be done, using a single, easily-inserted catheter, without opening up the chest. All that is needed are small "window" incisions through the ribs. These permit remote access approaches including direct aortic (main artery of the heart), femoral (thigh), sub-xiphoid (below the breastbone), or other trans-thoracic (chest) approaches.

By the beginning of the twenty-first century, use of minimally invasive technologies in cosmetic surgery, especially for the brow and eye area of the face as well as for breast augmentation, was considered state-of-the-art technology, and demand for such procedures was growing steadily. Again, the advantages were that endoscopic surgery offered faster healing, less surgical invasiveness, and was less harmful to surrounding tissue, all of which are of particular concern for patients undergoing cosmetic surgery. For example, an MIS brow lift requires just a few half-inch incisions in the scalp behind the hairline rather than larger incisions directly on the face in the brow area. After threading an endoscopic tube through one of the small incisions, the tiny instruments are inserted in another incision. Through remote viewing on a monitor, the surgeon then

pulls brow muscle and tissue taut, splices them internally, and exits.

Another growing application of MIS was in the area of organ transplants. Minimally invasive technology had advanced from simple exploratory laparoscopy followed by conventional surgery to actual surgical intervention during laparoscopy. This greatly reduced patient risk. In 2000, Canadian doctors performed a successful MIS kidney transplant on a married couple, with healing times cut to a matter of days. Kidney transplants previously required 12- to 18-inch surgical incisions through the abdominal muscles of the donor. With laparoscopic surgery, a small incision is made above the navel (where the kidney is to be channeled out), and four small holes are also made into the skin to insert the laparoscope and surgical instruments.

The MIS procedure called laparoscopic gastric bypass was developed for obese individuals who exceeded their ideal weight by 100 pounds or more. The procedure gained popularity after celebrities spoke favorably about it. In May 2002, a new Bariatric Surgical Weight Loss Program was launched at Sound Shore Medical Center in Westchester County, New York. The specially trained team there stressed that education before and after surgery enhanced success ratios.

A number of factors kept the growth of minimally invasive technology in check. Many surgeons remained resistant to using it, insisting that hands-on surgery of the kind in which they were trained was both practically and ethically superior. This was most true in the general surgery arena, in which surgical skills were the most lacking, since most early MIS products were geared toward specific procedures. In addition, the high costs of many MIS systems limited their marketing possibilities. Also, research and development created a long pipeline, and thus companies had to wait several years to realize profits from new products—a wait that not all companies were willing or able to withstand.

While at the Minimal Access Surgical Unit of the Imperial College School of Medicine at St. Mary's of London, Dr. Nick Taffinder conducted an in-depth evaluation of the Surgical Vision 3-D system. "You are typically looking at a flat TV monitor and operating a very thin instrument through very small holes. Those factors alone make it complex. Working in a three-dimensional space makes it very difficult," he explained.

One of the drawbacks to laparoscopy is the time required for proper training. Responding to the need for greater training of surgical residents, Ethicon Endo-Surgery introduced an interactive software and Web-linked curriculum entitled "Laparoscopy 101: A Resource for Resident Education." The curriculum was designed to assist hospitals in teaching the necessary skills and knowledge to residents.

In addition, in 2003, the Residency Review Committee of the American Medical Association began requiring different standards for documentation of training, which the curriculum generated automatically. The curriculum also included a recommended laboratory component for hands-on training in laparoscopic techniques.

Even experienced surgeons have difficulty with laparoscopic techniques. While patient injuries happen in less than 1 percent of surgeries, the injuries that do occur are largely due to a visual misperception. As scientific expert and former equipment designer Donald Kaplan told *The New York Times,* "It's like trying to tie a bow tie in the mirror."

Patient safety is a major concern related to laparoscopic surgery. A Hoover's Online article on new technologies explained that the risk is greater because the instrument is long, and stray current may be out of the surgeon's view. Encision of Boulder, Colorado, offered tools with an "active electrode monitoring" system to eliminate any risk of stray electrosurgical burns. Some hospital insurers reportedly offer a 10 percent discount to sites utilizing the system and instruments, believing that its use can prevent potential lawsuits.

While severe complications related to minimally invasive procedures were uncommon, some surgeons indicated that the number of accidental burns caused by faulty cutting wands was much higher than the number of reported cases. In the March 17, 2006, issue of *The New York Times,* one surgeon estimated that as many as 10,000 injuries and some 100 deaths result from laparoscopic surgery each year. Injuries of this kind are often undetected and cause problems for patients after surgery. One example is a small hole in a patient's colon that allows harmful bacteria to escape into the rest of the body. For this reason, many within the industry were calling for hospitals to purchase active electrode monitoring devices that caused equipment to turn off in the event of a short or electrical malfunction. However, some equipment companies argued that such devices were unnecessary, indicating that accidents often result from equipment that is overused. Heading into the late years of the twenty-first century's first decade, it appeared that this patient safety issue would continue to be on the health care industry's radar.

Orthopedics was one area where gradual progress was being made. Many orthopedic surgeons were using arthroscopes—thin, flexible fiber-optic scopes introduced into a joint space through a small incision to conduct diagnostic and/or treatment procedures—to perform spinal surgeries, including the removal of herniated disks. Total joint procedures were another emerging area within the orthopedic realm. One example is the "quad-sparing" knee replacement, in which surgeons avoid cutting into a patient's quadriceps tendon, thereby improving recovery time and range of motion and reducing postoperative pain.

PIONEERS IN THE FIELD

Endoscopic technology pioneer Karl Storz founded his medical instrument firm, Karl Storz GmbH & Co., in 1945. In 1960, he discovered that he could use a fiber-optic light cable to send light through an endoscope into the body. (Fiber-optics involves transmitting light through extremely thin fibers or rods.) Storz patented this process, called "cold light endoscopy." Next, inventors developed a remote electronic flash unit to enable endoscopes to take pictures inside body cavities. According to his company, Storz built the first extracorporeal (outside the body) electronic flash for endoscopy. In 1966, Storz teamed with Harold H. Hopkins to develop the Hopkins rod lens system, which an industry source called "the most important breakthrough in optics since the development of the conventional lens system by Max Nitze in 1879." It allowed inventors to reduce the endoscope's diameter while maintaining its photographic resolution. Years later, Storz's company improved the design with the Hopkins II optics system.

By the end of the 2000s' first decade, the most significant new developments in the minimally invasive surgery industry were in the area of robotics. According to a 2008 report by consultants Frost & Sullivan, robot-assisted surgery was a $813 million market in 2007, and a growth rate of 25.8 percent annually was expected through 2014. The report also noted that the initial costs of robotic surgery systems were a concern for some but, as cited in *Wireless News,* such systems have "sparked a revolution in the practice of medicine" and "the techniques and procedures that have been practiced for years [have] essentially become outmoded."

By 2008 many hospitals across the United States had centers for robotic surgery, and many of them used the $1.5 million da Vinci Surgical System, a robotic surgical system that coordinates a surgeon's manipulation of manual controls with operating tools inside the patient. The da Vinci robot has four arms, three for holding tools such as scalpels and scissors and one for holding a camera. The surgeon sits at a set of controls and manipulates the arms while looking at a 3-D image of the procedure.

In 2008, Boston Medical Center was one of the nine hospitals in the United States that used the da Vinci robot to perform minimally invasive coronary bypass surgery, a procedure that diverts blood around blocked arteries and is the most commonly performed operation by heart surgeons. A study by the University of Maryland showed that using the da Vinci system for bypass surgery reduced the patient's hospital stay and recovery time, resulted in fewer complications, and increased the chances that the new vessels would stay open. In addition, the study showed that the procedure saves costs because even though the cost of surgery is $8,000 more when using the da Vinci, the difference is more than made up by the shorter hospital stay and costs of treating complications. In 2009, the new da Vinci HDSI model was released.

Many physicians saw robotically assisted surgery as the direction in which a number of specialties were headed, even though systems were expensive and surgeries sometimes took longer to perform. Applications ranged from general and pediatric surgery to cardiac and oncology procedures. Further, the use of minimally-invasive surgery changed many traditional hospital-stay surgeries into those capable of being performed on an outpatient basis.

CURRENT CONDITIONS

In a 2009 industry report, "The Market for Minimally Invasive Medical Devices," BCC Research found that the global market was estimated at $15.8 billion for that year (it was $14.8 billion in 2008), reaching $23 billion by 2014. Surgical robots were the fastest growing equipment/device segment. Cardiothoracic surgeries represented the largest application segment, followed by orthopedic surgery, gastrointestinal surgery, and gynecologic surgery, in that order.

According to the National Institute of Biomedical Imaging and Bioengineering, the newest technology on the horizon in 2010 was flexible robotic surgery. In mid-2010, researchers at Columbia University in New York announced the creation of a surgical platform that was able to provide nimble movements as well as 3D visualization of surgical fields. The insertible robotic effector platform (IREP) was intended to address some of the limitations often experienced using the da Vinci robot. For example, more complex abdominal surgeries or those involving tight or twisted surgical sites remained a challenge for the long stick-like tools typically used during minimally invasive surgery. A surgical assistant was generally required to continually rotate the camera to ensure that the surgical instruments were always in view on the monitor in front of the surgeon. In addition to high costs and steep learning curves for surgeons, the conventional laparoscopic tools were long, thin, rigid instruments that needed to be positioned at the optimal angle to avoid instrument collision or distorted depth perception. Moreover, the da Vinci was too large to attach to a patient's bed, necessitating surgical assistants to disengage and re-engage the robotic system each time a patient was repositioned during surgery. As a result, only 30 percent of colon cancer surgeries were being performed by laparoscopy in 2010.

IREP, on the other hand, is smaller, flexible and multi-functional. The entire IREP is enclosed in a 15mm sheath and slides into a natural body opening or small laparoscopic incision, with two snake-like arms that move as easily as human fingers. The entire IREP weighs just 8 kg. According to experts, IREP will help usher in an emerging approach to surgery via single-port access. In some cases, no surgical incision will be required because IREP is small enough to be inserted in natural human orifices, i.e. natural orifice transluminal endoscopy, or NOTES. Furthermore, next generation IREPs will provide ultrasound deployment and other sensors to monitor conditions within the body during surgery, in addition to the present capability to cut, suction, and suture remotely.

At the April 2010 annual meeting of the Society of American Gastrointestinal and Endoscopic Surgeons, the latest trends in minimally invasive surgery tools were reusable devices, more product choices for single-incision laparoscopies, and products that assisted surgeons to maintain a clear and steady image while performing laparoscopies. In addition to increasingly smaller incisions for surgery, new developments in laser cutting and sealing tissue during surgery have also led to increasing use of robotics in outpatient surgical applications.

According to Gina Kolata in her February 2010 article for *The New York Times,* the jury was still out on whether robotic surgeries produced better outcomes than conventional surgery. Costs for robotic-assisted surgeries in 2010 were roughly $1500 to $2000 more per surgery (e.g., prostatic cancer surgery). However, increasingly, and with no assurance of a better outcome, more than 85 percent of men (73,000 of 85,000 who underwent prostate surgery) chose to have robot-assisted operations in 2009.

Also in 2009, Dr. Stuart Geffner performed the first robotics-assisted kidney transplant at St. Barnabas Medical Center in Livingston, New Jersey. Eight more such transplants were performed over the ensuing six months.

INDUSTRY LEADERS

As of 2010, two of the leading firms devoted to minimally invasive surgical technologies were Cincinnati-based Ethicon Endo-Surgery, an operating company of Johnson & Johnson, and Hamilton, Bermuda-based Covidien, which was known as United States Surgical Corp. until parent company Tyco's break-up in 2007. Ethicon's disposable surgical stapler, introduced in 1978 to compete against a similar Covidien product already on the market, sparked the long rivalry between these two firms. Johnson & Johnson was able to make great use of its vast product lines in conjunction with its Ethicon Endo-Surgery subsidiary to market bundled packages to hospitals and other customers. This critical mass gave the firm a great advantage in moving minimally invasive surgical products to market. During the first decade of the twenty-first century, Ethicon Endo-Surgery marketed its products in more than 50 countries. It also had training centers in Germany and Japan and the Endo-Surgery Institute, an educational facility in Cincinnati. In December 2009, Ethicon acquired Acclarent for roughly $785 million.

To compete with Ethicon, Covidien began bundling its products with Tyco's line of supplemental equipment, including electrosurgical generators and stereotactic tables. Whereas Covidien used to focus on the surgeon in the customer relationship, the heated competition changed the company's tactics and the firm began promoting itself as catering to the "whole-hospital customer." Covidien's minimally invasive surgical tools were especially strong in the field of women's health care. The company also was producing instruments used for spinal and cardiac procedures.

The competition between the two industry leaders culminated in yet another lawsuit between them when in early 2010, Covidien (successor company to Tyco Healthcare) filed suit against Ethicon, citing three patent infringements on a line of ultrasonic surgical devices. The suit somewhat repeated one filed in 2004 and dismissed in 2008. Ethicon reported $5.4 billion in 2009 revenues, while Covidien brought in $6.1 billion in revenues just from its medical device sales in its fiscal year 2009.

The endoscope segment's giant was Olympus Optical, a division of Olympus Corp. of Tokyo, Japan, which controlled a sizable share of the world market during the latter years of the twenty-first century's first decade. It is the leading maker of flexible fiberscopes and videoscopes used for examining the upper and lower gastrointestinal tract or the bronchial tubes. In the late 1990s and early years of the twenty-first century's first decade, the company rolled out a series of new products to complement its line of minimally invasive and endoscopic technologies, including its EVIS EXERA 160-Series Video System and the integrated information and management system EndoWorks. Olympus also makes endoscopic peripherals (connectable devices), including video monitors, computer support equipment, light sources, and video processors. In 2002, Olympus began using the Wavefront Coding technology produced by CDM Optics Inc., a technology which allowed the surgeon greater depth of field than other imaging systems. By 2006, the company offered a range of endoscopic products for virtually every surgical specialty, from general and pediatric procedures to neurosurgery, cardiology, and orthopedics.

ArthroCare, founded in 1993, developed and manufactured minimally invasive surgical products that incorporated its patented Coblation technology, using low-tempurature radiofrequency energy to carefully and precisely dissolve tissue rather than burn it, which minimized damage to healthy tissue. The company reported $331 million in revenues for 2009.

Based in Natick, Massachusetts, Boston Scientific Corporation produced a range of minimally invasive surgical devices, including guide wires, steerable catheters, and stents, which are used to hold open arteries. The company went on a purchasing spree in the mid- and late 1990s, greatly expanding its size and product line and propelling it to the industry's top ranks. Despite legal and financial difficulties in the late 1990s, partly caused by its numerous acquisitions, the company forged into the new century on strong ground. In 2006, Boston Scientific acquired Guidant Corporation, a developer of cardiovascular medical products, in a $27 billion deal.

Fujinon, part of Fuji Photo Optical Co. Ltd., of Omiya, Japan, makes a complete line of endoscopes including video colonoscopes, endoscopes, duodenoscopes (top of small intestines and pancreatic ducts), fiberscopes, laparoscopes, panendoscopes (bladder and urethra), and sigmoidoscopes. The company claims to make the thinnest and most flexible instruments, qualities of particular importance in pediatric procedures. Fujinon also makes a top-selling processor to carry the images gathered by its scopes. The company's major products include video laparoscope systems with high resolution and high magnification plus flexible or rigid design.

A major international player is Karl Storz Gmbh & Co. The company''s history is deeply rooted in minimally invasive surgery (MIS) as its founder, Karl Storz, was a pioneer in the development of endoscopes. The company remained family owned in the middle years of the first decade of the 2000s. At that time, two of the firm's major subsidiaries were Karl Storz Endoscopy-America, Inc. of Culver City, California, and Karl Storz Veterinary Endoscopy of America, Inc., which was a leader in expanding MIS to the veterinary services industry. Karl Storz Endoscopy designed the state-of-the-art, integrated operating facility at ValleyCare Medical Center in Pleasanton, California and also designed two electronically controlled surgical suites at St. Luke's Episcopal Hospital of Houston, Texas. At the 2002 American College of Surgeons Annual Meeting, Karl Storz Endoscopy launched Aida DVD with "advanced capabilities" including digital image capture and real-time recording of streaming video to DVD for publishing-quality images. In addition to its endoscopic devices, the company was a leader in video documentation and surgery illumination technologies, such as monitors, lights, cables, and video cameras. In 2006, the company's U.S. subsidiary was recognized by Frost & Sullivan with an award for market leadership.

Stryker Corporation of Kalamazoo, Michigan, maintained a payroll of 16,026 employees worldwide by the late first decade of the twenty-first century. The company researches, designs, and manufactures endoscopes through a California subsidiary called Stryker Endoscopy. Stryker operates in over 100 countries worldwide, deriving about 40 percent of its sales from overseas. The firm also manufactures a wide range of surgical tools and devices. In January 2003, Stryker Endoscopy signed an allograft (transplantation of an organ or tissue between two individuals of the same species but with different genes) tissue agreement with Regeneration Technologies, Inc. of Alachua, Florida. This agreement called for Stryker Endoscopy to be responsible for developing techniques and instrumentation for implantation of human allograft tissue in sports medicine surgeries, customer education, and marketing of available tissue.

In 2002, the largest U.S. firm specializing in endoscopic technology changed its name from Circon Corporation to ACMI Corporation to consolidate brand names. Circon had purchased the company in 1986 to capitalize on its sales force. American Cystoscope Makers, Inc. (ACMI) of Southborough, Massachusetts, was known for developing technologically advanced medical devices and led the way with many industry firsts. Circon was a subsidiary of Maxxim Medical, Inc., which acquired the company in early 1999. This followed Circon's solicitation in August 1998 of proposals for strategic partnerships or mergers and the defeat of a hostile takeover attempt by Covidien in September 1998. ACMI specialized in minimally invasive surgical instruments for urology, anesthesiology, and gynecology in 2007.

A smaller U.S. firm that was growing quickly and forging ahead with innovative new products was Intuitive Surgical, Inc. Based in Sunnyvale, California, the firm established itself as a haptics specialist. (On the home page of its Web site, Intuitive describes haptics as "the science of computer-aided touch sensitivity.") The company achieved revenues of $227.3 million in 2005, up nearly 64 percent from the previous year. In 2007, sales skyrocketed again, to $600.8 million. Much of the firm's exploding revenues can be attributed to the da Vinci Surgical System, which it developed. By 2008 the company had more than 800 da Vinci robots in hospitals worldwide.

Smith & Nephew Endoscopy Inc. (formerly Smith & Nephew Dyonics Inc.) of Andover, Massachusetts, was a worldwide health care company specializing in products to facilitate arthroscopy, visualization, and minimally invasive surgery. Its parent company, the diversified manufacturer of medical products Smith & Nephew plc of London, employed about 8,800 workers and generated revenues of $3.3 billion in 2007. In 2002, Smith & Nephew entered a strategic alliance with Computer Motion to interface the firm's Hermes Control Center with medical products. In 2003, *Hospital Materials Management* reported that Toronto Western Hospital installed a digital operating room designed by Smith & Nephew Endoscopy. This contract included training surgeons on the new arthroscopic instruments and equipment. In 2006, Smith & Nephew named Michael G. Frazzette as president of its endoscopy division.

RESEARCH AND TECHNOLOGY

In addition to the new IREPs introduced in 2010, several other new technologies and surgical tools surfaced during that year, particularly for endoscopic surgeries. A resusable clip applicator, the Challenger Ti-P, was introduced by Aesculap. Aragon Surgical introduced its Lektrafuse Caiman Tissue Cutting and Sealing Instrument, with larger articulating jaws that facilitated cutting and sealing up to 50mm of tissue with a single bite. Although indicated for use in bariatric, gynecologic, and colorectal procedures, the Caiman was being tested by a Dutch research group for intestinal surgeries, which, if successful, could have positive implications for eliminating the need for stapling the bowel in the future.

Also in 2010, CareFusion introduced its EnView Laparoscopic Control Device, which was designed to relieve surgical assistants from long-time holding of scopes. Ethicon Endo Surgery Division introduced its Endopath XCEL Trocar with Optiview. This tool prevents smudging on the scope and lens during the insertion and removal of laparoscopes. The Optiview wipes fluid and debris from the shaft and wisks them away into an absorbent ring.

Other new products introduced in 2009 and 2010 included the Bio-A Fistula Plug from Gore; the X-Cone from Karl Storz; the QuadPort and TriPort from Olympus, and the Radius T Surgical System from Tuebingen Scientific. The latter system uses a pair of resuable handheld manipulators with disposable endo effectors (graspers, needle holders) at the ends, similar to a surgical robot.

In May 2008, for the first time ever, a surgeon at the University of Calgary used a robot, called neuroArm, to remove a tumor from a patient's brain. Another example of innovative minimally invasive surgery was pituitary surgery performed at Thomas Jefferson University Hospital in which brain tumors were removed through a patient's nasal passages and sinus cavities, thereby eliminating the need for an external incision. According to a May 11, 2006, *Internet Wire* article, "Guided by the endoscope and enhanced computer navigation, surgeons open small holes in the base of the skull and membrane covering the brain to remove the tumor. Better visualization and access to these lesions have enabled improved resection of the tumor without causing damage to the brain and lower risk of complications and follow-up surgery."

Another neurosurgery breakthrough was the use of gamma (electromagnetic) "knives" to perform brain surgery without cutting open a patient's skull. The procedure, referred to as proton-beam therapy, involved using hundreds of small radioactive beams of varying intensities that could be conformed to different shapes and sizes. The beams could be targeted to destroy tumors, minimizing damage to surrounding tissue. This technique was the only option for patients who, due to the location of a tumor or other factors, were not candidates for traditional brain surgery.

Not only is minimally invasive technology a field ripe for research, but it also facilitates research into ever greater technologies as well as into more accurate understandings of anatomy and physiological disorders. The internal images provided by high-powered endoscopes offer researchers invaluable data from which to devise new treatments.

St. Peter's University Hospital in New Brunswick, New Jersey, took advantage of the educational applications of minimally invasive technologies and added a virtual training center specializing in MIS to its cutting-edge surgical center. In partnership with the University of Medicine and Dentistry of New Jersey-Robert Wood Johnson Medical School, St. Peter's equipped the facility with interactive workstations and teleconferencing equipment for easy consultations between students and their instructors. In this way, students can watch live feeds of MIS procedures and practice on both physical and three-dimensional models at their workstations. By late in the decade, several universities and hospitals had such training centers.

In addition, patients suffering from gastrointestinal difficulties, by the luck of sheer anatomy, no longer must have long cables maneuvered through their systems during MIS, a procedure that results in discomfort. A team of British and Israeli scientists in 2000 announced the creation of a micro-sized camera that is simply swallowed like a pill. As the camera moves through the digestive system, it takes pictures through the entire 20-foot pathway to the colon. The wireless capsule endoscope, as it is called, thus provides a detailed map of the gastrointestinal tract, the second leading location of cancers, which doctors can thus store and access for more precise diagnosis and, eventually, surgical plans.

Microelectromechanical systems (MEMS), also called micromachines, and nanotechnology, which were under extensive development in the first decade of the twenty-first century, also carried great promise for the medical industries. These tiny devices, embedded with circuitry, cameras, and programmable computer chips, could be designed to target specific areas of the body and, eventually, perform the surgery themselves, controlled by computer from outside the body entirely. (See also **'Micromachines/Nanotechnology.**)

The field of minimally invasive technology continues to be a very dynamic area of advancement. With each innovation in equipment comes a commensurate increase in breadth of application. The possibilities seem endless.

BIBLIOGRAPHY
"ArthroCare-Investor Relations-Corporate Overview." Available from http://www.arthrocare.com

BCC Research. "Market for Minimally Invasive Medical Devices," 2009. Available from http://www.bccresearch. com/report/HLCO51E.html.

Fargen, Jessica. "Bot's a Smooth Operator." *The Boston Herald,* 25 May 2008.

Feder, Barnaby J. "Surgical Device Poses a Rare but Serious Peril." *The New York Times,* 17 March 2006.

Finneran, Lisa. "Gamma Knife Offers Cutting-Edge Surgery— Without a Knife." *Daily Press,* 20 June 2006.

"Frost & Sullivan Says Era of Robotics Taking Shape in Healthcare Industry." *Wireless News,* 30 May 2008.

"Growing Popularity of Minimally Invasive Surgery Promotes Uptake of Related Devices and Boosts Market Prospects." *Business Wire,* 4 September 2007.

"IST Receives FDA Clearance of Paramount(TM) IBF System for Minimally Invasive Spine Surgery." *Internet Wire* 16 October 2007.

"J&J Strengthens Surgical Portfolio." *Market News,* March 2010. Available from http://www.istockanalyst.com/viewarticle/articleid/4247383.

Kolata, Gina. "Results Unproven, Robotic Surgery Wins Converts." *The New York Times,* 13 February 2010.

Lee, Jaimy. "$1.5m da Vinci Might Help Palomar Surgeons Create Masterpieces." *San Diego Business Journal,* 24 March 2008.

McCullough, Marie. "Some Doctors See Promise in Robotic Surgery." *Philadelphia Inquirer,* 15 May 2006.

Morain, Erin. "Orthopedic Surgeons Taking Minimally Invasive Approach." *The Des Moines Business Record,* 10 April 2006.

National Institute of Biomedical Imaging and Bioengineering. "On the Horizon-Flexible Robotic Surgery." 30 June 2010. Available from http://www.nibib.nih.gov/HealthEdu/eAdvances/30June10

"New Robot Technology Eases Kidney Transplants." CBS News, 22 January 2009.

"OR-Live.com Presents: Leading Edge Minimally Invasive Pituitary Surgery From Thomas Jefferson University Hospital; Breakthrough Procedure Allows Doctors to Remove Brain Tumors Through Nose and Nasal Sinuses." *Internet Wire,* 11 May 2006.

Renton, David. "What's New in Minimally Invasive Surgery." *Outpatient Surgery,* Vol XI, No. 7, July 2010.

Tennant, Scott. "Minimally Invasive Surgery Makes Inroads in Pediatrics." *Urology Times,* 15 May 2006.

"The Results of this Latest Data Analysis Indicate Ob/Gyn Surgery is Changing as New Minimally Invasive Procedures Become More Popular." *Business Wire,* 18 April 2008.

"Tiny, Careful Cuts: Robot Surgery." *The Economist,* 21 June 2008.

"University of Maryland Study Finds that Minimally Invasive Robotic Bypass Surgery Provides Health and Economic Benefits." *Ascribe Higher Education News Service,* 26 April 2008.

"UPDATE: Covidien Sues J&J Unit Ethicon Over Ultrasound Devices." *MassDevice,* 15 January 2010.

MOBILE APPS

SIC CODE(S)

4812

5731

5999

INDUSTRY SNAPSHOT

Mobile applications, commonly referred to as "apps," are software programs designed to run on mobile devices, including cell phones and smartphones. Consumers utilize apps for everything from playing games and checking the weather to staying current on the latest news and accessing social media sites. Apps even exist for searching library catalogs and locating apartments for rent or homes for sale. Businesses use "enterprise apps" to provide their employees with a wide range of work-related tools. Data from the research firm Gartner indicated that mobile users would spend more than $6 billion on mobile apps in 2010. A separate analysis conducted by Jupiter Research projected that indirect and direct revenue from mobile apps will exceed $25 billion by 2014.

ORGANIZATION AND STRUCTURE

Application Categories Approximately 100,000 apps were on the market by 2009, according to the July 20, 2009, issue of *World Entertainment News Network*. The publication indicated that by 2020 the number of available apps would approach the 10 million mark. Individual applications exist for virtually every conceivable purpose. Consumers utilize apps for everything from playing games and checking the weather to staying current on the latest news and accessing social media sites. Apps even

exist for searching library catalogs, reserving books, locating apartments for rent, and perusing property for sale.

Marketers and brand managers leverage custom apps to connect consumers with their products and services. For example, one brewery in the Midwest offered an app that allowed residents to see the types of beer that was available at its on-site pub. Benjamin Moore Paints offered a free app that enabled iPhone users to match colors from iPhone photos with more than 3,300 hues of the company's paints. Called Ben Color Capture, the app was developed in an effort to engage with a younger demographic. Directed Electronics offered a free "teaser" iPhone app that could be used to remotely start a car and turn on the heat or air conditioning (after purchasing associated in-car electronics that cost $500).

Large enterprises use apps to provide their workers with a wide range of business tools. These range from inventory and location-based services to customer relationship management and fleet vehicle management. One excellent example is the healthcare industry, which uses apps for a wide range of purposes. Healthcare apps include everything from medical calculators, reference programs, and decision support tools to drug databases, dictation programs, and tools for interfacing with insurance companies.

Apps fall within a dizzying array of categories, including, but not limited to:

- Books
- Business
- Education
- Entertainment

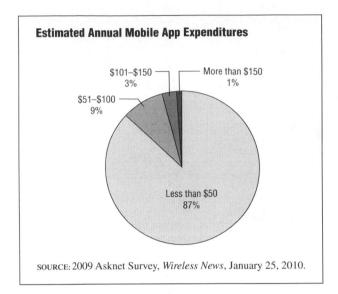

Estimated Annual Mobile App Expenditures

$101–$150
3%

More than $150
1%

$51–$100
9%

Less than $50
87%

SOURCE: 2009 Asknet Survey, *Wireless News*, January 25, 2010.

- Finance
- Games
- Health & Fitness
- Lifestyle
- Medical
- Music
- Navigation
- News
- Productivity
- Reference
- Social Networking
- Sports
- Travel
- Utilities
- Weather

Development Significant opportunity existed for mobile app developers during the 2010s. However, the industry climate was extremely competitive. As Deepak Swamy explained in the May 17, 2010, issue of *Total Telecom Online*: "Discovery remains an intractable problem for the bottom 60% of applications. Device fragmentation and app store variations require independent software vendors (ISVs) to take precious resources away from innovation and to put them on the appointment instead of development." Indeed, for many independent developers and development firms, success or failure was dictated by getting applications on the market quickly. In the July 20, 2009, issue of *World Entertainment News*

Network, one industry player indicated that the failure rate for application developers was nearly 90 percent.

Distribution Users were able to obtain mobile apps in a number of different ways. Distribution most commonly took place via "app stores." During the early 2010s these included Apple's Apps Store, Research in Motion's BlackBerry App World, Google's Android Market, and Microsoft's Windows Marketplace for Mobile. Other app stores were operated by mobile operators such as Sprint, which offered customers downloads via its Digital Lounge.

Finally, users obtained apps from independent app stores, such as Getjar. During the early twenty-first century the company operated the second-largest app store in the world. Getjar offered applications for all major mobile platforms, ranging from the iPhone and Windows Mobile to the Android and BlackBerry. By 2010 more than 1 million apps had been downloaded from GetJar, which offered more than 75,000 mobile applications.

Handsets & Devices Mobile apps are downloaded to, and used from, a large number of personal digital assistants (PDAs), smartphones, feature phones, and other mobile devices. According to *Total Telecom Online*, by mid-2010 more than 4 billion people were using hundreds of different mobile devices throughout the world. These devices utilized approximately 10 different operating systems, of which there were hundreds of different variations.

During the early 2010s the most popular devices on the market arguably were offered by Apple Computer. These included the iPhone, iPad, and iPod touch. In addition, Research in Motion's BlackBerry was widely used within both the consumer and enterprise markets. Other leading manufacturers at this time included Nokia Corp., LG Corp., Mio Technology Corp., Dell Inc., International Business Machines Corp., NEC Corp., Sharp Electronics Corp., Casio Computer Company Ltd., and Panasonic Corp.

BACKGROUND AND DEVELOPMENT

Short History of Portable Computing The Osborne I, developed in 1980 by Adam Osborne of Osborne Computer Corp., included innovations that led the way in the evolution of truly portable computers. Weighing 17 pounds, it had a detachable keyboard, a five-inch black-and-white display, and two floppy disk drives. It used a Zilog Z-80 microprocessor chip, an improved clone of Intel's 8080. The Osborne I not only pioneered portability, it was also credited with being the first to bundle software packages with the computer, an idea that became fundamental to selling hardware in the industry.

Tens of thousands of the Osborne I portable computers were sold before it became the victim of the company's own success. In 1983 the company announced that it would build an IBM-compatible portable called the Vixen, causing buyers to stop buying the Osborne I in anticipation of the new machine. The announcement, however, was premature, and without incoming orders to fund the new product's manufacture, Osborne was forced to file for bankruptcy protection. By the time the Vixen was ready to market, consumers had been wooed away by the products of a new leader, Compaq, that had been able to meet their demand.

According to Les Freed's *The History of Computers*, Compaq's opportunity to successfully take the portable computer market lead was largely due to a gaping hole in IBM's product line. In 1983 Compaq shipped the Compaq Transportable and Compaq Plus, both fully functional, IBM-compatible portable PCs weighing a not so svelte 30 pounds. During its first year in business the company sold 53,000 portables and took in revenues of $111.2 million, giving Compaq the highest first-year sales in the history of U.S. business.

In 1984 Gavilan Computer developed a truly portable machine that did not have to be plugged in. Industry commentator Tim Bajarin wrote: "The computer's clamshell design and battery-power capability made it the first serious mobile computing system." Gavilan, however, could not manufacture the computers in sufficient quantity and the company went out of business.

Apple Computer's PowerBook models, introduced in 1991, set a new standard for portables. They combined long battery life with excellent display quality and a built-in pointing device. The PowerBook 170 contained an optional internal modem slot, again redefining the meaning of a mobile office computer. Apple's Duo 210, released in 1992, featured the DuoDock, an innovation that allowed hookup to a docking station that might contain more system RAM, a larger hard drive, or more video RAM for a color monitor. The Duo could thus function fully as a desktop computer when in the DuoDock and as an excellent portable at other times.

Emergence of Handhelds In 1993 another Apple innovation was the Newton MessagePad, a new type of portable known as a personal digital assistant (PDA). It was the first mass market handheld computer and was offered as a personal information manager. The Newton solved the problem of keyboard size by using a stylus for input, but it promised more of this new pen-based technology than it could deliver. Apple promoted the Newton's ability to interpret handwriting with disastrous results because, at the time, its capability was relatively primitive.

By 1997, when the next-generation Newton, the MessagePad 2000, reached the market, its handwriting recognition was much improved. Reviewers praised the revamped MessagePad for its robust communication and computing features, but with Apple mired in losses, and profits from the Newton not imminent, in 1998 Apple dropped the curtain on the Newton line—the MessagePad, eMate (a Newton-based clamshell notebook for the education market), and the Newton operating system.

In the meantime, another competitor with greater staying power was emerging. In 1994 inventor Jeff Hawkins came up with a design for a new kind of PDA that would become the PalmPilot. At the time, he was working at a software firm developing handwriting recognition technology for handheld devices, but the sparse handhelds at the time lacked many useful features, and to Hawkins, an engineer, they were poorly designed. He believed an effective handheld device should be extremely light and portable, ought to synchronize readily with desktop computers, and should be simple in features and purpose. With his innovative design and support from the company's management, Hawkins helped transform the company into a hardware designer and maker, Palm Computing.

In 1995 the private company was sold to modem manufacturer U.S. Robotics in order to finance the product's debut. The first PalmPilot was shipped in early 1996, and more than 350,000 units had been sold by the year's end. Within another year, more than 1 million PalmPilots had been sold and the product began attracting a devoted following of users, software writers, and corporate partners. Palm became part of 3Com Corp. with its 1997 purchase of U.S. Robotics, and by that time Palm was becoming entrenched as the market leader in the nascent PDA category.

However, Palm wasn't alone. Numerous models of handhelds, palmtops, and other PDAs came on the market around the same time. These included computers running Microsoft's Windows CE operating system. Windows CE, although less functional than desktop Windows versions, was easy to learn for those familiar with the PC versions. Windows CE devices included modified versions of the popular Microsoft Word and Excel software, along with Microsoft's Internet Explorer browser. The Casio Cassiopeia, for instance, was able to transmit faxes, access e-mail, and receive information via a one-way pager in addition to being able to link and synchronize data through a docking station to a Windows 95 desktop computer. Hewlett-Packard introduced its 1000CX palmtop PC and Philips Electronics North America Corp. unveiled the Velo 1 in early 1997.

Early Mobile Applications Many of the earliest mobile apps were focused on the enterprise market. By late 1994 the advent of cellular digital packet data, which allowed mobile users to transmit data from remote locations, furthered the growth of mobile apps by third parties. Examples included software from Digital Equipment Corp. that enabled laptop users to access local area networks, a credit card and check-verification system from U.S. Wireless Data Inc., and a dispatching and vehicle-location system called Cadpak from Advanced Control Technology Inc.

By early 2000 the evolution of enterprise applications was gaining more momentum. San Mateo, California-based Siebel Systems Inc. was preparing to ship a mobile version of its customer relationship management software. Companies like Libertyville, Illinois-based PenDragon Inc. were developing customized mobile databases for the business market. Charles Schwab & Co. was working with Ericsson to research and develop Internet applications for mobile phones, including wireless trading applications.

The demand for mobile geographic information system (GIS) software also was heating up. By 2002 one of the first commercially available PDA apps with global positioning satellite (GPS) functionality was Personal Navigator, a Windows CE program developed by Pharos. Belgium-based Star Informatic had developed technology called WhereNeXt, which allowed wireless phones to track GPS-equipped vehicles. Finally, Microsoft was demonstrating its Microsoft Enterprise Location Server software, which enabled the development of location-based applications at the enterprise level.

Early Issues & Challenges During the early 2000s mobile app developers contented with a number of challenges. Factors such as small handheld screens, limited bandwidth, and differing standards between wireless devices often meant that it was necessary to focus on simplicity and functionality, as opposed to flashy programming. Other concerns emerged regarding ownership. For example, some industry players were concerned about how ownership rights of downloaded content would be transferred from one device to another, and how users would contend with lost applications.

During the mid-2000s consumers enjoyed a growing selection of mobile apps. For example, The Weather Channel unveiled a weather alerts tool that provided various weather warnings to mobile devices. Although ring tone downloads were the most popular wireless data app in 2004, the research firm IDC indicated that wireless gaming would assume the leadership slot in 2005, and that by 2008 the category would generate annual revenues of approximately $1.5 billion.

Google Acquires Android An important industry development took place in 2005 when Google acquired the mobile phone operating system developer, Android. Following the acquisition, the company began bolstering its portfolio of mobile software apps and making them compatible with various smartphones. Via a tie-up with Research in Motion, Google Mobile Maps and Google Talk IM applications became available on the Black-Berry. Other mobile apps developed by the company included an RSS reader, Gmail, a calendar, and search tools.

In addition to Research in Motion, Google also established partnerships with T-Mobile and Sprint Nextel in the United States. Internationally, the company made arrangements to have its apps included on handsets from China Mobile, Vodafone (Europe), and KDDI (Japan). By late 2007 rumors were circulating about the possibility that Google would develop its own smartphone.

Google's strategy evolved in September of 2008 when its Android operating system was introduced on T-Mobile's new G1 phone, along with a host of related applications available via the new Android Market. According to the October 24, 2008, issue of *The Online Reporter*, these included:

- AccuWeather.com
- BlueBrush
- BreadCrumbz
- Buzzd
- Cab4ME Light
- e-ventr
- imeem for Android
- Maverick
- MyCloset
- Myspace Mobile
- Plusmo College Football Live
- Plusmo Pro Football Live
- The Weather Channel
- TuneWiki

Mobile applications had been on the market for a number of years by 2008. However, some industry observers indicated that the average consumer still had a difficult time understanding how to shop for and download applications. Apple changed all of that by applying its popular iTunes store format to mobile apps. By early 2009 more than 500 million applications had been downloaded from the company's App Store.

CURRENT CONDITIONS

Data from the research firm Gartner revealed that mobile users would spend more than $6 billion on mobile apps in 2010. By this time apps had become a regular part of everyday life for billions of consumers and businesspeople across the globe. According to Nielsen's *App Playbook*, in 2010 the most popular apps focused on gaming, news, weather, and maps/navigation. Apps allowing users to connect to social media sites such as Facebook also were popular.

By 2009 commercials for Apple's pervasive and popular iPhone accurately touted, "There's an App for That." In fact, about 100,000 apps were on the market in 2009, according to the July 20, 2009, issue of *World Entertainment News Network*. The publication indicated that by 2020, the number of available apps would approach 10 million. Apple celebrated the one billionth download from its App Store in early 2009. Roughly one year later, approximately 3 billion apps had been downloaded for popular devices such as the iPhone, iPad, and iPod touch.

A major development took place in August of 2010 when the movie service Netflix rolled out an app for the Apple iPhone and iPod touch, allowing subscribers to stream movies and television episodes to their devices at no additional cost. An app allowing users to stream Netflix content to the Apple iPad had been introduced in April 2010. Following the August announcement, Netflix saw its stock price increase nearly 2 percent.

Enterprise users remained a key market for mobile apps. According to Frost & Sullivan, revenues for mobile workforce management, mobile sales force automation, mobile office, and enhanced fleet management applications alone totaled $2.84 billion in 2009. By 2015 revenues from such applications were forecast to reach $10.87 billion. Businesses stood to reap a return on investment from applications through reductions in employee overtime, speedier sales cycles, reduced paperwork, faster service response times, and improved billing accuracy.

Significant growth was forecast for the mobile app industry during the second and third decades of the twenty-first century. In the short term, a forecast from Chetan Sharma Consulting indicated that the "global mobile application economy" would be valued at $17.5 billion by 2012. By comparison, compact disc sales were expected to total $13.8 billion at that time. A separate analysis conducted by Jupiter Research projected indirect and direct revenues from mobile apps would exceed $25 billion by 2014.

INDUSTRY LEADERS

Apple Computer Inc. During the early 2010s, Cupertino, California-based Apple Computer remained a major player in the market for mobile devices and apps. This was evident by the success of the company's line of iPod portable music and video players, its Apple iTunes store, and the Apple App Store, from which users literally had downloaded billions of apps.

Apple introduced the iPod in 2002 and launched iTunes the following year. By 2004 iPod sales surpassed 2 million units. That year the company unveiled the iPod mini, which allowed users to store up to 1,000 songs, and iPod sales constituted 35 percent of the company's revenues. Apple's impact on the industry continued in 2005. That year the company replaced the iPod mini with the iPod nano, a media player that was thinner than a pencil but could hold 500 to 1,000 songs. In addition, Apple unveiled an iPod capable of playing video on a 2.5-inch color screen. Apple's iTunes service began offering approximately 2,000 music videos in 2005, as well as episodes of popular TV programs for $1.99. In only 20 days time iTunes sold more than 1 million videos.

In April of 2007 Apple announced that it had sold its 100 millionth iPod, which had become "the fastest selling music player in history," according to a company news release. The following year the company made a significant impact on the market by introducing its Apple App Store. Essentially, this involved the company applying its iTunes approach to mobile apps, making it easy for consumers to find and download them. By 2009 commercials for Apple's pervasive and popular iPhone accurately touted, "There's an App for That."

Apple celebrated the one billionth download from its App Store in early 2009. By 2010 approximately 3 billion apps had been downloaded for popular devices such as the iPhone, iPad, and iPod touch. In a company news release, CEO Steve Jobs remarked: "The revolutionary App Store offers iPhone and iPod touch users an experience unlike anything else available on other mobile devices, and we see no signs of the competition catching up anytime soon." In 2009 Apple's sales totaled $42.91 billion and the company employed 36,800 people. In late 2010 iPhone and iPod touch users in 77 countries were able to choose from a staggering number of apps in roughly 20 categories.

Google Inc. Google was established in 1995 by Larry Page and Sergey Brin, two Stanford University computer science graduate students. Page and Brin decided to develop a computer application that allowed users to sift through the largest data set in the world, the Internet, and retrieve relevant information. By 1997 the partners were using their dorm rooms as office space and searching for partners interested in licensing their technology. The following year, Page and Brin named their search engine technology "Google," an offshoot of the word googol, which is the number one followed by 100 zeros.

In 1998 Sun Microsystems founder Andy Bechtolsheim invested $100,000 in the new company, which was incorporated as Google Inc. By 2003 profits totaled $105.6 million on sales of $961.9 million. Google completed its initial public offering on August 19, 2004, selling its shares for $85 apiece via a Dutch auction on the NASDAQ. By the end of the day the firm's stock price had risen to $100, and more than 22 million shares had been traded.

An important industry development took place in 2005 when Google acquired the mobile phone operating system developer, Android. Following the acquisition, the company began bolstering its portfolio of mobile software apps and making them compatible with various smartphones. Via a tie-up with Research in Motion, Google Mobile Maps and Google Talk IM applications became available on the BlackBerry. Other mobile apps developed by the company included an RSS reader, Gmail, a calendar, and search tools.

In addition to Research in Motion, Google also established partnerships with T-Mobile and Sprint Nextel in the United States. Internationally, the company made arrangements to have its apps included on handsets from China Mobile, Vodafone (Europe), and KDDI (Japan). By late 2007 rumors were circulating about the possibility that Google would develop its own smartphone. The company's strategy evolved in September of 2008 when its Android operating system was introduced on T-Mobile's new G1 phone, along with a host of related applications available via the new Android Market.

Google employed 19,835 people in 2009. That year, the company's sales totaled $23.65 billion. In 2010 Google's Gmail, Google Calendar, Blogger, and Google Docs apps remained popular. The company hosted these applications, and stored user's data securely, allowing access from any Web-enabled device.

Research in Motion Ltd. Research in Motion Ltd. (RIM) is a mobile phone maker and provider of e-mail services. Through its BlackBerry brand of wireless devices, RIM pioneered the market for smartphones. The company survived extensive litigation over the patents to its technologies to remain a leader in the smartphone market. Initially marketed to corporations and businesspeople, the BlackBerry brand has expanded into the burgeoning consumer smartphone market, competing with Apple, Samsung, Nokia, and others.

Like most corporations, RIM saw its stock value drop during the recession of 2008 as decreased consumer spending affected sales. Despite the widespread economic uncertainty, RIM continued to forge ahead with its efforts to seize a larger share of the consumer market. In October 2008 it launched the BlackBerry Storm, the first BlackBerry device to feature a touch screen keyboard. Within months, RIM's bold strategy was paying substantial dividends. The Storm sold more than 1 million units within three months of its unveiling and the company's earnings increased 26 percent in the period between December 2008 and February 2009. Brisk sales led to an expansion of the RIM's workforce and by mid-2010 the company had 13,873 employees, up from about 9,000 in 2009 and 2,000 at the beginning of the decade. Sales in 2010 totaled $14.95 billion.

Palm Inc. In 2003 Sunnyvale, California-based Palm Inc. acquired Handspring Inc., a former competitor led by two of Palm's founders, Jeff Hawkins and Donna Dubinsky. Following the acquisition, Palm spun off its operating system business, which became PalmSource Inc.

Early in its history, Palm had an uneasy relationship with its parent, 3Com Corp., which acquired Palm through the 1997 buyout of U.S. Robotics. To give Palm greater autonomy and value separate from that of 3Com, primarily a networking equipment company, Palm was spun off from 3Com in 2000. Palm was criticized for a lack of innovation since its first products were introduced. It was slow to adopt color displays and other new features that competitors rolled out. Part of Palm's strategy was to keep its brand clear and devices simple, but skeptics assert the firm lost customers based on its limited product offerings.

In the early years of the first decade of the 2000s, Palm's generous lead in the market was diminished as new competitors shipped handhelds that had more features and in some cases were cheaper than Palm's line. During the middle years of the decade, Palm marketed its Zire line of handheld computers, which sported color screens and wireless Internet capabilities. In 2006 the company's PDA shipments dropped 29 percent as it focused more on smartphones, namely its Treo. That year, Gartner reported that Palm shipped about 1.97 million PDAs.

Palm's revenues totaled $735.9 million in 2009, when the company employed 939 people. In 2010 the company continued to market smartphones, including its Pixi and Pre models. In addition to direct sales, Palm made its devices available via tie-ups with the likes of Verizon Wireless, AT&T, and Sprint Nextel. A major development unfolded in 2010 when Hewlett-Packard parted with approximately $1.2 billion to acquire Palm. Following the conclusion of the deal, Palm became a subsidiary of Hewlett-Packard.

AMERICA AND THE WORLD

According to a report from Pyramid Research, mobile applications were expected to generate revenue of $139.6

billion in Europe from 2009 to 2014. The most significant market was Western Europe, where spending from mobile users was projected to account for $115.8 billion of the total. Mobile apps also were making strong inroads in China. After launching in 2009, China Mobile Ltd.'s Mobile Market app store offered 20,984 apps by mid-2010. The company indicated that its users and downloads had grown at a rate of 40 percent since the app store was first introduced.

RESEARCH AND TECHNOLOGY

An important development unfolded in early 2010 when a dedicated tradeshow was held for the mobile app industry in Las Vegas. AppCon provided developers, device manufacturers, and carriers with an opportunity to meet and discuss development issues, best practices, technology advancements, and more. The convention offered attendees the opportunity to participate in more than 100 educational sessions. AppCon was especially important because it was not platform-specific, as was the case with many existing developer forums.

In its January 25, 2010, issue, *Wireless News* shared the results of a survey conducted by the e-commerce distribution solutions provider Asknet. Based on responses from 400 smartphone users, the research found that 38 percent of users were frustrated by the high cost of applications. A reluctance to provide credit card information for app purchases was indicated by 29 percent of respondents. In addition, 34 percent of respondents said that app purchases were "not worth the time or effort."

BIBLIOGRAPHY

"Analysis: Apple Adapts iTunes Model to Mobile Apps." *Europe Intelligence Wire*, 7 March 2008.

"Apps Attack: Mobile Applications Offer PR Big Branding, Awareness Opportunities." *PR News*, 18 January 2010.

"Apps on Mobile Market Top 20,000." *SinoCast Daily Business Beat*, 11 June 2010.

"Asknet Survey: U.S. Consumers Frustrated by High Cost of Mobile Apps." *Wireless News*, 25 January 2010.

Barney, Doug. "Third-Party Cellular Mobile Apps Readied." *InfoWorld*, 21 November 1994.

Englehardt, Jim. "Mobile GIS Apps Soar." *Geospatial Solutions*, September 2000.

"Google Inc." *Notable Corporate Chronologies*. Online Edition. Farmington Hills, MI: Gale Group, 2009.

"Google Unplugged: gPhone or Not, Google's Apps Are Smartphone Ready, It's Partnering with Cellular Carriers, and the Company May Bid on Wireless Spectrum. Connect the Dots." *InformationWeek*, 29 September 2007.

"Handheld Computing Devices." *Encyclopedia of Emerging Industries*. Farmington Hills, MI: Gale Group, 2010.

McAllister, Sue. "Mobile Apps for Buying or Renting a Home." *San Jose Mercury News*, 28 April 2010.

"Mobile Apps to Hit $25 Billion by 2014; Handset Makers Will Receive the Bulk of the Revenue Selling Apps to Smartphones, but Carriers Have an Opportunity to Bring App Stores to Entry-Level and Feature Phones." *InformationWeek*, 29 April 2009.

"Mobile Apps Make Another Appearance at a Show of Their Very Own." *Tradeshow Week*, 22 March 2010.

"Mobile Apps Market Scales up from Zero to Billions." *NPR: Business Story of the Day*, 13 April 2010.

"Mobile Apps on the Rise." *Health Management Technology*, March 2010.

"Mobile Apps to Yield USD 139.6 bln in Europe in 2009-2014." *Europe Intelligence Wire*, 12 January 2010.

"Mobile Apps Will Be 'Bigger Than Internet.'" *World Entertainment News Network*, 20 July 2009.

"Mobile Apps Will Outsell CDs by 2012." *Europe Intelligence Wire*, 17 March 2010.

"Mobile Users Likely to Spend More Than USD 6b in 2010 on Mobile Apps: Gartner." *2.5G-4G*, February 2010.

"North America-Premium Mobile Apps Revenue to Hit USD 10.9 bln in 2015." *The America's Intelligence Wire*, 23 August 2010.

Pearse, Justin. "Industry Fears Rise over Mobile Apps Ownership." *New Media Age*, 17 October 2002.

Pepitone, Julianne. "Netflix Releases iPhone App, Stock Jumps." CNN Money, 26 August 2010. Available from www.cnnmoney.com.

"Pulling the Plug on Android Apps." *The Online Reporter*, 24 October 2008.

"Research in Motion Limited." *International Directory of Company Histories*, Vol. 106. St. James Press, 2010. Reproduced in Business and Company Resource Center. Farmington Hills, MI: Gale Group, 2010.

Swamy, Deepak. "Mobile Apps: From the Long Tail to the Holy Grail of Lifestyle Enablement." *Total Telecom Online*, 17 May 2010.

Theys, Julien. "Take Advantage of Mobile Applications: More Consumers Are Using Smartphones—So Mobile Apps Are a Great Way to Directly Connect with Your Customer. Four Experts Share the Best Strategies Marketers Can Use to Maximize the Use of This Channel." *DM News*, 2 March 2009.

"Wireless Gaming Seen as Top Mobile Data Apps." *Asia Africa Intelligence Wire*, 28 January 2005.

Zimmerman, Christine. "Mobile Apps Need Simplifying—Limited Bandwidth, Screen Sizes Mean Web Site Operators Must Adapt for Handheld Users." *InternetWeek*, 13 November 2000.

MOLECULAR DESIGN

——■——

SIC CODE(S)

8731

8733

INDUSTRY SNAPSHOT

Molecular design is a big bag of tricks comprised of the principles of biochemistry, medicinal chemistry, molecular biology, and computerized molecular modeling, with a pinch of mathematics and computer science thrown in for good measure, aimed at isolating a novel chemical compound, assessing its beneficial uses, and finding a means to synthesize it in a form optimal to the target use. Enormous advances in high-performance computing and visualization techniques have pushed molecular design to the forefront of biotechnology research. In place of random laboratory screening of chemical compounds, molecular design uses computational chemistry to produce research chemicals aimed at synthesizing new compounds for employment in a commercial market. The leading companies in the pharmaceutical, chemical, and agribusiness industries all make use of molecular design for integration into new products.

Molecular design greatly streamlines the painstaking and time-consuming process of weeding through enormous chemical "libraries" to find molecules appropriate for a specific application, a process that requires screening molecules one at a time. Scientists are now able to cut their time and effort considerably by using molecular design screening processes to isolate in minutes the precise chemical compounds that interact appropriately with their target. Meanwhile, software tailored to the process is employed to create a simulation of the chemical compound's action in its target situation, be it a pharmaceutical

medicine or an agricultural crop. Molecular design allows many of these advances to take place through genetic research. This is an area of rapidly increasing importance in medicine and industry, in part because extraordinary advances in computing make it possible to conduct accurate theoretical and experimental studies of enzymes, nucleic acids, and bio-molecular assemblies.

ORGANIZATION AND STRUCTURE

Biological activity is dependent on the three-dimensional geometry of specific functional groups. Biomolecular research has traditionally required synthesis and screening of large numbers of molecules to produce optimal activity profiles, producing an average of one compound a week. Combinatorial chemistry allows researchers to amass libraries of large populations of molecules (100,000 in a matter of weeks) for screening compounds. Similarly, advancements of modern computers, which have become fast, small, and affordable, allow researchers to visualize molecular structure and activity on screen rather than in a test tube. Moreover, advances in chemical models and program interfaces allow researchers to describe the mechanisms of biomolecular activity. Finally, high throughput robotic screens identify which compounds exhibit desired activity against the target. These potential lead candidates are then sold or licensed as information to the subsequent biotech companies for further product development and marketing in the individual sectors.

While computers allow the visualization of chemical interactions and large information databases, they have not entirely replaced experimentation in the lab. The final key to the technology that has made possible the massive libraries of potentially profitable biotech molecules each year is the process of combinatorial chemistry. First developed as a scheme to save time in drug research, the approach has evolved into the ability to create large numbers of organic compounds with the ability to tag them in such a way that those with optimal properties can be screened and identified. Combinatorial chemistry has reduced the time required to profile an optimum form of the compound from years to weeks.

College and university departments and institutes traditionally account for the majority of molecular design and research, although successful business applications had attracted a tremendous amount of attention by the middle years of the first decade of the 2000s and have enabled industry growth. The genetic engineering sector is responsible for much of this attention, with its promise of powerful new super drugs and boosted agricultural yields, although the latter generated a storm of controversy in the late 1990s (Also see the essay entitled Genetic Engineering). Major changes in molecular design technique have enabled numerous small research companies to operate with specialized core technologies and computer programs. Design companies then lease their software and technology. Alternately, they can carry out the molecular design that fuels the rest of the industry, working closely with international pharmaceutical companies.

Within the molecular design industry, individual molecular design companies tend to center on a patented specialized technology that can speed the search for compounds with properties that react favorably with a desired target. Once fully established, large corporations often acquire all or part of the smaller companies and their discovery processes.

The discovery and analysis of genes and their manifestations has come to be known as genomics. Coupled with other major technological advances in molecular design, the use of genomics to identify molecular targets revolutionized the molecular design industry in the 1990s. Giant undertakings, such as the Human Genome Project, offer an abundance of information accessible on highly sophisticated computerized databases. Having identified the biological target—an enzyme, hormone, growth factor, or other protein—the researcher has a point of entry for chemical manipulation.

Efficient and productive realization of molecular design techniques allows the biotech industry to profit from small molecule development and discovery in each of these areas. The pharmaceutical industry entirely depends upon the discovery and selective development of molecules possessing characteristics that may become profitable drugs. In addition, genetic engineering continuously uncovers interesting gene activity and needs large arrays of compounds to screen against gene products for potential activity. Developers of bioremediation processes use molecular design to discover advanced synthetic treatments and accessory compounds, such as nitrification inhibitors, to optimize conditions for microorganism activity.

BACKGROUND AND DEVELOPMENT

Humans have been using naturally occurring compounds to their benefit for thousands of years. Plants and animals provided food, medicine, and lubricating oils. New products were limited by traditional methods of screening naturally occurring substances. In contrast, the development of new substances based on knowledge of chemical properties could rarely be realized in practice. Once a novel compound with beneficial properties is isolated, it is often in a form that is unacceptable for its application, say, as a drug. It is beneficial to have access to knowledge about hundreds or thousands of chemicals that display similar beneficial properties and, among those, one form just possibly will be free from any undesirable properties.

The ability to do accurate theoretical and experimental studies of enzymes, nucleic acids, and bio-molecular assemblies is inherent to "designing" a molecule, but the idea of using living things for human benefit is far from new. The use of living organisms to make cheese and bread has been practiced since 7000 B.C. Modern molecular design grew out of this larger field of molecular biotechnology. The term "biotechnology" was coined in 1917 by Hungarian engineer Karl Ereky to describe "all lines of work by which products are produced from raw materials with the aid of living things."

The greatest problem facing molecular bio-technicians is the development of microorganisms and compounds into marketable products. Naturally occurring microorganisms rarely produce the results scientists need for commercial application. By exposing organisms to other factors, such as ultraviolet radiation, scientists induce genetic changes that might or might not produce a desired byproduct. With the recognition in 1944 that DNA (deoxyribonucleic acid, a chemical component of most living cells) held all the genetic material needed for a cell to reproduce itself, scientists began to think about creating organisms that would produce waste products that could serve as useful substances.

It was not until the late 1970s that researchers were able to apply genetic engineering techniques to molecular design. Due to the tedious nature of testing, the traditional genetic improvement regimens were time-consuming and costly. In addition, the best result that this traditional approach could yield was the improvement of an existing inherited property, rather than the expansion or creation of certain genetic capabilities. Molecular design, combined with genetic engineering, allowed these improvements to be made more efficiently.

The emergence of powerful microcomputers in the late 1970s allowed great advances in molecular biotechnology. In terms of molecular design in particular, computers proved to be important tools in the production of new chemicals. Computer databases allowed easy tracking and interpretation of huge numbers of characteristics. As microcomputing technologies improved during the 1980s, new computer programs were developed that allowed individual molecules to be displayed graphically on computer monitors. In the late 1990s, most advanced computer programs could create, edit, and print depictions of chemical molecules on the atomic level. (Also see the essay entitled Molecular Modeling.)

In 1978, the genetic research company Genentech, Inc. used a genetically modified *E. coli* bacterium to produce human insulin. The bacterial host cells acted as biological factories for the production of human insulin that was then purified and used by diabetics who were allergic to the commercially available porcine (pig) insulin. Genentech's product also made human insulin cheaper and more readily available to diabetics throughout the world.

Genentech was one of the most successful leaders in the molecular and genetic design industry in the 1980s. Its success inspired many imitators, only a few of which prospered. Promoters dreamed of a world in which genetically and molecularly engineered microorganisms would produce petroleum, clean up wastes, cure diseases, and repel pests. According to reports that appeared in newspapers, magazines, and on television at that time, the applications of molecular design were limitless. Many of those applications were being realized in the late 1990s, and while the field was rife with success stories, reactions were not as universally euphoric as predictions might have led some to expect.

Since a protein's shape determines whether and how it will interact with a molecule, pinpointing protein structures is a sort of holy grail for molecular design firms. Crystallography and nuclear magnetic resonance imaging have proven enormously helpful in "protein-structure prediction." Such techniques probe the crystals formed by proteins, thus revealing their structure. Scientists, however, have grown increasingly anxious for more reliable ways to determine the shape of proteins.

Three types of software were developed to try to pinpoint the protein structure in more accurate and less painstaking fashion. The first begins by assuming no prior knowledge of the protein except for its amino acids sequences and starting from scratch, or *ab initio*, as it is called. Building on the knowledge of amino acid sequences derived from genomic technology, the software tells the computer to reconstruct the protein one atom at a time. The forces between each atom are then measured to determine the way in which the protein folds and thus the shape it assumes.

The second type of software, comparative modeling, builds on the protein structures that have already been identified, comparing their amino acid sequences for similarities with the target protein. This results in an educated guess at the protein's structure, which is then augmented with further comparisons, producing an iterative process of protein structure prediction.

The final method proceeds from similar beginnings as comparative modeling, but the amino acid sequence of the target protein is graphed onto the known protein and compared with its sequences throughout its structure, at each point yielding comparative data. At the end of this process, the final composite comparison data are measured against other known protein structures.

Several companies offered molecular design services tailored to suit clients' needs. For example, Pharmacopeia Drug Discovery Inc. performed research services to develop drug discovery programs. The company generated large libraries for pharmaceutical research that offered structure activity data, the likelihood of rapid discovery of a suitable compound, and broad patent protection of identifiable libraries, thus slowing competitors' attempts to develop similar drugs. Another major player, Tripos Inc., specialized in software that created virtual combinatorial libraries. The company pinned its hopes for its strongest future growth on software and consulting.

Molecular design also alters the relationship between the various industries it touches. For instance, firms employing the most advanced molecular design techniques are no longer required to purchase enormous volumes of chemicals in order to conduct molecular research. As a result, firms specializing in combinatorial chemistry may find themselves compelled to form strategic alliances with companies and laboratories engaged in computerized design and structural biology.

The early 2000s produced a great deal of fertile ground on which to expand the application of molecular design techniques. For example, the Human Genome Project, headed by James Watson of the U.S. National Institutes of Health, was an international effort to identify the approximately 25,000 genes of the human genome and determine the sequence of chemical base pairs that make up DNA. The first complete draft was released in 2003. The Institute of Medicinal Molecular Design developed a new technique, known as Eigen-ID, which ran the genetic sequences through an encryption system and compressed the data, often with as many as several billion nucleotides, into strings of only 20 characters. Using these packaged, identifiable data sets, scientists could quickly scan the genomic sequences to identify potential genes that match those in their own databases, to which molecular screening was applied and new chemical compounds were formulated for drugs. Analysis of the mountains of data produced by the project was expected to continue into the second decade of the twenty-first century, and one of the goals was to transfer the learned technology to the private sector.

In addition, intricate new understandings of the classification and function of proteins resulted in a complete dictionary of protein families and their functions, according to some analysts. As a result, the molecular foundations of genetic variation came increasingly into focus, spurring more accurate and streamlined molecular design applications.

In 2007, New York University opened its Molecular Design Institute (MDI), which, according to a press release, "will engage in molecular engineering, in which it explores the design and synthesis of functional molecules and hierarchical systems created by 'directed self-assembly.' In this process, molecule-based building blocks are steered into prescribed, sometimes complex, architectures for the purposes of making new materials with advanced functions, ranging from energy efficient lighting to drug delivery to nanoscale separations."

One of the many breakthroughs in the molecular design industry occurred when James R. Heath of the California Institute of Technology and J. Fraser Stoddart of the University of California, Los Angeles, announced their creation of the most dense memory chip yet in 2007. The new chip, which measures one-2,000th of an inch on each side, can hold 1 billion bits of data per square centimeter, 40 times as much as current memory chips. Regarding the project, Heath told *The New York Times,* "Our goal always was to develop a manufacturing technique that works at the molecular scale."

CURRENT CONDITIONS

Clearly, the technology gaining the most attention by 2010 was pharmaceutical drug design. Partly because of a tight economy, partly because the Obama administration had expanded health coverage to all Americans, and partly because research facilitated such development, the bottom line was that the need for new drugs fueled the need for more molecular design to support that need. Therefore, the process of new drug discovery was undergoing a complete overhaul to not only make new drugs more cost-effective, but also to address increasing demands.

Conventional computer-aided drug design had employed virtual screenings of available chemical databases in commercial in-house or public-domain libraries and collections. yet on the cutting edge of technology was the increasing application of *de novo* drug design. This methodology facilitates the creation of molecules that do not exist in known compound databases. *De novo* design incorporates automated computation procedures that build new molecules by using atoms or fragments. The resulting molecular structures can therefore fit specified property constraints.

For example, a 2010 report from the Centers for Disease Control and Prevention (CDC) noted an 111 percent increase over the previous five years in emergency room visits related to abuse of prescription painkillers. Chronic pain accounts for more than $100 billion a year in direct health care costs, according to the American Pain Society. Of this, over $10 billion is spent annually in the United States alone on a classification of painkillers (analgesics) known as opioids. However, the U.S. Food and Drug Administration (FDA) cited prescription opioid painkillers as being at the center of a major public health crisis of addiction, abuse, overdose, and death. To the potential rescue came a small molecular design company known as Nektar Therapeutics. Using proprietary small molecule polymer conjugate technology, Nektar announced the creation of NKTR-181, an investigational drug candidate designed to treat pain but avoid not only the addictive qualities of opioid drugs, but also the euphoria and "highs" associated with opioid abuse and dependency. This next-generation drug with its novel molecular structure was uniquely designed to cross the blood-brain barrier at a substantially lower rate than other opioid drugs. NKTR-181 showed promising results in preclinical studies, noted Nektar Therapeutics in October 2010, and Nektar planned to begin Phase 1 clinical studies in early 2011.

Also in 2010, a computational-aided drug design web server was established on the Internet, known as "e-LEA3D," which integrated three complimentary tools to perform computer-aided drug design (CADD) based on molecular fragments. This tool will be used to invent new ligands that will optimize a user-specified scoring function. The e-LEA3D server was available at http://bioinfo.ipmc.cnrs.fr/lea.html.

In non-medical news, in February 2010, researchers at IBM's Semiconductor Research and Development Center announced that they had applied molecular design to develop a new environmentally-friendly compound involved in semiconductor chip manufacturing. The new "green chemistry" solution avoids the use of fluorine in semiconductor photolithography processes. IBM holds several patents on the new compounds and was in discussion with several chemical suppliers concerning their license.

INDUSTRY LEADERS

Specialized molecular design research services are carried out in both academic and commercial environments, with many partnerships and alliances formed between the two. For example, the Molecular Design Institute (MDI) at the University of California-San Francisco (UCSF) advances molecular design methods and works closely with industry. The National Institutes of Health have awarded MDI several grants covering structure-based molecular design. MDI also works to further drug discoveries.

Widely recognized as a leader in molecular design, Tripos, Inc.—renamed New Tripos International in 2007 when it was purchased by Vector Capital—was founded in 1979. Based in St. Louis, Missouri, the company has a history of success in the field of molecular imaging and design software. It is a leading provider of discovery chemistry, integrated discovery software products, software consulting services, and discovery research services to the pharmaceutical, biotechnology, agrochemical, and other life sciences industries. The firm also offers collaborative research services to life sciences companies. In 2008 Tripos had more than 1,000 customers in 46 countries, including the top pharmaceutical companies. Its product line includes more than 50 drug discovery research software products, the largest inventory of molecular design and analysis packages currently available.

With its Discovery informatics products software, Tripos enables customers to quickly identify and optimize new compounds that have the potential to become products. The tools make the research process more efficient by identifying physical and structural properties of molecules likely to make them suitable as drugs. The tools then use this information to design novel molecules that possess these properties. The centerpiece of the software suite is SYBYL, a platform for molecular design, analysis, and visualization. It provides a computational tool kit that simplifies and accelerates the discovery of drugs and new chemical entities.

Practically every pharmaceutical company uses Tripos's comparative molecular field analysis technology. Customers include scientific research organizations as well as biotech companies. Tripos has collaborated with the Central Research Division of Pfizer, Inc., to generate novel new software products geared toward pharmaceutical research. In the summer of 2000, Tripos agreed to utilize its discovery technologies to discover candidate drugs for metabolic and related diseases in conjunction with the Merck pharmaceutical subsidiary Lipha, S.A. In 2001, Tripos provided five novel lead series of drug-like compounds in a highly patented field to Lipha Pharmaceuticals. In 2002, it entered into collaborations with

several pharmaceutical and biotechnology companies, including a $100 million collaboration with Pfizer for chemical design and synthesis. By 2006, Tripos had completed more than 60 collaborative programs. In 2008, parent company Vector Capital also acquired Pharsight and expanded not only its library databases but also its design capabilities.

Pharmacopeia Drug Discovery Inc., previously a unit of Pharmacopeia Inc., combines three platform technologies of combinatorial chemistry, high throughput screening, and molecular modeling software to aid the development and discovery of life and material sciences products. Revenue is generated through software sales and service, chemical compound leasing, internal drug discovery, and collaborative drug discovery. Headquartered in Cranbury, New Jersey, Pharmacopeia has utilized its proprietary ECLiPS encoding technology to synthesize literally millions of small molecules. The company, which was founded in 1993, has benefited from collaborative agreements with agricultural and pharmaceutical companies such as Bayer Corp., Novartis AG, AstraZeneca, and Antigenics.

In May 2002, Pharmacopeia transferred nearly all of the assets, operations, and business of its drug discovery segment into a new, wholly owned subsidiary, Pharmacopeia Drug Discovery, Inc. (PDD), which integrates proprietary small molecule combinatorial and medicinal chemistry, high-throughput screening, in-vitro pharmacology, computational methods, and informatics to discover and optimize lead compounds. PPD applies its proprietary combinatorial chemistry technology, Encoded Combinatorial Libraries on Polymeric Support (ECLiPS), computational modeling, discovery biology, medicinal chemistry, ultra-high throughput screening and applied engineering to identify, enhance, and optimize potential drugs. The ECLiPS technology generates libraries of small-molecule compounds for pharmaceutical research. Pharmacopeia's scientists had synthesized more than 7 million diverse small molecules with drug-like characteristics.

RESEARCH AND TECHNOLOGY

In 2010, NASA scientists announced the development of molecular design strategies to address, and hopefully minimize, the environmental impact of greenhouse gas on global warming. After analyzing more than a dozen molecules involved in global warming, the researchers found that several fluorinated compounds tended to be more potent greenhouse gases than compounds containing chlorine and/or hydrogen. This discovery led to the ranking of greenhouse gases by strength/potency as global warming agents. Using this ranking system, scientists developed a screening method for industry to utilize in developing and producing chemical compounds that are less efficient at absorbing atmospheric radiated heat. This will minimize the effects of man-made materials that contribute to global warming.

Also in 2010, scientists from Japan announced that they had molecularly designed a computer-like device, only using organic molecules, that parallels the human brain. Just a few molecular layers thick, the organic computer can mimic certain aspects of human brain functions. Using a nanoscopic microscope, the scientists formed electronic bonds between molecules. Then they used a scanning tunneling micrscope with a nanoscopic tip to direct a slight voltage electric pulse, sending the molecules into different conducive states. To test their creation, the scientists simulated two phenomena that occur naturally: the way electrons move through material, and the way cancer spreads in a human body. Both simulations returned excellent results, i.e., responses paralleling that found in a brain. Other scientists and experts were skeptical of results and uncertain as to how useful the technique would be outside of laboratory experiments.

A few companies use molecular design software strictly to develop new commercial products. A great many more colleges and universities, however, use molecular design primarily to train students in chemistry. Still, there is some overlap between the two. The Department of Chemistry at the University of Houston, for instance, sponsors the Institute for Molecular Design (IMD), which exists to promote the exchange of information between field researchers. This information exchange helps with researching new computer tools for molecular design, attracting funds to support molecular design, and promoting computer-aided molecular design. Students as well as professional chemists utilize the programs and resources of the IMD. It is not a commercial program, however, and is therefore supported by grants from the government, private foundations, and companies in the industry.

The Molecular Design Institute (MDI) at the University of California-San Francisco (UCSF) is another example of the overlap between academia and commerce in molecular design. MDI was established in 1993 as an academic research institute to promote the discovery, design, and delivery of pharmaceutical agents. MDI seeks innovative partnerships between businesses and universities to expand their basic and applied research efforts and works closely with different agencies in the university, including the School of Medicine, the School of Pharmacy, and the biophysics program. It is also associated with the UCSF Computer Graphics Laboratory (CGL), which developed the MidasPlus program for use in molecular design. MidasPlus, an acronym for "molecular interactive display and simulation," is used both for training and for commercial applications.

In 2007, Wake Forest University's Center for Nanotechnology and Molecular Materials was making progress in the search for sustainable energy sources when scientists there increased the efficiency of plastic solar cells to more than 6 percent. Although traditional solar cells convert about 12 percent of the light that hits them into energy, plastic solar cells are much more lightweight and inexpensive. In order to be considered a viable technology, solar panels must be able to convert 8 percent of sunlight into energy, but David Carroll of Wake Forest commented in a *Space Daily* article that he "fully expect[s] to see higher numbers within the next two years, which may make plastic devices the photovoltaic of choice."

The University of California-San Francisco (UCSF) Computer Graphics Laboratory (CGL) also introduced a number of other programs for use in molecular design. One was AMBER, a suite of programs for performing a variety of molecular mechanics-based simulations on machines ranging from workstations to supercomputers and designed for researchers working with proteins and nucleic acids. DOCK/BUILDER/MOLSIM was a suite of three programs also distributed by the UCSF CGL that provided a way to screen large databases of chemical compounds that have features in common with receptor targets.

Other areas of UCSF associated with the Molecular Design Institute (MDI) have also produced software aimed to support their specific interests and needs. The UCSF Magnetic Resonance Laboratory, for instance, offered CORMA and MARDIGRAS, two programs designed to reduce error in creating molecular models. The Department of Cellular and Molecular Pharmacology, which works extensively with models of proteins, has developed four programs to help researchers working with amino acids and other protein structures. The MDI at UCSF also offers a corporate scholars program to disseminate information about molecular design and provides sabbatical positions for corporate chemists in UCSF laboratories.

Meanwhile, the push for faster, better screening technologies plunges forward. Protherics Molecular Design Ltd., a subsidiary of the U.K. firm Protherics PLC, completed its new DockCrunch project, which teamed Protherics with high performance computing manufacturer SGI. DockCrunch analyzed over one million chemical compounds for their effectiveness in treating a number of diseases associated with the female hormone estrogen. This represented a far more powerful application of computational analysis for a screening library than had previously been attempted, and the results portend significant cost savings for drug discovery.

BIBLIOGRAPHY

Baldi, A. "Computational Approaches for Drug Design and Discovery: An Overview." *Systems Review in Pharmacology,* October 2010.

Chang, Kenneth. "Researchers Go Molecular in Design of a Denser Chip." *The New York Times,* 25 January 2007.

Das, Saswato R. "A Molecular Computer That Mimics the Brain." *Spectrum,* 18 May 2010.

Douguet, Dominique. "e-LEA3d: A Computational-aided Drug Design Web Server." 17 April 2010. Available from http://www.ncbi.nih.gov/pmc/articles/PMC2896156/.

"Focusing on the Tiniest of the Small." *R & D,* July 2006.

"Human Genome Project Information." U.S. Department of Energy Department of Science, 24 July 2008. Available from http://www.ornl.gov.

"IBM Announces the Invention of New Compounds for Semiconductor Manufacturing that Offer Improved Environmental Benefits." IBM Press Room, 23 February 2010. Available from http://www-03.ibm.com/press/us/en/pressrelease/29609.wss.

"Molecular Design Institute." University of California-San Francisco, 2006. Available from http://mdi.ucsf.edu/.

"Nanotechnology Created by Dr. Ralph Merkle." Richardson, Texas: Zyvex Corp., 2006. Available from http://www.zyvex.com/nano.

"NASA Designs Molecular Strategies to Minimize Global Warming." Nationanl Aeronautics and Space Administration, 3 May 2010. Available from-: http://www.nasa. gov/centers.

"The New Tripos International Announces Beta Program For Its Popular SYBYL(R) Molecular Modeling Environment on Mac OS(R) X." *Business Wire,* 8 July 2008.

"NKTR-181, a Mu-Opiod Analgesic With a Novel Molecular Structure, Demonstrates Slower Entry Rate Into the Brain and Reduced CNS Side Effects." 15 October 2010. Available http://pharmalive.com.

"NYU Launches Molecular Design Institute with Lecture by National Medal of Science Winner, May 30." Press Release, New York University, 23 May 2007.

"Plastic Solar Cell Efficiency Breaks Record at Nanotechnology Center." *Space Daily,* 20 April 2007.

Rodden, Graeme. "The Future Is Still to Come." *Pulp & Paper,* April 2006.

"Spice-Based Compound May Kill Cancer Cells." *UPI NewsTrack,* 18 August 2008.

Wilson, Elizabeth. "Imaging Spin Noise." *Chemical & Engineering News,* 22 May 2006.

MOLECULAR MODELING

———■———

SIC CODE(S)

8731

8733

INDUSTRY SNAPSHOT

A powerful tool, molecular modeling uses computers to help predict the three-dimensional structures of molecules and elucidate their other physical and chemical properties. Its goal is to aid the rational design of compounds, including medicinal drugs, by bridging the gap between theoretical chemistry and synthetic chemistry. Theoretical chemistry employs concepts that do not always translate smoothly from the scratch pad to the bench top, and synthetic chemistry often relies on painstaking trial and error. Molecular modeling allows the display of three-dimensional (3-D) models of molecules that can be rotated on screen so users can perceive atomic and molecular interactions. In the hands of highly skilled professionals, molecular modeling can provide significant insight into chemical structures and processes.

Molecular modeling complements analytical and experimental work. However, just as power tools alone are not enough to build a house, computational methods alone are not enough to replace experimentation. No molecule has ever been conceived and created "from scratch" using molecular modeling alone. All molecular modeling relies on data first obtained from experiments. Still, molecular modeling serves an essential role. Time and money limit the number of experiments scientists can run, and simulations guide their research efforts and aid their interpretations.

The chemical, pharmaceutical, and biotechnology industries use molecular modeling extensively for materials research and drug development. The chemical industry, for instance, has used molecular modeling to create better catalysts, which make chemical reactions possible even under harsh conditions, as well as to synthesize substances from new fuels to industrial lubricants. Medicinal chemists, on the other hand, have used molecular modeling to design drugs that are more potent and less toxic than their precursors.

More than 50 percent of molecular modeling efforts are applied in pharmacology or biotechnology. Additional applications include polymers (about 30 percent) and general materials such as metals, clays, and cements (less than 20 percent).

ORGANIZATION AND STRUCTURE

The major worth of molecular modeling is its predictive value. Acting as a scratch pad to test ideas and graphically display molecules, it allows scientists to predict the properties of hypothetical compounds. It also can facilitate the analysis of experimental data and suggest useful trends. For example, in 1992, Hoechst Celanese of Somerville, New Jersey, began a program to bring molecular modeling to its bench chemists to get chemical insights in the shortest possible time. When chemists there used molecular modeling to develop polymers, they were able to reduce from 300 to 30 the number of chemical pairs they needed to examine. Similarly, guidance from molecular modeling helps the pharmaceutical industry streamline and accelerate the discovery and development of new drugs, making these processes less expensive.

589

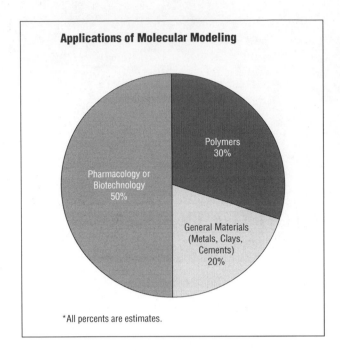

Applications of Molecular Modeling

Pharmacology or Biotechnology 50%

Polymers 30%

General Materials (Metals, Clays, Cements) 20%

*All percents are estimates.

Molecular modeling software treats molecules as a 3-D system of balls interconnected by springs. It applies mechanical constraints to the system to show the conformation (shape) that takes the least energy to maintain, to calculate the angle between two atoms bonded together in the molecule, or to reveal the location of electrostatic charges within the molecule.

Medicinal chemists may use this information to predict the biological performance of a compound, which guides the drug discovery process. Drugs work by interacting with biological molecules in the body, such as nucleic acids (DNA and RNA), enzymes, and receptors. How well a drug interacts with its biological target depends on a concept called complementarity. Just as a key must properly fit a lock to open a door, a drug must bind correctly at a specific site. Complementarity, the degree of "stickiness" of the drug to the target, influences the biological activity of the drug.

Molecular modeling aids drug design by facilitating two processes: lead generation and lead optimization. Lead generation is analogous to finding the key that can fit the lock. It determines the correct chemical structure that can bind to the desired biological target. To generate lead compounds, molecular modeling takes advantage of knowledge of the 3-D structure of a biological target. This knowledge is obtained experimentally: the target molecule is isolated, purified, and characterized using X-ray crystallography or nuclear magnetic resonance spectroscopy.

To find new lead compounds, scientists search 3-D databases of known chemical structures. During the middle years of the twenty-first century's first decade, these included commercial databases, such as those from Chemical Abstracts Service of Columbus, Ohio and Cambridge Crystallographic Data Centre of Cambridge, Great Britain, as well as databases available in the public domain plus in-house databases maintained by drug and chemical companies. Scientists also accessed chemical databases through the Internet. The Human Genome Project resulted in a large database of information becoming available on the Internet. San Diego-based Molecular Simulations Inc. released in March 1999 its WebLab Version 1.5 with improved features that, among other enhancements, allowed the biotech researcher to locate reading frames in a DNA sequence and translate them into protein sequences.

De novo drug design is an approach by which experimentally obtained knowledge of molecular properties is used to generate a lead compound. Based on the molecular properties of the region to which the drug binds, scientists can devise a chemical structure that will fit into the binding region. Molecular modeling can play an important role in creating a structure with a good fit. The chemical is then synthesized in the laboratory, tested, and optimized.

Lead optimization, the second method of designing drugs, is analogous to cutting a key to the exact shape needed to turn a lock. It fine tunes the degree of the interaction between the drug and the biological target. To optimize lead compounds, researchers try to correlate the relationship between a chemical structure and the biological effects it produces. This area of research is called "structure-activity analysis." It is the main focus for drug design in the twenty-first century, as it does not require knowledge of the biological target or its structure. First, the chemist makes a series of analogs, compounds that are structurally similar to the lead compound, and then he tests them in the laboratory. It is necessary to use a family of analogs that range in biological activity from inactive to active. The idea is to observe how changes in molecular properties, such as size, shape, electronic charge, and solubility, affect biological activity. Molecular modeling helps scientists decide what chemical modifications to make.

Optimizing the lead compound means maximizing its potency, minimizing its toxicity, and enhancing its delivery. Potency refers to how well a drug interacts with its biological target molecule. Toxicity and side effects result when drugs interact with biological molecules other than the desired target—in the lock and key analogy, the key opens more than one lock. Delivery deals with issues including the ability of the drug to reach its biological target in a large enough quantity to produce the desired effect. Sometimes, as when crossing the blood-brain barrier, this task is daunting. Molecular modification of the drug can affect all these properties, and modeling helps scientists decide what modifications to make.

It is important to note that molecular modeling seeks not to replace experimentation but to improve it. Virtually every aspect of drug design still depends on data obtained through experimentation. To build a structure-activity model, compounds have to be synthesized and tested. Biochemical studies must be conducted to identify the biological target molecules. Many molecular properties that drug designers need to explore are better measured experimentally than calculated.

BACKGROUND AND DEVELOPMENT

The pharmaceutical industry has been at the forefront of and remains the driving force behind computational chemistry. Traditional drug discovery relied on trial and error: extracts of natural substances were tested for their useful properties. In 1910, for example, Paul Ehrlich used a compound he obtained from a dye to create a drug for treating syphilis. Later, chemists made and tested large numbers of compounds and, when they identified an active compound, attempted to fine tune it into a substance that was clinically useful. This approach has been enormously successful in finding thousands of substances that turned out to be biologically active when tested in model systems. Beginning in the 1970s, however, this approach became more expensive and less successful in yielding new medicines. The cost of synthesis and testing, especially in animal studies and human clinical trials, has risen sharply. Competition among drug companies to be the first to the market with a new product is intense, and any tool that can facilitate that process is indispensable.

In 1965, the Massachusetts Institute of Technology introduced the first molecular modeling graphics system. By 1974, at least 19 universities and institutes had independently developed their own systems. Since then, many other organizations have developed systems, some of which are commercially available. For example, the National Institutes of Health (NIH) and the Environmental Protection Agency created the Chemical Information System; Brookhaven National Laboratories introduced Crystnet; NIH and Bolt, Beranek, and Newman produced Prophet; Washington University in St. Louis completed MMS-X. These systems help scientists search chemical databases, display and analyze molecular structures, study chemical interactions with their biological targets, and design drugs. To aid drug design efforts, Searle Co. of Chicago created the Moloch-2 molecular modeling system. Similarly, DuPont of Wilmington, Delaware produced Tribble, and Rohm & Haas of Philadelphia introduced Moly. These are but a few of the many modeling systems on the market.

Computational chemistry was a $2 billion industry in 1996 and experienced 25 percent annual growth through much of the 1990s. As computers got faster and scientists familiarized themselves with the software, the predictive power of molecular modeling grew. Commercial software for this field generated annual sales of about $50 million.

During the early years of the twenty-first century's first decade, researchers introduced software products that made viewing easier and that yielded more information. In 2003 the Digital Dynamic Depth Inc., in conjunction with the CACHe Group, developed the TriDef Visualizer, which enabled the CACHe software output to produce glasses-free stereoscopic 3-D displays in real time. This allowed researchers to see the true spatial relationships of molecular models without having to wear 3-D glasses. With the software, molecular models could be viewed simultaneously in 1-D and 3-D on separate screens.

In March of 2004, Accelrys released two new software tools. Because up to 60 percent of the failure of clinical drug trials is due to toxicity and other negative pharmacokinetic qualities, the effective identification of such issues ahead of time increases the likelihood of a successful trial. Topkat 6.2 was designed to forecast the toxicity of possible drug compounds, and it could be used with large data sets of 100,000 or higher. The Accord Chemistry Software Development Kit 6.0 allowed integration of chemical algorithms as well as data sources for chemical applications.

New technologies in the life sciences have allowed researchers to generate enormous libraries of molecular data through both computer programs and new laboratory methods. These molecular libraries provide starting points for experiment design in the development of compounds showing promise of usefulness and profitability in the biotech industry. Compounds with similar chemical properties can take on many forms, and a researcher must search through molecular libraries to find the optimum form of the compound for its ultimate use as, say, a drug or fertilizer. New software tools allow scientists to organize such massive amounts of data and exchange information. Novel compounds and processes can be simulated, developed, and analyzed. Researchers can interpret the properties of the molecular forms within those libraries in order to direct research efforts toward the most profitable results before they even enter the lab.

To tackle the massive undertaking of analyzing all of the chemical building blocks in terms of the rules of chemical behavior, screening vast numbers of compounds for activity with a target protein, and delivering the information in a form manageable by human scientists, many software programs rely on high power computer systems. The intricate interactive graphics displayed require high-resolution systems that are costly and may not be available in every lab, much less for every chemist. During the early years of the first decade of the twenty-first century, continued advances in personal computer hardware, coupled with low cost and greater availability, allowed molecular modeling applications to be run under Windows NT. Software providers for the industry responded by directing their efforts toward producing specific programs with high visualization in a standard Windows NT desktop environment. According to one DuPont Pharmaceutical Research Laboratories representative, the increasing availability of the Windows software at the workplace for each chemist was an important industry development.

While a great number of companies and learning institutions offer software programs and computational services designed to meet specific applications, sometimes it has been advantageous for pharmaceutical and biotechnology companies to build their own molecular modeling systems. Firms that have taken this approach include Bristol-Myers Squibb, Pharmacia & Upjohn, DuPont, Novo, GlaxoSmithKline, and Merck. For example, Merck decided to develop its own molecular modeling system to help its scientists study the geometry and reactivity of certain antibiotics. Scientists have successfully used it to design novel drug candidates, and the system has also aided the understanding of drugs' mechanisms of action.

Although by the middle years of the first decade of the 2000s molecular modeling was far from being able to simulate complex chemical reactions from A to Z, it remained a powerful research tool. A significant challenge faced by the industry was training those without computational backgrounds to obtain reliable results on computers. People must participate in extensive training to use molecular modeling properly and to familiarize themselves with strengths and weaknesses of various methods.

Heading into the second half of the twenty-first century's first decade, molecular modeling continued to make headway. Computers were getting faster, cheaper, more powerful, and more accessible. Software programs were able to yield more accurate information, as well as analyze larger molecules. Hybrid computers combined the power of supercomputers with massively parallel machines to solve big chemical problems.

In the pharmaceutical industry, exponential increases in computing power were being combined with new software applications and greater knowledge of protein structures to develop novel pharmaceuticals. As Kyle Strickland and other researchers noted in the 2005 *Bulletin of the South Carolina Academy of Science,* "Molecular modeling can give insight into the overall stability of bound ligands to protein structures, and therefore, contribute vital information concerning the aptitude of potential drugs."

Greater accessibility and quickly expanding databases, such as the Research Collaboratory for Structural Bioinformatics's protein data bank, were helping researchers to build upon the modeling efforts of others during the middle of the twenty-first century's first decade. Consortia formed with researchers in areas as diverse as pharmaceuticals, catalysts, and polymers have facilitated the spread of modeling knowledge. The result for chemists has been more quality time at the computer, which in turn allows more quality time in the lab.

New developments were occurring on a regular basis in the late years of the first decade of the 2000s in the molecular modeling industry. According to a February 20, 2008, *Business Wire* article, "Molecular modeling, with greater accuracy than ever, allows for the fastest and most economical way of experimenting before creating a new product or material." In a publication titled *Multiscale Simulation Methods for Materials,* Research and Markets reported on new computational chemistry techniques with graphics visualization for "simulating and predicting the structure, chemical processes, and properties of materials." These molecular models can be used for research in nano, organic, inorganic, and biomaterials.

In 2007 the Institute for Systems Biology and New York University announced a new model that, according to *Business Wire,* "rapidly characterizes and accurately predicts the molecular-level, mechanistic response of a free-living cell to genetic and environmental changes." The EGRIN model enables scientists to discover how complex biological systems work, a knowledge base that is necessary in order to reengineer organisms or "engineer cells back to health."

New software that enabled better and more advanced application of molecular models using computer-assisted design (CAD) were being developed in the late years of the first decade of the 2000s. In this way, engineers and scientists can design industrial products on the computer before creating the actual prototype. The knowledge necessary for future developments, according to a 2006 *Machine Design* article, will come from "the computational models such software provides, which describe nanomachines at the molecular level, in precise atomic detail." One such new software program, Nano-Engineer-1 by Nanorex of Bloomfield Hills, Michigan, combines physics, biology, and chemistry to create a program that allows the user to connect atoms "like Legos" to create virtual models. According to the company, Nano-Engineer-1 goes a step beyond traditional 3-D CAD programs, and the future of molecular modeling will be driven by nanotechnology.

The National Center for Biotechnology Information's (NCBI) Entrez is a comprehensive database that includes a database of experimentally determined 3-D biomolecular structures. One of the components is NCBI's structure database called MMDB (Molecular Modeling Database), a subset of 3-D structures obtained from the Protein Data Bank (PDB). MMDB includes ASN.1-formatted records. Designed to be flexible, it can archive conventional structural data as well as future descriptions of biomolecules. PDB is updated weekly and major releases are issued several times a year. The NCBI mirrors PDB for the purpose of making MMDB.

CURRENT CONDITIONS

Molecular modeling continued to make most advances in the field of medical science, particularly in new drug design. Expanded health care under the Obama administration, coupled with the increasing cost of pharmaceuticals, contributed to the steadfast and continued need for molecular modeling software. Computational drug design, however, got a shot in the arm in 2010, when billionnaire Bill Gates decided to invest $10 million in Schrodinger, a well-regarded but smaller computational chemistry entity. Given the complexities of molecular modeling, i.e., trying to "dock" a drug candidate computationally into its target protein, when the shapes of the molecules change in protein targets as well as in the presence of water molecules, etc., the company was most likely to use the funds for long-term research projects.

A development gaining worldwide attention in 2010 was the announcement, by Nanoviricides, Inc., that it had developed aa drug candidate, using sophisticated molecular modeling software, that showed significant efficacy in fighting Dengue Virus, a member of the Flaviviridae virus family, often spread by ticks and mosquitoes. Dengue Virus is related to Yellow Fever Virus, West Nile Virus, and Hepatitis C Virus. It was anticipated that the biggest market for this novel drug will be for treatment of Hepatitis C, the market for which was in the $ billions in the United States alone.

INDUSTRY LEADERS

Mergers and acquisitions comprise the dominant trend among the leaders in molecular modeling. Smaller start-up firms, once they have established a valuable product and a strong customer base, are often acquired by larger drug behemoths. These large companies have more money for research and development as well as advanced distribution and marketing systems, both of which are appealing to any "small" firm interested in the further scientific pursuit of molecular modeling.

In early 2010, New York-based Schrodinger Company announced that it would take over the continued

development, maintenance, and sales of PyMOL, a best-in-class interactive visualization and presentation molecular modeling software suite used by scientists worldwide. Its creator, Dr. Warren DeLano, passed away suddenly and unexpectedly in November 2009. However, prior to his death, DeLano had been working with Schrodinger about integrating products between companies, including the PyMOL software package. Schrodinger remained a private company in 2010; sales revenues were unavailable, but the company has indicated sales above $20 million.

Back in 2001, Accelrys, a wholly owned subsidiary of Pharmacopeia Inc., bought approximately 95 percent of the outstanding shares of Synomics Limited. Synomics, located in England, combined science, process, and information technology skills to offer life sciences research organizations more effective and shared access to data, applications, and knowledge. Pharmacopeia spun off its drug development arm, which adopted the name Pharmacopeia Drug, in 2004. At that time, Pharmacopeia Inc. changed its name to Accelrys Inc. The company reported "solid" performance for its full fiscal year 2009 of $83 million in revenues, and further announced a merger with scientific software firm Symyx.

Tripos Inc.—renamed the New Tripos International in 2007 when it was purchased by Vector Capital—was founded in 1979. Based in St. Louis, Missouri, the company has a history of success in the fields of molecular imaging and design software. Tripos is a leading provider of discovery chemistry, integrated discovery software products, software consulting services, and discovery research services to the pharmaceutical, biotechnology, agrochemical, and other life sciences industries. Tripos supplies software, sells third party hardware, and offers research services and molecular libraries to the pharmaceutical, biotech, and other life science industries. In 2006 the company had more than 1,000 customers in 46 countries, including the top pharmaceutical companies worldwide.

With its Discovery Informatics products software, Tripos enables customers to quickly identify and optimize new compounds that have the potential to become products. The tools make the research process more efficient by identifying physical and structural properties of molecules likely to make them suitable as drugs. The tools then use this information to design novel molecules that possess these properties. The centerpiece of the software suite is SYBYL, a platform for molecular design, analysis, and visualization. It provides a computational tool kit that simplifies and accelerates the discovery of drugs and new chemical entities. By 2006 the company's Discovery Research arm had grown from 12 staff members in 1997 to about 170. These scientists had completed some 60 collaborative projects with biotech and pharmaceutical firms.

RESEARCH AND TECHNOLOGY

Going into the second decade of the 2000s, the industry continued to benefit from new research software applications that leveraged the power of molecular modeling to speed up the process of new drug discovery. One of the most active areas of research in which molecular modeling is being applied is medicinal chemistry. In a path of chemical reactions that ultimately ends in the development of a disease, many biological molecules that can act as potential targets for drug intervention are involved. Molecules that interact specifically with receptors or enzymes, for instance, can act as leads for creating new drugs. Molecular modeling plays an important role in this process. For example, by using molecular modeling to study a small protein in snake venom that binds to and inactivates an angiotension-converting enzyme that helps regulate blood pressure, scientists have been able to create better drugs to treat hypertension.

AIDS researchers have also used molecular modeling to study proteases, protein-cutting enzymes required for the function of the human immunodeficiency virus (HIV). When developing protease inhibitors, drug designers used computers to generate a 3-D structure of a related protease in order to model the smaller HIV protease. They compared the structure of the active site to that of other biologically important molecules. Medicinal chemists often compare different structures with similar biological activities to detect non-obvious likenesses. These computer simulations provided enough insight into the probable features of the enzyme's active site to be useful in designing effective inhibitors.

In 2008 Australian scientists discovered a way to "switch off" the Gab2 molecule that is a key player in the development of breast cancer and some types of leukemia. In a 2008 *Women's Health Weekly* article, Roger Daly, leader of the project, said "We've identified a completely novel mechanism for switching off Gab2. This uses another molecule that attaches to Gab2 and acts as a kind of shield, preventing it from transmitting further proliferative signals."

Molecular modeling incorporates molecular nanotechnology, in which individual atoms could be manipulated and rearranged to produce new items. As Georgia Tech Professor Ralph C. Merkle explained, "In the future ... we'll be able to snap together the fundamental building blocks of nature easily, inexpensively and in most of the ways permitted by the laws of physics. This will be essential if we are to continue the revolution in computer hardware beyond about the next decade, and will also let us fabricate an entire new generation of products that are cleaner, stronger, lighter, and more precise."

One example was Quantum 3.1, a software suite for Linux and Windows released by Moscow-based Quantum Pharmaceuticals. According to the November 17, 2005 issue of *Product News Network,* "The Quantum software was developed using a new paradigm in molecular modeling—applying quantum and molecular physics instead of statistical scoring-function-like and QSAR-like methods. The key benefit of Quantum is the outstanding precision of molecular modeling and calculations. Using Quantum 3.1, researchers can calculate the IC50 of protein-ligand and protein-protein complexes, perform ligand docking, perform virtual screening of small-molecule libraries, analyze large-scale protein movements, perform de novo drug design and calculate the solvation energy and solubility."

Molecular modeling was being applied in a wide range of areas, including ones that might not immediately come to mind. One example was the pulp and paper industry, where, in 2008, molecular modeling was being used to improve the structure of chemicals used in papermaking. Specifically, researchers were concentrating on improving optical properties, the bonding of paper fibers, and even the use of molecular energy to increase the brightness of paper and reduce yellowing. Researchers held the industry's first molecular modeling symposium in 2005 and a second conference in 2008.

Correlating the 3-D shape of a molecule with its performance is also a useful activity in many research arenas. Scientists at Sandia National Laboratories in Albuquerque, New Mexico, developed their own molecular modeling system and used it to create synthetic substances that mimic natural enzymes' abilities to catalyze reactions. At Procter & Gamble, molecular modeling is used to develop enzymes that make detergents fast acting. Other organizations have used it to study superconductors. Amoco uses molecular modeling to find better fuels. The use of this technology is also growing in fields as diverse as electronic, optical, and magnetic materials. Indeed, the possibilities may be endless.

Molecular modeling was used in the research and development activities of many different industries, including industrial gases, computer hardware and software, specialty and commodity chemicals, photonic and electronic materials, food and personal care products, agricultural chemicals, and fuels, polymers, glass, and structured materials. Molecular modeling had proven to be an effective tool for such nanotechnology.

BIBLIOGRAPHY

"Accelrys Posts Modest revenue growth for Q4 and Full Year; Expects Symyx Merger to Close in July." 21 May 2010. Available from http://www.genomeweb.com/informatics.

"Accelrys Releases New Multiscale Modeling and Simulation Tools in Materials Studio(R) 4.3." *Internet Wire,* 17 June 2008.

Law, Derek. "Molecular Modelling's $10-Million Comeback?" *Nature News,* 7 May 2010.

"Model Developed that Predicts Molecular Response of Living Cells to Genetic or Environmental Change." *Business Wire,* 27 December 2007.

"Multiscale Simulation Methods for Nanomaterials Addresses a Range of Organic, Inorganic and Bio-Materials." *Business Wire,* 20 February 2008.

"Nano Viricides Reports that Significant Efficacy was Achieved in initial Studies on Dengus Virus." *Nanowerk News,* Press Release, 1 June 2010. Available from http://www.nanowerk.com/news/newsid=16518.php.

"Nanotechnology Created by Dr. Ralph Merkle." Zyvex Corp., 2006. Available from http://www.zyvex. com/nano.

"Noesis to Build upon OpenEye's Cheminformatics Toolkit OEChem." *Business Wire,* 16 June 2008.

Rodden, Graeme. "The Future Is Still to Come." *Pulp & Paper,* April 2006.

"Schrodinger - Products Guide - PyMOL." 8 January 2010. Available from http://www.schrodinger.com/products/14/25.

"SimBioSys Utilizes Revolutionary Hardware Technology to Open New Frontiers in Molecular Modeling." *PR Newswire,* 24 April 2008.

Sims, Mark. "Molecular Modeling in CAD: Are You Ready to Design a 'Molecular' Machine? Software that Is a Distant Cousin of Conventional Solid-Modeling Packages May Turn Today's Designers into Molecular Engineers." *Machine Design,* 28 September 2006.

"Star-P Helps MIT Scientists Clear Pollution from the Air." *Chem.Info,* April 2007.

MORTGAGE COMPANIES

———■———

SIC CODE(S)

6162

6163

INDUSTRY SNAPSHOT

Overall, mortgage companies represent a central component of the nation's housing and loan markets and in their behavior increasingly resemble players in other financial sectors. Companies in this industry are generally subsidiaries of large financial institutions, but mortgage companies themselves do not engage in banking functions such as accepting deposits or offering checking accounts. They concentrate specifically on mortgage loans, but within that market there is a great deal of variation.

Although the U.S. mortgage industry enjoyed the largest refinancing boom in its history in the early 2000s, the honeymoon was over in 2007 when interest rates increased. Many homeowners, who only qualified for "subprime" mortgage loans during the housing boom, could not make their house payments. Mortgage companies found themselves with stacks of foreclosure notices and homes that had declined in value. Indeed, many industry experts who earlier in the decade had predicted a subprime mortgage crisis were saying, "I told you so."

ORGANIZATION AND STRUCTURE

Many consumers may still be confused by the plethora of lending sources. Basically, however, people who shop for mortgage loans can go to one of three different types of lenders. First, there are the traditional financial institutions and their affiliates, which include most banks, thrifts (savings banks or saving and loan associations), and credit unions, nearly all of which make mortgage loans. Sometimes the financial institution itself offers the loan; sometimes the loan is offered via a mortgage company owned by the institution. If a bank directs a customer to a loan office somewhere else, chances are that office will be in a mortgage company owned by the bank. Financial institutions generally underwrite their own loans. That is, they use their own assets to fund the loan. Banks and thrifts may hold the new loan in their own portfolio until it is paid off (sometimes as long as 30 years), or they can sell the loan into the broader secondary market for mortgage loans.

The second group consists of the more specialized mortgage bankers and mortgage companies. These institutions offer the same sort of mortgage loans as financial institutions but without any other banking services. They, too, underwrite their own loans. The national mortgage companies in particular are fairly innovative about creating mortgage products with varying terms, floating interest rates, and other features that attract a wider range of customers.

According to the Mortgage Bankers Association of America (MBA), mortgage banking companies are the largest group of home mortgage lenders, followed by commercial banks and savings and loans. Mortgage banking companies operate mainly in the secondary mortgage market, using government and private institutions.

Finally, there are mortgage brokers, which are mortgage banks in that they are not financial institutions and can be part of national companies. However, there is one

30-Year Fixed Mortgage Rate Trends

October 2007	6.4 percent
October 2008	6.2 percent
October 2009	5.1 percent
October 2010	4.2 percent

SOURCE: "Interest Rate Trends-Historical Graphs for Mortgage Rates" 2010, http://www.Mortgage-X.com.

important distinction: mortgage brokers do not provide the money to make their loans. Instead, they play a matchmaking role by putting borrowers in touch with loan sources for a fee. Especially if a borrower has had credit problems in the past, a broker can be helpful in locating more flexible lenders. A broker makes its money by collecting a fee from the lender, the borrower, or both. In the best of circumstances, the lender and the broker split the points (the fees the borrower pays), so it should not cost more to borrow through a broker.

Mortgage firms account for about two-thirds of all originations. The second most important group by volume of mortgages is commercial banks, followed by the thrift industry (such as savings and loan associations), which as recently as 1990 dominated the industry. Other mortgage lenders include credit unions and life insurance companies.

Banks and thrifts may hold or sell newly originated mortgages, but mortgage companies generally sell their new loans almost immediately, often at the end of each month. This process involves what is known as the secondary mortgage market, in which large numbers of individual loans are bundled together according to characteristics such as their term in years and their interest rate. This large bundle is then used as the basis for a security or bond that is backed by the predictable payoff schedules of the underlying mortgages. These securities are then sold on the open market, normally to pension funds and other institutional investors who consider them a reliable long-term investment.

This process of "securitization" of mortgages has two profound effects on the market. First, since the secondary market makes cash available to buy up mortgage loans, it permits the influx of more money into the mortgage market. This action in turn frees up more money for loans to the consumers and is thus particularly helpful in financing loans at the lower end of the market, where credit histories may be suspect. The other important effect of securitization has been the growth of mortgage companies. Since these firms lack the deep pockets of banks and thrifts, they could not possibly bear the risks involved in maintaining each of these loans in their own portfolio. By selling off the loan (and the attendant risk)

to the secondary market, mortgage companies can offer a service to the consumer at little or no risk to themselves. This arrangement has fueled the rapid growth of private mortgage companies, which in turn has meant more choices for consumers.

The volume of mortgages sold into the secondary market varies with changes in the volume of fixed rate lending (as opposed to variable rate loans). The higher the percentage of fixed rate loans being made (such as in periods of low interest rates, when consumers want to lock in good rates for the long term), the easier it is to secure such loans. By 2004, with interest rates on the upswing, the secondary market was beginning to see less and less mortgage activity.

As in other industries experiencing soaring growth rates, mortgage companies come in all sizes and shapes. The cost of entry into loan origination remained low into the middle years of the first decade of the 2000s, and many of the smallest brokers were mere mom-and-pop storefronts. Nevertheless, the financial sources necessary to compete and succeed as a full service mortgage banker had increased dramatically. As a result, in terms of dollar volume, the industry was increasingly dominated by the largest players, which together accounted for tens of billions of dollars in home loan originations each year.

The low barriers to entry also generated some controversy in their own right. In 2000, the mortgage industry began to crack down on itself in an effort to eliminate fraud through a toughened self-regulatory program. Weary of declining consumer confidence amid increasing reports of fraud, the industry, led by the National Association of Mortgage Brokers, aimed to require national registration for all mortgage brokers. By the middle of the first decade of the 2000s, many states had licensing bodies that regulated mortgage companies. The Mortgage Industry Standards Maintenance Organization (MISMO) was established in 1999 by the Mortgage Bankers Association (MBA) to develop, promote, and maintain voluntary standards for the mortgage industry.

BACKGROUND AND DEVELOPMENT

Although mortgage lending has been around a long time, the modern mortgage industry dates back to the 1970s when a handful of firms began to focus in earnest on this financial sector, streamlining and standardizing their offerings for a consumer market increasingly interested in home ownership. Notoriously tied to the fluctuations of national interest rates, mortgage lending was, of course, highly cyclical, subject to wild swings in operations. For example, through the 1990s, originations rose steadily as the Federal Reserve tinkered with rates to stem the effects of global economic crisis and inflation, before heading south in 2000 as rates topped 8 percent. After the September 11, 2001, terrorist attacks on the United States, key industry players were challenged to maintain a continuous flow of capital to the U.S. mortgage market. The cooling U.S. economy brought interest rates down in the early years of the first decade of the 2000s, leading to a major refinancing boom. Through it all, however, the mortgage market remained robust. By 2000, approximately 70 percent of all mortgages were originated by lending brokerages rather than by banks and thrifts, up from 20 percent in the early 1990s.

The mortgage industry became even more competitive in the late 1990s, as companies operated with very low profit margins to remain competitive. The industry's emphasis on volume fueled the competition, which also began to lead to waves of consolidation within the industry. Most of the industry's profitable companies were large mortgage brokers who could slash their profit margins and glean their profits from the plethora of loans they issued. Smaller companies, on the other hand, struggled to stay afloat or exited the business as competition started to escalate in the mid-1990s.

Moreover, the greater competition in the industry gave rise to greater innovation as companies sought ways to differentiate their services from those of other companies. Online mortgage sites such as E-Loan Inc., Mortgage.com Inc., MortgageSelect.com, and Homestore.com, Inc. took off in the late 1990s and early years of the first decade of the 2000s. These sites allow home buyers to search for rates, compare rates, receive recommendations, and apply for mortgages over the Internet while saving up to 80 percent in traditional fees.

Meanwhile, as the online lending market heated up, international servicing posed significant competition to U.S. mortgage companies. In particular, lenders were under increased pressure to simplify the lending process and to make it more consumer-friendly, as opposed to the more intensive grilling customers traditionally received. Mortgage companies were thus faced with the competing demands of making the process simpler while hedging against potential delinquencies.

Prelude to the Subprime Mortgage Crisis Mortgage companies through this period also explored the subprime and "no equity" niche for a new avenue of growth by offering loans for debt consolidation, paying off existing loans, and home improvement. These companies catered to borrowers who did not qualify for Federal Housing Administration, Fannie Mae, or Freddie Mac mortgages because of poor credit history and bankruptcy. Typically, subprime lenders charge interest rates about 6 percent higher than traditional mortgage companies. Furthermore, instead of using traditional mortgage criteria for determining credit worthiness, these mortgage companies often relied on criteria more akin to those used by the finance industry, where the age of the previous debt, not just the amount, is considered. With low profit margins in the traditional mortgage market, companies turned to the subprime and no equity market, where profit margins—and risks—were much higher. In the early days of subprime lending, mortgage companies provided loans to people with poor credit that did not exceed 60 percent of the value of their homes. Lenders, however, increased these loans to as much as 70 percent of the value of their homes by the late 1990s.

The subprime sector, after emerging as the superstar segment of the mortgage industry in the mid- and late 1990s, suffered in late 1998 and the following year when "risky" became a dirty word on Wall Street in light of the Russian debt default and the world financial markets' dizzying volatility. Many subprime lenders flowed out of the business in a hurry, while others simply collapsed altogether and filed for bankruptcy. The blow was attributed to several factors exacerbating the social causes, including the over-exuberance of lenders descending on the storied subprime market in hopes of cashing in quickly, leading to mispriced loans. The dark days of subprime lending, however, had light on the horizon for the financial industry's larger players: the price of subprime loans was cheap, and major banks, thrifts, and mortgage companies were buying them up fast. Subprime lending looked to be one of the brightest sectors of mortgage lending, rising from just under $30 million in 1993 to $213 billion in 2002.

The sagging U.S. economy hardly weighed down the mortgage industry in the early years of the first decade of the 2000s. At the peak of the booming economy in 1999, loan originations totaled $1.29 trillion. Two years later, the industry registered originations of $2.03 trillion, and by 2002, the origination market stood at $2.48 trillion, according to data compiled by the Mortgage Bankers Association. The MBA estimated total residential originations in 2003 at a record high of $3.2 trillion, but that marked the end of the mortgage industry's boom in the early years of the first decade of the 2000s.

Enjoying record low interest rates, homeowners raced to their mortgage lenders to refinance their home loans through the early years of the first decade of the 2000s. Huge numbers of homeowners were locked into 30-year mortgages in the range of 5 percent interest. While this was the bread and butter of the early years of the decade's refinancing boom, the effects on the industry in the later years of the decade were harsh. With interest rates on the rise, refinancing became less attractive, and so loan performance diminished. Homeowners enjoying such low rates were less likely to refinance again or sell their current homes to move into more expensive models.

Following the record year of 2003, the mortgage industry cooled off in 2005 and into 2006 as interest rates increased and home values were no longer skyrocketing. Industry players looked to subprime mortgages to fuel growth, specifically targeting minorities, immigrants, and individuals with low to moderate incomes.

Alternative and subprime mortgages increased 28 percent in 2005, while the rest of the market remained relatively flat. According to a Mortgage Bankers Association survey, which included most of the industry's top 30 originators, more than $866 billion in first mortgages and $189 billion in second mortgages were originated during the second half of 2005 alone. During that time period, first mortgage originations increased 14 percent over the first half of the year, and second mortgage originations climbed 13 percent.

In a May 9, 2006, news release, MBA Chief Economist and Senior Vice President of Research and Business Development Doug Duncan explained, "As short-term rates increased over the second half of 2005, homeowners moved away from adjustable rate loans into fixed-rate loans. Fixed-rate loans are more attractive as short term interest rates rise to similar levels as long term rates. Not surprisingly, consumers respond to interest rate driven changes in opportunities in the marketplace."

While interest rates were rising during the middle years of the first decade of the 2000s, this was not without benefit for mortgage companies. Since the cost of new loans rises with interest rates, refinancing diminishes, resulting in less portfolio runoff. Moreover, servicing charges tend to rise with rates as well, leading to an improved revenue stream. These trends favor the larger lending companies who maintain greater economies of scale with which to hold on to customers and maintain viability. Higher interest rates usually lead to an incline in adjustable-rate mortgages (ARMs), as homeowners place their hopes in lower rates in the future. However, higher rates also tend to eat into origination profitability, and thus the firms most likely to weather years of boosted interest rates were those that maintained strong servicing operations.

Discrimination Discrimination continued to dog the industry and threaten its reputation. Gaining considerable attention in the late 1990s and early years of the first decade of the 2000s were increasing reports, confirmed by the findings of separate studies conducted by the Association of Community Organizations for Reform Now (ACORN) and the Urban Institute, of lingering racial bias in mortgage lending practices. The latter study reported that lenders in 1999 were less likely to provide minorities with information about loan products and generally quoted higher interest rates on mortgages to minorities than to white customers. The ACORN study, meanwhile, reported that blacks were denied loans 217 percent as often as whites, a trend that worsened in the late 1990s from 206 percent in 1995. Latino customers, likewise, were far more likely to be rejected for conventional mortgage loans than were whites, at a rate of 183 percent as often, up from 169 percent in 1995.

"Race continues to be an issue," said Massachusetts Community & Banking Council report author and University of Massachusetts economist James Campen, adding, "It is a bigger issue now than in 1990." According to the *Boston Business Journal,* the report also found that although blacks make up 24.5 percent of Boston's population, they received only 11.5 percent of loans issued. Latinos, who comprise 10.8 percent of the city's population, received 7.5 percent of all 2001 loans. Campen could not explain why blacks had a tougher time getting loans and why they experienced higher mortgage denial rates than Latinos.

The Research Institute for Housing America (RIHA) "Homeownership in the Immigrant Population" study, which documents immigration trends during the 1980s and 1990s and their effects on housing trends, found that a large gap initially exists in homeownership rates between immigrant groups and their correlative native-born households, and that that gap had been getting larger, in part reflecting the changing economic composition of new entrants. Another important finding was that the gap had closed over time, as immigrant households assimilated into housing markets. It was projected that this process would significantly boost housing and mortgage demand in the future.

Freddie Mac, in its efforts to alleviate charges of discriminatory lending, in April 2000 entered into a partnership with Jesse Jackson's Rainbow PUSH Coalition to promote minority homeownership, and also tightened restrictions on the subprime lending sector, which had generated complaints of predatory lending taking advantage of low income debtors.

In the early 2000s, mortgage companies grew quickly, thanks to the booming U.S. housing market. Consumers who perhaps were not qualified to obtain a home loan from a bank due to bad credit or low income were welcomed by the mortgage companies, and through subprime or adjustable rate mortgages, these homeowners purchased houses that, by 2007, were too much for them to handle financially. Home values declined, interest rates went up, and many people who had obtained a low-interest rate mortgage earlier in the decade became delinquent or defaulted on their home loans.

Stark statistics illustrated the severity of the situation in 2007 and 2008: RealtyTrac found that more than 2.2 million foreclosures were filed on approximately 1.3 million properties in 2007, an increase of 75 percent from 2006. According to *National Mortgage News,* in the first quarter of 2008, the overall delinquency rate, the number of loans entering foreclosure, and the foreclosure inventory all reached record highs. In July 2008, one in every 464 U.S. households received a foreclosure filing; bank repossessions went up 184 percent year-over-year; and default notices rose 53 percent. Statistics on the related job market showed that during the first half of 2008, more than 40,000 employees in the mortgage lending businesses lost their jobs when many companies either folded or laid off workers.

The undervaluation of real risk in the subprime market caused a ripple effect that affected the entire world economy. As of July 2008, banks and other financial institutions around the world, including mortgage companies, had experienced a total of $435 billion in losses.

According to the Mortgage Bankers Association (MBA), by August 2008, "the Federal Reserve's aggressive rate cuts and liquidity injections have helped alleviate the stress in some financial markets." Seventy-four percent of banks had tightened standards on prime mortgage loans and 86 percent of banks had done so for subprime mortgage loans. Despite some gains in the industry, however, several areas of mortgage financing had seen very little improvement since a year before when the global financial crisis began. New home sales continued to be down, although only by 17.1 percent in the second quarter of 2008 as compared to 44.9 percent in the first quarter. Existing home sales were down 3.2 percent in the second quarter, a significant improvement over the 25 percent figure shown in the last three quarters of 2007. Most significantly for mortgage companies, about 33 percent of sales in the first half of 2008 were foreclosures or distressed sales. The MBA noted, however, that the activity varied by state, with California experiencing the highest foreclosure rate: 41.1 percent of homes sold there in June 2008 were foreclosures. The MBA also expected declines in home sales and prices to continue through 2009 but at a more moderate rate.

CURRENT CONDITIONS

According to the National Association of Home Builders, residential real estate (including rent, mortgage payments, construction, remodeling, utilities, and brokers' fees) accounted for roughly 17 percent of gross domestic product in 2009. However, during that time, and well into 2010, the mortgage market was in a tailspin, taking down the real estate market with it. Even the lowest mortgage interest rates in decades (4.2 percent for a 30-year fixed loan in late 2010) could not attract new business because many prospective home owners were unemployed or otherwise drowning in debt. By mid-2010, more than 14 million persons were unemployed in the United States.

For existing mortgage business, roughly one in four homeowners, involving 10.7 million households nationwide, owed more mortgage debt than their houses were worth. Between 2008 and 2010, the housing market lost an estimated $4.9 *trillion* dollars, as 59 million homes had declined in value, reported Ben Tracy for CBS News in February 2010. Nationally, nearly six million households were foreclosed between 2007 and 2010, and this further brought down the value of other homes in the area as well as the value of entire neighborhoods. In July 2010, real estate data company Realty Trac reported that foreclosures had increased in 75 percent of the top U.S. metro areas. Las Vegas had the nation's highest metro foreclosure rate. Arizona, California, Florida, and Nevada led the country in cities with the highest numbers of foreclosures. Michigan, Idaho, and Utah also had high foreclosure rates. In 2010 alone, roughly 1.9 million homeowners received foreclosure/default notices, with an estimated full foreclosure, such as bank repossession, reaching one million of these. According to a report from Clear Capital, Inc., which tracked home prices across the United States, approximately 23 percent of homes on the market were bank-owned. Realty Trac senior vice-president Rick Sharga, in a July 2010 Reuters Press Release, opined that meaningful, sustainable home price appreciation was not expected to return until 2013.

New housing starts were equally dire in 2010, dropping to less than 500,000, or one-fourth of the 2 million they had been in 2005. The median price of a residential home in 2010, according to the National Association of Realtors, was $173,100.

There was light at the end of the tunnel. In mid-2010, housing values began to plateau, and there were even a few months where home prices actually rose, according to Standard & Poor's Case-Shiller indexes. Moreover, for those who were employed and had saintly credit histories, 30-year fixed mortgage rates had dropped from roughly 6.6 percent in September 2008 to 5.6 percent in June 2009 to 4.2 percent in October 2010. In the last quarter of 2010, the processing of foreclosures was stalled, and in fact, came to a halt for Bank of America, JPMorganChase, and GMAC, amid allegations that foreclosures had been hastily processed without due diligence, and in some cases, outright fraud. As of 2010, 24 states allowed foreclosure only through judical processes. The problem started when it was discovered that several banks and foreclosure processing firms had filed and/or signed court documents that contained unverified or false information, attempting to speed up the foreclosure process. Originally, the foreclosure moratorium affected only those state using judicial foreclosure processes. Later, all 50 state attorneys general, as well as several politicians, called for a moratorium, and in October 2010, the attorneys general launched a joint investigation into mortgage company mishandling of foreclosure processing. This, in combination with Obama administration efforts geared at helping homeowners work with their lenders, was expected to speed resolution of threatened foreclosures and facilitate more favorable remortgaging of properties for qualified homeowners temporarily experiencing financial difficulties.

The 2009 bail-out of Fannie Mae and Freddie Mac, generally faulted on the subprime mortgage market, was expected to be at least $160 billion and was classified as the biggest government bailout in American history. As of June 2010, Fanie Mae and Freddie Mac owned or guaranteed 53 percent of the nation's $10.7 trillion in residential mortgages, making them the largest stakeholders in the industry. As a result of the bailout, in 2010, American taxpayers owned 80 percent of Fannie and Freddie. Under the terms of the bailout, Fannie and Freddie were required to pay a ten percent annual dividend on the shares owned by taxpayers.

INDUSTRY LEADERS

Wells Fargo & Co. Wells Fargo & Co., the fifth largest bank in the country, moved to the top of the mortgage lending industry through its acquisition of Norwest Co. in 1998. By early 2000, Wells Fargo dissolved the Norwest name entirely but expanded its mortgage operations, forming a joint venture with American Financial Corp. and agreeing to sell most of its originations to Freddie Mac, while focusing on its approval expertise. The firm also purchased the mortgage servicing portfolios of GE Capital, First Union, and Bingham Financial. The Wells Fargo Home Mortgage Emerging Markets Department of Des Moines, Iowa was dedicated to increasing homeownership among America's low and moderate income families. The company had approximately 1,000 home mortgage store locations nationwide.

Countrywide Financial Corp. Countrywide Financial of Calabasas, California, was the third largest residential lender by loan volume in the United States in 2008. Countrywide is a subsidiary of Bank of America, which purchased the firm in 2008. The company services mortgages through two subsidiaries, Countrywide Bank and Countrywide Home Loans. In 2000, Countrywide reversed a long-standing strategy and began to hire commissioned people in its retail channel. Countrywide's focus was the traditional retail and wholesale loan origination market, though it built an extensive online presence as well. Moreover, the company

moved into the European market in 1999, when it agreed to service loans for the United Kingdom's Woolwich PLC.

Founded in 1969, Countrywide achieved its prominence in the industry by focusing solely on mortgages. Full Spectrum Lending Inc., founded in 1996, was a division of Countrywide that featured options for borrowers with less than perfect credit. The Full Spectrum Web site was launched specifically to ease the loan process for borrowers who are self-employed and have a harder time verifying their income, and those who have suffered financial hardships such as job loss, debt, or divorce.

GMAC Mortgage LLC GMAC Mortgage, based in Fort Washington, Pennsylvania, is a subsidiary of General Motors Acceptance Corp. (GMAC), one of the largest financial services companies in the world. GMAC Mortgage Corp. was formed in 1985. In the late years of the first decade of the 2000s, it originated first and second lien mortgages through a nationwide network of retail offices, direct lending centers, and the Internet brands of gmacmortgage.com and ditech.com.

Fannie Mae and Freddie Mac Although not technically part of the U.S. government, Fannie Mae's and Freddie Mac's government charters guarantee government backing in the event of a financial downturn. As a result, these companies enjoyed a great deal more flexibility, and bankers were willing to make loans at below-market levels, confident they would generate the returns.

All that changed in 2008 and 2009, when the U.S. government (Congress), faced with a national economic crisis with domino-effect consequences, extended credit to, and bought up mortgage-backed securities of, Fannie Mae and Freddie Mac, in what generally was termed the largest "government bailout" in U.S. history. At that time, millions of bad loans issued under supprime mortgages during the housing boom remained on their books, and delinquencies and foreclosures, as well as national unemployment, continued to rise. According to federal reports, in 2008, more than $500 billion of loans held or guaranteed by Fannie and Freddie were in subprime mortgages.

This was not the first controversy involving the two companies. Throughout the early 2000s, they drew an increasing amount of criticism. Critics claimed that the firms' relationship with the government put competitors at a disadvantage. Moreover, they claimed that both firms violated their charters by using the implicit backing of the government to diversify into market operations not explicitly covered by their charters. An audit of Freddie Mac found that the firm understated its earnings in the early years of the first decade of the 2000s to demonstrate smooth, steady earnings increases. The firm was forced to restate its earnings in 2003, and many critics called for both firms' charters to be revoked.

Fannie and Freddie came close to re-regulation in 2004, when the Bush administration moved to make the lenders more accountable to market forces by eliminating their exemption from U.S. bankruptcy laws, but the plans were scuttled in Congressional committee. For their part, Freddie Mac and Fannie Mae argued, along with their supporters, that the ultimate beneficiaries of their arrangement with the government were the millions of U.S. homeowners who couldn't afford to buy without the lower interest rates they provide.

The government-mandated companies Fannie Mae and Freddie Mac also played a significant role in the industry by ensuring that lenders had sufficient funds for low and moderate income, minority, and immigrant borrowers. These companies do not lend directly to home buyers but make sure mortgage companies have enough money to lend home buyers by purchasing mortgages from lenders. The firms grew dramatically in the 1990s and the early years of the first decade of the 2000s, with combined assets rising from $250 billion to $1.7 trillion in the 10 years ending in 2003.

Now a corporation owned by stockholders, Freddie Mac had been created by Congress in 1970 to ensure the availability of low cost mortgages. Like Fannie Mae, Freddie Mac—officially the Federal Home Loan Mortgage Corp.—serves the low and middle income markets as well as borrowers with special needs. Because of Freddie Mac, borrowers can take advantage of long term, fixed rate mortgages with a low down payment. Throughout its history, the company implemented new services and technologies to make obtaining mortgages easier.

RESEARCH & TECHNOLOGY

In the early 2000s, mortgage processing no longer took weeks, as it did in the past, but the industry nevertheless faced calls for speeding processing in order to keep up with the fast-paced marketplace. Automated underwriting, which received a boost with the onset of electronic signature imaging in 1999, could reduce the cost and speed of processing, but it could just as easily reduce the level of service, especially for customers less familiar with the mortgage process who may desire face-to-face service. Moreover, although processing costs, to the tune of about $4,600 each, were considered inflated throughout the industry, electronic imaging remained too costly to pose a viable alternative.

New tools were on the horizon to allow for more accurate estimations of real estate property values. Introduced in the late 1990s, automated valuation models (AVMs) had yet to take hold on a mass scale, although industry observers expected their deployment to skyrocket once market conditions were right. AVMs pool statistical data on real estate, including property characteristics and tax assessments, and weigh them against price and sales trends for properties with comparable features to yield a statistically precise valuation. Industry analysts expected the biggest selling point of AVMs would likely be their ability to generate improved risk positions, as loans that originated based on AVM valuation models acquired a track record of accuracy and safety.

The Mortgage Industry Standards Maintenance Organization (MISMO) eMortgage Workshop released the eMortgage Specifications Version 3.0 (the first version was released in 2003). The framework for entering paperless mortgages with electronic signatures centers on the concept of a Securable, Manageable, Archivable, Retrievable, Transferable (SMART) Document. The document binds data and signatures in a single electronic file. According to Freddie Mac Vice President of Asset Acquisition and Data Validation Jim Johnson, such systems should be based on open standards to simplify the technology integration process between all mortgage industry participants. Interconnecting of capabilities eliminated the re-keying of information and increased the integrity of mortgage data. MISMO played a key role in promoting the industry-wide usage of eXtensible Markup Language (XML) tags for data transfer. Similar to hypertext markup language (HTML) tags, XML used identifiers to tell a processor exactly what data was represented, which cut the time and expense of originating a mortgage loan.

BIBLIOGRAPHY

Adler, Lynn. "Foreclosures Up in 75 Percent of Toop U.S. Metro Areas." *Reuters Press Release*, 29 July 2010.

Cornwell, Ted. "Overdues Hit Record." *National Mortgage News*, 9 June 2008.

"Countrywide COO to Leave After Bank of America Acquisition." *Multi-Housing News*, 29 May 2008.

"Despite Housing Crisis, Mortgages Still Lead CU Loan Growth." *Banking Wire*, 13 August 2008.

"First Half 2008 Recap and Outlook." Washington, DC: Mortgage Bankers Association, 12 August 2008.

Garten, Jeffrey E. "Yet Another Domino Falls." *Newsweek International*, 28 July 2008.

"Home Foreclosure Filings Up 55 Percent in July." *Reuters*, 14 August 2008.

"Housing Crisis Getting Uglier in 2010." 2 February 2010. CBS Evening News Available from http://www. cbsnews.com/ stories/2010/02/02/eveningnews/main6167610.shtml.

"Housing Mess Spawns More Mortgage Fraud." *Investment News*, 28 July 2008.

"IndyMac May Not Be Last Bank to Fail, Analysts Say." *Investment News*, 21 July 2008.

"Interest Rate Trends-Historical Graphs for Mortgage Rates." Available from http://www.mortgages-x.com/trends.

Jalili, H. Michael. "In Brief: Mortgage Foreclosure Surge Predicted." *American Banker,* 12 May 2006.

Killian, Thomas. "Surviving The 2007 Financial Crisis." *US Banker,* March 2008.

"Long Delay in Freclosures Could Hurt Southern New Jersey Housing Market." *Press of Atlantic City,* 14 October 2010. Available from http://www.pressofatlanticcity.com/news/breaking/article_ff111508-dee-11df-9dc1-001cc4c002e0.html.

McMahon, Chris. "Recession Hurts: Many Analysts Claim the Current Subprime Crisis Has Led to the Greatest Economic Mess Since the Great Depression." *Futures,* July 2008.

Mook, Ben. "Moratorium on Foreclosures Triggers Housing Concerns Nationwide." *Arizona Capitol Times,* 14 October 2010.

"Mortgage Industry Job Cuts Surpass 40,000." Washington, DC: Associated Press, 2008.

"Mortgage Industry Less Than Enthusiastic About Housing Bill Provisions." *Multi-Housing News,* 9 May 2008.

"Mortgage Rates Increase: 30-Year Rate Hits Highest Level Since September." *Multi-Housing News,* 20 June 2008.

"Ohio AG Sues Freddie Mac over Subprime Mortgage Losses." *Mortgage Banking,* March 2008.

"Q3 2010 and September 2010 Foreclosure Reports." Reuters Press Release, 14 October 2010.

Silver-Greenberg, Jessica, Paula Lehman, and Jacob Stokes. "Things Aren't Tough All Over: Even Though U.S. Home Prices May Have Further to Fall, Plenty of Cities Are Defying the Subprime Slump." *Business Week,* 4 August 2008.

"U.S. Foreclosure Activity Increases 75 Percent in 2007." Irvine, CA: RealtyTrac, 29 January 2008.

"Weekly Commentary—Latest Data on Inflation and Housing Activity Show a Cooling Economy—Fed Will Likely Hold Rates Steady in September." Mortgage Bankers Association of America, 21 August 2006. Available from http://www.mortgagebankers.org/.

Woellert, Lorraine, and John Gittelsohn. "Fannie-Freddie Fix at $160 Billion With $1 Trillion Worst Case." *Bloomberg News.,* 13 June 2010. Available from http://www. bloomberg.com/news/2010-06-13.

MUTUAL FUNDS

—■—

SIC CODE(S)

6211

6221

6231

6282

6289

INDUSTRY SNAPSHOT

As one of the most popular investment vehicles in the United States, mutual funds take money from public investors and invest it as a collective institution. Investment decisions are made by a fund manager chosen by the board of directors. The fund manager is responsible for making the right picks to deliver strong returns to investors. While there are mutual funds for every type of investor, from the tycoon to the neophyte, they can be particularly attractive to inexperienced investors, not only because fund participants are not charged with direct control over investment but also because these funds limit risk exposure. Since mutual funds are spread out over a number of different investments, a washout in one will not deplete the entire investment pool.

Although U.S. mutual funds had held their own through the stock market bubble burst of 2000 and early in the sluggish economy that followed, shedding a few lackluster funds and losing a few million small investors even while assets hovered near historic highs, by 2002, a torrent of investors, both individual and institutional, had begun reducing holdings in mutual funds, including a heavy pull-out from money market funds, possibly to seek higher returns elsewhere. Retrenchment carried into

the following year, but while asset flows began to improve, a flurry of legal and ethical questions began to dog fund managers on issues ranging from asset valuation to improper trades. By 2004, federal and state regulators had charged several top-shelf fund companies with fraud, leaving a chain of fund managers and executives disgraced and unemployed, and Congress passed new legislation to curtail a number of practices seen as harmful to investors.

Fund companies responded to the crises with proposals to create a central clearinghouse for all trades, removing ambiguity and potential for so-called late trading that occurred after hours to the benefit of fund insiders. They likewise moved toward fair-value pricing of assets to eliminate arbitrage—the practice of taking advantage of a price imbalance between two or more markets to make a profit—between what the fund says a security is worth and its actual current price on the open market. Under a 2004 SEC regulation, firms were also to appoint a compliance officer to spearhead internal enforcement of legal requirements.

ORGANIZATION AND STRUCTURE

There are three broad categories of mutual funds. Money market funds normally invest in securities maturing in one year or less and are known as short-term funds. Stock funds and bond and income funds invest in securities to be held for the long term. Each category is further broken down depending on investors' goals. Money market mutual funds invest in either taxable or tax-exempt securities including Treasury bills, municipal securities, certificates of deposit of banks, and commercial paper. Bond

U.S. Mutual Fund Assets as of December 2009

Equity funds	44 percent
Money market funds	30 percent
Bond funds	20 percent
Hybrid funds	6 percent

SOURCE: 2010 Investment Company Fact Book.

and income funds look for growth of principal and/or income from bonds, Treasury bills, mortgage securities, company debt, municipal securities, and stocks. Stock or equity funds look for a combination of growth in the price of stocks and other securities and income, or dividends, of stocks.

There are also funds of funds—funds that pool money to invest in other mutual fund groups. These funds can be divided into the same categories as the funds they invest in. Thus there are funds that invest only in funds that invest only in technology stocks, and so on.

Mutual funds are managed professionally by those in the securities industry. They perform research on companies and securities plus keep tabs on general market conditions. Based on their research, managers decide which securities to add or delete from a fund to achieve investors' goals. An individual investor is known as a shareholder. A principal underwriter sells shares to shareholders, who include individuals and companies engaged in institutional investment such as through 401(k) plans. The precise services a fund offers are determined by the board of directors. While a mutual fund in theory spreads risk, risk is still associated with investing, including a possible loss of the principal investment. Just as with funds invested directly in the stock market, in bonds, or other securities, money invested in mutual funds is not insured by any federal agency.

Individual investors can buy shares in mutual funds through brokers, financial planners, bank representatives, insurance agents, or other investment professionals. Professionals can recommend funds based on clients' needs and goals and are compensated by commissions or fees. Investors may also buy shares directly, making decisions based upon their own research.

Most mutual funds list their prices with the NASDAQ. The price of a fund must be calculated every day by law. The price is the net asset value (NAV) plus any front-end sales charges. The NAV is determined by market value of the securities owned by the fund minus the liabilities and divided by the total number of shares owned by shareholders.

All U.S. mutual funds are regulated by the U.S. Securities and Exchange Commission (SEC) and by federal laws. Mutual funds must provide investors with a prospectus and shareholder report free of charge. A prospectus explains how to buy and sell shares; states the goals, strategies, and risks of the fund; and gives information on fees and expenses. The shareholder report contains financial statements and reviews the performance of the fund.

Four main laws also govern mutual funds. The Investment Company Act of 1940 requires twice-yearly filings with the SEC and the fund administrators must keep detailed financial records. The Securities Act of 1933 states that mutual funds must offer prospectuses to investors and must register the offerings of fund shares. The Securities Exchange Act of 1934 requires sellers of mutual funds, such as brokers, to register with the SEC and dictates seller and buyer relations. The Investment Advisers Act of 1940 details record-keeping requirements, requires registration of investment advisers, and includes anti-fraud provisions.

In 1996, the U.S. Congress passed the National Securities Markets Improvement Act. This legislation calls for uniform regulation of mutual funds. While preserving states' regulatory powers, mutual funds are regulated on the federal level as far as structure, operation, and review of prospectuses and advertising. The law lowers fees paid to the SEC by the securities industry and gives the SEC exclusive oversight of mutual fund advisers.

BACKGROUND AND DEVELOPMENT

In 1868, the Foreign and Colonial Government Trust in London, England set up the first mutual fund. It promised those of modest means the same chance at making money in securities as wealthier people. In the United States, those who invested in capital markets were still only the wealthiest few until the 1920s. Until then, middle-income people put their money into banks or bought stock in specific companies. The first mutual fund in the United States appeared in 1924 as the Massachusetts Investors Trust. The fund contained stocks of 45 companies and had $50,000 in assets. The stock market crash of 1929 forced Congress to act to protect investors. While risk is part of the industry, Congress passed laws to enable investors to gather as much information as possible about all types of securities, including mutual funds.

Once the country began recovering from the Great Depression of the 1930s, people turned to mutual funds as an alternative to investing directly in the stock market. The Investment Company Act of 1940 provided for the protection of investors through a fund's board of directors, charging the directors with ensuring a smooth convergence between the interests of the fund's investors and those of its managers. At the same time, the first international stock fund was offered. Funds remained relatively the same, containing mostly stocks, until the 1970s when funds began adding more bonds. Money market mutual funds were also created and tax-exempt funds were offered. By the 1990s, there were mutual funds for almost any investor's goals, including very specialized industry funds.

The choices facing investors have exploded since the creation of the first mutual fund. In 1940 there were fewer than 80 funds; in 1960, there were161 funds; in 1980, 564; and in 2000, 7,929. Assets grew from $500 million in 1940 to nearly $7 trillion in 2000. By 2003, there were 8,126 mutual funds available for investment, just slightly off from their all-time peak in 2001, according to the Investment Company Institute (ICI).

By the fall of 2000, the ICI reported that about 88 million Americans invested in mutual funds, representing an increase of 5 million shareholders from 1999. Company retirement plans gave mutual funds about half their business, while 34 percent of shareholders worked primarily through a broker, insurance agent, financial planner, or bank representative. The rest sought out funds themselves or through a discount broker. Generationally, baby boomers (born between 1946 and 1964) accounted for 51 percent of mutual fund shareholders, while those born prior to 1946 accounted for 27 percent, and Generation Xers (born between 1965 and 1980) accounted for 22 percent. The average shareholder in 1999 was 44 years old, married, and employed, with total mutual fund investments of $25,000. Median household income for the average shareholder was $55,000. In a little over half the U.S. households owning mutual funds, investment decisions were shared between men and women.

Investment professionals have added many services for investors over the years. Investors now receive information beyond the prospectus and annual report. Professionals provide tax information, retirement and general financial planning, toll-free 24-hour telephone service, newsletters, and facsimile and Internet access.

Mutual funds faced competition, however, from bankers and insurers who were fast encroaching on their territory. The repeal of the depression era Glass-Steagall Act with the late 1999 passage of the Gramm-Leach-Bliley Act, also known as the Financial Services Modernization Act, accelerated the pace at which such firms could engage in retail investment. To capitalize on their financial services business, banks and insurers have gobbled up brokerage firms with an eye toward the creation of financial "supermarkets"at which customers will conduct most or all of their financial business, including institutional investing. Wells Fargo Securities, for instance, rolled out a mutual fund marketplace in 1998 that generated over $500 billion in assets by 2000. In part related to these developments, the early years of

the first decade of the 2000s promised a wave of consolidation among mutual funds, as competition heightened and firms strove to remain competitive.

Emerging market funds also took off in 1999, reversing the previous year's dismal performance, which was largely due to the shockwaves from the Asian financial crisis. Having fallen 27.1 percent in 1998, emerging market funds shot up 70.8 percent in 1999 on fund flows totaling $702 million, led by the Lexington Worldwide Emerging Markets Fund with $300 million. Austerity programs and structural adjustment in developing countries, which lower the costs of doing business there, spurred terrific growth in this often risky sector, which remains subject to political and economic turmoil overseas. As the global financial system grows increasingly integrated, however, emerging market funds are likely to see a diminishment of their independence from domestic stock performance, as volatility in the United States reverberates around the world. By July 2000, emerging market fund assets totaled $141.3 billion, compared with only $14.3 billion ten years earlier. According to *Barron's,* global funds accounted for about half of total assets, while Asian regional fund assets amounted to $30.1 billion.

In the early years of the first decade of the 2000s, the industry faced an array of charges that fund managers and staff routinely abused their roles at investors' expense. Since some funds specialized in thinly traded (traded infrequently or in low volumes) holdings, funds often calculated their valuations themselves, a practice that some observers insisted was leading funds to succumb to the temptation to use those holdings to pay down debts, thus altering a fund's value without the knowledge of the average investor. As a result, valuations were increasingly seen as inaccurate, leading buyers to pay too much and sellers to make a killing.

Two practices in particular became the object of investigations and lawsuits orchestrated by state officials and the SEC. The first, known as late trading, involved hushed transactions outside normal market hours and frequently on terms favorable to fund employees or their favored clients. That practice was simply illegal. A second abuse related to taking advantage of short-term fluctuations in the price of an asset in different markets around the world. Called market timing, this activity was not illegal but in many cases was not in the interests of most fund investors and again was mainly used to benefit a few connected individuals unbeknownst to the general investing public.

These unethical activities came to the fore in 2003 when regulators announced investigations of several mutual fund companies. By the time they were finished, more than 15 fund companies were implicated in the abuses and a number of individuals were charged with securities fraud. Most prominently, Putnam Investments and Strong Funds were slapped with accusations of widespread improper activity. Both soon had senior management shakeups and within a few months, Strong, on the verge of failure, became absorbed by Wells Fargo.

In light of these problems, the SEC issued new regulations and a burst of legislation began to rumble through both houses of Congress in late 2003 and early 2004. The SEC addressed the abuses directly by specifying new procedures for handling end-of-day trades as well as so-called fair market pricing that would cut through the smoke surrounding foreign asset values.

Despite the tumult, most investors remained committed to funds, although some of the scandal-marred ones experienced great volatility. Public outcry aside, this underlying support was seen as a very healthy omen for the industry once the bad publicity died down and, in some cases, reparations were made. Nonetheless, a good number of marginal funds closed shop in 2003, following a trend of consolidation that predated the trading allegations.

Meanwhile, environmentally and socially conscious investors welcomed the rise of "ethical funds." As government deregulation flourishes, the responsibility to enforce business practices consistent with social welfare, environmental efficiency, and ethical standards becomes relegated increasingly to market forces. Ethical funds thus allow investors' money to speak their minds, as well as their consciences. Ethical funds are concentrated primarily on equities and have generally favored smaller or new firms, though that trend has grown less pronounced. As a recognized investment practice, socially responsible investment is fairly new, although some investors have long tried to remain cognizant of the social consequences of their investment patterns.

Meanwhile, diversification reigned among mutual fund investors. The Investment Company Institute and the Securities Industry Association (SIA) survey found that 22 percent of fund investors owned shares in seven or more stock funds, while an additional 26 percent maintained portfolios with four to six funds. Only 19 percent were invested in only one fund.

Although they have maintained a slightly more modest profile than the raging stock market, U.S. equity mutual funds have outperformed all U.S. stocks over the three, five, and 10 years up to 2000, when assets in such funds totaled $3.95 trillion, up from $3.1 trillion the year before. Funds that invested heavily in large capitalization U.S. companies continued to capture the lion's share of the new cash inflow compared with the flow of funds to small capitalization funds. By far the most popular type of fund, 90 percent of all fund investors put some money into equity funds, which generated an average return of 18 percent in 1999.

By 2002, according to a study on equity ownership done by the ICI and SIA, an estimated 52.7 million U.S households owned equities. The study indicated that the typical investor held an equity portfolio of moderate value. Nearly half of these investors had equity assets of less than $50,000. The SIA noted that 79 percent of equity owners participated in employer-sponsored retirement plans. The study also found that in 2001, more investors bought individual stock and stock mutual funds than sold investments (37 percent bought while 30 percent sold). That same year, 22 percent of mutual stock investors bought stock mutual funds while 16 percent sold. According to the study, by January 2002, 66 percent of equity investors owned stock mutual funds in retirement plans and 17 percent owned individual stock, including employer stock, in retirement plans.

Following the scandals of the early years of the first decade of the 2000s and predictions that the days of mutual funds were numbered, investors began channeling money back into them during the middle of the decade. According to the June 26, 2006, issue of *Business Week,* $255 billion flowed into mutual funds in 2005, followed by $145 billion through April 2006. Assets in mutual funds totaled $9.5 trillion by mid-2006, up from almost $7.0 trillion in 2000. Especially popular were asset allocation funds that enabled investors to spread their investments over an assortment of cash, bonds, and stocks.

Despite charges that mutual fund performance falls short of market indexes, *Business Week* reported that mutual funds outpaced the market between 2002 and 2005. According to the publication, while the Standard & Poor's 500 stock index increased 15.2 percent during this time period, stock funds earned an average of 16.9 percent.

The Investment Company Institute reported that U.S. mutual fund assets grew at a compound annual rate of 5.1 percent from 2000 to 2005, according to *Money Management Executive.* At this rate, the institute projected that fund assets could reach $11 trillion by 2010. While it was uncertain if such growth could be sustained, it seemed clear that mutual funds were here to stay—even though investors were also pouring a great deal of money into other options, such as hedge funds and exchange-traded funds.

While lower fees and increased regulatory surveillance were positive factors for mutual fund investors heading into the late years of the first decade of the 2000s, some observers still charged that investment brokers and advisors put too much emphasis on commissions instead of investment performance. In addition, investors had approximately 9,000 funds at their fingertips, making oversight a challenge.

According to the Investment Company Institute (ISI), in June 2008 total net assets of U.S. mutual funds equaled almost $12 trillion. Of this total, 40 percent were in domestic stock, 14 percent in international stock, 26 percent in money market funds, 14 percent in bond funds, and 6 percent in hybrid funds. In the previous year, approximately 88 million U.S. investors (51 million households) had added a record $883 billion to mutual funds. The ISI found that a majority of Americans (91 percent) used mutual funds to save for retirement, 52 percent used them to reduce taxable income, and 45 percent used them as savings for emergencies.

Competition was fierce in the industry as the United States neared the close of the 2000s' first decade. For example, according to the ISI, of the largest 25 fund companies in 1985, only 13 remained in this top group by 2007. Another indicator of the diversification of the industry is the Herfindahl-Hirschman index, which factors in both the number and the relative size of firms in the industry to measure competition. According to this index, scores below 1,000 indicate that an industry is unconcentrated; as of December 2009 the U.S. mutual fund industry had a score of approximately 457, compared with 440 in 2008.

CURRENT CONDITIONS

Going into 2010, the U.S. mutual fund industry managed $11.1 trillion in assets, accounting for roughly 48 percent of the worlds's $23 trillion in mutual fund assets, according to the *2010 Investment Company Fact Book.* Although investor demand for mutual funds had declined in 2009, total net assets for the year increased by $1.5 trillion from year-end 2008 levels. This was attributed to the rebound of stock values in 2009. Net withdrawals from all mutual fund types amounted to $150 billion in 2009, the largest on record in terms of total dollars, but by percentage, less (representing 1.4 percent of the average market value of assets) than the $23 billion withdrawal in 1988 (2.8 percent of average assets). The U.S. mutual fund market remained the largest in the world.

The improving conditions in financial markets stabilized in 2009, credited in large part to Obama administration efforts to provide liquidity and strength for financial institutions. Specifically, the Federal Reserve had maintained special credit and liquidity programs first instituted during 2008's financial crisis. this kept the feceral funds rate in a target range of 0 percent to 0.25 percent throughout 2009. After stocks bottomed out in March 2009 following more than a year of deep descent, the latter part of 2009 represented a bull market rally, with a gain of 65 percent in the S&P 500 index. Yet weakness in the labor market, modest income growth, lower housing values, and tight credit conditions for households and small businesses held the market in

check, and in fact, contributed to some market volatility in the first half of 2010.

For the full year of 2009, equity funds comprised 44 percent of U.S. mutual fund assets, according to the ICI *Fact Book.* Of these, domestic equity funds (investing primarily in U.S. corporations) held 33 percent of total industry assets, while international equity funds held another 11 percent. Money market funds accounted for 30 percent of industry assets, with bond funds (20 percent) and hybrid funds (6 percent) holding the remainder.

One of the weak areas in 2009 was retail money market funds, with inflow of $284 billion in 2007 and 2008, and outflow of $307 billion in 2009. This was attributed to the low yield short-term interest rates, which dipped below those on bank deposits over the entire year. This was the first such occurrence in 15 years.

In 2009, there were approximately 600 sponsors (firms or groups of firms) managing mutual fund assets in the United States. However, the largest 25 firms managed 74 percent of assets in 2009, up from 68 percent in 2000.

INDUSTRY LEADERS

Fidelity Investments, also known as FMR, is one of the world's leaders in the mutual fund industry, maintaining over 360 funds with some 23 million investors. Based in Boston, the company in recent years has taken steps to streamline its operations and performance. Having shed some of its non-fund assets, Fidelity has focused increasingly on picking the best stocks instead of concentrating on operational issues. The performance of FMR's funds has shown steady improvement since 1996 when its flagship fund Magellan was lagging behind the Standard & Poor's 500. Fidelity aggressively expanded its online presence, including its Powerstreet online brokerage where investors can trade and monitor their investments. In 2009, FMR managed more than $1.5 trillion in assets and underwent an employee layoff that year. It reported $11.48 billion in 2009 revenues.

Vanguard Group Inc., a notoriously conservative fund, focuses on investments of more than three years. That reputation paid off in 2003 when many investors fled funds perceived as riskier and flocked to Vanguard. Based in Malvern, Pennsylvania, outside Philadelphia, Vanguard has managed to attract a high level of investment largely by word of mouth, sharply cutting advertising and marketing costs. In another novel management twist, Vanguard outsources management of some of its funds to other companies. With more than 10,000 employees, the company managed total assets of more than $1 trillion.

Franklin Resources Inc. remained a major player in the mutual fund industry. The firm was aided by its heavy investment in international markets, amounting to one third of all investments. Franklin managed a family of more than 300 funds that invested in international and domestic stocks, taxable and tax-exempt money market instruments, and corporate, municipal, and U.S. government bonds. For its fiscal year 2009, the company had $553 billion in assets under management and reported revenues of $4.19 billion.

WORKFORCE

In addition to a college degree, a good bit of stamina will usually serve a securities representative well. Early in one's career, long hours, cold calling, and rejections can be expected as a client base is built. Many people drop out of the industry due to the tough nature of sales. Those who persevere usually stay in the field until retirement because of the amount of training and education undertaken and the large amounts of money that can be made.

In 2006 about 320,000 people were securities, commodities, or financial services sales agents, according to 2008-09 edition of the U.S. Bureau of Labor Statistics (BLS) *Occupational Outlook Handbook.* This was an increase from 281,000 in 2004. The BLS indicated that one of every six workers in this field was self-employed. Of the wage and salary workers, more than half worked for securities and commodities brokers, exchanges, and investment services companies, while one in five worked for commercial banks, savings institutions, and credit unions. Furthermore, the BLS predicted that the number of agents will grow 25 percent annually from 2006 to 2016. Median annual earnings of securities, commodities, and financial services sales agents was $68,500 in 2006.

New securities industry employees go through a training period while studying for licensing exams and waiting to become registered representatives of their firm. During this period the pay is low, usually an hourly wage or small salary; but after licensing and registration, employees will earn commissions against sales.

AMERICA AND THE WORLD

Worldwide, mutual fund assets were $23 trillion in 2009, down nearly $3 trillion from 2007 before the global economic crisis starting in 2008. The United States had the largest mutual fund market in the world, accounting for 48 percent of the total. European countries held roughly 34 percent of the market, followed by Africa and the Asia/Pacific with 14 percent and other regions with 5 percent. Worldwide, developing countries experienced similar patterns in market behavior as the United States in 2009, but emerging markets experienced significantly higher gains in stock prices than occurred in the United States and other developed countries.

RESEARCH AND TECHNOLOGY

The technological advances that have helped the mutual fund industry have mostly been in the area of computers. Computer hardware and software development assist the industry with trading by making it quicker and more accurate. Computer technology has enabled brokers to buy or sell securities closer to the price their clients want. The proliferation of computers in the home and the development of the Internet and the World Wide Web allow investment companies to reach more potential investors than ever before. Potential investors can access a company's Web site to find information about the firm's history, past performance, future strategies, and the types of funds offered. Once an account with a company is set up, investors may be able to access it through the company's Web site. Those investors who trade online were found to be considerably more affluent than the average old-fashioned trader, a significant factor spurring firms' aggressive moves to establish online brokerages.

BIBLIOGRAPHY

2008 Investment Company Fact Book, 48th ed. Washington, DC: Investment Company Institute, May 2008.

Balfour, Frederik. "Venture Capitalist's New Promised Land; China Is Hot—But the Best Plays May Lie Outside of Technology." *Business Week,* 16 January 2006.

Churchill, John. "Mutual Fund Performance Overstated; Says Study." *Registered Rep,* 30 March 2006.

"*Fortune* 500 2010: Top 1000 American Companies." *Money,* February 2010.

"Fund Assets Projected to Reach $11 Trillion by 2010." *Money Management Executive,* 8 May 2006.

Healy, Beth. "Fidelity Earnings Rose in '09." *Boston Globe,* 26 February 2010.

Investment Company Institute. "2010 Investment Company Fact Book." Available from http://www.icifactbook.com.

Pizzani, Lori. "Survivors: Casualties of the Harsh Summer of '07." *American Banker,* 27 September 2007.

Regnier, Pat. "Is Anyone Smart Left in Mutual Funds?" *Money,* 8 August 2007.

Steverman, Ben. "The Plight of the Value Investor." *Business Week Online,* 4 August 2008. Available from www.businessweek.com.

"Trends in Mutual Funds Investing, June 2008." Washington, DC: Investment Company Institute, 30 July 2008.

U.S. Department of Labor, Bureau of Labor Statistics. *Occupational Outlook Handbook, 2008-09 Edition.* Available from http://www.bls.gov/.

Young, Lauren. "Back in Action; Sure, the Markets are Jittery, but Mutual Funds are Doing a Better Job for Investors Since the Dot-Com Smashup." *Business Week,* 26 June 2006.

NATURAL AND ORGANIC GROCERIES

SIC CODE(S)

0100

0200

5411

INDUSTRY SNAPSHOT

Natural and organic food continues to be a successful and growing category in the grocery industry. The largest consumer of natural and organic food and beverages was the United States, which claimed almost 50 percent of the market. The European Union and Japan were also important markets.

While the natural and organic grocery market continues to be very promising, companies wanting to get in the game have to contend with a number of challenges, including products that have shorter shelf lives, complicated marketing strategies, having to compete with conventional food products, higher production costs, and selling higher priced products to cost conscious consumers. In fact, the high cost of organic foods remains one of the main roadblocks to industry growth.

The industry's phenomenal growth rate has been driven by increased awareness of organic and natural foods, rising consumer concern about the conventional food supply, available disposable income, and conventional food manufacturers and groceries introducing and selling organic and natural food products to increase their sales growth.

ORGANIZATION AND STRUCTURE

Natural foods, as defined by the *Nutrition Business Journal* (NBJ), "focus on the health benefits of foods derived from natural sources and that are, to varying degrees, free of pesticides, additives, preservatives and refined ingredients." Whole Foods Market, the world's largest chain of natural and organic supermarkets, defines natural foods as "free from artificial preservatives, colors, flavors and sweeteners, which means they have undergone minimal processing," and further states, "'Natural' often is misrepresented in product labeling to imply 'healthful' but 'natural' only means the product has undergone minimal processing. Unlike certified organic products, natural products have no certification or inspection requirements. Also, 'natural' does not necessarily relate to growing methods or use of preservatives." In other words, natural foods may contain genetically modified organisms.

Organic foods are grown without the use of potentially harmful synthetic pesticides, herbicides, and fungicides. Natural pesticides proven to be safe may be used. The primary goal of organic agriculture, according to the U.S. National Organic Standards Board (NOSB), is optimization of "health and productivity of interdependent communities of soil, life, plants, animals and people by seeking to restore, maintain and enhance ecological harmony."

Passage of the Organic Foods Production Act in 1990 paved the way for development of national organic standards, which were approved for implementation by a U.S. Department of Agriculture (USDA) "final rule" in December 2000 and became fully operational on October 21, 2002. This final rule fully implemented the Organic Foods Production Act and led to the formation of the National Organic Program (NOP), defining in detail the provisions governing production and handling of certified organic products in the United States.

U.S. Organic Food Sales for 2010	
Fruit and vegetables	$8.7 billion
Dairy	$3.8 billion
Beverages	$3.3 billion
Packaged/prepared foods	$3.2 billion
Breads and grains	$2.7 billion
Snack foods	$1.5 billion
Meat, poultry, fish	$1.0 billion
Condiments	$1.0 billion

Note: All figures are estimates.

SOURCE: USDA, Economic Research Service.

Previously, although organic practices were certified by state and private agencies, there was no requirement or assurance that the meaning of "organic" was the same in every state or among local certifiers. This confusion was cleared up by national standards of certification, which also afforded protections against mislabeling and fraud.

By the early years of the twenty-first century's first decade, the USDA had accredited 70 agencies to certify that organic operations had met the national organic standards. Growers who sold less than $5,000 per year were required to comply with the standards but did not need to become certified. The standards prohibited the use of toxic and persistent pesticides and fertilizers, sewage sludge, and genetically engineered organisms in organic production or processing. In addition, they specified that organic livestock must be fed 100 percent organic feed containing no antibiotics or growth hormones. Organic foods must be minimally processed without artificial ingredients, preservatives, or irradiation, and there are regulations governing their handling at various points along the distribution chain.

There are four organic labels that may be applied to organic products under the Organic Foods Production Act's national organic standards: 100 Percent Organic (the entire product content is organic); Organic (at least 95 percent of product's content is organic); Made With Organic Ingredients (at least 70 percent of a product's content is organic. Up to three ingredients can be listed with the phrase "made with organic"); and Less Than 70 Percent Organic (these products may identify organic content only on the product label's ingredients list).

Functional foods (FF) and nutraceuticals also are a significant presence in organic and natural food groceries. *Nutrition Business Journal* (NBJ) indicates that both are primarily marketing terms, and are not defined by U.S. or European law or in a dictionary. NBJ's overall definition of functional food is "food fortified with added or concentrated ingredients to a functional level, which improves health and/or performance, or products

marketed for their inherent functional qualities," including some enriched cereals, breads, sports drinks and bars, fortified snack foods, baby foods, prepared meals, soymilk, milk and yogurt, and more. NBJ also identifies "inherently functional foods" as "foods with naturally occurring functional properties, not the result of any manufacturing process, that are specifically marketed to consumers for their function attributes." As examples, the publication cites cranberry and prune juices, soy products, and herbal teas.

The term nutraceuticals is used by NBJ to cover anything consumed either primarily or in part for health reasons. NBJ divides nutraceuticals into five subsets: functional foods, natural/organic foods, dietary supplements, approximately 62 percent of "lesser-evil foods," and eight percent of "market standard foods." Lesser-evil foods are defined as foods altered by removal of ingredients such as fat, caffeine, salt, or calories. Market standard foods do not fit into the natural/organic, functional, or lesser-evil subsets and include products—including yogurt, orange juice, and chicken soup—that are consumed in the interest of improving or maintaining health. NBJ said it found that the term nutraceuticals more and more refers to ingredients used to fortify functional foods.

In the middle of the twenty-first century's first decade, natural, organic, functional, and nutraceutical foods and beverages, plus natural personal care products (dubbed cosmeceuticals), could be purchased in several types of retail outlets: natural/organic food supermarkets, independent natural/organic food stores, natural/organic food cooperatives, dietary supplement stores, conventional supermarkets, gourmet retailers like Trader Joe's, and super centers like Wal-Mart.

In 2003, the National Cooperative Business Association, a cooperative trade organization, indicated that there were about 500 retail cooperative food stores and about 75 retailer-owned cooperatives operating in the U.S. grocery industry. There also were cooperative buying clubs or preorder cooperatives, which to save money buy directly in bulk from wholesalers, dividing their order among themselves. Cooperatives are businesses owned, governed, and operated for the benefit of their members.

Additionally, although they may not be considered traditional groceries, there are more than 1,000 community-supported agriculture (CSA) farms in the United States that sell locally grown, pesticide-free produce to members who sign up in the winter or early spring and pay $300 to $500 for five months of a weekly share of fresh produce, herbs, and sometimes flowers. CSAs also sell to local natural/organic food stores, gourmet food shops, restaurants, and to farmers markets and roadside stands.

BACKGROUND AND DEVELOPMENT

In the early 1840s, the German chemist Justus Liebig, who believed that soil was static and needed minerals, ushered in "agricultural science" with his book *Organic Chemistry and Its Applications to Agriculture and Physiology* and his patented chemical fertilizer of mineral salts. By the mid-1880s, conventional Western agricultural philosophy centered on dominance over the environment, the concept that soil was sterile and used only to hold plants in place, and that crop production was merely a matter of chemistry. Near the end of his life, Liebig reversed his views and began asserting that organic matter was most important in soil management, but by then chemical farming was entrenched and nobody would listen.

During the 1880s, Charles Darwin published theories about the evolution of relationships between soil and plants, and a small number of Western farmers realized the importance of replenishing soil nutrients and the presence of soil animals, humus, and organic matter. In the early 1900s, a few individuals began to notice the relationship of decline in soil fertility to continued chemical use and began to explore natural alternatives that had existed for centuries. F. H. King, head of the U.S. Department of Agriculture's (USDA) Division of Soil Management, attempted to introduce the concept of sustainable agriculture he discovered while traveling through Asia and observing its successful practice on land that had been worked continually for 4,000 years. His 1911 book, *Farmers of Forty Centuries or Permanent Agriculture in China, Korea and Japan,* set forth and urged organic techniques of composting, crop rotation, mulching, and cover cropping in the United States. However, his book was largely ignored.

At about the same time, a German scholar named Rudolph Steiner introduced the concept of anthroposophy, a holistic combination of science, philosophy, and spirituality. Eight of his lectures on anthroposophic agriculture were published in a 1924 book entitled *Agriculture,* including one which introduced a form of organic agriculture and spiritual commitment he called Biodynamics, which did not become popular because it espoused the use of secret plant and animal material preparations and the timing of farming practices to coincide with phases of the moon. During the early years of the twenty-first century's first decade, biodynamic farming was being practiced to some extent in Europe. However, the book's practical techniques have had a significant influence on the evolution of the organic movement.

Also at that time, Sir Albert Howard developed a practical system of farming without chemicals during 30 years of agricultural research in India. From his experience, Howard concluded that chemicals degenerated plants, soil, animals, and people, and he developed layer composting to help organic matter become food for crops. In Great Britain, Lady Eve Balfour championed his ideas in her book, *The Living Soil,* and founded the Soil Association, England's first organic farming association.

World War II saw the first extensive use of petrochemicals. When the war ended, petrochemical farming began and became widespread in the United States. By the early years of the twenty-first century's first decade, the approach continued to be heavily used.

The organic movement in the United States coincided with the boom of U.S. chemical agriculture in the 1940s. Prior to 1940, the USDA did not oppose organic techniques. In fact, its 1938 yearbook of agriculture, entitled *Soils and Men,* actually was a fine text on organic farming. However, during the 1930s there was a "back to the land" movement of city dwellers moving to the country for a simpler life. One of its best-known leaders was Louis Bromfield, author of *The Rains Came* and *Mrs. Parkington.* In 1939, Bromfield bought several worn-out farms in Ohio and with William Albrecht, a brilliant soil scientist from the University of Missouri, established Malabar Farms and farmed there according to the principles of Sir Albert Howard, also conducting research and improvement.

During the 1940s and 1950s, Albrecht produced scientific papers on non-chemical soil management, many of which were still used by organic growers during the early years of the first decade of the twenty-first century, and Bromfield became very influential. In their book *Secrets of the Soil,* Peter Tompkins and Christopher Bird said that Bromfield would have become Secretary of Agriculture if Thomas Dewey had won the presidency instead of Harry Truman and "had every intention of derailing the fossil fuel technology that had taken command of the education machine, USDA extension programs and the farm press." Instead, they said, Truman fostered government-backed policies that "deliberately banished small farmers and fostered a dynamic increase in the use of chemical fertilizers and pesticides." This led to federal practices that began to discourage crop rotation, soil conservation, and reduced pesticide use.

In the early 1940s, agrichemical companies formed the Fertilization Institute. According to Charlie Walters, retired editor and publisher of *Acres, USA: A Voice for Eco-Agriculture,* through the institute they funded all U.S. agricultural colleges, which then taught chemical farming, and also funded much of the agricultural research of the time. Walters stated that if a research project revealed that a stronger, more potent pesticide fertilizer only induced more soil infertility, it never got published and that these agrichemical companies believed that crops could be genetically engineered to thrive in that infertile soil.

During that time, U.S. publisher J. I. Rodale became influenced by Sir Albert Howard's book *An Agricultural Testament* and began writing and speaking about organics. In 1940, he purchased a 60-acre experimental organic farm in Pennsylvania to illustrate his ideas. Also in 1940, Ehrenfried Pfeiffer, an Austrian biochemist and protégée of Rudolph Steiner, fled the Nazi regime and established the Kimberton Biodynamic Farm School in Kimberton, Pennsylvania, where many farmers came to learn organic farming. Rodale visited Pfeiffer, shared ideas with him, and in 1942 started publishing a magazine entitled *Organic Farming and Gardening*. The magazine became the highest-circulation gardening magazine in the world and very important in the development of the organic industry.

Rodale played a critical role in the development of popular interest in organic wartime gardening. However, because he lacked a formal agricultural science background and was sensationalistic in style, for much of his career, mainstreamers regarded him as an agricultural extremist, faddist, or crank. In his 1945 book *Pay Dirt,* Rodale took on conventional agricultural practices, including DDT. His later books and short-lived magazines were important sources of information and inspiration to U.S. organic pioneers, even though he had little success against prevailing attitudes.

PIONEERS IN THE FIELD

In 1946, Paul Keene, an early student at Pfeiffer's Kimberton Farm School, and his wife Betty started Walnut Acres. Their first success was an organic apple harvest, which they made into 200 quarts of apple butter. It was sampled by Clementine Paddleford, then the food editor at the *New York Herald Tribune,* who then did a feature story on the farm and the apple butter, which caused an influx of new customers. This was the first time a processed food was sold as organic and marked the humble birth of the organic food industry. Keene began a thriving mail order business shipping organic products such as root vegetables, canned peaches, and flour around the country. At its peak, the Walnut Acres catalog featured more than 250 organic items.

In 1953, the Natural Food Associates (NFA) was formed in Atlanta, Texas to connect scattered organic growers with fledgling markets and to disseminate nutritional and agricultural information. However, throughout the 1950s, organic foods were mostly sold at roadside stands and in a few early health food stores. The NFA magazine, *Natural Food and Farming,* at first had a difficult time directing readers to organic food locations. During the 1960s and 1970s, pioneer organic farmers

and interested consumers gradually created an emerging organic market. Frank Ford, an early NFA president and organic farmer, founded Arrowhead Mills in Hereford, Texas in 1960 and helped to develop the organic grains and cereals market through sales to small health food stores. A major breakthrough came in 1962 with the release of Rachel Carson's environmental classic *Silent Spring.* This book by a well-known and respected scientist indicted the widespread use of agrichemicals such as DDT as it detailed their pollution of land, air, water, and threats to animal and human life, alarming the country and contributing to the creation of a new and wider organic market.

By the late 1960s, environmentally conscious baby boomers wanted food without chemicals. Frank Ford saw that a more efficient distribution network was needed to meet the increasing demand for organic foods and began to traverse the country meeting with the principals of what he called the "new era" natural/organic food companies: Paul Hawken of Erewhon Trading Company in Boston; Bill Boldoc and Mike Potter of Eden Organic Foods in Ann Arbor, Michigan; and Irwin Carasso of Tree of Life in St. Augustine, Florida. These men and their companies were a major part of the development of organic food processing and distribution as small and midsize so-called "health food stores," independent and co-operative natural/organic stores, and supplement stores appeared in most cities and towns across the country. In 1971, Alice Waters opened Chez Panisse in Berkeley, California, and soon a new group of chefs began to search out and promote locally grown and all natural food.

Also during the 1960s and 1970s, young people again began moving to rural areas in pursuit of a simpler, agrarian lifestyle and found they lacked knowledge of organic farming. They turned to reading about farming without chemicals, including Rodale's published work and issues of Charlie Walters' *Acres, USA,* finding inspiration in Walters' straightforward questioning of "conventional wisdom" and his publishing of organic farming research and techniques for production-style agriculture. Helen and Scott Nearing also were pioneers of self-subsistent organic farming on their Maine farm and published many books and articles that greatly influenced the back-to-the-land movement of the 1960s and 1970s.

At this time, J. I. Rodale and organic farming/gardening were favorably featured in *Barron's, The Smithsonian,* and *Penthouse,* and Rodale appeared on the cover of the *New York Times Magazine.* As he was making a guest appearance on the Dick Cavett Show in 1971, Rodale suffered a massive coronary on stage and died. His son Robert, who had been working with him since 1949, not only took over Rodale Press but carried his father's vision forward by creating the Rodale Institute. Robert Rodale was killed in a 1990 car crash in Russia while establishing a Russian-language version of *The New Farmer.*

By 1990, organic sales were estimated at more than $1 billion. When asked if the years of commitment and innovation between 1940 and 1990 would turn the tiny organic industry around a corner where producing foods organically would become the dominating paradigm, Tom Stonebeck, a vice president of Rodale Press, commented that this was already happening, and he argued that sustainable agriculture had become the preferred form.

In its Market Overview 2003, *The Natural Foods Merchandiser* (NFM) reported that sales of all natural products, including natural and organic foods, nutritional supplements, and organic personal care products, totaled $36.4 billion. This was an increase of 6.6 percent from 2002. In that year, food, drug, and mass merchandisers sold $4.2 billion of both natural and organic food, a 15 percent hike from the previous year. At $10.4 billion, natural products retailers sold the most natural and organic food, achieving a 9 percent sales increase from 2001.

According to NFM, in 2002, about 60 percent of natural products retailers' sales came from food items, 44 percent of which were strictly organic. NFM also reported that several sub-categories were driving the organic segment's growth. These included produce, which saw a 33 percent sales increase from 2001; frozen/refrigerated goods (a 31 percent increase); and organic beer and wine (a 56 percent increase). In August 2003, Chicago-based research firm Synovate conducted a market study for natural foods retailer Whole Foods Market Inc. Entitled the "2003 Whole Foods Market Organic Foods Trend Tracker," the study found that while produce was the leading organic food category, organic snack sales were growing the fastest.

The Synovate/Whole Foods Market research was conducted roughly one year after the USDA's National Organic Program (NOP) began, which essentially imposed more stringent labeling requirements for organic products. In the wake of these new requirements, 54 percent of Americans said they had tried organic foods. Nearly 30 percent of respondents indicated that they were consuming more organic foods and beverages compared to the previous year. At 72 percent, produce was the top organic product category, followed by bread and bakery goods (30 percent), non-dairy beverages (29 percent), packaged goods (24 percent), dairy items (23 percent), meat (19 percent), frozen food items (17 percent), prepared foods (12 percent), and baby food (7 percent).

During the 1990s and the early years of the twenty-first century's first decade, USDA figures indicated that retail sales of organic foods increased about 23 percent per year—a pace that was five times faster than general food sales. A 2003 report issued by Packaged Facts, which evaluated sales of strictly organic foods and beverages, placed that category's 2002 sales at $11 billion—an increase of 1,000 percent from 1990. In early 2004, *DSN Retailing Today* revealed that the organic market increased to $13 billion in 2003 and was experiencing annual growth of 20 percent. At this rate, some estimates suggested that sales of organic food would reach $22 billion by 2010.

By 2004, a growing number of the original farmers and distributors who led the organic movement were selling their organic farms and businesses to large mainstream food corporations like Coca-Cola, Pepsi, Heinz, Kellogg, General Mills, Proctor & Gamble, and Kraft. These companies were intent on entering a burgeoning market and increasing profits. In addition to buying up small but highly popular natural/organic (N/O) brands, large corporations also were creating their own N/O foods and seeking shelf space from leading N/O grocery chains. However, it remained to be seen whether hardcore N/O consumers would accept the labels of such established brands, and whether big business had the expertise to produce N/O foods that also taste good. Some small organic farmers have reacted to corporate takeover by direct sales at farmers markets and to cooperatives, buying clubs (community-supported agriculture), high end and specialty local markets, and restaurants.

During the early years of the twenty-first century's first decade, some leaders in the organic movement worried that the National Organic Program in the 2002 Organic Foods Production Act was not strong enough; that it could enable corporate food producers to "industrialize" and in time diminish the meaning of organic; that it would be overseen by an apathetic and bureaucratic USDA, which chooses genetic engineering over sustainable agriculture and fails to properly review and accredit organic certifying organizations.

In February 2003, Congress approved the Fiscal Year 2003 Consolidated Budget Bill, which contained Section 771, a provision that threatened the integrity of organic labeling. Section 771 prevented any funds from being used to enforce the 100 percent organic feed requirement for certified livestock operations unless organically produced feed was commercially available at no more than twice the cost of conventionally produced feed. This was in direct contradiction to the National Organic Standards of October 2002, which clearly required that any meat or poultry labeled organic must be fed 100 percent organic feed.

On February 14, 2003, the *New York Times* reported that Section 771 was inserted at the last minute by House Speaker Dennis Hastert for Georgia Republican Representative Nathan Deal in a closed session on behalf of a Georgia poultry producer, Fieldale Farms. On February 27, Senator Patrick Leahy (D-Vermont), sponsor of the original Organic Foods Production Act in 1990, and 49 other bipartisan members of Congress introduced Senate Bill 457, the Organic Restoration Act, which would repeal the provision and restore the standard that organic livestock must be fed organic feed. On April 12, 2003, both the Senate and House approved passage of a Supplemental Appropriations Bill, which included an amendment repealing Section 771.

Natural and organic food was a successful and growing category heading into the second half of the first decade of the twenty-first century. However, estimates of its overall value varied considerably. In December 2005, *Frozen Food Digest* indicated that in the United States, consumers spent some $45.8 billion on natural and organic food in 2004, a figure that was expected to be 10 percent higher in 2005. According to *The Food Institute Report,* the Organic Trade Association estimated that U.S. retail sales of organic food products were a mere $13 million in 2005, with a growth rate of 5 to 10 percent projected over the next 20 years. Predictions from other analysts estimate that U.S. organic food sales will be $30 billion to $50 billion by 2025.

In an effort to address the challenge of the high cost of organic products, in late 2005 mainstream grocer Supervalu Inc. announced the development of its new Sunflower Market, a value-priced organic food outlet that *Progressive Grocer* described as "particularly groundbreaking." In its November 15, 2005, issue, the publication explained that the new chain of stores "will include organic wherever possible, as well as items that are minimally processed, with no artificial colorings, sweeteners, flavors, or preservatives. Featured departments will include grocery, frozen, dairy, produce and bulk foods, deli and cheese, all-natural bakery and cafe, hormone- and antibiotic-free meat and seafood, beer and wine, and wellness departments."

Supervalu's new concept marked the continuation of a fast-growing trend among conventional groceries to expand their selections of natural and organic foods. This trend was well underway by early 2004, when large supermarket chains like Safeway and Kroger were selling private label organic food, and other chains like Wegman's were reorganizing and expanding their natural and organic food sections to better compete with warehouse clubs and super centers. Even Wal-Mart, which had emerged as a national grocery giant, sold organic food products to its customers. By early 2006, Wal-Mart was doubling the number of organic food and beverage products sold at its super centers.

Concerns The USDA's organic labeling law continued to be a source of controversy within the industry during the

twenty-first century's first decade. A debate emerged over the issue of whether companies could use synthetic ingredients to process organic food products and still use the organic label, as opposed to indicating that a product was made with organic ingredients. When a federal appeals court upheld a blueberry farmer's lawsuit against the USDA for violating the Organic Foods Processing Act, the Organic Trade Association (OTA), whose members include major food companies such as General Mills and Dole, appealed to Congress to amend the act so that the use of synthetics would not affect labeling requirements. The Organic Consumers Association (OCA) also appealed to Congress through its activist network in an effort to preserve the act. However, in the end, Congress sided with the OTA.

While the OTA insisted that organic standards had not been violated and that all ingredients were clearly labeled for consumers, the decision was a source of outrage within the organic community. In the Spring 2006 issue of *Earth Island Journal,* Jason Mark wrote: "Dismay about the changes has been widespread." *Acres USA,* the oldest organic farming journal in the United States, wrote that a 'corporate mafia has seized control of the organic movement.' A *New York Times* editorial warned that the organic label is in danger of becoming 'meaningless.'"

The definition of what exactly can be classified as "organic" or "natural," especially, continued to be a source of controversy as well as a significant topic of discussion for the FDA and USDA during the latter part of the 2000s' first decade. The question seemed legitimate and important, considering the fact that the number of new food and beverage products claiming to be all natural or organic went from 1,665 in 2002 to 3,823 in 2006, according to research group Mintel. The demand for such products originated in part from consumers' health and safety concerns. According to the Mintel report, cited in the *Chicago Tribune,* "The desire for safe and pure foods, free from additives and preservatives, is a major driver when consumers consider choosing natural over mainstream food products." A 2007 article in *International Food Ingredients* noted that whereas Europeans were more likely to buy organic or natural because they are concerned about the integrity of their food, Americans are more motivated by a desire to "eat healthy." Euromonitor International found that dairy was the largest-selling organic product category in the United States, with sales of $5.1 billion in 2005, followed by bakery items ($2.9 billion) and baby food ($1.4 billion). The fastest growing categories were chilled processed foods (up 28 percent) and coffee (up 18 percent).

Despite the weak U.S. economy during the latter half of the 2000s' first decade, the organic and natural food industry continued to grow. According to the *Future Ingredient Trends in Food and Drinks,* the global market for organic foods and drinks will reach $58.9 billion in 2010, up from $31.8 billion in 2005. A study by the Natural Marketing Institute and the Nielsen Company showed similar findings—that people (20 percent of Americans) will continue to pay more for natural and organic, despite the state of the economy. One of the trends identified by the latter report, published in 2008, was that smaller, private-label organic brands were growing quickly. For example, Ian's Natural Foods (Lawrence, Massachusetts) cites an annual growth rate of 45 percent, and Nature's Path Foods (Richmond, Canada) grew 30 percent in the first half of 2008. Many other lesser known brands were finding their ways to the shelves of organic stores as well as stores such as Target and Wal-Mart.

Demand for organic and natural foods outpaced supply by as much as 10 percent in the United States in the latter part of the decade, according to industry experts, and some were concerned that unless manufacturers could gain better access to organic ingredients, the industry could suffer from resulting limitations. The rising costs of the end products were also a concern.

CURRENT CONDITIONS

In August 2010, industry leader Whole Foods Market Inc. announced results of its annual Food Shopping Trends Tracker online survey conducted (in June 2010) by Harris Interactive. The online survey found that organic foods were making a larger impact in consumers' shopping choices in 2010. A modest jump in the number of consumers purchasing natural and/or organic foods (75 percent in 2010, up from 73 percent in 2009) was eclipsed by a larger increase in the number of organic products they purchased (jumping from 20 percent to 27 percent of total grocery purchases). In a separate online survey of Baby Boomers, Harris Interactive found that more than four-fifths (84 percent) of adults were more concerned about what they ate and tended to read food labels closely. Finally, the surveys compared shopping needs or preferences in 2010 to 1980 (30 years prior). According to results, the top five items found in a pantry or refrigerator in 1980 were (in descending order) milk, canned or frozen vegetables, white bread, soda/pop, and iceberg lettuce. In 2010, the top five items were fresh fruit, milk, fresh vegetables, wheat or whole-grain bread, and canned or frozen vegetables. Spring or mixed lettuces showed the highest increase in popularity in 2010. On the other end, sugared cereals showed the largest decline in popularity.

In 2008 (the latest figures available, released by the USDA, Economic Research Service, ERS, in 2010), U.S. producers dedicated roughly 4.6 million acres of cropland,

rangeland, and pasture to certified organic production, which represented more than double the 1.8 million acres in 2000. Certified organic cropland jumped 51 percent from 2005 to 2008. The organic livestock sector grew even more rapidly, especially in the areas of organic dairy and eggs. Roughly 13,000 U.S. producers received organic certification through USDA affiliates in 2008, including those who offered secondary organic products such as cheeses, jams, and wines. California remained the leading state in certified organic cropland.

However, to put this in perspective, despite gains, only 3 percent of total U.S. fruit acreage and eight percent of U.S. vegetable acreage were dedicated to organic farming in 2008. Highest adoption/conversion rates were for berry crops, lettuces, and apples. Nationally, 2008 organic food sales in all categories, including livestock and dairy, were $3.16 billion. Production costs, regulatory challenges, and marketing issues, continued to challenge organic farmers, although 78 percent indicated they would maintain or increase organic production in the next five years.

INDUSTRY LEADERS

Whole Foods Market Inc. Whole Foods Market Inc. (WFM) owns and operates the largest chain of natural and organic foods supermarkets in the world. In 2010, it operated 270 stores in the United States and United Kingdom, and Canada. With 54,000 employees, the company reported 2009 revenues of $8 billion.

In addition to its retail locations, which averaged approximately 32,000 square feet (15 new stores in 2009), WFM operated a coffee-roasting operation, seafood processing facility, bakehouses, commissary kitchens, produce procurement and field inspection offices, and regional distribution centers.

WFM stores sell approximately 26,000 natural/organic food and non-food products with a heavy emphasis on perishable foods designed to appeal to natural/organic (N/O) and gourmet shoppers. They also offer a limited amount of conventional products that meet WFM standards. These products include produce, seafood, grocery, meat and poultry, bakery, prepared foods and catering, beverages, specialty (beer, wine, and cheese) items, nutritional supplements, vitamins, personal care products, household goods, and educational products such as books.

WFM quality standards include evaluation of every product sold; featured and prepared foods free from artificial preservatives, colors, flavors, and sweeteners; commitment to foods that are fresh, wholesome, and safe to eat; no genetically modified organisms in WFM private label products; seafood, humanely treated poultry and meat free of added growth hormones, antibiotics, nitrates, or other chemicals; as well as grains and grain products that have not been bleached or bromated. WFM does not sell irradiated food, and it sells only household and personal products that have been proven safe through non-animal testing.

In the early 2000s, WFM had constructed an 80,000-square-foot "flagship" store together with its corporate headquarters in Austin, Texas. Austin is where John Mackey, WFM co-founder, chairman, president, and CEO, opened SaferWay, a small health foods store in 1978. Craig Weller and Mark Skiles opened the Clarksville Natural Grocery in Austin in 1979. Mackey joined with Weller and Skiles in 1980 to re-open the two stores as Whole Foods Market, Inc. with Texas Health Distributors established as WFM's wholesale supplier. Expansion of WFM outside Austin began in August 1984 and has consisted of numerous purchases/acquisitions of natural/organic independent stores and chains as well as new store openings, becoming publicly traded on NASDAQ, twice experiencing two-for-one stock splits, and being included on *Fortune* magazine's One Hundred Best Companies to Work For List.

In August 2007, Whole Foods purchased its rival Wild Oats Market for $565 million. However, as of mid-2008, the merger was being challenged in the courts by the Federal Trade Commission (FTC), which claimed the purchase violated antitrust laws.

United Natural Foods Inc. With fiscal 2010 sales of $3.76 billion (up from $2.7 billion in 2007), United Natural Foods Inc. (UNF) is the nation's largest wholesale distributor of natural and organic foods. The company supplies more than 40,000 food products, nutritional supplements, and personal care items to the retail natural and organic industry, including natural supermarket chains, independent natural products retailers, and conventional supermarkets. This is accomplished through United Natural Foods in the eastern United States; Mountain People's Warehouse Inc. and Rainbow Natural Foods in the West; Blooming Prairie in the Midwest; and Albert's Organics, a wholesale distributor of organic produce in all regions. (In 2010, the company agreed to undertake the primary distribution for Whole Foods Market Distribution Inc. in the Rocky Mountain and Southwest regions.)

UNF owns the Hershey Import Company, one of the leading importers, processors, packagers, and wholesale distributors of nuts, dried fruit, seeds, trail mixes, and natural/organic confections. Through another subsidiary, the Natural Retail Group, UNF also owns and operates 12 natural products retail stores in the eastern United States.

On October 15, 2002, UNF acquired the privately held Blooming Prairie Cooperative, the largest volume distributor of natural and organic products in the Midwest, selling approximately 15,000 products to more than 2,700 retail formats including conventional supermarket chains, natural food supermarkets, independent retail operators, cooperatives, and buying clubs. On December 31, 2002, UNF announced its merger with Northeast Cooperatives, a privately held cooperative natural food distributor of more than 14,000 products to approximately 2,800 customers in the northeast United States. Finally, in 2004 the company acquired Select Nutrition Distributors.

Tree of Life Inc. A subsidiary of Koninklijke Wessanen, a Dutch food enterprise, Tree of Life markets and distributes natural and organic foods as well as specialty foods to both small and large retailers in the United States, Canada, and Europe. The company employs roughly 5,000 associates and emphasizes its "expertise in natural, specialty and organic foods, dietary supplements, as well as fine health and beauty products" and understanding of target customers, which stem from more than 30 years of operations. Tree of Life serves more than 20,000 retailers with approximately 100,000 products, including its own products sold under the trade names Harmony Farms, Peanut Wonder, Soy Wonder, and American Natural.

Trader Joe's Trader Joe's, based in Monrovia, California, began as a Los Angeles convenience store chain in 1958 and was purchased by German businessmen Karl and Theo Albrecht in 1979. As of 2010 the company owned more than 300 stores in 25 states and sold health food, organic produce, and dietary supplements, in addition to private label items, which account for 70 percent of sales.

WORKFORCE

The workforce encompasses both the wholesale and retail end of organic products. In 2008 (the latest figures available, released by the USDA, Economic Research Service, ERS, in 2010), USDA-accredited entities provided organic certification to nearly 13,000 U.S. producers. Wholesale distributors in 2010 included Albert's Organics; B&B of Indiana, a 100 percent certified organic distributor; Farm Fresh Connections, based in Maine; and Nature's Best, in the western states.

A unique quality of natural/organic (N/O) supermarket chains and independent N/O groceries and health food stores is the presence of employees, and sometimes owners, who have knowledge of and can educate customers about aspects and benefits of products. This type of educated employee is rarely found in gourmet or specialty stores and certainly not in conventional supermarkets. Another unique aspect of the N/O grocery industry is the network of growers, processors, and distributors, all USDA certified, who supply and enhance it.

AMERICA AND THE WORLD

According to the USDA, Economic Research Service, ERS, in 2008 (the latest figures available, released in 2010), U.S. producers dedicated less than one percent of total crop acreage for organic crops, far less than many other countries, including Switzerland (11 percent in 2007), Italy (9 percent), Uruguay (6 percent), the United Kingdom (4 percent), and Mexico (roughly 3 percent). This was attributed to several factors, an important one being the relatively limited resources available in the United States for farmers wishing to convert to organic farming, in addition to the weak economy.

In its March 16, 2006, issue, *just-food.com* shared results from its 2006 global market review, which indicated that on a global basis, the organic food and drink industry was growing at an annual rate of 15 to 22 percent. With a value of $36.7 billion in 2005, *just-food.com* expected the industry would be valued at $133.7 billion worldwide by 2012.

The same *just-food.com* market review also revealed that Europe constituted some 47 percent ($17.4 billion) of the organic food and drink industry in 2005. While sales were especially strong in Western Europe, strong growth was occurring in Poland, Lithuania, and Latvia. This supported previous findings about the strength of the European market. For example, according to the Soil Association's *Food and Farming Report 2003,* organic food sales in the United Kingdom were outpacing traditional food sales at a rate of two to one, growing 10 percent annually. Some 75 percent of babies were regularly given organic foods, and the value of organic milk and yogurt climbed approximately 12 and 13 percent respectively.

RESEARCH AND TECHNOLOGY

The Agricultural Research Service (ARS) is the principal in-house research agency of the U.S. Department of Agriculture. ARS has conducted research projects in agriculture, nutrition, technology, and the environment at ARS-managed research sites certified as organic farms as well as at small and large working organic farms. With a budget of $1.1 billion in 2007, the service employed 2,100 scientists and 6,000 other employees at some 100 research sites. At that time, the ARS was engaged in approximately 1,200 research projects.

In addition to the ARS, the USDA also engages in research activities via three other agencies: the Economic Research Service, the National Agricultural Statistics Service, and the Cooperative State Research, Education, and Extension Service (CSREES). In what *The New Farm* described as an "historic development," in 2008 the CSREES announced that $4.7 million would be available for the federal Integrated Organic Program. More specifically, funding pertained to two programs that originated during the late 1990s: the Organic Agriculture Research and Extension Initiative and the Organic Transitions Program. *The New Farm* explained that "the two programs will fund integrated research, education, and extension projects that address critical organic agriculture issues, priorities or problems."

BIBLIOGRAPHY

"About ARS." U.S. Department of Agriculture, Agricultural Research Service, 15 August 2008. Available from http://www.ars.usda.gov.

"About Whole Foods." Available from http://www.wholefoods markets.com.

"America's Organic Farmers Face Issues and Opportunities." *Amber Waves,* June 2010.

Ayling, Joe. "Are Organics really a Win-Win Investment?" *just-food.com,* 16 March 2006.

Bayles, Jaq. "Enjoying Sustained Growth: Organic Is No Longer Niche as Health and Ethical Concerns Reach the Mass Market Level." *Grocer,* 28 January 2006.

Cowling, Tania. "List of Wholesale Distributors of Natural Organic Products." 3 August 2010. Available from http://www.brighthub.com/environment/green-living/articles/66034.

Cummings, Betsy. "Despite Economic Dip, Organic Food Sales Soar." *Brandweek,* 9 June 2008.

"Executive Summary." *Organic Trade Association's 2007 Manufacturer Survey.* Organic Trade Association, 2008.

"The Global Organic Food Market Grew by 13.6% in 2006 to Reach a Value of $36.7 Billion." *Business Wire,* 13 August 2007.

Herrick, Clare. "Future Imperfect: Clare Herrick, Health and Wellness Products Industry Analyst at Euromonitor International, Looks to North America for Clues to the Future of the Global Organic Market." *International Food Ingredients,* April-May 2007.

"Industry Statistics and Projected Growth." Organic Trade Association, 2008. Available from www://ota.com/.

Mark, Jason. "Food Fight: Is the 'Organic' Label Being Amended to Uselessness?" *Earth Island Journal,* Spring 2006.

McTaggart, Jenny. "Organics: Stay the Course." *Progressive Grocer,* 1 March 2008.

"National Organic Program." U.S. Department of Agriculture, Agriculture Marketing Service. 15 August 2008. Available from http://www.ams.usda.gov.

"National Survey Shows Organic Foods Now Represent Larger Part of Total Food Purchases." Press Release, *PR Newswire,* 16 August 2010. Available from http://www.marketwatch.com/story/national-survey-shows-organic-foods.

"New USDA Data Offers In-depth Look at Organic Farming." Press Release, National Agricultural Statistics Service, USDA, 3 February 2010. Available from http://www.nass.usda.gov/Newsroom/

"Natural Food: Regulators, Industry, Consumer Groups Tangle Over Defining the Term." *Chicago Tribune,* 7 January 2008.

The Organic Report. Greenfield, MA: Organic Trade Association, 2008.

"United Natural Foods Announces Fiscal Year and Fourth Quarter Fiscal 2010 Results." *PR Newswire,* 8 September 2010.

"USA's Organic Alliance Poised for Growth, Says Equity Research Group Beacon." *Nutraceuticals International,* July 2008.

"Wal-Mart Organics." *Feedstuffs,* 20 March 2006.

"YoNaturals: Healthy Vending Machine Businesses Expected to Thrive Amidst Rising Food Prices." *Business Wire,* 16 June 2008.

NEW AGE PRODUCTS AND SERVICES

—————— ■ ——————

SIC CODE(S)

2099

8999

INDUSTRY SNAPSHOT

Comparable to alternative medicines, the philosophies and practices behind the New Age movement have been active in many forms worldwide for centuries. In the Western Hemisphere, the New Age movement draws much of its inspiration from Native American practices, Asian and Indian beliefs and customs, and the nine-teenth-century Utopian movement. The New Age industry draws its revenues from several diverse markets, including products and services ranging from incense and crystals to yoga and meditation classes. With the Internet providing increased awareness of and access to New Age methodologies and medicines, major insurance providers began to offer partial coverage of New Age treatments.

However, no longer an esoteric interest, the New Age industry has gone mainstream. Merchandisers and manufacturers have realized that just attaching the term "New Age" to products and services creates the percep-tion of newness, novelty, and forward-looking perspec-tive. Some examples of New Age products and services gaining popularity were in the areas of music, books, food and beverages, and health services.

ORGANIZATION AND STRUCTURE

For the most part, the New Age industry consists of numerous small businesses that furnish products and services to interested consumers. Excluded from the mix are those large, traditional firms (such as the Coca-Cola Co.) that came out with New Age products only after they became popular with a substantial segment of the market. By the mid- to late 1990s, many large stores sold trendy New Age products that were once available only in New Age establishments. The major exceptions were health food and grocery stores that carried New Age foodstuffs and food supplements. In the service sector, some consolidated meditation and yoga schools emerged on the scene in the late 1990s.

Conferences, Seminars, and Other Gatherings The rapid growth of the New Age industry can be attributed in part to the many conferences and seminars that characterize the movement. Featured speakers address topics such as the environment, dreams, nutrition, yoga, meditation, and spirituality. Among the most popular gurus on the circuit are author/physician Deepak Chopra and spiritual writer Marianne Williamson. Cost of attendance at one of their programs may well run into the hundreds of dollars. The Whole Life Expo, held annually in major cities such as San Francisco and Los Angeles, brings together hundreds of vendors, speakers, and practitioners of multiple New Age disciplines. Participants learn about the latest in everything from enzyme therapy to hair re-growth products, peruse the newest books, and go to seminars conducted by well-known personalities. Some New Age events are held at the same time as celebrations marking Earth Day and the spring and fall equinoxes, while others take their inspira-tion from ancient religious holidays of the Druids and Native Americans and include attempts to recreate the old rituals.

BACKGROUND AND DEVELOPMENT

The sensibilities propelling the New Age industry developed from a host of different sources. Helena Petrovna Blavatsky, founder of the theosophical movement, is often credited with inspiring the New Age movement as well. When Blavatsky died in May 1891, an editorial writer in the *New York Daily Tribune* declared, "No one in the present generation, it may be said, has done more toward reopening the long-sealed treasures of Eastern thought, wisdom, and philosophy. Her steps often led, indeed, where only a few initiates could follow, but the tone and tendency of all her writings were healthful, bracing, and stimulating." The Theosophical Society, which has followers around the world, espouses a doctrine that emphasizes direct and mystical contact with a divine power through meditation, incorporating elements of Buddhism and Brahmanism.

The New Age movement also has some historic antecedents in the hippie and counterculture movements of the 1960s. These movements did not constitute the largest or most consistent segment of New Agers, wrote Elliot Miller in his book, *A Crash Course on the New Age Movement.* He observed that New Age principles share some similarities with the 1960s movements. However, the respect for and appreciation of nature, the movement away from materialism, the interest in non-Western thought, culture, and medicine, and the desire to create a better way of living have not been embraced by all participants in the New Age industry. Miller also argued that Asian Hinduism and Buddhism have been key influences on the New Age movement, as well as concerns about health, personal growth, and environmental conservation and protection that germinated during the 1970s.

Even those ideas had first surfaced in the United States as early as the mid- and late nineteenth century. Philosophers and writers, such as Henry David Thoreau and Ralph Waldo Emerson of New England; wellness advocate Dr. John Harvey Kellogg of Battle Creek, Michigan; and the founders of the various Utopian communities across the country foreshadowed much of the later New Age movement. Around the same time, the mineral water springs in such places as Hot Springs, Arkansas, and Saratoga Springs, New York, led to the construction of resort complexes that became gathering places for many of the early progressive thinkers. All of this in turn stimulated an interest in organic foods (those free of chemicals and preservatives), recycling used materials, reducing natural resource consumption, fighting pollution, and cultivating respect for the environment.

Eventually, people began seeking spiritual fulfillment and self-authenticity outside of the traditional secular and religious channels. Miller noted that the people involved in these early movements also wanted to take responsibility for themselves and the planet, concerns similar to those that later prompted the environmental and spiritual quests on which New Agers embarked.

Some practices of the New Age movement became quite common in the United States during the 1960s and 1970s. Yoga and meditation, for example, had many devotees. Miller contended that the movement received very little attention until the mid-1980s when actress Shirley MacLaine began promoting her New Age beliefs on television and in her books. The mass media also took note in August 1987 after the Harmonic Convergence brought together approximately 20,000 New Agers to sites considered sacred worldwide for activities that included meditation, channeling, and rituals with crystals. The event prompted numerous articles and programs exploring the New Age movement, culminating in a *Time* magazine cover story that appeared in December 1987. The press coverage introduced a larger section of the public to the ideas, wares, services, practices, and foodstuffs associated with the New Age movement.

The confluence of these forces spawned the New Age industry. As more people started to share some of the beliefs and concerns of the original members of the New Age movement, the industry surrounding it grew. Demand for New Age-oriented products and services hit the market in full force during the late 1980s and continued to expand throughout the 1990s, especially as the millennium drew near. Consequently, many traditional businesses started offering New Age-related products, hoping to profit from the public's fascination with the not-so-new trend.

In the 1990s, major "traditional" food, beverage, and pharmaceutical manufacturers introduced their own versions of New Age products. Even the political arena felt the movement's influence: founded on New Age principles, the Natural Law party appeared on the ballot in 48 states for the 1996 elections.

Since private service providers and small business operations make up such a large part of the New Age industry, it is nearly impossible to come up with a sales figure for the entire market. In 1996 revenues from New Age industry products and services combined were estimated at nearly $22 billion, but in 1999 analysts estimated the global market for natural and organics products (a major component of the industry) at about $65 billion. In 2002, dietary supplements, a major product line in the market, were an $18 billion industry. The mainstream acceptance and subsequent entrenchment of the market and products is demonstrated in national drugstore chains, where shelf space is reserved for botanicals such as St. John's wort and gingko biloba.

Sales of health-related products in particular grew rapidly beginning in the early 1980s. According to the

National Center for Homeopathy, annual sales of homeopathic remedies in the United States were more than $200 million between 1997 and 1999 and projected to increase by 12 percent per year. Alternative medicine as a whole earned about $11 billion per year as early as 1990; and by the late 1990s, sales of all alternative medicines were estimated at between $21 billion and $34 billion annually. As reported by the National Center for Homeopathy, the complementary and alternative medicine marketplace exhibited an annual growth rate of close to 15 percent. By 2002, there were more than 2,000 homeopathic substances on the market.

The sales of books and food products classified as New Age were estimated to amount to as much as $9 billion by the late 1990s. New Age music sold well, too. Labels such as Windham Hill and Narada made up a significant part of the $86 million music industry in the late 1990s, according to *Forbes.*

By 2004, celebrities began to endorse New Age products as they became more widely accepted. Sylvester Stallone and Magic Johnson, for example, had signed on to endorse certain brands of nutritional supplements. Growth was exponential; from 1997 to 2002, the New Age beverage market alone grew nearly 89 percent. New Age products from books to convenience foods were showing no signs of decreasing in popularity, in spite of widespread negative press as with the ephedra scandal.

It is clear that while the majority of philosophies behind the New Age movement are centuries old, the burgeoning industry resulting from this movement was indeed only beginning to emerge.

Marketing New Age Products Typically, New Age products and services were marketed in small shops in major cities and towns. The distribution network for such items was limited and, for most vendors, expansion was an option they could not afford. During the mid to late 1990s, however, the Internet emerged as a major marketing tool for New Age vendors. Hundreds of sites offering candles, crystals, astrolites, incense, and other products have made their debut on the World Wide Web, thus enabling New Age suppliers to market their merchandise virtually everywhere without incurring significant additional expenses. Besides electronic New Age shops, the Internet hosted a number of sites advertising New Age services such as yoga, meditation instruction, and massage. Various New Age organizations also promoted themselves on the Internet and provided links to related sources of information.

Books Sales of New Age-oriented books dealing with religion and spirituality began to soar during the late 1980s, making it the fastest-growing publishing category

of the decade. The Book-of-the-Month Club even launched a New Age book club in 1995 called One Spirit that quickly became the most successful specialty book club in the firm's history. The genre remained on top during most of the 1990s, especially among female readers. In fact, between 60 and 70 percent of such titles are bought by women.

Quite a few U.S. best sellers fell within the New Age genre, according to the trade magazine *Publishers Weekly,* including *The Celestine Prophecy, The Seven Laws of Spiritual Success, Simple Abundance,* and *Conversations with God.* Books linking creativity with spirituality also did well in the United States. Upon its release in 1992, for example, *The Artist's Way* had only 5,500 copies in print; by 2000, nearly 1 million copies had been sold.

Titles that publishers once promoted as New Age have since been reclassified as psychology, philosophy, religion, health, or fiction, thus marking the assimilation of New Age ideas into mainstream culture. Nevertheless, some authors shun the New Age label, seeing it as a liability that could lead to lower sales because of some consumers' prejudices. For instance, *Publishers Weekly* reported that Bantam created a New Age label in 1980 but began to shy away from it by the mid-1990s because some authors did not want the New Age association. Alternative terms subsequently began to come into fashion, including "spiritual growth" and "personal growth," even if these covered only certain aspects of what was typically regarded as New Age. Since no one has been able to come up with another name for New Age books, it remains the only inclusive label available for such literature.

As the 1990s ended, the industry was undergoing some changes. Sales flattened, publishers of New Age materials consolidated, and alternative bookstores were facing a number of challenges, including increased competition from large chain operations and Internet booksellers.

Reflective of the situation was the 2001 merger of New Leaf Distributing Co. of Lithia Springs, Georgia, the largest distributor of New Age products in the world, with NewAgeCities.com. Prior to the merger, New Leaf Distributors was the largest and oldest wholesale distributor of New Age books and periodicals. Founded in 1975 and originally called Shakti Distributes, New Leaf started out by distributing the fledgling *New Age Journal* as well as Dr. Ann Wigmore's books on dietary medicine to health food stores and food co-ops in the Atlanta area. By 1976, the firm was bringing in only about $500 per week. Then a store was opened to supplement the distribution service, and in 1979 the company changed its name and sales began to rise. New Leaf posted a profit for the first time in 1983; by the late 1990s, annual sales topped $35 million.

By the time of the merger, New Leaf was generating revenues of approximately $25 million a year and had more than 6,000 retail stores. NewAgeCities.com of Boca Raton, Florida had been implementing an Internet-based consolidation of the New Age and alternative health markets through a growing network of Web sites. The plan was to combine the companies to create a new one that would generate higher revenues and profits than each would generate separately. The goal was to create the largest brick-and-mortar, business-to-business products and services company in the industry.

The growing focus on mind/body/spirit presented challenges for the sale of New Age books. Because the term applied to so many different categories, ranging from religion, self-help, and health to psychology and science, it became difficult to determine the best place to sell different titles in-store. In response, the publishing industry began to see the emergence of a new category called "conscious living." In the September 5, 2005, issue of *Publishers Weekly,* Llewellyn Publicity Manager Alison Aten explained: "You can have a conscious living business book, a yoga book, and so on. What they have in common is the idea that all the parts of your life are related and maybe have a higher spirit or purpose to them."

According to some industry experts, the upsurge in New Age book buying was tied to people's growing insecurity in an unstable world and the desire to find inner peace and strength. Beyond titles such as *The Da Vinci Code* and *What the Bleep Do We Know!?,* advanced, application-focused books on the Wiccan religion continued to be popular in 2006. The movement of many New Age books into the local Wal-Mart or Costco marked the subtle change in the public's perception of what New Age really is.

Beverages and Food Alternative beverages and natural foods are closely identified with the New Age movement. Natural foods are those deemed free of pesticides, preservatives, and artificial sweeteners, and that are produced without being cruel to animals. As with most other New Age products, they were often available at first only in smaller markets and specialty stores. By the year 2000, however, they enjoyed much wider distribution and acceptance.

New Age beverage manufacturers encountered several obstacles when they tried to tap into existing distribution networks or create new ones. According to John N. Frank in *Beverage Industry,* they had trouble getting their products into stores; and, if they managed to do so, the stores would often neglect New Age products in favor of traditional brands. Moreover, the well-established companies began developing their own products (such as Coca-Cola's Fruitopia) to take advantage of the growing demand for New Age products.

To address this problem, purveyors of New Age products had to choose from among several less than satisfactory options. They could, for instance, do business with small beverage distributors that served a strictly local market and thus miss national exposure, or they could seek out big beer distributors knowing that their products would not reach many convenience outlets and other small stores that did not sell beer. On the other hand, if they opted to go with food distributors instead, they risked bypassing the smaller stores that did not offer a large array of food items. No matter which option they chose, Frank argued, they also needed to come up with a niche marketing strategy or their products would not move quickly. Nevertheless, most New Age beverage and food operations were small and could not afford to promote their products on television or with other popular, expensive forms of advertising.

Despite these problems, New Age beverages managed to do extremely well during the 1990s. According to the trade publication *Beverage World,* so-called alternative beverages such as fruit juices, ready-to-drink teas and coffees, and sports drinks together reported sales of nearly $7 billion in 1999. From 1993 to 1999, the category experienced a 14 percent compound annual growth rate.

Retail sales of natural products experienced a 26 percent compound annual growth rate between 1994 and 1999, growing from $7.6 billion in 1994 to $19 billion by 1999. The total sales of natural products were estimated at $25.4 billion in 1998. This included Internet sales, sales by practitioners, and mail order sales.

Natural and organic foods also became a hit with consumers during this period. According to *Supermarket News,* many traditional food stores expanded their natural and organic food sections, and natural foods retailers such as Whole Foods Market and Wild Oats Markets grew rapidly. Furthermore, organic food producers began increasing the diversity of their products, with some companies even manufacturing organic baby and pet food. In 1995, for example, 1,015 new products debuted, compared to only 512 in 1991. As Cyndee Miller observed in *Marketing News,* beginning in 1991, organic food sales nearly doubled. She estimated that this portion of the industry earned $3 billion in 1996, and analysts estimated sales growth for the sector at over 20 percent throughout the 1990s. Sales of all types of organic products, a mere $178 million in 1980, blossomed into more than $6.6 billion by 2000, while sales of natural products exceeded $12 billion.

The numbers encouraged mainstream businesses to pursue the organic and natural foods market by way of mergers and acquisitions. Investor Roy E. Disney bought organic frozen vegetable pioneer Cascadian Farm in 1996. H. J. Heinz Co. purchased Earth's Best, a rapidly growing organic baby food company. Such expansion moved this emerging industry "off the natural foods screen and onto the global agribusiness screen," noted Bob Scowcroft, executive director of the Organic Farming Research Foundation in Santa Cruz, California, in a *Los Angeles Times* article.

However, overall sales declined for natural and organic products somewhat in the early part of the new century. While retailers experienced double-digit growth in the 1990s, they only saw an 8.3 percent growth in 2001. Natural and organic products sales by food and drug mass merchandisers increased 5.5 percent, while growth for all natural and organic product sales in retail and non-retail outlets increased 6.7 percent. Sales for natural food products in 2001 grew to 17.3 percent. The best performers for natural foods were nutrition bars and food service, including natural foods sold at delis, restaurants, and juice bars, and natural beverages. Best performers in the organic foods category were food service, snack foods, nondairy, and packaged grocery. Sales for supplements remained healthy, demonstrating double-digit growth in the sports and specialty categories. Popular sports supplements included powders, pills, and sports beverages. Specialty supplements included Ayurvedic products, hormones, and essential fatty acids.

Based on overwhelming evidence that trans-fats, manufactured during the hydrogenation process to extend food shelf life, were linked to a host of serious problems such as diabetes and heart disease, the National Academy of Sciences released a statement that there was no safe level of human consumption. The FDA gave a deadline of 2006 to food manufacturers to clearly indicate the amount of trans-fats in their products on food labels. Wild Oats Markets went one step further in 2004, and removed all products containing hydrogenated oils from their shelves.

By 2003, the desire in the United States for wellness, and consequently good-for-you foods, was proving nearly insatiable. Organic foods had also reached the mainstream. What was a $1 billion industry in 1990 had become an $11 billion industry in 2002. The natural foods industry as a whole reported sales of $32 billion in 2000, and the growth continued rapidly. Whole Foods Market had $1.1 billion in sales during the first quarter of 2004 alone.

A study by the Grocery Manufacturers of America found that light, lean, and diet brands were skyrocketing in annual growth. For snack foods, consumers were purchasing healthier substitutes for the traditional chips and crackers. The low-carb revolution was growing by leaps and bounds, with new products seemingly appearing overnight. There were 114 new high-protein products introduced in 2003 alone, nearly half of which were energy bars and meal substitute bars.

Health and Healing Services Health and healing services such as yoga, Tai Chi, and meditation have constituted an important element of the New Age industry since its beginnings. Yoga in particular has become very popular. According to *U.S. News & World Report,* the Clinton White House made yoga classes available to staff members. Large law firms and investment banks commission yogis (advanced yoga practitioners) to teach their employees. Many physicians recommend yoga to patients afflicted with diseases such as arthritis and diabetes, as well as those with cardiovascular ailments. In addition, some health insurance providers had started covering expenses related to yoga and meditation. Health care facilities had even started offering yoga and meditation classes, as do some private practitioners.

Paul L. Cerrato and Aria Amara reported in *RN* that one of every three people in the United States relied on some kind of holistic or non-Western therapy in 1997. Another study conducted that same year by a different researcher put the number at about 40 percent and observed that more than half of the patients were between 30 and 50 years of age. Not surprisingly, the number of professional practitioners of nontraditional medicine in the United States rose from 200 during the 1970s to 3,000 in 1998. Even national drugstore chains such as CVS, Kmart, and Walgreens started carrying homeopathic products in the late 1990s.

The New Age trend has even been reflected in the policies issued by several major insurance firms. By the end of the 1990s, for instance, Mutual of Omaha was covering chiropractic care, Prudential was paying for acupuncture, and Blue Cross of Washington and Alaska was offering a plan called "AlternaPath," which covered licensed naturopathic doctors. The book *New Choices in Natural Healing,* a publication of *Prevention* magazine, noted that at the end of the 1990s, the insurance plan that covered the widest array of alternative medicine practices was one offered by American Western Life Insurance Co. of Foster City, California. It reimbursed patients for homeopathy, Ayurveda, nutritional counseling, massage, and physical therapy as part of its wellness plan. The company also offers a full time "Wellness Line" with naturopathic doctors on call for their patients.

Much of what has come to be known as New Age or alternative medicine (increasingly referred to by the acronym CAM for complementary and alternative medicine) is not really new, nor did it all originate in Asia. Homeopathy developed in 18th century Germany. Chiropractic and naturopathy began in the United States, and people have been using herbs for healing all over the world for centuries. Practices such as homeopathy, herbalism, and midwifery were, in fact, part of mainstream medicine until the early 20th century, when members of the medical establishment began rejecting what they viewed as "nonstandard" practices. Nevertheless, as of the end of the 1990s, reported David Plank in *Vegetarian Times,* the World Health Organization estimated that 65 to 80 percent of what is regarded as standard health care elsewhere in the world would be defined by Americans as "alternative."

Homeopathic medicines remained very popular in Europe. For years they have been sold on drugstore shelves in France and Germany, and, in the United Kingdom, the government's national health insurance plan covers the cost of purchasing them. The use of herbal medicine is especially common in Germany. German physicians are far more willing than their American counterparts to recommend herbal medications to patients.

When the growing popularity of other New Age-oriented health regimens prompted scrutiny from the Western medical establishment, the results of their investigations proved favorable to holistic medicine. For instance, meditation was found to lower blood pressure, chiropractic care can eliminate certain kinds of back pain, and massage alleviates stress, anxiety, and pain, according to Cerrato and Amara in *RN.* In 1996, medical research revealed that acupuncture stimulates the excretion of analgesic and nerve-healing substances, wrote Doug Podolsky in *U.S. News & World Report.* That same year, the U.S. Food and Drug Administration (FDA) decreed that acupuncture needles could be considered medical instruments.

By 2004, the popularity of alternative herbal supplements had grown to the point that many of the plants harvested for use in such supplements were teetering on the brink of extinction. It was also reported in 2004 that hospitals were making use of alternative and complementary medicines with increasing frequency. As herbal remedies increased in popularity, however, the FDA began to subject them to intense examination. Some of the claims made by dietary supplements, for instance, have been found to be false. Consequently, manufacturers have become more careful about what they claim their products can do.

After the high-profile death on February 18, 2003, of Baltimore Orioles pitcher Steve Bechler, for example, there was a large outcry against ephedra and charges that dietary supplements were unregulated. The National Institutes of Health describes ephedra as a naturally occurring botanical (a plant part or extract) the active ingredient of which is an amphetamine-like compound that can powerfully stimulate the nervous system and

heart. It was marketed in dietary supplements to promote weight loss, increase energy, and enhance athletic performance. After a review, on February 6, 2004, the FDA issued a regulation officially banning ephedra in dietary supplements that would take effect on April 12, despite a 1994 law passed by Congress severely limiting the FDA's ability to regulate plant products unless it has proof of an unreasonable risk to the public health. The FDA is further limited in that it cannot require safety studies or acquire records of adverse side effects from a supplement manufacturer. Just the day before the FDA ban went into effect, an online company was still marketing such supplements as contributing to positive athletic performance.

On April 13, 2004, as reported in *The New York Times,* a federal judge denied the request of two ephedra manufacturers to halt the FDA ban until there was a full trial of their lawsuit. However, on April 14, 2005, *The New York Times* reported that a federal judge in Utah struck down the FDA ban on ephedra; and that although the judge's ruling pertained to Utah, it raised the question of whether the FDA could enforce its ephedra ban anywhere in the U.S. Ruling that the FDA "had failed to prove that ephedra at low doses was dangerous, and that it lacked the authority to ban the substance without such proof," the judge ordered the FDA to carry out low-dosage studies before creating new regulations for ephedra. Neither the president of the Nutraceutical Corporation, one of the manufacturers who brought the suit, nor any other maker of ephedra products has resumed selling ephedra, deeming it prudent to wait until the future of the controversial plant substance is resolved. The FDA appealed, and on August 17, 2006, the Federal Appeals Court reversed the ruling. Although Nutraceutical International Corp. sought to appeal, the Supreme Court refused to consider it, and the ban held.

In 2003, the FDA proposed a new regulation that would require current good manufacturing practices (CGMPs) in the manufacturing, packing, and holding of dietary supplements. The regulation was designed to help consumers obtain accurately labeled and unadulterated supplements. Specifically, the rule would establish new standards to help reduce risks associated with adulterated or misbranded dietary supplement products; industry-wide standards to ensure that dietary supplements are manufactured consistently for identity, purity, quality, strength, and composition; and minimum standards for the design and construction of physical plants that facilitate maintenance, cleaning, and proper manufacturing operations for quality control procedures, for testing final product or incoming and in-process materials, for handling consumer complaints, and for maintaining records. However, the idea was opposed by many in the industry, and in January 2006 the FDA officially withdrew the proposition.

New Age products continued to grow in both acceptance and popularity heading into the late years of the first decade of the 2000s. So-called holistic lifestyles were becoming more commonplace, as individuals began to look at the interrelationships between the various parts of their lives. This was reflected in the growing use of the term "mind/body/spirit" to describe things once looked upon as being New Age.

The use of New Age or alternative medicine continued to grow during the mid-decade, especially among older adults with chronic health problems that were not cured by traditional treatments. According to *The Futurist,* a study conducted by The Ohio State University revealed that among U.S. adults aged 50 and over, 71 percent used herbal medicine, acupuncture, or another form of alternative medicine in 2005. This represented an increase from 62 percent in 2002.

Industry observers have continued to voice concern about the safety and effectiveness of alternative medicines untested by traditional medical entities such as the FDA and to call for traditional health care providers to do a better job of familiarizing themselves with alternative medicines, the ways in which they are used, and the types of patients who use them. The American Society of Plastic Surgeons expressed concern because herbal supplements were being used by approximately 55 percent of plastic surgery patients, well above the rate of 24 percent for the general population.

Some alternative medicines may pose serious medical risks. For example, there is concern that Echinacea, an extract from the American coneflower, carries the risk of lowering a patient's immune response and preventing wounds from healing. Drugs.com, which describes itself as a prescription drug information site for consumers and professionals, states, "Echinacea is not recommended for use by people with multiple sclerosis, white blood cell disorders, collagen disorders, HIV/AIDS, autoimmune disorders or tuberculosis." In a 2003 study titled "Echinacea: A Safety Review," author Bruce Barrett stated that from a review of available scientific evidence, echinacea appears to be relatively safe, but he indicated in the summary section: "It should be remembered that any substance with pharmacological properties will almost certainly have accompanying toxicities. For instance, echinacea's demonstrated immunostimulating properties of macrophage activation and enhanced cytokine production are likely to be associated with immune-related adverse consequences, whether or not these have been demonstrated by current research. For instance, autoimmune diseases such as rheumatoid arthritis, lupus erythematosis, or multiple sclerosis could be triggered or accelerated. Similarly, common problems such as asthma, allergic rhinitis, or skin allergies could be activated or worsened. Or perhaps the immune system's natural-and-healthy manner of resisting infectious disease could be interfered with, leading to increased incidence or severity of bacterial or viral illness. Is there evidence to back up these speculations? No. Have these possibilities been ruled out? Not hardly. So, what is the bottom line? People with allergic, autoimmune or inflammatory disease (and their healthcare advisors) should think very carefully about the possible benefits and risks before dosing with this herbal medicine."

By the first decade of the 2000s, nearly 17 million Americans were discovering yoga, according to the research firm MRI, which indicated that participation had increased 100 percent from 2001 to 2005. Once viewed as a mystical endeavor, yoga was being offered in gyms, fitness centers, and a wide variety of other locations. MRI indicated that annual expenditures on clothing, DVDs, books, classes, equipment, and other products totaled almost $3 billion annually, which spelled great opportunity for industry players.

In addition to promoting relaxation, people were discovering that yoga provided cardiac health benefit's, as well as increased strength and greater flexibility. However, as with alternative medicine, industry observers were concerned about the possibility of physical injury that could result from yoga instructors with little training. For this reason, they suggested that consumers ensure that instructors were certified by the Yoga Alliance, a national credentialing organization.

All types of New Age products and services discussed above experienced growth as the use of the term enveloped new applications. For example, a 2008 book on brain wave vibration—based on an Asian form of yoga called Dahn Yoga, which, according to *PR Newswire,* "incorporates movement, music, and meditation to increase fitness, general health and wellness, and happiness"—was the sixteenth best-selling book on Amazon.com and ranked number one and number two, respectively, in the mental and spiritual healing category and the motivational, personal transformation, and personal health category. *Brain Wave Vibration: Getting Back into the Rhythm of a Happy, Healthy Life* by Ilchi Lee was just one of the popular New Age books published in the latter half of the decade; others included *A New Earth: Awakening to Your Life's Purposes* (2008) by Eckhart Tolle; *Eat, Pray, Love* (2007) by Elizabeth Gilbert; and *Midnights with the Mystic: A Little Guide to Freedom and Bliss* (2008) by Cheryl Simone.

Organic products were in high demand around the world in the late years of the first decade of the 2000s. According to one *Organic Monitor* report, international sales of organic goods more than doubled between 2000 and 2006, reaching $38.6 billion. In the United States, sales of organic food and beverages totaled nearly $20 billion in 2007. This was a significant increase as compared with the 1990 figure of $1 billion. According to the Organic Trade Association, the organic industry was expected to grow 18 percent annually through 2010. Sales of organic non-food items were also increasing, growing 26 percent in 2006.

Finally, more people were utilizing New Age health services. Integrative medicine—or that combining traditional and holistic methods—was becoming more common and available in hospitals around the United States. In fact, according to the American Hospital Association, as reported in *Health Governance Report,* one quarter of all hospitals offer an integrative medicine program. Other reports indicated alternative health care had become a $47 billion industry by 2008. In addition, some insurance programs began to cover New Age medical procedures, such as acupuncture.

Yoga as a component of a healthy lifestyle was also gaining increasing popularity. According to a study noted in the *Yoga Journal,* by 2008 almost 16 million Americans were practicing yoga, and 14 million had received yoga as a recommendation by their doctor or therapist. The same publication estimated that the amount spent on yoga classes and products had doubled in four years, reaching $5.7 billion in 2008. Also in 2008 the National Institutes of Health initiated the first ever "Yoga Week," adding to the already existing "Yoga Day" created by the Yoga Alliance. One of the more interesting developments in the latter part of the decade was the creation of "laughter yoga," whereby participants focus more on breathing than poses and posture. Laughing is used as an aerobic form of exercise as well as for stress relief. By 2008, laughing yoga was offered in 5,000 clubs worldwide.

CURRENT CONDITIONS

In her 2009 article, "The Dawn of New Age," author Emily Lambert covered some of the newest products in the widening scope of the industry. In addition to the traditional New Age interests in less familiar categories like Wiccan and Pagan products, more familiar ones related to yoga, astrology, and meditation were finding their ways into mainstream America. SoulJourney, a Butler, New Jersey, New Age store, stocked incense, oils, herbs, crystals, books, and Feng Shui products. Many gift retailers were carrying more products that could be classified as New Age, including candles, aromatherapy, inspirational books and CDs, stones, and jewelry. Some products had become so mainstream, noted Nora Monaco, owner of AngelStar in Morgan Hill, California, that one could even find them in Cracker Barrel. AngelStar had sold over 4 million of its angel worry stones, many

destined for troops in Iraq and Afghanistan as a reminder that things were going to be better and they could "give [their] worries to the angel." For those who appreciated NewAge humor, there were bumper stickers that read, "My Karma Just Ran Over Your Dogma," or "Practice Random Acts of Kindness." New Age music claimed to alter one's mood; New Age beverages touted healing and calming properties (mostly unproven).

The New Age label was added to many products or services wanting to represent the wave of the future. Often associated with "green" products, the term was increasingly used when referring to solar and wind power and other renewable energy sources. Private company Planet Resource Recovery, Inc. touted its "New-Age Products and Technologies" designed to enhance the recovery of the earth's natural resources, particularly metals, minerals, and hydrocarbons, that had been discarded through manufacturing and mining processes. In 2010, Gene Wize Natural Products announced its line of New Age nutritional supplements that were custom-made according to one's personal DNA. Upon ordering products from the company, customers received a DNA collection kit. They could then swab the cheeks of their mouths and return the swabs in the enclosed envelope. The samples were sent to Gene Wize Life Science labs. After analysis, the company then created personal DNA Supplements Online and recommended other special products related to the DNA results.

INDUSTRY LEADERS

Although overall the industry is fragmented and covers different sectors of the market, it is possible to identify some leaders in the area of natural and organic foods. The largest retailer of natural foods in the United States is Whole Foods Market, based in Austin, Texas. Beginning as a tiny natural foods store in 1980, it went on to pioneer the concept of selling natural foods in a supermarket-style atmosphere. In addition, it was ranked as one of *Fortune* magazine's "100 Best Companies to Work For" for the ninth year in a row in 2006.

Whole Foods Market Inc. (WFM) owns and operates the largest chain of natural and organic foods supermarkets in the world. In 2010, it operated 270 stores in the United States and United Kingdom, and Canada. With 54,000 employees, the company reported 2009 revenues of $8 billion.

In addition to its retail locations, which averaged approximately 32,000 square feet (15 new stores in 2009), WFM operated a coffee-roasting operation, seafood processing facility, bakehouses, commissary kitchens, produce procurement and field inspection offices, and regional distribution centers.

WFM stores sell approximately 26,000 natural/organic food and non-food products with a heavy emphasis on perishable foods designed to appeal to natural/organic (N/O) and gourmet shoppers. They also offer a limited amount of conventional products that meet WFM standards. These products include produce, seafood, grocery, meat and poultry, bakery, prepared foods and catering, beverages, specialty (beer, wine, and cheese) items, nutritional supplements, vitamins, personal care products, household goods, and educational products such as books.

Another industry leader was Trader Joe's, based in Monrovia, California. Trader Joe's began as a Los Angeles convenience store chain in 1958 and was purchased by German businessmen Karl and Theo Albrecht in 1979. As of 2008, the company owned 300 stores in 25 states and sold health food, organic produce, and dietary supplements, in addition to private-label items, which account for 70 percent of sales.

AMERICA AND THE WORLD

The New Age industry has won over many Americans, and people worldwide have embraced some of the movement's ideals and practices. According to *Marketing in Europe,* German demand for organic food started increasing during the 1980s, climbing 20 percent per year through the end of the decade. The market then slowed during the mid-1990s, posting gains of only about 10 to 15 percent per year. Organic food was also attracting a growing base of customers in France. A writer for *Eurofood* reported that the market increased by 15 percent each year beginning in the 1980s as French customers sought higher quality food and adopted healthier eating habits. However, the lack of an organized distribution system has hindered the industry's ability to expand even more.

As Yumi Kiyono noted in *Nikkei Weekly,* Japanese citizens have also heartily embraced the New Age movement. Spiritual books and other products have done well, as have so-called power stones, which facilitate meditation.

Sumit Sharma reported in the *Wall Street Journal* that in India, especially in Bombay, yoga, meditation, and other indigenous practices for health and stress reduction were prospering in the late 1990s. In 1996, some physicians were turning to classical yoga breathing exercises and laughing postures for their patients in the belief that they relieved stress. This spawned more than 100 laughing clubs across the country.

BIBLIOGRAPHY

"About Planet Resource Recovery, Inc." Planet Resources. Available from http://www.planetresources.net.

Baltes, Sharon. "Baby Boomers Bring Boost to Organic Food Sales." *Des Moines Business Record,* 8 May 2006.

Castillo, Andrea. "Yoga Makes Headway in Business Schools." *Business Week Online,* 16 July 2008. Available from www.businessweek.com.

"Date Announced for Yoga Day USA 2009." *Biotech Week,* 13 August 2008.

"DNA Nutritional Supplements for New Age." *ShapeUp America!,* 19 October 2010.

"Echinacea Drug Information." Drugs.com, August 2008. Available from http://www.drugs.com/.

"FDA Withdraws Direct Final Rule on Dietary Supplements that Contain Botanicals." *The Food Institute Report,* 26 January 2006.

"Herbal Supplements' Harmful Side Effects." *The Futurist,* May-June 2006.

"Industry Statistics and Projected Growth." Organic Trade Association, 2008. Available from www://ota.com/.

Lambert, Emily. "The Dawn of New Age." *Gift Shop Magazine,* Winter 2009.

Larkin, Maureen O. "Giving Patients an Alternative: Hospitals Find Success Integrating Holistic Medicine into Service Lines." *Health Governance Report,* September 2007.

"Laugh Yourself Healthy." *The St. Petersburg Times* (FL), 30 July 2008.

Monks, Richard. "Very Much a Growth Category." *Chain Drug Review,* 1 October 2007.

"No Hearing for NIC's Ephedra Ban Appeal." *Nutraceuticals International,* May 2007.

"Personal Health Book Jumps Up Amazon.com Rankings." *PR Newswire,* 14 August 2008.

Walzer, Emily. "A New Pose: Today's Vibrant Yoga Market Stretches into the Mainstream." *Sporting Goods Business,* March 2006.

"Whole Foods—Wild Oats Deal on Hold." *The Denver Post,* 30 July 2008.

NEW FOOD PRODUCTS

2099

INDUSTRY SNAPSHOT

The cozy scene of families gathered around the table each evening to share a home-cooked, made-from-scratch meal has been vanishing from the American dining horizon for some time. The reality of meal preparation is in flux. At the end of the twentieth century, almost one half of all U.S. food expenditures went for meals prepared outside the home and only one third of meals included at least one dish made the old-fashioned way. Americans don't want to invest more than 15 minutes in preparing their food, according to a Food Marketing Institute report. Seventy percent of households buy takeout at least once a month. Even the definition of food is changing rapidly. Meals can be prepared in minutes, since many packaged foods now eliminate the need for washing, slicing, and dicing.

Functional foods, also known as nutraceuticals, contain extra beneficial effects for "targeted" functions in the body. These products promise to rival medicines in their disease fighting and resisting capacities. The nutraceuticals market continued to be strong, thanks to factors such as the rising popularity of preventative medicine, skyrocketing healthcare costs, the aging of the baby boom generation, growing acceptance among the medical community, and higher quality raw materials.

While foods containing genetically engineered ingredients continued to be of concern to many consumers, their numbers continued to grow. This was reflected within the agriculture sector.

ORGANIZATION AND STRUCTURE

Before new food products hit stores nationwide, producers usually test market them in a limited geographical region. Companies monitor the success of the new products and determine whether they have market-staying or trend-setting power. If the products are deemed successful during the trial period, the companies then begin more extensive marketing. In order for new products to thrive once they are introduced, analysts note that companies must fortify them with a robust barrage of promotional strategies. Unless companies support new food products, they will never gain much attention from consumers, and if businesses let up on promoting new products prematurely, sales will start to flag and the new product will fade out of the market. After launching a new product, developers must track it—scrutinize the movement of the product and ascertain who buys it and why. Developers also must anticipate consumer reactions to the product and alter promotional campaigns to accommodate consumer response.

The U.S. Department of Agriculture (USDA), U.S. Food and Drug Administration (FDA), Center for Food Safety and Applied Nutrition, National Organic Standards Board, and an array of state, county, and municipal organizations that oversee the growing, production, and sale of foods all play a role in the regulation of new food items. The industry itself has an array of related trade organizations and groups such as the American Crop Protection Association and the Food Marketing Institute. Many commodities boast their own lobbying and marketing groups. The produce industry, for example, has the International Fresh-Cut Produce Association, United Fresh Fruit and Vegetable Association, Texas Produce Association, Produce

Marketing Association, Florida Fruit and Vegetable Association, Northwest Horticultural Council, and the Western Growers Association protecting its interests and marketing its products nationally and regionally.

Perhaps the most rigorous industry oversight involves the certification and monitoring of organic foods. As early as 1974, the USDA called for policies to govern the growing, processing, and marketing of organic foods, but no hard and fast rules resulted from these early exhortations. However, the USDA did provide a working definition. "Organically grown food" refers to produce not treated with chemical pesticides or fertilizers, and "organically processed food" includes produce not treated with synthetic preservatives, according to William Breene in *Prepared Foods*. Farm organizations started certification programs throughout the country beginning in the 1970s and 1980s. In 1990 Congress finally passed legislation toward creating standards for certifying organic food. The Farm Act of 1990 established the National Organic Standards Board, which tried to develop official standards for the organic foods industry. A host of certification agencies all over the country, however, still bore the brunt of the certification task using standards they created. By 1999, the USDA had issued guidelines for the certification of organic meat and poultry, but no final regulations to establish standards for all organic products. Further complicating issues related to the standards were whether foods genetically engineered, irradiated, or grown in soil fertilized with sewage sludge could be considered organic.

The National Organic Program Proposed Rule of 2000 developed national organic standards and established an organic certification program. The regulations include production and handling standards, labeling standards, certification standards, and accreditation standards. The use of genetic engineering, ionizing radiation, and sewage sludge in organic production and handling is prohibited. Imported agricultural products may be sold in the United States if they are certified under the regulations.

BACKGROUND AND DEVELOPMENT

With a slew of popular products such as the widening variety of home meal replacements on the market, food producers largely expanded or remarketed existing lines and did not launch many revolutionary products in the mid to late 1990s. A growing problem at the end of the decade was dwindling shelf space in stores. New product introductions slowed, but organic and all natural products showed significant gains. Meal kits and convenience foods continued to dominate, however.

Dinners, Entrees, and Mixes The drive to create products that capture market share of convenience and at least seemingly healthful food often resulted in the release of

hundreds of new dinner, entree, and mix offerings each year. Leading this category were frozen pizzas; *USA Today* reported sales of $2.6 billion by 2001. Most new products, however, were merely extensions of existing lines of entrees such as Stouffer, Lean Cuisine, Healthy Choice, and Budget Gourmet.

For traditional supermarkets, home meal replacement was the hottest item. However, many stores moved away from offering fully prepared meals, stressing pre-prepared meals in the refrigerated or frozen sections, meals that require only heating. Among the items located in these sections were already marinated meats, and packaged meals such as Skillet Sensations or Voila! one-dish dinners that include pasta, vegetables, and meat.

Interest in international cuisines remained strong, led as usual by Mexican and Italian, but Asian, Mediterranean, and Middle Eastern food products increased as well. One fully prepared meal item that did enjoy notable success was sushi. Larger supermarket chains, such as Jewel, Dominick's, and Wegman's, introduced to-go sushi, rolled, packaged, and placed on ice right before the shoppers' eyes. It proved to be a popular lunch option for office workers. Alongside traditional maki and California rolls, more adventurous combinations appeared. Sushi House offered Philly rolls (salmon and cream cheese), and Whole Foods featured shiitake rolls (shiitake mushrooms, avocados, and carrots encased in rice and seaweed).

Baby Food Due to the possibility of babies suffering harmful effects from farm chemical residue after consuming food processed with toxic chemicals, parents have grown more wary and cognizant of what they feed their children and how it is grown and processed. In addition, parents want healthful natural food for their babies, not food adulterated with unnecessary ingredients and treated with preservatives. Health food companies launched products to compete with the traditional baby food producers. Growing Healthy and Earth's Best were two of the most prominent alternative producers, offering unalloyed organic foods. Sales, however, slumped for these new contenders and baby health food never fully caught on. Furthermore, even though the Center for Science in the Public Interest reported that Gerber Products Co. diluted its products, the center failed to pique the public's interest and Gerber retained a majority market share. Nonetheless, Earth's Best had moderate but improving success, becoming the country's fourth leading producer of baby food. The key problem organic baby food producers face is offering competitive pricing. Nonetheless, Gerber began to market organic foods in its Tender Harvest line in order to retain market domination.

Packaged Prepared Produce A trend that started in the early 1990s and fared well by catering to both sensibilities of convenience and health consciousness was packaged salad. Its success led to the creation of numerous other new packaged produce releases. Introduced in 1994, salad kits continued to sell well throughout the decade. One of the most successful food categories in the 1990s was packaged produce. Although supermarkets traditionally offered many of these value-added products in order to promote or use up produce that neared its maximum storage limit, producers and distributors now wanted to participate in the market. The newest additions to packaged salads were edible flowers: marigolds, lavender, and rose petals.

In an effort to garner more fresh fruit sales, companies began to launch washed, sliced, and otherwise prepared fruits. For example, Fresh Express introduced Grape Escape—washed red seedless grapes removed from the stem in four-ounce packages. Fresh World Farms brought out its Necta Fresh Pineapples in a few different varieties: whole cored, chunked, and sliced. Some producers also offered pre-peeled fruit. Fruit of Groveland introduced the Heart Garden Fresh Cut Fruit line, providing an assortment of melons as well as grapes and pineapple. Global Fresh began marketing Fresh Cut Apples with Dip, which includes slices of Granny Smith or Fuji apples and reduced-fat caramel dip. Ready Pac Produce also introduced its ready-to-eat Fresh Melon Chunks featuring watermelon, cantaloupe, or honeydew.

Low Fat Although they declined in popularity in the late 1990s, the food industry created over 5,600 low-fat foods. Advances in food technology and the FDA's approval of Olean increased consumer options for fat-modified foods. A 1996 survey revealed 88 percent of Americans eat low-fat, reduced-fat, or fat-free foods. Rather than invent new fat-free foods, one trend was toward the reformulation of fat-free foods into better-tasting low-fat foods. Even small amounts of fat improve the sensory appeal of food, including texture and flavor.

Vending Machines The convenience and speed of vending machine cuisine has traditionally outranked its taste, but new lines of pizza, Mexican favorites, such as burritos and chimichangas, and soups and sandwiches edged out the usual coffee and chocolate bar fare traditionally provided by the machines. Shelf-stable entrees were introduced by DeLuca, Inc., Hormel Foods Corp., International Home Foods, Inc., and Jimmy Dean Foods. DeLuca, a subsidiary of Perdue Farms Inc., featured 12 different entrees including meat lasagna, eggplant lasagna, meatballs in meat sauce, macaroni and beef, sausage, peppers, and onions, American meat loaf, and baked ziti. Hormel and Dinty Moore extended their well-known canned products such as chili, beef stew, corned beef hash, scalloped potatoes, and beans and wieners to the

vending machine venue as well. Among soups, Maruchan Inc. of Irvine, California, provided instant ramen noodles and instant wonton in Styrofoam cups. Hormel and others also have soups available in ovenproof paper and/or foam cups. Oscar Mayer Lunchables and Charlie's Lunch Kit by Starkist Tuna rounded out the category.

Nutraceuticals Americans have been eating fortified foods since 1924, when manufacturers started adding iodine to salt to prevent the nutritional deficiency that causes goiters. However, the aging of the health-conscious and often affluent baby boomers has focused increasing attention on the development of nutraceuticals, also known as functional foods. Although a precise definition of functional foods is hard to pin down, they are often described as complete food items that provide an enhanced health benefit beyond the usual nutritional properties normally found in a food item. Products fitting this description— garlic, oat fiber, flax oil, berries, and soybean oil are examples—raked in an estimated $12.7 billion in 1999. Nutraceuticals continued to eclipse low-fat, no-fat, and sugar-free products. They are promoted as remedies or preventives for common ailments such as high cholesterol and osteoporosis, which predominantly strike people as they age. Many of these products competed with pharmaceuticals and were designed to replace vitamins or other diet aids. The nutrition industry itself was a $20 billion industry, and this encouraged mainstream food and pharmaceutical corporations to consider producing nutraceutical products.

On average, women exhibited greater awareness of the value and the health-related benefits of functional foods, yet consumed them less frequently than men. In addition, widespread appreciation of nutraceuticals has yet to penetrate the U.S. populace at large. According to a 2000 survey by the American Dietetic Association, 79 percent of those surveyed had not heard of functional foods, 68 percent defined them simply as "healthy" foods, while 17 percent felt that they either boosted energy or improved athletic performance. Leading consumers of functional foods had a high awareness of health topics and nutrition news. In addition, about 44 percent were 55 and over. The physical and performance benefits of some nutraceuticals, however, appealed most strongly to those at the ends of the age spectrum: 18 to 29-year-olds and healthy seniors 70 and older. In contrast, consumers in the 40 to 65-year-old group and seniors in poor health sought the medical and preventive functional benefits, according to Linda Gilbert, the president of HealthFocus Inc. of Des Moines, Iowa.

Antioxidants received particular attention for inclusion in functional foods. Clinical trials of the benefits of vitamins E and B are under way. Also under consideration were omega-3 fatty acids found in fish and certain vegetable oils since they may prevent ventricular fibrillation and sudden death. Pharmaceutical makers view functional foods as a way to help their products cross over from the pharmacy to the grocery store. For packaged-goods companies, nutraceuticals seem to be the next hot-selling, high-margin products in a traditionally very flat industry sector.

Among notable functional food releases were Benecol, a Johnson & Johnson margarine-like spread touted as lowering cholesterol levels by as much as 10 percent with regular use. In the first few months after its introduction, it had captured 2 percent of the market. It was joined by Unilever's Take Control, a similar spread with slightly lower performance abilities. Mead Johnson Nutritionals premiered Viactiv, chocolate-flavored, calcium-enriched chews, and EnfaGrow, a series of vitamin-fortified cereals and snacks for children. Novartis debuted its Aviva line in Europe, which consisted of orange drinks, biscuits, and muesli intended to strengthen bones and aid digestion. The company introduced the line in the United States in 2000. Cooke Pharma developed the first functional food for the management of vascular disease, the HeartBar. It contains the amino acid L-arginine, which, the company says, relieves angina, or heart-related chest pain, by dilating the coronary arteries. Gerber was developing a snack for pre-schoolers that was fortified with docosa hexaenoic acid, which is claimed to boost concentration. The additive already was being used in Japan.

Phytochemicals, which are extracts from plants, appeared in increasing numbers in functional foods. For example, Kellogg introduced its Ensemble line of frozen foods, desserts, and cereals that contain psyllium, a fiber that lowers cholesterol. Take Control spread featured soybean extract to lower cholesterol levels.

According to the Mintel International Group Ltd., functional food products were a $1.3 billion market in 2001. Bakery items and cereals were the largest functional foods category, bringing in $728 million in 2001. Bars, candy, and snacks amassed $259 million in sales that same year.

Functional foods do not lack for critics, however. The Center for Science in the Public Interest (CSPI) has charged that some functional foods do not live up to their health claims, often because they do not contain a great enough amount of their "functional" ingredient to deliver promised benefits or because the products require sustained consumption to achieve results, just as ordinary medicines do. Price constitutes another basis for complaint, as well as a barrier to widespread adoption of functional foods by U.S. consumers. Frequently, nutraceuticals cost five or six times the amount of non-enhanced counterparts.

In 2000, CSPI asked the FDA to stop the sale of more than 75 functional foods that contain ingredients not considered by the agency to be safe, such as St. John's wort, kava, ginko biloba, and ginseng. Furthermore, CSPI

called on the FDA to order manufacturers to stop making false and misleading claims about their products. CSPI felt that herbs are medicines and do not belong in foods. In response, food groups and manufacturers claimed that functional foods are regulated just like conventional foods and that there was enough regulation to ensure product safety, unadulterated ingredients, and accurate labeling.

That same year, the U.S. General Accounting Office (GAO) released a report criticizing how the FDA regulated functional foods. According to the GAO, the "FDA's efforts and federal laws provide limited assurances of the safety of functional foods." The GAO granted that "the extent to which unsafe functional foods reach consumers is unknown," but it concluded that the FDA should protect the public by discouraging misleading claims and requiring appropriate warning labels. In response to the all of the controversy, the Grocery Manufacturers of America, the world's largest association of food, beverage and consumer product companies, said that CSPI's intent to ban many functional foods was an overreaction. It was also pointed out that food manufacturers were constitutionally enabled to make health-related information available to consumers as long as the claims were true. Nevertheless, the FDA felt prompted to issue warning letters to some companies about their products.

In 2002, members of the American Council on Science and Health (ACSH) stated that many of the supposed health benefits of functional foods claimed by producers were not supported by substantial scientific information. In a report released that year, titled "Facts About 'Functional Foods,'" the ACSH evaluated the health effects of such foods and ranked them according to the strength of the evidence, separating the scientifically-supported claims from the unfounded ones. For instance, the report stated that evidence indicating that soy protein consumption lowered cholesterol levels was strong while evidence linking green tea to reduced risk of some types of cancer was fairly weak. The report informed consumers how to read and evaluate health claims made on food labels. In addition, it outlined the 13 health claims for foods or food ingredients approved by the FDA. These claims were based on the general health-enhancing properties of key ingredients in the food items.

Organics and Natural Foods Organic foods continued to draw strong interest from consumers. Sales grew nearly 20 percent annually through the 1990s. In contrast, ordinary grocery sales experienced only a 1 to 2 percent growth over the same period, according to the Grocery Manufacturers of America.

Organics also caught the eye of major food and pharmaceuticals manufacturers, who rushed to acquire prominent producers in this segment. For example, H.J.

Heinz Co. formed an organic and nutritional foods unit through investment in Hain Food Group. Kraft Foods, Inc, bought Boca Burger, the producer of soy-based meat alternatives. General Mills, Inc., purchased Small Planet Foods, which makes a line of frozen and canned organic produce. While such acquisitions boosted the visibility of organic items, they also probably threatened the market presence of the smaller, independent producers who traditionally characterized this sector.

In 2000, organic food sales in the United States reached $7.8 billion, according to the Organic Trade Association (OTA), as well as the report "Trends in the United States: Consumer Attitudes & the Supermarket, 2001," by the Food Marketing Institute. Sales of organic nondairy beverages grew by 26 percent in 2001, according to *Natural Foods Merchandiser.* The OTA predicted an annual growth rate of 24 percent between 2000 and 2005 for organic beverages. The Food Marketing Institute pointed out that in 2001, 71 percent of supermarkets carried organic and natural foods. That same year, according to the OTA, only 40 percent of organic food manufacturers' produce distribution went through health and natural food stores. That figure was down from 62 percent in 1998. Further, supermarkets accounted for 45 percent of organic food manufacturers' sales in 2001, said the OTA.

Genetically Modified Foods Undoubtedly the most controversial new foods were genetically modified (GM) foods. Critics broadcast fears of newly created viruses and allergens as a result of tampering with the genetic structure of food items, the long-term consequences of which were as yet unknown. Opponents also charged that patenting GM foods would lead to the domination of the world's food supply by a handful of large manufacturers.

Nevertheless, developing countries such as the People's Republic of China and India are heavy users of GM crops created by industry giants such as Monsanto and Novartis. China intended to put one half of all its harvest of rice, tomatoes, peppers, and potatoes into GM varieties within the next 5 to 10 years, citing both its lack of arable land and the lower pesticide and herbicide requirements of GM crops. In the United States, about 60 percent of all supermarket products contained GM canola oil, soybeans, or corn.

European representatives have called for labeling on all GM foods and advocate the establishment of an international supervisory panel to police the development and dissemination of GM foods. While the United States, with an enormous stake in GM foods, was traditionally resistant to labeling, in 2000 the proposed Genetically Engineered Food Right to Know Act (GEFRKA) was introduced in the U.S. Senate, although the act had not yet passed by early 2007.

Fans of GM foods may have found their champion in the form of "golden rice," a GM strain developed by Swiss professor Ingo Potrykus in Zurich. The rice, named for its golden hue, contains beta carotene (vitamin A), which the body needs for vision health. Potrykus developed the rice in an effort funded by the Swiss government and the Rockefeller Foundation to help combat vitamin A deficiency in the developing world, which kills about 2 million children each year and causes blindness in many others. Growers will be given the rice free.

The debate between advocates, who championed the increased productivity, and critics, who were concerned about long-term and not easily seen effects, continued unabated. By 2003, GM foods became a staple in the diets of U.S. consumers. Almost a third of all corn planted in Wisconsin came from genetically altered varieties, while about 80 percent of soybeans were genetically modified. Overall, according to the Council for Biotechnology Information, 40 different crops had been approved for commercial use. Even more, the crops were becoming ingredients in prepared foods such as soups, pizzas, and soft drinks.

Advocates claimed that genetically altered crops help farmers increase productivity and cut the use of farm chemicals. Opponents felt it was increasing an undesirable trend toward large-scale farming. Others worried about safety or simply the rightness about tampering with genetic structures. Long-term effects were also a strong consideration. Opponents fretted about the changes that may occur in humans and animals as well as the effect it would have on the natural cycle. Increased GM foods prompted calls for labeling. The Pew Initiative on Food and Biotechnology conducted a poll in 2001 that found that 75 percent of consumers wanted labeling that would indicate if food products were genetically altered. An international poll commissioned by the Discovery Channel for its program called "DNA: The Promise and the Price" revealed that 62 percent of people in eight countries believed that rules and regulations didn't keep pace with genetic research. It also revealed that 70 percent of those polled in the United States felt the same.

Pet Foods New food items aren't limited to human consumers. The $1 billion U.S. pet food market encompasses many novel products that resemble the special foods intended for pets' human counterparts. Since nearly as many pets as owners are overweight, for example, "lite" foods are included in most pet food brand lines. In 1999, the American Animal Feed Control Officials established standard calorie references for reduced-calorie pet foods.

Other special pet foods include formulas adapted for particular stages in the pet's life cycle such as puppyhood, old age, or pregnancy. Gourmet pet foods feature "human grade" ingredients and no fillers or artificial byproducts. Medical foods, such as low-protein mixes for pets with kidney ailments and dental products to reduce plaque on teeth, are regulated as foods, not drugs.

The next wave in specialty pet foods will likely be nutraceuticals for pets. These include dietary supplements, herbals for the stressed dog, and canine probiotics to aid digestion. Pet snacks constitute a popular product with pet owners. According to the Pet Products Manufacturers' Association, 8 of every 10 dog owners and 5 of every 10 cat owners regularly buy pet treats. Like other consumers of specialty foods, however, pet owners must exercise caution in their purchasing decisions. The long-term health effects of many pet products are not well known, since very few manufacturing guidelines have been established for these items. In addition, some dietary supplements may be entirely unnecessary for pet health or may even have negative effects.

Worldwide, packaged foods were a $1.4 trillion industry in 2004, according to the *Economist*. While a bevy of new food products continued to hit the market during the middle of the first decade of the 2000s, some analysts criticized the industry for a lack of innovation. This situation, which the *Economist* called "a crisis of creativity," was allowing supermarkets to garner a larger share of the market through the sale of private label food products. This especially was true of products targeted at health-conscious individuals.

The popularity of low-carbohydrate foods peaked in the first half of 2004. That year, the number of products in this category reached approximately 5,000, up from a mere 500 the previous year. While new products were still being introduced by industry leaders like Kraft, some observers indicated that interest in low-carbohydrate foods began to dwindle in late 2004, leaving some manufacturers with unsold product inventories that they donated to charities. One analyst theorized that quality and taste may have suffered as food companies rushed to roll out products amidst the "low-carb" hype. Nevertheless, others argued that low-carb foods would continue to occupy a niche in the health market, even if that niche is much smaller than it was in 2004.

The nutraceuticals market continued to be strong during the first decade of the 2000s, thanks to factors such as the rising popularity of preventative medicine, skyrocketing healthcare costs, the aging of the baby boom generation, growing acceptance among the medical community, and higher quality raw materials. Data from The Freedonia Group projected worldwide demand for nutraceuticals to reach $9.6 billion in 2008, up from $7.1 billion in 2003 and $5.2 billion in 1998. After growing at an annual rate of 6.3 percent from 1998 to 2003, a growth rate of 6.1 percent was expected from 2003 through 2008. Food additives such as soy isoflavones, lycopene, omega-3 fatty acids, and probiotics were expected to experience above average growth.

The number of foods containing genetically engineered ingredients also continued to grow. This was reflected within the agriculture sector. According to *Chemical Market Reporter*, the International Service for the Acquisition of Agri-biotech Applications reported that worldwide, 8.25 million farmers planted some 200 million acres of genetically engineered crops in 2004. This was an increase of 20 percent from the previous year and marked the second-highest growth in history. At 118 million acres, the United States accounted for the majority (59 percent) of genetically engineered crops. However, growth in developing countries was the strongest, outpacing growth in developed countries for the first time.

By 2006, organic food was the fastest growing segment of the food industry in North America. According to the Organic Trade Association, in the United States, the industry grew 16.2 percent in 2005 to reach $13.8 billion. Fruits and vegetables accounted for the largest portion of these sales at 39 percent, but the fastest growing segment of organic food products was in organic fresh meat sales, which grew by 55.4 percent. Statistics from *Natural Food Merchandiser* also reported significant growth in the sale of organic nutrition bars and beer and wine: both these segments saw a 30 percent increase in sales. In addition, revenue from the sale of organic pet products grew 37.5 percent.

The United States was not the only nation jumping on the organic bandwagon. The European Union outpaced the United States in number of farms and acres farmed organic, and together the European Union and the United States accounted for more than 95 percent of the world's retail sales of organic foods, which totaled $25 billion worldwide in 2005. In the first decade of the 2000s, the European Union had approximately 143,000 farms and more than 4.4 million hectares under organic production, whereas the United States had only 6,949 farms and about 1 million hectares farmed organically. The two also have different policies toward the organic food industry. Whereas the European Union encourages the growth of the organic sector through policies designed to increase the amount of land farmed organically and provide education, research, and marketing support, the United States takes more of a free-market approach, with policies mostly adopted through national standards and certification.

CURRENT CONDITIONS

In March 2009, First Lady Michelle Obama created a large organic garden on White House grounds, providing the impetus for a renewed national interest in home gardening across the country. According to the *Boomer Survive and Thrive Guide,*, 43 million U.S. households planned to grow their own fruits and vegetables in 2009. On the organic front, 2008 organic food and beverage sales were estimated at $32.9 billion, according to *Organic Consumers.* Despite economic cost or difficulty, consumers are willing to pay more for products grown without synthetic fertilizers, pesticides, GMOs, growth hormones, or sewage sludge.

Indeed, a return to all things natural appeared to have picked up steam at the end of the century's first decade. Partly spurred by incidents of widespread illness caused from tainted imported food (mostly fresh produce) in 2008, in combination with the national recall of several tainted meats and other food items, Americans became increasingly interested in reading food labels and understanding what they meant. This happened to coincide with new FDA food labeling requirements, most of which went into effect in January and/or July 2008. They included, but were not limited to, specific labeling requirements for qualified health claims (statements on food labels regarding a relationship between a food or food component and a disease or health-related condition). Also, nutrient content claims (containing terms such as "free," "lean," "extra lean," "high," "low," "good source," "reduced," "less," "light," "fewer," and "more,") must now meet statutory definitions.

Another trend in 2009 was the return to sugar and honey as sweetening ingredients in food products, instead of "high fructose corn syrup." ConAgra returned to using only sugar or honey in its Healthy Choice All Natural frozen entrees. Kraft Foods removed the corn sweetener from its salad dressings, and was working on its Lunchables line of portable meals and snacks.

In November 2009, the report "World Nutraceutical Ingredients: U.S. Industry Forecasts for 2013 & 2018," forecasted that the demand for nutraceutical ingredients worldwide would advance 6.2 percent annually to $21.8 billion in 2013, serving a $236 billion global nutritional product industry. Authors of the report noted that the world demand for nutrients and minerals would reach $12.6 billion in 2013, up 6.4 percent annually from 2008. Soy proteins and isoflavones, psyllium fibers, omega-3 fatty acids, probiotics, lycopene, calcium and magnesium were expected to see the fastest gains, based on widely accepted health benefits and expanding applications in meal supplements and functional foods and drinks.

According to Zenith International's February 2009 report, in 2008, consumption of nutraceutical beverages was estimated to have reached 3.7 billion litres, with a value of $11.5 billion. Zenith forecasted high single digit annual growth, with global volume sales set to reach 5.6 billion litres by 2013.

In 2008, the global probiotics market (including both foodstuffs and supplements) was worth more than $25.7 billion, representing more than 18 percent of the global functional foods market.

INDUSTRY LEADERS

As of November 2009, Nestle Foods remained the world's largest food and beverage company, as well as the largest processor in the United States and Canada. Its various operations in two countries aggressively expanded sales over the past decade through a mixture of organic growth and acquisitions. Its brands included Abuelita, Baby Ruth, Buitoni, Butterfinger, Carnation, Coffee-Mate, Crunch, Dibs, Dreyer's, Drumstick, Edy's, Eskimo Pie, Häagen-Dazs, Hot Pockets, Jenny Craig, Juicy Juice, La Lechera, Lean Cuisine, Lean Pockets, Libby's, Maggi, Nescafe, Nesquik, Nestle, Skinny Cow, Stouffer's, Taster's Choice, Toll House, and Wonka. A $101 billion global company, its Glendale, California U.S. operations had 2008 revenues of $26.5 billion, with 21,000 employees.

ConAgra Foods Inc., based in Nebraska, was a leading frozen food producer in the United States. The diversified food company produced some of the leading prepared food products in the United States. The company manufactured products for agriculture and prepared food items under various brand names such as Hunt's, Healthy Choice, Wesson, Rosarita, La Choy, Chun King, Peter Pan, Knott's Berry Farm, Orville Redenbacher's, Armour, Butterball, Hebrew National, and Van Camp's. ConAgra formed the CAG Functional Foods Division to take advantage of projected growth in that category. About half the company's revenues derive from its refrigerated foods operations while packaged foods brought in about 30 percent. ConAgra also ran one of the country's largest flour and corn-milling operations. In 1998 ConAgra rolled out its Advantage 10 vegetarian entrée line, and purchased meat snack maker GoodMark Foods. In 2000 the firm picked up high-profile brands Chef Boyardee and PAM cooking spray with its purchase of International Home Foods. The company sold its agricultural segments in order to concentrate on name-brand and value-added packaged foods. ConAgra, which employed 33,000 workers, finished its fiscal 2008 (ending in May 2009) with $11.5 billion in revenues.

AMERICA AND THE WORLD

As of 2009, the United States still lacked statutes or regulations requiring the identification of genetically modified (GM) ingredients to be listed on food labels. This put the nation years behind other world leaders, including The European Union, China, Australia/New Zealand, Japan, and Brazil, all of which had some form of regulation dating back as early as 2000 (Japan).

Many U.S. food trends and products originate elsewhere in the world. In many Asian cultures, diet and health are considered integrally linked, and herbal enhancements are routinely incorporated into everyday cuisine. Unique Japanese functional products include chewing gums and soft drinks that claim anti-allergy properties, a throat candy packaged in antibacterial film bags, and health/beauty drinks that contain collagen, an ingredient used in external skin care products.

As in the United States, in Europe the desire for convenience or indulgence combines with a concern for quality and health. In the United Kingdom, a cultural preference for snacking is creating a greater market for breakfast bars and other "on-the-go" foods. In Europe, functional foods include vitamin-fortified frozen vegetables from Agro, a division of Unilever, and "smart fat" Maval yogurt that contains appetite-suppressing palm oil extract. Spanish manufacturer Union Tostadora produces lines of coffee enriched with fiber, vitamins, and ginseng. According to analyst David Jago and others, European interest in natural, organic, and artisanal (handcrafted or traditional) food is developing in tandem with increasing ethical concerns about animal welfare and environmentally responsible food production. This was especially evident in the well-publicized European opposition to GM foods.

RESEARCH AND DEVELOPMENT

New items being researched and tested in 2009 included natural blue and green food colorants. Generally, natural colorings do not provide the same range of hues as are available with certified coloring. For example, anthocyanin pigments, derived from fruit or vegetables, exhibit a reversible molecular structural change when the pH of the environment changes. This causes a hue change from red to purple to blue, as the food matrix changes from acidic to basic. This characteristic can create issues for formulators wishing to use anthocyanins in products. In late 2008, there was an industry breakthrough that allowed developers to use a natural blue color at a lower pH level than conventional anthocyanin colorings. The patented blue color, offered by D.D. Williamson, was derived from red cabbage.

Other research in 2009 included the use of alternative "pulse," coatings (made of dry peas, chick peas, lentils, and beans) on foods in lieu of traditional wheat-based coatings for foods like tempura deep frying. Clinical studies in 2009 demonstrated that pulses contribute positively to the management and prevention of chronic diseases, such as diabetes and cardiovascular disease. According to a report from *Packaged Facts,* the gluten-free market grew at an average annual rate of 28 percent since 2004. At that time, it was valued at $580 million;

in 2008 the value was $1.56 billion. It was projected to be worth $2.6 billion by 2012.

BIBLIOGRAPHY

"Biotech Agriculture Reports Strong Growth." *Chemical Market Reporter,* 24 January 2005.

"Convenience Is Still King." *The Food Institute Report,* 11 December 2006.

De Guzman, Doris. "Nutraceuticals in Regulatory Spotlight." *CMR,* 13-19 June 2005.

Dimitri, Carolyn, and Lydia Oberholtzer. "EU and U.S. Organic Markets Face Strong Demand Under Different Policies." *Amber Waves,* February 2006. Available from www.ers. usda.gov/.

"Farley's Creates Baby Snack Line." *Marketing,* 1 December 2004.

"Food as Medicine Concept Gaining Steam." *Drug Store News,* 6 June 2005.

"Food Labeling—An Overview." National Agricultural Law Center. Updated March 2009. Available from http://www. nationalaglawcenter.org/assets/overviews/foodlabeling.html.

"Functional Soft Drinks a Major Force." *International Food Ingredients,* December 2004/January 2005.

Fusaro, Dave. "2009 Processsor of the Year: Nestle USA." *Processed Foods,* 30 November 2009.

"Global Market Review of Probiotics-Forecast to 2013." October 2009. Available from http://www.the-infoshop.com/report/jusf102546-review-of-probiotics.html.

"Global Nutraceutical Drinks Report 2009." Zenith International, February 2009. Available from http://www. marketresearch.com/map/prod/2271471.html.

"Global Nutraceutical Ingredients Market to hit $21.8 billion by 2013, says New Report." November 2009. Available from http://www.prlog.org/10408053-global-nutraceutical-ingredients-market-to-hit-218-billion-by-2013-says-new-report.html.

"Heinz Organic Baby Foods." 1 April 2007. Available from www.heinzbaby.com.

"Hoover's Company Capsules." *Hoover's Online,* 1 April 2007. Available from http://www.hoovers.com.

Hunter, Jo. "Fast Food Off the Shelf." *Packaging Today International,* February 2007.

"Industry Statistics and Projected Growth." Organic Trade Association: 2005.

Kjoeller, Katrine. "Next Stop, U.S." *Dairy Industries International,* February 2007.

Laux, Marsha. "Organic Food Trends Profile." Agricultural Marketing Resource Center, June 2006. Available from www.agmrc.org.

"Making a Meal of It." *Economist,* 7 May 2005.

Mannie, Elizabeth. "R&D: Natural Blues and Greens." *Processed Foods,* December 2008.

"Michelle Obama Planting White House Organic Vegetable Garden." *Boomer Survive and Thrive Guide,* March 2009. Available from http://boomersurvive-thriveguide.typepad.com.

"New Product Review." *Dairy Foods,* September 2004.

"Nutraceutical Demand to Reach US$9.6bn in 2008." *Manufacturing Chemist,* November 2004.

"Organic Food." April 2007. Available from http://en. wikipedia.org/.

"Organic Food." Organic Trade Association (OTA), updated 2009. Available from http://www.ota.com/organic/mt/business.html.

Parry, Caroline. "Heinz to Relaunch its Simply Organic Range." *Marketing Week,* 16 June 2005.

"R & D: Innovative Coating." *Processed Foods,* August 2009.

"Raising the Bar on Healthy Snacking." *Convenience Store News,* 12 January 2004.

Severson, Kim. "Sugar Is Back on Food Labels, This Time as a Selling Point." *New York Times,* 21 March 2009.

The Past, Present and Future of the Organic Industry. Organic Trade Association: 2006.

U.S. Department of Agriculture. "National Honey Report." 15 December 2009. Available from http://www.ams.usda.gov/mnreports/fvmhoney.pdf.

U.S. Organic Industry Overview. Organic Trade Association: 2006.

"World Nutraceutical Ingredients: U.S. Industry Forecasts for 2013 & 2018," November 2009. Available from http://www.reportbuyer.com/go/FED00497.

"The World of Organic Agriculture: Statistics and Emerging Trends 2007." February 23, 2007. Available from http://organicresearcher.wordpress.com.

NOISE CONTROL AND TECHNOLOGY

SIC CODE(S)

3825

INDUSTRY SNAPSHOT

Noise pollution is endemic in modern society. Anti-noise technology, also known as active noise control, active noise cancellation, or active structural-acoustic control, is a promising approach to coping with the overload of objectionable noise. For example, one noise control solution is to use speakers that silence disturbing noises by emitting an opposing noise. If the device works correctly, the new sound and the offensive one will have wave lengths that counter each other so that nothing is audible, or at least the offending noise is reduced.

Noise control has far-reaching applications ranging from aircraft and machinery to communications devices and office electronics. Even the Railroad Safety Reform Act contains provisions for noise control. By the later half of the first decade of the twenty-first century, noise control advancements were being driven by a variety of companies and researchers. Because of so many uses, this quiet industry is also a fragmented one, with such diverse participants as Bose Corp. (of high-end speaker notoriety), IBM Corp., Lucent Technologies, Matsushita Electric, and Owens Corning, as well as specialists such as Andrea Electronics and NCT Group.

Sources of Noise; Ways to Deal with It Technologies are needed to cope with various types of noise, particularly those connected with aircraft, trains, and motor vehicle traffic. Some solutions are of the more passive type, along the lines of soundproofing. Redesigning passenger compartments in cars and airplanes in order to cut down on noise for their occupants is an example of such methods, as is finding new materials effective in blocking noise within buildings and residences. Active noise cancellation technology can also be effective in such situations. An example is Barry Controls Aerospace's Active Tuned Mass Absorbers, which resonate at the same frequency as the engine compressors in a DC-9 airplane and thereby reduce cabin noise.

Airplanes and helicopters are among the most serious sources of noise in the United States, in urban settings and even in wilderness areas of national parks. Excessive noise emanating from airports often spurs years-long battles with city residents and institutions over building projects. Noise regulations adopted in the early 1990s stipulated that older planes had to be modified and new aircraft were to be designed with quieter engines by 1999. Lucent Technologies and Sikorsky Aircraft, in conjunction with the U.S. Naval Research Laboratory, have studied the use of smart materials to reduce helicopter rotor noise.

Cars and trucks are another racket to contend with, as anyone living near a freeway can attest. Proposed solutions include highway barriers of concrete, dirt, and even waterfalls to muffle noise. Alternative tire designs and on-vehicle silencing equipment have been explored. Researchers have likewise pondered new road-building materials such as porous asphalt to reduce the din of traffic. One noteworthy project is that of the Institute for Safe, Quiet, and Durable Highways at Purdue University. Backed by federal and private industry dollars, the institute has focused on complementary tire and pavement designs to eradicate noise.

Household appliances and power tools also add to environmental noise. Re-engineering, noise regulations, and anti-noise protection such as headsets are among the ways being used to tone down the clatters, whirrs, whines, and buzzing produced in residential areas. At Owens Corning, for example, acoustic engineers record the sounds of an appliance going through its operating cycles and then use different sound control systems to modify the noises. After the sounds are digitally edited, they are played to humans to get feedback on which have been most successfully quieted. Using this method along with computer simulation as part of the prototyping process saves half the time needed to develop a noise control system for an appliance.

BACKGROUND AND DEVELOPMENT

Anti-noise technology is far from new. In 1936, Paul Lueg patented one of the first working active noise control systems. His process of silencing sound oscillation received patents in the United States and Germany. Another pioneer in anti-noise technology was H. F. Olson, whose 1953 article on electronic sound absorbers was published in the *Journal of the Acoustical Society of America.*

The Noise Control Act of 1972 was passed to protect Americans from noise that threatened their health and well-being. It was amended by the Quiet Communities Act of 1978, Public Law 95-609, which required the administrator of the U.S. Environmental Protection Agency (EPA) to disseminate educational materials on the effects of noise on public health and the most effective means of noise control; to conduct or finance specified research projects on noise control; to administer a nationwide Quiet Communities Program designed to assist local governments in controlling noise levels; and to provide technical assistance to state and local governments in implementing noise control programs.

The Airport Noise and Capacity Act of 1990, Subtitle D of Public Law 101-508, required the establishment of a national aviation noise policy and issuance of regulations governing airport noise and access restrictions for stage two aircraft (weighing under 75,000 pounds). The act provided for the phase-out of older, noisier planes and for noise reduction to specified levels for new aircraft to go into effect in 1999, and it set civil penalties and reporting requirements for aircraft operators. It prohibited operation of certain domestic or imported civil subsonic turbojet aircraft unless such aircraft complied with Stage III noise levels. Subtitle B of the same law, known as the Aviation Safety and Capacity Expansion Act of 1990, called for environmental reviews before air traffic could be rerouted during an airport expansion.

The Office of Noise Abatement and Control Establishment Act of 1996 sought to reinstate the EPA's role in noise control after funding for it was eliminated in 1982. The primary duty of the office would be to coordinate federal noise abatement activities with state and local activity and other public and private agencies. It would also be responsible for updating and developing new noise standards, providing technical assistance to local communities, and promoting research and education on the impact of noise pollution. Initially, the Office of Noise Abatement and Control would study the physiological effects of airport noise in major metropolitan areas and surrounding communities in order to propose new measures to combat the impact of aircraft noise.

The National Park Scenic Overflight Concession Act of 1997 set guidelines for air traffic over national parks in order to eliminate intrusive noise. It proposed rules for use of quiet aircraft and minimum flight altitudes within national parks, flight-free zones, and, if necessary, flight bans to prevent commercial air tours in a park so as to preserve, protect, or restore the natural quiet of the park. It also created a schedule for any commercial air tour operator operating within a national park to convert the operator's fleet to quiet aircraft.

Because of the January 1, 1999, deadline for implementation of restrictions on aircraft noise, much activity in the aviation field was directed toward meeting the new noise control requirements, called the Stage III rules. Older airplanes, such as DC-8s and 727s, would be grounded if they were not retrofitted with "hush kits" to decrease noise. The Boeing Co. and Raisbeck Engineering, both of Seattle, Washington, were two companies developing solutions to the problem of retrofitting older aircraft and redesigning new ones to bring them into compliance with the Stage III regulations. In 1996, Raisbeck recertified the Boeing 727 to meet federal requirements. In January 1997, the Federal Aviation Administration (FAA) approved the installation of Lord Corp.'s NVX Active Noise and Vibration Control System in DC-9 models, making it the first active noise and vibration control system to receive FAA approval on a large commercial jet.

Aircraft remained a major source of noise pollution and thus lots of resources continued to be channeled into reducing aircraft noise. By 2000, hundreds of Boeing 727s and DC-9s had been fitted with hush kit mufflers. For the European Union, however, this was not an aggressive enough step toward noise muffling. In February 1999 the European Parliament approved a ban on airplanes that use hush kits—primarily those of U.S. carriers. Some interpreted the row between the European Unioin and the United States as more a political and economic dispute than a scientific or environmental disagreement.

Each side advocated technology that its companies had already embraced. In response, the United States threatened to ban Concorde flights into the country, and in 1999 won a temporary reprieve from the E.U. ban.

However, the activity pushed cool-headed observers to take more constructive action. Realizing that a lack of a global standard would only hinder all players in the long run, over 50 airlines worldwide—including all North and South American companies and a rising number of Asian, African, and European players—joined engine and aircraft manufacturers in establishing the Coalition for a Global Standard on Aviation Noise. The coalition worked to build a reasonable consensus to be approved by the International Civil Aviation Organization (ICAO) as the global standard.

In automotive applications, a few manufacturers have introduced new products to attack auto noise at various levels. Most common have been enhanced mufflers that can either cancel noise or at least curtail it some, but noise cancellation mufflers have tended to be costly and temperamental. This technology would not decrease the number of illegal muffler-less vehicles still on the highways, however. Others focused on reducing noise and vibration under the hood.

Noise pollution was coming from the unlikeliest of places. Patients of the world-renowned Mayo Clinic complained of noises that disturbed sleep. Even wind farms were not quiet in 2004. From Massachusetts to the United Kingdom, residents living near existing and proposed wind farms were speaking up on the noise pollution caused by the hum of the farms' turbines. Complaints about both physical and emotional effects of the noise were so widespread that the government in Great Britain was considering a study on the correlation between exposure to noise and overall health. Such studies were not new. In 2003, the Eighth International Congress on Noise as a Public Health Problem discussed current noise-affected health research.

By late 2003, the Noise Pollution Clearinghouse was calling for education on noise for children who have never known the world any other way but loud. In its newsletter, the company made the point that "A whole generation of kids learned not to litter from Woodsy Owl ('Give a hoot, don't pollute') and so did their parents. The anti-noise movement needs to create a cultural transformation." The concerns seemed legitimate, considering the findings of a 2003 study that discovered that background noise levels were 300 percent higher than in the 1970s.

By the middle years of the twenty-first century's first decade, the industry continued to explore large-scale noise control solutions. In the transportation arena, one example was the pursuit of quieter pavements. Some states were exploring the use of rubberized asphalt overlays. Working in partnership with the Federal Highway Administration and other groups, in 2006 the state of Arizona concluded its three-year Quiet Pavement Pilot Program, which involved the use of rubberized asphalt on some 115 miles of freeway in the Phoenix area. However, this material was not suitable in environments with climactic cycles that involved frequent freezing and thawing. By 2006, the concrete industry also was looking at ways to reduce noise by changing the texture of concrete.

Noise control initiatives also continued in the air transportation sector. In April 2006, *Airports International* reported that according to figures from the International Air Transport Association, from 1998 to 2004 the number of individuals exposed to aircraft noise had decreased approximately 35 percent on a global basis. In addition to efforts by manufacturers to produce quieter aircraft, airports also were taking action to reduce noise. One example was the Vancouver International Airport Authority's 2004–2008 Noise Management Plan, which included 17 different tactics to make the environment surrounding the airport a quieter place. These included the addition of a new engine "run-up" pad that directed the sound of airplane engines toward the ocean and not residential areas.

Efforts also continued to examine the role of noise in the workplace. In March 2006, *HR Focus* indicated that each year approximately 30 million U.S. workers were exposed to hazardous noise levels (those exceeding 85 decibels). Beyond obvious effects such as hearing damage, this exposure was blamed for lower productivity and morale. Examples of excessive noise include people shouting (85 to 95 decibels), and factory machines (more than 100 decibels). While these are more common examples, exposure to continuous noise from office equipment like copiers and fax machines, air conditioning units, and radios also can present problems for some workers.

Although noise control as an industry was still in its infancy, in the latter part of the first decade of the twenty-first century the issues of noise pollution and the health benefits of controlling it were receiving more attention. The Noise Pollution Clearinghouse, based in Montpelier, Vermont, for example, was a national non-profit organization dedicated to raise awareness and distribute resources about noise pollution, assist in efforts to reduce it, and strengthen related government laws and regulations. Another resource was the *Noise Regulation Report,* the only monthly noise control publication in the United States.

Although reducing noise was one of the objectives in the noise control industry, blocking various noise patterns—sometimes unpredictable ones—was also a way of dealing with the increasing racket caused by modern society. Another challenge for the industry was the cost of the technology that could provide the necessary conditions for noise reduction.

In Europe, the government was taking the issue of noise control in the transportation industry seriously, based in part perhaps on statistics such as those released by the environmental organization Transport & Environment that claim that 50,000 fatal heart attacks and 200,000 cases of cardiovascular disease are linked to traffic noise each year. In mid-2008 the European Commission was proposing guidelines that would require automakers to use tires that produce less noise. As reported in *Motor Authority,* the proposed regulations would require all tires fitted to new vehicles to have tire-pressure monitoring systems as well as lower rolling resistance and increased grip, while at the same time reducing noise levels by 67 percent. The auto industry and members of the European Tire and Rubber Manufacturers Association, however, were opposing the proposal, saying that quieter tires may not as able to stop a vehicle as quickly, thus decreasing the safety of the tires. According to automaker Daimler, trying to meet the Commission's requirements "would jeopardize safety and environmental issues." Some also opposed the fact that SUVS were exempted from the regulations.

Noise control also continued to be an issue in the United States. In mid-2007, New York City, which registered noise as the number one complaint of residents, enacted a new noise ordinance that, according to a 2008 *Occupational Hazards* article, "establishes important rules, guidelines and standards for governing noise in the city." The new law also addresses noise from a variety of sources, such as aircraft, construction sites, cars and motorcycles, garbage trucks, restaurants, and animals. Some experts predicted that other cities would follow New York's example and enact stricter noise control laws and guidelines.

The developments in noise control regulations provided an environment in which the noise control industry could grow. As more manufacturers, businesses, and other sectors of society were called on to reduce the noise, opportunities to tap into new markets arose for companies specializing in noise control.

CURRENT CONDITIONS

Ocean Noise First, a note about the planet's oceans. In 2009, the International Maritime Association began formal discussions on the steady increase of sonar and shipping noise in the world's oceans, and the effect on marine life (particularly whales, dolphins, and other larger sea mammals). A series of international workshops and seminars opened dialogue and showed promise for joint international efforts to reverse the steady rise in ocean background/ambient noise caused by increased international shipping over the years. After years of prototype testing, a high-profile project in Stellwagen Bank National Marine Sanctuary generated ground-breaking visualization of noise, through passive acoustic monitoring, for short and long-term listening at sea. A successful demonstration was conducted of the ships and whales outside Boston Harbor, inspiring new research and tenchologies to help identify not only which sounds were problematic and at what levels, but more importantly, which noise/sounds were important to marine life.

U.S. Navy training missions along U.S. coastlines, particularly those employing Naval Active Sonar EISs, continued to create waves of protest. One training initiative, the Undersea Warfare Training Range (USWTR) chose a site 50 miles off the coastline of northern Florida, allegedly interfering with key winter birthing grounds for the critically endangered North Atlantic Right Whales. Other training initiatives off the coasts of Alaska allegedly interfered with the designated critical habitat areas of many whale species and sea lions. Media coverage of large pods of beached and dying whales (etiology undetermined) aroused more public concern.

In January 2010, a consortium of environmental groups challenged Navy plans in federal court, focusing on processes and criteria under which permits were granted. The states of Florida and Georgia also announced concerns. The status and progress of the lawsuit could be tracked on the Web site of one of the plaintiffs, (http://www.humanesociety.org).

In unrelated news, according to John Farrell of the U.S. Arctic Research Commission, global warming and the melting of pelar ice in the Arctic Ocean has increased traffic from commercial fishing trawlers, zinc ore boats, oil and gas exploration rigs, sea floor mapping vessels, and tourist cruise ships. Farrell expressed concern that the increased noise levels may upset the ecosystem, especialy upon seal, walrus, and whale populations. Farrell presented his research at the March 2010 ASA Meeting.

Air Transportation In 2010, roughly 2.4 billion passsengers and 43 million tonnes of cargo were transported by airlines, according to the International Air Transport Association (IATA). In aviation engineering news, scientists were working on low-boom, high speed aircraft designs that would permit commercial supersonic travel over land (as of 2010, permitted only over oceans or in space). Central to new aircraft configurations was the design of the aircraft body, which altered the interaction of nose and tail sound waves (that collide to create sonic booms). The new design would create a sonic "puff" instead of a boom. In his presentation at the 159th ASA meeting in March 2010, Dr. Kenneth Plotkin, chief scientist with Wyle in Arlington, Virginia, surmised that within a decade, the first commercial application of the new design will be supersonic business jets, carrying 6-10 passengers, and traveling at speeds up to Mach 18. This will cut travel time between New York and California to under three hours, about half the time as in 2010.

City and Urban Noise With the increase in alternative fuel and electric vehicles on U.S. roads and streets came new and somewhat anticipated problems. Electric vehicles greatly reduce the background noise of running engines, in addition to reducing emissions and carbon pollutants. However, they run so silently that they have created their own hazards for bicyclists and persons who are sight-impaired. In 2008 and 2009, the National Federation of the Blind (NFB) lobbied the U.S. Congress to enact what was called the Pedestrian Safety Enhancement Act of 2009, co-sponsored by Senators John Kerry and Arlen Spector. The bill directed the Secretary of Transportation to study and then establish a motor vehicle safety standard that provided for a means of alerting blind and other pedestrians of approaching motor vehicles. Later in 2009, the National Highway Traffic Administration released a technical report, *Incidence of Pedestrian and Bicyclist Crashes by Hybrid Electric Passenger Vehicles,* DOT HS 811 204). As of 2010, non-mandated collaborations with automakers to voluntarily introduce artificial vehicle sounds were underway.

At the 159th annual meeting of the Acoustic Sciences Association in March 2010, Dr. Donald G. Albert, a scientist with the Engineer Research and Development Center Cold Regions Research and Engineering Laboratory in haaaaanover, New Hampshire, presented his research on the development of sensors to sort out complex sounds, vibrations, echoes, and signals in urban environments. After completing a series of seismic and acoustical measurements in Baltimore, Dr. Albert planned to develop computer algorithms corresponding with his measurements. Future applications include hospitals that may use remote systems as early-warning systems for traffic disasters; security systems capable of detecting idling engines or other suspect noises; and police or military use in detecting certain sounds or signals to respond to attacks or disasters. Of interest was the range of urban sounds recorded by Albert, down to 6 Hertz (well below the range of human hearing, between 100 and 10,000 Hertz) and well above that range as well. In other words, there is more urban noise than humans can even hear, which may have unknown effects or consequences on other forms of matter and/or living things.

Another presentation at the ASA meeting was by engineer Robert Otto, whose five-year research into hundreds of concrete pavement surfaces showed that resurfacing old noisy concrete with a technique known as diamond grinding resulted in a smoother, safer, and more silent road surface. Most road noise, Otto noted, comes from the interaction of tires and road. Otto further noted that several European countries already classified both tires and roads by their noise potential.

INDUSTRY LEADERS

The NCT Group Inc., formerly Noise Cancellation Technologies Inc., is a leading provider of noise and vibration reduction technology, and it is one of the most innovative companies. The Westport, Connecticut-based company designs, develops, licenses, produces, and distributes electronic systems that electronically reduce noise and vibration. The firm holds rights to hundreds of inventions, including applications in active noise reduction, active vibration reduction, active mufflers, active headsets, and multimedia audio.

NCT Group's subsidiaries included Artera Group Inc., Pro Tech Communications Inc., and NCT (Europe) Ltd. According to the company, its NCT (Europe) Ltd. subsidiary's ClearSpeech algorithm development group "has extensive experience in noise reduction, echo cancellation and signal conditioning. ClearSpeech technology is utilized in diverse applications including 3G phones, hands-free car kits, 'drive thru' intercoms, Formula 1 and NASCAR radio systems, business intercom products and radio communication devices."

NCT's Pro Tech subsidiary, based in Fort Pierce, Florida, offered NoiseBuster Audio technology that reduced electronic noise in entertainment headphones aboard airplanes as well as in consumer audio devices. It also offered NoiseBuster Safety technology used in safety earmuffs, as well as two-radio headsets. NCT uses patented active sound and signal wave management technology to reduce noise and improve sound quality. By the early years of the twenty-first century's first decade, it held approximately 598 patents and related rights. Licensing accounted for roughly half of NCT's revenues in the middle of the decade.

Another industry leader and maker of noise cancellation headsets is Andrea Electronics. Based in Bohemia, New York, and incorporated in 1934, the company offers microphone technologies (both software and hardware) to optimize voice user interface performance for devices in a number of categories, including auto PCs, automotive telematics systems, desktop dictation systems, Internet appliances, Internet telephony, personal digital assistants, videoconferencing applications, and voice-enabled Internet browsing.

The company seeks to differentiate itself from competitors by adapting its technology for use in a wide range of environments and platforms. Among its offerings is a product lineup of Active Noise Cancellation (ANC) and Noise Canceling (NC) PC headsets. These are used in call center settings and with wearable computers. According to Andrea Electronics, its "technological capability, coupled with growing relationships with industry leaders such as Intel Corporation, Analog Devices Inc. and Microsoft Corporation, have helped the company and its technologies to gain widespread acceptance and support from a broad range of speech solutions providers as well as with the end-user community."

Andrea Electronics has introduced a number of innovative technologies over the years. In 1997 the company unveiled its QuietWare 1000 anti-noise stereo headset for the computer market. In 1999 Andrea announced that it had received a patent for a head-mounted microphone. The firm's key customers and resellers have included the likes of IBM, Microsoft Corp., Kurzweil, Dragon Systems, and NEC.

Other firms trying to make the world a quieter place include Acoustical Solutions Inc.; Industrial Acoustics Co., Inc.; Industrial Noise Control Corp.; and Sennheiser Electronic. Products range from acoustical windows, diffusers, and foams to Universal Telephony Interface's (UTI's) telecommunications product that allows phone users to have a private conversation, even when other people are present.

RESEARCH AND TECHNOLOGY

In 2009, Lotus Engineering announced its agreement with Harman International to be granted exclusive rights for Active Noises Contril technologies. Jointly, they were refining the new Road Noise Cancellation and Engine Order cancellation systems for in-cabin vehicle noise improvement. They further developed the External Electronic Sound Synthesis which could be applied to external speaker systems to improve pedestrian safety. A synthesized sound is projected from front and rear speakers, making it instantly apparent that the vehicle was in motion.

Design engineers were working with ever more sophisticated tools to reduce the noise levels of everything from tools and home appliances to airplanes and cars. One example is Nearfield Acoustic Holography (NAH), a technology from Grosse Pointe Farms, Michigan-based SenSound that creates 3D visualizations of an object's sound values, such as intensity, pressure, and velocity.

As David J. Gaddis wrote in the August 2005 issue of *Appliance Design,* NAH enabled users to see these sound values "at the surface of an object and in the surrounding field in a single measurement with high spatial resolution, the broadest frequency range, and verifiable accuracy. It is a method that provides more insightful information than traditional approaches, thereby leading to faster diagnosis of problems and more cost effective solutions at any stage of a product's life cycle."

Controlling the noise from jet engines is a major problem, but engineers at Georgia Tech may have found one possible solution, according to Mark Hodges in *Technology Review.* By filling a liner with ceramic beads of assorted sizes and wrapping this liner around the engine, both low and high frequency noises were lessened; and the ceramic beads were able to withstand the high temperatures generated by the engine. This discovery could be used to reduce the noise of commercial jetliners traveling at supersonic speeds.

Pennsylvania State University's Center for Acoustics and Vibration, the National Aeronautics and Space Administration, and the Anti-Vibration Control Division of PCB Piezotronic announced the creation of a self-regulating vibration absorber that tracks changes in the frequency of undesirable noises and adjusts itself in response. This invention will have applications for noise control in industrial machinery, cars, and household appliances.

Professor Dimitri Papamoschou of the University of California-Irvine created a new technology to quiet supersonic jets, such as the Concorde, which have been permitted to land at only a few airports throughout the world because of the amount of noise they produce. His invention, the Mach Wave Eliminator, reduces the exhaust noise output of these aircraft.

Back on the ground, a 2003 study found that cities were about 330 percent noisier than rural areas. Outdoor advertising was challenged to draw attention to the products or services it hawked, but without being simply loud. A new technology, called Whispering Windows, was announced by *Marketing Week* in 2004. A "smart" technology, Whispering Windows was able to modify its own noise levels, changing to be heard over background noise by passersby but not becoming so loud as to be disturbing to those in the general vicinity of the shop windows.

BIBLIOGRAPHY

"159th ASA Meeting Puts Spotlight on Noise and Policy." April 2010. Available from htt://www.newswise.com/articles/view/563211.

Acoustic Ecology Institute. "AEI Ocean Noise 2009: Science, Policy, Legal Developments." August 2010. Available from http://www.slideshare.net/AcousticEcology/aei-ocean-noise-2009-science-policy-legal-developments.

"EU Tire Makers Oppose Tire Noise Regulations." *Motor Authority,* 23 June 2008.

"Identify and "Turn Down the Volume' on Workplace Noise." *HR Focus,* March 2006.

"Johns Hopkins Study Finds Noise Solutions." *Health Facilities Management,* February 2006.

Lewin, Tony. "Europe's Loud Debate over Quieter Tires." *Automotive News,* 3 March 2008.

McCormick, Carroll. "Vocal about Noise: Carroll McCormick Looks at Vancouver's Efforts to Reduce its Noise Footprint." *Airports International,* April 2006.

"New Maps Identify England's Noisiest Urban Areas." *Geographical,* August 2008.

"Noise Headlines." *Noise Regulation Report,* 25 July 2008.

O'Brien, John. "NYC Code Provides the Sound of Things to Come." *Occupational Hazards,* May 2008.

The Quiet Zone Newsletter, Winter 2008. Noise Pollution Clearinghouse. Available from http://www.nonoise.org/.

"Sonic Puff Technology May Speed Supersonic Flight Over Land." *Newswise,* April 2010.

"Technology Focus: Green Engines." *Aviation Maintenance,* 15 May 2008.

"What's Next: Active Noise Control." 17 April 2009. Available from http://www.cardomain.com.

NON-MEDICAL SENIOR CARE
AND PERSONAL SERVICES

SIC CODE(S)

8322

8059

8082

8361

INDUSTRY SNAPSHOT

Non-medical senior care includes an enormous range of services including consulting, day-to-day assistance with routine chores and personal care (such as eating and bathing), and more general welfare and social services. One of the most widespread sectors in this industry is the adult day care center, which follows the child day care model to provide social and medical attention to the elderly. Another strong sector is geriatric care management, in which consultants meet with families to design a care strategy for loved ones tailored to particular needs and financial capabilities.

For seniors not yet needing long-term care but in need of some daily attention, day-to-day care has been increasingly viewed as an intermediary step in a smooth transition to old age. Moreover, as baby boomers move into retirement years and begin to require non-medical care, a smaller percentage of those requiring such services will have family members capable of providing for them. Thus, the "professionalization" of non-medical senior care is likely to continue its strong upward trend.

ORGANIZATION AND STRUCTURE

Adult day care programs are offered in senior centers, community centers, and churches. These programs are sometimes attached to hospitals, nursing homes, or other health care institutions. In addition, residential care facilities might provide these services should the client's care needs extend to mental and other chronic care concerns. For the most part, they are nonprofit organizations. The centers provide opportunities for social interaction and exercise along with hot meals. Adult day care operations can also offer a range of services— including transportation to and from home; counseling and social services; grooming, hygiene, and laundry services; social activities; physical, occupational, and speech therapy; and others—to those seniors with cognitive or functional impairments.

Adult day care centers are recognized as a cost-effective way to help people in need of chronic care remain connected to their homes, community, family, and friends. The *National Adult Day Center Census,* compiled by the National Council on Aging's National Adult Day Services Association [NADSA], found that the adult day care center served a high proportion of individuals with disabilities who preferred to stay in their homes rather than enter nursing homes. According to a fact sheet from the National Adult Day Services Association, In 2010, the average daily cost for adult day care centers was approximately $60 to $75 a day.

According to Partners in Caregiving, 26 percent of existing day care centers opened in the late 1990s and the early years of the first decade of the 2000s. Nevertheless, the need is hardly met. According to the 2000 census, there were 3,407 adult day centers operating in the United States. The centers mostly served people with dementia, including Alzheimer's disease, or those in poor health. However, at the time, experts believed that more than 5,000 new centers would be needed in only a few years as the growing number

Largest Senior Care Franchises, By Units and Revenues (as of December 2009)

By unit	
Home Instead	585
Comfort Keepers	559
Visiting Angels	377
Home Helpers	325
Senior Helpers	270
By revenues	
Home Instead	$35.6 million
Visiting Angels	$ 9.6 million
Comfort Keepers	$ 9.4 million
Right At Home	$ 8.2 million
Home Helpers	$ 5.3 million
Senior Helpers	$ 5.2 million

SOURCE: *Franchise Business Review*, August 2010.

of aging baby boomers would need care. A 2003 national study funded by the Robert Woods Foundation found that 56 percent of U.S. counties did not have enough adult day centers to meet the growing need. In addition, the survey showed that many centers did not charge enough to continue without some kind of subsidy.

Intergenerational day care facilities, providing care for both children and elders, were on the rise by the end of the 1990s in the United States. These programs often began with intergenerational programming ventures in nursing homes and continued to expand. At a time when it was not uncommon to live across the country from other family members, grandparents and grandchildren often missed the interaction that was taken for granted in earlier generations. Older adults and children through school age were all beneficiaries of these expanded services. According to the American Association for Retired Persons (AARP), by 2000, about 280 facilities in the United States housed intergenerational care services, up from only about 50 in the early 1980s. A handful of these centers placed seniors and children in the same activities and areas for the entire day.

As this concept continued to evolve, an increasing number of care programs across the United States reconsidered their options. The baby boomers, often caught between caring for young children and aging parents, were also referred to as the "sandwich generation," with little time and busy careers of their own. Intergenerational day care sites showed promise to alleviate the burden of the situation. On-site corporate adult day care programs were not successful in this early stage, and they remained a rarity heading into the late years of the first decade of the 2000s. However, as the population of aging and retired workers grew, more businesses were expected to consider starting them as a benefit for employees.

Adult day care centers were transformed as the accompanying services of speech, physical, occupational, and drug therapy became more available, attracting Medicare and private-pay patients. Another development was the expansion of outpatient care and rehabilitation to complement nursing home services. Adult day service centers focused on assisting seniors with either minimal or extensive needs. Some centers specialized in certain types of patients, especially those with early onset dementia or Alzheimer's. Typical adult day service centers provided transportation, routine health care, meals, activities, and assistance with daily chores. The demand for more intense services was expected to increase in the twenty-first century with the aging of the U.S. population, and as changes in technology permit the delivery of medical services outside traditional hospitals.

The bulk of the nation's adult day care centers were small facilities based in the communities they served, and statistics on regional growth were difficult to determine accurately. Adult day care centers were run as for-profit, nonprofit, or state-run operations. Expenses were paid by various sources such as Medicaid, the participants, donations, grants, and private long-term care. Centers were typically run by a director, usually a nurse or social worker, with the assistance of administrative and office personnel, recreation and activity personnel, case managers and social workers, therapists, nurses, and medical staff. In centers run by nonprofit organizations such as community groups or churches, volunteers were crucial to providing services.

Adult day care facilities were often one component of a larger-scale continuum of care for senior adults. One example is a program operated by Adventist Healthcare in Takoma Park, Maryland, also in the suburban Washington, D.C., area, which grew out of a sub-acute-care nursing home. For a balance in the services, the nonprofit Adventist opened the day care center in Takoma Park in 1987. Such services were generally not exceptionally profitable, but they offered strong growth opportunities. Since for many people day care was only a first step for seniors in failing health, many assisted living and other continuing care facilities began day care centers with a view to the future business they could provide. If one was familiar with a long-term care center affiliated with the day care center, that long-term facility would become a reasonable choice when further care was chosen.

BACKGROUND AND DEVELOPMENT

The 1970s were flush with funding for older adult services in the United States. Federal and state monies flooded local areas as a result of the establishment of the National Institute on Aging in May 1972 during the administration of President Richard Nixon. Americans of the World War

II generation were beginning to retire. People were living longer, although not without health problems. Many older women, especially, had not worked outside the home and lived on very small retirement pensions or minimal Social Security benefits. Many of these men and women came from rural backgrounds and had moved to work in factories in the city where they had limited incomes, forcing them to live at or near poverty level. A new awareness of age—both its problems and its joys—swept the country. Money was made available for senior nutrition programs and senior centers, among them adult day care. Most adult day care centers were run by nursing homes for both social activities and medical rehabilitation that would prove a cost-effective alternative to long-term inpatient care.

Special library outreach services grew out the needs of older adults who were homebound or hearing or sight-impaired. Funds for large print books and arts-related programs for older adults were made available. Senior high-rise apartment buildings, many of them government-subsidized, were built in small towns and big cities. Local agencies on aging were set up under the auspices of state and federal programs. Church denominations started building retirement homes, along with private corporations. The dated notion of sending the aging population to "rest homes" was fading. Better health and more leisure time were cutting through stereotypes.

In addition, the demand for adult day care services developed as more people, especially women, tried to balance the demands of jobs with the needs of family members. For those living near and caring for aging parents, adult day care services provided a way to be sure of elders' safety and supervision during the workday. American Association of Retired Persons (AARP) statistics indicate that about three-fourths of caregivers to older people are women, and that more than 50 percent of these women are in the labor force and 41 percent of them also care for children. Day care facilities equipped to care for individuals with certain conditions, such as Alzheimer's disease, also provided a needed respite for their caregivers.

According to a 2000 survey conducted by the National Family Caregivers Association (NFCA), 26.6 percent of the adult population, or about 50 million people, had provided care for aged or ill family members. The NFCA also reported that men made up 44 percent of the care-giving population; in previous years, women made up about 75 percent of that population. Chronic Care in America indicated that despite the growing need, the pool of family caregivers was dwindling. In 1990, there were 11 potential caregivers for each person needing care. By 2050, it indicated, that ratio will be four to one.

Besides the emotional burden that care-giving places on individuals, it also creates a financial burden for society. The National Alliance for Care-giving conducted a study that showed that U.S. businesses lose between $11 billion and $29 billion each year due to employees' needs to care for loved ones 50 years of age and older. In order to alleviate some of the burdens on their employees—and to attract employees in the tight 1990s labor market—more and more firms began to offer elder care programs as part of their benefits packages. This often involved establishing on- or off-site adult care programs, especially at larger corporations, sometimes in conjunction with existing child day care facilities. In addition, firms provided coverage for geriatric care managers and home health care services. According to a study by MetLife Mature Market Institute in the fall of 1999, the number of employees responsible for care of at least one adult was expected to rise from 11 million to 15.6 million by the end of the first decade of the 2000s, representing about 10 percent of the work force. Companies reported that the assistance also helped boost productivity for their workers, who would not have to spend their working hours on the phone to various care centers.

In fact, a survey of 945 major U.S. employers, released in 2002 and conducted by Hewitt Associates, an international outsourcing and consulting firm, found that more and more work/life programs became available in the early part of the twenty-first century, despite the recession of 2001-2002. Elder care programs experienced steady growth during that period. According to the survey, half of all of the 945 employers who responded offered some form of elder care assistance, with dependent care spending accounts and resource/referral programs being most common. In addition, the availability of long-term care insurance grew 3 percent from 2001 to 2002, with 23 percent of companies providing this benefit to employees.

Short-term care center are geared toward families who need to have loved ones cared for while the family goes on vacation. Some day care facilities take care of seniors while their adult children or other caregivers get a much-needed vacation. The Fairfax Nursing Center, for instance, offers respite care along with its long-term services. The facility features such spa-like amenities as manicures and massages along with frequent visits from childcare groups. Other companies, such as Healthquest Travel Inc., aid travelers by arranging for adequate services to be provided at their destinations, thus allowing elders to more comfortably travel along with younger family members. For example, after meeting with clients and arranging precise needs and logistics, such companies will arrange for doctors or oxygen to be available at the point of destination.

Other services allow seniors to care for each other. California Blue Shield runs a program called CareXchange, in which seniors volunteer to provide basic services such as running errands or driving others to the doctor's office. Seniors thus offer those services they are capable of in exchange for the provision of tasks they cannot accomplish themselves.

Unfortunately, the non-medical senior care industry was hurt by findings of corruption. According to the *New York Times,* the federal inspector general of the U.S. Department of Health and Human Services reported in 1998 that about 90 percent of the nation's mental health centers simply provided social activities while billing for acute outpatient care.

In mid-2006, the National Adult Day Services Association reported that 23 percent of U.S. households provided care to a relative or friend over the age of 50. Contrary to many presumptions, families care for their elderly members far more often than nursing homes or other care facilities. In October 2005, *Crain's New York Business* reported that the number of adults providing unpaid care to an adult numbered 44.5 million. Of these, 59 percent were employed and 62 percent had been forced to adjust their work life. In 2006, there were more than 22 million households providing some type of elder care for a friend or relative. The future portended a voracious market for such services. According to the Health Insurance Association of America (HIAA), some 9 million seniors were expected to require long-term care in the foreseeable future. Demands on caregivers can be overwhelming, as most caregivers hold down full and/or part-time jobs. They often need support and help.

Conditions such as these fueled growing demand for non-medical senior care. In addition, employers have been forced to address this issue as it relates to their employees. According to a report from IOMA, a company that describes itself as a provider of business management information to senior and middle management professionals, a study from Metropolitan Life Insurance Co. and the National Alliance for Care-giving revealed that productivity losses associated with elder care issues cost businesses $11 billion to $29 billion annually. These costs were tied to everything from workday interruptions and absenteeism to the cost of replacing staff who leave the workforce to care for an aging parent.

Elder care was more visible on the corporate radar screen heading into the later years of the first decade of the 2000s, and companies were doing a better job of providing information about elder care issues to their employees. However, employers still had a long way to go to implement actual programs and benefits. According to IOMA, a 2005 survey from the Society for Human Resource Management found that a mere 1 percent of respondents had on-site elder care services, 3 percent provided emergency elder care services, and 11 percent offered elder care leave that exceeded requirements established by state and federal medical leave acts. Twenty-one percent offered elder care referral services.

To help potential patients and their families decide what type of care to seek, the federal government funded the Eldercare Locator, which provides information and referral services regarding local care agencies. Another resource is the Area Agencies on Aging (AAA), an organization that helps caregivers find other sources for the elderly, particularly those with limited incomes. The AAA provides information on home care agencies and volunteer groups that can help with transportation, household and yard chores, and respite for family caregivers. It can also help assess a senior's specific needs and then provide information about senior center programs for older persons with relatively minor problems associated with daily living and adult day care programs for those who have more serious problems.

Growth was characteristic among all sectors of the industry in the latter years of the 2000s' first decade. Demand for adult day care centers, for example, was growing at a rate of 5 to 15 percent annually. Part of the reason for the growth was the increase in the aging U.S. population. A study by the U.S. Department of Health and Human Services revealed that the senior population will increase dramatically from 2010 to 2030, when the largest part of the baby boomer generation reaches 65. It estimated that during this period, the ranks of the senior population will swell to about 70 million, more than twice the number recorded in 2000. In addition, Coordinated Care Solutions, which describes itself as a provider of information technology and services to health care plans, predicted that in roughly the same period, the demands placed on family and other informal caregivers will most likely increase and affect just about every family in the United States.

Adult Day Care Centers The majority of adult day care centers provide some type of nursing services. State licensing, certification, and accreditation standards for adult day care services vary, but most states require adherence to at least one category of such criteria. The character of adult day care centers also varies considerably. Some concentrate mainly on the provision of medical or therapy services, while others simply arrange social activities to keep seniors active and engaged. Whatever the service provided, the cost was lower than home care in nearly every situation. The majority of people served by the centers suffered from a condition such as Alzheimer's or dementia.

According to the National Adult Day Services Association, in 2008 there were 3,400 adult day care centers caring for 150,000 people. The majority of these centers (78 percent) were nonprofit, and 70 percent were affiliated with a larger organization. Of those receiving services in an adult day care center, about two-thirds were women, and the average age was 72.

One of the trends that was promoting the industry in the latter years of the first decade of the 2000s, according to a 2008 *Indianapolis Business Journal* article, was the increase in reimbursements for adult day care from organizations such as Medicaid, Area Agencies on Aging, and the Veterans Administration. In 2007 the federal branch of Medicare and Medicaid Services started a three-year pilot program that allows a portion of Medicare home health-care benefits to go toward adult day care. Thus, although private pay remained the most common method of payment, third-party payment was becoming more common.

Another development that granted the adult day care industry some recognition and autonomy occurred when MetLife, a major U.S. insurance company, included adult day care as a separate category in its annual report on costs in the long-term care industry. According to Kathy O'Brien of MetLife, adult day care "is becoming increasingly recognized within the long-term care community for the array of services available."

Nevertheless, the adult day care sector of the industry was still young. Tina McIntosh, founder of an adult day care center in Indianapolis, said, "Adult day service is where child care was in the '70s. It's just not very well-known."

Geriatric Care Consultancy The industry also developed a new type of service known as the geriatric care consultancy. Such consultants provide seniors and their families with information and expert advice on juggling the bevy of legal and financial concerns associated with senior care, including Medicare and Medicaid concerns. Consultancy agencies analyze family members' financial situations and help them determine an effective care strategy, be it home health care, nursing homes, day care services, or some other care arrangement. Consultants, also called care managers, also help the family secure placement into a care service, such as a nursing home or day care program, and arrange bookkeeping services for the family.

Many care managers have been certified through the National Academy of Certified Care Managers (NACCM) in Connecticut. Since it was established in 1994, about 1,000 care managers have taken the NACCM certification exam. Rona Bartelstone, a clinical social worker in south Florida, established the National Association of Professional Geriatric Care Managers, a Tucson, Arizona-based membership organization, in 1986. By 2006, the association had grown to include more than 2,000 members.

Geriatric care managers typically are expensive, charging between $200 and $500 for a consultation of about two or three hours. A geriatric care manager, usually a nurse or social worker, will consult with all the parties involved and help resolve differences based on detailed knowledge of different services available and an assessment of financial situations. Customers turn to geriatric care managers to gain an objective and expert outside opinion and to help relieve the tension that can stem from the difficult emotional decisions facing them. Geriatric care managers thus help adult children resolve a crisis effectively rather than hurriedly, or, in a best-case scenario, provide solutions before a crisis ever occurs. The president of the National Association of Geriatric Care Managers said that nearly two-thirds of the adult children looking for a geriatric care manager were living far away from the parent.

CURRENT CONDITIONS

According to a *Fact Sheet* published by the National Private Duty Association (NPDA), in 2011, more than 8,000 people will turn 65 each and every day. By the end of 2011, it is estimated that the senior population in the United States will reach nearly 49 million, growing to nearly 72 million by 2025 (quoting data from the U.S. Department of Health and Human Services and the State Department). The U.S. Census Bureau also projected that the population aged 85 and older could grow from 5.3 million in 2006 to roughly 21 million by 2050. Persons reaching age 65 have an average life expectancy of another 19 years (20.3 for females; 17.4 for males), reported the Administration on Aging. Finally, an AARP survey found that an overwhelming number of seniors, 89 percent, expressed a desire to go through their advanced years in their own homes for as long as possible. All of these facts and statistics set the stage for the sustained growth of this industry.

In *Entrepreneur* magazine's "2010 Trends: 10 and 1/2 Trends to Watch," private home care was the No. 1 growing industry from 2004 to 2009, expanding roughly seven percent a year (according to Ibis World). It further reported that in-home care employed 1.33 million people, and revenue was expected to exceed $72 billion by 2011.

In 2010, a sizable segment of the industry remained franchised. Core services provided by franchises focused on non-medical, in-home care for seniors, such as grooming, bathing, transportation services, and meal preparation. Some offered corollary medical care such as assisting with medications, wound care, or physical therapy. The entire industry was somewhat fragmented, with over 35 different franchise names in addition to non-franchised operations.

As of 2009, according to the NPDA, the average annual cost of one nursing home resident was $69,715. The average annual cost for one resident in an assisted living facility was $36,372. However, seniors who desired private duty home care could receive 20 hours of companionship home care each week for about $1,500 per month or $18,000 a year. A NPDA survey found that in 2009, the average cost for care ranged from $18.75 per hour for companionship services to $22.37 per hour for home health services.

INDUSTRY LEADERS

As of 2010, the senior home care industry remained largely fragmented but overall experiencing sustained growth. The vast majority of services continued to be provided by family members, private individuals/sole proprietors or local "mom and pop" business owners. Notwithstanding, there were more than 35 large franchise businesses competing for market share as well. Some of the businesses with the highest growth rates had been offering franchises for less than ten years, including Brightstar, Senior Helpers, and Synergy Homecare. Other big-name franchise operations included Home Instead, Comfort Keepers. Visiting Angels, and Right at Home. The industry also included non-franchised businesses including public companies such as Sunrise Senior Living and National Healthcare Corporation, both of which offered a full spectrum of services, from companionship to skilled care.

According to the National Adult Day Services Association, 78 percent of adult day care centers were still primarily private or not-for-profit institutions in 2008. Also, there was significant growth in the number of day care centers operating over the previous decade, and this was expected to continue. In 2008, Catholic Charities was one of the largest nonprofits in the category. Asbury Methodist Village in Gaithersburg, Maryland opened in September 1998 and launched a day care center for older adults in March 1999. Many church-related facilities such as these were leaders in the nonprofit sector for adult day care.

One of the largest for-profit companies in non-medical senior care was Brookdale Senior Living of Brentwood, Tennessee. Brookdale expanded its operations when it purchased American Retirement Corp. in 2006 for $1.2 billion. Brookdale offered assisted and independent living centers for seniors as well as adult day care centers.

Another industry leader was Louisville, Kentucky-based Almost Family Inc. The company operated 25 adult day care centers and 12 home health agencies and also provided housekeeping services and skilled home nursing. In 2007 it employed 3,200 workers and had revenues of $132.1 million. In September 2006, the firm exited the adult day care business when it sold that portion of its operation to Owings Mills, Maryland-based Active Day Corp. for $13.6 million in cash. Active Day operated what it described as the nation's "largest network of adult day health services centers, in-home personal care companies and outpatient rehabilitation facilities." In 2007 the company had 60 adult day care centers in seven states and plans to open 100 by 2010.

SarahCare Adult Day Care Centers Inc., based in Canton, Ohio, and founded in 1985, was a successful chain of centers that first offered franchise opportunities in 2001. Such franchise opportunities in the field were becoming more common in the latter part of the decade. By 2008 there were 48 SarahCare locations, and the company had plans to double that number by 2010.

WORKFORCE

In a 2009 *NPDA State of Caregiving Industry Survey* of its 1,200 member organizations, 83 percent of them indicated they would be adding employees (providing private pay in-home care for the elderly and disabled) to their staff in 2010. Approximately 70 percent of the employer organizations had been in business at least five years. Caregiver profiles revealed that 93 percent were female; 64 percent had previously cared for an elderly family member or friend; 19 percent had retired from another profession; and 17 percent were first-generation immigrants to the United States. The national average starting pay per hour ranged from $8.92 for companionship services to $11.78 for home halth services.

Opportunities for adult day care workers were expected to continue to expand as the aging population demanded more of such facilities and services. In the 2008-09 edition of its *Occupational Outlook Handbook,* the Bureau of Labor Statistics reported that 767,000 Americans were employed as personal and home care aides. The professional field of gerontology, in the areas of medicine and social work, was expanding as well. The number of geriatric social workers, geriatric nurses, and physicians who specialized in geriatrics continued to grow at the start of twenty-first century. One trend was employing active and healthy seniors to work with the elderly needing care or assistance.

BIBLIOGRAPHY

"2010 Trrends: 10 and 1/2 Trends to Watch." *Entrepreneur.*

"About NAPGCM." National Association of Professional Geriatric Care Managers, July 2008. Available from http://www.caremanager.org.

Administration on Aging. "Elders & Families."13 August 2008. Available from http://www.aoa.gov.

"Elder Care Options for a More Cost-Effective Approach." *Compensation & Benefits for Law Offices,* July 2006. Available from http://www.ioma.com.

Feldstein, Mary Jo. "Adult Day-Care Center Market Is Growing: Demographic Changes Are Fueling Demand." *St Louis Post-Dispatch*, 18 January 2008.

National Adult Day Services Association. "Adult Day Services: The Facts." 13 August 2008. Available from http://www.nadsa.org/.

National Private Duty Associaton. "Private Duty Home Care Industry Fact Sheet." 2009. Available from http://www.privatedutyhomecare.org/downloads/NPDA-FactSheet.pdf.

Olson, Scott. "Demand for Adult Day Care Rises with Aging Population." *Indianapolis Business Journal*, 4 February 2008.

Opdyke, Jeff. "Finding Day Care-For Your Parents: Choices Grow for Increasing Numbers of Baby Boomers Who Have Frail Relatives They Are Reluctant to Leave Alone." *Wall Street Journal*, 10 January 2008.

Roberts, Sally. "Employers Expand Assistance Offerings to Include Elder Care." *Business Insurance*, 19 June 2006.

"Special Report: Senior Care and Home Healthcare Franchises." *Franchise Business Review*, August 2010.

U.S. Bureau of Labor Statistics. *Occupational Outlook Handbook, 2008-09 Edition*. Washington, DC: 2008.

Whitaker, Barbara. "The Franchise Way to Play the Population Trend." *New York Times*, 29 March 2007.

"Workplace Flexibility Pivotal to Easing Employees' Elder Care Concerns." *Managing Benefits Plans*, July 2006. Available from http://www.ioma.com.

NUTRITIONAL SUPPLEMENTS

———— ■ ————

SIC CODE(S)

2833

2834

INDUSTRY SNAPSHOT

Despite being known for a diet rich in soft drinks and oversized fast-food burgers, the U.S. public has increasingly consumed products that promote dietary health. These nutritional supplements include well-known vitamins and minerals, as well as formerly counterculture herbal remedies and phytochemicals, and futuristic nutraceuticals.

The definition of nutritional supplements is broad and encompasses such diverse categories as phytochemicals, herbals, and nutraceuticals. The Office of Dietary Supplements (ODS) at the National Institutes of Health (NIH) describes dietary supplements as "products intended to supplement the diet, which contain one or more of the following: vitamins, minerals, amino acids, herbs, or other botanicals; or dietary substances used to supplement the diet by increasing total dietary intake; or concentrates, metabolites, constituents, extracts, or combinations of the above." In addition, supplements are "intended for ingestion as capsules, gelcaps, powders, or softgels." Supplements do not constitute conventional foods or the sole item of a meal.

By 2008, nutritional supplements had become a $22.5 billion industry. During the middle and latter years of the first decade of the twenty-first century, some 150 million Americans annually took one or more of the estimated 29,000 supplements that were available for sale. Consumer-direct methods, such as direct marketing, catalogs, sales representatives, the Internet, and infomercials account for the majority of supplement sales. Sales in food, drug, and mass-market stores contribute roughly 30 percent and specialty health food stores about 20 percent. The remainder is generated by sales through physicians, dieticians, and other professionals.

ORGANIZATION AND STRUCTURE

Nutritional supplements are produced by more than 1,000 private manufacturers as well as major drug and chemical companies. Sales have been especially strong over the Internet. About 95 percent of all companies, however, sell less than $20 million in products per year. The American Herbal Products Association (AHPA) is a national trade association that includes among its members thousands of companies that are importers, growers, manufacturers, and distributors of therapeutic herbs and herbal products. Located in Silver Springs, Maryland, the AHPA was founded in 1983.

Several other associations also provide a wealth of industry-related information including legislative and research updates. Notable among them are the American Botanical Council, Council for Responsible Nutrition, Ephedra Education Council, and National Nutritional Foods Association.

Phytochemicals overlap the vitamin field and are defined as plant substances used as food fortifiers and dietary supplements, including garlic, I3C, spices, soy, and herbal teas. About 4,000 different phytochemicals have been identified, but fewer than 200 have been carefully investigated for their health-giving properties. Well-known phytochemicals include indoles (in vegetables

Market Share of Nutrition Industry	
Supplements	61 percent
Household products	19 percent
Natural and organic foods	16 percent
Functional foods	4 percent

SOURCE: *Nutrition Business Journal*, 2010.

such as broccoli), protease inhibitors, and isoflavones in soybeans.

Nutraceuticals are loosely defined as foods that promote health or medical benefits, including disease prevention. The market's vague parameters make estimating their value and scope difficult. Often called functional foods, leading products in the market include among their ingredients soy isoflavones, tocotrienols, lutein, lycopene, gingko biloba, and St. John's wort. Other popular nutraceuticals are creatine monohydrate, androsteniodene, DHA (omega-3 fatty acid from fish), peptidase, and calcium citrate maleate.

Historically marketed through health food stores, direct mail, and network marketing, nutritional food supplements are also distributed through retail stores, pharmacies, discount stores, catalogs, multilevel marketing, and the Internet. The thousands of Kmart, Target, and Wal-Mart stores regularly selling nutritional supplements began installing displays adjacent to their pharmacies to expand herbal lines. Other chain stores such as Sam's Club and Costco installed pharmacies or nutritional supplement centers to take advantage of the booming market. With the visibility gained through chain stores, the relatively obscure herbals market caught the attention of many large over-the-counter brand companies, including Bayer Corp., which began using extensive marketing efforts, as well as nationally known and trusted brand name recognition, to attract non-users to its line of herbal products.

Industry Regulation The dietary supplements industry is regulated only loosely. Dietary supplements are considered a subset of foods under federal law and are regulated by the U.S. Food and Drug Administration (FDA) pursuant to the U.S. Food, Drug, and Cosmetic Act of 1938. The FDA has the authority to take action against any dietary supplement product found to be unsafe or making unsubstantiated or unapproved drug claims. The agency can also take action against supplements presenting significant risk of illness or injury. In addition, the Nutrition Labeling and Education Act of 1990 mandates that no health claims be allowed on food labels or advertisements unless the FDA finds "significant scientific agreement" for such claims. The U.S. Pharmacopoeia, a nonprofit group, was established to test supplements and assure compliance with scientific standards.

Informative point-of-purchase displays and the ability to make general claims about products were enabled by the 1994 Dietary Supplement Health and Education Act (DSHEA). The act defines dietary supplements—vitamins, minerals, and herbs—and the limits of information about them. A supplement must contain a premeasured amount that is in the form of a soft gel, powder, tablet, capsule, or liquid. DSHEA also permits substantiated, truthful statements that are not misleading on labels and in advertising. These statements may include claims about how the product benefits body structure and function but not any specific assertions that it prevents or cures disease. Supplement makers are supposed to send all labels to the FDA for review before using them; many, however, do not do so. In 2006 the FDA estimated that it had scrutinized only about 10 percent of the 22,500 labels it should have reviewed.

The limited regulatory framework established under the DSHEA has been widely criticized. Companies have avoided the extensive testing requirements of over-the-counter drugs by distributing their products as supplements. The FDA's vague definitions found within the dietary supplement category have prompted numerous manufacturers to challenge the 1994 act. The FDA treats herbs as food, which means they do not need to be proven effective, if they are safe. The vitamin supplement industry was not heavily regulated because vitamins were considered neither a food nor a drug, and few standards related to truth in advertising.

Regulatory activities regarding supplements are split between the FDA, which oversees product safety, manufacturing, and information, and the Federal Trade Commission (FTC), which regulates product advertising. In late 1998, the FTC issued advertising guidelines for the first time for the dietary supplement industry. The guidelines were posted on the FTC Web site on 18 November 1998 and were sent to industry trade associations. The guidelines dictate that supplement claims be truthful, not misleading, and that advertisers be able to support those claims with research. They also explain what kinds of claims supplement manufacturers can and cannot make. Action taken by the FTC was in part due to the industry's rapid growth during the late 1990s and also due to confusion on the part of supplement manufacturers after the Dietary Supplement Health and Education Act of 1994 limited the FDA's authority to regulate the industry.

New labels, mandated by the FDA in 1998, began to appear on supplement packaging in March 1999; all products manufactured after that date must bear them. The new labels contain Supplement Facts panels similar to the Nutrition Facts labels required on most packaged foods since 1994. The Supplement Facts panels include dosage information on 14 essential vitamins and other nutrients, as well as definitions of such terms as "high potency." They also must mention the presence of any additional ingredients, such as herbals and botanicals, which currently lack recommended daily intake guidelines.

Much important information, however, will not appear on the Supplement Facts panels. Maximum safe dosages, dangerous interactions with other substances and medications, and cautions for people for whom the supplements might be unsafe still are not required. Thus, the guidelines are far from complete. In addition, the panels can list ingredient amounts in relation to Daily Values (DVs) limits established in 1968, instead of Recommended Dietary Allowances (RDAs), because the RDAs are being revised. Even spokespeople for the supplement industry advised caution and the need for a high level of education about supplements when consumers use the new labels. John Hathcock, vice president of the Council for Responsible Nutrition, warned that the consumer has to "be inherently skeptical" when reading the Supplement Facts panels.

The industry itself was promoting the adoption of Good Manufacturing Practices (GMP) guidelines, which industry groups feel would bolster consumer confidence in product quality and help stave off further governmental regulation. The National Nutritional Foods Association, a California-based trade group, urged its members to undergo a voluntary, third party certification procedure as a requirement for continued membership.

A $4.1 million jury verdict was obtained against Metabolife International in November 2002. The company paid the amount to four people who claimed to have suffered strokes or had heart problems because they took the company's ephedra diet pills. According to the FDA, the Justice Department's related investigation of Metabolife began in August 2002. Ephedra would not be banned by the FDA until two years later, despite more than 150 deaths linked to it.

In February 2003, at the FDA's request, U.S. marshals seized approximately $19,000 worth of dietary supplement products from Global Source Management and Consulting of Sunrise, Florida. The FDA determined that these products claimed to treat a variety of medical conditions with unapproved drug claims in violation of the U.S. Food, Drug and, Cosmetic Act.

BACKGROUND AND DEVELOPMENT

The use of herbals and other botanicals as dietary supplements predates written history. In the West, the first known study of medicinal plants was produced by the Greek scientist Dioscorides in the first century A.D. Among modern early proponents of vitamins and micronutrients was the German chemist Hans von Euler-Chelpin (1873–1964), whose first work centered on fermentation. After World War I, Euler-Chelpin began his research into the chemistry of enzymes, particularly as to the role they played in the fermentation process. Apart from tracing phosphates through the fermentation sequence, he detailed the chemical makeup of co-zymase, a non-protein constituent involved in cellular respiration. In 1929 Euler-Chelpin became the director of the Vitamin Institute and Institute of Biochemistry at the University of Stockholm.

In more recent times, food supplement companies often originated from their founders' responses to physical adversity or from the personal discovery of a new product. These companies then grew phenomenally through multilevel marketing. For example, as the result of curing a stomach ulcer with capsicum, a spicy red-pepper powder, Eugene Hughes and his wife began making gelatin-filled red cayenne capsules and selling them to local health food stores in the mid-1960s. He added chaparral for digestion and goldenseal, a natural antibiotic. In 1972 they founded Hughes' Development Corp., which became Nature's Sunshine Products.

In the 1970s and 1980s, the United States witnessed a resurgence of general interest in herbal remedies. More than 50 percent of all pharmaceuticals were made from natural sources or synthetic analogs of natural products. Beginning in the mid-1990s, an increasing number of physicians started to recognize the medicinal value of herbs and foods in curing ailments.

Nutrition drinks and energy bars became popular in the mid-1990s. Boost, by Mead Johnson Nutritionals, debuted as an nutritional supplement drink for active adults who do not have the time to eat properly. Together, ReSource, Ensure, and Boost represent the leading liquid nutritional supplements, a category that accounted for $330 million in annual retail sales by the middle of the first decade of the 2000s.

Rapidly growing sectors of the nutritional supplement market have been mineral supplements, single vitamins (especially vitamins C and E), and combinations of vitamins and minerals targeted at particular population segments, such as menopausal women or those involved in athletic pursuits. Popular (and often controversial) supplements in the late 1990s included glucosamine and chondroitin, which claimed to combat the symptoms of arthritis; SAM-e (s-adenosylmethionine), naturally found in all human cells and which was touted as a joint lubricant and antidepressant; creatine and the steroid androstenedione, which gained national prominence as athletic performance enhancers when baseball stars Mark McGwire and Sammy Sosa admitted to using them after their famous home-run-hitting battle in 1998; and cholestin, made from fermented rice and believed to lower cholesterol levels.

The annual worldwide market for dietary supplements was estimated to be worth about $46 billion in 2000. That year, the vitamin and mineral market alone was valued at $17.8 billion, herbal and homeopathic products at $19.4 billion, and sports and specialty supplements at $8.8 billion, according to *Nutraceuticals World.* Americans comprised the largest national market for nutritional supplements. The *Nutrition Business Journal* projected overall supplement sales in the United States to reach $15.7 billion in 2000. It was estimated that about 40 percent of all Americans took a vitamin supplement regularly.

Although overall sector sales growth was slowing, household penetration by the industry equaled 71 percent in 1999, up from 68 percent in 1998, according to the Hartman Group. Leading products included those that strengthened bones and joints, antidepressants, energy boosters, sports supplements, and diet aids. Vitamins and minerals alone comprised 63 percent of all supplement sales. The overall category was revived by interest in products such as glucosamine, SAM-e, and creatine.

According to *Nutraceuticals World,* herbals experienced the greatest overall segment growth between 1994 and 1999, though that trend slowed in 2000. Sales of herbal formulas increased about 8 percent that year, roughly on par with vitamins and minerals. There was little change in product leaders from the previous year, as interest in vitamins C and E, gingko biloba, St. John's wort, ginseng, echinacea, and saw palmetto remained strong. In general, the field became more competitive, as the presence of major pharmaceutical firms expanded, and leading supplement makers merged. Among such ventures were those involving American Home Products Corp., Warner-Lambert, and Bayer Corp., all of which targeted providing greater offerings in mass market outlets.

Growth of supplement sales in the late 1990s was spurred by increased consumption by older consumers, the rising number of pharmacies in supermarkets, more display visibility, and health benefits substantiated by medical research. For example, because numerous studies verified that saw palmetto helps the prostate gland, its sales increased significantly. The herbal market also experienced a number of shifts in market share among various herb products. Sales of vitamin E, the health benefits of which were also supported by scientific studies, grew by about 5 percent per year. Calcium meanwhile remained the leading component of the nutritional supplement market, with sales of $361 million in 2000.

In May 1999, Roche Holding AG of Switzerland and BASF AG of Germany agreed to pay $725 million to the U.S. government to settle charges that alleged they participated in a nine-year global cartel that fixed prices for human and animal supplements. Roche had previously paid fines for fixing the price of citric acid. Assistant U.S. Attorney General Joel Klein described the situation as the "most pervasive and harmful criminal antitrust conspiracy ever uncovered." Rhone-Poulenc SA of France was instrumental in revealing the cartel; its cooperation led to immunity from prosecution for participation in the scheme.

In her U.S. soy market update, Dr. Kathie Wrick, an expert in food nutrition and health practice, reported that according to the 2002 Supplement Business Report from *Nutrition Business Journal,* soy isoflavones used in dietary supplements were worth approximately $34 million at retail, about double the value of 1999. Wrick said soy isoflavones were in competition with similar compounds isolated from red clover and black cohosh. The latter had substantial European data supporting its role in menopausal symptom relief.

As reported in *Nutrition Today,* after a congressional mandate, the Office of Dietary Supplements (ODS) of the National Institutes of Health (NIH) organized a conference/workshop in January 2000 to explore the state of knowledge about the important issues related to bioavailability of dietary supplements. One of the clearest findings from these discussions was that the use of dietary supplements in children from infancy through adolescence was increasing. It was also noted that little is known about the evidence base to support appropriate indications or the safety of these supplements for use by children.

About one-third of Americans turn to herbals to treat medical or physical conditions. In response, the National Institutes of Health launched the International Bibliographic Information on Dietary Supplements database. The database includes published international scientific literature free of charge via their Office of Dietary Supplements Web site. Looking ahead to the future of the study of dietary supplements, NIH published a report titled "Promoting Quality Science in Dietary Supplement Research, Education and Communication: A Strategic Plan for the Office of Dietary Supplements 2004-2009."

Some popular herbs were selling so well that their natural supply was becoming endangered due to overharvesting. Specifically, echinacea, goldenseal, American ginseng, and wild yam were becoming scarce and more expensive. Demand for St. John's wort and kava also exceeded supply. What was becoming more dangerous was that some products touted to have these ingredients were adulterated, and some contained none of the ingredients listed on their labels. According to *Chemist & Druggist,* nearly half of drugs and supplements had potential for interaction, 6 percent of which could be very serious.

In August 2002, the FDA announced a major agency-wide initiative in "Pharmaceutical Current Good Manufacturing Practices for the 21st Century: A Risk Based Approach." It was to be a two-year program that would apply to pharmaceuticals, including biological human drugs and veterinary drugs. In February 2003, the FDA announced that it had accomplished the initial objectives set in the ongoing initiative. By 2004, many in the industry were calling foul, claiming that the actual costs of the GMP (Good Manufacturing Practices) initiative were up to 10 times higher for individual companies ($1.2 billion total) than the FDA originally claimed ($78 million total). Consequently, the industry was asking the FDA to revise the GMP initiative in order to keep costs down and preserve the ability of many companies to stay in business.

After the 2003 death of Baltimore Oriole pitcher Steve Bechler, which was attributed in part to the supplements he had taken that contained ephedra, which was supposed to boost energy and aid in weight loss, the FDA sped up plans to ban the ingredient from the market. Despite the more than 150 deaths linked to the use of ephedra, not to mention the 16,000 reports on ephedra's negative effects, some in the industry claimed that ephedra was in fact safe if used as directed. According to Wes Siegner, an ephedra expert and advocate, "More than 16,000 deaths each year occur from the use of aspirin and similar drugs. Yet no one proposes banning aspirin." The FDA successfully banned ephedra in 2004 and was going after other steroid-type ingredients marketed as dietary supplements.

In the wake of the ephedra fiasco, many products were appearing in health food markets with labels boasting that they gave energy boosts and increased weight loss with ephedra. According to Ray Woosley, the University of Arizona's vice president for health sciences, who had been trying to get ephedra banned for more than 10 years before the FDA regulation came into effect, "It is very likely that the substitutes for ephedra are going to be just as toxic."

Approximately $20 billion in dietary supplements were sold in the U.S. alone during the middle years of the first decade of the 2000s. Each year, some 150 million Americans took one or more of the estimated 29,000 supplements that were available for sale. According to data from Information Resources Inc., reported in the November 28, 2005, issue of *MMR,* sales of nutritional supplements in drug, food, and discount stores

were estimated at $2.31 billion in October 2005, down 2.1 percent from October 2004. A number of factors made 2005 a difficult year for the industry. In addition to a gradual movement away from low-carb diets, reports emerged that challenged the efficacy of supplements such as echinacea (cold relief) and black cohosh (menopause relief). Additionally, bad publicity related to ephedra and other herbal supplements continued to impact the botanical and herbal category.

Despite these challenges, industry observers were hopeful that a turnaround was in store for the industry. The aging baby boomer segment was expected to be a key driver of new business, especially in the area of heart health supplements. In particular, supplement products such as fish oil and omega-3 fatty acids were forecast to be strong sellers. Beyond supplements, a number of food products incorporating omega-3s entered the market in 2006, including a yogurt product from Stonyfield Farm.

Beyond heart-related supplements, the nutrition bar category also was expected to drive growth for the industry during the latter part of the decade. Once a niche area of the supplement industry targeting athletes and fitness buffs, nutrition bars were appealing to a growing number of consumers for their nutritional value. Sales in this sector exceeded $3 billion during 2005 and continued to grow. Major packaged goods companies were moving to capitalize on this growth by acquiring well-known brands such as PowerBar (Nestle USA) and Balance Bar (Kraft Foods).

Following several years of collaboration with the National Institutes of Health's Office of Dietary Supplements and the FDA, in 2006 the National Institute of Standards and Technology (NIST) released the first in a series of Standard Reference Materials related to botanical dietary supplements. The materials were intended for use by researchers to ensure accurate analyses and by manufacturers for quality control purposes. While the initial materials pertained to products containing ephedra, releases were expected in the future that covered other supplements, such as bilberries, blueberries, and cranberries, as well as bitter orange, carrot extract, Ginkgo biloba, green tea, saw palmetto, and St John's wort.

While the NIST's reference materials were expected to benefit the industry through improved quality, experts still urged consumers to be cautious when consuming supplements, especially so-called exotic concoctions from foreign countries that often contained unknown or potentially harmful ingredients. In 2006 the FDA issued warnings related to supplements from Brazil that contained the active ingredients found in the prescription medications Librium and Prozac. Such concerns were prompting states to heighten their scrutiny of the industry. One example was the New York State Task Force on Life and the Law, which issued a 108-page report in late 2005 that called for "major new oversight initiatives aimed at protecting state consumers from dietary supplements that are unsafe and/or fail to live up to label claims," according to *Food Chemical News*.

A 2008 study by the Mercanti Group showed that the nutritional supplement industry was growing quickly due to a number of factors. One of these factors was the increasing acceptance of their use by the traditional medical field, in part because the industry has worked hard to gain credibility in the areas of research, education, and regulation. In addition, Americans were turning to nutritional supplements as alternative solutions to traditional health care options, which continued to increase in price. Other issues that pushed people toward using nutritional supplements as replacements for traditional pharmaceutical remedies were quality of care and distrust of pharmaceuticals. Whereas some people replaced their regular treatments with this more holistic option, others used supplements to complement their regular medicinal routines. In fact, according to the Mercanti Group's report, when considering what people used to replace or complement regular pharmaceutical treatments, nutritional supplements were the number-one product.

Another factor that was helping the industry was the emergence of the market for CAM (Complementary and Alternative Medicine) services, such as naturopathy, acupuncture, and traditional Chinese medicine. According to Eric Groman, author of the Mercanti report, "As consumers have become more interested in health and overall wellness, the market for products and services that provide a holistic approach has greatly increased." The number of practitioners in the holistic health care market has had a positive effect on growth in the industry. In addition, the report found that the nutritional supplement market is becoming more specialized, and companies are producing more products and combined formulas that target specific health conditions. According to Groman, as of 2008, "The market is certainly ripe for future growth."

Another study done in 2008 by Packaged Facts predicted that the nutritional supplements industry would grow 39 percent between 2008 and 2012 to reach $8.5 billion. This report also found that supplements targeted at specific conditions or groups (e.g., children, women) accounted for more than one third of sales in 2008 and was expected to continue to grow.

CURRENT CONDITIONS

An August 2010 release of a report by market research company, Packaged Facts, indicated that 2009 sales of nutritional supplements were estimated to have exceeded $9 billion in U.S. sales, increasing 8 percent over 2008 despite the tight economy. The sports nutrition and specialty supplement market were the two fastest growing segments in the industry, with a slight drop in growth for dietary supplements. Packaged Facts attributed the market growth to a combination of factors, including Americans' efforts to stay healthy to combat rising health care costs, as well as media and government efforts to call attention to product accountability and quality. The company also forecasted the market to exceed $13 billion in 2014.

According to the American Botanical Council, sales of herbal dietary supplements in the United States were estimated to have been greater than $5 billion in 2009. Sales in the mainstream market channels (drug stores, large retail chains, etc.) experienced the greatest growth in 2009 nutritional supplement sales, increasing 14 percent over 2008. Another report published by market research firm SPIN found that the five top-selling herbal supplements in the health and natural foods channel in 2009 were aloe (aloe vera), flaxseed oil, wheat and grasses, acai, and turmeric. In the food, drug, and mass market channel, the top-selling herbals were cranberry, soy, saw palmetto, garlic, and echinacea.

In May 2009, a major lawsuit was filed in federal district court in California, filed jointly by several county district attorneys, seeking a manufacturing injunction against 74 vitamin and supplement companies regarding the level of cancer-causing lead found in their products. This followed the release of a 2008 report by the FDA involving test results of multivitamin and mineral products for excessive amounts of lead. The lawsuit was filed under California Proposition 65, which required businesses to provide clear warnings that their products contained dangerous levels of lead. According to the complaint, toxic levels of lead (as in these products) cause damage to the nervous system, cancer, and reproductive harm.

In July 2009, the FDA issued a warning to consumers not to use body-building products that were being sold as nutritional supplements, as they may contain steroids or steroid-like substances that could cause kidney failure. It named eight specific supplements sold by one company, American Cellular Labs, including products called Mass Xtreme and Tren Xtreme, which FDA found to contain hidden steroids. The FDA further warned consumers not to purchase products labeled with code words such as "anabolic" and "tren" or phrases like "blocks estrogen" or "minimizes gyno" (referring to the effects of some bodybuilding products to enhance or diminish the effects of hormones). The FDA further acknowledged that it did not know how many products were affected by the warning. A full investigation into similar products marketed under other names followed.

INDUSTRY LEADERS

As of 2010, there were at least 2,000 supplement firms operating in the United States. They included Amway Products, with its popular line of Nutrilite nutritional supplements (the company reported $8.4 billion in 2009 sales); Atrium Innovations; NBTY Inc.; Neutraceuticals International; Whole Foods Markets; and Glanbia plc.

Among industry leaders is GNC Corp. (formerly General Nutrition Companies Inc.) of Pittsburgh, Pennsylvania. GNC, the number one specialty retailer of nutritional supplements, operates more than 6,150 retail outlets in the United States and Canada, as well as franchised stores in approximately 50 countries. The company operates an additional 1,350 stores within Rite Aid drugstores and produces products under the Rite Aid private label.

NBTY, headquartered in Bohemia, New York, is a leading supplier of vitamin, mineral, and nutritional supplements. In just 10 years, NBTY's employees grew from 400 to 2,000 and sales increased from $33 million to $281 million through aggressive automation, acquisitions, new product development, and advanced marketing. In May 1999, the company announced its acquisition of Dynamics Essentials, Inc., a distributor of nutritional supplements and skincare products, for $1 million. It produces, wholesales, and retails more than 22,000 products under such brand names as Nsature's Bounty, Solgar, Sundown, and Ester-C. The company operates some 500 Vitamin World stores in the United States and 80 Le Naturiste stores in Canada, as well as some 500 stores in the United Kingdom.

Cyanotech Corp., based in Kailua-Kona, Hawaii, produces natural products from microalgae nutritional supplements and is the world's largest commercial producer of natural astaxanthin from microalgae. A majority of its sales come from Spirulina Pacifica, a nutritional supplement made from vegetable algae. During the early years of the first decade of the 2000s, Cyanotech began delivering astaxanthin to the Rexall Sundown, GNC, and Unicity Network divisions of Royal Numico for use in specialty products.

Nature's Sunshine Products, Inc. (NSP) in Provo, Utah, is one of the major U.S. manufacturers of alternative health care products. As of 2008, members of the founding Hughes family owned 25 percent of the company. NSP offers more than 700 products, including a wide range of herbal supplements in many categories as well as personal care, water purification, healthful eating, and aromatherapy products. Nature's Sunshine also sells vitamins, personal care products, homeopathic remedies, and other health products. It also has operations in Asia, the Pacific Rim, Europe, and North and South America.

Rexall Sundown, Inc., of Bohemia, New York, sells the Sundown, Osteo Bi-Flex, CarbSolutions, and Pokemon Vitamins, in addition to a variety of other nutritional supplements to mass market stores, drug stores, health food stores, supermarkets, and through mail order. Rexall Sundown was a wholly owned subsidiary of NBTY, which acquired Sundown from Royal Numico, N.V. It was named "Manufacturer of the Year" in December 2000 by *Nutritional Outlook Magazine.* In February 2003, plans were announced for NBTY to buy the then struggling vitamin manufacturer. Royal Numico had been trying since November 2002 to unload Rexall, which had used layoffs and attrition to slim down from 1,200 employees in 2000 to about 1,000.

Herbalife Ltd. of Los Angeles, California, moved in the opposite direction of the rest of the industry by going private. By 2009, sales were approximately $2.32 billion and the firm employed more than 3,000 workers. A manufacturer of more than 160 natural and herbal products, Herbalife has more than 1.5 million independent distributors worldwide conducting business in 60 countries in Asia, the Pacific Rim, Europe, and the Americas. This distribution system is the only one the company has utilized since its origin. About one half of its sales traditionally came from its food and dietary supplements. In the first years of the twenty-first century's first decade, the company began to offer a wide range of scientifically advanced products, including a cosmetics line and a collection of products for children. Herbalife has evolved from a one-person operation to a $2 billion multinational corporation.

AMERICA AND THE WORLD

In nutrition products, the United States accounted for the majority of global sales in 2009, Western Europe followed, and Japan was third. China was expected to outpace Japan soon. Growing markets included Brazil, India, and Eastern Europe, according to *Nutritional Supplements-Edition 2010.* The prebiotics market was particularly active in Europe, with special focus on infant formula products, dairy, and beverages. Infant milk formula was also a strong segment of the market in China, with $4.1 billion in sales and an 18.03 percent compound annual growth rate (CAGR) between 2005 and 2009. Another high growth rate market was in the Indian herbal industry.

The European dietary supplements market in 2009 was dominated by just five countries (Germany, Italy, France, the United Kingdom and Norway) constituting 78 percent of market value, according to *Ingredients Network.* The German market grew just one percent in 2009, but sales were high in magnesium supplements and immune system-building supplements. Germany represented the highest European market for ginkgo biloba in 2009.

In Italy, consumers tended to limit supplements to specific needs, such as minerals lost in perspiration in hot weather or trendy probiotic supplements. Fiber-boosting supplements recorded the fastest growth in 2009. Probiotics sales were also high in France in 2009, despite a crushing blow to the overall market in 2008 and 2009 due to illegal imports, some of which had been found to be ineffective or unsafe. In Norway, fish oil continued to monopolize the supplement market; the popularity and apparent effectiveness of omega-3 for cardiovascular health was expected to keep this supplement in continued demand.

Despite resistance from the Alliance of Natural Health, as well as several consumer groups, in 2002, the European Union's Food Supplements Directive came into law, affecting the legality of about 300 ingredients, all but 28 vitamins and minerals combined. Companies were given until August 2005 to prove that their products no longer contained the banned vitamins and minerals.

Among the most closely regulated supplement industries is that of Germany, where nearly 40 percent of medicines are based on phytochemicals (plant chemicals). The German government hosts Commission E, a special committee on herbals that checks information about products from clinical trials, field studies, and medical literature. It issues product monographs about product identification, risks, and dosages. The European Scientific Co-operative on Phytotherapy planned to create similar monographs, and the World Health Organization launched two series of plant monographs.

RESEARCH AND TECHNOLOGY

Medicinal Herbs As the tight economy caused more Americans to lose health care insurance or coverage and aging Baby Boomers sought a more holistic approach to health, use of supplements doubled among senior citizens and the associated risks of self-medicating and self-diagnosing became of rising concern to medical professionals. A 2009 survey by Ipso Public Affairs for the Council for Responsible Nutrition found that 65 percent of adult Americans, or approximately 150 million persons, labeled themselves as supplement users. In a University of Chicago survey, up to 50 percent of patients scheduled for surgery were using herbal remedies that may have caused surgical complications if their physicians were not advised of the use. With heightened concern for the potential for drug-herb interactions, the American Pharmacists Association published its 16th edition of the *Handbook of Nonprescription Drugs* in April 2009. The textbook included a comprehensive examination of all self-care options, including nutritional and herbal supplements.

Medicinal Properties of Nutritional Supplements Research continued to define the health benefits of vitamins, other micronutrient supplements, and phytochemicals. A great deal of work was focused on the anticancer properties of vitamin E, vitamin C, and folic acid. A number of studies showed these were useful in fighting Alzheimer's disease, cancer, heart disease, and birth defects. Vitamin E was proven to have an important role in cognitive function, respiratory health, immune response, and the prevention of heart disease.

In addition, research at Cyanotech included development of an antioxidant supplement based on the microalgae astaxanthin, the antioxidant properties of which the company claimed to be up to 550 times more effective than vitamin E.

Lycopene, an up and coming phytochemical of the beta-carotene group that occurs naturally in red tomatoes, attracted attention as a promising antioxidant. Both BASF and Roche were developing lycopene products, which were believed to help prevent macular degeneration, prostate cancer, and heart disease. The world market for the product was estimated at $6 million to $8 million annually. Moreover, some industry leaders such as Herbalife appointed a medical advisory board of respected medical experts, scientists, nutritionists, and health care professionals who oversee the research and development of their products.

Meanwhile, in the wake of the ephedra scandal, other steroid products were facing banishment from the world of supplements. Such ingredients had been able to slip into supplement products due to a loophole in the 1990 Controlled Substances Act. The FDA announced in 2004 that ingredients such as androstenedione, known as andro, were not, in fact, dietary supplements at all and must be removed from the market. This news pleased most of the supplement industry, which was growing tired of the negative and detrimental press.

BIBLIOGRAPHY
"Dietary Supplement Industry Analysis: Research on Vitamins, Minerals, Herbs & Botanicals." *Nutrition Business Journal,* 2010. Available from http://www.nutritionbusinessjournal.com/supplements/.

"Dietary Supplements: Safe, Beneficial and Regulated." Council for Responsible Nutrition, 17 May 2005. Available from http://www.crnusa.org.

Geisler, Malinda. "Medicinal Herb Profile." Agricultural Marketing Resource Center, Iowa State University, April 2010.

Grammenou, Eleni. "Supplementing the Future." *International Food Ingredients,* April-May 2008.

"Herbalife to Build Production Base with USD 100mn in China." *Alestron,* 29 May 2006.

"Herbal Supplement Sales Increase to $5 Billion in Sales in the U.S." *Neutraceuticals World,* 7 May 2010.

"Indicators Point to Bright Future." *MMR,* 5 May 2008.

Kerr, Kathleen. "New Line of Vitamins Aimed at Needs of Blacks and Hispanics Puts Focus on Ethnicity's Role in Health: The Race to Market." *Newsday,* 14 April 2006.

Knape, Chris. "Amway Reports Record Sales of $8.4 Billion in 2009." *Grand Rapids Press,* 9 March 2010.

"Knowledge Before Use Is Necessary." *Chain Drug Review,* 10 April 2006.

"Market Trends: Dietary Supplements in Europe." *Ingredients Network,* 2010.

"Natural Solutions Gain Wider Distribution." *MMR,* 11 August 2008.

"New GM for Herbalife's China Operations." *China Retail News,* 28 December 2007.

"Nutritional Supplements a Fast-Growing Factor in Healthcare Field, Says Mercanti Group Report." *Business Wire,* 21 April 2008.

"Nutritional Supplements—Edition 2010." Abstract. Research and Markets, 3 September 2010. Available from http://www.researchandmarkets.com.

"Nutritional Supplements Market to Stay Healthy Amid Weak Economy." *Progressive Grocer,* 21 August 2008.

"Nutritional Supplements in the United States." 4th Edition, 2010. Abstract. Available from http://www.marketreserach.com/product/display.asp?productid=2642045.

"Researchers Plumb Supplements." *Chain Drug Review,* 14 July 2008.

Sahelian, Ray. "Vitamin Company Information and Their Products." 2010. Available from http://www.raysahelian.com.

Schmidt, Michael S. "FDA Issues Steroid Warning on Body-Buuilding Supplements." *New York Times,* 28 July 2009.

"Stock: Herbalife (HLF)." Available from http://www.wikinvest.com/stock/Herbalife_HLF.

There's Always Something New." *Chain Drug Review,* 14 July 2008.

"US Quality Standards Issued for Herbal Dietary Supplements by NIST." *Nutraceuticals International,* April 2006.

OCEAN ENERGY

SIC CODE(S)

1629

INDUSTRY SNAPSHOT

Ocean energy refers to the energy carried by ocean waves, tides, salinity, and the ocean temperatures. Although relatively new and still under development, ocean energy is said to be the next hope for replacing our reliance upon fuel energy by 2020. This change in energy source requires intellectual capital as research and development by energy companies progresses enough to create machinery, processes, and energy output to replace fuel or natural gas outputs. However, hopes are that ocean energy may bring in thousands of jobs over the next decade. This will occur as research and development (R&D) and technology improve, allowing us to harness the power of gale force winds and ocean waves to give power to electrical grids and a better way to conserve our nonrenewable resources.

Ocean energy may utilize temperatures in or above ocean waves to produce energy. It may also use the motion of the open sea to generate energy. From Ocean Energy in Ireland, a company that has been testing an Ocean Energy buoy in the Atlantic Ocean off the coast of Ireland for the past seven years, the idea of wave action to generate energy seems well within reach to replace all energy consumption on the west coast of Ireland by 2020. Hawaii's Natural Energy Laboratory has been studying the use of thermal energy production from the Pacific Ocean temperatures since 1994. A tidal energy plant in France makes enough energy to power 240,000 homes.

The idea of geothermal, kinetic, ocean thermal energy conversion (OTEC), and tidal energy from the ocean is not a new idea. In fact, history shows that ocean-fronting countries were utilizing some of these technologies since around the eleventh century. This makes the minor point that some of the best ideas to create energy may be those that have been tried and true, rather than those that look to be the least expensive and easiest.

ORGANIZATION AND STRUCTURE

Worries over finding newer and more diverse kinds of renewable energy have led to research and development for using ocean energy to produce power. The large mass of the oceans on our planet obviously seem prime for use to create great reserves of energy for countries worldwide. However, the actual logistics involved are still under consideration. The different kinds of energy production use different aspects of the ocean's power. The question remains: Which one is more effective? Which one is sustainable? Which one can be done safely and without great expense? There is not yet much regulatory guidance on these questions other than the Federal Energy Regulatory Commission (FERC) as entrepreneurs and small companies are the ones working on ocean energy projects currently. Until the R&D gets clear about which type of ocean energy is most effective, more and more companies will launch their technologies for testing. Ongoing tests of machinery with which to harness the power of waves takes place over many years. University and academic research labs can speed this process up slightly, but in 2010 we were still at least a decade away from actually using ocean energy to power our lives.

A few promising attempts were being tested, however. In the spring of 2009, the Sonoma County Water District in California applied to the FERC for three wave project preliminary permits. The projects will be located in state waters offshore Del Mar Landing (the northwestern portion of the county) and off Fort Ross farther to the south. Each of the three projects would begin as pilots in the 2 to 5 megawatt (MW) range, could potentially expand to commercial facilities in the 40 to 200 MW range, and would include substations, transmission lines, appurtenant facilities, and submersible electric cables. According to the California Energy Commission, "With these applications, the total number of FERC permits and applications for wave and tidal projects in California waters totals twelve."

BACKGROUND AND DEVELOPMENT

Tidal energy has been used since around the eleventh century on a small, local scale. Nevertheless, tides must rise and fall at least 16 feet for tidal energy to be successful. Geothermal energy from the ocean is still in its early testing phases. Ocean-based turbines are slated for 2012 off the coast of Maine. However, a big piece of energy legislation did not make it through the U.S. Senate in the summer of 2010, which frustrated efforts by energy companies looking to help our country and others capitalize on renewable energy sources. The big gains by the Republicans in the mid-term elections in November 2010 also frustrated any consensus on the issue as Republicans support the use of nuclear energy sources, as well as tidal and wind energy sources. However, because of the change in Washington, D.C., any chances for a pervasive energy bill must be the result of both parties working together in a bipartisan way.

Ocean thermal energy conversion (OTEC) or geo-thermal energy is not a new idea. Developed in the 1880s, OTEC relies on deep coldwater to get pulled up from the depths in order to power vast amounts of energy production. However, if OTEC does succeed, analysts expect it to be a very reliable source of billions of watts of electrical power. Wind turbines work well on land; planting the same sort of turbines into the Atlantic Ocean, it is hoped, will provide similar watts of electrical power for the Atlantic seaboard. However, the test of these sea-based turbines has not been completed.

PIONEERS IN THE FIELD

Matthew R. Simmons founded the Ocean Energy Institute in 2007. Ocean Energy Institute is a think tank and venture capital fund working on the challenges of U.S. offshore renewable energy. OEI looks at energy R&D and investment from a systems point of view; not just generation, but usage, storage, and transmission all working together as an interdependent set of opportunities and the next driving force of the international economy. Simmons received the Energy Ocean International 2010 Pioneer Award on June 9, 2010, before passing away in early August.

Florida Atlantic University's Center for Ocean Energy Technology (COET) received the Academic Pioneer Award from EnergyOcean International for significant contributions in the field of ocean energy research and technology. Dr. Karl Stevens, dean of the College of Engineering and Computer Science, oversees the COET, which has developed leading-edge work in ocean energy technologies and science. A current project of FAU includes a wind turbine project, utilizing the Gulf Stream change in temperatures.

Ted Johnson is a Lockheed Martin employee who was part of the original Ocean Thermal Energy Conversion (OTEC) team that developed, built, and deployed the first successful floating OTEC system in the 1980s. Johnson is currently OTEC program business development director and leads Lockheed Martin's efforts to bring modern, commercial utility-scaled OTEC plants to market. In 2008 Lockheed Martin was awarded a U.S. Department of Energy contract to demonstrate a modern fabrication approach for a cold water pipe, a key component of the OTEC system.

CURRENT CONDITIONS

With the lack of a comprehensive energy bill passing in the Senate in 2010, renewable energy resources are still somewhat "out there" and perhaps something of a pipe dream. However, many entrepreneurs and academic labs are going ahead with their R&D programs, which is good for the long haul. As these R&D efforts begin to give results, renewable energy sources will become clearer: Is it tidal energy, geothermal or OTEC energy, or ocean-powered wind turbines? Until further testing and R&D begin to prove themselves, however, we're still in need of as much varied and far-reaching R&D technologies as possible. In late 2010, the sky was the limit. Anyone with a good idea and a working prototype could apply. To some ocean energy proponents, the idea that we've made it to the moon several times and not yet found a way to harness the power of the ocean seems incongruous. Some argued that we know more about the surface of Mars than the bottom of our oceans. Thus, R&D efforts today will be our paths to follow tomorrow.

INDUSTRY LEADERS

Verdant Power began in 2000 and is based in New York City. The company pairs "emerging technology developers" with utility industry veterans with advanced experience in constructing and operating electricity generation facilities, focusing specifically on hydropower. Verdant Power is a recognized leader in the marine renewable energy industry, bringing to the table world-leading projects and technologies. Verdant's management team serves in leadership roles within a variety of industry organizations, as well as working with government entities and elected officials to progress the adoption of ocean energy technologies around the world.

In 1998 Verdant Power founders built and tested working prototypes of four different types of marine energy systems. This early history has allowed the company to determine the strengths and weaknesses of alternative designs, and has been a key motivator in the selection of the technologies Verdant seeks to implement now. In 2005 the company received a special Declaratory Order from the Federal Energy Regulatory Commission (FERC) to produce and deliver electricity to consumers during the testing phase of the RITE Project. Verdant Power received the 2010 Company Pioneer Award at the EnergyOcean International Conference. In 2006 the company was presented with the President's Award, the National Hydropower Association's highest honor.

Aquamarine Power was formed in 2005 as a wave energy company. Aquamarine has offices in Edinburgh, Scotland, and further operations in Orkney and Northern Ireland. The company is currently developing its main technology, a hydroelectric wave energy converter, known as Oyster. Aquamarine Power's goal is to develop commercial Oyster wave farms around the world.

In November 2009 the first demonstration-scale Oyster was successfully deployed at sea at the Orkney, Scotland-based European Marine Energy Centre. It then began producing power for the National Grid. The performance of Oyster is currently being monitored and results from those tests will give feedback for the design of the next-generation commercial-scale Oyster 2.

WORKFORCE

As R&D progresses to find the best way to harness the power of the ocean's energy, the best opportunities for jobs will be around an academic or for-profit research lab. Engineers, divers, fabricators, and energy specialists are often among the people most utilized for work in ocean energy.

Although things are still evolving, the desire is there to use the ocean's waves, tides, and thermal energy to power our own energy needs. The desire has been there for quite some time and there are academic labs and venture capital firms out there looking for people with a good idea. Coming up with a good idea means studying the field and learning what has worked and what has not. It means knowing a lot about oceanography, geography, and geology. It means knowing about weather patterns and how much tides can move from one continent to another. It means knowing how ocean currents affect the ocean's temperature.

A lot of people in ocean energy have a background in energy or in oceanography. They may be experts from another field that decided to throw their passion into ocean energy work. Above all, they know the history of the movement. They know the risks and how hard it has been to move our energy dependence from our usual sources to this. Additionally, they know the pressure on ocean energy experts to find better solutions that both the government and private enterprise can use in the future.

Some observers feel that the United States needs to pass some sort of renewably marine energy legislation to keep up with the rest of the world. Other countries, as has been shown in previous sections, are hard at work to develop technology to provide energy to their entire electrical grids. If successful, these other countries around the world may change their domestic oil usage and things could change in international political coalitions as the need for foreign oil decreases. This is a seemingly minor impetus for the development of a successful domestic renewal marine energy (ocean energy) technology to replace our dependence on foreign oil. Heading into 2011, it was unclear whether developments surrounding domestic energy would be political or based on independent R&D and technological advances.

AMERICA AND THE WORLD

In late 2010 some argued that the rest of the world had a somewhat better head start on ocean energy than the United States. France, above all, and Ireland, seemed to have a better grasp of what ocean energy could mean to their countries. After all, France has been utilizing tidal energy since around the eleventh century. Ireland is always looking for better ways to find energy for their island nation. Both countries have experiments going that have already been mentioned: Ocean Energy in Ireland has been testing an Ocean Energy buoy in the Atlantic Ocean off the coast of Ireland for the past seven years and a tidal energy plant in France makes enough energy to power 240,000 homes.

However, both the United States and the rest of the world (with the possible exception of the oil-producing Middle Eastern countries) understand that continuing to rely on nonrenewable resources of energy for much longer further impedes us from finding better resources and better ways of getting our hands on those resources. This impetus to find a long-term solution for the world's energy from the world's oceans is the main reason behind the push for ocean energy. It also touches on a sore subject pointed out often by oceanographers for the past 50 years: our oceans are less explored than the moon. We know less about the surface of our ocean's floor than we do about the surface of the moon. The last time we were at the bottom of the deepest point in our oceans in a manned submersible was 1960. What else is down there? What can we learn about our oceans to better utilize their power as a way to power our own energy needs?

Many ocean energy proponents estimate that ocean energy could be our savior in this regard. They estimate that there are billions of megawatts of energy available from simple wave or tidal energy and perhaps billions more from geothermal energy. There would be no need to build dangerous offshore oil-drilling operations into our ocean waters. In fact, many of the ocean energy experiments have no more than one operating part on them. There is nothing on these new ocean energy machines that would endanger animals or the ocean's ecosystem. This fact alone is a reason many ocean energy experts are pushing the research more than ever. It is time, they say, to finally learn the true potential of ocean energy.

RESEARCH AND TECHNOLOGY

From ocean-based air turbine installations and geothermal energy machinery to tidal energy capture, the technologies of ocean energy have been varied and diverse so far. In the future, what other technology will be brought to bear in order to harness the power of the oceans? Will we be able to pull extreme cold water from the depths in order to run energy grids back on land? Will we be able to harness the heat of a deep-water volcano to heat our homes? Will the tides bring us enough energy to power our cars in the future? Will waves give us the electricity that we require in 50 years? Those questions remain to be answered.

The prospect of discovery in front of us with ocean energy is actually quite exciting. These are the situations in which great breakthroughs have been made in the past and in which amazing scientists and researchers were able to point definitely to as the tipping point. Where is ocean energy's tipping point? When do we know enough to make it work?

It may not be right now, but we are not too far away, according to some researchers. The Ocean Energy Institute features a hopeful timeline on their Web site that points out that we may be only 10 years away from one of those breakthrough moments. If we truly are close, this is an exciting time to be interested in ocean energy. If we are still a few years away, then the more people who are interested in the prospects of renewable marine energy, the better. One day, the same waves that crash onto our closest beaches may be the same environmentally sustainable energy that powers our homes and cars and businesses and allows us to turn on the heater when the weather outside gets too cold.

BIBLIOGRAPHY

California Energy Commission, 2010. Available from http://www.energy.ca.gov/oceanenergy/index.html.

Charlier, Roger H., and Charles W. Finkl. *Ocean Energy: Tide and Tidal Power*. New York: Springer, 2009.

Khaligh, Alireza, and Omer C. Onar. *Energy Harvesting: Solar, Wind, and Ocean Energy Conversion Systems (Energy, Power Electronics, and Machines)* Danvers, Mass.: CRC Press, 2009.

McCormick, Michael E. *Ocean Wave Energy Conversion.* New York: Dover Publications, 2007.

Ocean Energy Council, 2010. Available from http://www.oceanenergycouncil.com.

Peppas, Lynn. *Ocean, Tidal, and Wave Energy: Power from the Sea.* New York: Crabtree Publishing Company, 2008.

U.S. Department of Energy. "Energy Savers: Ocean Energy Thermal Conversion." 2010. Available from http://www.energysavers.gov/renewable_energy/ocean/index.cfm/mytopic=50010.

OPTICAL SENSING AND INFRARED SENSORY DEVICES

■

SIC CODE(S)

3674

3577

3822

3761

3714

3827

3812

INDUSTRY SNAPSHOT

Bolstered by greater penetration of commercial markets, increased defense spending, and heightened demand from emerging economies, the optical and infrared sensing industry continued its forward momentum through the first decade of the twenty-first century with strong prospects. Although scientists originally developed optical sensing devices for the aerospace and defense industry, the technology ultimately crossed over many industry lines, finding applications in the medical, electronics, and automotive industries, among others. The ever-popular and ever-present television remote control, which uses an infrared sensor, shows the mass market potential of an optical sensing device that clicks with users. While the military continues to develop innovative and improved uses for optical sensing devices through government-funded research, other industries have developed and continue to develop their own commercial applications geared and priced for the masses. Sensors continue to pop up in a slew of consumer products such as cars, phones, pagers, watches, cameras, and computers.

Paul Saffo, a leading futurist, characterized the start of the twenty-first century as the decade of the sensor, just as the 1980s was the decade of the microprocessor. According to Saffo, sensors will eventually penetrate most aspects of life, making possible so-called intelligent homes and cars. However, the realization of this vision depends on the development of micro-machining processes that will enable the inexpensive mass production of more highly efficient and compact infrared sensors.

ORGANIZATION AND STRUCTURE

Infrared sensors, the most common type of optical sensors, detect objects or conditions by identifying the heat they emit. Infrared radiation (IR) is transmitted constantly through the atmosphere and is, in varying degrees, reflected or absorbed by objects. IR energy, which is absorbed, raises the temperature of the objects. The heat humans feel from a fire, sunlight, or a radiator is infrared.

Infrared sensors have a variety of applications—military, commercial, and otherwise. The guidance systems in heat-seeking missiles, for example, depend on infrared sensors, and sensors are the key technology in night vision systems, which the military was also instrumental in developing.

Sensors have also made a difference to ground troops. Soldiers on night guard duty at a camp during the North Atlantic Treaty Organization peacekeeping mission in Bosnia, for instance, often came outfitted with compact radios, night vision goggles, infrared sniper sights, and global positioning satellite range finders.

Infrared sensors have many civilian uses as well. Weather satellites carry infrared radiation (IR) sensors to track meteorological systems. They also track pollution. Polluted water, for example, has a higher temperature gradient, which satellite sensors easily detect. Earth and space-based telescopes integrate infrared sensors. Infrared systems are also integrated onto helicopters for finding people lost in wilderness areas and law enforcement agencies have modified versions designed to track criminals or escaped convicts. More and more, optical sensors are making their way into consumer markets. Digital cameras were made possible by optical sensors: the imaging system relies on optical sensor technology. "Smart" consumer devices, such as automatic light switches, lights that turn on automatically when someone enters a room, are smart because IR sensors "know" when someone is there.

Optical sensors are produced by a variety of company types. Historically, the biggest producers have been defense contractors who manufacture sensors for specific purposes—missile guidance systems, for example. Companies such as Northrop Grumman Corp. and Rockwell International Corp. continue to produce components for government projects, often in cooperation with other firms, while at the same time expanding into broader industrial applications such as robotics. Companies that make electronics for the industrial and consumer markets also produce sensors. These firms sell their sensors to other original equipment manufacturers for use in a broad variety of industrial and consumer applications.

As the technology becomes more highly developed and less expensive, specialist companies, as well as smaller start-up firms, are becoming involved in the development and manufacture of sensors. Camera companies, such as Olympus Optical and Polaroid, have made important advances in sensor technology that have led to the sophisticated auto-focus devices so popular with consumers. These firms continue to be an important force in the industry as they develop digital cameras that are dependent on optical sensors. Other smaller companies, often working with proprietary technology, produce sensors for diverse, highly specialized purposes as varied as night vision, environmental monitoring, or infrared telescopy.

BACKGROUND AND DEVELOPMENT

Because infrared sensors measure heat in objects, the first ones developed were essentially thermometers that relied on a change of temperature in the measuring device itself. These early devices led to the development of bolometers, which are still used to detect infrared radiation.

The first practical infrared sensor was developed in Germany during the 1930s when research capitalized on the infrared radiation (IR) sensitivity of lead sulfide. After World War II, American researchers followed suit, abandoning the materials they had been studying and instead concentrating on lead sulfide sensors. Early IR sensors

were limited to the short end of the IR spectrum. Other infrared-sensitive materials, however, soon helped extend sensitivity into the medium and eventually into longer wavelength ranges. The introduction of semiconductor alloys, such as mercury cadmium telluride, enabled infrared sensors to be fine-tuned to a specific wavelength for specific purposes.

In the early 1960s, photolithography—the repeatable imprinting of chemical or electronic patterns on silicon or other materials—made possible the first complex arrays of infrared sensors, some with focal planes of more than 1,000 elements. The refinement of such arrays would eventually make possible the focal systems for digital cameras. High volume production of IR sensor arrays using mercury cadmium telluride took off in the 1970s and these arrays have been the dominant technology ever since. They are used in a number of applications, including missile systems and weather satellites. Eventually silicon began to be used when it was discovered that IR-sensitive chemicals could be "grown" on a silicon substrate and used as sensors. Other advantages of silicon included its ready availability (it derives from sand), limited frequency response, and low thermal expansion quotient.

The first generation of infrared radiation (IR) sensors is represented by the arrays developed in the 1960s. The second generation began with electronic signal readouts that could integrate output from the many elements of an infrared array. That capability was first developed in the 1970s and reached maturity in the 1990s with large, fully integrated two-dimensional arrays. Such massive arrays are common on sensor-bearing satellites, but work was underway in the late 1990s to create miniature arrays on silicon chips using micro-electrical mechanical systems technology. Since the 1970s, the development of the infrared sensor has directly followed the development of the silicon integrated circuit. (Also see essays on Astronautics, Micromachines, Satellites, and Semiconductors.)

In 1993, the Infrared Data Association (IrDA) formed to establish a low cost, universal standard to enable all infrared-based cordless data communications to work together. IrDA envisioned a walk-up, point-to-point user model with data flying back and forth between a broad range of appliances from a variety of makers.

By 1998, IrDA reported that the IrDA standard port was rapidly becoming the most common cordless connection in the world. IrDA boasts more than 150 members, including 3Com Corp., Canon Inc., Dell Computer Corp., Hewlett-Packard Co., Motorola, Inc., IBM Corp., Sony Corp., and Xerox Corp. The IrDA port can be found in pagers, watches, cell phones, pay phones, printers, cameras, organizers, photo kiosks, communicators, and laptop and handheld computers.

Two basic types of infrared sensors have been developed. One detects energy (heat), the other detects photons (light). The energy sensor detects temperature changes caused by infrared radiation. An electrical current is monitored for changes, which results in proportion to external temperature. Energy type infrared radiation (IR) sensors are relatively inexpensive and are used in various applications from fire detection systems to automatic light switches. One technical limitation of energy sensors is that they must be insulated from the external environment to increase their sensitivity while at the same time be able to dissipate heat rapidly in order to respond quickly to changes.

One development in energy-type sensors involves micro-machining on silicon. Manufactured using photo-lithography, such sensors have extremely low power requirements yet match traditional sensors in performance. Microbolometers, devices that compare current and voltage in order to measure infrared radiation, have been developed. Micro-machined IR sensors have, by and large, not moved from the laboratory into commercial production, but one foreseen application is in night vision systems for military and civilian use.

Photon-type sensors react to the interaction of light with a semiconductor. Because they react to light rather than temperature, they respond to changes much faster than energy-type sensors. Photon sensors are easily manufactured in large two-dimensional arrays, a feature that has led to their application in advanced IR detection systems such as satellites. A major limitation to photon-type IR sensors is sensitivity to their own infrared radiation. To reduce such interference, they must be cooled to cryogenic temperatures, which requires added power and equipment. A focal point of IR sensor research is the development of sensors that don't require cooling. In 1996, after a year's work, Amber, a division of Raytheon, produced Sentinel, the world's first commercially available, microbolometer-based, uncooled, infrared imaging system. The development is eventually expected to revolutionize future production of infrared sensors.

In the past, most of the aerospace and defense industry's sales were to the government, primarily the U.S. Department of Defense, whose sensor purchases were symbolized by heat-seeking missiles and the "smart" weapons that burst into public view during the Persian Gulf War. Nevertheless, defense spending receded significantly in the 1990s—by about 50 percent between 1989 and 1998, and even more when compared to its height during the Reagan years. Consequently, aerospace and defense industry firms turned their focus to the civilian market. As a result, these manufacturers and developers sought civilian applications for technologies already developed for the military, as well as completely new sensors specifically for the civilian market.

In the late 1990s, a research consortium called ULTRA (Uncooled Low-Cost Technology Reinvestment Alliance) was formed by Honeywell, Texas Instruments, and Inframetrics to develop un-cooled focal plane array (UFPA) sensors. This technology has greater cost advantage over cryogenically cooled sensors, plus higher reliability, instant operation, and decreased systems costs. The sensor includes a signal conditioning circuit, analog-to-digital conversion, and signal processing functions, all arrayed on silicon chips—all the capabilities that define a smart IR sensor. The sensors are made from barium-strontium-titanate, which is a ferroelectric material. Ferroelectric materials are characterized by being crystalline materials having spontaneous electric polarization. Overseen in part by the Federal Aviation Administration, an initial application of the technology was for infrared-based inspection of aircraft hangar environments. Furthermore, the automotive and photography industries quickly adopted this technology.

Work continued on standard infrared radiation (IR) technologies and materials as well as on micro-machined IR sensors. Infrared sensors were increasingly being used to monitor environmental conditions such as oil pollution, forest fires, combustible vapors, and leaks. A new generation of household smoke detectors used an infrared sensor to detect the presence of lethal carbon monoxide. Development also was occurring on linear image sensors, the primary component of color scanners, and on new complementary metal oxide semiconductor (CMOS)-based image sensors for digital still cameras. CMOS sensors use low-power semiconductor microchips that help conserve energy in battery-powered devices. By 2000, CMOS sensors accounted for about 5 percent of the imaging sensor market. A new generation of high-resolution infrared cameras also emerged in the late 1990s and the early years of the first decade of the 2000s for use in machine vision systems.

The automotive industry was one of the first big customers for infrared and optical sensing devices as they became available at a competitive price. Infrared sensors were being integrated, for example, into automotive air bag systems to detect the presence of a child or small adult in a car seat, thus avoiding the inappropriate and dangerous deployment of an air bag. Other applications on the horizon include warning systems and adaptive cruise control. Unlike normal cruise control, which maintains a constant speed, adaptive cruise control would sense the presence of cars on the road ahead—by means of infrared sensors in one plan—and slow the car down to maintain a safe distance.

Furthermore, General Motors Corp. (GM) gave the public a peek at its new night vision system, based on un-cooled focal plane array (UFPA) technology, at the 1999 North American International Auto Show. The automaker became the first to offer night vision technology with the 2000 Cadillac Deville. GM touts the feature as a way to improve driving safety by enhancing the night-time driver's ability to detect potentially dangerous situations beyond the range of the headlamps without taking the driver's eyes off the road. In addition, this technology enables drivers to see three to five times farther down the road. GM mounted the infrared sensor behind the car's grille with a display for the sensor integrated into the dashboard. The 2000 Cadillac Evoq, a two-seat luxury roadster, sported both night vision and a rear obstacle detection system. The back-up aid used three sensors in the back bumper—one radar and two ultrasonic—to help avert back-up collisions.

Honda Motors and other automobile companies also were testing forward drive systems that used optical and infrared sensors to center the vehicle, change lanes, and avoid obstacles. Lockheed Martin was testing a forward-looking infrared camera adapted from its driverless military vehicles, and forward-looking radar systems also were being developed.

In early 2005, an agronomist with the Agricultural Research Service (ARS) was testing the use of optical sensors to gauge wheat quality. One challenge that farmers faced was that wheat quality varied throughout the same field. At the same time, wheat buyers require different levels of quality for different end uses. For example, cookies, crackers, and cakes usually call for low protein wheat, while breads require high protein wheat. The ARS developed a spectroscopic device that can measure wheat's protein content, as well as levels of oil, fat, moisture, and carbohydrates, during the harvesting process. The device, which employs near-infrared light and fiber optics to perform the measurement, is attached directly to a farmer's combine.

According to *Western Farm Press,* information from the ARS sensors also can be used to optimize the management of fertilizer applications. This is because a relationship exists between protein levels and the amount of nitrogen found in the soil. Benefits include environmental protection and cost savings through more efficient fertilizer use.

Fuel cells were another promising application for optical sensors during the middle of the first decade of the 2000s. According to *Machine Design,* researchers at Oak Ridge National Laboratory (ORNL) developed sensors that incorporate luminescence technology with fiber optics. These new sensors could be used for fuel cells that provide energy for everything from machines and buildings to the newest vehicles. In its February 3, 2005, issue, the publication explained: "Key to the success of the ORNL sensors is their ability to measure temperature and moisture within an operating fuel cell. This lets developers of proton-exchange membrane fuel cells verify computer

models of fuel-cell stocks to optimize performance. Furthermore, real time diagnostic sensors let designers increase stack power density by reducing operating margins and quickly identify the development of hot spots that could cause catastrophic failure."

One promising possibility involved using optical sensing to tap into hidden reserves in existing oil fields. Given the high fuel prices of the decade, oil companies were looking for ways to gain access to reserves. According to Paul Sanders of Weatherford International as reported in *Laser Focus World,* only about 30 percent of oil reserves are extracted; much of the oil reserve is mixed with sand and rock and is too expensive to separate out. Two-thirds of these oil reserves are "stuck" in the earth and must be heated to get out, which is where optical sensing comes in. By providing continuous multipoint pressure and temperature data, optical sensing can help oil producers be more efficient and better able to find and extract the oil reserves. Pat Edsell, president and CEO of NP Photonics, described the role of optical sensing in sea-bottom oil reserve monitoring in *Laser Focus World*: "The goal is to put a grid of optical fibers and sensors on the ocean floor to cover an entire reservoir (10 to 20 wells) and monitor the reservoir on a real-time basis. With this kind of active monitoring, people in the oil industry believe they can double the amount of reserves that are recovered." Optical sensing was also being used to monitor existing oil wells.

Another important developing application involves the use of optical sensing to manage electrical power grids in major cities. Service providers must monitor the flow of electricity during peak periods. Optical temperature sensing provides a way to continually monitor high-power cable temperatures and ensure they do not exceed maximum allowable temperatures, thus lessening the chance of power outages. According to Clemens Pohl of the Photonic Measurement Division of Agilent, service providers " want to be able to consistently measure the cable temperature and increase the utilization as needed. This is especially important in the United States, China, India, and other countries where the power infrastructure is underdesigned."

CURRENT CONDITIONS

Despite a slumping economy (and correlative dip) in late 2008 and early 2009, the global optoelectronics industry (also referred to as the photonics industry) continued to find new applications for its components/products, resulting in record sales nearing the end of the first decade. The trend toward convergence of applications led to a number of new products and devices that typically included displays, light-emitting diodes (LED), detectors, image sensors, and lasers. Consumer mobile phones and digital assistants, netbooks and notebook displays, GPS, and other handhelds drove the market. Added to this was the 2009 conversion from analog to high-definition digital television (HDTV), with many consumers splurging in new, wide screen TVs employing liquid crystal displays (LCD) (also used in mobile and camera phones). According to the Optoelectronics Industry Development Association (OIDA), the global market for optoelectronics-enabled products and components reached $745 billion in 2008 revenues, forecast to reach $1.3 trillion by 2020, with the biggest driver being LCD displays. Growing 5.5 percent from the 2007 market at $709 billion, the industry was projected to maintain a minimum compound annual growth rate (CAGR) of 5.3 percent through 2020.

Michael Lebby, president and CEO of OIDA, has raised national awareness of new and important issues in the photonics arena, such as the use of more photonics in broadband networks; the threat of fiber optic communication network-choking (especially in core systems as traffic continues to grow); technical challenges of photonic integrated circuits (PICs); new opportunities for photonic sensing, and energy efficient photonic solutions such as: thin film multijunction solar cells, plastic photonics (flexible lighting solutions), and novel applications of high brightness LEDs in consumer markets for solid state lighting.

In 2009, the green photonics technology, including the organic LED (OLED), became the technology expected to drive the next generation of consumer product displays (television, monitors, notebook displays, etc.). OLED displays are bright, thin, efficient, and labeled organic because they are made from carbon and hydrogen.

Within the optoelectronic-enabled products and components sector of the industry, the projected growth drivers for the second decade include solar, computing/processing, medical care, and consumer displays/TVs, according to OIDA.

According to Strategies Unlimited in its August 2009 report, *Image Sensors: Market Review and Forecast-2009,* the market for image sensors was expected to end 2009 with a decline to $6.4 billion, representing a drop of 11 percent from 2008 and the first decline since Strategies Unlimited began tracking the market in 1997.

INDUSTRY LEADERS

The most important companies in the optical sensor market are defense contractors that have been involved in cutting edge research for the government. Recent consolidation of the aerospace and defense industry, tied to federal spending cutbacks, has left only four major players in the industry: The Boeing Co., Lockheed Martin Corp.,

Raytheon Co., and Northrop Grumman Corp. Citing a concern about the lack of competition for military contracts, federal regulators barred further consolidation in 1998 when they protested the proposed merger of Lockheed Martin and Northrop Grumman.

The Boeing Company Boeing is the world's largest aerospace firm and in 2007 ranked as the second largest maker of commercial jets (behind Airbus) and second largest defense contractor (behind Lockheed Martin). The Chicago-based company manufactures planes, missiles, rockets, helicopters, space-faring vehicles, and advanced communications systems. After a series of acquisitions in the late 1990s, including McDonnell Douglas in 1997 and Hughes Electronics' satellite division in 1999, Boeing became the leading aerospace company. Buoyed by the acquisition of the space and defense unit of Rockwell International Corp. in 1996, Boeing also serves as the largest contractor to NASA. Boeing projects include communications satellites, missiles, the Space Shuttle (with Lockheed), and the International Space Station. Boeing's 2009 revenue guidance was $68 to $69 billion.

Lockheed Martin Corporation Lockheed Martin, the world's leading defense firm in 2007, is a major industry player through its Electronic Systems division. The company has made numerous contributions over the years, including the development of a remote sensing satellite that provides high resolution black-and-white imagery as well as multi-spectral images, to highlight chlorophyll content, chemical composition, surface water penetration, and other environmental features. The satellite's main advantage was a digital imaging sensor that can provide images with a resolution of one meter from 680 kilometers in altitude. The Maryland-based company also builds warplanes, rockets, and fire control systems and manages government projects. Government contracts make up about 70 percent of the company's sales. Total sales for Lockheed Martin stood at $42.7 billion in 2008 with 146,000 employees.

Raytheon Company Raytheon was another large aerospace and defense company in the middle of the first decade of the 2000s, specializing in missile systems, aircraft, and electronics. The company was a major industry player with its HISAR airborne surveillance system, which utilized forward-looking infrared sensors, as well as long-range optical sensors. HISAR had civil applications, as well as uses for national security, multi-mission radar, and the airborne and ground segments. Raytheon doubled in size when it bought the defense electronics division of Texas Instruments Inc. for $3 billion and the aerospace and defense division of Hughes for $9.5 billion from parent company General Motors in 1997. Also that year, Raytheon supplied a major sensing system for the refurbished Hubble Space Telescope. In 1998 the company began a major joint initiative with the U.S. Army to reduce the cost of night vision sensors and broaden their commercial applications. About 85 percent of the company's revenue comes from the U.S. government (defense related). The company posted revenues of $23.2 billion in 2008.

L-3 Communications Holdings New York-based L-3 Communications Holdings designs, manufactures, and sells a wide range of thermal imaging products and solutions serving the security, firefighting, public safety, transportation, industrial, and homeland security markets. Notable product applications are search and rescue, perimeter surveillance, industrial process monitoring, and automotive and truck night vision. May 2003 marked the introduction of the X100, a palm-sized thermal imaging camera, allowing safety and security officers to easily see people and objects that are virtually invisible to the naked eye, even when shrouded in darkness. It was used by 101st Airborne Division troops during Operation Iraqi Freedom. By mid-2005, L-3 marketed its uncooled infrared camera cores and products under the Thermal-Eye and NIGHTDRIVER brand names. Sales in 2008 totaled $14.9 billion with more than 60,000 employees.

Northrop Grumman Corporation Northrop Grumman became a powerhouse in defense electronics and systems integration with two acquisitions: the 1996 purchase of a defense and electronics arm from Westinghouse Electric Corp. and the 1997 acquisition of Logicon Inc., an information and battle-management systems maker. After its merger with Lockheed Martin was blocked, Northrop Grumman began to refocus its operations to remain competitive, which included putting some of its aircraft parts units up for sale. In December 2002 the company acquired TRW's military electronics business for $7.8 billion in stock plus assumption of approximately $4.8 billion in TRW debt. The additional purchases of Litton Industries and Newport News made Northrop Grumman the number three defense contractor. Northrop Grumman serves U.S. and international military, government, and commercial customers, and produces about 70 different types of sensors and systems. With 123,600 employees and operations in all 50 states and 25 countries, the company had sales of $33.9 billion in 2008.

AMERICA AND THE WORLD
The United States and Europe represent the largest consumers of infrared and other optical sensors, and U.S. companies manufacture the majority of the sensors used in the United States. Foreign companies have little visibility in the U.S. market, except perhaps in the area of digital camera sensors, a market segment in which Japanese companies such as Mitsubishi and Olympus Optical are very active. Nonetheless, innovative sensor technologies are being produced by small firms. For example, the French company Bureau Etudes Vision Stockplus developed an advanced visual recognition chip that mimics the human eye and can accept infrared, video, or radar signals.

Asia remained a key target for U.S. and European makers of optical sensors. They anticipated strong growth as these economies continue to recover, according to Frost & Sullivan. In addition, the Electronic Industries Association noted that Asia "will continue as the world's premier growth market." Frost & Sullivan expected China to become a significant player in the world sensor market. Other important markets during the early twenty-first century included Argentina and Brazil.

During the first decade of the 2000s, one strong market for optical sensors was the building automation sector, where building management systems (BMS) were being used to monitor functions and activity in old and new buildings alike. By relying on data from optical readers and sensors, building managers were able to monitor building functions from one centralized locations. In addition, they were able to obtain data on a building's performance. This latter task was increasingly important in the wake of environmental regulations such as the Kyoto Protocol, which required the tracking of energy consumption. In addition, by the beginning of 2005, the European Union was in the process of developing building performance reporting standards.

RESEARCH AND TECHNOLOGY
The year 2009 saw an explosion of interest in OLED technology (organic light emitting diodes made of carbon and hyrdrogen), with GE, Samsung, and LG stepping up their research budgets to accommodate the burgeoning market. The main applications for OLED were lighting and display panels (e.g., monitors).

Like most high-tech fields, research is the lifeblood of the optical sensor industry. During the first decade of the 2000s, a number of promising developments were underway—especially in the military sector. For example, the Department of Homeland Security and the Pentagon were concentrating on the development of both individual sensors and complete sensing systems that could identify bombs and land mines through the detection of explosive vapor traces. In addition, the U.S. Air Force had equipped most of its Predator unmanned aerial vehicles with infrared video cameras and high magnification optical sensors to zero in on enemy targets.

Developments also were under way at the Defense Advanced Research Projects Agency (DARPA), which was focused on pervasive sensing technology that could give U.S. troops significant advantages on the battlefield. As Jeff Hecht explained in the July 2004 issue of *Laser Focus World*, "DARPA is looking at exploiting emerging sensing techniques to identify and track potential targets on the battlefield. One example is the collection of three-dimensional data with laser radars that can reach through holes in the forest canopy and manipulating that data to view objects from other perspectives and identify enemy targets. Another example is the collection, correlation, and processing of images collected by unmanned aerial vehicles flying above the battlefield. Thomas M. Strat of DARPA envisions a future battlefield with 'droves of UAVs bristling with sensors,' able to watch everything that moves. Current staff and systems couldn't cope with the flood of image data, but Strat suggests that new processing technology could handle the load by tracking individual targets continually, rather than searching for them again and again."

In the same *Laser Focus World* article, Hecht noted that the industry also was focused on "sensor fusion," or using distributed optical sensors in a collective manner so that one picture can be formed from many different pieces of information. In this scenario, data from different sensors are combined to reach one conclusion, in the same way that someone might identify a problem with their automobile by hearing a particular noise and smelling something unusual.

Two key areas of research in the optical sensor industry are micro-electrical mechanical systems (MEMS) and un-cooled infrared sensors. The most important area of research affecting the optical sensor industry is the miniaturization/digitalization of sensor technology. Pressure sensors and accelerometers are already being micro-machined on silicon chips, and research is under way to extend micro-machining and its extremely cheap batch-processing capabilities to infrared sensors.

Bell Labs developed the world's first laser-based, semiconductor sensor. The sensor operates at room temperature and can detect minute amounts of trace gases or pollutants (potentially parts per billion). Its power and range are unprecedented for the mid-infrared region of the spectrum. It has been called a revolutionary development for sensor applications because it opens up a new field of un-cooled tunable infrared sensors.

BIBLIOGRAPHY

"And So It Begins." *Aviation Week & Space Technology,* 7 April 2003.

"Boeing's Huntington Beach, Calif.—Based Rocket Business Still Faces Probe." *Knight-Ridder/Tribune Business News,* 26 July 2003.

Databeans, Inc. *2009 Image Sensors.* Abstract, October 2009. Available from http://www.the-infoshop.com/report/data90290-image-sensor.html.

"Death by Data." *Forbes,* 6 January 2003.

"Does the Eiffel Tower Twist?" *Machine Design,* 6 January 2005.

"The National Institute for Standards and Technology (NIST; Washington, D.C.) and Utah State University (Logan, UT) Signed a Partnership Agreement to Develop and Calibrate Optical Sensors." *Laser Focus World,* May 2005.

Goodman, Glenn. "Watchful Eyes in the Sky." *Defense News,* 21 February 2005.

Hal, Kenji, and Hiroko Tashiro. "Potty Talk from Japan: The Country's Love of Gadgets and its Obsession with Cleanliness Have Taken Toilets High-Tech." *Business Week Online,* 3 January 2007. Available from www.businessweek.com.

Hect, Jeff. "Ever Vigilant, Optical Sensors Already Monitor Much of Our Daily Lives." *Laser Focus World,* July 2004.

"Hoover's Company Capsules." *Hoover's Online.* 1 April 2007. Available from http://www.hoovers.com.

"In the Focus: the Photonics Industry 3." OIDA Press Release. *Photonics,* 2009. Available from http://www.photonics21.org/download/In_the_focus.pdf.

Kincade, Kathy. "Biomedical Sensors Benefit from Biodefense Efforts." *Laser Focus World,* July 2006.

Lockheed. *Washington Technology Top 100,* Available from http://washington technology.com/toplists/top-100-lists/2009/1-lockheed-martin.aspx.

Mokhbery, Javad. "Making Sense of Orthopedic Technologies." *Medical Design Technology,* February 2007.

"The *Forbes* Platinum List Company of the Year, Northrup Grumman." *Forbes,* 6 January 2003.

Northrop Grumman. Available from http://washingtontechnology.com/toplists/top-100-lists/2009/3-northrop-grumman.aspx.

"Optical Sensors Enhance Oil and Gas Yields." *Laser Focus World,* September 2006.

"Optical Sensors Guide to High-Quality Wheat." *Western Farm Press,* 5 February 2005.

Overton, Gail. "Photonics and the Energy Crisis." *Laser Focus World,* September 2006.

"Pentagon Punishes Boeing for Rocket Trade Secret Scandal." *Knight-Ridder/Tribune Business News,* 25 July 2003.

"Sensors Could Improve Fuel-Cell Models." *Machine Design,* 3 February 2005.

"USAF Unit Alerts NASA to On-Orbit Hazards." *Aviation Week & Space Technology,* 17 February 2003.

"Worldwide Market for Building Management Systems to Cross $71 Billion by 2009." *Research Studies-Business Communications Inc.,* 11 January 2005.

OUTSOURCING

—■—

INDUSTRY SNAPSHOT

Outsourcing occurs when companies opt to have an outside party perform a task that was once handled in house. Examples of outsourcing range from manufacturing parts and products to high level professional functions like accounting, computer programming, engineering, and legal work. Outsourcing also extends to back end business processes, such as billing and accounts payable, as well as human resource functions like payroll and benefits administration. Outsourcing is a major strategic decision for organizations, because they must balance a loss of direct control over a process or function in exchange for cost savings, which can range from 15 to 40 percent, as well as heightened competitive advantage, the ability to provide more efficient service, and reduced time to market with new products and services.

When companies outsource a function or process to another country, the practice is called "offshoring" when far-away nations such as India are involved or "nearshoring" in the case of geographically closer countries like Mexico. Offshoring is popular because of the tremendous cost savings that can be achieved. For example, some estimates indicate that companies can save anywhere from 20 to 70 percent on labor by offshoring to low cost nations like India, China, and the Philippines.

U.S. companies had been outsourcing for several decades. After catching on during the early 1990s, outsourcing began to achieve explosive growth, especially in the manufacturing sector, where nearly 90 percent of U.S. industrial enterprises had outsourced at least one function by the turn of the new century, according to Cutting Edge Information, a Durham, North Carolina-based consultancy. During the early part of the decade, the practice was receiving a growing amount of attention. Critics blamed outsourcing for the so-called jobless recovery that was underway as the nation slowly emerged from an economic recession—as conditions improved, the number of unemployed workers remained relatively high. However, others countered that the number of jobs lost specifically to outsourcing was quite low and that job growth was hindered more by factors like rising productivity. In addition, they argued that as U.S. companies outsourced some employees, this allowed for the creation of new, higher level jobs, and that the loss of U.S. jobs to sources abroad was offset by foreign investment.

Although leading analysts and economists could not reach a consensus on the exact number of U.S. jobs outsourced in recent years, or on future projections, one thing seemed clear: outsourcing was a permanent and growing trend. The practice was especially prevalent in the information technology (IT), telemarketing/customer service, and health care fields.

ORGANIZATION AND STRUCTURE

Industry Players Large, multinational companies are at the very heart of the outsourcing industry, as they constitute the client base for a wide variety of service providers. The main reason companies often cite for choosing to outsource is because highly specialized service providers are often able to perform a function better and more efficiently than in-house staff. However, the outsourcing approach has a number of other advantages for them. Probably the most significant advantage is cost savings as a result of lower staffing levels, reduced operational costs, and a decline in capital expenditures. In addition, business enterprises claim they are able to better focus their resources on what they do best. It is also asserted that companies usually hold outsourcing vendors more accountable than in-house staff, which in theory ensures high quality work. Finally, it is claimed that outsourcing can provide a company with immediate access to resources that are not available in-house or which would be expensive to maintain. This view even extends to the use of contract employees, who can be quickly hired to form specialized task forces or departments.

However, outsourcing is not a panacea for every corporate challenge or problem. If not executed properly, the results can be negative. As the *Journal of Business Strategy* explained in its March-April 2004 issue, although there are many benefits associated with outsourcing, "many organizations are naive about the commitment and discipline it takes to reap these benefits. Organizations fail to realize the impacts on their people, processes, methods and tools as they proceed down the outsourcing path. This naive attitude results in outsourcing engagements that are too often disastrous rather than fruitful experiences for corporations. For instance, companies have outsourced legacy systems maintenance, application development, and business processes for the last decade and are still struggling to clearly measure cost savings, service levels and customer satisfaction."

While outsourcing service providers are sometimes located in the United States, they increasingly are located in Mexico, South America, or overseas, where lower operational costs make them attractive to U.S. firms. In its April 2004 issue, *Fast Company* indicated that according to research firm Gartner Inc., 40 percent of all

Fortune 500 companies were expected to have outsourced work to other nations by the year's end. U.S. firms such as Accenture and IBM Global Services, as well as India-based offshoring providers, continued to expand their operations in markets like China and Latin America. By 2007, Wipro, Ltd., a Bangalore outsourcer, had begun two centers in China and others in Romania, Brazil, and Canada.

Consultants are another critical component of the outsourcing industry. They provide strategic advice to companies that are considering or actively engaged in outsourcing. For this reason, Infosys—a leading Indian outsourcing services provider specializing in information technology (IT)—formed its own U.S.-based consulting subsidiary in April 2004. The firm was led by a team of business consulting heavyweights, including CEO Stephen Pratt, who in 2003 was dubbed one of the world's top 25 consultants by *Consulting Magazine.*

In addition to Infosys's new firm, many of the business world's older, established consulting players also are involved in the outsourcing game. Ernst & Young LLP was one leading global consultancy that helped companies to successfully implement and manage outsourcing initiatives. It accomplished this through its Business Risk Services unit, which helped companies perform risk assessments, engage in strategic planning, manage licensing, improve operational processes, evaluate third party vendors, and more. Ernst & Young worked with organizations to help them outsource specific functional elements or entire processes.

Accenture was another leading global consulting enterprise that assisted companies to use outsourcing as part of a strategy for maximizing performance. During the twenty-first century's first decade, the company offered consulting services in three main areas: business process outsourcing, application outsourcing, and technology infrastructure outsourcing.

Outsourcing consulting was not exclusive to large consulting firms. Smaller operations, such as Houston, Texas-based Backes Crocker LLC, also worked with companies to start new outsourcing initiatives or manage existing ones. Claiming to have simplified the outsourcing process, Backes Crocker offered clients something at each critical step. Its services included an offshore outsourcing audit, as well as business analysis and strategic resource planning. Backes Crocker also provided assistance selecting and evaluating vendors, negotiating contracts, managing projects and vendors, and providing ongoing evaluation.

In addition to advising companies on outsourcing matters, consulting firms also served as an information resource for leading newspapers and business magazines. They also educated businesspeople through newsletters, white papers, case studies, press releases, and presentations. For example, in 2004, McKinsey & Company, a leading consulting enterprise with roots dating back to 1926, hosted a leadership breakfast in New York for business executives that featured an expert panel discussion. Moderated by *New York Times* foreign affairs columnist Tom Friedman, the panel included Jeffrey Garten, dean of the Yale School of Management; Diana Farrell, director of the McKinsey Global Institute; and AFL-CIO Director of Corporate Affairs Ron Blackwell.

Domestic and offshore service providers are the third major component of the outsourcing industry in that they are responsible for performing outsourced tasks and processes for companies. By 2004, the fact that leading companies like Bank of America, IBM, Citibank, and General Electric were acquiring outsourcing providers or investing in them was a testament to their staying power. Because these entities are as diverse as the industries they serve and the tasks they perform, it is difficult to make generalizations about them as a large group. One way to gain deeper insight into the outsourcing industry is by looking at some of the major categories in which service providers operate.

Types of Outsourcing Generally speaking, outsourcing operates under one of two main models. Business process outsourcing (BPO) involves transferring the management of a function or service from a company's in-house staff to an outside service provider. The application service provider (ASP) model involves companies contracting with an outside firm that already provides a specialized function or service as opposed to transferring an existing function to them. The term application service provider (ASP) is often used to describe software-hosting arrangements but has been used more broadly in the context of outsourcing. Although these are presented as two distinct models for the sake of example, in actuality there is a great deal of variation in how outsourcing arrangements are made. Each situation is different and can vary depending on the nature of the function or service, the companies involved, and numerous other factors.

By the first decade of the twenty-first century, companies had been outsourcing manufacturing work to low cost nations for some time. However, a relatively recent development was the outsourcing of clerical, technical, and service level jobs. Even white-collar professionals like accountants, attorneys, and engineers were being outsourced in growing numbers. This trend was occurring as companies outsourced such "back office" functions as accounts receivable, claims processing, customer analytics, data processing, legal research, payment services, procurement, tax processing, and transaction processing.

In addition to the aforementioned back end processes, companies also were outsourcing various human resource management (HRM) functions during the early years of the twenty-first century's first decade. In some cases, entire HRM departments were being replaced with so-called professional employer organizations (PEOs), which assumed legal responsibility for a company's workers and managed the important details of hiring, compensation, and termination.

According to the Alexandria, Virginia-based National Association of Professional Employer Organizations (NAPEO), "Businesses today need help managing increasingly complex employee related matters such as health benefits, workers' compensation claims, payroll, payroll tax compliance, and unemployment insurance claims. They contract with a PEO to assume these responsibilities and provide expertise in human resources management. This allows the PEO client to concentrate on the operational and revenue-producing side of its operations." In 2006, NAPEO reported that there were approximately 700 PEOs operating in all 50 states, generating annual revenues of about $51 billion.

The IT industry was garnering widespread attention as a growing number of technology jobs were being "offshored," especially in the area of help desk and application development. Research issued by Foote Partners in 2003 estimated that 35 to 45 percent of IT workers in the United States and Canada would be replaced by a combination of part time workers, consultants, independent contractors, and offshore technicians by 2005. Although some claimed this prediction was somewhat aggressive, it was clear that a growing number of IT jobs were moving offshore.

Despite this emerging trend, some IT companies opted to keep work in-house at the risk of losing control. Still others experienced problems after outsourcing certain types of IT work. For example, some offshore employees have developed flawed applications that need extensive fixing back in the United States. On the help desk front, bad telephone connections and communication (language) barriers have angered customers. At the risk of losing business, this has prompted some software companies to back out of offshoring operations and revive higher-cost domestic operations.

Following the tech boom of the 1990s, when IT workers commanded high wages, the shift of IT jobs to low cost nations led to heated criticism by those who lost good paying jobs, as well as some politicians and media personalities. Indeed, some observers have said that high level IT jobs were slowly becoming analogous to those of textile workers.

By 2006, talk of IT offshoring was causing many students to avoid careers in this field. However, there was evidence that some areas of IT would continue to remain based on U.S. soil, and that the state of affairs was not as bad as some reports led the public to believe. In 2006, the Association for Computing Machinery released its ACM Job Migration study, which sought to separate fact from myth. In the February 2006 issue of *Communications of the ACM,* ACM President David A. Patterson explained that according to U.S. government figures, IT employment was at an all-time high. Patterson remarked that "Annual job losses to outsourcing have been no more than 2%-3% of the U.S. IT work force—and probably less."

By the twenty-first century's first decade, customer service call centers were being outsourced in greater numbers. Many U.S. and European firms—namely in the technology, financial services, and telecommunications industries—were opting to use call centers in Latin America, where employees worked for as little as $2.00 an hour. This especially was true for customer service calls that required Spanish-speaking representatives.

According to "Call Center Outsourcing in Latin America and the Caribbean to 2008," a report issued by research firm Datamonitor, the countries of Brazil, Mexico, and Argentina were fueling a compound annual growth rate of 16.8 percent for call center agent positions in Latin America. This was in comparison to slightly more than 15 percent in the Asia Pacific region and just above 7 percent in the market comprised of Africa, the Middle East, and Europe. In the United States, call center agent positions were growing at a paltry rate of less than 1 percent.

Although Datamonitor's report indicated that the United States was outsourcing some 10,600 customer service positions to Latin America each year, these represented only a small fraction of the industry's overall workforce. For example, the United States was home to nearly 2.9 million call center agent positions in 2004. Datamonitor estimated that a mere 0.9 percent of all U.S. call center jobs would be outsourced to Latin America each year by 2008, representing a total of 25,100 positions. In addition to Latin America, U.S. companies also were outsourcing call center positions to India and the Philippines. In May of 2004, *Forbes* referred to a reported loss of 250,000 call center positions to these nations, a number that is much higher than Datamonitor's estimations for the Latin American market.

The health care industry also was using outsourcing quite heavily by the middle of the twenty-first century's first decade. This especially was true of hospitals and large health care systems. However, with the exception of medical transcription services provided by Indian firms, many functions, including food services and supply chain management, were being outsourced to highly specialized domestic firms that offered greater levels of efficiency.

Beyond purely operational functions such as food service and materials management, health care providers were outsourcing some aspects of patient care and customer relations. One example involved medical contact centers or call lines that hospitals use to field calls from health care consumers seeking physician referrals or answers to general health questions. In 2006, Portland, Maine-based IntelliCare Inc. served more than 250 health systems, hospitals, physician practices, and health plans with what it called the nation's largest network of medical contact centers. By switching to IntelliCare, health care providers were able to offer expanded phone coverage to callers without incurring staffing costs. In addition, they were able to immediately scale call coverage during peak times.

On the patient care side, Mequon, Wisconsin-based Infinity HealthCare (IHC) specialized in the outsourced staffing and management of hospital emergency rooms and physician practices. In business for more than 25 years, the company offered hospitals a variety of related services including human resources, information management, and strategic planning. In addition to board-certified emergency physicians, radiologists, and occupational medicine/preventive health specialists, Infinity had a medical informatics division that concentrated on patient information systems.

BACKGROUND AND DEVELOPMENT

Examples of outsourcing can be found throughout global economic history. In a March 29, 2004, *Wall Street Journal* article, Bob Davis cited several cases, one of which involved the British textile industry of the 1830s. At that time, increased efficiency in Britain's textile mills made it so that Indian cloth makers could not compete, forcing India to obtain its textiles from Britain instead of producing items domestically.

By the twentieth and early twenty-first centuries, similar factors were at work, as skilled machinists saw their companies send jobs to developing nations with much lower labor costs. The same became true of skilled technology workers and even professionals such as engineers. Comparing past developments to early twenty-first century events, Davis remarked, "As Americans grapple with the fallout of shipping hundreds of thousands of jobs overseas, history echoes with many similar episodes—and lessons. Trade and technology can boost living standards for many people, by creating lower-priced goods. However, those same forces can destroy skilled jobs that workers thought never would be threatened."

Although U.S. companies had previously outsourced to some extent, the practice of outsourcing and offshoring exploded in popularity during the 1990s. Led by established multinational enterprises like General Electric and American Express, outsourcing during this time period received scant attention because of the prolific job growth that occurred along with the then booming economy.

In general, outsourcing became popular because it helped companies to improve efficiency, cut costs, and bolster their bottom lines. Although many outsourcing initiatives were implemented on shore, involving only U.S. companies, in time the number of nearshore and offshore implementations skyrocketed, especially in the IT sector. This was supported by several large trends that were unfolding at about the same time. First was the rapid evolution of India's technology market from the late 1970s to the 1990s. Another major development was the advent of the Internet and World Wide Web during the 1990s. This occurred in tandem with faster computers and an improved telecommunications infrastructure, making data transmission and processing more practical than ever before. Finally, the Y2K scare created an unprecedented demand for IT workers to fix potential problems, and India had an ample supply.

By the early years of the twenty-first century's first decade, many companies found global outsourcing necessary in order to compete and even survive. However, the practice was repeatedly criticized for hurting the U.S. job market as the nation recovered from an economic recession and many unemployed workers were unable to find new positions.

By 2004, some estimates placed the global outsourcing market's value at $350 billion. With much at stake, the debate over outsourcing's impact on the United States' jobless economic recovery continued. Some industry observers laid partial blame for this phenomenon on outsourcing, while proponents continued to argue that global trade caused growth in the U.S. economy that balanced the effects of any job loss. Those in favor of globalization said it led to "insourcing," a term used to describe foreign companies outsourcing to the United States, as well as a rise in purchased services from foreign nations.

Indeed, there were numbers to support the case for globalization. For example, in its April 12, 2004 issue, the *The Wall Street Journal* provided statistics from the U.S. Department of Commerce and the National Association of Software and Service Companies showing that the amount of U.S. services purchased by India increased from slightly more than $1 billion in 1992 to more than $3 billion in 2002. This increase followed the steady rise in Indian employees who perform services for offshore clients, a number that increased from 152,000 in 2000 to 505,000 in 2004. Furthermore, in its May 1, 2004 issue, *National Real Estate Investor* cited figures from the U.S. Department of Commerce indicating that

the United States performed $131 billion in services on behalf of foreign customers in 2003, outpacing services provided offshore for U.S. companies by $53 billion.

However, in the May 3, 2004, issue of *U.S. News & World Report,* former Assistant Treasury Secretary Paul Craig Roberts was critical of the term insourcing, stating: "This notion of insourcing is a propaganda device. What they're calling insourcing is nothing but just standard foreign investment." In the same article, writer and TV anchor Lou Dobbs pointed out that much of this foreign investment came not in the form of new plants and equipment from foreign enterprise but from the purchase of existing American assets. Dobbs also cited figures from the Economic Policy Institute revealing that "just 6.2 percent of the job growth by foreign firms in America is newly created jobs."

By 2004, resistance to offshoring existed at the federal and state levels. At the federal level, the U.S. Senate had approved a proposal in support of withholding government funding to companies that engaged in offshoring. In addition, some 30 states were in the process of developing bills in opposition to offshoring.

IT jobs represented a sizable share of the jobs companies were outsourcing in the early years of the twenty-first century's first decade. In December 2003 alone, IBM transferred almost 5,000 programming jobs to China and India. According to the aforementioned statistics from the U.S. Department of Commerce and the National Association of Software and Service Companies, of the 505,000 outsourcing jobs listed for India in 2004, more than 250,000 were IT workers. The statistics illustrated that the number of IT jobs being outsourced to India has increased steadily since 2000, when the total was slightly more than 100,000. While IT workers accounted for roughly two-thirds of all the outsourcing jobs listed in these figures for that year, by 2004 they accounted for about half.

The practice of offshoring remained at the forefront of the outsourcing industry heading into the later years of the first decade of the twenty-first century as economic globalization continued to grow at an unfettered pace. According to *Forbes,* in 2006 the McKinsey Global Institute estimated that offshore employment, including banking and information technology (IT) jobs, would total 1.2 million by 2008. This was double the number of jobs in 2003.

The debate regarding offshoring's impact on the U.S. economy continued to rage on. Opponents of the practice—including those who had lost their jobs because of offshoring—continued to criticize corporations for what they viewed as greed. However, others argued that globalization has been a windfall for many U.S. firms that have found new markets for their products and services. In May 2006, *Inc* reported that the United States exported $58 billion worth of surplus services in 2005 alone.

While there is no questioning the fact that offshoring has led to job loss for some workers, some reports indicate that, on a large scale, the impact has not been as severe in developed countries as news reports might lead one to believe. In its June 27, 2005, issue, *Fortune* detailed the results of a study from the McKinsey Global Institute, which found that while the potential existed for about one-tenth of all service jobs to be outsourced worldwide, by 2008 this figure was only expected to be 1 percent. Representing 4.1 million jobs, some would argue that this total is still large. However, the publication indicated that about 4.6 million people started new jobs in the United States.

Adding additional perspective to the situation, *Forbes* noted that "shockingly enough, the size of the available talent pool offshore isn't as large as you might think. It turns out that only a fraction of those dirt-cheap engineers, financiers, accountants, scientists, and other professionals churned out by universities in China, India, and elsewhere can be put to effective use by multinational corporations anytime soon. The big problems include inadequate foreign language proficiency, lack of practical skills, unwillingness to move for a job, and limited or no access to airports and other transportation networks."

In the April 12, 2004, issue of *The Wall Street Journal*, Mark Zandi, an economist with Economy.com, estimated that some 300,000 U.S. manufacturing and white collar jobs were being offshored each year—a number that he expected to reach 600,000 by 2010. Ravi Aron, a professor at the University of Pennsylvania's Wharton School, estimated that some 440,000 white collar jobs were outsourced to India and other countries between 2000 and 2004. Finally, John McCarthy of Cambridge, Massachusetts-based Forrester Research, estimated that less than 300,000 white collar jobs had been outsourced as of early 2004 but projected that as the use of outsourcing gradually increased, some 3.3 million jobs would be offshored by 2015.

A better understanding of the larger outsourcing workforce can be gained by looking at the types of jobs and job functions that were being outsourced or offshored in the early to middle years of the twenty-first century's first decade. In its April 2004 issue, *Fast Company* provided information that it compiled in conjunction with the University of California Berkeley Fisher Center for Real Estate and Urban Economics and Careerplanner.com regarding jobs that were most likely to be offshored, ranking them by risk level. According to Careerplanner.com President Michael T. Robinson, all

knowledge workers bore at least some risk for being offshored.

One emerging trend was a movement by offshoring providers to, in turn, offshore some of their own services. In 2006 Brazil, Chile, China, the Czech Republic, Hungary, Mauritius, and Uruguay were key offshoring markets for India-based outsourcing firms like Tata Consultancy Services, Infosys Technologies, and Wipro. Even U.S. companies like Accenture and IBM Global Services were opening new offices or increasing staff in markets like these. In addition to allowing them to serve a more global customer base, moving to markets such as these allowed providers to access a plentiful base of talented workers.

CURRENT CONDITIONS

In a December 2009 press release, global outsourcing leader Luxoft issued its 2010 predictions for the outsourcing industry. Identifying 2010 as a year marked by economic recovery, Luxoft noted that 2009 had been a year of substantial budget and staff cuts, but the volume of work remained the same, creating tremendous pressure for cost-savings and a re-thinking for new business models and strategies. This would manifest in part with companies shifting their focus from long-term contracts to project-based assignments with increased transparency. Luxoft also predicted that outsourcing clients would begin to shift from employing hundreds of different vendors to (instead) maintaining a short-list portfolio of strategic and versatile outsources.

Luxoft went on to list several trends and "hot" areas for 2010. First, it identified key areas where demand for outsourcing was expected to by dynamic. Investment banking was mentioned first and foremost, partly because of new government regulations being imposed. The energy field was another area, with the development of renewable energy technology and "smart" energy initiatives and devices. Another was technological advancements in social media, with a wave of new mobile and web applications, including Natural Language Processing technologies. Luxoft also predicted that cloud computing, especially SaaS applications and cloud platforms from Amazon and Google, would become an important platform for the outsourcing industry, particularly in the areas of client-vendor relationships and communications.

Said Kathleen Goolsby in her 2009 outlook for *Outsourcing Journal*, "Outsourcing will begin moving away from doing work in isolated pockets (buying an application from one provider, computing capacity from another, and outsourcing a business process to another) and move toward providers that can deliver all such aspects in one bundled offering at a pricing structure that suits the buyer's needs...This movement is beginning to happen now and will increase in niche areas over the next three to five years."

With respect to crunching the numbers, Canada-based XMG Global, in a report released in September 2009, valued the world's outsourcing market at $373 billion. The report showed a 14.4 percent growth expectation for 2009. Vincent Altez, senior analyst at XMG, noted that offshoring and outsourcing were "part of a natural ongoing economic revolution notwithstanding a financial crisis."

Revenues for worldwide cloud services, reported Gartner Inc. research firm in March 2009, were expected to surpass $56.3 billion by the end of the year, up from $46.4 billion in 2008. Cloud computing provides (as a free service) scalable and elastic IT-enabled capabilities to external customers using Internet technologies. The service represents a growing sector of the market expected to eventually replace direct payment and purchase for services. Instead, with the service provided free, revenues are generated from advertising. Google, Yahoo, Microsoft, and others are good examples of cloud-based services.

INDUSTRY LEADERS

Administaff Inc. With 2008 sales of $1.7 billion, Houston, Texas-based Administaff Inc. was among the leading professional employer organizations (PEOs) during the twenty-first century's first decade. According to the company, it managed some 96,000 workers for more than 5,000 small and medium-sized U.S. companies, serving as an off-site human resources department.

Administaff has been recognized by *Fortune* as one of America's "Most Admired Companies," and by *InformationWeek* for information technology innovation. In fact, the company's clients and worksite employees can receive assistance or access online employment information from any computer at any time.

In 2006, via its Personnel Management System, Administaff served clients from more than 40 sales offices and four regional service centers in 21 U.S. markets. Its range of human resources (HR) services included benefits management, employment administration, employer liability management, government compliance, owner support, performance management, recruiting and selection, and training and development.

Infosys Technologies Limited Infosys was an established leader in the realm of information technology offshoring, with 52,700 employees and revenues of roughly $4.4 billion in 2009. Based in Bangalore, India with U.S. headquarters in Fremont, California, Infosys also served a number of other international markets, including Australia, Belgium, Canada, France, Germany, Hong Kong, Japan, the Netherlands, Singapore, Sweden, Switzerland, the United Kingdom, and the United Arab

Emirates. According to Infosys, the company employs a "low-risk Global Delivery Model (GDM) to accelerate schedules with a high degree of time and cost predictability." Its range of IT services include product engineering, consulting, and application development. Infosys serves such industry sectors as aerospace, automotive, energy and utilities, engineering, financial services, health care, life sciences, manufacturing, retail and distribution, technology, telecommunications, and transportation. The company's clients include the likes of Airbus, Boeing, and Johnson Controls.

Infosys was established in 1981 and became a publicly traded Indian firm in 1992. The company was listed on the NASDAQ in 1999, at which time revenues surpassed $100 million. It achieved rapid growth heading into the early years of the twenty-first century's first decade, with revenues reaching $400 million in 2001 and rising above $1 billion only three years later. In April of 2004, Infosys announced the formation of a new U.S.-based consulting subsidiary called Infosys Consulting Inc., which was headed by some of corporate America's leading consultants, including its new CEO Stephen Pratt, who was named as one of the world's top consultants by *Consulting Magazine* in 2003. Other key players included former Deloitte Offshore CEO Raj Joshi; Paul Cole, who previously led global operations at the consultancy CGE&Y; and Romil Bahl, who once oversaw some 5,000 consultants at the consultancy owned by technology services firm EDS. According to Infosys Consulting, it offered a host of new services to the consulting field, such as proprietary industry analyses and up-front competitive edge assessments.

Owens & Minor Inc. With roots stretching back to 1882, Mechanicsville, Virginia-based Owens & Minor got its start as a wholesale drug company. It began distributing medical and surgical supplies on an exclusive basis in 1992, and by 2006 recorded sales of $5.5 billion on the strength of 3,700 employees. Although Owens & Minor distributes supplies to some 4,000 U.S. health care providers, it also provides inventory management and logistics services for hospitals via its OMSolutions offering. This allows hospitals to outsource key staff or even entire materials management departments, enabling them to achieve cost savings through greater efficiency.

WORKFORCE

Although individual service providers are often highly specialized, the larger outsourcing industry spans a wide range of industry sectors and types of work. In addition, many outsourcing providers offer services besides outsourcing. Because of these characteristics, and the fact that outsourcing initiatives have increasingly involved sending work to foreign countries, it is impossible to compile exact figures regarding the number of employees involved in outsourcing. However, economists and industry analysts have attempted to estimate the number of U.S. jobs being outsourced.

Fast Company placed airplane mechanics, artists, carpenters, civil engineers, interior designers, and recruiters on the low-risk end of the spectrum. Those professions bearing a moderate to high risk included automotive engineers, CAD (computer-aided design) technicians, computer systems analysts, copy editors and journalists, customer service representatives, database administrators, film editors, human resources specialists, insurance agents, lab technicians, medical transcriptionists, paralegals and legal assistants, and software developers. Finally, those jobs bearing an extremely high risk of being outsourced included accountants, call center operators, help desk specialists, industrial engineers, production control specialists, quality assurance engineers, and telemarketers.

AMERICA AND THE WORLD

According to a September 2009 report by XMG Global, India held 44.8 percent of the global market revenues in 2009, followed by China, accounting for 25.9 percent. The Philippines represented the third largest revenue-maker, accounting for 6.9 percent of the total offshore market.

Europe and the United States remained the main outsourcers, although there were parts of Europe in which outsourcing was just emerging, such as the Soviet bloc countries. Here labor was cheap enough that outsourcing to India or other areas did not offer great advantages. In fact, some companies were looking to Romania for possible outsource operations. Romania's pending admission to the European Union was expected to enhance its appeal to companies looking to outsource.

India remained the number-one location for outsourcing, with $17.7 billion in software and IT services exports in 2005. However, China was pursuing the industry aggressively. In 2006 the Chinese government earmarked ten cities for development as major outsourcing centers in an effort to draw business from companies that were outsourcing to India and other locations. The Chinese government hoped to quadruple its outsourcing exports by 2010. Outsource-related revenues for the entire country were worth around $900 million in 2006, less than many individual Indian companies were making annually on their own. One of the challenges for China was the fact that its outsourcing industry was still largely fragmented, whereas much of the work in India was centered on billion-dollar firms such as Infosys. Other countries that were hotspots for outsourcing in

2007 were Malaysia, Thailand, and Brazil, according to A.T. Kearney as reported in *Information Week.*

In 2009, multinational corporations—especially from the United States and Britain—were still very much attracted to India, where they could hire professional workers for a fraction of the salaries paid to entry level college graduates in their home countries. In 2005, India's total outsourcing exports reached $22 billion, the majority of which ($17.2 billion) came from back office services and software, according to the National Association of Software and Service Companies. Despite its popularity, India faced a number of challenges in meeting this strong international demand. For starters, stiff competition prevented service providers from hiking their prices significantly. Making matters more difficult was a high turnover rate, coupled with rising labor costs.

More than ever, China—where labor costs were anywhere from 30 to 40 percent cheaper than in the United States—was an attractive alternative to India. As Darwin Partners Senior Vice President Paul Buntrock remarked in the March 20, 2006 issue of *Newsweek,* "India has a great labor pool, but its society and infrastructure aren't keeping up with growth. China has a developed industrial economy. They've got insurance companies and banks and factories. What that means is Chinese workers have technical skills like Indians do, but in China you can find skilled people who understand your clients' specific business needs, too.".

BIBLIOGRAPHY

"2006: The Year of Living Globally." *eWeek,* 22 November 2006.

"Almost 90% of U.S. Industrial Companies Outsource." *Purchasing,* 19 February 2004.

"As IT Outsourcing Deals Grow, So Do Advisory Firms." *eWeek,* 16 January 2007.

"China to Challenge India as Top Outsourcing Destination." *InformationWeek,* 12 December 2006.

Cooney, Michael. "Outsourcing Bonanza 2006." *Network World,* 13 December 2006.

Davis, Bob. "Wealth of Nations: Finding Lessons Of Outsourcing In 4 Historical Tales—Technology, Trade, Migration Often Shook Job Market; Politics Can Slow Effects—Farmers Fall Prey to Railroads." *The Wall Street Journal,* 29 March 2004. Available from http://w4.stern.nyu.edu.

Despeignes, Peronet. "Offshoring: A Reality Check." *Fortune,* 27 June 2005.

Dobbs, Lou. "America's Do-Nothing Trade Policy: When Jobs Get Outsourced, It's Big Multinational Firms Who Benefit Most." *San Diego Business Journal,* 5 April 2004.

———. "Is Nothing Private Anymore?" *U.S. News & World Report,* 17 May 2004.

———. "The Myth of 'Insourcing.'" *U.S. News & World Report,* 3 May 2004.

Dolan, Kerry A. "Offshoring the Offshorers." *Forbes,* 17 April 2006.

"Don't Make Outsourcing a Scapegoat for Western Woes." *Business Week,* 10 May 2004.

Elstrom, Peter. "Outsourcing's Uneven Impact." *Business Week Online,* 22 February 2007. Available from www.business week.com.

"Fear of Job Losses from US Call Center Outsourcing to Latin America Is Much Ado About Nothing." TMCnet.com 24 May 2004. Available from www.tmcnet.com/.

Forbes, Steve. "Getting Worked Up." *Forbes,* 10 May 2004.

"Gartner Says Worldwide Cloud Services Revenue Will Grow 21.3 Percent in 2009." Press Release, 26 March 2009. Available from http://www.gartner.com/it/page.jsp%3Fid% 3D920712

"Globalization's Gloomy Guses Must Adapt." *Business Week Online,* 21 March 2006. Available from www.business week.com.

"Global Outsourcing Leader, Luxoft, Announces 2010 Industry Predictions." Press Release, 1 December 2009. Available from http://www.prnewswire.com/news-releases/global-outsourcing-leader-luxoft-announces-2010-industry-predictions-78213922. html.

Goolsby, Kathleen. "New Impacts on Outsourcing in 2009." *Outsourcing Journal,* November 2008.

"Growing Up: Outsourcing in India." *The Economist* (US) 22 May 2004.

Hilsenrath, Jon E. "Data Gap: Behind Outsourcing Debate: Few Hard Numbers." *The Wall Street Journal,* 12 April 2004.

"Hoover's Company Capsules." *Hoover's Online.* 15 April 2007. Available from http://www.hoovers.com.

Imeson, Michael. "Special Supplement: Outsourcing Strategies—Onwards and Outwards." *The Banker,* 1 December 2006.

"Infosys Profits Up 70% on Outsourcing Boom." *InformationWeek,* 13 April 2007.

King, Rachael. "Outsourcing: Beyond Bangalore." *Business Week Online,* 11 December 2006. Available from www.business week.com.

Malachuk, Daniel. "Offshoring Is a Two-Way Street." *National real Estate Investor,* 1 May 2004.

Margulius, David L. "It's a Small Outsourcing World." *Infoworld,* 17 April 2006.

"Mortgage Offshoring to India Goes Mainstream." *Mortgage Banking,* April 2006.

"Offshore Outsourcing Cost Advantages to Disappear by 2027, Study Says." *InformationWeek,* 15 March 2007.

"Outsourcing." In *Encyclopedia of Small Business.* Kevin Hillstrom and Laurie Collier Hillstrom, Eds. Vol. 2. 2nd ed. Detroit: Gale, 2002. 841-844. 2 vols. Gale Virtual Reference Library. 18 June 2004. Available from: http://galenet.galegroup.com/.

"Outsourcing Is Not a Bad Word." *Accounting Today,* 19 March 2007.

"Overseas Outsourcers Are Going Global." *American Banker,* 26 March 2007.

Patterson, David A. "Offshoring: Finally Facts vs. Folklore." *Communications of the ACM,* February 2006.

"PEO Industry Information." National Association of Professional Employer Organizations. 16 June 2004. Available from http://www.napeo.org/.

Perry, Joellen. "Apostle of Outsourcing." *U.S. News & World Report,* 19 April 2004.

Porter, Eduardo. "Outsourcing Is Becoming a Harder Sell in the U.S." *The New York Times,* 6 March 2004.

Power, Mike, Carlo Bonifazi, and Kevin C. Desouza. "The Ten Outsourcing Traps to Avoid." *Journal of Business Strategy,* March-April 2004.

Rai, Saritha. "World Business Briefing Asia: India: Outsourcing Said to Rise 34%." *The New York Times,* 3 June 2005.

Reingold, Jennifer. "A Brief (Recent) History of Offshoring." *Fast Company,* April 2004.

———. "Into Thin Air: These People Lost High-Tech Jobs to Low-Wage Countries. Try Telling Them That Offshoring Is a Good Thing in the Long Run." *Fast Company,* April 2004.

"Report: Offshoring to Have No Sudden Bad Effects." *eWeek,* 22 February 2007.

Rohde, David. "India's Communists Seek Capitalist Help." *The New York Times,* 16 May 2004.

Schmerken, Ivy. "Offshore Outsourcing: Is Your Data Safe?" *Wall Street & Technology,* May 2004.

Sparks, John. "Bull in the China Shop." *Newsweek,* 20 March 2006.

Thottam, Jyoti. "The Fuss Only Fuels the Outsourcing." *Time,* 24 May 2004.

"Top American Consultants Take Own Advice and Join Indian Firm." Infosys Technologies Ltd. 8 April 2004. Available from www.infosys.com.

Wellner, Alison Stein. "Turning the Tables." *Inc.,* May 2006.

Weston, Rusty. "BPO Grows as Companies Look to Save Money." *InformationWeek,* 17 May 2004. Available from www.informationweek.com/.

"Work Practices; HR Outsourcing Continues to Rise in US." *Personnel Today,* 17 May 2005.

Yu, Eileen. "World's Outsourcing Market Worth $373 Billion." *Business Week,* 25 September 2009.

OXYGEN THERAPY

——■——

SIC CODE(S)

8049

3841

7231

INDUSTRY SNAPSHOT

Having emerged from its long-term obscurity and shaken off much of its huckster-riddled image, oxygen therapy was an established, if shaky, market by the turn of the twenty-first century, used by doctors for intensive therapies; by New Age enthusiasts seeking new sources of energy, strength, and health; and by those trying to fend off aging and remain beautiful. Thus, that simple, universal element, oxygen, became the focus of a multibillion-dollar health care industry that captured the imagination of healers and charlatans alike. In all, the United States is home to more than 250 hyperbaric (greater than normal pressure) oxygen therapy (HBOT) facilities.

Perhaps the most common form of oxygen therapy was the hyperbaric chamber. Within small pods that look like something out of a science fiction movie, a person could sit and breathe enhanced oxygen for 15 minutes to an hour to quicken the healing process for wounds or injuries or simply to receive a boost of energy. Regular air is composed of 21 percent oxygen, and even if a person breathes pure oxygen, the body will consume only 21 percent unless the person is placed inside a pressurized chamber.

From a medical standpoint, hyperbaric oxygen therapy (HBOT) floods the body's cells with oxygen carried through the body's fluids rather than via the blood's hemoglobin, thereby stimulating the cells in areas of compromised blood supply. Upon sustaining a wound, for instance, oxygen levels in the blood near the wound are altered, thereby kicking bodily enzymes into action to attract cells appropriate for healing the wound. By applying extra oxygen, these cells are given enhanced energy to accelerate the healing process.

During the first decade of the twenty-first century, there was a growing acceptance of hyperbaric oxygen therapy within the mainstream medical community. This was evident in the development of new programs, as well as increased attention to oxygen therapy in professional literature for both physicians and registered nurses. Professionals acknowledged that hyperbaric treatments were effective for about a dozen applications, including the treatment of chronic, non-healing wounds and cancer patients undergoing radiation therapy. Outside the strictly medical field, a health and image-conscious society looked for ways to deter the aging process, especially among the 77 million baby boomers living in the United States in 2005.

ORGANIZATION AND STRUCTURE

Oxygen therapy is a segment of three major industries: health care, alternative medicine, and cosmetics. Oxygen therapy became the general term for any method by which oxygen was introduced into the human body in order to effect some manner of healing. For traditional medicine, hyperbaric oxygen chambers became standard equipment in many hospitals. After decades of seeing oxygen therapy work for decompression sickness and resulting air embolism, physicians began to experiment with other uses. Burns, carbon-monoxide poisoning, and serious flesh wounds benefited from these pressurized treatments. Other oxygen therapies for use in medicine became more advanced in such treatments as those for emphysema, asthma, and respiratory complications of newborn infants, to name a few. With the rise in the use of these therapies, the manufacture of new medical equipment surged to meet demand.

In the area of nontraditional medicine, or what came to be known as alternative medicine, oxygen therapies became popular, even if they were not medically advised. Hyperbaric therapy crossed over to alternative medicine. In fact, even before it received widespread acceptance in the medical community, hyperbaric therapy was promoted in health spas and sports clubs for serenity, skin rejuvenation, and other "miraculous" treatments. In addition, nutritional supplements said to purify blood, stabilize the body's metabolism, reduce stress, and remove toxins from the body were developed for oral use. Perhaps the most remarkable trend began with the opening of the first oxygen bar in Toronto, Canada during the mid-1990s. The cosmetics industry also got into the business of selling oxygen for skin treatments, whereby customers apply oxygenated moisturizers and breathe pure oxygen to maintain healthy skin.

Whatever the outcome of the debates over medical and health benefits, oxygen therapy is universally eyed as potentially dangerous if improperly administered. Hyperbaric chambers require extensive and precise monitoring as well as cleaning and maintenance.

Alternative medicine encompasses a broad spectrum of nontraditional practices using oxygen therapy. They might include the modern technology of the more widely accepted hyperbaric oxygen therapy (HBOT) medical procedure adapted for non-licensed homeopathic purposes, or they might include other oxygen therapies such as orally ingested nutritional supplements, ozone therapy, chelation therapy, hydrogen peroxide therapy, and forms of exercise therapy. In 1992, under the auspices of the National Institutes of Health (NIH), Congress established the Office of Alternative Medicine (OAM). That year, the NIH provided $14.5 million in research to explore alternative medical options not recognized by the established medical community. No specific regulations governing such practices or medicines were established, however.

The Office of Alternative Medicine (OAM) was eventually succeeded by the National Center for Complementary and Alternative Medicine (NCCAM) as Congress increased its financial support. By 2002, the NCCAM was provided with an annual budget of $105 million. Like the OAM, the NCCAM was set up to evaluate the effectiveness of alternative medicine. Many in the NIH, however, voiced opposition to the NCCAM,

feeling that such evaluations could be more objectively conducted within the NIH itself. Objectivity was a problem, they believed, as the NCCAM seemed staffed with individuals who had a personal interest in alternative medicine. Furthermore, Saul Green, a former professor of biochemistry at Sloan-Kettering Cancer Institute, conducted a study of OAM grants and reports to date and found that even though about $110 million in grants were given to alternative medical research, few studies were published and those that were published only concluded that more studies needed to be performed. Green concluded that the studies provided neither validation nor invalidation. In other words, Congress had wasted a great deal of money on the NCCAM. This caused critics of the NCCAM to suggest that standard double-blind tests could more effectively determine the effectiveness of alternative and complementary medical treatments.

In 1994, the Dietary Supplement Health and Education Act offered even more freedom to alternative medical providers by determining not to regulate this area through U.S. Food and Drug Administration (FDA) standards. However, organizations such as the American Medical Association took a closer look at the act and criticized the lack of dietary supplement regulation that resulted from its passage. As a result of the act, dietary supplements were classified as foods rather than drugs, and therefore they were not subject to the rigorous standards applied to drug products. In addition, standards for product quality and manufacturing practices didn't exist. In October of 2002, the U.S. Senate held a hearing on dietary supplement safety. The AMA testified, addressed its concerns, and suggested improvements.

Industry Regulation The health care system in the United States is highly regulated. The FDA sets national standards and guidelines for any medical treatment. Any oxygen therapy for use in an approved medical setting is subject to regulations regarding the licensing of qualified personnel, the safety and effectiveness of the equipment used, and the authorization of any medicine that might be used in administering treatment.

The AMA also offers its discretion in approving medical practices. In addition, professional societies for physicians, researchers, and other medical personnel set standards for conduct in the practice of utilizing the technology. Health maintenance organizations and major insurance companies, too, provide monitoring when determining appropriate oxygen therapies. Continued medical research into various therapies expands the market for these products and services annually. Finally, the licensing of cosmetologists under state testing programs also offers additional regulation of industry practices.

BACKGROUND AND DEVELOPMENT

In 1664, the first experiment using compressed air in a specially designed chamber was conducted in England, reportedly by a British physician by the name of Henshaw. Over a century later, after British scientist Joseph Priestley published his own discovery of oxygen in 1774, its utilization remained primarily the domain of physicians and scientists. The first reported use of oxygen as a therapy was by a doctor named Caillens in France in 1783. Details of this case are unknown. For most of the next 150 years, the use of oxygen for therapeutic purposes suffered from inconsistent research and trendiness, which earned it a reputation for quackery.

In 1874 in Geneva, Switzerland, however, a scientist named Jurine published his results of the daily oxygen inhalation treatments of a young woman in failing health due to tuberculosis or a condition causing similar deterioration. Throughout the entire nineteenth century, research and experimentation continued. Nothing proved significant until 1917, when physicians J. S. Haldane and J. Barcroft began to administer oxygen therapeutically, primarily to relieve respiratory illnesses.

In 1928, the progress of oxygen treatment in the form of hyperbaric oxygen therapy (HBOT) suffered a severe blow. Wealthy industrialist H. H. Timken of Canton, Ohio, known for his worldwide production of roller bearings, entered into a million dollar venture with Dr. O. J. Cunningham of Kansas City, Missouri, to build a primitive chamber called a "million dollar sanitarium" in the form of a giant steel ball. It was Cunningham's theory that diabetes, pernicious anemia, and cancer were due to an anaerobic form of pathogenic bacteria and could be cured with the use of concentrated oxygen therapy.

Despite his claims, Cunningham offered no proof of his theories. After a few years without success, the property fell into further disrepute, changing owners several times throughout the 1930s. In 1941 the huge steel ball was dismantled for use as scrap metal in the war effort. While advances continued in the use of bedside oxygen tanks and tents for varying degrees of life support, hyperbaric therapy would not begin recovering from the Cunningham folly for some time.

In 1939, the U.S. Navy began to treat deep sea divers suffering from decompression sickness, also known colloquially as the bends, with this specialized therapy. Different from the Cunningham experiment and others that simply used compressed air, these chamber treatments involved only compressed pure oxygen. During World War II, studies in high altitude sickness were also conducted using hyperbaric and other oxygen therapy technology. Acceptance of HBOT was slow to emerge. Studies continued into the 1960s and 1970s with claims

that it could treat anything from hair loss to senility, claims that were never fully supported. Other studies indicated that the therapy showed some measure of success in the treatment of burn patients, wounds, and serious infections such as gas gangrene.

The use of the hyperbaric oxygen chamber as a crossover between the worlds of traditional and alternative medicine became a widespread phenomenon in the 1980s. Famous pop star Michael Jackson reportedly slept in a hyperbaric chamber, a practice he continued long after treatment for facial burns he suffered in an accident while filming a television commercial. Beginning in the late 1980s, professional athletes used HBOT on a routine basis for treatment of charley horses, deep bruises, and even torn ligaments. Following right behind this development was the appearance of hyperbaric chambers known as hypoxic rooms in major gym facilities throughout the country. The claim by Nicholas Cohotin, vice president at Hypoxico, Inc., where the machine was made, was that his machine "will give you a 30-minute workout in just 15 minutes." He also made the claim that the machine could be effective simply by sitting inside of it. Another example was the Hyperbaric Oxygen Clinic in Santa Monica, which offered sessions in their chambers to those recovering from plastic surgery, adding further to the miracle claims of the treatments.

The origin of oxygen therapy in the world of alternative medicine is more difficult to pinpoint, although it did grow out of authentic medical research. The "wellness movement" that began in the nineteenth century throughout Europe and the United States gave birth to much of what eventually became known as the New Age Movement that emerged during the 1960s social revolution. European spas for health treatments were a centuries-old tradition. The ancient health and beauty treatments of China and the Far East, Egypt, and along the Mediterranean including everything from mud baths to breathing in mountain air were well-established, revered traditions long before anyone ever set sail for the new world of the Americas. The movement of the 1950s and 1960s toward eastern religions provided an opening to reconsider the Western traditions by which many Americans were raised, particularly after World War II. The prevalence of tuberculosis sanitariums, often placed in rural or mountain settings for the purer air, prompted the experimentation into the uses of oxygen.

Dietary herbal supplements were offered for better circulation—and that involved getting oxygen to flow more freely throughout the body. Into twentieth-century the United States, people amassed vast fortunes from tonics and treatments that offered no verifiable medical validity. Some treatments were harmless; others were not. Even as late as the 1980s, the FDA reported death and injury from the ingestion of hydrogen peroxide. Industrial strength hydrogen peroxide was illegally promoted to treat acquired immune deficiency syndrome (AIDS), some cancers, and at least 60 other conditions. The product was sold as "35 percent Food Grade Hydrogen Peroxide," which was diluted for use in "hyper-oxygenation therapy." The formula proved to be fatal to one child in Texas in 1989 and was particularly toxic to several other children due to its highly corrosive qualities.

Despite warnings of the harmful aspects of such nontraditional practices, the alternative medicine industry managed to grow into an $18 billion market by 1996. Even insurance companies began to look at various alternative treatments as viable and offered some reimbursement for certain procedures. A significant 35 percent of Californians polled in 1998 admitted to the use of high-dosage vitamins, once only a bastion of the alternative arsenal. The market for homeopathic remedies in California alone totaled $3.65 billion, up 100 percent from 1994 to 1998. California was long considered the forerunner in such experimentation.

Two interesting commercial venues opened for oxygen therapy by the 1990s. One was that of the oxygen bars opening first in Toronto, Canada, and shortly thereafter gaining serious popularity in Hollywood and New York. When *Science World* magazine first reported on the opening in Toronto in December 1996, customers could stop in for 20 minutes of pure oxygen, pumped in through the plastic plugs in their noses, for a mere $16. In January 1999, *Parade* magazine reported the latest celebrity craze: actor Woody Harrelson and his wife, along with holistic physician Dr. Richard DeAndrea, opened an organic food restaurant on Sunset Boulevard in Hollywood, where a 20-minute serving of oxygen there was available for $13. Other well-known television and film stars carried oxygen tanks with them to their sets.

Another area in which oxygen therapy began to climb into prominence was the cosmetics industry. The theory went that aging skin was a product of insufficient oxygen flowing to the cells in order for them to perform at a healthy, youthful rate. Geared especially for the rich and famous or otherwise well-to-do, an oxygen facial could cost $120.

Physicians remained skeptical of such treatments, however, warning that they relied on deceiving the customer into believing, contrary to available evidence, that the oxygen that is so necessary for life could actually provide a direct benefit to certain parts of the body, such as skin, if applied directly. Vendors of these treatments remained convinced, however, and their popularity seemed to bear out their claims, at least as far as business was concerned.

The industry's escalating popular support at the end of the twentieth century was largely attributable to two collective psychological factors. One was the general, and rising, distrust the population held for government and its regulations. Another was the progress medical researchers made throughout the twentieth century, helping people imagine that all diseases were curable and that the aging process itself was not as inevitable as it used to be.

Oxygen therapies in alternative medicine included specially designed deep breathing exercises (often followed with the assistance of a personal trainer), hydrogen peroxide therapy, oxidative therapy, "oxone" therapy, ionization, and the ingestion of oral stabilized oxygen products. Many of the oxygen compounds for ingestion in the form of dietary supplements continued to flood the market.

More socially oriented oxygen enthusiasts popped into oxygen bars to inhale oxygen cocktails, or quick bursts of pure oxygen, to receive a boost of energy and a general feeling of vigorous health. Oxygen cocktails combine about 40 percent strength oxygen with water and a fruit extract, which is then inhaled for 15 minutes to an hour through a mask or nasal prongs. While, again, doctors tended to ridicule the trend and deny the cocktails' efficacy, a number of customers continued to swear by it.

In addition to the often questionable health benefits, medical researchers warned of the still pervasive dangers of improper casual oxygen therapy, especially of the self-administered variety. Deaths resulting from patients falling asleep inside a chamber or other improperly supervised oxygen administration were not unheard of.

The Internet was inundated with sales of oxygen therapy products during the late 1990s and first decade of the 2000s. Established businesses and new start-ups appeared on the Internet and offered consumers thousands of products involving oxygen therapy. Among them were Crossroads' The Oxystore and Bio-Karmic Technologies, both California companies. Crossroads offered books, video and audio tapes, testing kits, oral oxygen, and a range of other products relating to oxygen and detoxification. The health value of these products was considered questionable, and many thus came with warnings even by the businesses themselves.

Another impact felt by this market was the unprecedented growth of health spas. The number began to grow so rapidly into the 1990s that it was nearly impossible to calculate. These spas included holistic health centers that could offer one-day, one-week, or extended stays for treatments. (Also see the essay entitled Health Spas.) Americans patronized many of the clinics that had opened in Mexico offering cancer treatments not approved in the United States. Even department stores began to cash in on the business of in-store therapeutic facials. As the world welcomed high technological advances, the U.S. public began to turn to health products that were born often of ancient health practices.

PIONEERS IN THE FIELD

A list of the earliest pioneers in the discovery of oxygen's therapeutic benefits would include Haldane and Barcroft, certainly, in the area of traditional medical treatments. The U.S. Navy itself was unparalleled in its use and investigation of hyperbaric oxygen therapy (HBOT), and that paved the way for other medical doctors and researchers to further its use. Authors of the book *Hyperbaric Oxygen Therapy,* Richard A. Neubauer, M.D., and Morton Walker, D.P.M., were devoted to the ongoing study of the benefits of that form of oxygen therapy. In his foreword to the book, well-known scientist Dr. Edward Teller, director of the Lawrence Livermore Laboratory in California, offered enthusiastic support for HBOT, and for the physicians' efforts in promoting its use. Teller was also critical of the United States for dragging its feet on the technology, and held that lives and bodies could be saved by administering HBOT to patients after major surgery.

One of the best-recognized authorities on oxygen therapy as an alternative medicine is Ed McCabe. Known as "Mr. Oxygen" because of his book, *O2xygen Therapies—A New Way of Approaching Disease,* he traveled the world promoting various forms of oxygen therapy. His activities were curtailed on April 7, 1998, when he was arrested by the U.S. Justice Department on counts of tax fraud.

During the first decade of the 2000s, there was a growing acceptance of hyperbaric oxygen therapy (HBOT) within the mainstream medical community. This was evident in the development of new programs, as well as increased attention to oxygen therapy in professional literature for both physicians and registered nurses. Professionals acknowledged that hyperbaric treatments were effective for about a dozen applications, including the treatment of chronic, non-healing wounds and cancer patients undergoing radiation therapy. One facility reported that because of hyperbaric treatments, as many as 70 percent of potential amputees were saved from having a limb removed.

The oxygen therapy industry received a boost in 2003, when Medicare and some private insurance companies began covering hyperbaric treatments. Following these developments, existing hyperbaric chambers began to see increased use, and hospitals began adding new chambers. Following the launch of its first hyperbaric therapy program, in 2004, Birmingham, Alabama-based

Baptist Health System announced plans to develop three new programs. In mid-2005, one of the nation's largest hyperbaric chambers was completed at Seattle's Virginia Mason Medical Center. Built at a cost of $6 million, the chamber was 46 feet in length and had individual chambers that could accommodate up to eight patients each.

Hyperbaric chambers were even being installed in small or financially strapped hospitals, thanks to private companies that offered turn-key solutions that provided chambers, staff, and transportation service for patients in exchange for a share of the substantial profits. Arrangements such as these proved to be a win for both parties.

Outside the strictly medical field, a health and image-conscious society looked for ways to deter the aging process, especially among the 77 million baby boomers living in the United States in 2005. Some 75 percent of boomers believe that it's important to look younger than one's calendar age. Oxygen therapy, as realized through alternative medicine options, was driven by market demand for products that promised benefits to health and well-being.

Oxygen facials, for instance, were purported to enhance cell production and repair, thereby improving the health and glow of skin. Cells take about 28 days to reach the skin's surface, though as people grow older, an increasing number of those cells do not survive that journey, leading to less healthy, drier skin. One cause of this general decay is the diminished oxygen load the body allows to enter the cellular system. Through oxygen therapy, proponents suggest that individuals can literally stave off the skin's aging process, retaining moisture and improving cell performance to produce youthful, glowing skin. Many salons therefore sell and use skin care products such as cleansers, face lotions, and masks, with encapsulated oxygen molecules.

The U.S. Census Bureau predicts that by 2030, the number of Americans over the age of 65 will reach more than 70 million, representing one-fifth of the entire population. There will be 9 million people over 85, and by 2050, some 40 percent of Americans will be 50 or older. From $42.7 billion in 2002, the research firm FIND/SVP Inc. forecast that estimated sales of anti-aging products and services would continue to grow, which may bode well for the non-medical oxygen therapy segment.

By 2007, an aging U.S. population and increased evidence of COPD (chronic obstructive pulmonary disease, also referred to as emphysema or chronic bronchitis) was causing increased interest in oxygen therapy, according to *Home Care Magazine.* Only about 50 percent of COPD cases are diagnosed, and often not until the patient has reached the later stages of the disease. COPD is the fourth leading cause of death in the United States, and the disease affects approximately 12 million Americans, with an additional 12 million undiagnosed. Oxygen therapy has been shown to delay the onset of more severe symptoms, but only 32 percent of COPD patients receive home oxygen treatment. In order to increase awareness of the disease, the National Heart, Lung and Blood Institute launched a public education campaign called "Learn More, Breathe Better." In addition, in 2007 the U.S. government began a six-year, $28 million project to study the use of home oxygen therapy for COPD patients. Earlier diagnosis and increased awareness of COPD was expected to increase the number of patients on oxygen therapy and demand for the necessary equipment.

CURRENT CONDITIONS

As of early 2009, the Undersea and Hyperbaric Medical Society, the professional organization in this field, recognized 13 conditions for which hyperbaric oxygen treatments were considered therapeutic. Eleven of those conditions have been approved by Medicare for reimbursement, indicating that solid evidence supported those uses.

The Medicare Home Oxygen Therapy Act of 2009 (H.R.3220) was introduced in Congress on July 15, 2009, after which it was referred to the House Ways and Means Committee. Later incorporated in part into the overall health care reform bill, it stood to amend Title XVIII (Medicare) of the Social Security Act to revise Medicare coverage and reimbursement requirements for home oxygen therapy services, providing separate coverage of home oxygen therapy services and payment for such services based on a single bundled payment rate. Under the new rules, Medicare would pay suppliers at the prevailing rate (an average of $200 a month, paid 80 percent by Medicare, 20 percent by patients) for the first three years after a patient began coverage. Suppliers would then be required to continue providing oxygen services to patients for an additional two years, but at sharply reduced payment rates. After that, patients would be entitled to receive new equipment, and Medicare would resume paying suppliers at the higher rate.

In an October 2009 press release, New Air, Inc. reported that during 2007, more than $1.6 billion was spent in the U.S. on ventilators, oxygen therapy systems, and airway management accessories outlined in Part 2 of the American Heart Association's presentation at its 2005 International Conference on Cardiopulmonary Resuscitation and Emergency Cardiovascular Care Science with Treatment, and later codified in one of its six published *Circulation Journals.* relating to the airway and ventilation in the United States. Anticipating growth at an annual rate of 6.3 percent, sales of these products would reach more than $1.9 billion by 2010.

INDUSTRY LEADERS

The business of oxygen therapy is part of a diverse number of professions, occupations, and industries. It includes medical professionals and trained technicians, academic researchers, cosmetologists, alternative health practitioners, medical equipment manufacturers, health spa owners, hospitals, and business owners who sell related products. Nevertheless, the key manufacturers of hyperbaric oxygen chambers are important to note. They include Environmental Tectonics Corp. of Southampton, Pennsylvania; Tampa Hyperbaric Enterprise Inc. of Tampa, Florida; and Sechrist Industries Inc. in Orange County, California.

Research and development of hyperbaric treatments is the focus of several laboratories and companies around the United States. They include the Ocean Hyperbaric Neurologic Center in Florida, also operating the American College of Hyperbaric Medicine from that facility; Biopure Corp. of Cambridge, Massachusetts; Baptist Medical Center in Jacksonville, Florida; Lifeforce in Baltimore, Maryland; Texas A & M University Hyperbaric Laboratory at College Station, Texas; and the Undersea Hyperbaric Medical Society Inc. of Kensington, Maryland.

Other standard oxygen equipment such as monitors, analyzers, and transmitters are products of a multitude of medical equipment companies and firms that deal simply with oxygen-related products. The Alpha Omega Instruments Corp. of Rhode Island is a rising company in this area of the industry, as is Sandia National Laboratories of Albuquerque, New Mexico.

WORKFORCE

As in many other aspects of the alternative medicine market, true projections for oxygen therapy have been difficult due to the nature of the business. Workers from chiropractors to herbal supplement specialists to health bookstore staff to production factory employees have reaped the benefits of this multibillion-dollar business. Because those who seek out alternative care tend to be affluent, well-educated members of the population with the resources to experiment, the economic implication was growth in exponential increments. This also was true of the cosmetics industry workforce, as oxygen therapy facials and similar body therapies have become a central source of oxygen therapy profits.

AMERICA AND THE WORLD

While the United States lagged behind the rest of the industrialized world in the use of hyperbaric therapy and alternative medicine, it was catching up near the end of the twentieth century. American wealth, education, and growing travel options helped to create more options in seeking health and beauty care. While many Americans continued to seek treatment at spas in Europe and Mexico, the growth of similar facilities in the United States had begun to offer them such opportunities closer to home. Because of the country's continued dominance in traditional health care services, the United States was considered likely to dominate the field, particularly in the manufacturing of equipment, as the possibilities for HBOT grew from increased research.

In many countries, meanwhile, oxygen therapy was finding a market embracing the treatment with open arms. Nearly all Japanese are within practical distance of one of Japan's 200 hyperbaric chambers. In Italy, doctors can even be sanctioned for failing to administer oxygen therapy for appropriate conditions.

Nevertheless, skepticism continued to hold the industry somewhat in check overseas as well, and will likely continue to do so for some years to come. In the United Kingdom, for instance, approximately 90,000 people suffer from multiple sclerosis (MS). More than 11,000 of these individuals have experimented with a hyperbaric oxygen chamber since the mid-1980s, but in light of the U.K. Multiple Sclerosis Society's judgment that the treatment was risky and expensive, doctors still often did not even bother to report the existence of oxygen therapy alternatives to those diagnosed with MS.

RESEARCH AND TECHNOLOGY

Research and development has been a major challenge facing oxygen therapy in traditional medicine. Since the technique has remained awash in controversy and skepticism, research grants have been relatively hard to come by. Private companies, such as Sechrist Industries Inc., a leader in the field of hyperbaric therapy equipment and other respiratory products, has provided much of the funding for further experimentation.

The challenges of HBOT extend further. The field of HBOT was relatively young by medical standards even at the start of the twenty-first century. Only since the 1960s had valid research and results been followed. Consequently, many doctors were graduated from medical school knowing little about this therapy. They might come to accept HBOT for certain conditions, such as wounds, burns, air emboli, carbon monoxide poisoning, and chronic bone infections, but the medical profession as a whole did not yet accept its use for many other conditions that hyperbaric doctors already recognized. These treatments included coma related to head injuries, bruising of the spinal cord, stroke, and multiple sclerosis. Other conditions that Neubauer and Walker noted were treatable with HBOT included cranial nerve syndromes,

peripheral neuropathy, various orthopedic conditions, gangrene, frostbite, diabetic retinopathy, cirrhosis, and Crohn's disease, to name a few.

Despite these challenges, increased research findings have benefited the industry and have led to new and potentially useful applications for oxygen therapy. About 100,000 patients were treated with hyperbaric oxygen therapy (HBOT) yearly by the late 1990s and the first decade of the 2000s. HBOT proved effective in slowing the swelling of nerve tissues, which led many industry hopefuls to conclude that it helps to slow the progress of such diseases as multiple sclerosis, in which internal scarring causes the body's immune system to disrupt signals to the brain by attacking those tissues.

Another area in which researchers have increasingly accepted oxygen therapy is infection prevention for post-surgery patients. A study performed by anesthesiologist Daniel I. Sessler and colleagues at the University of California-San Francisco tested 500 patients undergoing major surgery. Half were treated with 80 percent pure oxygen during post-surgery anesthesia while the other half received 30 percent pure oxygen. Only half as many, however, in the 80 percent group developed post-surgery infections. The researchers found that the higher oxygen doses enabled those patients' immune cells to capture and destroy infectious bacteria more effectively.

Having successfully tested his research on cats, Dr. Steven K. Fisher, director of the Neuroscience Research Institute at the University of California-Santa Barbara, concluded that oxygen therapy can reduce eye damage to patients with retinal detachment. Administered to patients as they await remedial surgery, Dr. Fisher held, oxygen can help save the eye's photoreceptor cells.

Hyperbaric oxygen therapy (HBOT) also has been viewed as providing effective treatment for hard-to-heal wounds such as diabetic ulcers of the leg and the foot, because it could stimulate capillary growth and increase the capacity of white blood cells. Diabetic ulcers result from poor circulation, low oxygen levels in the blood, and rigidity of the blood cells. Other areas HBOT has proved helpful with include treatment of osteomyelitis, traumatic crash injuries, injuries resulting from radiation therapy (an increasingly utilized treatment), and bloodless medicine and surgery (when patients choose not to have transfusions). In cases of radiation burns, which result in abrupt damage, the brain does not receive messages to send infection fighting and healing agents. HBOT can initiate this healing process because it can significantly increase oxygen pressure at the wound site. In bloodless surgery, HBOT can be applied before and after procedures to increase oxygen to the blood in those patients who don't wish to receive blood transfusions. Oxygen is carried throughout the body by red blood cells, which can only be replaced with a transfusion. The high pressure of the hyperbaric oxygen chamber forces oxygen into the plasma, which maintains oxygen levels in the parts of the body lacking in red blood cells.

In addition, HBOT is helpful in cases of toxic poisoning including carbon monoxide poisoning, and for conditions that create bubbles in the blood, including air embolisms suffered by divers and gas gangrene.

HBOT has been increasingly used to help treat Lyme disease, a serious bacterial infection transmitted by a tick bite. HBOT is especially helpful in cases where patients do not respond well to early treatment with antibiotics. In such cases, patients breathe in 100 percent oxygen at an atmospheric pressure of 2.4, a level that weakens and kills the Lyme spirochete.

A particularly cautious yet emerging field for oxygen therapy was pediatric care. A number of products were developed especially for postnatal infants. One such product provided long-term, patient-triggered, synchronized assisted ventilation in infants. A case study during the early 1990s by a team led by Nadarasa Visveshwara, M.D. of Valley Children's Hospital of Fresno, California, proved the procedure to be safe and effective in very low birth weight infants with uncomplicated respiratory failure. More recently, the National Institutes of Health Supplemental Therapeutic Oxygen for Prethreshold Retinopathy of Prematurity Trial found that liberal uses of oxygen resulted in decreased likelihood of surgery requirements for infants by limiting the harmful effects of postnatal injuries.

Large hyperbaric chambers ultimately may prove unnecessary for many injuries and conditions for which HBOT is employed. A partnership was formed between Sandia National Laboratories and Numotech Inc. aimed at the production of a new oxygen therapy vehicle known as topical hyperbaric oxygen treatment (THOT), which captures hyperbaric oxygen in a small, disposable plastic bag. Simply placing the bag around the affected wound or body part requiring attention allows the patient to breathe normal air while the area is bathed in high-pressure oxygen. The Sandia team will incorporate their patented internal pressure sensors in topical hyperbaric oxygen treatment (THOT) to enable easy readings and build in an automatic system shutdown if pressure levels rise to dangerous levels.

The research efforts of the two companies resulted in the development of a device called the Numobag, a spring-loaded pressure gauge that makes an oxygen therapy system available for even wider use. The Numobag applies THOT via a plastic bag hooked up to a standard pressurized oxygen tank. A mechanical sensor is attached to the outside of the bag. This sensor provides feedback about the pressure of oxygen in the system. The sensor makes the system easy to monitor and easy to use without highly specialized training.

Because the system employs oxygen, the sensor has no electrical parts, which eliminates the risks involved with heat or sparks. The system is also disposable, inexpensive, and easy to read. In topical hyperbaric oxygen treatment and the Numobag, only body parts requiring treatment are inserted into the bag. This eliminates the risk of pulmonary or central nervous system toxicity that can result from breathing high-pressure oxygen. The heightened oxygen content of the Numobag helps oxidize disease-causing organisms on the skin and in wounds and helps flesh to heal. It is especially effective in treating pressure ulcers, diabetic foot ulcers, severe burns, and other skin wounds.

In the meantime, Sandia and Numotech are working on system upgrades that will make the Numobag even safer and easier to use. The companies are also working on sensors that would use the "aroma" of a wound to assess its geometry, color, and depth. Such sensors would make the Numobag even more suitable for home use.

BIBLIOGRAPHY

Barry, Henry. "Hyperbaric Oxygen Therapy in Patients with Chronic Wounds." *American Family Physician,* 1 May 2005.

Bassing, Tom. "Baptist to Launch Three More Hyperbaric Programs." *Birmingham Business Journal,* 2 July 2004.

Brody, Jane E. "Oxygen Therapy Is Valuable, Sometimes." *The New York Times,* 9 March 2009.

Ehrenman, Gayle. "Healing Powers: A spring-loaded pressure gauge makes an oxygen therapy system available for wider use." Me Magazine 2003. Available from http://www.memagazine.org/medes03/healingp/healingp.html.

Gonzales, Victor. "Hospital Unveils Hyperbaric Chamber." *The Seattle Times,* 7 June 2005.

"Hoover's Company Capsules." *Hoover's Online.* 1 April 2007. Available from http://www.hoovers.com.

"H.R. 3220: Medicare Home Oxygen Therapy Act of 2009." Available from http://www.govtrack.us/congress/bill.xpd%3Fbill%3Dh111-3220.

"Inhalation Technology - Baby Breath." New Air Co. Press Release 6 October 2009. Available from http://www.scribd.com/doc/20690609/Inhalation-Technology-Baby-Breath.

McClinton, Denise H. "An Uncertain Air." *Home Care Magazine,* 1 December 2006.

McNamara, Damian. "HBOT May Lead to Improved Cognition in Cerebral Palsy." *Clinical Psychiatry News,* January 2007.

"Not Perfect, But Better." *Home Care Magazine,* 1 March 2007.

Scott, Gale. "Oxygen Therapy Offers Fresh Lift; Hyperbaric Chambers Save Limbs, Pump Up Revenues; Local Firm Provides the Means." *Crain's New York Business,* 3 January 2005.

"Studies Examine Home Oxygen Therapy." *Home Care Magazine,* 4 December 2006.

"Trends." *Home Care Magazine,* 1 February 2007.

Weil, Jennifer. "Growth Seen in Aging Population." *WWD,* 4 June 2004.

PARALLEL PROCESSING COMPUTERS

─────■─────

SIC CODE(S)

3571

INDUSTRY SNAPSHOT

Parallel computing simply means delegating a computing task to multiple processors (central processing units, or CPUs), each of which performs part of the operation in tandem with the rest. Parallel processing computers are of two basic types: vector and multiprocessing. In vector computers, a single, specialized processor can perform more than one operation at a time. Multiprocessing computers, by contrast, use many processors simultaneously to break difficult operations into pieces and complete those operations collectively. Multiprocessing systems were the most common computers in the industry.

The ongoing parade of ever faster personal computers (PCs) may cause some to overlook the true high-performance computer market with tremendously powerful, often multimillion-dollar machines. However, demand for massively parallel processing (MPP) computers, supercomputers, and other ultra-high-end computers certainly has not been exhausted.

Scientists, engineers, and other researchers depend on such rarified machines for a host of processing-intensive applications. Common high-end applications range from predicting hurricane movements to modeling nuclear warfare to exploring the human genome. These applications have a need for speed. It would literally take years, even decades, to run the same kinds of analyses on a single-processor system. For example, a supercomputer at the Los Alamos National Laboratory ran a record-setting series of engineering simulations in three days that would have taken a single processor almost 18 years to

complete. Accordingly, each hour of the supercomputer's time was worth 90 days of computing by lesser machines.

ORGANIZATION AND STRUCTURE

A rudimentary form of parallel processing is available on relatively inexpensive network servers (some costing less than $10,000) equipped with two or more microprocessors. These common devices, however, are not considered part of the high-end market. High performance systems often use hundreds or even thousands of microprocessors, and perhaps more importantly, rely on specially designed connectivity hardware and software to achieve dramatically faster speeds and greater capabilities.

The structure of the parallel and supercomputing market is driven in large part by hardware advances. While it is processor architecture that defines parallel processing, leaps and bounds in processor speed and miniaturization have made supercomputers much more compact and powerful than the room-size computers of the 1960s and 1970s. The power of the supercomputers of the early 1960s was available on many desktops at the end of the 1990s.

On the hardware side, parallel processing computers fall into several categories: supercomputers, often called "heavy iron"; clusters of small computers linked together to act as a single computer; and technical servers. These high-flying machines are produced by a small number of U.S. and Japanese companies, such as Silicon Graphics Inc., Cray Inc., IBM Corp., Hitachi Ltd., Fujitsu Ltd., and NEC Corp.

Most software used by supercomputers is developed by manufacturers specifically for their machines.

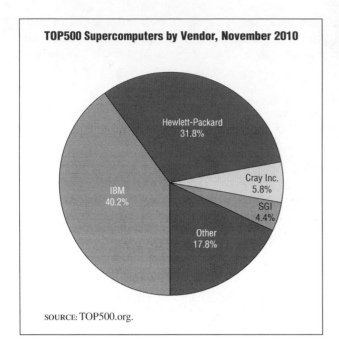

TOP500 Supercomputers by Vendor, November 2010

Hewlett-Packard
31.8%

Cray Inc.
5.8%

SGI
4.4%

Other
17.8%

IBM
40.2%

SOURCE: TOP500.org.

Generally, the investment in a supercomputer is for a particular purpose or range of purposes, and the software and hardware are chosen together to accomplish that purpose. Nevertheless, in some cases, off-the-shelf software is available for certain applications, such as graphics, mathematical simulations, and database applications.

BACKGROUND AND DEVELOPMENT

The first parallel computer architecture appeared in 1959 with the delivery of the IBM 7030, affectionately known as "Stretch." With a performance measurement of approximately 1 megaflops ("flops" being short for floating point operations), or 1 million instructions executed per second, the 7030 was the most formidable computing machine of its time. It was comparable in speed to the average desktop personal computer of 1992. It was delivered to Los Alamos National Laboratory to model nuclear explosions, but only eight 7030s were ever manufactured. Other government labs, such as Lawrence Livermore and the National Aeronautics and Space Administration (NASA), competed for high-speed computing machines to perform complex aeronautical and fluid dynamics calculations. The first single processor central processing unit (CPU), the Intel 4004, would not be introduced until 1971.

Control Data Corp. (CDC), founded in the late 1950s, developed the CDC 6600 in 1964 and the CDC 7600 in 1969, both exceeding a megaflop. Other giants of the early parallel processing supercomputing field included Burroughs, Sperry-Rand, and Texas Instruments. CDC was the starting place of a man who was later referred to as the father of the supercomputing industry: Seymour

Cray (1925–1996), who left the company in 1972 to found Cray Research. Cray Research dominated the supercomputer scene of the 1980s with its Freon-cooled Cray-1, Cray-2, and X-MP models. Soon new competitors arose to capture some of Cray's dominant market share. Convex, Sequent, and Alliant developed competing systems. However, for those who could afford the million-dollar price tags (mainly government laboratories and engineering departments at major research universities), a Cray computer was the first choice.

The late 1980s saw the production of the first non-U.S. parallel processing supercomputers for the general market. Companies such as Hitachi, NEC, Meiko, and Fujitsu began marketing computers to compete with Cray and CDC. The breakup of the former Soviet Union and the end of the Cold War caused a marked decline for supercomputers during most of the 1990s. University research that depended on heavy number crunching, such as oceanography and meteorology modeling, plus the growth of commercial applications such as power generation and transmission, securities and stock market data modeling, high definition television, and even virtual reality, kept the market alive. These and other high bandwidth applications relied on parallel rather than serial processing of data.

By the mid-1990s, led by the parallel and multiprocessing hardware of Intel Corp. and its P6 or PentiumPro chip, computer manufacturers such as IBM, Silicon Graphics, and Sun Microsystems, Inc., began to develop architectures to take advantage of greater throughput. Database giants Oracle Corp. and Sybase Inc. also used parallel architectures to quickly manipulate and retrieve records in relational databases. Their products represented the first forays of parallel processing and supercomputing into software products for standard to high-end business applications. This meant that parallel processing was nearing the desktop of the average personal computer.

Clustering Inexpensive Computers for High Performance

A significant trend in the supercomputing market is a series of initiatives that has combined ordinary PCs and network servers into a surprisingly powerful high performance system. In 1998, a team at Los Alamos announced their "supercomputer," which was actually a cluster of 68 PCs that could operate as a single computer and reach speeds up to 47 gigaflops (1 billion floating point operations per second). What was most noteworthy about it was the cost: approximately $313,000, roughly 10 percent of the cost of a conventional supercomputer. This computer, called Avalon, was a "Beowulf-class" computer, a development in parallel processing that began in 1994 among NASA scientists. Thomas Sterling and Don Becker, working at the Center of Excellence in Space Data and Information Sciences, a NASA contractor, put together 16 desktop computers using Ethernet connections and called it Beowulf. It was an instant success, and a movement began among government researchers that soon extended toward commercialization.

Beowulf clusters used off-the-shelf hardware and publicly available software, most significantly the Linux operating system, a version of Unix that is available free but requires considerable knowledge of computer networking to put together. In May 1999, EBIZ Enterprises, Inc. demonstrated a fully configured Beowulf Clustered Super Computer with a 16-node cluster that was priced at under $15,000. This machine ran a standard test problem in 12 seconds, compared to the three seconds required by the Cray T3E, which cost $5.5 million. According to the company, this made supercomputer power available to many people and organizations without the funds for a conventional supercomputer or the knowledge to build their own cluster.

Other groups, mostly affiliated with universities and research centers, have experimented with cluster configurations as well. In one interesting case, researchers at a South Korean university used parallel processing software over the Internet to simulate supercomputing functions on a group of 64-bit PCs.

Chips At the other end of the computing scale, individual chips were also being developed, incorporating parallel processing instruction within the chip. Making the most news at the end of the 1990s was the Merced IA-64 chip being jointly developed by Intel and Hewlett-Packard. A 64-bit processor, as opposed to a 32-bit Pentium-type processor, it was designed with "explicitly parallel instructions computing," or EPIC. This parallel processing within the chip would make it at least twice as fast as previous Intel chips, according to the designers. It would also incorporate previous generation instruction sets for backward compatibility.

Merced was not the first 64-bit processor, though. Digital Equipment Corp. introduced its 64-bit Alpha processor for its servers and workstations in 1993, but it did not have the impact on the industry that was expected of the Intel chip when it took hold. In the meantime, Elbrus International, a Russian computer company, announced in May 1999 the design of a processor that it claimed would operate faster than Merced. It also used internal parallel processing. Elbrus had taken out 70 patents on its design and was looking for a Western firm to help manufacture the chip.

Other Developments During the early 2000s, the fastest growing segment of the high performance market was for so-called technical servers. These high-end network servers, often running Unix, were devoted to a range of specialized tasks. An example is an image server for storing and transmitting medical images within a hospital system. Technical servers are more likely to be deployed in commercial and industrial settings rather than in pure research settings, which could be the reason that they were in greater demand than highbrow supercomputers.

Indeed, businesses represent a large and growing share of the high-performance market. Factors driving business use included heightened interest in data mining, especially scouring electronic commerce numbers for trends, and data visualization.

After the terrorist attacks on September 11, 2001, analysts predicted that the U.S. government would invest more heavily in supercomputers as the Department of Defense sought to upgrade its computing capabilities. An increase in spending by several national security agencies was expected to boost supercomputer market sales by $1.5 billion, according to IDC. In 2004, for example, a 2,132 CPU Linux cluster was being built for the Department of Defense.

Supercomputers were not immune to hackers, as the National Science Foundation, the Pittsburgh Supercomputing Center, the National Center for Atmospheric Research, the National Center for Supercomputing Applications, and many others found out in April 2004. Hackers reportedly used stolen passwords to investigate the weakness of the facilities' supercomputers.

Continued development pushed supercomputing into quadrillion flops (or petaflops) territory. New development efforts were led by an ambitious project announced in 1999 by IBM. Nicknamed BlueGene, the venerable computer maker's project produced a system that vastly outpaced all existing computers. BlueGene, a successor to its celebrated Deep Blue of the mid-1990s, was predicated to be 2 million times faster than a conventional PC and faster than a few hundred present-day supercomputers combined. BlueGene was completed in 2004 for California's Lawrence Livermore National Laboratory. A scaled-down version was 73rd on the TOP500 list for 2003, and at the size of a dishwasher, was one hundred twenty-eighth the size of the planned BlueGene.

BlueGene's design specifications included 64 connected boxes, or "racks," each as large as a kitchen refrigerator, and boasted more computing power than all of ASCI White (IBM's fourth-generation supercomputer for the U.S. Department of Energy's Accelerated Strategic Computing Initiative, which began in 1998). A rack housed eight motherboards with 64 chips, each one capable of a billion calculations per second. IBM claimed that at top performance, BlueGene would be 1,000 times more powerful than Deep Blue and 40 times faster than the 40 most powerful supercomputers in the world combined. By 2007, the BlueGene L ranked number two on the TOP500 list and had reached performance levels of 478.2 teraflops.

In 2003, the world's fastest computer was the Japanese supercomputer Earth Simulator, located in Yokohama, that could perform 35.86 trillion calculations per second, more than four and one-half times greater than the next fastest machine. Built by NEC and run by the Japanese government, the computer studies the climate and other aspects of the earth. Its emergence marked the first time that a supercomputer outside the United States topped the semi-annual list of the world's fastest computers. That year, the "ASCI Q" ranked second. The computer could run 13.88 trillion calculations per second and was built by Hewlett-Packard Co. for Los Alamos National Laboratory in New Mexico. In third place was a cluster system at Virginia Tech, the X Cluster, or Big Mac. Able to run 10.28 trillion calculations per second, the computer was built with Apple G5s and used a Mellanox network based on Infiband interconnect. Unlike most of the TOP500 list, the X Cluster was built in six months for approximately $5 million.

In fact, 2003 found 208 cluster systems on the TOP500 list of the world's fastest supercomputers, seven of which were in the top 10 of the list. Cluster systems were built with workstations or separate computers as building blocks that were then connected by internal networks. The most unusual cluster system on the 2003 list was built from Sony PlayStation 2 video game consoles. In 2003, IBM's newest supercomputer, which was seventy-third on the TOP500 list, used the same 2-Tflop chip that was planned for the next-generation video game consoles by both Sony and Nintendo.

The industry understood that a clustered system might not be the answer to all supercomputing needs. Experts distinguish between high performance systems that meet capacity needs, or large but relatively straightforward tasks, versus those that meet capability needs, which involve both large and complex tasks. In short, cluster systems tend to fare better meeting capacity needs, whereas more traditional (and expensive) machines with specialized chips are considered better candidates for capability needs. This distinction, however, has been played up by traditional manufacturers such as Cray, which stand to lose the most if cluster computing catches on in a big way.

The IBM BlueGene L helped the United States to surpass Japan and regain its leadership position in the supercomputer realm. Nevertheless, in what seemed to be a never-ending race, Japan was hard at work to produce an even faster computer. By 2011, that country expected to produce a supercomputer that could perform calculations at a blazing rate of more than 3 quadrillion floating point calculations per second (3 petaflops). Driving the

project to produce this machine were Hitachi Ltd.; NEC Corp.; Japan's Ministry of Education, Culture, Sports, Science, and Technology; and a number of Japanese Universities.

Many manufacturers claim on different grounds that their machines are the world's fastest. Some measure theoretical speeds that are never attained in practice; others measure peak operating speeds that are only rarely reached; still others gauge sustained operation speeds but tend to measure the speed during operations that their machines are particularly well suited to handle. This does not address the dilemma of processor capability versus specific interconnect capacities, which can dramatically affect end performance. In short, there are many variables that determine actual performance, so most observers are likely to encounter contradictory claims about speed and performance, particularly when the manufacturers are the source of the claims.

The supercomputer industry continued to face a number of challenges. One principal hurdle involved how quickly data moves back and forth from a supercomputer's processors. As Steve Ulfelder wrote in the March 6, 2006, issue of *Computerworld,* "Because supercomputing is the sharp end of the technology spear, these data-flow problems—still manageable in most corporate data centers—are quickly reaching critical mass in the world's top research facilities. Breakthroughs are needed, and experts acknowledge that answers are elusive."

One of the fastest supercomputers in the world was IBM's $120 million Roadrunner, built for the U.S. Department of Energy's (DOE) Los Alamos National Laboratory. Roadrunner achieved a peak performance of just over 1 petaflops (equal to 1 quadrillion calculations per second) and was the first supercomputer to reach this milestone. Also on the TOP500 supercomputer list, which was published twice a year and presented at the International Supercomputing Conference, was IBM's BlueGene L system, located at the U.S. Department of Energy's (DOE) Argonne National Laboratory. The BlueGene L demonstrated a performance level of 478.2 teraflops (1 teraflop equals a trillion calculations per second). Rounding out the top five on the list were the IBM BlueGene/P (450.3 teraflops) at the DOE's Argonne National Laboratory; the Sun SunBlade x6420 "Ranger" system (326 teraflops) at the Texas Advanced Computing Center at the University of Texas-Austin; and the Cray XT4 "Jaguar" (205 teraflops) at the DOE's Oak Ridge National Laboratory.

For the first time, the 2007 TOP500 list included energy efficiency calculations. The Green500 list, created in April 2005, allows a comparison of supercomputers based on performance per watt and illustrates the increasing importance of environmental issues in the industry. The Green500 placed an IBM system based in Germany, the BladeCenter QS22 Cluster, at the top of the list in June 2008. The Green500 web site also noted that the first sustained petaflop supercomputer, Roadrunner, "exhibits extraordinary energy efficiency" and that the top three Green500 systems "surpass the 400 MFLOPS/watt milestone for the first time." Also of note, all supercomputers in the top 10 2008 Green500 list had a higher flops/watt rating than the previous number-one Green500 system.

CURRENT CONDITIONS

Because massively parallel processing represents a process rather than product or service, industry revenues are hard to come by. Notwithstanding, according to IDC in 2010, the overall HPC market was down 11.6 percent in 2009. By competitive segment, IDC reported that HPC servers overall brought in $8.6 billion (industry leader Cray put it at $9.8 billion). Supercomputers (over $500K) accounted for $3.4 billion. IDC's latest forecast had HPC server revenue growing six to seven percent starting in 2010 and reaching $11 billion by 2013. Highly parallel programming challenges continued, as well as other issues involving power and cooling costs and software licensing costs.

In his 2010 article for *VentureBeat,* Ken Elefant, founding partner of Opus Capital, noted that (quoting scientist Andreas Weigand) humans generated more data in 2009 alone than in the entire history of our species up to that year. IT firm EMC projected that the quantity of digital information produced by humans will grow by a factor of 44 between 2009 and 2020. The question is not how to generate data, but rather how to rapidly organize and retrieve it. Massively parallel processing and supercomputers are not going anywhere soon.

According to late October 2010 claims, China's Tianhe-1 was to move ahead as the fastest supercomputer in the world. Using a Linux-based operations system, it was touted to be able to process 2,507 trillion calculations in one second. At the top of the list of TOP500 Supercomputing Sites (June 2010) were Jaguar (Cray) XT5-HE, with Opteron Six Core 2.6 GHz; the Nebulae (Dawning), with TC3600 Blade, Intel X5650, and NVIDIA Tesla C2050 GPU; the Roadrunner (BladeCenter) with QS22/LS21 Cluster, PowerXCell 8i 3.2 Ghz/Opteron DC 1.8 Ghz, Voltaire Infiniband; and Kraken XT5 (Cray) XT5-HE Opteron Six Core 2.6 Ghz. In 2009, the GPU-based Tianhe-1 debuted on the Green500's list as No.8.

The June 2010 Green500 List focused on accelerator-based supercomputers, which occupied the top eight slots. These computers were found to be three times more energy efficient than their non-accelerated counterparts on the list. Among these top eight, those based on the custom PowerXCell 8i processor from IBM, with

threee IBM quantum chromodynamics parallel computing on the cell (QPACE) machines. All equally tied for top place, and were located in Germany.

A relatively new processor technology in 2009 and 2010 was the GPU, or graphics processing unit, which contributed to more complex visual experiences. Indeed, according to a 2010 CNET report, NCSA Director Thom Dunning stated that the future of supercomputing could be summed up in three letters: GPU. As the world became more video oriented, for both data analysis and entertainment, GPU-based technology was becoming increasingly essential for the most competitive embedded hardware. Wide applications were anticipated. In the medical field, GPU technology was important for new monitor displays. In automotive applications, it contributed to better dashboard displays and information/entertainment transmission (e.g., the Sync technology in Ford Fusion, Taurus, and F150. In aerospace, GPU contributed to improved navigation through digital signal processing. GPU could also reduce costs and power consumption for data storage centers. In May 2010, Scientists announced they were using GPU-supercomputer technology to simulate life on earth, including economies, the financial system, and whole populations, for studies manipulating various hypothetical scenarios. Several companies were producing GPU products, including NVIDIA (a potential game-changer, with its Fermi architecture), AMD, and Intel.

Trends in the supercomputer industry were illustrated by characteristics of the computers listed in the TOP500 list. For example, 283 of the 500 machines use quad core processor based systems, whereas 203 use dual core processors. Most of the computers on the list—40.2 percent—were produced by IBM, with Hewlett Packard hosting the second most (31.8 percent). Other U.S. companies represented on the list include SGI, Cray, and Dell. The United States clearly represented the largest market, with 257 of the 500 top computers. The United Kingdom was second with 184, followed at a distance by Asia with 48.

INDUSTRY LEADERS

The high-performance computing industry is largely dominated by a handful of companies. Most of them are large, integrated computer companies with far-flung operations in other segments, such as IBM, Sun, and Hewlett-Packard. Other, more specialized players include Cray and Silicon Graphics Inc.

IBM Armonk, New York-based IBM Corp. was the world's largest computer company. It manufactures and sells computer services, hardware, and software, and provides customer solutions using advanced information technology. Practically synonymous with large computers for years, IBM built a market share of almost 80 percent in the

1960s and 1970s. It introduced the personal computer (PC) in 1981 but failed to capitalize on the growth of the low-end computer market and went into a steady decline as interest in mainframes stagnated and prices declined.

By the mid-1990s, however, IBM had regrouped, returning to profitability and rejuvenating its product and service lines. In 1997, an updated Deep Blue, IBM's enormous parallel processing computer, defeated World Chess Champion Garry Kasparov in a six-game rematch. (Kasparov won the first match in 1996.) The feat was mostly symbolic. However, it helped set the tone for the company's ambitious research and development program that would close out the 1990s with the massive BlueGene project.

By 2007, IBM's BlueGene L, located at the Lawrence Livermore National Laboratory (LLNL), ranked as the world's second fastest supercomputer. In June 2006, it set a world record in the scientific application realm when it sustained a performance level of 207.3 teraflops per second; and by 2007 it had reached speeds of 478.2 trillion calculations per second.

IBM produced a leading 210 (42 percent) of the TOP500 supercomputers in 2007, including four of the top 10. The company continued to be on the leading edge of technological developments in the industry in the late years of the first decade of the 2000s. In 2008 it partnered with the University of Toronto to develop an even faster and larger supercomputer, one that will be equivalent to "30,000 to 40,000 home computers linked together," according to Chris Pratt of IBM Canada. The computer, which is expected to be operational by summer 2009, will be able to hold data equivalent to that stored on 1 million DVDs and will perform at speeds of 360 trillion calculations per second. In September 2010, IBM acquired Marlborough, Massachusetts-based Netezza, which designed and marketed (internationally) data warehouse appliances and analytics applications.

Hewlett-Packard Co. Hewlett-Packard Co. (HP), of Palo Alto, California, is a top producer of computer systems for all markets. In the high end, it acquired Convex Computer in 1996 to offer the Exemplar line of parallel processing computers. HP also participates in the high end market through its N-Class and V-Class servers and its HyperPlex clustering platform, all of which run on the company's own chips. In May 2002, HP acquired Compaq Computer Corporation, a global provider of IT products, services, and solutions for enterprise customers. HP produced 166 (33 percent) of the TOP500 supercomputers in 2007, including the Cluster Platform 3000 BL460c system, which ranked eighth on the list and was installed in the Computational Research Laboratories in India.

Sun Microsystems Sun Microsystems Inc. is a major producer of technical servers and cluster systems using symmetric multiprocessing (SMP) technology. The Santa Clara, California, company was formed in the 1980s, when it earned a reputation for producing powerful, speedy Unix-based workstations for scientific and engineering applications. It also branched into servers, and got a big boost from SGI in the mid-1990s when Silicon Graphics, Inc. (SGI) sold off part of Cray Research's server business for a relative pittance. In subsequent years, Sun earned a hundredfold return on its investment. Sun also manufactures its own line of microprocessors (UltraSPARC), some of which are used by other high-performance system manufacturers, and other system components such as storage devices. Although the company was not represented in numbers near as well as IBM, HP, and others, it did own the number-four computer on the TOP500 list in 2007: the SunBlade x6420 Ranger system at the Texas Advanced Computing Center, University of Texas-Austin.

Intel Corp. Intel Corp., well known for its dominance of the processor market, has been selling parallel computers since about 1985. It built the multi-teraflops ASCI Red for the Sandia National Laboratories, but its Paragon line of parallel computers is its standard business offering. It also began shipping its Merced and Itanium 64-bit parallel processing microchips in late 2000. Some expected the Merced development to eventually bring parallel processing to the ordinary desktop computer. A key producer of processing chips, Intel is not a sizable producer of finished high performance computers.

Cray Inc. Seattle-based Cray Inc. designs, builds, sells, and services high performance computer systems and provides professional services that include furnishing solutions to its customers. The company has a long and colorful history in the supercomputing business, which it helped pioneer in the 1970s under the leadership of its eccentric and brilliant founder, Seymour Cray. Cray Research, operating out of Eagan, Minnesota, became a dominant leader in the 1980s but saw its supercomputer and parallel computer market share slide in the 1990s as government spending declined. Financial strife and indecision at Cray's helm left the company a willing target in a 1996 purchase bid by Silicon Graphics, Inc. (SGI). Later that year, Mr. Cray, who had formed a separate entity called Cray Computer Corp. a few years earlier, died at age 71 from injuries sustained in a car crash. The Cray T3E system, introduced that year, used up to 2,048 processors and was widely recognized as the first technically and commercially successful highly parallel system. It was ranked among the world's fastest supercomputers for sustained performance on real applications.

The merger of Cray Research and SGI proved an unhappy pairing, although arguably SGI profited more than from the arrangement than did Cray. The two companies' traditions did not mesh, and SGI never fully appreciated Cray's product line and marketing. Finally, in 1999, SGI made known its plans to sell Cray. It found a buyer named Tera Computer Co., a little known publicly traded designer of multi-threading high end systems. The buyout was completed in the spring of 2000, with the new entity taking the name Cray Inc.

The new company intended to focus on bringing out a new line of scalable supercomputers with both vector and MPP capabilities, backed by heavy funding from the U.S. Department of Defense. It also stated its intent to rebuild a sales force to sell its machines after having its sales channels all but ignored at SGI.

On April 1, 2000, Cray acquired the operating assets of the Cray Research business unit from Silicon Graphics, Inc. (SGI) and changed the company's name from Tera Computer Company to Cray Inc. The company acquired the Cray SV1 and T3E product lines and the code-named SV2 and other products under development. A month later, the company established an agreement with NEC Corporation to distribute and service NEC SX series vector supercomputers. The agreement provided it with exclusive distribution and servicing rights in the United States, Canada, and Mexico, and nonexclusive rights in the rest of the world. In December 2001, it formed a Professional Services organization to help provide solutions as well as computer systems to its customers. Services included consulting, integration, custom hardware and software engineering, advanced computer training, site engineering, data center operation and time-share computing services. In February 2002, it obtained PowerEdge servers from the Dell Computer Corporation with the goal of marketing high performance cluster solutions and services on a global basis. The company continued designing and building highly optimizing programming environments and performance management diagnostic software products. It also researched advanced algorithms and other approaches to improving application performance. In addition, it bought or licensed software technologies from third parties when necessary to provide appropriate support to its customers.

Cray produced the number five ranked supercomputer on the TOP500 list in 2007: the XT4 Jaguar, located at the DOE's Oak Ridge National Laboratory. That year, revenues totaled $186.1 million with 800 employees. In 2008, the company stepped out of its comfort zone by offering low-end machines equipped with Intel chips and Microsoft Windows software. Priced at $25,000, the new CX1 is meant to perform tasks that cannot be handled by a personal computer and is targeted toward businesses that perhaps cannot afford a supercomputer. According to Cray senior vice president Ian Miller, "It's the smallest thing we've done." Cray was facing competition in this arena from HP and SGI, which were producing similar machines. Its 2009 revenues were roughly $284 million.

Silicon Graphics, Inc. Silicon Graphics, Inc. (SGI) of Sunnyvale, California, creates computer products used in a variety of segments, including science and engineering, energy, and manufacturing, among others. The company serves large corporations as well as the government, and some of its most high-tech computers have created the special effects seen on the big screen. The fact that Disney and NASA are both clients illustrates the firm's range.

SGI held two spots in the top 10 of the TOP500 list in 2007. The system installed at the New Mexico Computing Applications Center in Rio Rancho and based on the Altix ICE 8200 model ranked seventh, and the GI Altix ICE 8200 system used by Total Exploration Production was tenth. The latter was also the largest system installed for an industrial customer.

Teradata Dayton, Ohio-based Teradata, a vendor specializing in data warehousing and analytics applications, was creating much industry buzz in 2009 and 2010 despite its small size. With a MPP system running on shared nothing architecture, Teradata had 21,500 employees and reported $4.6 billion in 2009 revenues.

WORKFORCE

Employees in the supercomputing and parallel processing computer industry generally have engineering or computer science backgrounds. Due to the theoretical work involved, a small percentage may come from mathematics or other hard science fields. Nonetheless, the growing multidisciplinary perspective used by many university research centers affects the work in parallel processing as well. According to the Caltech Concurrent Computation Project, which researched parallel computing from 1983 through 1990, a wide range of disciplines was recruited to tackle different aspects of the technology. It was also noted that the traditional inter-disciplinary field for the project, computational science, is not well understood or implemented either nationally or within the university structure.

According to the 2008-09 edition of the *Occupational Outlook Handbook,* published by the U.S. Bureau of Labor Statistics, in 2006, about 857,000 people in the United States were employed as computer software engineers, 542,000 as computer scientists and database administrators, 504,000 as computer systems analysts, and 435,000 as computer programmers. With the exception of the latter, all of these occupations were expected to experience above average job growth through 2016. Reasons for the decline in demand for computer programmers in the United States included advances in technology and the increasing ability of users to perform programming functions, as well as an increase in offshore outsourcing in the field.

RESEARCH AND TECHNOLOGY

A number of important initiatives drove progress in the supercomputing field. Among them was the High Productivity Computing Systems program. Headed by the Defense Advanced Research Projects Agency (DARPA), one component of the initiative's mission was to "provide a focused research and development program, creating new generations of high end programming environments, software tools, architectures, and hardware components in order to realize a new vision of high end computing, high productivity computing systems (HPCS) to address the issues of low efficiency, scalability, software tools and environments, and growing physical constraints."

Like other nations with a stake in the supercomputer game, the United States was heavily involved in developing next-generation systems. In mid-2006, the National Science Foundation was funding the development of a $200 million system that, when completed in 2010, would perform 1,000 trillion calculations per second. The potential applications for the new computer were numerous, ranging from economic modeling and genetic research to weather-related studies in the areas of earthquakes, global warming, and tornadoes.

An exciting industry development took place when the state of New York, IBM, and Rensselaer Polytechnic Institute joined in a $100 million partnership to create the world's most powerful university-based supercomputing center. Called the Computational Center for Nanotechnology Innovations and launched in late 2007, the new center is set to drive nanotechnology developments in the areas of semiconductors, arts, medicine, energy, and biotechnology. According to the May 11, 2006, issue of *The New York Times,* the center would be one of the top ten of its kind throughout the world.

There is much relevant research on parallel processing computers. While a significant amount of research considered hardware architecture, a growing body of research looked into the complexity of writing software for parallel hardware architectures. Scalability of parallel architectures varied, and some architectures handled certain mathematical problems—such as algorithms—better than others.

While supercomputers tend to be evaluated based on their central processing unit (CPU) throughput, input/output (I/O) requirements are a major consideration as well. Mapping the human genome, for example, requires just as much I/O throughput as CPU brute force due to the massive amount of data needed for input. Meteorological modeling can have billions of data points. Such "grand-challenge applications" push the frontiers of parallel processing research and development.

Fiber optics may offer a solution for both I/O and processing limitations. Researchers struggling with scaling problems in parallel architectures are working with light rather than electrical signals to transmit signals. For instance, a conventional electronic connection of ten processors requires 100 wires, and the number of wires rises exponentially as the number of processors increases. Fiber-optic technology, by contrast, has a theoretical potential of 2 terabits per second. The implementation, however, is expensive and daunting. Positioning systems for light pulses must be micro-accurate. Light beams through fiber-optic wires also suffer attenuation, or weakening, of a signal over longer distances. Lasers solve the problem, but with huge costs. Honeywell, Lucent Technologies, and Motorola, among others, have already invested research dollars into developing marketable optical computing solutions.

Cray announced a breakthrough technology in the industry in August 2008 when it revealed its ECOphlex (PHase-change Liquid EXchange), an energy-efficient liquid cooling system that allows computers to operate at speeds of multiple petaflops. According to *Worldwide Computer Products News,* the new technology is "room air neutral," meaning the temperature of the air that enters the computer system is similar to that exiting it. Computer systems with the new technology were expected to be available by the end of 2008.

Another research and development project begun in 2008 involved a collaboration among Intel, SGI, and the National Aeronautics and Space Administration (NASA) to create a computer system with a capacity of 1 petaflops by 2009 and 10 petaflops by 2012. The new system, "Pleiades," will be a 16-fold improvement over NASA's supercomputer Columbia, which operates at 88 teraflops at peak performance. NASA's S. Pete Worden told *EDN,* "Achieving such a monumental increase in performance will help fulfill NASA's increasing need for additional computing capacity and ... the computational performance and capacity for future missions."

BIBLIOGRAPHY

"31st TOP500 List of World's Most Powerful Supercomputers Topped by World's First Petaflop/s System." TOP500.org, 14 June 2008.

Ceruzzi, Paul. "The Mystery of the Massively Parallel Processor." *Air & Space,* 2 July 2010.

Clark, Don. "Cray Ventures into Small Computers." *Wall Street Journal,* 16 September 2008.

"The Complete IDC Intelligence Solution." 2009. Available from http://www.hpcuserforum.com/2009dearborn presentations.

"Cray Announces New Liquid Cooling Technology." *Worldwide Computer Products News,* 28 August 2008.

Elefant, Ken. "Startups find Strong Opportunities in 3 big DataMmarkets." *VentureBeat,* 13 September 2010.

"Embedded Technology Increasingly Reliant on GPUs." 14 October 2010. Available from http://www.vdc.com.

Feldman, Michael. "IBM Roadrunner Takes the Gold in the Petaflop Race." *HPCwire,* 9 June 2008. Available from http://hpcwire.com.

Feldman, Michael. "Top 10 Hits and Misses for 2009." *HPCwire,* 18 December 2009. Available from http://hpcwire.com.

"The Green500 List." June 2008. Available from http://www.green500.org.

"The Green500 List: Accelerators Raising the Fuel Efficiency of Supercomputers." June 2010. Available from http://www.hpcwire.com/offthewire/The-Green500-List-Accelerators-Raising-the-Fuel-Efficiency-of-Supercomputers/.

"High Productivity Computing." DARPA/IPTO, 15 September 2008. Available from http://www.darpa.mil/ipto/.

"IBM Achieves Performance Breakthrough in Massive Computer Networks." *Internet Wire,* 9 March 2006.

"IBM: BlueGene Saves Energy, Space." *eWeek,* 27 April 2006.

"IBM, U. of Toronto Building Supercomputer." *PC Magazine Online,* 14 August 2008.

"Largest Supercomputers to Simulate Life on Earth." *Science Daily,* 28 May 2010. Available from http://www.sciencedaily.com/releases/2010/05/100526134039.htm.

Miller, Matthew. "NASA Supercomputer to Get Boost." *Electronics News,* 1 June 2008.

"NCSA Director: GPU is The Future of Supercomputing." *Inside HPC,* October 2010. Available from http://insidehpc.com/2010/11/02/ncsa-director-gpu-is-the-future-of-supercomputing/

"Rensselaer Celebrates Grand Opening of World-Class Supercomputing Center." Rensselaer Polytechnic Institute, 7 September 2007.

"Supercomputing Turns Toward Productivity." *Computerworld,* 6 March 2006.

"TOP500 Supercomputing Sites." June 2010. Available from http://www.top500.org/.

U.S. Bureau of Labor Statistics. *Occupational Outlook Handbook, 2008–09 Edition,* 2008. Available from http://www.bls.gov/.

"Voltaire Solutions Tops on Green500 List." *Wireless News,* 22 August 2008.

PASSENGER RESTRAINT SYSTEMS

SIC CODE(S)

2399

3714

INDUSTRY SNAPSHOT

Consumer demand for safe autos, tight competition among carmakers, and technological advances have proven a potent mix where advanced passenger restraint systems are concerned. Going far beyond those old standbys, seat belts and newer restraint mechanisms such as air bags and child restraint equipment attempt to harness researchers' knowledge of crash physics in order to make safer cars, minivans, and sport utility vehicles (SUVs). Demand for advanced restraint systems continued throughout the twenty-first century's first decade. Despite a reduction in automotive manufacturing, there was a general increase in the addition of safety features to meet the growing consumer demand.

Front-end air bags work as a supplement to lap and shoulder belts in the event of an accident that propels the driver or passenger toward the steering wheel, dashboard, or windshield. Deployed by electronic sensors at the moment of a crash, these air bags inflate in a fraction of a second to cushion the forward-hurtling driver and passenger.

Even though air bags have been available commercially since at least the 1970s, it was not until the 1990s that their popularity surged. Some of the increase was due to federal regulations, which first mandated driver side air bags in the 1993 model year and later expanded the requirement to passenger side air bags in vehicles made during or after 1998. Competition in the auto industry and consumer demand have fueled additional growth, especially for side-impact systems. In 2007 the National Highway Transportation Safety Association (NHTSA) initiated new standards that require automakers to equip all vehicles with side-impact air bags by 2012.

Fueling growth further were government mandates requiring the use of smart air bags on all cars manufactured after 2006. The weight-sensing air bag systems are designed to react differently based on the passenger's weight and position in the seat. While figures from the NHTSA revealed that there were no air bag related deaths, air bags were still responsible for a number of injuries to drivers. Thus, improving air bag safety continued to be a hot topic within the automotive industry.

The use of seat belts and child safety seats continued to be areas of concern as well. Even if parents do buckle children up, risks are present in the form of the car seat not being properly installed and of the seat not providing adequate protection in the case of a crash. In a *Consumer Reports* study, 9 out of 12 car seats tested provided poor protection, even though they met the federal safety standards.

BACKGROUND AND DEVELOPMENT

Despite years of debate throughout the 1980s, it was not until 1993 that the federal government mandated that automobile manufacturers install air bags in all vehicles (with all new models compliant by 1999). Prior to that, air bags were installed in some European models and in a few domestic cars, usually in more expensive luxury models.

Top Automotive Safety System Manufacturers, 2009

	2009 revenue
TRW Automotive	$11.61 billion
Toyoda Gosei	$ 5.79 billion
Autoliv	$ 5.12 billion
Key Safety Systems	$ 1.00 billion

Air bags seized the imagination of the public, and carmakers, after years of avoiding any mention of safety issues for fear of scaring consumers, began to sell safety in their advertisements. Less than 1 percent of U.S.-made cars contained an air bag in the mid-1980s. By 1997, however, virtually all new vehicles sold in the United States had at least one, and 60 percent also had a passenger side air bag. As of September 1, 1998, government regulations required all passenger cars, vans, and light trucks to contain front dual air bags. Several states, including New York, Ohio, Arizona, Indiana, and Texas, ruled that consumers could sue car manufacturers for failing to equip cars with air bags, even if the cars were produced before laws were passed requiring them to be installed. Pennsylvania, Mississippi, and Idaho, however, subsequently ruled that car manufacturers could not be sued in such cases.

Government and industry figures indicated that air bags saved lives. Crashes resulted in roughly 1.4 million air bag deployments through 1996, including 1.2 million on the driver's side and 200,000 on the passenger side. Between 1986 and 1996 an estimated 2,000 lives were saved by air bags. Significantly, some 520 of those lives were saved in 1996 alone, indicating that as air bags became universal, their benefits grew.

Intense debate continued, however. First, safety experts maintained that side impact air bags were needed to save even more lives. Second, the occurrence of several deaths apparently due to air bags deploying so fast that they killed occupants led to questions about whether air bags needed to be depowered or even disengaged at the owner's request.

It was clear that while air bags mounted on the steering wheel or dashboard saved lives in head-on collisions, they did little for side-impact crashes. Indeed, the sensors telling an air bag to inflate were mounted on the front of the car and were not activated in the event of a side crash. The idea of a side-impact bag also ignited consumers' imaginations, and soon all the major car companies and their suppliers were rushing to develop systems. A variety of side-impact systems was proposed, but by 1998 only expensive luxury vehicles had them as standard features, and few people were requesting them as added options. Some side-impact bags inflate near the

driver's or passenger's knees; others pop out from near the headrest or from a door panel. Volvo was among the first car manufacturers to actually offer such a system. Later in the first decade of the 2000s, all car manufacturers would have an opportunity to utilize them, as federal regulations mandated their installation.

The second key question in the air bag debate involved whether air bags should be depowered or even switched off at the consumer's request. This question arose out of reports that air bags were deploying at minor low-speed bump crashes and striking occupants with such force as to injure or kill them. A review by the Centers for Disease Control and Prevention (CDC) looked at 32 such deaths that had occurred between 1993 and 1996. Young children and small or elderly women seemed to be at particular risk.

The CDC reported that of the 32 deaths, 21 had occurred among children who were not properly restrained. Nine were children who had been in rear-facing child safety seats in the front seat. The CDC found that while only one death occurred in 1993 when less than 1 percent of all vehicles had dual air bags, there were 18 such deaths during the first 11 months of 1996 when the percentage of dual air bags had risen to 11.4 percent. In addition, small or elderly women sometimes sat so close to the steering wheel that the inflating bag struck them instead of merely cushioning them as they fell forward.

As media reports of such incidents mounted, the safety industry rushed to placate fears. Air bags, they pointed out, had saved far more lives than they had taken. There was confusion and concern about air bags. Unfortunately, most of the concerns were misplaced, Brian O'Neill, president of the Insurance Institute for Highway Safety, told the *Washington Post*. The simple act of buckling up eliminates the risk of serious injury from an air bag for almost all adults, and putting children in the back seat eliminates the risk entirely for children. The benefits of air bags, particularly if one follows those instructions, greatly outweigh any risks.

Two solutions have been offered to eliminate the potential problems air bags can cause. One is to "depower" air bags so that they inflate 25 to 35 percent more slowly (first generation air bags deploy at a rate of 200 miles per hour). The answer to the question lies in determining the type of accident the industry hopes to guard against. Air bags were originally designed to save lives in high speed head-on collisions, during which occupants are thrown forward at such speeds that a bag needs to inflate almost instantaneously to do any good. However, a bag can inflate at a slightly slower rate and with less potential for injury from the bag if the accident is a slower fender-bender type. Beginning in 1997, the

NHTSA allowed automakers to depower frontal air bags and in 2001 issued an advanced ruling.

A cut-off switch that would allow an operator to disengage the passenger side air bag was also created. Safety regulators feared that consumers would switch off air bags due to unfounded worries about their defects and, thus, compromise their own safety; however, by 1997, some automakers were installing cut-off switches on the passenger side of some two-seaters and pickups, where babies or small children may be at risk in deployment. A few manufacturers, such as Subaru and Volvo, refused to produce cut-off switches, insisting that their cars are safest with the air bags fully operational.

In late 1997, the government's National Highway Traffic Safety Administration (NHTSA) began allowing Americans who met certain narrow height or age requirements to have a cut-off switch installed in their cars. The process is cumbersome, however, requiring a formal application and approval procedure with the NHTSA itself. By the middle of 1998, the federal government had issued 30,000 approvals for cut-off switches, but consumers soon found that government permission was not enough: many auto dealers refused to install cut-off switches, afraid they would be held liable should an injury occur as a result. According to the NHTSA, of the estimated 25,000 auto dealerships nationwide, only 400 were willing to install cut-off switches in 1998. The Automotive Service Association advised its members not to install the devices, out of safety and liability concerns.

By spring 1998, Ford Motor Co. announced that all of its cars as well as the Ford Windstar minivan would be outfitted with side air bags over the following two years. Side air bags were initially offered as an option on the Mercury Cougar coupe and then became standard on the Lincoln sedans and other Ford luxury models. The company promised that by 2000 side bags would be added to all other models.

Figures compiled by the Insurance Institute for Highway Safety suggested that 48 percent of cars and light trucks on U.S. roads in 2000 had driver side air bags and 35 percent had passenger air bags. Federal regulations required passenger vehicles to come equipped with both driver side and front seat passenger side air bags beginning in 1998 (1999 for light trucks). Thus, shipments of these air bags track closely with overall auto sales and were not expected to grow as rapidly as those of optional devices.

While the air bag debate continued to be the loudest in the passenger restraint field in the late 1990s, renewed attention was also turning to earlier mechanisms such as head restraints and seat belts. Starting in 1969, the federal government had required head restraints—a primary defense against whiplash injuries—to be installed in all automobiles. Two studies by the Insurance Institute for Highway Safety, however, found that by the late 1990s head restraints had morphed into more comfort-oriented "headrests," thus losing much of their protective function. In 1998, the NHTSA considered new regulations that would raise the height of head restraints and require them to lock in position so as to stay in place during an accident.

Car manufacturers in the late 1990s also revisited the idea of head restraint systems. In 1998, Saab became the first carmaker to offer "active" head restraints, which actually cradle a passenger's head in the event of an accident. Unlike air bags, the system, developed in part by General Motors Corp. (GM) and expected to become more widely available in GM cars, does not require professional repair or resetting after a crash.

With all the technological advances, however, simply "buckling up" remained the primary and most effective passenger restraint system in any vehicle. The NHTSA estimated that using seat belts reduced the risk of death in an accident by 45 percent for front seat occupants. Unfortunately, in the late 1990s, less than three-quarters of passengers reported wearing seat belts, even though every state but New Hampshire required it by law.

Air Bags Shown Effective Despite the small number of troubling mishaps with air bags, their overall benefits are well documented. As of 2000, the NHTSA estimated that air bags had saved about 5,300 lives in the United States since the agency first began monitoring their use in 1990. Most of the people saved, nearly 85 percent, were drivers, and the vast majority of them were not wearing seat belts. Nevertheless, seat belt statistics highlight why air bags are considered supplemental restraints: while air bags saved somewhere between 750 and 1,000 people a year in the late 1990s, seat belts were credited with saving 11,000 lives each year.

Dangers Reduced, Not Eliminated Fatalities associated with air bags remained a source of unease. As of early 2000, the NHTSA had confirmed 153 deaths attributed to air bags since 1990. Over half the victims were children, mostly young children who were not adequately restrained by either seat belts or child safety seats. There were signs, however, that public outcry since the mid-1990s was helping reduce air bag deaths. From a 1997 peak of 23 fatalities, the number of deaths of children who were not in rear-facing child safety seats fell to 11 in 1998 and 8 in 1999. Heightened public education on the dangers of air bags and on proper vehicle safety precautions for young children were believed to be factors. Regulators also believed redesigned air bags with less forceful deployment helped bring the count down. The threat of side impact air bags to children was comparatively unstudied, but they were believed to pose similar dangers and would require the vigilance of parents and automakers as the air bags entered the mainstream.

Standards Reached on Child-Safety Seats Child safety seats also provoked intense public debate in the late 1990s. This debate grew out of concerns that improperly restrained children, such as a baby placed in a rear-facing child safety seat in the front seat, were at greater risk from inflating air bags, as well as from a crash itself. The CDC report noted that children were more likely to move around or lean forward in the front passenger seat and that adult-sized shoulder belts may not fit properly. In addition, because children are shorter than adults, they may be more likely to have their heads or necks struck by inflating air bags. Smart bags would likely reduce this danger, but in the meantime, the NHTSA and other safety groups endorsed the recommendation that all children ride restrained in the back seat in appropriate safety seats or wear safety belts.

These safety concerns were a boon to manufacturers of child safety seats. Laws in all 50 states and the District of Columbia required that young children ride in safety seats. As consumers who rushed to buy the equipment soon learned, however, child safety seats could be confusing and easily misused. The *Wall Street Journal* reported that nearly 80 percent of child safety seats in cars and vans were used improperly, resulting in an estimated 600 deaths annually for children under the age of five. Further adding to the confusion was the multiplicity of models: dozens of child safety seats were on the market.

To correct such problems, in 1997 the NHTSA proposed rules backing a General Motors design that would change the ways child safety seats are attached to vehicles. The new design required vehicle makers to install fixtures that anchor child safety seats, through a series of straps and buckles, to the automobile. A drawback of the system is that it could raise the price of child safety seats, from approximately $55 to more than $100, which could discourage some consumers from buying them.

Some vehicle manufacturers responded to safety concerns by building child safety seats directly into the rear passenger seat of their vehicles. This, too, led to confusion. The *New York Times* reported that in July 1997, Chrysler Corp. was forced to send instructional videos to some 135,000 customers after receiving complaints that child seats built into its minivans malfunctioned. Complaints focused on whether restraints could retract and trap, or even choke, young children in their seats. No injuries or deaths were reported, but some parents were reported to have cut the belts away to free their children. Chrysler

maintained there was no defect in the seat and hoped that the videos would help resolve the problem. In 1998, General Motors produced a video called "Precious Cargo—Protecting the Children Who Ride with You" and offered it free to anyone at 4,000 Blockbuster Video stores around the country. The video showed parents how to correctly install various child safety restraint systems.

The NHTSA reported that child safety seats, when properly installed, reduce the risk of death in automobile accidents by 69 percent for children and 47 percent for toddlers. In 1996 alone, the agency asserted, an estimated 365 lives were saved by child safety restraint systems. More than half of all the children who died in car accidents in 1996 were completely unrestrained.

In addition to the proliferation of child safety seat regulations, a number of states in the late 1990s began requiring children to ride in the back seat. Children in Florida and Minnesota must ride in the back seat until they are 16; in Tennessee, they cannot ride in the front until they are 13. As often happens in the safety industry, the cautionary steps taken by these states were likely to "domino" throughout the country in the coming years.

Child safety seats also figured in a long-running debate in the airline industry. For decades, airlines permitted children under age 2 to ride for free if held in a parent's lap during flights. The National Transportation Safety Board had long recommended that aircraft restraint systems for toddlers be made mandatory. The Commission on Airline Safety and Security agreed with the recommendation and forwarded it to the Federal Aviation Administration (FAA). In the late 1990s, the FAA reviewed the proposal but expressed doubts about making such a requirement. Eventually the FAA settled on a strong recommendation that parents bring and use a car seat for children under 2. Children over the age of 2 are required to have their own seat.

Separately, a few initiatives have attempted to improve vehicle safety for children and address the weak points of existing child restraint equipment. Perhaps the biggest problem has been lack of standardization of child safety products and a dearth of information about how best to use them. The NHTSA's Uniform Child Restraint Anchorage (UCRA) ruling was aimed at standardizing some features and restraint techniques so that parents have an easier time understanding the best kinds of restraints and so that children are optimally protected. Issued in 1999, the UCRA ruling decreed a standard set of three anchorages (two seat-level bars and an upper ring) in all new vehicles by September 2002. Makers of the seats themselves were told to produce compatible units.

At the 2003 Society of Automotive Engineers (SAE) World Congress, New Lenox Baby Products of Dunnellon, Florida, stole the show when it introduced "The Tattle

Tale," which is a high-tech product with a soothing voice to guide users in proper usage of seats. Its five-point harness system met NHTSA standards.

Other Developments The International Organization for Standardization (ISO), a United Nations affiliate that promulgates nonbinding standards for private industry, adopted safety seat standards under the stewardship of Volvo, which led an ISO working group on the matter.

According to the Insurance Institute for Highway Safety, "some designs of seats and head restraints were reducing neck injuries among car occupants involved in rear end crashes." After the Institute conducted a study, it reported that "one definitive finding is a 43 percent reduction in neck injury claim rates for the Saab, General Motors and Nissan models with active head restraints, compared with similar cars before such restraints were introduced." In another study, it was reported that drivers of vehicles equipped with side air bags that included head protection were 53 percent less likely to die in accidents involving driver's side collision. Such collisions were responsible for nearly one-third of all accidental automotive deaths annually.

At least part of the credit for the reduction in serious injuries and deaths can be given to multistage air bags and smart air bags. These rely on sensors to determine the size and position of the seat occupant, as well as the speed of the collision, and adjust deployment accordingly. The government mandated that by 2006 all newly manufactured cars be equipped with this technology. For minivans and SUVs, some manufacturers also were introducing air curtains that drop out of the vehicle's headliner to cushion occupants during a rollover accident. By late 2005, such curtains were standard in a number of leading minivans, including the Honda Odyssey, Nissan Quest, and Toyota Sienna. These particular models were found to be the safest by the Insurance Institute for Highway Safety (IIHS).

Supplementing the smart air bags were smart seat belts. Armed with an array of sensors and other gadgetry, these belts instantly tighten upon collision to secure passengers into their seats and then loosen slightly to prevent whiplash and rib injuries. In this way, the seat belts, many of which are equipped with small air bags of their own, serve to cradle the occupant during the accident.

Despite these advancements, air bags still injured some drivers during automobile accidents. In 2006, arm and hand injuries were still quite common. Motorists who placed their hands on the middle of the steering wheel to honk the horn prior to a collision put themselves at the greatest risk for this category of injuries because air bag module covers are commonly located in the center of the steering wheel. Some industry players suggested that warning labels would prevent hand, arm, and shoulder injuries. However, others were skeptical that this approach would be effective since honking the horn to avoid a collision is human nature.

Moving into the second half of the decade, improving air bag safety continued to be a priority for the industry. Automotive engineers and insurance companies were both interested in reducing the number of drivers who were injured as a result of air bag deployment. One tactic was to de-power air bags so that they would not discharge with so much force. However, some insiders argued that this approach also reduced air bag performance. As the second half of the decade proceeded, it appeared that there was not one best way to improve air bag safety.

By the first decade of the 2000s, it had become apparent that air bags were here to stay, regardless of their drawbacks. According to figures from the Insurance Institute of Highway Safety (IIHS), as of July 1, 2008, 27,000 lives had been saved by frontal air bags since their inception. In a boon to the industry, in 2007 the National Highway Traffic Safety Administration (NHTSA) released new standards that require automakers to equip all vehicles with side curtain air bags by September 1, 2012. Vehicles weighing 8,500 to 10,000 pounds have until September 1, 2013. Side curtain air bags provide protection to the head and torso in side-impact crashes. The NHTSA noted that side-impact crashes account for 28 percent of all vehicle fatalities and stated that the new regulation will help to save 311 lives and prevent 361 serious injuries annually, especially brain-related injuries that often occur when a vehicle runs a stop sign and impacts the side of an oncoming car. The new regulations will also require automakers to install head protection for rear seat passengers. According to Nichole Nason of NHTSA, "With these rigorous new requirements, we are building on the strength of innovative and life-saving side-impact technologies that are already available to many new car buyers." To ensure that vehicles provide an adequate level of protection for all consumers, the NHTSA will require that side-impact crash tests use a dummy the size of a petite female, in addition to the traditional adult male model. Robert Shull of Public Citizen, a consumer advocacy organization, applauded the move by the NHTSA but said that more needs to be done in crash tests, especially regarding representation of children and the effects of SUVs and pickup trucks.

According to the IIHS, a safety belt air bag that would inflate the torso portion of the belt and thus provide protections to all belted passengers was on the horizon, as well as rear seat air bags and a pedestrian air bag, which would deploy on the outside of a vehicle. In 2010, Dutch bicyclists lobbied their government to mandate exterior air bags on all vehicles.

CURRENT CONDITIONS

In 2009, 10.4 million U.S. passenger vehicles were sold, down 21 percent from 2008. Despite the economic slump affecting car sales, there was a slight resurgence in the passenger restraint industry, based on the upcoming deadline of January 2012 for all new vehicles to have side airbags. The 111th Congressional House Report 111-564, in connection with the 2011 national budget, recommended funding allocations of $25 million for occupant protection incentive grants (authorized under 23 USC 405[a]), and $124.5 million for safety belt performance grants (23 USC 406). As of 2010, 14 states had passed primary seat belt laws in response to this program. A study released by the NHTSA found a 50 percent increase in risk of injury or death for passengers not wearing seat belts.

Moreover, according to the Insurance institute for Highway Safety, a 2009 study examining the long-term effects of the 1995 repeal of the national speed limit (leaving states to set their own limits) showed a three percent increase in road fatalities attributable to higher speeds, mostly on rural interstates. As of December 2009, 33 states had raised speed limits to 70 mph or higher on some portions of their road systems. Texas and Utah raised limits to 80 mph on certain rural interstates. Critics argued that for all the advancements made in industry safety technology, loosely-enforced speed and seat belt laws still diminished their true potential for saving lives.

If airbags ever proved their worth, it was with the 2009 and 2010 recall of millions of passenger vehicles, notably those manufactured by Toyota, for insidious and controversial sudden acceleration problems. Under pressure from the NHTSA, Toyota recalled more than 6 million vehicles in the United States and temporarily stopped production of new Toyota and Lexus models in early 2010. Disputed alleged causes and solutions continued for months.

Notwithstanding advances in restraint systems, in 2010, car crashes remained the leading cause of death for children 3 to 14 years old, based on the most recent data from the NHTSA. According to Martha Bidez, professor of safety engineering at the University of Alabama at Birmingham, child-restraint systems for rear seat passengers had failure rates near 50 percent. Despite extensive data compiled in her lab, showing improvement in safety through simple design changes, Bidez noted that the NHTSA continued to refuse adopting mandatory crash testing of child restraints in the rear seats of passenger cars sold in the United States. However, the congressional House Committee on Appropriations (House Report 111-564) directed NHTSA to report to the House and Senate Committees on Appropriations, not later than June 1, 2011, on the progress made in improving the LATCH restraint system (Lower Anchors and Tethers for Children), following a 2006 report documenting that only 35 percent of parents/caregivers were installing LATCH-equipped child resraints properly.

In August 2010, TRW Automotive Holdings Corporation unveiled its second generation Head Protection System for Convertibles (HPSC II). The new product operated via a small, lightweight pyrotechnic gas inflator with a diameter of only 20 mm. It worked together with the torso restraint system, and tooks into account different load cases and passenger sizes. With 18 convertible models in Europe alone (2010), the new airbag module concept was expected to be ready for vehicle launches in 2013.

Meanwhile, in late 2009, ARC Automotive Technologies, a producer of airbag inflator technologies, announced a new, "greener" alternative to engage airbag passive safety restraint systems. Labeled the EcoSafe Inflator, it employed a saltwater brine solution mixed with a small encapsulated pyrotechnic charge to activate airbags during traffic collisions. Not only did the new technology inflate the airbag with a non-toxic, low temperature, low particulate mixture, but it also emitted less particulate into the vehicle cabin.

Starting with the 2009 models, the Honda Element SUV featured new dog-friendly second row and cargo area pet restraint systems and a cushioned pet bed in the cargo area with an elevated platform, designed to meet the needs of traveling pet owners. The new family-friendly design concepts were introduced at the 2009 New York International Auto Show.

As of 2010, the global average for safety content per vehicle was $260, but emerging markets caused the amount to vary considerably from country to country. China's safety content per vehicle was just over $200, while India's was only $70.

INDUSTRY LEADERS

As of 2010, the airbag industry remained compartmentalized, in that no airbag manufacturer was capable of internally producing other components of the airbag system, such as sensors and MCUs, although many produced their own inflators and airbag covers. The United States' ARC Automotive and Japan's Daicel were among a handful of airbag inflator manufacturers, while ITG remained one of just a few airbag cover manufacturers. Key automotive safety system manufacturers in 2010 included AUTOLIV, TAKATA, Toyoda Gosei, KSS, and TRW Automotive Technologies. Autoliv dominated the market in North America, Europe, Asia-Pacific, India, and South America.

Autoliv Inc. Autoliv Inc., based in Stockholm, Sweden, was the number-one supplier of car safety equipment in 2010 and was a major supplier of air bags and seat belts in the United States (where it makes almost a third of its sales) and around the world. By 2004, the company held patents on over 3,000 products. Founded in 1956, the company was originally a seat belt manufacturer and gradually branched out into air bags and other restraint systems and components. It received a huge boost in the air bag market in 1996 when it merged its air bag business with that of Morton International, a top producer at the time. Autoliv was also a trailblazer in the market for air curtain devices, which are specialized side impact air bags. As of 2010, Autoliv held 40 percent market share of side-impact airbags. Autoliv had about 80 production facilities with almost 42,000 employees in 28 countries. There were also nine technical centers around the world, including 20 crash-test tracks. A company spokesman estimated that its products save 20,000 lives annually. Near the end of 2009, Autoliv acquired the business interests of Delphi automotive safety systems to further consolidate its market dominance. Its fiscal 2009 revenues were $5.12 billion.

Key Safety Systems Inc. Breed Technologies, of Lakeland, Florida, changed its name to Key Safety Systems in September 2003 and relocated to Sterling Heights, Michigan. The company manufactures seat belts, air bag systems, air bag inflators, and electronic crash sensors. The company was founded in 1987 by Allen K. Breed, an inventor inducted into the Automotive Hall of Fame in 1999 for work on sensor technology used in making air bags. Through a joint venture in the late 1990s with Siemens AG, Breed Technologies worked on "intelligent" restraint systems that would "provide optimum protection for all occupants in every crash scenario," according to company literature. A string of acquisitions and mounting debt, however, forced the firm into Chapter 11 bankruptcy in 1999 as it struggled to restructure its finances. In 2000, the company agreed to be acquired by the auto parts manufacturer Harvard Industries. In 2003, The Carlyle Group of Dallas purchased Breed and merged it into Key Automotive. It reported 2007 sales of $1.07 billion and had 8,700 employees.

TRW Automotive Holdings Corp. Blackstone Group, a private investment firm, purchased TRW Automotive from TRW Inc. in a deal valued at more than $4.7 billion. A 10 percent stake is held by Northrop Grumman, which merged with TRW in 2002 for its defense assets. TRW Automotive Holdings is a longtime leader in the passenger restraint business. The company makes components such as air bags, security electronics, and seat belts, for 40 different automakers; three of these account for more than 40 percent of sales: Volkswagen (17 percent), Ford (15 percent), and General Motors (11 percent).

The first vehicle to feature TRW's complete occupant restraint system was the 1998 Mercedes-Benz M-Class. The company was able to draw on the technical expertise of its aerospace and defense lines to keep its air bag technology on the cutting edge. The 1998 purchase of air bag and steering wheel operations specialist Magna International helped solidify and extend TRW's position in the field.

In 1999, TRW signed 12 production contracts with six different automakers worldwide to develop advanced, integrated safety systems featuring enhanced pretensioners, energy management systems, buckle switches, dual-stage inflators, an inflatable "tubular torso restraint," and head and knee air bags. Headquartered in Livonia, Michigan, the company, through its subsidiaries had more than 200 facilities in 26 countries and employed 60,000. It reported total revenues of $11.6 billion for 2009.

BIBLIOGRAPHY

"2009 New York: Honda Element Caters to the 74.8 Million Dogs in U.S." 9 April 2009. Available at http://www.egm-CarTech.com/2009/04/09/2009-new-york-honda-element-caters.

"Airbags." Insurance Institute for Highway Safety, July 2008. Available from http://www.iihs.org/research.

"ARC Automotive Announces New Inflator for Passive Restraint Systems—the EcoSafe Inflator." 14 September 2009. Available at http://defensenews-updates/.

"AUTOLIV, INC.(ALIVsdb.ST) Key Developments." Reuters Press Release. Available from http://www.reuters.com/finance/stocks/keyDevelopments/.

"Automotive Safety System Industry Report, 2009–2010." 23 October 2010. Adapted from *Global and China Automotive Safety System Industry Report, 2009-2010.* Available from http://www.pr.inside.com/.

Benton, Joe. "Curtain Airbags by 2013." 6 September 2007. Available from http://www.ConsumerAffairs.com.

"Child Restraint/Belt Use Laws." Insurance Institute for Highway Safety, 15 September 2008. Available from http://www.iihs.org.

"Committee Reports–111th Congress (2009–2010)—House Report 111-564." Available from http://thomas.loc.gov/cgi-bin/.

Counts of Frontal Air Bag Related Fatalities and Seriously Injured Persons. Washington, DC: NHTSA's National Center for Statistics & Analysis, January 2008.

Gordon, Jacques. "Automobile Air Bags." *Motor Age,* February 2006.

"High Dividend Stocks and Dividend Paying Stocks." Available from http://www.doubledividendstocks.com/.

International Frequency Sensor Association (IFSA). "World OEM Automotive Sensor Demand." Newsletter No. 7, July 2010. Available from http://www.sensorsportal.com/HTML/IFSA_Newsletter_July_2010.htm.

Kratzke, Stephen, and Adrian Lund. "Crash Test and Safety Research." *The Washington Post*, 24 January 2006. Available from www.washingtonpost.com.

"Nation's Top Highway Safety Official Calls on Manufacturers, Retailers and Consumer Groups to Make Child Safety Seats Easier to Install." National Highway Traffic Safety Administration, 8 February 2007.

"NHTSA Regulations Focus on Side Airbags." *BodyShop Business*, December 2007.

"Redesigned Air Bags Safeguard Both Children and Grown-Ups." *Status Report*, 9 June 2008. Available from http://www.iihs.org.

Schieffer, Keith. "Blowin' Smoke? Separating Fact from Fiction About Air Bags." *Automotive Body Repair News*, March 2006.

"Traffic Safety Facts." National Highway Traffic Safety Administration, 2007.

"Unintended Acceleration in Passsenger Vehicles." Congressional Research Service (CRS) Report for Congress, 2010. Available from http://www.crs.org.

"Lax U.S. Standards for Rear-seat Restraints Put Kids at Risk, UAB Expert Says." University of Alabama at Birmingham, October 18, 2010. Available from http://main.uab.edu/Sites/MediaRelations/articles/81114/.

Utter, Dennis. *The National Survey of the Use of Booster Seats.* Washington, DC: NHTSA's National Center for Statistics & Analysis, April 2008.

"What If This Were Your Child? Most Infant Car Seats Fail our New Front- and Side-Crash Tests." *Consumer Reports*, February 2007.

PET PRODUCTS AND SERVICES

————————————■————————————

SIC CODE(S)

0742

0752

2048

5149

5199

5999

0752

2047

INDUSTRY SNAPSHOT

According to the 2009–2010 National Pet Owners Survey conducted by the American Pet Products Association (APPA) (conducting such surveys since 1988), 62 percent of U.S. households owned a pet, which equaled 71.4 millions homes. Of this number, there were 45.6 million pet dogs and 38.2 million pet cats just in the United States alone. Add to this the birds, fish, rabbits, gerbils and hamsters, horses and ponies, reptiles and other small animals, and it is simple to see that the pet care industry is staggeringly broad and not going away any time soon.

The pet care industry also has a component to it that is lacking in most other industries: emotion. Perhaps no two incidents in recent history better exemplify the emotional attachment between pets and their owners than 2004's Hurricane Katrina (where people chose to remain stranded rather than leave their pets) and 2007's pet food recall, where thousands of animals became ill and several died after consuming pet food containing melamine and/or tainted wheat gluten. For the industry, that emotional

bond equates to this: no product is too good or too expensive for some pet owners, and this keeps the market dynamic, even in tough economic times.

Some attributed industry growth to the rise of such pet superstores as PETCO Animal Supplies Inc. and PetSmart Inc., which offer thousands of pet items at each location, including many premium and specialty products unavailable in supermarkets and general discount stores such as Wal-Mart. PetSmart has also delved into the service market in a bid to create a national brand for the traditionally localized market for animal shots, grooming, training, and the like. More recently, the Internet has emerged as a key battleground for retailers, launching several start-ups that hope to give chains such as PetSmart a run for their money.

ORGANIZATION AND STRUCTURE

The pet products and services business can be divided into three major segments: manufacturers, retailers, and services.

Manufacturers The manufacturing side is dominated by food makers such as Nestlé Purina PetCare Company and The Iams Co. Food accounts for around 70 percent of all pet product sales, and more than a third of total pet spending in the United States. Other important manufacturing niches include cat litter, aquarium equipment and supplies, bird supplies, pet cages and transporters, leashes and collars, and of course, toys.

Retailers The pet retailing business has three subdivisions: large national superstore chains, independent pet stores, and general line retailers such as supermarkets that carry pet supplies in addition to many other things. The first two subdivisions are sometimes collectively known as pet specialty retailers to distinguish them from supermarkets and general merchandise stores.

PetSmart Inc. and PETCO Animal Supplies Inc. are the largest national retailers of pet supplies. Using a superstore format that may include more than 10,000 different products, these stores can often charge lower prices than others because of their negotiating power with manufacturers and because of efficiencies in their inventory and distribution systems. Indeed, they even boast their own brand of products that are specially made for them, often by manufacturers of familiar branded pet products. In the late 1990s and early 2000, both chains were still expanding rapidly, opening dozens of new outlets each year.

The industry also has numerous independent specialty retailers that operate on a local or regional level. These pet stores may be found in downtown shopping centers as well as in the smaller regional malls throughout the country. In general, these stores do not fare as well when the big chains roll in, but because of the generally buoyant market for pet goods, many have been spared from demise. Independent retailers also include in their ranks a handful of offbeat endeavors such as restaurants and bakeries for pets.

Competing with the large pet retailers for consumers' pet supply dollars are supermarkets and the giant discount retailers such as Kmart and Wal-Mart, most of which aggressively market pet foods and a modicum of other basic pet supplies. In the past, specialty retailers have had an edge on such stores based on a wider breadth of offerings and, sometimes, on price. Because pet products are more profitable, however, than some of their other product lines, retailers such as Wal-Mart have been trying to move in on this territory, offering better prices and more selection.

Services Pet services include veterinary and health services, kennel and boarding services, and sundry minor activities such as pet grooming, training, walking, and sitting. Veterinary care is by far the biggest service category, representing about 48 percent of all pet expenditures. Most veterinary business is conducted by local operators. However, VCA Antech (formerly Veterinary Centers of America), is one major national chain. Although VCA had approximately 365 locations in 34 states during the first decade of the 2000s, its share is a small percentage of the total veterinary services market. The American Veterinary Medicine Association reported 23,632 U.S. veterinary practices; the average practice grossed $624,904 per year.

BACKGROUND AND DEVELOPMENT

Although U.S. companies have been meeting the needs of U.S. pet owners for decades, the major forces in the pet supply industry at the close of the 20th century were all of relatively recent vintage. Small independent retailers had been the norm until the build-up of nationwide chains and mega-stores in the 1980s and 1990s.

PetSmart Wises Up PetSmart, headquartered in Phoenix, traces its origins to the vision of a California-based pet supply wholesaler who decided in the 1980s that he could make a lot more money if he opened his own retail outlets. The wholesaler opened his first retail store in Las Vegas, Nevada, and hired Jim and Janice Dougherty to operate it. Called the Pet Food Supermarket, the Las Vegas outlet did a booming business, leading soon to the opening of four more stores in the Phoenix area. The Doughertys, managing the fledgling chain of Pet Food Supermarkets, met Ford Smith, a graduate of the Harvard Business School, and the trio decided to introduce the superstore format into the pet business. Using Toys "R" Us, Inc., as their model, they opened two PetFood Warehouses in Arizona in 1987. The following year, another seven stores were opened in Arizona, Colorado, and Texas.

PetFood Warehouse was re-named PetSmart in 1989. The company went public in 1993. By 2007, it had 600 retail stores. These stores carry a wide range of affordable pet supplies, offering more than 13,400 distinct items, including brand names, and a selection of private brands in a range of product categories. In addition, PetSmart provides a selection of value-added pet services such as grooming and training.

PETCO Takes a Slower Path PETCO Animal Supplies, the number two U.S. retailer of pet supplies, evolved from a San Diego-area veterinary supply store called Upco, which opened in 1965. When it decided to market a full range of pet supplies in the late 1970s, the company changed its name to PETCO. By 1988 the company had grown to about 40 stores and was purchased jointly by the Spectrum Group and the Thomas H. Lee Co. Shortly after the takeover, PETCO acquired two pet supply chains, more than tripling its number of stores.

In 2000, an investor group bought PETCO for about $600 million and PETCO went public in February 2002. The company became private again in 2007 in a $1.8 billion buyout deal with Texas Pacific and Leonard Green and Partners. In 2007, PETCO was the second top pet supply specialty retailer, not far behind PetSmart. It operated 780 stores in 49 states in a "superstore" format that offers about 10,000 pet-related items including premium cat and dog foods, collars, leashes, grooming products, toys, and animal habitats. Like its main competitor, it also offers related services including grooming, training, and veterinary services.

VCA Antech Finds Health in the Service Market One of the largest networks of full service animal hospitals in the United States is operated by VCA Antech (formerly Veterinary Centers of America Inc.). Founded in 1986, VCA's goal from the start was to become a leader in the field of veterinary services. In its second year, VCA acquired the West Los Angeles Veterinary Medical Group and has continued to grow through the acquisition of leading veterinary hospitals across the country. To finance its expansion, the company successfully completed its initial public offering of stock in October 1991.

The company joined with Heinz Pet Products in early 1993 to introduce a premium line of pet food called Vet's Choice. In 1996, VCA merged with Pets Rx and the Pet Practice. That same year, the company set up the largest veterinary diagnostic laboratory in the United States. Nine veterinary diagnostic laboratories across the country were consolidated to form Antech Diagnostics. VCA's laboratory services are available to veterinarians across the country, who also are encouraged to consult with VCA's staff of more than 50 board-certified veterinary specialists.

Food and Supplies Remain Strong, Innovative The array of pet products and services available to pet owners in the United States and abroad continues to grow. Among the products that debuted at the annual Pet Products Trade Show in Atlanta in the summer of 1998 were a number of interesting items likely to turn up soon on the shelves of pet stores across the country. These included Wordy Birdy, from Wordy Birdy Products, a $30 tape recorder that plays continuously (or until the tape wears out) a bird owner's recorded message of the phrase or phrases he would like his pet to learn. Another product sure to gladden the hearts of cat owners everywhere is CatFinder, offered by Pet Friendly for $40. This product is a radio remote device that attaches to the collar of a cat so that its owner can track it down in a pinch. Pet-Ag introduced its $7 Emergency Feeding Kit that contains everything one might need to feed an orphaned raccoon, kitten, porcupine, or other small mammal.

With the growing market in pet foods, specialized segments such as pet bakeries and herbal supplements for dogs and cats emerged in the late 1990s. A gourmet dog food manufacturer, Canine Caviar Inc. of Anaheim, California, went into business in 1996 and two years later had franchises all over California. Several canine bakery chains operated in California and the West, with business expected to grow nationally and internationally. Along with the late 1990s obsession with alternative medicine

for people came homeopathic and herbal veterinary medicine. While the number of nontraditional veterinarians is not known, the practice seemed to be growing. High tech medicine such as organ transplants, laser surgery, chemotherapy, and insertion of pacemakers was increasingly being used on animals as well.

More companies began developing products and services that would enable pets to participate in family oriented activities outside the home. This resulted in an unusual array of products such as life preservers, snowshoes, helmets, and other equipment made specifically for dogs. Along this line, human/canine summer camps began appearing in both the United States and Europe, offering places where owners and pets could engage in such activities as swimming and hiking. In fact, the term "owner" is being used less and less, as people with pets (and the companies that gear their marketing to them) are more fond of the term "pet parent." This shift in perception has opened up new opportunities for services and products and affects nearly every industry including pharmaceuticals, fashion, travel and luxury goods.

Retailers Claw for Market Share For the pet superstores such as PetSmart and PETCO, a significant percentage of their revenue is derived from the sale of pet foods. The competition for the pet food dollar tightened considerably after 1994, when Wal-Mart introduced a premium brand of pet food at a price notably lower than the major brands. Many of the other major discounters followed Wal-Mart's lead. From mid-1997 to mid-1998, sales of pet food at the major discount chains rose more than 16 percent. Regular supermarkets, which until the 1990s had been the primary source for U.S. pet food purchases, took note of the competition from the discounters and began introducing their own brands of pet food and sharply discounting some of the name brands they carried.

Perhaps the most surprising phenomenon in the pet supply market has been the resilience of the small, independent pet shops. Although many were predicted to fold under the pressure of competition from the pet superstores, most of these independent pet shops have demonstrated amazing staying power. The superstores generally don't deal in the sale of dogs and cats, although some of them participate actively in pet adoption programs. The small neighborhood pet shops almost all sell cats and dogs, in addition to fish, birds, and other small pets. Many pet owners, it turned out, felt more comfortable dealing with the pet stores from which they had originally acquired their pets, guaranteeing these smaller retailers a decent level of repeat business.

The dot-com boom of the late 1990s gave rise to Internet-only companies such as Pets.com, Petstore.com and Petopia.com. However, these new companies soon went out of business due to unrealistic or ineffective strategies. The major problem was thate-tailers failed to realize that pet food products, which represent a large portion of sales, were difficult to sell profitably when products had to be shipped to customers. However, even though the Internet-only concept didn't appear viable, the Internet remained a useful marketing tool, if only for a way to present catalogues to customers and as a method to bring customers into the actual brick and mortar stores. PetSmart even indicated that the most highly used feature on its site was its store locator. Nevertheless, Web sites could generate sales, specifically for items that were hard to stock in stores, such as 50-gallon fish tanks.

Pet owners were being targeted with branded products from the likes of Gucci, Harley Davidson, Paul Mitchell, and even Old Navy. According to the APPMA, a growing number of hotels were not only allowing pets to stay with their owners but offering special amenities such as pillows and plush doggie robes. High-end products included electric toothbrushes, fresh water fountains, and self-flushing litter boxes. Feline spas allowed cats to play in a toy gym and enjoy catnip, while dogs received massages and drank from fresh water fountains.

Growth Continues in Pet Insurance Pet insurance, which helps ease the financial responsibility of caring for pets, is a relatively new business that is expected to show growth as both the scope and the cost of veterinary care climbs sharply. The practice was already common in many European countries. In the United States, the top pet insurance company was the Veterinary Pet Insurance Co. (VPI) with 300,000 policies and 83 percent of market share. Founded in 1980, VPI is the oldest and largest provider of pet insurance in the United States. Like other similar companies, VPI will not cover known maladies specific to certain pet breeds—for instance, elbow dysplasia found mostly in large breed dogs, liver shunt found mostly in small breed dogs, or Von Willebrad's disease, a bleeding disorder found mostly in Dobermans and other large breed dogs. Generally, VPI's policies cost $240 to $360 per year. PetCare, another pet insurance provider, has been providing policies in the United States since 2001. Covering 46 states and Washington, D.C., the company insured approximately 400,000 pets during the middle of the first decade of the 2000s. PetCare doesn't cover typical pet maintenance like annual checkups or shots. It also does not cover congenital and hereditary problems. Another company, Pet Assure, covers all pets, animals of all ages and any health condition, regardless of pre-existing conditions. There are no health-related exclusions and the company helps owners save on food, boarding, training and vet bills.

A small but growing number of U.S. companies have begun offering pet-related benefits to their employees, including such firms as AT&T, Home Depot, Sears, Sprint, and Viacom.

Types of pet insurance policies and coverage vary. Some policies pay for all types of veterinary care, while others only cover accidents and illnesses. Some have pre-set annual or incident limits and some have deductibles. Premiums vary and can run anywhere from $99 a year to $500. Pet insurance is becoming increasingly necessary for owners wanting to prolong their pets' lives along with the quality of their lives as an alternative to economic euthanasia. Owners now have access to better care—newer technology and procedures—but this comes with a considerable price. Also, the price of standard medical care is increasing.

Setbacks In early 2007, the pet food portion of the pet supply industry faced a challenge when Menu Foods recalled dog and cat foods produced at two of its plants between December 2006 and March 2007. An FDA investigation revealed that the food contained wheat gluten that had been contaminated by melamine, a chemical used in plastics and fertilizers. The FDA worked with the distributor of the product, ChemNutra, of Las Vegas, Nevada, and the Chinese sources from which the product came, to find out how the wheat had become contaminated. Several other pet food companies voluntarily recalled products that may have become contaminated. The pet foods recalled included more than 100 brands ranging from store brands sold at Wal-Mart, Safeway, and Kroger to higher-end products made by Iams, Purina, Hill's, and Nutro. Thousands of pets who had ingested the bad food fell ill, and dozens died.

CURRENT CONDITIONS

According to the American Pet Products Association (APPA) (gathered from various market research sources), Americans spent an estimated $45.4 billion (not million) on their pets in 2009 (up from $43.2 billion in 2008). Broken down, $17.4 billion was spent on pet food; $10.2 billion on pet supplies and over-the-counter (OTC) medicine; $12.2 billion on veterinary services; $3.4 billion on pet grooming and boarding; and $2.2 billion on live animal purchases.

The APPA presented top pet product trends for 2009 as including natural litter, organic food options, and other earth-friendly pet products. Some new high-tech products in 2009 included computerized identification tags, digital aquarium kits, automatic doors and feeders, enhanced reptile terrarium lighting systems and touch-activated toys. Another trend was the growing market for DNA sampling to determine a pet's true pedigree/mix, especially popular for "pound puppies." Also, 2009 saw a rise in pet thefts nationally, especially those left unattended in vehicles (a dangerous practice to begin with) or (even) fenced backyards. As a consequence, more pet owners were getting their pets "micro-chipped" for identification purposes.

A trend mentioned by APPA was an increasing diverse set of retail outlets now selling pet products. These ranged from large food retailers like Kroger's to home improvement and hardware chains like Home Depot and Tractor Supply. Datamonitor reported that during the first 11 months of 2008, 270 new pet food products were launched.

In late 2008, Menu Foods Limited, Wal-Mart Stores Inc., Procter & Gamble Co., Nestle Purina PetCare Company, Target Corp., Petco Animal Supplies Inc., and Petsmart Inc. won a U.S. federal judge's approval to pay $24 million to end more than 100 lawsuits relating to their selling of melamine-tainted pet food in 2007. The companies will create a fund allowing consumers to recover as much as 100 percent of their financial damages for documented claims. Courts in Canada also needed to sign off on the settlement.

The pet food recall encouraged owners to convert to higher-priced foods that were perceived to be safer. This trend to premium food helped boost dollar sales for the category, despite the dramatic downturn in the economy, according to a report from Packaged Facts (PF) published in January 2009. U.S. pet food sales grew 5.5 percent for a cumulative 20.9 percent (CAGR of 4.9 percent) between 2004 and 2008, PF estimated in its latest edition of "Pet Food in the U.S." Dollar sales reflected consumer trading up and higher ingredient costs, not volume gains. Overall pound sales were slightly down and unit sales were down 6 percent in 2008, continuing the pattern seen in previous years, PF reported.

INDUSTRY LEADERS

Although supermarkets and the large discount chains compete in segments of the pet supply market, particularly pet foods and the most basic pet maintenance products such as collars, leashes, and flea sprays, the specialty pet retail segment is divided between two large superstore chains and hundreds of independent stores.

PetSmart The industry leader is PetSmart, headquartered in Phoenix, Arizona. After going public in 1993, it began to expand rapidly through acquisition, adding 40 stores in 1993, 50 more in 1994, and acquiring a Midwest chain of pet superstores, Westheimer Companies. PetSmart moved into Europe in 1996, but its stores didn't fare as well in

that market. In 2000, the firm sold its U.K. stores to Pets At Home for $40 million.

To jump-start growth, PetSmart began rolling out new equine departments at dozens of stores to tap into the horse care market, which has been traditionally ignored by many pet retailers. Pet food accounted for nearly half the company's revenues, and its vast array of pet supplies and services made up the rest.

PetSmart operated 900 outlets in the United States and Canada and employed 34,600 people. PetSmart provides pet food, supplies, accessories, and professional services. It focuses on providing customers with a one-stop shopping destination that offers lifetime care for pets. Nearly all of the company's stores offer complete pet training services and pet styling salons that provide grooming services. In addition, through its relationship with Banfield, The Pet Hospital, PetSmart offers veterinary care in approximately 545 of its stores. PetSmart also owned the PetsHotel concept, which offers boarding and day care for dogs and cats with 24-hour supervision, an on-site veterinarian, and air-conditioned rooms and suites. The company had plans for a total of 435 PetsHotels. PetSmart Company reported revenues of $5.065 billion in fiscal 2008.

PETCO Animal Supplies Inc. Number two in the pet supply market is PETCO Animal Supplies Inc., headquartered in San Diego. In 2006 the company was bought out by Leonard Green & Partners and Texas Pacific Group, and remains privately held. PETCO operated more than 780 stores in 49 states. Its "superstores" offer nearly 10,000 pet-related items, including premium cat and dog foods, collars, leashes, grooming products, toys, and animal habitats. It also offered grooming, training, and veterinary services, and employed 17,900 people.

VCA Antech In health care for pets, VCA Antech (formerly Veterinary Centers of America Inc.) leads the U.S. market with approximately 375 animal hospitals in 35 states. The company primarily operates animal hospitals and veterinary diagnostic laboratories in the United States. The animal hospitals offer general, medical and surgical services to pet animals. The veterinary laboratories offer diagnostic and reference tests to diagnose, monitor and treat diseases in animals. VCA's hospitals account for approximately 70 percent of the company's revenue. The hospitals' services range from basic services, such as vaccinations, sterilization, and routine exams, to specialized surgeries for most household pets.

In addition to its hospitals, VCA operates the country's largest network of veterinary laboratories. Its 30 diagnostic labs provide services to more than 15,000 animal hospitals in 50 states. The labs provide a full range of diagnostic services, including blood, urine, and tissue testing. VCA posted sales of $1.28 billion for 2008.

Procter & Gamble Co. The diversified consumer products behemoth Procter & Gamble Co., based in Cincinnati, made a startling entry into the premium food business in 1999 with its purchase of Iams Co., a leading premium food maker. Dayton, Ohio-based Iams, under the Iams and Eukanuba labels, controlled an estimated 27 percent of the premium foods market and had sales of more than $800 million. Procter & Gamble's strategy was to expand the Iams distribution channel to include mass retailers such as Wal-Mart. Previously, Iams was distributed only through veterinarians and pet stores. Eukanuba, Iams's top-notch label, was expected to remain in the specialty distribution channels.

WORKFORCE

Employment opportunities in the pet supply business range from entry level sales jobs and main office clerical positions to top level management positions with the leading superstore chains. Within the veterinary care segment of the pet industry, jobs range from support personnel through veterinary surgeons and specialists.

AMERICA AND THE WORLD

The pet industry is alive and well outside the United States, particularly in Canada and the United Kingdom. Britons in particular have been noted for their obsession with their pets. Pet insurance, a concept that had begun to catch on in the United States, is also making headway in Europe. In 2006 in the United Kingdom, 25 percent of dogs and 5 percent of cats had health insurance, whereas in Sweden, 50 percent of pet owners had insurance for their animals.

The market for pet products and services was also booming in the United Kingdom. According to data from Mintel, the market grew 30 percent between 1998 and 2004, reaching 3.8 billion pounds sterling. Growth of 18 index points was possible by 2010, according to Mintel. Growth of 30 percent is possible in the pet accessories category during this time frame. Despite the market boom, pet ownership in Britain has declined. Mintel reported that pet ownership levels fell from approximately 54 percent in 1999 to 51 percent in 2001 and 48 percent in 2004. This was partially due to a decline in the number of families with children (which influences pet ownership), as well as a growing number of single households and households in which men and women both work (affecting their ability to care for pets). Also cited were video games and television viewing, which compete for children's attention.

RESEARCH AND TECHNOLOGY

The pet industry, like almost every segment of the economy, is turning to high technology to develop products for pets and pet owners. One product certain to appeal to any pet owner who has ever been traumatized by the loss (temporary or permanent) of a pet that strayed away is offered by a Canadian firm. The PetNet microchip, barely larger than a grain of rice, is implanted under the skin of a pet for identification purposes. Pets that have been "chipped" are registered with PetNet, a registry of all pets that have been implanted with such a microchip. Anitech Enterprises Inc. of Markham, Ontario, which developed the PetNet microchip, said the technology makes it much easier to locate lost pets, sparing both pet owners and pets a lot of grief. In 2008 and 2009, probiotic and therapeutic pet foods were carried by virtually all major brands.

BIBLIOGRAPHY

"Addressing Pet Care Peeves." *Drug Store News,* 23 August 2004.

Bennett, Laura. "Pet Industry Trends in 2007." 16 January 2007. Available from www.smallbiztrends.com.

Harrison, Joan. "Buyers Sniff Out Pet-Care Deals." *Mergers & Acquisitions,* 1 May 2006.

"Hoover's Company Capsules." *Hoover's Online.* 15 April 2007. Available from http://www.hoovers.com.

"Industry Statistics." American Pet Products Manufacturers Association, 15 April 2007. Available from www.appma.org/.

"Industry Statistics and Trends: 2009–2010." American Pet Products Manufacturers Association. Available from http://www.americanpetproducts.org/press_industrytrends.asp.

"It's a Dog's Life for Britain's Pets." Mintel International Group Ltd., May 2005. Available from http://reports.mintel.com/.

Johannes, Amy. "Live from the Licensing Show: Disney Goes to the Dogs, Cats." *Promo,* 23 June 2006.

Lukovitz, Karlene. "Pet Food Recalls Actually Boosted Sales." *Marketing Daily,* 30 January 2009.

Mosquera, Nick. "Animal Lovers Putting Leash on Vet Care Bills with Pet Insurance." *New Orleans Citybusiness,* 4 April 2005.

Olson, Scott. "Insurers Go to the Dogs, Cats." *Indianapolis Business Journal,* 29 May 2006.

O'Connor, Margaret C. "Insurance Is Going to the Dogs (and Cats)." *National Underwriter Property & Casualty-Risk & Benefits Management,* 30 October 2006.

"Pampered Pet Market Continues to Make a Lot of Money." *Souvenirs, Gifts, and Novelties,* January 2007.

"Pets and Pet Care Take on New Status." *MMR,* 17 July 2006.

"PetSmart Company Reported Revenues of $5.065 billion in Fiscal 2008." Reuters Press Release, April 2009. Available from http://www.reuters.com/finance/stocks/.keyDevelopments%3Fsymbol%3DPETM.

"PetSmart History Timeline." 15 April 2007. Available from http://phx.corporate-ir.net/.

"Pet Trends Forecast." *Pet Product News,* April 2007.

Souers, Michael. "PetSmart's Animal Attractions." *Business Week Online,* 3 May 2005. Available from www.businessweek.com.

"Ten Key Facts from Mintel International's New Pet Food and Pet Care Retailing Report." *Pet Care Trust,* 20 June 2005. Available from www.petcare.org.uk/.

U.S. Food and Drug Administration. "Pet Food Recall." 20 April 2007. Available from www.fda.gov.

"U.S. Veterinarians." American Veterinary Medical Association, 3 July 2005. Available from www.avma.org/.

"Veterinary Pet Insurance Fact Sheet." Veterinary Pet Insurance Co., 3 July 2005. Available from http://press. petinsurance.com/.

von Hoffman, Constantine. "Upscale Amenities Go to the Dogs." *Brandweek,* 8 January 2007.

Wilensky, Dawn. "The Pet Set: Licensors Are Putting their Best Paws Forward as They Enter the Lucrative $34 Billion Pet Products and Services Industry." *License!,* June 2004.

PHARMACOGENOMICS

———■———

SIC CODE(S)

8731

INDUSTRY SNAPSHOT

The newest and hottest sector of the pharmaceutical industry takes offense at the notion that, deep down, all humans are pretty much the same. About 99.9 percent of the DNA strands spelling out an individual's genetic code is identical to that of the next person. However, it is on that tiny 0.1 percent variation in the human genetic makeup that those in the field of pharmacogenomics have pinned their hopes for the key to a revolution in health care.

Pharmacogenomics is the study of how human genetic variations, known as polymorphisms, affect the way in which pharmaceuticals react with patients suffering similar illnesses. Understanding that different patients with similar ailments or symptoms respond differently to the same drugs and diseases, pharmaceutical companies, using information about the human genome, have certainly come to recognize a potential gold mine when they see one.

Developments in molecular biology, molecular genetics, and genomics in the 50 years since Dr. James Watson discovered the DNA double helix spawned the field of pharmacogenomics and a shift, according to *The Journal of Commercial Biotechnology,* from the "chemical paradigm" to a "biological paradigm." Whereas through the 1970s drug development in the pharmaceutical industry primarily derived from advances in medical chemistry, the last quarter of the twentieth century witnessed a greatly expanded understanding of the physiological effects of biomolecules and genetics, pushing biology to the forefront of medical research.

The pharmacogenomics revolution promised an avalanche of new drugs, often referred to as tailor-made medications, targeting smaller and smaller markets. Investment money has poured in from a variety of sources, especially pharmaceutical firms, on the hunch that this burgeoning field will completely overhaul the way in which medicines are researched, developed, and prescribed.

Combining the research of the pharmaceutical industry and knowledge about the human genome, pharmacogenomics works toward the development of predictive medicine—treatments that identify the genes in question for the patient's condition and determine the nature of the patient's response, with an eye toward improving future medicines to more specifically target a patient's genetic profile.

Thus, pharmacogenomics constitutes a radical shift from the one-size-fits-all approach traditionally employed to treat diseases, often with high failure rates, and is thus highly favored by drug companies. The hit-or-miss nature of the pharmaceutical industry results in millions of dollars and years of time lost to doomed drug developments that fail in clinical trials and never receive regulatory approval. Moreover, even the best drugs on the market yield successful results in about only 80 percent of all targeted patients, while some are effective in as few as 20 percent.

Pharmacogenomics, however, promises to change all that. Since pharmacogenomics has as its starting point the particular genetic data that can end up causing the problems for drugs later (in the form of failed patient responses or adverse side effects), drug companies can be more assured of betting on a sure thing right from the start, thus realizing dramatic cost savings, and expanded

715

Global Demand for Orphan Drugs, 2005–2011		
	2005	**2011**
Biologics	$30,200 million	$53,400 million
Nonbiologics	$24,300 million	$28,400 million
Total	**$54,500 million**	**$81,800 million**

SOURCE: *Journal of Pharmacy & BioAllied Sciences*, 2010.

profit margins, in the process. However, while pharmacogenomics will reduce development costs, retail prices will likely increase significantly compared with traditional generalist medicines.

The field itself was poised for significant growth alongside these developments. By 2008, about 2,000 genes had been identified, and pharmacogenomics as a way to determine the best medical treatment for a particular individual was growing in acceptance among consumers, doctors, and insurers. The industry did face challenges, however, including the complexity of the process of finding the gene variations that affect drug response, the need to educate health care providers about the benefits of pharmacogenomics, and the lack of incentives for pharmaceutical companies to manufacture multiple pharmacogenomic products. Confidentiality also remained an issue in the industry. Although 91 percent of Americans surveyed by the *Wall Street Journal* supported genetic research on ways to prevent or treat diseases, 80 percent did not want health insurance companies to use genetic data to make decisions on who to insure and at what rate.

ORGANIZATION AND STRUCTURE

The most important fact of life for the pharmacogenomics industry is that different people's bodies respond differently to the same drugs. Absent that, the industry would not exist. People's systems metabolize and react to drugs differently, in some cases resulting in uncomfortable, harmful, or even fatal side effects. In fact, drug side effects constitute one of the leading causes of death in the United States, at approximately 106,000 fatal cases each year, and result in an additional 2.2 million nonfatal reactions. The primary regulatory oversight for pharmaceuticals, including those developed through pharmacogenomics, is performed by the U.S. Food and Drug Administration (FDA), which is required by federal law to rigorously review new drugs developed for specific genetic groupings.

Building especially on the massive Human Genome Project, genomics involves identifying and determining the function of specific genes. Pharmacogenomics simply takes this knowledge to the next step, applying it to the development of novel chemical compounds geared toward accommodating individual patients' specific genetic configurations, thereby accounting for defective or mutated genes that vary from what is considered a "normal" genetic profile.

Using the latest pharmacogenomics techniques, firms, based primarily within the biotechnology industry, develop DNA profiles of patients that can be stored and displayed on an electronic chip or similar platform in order to determine who will benefit from a specific drug. Generally, such companies are devoted either to the direct development of new drugs based on such information or to the storing and selling of the information itself, or both. Several leading pharmacogenomics firms maintain extensive databases, storing details on genetic sequences and their precise meaning. Drug firms then pay for access to a database and use the information to more accurately target specific patients in their research and development programs.

One of the most commonly employed techniques in pharmacogenomics involves the identification of tiny variations in DNA strains located in the minuscule DNA units called single nucleotide polymorphisms, or SNPs (pronounced "snips"). SNPs determine whether an individual is predisposed to certain diseases and whether he or she will respond positively, negatively, or not at all to a particular drug.

SNPs act as signposts on the genome map, occurring once every thousand nucleotides throughout the three-billion-nucleotide human genome. Thus there are approximately 3 million SNPs in the genome. A small proportion of SNPs produce amino acid alterations that carry some observable functional weight, and are thus the focus of pharmacogenomic attempts to isolate variations.

In order to study the function of SNPs, a physical genomic map of a healthy individual is compared with that of an individual suffering from a particular ailment. In this way, researchers can pinpoint differences in SNPs. A conspicuous SNP may tip researchers off to a potentially varied gene near the SNP that could be at the root of the ailment. Once troublesome genes are identified, pharmacogenomists can either target the gene directly with new drug compounds or can build on knowledge of the gene's function to alter existing compounds so as to better facilitate a patient's metabolism, absorption, or excretion of the medicine, thereby staving off harmful side effects.

For example, some immunosuppressive drugs developed for the treatment of cancer, including azathioprine and 6-mercaptopurine, can generate a potentially fatal toxin when they interact with mutant forms of the thiopurine methyltransferase gene. Pharmacogenomics can help drug makers take such factors into account before the development process. By understanding the nature of the mutant genes, drug firms can alter the chemical composition of the drugs so as to render them harmless to the system. Diagnostic tests for such genes therefore hold some of the earliest commercial promise for the genomics industry as a whole.

Research and development is the most important, and the most frustrating, component of the pharmaceuticals industry. Success stories are few and far between. Only about one out of every 10 drugs entering clinical trials ever sees the marketplace, while the remaining 90 percent either fail to attain regulatory approval or stall in unsuccessful clinical trials.

Drug companies also pay top dollar for the privilege of success in the form of hefty research and development expenditures, which they would obviously like to slash considerably. Analysts expect pharmacogenomics to be a key element in these efforts. By streamlining the development and regulatory process, pharmacogenomics could result in cost savings of about $60 million to $85 million for each approved drug. Furthermore, some analysts expect that genomics, combined with advances in combinatorial chemistry (synthesis of chemical compounds) and molecular design techniques, could cut the duration of the pre-clinical development stage by as much as half.

The prescription process will be similarly altered. For example, when prescribing an appropriate treatment to an individual cancer patient, doctors generally are forced to rely on a good deal of guesswork based on sorely inadequate information about a patient's predisposition to certain side effects. With a streamlined database of drug compounds and genetic details, however, combined with the patient's genetic profile, the guesswork can be greatly reduced, if not eliminated altogether.

BACKGROUND AND DEVELOPMENT

For decades, it has been well understood that genes underlie patients' reactions to medicines, and scientists known as pharmacogeneticists devoted themselves to the study of variations in drug responses between patients. Such studies, however, were generally confined to one gene at a time. It wasn't until the mid-1990s, when research into the human genome began to yield dramatic results, that pharmacogeneticists had a real, solid grounding on which to base their studies of a system's reaction with chemical compounds. Once the methods for studying the entire genome set, rather than only specific genes, were developed, the new field of pharmacogenomics was born, taking off around 1997.

The broadest back on which the pharmacogenomics industry hitched a ride was the Human Genome Project, the enormous, government-funded global effort to decode the entire 3-billion-digit sequence of the human genetic code. Begun in 1990, the project really bore fruit in the mid- and late 1990s as high-speed computers revealed ever larger bits of the code and research began into what exactly the code meant. A first incomplete draft was released in the summer of 2000. The project was declared officially complete on April 15, 2003, two hours after the project's self-imposed deadline. It resulted in an exquisitely detailed genetic blueprint underlying all human life. The final sequence, completed at a cost of $2.6 billion, provided the exact order of virtually all 3 billion letters of the human genetic code. The project also studied the genes of over 1,400 diseases for the exploration of new drug treatments.

In the meantime, however, dramatic new developments were underway. In the mid-1990s, the French genomics firm Genset S.A. mapped approximately 60,000 SNPs over the human genome, shortly thereafter teaming up with Abbott Laboratories Inc. to pinpoint variations aimed at eliminating the side effects of Abbott's Zyflo asthma drug. The development of DNA chips by Affymetrix, Inc. of Santa Clara, California propelled the industry ahead forcefully with the chips' ability to act as tiny laboratories capable of picking up microscopic variations in genetic data contained within a small sample of DNA.

One of the first practical applications of pharmacogenomics rolled out in the late 1990s when Judes Poirier at McGill University in Montreal isolated the cause of inconsistent reactions to drug treatments for Alzheimer's disease in inborn genetic variations. The risk of developing Alzheimer's disease is marked by variations of a gene known as ApolipoproteinE (ApoE), a fact determined years ago. Poirier, however, noted that variations in responses to drug treatments were rooted in the same genes. Patients carrying the E4 variety (ApoE4) failed to show rates of improvement from the Parke-Davis drug Cognex that were as successful as those in patients with the non-E4 versions (ApoE2 and three-gene complexes), and indeed often experienced worsening conditions. In early 1998, Poirier augmented his findings with the discovery that gender added to such variation, whereby women with non-E4 showed dramatic improvements while men of the same type experienced little change. These discoveries coincided with rapid developments in combinatorial chemistry and genetic screening, leading to a number of new applications for genomics in the pharmaceuticals industry.

Cooperation among pharmaceutical and biotechnology firms was arriving as the industry got on its feet. In 1999, 11 pharmaceutical companies announced the formation of a $45 million public, nonprofit, genome-mapping consortium in an effort to facilitate the pharmacogenomics revolution and get information on the crucial single nucleotide polymorphisms (SNPs) into the public domain. The SNP Consortium was originally devoted to the development of a map made of 300,000 SNPs, with an eye toward streamlining the process of bringing tailor-made drugs to market. By late 2000, the consortium was well underway, having identified over 1 million SNP variations, which was notable, considering its original goal was to reach 700,000 SNPs by early 2001. The first fruit to develop out of the SNP Consortium's SNP discoveries was the collaboration between Third Wave Technologies, Inc. and Novartis Pharmaceuticals Corp. to develop a panel of 10,000 SNP assays to be used to better understand genes and SNPs in order to target specific diseases and develop therapies.

Several leading industry research firms noted that pharmacogenomics and other biologically based pharmaceutical developments were edging into the mainstream. The biotechnology sector of the pharmaceutical industry, for years long on promise with little concrete to show for it, rode the breakthroughs of pharmacogenomics into increasing prominence. Sales of pharmacogenomically based cancer therapies, for instance, were expected to grow to represent about one-fifth of all global sales of cancer drugs by the late years of the first decade of the 2000s. However, market penetration was only just beginning. According to *Pharmaceutical Technology,* only 500 of the more than 30,000 human genes were targeted by the pharmaceutical industry in 2003, thus leaving an enormous swath of territory for pharmacogenomic products to cover.

A sure sign that pharmacogenomics was beginning to transform the drug industry landscape in the early and middle years of the first decade of the 2000s was the increasing tendency of major players and regulators to distinguish pharmacogenomics as a separate and revolutionary branch of medical research and development. The FDA in 2003 began to address the pharmacogenomics industry in its own terms rather than as an indistinguishable aspect of the pharmaceutical industry as a whole. That year, the agency issued preliminary guidelines, to be reviewed and formalized by the end of 2004, specifying when drug manufacturers basing their products on pharmacogenomic research are required to submit the genomic information detailing how the medicines in question affect people differently depending on their individual genetic sequences.

The goal, according to the FDA, was to provide a regulatory framework that would eliminate the possibility of running human clinical tests on individuals who could experience a negative reaction to the medication. In large part, the regulation centered on the labeling of pharmacogenomic drugs. If drug companies wished to label their drugs as having evolved from pharmacogenomic research, the FDA required that all such research information be

submitted before the drug could receive approval. For instance, in November 2003, the FDA approved an attention deficit disorder drug by Eli Lilly & Co. that informed patients that a genetic test was available to determine how they would likely react to the medication. Placating drug makers' concerns that such information would be used to limit the commercialization of potential blockbuster medications, the FDA defined limits on its use of such information. As a result, for instance, voluntarily submitted pharmacogenomic information that isn't specifically required by the FDA won't be used in the FDA's decision for approval, according to *The Wall Street Journal.*

Observers also saw a market opportunity in diagnostics, as mandatory diagnostic testing was expected to become part of the regulatory process by 2010. Success in the genomic-based diagnostic industry would come from a company's ability to target and position its diagnostic or diagnostic/therapeutic tandem products to the right disease markets. In the early part of the decade, only a small number of companies—including Myriad Genetics, Abbott Diagnostics, Quest Diagnostics, Celera Diagnostics, Millennium, and Roche Molecular Diagnostics—appeared interested in this potential market.

Not everyone was ecstatic over the encroachment of pharmacogenomics. Even the major drug companies approached the potential paradigm shift with some trepidation, since the very nature of pharmacogenomics fragmented markets. By definition, such research leads to the development of drugs that reach only a small proportion of the general population, and thus money spent on the research and development of pharmacogenomics eats into the resources that could be spent developing blockbuster medications. Some critics at first contended that pharmacogenomics would result in a market full of "orphan" drugs, defined as medicines reaching markets of fewer than 200,000 people. Traditionally, such minuscule drug markets were so unattractive to pharmaceutical firms that the FDA was inclined to offer tax breaks to firms producing them.

To make matters worse, all this came at a time when blockbusters were increasingly the drug industry's bread and butter. With low margins in the United States, price controls in Europe, and a number of lawsuits plaguing the leading industry players, efforts toward mega-sellers characterized the industry in the early years of the first decade of the 2000s. While pharmacogenomics research certainly eats into efforts toward the development of blockbusters, some industry analysts felt the case was overstated. In fact, *The Wall Street Journal* noted that the average turnover of conventional drugs runs about $338 million, whereas pharmacogenomics drugs generally come in at about $285 million, which over the average drug lifetime of 30 years amounts to a net present value for pharmacogenomics drugs at about $85 million higher than that for conventional drugs.

Moreover, the market may not fracture that extensively after all, as some proponents note that for any particular family of drugs created through pharmacogenomics, there may be only a handful of potential genetic profiles since, despite variation in DNA even among identical twins, human beings share almost all the same genetic information. Finally, proponents pointed out, the fragmentation would enable companies to target high-responding patients rather than all groups. This, they said, could provide benefits that outweigh the negatives.

Since the latest techniques and technologies in this young industry are scattered widely, strategic alliances flourished in the late 1990s and the early years of the twenty-first century's first decade. Pharmaceutical companies bought or partnered with biotechnology firms in droves. While many such deals were for a fairly long duration, usually three to five years, the erratic nature of the biotech industry gave due pause to some pharmaceutical giants, which insisted on clauses enabling them to exit the deal in a hurry if the development seemed destined to fail. Moreover, as the euphoria over the emerging developments subsides, drug companies are likely to become significantly more selective in their strategic alliances.

Pharmacogenomics could provide an added benefit to the pharmaceuticals industry by bringing back to life drugs that were shot down in clinical trials for their negative side effects on certain patients under the recognition that the drugs could in fact be marketed to patients with genetic profiles that were not at risk.

Heading into the late years of the first decade of the 2000s, the development of promising new pharmacogenomic treatments continued, holding great promise for the future. In mid-2005, a report from Business Communications Inc. revealed that the global pharmacogenomics market was valued at $1.24 billion in 2004. The firm projected that the industry was poised to grow at an average annual rate of 24.5 percent through 2009, reaching $3.7 billion.

As the field of personalized medicine evolved, industry analysts continued to debate the future of highly profitable blockbuster drugs with large markets. While some predicted their demise, others argued that this was not the case and pointed to examples like Herceptin, a breakthrough pharmacogenomic breast cancer drug from Genentech that was approved for patients with an over-expression of the abnormal, tumor-causing protein HER2.

Before patients can receive a prescription for Herceptin, they are required to undergo a mandatory pharmacogenetic test. This test was a sign of future developments within the health care industry, as providers must adapt to a new way of evaluating and prescribing drugs to patients. For example, rather than relying on average doses, factors such as ethnicity and genotypes will become important factors.

An important development occurred in March 2005 when the FDA issued "Guidance for Industry Pharmacogenomics Data Submissions," a long-awaited set of guidelines for industry players. According to the FDA, the guidelines are "intended to facilitate scientific progress in the field of pharmacogenomics and to facilitate the use of pharmacogenomic data in drug development. The guidance provides recommendations to sponsors holding investigational new drug applications (INDs), new drug applications (NDAs), and biologics license applications (BLAs) on when to submit pharmacogenomic data to the Agency during the drug or biological drug product development and review processes; what format and content to provide for submissions; and how and when the data will be used in regulatory decision making."

In the March 25, 2005, issue of *BIOWORLD Today*, Genaissance Pharmaceuticals Vice President of Medical Affairs Carol Reed commented on the new guidelines, stating, "I think that the FDA believes, based on data they've seen to date, that pharmacogenomics does hold the promise to deliver on personalized medicine. It's been touted for a long time, and people have been disappointed, but I think with this guidance and accompanying comments, they're saying, 'We do think it's a potential solution on both the efficacy and safety sides and we want to encourage you, drug developers, to do more of it.'"

Pharmacogenomics continued to expand into the late years of the first decade of the 2000s. At the end of 2007, the FDA had approved 20 treatments, several for certain types of cancer, that use genomic information to target use. In September 2008, the FDA accepted a new drug application from drug company ARCA biopharma, Inc. for bucindolol, a pharmacological drug used for the treatment of chronic heart failure. If approved, bucindolol could become the first genetically targeted cardiovascular treatment. Michael Bristow of ARCA biopharma said in a press release that "Clinical responses to bucindolol are substantially enhanced when administered to genetically targeted heart failure populations. This makes it possible for physicians to personalize treatment with the goal of improving patient outcomes, reducing hospitalization and avoiding the trial and error process that is common in treating heart failure patients today."

Concerns over Implications and Potential for Misuse
Like the wider study and implementation of gene technologies, however, pharmacogenomics made some people squeamish. Ethical considerations abound, and some

critics fear what such technology could potentially lend itself to. The ethical debate, however, centers on the control of the findings of such genetic testing known as medical response profiling. The range of access and ownership of such personal information will likely spur heated debate for years to come.

While early pharmacogenomics developments will require genetic testing primarily only for significant drug reactions, a series of such tests could result in the amassing of a great deal of genetic data on an individual, at which point very crucial privacy concerns arise. Critics fear the potential for such information to be used to label persons as "genetically deficient" and to discriminate along those lines.

Although the cost of genetic testing has traditionally been an obstacle in the industry, some experts believe it will become less of a barrier in the future. According to a May 2008 *Medical Laboratory Observer* article, the cost issue was being addressed through several avenues, one of which is the "thousand dollar genome" initiative: the National Institutes of Health's goal of being able to, by 2014, sequence an entire human genome for $1,000. A July 2008 *Global Agenda* article stated, "The way things are going, the $1,000 genome will be available long before then." To move things along, the X Prize Foundation is offering $10 million to the first private team to decode 100 human genomes within 10 days for less than $10,000 per genome. With such developments in the wings, the pharmacogenomics industry was set for huge growth.

CURRENT CONDITIONS

In the post-healthcare-reform climate of Washington, policy and political changes affected the industry in 2009 and 2010. The September 2009 resignation of Billy Tauzin as head of Pharmaceutical Research and Manufacturers of America (PhRMA) represented a potential shift in focus for pharmacogenomics. While heading PhRMA, Tauzin, a cancer survivor, pushed personalized medicine and research-based biopharmaceutical companies. Specifically, PhRMA backed such personalized medicine efforts as the Biomarker Consortium and the FDA's Critical Path initiative. Traditional drug makers resisted, arguing that pharmacogenomics was not yet ready "for prime time." PhRMA's new head, John Castellani, had stronger ties to traditional pharmaceutical leaders and business lobbying interests. The future direction of the organization was still uncharted, although industry insiders were optimistic that the push for more personalized medicines would continue as under Tauzin. Then came the November 2010 elections, after which came a party shift in Congress, again placing the future of new research funding for pharmacogenomics at risk. The biggest challenge facing pharmacogenomics in 2010 was funding for research.

Nevertheless, the healthcare reform bill, signed into law by President Barack Obama in March 2010, created a Patient-Centered Outcomes Research Institute. This independent entity was tasked with conducting research on the comparative risks and benefits of drugs, devices, and medical products on the market. With regard to personalized medicine, the new institute was expressly tasked with examining the utility and effectiveness of medical products and services in "various subpopulations" differentiated by race, ethnicity, gender, age, etc., as well as by genetic and molecular subtypes. Importantly, feedback from this initiative was slated to be used for health care coverage decisions, and the final determination would be made "through an iterative and transparent process which includes public comment and considers the effect on subpopulations." All this sounded promising for the future of pharmacogenomics. Additionally, part of the American Recovery and reinvestment Act provided for a $1.1 billion grant for comparative effectiveness research.

These overall promising developments as well as better acceptance of DNA-based "personalized" medicine, by both the pharmaceutical industry and the public at large, gave impetus to a heretofore somewhat tenuous market position. As of 2010, the pharmacogenomics industry had two active segments. A primary segment to emerge was the special application of pharmacogenomics to new cancer therapies and treatments. Secondly, there was an increased interest in its use for orphan drugs (those not attracting research and manufacturing interest from major pharmaceutical companies because they are designed to treat only small patient populations, e.g., those with rare diseases or conditions, or "orphan diseases"). These two segments are not mutually exclusive, as several rare cancers lack research funding and therefore fall under the umbrella of orphan diseases. Both of these segments represented huge market potential for the future of the industry. The global orphan drugs market reached $84.9 billion in 2009.

In September 2010, market research publisher Reportlinker.com announced the addition of a new market research study, *Cancer Profiling and Pathways: Technologies and Global Markets,* by the BCC Research Group. Genomics was the second largest application within this cancer profiling market for understanding gene function, biologic development, and disease progression involving tumor cells and surrounding tissue. Of course, cancer profiling developments directly impacted the future of pharmacogenomics, or drugs therapies personally developed for specific indiduals, according to their own gene profiles. According to BCC, the global market for cancer profiling Technologies was roughly $15 billion in 2009, with nearly $6 billion of it directly from genomics. The global cancer profiling market was projected to be worth $40 billion by 2015, growing at a compound annual growth rate (CAGR) of 20.8 percent. BCC noted that the market would be specifically driven by the growing demand for novel and specific biomarkers in the field of drug discovery.

The relationship between pharmacogenomics and orphan drug development cannot be overstated. The latest research tended to show that different patients with the same rare illness or disease did not respond equally to the same mass-marketed drug therapy, because of differences in their personal genetic makeup. Therefore, development of new drug protocols specifically tailored to their genetic responses appeared to be the key to success. Even in patient groups with similar genetic responses, their disease therapies were underfunded and underrepresented in the pharmacologic industry, which relied on mass-marketed, "one size fits all who have these symptoms" drugs. However, R&D funding for pharmacogenomics remained an issue for the foreseeable future. Under cost-benefit analysis, pharmacogenomics represented the development of drugs that benefited too few patients to make them profitable. In the alternative, their cost did not justify the extra few months of life they could or might give to a patient.

INDUSTRY LEADERS

Medco Health Solutions Neither a biopharmaceutical manufacturer nor a research leader, nonetheless, Medco Health Solutions plays a major role in the pharmacogenomics industry. It is one of the largest pharmacy benefits managers (PBMs) sought by governments, health plans, and employers to help contain rising health costs. As patents continue to expire on large, mass-marketed blockbuster drugs, ubiquitously mass-prescribed by physicians worldwide, many familiar brand-names had seen their best days. According to S&P's *The Outlook,* in 2010, about $9.1 billion of top-branded drugs lost their patents, with another $14.3 billion set to lose theirs in 2011. Less expensive generic drugs would replace the expired patents, and New Age personalized medicine would fill in the gap.

Seizing on this perceived opportunity, Medco began focusing on "smarter medicine." It has opened several therapeutic resource centers (TRCs, 15 opened as of January 2010), each one specializing in a specific chronic disease. In each TRC controlled environment, Medco drives patient adherence to prescription protocols, so that drug effectiveness and utilization studies have more meaning and reliability. Of particular focus to Medco is pharmacogenomics, because through TRCs, Medco can

help patients receive the most effective drugs, based on the patient's genetic makeup. Not only does this have an outright cost benefit, but it also has the dual benefit of preventing patients from taking ineffective medicines and preventing costly drug-related hospitalizations or side effects. In 2008 and 2009, Medco acquired over $13.4 billion in net new sales. Its total 2009 revenues were $59.8 billion, while 2010 revenues were estimated at $64.1 billion.

Takeda/Millennium Pharmaceuticals Inc. Based in Cambridge, Massachusetts, Millennium Pharmaceuticals focuses on three disease areas—cardiovascular, oncology, and inflammation—and it works on treatments and diagnostics for a range of conditions, including diabetes, obesity, and asthma. It has research and development deals with numerous leading pharmaceutical companies, including Schering-Plough. The company augments its research into SNPs, with a focus on genetic intermediaries such as proteins and RNA, looking for variations that can be targeted for treatment. Its major products include the INTEGRILIN (eptifibatide) injection for the treatment of angina and heart surgery patients, which brought in worldwide sales of $303.7 million in 2002. The following year, it received FDA approval for its most advanced drug to date, the proteasome inhibitor VELCADE (bortezomib) for injection, and developed another product targeting genetic mutations for certain patients with acutemyelogenous leukemia. Sales in 2007 reached $527.5 million with about 1,000 employees. In 2008, Takeda Pharmaceutical bought Millennium for $8.8 billion.

Incyte Corporation Incyte Corporation of Wilmington, Delaware, cut its teeth providing databases of gene sequences and related analytical software to drug companies and research firms by subscription. In recent years, however, the company branched into the inhibitor discovery and development sector. Founded in 1991, the company developed databases cataloging polymorphisms for every single gene for use in the development of individually tailored medicines. Incyte also developed a commercial portfolio of issued United States patents covering full-length human genes, the proteins they encode, and the antibodies directed against them, and developed an integrated platform of genomic technologies designed to aid in the understanding of the molecular basis of disease. It also built a client base of virtually all of the world's major pharmaceuticals firms that maintained subscriptions for access to Incyte's databases, particularly its library of expressed sequences linking its proprietary genetic information with biological analysis, known as LifeSeq.

At the end of 2002, the company changed its name from Incyte Genomics Inc. to Incyte Corp., reflecting its desire to become more competitive in the marketplace and among investors as a drug discovery company. In the process, the firm transformed much of its subscription base into drug development partnerships. To boost its competitiveness in this field, Incyte shed its unprofitable genomic product lines. With patents on 500 genes and hundreds of new patents pending, the company obtained a large insurance policy for future growth. In 2007, sales were $34.4 million, up from $7.8 million in 2005, and the company employed almost 200 people.

Human Genome Sciences, Inc. Human Genome Sciences (HGS) of Rockville, Maryland, was founded in 1992. It develops both drugs and proteins, and provides data to fuel its partners' drug discovery programs. HGS's proprietary portfolio includes drugs for cancer, heart disease, hepatitis C, and other ailments. The firm maintains partnerships with GlaxoSmithKline and others, and uses its gene-sequencing technology to develop its database of human and microbial genes, generating royalties when pharmaceutical firms manufacture drugs based on information derived from the database. In 2006, the company was focused on commercializing its two top products, a drug called LymphoStat-B for lupus and another called Albuferon for hepatitis C. In addition, it had completed construction of a large-scale manufacturing facility to produce drugs for its own research activities and for later commercial production. In mid-2006, the U.S. government purchased 20,000 doses of HGS' ABthrax, which was developed to treat anthrax disease. Sales totaled $41.9 million in 2007 with 770 employees.

Merck Serono International S.A. Merck Serono (formerly Serono S.A.), based in Geneva, Switzerland, catapulted to the top of the European pharmacogenomics field with its purchase of its rival Genset, based in Evry, France. Genset focused primarily on the information side of pharmacogenomics, contracting with drug companies to provide data to assist in the development of medicines for cancer, heart disease, mental illness, osteoporosis, and other illnesses, and had just begun to develop its own drugs. Focusing on genetic drug development, Serono was a world leader in the fight against infertility with its Gonal-F, which accounted for about 30 percent of Serono's total sales. The firm also maintained a strong pipeline for drugs to combat neurological, metabolic, and human growth disorders. Serono claimed some 40 percent of the non-U.S. market for multiple sclerosis (MS) drugs, thanks to its blockbuster Rebif. The drug entered the U.S. market in 2002 and by 2005 accounted for more than 50 percent of the company's sales. Merck Serono employed 4,826 people in 44 countries. It operated research sites in Geneva;

Rockland, Massachusetts; and Ivrea, Italy, and its main manufacturing sites were located in Switzerland, Italy, Spain, and France. In late 2009, the company announced that it would set up a global R&D center in China, creating 200 jobs by 2013. The emphasis of the new facility is on biomarkers and pharmacogenomics.

The Pharmaceutical Side The world's major pharmaceuticals firms play a pivotal role in the pharmacogenomics industry, representing the primary customer base for genomic research and often working in collaboration with pharmacogenomics specialists to bring drugs to market.

For example, GlaxoSmithKline was an early investor in pharmacogenomics, including its 1993 investment of $125 million in Human Genome Sciences, Inc. (HGS) in exchange for access to the HGS's database of genetic sequences. Glaxo upped its involvement by forming a partnership with Incyte Pharmaceuticals four years later, this time aimed at the production of gene-based diagnostic products. By the middle of the first decade of the 2000s, GlaxoSmithKline maintained partnerships with most of the major genomics researchers to research and develop treatments for a host of human ailments. Bristol-Myers Squibb, meanwhile, announced its intention to apply pharmacogenomics throughout its therapeutic operations. In the early years of the first decade of the 2000s, the firm joined forces with Millennium Pharmaceuticals to uncover the gene sequences of various tumors. As of 2010, one of its newly-approved orphan drugs was Lexiva (Fosamprenavir).

Nearly all the other big pharmaceuticals firms, including Roche, Novartis, Merck, and Pfizer Inc., also partner with pharmacogenomics firms for drug development. For example, in a $46 billion 2009 deal, Roche acquired Genetech, more specifically, the remaining 44 percent interest in Genetech that it did not already own.

AMERICA AND THE WORLD

The overwhelming bulk of the pharmacogenomics industry's development has taken place in the major industrialized countries, especially the United States. Several countries now have special governmental incentive programs to stimulate private-sector research and development into biotech genomics and pharmacogenomic treatments. This is expecially true for orphan diseases, where, in the United States, the FDA has charged the Office of Orphan Products Development with offering incentives for sponsors to develop products for rare diseases. Europe, Japan, Australia, India (pending), Taiwan, and Korea all have similar govermental incentives.

A report by Front Line Strategic Consulting estimated that in 2006, the United States represented some 60 percent of all pharmacogenomics revenues, while

Europe accounted for 25 percent and Japan claimed 10 percent. The increasing specialization and more focused targeting of drug treatments promised by pharmacogenomics, however, has many critics sounding alarm bells about the industry's relationship with less developed countries. As the pharmaceutical industry positioned itself for a massive shift toward pharmacogenomically developed, tailor-made drugs, some observers feared that since research and development of general, lower-cost drugs will inevitably decline in favor of more expensive target-market drugs, simple economics could lead companies to direct their efforts to particular genetic profiles in the wealthier nations where there exists a greater potential return. Critics fear that those in poorer nations could face a diminished supply of quality medications.

RESEARCH AND TECHNOLOGY

Developments in information technology are the cornerstone of advances in genomics and pharmacogenomics. To make for smoother, more efficient information flow, information technology networks and especially bioinformatics have been quickly developed, in the process integrating information on an industry-wide and cross-disciplinary scale. Bioinformatics is the computer data management that systematizes the discovery and analysis of pharmacogenomics research. Generally, huge databases of genetic sequences and descriptions permit quick and easy access, available over intranets—which operate like the Internet but restrict access to authorized users—for easy comparison and cross-referencing with emerging discoveries. Robot and computer technologies have also been deployed to scan the genes of patients in drug trials.

Bioinformatics integrates and simplifies the vast overflow of new information provided by such diverse fields as combinatorial chemistry, throughput sequencing and screening, DNA chip technology, and structure function analysis through the implementation of an industrial scale information technology platform. In this way, pharmacogenomics can further strip down the research, development, and regulatory processes. By installing intranets to integrate research and development databases, Market research firm Datamonitor estimated that the average amount of time a drug spends in research and development could drop from the current 14 years to 10.5 years.

In the March 2006 issue of *Medical Laboratory Observer,* Tina Hernandez-Boussard, Teri E. Klein, and Russ B. Altman commented, "In this post-genome era, many informatics challenges require the marriage of bioinformatics and clinical informatics. We are one step closer to a more unified laboratory and clinical setting, merging pharmacogenomic information into the clinical world."

Indeed, heading into the late years of the first decade of the 2000s, bioinformatics was a critical driver of the industry's growth and progress. "Bioinformatics Market Update 2006," a report released in July 2006 by the firm Research and Markets, predicted that the worldwide bioinformatics market would total $3 billion by 2010, fueled by annual growth of 15.8 percent. According to the report, the strongest growth was expected in the United States, Europe, and Japan.

Research into genomics also produced a greater understanding of how human diets interact with different genetic types, spawning a new subfield called nutritional genomics. Complementing pharmacogenomics, nutritional genomics was slated as a potentially explosive aspect of preventive care. According to *The Economist,* by the end of the decade, researchers would understand how to tailor diets to suit particular genetic sequences, thus staving off disease. The National Institutes of Health in Washington, D.C. in 2003 issued a $6.5 million grant to the University of California at Davis to launch the Center of Excellence for Nutritional Genomics.

Other developments included the creation of the Genetic Association Information Network (GAIN) in 2006, a collaboration among the National Institutes of Health, Pfizer Global Research and Development, and biotech firm Affymetrix of Santa Barbara, California. The objective of the initiative is to examine common genetic variations and compare them to those of eople who have certain chronic diseases. The first round of studies focused on six common diseases that affect the kidneys, brain, and skin. In 2007, the organization tackled attention deficit hyperactivity disorder, diabetic nephropathy in Type I diabetes, major depression, psoriasis, schizophrenia, and bipolar disorder, raising $26 million for research and genotyping 18,000 subjects. According to GAIN's web site, "Identifying genetic differences between the two groups will speed up the development of new methods to prevent, diagnose, treat and even cure common conditions."

BIBLIOGRAPHY

Annual Report 2007. Washington, DC: Foundation for the Institutes of Health, May 2008.

Brooks, Rebekah. "FDA Accepts New Drug Application for Bucindolol." ARCA Biopharma, 23 September 2008.

Edlin, Mari. "Pharmacogenomics Evolves Toward Personalized Medicine." *Managed Healthcare Executive,* October 2006.

"Genetic Association Information Network Announces Genotyping Awards for Six Common Diseases." Genetic Association Information Network, 10 October 2006.

"Getting Personal: Biotechnology." *The Economist,* 21 June 2008.

Hernandez-Boussard, Tina, Teri E. Klein, and Russ B. Altman. "Pharmacogenomics: The Relevance of Emerging Genotyping Technologies." *Medical Laboratory Observer,* March 2006.

Houlton, Sarah. "Pharma's year of Merger Mania." *Chemistry World,* 15 December 2009.

"It's in Your Genes—Maybe." *Global Agenda,* 18 July 2008.

"Medco Health Solutions." *The Outlook,* 22 February 2010.

Oleschuck, Curtis. "The Laboratory's Role in Pharmacogenetic Testing." *Medical Laboratory Observer,* May 2008.

"Personalized Medicine: A Revolution in Pharmacogenomics." *PR Newswire,* 29 March 2006.

Ray, Turna. "As Castellani Takes PhRMA's Helm, Where Does Personalized Medicine Advocacy Stand?" *Pharmacogenomics Reporter,* 11 August 2010.

"Reportlinker Adds Cancer Profiling and Pathways: Technologies and Global Markets." 23 September 2010.

Available from http://www.reportlinker.com/p0298002/Cancer-Profiling-and-Pathways-Technologies-and-Global-Markets.html.

Sharma. A., et al. "Orphan Drug: Development Trends and Strategies." *Journal of Pharmacy and BioAllied Sciences,* 20 February 2010.

Schultz, Nora. "Chemo Gets Personal." *Technology Review,* 23 September 2008.

Wechsler, Jill. "Personalized Medicine May Rationalize the Coverage of Specialty Therapies." *Biopharm International,* December 2007.

"What is Pharmacogenetics?" 30 July 2006. Available from http://www.royalsoc.ac.uk/.

PHOTONICS

INDUSTRY SNAPSHOT

Much as in the field of electronics before it, the applications for photonics technology were poised to kick-start a minor technological revolution as the first decade of the twenty-first century came to a close, extending from telecommunications to computers, from energy generation to imaging systems, and from home entertainment to optical storage. As the research was refined and the technology matured, the market possibilities looked enormous.

Photons travel faster than electrons—at the speed of light, to be precise—and light waves themselves can carry tremendous amounts of data, thus making photonics a source of extreme interest, investment, and development by major companies in a variety of industries. Telecommunications, data storage, computers, health care, and the military are just a few of the areas in which photonics components and processes enjoyed rapidly escalating application.

Although the sector faltered in the early 2000s, the area in which industry analysts expected the most substantial and revolutionary application of photonics technology was the field of telecommunications, specifically in optical fiber systems. Thanks largely to developments in photonics, telecommunications providers expanded carrying capacity at a dramatic pace, with even greater gains expected in the near future as the vast potential of photonics begins to be realized. Most analysts fully expected telecommunications operations, in the near future, to forsake electronics entirely in favor of photonics. In the meantime, however, most photonics technologies have both electronics and photonics technologies working in harmony as optoelectronics, with photons picking up the slack in those areas where electronic technology is sluggish.

According to the Insight Research Corporation, recent industry developments extend beyond telecommunications and into areas such as biochips, neuroscience, pharmaceuticals, cytometry (a technique for counting, studying, and sorting microscopic particles in a fluid stream), orthopedics, gene chips, prosthetic devices, ceramics, computer processing, imaging, and printing.

ORGANIZATION AND STRUCTURE

Photonics generates and harnesses light and other radiant energy forms, measured in photons, to power technological operations. The science of photonics replaces the electron, now dominant in electronics, with the photon. Photons are uncharged particles of light and are thus not affected by electromagnetic interference. Where electrons require barriers such as wires to keep them from interacting with one another, the photons in streams of light can cross paths with no adverse consequences. Scientists see in them an opportunity to move bits of data at speeds greater than anything previously known in the world of electronics. Photonics uses light for information processing and communication. Light is emitted, transmitted, deflected, amplified, and detected by sophisticated optical and electro-optical instruments and components, lasers, fiber-optics, and sophisticated hardware and systems.

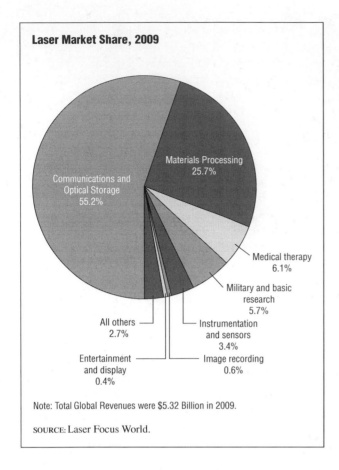

Laser Market Share, 2009

Communications and Optical Storage 55.2%

Materials Processing 25.7%

Medical therapy 6.1%

Military and basic research 5.7%

Instrumentation and sensors 3.4%

Image recording 0.6%

Entertainment and display 0.4%

All others 2.7%

Note: Total Global Revenues were $5.32 Billion in 2009.

SOURCE: Laser Focus World.

Photonics research in the early years of the first decade of the 2000s was geared toward communications, computer processing, and the generation of energy. Researchers experimented with optical memory, storage devices, computer buses (subsystems that transfer data or power between computer components inside a computer or between computers), optical network interfaces, and photon-based processors, all of which could drastically speed up communication and computing processes.

Although they are often passed through fiber-optic cable, photons can be beamed in all directions, thus providing a great number of parallel, interconnected data channels. Data transmission is "clean," with information traveling unhindered on independent channels of light. Given the neutral nature of photons, non-optical techniques are required for putting data onto these beams of light, and so-called photonic circuits still depend on electronic technology. Photonics also means more bandwidth, with photonic processes measured in trillions of hertz (terahertz) as opposed to the fewer than 10 billion hertz (gigahertz) reserved for electronics. Given this high bandwidth and capacity for interactivity and parallel information processing, photonics researchers envision devices that are cheaper, faster, and lighter than anything ever delivered by electronics.

Optical fiber is small, light, durable, resistant to corrosion, and difficult to tap. In addition, its broad bandwidth makes it the media of choice among long distance carriers. Among the crucial advances in photonics was the development of the optical fiber amplifier and error correction. With this technology, electrical impulses are sent to a local phone office where a switch modulates a laser to convert those impulses into optical form. Wave division multiplexing (WDM) is another technology helping to augment the capacity of optical fibers. With this technique, multiple laser pulses of different hues are sent simultaneously down a singular tiny fiber, increasing a fiber's capacity dozens of times.

Of those firms specializing in photonics technology, the vast majority were very small, distinguishing themselves primarily through technological differentiation. From there, the most common practice was to appeal to the major companies opening themselves to photonics operations in specific fields, such as telecommunications, and enter into a strategic alliance or position a company for acquisition. New photonics startups began to emerge as a Wall Street trend by early 2000.

BACKGROUND AND DEVELOPMENT

In the twentieth century, electronic technology revolutionized areas as varied as medicine, manufacturing, and defense, and sparked new industries such as computer science and telecommunications. By harnessing the electron, scientists are able to store, process, and transmit information through wires. Electrons are interacting, charged particles whose power, electricity, is manifested in electronic products such as the computer. The electronic integrated circuit (the chip), which often contains millions of rapid information-processing transistors, is the foundation for all electronic products—everything from computers to missiles to videocassette recorders.

While the advances wrought by electronics have been nothing short of revolutionary, electrons do have their shortcomings. Given the charged nature of electrons, the transmission of data runs the risk of "cross talk," noise sparked by their unwanted interaction. To be effective, electrons must pass through wires; and while a chip might hold millions of transistors, it can only accommodate hundreds of wires to transport the information it contains. In essence, there is more information being produced than there is capacity to transport it, so information traffic "clogs up." In order to overcome such "bottlenecks" in electronic processing, scientists integrated optoelectronics (a hybrid technology combining electronics and photonics) into electronic chips and circuits.

Researchers first explored photonics in the early 1950s, but experiments using light from the sun and from mercury arc lamps proved unsuccessful. The laser and the transistor were born a scant decade apart, yet it was the transistor that would triumph beginning in the 1960s. Early laser experiments for optical computing led many scientists to conclude that high heat dissipation and inadequate materials made photonics an improbable endeavor; but advancements in laser technology (in particular the use of the room temperature laser) encouraged more vigorous research into optics. With the advent of semiconductor lasers and optical fiber in the early 1970s, photonics research gathered momentum, particularly in the communications industry, where industry leaders saw the implications for high-speed data transmission. That need for speed, accompanied by the growing view that electronic computers left little room for evolution, sparked a renewed photonics industry that began to flourish only in the mid- to late 1990s.

At the close of the twentieth century, the Holy Grail of many photonics researchers remained the perfected "photonic crystal." Much as semiconductor chips can manipulate electricity, this artificial structure can transmit light, bend it, and make it turn corners with a minimal loss of light. Scientists have already been able to bend light in the laboratory, but photonic chips are still on the workbench. Despite the revolutionary applications of photonics in telecommunications, current communication systems require electronic circuits at either end. Light signals must pass through these circuits to be converted to electrical signals, a process that slows down the communication process. The development of all-photonic circuits was expected to bring tremendous increases in speed and efficiency.

In a major technological breakthrough, in 1999 Lucent Technologies Inc.'s Bell Laboratories unveiled a single laser time division multiplexing system that would quadruple information transmission to 40 gigabits per second—enough to send 500,000 phone calls per second over a single fiber-optic cable. At a time when companies were pushing toward a record of 1,000 fibers per one-inch cable, this meant radically faster and cheaper data transmission, which the industry needed to keep up with a growing number of consumers and their demands for high bandwidth capable of sending data, voice, and video on demand. (Also see the essays titled Telephony and Voice Mail Systems.)

In 2000, Princeton's Center for Photonics and Optoelectronic Materials (POEM) in Princeton New Jersey, responding to the telecommunications industry's interest in photonics' ability to increase capacity of equipment while reducing cost, partnered with Ultra Fast Optical Systems Inc. to develop optics to improve long-haul systems. POEM's Terahertz Optical Asymmetric Demultiplexer (TOAD) allowed the de-multiplexing of individual channels without optoelectronic conversion.

By 2001, it successfully tested rates of as much as 250 Gigabits/s or 250 billion gigabits per second. (Bits are the binary digits 0 or 1 used in the binary number system.) In turn, Ultra Fast used the technology to build fixed wavelength converters, tunable wavelength converters, all-optical "3R(reamplifying, reshaping, retiming)" regenerators, and optical time domain multiplexing (OTDM) transceivers.

Perhaps indicative of the industry's imminent success was the launching by several entrepreneurs of Incubic LLC in Mountain View, California, in the spring of 2000. Recognizing the shortage of incubators for the photonics industry, the partnership, incorporating the resources and know-how of photonics, telecommunications, and laser technology interests, was established to provide initial capital and management resources to photonics startups, whose numbers were snowballing by 2000. A number of industries were beginning to register the effects of photonics research, none more so than telecommunications.

The rush toward fiber-optic networking was expected to be the main impetus for the rapid expansion of photonics technology during the 2000s. Industry analysts at ElectroniCast Corp. predicted global sales of photonic switches and switch matrices of $16 billion in 2010, up from only $308 million at the start of the decade. The bulk of this increase will stem from booming demand in fiber-optic transport and access networks. Telecommunications applications spearheaded the movement of photonics technology out of the laboratory and into the commercial market. Demand for high-performance optical switches pushed communications firms into strategic alliances with firms grounded in photonics research.

Tough times in the larger telecommunications sector in the early years of the first decade of the 2000s put the brakes on photonics penetration in this market. Facing a severe shortage of cash, telecommunications firms stopped augmenting their networks with new fiber-optic lines, deciding instead that their networks were already wealthy enough in excess capacity to not require yet more lines. As a result of such conditions, industry analysts expected an increase in consolidation. By the middle of the first decade of the 2000s, industry leaders such as Corning and Nortel sold off parts of their photonics operations, while the ranks of smaller companies diminished due to absorption by larger competitors or shuttered doors. Meanwhile, the industry's telecommunications clients demanded a reduction in their supplier base to lower costs and boost the efficiency of their photonics networks.

Despite the lackluster telecommunications sector, market watchers insisted there was plenty of room for short-term growth. Demand for broadband continued to escalate, while the networks' core routers tended to require replacement at least every two years. Network traffic volumes increased at a rate of 35 percent per year through the early part of the first decade of the 2000s, with no letup on the horizon. With communications of all types continuing over these networks, the market for photonics components, if not entirely new fiber-optic lines, was highly likely to expand.

Given the ubiquity of the technology, individual consumers would receive a double advantage: drastically reduced communications charges and radically improved data throughput speeds. The most optimistic of photonics proponents contended that with the expansion of bandwidth to almost unthinkable levels, the cost of overseas telephone calls could be reduced to that of calls down the street, while users could even project entire holographic images of themselves into others' living rooms.

While the optical switches facilitating the capabilities of wave division multiplexing (WDM) were improving all the time, that very improvement was beginning to generate a sort of technological arms race that, observers surmised, the switches were destined to lose. Vendors, recognizing these advancements in switching capabilities, would be forced to expand their bandwidth continuously until the point when their demand outpaced the photonic switches' abilities to deliver. Ironically, then, a bottleneck would likely develop as a result of the implementation of the optical switches. Analysts expected this crunch to occur as the current generation of switches was overwhelmed by about the middle of the first decade of the 2000s.

In 2006, the Optoelectronics Industry Development Association (OIDA) revealed that new and novel investment areas in optoelectronics included advanced liquid crystal displays and thin film technology, high efficiency silicon solar cells, high efficiency thermal LED (light emitting diode) packaging, medical eye surgery, next generation fiber optical transceivers, and standardized laser diode fabrication. (A diode is an electronic component built into a chip to be used in several functions.)

Speaking to attendees at the 2006 Photon Forum in Boston on April 25, 2006, Dr. Michael Lebby, OIDA president, commented, "There will be a significant convergence of applications in the optoelectronics arena which will be led by flat panel displays penetrating many new markets over and above the replacement of the cathode ray tube (CRT) television. Portability will increase with smaller personal computers with virtual keyboards and tiny projection displays. New mobile functionality market opportunities will emerge in the medical and lighting industry."

Telecommunications Photonics was still an emerging technology within the telecommunications sector during the middle of the first decade of the 2000s. For data transmission, electrons were the most widely used medium as research pushed the capabilities of copper wire to the max. However, the development of a photonic communications infrastructure was in view, due to the inherent capacity limitations of copper wire.

In the November 1, 2005, issue of *Electronics News,* Kevin Krewell wrote, "The future really does look bright for photonic, but expect that engineers will continue to push copper technology to at least 10 Gbit/s. (Ten Gbit/s refers to 10 billion bits per second. A bit is a binary digit, 0 or 1, that represents the smallest element of computer storage and is used to transmit data.) Scaling network data beyond 10 Gbit/s will require optical technology, because there is little hope that copper cables can support 100-Gbit/s speeds. The transition will take place at 10 Gbit/s."

Optical Storage The more photonics research translates into affordable consumer products, the more individuals and institutions can expect to see revolutions in the way they store their information. Optical storage technology has grown considerably since the early 1980s. While CD-ROMS were still among the most ubiquitous optics products available during the middle of the first decade of the 2000s, DVD media (including DVD-R, DVD-RW, DVD+R, DVD+RW, and DVD-RAM) had made considerable inroads to becoming the storage medium of choice, especially for large amounts of data.

High-capacity DVD was introduced to consumers in mid-2006, offering discs with six times the storage capacity of a conventional DVD, including Toshiba's HD DVD (High Density Digital Versatile Disc) format and Sony's Blu-ray. Holographic storage was poised to move from the research lab into the marketplace.

An exciting new field for data storage combines photonics, electronics, and magnetism by examining the spin of an atom's nucleus. This field is known as "spintronics" or spin photonics. Rather than directing the flow of electrons, spintronics measures and manipulates their spin, adding another variable to electronic signals and thus vastly expanding the breadth of data that can be transmitted through photonic networks.

The first applications of spintronics in optical data storage experiments were made by IBM in 1997. By the middle of the first decade of the 2000s, spintronics was well on its way. IBM, with its project partner Infineon Technologies AG, was working to produce magnetic random-access memory (MRAM). By 2006, researchers from the University of Notre Dame had published research detailing how logic gates constructed from tiny magnets a few nanometers wide could replace the so-called logic gates in computer chips that are formed by groupings of transistors. Additional advancements were published by researchers from New York University and the Massachusetts Institute of Technology that year.

The bulk of spintronics funding in the United States flowed from the Defense Advanced Research Projects Agency (DARPA), which, among many other defense-related military projects, was also responsible for the development of the Internet. Some industry observers predicted that MRAM could wind up replacing all other forms of random access memory, and perhaps even disks themselves, as a means of data storage. Greatly alleviating one of the major computer processing bottlenecks—the interface with a disk—MRAM would most likely place optical storage on a single chip.

Photonic Computers For computers, optical photon switching holds a degree of promise commensurate with the fiber-optics revolution in telecommunications. The most attractive potential was in the realm of speed, of which there seems never to be enough when it comes to computing. For that reason, next-generation optical switching was a potential gold mine for the computer industry. Inspired by the possibilities of light, researchers dream of the day when computers consist of several processors communicating and connecting with one another in massive parallel interconnections based on photonics. The final goal of such technology is to refine it to the point that computations are performed at the speed of light. In addition to computer-to-computer fiber-optic links, photonics research is evolving to provide solutions at increasingly minute levels: links between circuit boards inside computers, chip-to-chip connections on individual circuit boards, and optical connections within the chips themselves.

Spintronics held out further hope in the world of photonic computers. Research at the Center for Spintronics and Quantum Computation at the University of California-Santa Barbara focused on the development of an optical information processor carrying information on light beams directly into the nucleus of an atom. By combining photonic and electronic components and processes, the computer's quantum memory would be dramatically faster and denser than semiconductor-based varieties. By alleviating the need to convert signals into varying types, maintaining all information on photonic light flows, memory and functions can be processed much more efficiently.

Photonic devices are similar to current semiconductor integrated circuits, so thanks to microcavity technology and the devices' planar structure, they can be built into current semiconductor wafers, integrating more

high-speed features on a single chip than electronics ever could. With the use of lenses, lasers, and holograms, some organizations are currently developing optical computers. The ultimate success of all-optical computing, however, will likely rest in the successful development of all-optical processors. (See also **Holography, Lasers and Laser Applications,** and **Parallel Processing Computers.**)

Video Displays Electro-optic technology has transformed television, with the traditional boxy television set being replaced by the flat panel display. This technology is also applied to computer monitors. The billion-dollar flat panel display industry exists thanks to beam-steering applications, a key component derived from photonics research. Electro-optics may also mean greater consumer choice and freedom from the restrictions of local cable television providers: with photonics technology, electrical TV signals turn into optical signals capable of traveling through fiber optics over long distances. If the industry's plans to deliver high-definition television with two-way communication pan out, many buildings and homes may see their traditional copper wire replaced by fiber cable—an expensive proposition that will require tearing out old network lines. According to Austin, Texas-based market information firm DisplaySearch, the flat panel display market was worth $40.4 billion, while between 2000 and 2007, the sector was expected to grow at an annual rate of 18 percent to achieve sales of $71.7 billion. (See also **Video Displays.**)

The nanophotonic device market—a subcategory within the larger photonics industry that involves the interaction of nanoscale structures with light—was a key driver in the advancement of flat panel and plasma display technology heading into the late years of the first decade of the 2000s. In particular, the light-emitting diodes used in such video displays constituted more than 80 percent of the overall nanophotonic market in the middle years of the first decade, and were projected to grow an average of 90 percent annually from 2004 to 2009, according to *Nanoparticle News.* In all, the total nanophotonics market was expected to reach $9.33 billion by 2009.

Military In addition to providing commercial products based on photonics technology, researchers are combining light beams and electrical pulses in various military-related applications. Given the durability of cable, and light's immunity to electromagnetic interference, weapons systems-based photons rather than electrons may be more reliable in battle conditions. A proposed high-speed optical digital computer network will have effects on avionics, satellites, and ground platforms. The fiber-optic, high-speed Synchronous Optical Network has been adapted for military data and voice transmission. The U.S. Air Force and AT&T worked toward perfecting a "ruggedized" (strengthened for better resistance to stress) optical connector for potential use in helicopters and tactical fighters.

The military has also shown an interest in photonic memory as a means of creating databases of interactive battlefield visualization systems. Existing synthetic aperture radar technology requires equipment so large that the electronics and their power supply must be carried in separate trucks. With photonic technology—particularly dense, system-on-a-chip photonics and free-space optical components—such battlefield tools could conceivably fit in one's hand.

By 2008, the technology that allowed holographic storage was cutting-edge in the photonics industry. Unlike technology that records one data bit at a time, holography allows the recording and reading of more than 1 million bits of data in one flash of light. InPhase Technologies and Maxell released a 300 GB holographic disc in 2007 and hoped to create a 1.6 terabit (TB) disc by 2011. (A 1 TB disc would hold more than 200 times more data than a single-sided DVD.) Because the holographic drive retailed for about $18,000, the market for it included television broadcasting and the like, rather than the general public. However, General Electric was working on producing a holographic storage system that would be marketed to consumers by 2012. Other companies involved in the technology included Bayer Innovation, which was developing the holographic data storage system known as PhenoStor. Wolfgang Schlichting of research firm IDC commented on the technology in *Computer Weekly,* saying, "We forecast steady growth and expect that it will have a chance to succeed existing media about 2010 and appeal to the high-end business user." He also noted that two or three more generations of Blu-ray technology will occur before the induction of holographic storage into the consumer market.

Another trend in the late years of the first decade of the 2000s was the "greening" of the industry. Manufacturers worked to develop technology that would reduce waste, pollution, and the amount of power used. Michael Lebby noted at the OIDA's Green Photonics forum in September 2008, "Optoelectronics will permeate all aspects of our lives, so green photonics is becoming a discipline." The OIDA predicted that the market for environmentally sound optoelectronic products will reach $100 billion by 2015.

CURRENT CONDITIONS

According to Michael Lebby, OIDA president in 2010, the global optoelectonics/photonics industry was "walking on eggshells" in 2009 but expected optimistic

recovery by the end of 2010. He noted that the trend toward convergence of applications created or expanded a number of optoelectronic device applications that typically included displays, light emitting diodes (LED), detectors, image sensors, and lasers. In 2008, the photonics-enabled and components market had reached $745 billion in overall revenues, and OIDA forecast slow and consistent growth for the next decade, reaching $1.3 trillion by 2020. The two largest revenue segments were consumer display/TV and computing/processing. For the 2009-2010 season, slight declines were predicted for automotive (1.9 percent), medical care/welfare (4.3 percent), and communications (15.3 percent).

There were several Key findings in the OIDA 2009 report. Flat panel display revenue was forecast to grow to nearly $180 billion over the next decade, driven predominately by the use of a-Si thin-film transistor liquid crystal displays for consumer products. White high-brightness light emitting diodes (LED) will fuel the LED market, driven by solid-state (or photonic) lighting, vehicular, and signs/displays. This market, rated by *Laser Focus World* to be worth $2 billion in 2009, was projected to reach $4 billion by 2012 and $11 billion by 2020. The optical communications market was expected to grow to $36 billion by 2020, thanks to optical networking equipment using dynamic optoelectronic components. In addition, solid-state lighting devices were expected to hold 30 percent of the lighting market by 2020, reaching over $7 billion. This would make this segment a fairly equal player to incandescent and fluorescent luminaires market shares. By 2012 there will be an almost universal ban on incandescent lighting technology, and LED solid state lighting was expected to take over as the major technology. Because of cost issues, organic light emitting diodes (OLED) were expected to penetrate the market more slowly. Total market value of photonics for 2009 was estimated at over $700 billion globally, according to a published analysis report by the National Research Council of Canada.

INDUSTRY LEADERS

There are literally thousands of companies using photonics, although not all are engaged exclusively in the field. Lucent Technologies Inc., Telcordia Technologies, CIENA Corp., and Nortel Networks Corp. are some of the major players in the photonics industry. Despite the presence of giant corporations dedicating part of their research and development costs to photonics, a substantial share of the cutting-edge research has been carried out by smaller photonics specialty firms.

Alcatel-Lucent Alcatel-Lucent, which was created as a result of a merger between Lucent Technologies and

Alcatel S.A. of France in 2006, is a telecommunications powerhouse, providing communications networks for communications service providers. The company is a top producer of software and telecommunications equipment, providing everything from wireless networks and switching and transmission equipment to telephones and business communication systems. Globally, Alcatel-Lucent is a leading developer of telecommunications power systems and digital signal processors. The company sells primarily to telecommunications network operators such as AT&T, Verizon, and BellSouth.

Alcatel-Lucent's products are chiefly the result of technology provided by Bell Labs, whose research efforts have included an ultra-dense wave division multiplexing system that uses a single laser to open up thousands of channels at a time. The optical switch reflected photons with 256 tiny mirrors situated on a silicon chip. In 2005 Bell Labs Physicist Rod Alferness, senior vice president of optical networking and photonics research, was recognized for making "seminal contributions to enabling photonics technologies and for visionary leadership in their application to networks and systems," according to the company. In 2009, the company reported revenues of Euro 15.157 billion, down 10.8 percent year-over-year. However, the explosive growth of mobile Internet was expected to drive the market back up. Company payroll included 76,410 employees.

Telcordia Technologies, Inc. Telcordia Technologies, formerly Bell Communications Research, was created after the breakup of AT&T in 1984 as a research institution for the so-called Baby Bells. The company changed its name to Telcordia in 1999, the year after it became a subsidiary of the defense contractor Science Applications International Corp. Telcordia provided software to about 80 percent of U.S. telecommunications networks and was a key provider of telecommunications software globally. The company dedicated one-tenth of its efforts to research, with its employees engaged mainly in consulting and software programming, though its focus was broadened in the late 1990s to include Internet-based technology. In 2005, Science Applications International sold the company to Warburg Pincus and Providence Equity. In 2010, Telcorida won several awards and industry recognitions, including being named on the 2010 Global Telecoms Business Power List; the 2010 Aegis Graham Bell Award; a 2010 NGN Leadership Award; a 2010 Billing and OSS World Excellence Award; and a 2010 Global Telecoms Business Innovation Award for its Telcordia Real-Time Charging product. The company reported 2009 revenues of $768 million with 3,245 employees.

Ciena Corp. Ciena, based in Linthicum, Maryland, was a rapidly growing telecom equipment maker, providing dense wave division multiplexing (DWDM) systems for leading telecommunications firms. Its DWDM systems give optical fiber the ability to carry up to 40 times more data than usual. The firm acquired the optical equipment companies ONI Systems and WaveSmith in the early years of the first decade of the 2000s, giving Ciena a stronger position in the market for metropolitan optical networks. Ciena more than halved its workforce in the early years of the first decade of the 2000s, maintaining a payroll of 1,816 employees by 2003. Revenues that year fell from $361.2 million to $283.1 million, of which 25 percent was derived from sales overseas. For 2009, the company reported revenues of $652.6 million, with more than 1,500 employees.

Nortel Networks Corp. Nortel Networks, based in Brampton, Ontario, Canada, was another dominant player in the optical transport equipment field. A string of acquisitions in the late 1990s and early part of the first decade of the 2000s propelled Nortel to the top of the optical telecommunications industry. The company boasted that roughly three-fourths of all Internet traffic is funneled through its equipment. Nortel operates two segments, Carrier Networks and Enterprise Networks. As wireless contracts in Europe and North America fell off in the early years of the first decade of the 2000s with the collapsing telecommunications market, Nortel made aggressive inroads into the Chinese market, where telecommunications growth was robust. During the early 2000s, the company's optical systems were used by more than 1,000 customers in 65 countries. Unfortunately, the company filed for bankruptcy in January 2009 and by August 2010 had sold substantially all of its businesses, which generated approximately $3 billion for its creditors.

AMERICA AND THE WORLD

The United States is one of the world's largest consumers of photonics technology and has been researching photonics for nearly half a century, but as of 2010, Asia remained the main manufacturing area, soon to also dominate the R&D segment as well. In some areas, however, the United States was rapidly shedding its clear dominance. Indeed, several foreign markets were viewed as potential gold mines to the companies most able to establish a presence early on. For example, a March 2006 study from the Consumer Electronics Association (CEA) found that broadband penetration exceeded the 50 percent mark in South Korea, Hong Kong, Singapore, and Taiwan, and was nearly 50 percent in Japan. The CEA study ranked the United States 15th worldwide, behind these and other countries, including the Netherlands,

Denmark, France, Sweden, and Canada. According to the OCRI, Canada had roughly 400 photonics companies generating close to $4.5 billion across the country.

RESEARCH AND TECHNOLOGY

While many photonic products were already on the market, much research remained to make photonics a more viable commercial option in the future. However, the industry was experiencing an increase in worldwide research and development activity.

In the spring of 2006, the University of Cambridge opened a new research facility to house its Centre for Advanced Photonics and Electronics. Around the same time, Ireland's Minister for Enterprise Trade and Employment announced the opening of the Photonics Systems Research and Development Centre. The new facility was located in Cork, Ireland, at Tyndall National Institute in University College Cork, and cost $11 million.

Researchers have investigated many different areas of photonics with many different techniques. Photonic crystals, photonic switches, photonic processors, and quantum information technology are just few examples of the technologies that have been or are being studied in laboratories worldwide.

Photonic Crystals The appeal of photons is also their handicap. Despite the greater freedom of movement that photons enjoy, they are not as easy to channel as electrons. Microelectronics researchers have been able to control electrons with the help of semiconductors: by using an electric field, scientists can control the movement of electrons across a semiconductor's "band gap." This technology has provided the base for minute solid state transistors and for the advancement of electronics in general. Photonics research, on the other hand, has lacked a similar light "semiconductor," and most of the 1990s was spent looking for a way to isolate and manipulate certain wavelengths of light.

One of the major barriers to developing photonics crystals was size. An effective crystal would have to be several times smaller than the ones used in integrated circuits. Researchers at Bell Communications Research used a drilling technique to design a crystal that filtered out certain wavelengths of microwave radiation. Others built photonic crystals from colloids (fine solid particles suspended in liquid). Electrical engineers and physicists at the Massachusetts Institute of Technology used X-ray lithography to build the first photonic crystal to function at an optical wavelength. By drilling strategically spaced microscopic holes in a silicon strip, they were able to trap light of the infrared wavelength—just what the telecommunications industry uses in fiber-optics. With this new technology, light can be bent and controlled much in the way that electrons are in integrated circuits. In March 2000, the Santa Clara, California-based firm Spectra-Switch Inc. introduced its WaveWalker photonic switch that incorporated liquid crystal cells to polarize light signals and direct them with an optical device.

Researchers at the Massachusetts Institute of Technology in 2003 discovered that a shockwave fired at photonic crystals induced a shift in the crystals' structure, narrowing the bandwidth and causing the crystals to alter the way in which they manipulate the path of light. By narrowing the bandwidth of a light wave, this technique raised the possibility of converting inefficient frequencies in a telecommunication photonic signal and alleviating the need for mirrors to redirect signal flows.

During the first decade of the 2000s, researchers were making significant progress in photonic crystal research. One example was a hollow-core photonic band gap fiber with walls constructed of photonic crystal developed by Cambridge, Massachusetts-based OmniGuide. The fiber had applications in the area of laser surgery, and was approved by the FDA in May of 2005.

Photonic Switching As internetworking capabilities become a primary concern among telecommunications service providers, the demand for optical backbone equipment will flourish. Companies such as NEC and Lucent took the lead in developing photonic routers to integrate into an open-switched core network. Speed, of course, remains the central concern for manufacturers of photonic switches. The most advanced optical switches in production in the early years of the first decade of the 2000s routed traffic on a packet-by-packet basis in a matter of milliseconds, but that was still far too slow for the expected demand in the coming years, according to the New York consulting firm Light Reading Inc., which contended that the process would need to be accomplished in nanoseconds.

Meanwhile, the purely photonic optical switch became a more practicable reality. The start-up Calient Networks developed an architecture known as scalable control of a re-arrangeable and extensible array of mirrors, through which the company planned to roll out an all-photonic network that bypasses the need for electronic infrastructure.

While telecommunications line orders fell off in the early years of the first decade of the 2000s, photonic switches could overcome cost obstacles by introducing immediate capital expenditure benefits. When combined with nano-scale design, photonic switches can handle multiple functions within a fiber-optic network at about one-fourth theper-port price of the electronic fabric systems generally used in such networks in the early years of the decade.

By 2006, the National Science Foundation was working on a five-year project called Optiputer that involved the use of photonic switches to boost the performance of computer networks. In particular, the project was focused on improving the bandwidth connecting research scientists. By taking advantage of optical fiber, the project hoped to improve the networked environment scientists used to collaborate.

For the time being, the competition between emerging all-optical photonic switching and the traditional optical-to-electrical-to-optical conversion will continue, with the potential benefits promised by an all-optical technology forestalled by the immature stage of development so far attained. There was universal agreement among industry players and analysts, however, that all-photonic switching technology would eventually emerge as the dominant format in fiber-optic telecommunications.

Quantum Information Technology In 1998, applied physicists at Stanford University reached a long-sought goal: they developed a "single-photon turnstile device," the first device capable of creating a beam of light composed of a steady stream of photons. By overcoming the noise caused by microscopic variations in ordinary light, the device paved the way for scientists to advance in such nascent, cutting-edge fields as quantum information technology. This research area brings new computation and encryption techniques with major implications for the future of mainstream computers and telecommunications devices. Quantum computers, for example, could solve problems millions of times more quickly than the most powerful supercomputer currently on the market. A research team from IBM Corp., the Massachusetts Institute of Technology, the University of California-Berkeley, and Oxford University has reportedly built the world's first computer modeled on the principles of quantum mechanics.

Photonics advocates dream of the day when information processing is entirely optical, whereby light is used to define the transmission of a signal beam. The final result, once again, is greater speed: with all-optical processors, computers, telecommunications equipment, and other devices will be able to operate without having to translate between electrons and photons. The main barriers to all-optical signal processing continue to be the properties of the materials it requires.

Evolving Processes Meanwhile, engineers made major breakthroughs in the manufacturing process that will allow optical network component designers substantially more control. For example, a partnership between Tohoku University in Japan and Photonic Lattice Inc. resulted in a process whereby silicon refractive indexes commonly used in the construction of semiconductors were employed to provide pinpoint accuracy in creating the patterns used to reflect and direct light. The researchers referred to the process as "autocloning." Since the optimal working of photonic equipment required accuracy at the smallest level possible, this nano-scale level of control could provide for vastly improved efficiencies.

Nanotechnology provided another major boost to manufacturing processes as well as potential photonic end uses. Although scores of research projects met with success in designing aspects of photonic components at the sub-wavelength level, by the middle years of the first decade of the 2000s, no such efforts yielded a manufacturable and integrated photonic circuit. The California Institute of Technology took the largest strides toward this goal by concentrating optical signals into nano-optic cavities where the signals are literally contained, since photons traveling below certain wavelengths are unable to travel through the photonic-bandgap material. The laws of quantum physics thus prevent any leakage, while the nanotechnological manipulation processes provide the means by which efficient photonic circuitry becomes a possibility. With such processes, manufacturers can greatly reduce the size of photonic circuits for integration into larger components in greater numbers, allowing for exponentially greater control.

In mid-2008, the University of California School of Engineering received a $4.3 million grant from DARPA to develop continuously tunable optical delays. With these systems, multiplexing could take place entirely in the photonic domain, without having to convert light streams into electronic signals and back again. According to *EDN*, researchers have successfully delayed an 80 GB per second (Gbps) data stream and multiplexed two 40-Gbps streams. In addition, researchers "hope to reach capacity in the hundreds of gigabits per second and aim to produce a system that can delay light by as much as 5 msec, which would represent a 50-fold improvement over the 100-nsec result they have published thus far."

BIBLIOGRAPHY

"A Logical Leap; Spintronics." *The Economist,* 14 January 2006.

Adshead, Antony. "Is Holography the Future for Storage?" *Computer Weekly,* 7 August 2007.

"Advance Nanotech and Partners Celebrate Grand Opening of New Research and Development Facility." *Business Wire,* 26 April 2006.

Anderson, Stephen G. "The Greening of Photonics." *Laser Focus World,* August 2008.

"Atal, Maha. "Spin Is In." *Forbes,* 15 September 2008.

Ciena. Press releases, 10 December 2009. Available from http://www.ciena.com/news/news_22377.htm.

"Colossal Storage Corp.—3D Atomic Holographic Optical Data Storage." Colossal Storage, 2010. Available from http://colossalstorage.net/colossal5.htm.

"Fourth Quarter and Full Year 2009 Results." Alcatel-Lucent, 11 February 2010. Available from http://www.alcatel-lucent.com/wps/portal/newsreleases.

Gaughan, Richard. "Photonic Switches Put the Internet on Steroids." *R & D,* January 2006.

"GE Moves to Holographic Data Storage." *Holography News,* May 2008.

"Holographic Lithography Enables Complicated 3-D Photonic Crystals." *Laser Focus World,* February 2008.

Lebby, Michael. "In the Focus: the Photonics Industry in the USA." *Photonics 21,* 2009. Available at http://www.photonics21.org/.

Marx, Bridget K. "Ireland Invests Millions in New Photonics Centre." *Optoelectronics Report,* 1 May 2006.

National Research Council. "Photonics Expertise Helps Clients Generate $500 Million in Revenue–Impact Analysis Reports." OCRI News Release, 27 October 2009 Available from http://ocrinews.wordpress.com/.

"New CEA Study Finds 43 Million American Households Now Have Broadband Internet Access." *Business Wire,* 30 March 2006.

"Nortel News Releases: Nortel Reports Financial Results for the Second Quarter 2010." Cleary-Nortel, 13 August 2010. Available from http://www.cleary-nortel.

"OIDA Holds Green Photonics Forum." *Business Wire,* 11 September 2008.

"OIDA Predicts Decade of Strong Growth in Worldwide Optoelectronics Market." Optoelectronics Industry Development Association, 1 May 2006. Available from http://www.oida.org/.

"OIDA Releases 9th Global Optoelectronics Market Data Summary." Optoelectronics Industry Development Association, 11 September 2008. Available from http://www.oida.org/.

Overton, Gail. "Photonic-Crystal Switch Is Ultracompact." *Laser Focus World,* March 2008.

Overton, Gail, Stephen G. Anderson, David A. Belforte, and Tom Hausken. "LASER MARKETPLACE 2010: How Wide is the Chasm?" *Laser Focus World,* 1 January 2010.

"Photonics Researchers Decelerate Light to Accelerate Data." *EDN ,* 21 August 2008.

"Quantum Scientists Study Spintronics." *UPI NewsTrack,* 12 July 2006.

"Telcordia Sees International Sales Growth But is Cautious." 18 October 2010. Available at http://vanillaplus.com/news/telecordia.

PHOTOVOLTAIC SYSTEMS

—■—

SIC CODE(S)

3674

3825

3699

INDUSTRY SNAPSHOT

The untapped energy potential of the sun is enormous. For instance, scientists have surmised that a single day's worth of sunlight, if properly harnessed and converted, could supply the entire energy needs of the United States for two years and that a daily dose of solar energy outpaces that of the world's entire fossil fuel energy by a ratio of 1,000 to 1. Photovoltaic (PV) systems act as the mediator between the sun and the desired energy by converting sunlight directly to electricity. Research and development in the closing years of the twentieth century pushed the technology within the grasp of those wishing to market it to a mass audience in the consumer and industrial worlds. PV systems were finding increasing employment in households, automobiles, and remote power systems and for telecommunications, lighting systems, and a range of other applications. More than 1 million homes around the world were powered by photovoltaic cells, according to *Appropriate Technology,* the bulk of them in developing countries that received significant funding for the introduction of solar power.

While the efficiency of electronic components for electrical systems improved rapidly throughout the early 2000s, the amount of power drawn from electric utilities continued to escalate and the solution to the increased energy demand was far from certain by mid-decade. Solar energy squared off with fuel cells, wind power, biomass, and other technologies for predominance in the renewable market. Although solar power was among the most hotly anticipated of all renewable energy sources, by the beginning of the twenty-first century, the sun accounted for only about 1 percent of all the renewable energy consumed in the United States.

Solar power continues to be less cost efficient than conventional power. A 50-kilowatt system, which is the size needed to power a small office building, costs approximately $350,000 to install. Even in sunny southern states, the 80,000 kilowatt hours produced per year, which would cost $7,200 at a retail rate of nine cents per kilowatt hour, only provide a 2 percent dividend. Demand for solar power in remote areas and government incentives allow the solar industry to survive until research breakthroughs or a continued rise in energy prices will make PV systems more competitive.

According to BCC Research, the global market will grow to $32 billion in 2012. RBC Capital Markets made a similar projection, with expectations that the demand for PV power would grow by 40 percent by 2011. Stuart Bush of RBC told *Space Daily,* "Today, solar energy costs nearly double what would be economical without subsidies, but solar energy companies are aggressively pursuing their Holy Grail: Organic competitiveness with grid electricity."

ORGANIZATION AND STRUCTURE

The term "photo" stems from the Greek word *phos,* which means light. "Volt" is named for Alessandro Volta (1745–1827), a pioneer in the study of electricity. "Photovoltaics," then, could literally mean light electricity.

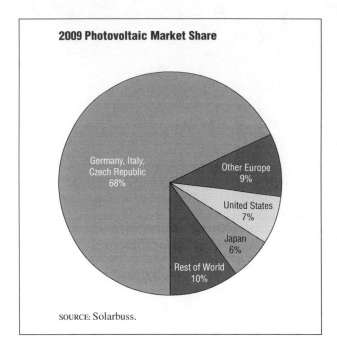

2009 Photovoltaic Market Share

Germany, Italy, Czech Republic 68%

Other Europe 9%

United States 7%

Japan 6%

Rest of World 10%

SOURCE: Solarbuss.

Solar power has long been recognized as a potentially inexhaustible, inexpensive source of energy. Within solar power, there are active and passive systems that include solar thermal, heating, cooling, and lighting, and photovoltaic or solar electric systems. Although both systems gather and contain energy, they distribute it in different ways. PV cells, panels, and arrays consist primarily of silicon, the second most abundant element on Earth, or other semiconductor materials. When these are combined with other materials, they exhibit electrical properties in the presence of sunlight, generating direct current (DC) electricity. Electrons are charged by the light and move through the silicon. This is known as the photovoltaic effect. Photovoltaic systems typically carry a life span of about 20 years, during which time maintenance and servicing are minimal, as there are no moving components. The typical PV panel in the early 2000s was about two feet by five feet and generated about 75 to 100 watts of electricity.

Of equal importance is the fact that there are few power generation technologies as environmentally friendly as PV systems. During operation, PV systems generate no noise, hazardous waste, or pollution. These systems are used in a wide variety of applications, including wireless and cellular communications, recreational vehicles and boats, off-grid homes, and crop irrigation systems. In developing countries, PV systems are used for water purification, water pumping, and vaccine refrigeration.

The overwhelming bulk of federal research funding for solar energy passed through the U.S. Department of Energy (DOE), particularly the National Renewable Energy Laboratory and the National Center for Photovoltaics (NCP). The latter was created to facilitate cooperative research efforts between the industry, government, and universities and establish guidelines to help bring about a solar power industry that, by 2030, would enjoy an annual growth rate of 25 percent and would maintain a central position in the U.S. and world energy markets. Most of the government funding went to universities and industry players to develop cheaper and more efficient semiconductor materials and components while at the same time boosting total capacity and production rates. Moreover, to bring about commercial success and thus ensure U.S. leadership of the PV industry, the NCP fostered the development of PV product standards, simplified maintenance procedures, and called for the elimination of legislative and regulatory obstacles to the development and promotion of PV technology.

Technology Experience to Accelerate Markets in Utility Photovoltaics (TEAM-UP) is a program designed to assist in developing commercial markets for a wide range of solar photovoltaic technologies. TEAM-UP, managed since 1994 by the Utility PhotoVoltaic Group, is in partnership with the utility industries and the Department of Energy (DOE). It provides cost sharing for selected PV business ventures in the United States; and because funding is provided by the U.S. government, TEAM-UP support is restricted to U.S. firms.

The Utility PhotoVoltaic Group is a nonprofit association of 90 electric utilities and electric service organizations in the United States, Canada, Europe, Australia, and the Caribbean, cooperating to accelerate the commercial use of solar electricity. The DOE's $5 million grant in 1998 was awarded to 14 solar electric businesses in the Utility PhotoVoltaic Group and also helped attain an additional $27 million in private funding to be used to support 1,000 systems in 12 states and Puerto Rico.

The industry has its share of concerns. Although efforts are being made to reduce costs, solar energy systems are still rather expensive. Nonetheless, by building upgraded, innovative photovoltaic systems and equipment, manufacturers are providing jobs and reducing the rate of consumption of polluting fossil fuels. Extensive use of solar energy technology will have a beneficial impact on air pollution and global climate change. PV technology can also help generate ethanol and methanol, which are themselves quickly gaining popularity as alternative fuel sources.

BACKGROUND AND DEVELOPMENT

The first experimenter to successfully convert sunlight into electricity was French physicist Edmond Becquerel (1820–1891), who noted the PV effect in 1839 when he built a device that could measure the intensity of light by observing the strength of an electric current between two metal plates. For over 110 years following the initial discovery of the PV effect, scientists experimented with different materials in an attempt to find a practical use for PV systems. In the late nineteenth century, scientists discovered that the metal selenium was particularly sensitive to sunlight, and during the 1880s, Charles Fritts constructed the first selenium solar cell. His device, however, was inefficient, converting less than 1 percent of the received light into usable electricity.

The Fritts selenium solar cell was mostly forgotten until the 1950s, when the drive to produce an efficient solar cell was renewed. It was known that the key to the photovoltaic cell lay in creating a semiconductor that would release electrons when exposed to radiation within the visible spectrum. During this time, researchers at the Bell Telephone Laboratories were developing similar semiconductors to be used in communication systems. By accident, Bell scientists Calvin Fuller and Daryl Chapin found the perfect semiconductor: a hybridized crystal called a "doped" cell, which was made of phosphorous and boron. The first solar cells using these new crystals debuted in 1954 and yielded a conversion efficiency of nearly 6 percent. Later improvements in the design increased the efficiency to almost 15 percent.

In 1957, Bell Telephone used a silicon solar cell to power a telephone repeater station in Georgia. The process was considered a success although it was still too inefficient to penetrate the general marketplace. The first real application of silicon solar cells came in 1958 when a solar array was used to provide electricity for the radio transmitter of *Vanguard 1,* the second U.S. satellite to orbit Earth. Solar cells have been used on almost every satellite launched since.

The oil crisis in the early 1970s and the nuclear accidents at Three Mile Island in New York and in Chernobyl in Ukraine, greatly enhanced the public's desire for alternative and renewable energies. As environmental consciousness grew, solar energy became the darling of the renewables category. It was not until the late twentieth century that solar energy became practical and economical enough to warrant its broad-scale marketing as one of the primary energy sources of the future. In the 1990s alone, the price of solar energy dropped 50 percent as technology continued to advance. It was during that period that PV applications went from a niche source of electricity to bringing solar technology to the threshold of big business. According to the Solar Energy Industries Association, over 10,000 homes in the United States were powered completely by solar energy in the late 1990s, and an additional 200,000 homes incorporated some form of photovoltaic system. The worldwide PV market in 2000 reached well over $1 billion.

The issuance of Executive Order 13123, along with the Million Solar Roofs Initiative, aimed at adding solar power systems to 1 million buildings throughout the United States by 2010. Shortly thereafter, a photovoltaic system was installed in the Pentagon as part of the massive renovation of the structure. The system was expected to displace about 48,000 pounds of carbon dioxide per year. The Million Solar Roofs Initiative offered a 15 percent tax credit with a $1,000 cap for solar thermal panels and a $2,000 cap for PV panels. The initiative had won over half a million commitments by the end of 1999. According to the Solar Energy Industries Association, the proposal for the million roofs would help deliver reliable PV-generated electricity to American consumers at a competitive price, lead to the construction of new plants in over 20 states, create 70,000 jobs in the PV industry, and increase the U.S. industry share from 40 to 60 percent.

Solar power still represented only about 1 percent of all electric power in the United States in 2003, primarily due to persistently high costs and the continuing availability of cheap energy via traditional sources. Thus there was little market-based incentive for customers to replace their existing energy technologies with photovoltaic systems. As a result, much of the growth in the deployment of solar power was expected to come from non-market forces—particularly from state and local government-sponsored initiatives. The industry's reliance on subsidies was thus unlikely to abate until at least late in the decade.

The deregulation of the utilities industries set back efforts toward implementation of PV systems by the nation's power companies in the late 1990s and early in the first decade of the twenty-first century by eliminating solar power incentives. As a result, according to *Power Engineering,* utilities were less willing to spend significant funds to develop technologies that might take years to bring to term and turn a profit.

Total solar cell production jumped 37 percent to reach 395 megawatts in 2001. By late 2002, according to the Earth Policy Institute, worldwide photovoltaic capacity exceeded 1,840 megawatts. The International Energy Agency further reported that PV capacity expanded some 900 percent between 1993 and 2003, during which time average PV panel costs fell from $5.69/peak watt to $3.46/peak watt, representing a 38 percent decline, according to the U.S. Department of Energy. Meanwhile, Arthur Rudin, the director of engineering for industry leader Sharp's solar operations, noted in 2003 that during his career in the industry beginning in the early 1970s—when the industry first started to gain momentum and significant funding—the average price for solar modules fell from about $200 per watt to only $5 per watt. While this highlighted the industry's progress in overcoming one of its highest hurdles in the route toward commercialization, it wasn't quite enough to induce consumers to overhaul their electrical systems. Industry analysts held that that per watt cost would need to sink closer to the $1.00 mark before the industry enjoyed serious market penetration.

By the start of the twenty-first century, there were over 100,000 people using solar power and living "off the grid," or independent of utility companies, in the United States, while worldwide, some 1.7 billion people lived outside of an electrical grid. Most solar systems in an average home are capable of producing 800 to 900 watts of power, enough to operate most basic electrical needs without the cost of monthly utility bills. By contrast, the start-up costs of powering new homes can be as high as $15,000.

Major oil and gas companies have committed large sums of money to develop new research and development outfits devoted to renewable energy. Royal Dutch/Shell Group, for instance, established Shell International Renewables in the late 1990s to study solar energy and biomass fuel, while British Petroleum (BP) established BP Solar, which opened a PV system operation in California. These firms' later incarnations emerged as major industry players in terms of both sales and research and development.

The efficiency of modern PV technology was noted by the accounting giant KPMG, which estimated that a large factory producing 5 million PV panels each year could power 250,000 households, thereby slashing energy costs by about 75 percent. Such a factory could, according to KPMG, be built at a cost of about $660 million.

Solar energy had yet to become a mainstay of the U.S. energy system. However, volatile energy markets in the early part of the decade, coupled with increasingly pronounced environmental concerns among a growing segment of the population, made for a sunny long-term outlook for the photovoltaic industry. With production costs inching downward and efficiencies rapidly improving, many observers expected that the long-awaited solar energy boom was just around the corner. Indeed, the market for photovoltaic (PV) cells was expanding rapidly. According to the San Francisco-based research group Clean Edge, shipments of PV cells grew at an average annual rate of 30 percent between 1999 and 2002, when sales reached $3.5 billion.

With the Energy Policy Act of 2005 offering tax incentives and photovoltaic efficiency improving, the demand for solar power continued to rise. The market for photovoltaics increased globally an average of 25 percent annually from 1996 to 2006; the foremost increase was seen from 2001 to 2006, with an annual growth rate of 35 percent, according to the Solar Energy Industries Association (SEIA). That translates into a doubling of installed solar power every four years, with comparable growth expected to continue.

The California Public Utilities Commission (PUC) allocated $300 million for solar photovoltaic technologies in December 2005, tripling its previous funding for solar power research, with the aim of building 3,000 megawatts of solar energy by 2015. The PUC proposes to offer customer incentives in the amount of $2.5 billion from 2007 through 2016 for existing residences, public buildings, industrial facilities, businesses, and agricultural facilities. Also available as incentives will be $350 million for builders and developers of new housing. This program makes California the state with the largest solar power investment.

In early 2006, only 20 percent of LEED-certified (Leadership in Energy and Environmental Design) projects incorporated PV systems. The major reason for this low percentage is the cost, especially for those projects not receiving tax benefits or low-peak-period power rates. However, by 2006, the cost of the systems began to drop, with a PV module costing approximately $6 per watt and being able to produce electricity for 25 to 30 cents per kilowatt hour. Five to 15 percent of sunlight can be converted into electricity utilizing commercial PV systems and they are expected to last at least 20 years.

The California PUC adopted the Solar Initiative in January 2006, which emulated the Million Solar Roofs plan. The Solar Initiative aspired to install 3,000 MV of solar power by 2016 with the help of customer incentives for installing PV or other solar power systems.

According to the Interstate Renewable Energy Council (IREA), more than 80,000 solar energy systems were installed in the United States in 2007, and the industry was expected to continue to grow due to rising energy costs, consumer demand, and financial incentives such as tax breaks from state and federal governments. Capacity of photovoltaic (PV) systems rose 48 percent as compared to 2006, and, although New Jersey, Nevada, Colorado, and California hold most of the market, PV systems were spreading to other states as well. California is the largest market for PV systems, with 69 percent of the market share in 2007. Other states in the top 10 included New York, Arizona, Hawaii, Connecticut, Massachusetts, and Oregon. Significantly, several states passed legislation in 2006 and 2007 that encouraged the use of solar energy. For example, in 2007 California began the $3 billion California Solar Initiative, a 10-year project that includes rebates given to public utilities customers that install and use solar systems.

Solar hot water installations also increased in 2007, due in part to a 2006 federal investment tax credit.

According to IREA, the installations of such systems quadrupled between 2005 and 2007. Although Hawaii has traditionally represented the largest market, the number of systems installed outside of Hawaii has risen dramatically. Florida and California are the second and third largest markets for solar hot water power. As of mid-2008, the industry was waiting to see whether federal tax credits that were set to expire at the end of the year would be renewed. Renewal of those would bode well for the industry.

CURRENT CONDITIONS

In the *Clean Energy Trends 2010* report produced by Clean Edge, the solar PV industry was worth roughly $30.7 billion in 2009 and was projected to grow to $98.9 billion by 2019. New solar PV installations reached 6 GW in 2009, representing a six-fold increase from five years earlier. However, rapidly declining solar PV prices resulted in a 20 percent revenue decline from 2008. In other words, solar prices dropped from an average of $7 peak watt installed in 2008 to $5.12 peak watt installed in 2009.

As for 2009, Solarbuzz, in its 2010 report, noted that world solar PV market installations reached a record high of 7.3 GW in 2009, representing a 20 percent jump from 2008. Global solar cell production reached 9.34 GW in 2009, with thin-film production accounting for 18 percent of that consolidated total. China and Taiwan produced nearly 50 percent of global cell production. Worldwide, Solarbuzz reported the PV industry generated $38.5 billion; the report was based on 112 countries across the globe.

In the United States, $100 billion of the $787 billion Stimulus bill under the Obama administration was slated for clean energy investments, including solar and wind power as well as alternate fuels. Before the bill's effects could be felt, U.S.-based venture capital investments in energy technologies had dropped from $3.2 billion in 2008 to just $2.2 billion in 2009. However, clean tech investment capital continued to rise.

Combined solar PV and wind power global industries accounted for 830,000 jobs in 2009, expected to grow to 3.3 million jobs by 2019.

The overall news was optimistic. Dr. Finlay Colville, senior analyst at Solarbuzz (London, England) noted that during 2010, more than 11 GW of new capacity was added, more than 18 GW of solar cells were produced, and the market as a whole almost doubled compared to 2009. There was palpable growth in equipment spending, and sales of crystalline silicon ingot-to-module and thin-film panels exceeding $10 billion for the first time.

By the second quarter of 2010, global PV demand rose 54 percent (to 3.82 GW) over the first quarter, reported Solarbuzz. It attributed the rush to install components in Germany ahead of tariff declines slated for mid-2010, combined with strong incentive programs across Europe. Germany accounted for 60 percent of second quarter global demand. Looking toward 2011, leading European markets, including Germany, will face large tariff reductions, and market demand is projected to be less than 50 percent of module production.

INDUSTRY LEADERS

According to Solarbuzz, the top seven polysilicon manufacturers in 2009 had 114,500 tonnes (per annum) capacity, up 92 percent from 2008; the top eight wafer manufacturers accounted for almost 33 percent of global wafer capacity in 2009. The excess of solar cell production over market demand resulted in weighted crystalline silicon module price averages to crash 38 percent over 2008 levels. In mid-2010, the top five cell manufacturers (by shipments) were First Solar, Suntech Power, JA Solar, Yingli Green Energy, and Trina Solar. Among the top 12 cell manufacturers, six were Chinese and accounted for 55 percent of shipments.

Shell Solar, the product of the 2001 merger between the solar operations of German electronic manufacturer Siemens and the London-based oil giant Royal Dutch/Shell and now owned and operated by Royal Dutch/Shell Group's Shell International Renewables division, was a leading supplier of solar panels, silicon components, and solar modules for residential and commercial applications. Based in Amsterdam, the firm produced about one-fifth of the total installed base of PV power worldwide.

Founded in 1977, Solarworld Industries America (formerly Siemens Solar Industries) was also an industry leader. The firm's merger with Shell Renewables made the latter a leader among the major petrochemical firms working on solar alternatives, investing $500 million per year in solar power. In fiscal year 2009, SOlarworld AG exceeded the $1 billion revenues mark for the first time.

BP Solar International LLC, built on the combining of BP Solar and Amoco's Solarex, claimed nearly 20 percent of the world's PV market in the earlyyears of the first decade of the 2000s, producing over 50 megawatts of solar products each year. Solarex, founded in 1973, was a unit of Amoco-Enron Solar and the largest U.S.-owned manufacturer of photovoltaic products. The company participated in some groundbreaking projects, such as supplying about 40,000 square feet of the PV modules that made up the roof array located at the 1996 Olympics swimming facility in Atlanta, Georgia. The National Renewable Energy Lab in Golden, Colorado, which is part of the U.S. Department of Energy (DOE), contracted with Solarex in August 1997 to conduct further research on thin-film photovoltaics. At the time of the merger, BP already owned about 10 percent of global PV production capacity. The firm partnered in 2003 with United Kingdom-based glass manufacturer Romag Holdings to develop a new generation of large PV glass panels to be mass-produced and implemented into building designs. BP Solar also teamed up with the U.S. Department of Energy's National Renewable Energy Laboratory to build a semi-transparent PV module that can serve as a roof or window by allowing sunlight to pass through while also absorbing and storing the solar energy for conversion into power. Headquartered in Linthicum, Maryland, the firm was a part of British Petroleum's Gas, Power and Renewables Business Stream.

Spire Corp. of Bedford, Massachusetts, with revenues of $69.9 million in 2009, was a small but crucial player in the photovoltaic systems industry. Spire provided products and services to photovoltaics, optoelectronics, and biomedical markets worldwide, including the PV cell testers, tabbing and stringing assemblers, and other components. Spire created a separate subsidiary, Spire Solar, Inc., in 2002 to handle all of the firm's solar operations. The company's PV systems were used in about 200 factories worldwide. Another subsidiary, Spire Solar Chicago, partnered with BP Solar to construct solar panels and fit them into photovoltaic products, and even offered workshops to train local building inspectors and electricians in the design and installation of PV systems.

GE Energy, a division of General Electric, catapulted to the forefront of the solar industry in 2004 with its purchase of industry leader AstroPower, Inc. A manufacturer of solar panels, cells, and modules for the industrial, residential, and commercial sectors, AstroPower garnered 96 percent of its revenues from solar electric power products, with the remainder coming from research contracts. Financial difficulties led to bankruptcy filings, followed by the sale of its assets to GE Energy.

Kyocera Solar, Inc., of Scottsdale, Arizona, manufactured solar electric systems primarily for use in rural areas where electrical grid distribution was lacking. Rural homes, telecommunications equipment, and other remote power sources utilized Kyocera's PV cells. Its parent company, the Japan-based Kyocera Company, began research into photovoltaics in 1973, and since rolling out its first residential systems in 1978, has installed solar power systems in nearly 20,000 homes worldwide.

AMERICA AND THE WORLD

As of 2010, European countries accounted for 77 percent of world demand for solar PV, manifesting in a demand for 5.6 GW. The top three European countries were Germany, Italy, and the Czech Republic, which collectively accounted for 4.07 GW. Italy became the second largest market in the world, but all three countries experienced soaring demand. The United States represented the third largest market, which grew to 485 MW, up 36 percent from 2008. Japan was fourth, growing 109 percent in one year. Spain actually declined in solar PV demand.

Japan is the leading country for installations of PV panels, but the cost is about four times as high in U.S. dollars than traditional sourcing from utility companies. However, the Japanese government subsidizes homeowners for nearly half the cost of a rooftop PV array. In total, the Japanese government allocated $271 million to PV development in 2001. The U.S. government, by comparison, spent only about $60 million on all solar programs in 2000. In Tokyo there were about 1.5 million buildings with solar water heating, more than in the entire United States. As of 2008, Japan was the largest exporter of PV cells and modules, overtaking the United States.

Australia continues to sit at the forefront of alternative and renewable energy applications. This is partly due to the geographic remoteness of areas in Australia where conventional electricity is not practicable. A joint venture between the University of South Wales and Pacific Power, known as Pacific Solar, was developing technology to set up the first manufacturing facility for PV products, with products on the market by 2002.

In the Democratic Republic of the Congo (formerly Zaire), Hospital Bulape treats 50,000 patients every year and depends exclusively on solar power for everything from X-ray machinery to air conditioning systems. In Morocco, solar panels are sold in open markets next to carpets and produce.

While developed countries led the photovoltaic industry, the customer base was primarily situated in developing regions where electricity was scarce. Ironically, 70 percent of the solar cells and solar power systems manufactured in the United States are exported to Third World countries. The export rate is expected to increase considerably, since about one-third of the world population lives without electricity. Although many of these countries have initiated aggressive electrification programs, costs are too high to build large power plants or extend the electrical grid to thousands of the remote villages without power. Consequently, household solar power systems may be an economically and environmentally sound alternative in these areas. Moreover, developing nations have outpaced their industrialized counterparts in the growth rates for energy consumption for over 20 years, and in the short term, growing Asian markets such as China and India are likely to lead the world in the increase of energy consumption.

RESEARCH AND TECHNOLOGY

Thanks to extensive research, photovoltaic systems have become no longer universally dependent on the sun. New PV systems, of which the first commercial models were in development, utilized heat energy, or infrared radiation, instead of solar energy, thereby allowing them to operate more efficiently and durably during nighttime or overcast conditions. Thermophotovoltaics, as these systems are called, must use natural gas or some other fuel to generate heat, but the semiconductor conversion nonetheless generates significantly more efficiently than diesel generators, leading to cost and pollution savings.

The Finnish energy firm Fortum Corp. is a leading innovator of building-integrated photovoltaic (BIPV) systems, which are integrated into the building's architecture. Fortum was formed by the merger of two state-run companies, the utility giant Imatran Volma Oy (IVO) and the oil, gas and chemical monopoly Neste. The Finnish government owns approximately 71 percent of Fortum. BIPV systems were a central area of research for the nonresidential PV applications market. BIPV systems are worked directly into the building's aesthetic and structural design, with excess energy fed into the central energy grid, which can also supply any necessary supplemental energy when the PV system fails to generate an amount sufficient to facilitate the building's normal functions. Fortum launched a pilot project in Zurich, Switzerland for the headquarters of the Swiss retailer Migros where the glass roof was integrated with PV cells.

Modern PV systems are being equipped with control inverters that can change normal solar energy into alternating current for use in households. Significantly, researchers are producing solar batteries that are in the 34 percent efficiency range, compared to earlier cells that were about 4 percent efficient. State-of-the-art direct motorized tracking devices that aim the PV cells directly at the sun at all times during the day are helping to improve systems by collecting more heat. Additionally, solar power and the PV industry are making inroads on traditional power-generating industries. Oil-fired power plants, for example, operate at only 35 percent efficiency.

One of the goals of PV system researchers is to improve the storage system currently in use. Another is to reduce the number of components in a system. The primary pieces of equipment in any solar system are the photovoltaic panels, which absorb and contain sunlight so that it begins conversion into useful power. Although they are made primarily of silicon, other materials have begun to be used, such as gallium arsenide, which was employed in the Russian space station Mir.

The number of panels needed in a given situation depends on the amount of energy required. For an average house, the number is determined by the kilowatts per hour actually used. Each panel generates about 50 watts of DC electricity for each hour of sunlight, and batteries are needed for the storage of the energy so that it can be used when needed. A power center must also be part of the system to regulate the flow of electricity going into the batteries so that they are not overcharged and to control the energy leaving the batteries. Inverters, which convert solar power into electricity, must also be obtained for a PV system. A generator is needed as a separate power source to serve as a backup if anything goes wrong and to replenish the system after a cloudy day.

The National Aeronautics and Space Administration has examined ways to increase the amount of energy to be stored. The agency is experimenting with the use of a solar power satellite (SPS), which can deliver enormous amounts of energy to Earth. This can be accomplished by building huge photovoltaic structures (estimated to be as large as Manhattan) that are designed to deliver five to ten gigawatts of electrical power. Just one of these monoliths would be sufficient to power Connecticut. The inventor of SPS, Dr. Peter Glaser, noted that they will be expensive to build but cheap to operate and environmentally safe.

Even the U.S. Army was going solar. In 2003, the Army announced it was funding photovoltaic developer Konarka to devise prototypes of lightweight plastic solar panels with semiconductors running on miniscule particles of titanium dioxide. Employing nanotechnological engineering, the catalyst is mounted on a film of photovoltaic dye that stimulates electrons, thereby generating power to be used as an ultra-light battery, thus easing the total battery weight a soldier carries into the field to power the increasing number of electronic gadgets utilized in combat. Significantly, Konarka's manufacturing process utilizes neither glass nor silicon, the only materials durable enough to withstand the high temperatures yielded in conventional photovoltaic production. Konarka's "cold sintering" process, according to *The Engineer,* allows for the use of less expensive and lighter plastics. By 2003, Konarka's PV cells registered efficiencies of about 6.5 percent, besting the levels of many thin-film silicon cells.

Nanotechnology was a major component in several other areas of PV development. Perhaps most significant was the employment of such technology to overhaul the manufacturing process for PV materials. Several manufacturers and research laboratories were busily devising factory processes to produce photo-reactive materials that are implanted on the catalyst itself, building the PV elements directly into long rolls of flexible plastic, thereby eliminating the bulky vacuum deposition process. (See the essay in this book titled *Micromachines/Nanotechnology.*)

A hybrid power plant, combining photovoltaic cells with a wind farm, is the source of energy for Atlantic City, New Jersey's wastewater treatment plant. By harnessing energy from the sun and the wind off the Atlantic Ocean, the hybrid plant produces enough electricity to power the equivalent of 3,800 homes, reducing dependence on fossil fuels by approximately 24,000 barrels of oil per year. This plant is one of the largest solar/wind plants in the world, generating approximately 40.8 million kilowatt hours of clean electricity annually. Two rooftop photovoltaic arrays, one carport-mounted PV array, and two PV arrays on the ground make up the solar energy portion of the hybrid plant.

In 2008, a new concentrating solar electricity plant, Solar One, began operation in Boulder City, Nevada. With a 64 MW capacity, this was the first new solar thermal electric plant constructed in the United States since the early 1990s, other than a smaller 1 MW plant in Arizona that went online in 2006.

Another development in the industry occurred in 2008 when the U.S. Department of Energy (DOE) announced it was investing $24 million for technological initiatives meant to promote and integrate PV systems into the U.S. power grid. John Mizrocho of the DOE told *PC Magazine Online,* "Our investment in these grid integration projects will lay the groundwork for high levels of solar photovoltaic market penetration to help meet the president's goal of making solar power cost-competitive with conventional sources of electricity."

BIBLIOGRAPHY

"California Public Utilities Commission Opens Rulemaking Process for Solar, Renewables." *Global Power Report,* 9 March 2006.

Colville, Finlay. "Hot Markets: Opportunities Within the Solar/Photovoltaics Industry." From Conference Agenda, Lasers & Photonics Marketplace 2011. Available from http://www.marketplaceseminar.com/globalnav/conference.htm.

"Energy Department Invests in Solar Tech." *PC Magazine Online,* 14 August 2008.

"Extensive Research on Growing PV Industry at Global and Country Level." *Space Daily,* 16 September 2008.

"Fast Solar Energy Facts." 15 September 2008. Available from http://www.solarbuzz.com.

"Global PV Demand Up 54% in Q2." *Photonics,* 27 September 2010.

"Green Energy Trends 2010." 30 march 2010. Available from http://www.renewable-energy-sources.com/2010/03/30/green-energy-trends-2010/.

"Growth in the Three Renewable Energy Sectors Last Year Was 11.4 % Over 2008, and Their UD$139 Billion in Aggregate Revenue Will Reach US$326 Billion by 2019." *Renewable Energy Focus,* March 2010.

"Investors Moving Into Rapidly Expanding Solar Power Industry." *Space Daily,* 10 May 2007.

"Largest Hybrid Solar-Wind Power Plant in U.S." *Environmental Design & Construction,* January/February 2006.

"Marketbuzz 2010: Annual World Solar PV Market Report." 2010. Available from http://www.solarbuzz.com/marketbuzz2010-intro.htm.

"New Solar Programs Underway." *Electric Perspectives,* March/April 2006.

"New Study Shows Extending Solar Tax Credits Will Create Jobs, Increase Investment." Solar Energy Industries Association, 15 September 2008.

Sherwood, Larry. *U.S. Solar Market Trends 2007.* Washington, DC: Interstate Renewable Energy Council, August 2008.

"The Solar Effect Boosts The European Inverters Market." *Space Daily* 5 March 2008.

Solar Generation V: 2008. Brussels: European Photovoltaic Industry Association, 2008.

"Solar Power Comes of Age." *Utility Week,* 12 September 2008.

"Solar Thermal Power Coming to a Boil." Earth Policy Institute, 22 July 2008. Available from http://www.earth-policy.org.

"SolarWorld AG Outperforms 1 Billion Revenue Forecast for 2009." March 2010. Available from http://www.solarworld.de/4301.html

U.S. Solar Industry Year in Review. Washington, DC: Solar Energy Industries Association, 2008.

Walsh, Bryan. "Solar Power's New Style." *Time,* 23 June 2008.

Yudelson, Jerry. "A New Sell for Photovoltaics." *Consulting— Specifying Engineer,* February 2006.

PHYSICAL FITNESS PRODUCTS

———■———

SIC CODE(S)

5941

INDUSTRY SNAPSHOT

The United States' obsession with looking good and staying healthy has remained a constant, even with economic downturns. According to the Sporting Goods Manufacturers Association (SGMA) in its "Manufacturers Sales by Category Report (2009 Edition)," manufacturers' (wholesale) sales of sporting goods equipment, fitness equipment, sports apparel, athletic footwear, and recreational transport items in the U.S. totaled $66.3 billion in 2008, only a slight 3.2 percent decrease from 2007, despite a drastic downturn in the economy.

"On the sales side, sports industry sales dipped below GDP for the first time since 2003, but the level of decline was not nearly as significant as it was for other durable goods industries," said Tom Cove, SGMA president, in a March 2009 press release. Indeed, at the same time (March 2009), the International Health, Racquet & Sportsclub Association (IHRSA) announced that nearly 22 percent (over 10 million), of the 45.5 million health club members were new, having joined a health club for the first time. Clearly, physical fitness would be the last to go when discretionary income was meager.

While overall, Americans have been and are expected to continue increasing their physical activity to get fit, the purchase of higher-end exercise equipment is tied rather tightly to general U.S. economic health. On an individual level, research has long showed that fitness activity, especially activity requiring heavy equipment, is fairly commensurate with income level. Paradoxically, such activity generally diminishes with age, although the latter

rule has grown far less pronounced in recent years. While advertisements for exercise equipment typically feature fit and toned young people, much of the growth in equipment sales has been generated by older customers.

Fueled by the U.S. Surgeon General's pronouncement that "physical activity is the key to good health for all Americans," individuals of all ages, but particularly the elderly, were investing both time and dollars in their own physical fitness. The American Council on Exercise (ACE), a nonprofit health and fitness organization, concluded that working out at work became popular as people tried to fit exercise into busy schedules. The ACE found that state-of-the-art facilities were showing up in major corporations in the United States, including Gap, Oracle, Clif Bar, and 3Com. Manufacturers of exercise products have tried to meet the needs and desires of potential customers by developing products that are not only efficient and simple to use, but also enjoyable and reasonably affordable.

ORGANIZATION AND STRUCTURE

Fitness items are typically sold by the manufacturers, either directly to retailers, where price mark-up occurs before sale, or via distributors who in turn sell to retailers. Often, high-end manufacturers give a retailer exclusive rights to sell their product in a certain region. Fitness products reach customers through a variety of outlets, the most notable being large sporting goods stores. Fitness products are also among the primary staples of late-night infomercials. Thirty-minute spots hawking Tae-Bo exercise videos, the Ab Rocker, and a host of other products were among the most successful infomercials in the late

743

1990s. The popularity of exercise videos continued into the first decade of the 2000s. Mail order and the Internet have also emerged as fresh marketing avenues for the promotion and sale of such products.

Producers of fitness products witnessed significant changes within the industry, as mergers, acquisitions, and initial public offerings (IPOs) occurred with relative frequency. The largest notable acquisition in the area of sporting goods was that of Spaulding Sports Worldwide by Kohlberg, Kravis, Roberts & Co. Estimated at over $1 billion, the deal was touted as the largest ever seen by the industry. Notable IPOs included those of Ridgeview Inc. and The North Face Inc. In 1998, Icon beat out two other bidders to acquire the well-known NordicTrack brand for $9.55 million when NordicTrack filed for bankruptcy. Icon awarded sole Nordic Track distribution rights, with the exception of about 20 NordicTrack stores acquired in the deal, to Sears, Roebuck & Co., Icon's best customer. Sears began to open NordicTrack specialty shops in stores across the country. Although NordicTrack's staple cross-country ski machines, one of the first major success stories in the exercise equipment market, suffered from declining sales in the mid and late 1990s, Icon greatly desired to capitalize on the astronomical brand name recognition. NordicTrack now enjoys strong sales from treadmills and weight equipment in addition to its ski machines. Other notable acquisitions included Cybex's purchase of Tectrix, Precor's acquisition of Pacific Fitness, and Schwinn's takeover of Hebb Industries as well as GT Bikes.

BACKGROUND AND DEVELOPMENT

In the late 1980s, the home exercise segment of the wholesale fitness market stood at $750 million and was growing fast. Factors contributing to the emergence of the home exercise phenomenon included convenience, proximity, the scarcity of available free time, and the added comfort and security of privacy—an issue of particular concern to those lacking confidence in either physical appearance or athletic ability. In 1988, *Forbes* magazine noted the comment of one expert who explained the reasoning behind people's preference for home exercise over health clubs, saying, "When you couple a new behavior with a new environment, like a health spa, it represents a double threat to people, so they prefer to stay home." By the early 1990s, this concept became a mantra in the ads of at least one exercise equipment manufacturer. The Trotter Co. beckoned the market with its theme, "For those who consider exercise a matter of privacy."

As membership in health clubs began to level off after a period of sustained growth, the major creators of exercise equipment realized the need to reorganize.

Companies such as Nautilus Sports/Medical Industries and Universal Gym Equipment found themselves joined by such competitors as Precor, Inc., in the race to grab sales. Precor succeeded in creating its own niche by catering to consumers willing to pay for high-quality equipment that would stand up to years of use. Whereas in the early 1980s a treadmill, for example, could be purchased for as little as $200, by the decade's end, a sturdier and better designed product could be bought for about $1,000, a price not considered unreasonable.

Interestingly, Nautilus, designated the "grandfather" of the exercise equipment companies by industry insiders, chose not to push its products aggressively into the home exercise market at that time. The firm, founded in 1970 by Arthur Jones, continued to focus on and provide its products primarily to health clubs and other commercial facilities. In 1998, however, the company's assets were acquired by Direct Focus, Inc., a direct marketing firm.

Adding to the convenience of home exercise equipment was the introduction of the exercise videotape. This segment of the industry faced significant challenges in initial distribution of its products in the early 1980s. Contributing to the difficulty of distribution was the lack of seriousness with which the industry viewed the coming aerobics boom. Industry pioneer Kathy Smith predicted that aerobics would be much more than a passing fad and that the industry would eventually realize this. It was a prophetic statement, since by 1992 Smith's 12 exercise videos combined sold more than 5 million copies. Names of other exercise gurus, particularly women, became common in American households by the 1990s. Models and actors, as well as professional trainers, cast their hats into the exercise video ring by the late 1990s, sometimes with mixed results. Among the most successful in this genre was Jane Fonda, who by 1989 made over 11 such tapes. While most exercise videos were initially geared toward aerobics and aerobic dancing, by the early 1990s, stress management, stretching, body sculpting, and toning were highlighted topics as well.

In 1999 hundreds of videotapes were available, though not necessarily on the shelves of large sporting goods stores. Discount retailers such as Target carry some of the more popular ones, but the mail order industry has the edge on exercise video sales. Video sales were relatively dormant in the mid-1990s compared to the 1980s boom when Jane Fonda had seemingly everyone in aerobics workouts. By the end of the decade, however, exercise videos had been rejuvenated, largely on the strength of the Tae-Bo exercise series by Hollywood's Billy Blanks, which derived its sales primarily through its blockbuster infomercial.

Frost & Sullivan revealed that fitness nutrition also emerged as a large and distinct category in the health and fitness industry in the early part of the twenty-first century. As far as home exercise equipment, the sales of treadmills, exercise bicycles, weight benches, and other apparatus reached $5.8 billion in 2000 versus $1.9 billion in 1990.

For most of the 1990s, growth in the sporting goods industry was fueled by the fitness products sector. About 49.6 million Americans used home exercise equipment at least once a week, while an additional 4.9 million used such equipment less often. The most popular home exercise equipment was free weights, used by about 42.8 million Americans; treadmills followed with 37.5 million, and stationary bikes placed third at 31 million.

Other product trends in the late 1990s and early years of the first decade of the 2000s included sales of such items as abdominal exercisers (also known as "ab trainers"); low-impact elliptical trainers; weight resistance machines; recumbent bikes, on which the user semi-reclines; and air walkers, flat-folding machines touted as providing "a complete workout" while inflicting no pounding impact on the body. While treadmills continued to reign as the best-selling equipment for home use, a resurgence in sales of exercise bikes began, in part due to the popularity of new group cardio classes such as the group cycling class known as Spinning. Heart rate monitors and body fat measuring devices became popular and continued to sell into 2000 in conjunction with larger equipment.

The industry's customer satisfaction component was expected to get a boost from the decision by Harris Black International, Ltd., and the American Council on Exercise (ACE) to issue customer surveys on home exercise equipment. By randomly polling owners nationwide on issues such as affordability, ease of use, and physical fitness benefits, the surveys would result in awards to manufacturers in categories such as "best of price" and "overall customer satisfaction," and would provide customers with a more comprehensive comparative view of the equipment market and manufacturers with greater detail on consumer wants and needs.

ACE reported that a primary objective for fitness products manufacturers was enhancing the personalization of their products. Treadmills, elliptical exercisers, and other equipment increasingly feature personal adjustability as well as heart rate monitors and programmable and adjustable training programs derived from health and strength data supplied by the user.

While sports participation declined in the late 1990s, physical fitness continued to be popular. Describing the phases of exercise trends, the Sporting Goods Manufacturers Association (SGMA) and the Fitness Products Council noted that while the 1970s were the running decade, in the 1980s everyone was into aerobics, and the 1990s were dominated by the exercise machine. By the middle of the first decade of the 2000s, the industry benefited from the exploding popularity of elliptical machines but was struggling to find next-generation, breakthrough products that were capable of inspiring people to exercise.

Following a stagnant period early in the decade, sales of physical fitness products began to improve along with the overall economy during the middle of the first decade of the 2000s. The SGMA reported that manufacturers' sales of sporting goods equipment, exercise equipment, sports apparel, licensed merchandise, and athletic footwear reached an estimated $74.6 billion in 2006. Of the $4.6 billion spent on exercise equipment, about 76 percent was from consumer spending, with the remainder accounted for by institutional purchases. Twenty-eight percent of consumer spending went to treadmills, followed by elliptical machines (20 percent), exercise cycles (11 percent), and home gyms (8 percent).

The SGMA projected that manufacturers' sales of sporting goods would continue to rise. One key market that supported future growth was the nation's aging baby boomer segment. According to the SGMA, those aged 41 to 57 numbered 77 million in 2005. In a January 17, 2005, news release, the association revealed that "Boomers are concerned about remaining healthy. They are a prime market for health club memberships and home exercise equipment. A recent study indicated that the number of Americans who exercise frequently grew from 51 million to 54 million between 1998 and 2003."

According to SGMA figures, by 2006 recreational swimming was the nation's most popular exercise activity, with 91.3 million participants, followed by recreational walking (87.6 million). Other popular activities included bowling (53.5 million), free weight lifting (48.6 million), treadmill exercise (47.9 million), running/jogging (37.8 million), and fitness walking (36.3 million). Notably, the number of people using treadmills had increased 29 percent since 1998, and although only about 16.6 million people used elliptical trainers in 2006, this represented a 331 percent increase from five years earlier.

In 2007 the American College of Sports Medicine published its top 10 predictions for health and fitness trends. The first was program development to reduce obesity among children, followed by the establishment of special fitness programs for older adults and an increase in the number of accredited education and certification programs for health/fitness professionals. Other trends included an increase in "functional fitness," which refers to using strength training to improve people's ability to perform the daily activities of life; a greater emphasis on core training and strength training; and an increased use of personal trainers.

CURRENT CONDITIONS

In March 2009, the International Health, Racquet & Sportsclub Association (IHRSA) announced that industry revenues reached $19.1 billion in 2008, an increase of three percent over 2007. It also reported that the number of health clubs increased by 1 percent in 2008, totaling 30,022 facilities in the United States. Individual health club memberships in the United States totaled 45.5 million in 2008. The modest increase in industry revenues came mostly from lessons, classes, or personal training sessions.

In SGMA's March 2009 report, "Manufacturers Sales by Category Report," industry sales were broken down by category. Accordingly, the report indicated that 2008 sales for sporting goods equipment dipped slightly to $20.8 billion in 2008. Exercise equipment was a $4.22 billion business, said the report, and treadmill sales accounted for 25.9 percent of that entire category. After treadmills, the next two largest fitness categories were elliptical machines ($892 million) and exercise cycles ($455 million). Consumer spending for exercise equipment accounted for 75 percent of the entire exercise equipment category.

Wholesale sales of sports apparel sales were $28.9 billion in 2008, a 2.2 percent decline from 2007. The largest segment of the sports apparel industry ($5.9 billion) was shirts/tops. Swimwear was the second largest segment of the sports apparel business at $2.4 billion. Athletic footwear sales were $12.39 billion in 2008.

The world market for physical fitness equipment was projected to near $12 billion by 2010, projected IHRSA. According to a report published by Global Industry Analysts Inc., the growth of the global market was driven by demand in European countries as well as increasing focus on fitness and healthy lifestyles by more affluent consumers in Asia-Pacific and Latin America. The United States represents the single largest regional market for physical fitness equipment, but the Asia-Pacific region was projected to emerge as the fastest growing regional market. In Europe, the fitness equipment market was projected to reach $3.4 billion by 2010, according to the report. In its 2008 report, Global Industry Analysts said the treadmill market was estimated at $2.43 billion in 2007, and the elliptical trainer market, which represented the fastest growing product segment in the global fitness equipment market, was estimated at $967 million for 2007.

INDUSTRY LEADERS

ICON Health & Fitness Inc. ICON, based in Logan, Utah, is one of the world's largest manufacturers and marketers of fitness equipment. With 11 locations around the globe, the company was one of the first U.S. fitness companies to set up international operations. Besides the United States, it has facilities in China, Europe, and Canada. Icon produces 3.9 million units of fitness equipment annually. The company manufactures all types of major exercise equipment: elliptical motion trainers, cross-country ski machines, treadmills, stationary bikes, rowers, strength trainers, weight sets, and other equipment under brand names including Weider, Reebok, ProForm, Weslo, IMAGE, Gold's Gym, Healthrider, and NordicTrack. It makes most of its products in Utah and sells them through retailers, infomercials, the Web, and its catalog. It also offers fitness accessories, spas, and commercial fitness gear. The company holds hundreds of patents and has many patent applications pending.

Icon was formed as Weslo in 1977 and through a series of business deals built up its fitness operations, becoming Icon Health & Fitness in 1994. Icon's channels of distribution include direct sales (via the Internet and toll-free 800 numbers), Workout Warehouse (the company's catalog), department stores (Sears represents approximately 40 percent of sales), mass merchandisers, sporting goods stores, specialty fitness retailers, catalog showrooms, and infomercials.

Precor Inc. Founded in 1980, Precor was established by improving the design of a European rowing machine. Today, Precor employs about 500 workers and makes fitness equipment that includes a line of elliptical trainers as well as cross trainers, treadmills, and cycles that are typically sold to commercial health clubs. In late 1998, Precor announced it had acquired Pacific Fitness Corp., a manufacturer of high-end cardiovascular and flexibility equipment, greatly expanding its equipment operations. Once a subsidiary of Premark International Inc., Precor was absorbed by Illinois Tool Works Inc. (ITW) in 1999 as part of the merger deal between ITW and Premark. In 2002, ITW sold Precor for $178 million to Amer Sports (formerly Amer Group). Amer Sports, which also has sports brands such as Wilson, Suunto, and Atomic, reported sales of $2.3 billion in 2008.

Cybex International Inc. Cybex, of Medway, Massachusetts, employed 556 people and posted sales of $147.9 million in 2008. The firm manufactures strength training and cardiovascular equipment for both consumer and commercial markets, focusing primarily on institutions such as health clubs, schools, and hotels. Cybex reaches the consumer market through independent retailers. The company unveiled its compact Cybex PG400 Personal Gym in 1998. Founded in 1973 as Trotter Inc., the company grew steadily until it merged with Cybex International Inc. in May 1997. Its strength training equipment, which uses weights for resistance, includes "selectorized" single station equipment, modular multistation units, the MG500 multigym, the FT360 functional trainer, plate-loaded equipment, and free-weight equipment.

Nautilus, Inc. Nautilus of Vancouver, Washington, makes and markets fitness equipment for commercial and home use, including strength equipment, free weights and benches, and exercise machines. Some of the firm's popular brands include Bowflex, Nautilus, StairMaster, Schwinn, and Trimline. Employing 1,500 people in 2008, Nautilus posted sales of $411.2 million.

RESEARCH AND TECHNOLOGY

Physical fitness through virtual reality became manifest in Nintendo's wildly popular Wii Fit games, which, in just two years, topped 20 million units sold worldwide by August 2009. The packaged video games, played on home televisions through a Nintendo game console, engage players to perform actual physical body movements while interactively playing sports games (e.g., tennis, bowling, golf) from an area directly in front of their television screens. One Wii video game also included a digital personal trainer to coach persons through exercises.

Fitness products manufacturers and retailers have expanded their presence on the Internet, setting up online stores. Even the equipment has taken on Internet capabilities. The Internet-based health and fitness concern Stayhealthy.com joined up with online insurance provider eHealthInsurance.com to market the CT1 Personal Calorie Tracker and BT1 Body Tracker, which monitor fitness information such as caloric levels, blood pressure, body fat, weight, and muscle mass, displaying the data directly over the Internet. The devices are pocket-sized electronic boxes resembling pagers that link to a central processing station. A user need only access the Stayhealthy.com Web site to see his/her latest statistics.

Manufacturers also sought out ways to make their staple products less monotonous and more motivating. For example, Icon's NordicTrack EXP 100 treadmill is a multimedia exerciser, offering music and a computerized personal trainer to assist workouts. The program is built on software called iFit.com, which is run on the Internet, videos, or compact discs. Web sites, too, assumed the roles of personal trainers. Recognizing the increasing fitness consciousness but limited available time among women, Joni Hyde, a Tae Kwon Do black belt and personal trainer, developed www.workoutsforwomen.com to offer personal training consultation, fitness articles, assessments, and workout programs available over the Internet.

BIBLIOGRAPHY

"2008 U.S. Health Club Revenues Total $19.1 billion, up 3%." Press Release, IHRSA, 31 March 2009. Available from http://cms.ihrsa.org/index.

Cybex International. December 2009. Available from http://www.ecybex.com.

"Equipment Market to Exceed Almost $12 Billion by 2010." Press Release, IHRSA, 5 March 2008. Available from http://clubindustry.com/news/fitness-equipment-market-0503/.

Florez, Gregory. "The Democratization of Technology and Product Is Here." *Fitness Business Pro,* September 2004.

"France-Sports Equipment." Datamonitor, September 2009. Available from http://wulibraries.typepad.com/files/sportsequpfrance.pdf.

"Hoover's Company Capsules." *Hoover's Online,* 2007. Available from www.hoovers.com.

International Health, Racquet and Sports Club Association. "U.S. Health Club Membership Reaches 42.7 Million in 2006." 25 April 2007. Available from http://cms.ihrsa.org.

MacMillan, Douglas. "Home Gyms Muscle Up." *Business Week Online,* 4 December 2006. Available from www.businessweek.com.

"National Briefing Science and Health: Heart Disease and Physical Fitness." *The New York Times,* 8 September 2004.

"New Home Fitness Revolutionizes Fitness Industry." 10 May 2007. Available from www.abc-of-fitness.com/.

Ryan, Thomas J. "A Strenuous Exercise: The Fitness Market Struggles to Stay Strong." *Sporting Goods Business,* October 2004.

Sporting Goods Manufacturers Association. "2007 SGMA Manufacturer Sales by Category." 15 May 2007. Available from www.sgma.com.

———. "Sales of Sporting Goods: On the Upswing." 17 January 2005. Available from www.sgma.com.

———. "SGMA Says Sales Of Equipment, Shoes & More Exceed $66 Billion." 16 March 2009. Available from http://www.sgma.com/.

———. "Sports Participation Topline Report, 2006 Edition." May 2006. Available from www.sgma.com.

"Survey Results Name Top 20 Trends In Health and Fitness Industry." 27 November 2006. Available from www.medicalnewstoday.com.

Varner, Christin. "Personal Trainer on Your Wrist." *Kiplinger's Personal Finance Magazine,* February 2007.

"Wii Fit Reaches 20 Million Copies Sold Milestone." Associated Press, 6 August 2009. Available from http://www.associatedcontent.com/article/2011474/.wii_fit_reaches_20_million_copies_sold.html

Wolf, Jessica. "Dance Workouts Give Fitness a New Twist." *Video Store,* 12 September 2004.

PREMIUM BOTTLED BEVERAGES

SIC CODE(S)

2086

5149

INDUSTRY SNAPSHOT

Dubbed "New Age" drinks, premium bottled beverages met the new millennium as a force to be reckoned with, drawing consumers' taste buds away from soft drinks and alcoholic beverages. This developing product category includes bottled water, enhanced and flavored bottled water, juice drinks, sports drinks, nutraceutical beverages, ready-to-drink (RTD) teas, energy drinks, and RTD iced coffee. Alcoholic beverages and soft drinks are excluded.

In 2007 in the United States, more bottled water was consumed than any otherNew Age beverage; that year Americans drank 8.8 billion gallons of bottled water, according to *Beverage World*'s "State of the Industry" 2008 report. Fruit beverages were second, with 3.8 billion gallons, followed by sports drinks (1.3 billion gallons), RTD tea (875 million gallons), flavored and enhanced water (546.5 million gallons), energy drinks (302.6 million gallons), and RTD coffee (45 million gallons). Although bottled water had the highest market share, the most growth was experienced by the flavored and enhanced water segment, which grew by more than 30 percent from 2006 to 2007. Energy drinks were the second fastest growing segment, with a 25 percent growth rate. Other categories experienced a slower growth trend: RTD tea, 15 percent; bottled water, 7 percent, sports drinks, 2.5 percent, and RTD coffee, about 1.5 percent. Consumption of fruit drinks actually declined 3 percent, and carbonated beverages lost out to the premium bottled beverages market by declining for the third year in a row.

ORGANIZATION AND STRUCTURE

Producers of premium bottled beverages include companies of all sizes, from beverage industry giants Coca-Cola Co. and PepsiCo Inc. to specialty firms such as Snapple Beverages and even small regional manufacturers. Distribution varies according to a company's array of products and how each is manufactured. Coca-Cola and PepsiCo dominate the distribution system in the United States by virtue of their size and market share.

Beverages are formulated and packaged using either a hot fill or cold fill processing method that is determined in part by the nature of the product in question. Hot fill, in which bottles are filled with hot liquid and immediately sealed, is the accepted method of bottling iced teas, for example. For cold-filled products, flavors are extracted from fruit or other ingredients while they are cold.

During the late 1990s, in response to the public's growing concern about *e. coli* and other food-borne diseases, manufacturers began paying extra attention to the bottling process in an effort to prevent contamination. Juice bottlers in particular have boosted quality control measures and turned for added safety to pasteurization, which kills potentially harmful bacteria.

BACKGROUND AND DEVELOPMENT

America's thirst for premium beverages developed in the early years of the new century. According to the Beverage Marketing Corp., U.S. per capita New Age beverage consumption increased 134 percent from 1994 to 2002, reaching approximately 16.9 gallons. In wholesale dollars, total revenues reached $11.6 billion in 2002, with the West and Midwest representing the strongest markets.

Market Trends in the Premium Bottled Beverage Industry by Percent Change from 2008 to 2009

Sports Drinks	−12.3%
Value-Added Water	−8.8%
Ready-to-Drink Coffee	−5.4%
Bottled Water	−2.5%
Ready-to-Drink Tea	−1.2%
Energy Drinks	−0.2%

SOURCE: Beverage Marketing Corporation.

By 2003, several categories were clear leaders within the New Age beverage segment. These included single-serve water (33.8 percent), single-serve fruit beverages (20.1 percent), sports beverages (18.3 percent), and ready-to-drink teas (12.3 percent). The remainder was rounded out by the likes of sparkling water, energy drinks, premium sodas, RTD coffee, vegetable and fruit juice blends, and other nutrient-enhanced beverages. In terms of volume growth, energy drinks increased a whopping 3,900 percent between 1997 and 2002, followed by vegetable and fruit blends (657.1 percent), single-serve water (260 percent), RTD coffee (100 percent), sports beverages (55.7 percent), and New Age dairy drinks (54 percent).

Bottled Water In 2003, bottled water was the second largest commercial beverage by category and by volume in the United States. According to the Beverage Market ing Corporation of New York, 2004 saw a continued upward spiral of sales. The bottled water market approached $9.2 billion in wholesale sales in 2004 in the United States, according to Beverage Marketing Corp., reaching new highs in volume as well as wholesale dollar sales. For the second year in a row, sales grew at a slower rate than volume, reflecting marketing strategies such as multi-packs of single-serve bottles and lowering prices to attract buyers. The bottled water category includes sparkling and nonsparkling water, domestic and imported, single-serve bottles (the so-called PET category, named for the plastic raw material used in manufacturing the bottles) and larger packages, and vended and direct-delivered waters. This total U.S. category volume rose 8.6 percent in 2004 over the 2003 volume level, exceeding 6.8 billion gallons. In 2004, more bottled water was consumed by U.S. residents than any other beverage except carbonated soft drinks (23.8 gallons per person).

In 2004, the bottled water market's single biggest component was domestic non-sparkling water, with 6.4 billion gallons, signifying 94.2 percent of total volume sold. Almost half the total volume of the non-sparkling segment sold in the United States in 2004 was the retail PET segment. Because of the strong market in the PET segment, leading PET companies further improved their position in the total U.S. bottled water market. This was especially true for Nestle Waters North America (NWNA), Pepsi-Cola (Aquafina), and Coca-Cola (the Dasani brand).

Evian, once considered the bottled water brand of choice for Hollywood and executives, experienced a 8 percent decrease in sales volume in 2004, while the bottled water market in general rose 18 percent, according to *Beverage Digest*. While globally maintaining the number-one spot by volume, Evian watched as less expensive, local brands, and new luxury brands such as Roll International's Fiji continued to chip away at its market share. To counteract the drop in volume sales due to what some consumers feel is an overpriced product, Evian contracted with a new public relations firm, 5W Public Relations, in New York.

Enhanced water was an especially strong category, with volume almost tripling between 2001 and 2002 alone. This category included products like Gatorade's Propel and Veryfine's Fruit20, a fruit-flavored spring water without sugar, caffeine, sodium, fat, carbohydrates, or calories. In 2004, flavored waters accounted for only 3 percent of wholesale revenues. Bottled water with a hint of flavor remained a small segment of the market in 2005, but was expected to grow as major beverage companies enter the market. A 2004 report in Beverage Marketing Corporation's *Focus Report* series predicted flavored water's share of sales would double by 2009.

Fruit Juices and Juice Drinks Fruit juices and juice drinks (beverages containing less than 100 percent fruit juice) were the third most popular type of beverage in the United States after carbonated soft drinks and bottled water in the early 2000s. They are typically available in single-serving portions that consumers might purchase in food service establishments and convenience stores or from vending machines. Although juice consumption declined during the 1980s, it picked up again during the 1990s and early 2000s. Health-conscious consumers, clever marketing, expanded distribution, and a wider variety of flavors are credited with reversing the downward trend and boosting sales. In 2003, research firm Mintel International Group reported that 38 percent of consumers were drinking fewer carbonated beverages in comparison to the previous year. Instead, many were opting for fruit juices and juice drinks, as well as bottled water.

In creating new flavors they hope will capture the public's fancy, juice makers experimented with juice blends as well as with single-fruit-juice drinks. The U.S. public's expanding awareness of nutrition boosted sales of some established products. For example, the health properties of purple grape juice, which contains the same anti-artery-clogging flavenoids as red wine, contributed to a 40 to 50 percent increase in sales of Welch's purple grape juice from 1995 to 1999.

Fortified smoothies are thick, fruit-flavored shakes with milk, yogurt, or soy milk as the base and sweetened with fruit juices. These beverages are often enhanced with the same additives as the health-oriented beverages. Smoothies can be purchased as ready-to-drink bottled beverages, with names such as Dannon Frusion, Tropicana Smoothies, Frulatte, Naked Foods, Odwalla Fruit Shakes, and Yocream Smoothies. On the other hand, restaurants and smoothie chains will often blend their personal adaptations at the bar.

Ready-to-Drink Tea Although ready-to-drink (RTD) tea had been on the market for several years, when brands such as Snapple and AriZona arrived on the scene, it had not caught on with consumers. Snapple and AriZona changed all that with single-serve, RTD beverages that actually tasted like brewed tea.

Snapple hit the national market in 1988. It enjoyed several good years during the early 1990s before sales fizzled in the middle of the decade, dropping 9 percent in 1995 and 8 percent in 1996. Purchased by Triarc Companies in 1997, Snapple recovered market share in 1998. AriZona Iced Tea was launched by Ferolito, Vultaggio & Sons in 1992 to compete with Snapple. Its unique packaging and competitive pricing helped draw consumers to the brand.

Lipton and Nestea, the traditional distributors of bottled iced tea, responded to their new competitors by forging alliances with PepsiCo and Coca-Cola, the undisputed leaders in the soft drink industry. With the distribution and marketing might of Pepsi and Coke behind them, they remained the top sellers of RTD teas. Lipton claimed about 28 percent market share in 2003 and Nestea 18 percent.

Sports Drinks Sports drinks experienced remarkable growth in the late 1990s and early years of the first decade of the 2000s, growing almost 56 percent between 1997 and 2002. PepsiCo's Gatorade, the granddaddy of the category, continued to maintain its overwhelming lead with 85 percent of the domestic sports drink market despite competition from Coca-Cola and other manufacturers. Gatorade constitutes a highly distinctive brand even beyond the beverage industry. PepsiCo acquired Gatorade in 2001, when it merged with Quaker Oats. Quaker Oats tailored the Gatorade line for a range of athletic abilities, from Frost (for less energetic exercisers) to Fierce (for the more so). It also developed a flavored

"workout water," Propel Fitness Water, with a lighter taste and fewer calories, to draw female consumers. PepsiCo furthered the evolution of Gatorade by developing new flavors of Gatorade Frost, rolling out Propel nationally in 2002, and developing new products like Gatorade Ice, All Stars (for children), and Gatorade Xtremo! for the Hispanic market.

Attracting more female consumers became a much larger concern. According to the Mintel International Group, an industry observer, consumption patterns always leaned heavily toward males, but the trend showed signs of changing as more female teens reportedly were drinking more and more sports drinks. This reflected female teens' ongoing interest in losing weight and increasing interest in exercise. Sports beverage producers also began targeting the fast-growing Hispanic population. Gatorade's Xtremo! was the first to appeal to this potential market with a line of more exotic and tropical flavors including mango and tropical. The effort was supported by bilingual packaging and Spanish language advertising. Coca-Cola's Powerade brand also began using Spanish language advertising to tap into this market.

Along with Powerade, another new brand was the All Sport Body Quencher by the Atlanta-based Monarch Company. More new products and another trend that began emerging were the so-called "energy drinks," including brands such as Adrenaline Rush and KMX Energy Drink. The first product in this line, and the recognized leader, was the Red Bull GmbH. Red Bull launched its one and only product in Europe, then entered the United States market in 1997. However, such energy drinks became involved in controversy, as they were often identified with nightclub usage and as a method to further enhance alcoholic drinks. In Norway, the government classified the Red Bull product as a medicine and banned sales in retail outlets. In Sweden, the public health agency issued a warning after Red Bull consumption became associated with the deaths of three young people. Red Bull itself fanned the flames somewhat by explicitly stating the benefits of its products as a means to improve performance, especially under increased stress or strain, by increasing endurance, improving concentration, and increasing reaction speed. To many, these claims sounded somewhat pharmaceutical. Not surprisingly, the most frequent users were club-goers looking to stay up all night, students who wanted to improve academic performance, and athletes. Indeed, product claims were being investigated around the world, and it was anticipated that U.S. regulatory authorities would also look into the matter. This examination could very well lead to increased regulation in the energy drink category. In addition, more companies were expected to enter the attractive market, which would then drive prices down and attract more consumers. Mintel indicated this development could lead to a more stable regulatory environment and aggressive enforcement.

In the early 2000s, Gatorade's chief competitors, Coca-Cola's Powerade and the Monarch Beverage Co.'s All Sport, together accounted for most of the remaining sports drink market, with Powerade holding approximately 13 percent of the market. Attempts by other companies to market sports drinks often failed.

In the United States, the sports beverage market showed an increase in volume in 2004, rising 12.4 percent. Volume rose 110.8 million over the 2003 level to a total of 890 million gallons (3.5 gallons per person). Growing at an even greater rate was revenue, increasing 12.7 percent from 2003. Wholesale dollars rose from $2.7 billion in 2003 to $3.1 billion in 2004, an increase of $345.1 million.

Sports drinks faced another challenge in their efforts to snag a bigger share of the beverage market: criticism from health professionals. While doctors and others in the medical field agree that encouraging athletes to drink more fluids is laudable, they doubt the nutritional benefits of sports drinks. In fact, the high sugar content of such products as Gatorade translates into more calories, and its acidic nature, coupled with the high sugar content, helps promote tooth decay.

Nutraceutical Drinks Nutraceuticals or functional foods constituted the rising stars of the premium beverage industry. All nutraceutical foods, whether solid or liquid, contain ingredients that are reputed to increase the product's health-boosting potential beyond whatever inherent nutritional value it already possesses. Although some nutraceutical ingredients straddle the line between herbs, dietary supplements, and drugs, promoters of functional foods are prohibited by law from making any explicit claims that their products treat or prevent specific diseases or medical conditions. They may, however, provide general statements about the product's ability to enhance bodily structures and functioning. Manufacturers who ignore these guidelines run the risk of having the product classified as a drug instead of a food and hence becoming subjected to the stringent and costly clinical trials procedure required for U.S. Food and Drug Administration approval to market the product.

Manufacturers like nutraceutical drinks because they can charge premium prices for them. However, while the ultra-bullish economy of the 1990s encouraged health-conscious, aging baby boomers to spend freely on items they perceived would help prolong their vitality and youth, weak economic conditions did slow down this segment's sales in the early years of the first decade of the 2000s.

Orange juice was among the first beverages to earn nutraceutical status, with the addition of calcium to brands such as PepsiCo's Tropicana and Coca-Cola's Minute Maid. Snapple introduced a new nutraceutical drink line, Elements, in the late 1990s. Each of the drinks is based on an elemental name, such as Sky. AriZona Beverages unveiled a new decaffeinated tea-based Rx line of herb-infused health drinks, such as Rx Memory and Rx Stress, to address specific health concerns. However, Bart Vinza, AriZona's vice president of national accounts, pointed out that the company made no claims concerning whether its beverages increased health. Quaker Oats entered a joint venture with the Consumer Health division of Switzerland's Novartis to create Altus Foods, a nutraceutical line under development for the North American market. Quaker also sought expansion into this sector on its own, bringing out Torq, a carbohydrate-laced fruit drink to boost energy, which also contains B vitamins and antioxidants. Soy, heralded for its anti-cancer and anti-heart-disease properties, popped up in South Beach Beverage's (SoBe) functional Soy Essentials, fruit-flavored elixirs supplemented with herbs.

By the early years of the 2000's first decade, nutraceuticals continued to make significant inroads with consumers. In fact, nutraceutical characteristics had spilled into virtually every premium beverage category. Water, dairy, juice drinks, RTD teas, and sports drinks had all made room for new functional product mates. Many manufacturers introduced functional beverages as extensions of existing product lines, and companies continued to explore new innovations, spot new nutritional trends, and keep their eye on different target populations.

Energy Drinks Energy drinks are fruity drinks containing hefty dosages of caffeine, along with additives such as taurine, ginseng, guarana, and mate. Manufacturers gear these drinks to the younger crowd, enticing them with names such as Adrenaline Rush, Ripped to the Max, Rock Star, Crunch, Xtazy, Hype, and SoBe Energy. The best-known brand and one of the first on the market is Red Bull, which is sometimes sold in bars to counteract the effects of alcohol. Nexcite Niagara Drink is a combination of South American herbs, such as damiana, yerba mate, schizandra, ginseng, and caffeine, and is marketed as Viagra in a bottle.

Hansen Beverage Company of Corona, California, introduced a taurine-added energy drink named Monster Energy in 1997. In 2004, the energy drink market reached the $991 million category in the U.S. with Hansen in the number two position behind industry leader Red Bull, which maintained a 54.4 percent share of the market. Catering to specific consumer lifestyles, Hansen introduced a low-carb version of Monster Energy and Monster Assault for the younger market. The number eight spot in the energy drink category was achieved by Lost, produced as a result of teamwork between Hansen and Lost Enterprises, a skateboard and apparel company in San Clemente, California. Lost targeted the 15- to 25-year-old demographic and included a low-calorie version named Lost Perfect 10 and a 50 percent juice variety named Lost Five-0. Lost's sales in 2004 reached $8.5 million, the first year it was on the market.

In 2004, energy drink/fruit juice hybrids were introduced, targeting a previously untapped demographic: health-conscious consumers who were still uncertain about energy drinks. Monster Khaos, with 70 percent juice and aimed at white-collar workers, was introduced by Hansen Beverage Co. in 2004. Following its success, other beverage makers jumped on the bandwagon, including Pepsi, who introduced MDX, featuring the citrus flavor of Mountain Dew. In 2006 Coca-Cola offered its sports drink/energy drink hybrid, Advance, under its Powerade subsidiary. It claims to boost hydration with ingredients such as the B-vitamins and electrolytes found in sports drinks and the taurine and caffeine that are found in energy drinks.

Although bottled water was the second most popular beverage in the United States (behind carbonated soft drinks), in 2007 that segment grew only about 7 percent, as compared to the double- and triple-digit growth rates experienced in the late 1990s and early 2000s. The decline in the sales was attributed to a slow economy and the increasing environmental awareness of Americans. Many consumers oppose the sale and consumption of bottled water, claiming that the emptied bottles are filling landfills and thousands of gallons of gasoline are being wasted by transporting a product that is readily available from the faucet in most U.S. homes. One of the reactions of the industry was to decrease the price of bottled water, a move based in part on data from such reports as the one completed by Brand Keys in early 2008 that found the number-one attribute consumers look for when purchasing bottled water is value. Producers also moved to enhance and flavor water, thus providing something more than "just plain water" to consumers. In fact, enhanced and flavored water grew by 30 percent in 2007 and showed an 18 percent growth rate in the first half of 2008. Other than private labels, of the regular PET bottled water brands, Pepsi's Aquafina led the pack.

U.S. sales of fruit drinks and juices declined in 2007 to $729 million, down about 7 percent from the previous year. The number-one product in the segment in 2007 was Hawaiian Punch, which showed a 58.1 million gallons consumption rate, followed by V8 Splash (22.8 million gallons). Other brands in the top 10 included Snapple, Welch's, and Tropicana.

Although RTD tea held only about a small share of the premium bottled beverage market, that segment grew 15 percent in 2007. Growth in this segment is attributed to the health and wellness trend, and the leading brand was AriZona, with sales of $291 million, followed by Lipton ($271.0 million) and Snapple ($133.2 billion). Although these brands held the top of the charts, industry experts predicted faster growth in specialty and premium brand teas, such as Honest Tea and Ito En. In addition, the number of RTD tea products available doubled between 2005 and 2007, with more choices concerning flavors, types, and natural and organic ingredients.

In 2007, although Gatorade remained the top sports drink in the United States, with $635.6 million in sales, Powerade experienced a more significant rise in sales, increasing almost 21 percent to $251.3 million. Other Gatorade brands such as Gatorade Rain, Frost, and All Stars completed the top five spots.

Without a doubt, nutraceuticals and energy drinks were the hottest spots in the industry in the late years of the first decade of the 2000s. According to Zenith International, as reported in *Beverage World,* consumption of energy drinks in the United States increased almost 600 percent between 2002 and 2007. The number one energy drink in the United States was Red Bull, accounting for 30.6 of the market share and $342.7 million in sales in 2007. Holding 17.5 percent and 13.5 percent of the market, respectively, were Monster Energy ($135.9 million in sales) and Rockstar ($96.2 million in sales). Full Throttle held the fourth spot, and AMP was fifth. In 2007, 185 new energy drinks were launched, and experts concluded that the market was saturated, leaving room only for "products that truly speak to specific needs of consumers—whether it be a female-targeted energy drink or one that uses a natural sweetener."

In the nutraceutical and functional beverages category, sales reached $9.7 billion in 2007. With Americans' focus on health and wellness, this segment was expected to continue to grow, with predictions of sales of more than $13 billion by 2012. One example of a new "recovery" product was Code Blue, called a "lifestyle beverage" by its creators. Code Blue contains reduced glutathione, an antitoxin the helps neutralize free radicals and detoxify the liver, as well as calcium, vitamins, and twice the electrolytes available in sports drinks. The turquoise blue drink is targeted toward people who " are out at night and getting up early to go to work. . . . This was created to help people recover," according to co-creator Jeff Frumin. Examples of other new beverages on the market in the late years of the first decade of the 2000s included Naked Juice's Protein Zone Banana Chocolate Smoothie, with 30 grams of soy and whey protein; vitaminwater's

B-Relaxed, which contains amino acids and advertises a calming effect; and PepsiCo's V Water, which comes in six flavors and incorporates vitamins, minerals, herbal extracts, zinc, selium, and ginseng. Research group Mintel found in a 2007 survey that 69 percent of consumers look for calcium in their beverages, 60 percent want antitoxins, and 52 percent desire green tea or green tea extract. Other ingredients that were in increased demand and thus being incorporated into nutraceutical beverages were fiber, omega-3, ginseng, pomegranate, and soy. Of the many new beverages being introduced, those with the greatest health benefits were predicted to be the most popular among U.S. consumers.

CURRENT CONDITIONS

Within the United States, a 2010 report by Beverage Marketing Corporation concluded that the U.S. beverage industry lost the equivalent of aggregate $11.8 billion in retail sales from the recessionary period of 2008 and 2009. The greatest losses occurred in the liquid refreshment beverages segment ($11 billion). Within this segment, the biggest setback was in sports beverages, with retail sales down 16 percent in 2009 (averaged to 12.3 percent over both 2008 and 2009). The second largest decline was in value-added bottled water, such as those, enhanced with vitamins and minerals (down 8.8 percent). There were slight increases in energy drinks and ready-to-drink tea. (Carbonated soft drinks, although excluded, remained, by far, the largest segment of the liquid refreshment beverages market, although they also declined in both volume and market share in 2009.)

As for premium bottled water, according to Beverage Marketing Corporation, Americans consumed, on average, 27.6 gallons of bottled water per person in 2009, up 11 gallons from 10 years prior (1999). Domestic non-sparkling water accounted for the largest majority of sales; sparkling water and imports accounted for less than one gallon per person.

In 2008, the bottled water industry began to decline, and this trend also continued through 2009, on an even larger scale (six percent). Bottled water volume declined 2.5 percent in 2009 after already dropping 1 percent in 2008. (By comparison, the industry had grown 10.8 percent in 2005.)

In revenues, bottled water sales were less than $10.6 billion in 2009, after having already declined to $11.2 billion in 2008 from $11.5 billion in 2007. In actual volume, domestic non-sparkling water represented the largest segment of the U.S. packaged water industry, accounting for 8.1 billion gallons in 2009. This represented 96.1 percent of total 2009 volume.

The retail premium PET segment (single serve premium water in disposable polyethylene terephthalate bottles) was flat in 2008 and declined in 2009 to roughly 5.2 billion gallons. Although partly due to the slumping economy, the PET segment was also fraught with adverse publicity regarding health risks associated with plastic bottles, both PET and polycarbonate BPA (Bis-phenol A) types. For example, bottle water dispensed in bottles made PET may also pack a substantial quantity of estrogen-mimicking pollution, according to researchers at Johann Wolfgang Goethe University in Frankfurt. Although the FDA continued to hold that neither bottle type imposed health risks when stored and shipped under normal operating conditions and consumed during the stated shelf life, some uneasiness remained among consumers. There was also adverse publicity regarding the amount of gasoline/fuel expended in shipping weight-heavy bottle water, considered by many a discretionary waste of energy during critical shortage times. Health and money-conscious consumers began to shift to other alternatives. For example, in 2009, the relatively small regional vending segment (involving refillable jug containers) actually grew after several years of decline.

2009 also saw declines in the other two (but much smaller) bottled water market segments: sparkling water and imported water. There were also declines in direct-delivery bottled water. U.S. home and office delivery slipped from volume of 1.3 billion gallons in 2008 to less than 1.2 billion gallons in 2009.

INDUSTRY LEADERS

As of 2010, four companies accounted for all of the top 10 refreshment beverage trademarks (buoyed partially by carbonated soft drinks, excluded from this category): Pepsi-Cola (five brands), Coca-Cola (four brands), Dr Pepper/Snapple, and Nestle. Nevertheless, Pepsi's overall sales volume was down 7.8 percent for 2009, and Coca-Cola was down 3 percent overall. Nestle Pure Life achieved the fastest growth among leading trademarks in 2009. The top three U.S. bottled water companies in 2009 were Nestle Waters North America, PepsiCo (Aquafina and Gatorade) and Coca-Cola (Dasani), accounting for nearly 60 percent (57.5) of all wholesale dollar sales. Nestle, with 35.4 percent of the market, had $3.8 billion in 2009 sales.

Snapple Beverage Corp., a subsidiary of Dr Pepper Snapple Group, was established in 1986 in Brooklyn, New York. Founders Lenny Marsh, Hymie Golden, and Arnie Greenberg regarded their product as an alternative to sweet soft drinks. The national success it achieved during the early 1990s can be traced in part to a humorous series of television advertisements featuring Wendy, the "Snapple Lady." She was a bona fide marketing department employee of the company who read and answered customers' letters to Snapple on the air. Sales soared, reaching over $700 million by 1994, the year Quaker Oats bought the firm for $1.7 billion. However, Quaker Oats soon sold Snapple to Triarc Companies after several years of declining sales that analysts blamed on distribution difficulties and a lack of promotion. A holding company with interests in several different industries, Triarc worked to turn the brand around, and total sales for 1999 inched up 5 percent to reach $854 million. It also introduced a number of new products at the end of the 1990s, including Whipper-Snapple smoothies, Snapple Farms juices, a line of herb-enhanced fruit drinks and teas called Elements, Mistic brand Italian Ice Smoothies, and Sun Valley Squeeze fruit-flavored drinks. In 2000, Triarc agreed to sell Snapple to Cadbury Schweppes. In 2001, Snapple brought in almost $1 billion in revenues. In 2003, the company secured an exclusive alternative advertising deal to become New York City's official beverage. For $166 million, Snapple obtained exclusive five-year distribution rights in New York public schools and buildings, on public transit systems, and more. In exchange, schools get a 30 percent cut on commissions and $3 million in donations to sports annually.

Ferolito, Vultaggio & Sons, purveyors of the Ari-Zona Iced Tea brand, started in business as beer distributors in Brooklyn, New York, during the 1970s. Their fleet eventually grew from one Volkswagen bus to 25 trucks. In 1992, they branched out to iced teas. Within two years, the AriZona brand was posting $300 million in sales. The company's innovative packaging, including larger than average portions and trendy "good for you" formulations featuring green teas and ginseng, helped build the AriZona brand.

WORKFORCE

Increased regulations and more sophisticated equipment in bottling plants created a need for better trained and more highly skilled employees in the beverage industry. Specialized courses of study, such as the Beverage Technician certification program at Florida International University, assure employers that their workers are properly educated.

Management level employees are expected to have degrees in the sciences or engineering, with follow-up training and education from trade-specific groups such as the International Society of Beverage Technologists. For areas such as quality control, employment requirements might demand that candidates possess a degree in microbiology, biology, chemistry, or field science. Additional experience in statistical process control, blending, flavors, and sanitation is considered a plus.

AMERICA AND THE WORLD

In the first decade of the 2000s, U.S. companies dominated the worldwide beverage industry. Among the exceptions were two firms based in Mexico: PanAmerican Beverage, a Coca-Cola-affiliated distributor, and Pepsi-Gemex. In addition, although Americans consumed the most New Age drinks, a 2008 report by Productscan predicted that the energy drink market in Europe would grow 4.5 percent by 2011 to reach $5 billion. Italy was expected to experience the fastest rate of growth (10 percent), followed by Sweden (7 percent).

One of the trends in the industry worldwide in the late years of the first decade of the 2000s involved the focus on health concerns. A study by Productscan found that of all new sports and energy beverages and foods introduced in 2007, 12 percent claimed to be high in vitamins and 7 percent were labeled as natural. The tendency of energy drink producers to add vitamins and organic ingredients to their beverages—with the idea of providing longer lasting energy benefits, rather than the short-term energy bursts provided by such ingredients as caffeine—was expected to increase in Europe as it followed the United States' lead.

Soft drinks continued to invade developing nations, stealing beverage consumers from more traditional beverages such as coffee and tea. In India, the world's largest consumer of tea, young people increasingly flocked to Western soft drinks, since they considered tea to be a "frumpy" drink of their elders. However, tea producers and marketers looked to the nutraceutical properties of the drink to reinvigorate the flagging market. Tata Tea, whose acquisition of Tetley Tea made it the world's second largest tea company, intended to introduce functional teas into the Indian market, and Hindustan Lever Ltd. test-marketed its mass brand tea A1 fortified with vitamins and minerals.

Beverage preferences vary widely from country to country. Americans tend to drink less fruit juice than Western Europeans, partly because of the popularity of soft drinks in the United States. Functional foods won increased consumer attention in the late 1990s, with dairy-based and vitamin-enhanced drinks especially popular in Germany, where the market segment grew by about 29 percent. In the Asian market, carbonated drinks were popular, but consumers also favored canned coffees and teas as well as mineral water. In Japan, for example, Georgia brand iced coffee, a Coca-Cola product, was a top-selling item.

RESEARCH AND TECHNOLOGY

Formulation and flavoring are ongoing preoccupations of premium beverage companies. With growing consumer demand for vitamins, minerals, and other health-related products, the challenge for flavoring companies trying to keep up with this trend is to provide beverage companies with nutritionally sound yet tasty products.

Many nutraceutical and flavoring ingredients in New Age beverages are difficult to work with because they have very strong flavors or odors, or because they add unaesthetic colorings to products. Food engineers both in the United States and abroad work to develop versions of these ingredients more amenable to combination in consumer beverages. In Europe, Zylepsis engaged in proprietary extraction work that permitted it to create black tea, a popular but hard-to-work-with flavor, as a white powder that is decaffeinated and becomes clear in beverage applications, thus eliminating the murky coloring it normally imparts to beverages. The U.S.-based Folexco/East Earth Herb focused on creating blends of herbs and botanicals for use in beverages, scrutinizing the 25 most commonly used botanicals to identify pleasing combinations of what the company termed "collateral" flavors. These included echinacea extract combined with citrus and the relaxation-inducing herb valerian, which has a particularly unpleasant smell. The firm devised a micro-encapsulation technology that permits the ingredient to be time-released to avoid unpleasant odors. In search of ever more exotic tastes, Givaudan Roure Flavours established a TasteTrek program to scout out new botanicals in the Central African rainforest that would be extracted for further investigation in Givaudan's Swiss and American laboratories.

Consumer demand for beverages to fulfill need states such as fun/social, meal accompaniment, relaxation/tranquility, comfort, and weight control drove beverage companies to expand their research into ever more healthful hybrids. A majority of the drinks being introduced in late decade contained some healthful ingredient. Weight loss was also an issue, and low-calorie energy drinks were being developed for active people who "don't want to put back the calories they just burned off," according to Michael La Kier, senior brand manager of Powerade.

One aspect of research and development in the industry in the late years of the first decade of the 2000s was the variety of new ingredients being incorporated into premium beverages. Some examples include alternative sweeteners, such as stevia, crystalline fructose, and erythritol; cupuacu, an ingredient from Africa that was thought to have many health benefits; and flaxseed, which contains omega-3 acids as well as ingredients that were thought to provide cosmetic benefits, such as aloe vera, green tea extract, and l-carnitine.

BIBLIOGRAPHY

"Balance Water Makes its U.S. Debut." *Beverage World,* 14 March 2008.

Bellas, Michael C. "Multitaskers: Try a Hybrid." *Beverage World,* 15 March 2006.

Beverage Marketing Corporation. "Bottled Water Confronts Persistent Challenges, New Report From Beverage Marketing Corporation Shows." Press Release, July 2010. Available from http://www.beveragemarketing.com/

———. "The U.S. Liquid Refreshment Beverage Market Declined by 2.7% in 2009, Beverage Marketing Corporation Reports." Press Release, 24 March 2010. Available from http://www.beveragemarketing.com/

———. "U.S. Beverage Industry Lost Billions in Recession, Beverage Marketing Corporation Report Concludes." Press Release, July 2010. Available from http://www.beveragemarketing.com/

"Bottled Fruit Drinks." *MMR,* 14 January 2008.

Cirillo, Jennifer. "Code Blue Can Help You Get Back to Life." *Beverage World,* 12 September 2008.

———. "Full Yet? New Age Beverages Look to Satisfy Consumers on the Inside and Out." *Beverage World,* 15 January 2008.

"Energy Drinks Producers Jump on Health Bandwagon." *just-drinks.com,* 5 September 2008.

"Global R&D Spotlight." *Beverage World,* June 2008.

"Global Top 10 Beverage Companies." Press Release, July 2010. Available from http://www.reportlinker.com/021815/Global-Top-10-Beverage-Companies-Industry.

Hein, Kenneth. "Has the Bottled Water Well Finally Run Dry?" *Brandweek ,* 8 September 2008.

Landi, Heather. "A Juice Guy Goes Back to Basics." *Beverage World,* 15 February 2006.

———. "Taste of What's to Come." *Beverage World,* 9 September 2008.

Landi, Heather. "Creating a Monster." *Beverage World,* 15 February 2006.

Raloff, Janet. "Bottled Water May Contain Hormones: Plastics." 12 March 2009. Available from http://www.sciencenews.org/.

"State of the Industry '08." *Beverage World.* April 2008.

Strenk, T.H. "To Your Health." *Foodservice Director,* 15 March 2006.

Wright, Rebecca. "Nutraceuticals Coast in the Beverage Market." *Nutraceuticals World,* July-August 2008.

PROFESSIONAL EMPLOYER ORGANIZATIONS

SIC CODE(S)

7363

INDUSTRY SNAPSHOT

Professional Employer Organizations (PEOs), which are firms engaged in employee leasing, assume the responsibility for a company's employees, placing them all on the PEO's payroll, handling all human resource and legal matters, and leasing the employees back to the company for a marked-up fee. There are four main areas of focus for a PEO: setting up payroll and taxes, providing human resources (HR) expertise, assisting with employment law, and managing employee health care benefits packages. PEOs can make available to smaller firms the ability to provide their employees with *Fortune* 500 level insurance and other human resources benefits, freeing managers and executives to focus on business strategies.

Despite some difficulties during its development years, by the early 2000s, the professional employer organization (PEO) industry emerged as the fastest growing business service in the United States, according to the Harvard Business Journal. The National Association of Professional Employer Organizations (NAPEO), based in Alexandria, Virginia, reported that an average member PEO grew, both in revenues and people, at approximately 20 percent annually during the same time period.

NAPEO had 400 member PEOs in all 50 states. According to the organization, NAPEO members represented about 90 percent of the industry's revenues. In addition, the NAPEO's Institute for Accreditation of Professional Employment Organizations (IAPEO) sets industry accreditation standards. To further shore up

the industry's reputation, NAPEO launched its Seal of Assurance for Professional Employer Organizations (SAFPEO) program in early 2000. The SAFPEO is awarded to participating PEOs to acknowledge that they meet the industry's financial and ethical standards.

ORGANIZATION AND STRUCTURE

Employee leasing firms are as varied in size and type as the client companies they represent. The biggest market for PEOs is among firms employing between 5 and 100 workers. Typically, a PEO will charge a fee to the company equal to between 3 and 6 percent of the client's payroll, as well as between 9 and 20 percent of the firm's gross wages for benefits and the PEO's margin. In most cases, the company signs a co-employment agreement with the PEO whereby the company becomes what is known as a "workside employer."

Employees still take their directions from the company's executives, who maintain control over all company policy and guidelines. Logistical employee concerns, however, such as paychecks, legal concerns, workers' compensation, and so on, are taken up with the PEO. Employees also receive the PEO's benefits package, which will generally include health and dental insurance, a 401(k) plan, assistance programs, credit union membership, and paid vacations after a specified period of employment.

One successful strategy lies in identifying and serving a particular industry niche. By targeting a particular type of client firm, a leasing company may specialize in terms of benefits offered, client size, payroll size, and risk ratios. PEOs may also assist in the training process for

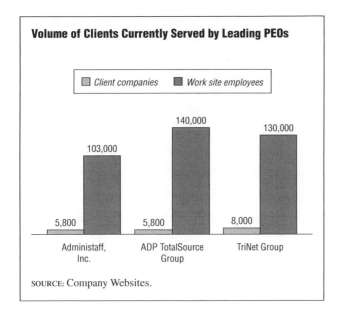

Volume of Clients Currently Served by Leading PEOs

◻ Client companies   ◼ Work site employees

Administaff, Inc.: 5,800 / 103,000
ADP TotalSource Group: 5,800 / 140,000
TriNet Group: 8,000 / 130,000

SOURCE: Company Websites.

companies, producing training manuals and policy guidelines customized for the client. Often, a PEO will also provide on-site inspections to monitor Occupational Safety and Health Administration (OSHA) compliance or other regulatory provisions.

Different client industries require different types of expertise from PEOs. Blue-collar manufacturing firms, for example, tend to employ people with lower average salaries but higher workers' compensation claims. White-collar employees in the computer software industry enjoy higher salaries and benefits, so a PEO needs to carve out a cost savings niche by relying on its economies of scale.

Key to the growing popularity of PEOs is the relief they offer in lifting administrative burdens from the shoulders of the client's managers. The U.S. Small Business Administration (SBA) put the average cost of regulation, tax compliance, and paperwork for smaller companies (fewer than 500 employees) at about $5,000 per employee versus $3,400 for bigger firms. The SBA further estimated that between 7 and 25 percent of the small business owner's time is spent on employee-related paperwork.

Small firms typically pay more for insurance and workers' compensation because their risk rating can be thrown off by a single unfortunate case; but in a leased environment, a PEO can merge a client's staff into very large pools of employees with a better overall risk rating. Therefore, a single workers' compensation claim will not have the same catastrophic effect on benefit costs. Many PEO clients are small manufacturers whose workers may suffer from a high number of repetitive strain injuries. PEO safety managers will analyze the patterns of work

and attempt to devise ergonomic solutions to avoid such problems. Often the solution may require a job rotation program or a change in the process or equipment involved. The key is to discover the root causes of injuries, then work with management and employees to eliminate those causes.

Many PEOs save their clients money by being very aggressive about return-to-work programs. When an employee is injured, the treating physician often places restrictions on when that employee may return to work. PEOs have been known to work directly with physicians to help them understand exactly what is required of specific employees. In such a case, a videotape of particular workplace procedures involved may serve this purpose. PEOs may also design a temporary "bridge" job that will allow the injured employee to return to lighter duty until fully recovered. Measures such as this have helped PEOs get employees back on the job sooner. This "pays benefits" in better morale, increased productivity, and lower workers' compensation costs.

BACKGROUND AND DEVELOPMENT

Analysts offer varied and often fanciful explanations for the historical roots of employee leasing. Some point to the mercenary soldiers employed by Britain during the American Revolution. Others trace the industry's origins to Alan Pinkerton, founder of the Pinkerton National Detective Agency in 1852, who leased security guards to the railroads to prevent theft and to recover stolen property. Since the 1940s, another pool of leased employees has been America's truck drivers. The Driver Employer Council of America reported that 30 percent of all private carriers use leased drivers, including many of the nation's largest firms.

In the 1970s, the employee leasing industry developed a negative reputation as an arrangement used only to dodge certain tax and other obligations. For example, during this period, many professional partnerships, such as those owned by physicians and dentists, viewed leasing only as a way to exclude clerical and other hourly help from the retirement plans of their more highly paid managers. The Internal Revenue Service (IRS) fought this arrangement in the tax courts, and in 1982, the Tax Equity and Fiscal Responsibility Act (TEFRA) was enacted to ban the practice outright. TEFRA held that leased employees could be excluded from the client company's own pension plan only if the client contributed a substantial amount of money (equal to 7.5 percent of the employee's pay) to a fully vested pension plan. This could have ended the controversy, but further legislative revisions and tax court rulings muddied the situation until the Tax Reform Act of 1986 finally ended the pension tax-related advantages of leasing employees. The Tax Reform Act was a boon for PEOs because it forced the leasing industry to come up with a more rational reason for its existence. From that time on, the best PEOs began to promote themselves as providing more and more of the client's total personnel needs.

The leasing industry still suffered its share of legal difficulties, however. In August 1989, embezzlement by managers sent CAP Staffing of North Carolina into bankruptcy, leaving leased employees with some $2.2 million in unpaid health claims. A few years later, Persona Management Corp., with nearly 100 client companies representing some 8,000 workers in Rhode Island and Massachusetts, was found by the IRS to have understated clients' payroll wages in 1992 and 1993 by $60 million, and to owe taxes of $13 million. To make matters worse, several larger companies were caught leasing some of their lower-paid workers to escalate pension benefits for the higher-paid employees, thus making the benefits package appear more attractive to potential clients.

The arrival of PEOs certainly confounded the regulatory climate. The industry was still rife with legal wrangling in the late 1990s, as the dust settled on issues related to the responsibility for regulatory compliance. For instance, the Occupational Safety and Health Review Commission issued a ruling in 1999 whereby the responsibility for OSHA compliance rests with the person or entity who maintains control over the workplace. The ruling stemmed from a dispute originating with an OSHA inspection of an Ohio ceramics manufacturer that resulted in violation citations for both the ceramics firm and its PEO, TEAM America Corp. TEAM America fought the citation on the grounds that it could not be held responsible for such on-site violations. In this case, the review commission held that although the PEO provided employment services and even agreed to run inspections for the company, TEAM America's involvement in the on-site compliance was "indirect or theoretical" and thus was outside the purview of the OSHA citation. Rather, the commission ruled, the ceramics firm was in control of the work environment and thus responsible for compliance.

These incidents, even while tarnishing the industry's reputation, provided an unexpected impetus to its growth. Many client companies that had a bad experience with an unscrupulous PEO found that the benefits of a leased arrangement so clearly outweighed the problems that they immediately sought to sign on with another, more reputable PEO. Numerous clients try one or more PEOs for a year or so before settling with one that meets their needs. With so many PEOs vying for attention, client companies are forced to exercise due diligence before signing on

with one of them. Since January 1996, the Institute for Accreditation of Professional Employment Organizations (IAPEO) has enforced its standards toward these ends. The process is costly, with annual accreditation fees ranging from $5,000 to $15,000.

Another issue comes in the form of competition from national firms such as Kelly Services, Inc., the temporary help agency that in 1994 entered the leasing industry by purchasing the California-based PEO Your Staff. For the industry, 2002 turned out to be a hard year, with several factors contributing. Some of the top names went out of business, including HR Logic and SES. According to the Staffing Industry Report, the National Association of Professional Employer Organizations (NAPEO) lost 150 members, as companies either shut down or consolidated. In Florida, insurance problems were the culprit. In August 2002, CNA Insurance stopped selling workers' compensation insurance to PEOs because of documented cases of insurance abuse. As a result, the Florida Department of Insurance shut down all PEOs without insurance, forcing four PEOs to shut down operations.

Other major PEOs that folded in 2002 included Employee Solutions, Inc. (ESI) of Phoenix, Arizona, TTC—Illinois, and Peopleworks of Little Rock, Arkansas. ESI was the most eye-opening, as the company was one of the industry leaders. Like many other PEOs, it targeted small and medium-size companies for its employee leasing services. ESI handled the administrative end of business (payroll, benefits, government regulations, tax services, etc.) for its 2,000 clients. At its height, it leased about 35,000 workers in 47 states, largely to clients in the transportation and service industries. The firm's revenues dipped slightly in 1999 to $939.8 million from $969.9 million in 1998, largely as a result of investment in the company pipeline and restructuring. However, the company's auditors issued a warning about its viability in 2000, causing Employee Solutions to be delisted from the NASDAQ. In 1996, ESI purchased assets of Leaseway Transportation, one of the nation's largest auto haulers and a major participant in the Teamster Trust Funds. The move eventually proved troublesome, when, less than five years later, ESI went bankrupt, with more than $5 million owed to the Central and New York Funds alone. As a result, more than 1,000 Teamster members lost their jobs.

In order to help, some members of the PEO industry sought to amend the tax codes to enable PEOs to serve as the employer for benefit purposes. PEOs already offered retirement plans, but that was a violation of the tax code, which required that retirement plans be offered by the real employer. The Professional Employer Organization Worker Benefits Act, sponsored by Representatives Rob

Portman (R-Ohio) and Benjamin Cardin (D-Maryland), along with Senators Graham (D-Florida) and Grassley (R-Iowa), was expected to fix the problem of noncompliance with the tax code. However, at the same time, it would repeal established common law rules that define employees and employers for purposes of taxes, pensions, health benefits, and other employee benefits.

Thanks largely to mergers and acquisitions, the number of PEOs nationwide shrank from 2,500 to less than 2,000 between 1997 and 2000, then to about 700 in 2004; but this trend belied the industry's long-term growth. In 1985, there were fewer than 100 PEOs employing about 10,000 workers. In 2002, about 2 to 3 million Americans found work through PEOs, and the PEO workforce earned about $18 billion in annual wages and benefits, according to the NAPEO. Florida, California, and Texas had the highest concentrations of PEO firms, with penetration in some regions reaching 30 to 40 percent.

A company of fewer than 20 employees is a typical client of a PEO. According to the SBA, these small companies would spend up to 80 percent more per regular employee than their larger counterparts on regulatory compliance, about $2,000 for each employee. This does not take into account the time involved; the SBA estimated that a full one-quarter of a business owner's time could be spent simply dealing with employee-related paperwork. Taking both time and money into account, a firm of fewer than 10 employees saved $5,000 by contracting with a PEO, and a company of 10 to 19 employees saved double that amount. PEOs offered the best of both worlds for many employers.

At the end of 2005, there were approximately 700 PEO companies nationwide providing a wide variety of employment services to business and industry, with an estimated $43 billion in gross revenues generated annually. An estimated 2 million employees were under contract with PEOs, according to the NAPEO. Revenues in 2006 rose to $51 billion.

For small to medium-sized companies especially, the benefits of maintaining a relationship with PEOs continued. Approximately 40 percent were able to upgrade their total employee benefit packages, according to the NAPEO. The U.S. Small Business Administration reported that small business employees' opportunities to have access to a 401(k) retirement account dropped from 28 to 19 percent; however, 95 percent of PEOs belonging to the NAPEO offer their contracted employees a 401(k) plan. Businesses with one to nine employees were able to save an average of $5,000 per year and seven hours per week, while larger firms with 50 to 99 employees averaged $32,000 per year saved, along with 34 hours saved each week. As a result, the main incentives for signing with a

PEO continued to be the savings in administrative costs, time spent, and headaches, and the industry was expected to continue to grow into the late 2000s.

By 2007, only 24 states regulated, licensed, or registered PEOs. Some states, such as Colorado, require persons employed by PEOs to sign an agreement acknowledging themselves as such. Such an arrangement can make companies a bit skittish about signing on with a PEO, which would then claim the right to hire and fire workers, resulting in a loss of control that some companies find too costly, in spite of the benefits a PEO can offer. PEO advocates counter, however, that making such moves without consulting with an employer would be ill advised for any PEO that hopes to keep getting business.

As of 2008, there were about 700 PEOs operating in 50 states. The industry saw an estimated 15 to 20 percent increase in revenues, reaching $61 billion in 2007. Although the average client of a U.S. PEO employs about 19 people, larger business are also beginning to use the services as well, according to the NAPEO. In a 2008 NAPEO press release, Greg Slamowitz of Ambrose Employer Group in New York, said, "The numbers have made it very clear that PEOs have come into their own. There's no end in sight to the growth, because we offer the services that more and more small businesses can't live without." Those services continued to include administrating payroll and filing workers compensation payments, as well as handling health benefits packages.

One of the trends in the industry was PEOs' use of the Internet to serve their clients. For example, Web-based information systems allow secure online access to payroll records and personnel information. In addition, PEOs were offering more and different types of benefits, such as travel discounts, college tuition reimbursements and scholarships, and health savings accounts. Some PEOs were also sponsoring continuing education credit courses on operations and regulations. Such classes were seen as a way to disseminate information as well as educate business professionals about the benefits of using a PEO.

CURRENT CONDITIONS

As the 2008 and 2009 recession took its hold on small businesses, coupled with the pending uncertainty of providing health benefits to employees (some for the first time) under the new health care reform package, PEOs stepped in to help. Because PEOs are larger organizations with many employees, they can better negotiate better benefits packages and reduced premiums with prospective group health care providers and insurers. The PEO industry was valued at $68 billion in 2008, and roughly the same for 2009.

According to the American Staffing Association (ASA), staffing agencies generated $53.5 billion in revenues in 2009. Another $7.9 billion came from permanent placements. The U.S. Department of Labor's Bureau of Labor Statistics, projected a 19 percent growth from 2008 to 2018, capitalizing on consistent employer needs to meet staffing variables.

In 2010, Nebraska (via LB 579, the 2010 Professional Employer Organization Registration Act) and Hawaii (Senate Bill 1026) became the latest states to codify into law the PEO industry. As of 2010, a total of 37 states had adopted versions of acts/laws that typically provided for the registration, licensing, and taxing of PEOs. Most states required PEOs to file annual statements with the Department of Labor.

INDUSTRY LEADERS

The nation's largest PEO in 2009 was Administaff, Inc., founded in 1986 and based in Kingwood, Texas. Administaff operated 31 offices in 21 major markets in the United States, focusing on small and medium-sized companies, providing them with a full service resources department. Administaff targets progressive, growth-oriented businesses with a workforce between 10 and 2,000 and demonstrating relatively low workers' compensation and unemployment risks. Most of its clients are white-collar industries, such as technology, accounting, real estate, and medical services, and their light manufacturing clients are the exception to that rule. In 2009, sales were $1.6 billion with more than 115,000 employees.

Another prominent and fast-growing PEO was ADP TotalSource Group of Miami, Florida, with almost 2,000 employees and revenues of $$8.9 billion for fiscal year 2010. In 2008, ADP TotalSource had 30 offices in 15 states.

In mid 2009, the TriNet Group, Inc. of California acquired Gevity HR, of Bradenton, Florida. Gevity managed 8,000 clients and 130,000 worksite employees. Gevity operates 40 offices in 20 states, including Florida, Texas, Georgia, Arizona, Minnesota, North Carolina, Tennessee, Alabama, Colorado, California, and New York. Products and services include assistance with employee recruiting, performance management, training and development, benefits administration, payroll administration, governmental compliance, risk management, unemployment administration, and health, welfare, and retirement benefits.

WORKFORCE

According to NAPEO, the typical PEO client employs 16 workers. These small businesses run the gamut from accountants to zookeepers and include every profession in between, from doctors and retailers to mechanics and funeral home directors. As a rule, those who work for such companies do not have access to the menu of benefits available to employees of larger organizations. Additionally, as reported by Rodney Ho in the *Wall Street Journal,* a survey by Dun & Bradstreet found that the number of small businesses offering employee benefits was decreasing.

PEO surveys indicated that employee satisfaction runs high because leased employees often enjoy a greater level of benefits than what was available to them prior to the leasing arrangement. According to NAPEO, all member companies offered health plans by 2000, compared to 45 percent of small firms nationally offering health insurance. Dental care was offered by 97 percent of NAPEO members, 80 percent offered vision coverage, nearly 90 percent offered short- and long-term disability insurance, and 92 percent offered life insurance. More than 80 percent offered a 401(k) retirement savings plan.

As the leasing industry grows, the need to find experienced and capable managers becomes increasingly important. While it is possible to hire good people from related industries (such as risk managers from the insurance profession), there will no doubt be shortages as the leasing industry expands. Given the skyrocketing growth rates of the industry, this means it is likely that some PEO firms will contract with clients but be unable to deliver the required services. This is expected to result in a shakeout and consolidation of the industry over the next decade.

RESEARCH AND TECHNOLOGY

Industry consolidation yielded unexpected benefits. PEOprofits.com is a firm made up of employee leasing industry veterans who came together to pool their expertise following the acquisitions of a number of PEOs in order to provide other PEOs with customized software and Internet solutions. In late 1999, PEOprofits.com teamed up with Ultimate Software, a provider of human resource and payroll e-business solutions, to offer Web-based payroll applications to PEO firms attempting to streamline their processing activities. This was the first such product specifically tailored to the employee leasing industry, whose players typically had to adapt general accounting and payroll software packages to their operations.

More PEOs began using the Internet as a way to provide information to their clients. Many PEOs advertised on the Internet, offering information about their services and the benefits of using them. Some PEOs also utilized the Web to provide a way for employees and clients to access payroll and benefit data online.

BIBLIOGRAPHY

Basso, Louis, and Barry Shorten. "PEO Industry Continues to Grow." *The CPA Journal,* August 2006.

Buchanan, Dennis. "PEOs Offer Big-Company Benefits to Small Businesses." *Journal: Employee Benefit Plan Review,* February 2006.

"Governor Lingle Signs PEO Act, 37th State to Standardize the $68 Billion Industry." 26 May 2010. Available from http://www.anythingresearch.com.

Harbert, Tam. "The Scoop on Outsourcing HR Using PEOs." 15 September 2008. Available from http://www.allbusiness.com.

"Health Benefits Model Brings Employers Big Cost Savings." San Jose *Business Journal,* 16 November 2009.

"Industry Facts." National Association for Professional Employer Organizations, 15 September 2008. Available from http://www.napeo.org.

Marquez, Jessica. "PEOs May Heat Competition in Middle Market." *Workforce Management,* 30 January 2006.

"Nebraska Becomes the 35th State to Codify the $68 Billion PEO Industry." 11 March 2010. Available from http://www.anythingresearch.com.

"Professional Employer Organization (PEO)." 15 September 2008. Available from http://www.entrepreneur.com.

"Professional Employer Organizations: A Boon to Small Businesses, Boom as More Companies Discover Benefits." National Association for Professional Employer Organizations, 8 January 2008. Available from http://www.napeo.org.

"Professional Employer Organizations and Their Suppliers Are Some of the Fastest-Growing Companies in America, Says *Inc.* Magazine in its New *Inc.* 5,000 List." National Association for Professional Employer Organizations, 1 October 2007. Available from http://www.napeo.org.

"Recent News About Professional Employer Organizations." Accessed October 2010 at http://www.anythingresearch.com.

Reynolds, Susan. "PEO One of Several Ways to Outsource HR." *Toledo Business Journal,* 1 April 2006.

Rodgers, Donna. "Information on Running a Staffing Agency." 20 May 2010. Available from http://www.ehow.com/about_6532185_information-running-staffing-agency-htm.

Tablac, Angela. "Small Businesses Turn to PEOs for Human Resources Help." *St. Louis Post-Dispatch,* 6 January 2008.

Winters, Howard. "Professional Employment Organizations Can Help Local Firms." *Las Vegas Business Press,* 13 March 2006.

PROFESSIONAL EXECUTIVE RECRUITING

———— ■ ————

SIC CODE(S)

7361

INDUSTRY SNAPSHOT

With annual salaries over $250,000, top-level executives are not exactly perusing the newspaper classifieds in search of new positions. Instead, professional executive recruiting services, also known as headhunting services, assist executives in finding their next positions, even when many of them are not actually looking for new jobs.

Back in the 1980s, nearly three-quarters of professionally-employed executives expected to change careers three or fewer times. However, reflecting the general changes in the U.S. business practices and economy over the last decades of the twentieth century, there was new understanding among top-level employees that career changes were likely. Fifty-three percent of executives now expected to change careers more than six times before retirement.

In addition to all the large, established companies that relied on executive recruiters for years, the well-funded Internet start-ups that sprouted like dandelions in the late 1990s created a huge demand for veteran executives to steer "dot-coms" to riches. In only a year or two, however, the industry faced a turnaround. The dot-com revolution turned out to be a big bust, the terrorist attacks of September 11, 2001 negatively impacted an already sluggish economy, and an ongoing recession changed the rosy picture very quickly. In 2001, a very bleak year for the industry, retainer fees plummeted 31 percent and firms posted single-digit revenue growth while experiencing double-digit losses, layoffs, and lost client firms. Market analysts estimated the industry lost $3 billion in two years.

The industry rebounded in mid-decade (2004–2008), but high unemployment at the end of the decade again held back growth. Financial services continued to hold the largest market share in the industry, followed by the industrial, consumer products, technology, life sciences and health care, nonprofit, and professional services sectors. The nonprofit sector experienced the most growth in terms of number of searches.

ORGANIZATION AND STRUCTURE

Executive recruiters, often called headhunters, seek and place management personnel domestically and internationally in a wide variety of positions and industries. Companies retain the services of an executive recruiter to access a global network of candidates far beyond the scope of an in-house human resources department and to locate a suitable candidate quickly and efficiently.

Executive search firms are non-licensed organizations that primarily place senior executives who earn a minimum of $50,000 per year. Top-level firms may restrict themselves to jobs paying over $100,000 annually. The differences between firms are disappearing as the industry sorts itself out and companies diversify.

When industry and business are operating at high levels, executive search services are in great demand. As downturns occur, businesses hire fewer managers, which cuts into the industry's employment levels and profits. Consequently, executive search firms are expanding their specialties to include such areas as business intelligence, outplacement, consulting, finance, benchmarking,

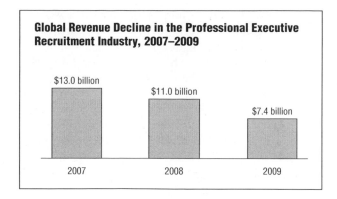

Global Revenue Decline in the Professional Executive Recruitment Industry, 2007–2009

$13.0 billion — 2007
$11.0 billion — 2008
$7.4 billion — 2009

employee testing, and temporary services. These additional services, combined with the expansion of the global market, provide an expanding opportunity for executive research firms.

The process of executive recruiting is multifaceted. The search firm and client company at the outset must prepare a written, detailed job description. The recruiter then conducts an extensive search, contacts prospective candidates, and performs reference checks. Client interviews are arranged with the top two or three prospects from the pool of candidates. The most promising candidate is selected.

Types of Headhunters The industry is divided into generalists and specialists. Some firms, such as Phyllis Solomon Executive Search Inc. based in Englewood Cliffs, New Jersey, concentrate on specific industries and clearly defined levels of management. Solomon focuses on middle to upper management personnel in the health care field. Smaller firms such as Solomon also tend to seek relatively localized niches within the industry. Larger companies such as Korn/Ferry International tend to be more diverse and serve a wider array of clients in widespread geographical areas. They also constantly seek new clients in diverse businesses. For example, A.T. Kearney Executive Search, which has been in business for more than 50 years, announced in 1997 that it was establishing an office in Santa Monica, California, to service the entertainment industry. Successful executive search firms constantly establish niches and respond rapidly to changes in the business world.

Executive recruiting is becoming increasingly specialized. Contemporary recruiters use state-of-the-art technology to ensure that the personnel recruited suitably fit the intended positions. They use tools such as computer software and paper-based tests to analyze items such as executives' skills and personality traits, then compare them to the requirements of the positions to be filled. Recruiters cannot trust luck, subjectivity, or hunches to select candidates. Clients can pay executive recruiting

firms as much as one-third of a candidate's first year's salary as compensation, which means neither side can afford mistakes in matching the right candidate to a specific job. Recruiters can earn as much as $750,000 and repeat business for the most high profile job searches.

A Small Matter of Money Firms generally work on either contingent or retained fee bases. Contingency means that the client pays no money until a person is placed. Firms that work on a contingency basis usually recruit junior or mid-level executives, and are paid only if the search is successful for the client. Contingency fees can be as much as half of the target position's annual salary.

Under the retained structure, the client typically pays one-third of the fee up front, another third halfway through the search, and the final third upon placement of a candidate. This fee can be as much as 33 percent of the position's annual compensation. The fee structure varies with the client's needs and the candidate's availability. In some cases, clients need people immediately and temporarily. In others, they can afford long lead times to replace outgoing personnel or for the assumption of newly created positions.

Industry experts estimate that one office needs to sustain between $1 million and$3 million in business per year. Income is based largely on location, however. For instance, fees for executive recruiters' services may vary greatly between major geographic locations such as New York and Miami.

Connections and Flexibility Money is only part of the picture. Executive recruiters also need access to candidates with diverse backgrounds and skills. Because U.S. companies increasingly form joint ventures with companies in other parts of the world, there is a need for executives who not only speak foreign languages but also understand foreign cultures as well. The search for executives who can do both is best conducted by specialists in the field.

Often, recruitment firms are called upon to place executives on a temporary basis. Many businesses today operate in a project mode in which they assign specialists to teams designed to complete a specific task. Once the task is completed, project members are reassigned or let go. Clients may need executives to fill in for short periods for key personnel. At other times, individuals may want to work only for a set period. These new practices have opened doors for recruitment firms to place executives on a temporary basis, which affects how they work. Placing temporary staff members generally means shorter time frames in identifying, testing, and placing executives. Clients seeking temporary personnel typically need them immediately. Consequently, recruiters sometimes must identify promising candidates quickly.

Ethical Worries An important issue in the late 1990s was recruiter ethics. In July 1997, John R. Walter resigned as president of AT&T Corp. after just seven months on the job. Although many laid sole responsibility at the feet of AT&T's board, some experts voiced concerns about the entire executive search system. As Judith Dobrzynski reported in the *New York Times,* the recruiters involved may not have heeded signs that the search was flawed, although many recruiters feel that the only way to ensure that this does not happen in the future is to fundamentally change the way recruiters are paid.

The Association of Executive Search Consultants (AESC), the leading trade group for retained search firms, maintains a code of ethics that members are supposed to follow, but critics say ethical guidelines are often set aside in the heat of a hunt. The AESC represents 160 member firms worldwide with a total of more than 700 offices and 3,000 consultants.

Kennedy Information, the publishers of *Executive Recruiter News,* an independent newsletter for the profession, says that clients must have a clear understanding of the search firm's replacement policy before booking a search. Search firms working on a contingency basis will usually guarantee a candidate for 60 days, while a search firm working on retainer will guarantee the candidate for a year or more. Should an executive leave before the duration of the time period, the firm should replace the candidate at a reduced or free rate.

BACKGROUND AND DEVELOPMENT

The emergence of the U.S. executive recruitment industry can be traced to the 1940s as businesses, growing after World War II, had a dearth of acceptable in-house candidates for promotions. For the most part, in the industry's first decades, the different types of recruiters were interchangeable. There was no sharp division of labor between personnel recruiters and executive search specialists.

In the early 1990s, a high-profile executive search helped reshape the industry. In early 1992, IBM Corp. launched a major search for a new chief executive. The corporation hired two top recruiters, Gerry Roche and Tom Neff, both of whom were acknowledged leaders in the field. (Both men have been included consistently in the top 250 executive recruiters in the United States.) This was an unusual move because Roche and Neff worked for different companies, Heidrick & Struggles International, Inc. and SpencerStuart respectively. IBM also sidestepped a practice common in the executive recruiting industry known as "client blocks," in which major executive search firms do not approach individuals

placed in jobs by competitors. Moreover, IBM was not shy about letting the world know how its search for a CEO was going. In fact, in a break with tradition, the corporation made public the names of executives who were ostensibly among the finalists for the position. The resulting publicity worked to the benefit of the executive search industry. For the first time, business experts and members of the public came face to face with an industry that had toiled in relative obscurity for most of its existence.

The publicity helped fuel growth in the executive recruitment industry as executives from companies of all sizes became acquainted with the model of professional recruiting firms. At the same time, other changes in business practices spurred greater demand for these services. The global market proved to have an impact on U.S. businesses, and recruiters found themselves involved in worldwide searches for executives to fill slots in multinational corporations. There was also a revolution in the U.S. workplace as corporations began downsizing thousands of people to become "leaner and meaner." Those laid off included many high-ranking executives. Executive recruiters picked up some of the slack by matching laid-off professionals with new positions.

Executive recruiters saw brisk growth in the late 1990s thanks to a booming U.S. economy, exceptionally low unemployment, and a rise in start-ups seeking first rate leadership. For example, the AESC reported that mid-1999 figures showed searches for e-commerce executives skyrocketed 1,407 percent from just a year earlier. Demand for top brass was also up sharply for telecommunications and general management positions. In the third quarter alone, member firms conducted some 3,500 searches.

The bubble quickly burst. A poor-performing stock market, combined with financial frugality of large companies, resulted in a $3 billion drop as recruiting became a $10 billion industry by 2001. That year saw fees slump 31 percent along with a huge drop in revenue growth. The sudden downturn was attributed to the terrorist attacks on the United States and an already weakened economy. Double-digit revenues of the late 1990s became double-digit losses in the early years of the first decade of the twenty-first century. In this bleak climate, one of the country's largest recruiting firms, Fort Worth-based Ray & Berndtson, filed for bankruptcy and was subsequently bought. The nation's top recruiting company, Heidrick & Struggles International, lost $63 million in seven quarters and was forced to cut 800 jobs, or one-third of its employees.

However, 2002 was slightly better, as revenue growth for some companies approached 50 percent. Nevertheless, combined retainer fees for the 25 largest recruiting firms fell below the $1 billion mark for the first time since 1997, and the industry as a whole saw a double-digit revenue decline for the second straight year. The slight improvement was attributed to a quick recovery in business activity for some firms and the acquisition of smaller, financially troubled search firms by larger, well-established companies.

After a couple of the worst years in more than a decade, executive recruiters were due for an upswing. Entering 2003, the general business trend of mergers, acquisitions, consolidations, and bankruptcies continued, creating a far higher pool of displaced executives than openings to fill. For example, Hite Executive Search near Cleveland, Ohio, reported receiving up to 100 unsolicited resumes each week, more than double the figures from 2000, and there were no open searches. Those in manufacturing industries were faring worse than anyone else, in keeping with the manufacturing sector of the U.S. economy as a whole.

However, by mid-2003, there was new hope for the economy in general and therefore new hope for the executive recruiting industry in particular. According to an Execunet, Inc., study, the majority of those in the industry were optimistic in mid-2003 that the outlook would soon be improving. In early summer, the executive job index was just under 190—100 equaled the abysmal 1997 year. By the fall, such optimism was rewarded as there was increasing demand for executives in industries across the board.

By 2005, the very elite business of professional executive recruiting had begun to expand its membership. Fresh faces, such as John Thompson at Heidrick & Struggles and James Citrin at Spencer Stuart, shook up the corporate world as they helped to place high-level executives in such companies as Hewlett-Packard; Bank One, now JP Morgan Chase; United; and Sprint Nextel. Andrea Redmond is one of the few top-level women in the business and Charles Tribbett is considered the highest-ranking African American. In an arena historically controlled by older white males, they feel that their relative youth, gender, and cultural perspective allow them to offer clients a different view. Their approach is to become insiders at a company to familiarize themselves with its problems, prospects, and culture in order to be able to suggest the perfect candidate. Joseph Daniel McCool, former editor of *Executive Recruiter News,* feels that the pair represents a fresh perspective in an industry that has become somewhat antiquated.

By 2006, it became even more apparent that the success of a company depended in large part on the quality and performance of its people. Moving ahead of its competition is primarily due to a company having the best executives. The goal, therefore, became to recruit the best from outside and develop the best from within. The impact of a wrong match can affect an organization in many ways and the cost of an error in an executive selection can quickly become apparent. One way to ensure a company finds the best fit for its specific needs in a scarce executive talent pool continued to be the employing of executive search companies.

By early 2006, many executive recruiting firms were targeting specific markets. For example, two former executives of A.T. Kearney, Russ Gerson and Maureen Brille, launched a company, the Gerson Group, aimed at providing executives for hedge funds and other financial services firms, such as asset management, investment banking, and wealth management companies.

A firm that specializes in serving the needs of Wal-Mart vendor teams is Cameron Smith & Associates based in Bentonville, Arkansas. Cameron Smith & Associates was founded in 1994, and in 2006 employed 15 people and served hundreds of client companies. Not only is the company interested in placing executives, but it is also concerned with retaining them because of the competitive vendor job market. The firm has seen an increased demand for experienced category managers, marketing, consumer insights, and a range of international positions.

Another family of companies that targets a specific field is FPL Advisory Group, based in Chicago, Illinois. The Group focuses entirely on providing corporate and managerial advisory services, such as human resources, management consulting, executive compensation, and finance service to real estate and financial services companies.

Despite the economic downturn in the United States in the late years of the first decade of the 2000s, the professional executive recruiting industry continued to thrive. Some of the reasons for the growth in the industry included an increased demand for high-quality talent, a limited pool of applicants, and continued economic expansion. According to figures released by the firm Accountants, Consultants, and Business Valuators, the industry was worth $13 billion in 2007, and there were more than 4,000 executive search firms in North America, 1,600 of which worked on a retainer basis. Overall, net revenues of executive recruiting firms increased 20 percent in the third quarter of 2007 as compared to a year earlier. Peter Felix, president of the Association of Executive Search Consultants (AESC), expressed optimism in the future of the industry, saying in a November 2007 press release, "Underlying trends in the global economy remain very favorable for executive search—these include the severe shortage of executive markets such as China, India, and Russia, and the growing shortage in Western economies due to the major demographic shifts as the baby boomers retire."

The limited number of people qualified for executive positions was one of the industry's major issues in 2008. According to a study by the AESC, 84 percent of recruiters surveyed said they were dealing with a shortage of talent. A majority also conceded that this shortage of qualified individuals would remain a problem at least through 2013.

Another trend that was affecting the industry was the increasing presence of Internet search firms. According to Nielsen/Net Ratings figures, more than 17 million job-searchers log onto career sites a month in the United States. Although most firms looking to fill high-level executive positions still prefer to use traditional recruiting companies, online services were expected to command an increasing share of the market in the future. Another trend that was expected to continue was the rise in number of mergers and acquisitions among professional executive recruiting firms.

CURRENT CONDITIONS

The AESC reported overall industry global revenues at $7.43 billion in 2009, plummeting 32.5 percent from their highest levels ever in 2008 ($11 billion). However, the fourth quarter of 2009 and into 2010 showed significant increases in the number of search requests, plus a slowdown in revenue declines. Senior executive search activity increased in Asia/Pacific, Central/South America, and Europe, but not in North America. During this time (2009) the financial services sector was replaced by the industrial sector as the leader, holding 25 percent of the market. Going into 2010, financial, industrial, and technology sectors were all showing renewed activity in search requests.

After a free-fall in 2009, the financial sector of the industry landed on its feet. The sharp stock market drop and banking crisis of 2008 and 2009 caused many personnel changes for the financial sector, especially for independent broker-dealers. Clients of brokers were reluctant to commit money to trading, and many were moving out of stocks into other investment alternatives. An ironic twist in the industry occurred, as big-name banks and insurance giants such as American International Group Inc. (AIG, subject of a massive government bailout) and ING Groep NV struggled to survive. The AIG and ING broker-dealer networks, renamed Advisor Group and Cetera Financial Group respectively, suffered major losses. For example, SagePoint Financial, an AIG broker-dealer, saw a revenue drop of 38.5 percent, with a net loss of $33.6 million, and FSC Securities Corp., another AIG firm, suffered gross revenues losses of 29.2 percent. However, this is what precisely caused the later boost in recruiting: it ultimately created internal scrambling of brokers.

"It was the perfect storm for recruiting in 2009," William C. Van Law III, senior vice president and national director of business development for Raymond James Financial Services, said in a 2010 article for *Investment News*. "The disruption in the industry played in our favor." His firm recruited 539 brokers in fiscal 2009. John Rooney, managing principal of Commonwealth Financial Network, noted that his firm had successfully recruited teams from a number of firms, including AIG's Royal Alliance Associates Inc. and ING's Financial Network Investment Group. "Brokers move when pain is intense. Last year, pain was intense," he said, adding that his firm had a "banner year" in 2009 recruiting. Eric Schwartz, chief executive of Cambridge Investment Research Inc., agreed and noted that Cambridge also had a record recruiting year in 2009.

INDUSTRY LEADERS

The world's largest executive search firm, Korn/Ferry International, headquartered in Los Angeles, California, has been in the executive search industry since 1969. The company operates worldwide with more than 80 offices in 35 countries and by 2005 had conducted over 100,000 senior level searches for clients around the world. The company's 500 consultants offer extensive backgrounds and specific expertise in a range of global industries, from investment banking and pharmaceuticals to retail, technology, energy, and entertainment. The company offers services ranging from corporate governance and CEO recruitment to executive search, middle management recruitment, strategic management assessment, and executive coaching and development. Korn/Ferry brought in global revenues of $600 million in 2009, down 11.3 percent from $676.1 million in 2008. The company served 4,238 clients in fiscal year 2009 from its database of more than 4 million executive candidates.

Heidrick & Struggles International, Inc. of Chicago, Illinois, is another major player and has been in the executive recruiting business since 1953. In 2005, the company had 57 locations and approximately 1,300 employees worldwide. Heidrick & Struggles recruits senior level executives for the business/professional services, consumer, education/nonprofit, financial services, health care, industrial, and technology fields on a global, multinational, national, and local level. Heidrick estimated its 2010 full-year revenue at $440 to $480 million.

Also prominent in the industry was A.T. Kearney Executive Search with offices in 30 countries. Founded in 1946, it is one of the longest-established search firms in the world. In January 2006, A.T. Kearney was acquired by an investment group led by international search executive Edward Kelley and was to undergo a name change later in the year. It did not. Later in 2009, the company was in talks to consider a merger with consulting firm Booz, but in July 2010, Booz withdrew. AT Kearney continued as "AT Kearney" and reported 2009 revenues of $786 million with a staff of 2,700 employees and 240 partners. The company recruits executives for the consumer goods and retail, education, government and not-for-profit, financial services, industrial markets, technology, and life sciences and health care fields.

WORKFORCE

The executive search industry does not employ large numbers of people, but its rapid growth has meant plenty of opportunities for people with the right skills. Many are sole proprietorships or small businesses. For example, the Curtiss Group employs 12 people and brings in about $1.5 million per year. Companies such as Curtiss employ recruiters, data processing and testing specialists, experts, and support people such as administrative assistants. Another example is the Compass Group of Birmingham, Michigan, which employs only 22 people, five of whom are full time employees. Most of its employees are retired executives from Ford Motor Company. The business, named one of the industry's top 50 firms by *Executive Recruiter News,* earns between $2 million and $5 million per year.

The majority of recruiters are well-educated people with advanced degrees. Many recruiters have MBAs because a business background helps recruiters understand their clients' needs. One of the hallmarks of successful executive recruiters is in-depth knowledge of the fields in which they specialize. Another is time in the industry. The average age of the top 250 executive recruiters is 55. They each average nearly 23 years in the business. Women and minorities make up a small but growing number of the industry's personnel. There are 28 women among the current top 250 recruiters but only a handful of minorities.

AMERICA AND THE WORLD

For the first time in 2009, the fourth quarter saw gains in senior executive search requests in Asia/Pacific/ Central / South America, and Europe. From 2006 to 2007, the Asia/ Pacific region saw the most growth in the industry (12 percent), as measured by an increase in the number of executive searches, followed by Europe (9.5 percent) and North America (8 percent). The Central and South America region experienced a decrease of 9 percent. North America retained 42 percent of the executive search market, whereas European countries accounted for 25 percent and the Asia/Pacific region, 16 percent.

Most of the top executive search firms in the United States have established offices throughout the world. For example, A. T. Kearney Executive Search has a multinational network of recruiting professionals with expertise in all principal industry and functional sectors. In fact, Kearney operates more than 60 offices in 30 countries. The Curtiss Group, based in Boca Raton, Florida, operates offices in Holland, Brazil, and Tokyo. This trend is expected to continue as the global market expands and multinational corporations continue to grow. As they do, U.S. executive search firms are likely to have a substantial impact on international searches. At the same time, non-U.S. firms such as Switzerland's Egon Zehnder International have moved aggressively to capture a bigger piece of the booming U.S. market.

RESEARCH AND TECHNOLOGY

Computers have revolutionized the world of executive recruiting. Firms compile and reference large databases containing the names of people who can fill particular jobs with particular companies. Many executive search firms operate proprietary computerized information systems and employ in-house specialists to implement, maintain, and enhance them. For example, Korn/Ferry International maintains a database of more than 4.4 million profiles and resumes of top candidates.

By the early 2000s, executive search specialists used software to help clients identify personality traits, simulate a day at the office, present models on how to conduct interviews properly, and a host of other tasks designed to facilitate the placement and hiring process. State-of-the-art software and hardware have enhanced recruiters' abilities to place the right people in the right positions.

The Internet poses both challenge and opportunity for the industry. For example, Korn/Ferry International launched Futurestep, an Internet service set up to recruit mid-level executives. Potential candidates log on to the system, answer informational questions, and respond to an assessment profile in lieu of submitting a resume. The information is screened electronically and videoconference interviews are held with candidates who match current client requirements. Prospective candidates must submit to a standard reference check. Monster.com is at the forefront of Internet recruiting services. Although some online recruiters were thought to be resume wholesalers because they solicited resumes via Web sites, many executive recruiters were expected to forge alliances with Internet content developers.

In 2008 the AESC announced that it would use technology created by VisualCV Inc., a Internet software company, to network and present candidate information to member firms. Through the VisualCV's program, candidates can present their credentials using video, charts, graphs, and other innovative mediums via the Internet. Peter Felix, president of AESC, said about VisualCV in a 2008 press release, "Finally a company has found a way through technology to allow individuals to fully amplify and present their credentials in a modern multi-media format, over the Internet."

BIBLIOGRAPHY

"2009 Ends on Upward Trend for Senior Executive Recruitment." AESC Press Release, 25 February 2010. Available from http://www.aesc.org/eweb/.

"AESC State of Industry Year-End Report Demonstrates Continued Worldwide Demand for Executive Talent." New York: Association of Executive Search Consultants, 3 March 2008. Available from http://www.aesc.org.

"Association of Executive Search Consultants and Visual CV Partner in Application of New Resume Technology." New York: Association of Executive Search Consultants, 28 April 2008. Available from http://www.aesc.org.

"AT Kearney Booz(es). Big Four Firm Stays Sober." 05 July 2010. Available from http://bigfouralumni.com

Barreto, Susan L. "Former Kearney Execs Launch Recruiting Shop." *Daily News,* 17 February 2006.

"Booz & Co Withdraws Offer for AT Kearney Inc." 06 July 2010. Available from http://www.alacrastore.com.

Crockett, Roger O. "The New Kingmakers." *Business Week,* 30 January 2006.

"Demand for Senior Executive Talent Continues Despite Turbulence in Financial Markets." Association of Executive Search Consultants, 19 May 2008. Available from http://www.aesc.org.

"Executive Jobs in Natural Resources and Engineering Expected to See Greatest Growth in Second Half of '08." New York: Association of Executive Search Consultants, 29 July 2008. Available from http://www.aesc.org.

"Executive Search Firm Survey." Vault, 17 April 2006. Available from http://www.vault.com/surveys/execsearch/executive.jsp.

Executive Search Industry Outlook Report 2008. New York: Association of Executive Search Consultants, 2008. Available from http://www.aesc.org.

"Executive Searches in Financial Services Steady But Overall Job Market to Remain Slow Until 2009." Association of Executive Search Consultants, 3 June 2008. Available from http://www.aesc.org.

Gottlieb, Mark S. *Executive Recruiting: An Industry Study.* Great Neck, NY: Accountants, Consultants & Business Valuators, 2006.

"Heidrick & Struggles Reports Fourth Quarter and 2007 Financial Results." Heidrick & Struggles, 26 February 2008. Available from http://phx.corporate-ir.net.

Kelly, Brian. "Broker-dealer Revenue Down 10%." *Investment News,* 23 April 2010. Available from http://www.investmentnews.com/article/20101423/REG/304259993.

"Korn/Ferry, La Z Boy Sales Rise." 15 June 2010. Daily Earnings available at http://www.ticker.com.

"Providing Vendors with Top-Tier Talent." *DSN Retailing Today,* First Quarter 2006.

Ruiz, Gina. "Recruiters See Strong Hiring Ahead Despite Recession Talk." *Workforce Management,* 4 February 2008.

"Search Firm Heidrick's Revenue Rises 28 Percent." *Workforce,* 30 April 2010. Available from http://www.workforce.com/section/news/article/search-firm-heicricks-revenue-rises-28-percent.php.

"Why Has The Executive Search Profession Grown So Extensively?" National Executive Personnel, 17 April 2006. Available from http://www.nationalexecutivepersonnel.com/.

PROSTHETICS AND ORTHOTICS

———————■———————

SIC CODE(S)

3842

8093

INDUSTRY SNAPSHOT

Prosthetics is a field of medical science that involves the design and creation of manufactured devices that replace something on or within the human body. Prosthescs are used to replace body parts that have been removed due to disease or accidents, as well as those missing because of birth defects. While most prosthetic devices are functional in nature, some—such as glass eyes and artificial breasts—are purely cosmetic. However, prostheses often have both cosmetic and functional properties.

Although the prosthetics field generally is associated with external devices such as artificial limbs, it technically overlaps with other medical specialties. For example, cardiothoracic surgery involves the use of artificial hearts and heart valves, and arthroplasty involves the installation of total and partial prosthetic joints like elbows, hips, fingers, knees, and shoulders. Another related field is prosthdontics, which deals with false teeth and supportive dental structures like bridges, crowns, and dentures.

Closely related to the prosthetics field, orthotics involves the design and fitting of various braces and external appliances that correct anatomical deformities and support paralyzed muscles. Orthotics help people to compensate for muscular or skeletal problems and move in more optimal ways.

According to some experts, in the early 2000s, the prosthetics industry was experiencing an increase in sales not seen since its inception during the Civil War. The market was expected to continue to grow well into the next decade. According to the American Orthotic & Prosthetic Association, this growth will likely be supported by a rise in chronic conditions such as diabetes and vascular disease, which can lead to amputation. Another reason for the rise in demand for prosthetics is improved body armor and prompt battlefield medical care in Iraq and Afghanistan. Soldiers who may have died in previous wars are being saved, but more have lost limbs. Approximately 600 military personnel in the two wars had been treated for injuries resulting in loss of legs, arms, feet, or hands, and some had lost more than one limb. Figures from the American Academy of Orthotists & Prosthetists call for the prosthetic care market to grow 50 percent by 2020, while orthotic care is expected to grow 25 percent during the same time period.

ORGANIZATION AND STRUCTURE

Manufacturers Prosthetic and orthotic device manufacturing is part of the larger surgical appliance and supplies industry, which in turn is a segment of the medical equipment and supply market. The American Orthotic & Prosthetic Association, a professional trade group representing patient care facilities and suppliers that manufacture, distribute, design, fabricate, fit, and supervise the use of orthoses (orthopedic braces) and prostheses (artificial limbs), had approximately 1,900 members in the early twenty-first century.

In addition to a wide range of prosthetic limbs, as well as orthoses for the spine, ankle, foot, back, shoulder, and hip, the industry produces and purchases a myriad of specialized components. These include various types of

Top Five Orthopedic Device Companies, 2009

	Revenue
Stryker	$7.0 billion
DePuy	$5.4 billion
Zimmer	$3.9 billion
Smith & Nephew	$3.7 billion
Synthes	$3.3 billion

SOURCE: Becker's Orthopedic & Spine Review.

adapters, assemblies, sockets, liners, gloves, locks, and suspensions. In addition, the industry uses special CAD/CAM (computer-aided design/computer-aided manufacturing) software for design purposes; different kinds of fabrication equipment; and materials such as leather, foam, grinding tools, and various resins and pigments.

PROVIDERS

Prosthetic manufacturers sell mainly to special labs and workshops. Staffed by trained and certified prosthetists and orthotists, these labs fill physicians' prescriptions for prostheses. The market for orthoses is somewhat different. Unlike most protheses, many orthotic devices are available without a prescription. In addition, only 30 percent of orthotic devices are sold to labs and workshops. The majority is sold to hospitals, pharmacies, physicians, and physiotherapists. Together, these providers serve as the main link between manufacturers and end users.

End Users In the United States, more than 1 million amputees comprise the market for traditional prostheses like artificial limbs, hands, and feet. During the early 2000s, the most common causes for amputation were chronic health conditions such as cardiovascular disease and diabetes as well as certain types of cancer. As the wars in Iraq and Afghanistan continued, soldiers injured in battle but saved on the battlefield due to body armor and superior medical care comprised a larger part of the market than ever before. Industrial, farm, or automobile accidents were to blame in a smaller number of cases. In addition, birth defects were responsible for some individuals being born without certain extremities.

The target population for orthotic devices includes individuals with a broad range of physical defects or weakened body parts. While some of these conditions are present at birth, others result from injuries, disease, or poor biomechanics.

Common Devices Technically, the term *prosthetic* can include a very broad range of internal and external devices, including artificial skin; facial parts such as artificial

noses; glass eyes; artificial knees, hips, wrists, and fingers; artificial organs and organ parts, including hearts and heart valves; and even hearing aids and various dental apparatuses. Some of these are highly specialized and fall within the jurisdiction of other medical fields. For example, cardiothoracic surgeons implant artificial hearts and heart valves, orthopedic surgeons perform joint replacement procedures, ocularists are professionals who specialize in working with artificial eyes, and anaplastologists craft artificial facial parts. However, the traditional prosthetic and orthotic market centers on artificial limbs and various types of orthoses.

Artificial limbs normally consist of preconstructed, interchangeable parts. For example, it is possible for an amputee to select different knee, leg, and foot components. Prosthetists then custom fit and adjust prostheses based on an amputee's individual needs. This process involves creating a mold from the amputee's residual limb, which is used to ensure a comfortable fit with the socket located at top of the prosthesis. Traditionally, this has been accomplished by producing a plaster cast of the residual limb, which is then filled with plaster and used to produce a laminated polyester or plastic socket. In the case of transtibial prostheses, which correspond to the leg, care is taken to ensure that an amputee will not bear weight on the distal end of the limb, which includes bony protrusions. For the sake of comfort, leg amputees bear weight on the softer areas of the limb. A computer program can be used to measure the amputee's limb, and a plastics process called squirt shaping is used to craft a final, tight-fitting polypropylene socket. Different methods are used to actually secure an artificial limb to an amputee.

Replacing the natural lower leg, thigh, forearm, or upper arm is a strut, which is constructed of a strong substance like titanium. The strut protrudes from the socket and is normally covered by foam rubber fashioned into the shape of the original limb. The outer covering of the prosthesis may consist of a lifelike silicone-based compound as opposed to materials like metal, leather, or wood, which were commonly used during the twentieth century. Amputees often select highly functional prostheses with hooks or pincher-like attachments to use for some tasks as well as more cosmetic-looking prostheses for other occasions.

By the early 2000s, amputees had several options for operating arm prostheses. One involved a harness and cable system, which used the person's body power to open and close the jaws of a mechanical pincher. Patients also could choose below-elbow prostheses that were myoelectric. According to the Northwestern University Prosthetics-Orthotics Center, in the case of myoelectric prostheses, "The signal to open or close is made by the presence or absence of small electrical charges in the muscles of the arm as it contracts. Small contacts that fit intimately against the skin detect the minute electrical pulses that race down a muscle as it contracts. When one is detected, circuitry tells the motor to open or close. More complex circuitry can even tell the hand how fast to open or to rotate at the wrist. These systems can use a hook or a hand and utilize an interface design that requires no harnessing. Although myoelectric arms are more cosmetic and technologically advanced, they are expensive, heavy, and require a certain amount of maintenance. For obvious reasons, the patient must avoid moisture when wearing the prosthesis."

Orthotic devices include a wide variety of braces, splints, and supports. The most common orthoses are used to treat various foot conditions, including plantar fasciitis (inflammation of connective tissue in the bottom of the foot), ingrown toenails, heel spurs, hammertoes, sesamoiditis (irritation or fracture of small bones running from the ball of the foot to the big toe), stress fractures, sprained ankles, inflammation or tearing of the Achilles tendon in the calf of the leg, runner's knee (pain from kneecap rubbing against the thighbone), bunions, flat feet, heel pain, and shin splints (injury to the front of the outer leg). Special orthotic helmets are available to help babies correct flat spots that develop on their skulls from sleeping on their backsides—a condition known as positional plagiocephaly. Orthoses also include rigid or flexible spinal braces that are used to control back pain, provide stabilization following back surgery, and prevent or correct spinal deformities such as spinal curvature or scoliosis.

Accrediting Bodies The main accrediting and certifying organization within the orthotics and prosthetics industry is the American Board for Certification in Orthotics and Prosthetics (ABC). Founded in 1948 and based in Alexandria, Virginia, the ABC maintains that its mission is to "encourage and promote the highest standards of professionalism in the delivery of orthotic and prosthetic services. The ABC advances the competency of practitioners, promotes the quality and effectiveness of orthotic and prosthetic care, and maintains the integrity of the profession. The ABC fulfills this mission by administering certification and other credentialing programs; establishing standards of organizational performance; mandating Professional Continuing Education to maintain competency; and administering a Professional Discipline Program."

In addition to the ABC, the Alexandria, Virginia-based National Commission on Orthotic & Prosthetic Education (NCOPE) is another accrediting body within the industry. The NCOPE focuses on ensuring the quality of and providing accreditation to orthotic and prosthetic educational and residency programs. It does this in conjunction with the Commission on Accreditation of Allied Health Education Programs (CAAHEP).

Associations Headquartered in Alexandria, Virginia, the American Academy of Orthotists and Prosthetists (AAOP) is the leading association for prosthetics and orthotics professionals who have been credentialed by the American Board for Certification in Orthotics and Prosthetics. Established in November 1970, its mission centers on promoting the highest patient care standards through education, advocacy, research, and literature.

The nonprofit National Association for the Advancement of Orthotics and Prosthetics (NAAOP) is another national association for orthotists and prosthetists. According to the NAAOP, its mission is "to aggressively pursue the vision and goals of the O&P community by affecting change in national policy through public education, advocacy, and timely communication." In addition to research, the association is actively involved in matters related to health care legislation, including issues involving managed care, the Veterans Administration, and Medicare and Medicaid policy. The NAAOP's origins date back to 1987, when it was formed to "help create a federal research and development program in orthotics and prosthetics which culminated in the establishment of the National Center for Medical Rehabilitation Research (NCMRR) at the National Institutes of Health." In addition to practitioners certified by the ABC, the NAAOP's membership base also includes accredited facilities as well as manufacturers and suppliers.

With roots stretching back to 1917, the American Orthotic & Prosthetic Association (AOPA) is a national association representing manufacturers, suppliers, and other firms involved in the design, manufacture, and custom fitting of prostheses and orthoses. Based in Alexandria, Virginia, the AOPA's mission is to "work for favorable treatment of the O&P business in laws, regulation and services; to help members improve their management and marketing skills; and to raise awareness and understanding of the industry and the association."

The orthotics and prosthetics industry also includes many state and regional organizations. Important international organizations include the International Society for Prosthetics and Orthotics (ISPO), the British Association of Prosthetists and Orthotists, the Canadian Association of Prosthetists and Orthotists, and the Hong Kong Society of Certified Prosthetists-Orthotists.

BACKGROUND AND DEVELOPMENT

According to the Northwestern University Prosthetics-Orthotics Center (NUPOC), the use of amputation surgery and prosthetics dates back to "the very dawning of human medical thought." Citing anthropological evidence of upper extremity amputees going back some 45,000 years, NUPOC explains, "In the three great western civilizations of Egypt, Greece, and Rome the first true rehabilitation aids that were recognized as prostheses were made. The Dark Ages produced prostheses for battle and hiding deformity. The Renaissance emerged and revitalized scientific development begun by the ancients."

On a similar note, the "History of Amputation Surgery and Prosthetics," in a chapter by A. Bennett Wilson, Jr. that appeared in the *Atlas of Limb Prosthetics: Surgical, Prosthetic, and Rehabilitation Principles,* explains that the use of crude prosthetics, such as forked sticks, likely dates back to the very dawn of civilization. However, the earliest record of an artificial limb pertains to a Persian soldier in 484 B.C. named Hegesistratus, who reportedly used a wooden foot after cutting off his natural one to escape from captors. In Capri, Italy, the oldest known prosthesis was discovered in 1858. Made of wood and copper, it was an artificial leg dating back to roughly 300 B.C. In approximately 600 B.C., artificial legs were used by the Roman Empire, and iron hands used by fifteenth-century knights have been displayed at the Stibbert Museum in Florence, Italy.

The French military surgeon Ambroise Pare is credited with establishing prosthetics as a science during the sixteenth century through his use of ligatures (thread used by surgeons to bind a blood vessel), which made amputation a successful lifesaving procedure, especially for soldiers wounded in battle. Subsequently, new forms of artificial limbs were developed to replace upper extremities. In sixteenth-century Europe, relatively sophisticated metal hands that employed springs and moving parts were developed. By the eighteenth century, developments included a functional hook, as well as a more cosmetic, leather-covered hand that was secured to an individual's forearm with a shell of wood or leather. Early artificial legs were little more than wooden pegs with saddle-like sockets.

Despite the increasing use of amputation, unsanitary conditions caused the death of many surgical patients, a fact that hindered the development of better prostheses. However, amputation surgery benefited from the introduction of the tourniquet in 1674 and Lord Lister's antiseptic technique in 1867, as well as the substances ether and chloroform. The industrial revolution and the Civil War impacted the prosthetic industry by spawning what the Northwestern University Prosthetic Orthotic Center (NUPOC) dubbed "a colorful array of humanitarians, scientists, and charlatans."

During the twentieth century, major wars propelled the evolution of the prosthetics field. In 1917, the Artificial Limb Manufacturers and Brace Association was formed after the Council of National Defense met with industry manufacturers to prepare for soldiers wounded in World War I. The use of prostheses grew in tandem with the massive number of injuries suffered by soldiers, and the public became more accepting of the devices. As prosthetic utilization increased, more effective designs and better materials were introduced, including improved mechanical joints and lightweight metals.

Improvements occurred at a rapid pace after World War II because veterans were dissatisfied with existing prosthetic technology. Many credit Normal Kirk, Surgeon General of the Army, for initiating an investigation by the National Academy of Sciences, which represented a quantum leap for prosthetic science. The Artificial Limb Program was sponsored by the Veterans Administration, HEW, and the Armed Services, and similar research was carried out by the Navy at Oakland Naval Hospital, the U.S. Army Air Force at Wright Field, Northup Aviation, Catranis, and New York University. Refinements in the area of socket designs and prosthetic materials included Northrup Aviation's introduction of thermosetting resins for developing custom sockets and components.

A period characterized by industry organization, education, and standardization began during the mid-1940s. When orthotists joined the Artificial Limb Manufacturers and Brace Association in 1946, the association changed its name to the Orthopaedic Appliances and Limb Manufacturers Association (OALMA). Within several years, orthopedic surgeons and industry practitioners established the American Board for Certification in Orthotics and Prosthetics (ABC), which became the profession's main accrediting and certifying organization. More formal industry education began during the late 1940s, marking a departure from the days when prosthetists learned mainly through apprenticeships. Educational pioneers included the University of California at Berkeley, which sponsored a series of pilot courses in prosthetics. In addition, OALMA and the Veterans Administration Prosthetics and Sensory Aids Service began offering local courses that used a team approach to train both prosthetists and orthopedic surgeons.

Prosthetic education continued to evolve, leading to the formation of formal, clinical, team-based courses in prosthetics at UCLA in 1956. In time, formal programs were introduced in other parts of the country: New York University in 1956 and Northwestern University in 1959. By the 1980s, some 12 universities offered formal certificate or baccalaureate programs. These institutions played a key role in furthering the fields of prosthetics and orthotics, leading to the development of stronger and more effective orthopedic devices through the remainder of the twentieth century.

The orthotics and prosthetics industry faced a number of challenges. In addition to rising administrative, material, and labor costs, practitioners were forced to contend with a challenging reimbursement environment. Together, these conditions created a situation in which it was difficult to simultaneously meet industry and patient care standards as well as those of insurance companies and other payors. In November 2003, some industry players were concerned about new Medicare reform legislation that had the potential to make a difficult situation even worse. The new legislation included a competitive bidding program for "off-the-shelf" orthotic devices as well as a three-year Medicare payment freeze on all prosthetic and orthotic services. These developments prompted a negative response from the American Orthotic & Prosthetic Association (AOPA), who estimated that the payment freeze would cost the industry more than $1 billion over a period of 10 years. On a positive note, the new legislation included accreditation and quality requirements related to Medicare payments for prosthetic and orthotic services. In addition, it prevented efforts by physical therapists to provide certain prosthetic and orthotic services to Medicare patients, which the AOPA saw as an encroachment upon its members' turf.

A breakthrough occurred when the Jackson, Mississippi-based firm Alatheia Prosthetics developed Dermatos—synthetic skin that looks, feels, and lasts like real skin. Its cofounder, Michael Kaczkowski, was a New York artist who moved to Mississippi in 1999 and spent five years researching and developing the technology before first fitting amputees in 2000. He uses medical-grade silicone to construct life-like skins that simulate the look of the three layers of human skin: the epidermis, dermis, and subcutaneous. Hours are devoted by the skin architects to make sure every detail is perfect for each patient, down to every crease, pore, and fingerprint. By 2005, satellite operations had been opened in Los Angeles, New York, and Greensboro, North Carolina, and 300 patients had been served worldwide.

Another major development was when the Defense Research Projects Agency (DARPA) awarded a $30.4 million contract to the Johns Hopkins Applied Physics Laboratory (APL) as one part of DARPA's two-part project to develop a prosthetic arm that would enable a user to feel and manipulate objects, lift up to 60 pounds, and perform normal tasks, even in the dark. Called DARPA's Revolutionizing Prosthetics 2009, the project hopes to design a prosthetic arm that connects directly into the peripheral and central nervous system so the wearer can operate the arm just like a biological arm. The second part of DARPA's project is an $18.1 million contract awarded to DEKA Research and Development Corporation of Manchester, New Hampshire, which is working on developing the arm's mechanical and cosmetic components. The final cost of this prosthetic arm is expected to be between $30,000 and $50,000.

In the past, the Johns Hopkins Applied Physics Laboratory (APL) helped to develop rechargeable, motor-driven prosthetic arms for people who were unable to use the body-powered type. The APL also perfected a mechanical arm that would spoon-feed paralyzed patients and the "C-leg," a computer-controlled leg that makes 50,000 measurements per second and allows soldiers to walk normally and return to active duty, even as paratroopers.

The challenge put forth by DARPA in its two-part Revolutionizing Prosthetics Program is to develop an arm that provides its wearers with sensory feedback from heat, cold, pressure, and proprioception (the signals that keep us aware of our limbs' position in space). The idea is to capture sensory data and feed it into the user's nervous system.

The DARPA Revolutionizing Prosthetics Program represents just part of the more than $70 million the Defense Department and Department of Veterans Affairs (VA) have spent on artificial limb research and development since 2001. In addition, the VA and the U.S. military purchased $1.1 million worth of prosthetic devices in 2006, up from $529,000 in 2000. The increase is attributed to the wars in Iraq and Afghanistan. As stated by Ian Fothergill of Iceland prosthetics manufacturer Ossur hf in *USA Today,* "The military expenditure on prosthetics is obviously booming, and it represents a more and more significant part of our business." However, Fothergill also noted that "it is still only a small part of our business." Growth in the industry is expected to focus more on the aging U.S. population and the need for orthotic devices such as braces and other assistive devices.

The issue of insurance coverage for prosthetics continued to be debated. Although some states had passed laws that required insurance companies to cover prosthetic care, there was no federal mandate as of mid-2008. One group, the Amputee Coalition of America (ACA), was lobbying for legislation that would establish a national standard for coverage of prosthetic benefits. The Prosthetic Parity Act of 2008, which was introduced in Congress in March 2008, would require insurance companies to cover prosthetic care as essential medical care. Many insurance companies either did not cover prosthetics or placed lifetime maximum caps on the amount that a person could claim for prosthetic devices. Insurance companies were fighting the legislation, claiming that it would increase costs and reduce the flexibility of certain plans.

In 2008, the prosthetics and orthotics industry was worth approximately $900 million. Sales of prosthetics increased from $340 million in 1996 to almost $600 million in 2007, according to federal data estimates. About 6,000 prosthetists—medical professionals who design and fit prostheses—served 1.9 million amputees within the United States, about 60 percent of which had lost a limb due to diabetes. A prosthetic device can cost between $2,500 and $50,000 and an adult usually needs to replace it every one to three years. As a child grows, he/she needs a new one every three to six months.

CURRENT CONDITIONS

According to industry research, about 100,000 Americans lose a limb to injury or disease every year. The American SOciety of Plastic Surgeons reported that about five million reconstructive plastic surgeries were performed in 2008. Resale or reuse of artificial limbs is prohibited in the United States, but New England Rehabilitation Hospital in Woburn, Massachusetts launched a new charitable overseas program in 2009. The hospital disassembles donated/discarded limbs and sends them to Limbs for Life, a national nonprofit organization that provides prosthetic limbs to amputees in foreign countries. The hospital received 35 limbs in its very first month.

In the orthopaedic prosthetics industry, 2009 global revenues for reconstructive devices (primarily joint replacements) were $7.0 billion in the United States, $13.3 billion globally. This figure did not include braces or bracing systems, reported *ORTHOWORLD* in 2010; those items were instead figured into a separate "other products" category worth another $3.2 billion in the United States, $4.9 billion globally. Spinal implants (and associated instrumentation) were worth another $5.2 billion in the United States, $7.1 globally in 2009. About 150 companies sold joint replacement products in 2010.

As of 2009, the global prosthetic heart valve market was slowly growing and expected to be worth $1.78 billion by 2016. The mechanical heart valve market saw a slow but steady decline, expected to be just $301 million by 2016. Conversely, global tissue heart valves were expected to represent the highest growth rate, reaching about $1.43 billion by 2016; technological (anti-calcification) developments in the durability of the tissue valves contributed to the growing market, and the launch of transcatheter valves will expand procedure volume among patients previously deemed too risky.

The U.S. dental prosthetic market (crowns, bridges, inlays/outlays, veneers, and dentures) was valued at more than $10.7 billion in 2009; in Europe (Austria, Benelux, France, Germany, Italy, Portugal, Russia, Scandinavia, Spain, Switzerland, and the United Kingdom), it was worth roughly $Euro 8.3 billion in 2008.

INDUSTRY LEADERS

Within the large orthopedic prosthetic and device segment of the industry, the top five in 2009, based on revenues, were Stryker Corp. (Kalamazoo, Michigan), with $7.0 billion; DePuy (Ranham, Massachussetts), with $5.4 billion; Zimmer Holdings (Warsaw, Indiana), with $3.9 billion; Smith & Nephew (London), with $3.7 billion; and Synthes (West Chester, Pennsylvania), with $3.3 billion. However, these industry leaders produced many other devices in addition to prostheses and implant devices. Those focusing more on prostheses are listed below.

Otto Bock Germany's Otto Bock Health Care was the world's largest manufacturer of prosthetics. With North American headquarters in Minneapolis, Minnesota, Otto Bock employed 3,800 workers worldwide and produced more than 25,000 different prosthetics and orthotic components and other devices. Otto Bock's so called C-Leg is the standard prosthetic device issued to U.S. soldiers who have lost a leg above the knee, according to the American Orthotics and Prosthetics Association. The device, which is controlled by a microprocessor, costs approximately $30,000 to $40,000 delivered and fitted. In 2009, the company announced a new joint venture with Victhom Human Bionics, a Quebec-based medical technology company after paying $11.5 billion to become a majority stakeholder in Victhom. The new venture has been named Neurostream Technologies. Otto Bock posted $200 million in 2008 revenues.

Ossur hf Iceland's Ossur hf was the second largest prosthetics manufacturer in 2008. Products ranged from prosthetic feet and knees to liners, sockets, and other components used in the production of artificial limbs, ankle, and knee braces. Based in Camarillo, California, the company's subsidiary Ossur Americas (formerly Ossur North America) brought in 62 percent of Ossur's 2009 sales, which totaled $331 million.

Ossur's base of approximately 680 employees worked from nine sites across the globe. In addition to its North American headquarters in California, the company operated Ossur Engineering Inc. in Michigan, Ossur Mauch Inc. in Ohio, and Ossur Generation II facilities in Seattle and Vancouver. All of these locations were engaged in manufacturing, and some also served as centers for customer service, research and development, and distribution. Its orthotic products included orthoses for the ankle/foot as well as knee braces and padding. Prosthetic products included the FLEX-FOOT high-performance carbon fiber foot, ICEROSS silicone liners, and artificial knees made of carbon fiber that included hydraulic function.

Becker Orthopedic Appliance Co. Based in Troy, Michigan, Becker Orthopedic Appliance Co. was also a leading manufacturer of orthotic devices and components including cervical, spinal, prefabricated, and thermoplastic orthoses; splints; knee joints; ankle and stirrup components; and more. The Otto K. Becker Co. was established in 1933 in Huntington, West Virginia by Otto Becker, a German mechanical engineer who came to the United States in 1929. In 1944, Becker sold his Huntington office, moved everything to Detroit, and renamed it the Becker Manufacturing Company.

Becker Metal Works was established in 1986 to make investment castings for orthotic components as well as castings for other industry sectors. Oregon Orthotic Systems was acquired in 1997. By 2004, the company operated Becker Oregon, Becker Orthopedic of Canada, and Rudolf Becker Orthopedic, B.V., in the Netherlands. In addition, it ran several patient care offices in the metropolitan Detroit area, which helped Becker Orthopedic stay in synch with the needs and concerns of practitioners.

Hanger Orthopedic Group Inc. Another industry leader was Bethesda, Maryland-based Hanger Orthopedic Group Inc. It was established in 1861 by James Edward Hanger, the inventor of the first artificial leg with an articulating joint, who lost his leg during the Civil War. It is one of the nation's largest providers of patient care services for orthotics and prosthetics. Hanger's operations run the gamut from manufacturing and distribution to patient care. In addition to providing orthotic and prosthetic (O&P) services in 619 wholly owned and operated Patient Care Centers in 44 states and the District of Columbia, the company runs OPNET, which is the nation's only managed care network devoted exclusively to prosthetics and orthotics. Hanger's distribution centers operate under the name Southern Prosthetic Supply (SPS).

WORKFORCE

In the early 2000s, there were approximately 5,000 certified prosthetists and orthotists in the United States as well as a number of technicians, assistants, and workers who specialized in fitting devices. These individuals worked in a variety of settings, including private practice, home health care agencies, specialty clinics, rehab centers, universities, hospitals, and nursing homes. By 2020, the American Academy of Orthotists & Prosthetists expects demand for prosthetic and orthotic care to rise approximately 50 percent and 25 percent, respectively.

Depending on the occupational role, employment within the prosthetics and orthotics field requires successful completion of a recognized educational program. While some schools offered certificate and associate degree programs, only a small handful of U.S. universities awarded bachelor's or master's degrees. These included the University of Washington School of Medicine, the Northwestern University Prosthetics-Orthotics Center, and the University of Texas at Southwestern Medical School. Caregivers are either registered or certified through the American Board of Certification in Orthotics and Prosthetics. Following graduation, practitioners complete residency training before working independently.

Despite the projected growth for prosthetic and orthotic care, some educators cited a lack of awareness as the main reason more students were not entering the profession. In fact, many of the individuals who choose careers within the prosthetic and orthotic field do so because of prior exposure to this kind of health care, either personally or through a friend or family member.

RESEARCH AND TECHNOLOGY

What once seemed like prosthetic science fiction was quickly becoming reality, as manufactured prosthetic components began to interact directly with the human body—a principle known as bionics.

The Electronica 2010 international Trade Fair for electronics showcased the world's first prosthetic leg that moved in reponse to the wearer's thoughts. It was developed by American biophysicist and MIT professor Hugh Herr in collaboration with Freescale Semiconductor, the Fraunhofer Institute for Manufacturing Engineering, and Automation IPA. Using electromyography (EMG) signals (produced when a muscle contracts), the prosthetic limb simulated the natural movement sequences of a leg. For demonstration purposes, the researchers operated an EMG pinball machine controlled by muscle tension.

This followed other news in 2009 after several research groups successfully developed "bionic" forearms and hands that were more advanced than previous versions, such as the addition of tactile sensations of heat or cold, and more finger dexterity for gripping, squeezing, and grasping.

By 2006, artificial limbs that accepted nerve signals from the human brain through a process called muscle reinnervation were being introduced. These bionic limbs contain sensory electrodes that recognize myoelectric signals from nerves (up to 50,000 per second) and translate them into artificial limb movements. Thus, it is possible for amputees to control artificial limbs in the same manner as natural limbs—with thought. An engineer at the Rehabilitation Institute of Chicago explained how a high-tech arm works to *O & P*: "The nerves grow into the chest muscles, so when the patient thinks 'Close hand,' a portion of the chest muscle contracts." This muscle contraction then sends signals to the nerve endings, which then 'communicate' with the artificial arm.

Significant advancements also were occurring with orthotic devices. In tandem with cheaper and more powerful computers, longer-lasting batteries, and advancements in the field of robotics, "active" orthotic devices were being developed that provided assistance to people who might not otherwise be able to walk, climb stairs, or even stand without assistance. These included devices such as PowerKnee from Moffett Field, California-based Tibion, and RoboKnee from Boston-based Yobotics. RoboKnee was the forerunner to the RoboWalker, an exoskeletal device that would supplement or replace the muscular functions of the lower body.

One step beyond the C-leg, the computerized prosthetic that appeared in 2004 and is especially used for the military in above-the-knee amputations, is a prosthetic device that will provide sensory feedback to its wearer, as well as have a completely natural appearance. The prosthetic was being developed by Johns Hopkins APL as part of a two-part program.

As the baby boomer generation ages, the need for joint replacements will continue to increase. The new material of choice for hips is diamond. A United Kingdom company called Element Six developed a diamond hip and hoped to have it on the market by 2010. The main cause of failure in an artificial hip is wear debris, caused by huge pressure on the metal ball in a polyethylene socket. Small pieces of the joint break away, causing bone loss and possibly osteoporosis. Diamond is an extremely hard material and this deterioration would not happen.

Named 2005 Innovator of the Year, Scott Sabolich Prosthetics & Research introduced the S.M.A.R.T. (Sabolich Martin Advanced Research Technologies) Hip Level Socket System, an anatomically contoured socket interface technology for hip-level amputees. People with this type of amputation often find it hard to wear a prosthetic and have a high rejection rate. The patent-pending S.M.A.R.T. system consists of high strength, lightweight carbon fiber support around a flexible, biocompatible thermoplastic socket, which contours around the patient's body for enhanced comfort, control, and appearance. Patients find this prosthesis easier to wear, due to its ability to help them move more easily.

BIBLIOGRAPHY

"About NAAOP." National Association for the Advancement of Orthotics and Prosthetics, 15 September 2008. Available from http://www.naaop.org.

"Amputees Fight Caps in Coverage for Prosthetics." Associated Press, 10 June 2008.

"AOPA Fact Sheet." American Orthotic and Prosthetic Association, 15 September 2008. Available from http://www.aopnet.org.

"Bionic Amputees Display Thought-Controlled UE Prostheses." *The O & P Edge,* 21 September 2006.

Blue, Rebecca. "Ranch Students Get a Lesson in Prosthetics." *The Bradenton Herald,* 19 January 2006.

Costello, Daniel. "Soaring Diabetes Rates Wake Prosthetics Industry." *Los Angeles Times,* 4 July 2007.

"DARPA's Cutting-Edge Programs Revolutionize Prosthetics." *The America's Intelligence Wire,* 8 February 2006.

Dishneau, David. "War Fuels Prosthetics Research Blitz." *USA Today,* 16 July 2007.

"European Markets for Dental Prosthetics and CAD-CAM 2009 16 Countries." 2009. Available from http://www.bioportfolio.com/store/product/932/.

"Intelligent Prosthetics for Natural Movements." *Electronic Component News,* 16 August 2010.

Long, Frank. "Work With What You've Got: Options for Amputees Are Better than Ever, as Therapists and Prosthetists Push the Limits of Function." *Rehab Management,* December 2007.

"Neurotech Jolts Otto Bock R&D." *Minneapolis/St. Paul Business Journal,* 28 December 2009.

"The Orthopaedic Industry Annual Report." July 2010. Available from http://www.orthoworld.com/site/docs/pdf/oiar/com.

Page, Leigh. "Top 5 Orthopedic Device Companies Based on 2009 Revenues." 9 September 2010. Available from http://www.beckersorthopedicandspine.comcom.

"Polymer May Allow Soldiers With Artificial Limbs to Feel Hot, Cold, Touch." *Science Daily,* 09 October 2009. Available from http://www.sciencedaily.com/releases/2009/10/091025194629.htm

"Portable Electricity, Life-Like Prosthetics On The Way." *Space Daily,* 20 November 2007.

"Prosthetic Heart Valves-Global Pipeline Analysis." October 2010. Available from http://www.researchandmarkets.com/reportinfo_id=3D1146871

Rovlance, Frank D. "Lab Pioneering Arms Controlled by Thought: Pentagon Taps APL to Create Prosthetics for Amputee Soldiers." *Baltimore Sun,* 1 April 2006.

Sheets, Morgan. "Victories Fueling the Fight in Congress." *The O & P Edge,* May 2008.

Shute, Nancy. "Will Upgrades Enhance Our Bodies? Engineers Are Building Strong Suits and Brainy Prosthetics." *U.S. News & World Report,* 4 August 2008.

"U.S. Market for Dental Prosthetics and CAD-CAM Devices 2009." 2010. Available from http://www.reportlinker.com/p0164165/U-S-Market-for-Dental-Prosthetics-and-CAD-CAM-Devices.html.

"Woburn Hospital Launches Program to Reuse Prosthetic Limbs." *Boston Globe,* 25 October 2009.

"World's Leading Supplier of Prostheses Celebrates 50 Years in the United States." Otto Bock Health Care, 21 February 2008. Available from http://www.ottobockus.com.

PUSH TECHNOLOGY

INDUSTRY SNAPSHOT

While accessing Web pages and e-mail uses a "pull" technology to download information each time in order to view it, push technology requires the user to register only once to obtain information automatically, as it becomes available, without further action on the part of the registered user. The technology is implemented as a software package or an online service, and the applications include so-called Webcasting or Netcasting (broadcasting content over the Internet) to defined audiences, as well as to more sophisticated corporate systems that automate sending timely and targeted information to the appropriate people.

The phrase "push technology" entered the technophile lexicon in the 1990s when a fledgling Internet service called PointCast Inc. began beaming news stories and other information tidbits to users' computer screens via the firm's proprietary, Internet-enabled application. Both the company and the concept were considered exceptionally promising, but PointCast failed to live up to expectations and was bought out in 1999 by Launchpad Technologies Inc.

Other push technology firms, though, continued to develop. Subsequent implementations of push technology offered what their proponents sometimes labeled as "polite" push features. Taking a cue from PointCast's dismal fate, developers of polite push technology incorporated such features as messaging priorities, time-phased distribution, and thinner, more agile programs.

By the early 2000s, push technology was being employed within the health care industry to improve patient safety through reduced medication errors, and by city and county governments to send targeted news bulletins to residents of specific geographic regions. Perhaps the most promising market existed within the corporate sector, where a strong need for highly selective market intelligence existed among professionals, both at their desktops and via mobile devices.

Later push technology was also being used in "smartphones," which allowed users mobile access to e-mail and the Internet.

BACKGROUND AND DEVELOPMENT

Pull technology, or actively searching out and "pulling" information from a Web site, remained the most commonly used technique for retrieving information from the Internet, and search engines such as Google, Yahoo!, HotBot, and Excite helped users locate sites.

Push technology concerns itself with the issue of who begins the search and how the information is delivered. Most people who use the Internet use push technology every day, when they send and receive e-mail. E-mail uses a very simple form of push technology. In other words, after people write e-mail, they then "push" it out over the Internet to the intended recipient.

PointCast, based in California, was the first company to see potential in delivering actual Web content to individuals instead of the other way around. The roots of the technology can be traced back to 1992, when Christopher and Gregg Hassett developed a product called *Journalist,* designed to deliver a customized

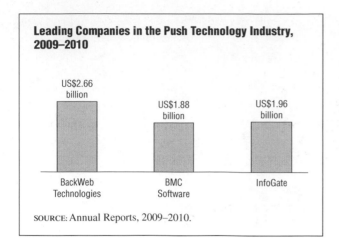

Leading Companies in the Push Technology Industry, 2009–2010

US$2.66 billion — BackWeb Technologies

US$1.88 billion — BMC Software

US$1.96 billion — InfoGate

SOURCE: Annual Reports, 2009–2010.

electronic newspaper to CompuServe and Prodigy customers. Although *Journalist* flopped, the Hassett brothers went on to develop a new way of delivering customized news, soon to become PointCast.

PointCast began sending news and advertising directly to computers in 1996. Shortly thereafter, several other Silicon Valley firms, including Marimba Inc. and BackWeb Technologies, Ltd., entered the market, each offering technologies to distribute and update software. Marimba was able to deliver World Wide Web content to all types of systems, mainly because its application, Castanet, was written in Java.

A "Netcast" or "Webcast" is a simple form of push-technology. A server broadcasts the program over the Internet and individual computer users can tune in to the channel, just like tuning in to a television or radio program. It has been applauded for costing less than traditional teleconferencing. The next step up from a Webcast was a push news and information service, which delivered to subscribers through an application running on their local computer. PointCast used this technology.

PointCast, however, soon ran into trouble as its hefty software and massive broadcasts began to clog companies' computer networks and disrupt subscribers' computing tasks. Since most of its content was considered frivolous, PointCast easily drew the ire of information technology managers, and the service's popularity began to ebb. After speculatively being valued at several hundred million dollars in its first years, PointCast was finally bought out in 1999 by Launchpad Technologies Inc. for a mere $7 million. The merged firm then changed its name to EntryPoint, offering a less invasive push information service, and the PointCast software and service were retired in early 2000.

Although PointCast faded from the scene, push technology was successfully embodied in a number of software products and services. The surviving companies learned from PointCast's mistakes. In essence, they competed with one another in using the least amount of network resources and providing the right amount of flexibility. Thus, applications such as BackWeb were intended to fit seamlessly into a company's existing systems and processes rather than rolling in with a one-size-fits-all product that disregarded users' work styles. For example, information distributed through BackWeb could be retrieved through an interface in the popular Microsoft Outlook e-mail package. That way, users could obtain information from the BackWeb system using a familiar tool that was regularly used for other purposes. By 2004, BackWeb was marketing itself as "The Offline Web Company," using its patented Polite synchronization technology to allow remote or mobile workers, even those with low-bandwidth Internet connections, to access volumes of content and applications that were normally Web based.

Software mechanisms for minimizing the network impact of push technology were growing ever more sophisticated. With leading packages such as BackWeb and Marimba's Castanet, network administrators could specify a maximum amount of system resources available to push activities. When the limit was reached, the software would wait until the bottleneck cleared before attempting to introduce new traffic. Under different settings, these types of programs could also be configured to detect idle time or idle connections within the network before proceeding with distributing content. Other bandwidth-conserving measures included file compression and, in case of a file transfer interruption, file transfers that could be restarted where they left off rather than starting the whole thing over again.

Beyond using push technology for broadcasting messages and user-oriented content, and, increasingly, for advertising, companies began to deploy push solutions for such tasks as software upgrades and system maintenance. For example, by 2004, leading companies in a variety of industry sectors—including retail, manufacturing, insurance, and financial services—used Marimba's product and service offerings to deploy, repair, upgrade, and remove software via their networks at the client and server levels. Some touted this method as a model for the future of software upgrades generally.

In addition to improving the ease and efficiency of software upgrades, push technology also was being used to save lives and improve safety. As health care providers relied more on electronic information systems to manage patient data rather than paper-based record systems, hospital and clinic pharmacies gained the ability to identify potential medication-related errors or conflicts and use push technology to alert clinicians quickly via e-mail or pager.

Push technology also found its way into the government sector, as some city and county governments began using it to send alerts and notices to residents via e-mail, pager, or voice mail. After registering online, residents were able to learn of government news specific to their geographic area, such as upcoming pesticide sprayings. Future applications included alerts that were more specific to individual residents, such as tax or license-related notices.

More traditional uses of push technology were far from dead. For example, by 2004, InfoGate Inc., which acquired Pointcast successor EntryPoint, was using its technology to serve up subscription-based content from the likes of CNN and *USA Today*. However, many observers argued that in order to be successful, these services had to deliver highly personalized information. This was one of the reasons attributed to the success of WeatherBug, which pushed local weather information to users' computer desktops. Fantasy football was another category that was likely to benefit from the use of push technology, as game participants required very specific information. The industry was especially excited about government and business customers, who were willing to pay as much as $500 per user for highly selective market intelligence delivered to mobile devices or computer desktops. One company's setup and licensing fees for enterprise level services ranged from $25,000 to $200,000.

The business-to-business sector looked to a communications channel called Rich Site Summary (RSS), which used extensible markup language (XML) to deliver subscription-based Internet content to users' desktops. An application known as a news aggregator was required to receive the content, which often consisted of a headline, summary, and link to the full content. Proponents argued that this channel weeded out annoying "spam" (junk mail or unwanted e-mail) that plagued traditional e-mail. While RSS was still an emerging channel, use by leading companies such as Apple Computer Inc., IBM Corp., Microsoft Corp., and Ziff Davis Media Inc. was an indication of its potential staying power.

In August 2005, Microsoft unveiled a preview of its Exchange Server update. This technology pushes e-mail directly from 0the e-mail server to a Windows mobile device. This service will no longer necessitate the use of Short Message Service to notify a mobile device to retrieve e-mail, but will e-mail directly from Exchange to the device, thus providing much faster and more efficient access to e-mail for Exchange users. However, the Exchange Server technology is only available to devices installed with Windows Mobile 5.0 Messaging and Security Feature Pack software, an early version of which is available from original equipment manufacturers (OEMs) that manufacture Windows mobile devices. In 2006, devices were shipped with the technology preinstalled.

Push technology was a major component of the cell phone called the BlackBerry. Developed by Toronto's Research in Motion (RIM), The BlackBerry is a communication tool that allows mobile professionals and individuals to send and receive e-mail as well as browse the Web wherever they go. The BlackBerry also had touchscreen, GPS (global positioning system), and WiFi capabilities.

Apple Inc.'s iPhone came on the scene in 2007. The iPhone had capabilities similar to the BlackBerry's, and in 2008, Apple introduced MobileMe, a subscription-based service that allows users to access e-mail, contacts, and calendars on a secure online server that pushes this information to clients via computer, iPhone, or iPod. By the late years of the decade, many companies were producing such phones, including Nokia, Samsung, Sony Ericsson, and Motorola.

These and other brands of so-called smartphones were becoming more common, as demand rose for devices that allowed consumers access to their e-mail and the Internet from a mobile, handheld instrument.

The most common operating systems for smartphones worldwide included Symbian OS (Nokia is its largest customer), the RIM BlackBerry operating system, Windows Mobile, and Linux. In mid-2008, these systems held approximately 57 percent, 17 percent, 12 percent, and 7 percent of the global market, respectively. iPhone OS, Palm OS, and Binary Runtime Environment for Wireless (BREW) held smaller percentages of the market share in 2008.

CURRENT CONDITIONS

While smartphones represented a fundamental shift in mobile communications, in 2010, they still only accounted for 19 percent ofthe total handset marketplace. However, London-based research group Informa Telecoms & Media projected that nearly 30 percent of wireless connecitons will be using 3G or higher wireless broadband and by 2014, almost half of the worlds's 6.7 billion mobile users will be using some combination of 3G and 3.5G technologies to access more and more data.

Perhaps the most widespread and far-reaching use of push technology in 2009 and 2010 was in the social networking arena, where Twitter and Facebook ruled. According to Techcrunch.com, by October 2010, there were about 90 million tweets per day sent instantly to family and friends and followers, up from 50 million just eight months prior (February 2010). Based on Real Time communication, Twitter operated via push technology through a constantly open IP connection, enabling mass communication to hundreds or thousands of followers with a single stroke. Likewise, FaceBook used similar technology to instantly message "friends" and family *en masse*. Twitter came to Blackberry users in mid-2010. In August 2010, Microsoft turned on push technology to allow users to use Exchange ActiveSync to synchronize their smartphones with Hotmail's email, contacts, calendar, and tasks. Google had already switched to Exchange ActiveSync in 2009.

In June 2010, software company uCirrus, a platform technology startup, announced it had raised $1.7 million of an expected $4.4 million equity round after it launched a new platform for MySpace game developers that brought push technology to Flash games. SK Telecom Ventures and ATA Ventures were investors in the company, formerly known as Groovy Corporation.

In October 2010, Microsoft announced that it was acquiring a small Silicon Valley company, Canesta, that specialized in gesture recognition technology. Such push technology allows users to control computers and other devices through hand movements and gestures, similar to the futuristic film, "Minority Report." Microsoft also began shipments of Kinect, which used gesture recognition to scan through game consoles and then make their on-screen avatars jump, run, dance, etc. (This technology was from a Canesta rival, PrimeSense.)

Microsoft was sued by industry leader Backweb Technologies Ltd. in March 2009 for patent infringement. In April 2009, Backweb amended its complaint to add Sybase and iAnywhere as defendants, several claims involving utilization and/or incorporation of push technology.

INDUSTRY LEADERS

BackWeb Technologies BackWeb Technologies Ltd. was a major push technology vendor based in San Jose, California, and Ramat Gan, Israel. BackWeb also had offices in Chicago, New York, Canada, and the United Kingdom, as well as several other countries. It provided business customers with Internet communications systems and applications for managing critical business operations such as customer service, competitive analysis, and sales. Eli Barkat, a former Israeli army paratrooper and founder of several other software ventures, was chairman of the company. BackWeb also had partnerships with many leading technology companies including Hewlett-Packard, IBM, Sun Microsystems, and others. It aspired to being at the center of an emerging multivendor standard for push applications, particularly those involving electronic commerce.

In 2004, BackWeb was marketing itself as "The Offline Web Company." The company employed its Polite Sync Server technology to serve up large volumes of content and applications to remote or mobile users— even those with low-bandwidth connections. In tandem with this strategy, BackWeb offered three key products. BackWeb Offline Access Server was aimed at users who were frequently disconnected from a corporate network but needed access to the applications and data found on intranets, portals, and the like. BackWeb e-Accelerator was billed as a "publishing and content management solution for online and offline content access." Finally, BackWeb Polite Sync Server allowed enterprises to efficiently push out software updates and changes. BackWeb licensed its software to more than 200 corporations. Its customers included AT&T, Eastman Kodak, Hewlett-Packard, IBM, and NBC. In 2008, the company shifted its priorities, shut down one-third of its U.S. operations, and opened a call center in Israel, though it plans to service its server-related products through 2010. BackWeb earned net revenues of $2.66 billion in 2008 and $1.2 billion for the first two quarters of 2009. Its 2008 Annual Report, released in January 2010, discussed business activities covering the period from January 2008 to November 2009.

BMC Software BMC Software (formerly Marimba) was founded by four members of Sun Microsystems' original Java team in Mountain View, California. BMC originally focused on content delivery, but by the late 1990s had turned its attention to developing applications enabling corporations to distribute and update software remotely via the Internet, corporate intranets, and extranets. BMC's suite of Castanet products used client-server technology to update and maintain off-the-shelf or custom applications. Castanet included powerful security features such as authentication and encryption, among others. Organizations could add new modules to the Castanet system as needs expanded. In addition to Castanet, the company also sold a line of software called Timbale for terminal server applications. In 1999, the company completed a public offering but posted a net loss on its $31 million in annual sales. BMC marketed products worldwide, and its Desktop/Mobile Management, Server Management, and Embedded Management product families allowed Global 2000 companies to better manage their IT resources, increase operational efficiency, and reduce IT (information technology) costs.

In April 2004, Marimba and BMC Software, Inc. announced a merger agreement, under which BMC Software acquired Marimba for a purchase price of $8.25 per share in cash. The transaction reflected a purchase price of approximately $239 million. The company then moved operations to Houston, Texas. In the fiscal year ending June 2009 it brought in $1.88 billion in revenues with about 6,000 employees.

InfoGate Inc. InfoGate's roots date back to 1995, when the company was established by Chairman and CEO Clifford Boro. However, the San Diego-based firm adopted the name InfoGate following the merger of Internet Financial Network (IFN) and EntryPoint, the successor organization to industry pioneer PointCast. EntryPoint Inc. had formed in 1999 following the acquisition of PointCast by Launchpad Technologies Inc. of San Diego. The firm discontinued using the PointCast name and service in early 2000, opting instead to build up its new brand identity. The InfoGate service was based on a premise similar to that of PointCast: online news and information delivered through a special program running on the subscriber's PC.

InfoGate is a division of iGate, based in Pittsburgh, Pennsylvania. As a whole, iGate had revenues of $307.3 million and 6,260 employees in 2007. InfoGate was purchased by Time Warner in 2003 and reported fiscal year revenues (for four quarters ending September 2010) of $1.96 billion.

AMERICA AND THE WORLD
In Sweden, Valinge announced its new side push technology in December 2009, which it claimed gave several advantages over 5G Original, such as easier installation and a lower license fee. More than 50 companies had already obtained license rights for the new technology, which was officially promoted at the Domotex 2010 trade fair.

U.S. companies had yet to make a big impact in the international market, particularly Europe, mostly due to slow and unreliable telephone lines, which sometimes ceased to function when receiving heavy volumes of information all at once. Because of this problem, one of the most successful companies was a Canadian company, Lanacom, Inc. Led by CEO Tony Davis, Lanacom's Headliner (launched in December 1996) "reads" Internet news sites and then delivers that information to registered users. The content is delivered to the desktop via a ticker-tape bar that runs on the top or bottom or vertically along the side of the screen. Information can also be delivered in the form of a screen saver or can be downloaded directly to the user's hard drive. Of the leaders in the U.S. market, BackWeb had the most success getting established in Europe.

Turkcell, the largest mobile communications operator in Turkey, was founded in February 1994, when Turkcell started Turkey's first Global Systems for Mobile Communications (GSM) network. Turkcell provided services to 25.6 million subscribers. In 2005, Turkcell deployed Visto Mobile with ConstantSync technology in order to deliver mass market push e-mail services to its customers' wireless devices. The technology, call TurkcellE-Postaci, is a personal mobile e-mail for mobile phone users. Customers using POP3 e-mail services can download the e-mail application from the Turkcell Website and immediately be able to send and receive e-mail on their mobile devices.

RESEARCH AND TECHNOLOGY
According to pushtechnology.com, as of October 2010, the latest project studies in push technology included one involving scalable Real-Time dashboards for a leading small capital/mid-capital-focused investment bank, and a next generation spread betting solution (via Diffusion technology) for Spreadfair to revolutionize its provision of data on its web site.

In February 2006, in an effort to compete with Research in Motion's BlackBerry, Microsoft introduced its first true e-mail service, Microsoft Direct Push, and paved the way for the cheapest Windows Mobile devices ever. Direct Push sends Outlook messages directly and instantly to mobile devices over the air (OTA) via a wireless account. Direct Push technology is a level above the Outlook Web Access or SMS (Short Message Service) currently available, which sends e-mail to a mobile device at predetermined intervals, but not in real time. Direct Push technology ties into Exchange servers without the need of additional software.

Also in 2006, a free software update was introduced for the Palm Treo 700w smartphone from Verizon Wireless that enables Direct Push technology using Windows Mobile Messaging and Security Feature Pack (MSFP). This technology offered users fast, automatic wireless updates of e-mail, contacts, and tasks and allowed IT managers to deliver the information directly from Exchange Server 2003 SP2 without third party licensing fees. It also offered up-to-the-minute updates.

As companies continued to produce more technologically advanced smartphones and other devices, consumers struggled to stay in a position of having "the best technology available." By September 2008, after having released many versions of the BlackBerry, including the Curve, Pearl, and Pearl Flip, RIM's flagship device was the BlackBerry Bold, which had live streaming video capabilities and a touch screen. It competed with the Windows Mobile 6.1 handsets and the iPhone 3G, among others.

BIBLIOGRAPHY
"5G Side Push Technology Had Great Success at the Leading Fairs 2010." 21 December 2009. Available from http://www.valinge.se/news/news.lasso?id=272

"Apple's MobileMe Replaces .Mac with Updated Services." *ExtremeTech.com,* 9 June 2008.

Arar, Yardena. "Battle of the Black Business Smartphones." *PC World,* November 2008.

Astor, Dave. "Universal Inks Deal to 'Push' Newspaper Content to Mobile Devices." *Editor & Publisher,* 19 September 2008.

"BackWeb Releases 2008 Annual Report and Financial Statement." 9 January 2010. Available from http://www.backweb.com/news-and-events/

"BlackBerry Maker RIM Posts $492 Million Profit For 2Q." *InformationWeek,* 25 September 2008.

Fitchard, Kevin. "Sprint: CDMA Direct Connect Ramps Up." *Telephony,* 12 May 2008.

Greer, Tyson. "Receive E-Mail Instantly with Direct Push Technology." Windows Mobile, 21 April 2006. Available from http://www.microsoft.com/.

Hamblen, Matt. "Microsoft Advances Wireless E-mail Plan." *Computerworld,* 20 February 2006.

"Hands On With Nokia's First Touchscreen Smartphone." *ExtremeTech.com,* 3 October 2008.

"Hotmail Supports Exchange ActiveSync Push Technology." *Information Week,* 31 August 2010.

"IBM, Visto Partner On Lotus Notes Traveler;." *InformationWeek,* 18 September 2007.

Johnson, Staurt J. "BackWeb Sues Microsoft Over Auto Update." *Internet News,* 25 march 2009.

Klein, Judy. "Push Technology Provider uCirrus Raises $1.7M." *VentureBeat,* 8 June 2010.

"Latest Project Case Studies." Available from http://www.pushtechnology.com.

Lendino, Jamie. "HP Unlocks a Powerful Smartphone." *PC Magazine,* October 2008.

Malik, Om. "Data Revenues Will Push Mobile Biz Past $1 Trillion." *Tech News,* 15 January 2010.

"Microsoft and RIM to Bring Windows Live Services to BlackBerry Smartphone Customers." Research in Motion, 12 May 2008.

"Nokia Brings Out iPhone 3G Competitor." *InformationWeek,* 2 October 2008.

"Real-Time Push Engine Efficiently Delivers Data." *Product News Network,* 1 July 2008.

Reedy, Sarah. "P2T's App Ambitions Widen Appeal." Telephony, 19 August 2008.

"Research In Motion's Costs Are on the Rise." *Business Week Online* 29 September 2008. Available from www.businessweek.com.

"A Touching Story at CES." *Business Week Online,* 10 January 2008. Available from www.businessweek.com.

"Twitter for Blackberry." 10 October 2010. Available from http://www.blackberry/twitter.

Vance, Ashlee. "Microsoft7rsquo;s Push Into Gesture Technology." *New York Times,* 29 October 2010.

"Visto Launches Push Mobile Social Networking Solution." *Total Telecom Online,* 9 September 2008.

QUICK CARE CLINICS

SIC CODE(S)

8011

INDUSTRY SNAPSHOT

Quick care clinics are retail medical facilities that usually are located within the pharmacy section of drugstores, grocery stores, or discount department stores, such as Wal-Mart or Target. They are referred to by a variety of names, such as walk in clinics, immediate care facilities, and convenient care centers. The medical and business communities refer to quick care clinics as retail health clinics.

Although some clinics are staffed by physicians, most are staffed by licensed nurse practitioners, health care professionals who are registered nurses with advanced training to diagnose and treat common medical conditions. In addition, nurse practitioners can administer vaccinations, perform diagnostic screenings, and prescribe medications. Nurse practitioners often have access to an off-site physician by phone for consultations. At quick care clinics, nurse practitioners provide routine medical care to patients 18 months and older with or without appointments.

Convenience and price are the reasons that most patients use quick care clinics. These facilities usually are open weekday evenings and on weekends when doctors' offices are closed and the emergency room is the only other option. They also are a useful option for people who do not have a primary care physician or who are away from home. With no expensive medical equipment or office space, immediate care facilities generally are inexpensive to operate and therefore can offer lower prices for the same services provided in a doctor's

office or emergency room. Most accept patients' insurance and are included in the preferred provider networks of insurance companies. Quick care clinics are intended to complement doctor's offices and usually have referral arrangements with local doctors.

ORGANIZATION AND STRUCTURE

The 2010 RAND Health technical report *Policy Implications of the Use of Retail Clinics* noted that about three-fourths of all quick care clinics are owned and operated by the retail pharmacy, grocery store, or discount department store within which they are housed. In some cases, the walk-in clinic is owned by a company that partners with the retail store to house it. Some quick care clinics are owned by health care providers, such as hospitals or physician's groups.

The business model for quick care centers is one of selected, basic medical service offered at extended hours, with or without an appointment, and provided at a low cost. Nurse practitioners and sometimes physician assistants provide care for common conditions, such as upper respiratory, ear, and bladder infections, using specific treatment guidelines. Some clinics focus on acute care only, while others provide additional services, such as weight loss programs, health screenings, general physicals, and vaccinations.

The price of medical care is held down at quick care clinics because the clinic comprises a small space, has a small staff, and houses no expensive medical equipment. In addition, most are run by nurse practitioners, who garner lower salaries than physicians. Results of a study published in *The Annals of Internal Medicine* on

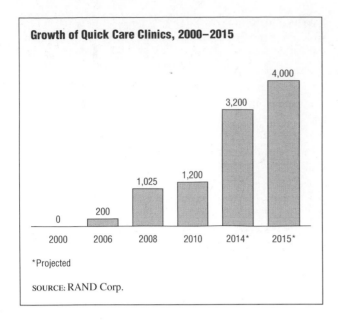

Growth of Quick Care Clinics, 2000–2015

4,000

3,200

1,200

1,025

200

0

2000   2006   2008   2010   2014*   2015*

*Projected

SOURCE: RAND Corp.

September 1, 2009, confirmed that the overall cost for medical care for three common illnesses at a walk-in clinic ($110) was lower than for the same care at a physician's office ($166), urgent care clinic ($156), or hospital emergency department ($570).

Convenient care clinics are located in a retail space, usually next to a pharmacy within a larger store. The California HealthCare Foundation, in *Health Care in the Express Lane: Retail Clinics Go Mainstream*, reported that retailers support quick care clinics in three ways: by either owning the clinics themselves (the in-house model), by partnering with a single operator (the exclusive-operator model), or by partnering with multiple operators (the multiple-operator model). The in-house model is exhibited by CVS, Walgreens, and Target, who own their clinics (MinuteClinic, Take Care Clinic, and Target Clinic, respectively). CVS and Walgreens purchased their clinics, and Target developed its own. The exclusive-operator model is exhibited by H.E. Butt Grocery Company (H-E-B). This Texas- and Louisiana-based grocery store chain has partnered with RediClinic (formerly Interfit Health). The multiple-operator model is exhibited by Wal-Mart, which works with eight operators, including Quick Health, Solantic, and My Healthy Access. According to the California HealthCare Foundation, Wal-Mart chooses operators by their fit with the community demographics.

BACKGROUND AND DEVELOPMENT

The Forerunner to Quick Care Clinics Established in 1989, Interfit Health can be thought of as the predecessor to the quick care clinic. Before quick care clinics were ever established, this business not only provided on-site employee health screenings for employer-sponsored programs but also screenings for the general public at retail outlets such as grocery stores and drug stores. In 1995 Interfit Health developed a Fitness Management division, but that division was made a separate entity in 2000. Interfit Health then evolved into the present-day quick care clinic RediClinic and partners with the grocery chain H-E-B.

QuickMedx/MinuteClinic: Pioneer in the Field According to the California HealthCare Foundation report *Health Care in the Express Lane: The Emergence of Retail Clinics*, the first quick care clinics opened their doors in 2000 in the Minneapolis-St. Paul region. The idea is attributed to businessman Rick Krieger when he was unable to get quick care for his son's sore throat. His successful clinics were called QuickMedx. Associated with the grocery chain Cub Foods, QuickMedx initially charged a $35 flat fee for basic healthcare services and did not accept insurance, but Krieger and his partners—two with medical degrees—decided to accept insurance in 2002. In addition they changed the name of the clinic chain to MinuteClinic.

The business grew, and in 2004 MinuteClinic became affiliated with Target stores in the Baltimore area. In 2005, with other retail medical clinics emerging in the marketplace, such as The Little Clinic, which arose in 2003 and was affiliated with Kroger grocery store chains, MinuteClinic partnered with CVS/Caremark. In 2006 CVS purchased the chain of retail medical clinics. According to Merchant Medicine, MinuteClinic has been the industry leader in retail health clinics since its inception and retained the top spot as of August 2010.

A Growth Spurt in Quick Care Clinics By 2006, not only were other retail medical clinics emerging in the marketplace, they were on the brink of a major growth spurt. Pamela Lewis Dolan, reporting for *American Medical News*, noted that the number of quick care clinics grew five-fold from October 2006 to September 2008, from 200 or so retail clinics in 2006 to about 1,025 in 2008. MinuteClinic operated 500 of those clinics.

Walgreens Enters the Market During those growth-spurt years, Walgreens entered the quick care clinic marketplace. In 2006 the pharmacy chain began offering in-store Health Corner Clinics in four major cities: Chicago, Kansas City, St. Louis, and Atlanta. In 2007 Walgreens acquired Take Care Health Systems, an employer-based health services provider that, in part, became their in-store Take Care Clinics. Walgreens' Take Care Clinics not only became the number two industry leader by December of that year, its market share also grew dramatically through 2008.

A Slow-Down in Growth According to the 2010 RAND Health technical report, quick care clinics were operating in 33 states in August 2008. However, nearly half of the approximately 1,025 clinics were in only five states: California, Florida, Illinois, Minnesota, and Texas. Growth in the number of retail medical clinics slowed after 2008 but still continued. RAND researchers and Merchant Medicine, a trade organization for retail health clinics, both estimated that there were about 1,200 retail medical clinics operating across the country in 2010.

CURRENT CONDITIONS

The Deloitte Center for Health Solutions suggests that years 2009 and 2010 were a pause between the quick care clinic growth spurt of 2006–2008 and a projected growth spurt from 2011–2014. Deloitte projects that by 2014 there will be about 3,200 clinics countrywide and reports a Merchant Medicine projection of 4,000 by 2015.

Profitability and Growth Deloitte reviewed results from a variety of studies on patient volume in quick care clinics and determined that between 7 percent and 17 percent of consumers had visited a retail health clinic within the past year for either themselves or their children. Although Deloitte considers this patient volume to be strong, it also characterizes the profitability of retail health clinics as marginal. Amy Merrick, in a September 10, 2009, article for the *Wall Street Journal*, reported that CVS' MinuteClinic expected to break even by 2012, about the time that Walgreens' Take Care clinics expected to become profitable.

Deloitte suggests that one of the keys to the survival and growth of quick care clinics is insurance coverage of patients. Deloitte-reported MinuteClinic and Harris Interactive data show that the proportion of patients visiting quick care centers who are covered by their insurance for those visits is rising.

Another key to the survival and growth of quick care clinics, suggests Deloitte, is the expansion of their services to include chronic disease management and medication management. Merrick agrees, suggesting that the retail health clinics have no choice but to expand their services into these areas and possibly others or they will remain unprofitable. Increasing the scope of their services, however, will put quick care clinics at odds with professional medical organizations, such as the American Academy of Family Physicians (AAFP) and the American Medical Association (AMA).

Quick Care Clinics and the Medical Home Organizations of medical professionals believe that retail health clinics should limit their services to basic care, such as tending to a sore throat or a sprained ankle, not only because clinic medical staff generally do not have the skills to provide expanded medical services, but also because they can erode the health care model of the medical home. The medical home can be thought of as the general practitioner's office, in which one or more physicians at one office manage the care for a patient. The general practitioner may refer patients to specialists, but the medical records from the specialists are sent to the general practitioner to assure coordination in care and comprehensive record-keeping. When patients visit walk-in clinics instead of their medical home, the coordination of medical care and the keeping of complete medical records can become compromised. As quick care clinics expand the scope of their businesses, the possibility of eroding the medical home increases.

The American Academy of Family Physicians in its January 2010 statement does not endorse retail health clinics. The organization explains that it "opposes expansion of their scope of service, in particular, to include the diagnosis, treatment and management of chronic medical conditions in this setting. The AAFP is committed to comprehensive, coordinated and continuing care for all persons (i.e., a medical home). The AAFP believes that the RHC model of care is not a medical home and has the potential to further fragment patient care." The 2010 RAND study suggests that more research is needed to determine how quick care clinics fit into the present medical system and the concept of a medical home.

Penelope Lemov, health columnist for *Governing Magazine*, explores the concept of disruptive innovation with physician and author Jason Hwang, and considers how the retail health clinic as a disruptive innovator might affect the concept of the medical home. The term "disruptive innovation" refers to an innovation that operates in ways different from the prior norm and, in so doing, forces others in that field to change their strategies and practices. In this case, the retail health clinic may force the medical community to rethink the concept of the medical home and how quick care clinics can fit into that concept. Hwang suggests that retail clinics can be viewed as a positive adjunct to the current medical system, helping primary care physicians who are already overworked and helping reduce lines at emergency rooms that are already overcrowded.

Although the October 3, 2010, Institute of Medicine (IOM) report, *The Future of Nursing: Leading Change, Advancing Health*, only mentions retail health clinics, the report strongly advocates the expansion of nursing practice as the country faces a shortage of physicians. The report stresses that nurses should practice to the full extent of their training and should receive additional training when possible. The report hinted at the expansion of the concept and structuring of the medical home, stating that "nurses should be full partners with physicians and other health care professionals, in redesigning health care in the United States."

John Agwunobi, president of Wal-Mart Stores' Health and Wellness Business Unit in Bentonville, Arkansas, and economic consultant Paul London agree that retail health clinics can have a place in an expanded medical home. In "Removing Costs From the Health Care Supply Chain: Lessons from Mass Retail," they explain how electronic medical records can be shared easily to help maintain continuity of patient care. In addition, most clinics already refer patients to local physicians when in-depth care is needed.

Preferred Attributes of Quick Care Clinics Although the AAFP does not endorse retail health clinics, the organization still provides a list of their preferred attributes, including a limited scope of service, a formal connection with physicians and patients' electronic health records to provide coordinated care, and a referral system to physicians when the patient's needs transcend the limited scope of the clinic.

INDUSTRY LEADERS

In *Retail Clinics Update and Implications*, the Deloitte Center for Health Solutions notes that MinuteClinic and Take Care were the market leaders in quick care clinics in 2009, with MinuteClinic holding 41 percent of the market share, and Take Care holding 31 percent. The Little Clinic was the third industry leader, but it held only 9 percent of the market share. Merchant Medicine showed these three remaining as the industry leaders in August 2010, with CVS/Caremark operating about 450 MinuteClinics and Walgreens operating about 375 Take Care clinics. The Little Clinic operated about 130 quick care centers in Kroger-owned grocery stores.

WORKFORCE

Nurse practitioners and physician's assistants generally are the health care professionals who staff retail health clinics. The Bureau of Labor Statistics defines the skills of the nurse practitioner as follows: "Diagnose and treat acute, episodic, or chronic illness, independently or as part of a healthcare team. May focus on health promotion and disease prevention. May order, perform, or interpret diagnostic tests such as lab work and X-rays. May prescribe medication. Must be registered nurses who have specialized graduate education." Physician assistants are generally college graduates who have some medical experience and who graduated from a specialized course of medical study. The work of physician assistants is similar to that of nurse practitioners, but as their title

suggests, physician assistants practice medicine under the supervision of a physician. They are not autonomous as are licensed nurse practitioners and can only practice in retail health clinics in which a physician is present some of the time.

If the number of walk-in clinics grows as projected, the demand for nurse practitioners and physician assistants will increase. *Money* magazine listed the job of nurse practitioner as the fourth-best job of 2009, citing the growth of walk-in clinics and the shortage of primary care physicians as contributing to development in the field. The article mentions, however, that a doctorate in nursing practice is increasingly becoming the expected level of education for the nurse practitioner. This degree requires three years of study in addition to a Master's degree the registered nurse already must have to become licensed as a nurse practitioner. The median salary for an experienced nurse practitioner was listed by *Money* as $85,200, and the top pay as $113,000. The 10-year job growth from 2006 to 2016 is projected to be 23 percent overall, not just in the retail health clinic market.

Money listed physician assistant as the second-best job in 2009, but added that the annual number of job openings in the field is still small. The median salary of an experienced physician assistant is $90,900, with the top pay being $124,000. The ten-year job growth from 2006 to 2016 is projected to be 27 percent overall.

AMERICA AND THE WORLD

The retail health clinic is also emerging in other countries around the world. The August 3, 2009, issue of *Chain Drug Review* notes that retail health clinics exist in Canada, for example. Like the U.S. model, many are staffed by nurse practitioners, but the Rexall drug store chain has walk-in clinics staffed by physicians. The doctors are independent of the drug store chain, but the drug store provides the physicians with some services. The physicians locate their clinics next to the drug store and sometimes within the store. *Chain Drug Review* notes that the Canadian government is highly supportive of retail health clinics staffed by physicians.

The Australian Medical Association, however, is not pleased with the idea of retail health clinics. Michael East of *Australian Doctor* quoted the Australian Medical Association as characterizing retail health clinics as "supermarket medicine." This negative response was triggered by the August 2010 franchising agreement between the Pharmacy Alliance Group and Revive Clinic to staff 186 pharmacies across Australia with nurse practitioners. Mark Gertskis, reporting for *Pharmacy News*, noted that Australian pharmacists already treat minor ailments but cannot prescribe medications. The Australian Medical Association views the employment of nurse practitioners in pharmacies as a potential conflict of interest between the two, because nurse practitioners can prescribe medications, thus linking the prescribing of medication with its selling in the pharmacy.

Although no worldwide statistics are available on retail health clinics, the high degree of patient satisfaction revealed in research results, such as those of Lauren P. Hunter, et al., published in the October 2009 issue of the *Journal of the American Academy of Nurse Practitioners*, suggests that retail clinics are likely to grow and prosper. In addition, retail health clinics appear to provide a lower-cost health care alternative for basic services, so this clinic model is likely to develop in countries around the world, as is already occurring.

At this time, however, nearly 90 percent of U.S. walk-in clinics are found in urban areas, according to results of research conducted by Rena Rudavsky and colleagues and published in the September 1, 2009, issue of the *Annals of Internal Medicine*. Craig Evan Pollack and Katrina Armstrong also determined that retail health clinics are located in more advantaged neighborhoods and published these research results in the May 25, 2009, issue of the *Archives of Internal Medicine*. If these characteristics of quick care clinics prevail worldwide, the clinics are likely to develop and spread most quickly in the urban, affluent areas of the world.

BIBLIOGRAPHY

"29-1171 Nurse Practitioners." *Standard Occupational Classification*, U.S. Department of Labor, Bureau of Labor Statistics, 11 March 2010. Available from http://www.bls.gov/soc/2010/soc291171.htm.

Agwunobi, John, and Paul A. London. "Removing Costs from the Health Care Supply Chain: Lessons from Mass Retail." *Health Affairs*, September/October 2009.

East, Michael. *Australian Doctor*, 21 August 2009.

Evans, Steven W. "Convenient Care Clinics: Making a Positive Change in Health Care." *Journal of the American Academy of Nurse Practitioners*, January 2010.

The Future of Nursing: Leading Change, Advancing Health. Institute of Medicine of the National Academies, October 2010. Available from http://www.iom.edu/~/media/Files/Report%20Files/2010/The-Future-of-Nursing/Future%20of%20Nursing%202010%20Report%20Brief%20v2.pdf.

Gertskis, Mark. "Pharmacists and Nurses Join Forces." *Pharmacy News*, 13 August 2009. Available from http://www.pharmacynews.com.au/article/pharmacists-and-nurses-join-forces/494284.aspx.

Hunter, Lauren P., Charles E. Weber, Anthony P. Morreale, and James H. Wall. "Patient Satisfaction with Retail Health Clinic Care." *Journal of the American Academy of Nurse Practitioners*, October 2009.

"Katz All About Health Care." *Chain Drug Review*, 3 August 2009.

Lemov, Penelope. "Creative Disruption." *Governing Magazine*, March 2009.

Mehrotra, Ateev, et al. "The Costs and Quality of Care for Three Common Illnesses at Retail Clinics as Compared to Other Medical Settings." *Annals of Internal Medicine*, 1 September 2009.

Merrick, Amy. "Retail Health Clinics Move to Treat Complex Illnesses, Rankling Doctors." *Wall Street Journal*, 10 September 2009. Available from http://online.wsj.com/article/SB125253798506197499.html.

Pollack, Craig Evan, and Katrina Armstrong. "The Geographic Accessibility of Retail Clinics for Underserved Populations." *Archives of Internal Medicine*, 25 May 2009.

"Retail Clinic Growth by Major Players." *Merchant Medicine*, 2010. Available from http://www.merchantmedicine.com/contentimages/GrowthByRetailClinicPlayers%209-1-10.png.

"Retail Clinics in the United States." *Merchant Medicine*, 2010. Available from http://www.merchantmedicine.com/contentimages/Retail ClinicGrowth%209-1-10.png.

Retail Clinics: Update and Implications. Deloitte Center for Health Solutions, 2009. Available from http://www.deloitte.com/assets/Dcom-UnitedStates/Local%20Assets/Documents/us_chs_RetailClinics_111209.pdf.

"Retail Health Clinics." American Academy of Family Physicians, January 2010. Available from http://www.aafp.org/online/en/home/policy/policies/r/retailhealthclinics.html.

Roher, James E., Kurt B. Angstman, and Gregory A. Bartel. "Impact of Retail Medicine on Standard Costs in Primary Care: A Semiparametric Analysis." *Population Health Management*, December 2009.

Rosato, Donna, Beth Braverman, and Alexis Jeffries. "The 50 Best Jobs in America." *Money*, November 2009. Available from http://money.cnn.com/magazines/moneymag/bestjobs/2009/index.html.

Rudavsky, Rena, Craig Evan Pollack, and Ateev Mehrotra. "The Geographic Distribution, Ownership, Prices, and Scope of Practice at Retail Clinics." *Annals of Internal Medicine*, 1 September 2009.

Scott, Mary Kate. *Health Care in the Express Lane: Retail Clinics Go Mainstream*. California HealthCare Foundation, September 2007. Available from http://www.chcf.org/~/media/Files/PDF/H/PDF%20HealthCareInTheExpressLaneRetailClinics2007.pdf.

———. *Health Care in the Express Lane: The Emergence of Retail Clinics*. California HealthCare Foundation, July 2006. Available from http://www.chcf.org/~/media/Files/PDF/H/PDF%20HealthCareInTheExpressLaneRetail Clinics.pdf.

Weinick, Robin M., et al. *Policy Implications of the Use of Retail Clinics*. RAND Corporation, 2010. Available from http://www.rand.org/pubs/technical_reports/2010/RAND_TR810.pdf.

Weinick, Robin M., Rachel M. Burns, and Ateev Mehrotra. "Many Emergency Department Visits Could Be Managed at Urgent Care Centers and Retail Clinics." *Health Affairs*, September 2010.

RADIO FREQUENCY IDENTIFICATION

—■—

SIC CODE(S)

3577

3625

3669

3674

7372

7379

7389

8748

INDUSTRY SNAPSHOT

In simple terms, radio frequency identification (RFID) technology involves the use of small radio tags that are able to communicate with a networked device known as a reader. These tags, which vary in size, price, and capability, consist of a digital memory chip and a transponder. They are affixed to, or embedded within, a wide range of items that manufacturers, retailers, and other parties wish to track. Much more than mere tracking devices, RFID tags contain actual data that is transmitted back to the reader. This data may include serial numbers and other specifications, such as the date and time that a product was manufactured or purchased.

Despite optimistic projections, some radio frequency identification (RFID) users indicated that full-blown implementations involving the manufacture, inbound delivery, and outbound shipment of entire product lines were still ten years away. This was because many organizations were evaluating the returns they would get from RFID investments. In addition to ROI (return on investment) concerns, during the twenty-first century's first decade, companies also were challenged with high RFID costs and the task of integrating RFID into existing systems without disrupting business. Another roadblock to the widespread adoption of RFID was the fact that many consumers and privacy advocates were concerned about the potential misuse of RFID by companies or government agencies. In particular, these groups were concerned about the potential to link the purchase of RFID-tagged items to a consumer's credit or loyalty card information, thereby enabling marketers to build detailed profiles of their purchasing habits. Some consumers also were alarmed by the prospect of being unknowingly tracked from a distance.

ORGANIZATION AND STRUCTURE

Technology Overview There are three main types of RFID tags: passive, semi-passive, and active, passive tags representing the smallest variety. At 0.4 mm x 0.4 mm, these tags could be made so small that they were essentially unnoticeable to the naked eye. As their name implies, passive tags do not contain an independent power source. Instead, they rely upon the energy emitted from the reader to transmit and receive data and must be within several feet of the reader to function. Powered by batteries, these coin-sized tags were somewhat larger, but could communicate at longer distances than passive tags (as far as 300 feet). These main classifications of RFID tags varied further depending on the frequency at which they operated. Microwave tags operated at a frequency of 2.45 gigahertz, followed by UHF tags (868 to 956 megahertz), high frequency tags (13.56 megahertz), and low frequency tags (125 to 134 kilohertz).

Market Overview During the middle years of the first decade of the 2000s, RFID was poised for explosive growth as leading retailers like Wal-Mart, as well as the U.S. Department of Defense, required their leading suppliers to begin using the technology. Leading industry players, covered within the Industry Leaders section of this essay, ranged from RFID tag and reader manufacturers to a host of consulting groups that assisted end users with various implementation issues.

Because radio frequency identification (RFID) tags can be used to track virtually anything, the end markets for RFID technology are virtually endless. However, organizations had to weigh costs against the benefits of using RFID. For example, while the potential existed to replace product bar codes with RFID chips, the cost to affix chips on individual, low-cost items such as packaged goods remained prohibitive. RFID technology was more practical at the pallet or shipping container level, or to track valuable assets and comparatively smaller quantities of expensive items.

The manufacturing sector has adopted radio frequency identification (RFID) in an attempt to reduce instances of lost inventory, improve operational efficiency, and even improve safety. Some companies lose hundreds of thousands of dollars—and in some cases, millions—when merchandise pallets are lost in shipping yards. In addition, time is often lost when staff is needed to hunt down lost or misplaced shipments of parts. The automotive industry is but one example of where RFID has been used to resolve issues like these quickly and easily. During the first decade of the 2000s, companies like AM General, which installed an RFID system in its Mishawaka, Indiana Hummer H2 plant, used RFID to streamline the delivery of parts. However, it was difficult to determine exactly how widespread the use of RFID was in this sector. *Automotive News* reported that many automakers were reluctant to discuss their use of the technology, since it was seen as a competitive advantage.

Leading tire manufacturers such as Goodyear also were incorporating RFID into their operations. In addition to meeting demands from customers like Wal-Mart and the Department of Defense, Goodyear sought to reduce shipping errors, improve inventory flow and visibility, and more cost effectively comply with the Transportation Recall Enhancement, Accountability, and the Documentation (TREAD) Act. Passed in 2000, the TREAD Act required tires to carry unique ID numbers (DOT numbers) that auto manufacturers linked with a vehicle's vehicle identification number (VIN).

Within the transportation sector, RFID has applications beyond the manufacturing process. While Goodyear planned to use disposable RFID tags on tires for light cars and trucks, it expected to use permanent RFID tags on the tires it made for heavy equipment. Combined with pressure and temperature sensors, RFID tags allow equipment owners to monitor the condition of tires and perform necessary maintenance. General Motors also used RFID technology in its OnStar system, which alerts emergency services when air bags deploy, helps authorities locate stolen vehicles, and remotely unlocks doors when keys are left inside.

Finally, states like Illinois used RFID tags in cars to reduce congestion on tollways. After installing an optional RFID device in their vehicle, travelers were able to drive through special toll lanes instead of stopping to pay. RFID readers recognized each vehicle's chip and deducted the appropriate toll from a credit card account. Other transportation-related uses include cards that customers employ to pay public transportation fares and baggage tracking by airlines.

The retail sector represents one of the largest markets for RFID. Pallets containing RFID tags can be identified by readers upon entering a distribution center. When RFID tags are affixed to boxes, it is possible for readers to identify when cases of products move from a store's warehouse to the sales floor. In this scenario, inventory can be closely tracked and replenished. When RFID chips eventually become commodity items, analysts foresee them being used to replace barcodes on individual products. This will enable customers to check themselves out at grocery and retail outlets by simply pushing their carts past a reader, which will instantly identify every item in a cart without needing to physically scan each one.

In addition to manufacturing and retail applications, RFID technology has the potential to save human lives. By 2005, RFID chips were commonly implanted into pets so that they could be easily identified by animal shelters or veterinarians if lost. While civil liberty groups oppose implantable RFID chips in humans, there is merit to the practice. For example, RFID can be used to identify lost Alzheimer's patients who may be unable to communicate their identity. However, RFID tags can save lives even if they don't identify the individual. From time to time, surgically implanted devices like pacemakers experience technical problems or are recalled by manufacturers. For various reasons, patients are not always able to locate the serial numbers of these devices to determine if they are affected by the recall. By adding an RFID tag to these kinds of surgical devices, it becomes possible to access all relevant details in an instant, eliminating the need to find a patient's medical record. The same general concept applies to medical ID bracelets, which notify emergency professionals about medical conditions an individual may have. Because individuals often choose not to wear their bracelets, emergency personnel may be unaware of serious conditions they may have. Since RFID chips can store the same data found on a bracelet, some health care industry observers foresee the day when emergency medical professionals or hospital admissions clerks will routinely scan patients with an RFID reader to obtain this critical information.

Health care organizations—namely hospitals, medical centers, and large clinic operations—also stood to benefit from RFID's location management capabilities. By affixing tags to equipment, staff, and patients, it became possible to know their whereabouts at all times. Acceptance by clinical staff as well as cost were two factors that stood to hinder explosive growth.

In addition to location management, RFID tags also were being used to avoid "wrong-site surgery." In January 2005, Vernon Hills, Illinois-based Zebra Technologies received Food and Drug Administration (FDA) approval to market its SurgiChip system, which produced RFID "smart labels" that were affixed to patients prior to their operation and used by operating room staff to verify the correct surgical site. In the interest of patient safety, the FDA also was spearheading an initiative to promote the use of RFID throughout the nation's drug supply chain. By tagging drugs with RFID tags it becomes possible to track their whereabouts from the manufacturer to the pharmacy, thereby reducing theft and counterfeiting, and also assisting in the event of a recall.

Beyond retail, manufacturing, and health care, radio frequency identification (RFID) has been adopted in many other industry sectors. For example, in the security field, ID badges have been equipped with RFID chips and used to control access to buildings. The corrections sector also has used RFID to track populations of inmates. Finally, libraries and bookstores have used RFID to manage and control collections of books.

Associations Based in Warrendale, Pennsylvania, the Association for Automatic Identification and Mobility (AIM) is one leading trade group within the RFID industry. Its 900 members are located in 43 countries and include RFID manufacturers and service providers as well as producers of related technologies such as bar codes, biometrics, electric article surveillance, and a variety of card technologies (smart cards, optical cards, contactless cards, and magnetic stripes). In addition to hosting an annual meeting and providing its members with print and electronic resources, AIM allowed members to participate in a number of work groups including the Standards Advisory Group, Health Care Work Group, RFID Privacy Work Group, Strategic Alliance Advisory Group, and Technical Symbology Committee.

A joint venture between the Uniform Code Council (UCC) and EAN International, non-profit EPCglobal Inc. seeks "to make organizations more effective by enabling true visibility of information about items in the supply chain." In support of this objective, the industry group oversees and develops standards for a technological development known as the EPCglobal Network. The EPCglobal Network was developed by a global research team called the Auto-ID Center, which was directed through the Massachusetts Institute of Technology and supported by a group of approximately 100 leading companies. According to EPCglobal, its RFID network consists of five main parts: an Electronic Product Code (EPC) used to identify individual items; an ID System consisting of EPC readers and tags; an Object Name Service (ONS) that computers use to locate data about an item containing an EPC code; Physical Markup Language (PML); and a software application called Savant that functions as the network's central nervous system. One final aspect of the network is EPCglobal's global EPCTM number registry service for electronic product codes. Early subscribers to the EPCglobal Network were allowed to participate in the Network Implementation Task Force (ITF), which was responsible for making the system a commercial reality.

BACKGROUND AND DEVELOPMENT

RFID's history is rooted in the development of radio detection and ranging (radar) by Scottish physicist Sir Robert Watson-Watt. During the mid-1930s, Watson-Watt developed radar for the British government to identify incoming German fighter planes during World War II. By calculating the time it takes to bounce a radio wave off of a moving object, radar makes it possible to pinpoint the object's location and distance. However, one limitation was that radar did not allow users to obtain more specific information about an object. This presented a challenge to the British, who were unable to distinguish between returning friendly planes and incoming enemy ones. In response, Watson-Watt worked in secret with the British government to develop an "active identify friend or foe" (IFF) system. In principle, IFF worked in the same manner as RFID. When British fighters were returning home, special on-board transmitters were activated by military radar stations. These transmitters then broadcast signals back to the radar stations identifying the aircraft as friendly.

According to *RFID Journal*, the first U.S. patent for an active RFID chip containing rewritable memory was filed by Mario W. Cardullo on January 23, 1973. Los Gatos, California inventor Charles Walton received a patent for a passive RFID device that same year. Using a card that contained a transponder encoded with a special ID number, Walton's device included a reader capable of unlocking a door without a key. Walton, who had started working with RFID in 1970, ultimately sold his invention to Schlage Lock. However, he continued to make contributions to the RFID industry, including use of the 13.56 MHz frequency that developed into an industry standard.

Government initiatives involving Los Alamos National Laboratory and the Department of Energy led to the use of RFID to track nuclear materials. This same technology was commercialized during the mid-1980s when several former Los Alamos employees started their own company and created RFID systems that tollways could use. This allowed travelers to drive through special lanes and have tolls debited from their credit card instead of stopping to pay with coins or cash. Los Alamos also developed RFID technology used by the agriculture sector to monitor livestock. By the early 1990s, higher-frequency RFID systems had been developed. Around this time, IBM unveiled an ultra-high frequency (UHF) system, which it sold to Intermec midway through the decade.

In 1999, Procter & Gamble and Gillette teamed with the Uniform Code Council (UCC) and EAN International to form the Auto-ID Center at the Massachusetts Institute of Technology (MIT). MIT Professors Sanjay Sarmathere and David Brock had been experimenting with affordable ways to affix RFID tags on individual products and link them to the Internet for tracking purposes. As *RFID Journal* explained, "Sarma and Brock essentially changed the way people thought about RFID in the supply chain. Previously, tags were a mobile database that carried information about the product or container they were on with them as they traveled. Sarma and Brock turned RFID into a networking technology by linking objects to the Internet through the tag. For businesses, this was an important change, because now a manufacturer could automatically let a business partner know when a shipment was leaving the dock at a manufacturing facility or warehouse and a retailer could automatically let the manufacturer know when the goods arrived."

By the first decade of the 2000s, the Auto-ID Center had established research facilities in such locations as Australia, China, Japan, Switzerland, and the United Kingdom. In addition to the U.S. Department of Defense (DOD), more than 100 organizations supported the Auto-ID Center's initiatives. The center subsequently developed many important technical and infrastructure components for RFID systems, including the Electronic Product Code (EPC) and Class 1 and Class 0 air interface protocols.

In 2003, the Auto-ID Center's technology was licensed to the Uniform Code Council (UCC). At this time, the UCC formed a joint venture with EAN International called EPCglobal. This new organization was created to bring RFID to the commercial world. Following these developments, the Auto-ID Center ceased to exist in October 2003. At that time, Auto-ID Labs assumed the research formerly performed by the Auto-ID Center. A second generation RFID standard was ratified by EPCglobal in December 2004, which stood to encourage the technology's widespread adoption.

By 2005, leading retailers such as Albertson's, Metro AG, Target, Tesco, and Wal-Mart were involved with the use of RFID technology. In fact, the DOD, Metro, and Wal-Mart required some of their vendors to use the technology as a condition of doing business with them.

The requirements of leading retailers and the DOD were expected to propel RFID initiatives from discussion to implementation. In October 2004, the research firm Gartner G2 indicated that some 18 percent of large European and U.S. retailers planned to test RFID tagging at the individual item level, a number that was expected to reach 50 percent between 2007 and 2009.

Despite these optimistic projections, some RFID users indicated that full-blown implementations involving the manufacture, inbound delivery, and outbound shipment of an entire product line were still 10 to 15 years away. This was because many organizations were still evaluating the returns they would get from RFID investments. In December 2004, *Chain Store Age* reported the results of consulting firm ABI Research's survey that found consumer packaged goods companies and retailers remained uncertain about RFID return on investment (ROI) as well as tag availability and performance. Twenty-three percent of respondents from all industries "cited ROI uncertainty as the main factor holding them back from a widespread RFID program. Other frequently cited obstacles were uncertainty regarding RFID standards (19 percent), the cost of tags and transponders (13 percent) and technological flux (13 percent). However, respondents were able to readily identify areas where RFID could benefit their companies. Thirteen percent said they think RFID would help track items at the pallet and reusable plastic container (RPC) levels. Another 12 percent said it would help manage the supply chain at the item and case levels, or at the container and trailer levels."

In addition to ROI concerns, companies also were challenged with high RFID costs and the task of integrating RFID into existing systems without disrupting the flow of business. An October 2004 Gartner research report entitled *Prepare for Disillusionment with RFID* indicated that as many as 50 percent of the RFID projects underway at that time were at risk of failing. Amidst these conditions, consultants and companies that could help on the integration front stood to benefit.

According to an October 2003 survey conducted by Cap Gemini Ernst & Young and SmartRevenue, consumers see a number of benefits resulting from RFID. Topping the list are faster recovery of stolen items, improved car anti-theft capabilities, savings due to lower costs, safer prescription drugs, and faster, more reliable product recalls. Nevertheless, many consumers are alarmed over a potential loss of privacy. In particular, concerns center around the potential to link the purchase of RFID-tagged items to a consumer's credit or loyalty card information, thereby enabling marketers to build detailed profiles of their purchasing habits. Consumers also were alarmed by the possibility of being unknowingly tracked from a distance.

On August 14, 2003, *CNET News.com* reported that consumers in the United Kingdom had protested outside of a Tesco supermarket chain store in Cambridge when they learned that RFID tags were being used to automatically take photographs of customers who removed packages of Gillette Mach 3 razor blades from the shelf and again when they exited the store with the product. Gillette claimed to have embedded the individual packages on a trial basis for supply chain purposes, while Tesco indicated it was experimenting with possible security benefits from RFID-tagged items. According to the article, Wal-Mart had cancelled a similar trial in a Boston-area store.

A separate *CNET News.com* story, released four days later, reported on a California State Senate hearing on RFID headed by Senator Debra Bowen and involving experts in the areas of consumer privacy and technology. According to the article, one witness suggested that not restricting RFID use "could lead to a world not unlike the fictional society portrayed in Steven Spielberg's science fiction thriller *Minority Report.* In that movie, set in 2054, iris scanning technology allowed billboards to recognize people and display personalized ads that called out their names. It also allowed law enforcement authorities to track people's whereabouts."

At the hearing, Privacy Rights Clearinghouse Director Beth Givens urged Senator Bowen to study RFID's "profound privacy and civil liberties implications" and called for the establishment of fair use guidelines whereby consumers are made aware of RFID-tagged items through the use of labels. In addition, Givens said consumers should have the option of deactivating the tags after purchasing an item. Much like a credit report, she also indicated that consumers should have the option to request reports from companies that contain any information collected about them via RFID. By 2005, EPCglobal's Guidelines on EPC for Consumer Products addressed most of Givens' concerns.

New uses for RFID tags were being discovered every day. For example, a patent granted in 2007 and held by Gentag, Inc. (Washington, DC) covers the uses of personal wireless devices such as PDAs, laptop computers, and cell phones as low-cost wireless readers for RFID sensors. According to a 2007 article in *Microwaves & RT,* "The patent provides the basis for the creation of a next-generation wireless technology that will put low-cost wireless readers in the hands of consumers, wireless networks, geolocation, and disposable wireless sensors for various market applications." Another example of a new use for RFID was being tested by Mems-ID Pty Ltd. of Melbourne, Australia, which had developed a microelectro-mechanical-systems (MEMS) chip that is mechanical rather than electronic. The chips can be placed directly onto medical devices, such as surgical instruments, and can withstand high temperatures and irradiation sterilization processes. Also in 2007, NXP Semiconductors and Kestrel Wireless were developing an antitheft mechanism for DVDs using passive RFID chips. According to Paul Atkinson, president of Kestrel Wireless, "10 to 15 percent of the disks—especially newly released films—shipped annually in the United States are believed to be stolen." Considering the fact that stolen DVDs cost sellers billions of dollars a year, the new technology was expected to be well received.

One of the emerging technologies in the middle of the first decade of the 2000s was the chipless RFID tag. Traditional RFID tags contain a silicon chip, which is part of the reason their costs are not practical for use on small items. However, according to a 2007 study by IDTechEx, chipless tags could eventually be printed directly on products and packaging for only one cent each. The study also reported that chipless tags are much more versatile and reliable than regular tags and that chipless tags could replace 10 trillion barcodes per year.

CURRENT CONDITIONS

In April 2009, IDTechEx released its new report, *RFID Forecasts, Players & Opportunities 2009-2019,* summarizing the global RFID market. Among its key findings was an estimated value of the global market at $5.56 billion, up from $5.25 billion in 2008. The major revenue-maker was RFID cards and their associated services. IDTechEx also projected continued growth for the industry, due in part to government initiatives such as for transportation, national ID (contactless cards and passports), military and animal tagging, etc. A total of roughly 2.35 billion RFID tags were sold in 2009, up from 1.97 billion in 2008.

With respect to applications trends, approximately 200 million RFID labels were used worldwide for apparel (including laundry) in 2009, reported IDTechEx. The tagging of animals (mostly pigs and sheep) reached 105 million, with strong growth expected as more territories legally require it, such as in China and Australasia.

In 2009, the tagging of pallets and cases/containers fell short of earlier projections. There were only 225 million passive UHF tags for this application, far below the multi-billion-tag forecast by some consumer goods companies. The decline of this application was credited to technical failures, i.e., poor read rates with high moisture content and metal products.

By value, IDTechEx found that $2.23 billion was spent on tags alone in 2008, at an average price of $1.13 per tag. With the launch of printed RFID in 2009 for transit ticketing and other applications, as well as the increase use of RFID labels rather than cards, the average price was expected to fall to $0.22 in 2014.

The leading frequency in 2008 remained HF (13.56MHz) said IDTechEx. In fact, HF RFID working at the ISO14443 specification was responsible for more than five times the expenditure on RFID to any other specification. This was in part due to large new applications such as for passports and RFID enabled phones. The market for 18000-6 passive UHF tags resulted in a market size of $145 million for the tags alone.

INDUSTRY LEADERS

Savi Technology Inc. Sunnyvale, California-based Savi Technology Inc. is a leader in the area of RFID networks that enable companies to manage assets, optimize inventories, achieve real time visibility, and secure their global supply chains. Founded in 1989, by 2005 the company had established regional offices in London, Johannesburg, Singapore, and Washington, D.C. Savi is the main technology provider for the world's largest wireless cargo monitoring network, operated by the U.S. Department of Defense (DOD). Its technology is used by the DOD "to track more than 35,000 conveyances daily across a global network of 1,400 locations in more than 45 countries." This tracking is achieved via a combination of barcoding and RFID as well as cellular and satellite communications systems. In addition to its work with the DOD, Savi also is the leading provider of RFID technology to the United Kingdom's Ministry of Defense.

Texas Instruments acquired Savi in 1995 but sold the company to Raytheon Corp. in 1997. Savi became a private company in May of 1999 when investors and company management bought the company from Raytheon. Since 2000, Savi has received numerous awards. In 2002 the company was included on *Red Herring*'s list of the "100 Companies Most Likely to Change the World." The following year, Savi received the National Defense Transportation Association Company of the Year Award and the European Retail Supply Chain Innovation Award, and was named a Technology Pioneer by the World Economic Forum. In 2009 it announced its winning of a $6.6 million order from the U.S.

Defense Department. The company employed roughly 250 employees; it held 13 fundamental patents on RFID technology and had approximately 20 more pending. The corporation reported 2008 sales of $42.7 billion.

Intermec Technologies Corp. Headquartered in Everett, Washington, Intermec Technologies Corp. is a leading provider of supply chain information products, services, and systems. Specifically, the company develops, manufactures, and integrates both wired and wireless automated data collection systems, including its Intellitag RFID and mobile computing systems. Intermec offers a full range of data capture devices in the RFID sector, including wands, scanners, imagers, charge coupled devices (CCDs), and laser scanners. Intermec's clients include 75 percent of *Fortune* 500 companies and 60 percent of the *Fortune* 100 in such industries as health care, manufacturing, logistics, field services, and retail. A division of industrial technologies provider UNOVA Inc., Intermec was formed by the combination of three companies: Intermec, Norand Corp., and United Barcode Industries. The company is well known for inventing the world's most widely used bar code symbology. Intermec's fiscal year 2008 revenues were $890.9 million, and the company employed 2,497 workers.

Texas Instruments With sales of nearly $12.5 billion and nearly 31,000 employees in 2008, Dallas-based Texas Instruments Inc. (TI) has been a major player in the RFID field since the 1990s. The company's RFID division, Texas Instruments RFid Systems, was established in 1991 as part of TI's Sensors & Controls Division. By the middle of the first decade of the 2000s, the company had evolved into the largest global integrated manufacturer of RFID reader systems and transponders. TI's scope of RFID offerings includes transponders, readers, antennas, software, and accessories. The company markets its products to a wide variety of end users for access control, airline baggage ID, automotive security, document tracking, express parcel ID, livestock ID, logistics and supply chain management, payment/loyalty, product authentication, retail, sports timing, and ticketing.

Consultants In addition to hardware and software companies, the burgeoning need for integration services supported a broad spectrum of consulting firms. These included large consulting enterprises like Accenture, Bearing Point, Cap Gemini, Ernst & Young, IBM, and Unisys, as well as a host of medium and small-sized firms. According to data released in December 2004 by research firm IDC, the market for RFID consulting, managed services, and implementation will reach $2 billion by 2008. Of the companies considering RFID projects, some 66 percent indicated that they would prefer to reply upon outside resources. These findings were good news for third party vendors and consultants with the knowledge and expertise to assist with integration and implementation issues.

RESEARCH AND TECHNOLOGY

Some new develoments in 2009 included an announcement that RURO Inc. had introduced a RFID component for its FreezerPro frozen sample management system, and project partners TERTIUM Technology and CAEN RFID presented a RFID UHF in their new range of BluePalm M series handheld terminals.

Implantable low-frequency RFID chips were one of the newest, and most controversial, applications of this emerging technology. In addition to being used to identify lost pets, some foreign law enforcement agencies have embedded chips into police officers for various purposes, including their recovery in the event of kidnapping. In 2004, VeriChip Corp., a subsidiary of Delray Beach, Florida-based Applied Digital, and Digital Angel Corp. obtained FDA approval to offer the world's first implantable RFID chip for medical use in humans. The VeriChip Health Information Microtransponder System included a rice grain-sized implantable microtransponder that individuals had implanted during an outpatient surgical operation. According to the company, "Each VeriChip contains a unique 16-digit verification number that is captured by briefly passing a proprietary scanner over the insertion site. The captured 16-digit number links to the database via encrypted Internet access. The previously stored information is then conveyed via the Internet to the registered requesting health care provider."

BIBLIOGRAPHY

Das, Raghu. "Chipless RFID." IDTechEx, 1 May 2007.

———. "RFID in 2006: A Story of Extremes." *Packaging Digest,* February 2007.

"FDA Clears VeriChip for Medical Applications in the United States." Verichip Corp. 6 February 2005. Available from www.4verichip.com/.

"FDA Thinks RFID Is Way to Go to Guard Rx Supply." *Chain Drug Review,* 20 December 2004.

Frederick, James. "RFID Outlook Not So Rosy." *Drug Store News,* 25 October 2004.

Friedrich, Nancy. "RFID Innovations Deepen Market Penetration." *Microwaves & RF,* January 2007.

"Frontline Conference Survey: Interest in RFID Is High." *Wireless News,* 22 September 2004.

"Full-Scale RFID Could Take a Decade." *eWeek,* 1 December 2004.

"Gartner: Retailers Embracing Item-Level RFID Faster Than Expected." *eWeek,* 1 October 2004.

"Guidelines on EPC for Consumer Products." EPCglobal Inc. 13 February 2005. Available from www.epcglobalinc.org/.

"The History of RFID Technology." *RFID Journal,* 2003. Available from www.rfidjournal.com/.

"Hoover's Company Capsules." *Hoover's Online,* 2007. Available from www.hoovers.com.

"Medical RFID Tagging Could Save Lives." *eWeek,* 15 October 2004.

Moran, Tim. "Radio Frequency Identification Is Growing Quietly." *Automotive News,* 28 June 2004.

"OnStar and StabiliTrak to Become Standard Equipment on GM Vehicles." General Motors. 30 January 2005. Available from http://www.onstargm.com/.

Pethokoukis, James M. "Big Box Meets Big Brother." *U.S. News & World Report,* 24 January 2005.

"Report: RFID Can Aid Health Care." *Health Data Management,* December 2004.

RFID Forecasts, Players & Opportunities 2009-2019, April 2009. Available from http://www.idtechex.com/research/articles/rfid_market_forecasts_2009_2019_00001377.asp.

"RFID Poised for Big Growth." *Business Communications Review,* February 2004.

"RFID Proving Useful Against Theft." *Access Control & Security Systems Integration,* 15 May 2007.

"RFID ROI Remains Uncertain." *Chain Store Age,* December 2004.

"RFID Spending Will Surpass $3 Billion in 2010." *Military & Aerospace Electronics,* May 2006.

"RFID System Cleared for Surgical Patients." *The BBI Newsletter,* January 2005.

"RFID's Return On Investment Tops List of Concerns; Companies Testing and Considering the Technology Look for Ways to Ensure Quantifiable Benefits." *InternetWeek,* 21 October 2004.

"Robert Watson-Watt." *Notable Scientists: From 1900 to the Present.* Gale Group, 2001. Reproduced in *Biography Resource Center.* Farmington Hills, Mich.: Thomson Gale. 2005. Available from http://galenet.galegroup.com/.

Roberti, Mark. "Goodyear Copes with RFID Challenges." *RFID Journal,* 5 November 2004. Available from www.rfidjournal.com/.

"Savi Wins $6.6 Million Order from U.S. Defense Department For RFID." Press Release, 22 October 2009.. Available from http://www.savi.com/about/press-releases/2009-10-22.php.

"The SN List: Top Benefits of RFID Seen by Consumers." *Supermarket News,* 27 December 2004.

Songini, Marc. "Passive RFID Tag Market to Hit $486M in 2013." *InfoWorld.com,* 14 May 2007.

"Stop RFID." Consumers Against Supermarket Privacy Invasion and Numbering. 5 February 2005. Available from www.spychips.com/.

"Strong Growth Expected In RFID Consulting Services." *InternetWeek,* 6 December 2004.

Texas Instruments. Available from http://investor.ti.com/releasedetail.cfm%3FReleaseID% 3D361491.

Trebilcock, Bob. "RFID: Is It for Real?" *Modern Materials Handling,* April 2004.

"Wal-Mart and Department of Defense." *Frontline Solutions,* April 2004.

Yoshida, Junko. "RFID Fix Promises to Thwart Packaged-DVD Thefts." *Electronic Engineering Times,* 14 May 2007.

RECOVERY AND EMERGENCY RELIEF SERVICES

———— ■ ————

SIC CODE(S)

8322

INDUSTRY SNAPSHOT

Whether the world today is experiencing an unprecedented wave of natural disasters, terrorist attacks, wars, and other emergencies, or whether people are simply more aware of such events because of blanket media coverage, there can be little doubt that a pressing need exists for emergency relief services in every corner of the world. Events in the twenty-first century's first decade, including the terrorist attacks of September 11, 2001; the earlier bombing of the Alfred P. Murrah Federal Building in Oklahoma City; the vast destruction wreaked by Hurricanes Katrina, Rita, and Wilma in 2005 and Hurricanes Gustav and Ike in 2008; major flooding and tornado activity in the Midwest in 2008 and 2010; and the 2010 Gulf of Mexico oil spill, thrust the U.S. emergency relief industry into the spotlight.

Although for purposes of government classification the providers of emergency relief services are lumped together as an industry, they do not comprise an industry in the popular sense of the word. Most of the organizations that make up the emergency and other relief services industry are either federal, state, or local government agencies or nonprofit relief organizations that derive most of their revenue from government support and charitable contributions, respectively. Because of the complex nature of emergency relief, many of these government agencies and nonprofit organizations work closely together to address the unique needs of communities struck by disaster.

Following Hurricane Katrina the Bush administration recommended measures to give the Department of Justice a greater role in disaster relief and require the White House to also play a larger part in coordinating efforts. Although the Federal Emergency Management Agency (FEMA) and the Department of Homeland Security (DHS) would continue to have the foremost responsibility of responding to natural and manmade disasters, they would be joined in disaster relief by several other departments. The Pentagon would take over in major catastrophes, such as a nuclear attack or multiple terrorist attacks. The military would be called in to provide logistical support (e.g., having troops deliver supplies and rescue victims). The Justice Department would be charged with disaster law enforcement along with the DHS, even in lesser emergencies. The medical teams that the Department of Health and Human Services (HHS) had supervised prior to their being moved to FEMA's authority following the establishment of the DHS would be put back under the auspices of the HHS. In addition, the Department of Housing and Urban Development (HUD) would be responsible for finding temporary housing and shelter for disaster victims instead of being handled by FEMA.

ORGANIZATION AND STRUCTURE

Under the definition of the North American Industry Classification System (NAICS), the agencies and establishments within the emergency and other relief services industry are "primarily engaged in providing food, shelter, clothing, medical relief, resettlement, and counseling to victims of domestic or international disasters or conflicts (e.g., wars)."

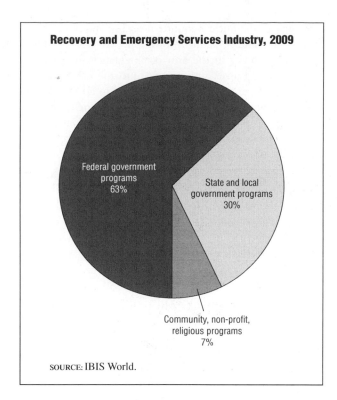

Recovery and Emergency Services Industry, 2009

Federal government programs
63%

State and local government programs
30%

Community, non-profit, religious programs
7%

SOURCE: IBIS World.

At the heart of the governmental emergency relief community in the United States is the Federal Emergency Management Agency (FEMA). The agency, formed in 1979 through the merger of multiple federal disaster and emergency relief activities into a single federal entity, coordinates the federal response to disasters of both natural and manmade origin. FEMA also works closely with state and local emergency relief agencies and with such nonprofit, nongovernmental organizations as the American Red Cross. FEMA, which in March 2003 became part of the new Department of Homeland Security, is charged with "responding to, planning for, recovering from, and mitigating against disasters." Every state in the union, along with the District of Columbia, Puerto Rico, Guam, and other U.S.-held territories, has its own emergency services agency. Similar governmental agencies are operated at both the local and regional level.

Of all the establishments classified as part of the emergency and other relief services industry, the vast majority are exempt from taxes. Such organizations include the American Red Cross, Catholic Relief Services, the Salvation Army, American Jewish World Service, World Relief, the International Rescue Committee, Lutheran World Relief, and the Volunteer Pilots Association.

While delivery of relief services in the wake of a disaster is the primary focus of the establishments in this industry, almost all of them expend a great deal of time, money, and energy looking for ways to either prevent or minimize the effects of such emergencies. Governmental agencies, as well as nonprofit humanitarian organizations involved in emergency relief, also regularly reassess their disaster management plans, which lay out advance strategies for the deployment of relief services in the event of an emergency.

BACKGROUND AND DEVELOPMENT

Disasters, particularly those of natural origin, have always triggered human compassion and desire to help those in need. On a purely person-to-person level, people have reached out to help each other in times of disaster for much of recorded history. However, organized emergency relief efforts are more recent. On the government side, federally supported response to disasters in the United States can be traced to the Congressional Act of 1803, enacted only two decades after the nation's founding fathers won independence from Great Britain. The legislation provided government assistance to a New Hampshire town in the wake of a disastrous fire. More than 100 versions of the 1803 Act were passed by Congress during the nineteenth and early twentieth centuries as subsequent disasters were mostly addressed by the federal government on a case-by-case basis until the 1930s and the presidency of Franklin D. Roosevelt.

In the latter half of the nineteenth century, the first of the nonprofit humanitarian organizations began to emerge. These early volunteer organizations, supported primarily by charitable contributions, included the International Red Cross and Red Crescent movement, founded in 1863, and the Salvation Army, founded in London in the 1860s by William Booth. An outgrowth of the International Red Cross, the American Red Cross was founded in 1881 by Clara Barton.

Against the backdrop of the Great Depression, Roosevelt's administration ushered in an era in which the federal government took a progressively larger role in addressing problems of all kinds. During the 1930s, the government's Reconstruction Finance Corporation was authorized to make loans to cover the repair or reconstruction of public facilities damaged or destroyed by earthquakes. This authority was later expanded to include financing for damage caused by other types of disasters. Shortly thereafter, the Bureau of Public Roads was given the authority to finance the reconstruction of bridges and highways destroyed by natural disasters, and the U.S. Army Corps of Engineers was given greater power to implement flood control projects. With numerous disaster relief functions assigned to a number of different federal agencies, it fell to the president to coordinate these sometimes overlapping operations.

Greater attempts to centralize federal responsibility for emergency disaster relief came in the 1960s and early 1970s, in the wake of massive natural disasters such as Hurricanes Carla, Betsy, Camille, and Agnes and catastrophic earthquakes in Alaska and California's San Fernando Valley. Congress passed an increasing amount of legislation addressing specific natural disasters and potential disaster threats, but federal disaster response operations remained alarmingly fragmented, with more than 100 different agencies involved in some aspect of disaster response. As complicated as it was to coordinate federal disaster response efforts, it was even more challenging for state and local emergency management agencies that were forced to deal with scores of different federal agencies. Finally, in 1979, in response to pressure from the National Governors Association, President Jimmy Carter issued an executive order merging a number of federal emergency agencies into the newly created Federal Emergency Management Agency (FEMA). Agencies absorbed by FEMA in the 1979 merger included the Federal Disaster Assistance Administration, Federal Insurance Administration, National Fire Prevention and Control Administration, National Weather Service Community Preparedness Program, and the Federal Preparedness Agency of the General Services Administration.

The terrorist attacks of September 11, 2001, had a profound impact on the emergency relief industry, not only in the United States but throughout much of the rest of the world as well. Besides putting an unprecedented strain on many of the providers of disaster relief services, the terrorist attacks in New York City and at the Pentagon just outside Washington, D.C., called public attention to the important role played by governmental and humanitarian disaster response teams. Although the catastrophic events energized fundraising campaigns for most of the humanitarian organizations involved in providing relief, the focus on the victims of the attacks on World Trade Center and Pentagon, and Shanksville, Pennsylvania (where a fourth hijacked plane crashed in spite of efforts of passengers to overtake the terrorists) diverted some of the charitable contributions that might have gone to other emergency relief efforts. The role of governmental agencies in responding to the attack on the United States prompted state and federal legislators to increase budget appropriations for these agencies.

Another important development in the wake of the attack on the United States was the establishment of the White House Office of Homeland Security by President George W. Bush. Less than a year after the establishment of the office, Bush proposed its elevation to cabinet level status. Under the terms of Bush's proposal, the newly created Department of Homeland Security (DHS) was charged with primary responsibility for four key governmental functions: border and transportation security; emergency preparedness and response; chemical, biological,

radiological, and nuclear countermeasures; and information analysis and infrastructure protection. To give the DHS ultimate authority in the area of emergency preparedness and response, FEMA was merged into the DHS in early 2003. The department was also assigned to administer the grant programs for firefighters, police, and emergency personnel previously managed by FEMA, the Department of Justice, and the Department of Health and Human Services.

In August 2003, the U.S. Northeast and Midwest experienced the worst and most massive power failure in the country's history. Along with the lengthy blackout of electricity, blood supplies were low due both to a drop in donations and an inability to collect blood from donors. Wyndgate Technologies Safe Trace Donor Management System was developed to aid blood centers in tracking, managing, and safeguarding of the blood supply.

In the fall of 2003, Hurricane Isabel devastated much of the eastern seaboard. The damage was so widespread and so severe that even in April 2004, hundreds of people still were unable to return home. At that time, the National Flood Insurance Program, in conjunction with FEMA, had paid out over $400 million to 24,000 victims. On the other coast, after California's devastating 2003 fires, more than $6 million in loans and $5 million in grants were disbursed by federal disaster relief agencies.

In early 2004, after train bombings in Madrid injured and killed nearly 2,000 people, the Rail Transportation Security Act was proposed to require the DHS to study the domestic rail system and report back on safety and security issues.

PIONEERS IN THE FIELD

Although almost all of the federal government's emergency response functions are today coordinated by a single agency, FEMA, for the first eight decades of the twentieth century, these responsibilities were shared by a number of different agencies. As the task of coordinating the activities of multiple relief agencies grew increasingly complex, efforts began in the middle of the twentieth century to centralize such federal efforts, although the responsibility remained within the executive office of the president. Agencies that preceded the 1979 formation of FEMA included the Office of Defense Mobilization (1953 to 1958), succeeded briefly by the Office of Defense and Civilian Mobilization (1958), and then the Office of Civil Defense Mobilization (1958 to 1961), the Office of Emergency Planning (1961 to 1968), and the Office of Emergency Preparedness (1968 to 1973). In 1968, federal disaster insurance functions were assigned to the Federal Insurance Administration, an agency of the Department for Housing and Urban Development (HUD). Five years later, in 1973, the Federal Disaster

Assistance Administration was formed as an agency of HUD to focus on the delivery of federal relief to communities struck by disaster. In 1979, all federal disaster assistance and insurance programs were merged under a single agency, FEMA, created by an executive order from President Jimmy Carter on March 31, 1979.

Pioneers in the area of nongovernmental humanitarian organizations included the Salvation Army and the International Red Cross, the American branch of which was founded by Clara Barton. The architect of the Salvation Army was William Booth, an English minister who abandoned the conventional pulpit to take his Christian message to the poor and homeless masses on the streets of London in the mid-19th century. Over time, he assembled a large team of volunteers spreading the word. In 1878, Booth referred to this team in his annual report as a "Salvation Army" and the name has stuck ever since. Although the primary goal of Booth's organization was to spread the Christian message, by the beginning of the twentieth century, it had launched its first major disaster relief operation in the wake of a devastating hurricane that struck the Texas coast near Galveston, killing more than 5,000 people. The Salvation Army continues to provide emergency relief after natural and manmade disasters.

Originally established in 1863 as the International Committee for the Relief of the Wounded and designed to assist those injured in war, the International Red Cross soon expanded through the efforts of its national chapters into an organization prepared to help prevent and relieve human suffering of all kinds. The American Association of the Red Cross was established in 1881 by army field nurse Clara Barton, who served as its president until 1904. The organization changed its name in 1893 to the American Red Cross. Barton spearheaded a change in the Red Cross charter, which gave the humanitarian organization its mission to provide aid not just in times of war but after such disasters as flood, famine, hurricane, cyclone, or pestilence.

The year 2005 was one of the worst and costliest disaster years on record, due to Hurricanes Katrina, Wilma, and others along the Gulf Coast and in the Midwest. The American Red Cross estimates that in any major disaster, 40 percent of businesses that close will never reopen. Because of the widespread devastation wrought by Hurricane Katrina, the Katrina Emergency Tax Relief Act of 2005 was enacted to allow penalty-free withdrawals from IRAs and other retirement funds by service center owners, to be used to keep their businesses open. In October 2006, the Gulf Coast Recovery and Disaster Preparedness Act of 2005 was introduced by Senator Judd Gregg to establish a Gulf Coast Recovery and Disaster Preparedness Agency to rebuild the infrastructure of the Gulf Coast area. The agency would be responsible for seeing that federal resources are used efficiently in efforts relating to disaster relief.

Harold Schaitberger, of the International Association of Fire Fighters, called on government officials to expand on the recommendation of the former 9/11 Commission, which called on the government to provide additional resources to firefighters and other "first responders" to enable them to carry out their jobs effectively in response to a disaster. Schaitberger proposed that measures should be taken to ensure more staffing, more equipment, more training, better communications, and more federal resources be made available in order to better save lives and protect privacy in time for the next event, whether manmade, accidental, intentional, or natural.

The National Disaster Medical System (NDMS) also came under fire in the aftermath of Hurricane Katrina for troubles the NDMS clinicians had in providing emergency medical care to sick and injured victims. The NDMS works to ensure that adequate medical resources are available after a disaster that overwhelms local health care resources, and to provide support to the military and Veterans Health Administration medical systems in treating casualties evacuated back to this country from armed conflicts abroad. A mixture of poor management, bureaucratic re-shuffling, and inadequate funding was blamed for its shortcomings after the various hurricanes in the fall of 2005. The NDMS, which was a division of the Department of Health and Human Services, was made a division of FEMA, now under the authority of the DHS. A source at Homeland Security was reported as saying that since everyone in DHS is in law enforcement, medical support and operations are not understood and just become lost. One of the recommended reforms was more funding and medical leadership with more control over medical assets.

The first six months of 2008 proved to be one of the deadliest and most costly in history in terms of natural disasters. In the approximately 400 natural disasters that occurred worldwide (300 of which were weather related), more than 150,000 people died and damage estimates reached $50 billion, according to a 2008 *Risk & Insurance* report. In the United States, in addition to the most active tornado season on record in the Midwest, which caused $955 million in damages, severe flooding affected several states, causing $1 billion in crop damage in Iowa alone. Hurricanes Ike and Gustav in the South and wildfires in the West also caused major damage and billions in losses. The 2008 Disaster Relief and Recovery Supplemental Appropriations Act allowed for funds to help repair the damage caused by these events, and in October 2008 the Department of Transportation released $679 million toward repair of roads and bridges in 28 states.

Many organizations stepped up to aid victims of the disasters, and in late 2008 the Red Cross launched the Campaign for Disaster Relief with a goal of $100 million.

The emergency and relief services industry was benefiting from advances in technology in the latter part of the 2000s' first decade. In 2008 a software program called Pathfinder allowed for faster response times and more efficient tracking of relief efforts via mobile devices. The program uses mobile electronic forms, global positioning systems (GPS), and Bluetooth technology. Due to the latter, the system works even when cellular and Internet services are not available, which is often the case when severe storms have caused major damage. Scott Lewis, founder of The Eagle Wings Foundation, a nonprofit relief organization, was the first to use Pathfinder and utilized it when coordinating relief efforts after Hurricane Ike in Texas. Lewis told *Space Daily,* "The technology has worked beautifully and is literally helping save lives." Previously, relief workers had to take notes by hand and then enter them into a computer database, which was time consuming and often resulted in duplication of efforts. With Pathfinder, a central command and control system allows for "multijurisdictional disaster reponse," and, with the use of GPS and wireless communication, allows relief workers to reach the most critical victims more quickly.

Nokia of Finland produced a similar software solution, Nokia Data Gathering, which is meant to help organizations gather data quickly via mobile devices in the case of such disasters as disease outbreaks. Gregory Elphinston of Nokia told *Space Daily,* "Information related to health, agriculture and environmental conditions is often recorded on paper, transported, and transcribed, in a process that can take months and result in errors. Nokia Data Gathering aims to improve accuracy and deliver information in near real-time, helping decision-makers to improve the delivery of social services." The software is available free of charge to public sector and nongovernmental organizations. The Amazonas State Health Department in Brazil will be the first organization to try out the program, using it to manage its dengue fever epidemic in late 2008.

CURRENT CONDITIONS

A late 2009 industry report by IBISWorld indicated that the U.S. Natural Disaster & Relief Services industry was worth roughly $8.3 billion in 2009, representing a 10 percent growth over 2008. Key industry statistics showed 2,652 establishments and 1,414 enterprises operating in 2009, with a total industry employment of 939,600. Federal government programs took the lion's share of the industry, roughly 62 to 63 percent. Another 29 to 30

percent constituted state and local government programs, and about 7 or 8 percent of the industry was represented by community, non-profit, and religious programs.

In February 2010, FEMA announced a freeze on funding for all recovery projects, excepting emergency work or individual assistance, because of depleted emergency accounts. An emergency $5.1 billion appropriation was being urged through Congress to replenish the fund. Meanwhile, recovery efforts from Hurricanes Katrina, Rita, Gustav, and Ike, the Midwest and Red River floods, winter storms in the Mid-Atlantic, and California wilddfires were all pending. In early 2010, an arbitration panel ruled against FEMA, ruling that Louisiana was entitled to receive an additional $474.7 million to replace Charity Hospital in New Orleans, still pending from Hurricane Katrina. Qualifying Gulf Coast projects were originally slated to be constructed by December 2010, but an appropriations amendment (because of the funding shortage) would push the deadline to December 2012. About 13,000 jobs and 77 housing projects for over 6,000 families were at stake.

House Bill 4899 of the 111th Congress (2009-2010), Supplemental Appropriations Act (which became Public Law 111-212 in July 2010) buoyed several governmental agencies and departments for the remainder of 2010. Appropriations related to emergencies and disaster relief included: the Foreign Agricultural Service's Food For Peace Title II Grants for emergency relief and assistance for Haiti; the Economic Development Administration for "disaster relief, recovery, and restoration of infrastructure in states that experienced damage from severe storms and flooding during March to May 2010"; the Department of Defense-Civil Section 401 under the Reclamation States Emergency Drought Relief Act of 1991 "for the optimization and conservation of project water supplies to assist drought-plagued areas of the West"; also Section 406 under the same Act, for the Secretary of the Army "to make dredged material available from maintenance dredging of existing federal navigation channels located in the Gulf Coast region to mitigate the impacts of the Deepwater Horizon Oil Spill in the Gulf of Mexico"; the Departments of the Treasury, Homeland Security, Labor, and State, for disaster response activites relating to Haiti following the earthquake of January 12, 2010; and other emergency and disaster relief efforts around the world.

INDUSTRY LEADERS

Federal Emergency Management Agency One of four main branches of the Department of Homeland Security (DHS), FEMA is charged with overseeing the department's responsibilities for emergency preparedness and response. Originally created by executive order in 1979,

FEMA retains the mission it was given at the time of its creation: "To lead America to prepare for, prevent, respond to, and recover from disasters with a vision of 'A Nation Prepared.'" With the importance of a strong federal disaster response emphasized by the terrorist attacks of September 11, 2001, President Bush proposed a fiscal 2004 budget of $5.9 billion for DHS's emergency preparedness and response operations, which FEMA directs. FEMA not only coordinates federal emergency response efforts but also works closely with state and local government relief agencies as well as volunteer humanitarian organizations such as the American Red Cross and the Salvation Army.

American Red Cross Headquartered in the nation's capital, the American Red Cross works through its network of state and local chapters and service delivery units to provide disaster relief throughout the United States. Active in emergency relief operations since its founding by Clara Barton in the late nineteenth century, each year the American Red Cross responds to approximately 70,000 disasters. Approximately 4 million people give blood through the Red Cross annually, making it the largest supplier of blood and blood products in the United States. In 2009, the Red Cross reported 35,000 employees and nearly 1 million volunteers in 900 locally supported chapters. It assisted more than 7 million persons in 2009, with net assets of $1.7 billion and operating revenues of $3.3 billion.

Although the Red Cross is not a government agency, the U.S. Congress in 1905 formalized the organization's authority in its charter to provide disaster relief. The American Red Cross charter authorizes the humanitarian organization to "carry on a system of national and international relief in time of peace and apply the same in mitigating the suffering caused by pestilence, famine, fire, floods, and other great national calamities, and to devise and carry on measures for preventing the same."

The American Red Cross has expanded its operations to offer service in five other areas: community services that help the needy; support and comfort for military members and their families; the collection, processing and distribution of blood and blood products; educational programs that promote health and safety; and international relief and development programs.

Salvation Army An evangelical arm of the universal Christian Church, the Salvation Army, based in Alexandria, Virginia, was founded in 1865 and was one of the world's largest charitable and service organizations by the first decade of the 2000s. Although its operations are not limited to disaster relief, most of its programs are directed toward providing relief in the wake of natural and manmade disasters. Its outreach includes more than 100 countries, with its officers preaching the Gospel in more than 160 languages. Its membership comprises 3,500 officers, 60,000 employees, 113,000 soldiers, 430,000 adherents, and more than 3.5 million volunteers. The Salvation Army expanded its services to address contemporary needs, such as disaster relief services, day care centers, summer camps, holiday assistance, services for the aging, AIDS education and residential services, medical facilities, shelters for battered women and children, family and career counseling, vocational training, correction services, and substance abuse rehabilitation. More than 30 million people a year are aided by services provided by the Salvation Army. Its fiscal year 2009 Annual Report indicated that it spent $3.12 billion serving almost 30 million people, up from $3.05 billion in 2008.

Other Organizations Other worldwide organizations related to emergency services and disaster relief include the International Association of Emergency Managers, a nonprofit educational organization designed to advance the emergency management profession; the Office for the Coordination of Humanitarian Affairs of the United Nations, which can deploy disaster relief teams; and the World Bank, which has spent more than $40 billion on disaster management activities since 1980.

WORKFORCE

In 2006 there were approximately 12,000 people employed as emergency management specialists in the United States, according to the Bureau of Labor Statistics' (BLS) *Occupational Outlook Handbook, 2008-09 Edition.* As defined by the BLS, emergency management specialists "coordinate disaster response or crisis management activities, provide disaster preparedness training, and prepare emergency plans and procedures for natural (e.g. hurricanes, floods, earthquakes), wartime, or technological (e.g., nuclear power plant emergencies, hazardous materials spills) disasters or hostage situations." The occupation was expected to grow about as fast as average through 2016.

AMERICA AND THE WORLD

Disasters, natural or manmade, are not unique to the United States but strike in virtually every corner of the world. Although the U.S. governmental agencies involved in emergency relief services confine their disaster response operations largely to the United States and its territories, they do sometimes provide their support and expertise to emergency relief services in other countries when the need arises. The same is true of such high-profile U.S.-based humanitarian organizations as the Salvation Army USA and the American Red Cross, both of which are the national chapters of organizations with branches throughout the world. Still other U.S.-based humanitarian organizations involved in providing disaster relief services focus primarily on the lesser-developed countries of the world. Catholic Relief Services, which maintains its world headquarters in Baltimore, Maryland, provides humanitarian and disaster relief services around the world, as does AmeriCares of New Canaan, Connecticut. The latter organization solicits donations of drugs, medical supplies, and other relief materials from American and international manufacturers. These donated goods are then delivered by AmeriCares to healthcare and welfare professionals in nearly 140 countries around the world.

The 2009–2010 World Emergency Relief Annual Report showed that 600 tons of cargo, worth $21 million, went to 25 countries during that timeframe. Some special projects included an expansion of its SafeWater programs in Africa and Central America (to fight parasites and worms) and assistance to severely wounded U.S. soldiers returning from war zones. About 94 percent of the non-profit's revenues went for disaste relief, and costs consumed just 6 percent in 2009. The International Development and Relief Foundation focused on the 2009 and 2010 earthquakes in Indonesia and Sumatra regions.

Headquartered in New York City, the International Rescue Committee was founded at the urging of Albert Einstein in the 1930s to help German citizens suffering under the policies of Adolf Hitler. Today the committee focuses its energies largely on the provision of relief services to refugees from racial, religious, and ethnic persecution, as well as those displaced by war and violence. Other U.S.-based humanitarian organizations providing a significant degree of disaster relief outside the country include Blessings International of Tulsa, Oklahoma; Lutheran World Relief of Baltimore; United Methodist Committee on Relief of New York City; American Jewish World Service of New York City; World Relief of Baltimore; and the Volunteer Pilots Association of Bridgeville, Pennsylvania.

The 75-year-old Kenyon International Emergency Services is a Texas-based company that provides emergency response services to government agencies and private companies anywhere in the world by coordinating emergency services connected with accidents, terrorist attacks and natural phenomena. The year 2005 was the busiest year in the company's history. It was called to Thailand to help deal with the aftermath of the tsunami that struck that part of the world, then summoned to Greece to help with the tragedy of the Helios Airways plane crash that took 121 lives. Immediately following the crash, the company was involved in the aftermath

of Hurricanes Katrina and Rita in the Gulf Coast area. A benefit that came from all those emergencies was that the company's experiences can be used by other recovery firms to improve their own emergency response efforts.

RESEARCH AND TECHNOLOGY

Although all establishments in the emergency relief community remain prepared to respond quickly to the effects of natural disaster, the focus of the early twenty-first century has been unprecedented attention on dealing with the consequences of manmade disasters, namely terrorist attacks. Only months after the devastating attacks on the United States on September 11, 2001, FEMA signed a memorandum of understanding with the Commerce Department's National Institute of Standards and Technology (NIST) designating NIST as a primary research and technical resource for FEMA. The goal of the agreement between FEMA and NIST is to strengthen collaboration between the two agencies and also buttress the federal government's abilities to improve homeland security and reduce national disaster losses.

Under the provisions of the FEMA-NIST accord, the two agencies will work jointly to reduce the loss of life and property and protect the nation's buildings and infrastructure from all types of hazards; advance the development of technology and methods to evaluate equipment for use by the nation's first responders and management communities; and ensure that FEMA can call on NIST quickly for help with scientific and technological services in disaster investigations, recovery planning, and support technologies. A non-regulatory agency of the U.S. Department of Commerce, NIST develops and promotes technology, measurements, and standards to enhance productivity, facilitate trade, and improve quality of life.

As part of its efforts to prepare for the rapid deployment of response teams in the event of disaster, FEMA has moved aggressively to enhance its information services. Released in 2002, the agency's Version 2.0 of its Information Technology Architecture (ITA) offers an overview of its strategy to create a truly robust information technology (IT) infrastructure. As the primary emergency coordinator for the federal government, FEA needs to be able to quickly set up fully IT-enabled field offices for hundreds of emergency managers, establish high-bandwidth connectivity to remote locations, and manage voice, data, and video services for both administrative and disaster response missions. At the heart of FEMA's IT infrastructure is the National Emergency Management Information System (NEMIS), which manages the allocation of disaster grants to individual victims as well as state and local governments.

FEMA also utilizes a software program called the HAZUS (Hazards U.S.), which was developed in 1997 and is used for risk assessment and loss estimation in disaster situations. The HAZUS-MH MR3 version used in the late years of the first decade of the 2000s was capable of dealing with flooding, hurricanes, and earthquakes. Other countries have adopted the model for use around the world.

The booming technological world of the twenty-first century's first decade was also bringing hackers, viruses, and other so-called "cyber attacks" to the forefront of concerns. In 2004, the DHS announced its national e-mail alert system to inform agencies how to protect their networks from both general and industry-specific attacks. DHS also launched the Protected Critical Infrastructure Information Program, which was designed to safeguard information the agency received about terrorism concerns.

Some of the legislation that was passed after the devastating hurricanes of the fall of 2005 included the Gulf Coast Recovery and Disaster Preparedness Act of 2005, which was designed to help rebuild/build the infrastructure of the Gulf Coast and produce proposals to give federal agencies from the Pentagon to the Justice Department a greater role in disaster relief, and the Katrina Emergency Tax Relief Act of 2005, to help businesses rebuild after disasters by withdrawing from retirement funds without tax penalties.

BIBLIOGRAPHY

"2009–2010 World Emergency Relief Annual Report." March 2010. Available from http://www.worldemergencyrelief.org/pdf.

"2009 Annual Report." American Red Cross. 2010. Available from http://www.RedCross.org/www-files/Documents/pdf.

"AAW Asks Senate to support Emergency Agriculture Relief Act." *Southwest Farm Press,* 15 September 2008.

"About Us." Federal Emergency Management Agency, 1 October 2008. Available from http://www.fema.gov/.

"About Us." The Salvation Army, 1 October 2008. Available from http://www.salvationarmyusa.org/.

Alpert, Bruce. "FEMA Money for Hurricane Recovery Projects is Running Out." *Times-Picayune,* 10 March 2010.

"American Medical Response Provides Largest EMS Deployment in U.S. History." *Business Wire,* 2 October 2008.

"Bill Summary and Status—111th Congress (2009–2010)—H.R. 4899-CRS Summary." Available from http://thomas.loc.gov/cgi-bin/bdquery/z?d111:HR04899/.

"Bush Proposes Shuffling Disaster Response Procedures." *Government Security,* 1 March 2006.

"The Deadly Six." *Risk & Insurance,* 1 September 2008.

"DOT Releases $679M Emergency Funds." *Traffic World,* 27 October 2008.

Elliott, Robert. "Masters of Disaster." *Security Management,* January 2006.

"HAZUS." Federal Emergency Management Association, 20 August 2008. Available from http://www.fema.gov.

IBISWorld. "Natural Disaster & Emergency Relief Industry Research in the US." No. 62423, 3 August 2009.

"Legislation: Rangel Weighs in on Disaster Relief, Tax Bills." *The Bond Buyer,* 25 September 2008.

"Nokia Launches Mobile Software to Aid Delivery of Critical Social Services." *Space Daily,* 29 September 2008.

"Red Cross Facts." American Red Cross, 1 October 2008. Available from http://www.redcross.org/.

The Salvation Army. "The Salvation Army Releases All-Online 2010 National Annual Report." 2010. Available from http://www.salvationarmyusa.org/usn/www_usn_2.nsf/vw-dynamic.

"Technology Revolutionizes Hurricane Relief Efforts." *Space Daily,* 29 September 2008.

U.S. Bureau of Labor Statistics. *Occupational Outlook Handbook, 2008-09 Edition.* Washington, D.C.: 2008.

RISK MANAGEMENT SERVICES

─■─

INDUSTRY SNAPSHOT

A wide-reaching spectrum of the business insurance sector, risk management has gained popularity as companies seek greater protection against unexpected losses, whether from natural disasters, lawsuits, political events, or even internal scandals. The relaxed regulatory climate in many industries also placed greater emphasis on risk assessment, which was increasingly a favored alternative to industry-wide regulatory standards and enforcement. Companies faced with such new-found responsibilities increasingly sought out professionals to sort out their exposures and position them for solid gains.

With so many risk categories, ranging from financial exposures to workers' compensation to environmental regulations, companies find it necessary to either hire managers or contract with companies who specialize in risk. The intricacies of business are simply becoming too much for a nonspecialist to efficiently and effectively deal with, and the costs are too great.

The worldwide financial crisis and economic downturn in the United States brought risk management to the top of many businesses' agendas, and risk management services became even more important to organizations' chances of survival. According to a 2008 survey by business advisers SAS, 60 percent of firms questioned were saving funds to use toward risk management strategies due to the global economic situation, and 59 percent were working with risk managers to put plans in place.

ORGANIZATION AND STRUCTURE

Any bid to secure or add to wealth entails some risk, which means that simply being in business is a risk in itself, consisting of a nearly unlimited number of specific risks depending on the particular business's structure and the climate in which it operates. Put simply, risk managers apply their knowledge of market conditions and a company's situation so as to minimize the amount of damage that could result from risk exposure. This usually involves appropriating exposure and insurance coverage in order to prevent or control losses in as efficient a manner as possible.

The risk manager is an insurance broker who advises clients on insurance and risk, an independent consultant on risk working for a fee, or a salaried employee who manages risk for the employer. The profession's largest trade group, the Risk and Insurance Management Society, Inc. (RIMS), based in New York, defines a risk management service provider as anyone who protects an organization's financial and physical assets; buys insurance/risk transfer products for an organization; manages an employee benefit program; administers a self-funded property/casualty and/or employee benefits insurance program; or buys risk control services from independent suppliers.

Risk managers and risk management services first identify what the organization potentially may lose. In a

U.S. Businesses Improving Continuity Planning, May 2010*

Business Continuity in Place	83%
Wireless Network Capabilities Part of Plan	63%
Employee Use of Mobile Devices a Factor in Choosing Plan	77%
Computing Infrastructure Virtualized	50%
Require Outside Suppliers to have BCPs in place	40%
Concern about Social Networks' Impact on Security	75%
Investing in New Technologies in 2010	70%

*Businesses surveyed had annual revenues above $10 million and most had locations outside the United States

SOURCE: AT&T.

disaster such as a chemical spill or fire, the company can lose physical property, such as buildings, vehicles, and equipment; it can lose income, since it is unable to do business while things are rebuilt or replaced; it can also lose personnel to a disaster. Employees would not necessarily need to die or be severely injured for the company to suffer losses. Whenever employees miss work and draw benefits, the employer pays for it. Another potential risk is liability. If the company produces something that accidentally harms its customers, the company could be liable for damages.

Risk control is intended to stop losses before they occur. One risk control technique is exposure avoidance, which means abandoning or not engaging in an activity that could bring a loss. For instance, a company might stop manufacturing children's pajamas with asbestos fibers. Loss prevention reduces the chance that loss could occur, while loss reduction involves efforts to lessen the severity of a loss, such as disaster planning. Another technique is the segregation of loss exposure: spreading valuable assets to avoid being wiped out by one bad move. Examples of segregation are splitting up the company's inventory in different warehouses or sending its delivery trucks along different routes so that if an accident occurs in one location, the company will not lose everything. Another form of risk control is contractual transfer, which shifts some legal and financial loss to another party. This is done by leasing or subcontracting risky activities such as toxic chemical transport to another firm, which then shares the liability for a mishap.

Risk financing means paying for the losses that *did* occur, and this is done by either transfer or retention. Companies transfer losses by sharing responsibility for risks with other parties, such as contractors, or by taking out insurance policies with commercial insurance providers. Insurance generally covers property risks, liability risks, and transportation risks. Transfers completed without commercial insurance carriers often involve paying into a mutual insurance arrangement or "pool" maintained by other organizations sharing similar risks. In contrast, companies retain losses by paying for their own losses themselves through establishment of special funds or taking out loans.

The simplest form of retention is current expensing of losses, which means paying for the loss like any other current expense. Other methods involve using an unfunded loss reserve, such as noting the loss as a potential liability to be paid later or using a funded loss reserve, which draws from a company fund set aside for that reason. The company might also borrow the money to pay for the loss. The most complex retention method involves the use of a captive insurer, a private insurance carrier owned by the company and used to insure itself and its international subsidiaries. Many U.S. Fortune 1000 companies own captive insurance companies, and set them up offshore in locations such as Bermuda.

BACKGROUND AND DEVELOPMENT

Risk management is a relatively new industry, though the practice of risk management is as old as business itself. The industry really developed in the 1980s and 1990s amidst surging economic booms. Insurance brokers in particular poured into risk management consulting as companies took advantage of strong markets to purchase less insurance, seek alternate financing sources such as captives, and lean towards longer term agreements with insurers, leaving brokers with less commission and thus hungry for new business.

Particularly among the economy's largest firms, executives are leaning toward the retention of greater amounts of risk in order to save on traditional insurance, a trend that carries with it a greater responsibility for and awareness of risk exposure and how to manage it. One of the most popular methods of funding alternative financing is through some form of self-insurance.

The cost of risk steadily declined through much of the economic expansion of the 1990s, partly as a result of improved "loss control." The trend, however, reversed in 1998 and 1999, when greater retained losses and flat premiums pushed the cost up to $5.71 per $1,000 of revenue, equal to the 1996 level, from its low point of $5.25 in 1997.

As risk managers analyzed potential new problems, the insurance industry responded with even more products. As more companies did business on the Internet, some mistakenly assumed their existing general liability policies covered losses accrued from electronic transactions. As the information superhighway expanded, more risk managers also had to plan for telecommuters. In addition, as more of the work force sat at computers,

55 percent of risk managers reported higher ergonomic repetitive motion claims, although 73 percent said their companies had programs to reduce the problem.

Leading up to the year 2000 date change and the unknown potential consequences of the Y2K computer bug, President Bill Clinton signed into law a bill, for which the Risk and Insurance Management Society (RIMS) lobbied heavily, to protect U.S. businesses from severe legal costs by limiting lawsuits related to the computer date change. While the more apocalyptic fears proved unfounded as the crucial date passed, the legislation freed up a good deal of risk managers' activities, which could have been devoted almost exclusively to Y2K risk management through late 1999 (and well into 2000, if things had indeed fallen apart).

The early 2000s brought austere conditions for the risk management industry, including high losses and unfavorable pricing. The terrorist attacks of September 11, 2001, raised consciousness about business liability in site-specific catastrophes and ushered in new categories of risk coverage. The destruction from those events triggered the biggest insurance losses in history. Under the Terrorism Risk Insurance Act of 2002, insurance carriers, with certain backing from the U.S. government, were required to offer several lines of policies to address officially designated acts of terrorism. While the industry watched closely, many risk managers did not find the terms of the new policies all that favorable and chose to decline such coverage. Terrorism most often fit into a much larger risk scenario so by 2003 quite a few managers reported that it was not their top concern because they had already made allowances for events of that nature.

As global trade flourishes, so do issues of intellectual property rights, such as trademarks, patents, and copyrights, and the means of securing their protection. Such intangible assets are assuming greater primacy in the global economy with the development of technology and the accelerating pace of patent grants. Licensing revenues from patents were expected to reach $500 billion in 2005 compared with $100 billion in 1998. The range of patents is also expanding, now including everything from software designs to production methods, rather than simply new, physical inventions.

The boundaries between previously demarcated professions such as loss adjusters and risk managers were also rapidly dissolving. Loss adjusters have witnessed their activities expand from simply sorting out losses following a claim to preventing the claim from occurring in the first place. In this case, firms are increasingly realizing the efficiency potential of more holistic risk management. Insurance companies hoping to maintain a strong footing are thus forced to diversify their services

to include the expedient allocation and coverage of various exposures.

In January 2003, *Best's Review* reported that American International Group's American International Companies was offering the Workplace Assurance product allowing insureds access to the services of Citigate Global Intelligence & Security, a security and workplace violence response company. The Workplace Violence Institute has estimated that costs of related incidents exceed $36 billion annually. Workplace Assurance covers consultant costs and related expenses such as lost salary, medical costs, informant rewards and security measures, plus dismemberment/ death benefits and business interruption. It was initially being introduced in the United States, the United Kingdom, and Europe.

The rising costs of workers' compensation premiums have been an ongoing concern of risk managers. In 2003, California's laws were a particular target of some risk managers, but new legislation in 2006 addressed some of the concerns. At that time, around 1,500 employee complaints were filed every day in the United States. New rules issued by the Occupational Safety and Health Administration (OSHA) extending benefits stemming from ergonomic injuries added to the number of claims. To reduce costs, many companies were taking more risk, delving into insurance schemes that reward claims reduction.

The financial services industries provide some of risk management's best customers. Domestic and international banking systems and enterprises, facing massive deregulation and increased credit issuing, fell under greater scrutiny as regulatory bodies, such as the U.S. Federal Reserve and the Basel Committee for Banking Supervision of the Bank for International Settlements, noted the need for enhanced supervision and standardization of credit risk practices lest the more fluid and globalized financial markets suffer instability as a result of poorly managed risk exposures. Spurring the regulatory bodies into action regarding credit risk management were the disastrous effects of the Asian financial crisis of the late 1990s. As speculative bubbles grew in Southeast Asia, many companies protected their credit in the local economies, thereby increasing their risk exposure to the troubled economy

The Risk and Insurance Management Society (RIMS) expects more small and mid-sized companies to add risk managers to their staffs or to include risk management as part of the responsibility of these companies' chief financial officers or treasurers. Because of the trend toward risk management services among companies of all sizes, more insurance brokers are charging fees for their services instead of receiving commissions for selling insurance products.

The Internet posed a number of new risks as well. Risk managers began to quantify the hazards that lurk on the information superhighway with such computer viruses as the "Love Bug," which was transported to millions of computers in 2000 and cost companies in excess of $15 billion worldwide. Since then, costs have escalated. In February 2004, for example, a barrage of viruses gummed up corporate networks and drained as much as $83 billion from companies in lost time and recovery expenses. Assurex International, a leading industry player, reported that one-fifth of the Fortune 500 companies were victims of computer hackers in the late 1990s. Three-fourths of all respondents to the survey conducted by the Computer Security Institute and the U.S. Federal Bureau of Investigation (FBI) reported serious security breaches in their computer systems in 1999. With e-commerce becoming an ever-increasing integrated component of firms' operations, risk managers are taking strides to prevent any disruption of business due to new computer-based disasters.

During the 1990s, insurance carriers marketed products covering all calamities. Several carriers offered kidnapping and extortion policies, especially designed to cover a company's top executives and their families when traveling or living abroad. Some of these policies paid $25 million to $50 million for hostage negotiations. American International Group Inc. also offered political risk insurance for companies doing business abroad in case their overseas locations were nationalized or confiscated by an unexpected new government.

With periodic mega mergers and acquisitions in most major industries, risk managers were increasingly brought in as consultants to develop solutions to problems and obstacles that cropped up during the consolidation process. For example, risk managers on the buying end must examine a target company's insurance policies, expenditures, loss experience, and other agreements and policies that could affect the management of its risk and then find solutions to any hurdles discovered in managing the prospective company's risks. Aon Corporation, based in Chicago, offers insurance against hostile takeovers for smaller companies, and the policy covers up to $5 million in legal expenses to thwart an unwanted buyer.

In spring 2003, an outbreak of Severe Acute Respiratory Syndrome (SARS) in Canada led to debate about whether property decontamination costs would be covered by insurance if facilities in the U.S. were ever subjected to a SARS cleanup. Although many industry experts said no, Aon argued in a report that Environmental Impairment Liability Insurance may offer coverage depending on "specific policy language and how it defines a pollution condition, since the International Organization for Standardization (ISO) has not developed an environmental liability policy."

The role of enterprise risk management, or ERM, had moved from being a trendy concept to becoming a necessary part of growing a business. An attempt to account for all forms of a company's risk, including operational, financial, employment, hazard, and strategic, under one portfolio, ERM was born of companies' evolving view of risk from separate exposures to a collective risk the company must face holistically. ERM began as more of a novelty, though the practice has expanded, led particularly by the financial services industries.

ERM has been described as "the systematic management of all of the direct and indirect risks within a bank." A survey by Deloitte & Touche revealed that around 81 percent of global financial institutions had established the new position of "chief risk officer," by 2006, up from 65 percent of companies in 2002. Seventy-five percent of the chief risk officers (CROs) report directly to the CEO, who realizes that the hands-on approach is the best way to manage a growing laundry list of risks surrounding banking. The interesting thing about ERM is that it expresses risk as an opportunity as well as a threat. When a penalty that comes with risk can be avoided, more risk can be taken, which can lead to more profit. Some of the goals of ERM are to run a bank where risk is mitigated, loss is compensated, employees share the company's values, and compliance is so expected that regulators sign off without having to check.

Enterprise risk management (ERM) became a top priority for many companies because of advances in technology, the accelerating pace of business, globalization, the possibility of terrorist attacks, and menaces that come out of nowhere—Hurricane Katrina, for example. Strong endorsements from chief regulators also propelled ERM onto the front burner for many companies. RIMS announced that they planned to become a "premiere resource and support organization" for ERM programs. In an e-mail survey of 1,054 deputy risk managers in March of 2005, nearly 38 percent of respondents either had an ERM program or were preparing to implement one.

In its October 2008 issue of *Risk Management,* the Risk and Insurance Management Society (RIMS) addressed risks that "ten years ago . . . were barely on the radar of most organizations." Some of these risks included hackers accessing companies' confidential files or infecting their networks with viruses, "cyberwarfare," blackouts, and "gray markets," whereby counterfeit goods are produced and sold over the Internet. Identity theft, whereby a person uses someone else's identity without his or her knowledge in order to commit crime, was also a major concern. In August 2008 federal authorities arrested a group of eleven hackers that had hacked into several major companies' computer systems and stole and sold more than 40 million credit and debit card numbers. Some of the companies affected included retailers OfficeMax, Barnes and Noble, Boston Market, and Sports Authorities, among others.

According to the Federal Trade Commission, more than 27 million Americans were victims of identity theft between 2003 and 2007, and by August 2008 the number of data breaches reported to the Identity Theft Resource Center, a nonprofit organization, had already surpassed 2007's figure. To combat these threats, companies turned increasingly to risk management firms for protection. However, even the organizations providing the protection were not totally safe. For example, during 2008 an identity theft protection company called LifeLock published its CEO's social security number in advertisements to emphasize how effective the company was at protecting his identity. However, during the campaign, the CEO's identity was stolen several times.

In 2008 the Federal Trade Commission added the "Red Flag" rules to the Fair and Accurate Transactions Act of 2003. The Red Flag rules imposed new regulations that required businesses to "define procedures for detecting, preventing, and mitigating identity theft," according to *Business Wire*. U.S. firms had until November 1 to become compliant with the new rules.

CURRENT CONDITIONS

At the close of the first decade (2010), the rise and sophistication of Internet communications for business transactions affected nearly all business enterprises, and computer security software could hardly keep up with new versions of worms, viruses, malware, spyware, and botware. Additionally, the global economic crisis of 2008 and 2009 placed multinational companies and global traders at heightened risk for foreign exchange rate fluctuations, compounded by foreign sovereign instability. Somalian pirates went on a rampage in 2009 and 2010, seizing international cargo vessels and demanding huge (multi-million dollar) ransoms. The 2010 U.S. Gulf Coast BP oil spill brought one-fourth of the country to nearly an economic standstill for three months, and international terrorist threats continued to grab headlines following several aborted attempts to harm Western countries and Western interests. All this caused many companies to develop what is termed "business continuity" plans as part of risk management assessment and response packages.

In a survey by the Business Continuity Institute conducted between November 20, 2009, and January 14, 2010, 94 percent of selected business respondents (220) said their organizations had experienced some level of disruption in the preceding 12 months. The top five events were swine flu, IT and/or Telecom disruption, adverse weather, lack of energy supply, and computer virus/cyber attacks.

For an AT&T study published in May 2010, surveyed businesses were chosen from those with annual revenues above $10 million and (most) also having locations outside the United States. Eighty-three percent of respondents stated that they had a business continuity plan in place, up 14 percent since 2005. A reported 63 percent of business included wireless network capabilities as part of their plan and 77 percent indicated that use of mobile devices by employees had been factored into their plans. About 50 percent had virtualized their computing infrastructure, and 40 percent required outside suppliers or vendors to have BCPs in place as a criterion for doing business with them. Roughly 75 percent of executives expressed concern about the increased use of social networking capabilities and mobile networks/devices and their potential impact on security threats. Seventy percent indicated they would be investing in new technologies during 2010.

Findings of a comprehensive 2010 edition of CSI's annual Computer Crime and Security Survey showed that respondents reported sharp rises in password sniffing, financial fraud, and malware infection. Notwithstanding, average losses resulting from security incidents again fell (from $289,000 to $234,244 per respondent), although still above 2006 figures. One-third of respondents' organizations were fraudulently represented as the senders of phishing messages, but 25 percent of overall respondents believed that the majority of their financial losses were due to non-malicious actions by insiders. A previous CSI survey had reported that the most prevalent security problem was insider abuse of network access or e-mail, an incident that 59 percent of the companies experienced. Virus incidents occurred at 52 percent of companies.

In its September 2009 "Top Cyber Security Risks" report, the SANS Institute noted that two risks dwarfed all others: client software that remained unpatched, and Web sites that were vulnerable. In the former, targeted e-mail attacks, such as spear phishing, were using commonly used programs, such as Adobe PDF Reader, QuickTime, Adobe Flash, and Microsoft Office, as the primary infection venues to compromise computers with Internet access. The infected computers were then used to propagate the infection and compromise other internal computers and sensitive servers. On average, noted the report, major organizations took at least twice as long to patch client vulnerabilities as they did to patch operating system vulnerabilities. Internet site, attacks against web applications constituted nearly two-thirds of attack attempts discovered on the Internet. Vulnerabilities, such as SQL Injection or Cross-Site Scripting, account for the majority. Web site owners failed to scan effectively and became unwitting vehicles to infect visitors who trusted their sites.

INDUSTRY LEADERS

One of the leading insurance brokerages offering risk management consulting was Marsh, Inc., a subsidiary of Marsh & McLennan Companies (MMC). Under MMC, Marsh operated as the retail brokerage unit, and Guy Carpenter & Co. was the reinsurance brokerage unit. Marsh had nearly 30,000 employees and annual revenues exceeding $5 billion. It offers global risk management, risk consulting, insurance brokering, financial solutions, and insurance program management services for businesses, public entities, associations, professional services organizations, and private clients in over 100 countries. Marsh generates over half of its revenues outside the United States, mainly in Asia, Europe, and South America. The company was aggressively working to gain mid-sized clients. *Risk Management* revealed that the insurance world's focus on the risks of maritime shipping were heightened by piracy in Southeast Asia and coastal Africa as well as terrorism in the Persian Gulf region and bad weather. In response, Marsh introduced an online service for marine cargo insurance customers called MarshCargo. Marsh Inc. reported 2009 revenues of $4.32 billion, while Guy Carpenter & Co. reported 2009 revenues of $911 million. MMC's risk consulting and technology segment reported a 27.7 percent drop in revenues of $668 million.

Aon Corporation, based in Chicago, whose name means "oneness" in Gaelic, is another large provider of risk management services, with 47,000 employees working in over 500 offices in 120 countries. Aon acquired the brokerage Alexander & Alexander Services, another risk management consultant, in 1996, and the combined firm provides risk management to companies worldwide through a subsidiary, Aon Risk Services, Inc. Like Marsh, Aon spent the rest of the 1990s in a consolidation frenzy, teaming with Zurich U.S. to establish RiskAttack, a risk management enterprise geared specifically toward mid-sized technology firms. The company was hit severely in the September 11, 2001, terrorist attacks, as it had a large presence in the World Trade Center and lost nearly 200 employees. In a letter dated September 10, 2005, Aon outlined the many tributes that had been made to lost colleagues. These included gifts and various fundraising activities, such as *Running to Remember,* a benefit established by marathon runners in New York and Chicago with participants and benefactors from around the globe. From such activities, Aon raised $3,250,000 for the Aon Memorial Education Fund, established to help families pay for the educational needs of victims' children. By 2006, 40 students had benefited by being able to go beyond secondary education and 10 had graduated. *Business Insurance* reported former New York Mayor Rudy Giuliani's firm had partnered with Aon to offer security and crisis management consulting services. In 2010, Aon announced a pending merger with Hewitt Associates, Inc., under a newly createed Aon Hewitt brand. The new brand offered not only risk mitigation but also the develooment and execution of a pension plan exit strategy through an independent platform. Aon Hewitt had 29,000 colleagues globally with combined revenues of $4.3 billion in 2009.

American International Group, Inc. (AIG) of New York, one of the world's largest international insurance organizations, has offices in 130 countries, and 40 percent of its revenues come from outside the United States. In 2007, AIG's revenues reached $110.0 billion and it employed 116,000 people. AIG suffered severely from the subprime mortgage crisis and in 2008 agreed to a $85 billion bailout by the U.S. government. (As of 2009, U.S. government loans to AIG totaled more than $180 billion.) However, by 2010, the company was gaining ground; assets under management grew to $235 billion as of March 31, 2010, and AIG reported $1.5 billion of net income.

A good deal of networking paid off for United States-based Assurex International in 1999 when it partnered with Europe's Synergy groups to create the world's largest private insurance brokerage group, specializing in risk management services and global insurance. Providing an umbrella organization for some of the largest independent brokerages around the world, the Assurex/Synergy alliance helps firms assess and manage global risks by drawing on the knowledge of its local partners in the context of the alliance's international specialization. Assurex, collectively with its partners, has more than 20,000 professionals serving at 130 independently owned insurance brokers on six continents, and generates annual premiums in excess of $21 billion.

WORKFORCE

In late 2008, the Risk and Insurance Management Society (RIMS), the industry's leading trade group, had 10,700 members engaged in all types of risk management around the world. Because their work has such sweeping financial implications for companies and because they need highly specialized knowledge and skills, risk managers command relatively high salaries. According to an annual survey of risk managers by Logic Associates, in 2003, risk professionals at companies with sales of $200 million or less earned an average of $88,875 a year. Companies with sales of $2 billion to $4 billion typically have risk management departments with professional workers who report to the chief financial officer. Companies with $4 billion to $7 billion in annual sales usually have risk management departments with four professional workers, while those with sales of over $7 billion have staffs of five or more. Risk managers' salaries at top companies average well over $200,000 and sizable bonuses are common as well. Moreover, about 90 percent of risk managers at the largest companies enjoyed stock options, compared with only 43 percent at companies with sales less than $200 million.

Other professional organizations include the Risk Management Association, which concentrates on risk in the financial services sector, and the Global Association of Risk Professionals, which has an international focus. A wealth of even more specialized bodies exist, including the Business Continuity Institute, the Fiduciary and Investment Risk Management Association, the Public Agency Risk Managers Association, and the Weather Risk Management Association.

AMERICA AND THE WORLD

U.S. risk managers often base a company's captive insurance office (one that can only write business for that company) in another state or country because of the tax advantage. The top U.S. states for captive insurance companies are Colorado, Illinois, Vermont, and Hawaii. Common offshore captive domiciles include Panama, Barbados, and Grand Cayman. The world leader for captive insurance companies is Bermuda with over 1,150 firms. Bermuda's liberal corporate tax laws also attract many global specialty insurance and reinsurance firms.

In a letter to the editor of *The Financial Times,* Compuware Vice President of the United Kingdom and Ireland Steve Jobson stressed the importance of having senior information technology (IT) management involved in risk management. "Business leaders are always quick to use IT to increase competitive advantages and make efficiency gains. However, they need to realise that IT is central to business operations and therefore put in place risk management strategies to ensure that IT failures become a thing of the past," wrote Jobson.

In 2006, following a high-profile investigation of the president of Livedoor Co., a Japanese Internet business, for violating securities laws, institutions in Asia and around the world began looking for custodians to assist in their risk management issues. About 80 percent of the 76 larger pension funds and nonprofit companies surveyed in 2005 said that although market risk is still a high priority, they plan to focus most of their attention on dealing with operational risks. Because it would be too costly and time-consuming for institutional investors to assess risk in-house, many are turning to firms that specialize in risk management analysis, such as Financial Insights, a Framingham, Massachusetts-based consulting firm.

RESEARCH AND TECHNOLOGY

Good risk managers should recognize their own risks as well as those of their clients. In that spirit, risk management institutions were trying to minimize their chances of losing or mishandling information crucial to their operations. A particularly popular remedy was the connected network backup (CNB) system from Connected Corp., which manages and protects electronic information assets. In the event of a computer or network malfunction, the CNB system is designed to retrieve lost information from its automatic backup copy. With the rapidly expanding percentage of work force engaged in telecommuting, and with more information stored electronically, such network protections are becoming an increasingly central part of a company's operating costs.

Along with the rise of e-commerce has come the inevitable rise of e-commerce fraud, another new risk source that companies have grown anxious about. Since firms are less able to avoid the Internet as a marketing source if they hope to remain competitive, the high fraud rate, estimated at between 4 and 25 percent of all online transactions, is nonetheless unable to keep them from the cyber marketplace. CyberSource Corp., a leading provider of online risk management services, developed its CyberSource Internet Fraud Screen to reduce the risk from this hazard. The program was designed to quickly calculate risk assessments and allow online merchants to convert orders to sales while minimizing customer service overhead.

Also in the later years of the first decade of the 2000s, companies were developing technological products to help protect against identity theft and fraud. For example, the Cyveillance Identity Theft Protection package was, according to an *InDefense* article, "a patented technology platform that helps organizations 'substantially reduce fraud claims' by proactively monitoring the Internet for compromised credit and debit card numbers, as well as sensitive personal information." This was just one of many risk management products offered on the market for both businesses and individuals. For example, in October 2008 Symantec Corp. announced that Data Loss Prevention Version 9.0, a software program designed to prevent data loss, would be available in early 2009. The new program addresses such increasing concerns as the effects of employees working remotely by covering data loss that begins at the endpoint.

BIBLIOGRAPHY

"AIG Reports $1.5 Billion of Nete Income." *Insurance News,* April 2010. Available from http://insurancenewsnet.com/article.aspx.

"Aon Completes Merger With Hewitt Associates." Press Release, 1 October 2010. Available from http://www.aon.com.

"Aon's Implemented Investment Consulting Reaches the $1 Billion Mark in Total U.S. Assets Under Management for 2010." Press Release, 26 August 2010. Available from http://www.aon.com.

"AT&T Study: U.S. Businesses Improving Continuity Planning."
28 May 2010. Available from http://www.prnewswire.

Bartlett, David, and Larry Smith. "Managing a Data Loss
Crisis." *Risk Management,* June 2008.

"The Business Case for BCM." Business Continuity Institute,
2010.

Coffin, Bill, Pearl Gabel, Morgan O'Rourke, and Jared Wade.
"Digital Risk Trends 2008." *Risk Management,* October 2008.

Computer Security Institute. *CSI/FBI Computer Crime and
Security Survey,* 2009. Available from http://gocsi.com/survey.

"Cyveillance Launches Web Service to Prevent Identify Theft."
InDefense, 13 December 2006.

"Global Financial Crisis Creates Unprecedented Need for
Enhanced Risk Management." *CNW Group,* 8 October 2008.

Groenfeldt, Tom. "Opportunities in Risk: Custodians Are
Offering Risk Assessment and Risk Management Services to
Institutional Investors." *Institutional Investor,* March 2006.

"International Business Continuity Program Management
Benchmarking Report." BC Management Inc., July 2009.

"MicroBilt Guarantees Red Flag Identity Theft Prevention."
Business Wire, 11 August 2008.

"MMC Reports Profit for 2009, Revenues Decline." *Business
Insurance,* 10 February 2010.

"Perceived Risk Management Failings Are Driving Spending
Spree." *Financial Adviser,* 25 September 2008.

Peterson, James R. "Ready for ERM: If Risk Management Is
New Religion, Enterprise Risk Management Is Its Mantra."
ABA Banking Journal, January 2006.

Quinley, Kevin. "Identity Theft: How Do We Manage the
Risk?" *Claims,* April 2007.

"Risk: Old-Style Risk Management Is No Longer Enough."
Credit Union Journal, 29 September 2008.

"Symantec Strengthens Protection Against Data Loss at the
Endpoint." *Internet Wire,* 7 October 2008.

Tuohy, Cyril. "ERM Makes Inroads with Carriers." *Risk &
Insurance,* 15 September 2008.

ROBOTICS AND INDUSTRIAL AUTOMATION

—■—

SIC CODE(S)

3541

3542

3535

3559

3569

INDUSTRY SNAPSHOT

Whether it was a matter of "Roomba," iRobot's little $200 self-propelled, self-guided vacuum cleaner, or the Rover Spirit, part of NASA's multimillion-dollar space exploration project of the surface on Mars, it was clear that the robots of the middle of the twenty-first century's first decade continued to perform functions once contemplated exclusively for humans. Previously relegated to executing specific tasks that were responsive to programmed commands, many new-age robots are now capable of acting as autonomous systems possessing their own independent artificial reasoning skills. This opens a whole new world of possible applications for this dynamic, competitive industry.

While the vast majority of robots so far are used in manufacturing, service robots are expected to be more commercially viable and meaningful. These devices won't resemble the intelligent android "bots" featured in movies and science fiction, but they will likely be harnessed in commercial settings for everyday tasks such as vacuuming and mowing lawns. In medicine, robotic limbs help amputees re-orient themselves to simple life functions such as walking or grasping, while in manufacturing, robotic machinery continues to replace human power in performing dangerous, tedious, or repetitive assembly line work.

ORGANIZATION AND STRUCTURE

Industry Makeup The robotics and industrial automation industry is made up of companies that produce robots and other industrial automation machines (including accessories such as "grippers" or "hands"); those that supply the software that controls them; and others, called system integrators, that bring the pieces together for a specific application for a specific customer. The 2009 issue of the *Robotics Industry Directory,* published by the Robotic Industries Association, listed 270 suppliers of robots and related automation products. The association's members included manufacturers, distributors, system integrators, accessory suppliers, research groups, and consultant firms.

A small number of large corporations, most headquartered outside the United States, manufacture most of the world's robots and industrial automation systems. The larger number of mid-size and small companies, however, focusing on the needs of a specific industry or application, has expanded the frontiers of robotics. Typically, the automation supplier and the customer work closely together to develop a system to meet the specific requirements of the application and site.

The industry's customers are primarily manufacturing companies, with the automotive industry being the largest segment. Each year, more and more manufacturers in other industries such as food processing, electronics, and consumer goods invest in robotics and other automation systems. Semiconductor manufacturers are another important market segment. These companies use robots for such applications as welding, assembling parts, and transporting materials in the manufacturing process. In general, robots appeal to industry in two situations: first, when they can perform a task faster and more accurately than humans (in some cases, tasks impossible or unsafe for humans), and secondly, when they are more cost-effective. Other fields, such as medicine, have increasingly taken interest in robotics technology.

Industry Nuts and Bolts Robots are classified by function as either industrial or non-industrial (domestic/service). Industrial robots are used primarily on assembly lines. Robots with grippers perform tasks such as loading and unloading presses and other machines. A second type can use its grippers to manipulate tools and spray paint, weld, grind, drill, or rivet. Non-industrial robots perform an entirely different range of services. For example, police departments use robots to detect bombs. This practice reduces the dangers that human officers might face in locating and defusing explosives. A Japanese university has developed a robot that simulates a human jawbone. The robot emulates human chewing motions, which the researchers hope will help them develop new dental treatments. A California-based manufacturer has invented a robot that performs hip replacements in dogs. Other companies have created robots that can patrol buildings as security guards, lift briefcases, open doors, pour drinks for wheelchair-bound people, and clean washrooms. Of course, the National Aeronautics and Space Administration used robots to traverse the Moon and Mars.

Thus far, there have been three generations of robots, each of which shows an increasing ability to accomplish more difficult tasks. Although some boast complex features, many amount to little more than electronic arms. In some cases, each ensuing generation of robots is simply a more state-of-the-art arm. For instance, there are robotic arms today equipped with tools to assist surgeons in performing delicate operations—a far cry from the primitive first generation of robots.

Industrial robots (such as information and painting robots and robots for education and automation in injection mold and welding lines) comprised the first generation of robots. Some were used in semiconductor and disk assembly, wafer inspection, and wafer disk carriers. The second generation gave birth to cleaning robots, security robots, and intelligent and assembly robots. As technology advanced, a third generation appeared. This group included more advanced service robots. This time, they did more than clean. They were personal robots. There were also medical/welfare robots used for rehabilitation and support for the elderly. In addition, this generation introduced cellular, navigational, biped, multi-arm and finger, and harvesting robots. Some featured artificial intelligence. There were also space robots,

micro-robots for bionics, robots to work in hazardous environments, and maintenance robots.

Robots are dependent to a great extent on developments in computers. Like computers, their intelligence control systems are based on microprocessors. These systems provide continuous two-way communication between the robot's microprocessor and the arms. Whether the robots are classified as "playback" or "sequence" types, they rely on their microprocessors for directions.

Playback robots are capable of memorizing and repeating movements programmed by human operators. Sequence robots are less expensive than playback robots since manufacturers build their programs directly into the machines. Often, these robots move from point to point or from one assembly station to another. In either case, they work at a lower cost than humans, which accounts for their growing popularity. Comparisons between humans and robots on a typical production line suggest that robots far outperform humans at less cost overall. Moreover, they can function in places that pose hazards to humans. These advantages account for the surge in the number of industrial robots currently in place and the increasing number predicted to be installed in the near future.

Researchers work constantly to upgrade the quality and efficiency of robots. They concentrate primarily on true robots for industrial use. A true robot operates independently and automatically from a self-contained program built into it. There is also a class of robots called telecherics, which are human-operated machines. These machines can possess many features of a true robot, but they are always under human direction by cable or radio links. They serve such purposes as handling radioactive or explosive materials and sample specimens on the ocean floor. In all cases, though, operators behind the scenes must manipulate them. They are not as numerous as true robots.

True robots are generally stationary industrial robots located in factories. Early models handled assignments such as welding or painting that posed hazards to humans. These robots tend to be cumbersome. Researchers have developed a new generation of light duty and inspection robots that address different problems. Modern true robots carry out monotonous, repetitive tasks with a high degree of precision. Some share work with human workers. Ironically, contemporary robots look nothing like the "creatures" portrayed in early movies, literature, and plays. Researchers have developed a new breed of robots with manipulators (the arms that define the machines' capabilities); controllers (the components that store information, instructions, and programs used to direct the manipulators' movements); and power supplies that drive the manipulators, which are smaller and more efficient than their forerunners. They have also improved on robots' degrees of freedom, geometrical configurations, and envelopes.

Degrees of Freedom A robot's applications and flexibility are determined by its number of degrees of freedom (the number of movements it can perform). Many industrial-type robots are limited by sequence nature. That is, they are restricted to a low number of movements. The degrees of freedom are related closely to the robot's geometrical configuration.

Geometrical Configuration Industrial robots feature four principal geometrical configurations: articulated, revolute or jointed-armed; spherical (also called polar coordinate); rectangular (or Cartesian); and cylindrical. They can also be vertically jointed, horizontally mounted, and/or gantry or overhead mounted.

Envelope A robot's envelope is the three-dimensional contour formed by the motion of the end effector (a device used to produce a desired change in an object in response to input, such as a gripper), or wrist, moved completely through the outer limits of motion.

As computers become more powerful, researchers make more changes to robots' degrees of freedom, geometrical configurations, and envelopes. That in turn means robots will become more flexible and capable of more advanced functions. In only one-quarter of a century, researchers have made remarkable strides in robotics technology. Thus the development of and need for advanced robots will continue to grow—as will the industrial automation industry.

BACKGROUND AND DEVELOPMENT

In the 1890s, Nikola Tesla built the first radio-controlled vehicles in response to his vision of smart mechanisms that could emulate human movements. These were known as "automatons" until 1921, when a Czech novelist and playwright, Karel Capek, featured robots in his play as *R.U.R.*, short for "Rossum's Universal Robots." The term "robot" comes from the Czech word *robota*, which translates loosely into "serf" or compulsory labor. The word caught people's fancy, but robots did not exist in any great number outside the human imagination. It was not until the 1940s that true robots became reality. They were closely tied to the invention of computers.

Serious robot research began in the late 1950s when George Devol and Joe Engelberger developed the first industrial modern robots, known as Unimates. Devol earned the first patents for parts transfer machines. Engelberger formed Unimation, Inc., the first company to market robots, and consequently he has been called the father of robotics.

In the late 1960s, researchers at the Stanford Research Institute produced the first robot prototype, an experimental robot called Shakey. This machine processed information via a small computer and was capable of arranging blocks into stacks through the use of a television camera, which it used as a visual sensor. By itself, Shakey was not especially useful. It did, however, encourage other researchers to pursue useful functions for robots.

General Motors Corp. (GM) teamed up with the Massachusetts Institute of Technology (MIT) in the mid-1970s to develop robots. Using GM funds, MIT researcher Victor Scheinman refined a motor-driven arm he had invented. His work led to the production of a programmable universal manipulator for assembly, which marked the beginning of the so-called robot age. Because success in developing industrial robots did not come easily, there were failures galore in the early stages of experimentation.

In the early 1980s, robotics was expected to be the "next industrial revolution." Zymark Corp. produced the first robots manufactured specifically for use in a laboratory in 1982. A few years later, Perkin-Elmer Corp. introduced the MasterLab and Fisher Scientific Co. offered the MAXX 5, but neither was successful and both projects were dropped. In 1985, U.S.-based companies reported orders for a record 6,200 robots. Large corporations, such as General Electric Co. (GE), IBM Corp., and Westinghouse, got into the robotics business, along with many smaller companies.

In the mid-1980s, however, the boom turned to bust when the huge market that had been predicted failed to materialize. The big-name companies shut down robot operations and many smaller companies merged or went out of business. The automobile industry accounted for more than 70 percent of robot orders, and cutbacks in that sector's capital investment had devastating consequences. New orders for robots fell to just 3,700 in 1987.

Between 1987 and 1992, robot manufacturers improved the reliability and performance of their products, which would help to establish them in industries other than automotive. In 1991, Zymark introduced the XP robot, which featured programmable speeds and operated three times faster than other units in existence. That same year, Hewlett-Packard (HP) developed its Optimized Robot for Chemical Analysis, which used a special methods development language to operate. These machines revolutionized the laboratory robot industry and set the stage for important advances in the field. Robots were also developed for assembly, material handling, and many other applications.

Consistently thinking out of the box led to more Zymark and HP innovations in recent years. Zymark earned applause for "Allegro," which interconnects approximately 26 different modules or workstations with at least one robotic arm. HP's "travel robot" has a head with several flat-panel displays that show distant co-workers' faces and facial expressions to colleagues attending meetings in other cities.

Major technological factors on the horizon that boded well for the industry in the middle of the first decade of the 2000s were the development of PC-based control systems stimulated by the simultaneous development of low-cost, PC-based vision systems. Vision systems, along with improved sensor technology, increase the possibilities for robot applications in currently labor-intensive processes. A survey of robotics professionals in *Robotics World* magazine reported that the shift away from proprietary control systems toward an open architecture would also be an important part of the future. *The Futurist Magazine* said Sony-made AIBO, a metal jointed dog responding to ear strokings and expressing excitement around its rubber ball, reflected a new generation of robots able to feel identity data as pleasure or pain and respond appropriately.

CURRENT CONDITIONS

In February 2009, the Robotics Industry Association (RIA) released its Robotics Trends report which projected that, despite declining orders from the automotive industry and a sharp drop in orders at the end of 2008, U.S. robotics products manufacturers were expected to do well for the full 2009 year if they expanded beyond automakers and into consumer robotics, non-automated heavy industry, and service robotics. (The auto industry accounts for 51 percent of all RIA sales, according to association figures.) Orders from North American companies in 2008 were 21 percent lower than in 2007, reported the RIA, although total revenue from them dropped only 16 percent. Orders from outside North America improved slightly in 2008; however, there was a sharper drop in orders placed by North American companies during the fourth quarter of 2008. Those orders were 26 percent lower in unit sales, and brought in revenue 33 percent lower than the same period during 2007, according to the RIA.

The International Federation of Robotics estimated that total global spending on robotics surpassed $18 billion in 2008, with RIA members reporting 2008 revenues of $997 billion from North American companies. Sales outside the auto industry were looking up, with an increase in orders of 9 percent compared to 2007. The largest increase was in the semiconductor/electronics market, which increased orders 63 percent. Following this were orders from plastics and rubber companies at 39 percent. While still trailing in total unit sales, non-automotive sales topped sales to the auto industry for the first time ever, RIA president Jeffrey Burnstein said.

In 2008, Wintergreen Research estimated that the defense industry, which spent $441 million on robots in 2007, will increase spending to $43.7 billion by 2014. Medical and surgical robotics products generated about $626.5 million in 2007 and will grow to $14 billion by 2014, according to Wintergreen.

INDUSTRY LEADERS

The largest manufacturers of robots and industrial automation machines are multinational corporations such as ABB Ltd. of Zurich, Switzerland; FANUC Ltd., and Yaskawa Electric Corp., both of Japan; Thyssen AG of Germany; and Elsag Bailey Process Automation N.V. of the Netherlands. FANUC, Yaskawa, and Thyssen have U.S. subsidiaries. Rockwell International is the largest U.S.-based manufacturer of automation products, but not robots per se.

ABB ABB Ltd. is regarded as the world's top producer of robotics equipment. It is considered to be ahead of the industry curve with software packages for increasing efficiency and productivity such as a high-precision robot control system for laser cutting. A sprawling $30 billion engineering and industrial concern, ABB has sizable robotics operations in the United States through its ABB Flexible Automation Inc. subsidiary and other holdings. In 2003, robotics comprised approximately 14 percent of its total revenues. The company benefited from strong world demand and its 1999 acquisition of Netherlands-based Elsag Bailey, a large automation machinery maker in its own right. ABB had 2008 revenues of $34.9 billion and employed 103,500 employees.

FANUC FANUC Robotics America, Inc., of Rochester Hills, Michigan, was a subsidiary of Japan-based FANUC Ltd., generally regarded as the world's second largest robot manufacturer. Originally called GMFANUC Robotics Corp., the firm was founded in 1982 as a joint venture between General Motors and FANUC Ltd. It became a wholly owned subsidiary of FANUC in 1992. While created in part to supply the auto industry, FANUC Robotics North America has diversified to serve most U.S. industries requiring robotics technology. The parent company has two other U.S. subsidiaries: FANUC America Corp. and GE FANUC Automation, a joint venture with General Electric. Besides its joint venture with GE in the U.S., FANUC operates subsidiaries in Asia, Europe and North America. Fujitsu owns approximately 36 percent of FANUC. JH Robotics has designed and manufactured assembly lines with up to

10 FANUC robots in various applications. FANUC created an easier-to-assemble paint spray robot, which uses pneumatics to shape air flow and atomize paint spray and combines the control of analog and digital I/O cards, as well as solenoid valves, into one module." In 2009, FANUC and GE agreed to split, with FANUC retaining CNC operations, reporting $5.1 billion in revenues for 2008.

Rockwell Automation Rockwell Automation, formerly known as Rockwell International Corp., once a big defense contractor, is the largest U.S.-based industrial automation company. Between 1984 and 1998, it made more than 50 acquisitions and divested itself of 30 operations, getting out of the airframe, automotive components, and semiconductor businesses. In the middle of the first decade of the 2000s, automation accounted for more than 60 percent of sales. The company employed 21,000 people and had revenues of $5.69 billion in 2008.

Motoman Motoman, Inc., a subsidiary of Yaskawa Electric Manufacturing Co. of Japan, celebrated its 15th anniversary in 2004, with more than 22,500 robot installations by that time. Founded in 1989, the West Carrollton, Ohio, company was the second largest robotics company in the Americas.

Adept Technology Although it suffered setbacks in 1999 (in July of that year, the company acquired BYE/Oasis Engineering, a microelectronics manufacturer, to help it branch into new lines of business), Adept Technology had installed over 20,000 robots worldwide by 2005 and remains one of the United States' largest industrial robot producers. The San Jose, California-based manufacturer makes selective compliance assembly robot arms, or highly flexible multi-jointed robotic arms, for materials handling, assembly, and packaging. Other products include palletizing robots, robotic vision devices, and software.

PRI Automation PRI Automation, Inc., of Billerica, Massachusetts, is the leading U.S. supplier of automation systems for computer chip manufacturers, with 90 percent of the market. Its hardware and software automate the movement of silicon wafers between different steps of the manufacturing process, reducing the risk of error and contamination. Intel Corp. accounts for 21 percent of its sales. Other major customers include Advanced Micro Devices, Samsung, and Motorola.

Brooks Automation Another major supplier to the chip industry is Brooks Automation, Inc. Its equipment uses vacuum technology to move, align, and hold the silicon wafers in the manufacturing process. The company supplies about 90 percent of the vacuum robots used in the semiconductor industry. It is an important resource as the industry transitions to 300m technology. Partnerships were established with the top 20 semiconductor manufacturers. Three-fourths of its sales derive from tool automation while the rest comes from its factory automation products.

Other Leaders Other important U.S. robotics companies include Cognex Corp., the world's leading manufacturer of hardware and software systems that function as robot eyes in industrial and new non-industrial applications, with more than 100,000 vision systems shipped. Gerber Scientific, Inc., makes automated manufacturing systems for the apparel, optical, sign-making, and printing industries. Integrated Surgical Systems, Inc., makes a computer-controlled robot used in hip and knee replacements as well as other surgeries. Caliper Technologies Corp. is a leader in microfludic lab-on-a-chip technology.

WORKFORCE

Automation and robotics have a mixed effect on employment. Proponents argue that the increasing use of robots will add jobs. After all, there must be humans to design, build, and repair them. Opponents suggest otherwise. They say that more robots performing tasks heretofore carried out by humans will eliminate jobs. Early evidence sides with the proponents. The industry has generated more jobs in manufacturing, sales, and computer maintenance than it has eliminated. Although there are no hard figures at this point to substantiate either claim, it must be remembered that the robotics industry is in its infancy. In addition, since it is allied closely with the computer industry, there may be a spillover effect between the two.

The industrial automation and robotics industry is also linked with other industries in a symbiotic manner. For example, there is a close relationship with the computer-aided design and computer-aided manufacturing, bionics, and laser industries. Jobs and career paths abound in all these industries. There is a growing need for robotics specialists in almost every industry, including electronics, shipbuilding, construction, automobile manufacturing, aerospace, computers, and medical technology. *Refrigerated & Frozen Foods* reported that "many manufacturers of standard palletizing machines are adding robots to their product line-up." Furthermore, usage by industry giants such as Proctor & Gamble was felt to ensure success and acceptance of the technology. Job titles include robot programmer, robotics engineer, robotics repairperson, robotics designer, mechanical engineer, robot sales representative, robotics assembly supervisor, and robotics software writer, to name a few.

However, with new jobs come increased demands for new skills. This is where the escalating use of industrial robots has an impact on the labor force.

Workers need new skills to cope with the new robots. There has been a reduction in the number of semi-skilled workers as a result of industrial automation. The labor force needed in an automated plant requires skilled workers such as maintenance engineers, electricians, toolmakers, and computer programmers. Without such people, industry and robots cannot function. Thus, the increase in industrial automation and robots has created a demand for more training, without which neither industry nor robots can survive.

Machine Design reported that Oak Ridge National Laboratory researchers were working on a telerobotic manipulation system with great hazardous waste applications that can be operated remotely. *Design Engineering,* Kawasaki Heavy Industries, and the National Institute for Advanced Industrial Technology publicly demonstrated a jointly developed humanoid robot that can operate a hydraulic excavator and provide the human operator with special views via its camera.

AMERICA AND THE WORLD

According to the Robotics Industry Association (RIA) in its February 2009 report, the Japan Robotics Association estimated the market for personal and lifestyle robots, (including everything from Roomba vacuum cleaners to robot toys) totaled approximately $3 billion in 2008 and is expected to surpass $15 billion by 2015. Notwithstanding, sales of industrial robots dropped significantly in Korea and Japan in 2008, according to the IFR, which identifies the two as among the most robot-dependent economies on Earth.

The robotics industry in China experienced 14 percent growth in 2008, while India grew by 11 percent. Although sales slowed during the first half of 2008, it was not enough to offset the growth. Europe also increased its purchases of robots in 2007 by 15 percent as part of an effort to further automate automotive manufacturing. IFR projected global growth to increase in the metalworking industry, beverages, glass, pharmaceutical, medical devices and photovoltaic industries.

RESEARCH AND TECHNOLOGY

At the 2009 China International Industry Fair (CIIF) industry leader ABB launched the Dragon IRB 120, the world's smallest robot ever, as well as the fastest six-axis industrial robot. Weighing just 25kg and mountable at any angle, even in an upside down or wall-mounted position, the Dragon was touted as achieving an outstanding degree of operating accuracy at 0.01mm, thinner than a single hair. It was the most accurate six-axis robot in the world. During the testing process complying with all ISO international standards, its technical performance in terms of accuracy was beyond the detectable limit of the laser-guided testing instrument in the laboratory.

While advances in robotics will be driven by potential applications, one thing is certain. Robots that will interact with humans will increasingly be constructed to resemble human beings in appearance and movement. The new breed of service robots will likely have artificial skin and muscles, in addition to the "seeing eye" capability already developed. In early 2004, the University of Tokyo reported advances in creating a flexible artificial skin constructed of several layers of a plastic film, a rubbery material, and a thin metallic layer. The artificial skin is embedded with 1,000 organic transistors that can sense pressure. "This will be bigger than the automobile market in 20 years," stated Dr. Takayasu Sakurai, professor at the University's Institute of Industrial Science, in a 2004 article appearing in the *Christian Science Monitor.* Dr. Sakurai said that as the artificial skin was perfected over the next 5 to 10 years, price would drop to approximately $10 per square foot.

BIBLIOGRAPHY

"ABB Launches China-developed Dragon Robot at the 2009 CIIF." *Robotics Trends,* 17 March 2009.

Alston, Barry. "This Robot Could Milk Your Cows While You Go Off to Work." *Farmers Guardian,* 17 January 2003.

Babyak, Richard J. "A Touch Better: Tactile Sensing Coming for Robotics." *Appliance Manufacturer,* May 2003.

Burnstein, Jeff. "North American Robotics Orders Rise 20 Percent in 2004." *Robotics Online,* 14 February 2005. Available from www.roboticsonline.com.

Campbell, Joe. "Assembly Robots 101." *Medical Design News,* 2003. Available from www.medicaldesignnews.com.

"Carnegie Mellon Cooks Up Internet-Ready Robot Recipes." *PC Magazine Online,* 25 April 2007.

Cristol, Hope. "Robots with Emotions." *The Futurist,* March/April 2003.

"The Face of Robotics in UK Industry: David Marshall, Business Manager, Robotics at ABB Discusses the State of Robot-Based Automation in the UK." *Automation,* February 2003.

FANUC International. Available from http://www.industryweek.com/research/iw1000/2009/IW1000Company.asp%3FInput%3D665.

Fowler, Jonathan. "U.N. Predicts Boom in Robot Labor." *CBS News,* 20 October 2004.

Fried, Ian. "HP Sends Bots to the Boardroom." CNET News, 23 May 2003. Available from http://news.cnet.com/.

"The Gentle Rise of the Machines." *The Economist,* 11 March 2004.

Higgins, Amy, and Sherri Koucky. "Best Workers for Hazardous Cleanup: Robots." *Machine Design,* 20 February 2003.

"Hoover's Company Capsules." *Hoover's Online,* 2007. Available from www.hoovers.com.

International Federation of Robotics (IFR). "The World Market of Industrial Robots." 2004.

Kanellos, Michael. "Invasion of the Robots: from Medicine to Military, Machines Finally Arrive." *CNET News,* 10 March 2004. Available from http://news.cnet.com/.

Koppal, Tanuja. "The Lasting Appeal of Allegro Technology." *Drug Discovery and Development,* 16 June 2003.

Kotelly, George. "Global Robotics Picked for Growth." *Vision Systems Design,* May 2003.

Maney, Kevin. "Basketball Buddies Build a Computerized Shot Doctor." *USA Today,* 7 February 2003.

"Manifold Simplifies Robot Design:Combined Digital and Analog I/O Saves Space and Wiring." *Design News,* 5 May 2003.

Mariner, Lee. "Robotics Competition Builds Student's Science Skills." *USA Today,* 2003.

"Non-Automotive Orders for Robots Rise in 2006, But Overall Sales Fall 30% in North America." *Robotics Online,* 23 February 2007. Available from www.roboticsonline.com.

"North American Robot Orders Jump 12% in First Quarter of 2007." *Robotics Online,* 21 May 2007. Available from www.roboticsonline.com.

"Orders Drop for U.S. Robot Makers; World Outlook Remains Strong ." *Robotics Trends,* 17 March 2009.

Powell, Cathy. "FANUC Robotics Announces FANUC LTD Produced More Than 120,000 Robots; Nearly 80,000 Installed in the Americas." 8 March 2004. Available from www.fanucrobotics.com/.

"Robot Labourer Unveiled." *Design Engineering,* February 2003.

"Robot Orders Rise in 2004." *Automation World,* 22 February 2005.

"Robotics Industry Sets New Records in 2005 as New Orders Jump 23% in North America." *Robotics Online,* 8 February 2006. Available from www.roboticsonline.com.

"Robotics Transforms Screening." *Drug Discovery and Development,* 16 June 2003.

"Robotized Induction Heating." *Induction Heating,* January 2003.

"Robots Are Coming." MSNBC, 21 March 2003. Available from http://www.msnbc.com.

"Robots Becoming Part of Everyday Life As Dish-Washing Robot Cell Will Demonstrate." *Robotics Online,* 18 May 2007. Available from www.roboticsonline.com.

"Robots Ordering Picking Up." *Material Handling Management,* April 2003.

Rockwell International . Available from http://finance.econsultant. com/rockwell-automation-2008-revenue-profit-2009-fortune-500-rank/.

"Technical Advances Increase Palletizing Possibilities: You Can Get Flexibility and Speed from the Same System but They May or May Not be a Robot." *Refrigerated & Frozen Foods,* April 2003.

Valigra, Lori. "Looking Technology in the Eye." *Christian Science Monitor,* 5 February 2004.

SATELLITES

━━━━━━━━━━━ ■ ━━━━━━━━━━━

SIC CODE(S)

3663

4899

INDUSTRY SNAPSHOT

The early 2000s represented a period of maturation borne of necessity for satellite makers as the commercial sector delivered some of its worst years in decades, forcing industry players to rethink their business models in order to remain viable and competitive through periods of industry retrenchment. Whereas through the 1980s and 1990s the industry could mostly count on a healthy log of new satellite contracts each year, the first decade of the new century proved that new orders could not always be counted on, as the low number of new satellite contracts befuddled expectations. Thus the euphoria of the 1990s gave way to malaise, in which key players diversified primarily by bolstering their satellite services operations. By the end of the first decade, the industry had recuperated somewhat, thanks partly to the satellite television segment, which accounted for almost 60 percent of revenues. Although a continued weak economy dampened commercial sales, government procurements on a global basis helped keep the industry in a growth phase with positive prospects ahead.

Broadcast Satellites Broadcast satellites send audio, video, and data signals directly to subscribers. Dominated by Boeing-owned DirecTV, direct broadcast satellite (DBS) television exploded in the late 1990s as equipment and subscription costs diminished and service was significantly improved. Unlike the telecommunications sector, the broadcast satellite market met with moderately good news in the early 2000s. For instance, a federal ruling, following an intensive industry lobbying campaign, finally allowed DBS companies to sell signals in local markets, and the major companies lost no time in breaking into the nation's major cities to transmit local broadcasts. Direct broadcast satellite television was aided in its ascendancy in the early 2000s by the integration of digital video recorders into DVRs. Together, DIRECTV and EchoStar, the broadcast satellite television leaders, penetrated 20 percent of U.S. multi-channel television households, with EchoStar reporting a 10.5 percent surge in subscribers in 2005, which translated into a 17.8 percent rise in revenues, to $8.4 billion, and a nearly eight-fold jump in net earnings, to $1.5 billion.

Among the bright spots for the industry was the booming satellite radio sector, which launched its first satellites in 2000 to compete with the heavily commercialized pop music and talk format of conventional radio. By running on a subscription basis, these firms offer a commercial-free mix of music, talk, and news programming over some 100 stations. Market leaders XM Satellite Radio and Sirius Satellite Radio merged in 2007, ending the year with a total of more than 9 million subscribers.

Internet Service Providers Satellites have also become a medium of Internet access, as researchers have sought faster ways of transmitting and downloading data. Internet access through satellite broadband services has become a viable option for rural areas without cable or DSL service, approximately 10 percent to 15 percent of the U.S. population. For these areas, satellite is an acceptable alternative, particularly since enhanced network

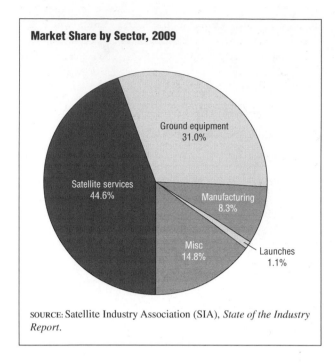

Market Share by Sector, 2009

Ground equipment
31.0%

Satellite services
44.6%

Manufacturing
8.3%

Misc
14.8%

Launches
1.1%

SOURCE: Satellite Industry Association (SIA), *State of the Industry Report*.

designs have minimized latency, the delay caused by the signal making a round trip into space and back to Earth. A satellite dish called a VSAT (very small aperture terminal) is installed outside the home or office and wired to a modem that plugs into the computer CPU. A connection is then made using wireless links to satellites in orbit over the equator. Unlike cable or DSL, satellite users must purchase their broadband access equipment. Internet access is then made available from virtually anywhere, as long as there is a view of the southern sky. Satellites deliver data at a much greater rate than any dial-up modem on the market but lag in speed behind cable and DSL.

Global Positioning Systems Global positioning systems (GPS) operate based on satellites and identify exact locations of users. GPS was developed and funded by the U.S. Department of Defense (DOD), although there are thousands of civil users as well. It runs on 24 satellites that orbit the earth in 12 hours. However, there are often more than 24 operational satellites at any given time, as new ones are launched to replace older satellites. Businesses have begun integrating the technology into a variety of products: cellular phones, dispatch hardware, and computers. Depending on the model, a GPS monitor can locate an object within 10 to 300 hundred feet of its actual position.

Global positioning systems (GPS) have also experienced increased commercial popularity. The most common application for GPS has been automobile navigation, though it is also used for aviation, marine, military,

tracking, and surveying purposes. According to an April 2003 *Automotive Industries* article, the Federal Communications Commission ruled mobile satellite operators can provide "ubiquitous" (available anywhere) coverage. Consequently, it awarded Boeing Satellite Systems frequencies needed to build a two-satellite system providing complete coverage for North America.

Other Applications Small satellites—classified as those weighing less than 2,000 pounds—were poised for substantial growth through the middle and late years of the twenty-first century's first decade. Up to that point, the main factor prohibiting widespread deployment of these satellites was their relatively weighty launch costs—it was cheaper to send one large satellite into orbit rather than three smaller versions. Over 170 such spacecraft were launched between 1990 and 2004, excluding those deployed for classified military operations. Universities and other research organizations and firms carried the greatest demand for such satellites, although defense agencies were also interested in the technology to utilize it for targeted operations, for which the smaller, cheaper equipment is more practical.

Consumer satellite communications helped facilitate the accelerating proliferation of distance education programs for students enrolled in everything from elementary school to graduate courses to continuing education. Satellites render distance, geography, and infrastructure almost entirely irrelevant for education, with simultaneous reception of signals across an area of millions of square miles. In place of the limited point-to-point transmission of land-based communications, satellites facilitate ideal point-to-multipoint communication, which is more suitable for education and training courses.

Defense projects have also goaded the satellite industry on by using satellites for such varied purposes as tracking the weather and spying. Additionally, in 1998, NASA began efforts to award a $600 million-a-year contract to a team of companies that will control or monitor more than 100 existing and planned NASA spacecraft. Two teams, one headed by Lockheed Martin and the other by Boeing Co., hoped to change the way NASA scientists gather information from research spacecraft.

ORGANIZATION AND STRUCTURE
Satellites serve as active repeaters of transmitted signals and therefore as an alternative method of sending information both short and long distances. Instead of wire, short-wave radio, cables, or fiber optics, communications satellites can send signals without interference across long distances and geographic boundaries. In addition, satellites are economical because their cost of operation does not depend on

distance. Satellites, moreover, can relay signals from one terrestrial transmitter to a number of receivers within the coverage vicinity. They can also transmit broadband signals and hence can send large quantities of data. With enough satellites in the proper configuration, they could cover any point on the globe. In practice, however, the International Telecommunications Union (ITU) and the U.S. Federal Communications Commission (FCC), regulatory bodies that oversee the development and operation of telecommunications technology, often restrict the coverage of satellites to a much more limited area.

Communications satellites contain equipment that receives signals from an Earth-based transmitter antenna, amplifies them, and sends them to Earth receiver stations. Hence, these features make satellites ideal for the one-to-many point transmissions of radio, television, data, and video.

Satellites can transmit and receive broadband microwave signals at a variety of different frequencies that are allocated for specific uses. The Ku-band (extending from 10.7 to 18 gigahertz) and the Ka-band (18 to 31 gigahertz) frequencies were expected to replace C-band (3.7 to 7.25 gigahertz) frequencies for Earth stations with immobile antennas or fixed satellite services in the mid-1990s. While the popularity of Ku-band transponders, or receivers, was beginning to overtake that of its predecessors, the C-band transponders, by the late 1990s, too many companies, organizations, and individuals had a significant investment in C-band technology, especially in Earth station C-band equipment. Moreover, the typical backyard satellite dish receives C-band frequencies and there are an estimated three million U.S. households with such receivers. In order to placate both sides, companies have developed and launched satellites with both C-band and Ku-band capabilities.

Space satellites are propelled into orbit by spacecraft or rocket boosters. Satellite services rely on different kinds of orbits depending on the kinds of tasks they perform and on the size of the satellites. The most frequently used orbits include low Earth orbits (LEOs), medium Earth orbits (MEOs), and geostationary orbits (GEOs). Many satellite projects under way in the late 1990s and the early 2000s called for low Earth orbiting satellites. MEOs cover altitudes of about 6,000 miles from Earth and work best for larger satellites. Many of the communications satellites in the late 1990s, however, used GEOs, which orbit at an altitude of 22,300 miles. From this point, a GEO satellite's rotation mirrors Earth's, causing the satellites to maintain a constant position relative to Earth. This orbit, however, can hold only about 150 satellites and was almost full.

The FCC and the ITU regulate satellite-related communications industries. The FCC focuses on issues concerning U.S. domestic use of satellites, while the ITU handles aspects of communications satellites with international ramifications. The FCC opened up the skies for U.S. satellites by rescinding the regulatory distinction between domestic and international satellites in a policy called Domestic International Satellite Consolidation in 1996. This policy allows satellite service providers access to international markets. The move, however, did not make the U.S. market more accessible to international satellite companies. On the other hand, the ITU allocates the use of various frequencies to different user groups and controls satellites in geostationary orbits (GEOs). The ITU makes its decisions concerning satellite use and radio frequencies at its World Administrative Radio Conferences.

BACKGROUND AND DEVELOPMENT

Russia launched the first successful satellite, the Sputnik, on October 4, 1957, taking the lead in space exploration. A few months later, on February 1, 1958, the United States launched its first satellite, becoming the second nation in space. On November 3, 1960, the National Aeronautics and Space Administration (NASA) launched its first satellite, Explorer 8, beginning the first of many NASA space expeditions.

Satellites first entered the commercial arena in the 1960s, providing alternative channels of data transmission for international telephone and telegraph services, competing with undersea cables. In the 1970s, companies started to deploy satellites within the United States for commercial purposes. These satellites not only transferred telephone signals for businesses, but also relayed network data.

In addition, television networks began implementing satellites to send and receive transcontinental relays of broadcast signals in the 1970s. Satellites ultimately had a revolutionary effect on television broadcasting. With satellites, networks could cull the best resources from all the stations in the network. Stations could transmit or receive signals from other network stations via satellites. Later, television stations acquired portable Earth stations, allowing them to travel from event to event, to broadcast live from events, and to rove around town looking for events to broadcast.

Throughout the 1990s, the industry restructured itself to capitalize on emerging consumer technologies incorporating satellite signals, and broadened from its weather, space, and military-centered operations, although those applications remained a cornerstone of satellite usage. The inundation of demand for cellular phones, voice message services, fax machines, and wireless communications devices fueled a massive surge in sales of low Earth orbit satellites. In the mid-1990s, it took over two and a half years for a satellite to be built and launched, but by 2000, the entire process generally required less than 18 months. Moreover, satellite manufacturers took broad steps to bring costs down so as to facilitate a more active consumer-based market, creating small satellites that cost less than $20 million, compared with the previous $100 million price tag.

Nevertheless, the industry hit some rather sizable speed bumps in 1999 and 2000, including the sudden failure of two promising young companies. Iridium World Communications Ltd., one of the most ambitious players in the satellite telecommunications sector, wound up in bankruptcy court. The telecommunications satellite boom that looked so unstoppable just a few years earlier was stuck in limbo by 2000.

Legislative difficulties also cut into the U.S. export market and ruffled the feathers of many industry executives. By 2000, the industry banded together to express its dissatisfaction with federal licensing policies. Since March 1999, the U.S. State Department has handled all licensing for the satellite industry, declaring that such equipment is classified as weaponry for export purposes. Previously, the task had been the responsibility of the U.S. Department of Commerce, which tended to be more permissive in its license grants. The switch came about after Congress feared Hughes and Loral might have given the Chinese missile defense system a boost when the companies investigated the failures of Chinese launchings of their satellites. Many industry executives complained that these stepped-up restrictions severely damaged their international presence, slowing sales even to U.S. allies. Several European and Japanese satellite manufacturers also strenuously objected to the U.S. government's action, arguing that it kept them from acquiring necessary components from their U.S. counterparts and that it effectively treated them as political enemies.

The satellite industry continued to flounder through the early 2000s, as evidenced by a drop-off in new satellite orders and a glut of orbiting spacecraft. This created an environment in which analysts expected a wave of consolidation, as smaller and struggling firms sought out better-leveraged peers for partnership in an attempt to stay afloat. By 2003, the sector began to accept the new market conditions, in which simply sending up a new satellite and waiting for orders to lease time on existing transponders would no longer suffice in a market with few space slots open for the existing customer base.

However, the communications satellite sector saw a recovery beginning in the middle of the decade. In 2004, revenues in the mobile sector rose to $1 billion, with the number of terminals exceeding the 1 million mark for the first time. 6.2 million people subscribed to Digital Audio Radio (Dars); that number rose to nearly 9 million by the end of 2004. By 2010, the number is forecasted to reach 40 million. The military is anticipated to contribute to the growth of commercial satellites, aided by the Pentagon's plans to spend $2 billion by 2010 to lease commercial bandwidth. In early 2005, more than 80 percent of the military's satellite communications coming out of the Persian Gulf region were being transmitted by commercial spacecraft.

The European consulting firm Euroconsult, which sponsors a prestigious annual forum, noted that about 50 percent of the commercial satellites circling the globe in 2003 would reach the end of their lifespan between 2006 and 2011, rendering prospects rosy for new contracts through the end of the decade. In 2005, total revenues for the fixed-service satellite (FSS) industry rose to $7.05 billion, up from $6.15 billion in 2003, according to Euroconsult's research report, "World Satellite Communications & Broadcasting Markets Survey—Market Forecasts for 2014."

While satellite capabilities and demand increased and strengthened, the glut of satellites in orbit created other, non-market obstacles as well. With all the space operations in the last few decades, the upper atmosphere was becoming inundated with cosmic debris. Thousands of rocket parts, shot satellites, and a host of other miscellaneous spacecraft components orbit around the galaxy, creating a perilous environment for new spacecraft. According to CNET News, in 2007 the U.S. Space Surveillance Network was tracking more than 13,000 human-made objects more than four inches in diameter that were orbiting the earth. In an effort to reduce the space clutter, in 2004 the U.S. Federal Communications Commission ruled that U.S. geostationary satellites launched after 18 March 2002 must be sent to a "satellite graveyard" in the earth's outer orbit once they were no longer needed or used.

In November 2005, a six-ton, Atlantic Ocean Region 1-4 Inmarsat satellite was launched that allowed broadband connections to magazine-sized portable transceivers. This satellite, along with two others, provided the platform for the Broadband Global Area Network (BGAN) service, which enabled battery-powered, portable terminals to support 492K bit/second data rates and separate voice traffic. As of 2008, BGAN served all parts of the world except the Pacific area, which was expected to receive service eventually.

Weather satellites have been used to track hurricanes for many years, but by the end of 2005, sophisticated sounding radars, passive radiometers, and other instruments on scientific satellites have been called upon to help with forecasting. Earth-observing satellites that were originally intended to monitor long-term climate trends helped forecasters in the fall of 2005 during the horrific Atlantic hurricane season. They improved meteorologists' predictions of the paths and intensities of the violent storms, allowing more than five days warning and even indicating changes in direction and intensity as they happened. In contrast, in 1900, forecasters had to rely on land-based weather stations and ships in the ocean for data that was very unreliable and spotty, at best. A joint Japanese/U.S. scientific satellite that had almost landed on NASA's cutting room floor due to financial issues, the Tropical Rainfall Measurement Mission (TRMM), provided invaluable storm-intensity data.

Global positioning systems also received a major upgrade in October 2005 with the launch of the Lockheed Martin GPS block IIR-M spacecraft with dual civilian channel capability. The multiple civil GPS channel capability will enable better position and location capability for low-power cell phones, added emergency service capabilities, and better tracking of ocean and atmospheric phenomena, all applications that relate directly to issues of disaster response raised by Hurricanes Katrina and Rita.

Broadcasting, including radio and television, continued to be the leading segment in the industry based on revenues. The satellite television and radio markets accounted for $57.5 billion of the total $73.9 billion in sales in the industry in 2007. High-speed satellite Internet services also represented a major growth area in the industry, as did mobile applications. In 2007, mobile satellite applications accounted for $2.1 billion in revenues, up from $1.3 billion in 2002.

A 2007 study by Euroconsult showed that 900 government and commercial satellites were launched worldwide between 1996 and 2006. The company predicted that an additional 960 satellites would be launched in the next decade (2007–2017), accounting for revenues of $145 billion ($104.5 billion for the satellites and $40.5 billion for launchers). Of these, 223 are expected to be commercial geostationary satellites, representing $43.1 billion in revenue. The average cost of launching a satellite in the former decade was $26,000; the cost of a launch is expected to drop to an average of $22,000 by 2017. Although the cost is predicted to go down, the size of the satellites will likely increase. The average mass of a satellite launched between 1996 and 2006 was 3.4 tons; in the following decade, this figure will increase to 3.8 tons, due mostly to the increasing number of transponders on board.

The amount of space available for placing new satellites was an issue in the industry. According to an October 2007 CNET News article, there were 240 working satellites in orbit. Bruce Elbert, president of Application Technology Strategy, said, "Most of the premium positions are already taken up. So if some new killer application is developed and we need a lot more satellites, it might be hard to accommodate them."

Another challenge to the industry in 2007 and 2008 was the competition from Earth-based wireless technologies, such as WiMAX. In addition, as reported in *Satellite Today*, WiMAX signals "pose a significant interference threat to satellite signals transmitted in the C-band frequency." The fight for access to the C-band spectrum continued.

Hybrid terrestrial/satellite services were being further explored. The hybrid system uses a ground tower network—the ancillary terrestrial component (ATC)—to boost the signal and eliminate the fade and interference issues that plagued first-generation mobile satellite service (MSS) networks. Boeing was awarded the contract for three satellites and their related ground systems that will replace a pair of older satellites covering Canada and the United States and will expand services to Latin America. Launch is scheduled for 2008–2009, with a price tag of $5.1 billion, which includes the three satellites, the launch, ground segment, and launch insurance.

CURRENT CONDITIONS

In its June 2010 State of the Satellite Industry Report, the Satellite Industry Association (SIA) reported an 11 percent growth from 2008 to 2009 in overall global satellite industry revenues. SIA reported that global revenues for the satellite industry were $160.9 billion for 2009. The industry grew 11.7 percent between 2004 and 2009, according to the SIA.

The report also showed that setellite manufacturing and launch services were the two fastest-growing sectors within the industry worldwide. However, the satellite services sector (the main demand driver) was the highest revenue-producer. Within that sector, satellite television led the sales, totaling $71.8 billion in 2009. Worldwide satellite manufacturing revenues were up 29 percent, with total sales jumping from $10.5 billion in 2008 to $13.5 billion in 2009. This growth spurt was attributed to larger and higher-value new spacecraft being launched. As to satellite launches, U.S. launch revenues grew from $1.1 billion in 2008 to $1.9 billion in 2009. Worldwide launch revenues were up by 18 percent in 2009.

Satellite TV and broadband, mobile satellite, and GPS services all contributed to a satellite ground equipment sector growth of 8 percent in 2009, with total revenues of $49.9 billion. The only industry decrease for 2009 was in employment; as of the 3rd quarter in 2009, down 5.5 percent across all four sectors.

Notwithstanding the overall positive global forecast for the industry, for the first time, according to research firm SNL Kagan, the number of U.S. cable, satellite, and telecommunication services dropped in the second quarter of 2010. Specifically, the television market lost 216,000 customers (compared to the gain of 378,000 one year prior). The number of total subscribers fell to 100.1 million in the second quarter, SNL Kagan reported. Although the firm pointed to economic factors and unemployment as contributing to subscriber declines, it also noted that the decline could signal a new market trend where subscribers turned to Internet-television for programming.

In the global mobile satellite TV market, Global Industry Analysts, Inc. announced, in February 2010, its newest report that forecasted an industry growth in revenue reaching $11 billion in 2015. The success was attributed to growing popularity of TV services, especially to mobile handhelds and phones that supported the general image quality and high data transferrates.

INDUSTRY LEADERS

The Boeing Company, which relocated to Chicago in 2001, is a diversified manufacturer of aerospace and defense products. Boeing's purchase of industry leader Hughes Space and Communications Co. from General Motors Corp. for $3.75 billion catapulted Boeing to the forefront of the satellite manufacturing industry. Its Boeing Satellite Systems subsidiary manufactures satellites for the commercial communications, military, meteorological, and scientific research sectors, having constructed over 200 systems. Boeing spent the late 1990s acquiring a variety of space-related enterprises to prepare for the acquisition of Hughes, which owned broadcast satellite leader DIRECTV. However, Boeing announced in 2003 that it was ceasing new launches of commercial systems to focus on its military government based lines, including satellites and other space offerings. In 2008 Boeing was competing for the Transformational Satellite Communications System program for the U.S. Air Force and for the next-generation Geostationary Operational Environmental Satellites (GOES R series) for NASA and the National Oceanic and Atmospheric Administration. Boeing employed more than 150,000 people in 2009 and brought in revenues of $68.3 billion.

Lockheed Martin, based in Bethesda, Maryland, provides the U.S. Defense Department with space and satellite technology and plays a role in the commercial satellite market. Lockheed received almost 80 percent of its business from government contacts; its Space Systems division brought in about 20 percent of sales, designing and producing satellites and satellite support systems as well as defensive missile systems and launch services. Sales in 2009 were $45.19 billion with 140,000 employees. Revenues for 2010 were expected to be the same ($44.9 billion to $45.9 billion).

Loral Space & Communications Ltd. is a high technology company headquartered in New York and specializing in satellite manufacturing and satellite services. Its operations are divided into two main divisions: fixed satellite services and satellite manufacturing and technology. Fixed satellite services include network services such as Internet and media services and managed communications networks as well as the leasing of transponder capacity to clients for various forms of satellite-based communications. Its Space Systems/Loral subsidiary handles the firm's manufacturing and technology components, designed and produced for telecommunications and weather systems. The company's clients included DIRECTV, DISH Network, and SIRIUS XM Radio.

AMERICA AND THE WORLD

North America, Europe, and Asia-Pacific dominated the global market for mobile satellite activity in 2009. The growth was driven by the conversion of television signals to digital formats and free Wi-Fi technologies such as MediaFLO and DVB-H. The market was expected to benefit from developing countries including Brazil, China and India. Leading companies in the global satellite-based mobile TV were Alcatel-Lucent, AT&T, DiBcom, DISH Network Corporation, KVH Industries Inc., Nagravision SA, and RaySat Inc.

While the United States commanded about 65 percent of the global satellite system market, a growing contingent of countries, including France, Russia, Japan, and the United Kingdom, played instrumental roles in the progress of the satellite industry. Companies from these countries acquired contracts to collaborate on some of the largest satellite projects on the drawing boards. Boeing was collaborating with Ukrainian, Russian, and Norwegian companies to create a mobile launch system, the Odyssey. In addition, these countries have thriving satellite industries of their own. Russia, for example, developed the Proton spacecraft, which can carry up to seven satellites in just one mission. In addition, France's Arianespace was among the world leaders for satellite launches. According to some analysts, the European and Japanese satellite industries have technological advantages over the U.S. industry in part because the governments in European countries and Japan have traditionally provided more support to satellite development. In May 2003, Lockheed Martin announced a contract with Japan's JSAT Corp. to build an A2100 geo-stationary telecommunications satellite. JCSAT-9 will provide services throughout Asia and Japan following its scheduled launch in 2005.

After several years of false starts, China's commercial satellite industry began to take off in 2003 as it shed its dependency on the United States in this sector. Southern Asia saw a 12 percent growth in transponders launched that year, largely to assist the burgeoning market for telecommunications in China and neighboring India, both of which were in the midst of rapid economic growth.

European satellite makers, like their U.S. counterparts, were thwarted by the commercial sector, while defense communications enjoyed respectable growth. The three leading European satellite firms—Alcatel Space, Astrium, and Alenia Spazio—experienced a retrenchment in sales of new satellite launches, but few orders for new spacecrafts. With the January 2005 launch of the Satcom Post-2000 satellite system by the North Atlantic Treaty Organization (NATO) comes improved satellite communication capabilities, which is important as NATO forces take on expeditionary missions far beyond the its traditional area of operations. Under the Satcom Post-2000 program, British, French and Italian governments are providing NATO, through what is known as "Capability Provision," with advanced satellite communication capabilities for 15 years after launching.

On December 28, 2005, Kazakhstan launched the Giove-A satellite—the biggest European space project ever. The Galileo In-Orbit Validation Element (Giove-A—the acronym is Italian for "Jove," the king of the Roman gods), will test several technologies for Galileo, a satellite-based navigation system. Barring any unforeseen setbacks, the system will be operational in 2008. In a news article in *Computing* magazine on January 19, 2006, it was announced that Giove-A had started transmitting, confirming the radio spectrum that will be used for the European GPS. Europeans are applauding the technological leap that will provide strategic and economic independence from the United States' GPS. However, since the project by the U.S. military is provided as a worldwide free service, some are objecting, contending that the $4.3-billion Giove-A project was unnecessary.

RESEARCH AND TECHNOLOGY

In addition to the satellites, the launches that send them into space are increasingly important. In the late years of the first decade of the 2000s, planned satellites exceeded the available number of launch pads. Companies, including Lockheed Martin, are developing reusable systems that should reduce the cost of a launch.

The United States and Europe launched SES Astra Satellite TV Company's 3D demo channel in early 2010. Europe used the 23.5 E orbital position on the Astra satellite television broadcast, hosted by the German Cable Operators Association (ANGA) in Cologne. In the United Kingdom, British Sky Broadcasting (BSkyB)

was using Astra 2A Satellite (28.2 E) to transmit kyHD 3D TV there and in Ireland.

Satellite producers and operators constantly look for ways to reduce costs while maintaining the technological advantages of satellites in order to make their products financially accessible to mass markets. Sea Venture, a bevy of international companies led by Boeing Commercial Space, has been developing a mobile offshore launching platform, the Odyssey, for satellites. The Odyssey was to provide the advantages of launching satellites at the equator, where Earth's rotation is the fastest and the path to geo-stationary transfer orbit—a stage of orbit prior to the final route to geo-stationary orbit—is the shortest. Therefore, launching satellites from equatorial points takes less energy than from other points.

The ability to receive television programs directly from space is made possible by way of a parabolic aerial, programming that will be available to consumers in 2009. Once programming is available, it is unlikely to be in English. Also, the possibility of "cultural invasion" by countries with powerful broadcast satellites into other countries is the cause of some political concerns. Commercial or politically unrestrained programming could be beamed from space to people in other countries, with or without that country's permission.

BIBLIOGRAPHY

"2010 State of the Satellite Industry Report Shows Continued Growth in 2009." Satellite Industry Association, 8 June 2010. Available from http://www.sia.org.

Bindra, Ashok. "Digital Terrestrial and Satellite Radio Markets Set for Growth." *RF Design,* 4 January 2007.

"Boeing Receives Satellite Industry Leadership Award." The Boeing Company, 12 June 2008.

"Boeing Reports Strong 2009 Revenue & Cash Flow on Solid Core Performance." Press Release, Boeing Company, 27 January 2010. Available from http://boeing.mediaroom.com/.

"Commercial Satellite Industry Revenues Jump 16 Percent in 2007." Space Mart, 12 June 2008.

"Cultural Invasion from Space." *New Scientist,* 25 February 2006.

"Dish Network News." Available from http://www.dishnetwork.com/news/acsi/aspx.

"HD Programming Services to Drive Growth in Uplink Industry, Says In-Stat." *Broadcast Engineering,* 9 January 2007.

Jones, Karen. "And Broadband for All." *Black Enterprise,* May 2006.

Kharif, Olga. "SIRIUS XM Is in a Serious Bind." *Business Week Online,* 18 September 2008. Available from www.businessweek.com.

Lardier, Christian. "Satellite Market Outlook Brightens." *Interavia Business & Technology,* Spring 2007.

Moran, Andrew. "Number of Subscribers to Cable, Satellite TV Services Fall in Q2." *DigitalJournal,* 26 August 2010.

"News—Galileo Starts to Transmit Signals." *Computing,* 19 January 2006.

Reardon, Marguerite. "The Age of the Satellite." CNET News, 2 October 2007. Available from http://news.cnet.com.

"SIA...A Positive Orbit For Satellite Industry Revenues." *SatNews Daily,* 8 June 2010.

"SIRIUS, XM Merger Completed, Creating U.S. Satellite Radio Giant." AFP, 29 July 2008.

State of the Industry Satellite Report. Satellite Industry Association, June 2008.

"SURG: WiMAX Can Interfere with C-Band Signals." *Satellite Today,* 4 March 2008.

Taverna, Michael A. "MSV, Inmarsat BGAN Show Strong Potential of Mobile Satellite Services." *Aviation Week & Space Technology,* 5 February 2006.

SOFTWARE AS A SERVICE

———— ■ ————

SIC CODE(S)

7372

INDUSTRY SNAPSHOT

Software as a Service (SaaS) is revolutionizing computing as we know it. SaaS is uprooting the way we traditionally think about computing by delivering software over the Internet, making it accessible from anywhere, at any time. SaaS is a new way of leveraging software applications—it shifts the burden of getting and keeping an enterprise application up and running, from the customer to the vendor. This enables customers to be able to focus on their core business objectives, and frees them from dedicating resources to support the enterprise application on an ongoing basis.

In his book *The Big Switch*, Nicholas Carr draws a parallel between what happened with the invention of electric utilities a hundred years ago to what is happening with computing today. As he explains, before the electricity grid, people had to generate their own power to run their machines. It wasn't until the late 1880s when people no longer had to worry about producing their own power, and instead could take advantage of the cost effective, powerful electric utility grid. What is happening now with SaaS is very similar to what happened with electricity—instead of accessing software on their personal computers, people are accessing services that are running on the provider's infrastructure and are accessed through a public network connection.

The landscape of personal computing, business computing, and the traditional way of offering software is getting rocked with the agile nature and low cost that SaaS has to offer. Those corporate users taking the leap are finding that SaaS consistently offers benefits that "far out-weigh any limitations. These benefits include:

- Quicker time to value
- Lower cost of ownership
- Higher return on investment
- Greater scalability and agility

ORGANIZATION AND STRUCTURE

Software as a Service (SaaS) enables businesses to shift their computing applications to the Internet. In the purest sense of the phrase, SaaS shifts the burden of housing and hosting data, and enables users to log in to their application from anywhere, at any time. True SaaS applications must be multi-tenant and single instance. That is, multiple users are using a single instance of the software as if it is their own. With all users running on the same software, the SaaS providers are able to make upgrades and developments to that one version and have it be pushed out to all users at once. One of the primary benefits of this is that users are never faced with an upgrade; these new features and customizations automatically get folded in to the base application.

One of the biggest characteristics of Software as a Service that sets it apart from any other software offering is that the software exists in a single instance; all users are running off of the same copy. That means, in most cases, that users are able to benefit from what is known as "The User Community." When one upgrade or fix is made to the single, master copy of the software,

827

Internet User Growth in Percentages, 2000 to 2010	
Africa	2,357.3%
Middle East	1,825.3%
Latin America/Caribbean	1,032.8%
Asia	621.8%
Europe	352.0%
Oceania/Australia	179.0%
North America	146.3%

SOURCE: Internet World Stats.

early to mid-2000s, the traditional ASP model does not eliminate:

- upfront costs
- extended deployment cycles
- remote accessibility issues
- need to acquire an up-front perpetual license
- multiple versions of the software

The traditional ASP model failed to satisfy business needs for corporate customers at the turn of the new century, which is why most ASPs founded in the dot-com era failed and disappeared. There are still companies that support the traditional ASP model, but they are struggling to stay afloat. In fact, many of the companies that support that ASP model in today's market attempt to pass their product off as a SaaS application; however much of the time that is not true. A common tell-tale sign of a true SaaS application is if there is a single version of the software. Many companies will market their product as SaaS, but in reality they are an ASP that is offering to house the servers that a company purchased.

However different Application Service Providers are from their descendants (Software as a Service), they share a common goal of enabling customers to outsource computer applications so they are able to focus on their core competencies. Based on that similarity, both can be considered indirect descendants of the "service bureaus" of the 1960s and 1970s. In turn, the service bureaus were trying to fulfill the vision of computing as a utility, which was "initially proposed by John McCarthy during a presentation at MIT in 1961."

PIONEERS IN THE FIELD

Salesforce.com is a company that has inspired new thinking and truly revolutionized an industry. Salesforce.com was started by Marc Benioff in a rented apartment in 1999 "with the goal of making enterprise software as easy to use as a Web site like Amazon.com." Benioff envisioned a world where enterprise software was no longer "exorbitantly expensive and onerous to implement." Benioff's vision changed the way the software industry works, and along the way Salesforce.com earned the distinction of being the first dot-com listed on the New York Stock Exchange.

Benioff started his career as an intern with Apple, and then moved into a full-time position at Oracle. Benioff started at Oracle when there was only about 200 people on staff; when founder and CEO Larry Ellison was a regular in the halls. According to Benioff, it was Larry's vision that inspired him. Ellison "envisioned a world of interconnected computers that could

every user is able to benefit—free of charge and disruption to their business. In every upgrade situation there is the company that "picks up the bill," for a benefit that everyone will feel. In theory, however, the company that foots the bill one time, will benefit free of charge other times.

An issue still looming over all benefits of Software as a Service is the issue of security. Many business owners wonder how their data is able to remain safe on the Internet in a time when Internet hacking is a very real thing. According to Forrester analyst Liz Herbert, "Security is the No. 1 reason preventing firms from moving to SaaS." What many potential users do not know is that security can actually be one of the major advantages of using many SaaS applications. Many of the SaaS providers actually have access to many more security resources than the average business. This usually enables the providers to provide features like tested firewalls, automated security sniffers, biometric control systems, security experts, and certified policies, procedures, and equipment. The combination of the abundant resources provides a very safe environment for data.

SaaS applications exist for a multitude of industries, from aerospace and defense to professional services, to medical and manufacturing, to electronics and beyond. As global businesses continue to indicate a need for a more cost-efficient, technologically savvy way to connect with their customers and do business, the list of SaaS offers is only going to grow.

BACKGROUND AND DEVELOPMENT

In many respects, Software as a Service is the brainchild of a previous generation of application service providers (ASPs). The traditional ASP model—also refered to as "hosted applications"—the "service provider is simply reselling and housing a traditional, on-premise application in its facilities to relieve the customer of the ongoing operational requirements." Unlike the current SaaS model, which didn't become popular until the easily share information across the planet at the touch of a button." With the help of the Internet, Benioff seemed to fulfill that goal with Salesforce.com and all that followed.

Marc Benioff was very successful at Oracle, but it was eventually Oracle's inability to "respond quickly or easily to new directions or opportunities. [He] found that limitation extremely challenging." Eventually Marc left to seek other opportunities elsewhere; this was when Salesforce.com was born.

The vision to make software "easier to purchase, simpler to use, and more democratic without the complexities of installation, maintenance, and constant upgrades," the vision of Salesforce.com had been brewing the in the mind of Marc Benioff since 1996. To make his dream of on-demand software (Software as a Service) a reality, Benioff spent the next several years planning and believed passionately in the computing revolution he was creating. In his book, *Behind the Cloud,* Benioff explains the steps he took to turn his dream into a reality. It was the next steps that he took that have truly transformed the software and business industries as we once knew them.

Salesforce.com started small, and has now transformed into more than a billion-dollar company. They have expanded their services to include much more than their original Customer Relationship Management (CRM) application; their offerings include the Platform as a Service (PaaS), Force.com, and literally hundreds of other SaaS applications that have been built to run on Force.com (both privately and by Force.com).

Software as a Service is an industry that is growing at a rapid pace and is at a stage that could almost categorize any adopters as "Pioneers in the Field." Software as a Service still represents a very small portion of the software industry, so every early adopter is a pioneer in the industry.

CURRENT CONDITIONS

In light of the recent economic downtown in the United States and the rest of the world, companies are looking everywhere to cut-costs, streamline operations, and gain a competitive edge. One of the first places companies are starting to look is their operations for software applications. Historically companies have invested in infrastructure that would enable them to house and run their own copies of the software that was necessary to run their business; in many cases this proved to be very costly. Costs add up quickly when one company is responsible for acquiring, deploying, updating, and maintaining legacy systems. Additionally, in many cases legacy applications lack the "features and functional capabilities [that] are essential in today's rapidly changing business environment."

Terms like "Globalizatoin" and "eCommerce" have become standard in most business sectors. Companies are looking for solutions to help them thrive as the business landscape changes from one inhibited by geographic barriers, to one that is free of geographic barriers to entry. The SaaS community is recognizing and latching on to this business paradigm shift and in light of the economic downturn, is experiencing high growth. A study released by Gartner showed that in 2009, worldwide SaaS sales sat at about $7.5 billion. In 2010, however, Gartner predicts worldwide SaaS sales be up 14.1 percent from 2009, coming in around $8.5 billion.

INDUSTRY LEADERS

Salesforce.com Salesforce.com is arguably the most influential company in the SaaS sphere. Salesforce.com (NYSE: CRM) was founded as a "groundbreaking idea" in 1999 and since has transformed into a "market and technology leader in enterprise cloud computing." Salesforce.com provides a customer relationship management (CRM) solution that helps companies "record, track, manage, analyze and share information regarding sales, customer service and support, and marketing operations." Salesforce.com is available in over 20 languages, and can be access from almost any Internet device (including many mobile platforms).

Salesforce.com includes CRM modules, such as:

- accounts and contacts
- marketing and leads
- analytics and forecasting
- workflows
- social networking

Salesforce.com filed an initial public offering on the New York Stock Exchange (NYSE) in December 2003. They were the first SaaS company to go public, and the first dot-com to trade on the NYSE. They ended their first day of public trading, Wednesday, June 23, 2004, at $17.20. Since then Salesforce.com has seen great success. Its five year growth rate is 49.24, while the rest of the industry is lagging behind at 13.96 percent. According to Reuters mean projections for Salesforce.com's fiscal year ending January 2010 is $1,293.81 billion.

Citrix Systems Inc. Citrix, founded in 1989, was one of the first companies to "exploit the potential of virtualization." Although many people typically associate Citrix with targeting the mass market, they actually started out by "creating products designed for low badwidth, high latency, and low power CPU environments," all which are main tenets of SaaS and virtualization.

Citrix offers a variety of products and solutions revolving around virtualization, cloud computing, and

Software as a Service. They offer several collaboration tools that are all SaaS based, including the well-known GoToMeeting and GoToWebinar. In a report released in mid-2010 by Frost & Sullivan, Citrix Online is recognized as the fastest growing provider among all top SaaS Web conferencing brands in 2009.

Since the quarter ending September 2009, Citrix has reported revenue slightly above analysis' estimates. Citrix' five-year sales growth rate is 16.84 percent, while the industry is slightly ahead at 22.84 percent.

Google Google debuted on the NASDAQ on August 19, 2004. Shares that were originally priced at $85 in 2004 have soared past $600 by the end of 2010. Similar to Salesforce.com, Google began as a start-up that was headquartered in a small, make-shift workspace. There are many facets of Google, including Google AdWords, Google Finance, Google Web Search, and a popular, free SaaS offering, Google Docs. Google Docs allows users to "create, view, edit and share documents, spreadsheets and presentations from anywhere using a browser." Google Docs are "available both as a free service to individuals, and a competitively priced service for companies or individuals who many require higher storage limits."

Intuit Intuit, maker of TurboTax, QuickBooks, and Quicken, joined the SaaS realm when it launched QuickBase in December of 2001. QuickBase, a Web-based customer relationship management (CRM) suite, offers a database of more than 400,000 applications built using a library of over 200 ready-to-use templates. It also offers the ability to build and integrate custom applications into existing systems. Like most other SaaS applications, QuickBase offers subscription-based memberships that can easily be scaled to meet individual business needs.

QuickBase opened the door to the SaaS space for Intuit and began to offer Web-based versions of its other, more popular software, such as QuickBooks Online and TurboTax Online. QuickBooks Online offers the QuickBooks Accounting software online for a small, subscription-based fee. Like any true SaaS application, QuickBooks Online is available from anywhere, at anytime, and requires no installation or upgrades. As Nicholas Carr points out in his book *The Big Switch*, "one of the most striking indicators of the rapid adoption of Web applications by consumers came during the 2007 U.S. tax season, when more Americans used the online version of Intuit's popular TurboTax software than used the traditional packaged version."

With its variety of business software solutions, Intuit competes in several business sectors. QuickBooks, and Intuit's other finance software solutions compete with large tax and finance firms, such as JP Morgan Chase, Bank of America, and Thomson Reuters. Their CRM software, QuickBase, competes with other large SaaS CRM providers such as Microsoft and Salesforce.com.

In 1993, just one year after introducing its QuickBooks accounting software, Intuit went public on the NASDAQ. The return on investment of 13.97 percent is higher than the 9.51 percent industry average.

Plex Systems In 2001, Plex Systems launched Plex Online, a SaaS solution with "comprehensive manufacturing [Enterprise Resource Planning] (ERP) software functions that cover the total manufacturing enterprise," including EDI, Quality Management, Shop Floor, HR, and CRM. Plex is transforming the approach manufacturers take to the cost, implementation, and use of ERP systems by offering:

- true SaaS with multi-tenant, single instance, rapidly evolving, and automatically updated versions and features
- no costly hardware, complex version control
- lower costs with no large capital outlay and an affordable subscription fee
- unlimited storage space and CPU power at no additional charge

Plex Systems was founded in 1995 and first offered Plex Online, as we know it today, in 2001. Ten years later Plex had approximately 500 customers, whose range in sales revenue is between $5 million and $2 billion. Their typical customers are mid-size at $25 to $100 million.

Plex Systems is a privately held company that is considered to be a pioneer in SaaS solution. They are, in many respects, leading the SaaS ERP industry ahead of legacies like Oracle and SAP.

WORKFORCE

The Software as a Service industry requires a diverse workforce just as any brick and mortar software company would. Similarly, the size of the required workforce depends entirely on the size of the company and customer demands. Unlike the traditional brick and mortar software company, however, with just a single-instance of the software running, it generally takes fewer employees to support an on-demand application as it does to support a traditional legacy application. For example, Plex Online, Plex Systems' ERP application, supports nearly 400 customers, in 38 countries simultaneously running their business on a single instance of the Plex software, all which is run on a single database. On a daily basis Plex Online has tens of thousands of customers log-in and use the software, all the while they are able to have just one or two employees support each functional area, such as Electronic Data Interchange (EDI).

The Plex Online employment requirements differ significantly from those of an on-premise, legacy system. Whereas an SaaS-based company is able to fully support the EDI needs of nearly 400 companies with just one person, an on-premise system would be required to have many more employees available to support that number of companies. One of the reasons for the difference is that with on-premise systems all data and software versions are stored on-site with the customer, with nearly 400 different copies of the same piece of software floating about, leaving room for nearly 400 opportunities for error and confusion. Additionally, with an on-premise system, each copy of the software is often so customized for each customer that it would be impossible for just one person to keep track of and be able to support all companies using it.

As Joseph Feiman points out in a paper published by Gartner in August 2010, "cloud computing and software as a service represent very significant opportunities for enterprises to save money, time, an resources. At the same time, however, SaaS also presents "significant threats for IT professionals' careers." The paper goes on to define and describe four levels of vulnerability for IT professionals as SaaS becomes more of a threat to the industry. The more narrow-focused a technical specialist is, the more vulnerable they are as the market changes. Conversely, the open, strategy-minded business professionals are less susceptible to vulnerability and more likely to find job security in the changing, cloud-based market.

Companies that have invested in Software as a Service often require the same type of employees as a more traditional brick and mortar software company (though they may not require as many of each resource). The number of employees required truly depends on the size of the company. Billion-dollar companies, such as Salesforce.com, require thousands of employees in many different departments. Salesforce.com's job categories include:

- finance
- global services
- IT
- marketing
- product marketing
- research and development
- sales
- foundation
- human resources
- University recruiting
- product management

The average salary and requirements, such as education and experience, vary for each of the jobs within the different job categories.

AMERICA AND THE WORLD

Historically, U.S.-based companies have led, and continue to lead, the SaaS industry. Many U.S.-based companies dominate the industry in innovation and utilization of SaaS. Software as a Service is a unique business asset as it not bound by the chains of geography; by nature, it enables users to connect from any place, at any time. Due in part to the lack of brick and mortar requirements for a SaaS-based operation to have an international presence, the SaaS industry exists in an international marketplace.

The utilization and adoption of SaaS by business owners, as well as an Internet presence, are critical components of the industry.

RESEARCH AND TECHNOLOGY

As beneficial as the idea of connectivity from any place, at any time sounds, the only way it is able to work is if business owners and users are able to be connected to a reliable Internet source. The correlation of Internet access and Saas is apparent in industry statistics.

According to a study released by Forrester, who surveyed nearly 3,000 technology decision makers worldwide, "emerging geographies—Latin America, China, India, Russia—are heavy adopters of [Software as a Service]." Survey results found that it was "the growing maturity of SaaS, combined with the buyers' desire for a solution that allows them to conserve cash, deploy quickly, and avoid long-term lock-in" that ultimately has demonstrated why SaaS continues to gain popularity.

Of the largest adopters named in the Forrester study, "Latin America led with the highest rate of SaaS adoption, with 30% of companies reporting SaaS use." Other emerging geographies that showed high adoption of SaaS included China, Hong Kong, India, and Russia. This group reported 21 percent SaaS usage. Based on data published by the U.S. Census Bureau and Nielsen-Online, all of these countries have shown huge growth in Internet use from 2000 to 2010:

- India—1520 percent
- China—1766.7 percent
- Hong Kong—113.7 percent
- India—1520 percent
- Russia—N/A

The exception for Internet user growth is in Hong Kong, whose user growth between 2000 and 2010 was only 113.7 percent. This is due in large part to the fact that Hong Kong's Internet penetration was already far above the world average at 68.8 percent.

As Internet penetration increases in countries all over the world, and firms recognize the business benefits that are gained with the SaaS model, it is inevitable that the popularity will increase as well. A study released by Gartner showed that in 2009, worldwide SaaS sales were at about $7.5 billion. In 2010, however, Gartner predicts worldwide SaaS sales would be up 14.1 percent from 2009, at around $8.5 billion. This rapid increase in the SaaS market means that in the future "on-demand applications will make up a larger percentage of total enterprise software sales." SaaS applications, which accounted for a little more than 10 percent of the total enterprise software market in 2009, are expected to represent at least 16 percent of worldwide software sales by 2014.

BIBLIOGRAPHY

"1880s: Birth of an Electric Power Industry." Smartgrid, May 17, 2010. Available from http://www.smartgrid.gov/history/1880.

Barrett, Larry. "SaaS Market Growing by Leaps and Bounds: Gartner." July 27, 2010. Available from http://itmanagement.earthweb.com/entdev/article.php/3895101/SaaS-Market-Growing-by-Leaps-and-Bounds-Gartner.htm.

Benioff, Marc, and Carlye Adler. *Behind the Cloud.* San Francisco: Jossey-Bass, 2009.

Carr, Nicholas. The Big Switch: Rewiring the World, from Edison to Google. New York: W.W. Norton & Company, Inc., 2009.

"Citrix Systems, Inc. (CTXS.O)." Reuters. Available from http://reuters.com/finance/stocks/companyProfile?symbol=CTXS.O.

Dell, Michael. Forward to *Behind the Cloud*, by Marc Benioff. San Francisco: Jossey-Bass, 2009.

Edmonston, Peter. "Google's I.P.O., Five Years Later." *New York Times*, August 19, 2009. Available from http://dealbook.blogs.nytimes.com/2009/08/19/googles-ipo-5-years-later/.

Feiman, Joseph. "How to Keep Your Job From Disappearing Into the Cloud." Gartner, August 26, 2010. Available from http://www.gartner.com/.

"Google Inc. (GOOG.O)." Reuters. Available from http://www.reuters.com/finance/stocks/companyProfile?symbol=GOOG.O.

"GoToMeeting and GoToWebinar Raise CitrixOnline to #2 in Global Web Conferencing Market." Citrix News, August 2, 2010. Available from http://www.citrix.com/English/NE/news/news.asp?newsID=2303637.

Herbert, Liz. "New Global SaaS Adoption Data Shows Emerging Geographies Embracing the Deployment Model." June 21, 2010. Available from http://blogs.forrester.com/liz_herbert/.

———. "SaaS Adoption 2010: Buyers See More Options But Must Balance TCO, Security, and Integration. June 14, 2010. Available from http://www.forrester.com/rb/Research/saas_adoption_2010_buyers_see_more _options/q/id/57006/t/2.

"Internet Usage Statistics: The Internet Big Picture." Internet World Stats. Available from http://www.internetworldstats.com/stats.htm.

"Intuit Inc (INTU.O)." Reuters. Available from http://reuters.com/finance/stocks/overview?symbol=INTU.O.

"Join the Cloud Crowd." Salesforce.com. Available from http://www.salesforce.com/company/careers/locations/.

"Median Salary by Job." Payscale.com. Available from http://www.payscale.com/research/US/Industry=IT_Consulting/Salary.

Moltzen, Edward F. "Intuit Goes SaaS With QuickBooks." November, 17, 2008. Available from http://www.crn.com/reviews/applications-os/212002586/intuit-goes-saas-with-quickbooks.htm.

"On Demand." Plex Online. Available from http://www.plex.com/ondemand/index.asp.

A Primer for Understanding and Maximizing the Value of SaaS Solutions. THINKstrategies. Available from http://thinkstrategies.icentera.com.

"Products & Solutions." Citrix. Available from http://www.citrix.com/English/ps2/products/product.asp?contentID=1857200.

"QuickBooks Online." Intuit. Available from http://oe.quickbooksonline.intuit.com.

Routon, John. *Cloud Computing Explained.* Recursive Limited, 2010.

"Salesforce.com, Inc (CRM)." Reuters. Available from http://www.reuters.com/finance/stocks/companyProfilesymbol=CRM.

Swanburg, Scott. "SaaS –What is it really?" The Citrix Blog, January 22, 2009. Available from http://community.citrix.com/pages/viewpage.action?pageId=55443502.

Symonds, Mark. "A Common Thread: Plex Online." Presented at PowerPlex 2010, held May 17-19, 2010 in Dearborn, MI.

"What is Web Hosting Service: Part 4." Eukhost.com. Available from http://blog.eukhost.com/webhosting/what-is-web-hosting-service-part-4/.

SECURITY PRODUCTS AND SERVICES

—■—

SIC CODE(S)

7381

7382

5043

INDUSTRY SNAPSHOT

Security is a multibillion-dollar industry, consisting of a diverse group of corporations that supply personnel and products designed to protect public and private property and individuals from a variety of problems such as theft, arson, and personal attacks. Services include security guards, private investigators, and consultants. Products range from armored cars to X-ray scanning devices to bank vaults. In addition, an area of significant growth and importance for the security industry has been the securing of intangibles, in particular intellectual property, computer-stored information or data, and computer networks. Throughout the world, it was an especially important industry in view of real and assumed threats to national security, petroleum pipelines, nuclear power plants, and the global economy, among others.

As the first decade of the twenty-first century came to a close, factors driving the industry included heightened public concern about crime, decreased government spending on crime and crime prevention, corporate downsizing, advances in security technology, and, because of the terrorist attacks of September 11, 2001, and others, international terrorism. Although the September 11 attacks did not translate into a uniform boom throughout the security industry, they did increase business within certain segments. For example, companies offering contract security services—including consulting and systems integration—were positioned to benefit from large contracts. This was especially the case for those serving government end-markets.

As of 2010, about 23 percent of U.S. households had some kind of home security system installed, and about 18 percent of the systems were professionally monitored, according to researcher Parks Associates. A majority of these systems are installed and monitored by large security firms such as ADT, Brinks (Broadview Security), and Protection One. However, new products were emerging on the market that allowed homeowners to install their own system, and some companies were offering home security packages "bundled" with other services such as Internet access and phone service. Self-monitoring was also becoming an option, as technology advances allowed notification of an alarm being set off or turned off via text messaging on a cell phone. Wireless systems, which eliminated the need to run wires through the house, were also becoming more common.

ORGANIZATION AND STRUCTURE

The security industry contains several distinct fields: civil and military service, public safety, private home and business security, data and information security, personal and consulting services, and a variety of guard services. The guard segment includes personnel such as bodyguards, border patrol officers, customs officials, private detectives, and park rangers. The industry contains many categories of services and products that are related by one common goal: the protection of individuals, groups, and property.

In general, numerous relatively small firms tend to dominate the product manufacturing segment of the

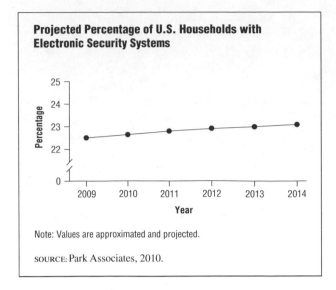

Projected Percentage of U.S. Households with Electronic Security Systems

Note: Values are approximated and projected.

SOURCE: Park Associates, 2010.

industry. Large firms, such as Security Services USA—a division of Sweden's Securitas AB that acquired Burns International, Pinkerton's, and six other U.S. security firms during the late 1990s and the early years of the twenty-first century's first decade—and Wackenhut Corp., dominated the guard segment of the industry, which provides executive protection, special events and strike coverage security, and patrol services, among others. Well-known companies, such as ADT and Brinks, led the home and industrial security systems industry. To demonstrate the volatility of the industry, though, the acquisition of ADT by Tyco International indicated the ongoing competition for position in this rapidly growing field.

The year 2005 became a banner year for cyber-villains, with data theft being only one of the computer security issues. Phishing (sending fraudulent e-mails for the purpose of obtaining personal or financial information), computer viruses aimed at businesses as well as personal computers, and data leaks were just some of the threats posed by hackers.

BACKGROUND AND DEVELOPMENT

The concept of a "police department" is relatively new. King Louis XIV of France maintained a small group of 40 inspectors in the seventeenth century. Their primary job was to report on individuals' movements, not necessarily provide security for them. Beginning in 1633, the city of London hired watchmen to guard its streets at night. That practice carried over to the United States well into the nineteenth century. In 1829, Sir Robert Peel (1788–1850) founded the first true police force in England by reorganizing the London metropolitan police force. The officers became known as "bobbies," in honor of Sir Robert.

The first organized U.S. police department came into existence in New York City in 1845. Boston became the next city to establish its own police force. Gradually, other cities followed suit. Private security, however, was relatively unknown until Allan Pinkerton (1819–1884) came along. Pinkerton is generally considered the father of private security. In 1850, he organized Pinkerton's National Detective Agency in Chicago. Eleven years later, he recovered a large sum of money stolen from the Adams Express Co. and uncovered a plot to assassinate President Lincoln. Those coups enhanced his reputation and accelerated the development of the private security industry, which was helped by the Industrial Revolution.

As the industry grew in the late nineteenth century in the United States, owners looked for ways to protect their property. This was especially true in the western sections of the United States as ranchers and manufacturers expanded throughout the territories. Not surprisingly, companies such as Pinkerton assumed much of the responsibility for protection of private goods and property. They took over the security for banks, department stores, museums, and other private buildings. That led to a spin-off industry of security system design (such as safes and vaults). Then, as homeowners began to see the value of personal property security, companies such as ADT formed to provide it. Concomitantly, there was an outgrowth of the industry into the twentieth century to provide security for government and privately owned facilities such as nuclear power facilities and oil pipelines. These demands created a need for better-trained protection personnel and more sophisticated security systems.

Starting in the late 1980s, technology made it possible for people to get away from traditional methods of buying products and banking. For example, people no longer needed to do their banking or shopping in person. They could do either of these by using automated teller machines (ATMs) or computers, which added to the need for and development of security systems. Naturally, if people chose to do their banking at 2:00 a.m. at out-of-the-way ATMs, they ran a risk of becoming victims of criminals. That risk called for heightened security measures provided by banks. In addition, there grew a need for security systems for computerized transactions made by businesses, banks, financial institutions, and private citizens. The increasing use of computers to conduct business of all kinds had a dramatic impact on the security industry, and companies emerged to fill the need. As a result, the commercial security services industry grew rapidly. In the early years of the twenty-first century's first decade, that growth showed no signs of slowing down. In fact, the security industry was one of the fastest growing—and most diverse—fields of employment in existence at that time.

The security industry expanded rapidly in the wake of highly publicized incidents such as the bombing of New York's World Trade Center in February 1993 and the bombing of the Oklahoma's Alfred Murrah Federal Building in April 1995. As a result of these incidents, the security firm Wackenhut, among others, grew by 20 percent, and the government called for legislation mandating more stringent security measures. Furthermore, because of employee outrage at the stream of corporate downsizing in the 1980s and 1990s, more industries turned to security firms to protect their executives from employee retaliation. Between 1980 and 1996, the number of security companies rose from 70,000 to 160,000 and the number of security employees grew from 975,000 to 2 million. Overall, security products and services mushroomed into a $100 billion industry by the close of the twentieth century, according to the *Los Angeles Business Journal.*

Besides providing technology to secure the Internet, security companies also began to use the Internet to market their products and services. For example, Secure-Rite.com, a division of Clark Security Products, a leading security products distributor with some 30,000 SKUs (stock keeping units or stocked items) in 2004, announced an alliance in 1999 with over 500 independent locksmiths from across the country to offer online marketing of a wide array of home security products. Orders taken online were completed by the nearest affiliated locksmiths. Also in 1999, JAWS Technologies Inc. announced an alliance with Offsite Data Services Ltd. to offer companies both online and off-site backup and recovery software to ensure that client companies have uninterrupted and secure access to their data.

The September 11, 2001, terrorist attacks on the United States created a new security technology market. In the wake of these events, companies in the Bay Area and in Silicon Valley in California focused on the potentially huge market of homeland security and counter-terrorism. Safeview Inc. in Menlo Park licensed a holographic imaging technology developed by the Pacific Northwest National Laboratory in Washington State. The technology was to be used to screen people in airports, illuminating them with high frequency radio waves that form a detailed picture on the screen. The system was capable of detecting plastic or ceramic weapons, plastic explosives, and other nonmetallic potential weapons. A prototype had been around since 1992, but it did not generate a lot of interest until after September 11, 2001. The Ancore Corp. in Santa Clara developed a machine that could scan any size object, from something as large as a truck to something as small as a shoe. Objects were scanned with neutrons. Again, the device attracted little attention until September 11, 2001. However, it soon captured the interest of the U.S. Customs Service.

In 2002, Varian Medical Systems of Palo Alto applied its medical imaging technology to X-ray devices that could scan cargo for explosives. Another Palo Alto firm, Tibco Software Inc., created applications that allow different networks to communicate and share information. Prior to September 11, 2001, the technology was mainly used in the business sector. After the terrorist attacks, the company began pursuing a deal with the government to retool its product, including adding more security measures, so that it suited the government's needs. Tibco eventually began installing the system for the Homeland Security Department.

Secugen Corp. of Sunnyvale, California, made biometric devices for computer security, focusing on fingerprint technology to secure computer systems. The company's technology attracted the attention of the government and was tested at several airports. Microfluidic Systems Inc. in Berkeley developed biodefense technology that could detect pathogens such as anthrax. The company attracted the attention of the U.S. government and large corporations as well as the British Consulate and British Aerospace.

Overall, U.S. companies spent an estimated $5.6 billion on computer security in 2000. According to a study by the Computer Security Institute and the U.S. Federal Bureau of Investigation (FBI), the 273 U.S. businesses surveyed had combined losses of $266 million in 1999 from Internet security breaches and some estimates indicated that total losses to computer crimes could be as high as $10 billion. Consequently, a growing area of increased need during the early part of the new decade was in software security processors for banking, the Internet, and enterprise security applications. These products used encryption technology embedded in hardware to help safeguard sensitive data that might be electronically communicated. The technology was used, for example, in direct deposit banking or credit card purchases over the Internet.

Other computer security technologies included firewalls and authentication. Firewalls are combinations of hardware and software that control access between different networks, allowing only authorized users to gain access to a network's resources. Authentication also involves both software and hardware, requiring users to enter passwords or have requisite certificates that are verified by a network before someone can gain access to its resources.

Theft of computer hardware was also of rising concern in the early years of the first decade of the twenty-first century. The insurance company Safeware Inc., for instance, pegged the number of thefts of laptop computers at almost 319,000 in 1999, up from 303,000 the year before. Therefore, companies developed and marketed products to prevent hardware theft. For instance,

Philadelphia Security Product's Flexguard Security System offered cable lock kits and PIN lock kits to prevent desktop and laptop model computers from being stolen while connected to systems hardware.

In late 2003, the security market was valued at $150 billion worldwide, according to *Mergers & Acquisitions.* Heightened public concern about crime, decreased government spending on crime and crime prevention, corporate downsizing, and advances in security technology continued to support the industry's growth.

In its *2003 Forecast Study, Security Distribution & Marketing* revealed that U.S. security dealers and system integrators saw revenues reach $22.3 billion in 2002, up nearly 10 percent over 2001 levels of $18.1 billion. In terms of product sales within this industry segment, burglar alarms accounted for 43 percent of revenues, followed by fire alarms (18 percent), video surveillance (16 percent), access control (9 percent), home systems other than burglary or fire (7 percent), integrated security systems (5 percent), and other products (2 percent). Revenue from services was led by the sale and installation of residential security systems (32 percent) followed by nonresidential sales and installation (28 percent), monitoring and leasing (17 percent), service and maintenance (12 percent), home systems sales and installation (9 percent), and other services (2 percent).

In the days before September 11, 2001, security budgets often were among the first to experience cuts. After the terrorist attacks, many corporate security directors increased their security budgets to accommodate more electronic security. However, it did not translate into a uniform boom throughout the security industry. Large defense contractors with the engineering expertise to assist the government with complex systems integration projects were positioned to reap more immediate rewards than traditional security product and service providers. In December 2003, industry analysts at Frost & Sullivan revealed that the U.S. government security market was worth almost $7.5 billion in 2002 and was expected to reach $16.0 billion by 2009.

Information technology (IT) security remained high on the corporate sector's radar heading into the middle of the twenty-first century's first decade, as virus attacks cost companies as much as $17 billion every year. In December 2003, the CERT Coordination Center (CERT/CC) at Carnegie Mellon University's Software Engineering Institute reported that cyber security incidents were up significantly. According to *Security Management,* in the first half of 2003, more than 76,400 cyber security incidents were reported. This number represented 93 percent of all attacks reported in 2002.

According to the *Los Angeles Business Journal,* the industry's revenues soared from $20 billion in 1980 to approximately $100 billion by 1999. In late 2003, *Mergers*

& Acquisitions reported that worldwide, the industry was worth some $150 billion. For this reason, companies were investing to protect their networks and data. Infonetics reported about 66 percent of respondents to a survey planned to buy so-called integrated security appliances—a new breed of security device that can include firewalls, virtual private networks (VPN), intrusion and detection prevention, vulnerability assessment, virus scanning, and content filtering—by 2005.

A *Security Distribution & Marketing* (SDM) report in May 2006 showed that the top 100 electronic security firms in 2005 captured $6.68 billion in revenue, about a 25 percent market share of the total $27 billion industry, with approximately 10.87 million subscribers. This was an increase of 4 percent from the year before. Forty of the SDM 100 companies achieved double-digit growth. Collectively, 2005 was the best revenue year since 1997. Sales in security systems improved from 2004 to 2005 in every market: residential, small business, commercial, and integrated systems. Residential sales, in particular, were strong, thanks to the very active real estate market.

A major security concern heading into the latter part of the decade continued to be cyber villainy. Major corporations, such as Citigroup and Time Warner, had sensitive data stolen from databases that were thought to be secure. However, data theft was only one of the major trends in security issues seen by security experts. Phishing, deceitful e-mail that encourages users to divulge personal or financial information, was expected to target customers of smaller organizations and beyond. Internet viruses, such as the worm Zotob, which exploited a vulnerability in Microsoft's Windows system, began to target businesses as well as home users. Although millions had been spent securing networks from intruders, company insiders and executives were the source of many data leaks in 2005. Wireless devices were an increasingly easy target for hackers to access people's private data. The newest form of spam attacks in the latter part of the decade was voice spam, made possible by VoIP (Voice-Over-Internet Protocol) applications, which allows telephone calls to be made using a broadband Internet connection instead of a regular (or analog) phone line. VoIP services lack strong encryption and are an easy target for spammers. Users' calls can be redirected or hijacked by advertisements.

In February 2005, in compliance with statutory mandates, the automated system US-VISIT Initiative was put into place by the Department of Homeland Security (DHS) to track the arrival and departure of certain foreign visitors to the U.S. The system captures biometric (specific and uniquely identifiable physical human characteristics, such as the retina, iris, acoustic spectrum of the voice) information when foreign visitors apply for a visa at a U.S. embassy or consulate or when they arrive at a U.S. port of entry. Upon arrival, they have their fingerprints and photographs taken for comparison to the US-VISIT database to ensure that they the same people who received the visa abroad. The biometric information is also checked against certain immigrant and criminal databases to be sure a visitor should be permitted to enter the United States On January 5, 2004, the US-VISIT system began operations at 14 seaports and 115 airports, with 50 of the busiest land border ports of entry added to the system at the end of December 2004. Initially, enrollment at land border ports of entry would be limited to secondary inspections. Mexicans with Border Crossing Cards would not be enrolled in the system at its outset unless they planed to be in the United States for over 72 hours or if they were traveling more than 25 miles.

CURRENT CONDITIONS

The results of SDM's "2010 Industry Forecast Study" showed a 7.8 percent industry decline in 2009. Revenues for that year were $44.6 billion, and were expected to drop another 1.6 percent (to $43.9 billion) for the full 2010 year. According to SDM, this was the first time that a revenue decrease had been reported since SDM started its study in 1981. The bad economy was cited as the primary factor in the revenue decline, particularly the falling real estate market.

With far fewer new homes being constructed, sales of new residential alarm systems suffered, in addition to large declines in all (new and used) home sales. If roughly 15 percent of the nearly six million homes foreclosed since 2007 had security monitoring, that would reprensent nearly 900,000 subscriptions lost. However, 2009 showed a six percent rise in monthly monitoring *rates,* and a two percent overall rise in revenues. Consequently, the residential burglar alarm and monitoring market was on target to experience roughly nine percent growth rates from 2010 through 2012, according to market researcher Parks Associates. It forecasted that revenues in this segment of the market (the residential intrusion and monitoring market) would reach at least $9 billion for 2010. Nearly 75 percent of this would come from monitoring revenues ($6.7 billion), another 20 percent from hardware purchases ($1.8 billion) and about six percent ($521 million) from installation labor.

Declining real estate values also caused a shift within the security systems industry, as companies retooled from residential into commercial properties. Notwithstanding, noted SDM, some regional markets held strong in 2009 and 2010. Texas, for example, remained a strong market, as did the Pacific Northwest.

The products segment of the industry held strong, as advances in technology continued unabated. In fact, the MSSP (managed security service provider) market saw revenues increase to $1.2 billion in 2009, according to

research firm Frost & Sullivan. The firm predicted this figure would rise to $3.9 billion by 2016. Large enterprises accounted for nearly 60 percent of all revenues, as they were perceived by their principals to be targets for ever-increasing attacks. A 2008 *Access Control & Security Systems ntegration* article stated that "Electronic access control systems have now pervaded the fabric of society and the market for security systems will continue on an upward trajectory. The market expects to grow at a tremendous pace and transform the ability to access buildings and computer networks."

The global revenues for security software were $14.8 billion in 2009, expected to reach $16.5 billion by the end of 2010. Within those revenues, the consumer sector was the largest element, representing $3.9 billion in 2009 and an expected $4.2 billion for the full year 2010 (mid-year forecast by Gartner Associates). The enterprise sector was the second largest, with $2.9 billion in 2009 and an anticipated $3 billion for 2010. Within the enterprise sector, identity and access management (IAM) was a leading source of revenues. According to Gartner, IAM clients spent roughly 8 percent of their security budgets on IAM software; the market was predicted to reach more than $12 billion by 2014.

In a September 2010 release from ABI Research, RFID systems (radio frequency identification, such as in barcodes) were expected to bring in more than $6 billion for 2011. This area included both traditional applications such as access control, automobile immobilization, e-ID/ID documents, etc., as well as some newer applications, including animal ID, baggage and cargo tracking and security, and contactless payment and ticketing. Part of the sector boost was from retail chain Walmart's multi-billion unit passive UHF RFID apparel tag and 15,000 handheld readers, sparking new interest in RFID for item-level tracking.

INDUSTRY LEADERS

Many companies in the security industry concentrate on specific niches, offering specialized services such as electronic debugging, background investigations, or anti-stalking operations. In the field of personal security services, the Anvil Group of London has been inconspicuously serving individuals and corporations since 1988 by providing executive protection against terrorism, extortion, and kidnapping, as well as investigative services for alleged celebrity stalking.

Top security companies, according to *Security Distribution & Marketing,* include ADT Security Services, Brink's Home Security, Protection One, HSM Electronic Protection Services, and Monitronics International.

G4S, formerly Group 4 Securicor, the world's second largest private-sector employer (behind supermarket chain Wal-Mart) is based in the United Kingdom and has activities in more than 100 countries. The Wackenhut Corporation, headquartered in Palm Beach Gardens, Florida, and founded by George Wackenhut, is the U.S.-based division of G4S. The massive company, with 595,000 employees, provided services ranging from cash/revenue transportation (by railway across the United Kingdom) to general security and protection. In 2009, G4S grew more as a result of U.K. government outsourcing, bringing an 18 percent growth in revenue at $7 billion pounds. Its profits also rose 20 percent to $417 million pounds ($632.5 million).

Wackenhut had 32,000 highly qualified employees dedicated to providing the organization with a competitive edge. Wackenhut rose to become one of the industry's largest security firms in the late 1990s. During this period, Wackenhut won key contracts that included providing services to AT&T, the Kennedy Space Center, and Bank of America. By 1999, it had received two new lucrative accounts: first, as primary security provider for IBM Corp. at its world headquarters and 37 other locations in 14 states, and second, as the provider of fire and emergency services for Ciba Specialty Chemicals commencing in May 1999 at Ciba's Alabama facility. In 2000, Wackenhut added the U.S. Embassy in El Salvador to its 20 other embassy clients. That same year, Wackenhut secured a five-year contract with the Federal Aviation Administration for the Atlantic City, New Jersey, International Airport.

Sweden-based Securitas is the world's second largest security firm. Years ago, it acquired the best-known company in the security business, Pinkerton's Inc., which named approximately half of the Fortune 500 companies as clients. The company's chief focus is on integrated security systems (i.e., combining high-tech electronic access control and monitoring tools). It also provides security personnel and consulting services, performs undercover work and fraud investigations, and offers executive protection and network security management. The firm's consulting arm offers on-site security system design and analysis and provides global risk assessments of terrorist and criminal activities. Specific services include searches for missing persons; patent and trademark infringement investigations; security system consulting; design engineering; project management; security system sales, installation, and service. Along with Burns International, American Protective Services Inc., and a number of other firms acquired by Securitas, Pinkerton became part of Securitas Security Services USA. guards. With more than 215,000 employees and a presence in approximately 30 countries, Securitas generated $8.2 billion in revenues in 2009. It also entered into a global agreement with UNI Global Union, committing to the well-being of the communities it operated in, and honoring the freedom of workers to form unions.

Tyco International Ltd. of Princeton, New Jersey, manufactures, designs, and sells electronic components, undersea cable, disposable medical supplies, fire suppression and detection equipment, security systems, and flow control products. In August 2001, Tyco scored a significant acquisition when it bought Sensormatic of Boca Raton, Florida, a global leader in electronic security. In 2005, Tyco's CEO Dennis Kozlowski was convicted of stealing millions of dollars from the company. In an attempt to make a fresh start, in 2007, executives divided the firm into three publicly held companies: Covidien Healthcare, Tyco Electronics, and Tyco International. Tyco International includes ADT Worldwide, Safety Products, and Fire Protection Services. In early 2010, Tyco International acquired Brink's Home Security (which was operating under the name of Braodview Security) for $2 billion in cash and stock.

One of the leading producers of security equipment was SafePak Corp., based in Portland, Oregon. SafePak develops and sells specialized deposit collection and ATM equipment to the banking industry, one of the leading users of security services. The company developed a deposit retrieval system for night depositories and ATMs that was considered the standard for the industry. SafePak's system dramatically reduced transportation and personnel costs involved in customer deposit collection and increased security for the deposits themselves. Moreover, it reduced dangers to bank customers and to the security personnel who were responsible for their safety, and increased the protection of banks' property and assets.

Other leading security firms included New York-based Guardsmark Inc. Employing large numbers of former FBI and U.S. Secret Service agents, Guardsmark provided security services, investigations, consulting, background screening, facility design, executive protection, and more. Allied Security Holdings, which began doing business as AlliedBarton Security Services after the 2004 purchase of Barton Protective Services, was one of largest private security firms in the United States in 2008. With headquarters in Pennsylvania, Allied served more than 3,300 customers in 100 offices. The company had 2007 sales of $1.2 billion. Doberman Security Products, based in Los Angeles and founded in 2001, offered security products for consumers, personal items, and homes. Its team of security professionals, engineers, and researchers spent three years developing, testing, and approving personal and home security devices, chosen for dependability, usability, durability, and effectiveness in addressing the specific security needs of home and daily life. In March 2006, Doberman began selling its Active and Home Security Lines at Target stores.

WORKFORCE

In the early 2000s, there were over 2.38 million people employed in the security services and equipment industry, including 1 million security guards (also called security technicians, patrollers, or bouncers); 132,000 production workers; 90,000 private investigators; and 16,500 armored car guards. There were also about 6,200 consultants and engineers in the field who designed and implemented security plans to protect personal property and goods. They generally worked closely with company officials to develop comprehensive security programs to fit individual clients' needs. They also generated policies and procedures on the effective destruction of critical documents and the protection of data processing and other machinery. Once their systems were implemented, they remained responsible for overseeing their effectiveness and amending the plans as needed.

As one indication of the seriousness of the security industry in meeting society's needs, educational requirements for consultants became quite rigid. In the first decade of the twenty-first century, many companies preferred to hire security consultants with at least a college degree. Ideally, consultants should have a well-rounded education, including courses in business management, communications, computers, sociology, and statistics. They should (but are not required to) have experience in police work, government, or other fields of crime prevention as well. The security industry needs a large variety of trained and experienced employees to develop and implement products and services required to combat sophisticated terrorists and criminals. *Security Management,* however, reported that some companies were forced to hire unskilled workers for security positions because of the shortage of skilled professionals. To compensate for the lack of experience, companies turned to computer-aided training programs that provided simulated security problems for trainees to resolve.

Private security workers were expected to be used increasingly to supplement or replace police officers in such activities as courtroom security, crowd control at airports, and at special events such as the Olympics, as state funding was reduced and companies continued to downsize. Meanwhile, others in the field were employed by firms developing and selling security systems.

AMERICA AND THE WORLD

European firms have made huge inroads into the U.S. security market. Sweden's Securitas acquired eight U.S. security companies in 1999 and 2000, including Pinkerton's Inc. and Burns International. German companies Siemens AG and Bosch AG acquired STGC and Detection Systems, respectively. Finally, Danish security firm Group 4 Falck A/S acquired Wackenhut Corp. in a $520

million deal. However, the Transportation Security Act had implications for this trend following the September 11, 2001, terrorist attacks. As Ida Corman explained in the October 1, 2003, issue of *Mergers & Acquisitions,* "Among other provisions, the far-reaching law precludes foreign-controlled companies from providing security at U.S. airports and requires domestic companies to run the security operations at all U.S. ports. These provisions stem from dissatisfaction in Congress and the government over security services provided at airports by foreign-based firms before 9/11."

The Asian economic crisis brought about political disquiet, as well as greater opportunities for security providers. In Indonesia, for example, the economic slump caused the country, which previously was relatively free of violence, to suffer from more frequent civil disturbances, riots, and looting, according to *Security Management.* As a result, more companies in Indonesia sought to install new security systems or enhance their existing systems. Furthermore, Chinese government agencies purchased CCTV (closed circuit TV) equipment to monitor the population as well as the traffic. In countries where labor is inexpensive, however, companies and organizations preferred hiring security guards to buying security equipment.

In Latin America, crimes such as abduction, hijacking, and armed robbery of production and warehouse facilities led to the need for greater security measures, including both products and services. Mexico and Brazil in particular increased their demand for security products and services, according to *Security Management.*

RESEARCH AND TECHNOLOGY

Los Angeles-based Applied DNA Sciences Inc. (ADNAS), specializing in intellectual property protection, has developed biotechnology products that use DNA to stop counterfeiters and other wrongdoers from accessing or stealing protected corporate data. ADNAS was recognized for the development of its Applied DNA Technology Access System. Working through the interaction of the company's Applied DNA Chip and Applied DNA Chip Reader, it has a wide range of possible applications in the government, financial, and retail sectors.

Another breakthrough technology involved biometric devices called access control iris identification systems. Such a system verifies a person's identity using images of the person's iris, the ring around the pupil of the eye. Iris scanning access control systems have been adopted by organizations and correctional institutions to ensure that only authorized people gain access to sensitive and restricted resources. Iris scanning, unlike other methods, such as photo identification and fingerprinting, cannot be circumvented easily. Photo identification requires a person to judge the resemblance of the photograph to the identification holder and fingerprints require a forensic expert to examine them. In contrast, an iris scan system is computerized and does not rely on human judgments.

Biometrics technology was expanding to include systems that recognized scent, facial features, and gait (the way a person walks). While biometric proponents sang the technology's praises, others argued that the systems were difficult to administer and that they often generated both false positive and false negative errors, thus holding more promise as a supplement to more traditional forms of security, such as passwords, card keys and the like, rather than a substitute.

Some new products that were highlighted at the April 2006 U.S. Law and Ready! Exposition in Washington included Customized Mobile Command Units, a command post to be utilized for disaster event coordination and communications and planned crowd control situations; the Biological Detection and Identification Device, the Defender TSR, a hand-held biological detection device with eight biological tests for HAZMAT crews in the field; and the R-300 Outdoor Perimeter Protection, a microwave barrier that is able to distinguish between a human and various animals in order to minimize false alarms, and has the capability to learn and adjust to changing weather and terrain conditions.

One of the new technologies in the home security systems segment of the industry in 2008 was the use of remote control. With products such as Schlage's Z-Wave lock, homeowners can unlock or lock their doors via the Internet. The system operates using radio frequency technology and a battery-operated keypad lock that communicates with a Web-enabled gateway.

BIBLIOGRAPHY

"Choices, Demand Drive Uptake In Access Control Market." *Access Control & Security Systems Integration,* 23 September 2008.

"Doberman Security Products Available at Target." *PrimeZone Media Network,* 29 March 2006.

"Global Security Service Revenues to Exceed $160 Billion in 2010." *SDM Magazine,* 1 March 2007.

Jacobson, Julie. "Tyco Buys Brink's Home Security for $2 Billion." *CE Pro,* 19 January 2010. Available from http://cepro.com/article/.

Magnuson, Stew. "Under Watch: Government Seeking Clear Path for Biometrics Data Use." *National Defense,* September 2008.

"Over 50 New Homeland Security Products Debuting at GovSec, U.S. Law and Ready 2006." *The America's Intelligence Wire,* 26-27 April 2006.

Parks, Tricia. "Why Residential is Ready to Rebound." *Security Sales & Integration,* 1 November 2010.

"Private 'Eyes,' Security Systems Thriving, Growing Businesses." *Colorado Springs Business Journal,* 15 August 2008.

"RFID Systems Revenue to Exceed $6 Billion in 2011, According to Research." *Security Products,* 17 September 2010. Available from http://www.secprodonline.com/articles/2010/09/17/rfid-ayatem-revenue-forecast-20100.aspx.

Scarborough, Melanie. "Turbo Tech: There's Technology, and Then There's Technology." *Community Banker,* September 2008.

Schwartz, Matthew. "Home Security Gets a Web Makeover." *InformationWeek,* 13 September 2008.

"SDM's 2010 Industry Forecast Study Are in: Total Annual Revenue Declined 7.8 Percent in 2009 to $44.67 Billion." *SDM Magazine,* 22 January 2010. Available from http://www.sdmmag.com.

"Stand for Security." Securitas Press Release, 10 November 2010. Available at http://www.seiu.org.

Stepanek, Laura. "Amidst Flux, the Beat Goes On." *SDM Magazine,* 1 January 2007.

Stoltzfus, Dwayne. "Home Security industry Growth Projected in 2010." 12 November 2010. Available from http://www.articlesnatch.com.

———. "Introducing the New SDM 100." *Security Distribution & Marketing,* 1 May 2007.

"UPDATE 2-G4S Eyes Govt Outsourcing Growth, Profit Up 20 Pct." Reuters Press Release, 16 March 2010. Available from http://www.reuters.com/article/idUSLDE62FOB920100316.

"U.S. Managed Security Services Market to Grow by Billions." *Access Control & Security Systems Integration,* 30 September 2008.

"US-VISIT Implementation Faces Challenges at Land Borders." Committee on Homeland Security Democratic Office, 14 May 2006. Available from http://hsc-democrats.house.gov/.

Wilson, Dean. "Security Software Revenues to Rise by 11.3 Percent in 2010." *Security,* 16 August 2010. Available from http://www.techyey.net/security/security-software-revenues-to-rise-by-11-percent-in-2010

Wofle, Daniel. "Some Security Concepts Getting a Second Chance." *American Banker,* 21 October 2008.

SEMICONDUCTORS

——■——

SIC CODE(S)

3674

INDUSTRY SNAPSHOT

The Semiconductor Industry Association (SIA) believes that the semiconductor industry sets the pace for global economic growth. This is because so many products in the world's economy depend on semiconductors. Insatiable demand for computers, wireless communications equipment, and countless other electronic gadgets has made it a vibrant and dynamic industry. In addition to vigorous sales of personal computers (PCs), which is one of the largest markets for semiconductors, growth in semiconductor manufacturing has been fueled by a multitude of consumer electronic devices such as digital audio players, wireless communications, digital cameras, automotive devices, and information appliances.

The performance of the international semiconductor industry has been uneven, with years of solid growth punctuated by periods of overcapacity and weak prices. The low points are felt mostly by the industry's older, more established product lines, such as dynamic random access memory (DRAM) chips (the inexpensive chips used for main memory in PCs), a notoriously commoditized segment usually with low profit margins. Nonetheless, a number of fast-moving emerging segments within the industry (recent examples being flash memory and digital signal processors) has helped the overall market survive and stay on the edge of developing technology. In addition, the growth of "fabless semiconductor companies," is predicted to overshadow traditional integrated device manufacturers (IDMs) by 2010. A fabless company farms out the actual manufacturing of wafer fabric chips, and instead focuses its capital on design and technology in order to stay competitive. Finally, tangible changes in the industry's makeup are expected by the "20-teens," (the second decade of the twenty-first century) due mostly to grand scale consolidation, which is predicted to cause 40 percent of semiconductor vendors in existence during the first decade to die out within 10 years.

ORGANIZATION AND STRUCTURE

The semiconductor industry is divided according to the type of semiconductor produced. Each type has a separate function. All semiconductors, however, are broadly similar. They are all made from materials that conduct electricity, such as copper, iron, and aluminum, and from insulators, such as rubber, glass, and wood. Semiconductors are important because they can change the way an electric current behaves, or even change one form of energy (such as light) into another form (such as electricity).

Transistors, perhaps the most important form of semiconductors, are particularly important because they can control the flow of a very large electric current by means of a very small electric current at another point on their surface. They can act like switches in conducting electric current. For example, some transistors conduct electricity well only over a certain voltage—the amount of effort needed to move electricity in a current from one place to another. When the threshold voltage is reached, the transistor stops resisting the current and becomes a conductor of the current. This ability of transistors to act as both resistors and conductors of electricity allows them to serve as switches. Different settings of different switches allow information to be stored and communicated. This basic property of semiconductor material allowed scientists to develop the microprocessors and microcomputers that have so influenced the modern industrial world.

All semiconductor chips are manufactured using basically similar processes. They are most commonly made from a silicon matrix composed of melted sand embedded with small crystals. Although other raw materials have been used to make semiconductors, including some plastics and ceramics, sand is most common. It is plentiful, inexpensive, and it works well. To make a semiconductor, a manufacturer melts sand into a column. Usually these columns are between six and eight inches in diameter, although recently they have expanded to 12 inches. The columns are cut into a series of thin wafers. Wafer manufacturing is usually separate from finished semiconductor manufacturing. Each wafer is then implanted or printed with a series of small circuits, which vary according to the function of the chip. The wafer is then cut into chips, which are sold to computer manufacturers, makers of electronic equipment, and hobbyists.

It is the imprinted circuits that make semiconductors function. They can be placed on the silicon matrix in a variety of ways. During the melting process, the manufacturer introduces impurities, called "dopants," in the form of crystals of phosphorus, aluminum, boron, or gallium, which change the semiconductor's ability to conduct electricity. This is commonly done by treating the wafer with chemicals. The first chemical makes it react like a piece of photographic paper. Next, a template called a photomask is placed over the wafer. The wafer is then treated with light-sensitive chemicals that cause tiny metal lines, some no thicker than 1/25 of a micron—finer than the finest human hair—to be deposited on its surface. Another way to imprint a circuit on a wafer is to flood the wafer with other dopants. The wafer is then heated to induce the dopant's atoms to line up in the desired pattern. Another way is to shoot atoms of the dopant directly into the surface of the wafer. All these processes can be repeated on several different levels, so that a single microchip may contain several layers of semiconductors within its surface.

Manufacturers divide semiconductors into two large categories: analog and digital. Analog semiconductors pass electricity in continuous waves of fluctuating voltage. They can amplify or regulate voltages, coordinate signals between different systems, or convert data from analog or linear signals into digital signals and back again. Analog integrated circuits are used in amplifiers, electronic musical instruments, and electronic analog computers. Digital semiconductors process information as a series of extremely high-speed pulses, using the ability of transistors to function as on/off switches. Each pulse that passes through the circuit switches a transistor "on" or "off." Thus digital circuitry requires only two voltage levels ("on" voltage and voltage) to communicate exact information quickly and accurately. High-speed microprocessors, such as Intel's Pentium processors, are capable of passing hundreds of millions of pulses per second, that can then be translated into other types of information, through binary (two-digit) communication languages. Digital semiconductors are subdivided into three functional types: memory chips, microprocessors, and logic chips.

Memory Chips Memory chips are made specifically to store information. Memory chips may be read-only memory (ROM) or random access memory (RAM). Some semiconductors (volatile memory chips) lose the information they store when their power is interrupted, while others (nonvolatile memory chips) can retain data through a loss of power. These concepts translate into different classes of memory semiconductors.

Dynamic random-access memory (DRAM) chips are most common in PCs. They store information quickly and cheaply, and allow it to be accessed relatively rapidly. The counterpart to the DRAM chip is the static random access memory (SRAM) semiconductor. SRAM performs the same functions as DRAM, but much faster. Unlike DRAM, SRAM does not require a constant electric current to operate. It can retain information with less current and operate much faster than DRAM. SRAM, however, is more complicated to manufacture and thus costs more than DRAM, so its use in computer systems is less common. Continually expanded processor power and function necessitates a corresponding upgrade in RAM modules. Extended data output random access memory modules may be required for faster machines that process greater quantities of digitized data simultaneously.

The flash memory chip is a nonvolatile semiconductor that can be erased and reprogrammed electrically. One example of a computer chip that uses flash memory is the binary input/output system (BIOS), a ROM chip that checks the hardware for system memory and the presence of installed devices such as disk drives. The BIOS directs the computer through the process of initial program load of the operating system. Flash memory chips are found in communications equipment as well as in computing devices.

Microprocessors Microprocessors are a specific type of chip used primarily in computers, but they are also important to the telecommunications, electronics, and automobile industries. They are sometimes called central processing units because they control and coordinate the processing of data from all other points of the computer.

They consist of a series of specialized integrated circuits contained in a single chip. Microprocessors are what make computers such powerful tools. Microprocessors can pack thousands or even millions of transistors into a very small area—in some cases, less than the size of a human fingernail. The best known of these microprocessors is the series manufactured by Intel, including the popular Pentium series.

Logic Devices A third category of semiconductors is logic devices. They control the ways in which information is transmitted and interpreted within a single electronic system. While most other types of semiconductors can be used in different types of equipment without major changes, logic devices usually have to be designed to fit into a particular system. There are three main categories of logic devices: complex programmable logic devices, field programmable logic devices, and application-specific integrated circuits (ASICs). The two programmable logic devices are fairly standard across the industry. Their value lies in the fact that manufacturers can modify them to suit their particular needs by using electrical codes. The ASICs have to be designed and constructed for a particular function and thus tend to be more expensive.

Encryption Devices Early in 1999, industry leader Intel acknowledged plans to develop a new application-specific integrated circuit (ASIC) called an encryption chip for a variety of applications including online banking and commerce transactions. Encryption technology originally emerged in the late 1990s as virtual private networks proliferated among business and industry. In order to achieve security over these networks, companies turned first to software packages but soon looked to hardware solutions for greater privacy. As a hardware component, the encryption chip would significantly expand the complexity of the array used to encrypt the data far beyond the original U.S. Data Encryption Standard that permits a maximum of 56 computer digits. In addition to the expanded array, the dedicated encryption chip would support multiple passes of the data through the chip before the process would be completed for transmission. Encryption chip technology would be useful in a variety of security applications, including the protection of copyrighted electronic materials, such as videotaped releases, from unauthorized duplication.

Another commercially important technology is the digital signal processor (DSP). A DSP's only function is to change an analog signal into a digital one. It's capable, however, of handling these signals at speeds up to 10 times faster than the average microprocessor. Digital signal processors (DSPs) have recently come down in price, and new technology allows them to be easily programmed. Although sales of DSPs amount to only a small portion of the semiconductor market, their sales have been growing at more than 20 percent a year. Some of the new applications in which DSPs could become important include voice-activated computers, videoconferencing, and downloading of digital television programs, movies, and games through consumers' television sets. Texas Instruments controls about 45 percent of the DSP manufacturing industry. The U.S. firm Lucent Technologies Inc. also ranks among the world's largest semiconductor manufacturers in the DSP market. The rest of the DSP industry is divided between several other firms, including Motorola.

BACKGROUND AND DEVELOPMENT

Semiconductors occur regularly in the natural environment. In 1874, Karl Ferdinand Braun used crystals of galena, an ore of lead, to make a simple semiconductor device to regulate electric current. Any atom that has more than three and fewer than six electrons in its outermost energy level can be a semiconductor. Inert gases such as helium and neon and rocklike materials such as mica have eight electrons in their outermost energy level and are very good insulators. Metals such as gold, silver, and copper are excellent conductors because they have only one electron in their outermost energy levels. The best semiconductors, such as silicon and germanium, have between three and six electrons. Even then, however, they have to be put through a manufacturing process in order to become commercially useful.

In the days before widespread development of semiconductors, scientists worked and experimented with other devices that could perform the same functions. Thomas Edison observed the principle behind the electron tube—the idea that an electric current would flow in only one direction through the device—as early as 1883. The electron tube was first developed in 1905 by Sir J. Ambrose Fleming, who used it to detect high-frequency radio waves. It works on the principle of heating or "cooking" electrons off a heated metal plate in order to affect current flow. Because this heating had to take place in a vacuum to prevent the plate from melting or oxidizing, these tubes were also called vacuum tubes. Electron tubes were common in early radio receivers and were common to nearly all telecommunications devices until the late 1950s and early 1960s. They are still seen in some microwave ovens, x-ray machines, and radar equipment.

Although the electron tube was indispensable in the development of the radio industry, it had its own problems. Electron tubes were bulky, inefficient, and fragile. In 1948, three scientists working at Bell Laboratories developed the first practical solid-state equivalent of the electron tube. Walter H. Brattain, John Bardeen, and William Shockley created the first transistors with the idea of replacing the tubes with something less fragile. The transistors were virtually unbreakable, gave off almost no heat, and were very small—in some cases, no larger than the tip of a man's finger. In 1952, one of the original developers, Shockley, further refined the transistor, making it less fragile and more reliable.

In 1958, Jack Kilby created the first integrated circuit (IC), a complex electronic device that incorporated one or more semiconductors. Kilby's integrated circuit (IC) combined transistors with other electronic devices, such as resistors and capacitors, to create a solid-state electronic device. It represented a great advance over existing electronic devices because it was less fragile and more compact. The miniaturization potential of the IC made possible the development of the microcomputer in the 1960s.

The history of computing took another great leap forward in 1971 when Intel created the first microprocessor. The microprocessor made possible the coordination of great numbers of integrated circuits into a single system. Only four years later, IBM Corp. introduced its first PC, and in 1976, Apple Computer Inc. introduced the first model in its popular Apple line. The PC had left the laboratory for the office, the classroom, and the home.

Even more astounding were the strides made as embedded systems permeated the manufacturing environment. Embedded systems are complete one-chip computers that perform a comprehensive spectrum of maintenance functions for the electronic operation of a device or appliance. By the mid-1990s, embedded systems were standard features on automobiles, security devices, household appliances, elevators, computer testing systems, and office machinery. The variety of potential applications for these systems will not be realized for years to come.

Aside from swift unit demand, the semiconductor recovery was under-girded by stronger prices. Whereas ample supply, soft international markets, and price competition took their toll on prices in the mid to late 1990s, by 1999 the industry found its products in relatively short supply and had to race to keep up with demand. Because of the inauspicious pricing climate, most manufacturers held the line on introducing new capacity, and few new fabrication plants were built.

The overall semiconductor market recovered in 1999 from a three-year lull. Surprising to many observers was the buoyancy of analog chips. These speedy, often task-specific semiconductors have often been viewed as holdovers from a bygone era, as chips facing extinction. On the contrary, soaring demand for computers, multimedia devices, and other electronics has kept a steady flow of analog chips coming from top makers such as Texas Instruments Inc., Philips Electronics, and Motorola,

Inc., as well as a bevy of smaller specialized producers. Analog chips in fact tend to have a complementary relationship with their digital brethren, and hence the more digital chips are needed, the more analog chips are needed. Newer digital cell phones, for instance, have required more analog semiconductors than older models.

In 2003, four industry leaders—ABB, Accenture, Intel, and Microsoft—announced they had formed an alliance to help manufacturers link plant floor operations and enterprise IT systems. The same year, Intel announced that many industry leaders had joined forces to support "the Advanced Switching" specification, the communications-oriented complement to the PCI Express Interconnect standard. Advanced Switching uses the same physical and link layers as PCI Express architecture to achieve widespread interoperability and availability of technology.

By 2005, personal computer sales represented about 30 percent of the semiconductor market. Other key semiconductor product categories included discreet components (including power transistors and radio frequency transistors found in wireless consumer products); opto-electronics (including image sensors used in camera phones and digital still cameras); and analog devices, microprocessors, microcontrollers, digital signal processors, MOS logic, DRAMs, and flash memory devices. According to *IT Facts,* 50.1 percent of chips sold in 2004 went into the consumer market.

Competition in the industry remained vitally important. The number of operational devices out of all those manufactured drastically cuts into revenues. In the 1980s, chip manufacturers accepted yields of 10 to 30 percent. In the first decade of the 2000s, it was necessary to sustain yields of 80 to 90 percent to remain competitive. Although it was by no means a field that just any company could enter—cutting edge digital chip fabrication plants cost easily a billion dollars or more to build—competition could be credited with many of the ongoing innovations in the industry as well as the persistent downward creep of semiconductor prices over time.

One of the most important trends in the semiconductor industry was the move toward miniaturization. According to *Personal Computer World,* Intel would ship its first x86 system-on-a-chip (SOC) in 2008. The new chip performs processes that were previously spread over four peripheral chips. The new processor, codenamed Tolapei, is expected to cut power by 20 percent compared to multi-chip designs and will reduce the total chip size by up to 45 percent, according to Pat Gelsinger, senior vice president of the Digital Enterprise Group. Reportedly the new chips will be used not only in personal computers but also media players and other electronic devices.

CURRENT CONDITIONS

Research firm Gartner, in a December 2009 report, estimated worldwide semiconductor sales for 2009 at $226 billion. Earlier in August, it had projected a 17 percent decline at just $212 billion, as compared to roughly $255 billion in 2008. In an earlier projection in November 2008, Gartner had expected a 2009 revenue increase to $282 billion. The Semiconductor Industry Association (SIA), in July 2009, had expected worldwide sales of $195.6 billion in 2009, down 21.3 percent from its estimate of $248.6 billion in 2008, more than 6 billion lower than Gartner's projection. These variances showed just how volatile and unpredictable a market it was, following the 2007–2009 global economic slump.

In any event, a decline was consistent with earlier indications. In December 2008, KPMG, LLP, a U.S. audit and tax advisory firm, published its global survey of 85 semiconductor senior level executives in conjunction with the Semiconductor Industry Association (SIA), including device, foundry, and fabless manufacturers. According to the results, growth projections for 2009 were pessimistic at that time. Fifty-two percent of those surveyed had expected revenues to decline, and 39 percent of them believed the decline would be greater than 6 percent.

According to IDC research firm in an October 2009 report, the worldwide semiconductor market for consumer devices actually declined a small 2.6 percent to $42.9 billion in 2008. This followed reported revenues of $44 billion in 2007.

There was one bright star in the market. Despite the disastrous final months of 2008, semiconductor sales of optoelectronics, MEMS-based accelerometers, CMOS image sensors, power transistors, and overall discrete devices reached record-high revenue levels. Collectively, optoelectronics, sensors, and discretes (O-S-D) sales reached an all-time high of $43 billion in 2008, reported market researcher Electronics.ca Publications. By 2013, the O-S-D markets will represent 17 percent of total semiconductor sales, it said.

INDUSTRY LEADERS

Intel Corporation Maker of the first microprocessor, Intel Corp. was the leader in sales of semiconductors industry-wide. In 1971 Intel's founders created the 4004 series microprocessor, which had 2,300 transistors and a processing speed of 60,000 instructions per second. Intel's modern Pentium series processors regularly contain more than 5 million transistors and access them at a processing speed of 400 million instructions per second or better. Intel has become a household word in the United States because of the popularity of its Pentium microprocessors and its commercials advertising "Intel Inside." The

company is also ranked number two globally (behind Samsung) for making flash memories, which are key components of electronic devices, including cell phones.

Intel dominates the industry in the sale of microprocessors, with more than 80 percent of the PC chip market. Its customers Dell and Hewlett-Packard together account for 35 percent of sales, The company employed 99,900 people, and had 2009 revenues of roughly $31.9 billion, holding 14 percent of the market.

Texas Instruments Texas Instruments Inc. (TI), a diversified electronics manufacturer, was one of the United States's largest makers of semiconductors. TI makes and sells an assortment of both digital and analog semiconductors, but perhaps its greatest strength lies in the fast-growing market for digital signal processing semiconductors. The company was increasingly focusing its semiconductor muscle on its digital light processor (DLP) technology for the creation of premium displays for personal computers, televisions, and movie theaters. TI used these devices in electronic toys in the 1970s, but they have emerged as important components of high-speed modems and telephone technology. In 2003, the company announced its selection of Richardson, Texas, as the site of its next major semiconductor plant. This facility is the second TI plant with the capability to build advanced semiconductors on 300-millimeter (12-inch diameter) silicon wafers. In 2009, TI employed 30,986 people and had estimated revenues of $9.57 billion.

Other Leaders Other semiconductor leaders, ranked in 2009 by Gartner, included Samsung (with 2009 revenues of $17.8 billion); Toshiba (with 2009 revenues of $9.74 billion; STMicroelectronics (with 2009 revenues of $8.4 billion); and Qualcomm (with $6.5 billion 2009 revenues. Only 3 of the top 10 semiconductor vendors saw revenue growth in 2009, reported Gartner. Two of them were memory manufacturers, Samsung and Hynix.

AMERICA AND THE WORLD

One factor keeping the semiconductor industry so globally oriented has been the outsourcing to other countries, mostly by U.S. fabless companies, of wafer fabrication. Two-thirds of all fabless wafer demand was met by Taiwan foundries. Singapore also played a key role, and China emerged as a formidable competitor. The latter's entry into the World Trade Organization (WTO) clearly facilitated that objective.

The Semiconductor Industry Association (SIA) reported that the migration of the electronics equipment market to the Asia Pacific region continued unabated. The market remained steady in Japan, at approximately 22 percent. Europe consumed 20 percent of the global market.

Although U.S. companies have a major stake in the world's semiconductor business, they represent less than a third of global sales. The chief competitors of U.S. manufacturers are Japanese producers such as NEC Corp., Toshiba Corp., and Hitachi, Ltd. Other top 10 semiconductor manufacturers are scattered across the world, including Samsung in South Korea. Three European companies—Philips Electronics, STMicroelectronics, and Infineon Technologies—were also major players.

RESEARCH AND TECHNOLOGY

The industry buzz word in the area of research and development was "nano-scaled technology." The need for joint research ventures to develop such technologies prompted Infineon, Intel, Philips, Samsung, and STMicroelectronics to sign on for a sub-45-nm research program at the Inter-university MicroElectronics Center in Belgium. By 2006 Intel and at least three other companies were producing 65-nm technology.

Solid State Technology applauded advances in technology for carbon nanotube devices, saying, "New materials and integration methods must be found for sub-10nm feature sizes on semiconductor devices. Carbon nanotubes have been widely proclaimed as part of a solution because of their extraordinary electrical and mechanical properties."

Key to producing more powerful semiconductors is increasing the number of transistors that can fit on a single chip. The number of transistors on a single chip controls the chip's power. In 1971, when Intel produced its first microprocessor, its transistors measured 10 microns in size, which made them much smaller than the original transistors first produced in 1948. Manufacturers regularly produce semiconductors containing circuits with lines less than 0.13 microns across. Leading-edge technology in 2005 was defined as less than 0.16 microns. Finer lines enable more transistors to be packed onto the same chip. The more transistors on a chip, the faster it can perform its functions.

Although semiconductor technology has advanced tremendously in the past 30 years, scientists are already predicting that there may be limits on how far semiconductor technology can progress. Even though his Moore's Law predicted the power of microchips could double every 18 months, Dr. Gordon Moore, one of the founders of Intel, has suggested more recently that such a progression may not last long. Moore foresees a limit to semiconductor power that may be reached in the next 10 years. In particular, he hinted that it may not be possible for line widths—the size of individual transistors on a single microchip—to be reduced to less than a tenth of a micron. That would limit how many transistors could be packed into a chip.

Researchers are trying to bypass this limit by placing semiconductors deeper inside a chip instead of in a small layer close to the surface, but this technology is not yet commercially viable. In 1999, Lawrence Berkeley National Laboratory announced that researcher Othon Monteiro developed a method of applying copper inlay to the semiconductor wafer instead of the common aluminum alloys in general use. The copper reportedly supported accelerated speeds with better insulation, greater stability, and potentially smaller circuit runs.

BIBLIOGRAPHY

"2006 Annual Report." May 2007. Available from www.sia-online.org/.

"ABB, Accenture, Intel, Microsoft Align to Help Manufacturers Connect Plant Operations to Enterprise Business Systems, New Alliance Enables 'Shop Floor to Top Floor' Connectivity Across Global Network of Plants to Enhance Business Visibility, Decision-Making, Financial Performance." *PrimeZone Media Network,* 3 March 2003.

Akass, Clive. "Miniaturisation Leads to All-in-One Chips." *Personal Computer World,* 17 May 2007.

"AMD, IBM Announce Semiconductor Manufacturing Technology Breakthrough." AMD Press Release, 13 December 2004. Available from www.amd.com/.

Beucke, Dan, and Arik Hesseldahl. "Taking the Pulse at Texas Instruments." *Business Week Online,* 16 May 2007. Available from www.businessweek.com.

Clark, Peter. "ST Chairman Reiterates Industry Consolidation is Coming." *EE Times,* 25 March 2005. Available from www.planetanalog.com/.

"Economy." Semiconductor Industry Association, March 2005. Available from www.sia-online.org/.

"Fabless Growth was Fabulous in 2004." *Silicon Valley/San Jose Business Journal,* 15 March 2005. Available from http://bizjournals.com/.

"First Quarter Global Chip Sales Grew by 3.2 Percent from 2006." Semiconductor Industry Association, 30 April 2007. Available from www.sia-online.org/.

"Gartner Says Worldwide Semiconductor Revenue on Pace to Decline 17 Percent in 2009." *DigitalTVNews,* 26 August 2009. Available from http://www.digitaltvnews.net/content?category_name=market-research.

"Hoover's Company Capsules." *Hoover's Online,* 2007. Available from www.hoovers.com.

"The Industry Handbook: The Semiconductor Industry." Investopedia, 15 May 2007. Available from www.investopedia.com.

"Infineon, Intel, Philips, Samsung, and STMicro Sign Up for IMEC's 45-nm Research Effort." *The Semiconductor Reporter,* 11 October 2003.

"Intel Invests In Chinese Social Network, Five Other Companies." *InformationWeek,* 10 May 2007.

"Industry Facts and Figures." Semiconductor Industry Association, 15 May 2007. Available from www.sia-online.org/.

Keyes, Edward. "Intel No Longer Alone at 65 nm." *Electronic Engineering Times,* 14 May 2007.

Krewell, Kevin. "PCs 2002: Big Gambles Await 2003; Despite the Slowdown, AMD and Intel Continue to Innovate." *Microprocessor Report,* February 2003.

"Market Share: Top 10 Semiconductor Consumers, 2006." Gartner, Inc., 12 February 2007. Available from www.gartner.com.

"Overall Market for Consumer Device Semiconductors Declines in 2008." IDC Research *DigitalTVNews,* 13 October 2009. Available from http://www.digitaltvnews.net/content?category_name=dvd.

Peters, Laura. "Double Gates Prompt Transistor Revolution." *Semiconductor International,* 1 March 2005.

"Return to Record Sales Seen in Opto, Sensors, and Power Discretes." Electronics.ca Publications Press Release, 28 March 2009. Available from http://www.pr.com/press-release/141507.

"Semiconductors." *IT Facts,* 7 March 2004 and 1 March 2005. Available from www.itfacts.biz/.

"Texas Instruments Earnings Could be Barometer for Semis...." 20 July 2009. Available at http://www.learningmarkets.com/index.php/200907203144/News-Feed/News-Feed/texas-instruments-earnings-could-be-barometer-for-semis-qcom-stm.html

"Worldwide Chip Market to Grow 8.6 percent in 2007, 12.1 percent in 2008." *World Semiconductor Trade Statistics,* 2007. Available from www.wsts.org.

"Worldwide Semiconductor Revenue Declined $29 Billion in 2009." *Cellular News,* December 2009.

"Worldwide Semiconductor Revenue Down in 2008-Qualcomm Bucks the Trend." *Cellular News,* Available at http://www.cellular-news.com/story/36921.php

Yager, Tom. "Inside Operton." *InfoWorld,* 9 May 2003.

SLEEP CLINICS

SIC CODE(S)

8011

8031

INDUSTRY SNAPSHOT

Sleep clinics provide a specialized location in which to study sleep disorders. There are two major types of sleep disorders: dyssomnias and parsomnias. A dyssomnia is a disorder of getting to sleep or staying asleep or of excessive sleepiness, whereas parasomnias are disorders of arousal or the interface between sleep and waking. Parasomnias may be induced or exacerbated by sleep but they are not disorders of the sleep stages as dyssomnias are.

Sleep clinics usually have a supervising physician, but the majority of the work will be completed by technicians. Patients might never see a physician while at the clinic, but that should not be a concern as experienced technicians can handle the routine work of sleep tests. A doctor will get the results after the test is completed and interpret them.

A study at a sleep clinic can be expensive, but many insurance programs will pay for it if referred by a primary physician. The doctor who has been handling the previous sleep disorder episodes should make the referral.

Upon arrival at the sleep clinic, patients will be asked to fill out a detailed history of sleep patterns and problems and list of medications and use of tobacco, alcohol, and caffeine. These forms point out any problem areas with regard to a patient's sleep as well as to protect the doctors from malpractice suits.

Most sleep clinics studies require overnight visits, and perhaps even more than one night. Apnea (breathing cessation) and narcolepsy (deep sleep attacks) can usually be diagnosed in one night, whereas insomnia often requires visits several nights in a row. (Patients are allowed to leave to go to work or school during the day.)

While at a sleep clinic, patients sleep with electrodes attached to various points on the body. The sleep test is similar to an electrocardiogram. The electrodes go on the head and eyes, chin, and chest. Depending on the type of study ordered by the doctor, the configurations can be different. Patients wear these electrodes in bed because they collect information during the night. A computer will record brain waves (indicating the phase of sleep), eye movement (indicating REM sleep), muscle tension, and breathing patterns.

There is often a camera (adjusted for low light) and an audio recorder in the room also. Sometimes the technicians will let a patient sleep until they wake up naturally, and sometimes they will wake patients at a preselected time.

When patients leave the sleep clinic, they don't receive any answers about their test. They have to wait until a doctor reads and analyzes the data.

ORGANIZATION AND STRUCTURE

Most people seeking treatment for sleep disorders end up at their regular doctor, who often does not know enough about sleep disorders to give them an effective treatment. Specialized care is often better found at sleep clinics, now a commodity around the United States, where the science of sleep and how to get patients more of it (and better sleep than they are currently getting) is the main focus.

Sleep clinics are often found in hospitals or in independent professional buildings near residential, suburban, and urban locales. They are often staffed by technicians who specialize in giving sleep tests—for example, the multiple sleep latency test (MSLT)—or checking to see if a patient's sleep can be improved by use of a continuous positive airway pressure (CPAP) machine. Technicians must possess accreditation by a sleep technician trainee program or a nationally accredited educational facility. Communication skills for sleep clinic technicians are necessary due to the interaction with patients and other health care professionals, and the ability to monitor nasal and oral airflow in patients is required.

Sleep clinics should not be seen as a solution to a sleep disorder, but rather a tool to get to a solution. Sleep clinic technicians do not diagnose but collect data to report to a primary care physician who will then interpret the results and offer a solution.

BACKGROUND AND DEVELOPMENT

The study of sleep itself did not get started until the 1920s, when scientists studied wakefulness and circadian rhythms. A 1913 book, *Le probleme physiologique du sommeil* by Henri Pieron, drew connections between sleep and psychological studies. His book is seen as the beginning of the modern sleep discovery movement. By the 1950s, Dr. Nathaniel Kleitman and his student, Dr. Eugene Aserinsky, had made the astonishing discovery of rapid eye movement (REM) during sleep.

Another of Kleitman's students furthered the study of sleep even more. Dr. William C. Dement, founder of the Stanford University Sleep Research Center in 1970, built upon Aserinsky's work on REM sleep by describing the "cyclical" nature of sleep in 1955. In 1957 and 1958, Dr. Dement described the relationship between REM sleep and dreaming. Also in 1958, Dr. Dement published a paper describing the sleep cycles experienced by cats. The idea that other species other than humans experienced sleep cycles took the study of sleep way past a side hobby for the medical profession.

In the past 40 years, sleep disorders have seen more and more attention both from the medical profession and from the general public. Statistics show that more children suffer from sleep disorders than adults. Thus, the study of sleep for the improved health of our future generation has taken on a new urgency. As a result, sleep clinics and other specialized clinics focusing solely on sleep now number in the thousands, according to the American Academy of Sleep Medicine. These clinics are accredited and highly specialized and usually accessed by referral only from a primary care physician.

Because of the misinformation given to doctors about sleep disorders, estimates range in the millions about how many children and adults have been misdiagnosed, under- or overmedicated, and/or simply left hanging unnecessarily.

PIONEERS IN THE FIELD

Henri Pieron (1881–1964) was the founder of French experimental psychology. Pieron was trained in philosophy and physiology, and became a leader in physiological studies of sensation and perception. He designed several ingenious optical and other instruments, and was also influential in personnel selection, vocational guidance, and animal psychology, as well as in psychophysics. His important works include *Thought and the Brain* (reprint 1999), *Vocabulaire de la psychologie* (1951; reprint 1990), and *Le probleme physiologique du sommeil,* which drew connections between sleep and psychological studies. This 1913 book is seen as the beginning of the modern sleep discovery movement.

Nathaniel Kleitman (1895–1999) was professor emeritus in Physiology at the University of Chicago. Kleitman is the author of the seminal 1939 book, *Sleep and Wakefulness,* and he is recognized as the father of American sleep research. Kleitman, and his student Eugene Aserinsky, discovered rapid eye movement (REM) sleep and demonstrated its correlation with dreaming and brain activity. Nathaniel Kleitman was born in Russia and emigrated to the United States in 1915. He obtained a PhD from the University of Chicago's department of physiology in 1923 (his thesis was titled, "Studies on the Physiology of Sleep") and joined the University of Chicago faculty in 1925. Two of his students later became well-known sleep researchers: Aserinsky and William Charles Dement.

William C. Dement (1928–) is known as one of the pioneer U.S. sleep researchers as well as founder of the Sleep Research Center, the world's first sleep laboratory, located at Stanford University. He is the world's leading authority on sleep, sleep deprivation, and the diagnosis and treatment of sleep disorders such as sleep apnea and narcolepsy.

In the 1950s, as a medical student at the University of Chicago, Dement was the first to intensively study the connection between rapid eye movement and dreaming. His fellow student Eugene Aserinsky mentioned to him that their professor, Dr. Kleitman, thought that rapid eye movements during sleep might be related to dreaming. Aserinsky, along with Dr. Kleitman, had already noticed the connection but had not considered it to be of interest. Because Dement had an interest in psychiatry, which in those days considered dreams to be important, he was excited by the idea. He began to work on sleep deprivation at Mount Sinai Hospital in the late 1950s and the early 1960s.

Dement was among the first researchers to study sleeping subjects with the electroencephalogram (EEG). Studying these recordings, he discovered and named the five stages of sleep. In collaboration with Dr. Christian Guilleminault, Dement proposed the measuring mechanism that is still used for the clinical definition of sleep apnea and the rating of its severity, the Apnea/Hyponea Index (AHI).

In 1975, Dement launched the American Sleep Disorders Association, now known as the American Academy of Sleep Medicine, and served as president for its first twelve years. In that same year, he and Mary Carskadon invented the Multiple Sleep Latency Test (MSLT), used to measure sleepiness, a test of how quickly people fall asleep during several daytime opportunities.

Dement served as chairman of the National Commission on Sleep Disorders Research, whose final report led directly to the creation of a new agency within the National Institutes of Health, the National Center on Sleep Disorders Research.

Dement teaches the popular "Sleep and Dreams" course at Stanford University. He has also been spending a great deal of time focusing on spreading information about the danger of driving when drowsy and obstructive sleep apnea. Dement is the author of numerous books, including *The Promise of Sleep* and *The Sleepwatchers,* and has written the first undergraduate textbook in the field. He lives with his family in northern California.

CURRENT CONDITIONS

Currently, there are over 2,000 sleep clinics accredited by the American Academy of Sleep Medicine. The study of sleep received official congressional support in 1992 and 1993 with the creation of the National Commission on Sleep Disorders Research, chaired by Dr. William C. Dement. The findings of the Commission include "a startling lack of information about sleep disorders among general practitioners." This lack of information has resulted in millions of misdiagnoses and mistreatments of patients, very often in situations where a little knowledge and the right treatment might have worked better had the doctor been better informed.

As a result of the Commission's work, legislation to create a National Center for Sleep Disorders Research passed into law in January 1993. With passage of this law, the study of sleep and its disorders and how it affects both humans and other species has entered the mainstream.

In neighborhoods and cities across the country, both hospital-based and independent sleep clinics have popped up to serve a community exhausted for answers. These clinics are the new front line of sleep research and will further knowledge and discovery well into the future.

Recent sleep clinics have opened across Ohio, New York, Wisconsin, and Washington. New York's Buffalo Medical Group points to recent study findings that sleep apnea is linked to cardiovascular disease as a main reason for the surge in sleep clinic availability across their area, the state of New York, and the rest of the United States.

INDUSTRY LEADERS

The Stanford Sleep Disorders Clinic is dedicated solely to the exploration of sleep and its disorders in humans. The Stanford Sleep Disorders Clinic and the basic research group at Stanford work with the Stanford University Center for Human Sleep Research located within the Stanford School of Medicine to design clinical studies. Together, they are capable of running short-term and long-term studies. State-of-the-art equipment is used to monitor human subjects in these studies.

Sleep Services of America, Inc. (SSA), provides sleep diagnostic services. Since 1983, its services span seven states and annually perform over 26,000 diagnostic studies for adults and children. SSA offers patients and physicians a trustworthy facility for diagnosing and treating sleep disorders. Jjointly owned by Vital Signs, Inc. (Totowa, NJ) and Johns Hopkins Medicine (Baltimore, MD), SSA provides comprehensive programs and services for patients, physicians, and hospitals. SSA states that its sleep professionals use state-of-the-art equipment to complete diagnostic testing and treatment of patients with sleep disorders. SSA can also provide educational in-services to medical health professionals, asserting, "These services lead to uncompromised quality, high patient and provider satisfaction, and superior results."

The American Academy of Sleep Medicine (AASM) was established in 1975 under the name of the Association of Sleep Disorders Centers. Currently, the AASM is the only professional society that dedicates itself solely to the medical subspecialty of sleep medicine. As the leading voice in the sleep medicine field, the AASM sets specialty-wide standards and promotes excellence in health care, education, and research.

The AASM membership is made up of more than 8,000 physicians, researchers, and other health care professionals. These members study, diagnose, and treat disorders of sleep and daytime alertness such as insomnia, narcolepsy, and obstructive sleep apnea.

WORKFORCE

For decades sleep disorders have been mis- and under-diagnosed by medical professionals, while specialized sleep clinics have been relegated to hack medicine and an easy way for entrepreneurs to make a quick buck. However, in the early twenty-first century, sleep clinics are a booming business. As sleep clinics proliferate, experienced staff and technicians to operate the tests at these sleep clinics will be in high demand.

What kind of skills are needed to work successfully at a sleep clinic? First and foremost, sleep clinic technicians must care about their patients, who often are frustrated and exhausted by their sleep problems. Technicians must possess an empathetic demeanor as they interact with patients who may have not had a good night's sleep in weeks or months or even years. Thus, technicians must have good communication skills in order to effectively hear the frustrations being expressed. How long has the situation been going on? How many hours of sleep on average does the patient get each night? What symptoms are exhibited?

Patients will also be asked to report personal information about their sleep, eating, and exercise habits. Patients often don't want to confess they still smoke the occasional cigarette or consume too much caffeine just before bed. Technicians must understand the propensity for patients to be frustrated at the idea that their eating, exercise, and sleeping habits may be a partial cause of their discomfort. A technician that can listen to what is actually being said without the patient actually saying it will be a sought-after employee.

Other skills can be gained by attending an accredited training program available at many community colleges and state universities around the country. Acceptable training programs teach students the basics about sleep disorders, including operating the testing machines and the right questions to ask to get the best information. However, technicians are not doctors; they are not going to interpret the results. They will simply provide the data for the doctor to later interpret the findings.

AMERICA AND THE WORLD

Sleep disorders affect 70 million Americans, nearly two-thirds of whom have a chronic disorder, according to the National Institutes of Health National Center on Sleep Disorders Research. Nevertheless, sleep clinics just now are becoming more mainstream in the United States. Sleep specialists remark that once again, U.S. doctors are playing catch-up to a science that should have received more legitimate attention before now.

In the United Kingdom, knowledge of sleep medicine and possibilities for diagnosis and treatment garner little attention from the medical professionals. *The Guardian* quotes the director of the Imperial College Healthcare Sleep Centre: "One problem is that there has been relatively little training in sleep medicine in this country—certainly there is no structured training for sleep physicians."

RESEARCH AND TECHNOLOGY

Sleep disorders have diverse symptoms, including:

- Primary insomnia: Chronic difficulty in falling asleep and/or maintaining sleep when no other cause is found for these symptoms.

- Bruxism: Involuntarily grinding or clenching of the teeth while sleeping.

- Delayed sleep phase syndrome (DSPS): inability to awaken and fall asleep at socially acceptable times but no problem with sleep maintenance, a disorder of circadian rhythms. (Other such disorders are advanced sleep phase syndrome (ASPS), non-24-hour sleep-wake syndrome (Non-24), and irregular sleep-wake rhythm, all much less common than DSPS, as well as transient jet lag and shift work sleep disorder.)

- Hypopnea syndrome: Abnormally shallow breathing or slow respiratory rate while sleeping.

- Narcolepsy: Excessive daytime sleepiness (EDS), often culminating in falling asleep spontaneously but unwillingly at inappropriate times.

- Cataplexy: a sudden weakness in the motor muscles that can result in collapse to the floor.

- Night terror: *Pavor nocturnus,* sleep terror disorder or abrupt awakening from sleep with behavior consistent with terror.

- Parasomnias: Disruptive sleep-related events involving inappropriate actions during sleep. Sleepwalking and night terrors are examples.

- Periodic limb movement disorder (PLMD): Sudden involuntary movement of arms and/or legs during sleep. For example, kicking the legs. Also known as nocturnal myoclonus. (See also Hypnic jerk, which is not a disorder.)

- Rapid eye movement behavior disorder (RBD): Acting out violent or dramatic dreams while in REM sleep.

- Restless leg syndrome (RLS): An irresistible urge to move legs. RLS sufferers often also have PLMD.

- Situational circadian rhythm sleep disorders: Shift work sleep disorder (SWSD) and jet lag.

- Obstructive sleep apnea: Obstruction of the airway during sleep, causing lack of sufficient deep sleep; often accompanied by snoring. Other forms of sleep apnea are less common.

- Sleep paralysis is characterized by temporary paralysis of the body shortly before or after sleep. Sleep paralysis may be accompanied by visual, auditory, or tactile hallucinations. Not a disorder unless severe. Often seen as part of narcolepsy.

- Sleepwalking or *somnambulism*: Engaging in activities that are normally associated with wakefulness (such as eating or dressing), which may include walking, without the conscious knowledge of the subject.

- Nocturia: A frequent need to get up and go to the bathroom to urinate at night. It differs from Enuresis, or bedwetting, in which the person does not arouse from sleep, but the bladder nevertheless empties.

- Somniphobia: A dread of sleep.

As research continues in the study of sleep disorders, cures for all these disorders may be found sooner rather than later. The emergence of specialty sleep clinics around the United States signal the medical profession's willingness to deal seriously with a growing disorder subspecialty.

BIBLIOGRAPHY

American Sleep Medicine Foundation. "Home Page." 2010. Available from http://www.discoversleep.org.

Drury, Tracey. "Sleep Disorder Business Awakens." *Buffalo Business First,* 2010. Available from http://bizjournals.com/buffalo/stories/2010/10/11/story10.html.

Journal of Clinical Sleep Medicine. "Home Page," 2010. http://www.aasmnet.org/JCSM.

Schwartz, Karen. "Sleep Centers for Kids Grow in Suburbs." *Chicago Tribune,* September 8, 2010. Available from http://articles.chicagotribune.com/2010-09-08/news/ct-x-w-0908-health-pediatric-sleep-20100908_1_sleep-centers-sleep-apnea-disorder-centers.

SLEEP. " Home Page," 2010. Available from http://www.journalsleep.org.

SMART CARDS

— ■ —

SIC CODE(S)

3674

3679

3572

INDUSTRY SNAPSHOT

After a decade of slumber, the U.S. smart card business began to catch up to its European and Asian industry counterparts in the first decade of the twenty-first century with everyone from Microsoft Corp. to American Express Co. to the Washington, D.C., subway system getting in on the action. While smart cards—credit-card-like devices containing integrated circuits for memory and processing power—have been the rage in Europe and Asia for years, introducing them in the United States had been slow and arduous. However, American Express led the way when it put marketing muscle behind its Blue smart card, and Visa, MasterCard, and others outside the financial industry began to follow suit. During the first decade of the 2000s, increased sophistication in technology produced an ever-expanding realm of possible uses, keeping the industry competitive and dynamic.

A smart card is a device that contains a microprocessor chip capable of storing large amounts of memory. Smart cards resemble and are usually the same size as credit cards, but without the magnetic stripe on the back. They are used for an increasingly diverse realm of applications, including financial transactions, security and identification purposes, retail purchasing, telephone accounts, the storing and maintenance of medical and other records, and for a variety of other purposes. Smart cards continue to replace their older magnetic stripe counterparts, which are more susceptible to hacking, counterfeiting, and fraudulent use, and hold only a fraction of the information found on smart cards.

Perhaps their ultimate power lies in the ability of one smart card to support multiple applications. Students at certain universities, for instance, can use a single card to gain access to areas of campus that are restricted to outsiders, to access library records and grade information, and to check on their financial accounts, not only at the tuition office but also at the student cafeteria. While multiple use cards offer myriad opportunities, they are difficult to implement outside contained environments such as a university or office campus. They require an infrastructure shared among all the supporting vendors and systems. The cafeteria, bookstore, and registrar all have to use compatible systems, but in coming years, many of these problems are likely to dissolve as network integration and connectivity increase.

Some analysts believe that shifting to a smart card economy would carry a cumulative price tag of $12 billion. Such costs would be borne mostly by industry unless companies find ways to make consumers willing to pay for the otherwise free plastic they tote in their wallets. Companies wishing to adopt smart cards must also contend with scant consumer awareness and, as a result, limited interest thus far.

ORGANIZATION AND STRUCTURE

The market is primarily dominated by two types of cards. The first—less expensive memory chip cards—are mainly used for the prepaid market—phone cards, copier and printing charges, mass transit fares, and so on. Memory cards store and deduct value as the card is used. A simple cash card or the telephone cards popular in Europe and East Asia are specific examples of memory cards.

The global market for the second type of card, the more sophisticated microprocessor chip cards, generally known as SIM (subscriber identity module) cards, began to grow at an unexpectedly rapid rate starting in 2003, as new applications began to emerge. These "intelligent" cards can perform complex functions and have the capacity to both read and write. Examples of intelligent cards are medical records cards that contain patients' vital statistics, prescription and allergy information, and medical histories. Some cards also include a digital image of the holder for identification.

Smart cards initially had three discrete functions: acting as electronic purses, as replacements for magnetic stripe technology, and as value transfer cards. The electronic purse function refers to systems designed to replace cash and coin with electronic credit. As a replacement for magnetic stripe technology, smart cards were designed to replace credit and debit cards and provide superior security. In addition, as value transfer cards, smart cards were designed to serve phone cards, copy cards, and so forth, where users transfer cash value to the computer chip cards. Newer cards also support multiple applications, but include applications well beyond these three.

There is also a variety of marketing applications for smart cards, including customer loyalty programs, in which the cardholder accrues points toward a gift from the issuer. An example is frequent flyer miles earned toward a free plane ticket. Sometimes smart cards themselves become the commodity, as with card collecting, a booming side industry. Banks and other card-issuing institutions ultimately benefit from such unused cards. A $5.00 card issued by NYNEX during the 1992 Democratic National Convention in New York City, for example, was valued at $2,500 five years later.

In 2001, two principal industry-related organizations merged to form the New York-based Smart Card Alliance (SCA). They were previously known as the Smart Card Forum (SCF) and the Smart Card Industrial Association (SCIA). The Smart Card Forum had promoted public policy initiatives in support of smart cards and worked to develop both cooperation and competition among members of the industry. The Smart Card Industrial Association (SCIA) was formed in 1989 and included manufacturers, integrators, resellers, users, issuers, consultants, and nonprofit and educational institutions involved in some aspect of the smart card industry. It sponsored CardTech/SecurTech, a conference for members of the advanced card and security technology industries; kept members and the public informed about developments within the industry; published a newsletter, *Smart Link*;

and educated the public about the developing smart card industry. The SCIA also provided links to principal financial card-issuing associations—Europay, MasterCard, and Visa—at its Web site. In order to kick-start sales in the laggard North American market, these two industry organizations joined together in 2000 to launch a $500,000 promotional effort in the United States and Canada over the following two years, primarily pitching the cards as a means for securing Internet transactions.

The International Smart Cards Associations Network is a global alliance allowing groups throughout the world to benefit by research conducted in other countries. It plans to organize meetings in conjunction with the biggest industry conferences, namely CardTech/SecurTech in the United States and Cartes in Paris.

In 2009, the SCA announced its inaugural group of industry experts who had passed the final certification exam and were designated as Certified Smart Card Industry Professionals. The certification process required applicants to demonstrate years of experience associated with smart card and associated technology; undergo interviews with references within the government and the industry; and pass a final three-part exam covering smart card fundamentals, security, cryptography, public key infrastructure, application data management, secure identification, mobile payments, pay TV, communication protocols, contactless interfaces, and near field communications. The United States Standards body, ANSI B10, writes the standards for smartcards.

BACKGROUND AND DEVELOPMENT

A key element in the development of the smart card was the microchip, which was invented by Texas Instruments Inc. engineer Jack Kilby and Fairchild Semiconductor Corp. engineer Robert N. Noyce in 1959. Until that time, there was a direct relationship between a computer's size and its power. When, in 1971, Intel Corp. scientist Ted Hoff created a tiny silicon chip capable of holding as much memory as ENIAC, an early computer that weighed 18 tons, it was clear that the information industry was about to undergo monumental change. Three years later, in 1974, Frenchman Roland Moreno conceived the idea of marrying chip technology with a credit-card-sized device, and the smart card was born. When in 1980 Arlen R. Lessin, an American, learned about the smart card, which was then virtually unknown in North America, he said, "I knew the moment I saw the card demonstrated that it would revolutionize the way we conduct both our business and personal lives." Lessin obtained the rights from Moreno to market the card in the United States and he founded the first U.S. company in the industry, SmartCard International, Inc.

Smart card technology spawned a demand for computer chips capable of fitting inside a card and undergoing the same wear and tear as magnetic stripe cards. In Europe, this technology was developing in the late 1970s and early 1980s as U.S. banks were just beginning to adopt the magnetic swipe card and as automated teller machines proliferated.

The United States' lag in smart card use had its roots, ironically, in the high quality of U.S. telecommunications services. Running checks on credit cards via the phone lines was easy for U.S. merchants, hence they felt little need for a card that would make it possible to instantly verify the customer's account information. In France, however, where phone services were not nearly as advanced as in the United States, smart cards were an appealing alternative.

Smart card use in the United States was minimal until the nation's two leading credit card companies, Visa and MasterCard, began to see them as a way to curtail credit card fraud. In the mid-1990s, such fraud in the United States accounted for some $500 million a year in losses and $1.7 billion annually worldwide.

In 1995, three large financial institutions helped foster a major development that paved the way for wider use of smart cards. Europay, MasterCard, and Visa, all credit card licensing institutions, developed a set of technical standards called the EMV specifications after their combined initials. These standards ensure that cards will be compatible with one another, preventing the proliferation of competing systems that could create costly failures analogous to Sony's ill-fated Betamax brand of videocassette technology.

Because of excitement over smart cards in the early 1990s, numerous companies flooded the market with smart card technology as the number of competitors rose by 250 percent between 1992 and 1997, according to *Electronic Business*. Production equipment for smart cards jumped from $2 million to $1.36 billion during this period as companies prepared for a smart card revolution. Nevertheless, despite the number of companies selling smart cards and smart card equipment, consumer demand remained limited.

The federal government took steps to increase the country's use of the new technology in the late 1990s. Under several government programs, federal employees began carrying smart cards that served as identification, credit cards, building access keys, and other functions. The federal government partnered with a number of firms to develop and manage such technology, including a pilot program run by Citibank.

The Internet was a leading factor in the rosy forecasts for U.S. smart cards. Following a string of high profile computer hackings in which hundreds of thousands of credit card numbers were stolen from online retailers, industry players planned to promote smart cards as a method for ensuring safe online shopping. Since online merchants would never actually receive the credit card numbers, just an authorization code, customers could rest easy.

In several articles, *Card Technology* pointed out that the U.S. government was boosting usage of chip cards by having some agencies move to the use of "chip-based ID cards for physical and computer access" applications. The Department of Defense was reportedly "in the early stages of a four-million-card rollout" program also known as the "Common Access Card" project. This card holds three digital certificates with authenticating capability for identification to networks and digital signatures and encrypting capability for electronic documents. The publication also claimed that U.S. government efforts to regroup after the September 11, 2001, terrorist attacks were accelerating efforts for several card projects, including ID programs for employees, workers in key industries, citizens, and foreign visitors.

Wanted: Standards and Security The smart card movement in the United States also gained momentum thanks in part to greater agreement on standards—and more powerful standards enforcers. One of the contributors was Microsoft with the 1999 debut of its Windows for Smart Cards operating system. The software, an extension based on the company's dominant operating system for personal computers (PCs), provides a common environment for smart card applications to run in. The Windows 2000 edition also included compatibility with some forms of smart card technology. Microsoft's products compete with the previously issued JavaCard and MultOS systems. Microsoft likewise has backed other smart card standards aimed at making them more universal.

Aside from getting its software onto smart cards and readers, Microsoft lobbied fervently to make smart card readers standard equipment with new PCs. The latter is a bid to bring electronic commerce (e-commerce) to a wider market because smart card transactions, managed locally by a card reader attached to the PC, are believed more secure than customary Web-based security methods, which usually involve submitting encoded credit card information over the Internet.

Retailers Aim for Smart Card Success Story In April 2002, *Card Technology* provided an industry insiders's look at Target's innovative plans for smart cards. One insider claimed the effort was supported by a $35 million Visa contribution. While Visa executives would not name the amount, their company's Target support was confirmed by them. As both a retailer and card issuer, Target was issuing chip-based credit cards and upgrading cash registers at nearly 1,000 stores, plus planning Target Web site and other merchant-linked incentives to enhance smart card usage.

Cardline revealed that Dallas-based Kinko's photocopy and office services chain had enTrac Technologies of Toronto "put a fake magnetic stripe on the back so people knew how to insert the card into the reader." This information, reflecting that Kinko's customers were unwittingly using smart cards, was obtained from enTrac Vice President Rob Anderson.

Additionally, industry experts ranked establishment of EMV, the global and cross-industry standard for chip-based debit or credit cards, as having a significant impact on growth of chip-based cards. In 2001, *The Banker* estimated that the EMV-based chip card had been implemented in 33 countries with the U.K. leading the way.

In response to Homeland Security Presidential Directive #12, the U.S. Government Printing Office (GPO) opened bids in 2004 in furtherance of continued plans to convert to an electronic passport system (ePASSPORT) using smart card technology. Furthermore, the U.S. government revealed plans for the purchase of 40 million microcontroller smart cards for the personal identity verification (PIV) of all federal employees and contractors starting in 2005.

The first decade of the 2000s saw an increasing number of uses for smart cards, fueling the industry's growth. Examples of innovative new uses included a program in New York City that would equip thousands of taxicabs with contactless payment readers, whereby riders could pay from the backseat with a wave of a card; the use of smart cards for pay TV services; and the use of smart cards for passports (called e-passports), which began in 2006 and was expected to involve 40 countries by the end of 2007.

Another new use for smart cards was for driver's licenses. In 2007, Gemalto, a leader in the industry, began to supply smart card driving licenses to consumers in Mexico. The contract between the firm and the Mexican government included the delivery of 900,000 driving licenses over a three-year period. Smart cards as driver's licenses are much more difficult to counterfeit. "The other major benefit of this smart card-based program," according to Jorge Domene, director of the Instituto de Control Vehicular, "lies in the information sharing capability since the chip allows for collecting and sharing information about the driver with other public Mexican institutions." The U.S. government was considering switching to smart card driver's licenses but had not implemented the program as of mid-2007. New rules released in March 2007, however, did allow some border states to add smart card chips to their driver's licenses to serve as border-crossing cards. The rule, known as Real ID, requires tamper-resistant driver's licenses for all 50 U.S. states by the end of 2009. The deadline had

been pushed back partly due to concerns by the state governments about the projected $11 billion implementation cost.

Smart cards were also becoming more sophisticated. According to a 2007 article in *Government Computer News,* "The next generation of smart cards are moving away from being stand-alone proprietary devices and will act more like full-fledged data servers." The cards of the future will be able to run a variety of fairly complex transactions due to increased storage space. Some of the newer cards have 1M or more of read-only memory (ROM), which can store an operating system, and enough flash memory to store programs. The newer cards can even draw information from the Internet and meld it with data on the card.

CURRENT CONDITIONS

As of mid-2009, nearly 7 billion smart cards were in use around the world according to Eurosmart, the worldwide association of the smart card security industry. It projected that global microcontroller smart card shipments would reach about 4.4 billion units by the end of 2009, representing a 5-9.6 percent increase from 2008 (4.18 billion units). Shipments of these more secure and capable microprocessor/microcontroller cards were expected to grow to 4.83 billion units for 2010. The biggest markets for the microprocessor smart cards were in telecommunications (nearly 75 percent) and financial services/retail. The industry research firm RNCOS, in its "Smart Card Market Forecast to 2012" report published in March 2009, noted that the global market for contactless smart cards stood at an estimated US$ 240 Million in 2008.

As microprocessor smart cards continued to replace memory cards, 2009 shipments of memory cards were just 740,000, expected to drop to 620 million in 2010, reported Eurosmart. The remaining markets for them were primarily telecommunications, government healthcare transactions, and transport (as in prepaid fare cards). Total global shipments of cell phone memory cards was flat, at 444 million cards, in 2008 and 2009, according to Strategy Analytics.

There were some major technical advances in 2009. In the telecommunications field, the UICC (SIM cards) became part of the LTE (4G) plans with early deployments, having already proved its worth as a service platform for 2G and 3G networks. The end-of-decade trend toward convergence of applications (i.e., inter-connected devices, such as cell phones, netbook PCs, GPS, MP3s, etc.) as well as the emergence of NFC (contactless) cards assured continued industry growth well into the future.

In the financial and retail sectors, contactless payment cards continued to be adopted worldwide. In manufacturing, the Machine-to-Machine (M2M) communications market experienced early votes of confidence in 2009 in areas like automotive diagnostics. EMV migration programs multiplied in 2009, in anticipation of the EMV adoption mandates in the medium term. Government identity and travel documents continued to go digital worldwide.

Memory cards now represent a small portion of the industry and do not have a significant impact on either volume or revenue, according to EuroSmart. Other (lesser) uses for both types of cards in 2009 were for corporate ID cards and Pay TV.

INDUSTRY LEADERS

Although many of the companies and institutions that use smart card applications are well known, such as Visa and MasterCard, those involved in manufacturing smart card technology are far from household names; Gemalto, for example. *Card Technology* claimed IBM's Zurich Lab Product Manager Michael Baentsch said issuers benefit as more manufacturers, including local companies, can offer smart cards. "You get, possibly, a more responsive environment than you had before when you had only a few sources for a complete package," Baentsch concluded.

Gemalto N.V., which was formed when industry leaders Axalto and Gemplus merged in 2006, is the largest maker of smart cards worldwide. With $1.4 billion in sales in 2008, the company employed about 10,000 people and operated in more than 50 countries. Gemalto produces cards and readers for a wide range of purposes, including parking, transit, mobile phones, finance, and medical information.

Oberthur Card Systems, part of the French firm Groupe Francois-Charles Oberthur, has been a fast-rising leader in smart card manufacturing. With its 1999 purchase of De La Rue plc of the United Kingdom, Oberthur became a leading maker of smart cards. The firm has industrial and commercial presence in 21 countries across five continents. As a leader in the financial sector, Oberthur sold 72 million banking smart cards in 2006. Clients include VISA and MasterCard. In September 2008, Oberthur announced its family controlled holding would spend up to 226 million euros ($331.2 million) to buy out minority shareholders in a debt-financed deal to prevent a shareholder takeover.

Chip manufacturers are major component suppliers to the smart card industry. Among chip manufacturers, the leader heading into the late years of the first decade of the 2000s was Motorola, Inc., with 20 percent of the industry, followed by Texas Instruments and SGS-Thomson with 15 percent each, and Siemens AG and Hitachi, Ltd. with 10 percent each. The remaining 30 percent of the chip market was held by all other companies involved, including Oki Semiconductor and Philips Semiconductor.

AMERICA AND THE WORLD

In the late years of the first decade of the 2000s, smart cards were one technological area in which the United States did not lead the world, although great strides had been made since the previous decade. According to a 2003 research study by the Freedonia Group, global demand for smart cards was expected to grow, mostly driven by conversion of debit/credit cards from magnetic stripe to smart card technology. That study placed the fastest growing market in Asia, followed by North America and Eastern Europe, with production remaining concentrated in Western Europe.

The Smart Card Alliance Latin America (SCALA) 2009 research report on EMV migration in Mexico and Brazil projected strong growth for EMV/chip cards and terminals. Brazil had issued 341 million EMV/chip cards in 2008, with a forecast of 145 million to be issued in 2009. Mexico had issued 82 million EMV/chip cards in 2008, with a forecast of 17 million for 2009.

"The card associations, Visa and Europay/Mastercard, mandated that any merchant accepting a non-chip card would be liable for any fraud against that card," said Director of Public Affairs for the United Kingdom's Association for Payment and Clearing Services (Apacs). *The Banker* asserted that government-led initiatives were spurring the introduction of EMV chip cards in Mexico and South Africa. Card usage to manage micro credit, encouraging entrepreneurial behavior in rural areas, plus the introduction of an electronic identity card tied in well with the Mexican president's mandate to improve education and banking opportunities for the masses.

Many countries continued to convert to contactless smart card technology for mass transit fares. By 2004, China had 80 cities using the technology, as did the global cities of Delhi, Osaka, Paris, Helsinki, London, Moscow, Rome, Singapore, Tokyo, and Warsaw. In the United States, Chicago, Newark, Washington, D.C., and Ventura County in California led the way, but Los Angeles, Atlanta, and New York were close behind.

RESEARCH AND TECHNOLOGY

In December 2009, the National Institute of Standards and Technology (NIST) announced its successful work in creating a handheld touch-screen device that may lead to mobile fingerprint ID work in the near future. NIST had been tasked by the FBI to develop a small, portable tool to identify fingerprints and faces for agents while out in the field, instead of the 20-pound rugged laptop plus fingerprint scanner they currently lugged around. It successfully created a small tool that could take pictures of fingerprints or faces and send the data wirelessly to a central hub for analysis, all with a minimum of touch strokes. The NIST team already had been collaborating with other security agencies on something called Mobile ID, a method to help officers identify people quickly and easily on the scene, instead of taking people back to headquarters to be fingerprinted. The next step for NIST is to integrate an actual finger print sensor into the demo program.

The industry was at an exciting crossroad in the first decade of the 2000s. On the one hand, worldwide demand had never been greater, with both public and private sector interest in smart card technology. The subscriber identity module (SIM) card had been reduced to the smallest size possible by the newer 3FF format. New cryptographic technology had enhanced its performance in security-sensitive applications, and its memory capability had been greatly increased.

However, the multi-media card (MMC), happened on the scene and threatened to steal away possible smart card growth. Not only were MMCs removable, like SIM cards, but they also were portable. The latest MMC cards had vast memory capacity that included flash memory. This technology was in high demand by the new camera-screen mobile phone industry, which effectively transformed handsets into mobile digital and micro-video cameras. In late 2004, Renesas Technology, a smart card microcircuit and flash module supplier, unveiled its new MMC card, the X-MobileCard, with a flash memory capacity of 128MB. The card also carried a crypto-controller and an MMC controller to interface with handsets, PDAs (personal digital assistants), or host PCs. The Nuremberg, Germany-based company IICS planned to take that technology a step further in developing customized electronic signature, payment, home banking and other applications on this platform. If and when that technology was perfected, the distinct markets held by smart cards versus MMCs would become more nebulous.

In response to the perceived market threat, DiskOn-Chip, a flash card manufacturer, paired itself with a crypto-processor supplier and planned to build a Mega-SIM to counter the MMC product line. SIM technology increasingly focused on developing contactless application, such as that used for the MasterCard PayPass, to compensate for lack of portability yet still inspire trust. The only thing then distinguishing SIM from MMC techonology would be cryptographic functionality.

Nevertheless, many analysts continued to tout distinct and separate roles for the two technologies, rather than competition or synergy. For example, the very fact that SIM card technology was not portable but only removable enhanced the security/authentication role of the card. Conversely, the primary role of MMCs and flash technology was to store or transport photos or images, where portability to other applications besides phones (e.g., PCs) would be desirable.

BIBLIOGRAPHY

"2007 to Break the 4 Billion Mark for Smart Cards Shipped." *Card Technology Today,* May 2007.

"4.4 billion Smartcards To Be Shipped This Year, According to Eurosmart Report." *SmartCard Trends,* 17 November 2009. Available from http://www.smartcardstrends.com/.

"Beep, Beep! Visa and Creative Mobile Technologies Partner to Bring Faster Payments to Thousands of New York Taxis." Smart Card Alliance, 12 June 2007. Available from www.smartcardalliance.org.

Cawsey, Tim, et al. "Is MMC Kidnapping the SIM Card Future?" *Smart Cards Trends* Newsletter, April/May 2004. Available from www.smartcardstrends.com/.

"Contactless Smart Card Market to Grow at 33 Percent." *PR Log,* 26 March 2009. Available from http://www.prlog.org/10205867-contactless-smart-card-market-to-grow-at-33.html.

"Engineers Designated as Certified Smart Card Industry Professionals." *ExPonent,* 25 November 2009. Available from http://www.exponent.com/Engineers-Designated-as-Certified-Smart-Card-Industry-Professionals-11-25-2009/.

"Gemalto Announces its Fourth Quarter and Full Year 2008 Revenue Results." *Smartcard Briefs* Available from http://www.ecommerce-journal.com/.

"Gemalto Delivers First Smart Card Driving License Program in Mexico." Smart Card Alliance, 13 June 2007. Available from www.smartcardalliance.org.

"Handheld Touch Screen Device May Lead to Mobile Fingerprint ID." *SmartCard Trends,* 24 December 2009. Available from http://www.smartcardstrends.com/.

"Hoover's Company Capsules." *Hoover's Online,* 2007. Available from www.hoovers.com.

Huber, Nick. "Traders Gear Up for Chip-and-Pin Future." *Computer Weekly,* 27 May 2003.

Jackson, Joab. "Cards Get Smarter: Tomorrow's Versions Will Act like Personal Web Servers." *Government Computer News,* 28 May 2007.

Jackson, William. "Smart Cards Play it Safe." *Government Computer News,* 28 May 2007.

"Is Asia Taking the Lead in Smartcards? " *Smart Cards Trends News,* SCT8, 30 October 2004. Available from www.smartcardstrends.com/.

"Issuers Buy More High-Security Banking Smart Cards." *Card Technology,* May 2007.

Meistermann, Nathalie. "UPDATE 3—France's Oberthur to Buy Out Minorities." Reuters Press Release, 23 September 2008. Available from http://www.reuters.com/article/idUSLN24978120080923.

"Newswatch: Americas." *Card Technology,* April 2007.

"Oberthur Card Systems, USA." 12 March 2005. Available from www.oberthurusa.com/.

"Profits Fall For Smart Card Vendors." *Card Technology,* April 2007.

"Smart Card Industry Will Hit New Records in 2007." Eurosmart, 19 April 2007. Available from www.eurosmart.com.

"Smart Card Alliance Wary Of Enhanced Driver's Licenses." *Government Security,* 3May 2007.

"Smart Card Market Information." Smart Card Alliance. Available from http://www.smartcardalliance.org/pages/publications-scala-emv-market-study.

"Smart Card Standard Incorporates GlobalPlatform Specification." *Card Technology,* May 2007.

"Strong Growth Predicted for 2005. " *Smartcard Briefs,* February 2005. Available from www.securitysa.com/.

"Why—and How—Corporate America Is Playing the Smart Card." *Access Control & Security Systems Integration,* 1 April 2007.

"World Smart Cards to 2006." Freedonia Group Report No. 1652, April 2003. Available from www.freedoniagroup.com.

SMOKING CESSATION PRODUCTS AND SERVICES

---■---

SIC CODE(S)

2834

8322

2111

INDUSTRY SNAPSHOT

With heated criticism of tobacco companies and attacks on the smoking habit coming from a variety of sources, including the Oval Office and the halls of Congress (with increased taxes for cigarette purchases), an estimated 70 percent of the 43 million smokers in the United States in 2010 expressed a desire to kick the habit; 40 percent (roughly 17 million) had made at least one serious attempt to do so. Nevertheless, almost one in five persons in the U.S. population was a smoker. Smoking was the cause of an incredible 5.4 million deaths each year worldwide.

According to the Centers for Disease Control and Prevention (CDC), tobacco smoking remained the leading cause of preventable deaths in the United States, responsible for more than 20 percent of all preventable deaths (438,000 each year) in the United States. In terms of lost productivity, direct medical costs, and premature death, smoking-related illnesses cost the nation about $193 billion annually. The U.S. Health Service Publication "Tracking Healthy People 2010" set a national goal of reducing tobacco use to 12 percent or less. However, according to the CEO of Pfizer, Inc. of New York City, the annual number of people dying globally will double from 5 to 10 million deaths by 2020 if current smoking patterns continue.

People's determination to "kick the habit" boded well for those in the business of helping them do just

that. According to Global Industry Analysts, a research firm, the global smoking cessation aids industry will grow 9.13 percent from 2011 through 2015. Major regional growth is expected from the Asia-Pacific (except Japan), the Middle East, Africa, and Latin America, which together should see a 13.81 percent growth. In the United States, the market for lozenges and tablets is expected to decline to $141.17 million by 2015, whereas in Europe, sales of nicotine patches may reach $341.35 million by 2012.

Nicotine replacement therapy (NRT) involves the ingestion of small amounts of nicotine through various vehicles—including transdermal (through the skin) patches, nasal spray, chewing gum, inhalants, and tablets—during the process of quitting in order to mitigate some of the more aggravating side effects of nicotine withdrawal. Extensive research concluded that smokers are far more likely to succeed at quitting with the aid of a nicotine replacement. Such products, usually classified as pharmaceuticals, are sold both by prescription and over the counter. In addition, combining use of a nicotine replacement product with a behavior modification program increased the chance of success still more, up to double the cessation rate according to some studies.

Notwithstanding honest attempts to help smokers quit, the industry has been plagued with criticism for high failure rates of smoking cessation products, and untoward side effects including serious behavior and mood problems. Nevertheless, new products enter the market every year, with the positive objective of assisting someone who needs a little help to quit.

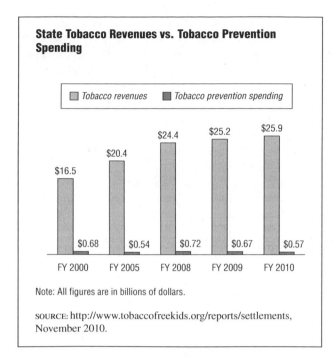

State Tobacco Revenues vs. Tobacco Prevention Spending

- Tobacco revenues
- Tobacco prevention spending

	FY 2000	FY 2005	FY 2008	FY 2009	FY 2010
Tobacco revenues	$16.5	$20.4	$24.4	$25.2	$25.9
Tobacco prevention spending	$0.68	$0.54	$0.72	$0.67	$0.57

Note: All figures are in billions of dollars.

SOURCE: http://www.tobaccofreekids.org/reports/settlements, November 2010.

ORGANIZATION AND STRUCTURE

Much of the marketing efforts of smoking cessation companies, including the introduction of hopeful new products, is engineered to coincide with calendar events, such as New Year's Day or the Great American Smokeout, when customers generally try to change their habits, and when building brand loyalty is at its greatest potential. Marketing of such products received a boost from the federal government in August 1999. While prescription drug advertising was already a $1.2 billion market, the U.S. Food and Drug Administration (FDA) issued a new ruling allowing direct marketing of pharmaceuticals on television and radio.

In an interesting financial reverse psychology, the Internal Revenue Service revoked its rule, officially acknowledging nicotine as an addictive and hazardous drug in September 1999. As a result, taxpayers could deduct the cost of smoking cessation programs and prescription drugs on their tax forms. Over-the-counter (OTC) therapies, however, remained nondeductible.

The smoking cessation business is actually divided into two segments, the largest of which is a branch of the pharmaceutical industry. The second segment consists of counseling services, hypnotherapists, and self-help smoking cessation programs such as SMOKENDERS.

The pharmaceuticals segment of the smoking cessation industry is made up mostly of large, diversified pharmaceutical companies, some of which are international in scope. The smoking cessation products of these companies in most cases represent only a small percentage of their overall production and business.

Within the pharmaceutical-based smoking cessation aids, there is a division between those marketed over the counter, such as Nicorette chewing gum and some of the transdermal nicotine patches, and other, more potent products, such as Zyban, nicotine nasal spray, and the nicotine inhaler, available in the United States only by prescription.

The services segment of the smoking cessation industry is often made up of groups formed by hospital and medical staff, volunteer organizations, addiction counselors, and psychologists. Often these groups offer personalized quitting advice or 12-step programs. Behavioral or supportive therapy can be done in groups, by telephone contacts, through written materials, and even individual counseling.

According to *Research Alert,* the smoking cessation industry transformed between the early 1990s and the early years of the first decade of the 2000s. It shifted from a retail emphasis to a medical approach with nicotine gum, new drugs, and nicotine patches (sold OTC) becoming more significant.

BACKGROUND AND DEVELOPMENT

In contemporary societies where there are smokers, some made a conscious decision to try to quit smoking. Not until the final decades of the twentieth century, however, did smokers actually get an array of products and methods that claimed to effectively treat nicotine withdrawal. Although there was undoubtedly some placebo effect from early over-the-counter (OTC) products, the FDA announced in June 1993 that all such products were ineffective and would be withdrawn from the market after existing supplies ran out. Most of these products were sold as chewing gum or oral medication and carried such brand names as Cigarrest, Bantron, Tabmint, and Nikoban.

More than a decade before the FDA's withdrawal of some of these OTC smoking deterrents, the first nicotine-replacement product in the form of a chewing gum made its debut. Nicorette was introduced originally by Marion Merrell Dow Inc. Each piece of gum contained 4 milligrams of nicotine. Chewing an average of six to nine pieces daily, a smoker could gradually cut down on the number of cigarettes smoked without suffering sharp withdrawal symptoms.

During the 1980s, pharmaceutical companies introduced a new nicotine-replacement delivery system, the transdermal patch. The patches, in varying strengths depending on the magnitude of the smoker's dependency, were applied directly to the skin and worn for 12 or more hours daily. After smokers had given up smoking and had gradually reduced the patch-delivered nicotine to its lowest level, they could stop using the patch and, it was hoped, would stay off cigarettes.

Counseling services also were available during the second half of the twentieth century, with most of the earliest programs relying heavily on hypnotherapy. Such services, many of them later affiliated with national and regional counseling services, continued to be available in the early years of the twenty-first century's first decade. In the 1960s, in the wake of the first urgent warning about the dangers of smoking, a number of stop-smoking programs, built around the concept of group therapy, appeared. Such therapy, which typically worked with a group of smokers over a period of several weeks, claimed to be more successful than individual efforts in helping smokers to quit.

The emergence of the fledgling smoking cessation industry occurred against the backdrop of an increasingly health-conscious U.S. public. Although health alarms about the use of tobacco products first sounded in the 1960s, in the 1980s and 1990s, smoking began to face strong social disapproval. This trend found its way into legislation that banned smoking in a wide range of public places. Additionally, smoking in the workplace became rare, with many places of business banning smoking altogether on their premises or limiting it to a few locations. In January 2003, California introduced a law that banned smoking within 25 feet of a playground. By 2008, many states and cities had enacted laws that banned smoking from a variety of venues, including restaurants, bars, hotels, and public outdoor spaces.

According to *The Journal of the American Medical Association* (JAMA), pharmaceutical companies toned down their marketing campaigns for smoking cessation products in the 1980s and 1990s due to pressure from tobacco suppliers, who threatened to cut off purchases from the companies' agriculture divisions.

The breakthrough in drug therapies aimed at smoking cessation came in 1984 with Marion Merrell Dow's introduction of its nicotine polacrilix gum, Nicorette. In 1992, another medium for nicotine replacement therapy was introduced: the transdermal patch. A number of companies, including Marion Merrell Dow and Parke-Davis, introduced the patches under such brand names as NicoDerm CQ, ProStep, Habitrol, and Nicotrol. The patches, available in a variety of strengths, were at first available only by prescription, as was Nicorette. Nicorette and NicoDerm CQ (also introduced by Marion Merrell Dow) were subsequently acquired by international pharmaceuticals giant SmithKline Beecham, based in the United Kingdom.

The near monopoly on smoking cessation products enjoyed by the merging Glaxo Wellcome PLC and SmithKline Beecham was threatened in 2000 by the rush to market of generic products as patents expired, but market leaders remained especially proprietary about their industry dominance. In the fall of 1999, SmithKline brought a lawsuit against California-based Watson Pharmaceuticals Inc., claiming that the user guide and audio-cassette packaged with Watson's FDA-approved polacrilix gum, a generic version of SmithKline's Nicorette, constituted a violation of SmithKline's copyright. SmithKline contended that the materials were too similar to those marketed with SmithKline's successful product. Watson protested that the materials were part of Nicorette's labeling. Under the Waxman-Hatch Act, generic products are required to use the innovator's labeling. Nonetheless, Watson was ordered by the Southern District of New York U.S. District Court to cease distribution of the product and to recall previously shipped quantities.

Despite growing product sales, some industry players decried retailers' frequent reluctance to more aggressively promote cessation products in their stores. Because of the relatively high cost of many of the products, retailers often kept them behind the counter or in a locked display case. Such restricted access, proponents claimed, discouraged prospective quitters from inspecting and buying them. SmithKline Beecham held that its own studies revealed that retail sales of smoking cessation products could increase from 44 percent to 73 percent by placing the merchandise up front with other retail items, though retailers had theft and space concerns to consider.

A series of new cessation products hit stores in the late 1990s, offering smokers new methods for breaking the habit. The nicotine in Nicotinal nasal spray, a product released in 1996, was absorbed through the user's nasal lining into the bloodstream. Like other nicotine-replacement therapies, the product was intended for use over relatively short durations—no more than six months. A little more than a year later, the FDA approved a Nicotrol nicotine inhaler, also available by prescription only. Users puffed on a plastic mouthpiece containing a nicotine cartridge in order to receive approximately four milligrams of nicotine, about one-third of the nicotine in a regular cigarette.

During the early 2000s, Nicorette and NicoDerm CQ, both marketed by GlaxoSmithKline, accounted for a very large percentage of industry sales. However, as industry players vied for customers in an ultra-competitive market, a number of new products were introduced, including sublingual wafers and bottled water containing nicotine. However, over-the-counter (OTC) sales also were fueled by the introduction of new flavors of smoking cessation gum. According to the *Wall Street Journal,* there were also strong sales of nicotine-laced lollipops that had not received federal regulatory approval.

The biggest leap forward in smoking cessation technology came in the late twentieth century in June 1997, when Glaxo Wellcome introduced Zyban into the prescription market. A tablet to be taken twice daily, Zyban offered a novel alternative to the gum, patch, and inhalant delivery systems. The drug, also marketed as an antidepressant called Wellbutrin SR, raises dopamine levels in the brain, thus reducing the smoker's craving. For smokers worried about an increase in weight, Zyban has the added appeal of helping to control appetite in the wake of smoking cessation, thus helping to alleviate the reluctance of potential quitters concerned about the weight gain often associated with smoking cessation.

Among the pioneers in the non-drug programs aimed at stopping smoking, perhaps the best known and one of the earliest successes was SMOKENDERS. Founded by Jacqueline Rogers in Phillipsburg, New Jersey, the program attracted a wide following and was built around the concept of group therapy. Smokers interested in quitting joined the program and paid a fee to SMOKENDERS. Weekly sessions over six or seven weeks could eventually lead smokers to stop smoking. In its original form, the program did not use any pharmaceuticals; later, those enrolled in SMOKENDERS had the option of supplementing their behavior modification techniques with pharmaceuticals. SMOKENDERS continued to attract a number of enrollees, and by 2000, included a program that an individual could follow outside the group setting.

Alternative therapies proved successful as well. Psychotherapist and hypnotist Dr. Steven Rosenberg developed a 20-minute aversion therapy antismoking session that met with a remarkable success rate of 85 percent.

Like other industries, by the new millennium, smoking cessation products and services were making room for themselves on the Internet. SmithKline developed their Committed Quitters program, which tallies data on individuals' smoking habits and processes the information to produce individually-tailored materials designed to help them quit. The 12-week program was offered free to purchasers of Nicorette, Nicorette Mint, or NicoDerm CQ, who could download a personalized program directly to their computers. Since studies have found that behavior modification programs greatly enhance the likelihood of success when followed in conjunction with nicotine replacement therapy, manufacturers increasingly sought ways to develop programs and tailor them to individual customers, for which the Internet could prove a perfect vehicle.

During the early years of the first decade of the twenty-first century, the availability of more inexpensive private label products and a reduction in the overall number of new smokers contributed to a declining market for smoking cessation products and services. However, by mid-2003, conditions appeared to be improving. In its June 17, 2003, issue, the *Wall Street Journal* cited data from Sanford C. Bernstein & Co., an investment research firm, showing that industry sales rose from approximately $600 million in 2001 to $700 million in 2002.

As competition heated up and industry players vied for fewer customers, a number of new products were introduced in 2003. While some were clearly aimed at the smoking cessation market, others were being marketed with the dual purpose of offering smokers an alternative way to ingest nicotine when circumstances did not permit them to smoke. For example, Westlake Village, California-based QT 5 Inc. began marketing NICOWater, a bottled water product that contained nicotine, in 2,600 Eckerd Drug Stores. The company sold NICOWater as a "homeopathic drug," which made it subject to FDA restrictions that were less stringent than for dietary supplements. A similar product, NIC Lite, was launched by NIC Time in 2006 and was initially sold in airports. The company encouraged flyers to consume the drink while in the air, thus soothing their need for cigarettes, which had been banned from domestic flights since 1998.

Other products aimed at active smokers and those wishing to quit included Nicotine Wafers—thin paper discs that quickly dissolved under users' tongues. Sold by a small Nashville, Tennessee, firm called Nicotinewafer.com, the wafers were only available via the Internet, and required a prescription from one of the company's doctors. Another product was the Vector Group's Quest brand of no-nicotine cigarettes. When preliminary research at Duke University suggested that Quest was effective in helping smokers kick the habit, the company moved ahead with plans for launching the product, which hit the market in 2003.

Advancements were also underway on the pharmaceutical front during the early years of the twenty-first century's first decade. For example, the *Wall Street Journal* reported that varenicline (later to be marketed under the brand name Chantix), a new smoking cessation drug from Pfizer, had helped 50 percent of users quit in a small clinical trial. In the same study, GlaxoSmithKline's Zyban (bupropion) had a 30 percent success rate.

Pfizer was inspired to develop varenicline following research conducted in the former Soviet Union during the 1960s. A weed known as "false tobacco" was used to produce a chemical called cytosine that produced similar results in users. However, its effects were not long lasting and frequent doses were required, so Pfizer set out to develop a synthetic version that could be taken less frequently.

Meanwhile, in 2006 the FDA approved Chantix (varenicline), Pfizer's new antismoking drug. Chantix works by tricking receptors in the brain into thinking that nicotine is present. However, it does not provide any pleasure for the user, unlike other cessation products that contain actual nicotine. According to Pfizer, studies show that 44 percent of those on Chantix quit by the end of 12 weeks, as compared to 18 percent who took a placebo. Although Chantix was initially popular and sold well, the honeymoon was over when research showed that some consumers who had taken it had suffered some serious neuropsychiatric side effects. A study by the Institute for Safe Medication Practices (ISMP) found that in the fourth quarter of 2007, the drug accounted for 988 serious injuries reported to the FDA, more than any other drug during the same time period. As a result of the ISMP report, the Federal Aviation Administration banned the use of Chantix by pilots.

Enough alarming evidence about Chantix had appeared, "including 39 reported suicides" 'by February 2008 for the FDA to issue a Public Health Advisory, warning that the drug could cause "changes in behavior, agitation, suicidal ideation, attempted and completed suicide." Although Pfizer earned $277 million from the drug in the first quarter of 2008, by the middle of the year sales had fallen drastically. In an attempt to counter all the negative press, Pfizer ran ads in newspapers and on television that emphasized the advantages of Chantix—and of quitting smoking—and launched a campaign called "My Time to Quit." In the campaign, Pfizer pointed out that 6.5 million people take the drug (5.5 million in the United States). The company also received a boost when the U.S. Public Service in August 2008 issued guidelines that recommended Chantix as a smoking-cessation product, despite its risks. The guidelines advocate use of the drug in combination with counseling and advise physicians to closely monitor patients for mood or behavior changes.

Pfizer faced potential competition from the French firm Sanofi-Synthelabo, which was developing a drug called rimonabant that also worked by affecting receptors in the brain. This drug was especially promising because it did not use nicotine to accomplish its objective. Like cigarettes, smoking cessation products containing nicotine may become addictive to users. For these products to be most effective, users had to gradually reduce their intake of nicotine until they had completely weaned themselves from the substance. Even when smoking cessation products are used, success rates after one year range from 15 to 25 percent. By 2008, rimonabant had been approved for use in Europe but not the United States.

By 2004, research regarding which smoking cessation products—including nicotine gum, patches, nasal sprays, inhalers, and prescription tablets—were the most effective continued to show that all were equally helpful and that no clear stand-out existed. In 2003, the *Journal of Family Practice* and *The Medical Letter* both published findings that supported this position. The former publication further indicated that all methods are effective at increasing cessation rates by 150 to 200 percent.

One development seemed especially promising for the smoking cessation products and services industry. In 2003, Washington became the first state to allow pharmacists to prescribe a wide range of smoking cessation products to customers, thereby eliminating doctor visits and increasing the potential for immediate sales. Developed jointly by the American Pharmacists Association and the Washington State Pharmacy Association, the initiative was intended to serve as a national model. By 2007, Florida had enacted a similar plan, and other states were considering it.

As an alternate to nicotine substitutes, such as gum, patches, and lozenges, SmithKline Beecham developed an improved nicotine lozenge, targeting people who want a faster-acting product than a patch or a better-tasting lozenge than the usual compressed tablets, which have a grainy, unpleasant texture and take too long to dissolve. In July of 2005, the company introduced its product: a lozenge in a glassy matrix, containing enough nicotine to reduce cravings and with a buffer to help with the grainy texture. The glassy matrix stabilizes the nicotine, can be formed into many shapes, and dissolves more rapidly than compressed tablets.

An ad campaign, QuitAssist, launched by the tobacco giant Philip Morris in September 2005, urged smokers to quit because, said Howard Willard, executive vice president of corporate responsibility, "we believe we have a role to play in communicating to smokers about the serious health effects of our products and resources that can help smokers quit." Cigarette manufacturers are not allowed by law to advertise their products. By advertising their QuitAssist program, Philip Morris managed to get its name on TV.

Another trend at the start of the twenty-first century was employer-assisted quit-smoking plans. For example, Matria Healthcare of Marietta, Georgia, provides employers the opportunity to offer their employees assistance in their quest to quit smoking. Their New Start for Smoking Cessation Program provides lifestyle support through educational materials and telephonic wellness counseling, covering topics such as managing side effects of nicotine withdrawal, improving unhealthy lifestyle habits that lead to smoking, and taking responsibility for their own physical and mental health. Matria believes that its mission is "to aid employers, health plans and the government's healthcare programs in the overwhelming task of transforming the healthcare system from within by developing better educated, motivated and self-enabled consumers."

Although the percentage of Americans who smoke fell from 30 percent in the early 1980s to about 21 percent in 2008, this decline does not necessarily coincide with a rise in sales of smoking cessation aids, according to *Drug Store News*. Data from the Nielsen Group shows that sales of smoking cessation products were down slightly (1.8 percent) to $495.4 million in 2007 as compared to the previous year. Sales of tobacco products rose 1.1 percent to $8.1 billion during the same time period; $7.3 billon of those sales were for cigarettes. The aforementioned article noted part of the reason may be that "today's smokers may dramatically underestimate the safety and efficacy of nicotine replacement therapy products for quitting smoking."

CURRENT CONDITIONS

As of 2010, the latest smoking cessation product to hit the market was electronic cigarettes, or "e-cigarettes," battery-operated cartridges which delivered an actual nicotine vapor (often flavored) but contained no tobacco product. Starter kits ran about $40 and contained cartridges, batteries, and atomizers. According to Bill Godshall, founder and executive director of Smokefree Pennsylvania, nearly 500,000 smokers had switched to e-cigarettes in the three years they had been available in the United States. He also stated, in a November 2010 *Bloomberg* press release, that other nicotine replacement therapies such as patches and gum had a "95 percent failure rate."

The holdup with e-cigarettes came in the form of the FDA, which wanted to regulate them. Most e-cigarettes were coming from China, and the FDA stated that it had blocked the importation of about 800 e-cigarette shipments since 2008. However, in 2010, the FSA found itself appealing a U.S. District Court ruling that the agency lacked authority to regulate e-cigarettes because they were recreational, not therapeutic. The industry, seeing competition, sided with the FDA, which argued that e-cigarettes may work with smokers the way methadone clinics worked with heroin addicts, by giving less harmful doses, and should therefore be regulated. As of late 2010, the FDA had won a delay of the decision pending a ruling from the U.S. Court of Appeals.

Meanwhile, according to the industry report *World Smoking Cessation Drug Market 2010-2025*, total revenues of smoking cessation products exceeded $1.6 billion (Rx products) in 2009. However, the U.S. Centers for Disease Control and Prevention (CDC) put the figure closer to $1.2 billion. Market researcher Global Industry Analysts, Inc. estimated the world market at $2.6 billion for 2010.

Of the smoking cessation products that were sold in the United States, nicotine gum was the most popular. According to *MMR*, 7.2 million packages of such gum, accounting for $282.7 million, were sold (excluding sales at Wal-Mart stores). This, however, represented a decrease in sales of 10.2 percent from the previous year. Sales of patches also decreased by almost 20 percent to 3.3 million units and $117.5 million. On the other hand, tablets saw a 19 percent increase in sales to 2.8 million units, bringing in $203.3 million.

In 2009, the FDA revised its regulations to now require Chantix and Zyban products (prescription only) to carry new safety information in a boxed warning on the product labeling for health care professionals, citing serious risks for users. Those risks included changes in behavior, depressed moods, hostility, and suicidal thoughts or actions.

In other news, the massive 1998 multi-state tobacco litigation settlement (in which several state governments sued the tobacco industry to pay for tobacco-related medical costs under state healthcare programs) included a provision that states would use a portion of annual settlement monies to fund tobacco prevention and cessation programs. However, a November 2010 report issued by several public entities, including the American Heart Association, the Campaign for Tobacco-Free Kids, the American Lung Association, and the American Cancer Society Cancer Action Network, found that states had cut funding for tobacco prevention and cessation programs to the lowest levels since 1999. In 2010, states cut funding for such programs by nine percent ($51 million) and by 28 percent ($199 million) in the prior three years. For fiscal year 2011, the states expected to collect $25.3 billion in revenues from the tobacco settlement and tobacco taxes, but were spending only 2 percent of it ($517 million) on prevention programs for youths and smoking cessation programs for adults. (The CDC had recommended a combined expenditure of $3.7 billion per year for all states.) Three states (Nevada, New Hampshire, and Ohio) provided no state funds for tobacco prevention in 2010. Meanwhile, the tobacco industry spent about $12.8 billion on advertising and marketing tobacco products in 2010.

INDUSTRY LEADERS

Perhaps the biggest news to hit the industry at the close of the twentieth century was the merger between market leaders SmithKline Beecham PLC and Glaxo Wellcome PLC to create GlaxoSmithKline (GSK)—a leading international research-based pharmaceutical company with a purpose to develop innovative medicines and products for people around the world. Headquartered in London and with offices in the United States, GSK had revenues of $45.8 billon and 100,000 employees in 2007. The company sold $144.6 million worth of its popular anti-smoking product Nicorette gum in 2009, holding 12 percent of the smoking cessation market, according to IMS Health Inc. It also marketed the NicoDerm CQ patch, and Commit lozenges. According to the irm, its over-the-counter smoking cessation aids had helped more than 7 million people quit smoking.

Founded in 1849, Pfizer Inc. of New York City markets an array of drugs for both humans and animals, along with a number of consumer products. Its Consumer Healthcare division markets over-the-counter drugs, including the Nicotrol Patch Nicotine Transdermal System. The firm also produces a nicotine nasal spray,Nicotrol NS. In 2006, Pfizer's new smoking cessation drug, Chantix (varenicline), was granted FDA approval. In October 2009, Pfizer acquired Wyeth for $68 billion. Sales for Chantix were $700 million in 2009; overall global sales for Pfizer were $50 billion in 2009.

Novartis AG, based in Basel, Switzerland, derives its name from *novae artes,* which is Latin for "new skills." It is the distributor of the Habitrol transdermal nicotine-replacement patch, which the company rolled out in 1999, and the Nicotinell flavored lozenge. Formed in 1996 by the $27 billion merger of Ciba-Geigy and Sandoz, Novartis operates through 360 independent affiliates in 140 countries and offers its products through its pharmaceuticals, consumer health, vaccines and diagnostics, and generics divisions.

WORKFORCE

The international pharmaceutical industry, which manufactures and markets most smoking cessation products, employs hundreds of thousands of people around the world. The jobs available in the industry range from clerical to management positions in the pharmaceutical companies' offices. For those with an interest in chemical and medical research, this industry offers a broad range of opportunities, for it is through these companies' ongoing research that new products are brought to market.

Employment levels in the non-drug smoking cessation services field are relatively low. Most of these operations involve individual counselors or small teams, the majority of whom are trained professionals. There is a fairly limited number of support jobs available in these operations.

AMERICA AND THE WORLD

Worldwide, as in the United States, smoking is the single biggest public health problem. It is the largest preventable cause of death and disability in the United Kingdom, killing 120,000 people each year—one in five deaths—and costing millions of dollars for the treatment of smoke-related illnesses. Each year, more than 2,000 cases of oral cancer alone are reported, as well as other health problems.

As of 2010, China remained the world's heaviest smoker. Although it raised its tobacco tax in mid-2009, both to raise revenue as well as curb smoking, the new tax was still considerably lower than in other countries. The China National Tobacco Company is the largest tobacco company in the world, and tobacco accounts for about 8 percent of total government revenues in that country, where an extimated 4 million workers rely on the industry for their livelihood.

A 2009 report from Global Industry Analysts cited major regional growth in cessation products anticipated in the Asia-Pacific (including China, India, Japan), Middle East, and Latin America, expecting a 13.8 percent CAGR (compounded annual growth rate) between 2011 and 2015. In Europe, sales of *Nicotine Pachesa* was projected to reach $341.3 million by 2012.

RESEARCH AND TECHNOLOGY

The results of a study involving the efficacy of smoking cessation products, published in the November 2009 issue of *Archives of General Psychiatry,* showed that a smoker trying to quit had the best odds for triumph by *combining* the use of a nicotine patch with the use of a nicotine lozenge. The study was the first ever that compared the effectiveness, alone or in combination, of popular smoking cessation products.

A vaccine for treatment of nicotine addition, called TA-NIC, was in the clinical trial stages in 2008 at Bermuda-based Celtic Pharmaceutical Holdings L.P. ("Celtic Pharma"). The firm is studying the effectiveness and safety of TA-NIC in helping people quit smoking when used together with current standard support treatments. The vaccine works by raising anti-nicotine antibodies, which will bind to nicotine in the bloodstream. Antibodies are too large to cross the blood-brain barrier, so nicotine that is bound by antibodies will be unable to get to the brain. Therefore, the pleasant stimulus that comes from smoking will be absent or reduced, diminishing the motivation to smoke again.

Cytos Biotechnology of Zurich, Switzerland, was also working on a nicotine vaccine, CYT002-NicQb, and in 2007 entered into an agreement with Novartis to develop, manufacture, and commercialize the drug. The drug works as an antibody to block nicotine from the brain.

Although teenage smoking is targeted by a variety of groups, the teen quitting rate is markedly low, in part because most cessation programs are engineered and marketed for adults. In the middle of the first decade of the 2000s, a number of scientists and preventive medicine specialists decried the common perception of teenage smokers as unwilling to quit as inconsistent with the facts. Rather, they held that, teenage smokers increasingly want to quit but find little support on the market or in their communities. Research conducted by Dr. Richard Hurt of the Mayo Clinic's Nicotine Dependence Center revealed that teenagers attempting to quit met with little success with the patch; only 11 of 101 teens were able to break the habit. Dr. Hurt surmised that this failure was in large part due to the absence of behavior intervention components in the study, which would support the cessation process with information about how to deal with a craving.

BIBLIOGRAPHY

"A New Vaccine for Nicotine Addiction." Huliq, 25 April 2007.

Arnold, Matthew. "Pfizer Pushes Back Amid Chantix Safety Worries." *Medical Marketing & Media,* July 2008.

Backinger, Cathy L., et al. "Building Consumer Demand for Tobacco-Cessation Products and Services." *American Journal of Prevenitive Medicine,* 2010.

"By 2012, Prescribing Pharmacists Could Influence $145 Billion in Drug Sales." *Bio-Medicine,* 20 October 2007.

"Celtic Pharma—Research Update." *Internet Wire,* 8 May 2006.

Chura, Lindsay. "Can Hypnosis Snuff Out a Smoker's Cigarette Habit?" *U.S. News & World Report,* 23 June 2008.

"Cigarette Smoking Statistics." American Heart Association, 13 October 2008. Available from http://www.americanheart.org/.

"Committed to Change." *PR Week,* 26 May 2008.

Dyess, Drucilla. "The Best Chance for Smoking Cessation: Patch & Lozenge Combo" *Health News,* 4 November 2009.

"FDA 101: Smoking Cessation Products." U.S. Food and Drug Administration, 26 January 2010. Available from http://www.fda.gov.

"FDA Issues Public Health Advisory on Chantix." U.S. Food and Drug Administration, 1 February 2008.

"GlaxoSmithKline a Potent Force in O-T-Cs." *Chain Drug Review,* 30 June 2008.

"Global Smoking Cessation Aids Market to Reach 2.6 Billion Dollars by 2010, According to a New Report by Global Industry Analysts, Inc." San Jose, CA: Global Industry Analysts, 23 April 2008. Available from http://www.strategyr.com.

Johnsen, Michael. "Smoking Cessation Sales Fall as Diet Aids Rise." *Drug Store News,* 21 April 2008.

"NIC Lite, NICTime's Newly Approved Nicotine Replacement Drink, Hits the Market to Help Cope with Smoking Bans." *Business Wire,* 12 June 2006.

"One Million Boxes of Over-the-Counter Smoking Cessation Products Sold in January 2008." *PR Newswire,* 4 February 2008.

Peterson, Molly. "Electronic Cigarettes' Nicotine Vapor Stokes U.S. Regulators." *Bloomberg News,* 2 November 2010. Available from http://www.bloomberg.com.

"Pfizer Drug's Woes Another 'Nail in the Coffin'" *The Star-Ledger* (Newark, NJ), 23 May 2008.

"Restrictions on Pfizer's Chantix as Reports of Neuropsych AEs Prompt Fresh Concerns." *Pharma Marketletter,* 2 June 2008.

Rubio, Lucas. "China, Thank You for Smoking." *US-China Today,* University of Southern California, 31 July 2009. Available from http://www.uschina.usc/edu/article.

"Smoking and Tobacco Use." Centers for Disease Control and Prevention, 7 April 2008.

"Smoking Cessation Drug Recommended Despite Controversy." *Healthcare Traveler,* August 2008.

"Smoking Cessation Products." *MMR,* 21 April 2008.

"State Tobacco Settlement: A Broken Promise to Our Children." Tobacco Free Kids, 17 November 2010. Available from http://ww.tobaccofreekids.org/reports/settlements/.

Terrie, Yvette C. "OTC Products for Smoking Cessation." *Pharmacy Times,* 17 August 2010.

"Tobacco Control." American Lung Association, State Legislated Actions on Tobacco Issues, 24 September 2008. Available from http://slati.lungusa.org.

"World Smoking Cessatio Drug Market 2010-2025." *PR Newswire,* 2010. Available from http://www.prnewswire.com.

SOCIAL MEDIA

—■—

SIC CODE(S)

7389

INDUSTRY SNAPSHOT

Although the term "social media" once referred to games and chat, by 2010 the term was defined as media for social interaction, using highly accessible and scalable publishing techniques. Social media uses Web-based technologies to turn communication into interactive dialogues. The opportunities available within social media continue to grow: either for social media managers, experts, and strategists or for social media programmers and coders.

As recently as 2005, the Internet was full of ignored brand messages, hidden e-mail addresses, and essentially a lot of talking in a space where no one was listening. MySpace, founded in 2003, and Facebook, which began in 2004, experienced rapid growth as social networks because, according to Reuters, almost 80 percent of the population was online in 2005, usually to check their e-mail and look at news or sports headlines. However, the idea of connection and community continued to grow.

By 2006 social media began to be tossed around as a term. Social networking sites began jockeying for power (MySpace was #1) and blogging platforms were ubiquitous. From 2007 onward, however, Facebook, Twitter, Flickr, Youtube, (later, Foursquare and Gowalla), and other assorted social media sites were in great demand. By 2010 Facebook had asserted itself as king of social media. Early that same year, the Library of Congress archived every public tweet posted on Twitter since March 2006, further elevating the importance of social media interactions.

As the demand for social media increased, so did the demand for strategists, social media theorists, and social media managers to harness the power of the medium for business/non-profit, government and elections, dating, and every other area of life. In addition, the demand for social media programmers and coders also increased, as more and more, social media users have increased the call for new and better social media networks, either for their open source or multifunctional capabilities.

Social media theorists appeared first as the medium began to gain traction: Doc Searls, Robert Scoble, Seth Godin, Chris Brogan, and David Meerman Scott all pointed out that the future of the Internet wouldn't be so much about one-way communication, but about two-way communication. Doc Searls was one of the authors of "The Cluetrain Manifesto: The End of Business as Usual" that began in 1999 as a Web site where the authors posted their theses while working at some of the largest companies in the world (e.g., Linux, Sun Microsystems, and NPR). These theses were often about how businesses lose touch with their customers. Then, in 2000, Robert Scoble began blogging from inside Microsoft, giving a more approachable, "insider's view" of the software giant with a nasty reputation. Finally, Seth Godin introduced the term "permission marketing" in 1999 to describe the move toward "social media" as a way for businesses to more effectively interact with their customers.

ORGANIZATION AND STRUCTURE

Social media has created a new department in many businesses (as well as a new category of business), not always directly related to or run inside of marketing

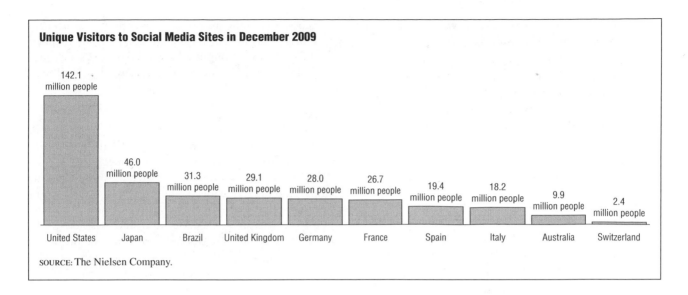

Unique Visitors to Social Media Sites in December 2009

142.1 million people — United States
46.0 million people — Japan
31.3 million people — Brazil
29.1 million people — United Kingdom
28.0 million people — Germany
26.7 million people — France
19.4 million people — Spain
18.2 million people — Italy
9.9 million people — Australia
2.4 million people — Switzerland

SOURCE: The Nielsen Company.

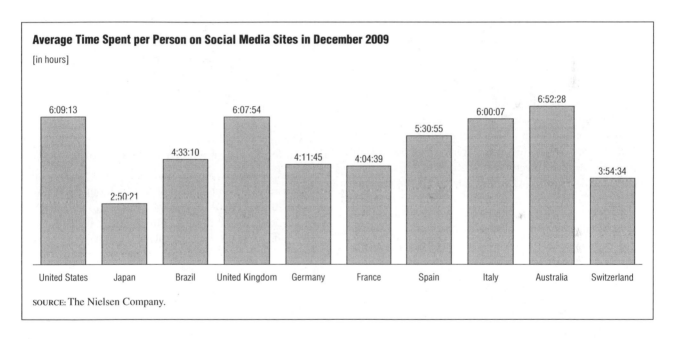

Average Time Spent per Person on Social Media Sites in December 2009

[in hours]

6:09:13 — United States
2:50:21 — Japan
4:33:10 — Brazil
6:07:54 — United Kingdom
4:11:45 — Germany
4:04:39 — France
5:30:55 — Spain
6:00:07 — Italy
6:52:28 — Australia
3:54:34 — Switzerland

SOURCE: The Nielsen Company.

departments, sales divisions, human resources departments, or any other predefined space in business. Social media occupies its own space; as a result, it is changing the way businesses work from the inside out. As businesses see the power of interacting with their customers and clients, the need for someone to keep an eye on those interactions is clear.

This is where social media strategists find opportunities. Social media strategists are either directly employed or work as consultants. They help businesses figure out a strategic social media approach: How best to interact with customers to 1.) get them to buy, 2.) get them to buy again, 3.) get them to refer businesses to their friends and family and acquaintances, and 4.) make sure they are 100 percent satisfied with their buying experience.

Social media manager is another title that is experiencing rapid growth. Jobs such as this are often priced well over six figures for larger corporations who are seeking top talent; in smaller companies, a marketing salary is appropriate. A social media manager usually is an employee who works with everyone in the company to develop their social media skills and to make sure every social media message that goes out on the Internet or verbally on the telephone matches the strategic message that the company seeks to embody. A social media manager often strategizes social media plans for the company and is often a theorist as well, keeping up with the latest books and articles and blogs to know what's working for other companies and what isn't worth the effort.

Social media theorists, strategists, and managers are likely to have experience as bloggers and use Twitter, Facebook, Foursquare/Gowalla, Flickr, and YouTube. On a regular basis, they either help other companies develop their social media strategy or develop one for their own companies. A lot of very successful social media theorists have worked inside of some of the largest companies in the world, which helps them to appear as more knowledgeable about social media. However, even bloggers with minimal experience (often journalists coming from print publishing to digital media) can land social media strategist or manager positions with large companies who want someone who has not worked for one of their competitors, but who can speak and talk and put forth an engaged message to their customers and clients.

Social media programmers and coders are those who often create the greatest innovation in this medium. Facebook co-creator Mark Zuckerberg and Wordpress programmer Matt Mullenweg have set the standard for social media networks and tools. Twitter co-founder Biz Stone and Gowalla CEO Josh Williams knew they were creating something new and truly amazing, but had no idea just how big both their network/tool would go. There is plenty of demand for employees who can code or program or even invent the world's next great social media network or tool. The best part about the medium is that while it's better to be close to venture capitalists located primarily in San Francisco; Austin, Texas; and New York City, a programmer/coder can work from almost anywhere in the country and still be at the top of his or her game.

There were no licensing agencies or associations for social media strategists, theorists, or managers during the early 2010s. However, many who work in these jobs attend BlogWorld, the world's largest conference on blogging, South by Southwest (SXSW) Interactive, a conference pertaining mostly to software development and startups, but that often caters to social media proponents, and more recently, BizTech Day, a one-day event in major cities geared toward working marketing professionals who want to brush up on their social media skills.

There also was no licensure or formalized training for social media programmers or coders or entrepreneurs; a lot of the top tools were created with minimal startup capital and developers only gained massive amounts of VC funding after releasing their product. Nevertheless, South by Southwest (SXSW) Interactive is a major conference held in Austin every March, as well as PodCamp. Rich Collins runs Lean Startup Circle, an e-mail list that allows discussion of new social media tools and their lean launches, stemming from the popularity of an underground bestseller, *Four Steps to an Epiphany*, by Stephen Gary Blank, which outlines how a programmer or coder could begin to build a social media network or tool on a lean budget.

BACKGROUND AND DEVELOPMENT

In 1999 Seth Godin introduced the term "permission marketing" in his book of the same name. The same year, "The Cluetrain Manifesto" was published by four employees of very large companies (e.g., Linux, Sun Microsystems, and NPR) as 95 theses aimed toward businesses seeking to move forward into this new world of social engagement. However, at the time, no one really knew exactly how "social" things would become. The idea of permission marketing and the Cluetrain Manifesto is that customers think in a certain way about the companies with which they do business.

Godin and the Cluetrain Manifesto authors brought that fact to the forefront of their vision of how business would run in the future. With permission marketing, no longer would companies be able to rely solely on ads or commercials or billboards (or even, at the time, banner ads on the Internet, which popped up as irritating blinking interruptions on Web pages). Instead, successful companies would seek to interact, to get permission, to listen to their customers in a way never really achieved before.

These pioneers warned that if business didn't take heed, customers would continue to block out these interruptions until they no longer even saw them and that, as a result, advertising using commercials, billboards, and banner ads would become obsolete. Ten years after these authors predicted it, loss of revenue from print advertising shuttered countless print magazines and forced the bankruptcy of countless retail corporations and smaller companies across the United States in 2008–2010. With the help of TiVo and DVR, the viewing of commercials is now 100 percent optional while watching television.

Social media has changed the way we interact with companies (as well as with each other); news comes from blogs and microblogging when in the past it came via newspapers and direct mail. E-mail has usurped regular mail and voice-mail in terms of daily and weekly volume. According to Newsday.com columnist Jamie Herzlich, "business users reported spending 19 percent of their workday, or close to two hours a day, on e-mail with no guarantee they actually read the messages most important to them. The average corporate user sends and receives about 156 messages per day." This matrix alone requires that companies get savvier with their social media messages. The onslaught of available information (which has been exacerbated by the introduction of social media) is such that a one-way message (whether in marketing, HR, corporate communications, or sales) will simply not get through. Social media offers companies the ability to interact with their customers and vendors, colleagues, and the world at large to qualify the message they send out. Social media managers, strategists, and theorists will blaze a trail through many varying messages and lead their company or clients along with a strategic plan.

PIONEERS IN THE FIELD

Seth Godin worked as a brand manager at Spinnaker Software and then a book packager before emerging on the scene as a social media pioneer with his introduction of permission marketing. Godin started YoYoDyne Inc., one of the first online marketing companies, sold it to Yahoo for $30 million in 1998, and became Yahoo's vice president of direct marketing until 2000. Godin writes books that call for more companies to pay attention to the emerging business model of social interaction and engagement, including *Permission Marketing, Unleashing the Ideavirus, Purple Cow, All Marketers are Liars, Tribes,* and *Linchpin.* In 2006 Godin launched Squidoo, a social media network that allows users to create lenses on topics they are interested in. Godin also was one of the founders of ChangeThis, a Web site that spread ideas through PDF files.

Doc Searls, one of the authors of the Cluetrain Manifesto, also is the senior editor of *Linux Journal.* Searls has been a well known blogger since October 1999. In an *Online Journalism Review* article, J.D. Lasica calls Searls "one of the deep thinkers in the blog movement." In his *New York Times* bestselling book, *The World is Flat,* Thomas L. Friedman calls Searls "one of the most respected technology writers in America."

Blogger and technology evangelist Robert Scoble was hired by Microsoft in 2003. Previously, Scoble already had discovered the power of blogging as a form of customer service while working for NEC as a sales support manager. Scoble was discovered through his NEC blog by Vic Gundotra (then general manager of Platform Evangelism at Microsoft) and subsequently was hired by the software giant as part of its Channel 9 MSDN video team. While Scoble was hired to show Microsoft in a favorable light, he had no qualms criticizing the company's practices and tech failings. This gave Scoble's blog a huge following and his subsequent book, *Naked Conversations: How Blogs are Changing the Way Businesses Talk with Customers,* written with Shel Israel in 2006, granted him worldwide success. Critics of Scoble cite his "egoblogger" status (someone whose blogging has a self-aggrandizing or narcissistic tone); however, there is no doubt Scoble is a social media pioneer.

Other pioneers include MySpace founders Brad Greenspan (who also founded the now-defunct eUniverse), Chris DeWolfe, Josh Berman, and Tom Anderson; Facebook co-founder Mark Zuckerberg; Wordpress founder Matt Mullenweg; Twitter founder Biz Stone, Youtube founders Steve Chen, Chad Hurley, and Jawed Karim; Foursqure founder Dennis Crowley; and Gowalla founder Josh Williams.

CURRENT CONDITIONS

In 2010 social media was the buzzword of marketing, PR, promotion, sales, HR, corporate communications, and branding. As the industry flowers, the opportunities for workers will continue to grow. However, the incredible gain of social media employment opportunities in 2010 alone was noteworthy against the backdrop of the lingering economic recession. As consultants, social media strategy firms are finding many clients. Every major brand has created a presence on Facebook or Twitter, started a blog, or began using videos to disseminate their brand message. A lot of companies have done this and then stopped, unsure what to do next. Strategists, both freelance and employed, will find plenty of chances to win work with those businesses. Theorists are losing traction and having to reframe their viewpoints. As the theory of how to use social media gives way to the reality of how to use social media, some observers argue that self-proclaimed "gurus" will fall away and go off to find another buzzword to follow. This means that the window for social media-savvy marketers is wide open. Opportunities for marketing professionals with social media experience drown out any opportunities for marketing jobs without social media.

Social media has pervaded every department in businesses, so much so that even HR now searches Google for Facebook profiles and Twitter streams of potential employees. In addition, C-level executives have Twitter and Facebook profiles (and blogs) from which they write about their philosophy or about the company's future. Any well-rounded employee will have a Twitter stream, a Facebook profile, and perhaps even a blog. At any time, employees may be asked to manage accounts on Twitter, Facebook, or other social media networks, and the company's blog (whether public or on the company intranet).

Microsoft hired a social media manager in the summer of 2010 with a starting salary of $150,000 per year. Other smaller companies hire marketing managers (which often also oversee social media activities) for more modest sums of $50,000 to $60,000 per year. As social media continues to be a buzzword, salaries for doing this work may stay inflated, but in time they will level out.

For consultants, hourly rates for social media strategy start at a very low end of $150/hour up to more than

$500/hour, depending on the length, commitment, and learning curve required by the job. Numerous specialty publications focusing on social media by companies producing newsletter content (including Smartbrief, Hubspot, and Sitepoint) help companies to get up to speed faster and make smarter decisions about the money they spend on social media training and consulting.

Ghostblogging and "ghost twittering" also was rampant in 2010; freelance journalists displaced by the print world fallout have turned to digital media opportunities, including blogging and Twittering for someone else. Jobs like these are commonplace, for pennies on the dollar, but there are still many companies out there looking for people who can write in a branded way (similar to advertising copy) on blogs, Twitter, and social media networks.

Programming and coding for social media provides plenty of opportunities for talented, technically-skilled workers, although the competition for these jobs requires workers to be at the top of their game. Top employers like Facebook, Twitter, Gowalla, and MySpace compete regularly for talent with Microsoft, Amazon, and Google. Top talent means more than just top dollar; it means the ability to pick the right team. Gowalla CEO and founder Josh Williams points out that he hires employees that work well together, providing plenty of extra perks to make work fun in place of trying to outbid or overpay to keep up with the competition. Amazon, on the other hand, pays high and thus has high expectations from its employees. Rumor has it the company burns through its employees quickly, pushing grueling work schedules and intense pressure on results.

INDUSTRY LEADERS

Facebook is a social media networking tool designed for games, chat, birthdays, fans of authors and products/brands, music groups, and celebrities. Started as a way for college students to keep up with each other (TheFacebook.com), creator Mark Zuckerberg had no idea that his simple networking tool would go so big. Midway through 2010, Facebook had more than 500 million active users (about one person for every 14 worldwide), making it one of the largest social media networks around. Nevertheless, Facebook has its faults. In 2010 privacy concerns led a group of Facebook users to delete their profiles and leave the service. Facebook has promised that it no longer changes privacy settings unilaterally, but being on Facebook presents challenges to privacy. Are profiles really private? Can anyone view your pictures? Are your activities on Facebook searchable on Google? If you delete your profile, is it really gone?

The ramifications of Facebook spread far beyond the current day. Employers often seek out employee Facebook profiles to see what kind of person they are, and employees must be careful to limit their Facebook time. Nevertheless, Facebook has connected the world. More people check Facebook first thing in the mornings than e-mail, and some Web sites are appearing in full on Facebook Markup Language (FMBL)-built pages so that Facebook users don't have to even leave the network to view their Web pages. Many industry experts have already called for a Facebook replacement that doesn't unilaterally change privacy settings and that is open source and easier to build other networks off of. How Facebook endures remains to be seen.

Twitter is a microblogging social media tool developed by Jack Dorsey, Evan Williams, and Biz Stone that allows users to follow other users in order to keep up with their location and activities. Users are able to follow lists of authors rather than only individual authors. The microblogging craze has led critics to worry that between texting and Tweeting, the new generation of communication is all about breadth and not so much about depth.

While Twitter may get a bad rap for being shallow, the power of the tool continues to grow. Chats using Twitter have grown so much that hundreds of mini-conferences are held weekly and monthly using on Twitter to discuss diverse subjects such as young adult authors and competitive horse shows. Integration of Twitter with both Facebook, Gowalla, and YouTube has allowed the sharing of content well beyond what the founders of any of the networks envisioned. The use of hashtags tries to organize the content loaded on Twitter. Hashtags follow the hash sign (#) and often are a combination of words or an acronym (#pubchat) or (#storyline). In 2010 the Library of Congress archived every Tweet ever sent on the service, which means teens who Tweet how much they love Britney Spears are now on the hook for loving her forever.

Gowalla is a geolocation tool used on Smartphones and tablet computers developed by the talented team at AlamoFire in Austin, Texas, and headed up by AlamoFire CEO Josh Williams. The goal of Gowalla (and Foursquare) is to allow users to check in at various geographic locations throughout the United States and the world in order to exchange icons, meet other users, and better explore the community they have traveled to or reside in. Gowalla is colorful and filled with icons for every category of location (food, arts, nature, museum, etc.) and can be integrated into other social media tools like Facebook and Twitter.

In 2010 both Gowalla and Foursquare experimented with both large (Adobe Creative Suite, Jimmy Choo) and small (Subway, local eateries) brands to test out how brick-and-mortar stores can utilize geolocation tools to gain more customers and build both urban and rural communities. On a recent road trip, users of Gowalla found a small, out-of-the-way town and covered it with Gowalla spots, encouraged by the local sheriff, in hopes that other travelers using Gowalla in the future will stop in for food, tourism sites, and exploring. Gowalla and Foursquare have a lot of growth ahead and it remains to be seen exactly how the geolocation tools will enhance the social media experience. At the beginning of the 2010s, it was primarily for entertainment.

WORKFORCE

Social media is increasingly diverse. The online environment makes it particularly attractive to people who live in rural areas and seek to be better connected with their peers and colleagues. In urban areas, social media provides a network for increased dialogue and innovation. The geolocation social media networks, Foursquare and Gowalla, have created both small and large cities as a vast map of potential interactions. Both services allow users to check in at nearby listed locations using smartphone GPS technology. Such geolocale services also allow people in the vicinity to locate and interact with each other. Twitter and Facebook allow for real-time interaction among a group of like-minded people using tweetchats or Facebook chat or groups. Finding people with similar interests has increased opportunities for Web-based entrepreneurs to expand opportunities and dialogues with many different kinds of people.

For businesses, social media still presents somewhat of a challenge. The first response may have been avoidance, then disinterest, then mild interest, then panic. By 2010 the power of the Internet and social networks to interact with customers had not yet made economic sense to some businesses, which saw no need to go online yet. As this trend changes and social media becomes more of a commonplace skill set (with most employees knowing how to use Twitter, blogs, and interact on social networks), business owners will begin to entrust the task to their employees.

As colleges are our future workforce training ground (and still coming up to speed with the Internet), we will continue to see many changes in the level of college graduate familiarity with social media and how a business can most use it for gaining new clients, interacting with current clients, hiring employees, communicating with current employees, and keeping up with innovation and trends. We'll also see increased focus on using current technologies and developing better technologies in order to keep up with the fast-developing world around us.

AMERICA AND THE WORLD

Social media is hardly a U.S.-based phenomenon. The entire world uses social media to advance causes, personal ideas, and business ventures. For social media, the world is extremely flat. Calcutta, India-based brothers created a firestorm after their popular Facebook game, Scrabulous (based on the board game Scrabble) was shut down by a lawsuit from Hasbro, which complained that the Facebook game impeded on its copyright. The court ruled in Hasbro's favor and brothers, Rajat Agarwalla, 27, and Jayant Agarwalla, 22, released the game once again on Facebook, only under the name Lexulous.

One of the most popular games played in the United States was created in India, which is not an isolated incident. Programmers and coders around the world are seizing the opportunity to get a head start in the U.S. technology market by building social media tools and networks. Darren Rowse, a blog network founder, resides in Australia. As Internet access expands to places where access has been limited, we will see increased cases just like these. The United States holds no monopoly on social media and programmers and coders who wish to enter into this medium must be able to compete on a worldwide playing field.

Not all countries welcome open competition in the social media space. In spring 2010 Google China pulled the plug. Because of infringements in China on their own Chinese search engine, Chinese government officials asked Google to suspend all availability in their country. However, many technology companies still have operations in China. Thus, a reverse of this ruling may be on the horizon. As the social media world flattens to include more countries, closing off entire populations may turn out to be the wrong decision.

RESEARCH AND TECHNOLOGY

The introduction of Apple's iPad will dramatically reshape the landscape of social media. Smartphones are ubiquitous; tablet computers are the future. Recent statistics indicate that the first online place people go in the morning is to Facebook. This is a change from the past when people checked e-mail first. As Facebook continues to grow and sustain its dominance as a social media network powerhouse, many question the need for external sites and are building mini sites within Facebook using FBML (Facebook Markup Language).

Twitter has doubled its usage and then doubled its usage again, causing experts to wonder if the social media service is sustainable for the long term. However, only 7 percent of the population online uses social media. research and development. In late 2010 there was a push for a new open source service to replace both Twitter and Facebook. Theoretically, this would more effectively allow innovative plug-ins, add-ons, and usage as more and more of the population joins the social media revolution.

BIBLIOGRAPHY

Comm, Joel. *Twitter Power 2.0: How to Dominate Your Market One Tweet at a Time.* New York: Wiley, 2010.

Herzlich, Jamie. "Small Business: Managing Company E-Mail." *Newsday,* 30 November 2009. Available from http://www.newsday.com/columnists/jamie-herzlich/small-business-managing-company-e-mail-1.1628906.

Rowse, Darren, and Chris Garret. *ProBlogger: Secrets for Blogging Your Way to a Six-Figure Income.* 2nd ed. New York: Wiley, 2010.

Safko, Lon. *The Social Media Bible.* 2nd ed. New York: Wiley, 2010.

Scott, David Meerman. *The New Rules of Marketing and PR: How to Use Social Media, Blogs, News Releases, Online Video, and Viral Marketing to Reach Buyers Directly.* 2nd ed. New York: Wiley, 2010.

SPECIALTY BAKERIES

SIC CODE(S)

2051

2052

5461

INDUSTRY SNAPSHOT

In 2010 retail bakeries generated more than $9.1 billion in sales, according to figures from Dun & Bradstreet's Marketing Solutions. After suffering through the economic recession of the late 2000s, the industry was looking forward to a recovery as 2010 neared a close. However, some of the developments in the early years of the twenty-first century had affected how retail bakeries conducted business. Some of the major trends influencing the industry included the increase in demand for small, individually sized products; the growing market for organic and allergen-free foods; and the incorporation of ethnic flavors and recipes into the mainstream bakery. In addition, Americans were demanding evidence of environmentally friendly practices from bakeries and other product suppliers. This demand resulted in changes to everything from the way bakeries powered their ovens to the types of materials they used to package their products.

The rise in Internet use and social networking in the early 2010s also was moving many retail bakeries to offer interactive Web sites, Facebook pages, and Twitter accounts. For example, according to *Supermarket News*, in January 2010 cupcake bakery Sprinkles in Los Angeles was tweeting a "secret" word every week, which customers could then use to cash in for a free cupcakes. The CupcakeStop, a mobile bakery in New York City, also relied heavily on Twitter and Facebook to generate business. Said owner Lev Ekster, "If I have an exciting new flavor that I want people to try, I'll tweet about it and get people excited. Twittering lets us manage inventory for the day, and show people what we're offering."

In addition, research indicated that Americans were plugging in and logging on more often. Retail bakeries—as well as other businesses—that capitalized on this trend were riding the market wave of the future. A 2008 study by the Boston-based marketing company Cone Inc., for example, showed that more than half of social media users "prefer and feel better served by brands and companies that they can interact with online."

ORGANIZATION AND STRUCTURE

This classification covers stand-alone retail bakeries that sell baked goods on-site or through special order. These establishments sell baked goods such as bagels, donuts, cookies, cupcakes, and bread over-the-counter; offer made-to-order or off-the-shelf items such as wedding cakes and other special-occasion baked goods; or do both. They also may offer lunch and breakfast items, coffee/tea, and other related products. While some retail bakeries focus on a specific product, others offer a wide range of baked goods. This classification does not include bakeries that are contained within another retail store, such as a grocery store or discount store.

According to Dun & Bradstreet, there were 33,385 retail bakeries in the United States in 2010. A majority were small establishments, with more than 61 percent employing only one to four people. The industry was served by several national trade associations, including

Top States in Number of Retail Bakeries, 2010

State	Approximate percentage of total establishments
California	15%
Texas	10%
New York	9%
Florida	6%
Massachusetts	5%
New Jersey	5%

SOURCE: Dun & Bradstreet's Marketing Solutions.

Retail Bakers of America, the American Bakers Association, and the American Society of Baking, as well as many regional and state organizations.

BACKGROUND AND DEVELOPMENT

Bread has been a staple of the human diet for thousands of years. The history of baking as a profession, however, can be traced to early Roman times. According to the American Bakers Association, a bakers' guild was formed around 168 B.C. in Rome, which established baking as its own profession. These first bakers were the only free people who worked a trade; all other tradespeople at the time were slaves. Bakers continued to hold a privileged position throughout the spread of civilization until the Industrial Revolution, which brought about technology that enabled bread to be produced at a price that was affordable by more than just the wealthy.

In addition, throughout history the importance of bread for the food supply was never underestimated by governing bodies. During World War I, for example, the U.S. government passed regulations on various aspects of the baking trade, such as price, ingredients, and even the shape of the bread. During World War II, when it was found that many of the male teenagers enlisting in the armed forces could not pass their physical examinations, the industry established enrichment standards for baked goods.

The operations of the retail bakery of the 2000s bear little resemblance to those of centuries past, when baked goods were kneaded by hand and baked in rough, clay-brick ovens. However, some aspects of the trade are still recognized as vital, including keeping recipes "secret." Other factors, such as using fresh ingredients and offering a large variety of options, were not major concerns until relatively recently in history.

In 2007 retail bakeries, as well as all other industries in the United States, faced a recession that would bring a severe drop in housing prices and a record number of foreclosures, an increase in unemployment, and a near-collapse of the automotive and financial services industries.

Although the bakery industry historically has been recession-resistant, according to *Modern Baking*, the economic recession of the late 2000s and the resulting "consumer frugality" took its toll on retail bakeries. With less extra cash, Americans cut down on trips to bakeries, an indulgence that some could no longer afford.

Some, however, looked at the recession as a positive influence on the bakery business. As stated by Ronald Krueger, a bakery merchandiser in Ohio, in the September 2010 issue of *Modern Baking*, "We've seen a lot of people looking for comfort foods—donuts, pound cakes and that kind of thing. They still find that bakery is an affordable treat." A June 2009 *Modern Baking* article had a similar premise: "Customers may not be able to afford a new car or a new TV, but they can afford a $2 cookie or $20 torte." Others noted the downturn in the economy as an opportunity. Todd Wagner of Wagner's European Bakery & Cafe in Olympia, Washington, told *Modern Baking*: "In a way it [the recession] has been beneficial. It woke us up. We are no longer complacent; we are not immune from downturns. We have changed our operations to adapt."

One of the ways some retail bakeries sought to capitalize on the market for small and affordable treats was by adding individual cupcakes to their shelves. The cupcake is an off-shoot of the individual pound cake, or "Queen cake," baked in England in the eighteenth century. According to food historian Andrew Smith, the first actual cupcake recipe was found in an American cookbook published in 1826. There are two theories for the origin of the cupcake's name. One relates to the amount of ingredients in a typical recipe (one cup of sugar, two cups of flour, and so on) and the other has to do with the fact that the cakes were originally baked in small, individual cups. Muffin tins became popular for baking cupcakes around the turn of the twentieth century. In addition, bakers appreciated the reduced amount of time it took to bake cupcakes as compared to a regular-sized cake.

Cupcakes became a popular item in U.S. bakeries in the late 1990s, boosted by an episode of the popular television series *Sex and the City* in which two of the characters visit over cupcakes at the Magnolia Bakery in New York City. By 2010 Magnolia had four locations in New York, one in Los Angeles, and one in Dubai. Los Angeles-based Sprinkles, however, which was founded in 2004, bills itself as the first cupcake-only bakery in the country. In 2010 the company had eight U.S. locations and plans for more.

A plethora of cupcake bakeries popped up around the country in the 2000s—spurring what many called a "cupcake craze." Other evidence of the growing popularity of the cupcake included the premiere of the Food Network television show "Cupcake Wars," in which four bakers competed to make the most original and tasty mini-cake; the sales numbers for Martha Stewart's new cookbook released in June 2009, *Martha Stewart's Cupcakes*, which spent 11 weeks on *The New York Times* bestseller list; and the creation of several Web sites and blogs about cupcakes, including Cupcakes Take the Cake.com and Cupcake-Business.com. In March 2010 Cupcake-Business.com claimed that cupcakes represented a $6 billion industry, with some stores, such as Magnolia Bakery, baking an average of 5,000 cupcakes a day.

By 2010 there were four basic types of cupcake bakeries, according to Elizabeth Olson of *The New York Times*: chains, such as Sprinkles; Web-based businesses that sold only online; bakeries that offered other items in addition to cupcakes; and the sole bakery. Some of these new bakeries took it a step further and created a specialty within the specialty: Examples included vegan-only cupcake bakeries and mobile cupcake bakeries (cupcake trucks). Some cupcake bakeries specialized in local or organic ingredients, whereas others stayed with the traditional ingredients and focused on creating the most unusual flavors or elaborate designs. Mintel Research predicted cupcake sales would increase 20 percent nationwide between 2010 and 2015, as compared to other baked goods, which were expected to show growth rates in the single digits.

CURRENT CONDITIONS

By 2010 many in the retail bakery industry were looking forward to economic recovery, as well as the return of more discretionary income for Americans. Some new developments, however, were changing the way bakeries did business, or at least what they offered on their shelves. One of these was the tendency of consumers to cut back on their portion sizes. As Steve Schulte, a bakery coordinator in Atlanta, told *Modern Baking* in September 2010: "Consumers are still eating bakery foods, but rather than have waste, they buy smaller portions. ... Before, somebody would come in and buy a cake, take it home and toss some. Now, they're buying the smaller cakes, but they may come back twice a week instead of just one time." This trend was one of the driving factors behind the cupcake craze. The desire for small but indulgent baked goods was also illustrated by the National Restaurant Association's Chefs Survey, in which bite-sized desserts were ranked number two among the top 10 eating trends of 2009.

Another trend that was continuing unabated into the 2010s was the overall health and wellness focus. Americans increasingly sought out healthier options, even in—or perhaps especially in—the bakery. For example, consumers looked for items that were baked with all-natural, organic, or locally grown ingredients, whole grains, and lower levels of fat, sugar, and sodium. The market for allergen-free and gluten-free baked goods was also growing. For example, a survey by *Modern Baking* showed that the percentage of in-store bakeries that experienced sales of organic and natural baked goods grew from 19 percent in 2006 to 38 percent in 2008, and that 20 percent of in-store bakeries sold gluten-free products, as compared to 3 percent in 2006. Overall sales of products containing natural ingredients and whole grains increased 45 percent between 2005 and 2008, according to Mintel. This trend was expected to continue, and many retail bakeries capitalized on it by dedicating whole shelves—and often the entire store—to offering these new "–free" products.

INDUSTRY LEADERS

Many of the leaders in this industry operated as both a bakery and/or café or coffee shop. For example, Starbucks Corp. of Seattle, Washington, was the world's number-one specialty coffee retailer and also sold baked goods. With 16,600 shops in more than 40 countries, Starbucks had sales of $9.77 billion in 2009. Total employment numbered 142,000.

Similarly, Panera Bread Company of Richmond Heights, Missouri, sold bagels, cookies, bread, and other bakery items in addition to offering a limited meal menu. In 2010 the firm had about 1,400 bakery/café sites in 40 states and Canada operating under the banners of Panera Bread, Saint Louis Bread Co., and Paradise Bakery & Café. About 580 of the stores were company owned, and the remainder were franchises. In 2009 Panera employed 12,100 people and recorded sales of $1.35 billion.

Einstein Noah Restaurant Group Inc. of Lakewood, Colorado, held the position as the United States' largest bagel bakery in 2010, operating under the banners of Einstein Bros. Bagels, Noah's New York Bagels, and Manhattan Bagel. With 690 locations in 35 states, Einstein Noah had sales of $408.5 million in 2009 with more than 7,000 employees.

Other major retail bakeries also operated as wholesale bakeries, such as Hostess Brands Inc. of Irving, Texas. Although Hostess sold its products to convenience stores, grocery stores, and other retailers, it also operated 700 bakery outlet stores around the country. Overall sales in 2009 reached $2.7 billion with 21,000 employees. Krispy Kreme Donuts Inc. of Winston-Salem, North Carolina, was another wholesaler that also had more than 580 donut stores in the United States and 20 other countries. With 3,570 employees in 2010, Krispy Kreme recorded annual sales of about $346.5 million.

Other industry leaders included Dunkin' Brands Inc., of Canton, Massachusetts. With 6,400 stores in the United States and about 3,000 more in 30 countries,

Dunkin' Donuts was the world's leading chain of dough-nut shops. Including sales from Dunkin' Brands other chain, Baskin-Robbins, sales were $6.9 billion in 2009. Similarly, Mrs. Fields' Original Cookies of Salt Lake City, Utah, operated two franchises: Mrs. Fields' Cookies and TCBY Frozen Yogurt. Mrs. Fields was one of the largest premium snack-food stand franchisors in the United States in 2010, with about 400 outlets in the United States and 100 more around the world. Another large franchiser in the retail bakery business was Cinna-bon Inc. of Atlanta, Georgia, with 750 outlets in the United States and overseas.

WORKFORCE

According to Dun & Bradstreet, 221,756 people were employed by the retail bakery industry in 2010. Califor-nia employed the most workers in the industry with 28,669, followed by New York with 20,435; Texas with 15,069; Massachusetts with 14,660; Florida with 13,112; New Jersey with 11,623; and Pennsylvania with 10,546.

U.S. Bureau of Labor Statistics figures showed that approximately 140,510 people were employed as bakers in the United States in 2009, including those employed by establishments other than retail bakeries. The average annual salary for a baker was $25,350, and demand for bakers was expected to remain stable through 2018.

RESEARCH AND TECHNOLOGY

Like many industries in the United States, retail bakeries dealt with the implications of the green movement in the late 2000s and early 2010s. One of the results of this movement was the introduction of the Leadership in Energy and Environmental Design (LEED) building cer-tification system. Established by the U.S. Green Building Council and verified by the Green Building Certification Institute (GBCI), the LEED certification is meant to encourage businesses to focus on energy and water sav-ings, emissions reduction, better indoor air quality, and other environment-related factors when designing build-ings. Different levels of certification are granted to build-ings designed with sustainability in mind.

Claire's on Cedros, a retail bakery and café in Solana Beach, California, became one of only five restaurants with LEED platinum certification, the highest rank, in 2010. Aspects of Claire's that contributed to its LEED rank included a vegetated roof, a pervious-concrete park-ing lot (allows water to be absorbed rather than run off), solar panels for energy production, low-flow and sensor-activated water fixtures, and various other indoor and outdoor energy- and water-saving features. Research on ways to make buildings, as well as practices in the retail bakery and other industries, was ongoing into the early 2010s.

While advances in technology were helping to create greener facilities and methods of production, they also were contributing to new methods of and materials for packaging bakery items. As a part of the green move-ment, many consumers looked for packaging that was environmentally friendly and did not involve excessive waste. In response, some bakeries created new options for packaging. For example, Pattycake Bakery in Columbus, Ohio, wraps its cookies in a plant-based material that is 100 percent biodegradable. Even the glue used to attach the labels is wheat-based and vegan, and the labels are printed with soy-based ink. According to *Modern Baking*, the company spent almost a year developing the new packaging, which involved finding sources that would provide the necessary materials. Owner Jennie Schein-bach told the magazine, "Many regular adhesives, includ-ing all-natural ones, are made with animal products, which didn't fit with our vegan operation. And the other vegan glues we found were made with chemicals."

Although Pattycake was an exception in terms of the extent to which its owners would go to be green, other bakeries were using more environmentally friendly pack-aging and bakeware as well, such as plain kraft paper bags and biodegradable paper molds for baking. Yummy Cup-cakes of Santa Monica, California, eliminated the waste of the paper liners with its Cupcake in a Jar, which consisted of layers of cupcake, icing, and toppings in a reusable mason jar. Other bakeries offered similar prod-ucts, as the trend toward reusable and biodegradable materials continued.

BIBLIOGRAPHY

"About Us." American Society of Baking, 22 October 2010. Available from http://www.asbe.org.

"Baked Product Trends." *Baking Management*, 23 April 2009.

"California Bakeries Awarded LEED Certification." *Modern Baking*, 1 April 2010.

"Hoover's Company Profiles." *Hoovers Online*, 22 October 2010. Available from http://www.hoovers.com.

"Cupcakes." All About Cupcakes, 22 October 2010. Available from http://www http://iml.jou.ufl.edu.

"Gotham Gets its Just Desserts: Not Every City Street Has a New Bakery. It Just Seems That Way." *Crain's New York Business*, 2 August 2010.

Heath, Thomas. "Cupcakeries Emerge as Washington's Sweet Spot in a Downturn." *Washington Post*, 26 August 2009.

"Industry News." Retail Bakers of America, 22 October 2010. Available from http://www.retailbakersofamerica.org.

"Keeping Sales Vibrant in a Stagnant Economy." *Modern Baking*, 1 September 2010.

"May 2009 National Industry-Specific Occupational Employment and Wage Estimates." Occupational Employment Statistics, 14 May 2010. Available from http://www.bls.gov.

"New Trends Impact Retail Bakeries in 2010." *Supermarket News*, 25 January 2010.

Occupational Outlook Handbook, 2010–11 Edition. Washington, DC: U.S. Department of Labor, Bureau of Labor Statistics, 17 December 2009. Available from http://www.bls.gov.

Olson, Elizabeth. "The Latest Entrepreneurial Fantasy Is Selling Cupcakes." *The New York Times*, 25 November 2009.

"Retail Bakeries." *Industry Reports*, 22 October 2010. Dun & Bradstreet. Available from http://www1. zapdata.com.

"Retail Bakers Upbeat in Down Economy." *Modern Baking*, 1 June 2009.

Solis, Brian. "The Business of Social Media: B2B and B2C Engagement by the Numbers," 8 January 2010. Available from http://www.briansolis.com.

"The History of Bread." American Bakers Association, 22 October 2010. Available from http://www.americanbakers. org.

"Think Outside the Bakery Box." *Modern Baking*, 1 February 2010.

SPECIALTY COFFEE

SIC CODE(S)

2095

5812

INDUSTRY SNAPSHOT

Contrary to popular belief, coffee did not originate in Brazil or Colombia; rather, it originated in Ethiopia. In the early 2000s, it was the world's second most traded commodity after oil. Specialty coffee has been defined as "a coffee that has no defects and has a distinctive flavor in the cup." The premium variety is Arabica coffee, which accounts for 70 percent of the world's coffee production. Specialty coffee remains one of the fastest-growing food service markets globally, due to the explosion of cafées and gourmet coffee retailers.

ORGANIZATION AND STRUCTURE

After growing in any of roughly 20 countries, coffee beans pass through many intermediaries and brokers before coming to industry firms in the United States. Usually, the beans arrive green, or un-roasted, whereupon industry firms buy and roast them in small batches. From that point, the beans reach consumers through several channels, including supermarkets, gourmet delis, fancy food stores, housewares/gift stores, mail order, mass merchandisers, the Internet, specialty coffee stores, and coffee cafées. In non-proprietary retail stores such as supermarkets, specialty coffee is prepackaged or in bulk, depending on the individual retailer's store format.

Industry firms often sell their beans through a combination of supermarkets, their own bean stores and/or cafées, mail order, and the Internet. The difference between a bean store and a cafée is that the former emphasizes selling beans (and assorted brewing gadgets) so consumers can make gourmet coffee at home while a cafée prepares single drinks for customers to consume on the premises or to take out. Many industry firms such as Starbucks sell whole beans as well as individual drinks at their stores and serve coffee drinks to consumers in two forms: the filtered drip coffee familiar to most Americans, and European-style espresso, a more concentrated form of the brew, which is harder for consumers to make at home. Shots of espresso are "pulled" from espresso machines by cafée workers called baristas, coffee bartenders of sorts. Most espresso beverages have one or more shots combined with steamed or foamed milk to make such drinks as cappuccinos, cafée mochas, or cafée au laits. Interestingly, a one-ounce espresso contains less caffeine than a regular cup of drip coffee. The water is in contact with the grounds for only 20 to 25 seconds, unlike drip coffee, in which the grounds are in contact with the water for several minutes. It takes 42 coffee beans to make an average-sized serving of espresso.

Although the coffee industry as a whole lacked standards for coffee brewing since 1975, the Specialty Coffee Association of America (SCAA) reinstituted such standards in the late 1990s. The SCAA's standards require that the coffee grounds to water ratio must fall between 3.25 and 4.25 ounces of ground coffee per every 64 ounces of water. Other standards cover water temperature and quality, brewing time, and coarseness or fineness of coffee grounds.

A study by the SCAA in the 1990s noted above-average consumption in the Pacific, Middle Atlantic, and New England states and found gourmet coffee drinkers tended to be slightly more affluent than average and that they lived or worked in large cities. Gourmet coffee consumption also rose with the drinker's educational level. Those who finished college bought 49 percent more gourmet coffee on average and those with some postgraduate education bought 71 percent more. They also found that households with children and two working parents bought 28 percent more gourmet coffee. The SCAA described its typical customer as "an educated urban resident with the disposable income to spend on fine coffee."

BACKGROUND AND DEVELOPMENT

Until the 1960s, nearly all Americans bought their coffee at the supermarket. During the late 1960s, some entrepreneurs opened shops carrying hard-to-find gourmet food items, such as specialty coffees, aimed at affluent consumers. Some of these businesses even roasted their own coffee to control the degree of roast and keep the coffee fresh. By 1969, the United States had about 50 specialty coffee stores. During the early 1970s, 100 gift/housewares stores and 1,200 specialty food stores carried gourmet coffee. In 1975, a killing frost in Brazil devastated the coffee crop, which raised coffee prices by 500 percent. Large roasters tried to calm consumer sticker shock by selling coffee in 13-ounce cans instead of the usual 16-ounce cans. Since consumers got less for their coffee dollar, some of them switched to the more flavorful gourmet blends, following a quality-versus-quantity consumer trend.

Throughout the 1970s, the industry experimented with roasting beans darker to make a smokier, more distinct coffee than the lighter supermarket roasts. Thus, many consumers came to associate dark roasted coffee with gourmet coffee and many specialty coffee companies developed proprietary house blends during the 1970s. Decaffeinated coffees became a popular seller during the 1980s, with 17 percent of the population drinking it by 1988. The demand for flavored coffees emerged in the mid-1980s, causing producers to add flavors such as cocoa, vanilla, or hazelnut in liquid or powder form to coffee beans. This required little capital investment and allowed specialty shops to sell flavored coffees at a higher price. Industry firms tried many different flavors and several became big hits, particularly by attracting new, younger coffee drinkers to the customer base.

Some coffee purists scoffed at flavored coffees, despite their apparent popularity. Starbucks, for example, refused to flavor its beans, but sold flavored syrup to add after brewing. Syrups provided retailers with more sales options than simply flavoring coffees. These could be used in Italian sodas, "granitas," and other drink concoctions popular with the 18- to 35-year-old café patron.

These drinks could also be sold at a premium. Standard flavors included vanilla, hazelnut, and raspberry, but companies such as Boyd Coffee expanded their lines to include crème brûlée and wild huckleberry flavored syrups, and Stasero added praline, marshmallow, and a combination of passion fruit, orange, and guava. Marketing syrup-flavored drinks proved to fuel creativity from employee and customer alike. Signature drinks offered by some retailers included Lemon Meringue Pie Italian Soda; Nutty Buddy, a mocha spiked with three nut-flavored syrups; and Starburst, with white chocolate and lemon syrups mixed in sparkling water.

Another trend included consumer requests for organic coffees, and more emphasis was placed by retailers on the beans' growing environment. One growing environmental and economic concern within the industry was the plight of wintering songbirds. The shade trees sheltering coffee bushes of Central and South America have long been home to migratory birds. Ornithological surveys have found 150 or more bird species living on traditional coffee plantations. Strong demand for coffee and advice from the U.S. government caused growers to convert their land to so-called sun plantations. The U.S. Agency for International Development spent $81 million in efforts to get growers to change planting methods to increase volume. Economic studies completed since dispute those assumptions, and the process of changing these once-fertile habitats from shade tree to sun plantations, started in 1978, has caused a decline in the migratory bird species population in these traditional locations.

Increased attention to the plight of the birds meant coffee drinkers began asking for shade-grown beans in an attempt to change the trend. Companies including Thanksgiving Coffee marketed specially labeled coffees to educate coffee lovers about the issue. According to a 1997 *Knight Ridder/Tribune News Service* article, most specialty coffee is actually shade grown. The SCAA said that most mass-market coffees are grown on sun plantations, where volume and price are a bigger factor.

Growth of the roaster/retailer segment shows how the industry evolved during the 1970s and 1980s. In 1979, there were about 50 coffee roaster/retailers in the United States; by 1989, there were 400. Growth of specialty coffee retail stores (no roasting on premises) was also dramatic as their number increased from 250 in 1979 to 1,000 by 1989.

The Competition As coffee prices rose, some analysts predicted that the specialty coffee business could only prosper. Since an ordinary cup of coffee was already considered expensive, specialty roasters and retailers believed consumers would spend slightly more for gourmet coffee. The array of products was never wider as retailers added more flavors to whole beans and variations to the basics of espresso and steamed milk. The more clever retailers added coffee shakes and iced tea concoctions, such as *chai*, to their menus, to outdo competitors who offered mere iced lattes. Since most specialty retailers also retailed whole beans, their stores added home espresso machines, coffee grinders, and other brewing supplies for add-on sales.

Many industry firms did all they could to increase market share. They ran catalog sales departments, added retail locations, and competed for new wholesale clients such as restaurant chains and supermarkets. Several industry firms started sites on the Internet during the 1990s to sell coffee beans over the Internet. Some roasters even created private label blends for their institutional customers. Starbucks Corp.'s Nordstrom Blend, for example, was created for the upscale department store chain. Courting corporate accounts became increasingly important because the principal place for drinking coffee in the late 1990s was the workplace.

The specialty coffee industry reaped sales of approximately $1.5 billion in the mid- to late 1990s, benefiting in part from an overall surge in coffee consumption in the United States. By 1999, 76 percent of the population consumed coffee, including espresso and gourmet coffee potables as well as coffee consumed by occasional drinkers, according to *Restaurant Business.* This number represented the highest level of consumption in the last 40 years, surpassing the 1962 peak of coffee consumption when 64 percent of the population consumed coffee. Moreover, the number of cups consumed also rose in 1999, climbing to 3.5 cups a day, up from three cups earlier in the decade. As a final indicator of this growth, one-third of coffee drinkers used larger, eight-ounce cups in 1999, up 10 percent from 1998, according to *Restaurant Business.*

Led by specialty coffees, whole bean sales by grocery, mass merchant, and drug stores rose 16 percent in 1999, hitting $264.8 million, according to Information Resources Inc., a marketing research company. These retailers reported that other coffee categories declined by 6.2 percent, as overall sales by grocery, mass merchant, and drug stores dipped to $2 billion. While ground coffee sales dropped, however, whole bean sales continued to do well, more than tripling their 1989 level, according to the SCAA. Starbucks was a major catalyst in the growth of whole bean sales because the company began selling its whole beans in these stores in 1998. By 1999, Starbucks accounted for almost 10 percent of the whole bean sales in these stores, with revenues of $23.8 million. Most affected was the Eight O'Clock brand. Its sales fell about 10 percent due in part to Starbucks' presence.

With strong demand for specialty coffee, more competitors entered the business during the late 1990s, with varied success. General Foods captured some market share from the smaller players with its line of Gevalia Coffees, sold only by mail order. Procter & Gamble, maker of Folgers, entered the specialty coffee fray in 1995 with its purchase of Millstone, which it distributes to about 7,000 stores. In 1999, Procter & Gamble even attempted to upgrade Folgers as a specialty coffee by selling whole coffee beans under the Folgers flag. In addition, another mass market coffee producer, Chock full o'Nuts Corp., bought an industry firm called Quikava in 1994. Based in Boston, Quikava is a chain of drive-through espresso shops that offers franchising. Quikava kept expanding and Chock full o'Nuts set a precedent for other established retailers to enter the market with its streamlined business approach and its careful expansion plans. Sara Lee Corp. expanded its presence in the industry in 1999 by acquiring Chock full o'Nuts.

The influx of coffeehouses also has driven the specialty coffee industry, since many cafées and coffeehouses sell specialty coffee primarily or exclusively. The number of cafés jumped to 12,000 in 1999, up from just 5,000 in 1995. One industry trend of the late 1990s was the consolidation of specialty coffee companies (or the rumors of such consolidation), as smaller competitors scrambled to compete with the industry giant, Starbucks Corp. For example, the nation's number two specialty coffee chain, Diedrich Coffee, acquired Coffee People in 1999 for $23 million, as well as Pannikin Coffee in 1997 for $2.8 million. In addition, Peabodys Coffee Inc. bought a number of smaller specialty coffeehouses, including Northern Lights Coffee, in 1999, and Capitol Coffee and Arrosto Coffee Co. in 2000.

In the fall of 2005, Burger King and McDonalds introduced upgraded coffee blends, brewing procedures, and packaging in an effort to compete with Starbucks and others in the breakfast business. Burger King launched its "BK Joe" branded made-to-order coffee program across the country in October, 2005, while McDonalds planned to began selling its new premium coffee early in 2006. As sellers of premium coffee, fast food restaurants are in a good position to deliver it quicker and cheaper. They are masters of convenience and are able to keep prices low.

New Developments Throughout 2003, the market continued its rapid expansion. One of the newest trends in the domestic market was in drive-through coffee stores. Starbucks had 540 drive-through stores in early 2004, all of which were seeing continual growth and long lines.

Some analysts said the industry trend toward consolidation indicated that the specialty coffee industry was maturing and that mergers and acquisitions brought needed capital. Ted Lingle, head of the SCAA, said in a published story, "We see growth peaking in this industry around the year 2010, and between now and then you'll see a slow but steady increase in the number of mergers. After that, I don't think you'll see merger mania tapering off until after the year 2020."

Such growth was not without concern, however. By early 2004, soaring dairy prices were expected to affect coffee stores in the prices of milk purchased for use in their specialty beverages as well as for the standard creamers. In addition, despite its widespread presence, Starbucks alone was purchasing only 2 percent of the coffee produced worldwide. However, because the specialty beans required by Starbucks and Diedrich and the other industry leaders were grown in far smaller quantities, the concern was that demand was rapidly exceeding supply, causing both increased prices and shortage. Starbucks was addressing the concern proactively, going directly to the source to ensure better quality coffee by opening a Costa Rican support office for coffee farmers and rewarding environmentally responsible farms through its CAFE Practices program.

In fact, "Fair Trade" practices were springing up in much of the coffee industry by 2004. The nonprofit organization Global Exchange had this to say about the import of Fair Trade Certified Coffee: "The chief concern of the Fair Trade movement has been to ensure that the vast majority of the world's coffee farmers (who are small holders) get a fair price for their harvests in order to achieve a decent living wage ($1.26/pound regardless of the volatile market); much needed credit at fair prices; and long term relationships. These fair payments are invested in health care, education, environmental stewardship, and economic independence." Green Mountain saw sales of its Fair Trade products grow 92 percent in 2003. Ahold USA launched its own brand of five Fair Trade coffee bean products in 1,200 of its grocery stores. Dunkin' Donuts, which in 2004 still had the number one U.S. spot in terms of coffee sold on a per cup basis, particularly in the New England area, was test-marketing a Fair Trade espresso brand.

In 2006, coffee trendsetters began buying coffee beans the way winemakers shop for top-quality grapes. Estate-grown beans, which are then roasted into lighter brews to bring out distinct flavors, began replacing the trademark charcoal-scented Northwest blended coffee. Blends are typically used to ensure enhanced flavor, but if an excellent coffee bean, called single-origin coffee, is found and brewed in a French press or Cona vacuum pot, there is no need to compromise with a blend. Some of these single-origin beans bear names that describe their origin. For example, Guatemala Huehuetenango Finca

Vista Hermosa Estate Reserve describes the bean right to the farm that grows it.

However, roasting these single-origins to a deep, dark one-size-fits-all brew is not the goal. To bring out the unique characteristics in the bean, custom coffee roasters experiment with time and temperature to highlight flavors and find the perfect balance of caramelized sugars to acidity, rather than simply roasting the beans dark, as specialty coffees are expected to be. A heavy roast can hide flaws in the coffee bean, so a medium roast of really good beans "is a revelation for people," according to Kenneth Davids, a Berkeley-based coffee expert.

The industry trade group Specialty Coffee Association of America (SCAA), in its *Retail in the USA 2006* report, showed that at the end of 2006, specialty coffee sales had reached $12.27 billion, up from $11.05 billion in 2005 and $8.3 billion in 2001. Sales were divided into several subgroups: 15,500 coffee cafées (retailers with seating) had sales of $8.53 billion; 3,600 coffee kiosks (retailers without seating), $1.08 billion; 2,900 coffee carts (mobile retailers) $400 million; and 1,900 coffee bean roasters/retailers (roasting on the premises), $1.76 billion. Sixteen percent of the U.S. adult population consumed specialty coffee on a daily basis, whereas 63 percent indulged occasionally. These figures illustrate the growth in popularity of specialty coffees, as only 13 percent and 59 percent of people reported daily and occasional consumption, respectively, in 2002.

Some industry experts claim the specialty coffee industry has continued to grow despite the economic downturn of the late years of the first decade of the 2000s, especially the smaller, community coffee shops and those that roast their own beans. Lindsay Vergin of Dunn Brothers Coffee told *Nation's Restaurant News* "People are interested in locally owned and roasted coffees. We roast coffee beans in each traditional location, and all our coffee served has been roasted within the past three days." Franchises were also acting on new trends in order to attract business, such as drive-ins, nontraditional units, and bundled offerings.

CURRENT CONDITIONS

Earlier predictions that the specialty coffee industry would survive the 2008-2009 economic downturn were correct because Americans were still willing to pay for good coffee. Results from The National Coffee Association's annual survey showed that at least 80 percent of coffee drinkers did not change their habits or tastes despite the economy. In 2009, specialty coffee accounted for $13.65 billion, or a full one-third, of the nation's $40 billion coffee industry.

Moreover, growth in value surpassed growth in volume. According to Daniele Giovannucci, a leading coffee consultant, the sales growth rate for the specialty coffee segment was four times that of traditional coffee. Specialty coffees were projected to top $18 billion by 2012.

Not only had consumers continued to enjoy their cup of coffee to help them through a weak economy, they became more proactive in their tastes and consumption. Fair Trade coffee sales grew 32 percent in 2008, and both Rainforest-certified and organic coffees had double-digit increases. In 2009, more than 93 million pounds of organic coffee were imported into the United States and Canada; in North America, the organic coffee market topped $1.4 billion in 2009, reported Giovannucci in the *North American Organic Coffee Industry Report 2010*. The report also revealed that the organic coffee market enjoyed an average annual growth rate of 21 percent between 2005 and 2009, compared with an estimated one percent annual growth of the conventional coffee industry.

In 2009, U.S. coffee drinkers, about 54 percent of the overall population, consumed, on average, nine pounds of coffee per person. The average independent coffee shop sold 230 cups per day. One in five coffee drinkers preferred expresso drinks. Even those who brewed at home were partaking of the opportunity to sample a wide assortment of specialty flavors and blends in single-cup serving sizes. Green Mountain Coffee Roasters reported selling 1.2 million Keurig single-cup brewers during just the first six months of 2009. The most exotic and expensive specialty coffee, according to the Specialty Coffee Association, was Kopi Luwak; others considered it to be one of the worst tasting.

INDUSTRY LEADERS

Starbucks Corp., based in Seattle, Washington, continued to lead the industry in 2010. The company began in 1971 with one store in Seattle. Three entrepreneurs— Gordon Bowker, Jerry Baldwin, and Zev Siegl—founded the original business. They named it after a character who loved coffee from Herman Melville's classic novel *Moby Dick,* and they developed the now-familiar mermaid logo. Starbucks originally sold bulk tea and specialty coffee beans by the pound. They did not add a coffee bar to sell drinks until 1984. The coffee bar idea came from Howard Schultz, who was the company's marketing director. Schultz quit the company in 1985 to start a chain of espresso cafés like those he had seen in Milan, Italy. He called his cafés Il Giornale, and they served Starbucks coffee. In 1987, Schultz raised money from private investors and bought Starbucks from its founders for $3.8 million. The venture paid off for Schultz, whose personal fortune was $100 million in 1997, 75 percent of which came from Starbucks stock.

During the late 1980s, Starbucks built a larger roasting plant, started a mail order catalog, and opened stores in British Columbia, Oregon, and the Chicago area. By 1992, the company grew to 165 stores and issued shares that were available on the NASDAQ. Their specialty sales division landed prized institutional accounts throughout the 1990s, including Nordstrom's coffee bars, United Airlines, Barnes & Noble, ITT/Sheraton Hotels, Westin Hotels, and Star Markets. Starbucks also offered some of their catalog items on the Internet through America Online. In 1994, Starbucks had 425 U.S. stores and bought a smaller competitor, the Coffee Connection, Inc. In 1995, the company also bought a minority stake in Noah's New York Bagels, Inc., a coffee and bagel chain based in Golden, Colorado.

Starbucks began joint ventures from 1995 to 1997 to get its coffee into other products, including Double Black Stout, a dark beer with a shot of espresso, developed with Redhook Ale Brewery; Frappucino, a bottled iced coffee beverage, developed with PepsiCo Inc.; and a line of Starbucks coffee-flavored ice creams marketed with Breyer's Grand Ice Cream, Inc. and sold in supermarkets. One of the company's few failures was a carbonated coffee beverage called Mazagran. Joint ventures extended to nonfood items as well, including the sale of music CDs in Starbucks stores, a concept developed with Capitol Records' Blue Note Jazz label. Furthermore, Starbucks sells its beans via mail order catalogs and the Internet.

Starbucks opened almost one new store per day in the late 1990s, including five on a single day in Toronto. During this period, Starbucks expanded to the Pacific Rim, opening stores in Hawaii, Japan, and Singapore. The expansion effort helped the company realize its goal of having 2,000 stores by the year 2000, which it handily exceeded by 800 cafées. Part of the company's expansion campaign also included the acquisition of Seattle Coffee Co. Seattle Coffee operates 68 cafés, primarily in the United Kingdom, under the names Seattle's Best Coffee and Torrefazione Italia, as well as a roasting and packaging facility. Furthermore, Seattle Coffee products can be found in about 1,600 grocery stores nationwide. Starbucks bought the company in order to penetrate the European market. Despite critics calling them the "golden arches" of the specialty coffee industry, the company's cash registers kept ringing; in 2000 Starbucks claimed to serve about 4 million customers per week.

In 1999, Starbucks posted sales of $1.68 billion and had about 2,800 retail locations throughout the world. By 2007, sales were $9.4 billion with 16,000 locations. Starbucks also distributed its specialty coffee to about 3,500 supermarkets. During the first decade of the 2000s, in addition to expanding its drive-through presence domestically, the company launched Music Cafés with Hewlett-Packard, where people can come in for their coffee fix and custom-burn their own music CDs. Some in the industry were dubious about the profitability of such a venture, but, according to the president of the International Recording Media Association, "You can never underestimate a company that convinced people to pay $5 for a cup of coffee."

In the early 2000s, Starbucks began a major transformation. President of the company Howard Schultz said in a July 1, 2008 press release, "We committed to transforming the company through a series of critical and strategic initiatives to improve the current state of our U.S. business and build the business for the long term." Part of this plan involved an extensive review of its U.S.-operated store portfolio, after which the firm announced that around 600 underperforming stores in the United States would be closed. In addition, only about 200 new stores were planned for 2009. Starbucks reported $10.7 billion in revenues for its fiscal year 2010, representing a record fourth quarter and overall revenue rise of 9.5 percent for the year.

One of Starbucks' publicly held competitors, Diedrich Coffee Inc. of Irvine, California, specializes in sourcing, roasting, and selling high quality coffees. Diedrich also sells its coffees through wholesale accounts, including office coffee service distributors, restaurants and specialty retailers, mail order, and the Internet.

Diedrich, founded in 1912, owns Central American plantations and is credited with designing and manufacturing "one of the world's most popular batch roasting machines," according to the company. In 1999, Diedrich acquired another leading specialty coffee company, Coffee People, Inc. Diedrich's coffee portfolio includes brands such as Diedrich Coffee, Gloria Jean's, and Coffee Plantation. Sales for the firm in 2007 reached $36.6 million, and it had 120 locations in 28 states. The company also sells to about 900 wholesale clients.

Caribou Coffee was started with a mere $200,000 in 1992, when Starbucks only had 116 stores nationwide, as the vision of newlyweds John and Kim Puckett, who opened the first shops in Minneapolis in 1993. Planned expansion was to take Caribou Coffee throughout the Southeast and Midwestern United States. In the late 1990s, Caribou Coffee had estimated sales of $75 million, but the company had operating capital problems that had plagued them almost from the start. In December 2000, although its investors had contributed over $40 million, it couldn't raise further operating capital and sold 70 percent of its stock (later it would become 87.8 percent) to a group of international investors led by the First Islamic Investment Bank, E.C., of Bahrain. The investment by this group enabled Caribou to continue the expansion of its store base in the United States. The bank described itself as purely a financial investment organization based in and regulated by the government of Bahrain, which is an ally of the United States in the Middle East and the headquarters of the U.S. Navy's 5th Fleet. The company's strategy for the first decade of the 2000s was expansion in its core Midwestern markets—such as jumping on the 2003-2004 "low carb" bandwagon by introducing its low-carb and low-calorie line for dieters—and exploration of the possibility of a public offering.

However, after the terrorist attacks of September 11, 2001, Internet and media attention focused on the fact that the First Islamic Investment Bank of Bahrain's heavy investments in U.S. companies were reviewed for compliance with Islamic religious tenets by the bank's Shari'ah advisory board, which at that time was chaired by an Islamic cleric and scholar named Yusef al-Qaradawi, who became controversial when his association with the Muslim Brotherhood, the Egyptian political group that spawned Ayman al-Zawahiri, Osama bin Laden's second in command, and Mohammed Atta, the leader of 9/11 terrorist attacks, came to light, along with reports of al-Qaradawi's endorsement of Hamas and suicide bombings against Israel and increasingly anti-American pronouncements. In 2002, al-Qaradawi retired from his position as chairman of First Islam's Shari'ah advisory board. Also, according to its "Urban Legends" reference page on Caribou Coffee, Snopes.com reported that in July 2002, the First Islamic Investment Bank hired a Washington, D.C., law firm to "review its charitable donations, and they have certified that no charitable contributions from Caribou's coffers go to groups banned under U.S. law." On March 15, 2005, the First Islamic Investment Bank changed its name to Arcapita, with wholly owned subsidiaries Crescent Capital Investments, Inc. in Atlanta, Georgia, and Crescent Capital Investments (Europe) Limited in the United Kingdom. On September 29, 2005, Caribou Coffee Company announced its initial public offering on the NASDAQ of 5.358 million shares of its common stock at $14.00 per share.

In 2010, Caribou Coffee, headquartered in Minneapolis, was the nation's second largest U.S. specialty coffee company with 535 coffeehouses (including 122 franchised/licensed) and more than 6,600 employees. On July 5, 2005, Caribou Coffee Company announced that it would "support sustainably produced coffee—and the communities and farms in coffee growing lands—through a new partnership with the Rainforest Alliance," an international nonprofit organization which certifies farms that meet the "highest standards for the conservation of natural resources and the rights and welfare of workers and local communities." Sales for 2009 were up 3.4 percent, at $262.5 million.

Second Cup Ltd., a Toronto-based firm, is Canada's largest specialty coffee cafée franchiser and its second largest retailer. It opened its first coffee café in Toronto in 1975 and in 2008 had 366 cafés across Canada, 90 percent of which were franchised, as well as 35 locations internationally. In 2008 the company opened a café in Waukesha, Wisconsin, which represented the firm's first store in the United States.

Another major player in the industry is Green Mountain Coffee Roasters, Inc., of Waterbury, Vermont. The firm sells gourmet coffee to catalog patrons and institutional customers, and dominated the market for single-serve specialty coffees in 2009. Although Green Mountain once ran about 12 cafés, it decided to divest itself of them in the late 1990s to focus on its core wholesale business. In the fall of 2003, the company scored a coup when Amtrak began selling the brand on its trains. By 2004, Green Mountain was a major participant in the "Fair Trade" coffee movement and was guaranteeing its Mexican coffee co-op $1.26 per pound, more than twice the world price. For fiscal year 2004, Green Mountain recorded sales in excess of $137 million, with the majority generated by its wholesale business, which served more than 7,000 customer accounts. By fiscal 2009, sales had risen 46 percent, reaching $500 million. The firm also produces a mail order catalog, which reaches customers nationally.

One of Starbucks' founders, Jerry Baldwin, retained and runs privately held Peet's Coffee and Tea, based in Emeryville, California. Peet's had 200 stores as of 2010, most of them in California (although it began to market packaged coffee on the East Coast). Peet's is not a major company, but it is a profitable one, maintaining its quality commitment while it gears up to keep pace with the market and grow its business. In 2009, its new Godiva-flavored esprresso drink was a huge hit. One of its fastest-growing areas was grocery sales; Pete's was also available through grocery stores, on the Internet, and by mail order. Riding on a high, in late 2009, Peet's bid $265 million to acquire Diedrich Coffee in an effort to enter the single-serve market dominated by Green Mountain.

Other industry leaders in the first decade of the 2000s included Coffee Tea & Bean Leaf (El Segundo, California), with 295 U.S. locations, 102 of which are franchised; Coffee Beanery (Flushing, Michigan), with 91 U.S. stores and 26 international; Dunn Brothers (Minneapolis, Minnesota), with 92 units; and Biggby Coffee (East Lansing, Michigan), with more than 100 stores and plans to open 22 more.

AMERICA AND THE WORLD

Gourmet coffee comes from about 20 different countries. Free trade between the United States and producer countries is vital to the industry, since the domestic crop is so small. The only gourmet coffee grown on U.S. soil comes from the Kona area on the island of Hawaii. However, Kona's crop is impractical for two reasons: price and authenticity. The coffee costs more than similar-tasting Latin American coffees because U.S. coffee pickers do not work for Third World wages. Since the beans are so expensive, scams have occasionally surfaced. For example, in 1996 a Berkeley, California, wholesaler got caught diluting Kona beans with cheaper Latin American beans, after having fooled consumers, and some in the industry, for years.

On the other end, the Organic Trade Association maintained statistics for coffees certified to Bird Friendly, Fair Trade, Rainforest Alliance, UTZ CERTIFIED, and Starbucks' Practices standards. Bolivia, Brazil, Costa Rica, El Salvador, and Nicaragua were among the countries having winning organic coffee farms in 2009. A Bolivian farm, Agrotakesi SA, received the highest ranking score for organic coffee, earning 93.96 points for its coffee in 2009.

Other specialty beans come from the Arab states and East Africa, including Yemen, Ethiopia, Kenya, Tanzania, and Zimbabwe. The final group of coffees comes from the Malay Archipelago, including such areas as Sumatra, Sulawesi, Java, and New Guinea. The most prominent coffee-growing region is Latin America. Brazil grows one-third of the world's coffee, but only a small portion of that is gourmet quality. The second largest coffee-producing country is Colombia, which produces the most consistent coffee, according to some analysts. Mexico, Ecuador, Peru, and Venezuela produce coffees most often used by specialty purveyors for blends, although better varieties from these countries are sometimes sold unblended. Some analysts believe Costa Rica grows the region's finest coffee, particularly the estate coffee, La Minita, from Tarrazu.

In 2009, a conference organization in Dubai hosted the Gulf Region's first specialty coffee exhibition alongside the UAE's first World Barista Championship sanctioned competition, deemed by industry insiders as a sign of things to come. In Asia, a longtime tea stronghold, specialty coffee has become a symbol of status and success for an upwardly mobile middle class. This could also be said for Eastern Europe and Russia. In 2009, Moscow commanded the highest average cost per cup of coffee in the world (nearly $11).

In January 2006, Australian and Canadian companies paid $6,580 for a 60 kg bag of Brazilian coffee at a specialty coffee auction. The record-breaking price was the equivalent of paying $49.75 per pound. Ten years earlier, world coffee importers were not convinced that Brazilian coffee producers could grow a top-quality bean on a par with Columbian coffees. However, technical investments in the plants have produced coffee in Brazil that is treated by coffee growers the same way grapes are treated, by paying special attention to the plant. In 2005, Brazil produced 800,000 bags of specialty coffee—10 percent of the 8 million bags consumed worldwide annually. Three percent was consumed domestically, while the rest was shipped abroad.

Germany has entered the realm of the U.S. style coffeehouse. As of 2010, Starbucks had 140 shops in Germany and another 48 in France that were attracting the upwardly-mobile 20- to 40-year-olds, while smaller, old-fashioned coffeehouses were fading away. German consumers are increasingly favoring the premium coffees imported from private estates and farms around the world.

BIBLIOGRAPHY

Bolton, Dan. "Ten 2010 Trends: Overview." *Specialty Coffee Retailer,* August 2009.

"Canadian Coffee Company Migrates to U.S." *Food Service Director,* 15 September 2008.

"Caribou Coffee Reports Fourth Quarter and Fiscal Year 2009 Revenues." January 2010 Available at http://restaurant news.com/.

"Coffee Industry Shifts Under Tough Economy." *Specialty Coffee Retailer,* March 2010.

Cole, Leslie. "The New Brew." *Knight Ridder/Tribune Business News,* 18 April 2006.

"DJ Brazilian Specialty Coffee Fetches $6,580 A 60-kg Bag." *FWN Financial News,* 12 January 2006.

Hadi, Mohammed. "Fighting Rumors, Companies Face Hard Choices, New Forums." *Dow Jones Newswires,* 24 August 2006. Available from http://money.cnn.com/.

"Kaffitar: A Hot Cup of Joe in Iceland." *Tea & Coffee Trade Journal,* June 2008.

McCabe, Jane. "Eyes on Starbucks." *Tea & Coffee Trade Journal,* September 2008.

Morris, David J., and Lon LaFlamme. "Warning! The Bell Curve Is Sounding: There Isn't Room for Amateurs in the Specialty Coffee Business Anymore!" *Tea & Coffee Trade Journal,* April 2008.

"Organic Coffee market Tops $1.4 Billion in North America, New Survey Shows." Press Release, 15 June 2010. Available from http://www.organicnewsroom.com.

"Premier Specialty Coffee Provider Revolutionizes Coffee Brewing With Innovative Technology Solution." *Internet Wire,* 8 October 2008.

Retail in the USA 2006. Long Beach, CA: Specialty Coffee Association of America, 2007.

"Starbucks Increases Number of U.S. Company-Operated Store Closures as Part of Transformation Strategy." *Business Wire,* 1 July 2008.

"Starbucks Reports Record Fourth Quarter and Fiscal 2010 Results." Press Release, 4 November 2010. Available from http://news.starbucks.com.

Sterrett, David. "McD's Eye-Opener: Its Double-Shot Task: Sell Fancy Coffee to Golden Arches Regulars, Lure Starbucks Fans." *Crain's Chicago Business,* 21 July 2008

Walkup, Carolyn. "Regional Coffeehouses Brew Expansion Plans." *Nation's Restaurant News,* 18 August 2008.

"What is Fair Trade Coffee All About?" *Global Exchange,* 19 August 2006. Available from http://www.globalexchange.org/.

"What is Specialty Coffee?" Speciality Coffee Association of America, 1 October 2008. Available from http://www.scaa.org/.

SPECIALTY GARDENING

———— ■ ————

SIC CODE(S)

5191

5193

INDUSTRY SNAPSHOT

There are many different kinds of specialty gardens. Specialty gardens include rose, water, rock, butterfly, koi pond, container, hummingbird, handicapped-focused (allows people with disabilities to enjoy gardening), hydroponic (plants grown without soil), organic, roof, or xeriscaping (plants grown without a steady supply of water).

Specialty gardening has grown in popularity over the past few years. This is due to a renewed interest in creating custom gardens that may be a bit different than the usual suburban flowerbeds. Urban spaces are now home to roof gardens, organic gardens, rock gardens, and other specialty gardens designed to better the experience for city dwellers.

The study of hydroponics and aeroponics came about early in the nineteenth century as a result of research seeking how to grow fresh vegetables using only water and minerals. Hydroponics is a subset of soilless gardening, but it uses no sand culture, whereas soilless gardening requires only that silt and clay are not used and sand culture is allowed. Aeroponics is sometimes considered a part of hyroponics because water is sometimes used as a growing medium. Aeroponics is where plants are grown without soil or an aggregate medium. The interest in both hydroponics and aeroponics has increased in recent years as hobbyist and urban farmers seek diverse ways to grow healthful foods or beautiful flowers for themselves or for others.

As environmental awareness expands, the focus on specialty gardens is becoming more than just a hobby. Organic gardening (including the use of natural pest control), biodynamic agriculture, and drip irrigation also has made a resurgence as people become more aware of their food, where it comes from, and how it affects their health. Retail outlets and online sites geared toward enthusiasts of specialty gardening have increased, as has interest in state universities that offer opportunities in general agriculture and agricultural management.

ORGANIZATION AND STRUCTURE

Specialty gardening information can be found in abundance Web sites, e-zines, and online forums. The growth of the Internet and the use of social media in the past five years has enabled enthusiasts to meet electronically and exchange information on specialty gardening. However, gardening centers, including large nationwide retail chains, also have gotten involved in the specialty gardening craze, offering plants and supplies and expert opinion and advice. In addition, bookstores offer books on the how and why of specialty gardening. Gardeners seeking out new and varied ideas can now use either free or minimal fee information with which to create their own specialty gardens.

Federal and state agencies may regulate the types of pesticides and herbicides that can be used in specialty gardens. States ban the propagation of certain plants. Some cities have weed laws to regulate the sort of plants that homeowners can grow in their yards, including acceptable heights and locations for certain plants. For those who rent, landlords can place limits on the use of yard space and deck. At the federal level, the Environmental Protection Agency (EPA) restricts the use of certain legal pesticides to licensed professionals. States also have the right to place stricter regulations on pesticide use. For example, phenoxy herbicides are illegal in some states, but not in others. The federal government maintains a list of invasive or noxious plants that are considered a threat to native species or agriculture. States can impose stricter regulations regarding the propagation of these or other plants. The United States Department of Agriculture (USDA) Web site includes links to regulations by state.

Many residential lawn and garden regulations, or "weed laws," date to the 1940s. City governments created weed laws in response to citizen concern that overgrown lots could harbor snakes, rats, and transients, cause a fire hazard, or more likely, lower neighboring property values. These weed laws impose height restrictions for plants and grasses or limit what types of plants can be grown in one's yard. For example, a state or city government can impose a ban on cultivating a specific noxious weed, invasive species, or even native wildflower. Some towns and cities also have laws that regulate if and where vegetables can be grown.

BACKGROUND AND DEVELOPMENT

The growing interest in specialty gardening represents an increase in better gardening, including gardening with a purpose (e.g., to attract butterflies or birds), gardening to help the environment (e.g., xeriscaping, organic and natural pest control, biodynamic agriculture), and gardening to take care of a singular landscape issue (e.g., rock, water, container). The resurgence of gardening and urban farms in recent years is a sign of the concerns regarding the food supply and how large the individual carbon footprint has become in recent years. Why must fresh fruits and vegetables be shipped from other states if they can be grown individually or locally? Why should chemically-based pest control be used when there are natural pest control solutions that will reduce the toxins in the soil, the air, and subsequently, in the water supply?

These concerns came about after the popular documentary, *Food, Inc.*, aired widely across the country. This documentary showed the horrific conditions in which some food is being raised and harvested. It led to concerns over fruits and vegetables and, as a result, encouraged individuals and communities to band together to increase the amount of locally-grown food. Community gardens are also on the rise; First Lady Michelle Obama's White House garden is a great inspiration for this. Community gardens in San Francisco and Seattle are also huge motivators for hobbyist gardeners to try their hand at growing their own food. However, specialty gardens also are an important part of balancing the delicate ecosystem.

Butterfly and dragonfly gardens and gardens filled with roses help insects and bird populations to get the food and sustenance they need to survive and thrive. Koi ponds encourage water-filled landscapes to develop an underwater ecosystem that can sustain life for natural water-loving plants and animals. This has nothing to do with what humans eat, but has a great impact on living things that must rely on nature to survive.

PIONEERS IN THE FIELD

Sir Francis Bacon's 1627 book, *Sylva Sylvarum*, introduced hydroponics to the world, even though water culture was discovered by someone else. Water culture became a popular interest in the years following Bacon's book. In 1699 John Woodward published his water culture experiments with spearmint. He discovered that plants that grew in less pure water sources grew better than in distilled water sources. By the early nineteenth century, soilless gardening was successfully mastered by using instead a mixture of nine essential ingredients. By 1929 the term hydroponics was finally introduced by University of California at Berkeley professor William Frederick Gericke and it quickly became a race to further develop techniques that could beat regular agriculture grown in soil and water. However, soon after Gericke's book, *Complete Guide to Soilless Gardening*, was published, two scientists, Dennis R. Hoaglund and Daniel I. Arnon, were assigned the task to disprove Gericke's claims of hydroponic techniques beating traditional crop growth yield. Hoaglund and Arnon succeeded, but actually developed better procedures and the Hoaglund techniques they developed are still in use today.

Alan Chadwick was an English master gardener and a leading innovator in organic and biodynamic/French intensive gardening techniques. A student of Rudoph Steiner, Chadwick is often cited as the inspiration for the "California Cuisine" movement. Chadwick's mentor, Rudolf Steiner, developed multiple theories throughout his career, including the Waldorf movement, biodynamic gardening, and anthroposophy (linked to Theosophy), and was influenced in his epistemological thinking by Johann Wolfgang Geothe, who believed that there was no limit to human knowledge. This belief led him to view gardening as a whole rather than as a separate process of earth's cycle of life.

CURRENT CONDITIONS

Many consumers want to know what pesticides and insecticides are used on their food and plants. Beginning back with Rachel Carson and her book, *Silent Spring*, consumer awareness of pesticides and other toxins used to grow plants and food has continued to grow to all-time high. Never before has society cared so much about where our food comes from and how it is grown. This trend also has led to the interest in specialty gardening, from growing a roof garden to encourage a bit of green in a stark, urban space, to maintaining a butterfly garden, to helping their delicate ecosystem and enjoying their beauty right in one's backyard. The idea of being able to grow a specialty garden as a hobby, and with the added bonus of helping the environment, is a huge draw. Even at stores such as Lowe's and Home Depot, one can see the many choices that are available, regardless of location or income.

The use of hydroponics has allowed people residing in faraway locations without arable land to grow their own fresh vegetables rather than having them flown in at great expense. Recent agricultural research and development is seen in the growing number of college students majoring in general agriculture even as farming in the United States continues to decrease year after year. Why the interest? The ability to grow food is an art and a science and the rising interest in developing this art and science via specialty gardening will continue to increase in the next few years.

INDUSTRY LEADERS

Jackson & Perkins (J & P) began in 1872, but roses were not the company's main product for quite some time. In 1896 the company hired E. Alvin Miller, who attempted to hybridize roses after finishing his regular work. In 1901 J & P marketed one of Miller's varieties, a climber rose called Dorothy Perkins, which became one of the most widely planted roses in the world. This success prompted J & P to add roses as one of its main products. The company began to hire full-time hybridizers, including Eugene Boerner, notable for his contributions to the Floribunda class of roses. Another hybridizer, William Warriner, developed 110 rose varieties. Sales grew to 40 million plants and from those 110 varieties came 20 All-American Rose selections.

The famous J & P mail order business came from the 1939 World's Fair in New York. J & P set up a display and when visitors purchased roses from them, they asked if J & P could mail the roses to their homes for them. Word spread of the convenience of roses by mail and this side of the business grew exponentially. Little Newark, New York, soon called itself the Rose Capital of America. J & P began to publish its famous rose mail order catalog and thousands of visitors came to see and buy the roses in person. In 1966 Harry and David, the nation's leading fruit gift company, purchased J & P and the company was relocated to California's San Joaquin Valley, just north of Bakersfield. More than 2 million roses and other plants are shipped to the company's customers every year.

The Water Garden & Koi Company started in 1997 on a small piece of rental property in Bayville, New Jersey, and grew into a popular brick-and-mortar/online retail space. The company specialized in koi and water garden features and its Bayville location boasts a 14,000-gallon tank with the 14-year-old koi, Cleopatra, as well as other koi specimens. The retail and online store offers water gardening products, domestic and imported koi, pond fish, water plants, and water garden cleaning supplies. The company is delighted to help DIY water garden enthusiasts and welcomes questions.

WORKFORCE

Specialty gardening fits mainly within the parameters of the traditional gardening industry. Landscaping companies often offer the ability to build specialty gardens for their clients, or may offer specialty gardens as an option when faced with a particular client request. Often, the landscaping is decided on at the same time as the home is built, bought, or sold. In addition, specialty gardens are seasonal projects. Because of the diverse climates across the United States, specialty gardening is a year-round business. Most of the specialty gardening work will continue to be completed during the spring and summer months. However, in temperate climates such as Texas, Arizona, or New Mexico, specialty gardening may be seen as more of a winter job.

Specialty gardening jobs are often at locations that offer landscaping materials or services, or through garden stores, whether big box retail chains or small mom-and-pop operations. The advent of the Internet in the 1990s and 2000s added specialty gardening Web sites from which all manner of specialty gardening equipment and supplies could be purchased year-round.

To get a job as a specialty gardener, one must possess a knowledge of agriculture and plants and demonstrate experience in creating, cultivating, and successfully operating such gardens. Often, employees who work as specialty gardeners will be hobbyists who have gardened for years, or who came from green construction or green architecture careers in which they were unhappy with simply sketching plans on paper.

Workers in specialty gardening must have a specialized understanding of plant life and ecosystem maintenance. They must understand the options of both pesticides versus natural pest control, as well as the intricacies of drip irrigation; especially in a butterfly garden or with a specific plant, so as to keep the delicate infrastructure in place. They must know about soil and minerals and growing mediums that may be encountered when putting in a specialty garden for a client. Above all, they must have an eye for aesthetics as the point of a specialty garden is its visual appeal. These are not difficult skills to learn, but they are necessary. Knowing what plants require sunshine or shade, which plants need more or less water, and how to mix and match them into the same garden is an art and science.

As the demand goes away from lawn care to plant and tree care, however, specialty gardeners will have a slight edge on the market. Consumers want to know how to best care for their plants and yard, as is evidenced by the multi-billion-dollar U.S. gardening industry. The demand for specialized information will only continue to grow as the years progress.

AMERICA AND THE WORLD

Specialty gardening around the world has grown at approximately the same pace as in the United States. As more and more urban spaces begin to house people and animals, the desire and need for gardens grows. Also, in some disparate climates, the opportunity for R&D and new technologies about gardening are gladly welcomed. How does one grow fresh vegetables without soil? How does one keep plants alive with minimal water? Which plants do the best in a sandy, shady environment? Which plants require more minerals than others?

Research and development is not solely the property of the United States. Other countries, especially developing countries with the assistance of the World Bank and the United Nations, are doing specialized research on crops and sustainable gardens to feed their populations. This technology is first and foremost for the survival of people and animals, as well as the environment, but their research helps all specialty gardeners. Learning about plants that thrive in sand and shade helps gardeners around the world know what to plant in such conditions after it helps produce edible crops.

RESEARCH AND TECHNOLOGY

Specialty gardening technologies are as diverse as hydroponics and aeroponics research; the theory of biodynamics; the art of organic, roof, and butterfly gardening; the skill of natural pest control and drip irrigation; and the beauty of rose hybridization and xeriscaping. As the energy-efficient trend continues in the United States, more and more consumers will take up gardening as a hobby and as a way to ensure their landscaping is reducing, not enlarging, their carbon footprint. As people become aware of the beauty of gardening and the ability to control water and pests naturally, without expending unnecessary resources to keep a beautiful yard, perhaps there will be less competition over green, expansive lawns and more focus on helping to create a strong ecosystem just outside the front or back door. In the years to come, our ideas about landscaping a suburban house may change significantly, which will increase the demand for specialty gardeners who can offer better options and who can help to create a beautiful footprint.

BIBLIOGRAPHY

Helm, Ben, and Kelly Billing. *The Water Gardener's Bible: A Step-by-Step Guide to Building, Planting, Stocking, and Maintaining a Backyard Water Garden.* Emmaus, PA: Rodale Books, 2008.

"How to Grow a Specialty Garden." The Learning Channel (TLC), 2010. Available from http://tlc.howstuffworks.com/home/how-to-grow-a-specialty-garden.htm.

Organic Gardening Catalogue, 2010. Available from http://www.organiccatalogue.com/catalog.

White, Hazel, and Philip Edinger. *Roses.* Menlo Park, CA: Sunset Books, 2002.

SPECIALTY TOURISM

■

SIC CODE(S)

7011

4512

INDUSTRY SNAPSHOT

From cycling to safaris and anthropological digs to spiritual retreats, the face of tourism changed dramatically in the last few decades. Most often called specialty tourism, this rapidly emerging segment began to revolutionize the leisure travel industry as a whole. Once geared toward only high-end customers who were able to pay large sums of money for extravagant and individualized tours, by the twenty-first century the industry had branched out, annually drawing in hundreds of thousands of "average" travelers, all interested in new and challenging ways to spend their leisure time.

In general, the bulk of specialty tours is targeted at specific groups—such as families, women, singles, or gays/lesbians—or specific activities such as cycling, hiking, kayaking, or gambling. This targeted approach has led to a great deal of diversity in the field, with more than 80,000 companies offering services worldwide. Specialty tourism is expected to continue to grow and develop and even emerge as a dominant force in the leisure travel industry well into the twenty-first century.

Despite some challenging developments around the world, specialty tourism seemed to take less of a hit than the industry overall. Indeed, some thrill-seeking adventure travelers were actually drawn to dangerous places such as Afghanistan and Iraq, in order to experience history in the making. Furthermore, overall membership in the American Society of Travel Agents decreased from 27,000 to 20,000, while the number of specialty agencies increased.

ORGANIZATION AND STRUCTURE

In general, the specialty travel industry has benefited from some emerging social, technological, and economic trends. Most importantly, travel has become easier, faster, and more important to twenty-first century lifestyles. The cost of air and surface travel has been going down. There are more roads, air routes, airplanes, and surface vehicles to transport travelers to destinations previously very difficult to reach. Information for travelers is more abundant and more available. There are more businesses offering specialty services. The expanding network of local providers of lodging, guides, transport, equipment, and those who otherwise facilitate exploration of areas without a formal tourist infrastructure is growing rapidly. A prosperous economy has afforded more people the high incomes and security to spend discretionary income on the exotic experiences that specialty travel provides. Finally, specialty travel responds to the public's increased interest in healthy, active, educational activities.

There is no single organization or publication that speaks for the specialty travel industry, though several private entities attempt to provide unifying promotional services based on common needs for insurance, working with political or environmental policies, or for commercial promotion. Some operators are members of such traditional travel associations as the American Society of Travel Agents. The Adventure Travel Society of Boulder, Colorado, a private organization, has attempted to provide a forum for discussing adventure travel trends and problems. Each year, the group holds a World Congress for adventure travel at a different venue around the world. The organization, however, has no position on travel policy, nor does it include any democratic participation of members in establishing guidelines or directions. Generally, organizers of specialty travel may work with airlines or other transportation companies and derive a portion of their earnings from ticket commissions. In the 1990s, however, airlines dramatically reduced commissions to agents and some operators left the matter of reaching remote trip destinations in the hands of the traveler.

The lack of a unifying body for this segment of the travel industry also leads to marketing confusion. Often, adventure travel land operators sell services through conventional travel agents, adventure agents, or directly to the consumer. This sometimes creates a dysfunctional marketing problem as diligent consumers may collect information from three or more sources describing the price and features of a single adventure experience with varying criteria. Most specialty travel companies have Web sites, which further complicate the problem of identifying and distinguishing services as unique. Generally, consumers pay a fixed retail price, which may include commission for booking agents and re-marketers at 10 to 35 percent, depending on booking volume and marketing commitment.

The retail costs of specialty travel vary greatly with destination, group size, duration, and types of service included. Cost of tips to guides on all trips is usually additional. Consumers of specialty travel tend to enjoy above-average wealth, but trips must still be priced competitively. Specialty travel groups from different companies often meet at campsites, favored hotels, trailheads, key locations, or remote airports, and participants compare notes on price, quality, leadership, and experience. Every company understands the paramount importance of customer loyalty derived from having the best trip at the best price.

Although lacking any formal, collective organization, specialty tourism is categorized according to certain functional characteristics or business types. Tourism promotion offices are often associated with national, state, or regional government agencies, and they usually promote all types of tourism. Inbound or receptive operators help groups of visitors or individual tourists and coordinate various portions of the overall itinerary, including lodging, transfers, activity reservations, guides, and meals. Inbound operators rely on local specialized service providers, who may be trekking, rafting, or diving operators; lodge, ski resort, and tour bus owners; or the owners and managers of any number of other services. Most agents and operators who organize and conduct these trips are not members of organizations such as the American Society of Travel Agents or the U.S. Tour Operators Association, who serve to set standards and track development of the broader leisure tourism industry.

In 2008 the Partnership for Global Sustainable Tourism Criteria, a group of 27 organizations in the private, public, and nonprofit sectors of the industry, created the first worldwide sustainable tourism criteria. The initiative was promoted by Ted Turner of the United Nations Foundation, the Rainforest Alliance, the United Nations Environment Programme, and the United Nations World Tourism Organization. As Turner noted in *Space Daily*, "Unfortunately, up to this point, the travel industry and tourists haven't had a common framework to let them know if they're really living up to that maxim. However, the Global Sustainable Tourism Criteria (GSTC) will change that. This is a win-win initiative—good for the environment and good for the world's tourism industry."

Specialty travel also relies on outbound operators, particularly in the case of foreign travel. Outbound operators design itineraries, print brochures, select inbound operators, specify services, negotiate prices, and promote services offered by their businesses as unique products for a national or international market. Often travelers who purchase vacation packages from outbound operators are not aware of this distinction. Outbound operators may rely on travel agents or independent trip organizers to fill trips. Each of the agents employed to reach the public may also specialize in some aspect of specialty travel, or more generally in leisure travel. Many travel agents have developed an interest or expertise in locating and evaluating special interest trips and the industry as a whole. Operators may try to fill trips through direct booking of clients and with the help of their own public relations agents. Increasingly, this purely promotional end of the specialty travel industry has proliferated to include the Internet, e-mail, video, magazines, database marketing, travel shows, and product or service cross-marketing schemes to reach prospective specialty travelers. All of these participate in the specialty travel industry, but none defines it individually. Operators of specialty travel trips distinguish events less by common standards than by the uniqueness of itineraries, leaders, style, qualifications, and value of services.

One of the best ways to assess the size and diversity of the industry is to attend one of the many adventure travel shows scheduled annually in large cities, including Chicago, Atlanta, Cincinnati, San Francisco, Baltimore, and New York. These shows bring together participants, providers, guides, tourist bureau and media publicists, adventure travel site operators, airlines, hotel and lodge owners, and others with interest in adventure group travel.

One can also gain a good sense of the diversity of this industry segment from the travel advertising sections of magazines such as *Outside, Sierra, Backpacker, Escape,* or *Men's Journal.*

New Business Start-Ups Because reputation and references are so important for acquiring customers, new operators should expect four to six lean years while getting started. Many who lack substantial start-up capital must keep a part time job until the business becomes established. Nevertheless, many newly established adventure travel companies do not survive into a second or third year. Due to the relatively high risk involved with travel to less developed countries, insurance to cover professional liability and accidents is very expensive, especially for new operators without a proven safety record. This, combined with the well-known litigious character of the American consumer, has ended the existence of many start-up specialty travel businesses.

Another frequent cause of business failure is related to limited business opportunity. Specialty operators, for example, often have problems if they can offer certain tours only during certain seasons and if the market they serve is too narrowly focused. Often, the specialty travel market is dispersed and hard to reach through traditional marketing avenues. Many excellent, well-planned, and fairly priced trips do not depart because the promoters failed to recruit enough participants in time to meet deposit or air reservation deadlines. When a specialty trip is sold to a broader market to achieve minimum enrollments, trip organizers and operators are often faced with participants who have varied expectations and purposes.

Sport Tourism Many people seek active vacations focusing on specific fitness activities. Biking, kayaking, golfing, horseback riding, trekking, climbing, orienteering (competitive compass navigation), and even marathons increasingly draw people from all around the world to organized tours or events that may take place in exotic locations. Rafting, ballooning, sailing, and walking trips may require less physical exertion but still demand a level of physical involvement, knowledge, and disciplined focus beyond the requirements of conventional leisure vacations. These types of vacations are typically organized by an individual or a company with knowledge of the sport and access to the specialized equipment required to perform the activity. They market expertise, access to optimal environments, the quality of their equipment and guides, and their ability to effectively coordinate necessary travel arrangements. Television programs on eco-challenges, in which teams from around world compete to navigate a difficult course over difficult and varied terrain, popularized a variety of sport tourism skills.

Adventure Tourism Adventure tourism is a broad term covering several smaller segments of specialty travel, all related to active pursuit of extreme sports, remote destinations, and unusual experiences. Increasing numbers of people are pursuing physically and intellectually challenging recreational experiences, both close to home and in remote regions. In response to the demand for special travel information and services, thousands of small businesses around the world emerged in the second half of the twentieth century.

Included are the more narrowly defined categories of adventure travel such as ecotourism, exploration cruising, trekking, mountaineering, rafting, kayaking, nature tourism, cultural tourism, scuba diving, dog sledding, and a variety of other recreational outdoor sports. Many organized tours include a combination of these and other activities. All of these activities require a greater amount of exertion, have a higher degree of risk, and place greater emphasis on the natural and cultural encounters of participants than conventional travel. Conversely, adventure tourism avoids or minimizes emphasis on luxury accommodations, nightlife, dining, relaxation, shopping, museums, and entertainment. More and more conventional tour and cruise operators, however, are expanding or redefining itineraries to include more active adventure activities as they detect market demand for authentic natural, cultural, and physical exploration on more spontaneous itineraries.

Adventure Racing Adventure racing, one of the world's newest and fastest growing diversions, takes adventure travel one step further, combining outdoor activities with competitions lasting for several hours, days, or even weeks. Adventure racing is 50 percent physical and 50 percent mental, as competitors must use strategy and analysis to complete tasks while trekking, biking, swimming, or rappelling. The emphasis in adventure racing is on teamwork rather than the individual and is one of the few sports where just completing a race is considered a victory. A race can consist of canoeing down white water rapids, followed by rappelling off a 100-foot cliff. Another race might involve traversing a treacherous path on a mountain bike or hiking and finding your way through a dense forest. It can be 10 miles or a hundred miles or more. By early 2006, there were 100 adventure racing clubs across the United States and the number of adventures racers was growing daily by leaps and bounds.

Ecotourism Another large segment of the specialty travel industry is ecotourism. While not completely distinct from adventure tourism, ecotourism focuses on the experience of nature and culture while also paying attention to the economic and environmental impacts of travel itself. The adventure component of ecotourism may be more intellectual than physical. Some ecotourism operators seek the highest accommodation standards possible and avoid placing clients in circumstances that demand excessive physical exertion or use of primitive accommodations. Others presume clients are fit and flexible and that they welcome or will at least tolerate the physical and intellectual challenges that accompany reaching pristine locations and/or cultures.

Ecotourism operators share a concern for enfranchising local communities in the economic process and benefits of tourism. Companies such as JOURNEYS International and International Expeditions also have nonprofit organizations or service divisions that help train local people in tourism-related fields and support schools, clinics, or local community projects. They view this as a way to help create a political and social environment for environmental preservation. Ecotourism is a process of learning, training, and improving the travel experience for participants and local hosts. It is also a way to move toward goals of sustainable activity and generate local community benefits without harming the local cultures or environments.

The recognized authority on ecotourism is the International Ecotourism Society. This organization has memberships in various classes ranging from travelers to operators to researchers, all concerned with improving the standards and effects of ecotourism. They publish many pamphlets and brochures of interest to anyone trying to get started in the ecotourism business.

Nature Tourism People more frequently formulate vacations around the primary objective of seeing and enjoying nature. Similar to ecotourism, nature tourism seeks nature for its own sake with less focus on human culture and less explicit concern for conservation or preservation. Bird watching, scuba diving, botany exploration, African wildlife safaris, sport fishing, whale watching, and other trips seek out nature and provide interpretation and education. Such trips may or may not support active conservation of the places they visit.

Spiritual Tourism In the second half of the twentieth century, increasing numbers of people joined similarly educated or religiously oriented travelers to further spiritual understanding. Organized pilgrimages to holy places in the Middle East had taken place for decades, but in the 1980s and 1990s, more tours promoted New Age spiritual orientations to visit ancient sites not usually associated with modern organized religion, such as the Mayan ruins of Central America or Stonehenge in England. Other trips adopted an agenda of self-realization similar to the vision quest of some Native American religions, but without its doctrinal components. Many Americans explored Buddhism or other Eastern beliefs by joining tours to important religious sites in Asia: the monasteries of Tibet and Nepal; the ashrams of Hindu India; Islamic monuments of Pakistan or central Asia; and the sacred sites of Native Americans in the United States.

Affinity Group Travel Demographic factors offer another way to focus specialty travel events. Participants may all be members of an organization, occupation, ethnic group, or have the same marital status. Operators organize trips for singles, families, grandparents and grandchildren, gays and lesbians, farmers, doctors, wine and food lovers, educators, students, and seniors. This kind of group definition determines an experience tailored to specific common expectations and group preferences. Sometimes groups have an occupational focus that defines the primary goals of the trip. Health professionals, for example, may choose to take a trip such as the Himalayan Health Expedition, on which they have a full program of contact with local clinics, local healers, and shamans. Similarly, some operators offer an extensive variety of trips specifically geared to physicians.

Groups of people embarking on specialized trips appreciate knowing fellow participants will have the same personal and lifestyle views. Gay and lesbian tours are quite common, often with adventure or ecotourist themes. Participants feel more comfort in knowing personal qualities such as sexual orientation or marital status will not create problems or confusion for other participants on the trip, allowing for more focus on the actual themes of the experience.

BACKGROUND AND DEVELOPMENT

The industry known as "specialty travel" was largely developed due to the increasing accessibility of once unknown, unattainable, or presumed hostile environments. Demystifying the dangers of wilderness, natural terrain, foreign travel, and wildlife created a psychological acceptance of the citizen as explorer and the traveler as student. Popular books, magazines, and movies about remote and wild places or attractive exotic locations also helped establish widespread desire to experience these places. Television programming on cable channels such as the Discovery Channel, the Travel Channel, the Learning Channel (TLC), and Animal Planet constantly remind viewers of the world they can explore. Additionally, specially designed clothing, luggage, medicines, and the spread of the English language have all facilitated adventure travel. Vastly expanded international air service made it easier and quicker to reach exotic locations. Peace Corps volunteers and other returned international workers brought back information on remote places and services for travelers. Increasingly, local residents of attractive adventure destinations acquired specialized activity knowledge, a hospitality infrastructure, and familiarity with international languages that allowed them to act as guides and hosts for foreign visitors.

Prior to the 1970s, when the first special interest travel companies developed, travel excursions to remote areas were truly an adventure, undertaken without the benefit of guide books, organized services, or knowledgeable local interpretation. Simply reaching foreign lands was an all-consuming activity and contracting area diseases was expected. In the 1970s and 1980s, pioneering companies such as Mountain Travel, EarthWatch, JOURNEYS, and American Wilderness Experience established consistent activity and information-based itineraries that took the logistic hassles out of exotic travel and made it safer and healthier. Nevertheless, many people viewed specialty travel as more demanding or more uncertain than it really was and early growth was slow. Gradually, popular perception came to match reality, which spurred growth for all types of specialty travel.

In the 1990s, political and nonprofit environmental and wildlife preservation organizations began an almost religious support of ecotourism. Previously, conservation organizations viewed tourism as a destructive force in natural habitats. Research, however, demonstrated the economic rationale for some tourist activity helping natural and cultural preservation. Organizations such as the World Wildlife Fund, Conservation International, Sierra Club, and Nature Conservancy sponsored trips for members. These groups derived significant funding from adventure advertising in publications, and they actively supported and facilitated development of accommodations in and adjacent to natural preserves where they conducted research.

This alliance between adventure travelers, local residents, and environmentalists served as significant rationale in development planning for new facilities. The Sierra Club has offered many trips that easily qualify as "adventure travel" or "eco-travel." In the late 1990s, organizations such as the World Wildlife Fund, Nature Conservancy, and Conservation International offered more comfortable, less physically demanding eco-travel. Some of these organizations were investing in large, luxurious, expensive lodges adjacent to the natural areas they sought to preserve. Travelers who desire pristine nature and culture experiences (and will pay well for it) provide tangible and direct measure of nature preservation benefits. This pattern became more convincing to policy makers than hypothetical and elusive rationales of preserving genetic diversity, protecting natural capital, balancing global gas emissions, or even reducing flooding from disturbed watersheds. Increasingly, adventure travel companies were closely aligned with efforts to preserve natural and cultural environments.

The growth of specialty travel as a broad industry in the 1980s and 1990s also reflected globalization of its underlying activities. In a world economy, people were more interested in seeing the rest of the world, not just their own community, in the context of their own experience and interests. The concepts of "world records," "wonders of the world," and "world-class experience" drew people to take up hobbies and pastimes that extended a sense of personal interest worldwide. Specialty travel providers had to understand not only tourism concepts, but also the underlying interests of their travelers.

Another important element in the development of an expanding specialty travel industry through the 1980s and 1990s was equipment innovation. It became possible to travel lighter, more comfortably, and more safely to previously hostile or inaccessible places. Safer climbing equipment, scuba gear, rafts, and other gear reduced risk and discomfort. Lighter, stronger fabrics, better medicines, improved maps, field guides, and custom luggage all added incentives to prospective travelers seeking to turn fantasies into actual exploration.

Economic prosperity in the United States, retirement security, the financial success of baby boomers, and the information revolution all served to expand the specialty tourism industry in the late 1990s. About 98 million U.S. adults took an adventure vacation in the second half of the 1990s, according to the Travel Industry Association of America's National Travel Survey. The Internet and the World Wide Web make information about travel more accessible to anyone with a computer. They also enable travelers to directly contact local operators in remote places, resulting in reduced use of U.S.-based travel organizers and agents. According to *Travel Weekly,* toward the end of the 1990s, airline ticket revenues declined drastically as airlines reduced commissions and completed their own sales. While some adventure travel promoters suggested that this was a reason to expect travel agents would sell more adventure travel (a high-priced product with at least a 10 percent commission to agents), fewer and fewer consumers were using travel agents to make their arrangements.

However, ironically, the same forces that expanded the industry constrained the growth of new and established companies. The full employment economy reduced the frequency and duration of American vacations, especially among the educated and high-income demographic groups. This shift limited the growth of international trips and more lengthy expeditionary travel. The average length of American vacations decreased. As baby boomers aged, they were more able to afford the relatively high price of organized adventure travel. The weakening effects of aging, however, constrained participation in more active and physically demanding activities such as trekking, skiing, mountaineering, and scuba diving.

Then the travel industry went on a roller coaster ride in the early part of the twenty-first century. Terrorism and the weakening economy caused the industry to suffer a bad year in 2001, which was followed by a mild recovery that soon dissipated. The global economy and tourism recovered in the latter half of 2002, but then experts anticipated another economic contraction in early 2003. The global unrest and anti-American sentiment as a result of the war in Iraq, as well as continued fears about terrorism, added to the uncertainty. One event that proved eye opening for prospective travelers was a 2002 nightclub bombing in Bali, a once popular and peaceful vacation spot. Nearly 200 people were killed in the attack, and most of them were tourists. In the aftermath, the U.S. State Department urged Americans to be cautious about traveling overseas. At the same time, the International Monetary Fund and the World Tourism Organization (WTO) both felt that worldwide tourism was not in any long-term danger.

In the early part of the twenty-first century's first decade, substantial difficulties arose to affect international vacations. Highly publicized stories of criminal or terrorist actions against tourists in Egypt, Uganda, Turkey, and Colombia created a generalized fear of foreign trips in travelers who might otherwise leave the United States. That fear compounded following the September 11, 2001, terrorist attacks on the United States. Concerns about economic and political instability around the world, as well as the U.S. military action against Iraq, also affected the industry. Even more, prospective travelers, once fearful of AIDS, cholera, virulent tuberculosis, and malaria in developing countries, now had a new disease to worry about, severe acute respiratory syndrome (SARS).

The war with Iraq caused an expected and sharp decrease in travel bookings, and industry players reported that many consumers were opting for safer travel destinations within domestic borders. Domestic locales that appealed to adventure travelers included Alaska, California, Florida, and Hawaii. However, for a certain segment of thrill-seeking specialty travelers, dangerous destinations like Afghanistan and Iraq were actually attractive. For example, travel guidebook publisher Lonely Planet dispatched a researcher to Afghanistan to explore the feasibility of a stand-alone guidebook for the country, as adventure-minded tourists hitched rides there with relief workers. Other war-torn regions such as the former Yugoslavia and Vietnam also were popular with some tourists. These destinations sold souvenirs like old weapons and pens made from bullet casings.

The appearance of severe acute respiratory syndrome (SARS) took the industry by surprise in the early years of the twenty-first century's first decade. The World Travel and Tourism Council (WTTC) said it expected world tourism to flatten because fears of SARS would cut tourist traffic to Asia. WTTC President Jean-Claude Baumgarten even said the estimated effect of SARS on the industry would be five times greater than that of the 9/11 attacks. Indeed, SARS had a devastating effect, both economically and in human casualties. According to the Centers for Disease Control and Prevention (CDC), by July of 2003, when transmission of SARS had been contained, more than 8,000 cases had been reported to the World Health Organization, along with 780 deaths. Worldwide, the United Nations estimated that some five million individuals would lose travel-related jobs in 2003 because of SARS and slack economic conditions. A SARS outbreak in Toronto, Ontario, also had dire consequences for Canada, with related economic costs tagged at approximately $2.1 billion in 2003.

On June 24, 2003, the World Health Organization (WHO) lifted its SARS-related travel warning—corresponding to Beijing, China's—which urged travelers to avoid all but the most necessary travel to affected areas. According to *Asia Africa Intelligence Wire,* China's State Administration of Tourism expected its industry to completely recover in 2004. However, by January 31, 2004, four new SARS cases had been identified by the Chinese Ministry of Health in the province of Guangdong. While this news was not enough to warrant a travel warning by the CDC or WHO, it had the potential to scare off would-be travelers to the region. The effects of SARS and other public health and safety concerns were often psychological and could lead travelers to avoid travel to an entire country, even when problems were isolated to specific geographic areas.

These concerns, coupled with the tendency toward shorter vacations for U.S. citizens, favored U.S.-based operators of domestic adventure experiences such as cycling, rafting, whale watching, canoeing, and skiing. Participation in these activities within the United States insulated customers from political risk and provided a complete adventure experience in a relatively short period. Similarly, Canada, Europe, Australia, and New Zealand tended to be viewed as safe, stable, healthy destinations, and these were expected to witness a higher rate of Americans visiting for specialty travel tours than less developed areas of the world.

The Internet poses a dilemma for specialty tourism operators. If they create a Web site accessible to the public, they very visibly compete with other agents selling the same trip. This is particularly true if tourism operators accept direct bookings through the Web site or if they publish a toll-free telephone number for reservations. Tourism operators are inclined to complement Web site information with traditional color brochures and catalogs, yet most operators want a credible Web presence. Given their largely information-based industry, many operators feel Internet promotion will be increasingly important in the 2000s and will provide an essential if not yet fully defined promotional tool.

By 2006, the Internet had proven to be an invaluable tool for the specialty traveler. There were hundreds of Web sites offering touring information and online booking for adventures from cooking lessons in Provence to learning Spanish while staying in a Mexican home to touring Turkey with an archaeology professor to learning to roll pasta from a Medici countess in her own Tuscan villa. Some Web sites act as clearinghouses of thousands of outfitters and tour operators so travelers can choose the vacation of their dreams that fits into their budget.

One Web site alone, Adventurevacation.com, featured 500 travel outfitters offering opportunities for worldwide adventure trips, with options for travelers of all fitness and experience levels. As popularity of action trips and adventure tours continues to sweep the nation at a phenomenal rate, such Web sites offered information, advice, and suggestions for enjoying the outdoors and experiencing an adventure tour that fits each individual's pace or special needs. Parents could find information on many Web sites to help them choose a vacation that the entire family will enjoy.

Several companies in Texas, Oklahoma, and Florida started offering "hurricane tours" in the fall of 2005, touting them as the "ultimate in storm chasing experiences." Created by self-confessed weather freaks who first went out on several trial runs, these tours are booked on a 48-hour-notice basis. Tourists are flown to a predicted landfall site, where they ride in vans equipped with The Weather Channel to a parking structure to wait for the storm to hit. After the storm passes, the tourists in the vans travel through the damaged area, having been versed in storm-chasing protocol that states that it is in very poor taste to boast about the experience to someone who has just lost everything. This type of tourism is admittedly controversial, according to David Gold, a tour organizer at Silver Lining, one of the companies offering hurricane tours. He says that contrary to what some people fear, he is not taking anyone into harm's way, that he does everything he can to avoid unnecessary risks, that clients are warned of the dangers, and that the purpose is not to celebrate the damages but just to experience them. So far, Silver Lining has taken 15 people on a hurricane tour.

PIONEERS IN THE FIELD

The merger of two of the oldest adventure travel companies formed Mountain Travel-Sobek (MTS) in 1991. MTS offered relatively high-priced group travel to all continents and was often considered a pioneer in both designing itineraries and promotional techniques. As of the early part of the first decade of the 2000s, it offered more than 100 trips around the world. The company changed ownership several times since its founding in 1967 and was, as of 2004, based in California.

JOURNEYS International, founded in 1978 by a former Peace Corps volunteer and his wife, specialized in active natural and cultural explorations of more than 60 worldwide destinations. Many of JOURNEYS trips support local conservation and cultural preservation projects. Local experts in each destination lead the group's programs. JOURNEYS is particularly known for Himalayan trekking, active African safaris, and small group adventure cruises.

American Wilderness Experience (AWE) is one of the oldest U.S. adventure travel companies. AWE describes its mission as promoting adventure travel with dedication to program quality and customer service and a commitment to support wilderness preservation, recycling, and ecologically sensitive tours. All AWE programs take place in North America.

As the decade advanced, the destinations of specialty tourists began to include more areas of risk and adventure, such as hurricane tours, space travel, or hurtling along a zip line, a steel cable suspended above a river or canyon. The interest of adventurers continued to be inspired by thoughts of excitement, adventure, and just the right touch of danger. Honeymooners who wanted to keep busy could reject the typical cruise or laying-on-the-beach option for the more adventurous destinations of Antarctica or Botswana. Hundreds of web sites cropped up in the middle of the decade, geared to those who want to find someplace new to go or a new adventure to pursue.

In September 2008, the Travel Promotion Act was passed by the House of Representatives. If passed, the legislation will create thousands of new jobs and attract millions of international visitors to the United States, according to the Travel Industry Association.

In 2008, a new type of specialty travel was causing controversy. According to a 2008 *Newsweek International* article, "slum tours" were "travel business's new growth industry." Tours to rundown and poverty-ridden sites were being led around the world and included shantytowns and slums in cities such as Rio de Janeiro, Moscow, Johannesburg, and Mexico City. For around $135, travelers can take Reality Tours' "Slum and Sightseeing Tour" to Dharavi, India, the largest slum in Asia. The tour includes visits to the red light district and the open-air laundry. Whereas providers of these tours tout advantages such as breaking down barriers between rich and poor and allowing those who are well off to develop a new appreciation and affinity for others unlike themselves, critics cite the new venture as a blatant exploitation of the poor.

Space travel was another new area of development in the specialty tourism industry. Virgin Galactic, a company created to undertake the challenge of developing space tourism for everyone, plans to operate its own privately built spaceships that will allow affordable suborbital space tourism. In 2004, Burt Rutan, one of the founders of Virgin Galactic, won the Ansari X Prize of $10 million offered by the X Prize Foundation for privately financing, building, and launching a spaceship able to carry three people to 100 kilometers (62.5 miles) and return safely to Earth. The same ship, SpaceShipOne, made three successful launches in 2004. Rutan's space craft design overcame the issues of reentry into the atmosphere faced by so many designers who have tried to create efficient, reusable space vehicles. His design is a spacecraft that, upon return to earth's atmosphere, changes from a sleek space plane to a "shuttlecock," to allow it to drift through the atmosphere without overheating. It then changes back into a conventional aircraft capable of landing.

By 2008 Virgin Galactic engineers had created a more advanced SpaceShipTwo and a carrier platform named WhiteKnightTwo. Potential space tourists will undergo a few days of medical assessments and preflight training before taking off for the "ET experience." According to Virgin Galactic's Web site, a space ticket will cost around $200,000, although the company is working to bring the price down so as to allow "many thousands of people to experience space for themselves." In November 2010, SpaceShipTwo successfully completed its third test flight high above the Mojave Air and Space Port in California. Designed to hold two pilots and six ticket-holding passengers, the price still held at $200,000 for a suborbital ride to the edge of space, with over 340 individuals on the wait list. Also in 2010, the Spaceship Company (TSC) broke ground for its new final assembly, integration and test hangar.

CURRENT CONDITIONS

In September 2010, the Boeing Company and Space Adventures, Ltd. announced a memorandum of agreement regarding a joint venture to offer transportation services to destinations in low Earth orbit (LEO) on Boeing commercial crew spacecraft. (Prior to this, Space Adventures had successfully contracted and flown seven spaceflight participants on eight missions to the International Space Station.) The plan was to market passenger seats on commercial flights aboard the Boeing spacecraft, with any excess seating capacity available to private individuals, companies, non-governmental organizations, and U.S. federal agencies other than NASA. Boeing will also continue to use the CST-100 spacecraft to provide crew transportation to the International Space Station. the

spacecraft can carry seven persons andd is able to fly on multiple launch vehicles. As of 2010, Space Adventures was the only company that provided orbital space flight opportunities to the world marketplace.

Overall, the global adventure market was worth approximately $89 billion in 2010. Tours ranged from a $1000 trip to Machu Picchu to a $35,000 luxury expedition to Antarctica. However, that was only part of the picture. 2010 also represented a time when many travelers donated their time and energy toward global causes, paying their own transportation to locations where they could contribute in their own way to change the world. In the United States, the Habitat for Humanity project in Louisiana was still drawing hundreds of laid-off as well as employed workers to pitch in and do their share to rebuild the area devastated by Hurricane Katrina five years earlier. Several Americans spent their vacation In Haiti, another area devastated by storms and floods. Americans did not want just adventure; they wanted meaningful adventure. An August 2010 report by Adventure Travel Trade Association and George Washington University found that adventure travelers were generally wealthier and more educated, and spent about one-third more than average travelers. They valued natural, cultural, and active experiences, and expressed their intent to travel more in coming years.

Green travel and sustainable tourism remained key buzzwords in promoting travel. In 2009, the overall U.S. travel industry as a whole lost 7 percent in revenues, from $770 billon in 2008 to just $704 billion in 2009. In addition to a poor economy, concerns about carbon emissions and global warming made both travelers and businesses rethink wasted fuel costs, both in terms of dollars and environmental harm. Airplanes cancelled flights in order to ensure that remaining flights were fully booked. Alternative transportation (other than single passenger car mode) was encouraged. A new subsegment of ecotourism was born: "voluntourism." active, hands-on volunteer vacations that addressed global issues. In that vein, the notorious "slum tour" business was actually on the rise in 2010, with one country (Brazil) openly promoting it. Peter Yesawich, CEO of a leading hospitality marketing agency, reported that 6 percent of all U.S. active travelers took a volunteer vacation in 2009. According to *Travel Weekly,* sustainable tourism could grow to 25 percent of the global travel market by 2012, bringing the value of the market to roughly $473 billion a year.

INDUSTRY LEADERS

The specialty travel industry is diverse and rather specialized, consisting of thousands of companies that provide unique and often individualized services. It is therefore difficult to identify truly dominant companies in the field. There are, however, leading firms within different categories.

One of the first specialty travel companies, Earth-Watch, is a unique nonprofit organization that helps sponsor and fund scientific research through expedition fees paid by travelers who are then allowed to join the expedition in a limited capacity. EarthWatch works with scientists who make support arrangements for volunteer assistants, and because it is a nonprofit organization, some of the trips' costs are tax deductible.

International Expeditions, based in Helena, Alabama, specializes in quality guided nature explorations with particular focus on tropical rain forests and the African savannahs. The company emphasizes strong academic leadership and invests in training for many local guides in travel destinations.

Wilderness Travels, founded in the late 1970s, offers quality group nature and cultural trips throughout the world. It has strong programs in the Galapagos, Peru, Turkey, and the Himalayas. Generally catering to the higher income market, these trips offer the best available standards of accommodation and dining in remote locations.

With more than 150 different bicycling, walking, hiking, and multi-sport vacations in more than 85 destinations around the world, Backroads has become a leading specialty travel provider. In 2006, Backroads added many new destinations and options, including Active Women Adventures, a women-only travel experience that brings women together for fitness, fun, and pampering, and Adventures Beyond, which includes some added element to a biking and/or walking tour to bring a region to life.

Abercrombie and Kent (A&K) of Oakbrook, Illinois, is an upscale company that bridges the conventional leisure travel market and specialty travel fields. Well known for cruises, safaris, and escorted trips to exotic locations, A&K is one of the most successful operators in the industry, marketing its programs worldwide through travel agents.

Victor Emanuel Nature Tours (VENT) specializes in birding tours. One of the oldest birding companies, VENT offers trips featuring expert birders and uses the best available accommodations for its relatively high-priced programs.

Founded in 1991, G.A.P. (the Great Adventure People) Adventures, is headquartered in Toronto, Ontario. By 2008 it serviced 85,000 tourists annually and offered more than 1,000 adventures in 100 countries. In 2007 it was awarded the number one "Do It All Outfitter on Earth" by *National Geographic Adventure*

magazine. Some of the company's new offerings in 2008 included festival and special photography trips.

WORKFORCE

By the early 2000s, there were roughly 83,000 adventure tour operators worldwide, according to the Adventure Travel Society. In 2004, the Specialty Travel Index, which includes only the larger companies selling to the U.S. travel industry, listed more than 500, most of which were based in North America. However, world events, combined with the stagnant global economy and a general fear of traveling, took their toll on the workforce. The United Nations International Labor Organization reported that 6.6 million tourism employees worldwide, or 1 out of every 12 workers, lost their jobs in 2001-2002. However, in 2006, the travel and tourism industry generated 4,590,000 jobs in the Middle East region, the equivalent of 10.1 percent of the total labor market in that area. By 2016, the travel industry is expected to provide 6.1 million jobs. In the United Arab Emirates, 294,000 jobs were created in 2006, equivalent to 11.7 percent of the overall labor market, and 376,000 jobs were expected to be provided in 2016.

The typical specialty travel operator is a small business employing the owner and two to five other people, none of whom is certified travel agent. There are no formal academic credentials required, although local licenses are required for some guides.

Most employees and owners of specialty travel companies do not spend time leading trips. While a single owner-operator-guide may be a basic model for operation, most people find that the challenge of running a profitable specialty travel business has more to do with understanding business, advertising, computers, communication, personnel management, and legal compliance than navigating difficult terrain. Most growing companies promoting international specialty travel require a competent staff of writers, salespeople, reservation agents, bookkeepers, and computer technicians to remain profitable. Many companies contract with guides as freelancers for individual trips or for a season of trips. Professional credentials, licenses, or training may be required.

While leading or guiding trips may be the most fun and hold the most glamour, guide pay and benefits are usually quite low, and the work can be physically and psychologically exhausting. Guide burnout is common, and extended guiding can be hard on personal relationships. In addition, the work is often seasonal, but more people seek guide positions than are available for many types of trips. Most companies hiring guides require demonstrated leadership and communication skills, authoritative knowledge of the skills or contents of the activity, and some previous experience in the field.

International specialty travel operators often hire local guides in destination countries, and company employees accompanying groups during international travel is relatively uncommon.

In order to promote and sell the services a specialty tourist business offers, staff must have first-hand knowledge of the tour activities and destinations. Being a specialized business requires more first-hand knowledge than generalized tour operators need. High quality, detailed written materials, reading lists, check lists, and pre-departure booklets must be constantly rewritten and revised to emphasize the capacity of the operator to provide a safe and satisfying trip.

Owners hiring staff for public or client contact positions must take care to educate the staff to represent the company's policies and products accurately. Satisfaction with the personal treatment a company affords the traveler is a major factor in the participant taking future trips or recommending the company to friends.

AMERICA AND THE WORLD

By the early 2000s, the war in Iraq had affected the international travel scene, and travel to regional Arab countries had decreased significantly. However, adventure travel in India prospered despite the war and concerns about SARS.

The challenge of permits, visas, acquiring local transport, and foreign languages and culture often compounds the adventure for travelers outside the United States and provides further incentive for the traveler to seek the help of a specialized operator. Responsible adventure travel operators provide extensive safety, medical, cultural, environmental, and ecological information to foreign-country-bound travelers to minimize problems, as many areas attractive to adventure travelers have no established local tourism industry. Accommodations, meals, standards of sanitation, legal and security services, and transportation fall far short of what would be reasonable minimum expectations in the United States.

Many international specialty travel operators pay special attention to the Travel Advisories and Warnings issued by the U.S. Department of State in planning or canceling trips to troubled areas. In addition, the advice and standards established by the Centers for Disease Control and Prevention in Atlanta often form a basis for the health and immunization suggestions given by operators to clients traveling overseas. Both of these organizations have Web sites and e-mail lists to which operators may subscribe for current information.

For Americans traveling overseas, the most popular adventure destinations in the first decade of the 2000s were the Himalayas for trekking, east and southern Africa for safaris, southern Europe for bicycling and sailing trips, Costa Rica and Belize for tropical nature tours, Peru for hiking and pre-Columbian culture experience, the Solomon Islands for cruise stopovers, and the Galapagos Islands of Ecuador and Antarctica for exploration cruises. Europe, perennially popular with conventional group tourists, also has a thriving specialty travel industry focusing on walking, bicycling, traditional cultural experiences, dining, and natural environment exploration.

In Latin America, destinations include Panama, where visitors combine tours of the Panama Canal with rain forest exploration. In Bolivia, the native cultures of the Andes, Amazon rain forest, and Inca ruins attract large numbers of visitors. The unique ecosystems and reverse seasons of Argentina and Chile and the spectacular scenery of Patagonia hold increasing interest for North American visitors.

Terrestrial limits were being pushed for future specialty trips, including circumpolar exploration cruises and icebreaker expeditions to the North Pole. Deep Ocean Expeditions, which offers shipwreck dive tours, took tourists to great ocean depths to see hydrothermal vents, undersea geysers, and bizarre sea creatures like eyeless shrimp. In Asia, companies are offering hiking trips to remote parts of Tibet and Yunnan, China, climbing in Kyrgystan, dinosaur digs in Mongolia, and sea kayaking in the Far East. In Africa, adventurous travelers can travel in Mozambique, Ethiopia, Mali, Burkina Faso, Chad, and the Ivory Coast. Kilimanjaro climbs are extremely popular. Niger, Sudan, Somalia, the Congo, Rwanda, Algeria, and Libya, however, were still beyond the interest of most travelers.

BIBLIOGRAPHY

"About Us." G.A.P. Adventures, 15 October 2008. Available from http://www.gapadventures.com.

"Adventurevacation.com Unveils Fresh Look, Features for Adventure Travel Planning." *PRNewswire,* 19 April 2006.

"Boeing and Space Adventures to Offer Commercial Spaceflight Opportunities." Press Release, 15 September 2010. Available from http://www.spaceadventures.com

Bramblett, Reid. "Specialty Tours Let You Choose Your Adventure—and Your Price Tag." *Daily Herald,* 19 May 2006.

"Brazil Promoting Slum Tours." 30 August 2010. Available from http://www.foxnews.com/.

David, Leonard. "Virgin Galactic's Spaceship Aces 3rd Glide Flight." 19 November 2010. Available from http://www.msnbc.msn.com/id/40274787.

"Dharavi Slum Tours." Reality Tours & Travel, 15 October 2008. Available from http://realitytoursandtravel.com.

Fink, Jennifer L.W. "Going Green with Eco-Adventures." *Locum Life,* July 2008.

"First-Ever Global Sustainable Tourism Criteria." *Space Daily,* 8 October 2008.

"Honeymoon on Ice, Sir?" *Travel Trade Gazette UK & Ireland,* 31 March 2006.

Jackson, Kristin. "Taking Flight in the Woods on a Whistler, B.C., Zipline." *Seattle Times,* 1 May 2006.

Klein, Karen E. "Adventure LIfe Thrives With Tours of Latin America's Best Spots." Bloomberg News, 21 October 2010.

Margolis, Mac. "Staying Among the Have-Nots." *Newsweek International,* 26 May 2008.

"Middle East: Tourism and Travel Industry Creates 4.59 Million Jobs." *Infoprod,* 1 May 2006.

"Mothership 'Eve' Rollout." Virgin Galactic, 28 July 2008. Available from http://www.virgingalactic.com/.

"New at Backroads." What's Hot, Cool and Fun." Backroads, 1 October 2008. Available from http://www. backroads.com/.

"Overview." Virgin Galactic, 15 October 2008. Available from http://www.virginGalactic.com.

Schwartz, Noaki. "'Hurricane Tours' The Latest Rage in Adventure Travel." *Miami Herald,* 29 March 2006.

Shum, Katrina. "Green Travel-Trends in Ecotourism." 26 January 2010. Available from http://www.lohas-asia.org/2010/.

Turen, Richard. "To Hell and Back for $6 and Change." *Travel Weekly,* 5 May 2008.

"UAE: Tourism and Travel Industry Creates 294,000 Jobs." *Infoprod,* 1 May 2006.

"U.S. House of Representatives Passes "The Travel Promotion Act of 2008." Travel Industry Association, 25 September 2008.

"U.S. Travel Expenditures Hit $600 Billion for the First Time." Travel Industry Association of America, 20 May 2006.

Velotta, Richard N. "Travel Expert: Environmental Policies Loom as Tourism Threat." *Las Vegas Sun,* 26 October 2010.

"Welcome." United States Adventure Racing Association, 20 May 2006. Available from http://www. usara.com/.

STEM CELL RESEARCH

SIC CODE(S)

8071

8733

8731

INDUSTRY SNAPSHOT

Some people view stem cell research as the means of creating "designer babies" while others see its potential to help find cures for deadly and often incurable diseases. Those diseases include Alzheimer's, diabetes, multiple sclerosis, and Parkinson's. Stem cell research gave the movie Superman Christopher Reeve hope that he might overcome paralysis and walk again, although he passed away in 2004 without having realized that dream. It has already made an impact throughout the world and will undoubtedly continue to do so in the future.

Despite the specious inference that stem cell research remained a contentious topic, in fact, only certain forms of research were under scrutiny and/or criticism. As Ariane Sains of *Europe* magazine pointed out, "Most stem cell research conducted in Europe and the U.S. was not controversial at all." Scientific experiments frequently involved stem cells from laboratory animals that were usually mice. Human sources widely considered to be acceptable were "placenta, fetal tissue obtained following spontaneous abortion (miscarriage), adult cells and even human fat."

The form of stem cell research that continues to spawn controversy revolves around usage of embryonic stem cells (ESCs) that are removed and harvested for research when an embryo is less than 15 days old. Related debate includes ethical, moral, political, and religious discussions reflecting beliefs about the origin of life. Sains claimed, "Those who believe that human life begins at conception argue that destroying a human embryo to obtain stem cells is tantamount to murder." A whole separate but collaterally related controversy involves the use of stem cell research to further the study of human cloning.

In response to the controversy, some bans have been issued and laws passed dramatically impacting stem cell research's progress in the United States. Other countries, where more freedom is allowed, have taken the lead. As an abundance of research reports and news items reflect, the stem cell research story is complicated and continues to evolve.

ORGANIZATION AND STRUCTURE

The Stem Cell Research Foundation (SCRF) defines stem cells as "primitive cells that can give rise to cells of multiple tissue types." The SCRF offers additional definitions for some types of these cells also known as progenitor cells. Totipotent cells are "master cells" with "genetic information needed to create all cells of the body plus the placenta that nourishes the human embryo." Pluripotent cells "are highly versatile and can give rise to any cell except the cells of the placenta." Multipotent cells "can give rise to several other cell types, but those types are limited in number." For example, hematopotetic cells are multipotent cells that can become diverse blood cells with the exception of brain cells. Last but certainly not least, terminally differentiated cells are "considered to be permanently committed to a specific function."

Issues related to stem cell research go well beyond the periphery of science and medicine. The quintessential issue of whether it is ethically or morally right to conduct research on an embryonic stem cell (ESC) taken from human embryos expressly created for such research, and especially in light of discoveries related to adult stem cells, has led to worldwide debate. Many voices from varied disciplines, including politics, philosophy, and education, have demanded to be heard on numerous related issues. Religious conservatives, especially Catholics, have been largely against stem cell research due to their belief that life starts at the moment of conception. They view an embryo as a living entity. The Vatican expressed its opposition and so have many predominately Catholic countries.

BACKGROUND AND DEVELOPMENT

Dreams of finding ways to help human beings live healthier and longer lives have propelled leaders in stem cell research along. The early research primarily involved working with mice. British researchers led the way by being the first to extract embryonic stem cells (ESCs) from mouse blastocysts.

In 1998, James Thompson and his University of Wisconsin team isolated human ESCs. That same year, John Gearhart and his Johns Hopkins University team announced their ability to isolate the human embryonic germ cell (EGC). The second team purified cells from the gonadel ridges of early aborteses.

According to *The Columbia Encyclopedia,* "Stem cells have been used experimentally to form the hematopoietic cells of bone marrow and heart, blood vessel, muscle and insulin-producing tissue. Embryonic germ line cells have been used to help paralyzed mice regain some of the ability to move."

The *The Columbia Encyclopedia* also stated that a 1994 National Institutes of Health (NIH) panel endorsed creating human embryos for use in certain experiments. Consequently, the U.S. Congress enacted a ban in 1995 on federal financing of research involving human embryos. In 1999, the Department of Health and Human Services ruled the 1995 ban did not apply to financing work with stem cells. Related financing guidelines were first issued in 2000 by the NIH.

The policy of President George W. Bush allowed unrestricted federal funds to be used for experiments on stem cells from human embryos only if they had been derived from embryos existing before August 9, 2001. This date appeared arbitrary, but in fact served to distinguish a distinct group of approved stem cell lines that were not originally grown for research purposes but came from existing excess embryos slated for disposal from in vitro fertilization clinics. The Bush policy further mandated that in order to receive federal funding, 1) there must have been informed consent from the donors; 2) the embryos must have been created for reproductive purposes and in excess of clinical need; 3) there must not have been any financial incentive from the donors; and 4) the embryos must not have been created for research purposes. Problems later arose when the number of cell lines turned out to be less than originally believed to be in existence. The *Washington Post* reported in March 2004 that at least 16 of the 78 approved lines had died or failed to reproduce in their laboratory dishes, or in the words of the NIH, "failed to expand into undifferentiated cell cultures." However, as of the middle of the first decade of the 2000s, no policy had replaced the existing one or permitted federal funding for research beyond that involving the authorized cell lines.

Distinguishing Cloning from Stem Cell Research "The idea of therapeutic cloning is to take adult cells from a person's body, create cloned embryos and extract embryonic stem cells that can turn into a wide range of tissues, all a perfect match for the patient," explained Sylvia Pagan Westphal in a 2002 article in *New Scientist.* She added, "But recent research suggests that stem cells in adults are just as versatile as embryonic ones, which might make cloning unnecessary."

In order to distinguish their work from strongly opposed reproductive cloning, stem cell research professionals preferred using the term "somatic cell nuclear transfer." As Laura Shanner pointed out in *Health Law Review,* "Using the phrase 'therapeutic cloning' as a comprehensive term for non-reproductive cloning ignores the 'genetic enhancement.' More important, the word 'therapeutic' means that research has already validated that the benefits of a treatment demonstrably outweigh risks."

"These past two years have only made it clearer that the promise of stem cell research is so strong that the restrictive policy must be changed," said Coalition for the Advancement of Medical Research (CAMR) President Michael Manganiello in 2003. CAMR led efforts to oppose a therapeutic cloning ban.

Crain's New York Business revealed that actor Michael J. Fox gave $650,000 from the foundation he started for the study of Parkinson's disease. The recipient, Lorenz Studer of Memorial Sloan-Kettering Cancer Center, had coaxed embryonic stem cells (ESCs) from mice into becoming dopamine-producing cells in the brain. The death of those cells can cause Parkinson's, which Fox testified has affected his life and career.

Business Week acknowledged the widely applauded work of Catherine Verfaillie at the University of

Minnesota. She demonstrated the enormous flexibility of certain adult cells. Verfaillie "extracted cells from bone marrow, grew them in petri dishes for up to two years and showed that they could turn into everything from liver and cartilage to brain cells."

Newsweek shared the story of National Institutes of Health (NIH) pediatric dental researcher and dentist Shi Songtao who spotted red material on his daughter's baby tooth that resulted in identification of Stem Cells from Human Exfoliated Deciduous (SHED) teeth. When six-year-old Julie lost the second tooth, Songtao and cow-orkers extracted the pulp and studied it in the lab. SHED teeth grow faster than stem cells in full-grown adults but can only transform into bone, nerve, and fat cells.

The Scientist reported that Intel Chairman Andy Grove donated $5 million to a matching fund to finance a new ESC program at the University of California, San Francisco. *Newsweek* revealed that Stanford announced receiving a $12 million anonymous donation to fund the new Institute For Cancer/Stem Cell Biology and Medicine. This generosity was evidence of private philanthropists reaching into their pockets and challenging others to step up the research.

The political, ethical, and cultural polarization of opinion over embryonic stem cell (ESC) research raged onward in full force through 2004 and 2005. The issue gained extensive media coverage during the 2004 U.S. presidential election campaigns between Senator John Kerry (D-MA) and incumbent President George W. Bush. The Bush administration firmly reiterated its position that ESC research posed an ethical question, and that taxpayer dollars would not be used to fund the destruction of human embryos, irrespective of their origin (including any newer disposals from in vitro clinics). Conversely, the Kerry platform called for a repeal of the existing restrictions and full federal embrace of stem cell research. His campaign platform was helped by the family of deceased President Ronald Reagan, who used the Democratic campaign to push reform. Nevertheless, Kerry lost the election, and it appeared that a majority of Americans did not embrace unrestricted research.

In early 2005, the British government granted approval to Professor Ian Wilmut of Edinburgh's Roslin Institute (the scientist behind the cloning of the sheep known as "Dolly") to clone human embryos for medical research. Despite substantial public outcry, the government was quick to point out that human reproductive cloning remained illegal, but approval could be granted where embryos were created as a source of stem cells to treat or cure disease (therapeutic cloning). Wilmut planned to use these stem cells for investigation into Motor Neurone Disease (MND).

The stem cell research industry includes biotechnology companies conducting studies throughout the world plus biopharmaceutical companies developing related products. As reported by Karen Young Kreeger in *The Scientist,* the Director of the United Kingdom Centre for Tissue Engineering Tim Hardingham said that researchers worldwide are combining the basic biology of tissue repair with the potential of stem cells. In *Visiongain*'s "Tissue Engineering and Stem Cell Technology Report 2003-2013," Dr. Ray Scraggs, PhD, a certified senior industry analyst, shared his views that this segment of the industry would be worth $10 billion by 2013. According to Scraggs, "Undoubtedly, the medical use of stem cells will revolutionise medicine and any company that can successfully develop this technology will be guaranteed substantial financial rewards." (See also **Tissue Engineering** for other companies involved in stem cell research.)

Scientists at the Whitehead Institute engineered a breakthrough in stem cell research in June 2007 when they discovered a way to create embryonic stem cells without an egg. According to the Stem Cell Research Foundation, "By genetically manipulating mature skin cells taken from a mouse, the scientists have transformed these cells back into a pluripotent state, one that appears identical to an embryonic stem cell in every way. No eggs were used, and no embryos destroyed." As Mary Carmichael commented in *Newsweek,* "The never-ending argument over embryonic stem cells has taken a turn that seems unprecedented: both sides look happy." Some experts, however, cautioned against attaching too much importance to the discovery and stated that scientists are still a long way from applying the technique to humans.

Those in favor of stem cell research were putting their hopes on a bill that loosened restrictions on federal funding for stem cell research that, as of mid-2007, had passed the House and was in the Senate. However, President Bush had already vetoed a similar bill in 2006 and stated that he would do the same for this bill. In 2007 the legal and moral intricacies involved in the industry were as yet to be untangled.

CURRENT CONDITIONS

According to the report "Cord Blood Stem Cells: A Global Market Overview," (*PRLog*), umbilical cord and placenta, once considered medical waste, emerged as valuable sources of stem cells. The cord blood stem cells show the potential to treat fatal diseases such as leukemia, cardiac attacks and debilitating diseases including Alzheimer's and Parkinson's. Cord blood stem cells are also widely used in therapies such as blood disorders, bone and tissue engineering, and dermatology. The report indicated that the global cord blood stem cell market for 2010 was estimated at about $4.5 billion. The market was expected to grow at a compounded annual rate (CAGR) of 27.3 through 2015 to reach $15 billion by 2015.

The industry suffered significantly greatly in revenues during 2008 and 2009. Partly due to shortages in grants and donations, several smaller concerns merged and broadened their research objectives. Others identified specific medical conditions they hoped to help with continued stem cell research.

Then, in March 2009, President Barack Obama signed Executive Order No. 13505, Removing Barriers to Responsible Scientific Research Involving Human Stem Cells, which expressly revoked the previous administration's restrictive Executive Order 13435 of June 2007. This was expected to provide not only more federal grant monies for research, but also raise the level of public knowledge of research projects and their status.

The 2009 Albert Lasko Basic Medical Research Award for advancements in genetic engineering research went to regenerative technology advances that do not rely on human reproductive embryos, but rather use transferred DNA coding capable of instructing special cells to form stem cells, which in turn, are coded to regenerate as specific organs or tissues. The related Lasko Clinical Medical Research Award went for stem cell research leading to a revolutionary cancer treatment for certain types of leukemia. The global market for such advancements, according to *Genetic Engineering & Biotechnology News,* was estimated at $700 million.

INDUSTRY LEADERS

Generally, the majority of industry leaders were losing revenues in 2008 and 2009, primarily due to the loss of grant monies following former bans on many forms of research over prior years, and softened donations.

CyThera/Novocell This biotechnology company focused on developing cell replacement therapies for the treatment of human degenerative disease. It creates cell-based products developed from embryonic stem cell (ESC) technologies, thereby overcoming limitations of sourcing and employing donated tissues. In 2001, CyThera announced its addition to the national registry of ESC lines by the U.S. National Institutes of Health (NIH). CyThera has nine ESC derivations that meet the White House criteria for federal funding and which were consequentially placed on the NIH registry. The initial focus was on development of functional islet cell transplants for the treatment of insulin-dependent diabetes. In 2002, the company reported completion of the Arcos Bioscience

acquisition. This acquisition gave CyThera the novel ESC technology, developed by Arcos Scientific Founder Dr. Jeanne Loring, that is different from the method patented by the University of Wisconsin. CyThera merged with Novocell Inc. in 2004.

Geron Corporation The Menlo Park, California, biopharmaceutical company Geron remains focused on developing and commercializing therapeutic and diagnostic products for applications in oncology and regenerative medicine plus research tools for drug discovery. It employs three validated and complementary technology platforms: telomerase, human embryonic stem cells (ESCs), and nuclear transfer. These technologies support multiple product opportunities for pioneering new approaches to improve cancer diagnosis and treatment, effecting tissue repair in chronic degenerative diseases and accelerating drug discovery and development. Product development programs are aligned along target markets to organize Geron into four specific business units: Oncology, Regenerative Medicine, R & D Technologies, and Nuclear Transfer: Ag/Xeno/Biologics. In January 2009, the FDA granted clearance of Geron's Investigational New Drug (IND) application for the clinical trial of GRNOPC1 in patients with acute spinal cord injury. The company reported $2.8 million revenues for 2008.

StemCell Technologies Headquartered in Vancouver, British Columbia, this company is a privately owned, market-driven biotechnology company. It provides highly specialized cell culture media and cell separation products that support and enable medical research in areas such as cancer, hematology, immunology, cell transplantation, gene therapy, and developmental biology. StemCell also offers training courses, coordinates a global proficiency testing program for hematopoietic progenitor assays, and contracts assay services to the biotechnology and pharmaceutical industry.

StemCells, Inc. StemCells, Inc., of Palo Alto, California, is engaged in identifying and isolating stem cells from a variety of medically important tissues including the brain, liver, and pancreas. Active research and development is conducted in the areas of the neural cell, liver stem cell, and pancreatic cell programs. The scientific founder/director is Irving L. Weissman. His biography says that he is a professor of cancer biology, pathology, and developmental biology at Stanford University. Weissman's Stanford University lab was the first to isolate in pure form any stem cell from any tissue in any species. In April 2009, the company acquired the Stem Cell Sciences (SCS) operations. As of 2009, the Company had exclusive rights to approximately

55 issued or allowed U.S. patents and approximately 200 granted or allowed non-U.S. patents.

ViaCell ViaCell is a clinical-stage biotechnology company with a cellular medicine pipeline that focuses in the areas of cancer, neurological diseases, infertility, diabetes, and muscular dystrophy. The Boston, Massachusetts, company is developing amplified, high-definition stem cell products based on its patented technology, Selective Amplification, for expanded populations of stem cells. The company has two divisions: the ViaCell Neuroscience Division, which develops cellular and molecular medicines for neurological diseases, and its ViaCord Division, which offers umbilical cord blood stem cell preservation services.

WORKFORCE

Experts who choose to work in the field of stem cell research are not like the stereotypically mad scientists working in isolated laboratories, nor are they scholarly geniuses locked in ivory towers. There is a lot of interaction with others relating to funding and advancing their research goals.

Stem cell research professionals' titles reflect that they come from diverse educational backgrounds and may wear multiple hats. The titles include scientific founder, scientist, cell biologist, doctor, laboratory technician, researcher and investigator. Furthermore, doctors who made noteworthy contributions to stem cell research included a dentist and liver pathologist. In an article in *Crain's New York Business,* Judith Messina acknowledged that most scientists she reported on did not start out as stem cell researchers: "They began working with stem cells while trying to answer fundamental questions in their specialties. Neil Theise wanted to see what tiny bile ducts in liver which drain fluid the body uses to digest fat looked like. The associate professor of pathology at New York University School of Medicine discovered the ducts contained stem cells from the bone marrow raising questions about the cells' ability to repair and regenerate diseased livers. Theise continued stem cell research after his discovery."

The political climate and public attitudes toward stem cell research often impact where professionals decide to work or continue their careers. There are opportunities throughout the world with varying degrees of freedom depending on bans and laws. Consequently, some stem cell professionals move their staff to another state or country, even if it requires ending alliances.

The Omaha World Herald reported that passage of the 2002 law banning usage of human embryos to create therapeutic stem cells had "a chilling effect" on recruitment for the University of Iowa's Carver College of Medicine. Jean Robillard, dean of the School, was credited with the following statement: "There's no question that, if I were a young investigator who had a chance to go to Illinois, Wisconsin or some state that is less restrictive, I would go there, not to Iowa." The newspaper also referenced a June 2003 announcement regarding one of the most prestigious cancer research teams, led by cell biologist Mary Hendrix, moving to Northwestern University after citing problems with the law.

According to a June 27, 2003 article by Eugene Russo titled "Stem Cell Research Climate" found on the Web site of *The Scientist,* during a Biotechnology Industry Organization conference in Washington, D.C., that week, U.S. biologist Diana Devore told a "global partners session" that she had left the U.S. to head the new National Center for Stem Cell Research in Australia. She said U.S. regulations influenced both her move and the creation of the center by the Australian government.

Erika Jonietz, an associate editor of *Technology Review,* noted in its June 2003 issue a trend where other countries are sending young people to the National Institutes of Health (NIH) for training but they are not staying in the U.S. afterward as their predecessors did. Instead, the young professionals are returning home to practice lessons learned in fields related to embryonic stem cells (ESCs), cell therapy or nuclear transfer where they anticipate more freedom.

AMERICA AND THE WORLD

As of the first decade of the new century, at least 32 countries, representing about 3.4 billion people (more than half the world"s population) had developed formal policies regarding human ESC research. Policies were distinguished as either "permissive" or "flexible." Countries having flexible policies permitted only derivations from fertility clinic donations, and often had other restrictions. Countries in that category included Australia, Brazil, Canada, Finland, France, Spain, Switzerland, The Netherlands, and Taiwan. Permissive policies allowed the more controversial somatic cell nuclear transfer (SCNT), also called therapeutic cloning. Countries with permissive policies included the United Kingdom, Belgium, Israel, India, China, Japan, South Korea, and Singapore. The Czech Republic appeared to be the next country awaiting passage of formal policy/law on the subject.

The United Nations (UN) itself became involved in the matter. After two years of unfruitful negotiations and deadlock among its members, the United Nations formally shelved human cloning treaties in 2004. A total ban had garnered the signature of 62 member states, but another 22 had supported a Belgian treaty that would have allowed cloning for stem cell research.

RESEARCH AND DEVELOPMENT

In 2003, the International Stem Cell Forum was launched in London. As reported by the organization, it is comprised of 14 funders of stem cell research around the world. Its stated objective is to encourage international collaboration and further funding support, with the overall aim of promoting accelerated progress in the global arena. By 2005, at least 32 countries had developed some form of permissive or flexible policy on human embryonic stem cell research. However, every one of these countries banned human reproductive cloning.

Several news sources claimed the European Union (E.U) had made stem cell research a top priority for science research spending. *Europe* contributing editor Ariane Sains reported that "the EU has financed research projects involving stem cells for a total of $24 million and funding continues in the latest framework research program that runs from this year through 2006." *The Lancet* in its July 12, 2003, issue said that the European Commission was adopting new guidelines regulating embryo usage in E.U.-funded research, the goal being to have guidelines in place before the moratorium expired at the end of 2003. The Associated Press, according to *Transplant News,* reported that E.U. countries could only obtain funding from the European Union if they used stored or frozen embryos left over from fertility treatments and created before June 27, 2002. That date reflected when the European Union adopted its 2003-2006 research program.

BIBLIOGRAPHY

"2009 Lasko Awards Recognize Promise of Stem Cells-Global Market Could Top $700 Million." *Genetic Engineering & Biotechnolgy News,* 14 September 2009.

"AAAS Policy Brief: 2004 Update." AAAS Center for Science, Technology, and Congress. 2005. Available from http://aaas.org/.

"Adult Stem Cells Aid in Repair of Neurological Damage Caused by Degeneration of Trauma, As Shown in Two Reports in *Journal of Hematotherapy & Stem Cell Research.*" *Business Wire,* 12 June 2003.

Barry, P. "Female Stem Cells Flourish: Sex Difference Could Affect Therapies." *Science News,* 14 April 2007.

"Boost for Stem Cell Research." *The Lancet,* 12 July 2003.

Breindl, Anette. "When Artificial Is Better Than Natural: Reprogramming Skin Cells Can Create Stem Cells From Scratch." *BIOWORLD Today,* 7 June 2007.

Carmichael, Mary. "An End to Debate or Deja Vu?" *Newsweek,* 18 June 2007.

"Cloning to Improve a Life vs. Cloning to Produce One." *Chicago Sun Times,* 20 June 2003.

Derfner, Larry. "Superhero Flies to Israel." *U.S. News & World Report,* 11 August 2003.

Embryonic Stem Cells Can Be Created Without Eggs." Stem Cell Research Foundation, 7 June 2007. Available from www.scrfinfo.org/.

"European Commission Adopts Stem Cell Research Guidelines; Plan Faces Opposition." *Transplant News,* 25 July 2003.

"Frequently Asked Questions." Stem Cell Research Foundation. 15 June 2007. Available from www.stemcellresearchfoundation.org.

Gertzen, Jason. "Pressure is on Stem Cell Firms." *Milwaukee Journal Sentinel,* 19 September 2004.

Gills, Justin, and Rick Weiss. "NIH: Few Stem Cell Colonies Available for Research." *Washington Post,* 3 March 2004.

"Global Cord Blood Stem Cells Market to Hit US$15 billion by 2015." Press Release, *PR Log,* 15 December 2009. Available from http://www.prlog.org/10453315-global-cord-blood-stem-cells-market-to-hit-us15-billion-by-2015.html.

Gottlieb, Scott, M.D. "California's Stem Cell Follies." *Forbes,* 1 November 2004.

Grygotis, Michele. "Bush Policy a Barrier to Advances in Human Embryonic Stem Cell Research, Say Scientists and Some in Congress." *Transplant News,* 30 May 2003.

Hagen, John D., Jr. "Bentham's Mummy and Stem Cells." *America,* 14 May 2007.

Hagan, Pat. "Stem Cell Forum Launched: Twelve Nations Sign Up for Project Designed to Speed Up Research." *The Scientist,* 17 July 2003.

Hoffman, William. "Stem Cells: Human Health, Global Competition and National Security." Available from http://mbbnet.umn.edu/.

"Hoover's Company Capsules." *Hoover's Online,* 2007. Available from www.hoovers.com.

"Iowa Law on Stem Cells Draws Criticism." *Omaha World Herald,* 11 September 2003.

"Is Stem Cell Reporting Telling the Real Story?" *Nieman Reports,* Summer 2003.

Jackson, Fred, and Jenny Parker. "Pro-Lifers Outraged as Britain Grants Dolly's Doc License to Clone." *IFRL Daily News,* 7 February 2005.

Jonietz, Erika. "Cloning, Stem Cells and Medicine's Future." *Technology Review,* June 2003.

Kreeger, Karen Young. "Hoping to Mend Their Sporting Ways: Researchers Turn to Gene Therapy, Tissue Engineering and More to Heal Sports Stars' Popped Knees and Torn Ligaments." *The Scientist,* 13 January 2003.

"Legislative Update: Stem Cell Research." National Institute of Health's Office of Legislative Policy and Analysis. 2005. Available from http://olpa.od.nih.gov/.

Leitzell, Katherine, and Chris Wilson. "A New Source for Stem Cells?" *U.S. News & World Report,* 18 June 2007.

Lemonick, Michael D. "Stem Cells in Limbo: Two Years After President Bush Said the U.S. Had All The Cell Lines It Needed, Where Did They Go?" *Time,* 11 August 2003.

Lewis, Ricki. "Sources for Adult Human Stem Cells." *The Scientist,* 16 June 2003.

"Life Technologies, Novocell Receive Stem Cell Agency Grants." *San Diego Business Journal,* 11 December 2008.

"Making Massachusetts Safe for Stem Cells." *Cell Therapy News,* May 2003.

"Nervous System: Hematopoietic Stem Cells Generate Neural Cells." *Cell Therapy News,* March 2003.

"News." Geron, 19 March 2005. Available from www.geron.com.

Office of the White House. 2009. "Executive Order No. 13505, Removing Barriers to Responsible Scientific Research

Involving Human Stem Cells." Available from http://www.whitehouse.gov/.

"Out of the Mouth of Babes." *National Right to Life News,* May 2003.

Oz, Mehmet C., M.D. "Breaking New Ground on Stem Cells." *Saturday Evening Post,* March-April 2007.

Philipkoski, Kristen. "U.N. Deadlocks on Cloning Ban." *Wired News,* 19 November 2004.

Russo, Eugene. "Stem Cell Research Climate." *The Scientist,* 27 June 2003.

Saskal, Rich. "California: Stem Cells Get $50M of Funds." *The Bond Buyer,* 8 June 2007.

"Spain Approves Stem Cell Research, With Conditions." Reuters, 25 July 2003.

Stem Cell Inc. Available from http://www.faqs.org/sec-filings/091105/STEMCELLS-INC_8-K/exhibit1.htm.

"Stem Cell Research." *Swiss News,* April 2003.

"Stem Cells & Tissue Engineering Market Worth $10 Billion by 2013." *Epharmaceuticalnews,* 18 May 2004.

"Stem Cells To Repair Damaged Heart Muscle." Stem Cell Research Foundation, 22 June 2007. Available from www.scrfinfo.org/.

"UK Government Increases Stem Cell Research Funds." *BioWorld Week,* 6 January 2003.

"ViaCell in the News." 13 March 2005. Available from www.viacellinc.com.

STORAGE NETWORKING

—■—

SIC CODE(S)

3572

INDUSTRY SNAPSHOT

Where corporate computer networks sprawl, and data storage and retrieval grow ever more unwieldy, the storage networking industry promises to restore some semblance of efficiency and reliability. Storage networking (or enterprise storage, as it is sometimes referred to) is the business of selling hardware, software, and services to organizations with complex data/information mass storage needs. As would be expected from an industry representing the compilation and condensation of mass data, it is an industry filled with a plethora of insider jargon and acronyms, a few of which are basic to an understanding of the technology and are discussed below.

The gist of storage networking is that specialized storage systems and software can do a better job at mundane file serving, backups, and other storage-related tasks in network environments than ordinary multipurpose network servers can. To wit, technologies such as storage area networks (SANs) and network-attached storage (NAS) devices are added to existing Unix, NetWare, and Windows NT networks in order to take some of the burden off application servers and other network resources, improving speed, accessibility, reliability, and even cost efficiency along the way.

One way or the other, the storage is networked by means of either Fibre Channel (FC) or Internet Protocol (IP) and, increasingly, through both (e.g., FCIP). Newer technology developed by the Internet Engineering Task Force (IETF) has opened the industry to smaller businesses and private concerns through the use of Internet Small Computer System Interface (ISCSI), which is an Internet Protocol-based storage area network (IP-based SAN). ISCSI is one of two main approaches to storage data transmission over IP networks. The other is the more limited Fibre Channel Internet Protocol (FCIP), a marriage of technologies that translates FC control codes and data into IP packets for transmission between geographically distant Fibre Channel storage area networks (FC SANS). Of the two, which do not completely overlap in applications, the ISCSI protocol is one of the leading technologies expected to rapidly enhance development of the SAN market.

With storage needs at data-laden companies now being tallied in terabytes, or trillions of bytes, the market for sophisticated storage systems, sometimes called enterprise storage, is flourishing. While these systems were originally aimed mostly at *Fortune* 1000 companies, storage networking vendors are beginning to target medium-sized organizations as well. According to Howard Goldstein in his Web editorial "Storage Networking: Perspectives on Terminology and Meaning," demand for such storage products and services in the twenty-first century's first decade was growing at about 40 to 50 percent annually.

ORGANIZATION AND STRUCTURE

Networks have always contained storage resources, but not all of these qualify as storage network devices. Storage networking describes a fairly narrow set of technologies centered around dedicated yet versatile storage appliances that are based on open standards, high performance, and nearly universal connectivity with different kinds of network operating systems and hardware. Although storage networks had many precursors, especially in the mainframe arena, the current notion of storage networking came about largely in the late 1990s.

The set of technologies includes hardware, software, and services. Specifically, storage networks usually come in one of two hardware configurations: network-attached storage (NAS) and storage area networks (SANs). These configurations consist of one or more—usually more—hardware devices that are attached to an existing computer network to provide greater storage capacity, greater manageability, and better performance. Storage networking also involves software for managing storage. Finally, services include consulting about storage needs, implementing and customizing a storage network, and, in the extreme, hosting and managing a storage network for a client. Each aspect of storage networking is described below.

Network-Attached Storage Network-attached storage (NAS) is a simple but powerful concept: let a speedy, focused appliance deal with storing and retrieving files so network servers can stick to the business of running applications and more advanced operations.

NAS devices, often called appliances or specialized servers, are the entry level gear in storage networking. Priced anywhere from $1,000 to $80,000 or more, NAS servers are often used to enhance network performance on a work group or department level. A single NAS server usually isn't enough to fix a big corporate network's storage woes. NAS systems can involve simply one such device hooked up to a local area network or any number of NAS devices strung together.

Either way, NAS systems are optimized for saving and retrieving user files and communicating with other machines. They run on simplified, nimble operating systems that don't get bogged down in running databases, delivering e-mail, or hosting the boss's solitaire tournaments.

Inside the box, NAS servers typically contain a microprocessor, a generous helping of RAM, an array of hard disk drives (although some use optical or tape drives), and a variety of external ports for connecting the NAS to the network. Most NAS hardware can be readily upgraded, say to add more storage capacity or additional network adapters. Top-notch systems use high speed connection architecture, such as Fibre Channel or Ultra SCSI, to keep the whole system running at peak speed. Higher-end NAS devices also include one or more mechanisms (software or hardware or both) for fault tolerance and error handling, meaning the system can recover quickly and successfully from a problem without losing data or going out of service for long stretches—or better yet, never go down in the first place.

NAS servers are also designed for easy connectivity with existing network resources. The software is meant to be easily administered—often through Web or Java-based utilities—and individual computers and servers can access the NAS much as they would any other shared resource on the network.

Storage Area Networks Storage area networks (SANs) fill many of the same broad functions as network attached storage (NAS) but do so on a much grander scale and are decidedly more complex. In fact, they can contain any number of separate interworking devices, so there's no precise definition of what constitutes a SAN.

Five things are needed to achieve the kind of reliability, interconnectivity, and speed associated with an effective SAN: (1) a pool of logically (although not necessarily physically) centralized storage devices, be they disk arrays, tape drives, or otherwise; (2) at least two network servers to access the storage pool; (3) at least one hub or switch to mediate traffic between the servers and the storage devices; (4) a high speed connection, usually via a Fibre Channel fiber-optic interface, between the hub and each of the servers and storage devices; and (5) software to manage it all. These are just the minimum requirements, and the way they're all put together has a huge impact on a SAN's performance and reliability.

Like NAS, a SAN frees up general network servers for more application processing, making networks run faster. By centralizing storage—a throwback to mainframe precepts—SANs also make network administration more efficient and in many cases have a lower total cost of ownership than conventional server-centric storage.

Whereas NAS servers are nearly plug-and-play devices, SANs often require a great deal of planning, consulting, and even integration work to implement. Indeed, heavy-duty SANs at big companies can easily cost several million dollars to set up. Clearly SANs are aimed at high volume storage needs, whether for legions of general office workers or a smaller number of storage-intensive users such as graphic artists and medical image technicians. SANs likewise differ in that the file system isn't contained on the storage device but on the server accessing the storage. SANs also have an extraordinary capacity to grow as needs change, known as scalability in the business, by adding more devices to the storage pool.

Software Software is mainly an issue for SANs, since NAS servers generally come with their own administration software. Most analysts believe software is key to realizing SANs' potential, although some also warn that management software for SANs is still underdeveloped.

SAN management software is the core of centralized storage administration. In addition to helping all the devices in the SAN function properly, these software utilities enable network administrators to configure SANs, allocate space effectively, and monitor storage resources.

Services The service side of the industry is mostly aimed at SAN implementation and maintenance. Some SAN vendors routinely sell service contracts along with the hardware. SAN services usually begin with consulting, which involves sizing up the client's current resources and present and future needs. The service vendor then formulates a network design that best uses resources and meets the client's needs.

Once a customer signs off on the plan, the work of implementing it begins. Implementation includes customizing old and new hardware so it all works with the SAN (for example, adding the appropriate network adapters), physically installing the new equipment and fiber-optic connections, and configuring software to run and administer the SAN. Most if not all of these tasks could be done by a customer's own information technology (IT) department. However, because SANs and the fiber optics that support them are relatively new technologies, service vendors may have expertise that internal staff lack.

Finally, service vendors perform ongoing maintenance and support of storage networks. This includes training, on-site repairs and troubleshooting, remote systems monitoring and problem detection, and phone-based technical support. Such services may be offered as part of the hardware sale or may be purchased separately.

BACKGROUND AND DEVELOPMENT

Although storage networking has roots in mainframe technology and other areas of network computing, the current concept came about in the late 1990s due to four developments: Large computer networks running Unix, NetWare, and Windows NT were hobbled by costly, overtaxed all-purpose servers and spiraling storage needs; storage device makers shifted away from proprietary technology toward open standards that allowed different vendors' machines to work together; standards groups and storage vendors agreed on new specifications for high speed fiber-optic data transfer, namely Fibre Channel, that could support the speed and flexibility needed to ease the burdens on networks; and storage vendors focused increasingly on high performance over mere functionality

Centralized storage was a common feature of mainframes from their inception. As businesses adopted distributed personal computer networking in the 1980s and 1990s, however, storage became increasingly fragmented and inefficient, parceled across different servers and sometimes different operating systems in what has come to be known as "islands of storage." Storage management was often done on a server by server basis, making it time-consuming and occasionally technically challenging. When existing servers were "maxed out," network managers added more storage capacity to individual servers or simply tacked on more servers, further fragmenting the organization's storage resources into an expansive archipelago.

Previous attempts at mass-storage networking met with mixed results. NAS-like file servers were used in Unix environments as early as the 1980s, but they had several deficiencies. They weren't particularly fast, were hard to manage, and tended to work only with specific kinds of systems. By the mid-1990s, more options and flexibility had come along, but performance and interoperability—the ability to work with all kinds of machines and software—were still limited.

Fiber-Optic Interface Key Emerging fiber-optic networking standards hastened the development of high performance storage networking. Work on the Fibre Channel fiber-optic computer interface standard began in 1988 under the auspices of the American National Standards Institute and later under a collaboration between IBM Corp., Hewlett-Packard Co., and Sun Microsystems, Inc. called the Fibre Channel Systems Initiative. A few Fibre Channel standards were crafted for various purposes. The most popular for storage devices was the Fibre Channel Arbitrated Loop (FC-AL).

By 1994 a blueprint was in place for what Fibre Channel could offer—and the offerings were considerable. The technology boasted up to one-gigabit-per-second data transfer rates (although 100 megabits was the standard in first generation interfaces), long distance connectivity up to 10 kilometers, and the ability to connect over a hundred devices in a single segment. By contrast, the aging, bulky, small computer system interface (SCSI) at the time supported speeds only up to 20 megabits per second (40 mbps more recently), a distance range of about 25 meters, and the ability to connect just 15 devices.

Importantly, Fibre Channel could also act both as a standard network communication interface and as a data channel for direct communication between a processor and a peripheral device. This was key to separating storage devices from processing on a network, paving the way for SANs and NAS servers. Fibre Channel also supported other communication protocols, including small computer system interface (SCSI) and the popular Internet

Protocol (IP), which made it highly compatible with existing technologies.

By 1996 enough manufacturers supported Fibre Channel and had begun to introduce devices to make it a commercially viable technology. Although it had helped create the Fibre Channel standards, IBM continued to tout a maverick interface called serial storage architecture (SSA). Despite IBM's clout, SSA was roundly seen as inferior to Fibre Channel—and even to SCSI—so few other manufacturers supported it. Nonetheless, IBM's competing interface contributed to uncertainty about Fibre Channel's future. Finally, in 1996, IBM entered a new collaboration with disk drive giant Seagate Technology, Inc. and system board manufacturer Adaptec, Inc. to meld SSA and the Fibre Channel Arbitrated Loop (FC-AL) into a new interface called Fibre Channel Enhanced Loop, or simply Fibre Channel Loop. While the features of the new interface had yet to be determined, IBM's action was interpreted as its long-awaited endorsement of Fibre Channel and helped build confidence about Fibre Channel both in the industry and in the marketplace.

Storage Networking Comes of Age For the next couple of years, storage vendors launched increasingly robust products using the emerging standards and began ramping up marketing as well. Meanwhile, the furious growth of the Internet and e-commerce had begun to multiply companies' storage problems. Web sites collected gigabyte upon gigabyte of traffic logs and potential customer data, all needing to be stored and analyzed. By some calculations, large companies' storage needs were doubling annually.

By the turn of the century, a recognizable storage networking industry was in place. Leading companies formed the Storage Networking Industry Association (SNIA), a Mountain View, California, trade group dedicated to promoting the technology and continuing collaboration on standards. In 2007 two other organizations, the Storage Networking User Group (SNUG) and the Association of Storage Networking Professionals (ASNP) merged as StorageNetworking.org.

Even though the industry had embraced Fibre Channel as its connectivity medium, particularly for SANs, rancorous debate continued about whether it was cost effective to deploy the pricey fiber optics. Fibre Channel's main opponent was Ethernet, the predominant network interface for local area networks. Ethernet underwent various upgrades over time, including the introduction of the upgraded Gigabit Ethernet standard. At this rate, some analysts said, Ethernet delivered performance comparable to Fibre Channel—and used cheaper technology that IT workers were more familiar with. In addition, future Ethernet specifications could potentially allow data transmissions of up to 10 gigabits per second (gbps), whereas the then current Fibre Channel road map went only to 2 gbps.

Separately, another connectivity standards initiative was close to being completed, this one with implications far beyond storage interfaces. In 1999, two rival camps developing standards for a new industry-wide high bandwidth input/output medium agreed on a technical framework called the InfiniBand Architecture. The Next Generation Input/Output group had been backed by Intel Corp., while the Future Input/Output group had Compaq, Hewlett-Packard, and IBM on its side. The 1999 truce ended a couple years of standoffs and signaled potentially sweeping changes for all forms of computer input/output connections. The new medium, which could support copper and fiber-optic cables, was expected to reach speeds up to 6 gbps, with room for growth in the future.

The InfiniBand Trade Association, the official trade group promulgating the standard, optimistically predicted that InfiniBand devices would begin hitting the market en masse in late 2001 but widespread adoption would likely take much longer. International Data Corp. expected about 100,000 servers would be supporting Infiniband by the end of 2001, with 800,000 servers signing on a year later.

eWeek predicted that standards would make it easier to manage heterogeneous storage infrastructures. The publication stated the Storage Networking Industry Association (SNIA)'s Storage Management Initiative Specification (unveiled in April 2003) would build on Common Information Model and Web-Based Enterprise Management, boosting storage management capabilities. SNIA is a not-for-profit organization consisting of more than 300 companies and individuals spanning the entire storage industry. In order to accelerate adoption of SNIA standards, the Storage Management Forum introduced new education programs for vendors, developers and end users. Activities were planned for the Storage Networking World Spring 2003 exhibition and the first Storage Management Initiative Specification (SMI-S) Developers Education course was scheduled in May at the SNIA Technology Center in Colorado Springs, Colorado.

Another interesting statistic, provided by Parks Associates in early 2005, was that 27 percent of households with home networking, and who also were digital entertainment enthusiasts, would be highly interested in network-attached storage. The survey gauged interest in a networked storage device, defined as a high capacity hard drive that could connect to the home network and enable multiple PCs, printers, and other digital devices (e.g., iPod), to store, share, and access content.

CURRENT CONDITIONS

Storage networking vendors were not faring well in early 2009 despite a strong market during 2008's slumping economy. At that time, the pressing need for disk space trumped IT spending concerns. However, when the other shoe later fell, storage vendors joined the ranks of the sufferers. The total market for external controller-based disk storage was $3.8 billion in the first quarter of 2009, research firm Gartner reported, down 11.1 percent from $4.2 billion in the first quarter of 2008. (The Gartner report did not include software and services revenue.)

In June 2009, market researcher IDC reported that global factory revenues for disk storage systems dropped 18.2 percent in a year, despite the fact that the total capacity of shipped disk storage systems grew nearly 15 percent. The cost of disk capacity on a per-terabyte basis continued to drop, also bad for suppliers but good for businesses. By some accounts, the storage market had become so competitive, storage vendors were offering discounts of between 40 and 70 percent.

IDC further reported that the total amount of disk capacity shipped on disk array systems rose by an encouraging 15.2 percent in the second quarter, to 2,345 petabytes. Although well below prior growth rates for storage, it boded well for 2009. Global disk array revenues in the second quarter of 2009 fell by 18.7 percent, to $5.7 billion. Liz Conner, research analyst for storage systems at IDC, in a statement accompanying the figures, said "The enterprise storage systems market continued to feel the impact of current economic conditions, posting its third straight year-over-year decline."

However, there were sectors in the market that continued to thrive. According to Conner, iSCSI SAN and FC SAN both showed strong year-over-year growth of 57.2 and 66.8 percent, respectively, in the entry level price range (up to $14.99 thousand $14.99 thousand) as customers continued to demand enterprise level network storage at a more economically friendly price. Likewise, midrange NAS with a price range between $15 thousand and $49.99 thousand enjoyed solid year-over-year growth of 20.7 percent as file-level data generation continued to be the hot topic of the year.

In overall storage system sales (including external and internal arrays), IBM was slightly ahead of Hewlett-Packard (see below) in mid-2009. Even so, IBM fell 12.6 percent in the second quarter, while HP, which sold internal arrays, fell by 28.4 percent in sympathy with server sales, which had declined by 30.4 percent in the second quarter. EMC ranked third in global storage sales, with a decline of 19.5 percent compared to the same period in 2008.

On the upside in mid-2009, said IDC, data protection and recover software sales for disk arrays saw 3 percent sequentially, with IBM, EMC (the leader), and Symantec all moving into positive territory on a sequential basis. NetApp ranked fourth in global storage software sales at that time.

INDUSTRY LEADERS

Near the end of 2009, Brocade and Cisco were the market leaders in the $2.4 billion storage networking market, according to market analyst Sramana Mitra. Brocade held a 71 percent share of storage networking market in 2008. It reported $1.9 billion in 2009 revenues, with data storage accounting for 58 percent of its total revenues, down from 84 percent in 2008. During Cisco's 2009 fiscal year, revenue decreased 8.7 percent to $36.1 billion, of which Cisco realized $13.50 billion in network services.

Several of the industry's biggest players were large, integrated computer manufacturers that often sold storage products as part of large new computer systems, such as mainframes or midrange servers, or as add-ons for customers who already own systems by the manufacturer. Hewlett-Packard was a top leader in the world disk and tape storage hardware market, followed closely by IBM. The next top three companies were EMC, Dell, and Hitachi.

A diverse mix of small, focused companies also produce storage networking products and services. One of the biggest of the independent manufacturers is also ranked number three in the world: EMC Corp. of Hopkinton, Massachusetts. Building SAN equipment was a natural extension for EMC, which had long made storage hardware for SAN-like configurations for mainframe systems. EMC sells its high-end equipment directly as well as through resellers and larger computer system manufacturers. Storage hardware accounted for 85 percent of EMC's revenues. Sales of two of its leading storage networking products, Connectrix (for SANs) and Celerra (for NAS), surged more than 40 percent. The company also markets storage software and services. To further solidify its place in the mid-range market, in 1999 EMC acquired Data General Corp., maker of the CLARiiON line of storage products. The following year, the company purchased SOFTWORKS, a maker of data storage software.

Network Appliance Corp., based in Sunnyvale, California, is a smaller producer of higher end storage networking devices. In the first decade of the 2000s, storage solutions for e-commerce activities made up a third of NetApp's sales. Most of NetApp's products are NAS servers. The company's NetCache Web-caching appliances deliver content more quickly by storing information physically closer to users. Customers included Boeing and Yahoo.

RESEARCH AND TECHNOLOGY

The emergence of intelligent fabrics, file systems, storage arrays and application-aware management software all point to the advent of what some refer to as programmable storage. While Fibre Channel (FC) had established itself as the technology of choice, where speed and low latency were important, Internet Protocol (IP) storage, especially around Internet Small Computer System Interface (ISCSI), holds great promise to deliver the benefits and features of a storage area network, but at a lower cost. Accordingly, the question facing researchers and technologists is whether there will continue to be a coexistence of technologies between ISCSI and FC. As of the middle of the first decade of the 2000s, there appeared to be distinct markets for both.

The Storage Networking Industry Association (SNIA) and the International Committee for Information Technology Standards (INCITS) announced in late 2004 that the Storage Management Initiative Specification (SMI-S) had been approved as the new INCITS standard. The new standard was designated as ASNI INCITS 388-2004, *American National Standard for Information Technology Storage Management.* The original standard focused on SANs, but was to be extended to include NAS, ISCSI, and other storage networking technologies. For the first time in the industry, products can be purchased that were built using a tested and standardized management interface.

BIBLIOGRAPHY

"Big Players Again Top World Storage Disk Markets." *eWeek,* 7 June 2007.

Brandon, John. "The Future of Storage." *PC Magazine,* 24 April 2007.

Brodkin, Jon. "Storage Vendors Take Lumps in Recession, But See Signs of Hope." *Network World,* 24 July 2009.

Connor, Deni. "From Punch Cards to iPods: A Short History of Data Storage." *Network World,* 14 June 2007.

———. "Storage User Groups Merge." *Network World,* 24 April 2007.

"Could FCoE Be The Next Industry Standard?" *TelecomWeb News Digest,* 17 April 2007.

"Crash Course: ISCSI." *SearchStorage,* 30 July 2004. Available from http://searchstorage.techtarget.com/.

"Deals." *CableFAX,* 4 March 2003.

"EMC CLARiiON Named 'Most Valuable Product's' *Business Wire,* 13 May 2003.

Fonseca, Brian. "IDC Lists Top 10 Storage Predictions for 2007." *Computer World,* 4 June 2007.

"General Motors CTO to Keynote Storage Networking World Fall 2003." *Business Wire,* 29 May 2003.

Goldstein, Howard A. "Storage Networking: Perspectives on Terminology and Meaning." 20 February 2003. Available from www.webtorials.com/.

Hill, Steven. "Storage & Servers—Virtual Servers, Quad-Core Systems: Coming Soon to a Data Center Near You." *Network Computing,* 21 December 2006.

"Hoover's Company Capsules." *Hoover's Online,* 2007. Available from www.hoovers.com.

"Incipient Launches with Broad Industry Support." *Business Wire,* 31 March 2003.

IT Facts. 1 June 2007. Available from www.itfacts.biz.

Johnson, Russ. "The Irrelevance of ISCSI Vs. FC in 2005." *SNIA Europe,* December 2004. Available from www.snseurope.com/.

King, Elliot. "Storage Hardware Market Flattens While Software Soars." *Enterprise Storage,* InstantDoc #45762, March 2005. Available from www.windowsitpro.com/.

Marks, Howard. "The Latest Standard We Don't Need." *Network Computing,* 28 May 2007.

Mitra, Sramana. "Changing Networking Sector Dynamics." 23 December 2009. Available from http://www.topix.com/com/ffiv/2009/12/changing-networking-sector-dynamics.

Morgan, Timothy Prickett. "Storage Hardware Crawls Out From Under Melted Economy." *Storage,* 9 September 2009.

Poelker, Christopher. "SAN Predictions for 2005: The Year of Programmable Storage." *SearchStorage,* 21 December 2004. Available from http://searchstorage.techtarget.com/.

Roos, Gina. "Deals Target Storage Networking." *Electronic Engineering Times,* 7 April 2003.

"SNIA IP Storage Forum Interview with David Dale." *SNIA Europe,* December 2004. Available from www.snseurope.com/.

"The SNIA Advances Storage Management Initiative with Delivery of Education Programs." *Business Wire,* 7 April 2003.

"The SNIA and INCITS Announce Approval of a New American National Standard for Storage Management." SNIA press release, 26 October 2004. Available from www.snia.org/.

"The SNIA Storage Management Initiative Unveils Storage Standard." *Business Wire,* 15 April 2003.

"The Storage Networking Conundrum." *eWeek,* 16 June 2003.

Storage Networking Industry Association. *New Technologies and Services for Responsible Data Storage.* 1 June 2007. Available from www.snia.org.

"When Life-or-Death Depends on the Storage Network." *Business Wire,* 14 April 2003.

Winterford, Brett. "Global Storage Revenues Sink." *IT News,* 5 June 2009. Available from http://www.itnews.com.au/News/146984,global-storage-revenues-sink.aspx.

SUPER DRUGS

SIC CODE(S)

2833

2834

2836

INDUSTRY SNAPSHOT

One of the most significant problems facing the health care and scientific communities is the continuous challenge of diseases becoming resistant to the drugs designed to cure them, especially for serious gram-positive infections. In developing countries, malaria and tuberculosis continue to devastate populations as they became resistant to current drugs. HIV/AIDS continued its rampage, particularly in Africa, and other major infectious diseases, including cholera, *e.coli,* and malaria, ravaged poorer nations where the conditions and infrastructure to stem the tide were not in place. Moreover, in a rapidly globalized world, industrialized countries can no longer rest easy in the knowledge that such diseases will remain confined to the world's most downtrodden. For example, a drug-resistant staphylococcus called MRSA (methicillin-resistant Staphylococcus aureus) began to spread in epidemic quantities. Although most people affected were hospitalized patients with weak immune systems, the disease, which is transferred through skin contact, had spread to public places as well, including schools. Even though a majority of the infections are minor, according to *CNN Money,* thousands of Americans have died from MRSA.

Another drug-resistant pandemic, known as Avian influenza ("bird flu"), an infectious disease affecting birds globally, is caused by many different viruses, or strains, including the H5N1 strain, which can be highly pathogenic, causing severe disease in birds. That is of concern to human health because it can also infect humans who are in close contact with infected birds. When a new influenza virus subtype emerges, infects humans, and spreads successfully among people, a pandemic can start. According to *Interpress Service,* the avian flu virus has continued to mutate. Takeshi Kasai of WHO stated, "The risk that avian influenza could cause the next pandemic remains the same. It has not changed at all since 2003."

Fears of a global avian flu pandemic and bioterrorist attacks in the near future also fueled an increased focus on drug manufacturing. While usually focusing on clinical and preclinical research, new drug development also involves improving manufacturing capabilities and overcoming production challenges. The previous year's problem of vaccine shortages led to policy changes, an increase in funding for new programs, and reduced regulatory and legal obstacles hindering new drug development. The National Institutes of Health (NIH) began supporting research into production methods for new vaccines, and the FDA began developing policies to hasten new vaccine approval while still ensuring that manufacturing facilities meet quality standards. Normally, in the production of seasonal flu vaccines, it takes six to eight months to identify prevalent flu strains, to develop effective vaccines, and to produce millions of doses. However, policymakers realized that it is becoming necessary to expand the manufacturing infrastructure to lay a foundation for responding quickly to the challenge of vaccine production in case of a national or global pandemic or a bioterrorism attack.

There was increasing evidence that humanity was entering into a new phase of interaction with infectious diseases. At least 30 new infectious diseases were discovered between 1970 and 2003, representing a rate of disease development unknown to humans since pre-historical times, according to Dr. Paul Epstein of the Center for Health and the Global Environment at Harvard Medical School. However, while research and development of medicines to combat infectious diseases was on the rise, efforts were widely viewed as incommensurate with the seriousness of the problem.

Ultimately, some experts have predicted the end of antibiotics, as research leans more toward nanotechnology and genetic manipulation to combat super organisms. While the pharmaceutical industry and its lobbyists strongly resisted this trend, several have incorporated pharmacogenomics (DNA-based personal medicine) (*see also*) into their drug development programs. In addition, surprisingly, the decrease in incidence of MRSA infections by 2010 was not attributed to the development of a new super antibiotic drug, but rather, a return to basic infection control, such as hand-washing by medical staff.

ORGANIZATION AND STRUCTURE

While part of the long-established pharmaceutical industry, "super drug" development is emerging in its own right. Although tremendous demand exists for these products, few had reached the market by the middle years of the twenty-first century's first decade. Most smaller companies had not yet turned a profit, existing on venture capital, government grants, and research and development (R & D).

The industry can be divided into two broad sectors. One consists of traditional pharmaceutical companies, large multinationals that have been manufacturing antibiotics since the 1950s. They possess "libraries" of hundreds of thousands of chemical compounds. Most of these compounds have been developed and tested, but have not been used in commercial pharmaceuticals or prototypes. They consist of chemical variants of commercial pharmaceutical ingredients or compounds that exhibit interesting or useful characteristics previously unexploited in medicines. Such compounds can be derived from animal or botanical (plant) sources, or,

increasingly, they may be designed at the molecular level to possess particular pharmaceutical properties. New technologies in drug design have increased tremendously the pace at which compounds are being added to these libraries. (See also **Molecular Design.**)

Traditionally, in new drug trials, compounds are tested on a pathological organism or condition on a mass-production scale until one compound exhibits a promising or desired result. It is then refined into a medication for human use. When bacteria that were resistant to a particular antibiotic emerged, the traditional response was to find another agent that would defuse the resistance and "piggyback" it onto the antibiotic, enabling it to function again. Since nearly all bacteria develop resistance to such combinations, drug research is moving away from simple modification toward such techniques as gene technology and automated drug screening to develop novel agents that bacteria have never encountered. Smaller high tech start-up companies, which began appearing in the 1980s and 1990s, use techniques such as genetic engineering to locate weak points in a pathogen's DNA. The techniques are usually based on the companies' own proprietary technologies, which they develop themselves or license from a university.

Small companies frequently form research partnerships with pharmaceutical firms. The small firms bring unique technology to the partnership and the larger companies bring their chemical library and company infrastructure. Pharmaceutical products resulting from such research are licensed exclusively to the larger partner, with the smaller receiving a licensing fee and royalty payments.

Regulation Super drugs must acquire FDA approval, sanctioning their safety and effectiveness for human use, before being sold in the United States. They thus undergo preclinical tests followed by three clinical trials on healthy and ill human subjects. The entire process can last 15 years. The FDA, however, has sought to reduce the length of time for final approval. A user fee program, refined under the Food and Drug Modernization Act of 1997, allows the FDA to hire more reviewers to speed up approvals. In 1998, 30 drugs received fast-track approval in an average of 11.7 months compared with a 30-month average per drug before user fees.

Two fast-track programs help facilitate patient access to experimental drugs. The expedited development and review program applies to drugs designed for patients with life-threatening diseases. The accelerated approval program is intended for new drugs that provide to patients therapeutic benefits which existing treatments lack. This program is generally limited to drugs for patients who are unresponsive to or intolerant of other available therapies.

BACKGROUND AND DEVELOPMENT

Attempts at vaccination are not new. Centuries ago, the Chinese vaccinated against smallpox by blowing material from pox scabs through a blowpipe into the noses of uninfected people. In Turkey, smallpox "parties" were held at which guests were given small doses of smallpox through their skin. This procedure was noticed by the wife of the British ambassador to Turkey, who introduced the method to England in 1721 during an outbreak of the disease. Some West Africans also used this method. When the 1721 outbreak was transferred to Boston, a slave from the Ivory Coast demonstrated the method to his master, the famous preacher Cotton Mather. Benjamin Franklin broadcast the technique in his newspaper. Edward Jenner, a British doctor, refined the technique in 1798, adapting its use to the less lethal cowpox. Taking inoculation material from lesions on the hand of a dairymaid, Jenner called his prophylactic measure vaccination, from the Latin word for cow (*vacca*).

Louis Pasteur (1822–1895) established the science of bacteriology. He also discovered fermentation and pasteurization, and demonstrated the benefits of vaccinating sheep against anthrax by using a heat-attenuated (weakened) strain of the disease. Robert Koch (1843–1910) discovered how to sterilize with dry heat and first isolated the agents of tuberculosis, anthrax, and cholera.

By accident, Alexander Fleming discovered penicillin in 1928 when he observed that *Penicillium notatum* inhibited growth of *Staphylococcus aureus*. By the 1950s, penicillin was recognized as a miracle drug. It was soon joined by other antibiotics, including the cephalosporins, tetracycline, streptomycin, erythromycin, and sulfa drugs.

By the 1970s, experts announced with satisfaction that epidemics such as smallpox and tuberculosis were on the way out due to the wonder drugs, including penicillin and tetracycline. Pharmaceutical manufacturers curtailed their R & D efforts, confident that existing remedies were adequate and fearful that the market was already saturated. This optimism proved premature, however. The discovery of acquired immunodeficiency syndrome (AIDS) in the early 1980s revealed all too clearly that pandemic infectious diseases had hardly been eradicated. Centuries-old killers such as tuberculosis (TB) and malaria also continued to kill many people, especially in the developing world. The World Health Organization (WHO) forecast in 1999 that one billion people would become infected with TB between 2000 and 2020. Even in the United States, it is estimated that 10 to 15 million people will be infected with latent TB; and at least 17,000 active cases were reported in 1999, according to the Centers for Disease Control and Prevention.

Increasing globalization seemed poised to spawn a new heyday for infectious disease. With more air travel each year, many microbes find a free ride to geographic areas far removed from their home turf. The sweeping internationalization of trade provided a means of transport as well. In 1991, a Chinese vessel emptied cholera-laced bilge water into a Chilean harbor, infecting local fish. A few weeks later, cholera appeared in Latin America where it had been unknown for a century. Within a year, the disease had spread to 11 adjacent countries. Population displacements from urbanization, deforestation, and warfare have exacerbated this dilemma. By the end of the 1990s, roughly 1 percent of the world's people were refugees of war, with infectious disease a common companion in refugee camps.

The antibiotic drug of last resort during the late 1990s was vancomycin. More than 95 percent of hospital-acquired *S. aureus* (*Staphylococcus aureus*) infections are resistant to penicillin or ampicillin. Vancomycin became the only effective drug for these cases. However, as early as 1989, hospitals began reporting rapid increases of vancomycin resistance in enterococci (intestinal bacteria) infections and realized that increased vancomycin-resistant enterococci (VRE) can lead to cross-resistance in *S. aureus infections*. Public health officials fear that humans could be rapidly approaching a window of vulnerability in which the existing antibiotics are no longer effective and not enough new ones have yet been developed to take their place.

The turn of the millennium thus refocused attention on the threat of infectious diseases and the need for a steady stream of new antimicrobial agents to attack them. Initiatives announced by the U.S. government and the World Health Organization (WHO), a large philanthropic donation from the Bill and Melinda Gates Foundation, and growing collaborations between old-line major pharmaceutical companies and younger biotech firms opened pathways for the development of new super drugs.

Evolving Causes, Increasing Threats In March 2003, the National Academy of Sciences, funded by the U.S. government, released its report, "Microbial Threats to Health: Emergence, Detection and Response," which assessed the emerging threat to humans from infectious diseases. The report noted that the prevalence and severity of such infections would likely increase in the twenty-first century as a result of the continued growth of large cities and international travel and commerce, exacerbated by deepening global poverty, ecological degradation, political strife causing refugee problems and destroyed social infrastructures, and famine.

Economic development and evolving world social patterns also contributed to the strengthening of infectious diseases. In June 2003, Dr. Paul Epstein of the Center for Health and the Global Environment at

Harvard Medical School testified before the U.S. Congress that global warming was creating conditions in which infectious diseases could more easily cluster, leading to severe outbreaks with the potential to spread across wide geographical areas. According to Dr. Epstein, the West Nile Virus that plagued the United States in the 1990s and the first decade of the twenty-first century was a classic, and foreboding, example of the ways in which ecological instability could create conditions favorable to the spread of infectious diseases. Rising temperatures and extreme weather conditions yielded a deepening cycle of floods and droughts, allowing the West Nile Virus to breed comfortably and rapidly, leading to a massive escalation in infections.

Other symptoms of economic globalization, such as the agricultural tendency toward large factory farms, also act as primary breeding grounds for the spread of disease, and, like the over-prescription of super drugs among humans, the excessive use of antibiotics and other disease-controlling chemicals on these farms has the long-term effect of producing stronger, more resistant strains of animal-borne diseases. Meanwhile, according to reports by leading health organizations, including the World Health Organization and the Centers for Disease Control and Prevention (CDC), humans are more vulnerable than ever to animal-borne infectious diseases. Whether contracting such diseases via direct contact, such as through the bite of a mosquito carrying an infectious disease from another animal, or via secondary contact, such as ingestion of contaminated food, humans were at increasing risk from other animals. The World Health Organization (WHO) reported that at least two-thirds of the more than 30 major diseases that arose since 1970 originated with animals.

The growing threat and awareness even elevated infectious diseases to the level of national security and foreign policy concerns. Bioterrorism moved to the fore-front of public health concerns in the early years of the first decade of the 2000s as well. After the September 11, 2001, terrorist attacks and the subsequent domestic anthrax scare, public health officials placed a renewed emphasis on infrastructure and medicine to counter a potential bioterrorist attack. In that vein, the federal government's National Institute of Allergy and Infectious Diseases awarded a $71.3 million contract to biotechnology firm Avecia to stockpile doses of its recombinant (genetically engineered) anthrax vaccine. Developed in cooperation with the Defence Science and Technology Laboratory in the United Kingdom, the vaccine was slated to induce immunity from inhalation of anthrax.

According to World Health Organization (WHO) reports on global infectious disease, about 300 million to 500 million cases of malaria occur each year, claiming about 1 million lives. Another 1.5 million succumb to tuberculosis. The number of worldwide HIV/AIDS infections topped 40 million. These trends were particularly pronounced in developing regions such as Africa and Southeast Asia. The WHO and UNICEF reported that about 1 million Africans die from malaria each year, over 90 percent of them children under five years of age, making it the second-leading infectious disease threat in Africa after HIV. Hepatitis C, generally acquired through blood transfusions or drug injections, has infected over 4 million Americans. First identified only in 1988, the onset of illness sometimes appears years after the original infection, and a widespread outbreak is feared between 2000 and 2020.

Cancer claims some 13 percent the world's total deaths each year, making it the third-leading killer after coronary and infectious diseases as a whole. With a huge market in both industrialized and developing countries, pharmaceutical and biotechnology firms poured significant R & D funding into devising anticancer super drugs. Most such drugs in the early years and middle of the first decade of the twenty-first century were cytoxics, built on molecules that were toxic to living cells. Although programmed to attack cancer, these drugs were still non-discriminatory, in that they also attack healthy cells.

The Over-Prescription Problem Nonetheless, coincident with these burgeoning fears came what many analysts saw as overcompensation among many health care providers and pharmaceutical companies. Ironically, success in the development of powerful antibiotics contributed directly to the rise of bacterial resistance to powerful medications, effectively creating stronger, more lethal diseases. The longer bacteria are exposed to a drug, the faster resistant strains are able to become dominant. Furthermore, bacteria can exchange genetic material via little packets of DNA called plasmids and thus pass resistance to as yet nonresistant strains. The over-prescription of super drugs and antibiotics thus emerged as a paramount concern among those monitoring the spread and development of infectious diseases.

Doctors and patients both contribute to the problem. Doctors may prescribe antibiotics when they are not indicated; for example, as treatment for the common cold, an illness caused by viruses, which do not respond to antibiotics. In addition, patients often stop taking antibiotics as soon as they start feeling better instead of continuing the full regimen prescribed. This gives resistant bacteria an opportunity to survive, multiply, and become dominant.

Pharmaceutical companies responded to drug resistance by fighting the problem one-on-one: if a bacterium developed an enzyme to digest an antibiotic, researchers combined two drugs, the original antibiotic and another, to short-circuit the enzyme. However, bacteria can develop resistance more quickly than scientists can react. This is particularly true in regard to patients with compromised immune systems.

The Industry Faces the Challenge Although developing nations bear the brunt of infectious diseases, the aging U.S. population and the spread of drug-resistant strains of staphylococcus, pneumonia, ande. coli indicate a need for new antimicrobial drugs. The Tufts Center for Drug Development estimated the average cost for developing a new medicine in 2000 was $802 million. Adjusted for inflation, that is 2.5 times more than research and development cost per approved new drug from previous studies. Future investment seems headed in the direction of pharmacogenomics to identify the sequences of disease-causing microbes for both antibiotic, antiviral and vaccine development. (See also **Pharmacogenomics**.) A high volume of patents expired at the end of 2004, and the field became significantly more competitive.

In 2003, according to industry researchers at Biopharm Insights, some 8.9 percent of the 497 biotechnology drugs in Phase 1 development were designed to combat HIV infection, with another 8 percent geared toward the battle against other infectious diseases. Fully 37 percent of Phase 1 drugs were for cancer. The ratio of approved drugs to investigative candidates, however, was particularly low, especially because the biotechnology sector was relatively new. Only 0.1 percent of cancer drugs in this sector received FDA approval. For HIV, 0.4 percent received such approval, and 0.2 percent of drugs for other infectious diseases made it that far.

In the pharmaceutical sector, among 320 companies, cancer accounted for 22.8 percent of the 580 drugs in the first phase of development, while HIV drugs totaled 13.6 percent, and other infectious diseases represented 11 percent of drug development. The approval percentage for drugs in the pharmaceutical sector showed a greater record of success. Fully 21.8 percent of drugs for infectious diseases received the FDA's seal of approval. For cancer, the figure stood at 4.6 percent and for HIV infections, 2 percent.

Other Developments The July 2004 Congress-approved Project BioShield legislation provides funding for government purchase of vaccines and medicines for national stockpiles and supports research and development funding for biopharmaceutical companies that are developing new treatments. The legislation also permits the FDA to authorize emergency use of unapproved new products and allows the agency to approve countermeasures based on animal testing.

One of the biggest concerns in the middle of the 2000's first decade was the fear that the avian flu virus could mutate and spread to humans, possibly killing millions worldwide. This threat, added to the possibility of bioterrorist attacks, caused Congress to consider new "Bio-Shield II" legislation to stimulate the development of countermeasures to biological threats and infectious diseases, knowing how such crises would strain the resources of national health care systems. In a further effort to prepare for a potential global influenza crisis in the near future, The Department of Health and Human Services (HHS) put into effect its Pandemic Influenza Preparedness and Response Plan in the fall of 2005. The plan was prepared to assist those responsible for public health and medical and emergency preparedness to respond to threats and occurrences of pandemic influenza.

At the forefront of medications aimed at treating patients ill with influenza are the antivirals Tamiflu (oseltamivir phosphate) and Relenza (zanamivir), approved by the FDA and recommended for stockpiling by the World Health Organization. Neither are vaccines, nor should they be used as substitutes for an annual influenza vaccine. They are medicines that attack the influenza virus and stop it from spreading inside the body. The drugs are indicated for the treatment of acute influenza in patients one year old and older (Tamiflu) or seven years old and older (Relenza) who have been symptomatic for no more than two days. Production of Tamiflu involves a complex process taking eight to twelve months from raw material to finished product, according to Dominick Iacuzio, the medical director of Roche Pharmaceuticals, the drug's manufacturer, based in Nutley, New Jersey.

In 2004, Roche doubled its production of Tamiflu at its European facility and planned to continue to increase production in 2006. Roche asked the U.S. Department of Health and Human Services (HHS) to increase its Tamiflu order to provide more than the 1 percent population coverage, 2.3 million courses, it had stockpiled in the fall of 2005. Other countries had purchased enough of the drug to treat 40 percent of their populations. On March 16, 2006, a *USA Today* article reported that Roche had delivered about 5 million treatment courses (two capsules a day for 10 days) to HHS and that 12.4 million more were ordered for delivery by the end of 2006. Roche CEO William Burns also revealed that its annual production capacity by the end of 2006 would be 400 million treatments, well in excess of all government orders to date, achieved by expansion of Roche facilities in the U.S. and Europe and partnerships with 15 other companies that will make some of the materials needed to produce Tamiflu, but warned that a shortage of orders from governments could force Roche to reduce future production. In 2008

Roche offered U.S. businesses a plan to reserve their own stockpile the drug in case of a pandemic.

Another area of manufacture pursued in the first decade of the 2000s was the development of cell-based vaccine production. This method would eliminate the need to use eggs, which is the basis for most traditional vaccine production in the United States and Europe. The HHS provided grants to Sanofi-Pasteur, based in Lyon, France, to test cellular and recombinant vaccine production methods, as well as to provide a year-round supply of eggs, in order to also produce vaccines in the traditional manner. Sanofi produced batches of the new vaccine to be tested in clinical trials and obtained a contract to produce 2 million doses of the vaccine.

A success story in the war on killer bugs is the development of Cubicin by Cubist Pharmaceuticals of Lexington, Massachusetts. Cubicin targets Staphylococcus aureus, or S. aureus, a bacterium that ranks high on the infectious disease "hit list." S. aureus is the second most common bacteria found in hospitalized patients whose blood becomes infected with bacteria. Annually, hospitals spend $9.7 billion treating the results of S. aureus infections. To prove the effectiveness of their new drug, Cubist Pharmaceuticals tested the drug against the S. aureus bacterium while it was actively in patients' bloodstreams. To conduct the study, Cubist screened 5,000 patients in 76 potential sites in six countries. The resulting study cost Cubist $100,000 per patient for the 246 patients enrolled in the trial internationally. By taking such a bold step, Cubist took nearly a four-year lead over its rivals, and obtained the FDA's first-ever approval of a drug to treat S. aureus bacteria in the bloodstream, which can lead to infective endocarditis, a disease that targets and inflames the heart.

In March of 2006, the Infectious Diseases Society of America (IDSA) published a list of six life-threatening, drug-resistant infections for which doctors have an insufficient supply of medicine. These diseases continue to become more drug-resistant, while development of new drugs is sluggish. It is not as profitable for a pharmaceutical company to develop new antibiotics as it is to provide treatments for chronic illnesses. Methicillin-resistant Staphylococcus aureus (MRSA) causes infections in hospitals and has started showing up in a more virulent form after being acquired outside of a hospital. Escherichia coli and Klebsiella cause often-fatal urinary and intestinal tract infections. Acinetobacter baumannii is a growing cause of hospital-acquired pneumonia with death rates of 20 to 50 percent. It also causes highly resistant wound infections in U.S. soldiers in Iraq and Afghanistan. Aspergillus is a fungus that has nearly a 60 percent mortality rate. Vancomycin-resistant enterococcus faecium (VRE) is a major cause of bloodstream infections, meningitis, and abdominal infections. Pseudomonas aeruginosa causes severe pneumonia and urinary tract infections, especially among cancer patients and people with compromised immune systems.

Infectious diseases remained a serious problem worldwide as the first decade of the 2000s neared a close. According to a 2008 *Genetic Engineering & Biotechnology News* article, bacterial infections contracted while patients are in a hospital are a leading cause of death in the United States, and it costs between $16,000 and $100,000 per patient to treat the infection. However, only about a dozen new antibiotics have been FDA approved since 1998, which is half of the number produced in the previous decade. The complexity and cost of producing such drugs are barriers; another factor may be a hesitation on the part of the FDA to approve new antibiotics after Ketek, an antibiotic to treat sinusitis and lung infections, caused unexpected side effects and resulted in three deaths from liver damage. Jeff Alder of Bayer Healthcare commented that many drug companies are focusing on creating drugs for such lifestyle conditions as male baldness and obesity rather than formulas that would cure or prevent diseases. He also said, "The problem is that we don't have a lot in our bag of tricks to counter this [drug-resistant infections], and it is imperative that we start developing new drugs now. The alternative is that we won't be able to fight back the rising tide of bacterial resistance."

In 2008, for the first time in 20 years, the Centers for Disease Control and Prevention and WHO recommended a complete reformulation of the influenza vaccine, after the three most common strains of the flu showed resistance to the Tamiflu and Relenza vaccines. The same year, the Food and Drug Administration recommended that warnings be added to the labels of these drugs regarding possibly psychiatric side effects, especially in children. Cases had been reported of children jumping from buildings and running into traffic, resulting in death, as well as other abnormal behavior, after taking Tamiflu, and officials in Japan warned physicians not to prescribe Tamiflu or Relenza to patients between the ages of 10 and 19.

One of the biggest breakthroughs in the industry was the creation of a vaccine against cervical cancer and other diseases caused by human papillomavirus (HPV), created by Merck & Company and granted FDA approval in 2006. Gardasil is given in three doses and is approved for use in women and girls ages nine and older. According to the FDA, cervical cancer is the second most common cancer in U.S. women and kills almost 4,000 women a year. The first usage study, conducted in 2008 by the Centers for Disease Prevention and Control, showed that about 25 percent of girls ages 13 to 17 had received the vaccine so far. Although some maintain that this is a good percentage for such a new drug, others hoped for it to be higher. Merck spent about $100 million advertising the drug in 2007 and received a return in sales of $1.5 billion.

CURRENT CONDITIONS

In the summer of 2010, the *Lancet* Journal of Infectious Diseases reported the spread of a new drug-resistant superbug coming from south Asia (India, Pakistan) that was "potentially a major global health problem." While some news agencies around the world reported "panic" over the possible consequences, Sarah Boseley, editor and columnist for the British newspaper the *Guardian,* said, "The era of antibiotics is coming to a close. In just a couple of generations, what once appeared to be miracle medicines have been beaten into ineffectiveness by the bacteria they were designed to knock out. Once, scientists hailed the end of infectious diseases. Now, the post-antibiotic apocalypse is within sight."

Meanwhile, in 2010, research and advisory firm Decision Resources reported that the MRSA drug market would increase from $631 million in 2009 to $752 million in 2019 in the United States, France, Germany, Italy, Spain, United Kingdom, and Japan. Two new therapeutic agents, ceftaroline and torezolid, were expected to capture one-third of the overall MRSA market by 2019. Most of the new MRSA therapies involved broad-spectrum agents, designed to treat new strains of the basic organism, as opposed to narrow-spectrum agents that had been the main approach. In 2010, the CDC announced a 16 percent drop in new cases of MRSA in nine metro areas from 2005 to 2008. This statistic followed a similar one in 2009 in which the CDc reported a drop in MRSA infections in hospital/medical facilities' intensive care units (ICU).

Still, the onslaught of new drug-resistant organisms marched on. In March 2010, the Duke Infection Control Outreach Network reported yet another new superbug on the rise, surpassing MRSA infection rates in community hospitals. Mainly causing gastro-intestinal problems, *C. difficile,* the multi-drug resistant bacterium, could cause life-threatening inflammation of the colon.

A 2010 survey of Chicago-area healthcare facilities revealed that from 2009 to 2010, there was a 30 percent increase in the spread of KPC, a type of antibiotic resistant organism originating from a common bacterium that had evolved into a superbug. At least 75 percent of those testing positive for KPC had been patients in a long-term care facility, such as a nursing home.

One of the causative factors for the development of drug-resistant organisms, but one which gets less publicity, has been the rampant use of antibiotics fed to cattle, sheep, pigs, chickens, and other feedstock animals factory-farmed for human consumption. According to the Union of Concerned Scientists, by 2010, some 70 percent of American antibiotics, twice as many as used on all the sick Americans across the country, were used in animal feed. The animals were not sick. Instead, the antibiotics, in smaller doses than would be given to sick animals, were added to their food to make them gain weight faster. Although the European Union banned routine use of antibiotics in animal feed several years prior, the practice has continued in the United States. In fact, FDA Commissioner Dr. Margaret Hamburg, in an October 2010 speech at the National Press Club, responded to a direct question about such use of antibiotics. She replied, "We are in the midst of very serious scrutiny of these issues and we have made recommendations in support of judicious use of antibiotics. Nobody wants to deny antibiotics to animals that need medical treatment. But the use in certain preventive contexts, where it is not clearly medically indicated, is of growing concern."

INDUSTRY LEADERS

London-based GlaxoSmithKline boasted such high-selling drugs as Advair, Amoxil, Augmentin, Valtrex, and Relenza. The firm derived about 11 percent of its revenues from antivirals, 10 percent from antibacterials, and another 5 percent from vaccines. The firm, formed from the high-profile merger in 2000 between Great Britain's Glaxo Wellcome and SmithKline Beecham, became the world's largest pharmaceutical company. Sales in 2009 topped GBP $28.4 billion, of which GBP $4.2 billion was from anti-virals and GBP $3.7 billion was from vaccines. The firm employed about 100,000 people.

To combat GlaxoSmithKline's market share, Pfizer and Pharmacia combined operations in 2003, leapfrogging to the top spot among pharmaceutical manufacturers. The two companies were themselves built from major mergers. Pfizer Inc. and Warner-Lambert joined forces in 1999, while Monsanto Co. and Pharmacia & Upjohn, Inc., combined operations the following year. While moving ahead as one company, New York-based Pfizer Inc., offered such top sellers as Lipitor, Celebrex, and Zoloft. In 2005, the FDA approved Zmax for treating sinus infections and pneumonia. Pfizer's revenues for 2009 reached $50 billion with 86,600 employees.

Other prominent players include Bristol-Myers Squibb Company, with global sales in 2009 of $18.8 billion and 42,000 employees. It funded the only comprehensive global study of bacterial resistance, based at the University of Iowa, and provided more than $600 million in free medicines to more than 800,000 people in the United States through donations to the Bristol-Myers Squibb Patient Assistance Foundation, Inc. The firm was particularly strong in the cancer drug market, for which it offered its top-selling Taxol, and the heart disease market, for which it sold Plavix, Pravachol, and Avapro. The firm purchased DuPont's pharmaceutical operations, acquiring its Sustiva drug that was a hallmark of AIDS therapy medications.

Merck & Company was the largest U.S. drug manufacturer in 2008. Besides such popular brands and top sellers as Excedrin, Cozaar, and Vytorin, Merck manufactured vaccines for mumps, measles, hepatitis, and shingles. In 2006 Merck was awarded FDA approval for the cervical cancer vaccine Gardasil. Merck's experimental AIDS vaccine, though several years from general use in the field, did not prevent infection outright but rather kept the virus in check by stimulating the immune system to attack the cells infected with HIV. Sales for Merck in 2007 were $27.4 billion with 59,800 employees.

Among biotech firms, Cubist Pharmaceuticals of Lexington, Massachusetts, identified as drug targets 20 enzymes bacteria used to bind amino acids into protein. Cubist has collaborative agreements with Bristol-Myers Squibb, Merck, Novartis, and Pfizer to develop anti-infective drugs in its target-based Synthetase Program. Its leading drug, Cubicin, has FDA approval for treatment of intravenous staph infections of the skin and blood.

Sangamo BioSciences, Inc., of Richmond, California, has collaborative agreements with numerous companies to use its Universal Gene Tools in their internal research and validation programs. Sangamo concentrates on research and development of transcription factors, proteins that turn genes on and off to regulate gene expression by recognizing specific DNA sequences. The firm's zinc finger DNA-binding proteins technology focuses on cancer, neurological disorders, infectious disease, and heart diseases. In 2008, its leading drug candidate SB-509 was in clinical trials for treatment of diabetic neuropathy.

Oscient Pharmaceuticals, formerly Genome Therapeutics of Waltham, Massachusetts, researches the genetic basis of disease and uses human and microbial data to develop drugs and diagnostics chiefly aimed at fighting drug-resistant bacterial and fungal infections. In 2004, Genome merged with Genesoft Pharmaceuticals and began selling the FDA-approved antibiotic FACTIVE, an antipneumonia and antibacterial bronchitis drug. Another of its drugs, ANTARA, is used to treat high cholesterol and triglycerides. Its two most important technologies are whole genome pathogen sequencing, which involves decoding and representing the genetic structure of a pathogen, and bio-informatics, which is the application of computers, software, and databases to the analysis of genomic research in order to compare sequences and identify a gene's function.

RESEARCH AND TECHNOLOGY

Late in 2010, researchers at the University of Strathclyde in Glasgow, Scotland, announced a pioneering lighting system designed to kill hospital superbugs (including MRSA) without the use of super drugs. The new technology decontaminated the air, exposing surfaces by bathing them in a narrow spectrum of visible light wavelengths known as HINS-light. the Light worked by exciting molecules contained within the bacteria, which, in turn, produced highly reactive chemical species that were lethal to bacteria, including MRSA and *C. difficile*.

In September 2009, the European Committee for Medicinal Products for Human Use recommended approval of GSK's H1N1 vaccine, Pandemrix, one month after which GSK announced orders for 149 million additional doses from governments around the world. total orders were for 440 million, worth $3.5 billion to GSK. However, by January 2010, governments found themselves with more doses than needed to meet demand, and GSK sales ended up being only half of the original orders.

Several tests were underway to add edible vaccines to genetically modified crops. Cornell University announced that it had embedded an antihepatitis-B vaccine into genetically modified potatoes, for example. Mice produced measles antibodies when fed edible vaccines in tobacco and lettuce in a project at Alfred Hospital in Sydney, Australia. Researchers are exploring applications for edible animal vaccines as well. ProdiGene of College Station, Texas, ran trials of genetically modified corn laced with a vaccine that fights the gastroenteritis virus in swine. This is a promising development, since the European Union maintained a ban on the use of antibiotics in animal feed out of concern that the practice contributes to the development of drug-resistant microbes in both animals and humans.

Molecular mapping and design technologies further enable researchers to examine infectious microbes' inner structures to isolate weaknesses and thus design drugs targeting those vulnerable points. Research based on the sequencing of the human genome and the genomes of viral strains offer further opportunities for the development of high-powered drugs tailored to the genetic makeup of both patients and the infections that ail them.

The U.S. government awarded Elusys Therapeutics of Pine Brook, New Jersey, $32 million to continue development of Anthim, its anthrax antibody therapeutic. In April 2008, the firm announced results of a primate study that showed a 75 percent survival rate when the subjects were given the drug after being infected with anthrax spores. The drug has been granted fast-track status by the FDA and is being developed under the FDA Animal Rule—a regulatory process designed specifically for the development of medical countermeasures to bioterror threats—stating that marketing approval of Anthim can be granted based on value in relevant animal trials with an acceptable safety risk profile in humans.

Millenia Hope, Inc. of Montreal, Quebec, continued its research and development of treatments for malaria and HIV/AIDS. These two major diseases continue to be a worldwide challenge, as resistance to existing drugs increases. Its flagship drug, Malarex/MMH 18, formerly known as Aspidos, has had successful tests in the treatment and prevention of malaria, and the company is continuing with further tests in the pursuit of final approval for consumer usage. Millenia also pursued a patent for its inhibitors of HIV RNase H, none of which have ever advanced to clinical trials. A successful drug that targets HIV RNase H will play a significant role in treating HIV/AIDS patients who have become resistant to current treatments. The market for HIV drugs in the first decade of the 2000s was approximately $6 billion and was estimated to reach $10 billion by 2010. The first successful orally bioavailable drug targeting HIV RNase H could be expected to achieve revenues of $350 million to $500 million per year.

BIBLIOGRAPHY

Blue, Laura. "The End of Antibiotics?" *Time,* 16 August 2010.

"Ceftobiprole Effective Against Drug-Resistant Pathogens in Animals." *Lab Business Week,* 7 May 2006.

Chase, Marilyn. "Incentives for New Antibiotics Urged." *Wall Street Journal Eastern Edition,* 1 March 2006.

"Dangerous Staph Infection MRSA Drops in U.S. Hospitals." *USA Today,* 12 August 2010.

"Elusys' Anthim Dramatically Improves Survival of Animals Treated After Active Anthrax Infection." *PR Newswire,* 22 April 2008.

"Emergence of a New Antibiotic Resistance Mechanism in India, Pakistan, and the UK: a Molecular, Biological, and Epidemiological Study." *The Lancet Journal of Infectious Disease,* published online 11 August 2010.

"Entirely New Flu Vaccine Needed, Says WHO." *Biopharm International,* April 2008.

"GSK's H1N1 Pandemrix Vaccine Receives Positive Opinion from European Regulators." GSK Press Release. Available from http://www.gsk.com/media/PressReleases/2009/2009.

"Health: Bird Flu Pandemic Is Still Possible, WHO Warns." *Interpress Service,* 8 October 2008.

Henderson, Diedtra. "New Front Developing in War on Killer Bugs." *Boston Globe,* 27 March 2006.

"Killing Antibiotic-Resistant Staph Bacteria With Fluorescent Light." *Medical News Daily,* 21 October 2010. Available from http://www.medicalnewstoday.co/articles/205219/php.

Magill-Lewis, Jillene. "Wanted: Superdrugs for Superbugs." *Modern Medicine,* 20 August 2007. Available from http://drugtopics.modernmedicine.com.

McGiffert, Lisa. "Summary of State Laws on Hospital Acquired Infections." Consumers Union, 5 October 2009. Available from http://www.medicalnewstoday.co/articles/205219/php.

McKenna, Maryn. "News Break: FDA Head Promises Very Serious Scrutiny of Farm Antibiotics." *Wired,* 7 October 2010.

"Merck Announces Fourth Quarter and Fiscal Year 2009 Financial Results." Merck Press Release, March 2010. Available from http://phx.corporate-ir-net.

Nesmith, Jeff. "Drug-Resistant Fatal Diseases Aliarm Scientists. Group Also Sounds Alarm Over Development of New Antibiotics." *The Atlanta Journal-Constitution,* 2 March 2006.

"New Superbug Surpasses MRSA Infection Rates in Community Hospitals." *Science Daily,* 22 March 2010.

Payne, January W. "Health Buzz: HPV Vaccine's Cost-Effectiveness and Other Health News." *U.S. News & World Report,* 21 August 2008.

Pearson, Sue. " Superbugs vs. Superdrugs: Race Goes On." *Genetic Engineering & Biotechnology News,* 1 June 2008.

"Pharmacology Watch: FDA Warnings Dominate Pharmaceutical News." *Infectious Disease Alert,* 1 January 2008.

"Quarter of U.S. Girls Get Cervical-Cancer Vaccine." *The Seattle Times,* 10 October 2008.

R&D Spending by U.S. Biopharmaceutical Companies Reaches Record $58.8 Billion in 2007." PhRMA, 24 March 2008.

"Relenza Information." Food and Drug Administration, 7 April 2008. Available from http://www. fda.gov.

"Roche Facilitates Corporate Pandemic Stockpiling of Tamiflu." *Biopharm International,* August 2008.

Smith, Aaron. "A New Round of Dangerous Staph Infections Has Biotechs Scrambling for New Antibiotics that Could Lead the Market." CNN, 14 February 2008. Available from http://www.CNNMoney.com.

"Survey Shows Rise in New Antibiotic-resistant Bacteria in Chicago Area." *Medical News Daily,* 23 October 2010. Available from http://www.medicalnewstoday.co/articles/205606/php.

SUPPLEMENTAL INSURANCE PLANS

—■—

SIC CODE(S)

6321

6324

INDUSTRY SNAPSHOT

Supplemental insurance fills the gaps left by other insurance coverage, mainly within the general categories of accident, health, and life insurance. A large segment of the supplemental insurance market serves the needs of Medicare beneficiaries looking for coverage broader than that offered by the federal insurance program for Americans over the age of 65. Although these "Medigap" policies account for the largest segment of supplemental insurance plans, supplemental insurers also sell policies to help pay for other coverage that is either not available or not fully compensated under regular insurance plans. An individual's needs for supplemental insurance are usually dictated by a variety of personal considerations: overall health, special risks occasioned by frequent travel or hazardous employment conditions, or a family history of such dread diseases as cancer or coronary heart disease. However, supplemental insurance is unpopular with some personal finance experts. Benefits advisor Virginia Povall of the Kooper Group blames its relatively high premiums and the difficulty in collecting for such things as paralysis or a coma.

Millions of Americans receive health and life insurance coverage as part of their benefits package at work. However, given their personal needs and ability to pay, many choose to supplement that insurance with additional coverage tailored to their individual circumstances. For example, a father of three may receive life insurance coverage of $100,000 from his employer but may want to increase the amount of his death benefit by purchasing supplemental coverage, often from the same insurer that supplies his primary life policy. A number of employers offer benefits packages that allow employees to supplement their basic employer-funded insurance by purchasing additional coverage. Such supplementary coverage may cover a broad range of specific situations. Popular supplementary coverage includes dental benefits, additional coverage for accident related expenses, supplemental life insurance, cancer care assistance, critical care insurance, sickness income insurance, and long-term care coverage. Some such supplemental coverage is made available to members of special interest groups and associations.

ORGANIZATION AND STRUCTURE

A segment of the overall insurance industry, the supplemental coverage market is served by many of the major insurers in the accident, health, and life insurance markets, most of which offer supplemental coverage as well as regular coverage through both individual and group policies. A few of the companies supplying supplemental insurance coverage specialize in such policies. Some of the major players in the latter category are American Family Life Assurance Company, better known by the acronym AFLAC, and some of the insurance-related subsidiaries of Conseco Inc. and Unum Group, such as Colonial.

CURRENT CONDITIONS

It is the business of supplemental insurers to offer coverage that is not supplied by other life, health, and accident insurance their customers may have. As the rising cost of

2010 Comparison of Medicare Supplemental Plans A through J

	Plan A	Plan B	Plan C	Plan D	Plan E	Plan F	Plan G	Plan H	Plan I	Plan J
Medicare Part A coinsurance	X	X	X	X	X	X	X	X	X	X
Medicare Part B coinsurance/copayment	X	X	X	X	X	X	X	X	X	X
Blood (first three pints)	X	X	X	X	X	X	X	X	X	X
Skilled nursing facility coinsurance			X	X	X	X	X	X	X	X
Part A deductible ($1,100 in 2010)		X	X	X	X	X	X	X	X	X
Part B deductible ($155 in 2010):			X			X				X
At-home recovery				X			X		X	X
Preventative care not covered by medicare					X					X

SOURCE: Senior Advisors Group, Medicare Supplement Center.

providing health and life coverage has forced increasing numbers of employers to cut back on the insurance they provide to their employees, the market for supplemental insurance has grown. Additionally, individuals with special health conditions or needs have found it necessary to purchase supplementary coverage that addresses such special circumstances. In the area of life insurance, employees with large families have often found it beneficial to increase their life insurance through supplemental coverage when they found the coverage provided through their employer was less than they felt essential to ensure the needs of their families.

Fueling growth within the supplemental insurance market during the last few decades of the twentieth century was the growing tendency of employers to cut back on their existing benefit programs either through curtailment of benefits or by increasing the cost of such benefits to employees. As more and more Americans found their safety nets unraveling, they turned to supplemental insurance plans to provide them with coverage for medical expenses and expanded life insurance. Of all the benefits provided by employers, according to the Employee Benefit Research Institute (EBRI), the fastest-growing segment by far has been health. EBRI breaks down employer spending on benefits into three main categories: retirement, health, and other. In 1960, employer spending for health benefits accounted for roughly 14.3 percent of all benefits outlays. The health component had grown to 22.2 percent by 1970, 26.6 percent by 1980, and 37.9 percent by 1990. By 1999, employers were spending 41.8 cents of every benefit dollar to provide health coverage for their employees. At first glance, these figures would tend to indicate sharp growth in health coverage. However, health care costs grew so quickly that the 1999 benefit dollar bought far less than it did only nine years earlier. In dollar terms, employers in 1999 spent $280.2 billion on health benefits, up from $188.6 billion in 1990. This represented an annual expenditure growth of approximately 4.5 percent between 1990 and 1999.

Illustrating the dramatic growth of health insurance costs over the last decades of the twentieth century are data from the Health Care Financing Administration (HCFA) of the U.S. Department of Health and Human Services. According to the administration's statistics, national health care expenditures grew more than seven times from the $255 billion total in 1980 to nearly $1.9 trillion in 2004—which was more than two and a half times the $717 billion spent in 1990. The $1.9 billion expenditure in 2004 represented approximately 16 percent of the gross domestic product (GDP), which was three times larger than in 1960. Health care spending is expected to pass the $2.6 trillion mark by 2010. HCFA reported that the fastest-growing component within health care spending is prescription drugs.

Health insurance plans fall into two broad categories: managed care networks and traditional health insurance. Under traditional health insurance plans, those insured may visit any doctor or hospital they want and receive coverage for any treatment covered under the policy. The cost for such coverage is higher than that for managed care plans, largely because traditional health insurance plans incorporate few cost saving or oversight measures. Managed care plans include health maintenance organizations (HMOs), exclusive provider organizations (EPOs), and preferred provider organizations (PPOs). All managed care plans seek to control health costs by limiting unnecessary treatment. Many HMO plans also offer point-of-service care, which allows those insured by the HMO to obtain reduced coverage for care outside the HMO network.

The largest single segment of the supplemental insurance market is that devoted to Medigap coverage, which helps meet some of the expenses not usually covered under Medicare. To fully understand the nature of Medigap coverage, it is necessary to provide a quick overview of Medicare—what it is and what it does and does not cover. Designed primarily for people 65 years and older, Medicare is a federal health insurance program that covers a majority, but not all, of its insureds' health care costs. Also covered by Medicare are certain people with disabilities. The two basic parts of Medicare coverage are Part A, which helps pay for inpatient hospital care, some skilled nursing facility care, hospice care, and limited home health care; and Part B, covering doctors' services, outpatient hospital care, and some other medical services that are not provided under Part A.

Private insurers sell Medigap policies to cover some of the medical expenses not routinely covered under either Part A or Part B of Medicare. Medigap polices are available in 12 standardized plans, ranging from A to L. In general, the further along in the alphabet, the better the coverage and the higher the premium. Under Medigap "open enrollment" rules, all applicants are guaranteed a Medigap policy regardless of current or past health history if they enroll in the program within carefully prescribed periods. The extent of Medigap coverage depends on the plan purchased. Generally speaking, however, Medigap policies cover some or all of the deductibles and copayments associated with health care services provided under Parts A and B of Medicare services as well as the cost of other services not covered at all under Medicare.

One insurer, Frontier Insurance Company of Rock Hill, New York, offers a natural health supplemental plan to members of the National Holistic Health Alliance. Frontier's plan covers such alternative medical therapies as acupuncture, biofeedback, massage and bodywork, homeopathic and herbal remedies, nutritional counseling, and chelation therapy.

Another major market for supplemental insurance sales is life insurance. Life insurers offer three main types of coverage: term, whole life, and endowment. Term life insurance, which is issued for a specified time period, offers life protection only for the specified period and has no cash value at the end of that term. Whole life coverage runs for the entirety of the insured's life, accumulating cash value over time. This cash value, always less than the face value of the life policy, can be paid when the contract matures or is surrendered. Endowment life policies run for a specified period of time and pay full face value at the period's end.

BACKGROUND AND DEVELOPMENT

Fundamental to any understanding of the supplemental insurance market is at least a brief overview of the history of insurance itself. The earliest forms of insurance emerged in ancient Babylonia where traders assumed the risks of caravan trade through loans that were repaid after the goods had arrived safely at their destination. Similar insurance-type schemes were utilized by the Phoenicians and Greeks to safeguard the value of their ocean-borne trade. The earliest life insurance was seen in ancient Rome, where burial clubs were established to provide funeral expenses for paying members. Eventually these clubs offered not only funeral expenses but also payments to survivors of the deceased member. In the United States, the first life insurance organization was founded in 1759 by the Presbyterian Synod of Philadelphia to provide coverage for the synod's ministers and their families. Ironically, although the Presbyterian Church was the first to establish a life insurance program in the United States, religious prejudice against the concept of life insurance inhibited its growth until the midpoint of the nineteenth century. As such prejudice fell away in the mid-1800s, life insurance experienced a boom in this country.

Health insurance is a relative newcomer in the United States. For much of the United States' early history, Americans received their medical care from traditional healers, herbalists, and midwives. Medicine had not yet emerged as the prestigious profession it is today, nor was the practice of medicine regulated. Such doctors as there were charged extremely low prices for those who had cash and often accepted prospective patients' promises of services or goods in return for medical treatment. Few hospitals existed. This all began to change in the early twentieth century. The practice of medicine gained prestige even as it came under state and federal regulation and licensing. Concurrent with medicine's rapidly growing prestige, more and more hospitals began to appear around the country. Before the turn of the century, the United States had only 200 hospitals. That figure had skyrocketed to 7,000 by 1930. Accompanying the sharp growth in the number of hospitals and medicine's increasing prestige was a sharp upturn in the cost of medical services.

As early as the 1920s, the Blue Cross network was born, providing its insureds with coverage in times of medical need in return for regular payments made during healthier times. Blue Cross enrolled a number of employers, convincing them that the benefits of having a healthy workforce would easily outweigh the expenses of setting up a health insurance program for their employees. At the time of the Great Depression, the vast majority of Americans found themselves unable to afford medical treatment, giving rise to a growing cry for solutions to the health care crisis.

In the realm of employer-provided health insurance benefits, Travelers Insurance Company was the first insurer to issue policies similar to those still issued today. In 1863, the company began to sell accident insurance to cover workers involved in railway mishaps. In time, Travelers expanded this coverage to include other forms of accident insurance. During the 1870s, companies in the mining, railroad, and other industries began to provide company doctors financed by deductions from workers' pay. In 1910, Montgomery Ward & Company entered into one of the first group insurance contracts in the United States. After Blue Cross first began to make inroads into the employer-provided health benefits market in the 1920s and 1930s, the industry witnessed the birth of many for-profit health insurers, which competed with Blue Cross for this business. By the late 1960s and the early 1970s, employer-provided health insurance coverage had grown so rapidly that nearly two-thirds of all Americans got their health insurance from work.

Beginning in the early 1990s and picking up speed in the mid-1990s has been a trend toward "demutualization" among life insurers, meaning that mutual insurance companies that heretofore had been owned by the policyholders are moving to transfer ownership into the hands of shareholders. Such major players as MetLife and John Hancock have already demutualized and taken their companies public, with others expected to follow.

One of the most troubling realities of health insurance coverage in the United States was the number of Americans who had no health insurance at all. According to data from the U.S. Census Bureau, 42 million Americans were without health coverage in 1999. Of the 232 million with health insurance, approximately 88 percent received their primary coverage through their employers. In the September 2000 issue of *Survey of Current Business,* the Department of Commerce reported that spending for medical care accounted for 15 cents of every dollar spent by Americans in 1999.

A newer policy introduced in mid-2001 by Colonial Life & Accident Insurance Company was typical of the move toward greater flexibility in employee benefits. Medical Bridge, a hospital confinement indemnity plan, supplemented existing major medical coverage by helping employees pay the medical and non-medical expenses—deductibles, copayments, child care, and transportation to and from the hospital—commonly associated with a hospital stay or outpatient surgery. Colonial made Medical Bridge available through employers as an optional add-on to company-funded health coverage. In introducing Medical Bridge, Monica Francis, Colonial's accident and disability product director, said, "Employers are facing rapidly rising health care costs, and many of them are forced to scale back benefits or offer plans with higher deductibles. The Medical Bridge policy gives employees a way to protect themselves against the resulting financial gap created by the rising costs."

PIONEERS IN THE FIELD

One of the pioneers in the U.S. life insurance market was the Metropolitan Life Insurance Company (now known as MetLife Inc.), which traces its roots back to the Civil War years. The company grew out of the National Union

Life and Limb Insurance Company, formed in 1863 by a group of New York City businessmen with an initial investment of $100,000. When it was founded, the company concentrated its coverage on compensation for disabilities suffered by Civil War soldiers. Five years after its establishment, the company turned its focus to life insurance, most of which was marketed to the middle class by a new company especially chartered for that purpose. The new company was dubbed "Metropolitan" because the New York City metropolitan area proved extremely fertile ground for the fledgling life insurance business. After weathering a severe business depression in the 1870s that put half of the 70 life insurers operating in New York State out of business, the company borrowed a marketing approach popular in England. Metropolitan began selling "workingman's" insurance door to door, using its sales force to collect the weekly premiums of five to ten cents for this inexpensive coverage. This new marketing approach proved phenomenally successful for Metropolitan, which by 1909 had become the largest U.S. life insurer in terms of insurance in force.

In the health and accident insurance market, Travelers Insurance Company, headquartered in Hartford, Connecticut, in 1863 introduced accident insurance for railroad workers injured in on-the-job mishaps, the first coverage of its kind in the United States. Travelers later expanded this insurance to cover accidents of other kinds. The fledgling field of health insurance, dominated during the latter half of the nineteenth century by a crazy quilt of coverages provided by non-profit fraternal organizations, attracted little interest from organized insurance companies until the very end of the century. One of the first stock insurance companies to become involved in health insurance was Aetna, which entered the market in 1899. At first, health coverage was offered only to people who already held or were in the process of purchasing an Aetna life or accident policy. Considered more of an incentive to life and accident sales than a viable insurance market in and of itself, health insurance was described in a 1903 Aetna publication as a business that "is not and never will be a source of profit in itself to the company." Health coverage was not sold to women at all, and only a limited number of men could pass the company's stringent physical and financial requirements to obtain such coverage. From these very reluctant beginnings, Aetna eventually developed into one of the country's largest providers of managed care benefits as well as dental, pharmacy, vision, and group insurance coverage.

Two of the hottest topics on Capitol Hill at the beginning of the twenty-first century were the need for some form of universal health coverage that would provide at least a minimal safety net for the millions of Americans who are now without any form of health insurance and the expansion of prescription drug coverage under Medicare. Because of the skyrocketing costs of prescription medicine, one of the most attractive forms of supplemental insurance in the new millennium was that which provided reimbursement for prescription drug expenditures. Prescription drugs account for the largest growth sector in health care spending, two-thirds of which is due to higher use as opposed to higher medicine cost. In 2003, Medicare enacted a prescription drug benefit that went into effect in 2006.

Under previous provisions governing Medicare, the federal health insurance program for those over the age of 65 did not cover 100 percent of the cost of medical services. Those covered under Medicare had to meet deductibles and make varying levels of co-payments depending on the specific services received. Medicare Part B is optional, and those choosing Part B coverage make a monthly contribution to the premium for this coverage. Although Medicare Parts A and B cover a number of medical services, there are some services that are not covered under the program. These include outpatient prescription drugs, eye care and glasses, dental services, and hearing aids. Supplemental Medicare coverage, also known as Medigap, fills a varying number of the gaps that are not filled by Medicare, depending on the level of Medigap coverage selected. In 2004, the monthly premium for enrollees in the Medicare Supplementary Medical Insurance, Part B, was $66.60; in 2006, it was $88.50

Under the multiple pressures of declining regulation, heightened competition, shifts in product demand, globalization, and demographics, the life insurance industry is undergoing radical changes. Perhaps the most notable change within the industry has been the growing trend toward consolidation. Smaller insurers, hard put to compete with their larger competitors, are seeking out larger merger partners, and even larger life insurers are being increasingly drawn into mergers with giant financial services companies, which combine such services as retail/commercial banking, brokerage, investment banking, and insurance.

In 2004, Colonial received almost 74,000 claims on its supplemental insurance, according to Monica Francis, assistant vice president of product marketing at Colonial. Eighty-three hundred were for superficial head injuries, such as cuts, bumps, and scrapes, amounting to 11.3 percent of all claims. Ankle injuries represented 3.6 percent of claims, while neck strains or sprains represented 3.3 percent. Statistics such as these are used to design and update insurance products. One of Colonial's products is $150 per-accident coverage for an emergency room visit. The money goes directly to the insured, who can use it for whatever he/she wants: toward the copayment, extra charges, or for anything else.

One of the biggest nightmares for Americans over 65 in 2005 was the complicated prescription drug coverage information concerning Medicare's Part D, which became available on January 1, 2006. Medicare Part D is designed to provide federal government prescription drug assistance to people on Medicare. Steering through all the competing plans to figure out which private health insurance plan to enroll in to get their prescription drugs paid for under Part D proved to be extremely confusing to seniors. Medicare subscribers have been presented with dozens of options. The plans cover some drugs, but not others; some offer supplemental insurance to cover the huge "doughnut hole" in the middle of the program; some plans re-price their options every day (for those seniors who wish to make the selection process a full-time job). The one option to help with the decision-making process, however, is Medicare's Plan Finder, found on the Medicare website. Unfortunately, only 23 to 30 percent of seniors ever go online.

At first glance, Plan D appears to be like any other insurance plan with a deductible and co-payments. However, when cumulative drug expenses reach $2,250, the plan no longer covers drug costs. Coverage begins again once cumulative expenses have exceeded $5,100. This gap has come to be known as the "doughnut hole." For example, if a person covered by Medicare Plan D spends $2,000 on prescription drugs in 2006, Medicare would cover 66 percent. However, for expenditures of $5,000, only 30 percent of prescription expenses will be paid by Medicare. For those with large drug expenses, there will be relatively low out-of-pocket expenses during the first several months of the year, until the "doughnut hole" is reached. At that point, their personal expenses will soar and, since the same prescriptions will most likely be needed in the next year, it would be the same in 2007.

Of course, the answer would be to get supplemental insurance to cover the gap in Plan D's coverage. Unfortunately, Plan D specifically prohibits purchasing supplemental gap insurance. For that reason, many seniors who have prescription drug insurance already have been advised not to sign up for Medicare Plan D.

In early spring of 2005, two major insurers introduced products to bridge the gap between traditional insurance coverage and the hefty additional expenses that critical illnesses can cause. MetLife, Inc., announced a package of critical illness products, available on an individual or group basis, that pays a lump sum of up to $100,000 for cancer, heart attack, stroke, or kidney failure, or if a coronary artery bypass graft or major organ transplant is needed. Colonial Supplemental Insurance launched a cancer product to be offered to employees at their work sites that pays benefits directly to the policyholder when cancer is diagnosed and treated. The product also pays for any one of seventeen cancer screening tests.

In October 2005, UnumProvident (which became Unum Group) presented MedSupport, a new voluntary supplemental insurance product aimed at helping employers and employees deal with the rising costs of medical care. MedSupport is designed to accompany an individual's employer-sponsored insurance by paying a lump sum benefit directly to the covered individual.

Medicare continued to be a major part of many older Americans' health insurance profile in the late years of the first decade of the 2000s. In 2008, the Medicare Improvements for Patients and Providers Act was enacted, which made some changes in the Medicare program regarding physician payment, therapy caps, and durable medical equipment bidding.

A 2008 study by America's Health Insurance Plans (AHIP) showed that the number of Medigap policy holders remained fairly constant throughout the first decade of the 2000s and that the number of Medigap policies in force increased 3 percent between 2004 and 2006. Karen Ignagni, president and CEO of AHIP, told *U.S. Newswire,* "Medigap provides beneficiaries with additional benefits not available through Medicare and allows seniors to more accurately budget for medical expenses." She also noted that 90 percent of the respondents in the AHIP study said they were satisfied with their Medigap coverage.

The economic slowdown in the United States during the late years of the first decade of the 2000s caused some employers to cease providing supplemental insurance for their employees. For example, in July 2008 General Motors, the largest car and truck manufacturer in the world, stopped paying its portion of supplemental insurance for retirees who also qualify for Medicare. According to *The Grand Rapids Press,* the Department of Labor also advised private-sector senior employees "not to bank on retiree health-care promises" and noted that employers are not required to supply supplemental insurance to their retirees. "When employers do offer retiree health benefits," said the memo, "nothing in federal law prevents them from cutting or eliminating those benefits—unless they have made a specific promise to maintain the benefits." According to David Smith, president of the Employers Association, employees who continue to receive such benefits include mostly government workers, teachers, and unionized factory workers. Smith said, "Most companies are trying to get out of it."

CURRENT CONDITIONS

Generally, health care reform under the Obama administration had little effect on supplemental insurance, but rather was directed at primary health coverage for Americans. Nevertheless, there were some changes in 2010 that affected supplemental insurance carriers and plans. A few involved the Medicare Medigap supplemental plans. Starting with policies effective on or after June 1, 2010, Hospice Part A coinsurance (outpatient prescription drugs and inpatient respite care) is now covered as a basic benefit. Plan K will cover 50 percent, and Plan L will cover 75 percent of costs. As for Part B coinsurance, Plans K,L, and N now require payment of a portion of Part B coinsurance and copayments, which may lower premiums. All other Medigap policies pay Part B coinsurance at 100 percent. Medigap Plans E,H, and I were no longer available for purchase after May 1, 2010. However, Plans M and N were new, and Plans D and G bought after June 1, 2010, had different benefits.

The weak economy of 2008 and 2009 had a collateral effect on the supplemental insurance industry. Employers were switching to lower-cost group health plans and/or plans that raised deductibles for employees. Employees were also footing more of the bill for continued health care coverage. Many employees were dropping supplemental plans or decreasing their benefits options as a cost-saving measure. To compensate, insurance companies were raising premiums. Further, they raised premiums to handle federal health care reforms that now extend coverage to previously uninsured groups. A 2010 study released by the federal Centers or Medicare and Medicaid Services projected that reforms that started in 2010 and 2011 would increase private insurance spending by $1.4 billion annually through 2013 although the number of policyholders would decrease, mostly because of the recession.

INDUSTRY LEADERS

AFLAC Inc. Millions of Americans know the American Family Life Assurance Company (AFLAC) of Columbus, Georgia, as the insurer with the talking duck in its television commercials. However, not as many Americans realize that what the company is advertising is supplemental insurance. In 2008 AFLAC was one of the largest sellers of supplemental life and health insurance in the United States. In addition, the firm has 14 million policies in force in Japan, where it has a 30-year history. AFLAC entered the supplemental insurance business in 1958 when it offered the world's first cancer expense insurance policies. The company, which has over 60,000 agents worldwide, markets a wide range of supplemental insurance, including term life policies, accident/disability insurance, cancer coverage, and coverage for the expenses of hospital intensive care, long-term care, hospital confinement indemnity, short-term disability, dental, and coverage tailored for the benefit of those suffering from specific health events such as heart attack, stroke, organ transplant, and coma. Sales in 2009 totaled $18.3 billion.

Unum Group Unum Group (formerly Unum Provident) is one of the largest providers of disability insurance in the United States and the United Kingdom. In addition to disability, it sells life and accidental death insurance. The firm has several subsidiaries, one of which, Colonial Supplemental Insurance (formerly Colonial Life & Accident), specializes in supplemental insurance. Colonial sells mostly through employers and offers disability, life, accident, and cancer insurance. In 2008 the firm operated in all 50 states except New York and had 2.5 million policies in force. Income from insurance premiums totaled $7.5 billion in 2009.

Conseco Company Conseco Company sells insurance and other products through three units: Bankers Life, Conseco Insurance Group, and Colonial Penn. The former two offer Medicare supplement and life insurance. Conseco claimed nearly 5 million customers in 2005. In 2009, sales for the company reached $4.3 billion.

WORKFORCE

According to the Bureau of Labor Statistics, about 436,000 people were employed as insurance sales agents in the United States in 2006. Approximately 50 percent worked for insurance agencies or brokerages, 23 percent were employed directly by insurance carriers, and 26 percent were self-employed. On average, insurance salespeople earned $43,870 annually. Employment in the profession was expected to grow about as fast as average through 2016, with preference given to college graduates.

AMERICA AND THE WORLD

A number of large U.S. supplemental insurers market coverage outside the United States. AFLAC, based in Columbus, Georgia, in 1974 became the second foreign company in history licensed to sell insurance in Japan. In the first decade of the twenty-first century, AFLAC Japan, which sells a variety of cancer and life insurance products, was the largest foreign insurer in Japan in terms of premium income. AFLAC insures approximately one-quarter of all Japanese households and ranks second in the number of individual policies in force among all of Japan's life insurers. Also active on the foreign front are the subsidiaries of Unum. The company's subsidiaries include Provident Life and Accident Insurance Company in Canada, Unum Japan Accident Insurance Company Ltd. in Japan, and Boston Compania Argentina de Seguros S.A. in South America. Unum also sells insurance in France, the Netherlands, and the United Kingdom.

Although France has a publicly financed health system providing universal coverage to all of the country's residents, approximately 85 percent of the French population purchases supplemental insurance to fill in the gaps that are either not covered or poorly covered by the nation's public health system. As with Medicare in the United States, the French public health system requires patient co-payment for many services and does not cover some health care treatments at all.

A further indication of the increasing globalization of the life and health insurance markets is the growing role of foreign-based insurers in the U.S. market. According to A.M. Best Company's listing of the top 10 U.S. life/health insurance groups and companies, two foreign-owned companies ranked among the top five. Ranked number four in terms of U.S. premiums written was ING Group, based in the Netherlands. AEGON USA Inc., the U.S. subsidiary of Dutch insurer AEGON N.V., ranked fifth.

RESEARCH AND TECHNOLOGY

A growing trend in the first decade of the 2000s in the insurance business was the increasing use of technology by agents in the field. For example, Colonial Supplemental Insurance provides its agents with Panasonic Toughbook laptops. Tim Sox of Colonial said in a 2008 *Best's Review* article, "We were ... one of the first companies to use laptop technology for enrollment purposes. And it's proven to be successful for us." Sox said the firm spends $2 million to $3 million a year purchasing technology. Although Toughbooks is a popular brand among insurance agents, it is not the only one, according to Donald Light of research firm Celent. According to Light, "The biggest trend has been to give your field adjusters and field producers their own notebooks with broadband capability," The other criteria besides fast connection to the Internet and mobility is durability, as agents must carry the PCs into sometimes hazardous and damaged environments. Experts predicted that insurance companies would allot even more funds in the future to IT in an effort to keep up with emerging technologies.

BIBLIOGRAPHY
"About AFLAC." AFLAC Press Release, 2 February 2010. Available from www.aflac.com/aboutaflac/pressroom/pressreleasestory.aspx?.

"A Shared Responsibility: Advancing Toward a More Accessible, Safe, and Affordable Health Care System for America." America's Health Insurance Plans, 29 May 2008. Available from http://www.hiaa.org.

"The Basics of Medicare." Employee Benefit Research Institute, May 2007. Available from http://www.ebri.org/.

Cavanaugh, Bonnie Brewer. "Soft on Hardware: As Technology Speeds Up Enrollment and Claims Filing, Insurers Dig Deep to Beat the Competition with Major Hardware Investments." *Best's Review,* November 2007.

"CMS Highlights." Department of Health and Human Services, Centers for Medicare and Medicaid Services, 15 October 2008. Available from http://www.cms.hhs.gov/.

"Conseco Trims CEO's Pay But Gives Exec Team Raises." 2 April 2010. Available from http://www.ibj.com.

"Fast Facts from EBRI." Employee Benefit Research Institute, 21 February 2008. Available from http://www.ebri.org/.

"GM Retirees Won't Be Last to Lose Health Coverage: Struggling Automaker Cuts Supplemental Insurance, Other Companies Expected to Follow." *The Grand Rapids Press,* 16 July 2008.

"Industry Overview." Insurance Information Institute, 2008. Available from http://www.iii.org.

Lavelle, Janet. "Why Job-based Insurance Costs are Soaring." San Diego *Union Tribune,* 9 September 2010.

"Medicare Medigap: What's New and Important in 2010?." Available from http://www.medicare.gov/publications/pubs/pdf/02110.

"Medicare Supplement Insurance." Senior Advisors Group, 2010. Available from http://www.mysenioradvisorsgroup.com/Medicare-Supplement_Center.

Nekola, Angie. "Advisors Need to Know Medicare Supplement Changes." *National Underwriter Life & Health,* 9 July 2007.

"New AHIP Study in Health Affairs Challenges Previous Assumptions About Medigap's Impact on Medicare Costs." *US Newswire,* 12 March 2008.

Occupational Outlook Handbook, 2008-09 Edition. Washington, DC: Bureau of Labor Statistics, 2008.

"Popular Medicare Plans to Change." *Milwaukee Journal Sentinel,* 20 July 2008.

"Unum-Financial Strength." Unum Press Release, 2 July 2010. Available from http://www.unum.co.uk/ho,=me/corporateinformation.

SYSTEMS INTEGRATION

———————— ■ ————————

SIC CODE(S)

7373

INDUSTRY SNAPSHOT

As companies scramble to develop electronic commerce (e-commerce) capabilities and better manage diverse information systems, the decades-old business of systems integration (SI) has been given new life. Two growth trends, e-commerce deployment and enterprise application integration, are responsible for a large infusion of revenue that the industry has enjoyed since 1996, while activities such as corporate mergers and new technology adoption have contributed as well.

Vigorous demand for SI and related services has changed the competitive dynamics among integrators. In some cases, smaller firms are gaining an edge in the market for rapid e-commerce integration, where they are seen as more flexible, more responsive, possibly more knowledgeable, and better able to meet tight deadlines. Meanwhile, large integrators such as Electronic Data Systems Corp. (EDS) and IBM Global Services bring tremendous resources and bargaining power to the table and are able to win larger, more complex contracts through their name recognition and stable brand image, even though they may subcontract the actual work to smaller, less well-known operatives. The industry has also seen a large number of mergers and acquisitions as companies seek the right mix of competencies and market access to best meet new demand.

Intense competition required companies to research increasingly complex solutions and to rapidly adopt new technology, including Web-based solutions. Companies such as IBM, in order to be competitive, had to begin offering advanced consulting and delivery expertise in end-to-end systems integration and custom application development. Innovation and expansion into new marketplaces must occur while overall costs must be reduced. On-demand e-business began driving the obligation to design, build, and manage the transformation to e-commerce, utilizing the ideas of custom development and legacy enabling, applications conversions, and platform consolidation, just to name a few.

ORGANIZATION AND STRUCTURE

Systems integration involves fitting together hardware and software to solve a business problem or create a competitive advantage. Often this occurs as part of deploying a new software application that was sold and installed by the integrator, who may also be called a reseller, but SI work can be performed at any point in a system's life cycle and by any service vendor that is retained to make two or more different systems interact as needed. Integration may also be performed by in-house staff instead of hiring an outside service.

One of the fastest-growing service areas within the information systems industry, systems integration was driven by fast-paced change in both business and technological environments during the 1980s and the 1990s. Drawing from traditional systems development approaches, systems integration nevertheless differs from this traditional systems model in a number of ways. The general assumption of most traditional systems development is that most, if not all, of the scope of the problem being attacked is within "design control" of the project. Traditional development assumes that the various parts of a system can be engineered to fit together and concentrates more on the development of applications and databases, giving little concern to interfacing those applications and databases. Systems integrators attack these development problems from the opposite direction, concentrating on building interfaces to make all system components work together.

Although it is separated from custom programming and other kinds of information technology (IT) services for statistical and analytical purposes, systems integration is in reality often done by firms that also perform such related services as custom application development, hardware and software installation, network management, and system maintenance.

The SI process usually comprises five steps: planning, design, development, implementation, and operation. SI brings about interaction between the hardware platform, software applications, and the operating system, and creates a base for all subsequent system-related uses and modifications.

Because systems integration can involve custom programming, as Alan R. Earls explained in *Computerworld,* the initial stage of the integration process is one of the most crucial. Clients must clearly specify exactly what capabilities they would like their systems to have and what the goals and requirements are. Systems integrators must also proceed carefully at this stage, ensuring that they fully comprehend client needs in order to deliver the expected service.

Furthermore, systems integrators and clients must take pains to draft thorough contracts that specify the tasks to be performed as well as the deadlines for those tasks. Earls urged companies to conduct a rigorous selection process to make sure they choose systems integrators with skills and fees amenable to their needs. The screening process should involve lawyers, technicians, and contract specialists so that all aspects of the SI contractor are examined prior to selecting a SI firm and signing a contract with the integrator.

Earls noted that companies should consider the location of the systems integrators as well. If both parties cannot solve a problem via the phone, then an on-site visit is warranted, which could cause significant delays if the systems integrator has to travel a long distance. In fact, on-site service and special attention make up some of the most important features systems integrators can offer, according to a *Computerworld* survey, which small, nearby SI firms may excel at providing.

Depending on client needs and project specifications, systems integrators may use prepackaged software exclusively. They may also need to design custom applications or outsource this task to a custom software developer. In addition, many systems integrators cater to specific markets, such as information system and manufacturing system

markets, and they specialize in certain kinds of technology and computer system-related skills. Therefore, companies and organizations seeking SI services select firms based on the firms' focal markets and aptitudes. SI firms usually have a team of systems integrators work on contracts, so a given firm may have specialists in various aspects of system integration and employ specialists in various computer environments such as Windows and Unix.

BACKGROUND AND DEVELOPMENT

With the proliferation of computers into homes and businesses during the 1980s and 1990s, the demand for diverse computer applications increased. In the beginning of the computer boom, custom software constituted the most prevalent kind of applications for businesses. Companies would contract software developers to create applications to suit individual needs. Computer programmers would design everything from workplace automation software to customer information databases. Custom development, however, had two significant drawbacks: cost and lack of standardization. Other than financial powerhouses, most companies could not afford custom software development except in financially prosperous times. Furthermore, without industry standards, custom software clients could have trouble upgrading software and ensuring that all divisions had the same operating systems and compatible software, which sometimes hindered interaction between various branches of a company.

By decree of the U.S. Justice Department in 1969, IBM Corp. had to start selling its software separately from its computer hardware, ending IBM's strong hold on the prepackaged software industry and opening the door for vigorous competition. Consequently, an excess of software developers sprouted in the wake of the Justice Department's decision. Prepackaged software offered an economical solution to the needs not only of small and medium-size businesses with tight budgets, but also to home computer users who used computers largely for uniform tasks such as word processing. Since software development required little capital investment, programmers could tinker away at novel and improved applications with very little financial risk. As a result, the prepackaged software industry blossomed in the 1980s and bore substantial fruit in the 1990s, producing high-quality products at much lower costs than custom-made counterparts. Therefore, the custom software industry began to slow down as the prepackaged software industry soared ahead. Nonetheless, because of their unique tasks, many businesses and organizations still required custom applications to increase the efficiency and functionality of company software. This need continued to feed the custom software industry.

Another need, however, emerged as well: systems integration. Integrators were required to build and link diverse systems for various organizational functions, often to interface large legacy systems on mainframes with more recent desktop computing environments. For example, a company might wish to access and manipulate data stored in a mainframe database from a Windows NT network. Such a project might involve creating intermediate programming, such as installing a middleware package, which allowed the Windows application to communicate with the mainframe application. Systems integration was beneficial anywhere companies needed to make unlike applications and platforms work together. This was especially true of massive proprietary applications, which were commonly used in government and large companies.

Cuts in federal spending in the early and mid-1990s reduced some opportunities for integrators serving the federal government, which was, at one point, the largest market for SI services. Nevertheless, as the number of federal employees decreased with government spending reductions, many systems integrators benefited as government agencies outsourced more projects. Thus, federal spending trends in the 1990s benefited the industry more than they hurt it. Streamlining of federal contract rules also changed the way federal contracts were obtained and under what terms, with a trend toward shorter, more task-specific contracts that rewarded high performance and penalized shoddy work.

Demand for systems integration (SI) services escalated markedly in the mid-1990s and remained strong. In 1998, U.S. Census Bureau figures pegged industry revenue at almost $32 billion a year, up some 20 percent from a year earlier. That amount included consulting and other work that is not considered part of systems integration. From 1996 to 1998 alone, according to government statistics, U.S. systems integrators' revenues jumped 50 percent, approaching $32 billion, including consulting and related work.

International Data Corp. (IDC), a market research firm, calculated U.S. industry revenue somewhat lower than the Census Bureau, at $22.5 billion in 1998, but agreed that SI was growing strongly, both in the United States and around the world. IDC estimated that the global market for SI in 1998 was worth $50 billion and growing at 13 percent a year.

In the early 2000s, significant corporate mergers reshaped the industry. In 2000, systems integration primarily involved a core of eight big companies, but that number had shrunk by 2002 as some companies left the IT consulting business, engaged in sell-offs, or merged. In October 2002, PricewaterhouseCoopers (PwC), once a major player, sold its consulting and technology services

business to IBM. In May 2002, KPMG, which spun off its KPMG Consulting arm in 2001, set out to acquire many of the consulting practices of Arthur Andersen, which was about to go under because of the Enron scandal. Reasons cited for such moves include the post-Enron regulatory environment, when Congress and the Securities Exchange Commission pushed for stricter laws to prevent conflicts of interest. Another more obvious reason was financial, as many firms saw a significant decrease in their IT consulting businesses due to the economic downturn. This resulted in a smaller market for the kind of major enterprise-wide integration projects typically conducted. These changes also impacted customers in significant ways. Most importantly, perhaps, it meant that most organizations would no longer contract with one company for both auditing services and IT consulting services.

The need for e-commerce and World Wide Web integration was one of the factors driving the growth in demand. As companies flocked to the Internet to reach customers, they often required the Internet interface to work with existing systems such as product catalog databases, order entry databases, and customer databases. Integrators are needed to bridge the World Wide Web system with those sorts of systems, and demand for some specialties within Web integration was expected to soon double.

By 2001, the growing number and size of Internet services posed a significant financial challenge to systems integrators. The major systems integrators began seeing Web services technology cutting into its revenues by snagging projects that involved low-level application integration programming. What drove this shift is that more companies began realizing that software components delivered over the Internet via standards-based technologies seemed as workable and yet simpler and less expensive than a large scale systems integration project, which could involve a lot of time and hundreds of people. A 2000 study conducted by Jupiter Media Metrix revealed that 60 percent of business executives interviewed intended to use Internet services for integrating internal applications during the next year. The obvious result of this was that systems integrators began examining what kind of opportunities would be available to them by providing Internet services. Accenture, for one, working closely with Microsoft, started to develop and work with tools to deliver Internet services. Forecasts about when the impact would be truly felt varied among observers. Some said significant changes would be felt within a year. Others said it would take at least five years.

In another industry trend, more financial institutions were turning to IT services firms to cut IT costs toward the end of 2002. The driving force behind this shift was the economy: more financial services needed to turn to outsourcing. In December 2002, JPMorgan

Chase selected IBM to handle a large amount of its technology infrastructure, including its data centers and voice and data networks. For the project, IBM planned to reduce JPMorgan Chase's 16,000 distributed servers by about half and move from 37 networks to a single voice and data network. That same month, IBM signed a $2.6 billion, 10-year agreement with Deutsche Bank to manage some of its computer centers. Other companies became involved in large outsourcing enterprises. Also in December 2002, Electronic Data Systems (EDS) signed multibillion-dollar deals with Bank of America and ABN Amro. In September of that year, Hewlett-Packard signed a seven-year, $1.5 billion outsourcing agreement with Canadian Imperial Bank of Commerce (CIBC) to manage much of its IT infrastructure.

It was estimated that systems integration services would account for $145 billion in revenues by 2005. Not surprisingly, getting in on integration for e-commerce systems had been a high priority at SI firms large and small. For some to shift in focus to the Internet was, in part, a matter of survival. By the end of 2003, one of the hottest SI growth opportunity areas was in identity management and security solutions.

There was a shift toward large, interoperable corporate applications such as enterprise resource planning packages. Companies have installed these powerful high-end applications to unify their data systems across different functional areas of the business, such as finance, human resources, and manufacturing, while still providing for the unique requirements of each area. Many also have industry-specific components intended for, say, telecommunications providers or financial services. These enterprise packages often require moderate customization for a particular client and often must be integrated to work with older systems. This kind of integration can extend not only to all of a company's major systems but it may also include linkage between supplier or customer systems to further streamline the supply chain.

By 2004, a new model for those in the SI industry was a movement away from selling stand-alone products and toward marketing total specialized solutions. A CRN market research study in 2003 revealed that more than half of the SI revenue for that year was from services. Part of the reason for the shift was in the trend for companies to purchase products directly from broadline distributors.

On another front, SI professionals were targeting the personal market, marketing IT solutions for the cutting-edge homes of 2004. A CRN study reported that those in the industry expected the home market to increase dramatically as more and more households required multiple computer, smart appliance, security system, wireless and broadband Internet connections, and remote technology integration.

In 2006, IBM announced that mainframe computers, which some feel will go the way of the dinosaur, were being reinvented as service-oriented architecture (SOA) hubs—a collection of services that allow applications to communicate and share data in order to extend the value of the applications and processes that currently run businesses. By making enhancements to its middleware and development products, IBM was making it easier to integrate mainframes running the z/OS operating system into SOA environments.

Although it has been believed for many years that mainframes will become nonexistent, Steven Mills, senior VP of IBM disagrees, estimating that System z mainframes globally process 80 billion transactions a day, a number expected to double by 2010. Mainframes can be difficult to integrate with new technologies, but Mills believes their capabilities—scalability, high-volume transaction processing, comprehensive security, input/output capacity, and the ability to simultaneously run multiple applications—make them useful for SOA and on-demand computing. In May 2006, IBM introduced its System z9 Business Class entry-level mainframe, with a $100,000 price tag, for smaller businesses. The System z9 can operate as hundreds of virtual servers and has a capacity-on-demand feature that allows processing capacity to be switched on and off for specific applications, which makes it especially suited to SOA computing.

Also in May 2006, Unisys launched its ES7000/one enterprise server, known as the SafeGuard Family. This system represented a unique central processing unit (CPU) architecture in the industry and was designed to protect data associated with a wide range of operating systems, including HP, IBM, Linux, and Microsoft. According to Unisys, the ES7000/one accomplished the highest performance of any Intel-based 16-processor server on the TPC-C benchmark with its ability to deliver 50 percent performance while costing 48 percent less than the comparable IBM system.

Despite the predictions that mainframes are a dying breed, according to a October 2008 *Wall Street & Technology* article, mainframe computing may be making a comeback. Philip Winslow, a software analyst for Credit Suisse, said, regarding the financial services industry, "Some types of users and applications need the reliability, security and scalability provided by mainframes. For them, it doesn't make sense to migrate off of the mainframe from either an architectural or economic perspective." According to Winslow, mainframe hardware spending by *Fortune* 1000 companies was forecast to grow in the mid-single-digit range. One of the reasons for the positive projections was IBM's introduction of specialty engines for running Linux and Java. Winslow commented, "With the new System z10, IBM has advanced the mainframe's compute-intensive capabilities." Others, however, disagreed with the idea of a mainframe comeback. Nik Simpson of the Burton Group said, "Many organizations with mainframes regard them as a necessary evil. If they can find a way to dispose of them without disruption at an acceptable cost, they will."

The shortage of talent due to the pending mass exodus of baby boomers to the ranks of retirement was also an issue in the industry in the late years of the first decade of the 2000s. IBM took this threat seriously enough to initiate, in cooperation with Micro Focus, a worldwide education program aimed at graduating 20,000 COBOL programmers by 2012. As of mid-2007, more than 300 educational institutions participated in IBM's Academic Initiative for System z.

In an effort to bring systems integration industry participants together, several organizations joined to form the Systems Integration Forum in October 2008. The main purpose of the forum, according to a press release by InnoVest Group, one of the founders, was to "cultivate collaboration and provide support for the Systems Integration and Information and Communication Technology (ICT) community." The organization planned to host an annual event where panelists and speakers would address key issues in the industry.

CURRENT CONDITIONS

In a November 2010 report, *Software Magazine* noted that overall growth for the Software 500 companies was flat "during the past year," with half of the top 10 companies reporting declines as their clients adjusted to the slow economy. Total 2010 Software 500 revenue was $491.7 billion. However, there was one area that did better than others: the trend of outsourcing critical IT functions continued, and systems integration/IT consulting outnumbered all other primary business sectors.

"Cost reduction and maximizing the return on the existing IT investments will continue to dictate the spending pattern of the SI services market in 2010," noted Ali Zaidi, IDC senior analyst, IT Consulting and Systems Integration Business Strategies, for IDC's *Worldwide and U.S. Systems Integration Services 2010-2014 Forecast.*

INDUSTRY LEADERS

IBM Global Services The reigning giant in the computer services business is IBM Global Services. This IBM division provides exhaustive IT services from consulting and design through implementation and management. It is commonly acknowledged as the world's largest systems integrator, although the company does not report its SI revenues separately from the rest of its diverse services. Total revenue for 2009 was $95.8 billion with about 350,000 employees.

In May 2001, in response to the increase in Internet services encroachment into the SI market, IBM implemented a wide-scale program to support production-ready infrastructure software and services to enable Internet services. This involved Internet standards and secure management of high-volume transactions and integrating complex business processes. In addition, IBM Global Services offered systems integration support to help businesses build Web services applications using IBM's infrastructure software. To support the growth of business process integration, IBM enabled all of its middleware infrastructure software with comprehensive support for open Internet standards to enable the development of Web services applications.

In October 2002, IBM purchased PwC Consulting in a deal worth $3.5 billion in cash and stock. IBM created a new unit, IBM Business Consulting Services, which was divided into three business lines: strategic outsourcing, business consulting, and integrated technology. The move enabled customers to utilize IBM Global's expertise in evaluating and building networks for e-commerce, customer relationship and supply chain management, and enterprise resource planning tasks.

HP Enterprise Services (Formerly Electronic Data Systems) IT industry leader HP purchased the former Electronic Data Systems Corp. (EDS) in 2008. Prior to that, EDS was the United States' largest integrator and second largest (behind IBM) in the world, as of late 2008. It too provided a full line of IT outsourcing services in addition to its SI business. EDS helped customers manage the reorganization of business processes by offering a comprehensive solution and service spectrum. With the EDS acquisition, HP's service business grew 68 percent. HP pulled in $114.6 billion in revenues for 2009. Of that, HP saw growth of 50.5 percent in software and services revenue, which reached $38.3 billion.

EDS had been reporting strong profits and double-digit earnings increases throughout 2001. However, things took a turn for the worse in 2002. Problems included sagging sales, a Securities and Exchange Commission (SEC) investigation, layoffs, losses of high profile deals, and the bankruptcy of several big clients. In the second quarter of 2002, EDS posted a net loss of $126 million compared with net income of $354 million in the first quarter. Total revenue rose 2 percent to $5.37 billion. Revenue for the third quarter of 2002 came in at $5.41 billion. The company had forecast it between $5.8 billion and $5.9 billion. The shortfall sparked the SEC probe. That year, EDS lost two big customers, WorldCom and US Airways, to bankruptcy. The resulting loss of revenue represented about $800 million a year. Also, the company's bottom line was negatively impacted by a $334 million cumulative pre-tax loss associated with a huge, multi-year Navy-Marine Corps Intranet (NMCI) project, which EDS won in October 2000. The deal was expected to be worth $6.9 billion over the life of the contract. However, the project fell about 18 months behind schedule, resulting in a loss of about $1.8 billion of expected revenue.

Things seemed to improve somewhat in 2003 when EDS signed a six and a half year contract with Telekomunikacja Polska S.A. (TPSA), the largest telecommunications company in Poland. The agreement was valued at $22 billion. EDS was responsible for implementation, system integration, and data migration for TPSA's new billing infrastructure, including maintenance of the overall solution. However, the company reported 2003 sales of $21.48 billion, which represented a loss of $1.7 billion in income.

Early results for 2006 showed that EDS had turned the financial corner. EDS also had contract signings worth $10 billion, up 45 percent from the previous year's $6.9 billion. The company secured two major contracts in early 2006: a $3.6 billion deal with General Motors and a $3.9 billion contract with the U.S. Department of the Navy. The second quarter was also strong, with the signing of a $1.7 billion contract for an IT infrastructure services agreement with Kraft Foods, Inc. Fifty thousand EDS employees completed almost 2 million training hours in 2005 in order to upgrade their skills and provide the company with a well-skilled, competitive workforce, able to keep up with the changing market.

Accenture Ltd. Another major company specializing in systems integration has been Accenture (ACN). In 2000, the company broke away from parent company Andersen Consulting, which eventually shut down as a result of the Enron scandal. ACN provides management and technology consulting services and solutions that help clients capitalize on business and technology opportunities. With more than 200 locations in 50 countries, ACN is the world's largest management and technology consulting firm. It provides consulting services as well as outsourced technology services across 15 industry groups. ACN's services are structured around five operating groups: communications and high tech, financial services, products, resources, and government.

As a result of the downturn in the economy in the early 2000s, ACN cut costs in its consulting operations and looked to outsourcing services for future growth. By 2008, revenues had grown to $23.4 billion with 186,000 employees, 4,600 of whom are senior executives. That year, the firm won a $22.1 million contract with the U.S. Air Force and a $26.2 million contract with the state of Kansas. In late 2009, it acquired the Symbian professional services of Nokia (maker of the Symbian smart phone operating system; this positioned Accenture to launch into providing services for mobile devices. By 2010, Accenture had 200,000 employees in 200 countries, bringing in $21.5 billion in revenues.

CGI With U.S. headquarters in Fairfax, Virginia, Canada's leading IT company, the CGI Group, purchased American Management Systems Inc. (AMS) in 2004 for $858 million. AMS then began to operate under the name CGI-AMS. Part of the transaction agreement included CACI International of Arlington, Virginia, purchasing the U.S. assets of AMS's military and intelligence unit for $415 million, thus reducing the cost of AMS to CGI to $443 million. The number of job cuts resulting from the purchase was not disclosed.

CGI is a global leader in information technology and business process services, with a history of on-time, on-budget delivery and a strong financial position. The firm designs and integrates technological solutions for a wide variety of businesses worldwide. It caters primarily to corporations and government agencies, offering business re-engineering, change management, and systems development, integration, and implementation services. The company as a whole earned $3.8 billion in revenues in fiscal 2009 and employed 26,000 people.

Perot Systems In 2009, Dell bought out Perot, and the combined entity is now known as DP Systems. Still based in Plano, Texas, the old Perot Systems Corp provides consulting and information technology services, such as systems management and integration, supply chain management, enterprise resource planning, e-commerce, and customer relationship management. Ross Perot and his family own about 25 percent of the company, which serves customers in a variety of markets. However, most of its clients are in financial services, health care, and manufacturing. In 2003, it increased its customer base and service offerings in its government services segment when it acquired Soza & Company, Ltd., a professional services company that provided information technology, management consulting, financial services, and environmental services primarily to public sector customers.

Unisys Unisys Corp. ranks as one of the highest SI companies in terms of technical aptitude and customer service. Incorporated in 1984, it is a global information technology services and solutions company that combines expertise in systems integration, outsourcing, infrastructure, server technology, and consulting. Servicing both corporate and government clients, the company has two business segments, services and technology. The services segment provides systems integration, outsourcing, infrastructure services, and core maintenance services. The technology segment provides enterprise-class servers and specialized technologies. In 2003, 76 percent of the company's revenue came from its services segment while 24 percent came from technology. The company also had strategic alliances with Microsoft, Hewlett-Packard, Sun Microsystems, PeopleSoft, Oracle, and Tandem.

Computer Sciences Corporation Founded in 1959, Computer Sciences Corp. (CSC) helps clients use IT more efficiently to improve operations and profitability. It offers a range of services to clients in the global commercial and government markets and specializes in the application of advanced and complex information technology. Specific services include IT and business process outsourcing, systems integration, and consulting/professional services. In 1998, CSC was the target of a hostile takeover bid by software vendor Computer Associates International, which had been aggressively branching into services. No deal was ever reached, however. In 2000, CSC had revenues of $9.37 billion; systems integration accounted for 24 percent of total revenues. In March 2003, CSC acquired DynCorp, an employee-owned technology and outsourcing firm in the federal IT services market. That year, the company reported $11.35 billion in revenues.

AMERICA AND THE WORLD

In the first decade of the 2000s, the Central Bank of Nigeria (CBN) urged 25 banks that met its minimum capitalization requirements to begin implementing the best integration facilities to improve operational efficiency and reliability of their information technology resources. Information and communication technology is seen as a very critical aspect of future mergers and acquisitions. Banks that were operating with different IT products would need to integrate applications, hardware infrastructure, data centers, financial systems, accounts, and various reports in order to ensure minimal disruption in the case of breakdown of their infrastructures, disaster, or terrorist attack.

RESEARCH AND TECHNOLOGY

Integrating the Internet into other applications constitutes a major area of research and development in the industry. Among other applications, the Internet has stimulated research into the development of integrated systems for Internet service providers (ISPs). As demand for Internet access escalated in the mid-1990s, a spate of telephone companies rushed to begin offering such service. SI firms such as Technology Applications, Inc., worked on developing systems to allow ISPs the efficiency of integrated Internet servers for network interface, online security, communications access, networking management, implementation, Web development, administration, and maintenance.

Internet services were so focused that SI was moving into the integration of grid computing with Internet services. New in 2004 from IBM and others were three parts to the WS-Resource Framework (WSRF), WS-notification, WS-Resource Properties, and WS-Resource Lifetime. The WSRF built statefulness—according to Caron Carlson writing in *eWeek*, the ability of a network to ensure that all requests from a given client are processed through the same server"—directly into Internet services, so the stack was compatible with the large scale resource-sharing, on-demand standards of existing open grid services infrastructure.

Software companies continued to roll out new system integration solutions. In June 2006, IBM launched the next-generation DB2 9 data server called Viper, which, according to the company's Web site, "deliver[s] the most significant database technology enhancements in more than two decades." The new server was a result of a five-year project involving more than 750 software developers in eight countries. In July of that year, the firm released the IBM System p5 595, a server capable of completing 4 million transactions per minute.

BIBLIOGRAPHY
"About EDS." Electronic Data Systems Corp., 11 November 2008. Available from http://www.eds.com/.

"About Us." Computer Sciences Corp., 11 November 2008. Available from http://www.csc.com/.

"CGI Reports F2008 EPS Growth of 31% and Signs $4.15 Billion in New Contracts, Up 30%." Montreal, Quebec, Canada: CGI, 10 November 2008.

Desmond, John P. "System Integrators, Outsourcers Gain Again as IT Guards In-House Resources." *Software Magazine*, November 2010.

"Formation of the Systems Integration Forum to Enhance Industry Collaboration and Dialogue." InnoVest Group, 13 October 2008.

Gabriel, Anne Rawland. "Mainframe Comeback?" *Wall Street & Technology* , 1 October 2008.

"History of IBM." IBM Global Service, 11 November 2008. Available from http://www-03.ibm.com.

Mari, Angelica. "City in Pressing Need of Skilled IT Matchmakers." *Computing*, 9 October 2008.

"Micro Focus, IBM Deliver Mainframe/COBOL Education Resources." *DMReview*, 3 May 2007. Available from www.dmreview.com.

"News." Accenture Ltd., 11 November 2008. Available from http://www.accenture.com/.

"SIA Interoperability Framework Approved as National Standard." Access Control & Security Systems Integration, 26 August 2008.

"Systems Integration." Unisys Corp., 11 November 2008. Available from http://www.unisys.com/.

"Unisys Launches ES7000 Server Platform Foundation." *The America's Intelligence Wire*, 10 May 2006.

"U.S. Department of Education Awards CSC Contract for IT System Development Services." Computer Sciences Corp., 20 October 2008.

Whiting, Rick. "Service Hubs: New Career Options for Mainframes." *InformationWeek*, 8 May 2006.

TABLET COMPUTERS

SIC CODE(S)

3571

3575

5045

5734

INDUSTRY SNAPSHOT

Tablet computers, also referred to as tablets or slates, are portable, flat-panel computers that users typically operate with a stylus or through a touch screen. Tablet-like devices, most of which offer handwriting recognition capabilities, have been on the market since the early 2000s. However, Microsoft accelerated their popularity by introducing a Tablet PC edition of its Windows XP operating system on November 7, 2002. Apple then revolutionized the tablet computer market on April 3, 2010, when it unveiled the Apple iPad, of which 1 million were sold within 28 days of the product's introduction.

By August of 2010 Research in Motion was preparing to launch a BlackBerry tablet, and Google's Android operating system was expected to be available on tablet devices from a number of different manufacturers. Hewlett-Packard also planned to release a tablet computer running its Palm webOS. Explosive growth was forecast for the tablet computer market. According to the July 26, 2010, issue of *eWeek*, Forrester Research indicated that sales of tablet computers would total 3.5 million units in 2010, 8.4 million units in 2011, and 59 million units by 2015.

ORGANIZATION AND STRUCTURE

The portable computer industry's distribution channels mirror those of the desktop PC industry, since many of the companies are the same. When customers want to buy notebook computers or any other hardware from industry leaders such as Toshiba, they typically go through resellers who take the orders; get the products from the manufacturer; and configure, deliver, and support them. Resellers' fees can add 10 to 20 percent to the price of a product.

Because the profit margin in the tablet computer segment is low and the competition so fierce, manufacturers tend to keep production just below demand level. At times this can backfire, which results in shortages, fulfillment backlogs, and long waits for products when production volume is miscalculated, or when there are shortages of new or popular components. Over the years, fierce competition from some of the direct sellers of mobile computers, such as Dell, has prompted many industry leaders to begin selling selections of their products directly to consumers.

BACKGROUND AND DEVELOPMENT

Although modern-day tablet computers came onto the scene during the early 2000s, their origins are rooted in the evolution of portable and handheld computing.

Short History of Portable Computing The Osborne I, developed in 1980 by Adam Osborne of Osborne Computer Corp., included innovations that led the way in the evolution of truly portable computers. Weighing 17 pounds, it had a detachable keyboard, a five-inch black-and-white display, and two floppy disk drives. It used a Zilog Z-80 microprocessor chip, an improved clone of Intel's 8080. The Osborne I not only pioneered portability, but it was also credited with being the first to bundle software packages with

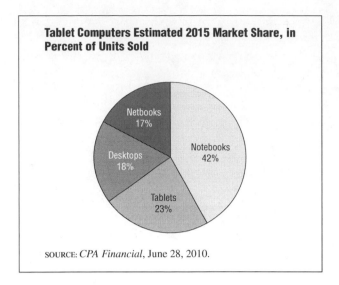

Tablet Computers Estimated 2015 Market Share, in Percent of Units Sold

Netbooks 17%
Desktops 18%
Notebooks 42%
Tablets 23%

SOURCE: *CPA Financial*, June 28, 2010.

the computer, an idea that became fundamental to selling hardware in the industry.

Tens of thousands of the Osborne I portable computers were sold before it became the victim of the company's own success. In 1983 the company announced that it would build an IBM-compatible portable called the Vixen, causing buyers to stop buying the Osborne I in anticipation of the new machine. The announcement, however, was premature, and without incoming orders to fund the new product's manufacture, Osborne was forced to file for bankruptcy protection. By the time the Vixen was ready to market, consumers had been wooed away by the products of a new leader, Compaq, that had been able to meet their demand.

According to Les Freed's *The History of Computers*, Compaq's opportunity to successfully take the portable computer market lead was largely due to a gaping hole in IBM's product line. In 1983 Compaq shipped the Compaq Transportable and Compaq Plus, both fully functional, IBM-compatible portable PCs weighing a not so svelte 30 pounds. During its first year in business the company sold 53,000 portables and took in revenues of $111.2 million, giving Compaq the highest first-year sales in the history of American business.

In 1984 Gavilan Computer developed a truly portable machine that did not have to be plugged in. Industry commentator Tim Bajarin wrote: "The computer's clamshell design and battery-power capability made it the first serious mobile computing system." Gavilan, however, could not manufacture the computers in sufficient quantity and the company went out of business.

Apple Computer's PowerBook models, introduced in 1991, set a new standard for portables. They combined long battery life with excellent display quality and a built-in pointing device. The PowerBook 170 contained

an optional internal modem slot, again redefining the meaning of a mobile office computer. Apple's Duo 210, released in 1992, featured the DuoDock, an innovation that allowed hookup to a docking station that might contain more system RAM, a larger hard drive, or more video RAM for a color monitor. The Duo could thus function fully as a desktop computer when in the Duo-Dock and as an excellent portable at other times.

Emergence of Handhelds In 1993 another Apple innovation was the Newton MessagePad, a new type of portable known as a personal digital assistant (PDA). It was the first mass market handheld computer and was offered as a personal information manager. The Newton solved the problem of keyboard size by using a stylus for input, but it promised more of this new pen-based technology than it could deliver. Apple promoted the Newton's ability to interpret handwriting with disastrous results because, at the time, its capability was relatively primitive.

By 1997, when the next-generation Newton, the MessagePad 2000, reached the market, its handwriting recognition was much improved. Reviewers praised the revamped MessagePad for its robust communication and computing features. However, with Apple mired in losses, and profits from the Newton not imminent, in 1998 Apple dropped the curtain on the Newton line—the MessagePad, eMate (a Newton-based clamshell notebook for the education market), and the Newton operating system.

In the meantime, another competitor with greater staying power was emerging. In 1994 inventor Jeff Hawkins came up with a design for a new kind of PDA that would become the PalmPilot. At the time, he was working at a software firm developing handwriting recognition technology for handheld devices, but the sparse handhelds at the time lacked many useful features, and to Hawkins, an engineer, they were poorly designed. He believed an effective handheld device should be extremely light and portable, ought to synchronize readily with desktop computers, and should be simple in features and purpose. With his innovative design and support from the company's management, Hawkins helped transform the company into a hardware designer and maker, Palm Computing.

In 1995 the private company was sold to modem manufacturer U.S. Robotics in order to finance the product's debut. The first PalmPilot was shipped in early 1996, and more than 350,000 units had been sold by the year's end. Within another year, more than 1 million PalmPilots had been sold and the product began attracting a devoted following of users, software writers, and corporate partners. Palm became part of 3Com Corp. with its 1997 purchase of U.S. Robotics, and by that time Palm was becoming entrenched as the market leader in the nascent PDA category.

However, Palm wasn't alone. Numerous models of handhelds, palmtops, and other PDAs came on the market around the same time. These included computers running Microsoft's Windows CE operating system. Windows CE, although less functional than desktop Windows versions, was easy to learn for those familiar with the PC versions. Windows CE devices included modified versions of the popular Microsoft Word and Excel software, along with Microsoft's Internet Explorer browser. The Casio Cassiopeia, for instance, was able to transmit faxes, access e-mail, and receive information via a one-way pager in addition to being able to link and synchronize data through a docking station to a Windows 95 desktop computer. Hewlett-Packard introduced its 1000CX palmtop PC and Philips Electronics North America Corp. unveiled the Velo 1 in early 1997.

Evolution of the Tablet When first introduced in 2000, tablet computers—lightweight, pen-based computers with handwriting recognition capabilities—cost about $2,000. Although features varied by model and manufacturer, these devices rivaled low-end laptops in the areas of performance and Internet connectivity. According to estimates from research firms such as Gartner and IDC, tablet computer sales were expected to account for less than 2 percent of all notebook sales in 2003.

Helping potential sales was the fact that Microsoft developed a Tablet PC edition of its Windows XP operating system, designed for use on tablet PCs from manufacturers like ViewSonic, Fujitsu, Hewlett-Packard, Acer, and Motion Computing. Bill Gates shared a Tablet PC prototype with attendees of the industry trade show Comdex in 2001. According to an article in the April 2, 2004, issue of *Computer Dealer News*, Gates predicted that the device, introduced on November 7, 2002, "would become the most popular personal computer within five years."

Early problems with tablet computers included everything from short battery lives to slow processor speeds. Nevertheless, the devices were slowly adopted at the enterprise level. Specifically, tablet computers caught on within industries such as transportation, consumer packaged goods, law, healthcare, and insurance, where portability was important.

By 2003 there were two different types of tablet computers on the market. The first was a "slate-style" flat tablet, which was not equipped with a keyboard. Instead of a mouse, users controlled the cursor and highlighted information with a special stylus. Utilizing a traditional keyboard was possible via a wireless or USB cable connection. Convertible-style tablet computers resembled laptops, but offered users a swivel-screen that folded on top of the device's keyboard to become a tablet. Some tablet computers were able to dock with a regular computer. Most devices included handwriting recognition software that, according to some observers,

offered an accuracy rate of approximately 85 percent to 90 percent.

Although tablet computers still represented a small percentage of the overall North American computer market in 2004, more manufacturers began introducing devices in the category. Examples included Fujitsu's LifeBook T3000 tablet PC, Acer's TravelMate C300, and Electrovaya's Scribbler SC-2010. By this time devices also had been introduced by the likes of Gateway, Compaq, NEC, and Toshiba. The *Computer Dealer News* article continued, with Acer predicting that tablet PC functionality would become integrated with 25 percent of its notebook shipments by 2009.

According to In-Stat, tablet PC sales totaled $1.2 billion in 2004. The following year the research firm indicated that sales would reach $5.9 billion by 2009. Indeed, by the late 2000s the tablet computer market was poised for explosive growth. Midway through 2009 rumors were circulating about a new tablet device reportedly under development by Apple that would bridge the gap between the company's iPod touch and MacBook devices.

CURRENT CONDITIONS

Apple revolutionized the tablet computer market on April 3, 2010, when it unveiled the Apple iPad. The trim, slate-like device, which cost between $499 and $829, offered consumers a large screen, a multi-touch user interface, and thousands of applications, or "apps." After debuting the iPad, Apple sold 1 million of the devices in only 28 days. In addition, customers had downloaded 12 million apps from the Apple App Store, as well as 1.5 million e-books from the Apple iBookstore.

Developments unfolded quickly. On April 30, 2010, Apple introduced a version of the iPad equipped with both WiFi access and 3G connectivity from AT&T. In late June sales had reached 3 million units. iPads were being sold at a rate of approximately 375,000 per day. In addition to the United States, the iPad was available in Canada, Italy, Germany, Japan, Australia, and France. Apple planned to offer the device in an additional nine countries in July. That month, the research firm iSuppli projected that Apple would ship 12.9 million units for the year. In addition, it forecast sales of 36.5 million units in 2011, and 50.4 million units in 2012.

Apple was not the only game in town, however. By August of 2010 Research in Motion was preparing to launch a BlackBerry tablet. Manufactured by Taiwan-based Quanta Computer, the $499 device was slated for a November roll-out. Estimated production paled in comparison to the iPad, with 2 million units scheduled for manufacture in 2010, followed by 8 million units in 2011, according to the August 13, 2010, issue of *The Online Reporter*. In addition to BlackBerry, Google's Android operating system was expected to be available on devices from a number of different manufacturers in 2010, including tablet PCs from Dell and Acer. Hewlett-Packard also planned to release a tablet PC running its Palm webOS.

Although its market dominance had been impacted by the availability of other operating systems, Microsoft continued to have a significant stake in the tablet market, and analysts acknowledged that the company would continue to be a noteworthy competitor. A number of leading manufacturers had new tablet computers in the works that were expected to run Microsoft's Windows 7 operating system.

According to some analysts, the main disadvantage that Apple's challengers faced was the lack of apps for their devices. "Success is pinned on the amount of apps you can offer tablet users," said IDC analyst Bob O'Donnell in the June 2010 issue of *PC World*. However, as the publication pointed out, other manufacturers were able to woo buyers by offering a greater range of sizes and shapes, as well as features not found on the iPad, including Adobe Flash, USB ports, and more.

Explosive growth was forecast for the tablet computer market. In its May 20, 2010, issue, *eWeek* cited data from the research firm IDC indicating that tablet computer shipments would reach 7.6 million in 2010. Fueled by a compound annual growth rate of 57.4 percent, shipments were expected to exceed 46 million by 2014. According to the July 26, 2010, issue of *eWeek*, Forrester Research indicated that sales of tablet computers would total 3.5 million in 2010, 8.4 million in 2011, and 59 million by 2015.

INDUSTRY LEADERS

Apple Computer Inc. During the early 2010s, Cupertino, California-based Apple Computer was a major player in the market for mobile devices and apps. This was evident by the success of the company's iPad tablet computer, as well as its line of iPod portable music and video players, the Apple iPhone, the Apple iTunes store, and the Apple App Store, from which users literally had downloaded billions of apps.

Apple introduced the iPod in 2002 and launched iTunes the following year. By 2004 iPod sales surpassed 2 million units. That year the company unveiled the iPod mini, which allowed users to store up to 1,000 songs, and iPod sales constituted 35 percent of the company's revenues. Apple's impact on the industry continued in 2005. That year the company replaced the iPod mini with the iPod nano, a media player that was thinner than a pencil but could hold 500 to 1,000 songs. In addition, Apple unveiled an iPod capable of playing video on a 2.5-inch color screen. Apple's iTunes service debuted in 2005, offering approximately 2,000 music videos and episodes of popular TV programs. In only 20 days, iTunes sold more than 1 million videos.

In April 2007 Apple announced that it had sold its 100 millionth iPod, which had become "the fastest selling music player in history," according to a company news release. The following year, the company made a significant impact on the market by introducing its Apple App Store. Essentially, it applied its iTunes approach to mobile apps, making it easy for consumers to find and download them.

Apple celebrated the one-billionth download from its App Store in early 2009. By 2010 approximately 3 billion apps had been downloaded for popular devices such as the iPad, iPhone, and iPod touch. In 2009 Apple's sales totaled $42.91 billion and the company employed 36,800 people. In late 2010 iPhone and iPod touch users in 77 countries were able to choose from a staggering number of apps in roughly 20 categories.

Apple revolutionized the tablet computer market on April 3, 2010, when it unveiled the Apple iPad. The trim, slate-like device, which cost between $499 and $829, offered consumers a large screen, a multi-touch user interface, and thousands of "apps." After debuting the iPad, Apple sold 1 million of the devices in only 28 days. In addition, customers had downloaded 12 million apps from the Apple App Store, as well as 1.5 million e-books from the Apple iBookstore. On April 30, 2010, Apple introduced a version of the iPad equipped with both WiFi access and 3G connectivity from AT&T. In late June sales had reached 3 million units. That month, the research firm iSuppli projected that Apple would ship 12.9 million units for the year. In addition, it forecast sales of 36.5 million units in 2011, and 50.4 million units in 2012.

Dell Computer Corp. Dell Computer Corp., of Round Rock, Texas, first gained its place in the computer industry as a direct seller of discounted IBM-compatible PCs to businesses. By the late 1990s Dell had started to embrace the consumer market as well, vigorously pushing its Web site as a convenient way for companies and individuals to order the exact system they wanted. In addition to desktop models, Dell makes notebooks and servers, and also offers a wide range of services, such as consulting, systems integration, support, and training. In 2010 the company reported revenues of $52.9 billion and employed 96,000 people worldwide.

Legendary for its efficient inventory and production systems, Dell climbed its way from being the world's seventh largest PC maker in 1992 to become the world's leading producer, with more than 14 percent of the market by 2001. In 2007 Dell lost its status as the world's largest manufacturer of personal computers, falling to second place. The following year, the company agreed to sell a limited selection of personal computers in Best Buy stores. In an effort to cut $3 billion in costs, the company announced plans to close one of its manufacturing facilities in Austin, Texas, and eliminate 8,900 jobs, representing about 10 percent of Dell's workforce.

During the late 2000s Michael Dell hinted at potential plans to develop a small-screen device that would compete with the Apple iPhone. By 2010 the company was generating excitement with its Dell Streak device, which sported a five-inch screen, Google's Android operating system, and offered a wide selection of apps available through the Android Marketplace. The device also was rugged, offering a damage-resistant Gorilla glass screen. By agreeing to a two-year data contract with AT&T, consumers could purchase a new Dell Streak for $299.99. Dell also offered users the Latitude XT2, which the company described as "The industry's first tablet PC with multi-touch screen technology." Via a multi-touch responsive screen, users were able to manipulate content with natural gestures such as pinching. Connectivity was enhanced through a LCD-based wireless antenna.

Microsoft Corp. Bill Gates started Microsoft in 1975 after he dropped out of Harvard at age 19 and founded "Microsoft" with friend Paul Allen in a hotel room in Albuquerque, New Mexico. In 1979 Gates moved Microsoft to his hometown, Bellevue, Washington, where he developed software that enabled users to write programs for personal computers. In 1980 Microsoft beat strong competitor Digital Research to write operating system software for IBM's new PC. Gates and Allen bought the rights to an existing speedy and efficient package, QDOS, which stood for "quick and dirty operating system" and had taken only two months to write, from Tim Paterson of Seattle Computer Products. Acquired for less than $100,000, they renamed the software MS-DOS.

Gates was considered to be the "the foremost applied economist of the second half of the twentieth century" by Steve Lohr, who gave credit to Gates and Microsoft for shaping the way people think about the behavior of technology markets. Microsoft had been described as being "a master practitioner of network effects and more" and had been identified as an expert in attracting consumers and software developers to technology. As the number of users of technology increased, the number of available products also increased. However, as the Internet gained popularity, Microsoft struggled to catch up to Google, which had become the Internet leader the way Microsoft led the PC segment.

Early on, sales within the tablet PC market benefited from the fact that Microsoft developed a Tablet PC edition of its Windows XP operating system, designed for use on tablet PCs from manufacturers like ViewSonic, Fujitsu,

Hewlett-Packard, Acer, and Motion Computing. Bill Gates shared a Tablet PC prototype with attendees of the industry trade show Comdex in 2001. According to an article in the April 2, 2004, issue of *Computer Dealer News*, Gates predicted that the device, introduced on November 7, 2002, "would become the most popular personal computer within five years."

In mid-2010 a number of leading manufacturers, including HP, Lenovo, Archos, and Toshiba, either offered or had plans to introduce tablet PCs running Microsoft's Windows 7 operating system. The Home Premium, Professional, Ultimate, and Enterprise editions of Windows 7 offered a new Math Input Panel for students that could be used for recognizing handwritten formulas. In addition, the system offered more accurate handwriting technology, custom dictionaries for those using specialized vocabularies, and improved pen input functionality for notetaking. In addition, some devices were able to take advantage of the operating system's ability to provide a pen-free experience, allowing users to manipulate content with their fingertips. One drawback to the Windows operating system, according to several industry observers, was the fact that Apple devices were perceived as having fewer security issues, in terms of threats from viruses.

Beyond Windows, Microsoft also had a product of its own in development. Named the Microsoft Courier, the device was described as "a folding dual-screen digital journal" in the June 2010 issue of *PC World*. In the article, Danny Allen indicated that the Courier had "the potential to match Apple's interface innovation...if it ever leaves the drawing board." In 2010 Microsoft remained the world's leading software company, with revenues of $62.48 billion and 89,000 employees worldwide.

Google Inc. Google was established in 1995 by Larry Page and Sergey Brin, two Stanford University computer science graduate students. Page and Brin decided to develop a computer application that allowed users to sift through the largest data set in the world, the Internet, and retrieve relevant information. By 1997 the partners were using their dorm rooms as office space and searching for partners interested in licensing their technology. The following year, Page and Brin named their search engine technology "Google," an offshoot of the word googol, which is the number one followed by 100 zeros.

In 1998 Sun Microsystems founder Andy Bechtolsheim invested $100,000 in the new company, which was incorporated as Google Inc. By 2003 profits totaled $105.6 million on sales of $961.9 million. Google completed its initial public offering on August 19, 2004, selling its shares for $85 each via a Dutch auction on the NASDAQ. By the end of the day the firm's stock price had risen to $100, and more than 22 million shares had been traded.

An important industry development took place in 2005 when Google acquired the mobile phone operating system developer, Android. Following the acquisition, the company began bolstering its portfolio of mobile software apps and making them compatible with various smartphones. Via a tie-up with Research in Motion, Google Mobile Maps and Google Talk IM applications became available on the BlackBerry. Other mobile apps developed by the company included an RSS reader, Gmail, a calendar, and search tools.

In addition to Research in Motion, Google also established partnerships with T-Mobile and Sprint Nextel in the United States. Internationally, the company made arrangements to have its apps included on handsets from China Mobile, Vodafone (Europe), and KDDI (Japan). By late 2007 rumors were circulating about the possibility that Google would develop its own smartphone. The company's strategy evolved in September of 2008 when its Android operating system was introduced on T-Mobile's new G1 phone, along with a host of related applications available via the new Android Market.

Google employed 19,835 people in 2009. That year, the company's sales totaled $23.65 billion. In late 2010 Google's Android operating system was slated to appear on a new tablet computer from Lenovo called LePad. The company also was rumored to be developing an Android-based tablet computer in conjunction with Verizon Wireless. Finally, Samsung was expected to introduce an Android-based tablet, featuring both wi-fi and 3G connectivity, named the Galaxy during the latter part of the year.

WORKFORCE

The computer industry employs large numbers of electrical engineers, programmers, assemblers, and technicians. Companies also hire large numbers of people for miscellaneous management, sales, and clerical positions.

Despite the sharp uptrend in the industry's output, U.S. employment in computer manufacturing has been declining since its peak in 1984. Between 1984 and 1995 the computer manufacturing industry lost 32 percent of its workforce, an average annual rate of 3 percent. The computer industry is one of the more highly automated manufacturing industries, and many manual assembly jobs have been eliminated. Other manufacturing and assembly work has been relocated overseas.

As of 2008 computer manufacturing employed 39,783 people, about 29 percent of whom were production workers. This reflects a dramatic decrease from earlier years. In 2000, for example, employment totaled 73,730 U.S. workers, about 34 percent of whom were production workers. In 1990 the industry employed as many as 278,500 people, with production workers making up just 25 percent.

Given the ongoing pressure on computer makers' revenues and profits, companies are expected to continue to introduce labor-saving automation and to outsource manufacturing activities to low-cost foreign producers. Furthermore, corporate alliances moderate the demand for research and development professionals.

The demand for computer programmers was expected to fall 3 percent from 2008 to 2018, according to the Bureau of Labor Statistics. The demand for electrical engineers was expected to slip about 2 percent by 2018. Manufacturing jobs, especially, were projected to disappear. The demand for electrical and electronic assemblers, for example, was expected to plummet 15 percent by 2018.

In its *Occupational Outlook Handbook, 2010-11 Edition*, the Bureau of Labor Statistics explained: "Although the use of information technology continues to expand rapidly, the manufacture of computer hardware is expected to be adversely affected by intense foreign competition. As computer and semiconductor manufacturers contract out more of their engineering needs to both domestic and foreign design firms, much of the growth in employment of hardware engineers is expected to take place in the computer systems design and related services industry."

AMERICA AND THE WORLD

The popularity of tablet computers is a global phenomenon, extending to developing markets. In early 2010 the organization One Laptop Per Child revealed plans to introduce a waterproof, flexible tablet computer that cost $75. Midway through the year, the Indian government announced plans to offer a Linux-based tablet computer for college students priced at $35. Around the same time, the manufacturing company VIA announced plans to introduce an Android-based tablet computer in China that would cost between $100 and $150. Finally, a survey conducted by Forsa revealed that German tablet PC sales would increase from 20,000 units in 2009 to 500,000 units in 2010. In addition, the research firm found that some 3 million Germans were interested in purchasing a tablet computer.

RESEARCH AND TECHNOLOGY

In its April 10, 2010, issue, *eWeek* reported that, according to Rapid Repair, between 5 percent and 10 percent of Apple iPads were expected to fail as a result of accidents. In the publication, Rapid Repair co-founder Aaron Vronko said: "The weight, size, and novel ways of using these devices will put them at risk for a higher rate of accidents, which are more damaging than what we are used to. Physics are not in the tablet's favor. While the fragile parts of the iPad are no less durable than their iPhone counterparts, a 10-inch and 24-ounce device is just a much bigger target for accident collisions and generates many times more force in the fall."

BIBLIOGRAPHY

"10 Reasons Why Windows Won't Win in the Tablet Market." *eWeek*, 1 June 2010.

Allen, Danny. "Apple's Rivals, Scramble to Make iPad Challengers." *PC World*, June 2010.

"Analysis: Apple Adapts iTunes Model to Mobile Apps." *Europe Intelligence Wire*, 7 March 2008.

"Android Running Lenovo Tablet to Launch in 2010 Report." *eWeek*, 20 July 2010.

"Apple Could Find Healthy Market for $700 Touch-Screen Tablet." *InformationWeek*, 21 May 2009.

"Apple iPad Design More Vulnerable to Accidents Falls." *eWeek*, 10 April 2010.

"Apple iPad Sales Reach 1 Million." *eWeek*, 3 May 2010.

"Apple iPad Success Could Boost Samsung Other Manufacturers." *eWeek*, 19 May 2010.

"Apple iPad Success Forces Revision in Forrester Estimates." *eWeek*, 26 July 2010.

"Apple Sells a Million iPads." *Linux Gram*, 10 May 2010.

"Apple Sells Three Million iPads in 80 Days." *Client Server News*, 28 June 2010.

"Apple Sold 327 Million iPads Earned 157 Billion." *eWeek*, 20 July 2010.

"Based on Apple iPad IDC Predicts Gangbuster Tablet Sales." *eWeek*, 20 May 2010.

"BlackBerry Tablet Due in November." *The Online Reporter*, 13 August 2010.

Cowan, James. "Take That, Apple: Our Tablet Is $75." *Canadian Business*, 19 January 2010.

Cyran, Robert. "As iPad Gains, Others Will Lose." *The New York Times*, 2 August 2010.

"Dell Computer Corp." *Notable Corporate Chronologies*, Online Ed. Farmington Hills, MI: Thomson Gale, 2009.

"Electronic Computers." *Encyclopedia of American Industries*, Online Ed. Farmington Hills, MI: Thomson Gale, 2007.

Goedert, Joseph. "New 'Tablet PCs' Could Boost Tablet Use in Health Care." *Health Data Management*, January 2003.

"Handheld Computing Devices." *Encyclopedia of Emerging Industries*, Online Ed. Farmington Hills, MI: Thomson Gale, 2010.

Himmelsbach, Vawn. "Tablet PCs: Nurturing a Fledgling Market; Despite a Slow Start, Sales of These Pen-based Units Are Starting to Take Off." *Computer Dealer News*, 2 April 2004.

"India Offers the World a $35 Tablet." *The Online Reporter*, 30 July 2010.

Kooser, Amanda C. "Take One Tablet...: Buyer's Guide: Give It a Good Look, and Call Us in the Morning If It's Right for Your Business." *Entrepreneur*, September 2003.

"Microsoft CEO Ballmer Pumps Cloud Tablets at WPC 2010." *eWeek*, 12 July 2010.

"Microsoft Could Be Strong Tablet Competitor Says Exec." *eWeek*, 1 June 2010.

"Packaged Software." *Encyclopedia of Global Industries*, Online Ed. Farmington Hills, MI: Thomson Gale, 2009.

"Samsung Galaxy Pad Tablet to Challenge Apple's iPad." *eWeek*, 30 August 2010.

"Tablet PC Faces Uncertain Future, Analyst Says; The Tablet PC Faces an Uncertain Future, as Microsoft Rolls Out its Next Generation Operating System for Small Computers." *InternetWeek*, 26 July 2005.

"Tablet PC Sales in Germany to Reach 500,000—Survey." *Europe Intelligence Wire*, 28 May 2010.

"Tablets to Outsell Netbooks by 2012." *CPI Financial*, 28 June 2010.

"Trouble in Tablet Land?" *eWeek*, 11 May 2004.

"Via Set to Launch Low-Priced Tablet PCs in 2nd Half: Report." *China Post*, 26 May 2010.

TELEMEDICINE

SIC CODE(S)

8099

4899

INDUSTRY SNAPSHOT

The telemedicine industry started out as a niche industry laden with problems: lack of trained professionals, limited broadband applications, lack of hardware and software devices, and concerns for medical privacy, just to name a few. However, by the end of the first decade of the 2000s, the industry had suddenly matured. Under the Obama administration, through the American Recovery and Reinvestment Act of 2009 (ARRA) Congress expressly provided for dedicated funds to support healthcare IT. As more Americans (as well as global customers) accessed broadband connections, telemedicine was clearly the way to the future, challenging traditional perceptions of medicine, accessibility, and doctor-patient relations.

Perhaps it is not surprising that medicine would follow the two major trends of the information age: high-speed communications and easy, immediate access to a wealth of information. While often broadly defined simply as the transfer of electronic medical data from one location to another, telemedicine really encompasses a broad range of emerging technologies, including telecommunications tools, information systems, and imaging technologies. Telemedicine is primarily intended to supplement the practice of conventional medicine and facilitate the exchange of information needed for diagnosis and treatment of illnesses. It has both obvious and subtle effects on the health care industry in general. One, it ostensibly helps to ease physician shortages as well as reduce overall health care costs. A key example is the remote monitoring of homebound patients. Another is teleradiology, which permits remote review and diagnosis by a licensed radiologist from electronically transmitted radiographic images, without the need to retain such expertise on site, "24/7," such as in rural emergency room settings.

Differing opinions as to the breadth and scope of the term "telemedicine" have made it nearly impossible to assess the true economic value of the industry. This has been further complicated by the transitional use of other terms along with telemedicine, such as "e-health" or "telehealth," which have become synonymous in the health care industry.

ORGANIZATION AND STRUCTURE

Telemedicine typically involves interactive, real time transactions (such as videoconferencing) that may require dedicated networks or even satellite links or "store-and-forward" systems that allow data, images, or patient information to be transmitted from a personal computer (PC) and inspected at the receiver's and sender's convenience. Transmission media include phone lines, coaxial or integrated services digital network lines, satellites, and other peripherals. Although complex dedicated networks provide the infrastructure for many institutional applications, telemedicine is rapidly evolving to encompass software and products for affordable desktop systems that can integrate voice, video, and data.

Applications range in complexity from the relatively simple transfer of digitized images or data via phone lines or the Internet to consultations and videoconferencing to the monitoring of patients at home or the direction of surgery or diagnostic procedures from a distance. Most applications have evolved from government-funded pilot programs, and a substantial proportion of telemedicine's advances were initially developed to meet the needs of military medicine and to improve health care in remote areas. Still in its youth, telemedicine is available primarily to large institutions such as medical centers and prisons, which utilize the technology in products and services for remote consultations, home health, teleradiology, telepathology, patient monitoring, distance education, and research.

The most popular application of telemedicine is the transmission of images in radiology, pathology, and dermatology, which do not require the patient's real-time involvement and can circumvent numerous legal problems created by cooperative diagnosis and treatment across state lines. The transmission of still images is also a well-established practice that Medicare and some other third parties will reimburse. Telemedicine in prisons, where the cost of patient transportation is exorbitant, has been highly successful. Interactive conferences for remote consults and distance education for practicing physicians and medical students are also becoming more widespread. *Health Care Management* pointed out that telemedicine offers a learning perspective that "can enable close observation of medical procedures and facilitate the diffusion of very intensive learning experiences." The publication also asserted that "telemedicine has a difficult relative value calculus." Thus, consideration must be given regarding whether there is economic justification for telemedicine technology.

Home Health With the number of U.S. senior citizens growing at a nearly exponential rate, home health spending continues to increase at a steady pace. Telemedical home health applications can range from phone-based call centers to integrated home telemonitoring systems that track the progress of chronically ill or recovering patients. In numerous pilot projects, at-home monitoring has been shown to reduce doctor and emergency visits and enable fewer home health nurses to see more patients more frequently in a shorter time. TeVital, a leading supplier of home-based monitoring equipment, estimated that per cost home health visits can be reduced by one third to one half through the use of sensing and video systems. Although home health telemedicine promised enormous potential savings, it had yet to establish itself as the accepted standard of practice, even in university-based programs in the United States, as of the middle of the first decade of the twenty-first century.

Rural Health An important and promising application for telemedicine technology, both globally and within the United States, has been its potential to reach geographically rural or isolated communities. The Health Resource and Services Administration (HRSA) of the U.S. Department of Health and Human Services (HHS), is tasked with overseeing telemedicine and telehealth concerns related to rural health settings within the United States. The most common applications are for diagnostic consults, data transmissions, and chronic disease management. Physicians in under-served rural areas are eligible for Medicare reimbursement for telemedicine services, with payment shared among practitioners. Although federal Medicaid law does not recognize telemedicine as a distinct service, services administered via telemedicine applications may be reimbursed at the state's option, according to a U.S. Department of Health and Human Services' Health Care Financing Administration Web page.

The HRSA's Office for the Advancement of Telehealth (OAT) is primarily a grants-based entity that provides funds and informational resources to eligible applicants. In its approval of grant awards, it focuses on rural health care or persons otherwise limited in access to proper care (e.g., the Alaskan Federal Health Care Access Network Telemedicine Project); under-represented populations (e.g., 40 telemedicine programs and partnerships within the Indian Health Service); innovative technology; and educational initiatives (such as instructional nursing guidelines for new mothers).

BACKGROUND AND DEVELOPMENT

Although interest in telemedicine was revived by the technological advances of the late 1990s, the use of communications technology to improve information sharing and to connect patients with doctors located elsewhere is not new. One of the first applications in the United States was a closed-circuit television system devised for a Nebraska state psychiatric institute in the 1950s. The National Aeronautics and Space Administration (NASA) began using telemetric devices to monitor the condition of astronauts in space in the 1960s and later to deliver health care to the Papago Indians of Arizona in the 1970s. Other early projects included a telemedicine station at Boston's Logan Airport to deliver emergency care to travelers and an experimental network that used satellite-based video to provide health care in isolated regions of Alaska.

International prototypes of low-cost telemedicine to link rural populations with health care providers included the Memorial University of Newfoundland's satellite-based audio and teleconferencing network that connected institutions throughout the province and was later linked to Kenya and five Caribbean nations. Using a government satellite, an Australian pilot project was begun in 1984 to provide health care to a remote group of islanders. In 1989 NASA established a satellite consultation network that used voice, video, and fax to aid earthquake victims in Soviet Armenia, and it was later extended to help burn victims after a railroad accident in Russia.

The U.S. government has actively supported a broad variety of mostly university-based demonstration projects for several decades, but many of its activities have never been systematically evaluated. After the National Information Infrastructure identified telemedicine as a key focus of information technology, joint agency ventures were reorganized to fulfill the requirements of the Telecommunications Reform Act of 1996, which mandated better reporting and evaluation of all federal telemedicine initiatives. Medicare was mandated to begin paying for some telemedicine consultations in 1999. Telecommunications carriers were required to provide service to rural health care providers, at rates comparable to those of urban areas in that state, with the support subsidy programs.

In December 2000, President Clinton signed legislation with strong bipartisan support that would greatly expand Medicare reimbursement for telemedicine services. The bill also greatly expanded the range of telemedical services covered by Medicare. The bill went into effect October 1, 2001. Because of the vagueness inherent in federal Medicaid law, states have the flexibility to reimburse the costs unique to telemedicine applications, such as technical support or line charges. As service caps become more universal and evidence of telemedicine's cost effectiveness accumulates, managed care organizations may begin reimbursing telemedicine more widely, or even requiring its use when direct patient-physician interaction is not essential.

In late 2002, the Centers for Medicare and Medicaid Services (CMS) announced specific criteria for telemedicine that must be met in order to receive Medicare payments. Specifically, the provider must use interactive audio and video to permit real time communication between the distant-site provider and the Medicare beneficiary. (Only a handful of states allowed payment for telemedicine services under Medicaid.) There has been a slow but steady increase in Medicare reimbursement for telemedicine since 2001.

Many visionary projections about the future of telemedicine have not been realized, and early grant-funded projects suffered from lack of focus. In addition, market projections are difficult because products and services are often part of larger investments in telecommunications technologies and health care delivery systems. Nevertheless, most industry projections were quite optimistic. The C. Everett Koop Institute estimated that as insurers recognize the savings provided by electronic links to patients and as technologies improve, telemedicine would become a $20 billion market consisting of software and hardware, biomedical equipment, and a standardized telecommunications infrastructure.

By 2009, at least 36 states and the District of Columbia had passed legislation expressly addressing telemedicine, according to a *Practical Health Law* publication. Georgia and Texas had the most comprehensive statutes, addressing not only licensure, but also exemptions from licensure for consulting services and/or irregular/infrequent practice.

Obstacles Although the cost of typical applications is quickly falling, telemedicine is not a common feature of the average medical practice. The most significant obstacles to its widespread use continue to be licensure constraints, malpractice concerns, lack of reimbursement, technical compatibility problems, and physician resistance.

Technology. Many interactive applications require high-bandwidth carriers and are dependent on switched public network, expensive media not yet balanced by the overall cost savings of many telemedicine applications. Although networking solutions for expensive real time teleconferencing and high level data exchange will continue to be critical, lack of integration and standards have discouraged many institutions from investing heavily in transitional or quickly obsolescent technology.

Liability. Electronically administered medical care that transcends a single jurisdiction poses significant new licensing, credentialing, and malpractice problems. Except for military physicians, who are licensed in one state but may practice anywhere, physicians who wish to practice telemedicine across state lines must be licensed wherever they provide care. Although reciprocal licensing schemes have been proposed by the Federation of State Medical Boards, they have thus far been rejected by the American Medical Association and other influential physicians' groups. Malpractice claims have also already been made for misdiagnoses by consulting physicians based on inadequate image transmission. *Medical Economics* claimed the growth of "national speciality programs" has changed standards of care to what a reasonable physician would do in the same specialty in a similar circumstance. Consequently, plaintiffs can utilize expert witnesses from anywhere in the country to testify regarding whether a standard was met.

Physician Resistance. In addition to malpractice concerns, logistical and political barriers also exist among individual practitioners who perceive increasingly centralized and cooperative medical care as a threat to their livelihood. Many physicians also express resistance to expensive technologies that cannot be easily integrated into an existing medical practice. Because patient records still exist substantially in paper form, data from electronic transactions must often be manually added to a medical record, adding another level of administrative labor. Rural physicians, among others, express reservations about giving up existing referral structures in favor of monopolistic networks mandated by large health care centers, and urban specialists accustomed to authority over their local resources express misgivings about relinquishing control over the quality of information available to them from distant sources. Many physicians cite inconvenience in existing telemedical consultation procedures and inconclusive evidence that telemedicine is in fact a better way to practice medicine.

A Canadian study published in the *Journal of the American Medical Association* in 2007 found that "home telemonitoring of chronic diseases appears to be a promising approach to patient management," especially for chronic pulmonary conditions, cardiac diseases, diabetes, and hypertension. The study also found that "home telemonitoring produces accurate and reliable data, empowers patients and influences their attitudes and behaviors, and may improve their medical condition." However, another study published the same year asserted that up to 45 million Americans age 60 and older may not be able to take advantage of telemedicine's benefits and improvements. A report by Parks Associates, as reported by *Medicine & Health,* found that many older Americans are not receptive to in-home health monitoring. Some of the possible reasons cited included a lack of interest and knowledge of technology, resistance to change in habits, and a feeling of invasion of privacy. The baby boomer generation, on the other hand—those 38 to 59 years old in the mid- to late first decade of the 2000s—is more technologically savvy and will "undoubtedly benefit from the recent and rapid advances in health-care technology."

CURRENT CONDITIONS

In just two years, 2008 and 2009, the telemedicine industry substantially expanded in visibility, scope, and support, thanks in large part to two developments. One was the increased availability of broadband Internet and communication connections for a majority of Americans, tying in with the 2009 conversion of analog to digital television signals. Secondly, the Obama administration (and Congress) provided nearly $20 billion in dedicated funds to the growth of the industry, both in geographic scope and expanded application.

In addition to the above comprehensive Act, Section 149 of the Medicare Improvements for Patients and Providers Act of 2008 added skilled nursing facilities to the list of eligible sites for reimbursement of health care services delivered via telemedicine. This was an important development and opened the door for further Medicare reimbursements in other areas. In 2008, Congress passed and the president signed the Ryan Haight Online Pharmacy Consumer Protection Act (P.L. 110-425), clamping down on the illegal sale and trafficking of prescription drugs over the Internet.

In December 2009, the American Telemedicine Association (ATA) provided comprehensive formal comment before the Federal Communication Commission (FCC) in support of a proposed national broadband plan (GN Docket 09-51) and a Medical Body Area Network (ET Docket 08-59) regarding healthcare delivery systems via telecommunications. The lack of uniform connectivity had thus far restricted universal acceptance of such a promise. However, the ATA was able to identify numerous comprehensive research studies and reports in support of expanded telemedicine.

As of 2009, PubMed, a bibliographic database of medical research maintained by the National Library of Medicine, contained more than 10,000 citations of published works relating to telemedicine or telehealth. The cumulative research tended to support the cost savings and efficacy of telemedicine in very palpable terms. For example, the cost to equip all U.S. emergency rooms with hybrid telehealth technologies could be covered just from savings from a reduction in transfers of patients between emergency departments, one broad study indicated. From a baseline of 2.2 million patients transported each year at a cost of $1.39 billion, hybrid telemedicine would have avoided 850,000 of the transports, at savings of $537 million a year. Another study showed avoidance of over 543,000 inmate transports in correctional facilities by the use of telemedicine. Nursing home transports would be reduced by over 387,000 transports yearly (from a baseline of 2.7 million transports), another study indicated, if hybrid telehealth technology was implemented, at an annual savings of $479 million. An example of substantial cost savings in disease management was shown in a 2008 study involving infants needing opthalmoscopy (scopic eye examinations), for conditions that would likely worsen over time (life years). For infants weighing less than 1500 grams, the costs (per quality-adjusted life year gained) were $3,193 with telemedicine, compared to $5,617 with standard opthalmoscopy.

Accordingly, the market for telemedicine devices and services was expected to generate nearly $3.6 billion in annual revenue within the next five years, with mobile services companies taking a sizeable chunk of that business, according to a 2009 report from market research firm Pike & Fischer (P&F). It also concluded that AT&T will have the largest presence in this market, followed closely by Verizon and Sprint Nextel.

INDUSTRY LEADERS

Service providers and device manufacturers are quickly stepping in as telemedicine moves from a grant-funded series of pilot projects to a mature industry incorporated into mainstream health care. Telecommunications providers such as BellSouth and AT&T are participating in pilot projects to provide networks capable of integrating voice, video, data, and advanced imaging.

American TeleCare Inc. (ATI) is prominent in the home health care market. Its Personal Telemedicine System works with a PC over phone lines to send and receive physiologic data. Images can be stored and filed with patient information and notes. In March 2000, ATI announced that it would be providing telemedicine equipment and services for a federally funded home telemedicine project for diabetes patients. The project was worth $28 million, the largest telemedicine grant ever funded by the U.S. government. The company formed a diabetes telemedicine partnership, called Informatics for Diabetes Education and Telemedicine (IDEATel), with Gentiva Health Services in late 2000. In 2002, HHC Health & Home Care, a division of the New York City Health and Hospitals Corporation, purchased 59 of ATI's home telehealth units. Sales in 2008 totaled $2.0 million.

PictureTel, another videoconferencing provider, offers high-end graphics and group conferencing and participates in several U.S. Department of Defense pilot projects. In 1999, Intel Corp. acquired 10 percent of PictureTel's equity at a cost of more than $30 million. The company produces videoconferencing units with a range of technology requirements, including integrated services digital network (ISDN), T1/E1, or ATM backbones. Applications include everything from operating room and emergency care to consultations via local Internet connections. Despite the boost from Intel's acquisition, the company faced growing doubts about its future, with continuing net losses. It was acquired by Polycom in 2001. Polycom develops, manufactures and markets a full range of high quality, easy-to-use, affordable voice and video communication products plus integrated communication solutions. Polycom, headquartered in Pleasanton, California, has seven U.S. offices and others throughout North America, Europe, Asia Pacific, Latin America, and the Caribbean.

MedVision, Inc., a software company, produces a utility for viewing MRI, x-ray, and other image and text data on any standard PC. The independent private company located in Minneapolis, Minnesota, develops software for medical practice management. Its customer base includes the Department of Defense, the University of Arizona, Canada's TechKnowledge, and the United Kingdom's United Medical Enterprises.

A relatively newer company on the scene was iMetrikus, based in Carlsbad, California, and formed in 1999. The company offers medical services to remote patients through its Internet-based MediCompass software. Patients can access results from devices such as blood glucose meters and blood pressure cuffs. The software also focuses on caring for patients with asthma, diabetes, hypertension, and AIDS.

AMERICA AND THE WORLD

According to a 2009 report by Global Industry Analysts, Inc., the global telemedicine market will exceed $18 billion by 2015. Some of the market drivers were an aging population, increased medical requirements in remote locations and technology advancements. The United States and Europe continued to dominate the world telemedicine market. Rising demand for quality healthcare and the need to contain escalating government expenditure on healthcare services was expected to push European governments towards adoption of e-health policies. The European software market was also poised to register double-digit compounded annual growth rates (CAGs) over through 2015.

Asia experienced a substantial rise in demand for telemedicine, primarily driven by the increasing healthcare costs and growth in aging population in the region (relatively faster compared to Europe and the United States). India and other developing countries, where quality of healthcare varies widely between urban and rural areas, have adopted telemedicine for bridging the rural-urban gap, offering enhanced access to medical care for its population. There has been a rapid rise in demand for teleradiology in Australia, with about 65 percent of radiologists relying on it.

Some of the key participants in the global telemedicine market included Aerotel Medical Systems Limited, AMD Telemedicine, Inc., Apollo PACS Inc., CARD GUARD Group, CardioNet Inc., Cerner Corporation, Cybernet Systems Corporation, GE Healthcare Ltd., Honeywell HomMed LLC, Invivo Corp., Johns Hopkins Medicine, Mennen Medical Corp., NightHawk Radiology Services LLC, Philips Healthcare, SHL TeleMedicine Ltd., Siemens Healthcare, Polycom, TANDBERG, TeleVital Inc., Templeton Readings LLC, United Therapeutics Corporation, Welch Allyn Protocol, Inc., and WorldCare International Inc., among others, according to Global Industry Analysts, Inc.

World Care Technologies, Inc., a Cambridge, Massachusetts, company, provides telemedicine and medical management services accessible through the Internet. In 1999 the company formed a strategic alliance with Data General Corp., a leading information systems provider, and MarkCare Medical Systems, Inc., a medical imaging systems distributor. The alliance combines telemedicine and personal archiving and communication systems to interconnect health care providers. Initial installation sites included hospitals and clinics in Spain, Portugal, and Romania.

Canada has a long history of providing networked medical services to its remote provinces. Some experts believe Canada's publicly financed health care system with government incentives helped advance the broad diffusion of telemedicine. *Telephony* reported that Dr. Mehran Anvari, from a performed the world's first telerobotic-assisted surgery over a public network from a surgery terminal at St. Joseph's Hospital in Hamilton, Ontario. The February 2003 acid reflux surgery helped a patient 250 miles away by, utilizing a multi-protocol-label-switching-based IP virtual private network linked to Bell Canada.

RESEARCH AND TECHNOLOGY

Perhaps the biggest concern for the advancement of telemedicine technology is that of medical privacy. Encryption of medical records and images communicated electronically remained a challenge in 2009.

The 42nd session of the Scientific and Technical Subcommittee of the United Nations Committee on the Peaceful Uses of Outer Space (COPUOS) was held in Vienna in early 2005. Space system-based disaster management support was one of the key agenda items, along with space system-based telemedicine. Member states were briefed on the application of telemedicine in health care, epidemiology, off-site radiology services, cardiac monitoring, medical consultations and specialist referrals, correctional care and tele-education. The subcommittee noted that space system-based telemedicine could provide significantly improved and cost-effective access to quality health care, transform the delivery of health care, and improve the health of millions of people throughout the world.

BIBLIOGRAPHY

"Advances in Telemedicine Wire Patient Care." *Employee Benefits News,* 1 May 2003.

American TeleCare, Inc. Announces New Product Release of its Multiuser Swipe Card Technology." Press Release, American TeleCare, 21 August 2006.

Becker, Cinda. "Dial-a-Doc Gets Boost: JCAHO Issues First Official Telemedicine Endorsement." *Modern Health Care,* 2 March 2003.

Bloch, Carolyn. *Federal Telemedicine, Telehealth & Informatics Report.* 2005. Available from www.federaltelemedicine.com/.

Bonfield, Tim. "Video Device Alters Home Nursing: System Lets Caretakers Conduct Checkups from Remote Sites." *Enquirer,* 4 August 2004.

Chin, Tyler. "Company Pushes Online Consultation in a Visual Direction." *American Medicine News,* 21 March 2005. Available from www.ama-assn.org/.

"Comments of the American Telemedicine Association before the Federal Communications Commission." *In the Matter of Healthcare Delivery Elements of National Broadband Plan NBP Public Notice #17,* 3 December 2009. Available from http://www.americantelemed.org/files/public/policy/FCC_12_2_2009.pdf.

Denes, Shary. "Cap Rock Telephone Opens Door to Telemedicine." *Rural Telecommunications,* March-April 2003.

Eron, Lawrence. "Treating Infections in the Home Yields Clinical, Economic Benefits." *Drug Benefit Trends,* 1 March 2007.

Eron, Lawrence, and Michelle Marineau. "Telemedicine: Treating Infections in the Home." *Infections in Medicine,* 1 November 2006.

"E-Visits Begin To Pay Off for Physicians." *Information Week,* 31 May 2004.

Gillespie, Greg. "A View From Afar: Vanderbuilt University Uses a Telemedicine Program to Help Diagnose a Devastating Eye Disease Before It's Too Late." *Health Data Management,* June 2003.

"Global Telemedicine Market to Exceed $18 Billion by 2015, According to New Report by Global Industry Analysts, Inc." *NewsGuide,* 4 June 2009. Available from http://www.newsguide. us/technology/networking/Global-Telemedicine-Market-to-Exceed-18-Billion-by-2015-According-to-New-Report-by-Global-Industry-Analysts-Inc/.

"HIDA Market Report." 2004. Available from www.mdsi.org/.

Hodgkinson, Jane. "Tech Solution to Night-time Doctor Shortage." *National Nine News,* 7 March 2005.

"Hoover's Company Capsules." *Hoover's Online,* 2007. Available from www.hoovers.com.

"Initiative Provides Free Electronic Prescribing." *Health Management Technology,* April 2007.

Johnson, Lee J. "Legal Risks of Telemedicine." *Medical Economics,* 10 January 2003.

Kvedar, Joseph C. "Physician Urges Employers to Get Connected to Telemedicine." *Employee Benefit News,* 1 August 2006.

Linkous, Jonathan D. "Telemedicine Information & Resources: Predicting the Market for Telemedicine." Available from www. atmeda.org/.

———. "The Challenge of Regulating Internet Prescribing." American Telemedicine Association White Paper, September 2009. Available from http://www.americantelemed.org/files/public/policy/Internet%20Prescribing%20and%20 Practice.pdf.

"Microsoft, Intel Partner in Telemedicine Venture." *ITworld.com,* 11 March 2005. Available from http://tie.telemed.org/.

Nagy, Benjamin. "Telemedicine's Depth Now Going Beyond Rural Areas." *Managed Healthcare Executive,* September 2006.

"New Study Finds Home Telehealth to be Promising for Patient Management of Chronic Diseases." *Health IT News,* 10 May 2007.

"News." American TeleCare, Inc., 2007. Available from www. americantelecare.com.

"November 2009 Brown Bag Write-Up State Changes in Telehealth Licensure Laws." Press Release, Center for TeleHealth and e-Health Law, November 2009. Available from http://www.telehealthlawcenter.org.

Reid, Jim. "A Telemedicine Primer: Understanding the Issues." 2005. Available from www.atsp.org/.

"Report: Telemedicine spending to approach $3.6B annually by 2014." *Health Imaging,* 11 October 2009. Available from http://www.healthimaging.com/_news/topic/telemedicine.

Robinson, David F., Grant T. Savage, and Kim Sydow Campbell. "Organizational Learning, Diffusion of Innovation and International Collaboration in Telemedicine." *Health Care Management Review,* January-March 2003.

"Rural Telemedicine Thrives Despite Lack of Broadband." *Government Health IT,* 17 April 2006.

"Telemedicine and Telehealth Articles." *Telemedicine Information Exchange,* 14 March 2005. Available from http://tie.telemed.org/.

"Telemedicine in the Ambulatory Setting: Trends, Opportunities and Challenges." First Consulting Group, 20 June 2007. Available from www.atsp.org.

"Telemedicine: Look Before You Leap." *Medical Laboratory Observer,* April 2003.

"Telepharmacy An Idea Whose Time Has Come." *Chain Drug Review,* 10 April 2006.

"U.K. Researchers Critical of Telemedicine but Bullish on Telecare." *E-Health Insider,* 7 March 2005.

U.S. Department of Health and Human Services, Indian Health Service. "Welcome to IHS Telemedicine." 15 June 2007. Available from www.his.gov/.

Wachter, Glenn. "How High Will Telemedicine Soar?" *For the Record,* 8 March 2004.

"What You Need to Know About Telemedicine." *Practical Health Law,* March/April 2004.

TELEPHONE SERVICES AND ACCESSORIES

SIC CODE(S)

5065

4812

INDUSTRY SNAPSHOT

As the telephone became a necessity, and as telephone penetration peaked, telephone companies began expanding their services and telephone equipment manufacturers began developing new accessories to make telephone use more convenient and to give users greater options. The wide array of telephone accessories and services was developed mainly by research and development teams at some of the country's better-known telecommunications companies. For the most part, telephone users avail themselves of these services through local service providers, although another telecommunications company may have developed the product or technology. Among the more popular telephone services and accessories are call blocking, call forwarding, caller ID, call waiting, call waiting ID, repeat dial, return call, signal ring, 900-call block, the cordless digital spread spectrum telephone, and conference calling.

The upsurge in U.S. telecommunications industry mega mergers was traced by many to the Telecommunications Reform Act of 1996. Intended to deregulate the industry and stimulate competition, the statute instead appeared to set off a massive wave of corporate mergers. Of the original seven Baby Bells, three remained by 2004: Verizon (the product of the merger of Bell Atlantic and GTE), SBC Communications (which absorbed Baby Bell sibling Pacific Telesis), and BellSouth. In 2005, SBC purchased former "Ma Bell" AT&T and adopted its name AT&T. In April 2008, AT&T acquired BellSouth.

These large telephone companies claimed a majority of the market in landline telephone service. AT&T served 22 states, with key markets in California, Texas, and Illinois, and all of the *Fortune 1000* companies. Verizon provided service in 28 states and Washington, DC. Sprint Nextel, which was formed when the number three and number five telecommunications companies merged in 2008, was the largest telephone company in the United States that was not born out of the Baby Bells. Qwest Communications was also a major local phone provider with service in 14 states. The former three companies held a large share of the wireless cellular phone market, which had grown to overcome landline telephone service in the weaker economy of 2009–2010. It is unlikely that, as the economy improves, Americans will revert to more landline services.

ORGANIZATION AND STRUCTURE

In the United States, the face of the telecommunications industry was forever altered in 1984 when the Justice Department's antitrust ruling broke the giant American Telephone & Telegraph (AT&T) into seven regional companies, or "Baby Bells": Ameritech, Bell Atlantic, BellSouth, NYNEX, Pacific Telesis, Southwestern Bell, and U.S. West. However, Bell Atlantic's acquisition in the late 1990s of Baby Bell sibling NYNEX for $25.7 billion doubled its size and made it the number two U.S. telecommunications service company after its former parent. Its merger with GTE Corp. in 2000 doubled the company's size again.

Mergers and acquisitions (M&As) continued to change the structure of the U.S. telecommunications

Personal Consumption Expenditures as a Percentage of Total Telephone and Internet Services, 1980–2009

Year	Landline	Cellular	Internet
1980	100%	0%	0%
1985	100%	0%	0%
1990	96%	4%	0%
1995	85%	13%	2%
2000	67%	22%	11%
2005	44%	39%	17%
2009	36%	44%	21%

SOURCE: Bureau of Economic Analysis.

industry throughout the second half of the 1990s and into the twenty-first century. The largest basic telephone service providers in the United States were AT&T, Verizon, and Sprint. Others included Qwest and Vonage. These and other companies such as Lucent Technologies and Nortel also developed and marketed some of the highly successful new add-on services and devices.

Almost all of these companies, including independents, offered customers a broad range of add-on services and accessories, including caller ID, call block, and call forwarding. In addition to these services, American consumers had a number of other products to choose from, such as the PowerDialer from Technology Arts of Massachusetts. PowerDialer was designed to automatically redial busy numbers as quickly as the local telephone company could process the calls, as fast as 25 times in a minute. The product, which retailed for $249 in the late 1990s, was marketed directly by Technology Arts and was not available through local telephone companies.

The future promises an even broader range of services for telephone consumers with the spread of fiber-optic wiring, which allows faster and better data transmission over telephone lines. A number of major telephone service providers also acquired an interest in television cable companies in order to offer television connections over telephone lines. Furthermore, the Internet and wireless telecommunications systems have played a significant role in the development of the industry.

BACKGROUND AND DEVELOPMENT

Telephone companies were left in a new competitive arena due to the upheaval in the U.S. telecommunications industry that resulted from the Justice Department's antitrust ruling in the mid-1980s. Home and business telephone users, who had previously rented equipment from the local telephone company, could now purchase their own equipment and pay local providers for hooking up to their networks. Although most telephone companies

offered a range of telephones for sale, consumers usually found they could get a better deal at the local discount chain or an electronics store.

Most telephone companies soon realized there was a virtual gold mine in marketing add-on products. Suddenly, services that previously had been available only to sophisticated business users were being sold to home service consumers. These included call forwarding ability and the ability to dial back the number of the last caller even if the phone was not answered. Some services were offered on a per-use basis. For example, telephone customers unable to get to a ringing phone in time could punch the star key and two numbers, typically six and nine, to activate this service, for which they would then be charged 75 cents or $1.00. Those who chose to have access to this service at all times paid a monthly fee for unlimited use.

Among the most popular services marketed by local telephone service providers in the late 1990s was call block, which allows telephone customers to block all calls from certain telephone numbers, and call forwarding, which routes all calls to another telephone number or to voice mail when the phone is busy or not answered. Also particularly popular is caller ID, the use of which requires a small box with a window to display a telephone number. This feature allows customers to determine the number (and sometimes the name of the caller) from which a call is coming.

The technology for cordless telephony improved significantly from the time this kind of equipment was first marketed. Reception on early cordless telephones left a great deal to be desired, and many purchasers of such early equipment soon abandoned it and returned to corded phones. In the late 1990s, digital spread spectrum technology vastly improved the reception and transmission quality of cordless telephones.

Entering the twenty-first century, the worldwide telecommunications industry offered a vast selection of premium telephone accessories and services. Furthermore, such established services as call waiting and caller ID had gained strong levels of penetration by this point. In addition, these accessories and services adapted to the prominence of wireless and Internet telecommunications technology as well as to changing user needs. Available from local telephone service providers, and in some cases from independent retailers, telephone accessories ran the gamut from caller ID boxes to a range of telephone instruments, both corded and cordless.

By the twenty-first century, the variety of telephone models available to consumers became increasingly expansive. In contrast, choices available in the 1980s would have been largely limited to console, wall, or princess telephones in black, white, or pink. After Ma Bell's control of telephones was loosened by deregulation, a typical discount store routinely began to stock a selection of about 50 cordless phones, 30 phones with cords, and at least a dozen cellular phones. That did not include the combination telephone/answering machines, of which one might find at least half a dozen. The consumer benefited from the increased competition in this marketplace as prices plummeted. By 2000, a 25-channel cordless telephone could be found at most discount retailers for less than $100, about half what it would have cost only a year earlier.

Furthermore, cordless telephones outsold corded phones in the late 1990s. Jim Barry, a spokesperson for the Consumer Electronics Manufacturers Association (CEMA), predicted that the gap between cordless and corded phone sales was likely to grow wider over time. "What you're getting with a cordless phone is convenience," Barry said. "And the technology of cordless telephones is getting better." Cordless telephones also proved to be a very popular gift idea. For example, Ameritech, owned by local service behemoth SBC Communications, reported that about 45 percent of all its cordless telephones are sold in November, just in time for Christmas gift giving.

Of the add-on telephone services and accessories, the three most popular features were call waiting, caller ID, and voice mail, in that order. Call waiting achieved significant penetration by the late 1990s. Pacific Bell, for example, reported that 50 percent of its customers subscribed to its call waiting service. Part of the appeal stems from the simplicity of obtaining and using this service, because call waiting service is compatible with any telephone. When a user with this service is on the telephone and someone else calls, an audible signal can be heard on the line. The user may click the receiver button or push "Flash" to answer the new call. No special equipment is needed for this service, although customers must pay a monthly fee to the local service provider. Moreover, by 2000, telephone companies merged two popular add-on services, call waiting and caller ID, which apprised users of their callers so that they could decide whether or not to take incoming calls while already on the phone. This service required a caller ID box, caller ID service, call waiting service, and the caller ID/call waiting service.

In addition, by the beginning of the twenty-first century, new call waiting technology had hit the market, enabling users to use call waiting services while online. Companies such as Callwave, Pagoo, Prodigy, and MSN were among the first to offer programs for call waiting service while using the Internet. Use of these programs cost $5.00 a month. In addition, Actiontec developed a call waiting modem that informs users of incoming calls and gives them the option of staying online or taking calls.

Built on the popular caller ID technology, a product called privacy manager was introduced in parts of Chicago and Detroit in the fall of 1998 by Ameritech. Caller ID was designed to help users screen out unwanted calls,

particularly from telemarketers and other sales personnel. Cagey telemarketing firms, however, managed to dodge this barrier by using legal means to block both their identities and telephone numbers. Privacy manager used caller ID technology to identify incoming calls from phone numbers that were either "unknown" or "unavailable." Such calls were intercepted by a recorded message that asks the caller to identify himself or herself. If the party placing the call chooses to disclose his or her identity, the call rings through to the privacy manager customer, who then hears a brief recording identifying the caller. The customer then has three options: accept the call, decline the call without explanation, or decline the call and have the privacy manager ask that the caller not call again. In introducing the product, Diane Primo, Ameritech's president of product management, said, "The message is loud and clear. Our customers simply want control over telemarketing."

By the end of the 1990s, the average household traded approximately 115 messages a week, according to a household messaging study by Pitney Bowes. In addition, the average household also received a plethora of telemarketing calls each week. According to *American Demographics,*, caller ID subscriptions quadrupled between 1995 and 1999 because of the influx of calls received. *American Demographics* also reported that about 40 percent of people between the ages of 16 and 74 in households with incomes of $25,000 or below used caller ID service. Unlike call waiting, caller ID service required special equipment, specifically a liquid crystal display (LCD) screen to display information about incoming calls. Some later models of phones, both corded and cordless, had a caller ID screen built in, and consumers who opted for this service could purchase a small caller ID box with such a screen. Customers paid a monthly fee for caller ID service and also paid a rental fee if they used a caller ID box supplied by the telephone company. In the late 1990s, telephone companies started offering this service via the Internet for managing calls while online. For example, Bell Atlantic (now Verizon) launched Internet Call Manager for $5.95 a month, which notified users of incoming calls while they surfed the Internet. Voice mail systems are covered in a separate essay in this book.

Increasingly popular were two-line phones that allowed customers to use a line hooked up to a computer modem as a second voice line when the computer was not in use. Other telephone accessories or features available on the market included storage for telephone numbers called frequently, speakers for hands-free telephone use, and an answering machine for those who prefer that to voice mail.

In the early 2000s, the main financial problems inundating the industry included more competition and a weak economy. The Baby Bells had been losing their local subscribers to carriers such as MCI because those companies could rent access equipment at fixed rates from the local companies. The smaller "upstart telecoms," known in the industry as competitive local exchanges, were serving 17.3 million, or 9 percent, of the 192 million access lines in 2001. That figure was up from 7.7 percent a year earlier. The new competition, though somewhat weak, was bringing prices down. The telecommunications industry was one sector that was significantly affected by the economic downturn. By 2002, it was evident that the companies making progress included Verizon, SBC, and BellSouth. On the other hand, Qwest was facing some trouble.

According to Verizon Vice-Chairman and President Lawrence Babbio, low prices on cellular, long distance, and high-speed Internet service had eroded profits and accelerated the troubles of the telecommunication business. For instance, Verizon maintained a virtual monopoly in the local phone business market but was showing visible signs of erosion. Verizon's access line growth rate slowed down in 2000 and posted losses in the first quarter of 2001. That rate of decline only continued. In the first quarter of 2002, the company's access lines declined by 1.1 percent. As such, Verizon turned its eye to the launch of digital subscriber lines (DSL), long distance, and wireless, to recover. By 2004, it was the clear leader in wireless services, with nearly 38 million subscribers.

One of the emerging trends in 2003 was that of service bundling. While bundling of such phone packages as call waiting plus caller ID had been the norm for some time, communications companies, many of which had merged in the frenzy after deregulation, began to package complete communication packages. Bundling of local, long distance, cellular, cable, and Internet services was seeing a tremendous upswing. A study by J.D. Power found that 40 percent of consumers purchased local and long distance bundles in 2003. Such bundling seemed to be a win-win situation, as it allowed the consumer to often get better rates than purchasing services a la carte, and it allowed the company to keep customers, who were 50 percent less likely to switch providers if they had bundled services.

By 2003, use of caller ID and call blocking services had changed. The national Do Not Call registry, which took effect on October 1, 2003, with 53 million registered phone numbers, significantly cut into the amount of unwanted telemarketing calls received. Such calls had often been the reason for subscriptions to the services in the first place. However, while caller ID services remained popular as they evolved in use and technology—with a DSL line, for instance, users could even check their caller ID on the television—use of the call block service declined. Call forwarding was also seeing a revolution. In 2003, subscribers to Cingular Wireless were able to

forward incoming calls to the landline phone number of their choice automatically.

Although the performance of cordless telephones sharply improved, the tried and true corded telephone continued to be first choice for many users because of its dependability and security. Other attractive features of corded phones are the lower price and the knowledge that they will still function in a power outage. However, cordless phones were still king in the early years of the twenty-first century's first decade.

There are a number of reasons for the sharp increase in popularity of the cordless telephone, not the least of which is significantly improved reception. The first cordless phones on the market allowed users to walk from one room of the house to another without dragging a telephone cord along with them, but they were subject to considerable interference, had a limited range, and lacked security. The first cordless phones transmitted sound from the handset to the telephone's base using an analog signal by which data is represented in continuously variable physical quantities. Neighboring cordless phone users often found snippets of other conversations breaking into their own. Even transmissions from household baby monitors sometimes interfered with cordless phone calls. However, cordless models in the early years of the first decade of the 2000s broadcast over frequencies that were less crowded and offered much clearer signals. Some new cordless phones used digital signals, reducing the possibility for intercepted conversations. Sounds are converted into computer code and then transmitted between the base and the handset.

In addition to increased dependability, cordless telephones in the early years of the first decade of the twenty-first century were available in a number of different models. Early cordless phones, operating on frequencies between 43 and 49 MHz, were highly susceptible to interference from computers, fluorescent lights, and other such devices. Transmissions at such low frequencies generally were not able to penetrate walls or other such obstructions. Most of the early cordless phones, now rarely available in stores, operated over 10 channels. If interference was encountered on one channel, the phone would switch automatically to the next.

Improved reception is available on 25-channel analog cordless phones, which manage to avoid interference by using more channels. Some of the 25-channel phones come with built-in caller ID. If longer range and still clearer reception is required, 900 MHz analog phones are a good choice, according to CEMA's Jim Barry. He said that some such telephones operate dependably at three-quarters of a mile from the base. He pointed out, however, that since the signal is uncoded, users run the risk of having their conversations intercepted. That danger can be avoided if users opt for a 900 MHz digital phone, which converts sounds into code for transmission from the handset to the base. To ensure even better reception, some 900 MHz phones use digital spread spectrum technology. If interference is encountered on one channel, the phone searches for a clear channel as far away as possible from the one that is blocked. This technology increases the clarity of reception and range. Finally, while the superior cordless phone of the early years of the first decade of the 2000s was the 2.4 GHz model, with twice the range of the 900 MHz models, by 2004 the premium product was the 5.8 GHz model. In addition, telephone equipment makers continued to include other features, such as multi-line capabilities and security features.

In a measure to reduce plastic pollution in landfills, Southwest Research Institute (SwRI), of San Antonio, Texas, collaborated in 2005 with a technology firm and NASA's Glenn Research Center to build a pilot plant to produce conductive biodegradable plastic pellets for use in the manufacture of biodegradable plastic cell phone cases. The new cases will degrade in landfills and will also incorporate E-911 location finding and electromagnetic interference-shielding capabilities. A company formed by the Spirit Lake Indian Tribe Reservation of Fort Totten, North Dakota, the Golden Eagle Wireless U.S.A. Co., undertook the work.

Chad West, president of Ascom Wireless Solutions of Gothenburg, Sweden, announced in early 2006 that they were expanding their Digital Enhanced Cordless Telecommunications (DECT) operations to the North American market. DECT is a European standard for digital portable phones, which is commonly used for domestic or corporate purposes but can also be used for wireless data transfers. DECT is similar to the Global System for Mobile Communications (GSM), which in the middle of the first decade of the 2000s was the most popular cellular system for mobile phones in the world, used by more than 1.8 billion people in more than 210 countries and territories. A major difference between the systems is cell radius. DECT cells have a radius of 25 to 100 meters, whereas GSM cells are 2 to 10 kilometers.

At the same time, at the January 2006 International CES trade show in Las Vegas, Motorola unveiled its "mobility solutions," a new family of connected cordless phone systems. On each handset of Motorola's C51 and SBV5400 expandable cordless phone systems is a "Connect To" button that will provide access to landline, Voice over Internet Protocol (VoIP) calling, cellular service, home intercom, live streaming video, shared family phone books, high-speed Internet, and push-to-talk-over-instant messaging. These cordless phones became available at the end of 2006 and were being marketed as a tool to allow families one-button access to the various ways they can communicate around their homes.

Later that year, newcomer Vonage of Holmdel, New Jersey, posted its best quarter in its short history (it began operations in March 2002). It added 328,279 lines for a total of almost 1.6 million subscriber line, and its users made more than 3 billion calls. Vonage's technology enables users to make and receive calls anywhere a broadband Internet connection is available, offering subscribers an experience similar to traditional telephone services. Vonage's services can be purchased online or at national retailers such as Wal-Mart, Target, and Best Buy. The service is available in the United States, Canada, and the United Kingdom and offers such traditional telephone services as call waiting, call forwarding, and voice mail for a flat monthly rate. In May 2006, Vonage offered its subscribers free unlimited calls to France, Italy, Ireland, Spain, and the United Kingdom. Its revenues for the first quarter of 2006 rose 192 percent to $119 million from $41 million in the first quarter of 2005. By 2007 it had sales of $828.2 million.

By the middle of the first decade of the 2000s, telephone users who wanted to save money on long distance calls, or who were unable to obtain a traditional phone contract, could purchase a prepaid phone card. With a prepaid phone card, calling minutes are purchased in advance and can be used anytime, for calls anywhere in the United States For international calls, prepaid minutes are used up at double the domestic rate. The user simply purchases the card, which is available at many stores, and when ready to activate it, calls the toll-free number shown on the card, enters a personal identification number, or PIN, which is also revealed on the card after scratching off a coating, and is then ready to dial a desired number. Because the minutes are purchased in advance, there are no monthly fees or hidden surcharges.

A new contender appeared in March 2002 when Vonage signed up its first residential customer. Vonage, headquartered in Holmdel, New Jersey, became a leading provider of broadband telephone services (Voice over Internet Protocol, or VoIP) with 2.5 million subscriber lines by 2008. The technology allows anyone with a touchtone telephone to make and receive calls wherever a broadband Internet connection is available.

The two largest telephone companies in the United States—AT&T and Verizon—seemed bent on getting larger in 2008. Verizon purchased Alltell Wireless for $28 billion, which increased its number of wireless subscribers to about 80 million. AT&T spent $275 million in November 2008 when it acquired Wayport, a network and applications management company that provides back-office management for Wi-Fi hot spots. Earlier that month, AT&T announced plans to buy wireless communications provider Centennial Communications for $944 million. These two purchases followed AT&T's buy-out of Bell South in April 2008. Not to be left out of the

M&A game, Spring spun off its WiMAX division to Clearwire to form a new $14.5 billion mobile broadband company.

Indeed, virtually all of the growth in the telephone industry in the late years of the first decade of the 2000s was concentrated in the mobile and wireless segments, and many believed the days of the landline telephone were limited. A 2008 J.D. Power and Associates study showed that one-quarter of U.S. wireless phone users "never pick up a traditional wired phone any more." Another report published in *RCR Wireless News* stated that, by September 2008, 20 million U.S. households had disconnected their landlines and were relying solely on cellular service. Thirty percent of those who used cell phones exclusively were under the age of 30. The same study predicted that one in five households in the United States would use only wireless phone service by 2009. Figures at Verizon, the nation's largest telecommunications provider in 2008, supported such predictions. The number of the company's landline subscribers fell 11.4 percent between June 2007 and June 2008 to 22.45 million, the largest such decline in its history.

CURRENT CONDITIONS

In 2010, a new phrase came into vogue: "There's an app for that." What it referred to was the seemingly unending list of new (software) applications one could download or install on mobile devices in order to access anything from visual directions to a restaurant, to Real Time scores at a football game, to instant messaging via Twitter, with or without photo or video clips attached. PDAs were a thing of the past, and for the most part, GPS devices almost were, since now there was an "app" for that, available for direct download/installation on mobile smartphones. Whereas the focus earlier in the decade had been on *accessories* for handhelds and mobile phones (e.g., chargers, stylish interchangeable cases or snap-on colors for phone faces, earphones, remote speakers, etc.), by 2010 the focus was on available applications.

Nonetheless, according to ABI Research worldwide revenues from accessories (puchased separately from any included in the box with a phone) were $26.5 billion in 2009, expected to reach $50 billion by 2015. The most popular products included carrying and protective cases for smartphones, and scratch protectors. Bluetooth headsets and memory cards were also big sellers.

3G and 4G technology was advancing so rapidly that, in its wake, associated problems began to attract more media attention. First, a renewed scare surfaced about radiation emitting from antennae from mobile phones. Then several states enacted new laws prohibiting "texting" while driving, following several widely-publicized fatal car crashes around the country. Finally, near the end of 2010, several media sources warned of privacy compromises through fake caller ID (for both wireless and landline accounts), in which hackers used someone else's caller ID to access not only voice mail messages, but also financial and other personal information.

On the good side of mobile phones, there were improvements in faster access for 911 emergency calls, and better technology to quickly identify and pinpoint the geographic location of a particular cell phone device, for use in both emergencies and crime-tracking (and parental monitoring). This technology was effective even when cell phones were not being used, such as when no calls were being placed or received.

Several reports published in early 2009 showed that, for the first time, U.S. households using just cell phones outpaced households using just landlines. Now that internet access was readily available in mobile devices, many telephone services became redundant (on both household landline and mobile phones) and persons opted for the convenience and mobility of cell phones. Some reports also alluded to households dropping landlines as a cost-saving measure during the tight economy. Moreover, by December 2009, mobile data transmission outnumbered voice traffic for the first time, according to wireless equipment vendor Ericsson.

In September 2010, the Federal Communications Commission (FCC), which regulates telephone and Internet services, released data on Internet access, focusing on broadband connection speeds. As of June 2009, there were 71 million fixed (as opposed to mobile) connections to households, of which only 44 percent met or exceeded the speed tier most closely approximating the universal availability target of 4 megabits per second downstream and 1 Mbps upstream, as set forth in the National Broadband Plan. The number of mobile wireless service subscribers with data plans for full Internet access increased to 35 million, up 40 percent in just six months. Cable modem connections remained the most popular, accounting for 41 million, a aDSL at 31 million. Four million subscribers used fiber connections, and one million used satellite Internet connections.

A fast-growing segment of the market was interconnected VoIP service. As of June 2009, there were 133 million traditional switched access lines in service and 23 million interconnected VoIP subscriptions, together representing about 157 million wireline retail local telephone service connections. Of these, 93 million were residential connections, and 64 million were business connections.

Overall, reported Datamonitor (using figures released by independent telecom analyst Ovum), total revenues for fixed line services worldwide were roughly $350 billion in 2010. These were expected to decline to $283 billion by 2014, mostly due to the increase in wireless services.

Revenues from mobile services worldwide were expected to increase by almost $100 billion between 2009 and 2012.

INDUSTRY LEADERS

In late 2005, SBC Communications, Inc. completed its acquisition of AT&T in a $16 billion transaction, at which point it adopted AT&T, Inc. as its corporate name. The merger propelled the new AT&T into a leadership position in the global telecommunications and networking market. In 2008 AT&T was a world leader in communications services. In the United States, AT&T Mobility (formerly Cingular Wireless) was one of the top two wireless carriers, with 70 million subscribers. In 2009 At&T had more than 300,000 employees worldwide and revenues of $123 billion, down from $124 billion in 2008.

Verizon Communications, formed by the merger of Bell Atlantic and GTE, is the largest of the surviving Baby Bells and remains a leading player in the market for telephone services and accessories. Its main competitive advantage is that it is the longest-lasting phone company in the heavily populated Northeast. Verizon provides local telephone service to approximately 40 million homes and businesses in a 29-state area stretching from Maine to Virginia, including the District of Columbia.

In 2003, Verizon became the second regional Bell company to allow long distance throughout its local calling region. That year, the company lost 3.8 percent of its local lines, a drop from 59.7 million in 2002 to 57.4 million, but it introduced plans to combine unlimited local and long distance calling in an effort to keep customers. In March 2008, Verizon had 39 million landline telephone customers and 67 million wireless customers. One year later, in March 2009, the number of landline customers dropped to 35 million, but wireless customers grew to 87 million. 2009 revenues were $62.1 billion.

Sprint Nextel Corp., like most players in the U.S. telecommunications market, has irons in a number of fires. Among the top three long distance providers in the United States, the company also provides local phone and Internet services. In 2000, regulators denied its acquisition by WorldCom (which later merged with MCI). In 2002, Sprint Corp. reported heavy losses, but finally managed to register a profit in the final quarter. By 2003, the company re-merged its SprintFON and SprintPCS divisions, and its one-year net income grew nearly 93 percent. On August 12, 2005, Sprint and Nextel Communications Inc. announced the completion of their merger transaction, forming Sprint Nextel Corporation. In May 2006, Sprint Nextel finalized the spin-off of its local telephone operations under the name of Embarq Corp., which allowed Sprint Nextel to mainly focus on building its position in the market for mobile communications products and services.

Based in Denver, Colorado, Qwest Communications International boosted its position in the telephone services market with its purchase in 2000 of Baby Bell U.S. West, which doubled the company's size. Qwest's acquisition of U.S. West gave it 25 million local phone service subscribers. It was hoped that the move would dispel U.S. West's reputation for poor service that earned it the nickname "U.S. Worst." In the spring of 2006, Qwest Communications Corp., an affiliate of Qwest Communications International, signed a three-year, multimillion-dollar contract with the state of Arizona to supply over 75 telecommunications products and services to state agencies, cities, counties, K-12 schools, colleges, and universities. Qwest had approximately 37,000 employees and sales of $12.3 billion in 2009.

WORKFORCE

It is virtually impossible to isolate the segments of the telecommunications industry responsible for some of the specialized services and accessories covered here. The industry as a whole is a major employer in the United States as well as in most other Western countries with a sophisticated communications infrastructure. The world's growing dependence on communications technology is likely to ensure that this sector remains a major employer. It is possible, however, that some of the rationalizations in the industry brought on by mergers and acquisitions may, from time to time, bring job reductions at some of the companies that are major players in this field.

Employment opportunities within the telecommunications industry run the gamut from entry-level clerical positions to researchers and engineers to high-paying management positions at the head of some of the industry's major players. For young people interested in participating in the technological revolution that continues to sweep this country and the world, the telecommunications industry is at the heart of this revolution, sponsoring much of the research that moved technological know-how forward during the late twentieth century.

RESEARCH AND TECHNOLOGY

One of the newer devices on the market in the late years of the first decade of the 2000s was the ComSwitch CS7500, manufactured by Command Communications. The ComSwitch is designed to make it possible for a phone, answering machine, fax, and modem to share a phone line. The device can automatically reject telemarketing calls and route the remaining incoming calls to the phone or fax. The ComSwitch will also send a message to a user at a remote location whenever he or she receives a voice message, fax, or data transmission.

Motorola, RCA, and Uniden all introduced cordless phone systems in 2006 that integrated home and cell phones with a touch of a button. Depending on the model, the handsets have buttons marked "Land," "Mobile," "Home," or "Cell." To make a call, the user pushes the button of the desired line and simply completes the call. The systems can also be programmed with different ring tones, to differentiate whether the call is coming in on the landline or cell phone. The systems include a base station with a cordless handset and a separate docking station for a cell phone. The base station is plugged into an electrical outlet and a phone jack. The docking station is plugged into an electrical outlet only, also charging the cell phone, and can be placed anywhere in the home—for instance, where reception is strongest.

Clearly, the technological capabilities of cell phones had surpassed expectations, and there was no end in sight to what they might do in the future. The introduction of the iPhone by Apple and the BlackBerry by Research in Motion, which allowed users to send and receive e-mail, browse the Internet, view video, and play music, among a host of other uses, set a new standard for the cell phone industry and showed that wireless was the wave of the future.

BIBLIOGRAPHY

"About Us." AT&T, 20 November 2008. Available from http://www.att.com.

"About Us." Sprint Nextel, 20 November 2008. Available from http://www2.spring.com.

"About Us." Verizon Communications, 20 November 2008. Available from http://www22.verizon.com.

"Aftermarket Mobile Phone Accessories Revenue to Cross $50 Billion in 2015." ABI News, Press Release, 24 September 2010. Available from http://www.mobilitiy.cbronline.com/news/aftermarket-mobile-phone-accessories-revenue-to-cross-50bn-in-2015-abi_240910.

"Americans Abandon Landlines For Wireless, Verizon Leads." *InformationWeek,* 2 October 2008.

"Ascom Launches DECT Solutions in American Market." *Wireless News,* 24 April 2006.

Blumberg, Stephen J., et al. "Wireless Services: Early Release of Estimates From the CDC." Centers for Disease control, Press Release, 3 September 2010. Available from http://www.cdc.gov/nchs/data/nhis/earlyrelease/wireless200905.htm.

"ComSwitch CS7500." Command Communications, 20 November 2008.Available from http://www.command communications.com.

"FCC Releases New Data on Internet Access Services." Federal Communications Commission, Press Release, 2 September 2010. Available from http://www.fcc. gov/wcb.stats.

"FCC Releases New Local Telephone Competition Data." Federal Communications Commission, Press Release, 3 September 2010. Available from http://www.fcc.gov/wcb.stats.

Fram, Alan. "Survey Says More Households Are Relying Solely on Cell Phones." *Capper's,* July 2008.

Gaylord, Chris. "As Recession Lingers, Cell Phones Take Over." *CS Monitor,* 7 May 2009.

Higginbotham, Stacey. "Mobile Milestone: Data Surpasses Voice Traffic." *Tech News,* 24 March 2010.

"Motorola Introduces Connected Cordless Phone Systems." *Wireless News,* 4 January 2006.

Nolan, Heather. "Number of U.S. Cell Phone Users Surpasses Landline users For the First Time." *Beaumont Enteprise,* 7 May 2009.

Reed, Brad. "AT&T Continues Wireless Services Spending Spree." *Network World,* 10 November 2008.

———. "FCC Approves Two Major Telecom Mergers." *Network World,* 5 November 2008.

Sidener, Jonathan. "Cell Phones Taking on Many Roles, Transforming Market, Generation." *Union-Tribune* (San Diego, CA), 27 January 2008.

"Study: By Next Year, 1 in 5 U.S. Households Will Be Wireless-Only." *RCR Wireless News,* 22 September 2008.

"Trends in Telephone Services." Federal Communication Commission, Press release, 3 September 2010. Available from http://www.fcc.gov/wcb.iatd/trends/html

"Verizon Suffers from Wall Street's Woes." *Business Week Online,* 29 July 2008. Available from www.businessweek.com.

Wildstrom, Stephen. "The Only Truly Smart Smartphones." *BusinessWeek,* 12 November 2008.

"The Year 2009, the Worst for Telecoms in a Decade, Finds Ovum." Press Release, 21 September 2010. Available from http://about.datamonitor.com/media/archives/4791.

TELEPHONY

———————■———————

SIC CODE(S)

4813

4812

INDUSTRY SNAPSHOT

Telephony—the science of converting voices and other sounds into electrical signals that can be transmitted by wire, fiber, or radio and reconverted to audible sound upon receipt—has been evolving at an astonishing rate, finding more and more ways to connect people more quickly and clearly. Bound primarily to the mammoth telecommunications industry, telephony was carried along for the whirlwind ride that industry experienced after deregulation, as mergers, acquisitions, and start-ups combined with an avalanche of technological innovation to produce a tempestuous market. In the arly 2000s, the industry was inundated with talk of convergence, or the integration of existing forms of telephony into a seamless whole.

There are a myriad of ways for data and voice signals to get from one place to another, including long distance phone calls, Voice over Internet Protocol (VoIP), Internet-based public phone networks, fax transmissions, and cable modems, to name a few. In addition to telecommunications firms, the computer and electronics industries figure prominently in the development of telephony, providing switches, networking equipment, and computer-telephone integration technology used in faxes, voice mail, call centers, voice recognition, video conferencing, and interactive voice response systems.

Mergers, acquisitions, and newcomers made the telephony industry keeps very fluid and unpredictable. SBC and AT&T became one; Sprint and Nextel merged, then spun off a WiMAX division to Clearwire; WorldCom became MCI, and then Verizon bought MCI. A newcomer in the Voice over Internet Protocol (VoIP) industry, Vonage came on to the scene in 2002 and by 2008 had 2.5 million subscribers.

ORGANIZATION AND STRUCTURE

The telephony industry consists of three main businesses: provision of services to consumers, corporations, and individuals; installing infrastructure, from production of hardware to deployment of software; and managing or providing business services for those business activities within the industry and to consumers such as Yellow Pages publishing and custom database maintenance.

Voice is encoded and decoded through the telephone itself into electrical signals. The signals are transmitted over a network of copper or fiber-optic cable, radio, or satellite transceivers and switches between one or more other telephones or networks. The majority of telephone services are designed for speech transmission, but with the advent of computerization and digitization, networks transmit other data as well. These include facsimile documents, audio and video, and big packets of secure data. Consumers want basic telephone service, cellular telephone service, and Internet connections; corporations need sophisticated telephony networks for broadband transmission of voice, data, and even video. Furthermore, they all want to transmit data at the fastest possible speed.

With over 600 million telephones throughout the world, it is small wonder that the telecommunications industry is as lucrative and as competitive as it is. Moreover, consumers, especially in industrialized countries

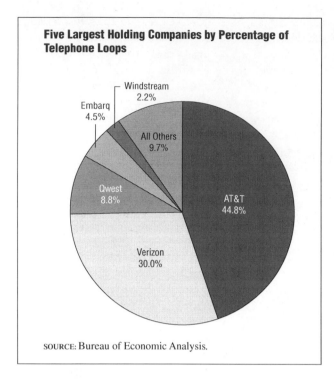

Five Largest Holding Companies by Percentage of Telephone Loops

- Windstream 2.2%
- Embarq 4.5%
- All Others 9.7%
- Qwest 8.8%
- Verizon 30.0%
- AT&T 44.8%

SOURCE: Bureau of Economic Analysis.

(particularly the United States), increasingly own several phones apiece, with telephones in several rooms throughout the house, cell phones, and so on. By the end of the twentieth century, analog lines, over which data is represented by continuously variable physical quantities, were being replaced or augmented with digital technology. Moreover, with the relaxation of the regulatory climate, competition was increasing to provide these customers with the fastest, most comprehensive service.

Telephony products cut a wide market swath. These included consumer products, from calling cards and handsets to sophisticated frame relay and network switching products to software and servers for high-end corporate users or service providers. Among the companies making telephony hardware and software available in the late 1990s were high-profile companies such as AT&T, Siemens Rolm Communications, Lucent Technologies, Northern Telecom, Pacific Bell, and Internet telephony players IDT and VocalTec Communications. Also active in this area were Mitel, NTT, Teleport Communications Group, NetFrame Systems, Rhetorex, PairGain Technologies, Cubix, and Madge Networks.

Governmental Agencies The telecommunications industry is regulated by the Federal Communications Commission (FCC). This independent agency, created in 1934, regulates interstate and international communications that originate in the United States and are transmitted via radio, TV, wire, cable, and satellite. As new technologies developed, this agency has undertaken the task of allocation of the electromagnetic spectrum for transmission of television and wireless communications signals. The FCC traditionally has attempted to maintain a balance between the stronger market players while ensuring markets remain open to competition.

At the state level, public utilities commissions provide another layer of regulation. These bodies, which do the bidding of state lawmakers, originally granted franchises to local service providers and regulated utilities, namely gas and power companies. The National Association of Regulatory Utility Commissioners is an umbrella group designed to make sure there are uniform regulations for public utilities. Other levels of government responsible for various regulations, primarily oversight of such things as franchise granting and infrastructure construction, exist at the county and municipal levels.

Standards Bodies and Trade Associations The predominant standards body for the telephony industry is the United Nations' International Telecommunication Union, based in Geneva. This body assists governments and the private sector alike by providing a forum for determining technical methods by which data is sent, such as the ratification of the V.90 standard for 56K modems. The American National Standards Institute approves and publishes U.S. telecommunications standards. An array of other bodies, such as the Institute of Electrical and Electronics Engineers, promulgates standards as well. The U.S. Telephone Association, Telecommunications Industry Association, Multimedia Telecommunications Association, and National Exchange Carrier Association are among the various industry trade organizations formed to protect the interests of member companies within the industry.

Impact of Regulation Regulation of the U.S. telecommunications market has primarily been shaped in the courts by antitrust actions brought against AT&T. In a 1949 case, the U.S. Department of Justice claimed that the Bell Operating Companies practiced illegal exclusion by purchasing goods from Western Electric, which was a part of the Bell system. The case, settled in 1956, resulted in AT&T holding on to Western Electric with the condition that they not enter the computer market. The second major antitrust suit, *United States v AT&T,* was initiated in 1974. The allegations included that AT&T monopolized the long distance market and again asserted that its relationship with Western Electric was illegal. The government demanded that AT&T divest its manufacturing and long distance businesses. The company broke up in 1982 after years of legal wrangling and formed seven regional Bell operating companies. The "Baby Bells" remained regulated monopolies, each with an exclusive franchise in its region.

Telecommunications Reform Act of 1996 Although the breakup of AT&T was the watershed legal event causing telephony to evolve and thrive, perhaps the most notable factor pushing its convergence with the computer industry was the Telecommunications Reform Act of 1996. Congress, through this legislation, removed barriers to competition throughout the telecommunications industry and effectively paved the way for the industry to seek cross-industry alliances such as with computing. Telecommunications reform was spearheaded by the guidance of Reed Hundt, chairman of the FCC, who shepherded the act through Congress during his tenure, before stepping down in November 1997.

President Bill Clinton hailed the act as a revolutionary piece of legislation ushering in a new era of technology to reshape how we work and communicate with each other. Ostensibly, the act was intended to unleash the industry from the chains, such as outdated laws and regulations, that were determined to hold it back, and to realize the virtues of the free market that were intended to push innovation, opportunities, and job creation.

Despite these promises, industry leaders chafed at regulatory challenges. Richard D. McCormick, chairman and chief operating officer of US West Inc., was among them. In a 1996 address, he told the U.S. Telephone Association that the FCC's new rules, far from creating a happy equilibrium and fairness, effectively gave the largest players free rein to steamroll smaller competitors, and insisted that the rules regarding industry interconnection were not competition but confiscation.

While McCormick's view may seem excessive to some observers, it was clear that the Telecommunications Reform Act had a somewhat more nuanced effect on the industry than President Clinton had predicted. The legislation resulted in corporate mergers and legal battles, rather than better and more competitive consumer communications services. Rather than creating new networks from the ground up, companies bought and sold customers to gain revenue, and bought companies to gain market position.

The resulting effect of the Telecommunications Reform Act of 1996 on telephony and other related communications businesses might take years to surface or afford comprehension of its impacts. Moreover, analysts were widely predicting future turmoil for the FCC and state regulators as they battled for regulatory turf. Effectively, these critics noted, the federal government had wrested away from states the right to determine telecommunications provisions and ownership patterns within their domains. Smaller local service providers, of course, were also none too pleased with the way the act was playing out.

Confusing issues further are taxes levied on telecommunications services. These include federal, state, and local charges for programs such as Universal Access, 911 service, and subsidies for school and hospital telephone service. Universal Access is a federal program designed to give rural residents and people in low-income brackets basic telephone service. What constitutes "basic" has been widely debated. The state of California, for example, in 1998, included a 0.41 percent charge to consumers to be used to discount school, library, and hospital bills. On one bill for one phone line in San Francisco, as many as 11 agencies intended to tax phone use.

New entrants to the telephony market are perceived by telecommunications companies to have an unfair competitive advantage. Primarily, the complaining has been directed at Internet service providers (ISPs) who are unregulated and not subject to the numerous taxes telecommunications firms have to pay. The regulation of ISP telephony was a heated political topic in the late 1990s. Regulatory restrictions on ISPs were being made on a select basis, solely on the complaints of telephone companies. With old technologies merging and new ones cropping up all the time, and with older ways of doing business becoming obsolete seemingly by the day, some players and analysts even argued that telephony should be relieved of all regulatory oversight altogether, arguing that the FCC had outlived its usefulness.

BACKGROUND AND DEVELOPMENT

The history of telephony is entwined with developments and advances in electronics, telephone, and computers for communication. "The telephone utterly evolutionized human communication," stated Isaac Asimov, who may have been exaggerating. It was the telegraph and the telephone that propelled the desire for increasingly faster and instantaneous means of communication. Alexander Graham Bell is credited with inventing the telephone, initially to send voice via telegraph. Bell patented the device in 1876. Thomas Edison was the first to improve on the invention.

Switching technologies have driven telephony development and deployment throughout the United States as it progressed from mechanical to analog to digital switching. The network and telephony devices are useless unless switching works properly to connect calls, whether for voice or data. In the early days, an operator manually plugged in and removed circuits from a switchboard to initiate and terminate calls. Alom B. Strowger, an irate undertaker whose business was being diverted to a competitor by a less than ethical operator, initiated the first technological growth in 1889. The Strowger system eliminated the need for a human to connect calls by utilizing mechanical devices to make a connection. This technology was standard throughout the United States for about 50 years.

Beginning in about the 1940s, a series of analog switches was developed to replace huge and cumbersome devices. The new devices included crossbar switches, the electronic switching system, and stored program control switches. Electronic switching systems were the first union of telephony and silicon. Computer technology was used within these systems to make operations efficient and thus reduce costs.

Regulation of the U.S. telecommunications market was shaped by antitrust actions brought against AT&T in 1949, 1956, and 1974. The company was finally broken up in 1982 after years of legal wrangling, forming seven regional Bell operating companies in 1984.

The 1970s, along with litigation against industry monolith AT&T, brought digital switching to the fore. These were faster, smaller, and more cost-efficient devices. A digital switch could accommodate between 1,000 and 10,000 subscribers on a network. These devices eventually automated and centralized maintenance. The late 1970s and 1980s were the age of fiber. The 1990s belonged to wireless, specifically digital wireless.

The telephone network was formed on twisted pair copper wires, but in the 1990s, various means became available to transmit large bundles of data economically without wires. This shift actually had its beginning in the 1980s, when Bell was broken up and MCI started out to build its microwave network. After the government determined that the long distance market for radio-based telephony was in fact competitive and, simultaneously, that the landline network amounted to a monopoly, new networks were immediately set up for wireless communication.

At that time, other emergent technologies included cellular systems and low power cellular or "personal communications services" networks. In addition, the cost to companies for these various technologies was vastly different and the economics of scale constantly widening. In 1993, the cost associated with creating infrastructure for cellular networks was estimated as $1,000 per subscriber, while traditional copper-wired landlines cost about $1,500, with the costs increasing. Transmission equipment developed in the 1990s, called Synchronous Option Network (SONET), was comprised of fiber-optic transport systems that increasingly provided the backbone for automated teller machines and broadband switching systems over which both voice and data can be carried. A steady, industry-wide transition toward an all-optical network was progressing in the late 1990s. At that time, however, the technology was not deemed cost effective to make these types of networks commercially available. According to *Telephony,* companies such as international carriers with large investments in fiber-optics were poised to be the first to employ these networks. Throughout this era, the industry became increasingly reliant on computers for all aspects of telephony operations.

Computing, photonics, satellites, and other technologies had become increasingly sophisticated, thus altering the foundation on which communications transmissions were made. Some telephony companies remained content to attempt to maximize their copper-wired infrastructure as long as possible without sacrificing service quality. Significant capital investments, after all, had been made. Additional investments would be absorbed through service rate hikes.

The telephone network was designed based on conjecture that each call was three minutes in duration with no more than nine minutes worth of calls made during peak use hours. By the middle of the 1990s, however, the snowballing use of the Internet resulted in phone lines routinely tied up for well over 15 minutes at a time. Because Internet service providers and subscriber-based online services had arranged for users to incur no charges for local calls, Web surfers could stay on indefinitely with no cost to them and there was no revenue for those local providers. The problem was further compounded by technology. While telephone companies had about $30 billion invested in the older circuit-switching infrastructure alone, packet switching technology was a digital, more efficient technology expected to go a long way toward solving network traffic problems.

Examples of the latter technologies include the asymmetric digital subscriber line (ADSL) and the integrated services digital network. According to the ADSL Forum, by 1999, there were over 100,000 ADSL systems installed throughout the world. Cahners In-Stat Group predicted the total number of digital subscriber lines worldwide would grow about 125 percent annually, much faster than the growth rate of cable modem subscribers, which was estimated at about 55 percent annually.

As a result, more companies were beginning to eye the mass purchase of ADSL technology as a viable option, particularly because it provided companies with a way to meet heightened consumer demand for high-speed access without ripping out their old copper wire networks. Several North American phone companies purchased enough ADSL equipment from the French firm Alcatel in 1999 to provide high-speed Internet access to 80,000 households.

Voice and data transmission networks were moving from traditional networks to specialized high bandwidth networks such as Internet Protocol (IP) networks. New-generation telephony networks were in the design stage to carry data and voice traffic by using IP networking. Internet phones that integrated mobile phone capabilities with e-mail and Web-based data access were being developed. Such devices were primarily based on the Wireless Application Protocol, a language adapted from standard HTTP specifically for wireless services. The creation of these types of networks and devices eliminated outdated copper line transmission and enabled businesses and individuals to simply mix and match an array of services, from traditional telephone conversations to conducting teleconferences.

By 1996, data traffic outpaced voice traffic on backbone networks, thereby providing a crucial reason for technological convergence in the telephony industry. The forecasts for 2020 put U.S. Internet use at 80 percent of the total population. Indeed the early adapters seemed to be large corporations most able to invest capital in these types of cutting-edge systems. Boeing and Ford Motor Co. were among those companies that deployed IP networks for their international internal communication needs.

The foremost buzzword throughout the telephony industry at the turn of the twentieth century was "convergence." Indicative of the accelerating convergence movement, computer telephony integration (CTI) was aided by enhanced technology for voice recognition, for use with messaging products, and for automatic call distribution. In coming years, moreover, hardware prices for CTI were expected to fall significantly, thereby relieving some of the pressure on companies to develop a production standard. CTI was generally a higher-margin system because it was geared mainly toward businesses. This technology was not expected to generate quite the level of excitement among major telecommunications firms, especially those focusing their operations on the individual consumer, since CTI is highly technical, even by modern telephony standards, and was thus expected to remain rarified, according to *Computer Reseller News.*

Demand for remote connectivity was greatly enhanced by the Internet, and the integration of wireless communications and Internet access was a very important priority among the major telecommunications and electronics firms. About one-third of the U.S. work force, amounting to 43 million individuals, were mobile—spending at least 20 percent of their working hours away from their workplace—in 1999, according to the Boston research firm the Yankee Group. In addition, as business shifted increasingly to online networks, this culminated in a market just waiting to explode. Some analysts, however, worried that the demand for perpetual connectivity, particularly in wireless technology, was outpacing the ability of companies to meet expectations. Nonetheless, virtually every company recognized that wireless Internet access was a crucial component of its convergence scheme, and the race was on to streamline the process in order to bring the data transmission up to par with standard, personal computer-based connections.

Mergers and increased competitiveness caused companies to vie for customers in every sector, down to the most substantial residential user. The new generation telecommunications company wants to run the entire gamut of telephony services packaged specifically for consumers. The frenetic drive toward convergence and the corresponding industry consolidation created some unusual partnerships.

Cable modem possibilities for connection to the elusive "final mile" meant matches were attempted with companies such as TCI, Cox, and Comcast to bring telephony services to consumers. In addition, companies in other market niches, such as utilities, attempted to get a piece of telephony for their investors by investing in hybrid companies.

Even cable companies were jumping into the mix in the early 2000s. In fact, by 2004, major companies such as Cox and Time Warner were joining communication giants such as SBC and AT&T in offering Voice over Internet Protocol (VoIP), a technology first offered in 1995 by Net2Phone that enabled telephone services such as inexpensive long distance to be available over the Internet. In its latest incarnation, VoIP enabled ordinary phone cords to connect directly to a high-speed Internet server. According to *Computer Reseller News,* a benefit of the terrorist attacks on September 11, 2001 was the demonstration that the Internet was still available to users, although traditional and cellular telephony were overworked and nonfunctional.

At of the end of 2003, there were 135,000 subscribers to Internet phone services, which were up to 20 or even 30 percent cheaper than traditional phone lines. By 2003, Net2Phone had split into two subsidiaries, one of which was devoted to the newer cable telephony market. It was predicted that the VoIP services from Net2Phone would bring in $250 million by 2008. According to *Fortune,* VoIP would not be in mainstream use until at least that year. In addition to the obvious questions of regulation, the technology had its problems, including transmission quality, voice over data priority, and the required broadband access. Nevertheless, it was predicted that the technology would eventually outrun traditional markets. By mid-2004, the transmission quality had already improved. Vonage was offering a 500-minute residential package with many additional features for under $15 per month in 2004.

Vonage was launched in March 2002, when it signed up its first residential customer. Vonage, headquartered in Holmdel, New Jersey, became the leading provider of broadband telephone services by early 2006, according to TeleGeography, a research firm. Its technology allows anyone with a touchtone telephone to make and receive calls wherever a broadband Internet connection is available. Vonage was founded by Jeffrey Citron, a former broker, who, in 2003, paid a penalty of $22.5 million to settle allegations of fraud and agreed to never work in securities again. He then turned his attention to making phone calls over the Internet—"Voice over Internet Protocol" (VoIP)—and, with tremendous amounts spent on marketing, by April of 2006 had convinced 1.6 million Americans to switch from their land line telephone company to Vonage's VoIP system. In 2006, there were 5.5 million VoIP subscribers.

On May 24, 2006, however, in spite of its phenomenal showing, Vonage made the worst debut on the stock market by a U.S. company in two years. Its offering of shares worth a total of $531 million dropped 13 percent by the end of the first day, leading analysts to wonder if VoIP was overhyped. Actually, VoIP technology has become even more in demand than anyone had predicted and because of that, Vonage found strong competition among other companies, even cable companies who offered cheap bundles of broadband Internet access, a requirement for VoIP that Vonage doesn't offer.

Another leader in the VoIP industry, Vapps, located in Hoboken, New Jersey, was a global provider of VoIP audio conferencing services and systems. Its proprietary VoIP conferencing platform provided audio conferencing to global service providers and corporations. In May 2006, Vapps announced the availability of its high-speed conferencing service on salesforce.com's AppExchange. Salesforce.com allowed its users to connect up to 500 conference callers within their Salesforce implementation for high-quality, low-cost audio conference calls, using regular phones or Skype communications services (a program for making free calls within the United States and Canada to all phones). In 2008, Vapps was purchased by Citrix Systems Inc. for $26.6 million.

In a major victory for a wide range of the tax-paying populace, including corporate and individual taxpayers, an embattled, archaic federal excise tax (FET) on land line and wireless phone bills was finally eliminated, according to a U.S. Treasury Department announcement made on May 25, 2006. Until then, the IRS had resisted demands that it stop collecting the FET, which was initially implemented to help finance the Spanish-American War in 1898. It was originally created to tax wealthy Americans who had the "luxury" of owning a telephone. In the announcement of the elimination of the FET, the Treasury stated that the tax on phone calls "is not compatible with today's modern information-age society" and that it is conceding the legal dispute over the FET on long-distance services and will no longer pursue litigation. The IRS issued refunds of the FET that were assessed on long-distance services from 2003 to 2006.

CURRENT CONDITIONS

Overall, reported Datamonitor (using figures released by independent telecom analyst Ovum), total revenues for fixed line telephone services worldwide were roughly $350 billion in 2010. These were expected to decline to $283 billion by 2014, mostly due to the increase in wireless services. Revenues from mobile services worldwide were expected to increase by almost $100 billion between 2009 and 2012.

In September 2010, the FCC released a series of reports on the state of telecom and telephony services in the United States. Its *Local Telephone Competition* report

contained comprehensive information about subscriptions to interconnected VoIP services as well as more traditional telephone lines. Significant findings included that, as of June 2009, there were 133 million traditional switched access lines in service in the United States, plus 23 million interconnected VoIP subscriptions, totaling 157 million wireline retail local telephone service connections. Of this total, 93 million were residential subscriptions, and 64 million were business connections. In addition, of this total (157 million), 13 percent were residential interconnected VoIP subscriptions, and 2 percent were business interconnected VoIP subscriptions.

Switched access lines were decreasing in 2009, while interconnected VoIP subscriptions were increasing twice as fast (up 10 percent in just the first six months of 2009). Of the 93 million wireline residential connections, 73.1 percent involved switched access lines owned by incumbent local exchange carriers (ILECs), 20 percent were non-ILEC interconnected VoIP subscriptions, 5.5 precent were non-ILEC switched access lines, and 0.6 percent were ILEC interconnected VoIP subscriptions. On the business side (64 million wireline), 68.71 percent involved switched access lines owned by incumbent local exchange carriers (ILECs), 25.6 precent were non-ILEC switched access lines, 5.1 percent were non-ILEC interconnected VoIP subscriptions, and 0.6 percent were ILEC interconnected VoIP subscriptions.

Eighty-three percent of interconnected VoIP subscribers received their service through a "broadband bundle," that included broadband Internet access service, with 17 percent of them receiving use of the subscription over any broadband connection to which they had access (e.g., while on travel or vacation), such as "nomadic functionality." A whopping 89 percent had broadband connections via cable modem, 10 percent via FTTP, DSL, or other wireline, and just 1 percent via fixed wireless or other connections.

INDUSTRY LEADERS

Long-Distance Providers With the advent of deregulation, increasing competition, and restructuring, AT&T broadened its focus to include wireless phone service, Internet access, and international and local telephone services. Meanwhile, the company was gobbling up cable companies, including TCI and MediaOne, in an effort to compete with Time Warner for the position of leading cable operator. AT&T struck a deal with British Telecommunications in 1999 to provide worldwide wireless service through the Advance alliance. AT&T Corp. was the leader in the U.S. long distance telephone carrier category in 2003, but was acquired by SBC in 2005, at which point it took AT&T Inc. as its corporate name. In 2009 AT&T was the world's leader in communications services, with more than 44.8 percent of the U.S. market. With more than 300,000 employees worldwide its 2009 revenues were $123 billion.

Sprint Nextel Corp. was the third leading long distance and wireless service provider. The company, which owns one of the largest fiber-optic networks, created neighborhood telephone stores with Radio Shack. In 1999, Sprint developed the Sprint Integrated On-Demand Network, which combined voice, video, and digital data transmissions through a single phone connection. After competitive negotiations, Sprint agreed to merge with WorldCom in 2000, but the U.S. Justice Department blocked the deal. In 2002, Sprint had heavy losses, but was able to rebound in the final quarter with a net profit of $630 million. In 2003, it had rejoined with its subsidiaries, SprintFON and SprintPCS, and its one-year net income rose almost 93 percent. In August of 2005, Sprint and Nextel Communications, Inc. announced the completion of their merger, forming Sprint Nextel Corporation, which in 2009 reported revenues of $32.3 billion with 60,000 employees and 48.8 million customers.

Qwest Communications International Inc., once an obscure telecommunications provider, grew to become the fourth largest long distance service provider in the United States by the end of the 1990s. Primarily operating in the western United States, the company constructed an 18,800-mile, fiber-optic network for more than 150 cities in the United States and Mexico. Qwest installs networks for companies such as Verizon alongside its own network and sells network capacity to various parties. In addition to its long distance operations, Qwest was a leading local phone service provider following its purchase of US West, and offered Internet access and multimedia services through its vast network. In 2009 Qwest reported revenues of $12.3 billion with approximately 37,000 employees.

Local Service Providers AT&T was the leading local phone service provider in the United States and provided local service in 22 states. Its other services included long distance, cable, Internet access, paging, and directory publishing, and it was a leader in DSL broadband service.

Verizon, the product of the purchase by Bell Atlantic of GTE Corp., was number two in local phone service in 2008. Bell Atlantic Corp. was among the local service provider companies that emerged from the AT&T breakup. This Baby Bell purchased NYNEX, another Baby Bell, in 1997 to lift it to the top of the local service industry, and its purchase of GTE solidified its lead in the industry. Verizon provided local phone service to 40 million customers in 28 states and the District of Columbia.

Wireless Services Vodafone was created in 1984 as a subsidiary of Racal Electronics PLC. In 1991, it became an independent company with the name of Vodafone Group PLC. Following its 1999 acquisition by AirTouch Communications, Inc., it became Vodafone AirTouch PLC. After that alliance, the company continued its acquisition spree, purchasing Germany's Mannesman for $180 billion. At that time, Vodafone AirTouch claimed some 39.1 million customers in 24 countries, and employed 12,640 workers. In 2000, it reverted to its former name of Vodafone Group PLC. In the United States, the company teamed up with Verizon and operated under the name Verizon Wireless. Worldwide, the company was the largest wireless phone service provider, with 200 million customers. Sales in 2009 reached $GBP 41 billion pounds British.

In the United States, AT&T Mobility (formerly Cingular Wireless) serviced 70 million wireless customers; Verizon operated the second largest wireless telephone service, Verizon Wireless, which had about 68 million customers.

Net2Phone was a world leader in delivering voice services over data networks. Founded in 1996, it provides VoIP, PacketCable (providing cable operators the ability to deliver high-quality primary line-type service), and wireless solutions globally. Net2Phone has serviced more than 100,000 users in the United States in addition to several hundred thousand overseas and has routed billions of VoIP minutes globally. In March of 2006, Net2Phone was merged with NTOP Acquisition, Inc., a wholly owned subsidiary of IDT Corporation of Newark, New Jersey, thereby also becoming wholly owned by IDT. A multinational carrier, IDT provides a range of telecommunications services to retail and wholesale customers worldwide, including integrated and competitively priced international and domestic long distance service and prepaid calling cards. Net2Phone accounted for $34.5 million of IDT's $1.8 billion in revenues in 2007.

AMERICA AND THE WORLD

BT Group was once the United Kingdom's government-run telephone company. The company offers a wide range of services, including international service, despite the fact that by the end of the 1990s, the firm generated nearly all its revenues in the United Kingdom. In 2008, BT was one of the world's leading providers of communications solutions, serving customers in Europe, the Americas, and the Asia Pacific region, and offering networked IT services, local, national and international telecommunications services, and higher-value broadband and Internet products and services. In the United Kingdom alone, BT served more than 22 million business and residential customers and provided network services to other licensed operators.

Deutsche Telekom AG is Europe's number one telecom company and one of the largest in the world. Its T-Home unit provides fixed-line network access services and was Germany's number one fixed-line phone operator, with 50 million access lines. The company's T-Mobile International served 14 million wireless phone subscribers, and its T-Online unit had 27 million customers, making it one of Europe's leading ISPs.

RESEARCH AND TECHNOLOGY

According to predictions by ABI Research, sophisticated IP telephone network systems will increasingly enable a range of new services in the travel and hospitality industry, especially in hotels and resorts. Such services totaled $869 million in 2008, but were forecasted to exceed $2 billion by the end of 2014. High-end hotels were the first to incorporate new telephony technology for customer service needs, but it was expected to expand into the mid-range hotel and resort market soon. Examples of applications included wireless phones provided by a hotel or resort, allowing poolside users to order drinks, food, or giftshop items by pushing a menu button. Another button would make a purchase, billed to the user's room. Service companies such as IBM and MTech were also offering workflow managed services for the hotel industry.

Technological advances in the industry have outpaced expectations. The changes have been amazingly rapid, from digital switching to fiber optics and beyond. Computers and the Internet play an increasingly important role in telephony through development and deployment of technologies such as voice-over networks, VoIP, Internet-based public phone networks, fax transmissions, and cable modems.

Server Message Block (SMB) is a protocol for sharing files, printers, serial ports, and communications abstractions such as named pipes and mail slots between computers. SMBs represent approximately 5 million businesses with over 40 million employees and more than $100 billion in spending on communications services. Consumers want to go with what is the least expensive and still works; therefore, the future of SMBs lies not just in VoIP and dedicated Internet access services. Future capabilities must also include managed services (including hosting application servers), desktop maintenance (via online maintenance tools), Web hosting, Web design and mobile VoIP service, which promises to be a catalyst in realizing true integration. Total communications service is the key for service providers, with SMBs expected to integrate mobile phones as another extension of the customer's VoIP system.

BIBLIOGRAPHY

Blumberg, Stephen J., et al. "Wireless Services: Early Release of Estimates From the CDC." Centers for Disease Control and Prevention, Press release, 3 September 2010. Available from http://www.cdc.gov/nchs/data/nhis/earlyrelease/wireless 200905.htm.

"Breaking News: Feds Finally End Telephony Excise Tax." *TelecomWeb News Digest,* 25 May 2006.

"Citrix Buys Vapps." *The New York Times,* 14 November 2008.

Clausen, Craig M. "SMBs More Than Small Talk." *Telephony Online,* 6 March 2006.

"FCC Releases New Data on Internet Access Services." Federal Communications Commission, Press Release, 2 September 2010. Available from http://www.fcc.gov/wcb.stats.

"FCC Releases New Local Telephone Competition Data." Federal Communications Commission, Press Release, 3 September 2010. Available from http://www.fcc.gov/wcb.stats.

Gaylord, Chris. "As Recession Lingers, Cell Phones Take Over." *CS Monitor,* 7 May 2009.

Hickey, Andrew R. "New VoIP, UC Wares Storm the Market." *VARbusiness,* 24 November 2008.

"IP Telephony Revenue in the Hospitality Industry Will Top $2 Billion in 2014." Prress Release, 22 January 2010. Available from http://www.abiresearch.com.

McKay, Martha. "Vonage Goes Public, Selling 20 Percent of Shares for $531M." *The Record,* 24 May 2006.

"More L.I. Firms Call on Internet-Based Phone." *Long Island Business News,* 5 November 2008.

"Report: VoIP-Connected Households to Grow by 8.5 Million by 2011." *VoIP Monitor,* 15 November 2008.

"Service Offers High Speed Conferencing Facility." *Product News Network,* 25 May 2006.

Sprint=Nextel. Available from http://www.investors.sprint.com.

"Telephony's 2008 Innovation Award Winners Say Persistence Pays Off." *Telephony,* 1 November 2008.

"Trends in Telephone Services." Federal Communications Commission, Press release, 3 September 2010. Available from http://www.fcc.gov/wcb.iatd/trends/html.

Vodafone. Available from http://www.telecom.com/17864/vodafone

"VoiceCon: Key Implementers Cite Hurdles to Unifying Communications." *InformationWeek,* 12 November 2008.

"VoIP Leads the Way in IBISWorld Top 10 List for 2008." *VoIP Monitor,* 15 November 2008. Available from http://www.voipmonitor.net.

"Vonage Unwanted; Internet Telephony." *The Economist,* 27 May 2006.

"The Year 2009, the Worst for Telecoms in a Decade, Finds Ovum." Datamonitor, Press Release, 21 September 2010. Available from http://about.datamonitor.com/media/archives/4791.

THERAPEUTIC EDUCATION SCHOOLS

—■—

SIC CODE(S)

8299

INDUSTRY SNAPSHOT

Therapeutic education schools offer rehabilitative programs for troubled youths. Ranging in age from 10 to 18, enrollees typically suffer from behavioral or discipline-related problems, as well as substance abuse. Varying in style and structure, these institutions also are known as therapeutic boarding schools, attitude adjustment schools, behavior modification schools, and in some cases, boot camps or wilderness schools. They can include community-based living programs, emotional growth boarding schools, and residential treatment academies, both in the public and private sector.

Therapeutic education schools differ from traditional reform schools in that a child's parents may be involved as part of the therapeutic process in the form of family counseling. Although children follow different admission pathways, their parents usually place them. In some cases, a judge may order a troubled adolescent to enroll in a therapeutic education school as an alternative to serving time in a correctional facility or psychiatric hospital. However, despite some similarities and overlap, these programs are different from juvenile detention centers, state-run "boot camps," and reform schools restricted to criminal offenders.

Because there are many types of institutions and programs available, the therapeutic industry offers parents who are facing tough choices a tremendous range of solutions to improve a child's future. Families stand a much better chance of turning a troubled child around and helping him or her toward a brighter future by dealing with the problems head on and employing one of the many therapeutic educational choices. However, in 2007 the U.S. Government Accountability Office conducted an investigation and revealed thousands of allegations of abuse and even death at therapeutic programs. The National Institutes of Health had already stated in late 2004 that "Programs that seek to prevent violence through fear and tough treatment do not work." Dealing with negative reports was one of the more significant challenges in the industry. By 2010, the general consensus was that regulation, rather than prohibition, was the best approach for objectively assessing the efficacy of such a loosely-organized industry.

ORGANIZATION AND STRUCTURE

Therapeutic education schools operate in many parts of the United States and the world. Programs serving U.S. families are common in the western part of the country, especially in states like Idaho, Utah, and Montana, where regulations are either lax or nonexistent, there is more wide open space. and it is easier to keep these troubled kids within the facility. However, programs also operate in Canada, Mexico, and more far-away locales including Costa Rica, the Czech Republic, Jamaica, and Western Samoa. In the case of foreign-based schools, government oversight or regulation is limited to the countries in which they operate. Government standards for such schools may not exist, or be very different from those in the United States.

By the early 2000s, therapeutic education schools numbered in the thousands, according to some estimates. While industry programs varied in their approach to rehabilitation, they all served the same target market: troubled children and adolescents. Numbering more than 10,000 per year, these enrollees typically suffer from

971

Parental Satisfaction with Aspen Wilderness Therapeutic Programs, by Survey Respondents, 2007–2010

Query	Before program	After program
Feared for child's safety	87%	22%
Didn't trust their child	86%	25%
Felt child was tearing family apart	78%	16%
Felt child would never get an education	86%	23%

SOURCE: CRC Health Group.

behavioral and discipline-related problems, and many struggle with a wide range of addictions, including drugs and alcohol.

As David L. Marcus explained in 2000 in *U.S. News & World Report,* "By several measures—including a decline in teen pregnancies and drunk-driving incidents—America's teenagers are doing better and better. But there is a sub-group that is in serious trouble, if not yet criminal trouble. These are the kids with discipline problems and Internet addictions, the ones who try everything from the drug ecstasy to sex with strangers, looking for a high, a connection, anything that might make them feel good. Psychologists say these kids share one trait: poor self-esteem. But in other ways they vary greatly. Some have parents too authoritarian and removed, others too lax—to the point of viewing pot-smoking as family recreation." In addition, many of the children who end up in therapeutic education schools come from middle class and upper class families where busy professional parents are often absent from the home.

While some children clearly are admitted to therapeutic education schools for the wrong reasons, such as what many would consider to be typical adolescent behavior, a great many have suffered emotional and psychological problems, including depression and anxiety, from a very young age. In some cases, these problems are very serious and lead to unpredictable and dangerous behavior.

Admission Pathways and Procedures Children are admitted to therapeutic education schools in a number of different ways. However, parents usually initiate the process—often as a last resort, when other measures fail. In order to reach desperate parents, many schools employ traditional, results-oriented marketing tactics like Web sites, videos, and targeted print advertising. In fact, in the May 9, 2003, *New York Times,* columnist Robert Weiner revealed that some parents send their children to therapeutic education programs based on little more than a glossy brochure or a Web site. Not taking the time to make actual site visits, these desperate parents sometimes end up placing their children in schools outside of U.S. borders, many of which rely on "minimum wage custodians more than teachers or therapists." In addition to marketing efforts, schools also develop

working relationships with front-line referral sources like psychiatrists, counselors, juvenile court judges, and educational consultants.

In their marketing communications, some schools mention the availability of special "escort services" that can be used to extract troubled youth from their homes and transport them to the school. These services are offered because many children would not willingly enter such a program. Extractions usually happen at night when children are asleep, and restraints like handcuffs are sometimes used. The legality of these extractions has been challenged in some state courts. Opponents—including grandparents of extracted adolescents and the adolescents themselves—have charged that they constitute kidnapping and a violation of civil rights, while proponents argue that they fall within the boundaries of parental authority.

In some cases, children are enrolled in therapeutic education schools by judges or state departments of correction. These "adjudicated" enrollees would otherwise be sentenced to psychiatric hospitals or traditional juvenile correctional facilities. One example of this type of enrollment is the RedCliff Ascent Outdoor Therapy Program in Utah, which admits offenders from the Utah Department of Corrections into its wilderness-based rehabilitation program in exchange for an annual fee of approximately $500,000.

School Types Therapeutic education schools, many of which are privately owned, are organized and structured in different ways. Because of their varying operational styles and treatment approaches, these institutions go by a range of names, including therapeutic boarding schools, specialty boarding schools, attitude adjustment schools, behavior modification schools, as well as boot camps or wilderness schools. Despite these differences, most schools share similar objectives. As *Chicago Tribune* reporter Bonnie Miller Rubin explained in the paper's January 14, 2004, issue, they "all seem to share the common goal of fostering self-control and self-esteem by removing distractions—peers, TV, computers—and putting youth in environments that promote good choices. Typically, the programs rely on a behavior modification system that rewards compliance and makes the students ultimately responsible for their own conduct. Ideally, as they progress through each level, they will gain new insight into how their actions affect others."

Therapeutic education programs can last two years or more, depending on a child's needs, progress, and his or her family's ability to pay. Program elements, which fit into highly structured schedules, frequently include classroom time, individual and family therapy sessions, physical labor, and, in some cases, wilderness survival exercises. In the case of reputable programs, specially trained and certified instructors, teachers, counselors, and therapists lead these activities. Additionally, a licensed medical doctor (often a psychiatrist) is involved, either as an employee or on a consultative or on-call basis, for the purpose of prescribing medication.

Of the different therapeutic education school varieties, wilderness schools have received significant media attention in recent years. These programs, many of which are based in mountainous or desert locations, use the simplicity and rigors of nature as a means of breaking through to troubled youth. In addition to building self-esteem and confidence, such programs also teach self-reliance and teamwork. As one camp operator explained, while adolescents may have been adept at using manipulative behavior with parents and other authority figures at home, they cannot use the same approach in dealing with the wilderness, where actions take precedence over words. In these camps, students spend as long as three months trekking through difficult terrain. In order to survive, they must master increasingly difficult sets of wilderness survival skills.

Operations Many therapeutic education schools are tight-lipped about the specifics of their operations. Some require participants and parents to remain quiet about their experiences, even going as far as insisting on an oath of secrecy. However, while every school is different, ranging from the prison-like to ones resembling college prep schools, many share certain operational similarities.

Most schools assess new program enrollees upon arrival to determine their level of educational attainment and identify existing psychological or emotional issues. Such assessments often lead students to be placed in categories according to their situation or needs. This information may be entered into a report, placed on a bulletin board, or stored in some kind of a system that allows the staff to quickly understand key information about a particular student. For example, students who are considered to be at risk for suicide may be given a particular designation, as are students who may attempt to exhibit especially resistant or disruptive behavior or attempt to run away.

Upon arriving, many students go through a difficult adjustment period during which they must come to terms with their new situation. This requires school staff to be extra vigilant, should the students attempt to escape or harm themselves or others. Students are then assigned to living quarters, which may be dorm rooms or, in the case of wilderness programs, small cottages or dorm units.

One main similarity is the highly structured use of students' time. In stark contrast to their lives prior to enrollment, every waking moment of an adolescent's day is spoken for in a therapeutic education program. There is little idle time for getting into trouble, and activities like watching television, listening to music, or even enjoying soda pop, are limited. In fact, such forms of enjoyment are often used as rewards for good behavior.

Academics are emphasized more at some therapeutic education schools than at others. Some focus mainly on breaking students down and teaching them to comply with strict rules and regulations, others offer educational videos or have curriculums based on correspondence classes, and some focus on providing students with a high-quality education. These latter schools believe that academic success will lead to improved behavior. After being assessed in areas like math, reading, spelling, and vocabulary, many students are assigned educational improvement goals if they come up short in a given subject area. For example, one school seeks to move students up two grade levels per year until they reach age-appropriate learning levels. At some schools, this is accomplished by teacher-to-student ratios that are smaller than those found in traditional public or private school settings.

For good reason, the rules governing student behavior are commonly very strict in most programs, and rule books at some schools are more than 50 pages long. In some settings, point systems are used, whereby every student begins the day with a given number of points. Violations like fighting or swearing cost points, and model behavior or extra academic effort provide opportunities for earning points. Some programs allow students to redeem points for on- or off-site recreational activities, depending on the student and the school's geographic location.

Beyond the loss of points, other disciplinary measures for bad behavior run the gamut. Reprimands may range from physically intense manual labor, like cutting wood or shoveling snow, to more extreme measures. For example, physically disruptive children may be subject to the use of restraints, handcuffs, mace, or stun guns. One program requires problem students to lie flat on a tile floor for one or more days, with short breaks to eat and use the bathroom.

Attributes of Reputable Programs On its Web site, the National Association of Therapeutic Schools and Programs (NATSAP) lists principles for ensuring the provision of ethical treatment. To qualify for NATSAP membership, schools agree to:"Be conscious of, and responsive to, the dignity, welfare, and worth of our program participants; honestly and accurately represent ownership, competence, experience, and scope of activities, and to not exploit potential clients' fears and vulnerabilities; respect the privacy, confidentiality, and autonomy of program participants within the context of our facilities and programs; be aware and respectful of cultural, familial, and societal backgrounds of our program participants; avoid dual or multiple relationships that may impair professional judgment, increase the risk of harm to program participants, or lead to exploitation; take reasonable steps to ensure a safe environment that addresses the emotional, spiritual, educational, and physical needs of our program participants; strive to maintain high standards of competence in our areas of expertise and to be mindful of our limitations; value continuous professional development, research, and scholarship; place primary emphasis on the welfare of our program participants in the development and implementation of our business practices; manage our finances to ensure that there are adequate resources to accomplish our mission; fully disclose to prospective candidates the nature of services, benefits, risks, and costs; and provide an appropriate professional referral if we are unable to continue service."

Problems and Challenges Despite the fact that many therapeutic education programs have good intentions, the industry is not without its problems. While dealing with extreme behavior calls for extreme measures, a number of schools have been criticized for employing methods that are psychologically or physically abusive, along with over-medicating children and running crowded facilities that force some students to sleep on the floor. Among the strongest critics are parents who claim schools lie about their methods and overstate their ability to deliver results.

Unfortunately, some students have died at therapeutic education schools. Wilderness-based programs have been exposed for withholding water and food as a form of punishment. In several cases, the rigors of these wilderness programs have led to death from dehydration or heat stroke. Ironically, abusive or questionable behavior at therapeutic education schools also has been directed at parents. At several different schools, parents attending mandatory seminars have indicated that facilitators used threats, intimidation, and sleep deprivation in an apparent attempt to gain control of their minds. These tactics have prompted some parents to withdraw their children from therapeutic education schools altogether.

Outcomes Formal research on the immediate and long-term success rates of therapeutic education schools is limited. Several studies concerning outdoor behavioral health care (OBH) programs have been conducted by Keith C. Russell, Ph.D., a professor at the University of New Hampshire. In addition to overseeing the university's graduate program in outdoor education, Russell formerly led the University of Idaho-Wilderness Research Center's Outdoor Behavioral Healthcare Research Cooperative (OBHRC).

One of Russell's studies, which followed 858 students in seven different outdoor behavioral heath care (OBH) programs from May 2000 to December 2000, revealed that participants had improved significantly at the time of discharge. Follow-up research published in 2002 examined a random sample of participant scores

from the time of admission, discharge, and 12 months after discharge. According to the follow-up study, entitled *A Longitudinal Assessment of Outcomes in Outdoor Behavioral Healthcare,* participants "had maintained outcomes from treatment, and had actually continued to improve up to one year after completion of treatment." The study also reported that based on self-reports, participants had apparently shown "improvement in organizing tasks, completing assignments in school, and learning how to handle frustration in appropriate ways." The research did indicate a decline in interpersonal skills when compared to the time of discharge.

Comments from parents, former students, and other industry observers seem to indicate that results vary considerably from program to program. Some are staunch believers in their effectiveness at transforming troubled children into productive members of society, telling success stories of students who learned how to control their anger, empathize with others, and gain awareness of the consequences linked to their behavior. The students and parents linked to these stories refer to therapeutic education schools as lifesavers. However, other accounts reveal that some students lie in order to make it through therapeutic education programs, telling facilitators and parents what they want to hear. Finally, some claim that therapeutic education schools actually do more harm than good, and that students emerge from programs as the victims of physical or psychological abuse.

Cost Therapeutic education schools are relatively expensive, costing anywhere from $20,000 to $60,000 a year, or an average of $5,000 per month. While wealthy parents often have the financial means to pay these costs, middle-income families frequently must make substantial sacrifices, like taking out second mortgages on their homes or dipping into savings intended for college or retirement.

For those adolescents whose enrollment in a therapeutic education school is mandated by a judge or state department of correction, the cost is often covered by a state, county, or local government, or even some health insurances. For example, the RedCliff Ascent Outdoor Therapy Program in Utah receives an annual fee of approximately $500,000 from the Utah Department of Corrections to accept students into its wilderness-based rehabilitation program.

Associations Founded in 1999, the Clearwater, Florida-based National Association of Therapeutic Schools and Programs (NATSAP) serves as "a national resource for programs and professionals assisting young people beleaguered by emotional and behavioral difficulties." Although the NATSAP is not an accrediting or licensing body, it lists several "Ethical Principles" by which their member programs—which include therapeutic schools, residential treatment programs, wilderness programs, outdoor therapeutic programs, young adult programs and home-based residential programs—must agree to abide. Members must renew annually, at which time each member is required to sign the NATSAP Ethical Principles, submit a copy of their current licensure and/or accreditation, and submit a self-report on any new principles that may have been established in the prior year. In this way, NATSAP and its members strive to make sure the industry provides the highest quality services to young people and their families.

On its Web site, the NATSAP offers a resource directory for professionals with information about participating programs, along with principles of good practice that full members must comply with and so-called associate members must aspire to. Specifically, these principles address adherence to state and federal laws, administrative practices and procedures, employee practices, admission and discharge policies, behavior management plans, the rights and responsibilities of program participants, access to health care services, safety, and incident reporting.

Another important industry organization is the non-profit Independent Educational Consultants Association (IECA). Founded in 1976 and headquartered in Fairfax, Virginia, the IECA represents the professional educational advisors who are instrumental in linking families with therapeutic education schools. According to the association, it "sponsors professional training institutes, workshops and conferences, publishes a directory of qualified consultants, offers information to students and their families regarding school selection issues, and works to ensure that those in the profession adhere to the highest ethical and business standards." Along these lines, the IECA formulated its principles of good practice—a stringent set of ethical guidelines to which members are expected to adhere. One principle prohibits consultants from receiving money from schools, thus ensuring that placements are made objectively. The IECA also operates the Independent Educational Consultants Association Foundation, which "supports projects that will benefit those involved in the process of making educational choices, including students, families, educational consultants, and other professionals."

BACKGROUND AND DEVELOPMENT

Troubled adolescents and children, and the most effective ways to deal with them, are timeless problems. Therapeutic education schools are in many ways a product of the larger juvenile justice system. Rehabilitative approaches for so-called wayward youth were quite stringent in the earliest days of American history. For example, in 1648, Massachusetts Colony passed a law recommending capital punishment for those children over age 16 who were guilty of cursing their natural parents.

In time, the nation's approach to dealing with troubled youth began to soften somewhat. A New York attorney named James W. Gerard was an early proponent of reforming troubled youth instead of punishing them. His efforts led to the establishment of the United States' first juvenile reformatory. Named the House of Refuge, it was established in 1825 by the New York Society for the Reformation of Juvenile Delinquents. According to *Scholastic Update,* the school relied on ldquo;rigorous days of prayer, work and study carried out almost entirely in silence." While kindness was supposed to be a central tenet of the reform process, the school often relied on tactics like whipping students, placing them in solitary confinement, or securing them with leg irons.

As the 1800s progressed, the nation's approach to rehabilitating troubled youth became more progressive, including small group or "family" systems at female reform schools in the mid-1850s. However, children often were placed in programs by judges or parents for typical teenage behavior like ldquo;incorrigibility" or "idleness."

In the late 1880s, an influx of poor immigrants into the United States led to a host of social problems and a subsequent rise in the nation's population of troubled youth. In 1899, Chicago became home to the nation's first juvenile court. By the mid-1920s, this special form of court, which held informal hearings and placed children and adolescents in reform schools instead of traditional correctional facilities, had spread to 46 states. In the 1930s, the juvenile justice system was burdened by young boys charged with vagrancy who were displaced by the economic circumstances of the Great Depression.

In time, the larger juvenile justice system began to take a broader view of the reasons behind anti-social or criminal behavior, looking beyond socio-economic conditions and concentrating more on individuals. This ultimately led to the development of therapeutic education programs. According to the October 2, 2000, issue of *U.S. News & World Report,* "Therapeutic schools were born of the educational innovations of the 1960s. For decades, troubled teens had been sent away to military academies or reform schools. Partly for insurance reasons, increasing numbers of truculent children ended up in psychiatric wards. But reports of violence and overmedication prompted parents to look for other options."

One of the very first therapeutic education institutions, the Brown Schools at San Marcos, was established in 1940 by author Bert Brown. Brown and his wife had previously operated one of the first rest homes for mentally disturbed individuals during the Great Depression, and an experience with a troubled girl moved them to establish a school for such children.

In 1968, a California merchant named Mel Wasserman founded another early program called CEDU, which eventually merged with the Brown Schools. According to CEDU, the program is based on "the principle of seeing yourself for who you are and doing something with it." The organization explains that "direct lines can be drawn from CEDU to a number of emotional growth boarding schools in existence today. These programs were actually started by former associates of CEDU and Wasserman."

By the early 1980s, a handful of therapeutic education schools were in operation. However, they quickly began to increase in numbers as society faced growing and more complicated social problems. Conservative estimates indicated that several hundred schools were in operation by the early 2000s, while other estimates placed this number at more than 1,000.

By 2004, therapeutic education schools were growing at an unprecedented rate. For example, one of the industry's leading firms, Aspen Education Group, saw its revenues soar from approximately $10 million in 1994 to nearly $100 million in 2003. This explosive growth was especially pronounced in Mexico and other foreign markets, where schools could operate more affordably and without the level of oversight found in the United States.

A number of unfortunate conditions supported the industry's strong growth. First, American youth struggled with an unprecedented number of social and emotional issues compared to earlier in the century. As a result of living in a more complicated, fragmented, and fast-paced society, conditions like bipolar disorders, depression, substance abuse, and eating disorders had become more prevalent. At the same time, many youth lacked access to strong support systems or resources to address these challenges, within or outside of their families.

In its September 6, 2003, issue, *Science News* shared the findings of a seven-year North Carolina study that found psychiatric ailments were common in one of every six children, and that one in every three children developed at least one psychiatric disorder by the age of 16. Citing results from a recent National Survey on Drug Use and Health, the October 2003 issue of *Contemporary Pediatrics* revealed that within the month preceding the survey, nearly 30 percent of respondents aged 12 to 20 admitted to consuming alcohol and more than 19 percent admitted to binge drinking. In March 2003, *Family Practice News* reported that adolescents and young adults were abusing prescription drugs in growing numbers— especially analgesics like Demerol and Vicodin.

Despite these troubling figures, an encouraging survey conducted by the Horatio Alger Association and reported in 2003 in *Capper's* found that nearly 75 percent of high school students "say they get along very well or extremely well with their parents or guardians." This survey may indicate that many parents and adolescents are capable of working through difficult problems without resorting to more extreme measures like therapeutic education programs.

Another factor contributing to the rise in therapeutic education programs is the advent of zero tolerance policies at schools. In the wake of school shootings and other violent behavior, zero tolerance policies have increased the likelihood that students will be severely punished for something that in the past may have been solved with a mere verbal or written warning. The April 2003 issue of *NEA Today* cited findings from Harvard University's Civil Rights Project indicating that "well-intentioned efforts have 'spun totally out of control,' expanding to include automatic or exceedingly harsh punishments for minor infractions that pose little or no threat to school safety." Indeed, such policies may place those guilty of minor violations in the company of more severe juvenile offenders or brand normal adolescents as problematic.

Amidst these conditions, therapeutic education schools were one answer for some troubled children. While many reputable programs were available, a number of schools continued to draw harsh criticism. Several had been formally charged—either by the U.S. State Department or by foreign authorities—for the abusive treatment of youth. One organization in particular, the World Wide Association of Specialty Programs and Schools (WWASPS), was at the center of some controversy. Operated by a small group of businesspeople, WWASPS is an umbrella organization based in St. George, Utah, that is affiliated with at least eight schools in the United States and abroad. Following the closure of two WWASPS-affiliated schools during the 1990s, Narvin Lichfield, operator of the Academy at Dundee Ranch in Costa Rica (a WWASPS affiliate) and brother of WWASPS founder Robert Lichfield, was jailed by Costa Rican authorities in 2003 amidst allegations that students were abused and that their civil liberties had been violated.

Therapeutic education programs continued to come under attack on charges of abuse, including beatings, food and sleep deprivation, and cruel and sadistic acts. Behavior modification programs affiliated with WWASPS faced allegations of abuse, and in September 2004, their Mexican affiliate, Casa by the Sea, near Ensanada, was shut down for suspected cases of abuse. WWASPS president Ken Kay said the charges were "unsubstantiated," but a panel was formed to study the issue.

Although therapeutic programs across the country for troubled teens had become a booming industry, there were little or no regulations or licensing requirements for these wilderness camps, schools, or military academies. Between 1980 and 2004, more than 30 teenagers died in camps for troubled teens, including a 14-year-old San Mateo County boy who died in an Arizona boot camp after being made to eat dirt, and 15-year-old Roberto Reyes, with numerous bruises, cuts, and ulcerations that were discovered after his death from being thrown into solitary confinement, refused use of a bathroom, and forced to lie in his own excrement for hours. In May 2004, several employees of Thayer Learning Center, a Missouri boot camp with about 100 students and which costs $50,000 per year, filed complaints with the sheriff's office, stating that students had been stripped to their underwear, tied up, and had ice water poured on them every hour, and a female student had been forced to sit in a tub of urine for several hours.

PIONEERS IN THE FIELD

Bert Brown Bert Brown is a recognized pioneer within the therapeutic education movement. Brown, an author, and his wife, started one of the first rest homes for mentally disturbed individuals during the Great Depression. After a moving experience with an emotionally troubled youth, the couple decided to start a school to reach out to this population.

According to the organization, "When asked why he and his wife started The Brown Schools, Bert Brown would often say, 'I don't believe a child is lost as long as one person in the world has faith in him.' He was also fond of saying, 'The Brown Schools was established on the rock of devotion to children and nurtured by love and loyalty... Always put the children first in the life of the Schools and make them happy, and the other parts of life will fall in place.'"

Bert Brown revealed some of the history behind the organization he and his wife founded in a book titled *Dedication: Hillview Unit*, explaining, "We bought some books on the subject and there were very few in those days. We read them over every night and we talked about our school and we had a good time. Mrs. Brown, being a former school teacher, made out schedules and talked about what we were going to teach them. We talked about their living habits, their eating, their rest periods, their social life, and how we were to entertain them. We were going to give every child a party with a birthday cake. We were going to give them picnics and take them riding in the country. We were going to take them to picture shows and teach them to swim."

In 1940, the Browns leased the former Spring Lake Hotel in Texas and their dream became a reality when the Brown Schools at San Marcos was established. In the aforementioned book, Bert Brown said, "We were young, we had a lot of faith, and our hearts were filled with love for all mankind. So right down there on the banks of the beautiful little San Marcos River the seeds were planted for The Brown Schools. They sprang up and they grew and they grew like a great tree. It sent its roots and branches out into every state in the union. There must have been something very much alive and growing in the schools to

have attracted so many people and hold them. So many people from so many far away places." By the beginning of the twenty-first century, the Brown Schools had evolved into an organization with more than 2,300 employees and revenues in excess of $200 million.

A shock wave went through the industry when the Brown Schools, with no prior notice, shut the doors to its operations in four states as of March 25, 2004. Parents had small hopes of recovering tuition money—which ran as high as $100,000 per year—after Brown filed for liquidation under Chapter 7 of the Bankruptcy Code. According to court filings, Brown owed over $40 million to 40 creditors and held assets of between $1 million and $10 million. Its major investors refused financing for any more loans, which led to the shutdown of the schools.

Mel Wasserman In 1967, a California merchant named Mel Wasserman began conversing with troubled teens who gathered, across from his furniture business, on the steps of the Palm Springs Public Library. These conversations quickly led Wasserman and his wife Brigitte to open up their house as a discussion forum where teens could talk and share their feelings and views with one another. Wasserman then sold his business, bought a ranch in Riverside, California, and started a therapeutic program called CEDU. That name, according to the organization, was derived from those group discussions and was based on "the principal of seeing yourself for who you are and doing something with it." Thus, "see and do" became CEDU.

According to CEDU, Wasserman's program "pioneered and defined emotional growth education by addressing the needs of troubled teens who were at risk of failing life. CEDU mastered the technique of reaching these youth by creating a structured environment where staff and students set the limits, provided positive reinforcement, and confronted each other openly when their integrity was flagging. This open dialogue, strong peer culture, and trust in human relationships created a safe haven for them to address emotional issues and rebuild their lives."

Wasserman died on April 28, 2002. In the May 2002 issue of *StrugglingTeens.com*, a long-time associate of Wasserman's named Dan Earle recalled, "Mel was actively tilling and planting an educational philosophy that would years later become a movement. Long before the world would become familiar with the phrase 'the child within,' Mel was creating an education whose core was dedicated to, in his words, 'the liberation of the child within' all of us. Three decades before the term 'Emotional Quotient' would appear, acknowledging the importance of emotions, Mel was pioneering the creation of an educational approach that would address equally the development of the individual's emotional knowledge, as well as one's intellectual capacity, civic participation, and personal responsibility. 'To know oneself,' to have the freedom to dream and the tools to achieve those dreams were an integral part of the education he felt everyone deserved."

The wilderness therapy segment of the industry was both popular and controversial. A new organization, the National Association of Therapeutic Wilderness Therapy Camping (NATWC), represented 50 therapeutic wilderness programs for youth in 2008 and published the *Journal of Therapeutic Wilderness Camping*. According to founder Larry Dean Olsen, "The goal was to identify the problems and propose solutions and establish standards. That went a long way toward eliminating the boot camps." According to *The America's Intelligence Wire,* "experiencing rugged nature on its own terms, stripped of modern conveniences and distractions, can have a transformative effect on a young life." The NATWC reports that 75 to 80 percent of participants experience significant improvement in the areas that bring them to the camp.

In 2006 a study by Canyon Research and Consulting claimed to be the first multiyear, large-scale clinical study on the effectiveness of private therapeutic residential programs. Aspen Education Group, one of the leaders in the industry, stated in *PR Newswire* that the study showed that "clinically driven, evidence-based therapeutic programs managed and staffed by licensed and qualified professionals can have a significant, positive impact on troubled adolescents who suffer from behavioral and emotional issues."

Despite such positive reports, allegations of abuse and mistreatment by some programs continued to be a problem for the industry. In 2007, the U.S. Government Accountability Office (GAO) investigated reports of abuse and death in residential treatment programs, including wilderness therapy schools and boot camps, and found "thousands of allegations of abuse" between 1990 and 2007. It also conducted extensive research into ten specific cases.

In July 2006, a participant at the Boulder Outdoor Survival School died of heat stroke and dehydration on the second day of a 28-day hike in the Utah desert. Hikers were given a lidless cup and could drink from natural sources along the way, but they had encountered no water sources for 10 hours. Parents of the man sued the school and eventually settled out of court. The U.S. Forest Service suspended the school's use of Dixie National Forest until it put into place new guidelines and started allowing students to carry water bottles.

Such incidents encouraged wilderness camps to be more careful. In September 2008, *The America's Intelligence Wire* reported that the 10 wilderness therapy camps in Utah had abandoned the boot camp framework for a "gentler, more targeted approach." Changes were taking place nationwide as well. In late 2008 Congress was considering legislation that would provide federal inspections and oversight of wilderness camps.

CURRENT CONDITIONS

In late 2010, a survey conducted by the Aspen Education Group (sent to 10,000 parents, with 1,300 responses as of October 2010) showed that an overwhelming 86 percent who sent their child to an Aspen Wilderness therapy program between 2007 and 2010 would recommend the program to other families in need. Prior to their child undergoing the treatment program, 87 percent of parents responded that they feared for their child's safety; the number was reduced to 22 percent following treatment. Similarly, 86 percent did not trust their child prior to treatment, with just 25 percent feeling that way after treatment. Furthermore, 78 percent felt their child was tearing their family apart, but after undergoing the treatment, just 16 percent felt that way. Other survey results showed a significant reduction in symptoms of pre-existing depression, anxiety, and stress after completing the program.

Still pending in the 111th Congress as of June 2010 was H.R. 911, the Stop Child Abuse in Residential Treatment Programs for Teens Act of 2009 (already passed by the House), with 23 sponsors. Although the bill was geared toward addressing numerous abuse and neglect issues involving permanent/long-term residential treatment facilities, it expressly included, within its scope, therapeutic boarding schools, boot camps, wilderness programs, and behavior modification facilities. A separate government accounting office (GAO) report conducted in 2008 found major gaps in the licensing and oversight of such programs, with some not covered at all under any state or federal law.

The bill would require the U.S. Department of Health and Human Services to inspect all such programs every two years and to issue civil penalties against programs that violated new standards. However, the bill required states, not the federal government, to set and enforce standards, starting within three years of the bill's passage. The pending lesislation also called for a toll-free national hotline for individuals to report cases of abuse. The bill had the support of the American Bar Association, the American Academy of Pediatrics, the American Psychological Association, the Child Welfare League of America, the Children's Defense Fund, Mental Health America, the National Child Abuse Coalition, and many other organizations.

INDUSTRY LEADERS

The majority of therapeutic educations schools are for-profit enterprises. Most are privately owned, either by partnerships, organizations that operate multiple programs in different locations, or individuals. Although many such schools exist in the United States, the most prominent is Aspen Education Group, Inc. Established in 1987, Cerritos, California-based Aspen Education Group Inc. serves the therapeutic education market with 31 programs in 11 states, including boarding schools, experiential outdoor education programs, weight-loss residential high schools, summer weight loss camps, and special education schools for children, teens, and young adults. Led by President and CEO Elliot Sainer, Aspen's mission is to provide "educational programs that promote academic and personal growth to youth and their families with the foundation of our success built upon quality, integrity, and dependability." According to Aspen, the company puts a strong emphasis on its educational programs and on hiring quality staff. In fact, this was one reason the organization changed its name from Aspen Youth Services to Aspen Education Group in 2001. In November 2006, Apsen became a division of CRC Health Group.

WORKFORCE

Therapeutic education schools employ a wide range of staff, including accounting and clerical support positions. Common administrative roles, which may or may not require college degrees, include program administrators, directors, and coordinators. Different levels of therapists, counselors, and caseworkers also are employed by the industry, along with instructors, teachers, field workers, and activity leaders. These positions may be filled by licensed clinical therapists and certified teachers. However, this varies from program to program and is not always the case. Salaries vary accordingly, depending on the program and an incumbent's education and experience. Many programs are located in remote areas and offer non-professional positions to local residents, who have few employment options, at minimum wage.

BIBLIOGRAPHY

"About Aspen." Aspen Education Group, 1 November 2008. Available from http://www.aspeneducation.com.

"About IECA." Independent Educational Consultants Association, 1 November 2008. Available from http://www.iecaonline.org.

"Aspen Education Group Applauds Results of Nation's First Large-Scale, Multi-Year Study on Private Therapeutic Residential Programs for Troubled Teens." *PR Newswire,* 26 April 2007.

Behrens, Ellen, and Kristin Satterfield. "Report of Findings from a Multicenter Study of Youth Outcomes in Private Residential Treatment." Canyon Research and Consulting, August 2006.

Brooklyn, Jenna. "Therapeutic Educational Programs and How They Help Struggling Teens." Available from http://ezinearticles.com.

"BYU Alumnus Sparks off Lucrative, Controversial Wilderness-Therapy Industry." *The America's Intelligence Wire,* 12 September 2008.

"Controversy Spurs Gentler Approach in Utah Wilderness-Therapy Camps." *The America's Intelligence Wire,* 13 September 2008.

"H.R. 911: the Stop Child Abuse in Residential Treatment Programs for Teens Act of 2009." Coalition Against Institutionalized Child Abuse, 27 June 2010. Available from http://www.caica.org/gao/htm.

Kutz, Gregory, and Andy O'Connell. *Residential Treatment Programs: Concerns Regarding Abuse and Death in Certain Programs for Troubled Youth.* Washington, DC: U.S. Government Accountability Office, 10 October 2007.

"NATSAP Principles of Good Practice." National Association of Therapeutic Schools and Programs, 15 November 2008. Available from http://www.natsap.org.

"Outcomes Research Study Reveals Vast Majority of Parents Would Recomment Wilderness Therapy Programs to Other Parents of Troubled Teens." *PR Web,* 27 October 2010. Available from http://www.prweb.com/releases/2010/10/prweb4707264.htm.

"Parents of Jersey Man Reach Settlement over Survival School Death." *The Star-Ledger,* (Newark, NJ), 13 November 2007.

Russell, Keith. *Summary of Research from 1999–2006 and Update to 2000 Survey of Behavioral Healthcare Programs in North America.* Minneapolis: University of Minnesota, May 2007.

"Selected Cases of Death, Abuse, and Deceptive Marketing." *General Accounting Office Reports & Testimony,* May 2008.

"State Licensure and Oversight Necessary: Therapeutic Schools and Programs Association Testifies on the Hill." National Association of Therapeutic Schools and Programs, 10 October 2007.

"Therapeutic Trek: Wilderness Therapy Programs Need Oversight." *The America's Intelligence Wire,* 17 September 2008.

"Wilderness Therapy Has Evolved." *The Salt Lake City Tribune,* 14 September 2008.

TISSUE ENGINEERING

—■—

SIC CODE(S)

8099

INDUSTRY SNAPSHOT

Although biomedically enhanced humans used to populate only 1970s television action shows and futuristic Hollywood offerings, the engineered production of human tissue was a reality by the twenty-first century—and the probability of engineering entire human organs, such as hearts and livers, loomed on the horizon. In the short term, tissue engineering—the field of biomedicine that helps to restore or replace organs and tissues that are damaged, affected by disease, or suffering from injury or congenital anomaly—results in replacements for artificial joints, such nonliving processed tissues as heart valves, and tissues taken from a patient's own body or that of a donor.

Tissue engineering is a fledgling, highly interdisciplinary field that straddles the disciplines of materials science and biology but draws on immunology, chemistry, and bioengineering as well. The aim of tissue engineering is to restore or replace human tissues or organs by introducing compatible, engineered, live cell tissue that becomes integrated into the recipient's body. Tissue engineering can decrease health care costs while improving the health and quality of life for people worldwide by revolutionizing health care treatment.

Tissue engineering is often referred to as regenerative medicine, although the latter refers exclusively to stem cell growth, while tissue engineering may employ other technologies, including the melding/integration of both organic and non-organic and/or non-human tissue components. However, by far, tissue engineering relies on tissue regeneration, utilizing human cell growth.

ORGANIZATION AND STRUCTURE

Most tissue engineering biotechnology companies are small, private startups engaged in research and development (R & D) in a nascent field with a high risk of failure. Because of the extensive interdisciplinary work the field requires, many firms collaborate with universities, larger pharmaceutical companies, or each other in conducting their R & D

Producing engineered tissues is a bit like growing houseplants. The specialist starts with a trellis-like scaffold (or matrix) made of collagen or biodegradable polymer, shapes it as necessary to facilitate development of the future tissue, seeds it with live cells, then nourishes the scaffold with growth factors to stimulate cell reproduction. The multiplying cells fill out the scaffold and grow into three-dimensional tissue. After being implanted in the body, intended tissue functions are recreated. Blood vessels attach themselves to the new tissue, the scaffold dissolves, and the tissue blends into the landscape. The procedure often uses stem cells, premature cells that were first identified in 1992. Implanting stem cells in appropriate places encourages them to grow into the intended type of cell, bone, tendon, or cartilage. Tissue-engineered systems can be either "open," and thus meant to be completely integrated into the recipient's body, or "closed" (encapsulated), to defend against rejection by the recipient's immune system. Controlled release of growth factors may aid in the formation of blood vessels to nourish the newly introduced tissue matrix or to spur tissue cell reproduction.

Funding for tissue engineering R & D comes from private foundations such as the Pugh Foundation, the Red Cross, the Howard Hughes Foundation, and the

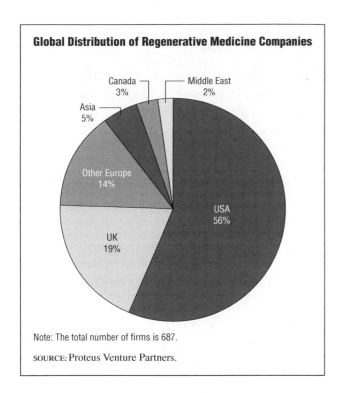

Global Distribution of Regenerative Medicine Companies

Canada 3%
Middle East 2%
Asia 5%
Other Europe 14%
USA 56%
UK 19%

Note: The total number of firms is 687.

SOURCE: Proteus Venture Partners.

Whittaker Foundation, and from governmental sources such as the National Science Foundation and the National Institutes of Health (NIH). In 1997, the NIH established a Bioengineering Consortium devoted to this emerging science.

BACKGROUND AND DEVELOPMENT

By the dawn of the twenty-first century, the field of tissue engineering had existed less than three decades. Groundwork was laid as early as 1933, when the European researcher Bisceglie inserted mouse tumor cells, which he had enclosed in a polymer membrane, into a pig's abdominal cavity. The pig's immune system failed to kill the cells.

Although the Kennedy administration backed some tissue engineering initiatives, the field really got its start in Boston at the Massachusetts Institute of Technology in the late 1970s. It resulted from the work of three research endeavors. Professor Howard Green pioneered research on skin (epithelial sheets and keratinocyte grafts). Professor Ioannis Yannas studied the creation of collagen scaffolds for skin repair. In conjunction withDr. John Burke, a burn doctor at Boston's Shriners Hospital, Yannas developed an implant that could be used to guide the reformation of skin tissue. The technique became known as the Burke-Yannas Method. The third project, conducted by Robert Langer and Eugene Bell, involved the application of synthetic polymers in cell lattices. By the 1980s, scientists were trying to grow skin replacements with cells embedded

in collagen gels. Those attempts led to the tissue-engineered skin products on the market today. In the same decade, the term "tissue engineering" was coined. In 1983, Langer and Dr. Joseph Vacanti developed a polymer scaffold for supporting tissue generation.

For its first 20 years, the focus of tissue engineering remained the development of skin products for burn wounds using autologous cells—those taken from the burn victim. The resultant tissue, which grafted well and was cosmetically acceptable, far surpassed the cadaver or pig skin tissues previously used for the purpose. The material was also adapted for chronic wounds, such as leg and foot ulcers.

Many research milestones were reached only in the 1990s—several backed by funding from Geron Corp. In August 1997, Nobel Prize recipient Thomas Cech of the University of Colorado-Boulder and his team isolated the human gene responsible for telomerase reverse transcriptase (rTRT), which knits together the fraying edges, or telomeres, of aging cells. Later the same year, Jerry Shay and Woodring Wright of the University of Texas's Southwest Medical Center actually introduced the rTRT gene into cells and demonstrated the process in action. This discovery benefited research aimed at extending the life span of new organs that may one day be engineered from a patient's own cells, which may be prematurely aged.

In 1998, both James Thompson of the University of Wisconsin and John Gearhart of Johns Hopkins University independently isolated human stem cells, the existence of which had previously only been surmised. Stem cells form an ideal raw material for tissue engineering research. By the end of the 1990s, scientists had also determined that adults as well as embryos possess stem cells that may carry on repair work on the body throughout life. This even proved to be true of adult neural stem cells, overturning the long-held belief that damage to the central nervous system (spinal cord and brain) was irreparable. The successful cloning of Dolly, the famous sheep, and the completed mapping of the human genome were breakthroughs with important implications for future field research as well.

Research and Products Still a nascent industry, only a handful of tissue engineering end products were approved by the U.S. Food and Drug Administration (FDA) for the U.S. market early in the first decade of the 2000s. The first such material widely available was engineered skin tissue, which is grown commercially in "factories" engaged in continuous production for ready product availability to hospitals and research facilities. The replacement skins have a long shelf life and are fairly durable. TransCyte, a skin product from Advanced Tissue Sciences (ATS), used donated human (allogeneic) dermal cells cultivated on a polyglycolic acid mesh. Rather than grafting onto a wound, the tissue covers it and emits wound-healing signals to the patient's body, thus speeding recovery.

ATS also announced in March 2000 the first scientific demonstration that engineered tissue could stimulate the formation of new blood vessels (angiogenesis), essential for regenerating damaged heart tissue. In conjunction with members of the University of Arizona, ATS researchers tissue-engineered an epicardial patch that induced angiogenesis within two weeks. The patch was a living, human-based product that secreted growth factors and proteins. Meanwhile, Organogenesis, Inc., a tissue regeneration company that describes itself as specializing in bioactive wound healing products designed to kick-start the body's natural healing process, bio-Aesthetics (tm) and biosurgery, produced Apligraf, a two-layered product that mimics the structure of human dermal and epidermal tissue. It is composed of a collagen matrix containing dermal cells (fibroblasts) overlaid with cultured epidermal cells (keratinocytes). In 1998, the product received approval for its use with venous leg ulcers, which affect nearly 2.6 million patients in the United States each year, primarily due to complications from diabetes and circulation disorders, which often lead to amputation.

By 2004, just four engineered tissue products had received federal approval, and none of them had yet met with commercial success. By that time, seven products failed or were aborted in the trial stage, while nine were still working their way through FDA trials. The middle of the first decade of the 2000s thus represented a period of readjustment for the tissue engineering industry. The extremely high cost of development and rigorous testing forced many key players out of the game, as the meager revenues generated by their products, coupled with the drying up of the pool of available venture capital, wreaked havoc on company balance sheets. Key industry players such as Advanced Tissue Sciences and Organogenesis filed for bankruptcy, and other firms were forced to drastically reduce their research and development budgets. In addition, tissue engineering touched on sensitive legal, political, and ethical questions that have yet to be addressed by governments and the courts, and these issues loomed over the industry's future.

Ongoing research centers on the matrices and cells used in tissue engineering. Most matrices are composed either of synthetics such as lactic-glycolic acid or olyacrylonitrile-polyvinyl or natural materials such as collagen and alginate. Bovine collagen was commonly used, raising alarms about possible contamination with mad cow disease and its human counterpart, Creutzfeldt-Jakob disease. While synthetics permit more control over matrix ductility, strength, and permeability, natural materials offer better cell adhesiveness. Research in this sector thus seeks to uncover matrix formulations that combine the best qualities of both. Matrices have been produced that are capable of being shaped to support the growth of blood vessel and intestinal tubes, ear and finger-shaped cartilage and bone, and heart valve leaflets. Cartilage from the patient's own body has been used to treat juvenile urinary reflux and urinary stress incontinence in adults.

Progress has even been made toward tackling the toughest challenge that confronts tissue engineers: engineering entire complex organs such as livers and hearts. Among the more promising technologies to bring this idea to fruition is what is known as "organ printing." Theoretically, organ printing could eventually lead to the manufacturing on demand of entire human bodies. Organ printing could function in much the manner as a highly sophisticated computer printer, according to *The Futurist,* using cell aggregates in the place of inks and thermoreversible gel for paper. Running from software including highly detailed information on human anatomy, the printer would build organs by layering rows of cells on top of each other.

Leading the causes for investment in organ printing and related technologies was the shortage of organs available for transplant in the first decade of the 2000s. With demand greatly outpacing the number of donors willing to offer their organs, the medical community looked with great interest at the ability to manufacture organs from the ground up. Another spur would be the emerging field of pharmacogenomics. A quickly emerging sector of the pharmaceutical industry in the middle years of the first decade of the 2000s, pharmacogenomics uses the knowledge of individuals' specific gene sequences to determine how they will react to particular drug treatments, and to develop new therapies accordingly. Organ printing would allow for pharmacogenomic research to utilize manufactured organs rather than live test subjects in some aspects of their clinical trials, greatly reducing the risks involved in using experimental drugs on live patients. Similarly, researchers could print, for example, live cancer tumors, and test the effectiveness of new drugs against them. (See also **Pharmacogenomics.**)

Other scientists worked on a potentially revolutionary sub-sector called injectable tissue engineering. Led by the biomedical engineer Jennifer Elisseeff and her colleagues at Johns Hopkins University, injectable tissue engineering involves the injection into joints of specially designed mixtures of polymers, cells, and growth stimulators that solidify and form healthy tissue. Some of the chief benefits of injectable tissue engineering included its much lower cost and reduced invasiveness when compared with full-scale tissue or organ transplants. Elisseeff's team successfully built cartilage by injecting cells and light-sensitive polymers into the backs of mice and feeding the cells with ultraviolet light shone through the skin. Follow-up studies using the same process injected into the knees of human cadavers were likewise successful.

Cell studies for tissue engineering usually examine specific cell types. Autologous (the same person is donor and recipient) cartilage transplants are in clinical use for rebuilding damaged knees. For engineered skin tissue, dermal (skin) cells from neonates (newborn babies less than four weeks old) are used. Researchers are seeking to identify single sources from which a variety of cells could be drawn. The answer may lie in human stem cells. These undifferentiated cells, which appear at the period of earliest formation of the human embryo, later develop into all the various cell types found in the body"s bone, blood, nerve, cartilage, liver, and so on. Stem cell research raised a public furor in the United States in the early 2000s because stem cells came from the umbilical cords of aborted fetuses or were obtained from fertility clinics in the form of unused fertilized frozen embryos. In 2001, the George W. Bush Administration banned use of federal research dollars for work using stem cells created through additional embryo destruction. With tensions high on both sides of the equation, debate and policy questions lingered.

Although initial results showed promise, further research was needed to solve technical problems of working with stem cells, such as methods to guarantee that stem cell batches were not contaminated with dermal cells, to prevent stem cells from sticking together during culturing, and to augment the production of mass quantities of stem cells that are needed for large scale tissue generation. Despite the political and legal wrangling and technical obstacles, the research firm Visiongain expected the market for stem cell products to reach $10 billion by 2013, even though there were no such products on the market by 2004.

Australian scientists and MIT bioengineers in early 2006 made a breakthrough in tissue engineering with "three-dimensional" construction, which was expected to revolutionize the treatment of such ailments as heart disease and cancer and may eventually lead to the creation of organs, including parts of the heart. Formerly, scientists were only able to create two-dimensional constructions of cells, such as skin cells, in a laboratory setting. Three-dimensional construction allows scientists to study cell organization in tissues and will potentially make it possible to re-grow cells to repair organs damaged by disease, accident, or aging.

Scientists at MIT use electricity to move cells into the desired position in a gel that resembles living tissue. Light is then used to lock the cells into place. By using a "micropatterning technique," they are able to place cells within 10 microns of each other—the same process used to create circuit patterns on electronic microchips. As of early 2006, the MIT scientists could form more than 20,000 cell clusters with exact sizes and shapes within a single gel. They also created cell layers that copy the structure of tissue inside the human body. Although it is expected that this technology will ultimately be used for tissue engineering in medical applications, it will first be used to study cell organization, cell function and communication in tissues, and how cells develop into organs or tumors.

In addition, in Melbourne, Australia, surgeons and scientists used a plastic chamber to grow three-dimensional cells. The chamber was used to implant a blood vessel with microsurgery, after which cells were mixed inside the chamber and allowed to grow into the environment created. As of early 2006, they had created breast tissue, fat muscle, pancreas tissues capable of producing insulin, and sinus tissue.

Although "printing" as a method of tissue engineering was not new in 2006, the method was modified by Gabor Forgacs, a biophysicist at the University of Missouri in Columbia. In the past, the technique involved using modified ink-jet printers which sprayed cells suspended in liquid. Forgacs, together with a company called Sciperio, has developed a device with print heads that extrude clumps of cells so that they spray out one at a time from a micropipette, resulting in a higher density of cells in the final printed structure. Droplets of "bioink," clumps of cells a few hundred micrometers in diameter, are placed next to each other, causing them to flow together, fuse, and form layers, rings, or other shapes. When layers of chicken heart cells were "printed," the structure began behaving like a normal chicken heart and started beating within nineteen hours. Bioprinting will allow a faster and cheaper method to engineer tissues.

More exciting news in tissue engineering involved engineered blood vessels grown from patients' own skin, reported at the December 2005 American Heart Association's scientific session. Cytograft Tissue Engineering of Novato, California announced at the session that three volunteer haemodialysis patients (patients needing a shunt between arteries and veins to access filtering machinery) received the engineered blood vessels. This advancement will provide opportunities for heart patients who are unable to have cardiac bypass surgery because they lack suitable veins for grafting. An invention of Cytograft, "sheet-based engineering," was used to produce the vessels. Fibroblasts and endothelial cells were harvested from the patient's hand, then cultured and encouraged to secrete extracellular matrix proteins. The fibroblasts produce the tough exterior of the vessels—the breakthrough which provided the necessary mechanical strength—while the endothelial cells grow into the lining. Cytograft CEO Todd McAllister states that the two-dimensional sheet of cells that results, can, after a few months, be shaped into a three-dimensional organ, such as a blood vessel. Other possibilities include the creation of new heart valves and tissue repairs.

Another success story out of the Massachusetts Institute of Technology (MIT) was the creation of skeletal muscle with its own blood supply that was implanted into live rats and mice. The lack of blood vessels in engineered tissue had been a major barrier for scientists trying to create replacement organs and tissues. Previously, very thin implants, such as skin, were successful because they used blood vessels from the underlying tissue. However, thicker implants, such as muscle, were not likely to survive very long because of the lack of their own blood vessels to deliver nourishment and eliminate waste. Robert Langer of MIT headed a group who successfully developed muscle cells in a lab dish that grew their own vascular network before being implanted in the body. After implantation in the abdominal muscle of a mouse, 41 percent of the engineered muscle's blood vessels connected with the mouse's vascular system. The engineered muscle tissue was grown on a biodegradable polymer scaffold by using three types of stem cells: human endothelial cells to form blood vessels, mouse muscle stem cells, and mouse fibroblasts to produce connective tissue and smooth muscle cells. The hope is that the technique could be used to produce organs with complex vascular systems, such as hearts and livers.

Regulatory and Financing Issues Beginning in 2001, in order to not break federal law, researchers in the private sector and in public universities began using millions in private money to obtain more cell lines in order to conduct stem cell research. For example, researchers at Harvard University used private money to clone embryos to use for stem cell research; and the University of Michigan's Medical School, Life Sciences Institute, and Molecular and Behavioral Neuroscience Institute funded a $10.5 million interdisciplinary stem cell biology center on campus.

In mid-2006, federal funding for stem cell research was still limited to research on 22 cell lines from human embryos available prior to President George W. Bush's announcement of this policy on August 9, 2001. (Bush initially said that more than 60 cell lines would be available, but many were tainted by mouse material.) Since 2001, public opinion steadily moved from the president's position that destruction of about 400,000 available frozen embryos awaiting disposal at fertility clinics was the immoral taking of human life toward the view of celebrities like former First Lady Nancy Reagan and the late actor Christopher Reeve that embryonic stem cells have the potential to treat and help find cures for disease conditions such as diabetes, spinal cord injuries, and Parkinson's disease and should be used in federally funded research for that purpose.

In late 2005, the House of Representatives passed a bill to alleviate financial constraints and to allow research on stem cells regardless of when they were derived,

increasing the possibility of a change in policy. President George W. Bush continued to oppose stem cell research, however, and called the House's vote a "great mistake." The Senate drafted an identical bill and passed it by a vote of 63 to 37 on July 18, 2006. President Bush vetoed the legislation on July 19, as he promised. It was the first veto of his administration. The bill then went back to the House, where a vote of 235 to 193 to overturn the veto fell short of the two-thirds majority needed, removing the need for a Senate override attempt.

The day after the president's veto, California Governor Arnold Schwarzenegger, who consistently disagreed with President Bush on stem cell research, referred to the veto as he announced that he had authorized the loan of $150 million from the state's general fund as grant money to scientists at the state's stem cell research arm, the California Institute for Regenerative Medicine, created when California voters in 2004 approved Proposition 71, a $3 billion bond measure, to be dispensed at $300 million a year for 10 years, for embryonic stem cell research, including cloning projects for research purposes only. According to an MSNBC online article, the measure was designed not only to circumvent the Bush funding restrictions but was by far the largest U.S. stem cell project to date. The $150 million loan was authorized because opponents of Proposition 71 sued to block the measure and it was still on appeal.

In March 2006, no doubt because of the passage of Proposition 71, four prestigious, San Diego-based research institutions—The Burnham Institute for Medical Research, the Salk Institute for Biological Studies, The Scripps Research Institute, and the University of California, San Diego—signed a formal agreement to work toward the establishment the San Diego Consortium for Regenerative Medicine. The Burnham Institute explained the Consortium's mission: "This historic alliance would marshal the intellectual resources of four world leaders in life sciences research, bringing scientists from each institution together to develop and conduct joint research and training programs in one of today's most promising areas of science. Regenerative medicine references the ability of stem cells to proliferate and become specific cell types, giving them the therapeutic potential for repairing and replacing tissue damaged by disease or injury. The objectives of the San Diego Consortium for Regenerative Medicine include establishing a jointly operated facility dedicated to stem cell research, and pursuing funding to support these collaborative projects."

Also following the Bush veto, Illinois Governor Rod Blagojevich offered $5 million in similar grants to scientists in his state; the Democratic candidate for Governor in Florida in 2006 said that if he was elected, stem cell research would be funded in Florida; and in Maryland's gubernatorial race, both the incumbent Republican governor and the Democratic hopeful supported stem cell research. In addition, on the November 2006 ballot in Missouri, a stem cell research initiative, cosponsored by the Democratic challenger for the U.S. Senate seat in Missouri, was strongly opposed by those advocating the right to life position, but was endorsed by over 2,000 doctors, nurses, and health care professionals, and by over 100 patient and medical groups, including the Missouri State Medical Association.

Controversy continued regarding the ethics of using embryonic cells for research. In late 2007 Japanese scientists and a research group at the University of Wisconsin at Madison simultaneously reported success at reprogramming adult skin cells to behave like embryonic stem cells; and in October 2008 scientists at Massachusetts General Hospital in Boston discovered a way to more safely revert adult cells to an embryonic state. However, some asserted that such discoveries did not negate the value of research on embryonic cells.

Researchers in the industry waited to see what would happen after the 2008 U.S. presidential elections. Whereas President Bush had vetoed the Stem Cell Research Enhancement Act, it was expected that then president-elect Obama would lift restrictions on stem cell research. During the previous five years, the National Institutes of Health had awarded $186 million in grants for embryonic stem cell research and $1 billion for those studying adult stem cells from sources such as skin and blood.

To address some of these pending but important issues, the FDA consolidated a number of programs to form the new Office of Cellular, Tissue, and Gene Therapies (OCTGT) and in September 2009 issues a new proposed rule for products that combined two or more regulated components, e.g., bioartificial organs, recombinant proteins, orthopedic implants that contained growth factors and anti-inflammatory drugs, etc.

Also in 2009, President Barack Obama reversed the more restrictive legislation enacted during the Bush administration and opened up research funds for scientists working with embryonic stem cells.

CURRENT CONDITIONS

In 2010, two research scientists filed suit in federal court to challenge President Obama's order that resumed federal funding of stem cell research. In August 2010, U.S. District Court Judge Royce Lamberth ruled that the research violated U.S. law because it involved the destruction of human embryos. A U.S. appeals court temporarily lifted the injunction and as of November 2010, final adjudication was still pending. As of 2010, eight states had statutes expressly prohibiting human cloning for reproductive purposes or for initiating a pregnancy, but

allowing research in this area. Those states were California, Connecticut, Illinois, Iowa, Masssachusetts, New Jersey, New York, and Rhode Island.

Various studies and reports published in 2010 placed the value of the global tissue-regenerative market at between $2 and $3 billion in 2009. The variance in revenue estimates was the result of varying inclusions/exclusions of product types and services included in the industry. For example, Medtronic's highly successful INFUSE product, a major contributor to global revenue, was a recombinant bone morphogenic protein product that involved cells *in vivo,* but was not a cellular product. Another major contributor to revenues was the segment of regenerative biomaterials, an important part of which was small intestine submucosa (SIS), but this was an extracellular product derived from pig tissue. Therefore, cell-based products, e.g., stem cell represented between one-fourth and one-third of the total market.

In any event, the tissue regenerative products market could expect a boom market for several years, according to market researcher Life Science Intelligence. It projected the market to grow as mudh as 16 percent yearly, reaching $11.8 billion by 2013. In another extensive industry report published in October 2010, Bureau AWEX of New York garnered studies and forecasts from several global industry analysts. Citing Mr. Robin Young, medical industry analyst from RRY Publications, the report quoted his projection that the U.S. regenerative medicine market would growm from $146.5 million in 2010 to over $8 billion by 2020. The fastest growing segments of the market were identified as orthopedics (joint replacement) and wound healing. The United States accounted for 90 percent of the global tissue engineering and regenerative medicine market and was expected to retain that place in the foreseeable future.

INDUSTRY LEADERS

Several companies within the United States were specialized in their research and/or component products; therefore, ranking them by size or revenue discounted their value to the industry. Several U.S. companies that were major players in the regenerative medicine/tissue engineering field in 2010 (with their specialties in parentheses) included Stryker Corporation (bone), Zimmer Inc., Kinetic Concepts, RTI Biologics Inc.(bone), Cryolife, Inc., NeoStem, Geron, Cytori Therapeutics (soft tissue), Osiris Therapeutics (bone), Athersys, Kensey Nash Corporation, LifeCell (skin), Advanced Biohealing (skin), Medtronics (which acquired Osteotech Inc. in August 2010), and Advanced Cell Technology.

Organogenesis Inc. of Canton, Massachusetts, (skin specialists) founded in 1985, struggled financially in the first decade of the 2000s. The company's primary commercial product, Apligraf, gained FDA approval in 1999, making it the first tissue engineering product to receive the agency's blessing. The tissue-engineered skin replacement was used for treating venous leg ulcers, and pharmaceutical giant Novartis claimed global marketing rights. In the late years of the first decade of the 2000s, Organogenesis was at work on the next generation of Apligraf, which would use all human materials. Other FDA-approved tissue replacement products in its portfolio included FortaPerm and FortaGen. Organogenesis's research agenda focused on Vitrix, a living cell soft tissue replacement for wound repair, a bio-artificial liver, and vascular grafts. By 2005, over 100,000 patients had been treated with their living cell-based therapy. Due to the sudden rise in sales of Apligraf in 2006, the company expanded their sales force for the third time in two years, employing 200 in the United States while also expanding into Switzerland. In 2009, the Massachussetts Life Sciences Board approved a $7.4 million investment grant to help Organogenesis implement the state's $1 billon life sciences initiative.

Genzyme Biosurgery, of Cambridge, Massachusetts (specializing in cartilage regeneration), is a separately traded division of Genzyme. Its Epicel Service grows skin grafts of patient skin; it can culture a body's worth of tissue from a postage-stamp-sized sample in four weeks. The company received FDA approval to grow autologous cartilage tissue and then implant it in human knees. Its main product is Carticel, used to heal knee cartilage. Other top products include Synvisc, also for knee cartilage; Seprafilm, used to prevent post-surgery tissue adhesions; and Epicel, a severe burn treatment. Genzyme's 2009 revenues reached $4.52 billion.

Forticell Bioscience (formerly Ortec International), a New York-based firm, received FDA approval for its Composite Cultured Skin (CCS), a wound dressing derived from a bovine collagen matrix seeded with skin cells, to treat epidermolysis bullosa, a skin disorder that creates severe blistering and sloughing. Forticell explored additional applications for CCS, including burns, skin ulcers, and reconstructive surgery. In June 2003, Forticell was granted patent protection for the cryopreservation process for its tissue-engineered product OrCel, intended to treat diabetic foot ulcers and a variety of other conditions The new patent, the fifth in Forticell's portfolio, will expire in 2020.

Integra LifeSciences of Plainsboro, New Jersey, is a diversified biosciences company that makes biological implants for brain, spinal, and orthopedic surgeries, and also skin products. The firm's Dermal Regeneration Template was its flagship proprietary tissue regeneration technology. Total revenues in 2009 reached $682.4 million.

The Canadian firm BioSyntech Inc. was established in 1995. BioSyntech patented the platform technology BST-Gel, which is a multifunctional, injectable thermosensitive and self-forming hydrogel that can be used for tissue repair or for targeted delivery of therapeutic agents. BST-Gel is considered a medical device by the FDA, and BioSyntech had several products in development late in the first decade of the 2000s, including those for cartilage repair, heel cushioning, and chronic wound healing. The firm also produced a natural biopolymer known as chitosan for tissue repair.

WORKFORCE

The U.S. Department of Labor expected the number of job openings in the booming biomedical engineering sector to grow 31.4 percent through 2010. New graduates, meanwhile, earned an average of approximately $50,000 per year to start. The industry demands well-educated and highly trained individuals with the talent to combine skills from several disciplines. Although a bachelor's degree will often suffice for workers in technical support, most research positions require postgraduate education, with advanced degrees in the life sciences, medicine, and engineering quite common. Many tissue engineering specialists possess postgraduate degrees in more than one field. Since it is a nascent industry, many of those who conduct tissue engineering research are professors at major research universities.

Given the potentially explosive ethical questions that tissue engineering raises, workers also must familiarize themselves with governmental regulations that affect developments in the field. Tissue engineering scientists must be able to collaborate with others as part of an R & D team, since virtually all industry breakthroughs have resulted from the combined efforts of several specialists whose work foci complement each other.

For management positions in the industry, knowledge of the life sciences, medicine, or engineering is still essential. A combination of master's degrees is most desirable: one in the sciences and the other a master's of business administration.

AMERICA AND THE WORLD

According to the 2010 *State of the U.S. Regenerative Medicine Industry* report, there were 687 regenerative medicine companies worldwide at that time, and 386 of them were located in the United States. Europe had the second highest number of companies ,with 226, primarily located within the United Kingdom. Despite the United States being recognized as a leader in cell therapy and tissue engineering, as well as home to so many companies, the U.S. tissue engineering market was expected to grow at a slower pace compared to Europe and other regions, noted *Tissue Engineering/Cell Therapy: Products, Technologies & Market Opportunities Worldwide, 2009-2018* issued by MedMarket Diligence.

The United States was widely considered the commercial leader in tissue engineering, but the industry quickly internationalized. More than 40 percent of the companies founded between 2000 and 2004 were located outside the United States. Research partnerships frequently cross international borders with scientists from leading universities throughout the world lending their expertise to ongoing research. The ethical challenges posed by stem cell-based research and growing human organs must be shared as well, since all governments will need to determine how they will grapple with new developments that are rapidly approaching. Canada introduced a Human Reproductive and Genetic Technologies bill that would permit embryos to be grown from eggs harvested from aborted fetuses for research, citing the need for fetal tissue to aid work that targeted treatments for Parkinson's and Alzheimer's, among other diseases. In the United Kingdom, the establishment of the new Building Up Biomaterials initiative in the Department of Trade and Industry aimed to increase the United Kingdom's presence in the industry.

The projected eventual availability of "farmed" human "spare parts" on the world market also raises the potential for organ and cell trafficking and the danger of diseases spreading through infected tissues. Global quality standards will be needed to assure safety and to adjudicate ethical and legal quandaries that will arise as tissue engineering moves from a fledgling, primarily research-oriented discipline to a full-blown commercial enterprise.

In an effort to position Europe at the forefront of tissue engineering and remove obstacles to its industry's development, in 2005, the European Commission proposed rules covering gene, cell and tissue-based therapies to guarantee public health while guaranteeing equal access for all European citizens to this new technology. The Commission gave the task of monitoring market authorization to the European Medicines Agency in London, who will set up a Committee for Advanced Therapies to evaluate new therapy products and to follow new developments in the field. It will also provide scientific advice.

RESEARCH AND TECHNOLOGY

Private industry, universities, and federal agencies all contribute to ongoing research in the field. Much current research centers on deciphering how cells interact and matching cells up with the right scaffold material to achieve desired results. Fertile ground for future work includes developing basic technologies for enabling viable cells to be mass produced for commercial applications; storage facilities to prolong cell and tissue viability;

technology for the manufacture of biocompatible materials; and the manufacture of products that will inhibit adverse reactions by the host recipient.

In 2010, Roche scientists used human heart tissue made from stem cells to re-test an antiviral drug that Roche had previously abandoned development of, because of irregular heartbeats in rodents and rabbits. The same effect was seen under laboratory conditions using the stem cell-generated heart cells. This opened a new door of opportunity to use stem cells to help predict adverse side effects from drugs still being developed. As of 2010, only Pfizer had set up a research unit (in Cambriddge, England) specifically dedicated to regenerative medicine.

Also in 2010, researchers announced the development of a technique for the self-assembly of cell-laden microgels on the interface of air and hydrophobic solutions. This facilitated fabrication of three-dimensional (3D) tissue constructs with controllable microscale features. Hydrogels had been in development for many years, but this new technique enhanced the regenerative process and kept tissue cells viable for longer periods, for use in creating long-term engineered tissues. The technique could be used for the rapid creation of tightly-packed tissue-like sheets with either single cell types or homogenously distributed cocultures.

Previously, in 2008, researchers at the Massachusetts Institute of Technology (MIT) discovered a way to attach synthetic patches—much like tiny "backpacks" to cells used for tissue engineering. The cell is allowed to function normally and interact with its external environment because the patch covers only part of its surface. Robert Cohen, one of the researchers in the project, commented in an MIT press release, "The goal is to perturb the cell as little as possible." The implications of the research were yet to be determined, but it is possible that "patches could be designed that allow researchers to align cells in a certain pattern, eliminating the need for a tissue scaffold."

Researchers have also unveiled some significant advances in engineering structures composed of simpler tissues such as cartilage. Harvard surgery professor Dr. Joseph Vacanti grew an ear from a cartilage-cell-seeded matrix embedded into a mouse's back. A U.S. and Japanese research team, headed by Dr. William Landis of Northeastern Ohio University's College of Medicine and Dr. Noritoka Isogia of Kenki University in Osaka, successfully grew an articulated, human-like finger joint on a mouse's back by wrapping bovine cells around a polymer scaffold. Within 20 weeks, blood vessels had formed in the joint. Initial future applications include the production of skeletal parts as replacements for toes and fingers. Liver-like tissues, bladders, and kidneys have also been engineered in animal studies.

Offering hope to people with diseased internal organs, researchers at the University of Queensland, Australia, have been able to grow new tissue in the body cavities of dogs and rats. This tissue can replace diseased tissue and provides a remedy for infection and rejection issues. The technology has been deemed a breakthrough in the human body's ability to grow its own spare parts.

Growing bone was particularly troublesome, as the matrix for the growth of bone, which included calcium and phosphate minerals along with protein fibers, tends to break down when placed under the mechanical pressure required to grow tissue. Jon Dobson and Alicia El Haj at the University of Keele in Great Britain devised a technique to overcome this problem, thus opening the possibility of widespread bone engineering, an extremely lucrative prospect. By attaching magnetic nanoparticles derived from a form of iron oxide to bone cells, the particles bond with the bone cell membrane. As the cells evolve and divide, the particles are passed on, thus allowing the genes for producing bone matrices to be stimulated and for the matrix to withstand the pressure involved in the growth process. Carnegie Mellon University researchers are engineering bone constructs in labs that may be used to repair bone loss related to a gunshot wound or car accident.

On October 12, 2006, a segment of the PBS News-Hour with Jim Lehrer looked at what is being done with advanced surgery and facial prosthetics to repair the severe injuries to the vulnerable faces of over 100 soldiers from insurgent weapons and explosives used in Iraq. Dr. Joe Rosen, a Dartmouth Medical Center plastic surgeon, was called in by the Walter Reed Army Hospital as a consultant in the case of Army Sergeant First Class Jeffrey Mittman, on duty in Iraq in July 2005 and driving a Humvee when an improvised explosive device (IED) came through the windshield and exploded, leaving Mittman without his left eye, a nose, lips, and most of his teeth. Dr. Rosen took pieces of bone from Mittman's forearm and ribs, and skin from his forehead, to make him a nose, lining in his mouth and nose, and an upper lip. Mittman faces future surgeries. Dr. Rosen told Mittman, "Plastic surgery is really a battle between beauty and blood supply, so we can only do so much at each stage without endangering what we've done. But if we're willing to be patient, sort of a two-year process, then each three months we can do another stage and make it better and better until you're satisfied. Now, one of the issues is that we can never make you normal again, but we can make you appear very good."

NewsHour health correspondent Susan Dentzer explained that the military is worried about more devastating facial wounds from Iraq or other conflicts in the future and is "frustrated that even the innovative surgical techniques, like those used on Jeffrey Mittman, will only get them so far." As a result, the Defense Advanced Research Projects Agency (DARPA) brought together physicians and scientists to explore future options for restoring a human face, one of whom was Dr. Anthony Atala, Director of the Wake Forest University Institute for Regenerative Medicine in North Carolina and considered a pioneer in tissue engineering. Atala and his team are taking bone, muscle, and blood vessels from people and growing them into tissues to be put back into the same people. "We would first start by growing a piece of bone for his face, and then a piece of muscle for his face, and then a skin for that particular area. And then we'd just really build upon the whole construct one step at a time. All we really need to bring these technologies faster to reality is a concerted national effort to be able to invest in these technologies that we know have a high potential of benefiting patients throughout the world," said Dr. Atala.

Also discussed at the DARPA workshop was an advanced facial prosthesis being built by engineer David Hanson in Dallas, Texas. Resembling a robot, "Jules" is made of a sophisticated skin-like material that Hanson calls "Frubber." A 9-volt battery powers tiny motors that work as facial muscles to give the robot facial expressions. Hanson feels that a robotic prosthetic could combine with tissue engineering techniques to create a composite face capable of even smiling, frowning, or chewing. He added, "If we can create these technologies to address our combat injuries, then we can alleviate so much misery in the world. We're at a time in history where these things are possible."

BIBLIOGRAPHY

Aldhous, Peter. "Print Me a Heart and a Set of Arteries." *New Scientist*, 15 April 2006.

"Australian Scientists Claim Breakthrough in Human Tissue Engineering." *Xinhua News Agency,* 7 June 2006.

Babbington, Charles. "Stem Cell Bill Gets Bush's First Veto." *The Washington Post*, 20 July 2006.

Barry, Patrick. "New Gene Delivery Method Takes Major Step Toward Safer Stem Cells." *Science News,* 25 October 2008.

Berger, Michael. "Tissue Engineering with Cell-laden Hyddrogels." *Nanowerks,* 28 April 2010.

Campbell, Alexia. "Respect Life Activists Debate Stem Cell Research Ethics." *Palm Beach Post,* 15 October 2006.

"Doctors Work to Restore Damaged Faces of Iraq War Soldiers." *PBS NewsHour With Jim Lehrer,* 12 October 2006. Available from http://www.pbs.org/.

"Four of the Nation's Preeminent Research Institutions Announce Stem Cell Research Alliance." Burnham Institute for Medical Research, 17 March 2006. Available from http://www.burnham.org/.

Gledhill, Lynda. "Governor OKs Stem Cell Research Funds. Schwarzenegger Authorizes Loans for $150 Million." *San Francisco Chronicle,* 21 July 2006.

Grace V. "Creating the Body's Microenvironment to Grow Artificial Organs." *National Defense,* March 2008.

Hendrick, Bill. "Stem Cell Research Targets Parkinson's." *The Atlanta Journal-Constitution,* 17 October 2006.

Mass Device Staff. "Report: Tissue Regeneration Market to Grow 16 Percent a Year to $118 Billion by 2013." *Mass Device,* 3 March 2009.

"Massachusetts Life Sciences Center Board Approves $7.4 Million Investment in Expansion of Organogenesis." Press Release, 27 January 2009.

Mayeux, Edith, et al. *State of the U.S. Regenerative Medicine Industry.* Bureau AWEX, October 2010.

"MIT Method Allows 3D Study of Cells; Work Could Impact Tissue Engineering." *Europe Intelligence Wire,* 24 April 2006.

Nerem, Robert M. *Regenerative Medicine: the Emergence of an Industry.* London: Royal Society Publishing, September 2010.

O'Reilly, Kevin B. "Elections Seen as Turning Point for Stem Cell Studies." *American Medical News,* 20 October 2008.

Pollack, Andrew. "Stem Cell Bill Seen as a Qualified Boon for Research." *The New York Times,* 19 July 2006.

"Stem Cells: The Hype and the Hope." 19 May 2010. Available from http://www.visiongain.com/

Stout, David. "In First Veto, Bush Blocks Stem Cell Bill." *The New York Times,* 19 July 2006.

Trafton, Anne. "Tiny Backpacks for Cells." Massachusetts Institute of Technology, 6 November 2008.

"U.S. 'Falling Behind' in Stem Cell Research." *Europe Intelligence Wire,* 1 June 2006.

Weintraub, Arlene. "The Waiting Game for Stem Cell Companies." *Business Week,* 6 October 2008.

Westphal, Wylvia Pagan. "Harvard Joins New U.S. Push in Stem Cells." *The Wall Street Journal Eastern Edition,* 7 June 2006.

USED COMPUTER EQUIPMENT RESELLING

SIC CODE(S)

5734

INDUSTRY SNAPSHOT

Often overlooked in the computer hardware business, the used equipment trade is fragmented but vibrant. In a world begging for electronic connectivity, the future for the industry appears bright on the surface. However, conflicting interests between for-profit and nonprofit entities have kept prices for refurbished hardware at modest levels. Moreover, breaches in security, which have left some end users of recycled computer products vulnerable to hackers, viruses, and identity compromises, or left them in possession of sensitive data from other previous owners, warrant more extensive regulation and control of the market. Moreover, concern for environmental waste from discarded information technology (IT) hardware ("e-waste") increasingly tugs at the sleeves of governmental agencies for more pressing attention and action.

Nevertheless, the industry continues with forward momentum, compensating for low profit margins with high volume and rapid turnover of components. Private and public initiatives to contain e-waste and recycle computers have cropped up in even the smallest of communities and countries, and an increasing number of countries have united to control and regulate the importation and exportation of used or refurbished computer hardware and software.

ORGANIZATION AND STRUCTURE

Sellers of used computer equipment are generally either retail stores or dealers. Although there are a few chains in the industry, notably Computer Renaissance, most retailers of used computers are small business owners. Retailers sell equipment of greatest interest to the consumer market: software, PCs, peripherals, and the occasional network card or memory chip for the do-it-yourself computer enthusiast. Dealers, on the other hand, sell all those things and more—including large systems for networking an entire company—but they do so in larger quantities. Typically, if consumers were to call a dealer and ask to buy or sell just one PC, the dealer would refer them to a retailer. Hence the difference between retailers and dealers is to some extent in what they sell, but more significantly in how they sell it. Dealers generally operate in an ordinary office, with a large storage and testing area in back, and do little of their business face to face. Rather, they are highly dependent on telephone communications. Generally they buy from and sell to other businesses, including other dealers. They make their money primarily because of the information they possess. They know that on one side, Company X needs a certain item and is willing to pay $1,000 for it and that on the other side, Dealer Y has the item priced at $750. The dealer in the middle, because he is able to link up the two companies, makes the $250 profit.

One of the leading trade organizations for used computer sellers is the Association of Service and Computer Dealers International (ASCDI), which is the result of the merger of two different trade groups founded in 1981 that represented dealers. The ASCDI's mission is to represent information technology companies, including used computer resellers, to promote ethical standards via their Code of Ethics, promote free-market legislation, provide educational opportunities, and create forums for the exchange of ideas.

More central to the life of the used computer business than industry associations, however, are arenas and forums where dealers can exchange information about available equipment. Retailers, and to a certain extent wholesale dealers, watch for news of liquidations and auctions, including those run by local governments or federal institutions. Salespeople and equipment brokers often communicate with each other over the telephone in a complex network of interactions that spans the globe. A dealer in the Midwest, for instance, may learn that a buyer in San Francisco needs 300 personal computers. So she calls her contact in Denmark, who then gets in touch with a supplier in Australia. The Australian supplier puts in a call to a dealer in Los Angeles, who has the equipment and sends it. Thus, the 300 PCs may travel around the world and back up the chain in order simply to travel from Los Angeles to San Francisco. Outsiders might ask why the Los Angeles dealer was not put directly in touch with the San Francisco end user, but to equipment dealers, the answer is obvious: without the profit that accrues to a dealer as middleman, his business would be unable to continue to exist; and the next time someone comes looking for equipment, he might be unable to locate it because there is no one to track it down.

Although voice interaction over the telephone remains a key element in arranging the movement of goods within the used computer industry, brokers also rely on weekly publications announcing equipment for sale and are dependent on information age technology to keep up to date on equipment offerings. A company with a large quantity of token rings to sell, for instance, might set up a fax broadcast to dealers and end users all over the United States or the world. The Internet is an emerging means of exchange as well. Numerous companies have their own Web sites, and there are sites as well for entities such as Daley Marketing Corp. (DMC), which sells primarily to dealers. Founded in 1980 as an IBM computer broker/lessor, DMC is in the business of providing timely, accurate, and detailed industry information through regular publication of its *DMC Computer Price List, DMC Broker and End-User Market Value Report,* and other items.

The market for used computer equipment is composed of three distinct segments: refurbished, used, and liquidated equipment. Refurbished equipment runs the gamut as far as quality is concerned, but all refurbished systems are previously owned computers that have been reconditioned. Many refurbished computer systems are sold with warranties. Used equipment, on the other hand, may or may not be reconditioned. Finally, liquidated computers generally represent last year's models that were never sold. According to Christine Arrington, an analyst for International Data Corp., the used computer market "has been evolving from a dumping ground for unwanted and under-powered systems to an acceptable source of low-cost hardware to fit a variety of budget and power ranges." She predicted increasing

competition between the new and used computer markets but said they will probably remain highly interdependent.

Starting in the late 1990s, cost-conscious school systems around the United States increasingly began to turn to refurbished personal computers to meet their needs in the classroom. The appearance on the used market of more and more used Pentium-based PCs has helped fuel this demand. Refurbished PCs are attractive to the folks running U.S. public schools for a number of reasons, not the least of which is the savings that can be realized. Many school systems operating under tight budgets are forced to cut corners on such basic supplies as paper and pencils, so an opportunity to save money on high end purchases such as computers and peripheral equipment is appealing. By going the used computer route, school boards can double or triple the number of computers they can put into the classroom. Of the growing school market, Brian Kushner, chief executive officer of ReCompute, an Austin, Texas-based company that markets refurbished PCs, said, "To get three to four times the computational resource for the same dollar—that's an enormous leverage. Schools don't need—and often don't want—powerful systems targeted at multimedia, engineering, and software compilation applications."

BACKGROUND AND DEVELOPMENT

In 1993 an article on used computers in the Stockholm-based periodical *Tomorrow* approached the subject from a characteristically "green" northern European angle: concern over the environmental impact of non-recyclable computer equipment. According to the article, the German Ministry of the Environment reported that western Germany alone generated some 800,000 metric tons of "electronic waste." This included batteries, cables, and other small items, but the bulk of it was in larger information and office systems. The situation pointed out the fact that computer equipment became obsolete at a quick rate, such that many companies considered it easier to dump such equipment into a landfill than to set about reselling it. The infrastructure for such reselling, in the form of a healthy computer resale industry was clearly only then developing—or at least people's awareness of it was still in its early stages.

There was a time when IBM literally dumped old PCs, PC/XTs, and PC/AT models offshore to create an artificial reef, but that day is long gone. In 1997, *Computerworld* magazine reported that the industry giant had begun selling refurbished equipment on the Internet. In fact, it was a 1956 U.S. Justice Department consent decree restraining IBM's actions in the used equipment market and other areas that laid the groundwork for the existence of the used computer industry. Of course, it would be many years before computers themselves became

Used Computer Equipment Reselling

widely available to ordinary consumers, but the explosion in PC use during the 1980s paved the way for the growth of used computer sales.

However, there was a period of lag, just as the used car business only came into its own approximately a decade after the advent of widespread sales of Fords and other models. For most of the 1980s and early 1990s, used equipment computer sales were primarily among dealers. Only later did the industry see the appearance of numerous storefront retail operations. A study by the Gartner Group, a research and analysis company, for the Computer Leasing and Remarketing Association at the end of 1993 found that volume had not grown for three years starting in 1991, a fact analysts attributed to caution on the part of consumers as well as to the economic recession.

By 1995, IBM was back in court challenging the 39-year-old Justice Department decree, but it faced strong opposition. One opponent, the very same judge who had presided over the original case—now 84 years old and still sitting on the bench—was removed from the case by a federal appeals court on the grounds that he could not be impartial. Another foe, Computer Leasing & Remarketing Association attorney Kevin Arguit, would not be so easily moved, though. According to the terms of the disputed decree, IBM was prevented from immediately reselling returned equipment. Instead, it had to wait 60 days and then offer it first to used equipment vendors at certain prices. These prices, which the company's representatives said were unreasonably high, further delayed sales of IBM's equipment. If the decree was lifted, Arguit responded, IBM would dominate the market. The dispute raged on.

With so much of the computer industry's attention fixed on the newest, fastest machines, it's little wonder that the used computer business has remained somewhat obscure. In the words of David Bernstein, head of the refurbishing vendor Access Direct Inc., the used business may be seen as the "ugly twin sister" of new computer sales.

There is some debate among analysts and industry veterans about what impact the ongoing erosion of new computer prices has on the remarketing segment. The standard logic is that given a choice between similarly priced, comparable machines, most buyers would opt for a new machine over an old. This prompts analysts such as Gabriel Griffith of International Data Corp. to predict a slowdown as new PC prices sink. Nevertheless, some in the business believe the relationship is more complex and that low prices on new equipment can boost demand for used devices as well.

Acclaimed computer recycler Rusty Johnson, executive director of Franklin, Indiana-based J & S Computer Assistance, collected 20,000 computers in varying states of disrepair according to an *Indianapolis Business Journal*

article. Although most of them had to be recycled, he placed approximately 4,000 with senior citizens, underprivileged students, police officers, veterans, and disabled people.

Crain's Detroit Business reported that nonprofit groups such as Think Detroit and Ann Arbor's Nonprofit Enterprise at Work redistribute old computers to those who can't afford them. These groups are being inundated with computers, resulting in the decision to stop advertising that they accept used computers. The publication also reported that there is a constant increase in businesses that buy used computers. U.S. Computer Exchange President Robert Campbell stated his company considers several variables: manufacturer, speed, configuration and monitor. The used computers are sold at its stores or parts are sold.

The *Greater Baton Rouge Business Report* spotlighted The Computer Regeneration Group. It is a new charitable organization specializing in refurbishing used computers and distributing them to needy communities. "Computers that we consider too slow to use are light years ahead of what is available in many areas around the world," William Stringer pointed out. The Greenwell Springs, Louisiana business is looking for Pentium class computers, preferably with CD-ROM drives and a modem.

With the rise in recycled and refurbished computer equipment comes the risk of inheriting someone else's computer problems. Worse yet (for the original owners), highly sensitive data may have been left on the computer disk drives. An investigation by the United Kingdom's University of Glamorgan's Information Security Research Group (ISRG) revealed that such breaches were found on items bought from various public sources, including eBay.

Some of the findings were published in an article for *Computing* in 2005. In two cases involving resold equipment from multinational companies, sufficient information was found on the disk drives to allow the security of both organizations to be breached. The data obtained also included staff records, e-mails and passwords, and financial data that was less than one year old. Further, there was enough information to allow a hacker to map the companies' computer systems. Seven of the examined disks contained enough information to allow a hacker to get into the organization. The data revealed what was behind a firewall and what was needed to overcome it, including passwords and user names. Another disk contained personal information on children from a primary school, including names, grades, school reports, letters to parents, and psychological information. "The single most striking thing that came out of this was that companies and organizations that are meant to be data-wiping are not, " said Dr. Andrew Blyth, head of the ISRG. (The

ENCYCLOPEDIA OF EMERGING INDUSTRIES, 6TH EDITION

international IT security standard, ISO/IEC 17799 states that storage devices containing sensitive data should be physically destroyed or the data securely overwritten rather than deleted by standard delete function.)

E-waste Several million computers are rendered obsolete by corporate standards each year, with less than 15 percent being recycled. An organization known as the Computer Takeback Campaign began to receive media attention in the early years of the first decade of the 2000s for its efforts in trying to promote brand owner responsibility for recycling efforts involving their products. In 2005, the Campaign rallied outside Apple Computer Headquarters in mock hazardous material safety suits, protesting company policies on e-waste and claiming that Apple lagged far behind such other leaders as Hewlett-Packard and Dell when it came to corporate accountability. According to the Campaign, when the millions of Apple computers and other electronic products hit the landfills and incinerators, millions of pounds of toxic lead and other hazardous materials penetrate the air, land and water.

Another initiative that could affect industry profits is grassroots pressure on computer manufacturers to make products with a longer life expectancy (by 3 to 5 years). According to findings published in 2004 by Eric D. Williams of United Nations University, adding a few years of life to a significant percentage of the 65 million computers sold in the United States annually would save 5 to 20 times more energy than recycling over each computer's life cycle. Williams found that producing a new computer took 1.8 cubic tons of water, fossil fuels, and chemicals that together weighed as much as an SUV.

A new use for old computers was gaining popularity, according to a 2007 article in *eWeek,* as more collectors were buying "retro" computers through such venues as eBay, other Internet sites, and swap meets, and appreciating them for both their historical as well as monetary value. Some used computers sell for a small price, whereas others that are considered more rare may go for several thousand dollars. Private demand and the increase in prices was also making it more difficult for museums to obtain certain models, according to John Toole of the Computer History Museum in Mountain View, California.

CURRENT CONDITIONS

The U.S. Environmental Protection Agency (EPA) reported that about 41.1 million desktop and laptop computers were discarded in 2007 (the latest year available). Overall, 205 million computer products (monitors, keyboards, printers, notebooks, copiers, etc.) were discarded that year (projected to reach 282 million in 2009). Of these, 157.3 million were trashed in dumps, and 48 million were recyled, representing less than one in five (18 percent).

According to a November 2009 article in *Business Week,* the e-waste industry was comprised of approximately 1200 mostly small companies that generated revenues of more than $3 billion in 2008. The article focused on Supreme Asset Management & Recovery, one of the nation's largest recyclers of electronic waste, located in New Jersey. Inside one of its warehouses, workers unloaded newly-arrived truckloads of old computer monitors, keyboards, printers, and TVs. The company maintained that it lawfully disposed of e-waste after neutralizing all hazardous contaminants. However, a 2009 probe by the U.S. Government Accountability Office found that "a large electronics recycler in New Jersey" (which *Business Week* identified as Supreme) was one of 43 U.S. companies that sought to sell e-waste for export to Asia, in apparent violation of the law. In China and elsewhere, electronic gear commonly is stripped for reusable microchips, copper, and silver; dangerous metals are dumped nearby, often close to farms or sources of drinking water. In the early 1990s, an international agreement known as the Basel Convention restricted trade in hazardous waste, but the United States never ratified the pact.

Meanwhile, as 2008 and 2009 saw explosive sales in netbooks and laptop computers, used laptops continued to sell, according to IT and telecom research firm Gartner Dataquest. It found that 86 million used computers were sold worldwide in 2007. Gartner also found that of the nearly 200 million PCs that were retired by corporations and institutions in 2007, fewer than half found their way into the secondary PC market. Gartner's 2008 update on these initial reports, *User Survey Analysis: Secondary PC Market Offers Growing Opportunity,* continued to support both the supply and demand growth projections, finding that "only one in five PCs suitable for reuse finds its way from a mature to a developing country market, even as demand for secondary PCs outstrips the available supply."

In a 2009 study examining the flow of used IT equipment from the United States to Peru, Dr. Ramzy Kahhat and Dr. Eric Williams, both of Arizona State University, reported that at least 85 percent of second-hand computers imported to Peru were reused, indicating a strong trend of used-computer adoption in developing markets worldwide, especially in major cities. The authors further noted that, as in the United States, a functioning used Pentium 4 computer was about half the cost of a comparable new computer.

INDUSTRY LEADERS

The largest sellers of used computer equipment include many of the companies that make it and lease it new. In addition to IBM's resale wing, Dell Computer Corp., Compaq Computer Corp., AT&T Systems Leasing Corp., and GE Capital are important players. At another tier are high volume dealers such as USA Computer in Long Island or Daktech in Fargo, North Dakota.

Business Wire reported that "Dell continues to encourage the reuse of computer technology as an important step in the product life cycle." Dell Exchange was expanded to include a recycling option. The program had previously allowed consumers to donate, auction or trade in used computers. "Our customers are looking for an easy way to dispose of old computers in an environmentally responsible manner. This program is easy to use and does not put a burden on our customers," claimed John Hamlin, vice president and general manager of Dell's U.S. consumer business. Dell also has a partnership with the National Cristina Foundation where donated systems are placed with nonprofit or public agencies in the consumer's local area. There is no cost for users of this program and the donation may be eligible for a tax deduction. In 2009, Dell boasted that it remained the only manufacturing company in the industry offering consumers free product recycling on a global basis.

Formed in 1988, Computer Renaissance (CR) is a chain of approximately 100 independent used computer franchises throughout the U.S. and Canada. This retail concept was franchised by Grow Biz International Inc. until Grow Biz sold it to Hollis Technologies LLC of Lakeland, Florida, in 1999 for $3 billion. Hollis was already a franchisee at several Florida outlets. An evolution of the business model allows CR to offer total computer solutions to small businesses and consumers. Most of CR's retail outlets show more computers than the superstores, displaying an average of 30 systems per store. Shoppers are encouraged to tinker with the equipment before making a decision to purchase. All stores take trade-ins. In June 2003, CR announced plans to open two new full service computer stores in the Miami-Fort Lauderdale area.

ReCompute International, based in Austin, Texas, refurbishes personal computers purchased from large companies that are upgrading their equipment and from PC manufacturers that are liquidating unsold units to make room for new models. Brian Kushner, ReCompute's CEO, said, "We're the undertakers of the PC industry." For many computer users, individual as well as corporate, the older technology in some of the used computers marketed by ReCompute and others in the industry is more than sufficient for their needs. "The vast majority of buyers out there are paying for way more computer than they need," according to Dale Yates, a systems administrator for McLane Co. based in Temple, Texas. Yates and others responsible for corporate computer buying decisions are finding that there's no need to supply someone whose responsibilities are largely confined to word processing, for example, with a computer designed to perform far more sophisticated functions.

Other companies in this industry include Second Source, with six stores in Delaware and Pennsylvania; Computer Exchange, which matches buyers and sellers for a 10 percent commission; Boston Computer Exchange, a phone-based buying and selling dealership; Rumarson Technologies Inc., a refurbisher; and U.S. Micro Corp., also a refurbisher. The Internet has several used computer selling sites, running from manufacturers who sell refurbished models to auctions.

WORKFORCE

Generally, a used computer operation, whether a wholesale dealer or a retail store, must employ at least one class of worker: salespeople. Salespeople, whether they work behind a counter or over the phone, may receive a salary, but usually commissions are used as an incentive for high performance. Because they generate the company's profit, salespeople are usually the most highly paid, and can often earn in the high five-digit figures, or even over $100,000 a year.

Also important are technical personnel, whose job is to evaluate equipment for problems and then fix those problems as they arise. Tech workers may earn $20 an hour or more. In addition, used computer businesses, depending on their size, may employ shipping and receiving personnel, inventory workers, and administrative assistants.

AMERICA AND THE WORLD

International trade in key markets of the used computer industry is controlled in large part by the Information Technology Agreement (ITA), a plurilateral trade agreement covering approximately 95 percent of world trade in defined IT products. Both new and used computer hardware and software are covered under the ITA.

One country specifically prohibiting the importation of used computers is India, which was fast becoming a dumping ground for electronic waste from the United States, Singapore, and South Korea, according to *ToxicLink*, based in New Delhi. Although prohibited, the computers end up in India as "charity" or "donations." *ToxicLink* has accused foreign companies of assisting Indian importers to bypass government regulations to bring these products into the country.

The used computer business continues to grow internationally, and buyers in emerging countries are thrilled to purchase slightly used U.S. equipment (generally less than three years old) at a discount. Trading goes on between the United States and the economic powerhouses of Western Europe and the Pacific Rim, but a future area of growth is likely to be "second-tier countries" such as developing nations in Eastern Europe, the

Middle East and Central Asia, East Asia (including China), and parts of Latin America and Africa.

China was an especially promising market for used computer equipment in the middle of the first decade of the 2000s, according to *Electronic Engineering Times*. Some estimated that between 40 percent and 60 percent of the computer equipment in China was used, and the demand for refurbished equipment was expected to continue. However, supply within China was dwindling, thus opening the door for overseas dealers. One drawback involves the weak network of service and parts providers in China.

Another international market that was booming at the beginning of the twenty-first century was Brazil, where the supply of used computers was in the millions. Many of these systems had been acquired from larger companies at cut rate prices, according to Loja dos Micros, a São Paulo-based seller of used systems. Another player in the Brazilian market is Celty Informatica, also based in São Paulo. Both companies predict that as the devaluation of the Brazilian currency increases the prices of new computers, the demand for used equipment will grow even stronger.

Advisory panels of Japanese industry and environment ministers agreed to establish a recycling system for personal computers used at homes separate from the ones for businesses. The system, which was scheduled to begin in fall 2003 at the earliest, would require consumers to pay recycling fees when they purchase new personal computers and dispose of their old equipment.

BIBLIOGRAPHY

"Apple Offers Computer Recycling." *American Metal Market*, 1 June 2006.

Ben-Horin, David. "Recycled Computer Initiative." *CompuMentor/TechSoup Project Development*, December 2004. Available from www.omidyar.net/.

Bland, Daren. "Why Second-Hand Equipment Is Key." *Computer Reseller News*, 9 October 2006.

Clendenin, Mike. "Chinese Shopping for Used Semiconductor Equipment." *Electronic Engineering Times*, 21 March 2005.

"Computer Renaissance Expands in South Florida." *Business Wire*, 18 June 2003.

Elgin, Ben, and Brian Grow. "E-waste: The Dirty Little Secret of Recycling Electronics." *Business, Week*, 4 November 2009. Available from http://www.businessweek.com/magazine/content/08_43/b4105000160974.htm.

"Facts and Figures on E Waste and Recycling." Available from http://www.computertakeback.com/Tools/Facts_and_Figures.pdf.

Larson, Polly. "When a Franchise System Needs CPR." *Franchising World*, January 2003.

Lynch, Jim. "Is the Used Computer Market Going Away?." *TechSoup*, 28 September 2009. Available from http://www.techsoup.org/learningcenter/hardware/page12182.cfm

Marion, Joseph. "IBM Keeps Residuals Up in a Grey World." Association of Service and Computer Dealers International, 2007. Available from www.ascdi.com.

———. "Used Equipment at Work." Association of Service and Computer Dealers International, 2007. Available from www.ascdi.com.

Messme, Eellen. "One Man's Trash Is Another's Cheap PC." *Network World*, 22 November 2004.

Morgan, Timothy Prickett. "Computer Trade Group Alleges Unfair Trading Practices at Sun." *Data Monitor*, 26 April 2007.

"New Homes for Old PCs." *eWeek*, 2 February 2007.

"Nonprofit Computer Recycling and Reuse Network" *The Times Union*. 20 March 2005. Available from www.recycles.org/.

Pope, Eric. "Used Computer Firm Finds Niche in Speed." *Detroit News*, 18 November 2004.

Schoenberger, Karl. "Apple E Waste Policy Trashed." *The San Jose Mercury News*, 11 January 2005.

Solomon, Howard. "Good as New: Refurbished PCs are Hot." *Computer Dealer News*, 18 April 2003.

"There's History and Money in Obsolete Computers." *eWeek*, 11 April 2007.

Toigo, Jon William. "Would You Buy a SAN from This Man?" *Network Computing*, 23 June 2005.

U.S. Department of Commerce, Division of International Trade Administration. Office of Technology and Electronic Commerce. "Customs, Taxes, and Documentation Requirements: IT Products and Services Imports (by country)." 18 March 2004.

———. "Information Technology Agreement." March 2004.

Warren, Peter. "Security at Risk From Failure to Wipe Disks." *Computing*, 17 February 2005.

World Computer Exchange. "Who We Are." 15 June 2007. Available from www.worldcomputerexchange.org.

VENTURE CAPITAL FIRMS

———————◼———————

SIC CODE(S)

6799

INDUSTRY SNAPSHOT

With the glossy sheen still coating the dot-com business model, venture capital (VC) firms in the late 1990s achieved enormous returns and were among the primary beneficiaries of the inflated technology bubble of the period. However, when the market bottomed out, these companies found themselves with scads of money lost to investments that would never pan out. At one time, the venture capital industry, one of the more glamorous sectors of finance in the late 1990s, cooled in a hurry following the declining technology sector—its bread and butter—in the early 2000s, which ushered in three straight years of losses after decades in the black. Still strong and extremely influential, however, the industry proceeded with greater caution and foresight than in its earlier carefree glory years, when firms threw enormous sums of money behind startup firms with no serious plan for long-term viability.

Venture capital is the equity invested in rapidly growing companies that investors believe hold excellent potential for future earnings. Venture capital firms thus fund enterprising startup companies trying to get off the ground. Concentrated particularly heavily in high-tech industries, venture capital is generally pooled by institutions or deep-pocketed individuals in the hopes of generating huge profits over the long term. Thus, venture capital firms are often exactly the financial break young, struggling entrepreneurs need to get their companies on their feet. However, during uncertain economic times, as in the volatile early 2000s, many venture capital firms had shifted their focus to more developed companies, preferring businesses that were expected to deliver returns sooner rather than later.

ORGANIZATION AND STRUCTURE

Once the exclusive perch of the extremely wealthy, the venture capital industry drifted ever closer to the mainstream through the 1990s and early years of the first decade of the 2000s, largely as a direct result of the Internet explosion. Major corporations and financial institutions increasingly forged their own venture capital wings or subsidiaries. Meanwhile, the major venture capital firms helped established organizations develop Internet-based companies. While still quite prohibitive owing to the lack of liquidity and long-term orientation, venture capital was drawing more average investors into the fold. On the other hand, the tremendous success of venture capitalists has shifted the industry dynamic 180 degrees. Gone are the days when eager opportunists would crawl, hat in hand, to venture capitalists seeking money. Nowadays, venture capital firms are scrambling to differentiate themselves amidst all the competition and the robust marketplace.

The venture capital industry is served by the National Venture Capital Association (NVCA). Established in 1973, the NVCA examines the intersection of the venture capital industry and the overall U.S. economy and facilitates the practice of funneling private equity to new business development. Two major research firms, VentureOne and Thomson Venture Economics, also supply information and analysis about the venture capital industry.

Most venture capital firms are private partnerships managed by small professional staffs or closely-help corporations.

Venture Capital Investment Comparison, 1995–2010			
Year	VC deals	Average amount of all VC deals	Total VC investment
1995	1,864	$ 3.9 million	$ 7.3 billion
2000	7,979	$12.5 million	$100.0 billion
2005	3,194	$ 7.0 million	$ 22.6 billion
2009	2,917	$ 6.2 million	$ 18.2 billion
2010*	2,498	$ 6.7 million	$ 16.7 billion

*These figures include deals in the first 9 months of 2010.

SOURCE: PricewaterhouseCoopers/National Venture Capital Association Money Tree Report.

Venture capital firms derive their capital from pension funds, endowments, foundations, sympathetic non-financial corporations, banks, insurance companies, governments, foreign investors, rich uncles, and the venture capitalists themselves. Through the 1980s and up to the mid-1990s, pension funds provided about half of all money for venture capital (VC) funds. That proportion was a primary casualty of the massive VC boom of the late 1990s, however, as individual investments jumped to 19 percent of the total VC pool. Foundations provided an additional 18 percent and non-financial corporations kicked in 13 percent.

The majority of venture capital firms are independent of other financial institutions, although a growing number are subsidiaries of commercial and investment banks, a trend that accelerated following the passage of the Financial Services Modernization Act of 1999. Other firms are affiliated with non-financial corporations seeking to diversify their assets.

According to the NVCA, venture capitalists typically devote themselves to financing emerging companies that promise fast and lucrative growth; purchase equity securities; help companies develop new products and bring them to market; engage in high-risk, high-reward financing; and maintain a long-term orientation. Although in recent years venture capital deals have grown larger, VC firms usually sprinkle a little money here and there among a great number of businesses, and then actively work with the companies' management teams over the long term to help bring the business plan to fruition and generate strong returns on their investments. The firm then pools all its company investments into a single fund, thereby limiting the company-by-company risk.

Investment portfolios also vary widely. Some venture capital firms are generalists, investing across industries and company types. Others specialize in certain industries or even industry segments, geographic regions, or companies of certain types, such as those in the late stages of development. High tech industry constitutes the overwhelming bulk of venture investment, but VC firms are spread far and wide, according to the NVCA, helping companies in industries from business services to construction, and firms with special characteristics, such as those that constitute socially responsible investment.

There are several different stages of company development for which a venture capital firm may provide financing. The formative stage involves getting the initial idea off the ground, from a solid plan on paper to an actual firm with a structure and a basis of operation. Formative stage companies pull in the largest share of venture financing, about 42 percent of the total. Investment at this stage is known as seed financing, the most common type of funding people think of when they consider venture capital. A company receiving seed financing generally has yet to become fully operational and probably has a product in development. Early-stage investment takes place when a company is well into its life cycle, perhaps looking to complete a current project or achieve new breakthroughs. Generally, early financing is directed at companies with a test or pilot product. Expansion financing fuels the renewed growth or widened reach of a product already on the market. The expansion stage calls for funding to push a well-grounded company to the next level of viability.

Eventually, a venture capital firm wants to realize a profit from its financial and management investment and will try to cash out. Once a venture-backed company gets on its feet, the most common financing step is to announce an initial public offering (IPO), the proceeds of which may be used to cash out the venture capital firm. This is not always the case, however. Some venture capital firms opt to stay in the game following the IPO, occasionally even forging a presence in the public company's management. Nevertheless, such guidance is not the main thrust of venture capitalists, who seek their fortunes primarily in moving companies out of the gestation process. Venture capital firms may also throw money behind a proposed merger and acquisition to facilitate the smooth consolidation of promising firms.

Another pillar of the venture capital industry is the VC "angel," who generally provides early financing to especially risky companies—those that are very young or that have poor financial histories. VC angels prepare a company for an IPO by providing the funds necessary to develop a new product or complete a key acquisition that will make the company viable for the public market. A VC angel will usually take a management position for as long as his/her money is invested. Angels are usually individual investors, a re-emerging sector of the industry, willing to devote both finances and management expertise to a struggling startup.

BACKGROUND AND DEVELOPMENT

While the practice of finding wealthy individuals or organizations to finance one's endeavors probably dates back, in various forms, to the earliest days of commerce, the modern venture capital industry emerged slowly from a tiny investment pool in the 1960s, with venture capital gradually evolving into a significant asset class. Prior to the 1960s, the venture capital industry was basically a number of tremendously wealthy individuals looking to make their mark funding innovative new companies. Particularly since World War II, the venture capital industry has constituted the financial fuel for high tech industry, and has, according to Dow Jones venture capital investment data provider VentureOne, financed entire new industries, such as biotechnology and overnight shipping, almost single-handedly bringing to life such giants as Apple, Microsoft, Intel, Genentech, and Netscape.

Nevertheless, venture capitalists have had a bumpy road on their way to their mythic success of the late 1990s. One of the most notable busts occurred in the early 1990s, when the slate of much-hyped biotechnology companies failed to live up to inflated promises, proving a washout at the IPO stage.

The overall annual rates of return are subject to massive fluctuations, from as little as 0.0 percent in off years, such as 1984 and 1990, to 60 percent in good years, such as 1980 and 1995, with the average usually hovering around 20 percent, although the late 1990s saw record returns of 85 percent.

The CIA Infiltrates the VC Market Venture capitalists fund the innovative companies of tomorrow, helping to bring to market the products that will change the average consumer's life for the better, but that is not all they do. With the announcement that the U.S. Central Intelligence Agency (CIA) would establish its own venture capital firm, In-Q-Tel, everybody's favorite conspiracy theory target launched its own high tech investment scheme. The name wraps the word "intelligence" around the letter "Q," the name of the purveyor of James Bond's high tech gadgetry. In addition to its cute pop culture nostalgia, the name signifies a certain reality. One of the firm's primary functions is to fund startup tech companies developing products for use in the CIA's vast spy and analyst networks. Beyond that, the CIA simply wants the best high tech gear that money can buy, including powerful search engines, language translation software, and even the ability to roam around the Internet in secret. The agency thus intends to transform the methods by which it gathers intelligence.

In this case, the government acted as the VC angel. Congress funneled $61 million to the nonprofit firm to get it on its feet, although skeptics were in abundance on Capitol Hill. Nevertheless, the program seemed to be generating some good business. In-Q-Tel's portfolio contained eight companies late in 2000, from small startups such as Graviton Inc. to such longtime government clients as Lockheed Martin Corp.

One of the CIA's first ventures fueled the growth of Silicon Valley software company PDH Inc., aimed at the development of technology capable of tracking and controlling the movement of digital information. The federal government was keeping a curious eye on In-Q-Tel. Should the venture capital firm prove to be successful, other departments and agencies could follow suit, in effect altering the interaction of government and business. The U.S. Postal Service and the National Aeronautics and Space Administration were contemplating similar business models.

In the meantime, In-Q-Tel made investments in several companies, including Browse3D, a Virginia company that enables Internet surfers to view several pages at once in virtual rooms that show what lies behind links, and Graviton of La Jolla, California, which makes networks of tiny sensors that communicate with each other and relay information to a user-friendly computer interface. Potential users include convenience stores needing to monitor refrigeration units. In the early years of the first decade of the 2000s, In-Q-Tel received about $30 million per year to spend on investments and technology analysis. All profits go right back into operations.

The terrorist attacksk on September 11, (9/11) had a significant impact on In-Q-Tel's direction. The organization felt a more urgent need to invest in developing technologies. In addition, the U.S. government's revitalized commitment to homeland security and defense would provide investment opportunities for companies producing appropriate technology. Post-9/11 investments included Stratify, one of the few companies that could find significant pieces of "unstructured data" (information dispersed throughout organizations in word processing files, e-mails and databases) and reassemble them in an understandable fashion. In-Q-Tel invested several million dollars in Stratify in 2001. Stratify's technology was of particular interest because the CIA needed to process enormous amounts of intelligence information more quickly. Similarly, In-Q-Tel invested $1 million in Tacit Knowledge Systems of Palo Alto, California, which has the ability to scan e-mail to determine which individuals in an organization have potentially helpful expertise that someone else should know about. In-Q-Tel also invested at least $1 million into Senturia's San Diego-based Mohomine, which makes software that gathers and categorizes information spread across various kinds of documents. Such technology can assist the CIA in monitoring overseas radio, newspaper and Internet reports.

In 2002, Gilman Louie, president and CEO of In-Q-Tel, appealed to information technology (IT) experts throughout corporate America to help the CIA's IT warriors access the best technology. Heading into the post-9/11 world, In-Q-Tel was especially interested in data and knowledge management systems due to an information overload. Louie's plea indicated that the CIA and In-Q-Tel were ready to work more openly with the private sector. In-Q-Tel was especially interested in companies that develop remote sensing technology or smart devices that attach to data collection tools such as meter readers. Such technology, Louie indicated, may prevent a situation such as someone entering an airport with a bomb in his shoe.

Venture Capital's Glory Years In the late 1990s and the early years of the first decade of the 2000s, venture capital basked in its most glorious era, drawing new players and new money at a fantastic pace while generating record returns. About 100 new venture capital firms cropped up in 1999, bringing the U.S. total to over 600. While some of the euphoria surrounding venture capital, which emboldened herds of individual investors and corporations to participate in VC funds, was a bit overstated, the industry certainly had enjoyed good times. According to the National Venture Capital Association, venture capital funds investing in early stage companies generated returns of 85 percent in 1999. The Standard & Poor's 500 (S&P 500) Stock Index, meanwhile, posted a 15 percent increase over the same period. Over a five-year period, the difference was less dramatic but still clearly tilted in favor of venture capital with 45 percent returns on early stage ventures compared with 28 percent gains for the S&P 500.

Indeed, the venture capital industry closed the twentieth century with a bang, greatly accelerating investment to a total of $36.4 billion in 1999, easily the most lucrative venture year on record, and outpacing the combined totals of the previous three years, according to VentureOne. The number of venture capital financings leaped 51 percent that year, while the total dollar amount behind those deals grew 155 percent. A total of about 4,000 companies received venture capital funding in 1999, up from about 2,900 the year before, while average funding rose from $5.2 million to $8.9 million.

Meanwhile, 248 venture-financed companies completed initial public offerings (IPOs) in 1999, according to VentureOne, bringing in $19.43 billion and doubling the record set in 1996 when the first wave of Internet companies hit the public market en masse. The median valuation of these IPOs also took off as well in 1999, reaching $316.6 million from $169.6 million in 1998. Venture capital also financed a total of 256 merger and acquisition deals in 1999, nearly tripling the totals for 1997 and 1998 for a total of $39.18 billion.

The central development behind the massive late 1990s flow of dollars into start-up financings was the Internet.

Venture-backed Internet companies alone rode their way to viability on $25 billion in venture capital in 1999, four times the 1998 total. Thus, Internet startups accounted for a whopping 69 percent of all venture capital investment in 1999 compared with 43 percent the year before. The other booming industries propping up venture capital investment in 1999 were telecommunications and networking segments such as fiber optics, representing 21 percent of all VC investment at $7.6 billion.

In addition to traditional venture capital firms, major commercial banks increasingly assumed a venture capital demeanor, tripling their venture capital investment to over $4 billion between 1996 and 1999 with no sign of a letup. One of the most attractive aspects of venture capital for banks is the boost in returns relative to loan interest that has accompanied the massive startup boom of the late 1990s. Amidst weakening bank stocks, the skyrocketing returns on venture investments have taken on greater importance as banks struggle to remain viable in their rapidly consolidating industry.

The industry through this period also experienced a massive influx of average investors into venture capital, indicative of the "can't miss" reputation the industry had acquired. While such investors still tend to be concentrated among the wealthier segments of the investing population, this trend has further relieved the super rich of their monopoly over venture capital. Not surprisingly, this new demographic changed the face of the industry somewhat. While venture capital firms typically stay in for the long haul, not expecting any significant returns for about five to seven years, the late 1990s technology and Internet boom popularized the industry with a number of new players with a lot less patience.

With a strong U.S. economic climate, ecstatic news stories about the New Economy, and the explosion of Internet dot-com start-ups, the venture capital industry was at its most robust in early 2000, with few signs of a letup save for analysts' prescient concerns over the long term stability of the Internet business model. In addition, a soaring stock market encouraged all sorts of get-rich-quick seekers, investors to throw money at the next great dot-com idea. However, the downturn in the technology markets in 2000 served as a painful reminder to venture capitalists that there was no such thing as a sure thing, and many players were ushered out of the game as quickly as they had entered. While hardly wiping out the venture capital industry, these events nonetheless injected some humility, forcing many to recall that fundamentals still mattered in a dot-com world.

Reality Sinks In The enthusiasm in the changed industry reached fever pitch when VCs raised $130 billion between the third quarter of 1999 and the end of 2000. Then the bottom dropped out and technology stocks collapsed. In the second quarter of 2001, VC firms only invested $11.2 billion, which fell well below the $27 billion average per quarter invested from April 1999 through October 2000. With the sudden slump of the technology sector, venture capital lost some, though by no means all, of its luster. Between April 1999, when the NASDAQ first started to fall, and the end of the year, nearly 20 VC funds of over $1 billion closed. According to research firm Thomson Venture Economics, for the fiscal year ending March 31, 2001, the value of U.S. venture funds fell 6.7 percent. It was the first time the industry experienced a 12-month negative return.

The industry realized it lost its sense of perspective during the boom years and had chased after any idea with fistfuls of dollars. Investors forgot the basic wisdom that only one in ten startups really have a chance of succeeding. Instead, they were looking to achieve success by throwing money at a new idea. Essentially, they were reawakened to the reality that not everything is going to fly.

VC Starts to Rebound Veteran venture capitalists came back from the experience a great deal shaken, but a good deal wiser. With less abundant investment opportunities, coupled with dramatically weakened returns on the investments that were made, the key word again became fundamentals. VC firms recovering from the shakeout promised a more conservative approach. Steering clear of firms soiled by excessive hype or overvalued Internet-based investments, fundraisers were looking to smaller market capitalization and more comprehensive business plans.

Fundraising finally began to pick up again in late 2003. The fourth quarter of 2003, for instance, saw venture capital firms raise nearly $5.16 billion, the best intake since the third quarter of 2001 and a 250 percent increase over the same period in 2002. The pace of venture-backed mergers and acquisitions likewise accelerated at the end of 2003. That year, according to Thomson Venture Economics and the National Venture Capital Association, 289 companies financed with venture capital were acquired for a total of $7.7 billion.

Such activity was especially important to the VC industry in the early years of the first decade of the 2000s, since, with the pool of initial public offerings run comparatively dry, mergers and acquisitions were one of the primary means of liquidity. VentureOne noted that the number of "restarts," or restructured financial transactions, also rose in 2003 to a seven-year high: venture capitalists put $1.1 billion into 114 of those deals. Finally, VentureOne reported that restructured financial transactions, another key source of industry liquidity, rose to their highest level in seven years in 2003, finishing that year with 114 venture-backed deals totaling $1.1 billion.

Although the vast majority of VC money in 2003 was funneled into later-stage investments, the industry began to look with interest again at startup companies for the first time since the tech bubble burst, even if those emerging companies received months' worth of intensive examination before receiving their venture financing. Reflecting the conservative industry mood, in the year and a half ending June 2003, just one-fifth of all U.S. venture deals were for early-stage financing, according to Thomson Venture Economics, representing the lowest proportion since 1977. In the three decades ending 2003, early-stage investments represented 34 percent of the total venture capital pool. Information technology remained the leading recipient of venture funding in 2003. That year, IT companies claimed 63 percent of all VC disbursements, according to Thomson Financial's *Venture Capital Journal,* with life sciences firms placing a distant second with 27.7 percent or $4.89 billion.

Despite the modest turnaround, however, there was still reason for caution. ThomsonVenture Economics reported total industry annual returns at negative 27.4 percent in 2003 and three-year returns at negative 20 percent. The industry included 113 funds raising about $10.8 billion, putting the industry at about the level of 1995. Moreover, the industry was more consolidated than ever. While those 113 funds represented a massive decline from the 629 venture capital firms that raised $105.4 billion in 2000, by 2003 just five companies accounted for nearly one third of all funding. Continuing the turnaround, venture-backed firms in 2005 reached a median valuation of $15.2 million, $3 million more than in 2004 and the highest in the past four years. While valuation for health care companies dropped $1.3 million in 2005 to $40.2 million, later stage IT companies rose nearly $8 million to $30.3 million.

A popular style of investing in the 1980s was corporate venturing, also called "direct investing," and it began coming back by 2005. While the typical venture capital goal is investment return, corporate venturing considers corporate strategic objectives as well as financial considerations. In addition, corporate venture programs usually invest their parent's capital; other venture investments use outside investors' money.

Media and entertainment companies became the benefactor of VC investments in growing numbers in 2006. The first quarter saw $396 million committed, compared to $275 in the same quarter of 2005. MovieBeam, a video-on-demand provider, was the recipient of entertainment's largest deal, with $52.5 million invested by Intel Capital, Norwest Venture Partners, and the Walt Disney Co., along with others. With $1.2 billion invested in the first quarter of 2006, the software industry was the beneficiary of the largest number of venture capital deals.

A company in Detroit, Oracle Capital Partners LLC, was the first venture capital firm in Michigan to focus on minority-owned businesses. Oracle officially opened for business in March 2006, after having raised $10 million to be used solely for minority-owned businesses, mainly in Southwest Michigan. To close out its first round of fundraising, Oracle hoped to raise enough from financial institutions and pension plans to become a top venture capital firm in the state. The largest such firm in 2006 was EDF Ventures of Ann Arbor, with $170 million under contract. According to Oracle's managing director, David Morris, "Minorities are an underserved niche." Of the $200 billion to $250 billion of venture capital invested in U.S. companies, only $4 billion to $5 billion are owned by minorities. Oracle intends to mainly invest in established companies that have demonstrated good leadership.

The Money Tree Survey, released in January 2006, reported that "late-stage"biotechnology, technology, and software sectors were the investment of choice for Colorado's venture capitalists. That survey agreed with one released the same week by accounting firm Ernst & Young, which stated that 75 deals in Colorado in 2005 totaled $612 million (most of which were late-stage businesses), up from $413 million in 2004, but still down from $633 million in 2003, and 2001, which had $1.3 billion in venture capital deals.

New York venture capitalists began hitting the fundraising trail in early 2006 in one of the strongest attempts in years to refill treasuries depleted during the internet boom. Most have been knocking on the doors of pension funds and other investors to raise investment capital to finance their plans to invest in local technology startups in the areas of media, online advertising, and health care, to name a few. Milestone Venture Partners, a Silicon Alley venture capital firm, had invested in 12 tech startups since 2002 and had only enough capital to do three more deals before its $13 million bank account emptied. In 2005, New York VC firms raised $3.1 billion, almost three times their total in 2002. Even so, that total is small compared to the glory days of the Internet boom in 2000, which saw fundraising efforts bring in $21.8 billion.

A few impressive successes in VC investing reignited investors' interest; for instance, Yahoo bought Del.icio.us, a social networking Web software firm, for $17 million, and the online marketing firm, Bigfoot, was bought by a large rival for $120 million in September 2005—a huge win for Hudson Ventures. With successes such as these becoming more frequent, VC firms were starting to reestablish images that had been badly tarnished in 2000.

By late 2008, the venture capital industry was shifting. Although the number of funds in the third quarter of that year decreased by 29 percent compared to the same period in 2007, the dollar value increased 6 percent. Mark Heesen, president of the National Venture Capital Association, said in an October 13, 2008, press release, "The third quarter fundraising statistics reflect the already anticipated trend that is likely to be pervasive in the coming year—fewer firms raising larger funds."

Fewer deals were being made in the merger and acquisition (M&A) segment of the industry as well. As of October 2008, 199 M&A deals had been completed for a total disclosed dollar value of $11.2 billion, down from 359 deals worth $28.4 billion in 2007. Most of the M&A activity in late 2008 was occurring in the information and technology sector. In the third quarter of 2008, 38 of the 56 deals that were made involved information and technology companies. Within that sector, computer software and services held the number-one spot in terms of number of companies targeted.

In 2008 the value of the average M&A disclosed deal was $154.3 million, which was not far from the average size in 2007 of $177.5 million. The statistic that was causing the most concern among many in the industry was the number of IPOs in 2008—only 6, as compared to 86 in 2007. In other words, only six venture-backed companies went public with their first sale of stock in 2008. The National Venture Capital Association called the situation "a capital markets crisis for the start-up community."

Despite the downturn in the economy and the low numbers in the industry, some remained optimistic. Said Tracy Lefteroff of Pricewaterhouse Coopers, "Venture capitalists have slugged through difficult economic times before, and this one should be no different."

CURRENT CONDITIONS

In 2009, there were approximately 794 venture capital firms in the United States, cumulatively managing approximately $179 billion in investment funds. The average venture fund size was $151 million. That year, according to the National Venture Capital Association, venture capitalists invested roughly $18 billion in nearly 2,400 companies. (Thomson Financial reported that venture capitalists invested $17.7 billion in 2,795 deals.) While 2009 was a year of overall investment declines (mostly double-digit), there was a two percent increase in seed stage financing, reflecting a little more confidence in the future entrpreneurial market.

The networking and equipment industry category suffered the least decline in investment, but even so, experienced a five percent decline in dollars in 2009, according to 2010 PricewaterhouseCooper National Venture Capital Association Report Data provided by Thomson Financial. Again in 2009, the software category remained the largest in terms of deals, but was the second largest, behind the biotechnology category, in terms of dollars. In 2009, venture capitalists invested $3.5 billion into 406 biotechnology deals and $3.1 billion in 619 software deals. The third largest category was in medical devices, with $2.5 billion going into 309 deals. Even clean technology experienced a significant decline, with just $1.9 billion going into 185 deals. Mergers and acquisitions (M&A) transactions dropped to 262 for the year.

By region, Silicon Valley (CA) attracted the most venture capital in 2009. The top three regions, Silicon Valley, New England, and the New York Metropolitan area, accounted for almost 60 percent of venture capital dollars and 52 percent of reported deals in 2009. California was the top state to attract funding, followed by Massachusetts, New York, and Texas.

The most active venture firms in 2009, according to Thomson Financial, were New Enterprise Associates, Kleiner Perkins Caulfield & Byers, and Polaris Venture Partners. The 2009 Venture Impact Study, produced by IHS Global Insight, found that companies which were originally venture-backed accounted for 12.1 million jobs and more than $2.9 trillion in revenue in the United States in 2008.

The first quarter of 2010 was off to a good start, according to *CB Insights*'s quarterly newsletter. For that first quarter, venture capitalists invested $5.8 billion in 731 companies, representing a significant improvement over the first quarter of 2009, with just $3.9 billion invested in 483 deals. Back in the game were green/clean technologies, jumping 55 percent in deals and 134 percent in dollars from the fourth quarter of 2009. New York and Massachusetts companies were beginning to close the gap with California in attracting new venture capital. In just the first quarter of 2010, there were eight venture-backed initial public offerings (IPOs) and signs of increasing M&A activity as well.

INDUSTRY LEADERS

Kleiner Perkins Caufield & Byers (KPCB), based in Menlo Park, California, has been a leading financial fuel provider to Silicon Valley. Since the company's inception in 1972, KPCB has supported hundreds of entrepreneurs in building over 475 companies, featuring such blockbusters as AOL, Compaq, Genentech, Netscape, Google, Juniper, Sun Microsystems, and Lotus. One of the firm's biggest dot-com success stories is its bankrolling of Amazon.com, Inc. By 2008 the company had about 100 companies in its portfolio. KPCB focuses its investments in four areas: information technology, life sciences, pandemic and biodefense, and green technology. In 2009, Kleiner Perkins was the leader in cleantech funding and was expected to complete 2010 with the same distinction. It was also an investor in two of 2009's top ten deals, for Silver Spring Networks Inc. and Pacific

Biosciences, Inc. Its 2010 deals included the start of a social fund with Amazon, Facebook, Shazam, and Zynga, launching a $250 million sFund at Facebook and placing its money on the U.S. virtual goods market for 2011.

Benchmark Capital Management became the first venture capital firm whose assets exceeded $1 billion, reaching that benchmark in 2000. The firm derived about one third of its investment pool from individuals, including its own partners. Also based in Menlo Park, California, Benchmark was another Silicon Valley giant, was an early financial backer of the hugely successful online auction company eBay Inc., and gave hefty backing to the Sunnyvale, California, networking Web site Friendster. Benchmark generally spent $3 million to $5 million in seed investments but also delved in at later stages, with investments in the later years of the first decade of the 2000s ranging from as little as $100,000 early on to as much as $15 million in late-stage investment.

Benchmark is interested in investing for the long haul, not "quick flips," and looks for entrepreneurs with a similar perspective. Its investment is geared mainly toward high-tech industries such as the Internet, semiconductors, software, and telecommunications. The company counts among its investors Bill Gates and the Ford Foundation. The firm manages over $3 billion in committed venture, most of which comes from university endowments, charitable foundations and entrepreneurs. In 2009, Benchmark shared in venture capital investment for one of the top ten venture-backed companies that year, Twitter, Inc.

New Enterprise Associates (NEA) of Baltimore, Maryland, had $8.5 billion under management in 2008 and had funded more than 500 companies in the information technology (IT) and medical sectors. With initial investments ranging from $200,000 to $20 million, New Enterprise has been devoted primarily to development-stage companies. Major winners in its portfolio history include 3Com Corp. and Vertex Pharmaceuticals Inc., highlighting its emphasis on high-tech, communications, and health care. More than 130 companies from New Enterprise's portfolio have gone public since the VC firm's founding in 1978, and the firm usually backs about 20 to 30 new companies annually. Despite the downturn in its focus sectors, New Enterprise still seeks and funds startups and has been one of the most active venture capital firms since the technology bust. Now it supports developing companies in health care and information technology. In 2009, New Enterprise Associates helped fund two of the top 10 U.S. venture capital investments-backed companies, Clovis Oncology Inc. and Workday, Inc.

Norwest Venture Partners of Palo Alto, California, is an affiliate of Wells Fargo and had invested in more than 350 companies and managed more than $650 million in the late years of the first decade of the 2000s. The firm's typical investment ranges from $10 million to $15 million in start-up or expansion-stage business, focusing on semiconductors, software, and communications.

Menlo Ventures in Menlo Park, California, is one of Silicon Valley's oldest venture capital partnerships with investment in more than 80 companies and $4 billion under management. Founded in 1976, the firm focuses on technology companies in software, security, communications, and Internet services. Menlo Ventures generally backs companies with $5 million to $30 million.

WORKFORCE

Professional venture capital fund managers, or general partners, are usually similar to mutual fund managers in that they assume control over the assets pooled by the investors and allocate them into a venture or into another fund, in most cases spreading out investments widely. Known as "gatekeepers," they enter into the firm as general partners, as opposed to the investors' limited partner status, and provide the resources and expertise the limited partners may lack. Venture capital firms recruit heavily from Wall Street investment banks and research departments. Compared with those positions, venture capital affords managers a great deal of independence, although the pay is a bit less.

AMERICA AND THE WORLD

China is a prime spot for venture capitalists due to the tax benefits foreign investors receive. However, by October 2008, industry experts were forecasting a downturn in the industry due to the global economic crisis. Investment during the third quarter of 2008 was down 12.1 percent from a year earlier, with $492.1 million invested in only 19 deals. This was the first time in five years the amount of investment decreased. One venture capitalist called the market in China "somewhere between uncertain and nonexistent" in a October 2008 Reuters article.

In Australia, the government committed $200 million in Australian dollars to venture capital over a five-year period beginning in 2006, expecting a matching amount from the private sector. As an incentive to venture capitalists, those who invest in early-stage companies will be exempt from income and capital gains tax. Private sector VC firms welcome the assistance from the government, but are concerned over some of the strings attached to the tax-exempt offer: funds cannot be over $100 million and can't be invested in any company worth over $50 million; and early-stage investors are required to divest their holdings once the company's assets reach $250 million.

VC firms in Thailand were optimistic about the future of "factoring services," which allow a company to sell off its accounts receivable in order to obtain ready cash. Small and medium-sized businesses especially welcomed this opportunity, particularly because banks had made loans for small businesses harder to obtain, according to the *Bangkok Post*. From 2001 to 2004, factoring more than doubled in the small- and medium-sized enterprise market, as it enables a company more flexibility in managing its short-term working capital, and its potential market is expected to remain hefty in light of the fact that small businesses account for most of the economic activity in Thailand.

BIBLIOGRAPHY

"Bigger Firms Grab Venture Capital." *Orange County Register,* 13 March 2006.

"College Endowments Deserting Venture Capital." *Business Week Online,* 21 November 2008. Available from www.businessweek.com.

Engleman, Eric. "Kleiner Perkins Starts Social Fund with Amazon, Facebook, Zynga." *TechFlash,* 21 October 2010. Available from http://www.techflash.com

Firms Closer to a Payoff Get Venture Capital." *The Denver Post,* 24 January 2006.

"Frequently Asked Questions About Venture Capital." National Venture Capital Association, 2009 . Available from http://www.ncva.org.

"Full Year 2009-Largest U.S. Venture Capital Investments." *Business Day,* 22 January 2010.

"Gloom Envelops Chinese Venture Capital Industry." Reuters, 29 October 2008.

Henderson, Tom. "VC Company to Target Minority-Owned Firms." *Crain's Detroit Business,* 27 March 2006.

"Latham Helps $50.6M Biotech Deal Survive Tough VC Climate." *The Recorder,* 20 November 2008.

Malone, Michael. "Is Venture Capital in Trouble?" ABCNews. com, 14 November 2008.

"National Money Tree Full Year Q4 2009." Pricewaterhouse-Coopers, National Venture Capital Association Report. Available from http://www.slideshare.net/evanwells/national-money-tree-full-year-q4-2009.

"No Venture-Backed IPOs Issued in the Second Quarter of 2008." National Venture Capital Association, 1 July 2008.

"Q1 2010 Sees Venturre Capitalists Invest $5.91B in 731 Companies." *CB Insights Newsletter.* Available from http://www.cbinsights.com.

Temkin, Sanchia. "Venture Capital Industry Enters New Phase." *Business Day,* 1 June 2006.

"Thailand: Venture Capital Firms Upbeat Over Factoring Service Business." *Thai Press Reports,* 10 March 2006.

"Venture-Backed IPO Drought Continues in the Third Quarter of 2008." National Venture Capital Association, 1 October 2008.

"VC Firms Seek Big Bucks; Gear Up to Invest in Tech Startups; Face Crowded Market." *Crain's New York Business,* 6 February 2006.

"VCs Tune in to Media." *Corporate Financing Week,* 1 May 2006.

"Venture Capital Firms Wary of Funding Hooks." *Australasian Business Intelligence,* 15 May 2006.

"Venture Capital Fundraising Activity Slows in the Third Quarter of 2008." National Venture Capital Association, 13 October 2008.

"Venture Capital Investment Holds in $7 Billion Range in Q3 2008 Despite Turmoil in the Financial Markets." National Venture Capital Association, 18 October 2008.

"Venture Capital Investors Hopeful Despite Economy." *Miami Daily Business Review,* 19 November 2008.

VIDEO DISPLAYS

―――――■―――――

SIC CODE(S)

3577

INDUSTRY SNAPSHOT

In the early 2000s, flat panel displays (FPDs) were the primary replacement technology for cathode ray tube (CRT) displays, which hitherto dominated the display market. The technology was simultaneously finding new applications in a wide array of consumer electronics—not only traditional television and computer screens but also smaller, portable devices such as cell phones, digital cameras, and other gadgetry. In 2007, the global sale of liquid crystal displays (LCDs), the most common form of FPD, surpassed those of CRT devices for the first time. Following behind were plasma panels and (way behind), the struggling OLED (organic light emitting diode) display panels.

Different market conditions influence demand for the various types of advanced displays, but especially in the consumer market, a common theme is pricing. Advanced displays commanded steep prices, often several thousand dollars per unit, and this delayed wider rollout. However, prices of LCDs later dropped. For televisions, mandatory conversion in the United States (and several other countries) from analog to digital signals in 2008 resulted in many consumers purchasing new television sets instead of converting their old CRTs, creating a temporary surge in new flat panel sales. However, while production was up—worldwide a record 117.9 million large LCD panels were shipped during the second quarter of 2008—demand soon fell, due to a slowing U.S. economy. This resulted in a drop in prices on most units. By 2010, the market had stabilized, with LCD models leading plasma flat panel screen models.

Clearly, the market buzz in FPDs, whether in televisions, monitors, mobile phones, digital cameras, even digital photo frames, was "3D," which came to life with LCD and plasma panel technology. The other newer technology dominating the industry involved touch screen display panels. OLED display represented an emerging and promising segment of the markets, with a CAGR (compound annual growth rate) of more than 25 percent projected between 2010 and 2020.

Digital TV Digital TV consists of several formats and standards, the most celebrated being high-definition digital TV (HDTV). Besides the HDTV formats, it also includes a series of formats known collectively as standard definition TV, which is more like conventional analog TV, in use since the 1940s, but offers additional features such as the ability to bundle multiple programs in one signal and potentially less distortion and interference.

HDTV marks a more dramatic departure from traditional TV. In contrast to analog TV with its 525 horizontal lines per frame, HDTV offers, depending on the format, either 720 or 1,080 horizontal lines, providing much clearer images and detail. HDTV can also provide wide format viewing, much as movie theaters do, and fewer signal distortions. A standard analog television receives modulated radio waves that it reconstructs into a nearly square picture. HDTV, on the other hand, receives signals digitally as binary electronic signals, which the receiver then translates into a stream of images virtually free from broadcast distortion. Like analog signals, digital signals can be transmitted by broadcast, cable, or satellite. HDTV provides a 16/9 width-to-height ratio compared to the 4/3 ratio of conventional TV. HDTV

Global TV Shipments, 2009

Technology	No. of units	Market share
LCD TV	50,700,000	74.8%
CRT TV	12,300,000	18.2%
Plasma TV	4,700,000	7.0%
RPTV	51,000	0.1%
OLED TV	4,000	0.0%

SOURCE: Display Search Quarterly Advanced Global TV Shipment and Forecast Report, February 2010.

also delivers digital sound, comparable in quality to an audio compact disc.

Digital TV hardware employs state-of-the-art computer technology to make it efficient and highly functional. Digital TV transmitters use computer technology to compress the signals for broadcast, allowing them to send two programs in one broadcast channel. Analog technology can deliver only one program per channel. Reciprocal technology must be present on the receiving end to interpret the digital signal.

Even though the Federal Communications Commission (FCC) decreed that all commercial broadcasts be offered digitally by 2002, and that all analog broadcasts must cease by 2006, bickering over standards made for an underwhelming debut by digital TV. Setting technical standards was complicated by the diverse range of business interests in the digital medium. In addition to television set manufacturers, other industries vying to have their positions heard included broadcasting stations, broadcast equipment makers, cable system operators, computer display manufacturers, and software developers. Often what was most beneficial to one of those industries was disadvantageous to others. For instance, computer hardware companies fought for a standard that would allow existing computer display technology to work readily with digital TV, but most broadcasters and traditional TV manufacturers preferred technology closer to existing TVs. Indeed, more than once, standards were all but agreed upon, only to have one or more parties to the agreement break ranks and lobby for changes. At the urging of companies involved, the FCC maintained a largely hands-off role, but regulators have been irked by the manufacturers' inability to resolve the disputes and get products on the market.

In November 2005, the U.S. Senate, in a budget bill, gave broadcasters until April 7, 2009, to end traditional analog transmissions and provided $3 billion to help those with older TV sets buy digital-to-analog converter boxes so they could receive a signal once conversion to digital becomes permanent. The month before, the House approved a December 31, 2008, deadline for analog and $1 billion for the converter boxes.

Some alternatives for receiving digital TV, however, do not involve buying a new display. Instead, some manufacturers have developed set-top conversion boxes that allow digital signals to be received by analog TVs. Such devices are necessary as analog broadcasting was phased out because the TV set replacement rate was expected to lag behind the adoption of digital standards.

Flat Panel Displays Liquid crystal displays (LCDs) are the most common form of flat panel display (FPD). LCDs work by having a layer of material that can regulate light and turn each picture element or pixel in an image on and off. Liquid crystal video displays comprise two primary kinds of laptop computer monitor technologies and constitute one of the costliest components of portable computers.

LCDs come in two main varieties: passive matrix and active matrix. Passive matrix LCD technology involves instructing the crystal valve to allow light to pass through, thereby addressing the individual pixels with the light to be displayed. However, active matrix LCDs became the addressing system of choice. This method directly addresses the pixels by placing thin film transistors (TFTs) underneath the liquid crystal itself, thereby allowing for greater signal control and superior image quality. Active display thin film transistor LCDs accounted for about 70 percent of all FPD sales in 2000; by 2006, that share reached 80 percent.

Gearing up for release in mid-2006, Toshiba showed working prototypes of its new surface-conduction electron-emitter display (SED) technology at the 2006 Consumer Electronics Show. SEDs are FPDs that use surface conduction electron emitters for every individual display pixel. The emitters "excite" a phosphor coating on the display panel, based on the same concept as cathode ray tubes (CRTs), allowing SEDs to combine the slim profile of LCDs with the high contrast ratios, refresh rates, and better picture quality of CRTs while using less power than LCDs.

The U.S. Display Consortium In addition to the industry giants, there were several prosperous companies in this industry segment, many of which were involved with the U.S. Display Consortium (USDC). Founded in 1993 as a government-industry response to the Flat Panel Display Initiative, USDC's mission was to ensure that this segment of the high-definition display industry remained "on the leading edge." The group was instrumental in creating and growing industry manufacturing infrastructures and funded more than 100 projects related to materials and components manufacturing between 1994 and 2004 with a total public/private investment in excess of $220 million. Those projects have been awarded to companies throughout the United States. In June 1998, the USDC was awarded an additional $10 million by the

Defense Advanced Research Projects Agency (DARPA) for continuing research for the U.S. flat panel display (FPD) industry.

Among its members, the USDC counts FPD manufacturers, developers, users, and equipment manufacturers and suppliers. In the 1990s, these included companies such as Candescent Technologies Corp., Compaq Computer, Planar-Standish, Texas Instruments, Three-Five Systems, and Universal Display Corp. After its annual High-Resolution Display Systems Summit in 2002, *Laser World* reported that USDC came to the following consensus: "Medical imaging, mapping/navigation and digital photography are the leading applications for high-resolution flat-panel displays, but widespread adoption will be contingent upon the industry's ability to resolve such key hurdles as color standardization and software development." In mid-2006, USDC member companies included Eastman Kodak, DuPont Displays, Hewlett-Packard, Fuji Film Dimatix, Dow Corning, Princeton University, and General Electric.

BACKGROUND AND DEVELOPMENT

Video display technology used in most desktop computers and TVs largely relied on one class of technology, the analog cathode ray tube (CRT), to present images. CRTs function by projecting a beam of electrons from one end of the tube to the other, where the electrons cause a layer of chemical phosphors to glow, revealing different colors. Manufacturers have employed this longstanding technology ever since the first TVs were made. The analog TV technology of the mid-1990s paralleled that of the 1940s and 1950s.

Early televisions of the late 1920s supported 90-line resolution with monochrome pictures that flickered across the screen. The technology improved, however, almost on a yearly basis in that period. Between 1931 and 1939, resolution expanded from 120 lines to 441 lines. RCA released a 441-line video display in 1939 that sold for $600, or about half the cost of a new car.

The National Television Standards Committee (NTSC) established the TV broadcast format in 1941 that governed the industry until the FCC's 1996 decree that TV broadcasters convert to digital TV transmission by 2006. The NTSC mandated that TV stations broadcast 525-line programs in the United States. With few alterations, this de facto standard remained for more than five decades, even though technology existed for higher-resolution broadcasting.

The modifications to the NTSC standard largely included making amendments for color broadcasting. Initially, the FCC adopted an ineffectual color wheel method for color broadcasting in 1950. CBS developed the color wheel technique, but it could produce only basic and inaccurate colors. The color wheel worked by creating the illusion of full color with a color wheel spinning inside the TV set, according to Joel Brinkley in the *New York Times*. In 1951, RCA introduced a different color system, which many companies and analysts extolled. Brinkley stated that RCA's electronic method created full-color images by shining three separate color images onto the screen. Consequently, the FCC repealed its original decision and made the RCA system the new standard.

In the 1970s and 1980s, companies such as Zenith Electronics Corp. and a number of Japanese companies led by the Japanese Broadcasting Corp. started to research new television formats using digital technology. These digital TV projects led to the development of both digital standard definition and digital HDTV. The goals of this research were to create televisions with better resolution and to imbue TV pictures with a near three-dimensional quality and faster image scanning. Japan premiered its HDTV capabilities at the 1984 Los Angeles Olympics and began a 1,125-line resolution direct broadcast service in 1989 called MUSE. Later, through a combined effort, the Japanese Broadcasting Company and Sony produced the regularly used HDTV system Hi-Vision, which promoted further development of HDTV technology.

Developers, however, could not integrate CRT displays into smaller electronic devices such as laptop computers, watches, calculators, and portable monitoring displays, because CRT displays require ample space for tubes; and the larger the screens became, the more unwieldy they were with CRT technology because the size of the tube increased with that of the screen.

U.S. electronics corporations developed alternative or advanced video displays by the end of the 1970s working with LCD, plasma, and electro-luminescent technologies. This research produced simple screens capable of presenting text and numbers as used in calculators and watches.

U.S. researchers, however, halted much of their research at this point, leaving the technology in an embryonic state, while Japanese companies continued to experiment with LCDs and developed active matrix LCDs for portable TVs in the 1980s. With this foundation in place, Japanese video display manufacturers such as Sharp Corp. and NEC Corp. enhanced and refined existing flat panel display (FPD) technology in the 1990s and conducted research on new flat panel and advanced video display technology.

Although squabbles over technical standards and high prices sidetracked sales of digital TV sets when they first came out in the late 1990s, manufacturers steamed ahead with launching new products aimed at the mass market. Although early sets introduced in 1998 and 1999 carried rich prices of $6,000 or more, newer models were going for more affordable rates. The Consumer Electronics Association reported that by the end of 1999, more than 100,000 digital-ready TVs had been sold in the United States. Cahners In-Stat estimated that total at 431,000 units at the end of 2000.

The sales figures are somewhat misleading, though, because most of the sets sold at that time were not capable of receiving a digital signal on their own. Separately, consumers would have to obtain a digital receiver that actually allowed them to harvest digital programming from the airwaves. While this division of technology allowed newer TVs to be more upgradeable, somewhat like computers, it also reflected the extent to which the technical standards were still in flux.

The standards fracas raged on into the twenty-first century. In 1999, Sinclair Broadcasting, a leading operator of TV stations, caused a stir with an aggressive campaign to revamp the broad standards already being put into practice by some manufacturers. The broadcaster argued that the existing standard made TV reception difficult in some urban areas and that it did not allow enough flexibility for broadcasting digitally to mobile devices. Meanwhile, cable operators and set manufacturers reached an accord on some of their differences in early 2000 but still had a way to go before reaching a comprehensive standard for delivering digital signals via cable.

The market for FPDs thrived as robust sales of portable computers and communications devices soared. After a slight sales dip from $24.6 billion in 2000 to $21.9 billion in 2001, attributed primarily to rapidly declining retail prices, sales took off in 2002. The rapid deployment of LCDs in desktop computer monitors was a primary engine of this growth. In 2000, only about 7 percent of PC monitors sold were LCDs, whereas just three years later, that share leaped to 40 percent. In the television segment, meanwhile, the penetration of FPDs was split between LCDs and plasma displays.

CRT sales inched downward each year alongside the blossoming demand for LCDs. Plasma display panels (PDPs), meanwhile, were especially strong in the markets for industrial displays and large (greater than 40 inches diagonally) displays. Plasma display panels remained high-end items in 2003, with televisions equipped with such technology running between $5,000 and $12,000. These displays tend to be significantly heavier than LCDs of comparable size. PDP sales totaled some $500 million in 2000, rising to an estimated total of $3 billion for 2003. In unit sales, plasma display panels rose from 2 percent to 8 percent of the total FPD sector. Flat panels used for portable computers accounted for a large chunk of worldwide sales, but the nascent market for stand-alone FPDs gained significant momentum through the early 2000s, although it was stronger in Japan than in the United States.

The dominance of thin film transistors in liquid crystal displays (TFT-LCDs) was expected to strengthen through the 2000s as the technology continued to penetrate the desktop monitor and premium television markets. Although TFT-LCDs were widely used in portable devices, other technologies also enjoyed a solid presence in these niches. Organic light-emitting displays (OLEDs) were introduced for use in handheld devices in March 2003, and their exceptionally high image quality positioned them as one of the key eventual rivals to TFT-LCDs in the wider market, though significant debugging and cost-reduction measures were required for OLEDs to live up to this potential.

While corporations were the largest customer base for FPDs, falling prices and improving technology ensured that consumers were emerging as the primary target. The opening of new plants designed to handle exceptionally large pieces of glass for the manufacture of displays was a primary catalyst in the dramatic decline in retail prices of FPDs. For example, DisplaySearch reported that retail prices of 15-inch diagonal displays fell 75 percent between 1999 and 2003, and 17-inch displays fell fully 85 percent over that period.

The large-format flat panels geared toward home entertainment drew public attention thanks to visible marketing campaigns by companies such as Philips Electronics N.V. Prices, however, remained in lofty territory—often above $10,000—and some media outlets reported consumer dissatisfaction with the units, which usually hung on the wall. Some people complained that flat panel TVs were hard to accommodate in homes and were unaesthetic. More to the heart of the problem, some believed the picture quality was not particularly good.

Some experts believed displays based on digital light processing (DLP) could steal market share from the more established LCD and plasma flat panels. DLP, which has been used since the mid-1990s in large-screen digital TVs and projectors for business, home, and professional venues and digital cinema, uses an optical semiconductor to manipulate light digitally, offering high resolution and a relatively compact design. More than 10 million systems were shipped to more than 75 manufacturers between 1996 and 2005.

Asia was the undisputed manufacturing center for video displays, particularly LCDs. Japanese and South Korean companies continued to lead FPD manufacturing, while other Asian countries such as Taiwan were also key players in the global flat FPD industry. In contrast to the United States, Japan invested billions of dollars in its flat panel industry, which allowed the Japanese industry to prosper quickly as demand for FPDs in laptop computers ballooned. This investment pushed the Japanese market to the forefront in both flat panel production and sales. By 2003, Korea surpassed Japan as the world's leading manufacturer of TFT-LCDs, and Samsung alone accounted for just over half of South Korea's sales.

In 2006, the Asian countries of South Korea, Japan, and Taiwan continued to lead in the production of FPD, in response to the tremendous demand for LCD and plasma discharge panel TVs coming out of Europe, North America, and China. The growth in popularity of digital television (DTV) and high-definition television (HDTV) spawned the development of support industries along with FPDs: broadcasting, telecommunications, chipset design and production, set-top box manufacturing, and software or middleware. Challenging the dominance of LCDs were the new technologies of organic light-emitting displays (OLEDs) and field emission displays (FED), thanks to advances in their manufacturing methods. However, the continued lack of cost-effective techniques of mass production, competition with the relatively low price of LCDs, the high cost of investment, and the lack of customer awareness of the newest technologies were all issues that new companies and technologies faced in the FPD industry.

Taiwan continued its climb toward leadership in the industry, manufacturing TFT-LCDs, TN/STN, PM, OLED, and AMOLED technologies. In 2006, production was up 37 percent from 2005, to a total of $40 billion, according to the Industrial Economics & Knowledge Center of the Industrial Technology Research Institute. Boosting the growth was the increasing demand for LCD TV and cell phone panel products as prices continued to drop; global demand for LCD TV reached 42 million units—worth about $17 billion. In 2006, Taiwan became the world's largest producer of TFT-LCDs, with more than a 40 percent market share.

Taiwan and China invested a combined 300 million yuan (US$37.22 million) to build two FPD production plants in Xiamen, in the Fujian Province of East China. Picture Tubes, Ltd. of Taiwan and Xiamen Overseas Chinese Electronic Co. made plans to build what was expected to be the world's biggest production plant for flat screen TVs.

The "Faroudja" chip, manufactured by Genesis Microchip of San Jose and introduced by Gateway in late 2005, allowed the image on its 21-inch monitor—Gateway's largest and highest definition flat panel monitor—to automatically straighten as the monitor is turned or twisted. The Faroudja won Emmy awards for video technology for its use in plasma TVs and high-end home theater systems. Its very clean video signal resulted from removing the jagged edges of standard video, allowing a clearer, sharper picture.

In 2005, Innovative Solutions and Support, Inc., of Exton, Pennsylvania, contracted with ABX Air, Inc. of Wilmington, Ohio, and the Canadian Department of National Defense (CDND) to install flat-panel cockpit displays in their respective Boeing 767 jets and C-130 airplanes. The FPDs did away with mechanical gauges, providing an improved user interface and significant logistics savings. New Boeing 757s and 767s were equipped with the FPDs, whereas older commercial and military planes could be retrofitted with them. The CDND placed an initial $42.4-million order for the FPDs in late 2005, replacing more than 40 electromechanical instruments.

Although many consumer electronics categories floundered as the economy stalled, the world market for FPDs skyrocketed. By 2003, worldwide sales in this category reached $40.4 billion. The total display module market, according to Banc of America Securities, was worth about $57.5 billion in 2002. In the United States, sales of LCD flat panel computer monitors overtook cathode ray tube (CRT) monitors for the first time in 2004, with sales of $21 billion, as prices slowly began falling on all size displays. LCDs took a 53 percent market share in the United States, compared to 46 percent for CRTs .

As the first decade of the twenty-first century neared a close, the U.S. video display industry, like many others, was dealing with the effects of a slowing economy. For example, the flat panel TV market experienced only a 21 percent growth in the third quarter of 2008, compared to around 41 percent for the previous six quarters. On the bright side, in 2008 HDTV sales surpassed those of standard definition TVs for the first time, and, according to *PC Magazine,* LCD television sales continued to climb, despite the downturn in the economy. One research firm, iSuppli, predicted that, worldwide, 241.2 million HDTV sets will be shipped by 2012, up from 97.1 million sets in 2007. On the other hand, shipment of standard definition TVs will drop to 23.1 million units by that time, down from 114.8 million units in 2007.

The drop in prices and demand in LCDs caused Sharp, one of the world's leading producers, to make plans to cut production by as much as 10 percent at its main production facility in Japan. According to a November 2008 Reuters news release, Sharp still expected to see sales of 11 million LCD TVs in fiscal year 2008. Samsung also had plans to reduce production, according to *PC World.*

Consumers were not the only ones paying lower prices for flat panels; original equipment manufacturers (OEMs) were paying less for the components that make up LCD TVs. OEMs, which produced about 23 percent of the 20.1 million LCD TVs shipped in the third quarter of 2007, paid about $223 for a 32-inch panel in 2007. According to Yoshio Tamura of DisplaySearch, "LCD panel makers face negative operating profits when panel prices are lower than the total cost. When the price approaches the cash cost, panel makers will suffer from cash out difficulties and take necessary steps to cut production and reduce capacity utilization." The average price of a 32-inch HD LCD TV in late 2008 was between $399 and $499.

As of August 2008, 28 percent of U.S. households owned at least one HDTV set, up from 8 percent in 2007. Consulting company Knowledge Networks predicted that figure would grow to 38 percent by 2009. The firm attributed the growth partly to the federal-mandated switch from analog to digital TV.

CURRENT CONDITIONS

2009 global sales of televisions were roughly $112 billion, reported Eric Schonfeld of *TechCrunch,* with 69 percent of them (or 140.5 million of the total estimated 205 million units) having LCD panels. Total television shipments had actually been in decline since mid-2008, as demand for CRTs continued to fall. Global revenues for TVs were roughly $101 billion in 2009, representing an estimated 10 percent decline from 2008, mostly due to price erosion. In fact, flat panel TVs dipped in price below $500, triggering a global surge in demand, especially in China. The 2010 World Cup Soccer tournament was also credited with breathing new life into the market.

According to market researcher DisplaySearch, the LCD TV sector grew by 50 percent year-over-year during the last quarter of 2009. Plasma televisions grew by six percent, while OLED, a fledgling technology, actually fell by one third. Between 2008 and 2009, sales of LCD televisions grew more than eight times faster than sales of plasma display televisions. Manufacturer Panasonic was working on bolstering sales by pushing it as the display technology of choice for 3D televisions. During the first seven months of 2010, the United States imported $1.5 billion worth of plasma televisions, the majority of them coming in from Mexico.

Touch screen technology in the panel market was expected to show a compound annual growth rate (CAGR) of 30 percent through 2013, with about 280 million units sold in 2009, and an expected demand of 800 million by 2013. Mobile phones dominated the touch screen market in 2009, taking a 52 percent share and expecting to take a 62 percent share by the end of 2010, thanks to smart phone sales, like Apple's iPhone. Other application areas for touch screen panels included PC monitors, electronic games, office and medical equipment, portable navigation handhelds, kiosk displays, and point-of-sale systems. Market revenues for touch screen panels were $2.5 billion in 2009, expected to grow to $7.4 billion by 2013.

Digital signage was on the rise in 2010, creating a niche market demand for larger than life panels. According to the *2101 Arbitron Digital Place-Based Video Study,* over two-thirds of adults and teens had seen a digital video display in a public venue in the preceding month.

OLED technology played an increasingly larger role, already bringing in $822 million in 2009, but expected to grow to $106 billion by 2020. As of 2010, 65 percent of OLED revenues were from displays in mobile phones. The anticipated growth of OLED in the market is expected from other larger display applications, including televisions, monitors, etc.

INDUSTRY LEADERS

South Korea's Samsung Electronics was the world's leading manufacturer of big-screen televisions and liquid crystal display (LCD) panels, holding approximately 19 percent of the market. In 2000, the company announced a joint venture with NEC Corp. to develop electro-luminescent (organic-EL) displays, while in 2002 it set up a $1.8 billion LCD production joint venture with Sony Corp. Its third-generation plasma displays rolled out in 2003, featuring both analog and digital inputs. Samsung was the fastest growing brand, according to research information from Interbrand, Inc., USA. In 2009, the company had revenues of $1117.6 billion and employed 250,000 people worldwide.

Royal Philips Electronics N.V. of the Netherlands was another major force in the world display industry. The fourth largest global monitor producer, Philips greatly expanded its investment in LCD technology, becoming the second largest manufacturer of LCDs in the world in 2006. Philips has long been a maker of TV sets and myriad other consumer electronics, and it amassed an imposing presence in the advanced display business. Philips markets electronic displays under its own and the Magnavox brands. The firm's partnership with Korea's LG Electronics (LGE), which saw sales of $24.6 billion in 2006, gave it a strong foothold in the booming Asian market as well as a major presence in the world's display manufacturing center. Phillips shed much of its non-core businesses, acquiring and forming joint ventures for its major operations.

NEC Corp. of Japan is a powerhouse in the market for advanced computer displays with a dominant share of the stand-alone LCD market and sizable shares in other categories. While the firm positioned itself aggressively as a solutions provider for information technology and data networks, the manufacture of electronic devices still made up 18 percent of its total revenues. Besides its video displays, NEC was a leading computer producer and a prominent manufacturer of semiconductors. NEC-Mitsubishi Electronics Display of America combined the desktop display monitor divisions of NEC Technologies and Mitsubishi Electronics Corporation. NEC splits ownership with Samsung of the Samsung NEC Mobile

Display Co. Ltd., a company formed to develop new electro-luminescent (organic-EL) displays. The firm sold its plasma display operations to Pioneer in 2004.

Sony Corp., an international electronics leader, competes in several segments of the advanced display business, including computer monitors, digital TVs, and specialty niches such as video headsets. It is also a top manufacturer of gaming consoles and DVD players. The company reported $78.9 billion in 2009 sales; subsidiary Sony Electronics was based in San Diego, California. Sony maintains a development partnership with Candescent Technologies to bring out next-generation light-emitting display (LED) technology for FPDs. Sony's restructuring efforts included a planned joint venture with Samsung to develop LCD panels.

Sharp Corp. was one of the first Japanese companies to follow up on initial U.S. research on flat panel displays (FPDs) in the 1970s. When U.S. companies such as Westinghouse and RCA halted their flat panel experimentation, Sharp began exploring the technology. In 2007 Sharp displayed a prototype of its largest flat panel TV yet, a 108-inch Aquos, at the Consumer Electronics Show in Las Vegas. The firm posted 2009 revenues of $13.6 billion with 53,708 employees. Along with LG Display and Chunghwa Picture Tubes of Taiwan, Sharp faced allegations of price-fixing LCD panels by the U.S. Justice Department in 2008. The firm pled guilty and was fined $120 million. The reason for the price-fixing schemes, according to industry experts, was to slow price decline. Richard Doherty of Envisioneering told the *International Herald Tribune,* "These companies were trying to get a toehold to protect profits in a very difficult market."

Toshiba Corp. of Japan was one of the largest FPD producers, as well as a leader in the portable personal computer market. Collaborating with IBM Corp., Toshiba manufactured advanced video displays for the computer and the consumer electronics industries. The merger between Toshiba's and Matsushita's LCD production operations yielded Toshiba Matsushita Display Technology. For the fiscal year ending March 2010, Toshiba employed 190,000 people and earned revenues of $71 billion.

Planar Systems, Inc. found its niche in instrumentation displays, gearing its products toward the health care sector as well as for use in commercial desktop monitors. In that vein, the firm purchased medical image display manufacturer DOME Imaging Systems for $61 million in 2002. About 40 percent of Planar's sales went to the commercial sector, whereas 35 percent were in the medical industries and 26 percent came from the industrial market. With customers including Siemens Medical, GE Medical Systems, Eastman Kodak, and Philips Medical Systems, Planar was North America's largest independent maker of industrial displays.

Corning Inc., based in Corning, New York, was an important industry component manufacturer. The firm's Information Display segment produced glass panels and funnels for LCD, flat panel, video cassette recorder, and cathode ray tube displays. While Corning's core telecommunications division staggered in the early 2000s, sales of its LCD equipment remained particularly strong. More than half of Corning's sales come from the Asia/Pacific region, particularly Taiwan and Japan.

RESEARCH AND TECHNOLOGY

At the FPD Internation 2010 Convention in Makuhari, Japan, LG Display showcased the world's thinnest 42-inch LED-backlit LCD television. Samsung showcased its 19-inch transparent 3D display, and AU Potronics introduced its world's largest 71-inch 3D television panel, that also had touch panel technology for interactive video game applications.

Sony and Samsung, in their joint venture called S-LCD, announced plans in April 2008 to build another eighth-generation TFT-LCD production line, this time in South Korea. According to a report by *The Inquirer,* by the second quarter of 2009 the facility will produce 60,000 TFT-LCD sheets of 2,200mm x 2,500mm glass per month. The company's second plant, in Kameyama, Japan, was the world's first to cut panels from eighth-generation glass substrates, which can yield eight 40-inch glass panels, as compared to three panels rendered from sixth-generation glass.

A Toronto-based electronics company, iFire, developed a pilot version of a thick-film dialectric electro-luminescent technology (TDEL) and began to manufacture it in 2007. TDEL technology is used to produce thinner, less expensive FLDs by using lightweight materials, thinner glass, and fewer electronics than plasma, with no backlight. The 37-inch HDTV set is 2 cm thick and weighs less than 2.2 pounds, according to *CNET News.* A sheet of blue phosphor, a blue light source, used as the source of energy, energizes fluorescent pigments that emit green or red light. The full color of an RGB (red, green, blue) video is displayed by combining the blue light source with the green and red light.

Another innovation that improved viewability in bright sunlight for electronics such as cash machines, mobile phones, and laptops was developed by scientists at Abertay University in Dundee, Scotland in conjunction with their counterparts at Greenwich University in London. They produced new thin film coatings for FPDs that are able to "sense" light levels and adjust the display output to maximize readability and efficiency. The thin film coating materials "combine several optical functions to produce a more-sensitive, higher-performance, more energy-efficient and lower-cost display," according to Colin Cartwright of Abertay University's School of Computing and Creative Technologies.

BIBLIOGRAPHY

"2010 Arbitron Digital Place-Based Video Study." Arbitron, 2010. Available from http://www.arbitron.com/study/digital_video_display_study.asp.

"Canadian Firm Creates New Low-Cost Flat Screen TV." *Broadcast Engineering,* 19 June 2006.

Chunghwa, D. "Flat-Panel Display Plants to be Built in Xiamen." *Business Daily Update,* 24 January 2006.

"DisplaySearch Revises Worldwide TV Forecasts: LCD TV Demand Outlook Raised After Good Q1 09 Result and Strong Outlook in China." DisplaySearch, 17 January 2009.

"Dundee Project Unveils a Bright Idea for Flat-Panel Display Screens." *Europe Intelligence Wire,* 19 April 2006.

"Flat Panel Sales Are Up, But Slowing." *PC Magazine,* 11 November 2008.

"FPD International 2010: LG Display Shows Thinnest 42-inch LED TV." *DigiTImes,* 12 November 2010.

"FPD International 2010: SMD Showcases 19-inch Transparent 3D Display." *DigiTImes,* 12 November 2010.

"Global LCD TV Shipments Reached 146M Units in 2009, Faster Growth Than 2008." DisplaySearch, 22 February 2010.

"Global Organic Light Emitting Diode (OLED) Display Market Holds Enormous revenue Potential and is Expected to Reach $10.6 Billion by 2020." *Electronics.ca,* 26 November 2010.

"Growth of DTV and IPTV Set to Boost Flat Panel Display, Set-Top Box and Chipsets Industries." *PR Newswire,* 2 June 2006.

"HDTV Prices May Be as Low as They Can Go." *PC Magazine Online,* 29 October 2008.

"HDTV Sales Overtake SD Models." *Broadcast Engineering,* 10 November 2008.

Les, Caren B. "Touch Screen Panel Market: Smooth Operations." *Photonoics Spectra,* May 2010.

"LG. Philips LCD Opens Joint Venture with Japanese Firm to Produce Glass for Flat Panels." *Yonhap News Agency of Korea,* 24 June 2006.

Lohr, Steve. "LG Display, Sharp, and Chunghwa Plead Guilty to Price Fixing." *International Herald Tribune,* 14 November 2008.

Magee, Mike. "Sony, Samsung Expand Eighth-Generation LCD Glass Line." *The Inquirer,* 25 April 2008.

Manufacturers Growth Chart . Available from http://www.prad.de/en/news/shownews_alg3399. html.

"News Flash: LCD TV Sales FIgures see 50-percent Increase in 2009." 23 February 2010. Available from http://Televisons.com.

Schonfeld, Eric. "The World Spent $112 Billion on 205 Million TVs This Year: 69 Percent Were LCD TVs." *TechCrunch,* 29 December 2009. Available from http://www.techcrunch.com/2009/12/29/tvs-2009.

"Sharp to Cut Output at Main LCD Plant Report." Reuters, 14 November 2008.

"Sharp Unveils 108-Inch Flat Panel TV." Associated Press, 8 January 2007.

"Thirty-Eight Percent of Households to Own HDTV Sets Next Year." *Broadcast Engineering,* 26 August 2008.

"Top Ten LCD TV OEM Set Manufacturers." Evertiz, 6 December 2007.

"U.S. Consumer Tech Sales Down In September." *Information Week,* 24 October 2008.

Workman, Daniel. "US Sales for Plasma Television by Country So Far in 2010." 9 September 2010. Available from http://www.suite101.com/content.

VIRTUAL REALITY

SIC CODE(S)

3571

3572

3575

3577

7372

INDUSTRY SNAPSHOT

Virtual reality (VR), as its name suggests, is a simulated version of reality wherein users feel they are "really" walking on a beach, flying a fighter jet, performing heart bypass surgery, or whatever else the VR software is programmed to do. Although virtual reality is commonly associated with science fiction and video games, it is a bona fide technology formed from a meld of computer hardware and software. While serious interest in virtual reality grew slowly, it gained momentum in the early years of the twenty-first century's first decade as sophisticated technology created new applications. Spurred by lower prices and greater capabilities, industries and professions began adopting VR technology for a variety of uses and functions, including training and design.

Jaron Lanier, founder of VPL Research Inc., was the first to coin the term "virtual reality." Other related terms include "artificial reality," coined by Myron Krueger in the 1970s; William Gibson's "cyberspace," which debuted in 1984; and such terms as "virtual worlds," "visual simulation," and "virtual environments," which first were used in the 1990s. The term "virtual reality" is today used in a wide variety of ways, often leading to some confusion. As originally coined by Lanier, the term was meant to describe total immersion in a three-dimensional (3D), computer-generated world.

Although its entertainment potential is fairly obvious and was the first area to be exploited by the fledgling VR industry, VR has more practical educational applications. For example, new terrorist acts created expanded interest of military and governmental entities in simulated defensive/offensive training aids utilizing VR. The industry in general is expected by its proponents to reshape the relationship between information technology and people, offering a variety of new and novel ways to communicate information and visualize processes. VR allows the creation of a 3D virtual environment that can be rooted in reality or abstract. Among the former could be such real systems as buildings, landscapes, human anatomy, crime scenes, automobile accidents, and spacecraft. Representations of abstract systems might include magnetic fields, mathematical systems, molecular models, and population densities.

ORGANIZATION AND STRUCTURE

Much of the discussion about VR technology focused on Virtual Reality Modeling Language (VRML) 2.0. VRML is a standard language for describing interactive 3D objects and worlds on the Internet. Like Hypertext Markup Language (HTML), the modeling language typically used on the World Wide Web, VRML is a Web-authoring software, but it also gives users the ability to create sophisticated 3D environments. It adds interaction, graphics, and extra dimensions to online communication.

A Virtual Reality Modeling Language (VRML) Consortium was formed as the official mouthpiece for VRML evolution to provide a forum for creating and promoting standards for VRML and 3D content on the Web. The consortium, a nonprofit group comprised of 65 organizations, approved VRML 97 as the International Organization for Standardization (ISO) standard in December 1997. In March of 1998, it worked on formalizing its organizational structure by forming an executive committee as well as task groups to work on marketing and specification issues. Although many of the larger technology companies, including Apple Computer, Cosmo Software (a Silicon Graphics company), Microsoft, Oracle, and Sony, had joined the consortium, other major players, including Sun Microsystems and Intel, did not lend their support to the consortium.

The W3D Consortium was instrumental in efforts to develop and implement a VRML97 ISO Standard for international stabilization and standardization of the technology. The consortium's technical activities also included the Extensible 3D (X3D) specification, which extended VRML97, using the Extensible Markup Language (XML). In 2003, the consortium continued its successful progress in implementing Extensible 3D (X3D) and developing commercial software to support 3D authoring and browsing. The X3D technology represented a major upgrade from VRML97, incorporating several advanced 3D techniques including advanced rendering and multi-texturing as well as Non-Uniform Rational B-Spline (NURBS) Surfaces, GeoSPatial referencing, Humanoid Animation. (H-Anim), and IEEE Distributed Interactive Simulation (DIS) networking.

BACKGROUND AND DEVELOPMENT

Computers have changed greatly since their inception. Early computers, in fact, lacked many of the elements users in the 1990s took for granted, such as memory and monitors. In the 1950s, computer scientists connected a typing board to a computer, and the notion of a monitor emerged soon afterward, followed in the early 1960s by a movable pointer, which was quickly nicknamed a "mouse" because of the tail-like wire attached to it. Later came the idea of a graphical user interface (GUI), which allowed users to talk to or "interface" with the computer. An example of a GUI is an icon that users click to access a particular function. The icon is the side of the interface that the user sees, whereas the computer responds to a set of commands activated when the user clicks on the icon.

The basic concept underlying virtual reality (VR) has been around for decades, although it began to take its present shape only in recent years. Simulators such as those used to train truck drivers and airline pilots were obvious forerunners of current virtual reality technology. It took the emergence of the computer and its ability to generate complex images and simulate interactive environments to

truly energize the VR concept and spark the birth of a new industry.

Many people helped lay the groundwork for VR. In 1950, Douglas Engelbart envisioned a world of small computers that people would use for communication—an utterly foreign concept at a time when computers were mammoth structures that might fill up an entire house and yet be capable of little more than simple addition and subtraction. In 1960, J. C. R. Licklider predicted that the human mind and the computer would work in close harmony in his essay entitled "Man-Computer Symbiosis." This too seemed doubtful in an age when programmers could communicate with the computer only through punched-hole tape.

By the 1960s, the notions that would later come to fruition as virtual reality were rapidly taking shape. In 1962 Morton Heilig built the Sensorama cubicle, which gave the user the illusion of driving a motorcycle. In 1965 Ivan Sutherland, "the father of computer graphics," had already imagined computer users being immersed in a separate reality created by graphics. In addition, Myron Krueger, a significant VR pioneer who in 1970 became the first to use the term "artificial reality," built the first of his many "responsive environments" in 1969. Called GLOWFLOW, it involved a platform surrounded by a screen. Viewers stood on the platform, and as they walked around, the shifting of their bodies' weight caused various pictures to appear on the screen.

From these early days, the development of VR was the product of a bizarre amalgam of players: computer scientists, many of whom worked in university research labs; unconventional visionaries; and military and civilian personnel from the U.S. Department of Defense and the National Aeronautics and Space Administration (NASA). The government was an important contributor to VR research. After the Soviets launched the first space satellite, *Sputnik,* in 1957, the U.S. government reacted by launching vast new programs in military and flight engineering and science. Out of this came the Defense Advanced Research Projects Agency, which developed the beginnings of the Internet, then called the Arpanet, and invested in what would become VR.

Futhermore, the military provided funding for J. C. R. Licklider, helping him to explore his ideas of "man-computer symbiosis." With its vast budget, the Defense Department facilitated the first use of a virtual reality system in the 1970s. NASA, on the other hand, had less money to spend, but its scientists were also interested in the possibilities for VR use in flight training and other aspects of space flight. Because of its limited budget, NASA was a key element in helping to develop relatively less expensive VR technology. NASA also explored the idea of telepresence, which would make it possible for someone to "do" something in one place while sitting in another. Following this concept, in July 1997, NASA programmers on earth were able to operate a vehicle that rolled over the surface of Mars and collected soil and rock samples.

Market expansion remained slow throughout much of the 1990s. One of the factors that contributed to VR's relatively slow growth was the legal battle involving VPL Research. The legal battle involved custody of the patent rights to much of the technology that defines VR. Since there was such uncertainty in the industry over the patents, interest in starting new companies waned during the four-year court battle (1993 to 1997).

That situation changed in 1998. By acquiring VPL, Sun Microsystems obtained the rights to the patent portfolio and technical assets of the company, which extend to networked 3D graphics, human-based body input, and 3D window systems. The acquisition provided stability in the volatile industry as a whole. According to Stuart Davidson, a partner in Labrador Ventures, a California high tech venture capital firm, "This will help virtual reality get out of the cottage-industry stage. At the very least, by establishing hardware and software standards for the technology, Sun Microsystems should end costly duplication of effort among companies developing VR."

In the late 1990s, VR applications started establishing a presence in wide-ranging segments of American life. The primary areas of VR penetration, however, were the entertainment, design and engineering, medicine, education and training, sales, and military industries.

Entertainment was an early area of VR application, and it remained significant in the early years of the first decade of the twenty-first century. For instance, one restaurant chain offered patrons the opportunity to experience virtual reality-based games, while another restaurant, Mars 2112, enabled customers the chance to experience what landing on Mars would be like. In addition, the Evans and Sutherland Computer Corp. developed a system in late 1996 that inserted the viewer into a virtual setting on live television, and research at Carnegie Mellon University involved a VR application that would make it possible for someone watching a sport on television to view the action from anywhere on the field of play. Moreover, Disney opened DisneyQuest, a family entertainment experience, at Downtown Disney in Orlando. DisneyQuest features futuristic games and rides that use motion-based simulators and VR environments. Disney partnered with Silicon Graphics, a leader in the VR field, for this project. DisneyQuest's Explore Zone is the entertainment world that features VR. Universal Studios also offers virtual reality rides at its theme parks, including the Amazing Adventures of Spider Man ride.

In the area of design and engineering, software for 3D modeling assists designers in creating prototypes. Although virtual reality technology struggled to find marketable applications, manufacturers teamed up with virtual reality developers to create virtual prototypes for the manufacturing industry. By replacing physical prototypes, manufacturers hoped to achieve greater cost efficiency and quicker transitions from model to market for new parts and products. The automotive, aerospace, and military industries expressed particular interest in the development of this technology. Because of prohibitive costs, industries have hesitated in using VR for prototype development. As VR costs dropped and VR systems became more powerful, however, VR technology gradually became a more viable technique for development.

VR prototype development involves engineers using large visualization centers, such as Silicon Graphics' Reality Center, to see the minute and realistic details of their designs. The result of this research has been software such as Engineering Animation Inc.'s VisConcept, which enables engineers to create and project virtual prototypes. VR gives architects the ability to design and "build" whole structures and allows their prospective clients to "walk through" them. Many software companies also offer programs for the general public that allow users to create residential floor plans the way professionals create them. Industrial engineers also create virtual factories with employees, robots, machines, and products to explore better ways to make the factories function.

Medical advances in VR technology include the National Institutes of Health's development of "virtual bronchoscopy," a virtual and noninvasive imaging of the bronchial tree within the human respiratory system. Other advances make it increasingly possible to study human anatomy without actually cutting open a cadaver and to improve surgical techniques through virtual operations. Coined "cybersurgery," VR is a crucial tool in neurosurgery whereby a 3D picture of the brain helps surgeons pinpoint the location of a brain tumor with extreme accuracy. In addition, developers have combined VR technology with robotics to advance cardiac surgery. The result is a VR system operated by a surgeon who controls a robot that performs the actual surgery. This technology makes cardiac surgery less invasive and speeds up recovery time. Furthermore, hospitals have implemented VR technology to help relieve patient stress prior to serious operations, offering them tranquil escapes from the operating room environment.

While VR advocates once proclaimed that VR would revolutionize training for many different professions, VR training remained limited to a small but growing number of professionals, most notably pilots, doctors, and military personnel. Educational applications of VR range from knowledge of purely theoretical or historical interest to highly practical applications. Rome Reborn, an ambitious project being developed at the University of California-Los Angeles, would walk users through versions of Rome from 850 B.C. to A.D. 450. VR also is used to help people from a wide variety of occupations—doctors, factory workers, fighter pilots—improve their work by simulating their activities. In the late 1990s and early years of the twenty-first century's first decade, the educational and training applications of VR continued to increase with the drop in VR technology prices and the improvement of performance.

Examples of VR applications in sales and marketing include uses in real estate such as Home Debut, which provides virtual tours of homes for sale. *In-Store Marketing* highlighted a few of the many VR applications for retail sales, including companies such as Luminova, creating electronic models of point-Of-purchase displays, packaging designs, and scenes reflecting how items would fit in when rolled out in stores. *Forbes* looked at VR technology enlisted by the marketing firm Coopers & Lybrand in an effort to predict the buying habits of 50,000 music consumers. In addition, the journal *I/S Analyzer Case Studies* predicted that an increasing number of businesses would use VR technology because VR authoring software was now compatible with most programming platforms and the cost of head-mounted displays and other equipment was dropping.

The military was one of VR's first advocates, using VR more frequently to simulate combat, and experiments were exploring ways it could be used in actual combat. Called Simnet, VR was used to train soldiers on real-to-life tank and helicopter training simulations for the U.S. Army. One promising area is that of telepresence, which allows remote command functions to orchestrate activities in a distant location. Furthermore, the Department of Defense is a major investor in VR technology. Fakespace, Inc. built a multimedia battle zone theatre so that the Army Research Laboratory could efficiently study how soldiers use equipment in combat.

Implement & Tractor pointed out that several trade publications had featured articles about Caterpillar engineers using computer programs for "three dimension" designs and John Deere's use of computer simulation sessions with farmers to refine tractors. It was also noted that John Deere has continued and expanded its relationship with the Virtual Reality Applications Center at Iowa State University.

In 2007 Iowa State University's Virtual Reality Applications Center opened what was called the most realistic VR room to date. "C6" is a 10-foot by 10-foot virtual reality cube that surrounds users in computer-generated 3D images and audio. C6 first opened in 2000 as the nation's first six-

side VR room but has undergone a $5 million upgrade since then. According to Iowa State, C6 now projects more than twice the resolution produced by any other VR room in the world and projects 16 times the pixels produced by the original C6. The room also sports eight channels of audio and ultrasonic motion tracking technology. Some of the varied fields in which C6 is being used include research, education, and training. On the lighter side, users can take a virtual trip to a tropical island and explore a sunken shipwreck.

Central to the development of new VR technology is the controversy surrounding immersion technology versus wearable display gear. The primary piece of equipment for the VR experience is the head-mounted display (HMD), a helmet hooked up to the computer that includes tiny monitors (television screens) to cover each eye. The screens each show slightly different views that, when viewed simultaneously, produce the illusion of looking at 3D objects. Also inside the HMD is a tracking device that follows the user's head movements and changes the on-screen images accordingly in order to maintain the sensation that one is operating within a fully spatial rather than a two-dimensional realm. The HMD also includes speakers to further enhance the experience. Virtual reality users often avail themselves of tactile devices, most commonly a sensor glove, which is connected to the computer just like the HMD. The glove senses movements of the user's hand and helps him or her to "move" within the virtual world seen through the screens on the headset. The headgear and the glove create an illusion of depth and the ability to manipulate objects. With prolonged use, these devices have proven to be awkward and uncomfortable. Head-mounted viewers such as Nintendo's Virtual Boy were expensive and ultimately unsuccessful. The most realistic computer-generated 3D world, however, is currently displayed using these wearable displays.

However, with the growing acceptance of VR in the marketplace came criticism. Some researchers found that people immersed in VR suffered side effects termed "cybersickness." The major problem with VR environments, according to these researchers, was the difficulty of adapting to the real world after a virtual experience. These adaptation problems included poor hand-eye coordination and poor eyesight. Other symptoms found were disorientation, nausea, and eyestrain. Furthermore, VR environments that required users to travel through a virtual landscape as a passive observer with little or no control of their movements seemed to cause the most severe forms of cybersickness.

PIONEERS IN THE FIELD

Jaron Lanier was a leader in the early development and commercialization of virtual reality technology and products. Lanier is called the pioneer of virtual reality and is recognized for coining the term. Virtual reality was the name he gave to the goggles, gloves, and software that allow people to interact with each other in worlds generated by 3D graphics. Lanier also developed software that made VR commercially viable.

Born in 1961, Lanier grew up in New Mexico, dropped out of high school, and set out to be a musician rather than a computer genius. Lanier was already developing the technology that would alter the future of humankind by the time he was in his twenties. Working with Atari in the early 1980s, he earned enough royalties from his Moondust video game to quit and start his own company. Legend has it that when *Scientific American* called to discuss a new programming language he had developed, the 22-year-old Lanier was embarrassed to tell them his company had no name so he made up the name VPL Research Inc. on the spot.

Lanier founded VPL Research in 1984 and headed the company until 1992. During that time, the company made many of the early advances that would later enable such interactive, networked 3D games as Doom and Quake. "VPL's groundbreaking efforts and research have become an important influence on many virtual reality and 3D graphics products that succeeded the company," according to Sun Microsystems, Inc., the company that later acquired VPL.

When Lanier left VPL in 1992 because of differences with Thomson-CFS, the French technology conglomerate that helped finance him, he gave up his patents. During the next four years, Greenleaf Medical financed VPL Systems. Greenleaf fought a four-year battle in bankruptcy court to keep Thomson from gaining exclusive control of the VPL patents. In February 1998, Sun Microsystems announced it had acquired VPL for an estimated $4 million. The deal settled debts and released approximately 35 patent applications, 12 of them already granted. The acquisition was looked on favorably by Wall Street and many in the VR industry.

Lanier has continued his involvement in the VR field as lead scientist for the National Tele-Immersion Initiative, a coalition of research universities working to create the next generation of VR applications on the Internet.

CURRENT CONDITIONS

In their 2009 published report, *Inside Virtual Goods: The U.S. Virtual Goods Market, 2009–2010,* Justin Smith and Charles Hudson said that while virtual goods had been driving revenues in Asia and Europe for years, 2009 would be remembered as the year virtual goods-based businesses began to scale in the United States, perhaps wholly disrupting entertainment, communication, and e-commerce infrastructure as we had known it. They estimated the total 2009 U.S. virtual goods market at just

over $1 billion. A few of the trends they noted in the report were (1) the explosion of the virtual goods market on social networks (which they considered one of the biggest stories of 2009); (2) the growth of virtual worlds and casual MMOs; (3) the success of MMOs and Free-to-Play Online Games; and (4) emerging applications in consoles, iPhone, and subscription MMOs.

A September 2009 article in *Eon Reality* focused on the VR sectors of 3D customer interaction management, interactive 3D virtual meeting , simulation based learning, and immersive 3D solutions. Summarizing various sources, the article noted that, according to Jon Peddie Research, the total CAD market was estimated to reach $8.2 billion by 2012. Of that, *Eon Reality* estimated that the 3D Customer Interaction Management market would be 10 percent of the CAD market by 2012, or approximately $800 million.

The simulation based learning market (SBL), as an extension of e-learning and changing learning environments, was rapidly expanding in applications for the military, education, and healthcare industries (e.g. simulated surgical procedures for interns and residents). On the fun side, simulation-based 3D learning experiences also included the video game industry with its interactive game experiences like the popular Nintendo Wii, Play-Station 3, and Xbox 360. The overall market for SBL was projected in 2009 to reach $1.5 billion by 2012.

However, perhaps the biggest money-maker for the industry in 2009 was the explosion of virtual desktop technology. In a report dated March 26, 2009 Gartner forecast that "Worldwide HVD [hosted virtual desktop] revenue would grow from about $1.5 billion in 2009, which is less than 1 percent of the worldwide professional PC market, to $65.7 billion in 2013, which will be equal to more than 40 percent of the worldwide professional PC market," having a compound growth rate (CAGR) from 2009 to 2013 of a astounding 113 percent each year. Part of its success will be due to the fact that it is a green technology, allowing companies to save money by increasing the life cycle of hardware, consolidating hardware, decreasing energy consumption, and recycling current hardware if necessary (such as turning current desktops into thin clients).

INDUSTRY LEADERS

Silicon Graphics Inc. Silicon Graphics Inc. (SGI) is one of the significant players in the VR field. The company is a leading supplier of visual computing and high performance systems. Its products include a broad range of computers, from desktop workstations to servers and high-end supercomputers. With corporate offices in Mountain View, California, and offices in 60 sites throughout the world, SGI manufactures and markets its systems to the communications, energy, entertainment, government, manufacturing, and science industries.

In 1994 SGI launched its Reality Center, a visualization facility for group virtual reality, which is used by hundreds of government and business employees. Furthermore, SGI provided VR technology to the new DisneyQuest entertainment complex in Orlando. Its core VR products include Onyx2 and InfiniteReality, which offer computer graphics and high performance for the VR experience. SGI also developed the Onyx2 InfiniteReality System, a virtual reality supercomputer, which is currently used by the National Center for Supercomputing Applications, a unit of the University of Illinois. This supercomputer allows researchers to process high-resolution visualizations of their applications as they run them.

The company celebrated its 10th anniversary of the SGI Reality Center Environment in July 2004. At that time, SGI reported a total of 670 SGI Reality Centers operating in key markets. These included oil and gas exploration, pharmaceutical research, product manufacturing, the sciences, museums, and academia. At the heart of every Reality Center facility was the SGI Onyx family of visual supercomputers, which could simultaneously process 3D graphics, imaging and video data in real time.

In 2009, SGI was acquired by Rackable Systems, the combination now known as Silicon Graphics. While SGI was not providing revenue or profit guidance for 2010, it expected sales for fiscal 2010 to be around $500 million.

Sun Microsystems, Inc. A chief competitor of SGI is Sun Microsystems. Although initially not a high-profile player in the virtual reality field, the company's 1998 acquisition of VPL Research changed that. In addition, Sun's operating systems are designed to be compatible with some of the leading VR authoring tools, including XvsLink and OrthoVista. Sun has been a leading manufacturer of graphics workstations used for mechanical computer-aided design (MCAD). Founded in 1982, Sun is a leading provider of hardware, software, and services for the Internet. Sun can be found in more than 150 countries around the world. Headquartered in Palo Alto, California, the company announced in April 2009 that it would be acquired by Oracle in January 2010. It posted 2008 revenues of $13.88 billion.

Autodesk Autodesk is the fourth largest personal computer (PC) software company worldwide. Its software products are focused on design solutions, visualization, and computer-aided automation software. Its Autocad, Autodesk, and Picture This software are used by architects, designers, engineers, animators, scientists, filmmakers, and educators to more easily conceptualize their ideas. Auto CAD2004 and Autodesk Revit 5 were honored with the CADENCE magazine Editors' Choice Award. CADENCE is the world's largest independent computer-aided design magazine. Industries served by Autodesk include manufacturing, utilities, civil engineering, media and entertainment. Based in San Rafael, California, Autodesk posted net revenues of $2.1 billion for fiscal 2008 with more than 4,000 employees. Its AutoCAD product line accounted for the vast majority of revenues, with more than five million worldwide users as of that year.

Other Leaders Government and university entities also play a role in VR, the most prominent of the former being the Department of Defense and NASA. Among the latter are the University of Illinois, home of the National Center for Supercomputing Applications, the University of Washington, and the University of North Carolina-Chapel Hill.

AMERICA AND THE WORLD

Some industry analysts expressed concern that America would fall behind other countries in the field of VR. This theme is familiar to those who observed the auto industry or various fields of electronics—Americans may have made the original innovations, but the Japanese were often more successful in developing and marketing the products. By the late 1990s, it appeared that Japan might well take the forefront in VR technology as well. Advantages enjoyed by the Japanese include the fact that Japanese industry in general—and high-tech industry in particular—operate according to national objectives, thus offering a modified form of the central planning espoused by command economies while enjoying the advantages of a free economy. The number of Japanese patent applications in the 1990s was double the number of those in the United States. Germany, France, and the United Kingdom also promise to be major players in the world of VR. As a result of Japanese efforts, the country boasts of an array of VR applications including entertainment, medicine, and training, which have reached strong levels of consumer acceptance.

Hong Kong Polytechnic University announced the installation of a $1.7 million virtual reality laboratory. The facility substantially enhanced the university's health education capabilities. Susie Lum, senior executive manager for nursing, said the facility "lowers risks associated with training on human patients and establishes standards and optimization of specific procedures."

To help prepare police officers in Australia's New South Wales to deal more effectively with such complex emergencies as hostage situations and major disasters, a VR training device called Minerva was introduced. The video-based equipment simulates real life crises and helps trainees to make split-second decisions. New South Wales Police Minister Paul Whelan, in introducing the VR trainer, likened its technology to simulators used in training race car drivers and airline pilots.

Canada's Royal LePage Relocation and Residential Real Estate divisions use videoconferencing to facilitate employee relocations for the Department of National

Defense and the Royal Canadian Mounted Police (RCMP) anywhere in Manitoba, Saskatchewan, Alberta, the Northwest Territories, and Nunavut. By using Novell technology, it was possible to establish virtual offices and communicate efficiently over great distances. *Computing Canada* also claimed the University of Toronto upgraded its videoconferencing system to facilitate assisting students while keeping professors at home. According to *Northern Ontario Business,* the Canadian mining industry has not realized the potential of VR technology. A VR lab at Laurentian University's Centre for Integrated Monitoring Technology in Sudbury had the capability to go through six months of discussions in 15 minutes.

RESEARCH AND DEVELOPMENT

THe VR industry had its own progeny by 2009, in the form of "Augmented Reality." This newly developing technology represented the capability to link the virtual world with the physical world through, for example, a "superman vision" in which a video image is superimposed with a 3D model of the same environment, along with the addition of hidden information accessible from sensors. From portable tablet PCs and glass free stereo displays to curved-screen and immersive rooms consisting of multi-channel projection walls, these new technologies are allowing people to move away from purely physical communication to augmented/mixed reality communications and interactions.

Researchers from the University of York and the University of Warwick in the United Kingdom were working on plans for a device able to manipulate five of a person's senses, to give the sensation of being somewhere else. While systems to control what a person sees and hears were well-established, touch, smell and taste were much harder to control realistically and still five to ten years away.

Many scientists have come to embrace the idea of immersing a user in a 3D environment on a computer screen without the use of wearable displays. Researchers are currently experimenting with these immersion VR environments. The National Center for Supercomputing Applications's computer animated virtual environment at the University of Illinois-Chicago is one such example. These environments completely surround the user, in effect transporting him or her to a different world through VR. The Laboratory for Integrated Medical Interface Technology at the University of Washington is another immersive environment. Other new immersive interface technologies are the Vision Dome from Alternate Realities Corp., Immersadesk from Pyramid Systems, and the Immersive Workbench from Fakespace.

Volumetric imaging was a new development researched by Parvis Soltan at the Naval Command, Control, and Ocean Surveillance Center in San Diego. Soltan's research used volumetric imaging devices, which place points of light in all three dimensions using a panel that is twisted into a helix. The image is projected onto the helix, which is spinning very fast to make it virtually invisible, and it can be viewed from the top as well as the sides. Soltan's device looked crude and was very loud, but the images it created were surprisingly good.

Another technology in development was the solid state crystal ball. Elizabeth Downing researched a whole new way to create 3D images by creating these images inside a solid piece of glass. The technology involves intersecting lasers in a fluoride-glass cube that contains elements that fluoresce when struck by these lasers. The energy created by the two intersecting beams releases visible photons, thus creating the image. Applications for the crystal ball technology include medicine, air traffic control, design engineering and, eventually, 3D television.

Researchers endeavored to add or improve tactile effect offered by VR environments. While visual simulation requires 15 to 20 frames per second to create the sensation of movement, the sensation of touch requires stimulation of the skin hundreds of times per second. Although rudimentary forms of touch virtual reality exist in video games, and pulse and vibrate when players encounter certain situations, researchers of companies, universities, and the military are trying to develop applications for defense and industry that have more realistic tactile effects.

BIBLIOGRAPHY

Amos, Kenigsberg. "Boot Camp Just Got Harder." *Discover,* August 2006.

Autodesk . Available from http://investors.autodesk.com/ phoenix.zhtml%3Fc%3D117861%26p%3Dirol-news Article%26ID%3D1003816%26highlight.

Autodesk Inc. "About Us—Company Profile." 21 March 2005. Available from http://media.corporate.ir.net/.

Barnes, Dan. "DAVOS: Office of the Future." *The Banker,* 1 January 2007.

Brutzman, Don. "X3D to International Standard." *Cover Pages,* 26 July 2004.

Ceurstemont, Sandrine. "Ultimate Virtual Reality Will Trigger Five Senses." *New Scientist,* 18 March.

Cole, Andrew. "Virtual Marketplace." *Telephony,* 11 December 2006.

"Company Fact Sheet." Silicon Graphics Inc., 21 March 2005. Available from www.sgi.com/.

"Digital Branding: Virtual Becomes Reality." *New Media Age,* 3 May 2007.

ECT News Business Desk. "Sun Microsoft Reports Profit." *MacNews,* 20 July 2004.

"Gartner predicts $65.7 billion in VDI revenue and 49 million users in 2013—Are you READY?" 11 November 2009. Available from http://www.gcloud3.com/2009/11/gartner/.

Helfer, Doris Small. "Virtual Reference in Libraries: Status and Issues." *Searcher,* February 2003.

Hilson, Gary. "Virtual Reality Comes of Age." *Computing Canada,* 28 February 2003.

Holahan, Catherine. "It's Carlton, Your Cyber Doorman." *Business Week Online,* 12 June 2007. Available from www.businessweek.com.

"Hoover's Company Capsules." *Hoover's Online,* 2007. Available from www.hoovers.com.

"How Large is the Virtual Reality Market Size ?" *Eon Rreality,* 25 September 2009.

"In the Boardroom." *Presentations,* May 2003.

"Inside Second Life's Data Centers." *InformationWeek,* 5 March 2007.

"Iowa State to Unveil the Most Realistic Virtual Reality Room in the World." *Space Daily,* 29 March 2007.

Lanier, Jaron. "Today, Virtual Games. Tomorrow, Virtual Worlds Where You Can Turn into DNA, Play a Piano, and Merge with your Computer." *Discover,* May 2007.

McCall, Margo. "Virtual Tradeshows Persist in Reality." *Tradeshow Week,* 2 June 2003.

McConnon, Aili, and Neil Gross. "Virtual Help for Real Pain." *Business Week,* 23 April 2007.

Mraz, Stephen. "Controls That Float in Midair." *Machine Design,* 5 June 2003.

"New VIS/SIM Report Now Available from Insight Media." *Insight Media,* 30 June 2004.

"On the Battlefield." *Presentations,* May 2003.

"Really Virtual Reality." *Science Daily,* 29 May 2009.

Rupley, Sebastian. "Virtual-Reality Renaissance." *PC Magazine,* July 2006.

Smith, Justin, and Charles Hudson. "Inside Virtual Goods: The U.S. Virtual Goods Market 2009–2010." Available from http://www.insidevirtualgoods.com.

Stacklin, Jeff. "Proposal Would Add Tech Touch to Art Appreciation at Museum." *Crain's Cleveland Business,* 9 June 2003.

"Sun Microsystems Reports Final Results for Full Fiscal Year." Sun Microsystems, 1 August 2008. Available from http://www.sun.com/aboutsun/pr/2008-08/sunflash.20080801.1.xml.

Van Voorhis, Bon., Jr "Virtual Reality…It's (Not) Only Make Believe." *Implement & Tractor,* January-February 2003.

"VRML (Virtual Reality Modeling Language) and X3D." *Cover Pages,* 2 August 2004. Available from www.coverpages.org/.

VOICE RECOGNITION SYSTEMS AND SOFTWARE

SIC CODE(S)

7372

3829

INDUSTRY SNAPSHOT

By the millenium, voice recognition (or speech recognition) systems had come into their own, taking hold in a number of industries that for years had looked upon the technology with a just-around-the-corner gaze. By improving on error rates in the translation of natural-voice input, voice recognition (VR) technology finally became efficient enough to enjoy widespread application and was poised to explode.

The uses for voice recognition (VR) systems and software are many and expanding quickly. One of the most prominent and established applications for VR technology is in the enhancement of office productivity. Several technologies are on the market allowing for quick and accurate voice dictation and for voice-based computer controls. Industrial applications afford companies streamlined inventory management and order processing.

VR systems are also an element of the biometrics industry, generating high level security systems through voice-based identification and verification. Banks and similar institutions were busily installing VR systems into their customer call centers, cutting down the account verification process. The convergence of wireless and other remote technologies with Internet applications also pushed the development of VR software for verification with electronic commerce.

The Internet played an enormous role in speeding the growth of the VR systems and software industry. As more and more people began to place a premium on perpetual connectivity, the rapidly changing work environment and fast-paced economy drove many to require Internet connections at all hours of the day and without restrictions as to location. As a result, VR technology sped to market to allow commuters and others to check stock quotes, news, and e-mail, and even perform routine business tasks via voice commands while en route between locations. Typical of the technology's drive toward more efficient office productivity, voice recognition systems were even cropping up in automobiles in an attempt to capitalize on perhaps the last untapped market for office connectivity.

BACKGROUND AND DEVELOPMENT

Judith Markowitz in *Using Speech Recognition* traced the development of speech recognition devices back to Alexander Graham Bell in the 1870s, though the result of his research was the telephone. Several decades later, a Hungarian scientist, Tihamer Nemes, sought a patent for a speech transcription apparatus that relied on the soundtracks of movies. Nemes wanted the device to recognize and transcribe speech sequences. The patent office, however, rejected the proposal. VR technology did not advance as quickly as Bell and Nemes had hoped. About 90 years after the initial endeavor to create a speech transcriber, AT&T Bell Laboratories finally developed a device that could recognize speech, especially digits, when uttered by a human voice. Matching a vocal stimulus with recorded patterns, the device required a lot of tuning before it could recognize someone's speech, yet it was said to have almost 99 percent accuracy once successfully tuned.

Research in the mid-1960s taught developers a lesson: voice recognition technology depended on perceiving subtle and complex oral input—abilities researchers could not reasonably hope to imbue their devices with, according to Markowitz. Consequently, researchers limited their focus to a series of lesser goals that one day might lead to a more comprehensive and powerful voice recognition system. They devoted their study to developing devices that could recognize a single person's voice, known as speaker-dependent technology. The devices used oral stimuli punctuated by small pauses to allow the machine to process the input and had small vocabularies of about 50 words. Speaker-dependent technology requires a training period: the speaker records sample pronunciations so that the device can create an archive of speech patterns and note a speaker's idiosyncratic inflections and cadences. Speakers must pause after each word with discrete devices. Hence, continuous speech is not possible with such technology and using a discrete word device demands patience.

The rudiments of continuous speech recognition did not come until the 1970s. This technology did not become functional until the 1980s and remained under refinement in the 1990s. Threshold Technologies, Inc., created the first commercial VR product in the early 1970s, according to Markowitz. Threshold's VIP 100 had a small vocabulary and used a discrete-word, speaker-dependent format, but, Markowitz reported, it proved moderately successful nonetheless.

Encouraged by these successes, the Advanced Research Projects Agency (ARPA) started to experiment with voice recognition technology. ARPA pushed for large vocabulary, continuous speech processing devices and helped launch the industry's collaboration with artificial intelligence research, according to Markowitz. ARPA also took a comprehensive approach to voice recognition technology, exploring the influence of word meaning, word structure, sentence structure, and contextual and social factors. By 1976, Markowitz related, ARPA created systems that had vocabularies of over 1,000 words, could process some continuous speech, could recognize the speech of several language users, had an artificial syntax, and recognized better than 90 percent of their input. ARPA contracted Carnegie Mellon University (CMU), Bolt Beranek and Newman, and the Massachusetts Institute of Technology to build these systems.

Markowitz reported that Carnegie Mellon University (CMU) developed one of the most successful early VR systems, Harpy, which could recognize over 1,000 words with an error rate of about 5 percent. CMU also implemented hidden Markov modeling (HMM) technology in its Dragon device, which generated or predicted letter sequences based on language immersion. HMM became a staple part of most of the major voice recognition applications that followed. By 1985, 1,000 word systems

were still considered large, especially for commercial products. However, Speech Systems, Inc., developed a product with an extremely large vocabulary for its time in 1986, the PE100, which could recognize as many as 20,000 words in continuous speech, and the system was not speaker-dependent. In the late 1980s, Dragon Systems raised the ante by creating a 30,000-word device, though it required discrete speech. Continuous speech voice recognition (VR) technology became much more viable in the 1980s, and so did technology that could tolerate some background noise. The 1980s also brought the advent of portable VR devices, according to Markowitz. The machines of the early 1980s sold for as much as several thousand dollars and had only small vocabularies, whereas those of the late 1980s sold for a few hundred dollars replete with vocabularies of over 1,000 words.

As personal computer (PC) prices fell in the mid-1990s, companies began to develop computer-based VR applications. In 1994, Philips Dictation Systems led the foray with software containing a large vocabulary that could process continuous speech. VR also began to expand its commercial potential at this point: companies integrated VR technology in videocassette recorder remote controls, air traffic control devices, and general computer software.

The accelerating growth of the industry, according to Ian Grayson of *Voice&Data,* was due to two main factors: improvement in recognition accuracy and a move by vendors to embrace open standards. In the past, VR systems had been constrained by small word dictionaries, with recognition rates hovering around 80 percent. This recognition rate was not acceptable for serious commercial or professional applications. However, by 2004, most recognition engines had vocabularies of more than 30,000 words, enough to cover most dialogues or interactions. By 2005 that figure had risen to 100,000 words. Moreover, the accuracy rates had improved to well into the high 90 percent levels.

Major software developers provided simple VR technology in many of their applications, including the Microsoft and Apple operating systems. The leading voice recognition products of the first decade of the 2000s united two components that were found only separately in the previous 5 to 10 years: large vocabularies and continuous recognition. Top of the line speech-to-text software, for example, wielded 60,000-word vocabularies and could process continuous speech. While these developments still did not quite allow for natural, everyday speech, clearly enunciated speech returned results of 98 percent accuracy through the top VR systems, which could usually keep up with relatively fast-speaking paces. Typically, the programs required a few "training" sessions to become accustomed to the user's voice, vocabulary, and syntax.

Business Not only had standard dictation software benefited from the advances in voice recognition (VR) technologies, but businesses also turned to voice recognition applications to perform many tasks including providing automated telephone service, selling and trading stocks and bonds, and providing general information. Banks, brokerages, credit corporations, telephone services, online databases, and other businesses chose VR technology because in addition to improved accuracy, it made fewer mistakes in general than did human counterparts, about 30 percent fewer on average. Most major airlines used VR technology for reservations and flight information, and telephone companies provided directory service by using interactive speech recognition software.

Customer contact centers utilized speech recognition technologies to improve productivity and customer service. The Gartner Group technology research firm predicted that during the first decade of the 2000s, 30 percent of the automated lines in contact centers responded to customers' speech. Agents rated the technology high because its efficiency in effectively answering and processing calls allowed them to focus on more complex customer service tasks. *Card Marketing* claimed inbound VR calls from consumers to card issuers were becoming significant marketing tools. According to the publication, Boston-based SpeechWorks International Vice President of Worldwide Marketing Steven Chambers said speech recognition technology would save marketers money by giving quick solutions to routine questions or by immediately sending callers to live operators for more complex issues or for cross-selling opportunities.

Clearly, more businesses turned to voice recognition systems to handle customer telephone calls. According to Datamonitor, spending on speech-enabled self-service applications will double to $1.2 billion in North America by 2008. Another estimate by Opus Research of San Francisco predicted the market for call center voice technology would double from 2006 to 2009, ending near $1.2 billion. Datamonitor claimed such automation delivers significant savings over offshore calls handled by call centers in places like India. In 2007 London-based bank Lloyds TSB announced plans to close its contact center in India, which was used to handle overflow calls from the United Kingdom, because the use of a VR phone system had eliminated the need for it.

Voice recognition (VR) systems in some cases even helped contribute to the long-fabled paperless work environment. Especially in industrial warehouses, the technology was eliminating the necessity for large stacks of order forms and inventory items. Workers could track items and orders while keeping their hands free, simply reading bar code numbers into portable microphone headsets. The central computer system then organized

the product information as necessary. Speech recognition has also been used in factories to control machinery, enter data, inspect parts, and take inventory, thereby opening up a wealth of employment opportunities previously closed to those with disabilities.

Lernout & Hauspie Speech Products, N.V., meanwhile, developed its own simultaneous translation system to translate from one language into another in a natural voice. With a voice-to-text system receiving the words and text-to-voice software sending them back out with a text-to-text translator in between, Lernout & Hauspie's system produced a translation with a delay of about only one second.

Banking and Security Banks rapidly embraced VR technology beginning in the late 1990s. High-level systems for banks and other security-dependent institutions usually could identify a voice after only a few spoken words. In such institutions, customers could be relieved of the requirements of normal security checks, including passwords, mothers' maiden names, and so on. In place of such processes, the customers' voices would simply be checked against a stored "voice bank" for verification.

Banking systems also benefited by shortening the duration of phone calls into the remote access system, which then freed up the lines for other calls and thus other business. According to some analysts, VR technology could reduce the cost per call to banks by 32 cents, translating into hundreds of thousands of dollars in savings over the course of a year. Guardian Life and the U.S. pension division of the Canadian-based Manulife Financial Corp. added VR technology to their 401(k) call centers. The Gartner Group, Inc. technology research firm noted that such call centers were primed for incorporation of such technology since customers frequently call to access basic account information quickly.

Fidelity Investments, known officially as FMR Corp., uses Nuance Communications technology for its Fidelity Automated Service Telephone system, relieving customers of the burden of remembering long account numbers and ticker symbols when checking account information and stock quotes and performing transactions. The system was designed to handle 750,000 to 1 million calls daily.

Telephone-Based Internet Capability The desire for perpetual Internet connectivity was a central driving force behind new developments in voice recognition technology. A number of companies developed systems whereby a central computer could recognize a customer's voice to deliver e-mail and Internet based information over telephones. For businesspeople in constant travel away from a computer, new technologies were under way that provided the ability to compose new e-mail messages over the telephone using VR applications and then send them as text.

The BeVocal service, meanwhile, used voice recognition software in conjunction with a central cellular phone service to allow subscribers to call and get real-time information, including directions and e-mail, from an almost conversational computer. Voice-operated direction systems typically made use of global positioning satellites that mapped out selected areas, picking up on the signal from the driver's system to figure out the best route to the desired location.

Automobiles In its "Automotive Voice Technology Market Outlook 2005," Strategy Analytics, an international research and consulting firm, predicted that nearly 50.3 million vehicles will have VR technology communications systems by 2010, representing a 30 to 40 percent market penetration. The capabilities of the installed VR systems will include such functions as dialing a cell phone, controlling the radio, programming navigation systems, and requesting emergency service. The most marketable strategy was predicted to be the development of more stringent hands-free safety initiatives, especially for cellular phone operation. Competition from non-VR applications, such as the BMW iDrive or touch screen navigation systems, would keep the industry at the cutting edge.

By 2001, many GM models already included OnStar's Virtual Advisor system to enable Web and e-mail access through cellular phones and voice recognition systems. Unlike Auto PC—Microsoft's in-car information and entertainment system with a speech interface—however, Virtual Advisor was wired to few of the automobile's actual systems, usually only the radio or other accessories.

Connectivity was not the only application for VR systems in automobiles. Visteon Automotive Systems developed a voice-activated computer system that was installed in the Jaguar S-Type to control the car's normal accessory functions, such as the heating and air conditioning systems and radio controls, in addition to voice-activated telephone dialing. However, while the Auto PC is fairly easily transferable between vehicles, Visteon's is more or less hardwired into the car's system and cannot be easily removed.

Internet "Speak" New VR-based special access applications for the disabled, introduced in 1998, included several speech-activated Web browsers and a talking Web browser from IBM Corp. Conversational Computing Corp., known as Conversa, launched Converse Web, an inexpensive (under $70) voice-activated Web browser that allowed any user with a multimedia computer to traverse the expanse of the Internet via oral commands without using a mouse or keyboard. Motorola, Inc., took

the concept one step further with its innovative Voice Markup Language (VoxML), a voice-activated language for voice-based browsers and Web pages. Motorola indicated its intent to submit VoxML to the World Wide Web Consortium for use as a standardized language. VoxML held the potential for Internet based telephone conversations, whereby users would converse with the Internet over standard telephone lines.

Medical Transcription Despite the anticipated continued growth of the industry, the medical community was more reticent in adopting the technology. It came in two versions. One, used by hospitals, was the transcriptionist-editor model, where medical transcriptionists were only required to review reports initially transcribed by machines (at a 40 percent cost savings). The other model required the physician to be the editor. The cost was not prohibitive.

The e-DOCS transcription service ran on AVRI's Voice Commander 99 software, provided services to physicians via the Internet, and offered 24-hour online turnaround for transcribed documents. Physicians earned discounts as high as 20 percent for realizing the highest accuracy rate of 95 to 100 percent. The discount incentives were an effort to encourage optimization of the technology, which required that dictators speak very clearly. AVRI offered to physicians contracts that included handheld dictation equipment along with the basic computer and printer. The Voice Commander software, conceived in 1994, was patented in 1997. By 2000, e-DOCS.net provided Internet-based medical transcription services to about 6,000 physicians in the United States.

Another industry giant, IBM, introduced new VR technology in 2007 that recognizes emotional cues in a person's voice, can interpret different dialects and phrasing, and allows for realistic commands for mobile devices. Many of the firm's new products work in several languages, with Arabic, English, and Mandarin the most popular due to business and government demand. According to *Information Week*, Travelers could soon be able to translate conversations with foreigners in an instant through laptops with microphones and software that functions pretty much like human interpreters," using IBM's new technology.

CURRENT CONDITIONS

In October 2009 *Consumer Search* magazine updated its Best voice recognition software list by concluding that Dragon NaturallySpeaking 10 Preferred was almost universally regarded in reviews as the best voice recognition software, with the potential for 97 to 99 percent accuracy. The Standard edition of Dragon NaturallySpeaking 10 works with AOL Instant Messenger, MS Word, Internet Explorer and WordPerfect, but not Excel. Windows

Vista and Windows 7 include Windows Speech Recognition at no additional charge. Reviewers point to MacSpeech Dictate as the best speech recognition choice for those using Macintosh operating systems.

Mobile speech recognition software continued to enjoy expanding markets and applications going into 2010. One of the biggest products to hit the North American market by storm, with millions of users in less than a year, was Vlingo. The era of mobile users being restricted to triple tapping and tiny keyboards was facing strong competition from VR. With Vlingo, after a simple download to their devices, consumers can talk to their mobile devices using ordinary speech to instantly send a text or an e-mail message, call a friend, create a note to themselves, or search the Internet. In 2009, Nokia was preloading Vlingo on the New Nokia N97 & Nokia E72 models.

In late 2008, OfCom, in its *Third International Communications Market Report* (summarized by BNet) found that mobile voice revenues were still larger than those from mobile data, but mobile data revenues were growing five times faster (using 2007 data). It further reported that total mobile voice revenues in the United Kingdom, France, Germany, Italy, the United States, Canada and Japan increased by 31 percent to $188 billion over a five-year period (2002-07), while corresponding data revenues increased by 171 percent to $52 billion. The rise was not such a surprise, the report noted, given the growth in SMS usage and other data services. The report put the global communications market at $1.3 trillion at that time.

After the 2008 and 2009 economic crisis, the automotive industry, scrambling for new gadgetry to attract consumers, focused on new VR technology to further develop vehicle response systems for basic voice commands. Acura, Audi, Honda, Infiniti, Lexus, and Subaru all announced 2010 models incorporating new VR technology for ignitions, security, GPS, etc.

In 2008, British market analyst Datamonitor reported that healthcare automation (primarily medical transcription and electronic medical records) was driving growth in the use of speech recognition software for transcription and dictation. It projected the market for healthcare speech recognition technology to hit $340 million by 2013. According to Nuance in 2008, $15 billion was spent on medical transcription in North America and Europe each year.

INDUSTRY LEADERS

Dragon Systems, Inc. of Newton, Massachusetts, had a total of nine voice recognition (VR) products on the market with more being developed. Founded in 1982, Dragon focused predominantly on speech-related technology. A key innovator, in 1984 Dragon's VR technology became the first to be integrated in a portable computer. The Advanced Research Projects Agency also commissioned Dragon to develop speaker-independent, continuous speech recognition applications in the mid-1980s. In 1990, medical application developers used Dragon's technology for a speech recognition information management system. By 1994, Dragon had increased its flagship DragonDictate's vocabulary to 60,000 words, the industry's largest at that time. In 1997, Dragon introduced current industry leader NaturallySpeaking, combining a large vocabulary with continuous speech recognition capabilities as the world's first general-purpose large vocabulary continuous speech recognition application. The company withdrew an offer to go public in 1999, and was purchased the following year by Lernout & Hauspie.

Microsoft entered the speech recognition market with the introduction of its Speech Server 2004 Standard Edition and Enterprise Edition, unveiled at the Speech TEK Conference in San Francisco in March 2004. With this product, developers can add speech capabilities to existing Web applications by adding code based on XML (Extensible Markup Language) and SALT (Speech Application Language Tags) technologies using Visual Studio. Net. In March 2007 Microsoft announced plans to acquire Tellme Networks in its effort to provide services that use voice technology to access information and services. More than 40 million people per month access Tellme's services, according to the company.

Silicon Valley VR firm Nuance (formerly SoftScan) was making headlines with its innovative products and global accessibility. Such big names as British Airways, Sprint PCS, UPS, Amtrak, Yahoo, and Onstar utilize software and support services of this leader. Nuance also built an invisible Web browser called Voyager to allow for voice-activated Web browsing directly over telephones. Most telephone-based Web browsers were activated by pushing telephone buttons and could display only a few lines at a time on a tiny screen. With the Voyager browser, users could navigate bookmarked Web sites purely by voice commands. Moreover, sending or receiving personalized information could be verified by voice recognition. Nuance Communications acquired Philips Speech Recognition Systems in late 2008 for $96.1 million to expand its healthcare-related business in Europe. The company stated that wireless communications was the fastest growing market for VR technology in the first decade of the 2000s. Said Peter Mahoney of Nuance, "Mobile is growing faster than the rest of our business...at 30 percent, while our overall business is growing at about 20 percent." The company reported fiscal 2009 revenues of $1.96 billion.

Vocollect, a global leader in voice-directed work, conducted business in 21 countries on five continents, Vocollect is known for its trademark products Vocollect,

Talkman, and Voice-Directed Work. *Inc.* magazine named the company in its 24th Annual *"Inc.500* List of America's Fastest Growing Private Companies" in 2004.

Fonix Corp. attempted to redefine VR technology by developing new approaches to voice recognition. Dissatisfied with the direction that voice recognition software was heading, Fonix sought alternative technology and models to replace some of the industry standards of the mid-1990s. One innovative product has been Fonix's VoiceCentral Lite that lets users access the information needed from a Pocket PC or a linked personal digital assistant (PDA). Another Fonix product, iSpeak, is a text-to-speech tool that reads e-mail and text files in a natural-sounding human voice. Incorporated in 1985, Fonix strives to develop speaker independent, real time, natural language software that can house large vocabularies and recognize speech with greater than 97 percent accuracy. The firm maintained licensing agreements with Infineon Technologies, Lucent Technologies, Nortel Networks Corp., and General Magic, Inc.Salt Lake City-based Fonix conducts research and creates VR technologies, which it then licenses to other companies. The company reported revenues of $1.3 billion for 2008.

IBM Corp., the world's largest computer firm, continued to have a strong presence in the industry. IBM's core voice recognition product during this period was ViaVoice, in its executive, office, and home versions. ViaVoice, a continuous speech program, features a 64,000-word base vocabulary, a 260,000-word backup dictionary, voice correction, and recognition of a wide range of voice frequencies. The ViaVoice Millennium model integrates automatically with the leading Web browsers, facilitatinge-mail and chat-room dictation. IBM also makes Simply Speaking and Simply Speaking Gold, VR word-processing applications.

The AT&T spinoff Lucent Technologies, carrying on the vision of Alexander Graham Bell, extensively developed voice recognition technology. Specific to VR technology, Lucent created security systems, voice processing technology, networking systems, and telephones. One of its key products was Conversant, an automated speech recognition application with a 2,000-word vocabulary that allows clients 24-hour access to their accounts. Lucent also developed speech recognition technology for faxes and computer networking and has developed Speech Application Platform, a programming platform for creating speech-based applications. It is based in Murray Hill, New Jersey.

RESEARCH AND TECHNOLOGY

In addition to battling traditional obstacles such as creating large vocabularies and implementing contextual information, the Speech Recognition Application Programming Interface Committee—which included IBM, Dragon, Lernout & Hauspie, and Philips Dictation Systems—also aimed at the development of a programming interface in order to standardize VR software. This programming interface would enable independent software developers to integrate VR technology into their applications.

The identification market also sought convergence between computer-based encryption systems and voice recognition systems. Currently, the Internet employs a public key infrastructure operating system encouraging public key cryptography. As the Internet incorporates voice-controlled activity, however, encryption must be available for VR technology if the development is not to hamper electronic commerce.

For security purposes in general, voice recognition encompasses the standard set by the Speaker Verification Application Programming Interface, which included the U.S. Department of Defense, the Internal Revenue Service, and the Immigration and Naturalization Service, among other organizations.

BIBLIOGRAPHY

"Automotive Voice Recognition Market Penetration Up Nearly 40 Percent by 2010, Says Strategic Analytics." *The Industry Analyst Reporter,* 31 March 2005.

Biswas, Soma. "Judge Clears Lernout's U.S. Liquidation." *The Daily Deal,* 2 June 2003.

Bova, Bob. "Look Mom, No Hands: Implementing Speech-Enabled Applications." *Law Enforcement Technology,* March 2007.

Brodkin, Jon. "Speech Recognition Technology Will Change the Way You Drive." *Network World,* 13 February 2007.

Cassavoy, Liane. "Speak Up." *Entrepreneur,* May 2003.

Chin, Tyler."Speech Impediment: Technology Getting Slow Start" *America's Medical News,* 14 June 2004.

Costlow, Terry. "Finally, a Listener: Cars Begin Adopting Voice Recognition that Understands You." *Design News,* 27 February 2006.

Evers, Joris. "Microsoft's Entry to Stir Speech Recognition Market." *InfoWorld,* 16 March 2004.

"Gartner Reports that Loquendo Has Highest Worldwide Speech Market Growth Rate." *SpeechTech,* 21 March 2005.

"Google Tests Directory Assistance for Phones." *eWeek,* 7April 2007.

"Hoover's Company Capsules." *Hoover's Online,* 2009. Available from www.hoovers.com.

Hu, David. "Newest Nintendo Handheld Console Will Support Voice Recognition." *Voice Application Publications,* May 2004.

"IBM Touts Speech Technology Enabling Real-Life Improvements." *InformationWeek,* 13 February 2007.

Morrison, Diane See. "Ofcom Report: Mobile Data Revenues Growing Five Times Faster Than Voice." 20 November 2008. Available from http://resources.bnet.com/topic/advertising+%2526+promotion+and+mobile+and+revenue.html.

"It's Official: Microsoft to Acquire Tellme Networks." *Newsweek,* 14 March 2007.

"Peabody, Mass.-Based ScanSoft Marks Milestone with Upgraded Dictation Program." *Knight Ridder/Tribune Business News,* 3 March 2003.

"The Perfect Pitch: Microsoft and Tellme Know the Secret of Good Business Communication." *Business Week Online,* 20 March 2007. Available from www.businessweek.com.

Pizzi, Richard. "Market for Healthcare Speech Recognition Technology to Hit $340 Million by 2013." *Healthcare IT News,* 30 June 2008.

Saran, Cliff. "IBM Talks Up Voice-Based." *Computer Weekly,* 15 August 2006.

"Speech Recognition Comes of Age." *Voice&Data Online,* August 2004.

Spring, Christopher. "Productivity Gains of Speech-Recognition Technology." *Health Management Technology,* January 2003.

"Vlingo Brings Mobile Voice Recognition Technology to Europe With Availability on the Ovi Store by Nokia." *PR Hub,* 1 September 2009. Available from www.newscom.com/cgi-bin/prnh/20090901/358224.

"Vocollect Closes 2004 With Record Growth." Vocollect Press Release, 15 February 2005. Available from www.vocollect.com/.

Wagley, John. "Reviving the Oral Tradition." *Institutional Investor,* February 2003.

"The Word in Voice Recognition Market is Consolidation." *RCR Wireless News,* 21 May 2007.

"Xbox 360 Video Game to Feature Voice Recognition." *ExtremeTech.com,* 19 December 2006.

Zolkos, Rodd. "Science Fact: Voice Systems Next Step in Customer Contact." *Business Insurance,* 1 April 2007.

WASTE MANAGEMENT

———————————■———————————

SIC CODE(S)

4212

4953

4959

7699

INDUSTRY SNAPSHOT

In a world in which almost everything seems to be disposable, the task of managing the collection and eventual disposal—or recycling—of this nation's ever-growing mountains of waste is a monumental one indeed. In 2007, the United States generated approximately 254 million tons of trash. Of this amount, 63.3 million tons were recovered for recycling. According to *Waste Age,* in 2008, solid waste management was a $40 billion industry.

The waste management industry faces the task not only of handling the solid waste from household, commercial, business, and institutional sources but also of safely disposing of a broad range of hazardous wastes, the volume of which is also growing almost exponentially. Under the definitions of the Resource Conservation and Recovery Act passed by Congress in 1976 and administered by the Environmental Protection Agency (EPA), hazardous wastes include disposable materials that burn readily or are corrosive or explosive. Wastes that contain specified amounts of toxic chemicals may also be considered hazardous. Hazardous wastes are found in a wide range of physical forms, including liquid, solid, and semisolid. According to the U.S. Census Bureau, more than 38 million tons of hazardous waste were produced in 2005 in the United States. Some of the more common generators of hazardous waste are auto repair shops, dry cleaners, hospitals, exterminators, photo processing centers, chemical manufacturers, petroleum refiners, and electroplating companies.

Clearly the biggest sector of the waste management industry is that involved in the handling of solid waste. In a study commissioned by the Environmental Research and Education Foundation (EREF), the solid waste sector was defined as those organizations that collect solid waste and handle it in various ways. Some of these are disposal, recycling, incineration, and composting. Solid waste, in the context of the EREF study, was considered to include all non-hazardous waste sent from its site of origin for final disposal, in whatever form. Included in this category are household wastes; commercial, business, or institutional waste; special waste; construction and demolition debris; regulated medical waste; yard waste; sludge; and scrap tires. Using this broader definition of solid waste from the EREF, the magnitude of the waste management task becomes clearer.

ORGANIZATION AND STRUCTURE

The waste management industry is divided into two major segments, the larger of which deals with the disposal and recycling of non-hazardous solid waste and the smaller of which is charged with the delicate responsibility of handling hazardous wastes. Each segment is further divided into operations in both the public and private sectors. The private sector includes both companies that are publicly held and those that are privately held, while the public sector includes municipalities (such as cities, towns, and counties) as well as solid waste districts and authorities that have been established by such municipalities.

The bulk of the 38 million tons of hazardous waste generated annually comes from commercial and industrial

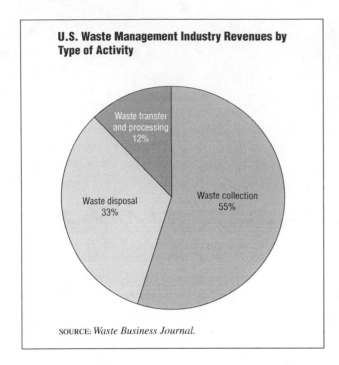

U.S. Waste Management Industry Revenues by Type of Activity

Waste transfer and processing 12%

Waste disposal 33%

Waste collection 55%

SOURCE: *Waste Business Journal.*

operations that deal in such materials. However, even the average household generates a fair amount of hazardous waste, most of it in the form of paint, mineral spirits (such as paint thinners, batteries, pesticides and herbicides), and used motor oil. Some public sector facilities handle hazardous wastes from homes and small businesses, but the lion's share of the hazardous waste management business is controlled by large companies that specialize in the safe disposal of such materials. The regulations of the Resource Conservation and Recovery Act (RCRA) govern the handling of hazardous wastes, including the operations of all commercial, industrial, and government facilities that generate, carry, process, store, or dispose of such waste. The regulations are designed to ensure that such hazardous waste is properly managed from the moment it is generated until it is eventually disposed of or destroyed.

BACKGROUND AND DEVELOPMENT

The first U.S. solid waste incinerator was built by the U.S. Army in 1885. Others quickly followed, and by the end of the 1930s, the United States had more than 700 such units. However, the focus was solely on the convenient disposal of waste materials and not the generation of energy. All that began to change after the passage in 1970 of the Resource Recovery Act, which provided resources and incentives for the development of new technologies to transform solid waste not only into energy but into alternative materials as well. Numerous methods of converting refuse-derived fuel (RDF) into energy were developed during the 1970s, including systems pioneered

by Combustion Power Company, Garrett Research & Development Company, Black Clawson, Monsanto, and St. Louis-Union Electric.

The evolution of the U.S. waste management industry from the beginning of the twentieth century was extremely dramatic, mirroring the radical changes in the nature of waste over the century or so. For much of the first half of the twentieth century, the main items in the waste stream were ashes from fireplaces and incinerators, textiles, metals, glass, paper, food waste, wood, and reusable products. In the early 1900s, most waste was collected by horse-drawn open wagons with high sideboards. As the century progressed, the horses were withdrawn from service in favor of the first so-called scavenger trucks, which, like their horse-drawn predecessors, featured open boxes with high sides. Up to 75 percent of all collected waste materials were recovered, with only 25 to 35 percent of the waste stream being ultimately disposed of. Recovered materials included textiles that were washed and sold to industry for use as rags; metals that were separated by grade and then sold to foundries and processors; and glass that was washed and sold to bootleggers, dairies, and wineries. Also recovered and given a second life were paper, food waste (sold for use as animal feed), and wood. Materials that were disposed of included ashes that were plowed into the soil and other nonrecoverables that were incinerated. Environmental concerns were virtually nonexistent.

The arrival on the scene of many revolutionary new products began to change the face of waste management after the end of World War II in 1945. In the 25 years between 1945 and the end of the 1960s, the waste stream swelled considerably with the addition of packaging for household convenience products, chemicals, pesticides, and commercial, construction, and industrial waste. Although waste collection during this period began with the same open scavenger trucks that had been used previously, they were soon replaced by the first closed box trucks and later by the earliest compaction body trucks. The amount of waste recovered dropped from a high of 75 percent to about half of all waste collected. Non-recoverable waste was generally disposed of in open burn dumps or municipal incinerators or barged out to sea to be dumped. In the late 1960s, as science and health researchers began to discover more about the adverse effects of air pollution, steps were taken to eliminate or at least reduce such pollution by eliminating such sources as open burning, backyard incinerators, and burn barrels. Landfills, which at best were loosely regulated previously, began to be held to more stringent sanitary standards as concerns mounted about public health and safety as well as environmental protection. The late 1960s also witnessed the beginning of a transition within the waste management industry, which prior to that time had been comprised almost exclusively of thousands of small, privately held companies.

During the 1970s and 1980s, as the volume of waste grew, so did concerns about the impact of waste disposal methods on the environment. In 1976, the Resource Conservation and Recovery Act (RCRA) was passed by the U.S. Congress as an amendment to the Solid Waste Disposal Act. The act and subsequent amendments gave the EPA authority over the handling, storage, treatment, and disposal of both solid waste and hazardous waste in all its various forms, including solid, semi-solid, liquid, and contained gas. This period witnessed the growing use of larger, high-efficiency compaction trucks in the collection of waste, which was made up largely of residential, commercial, and industrial waste. In 1970, about 7.5 percent of all waste collected was recycled; by 1980, the recovery rate had inched up to about 9 percent. During this two-decade period, the bulk of recovered materials consisted of metal, paper, and cardboard. Disposal facilities during this period included sanitary landfills and waste-to-energy incinerators.

In the 1990s and the early 2000s, the waste stream expanded at exponential rates, fueled by sharp increases in population and economic growth. Driven by exhortations from government and environmental authorities, recycling made significant strides. While only 17 percent of all waste was recovered in 1990, by 1997 that figure had almost doubled to 32 percent. The new push for the recycling of recoverable waste gave rise to a surge in programs to facilitate recovery efforts. Such programs included curbside recycling, buyback centers, recycling drop-offs, recycling centers, material recovery facilities, household hazardous waste collection programs, and construction and demolition waste processing facilities.

The waste management industry underwent substantial change, surviving price wars, massive consolidation efforts, shrinking profit margins, steadily more stringent regulation, and alarming high employee turnover rates. One of the hottest industries of the late 1980s and early 1990s, the industry began to experience the effects of overcapacity as more and more capital was invested, outpacing the demand for waste management services. To bring industry supply more in line with demand, the industry undertook to tighten its belt. Using the mergers and acquisitions route, many large companies moved aggressively to consolidate. Prominent among such moves in the late 1990s was the acquisition by WMI of Eastern Environmental Services in 1998 and the merger of BFI into Allied Waste Industries in 1999. Also active on the acquisitions front were European-based Vivendi and U.S. Liquids. Acting through its U.S. subsidiary, Onyx Environmental Services, Vivendi became the third largest player in the U.S. hazardous waste management business. To do so, the company acquired U.S. Filter, Superior Waste, Giant Cement Holdings, and select assets of WMI. One of the country's largest hazardous and non-hazardous wastewater treatment companies, U.S. Liquids also moved aggressively to expand its holdings, acquiring a number of smaller companies, including Romic Environmental Services, Waste Research & Recovery, and City Environmental.

In the wake of the industry's ambitious consolidation efforts, the price wars of the late 1980s and early 1990s were replaced by slowly increasing prices throughout the waste management business. The period witnessed a substantial increase in the number of service contracts awarded by large industrial and commercial companies to the waste management companies that provided them with the best service and not necessarily the lowest price.

PIONEERS IN THE FIELD

The business of waste management until the late 1960s and early 1970s was the realm of thousands of small companies, many of them family-owned. That all began to change in 1969 when cousins Tom Fatjo and Tom Deane, who had launched a garbage collection service they called American Refuse Systems (ARS) in 1967, acquired control of Browning-Ferris Machinery Company. Merging ARS into their new acquisition, the cousins renamed the larger company Browning-Ferris Industries (BFI). Refashioning BFI into a solid waste services company, they took the company public and in 1970 embarked on an ambitious acquisition drive, picking up numerous smaller companies in what was then more commonly called the garbage collection business. In the course of its drive to expand its hold on the waste management business, BFI acquired three companies owned by Harry Phillips, who came aboard at BFI as president and chief operating officer. By 1972, BFI had more than 4,200 employees and was operating in 26 states, Puerto Rico, and Canada. Before long, the company had grown into a multibillion-dollar global corporation. BFI in 1999 merged with Allied Waste Industries, under which name it continues to operate, the second-largest company in the waste management business.

Although Dean Buntrock first became involved in the waste management business in 1956, it was not until the early 1970s that he pulled together a network of family-owned operations into the giant Waste Management, Inc. (WMI), which went public in 1971. Shortly after the death of his father-in-law, Pete Huizenga, in the mid-1950s, Buntrock was persuaded to join the Huizenga family waste collection business. A little over a decade later, in 1968, he incorporated WMI as an umbrella organization under which the various Huizenga enterprises could be operated. After successfully pulling together all segments of the Huizenga family network into WMI, Buntrock took the company public in June 1971, raising $4 million in its initial offering that was used to buy equipment and retire debt. WMI in the first nine months of 1972 acquired 133 firms, bringing its total revenue for the year to $82 million. In 1998, WMI purchased Eastern Environmental Services, the nation's fifth largest waste hauler, in a $1.3 billion transaction. In 2004, WMI, based in Houston, was the largest U.S. waste management company with operations in all 50 states, the District of Columbia, Puerto Rico, Canada, and Mexico.

During the early 2000s, weak economic conditions led to a slump in the waste management industry. As consumers scaled back on spending, the level of waste they generated fell accordingly. In addition, the nation's levels of industrial and construction-related waste—which accounts for nearly a third of revenues for the industry's leading players—also decreased. Subsequently, landfills experienced overcapacity and falling prices.

Given the massive amount of waste the industry moves each year, one can imagine the negative effects of a prolonged delay in service. In the fall of 2003, approximately 8 million Chicago-area residents did not have to imagine such a dilemma; they got to experience it firsthand when 3,300 waste company employees represented by the Teamsters Union went on strike from October 1 to October 9. That July, the union had sought a 45 percent wage and benefits increase from the Chicago Area Refuse Haulers (CARH) Association, an organization representing 17 waste management firms. When workers went on strike, garbage piled up at the Chicago-area collection points, forcing city sanitation employees to step in. Federal mediation eventually reduced the Teamsters' desired increase to 30.5 percent. The strike led a group of residents to file a class action lawsuit against CARH in early 2004.

In the wake of heightened concerns about bioterrorism, the waste management industry was forced to contend with how to transport deadly biological agents such as anthrax. According to the August 1, 2003, issue of *Waste Age,* the Homeland Security Act of 2002 and the Public Health Security and Bio-terrorism Preparedness and Response Act of 2002 led Christine Todd Whitman, former administrator of the Environmental Protection Agency (EPA), to establish the National Homeland Security Research Center in Research Triangle Park, North Carolina. Its purpose is "to review disposal options for waste generated in a terrorist situation, including solid, hazardous and medical waste transport, treatment and disposal options." The publication also explained that "The EPA and leaders from the Washington, D.C.-based Association of State and Territorial Solid Waste Management Officials; Integrated Solid Waste Association; and National Solid Wastes Management Association, plus several waste companies are helping to identify areas of concern, develop guidance and offer waste management options."

Endeavors to increase recycling continued to be a major focus of the waste management industry, businesses, and individuals—in 2006, less than one-quarter of solid waste in the United States was being recycled; the rest was incinerated or buried in landfills. As part of the effort to positively affect statistics such as those, Electronic Recyclers of America (ERA) partnered with HMR, an Australia-based global surplus asset chain management service provider, in an effort to keep used computer and television components out of landfills. The ERA facility in Fresno is an electronic recycling location—the only one in the state with more than one cathode ray tube (CRT) crusher—that crushes and recycles CRTs and television sets. HMR recycles high-tech trash by transforming it into re-marketable commodities, extending the equipment's life and preventing it from entering landfills. According to John Bekiaris, HMR's U.S. CEO, "The most effective way to manage obsolete equipment is to either re-purpose it or recycle it."

At the same time, the San Francisco Bay Area Computer Recycling Project was launched by Goodwill Industries of San Francisco and Dell of Round Rock, Texas, as a pilot program for residents to drop off unwanted computers at no charge. Goodwill then collects the discards and separates materials with value to give to Dell's Asset Recovery Services. Proceeds from those sales are given to Goodwill and unsellable materials are recycled.

Honda's East Liberty plant in Ohio made major strides in its recycling efforts in the fall of 2005. Honda's central Ohio manufacturing operations had decreased their solid waste production by 66 percent and hazardous waste by 95 percent since the mid-1990s but continued to seek ways to make those numbers even better. Each month, the plant recycles some 700,000 to 800,000 gallons of industrial wastewater by a process of chlorination, followed by filtering; blue dye is then added, to distinguish it from drinking water. The recycled water is sent, via a special system of pipes, to designated holding tanks and used to operate toilets and urinals at that plant. The plant recycles approximately 9 million gallons of water a year, reducing Honda's usage of fresh water and decreasing the amount of wastewater that must be shipped to the city's treatment plant. Smaller programs have also been initiated to help increase the plant's percentages. For example, incorrectly threaded bolts, or those that fall on the floor, which were previously swept up and thrown away, are being swept up and put into a recycling bin, adding up to thousands of pounds of recyclables a year. Another way they have found to keep materials out of landfills is to use returnable containers for their packaging materials. An incentive program has also been initiated for employees, who can earn points for recycling efforts, which can be accumulated and turned in for a free new vehicle.

In mid-2005, the Department of Public Works of Denver's Denver Recycles expanded its residential recycling program by including seven new materials: corrugated cardboard, junk mail, paperboard, office paper, magazines and catalogs, phone books and brown paper bags. Denver residents were provided with larger, wheeled recycling carts to replace their current bins. The new program was expected to double the amount of material no longer being sent to landfills. Denver's Materials Recovery Facility (MFR) is capable of processing an estimated 30 tons of material an hour. At the outset, Recycle America Alliance (RAA), Denver's partner in the expanded program, processed 4,000 tons per month at the MFR; they hoped to raise that to 10,000 tons.

The waste management industry held its own in the slowing U.S. economy. Commenting on an October 2008 regional meeting, Bruce Parker, CEO of the National Solid Wastes Management Association, told *Waste News,* "Surprisingly, there was no whining or complaining about how the industry is doing. This industry is a little unique in the fact that we are recession-resilient." Ed Lang, treasurer of one of the industry leaders, Republic Services Inc., agreed and said that the industry generally experiences a steady and predictable flow of cash regardless, to some extent, of the state of the economy.

Recycling efforts continued in many industries. General Motors (GM), for example, announced plans in late 2008 to make half of its global manufacturing operations landfill-free by the end of 2010. In other words, all of the materials used at 80 plants will be either recycled or reused. As of October 2008, 43 of the firm's plants were landfill-free. According to Gary Cowager of GM, more than 96 percent of the waste materials at these sites is recycled or reused and 3 percent is converted to energy. GM's efforts have earned it almost $1 billion in recycled metal scrap sales and $16 million in revenues from the sale of recycled plastic, wood, cardboard, and other materials.

Electronic waste, or e-waste, was becoming a more significant problem for the industry. E-waste consists of broken or no longer used electronic devices or parts, such as computers, cell phones, televisions, and the like. According to the EPA and the TakeBack Coalition, the United States dumps between 300 million and 400 million electronic items a year. E-waste is considered toxic waste because, if not recycled or disposed of properly, it can be a source of toxins and carcinogens. Greenpeace International reported that less than 20 percent of the United States' e-waste is recycled, and much of it is exported to developing countries in Asia and Africa. Solutions to the problem were being sought by environmental organizations, makers of electronics, and the EPA.

CURRENT CONDITIONS

According to the *Waste Business Journal,* 2009 was a year of declining revenues for many major players in the industry, although total U.S. revenues were slightly up, $57.4 billion in 2009, compared with $56 billion in 2008. Collections of waste continued to hold the lion's share of the market, with 55 percent of revenues ($30.5 billion).

The disposal segment of the industry brought in the second highest revenues at $18.5 billion in 2009, followed by the transfer and processing segment, at $6.7 billion. The *Journal* projected full year revenues of $59.2 for 2010. In the "Waste Age 100 of 2010" listing, the top five U.S. solid waste firms were Waste Management, Republic Services Inc., Veolia Environmental Services North America Corp., Covanta Holding Corp., and Waste Connections Inc. Not far behind in ranking were Stericycle Inc., Clean Harbors Inc., and Safeety-Kleen Systems Inc. Several companies reported wince-worthy revenue declines in 2009, including industry leader Waste Management, down more than $1.5 billion from 2008 revenues. Other examples included Cincinnati-based Rumpke (No. 15 on the list) which lost about $8 million, and San Francisco-based Recology (No. 12 on the list) reported a $20 million decline in revenue.

The good news was that a substantial part of revenue loss was attributed to the rise in consumer and industrial recycling efforts. In the 2008 and 2009 tight economy, many for-profit as well as non-profit entities used recycling initiatives to raise revenues and/or donations; waste paper and plastic bottle drives were a few of the most common recyclables sought in these initiatives. The tight economy also caused less scrap metal to end up in landfills, with more of it redeemed for cash value. The Oscar-winning hit movie, "Slum Dog Millionaire" opened the eyes of many complacent consumers to the horrors of landfill sights and what they were doing to the earth, and the younger generation in particular was being targeted in many recycle-conscious campaigns around the world.

A 2010 market study by ABI Research, "e-Waste Recovery and Recycling," projected that the global market for e-waste recovery would grow from $5.7 billion in 2009 to about $14.7 billion by the end of 2014, representing a compound annual growth rate (CAGR) of 20.8 percent. Because e-waste posed such high risk to the world's ecosystem, contaminating soil, water, and air, and consequently, all human and wildlife, reclamation of valuable scrap materials from e-waste became a subsegment niche market within the broader industry. However, the economic downturn of 2008 and 2009 caused plummeting commodity prices, which reduced the demand for recycled materials. Notwithstanding, ABI practice director Larry Fischer, in a January 2010 ABI press release, noted, "The combined impact of the ongoing global economic reocery and strengthening e-waste recycling legislation worldwide will drive improved recycling/recovery rates in each of the next five years."

INDUSTRY LEADERS

Waste Management Inc. Headquartered in Houston, Texas, Waste Management Inc. (WMI) is the largest nonhazardous waste management company in the United States, reporting revenues of $11.79 billion in 2009 with 43,400 employees. WMI serves 21 million residential and commercial customers in the United States, Puerto Rico, Canada, and Mexico. WMI's North American operations can be divided into two major segments: North American Solid Waste (NASW), which is further divided into five geographic operating groups—Canada, Eastern, Midwest, Southern, and Western—and includes a national recycling operation; and Wheelabrator. NASW provides integrated waste management services, including collection, landfill, transfer, and recycling. Wheelabrator operates waste-to-energy facilities and independent power production plants in several states. In early 2006, WMI established a recycling and recovery division, called Recycle NZ, to serve commercial customers. In 2007 the company operated 277 landfills, 341 transfer stations, 99 material recovery facilities, 108 beneficial use landfill gas projects, and multiple waste-to-energy plants.

Allied Waste Industries Inc. Another industry leader is Allied Waste Industries, which is headquartered in Scottsdale, Arizona. In 2008, Allied operated 291 collection companies, 161 transfer stations, 161 active landfills, and 53 recycling facilities in 37 states. The company provides a wide range of services, including collection, transfer, recycling, and disposal and serves about 8 million customers.

Republic Services Inc. In 2009, Republic Services Inc. had revenues of $8.2 billion and 31,000 employees. The company, based in Fort Lauderdale, Florida, offers a wide variety of environmental services, including solid waste collection, transfer, disposal, and recycling. Republic's local operating companies, which are known as divisions, provide services to residential, commercial, industrial, and municipal customers. Operating in 21 states, the company has a network of 136 collection companies, which serve their customers through 94 transfer stations, 58 landfills, and more than 33 recycling centers. In 2008 Republic successfully moved to buy rival Allied Waste International for about $4.8 billion.

Safety-Kleen HoldCo Inc. Headquartered in Plano, Texas, Safety-Kleen HoldCo Inc. focuses on the clean-up and removal of hazardous waste for commercial and industrial customers. The company provides a broad array of environmental services, including the collection and recycling or disposal of both hazardous and non-hazardous wastes, parts cleaning, site remediation, soil decontamination, and wastewater processing. In 2008 it was the largest recovery and recycling company for used oil products in the United States. Formerly known as Safety-Kleen Corp., the company filed for bankruptcy protection in 2000. In December of 2003, the renamed organization announced that it had emerged from bankruptcy protection. With more than 200 facilities worldwide.

Casella Waste Systems Inc. Considerably smaller than its larger competitors, Casella Waste Systems nevertheless plays a significant role in the waste management business of the eastern United States. Headquartered in Rutland, Vermont, through its 34 solid waste collection businesses, the company serves nearly 293,000 residential customers, as well as 50,000 commercial and industrial customers. Casella's facilities include 38 recycling facilities, 30 transfer stations, 10 landfills, 33 transfer stations, 37 solid waste collection centers, and a waste-to-energy facility.

WORKFORCE

The bulk of the waste management industry's workforce is blue collar, working as collectors and processors of waste materials. In 2004, *Waste Age* reported that "mergers, buy-outs and other acquisitions within the waste industry have sent thousands of employees scurrying for new jobs." In June 2003 alone, industry leader Waste Management announced that it would cut 800 jobs as part of a plan to streamline operations. The EREF study indicated that approximately three-quarters of the industry's employees worked for private companies, 42 percent for privately held companies, and 32 percent for publicly held companies. The remaining 26 percent of the workforce was employed by the public sector.

AMERICA AND THE WORLD

The need to collect and properly dispose of waste is, of course, not just a U.S. concern but a major business around the world. Most of the major U.S. solid waste management companies confine their operations to this country and its neighbors, Canada and Mexico. Foreign involvement in the U.S. waste management industry has increased in recent years, notably through the investments of Vivendi in the American industry. Working through its U.S. subsidiary, Onyx Environmental Services, based in Lombard, Illinois, Vivendi moved aggressively to acquire U.S. companies in the waste management business. Its acquisitions have included Superior Waste, U.S. Filter, and Giant Cement Holdings. Vivendi also managed to acquire select assets of WMI, one of the largest U.S. waste management companies. With its U.S. acquisitions, Veolia Environment (formerly Vivendi), with approximately 300,000 employees and the arm of Vivendi that supplies environmental services and the parent of Onyx, became one of largest U.S. hazardous waste handlers. Now operating as Veolia Environmental Services North America Corp., the entity brought in 2009 revenues of $1.8 billion.

RESEARCH AND TECHNOLOGY

One of the most important technological trends in the industry was companies' efforts to develop "trash-to-gas" renewable energy. Such programs convert garbage into energy. One such program was launched by General Motors (GM) in conjunction with Coskata in early 2008. According to a GM news release, household garbage and old tires contain carbon, which can be converted to fuel. A more common method—and the one used by 445 trash-to-gas plants in the United States—is to use the methane gas from decomposing trash to produce power. This was how Waste Management planned to produce enough juice to power 700,000 homes by 2012. The company had 112 energy projects at landfills as of 2008 and planned to develop 60 more in the next five years.

Geoplasma of Atlanta, Georgia, planned to open the United States' first plasma refuse plant in 2011. According to a report by *Clean Technica,* the plant will recycle 1,500 tons of garbage a day and provide enough energy to power 50,000 homes. The process involves blasting garbage with a stream of superheated gas (plasma); the trash is then vaporized into pressurized gas, which spins a turbine to create electricity.

In an effort to provide the U.S. Department of Energy (DOE) an alternative method of disposing of liquid nuclear waste, Penn State University, together with the Savannah River National Laboratory, has created a process in which radioactive liquid waste is turned into a solid form—ziolitic ceramic, called a hydro ceramic—that is strong and durable over long periods and can be safely disposed of. In 2006, the DOE had approximately 80 million gallons of liquid radioactive wastes, called supemates, along with highly radioactive sludge, which settles to the bottoms of the underground tanks at the Hanford Nuclear Reservation in Richland, Washington, and at the Savannah River site in Aiken, South Carolina. In order to dispose of this "low-activity, high-alkali liquid waste," Penn State and Savannah researchers use extremely low temperatures to solidify and stabilize it, in an accelerated adaptation of rock formations that take place in nature. The previous method used by the DOE was to remove the liquid and the sludge from the tanks, clean the tanks, then fill them with a cement-like material before removing them from service. The researchers have said that this discovery could give the DOE a feasible option for treating the government's low activity wastes.

BIBLIOGRAPHY

"About Us." Allied Waste Industries, 1 November 2008. Available from http://investor.awin.com/.

"Denso is Seriously Green." *Automotive Design & Production,* April 2006.

"Effects of Crisis, Bailout Start to Unfurl: Trash Firms Are Somewhat Insulated." *Waste News,* 13 October 2008.

"E-Waste Recyclers Join Forces." *Electronics News,* 1 February 2006.

"From Trash to Gas: Breakthrough Fuel Technology Announced at the 2008 North American International Auto Show." General Motors, 13 January 2008.

"Global e-Waste Recovery/Reclamation Revenues to Reach $14.7 Billion by 2014." ABI Research Group, Press Release, 29 January 2010.

"Hazardous Waste Generated, Shipped, and Received by State and Other Area: 2005." *The 2008 Statistical Abstract.* U.S. Census Bureau, December 2006. Available from http://www.census.gov.

Johnson, Jim. "Auto Parts Firms Plan Waste Cuts." *Waste News,* 27 March 2006.

Jusko, Jill. "Putting Waste to Work." *Industry Week,* October 2008.

Kart, Jeff. "Whitefeather Landfill Will Turn Trash Gas into Energy with Mulitmillion Dollar Plan." *The Bay City Times,* 27 August 2008.

MacDonald, G. Jeffrey. "Don't Recycle E-Waste with Haste, Activists Warn." *USA Today,* 6 July 2008.

"More GM Plants To Go Landfill-Free." *Fleet Owner,* 1 October 2008.

"Municipal Solid Waste in the United States: 2007 Facts and Figures." Environmental Protection Agency, November 2008.

"New Research May Give the DOE More Options for Nuclear Waste Disposal." *Nuclear Waste News,* 4 May 2006.

Schwartz, Ariel. "Plasma Technology Turns Trash into Gas." *Clean Technica,* 10 November 2008. Available from http://cleantechnica.com.

"Summary of the Resource Conservation and Recovery Act." Environmental Protection Agency, 13 November 2008. Available from http://www.epa.gov.

"Ups, Downs of a Waste Deal." *Miami Herald* (Miami, FL), 15 November 2008.

"Waste Age 100 of 2010." Waste Age, 2010. Available from http://wasteage.com/waste-age-100/2010/.

"Waste Management Overview and Outlook 2009." *Waste Business Journal,* 9 March 2010.

"Where Does All the E-Waste Go?" Greenpeace International, 21 February 2008. Available from http://wwwl.greenpeace.org.

"WM to Help Landfill Owners Create own Gas Projects." *Waste News,* 13 October 2008.

WATER AND AIR FILTRATION AND PURIFICATION SYSTEMS

■———————

SIC CODE(S)

3564

3589

INDUSTRY SNAPSHOT

Increased consumer awareness and concern about environmental quality helped the residential water and air purification industries flourish during the first decade of the 2000s. Both industries are highly fragmented and are comprised of a large number of small companies manufacturing and distributing across various product lines. Nevertheless, a handful of companies, including divisions of industrial conglomerates, tended to dominate each industry.

Both industries grew rapidly in the early 2000s. Part of the reason for the growth was public understanding of the importance of water quality. According to the Water Quality Association (WQA), 60 percent of adults believe the quality of drinking water has an impact on their health and about 50 percent are concerned about contaminants in their drinking water.

Even with this growth, the industry still had plenty of room for expansion because of increased consumer consciousness and the efforts of retailers to encourage current users of water purification devices to upgrade to faucet-mounted, countertop, and under-sink models. In addition, some retailers tied water purification devices in with high-end and gourmet kitchenware, emphasizing fashionable and costlier models, according to *Home Furnishing News* (HFN), a weekly publication focused on retail trends and product analysis related to the home furnishings industry.

The air quality products industry was also on an upward trend. Sales of air purifiers, including fast-selling portable air cleaners, grew by more than 10 percent a year in the late 1990s. The need for air purification came to the forefront of the news following the disasters of Hurricane Katrina, the SARS outbreak, the news of a possible avian flu pandemic, and the anthrax terrorist attacks of the early 2000s. In 2008, BNP Media reported that the U.S. Environmental Protection Agency consistently rates indoor air pollution among the top five environmental health risks in the United States.

Both industries faced similar challenges for continued growth. Each segment of the industry sold products that could be used either at a particular location in a home or throughout the whole house. Encouraging consumers to upgrade inexpensive entry-level purchases to high-end, large-scale, or whole-house purification systems was the next challenge for these industries. Furthermore, each segment began introducing more sophisticated filtration devices, each capable of removing more harmful substances than its predecessor. Through various educational marketing techniques, the industry hoped to make consumers aware of the benefits and advantages of these new products. Additionally, consumer awareness of both air and water quality issues, especially in the home, continued to rise, due in large part to new regulations requiring the disclosure of such information and the consumer's ability to have his or her home tested for air and water purity.

ORGANIZATION AND STRUCTURE

Both the water and air purification industries are comprised of companies that produce finished units, component manufacturers, and assemblers of finished units.

Products are sold to industrial and commercial users as well as to residential homeowners. Although the largest industry leaders maintain their own networks of dealers and distributors, the large majority of firms sell products directly to retail outlets for resale.

Water Quality Products Industry Products sold by water industry participants include softeners, reverse osmosis units, ultraviolet units, distillation units, ozonators, carbon and noncarbon filters, filtration carafes, faucet-mounted models, countertop models, and personal filtration units. Components manufactured for those products include mineral tanks, valves, controllers, membranes, faucets, and filters. Retail operations in the industry generally have a high percentage of revenues, sometimes as high as 70 percent, derived from recurring sales of consumables such as servicing equipment, replacement parts, and filters.

The Water Quality Association (WQA) represents the household, commercial, industrial, and small community water treatment industry. The WQA is a not-for-profit international trade organization founded in 1950. In 2008, the agency had 2,500 members, all corporate manufacturers and retailers. A consumer survey commissioned by the WQA reported that the purchaser of water quality products and components is usually a dealership or original equipment manufacturer. As in many industries, assemblers and component manufacturers who make finished units sell more units to dealerships than to original equipment manufacturers.

The water quality products industry is not regulated by a government agency. Typically, however, units are labeled for retail sale with indications of the high quality of the filtration or purification system that has been installed. The National Sanitation Foundation International Standard 42 indicates a filter equipped for handling aesthetic problems such as taste, smell, and appearance, while Standard 53 indicates a filter equipped for handling basic health problems such as lead and organic compounds. Such filters normally indicate the specific contaminants they can handle. The most resistant filters, labeled as being certified "absolute one micron," are those that can filter parasites.

The U.S. Environmental Protection Agency (EPA) does not regulate the manufacture or distribution of water filter units; however, EPA policies and guidelines, as well as statutes such as the Safe Drinking Water Act of 1974, have had a great impact on the industry. The act contained water quality guidelines that many communities in the country failed to meet, and the 1996 reauthorization of the act made certain provisions more rigorous. Thus, while communities fail to meet federal water standards and the public grows more skeptical of the water it drinks, the water quality products industry benefits.

The Safe Drinking Water Act Amendment of 1996 was signed into law in August of that year. Congress overwhelmingly approved the bill, which authorized billions of dollars to improve deteriorating water systems. The funds represented a sharp increase in spending for water systems, both municipal and rural. The law also included a "right to know" provision that requires water authorities to disclose what chemicals and bacteria are in drinking water and requires public notice of any dangerous contaminants within 24 hours of discovery. The bill also imposes a duty on the EPA to develop and apply more rigorous standards to fight cryptosporidium and other common drinking water contaminants posing significant health risks. Beginning in 1999, water utility companies were required to report what elements were found in their water. This information would allow consumers to make better choices when purchasing home water filtration products, and the responsibility placed on the EPA reflects a shift in federal policy away from identifying new pollutants and toward controlling the most dangerous ones. The impact of the act is difficult to predict. Its passage, however, reflects a growing discontent among Americans about the quality of water. That discontent made itself felt in the booming sales figures for companies in the industry.

Air Quality Products Industry The air quality products industry manufactures and markets air filters and purifiers for both whole house applications and portable use. Within those two applications, there are three general types of air cleaners on the market: mechanical filters, electronic air cleaners, and ion generators.

Mechanical filters, which may be installed in whole house or portable devices, are of two major types. The first type, known as a flat or panel filter, normally consists of a dense medium, consisting of materials such as coarse glass fibers, animal hair, or synthetic fibers, which are then coated with a viscous substance such as oil to act as an adhesive for particulate material. Flat filters may also be made of "electret" media, which is comprised of a charged plastic film or fiber to which particles in the air are attracted. Although flat filters may collect large particles well, they remove only a small percentage of respirable-size particles.

The second type of mechanical filter is the pleated or extended surface filter. Due to its greater surface area, this type of filter generally achieves greater efficiency for capture of respirable-size particles than do flat filters. This allows an increase in packing density without a significant drop in air flow rate.

In electronic air cleaners, an electrical field traps charged particles. Electronic air cleaners are usually electrostatic precipitators or charged media filters. In electrostatic precipitators, particles are collected on a series of flat plates. In charged media filter devices, the particles are collected on fibers in a filter. In most electrostatic precipitators and in some charged media filters, the particles are ionized, or charged, before the collection process, resulting in a higher collection efficiency.

Like electronic air cleaners, ion generators use static charges to remove particles from indoor air. They act by charging the particles in a room so that they are attracted to walls, floors, or any surface. In some cases, these devices, which are only available as portable units, contain a collector to attract the charged particles back to the unit. Both electronic air cleaners and ion generators can produce ozone. Some systems on the market are hybrid devices containing two or more of the particle removal devices.

The residential air quality products industry was not regulated by a government agency, either, nor has the government published any guidelines or standards for use in determining how well an air cleaner works in removing pollutants from indoor air. Standards for rating particle removal by air cleaners, both whole house and portable, however, are published by trade associations and independent organizations. For example, the Association of Home Appliance Manufacturers developed an American National Standards Institute-approved standard for portable air cleaners. Whole-house systems can be analyzed by Standard 52-761 of the American Society of Heating, Refrigerating & Air Conditioning Engineers, a trade group. Both standards estimate the effectiveness of an air-cleaning device in removing particles from indoor air.

Like the water quality products industry, the manufacture and sale of air quality products was on the upswing in the late 1990s, a growth that continued into the twenty-first century. Both industries benefited from highly publicized findings of contaminants in homes and communities. The air quality industry, however, began its sharp increase in the early 1990s, meaning fewer companies were in that market than were in the water quality market.

Another major difference between the two industries lies in the perceived utility of the products themselves. While questions were raised as to whether the water quality of the vast majority of Americans is poor enough to require residential purification, testing typically showed that the products performed as advertised, reducing or eliminating the presence of various contaminants. As of the early 2000s, the question of effectiveness had not been answered for many air quality products. For example, by the end of the twentieth century, the EPA had not taken a position on the value of home air cleaners, despite its recognition of the ill effects of air pollution on human health. Furthermore, while standards exist for the quality of indoor air, standards for the products themselves are often difficult to compare across product lines.

BACKGROUND AND DEVELOPMENT

The water and air filtration and purification industries manufacture and sell systems and supplies that counter the effects of pollution and naturally occurring contaminants. Those effects range from the unhealthy and deadly to the aesthetic. Both industries have targeted the commercial and industrial markets for years, markets that are scrutinized by the EPA and the general public. More recent concerns about the safety of drinking water and the purity of indoor residential air were behind an increase in the retail market for those products. Both industries grew from being dominated by a few large manufacturers focusing on industrial and commercial applications to highly fragmented industries comprised of dozens of manufacturers, retailers, and distributors. Most were small businesses, all of whom vied for what appeared to be the United States' almost limitless appetite for contaminant-free living.

Public Concerns about Water Quality According to a trade group, the market for residential drinking water treatment nearly doubled from 1990 to 1995. By the end of the decade, the water purification industry was confronted with a public concerned about water quality and prepared to spend money to eliminate contaminants. The 1999 consumer survey commissioned by the Water Quality Association (WQA) revealed that the American public was increasingly suspicious of the tap water entering homes. Survey responses showed that three-quarters of consumers had some concern about their household water supply, one in five consumers was dissatisfied with the quality of his/her water supply, and one in three consumers felt that the water was not as safe as it should be. Despite these concerns, only one in four consumers reported ever having the water tested for contamination.

The WQA survey also revealed that consumer knowledge about water quality issues did not appear to be widespread. Forty-seven percent of respondents said that they wished they knew more about their household water supply. Twenty-three percent, however, said that they did not know how to obtain information. The survey results pointed to continued solid growth for the water quality industry. Among all respondents, adults between the ages of 18 and 44 were the most likely to believe household water was unsafe. Those consumers were also the least likely to know where to turn for information about their water. Increased reporting of water quality calamities in the 1990s, joined with the growing ubiquity of water purification devices in retail outlets, had an effect on this consumer group.

The U.S. consumer market was a sizable and growing market in the late 1990s. The WQA survey showed that due to increasing health concerns, about two-thirds of consumers were using either bottled water or a filtration device as a water treatment method compared to 53 percent in 1997. Thirty-eight percent of these consumers used a household water treatment device compared to 32 percent in 1997 and 27 percent in 1995. Sales of "entry level" devices, such as pour-through water carafes with filters, grew more quickly than any other type of water treatment device. The boom in entry level devices demonstrated that the industry's marketing target had been met.

The growth of entry-level sales also has repercussions in the location of retail purchases. While 29 percent of Americans making water quality purchases in 1997 still purchased home water treatment devices from local water treatment dealers, department and discount stores grew in popularity as the site of purchase. Up from 7 percent in 1995, sales of water quality products at those stores tripled to 21 percent. As the industry offered more inexpensive products that required little expertise to install or maintain, accessibility through general retail outlets became possible.

Growing Evidence of Water Quality Failings Most Americans receive water from a public water system where it has already been tested and treated under regulations derived from the Safe Drinking Water Act of 1974. Only those who get water from other sources, such as private wells or small water systems serving a relatively small number of customers, could not be as certain of the quality of their water. Nevertheless, well-publicized breakdowns of even the largest water systems cast uncertainty into the consumers' collective consciousness. For example, in the mid-1990s, more than a dozen communities in the Midwest were informed that their tap water had heightened concentrations of a weed killer. More than 100 people were killed by the waterborne contaminant *cryptosporidia* in Milwaukee in 1993. Additionally, in 1996, Washington, D.C., residents were given a "boil order" to combat unsafe bacteria levels. Sporadic reports of nitrate, which causes blue baby syndrome, as well as radon in drinking water, also spurred the public's concern.

Adding to Americans' suspicions were widely publicized findings and studies. In the summer of 1997, for example, the U.S. Geological Survey asked U.S. and Canadian residents to aid in the scientific investigation of deformed frogs, toads, and salamanders. Citizens were encouraged to report sightings of abnormal and malformed amphibians they saw while outdoors. Whether the deformities arose from waterborne contaminants or could affect human health had not been determined. It was known, however, that amphibians are highly sensitive to alterations in the aquatic environment.

Nationwide Responses to Water Quality Concerns American concerns about water quality were reflected in the actions of elected representatives. In October 1996, President Bill Clinton announced an environmental initiative that allocated $45 million over four years for the U.S. Geological Survey (USGS) to extend water quality testing to 75 cities, which increased the examining of 35 river basins and groundwater systems. The initiative also made data collected on the major rivers, water supply watersheds, and drinking water wells available to the public on the Internet. Through the USGS Water Resources Data Web site, consumers can get real time water data from 3,000 stations throughout the United States, daily stream flow reports from the National Water Information System, and records from the Water Quality Monitoring Network.

In addition, the Safe Drinking Water Act Amendment of 1996, which amended the Safe Drinking Water Act of 1974, created a revolving loan fund to aid states in rebuilding and maintaining deteriorating water systems. That federal effort provided funds where the U.S. public could see it in the form of a proposed budget giving every state at least $7 million. Up to $9.6 billion was authorized for payment to the states through 2003.

Water Products Sales Growth From the late 1990s to 2000, the water filtration products industry experienced robust growth, which was expected to continue well into the new decade. The public's concerns about water quality and aesthetics were widely held and widely publicized during this period, and its willingness to purchase items claiming to rectify the problems at the spigot and throughout the house was on the rise. Greater consumer consciousness about water quality and mandatory Consumer Confidence Reports fueled and are expected to continue to fuel the industry's growth.

Beginning in late 1999, the EPA required municipalities to send detailed reports on the drinking water they provide to their customers for compliance with the 1996 amendment to the Safe Drinking Water Act of 1974. Municipalities must submit these reports annually, and water purification system makers, manufacturers and retailers expect they will lead to greater consumer awareness and purifier sales. Makers and retailers use the Internet as an educational tool not only to demonstrate their purification wares and describe their features but also to apprise consumers of water quality and contamination issues, according to *Home Furnishing News.*

All types of water quality devices saw sales increases in that period. Not surprisingly, more inexpensive entry-level products saw the greatest sales boom. Equally significant, consumers across all income brackets were more willing to purchase water quality equipment for the home. Water filter penetration increased from 27 percent in 1995 to 32 percent in 1997 and to 38 percent in 1999, according to the National Consumer Water Quality Survey.

In 2001, water purification systems that featured conventional filtration media accounted for about 83 percent of sales, but analysts expected growth for this segment to be outpaced by the demand for reverse osmosis equipment and distillers. Reverse osmosis industry revenue was predicted to be driven by performance advantages, including the ability to process a broader range of contaminants compared to conventional filters. In addition, new portable filtration bottles were introduced into the market in the late 1990s, targeted to campers and sailors. These units contain a filter, secured inside the top of the bottle, which improves taste, cuts down on odor, and removes virtually all chlorine (99.8 percent), microscopic pathogens that cause gastrointestinal illness, detergents, pesticides, industrial and agricultural wastes, and heavy metals. The 30-ounce bottles filter 200 gallons, or more than 1,000 refills.

Deteriorating Air Quality At the end of the twentieth century, scientific experiments detected a reliable connection between human health problems and dirty air. Epidemiologists (doctors who study causes, distribution and control of disease in populations) estimated that the annual U.S. death toll from air pollution—through heart disease, asthma, bronchitis, stroke, and similar conditions—is 50,000. Faced with these figures, in 1977 the EPA proposed strengthening air pollution standards. The most comprehensive air pollution legislation is the Clean Air Act Amendment of 1970. Despite this law, approximately 121 million Americans live in areas where the air falls below health standards and 46 million live in areas where pollutants such as carbon monoxide, ozone, lead, nitrogen dioxide, and sulfur dioxide exceed maximum levels set by the EPA.

According to the EPA, the average American spends roughly 90 percent of his or her time indoors, where the air is more polluted than the outdoor air in even the largest and most industrialized cities. Furthermore, the American Lung Association found that 87 percent of Americans are unaware that air pollution may be worse indoors than outdoors. In the 1990s, the EPA called indoor air pollution one of the country's top five environmental issues. The EPA estimated that more than 50 percent of homes and offices suffered from highly polluted indoor air and the American Lung Association discovered that 40 percent of homeowners did not change the air filters for their air conditioners and heaters as recommended. The agency estimated that such pollution costs Americans tens of billions of dollars a year in direct medical expenses and lost productivity. An estimated one in five Americans suffered allergy-related illness at some point

during their lives, with indoor allergens responsible for a substantial number of those cases. Because of this, in 1993, the Institute of Medicine of the National Academy of Sciences urged a comprehensive effort to clean up the air in America's homes, schools, and businesses.

More findings in the 1990s made indoor air quality appear grim and in need of immediate relief. Along with AIDS and tuberculosis, asthma is one of the three chronic diseases with an increasing mortality rate. The National Institutes of Health called allergic disease one of America's most common and expensive health problems. Asthma and allergies alone cause over 130 million lost school days and 13.5 million lost workdays each year. Further, indoor allergens are blamed for much of the acute asthma in adults under the age of 50, according to the National Academy of Science.

Amid such well-publicized breakdowns in air quality, the residential air products industry thrived. Air purifier sales climbed 11 percent in 1996 to $340 million, marking five years of consecutive sales growth. Retail sales accounted for the majority of the revenues at $275 million, while alternative distribution channels accounted for $65 million. Overall, the industry sold about 3.2 million units. Some analysts believed air purifiers were among the most profitable small appliances due to the fact that they had a 40 percent profit margin, according to *HFN*.

Consumer Acceptance of Air Quality Products Growth in the industry in the late 1990s was primarily in the portable market. Variety among portable machines, however, grew greatly at that time as consumers demanded larger and more powerful units. Thus, the general trend in the market at that time was toward larger, console-sized models. Because installation of a whole house unit requires great expense and retrofitting of airflow sources, consumers appeared to want to solve air quality problems room by room with the largest units available, usually operated in bedrooms and other highly trafficked areas. Most users, about 75 percent of those surveyed, indicated they purchased air purifiers because of allergies.

In the late 1990s, one indicator of the public's growing disenchantment with its indoor air could be seen in a battle of standards over the air in commercial establishments. Commercial indoor air quality is set by local code, often adopted from guidelines set out by the American Society of Heating, Refrigerating & Air Conditioning Engineers (ASHRAE). In 1997, ASHRAE proposed a new industry standard for ventilation. Its proposal carried great weight because its then existing standard had become the most widely used and cited document for indoor air quality. The proposals by ASHRAE were far more rigorous and far-ranging than those in place. Of course, those standards, if adopted, would have no effect on residential air quality or products sold to consumers. The significant strengthening of the guidelines, however, gave an indication of the changes occurring on air issues: that more and more Americans find poor indoor air quality unacceptable and are prepared to pay greatly to improve their commercial and residential environments.

The ozone-producing qualities of some air cleaning systems was a technological concern for the industry at the start of the twenty-first century, as were studies showing that some electronic air cleaners themselves produce fine particulate material or that filters and other devices remove particles from the environment and then re-emit gases and odors from the collected particles. In addition, some materials used in the manufacturing of air cleaners may themselves emit chemicals into indoor air. For example, formaldehyde may be emitted if particleboard is used in the air cleaner housing. Another technological hurdle facing the air quality products industry at the beginning of the twenty-first century was the inability of many units to remove certain odors, primarily cigarette odors, from indoor environments. While most models are able to remove the particles from smoke, they are unable to remove the gaseous elements of cigarette residue. Some units are designed to scent the air, leading homeowners to believe the odor has been eradicated. Ion generators also were cause for concern. Studies showed a correlation between them and a heightened deposit of particles in the human lung.

Two new air quality products came on the market in the late 1990s that were expected to further increase sales. In 1998, Clean Air Systems installed filtration modules designed to eliminate cigarette smoke at Richmond International Airport. These filter modules operate by filtering out smoke, particles, and gases while returning clean air to the immediate environment. They are twice as efficient as previous filtration devices in absorbing 13 different chemical compounds found in cigarette smoke. Also in 1998, Environmental Elements Corp. was contracted by the EPA to develop a sterilizing filter capable of filtering more than 99 percent of micro-organisms, including those that cause tuberculosis and Legionnaires' disease. This filter enhanced the collection and destruction of such microorganisms that, along with inorganic particles, contributed heavily to indoor air pollution. These new units used electrically created plasma, which effectively destroys microorganisms without using chemicals or heat. Medical facilities, especially hospitals, greatly benefited from such technology.

Sales of both water and air purification systems were greatly influenced by units that could be used at a single location. Such point-of-use water purification systems were expected to demonstrate more rapid gains through 2006, compared to point-of-entry systems. At the same time, portable console air cleaners held the biggest share of sales of air cleaners.

In 2004, some communities were banning additives in the water supply, particularly fluoride, a movement pushed by the Citizens for Safe Drinking Water activist group. Sodium fluoride is often found to be contaminated with harmful chemicals at levels higher than EPA guidelines allow. The EPA published the 2003 Safe Drinking Water Information System, which reported that the general quality of U.S. drinking water had improved since the last report in 2000. Nonetheless, the market for water purification devices was continuing to rise, with many varied products for water filtration, ranging from pitchers that filter a few cups of water at a time to residential faucet mounts to full industrial sanitizing systems.

The water filtration industry was generating $10 billion annually by 2004. According to *The Daily Deal,* the water purification and filtration equipment industry worldwide was guaranteed to continue its growth due to the ever-increasing demand for drinkable water. A significant development in the industry is the growing availability of products for retail sale outside of locations normally associated with water treatment. As entry-level products are created and increased competition drives some prices down, more product niches will be marketed through department stores and other chain outlets. Some of these products enable individuals to test their own water to see if it contains contaminants. It is recommended that such a test be performed up to four times per year depending on the source of water and the health needs of the individual. With the increased technology of smart products and appliances, some manufacturers were producing products that automatically de-lime municipal water as it is used.

By 2003, the question of indoor air quality became a nagging one for thousands of the estimated 118,000 public schools across the country due to undergo renovation in the coming years, as well as for the future thousands that would need to be built to accommodate the growing population. The EPA reported that about 20 percent of Americans spend significant time in school buildings, and nearly two-thirds of those buildings have reported health problems linked to issues of poor or harmful indoor air quality.

The biggest demand among air cleaners was for electrostatic systems. Demand for such cleaners will be enhanced by an increasing popularity of electrostatic precipitators—collection devices that remove particles from the air using an induced electrostatic charge— because these devices generally do not require replacement filters, observers said.

Developments In the water quality products industry, two new rules were launched by the EPA in late 2005 aimed at decreasing gastrointestinal illnesses caused by microbial contaminants and lessening potential cancer risks linked to disinfectant byproducts in drinking water. One rule is targeted at reducing the incidence of disease-causing microorganisms from entering water supplies; the other establishes limits to the amount of potentially harmful "disinfection byproducts" (DBPs) that end up in drinking water.

The EPA also implemented updates to standards for arsenic in drinking water. The Safe Drinking Water Act, which sets standards for approximately 90 contaminants in drinking water, set the safe limit of arsenic at 50 parts per billion (ppb), but the EPA applied a 10 ppb standard that became effective January 23, 2006. Arsenic is an odorless and tasteless "semi-metal." It enters drinking water supplies from natural deposits in the earth or from agricultural and industrial practices and can cause such health issues as thickening and discoloration of the skin, stomach pain, nausea, vomiting, diarrhea, numbness in hands and feet, partial paralysis, and blindness. Arsenic has also been linked to cancer of the bladder, lungs, skin, kidney, nasal passages, liver, and prostate. The new standards are designed to protect consumers served by public water systems from the effects of long-term, chronic exposure to arsenic.

Levels of lead and copper in drinking water also came under the scrutiny of the EPA. The Lead and Copper Rule (the LCR or 1991 Rule) was established on June 7, 1991, and was aimed at minimizing lead and copper in drinking water, which results in a more neutral pH and reduces water corrosivity—which makes the water less corrosive and thus less hazardous. Lead and copper enter drinking water through plumbing materials and can lead to health problems ranging from stomach distress to brain damage. On January 12, 2000, and again in November 2004, the EPA published additional guidance for states and utilities to clarify several requirements of the regulations, to streamline requirements, and to promote consistent national implementation, in order to reduce the burden for water systems.

In 2006, hydroelectric dam owners and operators brought a case against the Clean Water Act (CWA), in which the definition of the term "discharge" was challenged. The Supreme Court upheld the authority of the state to require approval of hydroelectric dam licenses in regard to the CWA. Since the CWA was established with the purpose of protecting water quality from pollution in general, according to the Supreme Court, river water being restricted and then flowing through turbines falls into the category of altering water quality and therefore is subject to the standards and water quality requirements of the CWA.

The air quality products industry also experienced changes as well. Although indoor air—where most people spend about 90 percent of their time—has a great impact on health and well-being, it remained one of the least researched and understood health issues. In October 2005, Carrier Corp., the leading North American heating and air conditioning manufacturer, began research, together with the Syracuse Center of Excellence, in the area of indoor air quality and pledged $1.5 million to build a total indoor environmental quality lab at the Center.

Ever-increasing numbers of aging school buildings were presenting problems in ensuring safe indoor environments for children and teachers. According to Al Veeck, the executive director of the National Air Filtration Association (NAFA), the nation's 115,000 school buildings were among the dirtiest indoor facilities in the United States, in which some 55 million students, teachers, and support personnel were obliged to spend a great deal of time. New and existing school buildings began to be equipped with central system design two-stage filtration systems—MERV 7 and MERV 13—similar to those in office buildings. In the past, the system of choice, due to lower installation costs and ease of service, had been through-the-wall units. A central system design, although costlier to install—on average, approximately 50 percent higher—costs less in the overall life of the system.

School buses posed an especially vast health hazard to the 24 million children who rode them every day, spending on average an hour and a half each week day in a school bus. School buses drive move than 4 billion miles a year. Clean School Bus USA aimed to reduce childrens' exposure to diesel exhaust and limit the quantity of the air pollution created by diesel school buses.

By the middle of 2006, guests at hotels that had rooms certified as "Pure Allergy-Friendly" could be assured that the rooms were 99.9 percent free of allergens. In order to be so certified, guest rooms must be cleaned in a multi-step process: a thorough cleaning of the ducts, vents, circulation systems and all room surfaces; an application of a compound to prevent mold, yeast, and fungus from attaching to surfaces; the installation of air filters that kill viruses and bacteria; showerhead filters to eliminate chlorine; and hypoallergenic mattress and pillow covers. As of June 2006, there were 75 Pure Allergy-Friendly hotels in the U.S., and that number was expected to double by the end of the year.

The air and water purification and filtration industries were experiencing a "greening" trend. For example, more companies were seeking certification of their buildings and facilities from the U.S. Green Building Council's LEED (Leadership in Energy and Environmental Design). LEED certification focuses on improving water and indoor air quality and saving energy. Aaron Ayer of StrionAir in Louisville, Colorado, called LEED certification "the fastest growing trend in construction history" in a 2008 *Healthcare Purchasing News* article. He went on to say, "LEED registrations overall have grown at 100 percent every year for the last eight years. And it's not just new construction by any means. There is a substantial component of LEED that is focused on existing buildings." The GREEN-GUARD Environmental Institute also offered an air-quality certification program for building materials as well as furniture, cleaning solutions, textiles, and other indoor materials. GREENGUARD's Children & Schools Certification specifically applied to the air quality in educational institutions, which was becoming an increasing area of concern in the United States.

While the air quality industry was benefiting from more studies that showed that air quality affects consumers' health, the water quality industry was dealing with a heated debate about which was healthier, bottled or tap water, after the release of a study by the Environmental Working Group that found that 2 of the 10 brands of bottled water it tested contained contaminants, including fertilizer and bacteria. Environmental groups also urged consumers to stop drinking bottled water, with concerns about the plastic bottles clogging landfills. Although these campaigns against bottled water may have had an influence on consumers purchasing water filtration systems for their home faucets, another finding had an even greater possible impact. In March 2008, an investigation by the Associated Press (AP) revealed that at least 41 million Americans were ingesting pharmaceuticals from their drinking water. Drugs such as sex hormones, mood stabilizers, and antibiotics were found in the water in several U.S. metropolitan areas tested during a five-month period. Concern was heightened when in September 2008 the AP revised its original figures to state that 46 million—or as many as one in six—Americans could be affected. Related issues pointed to the adoption of more reverse osmosis treatment systems, as carbon systems were not capable of filtering such chemicals.

CURRENT CONDITIONS

In its 2010 report, *Water and Air Purification Systems and Products: Residential and Commercial,* research firm SBI Energy noted that the industry was still in a growth mode, but at a slower rate than pre-recession years (2008 and 2009). Bernie Galing, author of the report, further noted that comparatively few households [and businesses] owned air or water treatment products, therefore "[t]he market for air and water treatment products is also not saturated." Since the earth was obviously not becoming *less* polluted, the market would continue to grow worldwide. In fact, said the report, the residential water treatment market was projected to grow at a compound annual growth rate (CAGR) of 7 percent through 2015, and the industrial/commercial sector would grow at a 9 percent CAGR.

According to SBI, the consumer water purification/treatment market was worth a projected $12 billion in 2010, and was expected to approach $17 billion in global

sales by 2015, growing slower than the industrial market because of high unemployment and low consumer confidence. The industrial segment of the market was expected to drive growth, from a projected $22 billion in 2010 to an expected $33 billion by 2015.

Outdoor air treatment and purification products and services also suffered from a lackluster economy. The consumer market was expected to grow just by $1 billion between 2010 and 2015, th exceed $4 billion at that time. The industrial segment was forecasted to grow at a more rapid pace, from a projected $11 billion in 2010 to an expected $16 billion by 2015.

Indoor building HVAC systems for air filtering and purification did well, creating a market worth roughly $74 billion in 2010. Air filters for automobiles, vacuum cleaners, rooms, etc. brought in another $9.3 billion. Finally, fabric filters/bags used to capture industrial/manufacturing dust or particulate was worth about $8.7 billion in 2010.

Within the United States, according to the *Wall Street Journal,* the home water filtration products market was projected to grow 18 percent, from $2.47 billion in 2009 to $2.91 billion in 2012. Per capita bottled water consumption dropped 3.5 percent in 2009, as the market continued to shift toward home water filtration products.

Online assistance in choosing consumer products was greatly helped by Waterfilters.NET, which not only provided a wide selection of products but also created the online Water University to provide materials and educate buyers about water-related problems. The Minnesota-based company ran out of a dedicated warehouse and had close to $4 million in revenue in 2009. It laso launched into the social media market, developing a following on YouTube (55,000 views), Twitter (more than 25,000 followers), and Facebook (more than 750 fans) in 2009. Water.NET had more than 100,000 customers in 2009. market analyst Forrester projected that online sales of water filtration products would be roughly 8 percent of 2010 industry sales.

INDUSTRY LEADERS

Water Quality Industry Culligan International Company was one of the leaders in the water purification and filtration industry. Culligan, based in Rosemont, Illinois, was bought out by Clayton, Dubilier & Rice in 2004 for $610 million. Culligan manufactures water purification and treatment products for household, commercial, and industrial use. The company's products and services range from filters for tap water and household water softeners to advanced equipment and services for commercial and industrial applications.

Supporting its distribution network, Culligan maintains manufacturing facilities in the United States, Italy, Spain, and Canada. In addition, Culligan sells bottled water in the five-gallon bottled water market under names such as Elga, Everpure, and Bruner. In 1997 the company entered the consumer market selling filtration products directly to retailers. Culligan has been active in the water purification and treatment industry since 1936 and its brands are among the most recognized. Since the early 1980s, Culligan's residential water treatment systems have been installed in more than three million households in the United States, representing the largest installed base in the country, according to the company. In 1988, Culligan became the first company to be certified by the independent National Sanitation Foundation under its standard for residential reverse osmosis drinking water systems.

In 1997, Culligan created its new Consumer Market Division, which, through partnerships with other companies, sought quick access to niches of the retail market. The first products introduced by the division were faucet-mounted filters sold through department stores. The division expanded its product line by concentrating on the do-it-yourself market, selling under-counter systems, refrigerator water/ice maker filter systems, and a sediment and rust reduction whole house filtration system. The division also announced the introduction of a designer glass pitcher filtration system and two monitored faucet-mount systems. In 1997, Culligan entered into a marketing partnership with Health-O-Meter Products, Inc., the parent of Mr. Coffee, for plastic pour-through pitchers and with a major appliance manufacturer to provide a refrigerator water/ice maker filtration system. It also entered into a long-term agreement with Moen Inc. to develop Moen products incorporating Culligan water filtration assemblies. In 2009, it sold off its refillable water branch to PRMW Primo Water, wich reported fiscal 2010 sales of $69 million.

Through its Everpure division, Culligan also markets point-of-use filtration systems for homes and recreational vehicles such as Winnebago, Fleetwood, and Airstream. In 1997, Culligan Water Technologies merged with Ametek Inc. of Paoli, Pennsylvania, a global manufacturer of electrical and electromechanical products and a producer of parts for the residential water treatment market. In 1999, Culligan began selling and servicing Bruner water conditioning systems in a move to position itself for increased emphasis on the commercial market, especially the food service, lodging, and grocery industries.

Kinetico Inc. of Newbury, Ohio, was a leader in the production of under-counter reverse osmosis models, as well as carbon filters, entering the new decade with sales of roughly $50 million. Founded in 1970, the privately held company makes a line of products including a countertop filter model. Kinetico evolved from the Tangent Co., a small consulting design firm, eventually becoming a global organization of independent dealers, international distributors, and manufacturers' representatives in more than

100 countries. With 27 patents for water treatment and more than 1,100 industrial systems installed in 16 countries on five continents, the company has established a position of global leadership in the world of industrial water purification and recycling. The company uses a ceramic filter media developed by 3M Co., which Kinetico claims has proven very effective in the removal of microorganisms and contaminants such as methyl tertiary butyl ether (MTBE) from water. Because of the success of the ceramic filter, Kinetico now uses it in many of its applications, including residential, commercial, and industrial products.

Established in 1925, privately held EcoWater Systems Inc. claims to be the oldest and largest manufacturer of residential water treatment equipment in the world. The firm, headquartered in Woodbury, Minnesota, is a composite of three former companies. One of them, the Lindsay Co., obtained the first patent for water conditioning in 1925. Lindsay pioneered several industry firsts, such as automatic controls, high capacity resin, console units, iron-free systems, and rustproof fiberglass tanks. In 1981, Lindsay became a member of the Marmon Water Group, part of The Marmon Group of companies, an international association of autonomous manufacturing and service companies. In 1983, Lindsay purchased two other firms, after which the company was renamed EcoWater Systems in 1988. EcoWater was the first water treatment products manufacturer to become ISO-9001 certified by the International Organization for Standardization (IOS) of Geneva, Switzerland, to facilitate the distribution of EcoWater products to more than 1,400 independent water treatment dealers in the United States, Canada, Europe, Asia, and Africa.

In 1998, EcoWater Systems, Inc. entered into a working relationship with the Chesapeake Utilities Corporation, which began when Chesapeake acquired its first EcoWater dealership in March of that year. The two companies sought to identify and pursue opportunities to develop more aggressive, non-traditional methods of growth through growing the EcoWater dealer network. Chesapeake Utilities Corporation is a diversified utility company engaged in natural gas distribution and transmission, propane distribution and wholesale marketing, advanced information services, and water treatment services. Chesapeake also owns several businesses involved in water conditioning and treatment and bottled water services, including Sam Shannahan Well Co., Inc., Sharp Water, Inc., and Absolute Water. In 2000, the relationship with EcoWater continued expanding when Chesapeake acquired Carroll Water Systems, Inc. of Westminster, Maryland, an EcoWater Systems dealership.

Also in 2000, to attract more customers, EcoWater Systems developed a new line of products designed to be aesthetically pleasing and at the same time efficient, easy to use, and technologically innovative. The line included updated water softeners, conditioners, refiners and filters, as well as a new water conditioner and water refiner that featured a wireless remote monitor. Improved electronic controls include an easy to read and use digital dot matrix display that features a menu and provides access to information such as water rate, levels, and regeneration frequency. The company also added an advanced air-injected iron filter to complement its existing line of severe water problem-solving products.

BRITA, headquartered in Germany, is the global leader in the household water filter market, producing a variety of products such as pour-through water pitchers, tap filters, and squeeze-bottle filters. The BRTIA unit is the most visibly successful of the carafe units and established an early lead in the brand recognition battle..

Aqua Care Systems, Inc. of Coral Springs, Florida, designs, manufactures, and markets filtration and water purification systems under its subsidiaries KISS, Di-Tech Systems, and Midwest Water Technologies. The company organized its subsidiaries into two segments: industrial and municipal fluid handling and filtration, and commercial and residential water filtration and purification. Filtration and Separation Dynamics operates in the industrial and municipal fluid handling and filtration segment. It designs, manufactures, and markets a line of self-cleaning filtration and separation equipment for liquid slurries. KISS manufactures and distributes water filtration and purification products. Di-Tech Systems (DTSI) produces a line of water purification and ion exchange cartridges in the other segment.

The booming water purification market also served to lure large companies more known their for expertise in other areas. Entering the water treatment market in the late 1990s were appliance giant General Electric Co. (GE) and Honeywell International Inc., maker of thermostats and control products. GE's new line included water filtration and water softening products, which the company called "Smart-Water." According to GE, these systems allow homeowners to adjust the softness of the water throughout the home. According to GE, benefits include prolonged life of water-using appliances and plumbing, cleaner dishes and clothing, and increased water heater efficiency. Honeywell signaled its entrance into the water purification market in 1997 with its purchase of Filtercold Inc., a small Arizona-based maker of water purification systems with between $5 million and $10 million in annual sales. Honeywell primarily manufactures whole house systems designed to remove sediment such as sand and clay. Another industrial behemoth also jumped into the fray as Procter and Gamble acquired Recovery Engineering, maker of Pur water purifiers, for $300 million in 1999.

Air Quality Industry Honeywell International Inc. is a diversified technology and manufacturing company, offering aerospace products and services; control, sensing and security technologies for buildings, homes and industry; automotive products; specialty chemicals; fibers; and electronic and advanced materials. It was a leader in the air quality products industry in the first decade of the 2000s. Its Home and Building Control division manufactures and markets air quality systems. Sales for the division in 1999 were approximately $4 billion. The company expanded its product line in 1996 with its acquisition of the Duracraft Corp. of Southborough, Massachusetts, a company with annual sales of about $180 million. The following year, Honeywell's Home and Building Control division bought Phoenix Controls Corp., which specializes in precision airflow systems.

Other leaders in the industry include the Carrier Corp. of Farmington, Connecticut, a subsidiary of United Technologies Corp., and the Research Products Corp. of Madison, Wisconsin.

AMERICA AND THE WORLD

While the weak economy in the united States during 2008 and 2009 slowed the growth rate of the industry, there were many areas of the globe where clean, safe water was scarce but the economies were growing and people were able to afford purification technology. Such areas included China, India, and Indonesia in the Asia Pacific region, as well as countries like Brazil and South Africa. These areas were expected to drive the consumer market for water treatment.

Asia's Hyflux, a water-treatment company, was a leader in R & D, having developed Dragonfly, which condenses water in humid air to produce drinking water. Although Dragonfly was expensive and required significant levels of humidity, the company was optimistic for the product refinement process in 2004. The year before, Hyflux posted sales of $270 million.

Due to concentrations in population, industry, and agriculture, China and India's water requirements have escalated due to the point that the natural water supply can no longer accommodate the needs of the population without a major impact on the environment. China plans to allocate approximately $250 billion during the period of 2006 to 2009 toward its growing water demands, including supply, quality, technology, and infrastructure for its residential, industrial, and commercial markets.

Hendrx Corp., with offices in the United States and Canada, is a water technology company that researches, develops, manufactures, markets, and distributes water filtration and purification devices worldwide. Hendrx has begun targeting its products to meet the needs of developing countries, such as China and India. According to a Hendrx spokesperson, the needs of such countries are immense—from agricultural to industrial to wastewater treatment. Hendrx's main focus in the short term is on potable water.

RESEARCH AND TECHNOLOGY

Industry analysts expect the U.S. demand for water and air purification systems to continue to increase, along with total demand for purification systems and replacement parts (including filters and membranes). Anticipated technological developments include more efficient and user-friendly systems brought about through innovations such as faster and quieter operation, filter performance indicators, and a greater variety of purification systems. Driving the industry growth will be ongoing consumer concerns about the quality of water and indoor air as well as a sense of urgency to act on those concerns. Furthermore, it is expected that consumers already owning purification systems will upgrade to more efficient and better-performing equipment.

Water Quality Industry Research developments in the water purification industry ranged from the simple to the highly complex. All capitalized on America's fear of the water it drinks. On a local level, research that aided drinking water came from watershed management. One example was New York's purification of its water supply by microorganisms as the water percolated through the soil of the Catskills. Any municipality doubting the economic value of prevention rather than cure could look to New York's example. The city planned to spend $660 million to preserve that watershed. The alternative, a water treatment plant, would have cost $4 billion to build. On a national level, watershed management and source water protection was made a part of national policy in the Safe Drinking Water Act Amendment of 1996, which created a revolving fund to aid states in keeping water supplies in good condition.

Other new developments in the water quality industry included breakthrough products such as a water filter based on nanotechnology that removes carcinogens, developed at the Los Alamos National Laboratory; a filter developed by the Stevens Institute of Technology that removes arsenic; and a microbe discovered by researchers at the University of California at Davis that, when placed in water, "eats" the fuel additive MTBE.

The USDA, together with the EPA, co-hosted the second annual Water Quality Trading Conference in Pittsburgh n 2006. Water trading is essentially the buying and selling of water access entitlements, either on a permanent or temporary basis. A temporary arrangement can vary from months to several years. Water trading between users in an open market guarantees that water assigned for consumptive use progressively moves to higher value uses, resulting in greater production from the water, as well as environmental benefits, as water is traded from less productive areas and/or low value, low efficiency production to areas more suited to irrigation, using improved management practices on crops with higher priority. Water trading is an innovative approach to achieving cleaner water. The purpose of the Water Quality Trading Conference is to study the fundamentals and mechanics of trading, to scrutinize trading programs around the country, and to discuss the future of water trading.

Air Quality Industry One of the newest breakthroughs in the air quality industry was the use of nanotechnology in air cleaning systems. In 2007, for example, NanoTwin Technologies launched a product called NanoBreeze, which used nano-titanium dioxide crystals. The crystals, which are only 40 nanometers in size (one nanometer is equal to one-millionth of a millimeter), have semiconducting qualities when combined with light. When charged, the particles produce oxidizing agents that kill airborne germs and pollutants. An advantage of NanoBreeze, according to *Inside R&D,* is that it does not produce ozone gases, unlike some other ionizing air cleaners. The EPA does not recommend ozone generators for indoor air cleaning because ozone can be a lung irritant and even cause permanent lung damage.

In October 2008, the National Center for Energy Management and Building Technologies (NCEMBT), a nonprofit organization, began a six-year research program to address several issues in the air quality industry. Objectives included: advance the role of air cleaning, define a set of criteria for determining acceptable air quality, develop and test devices and methods used to measure air quality, and identify new products and services based on the research findings. The University of Nevada at Las Vegas, The University of Illinois at Chicago, Pennsylvania State University, and Syracuse University were NCEMBT's partners in the project.

A study by the Air Emissions Monitoring Protocol, conducted by Steve Hoff of Iowa State's Department of Agricultural and Biosystems Engineering, concluded that a cat's litter box, smoking, and everyday household cleaning products may have more of an impact on health and air quality in a home than nearby hog confinement facilities. Hoff measured the concentration of hydrogen sulfide at nine swine operations with herd sizes ranging from 1,200 to 4,800. The study showed that, contrary to common belief, the highest levels of ammonia found were not at the swine operations, but in the homes with smokers and/or pets. The results showed that the levels of hydrogen sulfide and ammonia at the swine operations were not at a level to be considered a risk, according to federally published guidelines. According to Hoff, "It shows that just because you smell it, it doesn't automatically mean it's a health threat." The highest concentration of ammonia was found in a home where both occupants smoked; the second highest was in a house with pets.

BIBLIOGRAPHY

"Air Cleaning and Control: An Air Purification Consortium Project of the National Center for Energy Management and Building Technologies." *Snips,* October 2008.

"Air Treatment in the United States Report Will Help Readers Make Strategic Decisions in the Ever Changing Household Air Quality Market." *Business Wire,* 9 January 2008.

Arnot, Charlie, and Cliff Gauldin. "Industry Study Looks at Indoor Air Quality." *Feedstuffs,* 3 April 2006.

Akridge, Jeannie. "Indoor Air Quality Affects Patient Care Quality." *Healthcare Purchasing News,* September 2008.

Donn, Jeff. "Bottled Water Has Contaminants Too, Study Finds." AP News, 15 October 2008.

"Drinking Water Standards." Environmental Protection Agency, 1 November 2008. Available from http://www.epa.gov/.

Grimaldi, Lisa. "Ousting Allergens." *Meetings & Conventions,* June 2006.

Hall, John R. "Filtration Solutions Can Improve School IAQ." *Air Conditioning, Heating & Refrigeration News,* 22 May 2006.

Mitra, Sramana. "Deal Radar 2010: WaterFilters.NET." 19 April 2010. Available from http://www.sramanamitra.com/2010/04/19/deal-radar-2010-waterfilters-net/.

"Nanotechnology Being Applied in Air Purification." *Inside R&D,* 14 September 2007.

"Pharmaceuticals in Water Back in Spotlight with New Data." Water Quality Association, 14 September 2008.

"Research in the News." Water Quality Association, 11 November 2008.

"Reverse Osmosis Systems Treat Pharmaceutical Drinking Water Contaminants." *Business Wire,* 11 March 2008.

Smith, Carl. "Setting a Green Framework: GREENGUARD Certification and LEED Rating System Have Established Standards for Indoor Environmental Quality." *Environmental Design & Construction,* August 2008.

"Top EPA Official Says Pharmaceuticals Worth Review." Water Quality Association, 19 September 2008.

"U.S. Supreme Court Upholds State Certification of Quality of Water Released from Hydroelectric Dams." *Monday Business Briefing,* 17 May 2006.

"Water and Air Purification Systems and Products: Residential and Commercial." SBI report No. SB2809842. SBI Energy, October 2010. Available from http://www.sbireports. com/Water-Air-Purification-2809842/.

"Worsening Global Water Quality and Scarcity Problems Drive Need for Improved Water Infrastructure, Filtration, Treatment and Delivery." *Internet Wire,* 22 June 2006.

"ZeroWater's Drinking Water Symposium 'How Can We Go Back to Tap?' Successfully Advances the Movement to Break the Public's Bottled Water Habit." *Science Letter,* 14 October 2008.

WEB DEVELOPERS

SIC CODE(S)

7371

INDUSTRY SNAPSHOT

Web development has come a long way since the World Wide Web was first brought to the public en masse in the mid-1990s. From long, bland pages featuring visually drab text and clumsily placed graphics to wild-eyed pages using every trick in the book with little attention to the finer virtues of subtlety, the World Wide Web has developed into a sophisticated portal to an endless supply of information and commerce. From 10-year-old tech savvies designing intricate sites devoted to their cats to the world's largest multinational corporations, Web pages continue to be an increasingly important source of public identification. The World Wide Web redefined everything from commercial transactions to communication to the daily vernacular. Behind it all are the developers who make the World Wide Web work.

By far, the factor most responsible for the rapid evolution of Internet site development was the onslaught of electronic commerce (e-commerce). Businesses seeking to hawk products over the Internet spurred the technology and the developers into overdrive in attempts to tailor World Wide Web sites and their capabilities to the companies' marketing and distribution needs. With each new generation of server products mitigating low-end headaches such as object management and database connectivity, the role of World Wide Web developers has rapidly shifted to the creation of sites that distinguish the company and its product. The net result has been a more differentiated World Wide Web environment.

Secondary to e-commerce, social networking, particularly its exponential expansion in Web applications near the end of the first decade of the millennium (e.g. Twitter, FaceBook, etc.) in turn widened databases for e-commerce applications. Third, the use of wireless web applications and interconnectivity of devices created an ever-evolving market expected to continue appreciable growth into the second decade.

ORGANIZATION AND STRUCTURE

Generally, the goal of a Web site is to combine optimal functionality with a unique and stimulating visual display. To achieve this, clients must clearly inform developers of what purposes their Web sites will serve and what features and information they should include. In return, developers must indicate what they can accomplish given their tools and the current state of technology so that clients do not expect more than developers can reasonably deliver.

Once the site is developed, the developer may take on the role of a Web site custodian, often called a Webmaster, depending on the contract and content of the Web site. If a company or organization wishes to keep its site up to date, then such a service is indispensable, whether performed by the developer, a third-party maintenance service, or the client.

Ownership of the Web site or its parts also depends on the contract between the developer and client. Some developers retain rights to Web pages and their graphics, but many clients prefer to own the copyright themselves. Ownership can be ambiguous if not negotiated in advance since most sites include content and ideas provided by the client but encoded and implanted by the developer. Hardware to support the site is usually a separate matter, often provided by third-party vendors.

Besides commissioning a Web site or purchasing it outright, organizations have two other options: renting a site or paying an initial fee and sharing the revenues the site generates. Renting is an economical method of getting on the Internet for companies with limited budgets or companies looking to test the efficacy of a Web site. Retailers planning to use Web sites for online commerce could benefit from paying a development fee, which may start at about $20,000, and then paying a percentage of their revenues to the developers. The latter option offers clients shared risk if the site fails to draw many sales.

While one developer can design simple Web sites consisting of a few pages, generally a whole team of Web developers must undertake the design of more complex sites, such as online stores or magazines. When working on larger projects, developers usually divide the labor by allocating specific tasks to specific developers. Thus, one developer composes graphics, another codes the functional aspects, and yet another prepares the encoded text. Furthermore, a project manager often coordinates and oversees the entire production of Web sites.

Pages on the World Wide Web are written using hypertext markup language (HTML) codes for the basic layout of the site. HTML codes indicate how the information should appear in a browser: centered, boldfaced, colored, and so forth. Each style feature is separately coded. For graphics, developers can place digital photographs and images on pages with HTML codes referencing the external graphics files. Dynamic Internet graphics can be developed through programming languages, such as Sun Microsystems, Inc.'s Java or Microsoft Corp.'s ActiveX. These languages allow the creation of active image applications, or applets, that rotate or change their form. Advanced Web authoring tools aid Web site development by allowing developers to use other programming languages such as Visual Basic or C++, or by automating parts of the design process, such as writing complex strings of commonly used HTML codes. For instance, a development tool might allow the designer to create a document using standard word-processing techniques that it converts to HTML.

The Internet Engineering Task Force (IETF) functions as an organization of vendors, designers, operators, and researchers concerned with the progress of Internet operation and development. Founded in 1986, the IETF consists of a series of work groups responsible for various aspects of Internet operation and architecture. In 1996, the World Wide Web Consortium (W3C), an international group of Internet researchers, with the backing of both Netscape Communications Corp. and Microsoft Corp., the bitterly embattled manufacturers of browser technology, started to assume responsibility for developing HTML and Web authoring standards. Founded in 1994, the W3C strives to develop the Internet as an accessible and freely available worldwide medium, not dependent on proprietary features or specifications. The consortium is headed by the Massachusetts Institute of Technology's Laboratory for Computer Science and the National Institute for Research in Computer Science and Control, a public French research institute.

As Internet development companies expanded their operations into providing online solutions to marketing needs and infrastructures, they increasingly squared off against major consulting firms. Since large consultancies generally contract with major technology firms such as IBM Corp. for such work, development companies are often able to out-price them.

The World Wide Web Consortium, an Internet research group, produced its "Architecture of the World Wide Web" document that identified and described HTML (the most-used software authoring language of World Wide Web pages) and Web authoring standards. It was the authoritative description of the World Wide Web's architecture. By publishing these standards for World Wide Web languages and protocols, W3C aims to avoid fragmentation of the market and the Web. W3C calls it "Web interoperability."

BACKGROUND AND DEVELOPMENT

If the Internet and the World Wide Web had to be traced back to one man, it would inevitably fall on the shoulders of Ted Nelson. Although many different people have developed and designed the World Wide Web and the Internet as it is today, they would all agree their ideas were based in some way on Nelson's vision.

Nelson is credited as the inventor of hypertext, a term he coined in 1965, which is the basis for HTML, the language for designing Web pages. In 1960, Nelson began to envision computer networks as the repository of all human documentation, with notions of hyperlinked text and media, an almost unheard of concept at the time.

Prior to the advent of graphic Internet capabilities associated with the World Wide Web, however, the Internet offered little to the average person or even to companies. Scholars, businesses, and the U.S. military made up the primary users of the Internet at that time. Use centered on exchange of information by posting text-only documents on browser-friendly directory trees called gophers and sending messages.

In 1990, Tim Berners-Lee created both HTML and the hypertext transfer protocol (HTTP) that enables the global transfer of information, effectively developing the World Wide Web as it is known today. Three years later, the graphical Web browser revolutionized the medium and helped launch the Internet into mainstream society in the United States and across the globe. The National Center for Supercomputing Applications at the University of Illinois at Urbana-Champaign developed the first browser, Mosaic, and licensed it to Spyglass, Inc., which in turn licensed it to other companies.

In 1995, as Web site development began to flourish as an industry, Kyle Shannon, cofounder of the Web design firm Agency.com Ltd., started the World Wide Web Artists Consortium to serve the needs and interests of Web site developers. The organization's focal points included advertising, digital imaging and graphics, e-commerce, Internet law, and database integration.

As more consumers subscribed to Internet service providers (ISPs), such as America Online, Microsoft Network, and Netcom, businesses and organizations began to use the Internet for more than internal company and organization communication. They found that they could promote and in some cases deliver their products and services via the World Wide Web. Unless they had a technically savvy staff, however, they could not expect to create a very exciting, functional, and informative Web site. Therefore, companies and organizations outsourced this task to competent agencies or individuals familiar with Web page creation. In addition, many software companies such as Microsoft and Novell developed HTML editing applications to allow users to create their own Web pages with templates and coding tools. Older programs required some familiarity with HTML and enabled HTML novices to create only fairly generic pages based on templates or automated code generators known as "wizards." While newer programs made Web authoring easier, most still lacked capabilities for automated creation of original logos, graphics, and images that are elements common to Web pages. Hence, while Web developers may have started out by creating a basic, no-nonsense Web site, they evolved alongside the technology and came to provide more advanced services and greater expertise in Web site design that commercial software cannot provide.

In 1999 and early 2000, a series of high-profile hackings into major commerce sites alarmed observers of the emerging electronic marketplace and focused developers' attention on heightening security measures. The Computer Emergency Response Team (CERT) Coordination Center at Carnegie Mellon University released a joint statement in February 2000 pertaining to the proliferation of software scripts that hackers can post to Web sites without the knowledge or approval of site operators. The scripts allow outsiders to access the systems to sabotage the infrastructure or intercept crucial information such as passwords or consumer profiles, including credit card numbers. To protect their sites, CERT advised developers to recode dynamically produced sites to filter content during download and to dynamically code and filter incoming data from order forms and other messages. IBM chief Louis Gerstner issued his own incentive to the e-commerce

community to drastically step up security measures, noting simply that if companies did not take such measures, then the government would, a development that would not be beneficial for businesses.

Analysts were also advising increased care in the construction of Web sites, since, according to Forrester Research, a site fix can cost between $8,500 and $17,000, while a complete overhaul can run as high as $1.56 million. To avoid such steep payments, observers noted, developers would do well to conduct a series of usability tests. Usability describes the access and information retrieval capabilities a user experiences when visiting a site. Developers were charged with maintaining constant cognizance of variations in users' technological capabilities.

Meanwhile, activists for the disabled increasingly pressured Congress to enact legislation to push Web site operators toward greater accessibility for those with disabilities, particularly the blind. Under Title III of the Americans with Disabilities Act, public accommodations are required to be handicap-accessible. Leading the activists was the W3C, which held that the Web can use computers to transmit information in a variety of ways, including streaming audio, that accommodate the needs of the disabled. The legal applicability to the Internet of the Title III provisions, which are generally geared toward physical structures such as schools, remained unclear in the early years of the twenty-first century's first decade, although some Internet industry proponents were calling for government-funded research to find the most effective way to implement such accessibility.

The Web development industry experienced a spate of consolidations in the late 1990s as a number of developers attempted to establish themselves as industry leaders. While there were about 40,000 Web developers overall, Forrester Research reported that only about 10 to 20 developers courted major corporate accounts. In order to pique the curiosity of big companies, Web developers merged to demonstrate that they are large and diverse enough to handle such accounts. For example, Web developers such as Agency.com and Razorfish made a plethora of acquisitions in the late 1990s, while USWeb/CKS, in perhaps a premonition of things to come, merged with the consultancy firm Whittman-Hart, Inc. in early 2000.

After the September 11, 2001, terrorist attacks, concerns about security issues for the industry were heightened. White Hat Security's WhiteHat Arsenal 2.0 was rated as being a good collection of basic tools for Quality of Service testing before applications go live to check for common vulnerabilities.

For several years, Web developers were torn between two competing browser standards: those of Netscape and those of Microsoft. Since each company's browser read similar coding in different ways because of the implementation of proprietary software technology, designers were forced to consider a variety of options to make their pages as accessible as possible for their intended audiences. They could either settle on a particular browser as the standard, creating duplicate pages while directing users to one or the other on the site's home page, or attempt to compromise the coding to produce as little friction as possible between the competing browsers and their users. Both Netscape and Microsoft submitted their standards to the W3C to release news to the effect that their browsers were on the way to standardization.

In 2000, the battle continued, but its rough edges were somewhat smoothed when both companies retooled their rendering engines—the components that actually interpret the coding—to be compatible with emerging W3C standards. In 2003, the W3C released its description of HTML and Web authoring standards. According to Kim Guenther, director of the University of Virginia (UVA) Health System Web Center and Webmaster for the UVA Health System, standards are the glue binding separate efforts together. Although back end standards may not be readily apparent to an end user, they guide site development with equally consistent functionality. The W3C report was the industry benchmark for Web architecture.

Due to the nature of the business, Web site development is a somewhat never-ending process, as the technology continues to develop. The e-commerce Web sites in particular, with a continual drive toward ease of use, were never seen as finished, but continually evolving. With a huge level of competition, only the easy-to-use sites would attract repeat visitors. Because the e-commerce-based Web site often drives a significant percentage of a company's sales, spending on Web development continued to increase, even when other IT spending went down.

High-end rich media (advanced technology special effects) capabilities afford Web developers the ability to create highly complex, visually stimulating, and interactive Web graphics and features. However, by 2000, professional developers tended to use rich media only sparingly, for several reasons. Perhaps most crucially, developers recognize that a relatively small proportion of the browsing population actually has the bandwidth capable of effectively reading or even downloading such complex displays. Despite the surging growth in e-commerce and Internet connectivity, the majority of the wired population did not use high-speed digital subscriber lines (DSL) or cable modems by 2004, although this impediment was significantly less pronounced for developers working on Web sites geared toward business-to-business activity. Moreover, current technology renders the delivery of rich media exceptionally complex, often requiring separate server infrastructure in order to be set up. Nonetheless, with increasingly integrated standards, rich media was expected to gain an increasing foothold on the Internet. By 2000, rich media was finding extensive application in e-commerce sites devoted to the online sale and distribution of music and video.

In general, Web developers were expected to also be designers by 2004, unlike their predecessors who simply had to be "techies" who could work with code. Companies such as IBM were unveiling software that automated many Web development tasks such as changing links and debugging code errors so that the developers could spend more time on the building and testing of applications—actual development—and less time on grunt work that could be handled with templates and other tools for automation.

The wide array of possibilities for accessing the Web allowed users, including the disabled, to choose the mode of interaction most suitable for their needs. With the use of the appropriate device, users can provide input by speech, handwriting, or keystrokes, while output can be presented via displays, prerecorded and synthetic speech, audio, or tactile mechanisms such as mobile phone vibrators and Braille strips. Speech, especially, works well with mobile devices, allowing the user to operate hands-free or one-handed. In 2005, W3C developed "the W3C Speech Interface Framework"—a set of markup specifications designed to develop applications that can be accessed from any telephone. The specifications apply to voice dialogs, speech synthesis, speech recognition, telephone call control for voice browsers, and any other mode of interactive voice response application, of particular interest to people with hearing or speaking disabilities.

CURRENT CONDITIONS

A May 2009 article by *Web Design* listed the top 21 web development trends for 2009. They included (1) rapid development platforms (e.g., CodeIgniter, Django, RoR); (2) Cloud Hosting(a very burgeoning industry as a whole); (3) distributed online storage, such as that offered by Amazon S3, which is designed to make Web scaling easy for developers, providing a Web service that can be used to store and retrieve any amount of data at any given time, from anywhere on the Internet; (4) CSS Sprites (especially for web games applications); (5) Framework/libraries that allow developers to write code elegantly. (For example, jQuery, a JavaScript framework, expanded the built-in features of JavaScript.); (6) browser/desktop offline applications based on Adobe Air (Adobe Integrated Runtime, a cross-platform runtime environment for building rich Internet applications. It uses Flash, Flex HTML and/or Ajax, and can be used online or desktop based.) Current applications based on Adobe Air in 2009 included AOL, eBay and Yahoo!; (7) flash HD streaming and HD flash streaming (with many websites, such as YouTube and Revision3, offering their content in HD thorough the flash player; (8) remote script use, such as loading scripts from a central location, like a direct link, which allows developers to call active server pages without having to refresh the page; and (9) using Application Programming Interfaces (APIs) to automate everything.

Despite the gloomy economy in 2008 and 2009, IT industry analyst Gartner reported that overall revenues from worldwide IT services, such as managed Web hosting and disaster recovery provision, increased 8.2 percent in 2008. The report, "Market Share: IT Services, Worldwide Rankings, 2008," indicated that total revenues for IT services increased from $745 billion in 2007 to $806 billion in 2008.

Web Host Industry Review's 2009 "Year in Review: Hosting Software and Technology" reminded consumers of some 2009 developments sometimes forgotten in the nonstop stream of daily online data. For example, right at year"s end, an attack directed at Neustar, the domain name system services provider for Amazon, Wal-Mart, and Expedia, and other large e-commerce companies, shut down several online Internet shopping sites the night before Christmas Eve, taking out sites completely or rendering them sluggish for about an hour, and leaving some last-minute shoppers scrambling. Even though spam levels were down from the same time in 2008, spammers and bot herders were expected to continue to plague the Internet until the industry lobbied for heavier prosecutions for their crimes, it reported.

In 2008, *ICT Statistics Newslog* (citing a report by Juniper Research) noted that global Mobile Web 2.0 revenues would reach $22.4 billion by 2013, up from US$5.5 billion in 2008. By embracing social networking and user-generated content (UGC), mobile search and mobile IM (Instant Messaging), Mobile Web 2.0 provided a framework for delivery of collaborative applications, further enhanced and contextualized by LBS (Location Based Services), the report concluded.

According to *Web Host Industry Review,*cloud computing did as much as any other technology, idea or product to define Web hosting in 2009. The review article said cloud computing was the buzzword that came up at every hosting event of the year.

INDUSTRY LEADERS

Based in New York, Agency.com successfully courted such major corporate clients as Metropolitan Life Insurance Co., American Express Co., Nike, Reuters, GTE, Visa, and T-Mobile UK. Kyle Shannon and Chan Suh founded the firm in 1995 with only $80 and two employees. In 1996, the advertising powerhouse Omnicom Group acquired Agency.com for its Communicade Division, its interactive marketing arm. In the following years, with strong corporate

backing, Agency.com acquired Online Magic, a Web design company based in the United Kingdom with clients such as the *Economist* and Simon & Schuster, as well as Interactive Solutions and Spiral Media. In 1998, Agency.com merged with Interactive Solutions, followed by an acquisition of Omnicom's Eagle River Interactive the following year, dramatically increasing its size before going public in late 1999.

Agency.com was particularly drawn to the emerging wireless e-commerce market, reorganizing to focus more heavily on the convergence of the World Wide Web and wireless telephones. The company was an early member of the association that developed the Wireless Access Protocol (WAP) mobile Internet access specification. Client feedback led to creation of a user-centric Web site, http://www.agency.com, in January 2003. Quality-HealthCare.org was launched in March 2003. The free site for the Institute for Healthcare Improvement was the first online global health care resource that allows healthcare professionals to share their expertise with their colleagues.

As of 2009, Agency.com had 11 international offices, including in Amsterdam, Boston, Chicago, Dallas, London, and San Francisco. It has garnered several industry awards, including December 2009 national awards by the Hospitality Sales and Marketing Association for its Web design and Search Engine Optimization (SEO) services; a 2009 Web Marketing Association Web Award; a 2009 Food Industry Standard of Excellence; a Cannes Lions 2009 award, and a New York Festivals 2009 Nike: Baby It's Cold Outside Bronze World Medal). With clients in the United States, Europe, and Asia, Agency.com employed 477 people in 10 global offices, and celebrated its tenth anniversary in 2005. Some of the firm's long-time clients include 3M, British Airways, Energizer, eBay, HP, Maidenform, and T-Mobile.

Razorfish, acquired by Microsoft in 2007, became one of the industry's leading companies in the late 1990s, designing sites as well as refitting them for e-commerce capability. After buying Sunbather, CHBI, Plastic, Spray, and Avalanche Systems, Razorfish added such clients as the *Financial Times* to its roster of Web design clients, which included the *Wall Street Journal,* Time Warner, Charles Schwab, and CBS. With these acquisitions, Razorfish took a key step toward providing coast-to-coast service in the United States and the globalization of the industry. In 1999, the company went public in an effort to raise additional money for expansion. Razorfish continued its aggressive acquisition campaign, boosting revenues and increasing its payroll to 1,500 employees. Avenue A/Razorfish is a wholly owned subsidiary of SBI. SBI focuses on helping clients develop meaningful customer relationships and improve business performance. At that time, it had operations in Australia, China, France, Germany, Hong Kong, Japan, and the United Kingdom. On August 9th, 2009, Microsoft sold the firm to Publicis Groupe. Razorfish's revenue was $380 million in 2008.

The USWeb/CKS merger with Whittman-Hart created the industry giant marchFIRST, Inc., signifying the date of the deal in 2000. The move was intended to integrate the creative World Wide Web capabilities of USWeb/CKS with Whittman-Hart's experience in working with firms on their development needs. USWeb went on an expansion spree in the late 1990s to become the industry's biggest player. Founded in 1995, USWeb had offices across the United States and earned the reputation of being one of the most experienced, qualified, and professional Internet consultants in the world. The developer specialized in helping businesses market themselves via the Internet by designing intranets, extranets, Web sites, and Internet commerce systems. The company operated in 14 countries worldwide and employed 3,900. In 2001, Divine Inc. acquired the central region business unit plus other offices and assets of marchFirst. Analysts said both Chicago-based companies struggled to survive during a time of downturn in demand for Web consultants after the infamous dot-com bottoming out in 2002. Divine sold most of its assets at a deep discount before filing for Chapter 11 bankruptcy in February 2003.

Digitas Inc., based in Boston and purchased in 2007 by French advertising conglomerate Publicis for $1.3 billion, has three operating agencies. One of these, Modern Media, provides Web site and intranet development, as well as other services. Modem Media has offices in the United States and London and serves such clients as General Motors, IBM, and Sprint.

WORKFORCE

Web site developers have launched their careers from a host of backgrounds. Some started out as graphic designers while others trained as computer programmers. Moreover, a significant contingent switched to Web site design from a multitude of unrelated fields. Knowledge of graphic design and computer programming facilitate Web site development, though many designers pick these skills up from Web development literature or from college courses on HTML and Web site design. Furthermore, certain Web authoring tools cater to novice programmers and require no familiarity with HTML, Java, or C++. Due to the rapid development of Web sites, however, education is something of a constant.

According to *The New York Times,* Web developers have typically earned about $30,000 a year for HTML authoring and $100,000 a year for advanced programming using CGI and Perl—programming languages for advanced site functions such as image maps, forms, and database queries. Long-term job market projections remain uncertain because software producers such as Microsoft, Adobe, and Novell continue to refine programs to streamline and simplify Web authoring. If such developments lead to

diminished value of such skills as HTML authoring, developers will be forced to market themselves on their creative expertise as it relates to page and infrastructure design, and the extent to which they can tailor that expertise to specific needs.

RESEARCH AND TECHNOLOGY

According to *Web Host Industry Review* (WHIR) in 2009, Open-Xchange technology made huge advances in web-based email and collaboration. R1Soft's CDP 3.0 emphasized the importance of data backup to enterprise customers interested in cloud computing. Parallels made it easier for web hosting businesses to manage their hosting and provide SaaS applications. VMware created what it called the first cloud operating system. Finally, Windows launched its latest server operating system release, adding features for new server infrastructures. Microsoft Exchange remained the choice email client for most business applications.

R1Soft Unveiled unveilled the next major update to its continuous data protection technology with the latest version of its CDP software at the cPanel Conference in October 2009. CDP Server 3.0 Standard Edition, the first release of R1Soft's CDP 3.0 products, offered users high-performance CDP backups on a single server without the need of a dedicated backup.

Parallels Panel 9 went into wide release in December 2008, as one of the top technologies of 2008 because of the immense power and control it gives to Web hosts, noted WHIR. Along with its Small Business Panel 10, released in 2009, the virtualization automation provider came out with a streamlined and accessible control panel application that could be used to let a hosting provider easily offer a full line of services.

BIBLIOGRAPHY

"21 Web Development Trends For 2009." Web Design Developments, 15 May 2009. Available from http://www.webdesigndev.com/web-development/21-web-development-trends-for-2009.

"About the World Wide Web Consortium (W3C)." World Wide Web Consortium (W3C), 7 July 2006. Available from www.w3.org/Consortium/.

"Agency.com Creates User-Centric Web Site Through Client Feedback." *Hoover's Online,* 17 January 2003. Available from http://www.hoovers.com.

"AJAX is the Future of Web App Development." *Network World,* 17 July 2006.

Andersson, David. "HTML5, XHTML2, and the Future of the Web." *Digital Web,* 10 April 2007.

"ASP.NET Mobile Controls." *Microsoft Corporation,* 2004. Available from asp.net/.

Barlas, Pete. "Shopping Sites Shell Out to Make Consumers Buy More." *Investor's Business Daily,* 21 October 2003.

"Design Software Offers Web Application Development Component." *Product News Network,* 20 June 2006.

"Facts." Agency.com, 8 July 2006. Available from http://agency.com/.

"Fusion 9.0. A Simple Yet Comprehensive tool for Web Developers." *Computer Reseller News,* 23 January 2006.

"Global Mobile Phone Subscription to Hit 3.5bn." *Business Day Website,* 24 May 2006. Available from www.businessday online.com/.

Hein, James. "A Look at Java and the Server Side of Web Development." *Asia Africa Intelligence Wire,* 3 September 2003.

"Hoover's Company Capsules." *Hoover's Online,* 2007. Available from www.hoovers.com.

IPTV Magazine, 9 August 2005. Available from www.iptvmagazine.com/.

Louderback, Jim. "A Whole New Web?" *PC Magazine,* 5 June 2007.

"Microsoft Learning Center Targets Beginner Programmers." *eWeek,* 1 March, 2007.

"Microsoft To Sell Razorfish to Publicis Groupe." CBS News, 29 June 2009. Available from http://www.cbsnews.com/stories/2009/06/29/paidcontent/main5120895.shtml.

"Mobile Web 2.0 Revenues to Reach $22.4 Billion by 2013. " *ICT Statistics Newslog,* 15 May 2008.

Scannell, Ed. "IBM Automates Web Development." *InfoWorld. com,* 14 August 2003.

"USWeb Internet Marketing." USWeb, 7 July 2006. Available from www.usweb.com/.

"W3C Technical Architecture Group Produces 'Architecture of the World Wide Web'." W3C. 10 December 2003. Available from www.w3.org/2003/12/tag-pressrelease.

Wagner, Mitch. "BEA Plans Technology for Incorporating XML in Java." *InternetWeek,* 27 January 2003.

White, Bobby. "Annapolis-Based Web Development Firm, Blog Sprite, Launches Free Marketing Tool for Businesses." *Daily Record,* 2 September 2003.

Wilson, Jason. "Web 2.0? Let's Recap." *Australian PC World,* June 2007.

Wright, Sarah Anne. "Amazon Aims for New Types of Web Developer." *Knight Ridder/Tribune Business News,* 18 January 2004.

"Year in Review: Hosting Software and Technology;" *Web Host Industry Review,* December 2009.

WEB PORTALS AND ONLINE COMMUNITIES

———————■———————

SIC CODE(S)

7370

INDUSTRY SNAPSHOT

Often considered synonymous with "search engines," Web portals are actually far broader, though most include search engines in their arsenals. Although Web portals fulfill several different functions, at their most basic, they act as a sort of gateway to the World Wide Web, providing a starting point through which users can choose the direction in which they wish to go with the aid of the portal's extensive categorization and search engines. In addition, they provide original content, such as news and business headlines, online communities, private e-mail services, and shopping sites, as well as other features, such as chat rooms and customization options.

As the Internet became increasingly central to the world of commerce, and vice versa, Web portals assumed a more commercial presence, acting not only as a central medium for companies to advertise and reach customers but also often acting as online merchants themselves. The impact that the Internet has had on commerce has been substantial, as e-commerce represents a growing percentage of revenues across various business sectors.

Online communities are often a part of Web portals or can be completely separate entities. Such communities provide space where those with common interests or characteristics—such as women, basketball lovers, musicians, or any other group—can meet virtually and exchange information and ideas through bulletin boards, chat rooms, and e-mail lists. Most major Web portals include at least some of these elements. Like Web portals, online communities proved a popular method of putting businesses in touch with each other.

ORGANIZATION AND STRUCTURE

Web portals come in a wide variety of sites. The most well known variety was the enormous generalist site, featuring a search engine, links pointing in all directions of the Internet, and an array of content for the average Internet surfer. Modern Internet portals generally include, but are not limited to, search engines. Since search engines simply allow users to go elsewhere, Web portals realized that to keep Internet users around on their sites, thereby attracting more advertising revenue, they needed to add value by expanding options and services. Depending on its precise focus and target audience, a Web portal typically augments its basic search engine and site categorization with additional services such as e-mail, chat rooms, virtual shopping centers, and directories.

Most Web portals began to open online malls in a full embrace of electronic commerce (e-commerce), while streamlining their existing shopping services by adding ease-of-use features. For example, Excite@Home's Excite Shopping Service was designed to provide users with the ability to seek out a range of products, compare prices, and keep abreast of product availability, while AOL, Inc.'s ShopAOL offered electronic wallets, in which customers could store credit card numbers and Web sites and easily toggle between product categories with a click of the mouse.

Along with the flourishing of e-commerce, a new breed of Web portals emerged. Known as vertical portals, they focus not on general subject areas for any and all audiences but on specific users looking for specific sites or categories. Mostly, vertical portals are concentrated in the business to business (B2B) e-commerce sector,

1055

putting suppliers in touch with buyers and creating communities within industries. B2B portals enable companies to instantly compare prices and availability across a range of suppliers, and facilitate faster ordering and delivery. Vertical portals have also been constructed outside the B2B realm, catering to customers looking for certain kinds of products. Fashionmall.com, for instance, was a vertical portal designed to assist customers seeking out name brand clothing.

Indeed, portals were beginning to emerge as the standard model by which businesses and information were organized. Companies began rearranging their manufacturing, advertising, and finance operations into a portal framework at the beginning of the twenty-first century, making applications simple to access and navigate. Business portals arranged corporate software and applications to perform their functions in the most efficient manner and facilitate the easy access of internal and external information. Software and Internet giants such as AOL and Netscape have helped build customized Web portals for corporations such as FedEx and Lucent to allow their employees quick access to company software and information from Netscape's NetCenter Web site. This practice stands to revolutionize the business computing process, replacing the standard personal computer desktop applications with Web-based portals.

BACKGROUND AND DEVELOPMENT

Most of the major Web portals started out as simple search engines. As a result of the perpetual battle to draw more users, these search engines, including Yahoo!, Infoseek, Lycos, HotBot, Excite, and others, enhanced their home pages with expanded features and information. They began to streamline their Web site indexes to offer news headlines, sports scores, wire services, technology-based links, travel pages, and an almost endless supply of other features that added value to their sites and invited users to stick around, drawing advertisers in their wake. By 1997, the leading Web portals such as Yahoo! recognized that many users felt simply overwhelmed with information and options when they hopped on the Web, and thus the portals began offering services such as My Yahoo! that allowed users to customize their options.

Web portals quickly became among the most famed of the dot-com companies. They greatly facilitated the onslaught of e-commerce, as companies eyeing their success at attracting Internet surfers fell over themselves to establish marketing deals with the portal firms, which commanded handsome fees for the service.

For the most part, up until mid-1998, dot-com companies knew their place: while the e-tailers engaged in commerce, the Web portals provided a site on which the merchants could hawk their goods. By 1999, things had begun to change, and Web portals began to aggressively promote new shopping sites and other e-commerce services directly on their own sites while still maintaining their marketing contracts with e-merchants. Excite, for instance, launched its Express Order site at which customers could make purchases from any of the company's affiliated vendors, while Lycos, Inc., initiated an online store where customers could use a single interface to shop from more than 200 retailers.

In the early years of the first decade of the twenty-first century, one of the most striking facts about Web portals, and indeed much of the dot-com juggernaut in general, was that extremely few of them were operating in the black. Investors had hardly soured on Web portals, however. Indeed, Web portals were the second best performing dot-com stock sector in 1999. For their part, the major Web portals were busily consolidating the dot-com industry in the late 1990s, buying up search engines and databases and forming alliances with established portals, Internet service providers, and e-tailers. For instance, Infoseek, one of the leading early Web portals, teamed up with the Walt Disney Co. to create the giant GO.com, while Excite was purchased by Internet service provider @Home to create Excite@Home. Jupiter Communications, Inc., meanwhile, estimated that e-commerce emerging from Web portals would account for 20 percent of all online purchases by 2002, or $8.7 billion, compared with about $2.4 billion in 1998.

Business to business (B2B) portals came into their own in 1999, providing companies with an extremely efficient way in which to procure equipment, supplies, and services, although the trend created a panic among manufacturing companies who feared the practice would undermine their operations and lead to diminished margins. While manufacturers scrambled for strategies to meet the rapidly shifting market conditions created by B2B portals, some jumped on board in full force, even creating portals of their own. DuPont helped prepare the launch of Yet2.com as an electronic marketplace for technology purchasing, and teamed up with the Redwood City, California-based ImproveNet Inc. to create a construction material portal and with Spec-Chem.com Inc. of Houston to build a site for chemicals.

Portals also tended to enjoy a surprising degree of loyalty. As customers became acclimated to one particular gateway's services and search methods, they often felt reluctant to deal with others. On the flip side of that loyalty was the "one-chance" mentality of users when it came to system crashes. Outside of the largest sites, users were quite often unforgiving of sites that delivered error messages and crashes. Thus, Web portals hoping to attract a lot of traffic were bound to extensively stress-test their systems to be sure they could handle the flood of site hits they hoped to generate.

Ironically, the borderless world of the Internet also helped local communities and businesses in some cases stave off competition from the encroachment of national chains and e-commerce giants. Local businesses have banded together to establish local portals as virtual neighborhoods in order to direct those in the community to the commerce, entertainment, and other Web sites and physical locations that will keep money and interest circulating inside the community. Ideally, local Web portals not only could keep small businesses alive in the New Economy and amidst the merger mania of the Old Economy, but could even help promote an active community life, providing links to local governments, organizations, and businesses, as well as keeping citizens on top of the local Little League standings or the results of the high school basketball team's game.

Local content was indeed one of the great prizes of the dot-com companies in 2000, and local portals found that they rarely had to make an effort to persuade local businesses to sign up, usually for a monthly fee that could range from about $30 to $400, depending on the level of service provided by the portal. Local newspapers, with mountains of local content, also got into the act and helped propel the local portal craze by simply uploading their extensive files to the World Wide Web. The *Boston Globe,* for instance, created Boston.com in 1995 to link to other media in the Boston area, although their brethren in the newspaper business were skeptical. It did not take long for the site to develop into a successful full-blown portal that most other media followed by the end of the twentieth century.

Media outlets in general quickly upgraded their Web sites to the portal model. The New York Times Co., Knight Ridder, and Dow Jones & Co. all announced plans to develop their sites into portals in 1999. It was hoped that in this way, traffic on their sites would boom and advertisers would come calling, providing the advertising revenue that lay at the heart of most newspaper companies' business.

Just as new Web portals were popping up continuously each year with more specific audiences and functions, online communities were created to bring together groupings of almost every conceivable variety. iVillage.com brought women together, Cancer.Home provided a place for cancer sufferers and their loved ones to exchange thoughts and feelings, and TheKnot.com helped engaged couples come together to share jitters and compare honeymoon and child plans. The Gay.com Network, formed by the merger of three online communities devoted to gay and lesbian Netizens, was one of the largest online communities.

Companies such as Participate.com specialized in helping businesses build online communities for business to business and business to customer applications. Online communities were attractive to businesses for obvious reasons, aside from getting potential customers under their domain. For instance,

companies could try to build brand loyalty by offering customers a place to share tips and opinions on the latest products, which effectively builds name recognition and word-of-mouth advertising.

By 2004, the majority of Internet users began to turn specifically to search engines rather than portals. Google was the clear leader, handling 200 million searches each day. According to search engine marketing firm 10E20, search was "the biggest thing online besides shopping and email." Yahoo! bought Overture, a search engine, and Inktomi, a search technology specialist. Microsoft launched its own search engine in 2004. By not including paid advertisers within search results but rather listing advertisers separately, like Google, the planned Microsoft search engine would be prepared to challenge its rival for most relevant, and therefore useful, search returns.

Even online shopping behemoth Amazon threw its search engine hat into the ring in April of 2004 with test marketing of its branded site A9, which offered such features as searching inside the books Amazon sells for specific references. Unlike other search engines, however, A9 is distinct from, yet intimately connected with, e-commerce. As with the main Amazon site, the A9 search engine was geared toward personalization; according to A9's chief executive Udi Manber, search is "about reading people's minds." Americans tend to stay with familiar products, however, and Internet sites, portals, and search engines are no exception. As one of the largest keyword buyers on Google, Amazon is already the recipient of much of Google's traffic. In addition, Microsoft has the undisputed advantage of being able to bundle its own branded search engine with its existing products, which includes browser Internet Explorer.

In 2004, Yahoo! began offering paid inclusions to advertisers, something that MSN was already doing. Unlike pay-per-performance listings, which place links to advertisers near the beginning of search results, the paid inclusions guarantee the advertiser a particular place in the search results. Additionally, these were not highlighted or marked in any way as paid inclusions, because the Federal Trade Commission only has such marking requirements for pay-per-performance ads.

Google stood alone in 2006 against a judicial ruling that would allow the Justice Department to obtain information on billions of search requests made by Internet users in their homes or offices. According to the Justice Department, they needed that information to help in their efforts to put into place a stronger shield law to keep children away from online porn. Yahoo!, MSN, and AOL all decided immediately to cooperate with the Justice Department's subpoena, insisting that it wouldn't compromise their customers' privacy. Google "just said no." On news of Google's stand against releasing its users' search information, Google's stock rose, proving that people are not only paying attention but are willing to reward those companies who are committed to protecting their clients' privacy.

A new search engine created by Microsoft in early 2006 for the U.S. General Services Administration (GSA) gave users access to more than 40 million federal documents and Web pages. Previously, users of the government's First-Gov Web portal could access only 8 million forms and pages. Online researchers are able to access government information using a variety of search engines, but the First-Gov portal searches only government information, which is helpful in filtering out irrelevant results when only government information is the subject being targeted.

Yahoo! joined CNet, owned by media company CNet Networks, in the competition for online tech advertising dollars on May 1, 2006, when it launched a new portal named Yahoo Tech, targeted mainly at technology aficionados. The online tech advertising market is one of the largest and fastest-growing markets, and CNet had it cornered for several years, growing its revenues 26 percent from 2004 to 2005 alone. Yahoo!'s site provides a vast variety of "gadget" reviews for items such as computers, cameras, MP3 players, and home theater systems. Such high profile companies as Hewlett-Packard, Panasonic, and Verizon Wireless quickly jumped on board, bringing the potential of up to $50 million in sales for Yahoo Tech in its first two years.

Online communities can be a major marketing tool for an online company, but a decision then has to made whether the community should be a private one—open only to those who register or are invited—or a public forum—open to anyone on the Web who wants to visit. These online communities can provide a place for customers to share new ideas or just gather to exchange thoughts and advice with people of similar interests. Public communities attract much larger numbers of users, but a higher percentage of people prefer private sites because of higher security, the creation of greater trust, personal accountability, and members-only access. A public online community might have 50,000 members, but only about 100 people (or 0.2 percent) may actively participate on a regular basis; a private community with 400 people is likely to see regular involvement of 300 of those members (75 percent). Members of private online communities tend to participate more in online blogs and conversations, post comments more often, and form connections with other members. Users of public communities are often hesitant to express opinions on such things as money, health care, children, or other private topics that can be seen by anyone.

In an effort to cash in on the popularity of online communities, companies have realized that online communities can be a valuable way to earn customer loyalty and, ultimately, more money for the company. In 2005,

Microsoft began testing that premise: their Xbox Live was made accessible at no charge; a new, free Web-logging service, MSN Spaces, was launched; and they tested a new, improved mapping service that will ultimately have restaurant reviews and other user contributions. Apple Computer has gone a step further by making available a 3,000-title directory of free audio broadcasts in its iTunes music program. Google and Yahoo! have both launched projects encouraging users to share photos of birthday parties, bike races, cooking demonstrations, etc., in an effort to boost customer interest and loyalty. Increased software sales are not expected to be an end product of such online communities. As more and more people are spending extended time at home on computers, these companies realize that what is being gained is loyalty, "buzz," and customer satisfaction.

Three major carrier-tracking Web portals, GT Nexus, Inttra, and CargoSmart, although created during the pinnacle of the dot-com era, began adding customers at a record pace by early 2006. Large U.S. exporters, with dozens of carriers, had to contend with all their respective Web sites to track shipments—with all the subsequent user IDs to remember, various user interfaces, and varied ways of tracking and sending information. GT Nexus boasted 40,000 users, attracting exporters and importers who had formerly used phones and faxes to collect and distribute information. Nexus covers the top 20 carriers, 70 of the top international third party logistics providers (3PLs), and ocean carriers with more than 90 percent of global capacity. Using the Nexus portal are approximately 12,000 organizations, including third party logistics providers, customs brokers, exporters, and carriers.

CargoSmart is the smallest portal with 38,000 registered users and four members: OOCL, Cosco, NYK Line, and Malaysia International Shipping Corp. Inttra's transaction volume is growing at 100 percent a year, according to Harry Sangree, senior VP of business development at Inttra.

According to figures from comScore reported in *DM News,* in March 2007 alone, nearly 20 billion sponsored links were served to U.S. Internet users from the top search engines. The top 10 paid search advertisers, which generated 16 percent of all sponsored links, were retail or comparison-shopping sites. The number-one site was e-Bay, with 802 million sponsored link exposures, followed by Smarter.com (366 million) and Shopping.com (357 million). The same article reported that although overall growth from search engines has slowed, Google continued to grow as a source of shopping traffic and remained the most prominent source for users looking for retail and classifieds as of mid-2007.

As the problems of hacking, spyware, and internet viruses continued to be on the rise, in April 2006, McAfee introduced McAfee Threat Center, its new online portal providing research on a wide array of security issues. The site offers virus updates, information on topics such as spam and phishing, and free tools, blogs and security articles.

CURRENT CONDITIONS

Easy access to Intenet links or sites for shopping or commercial purchasing is relevant to web portals, which rely on Internet advertising as their primary source of revenue. Industry researcher IWS reported that there were 1.6 billion total Internet users in 2008. Worldwide Internet advertising in 2008 was roughly $54 billion, said Plunkett Research (citing information from GroupM research). Internet advertising in the United States was about $25.5 billion, said IDC.

According to industry researcher TechCrunch in January 2009, there were 137 billion estimated total searches performed in the U.S. in 2008. However, according to com.Score, Americans logged in more than 9.6 billion online searches in 2009 (more than 300 million per day). By any calculation, Google took the lion's share.

Although figures change quickly in the industry, figures from comScore indicated that Google sites held roughly two-thirds (63 to 65 percent) of the U.S. search market in late 2008, with YouTube representing about 25 percent of all Google searches. Yahoo! sites were approximately in the lower 20s during the year, with Microsoft sites dropping two points to 8.3; Ask Network, 5.1 percent; and Time Warner Network, 5 percent. As stated in *PC World,* "Not many brands become verbs," but that is exactly what Google did in the new millennium. In fact, Google represented 90 percent of all U.S. search *growth* in 2008, according to TechCrunch.

In 2009, the newer kids on the block were "meta-search" engines, of which Info.com emerged as the most popular. The debate regarding broad search engines (e.g., Google) and vertical search engines (e.g., Shopping.com) typically centered around convenience rather than the relevancy that vertical search engines provided. Info.com appeared to satisfy the tradeoff by being a simple to use search platform that could access results from both traditional search engines and vertical search engines.

The mobile market was another happening place in the Web portal business. According to Sterling Market Intelligence and Opus Research, the number of U.S. mobile Internet users was expected to more than triple from 32 million in 2007 to 110 million in 2011. The big companies such as Microsoft, Google, and Yahoo! were all working to establish an Internet presence in the new market, as mobile advertising was certainly expected to be the "next big thing." ABI Research predicted global mobile marketing to increase sixfold in the next four years, from an approximately $3

billion business in 2007 to $19 billion in 2011. Indeed, said Danny Sullivan in *Advertising Age,* "The search wars are going mobile. The battle to dominate the third screen is heating up."

INDUSTRY LEADERS

Google, which had edged out Yahoo! as the number one search engine in the United States, had resisted becoming a full service Web portal in favor of specialization and narrow focus. It offers a host of sites, including shopping (Froogle), social networking (Orkut), and news, in addition to a planned private e-mail service called Gmail similar to Hotmail. However, Google kept its offerings separate and uncluttered for ease of use. Begun in 1998 by a pair of Stanford University graduate engineering students, Sergey Brin and Larry Page, Google quickly became a household word with hardly a marketing or advertising budget of any kind. In fact, the word "google" entered the U.S. vernacular as an action verb meaning to quickly research or look something up, as in, "Why don't we google that?" Google prided itself on doing little advertising, relying on word of mouth, and spending its money on research & development and technology. In late 2009, Google debuted GWT 2.0, a new tool for Web developers offering workflow improvements as well performance enhancements. GWT enabled developers to write an AJAX application in Java and then cross-compile the application into highly optimized JavaScript that ran across all browsers.

Google saw astonishing growth as academics, researchers, and journalists began using and praising the site. In reaction to other search engines and portals that returned paid advertisers in response to user searches, Google aimed to be relevant. Paid advertisers were included, but in highlighted listings in a separate section of the returned results. The formula worked, and by late 2003 the majority of Internet users turned specifically to search engines like Google rather than to Web portals. In December 2008, Google stock again rose above $600 a share, the first time in two years. At that time, the company reported 22,200 employees and ultimately saw sales of $21.8 billion in 2008.

Yahoo! was the number two search engine and one of the most popular Internet portals. The site features a search engine and directory to help users navigate the Internet. Yahoo! collects content from news, financial information, and streaming media sources, and offers registered users personalized Web pages, e-mail, chat rooms, and message boards. However, Yahoo! did not moonlight as an Internet service provider at the start. Yahoo! acquired GeoCities, which acted as a series of online neighborhoods for users to establish individual home pages. During 2002, the company entered an alliance with SBC to offer a co-branded Internet service to digital subscriber line (DSL) customers in a 13-state region and to dial-up subscribers nationwide. That same year, the company entered a distribution relationship with British Telecommunications plc (BT) to offer Yahoo! branded stand-alone premium service bundles. In March of that year, Yahoo! acquired Inktomi Corp., a provider of Web search and paid inclusion services.

By 2003, Yahoo! offered a comprehensive branded network of properties and services to consumers and businesses worldwide in five vertical areas: Search and Marketplace, Information and Content, Network and Platform Services, Enterprise Solutions, and Consumer Services. It also began offering Yahoo PayDirect as a way for consumers in the United States to send money overseas, as an alternative to other payment transfer services, such as PayPal and many banks. Later, the company made arrangements with wireless carriers and mobile device manufacturers to develop Yahoo! Mobile, which makes many of its featured network services available through wireless and/or alternative devices. Services include My Yahoo! Mobile Mail, Mobile Instant Messaging, Mobile Alerts, Finance, News, Weather, Calendar, Address Book, Movie Listings, Auctions, Yellow Pages, Driving Directions, and People Search, among others. Its biggest competition comes from AOL Time Warner and Microsoft. The company also faces competition from Amazon and eBay. Additionally, Yahoo! competes directly with other providers of Internet search and related search services including AltaVista, Fast Search, and Google, among others.

In 2008, Microsoft made an unsolicited $46 billion bid to purchase Yahoo! Ultimately, Microsoft withdrew the offer after Yahoo! refused its second offer of $33 per share, a $5 billion increase from its initial offer. Yahoo!'s main source of income, though other fees were extracted from its online auctions, e-commerce, and sponsorship agreements, remained advertising. The site's search engine organized some 1.2 million Web pages. In 2007 Yahoo! announced a major deal with Viacom that allows it exclusive rights to serve search and content-related text ads on about 36 Viacom Web sites, a move that was expected to increase Yahoo!'s already substantial advertising revenue. The company reported 2008 revenues of $7.2 billion.

AOL LLC (formerly America Online) is the world's leading Internet service provider, with 12 million U.S. subscribers and several million in Europe. It also maintains a leading Web portal with a wide range of content that has been greatly expanded and upgraded through its 2000 merger with media giant Time Warner. Based in Dulles, Virginia, and established in 1991, AOL is one of the oldest dot-coms. Seventy percent of the company's revenues derived from Internet service provider (ISP) subscription services, while the remainder was spread out over advertising, e-commerce, merchandising, and other sources. Its parent company was initially named

AOL Time Warner Inc., the large media and entertainment company. However, in the early years of the first decade of the twenty-first century, it changed its name to Time Warner. AOL Inc. was a 2009 spinoff from the parent company, and as of September 30, 2009, the AOL internet service had 5.4 million U.S users.

Time Warner's chief business interests are AOL, Web properties, Internet technologies and electronic commerce services, cable, filmed entertainment, cable and broadcast networks, music, CD and DVD manufacturing, and publishing. AOL itself provides interactive services, Web brands, Internet technologies, and electronic commerce services. Its operations include two worldwide Internet services, the AOL service and the CompuServe service; AOL for Broadband; AOL's music properties such as AOL Music Channel and Winamp; premium services such as MusicNet and AOL Call Alert; AOL Mobile services; and AOL's Web properties, such as AOL Instant Messenger, ICQ, Moviefone, MapQuest, and Netscape.

Software giant Microsoft Corp. counted the MSN.com portal as part of its empire. Microsoft rolled out the Microsoft Network (MSN) in 1995, finally embracing the Internet, and MSN.com emerged as a force in the Web portal industry by 1998. MSN.com featured gift certificates, buyers' guides, and an e-wallet known as a "Passport" to store credit card information and facilitate e-commerce, especially through its MSN marketplace. Microsoft was also building ways to link its software to the MSN portal.

Verticalnet, Inc. of Malvern, Pennsylvania, is a leader in the business to business portal sector, with more than 59 Web sites in 2006, spread across disparate industries. It provides collaborative supply chain solutions that enable companies to drive costs and inventory out of their supply base through more effective sourcing and supplier collaboration. Supply chain software applications include spending analysis, strategic sourcing, collaborative planning, and order management; and supply chain solutions include strategic sourcing, collaborative planning, and order management. Founded in 1995, the company bought its way into prominence through scores of Web site acquisitions over the years before going public in 1999. The portal was home to a number of industry-specific sites, including career centers, buyers guides, and news resources. The company also engaged in its own e-commerce and even held online auctions. Verticalnet expanded into Europe through a partnership with British Telecommunications and Internet Capital Group. Together, the three companies ran Verticalnet Europe. The bulk of the firm's revenue derived from advertising.

AMERICA AND THE WORLD

According to comScore Networks, 747 million people ages 15 and over used the Internet worldwide in January

2007, representing a 10 percent increase globally from January 2006. Fueling the growth was a surge of use in India, China, and Russia. The United States had the most users that month, with 153 million, but showed only a 2 percent growth. China, which experienced a 20 percent increase, was second with 86.7 million monthly users. The strongest growth, however, was seen in India, where the number of users that month increased 33 percent to 21.1 million.

Although it still trailed AOL and Yahoo! in subscribers, MSN became the top Internet portal in Europe. In that year, traffic to its free Web sites jumped 26 percent, to 34.3 million visitors per month, according to researcher NetRatings Inc. Traffic to the Yahoo! site grew only less than half as much, and AOL saw only a 4 percent gain. Partly because of its success in Europe, MSN's global revenues reached $1.1 billion in the six months ending December 31, 2002, a jump of 23 percent from the previous year. Part of MSN's strategy was to tailor content for each country.

At the same time, Yahoo! was making great inroads into the European market. In 2002, it formed a partnership with Sonera Zed Ltd., the largest independent mobile portal in Europe. Meanwhile, Terra Networks, S.A. was providing Internet access and local language interactive content and services to Spanish- and Portuguese-speaking residential and small office/home office customers in Spain, Brazil, Mexico, Peru, Chile, and Guatemala.

RESEARCH AND TECHNOLOGY

In July 2009, Open-source groupware provider Open-Xchange announced its "Social OX" concept, providing features that bridged isolated information such as email, contacts, calendars and documents. Under Social OX, all email and contact information is in one place, whether personal or business. It can aggregate Web mail from Google, Yahoo! and many others into a folder in Open-Xchange, plus automatically add and incorporate contact details from social networks such as Facebook, LinkedIn or Xing to the Open-Xchange address book. While Microsoft Exchange remained the choice email client for most business applications, Open-source added new features in 2009 that integrated all sorts of social features alongside business-class functionality, increasing its user base by 80 percent in 2009. In 2009 alone, Open-Xchange formed relationships with domain name registrars Dotster and NameCheap, as well as French web host Nexen-Alterway Hosting, and Asian SaaS distributor NTS.

Security was among the chief concerns of the Web portal industry, as it was for most Internet sectors. In early 2000, hackers were able to invade and disrupt the Yahoo! site, sending the industry, as well as legislators,

into a frenzy of activity trying to figure out the best way to ward off such invasions. While the issue was likely to be discussed on Capitol Hill for some time, portal companies could not afford to wait, so they began pouring vast amounts of money into the development of technology safeguards in an attempt to plug the security holes that hackers loved to exploit.

Some Web portals took an interactive approach to helping others with their technology troubles. AltaVista launched its own information technology (IT) help desk especially for IT professionals. The project was born of the partnership between AltaVista and online community Experts Exchange, a collection of IT eggheads. With common troubles categorized by topics such as Java and C++, AltaVista invited users to submit their queries, which were then answered by one of the Experts Exchange crew.

BIBLIOGRAPHY

"About Us." Time Warner, 17 July 2006. Available from http:// ir.timewarner.com/.

"Advertising and Branding Industry Overview." Plunkett Research, 2009. Available from http://www.plunkettresearch. com/ industries/AdvertisingandABranding/AdvertisingStatistics/.

"Amazon Starts Its Search Engine." *The America's Intelligence Wire,* 16 April 2004.

"April US Search Engine Ratings Published by comScore." *Internet Business News,* 19 May 2007.

Bertolucci, Jeff. "Search Engine Shoot-Out." *PC World,* June 2007.

"Big Firms Buy in to Web 2.0 Spin." *Financial Director,* 31 May 2007.

Boswell, Wendy. "The Web's Most Popular Search Engines of 2009." *The New York Times,* 2009. Available from http:// websearch.about.com/od/enginesanddirectories/tp/most-popular-search-engines.htm.

"Ensim and Submitnet Sign Strategic Agreement to Enable Web Hosters to Offer Search Engine Optimization Tools." *PR Newswire,* 12 April 2004.

"Facelift for FirstGov." *School Library Journal,* March 2006.

Field, Alan M. "Plugged In: Web Portals for Managing Shipments Have Survived and Thrived." *The Journal of Commerce,* 8 May 2006.

Google. Available from http://www.google.com/intl/en/press/ pressrel/revenues_q408.html.

"Google Gobbled Up 90 Percent Of All U.S. Search Growth In 2008." TechCrunch, 28 January 2009. Available from http:// www.techcrunch. com/2009/01/28/google-gobbled-up-90-percent-of-all-us-search-growth-in-2008/.

Harvey, Fiona. "New Media—Google Trawls for a Way to Stay Ahead of the Pack." *The Financial Times,* 30 March 2004.

Hessan, Diane, and Julie Wittes Schlack. "Online Communities Public vs. Private?" *Brandweek,* 15 May 2006.

"Hoover's Company Capsules." *Hoover's Online,* 2007. Available from www.hoovers.com.

Kharif, Olga. "Yahoo Woos the Tech User." *Business Week Online,* 2 May 2006. Available from www.businessweek.com.

"McAfee Portal Offers Virus Information." *Computerworld,* 17 April 2006.

"Microsoft Launches New Look MSN for Mobile Phones." *eWeek,* 18 June 18.

"MIT and SOHU to Cooperate in Search Engine Technology." *China Business News,* 15 April 2004.

"Number of Internet Users Up 10 Percent Worldwide." *The Sydney Morning Herald,* 7 March 2007.

O'Leary, Mick. "New Classification Engines Provide Alternative Web Search." *Information Today,* January 2007.

Peterson, Kim. "The Microsoft Connection; Online Communities." *The Seattle Times,* 1 August 2005.

Reinhardt, Andy, and Jay Green, "A Beacon of Hope for MSN." *BusinessWeek Online,* 7 April 2003. Available from www.businessweek.com.

Sherman, Chris. "Survey: Google, Yahoo Still Favorites in North America." 19 January 2006. Available from http://searchenginewatch.com.

Stilson, Janet. "Portals Make Plays for Upfront Dollars." *Advertising Age,* 14 May 2007.

Sullivan, Danny. "Mobile Search Is the Next Big Thing—For Real This Time." *Advertising Age,* 26 March 2007.

Tode, Chantal. "MSN, AOL Push Searchers to Retail." *DM News,* 11 June 2007.

"Unmarked Paid Search Results, Good or Bad?" *Investor's Business Daily,* 19 February 2004.

"US-Google Launches Personalized Search Engine Test Version." *The America's Intelligence Wire,* 30 March 2004.

"US-Microsoft to Launch New MSN Search Engine in July 2004." *The America's Intelligence Wire,* 23 March 2004.

Van Munching, Philip. "Google Searches for Privacy." *Brandweek,* 20 March 2006.

"Viacom Spurns Google for Yahoo." *Business Week Online,* 11 April 2007. Available from www.businessweek.com.

Waters, Richard. "Growing Pains for Google's Idealists." *The Financial Times,* 20 April 2004.

"World Internet Usage and Population Statistics." 10 June 2007. Available from www.internetworldstats.com/.

"Yahoo's Betting the Remittance Business Will Pay." *Investor's Business Daily,* 29 December 2003.

"Yahoo's Grand Mobile Ad Experiment." *Business Week Online,* 7 November 2006. Available from www.businessweek.com.

WEIGHT LOSS PRODUCTS & SERVICES

INDUSTRY SNAPSHOT

During the early 2000s, a very sizable market existed for weight loss products and services and showed no signs of faltering. According to data from the Centers for Disease Control and Prevention (CDC), the rate of obesity in the United States increased significantly between 1987 and 2007 (the last statistic available), and 49 states (all except Colorado) had an obesity prevalence rate of over 20 percent. Further CDC data showed that one-third of the U.S. population (more than 72 million adults) were considered clinically obese. Statistics supported a conclusion that the United States had become a society in which people ate larger portions more often and led more sedentary lifestyles. In addition, people consumed food that was convenient but of poor nutritional quality. As Yale University psychology professor Kelly D. Brownell explained in the *Toronto Star,* "Food is available everywhere all the time, like never before in history. Gas stations, drug stores, schools. Unhealthy food is cheap, convenient and tastes good, while just the opposite is true of healthy foods." The United States was not alone. By 2010, more than one billion people around the world were above an ideal weight.

In an attempt to lose or manage weight, consumers utilized a wide range of products and services including diet and exercise plans, nutritional supplements, pharmaceuticals, meal replacements, counseling, group support programs, gastric bypass surgery, and more. While many of these offerings were legitimate and helpful when properly used, some fraudulent products and services offered little more than false hope and failed to produce results. The U.S. Federal Trade Commission (FTC) took to task the producers of some of these items when in early 2008 it filed suit against four companies and one individual for making false claims about weight loss products. The defendants in the case included MedLab, Pinnacle Holdings, Metabolic Research Associates, and U.S.A. Health, which produced such products as Zyladex Plus, Questral AC, and Rapid Loss 245.

ORGANIZATION AND STRUCTURE

The Weight Loss Market According to the nonprofit Calorie Control Council, 29 percent of U.S. adults were on a diet in 2007. Historically, women have comprised the majority of those actively seeking to lose weight. A study conducted by Simmons Market Research Bureau during the first decade of the 2000s and reported in *American Demographics* found that 66 percent of dieters were female. The research also found that many women first consider dieting during their 20s and that most female dieters are between the ages of 55 and 64. Comparatively, men did not consider dieting until their sixties and were most likely to diet between the ages of 65 and 74. In general, dieters tended to have higher household incomes than non-dieters and live in rural rather than urban areas.

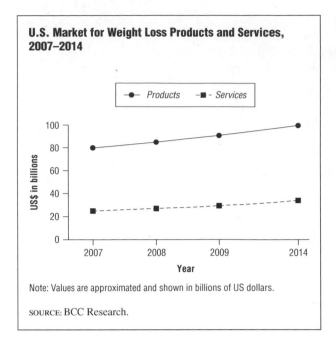

U.S. Market for Weight Loss Products and Services, 2007–2014

Note: Values are approximated and shown in billions of US dollars.

SOURCE: BCC Research.

With this in mind, many of the leading firms within the weight loss products and services industry have tailored their offerings and marketing messages to women. Approximately 90 to 95 percent of Weight Watchers' customers were women during the 1990s and first decade of the 2000s. One exception was Slim-Fast, which has actively marketed its meal replacement shakes and products to both men and women for more than a decade.

Traditional Product and Service Providers During the first decade of the 2000s, the weight loss products and services industry was dominated by companies that operated diet centers and sold products like prepared foods, meal replacement shakes, nutritional supplements, and informational products. While companies such as Slim-Fast Foods Co., Jenny Craig Inc., and Weight Watchers International Inc. had enjoyed an established market presence for many years, firms like Atkins Nutritionals Inc. and eDiets.com Inc. were newer players. Beyond these popular leaders, the industry contained thousands of other product manufacturers and service providers.

At first glance, some industry participants seem to fit nicely within a particular niche, like nutritional supplements. However, marketers of weight loss products and services often operate across multiple categories as they provide a wide range of offerings to consumers in order to address different aspects of the weight loss process.

Beyond more traditional weight loss product and service providers, the weight loss industry also included pharmaceutical manufacturers, healthcare providers, and professionals like psychologists who focused on behavior modification.

Pharmaceutical Manufacturers Although they had yet to discover a magic weight loss pill, leading pharmaceutical companies had marketed a number of successful drugs over the years. For many years, the appetite suppressants phentermine and fenfluramine were used successfully for short time periods during the treatment of obesity, along with the appetite suppressant dexfenfluramine. These prescription drugs were combined to produce weight loss drugs called fen-phen and dexfen-phen. However, all but phentermine were removed from the market in 1997, amidst reports that they caused heart valve damage.

The industry's experience with fen-phen caused a general reluctance among many doctors to prescribe weight loss drugs. In addition, some argued that the leading prescription drugs that remained on the market were not as effective as fen-phen had been. These included the likes of Meridia (Abbott Laboratories) and Xenical (Hoffman-LaRoche). Fluoxetine, the main ingredient in Eli Lilly's popular antidepressant drug Prozac, also gained attention when it failed to create weight gain in patients like other antidepressant medications, and in some cases led to weight loss. While a number of weight loss drugs were in the development pipeline, no major breakthroughs or "magic pills" were expected to appear on the market in the near future.

As of 2010, phentermine, which suppresses the appetite, remained the most commonly prescribed diet pill, accounting for about 50 percent of the market. Hydroxycut, an over-the-counter diet pill, was the top selling brand in 2009, at 1 million pills sold that year.

Healthcare Providers Healthcare providers also have a stake in the weight loss industry. While a number of traditional family physicians assist patients with weight loss issues, some physicians specialize in medical weight loss approaches that involve prescription drugs as well as diet and exercise programs. A more drastic medical approach, especially for those who are dangerously overweight, is gastric bypass surgery. This procedure can help patients lose 60 to 70 percent of their excess weight and reduce their risk of weight-related conditions and diseases like diabetes, high blood pressure, and even cancer. Such procedures cost anywhere from $20,000 to $30,000.

Some states could not keep up with demand for this procedure, as the number of candidates rapidly outpaced the number of surgeons available to perform the operation. Patients who received a gastric bypass reaped various benefits in addition to the weight loss. A 2005 study in a large comparative series of patients showed an 89 percent reduction in mortality over the five years following surgery, compared to a non-surgically treated group of patients. Other benefits directly related to the surgery and the subsequent weight loss were decreases in the incidence of cardiovascular disease, infections, cancer, hypertension, sleep apnea, diabetes, reflux disease, and back pain, to name a few.

Behavior Modification In addition to medical weight loss approaches, some individuals turn to psychologists for help. The Yale Center for Eating and Weight Disorders (YCEWD) is one example of an academic center devoted to conducting research and offering treatment and information to people with problems corresponding to body image, eating, food, and weight. Managed by the Yale University Department of Psychology, the CEWD's services include individual, family, and group outpatient psychotherapy sessions; consultations and evaluations for those considering bariatric (obesity-treating) surgery; and referrals to professionals within the fields of medicine and nutrition. In addition to obesity, YCEWD deals with eating disorders like binge eating, bulimia nervosa, and anorexia nervosa.

The YCEWD is headed by Yale University professor and psychology chair Kelly D. Brownell, Ph.D., who also serves as a professor of epidemiology and public health. Brownell is the author of 14 books and more than 200 articles and book chapters, and has received many awards for his work from the likes of the American Psychological Association, the New York Academy of Sciences, and Purdue University. YCEWD co-director Marlene B. Schwartz, Ph.D. provides treatment to patients suffering from eating disorders and obesity and serves as a research advisor for students at the undergraduate and graduate levels. According to the YCEWD, during the early years of the first decade of the 2000s, Schwartz's research focused on childhood eating patterns and how they were impacted by things like the environment and parental behavior.

The Internet By the first decade of the twenty-first century, the Internet played an important role in the weight loss industry. Companies such as Slim-Fast and Weight Watchers had established Web sites to support their brands. These sites included features like diet and fitness plans, recipes, grocery lists, journals, diaries, logs, weight charts, body mass index calculators, articles and newsletters, interactive tools, chat rooms, message boards, online meetings, and more.

Ediets.com, a publicly traded enterprise, offered consumers what it billed as "a global online diet, fitness and motivation destination." Established in 1996, by 2004, the Deerfield Beach, Florida-based company had recorded 1.3 million paid members and operated several Web sites including eDiets.com, eFitness.com, and DietSmart.com. In addition, the company had developed an international presence through affiliations with eDiets.de (Germany), eDietsUK.com (Ireland and the United Kingdom), and eDiets.com.es (Spain).

CaloriesCount.com was another online resource. Sponsored by the nonprofit Calorie Control Council, the site offered information and resources that helped individuals achieve and maintain healthy weight levels throughout their lifetimes. In May of 2003, the council reported that a study conducted by the Brown University Medical School, which appeared in the *Journal of the American Medical Association,* found Internet-based weight loss programs to be highly effective because they offered participants both convenience and privacy.

BACKGROUND AND DEVELOPMENT

Humankind has struggled with weight problems for thousands of years. However, obesity rates in the United States and other countries had reached alarming levels as people opted for food choices that were convenient but often unhealthy. In addition to an unprecedented oversupply of food items—stemming from twentieth century advancements in food packaging, preservation, and refrigeration—that caused people to eat more, there was a movement toward larger portions during meals and more sedentary lifestyles. Subsequently, the number of obese American adults between the ages of 20 and 74 more than doubled from 1960 to 2000, growing from slightly more than 13 percent to almost 31 percent. The number of obese or overweight children also increased dramatically. In 1980, some 5 percent of children between the ages of six and 19 were overweight. However, by the early 2000s, this number had risen to 15 percent.

Overweight individuals have turned to a variety of weight loss products and services for help over the years, ranging from diet programs and nutritional supplements to surgery. While some methods proved helpful, others produced mixed results or were harmful. For example, during the 1920s, upper class women took "weight loss capsules" that really were tapeworm eggs. In addition, during the 1960s and 1970s, addictive amphetamines were often prescribed to those seeking to lose weight.

The appetite suppressants phentermine and fenfluramine were introduced in 1959 and 1973, respectively. These two prescription drugs were combined to produce a weight loss drug called fen-phen. Another combination consisted of phentermine and exfenfluramine to produce dexfen-phen. These drugs were FDA-approved for use over periods of several weeks or less. However, doctors began prescribing them in an off-label fashion, and patients took the drugs for longer periods of time.

In July 1997, the Mayo Clinic reported that fen-phen use led to heart valve disease in 24 patients, causing the FDA to issue a public health advisory. Mayo's findings, which were published in the *New England Journal of Medicine,* were followed by similar reports showing heart valve disease in patients taking fen-phen as well as in those using only fenfluramine or dexfenfluramine. Phentermine was not named as a potentially harmful substance. This ultimately led the FDA to ask Interneuron Pharmaceuticals, which produced dexfenfluramine for American Home Products' subsidiary Wyeth-Ayerst Laboratories, to withdraw the drug. Wyeth, which sold dexfenfluramine under the name Redux, also was asked to withdraw the drug, along with its fenfluramine drug called Pondimin.

FDA Lead Deputy Commissioner Michael A. Friedman, M.D. called for immediate action and said the drugs presented an unacceptable health risk to patients. The FDA said its action was "based on new findings from doctors who have evaluated patients taking these two drugs with echocardiograms, a special procedure that can test the functioning of heart valves. These findings, the FDA said, indicated that approximately 30 percent of patients who were evaluated had abnormal echocardiograms, even though they had no symptoms. This was a much higher than expected percentage of abnormal test results."

In November 2000, the FDA also ordered that the drug phenylpropanolamine (PPA) be removed from the market when a Yale University study found a correlation between the substance—which was used as an ingredient in weight loss pills like Dexatrim and Acutrim, as well as in cold medicines like Dimetapp and Alka Seltzer Plus—and hemorrhagic strokes.

Beyond pharmaceuticals and a seemingly endless array of diets, more extreme approaches to weight loss began to appear in the later decades of the twentieth century. During the 1970s, surgeons removed entire sections of patients' intestinal tracts, with the idea that nutrients would pass through more quickly and with less absorption, thereby resulting in weight loss. However, this approach was abandoned when it failed to produce long-term weight loss in many patients and resulted in permanent diarrhea for some.

During the 1980s, another technique that ultimately proved unsuccessful involved inserting a special balloon made of polyurethane into a patient's stomach through the esophagus and then inflating it. Named the Garren-Edwards gastric bubble, this device was intended to make patients feel full so they would not have the urge to eat as much.

By the 1980s, a wide variety of commercial weight loss products and services had come onto the scene, comprising a burgeoning industry that enjoyed double-digit growth. By 1989, Marketdata Research reported the market was valued at almost $28 billion. While this figure increased to more than $30 billion in 1990, many industry players were then experiencing financial problems as growth in the number of new dieters slowed and an economic recession prompted many individuals to try low-cost or no-cost weight loss programs and techniques.

Amidst these conditions, Marketdata revealed that the leading commercial diet center chains, which achieved combined sales of approximately $2 billion in 1990, had reduced the number of their locations in place to 8,500 by mid-1991, a 10 percent decrease from 1989 levels. In addition, weight loss programs sponsored by doctors and hospitals saw revenues fall nearly 20 percent.

The diet industry's slowdown continued in the early and mid-1990s. In *Advertising Age,* Wendy Liebmann of retail marketing consultancy WSL said, "Both the diet counseling centers and the marketers of prepared diet products like Slim-Fast have seen steep sales declines recently. The reason is that people suddenly seem to be thinking differently about diet, health and weight loss, and chilling out on the idea of being thin at all costs." Industry leader Jenny Craig, which had achieved revenues of $491 million in 1993, saw its sales fall to $401 million by 1996.

By 1997, Marketdata placed the weight loss industry's value at $35 billion. Growth continued to occur, albeit at a slow pace. In its August 30, 1997, issue, *The Economist* reported that many of the newest overweight individuals also were poor, therefore having limited resources at their disposal for weight loss solutions. In addition, the publication argued that a broader problem corresponded to the quality and effectiveness of the industry's offerings, stating that many were worthless or required significant effort and willpower on the part of the user to produce any results. As *The Economist* explained, these conditions simply led to frustration and confusion among consumers. "Such things not only make consumers trust the industry even less, they also add to the general noise and confusion. Most of the evidence indicates that the slimming industry has an unusually high churn rate—with fat people jumping from one largely useless product or service to another in fairly short order. That is seldom a recipe for long-term health—for either the buyer or the seller."

Heading toward the twenty-first century, the weight loss products and services industry had yet to discover a stand-alone "silver bullet" for those seeking to lose weight and keep it off. A combination of exercise and a healthy diet consisting of low-calorie and low-fat foods appeared to be the most effective solution for most individuals. With this in mind, it was not surprising that diet sodas accounted for about half of the U.S. weight loss industry's revenues, with low-fat foods representing another leading category.

A great many of those seeking to lose weight opted for low-carbohydrate, high-protein regimens like the Atkins Diet, the South Beach Diet, Protein Power, and Sugar Busters. In March 2004, *Brandweek* cited research from Stamford, Connecticut-based J. Brown Agency that placed the number of Americans who had tried a low-carbohydrate diet at 36 percent, including 17 percent active low-carbohydrate dieters at the time of the study. More than 40 percent of low-carbohydrate dieters had college degrees, 70 percent did not have children, 55 percent were 45 years of age or older, and many tended to be in higher household income brackets. While these diets produced results for many, critics questioned their health value and noted that many people regained weight after returning to more normal eating habits.

The surge in low-carbohydrate diet popularity impacted companies that primarily sold higher-carbohydrate products. For example, Krispy Kreme, Papa John's Pizza Co., and Panera Bread Co. all faced declining stock prices in 2003. By early 2004, food industry trade groups were taking measures to promote the benefits of their respective food/agricultural industry segments. For example, the Wheat Foods Council was operating a campaign called the Grains of Truth About Fad Diets and Obesity, and the U.S. Potato Board was gearing up for a national $4.4 million promotional campaign called The Healthy Potato. In addition, the Florida Department of Citrus was in the midst of a $1.8 million campaign to counteract the bad name orange juice had acquired in low-carbohydrate circles.

By 2004, American Home Products and Wyeth-Ayerst Laboratories were still dealing with the fallout from fen-phen. For example, in March, a lawsuit was filed against American Home Products on behalf of 600 people in Tennessee and Mississippi. The following month, a Texas jury awarded an astonishing $1 billion to the family of a woman who died after taking the drug. While legal experts did not expect the award to stand, they indicated that the case could prompt the drug-maker to settle many of the lawsuits it faced. According to the Associated Press, Wyeth had reserved $16.6 billion to settle fen-phen-related lawsuits, which numbered in the tens of thousands. The company's legal costs were reportedly about $2 billion per year.

Fen-phen was not the only substance in the media spotlight over health risks. In December 2003, the FDA advised consumers to stop taking products that contained ephedra, an adrenaline-like stimulant used in weight loss products and supplements used for sports performance. This action followed the connection of more than 150 deaths to ephedra use, including professional baseball player Steve Belcher, a pitcher for the Baltimore Orioles. In December 2003, the FDA announced that it would ban ephedra, citing research indicating the substance posed a danger to the heart and circulatory system, raising blood pressure and leading to strokes.

In April 2004, the FDA's ephedra ban went into effect when a federal judge refused requests from the National Institute for Clinical Weight Loss and NVE

Pharmaceuticals for a temporary restraining order. Ephedra became the first dietary supplement to be banned by the FDA. Unlike the case with the pharmaceuticals, the Dietary Supplement Health and Education Act of 1994 states that the FDA must prove that a supplement is unsafe before taking such measures. Consumer advocates criticized this situation and called for a change in the legislation to prevent untested—and potentially dangerous—supplements from being marketed.

Dr. Robert Atkins created the Atkins Diet—and thus the birth of the low-carb phenomenon—and revolutionized dieting by telling people they could "get thin by eating fat," according to columnist Al Lewis in his *Denver Post* column of August 2, 2005. The diet plan advocated total avoidance of carbohydrates by eating protein-rich foods only: meat, bacon, eggs, etc. In 1989, Dr. Atkins took his diet corporate and created Nutritionals, Inc. Hundreds of small startup companies jumped on the bandwagon and began marketing low-carb everything. Next, Atkins began manufacturing its own line of low-carb food and "treats," such as Atkins Advantage Chocolate Delight shakes sweetened with Splenda; Atkins Advantage bars—Cookies and Creme, Chocolate Decadence, and Vanilla Fudge Swirl ice cream bars. Even those who didn't agree with Dr. Atkins' low-carb approach to dieting had to admire his success. He had the most popular diet ever devised, he turned his diet into an industry, and he became a very wealthy man. In April of 2003, Dr. Atkins died at age 72 of injuries sustained in a fall.

In February 2004, 9.1 percent of U.S. adults were on low-carb diets. By November, the percentage had dropped to 3.6, according to NPD Group, a marketing information firm. By the middle of 2005, the low-carb diet craze had officially run its course, when Atkins Nutritionals, Inc. filed for Chapter 11 bankruptcy in July. Although excessive carbohydrates were still a concern and there continued to be many low-carb products on the market, consumers were no longer as avid in avoiding carbs altogether. With the announcement of the U.S. Dietary Guidelines, many companies realized that the low-carb obsession was beginning to lose favor with dieters and began focusing more attention on grain-based foods. Many companies, understanding that knowledgeable consumers were looking more at healthy choices instead of fad diets, began offering a multitude of options containing par-baked wheat, whole wheat, multigrain, and whole grain breads, rolls, baguettes, buns, and other premium breads.

In early January 2006, Subway restaurants introduced a marketing campaign centered around Jared Fogelman, the chain's spokesperson and "weight-loss guru." Jared became Subway's spokesperson in 2000 after losing 245 pounds from eating Subway's low-fat sandwich choices. From January 2 to 8, 2006, between 3 p.m. and 11 p.m., the Fresh Resolutions Hotline was available to callers who could receive free support, advice, and resources from the American Dietetic Association. Also beginning January 2, by going to the Subwayfreshresolutions.com Web site, consumers could sign up for free daily phone reminders and motivational recordings from Jared himself throughout the month of January. Jared, at 6 feet, 2 inches tall, maintained his weight loss into 2006 and beyond, and continues to serve as an inspiration for others struggling with weight issues.

The general public has long known what it needs to do to lose weight and maintain that loss, but acting on that knowledge has continued to be an issue that doctors and dieticians face. However, by 2006, some major companies began to realize that the best interests of their customers could be served while still sustaining a profitable enterprise. A case in point was McDonald's, the world's largest restaurant chain, who began offering some healthier food choices. Its apple and walnut salad and apple dippers became so popular that McDonald's in early 2006 was the world's largest purchaser of fresh apples. Food manufacturers, in general, began to recognize the huge marketing possibilities even in the manufacture of processed foods prepared with healthier ingredients.

Insurance companies and healthcare professionals claimed that the cost of obesity-related ailments had risen 1,000 percent since 1990, which puts a financial strain on employers and their employees. Some employers began offering programs to their employees to help in their endeavors to lose weight and maintain healthy lifestyles. Insurance regulators in Florida, for example, introduced a "healthy lifestyle rebate" program to reward employers who are able to persuade employees to lose weight, quit smoking, or adapt similar healthier lifestyles. The program offered rebates of up to 10 percent off their premiums to employers with less than 50 employees.

In January 2008, *MMR* listed the top 10 diet aid/weight loss brands in drug stores, supermarkets, and discount stores (excluding Wal-Mart) for 2007. Leading the list was the industry's new golden child, Alli, with $91.0 million in sales and 1.6 million units sold. The only FDA-approved over-the-counter (OTC) weight loss product as of late 2008, Alli was produced by GlaxoSmithKline (GSK). According to the company's Web site, Alli works differently from other diet pills by preventing absorption of about 25 percent of the fat an individual eats. The program also includes an individually tailored online "action plan." Alli was the most successful OTC launch in GSK's history, reported *Brandweek* in December 2007, garnering more than half the sales in the OTC diet pill market. The firm exceeded its sales goals by 26 percent when it sold $49 million worth of the product in the first three months.

The other top products in 2007 in order of revenue, according to the *MMR* report, were Hydroxycut, which sold 1.3 million units for a total of $33.4 million; Relacore, which sold 700,00 units for $16.9 million; and Zantrex and Slimquick, which sold 500,000 units each for $14.0 million and $12.1 million, respectively. Rounding out the top 10 were MegaT, Metabolife, Smartburn, Cylaris, and NV Be Desired. Overall, Americans spent $358 million on weight control candy and tablets in 2007.

GlaxoSmithKline, in conjunction with three other organizations—the American Dietetic Association, the Obesity Society, and Shaping America's Health—shook up the industry in April 2008 when it formally asked the FDA to "determine that dietary supplements bearing claims that they promote, assist, or otherwise help in weight loss are 'disease claims' under Section 403(r)(6) of the FDCA [Federal Food, Drug, and Cosmetic Act]."If considered as such, these claims would be made illegal. As the manufacturer of Alli, GlaxoSmithKline obviously had a stake in the outcome of the proposal, which as of late 2008 was still undetermined. According to Loren Israelsen of the United National Products Alliance, if the petition does succeed, it will "officially open the door for even greater competition between pharmaceuticals and dietary supplements, spanning a variety of already accepted disease claims." Israelsen added, "Approval of this petition would suggest that the definition of disease has been changed. This would clearly be a victory for pharmaceutical products and a major loss for supplements."

CURRENT CONDITIONS

The global market for weight loss products and services was estimated at roughly $121 billion in 2009, accourding to BCC Research. It projected a compound annual growth rate (CAGR) of 2.2 percent for the industry through 2014, resulting in a projected market of about $134 billion at that time. Foods and beverages remained the largest segment of the ingested goods market, valued at roughly $79 billion in 2009. Within the foods and beverages segment, healthy eating trends, along with growing subsegments, were expected to contribute to the sustained growth, translated into expected revenues of $86 billion by 2014.

Nutraceuticals represented the second largest segment of the industry, contributing $3.6 billion in retail sales in 2009. This segment had a projected CAGR of 1.4 percent through 2014, translated into an expected $3.9 billion in revenues by then. Projections from MarketData Enterprises forecasted that prescription diet-drug revenue would grow at 13.5 percent, and diet books, cassettes, and exercise videos at 12.1 percent, annually through 2012.

Within the United States, according to Kalorama Information, more than 100 million people were actively involved in a weight loss or weight management plan at any one time during 2009. This suggested a sustained market for years to come. The Kalorama Information Report, *Obesity, Weight Loss and Diet Management Markets (Pharmaceutical, Surgical and Dietary Approaches),* placed the value of the U.S. weight loss market at $59 billion for 2010, up from $58.6 billion in 2009.

In April 2010 "Online Dieter Reseaerch Report" sponsored by CNBC.com indicated that the U.S. diet market was up two percent from the prior year. Market-Data research director John LaRosa tracked consumers' diet habits and reported that in the first quarter of 2010, over 80 percent of respondents wanted a low-cost, home-based diet plan. This included meal replacement products like Slim-Fast (Unilever), GNC's Weight Management Starter Kit, and various over-the-counter diet pills. Consumers were being inundated with infomercials, diet books, mail order offers, and solicitous websites, all adding to a vigorous and continued sustaining of the industry.

In a "View From the Top" report from *Publishers Weekly* that ranked top bestsselling hardcover books in 2009, *Master Your Metabolism: The 3 Diet Secrets to Naturally Balancing Your Hormones for a Hot and Healthy Body* ranked No. 12 in nonfiction. David Zinczenko's *Eat This, Not That! Best and Worst Foods* and Liz Vaccariello's *Flat Belly Diet Cookbook* were also selling well.

Another industry trend on its way up was direct-selling from multi-level marketing companies such as Medifast and Isagenix. Medifast's "Take Shape for Life" multi-level latform accounted for 60 percent of its business, generated by some 7,100 health coaches in 2009, up from just 3,400 in 2008. Other multi-level companies had thousands, even millions, of representatives, mostly looking for extra income or second jobs, and through them (and Medifast's 27 clinics) another 30 percent of revenues came in the form of shakes, snack bars, soups, and oatmeal.

INDUSTRY LEADERS

Weight Watchers International Inc. A long-time industry leader in the weight loss products and services industry, Woodbury, New York-based Weight Watchers International Inc. has been helping people lose or maintain their weight since its founding by Jean Nidetch in the 1960s. With operations in about 30 countries employing 49,000, the company recorded retail sales of $1.4 billion in 2009, including sales by its franchisees and licensees.

Weight Watchers' point system allows people to eat any foods they wish, as long as they stay within a given point range. Although Weight Watchers markets a number of different products, publications, and programs to the weight loss market, weekly meetings have always been a central part of its program. Some 50,000 of these meetings take place every week, attended by more than

1.5 million people and led by role models who have completed the Weight Watchers program.

In addition to selling its own magazine via subscription, at the news stand, and at weekly meetings, Weight Watchers' Web site offers a variety of online tools to help people in their weight loss journey. In addition, Weight Watchers Corporate Solutions offers companies different ways to provide the program to employees. These include Weight Watchers At Work meetings, Weight Watchers Local Meetings coupons that enable employees to attend meetings near the workplace, Weight Watchers Online subscriptions, and Weight Watchers At Home kits.

Weight Watchers experienced a difficult period during the mid-1990s, when it was part of the H.J. Heinz Co. However, European investment firm Artal Luxembourg took control of Weight Watchers in 1999 and named Linda Huett as president. A former Yale drama major, Huett had been promoted within the company to run its operation in Britain. Weight Watchers International Inc. went public on November 15, 2001, and saw its stock value skyrocket, almost doubling within the first year. As Weight Watchers' high-profile spokeswoman, Sarah Ferguson, the Duchess of York, played a significant role in bolstering the company's popularity.

Slim-Fast Foods Co. Based in West Palm Beach, Florida, Slim-Fast Foods Co.'s roots stretch back to the late 1940s when Daniel Abraham took the reins of Thompson Medical from his father. According to the company, "From the start, Abraham's philosophy was to identify niche products, aggressively market and distribute them, and build customer loyalties. Given financial constraints, he had to develop innovative techniques to market products such as creative advertising, free samples, and promotional labeling on packages." In 1977, Abraham developed the Slim-Fast meal replacement shake. Slim-Fast became its own company in 1990, in response to explosive growth within the meal replacement sector. In 2000, Slim-Fast Foods was purchased by Unilever, an international manufacturer of food, home care, and personal care products, for $2.6 billion. Slim-Fast sold 50 different products through retailers in the United States, Mexico, Canada, Ireland, the United Kingdom, and Germany.

Atkins Nutritionals Inc. Established by cardiologist Dr. Robert Atkins, Denver-based Atkins Nutritional Inc. offers a variety of food products and resources centered around its highly popular low-carbohydrate/high-protein diet, formerly called the Atkins Nutritional Approach. In the name of what it calls "controlled carbohydrate nutritional science," the company began offering food products like low-carbohydrate bread. According to the company, more than 50 studies had documented the effectiveness of a low-carb diet for losing weight. The company offered more than 50 different food products, ranging from essential oils to shakes, bars, and bake mixes. Atkins also marketed high-quality nutritional supplements and information products. Atkins Advantage food products were shelved in about 30,000 retail stores worldwide.

Jenny Craig Inc. Headquartered in Carlsbad, California, Jenny Craig Inc. is one of the world's leading weight management service companies. Jenny Craig operates approximately 650 classroom diet centers in the United States, Canada, Australia, New Zealand, Puerto Rico, and Guam, where it sells prepared food items and other weight loss products. The company was founded by Jenny and Sid Craig, who sold their enterprise to DB Capital Partners and ACI Capital Co. in 2002, at which time sales were estimated to be $300 million. In June 2006 the company was purchased by Nestle for $600 million. According to the company, Jenny Craig "offers a proven, comprehensive program that, through sound nutrition and simple activity, helps clients achieve the balance necessary for optimal weight loss and personal well-being." In addition to brick-and-mortar locations, Jenny Craig's program is available by phone and mail.

AMERICA AND THE WORLD

Obesity and weight-related problems are not unique to the United States. Some 1 billion people were reported to be obese or overweight worldwide, leading to the coining of a new word, "globesity." Rising obesity levels have been seen in Britain, Western Europe, Eastern Europe, Japan, and China. Even Africa and the Aborigines of Australia have seen rising rates of obesity and diabetes. Heart disease rates had increased 20-fold in as many years as dietary habits became less healthy.

RESEARCH AND TECHNOLOGY

In 2010, biopharmaceutical company Vivus was awaiting FDA approval for its new obesity drug, Qnexa. Several nutraceutical and biopharaceutical companies were being acquired by large traditional drug companies, aimed at developing new obesity drugs based on DNA and/or genetic manipulation.

Obesity, weight loss, and weight management remained complicated issues that continually inspire scientific research, from both medical and societal perspectives. Such research provides valuable insight to companies and professionals within the weight loss products and services industry as they seek to understand the root causes of weight problems and how to address them.

In 2007, products containing the new appetite suppressant hoodia appeared on the market. Hoodia is an extract from a plant found in the Kalahari Desert. Consumer products giant Unilever and biotech company

Phytopharm collaborated on research and development for hoodia gordonii, the plant that has long been used to curb hunger by tribes in the Kalahari in southern Africa. In 2006, after R&D established that the active ingredient could be successfully extracted from the plant, some prototype products containing the plant extract, such as drinks and food bars, were put into clinical trials. By 2007 a variety of products that included hoodia were available, including suckers ("Power Pops") and coffee creamer. Research was ongoing to determine just how safe and effective hoodia was in helping people eat less and lose weight. Investigations were also ongoing regarding certain products that claimed to contain hoodia but actually did not, or that did not include the part of the plant that actually suppressed the appetite. In addition, in response to a concern about a shortage of supply, Afriplex, a Cape Town company, planted more than 12 million acres of the plant between 2004 and 2007. This was " the largest independent commercial hoodia project worldwide," according to *Food Engineering & Ingredients*.

Meanwhile, the military was going online in an effort to help its personnel with their weight loss issues. Contrary to the general public's perception of a fit military with its personnel operating at a healthy weight, approximately 57 percent of the U.S. Air Force is considered either overweight or obese. Military personnel are reluctant to join weight loss programs because of the perceived stigma of being overweight in the military. As a result, the Air Force Substance Abuse Program Development, in a study of 452 overweight Air Force personnel, discovered that of those who participated in Minimal Contact Behavioral Internet Therapy (MCBIT), significantly more reached their weight loss goal than those who relied solely on usual programs, such as Weight Watchers or a military-sponsored program. MCBIT offers a comprehensive program, including a self-help book, two motivational phone calls, and an interactive Internet weight loss program, with weekly feedback of their food and exercise diaries. After 24 weeks, 23 percent of those who participated in MCBIT lost at least 5 percent of body weight, compared to only 7 percent of those who used only the usual, non-Internet weight loss programs. A further study revealed that the most effective weight loss programs involve face-to-face interaction, followed by Internet-based counseling, with a newsletter-based intervention program coming up a far third in effectiveness in losing and maintaining weight.

BIBLIOGRAPHY

"About Jenny Craig." Jenny Craig, 13 November 2008. Available from http://www.jennycraig.com.

"About Us." Weight Watchers International, 13 November 2008. Available from http://www.weightwatchers.com.

Alexander, Camila. "Hoodia: From the Desert into your Dessert?" *Food Engineering & Ingredients,* September 2007.

"Alli Throws the Book at 'Em." *Brandweek,* 10 December 2007.

"Atkins Gains as Studies Support Low-Carb Diets." *MMR,* 20 October 2008.

"China Medicine to Showcase Bethin Weight Loss Product at 2008 Natural Products Expo East Trade Show." *PR Newswire,* 13 October 2008.

Cohen, Robert. "Diet Pill Maker Targets Competition: Glaxo Urges FDA to Require Proof Supplements Work." *The Houston Chronicle,* 6 July 2008.

"Defining Success: The New Shape of the Diet Pill Market." *Chain Drug Review,* 19 February 2007.

"FTC Sues Diet Marketers." *Direct,* 10 February 2008.

"Hoodia—The New Obesity Breakthrough?" *Choice,* June 2007.

"Inside Drugmakers' War on Fat." *Business Week,* 8 March 2008.

Johnsen, Michael. "Diet Bars Aim to Gain Sales." *Drug Store News,* 23 June 2008.

Kalorama Information. "Obesity, Weight Loss and Diet Management Markets (Pharmaceutical, Surgical and Dietary Approaches)." December 2009. Available from http://www.reportlinker.com/p0167110

"Leaning into It." *Prepared Foods,* July 2008.

"Our Company." Atkins Nutritionals, 13 November 2008. Available from http://atkins.com.

"Preventing Overweight in USAF Personnel: Minimal Contact Program." U.S. National Institutes of Health, 13 November 2008. Available from http://clinicaltrials.gov.

Rao, Jessica. "It's The Year of the Value Diet." CNBC.com News, 18 June 2010.

"Reportlinker Adds Weight Loss Markets for Products and Services." 9 November 2010. Available from http://www.reportlinker.com/p0326192/Weight-Loss-Markets-for-Products-and_services.html.

Richman, Alan. "Weighty Matters." *Nutraceuticals World,* September 2008.

"Weight Watchers International (WTW)." Available from http://www.weight_watchers_international.com.

"There's Help for the Overweight." *MMR,* 14 January 2008.

"Today's Special . . . Weight-Loss Lollipops." *Maclean's,* 26 November 2007.

"Trends and Statistics." Calorie Control Council, August 2007.

"U.S. Obesity Trends, 1985–2007." Centers for Disease Control and Prevention, 28 July 2008.

"Weight Loss Markets for Products and Services." Report Code FOD027C. BCC Research, October 2010. Available from http://www.www.bccresearch.com/report/FOD027C.html.

"Weight-Loss Scams Slim Down Wallets. *Columbus Dispatch,* (Columbus, OH), 22 January 2008.

WIRELESS COMMUNICATIONS AND WAP

INDUSTRY SNAPSHOT

Known by related monikers such as mobile, cellular, and personal communications services, wireless communications services are a huge and fast-growing business. Consumers and businesses alike have been electronically tethering themselves in droves to wireless technology because of its convenience and increasing affordability. Although prices for wireless services dropped as they became mainstream, industry revenue has grown with market saturation. The market enjoyed a 300 percent increase between 1998 and 2008. The U.S. wireless industry is widely regarded as underdeveloped compared to those of Japan and Western Europe, signaling ample opportunities for continued expansion.

Digital and broadband services are two wireless segments that were experiencing sharp growth, and digital wireless services were increasing. Digital wireless services, which include personal communications services, have been available in the United States since the mid-1990s, but were not mainstream until the early 2000s. Digital technology represented the second generation (2G) of wireless communications; the first was various analog (defined by *Merriam-Webster's Collegiate Dictionary* as data represented by continuously variable physical quantities), systems that have been around for decades. Digital (defined by *Webster's* as calculation by numerical methods or by discrete units) encoding enables greater volumes of information to be sent and received by wireless devices and

is capable of delivering higher sound quality and other features found wanting in analog service.

The third generation (3G) of wireless communications is represented by mobile applications: wireless voice telephony, video calls, and broadband wireless (also known as WiFi). Using standards such as the nascent Wireless Application Protocol (WAP), 3G broadband services can deliver applications and data to wireless "smartphones" that double as handheld organizers, personal digital assistants (PDAs), or computers. WAPs that use displays and access the Internet utilize microbrowsers, browsers limited to small file sizes, to accommodate the low memory constraints of handheld devices and the low bandwidth limitations of a wireless handheld network. By 2010, 4G communications were ubiquitous, with 5G on the way.

Indeed, despite the industry's size and prominence, it is still characterized by a bewildering set of incongruent technologies. There is no single wireless standard or type of wireless service within the United States, much less the world. Major technical distinctions include whether a service uses analog or digital signals, what kind of signal separation scheme it employs to let multiple users share the same airwaves, and even what radio frequencies it uses. All these differences mean that portable phones and other wireless communications devices will work with some systems but not others, and in some locations but not all. This mélange of standards has resulted from technological change, proprietary competitive strategies of certain companies, and a failure to adopt wider standards before industry players invested heavily in any one technology. Resolutions have been proposed that could improve cross-system compatibility. Some industry insiders, however, dismiss the impact of competing standards as negligible, citing that pricing and features rather than cross-system compatibility are what drive new subscriptions.

ORGANIZATION AND STRUCTURE

The Federal Communications Commission (FCC) "sells air" by charging companies a fee to gain rights to a certain frequency. Beginning in 1994, for instance, the FCC auctioned off airspace for the new personal communications services (PCS) technology, and in 1998 and 1999 it added licenses for local multipoint distribution service. Such purchasers may in turn sell air to other parties for a profit. The FCC also regulates and sets guidelines for various aspects of the telecommunications industry such as cellular telephone service.

The six wireless divisions identified by the FCC—which are by no means equal in size and scope—are commercial mobile radio services, public mobile services, personal communications services, domestic public fixed radio services, private land mobile radio services, private operational fixed microwave services, and personal radio services. Of these, only the first three are normally considered part of the commercial wireless industry.

Commercial Mobile Radio Service Commercial mobile radio service includes the cellular telephone industry. Cellular telephone systems use low power radio-telephone transceivers. The cellular infrastructure in use in the United States at the end of the 1990s was largely analog, meaning that continuous electrical signals send and receive information. This differs from communications systems that use digital signals to send and receive messages. Digital systems create virtually exact replicas of signals because they are fed through computers that assign binary codes comprised of zeroes and ones to each unit of information. Analog systems create only very good copies of signals.

Geographic areas serviced by a cellular carrier are divided into small regions, sometimes only one mile across, called cells. Because of cooperation within the industry, it is possible for cellular service customers to be "handed off" from one service provider's antenna to another as the user passes from cell to cell.

The advantage of using a cellular system is frequency reuse. Because the FCC grants a limited number of channels, or frequencies, to the cellular telephone service industry, it would be impossible to have only one, or even a few, transceivers in each service area. Multiple cells allow the same frequency to be used by many callers in the same service area. Furthermore, each cell can be subdivided into sectors, usually three, using directional antennas. As a result, a single service area can have thousands of callers communicating on several hundred designated channels.

Public Mobile Services Public mobile services includes pagers, air to ground service (such as aircraft to control tower communications), offshore service (for sailing vessels), and rural radio-telephone service.

Personal Communications Service Personal communications service (PCS) is a departure from "traditional" wireless telecommunications that require high power and relatively large cells to accommodate phones moving rapidly through space in motor vehicles. PCS systems are digital and are maintained by a network of small transmitter-receiver antennas installed throughout a community, such as on buildings. The antennae are connected to a master telephone switch that is connected to a main telephone network. PCS systems use comparatively low-powered phones that operate at a higher radio frequency. As a result, the systems use smaller cells that allow a greater concentration of users. The net result of PCS differences is a cellular network with as much as 20 times the capacity of a standard cellular service area. This increased capacity allows PCS to spread costs over a potentially larger subscriber base. In addition, PCS phones weigh less and are cheaper to manufacture than their cellular counterparts.

Telecommunications Reform Act of 1996 The Telecommunications Reform Act, signed into law on February 8, 1996, swept away 62 years of regulation of the telecommunications industry. The legislation was intended to promote competition across the industry, thus resulting in the development of new technology, the creation of new business and new jobs, and ultimately lower prices. Local telephone companies, long-distance providers, wireless companies, and cable television operators were, in theory, free to offer all telecommunications services. Since all the major landline entities were already cellular providers, this did not have any immediate effect on the wireless industry, but the long-range goal of the major industry players was to provide "one-stop shopping" for consumer or business telecommunications needs. Mergers, acquisitions, and various kinds of joint ventures, already common in the wireless segment, drastically reshaped the broader telecommunications industry as companies tried to position themselves for future growth.

BACKGROUND AND DEVELOPMENT

The Detroit Police Department used one of the first mobile radio systems on April 7, 1928. The spectrum for radio transmission was broadened seven years later to include FM, or frequency modulation, signals. FM transmission technology paved the way for the mobile radio systems that were widely used during World War II. After the war, American Telephone and Telegraph (AT&T)—which at that time held a virtual monopoly over phone service in the United States—introduced the Improved Mobile Telephone Service, which made possible extremely limited cellular communication systems. The service was so restrictive that even by 1970, the Bell system in the city of New York could simultaneously sustain a total of only 12 mobile phone conversations.

Around 1980, under the guidance of AT&T, the first practical framework for mobile service in the United States, advanced mobile phone service (AMPS), was born. The FCC allocated space for AMPS in Washington, D.C., as a test market, but it was not until 1983 in the Chicago and Baltimore markets that companies provided relatively inexpensive, efficient consumer cellular service in the United States.

In the mid-1980s, cellular service grew rapidly in the industrialized world with the implementation of different networking systems in North America and parts of Europe and Japan. The first generation of technology quickly ran its course, expanding to the furthest reaches of the airspace spectrum allocated for it. This was particularly true in Europe, where in the mid- to late 1980s the second generation of mobile communications technology was born.

The first PCS licenses for the 51 major trading areas in the United States were auctioned off between December 1994 and March 1995. A total of 18 bidders won 99 licenses, generating $7.7 billion for the U.S. Treasury. Sprint Spectrum, an alliance of Sprint Corp. and several cable TV concerns, spent $2.1 billion for 29 licenses. AT&T Wireless took 21 licenses for $1.69 billion, and PrimeCo, a venture of AirTouch Communications, Bell Atlantic, NYNEX Corp., and US West Inc., spent $1.11 billion for 11 licenses.

The number of licenses purchased for each market put tremendous competitive pressure on everyone. Financial pressure was also great because of the cost of building the networks, along with the cost of the licenses. After purchasing these licenses, many PCS providers faced financial difficulty. Moreover, many communities opposed the construction of the many transmitting towers necessary for the low-power networks. The FCC, however, along with most industry observers, expected the investment to pay off abundantly within 10 years.

In the late 1990s, personal communications service (PCS) carriers began adopting new networks that included both wire and wireless technology. Known as the "hybrid approach," the blend of wire and wireless technology allows carriers to bypass the traditional stationary wireless local loop technology, according to *Telephony*. US West and BellSouth were among the first companies to choose the hybrid approach for their services. Europe had already widely developed this kind of integrated network.

In 1999 and 2000, average wireless prices appeared to finally reach a plateau after a decade of annual declines, as major carriers began to focus more on solidifying financial returns over luring in new customers with unsustainably low prices and promotions. Meanwhile, approximately one-third of existing customers changed carriers during 2000, a phenomenon known as customer churn, and a reflection of both more lenient subscriber contracts and greater customer willingness to shop around.

Maturity brings about a slowdown in growth, and that is what wireless cellular carriers began to see in 2002. While AT&T Wireless said it increased its number of subscribers by half a million, Verizon Wireless, the largest carrier in the country, reported customer numbers short of projections. In the first quarter of 2002, Verizon only added 186,000 customers instead of the expected number of 300,000. In the first quarter of 2001, Verizon had added 518,000 customers. In 2002, competition for subscribers increased and industry analysts were predicting that cellular markets had reached a saturation point. They pointed out that there were more than 130 million subscribers, which represented 44 percent of the U.S. population. In contrast to Verizon, VoiceStream gained almost half a million new customers in the first quarter of 2001. AT&T Wireless Group added 650,000 customers in the quarter, bringing its customer base to 19.5 million.

Among other factors driving growth were new services such as wireless data and Internet access and service bundling, in which a company's offerings in phone lines, Internet access, and cable television are sold together. In addition, there were prepaid and dispatch services. Prepaid services appealed to rate-sensitive customers who may have occasional need for a wireless phone but prefer not to pay a monthly subscription fee, while dispatch services offered intercom-like communications among coworkers, family members, or friends who are in frequent contact.

One technology that many carriers, device makers, and content providers were banking on was wireless application protocol (WAP). This communications standard was developed by a group of leading wireless hardware and service companies and was intended to provide a universal foundation on which wireless applications could be built. Using a programming scheme called wireless markup language, newer mobile phones and other devices could run wireless-oriented applications and transmit data over a common architecture that can be used in any number of digital wireless systems (CDMA, TDMA, GSM).

WAP required specially outfitted devices that did not begin commercial shipment until 2000. Nevertheless, with the backing of all the major wireless carriers and phone manufacturers, rollout was swift, especially in Europe, where cell phone penetration rates were vastly greater than in the United States.

Another complication in WAP's deployment was the problem that most of the early WAP devices, many of which hit the market a year later than anticipated, were not yet capable of the full range of WAP functions and activities. More sophisticated and powerful devices were developed that rendered early models obsolete or severely limited by comparison. In short, while WAP technology represented the third generation in mobile telephony, the first devices were not close to being the finest.

In the early 2000s, the wireless services industry had concentrated greater market share in the hands of a few multinational players such as Verizon Wireless—a collaboration of AirTouch, Vodafone, GTE, and Bell Atlantic Corp.'s wireless interests. Regional Bells SBC Communications Inc. and BellSouth Corp. also announced a merger of their wireless units in 2000, forming Cingular Wireless, and acquired AT&T Wireless in 2004.

Despite mergers and some warnings of market saturation, wireless industry growth continued, largely due to the ever-changing world of technology. The Strategis Group, a telecommunications market research firm, had predicted the wireless penetration rate would soar from about 28 percent of the population in 1999 to 56 percent by 2004. The Wireless Association reported approximately 135 million wireless users that year, which was more than 70 million higher than in 1997. The Cellular Telecommunications & Internet Association put the subscriber numbers at 158 million, reporting also that 92 percent of those subscribers had digital wireless services.

Perhaps the wireless technology causing the most stir in the early 2000s was broadband data access via wireless device. The data arena opens the possibility of accessing Web pages, sending and receiving e-mail and two-way text paging, and the potential to transmit data and application files without plugging into a conventional wired computer network. Moreover, fixed wireless broadband services, such as local multipoint distribution service (LMDS) and multichannel multipoint distribution service, can also support simultaneous voice and data transfer and, ultimately, advanced features such as video, although such capabilities are still at least a few years from widespread availability. In the meantime, local multipoint distribution service (LMDS) and similar services compete with such wired technologies as digital subscriber line (DSL) and cable for the high-speed data market.

Although naysayers had predicted the downfall of WAP, it began to appear as though reports of its demise were premature. By the end of December 2005, usage of multimedia messaging services (MMS) and WAP had skyrocketed. WAP browsing had risen to 32 percent, up from 17 percent in 2004. Sixty percent of mobile phone subscribers ages 18 to 24 sent MMSs compared to 37 percent in 2004. MMS is a standard for telephony (telephone transmission of sounds as electrical signals) messaging systems that allow sending messages that include multimedia objects (images, audio, video, and rich text) rather than just text. Third generation (3G) technology also began gaining momentum despite low customer satisfaction in its beginning stages. In 2005, Japan introduced 3G on a large commercial scale (it was the first country to do so) with about 40 percent of subscribers using 3G networks only. During 2006, the transition from 2G to 3G was expected to be mostly completed in Japan; upgrades to the next 3.5G stage with 3 Mbit/s data rates, was already underway.

With consumers becoming more comfortable with WAP, more companies began boosting their use of WAP Push—already being used as a technology to download such content as ringtones—to advertise their brands directly to users via mobile Internet sites as part of their marketing campaigns. WAP has the ability to display much more sophisticated and complex content than that available with the 160 characters of short messaging service (SMS) or even the slideshow format of multimedia messaging services (MMS). When a WAP bookmark is incorporated into an SMS message, the user simply clicks on it, a mobile web page loads, and an image is downloaded to his/her phone. The user pays for the cost of receiving the picture, which is delivered in the right format for each user's particular phone. Because of skyrocketing WAP usage by early 2005, advertisers became increasingly interested in mobile ads. More than 80 percent of Americans have a mobile phone, compared to 55 percent with Internet access; therefore, advertisers have realized WAP technology is a huge commercial opportunity.

Companies such as Levi's, McDonald's, and Vodafone began scrambling to stake a claim on the promising new market of placing and running ad campaigns on mobile Internet sites. Levi's introduced its 501s campaign in early 2005 using a WAP site as a integral aspect of its digital planning; McDonald's Incredibles used WAP with excellent results and no negative feedback from consumers; ESPN's WAP site received 500,000 unique visitors per day by October 2005, according to ESPN's vice president of Product Management and Emerging Sales, John Zaccario; and the Daily Telegraph launched its Mobile Fantasy League WAP service in late 2005 to give mobile users the same functionality as the highly successful online fantasy football game. To introduce it to consumers, it was offered as a free trial for one month, with the season running from October 2005 to May 2006. As the decade progressed, more advertising campaigns utilized WAP technology as part of their strategy.

In the Internet access segment of the business, WiFi, which allows wireless connection to the Internet within about 30 feet of a base station, was giving way to WiMAX, which extends the range to about 30 miles. The lack of industry-wide specification standards remained a problem for WiMAX. Rob Brownstein of LitePoint told *Electronic Engineering Times,* "There is really only one solution: Make sure WiMAX devices are tested in production in ways that ensure they truly meet the standard's specifications." The WiMAX Forum took steps to address the problem by offering a certification program for WiMAX products that meet certain criteria. Ron Resnick, president of the WiMAX Forum, said, "The Forum goes to great lengths to warn vendors that claims like 'WiMAX-like' and 'WiMAX-compliant'are not WiMAX Forum Certified, which means their equipment isn't interoperable with other vendors' equipment."

In the intensely competitive market of the early 2000s, wireless companies continued to grow and expand their businesses. In November 2008 AT&T announced plans to purchase wireless communications provider Centennial Communications for $944 million. At the time of the announcement, Centennial had about 1.1 million wireless subscribers, mostly in the Midwest. Earlier in the month, AT&T bought Wayport, a company that provides back-office management for Wi-Fi hot spots, for $275 million. According to *Network World,* these two additions will increase the quality and scope of AT&T's wireless services.

These major purchases by AT&T were somewhat overshadowed by Verizon's buy-out of Alltel Wireless in late 2008, a deal worth a reported $28 billion. After the merger, which the Federal Communications Commission approved, Verizon will have approximately 80 million wireless customers and more coverage in rural areas of the United States.

Sprint was not to be left out of the game. After spinning off its WiMAX (Worldwide Interoperability for Microwave Access) division to Clearwire, it made plans to "deploy a nationwide WiMAX network that will provide 4G coverage in both rural and urban markets," according to *Network World.* The new company, worth $14.5 billion and known as Clearwire, will also provide wireless broadband to businesses and consumers.

CURRENT CONDITIONS

The telecommunications industry had the worst year in a decade in 2009, experiencing a steady decline in the fixed line services sector. However, the wireless mobile sector contributed to a more positive outcome in 2010, growing an estimated six percent that year, and saving the industry. Mobile phone connections are projected to rise from 5 billion in 2010 to 7.1 billion in 2014, according to researcher Ovum's Global Telcoms Analyzer. Revenues from mobile phone services are projected to grow by nearly $100 billion by 2012. Much of the growth is attributed to emerging markets in Asia and Africa.

In 2009, the Associated Press reported that "the number of U.S. households opting for only cell phones ha[d] for the first time surpassed those that just ha[d] traditional landlines." An estimated 20 percent of U.S. homes relied exclusively on cell phones, whereare 17 percent used only traditional landlines, the report found. As an example of this switch, Verizon Communications Inc. had 39 million landline customers in 2008, but only 35 million in 2009. Conversely, its wireless customers grew from 67 million to 87 million during the same time (although 13 million of that total came from its acquisition of Alltell Corp.). In the first six months of 2009, the number of U.S. mobile wireless service subscriberswith data plans for full Internet access increased by 40 percent to 35 million.

Juniper Research reported in 2010 that LTE (Long Term Evolution, a next generation mobile wireless broadband technology) was beginning to generate appreciable revenues, and Juniper projected global service revenues by LTE mobile networks to reach $100 billion by 2014. Key market drivers were laptops, smartphones, and other devices. High traffic enterprise subscribers using Web, email, and video services were expected to be the earliest adopters of LTE.

For the first time, the amount of mobile data bits traveling around the world surpassed voice traffic in December 2009, according to wireless equipment vendor Ericsson. In order to do so, data traffic had to surpass 140,000 terabytes per month, which was the averaage for voice traffic. The data traffic was generated by an estimated 400 million smartphones, versus 4.6 billion mobile subscribers making voice calls. A large percentage of mobile data traffic was generated by social networking, particularly video clips, which consumed significantly more bytes than text data. With the popularity of Twitter and Facebook (100 million active users accessing through mobile devices), the demand for accessible broadband 24/7 was never greater.

While smartphones grabbed headlines (the IQE Group saw annual growth of 30 to 40 percent for several years to come), other applications of wireless technology were also making news, for example, with smart meters and point to point communications. These applications, in turn, stimulated the optoelectronics industry, for use in display screens for, e.g., finger navigation, short range data communications, etc.

INDUSTRY LEADERS

AT&T Mobility AT&T Mobility was the largest wireless communications provider in the United States. AT&T Mobility came about as a result of several mergers. In 2000, BellSouth Corp. and SBC Communications Inc., two regional Bells that had assembled sizable wireless services, merged and called the new firm Cingular

Wireless. Cingular was owned 60 percent by SBC and 40 percent by BellSouth and was a merging of the 11 brands controlled by its parent companies. SBC was already the third largest wireless carrier in its own right. The new firm had about 25 million wireless customers and sales of $15.5 billion, putting it second behind Verizon.

In March 2003, AT&T Wireless formed a joint venture with Cingular Wireless to provide Global System for Mobile Communication/General Packet Radio Services (GSM/GPRS) network coverage along approximately 4,000 miles of interstate highways in the Midwest, West, and Northeast, a venture that was the prelude to Cingular's 2004 acquisition of AT&T Wireless. In 2006, Cingular Wireless reported more than 54 million subscribers, taking Verizon Wireless's spot as the largest company in the wireless industry. In 2006, AT&T merged with BellSouth and changed Cingular's name to "the new AT&T." From there it became AT&T Wireless and then AT&T Mobility. In 2009 parent At&T had more than 300,000 employees worldwide and revenues of $123 billion, down from $124 billion in 2008

Verizon Wireless By 2008, Verizon Wireless was the nation's second largest wireless service provider with 68 million customers in the United States. Verizon Wireless was a joint venture of Vodafone AirTouch Plc (itself a merger of U.K. and U.S. wireless giants) and Bell Atlantic Corp., which absorbed GTE and its wireless unit in 2000. Once the merger was completed, Bell Atlantic and GTE took the Verizon name, which is a blend of the Latin *veritas* (truth) and "horizon." In May of 2003, it acquired 50 personal communications services (PCS) licenses and related network assets from Northcoast Communications LLC for approximately $750 million in cash. The licenses provided the company with additional growth capacity over large portions of the East Coast and Midwest. Verizon Wireless pointed out that the licenses overlap some of its most densely populated service areas, enabling it to provide network capacity to match growth in customer demand. In March 2003, Verizon Wireless and Lucent Technologies launched a super fast mobile data network in Washington, D.C., to provide businesses and consumers with data services at speeds of up to 2.4 megabits per second, a rate as fast or faster than those provided by cable or telephone wires. This enabled Verizon Wireless customers to access the high-speed commercial Evolution Data Only (EvDO) network by equipping their laptop PCs and personal digital assistants (PDAs) with 1xEVDO wireless modem cards. By providing secure mobile Internet Protocol (IP) virtual private network (VPN) connections on the network, business customers can access the Verizon Wireless network as an extension of their corporate local area network (LAN) or intranet. In this way, they could work from any location with the same speed and security they experienced at the office location, enabling them to download large files such as spreadsheets, inventory lists, and even video, in seconds.

In 2002, Verizon Wireless entered an agreement with America Online to offer AOL content and its instant messenger program on cell phones to its customers. With the deal, AOL had forged agreements with five of the six top wireless carriers to either give it prominent placement on the phone's deck or to sell the instant messenger service separately. Increasingly, carriers were adding wireless messaging and access to Internet portals like AOL to cell phones in the hopes of finding new sources of revenue. In this trend, AOL was behind its rivals Microsoft and Yahoo, which had already been making their content available to carriers. In fact, AOL's deal with Verizon Wireless meant that AOL services would share space on some cell phone decks or subscriber plans with Microsoft. Verizon Wireless offered its wireless Web subscribers a service called "VZW with MSN," which gives its users access to MSN Messenger, Hotmail, and Microsoft Net alerts, a calendar, and information such as news, stocks, sports, and weather. 2009 revenues for Verizon were $62.1 billion. In late 2010, Verizon introduced its new LTE 4G mobile wireless phone.

Sprint Nextel Sprint Nextel was formed when Sprint and Nextel Communications merged. Sprint was originally founded as a joint venture between long distance carrier Sprint Corp. and three large cable system operators. Sprint operated a national all-digital wireless network using code division multiple access (CDMA) technology. In 2002, the PCS Group, together with third party affiliates, operated PCS systems in over 300 metropolitan markets. The PCS Group supplemented its own network through affiliation arrangements with other companies that use CDMA. Experiencing a high customer change rate in 2002, Sprint PCS reduced its work force by 6 percent. In 2004, SprintPCS was re-joined to SprintFON.Although Spring Nextel has lagged behind competitors, it has a strong retail presence and one of the most modern networks in the United States. services. The company reported 2009 revenues of $32.3 billion with 60,000 employees and 48.8 million customers.

In 2010, TriQuint supplied the majority of wireless chips for smartphones including iPhone, Samsung Galaxy, and the Blackberry Tour.

AMERICA AND THE WORLD
Conservative estimates placed the number of global mobile subscribers at more than 4 billion in 2009. At the same time, the U.S. market was seen to be slowing down to a 40 percent rate. In fact, the United States trails a number of countries, notably those of Northern Europe, in the rate

and scope of wireless service deployment. In 2000, the use of cell phones in Scandinavian countries was so prevalent—at more than 60 percent of the population by some estimates—that some observers spoke of 100 percent penetration rates in the foreseeable future. In addition to wider adoption abroad, wireless services in Europe and parts of Asia also tend to be more technologically advanced than those of the United States. Wireless data services, for instance, were expected to be deployed faster in parts of Europe than in the United States.

The Asia-Pacific market was the largest cellular market in the world, with China leading the way. In 2010 alone, China and India added an estimated 329 million new mobile phone connections, which represented more than the total population of the United Kingdom, Germany, France, Italy, and Spain combined. Much of the projected growth of the global market (6 percent in 2010, a compound annual growth rate, CAGR, of 5 percent by 2014) is attributed to emerging markets in Asia and Africa.

As wealthy consumer and business markets such as those of Japan, Western Europe, and the United States approach saturation, multinational carriers are shifting their sights to other regions. Recognizing that half of the world's population lives more than 200 miles from the nearest telephone, many companies were striving to create a blanket service that could deliver inexpensive wireless telephone service to every person on the globe. Even if a company could capture just 1 to 2 percent of the global marketplace, it would enjoy a subscriber base of 50 to 100 million people.

RESEARCH AND TECHNOLOGY

By 2008, several companies were offering mobile Internet browsers, whereby users could access the Internet and e-mail via their cell phones. Examples were Opera Mobile, Internet Explorer Mobile by Microsoft, and the Black-Berry Browser, created especially for the BlackBerry smartphone by its creator, Research in Motion. MSN's Mobile aimed to include the same functionality as MSN's website—including city guides, news, and sports—as well as services such as Messenger, Spaces, and Mail. According to one report by Juniper Research and reported in *Database and Network Journal,* annual revenues from mobile Internet searches will reach $4.8 billion by 2013. However, the report also noted that users may be dissuaded by an overload of advertising, which could limit use.

Alatto, a mobile multimedia specialist company, introduced a new service called Tribes with four European network operators. Tribes is a content discovery service containing a three-button toolbar on the first scroll of a user's WAP screen, allowing the user to store

sites and forward links to friends' phones. Alatto claims that its algorithms personalize each user's profile automatically as they click on links, allowing Tribes to forward other similar sites to their phones. Because of the convenience of automatic browsing and sharing of WAP content, Alatto expected Tribes to double average user session times.

BIBLIOGRAPHY

Berg, Andrew. "Report: LTE Service Revenues to Reach $100 Billion by 2014." *Wireless Week,* 11 November 2010.

Dubie, Denise. "The New and Improved WAN Application Delivery Market." *Network World,* 2 January 2007.

Farley, Tom. "The Cell Phone Revolution." *Invention & Technology,* Winter 2007.

"FCC Releases New Data on Internet Access Services." Federal Communications Commission, Press Release, 2 September 2010. Available from http://www.fcc.gov/wcb.stats.

"FCC Releases New Local Telephone Competition Data." Federal Communications Commission, Press Release, 3 September 2010. Available from http://www.fcc.gov/wcb.stats.

Gaylord, Chris. "As Recession Lingers, Cell Phones Take OVer." *CS Monitor,* 7 May 2009.

Higginbotham, Stacey. "Mobile Milestone: Data Surpasses Voice Traffic." *Tech News,* 24 March 2010.

"IQE Profits Surge Thanks to Smartphones and Emerging Opto Markets." 1 September 2010. Available from http://www.compoundsemiconductor.net/csc/news.

"Mobile Search Revenues to Reach $4.8 Billion by 2013." *Database and Network Journal,* April 2008.

Mokhoff, Nicolas. "Extending Mobile Wireless Demands Conformance." *Electronic Engineering Times,* 27 October 2008.

Nystedt, Dan. "China Mobile Subscribers Top U.S. Population." *Info World,* 22 January 2007.

"Operators Relying Solely on Mobile Data for Growth." *Total Telecom Online,* 2 September 2008.

Reed, Brad. "AT&T Continues Wireless Services Spending Spree." *Network World,* 10 November 2008.

———. "FCC Approves Two Major Telecom Mergers." *Network World,* 5 November 2008.

"Skyrocketing Subscribers." CTIA, 11 November 2008. Available from http:/www.ctia.org.

"SMBs Driving Mobile Broadband Adoption." *Information Week,* 5 November 2008.

Sprint-Nextel. Available from http://www.investors.sprint.com.

"Trends in Telephone Services." Federal Communications Commission, Press release, 3 September 2010. Available from http://www.fcc.gov/wcb.iatd/trends/html.

"U.S. Wireless Quick Facts and Figures." CTIA, 11 November 2008. Available from http://www. ctia.org.

"Wireless Carriers Address an Open Future." *Information Week,* 11 September 2008.

"The Year 2009, the Worst for Telecoms in a Decade, Finds Ovum." Datamonitor, 21 September 2010. Available from http://about.datamonitor.com/media/archives/4791.

WOUND CARE

———■———

SIC CODE(S)

8011

8031

INDUSTRY SNAPSHOT

A wound is a break in the skin; the outer layer of skin is called the epidermis. Wounds are usually caused by cuts or scrapes. Each kind of wound may be treated differently, depending on how they happened and how serious they are. The following are the stages of the healing process in wound care:

- Inflammation. The injury phase, with bleeding, narrowing of the blood vessels, clot formation, and release of various chemical substances into the wound that will begin the healing process. Specialized cells will clear the wound of debris over the course of several days.

- Proliferation. This phase is the forming stage for a matrix or latticework of cells. On this matrix, new skin cells and blood vessels will form. It is the new small blood vessels, called capillaries, which give a healing wound its pink/purplish/red appearance. These new blood vessels supply the rebuilding cells with oxygen and nutrients to sustain the growth of the new cells and support the production of proteins (primarily collagen). The collagen acts as the framework for the new tissues. Collagen is the main substance in the final scar.

- Remodeling. This phase begins after two to three weeks. The collagen framework continues to build and organize, which makes the tissue strong. The blood vessel density decreases, and the wound loses its pinkish color. In the next six months, the area gets stronger, eventually regaining approximately 70 percent strength of the previously uninjured skin.

- Epithelialization. This is the process of laying down new skin, or epithelial cells, which form a protective barrier between the outer environment and the body. Their primary purpose is to protect against water loss and bacteria. Reconstruction of this layer begins within a few hours of the injury and is complete within 24 to 48 hours in a clean, stitched wound. Open wounds may take 7 to 10 days because the inflammatory process is prolonged, which contributes to scarring. Scarring occurs when the injury extends beyond the deep layer of the skin, called the dermis.

While wound care dates back to prehistoric times when hunter-gatherers utilized the best plants and herbs with which to heal topical injuries, current technologies continue to advance modern wound care.

ORGANIZATION AND STRUCTURE

While most wounds are usually caused by cuts or scrapes, approximately 5 million Americans suffer from chronic open sore wounds as a result of illness or bed rest. Several organizations in the United States operate with a direct purpose to discuss and apply the latest research in caring for wounds, whether chronic or accidental, including the American Academy of Wound Care; the Association for the Advancement of Wound Care; the Wound Care Education Institute; the Wound, Ostomy, and Continence Nurses Society; and the National Alliance of Wound Care.

Current medical journals on the subject include *Advances in Skin & Wound Care* and the *Journal of Wound Care.*

Wounds are classified as scrapes and abrasions, lacerations or cuts, and puncture wounds. Wound care includes two primary steps: stopping the bleeding and cleaning the wound. To stop bleeding, hold a bandage down with pressure and wait for the blood to clot. To clean the wound, use water with pressure, either a brisk running faucet or a handheld sprayer. However, do not ever scrub wounds.

For wounds bigger than a half-inch or where bleeding does not stop after 10 minutes, professional medical attention is needed. Waiting for even 8 to 12 hours after a severe wound to seek medical attention increases the risk of infection and should be avoided. If in doubt, visit your general practitioner's office or head for the nearest emergency room. The doctor at the emergency room or your own doctor will either use bandages, stitches, or a skin adhesive to close and cover the wound in order to speed up its healing. You also may need to update your tetanus shot if you haven't had one recently.

While these procedures seem straightforward and simple, wound care research continues in our modern medical community. Thanks to wound care research, wounds and our outer skin layer can be taken care of better and better as medical research progresses forward. Wound care is undertaken by both medical professionals and by laypeople, and modern research usually trickles down through the professional community first for R&D and vigorous testing. After being proved, the latest wound care procedures are then passed along to the general community in the latest antibiotic ointments, bandages, and first aid kits.

BACKGROUND AND DEVELOPMENT

The study of effective wound care has its roots in prehistoric time when hunter-gatherers noticed which plants and herbs were most effective in healing soft tissues. Wound care studies date back to ancient Egypt and Greece. The Ebers Papyrus, circa 1500 B.C., details the use of honey, animal grease, and lint as topical substances to heal wounds. Honey was noted for its antibacterial components, the lint provided a dressing, and the animal grease blocked other environmental exposure. Egyptians believed wound closure "preserved the soul." The Greeks were the first to note a distinction between different types of wounds, calling them "fresh" and "nonhealing." Galen of Pergamum, who served Roman gladiators, developed the idea of keeping the wound site moist to ensure successful closure.

During the Middle Ages and the Renaissance, nothing more of great significance was discovered. However, in the nineteenth century, Louis Pasteur and Joseph Lister both made discoveries that decreased the rate of mortality rates during medical procedures. Because of

Lister's discovery about using phenol to disinfect medical procedure equipment, Robert Wood Johnson developed his line of iodine-treated gauzes and bandage wrappings. These discoveries moved the application of wound site maintenance and infection prevention forward more than any research into wound care since the Egyptians and Greeks centuries before.

It was the 1950s when further innovations were made to the idea of wound site dressings with the development of synthetic wet polymer dressings. In the 1970s and 1980s, the modern field of wound care was born. In the 1990s, improvements in composite and hybrid polymers expanded the number of available materials for wound dressings. These improvements, coupled with related developments in tissue engineering, have created a new class of wound dressings that are called "living skin equivalents." Although they are missing key components of whole living skin, they are the future of wound dressings. These new polymers possess the potential to replicate the skin's cellular platforms that release the healing mechanisms essential for proper skin reconstruction.

PIONEERS IN THE FIELD

Louis Pasteur (December 27, 1822–September 28, 1895) was a French chemist and microbiologist. Pasteur is remembered for his remarkable discoveries in the causes and preventions of diseases. His breakthroughs reduced mortality from puerperal fever and he created the first vaccines for rabies and anthrax. His experiments supported the germ theory of disease. Pasteur was best known to the general public for inventing a method to stop milk and wine from causing sickness, a process that came to be called pasteurization. He is regarded as one of the three main founders of microbiology, together with Ferdinand Cohn and Robert Koch. This discovery revolutionized wound care because the idea that bacteria was a cause of illness was still very new at this time. Doctors often didn't stop to consider how bacteria exacerbated wounds to the point that they became life-threatening or killed the patient.

Aside from this main work, Pasteur also made many discoveries in the field of chemistry, most notably the molecular basis for the asymmetry of certain crystals. His body lies beneath the Institute Pasteur in Paris in a spectacular vault covered in depictions of his accomplishments in Byzantine mosaics.

Joseph Lister (April 5, 1827–February 10, 1912), known as Sir Joseph Lister between 1883 and 1897, was a British surgeon and a pioneer of antiseptic surgery, who promoted the idea of sterile surgery while working at the Glasgow Royal Infirmary. Lister successfully introduced carbolic acid (now known as phenol) to sterilize surgical instruments and to clean wounds, which led to reducing post-operative infections and made surgery safer for patients. This idea of a sterile environment for surgery was relatively unknown at the time, because doctors had not yet correlated the effects of bacteria to mortality rates both in surgical procedures and wound care.

Robert Wood Johnson (February 20, 1845–February 7, 1910) was an American entrepreneur and industrialist. He was also one of the three brothers who founded Johnson & Johnson. Before founding Johnson & Johnson, Robert Wood Johnson met George J. Seabury and they went into business together under the name of Seabury & Johnson. Both Seabury and Johnson were interested in Joseph Lister's discoveries and wanted to make products to assist in the surgery room. Johnson worked 12-hour days at Seabury & Johnson trying to invent aseptic (pathogen free) surgery equipment. By 1878, the firm was making $10,000 a month ($214,000 per month in 2006 dollars).

However, Seabury and Johnson couldn't agree on how to distribute the profits of the firm. In 1880, Johnson sold his shares to Seabury, and agreed to not go into the medical business for 10 years. In the meantime, James Wood Johnson and Edward Mead Johnson had started a family business called Johnson & Johnson. The firm was struggling to stay afloat, as it did not have enough capital. While the two brothers were going it alone, Seabury became unable to pay Robert Wood Johnson the monthly payments that had been agreed upon and agreed to let Robert Wood Johnson re-enter the medical industry provided he wouldn't have to pay the monthly payments anymore. Johnson agreed, and joined his brothers' firm, providing the capital for a fresh start.

The new partnership gave Johnson half of the company's shares in return for management of the company. His brothers would receive 30 percent of the company. Johnson worked all hours of the day, going back and forth from the factory in New Brunswick, New Jersey to the office in New York, and by early 1888, Johnson & Johnson was making $25,000 a month.

Johnson & Johnson is still in business and now one of the most famous sterile medical suppliers in the world.

CURRENT CONDITIONS

Along with polymer "living skin equivalents," other new developments in wound care have been focusing on handling patient concerns. Individuals with chronic wounds often report pain as the main concern in their lives, and the pain associated with chronic wounds should be handled as one of medicine's most important management priorities. Symptomatic treatment of pain as part of a patient-centered approach to wound care must be an essential consideration when treating the underlying etiology or cause of the wound.

Sufferers of chronic wounds include patients with ostomy bags, patients with diabetes, and patients who are bedridden or immobile. As the Baby Boomer generation continues to age, estimates about the need for professionals who know how to care for chronic wounds are broad-ranging and diverse. Some speculate that in the next decade, the medical community will experience a shortage of nursing staff for an aging population with advancing health problems, including chronic wounds as a result of diabetes, extended illnessed that requires bed rest, and the care of ostomy bags.

The main areas of research in these areas are focusing on keeping ostomy openings clean, caring for wounds as a result of diabetes, and ensuring the durability of skin tissue on bedridden patients. This research focuses on the next-generation polymers to replace skin tissues, dressings to provide relief from constant pressure, and procedures to keep skin healthy in spite of chronic wounds.

INDUSTRY LEADERS

Stryker was started in 1941, when Dr. Homer Stryker, an orthopedic surgeon from Kalamazoo, Michigan, discovered that certain medical products were not meeting his patients' needs. As a result, he invented new ones and his new company was used to produce, distribute, and sell them. Dr. Stryker's products were innovative from the start. The company's goal was to help patients lead healthier, more active lives through products and services that make surgery and recovery simpler, faster, and more effective.

Today, Stryker is a global leader in the medical technology industry. Company growth, it maintains, is based on an unparalleled variety of high-quality, innovative products and services that create cost-effective solutions and improve people's lives, achieved through the dedication of 15,000 employees worldwide.

Smith & Nephew was founded by Thomas James Smith as a pharmaceutical chemist shop in Hull, England. In 1896, Horatio Nelson Smith, the founder's nephew, entered into partnership with his uncle and the firm was renamed T.J. Smith and Nephew. They began to develop medical dressings. By 1906, the first overseas contracts were secured with Canadian Hospital Authorities. During the First World War, the firm expanded to fulfill the needs of wartime wound care; employees increased to over 1,200 during this time. In 1928 and 1930, the development of ELATOPLAST began and Plaster of Paris bandages were launched, respectively. In 1931, the firm officially became Smith & Nephew.

Recent developments include Dermograft and Acticoat, both of which assist physicians in dealing with high-risk injuries. Smith & Nephew is one of the major players in the wound care market, providing hospitals and medical care facilities with high-quality ointments and solutions to expedite healing.

MPM Medical Inc. was founded in 1981 by Clinton Howard to solve the mystery of the aloe vera plant's healing properties. Since then, MPM Medical Inc. has been dedicated toward establishing itself as a leader in wound care and pain management. This, the company says, means creating products based on scientific evidence, not marketing spin.

After years of study and more than $20 million in research, the MPM Medical team isolated the long-chain polysaccharide in aloe vera that proved to be instrumental in harnessing the plant's health-giving benefits. Howard later used his findings to create proprietary nutritional products under the auspices of RBC Life Sciences. Meanwhile, MPM used aspects of the research to develop state-of-the-art topical pain management products recognized as unique within the wound care and pain management industry. Since MPM joined RBC Life Sciences in 2001, they have focused their efforts on helping people worldwide to improve their quality of life.

WORKFORCE

The fact that there has been a nursing shortage for the past few years is nothing new. What is more worrisome is that a nursing shortage is expected to grow in the next decade as more and more of the Baby Boomer generation age into needing extended health care, with which comes the need for more wound care, whether for chronic wounds from an ostomy bag or from diabetes, or for other less serious wounds.

Current nurses have to keep up with the latest wound care research and care as part of their ongoing education. The most up-to-date R&D on handling both chronic and accidental wounds will be taught to nursing professionals first; later, the latest information trickles down to the general public.

AMERICA AND THE WORLD

Wound care is a continuing research around the world, not just in the United States. In Canada, the Canada Association of Wound Care holds annual conventions and offers continuing education classes for nurses and other medical professionals to learn about the latest innovations in treating and healing wounds. "The need for higher quality of patient care, better patient health outcomes and the ability to reallocate scarce health care dollars were highlighted throughout the CAWC's 16th Annual Professional Conference held November 4–7, 2010 in Calgary, Alberta. The conference included key health and public policy-related initiatives, including the following:

- Launch of CAWC's "Diabetes, Healthy Feet and You," a multimedia education program that could

help reduce the incidence of diabetes foot ulcers and in particular, its current amputation rate by 50 percent by 2015. Information will be available in 18 languages on the web and in 'how to' print materials. "Diabetes, Healthy Feet and You" will be Canada's "go to" program for on-line information and education to support effective self-monitoring, early detection, treatment and prevention of costly and potentially life-threatening diabetes foot wounds among Canadians with diabetes.

- Development of CAWC's Wound CARE Instrument, a new framework that establishes evidence-informed standards to self-appraise, identify and implement quality improvements in wound care and education programming. It will ensure that health care resources "support wound education programming to deliver positive patient health outcomes; evidence-based performance standards for care providers; and development of recommendations for governments to best use financial resources.".

RESEARCH AND TECHNOLOGY

The study of wound care necessitates producing natural and synthetic wound closure tools and supplies in order to lessen the chance of further infection and to accelerate the healing process. Current innovations in wound care are pointing the way toward further R&D with regard to natural wound closure, for example, skin grafts and the re-growth of natural skin. The ongoing controversy about stem cell research comes into play here. While stem cells are used primarily to help grow tissues from inside the body, a similar process may be the key in the future to growing outer skin layers later on.

Because there are so many new innovations in wound care research, the opportunities for workers interested in specializing in this, other than as nurses or medical professionals, are wide-ranging and varied. From doing research on different antibacterial chemical compounds to working in medical labs growing human tissue or stem cells, job seekers interested in working in wound care need to have specialized training in both microbiology or chemistry. Jobs in this sector require some sort of advanced degree at a minimum.

As chronic wounds become more and more of a health care burden and R&D continues to develop better and better solutions to treating and healing wounds, the years of simply "putting a bandage on it" may change very soon.

BIBLIOGRAPHY
"Bandaging Wounds." WebMD, 2010. Available from http://www.webmd.com/a-to-z-guides/wound-care-10/slideshow-bandaging-wounds.

Baranoski, Sharon, and Elizabeth A. Ayello. *Wound Care Essentials: Practice Principles.* Baltimore, MD: Lippincott, Williams & Wilkins, 2007.

Hess, Cathy Thomas. *Clinical Guide: Skin and Wound Care.* Baltimore, MD: Lippincott, Williams & Wilkins, 2007.

"Home Page." National Alliance of Wound Care, 2010. Available from http://www.nawccb.org/.

"Home Page." Wound, Ostomy and Continence Nurses Society, 2010. Available from http://www.wocn.org/.

"News." Canada Association of Wound Care, 2010. Available from http://cawc. net/index.php/about/members/news/16th-annual-professional-conference-draws-to-a-close/.

"Wound Care Do's and Don'ts." WebMD, 2010. http://www.webmd.com/a-to-z-guides/wound-care-10/slideshow-wound-care-dos-and-donts

XML

—■—

SIC CODE(S)

7371

7372

5734

5045

INDUSTRY SNAPSHOT

Extensible Markup Language (XML) has become the de facto standard for exchanging information over the Internet and for creating domain- and industry-specific markup vocabularies. Used for everything from content management, data mining, and access control to application integration, database management, and document presentation, XML's centerpiece is its flexibility and the ease with which a variety of protocols and applications can plug into it. As increasing amounts of sensitive information get stored in the form of XML, the importance of proper access control to those XML documents becomes more evident. XML has been lauded as one of the greatest technical milestones of the computer era, as it continues to realize its potential.

As a language designed to translate between a nearly infinite variety of data languages, protocols, and software, XML emerged as the common denominator—a universally applicable "Code of Integration"—between all those engaged in any form of electronic data exchange. XML allows documents to announce themselves, so to speak, as they travel across application and system boundaries. That is, XML not only enables documents to transmit data, but also defines that data so that outside applications will understand how to interpret it. Thus XML has been the primary means by which data is exchanged over large, distributed data-exchange environments, the lifeblood of the Information Age economy.

Markup languages such as Hypertext Markup Language (HTML) and Extensible Markup Language (XML) define a document's attributes by inserting "tags" around select bits of information. HTML uses a limited number of relatively inflexible tags that determine only the document's form. XML, however, is nearly infinite in the number of possible tags, and XML tags can influence the document's content as well as its form. XML empowers users to develop and define languages of their own that suit their specific needs while remaining compatible with others' XML creations. Therein lies the beauty, and usefulness, of XML in the World Wide Web environment of the future.

Although it is called a language, XML technically bears a fancier description: a meta-language. That is, it does not constitute the language in and of itself, but rather it acts as a grammar for the language, defining the language's rules and processes. It is for this reason that XML does not actually replace HTML but rather works alongside it. Since most companies over the years built Internet portals and e-marketplaces using a variety of frameworks in an effort to simply get the information or product into public view, one of XML's primary uses is to integrate all this information. XML furthermore allows for the seamless transfer between presentation media. That is, using the same set of criteria, XML can define content so as to appear in a particular way on a World Wide Web browser, for instance, and in a different way when printed on a hard copy.

ORGANIZATION AND STRUCTURE

Both XML and HTML are derived from an older format called Standard Generalized Markup Language (SGML), which was in use before the World Wide Web existed. HTML is a small subset of SGML, using only about 70 tags, mainly to indicate how a document should be displayed or how to link it to other documents. XML's tags, on the other hand, are not primarily presentation-oriented, and the meta-language itself exists independently of any database file format. Rather, XML provides a way to define and use new tags that describe various elements of a document. Any elements that are opened and closed properly (using start and end tags) are considered "well formed" and are acceptable. There can be an unlimited number of tags, including "nested" hierarchies (although not overlapping tags, that do not nest properly). So, for example, astudent's transcript might have tags indicating the student's name, student ID, and courses.

Along with the transcript would come a document type definition (DTD), a convention inherited from SGML, which describes how the document is organized. The document could be displayed in a browser or used with any other software capable of parsing it. A parser mediates between the document and the medium, such as a Web browser, both to ensure that the document is well formed and to present the information in the form tailored to that medium. Thus, the parser, rather than the application, actually reads the XML document. Parsers themselves are rendered in the XML format, usually conforming to the World Wide Web Consortium (W3C) XML standard. (The W3C is one of the major standards organizations for the Internet). The generic nature of XML lends itself to marking up database records and other structured information.

Since XML tags generally pertain to how information is organized, rather than how it is to be displayed, the same document may be presented in any number of ways. Different application software packages or scripts might produce HTML for a Web display, a Braille version, or a file formatted for printing, all from the same XML document.

XML is intended to complement HTML, not compete with it, but older HTML-based tools and applications are not compatible with the new technology. HTML conforms to a single document type definition (DTD), so it does not provide this description with every document. Rather, HTML tools are built to this single specification. XML documents use tags that are not part of HTML's fixed set; yet at the same time, XML is actually stricter about syntax rules, such as tags being properly closed. Newer software is being developed to take advantage of XML's capabilities. Web browsers are now able to support XML, and HTML specifications allow mixing of the two formats in a single document. Thus e-commerce, data interchange, and information discovery are becoming important applications of XML.

The document type definitions (DTDs), which describe the tags used in XML documents, can be provided in a number of ways. They can either be part of the document itself or reside in a separate file. Developers working with Standard Generalized Markup Language (SGML) have been generating application-specific DTDs for years, and many of these are available for public use. An XML convention called the "namespace" allows a document to reference a universal resource locator (URL) address where a set of agreed-upon tag names has been published. Namespaces can be created by organizations, industries, hobbyist groups, companies, or other entities interested in making a set of tags available for the type of data they work with. Using namespaces, information can be exchanged with all the capabilities inherent in XML and without generating confusion by inadvertent use of the same name in different ways.

All World Wide Web standards, including HTML and XML, are overseen by the World Wide Web Consortium (W3C). The W3C was founded in 1994 and is chaired by Tim Berners-Lee, who first conceived the World Wide Web and invented HTML. The W3C has more than 180 members, most of whom are commercial software developers. Standards discussions can be contentious because each company wants to gain a market advantage by distinguishing itself, even as it recognizes a need to maintain the inter-operability that drives the World Wide Web. Often a company will develop a technology, propose it to the W3C as a standard, and then market it by announcing that it is soon to be W3C-endorsed. In practice, inclusion in the popular Netscape or Microsoft Internet Explorer browsers has been at least as critical as W3C endorsement for advancing a technology.

For XML, agreeing on tag sets is an important area for cooperation between software vendors and other XML users. "Webcasting" or "push technology" applications, in which an "active channel" of information is sent directly to a user over the World Wide Web rather than having the user traverse links, were early adopters of XML.

BACKGROUND AND DEVELOPMENT

HTML was one of the most important developments in the history of information technologies. By facilitating the explosion of the World Wide Web, it changed the way modern societies distribute information and do business. A few short years, however, is a long time on the Internet. As the World Wide Web was expected to provide ever-increasing functionality and users struggled to find relevant information in a vast global network, HTML was beginning to show its age. Broken links—links that do not lead to an existing Web page—abound, limited document formatting makes some types of applications difficult, and search engines are getting bogged down in the sheer volume of documents on the Internet. Many technologies are being developed to address one or more of these problems.

XML was created to improve methods of organizing and finding data. Since tags can be tailored to a particular type of information, it can be navigated more efficiently. If entire industries or other groups agree on a set of tags, then search tools can be built to provide more relevant results when applied to the group's data stores. More data validation can be done by the browser, and all forms of publishing, including Internet, paper, and CD-ROM, can be done from the same XML document.

Development of XML began in September 1996. The W3C formed an XML Working Group, chaired by Jon Bosak of Sun Microsystems, and this group issued several draft specifications for review and comment. In December 1997, Version 1.0 of the XML specification, written by Tim Bray, was issued as a W3C recommendation at a meeting of the SGML/XML Conference in Washington, D.C. In February 1998, the W3C ratified XML as a standard. Software developers quickly perceived the potential of this technology. Tools were built to generate XML, and Internet software began to incorporate XML support. At a Seattle XML conference in March 1998, one month after adoption of the standard by the W3C, dozens of vendors announced new products. In the first year of XML's official existence, hundreds of SGML software packages were updated to support it.

Analysts were in near-universal agreement that XML was en route to becoming the standard language of the Web in particular and of data integration in general. By eliminating the need for and the utility of proprietary formats, XML was seen as a major boon to the quickly emerging business to business e-commerce industry. The impact of XML and the value of the industry were difficult to determine, but by the middle years of the first decade of the 2000s, several XML-based technologies began to rake in impressive sales. International Data Corporation of Framingham, Massachusetts, predicted that the market for native XML databases, for example, would blossom from $42 million in 2002 to about $77 million by 2007 as the major manufacturers of relational databases continue to embed XML into their offerings.

XML Diversifies The electronic business XML (ebXML), a schema designed specifically as a Web-based communications framework for intra-business transactions, was widely viewed as the next major XML form to emerge as the predominant business standard. Under development since 1999 by the United Nations Center for Facilitation of Procedures and Practices, Administration, Commerce, and Transport (UN/CEFACT) along with the Organization for the Advancement of Structured Information Standards (OASIS), a not-for-profit global consortium

dedicated to development and adoption of e-business standards for the Internet, by the middle years of the first decade of the 2000s, ebXML had yet to penetrate business to business communications as quickly as expected, particularly in the United States. Its adoption in overseas markets, especially in Europe, was much more immediate.

However, there were signs that the United States would soon catch up. The U.S. Department of Defense provided an engine for ebXML proliferation in 2004 when it announced its adoption of the standard for its electronic procurement portal. In this way, the Pentagon gave the impetus to all companies with which it does business to begin incorporating ebXML into their operations, which was expected to produce a ripple that would reach into a wide range of industries.

Indeed, there were signs that this was beginning to happen: General Motors in 2004 announced that it, too, would adopt ebXML as its global corporate information technology standard. As with other major platform shifts, the adoption of XML types on a broad scale, in the absence of legislation or broad mutual agreements, generally required the leadership of large enterprises to which other firms in several industries were connected. Thus, these announcements were expected to be a major boon to ebXML adoption.

The ebXML specifications cover six broad areas: architecture, collaboration, messaging, process, registration, and requirements. The framework brings all these areas into data transaction in a holistic manner, rather than the piecemeal fashion of traditional Web services. EbXML was set back in 2002 when retailing giant Wal-Mart chose an alternative specification, AS2, developed for Internet-based Electronic Data Interchange (EDI) transactions, for its migration to online business to business commerce, mandating that its suppliers do likewise, according to *Network World*. The Gartner Group noted that ebXML's specifications were only half complete in early 2004, thus exacerbating the delay.

Online financial data exchange was furthermore slowly becoming as globally integrated as the World Wide Web itself. The Extensible Business Reporting Language (XBRL) incorporates financial reporting standards into the XML framework so as to seamlessly integrate the particular measurements and currencies across different countries' financial systems, ideally creating a universal e-commerce market. An ancillary benefit for companies adopting the XBRL standard is a simplified integration of new financial information upon merging with or acquiring other companies. The XBRL Project Committee was endorsed by over 30 companies and organizations, including Microsoft and the American Institute of Certified Public Accountants, in April 2000.

The Extensible Style Language (XSL) describes how an XML document is formatted. XSL is a way to specify style sheets for XML documents, following the model of the cascading style sheets used with HTML. Software vendors Microsoft, ArborText, and Inso submitted a proposal for XSL to the W3C in August 1997, and the W3C created an XSL Working Group. XSL Version 1.0 was approved by the W3C in the summer of 1999. XSL was expected to complement and make up for the limitations of XML. As long as not all browsers support XML, developers may remain reluctant to shift to the new standard. In such cases, XSL can reformat the XML coding into an acceptable HTML format, which works with all browsers.

Open Financial Exchange is a framework for data exchange among financial institutions and with their customers. By moving to XML, banks can allow their customers the ability to download account statements, pay bills electronically, and basically manage their finances online. Originally based on SGML, the format required some modifications, such as end tags, to be compatible with XML. It integrates formats used by Microsoft, Intuit (which provides the popular financial software package Quicken), and electronic banking vendor CheckFree.

The Voice Extensible Markup Language (VXML) took advantage of the latest voice recognition technologies, readying e-commerce and other Web-based information for transmission via telephone. The VoiceXML Forum completed version 1.0 of the VoiceXML standard in early 2000. The forum, which counts among its 79 members IBM, Motorola, Lucent, and AT&T, submitted the specification to the W3C later that year for official ratification. By 2004, the W3C published VoiceXML 2.0 as the new industry standard, allowing for synthesized speech, telephony, digitized audio, and multimedia conversations, according to *New Media Age*. However, applications needed the ability to control interaction with the caller and the call itself. A new language known as Call Control XML (CCXML) was developed, which adds telephone call control capabilities to the platform. As stated in *Network World*, "Together, CCXML and VoiceXML make it possible to develop completely open-standards-based voice applications."

Specialized XML tags were also evolving in such fields as chemistry, astronomy, law, and genealogy. Chemical Markup Language, for example, provides a way of describing the structure of a molecule with advanced XML tags for the atoms, the bonds, and the isotopic constitution. A Mathematics Markup Language allows proper display and manipulation of mathematical symbols and equations for the first time since the inception of the World Wide Web. In addition, Legal XML allows parties involved in legal action to share data, such as information from warrants or subpoenas, integrating data for court records and case preparation.

Telecommunications firms got into the act as well. In 2004, AT&T introduced its WebService Connect XML-based integration service. Housed at the firm's data centers, the communications hub accepts incoming transmissions from AT&T's clients and translates them for other users. In this way, companies are relieved of managing tricky and expensive integration software, instead utilizing a messaging infrastructure with which they can publish information in their own formats. Other companies trying to capitalize on XML integration needs included Hubspan, GSX, and Sterling Commerce.

As XML technology approached its tenth anniversary, its potential was only beginning to be realized, with many issues yet to resolve and many pitfalls to be avoided. Standards, although necessary to the success of XML, must be balanced between simplicity and functionality. Too many standards being developed too soon can cause the failure of any new technology. It is essential that the correct set of standards be developed for the core technology and for industry-specific and domain-specific vocabularies. For those applications where interoperability is not important, XML is not an immediate requirement, nor is XML designed to replace rich application modeling. Therefore, XML deployment should be done in a sensible and practical manner.

An area that enthusiastically embraced XML to implement data sharing and semantic interoperability is in Healthcare and Life Sciences (HCLS), where, because there was no pre-existing data format, XML had a major impact. Information exchange of biomedical data is challenging because of the heterogeneous nature of the data: administrative information, clinical data, and genomic data, along with the use of an integrated health record for every individual patient. Therefore, data from many diverse systems must be generated, integrated, and made available at the point of care. XML supports the goal of HCLS to improve patient treatment and safety by being the universal data representation infrastructure that allows biomedical information integration within the industries of healthcare, pharmaceuticals, and bioinformatics.

Although originally released in 2002, by 2006, Research Information Extensible Markup Language (RIXML), designed to tag relevant research and sift out useful information from the avalanche of daily analyst reports, was not readily accepted by the securities industries or vendors at whom it was targeted, who anticipated limitations in its performance. Whereas the Extensible Business Reporting Language (XBRL) was created as an accounting standard, RIXML—governed by RIXML.org, a consortium of 20 buy-side and sell-side companies and research platform vendors—was targeted at equity and fixed-income research, as well as a variety of other research categories. In May 2009, RIXML.org released DRAFT 2.3 schema for a 30-day comment period.

According to *Network World,* "XML has become the *lingua franca* [simplified speech used for communication between people of different languages] of Internet applications." Because it is endorsed by the W3C, easy to customize, and text-based, it is understood by all types of computers, browsers, and applications. It was inevitable, then, that applications for XML would expand in the 2000s.

CURRENT CONDITIONS

As of 2009, hundreds of XML-based languages existed, but there were still just two versions. The first, XML 1.0, had undergone minor revisions without being given a new version number, and was currently in its fifth edition, as published on November 26, 2008. The second, XML 1.1, initially published in 2004, was in its second (August 2006) edition, but remained not widely implemented, being of use primarily for those who needed its special features, such as enabling the use of line-ending characters used on platforms.

Security breaches remained an issue in 2009. In July, multiple flaws in popular XML libraries were discovered, including those from Apache, Python, and Sun. By September 2009, Codenomicon, which dealt in security testing solutions, released a first-of-its-kind security testing product called Defensics for XML. In November 2009, it was discovered that Facebook and MySpace had a security hole in XML configuration files utilized for accessing Flash applications.

In December 2009, in a very important patent infringement case, the U.S. Court of Appeals for the Federal District ordered Microsoft to stop selling current versions of Word and Office (that contained protected XML technology) as of January 11, 2010. This was part of a ruling that upheld a jury verdict awarding Canadian developer i4i nearly $300 million in damages. However, in the alternative, Microsoft will delete the offending XML editing technology, dubbed "Custom XML," from Microsoft Word. Microsoft already had a patch available that stripped out the XML technology. The patch targeted large computer makers that factory-installed Microsoft Office on new PCs prior to shipment to dealers or customers. Microsoft's OEM Partner Center displayed a prominent notice and a link to a 13MB update, which stated in part, "Microsoft has released a supplement for Office 2007 (October 2009)...The following patch is *required* [emphasis in original] for the United States." It continued, "After this patch is installed, Word will no longer read the Custom XML elements contained within DOCX, DOCM, or XML files...These files will continue to open, but any Custom XML elements will be removed."

A few new XML applications were noteworthy. In October 2009, the National Archives and Records Administration and the U.S. Government Printing Office (GPO) announced a decision to publish the Federal Register in XML. The Federal Register is tantamount to the U.S. government's official newspaper; it follows the movements of different federal agencies and the executive branch, and publishes about 80,000 pages annually.

In mid-2009, members of the OASIS Election and Voter Services Technical Committee approved a Committee Draft of "Election Markup Language (EML) Specification Version 6.0 " and approved the document for public review through December 22, 2009. EML Version 6.0 described the background and purpose of the Election Markup Language, the electoral processes from which it derived its structure, and the security and audit mechanisms it was designed to support.

INDUSTRY LEADERS

Microsoft Microsoft has been instrumental in the development of XML technology and tools. Its XML-ready tool for building Web sites, BizTalk, was released in the summer of 2000. BizTalk was tailored toward the generation and exchange of e-commerce information and documents, including purchase orders and invoices, via XML tags. Beginning with Internet Explorer 4.0, Microsoft's browser used XML to schedule active channel information delivery and could process and display XML documents. Frontpage2000 also used XML to support Document Object Model (DOM), providing World Wide Web developers with the ability to specify documents by category. The company also marketed its MSXML tool, which parses an XML document into a hierarchical tree and provides Java programming language methods for manipulating the resulting structure.

Microsoft changed the name of its MSXML XML Parser to Microsoft XML Core Services and began releasing upgrades regularly. Not only did it support the W3C's final recommendation for XML Schema, but its XSLT engine for processing XML documents with XML style sheet transformations worked four to eight times faster. One interesting aspect of the release was that Microsoft declared External Data Representation (XDR) as a standard at a time when everyone else recognized XML Schema.

Microsoft sought to make XML more user-friendly. With its Office 11, the company claimed that XML would be more accessible for hundreds of millions of workstations. Microsoft's Jean Paoli, who was the co-editor of XML 1.0, called this the "XMLization" of Office. XML was already supported by Microsoft Back-Office products from Biztalk to CMS through its XML Server. The only thing missing was the ability for users to manipulate XML on their workstations. Microsoft's aim to bring XML into the mainstream seemed workable, as it employed, for the most part, standard technologies and it enabled the manipulation of arbitrary XML documents using customer-chosen schemas.

However, when Microsoft released Office 2003, customers found they were not getting all of the features they expected, as the company produced both a professional and standard version. Prior to the release, Microsoft touted Office 2003's support for Extensible Markup Language (XML). This feature was much anticipated, but it turned out that it was only available in the two high-end versions of the product, one of which was available only to businesses subscribing to Microsoft's volume licensing program. Two other features also were restricted: Windows Rights Management Services (RMS), a document protection technology, and Excel List, a feature for improving analysis of data lists. In 2009, later versions were prohibited, under court order, for patent infringements (see above).

Oracle Corp. Oracle Corp. was rapidly building XML into its offerings, developing publishing tools for storage and retrieval of XML data from the Oracle8i database. The company's XML parser went through several rapid upgrades through the early years of the first decade of the 2000s. In late 1999, Oracle released a free version of its Oracle XML Developers Kit, previously used only to access the database XML features. The system ran on Java, C++, and Oracle's own database scripting language. By 2000, Oracle had XML-enabled the entire Oracle Internet Platform and released the Oracle XML Schema Processor for Java.

At the time, the other major database manufacturers moved in a direction that further supported XML data and XML query languages in their products. However, it was Oracle who did it first with its XML DB engine. The XML DB was a combination of three technologies: a set of SQL functions that allows XML data to be manipulated as relational data; a native XML data type called XMLType that could store XML data either in an object-relational storage format that maintains the XML DOM (Document Object Model) or as the original text document; and a special hierarchical XML index type to speed access to hierarchies of XML files stored in Oracle9i's XML file repository. XML DB also supported XML Schema, the standard for defining the structure of XML documents. However, it did not support the next innovation: XQuery, an XML query language. Instead, XML DB used a combination of XPath and SQL to manipulate XML. The database included an Extensible Stylesheet Language Transformation engine. In 2006, Oracle introduced a Java-based product, Oracle XML Publisher 5.6.2, with the capability of defining, publishing, and scheduling reports using SQL and XML data sources. In

2009, the latest release version of Oracle's BI Publisher was 10.1.3.4.1.

IBM IBM was also at the forefront of XML's development, creating over 20 XML technologies by 2000. Its proposal for XML Schema offers a way to overcome the limitations of document type definitions (DTDs) by allowing data typing so that information, such as a date or integer, can be tagged and identified. IBM, Motorola, Lucent, and AT&T formed the Voice Extensible Markup Language Forum to develop further XML-based methods to access Web content by telephone. IBM submitted Speech Markup Language, and Motorola developed VoxML, an XML-based method for creating voice-activated Web sites and automated call centers for conducting business, in what Motorola called "v-commerce." Together with Lotus, IBM wrote the Simple Object Access Protocol specification for simple e-business XML exchange.

IBM's DB2 XML Extender and DB2 Information Integrator, updated and expanded versions, distinguished themselves from competitors' products by aiming for the smooth flow of data transmissions across a wide range of databases rather than allowing such transactions to communicate comfortably within a large, central database. These products combined DiscoveryLink, which allowed scientists to access multiple data sources' databases with a single query; DB2 Relational Connect, which provided DB2 with native read access to Microsoft's SQL Server, Oracle's Oracle and Sybase's Sybase; and Enterprise Information Portal, another querying tool. The three existing products were primarily used in the life sciences industries to search huge disparate database and data sources. In addition, they incorporated two pieces of XML technology developed by IBM: Xperanto, a code name for an XML foundation technology that supports XML within DB2; and XML query language based on the XQuery technology developed by IBM. Xperanto is IBM's major information integration initiative designed to enable aggregated access to structured and unstructured data from disparate sources such as relational databases, XML documents, flat files, spreadsheets and Web services. In 2006, IBM developed the RAD XML Wizard, a wizard-directed process to help users not familiar with XML syntax edit files. Being a generic technology, XML Wizard can be adjusted for the structure of any XML file.

RESEARCH AND TECHNOLOGY

The Stylus Studio 2010 XML was released in October 2009, featuring a suite of EDI dictionaries covering dozens of versions, including HL7, and providing comprehensive and innovative support for the newest XML technologies.

Like XML, dynamic HTML (DHTML) is an effort to improve on HTML, this time by allowing changing information to be presented to the user with fewer slow full-document downloads, resulting in greater control for the designer. The DHTML specification allows scripts to access structured data such as XML under program control. Dynamic HTML (DHTML) was first released in Internet Explorer 4.0. Later versions increased the use of DHTML by making all the elements of a Web page, such as graphics, text, buttons, and forms, dynamic. In addition, layout preferences were retained by the browser for return visits to the page.

DHTML is also known by the acronym AJAX: Asynchronous JavaScript and XML. Rather than a specific technology, AJAX describes a bundle of technologies that are often used together to build richer interactivity into Web applications by enabling those applications to interact asynchronously with a server. An example of an AJAX technique can be seen on the Google Map website (www.googlemaps.com). The "A" in AJAX means that the HTML the server sends to the browser contains client-side code running in the background, as well as the visible contents of the page. Although AJAX is popular with Web page developers because it is nonproprietary and utilizes known technologies, there is substantial testing and effort involved in building an AJAX application.

Because AJAX greatly increases the amount of XML network traffic being transmitted, security and corruption issues are major concerns. Therefore, Forum Systems, a Web services and service-oriented architecture security software provider, advises the use of XML content filtering and other security services to ensure protected AJAX applications. By basically turning a user's Web browser into a Web services portal, it can be exposed to corrupted data that may cause the browser to crash or perform badly.

BIBLIOGRAPHY

Adler, Sharon, Roberta Cochrane, John F. Morar, and Alfred Spector. "Technical Context and Cultural Consequences of XML." *IBM Systems Journal,* June 2006.

Alpert, Bill. "Born Again E-Commerce." *Barron's,* 1 September 2003.

Bednarz, Ann. "'Next EDI' Gains Key Proponent." *Network World,* 26 January 2004.

Clyman, John. "Better Web-App Interfaces with AJAX: A New Approach to Building Web Applications Promises a Richer Experience for Users." *PC Magazine,* 27 December 2005.

Desmond, Paul. "Butting Heads Over B2B." *Network World,* 22 December 2003.

Ewalt, David M. "AT&T Offers XML-Based Integration Service." *Information Week,* 15 March 2004.

"Facebook and MySpace Has A Security Hole In XML Config Files." *XMLPro News,* 18 November 2009. Available from http://www.xmlpronews.com/.

"Federal Register Becomes Available In XML." *XMLPro News,* 15 October 2009. Available from http://www.xmlpronews.com/.

Fontana, John. "California Lining Up to Consider Open Document Formats as State Standard." *Network World,* 1 March 2007.

———. "Microsoft, IBM in Slap-Fight over Open Document Formats: OpenXML, ODF at Heart of Tussle." *Network World,* 14 February, 2007.

"Forum Systems Issues AJAX Alert." *eWeek,* 6 February 2006.

Langley, Nick. "Increasing Range of Roles Expect Knowledge of XML." *Computer Weekly,* 19 September 2006.

"Microsoft Yanks Custom XML From Word, Offers Patch to OEMs." *Computer World,* 23 December 2009.

Middleton, Alastair. "Why XML Spells Advantage." *Supply Management,* 19 February 2004.

Miller, Rob. "The Devil is in the Details: The Revelation of XML Content Management." *Econtent,* April 2007.

Montalbano, Elizabeth. "U.S. Trails Other Nations in Adoption of ebXML." *CRN,* 12 January 2004.

Morejon, Mario. "Hurdles Abound in the Path to XML Integration." *CRN,* 20 October 2003.

"New York State Looks at Open Formats for Documents." *Information Week,* 8 June 2007.

Rittman, Mark. "Developer: Business Intelligence." *Oracle Technology Network,* June 2006.

"RIXML Stages Comeback in Changing Vendor Landscape." *Securities Industry News,* 26 June 2006.

Scheier, Robert L. "XML Gets Organized." *Computerworld,* 27 October 2003.

"Security Testing Product For XML Debuts." *XMLPro News,* 23 September 2009. Available from http://www.xmlpronews.com/.

Shabo, Amnon, Simona Rabinovici-Cohen, and Pnina Vortman. "Revolutionary Impact of XML on Biomedical Information Interoperability." *IBM Systems Journal,* June 2006.

Sliwa, Carol. "Surprise: XML-Based Document Formats Can Be Smaller." *Computerworld,* 12 March 2007.

Staton, Stephanie. "VoiceXML Solutions Are Easy to Find." *Speech Technology Magazine,* April 2007.

Udell, John. "Databases Get a Grip on XML." *InfoWorld,* 5 January 2004.

———. "Three Faces of e-Forms." *InfoWorld,* 26 January 2004.

"Understanding CCXML Standard." *Network World,* 22 March 2007.

"W3C Publishes New Web Standards for XML." *eWeek,* 25 January 2007.

"W3C Publishes Voice XML 2.0 as Industry Standard." *New Media Age,* 12 February 2004.

Wilcox, Joe. "Microsoft limits XML in Office 2003." *CNET News.com,* 14 April 2003. Available from http://asia.cnet.com/.

"XML Configuration Wizard." *IBM Research,* 25 July 2006. Available from www.haifa.il.ibm.com/.

"XML Library Flaws Found Far And Wide." *XMLPro News,* 21 July. Available from http://www.xmlpronews.com/.

Yoon, Jong P. "Presto Authorization: A Bitmap Indexing Scheme for High-Speed Access Control to XML Documents." *IEEE Transactions on Knowledge and Data Engineering,* July 2006.

SIC to NAICS Conversion Guide

The following listing cross-references four-digit 1987 Standard Industrial Classification (SIC) codes with six-digit 1997 North American Industry Classification System (NAICS) codes. Because the systems differ in specificity, some SIC categories correspond to more than one NAICS category. Please refer to the **Introduction** under "About Industry Classification" for more information.

AGRICULTURE, FORESTRY & FISHING

0111 Wheat *see* NAICS 111140: Wheat Farming

0112 Rice *see* NAICS 111160: Rice Farming

0115 Corn *see* NAICS 111150: Corn Farming

0116 Soybeans *see* NAICS 111110: Soybean Farming

0119 Cash Grains, NEC *see* NAICS 111130: Dry Pea and Bean Farming; NAICS 111120: Oilseed (except Soybean) Farming; NAICS 111150: Corn Farming; NAICS 111191: Oilseed and Grain Combination Farming; NAICS 111199: All Other Grain Farming

0131 Cotton *see* NAICS 111920: Cotton Farming

0132 Tobacco *see* NAICS 111910: Tobacco Farming

0133 Sugarcane and Sugar Beets *see* NAICS 111991: Sugar Beet Farming; NAICS 111930: Sugarcane Farming

0134 Irish Potatoes *see* NAICS 111211: Potato Farming

0139 Field Crops, Except Cash Grains, NEC *see* NAICS 111940: Hay Farming; NAICS 111992: Peanut Farming; NAICS 111219: Other Vegetable (except Potato) and Melon Farming; NAICS 111998: All Other Miscellaneous Crop Farming

0161 Vegetables and Melons *see* NAICS 111219: Other Vegetable (except Potato) and Melon Farming

0171 Berry Crops *see* NAICS 111333: Strawberry Farming; NAICS 111334: Berry (except Strawberry) Farming

0172 Grapes *see* NAICS 111332: Grape Vineyards

0173 Tree Nuts *see* NAICS 111335: Tree Nut Farming

0174 Citrus Fruits *see* NAICS 111310: Orange Groves; NAICS 111320: Citrus (except Orange) Groves

0175 Deciduous Tree Fruits *see* NAICS 111331: Apple Orchards; NAICS 111339: Other Noncitrus Fruit Farming

0179 Fruits and Tree Nuts, NEC *see* NAICS 111336: Fruit and Tree Nut Combination Farming; NAICS 111339: Other Noncitrus Fruit Farming

0181 Ornamental Floriculture and Nursery Products *see* NAICS 111422: Floriculture Production; NAICS 111421: Nursery and Tree Production

0182 Food Crops Grown Under Cover *see* NAICS 111411: Mushroom Production; NAICS 111419: Other Food Crops Grown Under Cover

0191 General Farms, Primarily Crop *see* NAICS 111998: All Other Miscellaneous Crop Farming

0211 Beef Cattle Feedlots *see* NAICS 112112: Cattle Feedlots

0212 Beef Cattle, Except Feedlots *see* NAICS 112111: Beef Cattle Ranching and Farming

0213 Hogs *see* NAICS 112210: Hog and Pig Farming

0214 Sheep and Goats *see* NAICS 112410: Sheep Farming; NAICS 112420: Goat Farming

0219 General Livestock, Except Dairy and Poultry *see* NAICS 112990: All Other Animal Production

0241 Dairy Farms *see* NAICS 112111: Beef Cattle Ranching and Farming; NAICS 112120: Dairy Cattle and Milk Production

0251 Broiler, Fryers, and Roaster Chickens *see* NAICS 112320: Broilers and Other Meat-Type Chicken Production

0252 Chicken Eggs *see* NAICS 112310: Chicken Egg Production

0253 Turkey and Turkey Eggs *see* NAICS 112330: Turkey Production

0254 Poultry Hatcheries *see* NAICS 112340: Poultry Hatcheries

0259 Poultry and Eggs, NEC *see* NAICS 112390: Other Poultry Production

0271 Fur-Bearing Animals and Rabbits *see* NAICS 112930: Fur-bearing Animal and Rabbit Production

0272 Horses and Other Equines *see* NAICS 112920: Horse and Other Equine Production

0273 Animal Aquaculture *see* NAICS 112511: Finfish Farming and Fish Hatcheries; NAICS 112512: Shellfish Farming; NAICS 112519: Other Animal Aquaculture

0279 Animal Specialties, NEC *see* NAICS 112910: Apiculture; NAICS 112990: All Other Animal Production

0291 General Farms, Primarily Livestock and Animal Specialties *see* NAICS 112990: All Other Animal Production

0711 Soil Preparation Services *see* NAICS 115112: Soil Preparation, Planting and Cultivating

0721 Crop Planting, Cultivating and Protecting; NAICS 481219: Other Nonscheduled Air Transportation; NAICS 115112: Soil Preparation, Planting, and Cultivating

0722 Crop Harvesting, Primarily by Machine *see* NAICS 115113: Crop Harvesting, Primarily By Machine

0723 Crop Preparation Services For Market, except Cotton Ginning *see* NAICS 115114: Postharvest Crop Activities (except Cotton Ginning)

0724 Cotton Ginning *see* NAICS 115111: Cotton Ginning

0741 Veterinary Service For Livestock *see* NAICS 541940: Veterinary Services

0742 Veterinary Services for Animal Specialties *see* NAICS 541940: Veterinary Services

0751 Livestock Services, Except Veterinary *see* NAICS 311611: Animal (except Poultry) Slaughtering NAICS 115210: Support Activities for Animal Production

0752 Animal Specialty Services, Except Veterinary; NAICS 115210: Support Activities for Animal Production; NAICS 812910: Pet Care (except Veterinary) Services

0761 Farm Labor Contractors and Crew Leaders *see* NAICS 115115: Farm Labor Contractors and Crew Leaders

0762 Farm Management Services *see* NAICS 115116: Farm Management Services

0781 Landscape Counseling and Planning *see* NAICS 541690: Other Scientific and Technical Consulting Services; NAICS 541320: Landscape Architectural Services

0782 Lawn and Garden Services *see* NAICS 561730: Landscaping Services

0783 Ornamental Shrub and Tree Services *see* NAICS 561730: Landscaping Services

0811 Timber Tracts *see* NAICS 111421: Nursery and Tree Production; NAICS 113110: Timber Tract Operations

0831 Forest Nurseries and Gathering of Forest Products; NAICS 111998: All Other Miscellaneous Crop Farming; NAICS 113210: Forest Nurseries and Gathering of Forest Products

0851 Forestry Services *see* NAICS 115310: Support Activities for Forestry

0912 Finfish *see* NAICS 114111: Finfish Fishing

0913 Shellfish *see* NAICS 114112: Shellfish Fishing

0919 Miscellaneous Marine Products *see* NAICS 114119: Other Marine Fishing; NAICS 111998: All Other Miscellaneous Crop Farming

0921 Fish Hatcheries and Preserves *see* NAICS 112511: Finfish Farming and Fish Hatcheries; NAICS 112512: Shellfish Farming

0971 Hunting, Trapping, and Game Propagation *see* NAICS 114210: Hunting and Trapping

MINING INDUSTRIES

1011 Iron Ores *see* NAICS 212210: Iron Ore Mining

1021 Copper Ores *see* NAICS 212234: Copper Ore and Nickel Ore Mining

1031 Lead and Zinc Ores *see* NAICS 212231: Lead Ore and Zinc Ore Mining

1041 Gold Ores *see* NAICS 212221: Gold Ore Mining

1044 Silver Ores *see* NAICS 212222: Silver Ore Mining

1061 Ferroalloy Ores, Except Vanadium *see* NAICS 212234: Copper Ore and Nickel Ore Mining; NAICS 212299: Other Metal Ore Mining

1081 Metal Mining Services *see* NAICS 213114: Support Activities for Metal Mining; NAICS 541360: Geophysical Surveying and Mapping Services

1094 Uranium-Radium-Vanadium Ores *see* NAICS 212291: Uranium-Radium-Vanadium Ore Mining

1099 Miscellaneous Metal Ores, NEC *see* NAICS 212299: Other Metal Ore Mining

1221 Bituminous Coal and Lignite Surface Mining *see* NAICS 212111: Bituminous Coal and Lignite Surface Mining

1222 Bituminous Coal Underground Mining *see* NAICS 212112: Bituminous Coal Underground Mining

1231 Anthracite Mining *see* NAICS 212113: Anthracite Mining

1241 Coal Mining Services *see* NAICS 213113: Support Activities for Coal Mining

1311 Crude Petroleum and Natural Gas *see* NAICS 211111: Crude Petroleum and Natural Gas Extraction

1321 Natural Gas Liquids *see* NAICS 211112: Natural Gas Liquid Extraction

1381 Drilling Oil and Gas Wells *see* NAICS 213111: Drilling Oil and Gas Wells

1382 Oil and Gas Field Exploration Services *see* NAICS 541360: Geophysical Surveying and Mapping

Services; NAICS 213112: Support Activities for Oil and Gas Field Exploration

1389 Oil and Gas Field Services, NEC *see* NAICS 213112: Support Activities for Oil and Gas Field Exploration

1411 Dimension Stone *see* NAICS 212311: Dimension Stone Mining and Quarry

1422 Crushed and Broken Limestone *see* NAICS 212312: Crushed and Broken Limestone Mining and Quarrying

1423 Crushed and Broken Granite *see* NAICS 212313: Crushed and Broken Granite Mining and Quarrying

1429 Crushed and Broken Stone, NEC *see* NAICS 212319: Other Crushed and Broken Stone Mining and Quarrying

1442 Construction Sand and Gravel *see* NAICS 212321: Construction Sand and Gravel Mining

1446 Industrial Sand *see* NAICS 212322: Industrial Sand Mining

1455 Kaolin and Ball Clay *see* NAICS 212324: Kaolin and Ball Clay Mining

1459 Clay, Ceramic, and Refractory Minerals, NEC *see* NAICS 212325: Clay and Ceramic and Refractory Minerals Mining

1474 Potash, Soda, and Borate Minerals *see* NAICS 212391: Potash, Soda, and Borate Mineral Mining

1475 Phosphate Rock *see* NAICS 212392: Phosphate Rock Mining

1479 Chemical and Fertilizer Mineral Mining, NEC *see* NAICS 212393: Other Chemical and Fertilizer Mineral Mining

1481 Nonmetallic Minerals Services Except Fuels *see* NAICS 213115: Support Activities for Non-metallic Minerals, (except Fuels); NAICS 541360: Geophysical Surveying and Mapping Services

1499 Miscellaneous Nonmetallic Minerals, Except Fuels *see* NAICS 212319: Other Crushed and Broken Stone Mining and Quarrying; NAICS 212399: All Other Non-Metallic Mineral Mining

CONSTRUCTION INDUSTRIES

1521 General Contractors-Single-Family Houses *see* NAICS 233210: Single-Family Housing Construction

1522 General Contractors-Residential Buildings *see* NAICS 233320: Commercial and Institutional Building Construction; NAICS 233220: Multi-Family Housing Construction

1531 Operative Builders *see* NAICS 233210: Single-Family Housing Construction; NAICS 233220: Multi-Family Housing Construction; NAICS 233310: Manufacturing and Light Industrial Building Construction; NAICS 233320:

Commercial and Institutional Building Construction

1541 General Contractors-Industrial Buildings and Warehouses *see* NAICS 233320: Commercial and Institutional Building Construction; NAICS 233310: Manufacturing and Light Industrial Building Construction

1542 General Contractors-Nonresidential Buildings, Other than Industrial Buildings and Warehouses *see* NAICS 233320: Commercial and Institutional Building Construction

1611 Highway and Street Construction, Except Elevated Highways *see* NAICS 234110: Highway and Street Construction

1622 Bridge, Tunnel, and Elevated Highway Construction *see* NAICS 234120: Bridge and Tunnel Construction

1623 Water, Sewer, Pipeline, and Communications and Power Line Construction *see* NAICS 234910: Water, Sewer and Pipeline Construction; NAICS 234920: Power and Communication Transmission Line Construction

1629 Heavy Construction, NEC *see* NAICS 234930: Industrial Nonbuilding Structure Construction; NAICS 234990: All Other Heavy Construction

1711 Plumbing, Heating, and Air-Conditioning *see* NAICS 235110: Plumbing, Heating and Air-Conditioning Contractors

1721 Painting and Paper Hanging *see* NAICS 235210: Painting and Wall Covering Contractors

1731 Electrical Work *see* NAICS 561621: Security Systems Services (except Locksmiths); NAICS 235310: Electrical Contractors

1741 Masonry, Stone Setting and Other Stone Work *see* NAICS 235410: Masonry and Stone Contractors

1742 Plastering, Drywall, Acoustical and Insulation Work *see* NAICS 235420: Drywall, Plastering, Acoustical and Insulation Contractors

1743 Terrazzo, Tile, Marble, and Mosaic Work *see* NAICS 235420: Drywall, Plastering, Acoustical and Insulation Contractors; NAICS 235430: Tile, Marble, Terrazzo and Mosaic Contractors

1751 Carpentry Work *see* NAICS 235510: Carpentry Contractors

1752 Floor Laying and Other Floor Work, NEC *see* NAICS 235520: Floor Laying and Other Floor Contractors

1761 Roofing, Siding, and Sheet Metal Work *see* NAICS 235610: Roofing, Siding, and Sheet Metal Contractors

1771 Concrete Work *see* NAICS 235420: Drywall, Plastering, Acoustical and Insulation Contractors; NAICS 235710: Concrete Contractors

1781 Water Well Drilling *see* NAICS 235810: Water Well Drilling Contractors

1791 Structural Steel Erection *see* NAICS 235910: Structural Steel Erection Contractors

1793 Glass and Glazing Work *see* NAICS 235920: Glass and Glazing Contractors

1794 Excavation Work *see* NAICS 235930: Excavation Contractors

1795 Wrecking and Demolition Work *see* NAICS 235940: Wrecking and Demolition Contractors

1796 Installation or Erection of Building Equipment, NEC *see* NAICS 235950: Building Equipment and Other Machinery Installation Contractors

1799 Special Trade Contractors, NEC *see* NAICS 235210: Painting and Wall Covering Contractors; NAICS 235920: Glass and Glazing Contractors; NAICS 562910: Remediation Services; NAICS 235990: All Other Special Trade Contractors

FOOD & KINDRED PRODUCTS

2011 Meat Packing Plants *see* NAICS 311611: Animal (except Poultry) Slaughtering

2013 Sausages and Other Prepared Meats *see* NAICS 311612: Meat Processed From Carcasses

2015 Poultry Slaughtering and Processing *see* NAICS 311615: Poultry Processing; NAICS 311999: All Other Miscellaneous Food Manufacturing

2021 Creamery Butter *see* NAICS 311512: Creamery Butter Manufacturing

2022 Natural, Processed, and Imitation Cheese *see* NAICS 311513: Cheese Manufacturing

2023 Dry, Condensed, and Evaporated Dairy Products *see* NAICS 311514: Dry, Condensed, and Evaporated Dairy Product Manufacturing

2024 Ice Cream and Frozen Desserts *see* NAICS 311520: Ice Cream and Frozen Dessert Manufacturing

2026 Fluid Milk *see* NAICS 311511: Fluid Milk Manufacturing

2032 Canned Specialties *see* NAICS 311422: Specialty Canning; NAICS 311999: All Other Miscellaneous Food Manufacturing

2033 Canned Fruits, Vegetables, Preserves, Jams, and Jellies *see* NAICS 311421: Fruit and Vegetable Canning

2034 Dried and Dehydrated Fruits, Vegetables, and Soup Mixes *see* NAICS 311423: Dried and Dehydrated Food Manufacturing; NAICS 311211: Flour Milling

2035 Pickled Fruits and Vegetables, Vegetables Sauces and Seasonings, and Salad Dressings *see* NAICS 311421: Fruit and Vegetable Canning; NAICS 311941: Mayonnaise, Dressing, and Other Prepared Sauce Manufacturing

2037 Frozen Fruits, Fruit Juices, and Vegetables *see* NAICS 311411: Frozen Fruit, Juice, and Vegetable Processing

2038 Frozen Specialties, NEC *see* NAICS 311412: Frozen Specialty Food Manufacturing

2041 Flour and Other Grain Mill Products *see* NAICS 311211: Flour Milling

2043 Cereal Breakfast Foods *see* NAICS 311920: Coffee and Tea Manufacturing; NAICS 311230: Breakfast Cereal Manufacturing

2044 Rice Milling *see* NAICS 311212: Rice Milling

2045 Prepared Flour Mixes and Doughs *see* NAICS 311822: Flour Mixes and Dough Manufacturing from Purchased Flour

2046 Wet Corn Milling *see* NAICS 311221: Wet Corn Milling

2047 Dog and Cat Food *see* NAICS 311111: Dog and Cat Food Manufacturing

2048 Prepared Feed and Feed Ingredients for Animals and Fowls, Except Dogs and Cats *see* NAICS 311611: Animal (except Poultry) Slaughtering; NAICS 311119: Other Animal Food Manufacturing

2051 Bread and Other Bakery Products, Except Cookies and Crackers *see* NAICS 311812: Commercial Bakeries

2052 Cookies and Crackers *see* NAICS 311821: Cookie and Cracker Manufacturing; NAICS 311919: Other Snack Food Manufacturing; NAICS 311812: Commercial Bakeries

2053 Frozen Bakery Products, Except Bread *see* NAICS 311813: Frozen Bakery Product Manufacturing

2061 Cane Sugar, Except Refining *see* NAICS 311311: Sugarcane Mills

2062 Cane Sugar Refining *see* NAICS 311312: Cane Sugar Refining

2063 Beet Sugar *see* NAICS 311313: Beet Sugar Manufacturing

2064 Candy and Other Confectionery Products *see* NAICS 311330: Confectionery Manufacturing from Purchased Chocolate; NAICS 311340: Non-Chocolate Confectionery Manufacturing

2066 Chocolate and Cocoa Products *see* NAICS 311320: Chocolate and Confectionery Manufacturing from Cacao Beans

2067 Chewing Gum *see* NAICS 311340: Non-Chocolate Confectionery Manufacturing

2068 Salted and Roasted Nuts and Seeds *see* NAICS 311911: Roasted Nuts and Peanut Butter Manufacturing

2074 Cottonseed Oil Mills *see* NAICS 311223: Other Oilseed Processing; NAICS 311225: Fats and Oils Refining and Blending

2075 Soybean Oil Mills *see* NAICS 311222: Soybean Processing; NAICS 311225: Fats and Oils Refining and Blending

2076 Vegetable Oil Mills, Except Corn, Cottonseed, and Soybeans *see* NAICS 311223: Other Oilseed Processing; NAICS 311225: Fats and Oils Refining and Blending

2077 Animal and Marine Fats and Oils *see* NAICS 311613: Rendering and Meat By-product Processing; NAICS 311711: Seafood Canning; NAICS 311712: Fresh and Frozen Seafood Processing; NAICS 311225: Fats and Oils Refining and Blending

2079 Shortening, Table Oils, Margarine, and Other Edible Fats and Oils, NEC *see* NAICS 311225: Fats and Oils Refining and Blending; NAICS 311222: Soybean Processing; NAICS 311223: Other Oilseed Processing

2082 Malt Beverages *see* NAICS 312120: Breweries

2083 Malt *see* NAICS 311213: Malt Manufacturing

2084 Wines, Brandy, and Brandy Spirits *see* NAICS 312130: Wineries

2085 Distilled and Blended Liquors *see* NAICS 312140: Distilleries

2086 Bottled and Canned Soft Drinks and Carbonated Waters *see* NAICS 312111: Soft Drink Manufacturing; NAICS 312112: Bottled Water Manufacturing

2087 Flavoring Extracts and Flavoring Syrups NEC *see* NAICS 311930: Flavoring Syrup and Concentrate Manufacturing; NAICS 311942: Spice and Extract Manufacturing; NAICS 311999: All Other Miscellaneous Food Manufacturing

2091 Canned and Cured Fish and Seafood *see* NAICS 311711: Seafood Canning

2092 Prepared Fresh or Frozen Fish and Seafoods *see* NAICS 311712: Fresh and Frozen Seafood Processing

2095 Roasted Coffee *see* NAICS 311920: Coffee and Tea Manufacturing; NAICS 311942: Spice and Extract Manufacturing

2096 Potato Chips, Corn Chips, and Similar Snacks *see* NAICS 311919: Other Snack Food Manufacturing

2097 Manufactured Ice *see* NAICS 312113: Ice Manufacturing

2098 Macaroni, Spaghetti, Vermicelli, and Noodles *see* NAICS 311823: Pasta Manufacturing

2099 Food Preparations, NEC *see* NAICS 311423: Dried and Dehydrated Food Manufacturing; NAICS 111998: All Other Miscellaneous Crop Farming; NAICS 311340: Non-Chocolate Confectionery Manufacturing; NAICS 311911: Roasted Nuts and Peanut Butter Manufacturing; NAICS 311991: Perishable Prepared Food Manufacturing; NAICS

311830: Tortilla Manufacturing; NAICS 311920: Coffee and Tea Manufacturing; NAICS 311941: Mayonnaise, Dressing, and Other Prepared Sauce Manufacturing; NAICS 311942: Spice and Extract Manufacturing; NAICS 311999: All Other Miscellaneous Food Manufacturing

TOBACCO PRODUCTS

2111 Cigarettes *see* NAICS 312221: Cigarette Manufacturing

2121 Cigars *see* NAICS 312229: Other Tobacco Product Manufacturing

2131 Chewing and Smoking Tobacco and Snuff *see* NAICS 312229: Other Tobacco Product Manufacturing

2141 Tobacco Stemming and Redrying *see* NAICS 312229: Other Tobacco Product Manufacturing; NAICS 312210: Tobacco Stemming and Redrying

TEXTILE MILL PRODUCTS

2211 Broadwoven Fabric Mills, Cotton *see* NAICS 313210: Broadwoven Fabric Mills

2221 Broadwoven Fabric Mills, Manmade Fiber and Silk *see* NAICS 313210: Broadwoven Fabric Mills

2231 Broadwoven Fabric Mills, Wool (Including Dyeing and Finishing) *see* NAICS 313210: Broadwoven Fabric Mills; NAICS 313311: Broadwoven Fabric Finishing Mills; NAICS 313312: Textile and Fabric Finishing (except Broadwoven Fabric) Mills

2241 Narrow Fabric and Other Smallware Mills: Cotton, Wool, Silk, and Manmade Fiber *see* NAICS 313221: Narrow Fabric Mills

2251 Women's Full-Length and Knee-Length Hosiery, Except Socks *see* NAICS 315111: Sheer Hosiery Mills

2252 Hosiery, NEC *see* NAICS 315111: Sheer Hosiery Mills; NAICS 315119: Other Hosiery and Sock Mills

2253 Knit Outerwear Mills *see* NAICS 315191: Outerwear Knitting Mills

2254 Knit Underwear and Nightwear Mills *see* NAICS 315192: Underwear and Nightwear Knitting Mills

2257 Weft Knit Fabric Mills *see* NAICS 313241: Weft Knit Fabric Mills; NAICS 313312: Textile and Fabric Finishing (except Broadwoven Fabric) Mills

2258 Lace and Warp Knit Fabric Mills *see* NAICS 313249: Other Knit Fabric and Lace Mills; NAICS 313312: Textile and Fabric Finishing (except Broadwoven Fabric) Mills

2259 Knitting Mills, NEC *see* NAICS 315191: Outerwear Knitting Mills; NAICS 315192: Underwear and Nightwear Knitting Mills; NAICS 313241: Weft Knit Fabric Mills; NAICS 313249: Other Knit Fabric and Lace Mills

2261 Finishers of Broadwoven Fabrics of Cotton *see* NAICS 313311: Broadwoven Fabric Finishing Mills

2262 Finishers of Broadwoven Fabrics of Manmade Fiber and Silk *see* NAICS 313311: Broadwoven Fabric Finishing Mills

2269 Finishers of Textiles, NEC *see* NAICS 313311: Broadwoven Fabric Finishing Mills; NAICS 313312: Textile and Fabric Finishing (except Broadwoven Fabric) Mills

2273 Carpets and Rugs *see* NAICS 314110: Carpet and Rug Mills

2281 Yarn Spinning Mills *see* NAICS 313111: Yarn Spinning Mills

2282 Yarn Texturizing, Throwing, Twisting, and Winding Mills *see* NAICS 313112: Yarn Texturing, Throwing and Twisting Mills; NAICS 313312: Textile and Fabric Finishing (except Broadwoven Fabric) Mills

2284 Thread Mills *see* NAICS 313113: Thread Mills; NAICS 313312: Textile and Fabric Finishing (except Broadwoven Fabric) Mills

2295 Coated Fabrics, Not Rubberized *see* NAICS 313320: Fabric Coating Mills

2296 Tire Cord and Fabrics *see* NAICS 314992: Tire Cord and Tire Fabric Mills

2297 Nonwoven Fabrics *see* NAICS 313230: Nonwoven Fabric Mills

2298 Cordage and Twine *see* NAICS 314991: Rope, Cordage and Twine Mills

2299 Textile Goods, NEC *see* NAICS 313210: Broadwoven Fabric Mills; NAICS 313230: Nonwoven Fabric Mills; NAICS 313312: Textile and Fabric Finishing (except Broadwoven Fabric) Mills; NAICS 313221: Narrow Fabric Mills; NAICS 313113: Thread Mills; NAICS 313111: Yarn Spinning Mills; NAICS 314999: All Other Miscellaneous Textile Product Mills

APPAREL & OTHER FINISHED PRODUCTS MADE FROM FABRICS & SIMILAR MATERIALS

2311 Men's and Boys' Suits, Coats and Overcoats *see* NAICS 315211: Men's and Boys' Cut and Sew Apparel Contractors; NAICS 315222: Men's and Boys' Cut and Sew Suit, Coat, and Overcoat Manufacturing

2321 Men's and Boys' Shirts, Except Work Shirts *see* NAICS 315211: Men's and Boys' Cut and Sew Apparel Contractors; NAICS 315223: Men's and Boys' Cut and Sew Shirt, (except Work Shirt) Manufacturing

2322 Men's and Boys' Underwear and Nightwear *see* NAICS 315211: Men's and Boys' Cut and Sew Apparel Contractors; NAICS 315221: Men's and Boys' Cut and Sew Underwear and Nightwear Manufacturing

2323 Men's and Boys' Neckwear *see* NAICS 315993: Men's and Boys' Neckwear Manufacturing

2325 Men's and Boys' Trousers and Slacks *see* NAICS 315211: Men's and Boys' Cut and Sew Apparel Contractors; NAICS 315224: Men's and Boys' Cut And Sew Trouser, Slack, And Jean Manufacturing

2326 Men's and Boys' Work Clothing *see* NAICS 315211: Men's and Boys' Cut and Sew Apparel Contractors; NAICS 315225: Men's and Boys' Cut and Sew Work Clothing Manufacturing

2329 Men's and Boys' Clothing, NEC *see* NAICS 315211: Men's and Boys' Cut and Sew Apparel Contractors; NAICS 315228: Men's and Boys' Cut and Sew Other Outerwear Manufacturing; NAICS 315299: All Other Cut and Sew Apparel Manufacturing

2331 Women's, Misses', and Juniors' Blouses and Shirts *see* NAICS 315212: Women's and Girls' Cut and Sew Apparel Contractors; NAICS 315232: Women's and Girls' Cut and Sew Blouse and Shirt Manufacturing

2335 Women's, Misses' and Junior's Dresses *see* NAICS 315212: Women's and Girls' Cut and Sew Apparel Contractors; NAICS 315233: Women's and Girls' Cut and Sew Dress Manufacturing

2337 Women's, Misses' and Juniors' Suits, Skirts and Coats *see* NAICS 315212: Women's and Girls' Cut and Sew Apparel Contractors; NAICS 315234: Women's and Girls' Cut and Sew Suit, Coat, Tailored Jacket, and Skirt Manufacturing

2339 Women's, Misses' and Juniors' Outerwear, NEC *see* NAICS 315999: Other Apparel Accessories and Other Apparel Manufacturing; NAICS 315212: Women's and Girls' Cut and Sew Apparel Contractors; NAICS 315299: All Other Cut and Sew Apparel Manufacturing; NAICS 315238: Women's and Girls' Cut and Sew Other Outerwear Manufacturing

2341 Women's, Misses, Children's, and Infants' Underwear and Nightwear *see* NAICS 315212: Women's and Girls' Cut and Sew Apparel Contractors; NAICS 315211: Men's and Boys' Cut and Sew Apparel Contractors; NAICS 315231: Women's and Girls' Cut and Sew Lingerie, Loungewear, and Nightwear Manufacturing; NAICS 315221: Men's and Boys' Cut and Sew Underwear and Nightwear Manufacturing; NAICS 315291: Infants' Cut and Sew Apparel Manufacturing

2342 Brassieres, Girdles, and Allied Garments *see* NAICS 315212: Women's and Girls' Cut and Sew Apparel Contractors; NAICS 315231: Women's and Girls'

Cut and Sew Lingerie, Loungewear, and Nightwear Manufacturing

2353   Hats, Caps, and Millinery *see* NAICS 315991: Hat, Cap, and Millinery Manufacturing

2361   Girls', Children's and Infants' Dresses, Blouses and Shirts *see* NAICS 315291: Infants' Cut and Sew Apparel Manufacturing; NAICS 315223: Men's and Boys' Cut and Sew Shirt (except Work Shirt) Manufacturing; NAICS 315211: Men's and Boys' Cut and Sew Apparel Contractors; NAICS 315232: Women's and Girls' Cut and Sew Blouse and Shirt Manufacturing; NAICS 315233: Women's and Girls' Cut and Sew Dress Manufacturing; NAICS 315212: Women's and Girls' Cut and Sew Apparel Contractors

2369   Girls', Children's and Infants' Outerwear, NEC *see* NAICS 315291: Infants' Cut and Sew Apparel Manufacturing; NAICS 315222: Men's and Boys' Cut and Sew Suit, Coat, and Overcoat Manufacturing; NAICS 315224: Men's and Boys' Cut and Sew Trouser, Slack, and Jean Manufacturing; NAICS 315228: Men's and Boys' Cut and Sew Other Outerwear Manufacturing; NAICS 315221: Men's and Boys' Cut and Sew Underwear and Nightwear Manufacturing; NAICS 315211: Men's and Boys' Cut and Sew Apparel Contractors; NAICS 315234: Women's and Girls' Cut and Sew Suit, Coat, Tailored Jacket, and Skirt Manufacturing; NAICS 315238: Women's and Girls' Cut and Sew Other Outerwear Manufacturing; NAICS 315231: Women's and Girls' Cut and Sew Lingerie, Loungewear, and Nightwear Manufacturing; NAICS 315212: Women's and Girls' Cut and Sew Apparel Contractors

2371   Fur Goods *see* NAICS 315292: Fur and Leather Apparel Manufacturing

2381   Dress and Work Gloves, Except Knit and All-Leather *see* NAICS 315992: Glove and Mitten Manufacturing

2384   Robes and Dressing Gowns *see* NAICS 315231: Women's and Girls' Cut and Sew Lingerie, Loungewear, and Nightwear Manufacturing; NAICS 315221: Men's and Boys' Cut and Sew Underwear and Nightwear Manufacturing; NAICS 315211: Men's and Boys' Cut and Sew Apparel Contractors; NAICS 315212: Women's and Girls' Cut and Sew Apparel Contractors

2385   Waterproof Outerwear *see* NAICS 315222: Men's and Boys' Cut and Sew Suit, Coat, and Overcoat Manufacturing; NAICS 315234: Women's and Girls' Cut and Sew Suit, Coat, Tailored Jacket, and Skirt Manufacturing; NAICS 315228: Men's and Boys' Cut and Sew Other Outerwear Manufacturing; NAICS 315238: Women's and Girls' Cut and Sew Other Outerwear Manufacturing; NAICS 315291: Infants' Cut and Sew Apparel Manufacturing; NAICS 315999: Other Apparel Accessories and Other Apparel Manufacturing; NAICS 315211: Men's and Boys' Cut and Sew Apparel Contractors; NAICS 315212: Women's and Girls' Cut and Sew Apparel Contractors

2386   Leather and Sheep-Lined Clothing *see* NAICS 315292: Fur and Leather Apparel Manufacturing

2387   Apparel Belts *see* NAICS 315999: Other Apparel Accessories and Other Apparel Manufacturing

2389   Apparel and Accessories, NEC *see* NAICS 315999: Other Apparel Accessories and Other Apparel Manufacturing; NAICS 315299: All Other Cut and Sew Apparel Manufacturing; NAICS 315231: Women's and Girls' Cut and Sew Lingerie, Loungewear, and Nightwear Manufacturing; NAICS 315212: Women's and Girls' Cut and Sew Apparel Contractors; NAICS 315211: Men's and Boys' Cut and Sew Apparel Contractors

2391   Curtains and Draperies *see* NAICS 314121: Curtain and Drapery Mills

2392   Housefurnishings, Except Curtains and Draperies *see* NAICS 314911: Textile Bag Mills; NAICS 339994: Broom, Brush and Mop Manufacturing; NAICS 314129: Other Household Textile Product Mills

2393   Textile Bags *see* NAICS 314911: Textile Bag Mills

2394   Canvas and Related Products *see* NAICS 314912: Canvas and Related Product Mills

2395   Pleating, Decorative and Novelty Stitching, and Tucking for the Trade *see* NAICS 314999: All Other Miscellaneous Textile Product Mills; NAICS 315211: Men's and Boys' Cut and Sew Apparel Contractors; NAICS 315212: Women's and Girls' Cut and Sew Apparel Contractors

2396   Automotive Trimmings, Apparel Findings, and Related Products *see* NAICS 336360: Motor Vehicle Fabric Accessories and Seat Manufacturing; NAICS 315999: Other Apparel Accessories, and Other Apparel Manufacturing; NAICS 323113: Commercial Screen Printing; NAICS 314999: All Other Miscellaneous Textile Product Mills

2397   Schiffli Machine Embroideries *see* NAICS 313222: Schiffli Machine Embroidery

2399   Fabricated Textile Products, NEC *see* NAICS 336360: Motor Vehicle Fabric Accessories and Seat Manufacturing; NAICS 315999: Other Apparel Accessories and Other Apparel Manufacturing; NAICS 314999: All Other Miscellaneous Textile Product Mills

LUMBER & WOOD PRODUCTS, EXCEPT FURNITURE

2411 Logging *see* NAICS 113310: Logging

2421 Sawmills and Planing Mills, General *see* NAICS 321912: Cut Stock, Resawing Lumber, and Planing; NAICS 321113: Sawmills; NAICS 321918: Other Millwork (including Flooring); NAICS 321999: All Other Miscellaneous Wood Product Manufacturing

2426 Hardwood Dimension and Flooring Mills *see* NAICS 321918: Other Millwork (including Flooring); NAICS 321999: All Other Miscellaneous Wood Product Manufacturing; NAICS 337215: Showcase, Partition, Shelving, and Locker Manufacturing; NAICS 321912: Cut Stock, Resawing Lumber, and Planing

2429 Special Product Sawmills, NEC *see* NAICS 321113: Sawmills; NAICS 321912: Cut Stock, Resawing Lumber, and Planing; NAICS 321999: All Other Miscellaneous Wood Product Manufacturing

2431 Millwork *see* NAICS 321911: Wood Window and Door Manufacturing; NAICS 321918: Other Millwork (including Flooring)

2434 Wood Kitchen Cabinets *see* NAICS 337110: Wood Kitchen Cabinet and Counter Top Manufacturing

2435 Hardwood Veneer and Plywood *see* NAICS 321211: Hardwood Veneer and Plywood Manufacturing

2436 Softwood Veneer and Plywood *see* NAICS 321212: Softwood Veneer and Plywood Manufacturing

2439 Structural Wood Members, NEC *see* NAICS 321912: Cut Stock, Resawing Lumber, and Planing; NAICS 321214: Truss Manufacturing; NAICS 321213: Engineered Wood Member (except Truss) Manufacturing

2441 Nailed and Lock Corner Wood Boxes and Shook *see* NAICS 321920: Wood Container and Pallet Manufacturing

2448 Wood Pallets and Skids *see* NAICS 321920: Wood Container and Pallet Manufacturing

2449 Wood Containers, NEC *see* NAICS 321920: Wood Container and Pallet Manufacturing

2451 Mobile Homes *see* NAICS 321991: Manufactured Home (Mobile Home) Manufacturing

2452 Prefabricated Wood Buildings and Components *see* NAICS 321992: Prefabricated Wood Building Manufacturing

2491 Wood Preserving *see* NAICS 321114: Wood Preservation

2493 Reconstituted Wood Products *see* NAICS 321219: Reconstituted Wood Product Manufacturing

2499 Wood Products, NEC *see* NAICS 339999: All Other Miscellaneous Manufacturing; NAICS 321920: Wood Container and Pallet Manufacturing; NAICS 321999: All Other Miscellaneous Wood Product Manufacturing

FURNITURE & FIXTURES

2511 Wood Household Furniture, Except Upholstered *see* NAICS 337122: Nonupholstered Wood Household Furniture Manufacturing

2512 Wood Household Furniture, Upholstered *see* NAICS 337121: Upholstered Wood Household Furniture Manufacturing

2514 Metal Household Furniture *see* NAICS 337124: Metal Household Furniture Manufacturing

2515 Mattresses, Foundations, and Convertible Beds *see* NAICS 337910: Mattress Manufacturing; NAICS 337121: Upholstered Wood Household Furniture Manufacturing

2517 Wood Television, Radio, Phonograph and Sewing Machine Cabinets *see* NAICS 337129: Wood Television, Radio, and Sewing Machine Cabinet Manufacturing

2519 Household Furniture, NEC *see* NAICS 337125: Household Furniture (except Wood and Metal) Manufacturing

2521 Wood Office Furniture *see* NAICS 337211: Wood Office Furniture Manufacturing

2522 Office Furniture, Except Wood *see* NAICS 337214: Nonwood Office Furniture Manufacturing

2531 Public Building and Related Furniture *see* NAICS 336360: Motor Vehicle Fabric Accessories and Seat Manufacturing; NAICS 337127: Institutional Furniture Manufacturing; NAICS 339942: Lead Pencil and Art Good Manufacturing

2541 Wood Office and Store Fixtures, Partitions, Shelving, and Lockers *see* NAICS 337110: Wood Kitchen Cabinet and Counter Top Manufacturing; NAICS 337212: Custom Architectural Woodwork, Millwork, and Fixtures; NAICS 337215: Showcase, Partition, Shelving, and Locker Manufacturing

2542 Office and Store Fixtures, Partitions Shelving, and Lockers, Except Wood *see* NAICS 337215: Showcase, Partition, Shelving, and Locker Manufacturing

2591 Drapery Hardware and Window Blinds and Shades *see* NAICS 337920: Blind and Shade Manufacturing

2599 Furniture and Fixtures, NEC *see* NAICS 339113: Surgical Appliance and Supplies Manufacturing; NAICS 337127: Institutional Furniture Manufacturing

PAPER & ALLIED PRODUCTS

2611 Pulp Mills *see* NAICS 322110: Pulp Mills; NAICS 322121: Paper (except Newsprint) Mills; NAICS 322130: Paperboard Mills

2621 Paper Mills *see* NAICS 322121: Paper (except Newsprint) Mills; NAICS 322122: Newsprint Mills

2631 Paperboard Mills *see* NAICS 322130: Paperboard Mills

2652 Setup Paperboard Boxes *see* NAICS 322213: Setup Paperboard Box Manufacturing

2653 Corrugated and Solid Fiber Boxes *see* NAICS 322211: Corrugated and Solid Fiber Box Manufacturing

2655 Fiber Cans, Tubes, Drums, and Similar Products *see* NAICS 322214: Fiber Can, Tube, Drum, and Similar Products Manufacturing

2656 Sanitary Food Containers, Except Folding *see* NAICS 322215: Non-Folding Sanitary Food Container Manufacturing

2657 Folding Paperboard Boxes, Including Sanitary *see* NAICS 322212: Folding Paperboard Box Manufacturing

2671 Packaging Paper and Plastics Film *see* NAICS 322221: Coated and Laminated Packaging Paper and Plastics Film Manufacturing; NAICS 326112: Unsupported Plastics Packaging Film and Sheet Manufacturing

2672 Coated and Laminated Paper, NEC *see* NAICS 322222: Coated and Laminated Paper Manufacturing

2673 Plastics, Foil, and Coated Paper Bags *see* NAICS 322223: Plastics, Foil, and Coated Paper Bag Manufacturing; NAICS 326111: Unsupported Plastics Bag Manufacturing

2674 Uncoated Paper and Multiwall Bags *see* NAICS 322224: Uncoated Paper and Multiwall Bag Manufacturing

2675 Die-Cut Paper and Paperboard and Cardboard *see* NAICS 322231: Die-Cut Paper and Paperboard Office Supplies Manufacturing; NAICS 322292: Surface-Coated Paperboard Manufacturing; NAICS 322298: All Other Converted Paper Product Manufacturing

2676 Sanitary Paper Products *see* NAICS 322291: Sanitary Paper Product Manufacturing

2677 Envelopes *see* NAICS 322232: Envelope Manufacturing

2678 Stationery, Tablets, and Related Products *see* NAICS 322233: Stationery, Tablet, and Related Product Manufacturing

2679 Converted Paper and Paperboard Products, NEC *see* NAICS 322215: Non-Folding Sanitary Food Container Manufacturing; NAICS 322222: Coated and Laminated Paper Manufacturing; NAICS 322231: Die-Cut Paper and Paperboard Office Supplies Manufacturing; NAICS 322298: All Other Converted Paper Product Manufacturing

PRINTING, PUBLISHING, & ALLIED INDUSTRIES

2711 Newspapers: Publishing, or Publishing and Printing *see* NAICS 511110: Newspaper Publishers

2721 Periodicals: Publishing, or Publishing and Printing *see* NAICS 511120: Periodical Publishers

2731 Books: Publishing, or Publishing and Printing *see* NAICS 512230: Music Publishers; NAICS 511130: Book Publishers

2732 Book Printing *see* NAICS 323117: Book Printing

2741 Miscellaneous Publishing *see* NAICS 511140: Database and Directory Publishers; NAICS 512230: Music Publishers; NAICS 511199: All Other Publishers

2752 Commercial Printing, Lithographic *see* NAICS 323114: Quick Printing; NAICS 323110: Commercial Lithographic Printing

2754 Commercial Printing, Gravure *see* NAICS 323111: Commercial Gravure Printing

2759 Commercial Printing, NEC *see* NAICS 323113: Commercial Screen Printing; NAICS 323112: Commercial Flexographic Printing; NAICS 323114: Quick Printing; NAICS 323115: Digital Printing; NAICS 323119: Other Commercial Printing

2761 Manifold Business Forms *see* NAICS 323116: Manifold Business Form Printing

2771 Greeting Cards *see* NAICS 323110: Commercial Lithographic Printing; NAICS 323111: Commercial Gravure Printing; NAICS 323112: Commercial Flexographic Printing; NAICS 323113: Commercial Screen Printing; NAICS 323119: Other Commercial Printing; NAICS 511191: Greeting Card Publishers

2782 Blankbooks, Loose-leaf Binders and Devices *see* NAICS 323110: Commercial Lithographic Printing; NAICS 323111: Commercial Gravure Printing; NAICS 323112: Commercial Flexographic Printing; NAICS 323113: Commercial Screen Printing; NAICS 323119: Other Commercial Printing; NAICS 323118: Blankbook, Loose-leaf Binder and Device Manufacturing

2789 Bookbinding and Related Work *see* NAICS 323121: Tradebinding and Related Work

2791 Typesetting *see* NAICS 323122: Prepress Services

2796 Platemaking and Related Services *see* NAICS 323122: Prepress Services

CHEMICALS & ALLIED PRODUCTS

2812 Alkalies and Chlorine *see* NAICS 325181: Alkalies and Chlorine Manufacturing

2813 Industrial Gases *see* NAICS 325120: Industrial Gas Manufacturing

2816 Inorganic Pigments *see* NAICS 325131: Inorganic Dye and Pigment Manufacturing; NAICS 325182: Carbon Black Manufacturing

2819 Industrial Inorganic Chemicals, NEC *see* NAICS 325998: All Other Miscellaneous Chemical Product Manufacturing; NAICS 331311: Aluminum Refining; NAICS 325131: Inorganic Dye and Pigment Manufacturing; NAICS 325188: All Other Inorganic Chemical Manufacturing

2821 Plastics Material Synthetic Resins, and Nonvulcanizable Elastomers *see* NAICS 325211: Plastics Material and Resin Manufacturing

2822 Synthetic Rubber *see* NAICS 325212: Synthetic Rubber Manufacturing

2823 Cellulosic Manmade Fibers *see* NAICS 325221: Cellulosic Manmade Fiber Manufacturing

2824 Manmade Organic Fibers, Except Cellulosic *see* NAICS 325222: Noncellulosic Organic Fiber Manufacturing

2833 Medicinal Chemicals and Botanical Products *see* NAICS 325411: Medicinal and Botanical Manufacturing

2834 Pharmaceutical Preparations *see* NAICS 325412: Pharmaceutical Preparation Manufacturing

2835 In Vitro and In Vivo Diagnostic Substances *see* NAICS 325412: Pharmaceutical Preparation Manufacturing; NAICS 325413: In-Vitro Diagnostic Substance Manufacturing

2836 Biological Products, Except Diagnostic Substances *see* NAICS 325414: Biological Product (except Diagnostic) Manufacturing

2841 Soaps and Other Detergents, Except Specialty Cleaners *see* NAICS 325611: Soap and Other Detergent Manufacturing

2842 Specialty Cleaning, Polishing, and Sanitary Preparations *see* NAICS 325612: Polish and Other Sanitation Good Manufacturing

2843 Surface Active Agents, Finishing Agents, Sulfonated Oils, and Assistants *see* NAICS 325613: Surface Active Agent Manufacturing

2844 Perfumes, Cosmetics, and Other Toilet Preparations *see* NAICS 325620: Toilet Preparation Manufacturing; NAICS 325611: Soap and Other Detergent Manufacturing

2851 Paints, Varnishes, Lacquers, Enamels, and Allied Products *see* NAICS 325510: Paint and Coating Manufacturing

2861 Gum and Wood Chemicals *see* NAICS 325191: Gum and Wood Chemical Manufacturing

2865 Cyclic Organic Crudes and Intermediates, and Organic Dyes and Pigments *see* NAICS 325110: Petrochemical Manufacturing; NAICS 325132: Organic Dye and Pigment Manufacturing; NAICS

325192: Cyclic Crude and Intermediate Manufacturing

2869 Industrial Organic Chemicals, NEC *see* NAICS 325110: Petrochemical Manufacturing; NAICS 325188: All Other Inorganic Chemical Manufacturing; NAICS 325193: Ethyl Alcohol Manufacturing; NAICS 325120: Industrial Gas Manufacturing; NAICS 325199: All Other Basic Organic Chemical Manufacturing

2873 Nitrogenous Fertilizers *see* NAICS 325311: Nitrogenous Fertilizer Manufacturing

2874 Phosphatic Fertilizers *see* NAICS 325312: Phosphatic Fertilizer Manufacturing

2875 Fertilizers, Mixing Only *see* NAICS 325314: Fertilizer (Mixing Only) Manufacturing

2879 Pesticides and Agricultural Chemicals, NEC *see* NAICS 325320: Pesticide and Other Agricultural Chemical Manufacturing

2891 Adhesives and Sealants *see* NAICS 325520: Adhesive and Sealant Manufacturing

2892 Explosives *see* NAICS 325920: Explosives Manufacturing

2893 Printing Ink *see* NAICS 325910: Printing Ink Manufacturing

2895 Carbon Black *see* NAICS 325182: Carbon Black Manufacturing

2899 Chemicals and Chemical Preparations, NEC *see* NAICS 325510: Paint and Coating Manufacturing; NAICS 311942: Spice and Extract Manufacturing; NAICS 325199: All Other Basic Organic Chemical Manufacturing; NAICS 325998: All Other Miscellaneous Chemical Product Manufacturing

PETROLEUM REFINING & RELATED INDUSTRIES

2911 Petroleum Refining *see* NAICS 324110: Petroleum Refineries

2951 Asphalt Paving Mixtures and Blocks *see* NAICS 324121: Asphalt Paving Mixture and Block Manufacturing

2952 Asphalt Felts and Coatings *see* NAICS 324122: Asphalt Shingle and Coating Materials Manufacturing

2992 Lubricating Oils and Greases *see* NAICS 324191: Petroleum Lubricating Oil and Grease Manufacturing

2999 Products of Petroleum and Coal, NEC *see* NAICS 324199: All Other Petroleum and Coal Products Manufacturing

RUBBER & MISCELLANEOUS PLASTICS PRODUCTS

3011 Tires and Inner Tubes *see* NAICS 326211: Tire Manufacturing (except Retreading)

3021 Rubber and Plastics Footwear *see* NAICS 316211: Rubber and Plastics Footwear Manufacturing

3052 Rubber and Plastics Hose and Belting *see* NAICS 326220: Rubber and Plastics Hoses and Belting Manufacturing

3053 Gaskets, Packing, and Sealing Devices *see* NAICS 339991: Gasket, Packing, and Sealing Device Manufacturing

3061 Molded, Extruded, and Lathe-Cut Mechanical Rubber Products *see* NAICS 326291: Rubber Product Manufacturing for Mechanical Use

3069 Fabricated Rubber Products, NEC *see* NAICS 313320: Fabric Coating Mills; NAICS 326192: Resilient Floor Covering Manufacturing; NAICS 326299: All Other Rubber Product Manufacturing

3081 Unsupported Plastics Film and Sheet *see* NAICS 326113: Unsupported Plastics Film and Sheet (except Packaging) Manufacturing

3082 Unsupported Plastics Profile Shapes *see* NAICS 326121: Unsupported Plastics Profile Shape Manufacturing

3083 Laminated Plastics Plate, Sheet, and Profile Shapes *see* NAICS 326130: Laminated Plastics Plate, Sheet, and Shape Manufacturing

3084 Plastic Pipe *see* NAICS 326122: Plastics Pipe and Pipe Fitting Manufacturing

3085 Plastics Bottles *see* NAICS 326160: Plastics Bottle Manufacturing

3086 Plastics Foam Products *see* NAICS 326150: Urethane and Other Foam Product (except Polystyrene) Manufacturing; NAICS 326140: Polystyrene Foam Product Manufacturing

3087 Custom Compounding of Purchased Plastics Resins *see* NAICS 325991: Custom Compounding of Purchased Resin

3088 Plastics Plumbing Fixtures *see* NAICS 326191: Plastics Plumbing Fixtures Manufacturing

3089 Plastics Products, NEC *see* NAICS 326122: Plastics Pipe and Pipe Fitting Manufacturing; NAICS 326121: Unsupported Plastics Profile Shape Manufacturing; NAICS 326199: All Other Plastics Product Manufacturing

LEATHER & LEATHER PRODUCTS

3111 Leather Tanning and Finishing *see* NAICS 316110: Leather and Hide Tanning and Finishing

3131 Boot and Shoe Cut Stock and Findings *see* NAICS 321999: All Other Miscellaneous Wood Product Manufacturing; NAICS 339993: Fastener, Button, Needle, and Pin Manufacturing; NAICS 316999: All Other Leather Good Manufacturing

3142 House Slippers *see* NAICS 316212: House Slipper Manufacturing

3143 Men's Footwear, Except Athletic *see* NAICS 316213: Men's Footwear (except Athletic) Manufacturing

3144 Women's Footwear, Except Athletic *see* NAICS 316214: Women's Footwear (except Athletic) Manufacturing

3149 Footwear, Except Rubber, NEC *see* NAICS 316219: Other Footwear Manufacturing

3151 Leather Gloves and Mittens *see* NAICS 315992: Glove and Mitten Manufacturing

3161 Luggage *see* NAICS 316991: Luggage Manufacturing

3171 Women's Handbags and Purses *see* NAICS 316992: Women's Handbag and Purse Manufacturing

3172 Personal Leather Goods, Except Women's Handbags and Purses *see* NAICS 316993: Personal Leather Good (except Women's Handbag and Purse) Manufacturing

3199 Leather Goods, NEC *see* NAICS 316999: All Other Leather Good Manufacturing

STONE, CLAY, GLASS, & CONCRETE PRODUCTS

3211 Flat Glass *see* NAICS 327211: Flat Glass Manufacturing

3221 Glass Containers *see* NAICS 327213: Glass Container Manufacturing

3229 Pressed and Blown Glass and Glassware, NEC *see* NAICS 327212: Other Pressed and Blown Glass and Glassware Manufacturing

3231 Glass Products, Made of Purchased Glass *see* NAICS 327215: Glass Product Manufacturing Made of Purchased Glass

3241 Cement, Hydraulic *see* NAICS 327310: Cement Manufacturing

3251 Brick and Structural Clay Tile *see* NAICS 327121: Brick and Structural Clay Tile Manufacturing

3253 Ceramic Wall and Floor Tile *see* NAICS 327122: Ceramic Wall and Floor Tile Manufacturing

3255 Clay Refractories *see* NAICS 327124: Clay Refractory Manufacturing

3259 Structural Clay Products, NEC *see* NAICS 327123: Other Structural Clay Product Manufacturing

3261 Vitreous China Plumbing Fixtures and China and Earthenware Fittings and Bathroom Accessories *see* NAICS 327111: Vitreous China Plumbing Fixture and China and Earthenware Fitting and Bathroom Accessories Manufacturing

3262 Vitreous China Table and Kitchen Articles *see* NAICS 327112: Vitreous China, Fine Earthenware and Other Pottery Product Manufacturing

3263 Fine Earthenware (Whiteware) Table and Kitchen Articles *see* NAICS 327112: Vitreous China, Fine Earthenware and Other Pottery Product Manufacturing

3264 Porcelain Electrical Supplies *see* NAICS 327113: Porcelain Electrical Supply Manufacturing

3269 Pottery Products, NEC *see* NAICS 327112: Vitreous China, Fine Earthenware, and Other Pottery Product Manufacturing

3271 Concrete Block and Brick *see* NAICS 327331: Concrete Block and Brick Manufacturing

3272 Concrete Products, Except Block and Brick *see* NAICS 327999: All Other Miscellaneous Nonmetallic Mineral Product Manufacturing; NAICS 327332: Concrete Pipe Manufacturing; NAICS 327390: Other Concrete Product Manufacturing

3273 Ready-Mixed Concrete *see* NAICS 327320: Ready-Mix Concrete Manufacturing

3274 Lime *see* NAICS 327410: Lime Manufacturing

3275 Gypsum Products *see* NAICS 327420: Gypsum and Gypsum Product Manufacturing

3281 Cut Stone and Stone Products *see* NAICS 327991: Cut Stone and Stone Product Manufacturing

3291 Abrasive Products *see* NAICS 332999: All Other Miscellaneous Fabricated Metal Product Manufacturing; NAICS 327910: Abrasive Product Manufacturing

3292 Asbestos Products *see* NAICS 336340: Motor Vehicle Brake System Manufacturing; NAICS 327999: All Other Miscellaneous Nonmetallic Mineral Product Manufacturing

3295 Minerals and Earths, Ground or Otherwise Treated *see* NAICS 327992: Ground or Treated Mineral and Earth Manufacturing

3296 Mineral Wool *see* NAICS 327993: Mineral Wool Manufacturing

3297 Nonclay Refractories *see* NAICS 327125: Nonclay Refractory Manufacturing

3299 Nonmetallic Mineral Products, NEC *see* NAICS 327420: Gypsum and Gypsum Product Manufacturing; NAICS 327999: All Other Miscellaneous Nonmetallic Mineral Product Manufacturing

PRIMARY METALS INDUSTRIES

3312 Steel Works, Blast Furnaces (Including Coke Ovens), and Rolling Mills *see* NAICS 324199: All Other Petroleum and Coal Products Manufacturing; NAICS 331111: Iron and Steel Mills

3313 Electrometallurgical Products, Except Steel *see* NAICS 331112: Electrometallurgical Ferroalloy Product Manufacturing; NAICS 331492: Secondary Smelting, Refining, and Alloying of Nonferrous Metals (except Copper and Aluminum)

3315 Steel Wiredrawing and Steel Nails and Spikes *see* NAICS 331222: Steel Wire Drawing; NAICS 332618: Other Fabricated Wire Product Manufacturing

3316 Cold-Rolled Steel Sheet, Strip, and Bars *see* NAICS 331221: Cold-Rolled Steel Shape Manufacturing

3317 Steel Pipe and Tubes *see* NAICS 331210: Iron and Steel Pipes and Tubes Manufacturing from Purchased Steel

3321 Gray and Ductile Iron Foundries *see* NAICS 331511: Iron Foundries

3322 Malleable Iron Foundries *see* NAICS 331511: Iron Foundries

3324 Steel Investment Foundries *see* NAICS 331512: Steel Investment Foundries

3325 Steel Foundries, NEC *see* NAICS 331513: Steel Foundries (except Investment)

3331 Primary Smelting and Refining of Copper *see* NAICS 331411: Primary Smelting and Refining of Copper

3334 Primary Production of Aluminum *see* NAICS 331312: Primary Aluminum Production

3339 Primary Smelting and Refining of Nonferrous Metals, Except Copper and Aluminum *see* NAICS 331419: Primary Smelting and Refining of Nonferrous Metals (except Copper and Aluminum)

3341 Secondary Smelting and Refining of Nonferrous Metals *see* NAICS 331314: Secondary Smelting and Alloying of Aluminum; NAICS 331423: Secondary Smelting, Refining, and Alloying of Copper; NAICS 331492: Secondary Smelting, Refining, and Alloying of Nonferrous Metals (except Copper and Aluminum)

3351 Rolling, Drawing, and Extruding of Copper *see* NAICS 331421: Copper (except Wire) Rolling, Drawing, and Extruding

3353 Aluminum Sheet, Plate, and Foil *see* NAICS 331315: Aluminum Sheet, Plate, and Foil Manufacturing

3354 Aluminum Extruded Products *see* NAICS 331316: Aluminum Extruded Product Manufacturing

3355 Aluminum Rolling and Drawing, NEC *see* NAICS 331319: Other Aluminum Rolling and Drawing

3356 Rolling, Drawing, and Extruding of Nonferrous Metals, Except Copper and Aluminum *see* NAICS 331491: Nonferrous Metal (except Copper and Aluminum) Rolling, Drawing, and Extruding

3357 Drawing and Insulating of Nonferrous Wire *see* NAICS 331319: Other Aluminum Rolling and Drawing; NAICS 331422: Copper Wire Drawing; NAICS 331491: Nonferrous Metal (except Copper and Aluminum) Rolling, Drawing, and Extruding; NAICS 335921: Fiber Optic Cable Manufacturing; NAICS 335929: Other Communication and Energy Wire Manufacturing

3363 Aluminum Die-Castings *see* NAICS 331521: Aluminum Die-Castings

3364 Nonferrous Die-Castings, Except Aluminum *see* NAICS 331522: Nonferrous (except Aluminum) Die-Castings

3365 Aluminum Foundries *see* NAICS 331524: Aluminum Foundries

3366 Copper Foundries *see* NAICS 331525: Copper Foundries

3369 Nonferrous Foundries, Except Aluminum and Copper *see* NAICS 331528: Other Nonferrous Foundries

3398 Metal Heat Treating *see* NAICS 332811: Metal Heat Treating

3399 Primary Metal Products, NEC *see* NAICS 331111: Iron and Steel Mills; NAICS 331314: Secondary Smelting and Alloying of Aluminum; NAICS 331423: Secondary Smelting, Refining and Alloying of Copper; NAICS 331492: Secondary Smelting, Refining, and Alloying of Nonferrous Metals (except Copper and Aluminum); NAICS 332618: Other Fabricated Wire Product Manufacturing; NAICS 332813: Electroplating, Plating, Polishing, Anodizing, and Coloring

FABRICATED METAL PRODUCTS, EXCEPT MACHINERY & TRANSPORTATION EQUIPMENT

3411 Metal Cans *see* NAICS 332431: Metal Can Manufacturing

3412 Metal Shipping Barrels, Drums, Kegs and Pails *see* NAICS 332439: Other Metal Container Manufacturing

3421 Cutlery *see* NAICS 332211: Cutlery and Flatware (except Precious) Manufacturing

3423 Hand and Edge Tools, Except Machine Tools and Handsaws *see* NAICS 332212: Hand and Edge Tool Manufacturing

3425 Saw Blades and Handsaws *see* NAICS 332213: Saw Blade and Handsaw Manufacturing

3429 Hardware, NEC *see* NAICS 332439: Other Metal Container Manufacturing; NAICS 332919: Other Metal Valve and Pipe Fitting Manufacturing; NAICS 332510: Hardware Manufacturing

3431 Enameled Iron and Metal Sanitary Ware *see* NAICS 332998: Enameled Iron and Metal Sanitary Ware Manufacturing

3432 Plumbing Fixture Fittings and Trim *see* NAICS 332913: Plumbing Fixture Fitting and Trim Manufacturing; NAICS 332999: All Other Miscellaneous Fabricated Metal Product Manufacturing

3433 Heating Equipment, Except Electric and Warm Air Furnaces *see* NAICS 333414: Heating Equipment (except Electric and Warm Air Furnaces) Manufacturing

3441 Fabricated Structural Metal *see* NAICS 332312: Fabricated Structural Metal Manufacturing

3442 Metal Doors, Sash, Frames, Molding, and Trim Manufacturing *see* NAICS 332321: Metal Window and Door Manufacturing

3443 Fabricated Plate Work (Boiler Shops) *see* NAICS 332313: Plate Work Manufacturing; NAICS 332410: Power Boiler and Heat Exchanger Manufacturing; NAICS 332420: Metal Tank (Heavy Gauge) Manufacturing; NAICS 333415: Air-Conditioning and Warm Air Heating Equipment and Commercial and Industrial Refrigeration Equipment Manufacturing

3444 Sheet Metal Work *see* NAICS 332322: Sheet Metal Work Manufacturing; NAICS 332439: Other Metal Container Manufacturing

3446 Architectural and Ornamental Metal Work *see* NAICS 332323: Ornamental and Architectural Metal Work Manufacturing

3448 Prefabricated Metal Buildings and Components *see* NAICS 332311: Prefabricated Metal Building and Component Manufacturing

3449 Miscellaneous Structural Metal Work *see* NAICS 332114: Custom Roll Forming; NAICS 332312: Fabricated Structural Metal Manufacturing; NAICS 332321: Metal Window and Door Manufacturing; NAICS 332323: Ornamental and Architectural Metal Work Manufacturing

3451 Screw Machine Products *see* NAICS 332721: Precision Turned Product Manufacturing

3452 Bolts, Nuts, Screws, Rivets, and Washers *see* NAICS 332722: Bolt, Nut, Screw, Rivet, and Washer Manufacturing

3462 Iron and Steel Forgings *see* NAICS 332111: Iron and Steel Forging

3463 Nonferrous Forgings *see* NAICS 332112: Nonferrous Forging

3465 Automotive Stamping *see* NAICS 336370: Motor Vehicle Metal Stamping

3466 Crowns and Closures *see* NAICS 332115: Crown and Closure Manufacturing

3469 Metal Stamping, NEC *see* NAICS 339911: Jewelry (including Precious Metal) Manufacturing; NAICS 332116: Metal Stamping; NAICS 332214: Kitchen Utensil, Pot, and Pan Manufacturing

3471 Electroplating, Plating, Polishing, Anodizing, and Coloring *see* NAICS 332813: Electroplating, Plating, Polishing, Anodizing, and Coloring

3479 Coating, Engraving, and Allied Services, NEC *see* NAICS 339914: Costume Jewelry and Novelty Manufacturing; NAICS 339911: Jewelry (including Precious Metal) Manufacturing; NAICS

339912: Silverware and Plated Ware Manufacturing; NAICS 332812: Metal Coating, Engraving, and Allied Services (except Jewelry and Silverware) to Manufacturing

3482 Small Arms Ammunition *see* NAICS 332992: Small Arms Ammunition Manufacturing

3483 Ammunition, Except for Small Arms *see* NAICS 332993: Ammunition (except Small Arms) Manufacturing

3484 Small Arms *see* NAICS 332994: Small Arms Manufacturing

3489 Ordnance and Accessories, NEC *see* NAICS 332995: Other Ordnance and Accessories Manufacturing

3491 Industrial Valves *see* NAICS 332911: Industrial Valve Manufacturing

3492 Fluid Power Valves and Hose Fittings *see* NAICS 332912: Fluid Power Valve and Hose Fitting Manufacturing

3493 Steel Springs, Except Wire *see* NAICS 332611: Steel Spring (except Wire) Manufacturing

3494 Valves and Pipe Fittings, NEC *see* NAICS 332919: Other Metal Valve and Pipe Fitting Manufacturing; NAICS 332999: All Other Miscellaneous Fabricated Metal Product Manufacturing

3495 Wire Springs *see* NAICS 332612: Wire Spring Manufacturing; NAICS 334518: Watch, Clock, and Part Manufacturing

3496 Miscellaneous Fabricated Wire Products *see* NAICS 332618: Other Fabricated Wire Product Manufacturing

3497 Metal Foil and Leaf *see* NAICS 322225: Laminated Aluminum Foil Manufacturing for Flexible Packaging Uses; NAICS 332999: All Other Miscellaneous Fabricated Metal Product Manufacturing

3498 Fabricated Pipe and Pipe Fittings *see* NAICS 332996: Fabricated Pipe and Pipe Fitting Manufacturing

3499 Fabricated Metal Products, NEC *see* NAICS 337215: Showcase, Partition, Shelving, and Locker Manufacturing; NAICS 332117: Powder Metallurgy Part Manufacturing; NAICS 332439: Other Metal Container Manufacturing; NAICS 332510: Hardware Manufacturing; NAICS 332919: Other Metal Valve and Pipe Fitting Manufacturing; NAICS 339914: Costume Jewelry and Novelty Manufacturing; NAICS 332999: All Other Miscellaneous Fabricated Metal Product Manufacturing

INDUSTRIAL & COMMERCIAL MACHINERY & COMPUTER EQUIPMENT

3511 Steam, Gas, and Hydraulic Turbines, and Turbine Generator Set Units *see* NAICS 333611: Turbine and Turbine Generator Set Unit Manufacturing

3519 Internal Combustion Engines, NEC *see* NAICS 336399: All Other Motor Vehicle Parts Manufacturing; NAICS 333618: Other Engine Equipment Manufacturing

3523 Farm Machinery and Equipment *see* NAICS 333111: Farm Machinery and Equipment Manufacturing; NAICS 332323: Ornamental and Architectural Metal Work Manufacturing; NAICS 332212: Hand and Edge Tool Manufacturing; NAICS 333922: Conveyor and Conveying Equipment Manufacturing

3524 Lawn and Garden Tractors and Home Lawn and Garden Equipment *see* NAICS 333112: Lawn and Garden Tractor and Home Lawn and Garden Equipment Manufacturing; NAICS 332212: Hand and Edge Tool Manufacturing

3531 Construction Machinery and Equipment *see* NAICS 336510: Railroad Rolling Stock Manufacturing; NAICS 333923: Overhead Traveling Crane, Hoist, and Monorail System Manufacturing; NAICS 333120: Construction Machinery Manufacturing

3532 Mining Machinery and Equipment, Except Oil and Gas Field Machinery and Equipment *see* NAICS 333131: Mining Machinery and Equipment Manufacturing

3533 Oil and Gas Field Machinery and Equipment *see* NAICS 333132: Oil and Gas Field Machinery and Equipment Manufacturing

3534 Elevators and Moving Stairways *see* NAICS 333921: Elevator and Moving Stairway Manufacturing

3535 Conveyors and Conveying Equipment *see* NAICS 333922: Conveyor and Conveying Equipment Manufacturing

3536 Overhead Traveling Cranes, Hoists, and Monorail Systems *see* NAICS 333923: Overhead Traveling Crane, Hoist, and Monorail System Manufacturing

3537 Industrial Trucks, Tractors, Trailers, and Stackers *see* NAICS 333924: Industrial Truck, Tractor, Trailer, and Stacker Machinery Manufacturing; NAICS 332999: All Other Miscellaneous Fabricated Metal Product Manufacturing; NAICS 332439: Other Metal Container Manufacturing

3541 Machine Tools, Metal Cutting Type *see* NAICS 333512: Machine Tool (Metal Cutting Types) Manufacturing

3542 Machine Tools, Metal Forming Type *see* NAICS 333513: Machine Tool (Metal Forming Types) Manufacturing

3543 Industrial Patterns *see* NAICS 332997: Industrial Pattern Manufacturing

3544 Special Dies and Tools, Die Sets, Jigs and Fixtures, and Industrial Molds *see* NAICS 333514: Special Die and Tool, Die Set, Jig, and Fixture Manufacturing; NAICS 333511: Industrial Mold Manufacturing

3545 Cutting Tools, Machine Tool Accessories, and Machinists' Precision Measuring Devices *see* NAICS 333515: Cutting Tool and Machine Tool Accessory Manufacturing; NAICS 332212: Hand and Edge Tool Manufacturing

3546 Power-Driven Handtools *see* NAICS 333991: Power-Driven Hand Tool Manufacturing

3547 Rolling Mill Machinery and Equipment *see* NAICS 333516: Rolling Mill Machinery and Equipment Manufacturing

3548 Electric and Gas Welding and Soldering Equipment *see* NAICS 333992: Welding and Soldering Equipment Manufacturing; NAICS 335311: Power, Distribution, and Specialty Transformer Manufacturing

3549 Metalworking Machinery, NEC *see* NAICS 333518: Other Metalworking Machinery Manufacturing

3552 Textile Machinery *see* NAICS 333292: Textile Machinery Manufacturing

3553 Woodworking Machinery *see* NAICS 333210: Sawmill and Woodworking Machinery Manufacturing

3554 Paper Industries Machinery *see* NAICS 333291: Paper Industry Machinery Manufacturing

3555 Printing Trades Machinery and Equipment *see* NAICS 333293: Printing Machinery and Equipment Manufacturing

3556 Food Products Machinery *see* NAICS 333294: Food Product Machinery Manufacturing

3559 Special Industry Machinery, NEC *see* NAICS 333220: Rubber and Plastics Industry Machinery Manufacturing; NAICS 333319: Other Commercial and Service Industry Machinery Manufacturing; NAICS 333295: Semiconductor Manufacturing Machinery; NAICS 333298: All Other Industrial Machinery Manufacturing

3561 Pumps and Pumping Equipment *see* NAICS 333911: Pump and Pumping Equipment Manufacturing

3562 Ball and Roller Bearings *see* NAICS 332991: Ball and Roller Bearing Manufacturing

3563 Air and Gas Compressors *see* NAICS 333912: Air and Gas Compressor Manufacturing

3564 Industrial and Commercial Fans and Blowers and Air Purification Equipment *see* NAICS 333411: Air Purification Equipment Manufacturing; NAICS

333412: Industrial and Commercial Fan and Blower Manufacturing

3565 Packaging Machinery *see* NAICS 333993: Packaging Machinery Manufacturing

3566 Speed Changers, Industrial High-Speed Drives, and Gears *see* NAICS 333612: Speed Changer, Industrial High-Speed Drive, and Gear Manufacturing

3567 Industrial Process Furnaces and Ovens *see* NAICS 333994: Industrial Process Furnace and Oven Manufacturing

3568 Mechanical Power Transmission Equipment, NEC *see* NAICS 333613: Mechanical Power Transmission Equipment Manufacturing

3569 General Industrial Machinery and Equipment, NEC *see* NAICS 333999: All Other General Purpose Machinery Manufacturing

3571 Electronic Computers *see* NAICS 334111: Electronic Computer Manufacturing

3572 Computer Storage Devices *see* NAICS 334112: Computer Storage Device Manufacturing

3575 Computer Terminals *see* NAICS 334113: Computer Terminal Manufacturing

3577 Computer Peripheral Equipment, NEC *see* NAICS 334119: Other Computer Peripheral Equipment Manufacturing

3578 Calculating and Accounting Machines, Except Electronic Computers *see* NAICS 334119: Other Computer Peripheral Equipment Manufacturing; NAICS 333313: Office Machinery Manufacturing

3579 Office Machines, NEC *see* NAICS 339942: Lead Pencil and Art Good Manufacturing; NAICS 334518: Watch, Clock, and Part Manufacturing; NAICS 333313: Office Machinery Manufacturing

3581 Automatic Vending Machines *see* NAICS 333311: Automatic Vending Machine Manufacturing

3582 Commercial Laundry, Drycleaning, and Pressing Machines *see* NAICS 333312: Commercial Laundry, Drycleaning, and Pressing Machine Manufacturing

3585 Air-Conditioning and Warm Air Heating Equipment and Commercial and Industrial Refrigeration Equipment *see* NAICS 336391: Motor Vehicle Air Conditioning Manufacturing; NAICS 333415: Air Conditioning and Warm Air Heating Equipment and Commercial and Industrial Refrigeration Equipment Manufacturing

3586 Measuring and Dispensing Pumps *see* NAICS 333913: Measuring and Dispensing Pump Manufacturing

3589 Service Industry Machinery, NEC *see* NAICS 333319: Other Commercial and Service Industry Machinery Manufacturing

3592 Carburetors, Pistons, Piston Rings and Valves *see* NAICS 336311: Carburetor, Piston, Piston Ring and Valve Manufacturing

3593 Fluid Power Cylinders and Actuators *see* NAICS 333995: Fluid Power Cylinder and Actuator Manufacturing

3594 Fluid Power Pumps and Motors *see* NAICS 333996: Fluid Power Pump and Motor Manufacturing

3596 Scales and Balances, Except Laboratory *see* NAICS 333997: Scale and Balance (except Laboratory) Manufacturing

3599 Industrial and Commercial Machinery and Equipment, NEC *see* NAICS 336399: All Other Motor Vehicle Part Manufacturing; NAICS 332999: All Other Miscellaneous Fabricated Metal Product Manufacturing; NAICS 333319: Other Commercial and Service Industry Machinery Manufacturing; NAICS 332710: Machine Shops; NAICS 333999: All Other General Purpose Machinery Manufacturing

ELECTRONIC & OTHER ELECTRICAL EQUIPMENT & COMPONENTS, EXCEPT COMPUTER EQUIPMENT

3612 Power, Distribution, and Specialty Transformers *see* NAICS 335311: Power, Distribution, and Specialty Transformer Manufacturing

3613 Switchgear and Switchboard Apparatus *see* NAICS 335313: Switchgear and Switchboard Apparatus Manufacturing

3621 Motors and Generators *see* NAICS 335312: Motor and Generator Manufacturing

3624 Carbon and Graphite Products *see* NAICS 335991: Carbon and Graphite Product Manufacturing

3625 Relays and Industrial Controls *see* NAICS 335314: Relay and Industrial Control Manufacturing

3629 Electrical Industrial Apparatus, NEC *see* NAICS 335999: All Other Miscellaneous Electrical Equipment and Component Manufacturing

3631 Household Cooking Equipment *see* NAICS 335221: Household Cooking Appliance Manufacturing

3632 Household Refrigerators and Home and Farm Freezers *see* NAICS 335222: Household Refrigerator and Home and Farm Freezer Manufacturing

3633 Household Laundry Equipment *see* NAICS 335224: Household Laundry Equipment Manufacturing

3634 Electric Housewares and Fans *see* NAICS 335211: Electric Houseware and Fan Manufacturing; NAICS 333414: Heating Equipment (except Electric and Warm Air Furnaces) Manufacturing

3635 Household Vacuum Cleaners *see* NAICS 335212: Household Vacuum Cleaner Manufacturing

3639 Household Appliances, NEC *see* NAICS 335212: Household Vacuum Cleaner Manufacturing; NAICS 333298: All Other Industrial Machinery Manufacturing; NAICS 335228: Other Household Appliance Manufacturing

3641 Electric Lamp Bulbs and Tubes *see* NAICS 335110: Electric Lamp Bulb and Part Manufacturing

3643 Current-Carrying Wiring Devices *see* NAICS 335931: Current-Carrying Wiring Device Manufacturing

3644 Noncurrent-Carrying Wiring Devices *see* NAICS 335932: Noncurrent-Carrying Wiring Device Manufacturing

3645 Residential Electric Lighting Fixtures *see* NAICS 335121: Residential Electric Lighting Fixture Manufacturing

3646 Commercial, Industrial, and Institutional Electric Lighting Fixtures *see* NAICS 335122: Commercial, Industrial, and Institutional Electric Lighting Fixture Manufacturing

3647 Vehicular Lighting Equipment *see* NAICS 336321: Vehicular Lighting Equipment Manufacturing

3648 Lighting Equipment, NEC *see* NAICS 335129: Other Lighting Equipment Manufacturing

3651 Household Audio and Video Equipment *see* NAICS 334310: Audio and Video Equipment Manufacturing

3652 Phonograph Records and Prerecorded Audio Tapes and Disks *see* NAICS 334612: Prerecorded Compact Disc (Except Software), Tape and Record Reproducing; NAICS 512220: Integrated Record Production/Distribution

3661 Telephone and Telegraph Apparatus *see* NAICS 334210: Telephone Apparatus Manufacturing; NAICS 334416: Electronic Coil, Transformer, and Other Inductor Manufacturing; NAICS 334418: Printed Circuit/Electronics Assembly Manufacturing

3663 Radio and Television Broadcasting and Communication Equipment *see* NAICS 334220: Radio and Television Broadcasting and Wireless Communications Equipment Manufacturing

3669 Communications Equipment, NEC *see* NAICS 334290: Other Communication Equipment Manufacturing

3671 Electron Tubes *see* NAICS 334411: Electron Tube Manufacturing

3672 Printed Circuit Boards *see* NAICS 334412: Printed Circuit Board Manufacturing

3674 Semiconductors and Related Devices *see* NAICS 334413: Semiconductor and Related Device Manufacturing

3675 Electronic Capacitors *see* NAICS 334414: Electronic Capacitor Manufacturing

3676 Electronic Resistors *see* NAICS 334415: Electronic Resistor Manufacturing

3677 Electronic Coils, Transformers, and Other Inductors *see* NAICS 334416: Electronic Coil, Transformer, and Other Inductor Manufacturing

3678 Electronic Connectors *see* NAICS 334417: Electronic Connector Manufacturing

3679 Electronic Components, NEC *see* NAICS 334220: Radio and Television Broadcasting and Wireless Communications Equipment Manufacturing; NAICS 334418: Printed Circuit/Electronics Assembly Manufacturing; NAICS 336322: Other Motor Vehicle Electrical and Electronic Equipment Manufacturing; NAICS 334419: Other Electronic Component Manufacturing

3691 Storage Batteries *see* NAICS 335911: Storage Battery Manufacturing

3692 Primary Batteries, Dry and Wet *see* NAICS 335912: Dry and Wet Primary Battery Manufacturing

3694 Electrical Equipment for Internal Combustion Engines *see* NAICS 336322: Other Motor Vehicle Electrical and Electronic Equipment Manufacturing

3695 Magnetic and Optical Recording Media *see* NAICS 334613: Magnetic and Optical Recording Media Manufacturing

3699 Electrical Machinery, Equipment, and Supplies, NEC *see* NAICS 333319: Other Commercial and Service Industry Machinery Manufacturing; NAICS 333618: Other Engine Equipment Manufacturing; NAICS 334119: Other Computer Peripheral Equipment Manufacturing; NAICS 335129: Other Lighting Equipment Manufacturing; NAICS 335999: All Other Miscellaneous Electrical Equipment and Component Manufacturing

TRANSPORTATION EQUIPMENT

3711 Motor Vehicles and Passenger Car Bodies *see* NAICS 336111: Automobile Manufacturing; NAICS 336112: Light Truck and Utility Vehicle Manufacturing; NAICS 336120: Heavy Duty Truck Manufacturing; NAICS 336211: Motor Vehicle Body Manufacturing; NAICS 336992: Military Armored Vehicle, Tank, and Tank Component Manufacturing

3713 Truck and Bus Bodies *see* NAICS 336211: Motor Vehicle Body Manufacturing

3714 Motor Vehicle Parts and Accessories *see* NAICS 336211: Motor Vehicle Body Manufacturing; NAICS 336312: Gasoline Engine and Engine Parts Manufacturing; NAICS 336322: Other Motor Vehicle Electrical and Electronic Equipment

Manufacturing; NAICS 336330: Motor Vehicle Steering and Suspension Components (except Spring) Manufacturing; NAICS 336340: Motor Vehicle Brake System Manufacturing; NAICS 336350: Motor Vehicle Transmission and Power Train Part Manufacturing; NAICS 336399: All Other Motor Vehicle Parts Manufacturing

3715 Truck Trailers *see* NAICS 336212: Truck Trailer Manufacturing

3716 Motor Homes *see* NAICS 336213: Motor Home Manufacturing

3721 Aircraft *see* NAICS 336411: Aircraft Manufacturing

3724 Aircraft Engines and Engine Parts *see* NAICS 336412: Aircraft Engine and Engine Parts Manufacturing

3728 Aircraft Parts and Auxiliary Equipment, NEC *see* NAICS 332912: Fluid Power Valve and Hose Fitting Manufacturing; NAICS 336413: Other Aircraft Part and Auxiliary Equipment Manufacturing

3731 Ship Building and Repairing *see* NAICS 336611: Ship Building and Repairing

3732 Boat Building and Repairing *see* NAICS 811490: Other Personal and Household Goods Repair and Maintenance; NAICS 336612: Boat Building

3743 Railroad Equipment *see* NAICS 333911: Pump and Pumping Equipment Manufacturing; NAICS 336510: Railroad Rolling Stock Manufacturing

3751 Motorcycles, Bicycles, and Parts *see* NAICS 336991: Motorcycle, Bicycle, and Parts Manufacturing

3761 Guided Missiles and Space Vehicles *see* NAICS 336414: Guided Missile and Space Vehicle Manufacturing

3764 Guided Missile and Space Vehicle Propulsion Units and Propulsion Unit Parts *see* NAICS 336415: Guided Missile and Space Vehicle Propulsion Unit and Propulsion Unit Parts Manufacturing

3769 Guided Missile Space Vehicle Parts and Auxiliary Equipment, NEC *see* NAICS 336419: Other Guided Missile and Space Vehicle Parts and Auxiliary Equipment Manufacturing

3792 Travel Trailers and Campers *see* NAICS 336214: Travel Trailer and Camper Manufacturing

3795 Tanks and Tank Components *see* NAICS 336992: Military Armored Vehicle, Tank, and Tank Component Manufacturing

3799 Transportation Equipment, NEC *see* NAICS 336214: Travel Trailer and Camper Manufacturing; NAICS 332212: Hand and Edge Tool Manufacturing; NAICS 336999: All Other Transportation Equipment Manufacturing

MEASURING, ANALYZING, & CONTROLLING INSTRUMENTS

3812   Search, Detection, Navigation, Guidance, Aeronautical, and Nautical Systems and Instruments *see* NAICS 334511: Search, Detection, Navigation, Guidance, Aeronautical, and Nautical System and Instrument Manufacturing

3821   Laboratory Apparatus and Furniture *see* NAICS 339111: Laboratory Apparatus and Furniture Manufacturing

3822   Automatic Controls for Regulating Residential and Commercial Environments and Appliances *see* NAICS 334512: Automatic Environmental Control Manufacturing for Regulating Residential, Commercial, and Appliance Use

3823   Industrial Instruments for Measurement, Display, and Control of Process Variables; and Related Products *see* NAICS 334513: Instruments and Related Product Manufacturing for Measuring Displaying, and Controlling Industrial Process Variables

3824   Totalizing Fluid Meters and Counting Devices *see* NAICS 334514: Totalizing Fluid Meter and Counting Device Manufacturing

3825   Instruments for Measuring and Testing of Electricity and Electrical Signals *see* NAICS 334416: Electronic Coil, Transformer, and Other Inductor Manufacturing; NAICS 334515: Instrument Manufacturing for Measuring and Testing Electricity and Electrical Signals

3826   Laboratory Analytical Instruments *see* NAICS 334516: Analytical Laboratory Instrument Manufacturing

3827   Optical Instruments and Lenses *see* NAICS 333314: Optical Instrument and Lens Manufacturing

3829   Measuring and Controlling Devices, NEC *see* NAICS 339112: Surgical and Medical Instrument Manufacturing; NAICS 334519: Other Measuring and Controlling Device Manufacturing

3841   Surgical and Medical Instruments and Apparatus *see* NAICS 339112: Surgical and Medical Instrument Manufacturing

3842   Orthopedic, Prosthetic, and Surgical Appliances and Supplies *see* NAICS 339113: Surgical Appliance and Supplies Manufacturing; NAICS 334510: Electromedical and Electrotherapeutic Apparatus Manufacturing

3843   Dental Equipment and Supplies *see* NAICS 339114: Dental Equipment and Supplies Manufacturing

3844   X-Ray Apparatus and Tubes and Related Irradiation Apparatus *see* NAICS 334517: Irradiation Apparatus Manufacturing

3845   Electromedical and Electrotherapeutic Apparatus *see* NAICS 334517: Irradiation Apparatus Manufacturing; NAICS 334510: Electromedical and Electrotherapeutic Apparatus Manufacturing

3851   Ophthalmic Goods *see* NAICS 339115: Ophthalmic Goods Manufacturing

3861   Photographic Equipment and Supplies *see* NAICS 333315: Photographic and Photocopying Equipment Manufacturing; NAICS 325992: Photographic Film, Paper, Plate and Chemical Manufacturing

3873   Watches, Clocks, Clockwork Operated Devices and Parts *see* NAICS 334518: Watch, Clock, and Part Manufacturing

MISCELLANEOUS MANUFACTURING INDUSTRIES

3911   Jewelry, Precious Metal *see* NAICS 339911: Jewelry (Including Precious Metal) Manufacturing

3914   Silverware, Plated Ware, and Stainless Steel Ware *see* NAICS 332211: Cutlery and Flatware (except Precious) Manufacturing; NAICS 339912: Silverware and Plated Ware Manufacturing

3915   Jewelers' Findings and Materials, and Lapidary Work *see* NAICS 339913: Jewelers' Material and Lapidary Work Manufacturing

3931   Musical Instruments *see* NAICS 339992: Musical Instrument Manufacturing

3942   Dolls and Stuffed Toys *see* NAICS 339931: Doll and Stuffed Toy Manufacturing

3944   Games, Toys, and Children's Vehicles, Except Dolls and Bicycles *see* NAICS 336991: Motorcycle, Bicycle, and Parts Manufacturing; NAICS 339932: Game, Toy, and Children's Vehicle Manufacturing

3949   Sporting and Athletic Goods, NEC *see* NAICS 339920: Sporting and Athletic Good Manufacturing

3951   Pens, Mechanical Pencils, and Parts *see* NAICS 339941: Pen and Mechanical Pencil Manufacturing

3952   Lead Pencils, Crayons, and Artist's Materials *see* NAICS 337127: Institutional Furniture Manufacturing; NAICS 325998: All Other Miscellaneous Chemical Product Manufacturing; NAICS 339942: Lead Pencil and Art Good Manufacturing

3953   Marking Devices *see* NAICS 339943: Marking Device Manufacturing

3955   Carbon Paper and Inked Ribbons *see* NAICS 339944: Carbon Paper and Inked Ribbon Manufacturing

3961   Costume Jewelry and Costume Novelties, Except Precious Metals *see* NAICS 339914: Costume Jewelry and Novelty Manufacturing

3965 Fasteners, Buttons, Needles, and Pins *see* NAICS 339993: Fastener, Button, Needle and Pin Manufacturing

3991 Brooms and Brushes *see* NAICS 339994: Broom, Brush and Mop Manufacturing

3993 Signs and Advertising Specialties *see* NAICS 339950: Sign Manufacturing

3995 Burial Caskets *see* NAICS 339995: Burial Casket Manufacturing

3996 Linoleum, Asphalted-Felt-Base, and Other Hard Surface Floor Coverings, NEC *see* NAICS 326192: Resilient Floor Covering Manufacturing

3999 Manufacturing Industries, NEC *see* NAICS 337127: Institutional Furniture Manufacturing; NAICS 321999: All Other Miscellaneous Wood Product Manufacturing; NAICS 316110: Leather and Hide Tanning and Finishing; NAICS 335121: Residential Electric Lighting Fixture Manufacturing; NAICS 325998: All Other Miscellaneous Chemical Product Manufacturing; NAICS 332999: All Other Miscellaneous Fabricated Metal Product Manufacturing; NAICS 326199: All Other Plastics Product Manufacturing; NAICS 323112: Commercial Flexographic Printing; NAICS 323111: Commercial Gravure Printing; NAICS 323110: Commercial Lithographic Printing; NAICS 323113: Commercial Screen Printing; NAICS 323119: Other Commercial Printing; NAICS 332212: Hand and Edge Tool Manufacturing; NAICS 339999: All Other Miscellaneous Manufacturing

TRANSPORTATION, COMMUNICATIONS, ELECTRIC, GAS, & SANITARY SERVICES

4011 Railroads, Line-haul Operating *see* NAICS 482111: Line-Haul Railroads

4013 Railroad Switching and Terminal Establishments *see* NAICS 482112: Short Line Railroads; NAICS 488210: Support Activities for Rail Transportation

4111 Local and Suburban Transit *see* NAICS 485111: Mixed Mode Transit Systems; NAICS 485112: Commuter Rail Systems; NAICS 485113: Bus and Motor Vehicle Transit Systems; NAICS 485119: Other Urban Transit Systems; NAICS 485999: All Other Transit and Ground Passenger Transportation

4119 Local Passenger Transportation, NEC *see* NAICS 621910: Ambulance Service; NAICS 485410: School and Employee Bus Industry; NAICS 487110: Scenic and Sightseeing Transportation; NAICS 485991: Special Needs Transportation; NAICS 485999: All Other Transit and Ground

Passenger Transportation; NAICS 485320: Limousine Service

4121 Taxicabs *see* NAICS 485310: Taxi Service

4131 Intercity and Rural Bus Transportation *see* NAICS 485210: Interurban and Rural Bus Lines

4141 Local Bus Charter Service *see* NAICS 485510: Charter Bus Industry

4142 Bus Charter Service, Except Local *see* NAICS 485510: Charter Bus Industry

4151 School Buses *see* NAICS 485410: School and Employee Bus Industry

4173 Terminal and Service Facilities for Motor Vehicle Passenger Transportation *see* NAICS 488490: Other Support Activities for Road Transportation

4212 Local Trucking Without Storage *see* NAICS 562111: Solid Waste Collection; NAICS 562112: Hazardous Waste Collection; NAICS 562119: Other Waste Collection; NAICS 484110: General Freight Trucking, Local; NAICS 484210: Used Household and Office Goods Moving; NAICS 484220: Specialized Freight (except Used Goods) Trucking, Local

4213 Trucking, Except Local *see* NAICS 484121: General Freight Trucking, Long-Distance, Truckload; NAICS 484122: General Freight Trucking, Long-Distance, Less Than Truckload; NAICS 484210: Used Household and Office Goods Moving; NAICS 484230: Specialized Freight (except Used Goods) Trucking, Long-Distance

4214 Local Trucking with Storage *see* NAICS 484110: General Freight Trucking, Local; NAICS 484210: Used Household and Office Goods Moving; NAICS 484220: Specialized Freight (except Used Goods) Trucking, Local

4215 Couriers Services Except by Air *see* NAICS 492110: Couriers; NAICS 492210: Local Messengers and Local Delivery

4221 Farm Product Warehousing and Storage *see* NAICS 493130: Farm Product Storage Facilities

4222 Refrigerated Warehousing and Storage *see* NAICS 493120: Refrigerated Storage Facilities

4225 General Warehousing and Storage *see* NAICS 493110: General Warehousing and Storage Facilities; NAICS 531130: Lessors of Mini-warehouses and Self Storage Units

4226 Special Warehousing and Storage, NEC *see* NAICS 493120: Refrigerated Storage Facilities; NAICS 493110: General Warehousing and Storage Facilities; NAICS 493190: All Other Warehousing and Storage Facilities

4231 Terminal and Joint Terminal Maintenance Facilities for Motor Freight Transportation *see* NAICS 488490: Other Support Activities for Road Transportation

4311 United States Postal Service *see* NAICS 491110: Postal Service

4412 Deep Sea Foreign Transportation of Freight *see* NAICS 483111: Deep Sea Freight Transportation

4424 Deep Sea Domestic Transportation of Freight *see* NAICS 483113: Coastal and Great Lakes Freight Transportation

4432 Freight Transportation on the Great Lakes-St. Lawrence Seaway *see* NAICS 483113: Coastal and Great Lakes Freight Transportation

4449 Water Transportation of Freight, NEC *see* NAICS 483211: Inland Water Freight Transportation

4481 Deep Sea Transportation of Passengers, Except by Ferry *see* NAICS 483112: Deep Sea Passenger Transportation; NAICS 483114: Coastal and Great Lakes Passenger Transportation

4482 Ferries *see* NAICS 483114: Coastal and Great Lakes Passenger Transportation; NAICS 483212: Inland Water Passenger Transportation

4489 Water Transportation of Passengers, NEC *see* NAICS 483212: Inland Water Passenger Transportation; NAICS 487210: Scenic and Sightseeing Transportation, Water

4491 Marine Cargo Handling *see* NAICS 488310: Port and Harbor Operations; NAICS 488320: Marine Cargo Handling

4492 Towing and Tugboat Services *see* NAICS 483113: Coastal and Great Lakes Freight Transportation; NAICS 483211: Inland Water Freight Transportation; NAICS 488330: Navigational Services to Shipping

4493 Marinas *see* NAICS 713930: Marinas

4499 Water Transportation Services, NEC *see* NAICS 532411: Commercial Air, Rail, and Water Transportation Equipment Rental and Leasing; NAICS 488310: Port and Harbor Operations; NAICS 488330: Navigational Services to Shipping; NAICS 488390: Other Support Activities for Water Transportation

4512 Air Transportation, Scheduled *see* NAICS 481111: Scheduled Passenger Air Transportation; NAICS 481112: Scheduled Freight Air Transportation

4513 Air Courier Services *see* NAICS 492110: Couriers

4522 Air Transportation, Nonscheduled *see* NAICS 621910: Ambulance Services; NAICS 481212: Nonscheduled Chartered Freight Air Transportation; NAICS 481211: Nonscheduled Chartered Passenger Air Transportation; NAICS 487990: Scenic and Sightseeing Transportation

4581 Airports, Flying Fields, and Airport Terminal Services *see* NAICS 488111: Air Traffic Control; NAICS 488119: Other Airport Operations; NAICS 561720: Janitorial Services; NAICS

488190: Other Support Activities for Air Transportation

4612 Crude Petroleum Pipelines *see* NAICS 486110: Pipeline Transportation of Crude Oil

4613 Refined Petroleum Pipelines *see* NAICS 486910: Pipeline Transportation of Refined Petroleum Products

4619 Pipelines, NEC *see* NAICS 486990: All Other Pipeline Transportation

4724 Travel Agencies *see* NAICS 561510: Travel Agencies

4725 Tour Operators *see* NAICS 561520: Tour Operators

4729 Arrangement of Passenger Transportation, NEC *see* NAICS 488999: All Other Support Activities for Transportation; NAICS 561599: All Other Travel Arrangement and Reservation Services

4731 Arrangement of Transportation of Freight and Cargo *see* NAICS 541618: Other Management Consulting Services; NAICS 488510: Freight Transportation Arrangement

4741 Rental of Railroad Cars *see* NAICS 532411: Commercial Air, Rail, and Water Transportation Equipment Rental and Leasing; NAICS 488210: Support Activities for Rail Transportation

4783 Packing and Crating *see* NAICS 488991: Packing and Crating

4785 Fixed Facilities and Inspection and Weighing Services for Motor Vehicle Transportation *see* NAICS 488390: Other Support Activities for Water Transportation; NAICS 488490: Other Support Activities for Road Transportation

4789 Transportation Services, NEC *see* NAICS 488999: All Other Support Activities for Transportation *see* NAICS 487110: Scenic and Sightseeing Transportation, Land; NAICS 488210: Support Activities for Rail Transportation

4812 Radiotelephone Communications *see* NAICS 513321: Paging; NAICS 513322: Cellular and Other Wireless Telecommunications; NAICS 513330: Telecommunications Resellers

4813 Telephone Communications, Except Radiotelephone *see* NAICS 513310: Wired Telecommunications Carriers; NAICS 513330: Telecommunications Resellers

4822 Telegraph and Other Message Communications *see* NAICS 513310: Wired Telecommunications Carriers

4832 Radio Broadcasting Stations *see* NAICS 513111: Radio Networks; NAICS 513112: Radio Stations

4833 Television Broadcasting Stations *see* NAICS 513120: Television Broadcasting

4841 Cable and Other Pay Television Services *see* NAICS 513210: Cable Networks; NAICS 513220: Cable and Other Program Distribution

4899 Communications Services, NEC *see* NAICS 513322: Cellular and Other Wireless Telecommunications; NAICS 513340: Satellite Telecommunications; NAICS 513390: Other Telecommunications

4911 Electric Services *see* NAICS 221111: Hydroelectric Power Generation; NAICS 221112: Fossil Fuel Electric Power Generation; NAICS 221113: Nuclear Electric Power Generation; NAICS 221119: Other Electric Power Generation; NAICS 221121: Electric Bulk Power Transmission and Control; NAICS 221122: Electric Power Distribution

4922 Natural Gas Transmission *see* NAICS 486210: Pipeline Transportation of Natural Gas

4923 Natural Gas Transmission and Distribution *see* NAICS 221210: Natural Gas Distribution; NAICS 486210: Pipeline Transportation of Natural Gas

4924 Natural Gas Distribution *see* NAICS 221210: Natural Gas Distribution

4925 Mixed, Manufactured, or Liquefied Petroleum Gas Production and/or Distribution *see* NAICS 221210: Natural Gas Distribution

4931 Electric and Other Services Combined *see* NAICS 221111: Hydroelectric Power Generation; NAICS 221112: Fossil Fuel Electric Power Generation; NAICS 221113: Nuclear Electric Power Generation; NAICS 221119: Other Electric Power Generation; NAICS 221121: Electric Bulk Power Transmission and Control; NAICS 221122: Electric Power Distribution; NAICS 221210: Natural Gas Distribution

4932 Gas and Other Services Combined *see* NAICS 221210: Natural Gas Distribution

4939 Combination Utilities, NEC *see* NAICS 221111: Hydroelectric Power Generation; NAICS 221112: Fossil Fuel Electric Power Generation; NAICS 221113: Nuclear Electric Power Generation; NAICS 221119: Other Electric Power Generation; NAICS 221121: Electric Bulk Power Transmission and Control; NAICS 221122: Electric Power Distribution; NAICS 221210: Natural Gas Distribution

4941 Water Supply *see* NAICS 221310: Water Supply and Irrigation Systems

4952 Sewerage Systems *see* NAICS 221320: Sewage Treatment Facilities

4953 Refuse Systems *see* NAICS 562111: Solid Waste Collection; NAICS 562112: Hazardous Waste Collection; NAICS 562920: Materials Recovery Facilities; NAICS 562119: Other Waste Collection; NAICS 562211: Hazardous Waste Treatment and Disposal; NAICS 562212: Solid Waste Landfills; NAICS 562213: Solid Waste Combustors and Incinerators; NAICS 562219: Other Nonhazardous Waste Treatment and Disposal

4959 Sanitary Services, NEC *see* NAICS 488119: Other Airport Operations; NAICS 562910: Remediation Services; NAICS 561710: Exterminating and Pest Control Services; NAICS 562998: All Other Miscellaneous Waste Management

4961 Steam and Air-Conditioning Supply *see* NAICS 221330: Steam and Air-Conditioning Supply

4971 Irrigation Systems *see* NAICS 221310: Water Supply and Irrigation Systems

WHOLESALE TRADE

5012 Automobiles and Other Motor Vehicles *see* NAICS 421110: Automobile and Other Motor Vehicle Wholesalers

5013 Motor Vehicle Supplies and New Parts *see* NAICS 441310: Automotive Parts and Accessories Stores; NAICS 421120: Motor Vehicle Supplies and New Part Wholesalers

5014 Tires and Tubes *see* NAICS 441320: Tire Dealers; NAICS 421130: Tire and Tube Wholesalers

5015 Motor Vehicle Parts, Used *see* NAICS 421140: Motor Vehicle Part (Used) Wholesalers

5021 Furniture *see* NAICS 442110: Furniture Stores; NAICS 421210: Furniture Wholesalers

5023 Home Furnishings *see* NAICS 442210: Floor Covering Stores; NAICS 421220: Home Furnishing Wholesalers

5031 Lumber, Plywood, Millwork, and Wood Panels *see* NAICS 444190: Other Building Material Dealers; NAICS 421310: Lumber, Plywood, Millwork, and Wood Panel Wholesalers

5032 Brick, Stone and Related Construction Materials *see* NAICS 444190: Other Building Material Dealers; NAICS 421320: Brick, Stone and Related Construction Material Wholesalers

5033 Roofing, Siding, and Insulation Materials *see* NAICS 421330: Roofing, Siding, and Insulation Material Wholesalers

5039 Construction Materials, NEC *see* NAICS 444190: Other Building Material Dealers; NAICS 421390: Other Construction Material Wholesalers

5043 Photographic Equipment and Supplies *see* NAICS 421410: Photographic Equipment and Supplies Wholesalers

5044 Office Equipment *see* NAICS 421420: Office Equipment Wholesalers

5045 Computers and Computer Peripheral Equipment and Software *see* NAICS 421430: Computer and Computer Peripheral Equipment and Software Wholesalers; NAICS 443120: Computer and Software Stores

5046 Commercial Equipment, NEC *see* NAICS 421440: Other Commercial Equipment Wholesalers

5047 Medical, Dental, and Hospital Equipment and Supplies *see* NAICS 421450: Medical, Dental and Hospital Equipment and Supplies Wholesalers; NAICS 446199: All Other Health and Personal Care Stores

5048 Ophthalmic Goods *see* NAICS 421460: Ophthalmic Goods Wholesalers

5049 Professional Equipment and Supplies, NEC *see* NAICS 421490: Other Professional Equipment and Supplies Wholesalers; NAICS 453210: Office Supplies and Stationery Stores

5051 Metals Service Centers and Offices *see* NAICS 421510: Metals Service Centers and Offices

5052 Coal and Other Minerals and Ores *see* NAICS 421520: Coal and Other Mineral and Ore Wholesalers

5063 Electrical Apparatus and Equipment Wiring Supplies, and Construction Materials *see* NAICS 444190: Other Building Material Dealers; NAICS 421610: Electrical Apparatus and Equipment, Wiring Supplies and Construction Material Wholesalers

5064 Electrical Appliances, Television and Radio Sets *see* NAICS 421620: Electrical Appliance, Television and Radio Set Wholesalers

5065 Electronic Parts and Equipment, Not Elsewhere Classified *see* NAICS 421690: Other Electronic Parts and Equipment Wholesalers

5072 Hardware *see* NAICS 421710: Hardware Wholesalers

5074 Plumbing and Heating Equipment and Supplies (Hydronics) *see* NAICS 444190: Other Building Material Dealers; NAICS 421720: Plumbing and Heating Equipment and Supplies (Hydronics) Wholesalers

5075 Warm Air Heating and Air-Conditioning Equipment and Supplies *see* NAICS 421730: Warm Air Heating and Air-Conditioning Equipment and Supplies Wholesalers

5078 Refrigeration Equipment and Supplies *see* NAICS 421740: Refrigeration Equipment and Supplies Wholesalers

5082 Construction and Mining (Except Petroleum) Machinery and Equipment *see* NAICS 421810: Construction and Mining (except Petroleum) Machinery and Equipment Wholesalers

5083 Farm and Garden Machinery and Equipment *see* NAICS 421820: Farm and Garden Machinery and Equipment Wholesalers; NAICS 444210: Outdoor Power Equipment Stores

5084 Industrial Machinery and Equipment *see* NAICS 421830: Industrial Machinery and Equipment Wholesalers

5085 Industrial Supplies *see* NAICS 421830: Industrial Machinery and Equipment Wholesalers; NAICS 421840: Industrial Supplies Wholesalers

5087 Service Establishment Equipment and Supplies *see* NAICS 421850: Service Establishment Equipment and Supplies Wholesalers; NAICS 446120: Cosmetics, Beauty Supplies, and Perfume Stores

5088 Transportation Equipment and Supplies, Except Motor Vehicles *see* NAICS 421860: Transportation Equipment and Supplies (except Motor Vehicles) Wholesalers

5091 Sporting and Recreational Goods and Supplies *see* NAICS 421910: Sporting and Recreational Goods and Supplies Wholesalers

5092 Toys and Hobby Goods and Supplies *see* NAICS 421920: Toy and Hobby Goods and Supplies Wholesalers

5093 Scrap and Waste Materials *see* NAICS 421930: Recyclable Material Wholesalers

5094 Jewelry, Watches, Precious Stones, and Precious Metals *see* NAICS 421940: Jewelry, Watch, Precious Stone, and Precious Metal Wholesalers

5099 Durable Goods, NEC *see* NAICS 421990: Other Miscellaneous Durable Goods Wholesalers

5111 Printing and Writing Paper *see* NAICS 422110: Printing and Writing Paper Wholesalers

5112 Stationery and Office Supplies *see* NAICS 453210: Office Supplies and Stationery Stores; NAICS 422120: Stationery and Office Supplies Wholesalers

5113 Industrial and Personal Service Paper *see* NAICS 422130: Industrial and Personal Service Paper Wholesalers

5122 Drugs, Drug Proprietaries, and Druggists' Sundries *see* NAICS 422210: Drugs, Drug Proprietaries, and Druggists' Sundries Wholesalers

5131 Piece Goods, Notions, and Other Dry Goods *see* NAICS 313311: Broadwoven Fabric Finishing Mills; NAICS 313312: Textile and Fabric Finishing (except Broadwoven Fabric) Mills; NAICS 422310: Piece Goods, Notions, and Other Dry Goods Wholesalers

5136 Men's and Boys' Clothing and Furnishings *see* NAICS 422320: Men's and Boys' Clothing and Furnishings Wholesalers

5137 Women's Children's and Infants' Clothing and Accessories *see* NAICS 422330: Women's, Children's, and Infants' Clothing and Accessories Wholesalers

5139 Footwear *see* NAICS 422340: Footwear Wholesalers

5141 Groceries, General Line *see* NAICS 422410: General Line Grocery Wholesalers

5142 Packaged Frozen Foods *see* NAICS 422420: Packaged Frozen Food Wholesalers

5143 Dairy Products, Except Dried or Canned *see* NAICS 422430: Dairy Products (except Dried or Canned) Wholesalers

5144 Poultry and Poultry Products *see* NAICS 422440: Poultry and Poultry Product Wholesalers

5145 Confectionery *see* NAICS 422450: Confectionery Wholesalers

5146 Fish and Seafoods *see* NAICS 422460: Fish and Seafood Wholesalers

5147 Meats and Meat Products *see* NAICS 311612: Meat Processed from Carcasses; NAICS 422470: Meat and Meat Product Wholesalers

5148 Fresh Fruits and Vegetables *see* NAICS 422480: Fresh Fruit and Vegetable Wholesalers

5149 Groceries and Related Products, NEC *see* NAICS 422490: Other Grocery and Related Product Wholesalers

5153 Grain and Field Beans *see* NAICS 422510: Grain and Field Bean Wholesalers

5154 Livestock *see* NAICS 422520: Livestock Wholesalers

5159 Farm-Product Raw Materials, NEC *see* NAICS 422590: Other Farm Product Raw Material Wholesalers

5162 Plastics Materials and Basic Forms and Shapes *see* NAICS 422610: Plastics Materials and Basic Forms and Shapes Wholesalers

5169 Chemicals and Allied Products, NEC *see* NAICS 422690: Other Chemical and Allied Products Wholesalers

5171 Petroleum Bulk Stations and Terminals *see* NAICS 454311: Heating Oil Dealers; NAICS 454312: Liquefied Petroleum Gas (Bottled Gas) Dealers; NAICS 422710: Petroleum Bulk Stations and Terminals

5172 Petroleum and Petroleum Products Wholesalers, Except Bulk Stations and Terminals *see* NAICS 422720: Petroleum and Petroleum Products Wholesalers (except Bulk Stations and Terminals)

5181 Beer and Ale *see* NAICS 422810: Beer and Ale Wholesalers

5182 Wine and Distilled Alcoholic Beverages *see* NAICS 422820: Wine and Distilled Alcoholic Beverage Wholesalers

5191 Farm Supplies *see* NAICS 444220: Nursery and Garden Centers; NAICS 422910: Farm Supplies Wholesalers

5192 Books, Periodicals, and Newspapers *see* NAICS 422920: Book, Periodical and Newspaper Wholesalers

5193 Flowers, Nursery Stock, and Florists' Supplies *see* NAICS 422930: Flower, Nursery Stock and Florists' Supplies Wholesalers; NAICS 444220: Nursery and Garden Centers

5194 Tobacco and Tobacco Products *see* NAICS 422940: Tobacco and Tobacco Product Wholesalers

5198 Paint, Varnishes, and Supplies *see* NAICS 422950: Paint, Varnish and Supplies Wholesalers; NAICS 444120: Paint and Wallpaper Stores

5199 Nondurable Goods, NEC *see* NAICS 541890: Other Services Related to Advertising; NAICS 422990: Other Miscellaneous Nondurable Goods Wholesalers

RETAIL TRADE

5211 Lumber and Other Building Materials Dealers *see* NAICS 444110: Home Centers; NAICS 421310: Lumber, Plywood, Millwork, and Wood Panel Wholesalers; NAICS 444190: Other Building Material Dealers

5231 Paint, Glass, and Wallpaper Stores *see* NAICS 422950: Paint, Varnish, and Supplies Wholesalers; NAICS 444190: Other Building Material Dealers; NAICS 444120: Paint and Wallpaper Stores

5251 Hardware Stores *see* NAICS 444130: Hardware Stores

5261 Retail Nurseries *see* NAICS 444220: Nursery and Garden Centers; NAICS 453998: All Other Miscellaneous Store Retailers (except Tobacco Stores); NAICS 444210: Outdoor Power Equipment Stores

5271 Mobile Home Dealers *see* NAICS 453930: Manufactured (Mobile) Home Dealers

5311 Department Stores *see* NAICS 452110: Department Stores

5331 Variety Stores *see* NAICS 452990: All Other General Merchandise Stores

5399 Miscellaneous General Merchandise Stores *see* NAICS 452910: Warehouse Clubs and Superstores; NAICS 452990: All Other General Merchandise Stores

5411 Grocery Stores *see* NAICS 447110: Gasoline Stations with Convenience Stores; NAICS 445110: Supermarkets and Other Grocery (except Convenience) Stores; NAICS 452910: Warehouse Clubs and Superstores; NAICS 445120: Convenience Stores

5421 Meat and Fish (Seafood) Markets, Including Freezer Provisioners *see* NAICS 454390: Other Direct Selling Establishments; NAICS 445210: Meat Markets; NAICS 445220: Fish and Seafood Markets

5431 Fruit and Vegetable Markets *see* NAICS 445230: Fruit and Vegetable Markets

5441 Candy, Nut, and Confectionery Stores *see* NAICS 445292: Confectionery and Nut Stores

5451 Dairy Products Stores *see* NAICS 445299: All Other Specialty Food Stores

5461 Retail Bakeries *see* NAICS 722213: Snack and Nonalcoholic Beverage Bars; NAICS 311811: Retail Bakeries; NAICS 445291: Baked Goods Stores

5499 Miscellaneous Food Stores *see* NAICS 445210: Meat Markets; NAICS 722211: Limited-Service Restaurants; NAICS 446191: Food (Health) Supplement Stores; NAICS 445299: All Other Specialty Food Stores

5511 Motor Vehicle Dealers (New and Used) *see* NAICS 441110: New Car Dealers

5521 Motor Vehicle Dealers (Used Only) *see* NAICS 441120: Used Car Dealers

5531 Auto and Home Supply Stores *see* NAICS 441320: Tire Dealers; NAICS 441310: Automotive Parts and Accessories Stores

5541 Gasoline Service Stations *see* NAICS 447110: Gasoline Stations with Convenience Stores; NAICS 447190: Other Gasoline Stations

5551 Boat Dealers *see* NAICS 441222: Boat Dealers

5561 Recreational Vehicle Dealers *see* NAICS 441210: Recreational Vehicle Dealers

5571 Motorcycle Dealers *see* NAICS 441221: Motorcycle Dealers

5599 Automotive Dealers, NEC *see* NAICS 441229: All Other Motor Vehicle Dealers

5611 Men's and Boys' Clothing and Accessory Stores *see* NAICS 448110: Men's Clothing Stores; NAICS 448150: Clothing Accessories Stores

5621 Women's Clothing Stores *see* NAICS 448120: Women's Clothing Stores

5632 Women's Accessory and Specialty Stores *see* NAICS 448190: Other Clothing Stores; NAICS 448150: Clothing Accessories Stores

5641 Children's and Infants' Wear Stores *see* NAICS 448130: Children's and Infants' Clothing Stores

5651 Family Clothing Stores *see* NAICS 448140: Family Clothing Stores

5661 Shoe Stores *see* NAICS 448210: Shoe Stores

5699 Miscellaneous Apparel and Accessory Stores *see* NAICS 448190: Other Clothing Stores; NAICS 448150: Clothing Accessories Stores

5712 Furniture Stores *see* NAICS 337122: Nonupholstered Wood Household Furniture Manufacturing; NAICS 337110: Wood Kitchen Cabinet and Counter Top Manufacturing; NAICS 337121: Upholstered Wood Household Furniture Manufacturing; NAICS 442110: Furniture Stores

5713 Floor Covering Stores *see* NAICS 442210: Floor Covering Stores

5714 Drapery, Curtain, and Upholstery Stores *see* NAICS 442291: Window Treatment Stores; NAICS

451130: Sewing, Needlework, and Piece Goods Stores; NAICS 314121: Curtain and Drapery Mills

5719 Miscellaneous Homefurnishings Stores *see* NAICS 442291: Window Treatment Stores; NAICS 442299: All Other Home Furnishings Stores

5722 Household Appliance Stores *see* NAICS 443111: Household Appliance Stores

5731 Radio, Television, and Consumer Electronics Stores *see* NAICS 443112: Radio, Television, and Other Electronics Stores; NAICS 441310: Automotive Parts and Accessories Stores

5734 Computer and Computer Software Stores *see* NAICS 443120: Computer and Software Stores

5735 Record and Prerecorded Tape Stores *see* NAICS 451220: Prerecorded Tape, Compact Disc, and Record Stores

5736 Musical Instrument Stores *see* NAICS 451140: Musical Instrument and Supplies Stores

5812 Eating and Drinking Places *see* NAICS 722110: Full-Service Restaurants; NAICS 722211: Limited-Service Restaurants; NAICS 722212: Cafeterias; NAICS 722213: Snack and Nonalcoholic Beverage Bars; NAICS 722310: Foodservice Contractors; NAICS 722320: Caterers; NAICS 711110: Theater Companies and Dinner Theaters

5813 Drinking Places (Alcoholic Beverages) *see* NAICS 722410: Drinking Places (Alcoholic Beverages)

5912 Drug Stores and Proprietary Stores *see* NAICS 446110: Pharmacies and Drug Stores

5921 Liquor Stores *see* NAICS 445310: Beer, Wine and Liquor Stores

5932 Used Merchandise Stores *see* NAICS 522298: All Other Non-Depository Credit Intermediation; NAICS 453310: Used Merchandise Stores

5941 Sporting Goods Stores and Bicycle Shops *see* NAICS 451110: Sporting Goods Stores

5942 Book Stores *see* NAICS 451211: Book Stores

5943 Stationery Stores *see* NAICS 453210: Office Supplies and Stationery Stores

5944 Jewelry Stores *see* NAICS 448310: Jewelry Stores

5945 Hobby, Toy, and Game Shops *see* NAICS 451120: Hobby, Toy and Game Stores

5946 Camera and Photographic Supply Stores *see* NAICS 443130: Camera and Photographic Supplies Stores

5947 Gift, Novelty, and Souvenir Shops *see* NAICS 453220: Gift, Novelty, and Souvenir Stores

5948 Luggage and Leather Goods Stores *see* NAICS 448320: Luggage and Leather Goods Stores

5949 Sewing, Needlework, and Piece Goods Stores *see* NAICS 451130: Sewing, Needlework, and Piece Goods Stores

5961 Catalog and Mail-Order Houses *see* NAICS 454110: Electronic Shopping and Mail-Order Houses

5962 Automatic Merchandising Machine Operator *see* NAICS 454210: Vending Machine Operators

5963 Direct Selling Establishments *see* NAICS 722330: Mobile Caterers; NAICS 454390: Other Direct Selling Establishments

5983 Fuel Oil Dealers *see* NAICS 454311: Heating Oil Dealers

5984 Liquefied Petroleum Gas (Bottled Gas) Dealers *see* NAICS 454312: Liquefied Petroleum Gas (Bottled Gas) Dealers

5989 Fuel Dealers, NEC *see* NAICS 454319: Other Fuel Dealers

5992 Florists *see* NAICS 453110: Florists

5993 Tobacco Stores and Stands *see* NAICS 453991: Tobacco Stores

5994 News Dealers and Newsstands *see* NAICS 451212: News Dealers and Newsstands

5995 Optical Goods Stores *see* NAICS 339115: Ophthalmic Goods Manufacturing; NAICS 446130: Optical Goods Stores

5999 Miscellaneous Retail Stores, NEC *see* NAICS 446120: Cosmetics, Beauty Supplies, and Perfume Stores; NAICS 446199: All Other Health and Personal Care Stores; NAICS 453910: Pet and Pet Supplies Stores; NAICS 453920: Art Dealers; NAICS 443111: Household Appliance Stores; NAICS 443112: Radio, Television, and Other Electronics Stores; NAICS 448310: Jewelry Stores; NAICS 453998: All Other Miscellaneous Store Retailers (except Tobacco Stores)

FINANCE, INSURANCE, & REAL ESTATE

6011 Federal Reserve Banks *see* NAICS 521110: Monetary Authorities-Central Banks

6019 Central Reserve Depository Institutions, NEC *see* NAICS 522320: Financial Transactions Processing, Reserve, and Clearing House Activities

6021 National Commercial Banks *see* NAICS 522110: Commercial Banking; NAICS 522210: Credit Card Issuing; NAICS 523991: Trust, Fiduciary, and Custody Activities

6022 State Commercial Banks *see* NAICS 522110: Commercial Banking; NAICS 522210: Credit Card Issuing; NAICS 522190: Other Depository Intermediation; NAICS 523991: Trust, Fiduciary, and Custody Activities

6029 Commercial Banks, NEC *see* NAICS 522110: Commercial Banking

6035 Savings Institutions, Federally Chartered *see* NAICS 522120: Savings Institutions

6036 Savings institutions, Not Federally Chartered *see* NAICS 522120: Savings Institutions

6061 Credit Unions, Federally Chartered *see* NAICS 522130: Credit Unions

6062 Credit Unions, Not Federally Chartered *see* NAICS 522130: Credit Unions

6081 Branches and Agencies of Foreign Banks *see* NAICS 522293: International Trade Financing; NAICS 522110: Commercial Banking; NAICS 522298: All Other Non-Depository Credit Intermediation

6082 Foreign Trade and International Banking Institutions *see* NAICS 522293: International Trade Financing

6091 Nondeposit Trust Facilities *see* NAICS 523991: Trust, Fiduciary, and Custody Activities

6099 Functions Related to Deposit Banking, NEC *see* NAICS 522320: Financial Transactions Processing, Reserve, and Clearing House Activities; NAICS 523130: Commodity Contracts Dealing; NAICS 523991: Trust, Fiduciary, and Custody Activities; NAICS 523999: Miscellaneous Financial Investment Activities; NAICS 522390: Other Activities Related to Credit Intermediation

6111 Federal and Federally Sponsored Credit Agencies *see* NAICS 522293: International Trade Financing; NAICS 522294: Secondary Market Financing; NAICS 522298: All Other Non-Depository Credit Intermediation

6141 Personal Credit Institutions *see* NAICS 522210: Credit Card Issuing; NAICS 522220: Sales Financing; NAICS 522291: Consumer Lending

6153 Short-Term Business Credit Institutions, Except Agricultural *see* NAICS 522220: Sales Financing; NAICS 522320: Financial Transactions Processing, Reserve, and Clearing House Activities; NAICS 522298: All Other Non-Depository Credit Intermediation

6159 Miscellaneous Business Credit Institutions *see* NAICS 522220: Sales Financing; NAICS 522293: International Trade Financing; NAICS 522298: All Other Non-Depository Credit Intermediation

6162 Mortgage Bankers and Loan Correspondents *see* NAICS 522292: Real Estate Credit; NAICS 522390: Other Activities Related to Credit Intermediation

6163 Loan Brokers *see* NAICS 522310: Mortgage and Other Loan Brokers

6211 Security Brokers, Dealers, and Flotation Companies *see* NAICS 523110: Investment Banking and Securities Dealing; NAICS 523120: Securities Brokerage; NAICS 523910: Miscellaneous Intermediation; NAICS 523999: Miscellaneous Financial Investment Activities

6221 Commodity Contracts Brokers and Dealers *see* NAICS 523130: Commodity Contracts Dealing; NAICS 523140: Commodity Brokerage

6231 Security and Commodity Exchanges *see* NAICS 523210: Securities and Commodity Exchanges

6282 Investment Advice *see* NAICS 523920: Portfolio Management; NAICS 523930: Investment Advice

6289 Services Allied With the Exchange of Securities or Commodities, NEC *see* NAICS 523991: Trust, Fiduciary, and Custody Activities; NAICS 523999: Miscellaneous Financial Investment Activities

6311 Life Insurance *see* NAICS 524113: Direct Life Insurance Carriers; NAICS 524130: Reinsurance Carriers

6321 Accident and Health Insurance *see* NAICS 524114: Direct Health and Medical Insurance Carriers; NAICS 525190: Other Insurance and Employee Benefit Funds; NAICS 524130: Reinsurance Carriers

6324 Hospital and Medical Service Plans *see* NAICS 524114: Direct Health and Medical Insurance Carriers; NAICS 525190: Other Insurance and Employee Benefit Funds; NAICS 524130: Reinsurance Carriers

6331 Fire, Marine, and Casualty Insurance *see* NAICS 524126: Direct Property and Casualty Insurance Carriers; NAICS 525190: Other Insurance and Employee Benefit Funds; NAICS 524130: Reinsurance Carriers

6351 Surety Insurance *see* NAICS 524126: Direct Property and Casualty Insurance Carriers; NAICS 524130: Reinsurance Carriers

6361 Title Insurance *see* NAICS 524127: Direct Title Insurance Carriers; NAICS 524130: Reinsurance Carriers

6371 Pension, Health, and Welfare Funds *see* NAICS 523920: Portfolio Management; NAICS 524292: Third Party Administration for Insurance and Pension Funds; NAICS 525110: Pension Funds; NAICS 525120: Health and Welfare Funds

6399 Insurance Carriers, NEC *see* NAICS 524128: Other Direct Insurance Carriers (except Life, Health, and Medical)

6411 Insurance Agents, Brokers, and Service *see* NAICS 524210: Insurance Agencies and Brokerages; NAICS 524291: Claims Adjusters; NAICS 524292: Third Party Administrators for Insurance and Pension Funds; NAICS 524298: All Other Insurance Related Activities

6512 Operators of Nonresidential Buildings *see* NAICS 711310: Promoters of Performing Arts, Sports and Similar Events with Facilities; NAICS 531120: Lessors of Nonresidential Buildings (except Mini-warehouses)

6513 Operators of Apartment Buildings *see* NAICS 531110: Lessors of Residential Buildings and Dwellings

6514 Operators of Dwellings Other Than Apartment Buildings *see* NAICS 531110: Lessors of Residential Buildings and Dwellings

6515 Operators of Residential Mobile Home Sites *see* NAICS 531190: Lessors of Other Real Estate Property

6517 Lessors of Railroad Property *see* NAICS 531190: Lessors of Other Real Estate Property

6519 Lessors of Real Property, NEC *see* NAICS 531190: Lessors of Other Real Estate Property

6531 Real Estate Agents and Managers *see* NAICS 531210: Offices of Real Estate Agents and Brokers; NAICS 813990: Other Similar Organizations; NAICS 531311: Residential Property Managers; NAICS 531312: Nonresidential Property Managers; NAICS 531320: Offices of Real Estate Appraisers; NAICS 812220: Cemeteries and Crematories; NAICS 531390: Other Activities Related to Real Estate

6541 Title Abstract Offices *see* NAICS 541191: Title Abstract and Settlement Offices

6552 Land Subdividers and Developers, Except Cemeteries *see* NAICS 233110: Land Subdivision and Land Development

6553 Cemetery Subdividers and Developers *see* NAICS 812220: Cemeteries and Crematories

6712 Offices of Bank Holding Companies *see* NAICS 551111: Offices of Bank Holding Companies

6719 Offices of Holding Companies, NEC *see* NAICS 551112: Offices of Other Holding Companies

6722 Management Investment Offices, Open-End *see* NAICS 525910: Open-End Investment Funds

6726 Unit Investment Trusts, Face-Amount Certificate Offices, and Closed-End Management Investment Offices *see* NAICS 525990: Other Financial Vehicles

6732 Education, Religious, and Charitable Trusts *see* NAICS 813211: Grantmaking Foundations

6733 Trusts, Except Educational, Religious, and Charitable *see* NAICS 523920: Portfolio Management; NAICS 523991: Trust, Fiduciary, and Custody Services; NAICS 525190: Other Insurance and Employee Benefit Funds; NAICS 525920: Trusts, Estates, and Agency Accounts

6792 Oil Royalty Traders *see* NAICS 523999: Miscellaneous Financial Investment Activities; NAICS 533110: Owners and Lessors of Other Non-Financial Assets

6794 Patent Owners and Lessors *see* NAICS 533110: Owners and Lessors of Other Non-Financial Assets

6798 Real Estate Investment Trusts *see* NAICS 525930: Real Estate Investment Trusts

6799   Investors, NEC *see* NAICS 523910: Miscellaneous Intermediation; NAICS 523920: Portfolio Management; NAICS 523130: Commodity Contracts Dealing; NAICS 523999: Miscellaneous Financial Investment Activities

SERVICE INDUSTRIES

7011   Hotels and Motels *see* NAICS 721110: Hotels (except Casino Hotels) and Motels; NAICS 721120: Casino Hotels; NAICS 721191: Bed and Breakfast Inns; NAICS 721199: All Other Traveler Accommodations

7021   Rooming and Boarding Houses *see* NAICS 721310: Rooming and Boarding Houses

7032   Sporting and Recreational Camps *see* NAICS 721214: Recreational and Vacation Camps

7033   Recreational Vehicle Parks and Campsites *see* NAICS 721211: RV (Recreational Vehicle) Parks and Campgrounds

7041   Organization Hotels and Lodging Houses, on Membership Basis *see* NAICS 721110: Hotels (except Casino Hotels) and Motels; NAICS 721310: Rooming and Boarding Houses

7211   Power Laundries, Family and Commercial *see* NAICS 812321: Laundries, Family and Commercial

7212   Garment Pressing, and Agents for Laundries *see* NAICS 812391: Garment Pressing and Agents for Laundries

7213   Linen Supply *see* NAICS 812331: Linen Supply

7215   Coin-Operated Laundry and Drycleaning *see* NAICS 812310: Coin-Operated Laundries and Drycleaners

7216   Drycleaning Plants, Except Rug Cleaning *see* NAICS 812322: Drycleaning Plants

7217   Carpet and Upholstery Cleaning *see* NAICS 561740: Carpet and Upholstery Cleaning Services

7218   Industrial Launderers *see* NAICS 812332: Industrial Launderers

7219   Laundry and Garment Services, NEC *see* NAICS 812331: Linen Supply; NAICS 811490: Other Personal and Household Goods Repair and Maintenance; NAICS 812399: All Other Laundry Services

7221   Photographic Studios, Portrait *see* NAICS 541921: Photographic Studios, Portrait

7231   Beauty Shops *see* NAICS 812112: Beauty Salons; NAICS 812113: Nail Salons; NAICS 611511: Cosmetology and Barber Schools

7241   Barber Shops *see* NAICS 812111: Barber Shops; NAICS 611511: Cosmetology and Barber Schools

7251   Shoe Repair Shops and Shoeshine Parlors *see* NAICS 811430: Footwear and Leather Goods Repair

7261   Funeral Services and Crematories *see* NAICS 812210: Funeral Homes; NAICS 812220: Cemeteries and Crematories

7291   Tax Return Preparation Services *see* NAICS 541213: Tax Preparation Services

7299   Miscellaneous Personal Services, NEC *see* NAICS 624410: Child Day Care Services; NAICS 812191: Diet and Weight Reducing Centers; NAICS 532220: Formal Wear and Costumes Rental; NAICS 812199: Other Personal Care Services; NAICS 812990: All Other Personal Services

7311   Advertising Agencies *see* NAICS 541810: Advertising Agencies

7312   Outdoor Advertising Services *see* NAICS 541850: Display Advertising

7313   Radio, Television, and Publishers' Advertising Representatives *see* NAICS 541840: Media Representatives

7319   Advertising, NEC *see* NAICS 481219: Other Nonscheduled Air Transportation; NAICS 541830: Media Buying Agencies; NAICS 541850: Display Advertising; NAICS 541870: Advertising Material Distribution Services; NAICS 541890: Other Services Related to Advertising

7322   Adjustment and Collection Services *see* NAICS 561440: Collection Agencies; NAICS 561491: Repossession Services

7323   Credit Reporting Services *see* NAICS 561450: Credit Bureaus

7331   Direct Mail Advertising Services *see* NAICS 541860: Direct Mail Advertising

7334   Photocopying and Duplicating Services *see* NAICS 561431: Other Business Service Centers (including Copy Shops)

7335   Commercial Photography *see* NAICS 481219: Other Nonscheduled Air Transportation; NAICS 541922: Commercial Photography

7336   Commercial Art and Graphic Design *see* NAICS 541430: Graphic Design Services

7338   Secretarial and Court Reporting Services *see* NAICS 561410: Document Preparation Services; NAICS 561492: Court Reporting and Stenotype Services

7342   Disinfecting and Pest Control Services *see* NAICS 561720: Janitorial Services; NAICS 561710: Exterminating and Pest Control Services

7349   Building Cleaning and Maintenance Services, NEC *see* NAICS 561720: Janitorial Services

7352   Medical Equipment Rental and Leasing *see* NAICS 532291: Home Health Equipment Rental; NAICS 532490: Other Commercial and Industrial Machinery and Equipment Rental and Leasing

7353 Heavy Construction Equipment Rental and Leasing *see* NAICS 234990: All Other Heavy Construction; NAICS 532412: Construction, Mining and Forestry Machinery and Equipment Rental and Leasing

7359 Equipment Rental and Leasing, NEC *see* NAICS 532210: Consumer Electronics and Appliances Rental; NAICS 532310: General Rental Centers; NAICS 532299: All Other Consumer Goods Rental; NAICS 532412: Construction, Mining and Forestry Machinery and Equipment Rental and Leasing; NAICS 532411: Commercial Air, Rail, and Water Transportation Equipment Rental and Leasing; NAICS 562991: Septic Tank and Related Services; NAICS 532420: Office Machinery and Equipment Rental and Leasing; NAICS 532490: Other Commercial and Industrial Machinery and Equipment Rental and Leasing

7361 Employment Agencies *see* NAICS 541612: Human Resources and Executive Search Consulting Services; NAICS 561310: Employment Placement Agencies

7363 Help Supply Services *see* NAICS 561320: Temporary Help Services; NAICS 561330: Employee Leasing Services

7371 Computer Programming Services *see* NAICS 541511: Custom Computer Programming Services

7372 Prepackaged Software *see* NAICS 511210: Software Publishers; NAICS 334611: Software Reproducing

7373 Computer Integrated Systems Design *see* NAICS 541512: Computer Systems Design Services

7374 Computer Processing and Data Preparation and Processing Services *see* NAICS 514210: Data Processing Services

7375 Information Retrieval Services *see* NAICS 514191: On-Line Information Services

7376 Computer Facilities Management Services *see* NAICS 541513: Computer Facilities Management Services

7377 Computer Rental and Leasing *see* NAICS 532420: Office Machinery and Equipment Rental and Leasing

7378 Computer Maintenance and Repair *see* NAICS 443120: Computer and Software Stores; NAICS 811212: Computer and Office Machine Repair and Maintenance

7379 Computer Related Services, NEC *see* NAICS 541512: Computer Systems Design Services; NAICS 541519: Other Computer Related Services

7381 Detective, Guard, and Armored Car Services *see* NAICS 561611: Investigation Services; NAICS 561612: Security Guards and Patrol Services; NAICS 561613: Armored Car Services

7382 Security Systems Services *see* NAICS 561621: Security Systems Services (except Locksmiths)

7383 News Syndicates *see* NAICS 514110: New Syndicates

7384 Photofinishing Laboratories *see* NAICS 812921: Photo Finishing Laboratories (except One-Hour); NAICS 812922: One-Hour Photo Finishing

7389 Business Services, NEC *see* NAICS 512240: Sound Recording Studios; NAICS 512290: Other Sound Recording Industries; NAICS 541199: Other Legal Services; NAICS 812990: All Other Personal Services; NAICS 541370: Surveying and Mapping (except Geophysical) Services; NAICS 541410: Interior Design Services; NAICS 541420: Industrial Design Services; NAICS 541340: Drafting Services; NAICS 541490: Other Specialized Design Services; NAICS 541890: Other Services Related to Advertising; NAICS 541930: Translation and Interpretation Services; NAICS 541350: Building Inspection Services; NAICS 541990: All Other Professional, Scientific and Technical Services; NAICS 711410: Agents and Managers for Artists, Athletes, Entertainers and Other Public Figures; NAICS 561421: Telephone Answering Services; NAICS 561422: Telemarketing Bureaus; NAICS 561439: Private Mail Centers; NAICS 561431: Other Business Service Centers (including Copy Shops); NAICS 561491: Repossession Services; NAICS 561910: Packaging and Labeling Services; NAICS 561790: Other Services to Buildings and Dwellings; NAICS 561599: All Other Travel Arrangement and Reservation Services; NAICS 561920: Convention and Trade Show Organizers; NAICS 561591: Convention and Visitors Bureaus; NAICS 522320: Financial Transactions, Processing, Reserve and Clearing House Activities; NAICS 561499: All Other Business Support Services; NAICS 561990: All Other Support Services

7513 Truck Rental and Leasing, Without Drivers *see* NAICS 532120: Truck, Utility Trailer and RV (Recreational Vehicle) Rental and Leasing

7514 Passenger Car Rental *see* NAICS 532111: Passenger Cars Rental

7515 Passenger Car Leasing *see* NAICS 532112: Passenger Cars Leasing

7519 Utility Trailer and Recreational Vehicle Rental *see* NAICS 532120: Truck, Utility Trailer and RV (Recreational Vehicles) Rental and Leasing

7521 Automobile Parking *see* NAICS 812930: Parking Lots and Garages

7532 Top, Body, and Upholstery Repair Shops and Paint Shops *see* NAICS 811121: Automotive Body, Paint, and Upholstery Repair and Maintenance

7533 Automotive Exhaust System Repair Shops *see* NAICS 811112: Automotive Exhaust System Repair

7534 Tire Retreading and Repair Shops *see* NAICS 326212: Tire Retreading; NAICS 811198: All Other Automotive Repair and Maintenance

7536 Automotive Glass Replacement Shops *see* NAICS 811122: Automotive Glass Replacement Shops

7537 Automotive Transmission Repair Shops *see* NAICS 811113: Automotive Transmission Repair

7538 General Automotive Repair Shops *see* NAICS 811111: General Automotive Repair

7539 Automotive Repair Shops, NEC *see* NAICS 811118: Other Automotive Mechanical and Electrical Repair and Maintenance

7542 Carwashes *see* NAICS 811192: Car Washes

7549 Automotive Services, Except Repair and Carwashes *see* NAICS 811191: Automotive Oil Change and Lubrication Shops; NAICS 488410: Motor Vehicle Towing; NAICS 811198: All Other Automotive Repair and Maintenance

7622 Radio and Television Repair Shops *see* NAICS 811211: Consumer Electronics Repair and Maintenance; NAICS 811213: Communication Equipment Repair and Maintenance; NAICS 443112: Radio, Television and Other Electronics Stores

7623 Refrigeration and Air-Conditioning Services and Repair Shops *see* NAICS 443111: Household Appliance Stores; NAICS 811310: Commercial and Industrial Machinery and Equipment (except Automotive and Electronic) Repair and Maintenance; NAICS 811412: Appliance Repair and Maintenance

7629 Electrical and Electronic Repair Shops, NEC *see* NAICS 443111: Household Appliance Stores; NAICS 811212: Computer and Office Machine Repair and Maintenance; *see* NAICS 811213: Communication Equipment Repair and Maintenance; NAICS 811219: Other Electronic and Precision Equipment Repair and Maintenance; NAICS 811412: Appliance Repair and Maintenance; NAICS 811211: Consumer Electronics Repair and Maintenance

7631 Watch, Clock, and Jewelry Repair *see* NAICS 811490: Other Personal and Household Goods Repair and Maintenance

7641 Reupholster and Furniture Repair *see* NAICS 811420: Reupholstery and Furniture Repair

7692 Welding Repair *see* NAICS 811490: Other Personal and Household Goods Repair and Maintenance

7694 Armature Rewinding Shops *see* NAICS 811310: Commercial and Industrial Machinery and Equipment (except Automotive and Electronic) Repair and Maintenance; NAICS 335312: Motor and Generator Manufacturing

7699 Repair Shops and Related Services, NEC *see* NAICS 561622: Locksmiths; NAICS 562991: Septic Tank and Related Services; NAICS 561790: Other Services to Buildings and Dwellings; NAICS 488390: Other Support Activities for Water Transportation; NAICS 451110: Sporting Goods Stores; NAICS 811310: Commercial and Industrial Machinery and Equipment (except Automotive and Electronic) Repair and Maintenance; NAICS 115210: Support Activities for Animal Production; NAICS 811212: Computer and Office Machine Repair and Maintenance; NAICS 811219: Other Electronic and Precision Equipment Repair and Maintenance; NAICS 811411: Home and Garden Equipment Repair and Maintenance; NAICS 811412: Appliance Repair and Maintenance; NAICS 811430: Footwear and Leather Goods Repair; NAICS 811490: Other Personal and Household Goods Repair and Maintenance

7812 Motion Picture and Video Tape Production *see* NAICS 512110: Motion Picture and Video Production

7819 Services Allied to Motion Picture Production *see* NAICS 512191: Teleproduction and Other Post-Production Services; NAICS 561310: Employment Placement Agencies; NAICS 532220: Formal Wear and Costumes Rental; NAICS 532490: Other Commercial and Industrial Machinery and Equipment Rental and Leasing; NAICS 541214: Payroll Services; NAICS 711510: Independent Artists, Writers, and Performers; NAICS 334612: Prerecorded Compact Disc (Except Software), Tape, and Record Manufacturing; NAICS 512199: Other Motion Picture and Video Industries

7822 Motion Picture and Video Tape Distribution *see* NAICS 421990: Other Miscellaneous Durable Goods Wholesalers; NAICS 512120: Motion Picture and Video Distribution

7829 Services Allied to Motion Picture Distribution *see* NAICS 512199: Other Motion Picture and Video Industries; NAICS 512120: Motion Picture and Video Distribution

7832 Motion Picture Theaters, Except Drive-In *see* NAICS 512131: Motion Picture Theaters, Except Drive-In

7833 Drive-In Motion Picture Theaters *see* NAICS 512132: Drive-In Motion Picture Theaters

7841 Video Tape Rental *see* NAICS 532230: Video Tapes and Disc Rental

7911 Dance Studios, Schools, and Halls *see* NAICS 713990: All Other Amusement and Recreation Industries; NAICS 611610: Fine Arts Schools

7922 Theatrical Producers (Except Motion Picture) and Miscellaneous Theatrical Services *see* NAICS

561310: Employment Placement Agencies; NAICS 711110: Theater Companies and Dinner Theaters; NAICS 711410: Agents and Managers for Artists, Athletes, Entertainers and Other Public Figures; NAICS 711120: Dance Companies; NAICS 711310: Promoters of Performing Arts, Sports, and Similar Events with Facilities; NAICS 711320: Promoters of Performing Arts, Sports, and Similar Events without Facilities; NAICS 512290: Other Sound Recording Industries; NAICS 532490: Other Commercial and Industrial Machinery and Equipment Rental and Leasing

7929   Bands, Orchestras, Actors, and Other Entertainers and Entertainment Groups *see* NAICS 711130: Musical Groups and Artists; NAICS 711510: Independent Artists, Writers, and Performers; NAICS 711190: Other Performing Arts Companies

7933   Bowling Centers *see* NAICS 713950: Bowling Centers

7941   Professional Sports Clubs and Promoters *see* NAICS 711211: Sports Teams and Clubs; NAICS 711410: Agents and Managers for Artists, Athletes, Entertainers, and Other Public Figures; NAICS 711320: Promoters of Performing Arts, Sports, and Similar Events without Facilities; NAICS 711310: Promoters of Performing Arts, Sports, and Similar Events with Facilities; NAICS 711219: Other Spectator Sports

7948   Racing, Including Track Operations *see* NAICS 711212: Race Tracks; NAICS 711219: Other Spectator Sports

7991   Physical Fitness Facilities *see* NAICS 713940: Fitness and Recreational Sports Centers

7992   Public Golf Courses *see* NAICS 713910: Golf Courses and Country Clubs

7993   Coin Operated Amusement Devices *see* NAICS 713120: Amusement Arcades; NAICS 713290: Other Gambling Industries; NAICS 713990: All Other Amusement and Recreation Industries

7996   Amusement Parks *see* NAICS 713110: Amusement and Theme Parks

7997   Membership Sports and Recreation Clubs *see* NAICS 713910: Golf Courses and Country Clubs; NAICS 713940: Fitness and Recreational Sports Centers; NAICS 713990: All Other Amusement and Recreation Industries

7999   Amusement and Recreation Services, NEC *see* NAICS 561599: All Other Travel Arrangement and Reservation Services; NAICS 487990: Scenic and Sightseeing Transportation, Other; NAICS 711190: Other Performing Arts Companies; NAICS 711219: Other Spectator Sports; NAICS 713920: Skiing Facilities; NAICS 713940: Fitness

and Recreational Sports Centers; NAICS 713210: Casinos (except Casino Hotels); NAICS 713290: Other Gambling Industries; NAICS 712190: Nature Parks and Other Similar Institutions; NAICS 611620: Sports and Recreation Instruction; NAICS 532292: Recreational Goods Rental; NAICS 487110: Scenic and Sightseeing Transportation, Land; NAICS 487210: Scenic and Sightseeing Transportation, Water; NAICS 713990: All Other Amusement and Recreation Industries

8011   Offices and Clinics of Doctors of Medicine *see* NAICS 621493: Freestanding Ambulatory Surgical and Emergency Centers; NAICS 621491: HMO Medical Centers; NAICS 621112: Offices of Physicians; NAICS 621111: Offices of Physicians (except Mental Health Specialists)

8021   Offices and Clinics of Dentists *see* NAICS 621210: Offices of Dentists

8031   Offices and Clinics of Doctors of Osteopathy *see* NAICS 621111: Offices of Physicians (except Mental Health Specialists); NAICS 621112: Offices of Physicians, Mental Health Specialists

8041   Offices and Clinics of Chiropractors *see* NAICS 621310: Offices of Chiropractors

8042   Offices and Clinics of Optometrists *see* NAICS 621320: Offices of Optometrists

8043   Offices and Clinics of Podiatrists *see* NAICS 621391: Offices of Podiatrists

8049   Offices and Clinics of Health Practitioners, NEC *see* NAICS 621330: Offices of Mental Health Practitioners (except Physicians); NAICS 621340: Offices of Physical, Occupational, and Speech Therapists and Audiologists; NAICS 621399: Offices of All Other Miscellaneous Health Practitioners

8051   Skilled Nursing Care Facilities *see* NAICS 623311: Continuing Care Retirement Communities; NAICS 623110: Nursing Care Facilities

8052   Intermediate Care Facilities *see* NAICS 623311: Continuing Care Retirement Communities; NAICS 623210: Residential Mental Retardation Facilities; NAICS 623110: Nursing Care Facilities

8059   Nursing and Personal Care Facilities, NEC *see* NAICS 623311: Continuing Care Retirement Communities; NAICS 623110: Nursing Care Facilities

8062   General Medical and Surgical Hospitals *see* NAICS 622110: General Medical and Surgical Hospitals

8063   Psychiatric Hospitals *see* NAICS 622210: Psychiatric and Substance Abuse Hospitals

8069   Specialty Hospitals, Except Psychiatric *see* NAICS 622110: General Medical and Surgical Hospitals; NAICS 622210: Psychiatric and Substance Abuse

Hospitals; NAICS 622310: Specialty (except Psychiatric and Substance Abuse) Hospitals

8071 Medical Laboratories *see* NAICS 621512: Diagnostic Imaging Centers; NAICS 621511: Medical Laboratories

8072 Dental Laboratories *see* NAICS 339116: Dental Laboratories

8082 Home Health Care Services *see* NAICS 621610: Home Health Care Services

8092 Kidney Dialysis Centers *see* NAICS 621492: Kidney Dialysis Centers

8093 Specialty Outpatient Facilities, NEC *see* NAICS 621410: Family Planning Centers; NAICS 621420: Outpatient Mental Health and Substance Abuse Centers; NAICS 621498: All Other Outpatient Care Facilities

8099 Health and Allied Services, NEC *see* NAICS 621991: Blood and Organ Banks; NAICS 541430: Graphic Design Services; NAICS 541922: Commercial Photography; NAICS 621410: Family Planning Centers; NAICS 621999: All Other Miscellaneous Ambulatory Health Care Services

8111 Legal Services *see* NAICS 541110: Offices of Lawyers

8211 Elementary and Secondary Schools *see* NAICS 611110: Elementary and Secondary Schools

8221 Colleges, Universities, and Professional Schools *see* NAICS 611310: Colleges, Universities, and Professional Schools

8222 Junior Colleges and Technical Institutes *see* NAICS 611210: Junior Colleges

8231 Libraries *see* NAICS 514120: Libraries and Archives

8243 Data Processing Schools *see* NAICS 611519: Other Technical and Trade Schools; NAICS 611420: Computer Training

8244 Business and Secretarial Schools *see* NAICS 611410: Business and Secretarial Schools

8249 Vocational Schools, NEC *see* NAICS 611513: Apprenticeship Training; NAICS 611512: Flight Training; NAICS 611519: Other Technical and Trade Schools

8299 Schools and Educational Services, NEC *see* NAICS 611512: Flight Training; NAICS 611692: Automobile Driving Schools; NAICS 611710: Educational Support Services; NAICS 611691: Exam Preparation and Tutoring; NAICS 611610: Fine Arts Schools; NAICS 611630: Language Schools; NAICS 611430: Professional and Management Development Training Schools; NAICS 611699: All Other Miscellaneous Schools and Instruction

8322 Individual and Family Social Services *see* NAICS 624110: Child and Youth Services; NAICS 624210: Community Food Services; NAICS

624229: Other Community Housing Services; NAICS 624230: Emergency and Other Relief Services; NAICS 624120: Services for the Elderly and Persons with Disabilities; NAICS 624221: Temporary Shelter; NAICS 922150: Parole Offices and Probation Offices; NAICS 624190: Other Individual and Family Services

8331 Job Training and Vocational Rehabilitation Services *see* NAICS 624310: Vocational Rehabilitation Services

8351 Child Day Care Services *see* NAICS 624410: Child Day Care Services

8361 Residential Care *see* NAICS 623312: Homes for the Elderly; NAICS 623220: Residential Mental Health and Substance Abuse Facilities; NAICS 623990: Other Residential Care Facilities

8399 Social Services, NEC *see* NAICS 813212: Voluntary Health Organizations; NAICS 813219: Other Grantmaking and Giving Services; NAICS 813311: Human Rights Organizations; NAICS 813312: Environment, Conservation and Wildlife Organizations; NAICS 813319: Other Social Advocacy Organizations

8412 Museums and Art Galleries *see* NAICS 712110: Museums; NAICS 712120: Historical Sites

8422 Arboreta and Botanical or Zoological Gardens *see* NAICS 712130: Zoos and Botanical Gardens; NAICS 712190: Nature Parks and Other Similar Institutions

8611 Business Associations *see* NAICS 813910: Business Associations

8621 Professional Membership Organizations *see* NAICS 813920: Professional Organizations

8631 Labor Unions and Similar Labor Organizations *see* NAICS 813930: Labor Unions and Similar Labor Organizations

8641 Civic, Social, and Fraternal Associations *see* NAICS 813410: Civic and Social Organizations; NAICS 813990: Other Similar Organizations; NAICS 921150: American Indian and Alaska Native Tribal Governments; NAICS 624110: Child and Youth Services

8651 Political Organizations *see* NAICS 813940: Political Organizations

8661 Religious Organizations *see* NAICS 813110: Religious Organizations

8699 Membership Organizations, NEC *see* NAICS 813410: Civic and Social Organizations; NAICS 813910: Business Associations; NAICS 813312: Environment, Conservation, and Wildlife Organizations; NAICS 561599: All Other Travel Arrangement and Reservation Services; NAICS 813990: Other Similar Organizations

8711 Engineering Services *see* NAICS 541330: Engineering Services

8712 Architectural Services *see* NAICS 541310: Architectural Services

8713 Surveying Services *see* NAICS 541360: Geophysical Surveying and Mapping Services; NAICS 541370: Surveying and Mapping (except Geophysical) Services

8721 Accounting, Auditing, and Bookkeeping Services *see* NAICS 541211: Offices of Certified Public Accountants; NAICS 541214: Payroll Services; NAICS 541219: Other Accounting Services

8731 Commercial Physical and Biological Research *see* NAICS 541710: Research and Development in the Physical Sciences and Engineering Sciences; NAICS 541720: Research and Development in the Life Sciences

8732 Commercial Economic, Sociological, and Educational Research *see* NAICS 541730: Research and Development in the Social Sciences and Humanities; NAICS 541910: Marketing Research and Public Opinion Polling

8733 Noncommercial Research Organizations *see* NAICS 541710: Research and Development in the Physical Sciences and Engineering Sciences; NAICS 541720: Research and Development in the Life Sciences; NAICS 541730: Research and Development in the Social Sciences and Humanities

8734 Testing Laboratories *see* NAICS 541940: Veterinary Services; NAICS 541380: Testing Laboratories

8741 Management Services *see* NAICS 561110: Office Administrative Services

8742 Management Consulting Services *see* NAICS 541611: Administrative Management and General Management Consulting Services; NAICS 541612: Human Resources and Executive Search Consulting Services; NAICS 541613: Marketing Consulting Services; NAICS 541614: Process, Physical, Distribution, and Logistics Consulting

8743 Public Relations Services *see* NAICS 541820: Public Relations Services

8744 Facilities Support Management Services *see* NAICS 561210: Facilities Support Services

8748 Business Consulting Services, NEC *see* NAICS 611710: Educational Support Services; NAICS 541618: Other Management Consulting Services; NAICS 541690: Other Scientific and Technical Consulting Services

8811 Private Households *see* NAICS 814110: Private Households

8999 Services, NEC *see* NAICS 711510: Independent Artists, Writers, and Performers; NAICS 512210: Record Production; NAICS 541690: Other Scientific and Technical Consulting Services;

NAICS 512230: Music Publishers; NAICS 541612: Human Resources and Executive Search Consulting Services; NAICS 514199: All Other Information Services; NAICS 541620: Environmental Consulting Services

PUBLIC ADMINISTRATION

9111 Executive Offices *see* NAICS 921110: Executive Offices

9121 Legislative Bodies *see* NAICS 921120: Legislative Bodies

9131 Executive and Legislative Offices, Combined *see* NAICS 921140: Executive and Legislative Offices, Combined

9199 General Government, NEC *see* NAICS 921190: All Other General Government

9211 Courts *see* NAICS 922110: Courts

9221 Police Protection *see* NAICS 922120: Police Protection

9222 Legal Counsel and Prosecution *see* NAICS 922130: Legal Counsel and Prosecution

9223 Correctional Institutions *see* NAICS 922140: Correctional Institutions

9224 Fire Protection *see* NAICS 922160: Fire Protection

9229 Public Order and Safety, NEC *see* NAICS 922190: All Other Justice, Public Order, and Safety

9311 Public Finance, Taxation, and Monetary Policy *see* NAICS 921130: Public Finance

9411 Administration of Educational Programs *see* NAICS 923110: Administration of Education Programs

9431 Administration of Public Health Programs *see* NAICS 923120: Administration of Public Health Programs

9441 Administration of Social, Human Resource, and Income Maintenance Programs *see* NAICS 923130: Administration of Social, Human Resource, and Income Maintenance Programs

9451 Administration of Veteran's Affairs, Except Health Insurance *see* NAICS 923140: Administration of Veteran's Affairs

9511 Air and Water Resource and Solid Waste Management *see* NAICS 924110: Air and Water Resource and Solid Waste Management

9512 Land, Mineral, Wildlife, and Forest Conservation *see* NAICS 924120: Land, Mineral, Wildlife, and Forest Conservation

9531 Administration of Housing Programs *see* NAICS 925110: Administration of Housing Programs

9532 Administration of Urban Planning and Community and Rural Development *see* NAICS 925120: Administration of Urban Planning and Community and Rural Development

9611 Administration of General Economic Programs *see* NAICS 926110: Administration of General Economic Programs

9621   Regulations and Administration of Transportation Programs *see* NAICS 488111: Air Traffic Control; NAICS 926120: Regulation and Administration of Transportation Programs

9631   Regulation and Administration of Communications, Electric, Gas, and Other Utilities *see* NAICS 926130: Regulation and Administration of Communications, Electric, Gas, and Other Utilities

9641   Regulation of Agricultural Marketing and Commodities *see* NAICS 926140: Regulation of Agricultural Marketing and Commodities

9651   Regulation, Licensing, and Inspection of Miscellaneous Commercial Sectors *see* NAICS 926150: Regulation, Licensing, and Inspection of Miscellaneous Commercial Sectors

9661   Space Research and Technology *see* NAICS 927110: Space Research and Technology

9711   National Security *see* NAICS 928110: National Security

9721   International Affairs *see* NAICS 928120: International Affairs

9999   Nonclassified Establishments *see* NAICS 999990: Unclassified Establishments

NAICS to SIC Conversion Guide

The following listing cross-references six-digit 1997 North American Industry Classification System (NAICS) codes with four-digit 1987 Standard Industrial Classification (SIC) codes. Because the systems differ in specificity, some NAICS categories correspond to more than one SIC category.

AGRICULTURE, FORESTRY, FISHING, & HUNTING

111110   Soybean Farming *see* SIC 0116: Soybeans

111120   Oilseed (except Soybean) Farming *see* SIC 0119: Cash Grains, NEC

111130   Dry Pea and Bean Farming *see* SIC 0119: Cash Grains, NEC

111140   Wheat Farming *see* SIC 0111: Wheat

111150   Corn Farming *see* SIC 0115: Corn

111150   Corn Farming *see* SIC 0119: Cash Grains, NEC

111160   Rice Farming *see* SIC 0112: Rice

111191   Oilseed and Grain Combination Farming *see* SIC 0119: Cash Grains, NEC

111199   All Other Grain Farming *see* SIC 0119: Cash Grains, NEC

111211   Potato Farming *see* SIC 0134: Irish Potatoes

111219   Other Vegetable (except Potato) and Melon Farming *see* SIC 0139: Field Crops, Except Cash Grains, NEC; SIC 0161: Vegetables and Melons

111310   Orange Groves *see* SIC 0174: Citrus Fruits

111320   Citrus (except Orange) Groves *see* SIC 0174: Citrus Fruits

111331   Apple Orchards *see* SIC 0175: Deciduous Tree Fruits

111332   Grape Vineyards *see* SIC 0172: Grapes

111333   Strawberry Farming *see* SIC 0171: Berry Crops

111334   Berry (except Strawberry) Farming *see* SIC 0171: Berry Crops

111335   Tree Nut Farming *see* SIC 0173: Tree Nuts

111336   Fruit and Tree Nut Combination Farming *see* SIC 0179: Fruits and Tree Nuts, NEC

111339   Other Noncitrus Fruit Farming *see* SIC 0175: Deciduous Tree Fruits; SIC 0179: Fruits and Tree Nuts, NEC

111411   Mushroom Production *see* SIC 0182: Food Crops Grown Under Cover

111419   Other Food Crops Grown Under Cover *see* SIC 0182: Food Crops Grown Under Cover

111421   Nursery and Tree Production *see* SIC 0181: Ornamental Floriculture and Nursery Products; SIC 0811: Timber Tracts

111422   Floriculture Production *see* SIC 0181: Ornamental Floriculture and Nursery Products

111910   Tobacco Farming *see* SIC 0132: Tobacco

111920   Cotton farming *see* SIC 0131: Cotton

111930   Sugarcane Farming *see* SIC 0133: Sugarcane and Sugar Beets

111940   Hay Farming *see* SIC 0139: Field Crops, Except Cash Grains, NEC

111991   Sugar Beet Farming *see* SIC 0133: Sugarcane and Sugar Beets

111992   Peanut Farming *see* SIC 0139: Field Crops, Except Cash Grains, NEC

111998   All Other Miscellaneous Crop Farming *see* SIC 0139: Field Crops, Except Cash Grains, NEC; SIC 0191: General Farms, Primarily Crop; SIC 0831: Forest Nurseries and Gathering of Forest Products; SIC 0919: Miscellaneous Marine Products; SIC 2099: Food Preparations, NEC

112111   Beef Cattle Ranching and Farming *see* SIC 0212: Beef Cattle, Except Feedlots; SIC 0241: Dairy Farms

112112   Cattle Feedlots *see* SIC 0211: Beef Cattle Feedlots

112120   Dairy Cattle and Milk Production *see* SIC 0241: Dairy Farms

112210 Hog and Pig Farming *see* SIC 0213: Hogs

112310 Chicken Egg Production *see* SIC 0252: Chicken Eggs

112320 Broilers and Other Meat-Type Chicken Production *see* SIC 0251: Broiler, Fryers, and Roaster Chickens

112330 Turkey Production *see* SIC 0253: Turkey and Turkey Eggs

112340 Poultry Hatcheries *see* SIC 0254: Poultry Hatcheries

112390 Other Poultry Production *see* SIC 0259: Poultry and Eggs, NEC

112410 Sheep Farming *see* SIC 0214: Sheep and Goats

112420 Goat Farming *see* SIC 0214: Sheep and Goats

112511 Finfish Farming and Fish Hatcheries *see* SIC 0273: Animal Aquaculture; SIC 0921: Fish Hatcheries and Preserves

112512 Shellfish Farming *see* SIC 0273: Animal Aquaculture; SIC 0921: Fish Hatcheries and Preserves

112519 Other Animal Aquaculture *see* SIC 0273: Animal Aquaculture

112910 Apiculture *see* SIC 0279: Animal Specialties, NEC

112920 Horse and Other Equine Production *see* SIC 0272: Horses and Other Equines

112930 Fur-bearing Animal and Rabbit Production *see* SIC 0271: Fur-Bearing Animals and Rabbits

112990 All Other Animal Production *see* SIC 0219: General Livestock, Except Dairy and Poultry; SIC 0279: Animal Specialties, NEC; SIC 0291: General Farms, Primarily Livestock and Animal Specialties

113110 Timber Tract Operations *see* SIC 0811: Timber Tracts

113210 Forest Nurseries and Gathering of Forest Products *see* SIC 0831: Forest Nurseries and Gathering of Forest Products

113310 Logging *see* SIC 2411: Logging

114111 Finfish Fishing *see* SIC 0912: Finfish

114112 Shellfish Fishing *see* SIC 0913: Shellfish

114119 Other Marine Fishing *see* SIC 0919: Miscellaneous Marine Products

114210 Hunting and Trapping *see* SIC 0971: Hunting, Trapping, and Game Propagation

115111 Cotton Ginning *see* SIC 0724: Cotton Ginning

115112 Soil Preparation, Planting and Cultivating *see* SIC 0711: Soil Preparation Services; SIC 0721: Crop Planting, Cultivating and Protecting

115113 Crop Harvesting, Primarily By Machine *see* SIC 0722: Crop Harvesting, Primarily by Machine

115114 Postharvest Crop Activities (except Cotton Ginning) *see* SIC 0723: Crop Preparation Services For Market, except Cotton Ginning

115115 Farm Labor Contractors and Crew Leaders *see* SIC 0761: Farm Labor Contractors and Crew Leaders

115116 Farm Management Services *see* SIC 0762: Farm Management Services

115210 Support Activities for Animal Production *see* SIC 0751: Livestock Services, Except Veterinary; SIC 0752: Animal Specialty Services, Except Veterinary; SIC 7699: Repair Shops and Related Services, NEC

115310 Support Activities for Forestry *see* SIC 0851: Forestry Services

MINING

211111 Crude Petroleum and Natural Gas Extraction *see* SIC 1311: Crude Petroleum and Natural Gas

211112 Natural Gas Liquid Extraction *see* SIC 1321: Natural Gas Liquids

212111 Bituminous Coal and Lignite Surface Mining *see* SIC 1221: Bituminous Coal and Lignite Surface Mining

212112 Bituminous Coal Underground Mining *see* SIC 1222: Bituminous Coal Underground Mining

212113 Anthracite Mining *see* SIC 1231: Anthracite Mining

212210 Iron Ore Mining *see* SIC 1011: Iron Ores

212221 Gold Ore Mining *see* SIC 1041: Gold Ores

212222 Silver Ore Mining *see* SIC 1044: Silver Ores

212231 Lead Ore and Zinc Ore Mining *see* SIC 1031: Lead and Zinc Ores

212234 Copper Ore and Nickel Ore Mining *see* SIC 1021: Copper Ores; SIC 1061: Ferroalloy Ores, Except Vanadium

212291 Uranium-Radium-Vanadium Ore Mining *see* SIC 1094: Uranium-Radium-Vanadium Ores

212299 Other Metal Ore Mining *see* SIC 1061: Ferroalloy Ores, Except Vanadium; SIC 1099: Miscellaneous Metal Ores, NEC

212311 Dimension Stone Mining and Quarry *see* SIC 1411: Dimension Stone

212312 Crushed and Broken Limestone Mining and Quarrying *see* SIC 1422: Crushed and Broken Limestone

212313 Crushed and Broken Granite Mining and Quarrying *see* SIC 1423: Crushed and Broken Granite

212319 Other Crushed and Broken Stone Mining and Quarrying *see* SIC 1429: Crushed and Broken Stone, NEC; SIC 1499: Miscellaneous Nonmetallic Minerals, Except Fuels

212321 Construction Sand and Gravel Mining *see* SIC 1442: Construction Sand and Gravel

212322 Industrial Sand Mining *see* SIC 1446: Industrial Sand

212324 Kaolin and Ball Clay Mining *see* SIC 1455: Kaolin and Ball Clay

212325 Clay and Ceramic and Refractory Minerals Mining *see* SIC 1459: Clay, Ceramic, and Refractory Minerals, NEC

212391 Potash, Soda, and Borate Mineral Mining *see* SIC 1474: Potash, Soda, and Borate Minerals

212392 Phosphate Rock Mining *see* SIC 1475: Phosphate Rock

212393 Other Chemical and Fertilizer Mineral Mining *see* SIC 1479: Chemical and Fertilizer Mineral Mining, NEC

212399 All Other Non-Metallic Mineral Mining *see* SIC 1499: Miscellaneous Nonmetallic Minerals, Except Fuels

213111 Drilling Oil and Gas Wells *see* SIC 1381: Drilling Oil and Gas Wells

213112 Support Activities for Oil and Gas Field Exploration *see* SIC 1382: Oil and Gas Field Exploration Services; SIC 1389: Oil and Gas Field Services, NEC

213113 Support Activities for Coal Mining *see* SIC 1241: Coal Mining Services

213114 Support Activities for Metal Mining *see* SIC 1081: Metal Mining Services

213115 Support Activities for Non-metallic Minerals, (except Fuels) *see* SIC 1481: Nonmetallic Minerals Services Except Fuels

UTILITIES

221111 Hydroelectric Power Generation *see* SIC 4911: Electric Services; SIC 4931: Electric and Other Services Combined; SIC 4939: Combination Utilities, NEC

221112 Fossil Fuel Electric Power Generation *see* SIC 4911: Electric Services; SIC 4931: Electric and Other Services Combined; SIC 4939: Combination Utilities, NEC

221113 Nuclear Electric Power Generation *see* SIC 4911: Electric Services; SIC 4931: Electric and Other Services Combined; SIC 4939: Combination Utilities, NEC

221119 Other Electric Power Generation *see* SIC 4911: Electric Services; SIC 4931: Electric and Other Services Combined; SIC 4939: Combination Utilities, NEC

221121 Electric Bulk Power Transmission and Control *see* SIC 4911: Electric Services; SIC 4931: Electric and Other Services Combined; SIC 4939: Combination Utilities, NEC

221122 Electric Power Distribution *see* SIC 4911: Electric Services; SIC 4931: Electric and Other Services Combined; SIC 4939: Combination Utilities, NEC

221210 Natural Gas Distribution *see* SIC 4923: Natural Gas Transmission and Distribution; SIC 4924: Natural Gas Distribution; SIC 4925: Mixed, Manufactured, or Liquefied Petroleum Gas Production and/or Distribution; SIC 4931: Electric and Other Services Combined; SIC 4932: Gas and Other Services Combined; SIC 4939: Combination Utilities, NEC

221310 Water Supply and Irrigation Systems *see* SIC 4941: Water Supply; SIC 4971: Irrigation Systems

221320 Sewage Treatment Facilities *see* SIC 4952: Sewerage Systems

221330 Steam and Air-Conditioning Supply *see* SIC 4961: Steam and Air-Conditioning Supply

CONSTRUCTION

233110 Land Subdivision and Land Development *see* SIC 6552: Land Subdividers and Developers, Except Cemeteries; SIC 1521: General Contractors-Single-Family Houses; SIC 1531: Operative Builders

233220 Multi-Family Housing Construction *see* SIC 1522: General Contractors-Residential Buildings, Other Than Single-Family; SIC 1531: Operative Builders

233310 Manufacturing and Light Industrial Building Construction *see* SIC 1531: Operative Builders; SIC 1541: General Contractors-Industrial Buildings and Warehouses

233320 Commercial and Institutional Building Construction *see* SIC 1522: General Contractors-Residential Buildings, Other Than Single-Family; SIC 1531: Operative Builders; SIC 1541: General Contractors-Industrial Buildings and Warehouses; SIC 1542: General Contractors-Nonresidential Buildings, Other than Industrial Buildings and Warehouses

234110 Highway and Street Construction *see* SIC 1611: Highway and Street Construction, Except Elevated Highways

234120 Bridge and Tunnel Construction *see* SIC 1622: Bridge, Tunnel, and Elevated Highway Construction

234910 Water, Sewer and Pipeline Construction *see* SIC 1623: Water, Sewer, Pipeline, and Communications and Power Line Construction

234920 Power and Communication Transmission Line Construction *see* SIC 1623: Water, Sewer, Pipeline, and Communications and Power Line Construction

234930   Industrial Nonbuilding Structure Construction *see* SIC 1629: Heavy Construction, NEC

234990   All Other Heavy Construction *see* SIC 1629: Heavy Construction, NEC; SIC 7353: Heavy Construction Equipment Rental and Leasing

235110   Plumbing, Heating and Air-Conditioning Contractors *see* SIC 1711: Plumbing, Heating, and Air-Conditioning

235210   Painting and Wall Covering Contractors *see* SIC 1721: Painting and Paper Hanging; SIC 1799: Special Trade Contractors, NEC

235310   Electrical Contractors *see* SIC 1731: Electrical Work

235410   Masonry and Stone Contractors *see* SIC 1741: Masonry, Stone Setting and Other Stone Work

235420   Drywall, Plastering, Acoustical, and Insulation Contractors *see* SIC 1742: Plastering, Drywall, Acoustical and Insulation Work; SIC 1743: Terrazzo, Tile, Marble, and Mosaic Work; SIC 1771: Concrete Work

235430   Tile, Marble, Terrazzo and Mosaic Contractors *see* SIC 1743: Terrazzo, Tile, Marble, and Mosaic Work

235510   Carpentry Contractors *see* SIC 1751: Carpentry Work

235520   Floor Laying and Other Floor Contractors *see* SIC 1752: Floor Laying and Other Floor Work, NEC

235610   Roofing, Siding, and Sheet Metal Contractors *see* SIC 1761: Roofing, Siding, and Sheet Metal Work

235710   Concrete Contractors *see* SIC 1771: Concrete Work

235810   Water Well Drilling Contractors *see* SIC 1781: Water Well Drilling

235910   Structural Steel Erection Contractors *see* SIC 1791: Structural Steel Erection

235920   Glass and Glazing Contractors *see* SIC 1793: Glass and Glazing Work; SIC 1799: Special Trade Contractors, NEC

235930   Excavation Contractors *see* SIC 1794: Excavation Work

235940   Wrecking and Demolition Contractors *see* SIC 1795: Wrecking and Demolition Work

235950   Building Equipment and Other Machinery Installation Contractors *see* SIC 1796: Installation or Erection of Building Equipment, NEC

235990   All Other Special Trade Contractors *see* SIC 1799: Special Trade Contractors, NEC

FOOD MANUFACTURING

311111   Dog and Cat Food Manufacturing *see* SIC 2047: Dog and Cat Food

311119   Other Animal Food Manufacturing *see* SIC 2048: Prepared Feed and Feed Ingredients for Animals and Fowls, Except Dogs and Cats

311211   Flour Milling *see* SIC 2034: Dried and Dehydrated Fruits, Vegetables, and Soup Mixes; SIC 2041: Flour and Other Grain Mill Products

311212   Rice Milling *see* SIC 2044: Rice Milling

311213   Malt Manufacturing *see* SIC 2083: Malt

311221   Wet Corn Milling *see* SIC 2046: Wet Corn Milling

311222   Soybean Processing *see* SIC 2075: Soybean Oil Mills; SIC 2079: Shortening, Table Oils, Margarine, and Other Edible Fats and Oils, NEC

311223   Other Oilseed Processing *see* SIC 2074: Cottonseed Oil Mills; SIC 2076: Vegetable Oil Mills, Except Corn, Cottonseed, and Soybeans; SIC 2079: Shortening, Table Oils, Margarine, and Other Edible Fats and Oils, NEC

311225   Fats and Oils Refining and Blending *see* SIC 2074: Cottonseed Oil Mills; SIC 2075: Soybean Oil Mills; SIC 2076: Vegetable Oil Mills, Except Corn, Cottonseed, and Soybeans; SIC 2077: Animal and Marine Fats and Oils; SIC 2079: Shortening, Table Oils, Margarine, and Other Edible Fats and Oils, NEC

311230   Breakfast Cereal Manufacturing *see* SIC 2043: Cereal Breakfast Foods

311311   Sugarcane Mills *see* SIC 2061: Cane Sugar, Except Refining

311312   Cane Sugar Refining *see* SIC 2062: Cane Sugar Refining

311313   Beet Sugar Manufacturing *see* SIC 2063: Beet Sugar

311320   Chocolate and Confectionery Manufacturing from Cacao Beans *see* SIC 2066: Chocolate and Cocoa Products

311330   Confectionery Manufacturing from Purchased Chocolate *see* SIC 2064: Candy and Other Confectionery Products

311340   Non-Chocolate Confectionery Manufacturing *see* SIC 2064: Candy and Other Confectionery Products; SIC 2067: Chewing Gum; SIC 2099: Food Preparations, NEC

311411   Frozen Fruit, Juice, and Vegetable Processing *see* SIC 2037: Frozen Fruits, Fruit Juices, and Vegetables

311412   Frozen Specialty Food Manufacturing *see* SIC 2038: Frozen Specialties, NEC

311421   Fruit and Vegetable Canning *see* SIC 2033: Canned Fruits, Vegetables, Preserves, Jams, and Jellies; SIC 2035: Pickled Fruits and Vegetables, Vegetables Sauces and Seasonings, and Salad Dressings

311422   Specialty Canning *see* SIC 2032: Canned Specialties

311423   Dried and Dehydrated Food Manufacturing *see* SIC 2034: Dried and Dehydrated Fruits, Vegetables, and Soup Mixes; SIC 2099: Food Preparations, NEC

311511   Fluid Milk Manufacturing *see* SIC 2026: Fluid Milk

311512   Creamery Butter Manufacturing *see* SIC 2021: Creamery Butter

311513   Cheese Manufacturing *see* SIC 2022: Natural, Processed, and Imitation Cheese

311514   Dry, Condensed, and Evaporated Dairy Product Manufacturing *see* SIC 2023: Dry, Condensed, and Evaporated Dairy Products

311520   Ice Cream and Frozen Dessert Manufacturing *see* SIC 2024: Ice Cream and Frozen Desserts

311611   Animal (except Poultry) Slaughtering *see* SIC 0751: Livestock Services, Except Veterinary; SIC 2011: Meat Packing Plants; SIC 2048: Prepared Feed and Feed Ingredients for Animals and Fowls, Except Dogs and Cats

311612   Meat Processed From Carcasses *see* SIC 2013: Sausages and Other Prepared Meats; SIC 5147: Meats and Meat Products

311613   Rendering and Meat By-product Processing *see* SIC 2077: Animal and Marine Fats and Oils

311615   Poultry Processing *see* SIC 2015: Poultry Slaughtering and Processing

311711   Seafood Canning *see* SIC 2077: Animal and Marine Fats and Oils; SIC 2091: Canned and Cured Fish and Seafood

311712   Fresh and Frozen Seafood Processing *see* SIC 2077: Animal and Marine Fats and Oils; SIC 2092: Prepared Fresh or Frozen Fish and Seafoods

311811   Retail Bakeries *see* SIC 5461: Retail Bakeries

311812   Commercial Bakeries *see* SIC 2051: Bread and Other Bakery Products, Except Cookies and Crackers; SIC 2052: Cookies and Crackers

311813   Frozen Bakery Product Manufacturing *see* SIC 2053: Frozen Bakery Products, Except Bread

311821   Cookie and Cracker Manufacturing *see* SIC 2052: Cookies and Crackers

311822   Flour Mixes and Dough Manufacturing from Purchased Flour *see* SIC 2045: Prepared Flour Mixes and Doughs

311823   Pasta Manufacturing *see* SIC 2098: Macaroni, Spaghetti, Vermicelli, and Noodles

311830   Tortilla Manufacturing *see* SIC 2099: Food Preparations, NEC

311911   Roasted Nuts and Peanut Butter Manufacturing *see* SIC 2068: Salted and Roasted Nuts and Seeds; SIC 2099: Food Preparations, NEC

311919   Other Snack Food Manufacturing *see* SIC 2052: Cookies and Crackers; SIC 2096: Potato Chips, Corn Chips, and Similar Snacks

311920   Coffee and Tea Manufacturing *see* SIC 2043: Cereal Breakfast Foods; SIC 2095: Roasted Coffee; SIC 2099: Food Preparations, NEC

311930   Flavoring Syrup and Concentrate Manufacturing *see* SIC 2087: Flavoring Extracts and Flavoring Syrups NEC

311941   Mayonnaise, Dressing, and Other Prepared Sauce Manufacturing *see* SIC 2035: Pickled Fruits and Vegetables, Vegetables Sauces and Seasonings, and Salad Dressings; SIC 2099: Food Preparations, NEC

311942   Spice and Extract Manufacturing *see* SIC 2087: Flavoring Extracts and Flavoring Syrups NEC; SIC 2095: Roasted Coffee; SIC 2099: Food Preparations, NEC; SIC 2899: Chemicals and Chemical Preparations, NEC

311991   Perishable Prepared Food Manufacturing *see* SIC 2099: Food Preparations, NEC

311999   All Other Miscellaneous Food Manufacturing *see* SIC 2015: Poultry Slaughtering and Processing; SIC 2032: Canned Specialties; SIC 2087: Flavoring Extracts and Flavoring Syrups NEC; SIC 2099: Food Preparations, NEC

BEVERAGE & TOBACCO PRODUCT MANUFACTURING

312111   Soft Drink Manufacturing *see* SIC 2086: Bottled and Canned Soft Drinks and Carbonated Waters

312112   Bottled Water Manufacturing *see* SIC 2086: Bottled and Canned Soft Drinks and Carbonated Waters

312113   Ice Manufacturing *see* SIC 2097: Manufactured Ice

312120   Breweries *see* SIC 2082: Malt Beverages

312130   Wineries *see* SIC 2084: Wines, Brandy, and Brandy Spirits

312140   Distilleries *see* SIC 2085: Distilled and Blended Liquors

312210   Tobacco Stemming and Redrying *see* SIC 2141: Tobacco Stemming and Redrying

312221   Cigarette Manufacturing *see* SIC 2111: Cigarettes

312229   Other Tobacco Product Manufacturing *see* SIC 2121: Cigars; SIC 2131: Chewing and Smoking Tobacco and Snuff; SIC 2141: Tobacco Stemming and Redrying

TEXTILE MILLS

313111   Yarn Spinning Mills *see* SIC 2281: Yarn Spinning Mills; SIC 2299: Textile Goods, NEC

313112   Yarn Texturing, Throwing and Twisting Mills *see* SIC 2282: Yarn Texturizing, Throwing, Twisting, and Winding Mills

313113   Thread Mills *see* SIC 2284: Thread Mills; SIC 2299: Textile Goods, NEC

313210   Broadwoven Fabric Mills *see* SIC 2211: Broadwoven Fabric Mills, Cotton; SIC 2221: Broadwoven Fabric Mills, Manmade Fiber and Silk; SIC 2231: Broadwoven Fabric Mills, Wool (Including Dyeing and Finishing); SIC 2299: Textile Goods, NEC

313221   Narrow Fabric Mills *see* SIC 2241: Narrow Fabric and Other Smallware Mills: Cotton, Wool, Silk, and Manmade Fiber; SIC 2299: Textile Goods, NEC

313222   Schiffli Machine Embroidery *see* SIC 2397: Schiffli Machine Embroideries

313230   Nonwoven Fabric Mills *see* SIC 2297: Nonwoven Fabrics; SIC 2299: Textile Goods, NEC

313241   Weft Knit Fabric Mills *see* SIC 2257: Weft Knit Fabric Mills; SIC 2259: Knitting Mills, NEC

313249   Other Knit Fabric and Lace Mills *see* SIC 2258: Lace and Warp Knit Fabric Mills; SIC 2259: Knitting Mills, NEC

313311   Broadwoven Fabric Finishing Mills *see* SIC 2231: Broadwoven Fabric Mills, Wool (Including Dyeing and Finishing); SIC 2261: Finishers of Broadwoven Fabrics of Cotton; SIC 2262: Finishers of Broadwoven Fabrics of Manmade Fiber and Silk; SIC 2269: Finishers of Textiles, NEC; SIC 5131: Piece Goods, Notions, and Other Dry Goods

313312   Textile and Fabric Finishing (except Broadwoven Fabric) Mills *see* SIC 2231: Broadwoven Fabric Mills, Wool (Including Dyeing and Finishing); SIC 2257: Weft Knit Fabric Mills; SIC 2258: Lace and Warp Knit Fabric Mills; SIC 2269: Finishers of Textiles, NEC; SIC 2282: Yarn Texturizing, Throwing, Twisting, and Winding Mills; SIC 2284: Thread Mills; SIC 2299: Textile Goods, NEC; SIC 5131: Piece Goods, Notions, and Other Dry Goods

313320   Fabric Coating Mills *see* SIC 2295: Coated Fabrics, Not Rubberized; SIC 3069: Fabricated Rubber Products, NEC

TEXTILE PRODUCT MILLS

314110   Carpet and Rug Mills *see* SIC 2273: Carpets and Rugs

314121   Curtain and Drapery Mills *see* SIC 2391: Curtains and Draperies; SIC 5714: Drapery, Curtain, and Upholstery Stores

314129   Other Household Textile Product Mills *see* SIC 2392: Housefurnishings, Except Curtains and Draperies

314911   Textile Bag Mills *see* SIC 2392: Housefurnishings, Except Curtains and Draperies; SIC 2393: Textile Bags

314912   Canvas and Related Product Mills *see* SIC 2394: Canvas and Related Products

314991   Rope, Cordage and Twine Mills *see* SIC 2298: Cordage and Twine

314992   Tire Cord and Tire Fabric Mills *see* SIC 2296: Tire Cord and Fabrics

314999   All Other Miscellaneous Textile Product Mills *see* SIC 2299: Textile Goods, NEC; SIC 2395: Pleating, Decorative and Novelty Stitching, and Tucking for the Trade; SIC 2396: Automotive Trimmings, Apparel Findings, and Related Products; SIC 2399: Fabricated Textile Products, NEC

APPAREL MANUFACTURING

315111   Sheer Hosiery Mills *see* SIC 2251: Women's Full-Length and Knee-Length Hosiery, Except Socks; SIC 2252: Hosiery, NEC

315119   Other Hosiery and Sock Mills *see* SIC 2252:, Hosiery, NEC

315191   Outerwear Knitting Mills *see* SIC 2253: Knit Outerwear Mills; SIC 2259: Knitting Mills, NEC

315192   Underwear and Nightwear Knitting Mills *see* SIC 2254: Knit Underwear and Nightwear Mills; SIC 2259: Knitting Mills, NEC

315211   Men's and Boys' Cut and Sew Apparel Contractors *see* SIC 2311: Men's and Boys' Suits, Coats and Overcoats; SIC 2321: Men's and Boys' Shirts, Except Work Shirts; SIC 2322: Men's and Boys' Underwear and Nightwear; SIC 2325: Men's and Boys' Trousers and Slacks; SIC 2326: Men's and Boys' Work Clothing; SIC 2329: Men's and Boys' Clothing, NEC; SIC 2341: Women's, Misses, Children's, and Infants' Underwear and Nightwear; SIC 2361: Girls', Children's and Infants' Dresses, Blouses and Shirts; SIC 2369: Girls', Children's and Infants' Outerwear, NEC; SIC 2384: Robes and Dressing Gowns; SIC 2385: Waterproof Outerwear; SIC 2389: Apparel and Accessories, NEC; SIC 2395: Pleating, Decorative and Novelty Stitching, and Tucking for the Trade

315212   Women's and Girls' Cut and Sew Apparel Contractors *see* SIC 2331: Women's, Misses', and Juniors' Blouses and Shirts; SIC 2335: Women's, Misses', and Junior's Dresses; SIC 2337: Women's, Misses', and Juniors' Suits, Skirts and Coats; SIC 2339: Women's, Misses', and Juniors' Outerwear, NEC; SIC 2341:

Women's, Misses, Children's, and Infants' Underwear and Nightwear; SIC 2342: Brassieres, Girdles, and Allied Garments; SIC 2361: Girls', Children's, and Infants' Dresses, Blouses, and Shirts; SIC 2369: Girls', Children's, and Infants' Outerwear, NEC; SIC 2384: Robes and Dressing Gowns; SIC 2385: Waterproof Outerwear; SIC 2389: Apparel and Accessories, NEC; SIC 2395: Pleating, Decorative and Novelty Stitching, and Tucking for the Trade

315221   Men's and Boys' Cut and Sew Underwear and Nightwear Manufacturing *see* SIC 2322: Men's and Boys' Underwear and Nightwear; SIC 2341: Women's, Misses, Children's, and Infants' Underwear and Nightwear; SIC 2369: Girls', Children's and Infants' Outerwear, NEC; SIC 2384: Robes and Dressing Gowns

315222   Men's and Boys' Cut and Sew Suit, Coat, and Overcoat Manufacturing *see* SIC 2311: Men's and Boys' Suits, Coats and Overcoats; SIC 2369: Girls', Children's and Infants' Outerwear, NEC; SIC 2385: Waterproof Outerwear

315223   Men's and Boys' Cut and Sew Shirt, (except Work Shirt) Manufacturing *see* SIC 2321: Men's and Boys' Shirts, Except Work Shirts; SIC 2361: Girls', Children's and Infants' Dresses, Blouses and Shirts

315224   Men's and Boys' Cut And Sew Trouser, Slack, And Jean Manufacturing *see* SIC 2325: Men's and Boys' Trousers and Slacks; SIC 2369: Girls', Children's and Infants' Outerwear, NEC

315225   Men's and Boys' Cut and Sew Work Clothing Manufacturing *see* SIC 2326: Men's and Boys' Work Clothing

315228   Men's and Boys' Cut and Sew Other Outerwear Manufacturing *see* SIC 2329: Men's and Boys' Clothing, NEC; SIC 2369: Girls', Children's and Infants' Outerwear, NEC; SIC 2385: Waterproof Outerwear

315231   Women's and Girls' Cut and Sew Lingerie, Loungewear, and Nightwear Manufacturing *see* SIC 2341: Women's, Misses, Children's, and Infants' Underwear and Nightwear; SIC 2342: Brassieres, Girdles, and Allied Garments; SIC 2369: Girls', Children's and Infants' Outerwear, NEC; SIC 2384: Robes and Dressing Gowns; SIC 2389: Apparel and Accessories, NEC

315232   Women's and Girls' Cut and Sew Blouse and Shirt Manufacturing *see* SIC 2331: Women's, Misses', and Juniors' Blouses and Shirts; SIC 2361: Girls', Children's and Infants' Dresses, Blouses and Shirts

315233   Women's and Girls' Cut and Sew Dress Manufacturing *see* SIC 2335: Women's, Misses'

and Junior's Dresses; SIC 2361: Girls', Children's and Infants' Dresses, Blouses and Shirts

315234   Women's and Girls' Cut and Sew Suit, Coat, Tailored Jacket, and Skirt Manufacturing *see* SIC 2337: Women's, Misses' and Juniors' Suits, Skirts and Coats; SIC 2369: Girls', Children's and Infants' Outerwear, NEC; SIC 2385: Waterproof Outerwear

315238   Women's and Girls' Cut and Sew Other Outerwear Manufacturing *see* SIC 2339: Women's, Misses' and Juniors' Outerwear, NEC; SIC 2369: Girls', Children's and Infants' Outerwear, NEC; SIC 2385: Waterproof Outerwear

315291   Infants' Cut and Sew Apparel Manufacturing *see* SIC 2341: Women's, Misses, Children's, and Infants' Underwear and Nightwear; SIC 2361: Girls', Children's and Infants' Dresses, Blouses and Shirts; SIC 2369: Girls', Children's and Infants' Outerwear, NEC; SIC 2385: Waterproof Outerwear

315292   Fur and Leather Apparel Manufacturing *see* SIC 2371: Fur Goods; SIC 2386: Leather and Sheep-Lined Clothing

315299   All Other Cut and Sew Apparel Manufacturing *see* SIC 2329: Men's and Boys' Clothing, NEC; SIC 2339: Women's, Misses' and Juniors' Outerwear, NEC; SIC 2389: Apparel and Accessories, NEC

315991   Hat, Cap, and Millinery Manufacturing *see* SIC 2353: Hats, Caps, and Millinery

315992   Glove and Mitten Manufacturing *see* SIC 2381: Dress and Work Gloves, Except Knit and All-Leather; SIC 3151: Leather Gloves and Mittens

315993   Men's and Boys' Neckwear Manufacturing *see* SIC 2323: Men's and Boys' Neckwear

315999   Other Apparel Accessories and Other Apparel Manufacturing *see* SIC 2339: Women's, Misses' and Juniors' Outerwear, NEC; SIC 2385: Waterproof Outerwear; SIC 2387: Apparel Belts; SIC 2389: Apparel and Accessories, NEC; SIC 2396: Automotive Trimmings, Apparel Findings, and Related Products; SIC 2399: Fabricated Textile Products, NEC

LEATHER & ALLIED PRODUCT MANUFACTURING

316110   Leather and Hide Tanning and Finishing *see* SIC 3111: Leather Tanning and Finishing; SIC 3999: Manufacturing Industries, NEC

316211   Rubber and Plastics Footwear Manufacturing *see* SIC 3021: Rubber and Plastics Footwear

316212   House Slipper Manufacturing *see* SIC 3142: House Slippers

316213 Men's Footwear (except Athletic) Manufacturing *see* SIC 3143: Men's Footwear, Except Athletic

316214 Women's Footwear (except Athletic) Manufacturing *see* SIC 3144: Women's Footwear, Except Athletic

316219 Other Footwear Manufacturing *see* SIC 3149: Footwear, Except Rubber, NEC

316991 Luggage Manufacturing *see* SIC 3161: Luggage

316992 Women's Handbag and Purse Manufacturing *see* SIC 3171: Women's Handbags and Purses

316993 Personal Leather Good (except Women's Handbag and Purse) Manufacturing *see* SIC 3172: Personal Leather Goods, Except Women's Handbags and Purses

316999 All Other Leather Good Manufacturing *see* SIC 3131: Boot and Shoe Cut Stock and Findings; SIC 3199: Leather Goods, NEC

WOOD PRODUCT MANUFACTURING

321113 Sawmills *see* SIC 2421: Sawmills and Planing Mills, General; SIC 2429: Special Product Sawmills, NEC

321114 Wood Preservation *see* SIC 2491: Wood Preserving

321211 Hardwood Veneer and Plywood Manufacturing *see* SIC 2435: Hardwood Veneer and Plywood

321212 Softwood Veneer and Plywood Manufacturing *see* SIC 2436: Softwood Veneer and Plywood

321213 Engineered Wood Member (except Truss) Manufacturing *see* SIC 2439: Structural Wood Members, NEC

321214 Truss Manufacturing *see* SIC 2439: Structural Wood Members, NEC

321219 Reconstituted Wood Product Manufacturing *see* SIC 2493: Reconstituted Wood Products

321911 Wood Window and Door Manufacturing *see* SIC 2431: Millwork

321912 Cut Stock, Resawing Lumber, and Planing *see* SIC 2421: Sawmills and Planing Mills, General; SIC 2426: Hardwood Dimension and Flooring Mills; SIC 2429: Special Product Sawmills, NEC; SIC 2439: Structural Wood Members, NEC

321918 Other Millwork (including Flooring) *see* SIC 2421: Sawmills and Planing Mills, General; SIC 2426: Hardwood Dimension and Flooring Mills; SIC 2431: Millwork

321920 Wood Container and Pallet Manufacturing *see* SIC 2441: Nailed and Lock Corner Wood Boxes and Shook; SIC 2448: Wood Pallets and Skids; SIC 2449: Wood Containers, NEC; SIC 2499: Wood Products, NEC

321991 Manufactured Home (Mobile Home) Manufacturing *see* SIC 2451: Mobile Homes

321992 Prefabricated Wood Building Manufacturing *see* SIC 2452: Prefabricated Wood Buildings and Components

321999 All Other Miscellaneous Wood Product Manufacturing *see* SIC 2421: Sawmills and Planing Mills, General; SIC 2426: Hardwood Dimension and Flooring Mills; SIC 2429: Special Product Sawmills, NEC; SIC 2499: Wood Products, NEC; SIC 3131: Boot and Shoe Cut Stock and Findings; SIC 3999: Manufacturing Industries, NEC

PAPER MANUFACTURING

322110 Pulp Mills *see* SIC 2611: Pulp Mills

322121 Paper (except Newsprint) Mills *see* SIC 2611: Pulp Mills

322121 Paper (except Newsprint) Mills *see* SIC 2621: Paper Mills

322122 Newsprint Mills *see* SIC 2621: Paper Mills

322130 Paperboard Mills *see* SIC 2611: Pulp Mills

322130 Paperboard Mills *see* SIC 2631: Paperboard Mills

322211 Corrugated and Solid Fiber Box Manufacturing *see* SIC 2653: Corrugated and Solid Fiber Boxes

322212 Folding Paperboard Box Manufacturing *see* SIC 2657: Folding Paperboard Boxes, Including Sanitary

322213 Setup Paperboard Box Manufacturing *see* SIC 2652: Setup Paperboard Boxes

322214 Fiber Can, Tube, Drum, and Similar Products Manufacturing *see* SIC 2655: Fiber Cans, Tubes, Drums, and Similar Products

322215 Non-Folding Sanitary Food Container Manufacturing *see* SIC 2656: Sanitary Food Containers, Except Folding; SIC 2679: Converted Paper and Paperboard Products, NEC

322221 Coated and Laminated Packaging Paper and Plastics Film Manufacturing *see* SIC 2671: Packaging Paper and Plastics Film, Coated and Laminated

322222 Coated and Laminated Paper Manufacturing *see* SIC 2672: Coated and Laminated Paper, NEC; SIC 2679: Converted Paper and Paperboard Products, NEC

322223 Plastics, Foil, and Coated Paper Bag Manufacturing *see* SIC 2673: Plastics, Foil, and Coated Paper Bags

322224 Uncoated Paper and Multiwall Bag Manufacturing *see* SIC 2674: Uncoated Paper and Multiwall Bags

322225 Laminated Aluminum Foil Manufacturing for Flexible Packaging Uses *see* SIC 3497: Metal Foil and Leaf

322231 Die-Cut Paper and Paperboard Office Supplies Manufacturing *see* SIC 2675: Die-Cut Paper and Paperboard and Cardboard; SIC 2679: Converted Paper and Paperboard Products, NEC

322232 Envelope Manufacturing *see* SIC 2677: Envelopes

322233 Stationery, Tablet, and Related Product Manufacturing *see* SIC 2678: Stationery, Tablets, and Related Products

322291 Sanitary Paper Product Manufacturing *see* SIC 2676: Sanitary Paper Products

322292 Surface-Coated Paperboard Manufacturing *see* SIC 2675: Die-Cut Paper and Paperboard and Cardboard

322298 All Other Converted Paper Product Manufacturing *see* SIC 2675: Die-Cut Paper and Paperboard and Cardboard; SIC 2679: Converted Paper and Paperboard Products, NEC

PRINTING & RELATED SUPPORT ACTIVITIES

323110 Commercial Lithographic Printing *see* SIC 2752: Commercial Printing, Lithographic; SIC 2771: Greeting Cards; SIC 2782: Blankbooks, Loose-leaf Binders and Devices; SIC 3999: Manufacturing Industries, NEC

323111 Commercial Gravure Printing *see* SIC 2754: Commercial Prinring, Gravure; SIC 2771: Greeting Cards; SIC 2782: Blankbooks, Loose-leaf Binders and Devices; SIC 3999: Manufacturing Industries, NEC

323112 Commercial Flexographic Printing *see* SIC 2759: Commercial Printing, NEC; SIC 2771: Greeting Cards; SIC 2782: Blankbooks, Loose-leaf Binders and Devices

323112 Commercial Flexographic Printing *see* SIC 3999: Manufacturing Industries, NEC

323113 Commercial Screen Printing *see* SIC 2396: Automotive Trimmings, Apparel Findings, and Related Products; SIC 2759: Commercial Printing, NEC; SIC 2771: Greeting Cards; SIC 2782: Blankbooks, Loose-leaf Binders and Devices; SIC 3999: Manufacturing Industries, NEC

323114 Quick Printing *see* SIC 2752: Commercial Printing, Lithographic; SIC 2759: Commercial Printing, NEC

323115 Digital Printing *see* SIC 2759: Commercial Printing, NEC

323116 Manifold Business Form Printing *see* SIC 2761: Manifold Business Forms

323117 Book Printing *see* SIC 2732: Book Printing

323118 Blankbook, Loose-leaf Binder and Device Manufacturing *see* SIC 2782: Blankbooks, Loose-leaf Binders and Devices

323119 Other Commercial Printing *see* SIC 2759: Commercial Printing, NEC; SIC 2771: Greeting Cards; SIC 2782: Blankbooks, Loose-leaf Binders and Devices; SIC 3999: Manufacturing Industries, NEC

323121 Tradebinding and Related Work *see* SIC 2789: Bookbinding and Related Work

323122 Prepress Services *see* SIC 2791: Typesetting; SIC 2796: Platemaking and Related Services

PETROLEUM & COAL PRODUCTS MANUFACTURING

324110 Petroleum Refineries *see* SIC 2911: Petroleum Refining

324121 Asphalt Paving Mixture and Block Manufacturing *see* SIC 2951: Asphalt Paving Mixtures and Blocks

324122 Asphalt Shingle and Coating Materials Manufacturing *see* SIC 2952: Asphalt Felts and Coatings

324191 Petroleum Lubricating Oil and Grease Manufacturing *see* SIC 2992: Lubricating Oils and Greases

324199 All Other Petroleum and Coal Products Manufacturing *see* SIC 2999: Products of Petroleum and Coal, NEC; SIC 3312: Steel Works, Blast Furnaces (Including Coke Ovens), and Rolling Mills

CHEMICAL MANUFACTURING

325110 Petrochemical Manufacturing *see* SIC 2865: Cyclic Organic Crudes and Intermediates, and Organic Dyes and Pigments; SIC 2869: Industrial Organic Chemicals, NEC

325120 Industrial Gas Manufacturing *see* SIC 2813: Industrial Gases; SIC 2869: Industrial Organic Chemicals, NEC

325131 Inorganic Dye and Pigment Manufacturing *see* SIC 2816: Inorganic Pigments; SIC 2819: Industrial Inorganic Chemicals, NEC

325132 Organic Dye and Pigment Manufacturing *see* SIC 2865: Cyclic Organic Crudes and Intermediates, and Organic Dyes and Pigments

325181 Alkalies and Chlorine Manufacturing *see* SIC 2812: Alkalies and Chlorine

325182 Carbon Black Manufacturing *see* SIC 2816: Inorganic Pigments; SIC 2895: Carbon Black

325188 All Other Inorganic Chemical Manufacturing *see* SIC 2819: Industrial Inorganic Chemicals,

NEC; SIC 2869: Industrial Organic Chemicals, NEC

325191 Gum and Wood Chemical Manufacturing *see* SIC 2861: Gum and Wood Chemicals

325192 Cyclic Crude and Intermediate Manufacturing *see* SIC 2865: Cyclic Organic Crudes and Intermediates, and Organic Dyes and Pigments

325193 Ethyl Alcohol Manufacturing *see* SIC 2869: Industrial Organic Chemicals, NEC

325199 All Other Basic Organic Chemical Manufacturing *see* SIC 2869: Industrial Organic Chemicals, NEC; SIC 2899: Chemicals and Chemical Preparations, NEC

325211 Plastics Material and Resin Manufacturing *see* SIC 2821: Plastics Material Synthetic Resins, and Nonvulcanizable Elastomers

325212 Synthetic Rubber Manufacturing *see* SIC 2822: Synthetic Rubber

325221 Cellulosic Manmade Fiber Manufacturing *see* SIC 2823: Cellulosic Manmade Fibers

325222 Noncellulosic Organic Fiber Manufacturing *see* SIC 2824: Manmade Organic Fibers, Except Cellulosic

325311 Nitrogenous Fertilizer Manufacturing *see* SIC 2873: Nitrogenous Fertilizers

325312 Phosphatic Fertilizer Manufacturing *see* SIC 2874: Phosphatic Fertilizers

325314 Fertilizer (Mixing Only) Manufacturing *see* SIC 2875: Fertilizers, Mixing Only

325320 Pesticide and Other Agricultural Chemical Manufacturing *see* SIC 2879: Pesticides and Agricultural Chemicals, NEC

325411 Medicinal and Botanical Manufacturing *see* SIC 2833: Medicinal Chemicals and Botanical Products

325412 Pharmaceutical Preparation Manufacturing *see* SIC 2834: Pharmaceutical Preparations; SIC 2835: In Vitro and In Vivo Diagnostic Substances

325413 In-Vitro Diagnostic Substance Manufacturing *see* SIC 2835: In Vitro and In Vivo Diagnostic Substances

325414 Biological Product (except Diagnostic) Manufacturing *see* SIC 2836: Biological Products, Except Diagnostic Substances

325510 Paint and Coating Manufacturing *see* SIC 2851: Paints, Varnishes, Lacquers, Enamels, and Allied Products; SIC 2899: Chemicals and Chemical Preparations, NEC

325520 Adhesive and Sealant Manufacturing *see* SIC 2891: Adhesives and Sealants

325611 Soap and Other Detergent Manufacturing *see* SIC 2841: Soaps and Other Detergents, Except

Specialty Cleaners; SIC 2844: Perfumes, Cosmetics, and Other Toilet Preparations

325612 Polish and Other Sanitation Good Manufacturing *see* SIC 2842: Specialty Cleaning, Polishing, and Sanitary Preparations

325613 Surface Active Agent Manufacturing *see* SIC 2843: Surface Active Agents, Finishing Agents, Sulfonated Oils, and Assistants

325620 Toilet Preparation Manufacturing *see* SIC 2844: Perfumes, Cosmetics, and Other Toilet Preparations

325910 Printing Ink Manufacturing *see* SIC 2893: Printing Ink

325920 Explosives Manufacturing *see* SIC 2892: Explosives

325991 Custom Compounding of Purchased Resin *see* SIC 3087: Custom Compounding of Purchased Plastics Resins

325992 Photographic Film, Paper, Plate and Chemical Manufacturing *see* SIC 3861: Photographic Equipment and Supplies

325998 All Other Miscellaneous Chemical Product Manufacturing *see* SIC 2819: Industrial Inorganic Chemicals, NEC; SIC 2899: Chemicals and Chemical Preparations, NEC; SIC 3952: Lead Pencils, Crayons, and Artist's Materials; SIC 3999: Manufacturing Industries, NEC

PLASTICS & RUBBER PRODUCTS MANUFACTURING

326111 Unsupported Plastics Bag Manufacturing *see* SIC 2673: Plastics, Foil, and Coated Paper Bags

326112 Unsupported Plastics Packaging Film and Sheet Manufacturing *see* SIC 2671: Packaging Paper and Plastics Film, Coated and Laminated

326113 Unsupported Plastics Film and Sheet (except Packaging) Manufacturing *see* SIC 3081: Unsupported Plastics Film and Sheet

326121 Unsupported Plastics Profile Shape Manufacturing *see* SIC 3082: Unsupported Plastics Profile Shapes; SIC 3089: Plastics Products, NEC

326122 Plastics Pipe and Pipe Fitting Manufacturing *see* SIC 3084: Plastic Pipe; SIC 3089: Plastics Products, NEC

326130 Laminated Plastics Plate, Sheet, and Shape Manufacturing *see* SIC 3083: Laminated Plastics Plate, Sheet, and Profile Shapes

326140 Polystyrene Foam Product Manufacturing *see* SIC 3086: Plastics Foam Products

326150 Urethane and Other Foam Product (except Polystyrene) Manufacturing *see* SIC 3086: Plastics Foam Products

326160   Plastics Bottle Manufacturing *see* SIC 3085: Plastics Bottles

326191   Plastics Plumbing Fixtures Manufacturing *see* SIC 3088: Plastics Plumbing Fixtures

326192   Resilient Floor Covering Manufacturing *see* SIC 3069: Fabricated Rubber Products, NEC; SIC 3996: Linoleum, Asphalted-Felt-Base, and Other Hard Surface Floor Coverings, NEC

326199   All Other Plastics Product Manufacturing *see* SIC 3089: Plastics Products, NEC; SIC 3999: Manufacturing Industries, NEC

326211   Tire Manufacturing (except Retreading) *see* SIC 3011: Tires and Inner Tubes

326212   Tire Retreading *see* SIC 7534: Tire Retreading and Repair Shops

326220   Rubber and Plastics Hoses and Belting Manufacturing *see* SIC 3052: Rubber and Plastics Hose and Belting

326291   Rubber Product Manufacturing for Mechanical Use *see* SIC 3061: Molded, Extruded, and Lathe-Cut Mechanical Rubber Products

326299   All Other Rubber Product Manufacturing *see* SIC 3069: Fabricated Rubber Products, NEC

NONMETALLIC MINERAL PRODUCT MANUFACTURING

327111   Vitreous China Plumbing Fixture and China and Earthenware Fitting and Bathroom Accessories Manufacturing *see* SIC 3261: Vitreous China Plumbing Fixtures and China and Earthenware Fittings and Bathroom Accessories

327112   Vitreous China, Fine Earthenware and Other Pottery Product Manufacturing *see* SIC 3262: Vitreous China Table and Kitchen Articles; SIC 3263: Fine Earthenware (Whiteware) Table and Kitchen Articles; SIC 3269: Pottery Products, NEC

327113   Porcelain Electrical Supply Manufacturing *see* SIC 3264: Porcelain Electrical Supplies

327121   Brick and Structural Clay Tile Manufacturing *see* SIC 3251: Brick and Structural Clay Tile

327122   Ceramic Wall and Floor Tile Manufacturing *see* SIC 3253: Ceramic Wall and Floor Tile

327123   Other Structural Clay Product Manufacturing *see* SIC 3259: Structural Clay Products, NEC

327124   Clay Refractory Manufacturing *see* SIC 3255: Clay Refractories

327125   Nonclay Refractory Manufacturing *see* SIC 3297: Nonclay Refractories

327211   Flat Glass Manufacturing *see* SIC 3211: Flat Glass

327212   Other Pressed and Blown Glass and Glassware Manufacturing *see* SIC 3229: Pressed and Blown Glass and Glassware, NEC

327213   Glass Container Manufacturing *see* SIC 3221: Glass Containers

327215   Glass Product Manufacturing Made of Purchased Glass *see* SIC 3231: Glass Products, Made of Purchased Glass

327310   Cement Manufacturing *see* SIC 3241: Cement, Hydraulic

327320   Ready-Mix Concrete Manufacturing *see* SIC 3273: Ready-Mixed Concrete

327331   Concrete Block and Brick Manufacturing *see* SIC 3271: Concrete Block and Brick

327332   Concrete Pipe Manufacturing *see* SIC 3272: Concrete Products, Except Block and Brick

327390   Other Concrete Product Manufacturing *see* SIC 3272: Concrete Products, Except Block and Brick

327410   Lime Manufacturing *see* SIC 3274: Lime

327420   Gypsum and Gypsum Product Manufacturing *see* SIC 3275: Gypsum Products; SIC 3299: Nonmetallic Mineral Products, NEC

327910   Abrasive Product Manufacturing *see* SIC 3291: Abrasive Products

327991   Cut Stone and Stone Product Manufacturing *see* SIC 3281: Cut Stone and Stone Products

327992   Ground or Treated Mineral and Earth Manufacturing *see* SIC 3295: Minerals and Earths, Ground or Otherwise Treated

327993   Mineral Wool Manufacturing *see* SIC 3296: Mineral Wool

327999   All Other Miscellaneous Nonmetallic Mineral Product Manufacturing *see* SIC 3272: Concrete Products, Except Block and Brick; SIC 3292: Asbestos Products; SIC 3299: Nonmetallic Mineral Products, NEC

PRIMARY METAL MANUFACTURING

331111   Iron and Steel Mills *see* SIC 3312: Steel Works, Blast Furnaces (Including Coke Ovens), and Rolling Mills; SIC 3399: Primary Metal Products, NEC

331112   Electrometallurgical Ferroalloy Product Manufacturing *see* SIC 3313: Electrometallurgical Products, Except Steel

331210   Iron and Steel Pipes and Tubes Manufacturing from Purchased Steel *see* SIC 3317: Steel Pipe and Tubes

331221   Cold-Rolled Steel Shape Manufacturing *see* SIC 3316: Cold-Rolled Steel Sheet, Strip, and Bars

331222   Steel Wire Drawing *see* SIC 3315: Steel Wiredrawing and Steel Nails and Spikes

331311 Aluminum Refining *see* SIC 2819: Industrial Inorganic Chemicals, NEC

331312 Primary Aluminum Production *see* SIC 3334: Primary Production of Aluminum

331314 Secondary Smelting and Alloying of Aluminum *see* SIC 3341: Secondary Smelting and Refining of Nonferrous Metals; SIC 3399: Primary Metal Products, NEC

331315 Aluminum Sheet, Plate, and Foil Manufacturing *see* SIC 3353: Aluminum Sheet, Plate, and Foil

331316 Aluminum Extruded Product Manufacturing *see* SIC 3354: Aluminum Extruded Products

331319 Other Aluminum Rolling and Drawing, *see* SIC 3355: Aluminum Rolling and Drawing, NEC; SIC 3357: Drawing and Insulating of Nonferrous Wire

331411 Primary Smelting and Refining of Copper *see* SIC 3331: Primary Smelting and Refining of Copper

331419 Primary Smelting and Refining of Nonferrous Metals (except Copper and Aluminum) *see* SIC 3339: Primary Smelting and Refining of Nonferrous Metals, Except Copper and Aluminum

331421 Copper (except Wire) Rolling, Drawing, and Extruding *see* SIC 3351: Rolling, Drawing, and Extruding of Copper

331422 Copper Wire Drawing *see* SIC 3357: Drawing and Insulating of Nonferrous Wire

331423 Secondary Smelting, Refining, and Alloying of Copper *see* SIC 3341: Secondary Smelting and Refining of Nonferrous Metals; SIC 3399: Primary Metal Products, NEC

331491 Nonferrous Metal (except Copper and Aluminum) Rolling. Drawing, and Extruding *see* SIC 3356: Rolling, Drawing, and Extruding of Nonferrous Metals, Except Copper and Aluminum; SIC 3357: Drawing and Insulating of Nonferrous Wire

331492 Secondary Smelting, Refining, and Alloying of Nonferrous Metals (except Copper and Aluminum) *see* SIC 3313: Electrometallurgical Products, Except Steel; SIC 3341: Secondary Smelting and Refining of Nonferrous Metals; SIC 3399: Primary Metal Products, NEC

331511 Iron Foundries *see* SIC 3321: Gray and Ductile Iron Foundries; SIC 3322: Malleable Iron Foundries

331512 Steel Investment Foundries *see* SIC 3324: Steel Investment Foundries

331513 Steel Foundries (except Investment) *see* SIC 3325: Steel Foundries, NEC

331521 Aluminum Die-Castings *see* SIC 3363: Aluminum Die-Castings

331522 Nonferrous (except Aluminum) Die-Castings *see* SIC 3364: Nonferrous Die-Castings, Except Aluminum

331524 Aluminum Foundries *see* SIC 3365: Aluminum Foundries

331525 Copper Foundries *see* SIC 3366: Copper Foundries

331528 Other Nonferrous Foundries *see* SIC 3369: Nonferrous Foundries, Except Aluminum and Copper

FABRICATED METAL PRODUCT MANUFACTURING

332111 Iron and Steel Forging *see* SIC 3462: Iron and Steel Forgings

332112 Nonferrous Forging *see* SIC 3463: Nonferrous Forgings

332114 Custom Roll Forming *see* SIC 3449: Miscellaneous Structural Metal Work

332115 Crown and Closure Manufacturing *see* SIC 3466: Crowns and Closures

332116 Metal Stamping *see* SIC 3469: Metal Stamping, NEC

332117 Powder Metallurgy Part Manufacturing *see* SIC 3499: Fabricated Metal Products, NEC

332211 Cutlery and Flatware (except Precious) Manufacturing *see* SIC 3421: Cutlery; SIC 3914: Silverware, Plated Ware, and Stainless Steel Ware

332212 Hand and Edge Tool Manufacturing *see* SIC 3423: Hand and Edge Tools, Except Machine Tools and Handsaws; SIC 3523: Farm Machinery and Equipment; SIC 3524: Lawn and Garden Tractors and Home Lawn and Garden Equipment; SIC 3545: Cutting Tools, Machine Tool Accessories, and Machinists' Precision Measuring Devices; SIC 3799: Transportation Equipment, NEC; SIC 3999: Manufacturing Industries, NEC

332213 Saw Blade and Handsaw Manufacturing *see* SIC 3425: Saw Blades and Handsaws

332214 Kitchen Utensil, Pot and Pan Manufacturing *see* SIC 3469: Metal Stamping, NEC

332311 Prefabricated Metal Building and Component Manufacturing *see* SIC 3448: Prefabricated Metal Buildings and Components

332312 Fabricated Structural Metal Manufacturing *see* SIC 3441: Fabricated Structural Metal; SIC 3449: Miscellaneous Structural Metal Work

332313 Plate Work Manufacturing *see* SIC 3443: Fabricated Plate Work (Boiler Shops)

332321 Metal Window and Door Manufacturing *see* SIC 3442: Metal Doors, Sash, Frames, Molding, and

Trim Manufacturing; SIC 3449: Miscellaneous Structural Metal Work

332322 Sheet Metal Work Manufacturing *see* SIC 3444: Sheet Metal Work

332323 Ornamental and Architectural Metal Work Manufacturing *see* SIC 3446: Architectural and Ornamental Metal Work; SIC 3449: Miscellaneous Structural Metal Work; SIC 3523: Farm Machinery and Equipment

332410 Power Boiler and Heat Exchanger Manufacturing *see* SIC 3443: Fabricated Plate Work (Boiler Shops)

332420 Metal Tank (Heavy Gauge) Manufacturing *see* SIC 3443: Fabricated Plate Work (Boiler Shops)

332431 Metal Can Manufacturing *see* SIC 3411: Metal Cans

332439 Other Metal Container Manufacturing *see* SIC 3412: Metal Shipping Barrels, Drums, Kegs and Pails; SIC 3429: Hardware, NEC; SIC 3444: Sheet Metal Work; SIC 3499: Fabricated Metal Products, NEC; SIC 3537: Industrial Trucks, Tractors, Trailers, and Stackers

332510 Hardware Manufacturing *see* SIC 3429: Hardware, NEC; SIC 3499: Fabricated Metal Products, NEC

332611 Steel Spring (except Wire) Manufacturing *see* SIC 3493: Steel Springs, Except Wire

332612 Wire Spring Manufacturing *see* SIC 3495: Wire Springs

332618 Other Fabricated Wire Product Manufacturing *see* SIC 3315: Steel Wiredrawing and Steel Nails and Spikes; SIC 3399: Primary Metal Products, NEC; SIC 3496: Miscellaneous Fabricated Wire Products

332710 Machine Shops *see* SIC 3599: Industrial and Commercial Machinery and Equipment, NEC

332721 Precision Turned Product Manufacturing *see* SIC 3451: Screw Machine Products

332722 Bolt, Nut, Screw, Rivet, and Washer Manufacturing *see* SIC 3452: Bolts, Nuts, Screws, Rivets, and Washers

332811 Metal Heat Treating *see* SIC 3398: Metal Heat Treating

332812 Metal Coating, Engraving, and Allied Services (except Jewelry and Silverware) to Manufacturing *see* SIC 3479: Coating, Engraving, and Allied Services, NEC

332813 Electroplating, Plating, Polishing, Anodizing, and Coloring *see* SIC 3399: Primary Metal Products, NEC; SIC 3471: Electroplating, Plating, Polishing, Anodizing, and Coloring

332911 Industrial Valve Manufacturing *see* SIC 3491: Industrial Valves

332912 Fluid Power Valve and Hose Fitting Manufacturing *see* SIC 3492: Fluid Power Valves and Hose Fittings; SIC 3728: Aircraft Parts and Auxiliary Equipment, NEC

332913 Plumbing Fixture Fitting and Trim Manufacturing *see* SIC 3432: Plumbing Fixture Fittings and Trim

332919 Other Metal Valve and Pipe Fitting Manufacturing *see* SIC 3429: Hardware, NEC; SIC 3494: Valves and Pipe Fittings, NEC; SIC 3499: Fabricated Metal Products, NEC

332991 Ball and Roller Bearing Manufacturing *see* SIC 3562: Ball and Roller Bearings

332992 Small Arms Ammunition Manufacturing *see* SIC 3482: Small Arms Ammunition

332993 Ammunition (except Small Arms) Manufacturing *see* SIC 3483: Ammunition, Except for Small Arms

332994 Small Arms Manufacturing *see* SIC 3484: Small Arms

332995 Other Ordnance and Accessories Manufacturing *see* SIC 3489: Ordnance and Accessories, NEC

332996 Fabricated Pipe and Pipe Fitting Manufacturing *see* SIC 3498: Fabricated Pipe and Pipe Fittings

332997 Industrial Pattern Manufacturing *see* SIC 3543: Industrial Patterns

332998 Enameled Iron and Metal Sanitary Ware Manufacturing *see* SIC 3431: Enameled Iron and Metal Sanitary Ware

332999 All Other Miscellaneous Fabricated Metal Product Manufacturing *see* SIC 3291: Abrasive Products; SIC 3432: Plumbing Fixture Fittings and Trim; SIC 3494: Valves and Pipe Fittings, NEC; SIC 3497: Metal Foil and Leaf; SIC 3499: Fabricated Metal Products, NEC; SIC 3537: Industrial Trucks, Tractors, Trailers, and Stackers; SIC 3599: Industrial and Commercial Machinery and Equipment, NEC; SIC 3999: Manufacturing Industries, NEC

MACHINERY MANUFACTURING

333111 Farm Machinery and Equipment Manufacturing *see* SIC 3523: Farm Machinery and Equipment

333112 Lawn and Garden Tractor and Home Lawn and Garden Equipment Manufacturing *see* SIC 3524: Lawn and Garden Tractors and Home Lawn and Garden Equipment

333120 Construction Machinery Manufacturing *see* SIC 3531: Construction Machinery and Equipment

333131 Mining Machinery and Equipment Manufacturing *see* SIC 3532: Mining Machinery and Equipment, Except Oil and Gas Field Machinery and Equipment

333132 Oil and Gas Field Machinery and Equipment Manufacturing *see* SIC 3533: Oil and Gas Field Machinery and Equipment

333210 Sawmill and Woodworking Machinery Manufacturing *see* SIC 3553: Woodworking Machinery

333220 Rubber and Plastics Industry Machinery Manufacturing *see* SIC 3559: Special Industry Machinery, NEC

333291 Paper Industry Machinery Manufacturing *see* SIC 3554: Paper Industries Machinery

333292 Textile Machinery Manufacturing *see* SIC 3552: Textile Machinery

333293 Printing Machinery and Equipment Manufacturing *see* SIC 3555: Printing Trades Machinery and Equipment

333294 Food Product Machinery Manufacturing *see* SIC 3556: Food Products Machinery

333295 Semiconductor Manufacturing Machinery *see* SIC 3559: Special Industry Machinery, NEC

333298 All Other Industrial Machinery Manufacturing *see* SIC 3559: Special Industry Machinery, NEC; SIC 3639: Household Appliances, NEC

333311 Automatic Vending Machine Manufacturing *see* SIC 3581: Automatic Vending Machines

333312 Commercial Laundry, Drycleaning, and Pressing Machine Manufacturing *see* SIC 3582: Commercial Laundry, Drycleaning, and Pressing Machines

333313 Office Machinery Manufacturing *see* SIC 3578: Calculating and Accounting Machines, Except Electronic Computers; SIC 3579: Office Machines, NEC

333314 Optical Instrument and Lens Manufacturing *see* SIC 3827: Optical Instruments and Lenses

333315 Photographic and Photocopying Equipment Manufacturing *see* SIC 3861: Photographic Equipment and Supplies

333319 Other Commercial and Service Industry Machinery Manufacturing *see* SIC 3559: Special Industry Machinery, NEC; SIC 3589: Service Industry Machinery, NEC; SIC 3599: Industrial and Commercial Machinery and Equipment, NEC; SIC 3699: Electrical Machinery, Equipment, and Supplies, NEC

333411 Air Purification Equipment Manufacturing *see* SIC 3564: Industrial and Commercial Fans and Blowers and Air Purification Equipment

333412 Industrial and Commercial Fan and Blower Manufacturing *see* SIC 3564: Industrial and Commercial Fans and Blowers and Air Purification Equipment

333414 Heating Equipment (except Electric and Warm Air Furnaces) Manufacturing *see* SIC 3433: Heating Equipment, Except Electric and Warm Air Furnaces; SIC 3634: Electric Housewares and Fans

333415 Air-Conditioning and Warm Air Heating Equipment and Commercial and Industrial Refrigeration Equipment Manufacturing *see* SIC 3443: Fabricated Plate Work (Boiler Shops); SIC 3585: Air-Conditioning and Warm Air Heating Equipment and Commercial and Industrial Refrigeration Equipment

333511 Industrial Mold Manufacturing *see* SIC 3544: Special Dies and Tools, Die Sets, Jigs and Fixtures, and Industrial Molds

333512 Machine Tool (Metal Cutting Types) Manufacturing *see* SIC 3541: Machine Tools, Metal Cutting Type

333513 Machine Tool (Metal Forming Types) Manufacturing *see* SIC 3542: Machine Tools, Metal Forming Type

333514 Special Die and Tool, Die Set, Jig, and Fixture Manufacturing *see* SIC 3544: Special Dies and Tools, Die Sets, Jigs and Fixtures, and Industrial Molds

333515 Cutting Tool and Machine Tool Accessory Manufacturing *see* SIC 3545: Cutting Tools, Machine Tool Accessories, and Machinists' Precision Measuring Devices

333516 Rolling Mill Machinery and Equipment Manufacturing *see* SIC 3547: Rolling Mill Machinery and Equipment

333518 Other Metalworking Machinery Manufacturing *see* SIC 3549: Metalworking Machinery, NEC

333611 Turbine and Turbine Generator Set Unit Manufacturing *see* SIC 3511: Steam, Gas, and Hydraulic Turbines, and Turbine Generator Set Units

333612 Speed Changer, Industrial High-Speed Drive, and Gear Manufacturing *see* SIC 3566: Speed Changers, Industrial High-Speed Drives, and Gears

333613 Mechanical Power Transmission Equipment Manufacturing *see* SIC 3568: Mechanical Power Transmission Equipment, NEC

333618 Other Engine Equipment Manufacturing *see* SIC 3519: Internal Combustion Engines, NEC; SIC 3699: Electrical Machinery, Equipment, and Supplies, NEC

333911 Pump and Pumping Equipment Manufacturing *see* SIC 3561: Pumps and Pumping Equipment; SIC 3743: Railroad Equipment

333912 Air and Gas Compressor Manufacturing *see* SIC 3563: Air and Gas Compressors

333913 Measuring and Dispensing Pump Manufacturing *see* SIC 3586: Measuring and Dispensing Pumps

333921 Elevator and Moving Stairway Manufacturing *see* SIC 3534: Elevators and Moving Stairways

333922 Conveyor and Conveying Equipment Manufacturing *see* SIC 3523: Farm Machinery and Equipment; SIC 3535: Conveyors and Conveying Equipment

333923 Overhead Traveling Crane, Hoist, and Monorail System Manufacturing *see* SIC 3531: Construction Machinery and Equipment; SIC 3536: Overhead Traveling Cranes, Hoists and Monorail Systems

333924 Industrial Truck, Tractor, Trailer, and Stacker Machinery Manufacturing *see* SIC 3537: Industrial Trucks, Tractors, Trailers, and Stackers

333991 Power-Driven Hand Tool Manufacturing *see* SIC 3546: Power-Driven Handtools

333992 Welding and Soldering Equipment Manufacturing *see* SIC 3548: Electric and Gas Welding and Soldering Equipment

333993 Packaging Machinery Manufacturing *see* SIC 3565: Packaging Machinery

333994 Industrial Process Furnace and Oven Manufacturing *see* SIC 3567: Industrial Process Furnaces and Ovens

333995 Fluid Power Cylinder and Actuator Manufacturing *see* SIC 3593: Fluid Power Cylinders and Actuators

333996 Fluid Power Pump and Motor Manufacturing *see* SIC 3594: Fluid Power Pumps and Motors

333997 Scale and Balance (except Laboratory) Manufacturing *see* SIC 3596: Scales and Balances, Except Laboratory

333999 All Other General Purpose Machinery Manufacturing *see* SIC 3569: General Industrial Machinery and Equipment, NEC; SIC 3599: Industrial and Commercial Machinery and Equipment, NEC

COMPUTER & ELECTRONIC PRODUCT MANUFACTURING

334111 Electronic Computer Manufacturing *see* SIC 3571: Electronic Computers

334112 Computer Storage Device Manufacturing *see* SIC 3572: Computer Storage Devices

334113 Computer Terminal Manufacturing *see* SIC 3575: Computer Terminals

334119 Other Computer Peripheral Equipment Manufacturing *see* SIC 3577: Computer Peripheral Equipment, NEC; SIC 3578: Calculating and Accounting Machines, Except Electronic Computers; SIC 3699: Electrical Machinery, Equipment, and Supplies, NEC

334210 Telephone Apparatus Manufacturing *see* SIC 3661: Telephone and Telegraph Apparatus

334220 Radio and Television Broadcasting and Wireless Communications Equipment Manufacturing *see* SIC 3663: Radio and Television Broadcasting and Communication Equipment; SIC 3679: Electronic Components, NEC

334290 Other Communication Equipment Manufacturing *see* SIC 3669: Communications Equipment, NEC

334310 Audio and Video Equipment Manufacturing *see* SIC 3651: Household Audio and Video Equipment

334411 Electron Tube Manufacturing *see* SIC 3671: Electron Tubes

334412 Printed Circuit Board Manufacturing *see* SIC 3672: Printed Circuit Boards

334413 Semiconductor and Related Device Manufacturing *see* SIC 3674: Semiconductors and Related Devices

334414 Electronic Capacitor Manufacturing *see* SIC 3675: Electronic Capacitors

334415 Electronic Resistor Manufacturing *see* SIC 3676: Electronic Resistors

334416 Electronic Coil, Transformer, and Other Inductor Manufacturing *see* SIC 3661: Telephone and Telegraph Apparatus; SIC 3677: Electronic Coils, Transformers, and Other Inductors; SIC 3825: Instruments for Measuring and Testing of Electricity and Electrical Signals

334417 Electronic Connector Manufacturing *see* SIC 3678: Electronic Connectors

334418 Printed Circuit/Electronics Assembly Manufacturing *see* SIC 3661: Telephone and Telegraph Apparatus; SIC 3679: Electronic Components, NEC

334419 Other Electronic Component Manufacturing *see* SIC 3679: Electronic Components, NEC

334510 Electromedical and Electrotherapeutic Apparatus Manufacturing *see* SIC 3842: Orthopedic, Prosthetic, and Surgical Appliances and Supplies; SIC 3845: Electromedical and Electrotherapeutic Apparatus

334511 Search, Detection, Navigation, Guidance, Aeronautical, and Nautical System and Instrument Manufacturing *see* SIC 3812: Search, Detection, Navigation, Guidance, Aeronautical, and Nautical Systems and Instruments

334512 Automatic Environmental Control Manufacturing for Regulating Residential, Commercial, and Appliance Use *see* SIC 3822:

Automatic Controls for Regulating Residential and Commercial Environments and Appliances

334513 Instruments and Related Product Manufacturing for Measuring Displaying, and Controlling Industrial Process Variables *see* SIC 3823: Industrial Instruments for Measurement, Display, and Control of Process Variables; and Related Products

334514 Totalizing Fluid Meter and Counting Device Manufacturing *see* SIC 3824: Totalizing Fluid Meters and Counting Devices

334515 Instrument Manufacturing for Measuring and Testing Electricity and Electrical Signals *see* SIC 3825: Instruments for Measuring and Testing of Electricity and Electrical Signals

334516 Analytical Laboratory Instrument Manufacturing *see* SIC 3826: Laboratory Analytical Instruments

334517 Irradiation Apparatus Manufacturing *see* SIC 3844: X-Ray Apparatus and Tubes and Related Irradiation Apparatus; SIC 3845: Electromedical and Electrotherapeutic Apparatus

334518 Watch, Clock, and Part Manufacturing *see* SIC 3495: Wire Springs; SIC 3579: Office Machines, NEC; SIC 3873: Watches, Clocks, Clockwork Operated Devices and Parts

334519 Other Measuring and Controlling Device Manufacturing *see* SIC 3829: Measuring and Controlling Devices, NEC

334611 Software Reproducing *see* SIC 7372: Prepackaged Software

334612 Prerecorded Compact Disc (Except Software), Tape and Record Reproducing *see* SIC 3652: Phonograph Records and Prerecorded Audio Tapes and Disks; SIC 7819: Services Allied to Motion Picture Production

334613 Magnetic and Optical Recording Media Manufacturing *see* SIC 3695: Magnetic and Optical Recording Media

ELECTRICAL EQUIPMENT, APPLIANCE, & COMPONENT MANUFACTURING

335110 Electric Lamp Bulb and Part Manufacturing *see* SIC 3641: Electric Lamp Bulbs and Tubes

335121 Residential Electric Lighting Fixture Manufacturing *see* SIC 3645: Residential Electric Lighting Fixtures; SIC 3999: Manufacturing Industries, NEC

335122 Commercial, Industrial, and Institutional Electric Lighting Fixture Manufacturing *see* SIC 3646: Commercial, Industrial, and Institutional Electric Lighting Fixtures

335129 Other Lighting Equipment Manufacturing *see* SIC 3648: Lighting Equipment, NEC; SIC 3699: Electrical Machinery, Equipment, and Supplies, NEC

335211 Electric Houseware and Fan Manufacturing *see* SIC 3634: Electric Housewares and Fans

335212 Household Vacuum Cleaner Manufacturing *see* SIC 3635: Household Vacuum Cleaners; SIC 3639: Household Appliances, NEC

335221 Household Cooking Appliance Manufacturing *see* SIC 3631: Household Cooking Equipment

335222 Household Refrigerator and Home and Farm Freezer Manufacturing *see* SIC 3632: Household Refrigerators and Home and Farm Freezers

335224 Household Laundry Equipment Manufacturing *see* SIC 3633: Household Laundry Equipment

335228 Other Household Appliance Manufacturing *see* SIC 3639: Household Appliances, NEC

335311 Power, Distribution, and Specialty Transformer Manufacturing *see* SIC 3548: Electric and Gas Welding and Soldering Equipment; SIC 3612: Power, Distribution, and Specialty Transformers

335312 Motor and Generator Manufacturing *see* SIC 3621: Motors and Generators; SIC 7694: Armature Rewinding Shops

335313 Switchgear and Switchboard Apparatus Manufacturing *see* SIC 3613: Switchgear and Switchboard Apparatus

335314 Relay and Industrial Control Manufacturing *see* SIC 3625: Relays and Industrial Controls

335911 Storage Battery Manufacturing *see* SIC 3691: Storage Batteries

335912 Dry and Wet Primary Battery Manufacturing *see* SIC 3692: Primary Batteries, Dry and Wet

335921 Fiber Optic Cable Manufacturing *see* SIC 3357: Drawing and Insulating of Nonferrous Wire

335929 Other Communication and Energy Wire Manufacturing *see* SIC 3357: Drawing and Insulating of Nonferrous Wire

335931 Current-Carrying Wiring Device Manufacturing *see* SIC 3643: Current-Carrying Wiring Devices

335932 Noncurrent-Carrying Wiring Device Manufacturing *see* SIC 3644: Noncurrent-Carrying Wiring Devices

335991 Carbon and Graphite Product Manufacturing *see* SIC 3624: Carbon and Graphite Products

335999 All Other Miscellaneous Electrical Equipment and Component Manufacturing *see* SIC 3629: Electrical Industrial Apparatus, NEC; SIC 3699: Electrical Machinery, Equipment, and Supplies, NEC

TRANSPORTATION EQUIPMENT MANUFACTURING

336111 Automobile Manufacturing *see* SIC 3711: Motor Vehicles and Passenger Car Bodies

336112 Light Truck and Utility Vehicle Manufacturing *see* SIC 3711: Motor Vehicles and Passenger Car Bodies

336120 Heavy Duty Truck Manufacturing *see* SIC 3711: Motor Vehicles and Passenger Car Bodies

336211 Motor Vehicle Body Manufacturing *see* SIC 3711: Motor Vehicles and Passenger Car Bodies; SIC 3713: Truck and Bus Bodies; SIC 3714: Motor Vehicle Parts and Accessories

336212 Truck Trailer Manufacturing *see* SIC 3715: Truck Trailers

336213 Motor Home Manufacturing *see* SIC 3716: Motor Homes

336214 Travel Trailer and Camper Manufacturing *see* SIC 3792: Travel Trailers and Campers; SIC 3799: Transportation Equipment, NEC

336311 Carburetor, Piston, Piston Ring and Valve Manufacturing *see* SIC 3592: Carburetors, Pistons, Piston Rings and Valves

336312 Gasoline Engine and Engine Parts Manufacturing *see* SIC 3714: Motor Vehicle Parts and Accessories

336321 Vehicular Lighting Equipment Manufacturing *see* SIC 3647: Vehicular Lighting Equipment

336322 Other Motor Vehicle Electrical and Electronic Equipment Manufacturing *see* SIC 3679: Electronic Components, NEC; SIC 3694: Electrical Equipment for Internal Combustion Engines; SIC 3714: Motor Vehicle Parts and Accessories

336330 Motor Vehicle Steering and Suspension Components (except Spring) Manufacturing *see* SIC 3714: Motor Vehicle Parts and Accessories

336340 Motor Vehicle Brake System Manufacturing *see* SIC 3292: Asbestos Products; SIC 3714: Motor Vehicle Parts and Accessories

336350 Motor Vehicle Transmission and Power Train Part Manufacturing *see* SIC 3714: Motor Vehicle Parts and Accessories

336360 Motor Vehicle Fabric Accessories and Seat Manufacturing *see* SIC 2396: Automotive Trimmings, Apparel Findings, and Related Products; SIC 2399: Fabricated Textile Products, NEC; SIC 2531: Public Building and Related Furniture

336370 Motor Vehicle Metal Stamping *see* SIC 3465: Automotive Stamping

336391 Motor Vehicle Air Conditioning Manufacturing *see* SIC 3585: Air-Conditioning and Warm Air Heating Equipment and Commercial and Industrial Refrigeration Equipment

336399 All Other Motor Vehicle Parts Manufacturing *see* SIC 3519: Internal Combustion Engines, NEC; SIC 3599: Industrial and Commercial Machinery and Equipment, NEC; SIC 3714: Motor Vehicle Parts and Accessories

336411 Aircraft Manufacturing *see* SIC 3721: Aircraft

336412 Aircraft Engine and Engine Parts Manufacturing *see* SIC 3724: Aircraft Engines and Engine Parts

336413 Other Aircraft Part and Auxiliary Equipment Manufacturing *see* SIC 3728: Aircraft Parts and Auxiliary Equipment, NEC

336414 Guided Missile and Space Vehicle Manufacturing *see* SIC 3761: Guided Missiles and Space Vehicles

336415 Guided Missile and Space Vehicle Propulsion Unit and Propulsion Unit Parts Manufacturing *see* SIC 3764: Guided Missile and Space Vehicle Propulsion Units and Propulsion Unit Parts

336419 Other Guided Missile and Space Vehicle Parts and Auxiliary Equipment Manufacturing *see* SIC 3769: Guided Missile Space Vehicle Parts and Auxiliary Equipment, NEC

336510 Railroad Rolling Stock Manufacturing *see* SIC 3531: Construction Machinery and Equipment; SIC 3743: Railroad Equipment

336611 Ship Building and Repairing *see* SIC 3731: Ship Building and Repairing

336612 Boat Building *see* SIC 3732: Boat Building and Repairing

336991 Motorcycle, Bicycle, and Parts Manufacturing *see* SIC 3751: Motorcycles, Bicycles, and Parts; SIC 3944: Games, Toys, and Children's Vehicles, Except Dolls and Bicycles

336992 Military Armored Vehicle, Tank, and Tank Component Manufacturing *see* SIC 3711: Motor Vehicles and Passenger Car Bodies; SIC 3795: Tanks and Tank Components

336999 All Other Transportation Equipment Manufacturing *see* SIC 3799: Transportation Equipment, NEC

FURNITURE & RELATED PRODUCT MANUFACTURING

337110 Wood Kitchen Cabinet and Counter Top Manufacturing *see* SIC 2434: Wood Kitchen Cabinets; SIC 2541: Wood Office and Store Fixtures, Partitions, Shelving, and Lockers; SIC 5712: Furniture Stores

337121 Upholstered Wood Household Furniture Manufacturing *see* SIC 2512: Wood Household Furniture, Upholstered; SIC 2515: Mattresses, Foundations, and Convertible Beds; SIC 5712: Furniture Stores

337122 Nonupholstered Wood Household Furniture Manufacturing *see* SIC 2511: Wood Household Furniture, Except Upholstered; SIC 5712: Furniture Stores

337124 Metal Household Furniture Manufacturing *see* SIC 2514: Metal Household Furniture

337125 Household Furniture (except Wood and Metal) Manufacturing *see* SIC 2519: Household Furniture, NEC

337127 Institutional Furniture Manufacturing *see* SIC 2531: Public Building and Related Furniture; SIC 2599: Furniture and Fixtures, NEC; SIC 3952: Lead Pencils, Crayons, and Artist's Materials; SIC 3999: Manufacturing Industries, NEC

337129 Wood Television, Radio, and Sewing Machine Cabinet Manufacturing *see* SIC 2517: Wood Television, Radio, Phonograph and Sewing Machine Cabinets

337211 Wood Office Furniture Manufacturing *see* SIC 2521: Wood Office Furniture

337212 Custom Architectural Woodwork, Millwork, and Fixtures *see* SIC 2541: Wood Office and Store Fixtures, Partitions, Shelving, and Lockers

337214 Nonwood Office Furniture Manufacturing *see* SIC 2522: Office Furniture, Except Wood

337215 Showcase, Partition, Shelving, and Locker Manufacturing *see* SIC 2426: Hardwood Dimension and Flooring Mills; SIC 2541: Wood Office and Store Fixtures, Partitions, Shelving, and Lockers; SIC 2542: Office and Store Fixtures, Partitions Shelving, and Lockers, Except Wood; SIC 3499: Fabricated Metal Products, NEC

337910 Mattress Manufacturing *see* SIC 2515: Mattresses, Foundations, and Convertible Beds

337920 Blind and Shade Manufacturing *see* SIC 2591: Drapery Hardware and Window Blinds and Shades

MISCELLANEOUS MANUFACTURING

339111 Laboratory Apparatus and Furniture Manufacturing *see* SIC 3821: Laboratory Apparatus and Furniture

339112 Surgical and Medical Instrument Manufacturing *see* SIC 3829: Measuring and Controlling Devices, NEC; SIC 3841: Surgical and Medical Instruments and Apparatus

339113 Surgical Appliance and Supplies Manufacturing *see* SIC 2599: Furniture and Fixtures, NEC; SIC 3842: Orthopedic, Prosthetic, and Surgical Appliances and Supplies

339114 Dental Equipment and Supplies Manufacturing *see* SIC 3843: Dental Equipment and Supplies

339115 Ophthalmic Goods Manufacturing *see* SIC 3851: Ophthalmic Goods; SIC 5995: Optical Goods Stores

339116 Dental Laboratories *see* SIC 8072: Dental Laboratories

339911 Jewelry (including Precious Metal) Manufacturing, *see* SIC 3469: Metal Stamping, NEC; SIC 3479: Coating, Engraving, and Allied Services, NEC; SIC 3911: Jewelry, Precious Metal

339912 Silverware and Plated Ware Manufacturing *see* SIC 3479: Coating, Engraving, and Allied Services, NEC; SIC 3914: Silverware, Plated Ware, and Stainless Steel Ware

339913 Jewelers' Material and Lapidary Work Manufacturing *see* SIC 3915: Jewelers' Findings and Materials, and Lapidary Work

339914 Costume Jewelry and Novelty Manufacturing *see* SIC 3479: Coating, Engraving, and Allied Services, NEC; SIC 3499: Fabricated Metal Products, NEC; SIC 3961: Costume Jewelry and Costume Novelties, Except Precious Metals

339920 Sporting and Athletic Good Manufacturing *see* SIC 3949: Sporting and Athletic Goods, NEC

339931 Doll and Stuffed Toy Manufacturing *see* SIC 3942: Dolls and Stuffed Toys

339932 Game, Toy, and Children's Vehicle Manufacturing *see* SIC 3944: Games, Toys, and Children's Vehicles, Except Dolls and Bicycles

339941 Pen and Mechanical Pencil Manufacturing *see* SIC 3951: Pens, Mechanical Pencils and Parts

339942 Lead Pencil and Art Good Manufacturing *see* SIC 2531: Public Building and Related Furniture; SIC 3579: Office Machines, NEC; SIC 3952: Lead Pencils, Crayons, and Artist's Materials

339943 Marking Device Manufacturing *see* SIC 3953: Marking Devices

339944 Carbon Paper and Inked Ribbon Manufacturing *see* SIC 3955: Carbon Paper and Inked Ribbons

339950 Sign Manufacturing *see* SIC 3993: Signs and Advertising Specialties

339991 Gasket, Packing, and Sealing Device Manufacturing *see* SIC 3053: Gaskets, Packing, and Sealing Devices

339992 Musical Instrument Manufacturing *see* SIC 3931: Musical Instruments

339993 Fastener, Button, Needle, and Pin Manufacturing *see* SIC 3131: Boot and Shoe Cut Stock and Findings; SIC 3965: Fasteners, Buttons, Needles, and Pins

339994 Broom, Brush and Mop Manufacturing *see* SIC 2392: Housefurnishings, Except Curtains and Draperies; SIC 3991: Brooms and Brushes

339995 Burial Casket Manufacturing *see* SIC 3995: Burial Caskets

339999 All Other Miscellaneous Manufacturing *see* SIC 2499: Wood Products, NEC; SIC 3999: Manufacturing Industries, NEC

WHOLESALE TRADE

421110 Automobile and Other Motor Vehicle Wholesalers *see* SIC 5012: Automobiles and Other Motor Vehicles; SIC 5013: Motor Vehicle Supplies and New Parts

421130 Tire and Tube Wholesalers *see* SIC 5014: Tires and Tubes

421140 Motor Vehicle Part (Used) Wholesalers *see* SIC 5015: Motor Vehicle Parts, Used

421210 Furniture Wholesalers *see* SIC 5021: Furniture

421220 Home Furnishing Wholesalers *see* SIC 5023: Home Furnishings

421310 Lumber, Plywood, Millwork, and Wood Panel Wholesalers *see* SIC 5031: Lumber, Plywood, Millwork, and Wood Panels; SIC 5211: Lumber and Other Building Materials Dealers

421320 Brick, Stone and Related Construction Material Wholesalers *see* SIC 5032: Brick, Stone and Related Construction Materials

421330 Roofing, Siding, and Insulation Material Wholesalers *see* SIC 5033: Roofing, Siding, and Insulation Materials

421390 Other Construction Material Wholesalers *see* SIC 5039: Construction Materials, NEC

421410 Photographic Equipment and Supplies Wholesalers *see* SIC 5043: Photographic Equipment and Supplies

421420 Office Equipment Wholesalers *see* SIC 5044: Office Equipment

421430 Computer and Computer Peripheral Equipment and Software Wholesalers *see* SIC 5045: Computers and Computer Peripheral Equipment and Software

421440 Other Commercial Equipment Wholesalers *see* SIC 5046: Commercial Equipment, NEC

421450 Medical, Dental and Hospital Equipment and Supplies Wholesalers *see* SIC 5047: Medical, Dental, and Hospital Equipment and Supplies

421460 Ophthalmic Goods Wholesalers *see* SIC 5048: Ophthalmic Goods

421490 Other Professional Equipment and Supplies Wholesalers *see* SIC 5049: Professional Equipment and Supplies, NEC

421510 Metals Service Centers and Offices *see* SIC 5051: Metals Service Centers and Offices

421520 Coal and Other Mineral and Ore Wholesalers *see* SIC 5052: Coal and Other Minerals and Ores

421610 Electrical Apparatus and Equipment, Wiring Supplies and Construction Material Wholesalers *see* SIC 5063: Electrical Apparatus and Equipment Wiring Supplies, and Construction Materials

421620 Electrical Appliance, Television and Radio Set Wholesalers *see* SIC 5064: Electrical Appliances, Television and Radio Sets

421690 Other Electronic Parts and Equipment Wholesalers *see* SIC 5065: Electronic Parts and Equipment, Not Elsewhere Classified

421710 Hardware Wholesalers *see* SIC 5072: Hardware

421720 Plumbing and Heating Equipment and Supplies (Hydronics) Wholesalers *see* SIC 5074: Plumbing and Heating Equipment and Supplies (Hydronics)

421730 Warm Air Heating and Air-Conditioning Equipment and Supplies Wholesalers *see* SIC 5075: Warm Air Heating and Air-Conditioning Equipment and Supplies

421740 Refrigeration Equipment and Supplies Wholesalers *see* SIC 5078: Refrigeration Equipment and Supplies

421810 Construction and Mining (except Petroleum) Machinery and Equipment Wholesalers *see* SIC 5082: Construction and Mining (Except Petroleum) Machinery and Equipment

421820 Farm and Garden Machinery and Equipment Wholesalers *see* SIC 5083: Farm and Garden Machinery and Equipment

421830 Industrial Machinery and Equipment Wholesalers *see* SIC 5084: Industrial Machinery and Equipment; SIC 5085: Industrial Supplies

421840 Industrial Supplies Wholesalers *see* SIC 5085: Industrial Supplies

421850 Service Establishment Equipment and Supplies Wholesalers *see* SIC 5087: Service Establishment Equipment and Supplies

421860 Transportation Equipment and Supplies (except Motor Vehicles) Wholesalers *see* SIC 5088: Transportation Equipment and Supplies, Except Motor Vehicles

421910 Sporting and Recreational Goods and Supplies Wholesalers *see* SIC 5091: Sporting and Recreational Goods and Supplies

421920 Toy and Hobby Goods and Supplies Wholesalers *see* SIC 5092: Toys and Hobby Goods and Supplies

421930 Recyclable Material Wholesalers *see* SIC 5093: Scrap and Waste Materials

421940   Jewelry, Watch , Precious Stone, and Precious Metal Wholesalers *see* SIC 5094: Jewelry, Watches, Precious Stones, and Precious Metals

421990   Other Miscellaneous Durable Goods Wholesalers *see* SIC 5099: Durable Goods, NEC; SIC 7822: Motion Picture and Video Tape Distribution

422110   Printing and Writing Paper Wholesalers *see* SIC 5111: Printing and Writing Paper

422120   Stationery and Office Supplies Wholesalers *see* SIC 5112: Stationery and Office Supplies

422130   Industrial and Personal Service Paper Wholesalers *see* SIC 5113: Industrial and Personal Service Paper

422210   Drugs, Drug Proprietaries, and Druggists' Sundries Wholesalers *see* SIC 5122: Drugs, Drug Proprietaries, and Druggists' Sundries

422310   Piece Goods, Notions, and Other Dry Goods Wholesalers *see* SIC 5131: Piece Goods, Notions, and Other Dry Goods

422320   Men's and Boys' Clothing and Furnishings Wholesalers *see* SIC 5136: Men's and Boys' Clothing and Furnishings

422330   Women's, Children's, and Infants' Clothing and Accessories Wholesalers *see* SIC 5137: Women's Children's and Infants' Clothing and Accessories

422340   Footwear Wholesalers *see* SIC 5139: Footwear

422410   General Line Grocery Wholesalers *see* SIC 5141: Groceries, General Line

422420   Packaged Frozen Food Wholesalers *see* SIC 5142: Packaged Frozen Foods

422430   Dairy Products (except Dried or Canned) Wholesalers *see* SIC 5143: Dairy Products, Except Dried or Canned

422440   Poultry and Poultry Product Wholesalers *see* SIC 5144: Poultry and Poultry Products

422450   Confectionery Wholesalers *see* SIC 5145: Confectionery

422460   Fish and Seafood Wholesalers *see* SIC 5146: Fish and Seafoods

422470   Meat and Meat Product Wholesalers *see* SIC 5147: Meats and Meat Products

422480   Fresh Fruit and Vegetable Wholesalers *see* SIC 5148: Fresh Fruits and Vegetables

422490   Other Grocery and Related Product Wholesalers *see* SIC 5149: Groceries and Related Products, NEC

422510   Grain and Field Bean Wholesalers *see* SIC 5153: Grain and Field Beans

422520   Livestock Wholesalers *see* SIC 5154: Livestock

422590   Other Farm Product Raw Material Wholesalers *see* SIC 5159: Farm-Product Raw Materials, NEC

422610   Plastics Materials and Basic Forms and Shapes Wholesalers *see* SIC 5162: Plastics Materials and Basic Forms and Shapes

422690   Other Chemical and Allied Products Wholesalers *see* SIC 5169: Chemicals and Allied Products, NEC

422710   Petroleum Bulk Stations and Terminals *see* SIC 5171: Petroleum Bulk Stations and Terminals

422720   Petroleum and Petroleum Products Wholesalers (except Bulk Stations and Terminals) *see* SIC 5172: Petroleum and Petroleum Products Wholesalers, Except Bulk Stations and Terminals

422810   Beer and Ale Wholesalers *see* SIC 5181: Beer and Ale

422820   Wine and Distilled Alcoholic Beverage Wholesalers *see* SIC 5182: Wine and Distilled Alcoholic Beverages

422910   Farm Supplies Wholesalers *see* SIC 5191: Farm Supplies

422920   Book, Periodical and Newspaper Wholesalers *see* SIC 5192: Books, Periodicals, and Newspapers

422930   Flower, Nursery Stock and Florists' Supplies Wholesalers *see* SIC 5193: Flowers, Nursery Stock, and Florists' Supplies

422940   Tobacco and Tobacco Product Wholesalers *see* SIC 5194: Tobacco and Tobacco Products

422950   Paint, Varnish and Supplies Wholesalers *see* SIC 5198: Paint, Varnishes, and Supplies; SIC 5231: Paint, Glass, and Wallpaper Stores

422990   Other Miscellaneous Nondurable Goods Wholesalers *see* SIC 5199: Nondurable Goods, NEC

RETAIL TRADE

441110   New Car Dealers *see* SIC 5511: Motor Vehicle Dealers (New and Used)

441120   Used Car Dealers *see* SIC 5521: Motor Vehicle Dealers (Used Only)

441210   Recreational Vehicle Dealers *see* SIC 5561: Recreational Vehicle Dealers

441221   Motorcycle Dealers *see* SIC 5571: Motorcycle Dealers

441222   Boat Dealers *see* SIC 5551: Boat Dealers

441229   All Other Motor Vehicle Dealers *see* SIC 5599: Automotive Dealers, NEC

441310   Automotive Parts and Accessories Stores *see* SIC 5013: Motor Vehicle Supplies and New Parts; SIC 5531: Auto and Home Supply Stores

441310   Automotive Parts and Accessories Stores *see* SIC 5731: Radio, Television, and Consumer Electronics Stores

441320 Tire Dealers *see* SIC 5014: Tires and Tubes; SIC 5531: Auto and Home Supply Stores

442110 Furniture Stores *see* SIC 5021: Furniture; SIC 5712: Furniture Stores

442210 Floor Covering Stores *see* SIC 5023: Home Furnishings; SIC 5713: Floor Covering Stores

442291 Window Treatment Stores *see* SIC 5714: Drapery, Curtain, and Upholstery Stores; SIC 5719: Miscellaneous Homefurnishings Stores

442299 All Other Home Furnishings Stores *see* SIC 5719: Miscellaneous Homefurnishings Stores; SIC 5722: Household Appliance Stores

443111 Household Appliance Stores *see* SIC 5999: Miscellaneous Retail Stores, NEC; SIC 7623: Refrigeration and Air-Conditioning Services and Repair Shops; SIC 7629: Electrical and Electronic Repair Shops, NEC

443112 Radio, Television, and Other Electronics Stores *see* SIC 5731: Radio, Television, and Consumer Electronics Stores; SIC 5999: Miscellaneous Retail Stores, NEC; SIC 7622: Radio and Television Repair Shops

443120 Computer and Software Stores *see* SIC 5045: Computers and Computer Peripheral Equipment and Software; SIC 5734: Computer and Computer Software Stores; SIC 7378: Computer Maintenance and Repair

443130 Camera and Photographic Supplies Stores *see* SIC 5946: Camera and Photographic Supply Stores

444110 Home Centers *see* SIC 5211: Lumber and Other Building Materials Dealers

444120 Paint and Wallpaper Stores *see* SIC 5198: Paint, Varnishes, and Supplies; SIC 5231: Paint, Glass, and Wallpaper Stores

444130 Hardware Stores *see* SIC 5251: Hardware Stores

444190 Other Building Material Dealers *see* SIC 5031: Lumber, Plywood, Millwork, and Wood Panels; SIC 5032: Brick, Stone and Related Construction Materials; SIC 5039: Construction Materials, NEC; SIC 5063: Electrical Apparatus and Equipment Wiring Supplies, and Construction Materials; SIC 5074: Plumbing and Heating Equipment and Supplies (Hydronics); SIC 5211: Lumber and Other Building Materials Dealers; SIC 5231: Paint, Glass, and Wallpaper Stores

444210 Outdoor Power Equipment Stores *see* SIC 5083: Farm and Garden Machinery and Equipment; SIC 5261: Retail Nurseries, Lawn and Garden Supply Stores

444220 Nursery and Garden Centers *see* SIC 5191: Farm Supplies; SIC 5193: Flowers, Nursery Stock, and Florists' Supplies; SIC 5261: Retail Nurseries, Lawn and Garden Supply Stores

445110 Supermarkets and Other Grocery (except Convenience) Stores *see* SIC 5411: Grocery Stores

445120 Convenience Stores *see* SIC 5411: Grocery Stores

445210 Meat Markets *see* SIC 5421: Meat and Fish (Seafood) Markets, Including Freezer Provisioners; SIC 5499: Miscellaneous Food Stores

445220 Fish and Seafood Markets *see* SIC 5421: Meat and Fish (Seafood) Markets, Including Freezer Provisioners

445230 Fruit and Vegetable Markets *see* SIC 5431: Fruit and Vegetable Markets

445291 Baked Goods Stores *see* SIC 5461: Retail Bakeries

445292 Confectionery and Nut Stores *see* SIC 5441: Candy, Nut, and Confectionery Stores

445299 All Other Specialty Food Stores *see* SIC 5451: Dairy Products Stores; SIC 5499: Miscellaneous Food Stores

445310 Beer, Wine and Liquor Stores *see* SIC 5921: Liquor Stores

446110 Pharmacies and Drug Stores *see* SIC 5912: Drug Stores and Proprietary Stores

446120 Cosmetics, Beauty Supplies, and Perfume Stores *see* SIC 5087: Service Establishment Equipment and Supplies

446120 Cosmetics, Beauty Supplies, and Perfume Stores *see* SIC 5999: Miscellaneous Retail Stores, NEC

446130 Optical Goods Stores *see* SIC 5995: Optical Goods Stores

446191 Food (Health) Supplement Stores *see* SIC 5499: Miscellaneous Food Stores

446199 All Other Health and Personal Care Stores *see* SIC 5047: Medical, Dental, and Hospital Equipment and Supplies; SIC 5999: Miscellaneous Retail Stores, NEC

447110 Gasoline Stations with Convenience Stores *see* SIC 5411: Grocery Stores; SIC 5541: Gasoline Service Stations

447190 Other Gasoline Stations *see* SIC 5541: Gasoline Service Stations

448110 Men's Clothing Stores *see* SIC 5611: Men's and Boys' Clothing and Accessory Stores

448120 Women's Clothing Stores *see* SIC 5621: Women's Clothing Stores

448130 Children's and Infants' Clothing Stores *see* SIC 5641: Children's and Infants' Wear Stores

448140 Family Clothing Stores *see* SIC 5651: Family Clothing Stores

448150 Clothing Accessories Stores *see* SIC 5611: Men's and Boys' Clothing and Accessory Stores; SIC

5632: Women's Accessory and Specialty Stores; SIC 5699: Miscellaneous Apparel and Accessory Stores

448190 Other Clothing Stores *see* SIC 5632: Women's Accessory and Specialty Stores; SIC 5699: Miscellaneous Apparel and Accessory Stores

448210 Shoe Stores *see* SIC 5661: Shoe Stores

448310 Jewelry Stores *see* SIC 5944: Jewelry Stores; SIC 5999: Miscellaneous Retail Stores, NEC

448320 Luggage and Leather Goods Stores *see* SIC 5948: Luggage and Leather Goods Stores

451110 Sporting Goods Stores *see* SIC 5941: Sporting Goods Stores and Bicycle Shops; SIC 7699: Repair Shops and Related Services, NEC

451120 Hobby, Toy and Game Stores *see* SIC 5945: Hobby, Toy, and Game Shops

451130 Sewing, Needlework and Piece Goods Stores *see* SIC 5714: Drapery, Curtain, and Upholstery Stores; SIC 5949: Sewing, Needlework, and Piece Goods Stores

451140 Musical Instrument and Supplies Stores *see* SIC 5736: Musical Instrument Stores

451211 Book Stores *see* SIC 5942: Book Stores

451212 News Dealers and Newsstands *see* SIC 5994: News Dealers and Newsstands

451220 Prerecorded Tape, Compact Disc and Record Stores *see* SIC 5735: Record and Prerecorded Tape Stores

452110 Department Stores *see* SIC 5311: Department Stores

452910 Warehouse Clubs and Superstores *see* SIC 5399: Miscellaneous General Merchandise Stores; SIC 5411: Grocery Stores

452990 All Other General Merchandise Stores *see* SIC 5331: Variety Stores; SIC 5399: Miscellaneous General Merchandise Stores

453110 Florists *see* SIC 5992: Florists

453210 Office Supplies and Stationery Stores *see* SIC 5049: Professional Equipment and Supplies, NEC; SIC 5112: Stationery and Office Supplies; SIC 5943: Stationery Stores

453220 Gift, Novelty and Souvenir Stores *see* SIC 5947: Gift, Novelty, and Souvenir Shops

453310 Used Merchandise Stores *see* SIC 5932: Used Merchandise Stores

453910 Pet and Pet Supplies Stores *see* SIC 5999: Miscellaneous Retail Stores, NEC

453920 Art Dealers *see* SIC 5999: Miscellaneous Retail Stores, NEC

453930 Manufactured (Mobile) Home Dealers *see* SIC 5271: Mobile Home Dealers

453991 Tobacco Stores *see* SIC 5993: Tobacco Stores and Stands

453998 All Other Miscellaneous Store Retailers (except Tobacco Stores) *see* SIC 5261: Retail Nurseries, Lawn and Garden Supply Stores; SIC 5999: Miscellaneous Retail Stores, NEC

454110 Electronic Shopping and Mail-Order Houses *see* SIC 5961: Catalog and Mail-Order Houses

454210 Vending Machine Operators *see* SIC 5962: Automatic Merchandising Machine Operator

454311 Heating Oil Dealers *see* SIC 5171: Petroleum Bulk Stations and Terminals; SIC 5983: Fuel Oil Dealers

454312 Liquefied Petroleum Gas (Bottled Gas) Dealers *see* SIC 5171: Petroleum Bulk Stations and Terminals; SIC 5984: Liquefied Petroleum Gas (Bottled Gas) Dealers

454319 Other Fuel Dealers *see* SIC 5989: Fuel Dealers, NEC

454390 Other Direct Selling Establishments *see* SIC 5421: Meat and Fish (Seafood) Markets, Including Freezer Provisioners; SIC 5963: Direct Selling Establishments

TRANSPORTATION & WAREHOUSING

481111 Scheduled Passenger Air Transportation *see* SIC 4512: Air Transportation, Scheduled

481112 Scheduled Freight Air Transportation *see* SIC 4512: Air Transportation, Scheduled

481211 Nonscheduled Chartered Passenger Air Transportation *see* SIC 4522: Air Transportation, Nonscheduled

481212 Nonscheduled Chartered Freight Air Transportation *see* SIC 4522: Air Transportation, Nonscheduled

481219 Other Nonscheduled Air Transportation *see* SIC 0721: Crop Planting, Cultivating and Protecting; SIC 7319: Advertising, NEC; SIC 7335: Commercial Photography

482111 Line-Haul Railroads *see* SIC 4011: Railroads, Line-haul Operating

482112 Short Line Railroads *see* SIC 4013: Railroad Switching and Terminal Establishments

483111 Deep Sea Freight Transportation *see* SIC 4412: Deep Sea Foreign Transportation of Freight

483112 Deep Sea Passenger Transportation *see* SIC 4481: Deep Sea Transportation of Passengers, Except by Ferry

483113 Coastal and Great Lakes Freight Transportation *see* SIC 4424: Deep Sea Domestic Transportation of Freight; SIC 4432: Freight Transportation on the Great Lakes-St. Lawrence Seaway; SIC 4492: Towing and Tugboat Services

483114 Coastal and Great Lakes Passenger Transportation *see* SIC 4481: Deep Sea Transportation of Passengers, Except by Ferry; SIC 4482: Ferries

483211 Inland Water Freight Transportation *see* SIC 4449: Water Transportation of Freight, NEC; SIC 4492: Towing and Tugboat Services

483212 Inland Water Passenger Transportation *see* SIC 4482: Ferries; SIC 4489: Water Transportation of Passengers, NEC

484110 General Freight Trucking, Local *see* SIC 4212: Local Trucking Without Storage; SIC 4214: Local Trucking with Storage

484121 General Freight Trucking, Long-Distance, Truckload *see* SIC 4213: Trucking, Except Local

484122 General Freight Trucking, Long-Distance, Less Than Truckload *see* SIC 4213: Trucking, Except Local

484210 Used Household and Office Goods Moving *see* SIC 4212: Local Trucking Without Storage; SIC 4213: Trucking, Except Local; SIC 4214: Local Trucking with Storage

484220 Specialized Freight (except Used Goods) Trucking, Local *see* SIC 4212: Local Trucking Without Storage; SIC 4214: Local Trucking with Storage

484230 Specialized Freight (except Used Goods) Trucking, Long-Distance *see* SIC 4213: Trucking, Except Local

485111 Mixed Mode Transit Systems *see* SIC 4111: Local and Suburban Transit

485112 Commuter Rail Systems *see* SIC 4111: Local and Suburban Transit

485113 Bus and Motor Vehicle Transit Systems *see* SIC 4111: Local and Suburban Transit

485119 Other Urban Transit Systems *see* SIC 4111: Local and Suburban Transit

485210 Interurban and Rural Bus Lines *see* SIC 4131: Intercity and Rural Bus Transportation

485310 Taxi Service *see* SIC 4121: Taxicabs

485320 Limousine Service *see* SIC 4119: Local Passenger Transportation, NEC

485410 School and Employee Bus Industry *see* SIC 4119: Local Passenger Transportation, NEC; SIC 4151: School Buses

485510 Charter Bus Industry *see* SIC 4141: Local Bus Charter Service; SIC 4142: Bus Charter Service, Except Local

485991 Special Needs Transportation *see* SIC 4119: Local Passenger Transportation, NEC

485999 All Other Transit and Ground Passenger Transportation *see* SIC 4111: Local and Suburban Transit; SIC 4119: Local Passenger Transportation, NEC

486110 Pipeline Transportation of Crude Oil *see* SIC 4612: Crude Petroleum Pipelines

486210 Pipeline Transportation of Natural Gas *see* SIC 4922: Natural Gas Transmission; SIC 4923: Natural Gas Transmission and Distribution

486910 Pipeline Transportation of Refined Petroleum Products *see* SIC 4613: Refined Petroleum Pipelines

486990 All Other Pipeline Transportation *see* SIC 4619: Pipelines, NEC

487110 Scenic and Sightseeing Transportation, Land *see* SIC 4119: Local Passenger Transportation, NEC; SIC 4789: Transportation Services, NEC; SIC 7999: Amusement and Recreation Services, NEC

487210 Scenic and Sightseeing Transportation, Water *see* SIC 4489: Water Transportation of Passengers, NEC; SIC 7999: Amusement and Recreation Services, NEC

487990 Scenic and Sightseeing Transportation, Other *see* SIC 4522: Air Transportation, Nonscheduled; SIC 7999: Amusement and Recreation Services, NEC

488111 Air Traffic Control *see* SIC 4581: Airports, Flying Fields, and Airport Terminal Services; SIC 9621: Regulations and Administration of Transportation Programs

488119 Other Airport Operations *see* SIC 4581: Airports, Flying Fields, and Airport Terminal Services; SIC 4959: Sanitary Services, NEC

488190 Other Support Activities for Air Transportation *see* SIC 4581: Airports, Flying Fields, and Airport Terminal Services

488210 Support Activities for Rail Transportation *see* SIC 4013: Railroad Switching and Terminal Establishments; SIC 4741: Rental of Railroad Cars; SIC 4789: Transportation Services, NEC

488310 Port and Harbor Operations *see* SIC 4491: Marine Cargo Handling; SIC 4499: Water Transportation Services, NEC

488320 Marine Cargo Handling *see* SIC 4491: Marine Cargo Handling

488330 Navigational Services to Shipping *see* SIC 4492: Towing and Tugboat Services; SIC 4499: Water Transportation Services, NEC

488390 Other Support Activities for Water Transportation *see* SIC 4499: Water Transportation Services, NEC; SIC 4785: Fixed Facilities and Inspection and Weighing Services for Motor Vehicle Transportation; SIC 7699: Repair Shops and Related Services, NEC

488410 Motor Vehicle Towing *see* SIC 7549: Automotive Services, Except Repair and Carwashes

488490 Other Support Activities for Road Transportation *see* SIC 4173: Terminal and Service Facilities for Motor Vehicle Passenger Transportation; SIC 4231: Terminal and Joint Terminal Maintenance Facilities for Motor Freight Transportation; SIC 4785: Fixed Facilities and Inspection and Weighing Services for Motor Vehicle Transportation

488510 Freight Transportation Arrangement *see* SIC 4731: Arrangement of Transportation of Freight and Cargo

488991 Packing and Crating *see* SIC 4783: Packing and Crating

488999 All Other Support Activities for Transportation *see* SIC 4729: Arrangement of Passenger Transportation, NEC; SIC 4789: Transportation Services, NEC

491110 Postal Service *see* SIC 4311: United States Postal Service

492110 Couriers *see* SIC 4215: Couriers Services Except by Air; SIC 4513: Air Courier Services

492210 Local Messengers and Local Delivery *see* SIC 4215: Couriers Services Except by Air

493110 General Warehousing and Storage Facilities *see* SIC 4225: General Warehousing and Storage; SIC 4226: Special Warehousing and Storage, NEC

493120 Refrigerated Storage Facilities *see* SIC 4222: Refrigerated Warehousing and Storage; SIC 4226: Special Warehousing and Storage, NEC

493130 Farm Product Storage Facilities *see* SIC 4221: Farm Product Warehousing and Storage

493190 All Other Warehousing and Storage Facilities *see* SIC 4226: Special Warehousing and Storage, NEC

INFORMATION

511110 Newspaper Publishers *see* SIC 2711: Newspapers: Publishing, or Publishing and Printing

511120 Periodical Publishers *see* SIC 2721: Periodicals: Publishing, or Publishing and Printing

511130 Book Publishers *see* SIC 2731: Books: Publishing, or Publishing and Printing

511140 Database and Directory Publishers *see* SIC 2741: Miscellaneous Publishing

511191 Greeting Card Publishers *see* SIC 2771: Greeting Cards

511199 All Other Publishers *see* SIC 2741: Miscellaneous Publishing

511210 Software Publishers *see* SIC 7372: Prepackaged Software

512110 Motion Picture and Video Production *see* SIC 7812: Motion Picture and Video Tape Production

512120 Motion Picture and Video Distribution *see* SIC 7822: Motion Picture and Video Tape Distribution; SIC 7829: Services Allied to Motion Picture Distribution

512131 Motion Picture Theaters, Except Drive-In *see* SIC 7832: Motion Picture Theaters, Except Drive-In

512132 Drive-In Motion Picture Theaters *see* SIC 7833: Drive-In Motion Picture Theaters

512191 Teleproduction and Other Post-Production Services *see* SIC 7819: Services Allied to Motion Picture Production

512199 Other Motion Picture and Video Industries *see* SIC 7819: Services Allied to Motion Picture Production; SIC 7829: Services Allied to Motion Picture Distribution

512210 Record Production *see* SIC 8999: Services, NEC

512220 Integrated Record Production/Distribution *see* SIC 3652: Phonograph Records and Prerecorded Audio Tapes and Disks

512230 Music Publishers *see* SIC 2731: Books: Publishing, or Publishing and Printing; SIC 2741: Miscellaneous Publishing; SIC 8999: Services, NEC

512240 Sound Recording Studios *see* SIC 7389: Business Services, NEC

512290 Other Sound Recording Industries *see* SIC 7389: Business Services, NEC; SIC 7922: Theatrical Producers (Except Motion Picture) and Miscellaneous Theatrical Services

513111 Radio Networks *see* SIC 4832: Radio Broadcasting Stations

513112 Radio Stations *see* SIC 4832: Radio Broadcasting Stations

513120 Television Broadcasting *see* SIC 4833: Television Broadcasting Stations

513210 Cable Networks *see* SIC 4841: Cable and Other Pay Television Services

513220 Cable and Other Program Distribution *see* SIC 4841: Cable and Other Pay Television Services

513310 Wired Telecommunications Carriers *see* SIC 4813: Telephone Communications, Except Radiotelephone; SIC 4822: Telegraph and Other Message Communications

513321 Paging *see* SIC 4812: Radiotelephone Communications

513322 Cellular and Other Wireless Telecommunications *see* SIC 4812: Radiotelephone Communications; SIC 4899: Communications Services, NEC

513330　Telecommunications Resellers *see* SIC 4812: Radiotelephone Communications; SIC 4813: Telephone Communications, Except Radiotelephone

513340　Satellite Telecommunications *see* SIC 4899: Communications Services, NEC

513390　Other Telecommunications *see* SIC 4899: Communications Services, NEC

514110　New Syndicates *see* SIC 7383: News Syndicates

514120　Libraries and Archives *see* SIC 8231: Libraries

514191　On-Line Information Services *see* SIC 7375: Information Retrieval Services

514199　All Other Information Services *see* SIC 8999: Services, NEC

514210　Data Processing Services *see* SIC 7374: Computer Processing and Data Preparation and Processing Services

FINANCE & INSURANCE

521110　Monetary Authorities-Central Banks *see* SIC 6011: Federal Reserve Banks

522110　Commercial Banking *see* SIC 6021: National Commercial Banks; SIC 6022: State Commercial Banks; SIC 6029: Commercial Banks, NEC; SIC 6081: Branches and Agencies of Foreign Banks

522120　Savings Institutions *see* SIC 6035: Savings Institutions, Federally Chartered; SIC 6036: Savings institutions, Not Federally Chartered

522130　Credit Unions *see* SIC 6061: Credit Unions, Federally Chartered; SIC 6062: Credit Unions, Not Federally Chartered

522190　Other Depository Intermediation *see* SIC 6022: State Commercial Banks

522210　Credit Card Issuing *see* SIC 6021: National Commercial Banks; SIC 6022: State Commercial Banks; SIC 6141: Personal Credit Institutions

522220　Sales Financing *see* SIC 6141: Personal Credit Institutions; SIC 6153: Short-Term Business Credit Institutions, Except Agricultural; SIC 6159: Miscellaneous Business Credit Institutions

522291　Consumer Lending *see* SIC 6141: Personal Credit Institutions

522292　Real Estate Credit *see* SIC 6162: Mortgage Bankers and Loan Correspondents

522293　International Trade Financing *see* SIC 6081: Branches and Agencies of Foreign Banks; SIC 6082: Foreign Trade and International Banking Institutions; SIC 6111: Federal and Federally Sponsored Credit Agencies; SIC 6159: Miscellaneous Business Credit Institutions

522294　Secondary Market Financing *see* SIC 6111: Federal and Federally Sponsored Credit Agencies

522298　All Other Non-Depository Credit Intermediation *see* SIC 5932: Used Merchandise Stores; SIC 6081: Branches and Agencies of Foreign Banks; SIC 6111: Federal and Federally Sponsored Credit Agencies; SIC 6153: Short-Term Business Credit Institutions, Except Agricultural; SIC 6159: Miscellaneous Business Credit Institutions

522310　Mortgage and Other Loan Brokers *see* SIC 6163: Loan Brokers

522320　Financial Transactions Processing, Reserve, and Clearing House Activities *see* SIC 6019: Central Reserve Depository Institutions, NEC; SIC 6099: Functions Related to Deposit Banking, NEC; SIC 6153: Short-Term Business Credit Institutions, Except Agricultural; SIC 7389: Business Services, NEC

522390　Other Activities Related to Credit Intermediation *see* SIC 6099: Functions Related to Deposit Banking, NEC; SIC 6162: Mortgage Bankers and Loan Correspondents

523110　Investment Banking and Securities Dealing *see* SIC 6211: Security Brokers, Dealers, and Flotation Companies

523120　Securities Brokerage *see* SIC 6211: Security Brokers, Dealers, and Flotation Companies

523130　Commodity Contracts Dealing *see* SIC 6099: Functions Related to Deposit Banking, NEC; SIC 6221: Commodity Contracts Brokers and Dealers; SIC 6799: Investors, NEC

523140　Commodity Brokerage *see* SIC 6221: Commodity Contracts Brokers and Dealers

523210　Securities and Commodity Exchanges *see* SIC 6231: Security and Commodity Exchanges

523910　Miscellaneous Intermediation *see* SIC 6211: Security Brokers, Dealers, and Flotation Companies; SIC 6799: Investors, NEC

523920　Portfolio Management *see* SIC 6282: Investment Advice; SIC 6371: Pension, Health, and Welfare Funds; SIC 6733: Trusts, Except Educational, Religious, and Charitable; SIC 6799: Investors, NEC

523930　Investment Advice *see* SIC 6282: Investment Advice

523991　Trust, Fiduciary and Custody Activities *see* SIC 6021: National Commercial Banks; SIC 6022: State Commercial Banks; SIC 6091: Nondeposit Trust Facilities; SIC 6099: Functions Related to Deposit Banking, NEC; SIC 6289: Services Allied With the Exchange of Securities or Commodities, NEC; SIC 6733: Trusts, Except Educational, Religious, and Charitable

523999 Miscellaneous Financial Investment Activities *see* SIC 6099: Functions Related to Deposit Banking, NEC; SIC 6211: Security Brokers, Dealers, and Flotation Companies; SIC 6289: Services Allied With the Exchange of Securities or Commodities, NEC; SIC 6792: Oil Royalty Traders; SIC 6799: Investors, NEC

524113 Direct Life Insurance Carriers *see* SIC 6311: Life Insurance

524114 Direct Health and Medical Insurance Carriers *see* SIC 6321: Accident and Health Insurance; SIC 6324: Hospital and Medical Service Plans

524126 Direct Property and Casualty Insurance Carriers *see* SIC 6331: Fire, Marine, and Casualty Insurance; SIC 6351: Surety Insurance

524127 Direct Title Insurance Carriers *see* SIC 6361: Title Insurance

524128 Other Direct Insurance Carriers (except Life, Health, and Medical) *see* SIC 6399: Insurance Carriers, NEC

524130 Reinsurance Carriers *see* SIC 6311: Life Insurance; SIC 6321: Accident and Health Insurance; SIC 6324: Hospital and Medical Service Plans; SIC 6331: Fire, Marine, and Casualty Insurance; SIC 6351: Surety Insurance; SIC 6361: Title Insurance

524210 Insurance Agencies and Brokerages *see* SIC 6411: Insurance Agents, Brokers, and Service

524291 Claims Adjusters *see* SIC 6411: Insurance Agents, Brokers, and Service

524292 Third Party Administration for Insurance and Pension Funds *see* SIC 6371: Pension, Health, and Welfare Funds; SIC 6411: Insurance Agents, Brokers, and Service

524298 All Other Insurance Related Activities *see* SIC 6411: Insurance Agents, Brokers, and Service

525110 Pension Funds *see* SIC 6371: Pension, Health, and Welfare Funds

525120 Health and Welfare Funds *see* SIC 6371: Pension, Health, and Welfare Funds

525190 Other Insurance and Employee Benefit Funds *see* SIC 6321: Accident and Health Insurance; SIC 6324: Hospital and Medical Service Plans; SIC 6331: Fire, Marine, and Casualty Insurance; SIC 6733: Trusts, Except Educational, Religious, and Charitable

525910 Open-End Investment Funds *see* SIC 6722: Management Investment Offices, Open-End

525920 Trusts, Estates, and Agency Accounts *see* SIC 6733: Trusts, Except Educational, Religious, and Charitable

525930 Real Estate Investment Trusts *see* SIC 6798: Real Estate Investment Trusts

525990 Other Financial Vehicles *see* SIC 6726: Unit Investment Trusts, Face-Amount Certificate Offices, and Closed-End Management Investment Offices

REAL ESTATE & RENTAL & LEASING

531110 Lessors of Residential Buildings and Dwellings *see* SIC 6513: Operators of Apartment Buildings; SIC 6514: Operators of Dwellings Other Than Apartment Buildings

531120 Lessors of Nonresidential Buildings (except Mini-warehouses) *see* SIC 6512: Operators of Nonresidential Buildings

531130 Lessors of Mini-warehouses and Self Storage Units *see* SIC 4225: General Warehousing and Storage

531190 Lessors of Other Real Estate Property *see* SIC 6515: Operators of Residential Mobile Home Sites; SIC 6517: Lessors of Railroad Property; SIC 6519: Lessors of Real Property, NEC

531210 Offices of Real Estate Agents and Brokers *see* SIC 6531: Real Estate Agents and Managers

531311 Residential Property Managers *see* SIC 6531: Real Estate Agents and Managers

531312 Nonresidential Property Managers *see* SIC 6531: Real Estate Agents and Managers

531320 Offices of Real Estate Appraisers *see* SIC 6531: Real Estate Agents and Managers

531390 Other Activities Related to Real Estate *see* SIC 6531: Real Estate Agents and Managers

532111 Passenger Cars Rental *see* SIC 7514: Passenger Car Rental

532112 Passenger Cars Leasing *see* SIC 7515: Passenger Car Leasing

532120 Truck, Utility Trailer and RV (Recreational Vehicle) Rental and Leasing *see* SIC 7513: Truck Rental and Leasing, Without Drivers; SIC 7519: Utility Trailer and Recreational Vehicle Rental

532210 Consumer Electronics and Appliances Rental *see* SIC 7359: Equipment Rental and Leasing, NEC

532220 Formal Wear and Costumes Rental *see* SIC 7299: Miscellaneous Personal Services, NEC; SIC 7819: Services Allied to Motion Picture Production

532230 Video Tapes and Disc Rental *see* SIC 7841: Video Tape Rental

532291 Home Health Equipment Rental *see* SIC 7352: Medical Equipment Rental and Leasing

532292 Recreational Goods Rental *see* SIC 7999: Amusement and Recreation Services, NEC

532299 All Other Consumer Goods Rental *see* SIC 7359: Equipment Rental and Leasing, NEC

532310 General Rental Centers *see* SIC 7359: Equipment Rental and Leasing, NEC

532411 Commercial Air, Rail, and Water Transportation Equipment Rental and Leasing *see* SIC 4499: Water Transportation Services, NEC; SIC 4741: Rental of Railroad Cars; SIC 7359: Equipment Rental and Leasing, NEC

532412 Construction, Mining and Forestry Machinery and Equipment Rental and Leasing *see* SIC 7353: Heavy Construction Equipment Rental and Leasing; SIC 7359: Equipment Rental and Leasing, NEC

532420 Office Machinery and Equipment Rental and Leasing *see* SIC 7359: Equipment Rental and Leasing, NEC; SIC 7377: Computer Rental and Leasing

532490 Other Commercial and Industrial Machinery and Equipment Rental and Leasing *see* SIC 7352: Medical Equipment Rental and Leasing; SIC 7359: Equipment Rental and Leasing, NEC; SIC 7819: Services Allied to Motion Picture Production; SIC 7922: Theatrical Producers (Except Motion Picture) and Miscellaneous Theatrical Services

533110 Owners and Lessors of Other Non-Financial Assets *see* SIC 6792: Oil Royalty Traders; SIC 6794: Patent Owners and Lessors

PROFESSIONAL, SCIENTIFIC, & TECHNICAL SERVICES

541110 Offices of Lawyers *see* SIC 8111: Legal Services

541191 Title Abstract and Settlement Offices *see* SIC 6541: Title Abstract Offices

541199 Other Legal Services *see* SIC 7389: Business Services, NEC

541211 Offices of Certified Public Accountants *see* SIC 8721: Accounting, Auditing, and Bookkeeping Services

541213 Tax Preparation Services *see* SIC 7291: Tax Return Preparation Services

541214 Payroll Services *see* SIC 7819: Services Allied to Motion Picture Production; SIC 8721: Accounting, Auditing, and Bookkeeping Services

541219 Other Accounting Services *see* SIC 8721: Accounting, Auditing, and Bookkeeping Services

541310 Architectural Services *see* SIC 8712: Architectural Services

541320 Landscape Architectural Services *see* SIC 0781: Landscape Counseling and Planning

541330 Engineering Services *see* SIC 8711: Engineering Services

541340 Drafting Services *see* SIC 7389: Business Services, NEC

541350 Building Inspection Services *see* SIC 7389: Business Services, NEC

541360 Geophysical Surveying and Mapping Services *see* SIC 1081: Metal Mining Services; SIC 1382: Oil and Gas Field Exploration Services; SIC 1481: Nonmetallic Minerals Services Except Fuels; SIC 8713: Surveying Services

541370 Surveying and Mapping (except Geophysical) Services *see* SIC 7389: Business Services, NEC; SIC 8713: Surveying Services

541380 Testing Laboratories *see* SIC 8734: Testing Laboratories

541410 Interior Design Services *see* SIC 7389: Business Services, NEC

541420 Industrial Design Services *see* SIC 7389: Business Services, NEC

541430 Graphic Design Services *see* SIC 7336: Commercial Art and Graphic Design; SIC 8099: Health and Allied Services, NEC

541490 Other Specialized Design Services *see* SIC 7389: Business Services, NEC

541511 Custom Computer Programming Services *see* SIC 7371: Computer Programming Services

541512 Computer Systems Design Services *see* SIC 7373: Computer Integrated Systems Design; SIC 7379: Computer Related Services, NEC

541513 Computer Facilities Management Services *see* SIC 7376: Computer Facilities Management Services

541519 Other Computer Related Services *see* SIC 7379: Computer Related Services, NEC

541611 Administrative Management and General Management Consulting Services *see* SIC 8742: Management Consulting Services

541612 Human Resources and Executive Search Consulting Services *see* SIC 7361: Employment Agencies; SIC 8742: Management Consulting Services; SIC 8999: Services, NEC

541613 Marketing Consulting Services *see* SIC 8742: Management Consulting Services

541614 Process, Physical, Distribution and Logistics Consulting *see* SIC 8742: Management Consulting Services

541618 Other Management Consulting Services *see* SIC 4731: Arrangement of Transportation of Freight and Cargo; SIC 8748: Business Consulting Services, NEC

541620 Environmental Consulting Services *see* SIC 8999: Services, NEC

541690 Other Scientific and Technical Consulting Services *see* SIC 0781: Landscape Counseling and Planning; SIC 8748: Business Consulting Services, NEC; SIC 8999: Services, NEC

541710 Research and Development in the Physical Sciences and Engineering Sciences *see* SIC 8731: Commercial Physical and Biological Research; SIC 8733: Noncommercial Research Organizations

541720 Research and Development in the Life Sciences *see* SIC 8731: Commercial Physical and Biological Research; SIC 8733: Noncommercial Research Organizations

541730 Research and Development in the Social Sciences and Humanities *see* SIC 8732: Commercial Economic, Sociological, and Educational Research; SIC 8733: Noncommercial Research Organizations

541810 Advertising Agencies *see* SIC 7311: Advertising Agencies

541820 Public Relations Services *see* SIC 8743: Public Relations Services

541830 Media Buying Agencies *see* SIC 7319: Advertising, NEC

541840 Media Representatives *see* SIC 7313: Radio, Television, and Publishers' Advertising Representatives

541850 Display Advertising *see* SIC 7312: Outdoor Advertising Services; SIC 7319: Advertising, NEC

541860 Direct Mail Advertising *see* SIC 7331: Direct Mail Advertising Services

541870 Advertising Material Distribution Services *see* SIC 7319: Advertising, NEC

541890 Other Services Related to Advertising *see* SIC 5199: Nondurable Goods, NEC; SIC 7319: Advertising, NEC; SIC 7389: Business Services, NEC

541910 Marketing Research and Public Opinion Polling *see* SIC 8732: Commercial Economic, Sociological, and Educational Research

541921 Photographic Studios, Portrait *see* SIC 7221: Photographic Studios, Portrait

541922 Commercial Photography *see* SIC 7335: Commercial Photography; SIC 8099: Health and Allied Services, NEC

541930 Translation and Interpretation Services *see* SIC 7389: Business Services, NEC

541940 Veterinary Services *see* SIC 0741: Veterinary Service For Livestock; SIC 0742: Veterinary Services for Animal Specialties; SIC 8734: Testing Laboratories

541990 All Other Professional, Scientific and Technical Services *see* SIC 7389: Business Services, NEC

MANAGEMENT OF COMPANIES & ENTERPRISES

551111 Offices of Bank Holding Companies *see* SIC 6712: Offices of Bank Holding Companies

551112 Offices of Other Holding Companies *see* SIC 6719: Offices of Holding Companies, NEC

ADMINISTRATIVE & SUPPORT, WASTE MANAGEMENT & REMEDIATION SERVICES

561110 Office Administrative Services *see* SIC 8741: Management Services (Except Construction Management Services)

561210 Facilities Support Services *see* SIC 8744: Facilities Support Management Services

561310 Employment Placement Agencies *see* SIC 7361: Employment Agencies; SIC 7819: Services Allied to Motion Picture Production; SIC 7922: Theatrical Producers (Except Motion Picture) and Miscellaneous Theatrical Services

561320 Temporary Help Services *see* SIC 7363: Help Supply Services

561330 Employee Leasing Services *see* SIC 7363: Help Supply Services

561410 Document Preparation Services *see* SIC 7338: Secretarial and Court Reporting Services

561421 Telephone Answering Services *see* SIC 7389: Business Services, NEC

561422 Telemarketing Bureaus *see* SIC 7389: Business Services, NEC

561431 Other Business Service Centers (including Copy Shops) *see* SIC 7389: Business Services, NEC; SIC 7334: Photocopying and Duplicating Services

561439 Private Mail Centers *see* SIC 7389: Business Services, NEC

561440 Collection Agencies *see* SIC 7322: Adjustment and Collection Services

561450 Credit Bureaus *see* SIC 7323: Credit Reporting Services

561491 Repossession Services *see* SIC 7322: Adjustment and Collection Services; SIC 7389: Business Services, NEC

561492 Court Reporting and Stenotype Services *see* SIC 7338: Secretarial and Court Reporting Services

561499 All Other Business Support Services *see* SIC 7389: Business Services, NEC

561510 Travel Agencies *see* SIC 4724: Travel Agencies

561520 Tour Operators *see* SIC 4725: Tour Operators

561591 Convention and Visitors Bureaus *see* SIC 7389: Business Services, NEC

561599 All Other Travel Arrangement and Reservation Services *see* SIC 4729: Arrangement of Passenger Transportation, NEC; SIC 7389: Business

Services, NEC; SIC 7999: Amusement and Recreation Services, NEC; SIC 8699: Membership Organizations, NEC

561611 Investigation Services *see* SIC 7381: Detective, Guard, and Armored Car Services

561612 Security Guards and Patrol Services *see* SIC 7381: Detective, Guard, and Armored Car Services

561613 Armored Car Services *see* SIC 7381: Detective, Guard, and Armored Car Services

561621 Security Systems Services (except Locksmiths) *see* SIC 1731: Electrical Work; SIC 7382: Security Systems Services

561622 Locksmiths *see* SIC 7699: Repair Shops and Related Services, NEC

561710 Exterminating and Pest Control Services *see* SIC 4959: Sanitary Services, NEC; SIC 7342: Disinfecting and Pest Control Services

561720 Janitorial Services *see* SIC 4581: Airports, Flying Fields, and Airport Terminal Services; SIC 7342: Disinfecting and Pest Control Services; SIC 7349: Building Cleaning and Maintenance Services, NEC

561730 Landscaping Services *see* SIC 0782: Lawn and Garden Services; SIC 0783: Ornamental Shrub and Tree Services

561740 Carpet and Upholstery Cleaning Services *see* SIC 7217: Carpet and Upholstery Cleaning

561790 Other Services to Buildings and Dwellings *see* SIC 7389: Business Services, NEC; SIC 7699: Repair Shops and Related Services, NEC

561910 Packaging and Labeling Services *see* SIC 7389: Business Services, NEC

561920 Convention and Trade Show Organizers *see* SIC 7389: Business Services, NEC

561990 All Other Support Services *see* SIC 7389: Business Services, NEC

562111 Solid Waste Collection *see* SIC 4212: Local Trucking Without Storage; SIC 4953: Refuse Systems

562112 Hazardous Waste Collection *see* SIC 4212: Local Trucking Without Storage; SIC 4953: Refuse Systems

562119 Other Waste Collection *see* SIC 4212: Local Trucking Without Storage; SIC 4953: Refuse Systems

562211 Hazardous Waste Treatment and Disposal *see* SIC 4953: Refuse Systems

562212 Solid Waste Landfills *see* SIC 4953: Refuse Systems

562213 Solid Waste Combustors and Incinerators *see* SIC 4953: Refuse Systems

562219 Other Nonhazardous Waste Treatment and Disposal *see* SIC 4953: Refuse Systems

562910 Remediation Services *see* SIC 1799: Special Trade Contractors, NEC; SIC 4959: Sanitary Services, NEC

562920 Materials Recovery Facilities *see* SIC 4953: Refuse Systems

562991 Septic Tank and Related Services *see* SIC 7359: Equipment Rental and Leasing, NEC; SIC 7699: Repair Shops and Related Services, NEC

562998 All Other Miscellaneous Waste Management *see* SIC 4959: Sanitary Services, NEC

EDUCATIONAL SERVICES

611110 Elementary and Secondary Schools *see* SIC 8211: Elementary and Secondary Schools

611210 Junior Colleges *see* SIC 8222: Junior Colleges and Technical Institutes

611310 Colleges, Universities and Professional Schools *see* SIC 8221: Colleges, Universities, and Professional Schools

611410 Business and Secretarial Schools *see* SIC 8244: Business and Secretarial Schools

611420 Computer Training *see* SIC 8243: Data Processing Schools

611430 Professional and Management Development Training Schools *see* SIC 8299: Schools and Educational Services, NEC

611511 Cosmetology and Barber Schools *see* SIC 7231: Beauty Shops; SIC 7241: Barber Shops

611512 Flight Training *see* SIC 8249: Vocational Schools, NEC; SIC 8299: Schools and Educational Services, NEC

611513 Apprenticeship Training *see* SIC 8249: Vocational Schools, NEC

611519 Other Technical and Trade Schools *see* SIC 8243: Data Processing Schools; SIC 8249: Vocational Schools, NEC

611610 Fine Arts Schools *see* SIC 7911: Dance Studios, Schools, and Halls; SIC 8299: Schools and Educational Services, NEC

611620 Sports and Recreation Instruction *see* SIC 7999: Amusement and Recreation Services, NEC

611630 Language Schools *see* SIC 8299: Schools and Educational Services, NEC

611691 Exam Preparation and Tutoring *see* SIC 8299: Schools and Educational Services, NEC

611692 Automobile Driving Schools *see* SIC 8299: Schools and Educational Services, NEC

611699 All Other Miscellaneous Schools and Instruction *see* SIC 8299: Schools and Educational Services, NEC

611710 Educational Support Services *see* SIC 8299: Schools and Educational Services, NEC; SIC 8748: Business Consulting Services, NEC

HEALTH CARE & SOCIAL ASSISTANCE

621111 Offices of Physicians (except Mental Health Specialists) *see* SIC 8011: Offices and Clinics of Doctors of Medicine; SIC 8031: Offices and Clinics of Doctors of Osteopathy

621112 Offices of Physicians, Mental Health Specialists *see* SIC 8011: Offices and Clinics of Doctors of Medicine; SIC 8031: Offices and Clinics of Doctors of Osteopathy

621210 Offices of Dentists *see* SIC 8021: Offices and Clinics of Dentists

621310 Offices of Chiropractors *see* SIC 8041: Offices and Clinics of Chiropractors

621320 Offices of Optometrists *see* SIC 8042: Offices and Clinics of Optometrists

621330 Offices of Mental Health Practitioners (except Physicians) *see* SIC 8049: Offices and Clinics of Health Practitioners, NEC

621340 Offices of Physical, Occupational, and Speech Therapists and Audiologists *see* SIC 8049: Offices and Clinics of Health Practitioners, NEC

621391 Offices of Podiatrists *see* SIC 8043: Offices and Clinics of Podiatrists

621399 Offices of All Other Miscellaneous Health Practitioners *see* SIC 8049: Offices and Clinics of Health Practitioners, NEC

621410 Family Planning Centers *see* SIC 8093: Specialty Outpatient Facilities, NEC; SIC 8099: Health and Allied Services, NEC

621420 Outpatient Mental Health and Substance Abuse Centers *see* SIC 8093: Specialty Outpatient Facilities, NEC

621491 HMO Medical Centers *see* SIC 8011: Offices and Clinics of Doctors of Medicine

621492 Kidney Dialysis Centers *see* SIC 8092: Kidney Dialysis Centers

621493 Freestanding Ambulatory Surgical and Emergency Centers *see* SIC 8011: Offices and Clinics of Doctors of Medicine

621498 All Other Outpatient Care Facilities *see* SIC 8093: Specialty Outpatient Facilities, NEC

621511 Medical Laboratories *see* SIC 8071: Medical Laboratories

621512 Diagnostic Imaging Centers *see* SIC 8071: Medical Laboratories

621610 Home Health Care Services *see* SIC 8082: Home Health Care Services

621910 Ambulance Service *see* SIC 4119: Local Passenger Transportation, NEC; SIC 4522: Air Transportation, Nonscheduled

621991 Blood and Organ Banks *see* SIC 8099: Health and Allied Services, NEC

621999 All Other Miscellaneous Ambulatory Health Care Services *see* SIC 8099: Health and Allied Services, NEC

622110 General Medical and Surgical Hospitals *see* SIC 8062: General Medical and Surgical Hospitals; SIC 8069: Specialty Hospitals, Except Psychiatric

622210 Psychiatric and Substance Abuse Hospitals *see* SIC 8063: Psychiatric Hospitals; SIC 8069: Specialty Hospitals, Except Psychiatric

622310 Specialty (except Psychiatric and Substance Abuse) Hospitals *see* SIC 8069: Specialty Hospitals, Except Psychiatric

623110 Nursing Care Facilities *see* SIC 8051: Skilled Nursing Care Facilities; SIC 8052: Intermediate Care Facilities; SIC 8059: Nursing and Personal Care Facilities, NEC

623210 Residential Mental Retardation Facilities *see* SIC 8052: Intermediate Care Facilities

623220 Residential Mental Health and Substance Abuse Facilities *see* SIC 8361: Residential Care

623311 Continuing Care Retirement Communities *see* SIC 8051: Skilled Nursing Care Facilities; SIC 8052: Intermediate Care Facilities; SIC 8059: Nursing and Personal Care Facilities, NEC

623312 Homes for the Elderly *see* SIC 8361: Residential Care

623990 Other Residential Care Facilities *see* SIC 8361: Residential Care

624110 Child and Youth Services *see* SIC 8322: Individual and Family Social Services; SIC 8641: Civic, Social, and Fraternal Associations

624120 Services for the Elderly and Persons with Disabilities *see* SIC 8322: Individual and Family Social Services

624190 Other Individual and Family Services *see* SIC 8322: Individual and Family Social Services

624210 Community Food Services *see* SIC 8322: Individual and Family Social Services

624221 Temporary Shelter *see* SIC 8322: Individual and Family Social Services

624229 Other Community Housing Services *see* SIC 8322: Individual and Family Social Services

624230 Emergency and Other Relief Services *see* SIC 8322: Individual and Family Social Services

624310 Vocational Rehabilitation Services *see* SIC 8331: Job Training and Vocational Rehabilitation Services

624410 Child Day Care Services *see* SIC 7299: Miscellaneous Personal Services, NEC; SIC 8351: Child Day Care Services

ARTS, ENTERTAINMENT, & RECREATION

711110   Theater Companies and Dinner Theaters *see* SIC 5812: Eating and Drinking Places; SIC 7922: Theatrical Producers (Except Motion Picture) and Miscellaneous Theatrical Services

711120   Dance Companies *see* SIC 7922: Theatrical Producers (Except Motion Picture) and Miscellaneous Theatrical Services

711130   Musical Groups and Artists *see* SIC 7929: Bands, Orchestras, Actors, and Other Entertainers and Entertainment Groups

711190   Other Performing Arts Companies *see* SIC 7929: Bands, Orchestras, Actors, and Other Entertainers and Entertainment Groups; SIC 7999: Amusement and Recreation Services, NEC

711211   Sports Teams and Clubs *see* SIC 7941: Professional Sports Clubs and Promoters

711212   Race Tracks *see* SIC 7948: Racing, Including Track Operations

711219   Other Spectator Sports *see* SIC 7941: Professional Sports Clubs and Promoters; SIC 7948: Racing, Including Track Operations; SIC 7999: Amusement and Recreation Services, NEC

711310   Promoters of Performing Arts, Sports, and Similar Events with Facilities *see* SIC 6512: Operators of Nonresidential Buildings; SIC 7922: Theatrical Producers (Except Motion Picture) and Miscellaneous Theatrical Services; SIC 7941: Professional Sports Clubs and Promoters

711320   Promoters of Performing Arts, Sports, and Similar Events without Facilities *see* SIC 7922: Theatrical Producers (Except Motion Picture) and Miscellaneous Theatrical Services; SIC 7941: Professional Sports Clubs and Promoters

711410   Agents and Managers for Artists, Athletes, Entertainers and Other Public Figures *see* SIC 7389: Business Services, NEC; SIC 7922: Theatrical Producers (Except Motion Picture) and Miscellaneous Theatrical Services; SIC 7941: Professional Sports Clubs and Promoters

711510   Independent Artists, Writers, and Performers *see* SIC 7819: Services Allied to Motion Picture Production; SIC 7929: Bands, Orchestras, Actors, and Other Entertainers and Entertainment Groups; SIC 8999: Services, NEC

712110   Museums *see* SIC 8412: Museums and Art Galleries

712120   Historical Sites *see* SIC 8412: Museums and Art Galleries

712130   Zoos and Botanical Gardens *see* SIC 8422: Arboreta and Botanical or Zoological Gardens

712190   Nature Parks and Other Similar Institutions *see* SIC 7999: Amusement and Recreation Services, NEC; SIC 8422: Arboreta and Botanical or Zoological Gardens

713110   Amusement and Theme Parks *see* SIC 7996: Amusement Parks

713120   Amusement Arcades *see* SIC 7993: Coin Operated Amusement Devices

713210   Casinos (except Casino Hotels) *see* SIC 7999: Amusement and Recreation Services, NEC

713290   Other Gambling Industries *see* SIC 7993: Coin Operated Amusement Devices; SIC 7999: Amusement and Recreation Services, NEC

713910   Golf Courses and Country Clubs *see* SIC 7992: Public Golf Courses; SIC 7997: Membership Sports and Recreation Clubs

713920   Skiing Facilities *see* SIC 7999: Amusement and Recreation Services, NEC

713930   Marinas *see* SIC 4493: Marinas

713940   Fitness and Recreational Sports Centers *see* SIC 7991: Physical Fitness Facilities; SIC 7997: Membership Sports and Recreation Clubs; SIC 7999: Amusement and Recreation Services, NEC

713950   Bowling Centers *see* SIC 7933: Bowling Centers

713990   All Other Amusement and Recreation Industries *see* SIC 7911: Dance Studios, Schools, and Halls; SIC 7993: Coin Operated Amusement Devices; SIC 7997: Membership Sports and Recreation Clubs; SIC 7999: Amusement and Recreation Services, NEC

ACCOMODATION & FOODSERVICES

721110   Hotels (except Casino Hotels) and Motels *see* SIC 7011: Hotels and Motels; SIC 7041: Organization Hotels and Lodging Houses, on Membership Basis

721120   Casino Hotels *see* SIC 7011: Hotels and Motels

721191   Bed and Breakfast Inns *see* SIC 7011: Hotels and Motels

721199   All Other Traveler Accommodations *see* SIC 7011: Hotels and Motels

721211   RV (Recreational Vehicle) Parks and Campgrounds *see* SIC 7033: Recreational Vehicle Parks and Campsites

721214   Recreational and Vacation Camps *see* SIC 7032: Sporting and Recreational Camps

721310   Rooming and Boarding Houses *see* SIC 7021: Rooming and Boarding Houses; SIC 7041: Organization Hotels and Lodging Houses, on Membership Basis

722110 Full-Service Restaurants *see* SIC 5812: Eating and Drinking Places

722211 Limited-Service Restaurants *see* SIC 5499: Miscellaneous Food Stores; SIC 5812: Eating and Drinking Places

722212 Cafeterias *see* SIC 5812: Eating and Drinking Places

722213 Snack and Nonalcoholic Beverage Bars *see* SIC 5461: Retail Bakeries; SIC 5812: Eating and Drinking Places

722310 Foodservice Contractors *see* SIC 5812: Eating and Drinking Places

722320 Caterers *see* SIC 5812: Eating and Drinking Places

722330 Mobile Caterers *see* SIC 5963: Direct Selling Establishments

722410 Drinking Places (Alcoholic Beverages) *see* SIC 5813: Drinking Places (Alcoholic Beverages)

OTHER SERVICES

811111 General Automotive Repair *see* SIC 7538: General Automotive Repair Shops

811112 Automotive Exhaust System Repair *see* SIC 7533: Automotive Exhaust System Repair Shops

811113 Automotive Transmission Repair *see* SIC 7537: Automotive Transmission Repair Shops

811118 Other Automotive Mechanical and Electrical Repair and Maintenance *see* SIC 7539: Automotive Repair Shops, NEC

811121 Automotive Body, Paint, and Upholstery Repair and Maintenance *see* SIC 7532: Top, Body, and Upholstery Repair Shops and Paint Shops

811122 Automotive Glass Replacement Shops *see* SIC 7536: Automotive Glass Replacement Shops

811191 Automotive Oil Change and Lubrication Shops *see* SIC 7549: Automotive Services, Except Repair and Carwashes

811192 Car Washes *see* SIC 7542: Carwashes

811198 All Other Automotive Repair and Maintenance *see* SIC 7534: Tire Retreading and Repair Shops; SIC 7549: Automotive Services, Except Repair and Carwashes

811211 Consumer Electronics Repair and Maintenance *see* SIC 7622: Radio and Television Repair Shops; SIC 7629: Electrical and Electronic Repair Shops, NEC

811212 Computer and Office Machine Repair and Maintenance *see* SIC 7378: Computer Maintenance and Repair; SIC 7629: Electrical and Electronic Repair Shops, NEC; SIC 7699: Repair Shops and Related Services, NEC

811213 Communication Equipment Repair and Maintenance *see* SIC 7622: Radio and Television Repair Shops; SIC 7629: Electrical and Electronic Repair Shops, NEC

811219 Other Electronic and Precision Equipment Repair and Maintenance *see* SIC 7629: Electrical and Electronic Repair Shops, NEC; SIC 7699: Repair Shops and Related Services, NEC

811310 Commercial and Industrial Machinery and Equipment (except Automotive and Electronic) Repair and Maintenance *see* SIC 7623: Refrigeration and Air-Conditioning Services and Repair Shops; SIC 7694: Armature Rewinding Shops; SIC 7699: Repair Shops and Related Services, NEC

811411 Home and Garden Equipment Repair and Maintenance *see* SIC 7699: Repair Shops and Related Services, NEC

811412 Appliance Repair and Maintenance *see* SIC 7623: Refrigeration and Air-Conditioning Services and Repair Shops; SIC 7629: Electrical and Electronic Repair Shops, NEC; SIC 7699: Repair Shops and Related Services, NEC

811420 Reupholstery and Furniture Repair *see* SIC 7641: Reupholster and Furniture Repair

811430 Footwear and Leather Goods Repair *see* SIC 7251: Shoe Repair Shops and Shoeshine Parlors; SIC 7699: Repair Shops and Related Services, NEC

811490 Other Personal and Household Goods Repair and Maintenance *see* SIC 3732: Boat Building and Repairing; SIC 7219: Laundry and Garment Services, NEC; SIC 7631: Watch, Clock, and Jewelry Repair; SIC 7692: Welding Repair; SIC 7699: Repair Shops and Related Services, NEC

812111 Barber Shops *see* SIC 7241: Barber Shops

812112 Beauty Salons *see* SIC 7231: Beauty Shops

812113 Nail Salons *see* SIC 7231: Beauty Shops

812191 Diet and Weight Reducing Centers *see* SIC 7299: Miscellaneous Personal Services, NEC

812199 Other Personal Care Services *see* SIC 7299: Miscellaneous Personal Services, NEC

812210 Funeral Homes *see* SIC 7261: Funeral Services and Crematories

812220 Cemeteries and Crematories *see* SIC 6531: Real Estate Agents and Managers; SIC 6553: Cemetery Subdividers and Developers

812220 Cemeteries and Crematories *see* SIC 7261: Funeral Services and Crematories

812310 Coin-Operated Laundries and Drycleaners *see* SIC 7215: Coin-Operated Laundry and Drycleaning

812321 Laundries, Family and Commercial *see* SIC 7211: Power Laundries, Family and Commercial

812322 Drycleaning Plants *see* SIC 7216: Drycleaning Plants, Except Rug Cleaning

812331 Linen Supply *see* SIC 7213: Linen Supply; SIC 7219: Laundry and Garment Services, NEC

812332 Industrial Launderers *see* SIC 7218: Industrial Launderers

812391 Garment Pressing and Agents for Laundries *see* SIC 7212: Garment Pressing, and Agents for Laundries

812399 All Other Laundry Services *see* SIC 7219: Laundry and Garment Services, NEC

812910 Pet Care (except Veterinary) Services *see* SIC 0752: Animal Specialty Services, Except Veterinary

812921 Photo Finishing Laboratories (except One-Hour) *see* SIC 7384: Photofinishing Laboratories

812922 One-Hour Photo Finishing *see* SIC 7384: Photofinishing Laboratories

812930 Parking Lots and Garages *see* SIC 7521: Automobile Parking

812990 All Other Personal Services *see* SIC 7299: Miscellaneous Personal Services, NEC; SIC 7389: Business Services, NEC

813110 Religious Organizations *see* SIC 8661: Religious Organizations

813211 Grantmaking Foundations *see* SIC 6732: Education, Religious, and Charitable Trusts

813212 Voluntary Health Organizations *see* SIC 8399: Social Services, NEC

813219 Other Grantmaking and Giving Services *see* SIC 8399: Social Services, NEC

813311 Human Rights Organizations *see* SIC 8399: Social Services, NEC

813312 Environment, Conservation and Wildlife Organizations *see* SIC 8399: Social Services, NEC; SIC 8699: Membership Organizations, NEC

813319 Other Social Advocacy Organizations *see* SIC 8399: Social Services, NEC

813410 Civic and Social Organizations *see* SIC 8641: Civic, Social, and Fraternal Associations; SIC 8699: Membership Organizations, NEC

813910 Business Associations *see* SIC 8611: Business Associations; SIC 8699: Membership Organizations, NEC

813920 Professional Organizations *see* SIC 8621: Professional Membership Organizations

813930 Labor Unions and Similar Labor Organizations *see* SIC 8631: Labor Unions and Similar Labor Organizations

813940 Political Organizations *see* SIC 8651: Political Organizations

813990 Other Similar Organizations *see* SIC 6531: Real Estate Agents and Managers; SIC 8641: Civic, Social, and Fraternal Associations; SIC 8699: Membership Organizations, NEC

814110 Private Households *see* SIC 8811: Private Households

PUBLIC ADMINISTRATION

921110 Executive Offices *see* SIC 9111: Executive Offices

921120 Legislative Bodies *see* SIC 9121: Legislative Bodies

921130 Public Finance *see* SIC 9311: Public Finance, Taxation, and Monetary Policy

921140 Executive and Legislative Offices, Combined *see* SIC 9131: Executive and Legislative Offices, Combined

921150 American Indian and Alaska Native Tribal Governments *see* SIC 8641: Civic, Social, and Fraternal Associations

921190 All Other General Government *see* SIC 9199: General Government, NEC

922110 Courts *see* SIC 9211: Courts

922120 Police Protection *see* SIC 9221: Police Protection

922130 Legal Counsel and Prosecution *see* SIC 9222: Legal Counsel and Prosecution

922140 Correctional Institutions *see* SIC 9223: Correctional Institutions

922150 Parole Offices and Probation Offices *see* SIC 8322: Individual and Family Social Services

922160 Fire Protection *see* SIC 9224: Fire Protection

922190 All Other Justice, Public Order, and Safety *see* SIC 9229: Public Order and Safety, NEC

923110 Administration of Education Programs *see* SIC 9411: Administration of Educational Programs

923120 Administration of Public Health Programs *see* SIC 9431: Administration of Public Health Programs

923130 Administration of Social, Human Resource and Income Maintenance Programs *see* SIC 9441: Administration of Social, Human Resource and Income Maintenance Programs

923140 Administration of Veteran's Affairs *see* SIC 9451: Administration of Veteran's Affairs, Except Health Insurance

924110 Air and Water Resource and Solid Waste Management *see* SIC 9511: Air and Water Resource and Solid Waste Management

924120 Land, Mineral, Wildlife, and Forest Conservation *see* SIC 9512: Land, Mineral, Wildlife, and Forest Conservation

925110 Administration of Housing Programs *see* SIC 9531: Administration of Housing Programs

925120 Administration of Urban Planning and Community and Rural Development *see* SIC 9532: Administration of Urban Planning and Community and Rural Development

926110 Administration of General Economic Programs *see* SIC 9611: Administration of General Economic Programs

926120   Regulation and Administration of Transportation Programs *see* SIC 9621: Regulations and Administration of Transportation Programs

926130   Regulation and Administration of Communications, Electric, Gas, and Other Utilities *see* SIC 9631: Regulation and Administration of Communications, Electric, Gas, and Other Utilities

926140   Regulation of Agricultural Marketing and Commodities *see* SIC 9641: Regulation of Agricultural Marketing and Commodities

926150   Regulation, Licensing, and Inspection of Miscellaneous Commercial Sectors *see* SIC 9651: Regulation, Licensing, and Inspection of Miscellaneous Commercial Sectors

927110   Space Research and Technology *see* SIC 9661: Space Research and Technology

928110   National Security *see* SIC 9711: National Security

928120   International Affairs *see* SIC 9721: International Affairs

999990   Unclassified Establishments *see* SIC 9999: Nonclassified Establishments

Industry Index

General Index

ARDA (Advanced Research and Development Activity), 200, 201, 1023

Area Agencies on Aging (AAA), 649

Argenbright Security firm, 94

Argentina
computer security industry, 181
direct broadcast satellite TV, 236
genetic engineering, 384, 389
optical sensing/IR devices, 672
outsourcing, 677
specialty tourism, 901
supplemental insurance plans, 931

Argonne National Laboratory, 694

Ariba Inc., 249

AriZona Iced Tea brand, 750, 751, 752, 754

Arnon, Daniel I., 889

Arrosto Coffee Co., 882

Arrowhead Mills, 614

Ars Technica Web site, 276

Artera Group Inc., 643

ArthroCare Corp., 571

Arthur Andersen accounting firm, 192, 492

Artificial intelligence, **73–80**
America and the world, 80
background/development, 74–76
current conditions, 77–78
data mining and, 199
industry leaders, 78–79
industry snapshot, 73
organization/structure, 73–74
pioneers, 76–77
research and technology, 79–80

Artificial Limb Manufacturers and Brace Association (U.S.), 772

Artificial Limb Program (Veterans Administration), 772

Arts and Crafts Movement (U.S.), 84

Arts and crafts stores, **81–87**
background/development, 83–86
current conditions, 86
industry leaders, 86–87
industry snapshot, **81–87**
organization/structure, 81–83

AS/400 mainframe computer, 478

Asahi Optical Company, 219

ASCDI (Association of Service and Computer Dealers International (ASCDI), 991

Ascend Communications, 172

Ascenda Environmental Science Corporation (AES), 111

Ascent Healthcare Solutions, 454

Asensio & Company investment firm, 548

Aserinsky, Dr. Eugene, 849

Asia Pacific Coatings Journal, 560

Asia-Pacific region
computer network support services, 172
digital imaging industry, 219
digital satellite broadcasting system, 236
e-commerce/B2B, 249
executive search firms, 766, 767
exercise equipment industry, 746
fiber optics industry, 342
gambling casinos and resorts, 365
geographic information systems, 400
global AI market, 77
high speed internet services, 431
nutritional supplements, 659
outsourcing and, 677
passenger restraint systems, 705
satellites, 824
selling used computer equipment, 995
semiprocessor industry, 845
smoking cessation products and services, 860, 866
telemedicine industry, 952
wireless communications and WAP, 1078

Asia Pacific Satellite Communications (APSCC), 236

Asian Investors magazine, 293

ASICS (application-specific integrated circuits). *See* Semiconductors

ASP (application service providers) Industry Consortium, 67–69

Aspen Education Group, Inc. (AEG), 978–979

Assisted Living Concepts, Inc., 3

Assisted reproductive technology (ART), 328, 331–332

Associated Bond and Insurance Agency, 115

Association for Automatic Identification and Mobility (AIM), 791

Association for Computing Machinery (ACM), 77, 79, 677

Association for Financial Counseling and Planning Education (AFCPE), 347

Association for Payment and Clearing Services (Apacs, UK), 857

Association for the Advancement of Artificial Intelligence (AAAI), 74

Association for the Advancement of Wound Care, 1079

Association for the Study of Peak Oil and Gas (ASPO) Conference (U.S.), 31

Association of American University Presses (AAUP), 300

Association of Computing Machinery, 74

Association of Contingency Planners (ACP), 124, 127

Association of Crafts & Creative Industries (ACCI), 82

Association of Executive Search Consultants (AESC), 764, 765, 766, 767

Association of Home Appliance Manufacturers, 1037

Association of Professional Genealogists (APGEN), 376, 377

Association of Retail Environments (A.R.E.), 411

Association of Sleep Disorders Centers, 850

AstraZeneca, 586

Astro Boy products, 528

AstroPower Inc., 740

A.T. Kearney Executive Search, 763, 765, 766–767

ATA Ventures, 780

Atari Inc., 369, 370, 372, 1018

Athersys, 985

Atkins Nutritionals Inc., 1064, 1066, 1069–1070

Atlantic City (NJ) gambling casinos, 363, 366

Atlantic Journal Constitution articles, 200, 202

Atlantic Ocean Region 1-4 Inmarsat satellite, 822

Atlas, Ronald M., 110

Atlas of Limb Prosthetics: Surgical, Prosthetic, and Rehabilitation Principles (Wilson), 772

"Atlas to Accompany the Second Report of the Irish Railway Commissioners," 394

Atrium Innovations, 659

ATSA (Aviation and Transportation Security Act, 2001), 89–90, 91

AT&T Inc., 68, 73, 126, 129–130, 131, 137, 169, 172, 236, 430, 470, 486, 488, 824, 955–956, 959, 961, 1022, 1076–1077

"Austin Powers" merchandise, 525

Australia
anti-bacterial products, 64
arts and crafts industry, 87
bioremediation industry, 110
business emergency planning, 132
computer security industry, 181
digital audio entertainment, 210
distance learning, 239

Dorsey, Jack, 872

Doughtery, Jim and Janice, 709

Dow AgroSciences, 390

Dow Corning, 1008

Download.com, 281

DP (Dell-Perot) Systems, 938

Dr. Pepper Snapple Group, 753

Dragon NaturallySpeaking software (Nuance), 1025

Dragon Systems, Inc., 1026

DRAM (dynamic random access memory) chips. *See* Semiconductors

DreamWorks SKG Inc., 163, 165, 529

Drexler, K. Eric, 546

DRI International newsletter, 127

Driscoll, Margaret, 241

DRTV (direct response TV), 469, 472–473

Drug Enforcement Administration (DEA), 305

Drypers Corporation (diapers), 63

DSN Retailing Today magazine, 85

DTE Energy Co., 356

DuBarry-Hay, Denise, 473

Duke, Mike, 407

Duke University Infection Control Outreach Network, 922

Dulles International Airport (Washington, D.C.), 91

Duncan, Doug, 599

Dunkin' Brands Inc., 863, 877–878

Dunn Brothers Coffee, 883, 886

DuPont Corp., 592

DuPont Displays, 1008

Durable medical equipment (DME). *See* Home health care services

DVG-H Wi-Fi technology, 824

Dynamic Associates Inc., 559

Dynamic Hypertext Markup Language (DHTML), 1090–1091

Dynamic Systems Development Model (DSDM), of agile software development, 10, 11

E

e-books. *See* Electronic publishing

E-commerce: business to business, 102, **245–249**
America and the world, 249
background/development, 246–247
current conditions, 248–249
industry leaders, 249
industry snapshot, 245
organization/structure, 245–246
pioneers in the field, 247–248

E-commerce: consumer products, **251–257**
America and the world, 257
background/development, 253–256
current conditions, 256
industry leaders, 256–257
industry snapshot, 251
organization/structure, 251–253
research and technology, 257

E-commerce: online auctions, **259–263**
America and the world, 262
background/development, 260–261
current conditions, 261
industry leaders, 261–262
industry snapshot, 259
organization/structure, 259–260
research and technology, 262–263

E-commerce: online brokerages, **264–269**
background/development, 265–268
current conditions, 268
industry leaders, 268–269
industry snapshot, 264
organization/structure, 264–265

E-commerce: online grocery shopping, **270–275**
background/development, 271–274
current conditions, 274
industry leaders, 274–275
industry snapshot, 270
organization/structure, 270–271

E-commerce: online music and film distribution, **276–282**
America and the world, 281–282
background/development, 277–280
current conditions, 280
industry leaders, 280–281
industry snapshot, 276
organization/structure, 276–277

E-commerce in the U.S.: Retail Trends (eMarketer), 254–255

e-DOCS transcription service, 1025

E-Loan Inc., 598

E-Sign Act (Electronic Signatures in Global and National Commerce Act, 2000), 305

E-surance, 280

E-VEHICLE Co., 288

E-waste, 216, 994

EAI (Education Alternatives Inc.), 142

EAN International, 791, 792

Early Alert Alzheimer's home screening test, 534

Earth Day, 621

Earth Island Journal, 616

Earth Policy Institute, 737

Earth Simulator super computer (Japan), 694

Earth Viewer program (Google), 396

EarthLink Inc., 426, 430–431, 483, 488

Earthquakes. *See* Recovery and emergency relief services

EarthWatch Travel Co., 896

East, Michael, 786

Eastern Europe
bioremediation industry, 110
environmental remediation, 317
IT consulting, 496
nutritional supplements, 659
specialty coffee industry, 886
therapeutic education schools, 971
weight loss industry, 1070

Eastman Kodak Co., 217, 219, 220, 1008

Eat, Pray, Love (Gilbert), 627

Eatboutique.com Web site, 119

EBIZ Enterprises Inc., 693

EBRI (Employee Benefit Research Institute), 926

ebXML (electronic business XML), 1087

Echo digital music service, 211

EchoStar DBS, 233–234, 235, 236, 237, 819

Eckerd Drug Stores, 863

ECLiPS encoding technology (ECLiPS), 586

The Ecology of Commerce (Hawken), 403

Economic Development Administration (EDA), 316

Economic Espionage Act (U.S., 1996), 154–155

Economic Research Service (ERS), 619

The Economist Group, 158

The Economist magazine, 158, 296

Ecotourism, 894–895

EcoWater Systems Inc., 1044

EDAP Technomed Group, 559

Eden Organic Foods, 614

eDiets.com Inc., 1064, 1065

Edison Schools, Inc., 142, 148, 150

EdisonLearning, Inc., 145–146

EDS (Electronic Data Systems Corp.), 69, 126

Edsell, Pat, 670

Educate Corporate Centers, 151

Educate Online, 151

Educating Entrepreneurs Through Technology Act, 312

distance learning, 241–242
electric vehicles, 287
fertility medicine: products and services, 334
gambling resorts and casinos, 366
geographic information systems, 400
green construction, 404
health spas, 424
high speed internet service providers, 431
high tech PR firms, 436
holography, 443
home health care services, 450
infant and preschool products, 467
mass merchandising, 530–531
medical tourism, 542
natural and organic groceries, 618–619
pet products and services, 713
quick care clinics, 786
recovery and emergency relief services, 801
reselling used computer equipment, 995
risk management services, 809–810
robotics and industrial automation, 816–817
smoking cessation products and services, 866
social media, 873
software as a service, 830–831
specialty tourism, 900–901
stem cell research, 907
supplemental insurance plans, 931
tablet computers, 946
telephone services and accessories, 961
tissue engineering, 986
venture capital firms, 1004
waste management, 1034
web developers, 1053
wound care, 1082
Working Wisdom (Leonard), 513
Workplace Violence Institute, 806
World Administrative Radio Conferences, 821
World Alliance for Patient Safety, 540
World Barista Championship, 886
World Business Council for Sustainable Development, 402
World Care Technologies Inc., 952
World Communications, 473
World Emergency Relief Annual Report (2009-2010), 802
World Entertainment News Network magazine, 575, 576, 579
World Health Organization (WHO)
alternative health care definition, 626
Collaborating Centre, 541

disease outbreak coordination, 542, 897, 916
global infectious disease report, 919
influenza vaccine recommendations, 921
malaria data, 919
TB predictions (1999), 918
World Intellectual Property Organization (WIPO), 209
World Population Data Sheet (Population Reference Bureau), 1
World Relief, 797
"World Satellite Communications & Broadcasting Markets Survey (2014)" (Euroconsult report), 822
World Smoking Cessation Drug Market 2010-2025 report, 865
World Trade Center attack. *See* September 11, 2001 attack (Word Trade Center)
World Wide Association of Specialty Programs and Schools (WWASPS), 976
World Wide Web. *See* Internet
World Wide Web Artists Consortium, 1050
WorldCare International Inc., 952
Worldwide Computer Products News, 698
"Worldwide Market for Anti-Infectives" (Kalorama Information, 2009), 65
Wound, Ostomy, and Continence Nurses Society, 1079
Wound care, **1079–1082**
Wound Care Education Institute, 1079
WQA (Water Quality Association), 1036–1037, 1038
Wrapper Inc., 371
Wrick, Dr. Kathie, 656
WSJ.com, 298
WWASPS (World Wide Association of Specialty Programs and Schools), 976
Wyatt, Pat, 527
Wyatt Matas and Associates, 495
Wyeth-Ayerst Laboratories, 1067
Wyndham Hotels, 137
Wynn, Stephen A., 363

X

X Games (ESPN), 324
Xactly Analytics, 203
XBRL (Extensible Business Reporting Language), 1087–1088
Xerox Corporation, 73, 668
XM Satellite Radio, 819

XMG Global, 680, 681
XML (Extensible Markup Language), 242, 248, 480, 502, 602, 779, 1015, 1026, **1085–1091**
background/development, 1086–1089
current conditions, 1089
industry leaders, 1089–1090
industry snapshot, 1085
organization/structure, 1085–1086
research and technology, 1090–1091
XyclonyX microbial technology company, 109

Y

Yahoo!, 68, 79, 176, 256, 257, 259–260, 262, 279, 281, 400, 478, 489, 498, 777, 1051, 1056–1061, 1059–1060
Yale Center for Eating and Weight Disorders (YCEWD), 1065
Yamauchi, Fusajiro, 372
Yankee Group (computer security), 177
Yaskawa Electric Corp., 815, 816
Yeang, Dr. Ken, 404
Yellow Corp., 519
Yingli Green Energy, 739
Y2K risk management, 806
Yoga Alliance, 628
Yoga Journal, 628
Yoga practices. *See* New Age products and services
Yole Development (France), 549
Yourdan, Ed, 494
YouTube, 72, 279, 487, 868, 870–872, 871, 1043, 1052, 1059
YoYoDyne Inc., 871
yStats.com market research firm, 257
Yuke's, 372
Yummy Cupcakes, 878

Z

Zargis Medical, 455
Zebra Imaging, 439, 443
Zebra Technologies, 791
Zeldin, Cindy, 195
Zenith Electronics Corp., 1008
Zero Emissions Vehicles (ZEVs), 55, 285
Zhou, Wu, 171
Zimmer Holdings, 774
Zimmer Inc., 985
Zix Corporation, 307
Zogby International, 373
Zuckerberg, Mark, 870, 871, 872
Zuech, Nello, 508
Zyban anti-smoking drugs, 863, 865
Zymark Corp., 814–815